S0-BQX-816

ARCTIC OCEAN

RUSSIAN FEDERATION

SWEDEN
FINLAND
ESTONIA
LATVIA
LITHUANIA
POLAND
BELARUS
NY
CZ. REP.
SLK.
MOLDOVA
AUS.
HUNG.
UKRAINE
CR.
ROMANIA
YUG.
BULGARIA
B.H.
MAC.
ALB.
GREECE
TURKEY
GEORGIA
ARMENIA
AZERBAIJAN
NISIA
MALTA
CYPRUS
SYRIA
LEBANON
ISRAEL
IRAQ
JORDAN
KUWAIT
BAHRAIN
LIBYA
EGYPT
SAUDI ARABIA
QATAR
UNITED ARAB
EMIRATES
OMAN
IRAN
YEMEN
DJIBOUTI

KAZAKHSTAN
UZBEKISTAN
KYRGYZSTAN
TURKMENISTAN
TAJIKISTAN
AFGHANISTAN
PAKISTAN

MONGOLIA

CHINA

N. KOREA
S. KOREA
JAPAN

PACIFIC OCEAN

NEPAL
BHUTAN
BANGLADESH
INDIA
MYANMAR
(BURMA)
TAIWAN

MALDIVES
SRI
LANKA

LAOS
VIETNAM
THAILAND
CAMBODIA

PHILIPPINES

Mariana Is.
(U.S.)

Guam
(U.S.)

MARSHALL
IS.

CHAD
SUDAN
ERITREA
CENTRAL
AFRICAN REP.
MEROON
UGANDA
RWANDA
KENYA
CONGO
DEM. REP. OF
THE CONGO
BURUNDI
TANZANIA
COMOROS
SEYCHELLES
ETHIOPIA
SOMALIA

BRUNEI
MALAYSIA
PALAU
FEDERATED STATES
OF MICRONESIA

SINGAPORE

INDONESIA

NAURU
KIRIBATI
TUVALU
PAPUA
NEW
GUINEA
SOLOMON
IS.

INDIAN OCEAN

ANGOLA
ZAMBIA
MALAWI
ZIMBABWE
MADAGASCAR
NAMIBIA
BOTSWANA
MOZAMBIQUE
SWAZILAND
SOUTH
AFRICA
LESOTHO

MAURITIUS

VANUATU
FIJI

New Caledonia
(Fr.)

AUSTRALIA

NEW
ZEALAND

Tasmania
(Aust.)

Abbreviations	
ALB.	ALBANIA
AUS.	AUSTRIA
BEL.	BELGIUM
B.H.	BOSNIA AND HERZEGOVINA
CR.	CROATIA
CZ. REP.	CZECH REPUBLIC
DEN.	DENMARK
HUNG.	HUNGARY
LUX.	LUXEMBOURG
MAC.	MACEDONIA
NETH.	NETHERLANDS
SLK.	SLOVAKIA
SLN.	SLOVENIA
SWITZ.	SWITZERLAND
YUG.	YUGOSLAVIA

N
W E
S

NTARCTICA

20°E   40°E   60°E   80°E   100°E   120°E   140°E   160°E

THE MAKING OF THE WEST

PEOPLES AND CULTURES

THE MAKING OF THE WEST

PEOPLES AND CULTURES

LYNN HUNT
University of California at Los Angeles

THOMAS R. MARTIN
College of the Holy Cross

BARBARA H. ROSENWEIN
Loyola University Chicago

R. PO-CHIA HSIA
New York University

BONNIE G. SMITH
Rutgers University

BEDFORD/ST. MARTIN'S   Boston ◆ New York

FOR BEDFORD/ST. MARTIN'S

Executive Editor: Katherine E. Kurzman
Senior Development Editor: Elizabeth M. Welch
Project Manager: Tina Samaha
Production Supervisor: Catherine Hetmansky
Map Development Editors: Heidi Hood, Laura Arcari
Editorial Assistants: Sarah Barrash, Molly E. Kalkstein
Marketing Manager: Jenna Bookin Barry
Assistant Production Editor: Coleen O'Hanley
Copyeditor: Barbara G. Flanagan
Text Designer: Wanda Kossak
Cover Designer: Donna Lee Dennison
Photo Researchers: Carole Frohlich and Martha Shethar, The Visual Connection
Proofreaders: Mary Lou Wilshaw-Watts, Jan Cocker
Indexer: Maro Riofrancos
Composition: York Graphic Services, Inc.
Cartography: Mapping Specialists Limited
Printing and Binding: R.R. Donnelley & Sons Company

President: Charles H. Christensen
Editorial Director: Joan E. Feinberg
Director of Marketing: Karen Melton
Director of Editing, Design, and Production: Marcia Cohen
Managing Editor: Elizabeth Schaaf

Library of Congress Control Number: 00–133169
Copyright © 2001 by Bedford/St. Martin's

Manufactured in the United States of America.

5   4   3   2   1   0
f   e   d   c   b   a

For information, contact: Bedford/St. Martin's, 75 Arlington Street, Boston, MA 02116
617-399-4000
www.bedfordstmartins.com

ISBN: 0–312–18370–4 (hardcover complete edition)
ISBN: 0–312–18369–0 (paperback Volume I)
ISBN: 0–312–18368–2 (paperback Volume II)
ISBN: 0–312–18365–8 (paperback Volume A)
ISBN: 0–312–18364–X (paperback Volume B)
ISBN: 0–312–18363–1 (paperback Volume C)

Cover Art: Top left; title page spread (details): *Les Desmoiselles d'Avignon.* Pablo Picasso, Paris (June–July 1907). The Museum of Modern Art, New York. Acquired through the Lillie P. Bliss Bequest. Photograph © 2000 the Museum of Modern Art, New York. Bottom left: Otto III receiving homage from the four corners of his kingdom. Bavarian State Library, Munich. Courtesy of Art Resource. Right: *George Gordon Byron, 6th Baron Byron* (1788–1824). By Thomas Phillips (1770–1845). Courtesy of the National Portrait Gallery, London.

A Conversation with Lynn Hunt

A RENOWNED SCHOLAR OF THE FRENCH REVOLUTION who has trained a generation of graduate students at the University of California at Berkeley, the University of Pennsylvania, and now as Eugen Weber Professor of Modern European History at the University of California at Los Angeles, Lynn Hunt has long been committed to the centrality of the Western civilization survey course to undergraduate education. In this conversation she explains why she and her coauthors Thomas R. Martin, Barbara H. Rosenwein, R. Po-chia Hsia, and Bonnie G. Smith wrote *The Making of the West: Peoples and Cultures.*

Q **You taught the Western civilization survey for many years before deciding to write a textbook for the course. What inspired you to undertake such a time-consuming project at this point in your career?**

A When I started teaching Western civ in the 1970s, I found the prospect daunting. How can any one person make sense of such a long time span—in my case, the West from the sixteenth century to the present? In addition, historical research was undergoing major changes: social history produced much new information about the lower classes, women, and minorities; then cultural historians began to draw attention to the importance of religious festivals, political rituals, and a variety of cultural expressions. How could these new subjects, new findings, and new methods be incorporated into the narrative of Western historical development?

Every generation needs new textbooks that synthesize the most recent findings. But after 1989 the need for a new vision became especially acute. Not only did new information need to be integrated in a course that was already jam-packed with important material about political personalities, events, and movements, but the very notion of the West was beginning to change. Just as immigration was creating a United States that was much more multiethnic and multicultural than ever before, so too historians had become much more interested in the interactions between the West and the rest of the world. Textbooks conceived and written during the era of the cold war had been oriented toward explaining the conflict between the West and their eastern-bloc opponents, eastern Europe and the Soviet Union. In the post-1989 world,

"Every generation needs new textbooks that synthesize the most recent findings."

political conflicts no longer fit into that neat mold: conflict takes place on a global stage at a time when many important social, economic, and cultural trends have became global. The new histories had to reflect these momentous changes. Since my coauthors and I have all been personally involved in the new approaches to historical research and in the effort to understand the West in a world setting, we felt we would make an effective team for integrating these perspectives and showing how they offer a more coherent and convincing view of the important issues in Western civ.

Q Textbooks for the course typically contain "Western Civilization" in the title. Why is your book named *The Making of the West: Peoples and Cultures?* What are its themes and objectives, and how are they realized?

A Our title makes two important points about our approach: (1) that the history of the West is the story of a process that is still ongoing, not a finished result with only one fixed meaning; and (2) that "the West" includes many different peoples and cultures, that is, that there is no one Western people or culture that has existed from the beginning until now. Although our book emphasizes the best of recent social and cultural history—hence our subtitle, *Peoples and Cultures*—it integrates that new material into a solid chronological framework that does full justice to political, military, and diplomatic history. We try to suggest the richness of themes available for discussion and challenge students to think critically without limiting instructors to just one or two points of view. My coauthors and I have learned from our own teaching that students need a compelling chronological narrative, one with enough familiar benchmarks to make the material readily assimilable, but also one with enough flexibility to incorporate the new varieties of historical research. We aimed for a strong central story line that could integrate the findings of social and cultural history into the more familiar accounts of wars, diplomacy, and high politics, yet we also endeavored to include the experiences of many

"Although our book emphasizes the best of recent social and cultural history—hence our subtitle, Peoples and Cultures—*it integrates that new material into a solid chronological framework that does full justice to political, military, and diplomatic history."*

individual women and men. Nothing makes sense in history if it cannot be related back to the actual experiences of real people. For this reason we begin each chapter with an anecdote about an individual and his or her particular experience and then incorporate that information into the discussion of

"Nothing makes sense in history if it cannot be re-lated back to the actual experiences of real people."

general themes and trends. It is, after all, the interaction between public events and private experiences that makes history of enduring interest to students. Among the ordinary people we chose for special attention, we focused in particular on those who had contacts with the world outside the West, from missionaries and soldiers to naturalists and painters.

Q Four other well-known historians join you on the author team: Thomas Martin, Barbara Rosenwein, R. Po-chia Hsia, and Bonnie Smith. How did the author team come into being? Knowing the potential dangers of a multiauthored textbook, how did you all work together to ensure a single, cohesive work?

A No one scholar can hope to offer a truly authoritative and balanced synthesis of the rich materials available on the whole course of Western history. It is hard enough for one person to teach a semester of Western civ! This kind of undertaking requires collaboration among colleagues of great expertise who can bring to their writing the experience that comes from years of teaching different kinds of students. Our team is made up of just these kinds of scholars and teachers. Each author has an international reputation for research that has helped to shape the agenda for history in the new century. Each one has taught a wide range of students with different levels of skills. We have worked intensively together over the years—meeting often, reading one another's chapters—to develop a clearly focused, integrated narrative that combines the best of new social and cultural approaches with the traditional political narrative and seeks to put Western history in a worldwide context. We have benefited as well from an exceptionally intensive review process that has provided us with helpful input from scores of scholars and teachers with expertise different from our own. They and our editors at Bedford/St. Martin's have helped ensure that the text offers a coherent, continuous narrative. Reading the book, even I can't detect a change in authorship from chapter to chapter!

"This kind of undertaking requires collaboration among colleagues of great expertise who can bring to their writing the experience that comes from years of teaching different kinds of students."

Q   The authors—you in particular—are known for cutting-edge scholarship. In what ways does *The Making of the West* reflect your research and interpretations?

A   From long experience in teaching, we know that students can grasp the most recent advances in scholarship only if those advances can be put in a clear framework that builds on what the students already find familiar. And we also know, like all of our fellow Western civ instructors, that new materials have to be carefully calibrated so as not to overwhelm students who might not be familiar at all with Western history or the methods of historical criticism. For this reason, we have confined much of the explicit discussion of methods and interpretations to the features, which instructors can use or not as they see fit. The narrative itself reflects the authors' most recent research, but it never neglects to explain the relevance of social, cultural, gender, or minority history to the central political problems of an age. Our team has a distinct advantage in this regard because each of us works on topics that have clear relevance for the most "traditional" kinds of political or economic history. In my work on the cultural aspects of the French Revolution, for example, I have always tried to use those approaches to illuminate the most traditional questions: How is a new form of power created? What makes people change their minds and endorse new ideas? Tom Martin, our specialist on ancient history, has considered equally fundamental issues in his study of ancient Greek coinage. How did coins originate in Western civilization? What is the function of money in a society? How are money and power related? As a consequence of these kinds of linkages, we as a team are particularly well placed to show how social and cultural developments can illuminate the most enduring questions of history.

"As a consequence of these kinds of linkages, we as a team are particularly well placed to show how social and cultural developments can illuminate the most enduring questions of history."

Q   *The Making of the West: Peoples and Cultures* represents a major revision of *The Challenge of the West* (Heath, 1995). From the narrative itself to features, pedagogy, maps, and artwork, the book has changed dramatically. Can you describe these revisions and explain why the authors made them? Let's start with the narrative.

A   There is no better way to find out what works and what doesn't than by trying out an approach. Since *Challenge* was published in 1995, we have had the opportunity to teach the book and to get feedback from scores of colleagues around the country who have used it. We now have a much surer sense of how to make our case. *The Making of the West* offers much clearer signposts of the development of the argument along the way. For example, we added a third level of chapter heading to signal supporting as well as main ideas and developments, and we worked hard to provide clear and compelling chapter and section introductions

> "Much of our excitement in this project arose from its very nature: textbook writing, unlike the scholarly books to which we were accustomed, offers historians the rare chance to revise the original work, to keep it fresh, and to make it better."

and summaries. Although we maintained our strong chronological organization, we loosened it here and there—the scientific revolution provides one example, the World Wars of the twentieth century another —to allow the completion of a story in progress, to streamline discussion, and to underline the main themes in our narrative. While offering a clearer sense of our overall direction, we also incorporated even more material on the West's interactions with the rest of the world. And of course we brought in the new research published since 1995. Much of our excitement in this project arose from its very nature: textbook writing, unlike the scholarly books to which we were accustomed, offers historians the rare chance to revise the original work, to keep it fresh, and to make it better.

Q   **New to the book are extensive pedagogical support, recurring special features, and large map and art programs. Knowing the time pressures that teachers and students face, why did you decide to devote many pages to these elements?**

A   More and more is required of students these days (and not just in Western civ), and we know from our own teaching that students need all the help they can get in assimilating information, acquiring skills, learning about historical debate, and sampling the very newest approaches. It is a truism now, but an important one, that education must foster the ability to keep on learning how to adapt to new requirements in the future. Frankly, in *Challenge* we stuck too much to the traditional approach, expecting students to comprehend by simply reading straight through. In *The Making of the West*, we try to teach both traditional skills and new perspectives with the aim of preparing students to grasp the past and understand the history that is yet to come. For example, mastery of chronology is perhaps the most fundamental task for history students: to help them accomplish it, each chapter in our text opens with a comparative timeline that allows students to see at a glance how politics and diplomacy, economic and social trends, and intellectual, religious and cultural developments interact. A list of important dates near the close of each chapter provides a view of key events, while topic-specific timelines outline particular themes and processes. Even the running heads at the top of pages support our effort to help students keep track of chronology and stay focused on their reading by linking subject matter to time frame.

"We try to teach both traditional skills and new perspectives with the aim of preparing students to grasp the past and understand the history that is yet to come."

But like a clear narrative synthesis, strong pedagogical support is not enough on its own to encourage active learning. Setting out to revise *Challenge*, we paid special care to the boxed feature program, eager to hold to our goal of maximum flexibility for teachers while offering student readers the best introduction to historical thinking available in a survey text. We are very proud of the result: an integrated set of features that genuinely extend the narrative by revealing the process of interpretation, providing a solid introduction to the principles of historical argument, and capturing the excitement of historical investigation. The **Contrasting Views** feature, for example, provides three or four often conflicting eyewitness accounts of a central event, person, or development, such as the English civil war, Martin Luther, late-nineteenth-century migration. But it does not just present these views inertly. Introductory paragraphs provide needed context for the primary sources, and questions for debate help students focus on the big questions and alert them at the same time to the ways that history is susceptible to ongoing reinterpretation.

The **New Sources, New Perspectives** feature shows students how historians continue to develop new kinds of evidence about the past—from tree rings to Holocaust museums. This feature will fascinate students with unexpected information and also prompt them to consider how new evidence leads to new interpretations. Curious students will find suggested references for further study of these issues. Questions for Debate that appear at the end of the feature might spark a class discussion about the relationship between evidence and interpretation in our understanding of history.

Too often, textbooks seem to assume that students already know the meaning of some of the most important and contested terms in the history of the West: feudalism, the Renaissance, progress, and revolution, not to mention civilization itself. We do not make this assumption. Instead we offer a **Terms of History** feature in which we explain the meaning of these terms and show how those meanings have developed—and changed—over time. Thus, for example, the discussion of *progress* shows how the term took root in the eighteenth century and has been contested in the twentieth. For the student who is struggling to make sense of Western history, this feature explains the meaning of key terms. For a more sophisticated student, this feature can shed yet more light on the question of historical interpretation.

Since we want to emphasize the interactions between the West and the broader world, a short illustrated feature, **Did You Know?**, offers unexpected and sometimes even startling examples of cultural interchange ranging from the invention of "smoking" (derived from the New World) to the creation of polo (adapted from South Asia). History can be fun as well as provocative, after all! From our many years of teaching, we know that students learn best when they are engaged by the material.

Now, more than ever, quantitative or statistical literacy is vitally important. The **Taking Measure** feature, which appears in every chapter, highlights a chart, table, graph, or map of historical statistics that illuminates an important political, social, or cultural development. Learning how to read such information is crucial preparation for students, no matter what their eventual field of study.

"We learned from our experience with Challenge *that the look of the textbook plays a vital role in capturing students' interest."*

Q **Your rationale for extensive pedagogy and features is clear; what about the space devoted to art and maps?**

A We learned from our experience with *Challenge* that the look of the textbook plays a vital role in capturing students' interest, and we were pleased to work with a publisher who similarly understood the importance of a striking, full-color design and rich art and map programs. Students have become much more attuned to visual sources of information, yet they do not always receive systematic instruction in how to "read" such visual sources. Our captions aim to help them learn how to make the most of these visually attractive and informative materials. Over 480 illustrations not only reinforce the text but show the varieties of primary sources from which historians build their narratives and interpretations. We are proud as well of our map program: fundamental to any good history book, maps take on special importance in a text intended to stress interactions between the West and the wider world, and we worked intensively with our publisher to provide the most comprehensive map program available in a survey text. Thus we offer in each chapter 4–5 full-size maps, 2–4 "spot maps"—that is, small maps on single but crucial issues that are exactly located in related discussion—and, another first for our map program, "summary maps" at the end of each chapter, which individually provide a snapshot of the West at the close of a transformative period and collectively help students visualize the West's changing contours over time.

Q You and your coauthors have written many well-received and influential scholarly works. What response to *The Making of the West: Peoples and Cultures* would please you most?

A We aim to communicate the vitality and excitement as well as the fundamental importance of history. The highest compliment we could receive would be to hear that reading this textbook has encouraged students to take more history courses, major in history, perhaps even want to become historians themselves. We also hope that our text helps instructors overcome the obstacles in teaching this course and perhaps even revives their own interest in the materials covered here. History is never an entirely settled matter; it is always in process. If we have succeeded in conveying some of the vibrancy of the past and the thrill of historical investigation, we will be encouraged to start rethinking and revising—as historians always must—once again.

"History is never an entirely settled matter; it is always in process."

❖ Supplements

The authors of *The Making of the West: Peoples and Cultures* oversaw development of the well-integrated ancillary program that supports their text. A comprehensive collection of print and electronic resources for students and instructors provides a host of practical learning and teaching aids.

For Students

Study Guide to Accompany **The Making of the West: Peoples and Cultures**—Volumes I (to 1740) and II (since 1560)—by Victoria Thompson, Arizona State University. This carefully developed study guide offers overview and review materials to help students master content and learn to analyze it. For each chapter in the textbook, the study guide offers a summary; an expanded outline with matching exercises; a glossary of important terms with related questions; multiple-choice and short-answer questions; and map, illustration, and documents exercises that help students synthesize the material they have learned as well as appreciate the skills historians use to understand the past. Answers for all questions and exercises, with references to relevant pages in the textbook, are provided.

The *Online Study Guide for* **The Making of the West: Peoples and Cultures** is like none other: thoroughly integrated with the text and based on the print study guide, the online study guide takes advantage of the Internet to offer structured and easily accessed help for each chapter and innovative multimedia exercises designed to reinforce themes and content. For each chapter, an initial multiple-choice test assesses student comprehension of the material and a Recommended Study Plan suggests specific exercises that cover the subject areas they still need to master. Three multiple-choice tests per chapter help students improve their command of the material. Additional exercises encourage students to think about chapter themes as well as to develop skills of analysis.

Using the highly acclaimed course-tools software developed by QuestionMark, the online study guide for *The Making of the West* allows students to keep track of their performance chapter by chapter.

Sources of **The Making of the West: Peoples and Cultures**—Volumes I (to 1740) and II (since 1560)—by Katharine Lualdi, Colby College. For each chapter in *The Making of the West*, this companion sourcebook features four important political, social, or cultural documents that either reinforce or extend text discussion. Short chapter summaries, headnotes, and discussion questions highlight chapter themes and encourage students to think critically about these primary sources.

The Bedford Series in History and Culture—Advisory Editors Natalie Z. Davis, Princeton University; Ernest R. May, Harvard University; David W. Blight, Amherst College. Any of the volumes from this highly acclaimed series of brief, inexpensive, document-based supplements can be packaged with *The Making of the West* at a reduced price. The fourteen European history titles include *Spartacus and the Slave Wars, Utopia, Candide, The French Revolution and Human Rights,* and *The Communist Manifesto.*

For Instructors

Instructor's Resource Manual for **The Making of the West: Peoples and Cultures**—Volumes I (to 1740) and II (since 1560)—by Michael Richards, Sweet Briar College. This comprehensive collection of tools offers both the first-time and the experienced instructor extensive teaching information for each chapter in the textbook: outlines of chapter themes, chapter summaries, lecture and discussion topics, ideas for in-class work with maps and illustrations, writing and classroom presentation assignments, and research topic suggestions. The manual also includes seven essays for instructors with titles such as "What Is Western Civilization?," "Teaching Western Civilization with Computers and Web Sites," and "Literature and the Western Civilization Classroom," as well as over a dozen reprints of frequently assigned primary sources for easy access and distribution.

Test Items to Accompany **The Making of the West: Peoples and Cultures**—Volumes I (to 1740) and II (since 1560)—by Tamara Hunt, Loyola Marymount University. In addition to twenty fill-in-the-blank, fifteen multiple-choice, ten short-answer, and four essay questions, this test bank includes for each chapter in the text a relationship-causation exercise, which asks students to place five events in chronological order and to explain a common theme that runs through them, and four map and documents exercises that test students' comprehension of chapter material and their ability to use sources. Answers for identification, multiple-choice, and short-answer questions, with references to relevant pages in the textbook, are provided. So that instructors may customize their tests to suit their classes, the answer key labels multiple-choice questions by difficulty.

The test bank is available in book format, with perforated pages for easy removal, or in Macintosh and Windows formats on disk. Easy-to-use software allows instructors to create and administer tests on paper or over a network. Instructors can generate exams and quizzes from the print test bank or write their own. A grade management function helps keep track of student progress.

Map Transparencies. A set of approximately 145 full-color acetate transparencies, free to adopters, includes all the full-size maps in the text.

CD-ROM with Presentation Manager Pro. For instructors who wish to use electronic media in the classroom, this new CD includes images, maps, and graphs from *The Making of the West: Peoples and Cultures* in an easy-to-use format that allows instructors to customize their presentations. The CD-ROM may be used with Presentation Manager Pro or with PowerPoint for instructors who wish to add their own slides to a presentation.

Using the Bedford Series in the Western Civilization Survey by Maura O'Connor. Recognizing that many instructors use a survey text in conjunction with supplements, Bedford/St. Martin's has made the fourteen Bedford Series volumes available at a discount to adopters of *The Making of the West: Peoples and Cultures.* This short guide gives practical suggestions for using volumes from the Bedford Series in History and Culture with *The Making of the West.* The guide not only supplies links between the text and the supplements but also provides ideas for starting discussions focused on a single primary-source volume.

The **Web Site for The Making of the West: Peoples and Cultures.** At http://www.bedfordstmartins .com/makingwest, instructors will find our useful Syllabus Manager as well as annotated pedagogical links with teaching suggestions tied to *The Making of the West.* A print guide is available for instructors looking for guidance in setting up their own Web sites.

❖ Acknowledgments

From the first draft to the last, the authors have benefited from repeated critical readings by many talented scholars and teachers. Our thanks to the following instructors, whose comments often challenged us to rethink or justify our interpretations and always provided a check on accuracy down to the smallest detail.

Dorothy Abrahamse, *California State University at Long Beach*

F. E. Beeman, *Middle Tennessee State University*

Martin Berger, *Youngstown State University*

Raymond Birn, *University of Oregon*

Charmarie J. Blaisdell, *Northeastern University*

Keith Bradley, *University of Victoria*

Paul Breines, *Boston College*

Caroline Castiglione, *University of Texas at Austin*

Carolyn A. Conley, *University of Alabama*

William Connell, *Seton Hall University*

Jo Ann H. Moran Cruz, *Georgetown University*

John P. Daly, *Louisiana Tech University*

Suzanne Desan, *University of Wisconsin at Madison*

Michael F. Doyle, *Ocean County College*

Jean C. England, *Northeastern Louisiana University*

Steven Epstein, *University of Colorado at Boulder*

Steven Fanning, *University of Illinois at Chicago*

Laura Frader, *Northeastern University*

Alison Futrell, *University of Arizona*

Gretchen Galbraith, *Grand Valley State University*

Timothy E. Gregory, *Ohio State University*

Katherine Haldane Grenier, *The Citadel*

Martha Hanna, *University of Colorado at Boulder*

Julie Hardwick, *Texas Christian University*

Kenneth W. Harl, *Tulane University*

Charles Hedrick, *University of California at Santa Cruz*

Robert L. Hohlfelder, *University of Colorado at Boulder*

Maryanne Horowitz, *Occidental College*

Gary Kates, *Trinity University*

Ellis L. Knox, *Boise State University*

Lawrence Langer, *University of Connecticut*

Keith P. Luria, *North Carolina State University*

Judith P. Meyer, *University of Connecticut*

Maureen C. Miller, *Hamilton College*

Stuart S. Miller, *University of Connecticut*

Dr. Frederick Murphy, *Western Kentucky University*

James Murray, *University of Cincinnati*

Phillip C. Naylor, *Marquette University*

Carolyn Nelson, *University of Kansas*

Richard C. Nelson, *Augsburg College*

John Nichols, *University of Oregon*

Byron J. Nordstrom, *Gustavus Adolphus College*

Maura O'Connor, *University of Cincinnati*

Lawrence Okamura, *University of Missouri at Columbia*

Dolores Davison Peterson, *Foothill College*

Carl F. Petry, *Northwestern University*

Carole A. Putko, *San Diego State University*

Michael Richards, *Sweet Briar College*

Barbara Saylor Rodgers, *University of Vermont*

Sally Scully, *San Francisco State University*

Jane Slaughter, *University of New Mexico*

Donald Sullivan, *University of New Mexico*

Victoria Thompson, *Arizona State University*

Sue Sheridan Walker, *Northeastern Illinois University*

John E. Weakland, *Ball State University*

Theodore R. Weeks, *Southern Illinois University at Carbondale*

Merry Wiesner-Hanks, *University of Wisconsin at Milwaukee*

Each of us has also benefited from the close readings and valuable criticisms of our coauthors, though we all assume responsibility for our own chapters. Thomas Martin has written Chapters 1–7; Barbara Rosenwein, Chapters 8–12; Ronnie Hsia, Chapters 13–15; Lynn Hunt, Chapters 16–22; and Bonnie Smith, Chapters 23–30.

Many colleagues, friends, and family members have helped us develop this work as well. Lynn Hunt wishes to thank in particular Anne Engel, Margaret Jacob, Rick Weiche, and Melissa Verlet for their help with various aspects of this project. Tom Martin and Ronnie Hsia express warm thanks to their families for their forbearance and support. Barbara Rosenwein extends special gratitude to Steven Epstein, Naomi Honeth, Maureen Miller, and Frank, Jess, and Tom Rosenwein. Bonnie Smith thanks Julie Taddeo, Cathy Mason, Scott Glotzer, Tamara Matheson, and Todd Shepard for research assistance.

We also wish to acknowledge and thank the publishing team who did so much to bring this book into being. Katherine E. Kurzman, executive editor for history, introduced us to Bedford/St. Martin's and guided our efforts throughout the project. Charles H. Christensen, president, and Joan E. Feinberg, editorial director, shared generous resources, mutual vision, and, best, confidence in the project and in us. Special thanks are due to many other individuals: Tina Samaha, our project manager, who with great skill and professionalism pulled all the pieces together with the help of Coleen O'Hanley, assistant production editor; photo researchers Carole Frohlich and Martha Shethar and map editors Heidi Hood and Laura Arcari, who did so much to help us realize our goals for the book's art and map programs; our original development editor, Ellen Kuhl, and the fine editors she brought to the project, Louise Townsend, Barbara Muller, and Jane Tufts; editorial assistants Sarah Barrash and Molly Kalkstein, who helped in myriad ways on many essential tasks; and our superb copyeditor, Barbara Flanagan. Last and above all, we thank Elizabeth M. Welch, senior development editor, who provided just the right doses of encouragement, prodding, and concrete suggestions for improvement. Her intelligence, skill, and determination proved to be crucial at every step of the process.

Our students' questions and concerns have shaped much of this work, and we welcome all our readers' suggestions, queries, and criticisms. Please contact us at our respective institutions or through our Web site: www.bedfordstmartins.com/makingwest.

L.H.   T.R.M.   B.H.R.   R.P.H.   B.G.S.

Brief Contents

Contents

Foundations of Western Civilization, to 1000 B.C.   3

New Paths for Western Civilization, c. 1000–500 B.C. *45*

The Greek Golden Age, c. 500–400 B.C. *83*

Maps and Figures

FIGURES

Special Features

TERMS OF HISTORY

DID YOU KNOW?

TAKING MEASURE

The B.C./A.D. System for Dates

"When were you born?" "What year is it?" We customarily answer questions like these with a number, such as "1983" or "2000." Our replies are usually automatic, taking for granted the numerous assumptions Westerners make about dates. But to what do numbers such as 1983 and 2000 actually refer? In this book the numbers used to specify dates follow the system most common in the Western secular world. This system reckons the dates of solar years by counting backward and forward from the traditional date of the birth of Jesus Christ, over two thousand years ago.

Using this method, numbers followed by the abbreviation B.C., standing for "before Christ," indicate the number of years counting backward from the birth of Jesus. The larger the number after B.C., the earlier in history is the year to which it refers. The date 431 B.C., for example, refers to a year 431 years before the birth of Jesus and therefore comes earlier in time than the dates 430 B.C., 429 B.C., and so on. The same calculation applies to numbering other time intervals calculated on the decimal system: those of ten years (a decade), of one hundred years (a century), and of one thousand years (a millennium). For example, the decade of the 440s B.C. (449 B.C. to 440 B.C.) is earlier than the decade of the 430s B.C. (439 to 430 B.C.). "Fifth century B.C." refers to the fifth period of 100 years reckoning backward from the birth of Jesus and covers the years 500 B.C. to 401 B.C. It is earlier in history than the fourth century B.C. (400 B.C. to 301 B.C.), which followed the fifth century B.C. Because this system has no year "zero," the first century B.C. covers the years 100 B.C. to 1 B.C. As for millennia, the second millennium B.C. refers to the years 2000 B.C. to 1001 B.C., the third millennium to the years 3000 B.C. to 2001 B.C., and so on.

To indicate years counted forward from the traditional date of Jesus' birth, numbers are sometimes preceded by the abbreviation A.D., standing for the Latin phrase *anno Domini* ("in the year of the Lord"). The date A.D. 1492, for example, translates as "in the year of the Lord 1492," meaning 1492 years after the reported birth of Jesus. Writing dates with A.D. following the number, as in 1492 A.D., makes no sense because it would amount to saying "1492 in the year of the Lord." It is, however, customary to indicate centuries by placing the abbreviation A.D. after the number. Therefore "first century A.D." refers to the period from A.D. 1 to A.D. 100. For numbers indicating dates after the birth of Jesus, the smaller the number, the earlier the date in history. The fourth century A.D. (A.D. 301 to A.D. 400) comes before the fifth century A.D. (A.D. 401 to A.D. 500). The year A.D. 312 is a date in the early fourth century A.D., and A.D. 395 is a date late in the same century. When numbers are given without either B.C. or A.D., they are presumed to be dates after the birth of Jesus. For example, *eighteenth century* with no abbreviation accompanying it refers to the years A.D. 1701 to A.D. 1800.

No standard system of numbering years, such as the B.C./A.D. method, existed in antiquity. Different people in different parts of the world identified years with varying names and numbers. Consequently, it was difficult to match up the years in any particular local system with those in a different system. Each city of ancient Greece, for example, had its own method for keeping track of the years. The ancient Greek historian Thucydides therefore faced a problem in presenting a chronology for the war between Athens and Sparta, which began (by our reckoning) in 431 B.C. To try to explain to as many of his readers as possible the date the war had begun, he described its first year by three different local systems: "the year when Chrysis was in the forty-eighth year of her priesthood at Argos, and Aenesias was overseer at Sparta, and Pythodorus was magistrate at Athens."

A monk named Dionysius, who lived in Rome in the sixth century A.D., invented the system of reckoning dates forward from the birth of Jesus. Calling himself "Exiguus" (Latin for "the little" or "the small") as a mark of humility, he placed Jesus' birth 754 years after the foundation of ancient Rome. Others then and now believe his date for Jesus' birth was in fact several years too late. Many scholars today figure that Jesus was born in what would be 4 B.C. according to Dionysius's system, although a date a year or so earlier also seems possible.

Counting backward from the supposed date of Jesus' birth to indicate dates earlier than that event represented a natural complement to reckoning forward for dates after it. The English historian and theologian Bede in the early eighth century was the first to use both forward and backward reckoning from the birth of Jesus in a historical work, and this system gradually gained wider acceptance because it provided a basis for standardizing the many local calendars used in the Western Christian world. Nevertheless, B.C. and A.D. were not used regularly until the end of the eighteenth century.

The system of numbering years from the birth of Jesus is not the only one still used. The Jewish calendar of years, for example, counts forward from the date given to the creation of the world, which would be calculated as 3761 B.C. under the B.C./A.D. system. Years are designated A.M., an abbreviation of the Latin *anno mundi*, "in the year of the world under this system." The Islamic calendar counts forward from the date of the prophet Muhammad's flight from Mecca, called the *Hijra*, in what would be the year A.D. 622 under the B.C./A.D. system. The abbreviation A.H. (standing for the Latin phrase *anno Hegirae*, "in the year of the Hijra") indicates dates calculated by this system. Today the abbreviations B.C.E. ("before the common era") and C.E. ("of the common era") are often used in place of B.C. and A.D., respectively, to allow the retention of numerical dates as reckoned by the B.C./A.D. system without the Christian reference implied by this system. Anthropology commonly reckons distant dates as "before the present" (abbreviated B.P.).

History is often defined as the study of change over time; hence the importance of dates for the historian. But just as historians argue over which dates are most significant, they disagree over which dating system to follow. Their debate reveals perhaps the most enduring fact of history—its vitality.

About the Authors

LYNN HUNT, Eugen Weber Professor of Modern European History at the University of California at Los Angeles, received her B.A. from Carleton College and her M.A. and Ph.D. from Stanford University. She is the author of *Revolution and Urban Politics in Provincial France* (1978); *Politics, Culture, and Class in the French Revolution* (1984); and *The Family Romance of the French Revolution* (1992). She is also the coauthor of *Telling the Truth about History* (1994); editor of *The New Cultural History* (1989); editor and translator of *The French Revolution and Human Rights* (1996); and coeditor of *Histories: French Constructions of the Past* (1995) and *Beyond the Cultural Turn* (1999). She has been awarded fellowships by the Guggenheim Foundation and the National Endowment for the Humanities and is a fellow of the American Academy of Arts and Sciences. She is currently preparing a CD-ROM of documents, images, and songs from the French Revolution and a book on the origins of human rights.

THOMAS R. MARTIN, Jeremiah O'Connor Professor in Classics at the College of the Holy Cross, earned his B.A. at Princeton University and his M.A. and Ph.D. at Harvard University. He is the author of *Sovereignty and Coinage in Classical Greece* (1985) and *Ancient Greece* (1996, 2000) and one of the originators of *Perseus 1.0: Interactive Sources and Studies on Ancient Greece* (1992, 1996) and www.perseus.tufts.edu, which, among other awards, was named the EDUCOM Best Software in Social Sciences (History) in 1992. He also wrote the lead article on ancient Greece for the revised edition of the Encarta electronic encyclopedia. He serves on the editorial board of STOA (www.stoa.org) and as codirector of its DEMOS project (online resources on ancient Athenian democracy). A recipient of fellowships from the National Endowment for the Humanities and the American Council of Learned Societies, he is currently conducting research on the history and significance of freedom of speech in Athenian democracy.

BARBARA H. ROSENWEIN, professor of history at Loyola University Chicago, earned her B.A., M.A., and Ph.D. at the University of Chicago. She is the author of *Rhinoceros Bound: Cluny in the Tenth Century* (1982); *To Be the Neighbor of Saint Peter: The Social Meaning of Cluny's Property, 909–1049* (1989); and *Negotiating Space: Power, Restraint, and Privileges of Immunity in Early Medieval Europe* (1999). She is the editor of *Anger's Past: The Social Uses of an Emotion in the Middle Ages* (1998) and coeditor of *Debating the Middle Ages: Issues and Readings* (1998) and *Monks and Nuns, Saints and Outcasts: Religion in Medieval Society* (2000). A recipient of Guggenheim and National Endowment for the Humanities fellowships, she is currently working on a history of emotions in the early Middle Ages.

R. PO-CHIA HSIA, professor of history at New York University, received his B.A. from Swarthmore College and his M.A. and Ph.D. from Yale University. He is the author of *Society and Religion in Münster, 1535–1618* (1984); *The Myth of Ritual Murder: Jews and Magic in Reformation Germany* (1988); *The German People and the Reformation* (1998); *Social Discipline in the Reformation: Central Europe, 1550–1750* (1989); *Trent 1475: Stories of a Ritual Murder Trial* (1992); and *The World of the Catholic Renewal* (1997). He has been awarded fellowships by the Woodrow Wilson International Society of Scholars, the National Endowment for the Humanities, the Guggenheim Foundation, the Davis Center of Princeton University, and the Mellon Foundation. Currently he is working on sixteenth-to-eighteenth-century cultural contacts between Europe and Asia.

BONNIE G. SMITH, professor of history at Rutgers University, earned her B.A. at Smith College and her Ph.D. at the University of Rochester. She is the author of *Ladies of the Leisure Class* (1981); *Confessions of a Concierge: Madame Lucie's History of Twentieth-Century France* (1985); *Changing Lives: Women in European History since 1700* (1989); *The Gender of History: Men, Women, and Historical Practice* (1998); and *Imperialism* (2000). She is also the coauthor and translator of *What Is Property?* (1994); editor of *Global Feminisms since 1945* (2000); and coeditor of *History and the Texture of Modern Life: Selected Writings of Lucy Maynard Salmon*. She has received fellowships from the Guggenheim Foundation, the National Endowment for the Humanities, the National Humanities Center, the Davis Center of Princeton University, and the American Council of Learned Societies. Currently she is studying the globalization of European culture and society after World War II.

THE MAKING OF THE WEST

PEOPLES AND CULTURES

1

Foundations of Western Civilization

To 1000 B.C.

Egyptian Painted Sarcophagus
*This brilliantly painted sarco-
phagus held the mummified
corpse of an ancient Egyptian
named Khonsu or Khons, who
died in his fifties — a ripe old
age for his era — and was buried
alongside his family members in
their tomb at Deir el Medina
outside Thebes, probably in the
1200s B.C. Like his father, he was
an artisan who had worked on
the royal tombs in the Valley of
the Kings just west of the Nile.
The goddesses shown here on
one end of the sarcophagus were
believed to offer protection in
the afterlife; the green tint of
their skin — the color of healthy,
growing plants — symbolizes
their powers of rejuvenation.*
Ken S. Graetz.

ACCORDING TO THE MESOPOTAMIAN *EPIC OF CREATION*, a violent struggle among the gods created the universe. The hugely powerful goddess Tiamat threatened to destroy the other gods in anger at the murder of her husband, Apsu. In a meeting inflamed by bottomless beakers of beer and wine, the gods agreed to hail the male god Marduk as king of the universe, if he could save them. Marduk promptly unleashed his fearsome powers—"four were his eyes, four were his ears; when his lips moved, fire blazed forth"—in a gory battle that destroyed Tiamat and her army of snaky monsters. Marduk then fashioned human beings out of the blood of Tiamat's chief monster. He created people so that they could serve and entertain their divine masters. This myth taught people that they had far less power than the gods, that they had to win the favor of the gods to avoid punishment, and that they had to work hard to please the gods by offering them gifts.

The precariousness of life implied by this story about human origins rings true: before civilization, in the Stone Age tens and tens of thousands of years ago, people had to roam around to hunt and gather food in the wild, using tools made from stone, bone, and wood. They were constantly on the move, hoping to find enough to feed their families and still have something left over for offerings to the supernatural forces they believed controlled nature. Technological change altered this way of life fundamentally, if slowly, beginning about ten to twelve thousand years ago, when people in southwestern Asia developed agriculture and domesticated animals.

40,000 B.C.			1000 B.C.

Politics and War

First cities in Mesopotamia			Hittite kingdom emerges in Anatolia
	Egyptian Old Kingdom	Egyptian Middle Kingdom	Egyptian New Kingdom
	First Empire in Akkadia	Mycenaean civilization in Greece	
	Minoan civilization begins on Crete	Violence in eastern Mediterranean	

Society and Economy

Bronze metallurgy develops throughout Near East

Modern humans migrate from Africa to Southwest Asia and Europe

Agriculture invented in the Fertile Crescent and spreads throughout Europe

Animals domesticated throughout Near East and Europe

Wheel invented in Sumer

Culture, Religion, and Intellectual Life

Cuneiform invented in Sumer

Hammurabi's Law Code

Early elements of
Epic of Gilgamesh

Alphabet invented
in Canaan

These revolutionary developments opened the way to civilization by creating the first permanent settlements and enough surpluses to allow many people to work full-time at crafts, not just farming. Gradually, settlements grew larger, until around 4000–3000 B.C. the first cities formed in Mesopotamia (modern Iraq). Thus began the earliest civilization: life based in cities that functioned as political states. That is, people lived in separate territories marked off by boundaries and organized under governments with rulers, taxes, and a local sense of identity. In their daily lives, they grew crops with irrigation, crafted a wide array of products, traded far and wide, built temples to worship the gods, used the new technology of writing to do accounting and record their literature, and fought other states to win glory and to control areas where valuable metals could be found for use in the new technology of metallurgy.

As symbolized by the Marduk creation myth, religious concerns permeated early civilization. This characteristic appeared prominently in the special religious status of Mesopotamia's rulers, who were responsible for creating order on earth by establishing laws and making sure the people honored the gods. The same was true in Egypt, where civilization emerged about 3100–3000 B.C., when the land became a unified state under a central authority. The Egyptians' deep religious conservatism, combined with their extraordinary architectural skills, inspired them to build fabulous temples and the pyramids. By 2000 B.C., civilizations also appeared in Anatolia (today Turkey), on islands in the eastern Mediterranean Sea, and in Greece; all of them learned from the older civilizations of Mesopotamia and Egypt. Comparable civilizations also emerged, at different times starting about 2500 B.C., in India, China, and the Americas—whether through independent development or some process of mutual influence we do not know at present. We are sure, however, that the early civilizations of Mesopotamia, Egypt, Minoan Crete, and Mycenaean Greece began the history of Western civilization and that a violent period of crisis from about 1200 to 1000 B.C. threatened to end its story.

These early civilizations developed and changed as a result of both intended and unintended consequences. More sophisticated metallurgical technology, for example, created ever better tools and weapons, but it also increased differences in status among people. Just as the gods insisted on their superiority to human beings, so too did people develop status differences, or *hierarchy,* among themselves. These early civilizations also thrived on cultural interaction. From the earliest times, trade and war brought different peoples into contact, peacefully and violently. Very often, this interaction spurred people to learn from one another and to adapt for themselves the traditions, beliefs, and technologies of others.

❖ Before Civilization

Human beings existed for a long time before they created what we call civilization. (We refer to the people who lived before civilization as "prehistoric" because they did not know how to write and therefore left no historical records.) People whose brains and bodies were close to ours today (*Homo sapiens,* or "wise human being," the immediate ancestor of modern human beings, *Homo sapiens sapiens*) first

appeared about four hundred thousand years ago in Stone Age Africa. Anthropologists and archaeologists divide the Stone Age into an ancient period, the Paleolithic ("Old Stone"), whose beginning reaches back to the appearance of *Homo sapiens,* and a more recent period, the Neolithic ("New Stone"), which began about ten to twelve thousand years ago, when the modern pattern of life based on agriculture began to emerge. Paleolithic peoples had to find their food because they did not know how to produce it. Still, important characteristics of their lives—especially their division of labor according to gender, their desire for trade, and their love of art as part of religion—established patterns that persisted in Western civilization. Paleolithic hunter-gatherers passed on to later societies their successful strategies for survival in a harsh world.

People in the Neolithic period dramatically changed the ways they acquired food by inventing agriculture and domesticating animals. These innovations had enormous, permanent effects on human life by leading people to live in settled communities, enabling them to produce surpluses of food to support full-time crafts workers, and tying work and prestige more closely to gender. So radical were these developments that they have earned the name "Neolithic Revolution," though this was a revolution that happened gradually.

Paleolithic Life, to c. 10,000 B.C.

Humans in the Paleolithic period lived a very different life from the settled existence most of us take for granted today: they roamed all their lives, moving around in a constant, risky search for food. They hunted wild game for meat, fished in lakes and rivers, collected shellfish, and gathered anything edible, from wild plants, roots, fruits, and nuts to animal dung. Because they survived by hunting and gathering their food, we refer to these early humans as *hunter-gatherers.*

When human beings anatomically identical with modern people (*Homo sapiens sapiens*) first migrated from their homeland in Africa through southwestern Asia into Europe, beginning about 40,000 B.C., they encountered human populations of an earlier type that had arrived there long before. Gradually, the modern human type, commonly called Cro-Magnon after the rock shelter in southern France where their remains have been found,

A Paleolithic Shelter
This is a reconstruction of a hut that Paleolithic people built about 15,000 years ago from the bones of giant mammoths in what is now Ukraine. Animal hides would have been used to cover the structure, like a tent on poles. It was big enough for a small group to huddle inside to survive cold weather.
Novosti (London).

to be particularly good for gathering wild plants. Caves or rough dwellings made from branches and animal skins sheltered them from harsh weather. Occasionally, hunter-gatherers built more elaborate shelters, such as the domelike hut found in western Russia that was constructed from the bones of mammoths. Still, even though hunter-gatherers might return year after year to the same places where they had found food in the past, they had to roam to survive.

Hunter-Gatherer Society. Stone Age groups divided their principal labor—finding food—between men and women. Because women of childbearing age had to nurse their young, they rarely roamed far from their camp on hunts. They and the smaller children gathered food closer to home by foraging for edible plants, especially roots, nuts, and berries, and trapping small animals, such as frogs and rabbits. The plant food they collected constituted the bulk of the diet of hunter-gatherer populations. Women past childbearing age made especially important contributions to the group because, unburdened by infants, they could move around widely to help wherever needed. Men probably did most of the hunting of large and sometimes dangerous animals, often far from camp. Recent archaeological evidence shows that women participated too, especially when groups ensnared game in nets. These hunts were the main source of meat as well as skins for clothing and tents.

Paleolithic peoples probably did not divide power strictly according to gender, because both men and women made essential contributions to supporting the group. Many hunter-gatherer groups may have been largely egalitarian, meaning all adults enjoyed a rough equality in making decisions for their group. Furthermore, hunter-gatherer society had no legal and political institutions in the modern sense. At the same time, differences in social status existed. Since slaying large game was dangerous, men probably acquired status from their prominent role in this vital activity. Older people of both genders enjoyed prestige because of their wisdom from long experience and because their age made them special at a time when, according to historical demographers, illness and accidents killed most people before age thirty.

replaced the earlier types, such as the Neanderthals, so named because archaeologists first found their bones in Germany's Neanderthal valley. Although *Homo sapiens sapiens* had developed spoken language, the invention of writing still lay tens of thousands of years in the future. These early hunter-gatherers therefore left no documents to tell us about their lives; only anthropology and archaeology can give us a glimpse.

Anthropologists reconstruct the patterns of Paleolithic life from information about the hunter-gatherer populations that survived into modern times, such as the !Kung in Africa, the Aborigines in Australia, and the Coahuiltecans in the American Southwest. Paleolithic peoples probably banded together in groups of twenty to fifty. They hunted and foraged for food, which they shared among themselves, and tended to stay within a loosely defined region to reduce conflict with others. Because no one had yet domesticated oxen or horses or built wheeled vehicles for transport, hunter-gatherers had to walk everywhere, carrying their belongings with them. They used their knowledge of wild animals to plan ahead for cooperative hunts at favorite locations. Although they made no permanent homes, they camped in spots shown from past experience

Especially rich Paleolithic graves containing weapons, tools, animal figurines, ivory beads, and bracelets also suggest social differences among individuals. We can surmise that persons buried with such elaborate care and expenditure enjoyed superior wealth, power, or status. These special burials may indicate that some groups organized themselves into hierarchies.

Trade, Technology, and Religion. The goods found in Paleolithic burial places show that hunter-gatherers acquired attractive and useful resources and objects from outside their own territory. They obtained such things often by trading goods with other groups whom they encountered in their roaming. Materials exchanged in this way could travel great distances from their point of origin. Seashells used as jewelry, for example, made their way far inland through repeated swaps from one group to another. Known from at least the late Paleolithic period, this activity represented the earliest stage in the development of long-distance trade, which would later forge far-reaching connections among separate parts of the world.

Trade spread crucial knowledge and skills as well as valuable resources and materials. The ability to make fire, for example, helped people survive the extended winters of recurring ice ages, when the northern European glaciers moved much farther south than usual. Control of fire also helped hunter-gatherers improve their nutrition by cooking foods. Cooking was an important technological innovation because it made edible and nutritious food out of some plants, such as wild grain, that were indigestible raw. Creating tools for cutting and digging also improved hunting and food preparation; careful work could chip stones into blades and sharpen sticks and bones into spears and trowels.

Hunter-gatherers developed skill in art as well as technology. Late Paleolithic cave paintings found in Spain and France display striking artistic ability and hint at religious beliefs. Using strong, dark lines and earthy colors, artists of this period painted on the walls of caves that had been set aside as special places, not to be used as day-to-day shelters. The paintings, which depict primarily large wild animals, suggest that these powerful beasts and the dangerous hunts that killed them played a significant role in the life and religion of prehistoric people. Paleolithic artists also sculpted statuettes of human figures, most likely for religious purposes. For example, female statuettes with extra-large breasts, abdomens, buttocks, and thighs have turned up in excavations of Paleolithic sites all over Europe. The exaggerated features of these figurines suggest that the people to whom they belonged had a special set of beliefs and community rituals about fertility and birth. The care with which they buried their dead, decorating the corpses with red paint, flowers, and seashells, indicates a concern with the mystery of death and perhaps some belief about an afterlife.

Prehistoric "Venus" figurine
Archaeologists have discovered small female figures, like this one from Romania, in many late Paleolithic and Neolithic sites in Europe. Since they predate writing, we cannot be sure of their significance, but many scholars assume that their hefty proportions are meant to signal a special concern for fertility. That is, these female figures represent prehistoric peoples' vision of rare good fortune: having enough food to become fat and produce healthy children. The statuettes are called "Venus" figurines after the Roman goddess of love.
Erich Lessing/Art Resource, NY.

Despite their knowledge of nature and technological skills, Paleolithic hunter-gatherers lived precarious lives dominated by the relentless search for food. Survival was a risky business. Groups endured only if their members learned to cooperate in securing food and shelter, to profit from technological innovations like the use of fire and toolmaking, and to teach their children the knowledge, social traditions, and beliefs that had helped make their society viable.

The Neolithic Revolution, c. 10,000–4000 B.C.

Domestication of plants and animals radically altered the relationship between people and their environment: it encouraged population growth, transformed hunter-gatherer society, and eventually made civilization possible. These revolutionary innovations in human life began about ten to twelve thousand years ago in the Neolithic period in the Near East.* This was one of the world's rare geographical regions where the right combination of wild plants and animals suitable for domestication coexisted—wheat, barley, peas, and lentils together with sheep, goats, swine, and cattle. Climatological scientists, who try to determine major ancient weather changes based on the pattern of plant material found in excavations and fossilized tree rings, think that about twelve thousand years ago the Near

---

*The meaning of the term *Near East*, like *Middle East*, has changed over time. Both terms originally reflected a European geographic point of view. During the nineteenth century, *Middle East* usually meant the area from Iran to Burma, especially the Indian subcontinent (then part of the British Empire); the *Near East* comprised the Balkan peninsula (today the territory of the formerly united Yugoslavia, Albania, Greece, Bulgaria, Romania, and the European portion of Turkey) and the eastern Mediterranean. The term *Far East* referred to the Asian lands that border the Pacific Ocean.

Today the term *Middle East* usually refers to the area encompassing the Arabic-speaking countries of the eastern Mediterranean region, Israel, Iran, Turkey, Cyprus, and much of North Africa. Ancient historians, by contrast, commonly use the term *ancient Near East* to designate Anatolia (often called Asia Minor, today occupied by the Asian portion of Turkey), Cyprus, the lands around the eastern end of the Mediterranean, the Arabian peninsula, Mesopotamia (the lands north of the Persian Gulf, today Iraq and Iran), and Egypt. Some historians exclude Egypt from this group on strict geographic grounds because it is in Africa, while the rest of the region lies in Asia. In this book we will observe the common usage of the term *Near East* to mean the lands of southwestern Asia and Egypt.

East's mountain regions became milder and wetter than they had been previously. This climate change promoted the growth of fields of wild grains in the foothills of the Fertile Crescent, an arc of relatively well-watered territory bounded by desert and mountain ranges that curved up from what is today the Jordan valley in Israel, through eastern Turkey, and down into the foothills and plains of Iraq and Iran (Map 1.1).

Since hunting had severely reduced the number of large game animals, people began to gather more and more wild grains, made more abundant by the better weather. The increased food supply in turn spurred population growth, a process also encouraged by the milder climate. The more hungry mouths born, the greater the corresponding need to exploit the food supply efficiently. After thousands of years of trial and error, people domesticated plants by sowing seeds from one crop to produce another, thus inventing agriculture. Because Neolithic women, as foragers for plant food, had the greater knowledge of plants, they probably played the major role in the invention of agriculture and the tools needed to practice it, such as digging sticks and grinding stones. In this early stage of farming, women did most agricultural labor, while men continued to hunt the dwindling supplies of large game animals. (See "New Sources, New Perspectives," page 10.)

During this same period, people also domesticated animals by taming, herding, and breeding them for food. The sheep was the first animal raised for meat, beginning about 8500 B.C. (People had tamed dogs much earlier but usually did not eat them.) Domesticated animals became widespread throughout the Near East by about 7000 B.C. Some people continued to move around to find grazing land for their animals, living as *pastoralists* but also cultivating small, temporary plots from time to time when they found a suitable area. Others, relying on permanent fields, tended small herds close to their farms. At this stage men, women, and children alike could be herders. They tended their herds as a source of meat, but they had not yet learned to exploit them for milk and wool.

Life in Settled Communities. To raise regular crops, people had to reside in a permanent location. Settling down marked a turning point in the relation between people and their environment as the

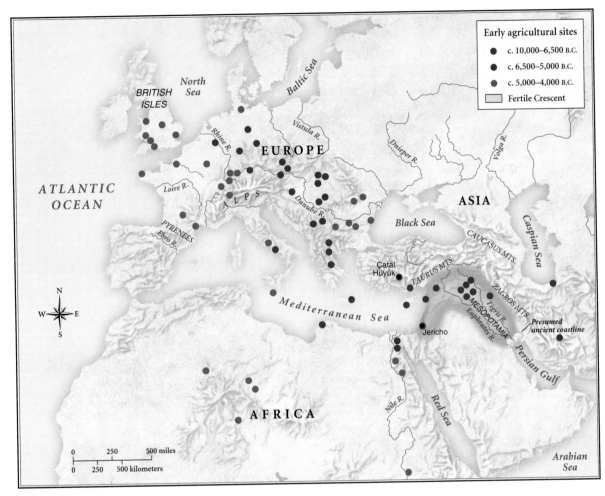

MAP 1.1 **The Development of Agriculture**
From about 10,000 to 8000 B.C., people first learned to plant seeds to grow nourishing plants in
the foothills of the semicircle of mountains that curved up and around from the eastern end of the
Mediterranean down to Mesopotamia, where reliable rainfall and moderate temperatures prevailed.
The invention of irrigation later allowed them to grow lush crops in the hot plains below, providing
resources that eventually spurred the emergence of the first large cities by about 4000 B.C.

knowledge of agriculture gradually spread. This process changed the landscape and relocated wildlife, as farmers cut down forests and diverted streams to grow crops. By 4000 B.C., people from the Fertile Crescent to the shores of the Atlantic Ocean practiced agriculture. They learned it from farmers slowly migrating westward from the Near East, who brought domesticated plants and animals into areas of Europe where they had not existed before. People's lives were never the same after they settled in agricultural communities. Now that farmers and herders produced a surplus of food to support

others, specialists in architecture, art, crafts, and trade could develop as never before, as could a more complex social hierarchy.

Many archaeological sites reveal the profound effects of the Neolithic Revolution on human life. One site currently under intensive study arose at Çatal Hüyük (pronounced "chatal hooyook") in what is today Turkey, northwest of the Fertile Crescent; there had been earlier large settlements in the Near East, for example at Jericho in Israel, but continuing excavation has made Çatal Hüyük especially instructive. By 6500 B.C., its inhabitants had built

Daily Bread, Damaged Bones, and Cracked Teeth

The invention of agriculture radically changed human life in many ways. Some of them historians have long recognized. Above all, by allowing Neolithic people to produce a more predictable and abundant supply of food, agricultural technology improved productivity, which in turn allowed the population to expand and eventually led to growing craft specialization and the development of cities and civilization.

Recent scientific research in biological anthropology and osteological archaeology (the study of ancient bones and teeth) has uncovered dramatic evidence of the physical price paid by the individuals who first made agriculture the basis of daily subsistence. Excavators at Tell Abu Hureyra in Syria have found bones and teeth from people living about 6000 B.C. The most startling evidence of what this new technology demanded appeared on the bones of their big toes, which osteologists point to the people's usual posture. The bones showed clear proof of extreme and prolonged dorsiflexion—bending the front of the foot up toward the shin. The ends of the bones became flatter and broader than normal through the constant pressure of being bent in the same position for long periods of time. The big toes exhibited the most obvious signs of this wear and tear because they are the main pressure point in dorsiflexion of the foot.

What activity could the people have been pursuing so doggedly that it deformed their bones? The only posture that creates such severe bending

Bones from Tel Abu Hureyra, Syria
These views of the first metatarsals (big toes) of a middle-aged man reveal severe arthritic changes to the big toe joint. Osteologists interpret this deformity as evidence of extreme and prolonged dorsification, or bending, of the foot.
Dr. Theya Molleson, Department of Paleontology, British Museum.

of the foot is kneeling for extended periods. Confirmation that kneeling was common came from several cases of arthritic changes in knee joints and lower spines seen in skeletons at the site; kneeling a lot causes this sort of arthritis.

But why were the people kneeling for so long? Other bone evidence offered the first clue to solving this mystery. The skeletons showed strongly developed attachment points for the deltoid muscle on the humerus (the bone in the upper arm) and prominent growth in the lower arm bones. These characteristics mean that the people had especially strong deltoids for pushing their shoulders back and forth and powerful biceps for rotating their forearms. Whatever they were doing made them use their shoulders and arms vigorously.

mud-brick houses nestled chockablock with one another to form a permanent farming community. They constructed their houses in the basically rectangular shape still common today, but they put no doors in their outer walls. Instead, they entered their homes by climbing down a ladder through a hole in the flat roof. Because this hole also served as a vent for smoke from the family fire, getting into a house at Çatal Hüyük could be a grimy business. But not having doors meant that the walls of the community's outermost homes could form a fortification wall.

The settlers at Çatal Hüyük produced their own food, growing wheat, barley, peas, and other

Sculpture from Giza, Egypt
In this statuette, a woman grinds grain into flour. The sculptor shows her rubbing her severely flexed right foot with the toes of her left foot, doubtless to ease the throbbing resulting from hours of kneeling.
The Oriental Institute, University of Chicago.

The skeletons' teeth provided the next clue. Everyone except the very youngest individuals had deeply worn and often fractured teeth. This damage indicated that they regularly chewed food full of rock dust, which probably resulted from grain being ground in rock bowls.

The final clue came from art. Later paintings and sculptures from the region show people, usually women, kneeling down to grind grain into flour by pushing and rotating a stone roller back and forth on heavy slabs of rock tilted away from them. This posture is exactly what would cause deformation of the big toes and arthritis in the knees and lower back. People grinding grain this way would have to push off hard from their toes with every stroke down the rock, as well as vigorously

use the muscles of their shoulders and forearms to apply pressure to the roller. In addition, the flour would pick up tiny particles from the wearing down of the stones used to grind it; bread made from it would have a sandy consistency hard on teeth. That Neolithic people worked so constantly and so hard at processing the grain they grew, no matter the toll on their bones and their teeth, shows how vital this supply of food had become to them.

At this Syrian site, everyone's bones—men's, women's, and even children's—show the same signs of the kneeling and grinding activity. Evidently the production of flour for bread was so consuming that no gender division of this labor was possible or desirable, as it seems to have become in later times. Regardless of who performed it, this new technology that literally provided the stuff of life for the community took its toll in individual pain and hardship.

QUESTIONS FOR DEBATE
1. Does the introduction of new technology to increase productivity and better human life usually involve new pains and stresses as well?
2. How do you decide what price—financial, physical, emotional—is worth paying for new technology? Who will make those decisions?

FURTHER READING
G. Hillman. "Traditional Husbandry and Processing of Archaic Cereals in Recent Times: The Operations, Products, and Equipment Which Might Feature in Sumerian Texts." *Bulletin on Sumerian Agriculture* 1 (1984): 114–52.

Theya Molleson. "Seed Preparation in the Mesolithic: The Osteological Evidence." *Antiquity* 63 (1989): 358.

A. M. T. Moore. "The Excavation of Tell Abu Hureyra in Syria: A Preliminary Report." *Proceedings of the Prehistoric Society* 41 (1975): 50–71.

vegetables. They diverted water from a nearby river to irrigate their fields, a technology that would be essential to the spread of civilization throughout the Near East. Domesticated cattle provided their main supply of meat and, by this time, hides and milk. (Sheep and goats were more common elsewhere in the Near East.) Wall paintings of hunting scenes

show that men still pursued game. Unlike hunter-gatherers, however, these villagers no longer depended exclusively on the perilous luck of the hunt to acquire meat and leather. At its height, the population of Çatal Hüyük probably reached six thousand, until a volcano destroyed the settlement about a thousand years after its foundation.

Trade was crucial in the economy of Neolithic settlements because it brought in desirable resources not available locally, such as seashells to wear as ornaments and special flint to shape into ceremonial daggers. The villagers at Çatal Hüyük, for example, acquired these prized materials by trading obsidian, a local volcanic glass whose glossy luster and capacity to hold a sharp edge made it valuable. The trade that villagers negotiated with other settlements meant that their world was not made up of isolated communities. On the contrary, they already had started down the path of economic interconnection among far-flung communities—a pattern familiar in our world today.

Neolithic Society. Because Neolithic farmers produced enough food to support the village without everyone having to work in the fields or herd cattle, other people could work full-time at new occupations. Specialized crafts workers made tools, containers, and ornaments using traditional materials—wood, bone, hide, and stone—but they also started working with the material of the future: metal. Metalworkers at Çatal Hüyük, for example, knew how to smelt copper in high-temperature furnaces. Other workers in the settlement specialized in weaving textiles; the scraps of cloth discovered there are the oldest examples of this craft yet found. Like other early technological innovations, metallurgy and the production of cloth developed independently in many other places in the Near East.

The Neolithic Revolution created a new division of labor by gender, which increased social hierarchy. Men began to dominate agriculture, many crafts, and long-distance trade, while women took up new tasks at home. Sometime after about 4000 B.C., farmers started using wooden plows pulled by oxen to cultivate rough land. Women continued to contribute to farming by digging with hoes and sticks, but men did the plowing because it required great physical strength. They also began to take over herding because animals were being tended in larger groups that had to be led farther and farther from the base settlement to find enough new grazing land. Men, free from having to bear and nurse children, took on this time-consuming task. The responsibility for new domestic tasks fell to women and older children. For example, they now turned milk into cheese and yogurt and made their families' clothing by spinning and weaving wool.

This division of labor by gender arose as an efficient response to the conditions and technologies of the time. Men's physical strength and mobility allowed them to provide the group with valuable items that women had less opportunity to secure, above all meat and trade goods; in this way, men's tasks gained greater prestige than women's. Hierarchical societies dominated by men would characterize Western history from this time forward.

❖ Mesopotamia, Home of the First Civilization, c. 4000–1000 B.C.

Historians traditionally define the features of civilization as cities with dense populations and large buildings for community purposes, formal political systems, diverse crafts, and the knowledge of writing. (See "Terms of History," page 14.) By this definition, the world's first civilization arose about 4000–3000 B.C. in Mesopotamia, the region between the Euphrates and Tigris Rivers (today southern Iraq), because it is there that archaeologists find the earliest settlements that they regard as cities. The residents of early Mesopotamian cities built great monuments to honor their gods as their divine masters, lived in a hierarchical society with slaves at the bottom and kings at the top, and invented writing to keep track of economic transactions and record their stories and beliefs. The rulers of these cities constantly battled one another for glory, territory, and, especially, access to metal ores.

The invention of bronze, an alloy of copper and tin, in this period has led historians to label it the Bronze Age (approximately 4000–1000 B.C.). The drive to acquire metals from distant sources helped create the first empire, a political unit that includes a number of formerly independent territories or peoples now ruled by a single sovereign leader. The ownership of objects produced by the new technology of metallurgy increased the division in society between men and women and rich and poor. Long-distance commerce grew to satisfy people's desire for goods and materials not available in their homelands, while rulers created systems of law to show the gods that they were promoting justice in their increasingly complex societies and to govern their subjects.

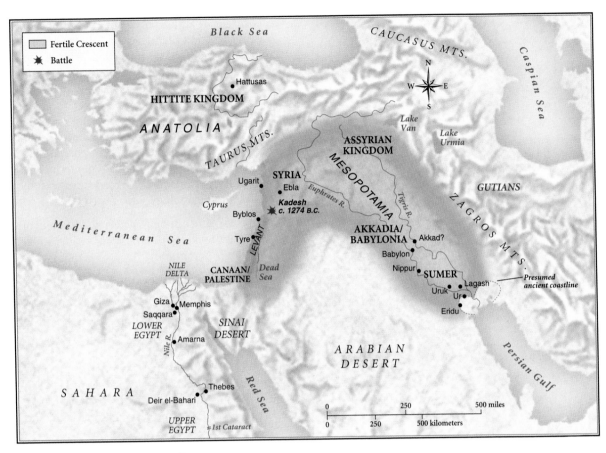

MAP 1.2 The Ancient Near East

The large region we call the ancient Near East encompassed a variety of landscapes, climates, peoples, and languages; monarchy was the usual form of government. Trade by land and sea for natural resources, especially metals, kept the peoples of the region in constant contact with one another, as did the wars of conquest that the region's kings regularly launched.

Cities and Society, c. 4000–2350 B.C.

The first cities and thus the first civilization emerged in Mesopotamia because its inhabitants figured out how to raise crops on the fertile but dry land between and around the Tigris and Euphrates Rivers (Map 1.2). Agriculture had begun in the well-watered hills of the Fertile Crescent, but they offered too little habitable land to support the growth of cities. The plains along the rivers were huge, but they presented serious challenges to farmers: little rain fell, temperatures soared to 120 degrees Fahrenheit, and devastating floods occurred unpredictably. Mesopotamians turned this difficult environment into lush farmland by irrigating the plains with water from the rivers. Intricate canal systems that required constant maintenance turned the desert green with agriculture and helped limit flooding. The surpluses of food produced by Mesopotamian farmers allowed the population to swell, the number of crafts producers to increase rapidly, and cities to emerge.

The necessity of maintaining the canals promoted central organization in Mesopotamian cities, which controlled agricultural land outside their fortification walls and built great temples inside them. This arrangement—an urban center exercising political and economic control over the countryside around it—is called a *city-state*. Mesopotamian city-states were independent communities that competed for land and resources. Travelers from one to another would first come to the irrigated

Civilization

Our term *civilization* is derived from the Latin word *civilis*. For ancient Romans, *civilis* meant "suitable for a private citizen" and "behaving like an ordinary, unpretentious person." To be "un-*civilis*" was to behave in a showy and arrogant way that suggested you thought yourself superior to others.

It is ironic, then, that the modern term *civilization* was developed to express the judgment that becoming civilized meant achieving a superior way of life. Consider, for example, these definitions from one of today's most widely used reference works, *The Random House Webster's College Dictionary*.[1]

---

[1]*The Random House Webster's College Dictionary.* 2nd ed. (New York, 1997), 240.

civilization: 1. an advanced state of human society, in which a high level of culture, science, and government has been reached. 2. those people or nations that have reached such a state. 3. any type of culture, society, etc. of a specific place, time, or group: *Greek civilization.* 4. the act or process of civilizing or being civilized. 5. cultural and intellectual refinement. 6. cities or populated areas in general, as opposed to unpopulated or wilderness areas. 7. modern comforts and conveniences, as made possible by science and technology.

civilize: to bring out of a savage, uneducated, or rude state; make civil; enlighten; refine: *Rome civilized the barbarians.*

civilized: 1. having an advanced or humane culture, society, etc. 2. polite, well-bred; redefined.

The common thread in almost all these entries is the sense that *civilization* implies an "advanced," "refined" way of life compared to a "savage" or "rude" way. Ancient peoples were perfectly comfortable making this sort of comparison between themselves and others whom they saw as crude; the urban dwellers of the Near East, Greece, and

green fields on the outskirts of the city, the villages housing agricultural workers, and then the city's fortress walls and high buildings in the distance. Outside the entrance, travelers would find a bustling center of trade, either a harbor on the river or a marketplace on the overland routes leading to the city. Inside the walls, their eyes would be drawn to the royal family's palace and, above all, to the immense temples of the gods.

Mesopotamian Religion and Mythology. Mesopotamians believed that their survival in a harsh and unpredictable environment depended on the goodwill of the gods, whom people had to please with sacrifices, rituals, and magnificent temples. Each city-state honored a particular major deity as its special protector, but, as polytheists, Mesopotamians worshiped multiple gods, who were

thought to have power in different areas affecting human existence, such as the weather, war, and fertility. The more critical a divinity's sphere of influence on people, the more important was the god.

To be close to the gods, Mesopotamian city dwellers built great ziggurats (temple towers), which soared up to ten stories high and dominated the urban skyline. Realizing that human beings could not control nature, Mesopotamians viewed the gods as their absolute masters, to whom they owed total devotion. They believed their deities looked like human beings and had human emotions, especially anger. After all, their mythology taught that divine rage had led to the creation of the world. If human beings offended them, Mesopotamian divinities such as Enlil, god of the sky, and Inanna (also called Ishtar), goddess of love and war, would punish worshipers by causing disasters, like floods and famine.

Rome were particularly prone to apply this judgment to those who did not build cities. Much later, this notion of superiority became especially prominent in European thought after voyagers to the New World and colonial settlers reported on what they saw as the "savage" or "barbarous" life of the peoples they called Indians. Because Europeans of the times saw Indian life as lacking discipline, government, and, above all, Christianity, it seemed to them to be primitive and raw and therefore an inversion of their idea of civilized life.

Therefore, the term *civilization* entered the English language in a "sense opposed to *barbarity*," as James Boswell in 1772 advised Samuel Johnson to define it in the latter's famous and influential *Dictionary of the English Language*. It became common to compare "the lower races of man" with "civilized peoples."[2] The word's built-in sense of comparative superiority became so accepted that it could even be used to express this

notion in nonhuman contexts, such as in the startling comparison ". . . some communities of ants are more advanced in civilization than others."[3]

Historians in recent times have been reluctant to confront explicitly the difficult issues that the term raises. Tellingly, there is no mention of the topic in the standard guide to scholarly work issued by the major professional organization for historians.[4]

Ultimately, the failure to consider what the term should mean can lead to its being used without much definitional content at all, as in No. 3 under *civilization*. Does the term have any deep meaning if it can be defined as "any type of culture, society, etc. of a specific place, time, or group"? This empty definition reveals that giving meaning to the crucial term *civilization* and investigating the issues raised in the process still present daunting challenges to all students of history.

---

[2]Sir John Lubbock, *The Origin of Civilisation and The Primitive Condition of Man. Mental and Social Condition of Savages.* 5th ed. (New York, 1889), 1–2.

[3]Sir John Lubbock, *On the Origin and Metamorphoses of Insects.* 2nd ed. (London, 1874), 13.

[4]*The American Historical Association's Guide to Historical Literature.* 3rd ed. (New York, 1995).

Mythical stories such as the *Epic of Creation* emphasized the gods' awesome power and the limits of human control over the circumstances of life. The *Epic of Gilgamesh,* another long poem known from many versions, related the adventures of the hero Gilgamesh, who sought to cheat death and achieve immortality. As king of the city of Uruk, he forced the city's young men to construct a temple and fortification wall and all the young women to sleep with him. When the distressed inhabitants implored the mother of the gods, Aruru, to grant them a rival to Gilgamesh, she created a man of nature, Enkidu, "hairy all over . . . dressed as cattle are." A week of sex with a prostitute tamed this brute, preparing him for civilization: "Enkidu was weaker; he ran slower than before. But he had gained judgment, was wiser." After wrestling to a draw, he and Gilgamesh became friends and set out to conquer

Humbaba (or Huwawa), the ugly giant of the Pine Forest. The two comrades also defeated the Bull of Heaven, but the gods doomed Enkidu to die not long after this moment of triumph. In despair over human frailty, Gilgamesh tried to find the secret of immortality, only to have his quest foiled by a thieving snake. He subsequently realized that immortality for human beings comes only from the fame generated by their achievements, above all building a great city such as Uruk, which encompassed "three square miles and its open ground." Only memory and gods live forever, he found.

A late version of the *Epic of Gilgamesh* included a description of a huge flood that covered the earth, recalling the devastating inundations that often struck Mesopotamia. When the gods sent the flood, they warned one man, Utnapishtim, of the impending disaster, telling him to build a boat. He

The Ziggurat of Ur in Sumer
King Ur-Nammu and his son Shulgi built this massive temple as an architectural marvel for their city of Ur (in what is today southern Iraq) in the early twenty-first century B.C. It had three massive terraces, one above another and connected by stairways, constructed with a mud-brick core covered with a skin of baked brick, glued together with tar. Its walls were more than seven feet thick to sustain its enormous weight. Its total height is uncertain, but the first terrace alone soared some forty-five feet above the ground.
Hirmer Fotoarchiv.

loaded his vessel with his relatives, artisans, possessions, domesticated and wild animals, and "everything there was." After a week of torrential rains, he and his passengers disembarked to repopulate and rebuild the earth. This story recalled the frequently devastating floods of the Tigris and Euphrates Rivers and foreshadowed the later biblical account of the flood and the story of Noah's ark. The themes of Mesopotamian mythology, which lived on in poetry and song, also powerfully influenced the mythology of distant peoples, most notably the Greeks in later times.

Since religion meant so much to Mesopotamians, the priest or priestess of a city's chief deity enjoyed extremely high status. Perhaps the most important duty of Mesopotamian priests was to discover the will of the gods by divination. To perform this function, they studied natural signs by tracking the patterns of the stars, interpreting dreams, and cutting open animals to examine their organs for deformities signaling trouble ahead. These inspections helped the people decide when and how to please their gods, whether by giving them wondrous gifts placed in their sanctuaries or by celebrating festivals in their honor. During the New Year holiday, for example, the reenactment of the story of the marriage of the goddess Inanna and the god Dumuzi was believed to ensure successful reproduction by the city's residents for the coming year.

The Cities of Sumer. The people of Sumer, the name for southern Mesopotamia, built the earliest cities. Unlike their neighbors, the Sumerians spoke a tongue that was not a member of the Semitic family of languages; its origins are unknown. By 3000 B.C., they had created sizable walled cities, such as Uruk, Eridu, and Ur, in twelve city-states, which fought repeated wars over territory. By about 2500 B.C., the Sumerian cities had grown to twenty thousand residents or more. The mud-brick houses consisted of rooms grouped around an open court. Most people lived in only one or two rooms, but the wealthy constructed two-story dwellings that had a dozen or more rooms. Rich and poor alike suffered the ill effects of a domestic water supply often contaminated by sewage because no system of waste disposal existed; pigs and dogs scavenged in the streets and areas where garbage was unceremoniously dumped.

The prosperity of Sumerian cities came from agriculture and trade. They constantly bartered grain, vegetable oil, woolens, and leather with one another and with foreign regions, from which they acquired natural resources not found in Sumer, such as metals, timber, and precious stones. Sumerian traders traveled as far east as India, sailing for weeks to reach that distant land, where the Indus civilization's large cities emerged about five hundred years after Sumer's. Technological innovation also strengthened the early Mesopotamian economy, especially around 3000 B.C. when Sumerians invented the wheel in a form sturdy enough to be used on carts for transport. Temples predominated in the Sumerian economy because they controlled large farms and gangs of laborers, whose work supported the ziggurats and their religious activities. Priests and priestesses supervised the temples' considerable property and economic activity. Some private households also amassed significant economic power by working large fields.

Slaves and Kings in Sumer. Slavery existed in many forms in the ancient Near East, and no single description can cover all the social and legal consequences. Both temples and private individuals could own slaves. People lost their freedom by being captured in war, by being born to slaves, by voluntarily selling themselves or their children to escape starvation, or by being sold by their creditors to satisfy debts. Foreigners enslaved as captives in war or by raiding parties were considered inferior to citizens who fell into slavery to pay off debts. Children whose parents dedicated them as servants to the gods, although counted as slaves, could rise to prominent positions in the temple administrations. In general, however, slavery was a state of near-total dependency on other people and of legal exclusion from normal social relations; slaves usually worked without compensation and lacked almost all legal rights. Although slaves sometimes formed relationships with free persons and frequently married each other and had families, they had no guarantee that their family members would not be sold. They could be bought, sold, beaten, or even killed by their masters because they counted as property, not people. Apparently, people accepted slavery as a fact of nature, and there is no evidence of any sentiment for abolishing it.

Slaves worked in domestic service, craft production, and farming, but their economic significance compared with that of free workers in early Mesopotamia is still disputed. Most state labor

seems to have been performed by free persons who paid their taxes with labor rather than with money (which consisted of measured amounts of food or precious metal; coins were not invented until about 700 B.C. in Anatolia). Gaining freedom was only a faint possibility for most slaves, but under certain conditions they could be set free: masters' wills could liberate them, or they could purchase their freedom from the earnings they could sometimes accumulate.

At the opposite end of the social hierarchy from slaves were the kings. Mesopotamians probably had kings heading their cities from the first. A king formed a council of older men as his advisers and acknowledged the gods as his ruler—a notion that made the state a theocracy (government by gods) and gave the priests and priestesses some influence in political matters. The king's supreme responsibility was to defend his people against the anger of the gods and attacks from rival cities eager to seize their riches and their irrigated land. In return, he extracted surpluses from the working population to support his family, court, palace, army, and officials. If the surpluses came in regularly, the king mostly left the people alone to live their daily lives.

As befitted his status atop the hierarchy, a Sumerian king and his family lived in an elaborate palace that rivaled the scale of the great temples. The palace served as the administrative center for the city and its surrounding territory, and it also stored the rulers' enormous wealth. A significant portion of the community's economic surplus was dedicated to displaying the royal family's superior status. Archaeological excavation of the immense royal cemetery in Ur, for example, has revealed the dazzling extent of the rulers' riches—spectacular possessions crafted in gold, silver, and precious stones. These graves also yielded grislier evidence of the exalted status of the king and queen: the bodies of the servants sacrificed to serve their royal masters after death.

The spectacle of wealth and power that characterized Sumerian kingship reveals how great the gap was between the upper and lower ranks of Sumerian society. Moreover, patriarchy—domination by men in political, social, and economic life—was already established in these first cities. Although a Sumerian queen was respected because she was the wife of the king and the mother of the royal children, the king held the supreme power.

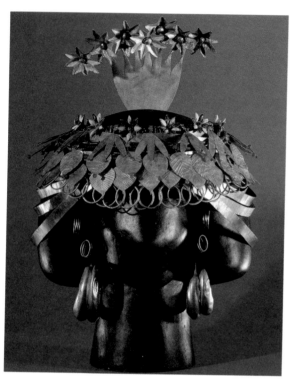

Royal Grave Goods from Ur in Sumer
The royal family in Ur amassed tremendous riches, to judge from the expensive goods that they put into their graves. Royal women wore spectacular jewelry of gold and the deep-blue stone lapis lazuli. One tomb alone yielded the bodies of sixty-eight women wearing jewelry including this complex head-dress; most of them were presumably the attendants of the queen and had been sacrificed to serve her in the afterlife.
University of Pennsylvania Museum, Philadephia.

A Cuneiform Letter in Its Envelope
Written about 1900 B.C., this cuneiform text records a merchant's complaint that a shipment of copper contained less metal than he had expected. His letter, impressed on a clay tablet several inches long, was enclosed in an outer clay shell, which was then marked with the sender's private seal. This envelope protected the inner text from tampering or breakage.
British Museum.

The Invention of Writing. As the populations of their cities grew and economic transactions became more complicated, the Sumerians invented writing to do accounting. Before writing, people drew small pictures on clay tablets to represent objects. At first, these pictographs symbolized concrete objects only, such as a cow. Eventually, nonpictorial symbols and marks were added to the pictographs to stand for the sounds of spoken language. Sumerian writing was not an alphabet, in which a symbol represents the sound of a single letter, but a mixed system of phonetic symbols and pictographs that represented the sounds of entire syllables and often entire words.

The Sumerians' fully developed script is now called *cuneiform* (from *cuneus*, Latin for "wedge") because it used wedge-shaped marks impressed into

clay tablets to record spoken language (Figure 1.1). Other peoples in this region subsequently adopted cuneiform to write their own, different languages. For a long time, writing was largely a professional skill mastered by only a few men and women, known as scribes, and was used mostly in accounting. Schools sprang up to teach the new technology to aspiring scribes, who could find jobs writing down official records. Kings, priests, and wealthy landowners could thus control their workers even more strictly because they could keep precise track of who had paid, who still owed, and how much.

Before long, writing proved useful for purposes other than accounting. The scribal schools extended their curriculum to cover specialized knowledge in nature lore, mathematics, and foreign languages.

Writing also created a new way to hand down stories and beliefs, previously preserved only in memory and speech. Written literature provided a powerful new tool for passing on a culture's traditions to later generations. The world's oldest written poetry by a known author was composed by Enheduanna in the twenty-third century B.C. She was a priestess, prophetess, and princess, the daughter of King Sargon of the city of Akkad. Her poetry, written in Sumerian, praised the awesome power of the life-giving goddess of love, Inanna: "the great gods scattered from you like fluttering bats, unable to face your intimidating gaze . . . knowing and wise queen of all the lands, who makes all creatures and people multiply." Later princesses, who wrote love songs, lullabies, dirges, and prayers, continued the Mesopotamian tradition of royal women as authors and composers.

Metals and the Akkadian Empire, c. 2350–2200 B.C.

While cities were emerging in Mesopotamia, metalworkers in the Near East and around the Mediterranean world developed metallurgical technology to work with lead, silver, gold, and bronze. These technological innovations indirectly fueled the creation of the world's first empire, in Akkadia.

Devising innovative ways to smelt ore and to make metal alloys at high temperatures, Bronze Age smiths fashioned new luxury goods and better tools for agriculture, construction, and, above all, weapons. Pure copper, which had been available for some time, had offered few advantages over stone because it easily lost its shape and edge; bronze, by contrast, a copper-tin alloy hard enough to hold a razor edge, enabled smiths to produce durable and deadly metal daggers, swords, and spearheads. Bronze weaponry soon became standard equipment for every prosperous man.

Rich men found a new way to display their wealth and status by commissioning metalworkers to decorate their swords and daggers with lavish and expensive engravings and inlays, as on costly guns today. Metal weapons also underscored the differences between men and women in society, because they signified the masculine roles of hunter and warrior that had emerged long ago in the division of labor among hunter-gatherers. The development of metallurgy had other social consequences as well. People now expected to acquire wealth not just in foodstuffs, animals, or land, but in metals. Their desire to accumulate wealth and to possess status symbols stimulated demand for metals and for the skilled workers who could create lavishly adorned weapons for men and exquisitely crafted jewelry

c. 3100 B.C.	c. 3000 B.C.	c. 2500 B.C.	c. 2100 B.C.	c. 700 B.C. (Neo-Assyrian)	Sumerian reading + meaning
					SAG Head
					NINDA bread
					GU$_7$ eat
					AB$_2$ cow
					APIN plough
					SUHUR carp

FIGURE 1.1 Cuneiform Writing

The earliest known form of writing developed in different locations in Mesopotamia in the late 3000s B.C. when meaning and sound were associated with signs such as these. The scribes who mastered the system used sticks or reeds to press dense rows of small wedge-shaped marks into damp clay tablets or chisels to engrave them on stone. Cuneiform was used for at least fifteen Near Eastern languages and continued to be written for three thousand years.

made from exotic materials for both women and men. Growing numbers of crafts workers swelled the size of Bronze Age cities.

Mesopotamian monarchs craved a reliable supply of metals, a desire that, as part of their constant quest for glory, led to empire. If a king lacked deposits of ore in his territory, he could acquire it in two ways: trade or conquest. Ambition induced rulers to take rather than to trade, and they started wars to capture territory where ore mines could be found. The first empire began about 2350 B.C., when Sargon, king of the city of Akkad, launched invasions far to the north and south of his homeland in mid-Mesopotamia. His violent campaigns overcame Sumer and the regions all the way westward to the Mediterranean Sea. Since Akkadians expressed their ideas about their own history in poetry and believed that the gods determined their fate, it was particularly fitting that a poet of about 2000 B.C. credited Sargon's success to the favor of the god Enlil: "to Sargon the king of Akkad, from below to above, Enlil had given him lordship and kingship."

The Akkadian Empire, c. 2350–2200 B.C.

Sargon's energetic grandson Naram-Sin continued the family tradition of conquering distant places. By 2250 B.C., he had severely damaged Ebla, a large city whose site has only recently been discovered in modern Syria, more than five hundred miles from Naram-Sin's home base in Mesopotamia. Archaeologists have unearthed many cuneiform tablets at Ebla, some of them in more than one language. These discoveries suggest that Ebla thrived as an early center for learning.

Indirectly, the process of building an empire by force helped extend Mesopotamian literature and art throughout the Near East. Although the Akkadians, like many other peoples of the Near East, spoke what we call a Semitic language unrelated to Sumerian, in the process of conquest they took over most of the characteristics of Sumerian religion, literature, and culture. The other peoples whom the Akkadians overran were then exposed to Sumerian beliefs and traditions, which they in turn

adapted to suit their own purposes. In this way, war promoted cultural interaction between peoples, although that was not the goal of the Akkadian empire builders.

The Akkadian empire created by the drive to acquire metals failed to last. Attacks from neighboring hill peoples, the Gutians, ended Akkadian dominance in Sumer around 2200 B.C. The poet who had explained Sargon's empire as a benefit of divine favor gave an equally theological explanation for the vast devastation inflicted on the Akkadian empire by the Gutians. King Naram-Sin, the poet explained, grew enraged at the god Enlil when his capital's prosperity waned. Crazed by anger, he reduced Enlil's main temple in Nippur to "dust like a mountain mined for silver." In retribution, Enlil punished the Akkadians by sending the fierce Gutians swooping down from their "land that rejects outside control, with the intelligence of human beings but with the form and stumbling words of a dog." This religious explanation for military defeat reflected the deep-seated Mesopotamian belief that human life remained extremely precarious in the face of divine power: no matter how large its populations or how high its cities' walls, the world's earliest empire could not escape a divinely ordained fate.

Mesopotamian Legacies, c. 2200–1000 B.C.

Two kingdoms, Assyria and Babylonia, developed in the second millennium B.C. to fill the void of power left by the fall of the Akkadian empire. Although they became militarily powerful for a time, their lasting importance for Western civilization would be in their innovations in commerce, law, and learning. These achievements are all the more remarkable because they came during a long period of grave difficulties for Mesopotamian cities caused by agricultural pollution. Intensive irrigation had promoted centralized government and cities with large populations, but over time irrigation had the unintended consequence of increasing the salt level of the soil so much that eventually crop yields fell. The resulting economic stress undermined the political stability of Mesopotamia for centuries, beginning about 2000 B.C. Even in the face of these problems, Assyria and Babylonia made innovations that had lasting effects.

The Assyrians and Long-Distance Commerce.
The Assyrians, a Semitic people descended from the Akkadians, lived in northern Mesopotamia, between the peoples of Mesopotamia and those of Anatolia to the west. They took advantage of this geography to build an independent kingdom whose prosperity depended on long-distance trade. The city-states of Anatolia had become the principal source of wood, copper, silver, and gold for the city-states of Mesopotamia. By acting as middlemen in the trade between Anatolia and Mesopotamia, the Assyrians became the leading merchants of the Near East. Adapting to their country's lack of natural resources, the Assyrians produced woolen textiles to export to Anatolia in exchange for its raw materials, which they in turn sold to the rest of Mesopotamia.

Previous Mesopotamian societies had operated mainly under state monopolies, which redistributed goods between people according to the king's orders, rather than through buying and selling, and controlled trade in the king's interest. This redistributive economic system never totally disappeared in Mesopotamia, but by 1900 B.C. the Assyrian kings were allowing private individuals to transact large commercial deals on their own initiative. Assyrian investors provided funds to traders to purchase an export cargo of cloth. The traders then formed donkey caravans to travel the hundreds of rocky and dangerous miles to Anatolia, where, if they survived the journey, they could make huge profits to be split with their investors. Regulators existed to deal with trader fraud and losses in transit. The financial arrangements motivated the participants to maximize profits as a reward for the risk of the business.

Hammurabi of Babylon and Written Law. The expansion of private commerce and property ownership in Mesopotamia created a pressing need to guarantee fairness and reliability in contracts and other business agreements. It was the king's sacred duty to make divine justice known to his subjects by rendering judgments in all sorts of cases, from commercial disputes to crime. Once written down, the record of the king's decisions amounted to what historians today call a "law code," even though the Mesopotamians did not use that term. King Hammurabi (r. c. 1792–1750 B.C.) of Babylon, a great city on the Euphrates River, instituted the most famous set of written Mesopotamian laws.

Like his Mesopotamian predecessors in law-making, Hammurabi proclaimed that his goal was to promote "the principles of truth and equity" and to protect the less powerful members of society from exploitation. His code legally divided society into three categories: free persons, commoners, and slaves. We do not know what made the first two categories different, but they corresponded to a social hierarchy. An attacker who caused a pregnant woman of the free class to miscarry, for example, paid twice the fine levied for the same offense against a woman in the commoner class. In the case of physical injury between social equals, the code specified "an eye for an eye" (an expression still used today). But a member of the free class who killed a commoner was not executed, only fined.

Most of the laws concerned the king's interests as a property owner who leased innumerable tracts of land to tenants in return for rent or services. The laws imposed severe penalties for offenses against property, including mutilation or a gruesome death for crimes as varied as theft, wrongful sales, and careless construction. Women had

The Kingdom of Assyria, c. 1900 B.C.

limited legal rights in this patriarchal society, but they could make business contracts and appear in court. A wife could divorce her husband for cruelty; a husband could divorce his wife for any reason. The inequality of the divorce laws was tempered in practice, however, because a woman could recover the property she had brought to her marriage, a considerable disincentive for a man to end his marriage.

Hammurabi's laws publicized a royal ideal; they did not necessarily reflect everyday reality. Indeed, Babylonian documents show that legal penalties were often less severe than the code specified. The people themselves assembled in courts to determine most cases by their own judgments. Why, then, did Hammurabi have his laws written down? He announces his reasons at the beginning and end of his code: to show Shamash, the Babylonian sun god and god of justice, that he had fulfilled the social responsibility imposed on him as a divinely installed monarch—to ensure justice and the moral and material welfare of his people: "So that the powerful may not oppress the powerless, to provide justice for the orphan and the widow . . . let the victim of injustice see the law which applies to him, let his heart be put at ease." The king's moral responsibility for his society's welfare corresponded to the strictly hierarchical and religious vision of society accepted by all Mesopotamian peoples.

City Life and Learning.   The situations and conflicts covered by Hammurabi's laws illuminate many aspects of the lives of city dwellers in Mesopotamia's Bronze Age kingdoms. For example, crimes of burglary and assault apparently plagued urban residents. Marriages were arranged by the groom and the bride's father, who sealed the agreement with a legal contract. The detailed laws on surgery in the code of Hammurabi make clear that doctors practiced in the cities. Because people believed that angry gods or evil spirits caused serious diseases, Mesopotamian medicine included magic as well as treatment with potions and diet. A doctor might prescribe an incantation as part of his therapy. Magicians or exorcists offered medical treatment that depended primarily on spells and on interpreting signs, such as the patient's dreams or hallucinations.

Archaeological excavations and written documents supplement the information on urban life derived from the code. Cities had many taverns and wine shops, often run by women proprietors, attesting to the city dwellers' enjoyment of alcoholic drinks and a convivial atmosphere. Contaminated drinking water caused many illnesses because sewage disposal was rudimentary. Relief from the odors and crowding of the streets could be found in the open spaces set aside for city parks. The oldest known map in the world, an inscribed clay tablet showing the outlines of the Babylonian city of Nippur about 1500 B.C., indicates a substantial area designated for this purpose.

Creating maps required sophisticated techniques of measurement and knowledge of spatial relationships. Mesopotamian achievements in mathematics and astronomy had a profound effect that endures to this day. Mathematicians knew how to employ algebraic processes to solve complex problems, and they could derive the roots of numbers. They invented place-value notation for numbers. For example, in a decimal system, the position of a numeral in a list shows whether it indicates ones, tens, hundreds, and so on. We have also inherited from Mesopotamia the system of reckoning based on sixty, still used in the division of hours and minutes and degrees of a circle. Mesopotamian expertise in recording the paths of the stars and planets probably arose from the desire to make predictions about the future, based on the astrological belief that the movement of celestial bodies directly affects human life. Astrology never lost its popularity in Mesopotamia, and the charts and tables compiled by Mesopotamian stargazers laid the basis for later advances in astronomical knowledge.

❖ Civilization in Ancient Egypt and the Levant, c. 3100–1000 B.C.

Africa was home to the second great civilization to shape the West—Egypt, which was located close enough to Mesopotamia to learn from its peoples but geographically protected enough to develop its own distinct culture. Egyptians created a wealthy, profoundly religious, and strongly traditional civilization ruled by kings. Unlike Mesopotamia, Egypt became a united state, whose prosperity and stability depended on the king's success in maintaining strong central authority. The Egyptians' deep concern for the immortality of their souls and the afterlife motivated the construction of some of the most imposing tombs in history, the pyramids, while their architecture and art inspired later Mediterranean peoples, especially the Greeks.

The civilization of the Levant* (the lands along the eastern coast of the Mediterranean) never rivaled the splendor of Egypt, but it nonetheless transmitted lasting legacies to Western civilization, among them the first alphabet and the religion of the Hebrews (or Israelites). Their monotheism, Judaism, took a long time to develop and reflected influences from their polytheistic neighbors in Canaan (ancient Palestine), but it initiated the most important religious movements in Western history.

---

*The name *Levant*, French for "rising (sun)"—that is, the East—reflects the European perspective on the area's location.

The Old Kingdom in Egypt, c. 2686–2181 B.C.

Geography was kind to the Egyptians: the Nile River irrigated their farms, the deserts beyond their rich fields yielded metal ores and protected them from invasion, their Mediterranean ports supported seaborne commerce, and their southern neighbors in Africa offered trade and cultural interaction. The first large-scale Egyptian state emerged about 3100–3000 B.C. when King Menes united the previously separate territories of Upper (southern) Egypt and Lower (northern) Egypt. (*Upper* and *Lower* derive from the direction of the Nile River, which begins south of Egypt and flows northward to the Mediterranean.) By c. 2686 B.C., his successors had forged a strong, centralized state, known as the Old Kingdom, which lasted until c. 2181 B.C. (Map 1.3).*

Menes's unification created a habitable territory resembling a long green ribbon, zigzagging seven hundred miles southward from the Mediterranean Sea along the Nile. Lush agricultural fields extending several miles away from the river's banks formed this fertile strip. Under normal weather conditions, the Nile created Egypt's fertility by overflowing its channel for at least several weeks each year, when melting snow from the mountains of central Africa swelled its volume of water. This annual flood enriched the soil with nutrients from the river's silt and prevented the accumulation of harmful deposits of mineral salts. Unlike the random and catastrophic floods of the rivers of Mesopotamia, the flooding of the Nile recurred at the same season and benefited its land. Trouble came from the Nile only if dry weather in the mountains kept its flood from occurring and therefore reduced the year's crops to dust.

Deserts east and west of the river protected Egypt from attack by land, except through the Nile's delta at its mouth and its valley on the

southern frontier with Nubia. The surpluses that a multitude of hardworking farmers produced in the lush Nile valley made Egypt prosperous. Date palms, vegetables, grasses for pasturing animals, and grain grew in abundance. From their ample supplies of grain the Egyptians made bread and beer, a staple beverage.

Egypt's population included a diversity of people, whose skin color ranged from light to very dark. A significant proportion of ancient Egyptians would be regarded as black by modern racial classification,

MAP 1.3 Ancient Egypt
The Nile River, closely embraced by arid deserts, provided Egyptians with water to irrigate their fields and a highway for traveling north to the Mediterranean Sea and south to Nubia. The only easy land route into and out of Egypt lay through the northern Sinai peninsula into the coastal area of the Levant; Egyptian kings therefore always fought to control these areas to secure the safety of their land.

*Scholars still dispute the precise dates for ancient Egyptian history because the evidence is often contradictory, even when related to ancient observations of celestial events. For explanations of the problem, see A. Bernard Knapp, *The History and Culture of Ancient Western Asia and Egypt*, 9–10, and Trevor Bryce, *The Kingdom of the Hittites*, 408–15. The approximate chronology given here is simply one of several reasonable schemes; it can be found conveniently tabulated in T. G. H. James, *An Introduction to Ancient Egypt* (1979), 263–66.

which ancient people did not observe. The heated modern controversy over whether Egyptians were people of color is therefore anachronistic; if asked, ancient Egyptians would presumably have answered that they were an African population identifying themselves by geography, language, religion, and traditions. Later peoples, especially the Greeks, admired Egyptian civilization for its great antiquity and piety; there is merit to the modern accusation that some nineteenth-century historians minimized the Egyptian contribution to Western civilization, but it is important to remember that ancient peoples did not.

At the origins of their civilization, Egyptians learned from other peoples, such as the Mesopotamians and, especially, their southern African neighbors the Nubians. For example, the Egyptians may have originally learned the technology of writing from the Sumerians, but they developed their own scripts rather than using cuneiform. To write formal and official texts they used an ornate pictographic script known as *hieroglyphs* (Figure 1.2). They also developed other scripts for everyday purposes.

By Menes's time, the people of Nubia had already built extensive settlements and produced complex art. At places such as Afyeh near the Nile's First Cataract, a social elite lived in dwellings much grander than the small huts housing most of the population. Egyptians constantly interacted with Nubians while trading for raw materials such as gold, ivory, and animal skins, and some scholars today think that a hierarchical political and social organization in Nubia influenced the development of Egypt's politically centralized Old Kingdom. Eventually, however, Egypt's power overshadowed that of its southern neighbor.

Religion and Central Authority.   The waxing and waning of strong, central authority determined the course of Egyptian political history. When the kings were strong, as during the Old Kingdom, the country was stable and rich, with flourishing international trade, especially along the Levant coast (modern Syria, Lebanon, and Israel). However, when the governors of different regions or the many priests of the state religion refused to support the king, political instability resulted. Above all, the king's power and success depended on his properly fulfilling his religious obligations.

Like the Mesopotamians, Egyptians both royal and ordinary centered their lives on religion. Therefore, the priests who administered the country's temples, sacrifices, and religious festivals gained a prominent place in social and political life, second only to the royal family. Egyptians worshiped a great variety of gods, who were often shown in paintings and sculpture as creatures with both human and animal features, such as the head of a jackal or a bird atop a human body. This style of depicting deities did not mean that people worshiped animals but rather expressed their belief that each god had a particular animal as the bearer of the divine soul. A picture or a statue of a divinity had to include the animal so the depiction would not lack a soul. Egyptian religion told complicated stories about the daily lives of the gods to explain their powers and their significance for human beings. At the most basic level, deities were associated with powerful natural objects, emotions, qualities, and technologies, such as Re, the sun god, Isis, the goddess of love and fertility, and Thoth, god of wisdom and the inventor of writing.

Egyptians regarded their king as a god in human form. At the same time, they recognized that the actual king on the throne was mortal. Therefore, they differentiated between the human existence of the individual king and the divine origin of monarchy. In the Egyptian view, their system of rule was divine because it represented on earth the supernatural, eternal force that created harmony and stability in human life. This force was called *ma'at,* often translated as "truth" or "justice" or "correct balance." It was the king's responsibility as a divine being to rule according to *ma'at* by keeping the forces of nature in balance for the benefit of his people. The Egyptian kings' exalted religious status distinguished them from Sumerian kings, who ruled as strictly human lords, even though their cities were devoted to the gods.

An Egyptian king ensured the welfare of his country by following certain rituals. For example, he regulated his daily activities very strictly. He had to have a specific time to take a bath, go for a walk, or make love to his wife. Above all, the king was obliged to protect his country's fertility by summoning the divine power necessary to make the Nile flood every year. If he failed to make the flood happen, he gravely weakened his control. A king's inability to produce annual floods and thus to keep

Hieroglyph	Meaning	Sound value
	vulture	glottal stop
	flowering reed	consonantal I
	forearm and hand	ayin
	quail chick	W
	foot	B
	stool	P
	horned viper	F
	owl	M
	water	N
	mouth	R
	reed shelter	H
	twisted flax	slightly guttural
	placenta (?)	H as in "loch"
	animal's belly	slightly softer than h
	door bolt	S
	folded cloth	S
	pool	SH
	hill	Q
	basket with handle	K
	jar stand	G
	loaf	T

FIGURE 1.2 Egyptian Hieroglyphs

Ancient Egyptians developed their own system of writing about 3100 B.C., using pictures such as these. Because this formal script was used mainly for religious inscriptions on buildings and sacred objects, Greeks referred to it as "the sacred carved letters" (ta hieroglyphica), from which comes the modern term hieroglyphs.

Giraudon/Art Resource, NY.

Egyptian Hieroglyphic Writing

This pictorial writing system continued until about A.D. 400, when Arabic replaced Egyptian as the land's spoken language, except in the liturgy of the Coptic church, where it survives today. Egyptian hieroglyphs employ around seven hundred pictures in three categories: ideograms (signs indicating things or ideas), phonograms (signs indicating sounds), and determinatives (signs clarifying the meaning of the other signs). Eventually (the chronology is unsure), Egyptians also developed the handwritten cursive script called demotic *(Greek for "of the people"), a much simpler and quicker form of writing.*

Victor Boswell, Jr. © National Geographic Society Image Collection.

his people well fed showed he lacked the religious force necessary for ruling: he had lost his *ma'at*. He might then lose his kingdom.

Pyramids and the Afterlife.   Successful Old Kingdom rulers used expensive building programs to demonstrate their piety and exhibit their status atop the social hierarchy. Unlike their Mesopotamian counterparts ruling independent states in a divided land, they built only a few large cities in their united country. The first capital of the united country, Memphis (south of modern Cairo), grew into a metropolis packed with mammoth structures. It was in the suburbs of Memphis that these kings erected the most stunning manifestations of their status and their religion—their huge tombs.

These tombs—the pyramids—formed the centerpieces of elaborate groups of buildings for royal funerals and religious ceremonies. Although the pyramids were not the first monuments in the world built from enormous, worked stones (that honor goes to temples on the Mediterranean island of Malta), they rank as the grandest. The Old Kingdom rulers spent vast sums of money and labor on these huge complexes because they cared so much about protecting their mummified bodies for existence in the afterlife. Imhotep, chief architect of King Djoser around 2650 B.C., became famous for overseeing the construction of the first monumental tomb, the Step Pyramid at Saqqara. Around 2575 B.C., King Cheops commissioned the biggest of them all—the Great

Pyramid at Giza. At about 480 feet high, it stands taller than a forty-story skyscraper. Covering over thirteen acres and 760 feet long on each side, it required more than two million blocks of limestone, some of which weighed fifteen tons apiece; quarried in the desert, they were floated to the site on river barges and dragged on rollers and sleds up earthen ramps into position.

The kings' lavish preparations for death reflect the strong Egyptian belief in an afterlife. A hieroglyphic text dating around 2300 B.C., addressed to the god Atum, expresses the hope that an Old Kingdom ruler will have a secure afterlife: "O Atum, put your arms around King Nefer-ka-Re, around this construction work, around this pyramid. . . . May you guard lest anything happen to him evilly throughout the course of eternity." The royal family equipped their tombs to provide them with elaborate delights for their existence in the world of the dead. Gilded furniture, sparkling jewelry, exquisite objects of all kinds—the dead kings had all this and more placed beside their coffins, in which rested their mummies. Archaeologists have even uncovered two full-sized cedar ships buried next to the Great Pyramid, meant to carry King Cheops on his journey into eternity.

Hierarchy and Order in Egyptian Society.   Since Old Kingdom rulers made their administration more centralized and authoritarian to organize the labor for their mammoth construction projects,

The Pyramids at Giza in Egypt
The kings of the Egyptian Old Kingdom constructed massive stone pyramids for their tombs, the centerpieces of large complexes of temples and courtyards stretching down to the banks of the Nile or along a canal leading to the river. The inner burial chambers lay at the end of long, narrow tunnels snaking through the pyramids' interiors. The biggest pyramid shown here is the so-called Great Pyramid of King Cheops, erected about 2575 B.C. Farrell Grehean/NGS Image Collection.

Egyptian society evolved into a very structured hierarchy. The king and queen, whose role included producing children to continue the ruling dynasty, topped the social order. Brothers and sisters in the royal family could marry each other, perhaps because such matches were believed necessary to preserve the purity of the royal line or to imitate the marriages of the gods. The priests, royal administrators, provincial governors, and commanders of the army came next in the hierarchy, but they ranked far below the king and queen. The common people, who did all the manual labor, constituted the massive base of this figurative pyramid of free people in Egypt. (Slaves captured in foreign wars worked for the royal family and the temples in the Old Kingdom, but privately owned slaves working in free persons' homes or on their farms did not become prevalent until after the Old Kingdom.) Although not slaves, free workers had heavy obligations to the state. For example, they were the principal workers on the pyramids, under orders of the kings, whom no one could disobey. On occasion the workers received wages, but mostly their labor was a way of paying taxes. Rates of taxation reached twenty percent on the produce of free farmers.

Women generally had the same legal rights as free men in ancient Egypt. They could own land and slaves, inherit property, pursue lawsuits, transact business, and initiate divorces. Old Kingdom portrait statues vividly express the equal status of wife and husband: each figure is the same size and sits on the same kind of chair. Men dominated public life, while Egyptian women devoted themselves mainly to private life, managing their households and property. When their husbands went to war or were killed in battle, however, women often took on men's work. As a result, some women held government posts, served as priestesses, managed farms, and practiced medicine.

The formalism of Egypt's art illustrates how much its civilization valued order and predictability. Almost all its sculpture and painting come from tombs or temples, testimony to its people's consuming interest in maintaining proper relations with the gods. Old Kingdom artists excelled in stonework, from carved ornamental jars to massive portrait statues of the kings. These statues represent the subject either standing stiffly with the left leg advanced or sitting on a chair or throne, stable and poised. The concern for decorum also appears in the Old Kingdom literature the Egyptians called *Instructions,* known today as *wisdom literature.* These texts conveyed instructions for appropriate behavior for high officials. In the *Instruction of Ptahhotep,* for example, the king advises his minister Ptahhotep to tell his son, who will succeed him in office, not to be arrogant or overconfident just because he is well educated and to seek advice from ignorant people as well as the wise.

The Middle and New Kingdoms in Egypt, c. 2050–1085 B.C.

The Old Kingdom's ordered stability began to disintegrate when, beginning about 2350 B.C., climate changes caused the annual Nile flood to shrink. The ensuing famines discredited the regime—it had lost its *ma'at*—and destroyed the country's unity because regional governors increased their power at the expense of the kings, who had failed in their religious duty to provide prosperity. The governors, who had supported the kings while times were good, now seized independence for their regions. Starvation and civil unrest during the First Intermediate Period (c. 2181–2050 B.C.) thwarted attempts by the princes of Thebes in Upper Egypt to reestablish political unity.

The Middle Kingdom. King Mentuhotep II finally reunited Egypt, initiating the Middle Kingdom (c. 2050–1786 B.C.). The monarchs of the Middle Kingdom gradually restored the strong central authority their Old Kingdom predecessors had lost. They pushed the boundaries of Egypt farther south, while to the north they expanded diplomatic and trade contacts in ancient Palestine and Syria and with the island of Crete.

During this second period of unity, the Egyptians felt a warm pride in their homeland, as their vigorous literature demonstrates. The Egyptian narrator of the Middle Kingdom tale *The Story of Sinuhe,* for example, reports that he lived luxuriously during a forced stay in Syria but still pined to return: "Whichever deity you are who ordered my exile, have mercy and bring me home! Please allow me to see the land where my heart dwells! Nothing is more important than that my body be buried in the country where I was born!" For him, love for Egypt outranks even personal riches.

From Hyksos Invasion to New Kingdom. The Middle Kingdom fell apart when nature again undermined the kings' hold on a unified Egypt: famines caused by irregular Nile floods destroyed their power. Another long period of disunity ensued, the Second Intermediate Period (c. 1786–1567 B.C.), during which a foreign invasion violently disrupted the Egyptians' ordered world. Taking advantage of the land's political weakness, a Semitic people from the Syria-Palestine region took over Lower Egypt around 1670 B.C. The Egyptians called these foreigners the Hyksos. Recent archaeological discoveries have emphasized the role of the Hyksos settlers in transplanting elements of foreign culture to Egypt. These invaders introduced such innovations as bronze-making technology, horses and war chariots, more powerful bows, new musical instruments, hump-backed cattle, and olive trees; they also promoted regular contact with other Near Eastern states. As with the empire of the Akkadians, so too in this case did violent invasion indirectly promote cultural interchange.

Eventually, the leaders of Thebes once again reunited Egypt by liberating their land from the Hyksos around 1567 B.C. and initiating the New Kingdom (c. 1567–1085 B.C.). The kings of this period, known as *pharaohs* (meaning "the Great House," that is, the royal palace and estate), rebuilt central authority by restricting the power of regional governors. At the same time, recognizing from the Hyksos invasion that knowledge of the rest of the world was necessary for safety, they established regular diplomatic contacts with neighboring monarchs. In fact, the pharaohs regularly exchanged letters on matters of state with their "brother kings," as they called them, elsewhere in the Near East.

Warrior Pharaohs. In addition to diplomacy directed at forging defensive alliances with kingdoms in Mesopotamia and Anatolia, the New Kingdom kings used foreign wars to promote Egypt's interests. They earned the title "warrior pharaohs" by waging many campaigns abroad and modifying their royal religious stature by presenting themselves as the incarnations of a warrior god. They invaded Nubia and the Sudan to the south to win access to gold and other precious materials, while they fought in Palestine and Syria to seize the Levant and thus the land route to Egypt.

Massive riches supported the power of the warrior pharaohs. Egyptian traders exchanged local fine goods, such as ivory, for foreign luxury goods, such as wine and olive oil transported in painted pottery from Greece. Egyptian royalty displayed their wealth most conspicuously in the enormous sums they spent to build temples of stone. Queen Hatshepsut in the fifteenth century B.C., for example, built the massive complex at Deir el Bahri near Thebes, including a temple dedicated to the god Amen and to a cult that would worship her as a deity after her death. After her husband (who was also her half-brother) died, Hatshepsut proclaimed herself "female king" as co-ruler with her young stepson. In this way, she shrewdly sidestepped Egyptian political ideology, which made no provision for a queen to reign in her own right. She therefore had herself often represented in official art as a man, sporting a king's beard and male clothing.

Religious Tradition and Upheaval. The many gods of Egyptian polytheism oversaw all aspects of life and death, with particular emphasis on the afterlife. Glorious temples honored the traditional gods, and their cults were integral to the religious life of the general population as well as the leaders. The principal festivals of the gods, for example, involved lavish public celebrations. A calendar based on the moon governed the dates of religious ceremonies. (The Egyptians also developed a calendar for administrative and fiscal purposes that had 365 days, divided into 12 months of 30 days each, with the extra 5 days added before the start of the next year. Our modern calendar derives from it.)

The early New Kingdom pharaohs from Thebes promoted their state god Amen-Re until he overshadowed the other gods. This Theban cult incorporated and subordinated the other gods without denying either their existence or the continued importance of their priests. The pharaoh Amenhotep IV, also known as Akhenaten, went a step further, however, during his reign in the fourteenth century B.C. because he believed so fervently that traditional belief had become misguided. He reformed official religion by making the cult of Aten, who represented the shining disk of the sun, the centerpiece of official religion. This new cult excluded the other deities and their supporters, although it should probably not be regarded as pure monotheism (belief in the

Queen Hatshepsut of Egypt as Pharaoh
This famous New Kingdom monarch of the fifteenth century B.C. had to adopt the male trappings of Egyptian kingship to claim legitimacy because her land's tradition had no place for women as sole rulers. Here she is depicted wearing the distinctive garb of a pharaoh. She had this statue placed in a temple she built outside Thebes in Upper Egypt. Metropolitan Museum of Art, Rogers Fund and contribution from Edward Harkness, 1929.

existence of only one god, as in Judaism, Christianity, and Islam) because Akhenaten did not revoke the divine status of the king; the population presumably went on venerating their ruler as before.

To showcase his reforms and the concentration of power that they brought him, he built a new capital for his god at Amarna (see Map 1.3). He tried to force his revised religion on the priests of the old cults, who resisted stubbornly. His wife, Queen Nefertiti, tried to restrain him when she realized the hostility that his changes were causing in a population who treasured stability and order. Unfortunately for everyone, Akhenaten's zeal grew so passionate that he neglected the practical affairs of ruling the kingdom. Ultimately, his failure to attend to government business created financial distress, a weakened national defense, and intense unhappiness with his reign. His religious reform died with him; during the reign of his successor Tutankhamun (r. 1361–1352 B.C.), famous today through the discovery in 1922 of his rich, unlooted tomb, the cult of Amen-Re reclaimed its leading role. The crisis created by Akhenaten's attempted reform emphasizes the overwhelming importance of religious conservatism in Egyptian life.

Life and Belief in the New Kingdom. Despite the period's many upheavals, the rhythm of ordinary Egyptians' daily lives still revolved around the relation between their labor and the annual flood of the Nile. During the months when the river stayed between its banks, they worked their fields, rising very early in the morning to avoid the searing heat. Their obligation to labor on royal building projects came due when the flooding halted agricultural work and freed them to move to workers' quarters erected next to the building sites. Although slaves became more common as household workers in the New Kingdom, free workers, doing service instead of paying taxes in money, performed most of the labor on the mammoth royal construction projects of this period. Surviving texts reveal that they lightened their labors by singing songs and telling adventure stories. They had a lot of labor to do: the majority of temples remaining in Egypt today come from the New Kingdom. The architecture of these rectangular buildings of stone studded with soaring, sculpted columns anticipated the style of the later temples of Greece.

Ordinary people devoted much attention to deities outside the royal cults, especially to gods they hoped would protect them in their daily lives. They venerated Bes, for instance, a dwarf with the features of a lion, as a protector of the household. They carved his image on amulets, beds, headrests, and the handles of mirrors. People also continued to spend much time and effort preparing for the next life. Those who could afford it arranged to have their bodies mummified and their tombs outfitted with all the goods needed for the journey to their new existence. An essential piece of equipment for a mummy was a copy of the *Book of the Dead,* a collection of magic spells to ward off dangers and ensure a successful verdict in the divine judgment that people believed every soul had to pass to avoid experiencing death a second time. The text enumerated a long list of sins that the dead person had to be able to deny before the gods, including "I have not committed crimes against people; I have not mistreated cattle; I have not robbed the poor; I have not caused pain; I have not caused tears." If the verdict on their lives was positive, dead persons underwent a mystical union with the god Osiris, the head judge of souls.

Magic, both written and oral, played a large role in the lives of Egyptians. They sought spells and charms from professional magicians to ward off demons, smooth the rocky course of love, exact revenge on enemies, and find relief from disease and injury. Egyptian doctors knew many medicinal herbs, knowledge that was passed on to later civilizations, and they could perform demanding surgeries, including opening the skull. Still, no doctor could cure infection, and, as in the past, sick people continued to rely on the help of supernatural forces through prayers and spells.

The Legacy of the Levant, c. 3000–1000 B.C.

The peoples of the Levant played a large role in the history of Western civilization because their location on the eastern coast of the Mediterranean put them at a crossroads of cultural interaction, allowing their commercial and intellectual energies to thrive. The Canaanites and the Hebrews never rivaled the political and military power of the Egyptians, who in fact sometimes dominated them, but their innovations in writing technology and religion made them enduringly influential.

The "Opening of the Mouth" Ceremony in an Egyptian Funeral
This picture from a papyrus scroll containing the Egyptian Book of the Dead, *the magical instructions for the afterlife, shows the priests, mourners, and the god Anubis performing the Opening of the Mouth funeral ceremony. In this ritual, the deceased's mummy was touched on the mouth by sacred instruments, which released the person's individual personality (*ba*) to join the rest of his or her spirit for a happy new existence in the next world.*
British Museum.

Canaanites, Commerce, and the Alphabet. The Canaanites dominated the Levant in this period, which is therefore referred to as Canaan. By around 3000 B.C., they had built an urban civilization. Their independent city-states, such as the bustling ports of Ugarit, Byblos, and Tyre, grew rich from maritime commerce in the second millennium B.C., especially from trading metals and exporting timber from the Lebanese foothills; and they expanded their populations by absorbing merchants from many lands.

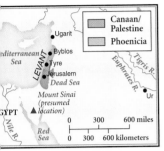

The Ancient Levant Some scholars believe that the Canaanite communities provided an antecedent for the later city-states of Greece.

The interaction of traders and travelers from many different cultures in the Levant encouraged innovation in the recording of business transactions. This lively, multilingual environment produced an overwhelmingly important innovation in writing technology about 1600 B.C.: the alphabet. In this new system, a picture—a letter—stood for only one sound in the language—a marvelously simple improvement over cumbersome cuneiform and hieroglyphic scripts. The alphabet developed in the Levant later became the basis for the Greek and Roman alphabets and hence of modern Western alphabets. Few intellectual achievements have had as great an impact on later times.

The Hebrews and the Bible. The enduring legacy of the Hebrews to Western civilization comes from the significance of the book that became their sacred scripture, the Hebrew Bible (known to Christians as the Old Testament). This primary text deeply affected the formation of not only Judaism but also Christianity and, later, Islam. Unfortunately, no source provides clear information on the origins of the Hebrews or of their religion. The Bible tells stories to explain God's moral plan for the universe, not to give a full historical account of the Hebrews, and archaeology has not yielded a clear picture.

The Hebrew Bible reports that the patriarch Abraham and his followers left the Mesopotamian city of Ur to migrate to ancient Palestine, at the southeast corner of the Mediterranean Sea. Because other Semitic peoples, such as the Amorites and Aramaeans, are known to have moved throughout the Fertile Crescent in the early second millennium, the story of Abraham's journey perhaps reflects this era and can be dated about 1900 B.C. Once in Palestine, the Hebrews continued their traditional existence as seminomads, tending flocks of animals on the region's scanty grasslands and living in temporary tent settlements. They occasionally planted barley or wheat for a season or two and then moved on to new pastures. Traditionally believed to have been divided into twelve tribes, they never settled down or formed a political state in this period. Organized political and military power in the region remained in the hands of the Canaanites.

Abraham's son Isaac led his pastoral people to live in various locations, to avoid disputes with local Canaanites over grazing rights. Isaac's son Jacob, the story continues, moved to Egypt late in life when his son Joseph brought Jacob and other relatives there to escape famine in Palestine. Joseph had used his intelligence and charisma to rise to an important position in the Egyptian administration. The biblical story of the movement of a band of Hebrews to Egypt represents a crucial event in their early history; it may reflect a time when drought forced some Hebrews to migrate gradually from southwest Asia into the Nile delta of Egypt. They probably drifted in gradually during the seventeenth or sixteenth century B.C. because, unlike the Hyksos, these Hebrew immigrants lacked military might. By the thirteenth century B.C., the pharaohs had conscripted the Hebrew men into slave labor gangs for farming and for construction work on large building projects.

According to the book of Exodus, the Hebrew deity Yahweh instructed Moses to lead the Hebrews out of bondage in Egypt against the will of the king, who may have been Ramesses II, around the mid-thirteenth century B.C. Yahweh sent ten plagues to compel the pharaoh to free the Hebrews, but the king still tried to recapture them during their flight. Yahweh therefore miraculously parted the Red Sea to allow them to escape eastward; the water swirled back together as the pharaoh's army tried to follow, drowning the Egyptians.

Covenant and Law. The biblical narrative then relates a seminal event in the history of the Hebrews: the formalizing of a covenant between them and

Pottery Stand with Sculpted Musicians from the Levant
This sculpted stand from about 1000 B.C., a little over a foot high, has five musicians playing different instruments leaning out from "windows" in the pedestal. The traces of incised and painted decoration preserved on it reflect a mixture of Canaanite and Mycenaean artistic styles, the result of the kind of cultural interchange that took place often in the Levant, the crossroads of the ancient Near East. Since music played an important role in religion and court ceremonies, this piece may have belonged to a temple or a palace. Israel Museum, Jerusalem. Artifact Collection of the Israel Antiquities Authority.

their deity, who revealed himself to Moses on Mount Sinai in the desert northeast of Egypt. The covenant consisted of an agreement between the Hebrews and Yahweh that, in return for their promise to worship him as their only God and to live by his laws, he would make them his chosen people and lead them into a promised land of safety and prosperity. This

binding agreement demanded human obedience to divine law and promised punishment for unrighteousness. As God described himself to Moses, he was "compassionate and gracious, patient, ever constant and true . . . forgiving wickedness, rebellion, and sin, and not sweeping the guilty clean away; but one who punishes sons and grandsons to the third and fourth generation for their fathers' iniquity" (Exodus 34:6–7). In two places the Hebrew Bible sets forth the religious and moral code the Hebrews had to follow: the Ten Commandments, the first three of which required the exclusive worship of Yahweh, followed by commandments to honor one's parents, to observe the seventh day of the week (the Sabbath) as a day free of work, and to abstain from murder, adultery, theft, lying, and covetousness; and the Pentateuch (the first five books of the Hebrew Bible), or Torah.

Most of the Pentateuchal laws shared the traditional form and much content of earlier Mesopotamian laws such as those of Hammurabi: if someone does a certain thing to another person, then a specified punishment is imposed on the perpetrator. For example, both Hammurabi's and Hebrew law covered the case of an ox that had gored a person; the owner was penalized only if he had been warned about his beast's tendency to gore and had done nothing to restrain it. Also like Hammurabi's laws, Hebrew law expressed an interest in the welfare of the poor as well as the rich. In addition, it secured protection for the lower classes and people without power, such as strangers, widows, and orphans.

Hebrew law differed from Mesopotamian law, however, in that the same rules applied to all, without regard to position in the social hierarchy, and the severity of punishments did not depend on a person's social class. Hebrew law also did not allow vicarious punishment—a Mesopotamian tradition ordering, for example, that a rapist's wife be raped or that the son of a builder be killed if his father's work negligently caused the death of someone else's son. Hebrew women and children had certain legal protection, although their rights were less extensive than men's. For example, wives had less freedom to divorce their husbands than husbands had to divorce their wives, much as in the laws of Hammurabi. Crimes against property never carried the death penalty, as they frequently did in other Near

Eastern societies. Hebrew laws also protected slaves against flagrant mistreatment by their masters. Slaves who lost an eye or even a tooth from a beating were to be freed. Like free people, slaves enjoyed the right to rest on the Sabbath, the holy day of the seven-day Hebrew week.

Hebrew Monotheism. Because the earliest parts of the Hebrew Bible were probably composed about 950 B.C., over three hundred years after the exodus from Egypt, their account of the Hebrew covenant and laws deals with a distant, undocumented time. Many uncertainties persist in our understanding of the process by which the Hebrews acquired their distinctive religion and way of life, but it seems clear that both took much longer to evolve than the biblical account describes. Like their neighbors in Canaan, the early Hebrews worshiped a variety of gods, including spirits believed to reside in natural objects such as trees and stones. Yahweh may have originally been the deity of the tribe of Midian, to which Moses's father-in-law belonged. The form of the covenant with Yahweh conformed to the ancient Near Eastern tradition of treaties between a superior and subordinates, but its content differed from that of other ancient Near Eastern religions because it made Yahweh the exclusive deity of his people. In the time of Moses, Yahweh religion was not yet the pure monotheism it would later become because it did not deny the existence of other gods. Because in the ensuing centuries some Hebrews worshiped other gods as well, such as Baal of Canaan, it seems that the covenant with Yahweh and fully formed Hebrew monotheism did not emerge until well after 1000 B.C.

The Hebrews who fled from Egypt with Moses made their way back to Palestine, but they were still exposed to attacks by the Egyptian army. The first documentation of their return to Palestine comes from an inscribed monument erected by the pharaoh Merneptah in the late thirteenth century B.C. to commemorate his victory in a military expedition there. The Hebrew tribes joined their relatives who had remained in Palestine and somehow carved out separate territories for themselves there. The twelve tribes remained politically distinct under the direction of separate leaders, called judges, until the eleventh century, when their first monarchy emerged.

❖ Civilization in Bronze-Age Greece and Anatolia, c. 2200–1000 B.C.

The first civilizations in the Mediterranean region arose not long before 2000 B.C. on the islands of the Aegean Sea and especially on the large island of Crete, home to the peaceful and artistic civilization of the Minoans. Somewhat later, civilizations also developed in Anatolia, dominated by the Hittite kingdom, and on the Greek mainland, where Mycenaean civilization grew rich from raiding and trade. These peoples had advanced technologies, elaborate architecture, striking art, a marked taste for luxury, and extensive trade contacts with Egypt and the Near East. They also inhabited a dangerous world where regional disruptions in the period from about 1200 to 1000 B.C. ultimately overwhelmed their prosperous cultures. Nevertheless, their accomplishments paved the way for the later civilization of Greece, which would dramatically influence the course of Western history.

It makes sense that the earliest Mediterranean civilizations arose on islands located in the middle of antiquity's highway, the sea. People, trade goods, and ideas from other places could reach islands easily. As early as 6000 B.C., people from Anatolia began migrating westward and southward to inhabit islands in the Mediterranean Sea. By about 2200 B.C., the rich civilization of the Minoans had emerged on the island of Crete. The Anatolian peoples who stayed on the mainland also developed civilizations, of which the most aggressive and ambitious was the kingdom of the Hittites.

Minoan Crete, c. 2200–1400 B.C.

With its large, fertile plains, adequate rainfall, and sheltered ports for fishing and seaborne trade, Crete offered a fine home for settlers (Map 1.4). By 2200 B.C., the inhabitants of Crete created what scholars have named a *palace society,* in recognition of its sprawling, many-chambered buildings that appear to have been the residences of rulers and the centers of political, economic, and religious administration. The Cretan rulers combined the functions of chief and priest, dominating both politics and religion but not having the unchallenged power of kings. The palaces seem to have been largely independent, with no one imposing unity on the island.

We call this civilization *Minoan* because a famous archaeologist, Arthur Evans (1851–1941), searched there for traces of King Minos of Crete, renowned in Greek myth as a fierce ruler who built the first great navy. The so-called palaces housed the rulers, their families, and their servants. The general population clustered around the palaces in houses adjacent to one another; some of these settlements reached the size of cities, with thousands of inhabitants. The most famous one was Knossos, which Evans thought had been Minos's headquarters. Other, smaller settlements dotted outlying areas. Cretans wrote in a script today called Linear A; their language remains only partially deciphered, but recent research suggests, despite the long-held assumption to the contrary, that Minoan may have been a member of the Indo-European family of languages, the ancestor of many languages, including Greek, Latin, and, much later, English.

The emergence in Minoan farming of what is called *Mediterranean polyculture*—the cultivation of olives and grapes as well as grain in one agricultural system—profoundly affected Minoan society. The idea was to make the best use of a farmer's labor by growing crops together that required intense work at different seasons. This system, which still dominates Mediterranean agriculture, had two important consequences: the combination of crops provided a very healthy diet and thus stimulated population growth, and agriculture became both diversified and specialized, producing valuable new products such as olive oil and wine.

As in Mesopotamia and Egypt, so too on Crete the production of agricultural surpluses led to growth in specialized crafts. Because old methods were inadequate for storing and transporting surplus food, artisans began to invent and manufacture huge storage jars that could accommodate these products, in the process creating another specialized industry. Crafts workers, producing their sophisticated wares using time-consuming techniques, no longer had time to grow their own food or make the goods, such as clothes and lamps, they needed for everyday life. Instead, they had to exchange the products they made for food and other goods. In this way, Cretan society experienced increasing economic interdependence.

The vast storage areas of Cretan palaces suggest that Minoan rulers, like some Mesopotamian kings before them, may have controlled this interdependence by creating an economic system based on

MAP 1.4 Greece and the Aegean Sea, c. 1500 B.C.
Mountains, islands, and sea defined the geography of Greece. The distances between settlements were mostly short but rough terrain and seasonally stormy sailing made travel a chore. The distance from the mainland to the largest island in this region, Crete, where Minoan civilization arose, was sufficiently long to keep Cretans isolated from the turmoil of most of later Greek history.

Wall Painting from the Palace at Knossos
Minoan artists painted with vivid colors on plaster to enliven the walls of buildings. They depicted a wide variety of subjects, from lively animals and flowering plants to young boxers and women of the court in splendid dress. Unfortunately, time and earthquakes have severely damaged most Minoan wall paintings, and the versions we see today are largely reconstructions painted around surviving fragments of the originals. The paintings from the Knossos palace, for example, were reconstructed as part of the overall plan of the original excavator, Arthur Evans, to rebuild the entire structure from fragmentary remains.
Julia M. Fair.

redistribution. The Knossos palace, for example, held hundreds of gigantic jars capable of holding 240,000 gallons of olive oil and wine. Bowls, cups, and dippers crammed storerooms nearby. If the palace was truly the dispatch point in a redistributive economy, officials would have decided how much each farmer or crafts producer had to contribute to the palace storehouse and how much of those contributions would then be redistributed to each person in the community for basic subsistence or as an extra reward. In this way, people gave the products of their labor to the local authority, which redistributed them as it saw fit. There would have been almost no free markets.

Whatever its exact nature, the Minoan economy apparently worked smoothly and peacefully for centuries, until at least 1400 B.C. Although contemporary settlements elsewhere around the Aegean Sea and in Anatolia had elaborate defensive walls, Crete had none. The palaces, towns, and even isolated country houses apparently saw no need to fortify themselves against one another. The remains of the newer palaces—such as the one at Knossos with its hundreds of rooms in five stories, indoor plumbing, and colorful scenes painted on the walls—have led some to the controversial conclusion that Minoans were exceptionally peaceful; others point out that they dominated neighboring Aegean islands, and recent discoveries of tombs have revealed weapons caches. The prominence of women in palace frescoes and the numerous figurines of buxom goddesses found on Cretan sites have also prompted speculation that Minoan society was female-dominated, but no texts have come to light to verify this. Minoan art certainly depicts women prominently and nobly, but the same is true of other contemporary civilizations, which men controlled. More archaeological research is needed to resolve the controversies over the nature of Minoan civilization.

Hittite Royal Couple Worshiping the Weather God
This relief sculpture from Alaca Hüyük in north central Anatolia shows a Hittite king and queen worshiping the Weather god, as he was called, who is represented here by his sacred animal, the bull, standing on an altar. In Hittite mythology, the Weather god was thought to ride over the mountains in a chariot pulled by bulls. He was a divine hero who overcame evil by slaying a great dragon. At first the monster defeated him, but the goddess Inaras tricked the dragon into getting drunk so that the Weather god could kill him.
Hirmer Fotoarchiv.

The Hittite Kingdom, c. 1750–1200 B.C.

Migrating from the Caucasus area, between the Black and Caspian Seas, and overcoming indigenous peoples, the Hittites became the most powerful people of central Anatolia by about 1750 B.C. (or somewhat later; the chronology is in dispute). (See Map 1.2.) They flourished because they inhabited a fertile, upland plateau in the peninsula's center and excelled in war and diplomacy. They built a kingdom whose power and splendor rivaled those of Crete by controlling trade in their region and southward into the Levant, the commercial crossroads of the eastern Mediterranean. The Hittites even threatened the security of Egypt with their military campaigns into that state's Levantine possessions.

Since the Hittites spoke an Indo-European language, they belonged to the linguistic family that eventually populated most of Europe. The original Indo-European speakers, who were pastoralists and raiders, had migrated as separate groups into Anatolia and Europe, including Greece, from somewhere in western Asia. Recent archaeological discoveries there of graves of women buried with weapons suggest that women in these groups originally occupied positions of leadership in war and peace alongside men; the prominence of Hittite queens in documents, royal letters, and foreign treaties perhaps sprang from that tradition.

As in Mesopotamia, Egypt, the Levant, and Minoan Crete, Hittite rule was directly linked to religion. Hittite religion combined worship of the gods of Indo-European religion with worship of deities inherited from the original Anatolian population. The king served as high priest of the storm god, and Hittite belief therefore demanded that he maintain a strict purity in his life. His drinking water, for example, always had to be strained. So strong was this insistence on purity that the king's water carrier was executed if so much as one hair was found in the water. Like Egyptian kings, Hittite rulers felt responsible for maintaining divine goodwill toward their subjects. King Mursili II (r. 1321–1295 B.C.), for example, issued a set of prayers begging the gods to end a plague: "What is this, o gods, that you have done? Our land is dying. . . . We have lost our wits, and we can do nothing right. O gods, whatever sin you behold, either let a prophet come forth to identify it . . . or let us see it in a dream!"

The kings conducted many religious ceremonies in the kingdom's capital, Hattusas, which grew into one of the most impressive cities of its era. Ringed by massive defensive walls and towers of stone, it had huge palaces set on straight, gravel-paved streets. Sculptures of animals, warriors, and, especially, the royal rulers decorated public spaces. The Hittite kings maintained their rule by forging personal alliances—cemented by marriages and oaths of loyalty—with the noble families of the kingdom.

The Hittite rulers aggressively employed their troops to expand their power. In the periods during which ties between the king and the nobility remained strong and the kingdom therefore preserved its unity, they launched extremely ambitious military campaigns. In 1595 B.C., for example, the royal army raided as far as Babylon, destroying that kingdom. Scholars no longer accept the once popular idea that the Hittites owed their success in war to a special knowledge of making weapons from iron, although their craftsmen did smelt iron from which they made ceremonial implements. (Weapons made from iron did not become common in the Mediterranean world until well after 1200 B.C.—at the end of the Hittite kingdom.) Their army excelled in the use of chariots, and perhaps this skill gave them an edge.

The economic strength of the Hittite kingdom depended on controlling long-distance trade routes by which it secured essential raw materials, especially metals. The Hittites particularly wanted to dominate the lucrative trade in and out of Mesopotamia and Egypt. A key part of their strategy was the invasion of the Levant, the principal trade highway to Egypt and the commercial crossroads of the region. The Egyptian New Kingdom pharaohs fiercely resisted Hittite expansion because they wanted to keep these formidable warriors as far from their border as possible. But the Anatolian kingdom was too strong, and in the bloody battle of Kadesh about 1274 B.C., the Hittites prevented the Egyptians from recovering their Syrian possessions. Diplomacy finally settled the issue when, around 1259 B.C., the Hittite king Hattusili III made a treaty with the Egyptian king Ramesses II and gave him his daughter to marry to seal the agreement. Remarkably, both Egyptian and Hittite copies of this landmark in diplomatic history survive. In it the two monarchs pledged to be "at peace and brothers forever."

Mycenaean Greece, c. 1800–1000 B.C.

The Greeks were Indo-European speakers whose ancestors had moved into the region by 8000 B.C.; their first mainland civilization arose about the same time as the Hittite kingdom, in the early second millennium B.C. Its modern designation—Mycenaean—comes from the hilltop site of Mycenae in the Peloponnese (the large peninsula forming southern Greece), which had a fortified settlement dominated by a palace and dotted with rich tombs (see Map 1.4). Neither it nor any other community ever ruled Bronze Age Greece as a united state, however. Instead, Mycenaean settlements vied with one another in a fierce competition for natural resources and territory. Since the hilly terrain of Greece had little fertile land but many useful ports, its settlements tended to spring up near the coast. Greeks from the earliest times depended on the sea: for food, for trade with one another and foreign lands, and for naval raids on rich targets. The Mycenaean economy was certainly redistributive, as palace records discovered on clay tablets show: scribes kept elaborate lists of goods received and goods paid out, tirelessly recording stored material, livestock, land holdings, and personnel. They wrote down everything, from chariots to perfumes, even broken equipment taken out of service. The records of goods distributed from the storerooms covered ritual offerings to the gods, rations to personnel, and raw materials for crafts production, such as metal issued to bronze smiths.

The first excavator of Mycenae, the nineteenth-century German millionaire Heinrich Schliemann, made the site famous by discovering treasure-filled graves there. The burial objects revealed a warrior culture organized in independent settlements and ruled by aggressive kings. Constructed as stone-lined shafts, the graves contained entombed dead, who had taken hordes of valuables with them: golden jewelry, including heavy necklaces festooned with pendants, gold and silver vessels, bronze weapons decorated with scenes of wild animals inlaid in precious metals, and delicately painted pottery.

In his excitement at finding treasure, Schliemann proudly informed the international press that he had found the grave of Agamemnon, the legendary king who commanded the Greek army against Troy, a city in northwestern Anatolia, in the Trojan War, which Greece's first and most famous poet, Homer, had immortalized in his epic poem *The Iliad;* archaeologists now know the shaft graves date to around 1700–1600 B.C., long before the Trojan War could have taken place. Schliemann, who earlier paid for his own excavation at Troy to prove to skeptical scholars that the city had really existed, infuriated scholars with his self-promotion. But his passion to confirm that Greek myth preserved a kernel of historical truth spurred him on to the work at Mycenae, which provided the most spectacular evidence for mainland Greece's earliest civilization.

Interaction with Minoan Crete. Mycenaean rulers enriched themselves by dominating local farmers, conducting raids near and far, and participating in seaborne trade. International commerce in this period promoted vigorous cultural interaction and mingling, as underwater archaeology dramatically reveals. Divers have discovered, for example, that a late-fourteenth-century B.C. shipwreck off Uluburun in Turkey carried such a mixed cargo and varied personal possessions—from Canaan, Cyprus, Greece, Egypt, Babylon, and elsewhere in the Near

East—that attaching a single "nationality" to this tramp freighter makes no sense.

A special kind of burial chamber, called *tholos* tombs—spectacular underground domed chambers built in beehive shapes with closely fitted stones—shows how rich Mycenaeans had become by about 1500 B.C. The architectural details of the tholos tombs and the style of the burial goods found in them testify to the far-flung raiding and trading that Mycenaean rulers conducted throughout the eastern Mediterranean; but above all they show a close connection with the civilization of Minoan Crete. That is, the art and goods of the Mycenaeans display many motifs clearly inspired by Cretan designs.

At the same time, the two civilizations remained distinctly different in important ways. The Mycenaeans spoke Greek and made burnt offerings to the

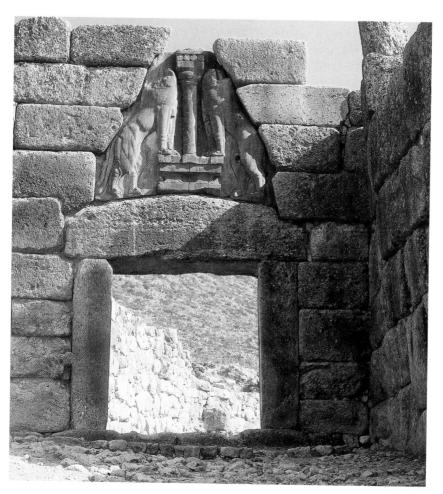

The Lion Gate to the Citadel at Mycenae
The hilltop fortress and palace at Mycenae was the capital of Bronze Age Greece's most famous kingdom. Above its main gate stood a sculpture of lions flanking a column, a design imitating the royal art of the Near East that shows that the Mycenaean kings admired the power and traditions of that region. In the circle of graves beyond the gate, Heinrich Schliemann found the treasure that he thought had belonged to King Agamemnon, the leader of the Greeks in the Trojan War.
Dimitrios Harissiades/Benatri Museum.

gods; the Minoans did neither. The Minoans scattered sanctuaries across the landscape in caves, on mountaintops, and in country villas; the mainlanders did none of this. When the Mycenaeans started building palaces in the fourteenth century B.C., unlike the Minoans they designed them around *megarons*—rooms with prominent ceremonial hearths and thrones for the rulers. Some Mycenaean palaces had more than one megaron, which could soar two stories high with columns to support a roof above the second-floor balconies.

The Mycenaeans, then, were from their origins a separate people. A startling find of documents in the palace at Knossos, however, shows that Mycenaeans eventually achieved dominance over Crete, possibly in a war over commercial rivalry in the Mediterranean. These were tablets written in a script called Linear B, which was a pictographic script based on Minoan Linear A. A brilliant twentieth-century architect named Michael Ventris, however, proved that Linear B was used to write not Minoan, but a different language: Greek. Because the Linear B tablets dated from before the final destruction of Knossos in about 1370 B.C., they revealed that the palace administration had been keeping its records in a foreign language for some time and that Mycenaeans were controlling Crete well before the end of Minoan civilization.

In the end, then, the Mycenaeans conquered the culture whose art they had so highly admired; by the middle of the fourteenth century B.C., they had displaced the Minoans as the Aegean's preeminent civilization. The Greeks later recalled this reversal of power in the myth about Theseus of Athens defeating the half-man, half-bull Minotaur of King Minos: when the Cretan king forced the Athenians to send youths for the monster to devour in his labyrinth, Theseus slew the beast and found his way to freedom by backtracking along the thread that the king's daughter Ariadne, who had fallen in love with the dashing hero, had told him to leave to mark his way in the maze.

War in Mycenaean Society. By the time Mycenaeans took over Crete, war at home and abroad was the principal concern of well-off Mycenaean men, a tradition that they passed on to later Greek civilization. Contents of Bronze Age tombs in Greece reveal that no wealthy man went to his grave

without his war equipment. The expense of these grave goods shows that armor and weapons were so central to a Mycenaean male's identity that he could not do without them, even in death. Warriors rode into battle in expensive hardware—lightweight, two-wheeled chariots pulled by horses. These revolutionary vehicles, sometimes assumed to have been introduced by Indo-Europeans migrating from Central Asia, first appeared in various Mediterranean and Near Eastern societies not long after 2000 B.C.; the first picture of such a chariot in the Aegean region occurs on a Mycenaean grave marker from about 1500 B.C. Wealthy people evidently desired this new form of transportation not only for war but also as proof of their social status.

The Mycenaeans seem to have spent more on war than on religion. In any case, they did not construct any large religious buildings like the giant ziggurats and pyramids of Mesopotamia and Egypt. Mycenaeans passed on many divinities to the Greeks of later times, as we can tell from the names of gods found in the Linear B tablets, but their own civilization's most important divinities were male gods concerned with war.

The Calamities of c. 1200–1000 B.C. A state of political equilibrium, in which kings corresponded with one another and traders traveled all over the area, characterized the Mediterranean and Near Eastern world around 1300 B.C. Within a century, however, calamity had struck not only small, loosely organized groups such as the Hebrews in Canaan, but also almost every major political state, including Egypt, some kingdoms of Mesopotamia, and the Hittite and Mycenaean kingdoms. Explaining all the catastrophes that occurred in the period 1200–1000 B.C. remains one of the most fascinating puzzles in ancient Western history.

The best clue to what happened comes from Egyptian and Hittite records, which document foreign invasions in this period, especially from the sea. According to his own inscribed account, the pharaoh Ramesses III around 1182 B.C. defeated a fearsome coalition of seaborne invaders from the north, who had fought their way to the edge of Egypt. These Sea Peoples, as they are called, comprised many different groups. Some had been mercenary soldiers in the armies of rulers whom they deserted; some were raiders by profession. Many

IMPORTANT DATES

c. 40,000 B.C.   *Homo sapiens sapiens* enters Europe from Africa via southwestern Asia

c. 10,000–8000 B.C.   Development of agriculture and domestication of animals

c. 6500–5500 B.C.   Settlement at Çatal Hüyük in Anatolia

c. 4000–1000 B.C.   Bronze Age in southwestern Asia, Egypt, and Europe

c. 4000–3000 B.C.   First cities established and writing developed in Mesopotamia

c. 3100–3000 B.C.   Political unification of Upper and Lower Egypt into one kingdom

c. 3000 B.C.   The wheel invented in Sumer

c. 2686–2181 B.C.   Old Kingdom in Egypt

c. 2350 B.C.   Sargon establishes the world's first empire in Akkadia in Mesopotamia

c. 2200 B.C.   Gutians destroy the Akkadian empire

c. 2200 B.C.   Earliest Minoan palaces on Crete

c. 2050–1786 B.C.   Middle Kingdom in Egypt

c. 1792–1750 B.C.   Reign of Hammurabi, king of Babylon in Mesopotamia

c. 1750 B.C.   Beginning of Hittite kingdom in Anatolia

c. 1670 B.C.   Hyksos take over Egypt

c. 1600–1400 B.C.   Hebrews migrate into Egypt

c. 1567–1085 B.C.   New Kingdom in Egypt

c. 1600 B.C.   Alphabet invented in Canaan

c. 1400 B.C.   Earliest Mycenaean palaces in Greece; Mycenaeans take over Minoan Crete

c. 1274 B.C.   Battle of Ramesses II with the Hittites at Kadesh in Syria

Early or mid-thirteenth century (?) B.C.   Exodus of Hebrews from Egypt

c. 1200–1000 B.C.   Disturbances across the eastern Mediterranean region end many kingdoms

may have been Greeks; the story of the army attacking Troy probably recalls such marauders.

Apparently no single, unified group of Sea Peoples launched a single tidal wave of violence. Rather, many different bands devastated the region. A chain reaction of attacks and flights in a recurring and expanding cycle put even more bands on the move. The turmoil reached far inland. The Kassite kingdom in Babylonia collapsed, and the Assyrians were confined to their homeland. Invasions by the Semitic peoples known as Aramaeans and Chaldeans devastated western Asia and Syria.

The reasons for these widespread calamities remain mysterious, but their dire consequences in the eastern Mediterranean region are clear. The once mighty Hittite kingdom fell about 1200 B.C., when raiders finally cut off its trade routes for raw materials. Invaders razed its capital city, Hattusas, which never revived. Egypt's New Kingdom repelled the Sea Peoples with a tremendous military effort, but these raiders reduced the Egyptian long-distance trade network to a shambles. Power struggles between the pharaohs and the priests only made the situation worse. By about 1050 B.C., Egypt had shrunk to its original territorial core along the Nile's banks. The calamities ruined Egypt's credit. For example, when the eleventh-century B.C. Theban temple official Wenamun traveled to Byblos in Phoenicia to buy cedar for a ceremonial boat, the city's ruler demanded cash in advance. Although the Egyptian monarchy struggled on after the end of the New Kingdom in 1085 B.C., ongoing power struggles between pharaohs and priests, and with frequent attacks from abroad, prevented the reestablishment of centralized authority. No Egyptian dynasty ever again became an aggressive international power.

The calamities of this time also afflicted the copper-rich island of Cyprus in the eastern Mediterranean and the flourishing cities of the Levant. Raiders from the north, called Philistines, settled in Palestine and attacked the Canaanites and the Hebrews repeatedly in the eleventh century B.C. The Hebrew tribes appointed the judges in an attempt to unify their loose confederation during this period of near anarchy. One of these judges, Deborah, led an Israelite coalition force to victory over a Canaanite army, but the situation of the Hebrews remained precarious.

In Greece, the troubles were homegrown. The Mycenaeans reached the zenith of their power about 1400–1250 B.C. The enormous domed tomb at Mycenae, called the Treasury of Atreus, testifies to the riches of this period. The tomb's elaborately decorated facade and soaring roof reveal the self-confidence of the Mycenaean warrior princes. The last phase of the extensive palace at Pylos on the west coast of the Peloponnese also dates from this time. It boasted glorious wall paintings, storerooms bursting with food, and a royal bathroom with a built-in tub and intricate plumbing. But these prosperous Mycenaeans did not escape the widespread calamities of the period beginning about 1200 B.C. Linear B

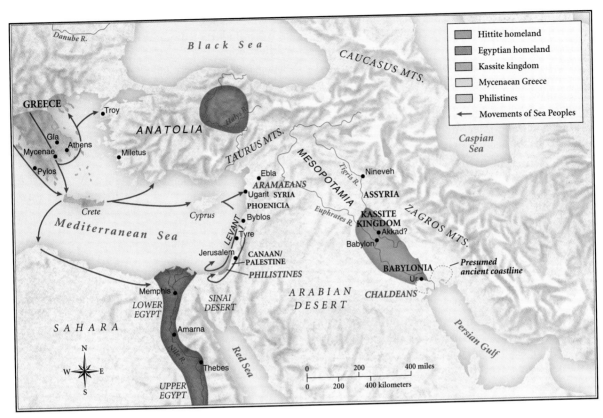

MAPPING THE WEST The Calamities of 1200–1000 B.C.
Bands of wandering warriors and raiders set the eastern Mediterranean aflame at the end of the Bronze Age. This violence displaced many people and ended the power of the kingdoms of the Egyptians, the Hittites, and the Mycenaeans. Even some of the Near Eastern states well inland from the Levant felt the effects of this period of unrest, whose causes remain mysterious.

tablets record the disposition of troops to the coast to guard the palace at Pylos at this time. The palace inhabitants of eastern Greece now constructed such massive defensive walls that the later Greeks thought giants had built them. Such fortifications would have protected coastal palaces against seafaring attackers, who could have been either outsiders or Greeks. The wall around the inland palace at Gla in central Greece, however, which foreign raiders could not easily reach, confirms that above all the Mycenaeans had to defend themselves against other Mycenaeans.

It seems, then, that in Greece Sea Peoples did relatively little damage but that internal turmoil and major earthquakes destroyed Mycenaean civilization; archaeology offers no evidence for the ancient tradition that Dorian Greeks invading from the north caused the destruction. Near-constant civil war by jealous rulers overburdened the elaborate ad-

ministrative balancing act necessary for the palaces' redistributive economies and hindered recovery from earthquake damage. The failure of the palace economies devastated most Mycenaeans, who depended on the redistributive system for their subsistence. This calamity uprooted many Greeks from their homes and forced them to wander abroad in search of new places to settle. Like people from the earliest times, these ancestors of Western civilization had to move to try to build a better life.

Conclusion

Fundamental characteristics of Western civilization slowly emerged in the long period from the Stone Age to 1000 B.C. Most important, the Neolithic Revolution transformed human life into a settled existence, culminating in cities arising in Mesopotamia by 4000–3000 B.C. Hierarchy had characterized society to some degree from the very beginning, but it grew more pronounced once civilization emerged.

Trade and war were constants, both aiming in different ways at profit and glory. Indirectly, they often generated energetic cultural interaction, with distinct civilizations learning from one another. The importance of technological innovation and the centrality of religion were also prominent characteristics of this long period. Developments such as the invention of metallurgy, monumental architecture, mathematics, and alphabetic writing would greatly affect the future, while the emergence of monotheism set the stage for the leading faiths of later Western history.

The Mediterranean Sea was a two-edged sword for the early civilizations that grew up around and near it: As a highway for transporting goods and ideas, it was a boon; as an artery for conveying attackers, it could be a bane. Ironically, the raids of the Sea Peoples that smashed the prosperity of the eastern Mediterranean region during the years 1200–1000 B.C. also set in motion the forces that led to the next step in our story, the resurgence of Greece. Strife among Mycenaean rulers turned the regional unrest of those centuries into a local catastrophe; fighting each other for dominance, they so weakened their monarchies that they could not recover after natural disasters. To an outside observer, Greek society by 1000 B.C. might have seemed destined for irreversible economic and social decline, even oblivion. The next chapter shows how wrong this prediction would have been. After a dark period of economic and population decline, Greeks would invent a new form of social and political organization and breathe renewed life into their culture with inspiration from their neighbors in the Near East and Egypt.

Suggested References

Before Civilization

Archaeological excavation and new scientific techniques for analyzing organic materials, such as paleoethnobotany, are providing a better understanding of the long period in the Stone Age during which human life changed radically from that of hunter-gatherers to that of settled agriculturists. The origins of religion probably lie deep in this period, but, with-

out written sources to enlighten us, we have to speculate, as in Walter Burkert's provocative linking of biological facts to religious beliefs.

Banning, E. B. "The Neolithic Period: Triumphs of Architecture, Agriculture, and Art," *Near Eastern Archaeology* 61 (1998): 188–237.

Barber, Elizabeth Wayland. *Women's Work: The First 20,000 Years. Women, Cloth, and Society in Early Times.* 1994.

Burkert, Walter. *Creation of the Sacred: Tracks of Biology in Early Religions.* 1996.

Çatal Hüyük archaeological site: http://catal.arch.cam.ac.uk/catal/catal.html.

Cunliffe, Barry, ed. *The Oxford Illustrated Prehistory of Europe.* 1994.

Ehrenberg, Margaret. *Women in Prehistory.* 1989.

Fagan, Brian M. *People of the Earth: An Introduction to World Prehistory.* 9th ed. 1997.

Lerner, Gerda. *The Creation of Patriarchy.* 1986.

Phillipson, David W. *African Archaeology.* 2nd ed. 1993.

Rudgley, Richard. *The Lost Civilizations of the Stone Age.* 1999.

Warnock, Peter. "The History of Paleoethnobotany in the Near East," *Near Eastern Archaeology* 61 (1998): 238–52.

Wenke, Robert J. *Patterns in Prehistory: Humankind's First Three Million Years.* 4th ed. 1999.

Mesopotamia, Home of the First Civilization, c. 4000–1500 B.C.

Contemporary political events have drastically limited archaeological exploration in Mesopotamia (present-day Iraq) and severely damaged its ancient remains. Recent research therefore has concentrated on studying already excavated material and texts to understand the complex social and economic history of the region in early times. Recent translations and analysis of Mesopotamian myth have made this literature more accessible.

Ancient Near Eastern sites: http://www-oi.uchicago.edu/OI/DEPT/RA/ABZU/ABZU.HTML.

Black, Jeremy, and Anthony Green. *Gods, Demons, and Symbols of Ancient Mesopotamia: An Illustrated Dictionary.* 1992.

Crawford, Harriet. *Sumer and the Sumerians.* 1991.

Dalley, Stephanie, trans. *Myths from Mesopotamia: Creation, The Flood, Gilgamesh, and Others.* 1991.

Kings of Mesopotamian cities: http://www.mpiwg-berlin.mpg.de/Yearnames/yearnames.htm.

Kuhrt, Amélie. *The Ancient Near East, c. 3000–330 B.C.* Vol. 1. 1995.

McCall, Henrietta. *Mesopotamian Myths.* 1990.

Mieroop, Marc van de. *The Ancient Mesopotamian City.* 1997.

Nissen, Hans J. *The Early History of the Ancient Near East, 9000–2000 B.C.* Trans. Elizabeth Lutzeier, with Kenneth J. Northcutt. 1988.

Oates, Joan. *Babylon.* Rev. ed. 1986.

Postgate, J. N. *Early Mesopotamia: Society and Economy at the Dawn of History.* 1994.

Roux, Georges. *Ancient Iraq.* 3rd ed. 1992.

Silver, Morris. *Economic Structures of the Ancient Near East.* 1985.

Snell, Daniel C. *Life in the Ancient Near East, 3100–332 B.C.E.* 1997.

Walker, C. B. F. *Cuneiform.* 1987.

Civilization in Ancient Egypt and the Levant, c. 3100–1000 B.C.

Recent archaeological research has revealed much new information about the ancient kingdom of Nubia, south of Egypt, as well as sub-Saharan Africa. Publications on every aspect of ancient Egyptian life continue to pour out, with especially thorough work on famous queens. Scholars studying the Levant increasingly emphasize the interaction of its various cultures in trade and in war.

Aldred, Cyril. *The Egyptians.* Rev. ed. 1984.

Aubet, Maria Eugenia. *The Phoenicians and the West: Politics, Colonies, and Trade.* 1993.

Delgado, James P., ed. *Encyclopedia of Underwater and Maritime Archaeology.* 1998.

Foster, John. L. *Echoes of Egyptian Voices: An Anthology of Ancient Egyptian Poetry.* 1992.

Hart, George. *Egyptian Myths.* 1990.

Healey, John F. *The Early Alphabet.* 1990.

Kendall, Timothy. *Kerma and the Kingdom of Kush, 2500–1500 B.C.: The Archaeological Discovery of an Ancient Nubian Empire.* 1997.

Knapp, A. Bernard. *The History and Culture of Ancient Western Asia and Egypt.* 1988.

Lesko, Barbara. S., ed. *Women's Earliest Records: From Ancient Egypt and Western Asia.* 1989.

Meeks, Dimitri, and Christine Favard-Meeks. *Daily Life of the Egyptian Gods.* Trans. G. M. Goshgarian. 1996.

Miller, J. Maxwell, and John H. Hayes. *A History of Ancient Israel and Judah.* 1986.

Newby, P. H. *Warrior Pharaohs: The Rise and Fall of the Egyptian Empire.* 1980.

Nunn, John F. *Ancient Egyptian Medicine.* 1996.

Parkinson, R. B. *Voices from Ancient Egypt: An Anthology of Middle Kingdom Writings.* 1991.

Redford, Donald B. *Egypt, Canaan, and Israel in Ancient Times.* 1992.

Redford, Donald B., ed. *The Oxford Encyclopedia of Ancient Egypt.* 2000.

Rice, Michael. *Egypt's Making: The Origins of Ancient Egypt, 5000–2000 B.C.* 1990.

Robins, Gay. *Women in Ancient Egypt.* 1993.

Royal tomb of the sons of Pharaoh Ramesses II: http://www.kv5.com.

Stead, Miriam. *Egyptian Life.* 1986.

Tubb, Jonathan N. *Canaanites.* 1998.

Tyldesley, Joyce. *Hatshepsut: The Female Pharaoh.* 1996.

———. *Nefertiti: Egypt's Sun Queen.* 1998.

Virtual Museum of Nautical Archaeology (including the Uluburun shipwreck): http://nautarch.tamu.edu/ina/vm.htm.

Weiss, Harvey. *Ebla to Damascus: Art and Archaeology of Ancient Syria.* 1985.

Wildung, Dietrich, ed. *Sudan: Ancient Kingdoms of the Nile.* Trans. Peter Der Manuelian and Kathleen Guillaume. 1997.

Wilkinson, R. H. *Symbol and Magic in Egyptian Art.* 1994.

Civilization in Bronze Age Greece and Anatolia, c. 2200–1000 B.C.

Archaeology continues to uncover the best evidence for the emergence of Greek and Anatolian civilization. Intensive study of Minoan civilization has raised many questions about traditional interpretations of it as more peaceful than its Mediterranean neighbors. Controversy also persists about the course and causes of the tumult of the period 1200–1000 B.C., such as that concerning Robert Drews's explanation for the calamities, which posits a change in military technology that made chariot warfare obsolete.

Aegean Bronze Age: http://devlab.dartmouth.edu/history/bronze_age.

Bryce, Trevor. *The Kingdom of the Hittites.* 1998.

Chadwick, John. *The Mycenaean World.* 1976.

Crete: http://harpy.uccs.edu/greek/crete.html.

Dickinson, Oliver. *The Aegean Bronze Age.* 1994.

Drews, Robert. *The Coming of the Greeks: Indo-European Conquests in the Aegean and the Near East.* 1988.

———. *The End of the Bronze Age: Changes in Warfare and the Catastrophe ca. 1200 B.C.* 1993.

Farnoux, Alexandre. *Knossos: Searching for the Legendary Palace of King Minos.* Trans. David J. Baker. 1996.

Fitton, J. Lesley. *The Discovery of the Greek Bronze Age.* 1995.

Gurney, O. R. *The Hittites.* Rev. ed. 1990.

Macqueen, J. G. *The Hittites and Their Contemporaries in Asia Minor.* Rev. ed. 1986.

Mycenae: http://harpy.uccs.edu/greek/mycenae.html.

Sanders, N. K. *The Sea Peoples: Warriors of the Ancient Mediterranean, 1250–1150 B.C.* Rev. ed. 1985.

Willetts, R. F. *The Civilization of Ancient Crete.* 1977.

2

New Paths for Western Civilization

c. 1000–500 B.C.

Black-Figure Vase from Corinth

This vase was made in Corinth about 600 B.C. and then shipped to the island of Rhodes, where it was found. The drawing is in the so-called black-figure style, in which artists carved details into the dark-baked clay. In the late sixth century B.C., this style gave way to red-figure, in which artists painted details in black on a reddish background instead of engraving them; the result was much finer work (compare this vase painting with that on page 64). The animals and mythical creatures on this vase follow Near Eastern models, which inspired Archaic Age Greek artists to put people and animals into their designs again after their absence during the Dark Age.
British Museum.

A FIFTH-CENTURY B.C. GREEK, HERODOTUS, blazed a new path for Western civilization by writing the first book-length narrative history. He believed that describing the different customs of peoples was a central part of history. Accordingly, he told a story about some Greeks meeting a delegation from India to compare their customs for proper treatment of their parents' corpses during funerals. When the Greeks were asked how much they would take to eat their parents' bodies, as the Indians did, they insisted that no amount of money could make them do that. The Indians in turn were asked what payment would be required to make them cremate their parents, the way the Greeks did. The Indians immediately shouted, "Don't even mention such a horror!"

Herodotus told this tale to illustrate the diversity of peoples and cultures in the far-flung world of ancient Western civilization. By bringing together two groups whose homelands lay thousands of miles apart, the story also reveals the contacts between different peoples that characterized this world. As far back in the past as we can see, people had sought out this sort of interaction, above all to trade and to discover technological innovations in other places. Inevitably, contact exposed people to others' ideas as well as their goods. New paths for civilization emerged as people traded, traveled, innovated, and adapted what they learned from others to their own purposes.

The widespread violence of the Sea Peoples period, which lasted from about 1200 to 1000 B.C., threatened to cut off such contacts by making the Mediterranean world too dangerous and unstable. But the craving of the region's peoples for trade and the cross-cultural contact it brought were too strong to be snuffed out by even violent turmoil

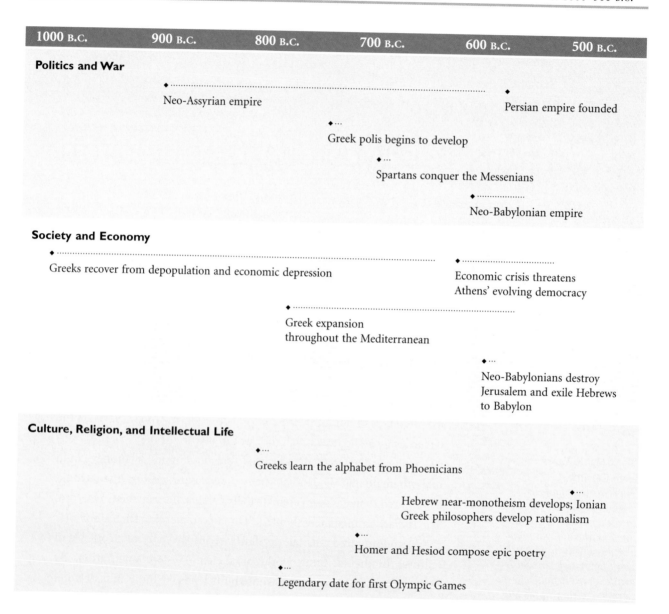

1000 B.C.	900 B.C.	800 B.C.	700 B.C.	600 B.C.	500 B.C.

Politics and War

Neo-Assyrian empire

Persian empire founded

Greek polis begins to develop

Spartans conquer the Messenians

Neo-Babylonian empire

Society and Economy

Greeks recover from depopulation and economic depression

Economic crisis threatens Athens' evolving democracy

Greek expansion throughout the Mediterranean

Neo-Babylonians destroy Jerusalem and exile Hebrews to Babylon

Culture, Religion, and Intellectual Life

Greeks learn the alphabet from Phoenicians

Hebrew near-monotheism develops; Ionian Greek philosophers develop rationalism

Homer and Hesiod compose epic poetry

Legendary date for first Olympic Games

and severe international economic distress. This drive increased as conditions improved after 1000 B.C. The Near East recovered quickly and went on much as before, maintaining its traditional form of social and political organization, monarchy. As they had always done, Near Eastern kings in this period continued to extract surpluses from subject populations to support their palaces and their armies. Also following tradition, the highest aspiration of a Near Eastern king remained the conquest of a large empire to win glory, exploit the labor of conquered peoples, seize raw materials, and conduct long-distance trade.

In Greece, by contrast, the period from 1000 to 500 B.C. differed radically from the past. The war and economic collapse of 1200–1000 B.C. had put a complete end to the social and political organization of Minoan and Mycenaean Greece. No more powerful rulers existed to demand surpluses from subjects. During the recovery from poverty and depopulation in most areas, Greeks maintained trade and cross-cultural contact with the older civilizations of the Near East; their art and mythology reveal that they imported ideas as well as goods.

By the eighth century B.C., Greeks had begun to create a new form of organization, the *polis* (an independent city-state). It made citizenship and freedom the basis for society and politics, with legal—but not political—rights for women and with slavery the fate of those treated as property instead of as people. The Greek city-state depended on agreement among male citizens to share power in governing, except when a tyrant ruled, and in contributing surpluses for common purposes. The extent of the sharing varied, with small groups of upper-class men dominating in some places. In other places, however, the sharing of power included all free men, even the poor, and thus the world's first democracy was born.

One experience that Greeks and Near Eastern peoples shared in this period was the frequent presence of war in their lives. In Greece, the long process of creating independent city-states created violent clashes over the mainland's limited supply of fertile land, while in the Near East the drive for empire made war as common as sunshine. With the clash of arms constantly ringing in their ears, thinkers in the Near East and Greece developed new patterns in religion and thought that make up the foremost legacies of this period to later Western civilization: the Persians' Zoroastrian beliefs about life as a struggle between good and evil, Hebrew monotheism, and Greek philosophy's rationalism in place of mythological explanations of nature.

❖ From Dark Age to Empire in the Near East

The violent raids and unrest of the period 1200–1000 B.C. had weakened or obliterated many communities and populations in the eastern Mediterranean. We know little about the period of recovery that followed because few sources exist to supplement the information provided by archaeology. Both because economic conditions were so gloomy for so many people and because our view of what happened is so dim, historians often refer to the era in which conditions were hardest for a particular region as its Dark Age. In the Near East, recent archaeological excavation suggests that its Dark Age lasted less than a century, a much shorter period than Greece experienced.

By 900 B.C., a powerful and centralized Assyrian kingdom had once again emerged in Meso-

potamia. From this base, the Assyrians ruthlessly carved out a new empire even larger than the one their ancestors had long ago created. The riches and power of this Neo-Assyrian empire later inspired first the Babylonians and then the Persians to try to fill the void created when Assyrian power collapsed. This constant striving for imperial wealth and territory kept the Near East on the same path politically and militarily that the region had followed in the past. Ironically, the relatively powerless Hebrews established a new path for civilization during this period: Influencing the future by a change in their religion rather than bloodshed, they developed monotheism and produced the Hebrew Bible, known to Christians as the Old Testament.

The New Empire of Assyria, c. 900–612 B.C.

The collapse of the Hittite kingdom in Anatolia and the Levant by 1000 B.C. created a power vacuum. The aggressive warriors of Assyria leapt into this gap to seize supplies of metal and try to control trade routes by land and sea. Beginning around 900 B.C., the armies of what historians call the Neo-Assyrian ("New Assyrian") kingdom relentlessly drove westward against the Aramaean states in Syria until they punched through to the Mediterranean coast (Map 2.1). Neo-Assyrian monarchs pursued a determined policy of foreign expansion. In the eighth century B.C., they extended their control into southern Mesopotamia by conquering Babylon, while in the seventh century they added Egypt to their empire. This conquest offered dramatic proof of the weakness that had plagued Egypt since the New Kingdom had fallen in 1085 B.C.

Military Might and Imperial Brutality. The values of violence pervaded Neo-Assyrian society, which seems to have been dominated by male warriors. Unlike earlier armies, the Neo-Assyrians made foot soldiers their principal striking force instead of cavalry. Trained infantrymen excelled in the use of military technology such as siege towers and battering rams, while swift chariots carried archers. Campaigns against foreign lands brought in revenues to supplement the domestic economy, which was based on agriculture, raising animals, and long-distance trade. Conquered peoples not deported to Assyria had to pay annual tribute to support the kingdom's prosperity, supplying raw materials and luxury goods such as incense, wine, dyed linens, glasswork, and ivory.

Neo-Assyrian kings treated conquered peoples brutally, torturing and executing captives to keep order by instilling fear. They also routinely herded large numbers of people from their homelands to Assyria to make them work on huge building projects—temples and palaces—in main cities. One unexpected consequence of this rough policy was that the kings undermined their native language: so many Aramaeans were deported from Canaan to Assyria that Aramaic had largely replaced Assyrian as the land's everyday language by the eighth century B.C.

Neo-Assyrian Life and Religion. When not making war, Neo-Assyrian men spent much time hunting wild animals, the more dangerous the quarry the better. The king, for example, hunted lions as proof of his vigor and power. Royal lion hunts provided a favorite subject for sculptors, who mastered the

MAP 2.1 Expansion of the Neo-Assyrian Empire, c. 900–650 B.C.
Like their Akkadian, Assyrian, and Babylonian predecessors, the Neo-Assyrian kings dominated a vast region of the Near East to secure a supply of metals, access to trade routes on land and sea, and imperial glory; they built the largest empire the world had yet seen. Also like their predecessors, they treated disobedient subjects harshly and intolerantly to try to prevent their diverse territories from rebelling.

artistic technique of carving long relief sculptures that narrated a connected story. Although the Neo-Assyrian imperial administration devoted much effort to preserving documents in its archives, literacy apparently mattered far less to the kingdom's males than war, hunting, and practical technology. Sennacherib (r. 704–681 B.C.), for example, boasted that he invented new irrigation equipment and a novel method of metal casting. Ashurbanipal (r. 680–626 B.C.) is the only king to proclaim his scholarly accomplishments: "I have read complicated texts, whose versions in Sumerian are obscure and in Akkadian hard to understand. I do research on the cuneiform texts on stone from before the Flood." Women of the social elite probably had a chance to become literate, but even they were excluded from the male dominions of hunting and war.

Public religion, which included deities adopted from Babylonian religion, reflected the prominence of war in Assyrian culture: even the cult of Ishtar (the Babylonian name for Inanna), the goddess of love and fertility, glorified warfare. The Neo-Assyrians' passion for monumental architecture manifested itself in huge temples erected to the gods. The temples' staffs of priests and slaves grew so numerous that the revenues from temple lands were no longer enough to support them, and the kings had to supply extra funds from the spoils of conquest.

The Neo-Assyrian kings' harshness made even their own people dislike their rule, especially the social elite. Rebellions were common throughout the history of the kingdom, and in the seventh century B.C. it finally faced too many rebels to overcome. The Medes, an Iranian people, and the Chaldeans, a Semitic people who had driven the Assyrians from Babylonia, combined forces to invade the weakened kingdom. They destroyed its capital at Nineveh in 612 B.C. and ended the Neo-Assyrian kings' golden dreams of empire.

The Neo-Babylonian Empire, c. 605–562 B.C.

Since the Chaldeans had headed the allies who overthrew the vast Neo-Assyrian empire, they acquired the lion's share of the fallen enemy's territory. Sprung from seminomadic herders along the Persian Gulf, they went on to establish what we call the Neo-Babylonian empire, which became the most powerful in Babylonian history and perpetuated

Neo-Assyrian History in Metal
*Shalmaneser III, ruler of the Neo-Assyrian empire
(858–824 B.C.), followed the tradition of his predecessors
on the throne by commemorating his conquests in relief
sculptures; these and other scenes prominently decorated
a wooden gate of a palace near Nimrud. (These bands are
circular because they were attached to a spindle on which
one of the gate's doors revolved.) Shalmaneser apparently
set a new precedent by having these scenes crafted in metal,
for previous royal historical reliefs had been carved in
stone. The metalworkers were highly skilled: the bands
are less than 0.06 inches thick.*
British Museum.

imperial monarchy as the standard form of government in the Near East. King Nebuchadnezzar II (r. 605–562 B.C.) made the Neo-Babylonians the Near East's leading power by driving the Egyptian army from Syria at the battle of Carchemish in 605 B.C. Nebuchadnezzar spent lavishly to turn Babylon into an architectural showplace, rebuilding the great temple of its chief god, Marduk, creating the famous Hanging Gardens—so named because lush plants drooped over its terraced sides—and constructing an elaborate city gate dedicated to the goddess Ishtar. Blue-glazed bricks and lions molded in yellow, red, and white decorated the gate's walls, which soared thirty-six feet high.

The Chaldeans adopted traditional Babylonian culture and preserved much ancient Mesopotamian literature, such as the *Epic of Gilgamesh* and other famous myths. They also created many new works of prose and poetry, which educated people, a minority of the population, would often read aloud publicly for the enjoyment of the illiterate. Particularly popular were fables, proverbs, essays, and prophecies that taught morality and proper behavior. This so-called wisdom literature, a Near Eastern tradition going back at least to the Egyptian Old Kingdom, would greatly influence the later religious writings of the Hebrews.

The Chaldeans also passed on their knowledge to others outside their region. Their advances in astronomy became so influential that the word *Chaldean* became the Greeks' word for *astronomer*. As in the past, the primary motivation for observing the stars was the belief that the gods communicated their will to humans through natural phenomena, such as celestial movements and eclipses, abnormal births, the way smoke curled upward from a fire, and the trails of ants. The interpretation of these phenomena as messages from the gods exemplified the mixture of science and religion characteristic of ancient Near Eastern thought and proved influential on the Greeks.

The Persian Empire, c. 557–500 B.C.

Throwing off Median rule of Persia (today Iran), Cyrus (r. c. 557–530 B.C.) founded the Near East's next great kingdom through his skills as a general and a diplomat who respected others' religious beliefs. He continued the region's tradition of kings fighting to control territorial empires by conquering Babylon in 539 B.C.; a rebellion there had weakened the Chaldean dynasty when King Nabonidus (r. c. 555–539 B.C.) had provoked a revolt among the priests of Marduk by promoting the cult of Sin, the moon god of the Mesopotamian city of Harran. Cyrus capitalized on this religious strife by presenting himself as the restorer of traditional Babylonian religion, thereby winning local support; an ancient inscription has him proclaim: "Marduk, the great lord, caused Babylon's generous residents to adore me." He also won the gratitude of the exiled Hebrews by allowing any who wished to return to Jerusalem, their spiritual capital.

His successors expanded Persian rule on the same principles of military strength and cultural tolerance; at its greatest extent, the empire extended from Anatolia, the Levant, and Egypt on the west to

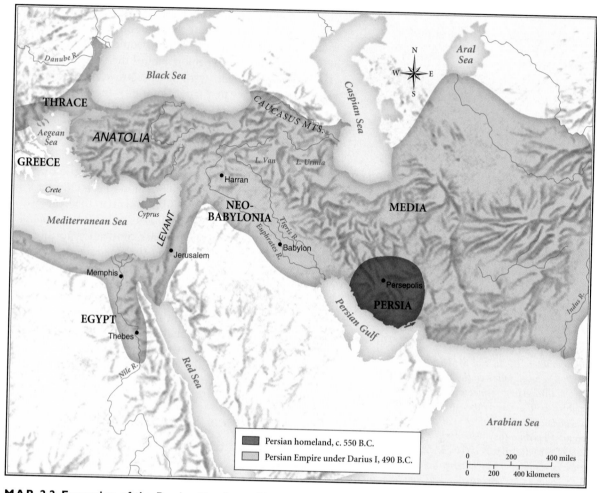

MAP 2.2 Expansion of the Persian Empire, c. 550–490 B.C.
Cyrus (r. c. 557–530 B.C.) initiated the Persian empire, which his successors expanded to be even larger than the Neo-Assyrian empire that it replaced. By the later years of Darius's reign (r. 522–486 B.C.), the Persian empire had expanded eastward as far as the western edge of India, while to the west it reached Thrace, the eastern edge of Europe. Unlike their imperial predecessors, the Persian kings won their subjects' loyalty with tolerance and religious freedom, although they treated rebels very harshly.

Pakistan on the east (Map 2.2). The Persian kings interfered in their subjects' affairs as little as possible. At the same time, they emphasized the distance in status between king and subject by the magnificence of their court and the severity of the punishments inflicted on wrongdoers. The kings' faith that they had a divine right to rule everyone in the world could provoke great conflicts, above all the war between Persians and Greeks that would break out around 500 B.C.

Royal Magnificence and Decentralized Rule.   The revenues of its realm made the Persian monarchy wealthy beyond imagination, and everything about the king emphasized his grandeur. His purple robes were more splendid than anyone's; the red carpets spread for him to walk upon could not be trod by anyone else; his servants held their hands before their mouths in his presence so that he would not have to breathe the same air as they; in the sculpture adorning his immense palace at Persepolis, he appeared larger than any other human. To display his concern for his loyal subjects, as well as the gargantuan scale of his resources, the king provided meals for some fifteen thousand nobles, courtiers, and other followers every day—although he himself ate hidden from the view of his guests. Those who committed serious offenses against his laws or his dignity the king punished brutally, by mutilating their bodies and executing their families. Contemporary Greeks, in awe of the Persian monarch's power and his lavish style of life, referred to him as "The Great King."

So long as his subjects—numbering in the millions and of many different ethnicities—remained peaceful, the king left them largely unrestrained to live and worship as they pleased. The empire's smoothly functioning administrative structure sprang from Assyrian precedents: provincial governors (*satraps*) ruled enormous territories with little if any direct interference from the kings. In this decentralized system, the governors' duties included keeping order, enrolling troops when needed, and sending revenues to the royal treasury.

Darius I (r. 522–486 B.C.) vastly extended Cyrus's conquests by pushing Persian power eastward to the Indus valley and westward to Thrace. Organizing this vast territory into provinces, he assigned each region taxes payable in the medium best suited to its local economy—precious metals, grain, horses, slaves. In addition, he required each region to send soldiers to staff the royal army. A network of roads and a courier system for royal mail facilitated communications among the far-flung provincial centers; Herodotus reports that neither snow, rain, heat, nor darkness slowed the couriers from completing their routes as swiftly as possible, a feat later transformed into the U.S. Postal Service motto.

Zoroastrian Religion. Ruling as absolute autocrats and therefore possessing the power to make the rules for everyone else, the Persian kings believed they were superior to all humans. They regarded themselves not as gods but as the agents of Ahura Mazda, the supreme god of Persia. As Darius said in his autobiography carved into a mountainside in three languages, "Ahura Mazda gave me kingship . . . by the will of Ahura Mazda the provinces respected my laws."

Based on the teachings of the legendary prophet Zarathustra and called Zoroastrianism from the Greek name for this holy man, Persian religion made Ahura Mazda the center of its devotion. It seems, however, not to have been pure monotheism (belief in the existence of only one god). Its most important doctrine was a moral dualism: perceiving

The Great King of Persia
Like their Assyrian predecessors, the Persian kings decorated their palaces with large relief sculptures emphasizing royal dignity and success. This one from Persepolis shows officials and petitioners giving the king proper respect when entering his presence. To symbolize their elevated status, the king and his son, who stands behind the throne, are depicted as larger than everyone else.
Courtesy of the Oriental Institute of the University of Chicago.

the world as the arena for an ongoing battle between the opposing forces of good and evil. Ahura Mazda's two children, according to Persian belief, made different moral choices, one choosing the way of the truth and the other the way of the lie. Like these divine beings, humans could freely decide between purity and impurity, and their judgment had consequences: Zoroastrianism promised that salvation would be the fate of those following the way of the truth, while damnation would punish those electing the way of the lie. The Persian religious emphasis on ethical behavior had a lasting influence on others, most strikingly on the Hebrews.

The Consolidation of Hebrew Monotheism, c. 1000–539 B.C.

The Hebrews achieved their first truly national organization with the creation of a monarchy in the late eleventh century B.C. Saul became their first king by fighting to limit Philistine power in Palestine, and his successors David (r. 1010–970 B.C.) and Solomon (r. c. 961–922 B.C.) brought the united nation to the height of its prosperity. Its national wealth, largely derived from import-export commerce conducted through its cities, was displayed above all in the great temple richly decorated with gold leaf that Solomon built in Jerusalem to be the house of the Hebrews' god, Yahweh. This temple was their premier religious monument.

After Solomon's death, the monarchy split into two kingdoms: Israel in the north and Judah in the south. The more powerful Mesopotamians later subjugated these kingdoms. Tiglath-pileser III of Assyria forced much of Palestine to become a tribute-paying, subject territory, destroying Israel in 722 B.C. and deporting its population to Assyria. In 597 B.C., the neo-Babylonian king Nebuchadnezzar II conquered Judah and captured its capital, Jerusalem. Ten years later he destroyed its temple to Yahweh and banished the Hebrew leaders and much of the population to Babylon. The Hebrews always remembered the sorrow of this exile.

When the Persian king Cyrus overthrew the Babylonians in 539 B.C., he permitted the Hebrews to return to Palestine, which was called *Yehud* from the name of the southern Hebrew kingdom Judah. From this geographical term came the name *Jews,* a designation for the Hebrews after their Babylonian exile. Cyrus allowed them to rebuild their main temple in Jerusalem and to practice their religion. After returning from exile, the Jews were forever after a people subject to the political domination of various Near Eastern powers, save for a period of independence during the second and first centuries B.C.

Jewish prophets, both men and women, preached that their defeats were divine punishment for neglecting the Sinai covenant and mistreating their poor. Some prophets also predicted the coming end of the present world following a great crisis, a judgment by Yahweh, and salvation leading to a new and better world. This apocalypticism ("uncovering" of the future), reminiscent of Babylonian prophetic wisdom literature, would greatly influence Christianity later. Yahweh would save the Hebrew nation, the prophets thundered, only if Jews learned to observe divine law strictly.

To ensure proper observance, Jewish religious leaders developed firm regulations requiring their people to maintain ritual and ethical purity in all aspects of life. Women enjoyed great honor as mothers, but fathers had legal power over the household, subject to intervention by the male elders of the community. Only men could initiate divorce proceedings. Marrying non-Jews was forbidden, as was working on the Sabbath (the week's holy day). Ethics applied not only to obvious crimes but also to financial dealings; cheating in business transactions was condemned. Taxes and offerings had to be paid to support and honor the sanctuary of Yahweh, and debts had to be forgiven every seventh year.

The Jews' hardships had taught them that their religious traditions and laws gave them the strength to survive even when separated from their homeland. They came to believe above all that Yahweh was the only god and that to abide by divine will they had to behave ethically toward everyone, rich and poor alike. They thus created the first complete monotheism, with laws based on ethics. Jews retained their identity by following this religion, regardless of their personal fate or their geographical location. A remarkable outcome of these religious developments was that those who did not return to their homeland, but chose to remain in Babylon or Persia or Egypt, could maintain their Jewish identity while living among foreigners. In this way, the Diaspora ("dispersion of population") came to characterize the history of the Jewish people.

Hebrew monotheism as it developed during and after the period of exile in Babylon made the preservation and understanding of a sacred text, the Bible, the center of religious life. The chief priests compiled an authoritative scripture by forming the Torah, the first five books of the Hebrew Bible, to which were eventually added the books of the prophets, such as Isaiah. Making scripture the focus of religion proved the most crucial development for the history not only of Judaism, but also of Christianity and Islam, because these later religions made their own sacred texts, the Christian Bible and the Qur'an respectively, the centers of their belief and practice.

Although the ancient Hebrews never formed a powerful nation, their religious ideas created a new path for Western civilization. Through the continuing vitality of Judaism and its impact on the doctrines of Christianity and Islam, the early Jews passed on ideas whose effects—the belief in monotheism and the notion of a covenant bestowing a divinely ordained destiny on a people if they obey

divine will—have endured to this day. These religious concepts constitute one of the most significant legacies to Western civilization from the Near East in the period 1000–500 B.C.

❖ Remaking Greek Civilization

For all practical purposes, the unrest of 1200–1000 B.C. cost the Greeks the distinguishing marks of civilization: they no longer had large settlements, palaces, or writing. These losses led to their Dark Age (c. 1000–750 B.C.), during which they had to remake their civilization by emerging from poverty and depopulation. Trade, cultural interaction, and technological innovation led to recovery: contact with the Near East promoted intellectual, artistic, and economic revival, while the introduction of metallurgy for making iron made farming more efficient. As conditions improved, a social elite distinguished by wealth and the competitive value of excellence derived from Homeric poetry replaced the lost hierarchy of Mycenaean times. In the eighth century B.C., the creation of the Olympic Games and the emphasis on justice in Hesiod's poetry promoted the communal values that fueled the story of Greek civilization following the Dark Age.

The Greek Dark Age, c. 1000–750 B.C.

The depressed economic conditions in Greece after the fall of Mycenaean civilization typify the desperately reduced circumstances so many people in the Mediterranean and the Near East had to endure during the worst years of their Dark Ages. One of the most startling indications of the severity of life in the Dark Age in Greece is that Greeks apparently lost their knowledge of writing when Mycenaean civilization fell. The Linear B script they had used was difficult to master and probably known only by a few scribes, who used writing exclusively to track the flow of goods in and out of the palaces. When the redistributive economy of Mycenaean Greece collapsed, the Greeks no longer needed scribes or writing. Oral transmission kept Greek cultural tradition alive.

Archaeological excavations have shown that the Greeks cultivated much less land and had many

Goddess Figurines from Judah
Many small statues of this type, called "Astarte figurines" after a popular Canaanite goddess, have been found in private houses in Judah dating from about 800 to 600 B.C. Hebrews evidently kept them as magical tokens to promote fertility and prosperity. The prophets fiercely condemned the worship of such figures as part of the development of Hebrew monotheism and the abandoning of polytheism.
© Israel Museum, Jerusalem. Artifact Collection of the Israel Antiquities Authority.

fewer settlements in the early Dark Age than at the height of Mycenaean prosperity (Map 2.3). No longer did powerful rulers ensconced in stone fortresses control redistributive economies that provided a tolerable standard of living for their subjects. The number of ships carrying Greek adventurers, raiders, and traders dwindled. Developed political states ceased to exist, and the people eked out their existence as herders, shepherds, and subsistence farmers bunched in tiny settlements—as few as twenty people in many cases. As the Greek population dwindled, less land was cultivated, and food production declined, causing the population to drop further. These two processes reinforced one another in a vicious circle, multiplying the negative effects of both.

The Greek agricultural economy remained complex despite the withering away of many traditional forms of agriculture. Since more Greeks than ever before made their living by herding animals, people became more mobile: they needed to move their herds to new pastures once the animals had overgrazed their current location. Lucky herders

MAP 2.3 Dark-Age Greece
Recent archaeological research indicates that Greece was not as impoverished or as depopulated after the fall of the Mycenaean kingdoms as once assumed. Still, during the Dark Age, Greeks lived in significantly fewer and smaller population centers than in the Bronze Age; it took centuries for the region as a whole to revive.

might find a new spot where they could grow a crop of grain if they stayed long enough. As a result of this less settled lifestyle, people built only simple huts and got along with few possessions. Unlike their Bronze Age forebears, Greeks in the Dark Age had no monumental architecture, and they even lost an old tradition in their everyday art: they stopped painting people and animals in their principal art form, ceramics.

Trade, Innovation, and Recovery. The troubles of the Dark Age reduced but did not end Greece's trade with the civilizations of the eastern Mediterranean; this contact taught Greeks to write again about 800 B.C. when they learned the alphabet from the Phoenicians, energetic seafaring traders whose homeland was in Canaan (and whose name, *Phoenicians*, may have derived from the Greek term for the valuable purple dye they extracted from shellfish). They changed and added letters to achieve independent representation of vowel sounds so they could express their language and record their literature, beginning with the eighth-century B.C. poems of Homer and Hesiod. Eastern art inspired them once more to include lively pictures of animals and people in their paintings. By making available rare goods such as gold jewelry and gems from Egypt and Syria, seaborne commerce encouraged elite Greeks to produce surpluses to trade for such luxuries.

Most important, trade brought the new technology of iron metallurgy. The violence of the Sea Peoples period had interrupted the traditional trading routes for tin, which was needed to make bronze weapons and tools. To make up for this loss, metalsmiths in the eastern Mediterranean devised technology to smelt iron ore. Greeks then learned this skill through their eastern trade contacts and mined their own ore, which was common in Greece. Iron eventually replaced bronze in many uses, above all for agricultural tools, swords, and spear points. Bronze was still used for shields and armor, however, perhaps because it was easier to shape into thinner, curved pieces.

Eventually, the lower cost of iron tools meant that more people could afford them; and because iron is harder than bronze, implements now kept their sharp edges longer. Better and more plentiful farming implements of iron eventually helped increase food production, which supported a larger population. In this way, imported technology improved the chances of ordinary people for survival and thus helped Greece recover from the depopulation of the Dark Age.

The Social Elite and the Homeric Ideal. Since the powerful rulers of Mycenaean Greece had disappeared, there was an open field for competition for leadership positions in Dark Age society. The men and women who proved themselves excellent in action, words, charisma, and religious knowledge became the social elite. Excellence—*aretê* in Greek—was a competitive value: high social status stemmed from a family's men and women outdoing others. Men displayed *aretê* above all through prowess in war and persuasiveness in speech; the highest *aretê* for women was savvy management of a bustling household of children, slaves, and the family's storerooms. Members of the elite also accumulated wealth by controlling agricultural land which people of lower status worked for them as tenants or slaves.

The Greek Dark Age, c. 1000–700 B.C.

c. 1000 B.C. Almost all important Mycenaean sites except Athens destroyed by now

c. 1000–900 B.C. Greatest depopulation and economic loss

900–800 B.C. Early revival of population and agriculture; iron now beginning to be used for tools and weapons

c. 800 B.C. Greek trading contacts initiated with Al Mina in Syria

776 B.C. First Olympic Games held

c. 775 B.C. Euboeans found trading post on Ischia in the Bay of Naples

c. 750–700 B.C. Homeric poetry recorded in writing after Greeks learn to write again; Hesiod composes his poetry; Oracle of Apollo at Delphi already famous

A Rich Woman's Model Granary from the Dark Age
This clay model of storage containers for grain was found in a woman's tomb in Athens from about 850 B.C. It apparently symbolizes the surpluses that the woman and her family were able to accumulate and indicates that she was wealthy by the standards of her time. We can therefore deduce that economic conditions had begun to improve for at least some Athenians already at this point in the Dark Age. The geometric designs painted on the pottery are characteristic of Greek art in this period, when human and animal figures were left out. By the Archaic Age, this had changed under Near Eastern influence. Contrast the lively animals painted some two hundred years later on the Corinthian vase illustrated at the opening of this chapter (page 44).
American School of Classical Studies at Athens: Agora Excavation.

The poetry of Homer, which became Greece's most famous literature, provided the elite with its ideals. The Greeks believed that Homer was a blind poet from the region called Ionia (today Turkey's western coast), who composed the epics *The Iliad* and *The Odyssey*. Most modern scholars believe that Homer was the last in a long line of poets who, influenced by Near Eastern mythology, had been singing these stories for centuries, orally transmitting cultural values from one generation to the next. *The Iliad* tells the story of the Greek army in the Trojan War. Camped before the walls of Troy for ten years, the heroes of the army compete for glory and riches by raiding the countryside, dueling Troy's best fighters, and quarreling with one another over status and booty. The greatest Greek hero is Achilles, who proves his surpassing excellence by choosing to die young in battle rather than accept the gods' offer to return home safely but without glory. *The Odyssey* recounts the hero Odysseus's ten-year adventure finding his way home after the fall of Troy and the struggle of his wife, Penelope, to protect their household from the schemes and threats of their family's rivals for status and wealth. Penelope proves herself the best of women, showing her *aretê* by outwitting envious neighbors and thereby preserving her family's prosperity for her husband's return.

In both *The Iliad* and *The Odyssey*, Homer reveals how the white-hot emotions inflamed by the individual's quest for excellence could provoke a disturbing level of inhumanity. As Achilles prepares to duel Hector, the prince of Troy, he brutally rejects the Trojan's proposal for the winner to return the loser's corpse to his family and friends: "Do wolves and lambs agree to cooperate? No, they hate each other to the roots of their being." The victor, Achilles, mutilates Hector's body. When Hecuba, the queen of Troy, sees this outrage, she bitterly shouts "I wish I could sink my teeth into his liver in his guts to eat it raw." The endings of both poems suggest that the gods could help people achieve reconciliation after violent conflict, but the level of suffering Homer attributes to the human condition makes it clear that excellence comes at a high price.

Achilles, Odysseus, and Penelope are fictional, but they had real-life counterparts. That is, there was a Dark Age social elite, to judge from some rich burials from this period that archaeologists have discovered. At Lefkandi on the island of Euboea, for example, a tenth-century B.C. couple took such enormous riches with them to the next world that the woman's body was dripping with gold ornaments. About 900 B.C., a man at Athens had many weapons of iron buried with him. Fifty years later, an Athenian woman had her grave filled with jewelry from the Near East and a model of the storehouse for all her grain. These people had done well in the competition for status and wealth; most people of the time were, by comparison, paupers. They had to scratch out a living as best they could, while only dreaming of the heroic deeds and rich goods they heard about in Homer's poems.

The Values of the Olympic Games

By the eighth century B.C., Greece's recovery was assured. The most vivid evidence for its renewed vigor was the founding of the Olympic Games, traditionally dated to 776 B.C., as a showcase for the competitive value of *aretê*. The fifth-century B.C. poet Pindar made the purpose of the games clear in praising a family of victors: "Hiding the nature you are born with is impossible. The seasons rich in their flowers have many times bestowed on you, sons of Aletes, the brightness that victory brings, when you achieved the heights of excellence in the sacred games."

Every four years, the games took place as part of a religious festival held at Olympia, in the northwest Peloponnese, in a huge sanctuary dedicated to Zeus, the king of the gods. There, athletes from elite families vied in sports recalling the *aretê* needed for war: running, wrestling, jumping, and throwing. Horse and chariot racing were added to the program later, but the main event remained a two-hundred-yard sprint, the *stadion*. Athletes competed as individuals, not on national teams as in the modern Olympic Games. Only first prizes were awarded; winners received no financial rewards, only a garland made from wild olive leaves to symbolize the prestige of victory.

Crowds of men flocked to the games; admission was free and the sanctuary at Olympia was configured to accommodate the crowds that assembled. Women were barred on pain of death, but they had their own separate Olympic festival on a different date in honor of Hera, queen of the gods; only unmarried women could compete. Eventually, full-time athletes dominated the Olympics, earning their

Athletic Competition
Greek vase painters loved to depict male athletes in action or training, perhaps in part because they were customers who would buy pottery with such scenes. As in this scene of an Athenian foot race c. 530 B.C., the athletes were usually shown nude, which is how they competed, revealing their superb physical condition and strong musculature. Being in excellent shape was a man's ideal for several reasons: it was regarded as beautiful, it enabled him to strive for individual glory in athletic competitions, and it allowed him to fulfill his community responsibility by fighting as a well-conditioned soldier in the city-state's citizen militia.
The Metropolitan Museum of Art, Rogers Fund, 1914.

living from appearance fees and prizes at games held throughout the Greek world. The most famous winner was Milo, from Croton in Italy. Six-time Olympic wrestling champion, he stunned audiences with demonstrations of strength such as holding his breath until veins expanded so much that they would snap a cord tied around his head.

Although the Olympics existed to glorify individual excellence, one feature of their organization reveals an important trend under way in Greek society: the Olympics were pan-Hellenic. That is, they were open to any socially elite Greek male good enough to compete and to any male spectator who could journey there. For the times, these rules constituted beginning steps toward a concept of Greek identity that was not purely individual. Remarkably for a land so often torn by war, once every four years an international truce of several weeks was declared so that competitors and fans from all Greek communities could travel to and from Olympia in security. By the mid-eighth century B.C., the pan-Hellenic games channeled the competition for excellence—an individual, not a communal, value—into a new context of social cooperation and communal interest, essential preconditions for the creation of Greece's new political form, the city-state.

Hesiod and Divine Justice in Greek Myth

Developing communal, cooperative values was necessary for Greeks to remake their civilization, and they were inspired in this difficult process by their belief in divine justice. Throughout the history of ancient Greece, religion provided the context for almost all communal activity, from sports to war. Greek religion had no scriptural canon. Its heart was the vast and diverse store of *myths* (Greek for "stories") about the gods and goddesses and their relationships to humans, which poets began to write down in the eighth century B.C. after Greeks re-learned the technology of writing.

The poetry of Hesiod reveals how religious myths contributed to the feeling of community that underlay the creation of Greece's new social and political structure. A contemporary of Homer in the eighth century B.C. and nearly as famous in his time, Hesiod wrote vivid stories of the mythical past that had their origins in Near Eastern myths like those of the Mesopotamian *Epic of Creation*. His stories carry the message that existence, even for deities, entailed struggle, sorrow, and violence. They also show that a concern for justice was a component of the divine order of the universe from the beginning. His poetry describing the strife between elite leaders and ordinary people in his own time emphasizes the need to instill justice in Greek society.

Hesiod's epic poem *Theogony* ("Genealogy of the Gods") recounts the birth of the race of gods from primeval Chaos ("void" or "vacuum") and Earth, the mother of Sky and numerous other off-spring. Hesiod explains that when Sky begins to imprison his siblings, Earth persuades her fiercest son, Kronos, to overthrow him violently because "Sky first contrived to do shameful things." When Kronos later begins to swallow up all his own children to avoid sharing power with them, his wife, Rhea (who was also his sister), has their son Zeus forcefully depose his father in retribution.

In his poem on conditions in his own world, *Works and Days,* Hesiod identifies Zeus as the source of justice in human affairs, describing justice as a divine quality intended to punish evildoers: "For Zeus ordained that fishes and wild beasts and birds should eat each other, for they have no justice; but to human beings he has given justice, which is far the best." Men from the social elite dominated the distribution of justice in Hesiod's day. They controlled their family members and household servants. Hesiod emphasizes that a leader should demonstrate excellence by employing persuasion instead of force: "When his people in their assembly get on the wrong track, he gently sets matters right, persuading them with soft words."

Hesiod complains that many elite leaders in his time fell short of this ideal, creating a state of high tension between themselves and the ordinary people, the peasants (free proprietors of small farms owning a slave or two, oxen to work their fields, and a limited amount of goods acquired by trading the surplus of their crops). Assuming the perspective of a peasant farming a small holding, Hesiod insists that the divine origin of justice should be a warning to "bribe-devouring chiefs," who settle disputes among their followers and neighbors "with crooked judgments." This feeling of outrage that commoners felt at not receiving equal treatment served as yet another stimulus for the gradual movement toward a new form of social and political organization in Greece.

❖ The Creation of the Greek *Polis,* c. 750–500 B.C.

Since Greece had recovered economically and begun to create a new form of social and political organization by the mid-eighth century B.C., historians use this date as the end of the Dark Age and the beginning of the Archaic Age (c. 750–500 B.C.). The new form was the *polis,* usually translated "city-state," an independent community of citizens inhabiting a city and the countryside around it. Greece's geography, dominated by mountains and islands, promoted the creation of city-states as separate communities. During this same period, Greeks also dispersed widely in settlements around the Mediterranean in a process traditionally, but problematically, called "colonization." Individuals' entrepreneurial drive for profit from trade, especially in raw materials, and free farmland probably started this process of founding new settlements, especially in the western Mediterranean.

Putting their ideas on divine justice into practice, Greeks developed the concept of citizenship and sharing of power as the defining characteristics of their city-states, which distinguished them from the city-states of Mesopotamia. Surprisingly for the ancient world, in the fully developed city-state poor citizens enjoyed a rough legal and political equality with the rich. Not so surprisingly, women failed to attain equality with men, and slaves remained completely excluded from the benefits of the city-state's new emphasis on communal interests. The stress on the welfare of the community as a whole created a continuing tension between the interests of the elite and the interests of ordinary people.

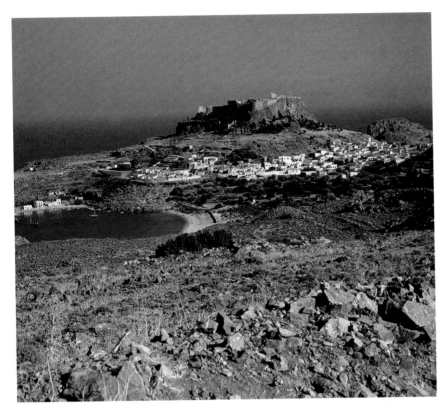

The Acropolis and Harbor of Lindos

The topography of Lindos, one of several city-states on the large island of Rhodes, illustrates the ideal setting for a Greek settlement. A high, rocky outcropping served as its citadel (acropolis) and religious center; its sheer sides made it easy to defend in an emergency. The nearly circular harbor below offered ships protection from storms and a safe place for loading and unloading passengers and cargo.
E. Hosking/Bruce Coleman, Inc.

The Physical Environment of the City-State

The ancient Greeks never constituted a nation in the modern political sense because their hundreds of separate and fiercely independent city-states lacked a unifying organization. Greeks identified with one another culturally, however, because they spoke the same language and worshiped the same deities. (See "Did You Know?," page 61.) Their homeland lay in and around the Aegean Sea, a part of the Mediterranean dotted with numerous islands, both large and small, with the southern Balkan peninsula on the west and the coast of Anatolia on the east (Map 2.4).

By isolating the city-states and making communication difficult, the mountainous geography of Greece contributed to the tradition of feisty separateness, indeed of noncooperation, among the city-states. A single island could be home to multiple city-states; Lesbos, for example, had five. Because few city-states had enough good farmland to support a large population, settlements numbering only several hundred to several thousand were the rule

even after the rise in the Greek population at the end of the Dark Age.

Most Greeks never traveled very far from home; what long-distance travelers there were journeyed by sea. Greece's rivers were practically useless as avenues for trade and communication because most of them dried up during the annual periods of little or no rainfall. Overland transport was slow and expensive because rudimentary dirt paths and dry riverbeds in summer served as the only roads in Greece's craggy terrain. The most plentiful resource of the mainland's mountains was timber for building houses and ships. Some deposits of metal ore were also scattered throughout Greek territory, as were clays suitable for pottery and sculpture. Various quarries of fine stone such as marble provided material for special buildings and works of art. The uneven distribution of these resources meant that some areas were considerably wealthier than others.

Although none of the mountains wrinkling the Greek landscape rose higher than ten thousand feet, their steep slopes restricted agriculture. Only 20 to 30 percent of the total land area could be farmed.

The scarcity of level terrain in most areas ruled out large-scale raising of cattle and horses; so pigs, sheep, and goats were the common livestock. The domestic chicken had also been introduced from the Near East by the seventh century B.C. The Mediterranean climate (intermittent heavy rain during a few months and hot, dry summers) limited a farmer's options, as did the fragility of the environment: grazing livestock, for example, could be so hard on plant life that winter downpours would wash away the limited topsoil. Because the amount of annual precipitation varied so much, farming was a precarious business of boom and bust. Farmers grew more barley, the cereal staple of the Greek diet, than wheat, which people preferred but was more expensive to cultivate. Wine grapes and olives were the other most important crops.

Trade and "Colonization"

The *polis* emerged during a time when Greeks were once again in frequent contact with Egypt and the Near East by sea. Greeks in this period had many opportunities for cross-cultural contact as the desire for trade and land roused them to move around the Mediterranean. Greece's geography made sea travel convenient: so jagged was its coastline that almost all its communities lay within forty miles of the Mediterranean Sea. But sailing meant dangers from pirates and, especially, storms; prevailing winds and fierce gales almost ruled out sea travel during winter. When they could, sailors hugged the coast, hopped from island to island, and put in to shore at night; but the drive for profit made long, nonstop voyages necessary over the open waters. As Hesiod commented, merchants needing to make a living took to the sea "because an income means life to poor mortals, but it is a terrible fate to die among the waves."

As it had for centuries, the search for metals and other scarce resources drove traders far from home in this era. The *Odyssey* describes the basic strategy of this commodity trading, when the goddess Athena appears disguised as a metal trader: "I am here . . . with my ship and crew on our way across the wine-dark sea to foreign lands in search of copper; I am carrying iron now." By 800 B.C., the Mediterranean was swarming with entrepreneurs of

MAP 2.4 Archaic Greece, c. 750–500 B.C.
The Greek heartland lay in and around the Aegean Sea, in what is today the nation of Greece and the western edge of the nation of Turkey (ancient Anatolia). The "mainland," where Athens, Corinth, and Sparta are located, is the southernmost tip of the mountainous Balkan peninsula. The many islands of the Aegean area were home mainly to small city-states, with the exception of the large islands just off the western Anatolian coast, which were home to populous ones.

DID YOU KNOW?

The First Money with Pictures

The Goddess Athena, Athens
(American Numismatic Society)

Minotaur, Crete
(American Numismatic Society)

Satyr Carrying off Nymph, Thasos
(American Numismatic Society)

When someone today asks "Do you have any money on you?" he or she is referring to currency: coins and bills with pictures and words identifying their source and value. As familiar as this form of money now seems, people got along without it for thousands of years before the first currency, coins minted about 600 B.C. at the intersection of Near Eastern and Greek culture in Anatolia. Before that, Near Eastern civilization used money in many other forms, from measured amounts of grain to small, unmarked pieces or rings of weighed metal.

Coinage soon became the principal form of money in ancient Greece, but it did not replace the noncoinage money of the Near East while that region's traditional kingdoms continued strong. The clue why lies in the difference with earlier money: coins carried images and letters conveying messages. The most important was the coin's origin—the state that minted it—because that information told people where they could be certain the money would be honored. Greeks needed this guarantee because they lacked a central political authority like Near Eastern monarchy to protect the integrity of unmarked money.

Greek coins displayed a dizzying and sometimes disturbing diversity of images, from gods and goddesses to monsters such as the half-man, half-bull Minotaur to scenes of satyrs ravishing nymphs. The pictures often had religious significance to demonstrate the importance Greeks attributed to currency's social impact; realizing that coinage had enormous potential to promote both prosperity and crime, the Greeks punished counterfeiting with death and locked away false coins in temples so the gods could keep them forever out of human society.

many nationalities. The Phoenicians proved exceptionally successful, establishing footholds as far west as Spain's Atlantic coast to gain access to inland mines there. Their North African settlement at Carthage (modern Tunis) would become one of the Mediterranean's most powerful cities in later times, dominating commerce west of Italy.

Greeks energetically joined this wave-tossed contest for profit as the scale of trade soared near the end of the Dark Age: archaeologists have found only two tenth-century B.C. Greek pots that were carried abroad, while eighth-century pottery turns up at more than eighty foreign sites. Starting around 775 B.C., numbers of Greeks began to settle far from their homeland, sometimes living in others' settlements, such as those of the Phoenicians in the western Mediterranean, and sometimes establishing trading posts of their own, as at Pithecusae in the

MAP 2.5 Phoenician and Greek Expansion, c. 750–500 B.C.

The Phoenicians, setting out from their homeland in the Levant, were early explorers and settlers of the western Mediterranean; by 800 B.C. they had already founded the city of Carthage, which would become the main commercial power in the region. During the Archaic Age, groups of adventurous Greeks followed the Phoenicians' lead and settled all around the Mediterranean, hoping to improve their economic prospects by trade and farming. Sometimes they moved into previously established Phoenician settlements, sometimes they founded their own. Eventually, some Greek city-states in the heartland established formal ties with new settlements or sent out their own expeditions to try to establish "colonies" (new, independent city-states that were supposed to remain loyal to their "mother city").

Bay of Naples. Everywhere they traded energetically with the local populations, such as the Etruscans in central Italy, who imported large amounts of Greek goods, as the vases found in their tombs reveal. Greeks staying abroad for the long term would also cultivate vacant land, gradually building permanent communities. A shortage of arable territory in Greece drove some poor citizens abroad to find farmland of their own. Because apparently only males left home on trading and land-hunting expeditions, they had to find wives in the areas where they settled, either through peaceful negotiation or by kidnapping.

By about 580 B.C., Greeks had settled in practically every available location in Spain, present-day southern France, southern Italy and Sicily, North Africa, and the Black Sea coast (Map. 2.5). Greek culture thus became particularly well known around

the western and northern Mediterranean. The settlements in southern Italy and Sicily, such as Naples and Syracuse, eventually became so large and powerful that this region was called "Great Greece" (*Magna Graecia*); its communities became rivals of Carthage for commercial dominance in the western Mediterranean.

Greek settlement in the east was less prevalent, perhaps because the monarchies there restricted foreign immigration. Still, a trading station had sprung up at Al Mina in Syria by 800 B.C., while King Psammetichus I of Egypt (r. 664–610 B.C.) permitted a similar foundation at Naucratis. These close contacts with eastern Mediterranean civilizations paid cultural as well as economic dividends. In addition to inspiring Greeks to reintroduce figures into their painting, Near Eastern art gave Greeks models for statues: they began sculpting images that stood stiffly and stared straight ahead, imitating Egyptian statuary. When the improving economy of the later Archaic Age allowed Greeks again to afford monumental architecture in stone, their rectangular temples on platforms with columns reflected Egyptian architectural designs.

Historians have traditionally called the settlement process of this era "Greek colonization," but recent research emphasizes the inappropriateness of this term, which recalls the foreign colonies established and administered by European imperial powers in the modern period. Close study of the archaeological and textual evidence for these Greek settlements suggests that private entrepreneurship initiated most of them; official state involvement was minimal, at least in the beginning. Most commonly, a city-state in the homeland would establish ties with a settlement originally set up by its citizens and claim it as its "colony" only after the community had grown into an economic success. Few instances are clearly recorded in which a Greek "mother city" officially sent out a group to establish a formally organized "colony" abroad.

Citizenship and Freedom in the City-State

Whatever term we give to the widespread dispersal of Greeks outside their homeland in the Archaic period, it seems fair to give the label "state-building" to the creation of the *polis* because this new form of organization filled the political vacuum left by the fall of Mycenaean civilization. It was unique because it was based on the concept of citizenship for all its free inhabitants and, usually, shared governance for all its free men. Some historians argue that knowledge of the older cities of the island of Cyprus and of Phoenicia in the Levant influenced the Greeks in creating their city-states; since those eastern states were headed by monarchs ruling over subjects, however, this theory cannot explain the origin of citizenship and shared power as the defining characteristics of the Greek city-state. The most famous ancient analyst of Greek politics and society, the philosopher Aristotle (384–322 B.C.), insisted that the forces of nature had created the city-state: "Humans are beings who by nature live in a city-state." Anyone who existed outside such a community, Aristotle only half-jokingly maintained, must be either a beast or a deity.

Religion in the City-State. City-states were officially religious communities: as well as worshiping the many deities of Greek polytheism, each place honored a particular god or goddess, such as Athena at Athens, as its protector and patron. Different communities could choose the same deity: Sparta, Athens's chief rival in later times, also chose Athena as its patron. The twelve most important gods were envisioned assembling for banquets atop Mount Olympus, the highest peak in mainland Greece. Zeus headed this pantheon; joining them were Hera,

Archaic Greek Freestanding Sculpture
Greek sculptors in the early Archaic Age took inspiration for the style of their freestanding statues from Egyptian art. Carved from marble, the statues stand stiffly erect, with a frozen, if pleasant, expression on their faces. This damaged statue from the late Archaic period shows the elegant and colorful clothing, elaborate hairstyle, and slight smile that distinguished sculptural portraiture of women in this era; males were shown with the bodies of athletes and warriors in top physical condition. All the statues were painted, but the color has been mostly lost over time. By the end of the Archaic Age, Greek artists were producing statues in much less rigid poses.
Hirmer Fotoarchiv.

A Greek Woman at an Altar

This red-figure vase painting (contrast the black-figure vase on page 44) from the center of a large drinking cup shows a woman in rich clothing pouring a libation to the gods onto a flaming altar. In her other arm, she carries a religious object that we cannot securely identify. This scene illustrates the most important and frequent role of women in Greek public life: participating in religious ceremonies, both at home and in community festivals.

The Toledo Museum of Art, Toledo, Ohio; Purchased with funds from the Libbey Endowment, Gift of Edward Drummond Libbey.

his wife; Aphrodite, goddess of love; Apollo, sun god; Ares, war god; Artemis, moon goddess; Athena, goddess of wisdom and war; Demeter, earth goddess; Dionysus, god of pleasure, wine, and disorder; Hephaestus, fire god; Hermes, messenger god; and Poseidon, sea god. Like the prickly warriors of Homer's stories, the Olympian gods resented any slights to their honor. "I am well aware that the gods are competitively envious and disruptive towards humans," remarked the sixth-century Athenian statesman Solon. The Greeks believed that their gods occasionally experienced temporary pain or sadness in their dealings with one another but essentially were immune to permanent suffering because they were immortal.

The core belief of Greek religion was that humans, both as individuals and as groups, must honor the gods to thank them for blessings received and to receive blessings in return. Furthermore, the Greeks believed that the gods sent both good and

bad into the world. As a result, they did not expect to reach paradise at some future time when evil forces would finally be vanquished forever. Their assessment of existence made no allowance for change in the relationship between the human and the divine. That relationship included sorrow as well as joy, punishment in the here and now, and an uncertain hope for favored treatment in this life and in the underworld after death.

The idea of reciprocity between gods and humans underlay the Greek understanding of the nature of the gods. Deities did not love humans, though in some mythological stories they took earthly lovers and produced half-divine children. Rather, they supported humans who paid them honor and did not offend them. Gods offended by humans could punish them by sending calamities such as famine, earthquake, epidemic disease, or defeat in war.

City-states honored gods especially by sacrificing animals such as cattle, sheep, goats, and pigs, but they also decorated the gods' sanctuaries with works of art and held festivals of songs, dances, prayers, and processions. A seventh-century B.C. bronze statuette, which a man named Mantiklos gave to a (now unknown) sanctuary of Apollo to honor the god, makes clear why individuals gave such gifts. On its legs Mantiklos inscribed his understanding of the transaction: "Mantiklos gave this from his share to the Far Darter of the Silver Bow [Apollo]; now you, Apollo, do something for me in return."

The greatest difficulty for humans lay in anticipating what might offend a deity. Mythology hinted at the gods' expectations of a moral order mandating at least a few rules for proper human behavior. For example, the Greeks told stories of the gods demanding hospitality for strangers, proper burial for family members, and punishment for human arrogance and murderous violence. Oracles, dreams, divination, and the prophecies of seers were all regarded as clues to what humans might have done to anger the gods. Offenses could be acts such as performing a sacrifice improperly, violating the sanctity of a temple area, or breaking an oath or sworn agreement. People believed that the deities were especially concerned with certain transgressions, such as violating oaths, but generally uninterested in common crimes, which humans had to police themselves. Homicide was such a serious offense, however, that the gods were thought to punish it by casting a *miasma* (ritual contamination) upon the murderer and upon all those around him or her. Unless the members of the affected group purified themselves by punishing the murderer, they could all expect to suffer divine punishment, such as bad harvests or disease.

The community and individuals alike paid homage and respect to the deities through *cults*, which were prescribed sets of religious activities overseen by priests and priestesses and publicly funded. To carry out their duties, people prayed, sang hymns of praise, offered sacrifices, and presented gifts at the deity's sanctuary. In these holy places a person could honor and thank the deities for blessings and beg them for relief when misfortune had struck the community or the petitioner. Individuals could also offer sacrifices at home with the household gathered around; sometimes the family's slaves were allowed to participate.

Priests and priestesses chosen from the citizen body conducted the sacrifices of public cults; they did not seek to use their positions to influence political or social matters. Their special knowledge consisted in knowing how to perform traditional religious rites. They were not guardians of correct religious thinking, as are some clergy today, because Greek polytheism had no scripture or uniform set of beliefs and practices. It required its adherents only to support the community's local rituals honoring its gods and to avoid ritual contamination by not saying and doing the wrong things.

The Principle of Citizenship for Rich and Poor. Greeks devised the concept of citizenship to organize their new communities. As a general principle, citizenship meant free people agreeing to form a political community that would be a partnership of privileges and duties in common affairs under the rule of law. It was a distinctive organizing concept because it assumed a certain basic level of political and legal equality, above all the expectation of equal treatment under the law for citizens regardless of their social status or wealth. Women had the protection of the law, but they were barred from participation in politics on the grounds that female judgment was inferior to male. Regulations governing their sexual behavior and control of property were stricter than for men. The most dramatic demonstration of political equality in a Greek city-state was having all free, adult male citizens share in

governance by attending and voting in a political assembly, where the laws and policies of the community were ratified. Not all city-states reached this level of equality, however.

Because every city-state was independent and made its own laws, the degree of power sharing was closer to equality in some places than in others. In city-states where the social elite had a stranglehold on politics, small groups or even a single family dominated. At the other end of the scale, some city-states instituted direct democracy, which gave all free men the right to propose laws and policies in the assembly and to serve on juries. Even in democratic city-states, citizens did not enjoy perfect political equality, however. The right to hold office, for example, could be restricted to citizens possessing a certain amount of property because usually no pay was provided. Although it took many years for law to replace traditions of personal revenge and blood feuds, eventually the court system prevailed, in which all male citizens were treated the same.

Because a strong social hierarchy and legal inequality had characterized the history of the ancient Near East and Greece in earlier times, it is remarkable that a notion of equality, no matter how incomplete it was in practice, became a principle for the reorganization of Greek society and politics in the Archaic Age. The city-state—with its emphasis on equal protection of the laws for rich and poor alike—remained the preeminent form of political and social organization in Greece until the beginning of the Roman Empire eight centuries later.

Throughout that long period, the free poor enjoyed the privileges and duties of citizenship alongside the rich. How they gained that status remains an important mystery. The greatest population increase in the late Dark Age and the Archaic Age came in the ranks of the poorer section of the population. These families raised more children to help farm more land, which had been vacant after the depopulation brought on by the worst of the Dark Age. (See "Taking Measure," page 66.) There was no precedent for extending the principle of even a limited political and legal equality to include this growing number of poorer people, but the Greek city-state did so.

For a long time, historians attributed the general widening of political rights in the city-state to a so-called hoplite revolution, but recent research has undermined the plausibility of this theory. *Hoplites* were infantrymen who wore metal body armor;

they constituted the main strike force of the militia that defended each city-state in this period. The hoplites marched into combat shoulder to shoulder in a rectangular formation called a *phalanx*. Staying in line and working as part of the group were the secrets to successful phalanx tactics. In the words of the seventh-century B.C. poet Archilochus, a good hoplite was "a short man firmly placed upon his legs, with a courageous heart, not to be uprooted from the spot where he plants his feet." Greeks had fought in phalanxes for a long time, but until the eighth century B.C. only the elite and a few of their followers could afford hoplite equipment. In the eighth century B.C., however, a growing number of men had become prosperous enough to buy metal weapons, especially because the use of iron had made them more readily available. Presumably these new hoplites, because they bought their own equip-

ment and trained hard to learn phalanx tactics to defend their community, felt they should also enjoy political rights. According to the theory of a hoplite revolution, these new hoplites forced the social elite to share political power by threatening to refuse to fight, which would cripple military defense.

The theory correctly assumes that new hoplites had the power to demand and receive a voice in politics. But the hoplites were not poor. How, then, did poor men, too, win political rights? If contributing to the city-state's defense as a hoplite was the only grounds for meriting the political rights of citizenship, the social elite and the hoplites had no obvious reason to grant poor men anything. Yet poor men did become politically empowered in many city-states, with some variations. All male citizens, regardless of their wealth, eventually were entitled to attend and vote in the communal assemblies that

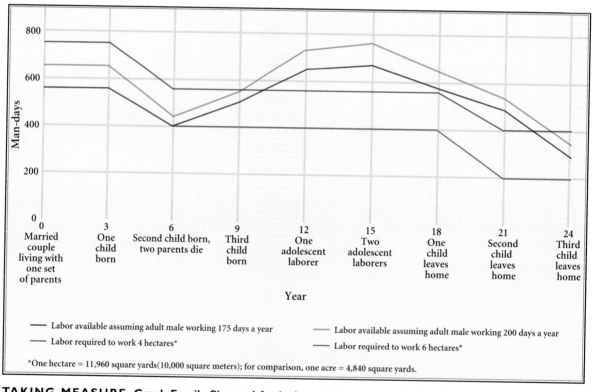

Married couple living with one set of parents | One child born | Second child born, two parents die | Third child born | One adolescent laborer | Two adolescent laborers | One child leaves home | Second child leaves home | Third child leaves home

Year

—— Labor available assuming adult male working 175 days a year   —— Labor available assuming adult male working 200 days a year

—— Labor required to work 4 hectares*   —— Labor required to work 6 hectares*

*One hectare = 11,960 square yards (10,000 square meters); for comparison, one acre = 4,840 square yards.

TAKING MEASURE Greek Family Size and Agricultural Labor in the Archaic Age
Modern demographers have calculated the changing relationship in the Archaic Age between a farm family's productive capacity to work the land and the number of people in the family over time. The graph makes it obvious why healthy teenage children were so valuable to the family's well-being: when the family had two adolescent laborers available, it could farm more than 50 percent more land, increasing its productivity significantly and thus making life more prosperous.
Adapted from Thomas W. Gallant, *Risk and Survival in Ancient Greece: Reconstructing the Rural Domestic Economy* (1991), fig. 4.10. Reprinted with the permission of Stanford University Press.

ratified policy decisions for many city-states. The hoplite revolution fails to explain completely the development of the city-state mostly because it cannot account for the extension of rights to poor men. Furthermore, archaeology shows that not many men were wealthy enough to afford hoplite armor until the middle of the seventh century B.C., well after the initial formation of the city-state.

No completely satisfactory alternative or extension to the theory of a hoplite revolution as the reason for the rise of city-states yet exists. Perhaps hoplite armor was less expensive than usually thought, or, more likely, poor men earned respect by fighting as lightly armed skirmishers, disrupting an enemy's heavy infantry by launching barrages of rocks. The laboring free poor—the workers in agriculture, trade, and crafts—also contributed to the city-state's economic strength, but it is hard to see how their value as laborers could have been translated into political rights. Perhaps tyrants (sole rulers who seized power for their families unconstitutionally in some city-states) boosted the status of poor men. Tyrants could have granted greater political rights to poor or disfranchised men as a means of marshaling popular support.

Another, more speculative possibility is that the social elite and hoplites had simply become less cohesive as a political group, thereby weakening opposition to the growing idea among poor men that it was unjust to be excluded from political participation. According to this view, when the poor agitated for power, the elite and the hoplites had no united front to oppose them, so compromise was necessary to prevent destructive civil unrest. In any case, the wealthier elements in society certainly did not extend rights of citizenship to the poor out of any romanticized vision of poverty as spiritually noble. As one contemporary put it, "Money is the man; no poor man ever counts as good or honorable." Tension between haves and have-nots never disappeared in the city-state. Whatever the reason for the inclusion of the poor as citizens with a rough equality of political and legal rights with the rich, this unprecedented decision constituted the most innovative feature of Greek society in the Archaic Age.

The Expansion of Slavery. As ideas of inclusiveness for free citizens strengthened, so too did the practice of slavery become ever more widespread in Greece; the more prominent the notion of freedom,

A Hoplite's Breastplate
This bronze armor protected the chest of a sixth-century B.C. hoplite. It had to be fitted to his individual body; the design is meant to match the musculature of his chest. The soldier would have worn a cloth or leather shirt underneath to prevent the worst chafing, but such a heavy and hot device could never be comfortable. A slave would have carried the soldier's armor for him until the moment of battle, when he would have donned his protective gear just before facing the enemy. Ekdotike.

the more common it became to distinguish it from unfreedom. Many slaves were war captives; pirates or raiders seized others in the rough regions to the north and east of Greek territory. The fierce bands in these areas even captured and sold one another to slave dealers. Greeks also enslaved other Greeks, mainly after defeat in war. Rich families prized Greek-speaking captives with some education because they could be used as tutors for children—no schools existed in this period.

City-states as well as individuals owned slaves. Public slaves enjoyed a measure of independence, living on their own and performing specialized tasks. In Athens, for example, some were trained to look for counterfeit coinage. Temple slaves "belonged" to the deity of the sanctuary, for whom they worked as servants.

By the fifth century B.C., slaves accounted for up to one-third of the total population in some city-states. Eventually slaves became cheap enough that people of even moderate means could afford one or two. Even so, small landowners and their families continued to do much work themselves, sometimes hiring free laborers. Not even wealthy Greek landowners acquired large numbers of agricultural slaves because maintaining gangs of hundreds of enslaved workers year round would have been uneconomical: most crops required short periods of intense labor punctuated by long stretches of inactivity, and owners did not want to feed and house slaves who had no work.

To keep slaves busy, owners assigned them all kinds of jobs. Those in the household, often women, had the least dangerous existence: they cleaned, cooked, fetched water from public fountains, helped the wife with the weaving, watched the children, accompanied the husband as he did the marketing, and performed other domestic chores. Neither they nor males could refuse if their masters demanded sexual favors. Owners often labored alongside their slaves in small manufacturing businesses and on farms, although rich landowners might appoint a slave supervisor to oversee work in the fields. Those who toiled in the narrow, landslide-prone tunnels of Greece's few silver and gold mines had the worst lot: many died doing this dangerous, dark, and back-breaking work.

Owners could punish, even kill, their slaves with impunity. But beating good workers severely enough to cripple them or executing able-bodied slaves was probably limited because it made no economic sense—in essence the master would be destroying his property. Under the best conditions, household workers with humane masters lived lives free of violent punishment; they might even be allowed to join their owners' families on excursions and attend religious rituals. However, without the right to a family of their own, without property, and without legal or political rights, they remained alienated from regular society. In the words of an ancient commentator, slaves lived lives of "work, punishment, and food." Sometimes owners liberated their slaves, and some promised freedom at a future date to encourage their slaves to work hard. Those slaves who gained their freedom did not become citizens in Greek city-states but instead mixed into the population of noncitizens officially allowed to live in the community (called *metics*). Freed slaves were still expected to help out their former masters when called upon as thanks for their masters' liberating them and thus transforming them into people instead of property.

Despite the bitter nature of their lives, Greek slaves almost never revolted on a large scale except in Sparta, perhaps because elsewhere they were of too many different origins and nationalities and too scattered to organize. No one is known to have called for the abolition of slavery. The expansion of slavery in the Archaic Age reduced more and more unfree persons to a state of absolute dependence; as Aristotle later put it, slaves were "living tools."

Women's Lives. Women counted as citizens legally, socially, and religiously, although only men had the right to participate in city-state politics and to vote. Despite its limitations, women's citizenship was an important source of security and status because it guaranteed access to the justice system and a respected role in the city-state's public religious activity. Citizen women had legal protection against being kidnapped for sale into slavery, and they had recourse to the courts in disputes over property, although they usually had to have a man speak for them. Before her marriage, a woman's father served as her legal guardian; after marriage, her husband assumed the same role. The traditional paternalism of Greek society, with men acting as "fathers" to regulate the lives of women and safeguard their interests as defined by men, demanded that all women have male guardians to protect them physically and legally.

The emergence of widespread slavery in the city-state made households bigger and added new responsibilities for women. While their husbands farmed, participated in politics, and met with their male friends, well-off wives managed the household: raising the children, supervising the preservation and preparation of food, keeping the family's financial accounts, weaving fabric for clothing, directing the work of the slaves, and tending them when they were ill. Poor women worked outside the home, hoeing and reaping in the fields and selling produce and small goods such as ribbons and trinkets in the market that occupied the center of every settlement. Women's labor ensured the family's economic self-sufficiency and allowed the male citizens the time to participate in public life.

Vase Painting of a Bride's Preparation

This special piece of pottery was an epinetron, designed to fit over a woman's thigh to protect it while she sat down to spin wool. As a woman's tool, it appropriately carried a picture from a woman's life: a bride being helped to prepare for her wedding by her family, friends, and servants. The inscriptions indicate that this is the mythological bride Alcestis, famous for sacrificing herself to save her husband and then being rescued from Death by the hero Heracles. This red-figure epinetron dates from the late fifth century B.C.
Deutsches Archaologisches Institut-Athen.

Women's religious functions gave them freedom of movement and prestige. Women rich and poor alike left the home to attend funerals, state festivals, and public rituals. They had access, for example, to the initiation rights of the popular cult of Demeter at Eleusis, near Athens. This internationally renowned cult may have served as a sort of safety valve for the pressures created by the precariousness of life, because it promised protection from evil and a better fate in the afterworld for everyone, regardless of class or gender. Women had control over cults reserved exclusively for them and also performed important duties in various nonrestricted official cults; at Athens, for example, by the fifth century B.C. they officiated as priestesses for more than forty different deities, with benefits such as salaries paid by the state.

Marriages were arranged, and everyone was expected to marry. A woman's guardian—her father or, if he was dead, her uncle or her brother—would commonly engage her to another man's son while she was still a child, perhaps as young as five. The engagement was an important public event conducted in the presence of witnesses. The guardian on this occasion repeated the phrase that expressed the primary aim of the marriage: "I give you this woman for the plowing [procreation] of legitimate children." The wedding itself customarily took place when the girl was in her early teens and the groom ten to fifteen years older. Hesiod advised a man to marry a virgin in the fifth year after her first menstruation, when he himself was "not much younger than thirty and not much older." A legal wedding consisted of the bride moving to her husband's dwelling; the procession to his house served as the ceremony. The woman brought to the marriage a dowry of property (perhaps land yielding an income, if she was wealthy) and personal possessions that formed part of the new household's assets and could be inherited by her children. Her husband was legally obliged to preserve the dowry and to return it in case of a divorce. A husband could expel his wife from his home; a wife, in theory, could leave her husband on her own initiative to return to the guardianship of her male relatives, but her husband could force her to stay.

Except in certain cases in Sparta, monogamy was the rule in ancient Greece, as was a nuclear family (that is, husband, wife, and children living together without other relatives in the same house). Citizen men, including husbands, could have sexual relations without penalty with slaves, foreign concubines, female prostitutes, or willing pre-adult citizen males. Citizen women, single or married, had no such freedom. Sex between a wife and anyone other than her husband carried harsh penalties for both parties, except in Sparta.

Greek citizen men placed Greek citizen women under their guardianship both to regulate marriage and procreation and to maintain family property. According to Greek mythology, women were a necessary evil: men needed them to have a family but could expect troubles as the price. Zeus supposedly created the first woman, Pandora, as a punishment for men in his vendetta against Prometheus for giving fire to humans. Like the biblical Eve giving Adam forbidden fruit from the Tree of Knowledge, Pandora loosed "evils and diseases" into the previously trouble-free world when curiosity overcame her. To see what was in a container that had come as a gift from the gods, Pandora lifted its lid and accidentally freed the evils that had been penned inside. Only hope still remained in the container when she finally slammed the lid back down. Many Greek men probably shared Hesiod's opinions about women: he described them as "big trouble" but thought any man who refused to marry to escape the "troublesome deeds of women" would come to "destructive old age" alone, with no heirs. In other words, a man needed a wife so he could sire children who would later care for him and preserve his property after his death. This paternalistic attitude allowed men to control human reproduction and consequently the distribution of property in Greece's new form of social and political organization.

❖ New Directions for the Greek City-State

During the Archaic Age, the hundreds of Greek city-states developed three strikingly diverse forms of society and government: oligarchy, tyranny, and democracy. Each of the three had its own variants; Sparta, for example, provided Greece's most famous example of an *oligarchy,* in which a small number of men kept political power in their hands, but its arrangements were crafted to fit its peculiar situation. Corinth had the best-known *tyranny,* in which one man seized control of the city-state, ruling it for the advantage of his family and loyal supporters.

And Athens instituted the world's first *democracy* ("rule by the people") by allowing all male citizens to participate in governing. Although some assemblies of men had influenced kings in certain early states in the ancient Near East, never had any group of people been invested with the amount of political power the Greek democracies gave their male citizens.

These varied paths of political and social development illustrate the great challenge Greeks faced as they struggled to construct new ways of life during the Archaic Age. In the course of this endeavor they also created new paths of thought by formulating different ways of understanding the physical world, their relations to it, and their relationships with one another.

The Oligarchy of Sparta

Sparta was a city-state in which military readiness overrode all other concerns. During the Archaic Age, it developed the mightiest infantry force in Greece. Its citizens were renowned for their self-discipline—a cultural value that manifested their militaristic bent. The urban center nestled in an easily defended valley on the Peloponnese peninsula twenty-five miles from the Mediterranean coast. This relative isolation from the sea kept the Spartans from becoming adept sailors, and their interests and their strength lay on land.

In keeping with military principles, a small group of men commanded Spartan government. This version of oligarchy included three components in its ruling body. First came the two hereditary military leaders of high prestige called kings, who served as the state's religious heads and the generals of its army. Despite their title, they were not monarchs but only part of the ruling oligarchy. The

Sparta and Corinth, c. 750 – 500 B.C.

other two parts consisted of a council of twenty-eight men over sixty years old ("the elders") and five annually elected magistrates called *ephors* ("overseers").

As a concession to the principle of shared governance, legislation had to be submitted to an assembly of all the free adult males, called Equals. The assembly had only limited power to amend the proposals put before it, however, and the council retained the right to withdraw a proposal when the reaction to it in the assembly seemed negative: "If the people speak crookedly," according to Spartan tradition, "the elders and the leaders of the people shall be withdrawers." The council could then resubmit the proposal after marshaling support for its passage.

Spartan society demanded strict compliance with the laws, major and minor. When the ephors entered office, for example, they issued an official proclamation to the men of Sparta: "Shave your mustache and obey the laws." The importance of their legal code was emphasized by the official story that it had been handed down by the god Apollo. Unlike other Greeks, the Spartans never wrote down their laws. Instead, they preserved their system from generation to generation with a unique, highly structured way of life. All Spartan citizens were expected to put service to their city-state before personal concerns because their state's survival was continually threatened by its own economic foundation, the great mass of slaves called *helots* who did almost all the work for citizens.

The Helots. Helots were captives from neighboring towns and regions that the Spartans conquered, especially the fertile plain of Messenia to the west, which they overran by c. 700 B.C. The total helot population outstripped that of Sparta. The despair felt by helots is reflected in the Messenian legend of Aristodemus, who sacrificed his beloved daughter to the gods of the underworld in an attempt to enlist their aid against the invading Spartans. When his campaign of resistance at last failed, in grief he slew himself on her grave. Deprived of their freedom and their city-states, helots were always on the lookout for a chance to revolt against their Spartan overlords.

Like public slaves in other city-states, helots were not owned by individual Spartans but rather belonged to the whole community, which alone could free them. Helots had a semblance of family life because they were expected to produce children to maintain their population. They labored as farmers and household slaves so Spartan citizens would not have to do such "demeaning" work. Spartan men in fact wore their hair very long to show they were "gentlemen" rather than laborers, for whom long hair was inconvenient.

In their private lives, helots could keep some personal possessions and practice their religion, as could slaves generally in Greece. Publicly, however, helots lived under the constant threat of officially sanctioned violence. Every year the ephors formally declared war between Sparta and the helots, allowing any Spartan to kill a helot without legal penalty or fear of offending the gods by unsanctioned murder. By beating the helots frequently, forcing them to get drunk in public as an object lesson to young Spartans, making them wear dog-skin caps, and generally humiliating them, the Spartans consistently emphasized the "otherness" of the helots. In this way Spartans erected a moral barrier to justify their harsh abuse of fellow Greeks. Contrasting the freedom of Spartan citizens from ordinary work with the lot of the helots, the later Athenian Critias observed, "Sparta is the home of the freest of the Greeks, and of the most enslaved."

Spartan Communal Life. Because helots worked the fields, male citizens, from childhood, could devote themselves to full-time preparation for war, training to protect their state from hostile neighbors and its own slaves. Boys lived at home only until their seventh year, when they were sent to live in communal barracks with other males until they were thirty. They spent most of their time exercising, hunting, practicing with weapons, and being acculturated to Spartan values by listening to tales of bravery and heroism at common meals, where adult males ate much of the time instead of at home. Discipline was strict, and the boys were purposely underfed so they would learn stealth by stealing food. If they were caught, punishment and disgrace followed immediately. One famous Spartan tale taught how seriously boys were supposed to fear such failure: having successfully stolen a fox, which he was hiding under his clothing, a Spartan youth died because he let the panicked animal rip out his insides rather than be detected in the theft. Spartan males who could not survive the tough conditions of their childhood training fell into social disgrace and were not certified as Equals.

The experience of spending so much time in shared quarters schooled Sparta's young men in the

Hunt Painting in a Spartan Cup
This black-figure drinking cup with a picture of a hunt on its interior was made in Sparta about 560 B.C. Hunting large, dangerous wild game was an important activity for Spartan men to show their courage and acquire meat for their communal meals. The painter has chosen a "porthole" style, as if we were looking through a circular window at the scene beyond. The fish below the ground line may indicate a seashore, or they may just be a way for the painter to fill open space decoratively, a technique characteristic of Greek art in this period. By the classical period, Spartans had largely stopped creating art like this, perhaps reflecting the increased military focus of their society.
Photo Reunion Des Musées Nationaux – H. Lewandowski.

values of their society. In short, a communal existence took the place of a Spartan boy's family and school when he was growing up and remained his main social environment once he reached adulthood. There he learned to call all older men "father" to emphasize that his primary loyalty was to the group and not to his biological family. The environment trained him for the one honorable occupation for Spartan men: an obedient soldier. The seventh-century B.C. poet Tyrtaeus expressed the Spartan male ideal: "Know that it is good for the city-state and the whole people when a man takes his place in the front row of warriors and stands his ground without flinching."

An adolescent boy's life often involved what in today's terminology would be called a homosexual relationship. That is, he would be chosen as a special favorite by an older male to build bonds of affection, often including sexual relations, for another man at whose side he would one day march into deadly battle. Greek sexual customs included this form of homosexuality, a fact that the first modern histories of Greece suppressed out of repulsion at what was seen as a form of child abuse. Interestingly, the Athenian author Xenophon (c. 430–355 B.C.), in his work on the Spartan way of life, denied

against the evidence that sex with boys existed in Sparta because he thought it demeaning to the Spartans' reputation for virtue; evidently not every Greek approved of the physical side of such a relationship. In any case, the elder partner ("the lover") was supposed to help educate the young man ("the beloved") in politics and community values and not just exploit him for physical pleasure. The relationship would not be lasting or exclusive: "beloveds" would grow up to get married, as their "lovers" were, and would eventually become the older member of a new pair. Homoerotic sex between adult males was considered disgraceful, as it was for women of all ages.

Spartan women were known throughout the Greek world for their relative liberty. They could own property, including land. Women were expected to use their freedom from farm labor provided by the helot system to keep themselves physically fit, so they could bear healthy children to keep up the population and raise them to live strictly by Spartan values. One mother became legendary, for example, for handing her son his shield on the eve of battle and admonishing him, "Come back with it or on it." Since their husbands were so rarely at home, women directed the households, which included servants, daughters, and sons until they left for their communal training. Consequently, Spartan women exercised more power in the household than did women elsewhere in Greece.

Sparta's population was never large; adult males—who made up the army—numbered between eight and ten thousand in this period. Over time, the problem of producing enough children to keep the Spartan army from shrinking became acute, probably because losses in war far outnumbered births. Men were therefore legally required to marry, and bachelors were subjected to fines and public ridicule. If all parties agreed, a woman could legitimately have children by a man other than her husband. The male ideal for Spartan women appears in the late seventh century B.C. in the work of Alcman, a poet who wrote songs performed by female and male choruses. The dazzling leader of a women's chorus, he wrote, "stands out as if, among a herd of cows, someone placed a firmly built horse with ringing hooves, a prize winner from winged dreams."

Because the Spartans' well-being depended on the systematic exploitation of enslaved Greeks, their oligarchic system cultivated a staunch militarism and conservative values. Change meant danger; they were therefore suspicious of foreigners and hostile to intellectual pursuits that questioned tradition. Some Greeks, even from other oligarchic city-states, criticized the Spartan way of life as repressive and monotonous, but they admired the Spartans' unswerving respect for their laws as a guide to life in hostile surroundings.

Tyranny in Corinth

In some city-states, competition between members of the social elite for political leadership became so bitter that a single family would suppress all its rivals and establish itself in power for a time. The leader of the victorious family thus became a tyrant, a dictator backed by his relatives and other supporters hoping to feed off the scraps from his table, so to speak. Greek tyranny was a distinctive type of sole rule that could be benevolent or harsh and tended to be temporary: tyrants were usually members of the social elite, who rallied support for their takeovers among ordinary citizens but often had difficulty passing their popularity on to their heirs. In city-states where landless men lacked full citizenship or felt substantially disfranchised in political life, tyrants could garner backing by extending citizenship and other privileges to these groups.

Tyrants usually preserved the existing laws and political institutions of their city-states. If a city-state had an assembly, for example, the tyrant would allow it to continue to meet, though not to act against his wishes. Successful tyrants kept their elite rivals at bay by cultivating the goodwill of the masses with economic policies favoring their interests, such as public employment schemes. Other members of the social elite would then not act against the tyrant and his family for fear of provoking the common people to violence. Although today the English word *tyrant* labels a brutal or unwanted leader, tyrants in Archaic Greece did not always fit that description. Ordinary Greeks evaluated tyrants based on their behavior, opposing the ruthless and violent ones but welcoming the fair and helpful ones.

The most famous early tyranny arose at Corinth in 657 B.C., when the family of Cypselus rebelled against the harshly oligarchic leadership being exercised by members of the social elite. This takeover attracted wide attention in the Greek world because Corinth was such an important city-state. Its location on the isthmus controlling land access to the Peloponnese and a huge amount of seaborne trade had made it the most prosperous city-state of the Archaic Age (see Map 2.4). Cypselus gained support for his political coup by rallying popular support: "He became one of the most admired of Corinth's citizens because he was courageous, prudent, and helpful to the people, unlike the oligarchs in power, who were insolent and violent," according to a later historian. He later ruthlessly suppressed rivals, but his popularity remained so high that he could govern without the protection of a bodyguard.

When Cypselus died in 625 B.C., his son Periander succeeded him. Like his father, Periander aggressively continued Corinth's economic expansion by founding colonies on the coasts both northwest and northeast of Greek territory to increase trade. He also pursued commercial contacts with Egypt. The city's prosperity encouraged crafts, art, and architecture to flourish. Unlike his father, however, Periander lost popular support by ruling harshly. He held on to power until his death in 585 B.C., but the hostility that persisted against him led to the overthrow of his heir and successor, Psammetichus,

The Archaic Temple of Apollo at Corinth
Built in the sixth century B.C. at the foot of the city's looming acropolis, this is one of the earliest surviving stone temples from Greece. It was done in Doric style, with its columns resting directly on the foundation and topped by flattened disks. Earthquakes over the centuries have destroyed most of it.
Anne van de Vaeren/The Image Bank.

within a short time. The social elite thereupon installed a government based on a board of magistrates and a council.

By working in the economic interests of the masses, some tyrannies, like that founded by Cypselus, maintained their popularity for more than a generation or two. Other tyrants soon experienced bitter opposition from jealous rivals or provoked civil war by ruling brutally and grabbing more than a fair share of their city-state's wealth. Around 600 B.C., the poet Alcaeus described how fierce such conflict could become: "Let's forget our anger; let's quit our heart-devouring strife and civil war, which some god has stirred up among us, ruining the people but bestowing the glory on our tyrant for which he prays."

Early Democracy at Athens

A tyrant usually tried to secure his rule by improving the economic lot of the masses and by preserving the appearance of consulting them, but he did not truly share political power with them. Only democracy, which Greeks invented, empowered ordinary citizens politically. Athens, located at the southeastern corner of central Greece, became the most famous of the democratic city-states because its government gave political rights to the greatest

number of people, its urban center housed magnificent temples and public buildings, and its military forces eventually became strong enough to force numerous other city-states to knuckle under to Athenian power—democracy at home did not exclude imperialism abroad. The innovative Athenian system took a long time and endured considerable strife before reaching its fullest development in the mid-fifth century B.C., but even its tentative beginnings in the Archaic Age were remarkable because it granted all male citizens the possibility of participating meaningfully in making laws and administering justice. Democracy has remained so important in Western civilization that understanding why and how Athenian democracy worked remains a vital historical quest.

Athens and Central Greece, c. 750 – 500 B.C.

By the late seventh century B.C., Athens had taken the first steps toward democracy. One crucial factor in opening this new path for Western civilization was that Athens early on developed a strong and populous middle class. As economic conditions improved rapidly from about 800 to 700 B.C., the Athenian population apparently expanded at a phenomenal rate. The ready availability of good farmland in their territory and opportunities for seaborne trade along the long coastline allowed many families to achieve modest prosperity. These hardworking entrepreneurs evidently felt that their self-won economic success entitled them to a say in government, believing that justice demanded at least limited political equality with the elite. The power and political cohesiveness forged by the Athenian masses were evident as early as 632 B.C., when the people rallied "from the fields in a body," according to a later historian, to foil the attempt by an elite Athenian named Cylon to install a tyranny.

By the seventh century B.C., all freeborn adult male citizens of Athens could attend the assembly to discuss community affairs, especially decisions on peace and war; when the assembly began passing laws is not clear, but it eventually acquired this power. It also elected magistrates called *archons,* who headed the government and the judicial system by rendering verdicts in disputes and criminal accusations. At this time, members of the elite still dominated Athenian political life, especially by using their wealth and status to win the archon elections and sustain themselves in office, as they received no pay at this early stage. The right of middle-class and poor men to serve in the assembly had only limited value at first because the assembly probably met rarely, leaving the magistrates to operate mostly on their own.

An economic crisis near the end of the seventh century B.C. caused Athens's infant democracy to stumble badly. The details are obscure, but the first attempt to solve the problem was the emergency appointment of a man named Draco ("the Snake") to a special position created to revise the law code. Unfortunately, Draco's changes proved futile. By 600 B.C., the situation had become desperate, with poorer farmers forced to borrow constantly from richer neighbors and deeply mortgage their land just to survive. Finally, the crisis became so acute that impoverished citizens were even being sold into slavery to pay off debts, and civil war threatened to break out.

Solon's Democratic Reforms. In desperation, the Athenians once again made an emergency appointment to try to resolve the crisis. This time, in

594 B.C., the rich and the poor agreed on a distinguished war hero named Solon to be sole archon. To head off the immediate threat of violence in the citizen body, Solon gave each side something of what it wanted, a compromise called the "shaking off of obligations." This canceled debts, which helped the poor but displeased the rich; his decision not to redistribute land did the opposite. Less controversial were his permanent ban on selling citizens into slavery to settle debts and his liberation of citizens who had become slaves in this way. Eliminating debt slavery was an innovative and significant recognition of what today would be called citizen rights, and Solon celebrated his success in verses he wrote: "To Athens, their home established by the gods, I brought back many who had been sold into slavery, some justly, some not."

In an effort to provide long-term stability, Solon created a four-part ranking of citizens by wealth to balance political power between rich and poor. The higher a man's ranking, the higher the government office for which he was eligible; men at the lowest level, called *laborers,* were not eligible for any post. Solon did, however, reaffirm their right to participate in the legislative assembly. His creation of a council proved especially significant in the long term for making the assembly more efficient and influential: his version was made up of four hundred men to prepare an agenda for discussion in the assembly and prevented the social elite from capturing too many council seats by having its members chosen annually by lottery. Solon's classification scheme was another step toward democracy because it allowed for upward social mobility: if a man increased his wealth, he could move up the scale of eligibility for office.

Equally important for the development of a more democratic judicial system was Solon's ruling that any male citizen could bring charges on behalf of any victim of a crime on a wide variety of offenses. Furthermore, people who believed a magistrate had rendered unfair judgments against them now had the right to appeal their case to the assembly. With these two measures, Solon involved ordinary citizens, not just the predominantly elite magistrates, in the administration of justice. He balanced these reforms, however, by granting broader powers to the "Council which meets on the Hill of the god of war Ares," a judicial body we call the Areopagus Council. This body of ex-archons could wield great power, because its members judged the most serious cases—in particular, any accusations against archons themselves.

Solon's reforms broke his world's traditional pattern of government: they began the process at Athens of extending power broadly through the citizen body and created a system of law applying equally to all the community's free men. An anecdote reported by the later biographer Plutarch offers a typical reaction to Solon's innovations: when a visiting foreign king, Anacharsis from Scythia, discovered what Solon was doing, he burst into laughter, scoffing at Athenian democracy. Observing the procedure in the Athenian assembly, the king expressed his amazement that elite politicians could only recommend policy in their speeches, while the male citizens as a whole voted on what to do: "I find it astonishing," he remarked, "that here wise men speak on public affairs, while fools decide them." The king then added, "Do you actually believe your fellow citizens' injustice and greed can be kept in check this way? Written laws are more like spiders' webs than anything else: they tie up the weak and the small fry who get stuck in them, but the rich and the powerful tear them to shreds." Solon replied to these objections by explaining his view of communal values as the guarantee of the rule of law: "People abide by their agreements when neither side has anything to gain by breaking them. I am writing laws for the Athenians in such a way that they will clearly see it is to everyone's advantage to obey the laws rather than to break them."

Some elite Athenians vehemently disagreed with Solon because they wanted oligarchy. Jealousy of one another kept opponents of democracy from uniting, however, and the unrest they caused opened the door to a period of tyranny. One of them, Peisistratus, helped by his upper-class friends and the poor whose interests he championed, made himself sole ruler in 546 B.C. Like the earlier tyrants of Corinth, he promoted the economic, cultural, and architectural development of Athens and made his family popular with the masses. He helped poorer men, for example, by hiring them to build roads and work on such major public works as a great temple to Zeus and fountains to increase the supply of drinking water.

As in Corinth, the tyrant's family could not maintain public goodwill after his death. Hippias,

Peisistratus's eldest son, ruled ever more harshly, and a rival family, the Alcmaeonids, roused strong opposition by denouncing him as unjust toward the masses. His rivals convinced the Spartans, the strongest Greek military power and the self-proclaimed champions of Greek freedom, to "liberate" Athens from tyranny by expelling Hippias and his family in 510 B.C.

Cleisthenes, "Father of Athenian Democracy." The liberation opened the way to the definitive stage in the origin of Athenian democracy, the reforms of Cleisthenes. A leading Alcmaeonid, he found that the only way he could gain a political following was to win support among the masses by promising greater democracy. Ordinary people were so strongly in favor of his reforms that they banded together to repel a Spartan army, which Cleisthenes's bitterest rival had convinced Sparta's leaders to send once again, this time to support the enemies of democracy. The reversal of policy destroyed the goodwill at Athens for Sparta that the liberation had earned.

Cleisthenes delivered on his promises to the people, and he was remembered by later Athenians as the "father" of their developed democracy. His reorganization was complex, but by about 500 B.C. he had devised a democratic system that ensured direct participation by as many adult male citizens as possible. He started by forming the constituent units, called *demes* ("peoples"), of the city-state's political organization from the scores of country villages and the neighborhoods of the urban center. Then he took a crucial step toward increased democracy by having the demes annually choose council members by lottery in proportion to the size of their populations. To allow for greater participation, Solon's Council of 400 became the Council of 500. Finally, Cleisthenes required candidates for public office to be spread widely throughout the demes.

That he could institute such a system successfully in a time of turmoil and that it could endure, as it did, means that he must have been building on preexisting conditions favorable to democracy. As a member of the elite looking for popular support, Cleisthenes certainly had reason to establish the kind of system he thought ordinary people wanted. His decision to base his system on the demes, most of which were country villages, suggests that some democratic notions may have stemmed from the traditions of village life: each man was entitled to his say in running local affairs and had to persuade others of the wisdom of his recommendations. It would take another fifty years of political struggle before Athens's democracy reached its fullest form, but Cleisthenes's reforms set it on the way to that final stage.

New Ways of Thought and Expression

The idea that persuasion, rather than force or status, should constitute the mechanism for making political decisions in the emerging Athenian democracy fit well with the spirit of intellectual change rippling through Greece in the late Archaic Age. In city-states all over the Greek world, new ways of thought inspired artists, poets, and philosophers. The Greeks' ongoing contacts with the Near East gave them traditions to learn from and, in some cases, to alter dramatically.

Art and Literature.   In the early Archaic period, Greek artists had taken inspiration from the Near East as they started to expand the geometric patterns of the Dark Age with pictures of animals and people and as they sculpted statues of people and gods. By the sixth century B.C., they had introduced imaginative innovations of their own. In ceramics, painters experimented with different clays and colors to depict vivid scenes from mythology and daily life. They became expert at rendering fully three-dimensional figures—whether goddesses, warriors, or monsters from myth—in an increasingly realistic style. Sculptors made their statues less stiff and more varied, from gracefully clothed young women to muscular male nudes. Sculptures decorating temples were posed to tell stories relevant to the deity. In every case statues gleamed with bright paint.

Archaic Age poets were equally innovative. Near Eastern literature had long used poetry to express deeply personal emotions; Greeks now added to this tradition with a new form of poetry, called *lyric*, that developed from popular song. Characterized by rhythmic diversity and always performed to the accompaniment of the lyre (a kind of harp that gives its name to the poetry), Greek lyric poems were much shorter than the epics of Homer or

Vase Painting of a Music Lesson
This sixth-century-B.C. red-figure vase shows a young man (seated on the left, without a beard) holding a lyre and watching an older, bearded man play the same instrument, while an adolescent boy and an older man listen. They all wear wreaths to show they are in a festive mood. The youth is evidently a pupil learning to play. Instruction in performing music and singing lyric poetry was considered an essential part of an upper-class Greek male's education. The teacher's lyre has a sounding board made from a turtle shell, as was customary for this instrument.
Staatliche Antikensammlungen und Glypothek.

Hesiod and included many forms and subjects. Some lyric poets wrote choral songs for groups to perform on public occasions to honor the deities, to celebrate famous events in a city-state's history, for wedding processions, and to praise victors in athletic contests.

Poets writing songs for solo performance at social occasions stressed a personal level of expression on a variety of topics. Solon, for example, wrote poems setting forth his political views and justifying his reforms. Others deliberately adopted a critical attitude toward traditional values, such as strength in war. For example, Sappho, a lyric poet from Lesbos born about 630 B.C. and famous for her poems on love, wrote, "Some would say the most beautiful thing on our dark earth is an army of cavalry, others of infantry, others of ships, but I say it's whatever a person loves." In this poem Sappho was expressing her longing for a woman she loved, who was now far away. Archilochus of Paros, who probably lived in the early seventh century B.C., became famous for poems on themes as diverse as mockery of soldiering, friends lost at sea, and love gone astray. He became infamous for the unheroic sentiment in his lines about throwing down his shield in battle so he could run away to save his life: "Oh, the hell with it; I can get another one just as good." The bitter power of his ridicule reportedly caused a father and his two daughters to commit suicide when the poet mocked them after the father had ended Archilochus's affair with one of his daughters. Lyric poets' focus on the individual's feelings represented a new stage in Greek literary sensibilities, one that continues to inspire much poetry today.

Philosophy and Science. The study of philosophy in Greece began in this period when thinkers whom we now call pre-Socratic ("before Socrates") philosophers created prose writing to express their new ways of thought. These thinkers developed radically new explanations of the human world and its relation to the gods and goddesses. Most of these philosophers lived in Ionia, the western coast of what is today Turkey. This location placed them in

Ionia and the Aegean, c. 750 – 500 B.C.

close contact with Near Eastern knowledge, especially astronomy, mathematics, and myth; indeed, the Persian king Cyrus compelled their city-states to become subjects of his Persian empire in 546 B.C. Because at this period there were no formal schools, early philosophers made their ideas known by teaching pupils privately and giving public lectures. Some of them also composed poetry to explain their theories, which they presented in public performances. People who studied with these philosophers or heard their presentations then helped spread the new ideas.

Working from information about the regular movements of the stars and planets previously discovered by Babylonian astronomers, Ionian Greek philosophers such as Thales (c. 625–545 B.C.) and

Anaximander (c. 610–540 B.C.) of Miletus reached revolutionary conclusions about the nature of the physical world. They reasoned that the universe was regulated by a set of laws of nature rather than by the arbitrary intervention of divine beings. Pythagoras, who emigrated from the island of Samos to the Greek city-state Croton in southern Italy about 530 B.C., taught that patterns and relationships of numbers explained the entire world and began the systematic study of mathematics and the numerical aspects of musical harmony.

Ionian philosophers insisted that the workings of the universe could be revealed because natural phenomena were neither random nor arbitrary. They named the universe *cosmos*, meaning an orderly arrangement that is beautiful. The order of the cosmos encompassed not only the motions of heavenly bodies but also the weather, the growth of plants and animals, human health and well-being, and so on. Because the universe was ordered, it was intelligible; because it was intelligible, events could be explained by thought and research. They therefore looked for the first or universal cause of things, a problem that scientists still pursue. The philosophers who deduced this view of the cosmos believed they needed to give reasons for their conclusions and to persuade others by arguments based on evidence. They believed, in other words, in *logic.* This mode of thought, called *rationalism,* represented a crucial first step toward science and philosophy as these disciplines endure today. The rule-based view of the causes of events and physical phenomena developed by these philosophers contrasted sharply with the traditional mythological view of causation. Naturally, many people had difficulty accepting such a startling change in their understanding of the world, and the older tradition explaining events as the work of deities lived on alongside the new approach.

The ideas of the Ionian philosophers probably spread slowly because no means of mass communication existed, and magic remained an important preoccupation in the lives of the majority of ordinary people. Even so, these philosophers had initiated a tremendous development in intellectual history that deeply influenced later times: the separation of scientific thinking from myth and religion, the birth of rationalism. In this way, the Ionian philosophers parted company with the traditional ways of thinking of the ancient Near East as found

c. 1000–500 B.C.

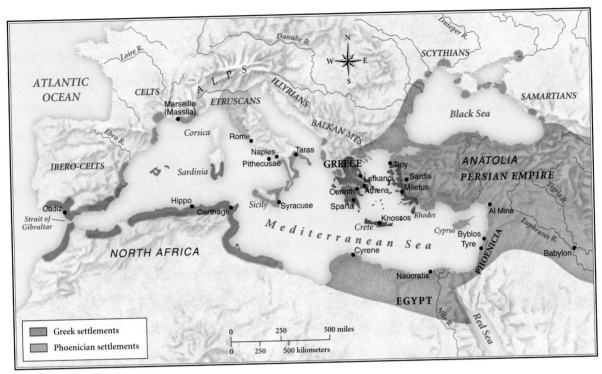

MAPPING THE WEST Mediterranean Civilizations, c. 500 B.C.

At the end of the sixth century B.C., the Persian empire was far and away the most powerful civilization touching the Mediterranean. Its riches and its unity gave it resources that no Phoenician or Greek city could match. The Phoenicians dominated economically in the western Mediterranean, while the Greek city-states in Sicily and southern Italy rivaled the power of those in the heartland. In Italy, the Etruscans were the most powerful civilization; the Romans were still a small community struggling to replace monarchy with a republic.

in its rich mythology and imitated in the myths of early Greece.

The idea that people must give reasons to explain their beliefs, rather than just make assertions others must believe without evidence, was the most important achievement of the early Ionian philosophers. This insistence on rationality, coupled with the belief that the world could be understood as something other than the plaything of divine whims, gave people hope that they could improve their lives through their own efforts. As Xenophanes from Colophon (c. 580–480 B.C.) put it, "The gods have not revealed all things from the beginning to mortals, but, by seeking, human beings find out, in time, what is better." This saying well expressed the value Archaic Age Greeks came to attach to intellectual freedom, corresponding to the value given to political freedom in the city-state, unequally distributed though it may have been.

Conclusion

Over different spans of time and with different results, both the Near East and Greece recovered from their Dark Ages, which the troubles of the period 1200–1000 B.C. had caused. The Near East quickly revived its traditional pattern of social and political organization: wide empire under a strong central authority. The Neo-Assyrians, then the Neo-Babylonians, and then the Persians succeeded one another as holders of great empires from Mesopotamia to the Mediterranean. The moral dualism of Persian religion, Zoroastrianism, had a great influence on later religions in Western civilization, most importantly on that of the Hebrews. Judaism developed into the first complete monotheism and produced the Hebrew Bible while its people suffered exile and loss of their political independence.

IMPORTANT DATES

Late eleventh century B.C. Saul becomes ancient Israel's first king, followed by David and Solomon in the tenth century B.C.

c. 1000–750 B.C. Greece experiences its Dark Age

c. 900 B.C. Neo-Assyrians create an empire

814 B.C. Traditional date of founding of Carthage in North Africa by Phoenicians, who go on to establish trading stations in the western Mediterranean

776 B.C. Traditional date of First Olympic Games in Greece

c. 775–550 B.C. Greeks establish many new settlements around the Mediterranean

c. 750 B.C. Greeks begin to create city-states

c. 700 B.C. Spartans complete the conquest of Messenia, making its inhabitants into slaves (helots)

657–c. 580 B.C. Cypselus and his descendants rule Corinth as tyrants

612 B.C. Babylonian-led army destroys the neo-Assyrian capital, Nineveh

604–562 B.C. Nebuchadnezzar II creates the Neo-Babylonian empire and exiles most Hebrews to Babylon

594 B.C. Athenians appoint Solon to recodify their laws to try to end social unrest

560 B.C. Cyrus founds the Persian empire

539 B.C. Cyrus allows exiled Hebrews to return from Babylon to Palestine

510 B.C. Athenian aristocrats and the Spartan army free Athens from tyranny

508 B.C. Cleisthenes begins to reform Athenian democracy

The Dark Age devastated Greece, but its recovery led to significant changes. A rapidly growing population developed a sense of communal interests and divine justice that led to the creation of the polis. This new form of social and political organization, based on the concepts of citizenship and shared power, treasured the notion of personal freedom, which was not, however, extended fully to women or at all to slaves. Greek city-states came in a diversity of forms in different places and at different times; the most significant of these for later history was democracy, which arose for the first time

at Athens. Equally revolutionary was the change in ways of thought inspired by Greek philosophers in the Archaic Age. By arguing that the universe was based on laws of nature, which humans could explain through reason and research, they established rationalism as the conceptual basis for science and philosophy.

Thus it was during the Archaic Age of Greece that the values that have so profoundly affected Western civilization began to emerge. But the Greek world and its new values would soon face a grave threat from the awesome empire of Persia.

Suggested References

From Dark Age to Empire in the Near East

The scholarly surveys of Amélie Kuhrt and Daniel Snell stand out in recent work that makes this period much more accessible; they take an integrative approach to archaeological and textual evidence and extend chronological coverage down to the eve of Alexander the Great's conquest in the late fourth century B.C. The significance of Persian religion for later faiths has also been an active field of study.

Brosius, Maria. *Women in Ancient Persia (559–331 B.C.)*. 1996.

Cohn, Norman. *Cosmos, Chaos, and the World to Come: The Ancient Roots of Apocalyptic Faith*. 1993.

Cook, J. M. *The Persian Empire*. 1983.

Fagan, Brian, ed. *The Oxford Companion to Archaeology*. 1996.

Finegan, Jack. *Archaeological History of the Ancient Near East*. 1979.

Frye, Richard N. *The History of Ancient Iran*. 1984.

Knapp, A. Bernard. *The History and Culture of Ancient Western Asia and Egypt*. 1988.

Kuhrt, Amélie. *The Ancient Near East c. 3000–330 B.C.* Vol. 2. 1995.

Lloyd, Seton. *The Archaeology of Mesopotamia: From the Stone Age to the Persian Conquest*. Rev. ed. 1984.

Malandra, William W. *An Introduction to Ancient Iranian Religion: Readings from the Avesta and the Achaemenid Inscriptions*. 1983.

Nigosian, S. A. *The Zoroastrian Faith: Tradition and Modern Research*. 1993.

Olmstead, A. T. *History of the Persian Empire*. 1948.

Persepolis and Ancient Iran: http://www-oi.uchicago.edu/OI/MUS/PA/IRAN/PAAI/PAAI_Persepolis.html.

Reade, Julian. *Assyrian Sculpture*. 1983.

Roux, Georges. *Ancient Iraq*. 3rd ed. 1992.

Snell, Daniel C. *Life in the Ancient Near East, 3100–332 B.C.E.* 1997.

Remaking Greek Civilization

Scholarship on the Dark Age, such as by Sarah Morris, emphasizes that it was not as dark as sometimes asserted in the past, above all because Greece was never completely cut off from contact with the Near East. The Archaic Age is emphatically seen as a period of tremendous activity and change, but the trustworthiness of the (later) ancient sources that inform us about it is being much debated, for example, concerning the date of the first Olympic Games (see the article by Hugh Lee in the collection edited by Rashcke).

Ancient Olympic Games: http://olympics.tufts.edu.

Donlan, Walter. *The Aristocratic Ideal in Ancient Greece: Attitudes of Superiority from Homer to the End of the Fifth Century B.C.* 1980.

Finley, M. I., and H. W. Pleket. *The Olympic Games: The First Thousand Years.* 1976.

Hanson, Victor Davis. *The Other Greeks: The Family Farm and the Agrarian Roots of Western Civilization.* 1995.

Morris, Sarah P. *Daidalos and the Origins of Greek Art.* 1992.

Murray, Oswyn. *Early Greece.* 2nd. ed. 1993.

Olympia: http://harpy.uccs.edu/greek/olympia.html.

Osborne, Robin. *Greece in the Making, 1200–479 B.C.* 1996.

Raschke, Wendy J., ed. *The Archaeology of the Olympics: The Olympics and Other Festivals in Antiquity.* 1988.

Snodgrass, Anthony. *The Dark Age of Greece.* 1971.

Steiner, Deborah Tarn. *The Tyrant's Writ: Myths and Images of Writing in Ancient Greece.* 1994.

Swaddling, Judith. *The Ancient Olympic Games.* 1980.

The Creation of the Greek *Polis*

More and more scholars are realizing that the Greek city-state did not spring up in a cultural vacuum, but the scarcity of sources for this period makes it difficult to weigh the various influences with confidence; see, for example, the differing approaches of Morris, Polignac, and Starr. Recent research persuasively argues for a greater role for individual entrepreneurs in what is usually regarded as state-initiated colonization (see the article by Robin Osborne in the collection edited by Fisher and van Wees).

Boardman, John. *The Greeks Overseas: Their Early Colonies and Trade.* New ed. 1980.

Burkert, Walter. *The Orientalizing Revolution: The Near Eastern Influence on Greek Culture in the Early Archaic Age.* Trans. Margaret E. Pinder and Walter Burkert. 1992.

Fisher, Nick, and Hans van Wees, eds. *Archaic Greece: New Approaches and Evidence.* 1998.

Garlan, Yvon. *Slavery in Ancient Greece.* Rev. ed. Trans. Janet Lloyd. 1988.

Garland, Robert. *Religion and the Greeks.* 1994.

Morris, Ian. *Burial and Ancient Society: The Rise of the Greek City-State.* 1987.

Polignac, François de. *Cults, Territory, and the Origins of the Greek City-State.* Trans. Janet Lloyd. 1995.

Snodgrass, Anthony. *Archaic Greece: The Age of Experiment.* 1980.

Starr, Chester. *Individual and Community: The Rise of the Polis, 800–500 B.C.* 1986.

Diversity in City-State Society, Government, and Thought

A strong trend is to try to lessen the focus on Athens and Sparta in modern historical accounts of the emerging Greek city-state and bring in as many other places as possible from the hundreds and hundreds that existed. As usual in ancient history, the limited number of extant sources makes this quest very difficult, even for the basic chronology and events of political history. Since precise dating is less crucial in social and cultural history, scholarship in those areas for this period has been productive and provocative, as in the study of sexuality.

Anhalt, Emily Katz. *Solon the Singer: Politics and Poetics.* 1993.

Archaic Greek Sculpture: http://harpy.uccs.edu/greek/archaicsculpt.html.

Barnes, Jonathan. *Early Greek Philosophy.* 1987.

Cartledge, Paul. *Sparta and Lakonia: A Regional History, 1300–362 B.C.* 1979.

Emlyn-Jones, C. J. *The Ionians and Hellenism: A Study of the Cultural Achievements of Early Greek Inhabitants of Asia Minor.* 1980.

Fitzhardinge, L. F. *The Spartans.* 1980.

Fornara, Charles W., and Loren J. Samons II. *Athens from Cleisthenes to Pericles.* 1991.

Halperin, David. M. *One Hundred Years of Homosexuality and Other Essays on Greek Love.* 1990.

Hurwitt, Jeffrey M. *The Art and Culture of Early Greece, 1100–480 B.C.* 1985.

Kennell, Nigel M. *The Gymnasium of Virtue: Education and Culture in Ancient Sparta.* 1995.

McGlew, James F. *Tyranny and Political Culture in Ancient Greece.* 1993.

Meier, Christian. *The Greek Discovery of Politics.* Trans. David McLintock. 1990.

Ober, Josiah, and Charles W. Hedrick. *The Birth of Democracy: An Exhibition Celebrating the 2500th Anniversary of Democracy.* 1993.

Sergent, Bernard. *Homosexuality in Greek Myth.* Trans. Arthur Goldhammer. 1986.

Smith, J. A. *Athens under the Tyrants.* 1989.

The Greek Golden Age

c. 500–400 B.C.

**The Sculptural Style
of the Greek Golden Age**
*This sculpture of a male nude
was cast in bronze in the fifth
century B.C.; bronze was preferred over marble for top-rank
statues. The relaxed pose displays the asymmetry — the head
looking to one side, the arms in
different positions, the torso
tilted — that made statues from
the Classical period appear less
stiff than Archaic period ones.
The lifelike body nonetheless
displays an idealized physique.
Complete bronze statues such as
this one have rarely survived
because they were commonly
melted down for their metal
in the medieval and early
modern periods.*
Erich Lessing/Art Resource, NY.

T HE GREATEST EXTERNAL DANGER ever to threaten ancient Greece
began with a diplomatic fiasco. In 507 B.C., the Athenians sent
ambassadors to the Persian king, Darius I (r. 522–486 B.C.), to
ask for a protective alliance against the Spartans. The Persian empire
was at the time the greatest power in the ancient world. The diplomats
met with one of the king's governors at Sardis, the Persian regional headquarters in western Anatolia (modern Turkey). After the royal administrator listened to their plea, he reportedly replied, "But who in the
world are you and where do you live?"

This incident reveals the forces motivating the conflicts that would
dominate the military and political history of mainland Greece during
the fifth century B.C. First, the two major powers in mainland Greece—
Athens and Sparta—remained wary of each other. Second, the kingdom
of Persia had expanded far enough west that the Greek city-states in
Ionia (today western Turkey) had become its subjects. Yet neither the
Persians nor the mainland Greeks knew much about each other. Their
mutual ignorance opened the door to explosive wars.

Although the fifth century B.C. was a time of almost constant
warfare, first between Greeks and Persians and then between Greek
city-states themselves, it also encompassed Greece's most enduring
cultural and artistic achievements. Athenian accomplishments of the
fifth century B.C. had such a profound impact that historians call this
period a Golden Age. This Golden Age opens the Classical Age of
Greek history, a modern designation that covers the period from
about 500 B.C. to the death of Alexander the Great in 323 B.C.

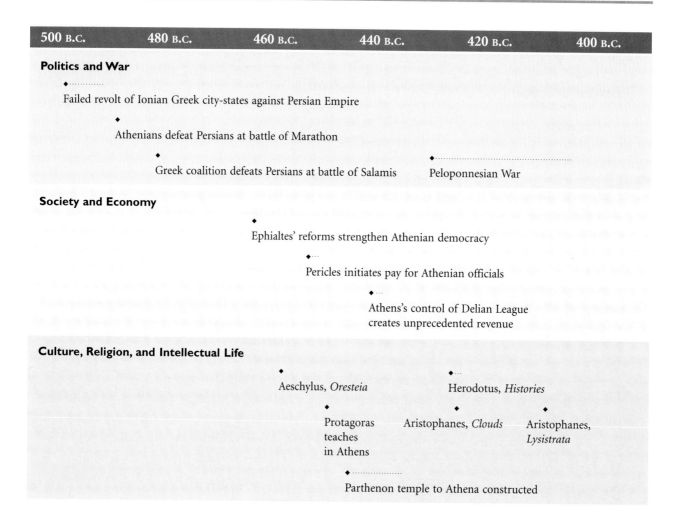

| 500 B.C. | 480 B.C. | 460 B.C. | 440 B.C. | 420 B.C. | 400 B.C. |

Politics and War

Failed revolt of Ionian Greek city-states against Persian Empire

Athenians defeat Persians at battle of Marathon

Greek coalition defeats Persians at battle of Salamis

Peloponnesian War

Society and Economy

Ephialtes' reforms strengthen Athenian democracy

Pericles initiates pay for Athenian officials

Athens's control of Delian League creates unprecedented revenue

Culture, Religion, and Intellectual Life

Aeschylus, *Oresteia*

Herodotus, *Histories*

Protagoras teaches in Athens

Aristophanes, *Clouds*

Aristophanes, *Lysistrata*

Parthenon temple to Athena constructed

Despite the pressures of war, Athenians in the Golden Age created the preeminent society in ancient Greece, developing sweeping democracy at home while establishing an empire abroad and achieving enormous prosperity and world-famous artistic and cultural accomplishments. More than any other city-state, Golden Age Athens was home to innovations in drama, art, architecture, and thought that have had a lasting influence on Western civilization. Some of these changes created tensions at the time, however, because they conflicted with ancient traditions, such as the competitive desire of the social elite to dominate government and many people's religious fear that Greeks would offend the gods by abandoning old beliefs and practices.

The Peloponnesian War, a protracted struggle between Athens and Sparta, finished the Golden Age in the closing decades of the fifth century B.C. This period of cultural blossoming therefore both began and ended with destructive wars, with Greeks standing together in the first one and tearing each other apart in the concluding one.

❖ Clash between Persia and Greece, 499–479 B.C.

The most famous series of wars in ancient Greek history had its roots in the Athenian-Persian meeting at Sardis in 507 B.C. There the Athenian ambassadors gave in to the customary Persian terms for an alliance: presenting tokens of earth and water to the king's representative, thereby recognizing Persian superiority. Although outraged at this symbolic submission to a foreign power, the Athenian assembly never openly rejected the alliance; King Darius therefore believed that Athens had accepted his terms. This misunderstanding opened the door to a chain of events culminating in two invasions of Greece by the enormous military forces of Persia. The Persian kingdom outstripped Greece in every category of material resources, from precious metals to soldiers. The clash between Persia and Greece pitted the equivalent of an elephant against a small swarm of mosquitoes. In such a conflict a Greek victory seemed improbable, to say the least. Equally unexpected—given the tendency toward disunity of the independent Greek city-states—was that a coalition of city-states would eventually, if temporarily, unite to repel the common enemy.

The Persian Wars Begin

Hostilities began in 499 B.C. with a revolt of the Ionian Greek city-states against the Persian-installed tyrannies ruling them. Troops sent by Athens to aid the rebels proceeded as far as Sardis, which they burned. A Persian counterattack sent them fleeing home and crushed the revolt by 494 B.C. (Map 3.1).

King Darius erupted when he learned that the Athenians had aided the Ionian revolt: not only had they dared attack his kingdom, but they had done it after, as far as he knew, agreeing to be loyal to him. To remind himself to punish this betrayal, Darius ordered a slave to say to him three times at every meal, "Sire, remember the Athenians." In 490 B.C., he dispatched a fleet with orders to punish Athens by reinstalling the elderly Hippias as its puppet tyrant.

This Persian force expected the city-state to surrender without a fight. The Athenians, however, confronted the invaders near the village of Marathon, on the northeastern coast of Athenian territory. Everyone believed the foreigners would win. The Athenian soldiers, who had never before seen Persians, grew anxious merely at the sight of their outlandish (to Greek eyes) outfits—they wore pants instead of the short tunics and bare legs that Greeks regarded as manly dress. Nevertheless, the Athenian generals never let their men lose heart or back down.

Planning their tactics to minimize the time their soldiers would be exposed to the menacing arrows of Persian archers, the commanders sent their hoplites straight toward the enemy line at a dead run. The Greeks dashed across the Marathon plain in their clanking metal armor (all seventy pounds of it) under a hail of arrows. Once engaged in hand-to-hand combat with the Persians, the Greek hoplites benefited from their heavier weapons. After a furious struggle, they drove the Persians back into a swamp; all who failed to escape to their ships were killed.

The Athenian army then hurried the twenty-six miles from Marathon to Athens to guard the city against a Persian naval attack. (Today's marathon races commemorate the legendary exploit of a runner who had been sent ahead to announce the victory, after which he dropped dead from the effort.) When the Persians saw the city defended, they sailed home. The Athenians rejoiced in disbelief. The Persians, whom they had feared as invincible, had retreated. For decades thereafter, the greatest honor a family could claim was to say it had furnished a "Marathon fighter."

The symbolic importance of the battle of Marathon far outweighed its military significance. The defeat of his punitive expedition enraged Darius because it injured his prestige, not because it threatened his kingdom's security. The Athenians had dramatically demonstrated their commitment to preserving their freedom. The unexpected victory at Marathon boosted Athenian self-confidence, and the city-state's citizens thereafter boasted that they had withstood the feared Persians on their own, without Sparta's help.

The Great Invasion of 480–479 B.C.

The Marathon victory helped Greeks find the will to resist the second, gigantic Persian invasion of Greece in 480 B.C., led by Darius's son Xerxes I (r. 486–465 B.C.). So immense was his army, the Greeks claimed, that it required seven days and seven nights of continuous marching to cross a temporary bridge over the Hellespont strait, the narrow passage of sea between Anatolia and mainland Greece. Xerxes expected the Greek city-states to surrender immediately once they learned the size of his forces. Some did, but thirty-one city-states allied to fight the Persians. This coalition, known as

MAP 3.1 The Persian Wars, 499–479 B.C.
Following the example of the founder of the Persian kingdom, Cyrus the Great (d. 530 B.C.), Cambyses (r. 530–522 B.C.) and Darius (r. 522–486 B.C.) energetically worked to expand their empire eastward and westward. Darius in fact invaded Thrace more than fifteen years before the conflict against the Greeks that we call the Persian Wars. The Persians' unexpected defeat in Greece put an end to their attempt to extend their power into Europe.

the Hellenic League, accomplished the incredible: protecting their homeland and their independence from the world's strongest power. They did this without the aid of the vigorous city-states in Italy and Sicily, such as Syracuse, the powerful ruler of a regional empire; the western Greeks declined to join the league because they were occupied defending themselves against Carthage, a Phoenician foundation in North Africa that was aggressively trying to monopolize commerce in their area.

The Greek coalition chose Sparta as its leader because of its formidable hoplite army. The Spartans showed their courage when three hundred of their men, led by one of their kings, Leonidas, held off Xerxes' huge army for several days at the narrow pass called Thermopylae ("warm gates") in central Greece. A hoplite summed up the Spartans' bravery with his reputed response to the observation that the Persian archers were so numerous that their arrows darkened the sky in battle. "That's good news," said the Spartan warrior. "We'll fight in the shade." They all went down fighting.

When the Persians marched south, the Athenians evacuated their population instead of surrendering. They believed their city-state and its freedom would survive so long as its people did, regardless of what happened to their property. The Persians promptly burned the empty city. In the summer of 480 B.C., Themistocles of Athens maneuvered the other, less aggressive Greek leaders into facing the larger Persian navy in a sea battle in the narrow channel between the island of Salamis and the west coast of Athenian territory. The narrowness of the channel prevented the Persians from using all their ships at once and let the heavier Greek ships win victory by ramming the flimsier Persian craft. When Xerxes observed that the most energetic of his naval commanders appeared to be the one woman among them, Artemisia, ruler of Caria (the southwest corner of Anatolia), he remarked, "My men have become women, and my women, men." In 479 B.C., the Greek infantry headed by the Spartans defeated the remaining Persian land forces at Plataea.

The Greeks' superior weapons and resourceful use of their topography to counterbalance the Persians' greater numbers help explain their military victories. But what is remarkable about the Persian Wars is the decision of the thirty-one Greek city-states to form a coalition in the first place. They could easily have surrendered and agreed to become Persian subjects to save themselves; for most of them, Persian rule would have meant only minimal interference in their internal affairs. Instead, they chose to fight for absolute independence and triumphed together against seemingly overwhelming odds. Because the Greek forces included not only the social elite and hoplites but also thousands of poorer men who rowed the warships, the effort against the Persians cut across social and economic

Leonidas, Hero of the Battle of Thermopylae

One of the two kings of Sparta at the time, Leonidas in 480 B.C. led the small force of Spartans and other Greeks sent to block the advance of the massive Persian army at the narrow pass of Thermopylae in central Greece. According to the Greek historian Herodotus, a contemporary of the Persian wars, this heroic action was meant to inspire wavering Greek city-states to remain in the Hellenic alliance against Persia. The defenders fell and were buried where they fought, inspiring the lines of poetry inscribed over the graves of Leonidas's men:

> *Go tell the Spartans, you*
> *strangers who pass by,*
> *That here obeying their orders*
> *we lie.*

Deutsches Archaologisches Institut–Athens.

divisions. The Hellenic League's decision to fight the Persian Wars demonstrated not only courage but a deep commitment to the ideal of political freedom that had emerged in the Archaic Age.

❖ Athenian Confidence in the Golden Age

The struggle against the Persians generated a rare instance of city-state cooperation in ancient Greek history. The two most powerful city-states, Athens and Sparta, put aside their mutual hostility in the interest of a united effort. Victory undid the alliance, however, despite the lobbying of pro-Spartan Athenians who believed the two city-states should be partners rather than rivals. Out of this fractured partnership arose the so-called Athenian empire, a modern label to describe Athens's new vision of itself that gradually emerged by the mid-fifth century B.C. No longer were Athenians satisfied being an equal member of a voluntary coalition of Greek city-states: they fancied a much grander role for themselves. The growth of Athenian power internationally went hand in hand with increasing democracy and vast spending on public buildings, art, and festivals.

The Establishment of the Athenian Empire

Following the Persian Wars, Sparta and Athens both built up their own allies to strengthen their positions against each other. Relying on longstanding treaties with city-states located mainly on the Peloponnese peninsula, Sparta tended to lead forces stronger in infantry than in warships, with the notable exception of Corinth, a naval power. The Spartan alliance, which modern historians refer to as the Peloponnesian League, had an assembly to determine policy, but no action could be taken unless the Spartan leaders approved.

By 477 B.C., under the leadership of the Athenian aristocrat Aristides (c. 525–465 B.C.), Athens allied with city-states in the areas most exposed to possible Persian retaliation—in northern Greece, on the islands of the Aegean Sea, and along the western coast of Anatolia. Athenian allies, who usually had stronger navies than infantries, swore a solemn oath never to desert the coalition. This alliance, today referred to as the Delian League because its treasury was originally located on the island of Delos, also had an assembly to set policy. Theoretically, every member had an equal say in making decisions, but in practice Athens was in charge.

The Delian and Peloponnesian Leagues

The Athenians came to dominate this "democracy" as a result of the special arrangements made to finance the alliance's naval operations. Each member city-state paid annual "dues" based on its size and prosperity. Because compulsory, these dues were really "tribute." Larger member states were to supply entire triremes (warships) complete with crews and their pay; smaller states could share the cost of a ship and crew or simply contribute cash.

Over time, more and more Delian League members paid their dues in cash rather than by furnishing warships. It was beyond their capacities to build ships as specialized as triremes and to train crews (170 rowers were needed); the recent reconstruction of a full-size, seaworthy Greek warship has demonstrated the great difficulty of the construction project and of crew training. Athens, far larger than most of the allies, had the shipyards and skilled workers to build triremes as well as an abundance of men eager to earn pay as rowers. Many oarsmen came from the poorest class in society, and they earned not only money but also political influence in Athenian democracy as naval strength became the city-state's principal source of military power. Without them, Athens had no navy.

The decision of many Delian League allies to let Athens supply warships eventually left them without any navies of their own. Therefore, they had no effective recourse if they disagreed with decisions made for the league by Athens. The Athenian assembly could simply order the superior Athenian fleet to compel discontented allies to comply with league policy and continue paying their annual tribute. As the Athenian historian Thucydides observed, rebellious allies "lost their independence," and the Athenians were "no longer as popular as they used to be." This unpopularity was the price Athens paid for making itself the dominant power in the coalition and the major naval power in the eastern Mediterranean.

By about 460 B.C., twenty years after the battle of Salamis, the Delian League's fleet had expelled almost all the Persian garrisons that had continued to hold out in some city-states along the northeastern Aegean coast. The alliance drove the enemy fleet from the Aegean Sea, ending the Persian threat to Greece for the next fifty years. Athens meanwhile grew rich from its share of the spoils captured from Persian outposts and the tribute paid by Delian League members.

The Athenian assembly decided how to spend this income. Rich and poor alike had a stake in keeping the fleet active and the league members paying for it. The numerous lower-class Athenian men who rowed the Delian League's ships came to depend on the income they earned on league expeditions. Members of the social elite enhanced their social status by commanding successful league campaigns and spending their portion of the spoils on public festivals and buildings. Wealthy and prominent men were expected to make financial contributions to the common good to win popular support. They did not form political parties in the modern sense but gathered informal circles of friends and followers to support their agendas. Disputes in the social elite

A Modern Reconstruction of a Greek Warship
This full-scale reconstruction of an ancient trireme (the largest warship of the Classical period, with three banks of oars on each side) has been commissioned in today's Royal Greek Navy. A trireme had a bronze ram on its bow that projected just below the water line and that was used to puncture enemy vessels. Sea trials with volunteer rowers have shown that ancient oarsmen must have had a very high level of aerobic fitness and muscular strength to propel the ships at more than nine knots at full ramming speed.
Trireme Trust.

often stemmed more from competition for public offices and influence in the assembly than from disagreements over policy matters. Arguments about policy tended to revolve around how Athens should exercise its growing power internationally, not whether it was right to treat allies as subjects.

As this originally democratic alliance was transformed into an empire commanded by a democratic city-state, Sparta and the rest of the Peloponnesian League denounced the change as the equivalent of enslavement, the very issue over which Athens had once stood shoulder to shoulder with these same allies against the Persians. The Athenians insisted that their conversion from partner to dominant leader was justified because it kept the Delian League strong enough to protect Greece from the Persians.

Radical Democracy and Pericles' Leadership

As the Delian League grew, the poorer men who powered the Athenian fleet came to recognize that they provided a cornerstone of Athenian security and prosperity. They felt the time had come to increase their political power by making the judicial system of Athens just as democratic as the process of passing laws in the assembly, which was open to all male citizens over eighteen years of age. The leaders of this demand for judicial change were members of the elite, who competed for popular support for their elective offices. One of Athens's most socially prominent citizens, Pericles (c. 495–429 B.C.), became the leading politician of the Golden Age by supporting the people's call for greater democracy.

Creating Radical Democracy. In the mid-fifth century B.C., Athenian democracy gradually became so sweeping, compared with most governments in the ancient world, that today it is called "radical." Its principles were clear: direct and widespread participation by male citizens in the assembly to make laws and policy; random selection and rotation in office of the members of Cleisthenes' Council of 500, most magistrates, and jurors; elaborate precautions to prevent corruption; equal protection under the law for citizens regardless of wealth; and the majority's authority over any minority or individual. At the same time, excellence was recognized by making the top public offices—the board of ten "generals," with far-reaching oversight of the city-state's military and financial affairs—elective annually and without limits on how many terms a man could serve.

Reforming the judicial system became a central step in creating radical democracy. Ever since Cleisthenes' reforms, the archons (magistrates of the city-state) and the Areopagus Council of ex-archons had rendered most judicial verdicts. Although archons were now chosen annually by lottery to make their selection truly democratic, they and the Areopagus members were still susceptible to bribery and pressure from the social elite. Since democratically enacted laws meant little if they were not applied fairly, the masses demanded reforms to insulate legal cases from the influence of unscrupulous members of the elite.

As previously with Cleisthenes' reforms, the opportunity for change arose when a prominent member of the elite sought the support of the people against a rival from his own class. In 461 B.C., a politician named Ephialtes got the upper hand in just such a struggle for status by sponsoring measures to establish a new court system. Ephialtes' reforms made it virtually impossible to bribe or pressure jurors because they were selected by lottery from male citizens over thirty years old, the selection was made only on the day of the trial, all trials were concluded in one day, and juries were large (from several hundred to several thousand). No judges presided; only one official was present—to keep fistfights from breaking out. Jurors made up their minds after hearing speeches by the persons involved. The accuser and the accused were required to speak for themselves, although they might pay someone else to compose their speeches and ask others to speak in support of their arguments. A majority vote of the jurors ruled, and no appeals were allowed.

The Importance of Majority Rule. Majority rule, especially in enforcing public accountability, was the operative principle for making decisions in Athenian radical democracy. Any citizen could call for a trial to judge an official's conduct in office. A striking example of majority rule was the procedure called *ostracism* (from *ostracon*, meaning a "piece of broken pottery," the material used for casting ballots). Once a year, all male citizens were eligible to cast a ballot on which they scratched the name of one man they thought should be ostracized (exiled for ten years). If at least six thousand ballots were cast, the man whose name appeared on the greatest number was expelled from Athenian territory. He suffered no other penalty, and his family and property could remain behind undisturbed. Ostracism was not a criminal penalty, and men returning from their exile had undiminished rights as citizens.

Since this process was meant to protect radical democracy, a man could be ostracized if he became so prominent that his personal popularity seemed a threat to the interests of the majority. An anecdote about the politician Aristides illustrates this situation. He was nicknamed "the Just" because he had proved himself so fair-minded in setting the original level of dues for the Delian League members.

Potsherd Ballots for Ostracism

These two shards (ostraka) were broken from the same pot (as the breakage line shows) to be inscribed for use as ballots in an ostracism at Athens in the Classical period. The lower fragment carries the name of Themistocles, the controversial Athenian leader who engineered the Greek fleet's successful stand against the Persian navy off the island of Salamis in 480 B.C.; the upper one bears the name of the Delian League's most famous general against the Persians, Cimon. Political strife led to Themistocles' ostracism sometime in the late 470s B.C. and Cimon's in 461 B.C. Therefore, if these two ballots were intended for the same ostracism, it must have been Themistocles' or an earlier one when he was still in Athens. Deutsches Archäologisches Institut–Athens.

On the day of the balloting, an illiterate man from the countryside handed Aristides a pottery fragment and asked him to scratch the name of the man's choice for ostracism on it.

> "Certainly," said Aristides. "Which name shall I write?"
> "Aristides," replied the countryman.
> "Very well," remarked Aristides as he proceeded to inscribe his own name. "But tell me, why do you want to ostracize Aristides? What has he done to you?"
> "Oh, nothing. I don't even know him," sputtered the man. "I just can't stand hearing everybody refer to him as 'the Just.'"

True or not, this tale demonstrates that Athenians assumed that the right way to protect democracy was always to trust the majority vote of freeborn, adult male citizens, without any restrictions on a man's ability to decide what he thought was best for democracy. This conviction required making allowances for irresponsible types like the illiterate man who complained about Aristides. It rested on the belief that the cumulative political wisdom of the majority of voters would outweigh the eccentricity and ignorance of a few. It also showed that men seeking the high status of political success in Athenian democracy had to be ready to pay the equally high price that envy or scapegoating could bring.

Pericles' Leadership. Like his distant relative Cleisthenes, Pericles became the most influential Athenian politician of his era by devising innovations to strengthen the egalitarian tendencies of Athenian democracy. The most spellbinding public speaker of the Golden Age, Pericles repeatedly persuaded the assembly to pass laws increasing its political power. In return, he gained such popularity that he regularly won election to the annual board of ten generals.

Pericles' most important democratic innovation, pay for service in public offices filled by lottery, made it possible for poorer men to leave their regular work to serve in government. Early in the 450s B.C., he convinced the assembly to use state revenues to pay a daily stipend to men who served in the Council of 500, on juries, and in numerous other posts. The amount that councilors and others received was not lavish, no more than an ordinary worker could earn in a day. The highest officials, the generals, received no pay because the prestige of their position was considered its own reward.

In 451 B.C., Pericles strengthened the definition of citizen identity, which even the poor possessed under democracy: he sponsored a law making citizenship more exclusive and enhancing the status of Athenian mothers. This law mandated that from now on citizenship would be conferred only on children whose mother and father were both Athenian by birth. Previously, the children of Athenian men who married non-Athenian women had been granted citizenship, and upper-class men had often married rich foreign women. Ironically, Pericles' own maternal grandfather had done just that. After this law, however, men avoided seeking wives outside the citizen body.

Finally, Pericles supported the interests of poorer men by recommending frequent naval campaigns against Spartan and Corinthian interests in Greece and against Persian control of Cyprus, Egypt, and the eastern Mediterranean. Rowers earned pay and booty in these wars. Athenian confidence reached such a fever pitch in this period that the assembly voted to carry on as many as three different major expeditions at the same time. The Athenians' ambitions at last outstripped their resources, however, and they had to pull back from the eastern Mediterranean after 450 B.C. and stop fighting the Peloponnesian League. In the winter of 446–445 B.C., Pericles engineered a peace treaty with Sparta designed to freeze the balance of power in Greece for thirty years and thus preserve Athenian control of the Delian League. Pericles made this agreement and changed his aggressive foreign policy because he realized that preserving radical democracy at home depended on his city-state not losing its power over its allies.

The Urban Landscape of Athens

The Golden Age in the time of Pericles brought Athens prosperity from Delian League dues, war booty, and taxes on booming seaborne trade. Its empire consisted of a far-flung array of ports for merchants to use in safety, with Athens providing the largest market as well as the legal system for resolving disputes. The city's growing vitality as a commercial center attracted cargo, merchants, and crafts producers from around the Mediterranean world and sent local products far afield; Etruscan civilization in central Italy, for example, imported large amounts of decorated pottery for wine drinking in Greek fashion at dinner parties. The increased economic activity of the mid-fifth century B.C. brought Athens to the height of its prosperity.

The new riches flowed mainly into public building projects, art, and festivals rather than private luxury. People's homes, in both the city and the countryside, retained their traditional modest size. Farmhouses were usually clustered in villages, while homes in the city wedged higgledy-piggledy against one another along narrow, winding streets. All residences followed the same basic design: bedrooms, storerooms, and dining rooms grouped around small, open-air courtyards. Wall paintings or works of art were not yet common as decorations for private homes. Sparse and simple furnishings were the rule. Sanitary facilities usually consisted of a pit dug just outside the front door, which was emptied by collectors paid to dump the contents outside the city at a distance set by law. Poorer people rented small apartments.

Generals who won enormous booty leading Delian League forces against Persian outposts in the eastern Mediterranean used this wealth to beautify the city, not to build themselves mansions. In this way, Athens acquired landscaping with shade trees, running tracks for exercise, and gathering places such as the renowned Painted Stoa. *Stoas* were narrow buildings open along one side whose purpose was to provide shelter from sun or rain. One successful general's family built the Painted Stoa in the heart of the city, on the edge of the central market square, the *agora*. The crowds who came to the agora daily to shop and chat about politics would cluster inside this shelter. There they could gaze on its bright paintings, which depicted the glorious exploits of the general's family and thus publicized its dedication to the city-state. Wealthy citizens also paid for other major public expenses, such as

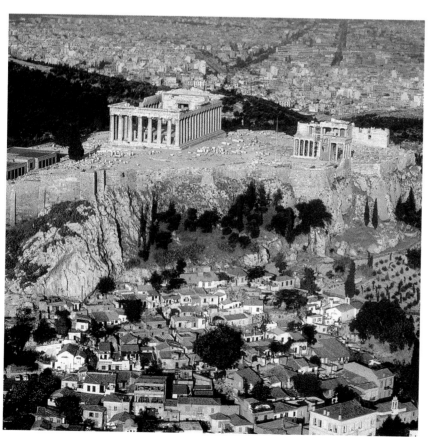

The Acropolis of Athens
Like most Greek city-states, Athens grew up around a prominent hill (acropolis), whose summit served as a special sanctuary for the gods and as a fortress to which the population could retreat when an enemy attacked. The invading Persians burned the buildings on the Athenian acropolis in 480 B.C.; the Athenians left the charred remains in place for thirty years to remind themselves of the sacrifice they had made for their freedom. In the 440s, they began erecting magnificent temples and other public buildings there that made their city famous then and now for its monumental marble architecture.
Michael Freeman/Bruce Coleman, Ltd.

equipment for warships and entertainment at city festivals. This custom was essential because Athens, like most Greek city-states, had no regular direct taxes on income or property.

Huge buildings paid for by public funds constituted the most conspicuous new architecture in Golden Age Athens (Map 3.2). In 447 B.C., Pericles instigated the city's greatest building project ever, on the rocky hill at the center of the city called the *acropolis*. The project's centerpieces were a mammoth gate building with columns straddling the western entrance of the acropolis and a new temple of Athena housing a huge statue of the goddess. Comparing the value of a day's wage then and now, we can calculate that these buildings easily cost more than the modern equivalent of a billion dollars, a phenomenal sum for a Greek city-state. Pericles' political rivals railed at him for squandering public funds. Scholars disagree about whether the assembly used Delian League dues to help finance the program; it is certain that substantial funds were taken

from sales taxes, harbor taxes, and the financial reserves of the sanctuaries of the goddess Athena, which private donations and public support had provided.

The Parthenon. The vast new temple built for Athena became Greece's most famous building, known as the Parthenon ("the house of the virgin goddess"). As the patron goddess of Athens, Athena had long had another sanctuary on the acropolis. Its focus was an olive tree regarded as the goddess's sacred symbol as protector of the city-state's economic health. The Parthenon honored her in a different capacity: a warrior serving as the divine champion of Athenian military power. Inside the temple stood a gold and ivory statue nearly forty feet high depicting the goddess in battle armor, holding in her outstretched hand a six-foot statue of the figure of Victory (Nike in Greek).

Like all Greek temples, the Parthenon was meant as a house for its divinity, not as a gathering

MAP 3.2 Fifth-Century Athens
The urban center of Athens with the agora and acropolis at its heart measured about one square mile, surrounded by a stone wall with a circuit of some four miles. Fifteen large gates flanked by towers and various smaller doors allowed traffic in and out of the city; much of the Athenian population lived in the many villages (demes) of the surrounding countryside. Most of the city's water supply came from wells and springs inside the walls, but, unusually for a Greek city, Athens also had water piped in from outside. Most streets were narrow (no more than fifteen or twenty feet wide) and winding, with houses crowding in on both sides.

FIGURE 3.1 Styles of Greek Capitals
The Greeks decorated the tops ("capitals") of columns in these three styles to fit the different architectural "canons" (their word for precise mathematical systems of proportions) that they devised for designing buildings.

DORIC   IONIC   CORINTHIAN

place for worshipers. Its design followed standard temple architecture: a rectangular box on a raised platform, a plan the Greeks probably derived from the stone temples of Egypt. The box, which had only one small door at the front, was fenced in by columns all around. The Parthenon's columns were carved in the simple style called Doric, in contrast to the more elaborate Ionic and Corinthian styles that have often been imitated in modern buildings (Figure 3.1). Only priests and priestesses could enter the temple usually; public religious ceremonies took place out front.

The Parthenon was intended to proclaim the self-confidence of Golden Age Athens. Constructed from twenty thousand tons of Attic marble, it stretched nearly 230 feet in length and 100 feet wide, with eight columns across the ends instead of the six normally found in Doric style and seventeen instead of thirteen along the sides. Its massive size conveyed an impression of power. The temple's sophisticated architecture demonstrated Athenian ability to construct order that was both apparent and real: because perfectly rectilinear architecture appears curved to the human eye, subtle curves and inclines were built into the Parthenon to produce an illusion of completely straight lines and emphasize its massiveness.

The elaborate sculptural frieze of the Parthenon announced the temple's most innovative and confident message: Athens's citizens possessed the special goodwill of the gods. The frieze, a continuous band of figures, was carved in relief around the top of the walls inside the porch along the edges of the building's platform. This sort of decoration usually appeared only on Ionic-style buildings. Adding it to a Doric-style temple was a striking departure meant to attract attention. The Parthenon's frieze por-

trayed Athenian men, women, and children in a parade in the presence of the gods, most likely during the Panathenaia festival, the city's most important ceremony honoring Athena. Depicting the procession in motion, like a filmstrip in stone, the frieze included youths riding spirited horses and women carrying sacred implements. As usual on Greek temples, brightly colored paint and shiny metal attachments enlivened the figures of people and animals.

No other city-state had ever gone beyond the traditional function of temples—glorifying and paying homage to the community's special deities—by adorning a temple with representations of its citizens. The Parthenon frieze made a unique statement about how Athenians perceived their relationship to the gods. Even if the deities carved in the frieze were understood to be separated from and perhaps invisible to the humans in the procession, a temple adorned with pictures of citizens, albeit idealized citizens of perfect physique and beauty, amounted to a claim of special intimacy between the city-state and the gods. This assertion reflected the Athenians' interpretation of their success in helping turn back the Persians, in achieving leadership of a powerful naval alliance, and in amassing wealth that made Athens richer than all its neighbors in mainland Greece. Their success, the Athenians would have said, proved that the gods were on their side.

The Message of Sculpture. Like the design of the Parthenon frieze, the changes that Golden Age artists made in freestanding sculpture broke with tradition. Archaic Age (c. 750–500 B.C.) statues had impressed viewers with their stiff posture and straight-ahead stance, imitating the unchanging style of Egyptian statuary. Archaic male statues had only one pose: striding forward with their left legs, arms held rigidly at their sides. This style gave them an appearance of stability; not even a hard shove seemed likely to budge them. By the time of the Persian Wars, however, Greek sculptors began to create a variety of poses to put statues into motion. The spirited movement portrayed by this new style suggested the confident energy of the times but also hinted at the possibility of instability: Golden Age statues took more chances with their balance.

Not everything changed. Sculptors still usually portrayed human males nude, as athletes or warriors, while clothing females in fine robes. Changes did come, however, in their physiques and postures, which became more naturalistic in portraying perfect bodies. These innovations suggested that humans could take pride in their idealized potential for natural beauty and mobility. Male statues now could have bent arms and the body's weight on either leg. Their musculature was anatomically correct rather than sketchy and impressionistic, as had been the style in the sixth century B.C. Female statues, too, had more relaxed poses and clothing,

which hung in a way that hinted at the shape of the curves underneath instead of disguising them. The faces of classical sculptures were self-confidently calm rather than smiling like archaic figures.

In every case, Golden Age statues were meant to be seen by the public, whether they were paid for with private or government funds. In this sense, both categories served a public function: broadcasting a message to an audience. Greeks who ordered pieces of private art did not yet use them to decorate the interiors of their homes. Instead, they displayed them in public, for a variety of purposes. Privately commissioned statues of gods could be placed in a sanctuary as symbols of devotion. In the tradition of offering lovely crafted objects to divinities as commemorations of important personal experiences, such as economic success or victory in athletic contests, people also donated sculptures of physically beautiful humans to the sanctuaries of the gods. Wealthy families commissioned statues of their deceased members, especially if they had died young in war, to be placed above their graves as memorials of their virtue.

Scene from the Parthenon Frieze
The Parthenon, the Athenian temple honoring Athena as a warrior goddess and patron of the Delian League, dominated the summit of the city's acropolis. A frieze, of which this is a small section, ran around the top of the temple's outside wall. It is a testimony to Athenian confidence in divine favor that the frieze appears to show ordinary people in the same context as the immortal gods: the deities are observing the citizens as they participate in the Panathenaic festival's procession to the Parthenon. The elaborate folds of the figure's garments display the richness of style characteristic of clothed figures in Classical period sculpture.
British Museum.

❖ Tradition and Innovation in Athens's Golden Age

Fifth-century B.C. Athens created unprecedented accomplishments in architecture, art, drama, and intellectual life, but many central aspects of its social and religious life remained unchanged. The result was a heightened tension between the love of innovation and the strength of tradition, especially in religion. Tradition also continued to determine the limited role allowed women in public life, but they continued to play essential roles in managing the household, participating in religious ceremonies, and, for poorer women, working in commerce and agriculture to help support their families. A far-reaching source of tension arose from innovative intellectual developments: the startling ideas of teachers called *sophists* and the ethical views of the philosopher Socrates. The most visible response to the tension produced by these new developments was the increased importance of tragic and comedic drama as publicly supported art forms examining problems in city-state life.

Religious Tradition in a Period of Change

Greeks maintained their religious traditions by participating in the sacrifices and public festivals of the city-state's cults and by seeking a personal relationship with the gods in the rituals of hero cults and mystery cults. Each cult—the set of prayers and other forms of worship connected with a particular divinity—had its own rituals, but sacrifice provided the focus. Sacrifices ranged from the bloodless offering of fruits, vegetables, and small cakes to the slaughter of large animals. The speechwriter Lysias (c. 445–380 B.C.), a Syracusan residing in Athens, explained the necessity for public sacrifice in an address composed for an Athenian official: "Our ancestors handed down to us the most powerful and prosperous community in Greece by performing the prescribed sacrifices. It is therefore proper for us to offer the same sacrifices as they, if only for the sake of the success which has resulted from those rites." The sacrifice of a large animal provided an occasion for the community to assemble and reaffirm its ties to the divine world and, by sharing the roasted meat of the sacrificed beast, for the worshipers to benefit personally from a good relationship with the gods. The feasting that followed a large-animal sacrifice was especially significant because meat was rare in most Greeks' diet.

The bloody process of killing the victim followed strict rules to avoid ritual contamination. The victim had to be an unblemished domestic animal, specially decorated with garlands and induced to approach the altar as if of its own free will. The assembled crowd maintained strict silence to avoid possibly impure remarks. The sacrificer sprinkled water on the victim's head so it would, in shaking its head in response, appear to consent to its death. After washing his hands, the sacrificer scattered barley grains on the altar fire and the animal's head and then cut a lock of the animal's hair and threw it on the fire. Following a prayer, he swiftly cut the animal's throat while musicians played flutelike pipes and female worshipers screamed, presumably to express the group's ritual sorrow at the victim's death. The carcass was then butchered, with some portions thrown on the altar fire so their aromatic smoke could waft its way upward to the god of the cult. The rest of the meat was then cooked for the worshipers to eat.

Public festivals featured not just large-animal sacrifice but also elaborate rituals, such as parades, open to the entire community. Athens boasted of having the most festivals—some large, some small—in all of Greece, with nearly half the days of the year featuring one. Not everyone attended all the festivals; hired laborers' contracts specified how many days off they received to attend religious ceremonies. Major occasions such as the Panathenaia festival, whose procession was probably portrayed on the Parthenon frieze, attracted large crowds of both women and men. It honored Athena not only with sacrifices and parades but also with contests in music, dancing, poetry, and athletics. Valuable prizes were awarded to the winners. Some festivals were for women only: one was the three-day festival for married women in honor of Demeter, goddess of agriculture and fertility.

In keeping with ancient tradition, Golden Age Greek religion encompassed many activities besides the civic cults of the twelve Olympian gods. People took a keen interest in religious actions meant to improve their personal relations with the divine.

Cup with Symbols to Avert Evil
Ancient Greeks had a healthy respect for the ability of nature and their fellow human beings to do them harm. Like prayer, magical symbols were thought to have power to ward off bad luck and other evils. Sometimes items from everyday life, such as this cup, were decorated with these symbols as a way of providing the object's owner with some hope of averting evil fortune both large and small. Here the god Dionysus is seated between two large eyes as sources of magical power.
Kannellopoulos Museum/Archaeological Receipts Fund.

Families marked significant moments such as birth, marriage, and death with prayers, rituals, and sacrifices. They honored their ancestors with offerings made at their tombs, consulted seers about the meanings of dreams and omens, and sought out magicians for spells to improve their love lives or curses to harm their enemies. Particularly important to individuals, as well as the community, were hero cults and mystery cults. The former were rituals performed at the tomb of an extraordinarily famous man or woman. Heroes' remains were thought to retain special power to reveal the future by inspiring oracles, to heal illnesses and injuries, and to provide protection in battle. The only hero to whom

cults were established all over the Greek world was the strongman Heracles (or Hercules, as his name was later spelled by the Romans). His superhuman feats gave him an appeal as a protector in many city-states.

The Athenian mystery cult of Demeter and her daughter Kore (also called Persephone), headquartered in the village of Eleusis, attracted followers from all parts of the world because it offered the hope of protection in this life and the afterlife. The central rite of this cult was the Mysteries: a series of initiation ceremonies into the secret knowledge of the cult. So important were the Eleusinian Mysteries that the Greek states observed an international truce—as with the Olympic Games—to allow travel to and from the festival even from distant corners of the Greek world. The Mysteries were open to all free Greek-speaking people everywhere—women and men, adults and children—if they were free of ritual contamination (for example, if they had not been convicted for murder, committed sacrilege, or had recent contact with the blood of a birth or with a corpse). Some slaves who worked in the sanctuary were also eligible. Initiation proceeded in several stages, but the main part took place during an annual festival lasting almost two weeks, which culminated in the revelation of Demeter's central secret after a day of fasting. The most eloquent proof of the sanctity attached to the Mysteries of Demeter and Kore is that no one ever revealed the secret throughout the thousand years during which the rites were celebrated. Indirect reports reveal that it promised initiates a better life on earth and a better fate after death. In the words of the poem *The Hymn to Demeter,* "Richly blessed is the mortal who has seen these rites; but whoever is not an initiate and has no share in them, that one never has an equal portion after death, down in the gloomy darkness."

The Eleusinian Mysteries were not the only mystery cult of the Greek world, nor were they unique in their concern with what lay beyond death. Mystery cults also emphasized protection for initiates in their current lives, whether against ghosts, illness, poverty, shipwrecks, or the countless other dangers of life. Divine protection was accorded, however, as a reward for appropriate worship, not by any abstract belief in the gods. For the ancient Greeks, gods expected honors and rites, and their religion required action from its worshipers. Greeks had to pray and sing hymns honoring the gods, perform sacrifices, and undergo ritual purification. These rites were a response to the precarious conditions of human life in a world in which early death from disease, accident, or war was commonplace. Preserving religious tradition mattered deeply to most people because they saw it as the safeguard.

Social Tradition and Athenian Women

Women in Golden Age Athens patiently maintained social traditions. Upper-class women devoted their lives to running their households, meeting female friends, and participating in the city-state's religious cults. Poorer women helped support themselves and their families, often as small-scale merchants and crafts producers. Legally, women's control of their own property and their ability to act on their own behalf in matters of law were still restricted.

The power and status of Athenian women came from their roles in the family and in religion. Their exclusion from politics, however, meant that their contributions to the city-state might well be overlooked by men.

Property, Inheritance, and Marriage. Euripides' heroine Medea in the play of 431 B.C. of that same name insists that women who bear children are due respect at least commensurate with that granted men who fight as hoplites, a reasonable claim given the high risks of childbirth under the medical conditions of antiquity:

People say that we women lead a safe life at home, while men have to go to war. What fools they are! I would much rather fight in the phalanx three times than give birth to a child even once.

Drama well emphasized the areas in which Athenian women contributed to the community: publicly by acting as priestesses and privately by bearing and raising legitimate children, the future citizens of the city-state, and by managing the household's property. (See "Contrasting Views," page 100.) Women had certain property rights in Golden Age Athens, although these rights were granted more to benefit men than to acknowledge women's legal claims. Women could control property, even land—the most valued possession in

Greek society—through inheritance and dowry, although they faced more legal restrictions than men did when attempting to sell it or give it away as gifts.

Women, like men, were supposed to preserve their property to hand down to their children. Daughters did not inherit anything from their father on his death if he had any living sons, but perhaps one household in five had only daughters, to whom the father's property fell. A daughter's share in her father's estate usually came to her in her dowry at marriage. Husband and wife co-owned the household's common property, which was apportioned to its separate owners only if the marriage was dissolved. The husband was legally responsible for preserving the dowry and using it for the support and comfort of his wife and any children she bore. A man often had to put up valuable land of his own as collateral to guarantee the safety of his wife's dowry if, for example, she brought to the marriage money or farm animals that he was to manage. Upon her death, her children inherited the dowry. As with the rules governing women's rights to inheritances, customary dowry arrangements supported the society's goal of enabling males to establish and maintain households, because daughters' dowries were usually less valuable than their brothers' inheritances and therefore the bulk of a father's property was attached to his sons.

The same goal motivated Athenian laws concerning heiresses. If a father died leaving only a daughter, his property went to her, but she did not own it in the sense of being able to dispose of it as she pleased. Instead, her father's closest male relative—her official guardian after her father's death—was required to marry her, with the aim of producing a son. The inherited property then belonged to that son when he reached adulthood. This rule applied regardless of whether the heiress was already married (without any sons) or whether the male relative already had a wife. The heiress and the male relative were both supposed to divorce their present spouses and marry each other, although in practice the rule could be circumvented by legal subterfuge.

This rule preserved the father's line and kept the property in his family. The practice also prevented rich men from getting richer by engineering deals with wealthy heiresses' guardians to marry them and therefore merge estates. Above all it prevented property from piling up in the hands of unmarried women. At Sparta, the renowned scholar

Aristotle (384–322 B.C.) reported, precisely this agglomeration of wealth took place as women inherited land or received it in their dowries without—to Aristotle's way of thinking—adequate regulations promoting remarriage. He claimed that women had come to own 40 percent of Spartan territory. Athenian men regulated women's access to property and therefore to power more strictly.

Women's Daily Lives.   Athenian women from the urban propertied class were expected to avoid close contact with men who were not family members or good friends. They were supposed to spend much of their time in their own homes or the homes of women friends. Women dressed and slept in rooms set aside for them, but these rooms usually opened onto a walled courtyard where they could walk in the open air, talk, supervise the family's slaves, and interact with other members of the household, male and female. Here in her "territory" a woman would spin wool for clothing while chatting with visiting friends, play with her children, and give her opinions on various matters to the men of the house as they came and went. Poor women had little time for such activities because they, like their husbands, sons, and brothers, had to leave their homes, usually crowded rental apartments, to work. They often set up small stalls to sell bread, vegetables, simple clothing, or trinkets.

A woman with servants who answered the door herself would be reproached as careless of her reputation. A proper woman left her home only for an appropriate reason. Fortunately, Athenian life offered many occasions for women to get out: religious festivals, funerals, childbirths at the houses of relatives and friends, and trips to workshops to buy shoes or other domestic articles. Sometimes her husband escorted her, but more often a woman was accompanied only by a servant and had opportunity to act independently. Social protocol required men not to speak the names of respectable women in public conversations and speeches in court unless absolutely necessary.

Because they stayed inside or in the shade so much, rich women maintained very pale complexions. This pallor was much admired as a sign of an enviable life of leisure and wealth. Women regularly used powdered white lead to give themselves a suitably pallid look. Presumably, many upper-class women viewed their limited contact with men outside the household as a badge of superior social status. In a gender-segregated society such as that of upper-class Athens, a woman's primary personal relationships were probably with her children and other women with whom she spent most of her time.

Men restricted women's freedom of movement partly to reduce uncertainty about the paternity of their children and to protect the virginity of their

Vase Painting of a Woman Buying Shoes
Greek vases were frequently decorated with scenes from daily life instead of mythological stories. Here, a woman is being fitted for a pair of custom-made shoes by a craftsman and his apprentice. Her husband has accompanied her, as was usual for such expeditions, and, to judge from his gesture, is participating in the discussion of the purchase. This vase was painted in so-called black-figure technique, in which the figures are dark and have their details incised on a background of red clay.
H. L. Pierce Fund. Courtesy Museum of Fine Arts, Boston.

The Nature of Women and Marriage

Greeks strongly believed that women had different natures from men, but they disagreed on how those differences played out in everyday life; both men and women were capable of excellence, but in their own ways (Documents 1 and 2). Marriage was supposed to bring these natures together in a partnership of complementary strengths (Document 3). Husband and wife therefore owed each other obligations of support and loyalty that written contracts spelled out and made legally binding (Document 4).

1. The Political Leader Pericles Addressing the Athenians at the Funeral of Soldiers Who Died in the First Year of the Peloponnesian War (431–430 B.C.)

According to Thucydides, the famously stern Pericles concluded his Funeral Oration, a solemn public occasion commemorating the valor and virtues expected of citizens, with these terse remarks to the women in the audience. His comments reveal two ancient Greek assumptions: women had a different nature from men and best served social harmony by not becoming subjects of gossip. He therefore kept his comments to and about them to a bare minimum in an otherwise long speech.

If it is also appropriate here for me to say something about what constitutes excellence for women, I will signal all my thinking with this short piece of advice to those of you present who are now widows of the war dead: your reputation will be great if you don't fall short of your innate nature and men talk about you the least whether in praise of your excellence or blaming your faults.

Source: Thucydides, *History of the Peloponnesian War,* bk. 2.45 (translation by author).

2. Melanippe, the Heroine of Melanippe the Captive, a Late-Fifth-Century-B.C. Tragedy by Euripides, Explaining Why Men's Criticism of Women Is Baseless

The Athenian playwright Euripides often portrayed female characters as denouncing men for misunderstanding and criticizing women. In mythology, Melanippe is a mother who overcomes hardship and treachery to save her family and fight for justice. Preserved only on damaged papyrus scraps, Melanippe's speech unfortunately breaks off before finishing.

Men's blame and criticism of women are empty, like the twanging sound a bow string makes without an arrow. Women are superior to men, and I'll demonstrate it. They make contracts with no need of witnesses [to swear they are honest]. They manage their households and keep safe the valuable possessions, shipped from abroad, that they have inside their homes; bereft of a woman, no household is elegant or happy. And then in the matter of people's relationship with the gods—this I judge to be most important of all—there we have the greatest role. For women prophesy the will of Apollo in his oracles, and at the hallowed oracle of Dodona by the sacred oak tree a woman reveals the will of Zeus to all Greeks who seek it. And then there are the sacred rites of initiation performed for the Fates and the Goddesses Without Names: these can't be done with holiness by men, but women make them flourish in every way. In this way women's role in religion is right and proper.

Therefore, should anyone denigrate women? Won't those men stop their empty fault-finding, the ones who strongly believe that all women should be blamed if a single one is found to be bad? I will make a distinction with the following argument: nothing is worse than a bad woman, but nothing is more surpassingly superior than a worthy one; their natures are not the same.

Source: Euripides, *Melanippe the Captive,* fragment 660 Mette (translation by author).

3. The Philosopher Socrates Discussing Gender Roles in Marriage with a New Husband (toward the End of the Fifth Century B.C.)

Socrates, who was dedicated to discovering the nature of human virtue, often discussed family life because it revealed the qualities of women as well as men. When his upper-class friend Ischomachus married a young wife, as was common, the philosopher quizzed him about their marriage; the new husband, according to Xenophon, explained it was a partnership based on the complementary natures of male and female.

ISCHOMACHUS: I said to her: . . . I for my sake and your parents for your sake [arranged our marriage] by considering who would be the best partner for forming a household and having children. I chose you, and your parents chose me as the best they could find. If god should give us children, we will then plan how to raise them in the best possible way. For our partnership provides us this good: the best mutual support and the best maintenance in our old age. We have this sharing now in our household, because I've contributed all that I own to the common resources of the household, and so have you. We're not going to count up who brought more property, because the one who turns out to be the better partner in a marriage has made the greater contribution.

ISCHOMACHUS'S WIFE (no name is given): But how will I be able to partner you? What ability do I have? Everything rests on you. My mother told me my job was to behave with thoughtful moderation.

ISCHOMACHUS: Well, my father told me the same thing. Thoughtful moderation for a man as for a woman means behaving in such a way that their possessions will be in the best possible condition and will increase as much as possible by fine and just means. . . . So, you must do what the gods made you naturally capable of and what our law enjoins. . . . With great forethought the gods have yoked together male and female so that they can form the most beneficial partnership. This yoking together keeps living creatures from disappearing by producing children, and it provides offspring to look after parents in their old age, at least for people. [He then explains that human survival requires outdoor work—to raise crops and livestock—and indoor work—to preserve food, raise infants, and manufacture clothing.] And since the work both outside and inside required effort and care, god, it seems to me, from the start fashioned women's nature for indoor work and men's for outdoor. Therefore he made men's bodies and spirits more able to endure cold and heat and travel and marches, giving them the outside jobs, while assigning indoor tasks to women, it seems, because their bodies are less hardy. . . .

But since both men and women have to manage things, he gave them equal shares in memory and attentiveness; you can't tell which gender has more of these qualities. And god gave both an equal ability to practice self-control, with the power to benefit the most from this quality going to whoever is better at it—whether man or woman. Precisely because they have different natures, they have greater need of each other and their yoking together is the most beneficial, with the one being capable where the other one is lacking. And as god has made them partners for their children, the law makes them partners for the household.

Source: Xenophon, *Oeconomicus* 7.10–30 (translation by author).

4. A Greek Marriage Contract from Elephantine in Egypt Stating the Legal Obligations of Husband and Wife (311–310 B.C.)

Greeks living abroad customarily drew up written contracts to define the duties of each partner in a marriage because they wanted their traditional expectations to remain legally binding regardless of the local laws. The earliest surviving such contract comes from the site of a Greek military garrison far up the Nile.

Marriage contract of Heraclides and Demetria.

Heraclides [of Temnos] takes as his lawful wife Demetria of Cos from her father Leptines of Cos and her mother Philotis. He is a free person; she is a free person. She brings a dowry of clothing and jewelry worth 1,000 drachmas. Heraclides must provide Demetria with everything appropriate for a freeborn wife. We will live together in whatever location Leptines and Heraclides together decide is best.

If Demetria is apprehended doing anything bad that shames her husband, she will forfeit all her dowry; Heraclides will have to prove any allegations against her in the presence of three men, whom they both must approve. It will be illegal for Heraclides to bring home another wife to Demetria's harm or to father children by another woman or to do anything bad to Demetria for any reason. If he is apprehended doing any of these things and Demetria proves it in the presence of three men whom they both approve, Heraclides must return

her dowry in full and pay her 1,000 drachmas additional. Demetria and those who help her in getting this payment will have legal standing to act against Heraclides and all his property on land and sea.... Each shall have the right to keep a personal copy of this contract. [A list of witnesses follows.]

Source: *Elephantine Papyri*, ed. O. Rubensohn (Berlin, 1907), no. 1 (translation by author).

QUESTIONS FOR DEBATE

1. What evidence for the differing natures of women and men do these documents offer? Which arguments do you find convincing?
2. What are the advantages and disadvantages of a written contract between marriage partners? Have they changed over time?

---

daughters by limiting opportunities for seducers and rapists. Given that citizenship defined the political structure of the city-state and a man's personal freedom, Greeks felt it crucial to ensure that a boy truly was his father's son and not the offspring of some other man, who might be a foreigner or a slave. Furthermore, the preference for keeping property in the father's line meant that the sons who inherited a father's property needed to be legitimate. Women who bore legitimate children immediately earned higher status and greater freedom in the family, as an Athenian man explained in this excerpt from a court case:

> After my marriage, I initially refrained from bothering my wife very much, but neither did I allow her too much independence. I kept an eye on her. . . . But after she had a baby, I started to trust her more and put her in charge of all my things, believing we now had the closest of relationships.

Bearing male children brought special honors to a woman because sons meant security for parents. Sons could appear in court in support of their parents in lawsuits and protect them in the streets of Athens, which for most of its history had no regular police force. By law, sons were required to support elderly parents. So intense was the pressure to produce sons that stories of women who smuggled in male babies born to slaves and passed them off as their own

were common. Such tales, whose truth is hard to gauge, were credible because husbands customarily stayed away at childbirth.

Extraordinary Women. A small number of Athenian women were able to escape traditional restrictions because they gave up the usual expectations of marrying or were too rich to be cowed by men. The most renowned of the former group were called *companions*. Often foreigners, they were physically attractive, witty in conversation, and able to sing and play musical instruments. They often entertained at symposia (men's dinner parties to which wives were not invited), and sometimes they sold sexual favors for a high price. Their independent existence strongly distinguished companions from citizen women, as did the freedom to control their own sexuality. Equally distinctive was their cultivated ability to converse with men in public. Companions charmed men with their witty, bantering conversation. Their characteristic skill at clever taunts and verbal snubs allowed companions a freedom of speech denied to "proper" women.

Some companions lived precarious lives subject to exploitation and even violence at the hands of their male customers, but the most accomplished could attract lovers from the highest levels of society and become sufficiently rich to live in luxury on their own. The most famous such woman was

Aspasia from Miletus, who became Pericles' lover and bore him a son. She dazzled Athens's upper-class males with her brilliant conversation and confidence; ironically, Pericles' desire to make her an "honest woman" by marrying her was blocked by his own law of 451 B.C. restricting citizenship.

Only the very wealthiest citizen women could speak to men publicly with the frankness that companions enjoyed. One such was Elpinike, a member of a superrich Athenian family of great military distinction. She once openly rebuked Pericles for having boasted about the Athenian conquest of a rebellious ally. When some other Athenian women praised Pericles for his success, Elpinike sarcastically remarked, "This really is wonderful, Pericles, . . . that you have caused the loss of many good citizens, not in battle against Phoenicians or Persians, like my brother Cimon, but in suppressing an allied city of fellow Greeks."

Other sources report that ordinary women, too, remained engaged and interested in issues affecting the city-state as a whole. They often had strong opinions on politics and public policy, but they had to express their views privately to their husbands, children, and relatives.

Slaves and Metics. Slaves and metics (foreigners granted permanent residency permits) were "outsiders" living inside Greek society. Traditional social and legal restrictions on slaves remained in force in the Golden Age. Individuals and the city-state alike owned slaves, who could be purchased from traders or bred in the household. Unwanted newborns abandoned by their parents (the practice called *infant exposure*) were often picked up by others and raised as slaves. Athens's commercial growth in this period increased the demand for slaves; although no reliable statistics survive, slaves probably made up 100,000 or more of the city-state's estimated 250,000 residents in Pericles' time. Slaves worked in homes, on farms, in crafts shops, and, if they were really unfortunate, in the cramped and dangerous silver mines whose riches boosted Athens's prosperity. Unlike at Sparta, Athens's slaves never rebelled, probably because they originated from too many different places to be able to unite. Many mining slaves did run away to the Spartan base established in Athenian territory during the Peloponnesian War; the Spartans later resold them.

Golden Age Athens's wealth and cultural vitality attracted numerous metics, who flocked to the

Vase Painting of a Symposium
Upper-class Greek men often spent their evenings at symposia, drinking parties that always included much conversation and usually featured music and entertainers; wives were not included. The discussions could range widely, from literature to politics to philosophy. Here, a female musician, whose nudity shows she is a hired prostitute, entertains the guests, who recline on couches, as was customary. The man on the right is about to fling the dregs of his wine, playing a messy game called kottabos.
Master and Fellows of Corpus Christi College, Cambridge, The Parker Library.

city from all around the Mediterranean, hoping for business success as importers, crafts producers, entertainers, and laborers. By the start of the Peloponnesian War in 431 B.C., they constituted perhaps half the free population, which now stood at more than 100,000 men, women, and children. Metics had to pay for the privilege of living and working in Athens through a special foreigners' tax and military service. Citizens had ambivalent feelings about metics, valuing their contributions to the city's prosperity but almost never offering them citizenship. Like other Greeks, Athenians preserved their traditional community feeling by regarding people as "outsiders" regardless of how long they had resided in the city-state.

Metics therefore sometimes found themselves relegated to ways of life outside the mainstream, such as prostitution. Men, unlike women, were not penalized for sexual activity outside marriage. "Certainly you don't think men beget children out of sexual desire?" wrote the upper-class author Xenophon. "The streets and the brothels are swarming with ways to take care of that." Men could have sex with female or male slaves, who could not refuse their masters, or they could patronize various classes of prostitutes, depending on how much money they wanted to spend.

Intellectual Innovation

Athenians learned the rules of respectable behavior in the family and in the course of everyday life. Education, which was a private matter, stressed the preservation of old ways and resisted innovation. When teachers called *sophists* appeared in the later fifth century B.C. and proclaimed startling new ideas, they upset many people, who feared that new ways of thinking would undermine tradition and anger the gods. The ethical views of the philosopher Socrates had the same effect.

Innovations in historical writing and medicine also took place; their impact on ordinary people is hard to assess. It is certain, however, that misgivings about the new trends in education and philosophy had definitely heightened the political tension in Athens by the 430s B.C. These intellectual developments had a wide-ranging effect because the political, intellectual, and religious dimensions of life in ancient Athens were so intertwined. A person could discuss the city-state's domestic and foreign policies on one occasion, novel theories of the nature of the universe on another, and the disposition of the gods to the community every day.

Education.   Public schools did not exist in Golden Age Athens. Only well-to-do families could afford to pay teachers, to whom they sent their sons to learn to read, write, perhaps sing or play a musical instrument, and train for athletics and military service. Physical fitness was considered vital for men, who could be called up for military service from age eighteen to sixty. Therefore, men exercised daily in public open-air facilities paid for by wealthy families. Men frequently discussed politics and exchanged news at these *gymnasia*. The daughters of wealthy families usually learned to read, write, and do simple arithmetic at home; a woman with these skills would be better prepared to manage a household and help her future husband run their estate.

Poorer girls and boys learned a trade and perhaps some rudiments of literacy by assisting their parents in their daily work or, if they were fortunate, by being apprenticed to skilled crafts producers. Scholars disagree about the level of literacy, but it seems unlikely that it can have been high outside the ranks of the prosperous. Poor reading ability did not hinder most people, who could find someone to read aloud any written texts they needed to understand. The predominance of oral rather than written communication meant that people were accustomed to absorbing information by ear, and Greeks were very fond of songs, speeches, narrated stories, and lively conversation.

Young men from prosperous families traditionally acquired the advanced skills to participate successfully in the public life of Athenian democracy by observing their fathers, uncles, and other older men as they debated in the Council of 500 and the assembly, served as magistrates, and spoke in court. In many cases an older man would choose an adolescent boy as his special favorite to educate. The boy would learn about public life by spending his time in the company of the older man and his adult friends. During the day the boy would observe his mentor talking politics in the agora, help him perform his duties in public office, and work out with him in a gymnasium. Their evenings would be spent at a symposium, which would encompass a range of behavior from serious political and philosophical discussion to riotous partying.

Such a mentor-protégé relationship could lead to sexual relations as an expression of the bond between the boy and the older male, who would normally be married. Although both male homosexuality outside a mentor-protégé relationship and female homosexuality in general were regarded as wrong throughout the Greek world, sexual relations between older mentors and younger protégés were considered acceptable in many, though not all, city-states; these differing attitudes about homosexual behavior reflected the complexity of Greek ideas of masculinity, about what made a man a man and what unmade him. In any case, a mentor was never supposed to exploit his younger companion physically or neglect his political education. If this ideal was observed, Athenian society accepted the relationship as part of a complicated range of bonds among males, from political and military activity, to training of mind and body, to sexual activity.

Sophists and the Threat to Tradition. By the time radical democracy was established in Athens, young men who sought to polish their political skills of persuasive speech had access to a new kind of teacher. These teachers were called *sophists* ("wise men"), a label that later acquired a negative connotation (preserved in the English word *sophistry*), because they were so clever at public speaking and philosophical debates. The earliest sophists emerged in parts of the Greek world outside Athens. From about 450 B.C. on, they began to travel to Athens, which was then at the height of its prosperity, to search for pupils who could pay the hefty prices they charged for their instruction. Sophists created controversy because they taught new skills of public speaking and new ways of looking at the nature of human existence and religion that challenged traditional beliefs.

The sophists taught the skill that every ambitious young man needed to become influential in Athens's radical democracy: public speaking to persuade his fellow citizens in the debates of the assembly and the councils or in lawsuits before large juries. Wealthy young men therefore flocked to the dazzling demonstrations these itinerant teachers put on to showcase their eloquence and persuasive ability. For those unwilling or unable to master the new rhetorical skills, the sophists charged stiff fees to write speeches the purchasers could deliver as their own compositions.

The sophists alarmed many traditionally minded men, who thought their facility with words might be used (by them or by their pupils) to undermine communal social and political traditions in favor of individual interests. In ancient Greek culture, where codes of proper behavior, moral standards, and religious ideals were expressed and transmitted orally from generation to generation, a persuasive and charismatic speaker could potentially wield as much power as an army of warriors. Sophists made people nervous because political leaders, such as Pericles, flocked to hear them. Many citizens feared that selfish politicians would use the silver-tongued style of the sophists to mislead the assembly and the councils.

The sophists especially upset people because they taught new ideas about the nature of human existence and religion that contradicted commonly held beliefs. An especially controversial sophist was Protagoras, a contemporary of Pericles from Abdera in northern Greece. Protagoras immigrated to Athens around 450 B.C., when he was about forty, and spent most of his career there. His views proved very upsetting, especially his agnosticism, the belief that supernatural phenomena are unknowable: "Whether the gods exist I cannot discover, nor what their form is like, for there are many impediments to knowledge, [such as] the obscurity of the subject and the brevity of human life." Statements like this implied that conventional religion had no meaning, and people worried that they might provoke divine anger.

Equally controversial was Protagoras's denial of an absolute standard of truth, his assertion that every issue had two, irreconcilable sides. For example, if one person feeling a breeze thinks it warm, whereas another person thinks it cool, neither judgment can be absolutely correct because the wind simply is warm to one and cool to the other. Protagoras summed up his subjectivism—the belief that there is no absolute reality behind and independent of appearances—in the much-quoted opening of his work *Truth*: "Man is the measure of all things, of the things that are that they are, and of the things that are not that they are not." *Man* (*anthropos* in Greek, hence our word *anthropology*) in this passage refers to the individual human, male or female, whom Protagoras makes the sole judge of his or her own impressions.

These ideas, which other sophists expressed in different ways, aroused special concern: that human institutions and values were only matters of convention, custom, or law (*nomos*) and not products of nature (*physis*) and that because truth was subjective, speakers should be able to argue either side of a question with equal persuasiveness. The first view implied that traditional human institutions were arbitrary rather than grounded in nature, and the second made morality irrelevant to rhetoric. The combination of the two ideas amounted to moral relativism, which threatened the shared public values of the democratic city-state.

Protagoras, however, insisted that his doctrines were not hostile to democracy, arguing that every person had an innate capability for "excellence" and that human survival depended on the rule of law based on a sense of justice. Members of the community, he explained, must be persuaded to obey the laws not because they were based on absolute truth, which does not exist, but because it was advantageous for people to live by them. A thief, for example, who might claim a law against stealing was pointless, would have to be persuaded that the law forbidding theft was to his advantage because it protected his own property and the community in which he, like all humans, had to live in order to survive.

These were not the only disturbing ideas taught by sophists. Anaxagoras of Clazomenae and Leucippus of Miletus, for example, propounded unsettling new theories about the nature of the cosmos in response to the provocative physics of the Ionian thinkers of the sixth century B.C. Anaxagoras's thinking offended believers in traditional religion. For example, he argued that the sun was nothing more than a lump of flaming rock, not a divine entity. Leucippus, whose doctrines were made famous by his pupil Democritus of Abdera, invented an atomic theory of matter to explain how change was possible and indeed constant. Everything, he argued, consisted of tiny, invisible particles in eternal motion. Their random collisions caused them to combine and recombine in an infinite variety of forms. This physical explanation of the source of change, like Anaxagoras's analysis of the nature of the sun, seemed to deny the validity of traditional religion, which explained events as the outcome of divine forces.

The techniques of persuasion and ways of thought taught by Protagoras and his fellow sophists enabled a man to advance his opinions on policy

with great effect or defend himself staunchly in court. Because only wealthy men could afford instruction from sophists, however, this new education worked against the egalitarian principles of Athenian democracy by giving an advantage to the rich. In addition, moral relativism and the physical explanation of the universe struck many Athenians as dangerous: they feared that the teachings of the sophists would offend the gods and therefore erode the divine favor they believed Athens enjoyed. Just like a murderer, a teacher spouting sacrilegious doctrines could bring *miasma* (ritual contamination), and therefore divine punishment on the whole community.

Socrates and Ethics. The provocative ideas of Socrates (469–399 B.C.), the most famous philosopher of the Golden Age, added to the consternation his fellow Athenians were feeling at this time. He was not a sophist and offered no courses, but his views became well known. Socrates devoted his life to conversation combating the notion that justice should be equated with the power to work one's will. His passionate concern to discover valid guidelines for leading a just life and to prove that justice is better than injustice under all circumstances gave a new direction to Greek philosophy: an emphasis on ethics. Although other thinkers before him had dealt with moral issues, especially the poets and dramatists, Socrates was the first philosopher to make ethics and morality his central concern.

Socrates lived a life that inevitably attracted attention. He paid so little heed to his physical appearance and clothes that he seemed eccentric. Sporting a stomach, in his words, "somewhat too large to be convenient," he wore the same nondescript cloak summer and winter and scorned shoes no matter how cold the weather. His physical stamina was legendary, both from his tirelessness when he served as a soldier in Athens's infantry and from his ability to outdrink anyone at a symposium. Unlike the sophists, he lived in poverty and disdained material possessions, somehow managing to support a wife and several children. He may have inherited some money, but he certainly received gifts from wealthy admirers.

Socrates spent his time in conversations all over town: participating in a symposium, strolling in the agora, or watching young men exercise in a gymnasium. In this characteristic he resembled his fellow Athenians, who placed great value on the importance and pleasure of speaking with one another at length. He wrote nothing; our knowledge of his ideas comes from others' writings, especially those of his pupil Plato (c. 428–348 B.C.). Plato portrays Socrates as a relentless questioner of his fellow citizens, foreign friends, and leading sophists. Socrates' questions had the goal of making his conversational partners doubt the basic assumptions of their way of life. Giving few answers, Socrates never

Statuette of the Philosopher Socrates
The controversial Socrates, the most famous philosopher of Athens in the fifth century B.C., joked that he had a homely face and a bulging stomach. This small statue is an artist's impression of what Socrates looked like; we cannot be sure of the truth. Socrates was renowned for his irony, and he may have purposely exaggerated his physical unattractiveness to show his disdain for ordinary standards of beauty and his own emphasis on the quality of one's soul as the true measure of a person's worth.
British Museum.

directly instructed anyone; instead, he led them to draw conclusions in response to his probing questions and refutations of their cherished assumptions.

This indirect method of searching for the truth often left people uncomfortably baffled because they were forced to conclude that they were ignorant of what they had assumed they knew very well. Socrates' questions showed that the way they lived their lives—pursuing success in politics or business or art—was an excuse for avoiding genuine virtue. Socrates insisted that he was ignorant of the best definition of virtue but that his wisdom consisted of knowing that he did not know. He vowed he was trying to improve, not undermine, people's beliefs in morality, even though, as a friend put it, a conversation with Socrates made a man feel numb—just as if he had been stung by a stingray. Socrates especially wanted to discover through reasoning the universal standards that justified individual morality. He fiercely attacked the sophists, who proclaimed conventional morality to be the "fetters that bind nature." This view, he protested, equated human happiness with power and "getting more."

Socrates passionately believed that just behavior was better for people than injustice and that morality was invaluable because it created happiness. Essentially, he argued that just behavior, or virtue, was identical to knowledge and that true knowledge of justice would inevitably lead people to choose good over evil. They would therefore have truly happy lives, regardless of how rich or poor they were. Since Socrates believed that moral knowledge was all a person needed for the good life, he argued that no one knowingly behaved unjustly and that behaving justly was always in the individual's interest. It was simply ignorant to believe that the best life was the life of unlimited power to pursue whatever one desired. The most desirable human life was concerned with virtue and guided by reason, not by dreams of personal gain.

Socrates' effect on many people was as disturbing as the relativistic doctrines of the sophists. His refutation of his fellow citizens' ideas about the importance of wealth and public success made some men extremely upset. Unhappiest of all were the fathers whose sons, after listening to Socrates reduce someone to utter bewilderment, came home to try the same technique on their parents by arguing that the accomplishments their family held dear were old-fashioned and worthless. Men who experienced this reversal of the traditional educational hierarchy—the son was supposed to be educated by the father—felt that Socrates was undermining the stability of society by making young men question Athenian traditions. We cannot say with certainty what Athenian women thought of Socrates or he of them. His thoughts about human capabilities and behavior could be applied to women as well as to men, and he probably believed that women and men both had the same basic capacity for justice.

The feeling that Socrates presented a danger to conventional society gave the comic playwright Aristophanes the inspiration for his play *Clouds* (423 B.C.). He portrayed Socrates as a cynical sophist who, for a fee, offered instruction in the Protagorean technique of making the weaker argument the stronger. When the curriculum of Socrates' Thinking Shop transforms a youth into a public speaker arguing that a son has the right to beat his parents, his father burns down Socrates' school. None of these plot details was real; what was genuine was the fear that Socrates' uncompromising views on individual morality endangered the traditional practices of the community at a time when new ways of thought were springing up fast and furiously.

Historical Writing. One especially significant intellectual innovation that emerged in this period was historical writing as a critical vision of the past. Herodotus of Halicarnassus (c. 485–425 B.C.) and Thucydides of Athens (c. 455–399 B.C.) became Greece's most famous historians and established Western civilization's tradition of history writing. Herodotus wrote the groundbreaking work called *Histories* (meaning "inquiries" in Greek) to explain the Persian Wars as a clash between East and West; by Roman times he had been christened "Father of History." Herodotus achieved an unprecedented depth for his book by giving it a wide geographical scope, an investigative approach to evidence, and a lively narrative. Herodotus searched for the origins of the Persian-Greek conflict both by delving deep into the past and by examining the cultural traditions of all the peoples involved. He recognized the relevance and the delight of studying other cultures as a component of historical investigation.

Thucydides took another giant step in this process by writing contemporary history influenced by what today is called political science. His *History of the Peloponnesian War* made power politics, not

divine intervention, history's primary force. Deeply affected by the war's brutality, he brilliantly used his personal experiences as a politician and military commander to make his narrative vivid and frank in describing human moral failings. His insistence that historians should spare no effort in seeking out the most reliable sources and evaluating their testimony with objectivity set a high standard for later writers.

Hippocrates and Medicine. Hippocrates of Cos, a fifth-century contemporary of Thucydides, is remembered today in the oath bearing his name that doctors swear at the beginning of their professional careers. Details about the life and thought of this most famous of all Greek doctors are sketchy, but he made great strides in putting medical diagnosis and treatment on a scientific basis. Earlier medical practices had depended on magic and ritual. Hippocrates

Vase Painting of a Doctor at Work
This piece of pottery, apparently used to hold perfume or ointment, was decorated with a picture of a physician treating a patient's arm. The prevalence of war gave Greek doctors much experience with wounds and trauma, and they could stop bleeding, set bones, perform minor surgery, and offer some pain relief with drugs derived from plants. Still, the effectiveness of their treatment was limited because they had no cure for infections.
Photo Réunion des Musées Nationaux–Herve Lewandowski.

Theater of Dionysus at Athens
Seating some fourteen to fifteen thousand people outside on a hillside next to the Athenian acropolis, this theater honored the god Dionysus. Tragedies, satyr plays, and comedies were produced there in daytime festivals that riveted the attention of the city. The seating and stone stage building founda- tions that are visible today are remnants of much later changes in the theater and do not belong to the Classical period, when the seating, the stage, and the scenery were not yet permanent installations.
John Elk III/Bruce Coleman, Inc., New York.

viewed the human body as an organism whose parts must be understood as segments of the whole. Some attributed to him the view, popular in later times, that four humors (fluids) made up the human body: blood, phlegm, black bile, and yellow bile. Health depended on keeping the proper balance among them; being healthy was to be in "good humor." This intellectual system corresponded to the division of the inanimate world into four parts: the elements earth, air, fire, and water.

Hippocrates taught that the physician's most important duty was to base his knowledge on care- ful observation of patients and their response to remedies. Clinical experience, not theory, he in- sisted, was the best guide to effective treatments. Although various cults in Greek religion offered healing to petitioners, Hippocratic medical doctrine apparently made little or no mention of a divine role in sickness and its cures.

The Development of Greek Tragedy

The complex relationship between gods and hu- mans formed the basis of Golden Age Athens's most influential cultural innovation: tragic drama. Greek plays, still read and produced onstage, were pre- sented over three days at the major annual festival of the god Dionysus, which was held in the spring and included a drama contest, in keeping with the competitive spirit characteristic of many events honoring the gods. By presenting shocking stories relevant to broad issues creating tension in the city- state, tragedy inspired its large audiences to ponder the danger that ignorance, arrogance, and violence presented to Athens's democratic society. Following the tradition of Homer and Hesiod, Golden Age playwrights explored topics ranging from individ- ual freedom and responsibility in the *polis* to the underlying nature of good and evil.

Every year, one of Athens's magistrates chose three competing authors to present four plays each: three tragedies in a row (a trilogy), followed by a semicomic play featuring satyrs (mythical half-man, half-animal beings) to end the day on a lighter note. The term *tragedy*—derived, for reasons now lost, from the Greek words for "goat" and "song"— referred to plays with plots that involved fierce conflict and characters who represented powerful forces. Tragedies were written in verse and used solemn language; they were often based on stories about the violent consequences of the interaction between gods and humans. The plots often ended with a resolution to the trouble—but only after considerable suffering.

The performance of Athenian tragedies bore little resemblance to modern theater productions. They took place during the daytime in an outdoor theater sacred to Dionysus, built into the southern slope of Athens's acropolis. This theater held about fourteen thousand spectators overlooking an open, circular area in front of a slightly raised stage. Every tragedy had to have eighteen cast members, all of whom were men: three actors to play the speaking roles (both male and female characters) and fifteen chorus members. Although the chorus leader sometimes engaged in dialogue with the actors, the chorus primarily performed songs and dances in the circular area in front of the stage, called the *orchestra*.

Even though scenery on the stage was sparse, a good tragedy presented a vivid spectacle. The chorus wore elaborate, decorative costumes and performed intricate dance routines. The actors, who wore masks, used broad gestures and booming voices to reach the upper tier of seats. A powerful voice was crucial to a tragic actor because words represented the heart of a tragedy, in which dialogue and long speeches were far more common than physical action. Special effects were, however, part of the spectacle. For example, a crane allowed actors playing the roles of gods to fly suddenly onto the stage. The actors playing lead roles, called the *protagonists* ("first competitors"), competed against one another for the designation of best actor. So important was a first-rate protagonist to a successful tragedy that actors were assigned by lottery to the competing playwrights to give all three an equal chance to have the finest cast. Great protagonists became enormously popular, although they were not usually members of the social elite.

Many playwrights were from the elite because only men of some wealth could afford the amount of time and learning this work demanded: as author, director, producer, musical composer, choreographer, and sometimes even actor. The prizes awarded in the tragedy competition were modest. As citizens, playwrights also fulfilled the normal military and political obligations of Athenian men. The best-known Athenian tragedians—Aeschylus (525–456 B.C.), Sophocles (c. 496–406 B.C.), and Euripides (c. 485–406 B.C.)—all served in the army, held public office at some point in their careers, or did both.

Athenian tragedy was a public art form. Not only were its performances subsidized with public funds, its plots explored the ethical quandaries of humans in conflict with the gods and with one another in a city-state. Even though most tragedies were based on stories that referred to a legendary time before city-states existed, such as tales of the Trojan War, the moral issues the plays illuminated always pertained to the society and obligations of citizens in a city-state. To take only a few examples: Aeschylus in his trilogy *Oresteia* (458 B.C.) uses the story of how the gods stopped the murderous violence in the family of Orestes, son of the Greek leader against Troy, to explain the necessity and the sanctity of democratic Athens's court system. The plays suggest that human beings have to learn by suffering but that the gods will provide justice in the long run. Sophocles' *Antigone* (441 B.C.) presents the sad story of the family of Oedipus of Thebes as a drama of harsh conflict between a courageous woman, Antigone, who insists on her family's moral obligation to bury its dead in obedience to divine command, and her uncle Creon, the city-state's stern male leader, who defends the need to preserve order and protect community values by prohibiting the burial of traitors. In a horrifying story of anger and suicide centered on one of the most famous heroines of Western literature, Sophocles deliberately exposes the right and wrong on each side of the conflict, and the play

Theaters of Classical Greece

offers no easy resolution of the competing interests of divinely sanctioned moral tradition and the political rules of the state. Euripides' *Medea* (431 B.C.) implies that the political order of a city-state depends on men treating their wives and families with honor and trust: when Medea's husband betrays her for a younger woman, she takes revenge by destroying their children and the community's political leadership with her magical power.

We cannot reconstruct precisely how the audiences of the drama competition of the Dionysian festival understood the messages of tragedies. At the very least, however, they must have been aware that the central characters of the plays were figures who fell into disaster from positions of power and prestige. The characters' reversals of fortune came about not because they were absolute villains but because, as humans, they were susceptible to a lethal mixture of error, ignorance, and *hubris* (violent arrogance). The Athenian empire was at its height when audiences at Athens attended the tragedies of these three great playwrights. Thoughtful spectators may have reflected on the possibility that Athens's current power and prestige, managed as it was by humans, remained hostage to the same forces that controlled the fates of the heroes and heroines of tragedy. Tragedies certainly appealed to audiences because they were compelling, but they also had an educational function: to remind male citizens, who made policy for the city-state, that success engendered complex moral problems that could not be solved casually or arrogantly.

The Development of Greek Comedy

Athens developed theatrical comedy as another distinctive form of public art. Like tragedies, comedies were written in verse, were performed in a competition in the city's large outdoor theater during festivals honoring the god Dionysus, and were subsidized with public funds. Unlike tragedies, comedies made direct comments about public policy, criticized current politicians and intellectuals by name, and devised plots of outrageous fantasy to make its points. Comic choruses of twenty-four actors, for example, could feature characters colorfully dressed as talking birds or dancing clouds.

The immediate purpose of a comic playwright was to win the award for the festival's best comedy by creating beautiful poetry, raising laughs with constant jokes and puns, and skewering political leaders. Much of the humor concerned sex and bodily functions, delivered in a stream of imaginative profanity. Well-known actual men were targets for insults as cowardly or sexually effeminate. Women characters portrayed as figures of fun and ridicule, however, seem to have been fictional.

The remarkable freedom of speech given this public art promoted frank, even brutal, commentary on current issues and personalities. Even during wartime, comic playwrights presented plays that criticized the city-state's policy and recommended making peace immediately. It cannot be an accident that this energetic, critical drama emerged in Athens at the same time as radical democracy, in the mid-fifth century B.C. The feeling that all citizens should have a stake in determining their government's policies evidently fueled a passion for using biting humor to keep the community's leaders from becoming arrogant and aloof.

Athenian comedies often blamed particular political leaders for government policies that had been approved by the assembly, similar to the way

Statuettes of Comic Actors
Although these little statues portray comic actors dressed in the kinds of masks and costumes that came into vogue later than the style of comedy that Aristophanes and his contemporaries wrote in the fifth century B.C. (for which no contemporary such pieces exist), they give a vivid sense of the exaggerated buffoonery that characterized the acting in Greek comedy. In Aristophanes' day, the grotesque unreality of comic costumes would have been even more striking because the male actors wore large leather phalluses attached below their waists that could be props for all sorts of ribald jokes.
Staatliche Museen zu Berlin-Preußicher Kulturbesitz Antiken-sammlung.

IMPORTANT DATES

c. 499–494 B.C.   Ionian revolt against Persian control

490 B.C.   King Darius sends Persian force against Athens; battle of Marathon

480 B.C.   King Xerxes leads Persian invasion of Greece; battles of Thermopylae and Salamis

477 B.C.   Athens assumes leadership of the Delian League

461 B.C.   Ephialtes passes political and judicial reforms to strengthen Athenian democracy

458 B.C.   Aeschylus presents the trilogy *Oresteia*

450 B.C.   The sophist Protagoras comes to Athens

447 B.C.   Pericles starts construction of the Parthenon

446 B.C.   Athens and Sparta sign a peace treaty meant to last thirty years

431 B.C.   The Peloponnesian War begins between Athens and Sparta

425 B.C.   Herodotus finishes the *Histories*

415–413 B.C.   Alcibiades leads Athenian expedition against Sparta's allies in Sicily

411 B.C.   Aristophanes presents the comedy Lysistrata.

404 B.C.   Athens surrenders to Sparta

404–403 B.C.   The Thirty Tyrants suspend democracy at Athens and conduct a reign of terror

403 B.C.   Athenians overthrow the Thirty Tyrants and restore democracy

ostracism singled out individuals for punishment. As the leading politician of radical democracy, Pericles came in for fierce criticism in comedy. Comic playwrights mocked his policies, his love life, and his looks ("Old Tuber Head" was a favorite insult). Cleon, the most prominent politician after Pericles, was so outraged by the way Aristophanes (c. 455–385 B.C.), Athens's most famous comic playwright, portrayed him onstage that he sued the author. When Cleon lost the case, Aristophanes responded by pitilessly parodying him as a slavish foreign slob in *The Knights* (424 B.C.).

The most remarkable of Aristophanes' comedies are those in which the main characters are powerful women who compel the men of Athens to change their policy to preserve family life and the city-state. Most famous is *Lysistrata* (411 B.C.), named after the female lead character of the play. In it, the women of Athens and Sparta unite to force their husbands to end the Peloponnesian War. To make the men agree to a peace treaty, they first seize the acropolis, where Athens's financial reserves are kept, to prevent the men from squandering them further on the war. They then beat back an attack on their position by the old men who have remained in Athens while the younger men are out on campaign. When their husbands return from battle, the women refuse to have sex with them. This strike, which is portrayed in a series of risqué episodes, finally coerces the men of Athens and Sparta to agree to a treaty.

Lysistrata presents women acting bravely and aggressively against men who seem bent on destroying their traditional family life—they are staying away from home for long stretches while on military campaign and are ruining the city-state by prolonging a pointless war. Lysistrata insists that women have the intelligence and judgment to make political decisions: "I am a woman, and, yes, I have brains. And I'm not badly off for judgment. Nor has my education been bad, coming as it has from my listening often to the conversations of my father and the elders among the men." Her old-fashioned training and good sense allow her to see what needs to be done to protect the community. Like the heroines of tragedy, Lysistrata is a reactionary; she wants to put things back the way they were. To do that, however, she has to act like an impatient revolutionary. That irony well sums up the challenge that Golden Age Athens faced in trying to balance its reliance on tradition with the dynamism of the period's innovation in so many fields.

❖ The End of the Golden Age

A war between Athens and Sparta that lasted a generation (431–404 B.C.) ended the Athenian Golden Age. Called "Peloponnesian" today because it pitted Sparta's Peloponnese-based alliance against Athens's alliance, it arose at least in part as a result of Pericles' policies. The most powerful politician in Athens—he won election as a general for fifteen years in a row beginning in 443 B.C.—Pericles nevertheless had to withstand severe criticism of the enormous public spending on his building program and harsh measures against Delian League allies that his rivals said sullied Athens's reputation. He faced his greatest challenge, however, when relations with Sparta worsened in the mid-430s B.C. over Athenian actions against Corinth and Megara, crucial Spartan allies. Finally, Corinth told Sparta to attack Athens or Corinth would change sides to the Athenian alliance. Sparta's leaders therefore gave Athens an ultimatum—stop mistreating our allies—which Pericles convinced the Athenian assembly to reject as unfair because Sparta was refusing arbitration of the disputes. In this way, the relations of Athens and Sparta with lesser city-states propelled the two powers over the brink into war. Pericles' critics claimed he was insisting on war against Sparta to revive his fading popularity. By 431 B.C., the thirty-year peace made in 445 B.C. had been shattered beyond repair.

The Peloponnesian War, 431–404 B.C.

Dragging on longer than any previous war in Greek history, the Peloponnesian War took place above all because Spartan leaders feared that the Athenians would use their superior long-distance offensive weaponry—the naval forces of the Delian League—to destroy Spartan control over the Peloponnesian League. (See "Taking Measure," opposite.) The duration of the struggle reveals the unpredictability of war and the consequences of the repeated reluctance of the Athenian assembly to negotiate peace terms instead of dictating them.

Thucydides dramatically revealed the absolute refusal of the Athenians to find a compromise solution with these words of Pericles to the assembly:

> If we do go to war, harbor no thought that you went to war over a trivial affair. For you this trifling matter is the assurance and the proof of your determination. If you yield to their demands, they will immediately confront you with some larger demand, since they will think that you only gave way on the first point out of fear. But if you stand firm, you will show them that they have to deal with you as equals. . . . When our equals, without agreeing to arbitration of the matter under dispute, make claims on us as neighbors and state those claims as commands, it would be no better than slavery to give in to them, no matter how large or how small the claim may be.

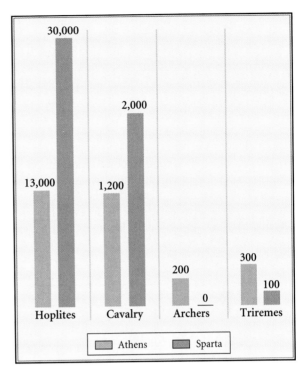

TAKING MEASURE Military Forces of Athens and Sparta at the Beginning of the Peloponnesian War (431 B.C.)

These figures give estimates of the relative strengths of the military forces of the Athenian side and the Spartan side when the Peloponnesian War broke out in 431 B.C. The numbers come from ancient historical sources, above all the Athenian general and historian Thucydides, who fought in the war. The bar graphs starkly reveal the different characteristics of the competing forces: Athens relied on its navy of triremes and its archers (the fifth-century equivalent of artillery and snipers), while Sparta was preeminent in the forces need for pitched land battles, hoplites (heavily armed infantry) and cavalry (shock troops used to disrupt opposing phalanxes). These differences dictated the differing strategies and tactics of the two sides, Athens trying guerrilla-fashion by launching surprise raids from the sea and Sparta trying to force decisive confrontations on the battlefield.
From Pamela Bradley, *Ancient Greece: Using Evidence* (Melbourne: Edward Arnold, 1990), 229.

Pericles advised Athens to use its superior navy to raid enemy lands while avoiding pitched battles with the Spartan infantry, even when they invaded the Athenian countryside and destroyed citizens' property there. In the end, he predicted, the superior resources of Athens would enable it to win a war of attrition. With his unyielding leadership, this strategy might have prevailed, but chance intervened. From 430 to 426 B.C., an epidemic disease ravaged Athens's population, killing thousands—including Pericles in 429 B.C. The Athenians fought on, but they lost the clear direction that Pericles' prudent strategy had required. The generals after him followed increasingly risky plans, culminating in an overambitious campaign against Sparta's allies in Sicily, far to the west. Dazzling the assembly in 415 B.C. with the dream of conquering that rich island, Alcibiades, the most innovative and brashest commander of the war, persuaded the Athenians to launch their largest naval expedition ever. His political rivals got him recalled from his command,

however, and the invasion force suffered a catastrophic defeat in 413 B.C. (Map 3.3).

The Spartans then launched the final phase of the war by establishing a permanent base of operations in the Athenian countryside for year-round raids. The agricultural economy was devastated, and revenues fell drastically when twenty thousand slave workers crippled production in Athens's publicly owned silver mines by deserting to the enemy. Distress over the war's course led to an oligarchic coup that briefly overturned the democracy in 411 B.C., but the citizens soon restored traditional government and fought on. The end came when Persia sent money to help the Spartans finally build a strong navy. Aggressive Spartan

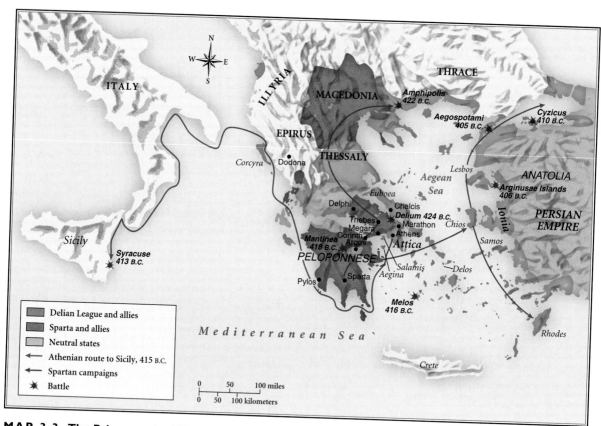

MAP 3.3 The Peloponnesian War, 431–404 B.C.
For the first ten years, the war's battles took place largely in mainland Greece; Sparta, whose armies usually avoided distant campaigns, shocked Athens when its general Brasidas led successful attacks against Athenian forces in northeast Greece. Athens stunned the entire Greek world in the war's next phase by launching a huge naval expedition against Spartan allies in far-off Sicily. The last ten years of the war saw the action move to the east, on and along the western coast of Anatolia and its islands, on the boundary of the Persian Empire, which helped the Spartans build a navy there to defeat the famous Athenian fleet.

action at sea forced Athens to surrender in 404 B.C. After twenty-seven years of near-continuous war, the Athenians were at the mercy of their enemies.

Athens Humbled

The Spartans soon installed a regime of anti-democratic Athenians, members of the social elite who became known as the Thirty Tyrants. Brutally suppressing democratic opposition, these oligarchs embarked on an eight-month period of terror in 404–403 B.C. The speechwriter Lysias, for example, reported that Spartan henchmen seized his brother for execution as a way of stealing the family's valu-

ables, down to the gold earrings ripped from the ears of his brother's wife. An Athenian democratic resistance movement soon arose and expelled the Thirty Tyrants after a series of bloody street battles. Fortunately for the democrats, a split in the Spartan leadership, fueled by the competing ambitions of its two most prominent men, prevented effective Spartan military support for the tyrants.

To settle the internal strife that threatened to tear Athens apart, the newly restored democracy proclaimed the first known amnesty in Western history, a truce agreement forbidding any official charges or recriminations stemming from the crimes of 404–403 B.C. Athens's government was

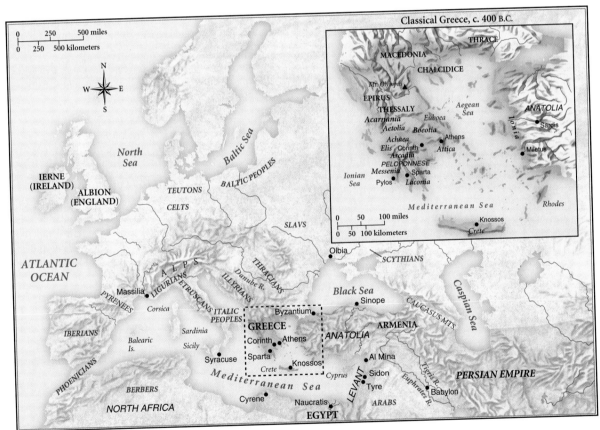

MAPPING THE WEST Greece, Europe, and the Mediterranean, c. 400 B.C.
No single power controlled the Mediterranean region at the end of the fifth century B.C. In the west, the Phoenician city of Carthage and the Greek cities of Sicily and southern Italy were rivals for the riches to be won by trade. In the east, the Spartans, emboldened by their recent victory over Athens in the Peloponnesian War, tried to become an international power outside the mainland for the first time in their history by sending campaigns into Anatolia. This aggressive action aroused stiff opposition from the Persians because it was a threat to their westernmost imperial provinces. There was to be no peace and quiet in the Mediterranean even after the twenty-seven years of the Peloponnesian War.

once again a functioning democracy, but its financial and military strength was shattered. Worse, its society harbored the memory of a bitter divisiveness that no amnesty could dispel. The end of the Golden Age left Athenians worriedly wondering how to remake their lives and restore the luster that their city-state's innovative accomplishments had produced in that wondrous period.

Conclusion

Athens's Golden Age in the fifth century B.C. was a time of prosperity, political stability, international power, and artistic and cultural accomplishment. Its citizens had won great glory in the unexpected victory of the Greek alliance against the Persians at the beginning of the century. This stunning triumph occurred, the Athenians believed, because the gods smiled upon them with special favor and because they displayed superior courage, intelligence, and virtue.

Athens soon rivaled Sparta for the leadership of the Greek world, and by the mid-fifth century it was enjoying unprecedented confidence and prosperity. As the money poured in, the city-state built glorious temples, instituted pay for service in many government offices, and assembled the Mediterranean's most powerful navy. The poorer men who rowed the ships demanded greater democracy, leading to a judicial system guaranteeing fair treatment for all. Pericles became the most famous politician of the Golden Age by leading the drive for radical democracy.

Religious practice and women's lives maintained their traditional boundaries, but the scale of intellectual change was as dramatic as that in politics. Art and architecture broke out of old forms, promoting an impression of precarious motion rather than stability. Tragedy and comedy developed at Athens as public art forms commenting on contemporary social and political issues. Sophists' relativistic views of the universe and morality disturbed traditionally minded people, as did Socrates' strict ethics denying the value of the ordinary pursuit of wealth and success.

Wars framed the Golden Age. The Persian Wars sent the Athenians soaring to imperial power and prosperity, but their high-handed treatment of allies and enemies helped bring on the disastrous Peloponnesian War. Its nearly three decades of

battle brought the stars of the Greek Golden Age thudding back to earth: the Athenians in 400 B.C. found themselves in the same situation as in 500 B.C., fearful of Spartan power and worried whether the world's first democracy could survive. As it turned out, the next great threat to Greek stability and independence would once again come from outside, not from the east this time but from the north.

Suggested References

Clash between Persia and Greece, 499–479 B.C.

Recent scholarship emphasizes how the ancient Greeks tried to understand their own identity by contrasting themselves with others, especially the non-Greek-speaking peoples ("barbarians") of the Near East. It also stresses the differing approaches to war characteristic of the Greek city-states and the Persian empire.

Georges, Pericles. *Barbarian Asia and the Greek Experience: From the Archaic Period to the Age of Xenophon.* 1994.

Green, Peter. *The Greco-Persian Wars.* 1996.

Lazenby, J. F. *The Defence of Greece, 490–479 B.C.* 1993.

Olmstead, A. T. *History of the Persian Empire.* 1948.

Smith, John Sharwood. *Greece and the Persians.* 1990.

Athenian Confidence in the Golden Age

In addition to placing ancient Athenian government in the context of political theory on democracy, scholars are increasingly exploring its significance for modern democratic government. Online resources are also now available and important for studying the full context of Golden Age Athenian history.

Athenian democracy: http://www.perseus.tufts.edu/~hartzler/agora/site/demo/index.html.

Camp, John M. *The Athenian Agora: Excavations in the Heart of Classical Athens.* 1986.

Loomis, William T. *Wages, Welfare Costs, and Inflation in Classical Athens.* 1998.

Ober, Josiah, and Charles W. Hedrick, eds. *The Birth of Democracy: An Exhibition Celebrating the 2500th Anniversary of Democracy.* 1993.

———. *Dēmokratia: A Conversation on Democracies, Ancient and Modern.* 1996.

Parthenon: http://www.perseus.tufts.edu/cgi-bin/architindex?lookup=Athens,+Parthenon.

Pollitt, J. J. *Art and Experience in Classical Greece.* 1972.

Samons, Loren. J., III, ed. *Athenian Democracy and Imperialism.* 1998.

Thorley, John. *Athenian Democracy.* 1996.

Tradition and Innovation in Athens's Golden Age

After long neglect, historians have begun seriously discussing the meaning of the customs of Greek daily life and religion; fierce debates have ensued about how to measure and evaluate the difference between their habits and understandings and contemporary Western mores. Davidson, for example, has rebutted the popular view that Greeks considered sex a game of aggressive domination with winners and losers; that is a modern, not an ancient, idea.

Cartledge, Paul. *Aristophanes and His Theatre of the Absurd.* 1990.

Davidson, James. *Courtesans and Fishcakes: The Consuming Passions of Classical Athens.* 1998.

Easterling, P. E., and J. V. Muir, eds. *Greek Religion and Society.* 1985.

Farrar, Cynthia. *The Origins of Democratic Thinking: The Invention of Politics in Classical Athens.* 1988.

Ferguson, John. *Morals and Values in Ancient Greece.* 1989.

Fisher, N. R. E. *Slavery in Classical Greece.* 1995.

Garland, Robert. *Daily Life of the Ancient Greeks.* 1998.

———. *Religion and the Greeks.* 1994.

Garner, Richard. *Law and Society in Classical Athens.* 1987.

Goldhill, Simon. *Reading Greek Tragedy.* 1986.

Greek daily life: **http://www.museum.upenn.edu/Greek _World/Daily_life/index.html**.

Hall, Edith. *Inventing the Barbarian: Greek Self-Definition through Tragedy.* 1989.

Hanson, Victor Davis. *The Other Greeks: The Family Farm and the Agrarian Roots of Western Civilization.* 1995.

Kerferd, G. B. *The Sophistic Movement.* 1981.

Lefkowitz, Mary R., and Maureen B. Fant. *Women's Life in Greece and Rome: A Source Book in Translation.* 1982.

Morris, Ian, ed. *Classical Greece: Ancient Histories and Modern Archaeologies.* 1994.

Parker, Robert. *Athenian Religion: A History.* 1996.

Patterson, Cynthia B. *The Family in Greek History.* 1998.

Sealey, Raphael. *Women and Law in Classical Greece.* 1990.

The End of the Golden Age

The Spartan victory in the Peloponnesian War in 404 B.C. ended the Golden Age of Athens. Controversy continues to this day over how to explain the Athenian defeat: was it caused by political disunity and failure of leadership at Athens, or by Sparta's success in winning Persian financial support? Deciding the issue is difficult because our best source for the war, Thucydides, unfortunately breaks off in 411 B.C. At least Strassler's wonderfully helpful edition of that author now allows easy access to what we do have.

Kagan, Donald. *The Archidamian War.* 1974.

———. *The Fall of the Athenian Empire.* 1987.

———. *The Outbreak of the Peloponnesian War.* 1969.

———. *The Peace of Nicias and the Sicilian Expedition.* 1981.

Lazenby, J. F. *The Spartan Army.* 1985.

Strassler, Robert B., ed. *The Landmark Thucydides: A Comprehensive Guide to the Peloponnesian War.* 1996.

4

From the Classical to the Hellenistic World

c. 400–30 B.C.

Dancing Figure on Gilded Bowl
The large metal crater (wine bowl) on which this exuberant dancer appears was found at Derveni in Macedonia. Fashioned from gilded bronze, it probably dates from the 330s B.C. The intricate detail of the design shows the high level of skill characteristic of Greek metalworking; vases crafted in precious metals were favorite luxury items for the social elite. The imagery on this bowl was appropriate for wine drinking, a prominent feature of Macedonian life, because it portrayed worshipers of Dionysus, the god of wine, in a state of ecstatic joy.
Thessalonike, Archaeological Museum, © Archaeological Receipts Fund.

BOUT 255 B.C., AN EGYPTIAN CAMEL TRADER far from home paid a bilingual scribe to write an emotional letter to send to his Greek employer, Zeno, back in Egypt, to complain about his treatment by Zeno's Greek assistant, Krotos: "You know that when you left me in Syria with Krotos I followed all your instructions concerning the camels and behaved blamelessly towards you. But Krotos has ignored your orders to pay me my salary; I've received nothing despite asking him for my money over and over. He just tells me to go away. I waited a long time for you to come, but when I no longer had the necessities of life and couldn't get help anywhere, I had to run away to Syria to keep from starving to death. . . . I am desperate summer and winter. . . . They have treated me with contempt because I am not a Greek. I therefore beg you, please, command them to pay me my salary so that I won't go hungry just because I don't know how to speak Greek."

The letter writer's name and ethnic identity have been lost from the papyrus that the scribe used, but the trader's desperate plea makes it clear that his not being Greek contributed to his mistreatment. His plight—having to find a way to communicate persuasively with a foreigner holding power in his homeland—reveals the kind of new challenges that characterized the eastern Mediterranean world after it moved from the Classical period (500–323 B.C.) to the Hellenistic period (323–30 B.C.). These challenges were created by the large-scale movement of Greeks into the Near East and the resulting interaction between the local cultures and the culture of the newcomers. War initiated these

119

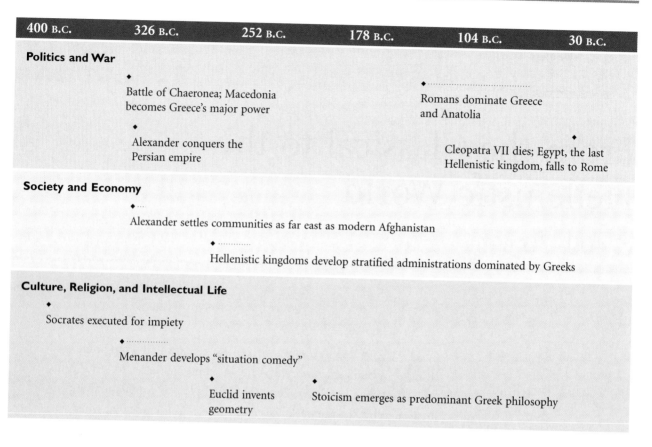

400 B.C.	326 B.C.	252 B.C.	178 B.C.	104 B.C.	30 B.C.

Politics and War

Battle of Chaeronea; Macedonia becomes Greece's major power

Romans dominate Greece and Anatolia

Alexander conquers the Persian empire

Cleopatra VII dies; Egypt, the last Hellenistic kingdom, falls to Rome

Society and Economy

Alexander settles communities as far east as modern Afghanistan

Hellenistic kingdoms develop stratified administrations dominated by Greeks

Culture, Religion, and Intellectual Life

Socrates executed for impiety

Menander develops "situation comedy"

Euclid invents geometry

Stoicism emerges as predominant Greek philosophy

changes. The long Peloponnesian War had turned many Greeks into full-time soldiers, and after it ended in 404 B.C., thousands of them became mercenaries serving Near Eastern rulers. The number of Greeks moving to the Near East took a huge leap when Alexander the Great conquered all of the Persian empire and beyond, from Egypt to the Indus valley, in the decade before his death in 323 B.C. and left behind colonies of Greeks everywhere he marched.

Alexander's successors revived monarchy in the Greek world by carving up Macedonian and Near Eastern territory into separate kingdoms, whose wealth made them the dominant political structures of the age and reduced the old city-states of Greece to second-rate powers. The *polis* retained its local political and social institutions, but it lost its independence in foreign policy: the newly made Hellenistic kings decided international politics now. They imported Greeks to fill royal offices, man their armies, and run businesses, which led to tension with their non-Greek subjects, such as the forlorn camel trader. Immigrant Greeks, such as Zeno in

Egypt, formed a social and political elite that dominated the kingdoms' local populations. Egyptians or Syrians or Mesopotamians who wanted to rise in society had to win the support of these Greeks and learn their language. Otherwise, they might find themselves as powerless as the hungry camel merchant.

Over time, however, the enduring local cultures of the Near East interacted with the culture of the Greek overlords to produce a new, multicultural synthesis. Locals married Greeks, shared their religious traditions with the newcomers, taught them their agricultural and scientific knowledge, and, on occasion, learned Greek to win administrative jobs. Although Hellenistic royal society always remained layered, with Greeks at the top, and never eliminated tension between rulers and ruled, it did achieve a stability that promoted innovations in art, science, philosophy, and religion based on a combination of Greek and Near Eastern traditions. The end of the Hellenistic kingdoms came in the first century B.C., after the Romans had expanded from their home in Italy to overthrow them all. The complex mixing of peoples and ideas that characterized the Hellenistic period, however, greatly influenced Roman civilization and, therefore, later Western civilization; the period's artistic, scientific, philosophical, and religious innovations provided a legacy that persisted even after the glory of Greece's Golden Age had faded, especially since Hellenistic religious developments provided the background for Christianity. In this way, the cultural interaction of the Hellenistic period proved to be its greatest influence on the history of the Mediterranean world.

❖ The Decline of Classical Greece, c. 400–350 B.C.

The fifth century B.C. had been the Golden Age of Greece, but the Peloponnesian War (431–404 B.C.) had put a violent end to that most prosperous part of the Classical period. After Athens's defeat in the war, its economy recovered sufficiently for most people to regain a tolerable standard of living. The stability of daily life, however, could not conceal the bitterness that democratic Athenians felt toward those whom they blamed for the violent rule of the Thirty Tyrants. This tension led to the execution of Socrates; his fate spurred Plato and Aristotle to create Greece's most famous philosophies about right and wrong and how human beings should live.

The Spartans tried to use their Peloponnesian War victory to turn themselves into an international power. Their high-handed behavior and their collaboration with the Persian empire stirred up fierce resistance from the Greek city-states, especially Thebes and Athens. By the 350s B.C., the bloody squabbling of the Greeks had so weakened all of them that they lacked the strength and the will to block the ambitious expansion of their neighbors from the north, the Macedonians. This decline set the stage for the fall of Classical Greece.

Restoring Daily Life in Postwar Athens

The Peloponnesian War had ruined the lives of the many Athenians who lived in the countryside because the Spartan invaders had wrecked their homes. The crowded conditions in the city and the devastated economy produced friction between city dwellers and the refugees from the rural areas. Es-

pecially hard hit were moderately well-off women whose husbands and brothers had died during the conflict. Such women had traditionally done weaving at home for their own families and supervised the work of household slaves, but the men had earned the family's income by farming or practicing a trade. With no one to provide for them and their children, widowed women were forced to work outside the home to support their families. The only jobs open to them were low-paying occupations traditional for women, such as wet nurses or weavers or laborers in such areas as vineyard work, for which not enough men were available to meet the need.

Over time, resourceful Athenians found ways to profit from women's skills. The family of Socrates' friend Aristarchus, for example, became poverty-stricken because several widowed sisters, nieces, and female cousins had to move in. Aristarchus found himself unable to support a household of fourteen, not counting the slaves. Socrates reminded his friend that his female relatives knew how to

Vase Painting of Women Fetching Water
This vase painting depicts a scene from everyday life in a well-appointed city-state: women filling water jugs to take back to their homes from the gushing spouts at an elaborate public fountain. It was the duty of the freeborn and slave women in the household to gather water for drinking, cooking, washing, and cleaning, as virtually no Greek homes had running water. Prosperous cities built attractive fountain houses such as this one, where a regular supply of fresh water would be available from springs or piped in through aqueducts; these were popular spots for women's conversations outside the house. The women in this scene wear the long robes and hair coverings characteristic of the time.
William Francis Warden Fund. Courtesy of the Museum of Fine Arts, Boston.

make men's and women's cloaks, shirts, capes, and smocks, "the work considered the best and most fitting for women." Although the women had previously made clothing only for the family, Socrates suggested they now begin to sell it for profit. Other families sewed clothing or baked bread for sale, and Aristarchus could tell the women in his house to do the same. The plan succeeded financially, but the women complained that Aristarchus was now the only member of the household who ate without working. Socrates advised his friend to reply that the women should think of him as sheep did a guard dog—he earned his share of the food by keeping the wolves away.

This period saw the decline of productivity in Athens's single-biggest enterprise—the state-owned silver mines, which were leased to private citizens exploiting gangs of slave miners. But the economy improved because private business owners and households once again energetically engaged in trade and produced manufactured goods in their homes and small shops, such as metal foundries and pottery workshops. The return of prosperity, coupled with the flexibility in work roles for men and women that the needs of war had promoted, apparently led to limited change in gender-defined occupations: the earliest evidence for men working alongside women in cloth production occurs in this period, when commercial weaving shops sprang up for the first time. Previously, only women had made cloth and had done so at home. Later in the fourth century B.C., there is also evidence that a few women made careers in the arts, especially painting and music, which men had traditionally dominated.

Greek businesses, usually run by families, did not grow large; the largest known from this time was a shield-making company that employed 120 slaves. Athens's economic health received a further boost when the Long Walls connecting the city with the port, destroyed at the end of the war, were rebuilt by 393 B.C. These fortifications protected the ships importing grain to feed the city and once again made it safe for traders going in and out of Athens; a brisk international commerce therefore resumed in grain, wine, pottery, and some silver from Athens's mines. The refortified harbor also allowed Athens to begin to rebuild its navy, which increased employment opportunities for poor men.

Even the improved postwar economy did not provide an easy life for most working people, how-

ever. Most workers earned just enough to feed and clothe their families. They usually had only two meals a day, a light lunch in midmorning and a heavier meal in the evening. Bread baked from barley provided the main part of their diet; only rich people could afford wheat bread. A family bought its bread from small bakery stands, often run by women, or made it at home, with the wife directing and helping the household slaves to grind the grain, shape the dough, and bake it in a pottery oven heated by charcoal. Those few households wealthy enough to afford meat from time to time boiled it or grilled it over coals. Most people ate greens, beans, onions, garlic, olives, fruit, and cheese with their bread; they had meat only at animal sacrifices paid for by the state. The wine everyone drank, usually much diluted with water, came mainly from local vineyards. Water was fetched from public fountains and brought to the house in jugs, a task the women of the household performed or made sure the household slaves did. All but the poorest families continued to have at least one or two slaves to do household chores and look after the children.

Within a few years after the end of the war, the daily lives of most Athenians had returned to old patterns. People did not soon forget the horror of the reign of the Thirty Tyrants, however, and their bitter feelings created tensions that economic stability did not relieve.

The Condemnation of Socrates, 399 B.C.

The philosopher Socrates became the most famous victim of the bitterness dividing Athenians after the Peloponnesian War. Since the official amnesty blocked prosecutions for crimes committed under the Thirty Tyrants, angry Athenians had to find other charges to bring against those whom they wanted to punish. Several prominent democratic Athenians felt this way about Socrates: they blamed him because his follower Critias had been one of the most violent members of the Thirty. Socrates had committed no crimes; in fact, he had put himself at risk in 403 B.C. by refusing to cooperate with the tyrants. But the philosopher's enemies felt he was guilty because they believed his philosophy helped turn Critias into a traitor.

Since Socrates' opponents could not accuse him of a political crime, they charged him with impiety. His accusers had to convince the jurors that Socrates had behaved in a way that angered the gods and therefore threatened to bring divine punishment on the city. As usual in Athenian trials, no judge presided to rule on what evidence was admissible or how the law should be applied. Socrates' accusers argued their case before a jury of 501 male citizens, who had been chosen by lottery from that year's pool of eligible men. Their case featured both a religious and a moral component: they accused Socrates of not believing in the city-state's gods and of introducing new divinities and also of luring young men away from Athenian moral traditions. When Socrates spoke in his own defense, he did not beg for sympathy, as jurors expected in serious cases, but instead repeated his unyielding dedication to goading his fellow citizens into examining their preconceptions. He vowed to remain their stinging gadfly no matter what the consequences.

After the jury narrowly voted to convict, standard Athenian legal procedure required the jurors to decide between alternative penalties proposed by the prosecutors and the defendant. The prosecutors proposed death. In such instances the defendant was then expected to offer exile as an alternative, which the jury usually accepted. Socrates, however, replied that he deserved a reward rather than a punishment, until his friends at the trial prevailed upon him to propose a fine as his penalty. The jury chose death. Socrates accepted his sentence calmly because, as he put it, "no evil can befall a good man either in life or in death." He was executed in the customary way, with a poisonous drink concocted from powdered hemlock. The silencing of Socrates turned out not to be the solution for Athens's postwar tension. Ancient sources report that many Athenians soon came to regret the execution of Socrates as a tragic mistake and a severe blow to their reputation.

The Philosophy of Plato and Aristotle

The fate of Socrates in democratic Athens turned the world upside down for his most famous follower, Plato (c. 429–348 B.C.). From a well-to-do family, Plato at the start of his career tried to right what he saw as the wrongs of democracy by promoting his ideas for better government—the rule of an educated and philosophical tyrant. His service as a political adviser to Dionysius, ruler of Syracuse in Sicily, however, crushed Plato's hopes that politics was the answer to the troubles created by war

and people's desire for revenge; abandoning the life of a public career, marriage, and children that a man was expected to follow, he devoted himself to philosophy and a life of contemplation, pondering the nature of the world in which such an evil fate could have befallen such a good man as Socrates. He established a philosophical school, the Academy, in Athens c. 386 B.C. Not a school or college in the modern sense but rather an informal association of people who studied philosophy, mathematics, and theoretical astronomy under Plato's guidance, the Academy attracted intellectuals to Athens for nine hundred years after its founder's death.

Plato's highly abstract ideas on ethics and politics have remained central to philosophy and political science since his day, but his legacy also included inspiring his most famous pupil, Aristotle (384–322 B.C.). The son of a wealthy doctor in northern Greece, Aristotle came to study in the Academy at the age of seventeen. After Plato's death, he became an itinerant scholar for more than a decade; from 342 to 335 B.C., he earned a living by tutoring the young Alexander the Great in Macedonia. Then returning to Athens, Aristotle created his own practical philosophy for life,

Plato's Academy, established c. 386 B.C., and nearby Athens

based on scientific knowledge and theories, and founded his own school, the Lyceum. His vast writings made him one of the most influential thinkers in Western history. Since Socrates' sad fate

Mosaic of Plato's Academy
*This mosaic from the Roman period depicts philosophers —
identified by their beards — at Plato's school (called the Academy after the name of a local mythological hero) in Athens
holding discussions among themselves. The Academy, founded
probably in 386 B.C., became one of Greece's most famous and
long-lasting institutions, attracting scholars and students for
a thousand years until it closed under the Byzantine emperor Justinian in A.D. 529. The columns and the tree depicted in the mosaic express the harmonious blend of the
natural and built environment of the Academy, which was
meant to promote productive and pleasant discussions.*
Erich Lessing/Art Resource, NY.

provoked the chain of events that produced the
philosophy of Plato and Aristotle, Socrates' death—
as he intended—indirectly made an enormous
contribution to the intellectual vitality of Western
civilization.

Plato's Ethical Thought.   Plato's interests ranged
widely, covering astronomy, mathematics, and
metaphysics as well as ethics and political philosophy. He presented his ideas in dialogues, which often featured Socrates conversing with a variety of
people. Plato intended his dialogues to provoke
readers into thoughtful reflection rather than to prescribe a predetermined set of beliefs. His views apparently changed over time—nowhere did he
present one cohesive set of doctrines. Nevertheless,

he always maintained one essential idea: moral qualities in their ultimate reality are universal and absolute, not relative.

Plato taught that we cannot define and understand absolute qualities such as goodness, justice,
beauty, or equality by our experience of them in our
lives. Any earthly examples will in some other context display the opposite quality. For example, always returning what one has borrowed might seem
just. But what if a person who has borrowed a
friend's weapon is confronted by that friend, who
wants the weapon back to commit murder? In this
case returning the borrowed item would be unjust.
Examples of equality are also only relative. The
equality of a stick two feet long, for example, is evident when it is compared with another two-foot
stick. Paired with a three-foot stick, however, it is
unequal. In sum, in the world that humans experience with their senses, every virtue and every quality is relative to some extent.

In some of his works, Plato referred to the ultimate realities of the absolute virtues as Forms (or
Ideas); among them were Goodness, Justice, Beauty,
and Equality. He argued that the Forms are invisible,
invariable, and eternal entities located in a higher
realm beyond the daily world. According to Plato, the
Forms are the only true reality; what we experience
through our senses in everyday life are only dim and
imperfect representations of these metaphysical realities, as if, he said, we were watching their shadows
cast on the wall of a cave. Plato's views on the nature
and significance of Forms altered throughout his career, and his later works seem quite divorced from
this theory. Nevertheless, Forms exemplify both the
complexity and the wide range of Plato's thought. His
theory of Forms elevated metaphysics—the consideration of the ultimate nature of reality beyond the
reach of the human senses—to a central and enduring issue for philosophers.

Plato's idea that humans possess immortal souls
distinct from their bodies established the concept
of *dualism,* a separation between spiritual and physical being. This notion influenced much of later
philosophical and religious thought. Plato also wrote
that the preexisting knowledge possessed by the immortal human soul is in truth the knowledge known
to the supreme deity. Plato called this god the Demiurge ("craftsman") because the deity used knowledge of the Forms to craft the world of living beings
from raw matter. According to Plato, because a

knowing, rational god created the world, the world has order. Furthermore, the world's beings have goals, as evidenced by animals adapting to their environments in order to thrive. The Demiurge wanted to reproduce the perfect order of the Forms in the material world, but the world turned out imperfect because matter is imperfect. Plato believed the proper goal for humans is to seek perfect order and purity in their own souls by using rational thoughts to control their irrational desires, which are harmful. The desire to drink wine to excess, for example, is irrational because the drinker fails to consider the hangover to come the next day. Those who give in to irrational desires fail to consider the future of both their body and soul. Finally, because the soul is immortal and the body is not, our present, impure existence is only one passing piece in our cosmic existence.

Plato's *Republic*.   Plato presented the most famous version of his utopian political vision in his dialogue *The Republic*. This work, whose title would be more accurate as *System of Government*, primarily concerns the nature of justice and the reasons people should be just instead of unjust. For Plato, justice is unattainable in a democracy. He therefore had no love for contemporary Athenian government: the condemnation of Socrates convinced him that citizens were incapable of rising above narrow self-interest to knowledge of any universal truth unless they were ruled by an enlightened oligarchy or monarch.

For Plato, a just society needs a proper hierarchy, like that of Sparta. In *The Republic*, he sketches his ideal society ordered by division into three classes of people, distinguished by their ability to grasp the truth of Forms; some modern critics regard his utopian scheme as overauthoritarian. The highest class constitutes the rulers, or "guardians," as Plato calls them, who must be educated in mathematics, astronomy, and metaphysics. Next come the "auxiliaries," whose function is to defend the community. The lowest class comprises the "producers," who grow the food and make the objects the whole population requires. Each part contributes to society by fulfilling its proper function.

According to Plato's *Republic*, women as well as men can be guardians because they possess the same virtues and abilities as men, except for a disparity in physical strength between the average woman and

the average man. To minimize distraction, guardians are to have neither private property nor nuclear families. Male and female guardians are to live in houses shared in common, to eat in the same mess halls, and to exercise in the same gymnasiums. They are to have sexual relations with various partners so that the best women can mate with the best men to produce the best children. The children are to be raised together in a common environment by special caretakers. The guardians who achieve the highest level of knowledge in Plato's ideal society qualify to rule over the utopia as philosopher-kings.

Plato did not think that human beings could actually create such a society, but he did believe that imagining it was an important way to help people teach themselves to live justly. For this reason above all, he passionately believed the study of philosophy mattered to human life.

Aristotle, Scientist and Philosopher.   Aristotle's great reputation as a thinker in science and philosophy rests on his emphasis on scientific investigation of the natural world and the development of rigorous systems of logical argument. He regarded science and philosophy not as abstract subjects isolated from the concerns of ordinary existence but as the disciplined search for knowledge in every aspect of life. That search epitomized the kind of rational human activity that alone could bring the good life and genuine happiness. Like Plato, Aristotle criticized democracy because it allowed

Aristotle's Lyceum, established 335 b.c.

uneducated instead of "better" people to control politics. He nevertheless chose Athens as the site of his school, the Lyceum (founded 335 b.c.), because the city's cosmopolitan atmosphere attracted the curious and wealthy young men he needed as pupils; he would have preferred a monarchy for its location, but at the time none existed rich and cultured enough to be a magnet for the elite Greeks he instructed. Later called the Peripatetic School, instead of Lyceum, after the covered walkway (*peripatos*) where its students carried on conversations out of the glare of the Mediterranean sun, his Athenian school became world famous. There, Aristotle lectured with dazzling intelligence and energy on nearly every branch of learning: biology, medicine, anatomy, psychology, meteorology, physics, chemistry, mathematics, music, metaphysics, rhetoric, political science, ethics, and literary criticism. He also worked out a sophisticated system of logic for precise argumentation. Creating a careful system to identify the forms of valid arguments, Aristotle established grounds for distinguishing a logically sound case from a merely persuasive one.

Aristotle insisted on explanations based on common sense rather than metaphysics. He denied the validity of Plato's theory of Forms, for example, on the grounds that the separate existence Plato postulated for them did not make sense. Furthermore, Aristotle believed that the best way to understand objects and beings was to observe them in their natural settings. His coupling of detailed investigation with perceptive reasoning worked especially well in such physical sciences as biology, botany, and zoology. For example, as the first scientist to try to collect and classify all the available information on the animal species, Aristotle recorded facts about more than five hundred different kinds of animals, including insects. Many of his findings represented significant advances in learning. His recognition that whales and dolphins are mammals, for example, which later writers on animals overlooked, was not rediscovered for another two thousand years.

Some of Aristotle's views justified inequalities characteristic of his time. He regarded slavery as natural, arguing that some people were by nature bound to be slaves because their souls lacked the rational part that should rule in a human. He also concluded, based on faulty notions of biology, that women were by nature inferior to men. He wrongly believed, for example, that in procreation the male's semen actively gave the fetus its design, whereas the female passively provided its matter. He justified his assertion that females were less courageous than males by dubious evidence about animals, such as the report that a male squid would stay by as if to help when its mate was speared but that a female squid would swim away when the male was impaled. Erroneous and inconclusive biological information such as this led Aristotle to evaluate females as incomplete males, a conclusion with disastrous results for later thought. At the same time, he believed that human communities could be successful and happy only if women and men both contributed.

In ethics, Aristotle emphasized the need to develop habits of just behavior. People should achieve self-control by training their minds to win out over instincts and passions. Self-control did not mean denying human desires and appetites; rather, it meant striking a balance between suppressing and heedlessly indulging physical yearnings, of finding "the mean." Aristotle claimed that the mind should rule in finding this balance because the intellect is the finest human quality and the mind is the true self—indeed, the godlike part of a person.

Aristotle did the study of ethics a great service by insisting that standards of right and wrong have merit only if they are grounded in character and aligned with the good in human nature and do not simply consist of lists of abstract reasons for behaving in one way rather than another. That is, an ethical system must be relevant to the actual moral situations people experience. In his ethical thought, as in all his scholarship, Aristotle distinguished himself by insisting that the life of the mind and experience of the real world are inseparable components in the quest to define a worthwhile existence for human beings.

The Disunity of Greece

During the same period in which Plato taught and Aristotle began his studies—the fifty years following the Peloponnesian War—the rival city-states of Sparta, Thebes, and Athens each in turn tried to dominate Greece. None succeeded. Their struggles with one another sapped their strength and left Greece susceptible to outside interference, which eventually undermined the political independence of the Classical city-states.

The Spartans did the most to provoke this fatal disunity by trying to conquer other city-states. Their general Lysander pursued an aggressive policy in Anatolia and northern Greece in the 390s B.C., and other Spartan commanders meddled in Sicily. Thebes, Athens, Corinth, and Argos thereupon formed an anti-Spartan coalition because Spartan aggression threatened their interests at home and abroad. The Spartans checkmated the alliance by coming to terms with the Persian king. In a blatant renunciation of their traditional claim to defend Greek freedom, the Spartans acknowledged the Persian ruler's right to control the Greek city-states of Anatolia—in return for permission to pursue their own interests in Greece without Persian interference. This agreement of 386 B.C., called the King's Peace, effectively sold out the Greeks of Anatolia and returned them to their dependent status of a century past, before the Greek victory in the Persian Wars.

The Athenians rebuilt their military strength to combat Sparta. The reconstructed Long Walls restored Athens's invulnerability to invasion, and a new kind of foot soldier—the *peltast,* armed with a light leather shield, javelins, and sword—fighting alongside hoplites gave Athenian ground forces more tactical mobility and flexibility. Most important, Athens's navy regained its offensive strength, and by 377 B.C. the city-state had again become the leader of a naval alliance of Greek city-states. But this time the league members insisted that their rights be specified in writing to prevent a recurrence of high-handed Athenian behavior.

The Thebans, fighting hard to block Spartan domination of Greece, became the region's main power in the 370s B.C. Their army dashed Sparta's hopes for lasting power by decisively defeating an invasion force at Leuctra in Boeotia in 371 B.C. and then invading the Spartan homeland in the Peloponnese. They destroyed Spartan power forever by freeing many helots. This Theban success so frightened the Athenians, whose city was only forty miles from Thebes, that they made a temporary alliance with their hated enemies the Spartans. Their combined armies confronted the Thebans in the battle of Mantinea in the Peloponnese in 362 B.C., where Thebes won the battle but lost the war when its best general was killed and no capable replacement could be found.

The battle of Mantinea left the Greek city-states in impotent disunity. The contemporary historian Xenophon succinctly summed up the situation after 362 B.C.: "Everyone had supposed that the winners of this battle would be Greece's rulers and its losers their subjects; but there was only more confusion and disturbance in Greece after it than before." The truth of his analysis was confirmed when the Athenian naval alliance fell apart in a war between Athens and its allies over the close ties some allies were developing with Persia and Macedonia.

All the efforts of the various major Greek city-states to win control over mainland Greece in this period failed. By the mid 350s B.C., no Greek city-

state had the power or the status to rule anything except its own territory; this state of mutual weakness made effective foreign policy, which depended on astute diplomacy and resolute military power, only a distant memory. The Greek city-states' struggle for supremacy over one another that had begun long before in the Peloponnesian War had thus finally petered out in a stalemate of exhaustion. By failing to cooperate, they opened the way for the rise of a new power—the kingdom of Macedonia—that would threaten their cherished independence.

❖ The Rise of Macedonia, 359–323 B.C.

The kingdom of Macedonia, taking advantage of the futile wars the Greek city-states waged against one another in the first half of the fourth century B.C., turned itself into an international superpower. That this formerly minor kingdom would seize the leadership of Greece and conquer the Persian empire ranks as one of the greatest surprises in ancient military and political history. Two aggressive and charismatic kings produced this amazing transformation: Philip II (r. 359–336 B.C.) and his son Alexander the Great (r. 336–323 B.C.). Their extensive conquests marked the end of the Classical period and paved the way for the changes and cultural interactions of the Hellenistic age.

The Background of Macedonian Power

The power of the Macedonians sprang from the characteristics of their monarchy and their ethnic pride. Macedonian kings did not rule in isolation—they had to listen to their people, who were used to freedom of speech in telling their monarchs what needed to be improved. Moreover, a king could govern effectively only as long as he maintained the support of the most powerful nobles, who counted as the king's social equals and controlled large bands of followers. Fighting, hunting, and heavy drinking were these men's favorite pastimes. The king was expected to demonstrate his prowess in these activities to show he was capable of heading the state. Queens and royal mothers received respect in this male-dominated society because they came from powerful families in the nobility or the ruling houses of lands bordering Macedonia. In the king's absence these royal women often vied with the king's designated representative for power at court.

Macedonians, who thought of themselves as Greek by blood, took great pride in their identity. They had their own language, related to Greek but not comprehensible to Greeks; the nobles who dominated their society routinely learned to speak Greek. Macedonians looked down on their relatives to the south as a soft lot unequal to the adversities of life in the north. The Greeks reciprocated this scorn. The famed Athenian orator Demosthenes (384–322 B.C.) lambasted Philip II as "not only not a Greek nor related to the Greeks, but not even a barbarian from a land worth mentioning; no, he's a pestilence from Macedonia, a region where you can't even buy a slave worth his salt." Hostile feelings of this kind made peaceful relations between Macedonians and Greeks impossible.

The Career of Philip II, 359–336 B.C.

Philip II forged Macedonia into an international power against heavy odds. Before his reign, strife in the royal family and disputes among the nobles had been so common that Macedonia had never united sufficiently to mobilize its full military strength. Indeed, kings so feared violence from their own countrymen that they stationed bodyguards outside the royal bedroom. Princes married earlier than did ordinary men, soon after the age of twenty, because the instability of the kingship demanded male heirs as soon as possible.

A military disaster in 359 B.C. brought Philip to the throne at a desperate moment. The Illyrians, hostile neighbors to the north, had just slaughtered Philip's predecessor and four thousand troops. Philip immediately persuaded the nobles to recognize him as king in place of his infant nephew. Philip then restored the army's confidence by teaching the hoplites an unstoppable new tactic with their thrusting spears, which reached fourteen to sixteen feet long and took two hands to wield: arranging them in the traditional phalanx formation, he created deep blocks of soldiers whose front lines bristled with outstretched spears like a lethal porcupine. By moving as a unit, the phalanx armed with such long spears could push aside opposing forces. Deploying cavalry as a strike force to soften up the enemy and protect the infantry's flanks, Philip's reorganized army

Statue of the Orator Demosthenes

The Athenian political leader Demosthenes (384–322 B.C.) became the most famous orator in the Greek world by opposing the expansionist actions of the Macedonian king Philip and his son Alexander the Great. This statue is a marble copy from the Roman period of a Greek original that would have been cast in bronze. It showed Demosthenes holding a scroll to symbolize his great learning; his speeches, whether given before the democratic assembly or in a court, were delivered without reading from a text. The statue also shows him in fine physical condition; he reportedly practiced delivering speeches while jogging to improve his lung power. Scala/Art Resource, NY.

promptly routed the Illyrians and defeated his local rivals for the kingship.

Philip then embarked on a whirlwind of diplomacy, bribery, and military action to force the Greek city-states to acknowledge his superiority. A Greek contemporary, the historian Theopompus of Chios, labeled Philip "insatiable and extravagant; he did everything in a hurry . . . he never spared the time to reckon up his income and expenditure." By the late 340s B.C., Philip had cajoled or coerced most of northern Greece to follow his lead in foreign policy. Seeking the glory of avenging Greece and fearing the potentially destabilizing effect his reinvigorated army would have on his kingdom if the soldiers had nothing to do, his goal became to lead a united Macedonian and Greek army against the Persian empire.

To launch his grandiose invasion, however, he needed to strengthen his alliance by adding to it the forces of southern Greece. He found in Greek history the justification for attacking Persia: revenge for the Persian Wars. But some Greeks remained unconvinced. At Athens, Demosthenes used stirring rhetoric to criticize Greeks for their failure to resist Philip. They stood by, he thundered, "as if Philip were a hailstorm, praying that he would not come their way, but not trying to do anything to head him off." Finally, Athens and Thebes headed a coalition of southern Greek city-states to try to block Philip's plans, but in 338 B.C. Philip and his Greek allies trounced the coalition's forces at the battle of Chaeronea in Boeotia (Map 4.1). The defeated city-states retained their internal freedom, but Philip compelled them to join an alliance under his undisputed leadership. The course of later history showed the battle of Chaeronea to be a decisive turning point in Greek history: never again would the city-states of Greece make foreign policy for themselves without considering, and usually following, the wishes of outside powers. The Greek city-states no longer were independent actors in international politics, though they did remain the basic economic and social units of Greece. Soon after, Philip's son Alexander III stepped onto center stage.

Alexander the Great, 336–323 B.C.

Violence marked the reign of Alexander. It began in 336 B.C. when a Macedonian assassinated Philip. Unconfirmed rumors speculated that Alexander's

MAP 4.1 Expansion of Macedonia under Philip II, 359–336 B.C.

Two factors, one geographic and one cultural, directed Macedonian expansion southward: mountainous terrain and warlike people lay to the north, while the Macedonian royal house saw itself as ethnically Greek and therefore rightfully linked to Greece to the south. King Philip II made himself the leader of Greece by convincing the Thessalians in the 340s B.C. to follow him and by defeating a Greek coalition led by Athens at the battle of Chaeronea in 338 B.C. Sparta, far from Macedonia in the southern Peloponnese, kept out of the fray; its dwindling population had made it too weak to matter.

mother, Olympias, had instigated the murder to procure the throne for her son, now twenty years old. He promptly murdered potential rivals for the crown and forced the nobles to recognize him as king. Next, in several lightning-fast wars, he subdued Macedonia's traditional enemies to the west and north. Then Alexander compelled the southern Greeks, who had defected from their forced alliance with Macedonia at the news of Philip's death, to rejoin. To demonstrate the price of disloyalty, in 335 B.C. Alexander destroyed Thebes for rebelling.

Conquest of the Persian Empire. The following year he embarked on the most astonishing military campaign in ancient history by leading a

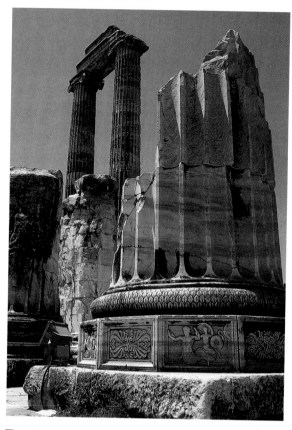

Temple of Apollo at Didyma
This massive temple at Didyma on the western coast of Anatolia (modern Turkey) was built in the time of Alexander the Great to replace a temple that had been destroyed by the Persians in 494 B.C. It housed a famous oracle of Apollo, to which people flocked to seek advice from the god. Its huge scale—129 yards long by 66 yards wide, surrounded by a veritable forest of 120 columns—stressed the shrine's importance, which lasted until the first Christian Roman emperor, Constantine, forced it to close in the early fourth century.
Robert Frereck/Odyssey/Chicago.

Macedonian and Greek army against the Persian empire in the Near East to fulfill his father's dream of avenging Greece. Alexander's astounding success in conquering all the lands from Turkey to Egypt to Uzbekistan while still in his twenties earned him the title "the Great" in later ages and inspired legends about him among countless peoples. In his own time his greatness consisted of his ability to motivate his men to follow him into hostile, unknown regions and to use cavalry charges to disrupt the enemy's infantry. Alexander inspired his troops with his reckless disregard for his own safety. He often rode his warhorse Bucephalus ("Oxhead") into the

heart of the enemy's front line at the head of his men, sharing the danger of the common soldier. No one could miss him in his plumed helmet, vividly colored cloak, and armor polished to reflect the sun. He was so intent on conquering distant lands that he rejected advice to delay his departure from Macedonia until he had married and fathered an heir. He further alarmed his principal adviser by giving away virtually all his land and property in order to strengthen the army, thereby creating new landowners who would furnish troops. "What," the adviser asked, "do you have left for yourself?" "My hopes," Alexander replied. Those hopes centered on constructing an image of himself as a warrior as splendid as the incomparable Achilles of Homer's *Iliad*; he always kept a copy of the *Iliad* and a dagger under his pillow. Alexander's aspirations and behavior were the ultimate expression of Homer's vision of the glorious conquering warrior, still the prevailing ideal of male Greek culture.

Alexander repeatedly displayed his heroic ambitions as his army advanced relentlessly eastward through Persian territory. In Anatolia, he visited Gordion, where an oracle had promised the lordship of Asia to whoever could loose a seemingly impenetrable knot of rope tying the yoke of an ancient chariot preserved in the city. The young king, so the story goes, cut the Gordian knot with his sword. When his army later forced the Persian king, Darius III, to abandon his wives and daughters when he fled from the battlefield to avoid capture, Alexander treated the women with great chivalry. His honorable behavior toward the Persian royal women after their capture reportedly enhanced his reputation among the peoples of the Persian empire.

Alexander complemented his heroic bravery and code of honor with a keen eye for the latest in military technology. When Tyre, a heavily fortified city on an island off the coast of the Levant, refused to surrender to him in 332 B.C., he built a long, massive stone pier as a platform for artillery towers, armored battering rams, and catapults flinging boulders to breach the walls of the city. The capture of Tyre rang the death knell of supposedly impregnable walled city-states. Although effective attacks on cities with defensive walls remained rare even after Alexander, his success at Tyre increased the terror of a siege for a city's general population. No longer could a city-state's citizens confidently assume they could withstand their enemies' technology indefinitely.

The fear that armed warriors might actually penetrate into the city made it much harder for city-states to remain united in the face of attacks.

Alexander's actions after he conquered Egypt and the Persian heartland revealed his strategy for ruling a vast empire: establish colonies of Greeks and Macedonians in conquered territory and keep the traditional administrative system in place. In Egypt, he started his founding of cities by establishing a new one on the coast, to the west of the Nile River, naming it Alexandria after himself. In Persia, he proclaimed himself the king of Asia and left the existing governing units intact, even retaining some high-ranking Persian administrators. For the local populations of the Persian empire, therefore, the succession of a Macedonian to the Persian throne changed their lives very little. They continued to send the same taxes to a remote master, whom they rarely if ever saw.

The Expedition to India and Back.

So fierce was Alexander's heroic love of conquest and adventure that he next led his army farther east into territory hardly known to the Greeks (Map 4.2). His goal seems to have been to outdo even the heroes of legend by marching to the end of the world. Paring his army to reduce the need for supplies, he led it northeast into the trackless steppes of Bactria and Sogdiana (modern Afghanistan and Uzbekistan). On the Jaxartes River (Syr Darya), he founded a city called Alexandria the Furthest to show that he had penetrated deeper into this region than even Cyrus, the founder of the Persian empire. When it proved impossible to subdue the highly mobile locals, however, Alexander settled for an alliance sealed by a marriage to the Bactrian princess Roxane. He then headed east into India. Seventy days of marching through monsoon rains extinguished his soldiers' fire for conquest. In the spring of 326 B.C., they

Mosaic of Alexander the Great at the Battle of Issus

This large mosaic, which served as a floor in an upscale Roman house, was a copy of a famous earlier painting of the battle of Issus of 333 B.C. It shows Alexander the Great on his warhorse Bucephalus confronting the Persian king Darius in his chariot. The latter reaches out in compassion for his warriors who are selflessly throwing themselves in the way to protect him. The original artist was an extremely skilled painter, as revealed by the dramatic foreshortening of the horse right in front of Darius and by the startling effect of the face of the dying warrior reflected in the polished shield just to the right of the horse.
Erich Lessing/Art Resource, NY.

MAP 4.2 Conquests of Alexander the Great, 336–323 B.C.

The scale of Alexander's military campaigns in Asia made him a legend; from the time he led his army out of Macedonia and Greece in 334 B.C. until his death in Babylon in 323 B.C., he was continually on the move. His careful intelligence gathering combined with his charismatic and brilliant generalship generated an unbroken string of victories; his skillful choice of regional administrators, founding of garrison cities, and preservation of local governing structures kept his conquests stable after he moved on.

mutinied on the banks of the Hyphasis River in western India and forced Alexander to turn back. The return journey cost many casualties; the survivors finally reached safety back in Persia in 324 B.C. Alexander promptly began planning an invasion of the Arabian peninsula and, after that, of all North Africa west of Egypt.

By the time Alexander returned to Persia, he had dropped all pretense of ruling over the Greeks as anything other than an absolute monarch. Despite his earlier promise to respect the internal freedom of the Greek city-states, he ordered them to restore citizenship to the many war-created exiles whose status as wandering, stateless persons was creating unrest. Even more striking was his announcement that he wished to receive the honors due a god. Initially dumbfounded by this request, the leaders of most Greek city-states soon complied by sending honorary religious delegations to him. The Spartan Damis pithily expressed the only prudent position on Alexander's deification: "If Alexan-

der wishes to be a god, then we'll agree that he be called a god."

Personal rather than political motives best explain Alexander's request. He almost certainly had come to believe he was actually the son of Zeus; after all, Greek mythology contained many stories of Zeus mating with a human female and producing children. Most of Zeus's legendary offspring were mortal, but Alexander's conquests proved he had surpassed them. His feats were superhuman because they exceeded the bounds of human possibility. Since Alexander's accomplishments demonstrated that he had achieved godlike power, he therefore must be a god himself. Alexander's divinity was, in ancient terms, a natural consequence of his power.

Alexander's premature death from a fever and heavy drinking on June 10, 323 B.C., ended his plan to conquer Arabia and North Africa. He had been suffering for months from depression brought on by the death of his best friend, Hephaistion. Close since their boyhood, Alexander and Hephaistion were probably lovers. Like Pericles, Alexander had made no plans about what should happen if he died unexpectedly. Roxane gave birth to their first child a few months after Alexander's death. The story goes that when at Alexander's deathbed his commanders asked him to whom he bequeathed his kingdom, he replied, "To the most powerful."

Alexander's Impact. Modern scholars disagree on almost everything about Alexander, from whether his claim to divinity was meant to justify his increasingly authoritarian attitude toward the Greek city-states to what his expedition was meant to achieve. They also offer different assessments of his character, ranging from bloodthirsty monster interested solely in endless conquest to romantic visionary intent on creating a multiethnic world open to all cultures. The ancient sources suggest that Alexander's overall aims can best be explained as interlinked goals: the conquest and administration of the known world and the exploration and possible colonization of new territory beyond. Conquest through military action was a time-honored pursuit for Macedonian aristocrats like Alexander and suited his restless, ruthless, and incredibly energetic nature. He included non-Macedonians in his administration and army because he needed their expertise. Alexander's explorations benefited numerous scientific fields, from geography to botany, because he took along scientifically minded writers to collect and catalog the new knowledge they acquired; he regularly sent reams of new scientific information to his old tutor Aristotle, who used it to write influential treatises. The far-flung cities that Alexander founded served as loyal outposts for keeping the peace in conquered territory and providing warnings to headquarters in case of local uprisings. They also created new opportunities for trade in valuable goods such as spices that were not produced in the Mediterranean region.

The Athenian orator Aeschines (c. 397–322 B.C.) well expressed the bewildered reaction of many people to the events of Alexander's lifetime: "What strange and unexpected event has not occurred in our time? The life we have lived is no ordinary human one, but we were born to be an object of wonder to posterity." Alexander certainly attained legendary status in later times. Stories of fabulous exploits attributed to him became popular folktales throughout the ancient world, even reaching distant

regions where Alexander had never set foot, such as southern Africa. The popularity of the legend of Alexander as a symbol of the heights a warrior-hero could achieve was one of his most persistent legacies to later ages. That the worlds of Greece and the Near East had been brought into closer contact than ever before represented another long-lasting effect of his astonishing career, which drew the curtain on the Classical period and opened the next act in the drama of Western history, the Hellenistic period.

❖ The Hellenistic Kingdoms, 323–30 B.C.

The word *Hellenistic* was coined in the nineteenth century to designate the period of Greek and Near Eastern history from the death of Alexander the Great in 323 B.C. to the death of Cleopatra VII, the last Macedonian queen of Egypt, in 30 B.C. The term *Hellenistic* conveys the idea that a mixed, cosmopolitan form of social and cultural life combining Hellenic (that is, Greek) and indigenous traditions emerged in the eastern Mediterranean region in the aftermath of Alexander's expedition. The innovative political, cultural, and economic developments of this period arose from the interaction of Greek and Near Eastern civilizations. The process, set in motion by war, was filled with tension between conquerors and subjects and produced uneven results: Greek ideas and practices had their greatest impact on the urban populations of Egypt and southwestern Asia, while the many people who farmed in the countryside and rarely visited the cities had much less contact with Greek ways of life. Still, the legacy of the Hellenistic world was long-lasting, especially in its later influence on the Romans.

The dominant political structures of the Hellenistic period were new kingdoms, which reintroduced monarchy into Greek history; kings had been rare in Greece since the fall of Mycenaean civilization nearly a thousand years earlier. The new kingdoms were created by commanders from Alexander's army who seized portions of his empire for themselves after his death and proclaimed themselves kings. After more than twenty years of struggle, their families established themselves as the dynasties ruling the Hellenistic kingdoms and accumulated the power to compel the Greek city-states to shape their foreign policies according to the kings' wishes; from then on, *polis* citizens could make independent decisions only on local matters.

The Creation of "Successor Kings"

Alexander the Great left no heir in place; his only legitimate son, Alexander IV, was born several months after his death. His mother, Olympias, tried for several years to establish her grandson as the Macedonian king under her protection, but her plan failed because Alexander's former army commanders wanted to rule instead. In 316 B.C., they executed Olympias for rebellion and in about 311 B.C. they murdered the boy and his mother, Roxane, in cold blood; having eradicated the royal family, they divided Alexander's conquests among themselves. Antigonus (c. 382–301 B.C.) took over in Anatolia, the Near East, Macedonia, and Greece; Seleucus (c. 358–281 B.C.) in Babylonia and the East as far as India; and Ptolemy (c. 367–282 B.C.) in Egypt.

Because these men assumed control of the largest parts of Alexander's conquests, they were referred to as the "successor kings."

These new rulers—the Hellenistic kings—had to create their own form of kingship because they did not inherit their positions legitimately: they were self-proclaimed monarchs with neither blood relationship to any traditional royal family line nor any special claim to a particular territory. For this reason historians often characterize their type of rule as "personal monarchy." They transformed themselves and their sons into kings by using their military might, their prestige, and their ambition. In the beginning, their biggest enemies were one another, as the new royal families repeatedly fought in the decades after Alexander's death, trying to slice off more territory for their individual kingdoms.

By the middle of the third century B.C., the three Hellenistic kingdoms had reached a balance of power that precluded their expanding much beyond their core territories (Map 4.3). The Antigonids had

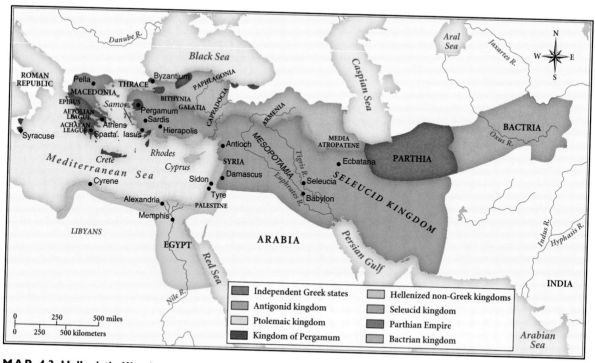

MAP 4.3 Hellenistic Kingdoms, c. 240 B.C.
Although the traditional Greek city-states retained their formal independence in the Hellenistic period, monarchy became the dominant political system in the areas of Alexander's former conquests. By about eighty years after his death in 323 B.C., the most striking changes to the three major kingdoms originally established by his successors were that the Seleucids had given up their easternmost territories and the kingdom of Pergamum had carved out an independent local reign in western Anatolia.

been reduced to a kingdom in Macedonia, but they also controlled mainland Greece, whose city-states had to follow royal foreign policy, even though they retained their internal freedom. The Seleucids ruled in Syria and Mesopotamia, but they had been forced to cede their easternmost territory early on to the Indian king Chandragupta (r. 323–299 B.C.), founder of the Mauryan dynasty. They also lost most of Persia to the Parthians, a northern Iranian people. The Ptolemies retained control of the rich land of Egypt.

These territorial arrangements were never completely stable because Hellenistic monarchs never stopped being competitive. Conflicts frequently arose over contested border areas. The armies of the Ptolemaic and Seleucid kingdoms, for example, periodically engaged in a violent tug-of-war over the lands of the Levant, just as the Egyptians and Hittites had done centuries earlier. Sometimes the struggles between the major kingdoms left openings for smaller, regional kingdoms to establish themselves. The most famous of these was the kingdom of the Attalids in western Anatolia, with the wealthy city of Pergamum as its capital. In Bactria in Central Asia (in modern Afghanistan), the Greeks—originally colonists settled by Alexander—broke off from the Seleucid kingdom in the mid-third century B.C. to found their own regional kingdom, which flourished for a time from the trade in luxury goods between India and China and the Mediterranean world.

The Hellenistic kings adopted different strategies to meet the goal shared by all new political regimes: to establish a tradition of legitimacy for their rule. Legitimacy was essential if they were to found a royal line that had a chance of enduring beyond their deaths. Whenever possible, the kings tried to incorporate local traditions into their rule. For the Seleucids, for example, this meant combining Macedonian with Near Eastern royal customs; for the Ptolemies, Macedonian with Egyptian. All the kingdoms sought to strengthen their legitimacy from the female as well as the male side. For this reason, Hellenistic queens enjoyed a high social status as the representatives of distinguished families and then became the mothers of a line of royal descendants. In the end, of course, the rulers' positions ultimately rested on their personal ability and their power. A letter from the city of Ilion (on the site of ancient Troy) summed up the situation with the writer praising the Seleveid king Antiochus I (c. 324–261 B.C.):

Altar of Zeus at Pergamum
Eumenes II, king of Pergamum in western Anatolia from 197 to 158 B.C., turned his city into a prosperous capital and a cultural showplace by craftily navigating his small kingdom through the competing demands made by the great powers of the time, the Seleucid empire and the Roman republic. Allying with the Romans, he profited from their intervention against the Seleucids. In the 170s B.C., he initiated a grand building program that had this huge, sculpted altar to Zeus as its centerpiece; the energetically composed sculptures portrayed the victory of divinely inspired civilization over barbarism. Their striking style greatly influenced later artists. Art Resource, NY.

"His rule depends mostly on his own excellence [*aretê*], and on the goodwill of his friends and on his forces."

The Structure of Hellenistic Kingdoms

The Hellenistic kingdoms amounted to foreign rule over indigenous populations by kings and queens of Macedonian descent. Although monarchs had to maintain harmony with the favored Greek and Macedonian immigrants and local urban elites in their kingdoms, royal power was the ultimate source of control over the kingdoms' subjects, in keeping with the tradition of Near Eastern monarchy that Hellenistic kingdoms adopted. This tradition persisted above all in meting out justice. Seleucus, for one, claimed this right as a universal truth: "It is not the customs of the Persians and other people that I impose upon you, but the law which is common to everyone, that what is decreed by the king is always just." Hellenistic kings of course had to do more to survive than simply assert a right to rule. The survival of their dynasties depended on their ability to create strong armies, effective administrations, and cooperative urban elites.

Royal Military Forces and Administration. Hellenistic royal armies and navies provided security against internal unrest as well as external enemies. Professional soldiers manned these forces. To develop their military might, the Seleucid and Ptolemaic kings vigorously promoted immigration by Greeks and Macedonians, who received land grants in return for military service. When this source of manpower gave out, the kings had to employ more local men as troops. Military expenditures eventually became a problem because the kings faced continual pressure to pay large numbers of mercenaries and because military technology had become so expensive. To compete effectively, a Hellenistic king had to provide giant artillery, such as catapults capable of flinging a projectile weighing 170 pounds a distance of nearly two hundred yards. His navy cost a fortune because warships were now larger than triremes, requiring hundreds of men as crews. Elephants, employed for their shock effect when charging enemy troops, were also extremely costly to maintain.

Hellenistic kings had to create large administrations to collect the revenues they needed. Initially, they recruited mostly Greek and Macedonian immigrants to fill high-level administrative posts to carry out royal orders. Following Alexander the Great's example, however, the Seleucids and the Ptolemies also employed non-Greeks in the middle and lower levels of their administrations, where it was necessary for officials to be able to deal with the subject populations and speak their languages. Local men who aspired to a government career

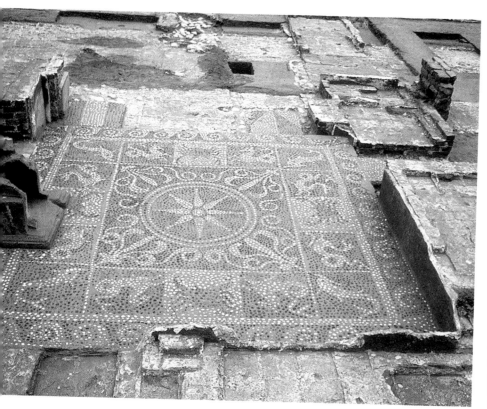

Mosaic Floor from Ai Khanoum

This mosaic floor was excavated at the site of a city founded by Greeks and Macedonians in Afghanistan about 300 B.C.; since its original name is unknown, it is referred to by its modern one, Ai Khanoum. Like the other cities that Alexander the Great and the successor kings founded in the Near East and Asia, this one was built to serve as a defense point and an administrative center. To try to make its immigrant population feel more at home, the Greeks designed its buildings to replicate the Greek way of life, far from the homeland. Decorating floors with designs constructed from pebbles or colored pieces of stone was a favorite technique for giving visual interest to a room, while also providing a very durable surface. Paul Bernard/Hellenisme et Civilizations Orientales.

bettered their chances if they learned to read and write Greek in addition to their native language. This bilingualism qualified them to fill positions communicating the orders of the highest-ranking officials, all Greeks and Macedonians, to the indigenous farmers, builders, and crafts producers. Even if non-Greeks had successful careers in government, however, only rarely were they admitted to the highest ranks of royal society because Greeks and Macedonians generally saw themselves as too superior to mix with locals. For this reason, Greeks and non-Greeks tended to live in separate communities.

Administrators' principal jobs were to maintain order and to direct the kingdoms' tax systems. In many ways the goals and structures of Hellenistic royal administrations recalled those of the earlier Assyrian, Babylonian, and Persian empires. Officials kept order among their kingdoms' subjects by mediating between disputing parties whenever possible, but they could call on soldiers to serve as police if necessary. The very complex Ptolemaic royal administration was based on methods of central planning and control inherited from much earlier periods of Egyptian history. Officials continued to administer royal monopolies, such as that on vegetable oil, to maximize the king's revenue. They also decided how much land farmers should sow in oil-bearing plants, supervised production and distribution of the oil, and set prices for every stage of the oil business. The king, through his officials, also often entered into partnerships with private investors to produce more revenue.

Cities and Urban Elites. Cities were the economic and social hubs of the Hellenistic kingdoms. Many Greeks and Macedonians lived in new cities founded by Alexander and the Hellenistic kings in Egypt and the Near East, and they also moved to old cities. Hellenistic kings promoted this urban immigration to build a constituency supportive of their policies. They adorned their new cities with the traditional features of classical Greek city-states, such as gymnasia and theaters. The price of these amenities was dependence on the king. Although these cities often retained the political institutions of the *polis,* such as councils and assemblies for citizen men, the requirement to follow royal policy limited their freedom; they certainly made no independent decisions on international affairs. In addition, the cities also often had to pay taxes directly to the king.

Interior of the Council House at Priene
Priene, an ancient Ionian city in western Anatolia that had fallen on hard times, was refounded as a planned community in the time of Alexander the Great in the later fourth century B.C. Inside the city's wall, streets followed a grid pattern aligned with the points of the compass. The agora (central gathering area and market) was at the center of the grid, flanked by public buildings such as the council house (bouleuterion) on a rectangular plan. The council house had an altar at its center and seats for several hundred. Residential areas abutted the public center.
Scala/Art Resource, NY.

The reemergence of monarchy therefore severely circumscribed the self-sufficiency and independence of the traditional Greek *polis.* At the same time, it created a new relationship between rulers and the social elites because the crucial factor in the organization of the Hellenistic kingdoms was the system of mutual rewards by which the kings and their leading urban subjects became partners in government and public finance. The kings treated the cities considerately because they needed the goodwill of the wealthiest and most influential city dwellers—the Greek and Macedonian urban elites—to keep order in the cities and ensure a steady flow of tax revenues. Wealthy people had the crucial responsibility of collecting taxes from the surrounding countryside as well as from their city and sending the money on to the royal treasury; the royal military and administration, despite their size and cost, were too small to perform all these duties themselves. The kings honored and flattered the members of the cities' social elites to secure their help. When writing to a city's council, therefore, the king would express himself in the form of a polite request; the recipients knew he expected his wishes to be fulfilled as if they were commands.

This system continued the Greek tradition of the wealthy elite making contributions for the common good in a new way, through the social interaction of the kings and the urban upper classes. Cooperative cities received gifts from the king to pay for expensive public works like theaters and temples or rebuilding after natural disasters such as earthquakes. The wealthy men and women of the urban elite in turn helped keep the general population peaceful by subsidizing teachers and doctors, constructing public works, and providing donations and loans that secured a reliable supply of grain to feed the city's residents.

This organizational system also required the kings to establish relationships with well-to-do non-Greeks living in the old, established cities of Anatolia and the Near East, such as Sardis, Tyre, and Babylon. The kings had to develop cordial relations with the leading citizens of such cities because they could not keep their vast kingdoms peaceful and profitable without the help of local elites. In addition, non-Greeks and non-Macedonians from eastern regions began moving westward to the new Hellenistic Greek cities in increasing numbers. Jews in particular moved from Palestine to Anatolia, Greece, and Egypt. The Jewish community eventually became an influential minority in Egyptian Alexandria, the most important Hellenistic city. In Egypt the king also had to come to terms with the priests who controlled the temples of the traditional Egyptian gods because the temples owned large tracts of rich land worked by tenant farmers.

The Layers of Hellenistic Societies

Hellenistic society in the eastern Mediterranean world was clearly divided into separate layers. The royal family and the king's friends topped the hierarchy. The Greek and Macedonian elites of the major cities ranked next. Just under them came the indigenous wealthy elites of the cities, the leaders of large minority urban populations, and the traditional lords and princes of local groups who maintained their ancestral domains in more rural regions.

Lowest of the free population were the masses of small merchants, artisans, and laborers. Slaves remained where they had always been, outside the bounds of society. (See "Taking Measure," page 139.)

The growth of the kingdoms apparently increased the demand for slave labor throughout the eastern Mediterranean: the centrally located island of Delos established a market where up to ten thousand slaves a day were bought and sold. The fortunate ones would be chosen as servants for the royal court and would live physically comfortable lives, so long as they pleased their owners; the luckless ones would toil, and often die, in the mines. Enslaved children often were taken far from home and set to work; for example, a sales contract from 259 B.C. shows that Zeno, to whom the camel trader wrote, bought a girl about seven years old named Sphragis ("Gemstone") to put her to work in an Egyptian textile factory. This was not her first job: originally from Sidon in the Levant, she had previously been the slave of a Greek mercenary soldier employed by Toubias, a Jewish cavalry commander in the Transjordan region.

The Poor. Even with power based in the cities, most of the population continued to live where people always had—in small villages in the countryside. Poor people performed the overwhelming bulk of the labor required to support the economies of the Hellenistic kingdoms. Agriculture remained the economic base, and conditions for farmers and field workers changed little over time. Many worked on the royal family's huge agricultural estates, but around cities that retained their countryside, free peasants still worked their own small plots as well as the larger farms of wealthy landowners. Rural people rose with the sun and began working before the heat became unbearable, raising the same kinds of crops and animals as their ancestors had with the same simple hand tools. Perhaps as many as 80 percent of all adult men and women, free as well as slave, had to work the land to produce enough food to sustain the population. In the cities, poor women and men could work as small merchants, peddlers, and artisans, producing and selling goods such as tools, pottery, clothing, and furniture. Men could sign on as deckhands on the merchant ships that sailed the Mediterranean Sea and Indian Ocean.

Poverty often meant hunger, even in fertile lands such as Egypt. Papyrus documents reveal, for

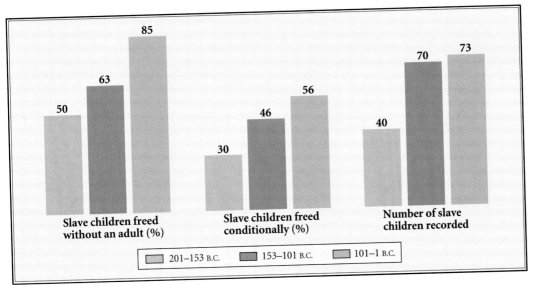

TAKING MEASURE Records of Slave Children Freed at Delphi, 201–1 B.C.
*Inscriptions from the temple of Apollo at Delphi in central Greece in the Hellenistic period record
the prices that slaves paid to obtain their freedom, either fully or conditionally (being freed conditionally, which was less expensive, meant the former slave still had to work for his or her former
owner until the latter's death). The records reveal that from 201 to 1 B.C., more and more children
remained in slavery even after their parents had bought their own freedom. Since the increasing
demand for slaves to work on large estates in Italy in this period made prices for slaves rise, it seems
that many slave parents could not afford to buy their children's freedom until years after they had
purchased freedom for themselves.*
Source: Adapted from Keith Hopkins, *Conquerors and Slaves: Sociological Studies in Roman History* (Cambridge:
Cambridge University Press, 1978), 166, Table III.6. Reprinted with permission of Cambridge University Press.

example, that villagers at Kerkeosiris in the late second century B.C. had enough food for about 2,200
calories each per day in grain, supplemented by an
unknown amount of lentils, onions, and other vegetables. They thus risked not getting adequate daily
nourishment: physically active adults require about
2,500 to 3,600 or more calories depending on size,
gender, and the intensity of their activity. Slaves
in the American South in 1860, by comparison,
received an average of 4,185 calories on a diet of
mostly corn and pork, while the general United
States population in 1879 consumed about 3,741
calories every day.

In the Seleucid and Ptolemaic kingdoms, a large
portion of the rural population existed in a state of
dependency somewhere between free and slave. The
"peoples," as they were called, farmed the estates belonging to the king, who owned the most land in
the kingdom. The peoples were not landowners but
compulsory tenants. Although they could not be
sold like slaves, they were not allowed to move away

or abandon their tenancies. They owed a certain
quota of produce per area of land to the king, similar to rent to a landlord. The rent was sufficiently
heavy that these tenant farmers had virtually no
chance of improving their economic lot in life.

Conditions for Women. The social and political
status of women in the Hellenistic world depended
on the social layer to which they belonged. Hellenistic queens, like their Macedonian predecessors,
commanded enormous riches and received honors
commensurate with their elevated rank. They usually exercised power only to the extent that they
could influence their husbands' decisions, but they
ruled on their own when no male heir existed. Because the Ptolemaic royal family observed the
Egyptian royal tradition of brother-sister marriage,
daughters as well as sons could rule. For example,
Arsinoe II (c. 316–270 B.C.), the daughter of
Ptolemy I, first married the Macedonian successor
king Lysimachus, who gave her four towns as her

personal domain. After Lysimachus's death she married her brother Ptolemy II of Egypt and exerted at least as much influence on policy as he did. The virtues publicly praised in a queen reflected traditional Greek values for women. When the city of Hierapolis around 165 B.C. passed a decree in honor of Queen Apollonis of Pergamum, for example, it praised her piety toward the gods, her reverence toward her parents, her distinguished conduct toward her husband, and her harmonious relations with her "beautiful children born in wedlock."

Some queens paid special attention to the condition of women. About 195 B.C., for example, the Seleucid queen Laodice gave a ten-year endowment to the city of Iasus in southwestern Anatolia to provide dowries for needy girls. That Laodice funded dowries shows that she recognized the importance to women of controlling property, the surest guarantee of a certain respect and a measure of power in their households.

Most women still remained under the control of men. "Who can judge better than a father what is to his daughter's interest?" remained the dominant creed of fathers with daughters; once a woman married, *husband* and *wife's* replaced *father* and *daughter's* in the creed. Most of the time, elite women continued to live separated from men outside of their families; poor women still worked in public. Greeks continued to abandon infants they could not or would not raise—girls more often than boys—but other populations, such as the Egyptians and the Jews, did not practice abandonment, or exposure, as it is often called. Exposure differed from infanticide because the parents expected someone else to find the child and rear it, albeit usually as a slave. The third-century B.C. comic poet Posidippos overstated the case by saying, "A son, one always raises even if one is poor; a daughter, one exposes, even if one is rich." Daughters of wealthy parents were not usually abandoned, but it has been estimated that up to 10 percent of other infant girls were.

In some limited ways, however, women achieved greater control over their own lives in the Hellenistic period. The rare woman of exceptional wealth could enter public life, for example, by making donations or loans to her city and being rewarded with an official post in her community's government. Such posts were less prestigious and important than in the days of the independent city-

Egyptian Style Statue of Queen Arsinoe II
Arsinoe II (c. 316–270 B.C.), daughter of Alexander's general Ptolemy, was one of the most remarkable women of the Hellenistic period. After surviving twenty-five years of political turmoil, dynastic intrigue, and family murders, she married her brother Ptolemy II to unify the monarchy. Hailed as Philadelphoi *("Brother-Loving"), the couple set a precedent for brother-sister marriages in the Macedonian dynasty, the Ptolemies, that ruled Egypt until the death of Cleopatra VII in 30 B.C. Arsinoe was the first Ptolemaic ruler whose image was placed in Egyptian temples as a "temple-sharing goddess." This eight-foot-tall, red granite statue portrays her in the traditional sculptural style of the pharaohs.*
Vatican Museums.

states, because the king and his top administrators now controlled the real power. In Egypt, women acquired greater say in the conditions of marriage because contracts, the standard procedure, gradually evolved from an agreement between the groom and the bride's parents to one in which the bride made her own arrangements with the groom.

The Wealthy. During the Hellenistic period, the wealthy showed increasing concern for the welfare of the less fortunate. In this, they were following the example of the royal families, who emphasized philanthropy as part of their cultivation of an image of great generosity befitting kings and queens. On the island of Samos, for example, wealthy citizens funded a foundation to pay for distributing free grain to all the citizens so that food shortages would no longer trouble their city. State-sponsored schools for educating children, often funded by wealthy donors, also sprang up in various Hellenistic cities. In some places, girls as well as boys could attend school. Many cities also began ensuring the availability of doctors by sponsoring their practices: patients still had to pay for medical attention, but at least they could count on finding a doctor.

The donors who made these services possible were paid back by the respect and honor they earned from their fellow citizens. Philanthropy even touched international relations occasionally. When an earthquake devastated Rhodes, many cities joined kings and queens in sending donations to help the Rhodians recover. In return, the Rhodians showered honors on their benefactors by appointing them to prestigious municipal offices and erecting highly visible inscriptions expressing the city's gratitude. In this system, the welfare of the masses depended more and more on the generosity and goodwill of the rich; without democracy, the poor had no political power to demand reforms. This strongly hierarchical arrangement reflected the "top-down" structure of society characteristic of the Hellenistic age.

The End of the Hellenistic Kingdoms

All the Hellenistic kingdoms and their peoples eventually fell to the Romans. The trouble began when Philip V (238–179 B.C.), descendant of Antigonus and king of Macedonia, made a treaty in 215 B.C. to help Hannibal of Carthage in a war against Rome (the Second Punic War); after the Romans won in 201 B.C., they sent an army to take revenge on Philip. Repeatedly drawn into the squabbles of the city-states to try to create peace on their eastern frontier, Rome dominated Macedonia and Greece militarily by the middle of the second century B.C. Smaller powers, such as the city-state of Rhodes and the Attalid kings in Pergamum, convinced the Romans that preserving their safety required them to intervene farther east in the Mediterranean as a counterbalance to the Seleucid and Ptolemaic kingdoms. Despite losses of territory and troubles from both internal uprisings and external enemies, the

Seleucid kingdom remained a power in the Near East until its final part fell to the Romans in 64 B.C.

The Ptolemaic kingdom in Egypt survived the longest. Eventually, however, its royal family split into warring factions, and the resulting disunity and weakness forced the Egyptian kings to summon Roman support against rivals. The end came when the famous queen Cleopatra, a descendant of Ptolemy and the last Macedonian to rule Egypt, chose the losing side in the civil war between Mark Antony and the future emperor Augustus in the late first century B.C. An invading Roman army ended her reign and the long succession of Ptolemaic rulers in 30 B.C. In this way, Rome became the heir to all the Hellenistic kingdoms (Map 4.3).

❖ Hellenistic Culture

Hellenistic culture reflected three principal characteristics of the age: the overwhelming impact of royal wealth, a concentration on private rather than public matters, and the increased interaction of diverse peoples. In keeping with the era's hierarchical trends, the kings almost single-handedly determined developments in literature, art, science, and philosophy—depending on what fields and what scholars and artists they supported financially. Their status as sole rulers and the source of law meant that authors and artists did not have freedom to criticize public policy and thus concentrated on individual emotion and aspects of private life. Still, royal patronage did produce an expansion and diversification of knowledge.

Cultural interaction between Greek and Near Eastern traditions happened most prominently in language and religion. These developments eventually became extremely influential in Roman culture; in this way, "captive Greece captured its fierce victor," as the Roman poet Horace (65–8 B.C.) expressed the effect of Hellenistic culture on his own.

The Arts under Royal Patronage

The Hellenistic kings became the patrons of scholarship and the arts on a vast scale, competing with one another to lure the best scholars and artists to their capitals with lavish salaries and other benefits. They spent money in this way because they wanted to increase the international reputation of their courts by having these famous people produce books, poems, sculpture, and other prestigious creations under their patronage. This expenditure paid for many intellectual innovations, but for little applied technology except for military use.

The Ptolemies assembled the Hellenistic world's most intellectually distinguished court by turning Alexandria into the Mediterranean's leading center of the arts. There they established the world's first scholarly research institute. Its massive library had the ambitious goal of trying to collect all the books (that is, manuscripts) in the world; it grew to hold a half-million scrolls, an enormous number for the time. Linked to it was a building in which the hired scholars dined together and produced encyclopedias of knowledge such as *The Wonders of the World* and *On the Rivers of Europe* by Callimachus, a learned prose writer as well as a poet. The name of this building, the Museum (meaning "place of the Muses," the Greek goddesses of learning and the arts), is still used to designate institutions that preserve and promote knowledge. The output of the Alexandrian scholars was prodigious. Their champion was Didymus (c. 80–10 B.C.), nicknamed "Brass Guts" for his indefatigable writing of nearly four thousand learned books; it is a sad commentary on the poor preservation rate of ancient sources that not a single one has survived.

Literature Turns Inward. The writers and artists whom Hellenistic kings paid necessarily had to please their patrons with their works. The poet Theocritus (c. 300–260 B.C.), for example, relocated from his home in Syracuse to the Ptolemaic court. In a poem expressly praising his patron, Ptolemy II, he spelled out the quid pro quo of Hellenistic literary patronage: "The spokesmen of the Muses [that is, poets] celebrate Ptolemy in return for his benefactions." Poets such as Theocritus succeeded by avoiding political subjects and stressing the division in society between the intellectual elite—to which the kings belonged—and the uneducated masses. Their poetry centered on individual emotions and broke new ground in demanding great intellectual effort as well as emotional engagement from the audience. Only people with a deep literary education could appreciate the allusions and complex references to mythology that these poets employed in their elegant poems.

Theocritus was the first Greek poet to express the divide between town and countryside, a poetic stance corresponding to a growing Hellenistic reality. The *Idylls*, his pastoral poems, emphasized the discontinuity between the environment of the city and the bucolic life of the country dweller, reflecting the fundamental social division of the Ptolemaic kingdom between the food consumers of the town and the food producers of the countryside. He presented a city dweller's idealized dream that country life must be peaceful and stress-free; this fiction deeply influenced later literature.

None of the women poets known from the Hellenistic period seem to have enjoyed royal patronage. They excelled in writing epigrams, a style of short poems originally used for funeral epitaphs. Elegantly worded poems written by women from diverse regions of the Hellenistic world—Anyte of Tegea in the Peloponnese, Nossis of Locri in southern Italy, Moero of Byzantium—still survive. Women, from courtesans to respectable matrons, figured as frequent subjects in their work and expressed a wide variety of personal feelings, love above all. Nossis's poem on the power of Eros, for example, proclaimed, "Nothing is sweeter than Eros. All other delights are second to it—from my mouth I spit out even honey. And this Nossis says: whoever Aphrodite has not kissed knows not what sort of flowers are her roses." No Hellenistic literature better conveys the depth of human emotion than the epigrams of women poets.

The Hellenistic theater, too, largely shifted its focus to stories of individual emotion; no longer did dramatists offer open critiques of politics or contemporary leaders, as they had in the Classical Greek theater. Comic dramatists like Menander (c. 342–289 B.C.) now presented plays with timeless plots concerning the trials and tribulations of fictional lovers. These comedies of manners, as they are called, proved enormously popular because, like modern situation comedies, they offered a humorous view of situations and feelings that occur in daily life. Recent papyrus finds have allowed us to recover almost complete plays of Menander, the most famous Hellenistic playwright, and to appreciate his subtle skill in depicting human personality. He presented his first comedy at Athens in 324 or 323 B.C. (See "New Sources, New Perspectives," page 144.) Almost no tragedy written in this period has survived, but we know that Hellenistic tragedy could take a multicultural approach: Ezechiel, a Jew living in Alexandria, wrote *Exodus*, a tragedy in Greek about Moses leading the Hebrews out of captivity in Egypt.

Human Expression in Sculpture and Painting. Like their literary contemporaries, Hellenistic sculptors and painters featured human emotions prominently in their works. Classical artists had consistently imbued their subjects' faces with a serenity that represented an ideal rather than reality. Numerous examples, usually surviving only in later copies, show that Hellenistic artists tried to depict individual emotions more naturally in a variety of types. In portrait sculpture, Lysippus's famous bust of Alexander the Great captured the young commander's passionate dreaminess. A sculpture from Pergamum (right) by an unknown artist commemorated the third-century B.C. Attalid victory over the plundering Gauls (one of the Celtic peoples from what is now France) by showing a defeated Gallic warrior stabbing himself after having killed his wife to prevent her enslavement by the victors. A large-scale painting of Alexander battling with the Persian king Darius (see page 131) portrayed Alexander's intense concentration and Darius's horrified expression. The artist, who was probably either Philoxenus of Eretria or a Greek woman from Egypt named Helena (one of the first female artists known), used foreshortening and strong contrasts between shadows and highlights to accentuate the emotional impact of the picture.

To appreciate fully the appeal of Hellenistic sculpture, we must remember that, like earlier Greek sculpture, it was painted in bright colors. But Hellenistic art differed from classical art in its social context. Works of classical art had been commissioned by the city-states for public display or by wealthy individuals to donate to their city-state as a work of public art. Now sculptors and painters created their works more and more as commissions from royalty and from the urban elites who wanted to show they had artistic taste like their social superiors in the royal family. The increasing diversity of subjects that emerged in Hellenistic art presumably represented a trend approved by kings, queens, and the elites. Sculpture best reveals this new preference for depiction of humans in a wide variety of poses, mostly from private life (again in contrast

Dying Celts
Hellenistic artists excelled in portraying deeply emotional scenes, such as this murder-suicide of a Celtic warrior who is in the act of slaying himself after killing his wife, to prevent their capture by the enemy after defeat in battle. Celtic women followed their men to the battlefield and willingly exposed themselves to the same dangers. The original of this composition was in bronze, forming part of a large sculptural group that Attalus I, king of Pergamum from 241 to 197 B.C., set up on his acropolis to commemorate his defeat around 230 B.C. of the Celts, called Galatians, who had moved into Anatolia in the 270s B.C. to conduct raids throughout the area. It is striking that Attalus celebrated his victory by erecting a monument portraying the defeated enemy as brave and noble.
Erich Lessing/Art Resource, NY.

Papyrus Finds and Menander's Comedies

Fourth-century B.C. Greece invented the kind of comedy that lives on as the most popular form of humor on today's most common entertainment medium—television sitcoms. In the aftermath of the Peloponnesian War, Greek authors began creating comic plays that concentrated on the conflicts between human personality types as they suffered through the trials and tribulations of daily life, especially the rocky course of love and marriage. Forsaking the bawdy political satire characteristic of earlier Greek comedy, playwrights now penned comic stories for the stage featuring stereotyped characters such as addled lovers, cantankerous fathers, rascally servants, and boastful soldiers. Confusions of identity leading to hilarious misunderstandings were a regular plot device, while jokes about marriage were a staple; typical were one-liners such as

FIRST MAN: "He's married, you know."
SECOND MAN: "What's that you say? Actually married? How can that be? I just left him alive and walking around!" (Antiphanes, fragment 221 Koch)

The comedies' titles hinted at their approach and tone: *The Country Boob, Pot-Belly, The Stolen Girl, The Bad-Tempered Man.*

By the end of the fourth century, these comedies had become wildly popular; audiences wanted no more of explicit political comedy. Greek comic plays about daily life and social mix-ups inspired many imitations, especially Roman comedies, which eventually inspired William Shakespeare (1564–1616) in England and Molière (1622–1673) in France; comedies like theirs in turn eventually led to today's sitcoms.

The most successful and famous author of this form of Greek comedy was Menander (343–291 B.C.) of Athens. Ancient critics ranked him as "second only to Homer" for the quality of his po-

Pompeian Wall Painting of Menander
Four centuries after Menander's death, a wealthy Roman commissioned this painting of the playwright for a wall in his house at Pompeii, near Naples. Evidently the owner meant to proclaim his love for Greek drama because the room's other walls — now very damaged — were probably decorated with images of the tragedian Euripides and possibly the Muses of Tragedy and Comedy. This figure was identified by faded lettering on the scroll: "Menander: he was the first to write New Comedy." The ivy wreath on his head symbolizes the poet's victory in the contests of comedies presented at the festivals of the god Dionysus, the patron of drama.
Scala/Art Resource, NY.

etry and praised him as "a mirror of life" for his plots. Despite antiquity's unanimous "two thumbs up" for Menander's comedies, however, none of them survived into modern times in the way other ancient works did. That is, works of Greek and Roman literature had to be slowly recopied over and over by hand for centuries if they were not to disappear, until finally the invention of the printing press in the fifteenth century made mass production of books possible. For unknown reasons, people at some point stopped recopying Menander's comedies (as well as those of his contemporaries in this genre), and his works seemed lost to us forever. Therefore, until quite recently, although we knew Menander had been a star, we could not read the material that had made him so famous.

This situation changed dramatically when scholars began finding ancient paper—papyrus—that survived buried in the dry sands of Egypt. In antiquity, Egyptians had processed the reeds of the papyrus plant to make a thick, brownish paper for writing down everything from literature to letters to tax receipts. When papyrus texts were damaged or no longer needed, they were thrown out with the garbage or used to wrap mummies to help preserve the dried-out corpses for the afterlife. The super-arid climate of the Egyptian desert kept this waste paper from rotting away. By excavating ancient Egyptian trash dumps and unwrapping mummies, scholars have now found thousands and thousands of pieces of ancient papyrus containing texts of all kinds.

Script on Papyrus
The script on this papyrus fragment by Menander rates as very clear compared with the more crabbed handwriting often found in such texts. Its condition is also remarkably good, with only small gaps. Reconstructing a text from small papyrus fragments is like assembling a giant jigsaw puzzle without any guide to what it should look like.

Incredibly, these discoveries have returned Menander to us from more than two thousand years ago: over the last several decades, painstaking study of often severely damaged papyrus sheets has uncovered texts of his comedies. When the so-called Bodmer Papyrus proved to contain a nearly complete copy of *The Bad-Tempered Man,* we could once again enjoy a Menander comedy for the first time since antiquity. Further detective work has yielded more, and today we can also read most of *The Girl from Samos* and parts of other plays. In this way, Menander's memorable and influential characters, stories, and jokes have been restored from the dead.

Rediscovering ancient comedy (or any other kind of writing) on papyrus is challenging. The handwriting on the papyrus is often crabbed and difficult to decipher, there are no gaps between words, punctuation is minimal at best, changes in speakers are indicated just by colons or dashes rather than by names, and there are no stage directions. The papyrus can be burned or torn into pieces or pierced by holes chewed by mice and insects. One part of a play can turn up in the wrapping of one mummy and another part in a different one. Incompletely preserved scenes and lines can be hard to understand.

The hard work required to make sense of papyrus texts pays off wonderfully, however, with discoveries like those that recovered Menander's comedies. In this case, the collaboration of archaeologists, historians, and literary scholars has brought back to life the distant beginnings of what remains our most enduring and crowd-pleasing form of comedy.

QUESTIONS FOR DEBATE

1. What makes situation comedy so appealing?
2. Why would Greeks living in the fourth century B.C. prefer situation comedy to political satire or darker forms of humor?

FURTHER READING

Roger Bagnall, *Reading Papyri, Writing Ancient History.* 1995.

Menander: Plays and Fragments. Translated with an introduction by Norma Miller. 1987.

Richard Parkinson and Stephen Quirke, *Papyrus.* 1995.

Praxiteles' Statue of Aphrodite

The Athenian sculptor Praxiteles, whose career spanned approximately 375 – 330 B.C., became internationally renowned for his marble statues. He excelled at making stone resemble the softness of flesh and producing perfect surface finishes, which he employed the painter Nicias to embellish with color. His masterpiece was the Venus made for the city-state of Cnidos in southwestern Anatolia; the original is lost, but many Roman-era copies of the type illustrated here were made. The statue was displayed in a colonnaded, circular shrine set in a garden; it was the first time that the goddess of love had been portrayed completely nude. Gossips spread the rumor that Praxiteles had used his lover Phryne as his model for the world-famous statue.
Nimatallah/Art Resource, NY.

with classical art). Hellenistic sculptors portrayed subjects never before shown: foreigners (such as the dying Gaul), drunkards, battered athletes, wrinkled old people. The female nude became a particular favorite. A statue of Aphrodite, which Praxiteles sculpted completely nude as an innovation in depicting this goddess, became so renowned as a religious object and tourist attraction in the city of Cnidos, which had commissioned it, that the king of Bithynia later offered to pay off the citizens' entire public debt if he could have the work of art. They refused.

Philosophy for a New Age

New philosophies arose in the Hellenistic period, all asking the same question: what is the best way for humans to live? They recommended different paths to the same answer: individual humans must attain personal tranquillity to achieve freedom from the turbulence of outside forces, especially chance. For Greeks in particular, the changes in political and social life accompanying the rise to dominance of the Macedonian and, later, the Hellenistic kings made this focus necessary. Outside forces in the persons of aggressive kings had robbed the city-states of their freedom of action internationally, and the fates of city-states as well as individuals now rested in the hands of distant, often capricious monarchs. More than ever before, human life and opportunities for free choice seemed poised to career out of the control of individuals. It therefore made sense, at least for those wealthy enough to spend time philosophizing, to look for personal, private solutions to the unsettling new conditions of life in the Hellenistic age.

Few Hellenistic thinkers concentrated on metaphysics. Instead they focused on philosophical materialism, a doctrine asserting that only things made up of matter truly existed. It therefore denied the concept of soul that Plato described and ignored any suggestion that such nonmaterial phenomena could exist. Hellenistic philosophy was regularly divided into three related areas: *logic*, the process for discovering truth; *physics*, the fundamental truth about the nature of existence; and *ethics*, the way humans should achieve happiness and well-being as a consequence of logic and physics. The era's philosophical thought greatly influenced Roman thinkers and, thus, the many important Western philosophers who in turn later read their works.

Epicureanism. One of the two most significant new philosophical schools of thought was Epicureanism. It took its name from its founder, Epicurus (341–271 B.C.), who about 307 B.C. settled his followers in Athens in a house amidst a verdant garden (hence "the Garden" as the name of his school). Under Epicurus the study of philosophy assumed a social form that broke with tradition, because he admitted women and slaves as regular members of his group. His lover, the courtesan Leontion, became well known for her treatise criticizing the views of Theophrastus (c. 370–285 B.C.), Aristotle's most famous pupil.

People should above all be free of worry about death, Epicurus taught. Because all matter consists of microscopic atoms in random movement, death is nothing more than the painless separating of the body's atoms. Moreover, all human knowledge must be empirical, that is, derived from experience and perception. Phenomena that most people perceive as the work of the gods, such as thunder, do not result from divine intervention in the world. The gods live far away in perfect tranquillity, paying no attention to human affairs. People therefore have nothing to fear from the gods, in life or in death.

Epicurus believed people should pursue pleasure, but his notion of true pleasure had a special definition: he insisted that it consisted of an "absence of disturbance" from pain and the everyday turbulence, passions, and desires of ordinary existence. A sober life spent in the society of friends apart from the cares of the common world could best provide this essential peace of mind. His teaching represented a serious challenge to the traditional ideal of Greek citizenship, which required men of means to participate in local politics and citizen women to engage in public religious cults.

Stoicism. Stoicism, the other important new Hellenistic philosophy, recommended a less isolationist path for individuals. Its name derived from the Painted Stoa in Athens, where Stoic philosophers discussed their doctrines. Zeno (c. 333–262 B.C.) from Citium on Cyprus founded Stoicism, but Chrysippus (c. 280–206 B.C.) from Cilicia in Anatolia did the most to make it a comprehensive guide

to life. Stoics believed that life was fated but that people should still make the pursuit of virtue their goal. Virtue, they said, consisted of putting oneself in harmony with the divine, rational force of universal Nature by cultivating the virtues of good sense, justice, courage, and temperance. These doctrines applied to women as well as men. In fact, the Stoics advocated equal citizenship for women and doing away with the conventions of marriage and families as the Greeks knew them. Zeno even proposed unisex clothing as a way to obliterate unnecessary distinctions between women and men.

The belief that everything that happened was fated created the question of whether humans truly have free will. Employing some of the subtlest reasoning ever applied to this fundamental issue, Stoic philosophers concluded that purposeful human actions did have significance. Nature, itself good, did not prevent vice from occurring, because virtue would otherwise have no meaning. What mattered in life was the striving for good, not the result. A person should therefore take action against evil by, for example, participating in politics. To be a Stoic also meant to shun desire and anger while enduring pain and sorrow calmly, an attitude that yields the modern meaning of the word *stoic*. Through endurance and self-control, adherents of Stoic philosophy attained tranquillity. They did not fear death because they believed that people lived over and over again infinitely in identical fashion to their present lives. This repetition would occur as the world would be destroyed by fire periodically and then re-formed after the conflagration.

Competing Philosophies. Numerous other philosophies emerged in the Hellenistic period to compete with the two leading schools. Some of these philosophies carried on the work of earlier giants such as Plato and Pythagoras. Still others struck out in idiosyncratic directions. Skeptics, for example, aimed at the same state of personal imperturbability as did Epicureans, but from a completely different premise. Following the doctrines of Pyrrho (c. 360–270 B.C.) from Elis in the Peloponnese, they believed that secure knowledge about anything was impossible because the human senses yield contradictory information about the world. All people can do, they insisted, is depend on appearances while suspending judgment about their reality. Pyrrho's thought had

Gemstone Showing Diogenes in His Jar

This engraved gem from the Roman period shows the famous philosopher Diogenes (c. 412–324 B.C.) living in a large storage jar and having a discussion with a man who holds a scroll. Diogenes was born at Sinope on the Black Sea but was exiled in a dispute over monetary fraud; he spent most of his life at Athens and Corinth, becoming famous as the founder of Cynic ("doglike") philosophy. He espoused an ascetic life of poverty ruled by nature, not law or tradition. His "shamelessness" in defying social convention was said to be the lifestyle of a dog, hence the name given to his philosophical views and the dog usually shown beside him in art, as in this engraving.
Thorvaldsen Museum, Copenhagen.

been influenced by the Indian ascetic wise men (the magi) he met while a member of Alexander the Great's entourage. The basic premise of skepticism inevitably precluded any unity of doctrine.

Cynics ostentatiously rejected every convention of ordinary life, especially wealth and material comfort. They believed that humans should aim for complete self-sufficiency. Whatever was natural was good and could be done without shame before anyone; according to this idea, even public defecation and fornication were acceptable. Women and men alike were free to follow their sexual inclinations. Above all, Cynics were to disdain the pleasures and luxuries of a comfortable life. The most famous early Cynic, Diogenes (d. 323 B.C.) from Sinope on the Black Sea, was reputed to wear borrowed clothing and sleep in a big storage jar. Almost as notorious was Hipparchia, a Cynic of the late fourth century B.C. She once bested an obnoxious philo-

sophical opponent named Theodorus the Atheist with the following argument: "That which would not be considered wrong if done by Theodorus would also not be considered wrong if done by Hipparchia. Now if Theodorus strikes himself, he does no wrong. Therefore, if Hipparchia strikes Theodorus, she does no wrong." The name *Cynic*, which meant "like a dog," reflected the common evaluation of this ascetic and unconventional way of life.

Greek philosophy in the Hellenistic period reached a wider audience than ever before. Although the working poor had neither the leisure nor the resources to attend philosophers' lectures, the more affluent members of society studied philosophy in growing numbers. Theophrastus lectured to crowds of up to two thousand in Athens. Most philosophy students continued to be men, but women could now join the groups attached to certain philosophers. Kings competed to attract famous thinkers to their courts, and Greek settlers took their interest in philosophy with them, even to the most remote Hellenistic cities. Archaeologists excavating a city located thousands of miles from Greece on the Oxus River in Afghanistan, for example, turned up a Greek philosophical text as well as inscriptions of moral advice imputed to Apollo's oracle at Delphi.

Innovation in the Sciences

Scientific investigation of the physical world became a specialty separate from philosophy in the Hellenistic period. Science so benefited from its widening divorce from philosophical schools that historians have called this era the Golden Age of ancient science. Various factors contributed to a flourishing of thought and discovery: the expeditions of Alexander had encouraged curiosity and increased knowledge about the extent and differing features of the world, royal patronage supported scientists financially, and the concentration of scientists in Alexandria promoted a fertile exchange of ideas that could not otherwise have taken place.

Advances in Geometry and Mathematics. The greatest advances came in geometry and mathematics. Euclid, who taught at Alexandria around 300 B.C., made revolutionary progress in the analysis of two- and three-dimensional space. The utility of Euclidean geometry still endures. Archimedes of

Syracuse (287–212 B.C.) was a mathematical genius who calculated the approximate value of pi and devised a way to manipulate very large numbers. He also invented hydrostatics (the science of the equilibrium of a fluid system) and mechanical devices such as a screw for lifting water to a higher elevation. Archimedes' shout of delight "I have found it" (*heureka* in Greek) when he solved a problem while soaking in his bathtub has been immortalized in the modern expression "Eureka!"

The sophistication of Hellenistic mathematics affected other fields that also required complex computation. Aristarchus of Samos early in the third century B.C. became the first to propose the correct model of the solar system: he argued that the earth revolved around the sun, which he also identified as being far larger and far more distant than it appeared. Later astronomers rejected Aristarchus's heliocentric model in favor of the traditional geocentric one (with the earth at the center) because calculations based on the orbit he calculated for the earth failed to correspond to the observed positions of celestial objects. Aristarchus had made a simple mistake: he had assumed a circular orbit instead of an elliptical one. Eratosthenes of Cyrene (c. 275–194 B.C.) pioneered mathematical geography. He calculated the circumference of the earth with astonishing accuracy by simultaneously measuring the length of the shadows of widely separated but identically tall structures. The basic ideas and procedures of these Hellenistic researchers gave Western scientific thought an important start toward the essential process of reconciling theory with observed data through measurement and experimentation.

Scientific Discoveries. Hellenistic science maintained a spirit of discovery despite the enormous difficulties imposed by technical limitations. Rigorous scientific experimentation was not possible because no technology existed for the precise measurement of very short intervals of time. Measuring tiny quantities of matter was also next to impossible. The science of the age was as quantitative as it could be given these limitations. Ctesibius of Alexandria (b. c. 310 B.C.), a contemporary of Aristarchus, invented the scientific field of pneumatics by creating machines operated by air pressure. He also built a working water pump, an organ powered by water, and the first accurate water clock. A later Alexandrian, Hero, continued the Hellenistic tradition of mechanical ingenuity by building a rotating sphere powered by steam. As in most of Hellenistic science, these inventions did not lead to viable applications in daily life. The scientists and their royal patrons were more interested in new theoretical discoveries than in practical results, and the metallurgical technology to produce the pipes, fittings, and screws needed to build powerful machines did not yet exist.

Military technology was the one area in which Hellenistic science produced noteworthy applications. The kings hired engineers to design powerful catapults and wheeled siege towers many stories high, which were capable of battering down the defenses of walled cities. The most famous large-scale application of technology for nonmilitary purposes was the construction of a lighthouse three hundred feet tall (the Pharos) for the harbor at Alexandria. Using polished metal mirrors to reflect the light from a large bonfire, it shone many miles out over the sea. Awestruck sailors regarded it as one of the wonders of the world.

The Origins of Anatomy. Medicine also benefited from the thirst for new knowledge characteristic of Hellenistic science. The increased contact between Greeks and people of the Near East in this period

Bronze Astronomical Calculator
These fragments of a Hellenistic bronze astronomical calculator were discovered underwater in an ancient shipwreck off Anticythera, below the Peloponnese in southern Greece. The device was being transported to Italy in the early first century B.C. as part of a shipment of metalwork and other valuable objects. The product of sophisticated applied engineering and astronomical knowledge, it used a complex set of intermeshed gears, turned by hand, to control rotating dials that indicated the position of celestial phenomena.
National Archaeological Museum, Athens. Archaeological Receipts Fund.

made the medical knowledge of the ancient civilizations of Mesopotamia and Egypt better known in the West and gave an impetus to the study of human health and illness. Around 325 B.C., Praxagoras of Cos discovered the value of measuring the pulse in diagnosing illness. A bit later, Herophilus of Chalcedon (b. c. 300 B.C.), working in Alexandria, became the first scientist in the West to study anatomy by dissecting human cadavers and, it was rumored, condemned criminals while they were still alive; he had access to these subjects because the king authorized his research. Some of the anatomical terms Herophilus invented are still used. Other Hellenistic advances in understanding anatomy included the discovery of the nerves and nervous system.

As in science, however, Hellenistic medicine was limited by its inability to measure and observe phenomena not visible to the naked eye. Unable to see what really occurred under the skin in living patients, for example, doctors thought many illnesses in women were caused by displacements of the womb, which they wrongly believed could move around in the body. These mistaken ideas could not be corrected because the technology to evaluate them was absent.

A New East-West Culture

Wealthy non-Greeks increasingly adopted Greek habits as they adapted to the new social hierarchy of the Hellenistic world. Diotimus of Sidon, for example, took a Greek name and pursued the premier Greek sport, chariot racing. He traveled to Nemea in the Peloponnese to enter his chariot in the race at the prestigious festival of Zeus. He announced his victory in an inscription written in Greek, which had become the language of international commerce and culture in the Hellenistic world. The explosion in the use of the Greek language in the form called *koine* ("shared" or "common") reflected the emergence of an international culture based on Greek models; this was the reason that the Egyptian camel trader stranded in Syria had to communicate in Greek with a high-level official such as Zeno. The most striking evidence of this cultural development comes from Afghanistan. There, King Ashoka (r. c. 268–232 B.C.), who ruled most of the Indian subcontinent, used Greek as one of the languages in his public inscriptions to announce his

efforts to introduce his subjects to Buddhist traditions of self-control, such as abstinence from eating meat. Local languages did not disappear in the Hellenistic kingdoms, however. In one region of Anatolia, for example, people spoke twenty-two different languages. This sort of diversity remained the norm in the world that the Hellenistic kings ruled.

Transformations in Religion. The diversity of religious practice matched the variety of so many other areas of Hellenistic life. The traditional cults of Greek religion remained very popular, but new cults, such as those that deified ruling kings, responded to changing political and social conditions. Preexisting cults that previously had only local significance, such as that of the Greek healing deity Asclepius or the mystery cult of the Egyptian goddess Isis, grew prominent all over the Hellenistic world. In many cases, Greek cults and local cults from the eastern Mediterranean influenced each other. Their beliefs meshed well because their cults shared many assumptions about how to remedy the troubles of human life. In other instances, local cults and Greek cults existed side by side, with some overlap. The inhabitants of villages in the Fayum district of Egypt, for example, continued worshiping their traditional crocodile god and mummifying their dead according to the old ways but also paid homage to Greek deities. In the tradition of polytheistic religion, people could worship in both old and new cults.

New cults picked up a prominent theme of Hellenistic thought: a concern for the relationship between the individual and what seemed the controlling, unpredictable power of the divinities Luck and Chance. Although Greek religion had always addressed randomness at some level, the chaotic course of Greek history since the Peloponnesian War had made human existence appear more unpredictable than ever. Since advances in astronomy revealed the mathematical precision of the celestial sphere of the universe, religion now had to address the seeming disconnection between that heavenly uniformity and the shapeless chaos of life on earth. One increasingly popular approach to bridging that gap was to rely on astrology for advice deduced from the movement of the stars and planets, thought of as divinities. Another very common choice was to worship Tyche (Chance) as a god in the hope of securing good luck in life.

The most revolutionary approach in seeking protection from the capricious tricks of Chance or Luck was to pray for salvation from deified kings, who enjoyed divine status in what are known as *ruler cults*. Various populations established these cults in recognition of great benefactions. The Athenians, for example, deified the Macedonians Antigonus and his son Demetrius as savior gods in 307 B.C., when they liberated the city and bestowed magnificent gifts on it. Like most ruler cults, this one expressed both spontaneous gratitude and a desire to flatter the rulers in the hope of obtaining additional favors. Many cities in the Ptolemaic and Seleucid kingdoms instituted ruler cults for their kings and queens. An inscription put up by Egyptian priests in 238 B.C. concretely described the qualities appropriate for a divine king and queen:

> *King Ptolemy III and Queen Berenice, his sister and wife, the Benefactor Gods, . . . have provided good government . . . and [after a drought] sacrificed a large amount of their revenues for the salvation of the population, and by importing grain . . . they saved the inhabitants of Egypt.*

As these words make clear, the Hellenistic monarchs' tremendous power and wealth gave them the status of gods to the ordinary people who depended on their generosity and protection in times of danger. The idea that a human being could be a god, present on earth to be a "savior" delivering people from evils, was now firmly established and would prove influential later in Roman imperial religion and Christianity.

Healing divinities offered another form of protection to anxious individuals. Scientific Greek medicine had rejected the notion of supernatural causes and cures for disease ever since Hippocrates had established his medical school on the Aegean island of Cos in the late fifth century B.C. Nevertheless, the cult of Asclepius, who offered cures for illness and injury at his many shrines, grew popular during the Hellenistic period. Suppliants seeking Asclepius's help would sleep in special dormitories at his shrines to await dreams in which he prescribed healing treatments. These prescriptions emphasized diet and exercise, but numerous inscriptions set up by grateful patients also testified to miraculous cures and surgery performed while the sufferer slept. The following example is typical:

> *Ambrosia of Athens was blind in one eye. . . . She . . . ridiculed some of the cures [described in inscriptions in the sanctuary] as being incredible and impossible. . . . But when she went to sleep, she saw a vision; she thought the god was standing next to her. . . . He split open the diseased eye and poured in a medicine. When day came she left cured.*

People's faith in divine healing gave them hope that they could overcome the constant danger of illness, which seemed to strike at random.

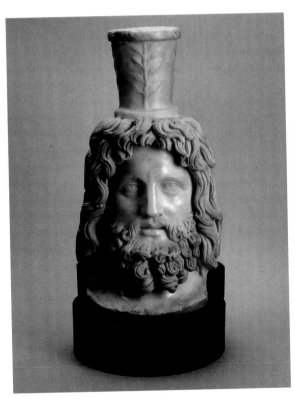

Bust of the Greco-Egyptian God Sarapis
This marble head was found in a Roman-era temple in England, demonstrating the enduring and widespread appeal of this deity. Originally an Egyptian conjunction of Osiris, the consort of Isis, and the sacred Apis bull, Sarapis was adopted in the early Hellenistic period by the Ptolemaic royal family as its patron god guaranteeing their rule. Eventually, the cult of Sarapis was spread around the Hellenistic world by groups of devotees who met for worship and feasting. They identified him as a transcendent god combining the powers of Zeus with those of other divinities and looked to him for miracles. He was commonly portrayed with a food container or measure on his head, as here, to signify his concern for human prosperity in this world and in the afterlife. Museum of London Photographic Library.

IMPORTANT DATES

399 B.C.   Trial and execution of Socrates at Athens

390s–370s B.C.   Sparta attacks city-states in Anatolia and Greece

386 B.C.   Sparta makes a peace with Persia ceding control over the Anatolian Greek city-states; the philosopher Plato founds the Academy in Athens

371 B.C.   Thebes defeats Sparta at the battle of Leuctra in Boeotia

359 B.C.   Philip II becomes Macedonian king and successfully reorganizes the army

338 B.C.   Philip II defeats a Greek alliance at the battle of Chaeronea to become the leading power in Greece

336 B.C.   Philip II is murdered; Alexander becomes king

335 B.C.   The philosopher Aristotle founds the Lyceum in Athens

334 B.C.   Alexander leads an army of Greeks and Macedonians against the Persian empire

331 B.C.   Alexander takes Egypt and founds Alexandria

326 B.C.   Alexander's army mutinies at the Hyphasis River in India

324 or 323 B.C.   The dramatist Menander presents his first comedy at Athens

323 B.C.   Alexander dies in Babylon

c. 307 B.C.   The philosopher Epicurus founds "the Garden" in Athens

306–304 B.C.   The successors of Alexander declare themselves to be kings

263–241 B.C.   Eumenes I founds the independent Attalid kingdom in Anatolia

239–130 B.C.   Independent Greek kingdom in Bactria

214–205 B.C.   Philip V, king of Macedonia, fights the Second Punic War against Rome

167 B.C.   Jewish revolt in Jerusalem

64 B.C.   Rome takes over the last part of the Seleucid empire

30 B.C.   Death of Cleopatra VII, queen of Egypt, and takeover of the Ptolemaic empire by Rome

Mystery cults proffered secret knowledge as a key to worldly and physical salvation. The cults of the Greek god Dionysus and, in particular, the Egyptian goddess Isis gained many followers in this period. The popularity of Isis, whose powers ex-

tended over every area of human life, received a boost from King Ptolemy I, who established a headquarters for her cult in Alexandria. He also refashioned the Egyptian deity Osiris in a Greek mold as the new god Sarapis, whose job was to serve as Isis's consort. Sarapis reportedly performed miracles of rescue from shipwreck and illness. The cult of Isis, who became the most popular female divinity in the Mediterranean, involved extensive rituals and festivals incorporating features of Egyptian religion mixed with Greek elements. Disciples of Isis apparently hoped to achieve personal purification as well as the aid of the goddess in overcoming the sometimes demonic influence of Chance on human life. That an Egyptian deity like Isis could achieve enormous popularity among Greeks (and Romans in later times) alongside the traditional gods of Greek religion is the best evidence of the cultural cross-fertilization of the Hellenistic world.

Hellenistic Judaism.   The history of Judaism in the Hellenistic period shows especially striking evidence of cultural interaction. King Ptolemy II had the Hebrew Bible translated into Greek (the Septuagint) in Alexandria in the early third century B.C. Many Jews, especially those living in the large Jewish communities that had grown up in Hellenistic cities outside Palestine, adopted the Greek language and many aspects of Greek culture. Nevertheless, these Hellenized Jews largely retained the ritual practices and habits of life that defined traditional Judaism, and they refused to worship Greek gods. Hellenistic politics also affected the Jewish community in Palestine, which was controlled militarily and politically first by the Ptolemies and then by the Seleucids. Both allowed the Jews to live according to their ancestral tradition under the political leadership of a high priest in Jerusalem.

Internal dissension among Jews erupted in second-century B.C. Palestine over the amount of Greek influence that was compatible with traditional Judaism. The Seleucid king Antiochus IV (r. 175–163 B.C.) intervened in the conflict in support of an extreme Hellenizing faction of Jerusalem Jews, who had taken over the high priesthood. In 167 B.C., Antiochus converted the main Jewish temple there into a Greek temple and outlawed the practice of Jewish religious rites, such as observing the Sabbath and circumcision. A revolt led by Judah

MAPPING THE WEST Dissolution of the Hellenistic World, to 30 B.C.

By 30 B.C. (the death of Cleopatra VII, the last Ptolemaic monarch of Egypt), the Roman republic had conquered or absorbed the Hellenistic kingdoms of the eastern Mediterranean. Competition for the tremendous wealth that this expansion captured helped fuel bitter and divisive feuds between Rome's most ambitious generals and political leaders. This territory became the eastern half of the Roman Empire, with only minor changes in extent over time.

the Maccabee eventually won Jewish independence from the Seleucids after twenty-five years of war. The most famous episode of this revolt was the retaking of the Jerusalem temple and its rededication to the worship of the Jewish god, Yahweh: a triumphant moment commemorated by Jews ever since on the holiday of Hanukkah. That Greek culture attracted some Jews in the first place, however, provides a striking example of the transformations that affected many—though far from all—people of the Hellenistic world. By the time of the Roman Empire, one of those transformations would be Christianity, whose theology had roots in the cultural interaction of Hellenistic Jews and Greeks and their ideas on apocalypticism and divine human beings.

Conclusion

Between about 400 and 325 B.C.—the three-quarters of a century following the Peloponnesian War—the Classical period for Greece came to an end. The violence and bitterness of the war and its aftermath led ordinary people as well as philosophers to question the basis of morality. The characteristic disunity of Greek international politics proved disastrous because the Macedonian kingdom developed aggressive leaders, Philip II (r. 359–336 B.C.) and Alexander the Great (r. 336–323 B.C.), who made themselves the masters of the squabbling city-states to their south. Inspired by Greek heroic ideas, Alexander the Great conquered the entire Persian empire and set in motion the momentous political, social, and cultural changes of the Hellenistic period.

When Alexander's generals transformed themselves into Hellenistic kings, they not only made use of the governmental structures they found already established in the lands they conquered but also added an administrative system staffed by Greeks and Macedonians. Local elites as well as Greeks and Macedonians cooperated with the Hellenistic monarchs in governing and financing their society, which was divided along hierarchical ethnic lines. To enhance their image of magnificence, the kings and queens of the Hellenistic world supported writers, artists, scholars, philosophers, and scientists, thereby encouraging the distinctive energy of Hellenistic intellectual life. The traditional city-states continued to exist in Hellenistic Greece, but their freedom extended only to local affairs; their foreign policy was constrained by the need to stay on good terms with powerful monarchs.

The diversity of the Hellenistic world encompassed much that was new, especially because cultural interaction between different peoples was more common than ever before. An inevitable outgrowth of the greater opportunities created by change and diversity was an added anxiety about the role of chance in life. In response, people looked to new religious experiences to satisfy their yearning for protection from perils. In the midst of so much novelty, however, the most fundamental elements of the ancient world remained unchanged—the labor, the poverty, and the necessarily limited horizons of the mass of ordinary people working in its fields, vineyards, and pastures.

What did change was the culture of Rome once it came into close contact with the fertile traditions of the Hellenistic kingdoms that it replaced as the Mediterranean's dominant political state. That rise to power, however, took centuries because Rome originated as a tiny, insignificant place that no one except Romans ever expected to amount to anything on the world stage.

Suggested References

The Decline of Classical Greece, c. 400–350 B.C.

Fortunately, we have good ancient sources on which to base our history of the frequent wars and shifting alliances among Greek city-states in the fourth century B.C. Moreover, the works of Plato and Aristotle, unlike those of many ancient authors, have survived almost intact so that we can study their thought in detail.

Adcock, F. E. *The Greek and Macedonian Art of War.* 1957.

Barnes, Jonathan. *Aristotle.* 1982.

Garnsey, Peter. *Ideas of Slavery from Aristotle to Augustine.* 1996.

Gosling, J. C. B. *Plato.* 1973.

Greek archaeology: http://archnet.uconn.edu/regions/europe.php3.

Hornblower, Simon. *The Greek World, 479–323 B.C.* 1983.

McKechnie, Paul. *Outsiders in the Greek Cities in the Fourth Century B.C.* 1989.

Strauss, Barry S. *Athens after the Peloponnesian War: Class, Faction, and Policy, 403–386 B.C.* 1986.

Tritle, Lawrence A., ed. *The Greek World in the Fourth Century: From the Fall of the Athenian Empire to the Successors of Alexander.* 1997.

The Rise of Macedonia, 359–323 B.C.

In 1977, Manolis Andronicos greatly enhanced our knowledge of ancient Macedonia by discovering the rich tombs of the royal family in the time of Philip, Alexander, and the successor kings, but dispute still rages over the identification of who was buried where. Scholars are also energetically debating Alexander's character; for Bosworth, for example, he was a natural-born killer, while O'Brien sees him as overcome by alcoholism.

Andronicos, Manolis. *Vergina: The Royal Tombs and the Ancient City.* 1989.

Borza, Eugene N. *In the Shadow of Olympus: The Emergence of Macedon.* 1990.

Bosworth, A. B. *Alexander and the East: The Tragedy of Triumph.* 1996.

———. *Conquest and Empire: The Reign of Alexander the Great.* 1988.

Ellis, J. R. *Philip II and Macedonian Imperialism.* 1976.

Ginouvès, René, ed. *Macedonia: From Philip II to the Roman Conquest.* 1994.

Green, Peter. *Alexander of Macedon, 356–323 B.C. A Historical Biography.* 1991.

Hamilton, J. R. *Alexander the Great.* 1973.

Macedonian royal tombs at Vergina: http://alexander.macedonia.culture.gr/2/21/211/21117a/e211qa07.html.

O'Brien, John Maxwell. *Alexander the Great, the Invisible Enemy: A Biography.* 1992.

Roisman, Joseph. *Alexander the Great: Ancient and Modern Perspectives.* 1995.

The Hellenistic Kingdoms, 323–30 B.C.

Recent research, especially that of Susan Sherwin-White and Amélie Kuhrt, stresses the innovative responses of the successor kings to the challenges of ruling multicultural empires. Underwater archaeology has begun to reveal ancient Alexandria in Egypt, whose harbor district has sunk below the level of today's Mediterranean Sea.

Bowman, Alan K. *Egypt after the Pharaohs: 332 B.C.–A.D. 642.* 1986.

The Cambridge Ancient History. 2nd ed. Vol. 7, pt. 1, *The Hellenistic World.* 1984.

Cartledge, Paul, and Antony Spawforth. *Hellenistic and Roman Sparta: A Tale of Two Cities.* 1989.

Ellis, Walter M. *Ptolemy of Egypt.* 1994.

Empereur, Jean-Yves. *Alexandria Rediscovered.* 1998.

Grainger, John D. *Seleukos Nikator: Constructing a Hellenistic Kingdom.* 1990.

Grant, Michael. *From Alexander to Cleopatra: The Hellenistic World.* 1982.

Green, Peter. *Alexander to Actium: The Historical Evolution of the Hellenistic Age.* 1990.

Habicht, Christian. *Athens from Alexander to Antony.* Trans. Deborah Lucas Schneider. 1997.

Lewis, Naphtali. *Greeks in Ptolemaic Egypt.* 1986.

Ptolemaic Egypt: http://www.houseofptoley.org.

Sherwin-White, Susan, and Amélie Kuhrt. *From Samarkhand to Sardis: A New Approach to the Seleucid Empire.* 1993.

Tarn, W. W. *Hellenistic Civilisation.* 3rd ed. Rev. G. T. Griffith. 1961.

Hellenistic Culture

Modern scholarship has rejected the old view that Hellenistic culture was decadent and "impure" because it mixed Greek and Near Eastern tradition and therefore was less valuable and interesting than Classical Greek culture. Instead, scholars now tend to identify the imaginative ways in which Hellenistic thinkers and artists combined the old and the new, the familiar and the foreign. Studying Hellenistic philosophers for the intrinsic interest of their ideas has become common, for example, as opposed to seeing them merely as inferior successors to Plato and Aristotle.

Ancient Alexandria in Egypt: http://pharos.bu.edu/Egypt/Alexandria.

Cartledge, Paul, et al., eds. *Hellenistic Constructs: Essays in Culture, History, and Historiography.* 1997.

Green, Peter, ed. *Hellenistic History and Culture.* 1993.

Gruen, Erich S. *Heritage and Hellenism: The Reinvention of Jewish Tradition.* 1998.

Hellenistic artifacts: http://www.museum.upenn.edu/greek_World/Land_time/Hellenistic.html.

Koester, Helmut. *Introduction to the New Testament:* Vol. 1, *History, Culture, and Religion of the Hellenistic Age.* 1982.

Long, A. A. *Hellenistic Philosophy: Stoics, Epicureans, Sceptics.* 2nd ed. 1986.

Martin, Luther. *Hellenistic Religions: An Introduction.* 1987.

Mikalson, Jon D. *Religion in Hellenistic Athens.* 1998.

Momigliano, Arnaldo. *Alien Wisdom: The Limits of Hellenization.* 1975.

Phillips, E. D. *Greek Medicine.* 1973.

Pollitt, J. J. *Art in the Hellenistic Age.* 1986.

Pomeroy, Sarah B. *Women in Hellenistic Egypt: From Alexander to Cleopatra.* Rev. ed. 1990.

Ridgway, Brunilde Sismondo. *Hellenistic Sculpture I: The Styles of ca. 331–200 B.C.* 1990.

Schäfer, Peter. *Judeophobia: Attitudes toward the Jews in the Ancient World.* 1997.

Sharples, R. W. *Stoics, Epicureans, and Sceptics: An Introduction to Hellenistic Philosophy.* 1996.

Snyder, Jane M. *The Woman and the Lyre: Women Writers in Classical Greece and Rome.* 1989.

Tcherikover, Victor. *Hellenistic Civilization and the Jews.* Trans. S. Applebaum. 1975.

Walbank, F. W. *The Hellenistic World.* Rev. ed. 1992.

White, K. D. *Greek and Roman Technology.* 1984.

Witt, R. E. *Isis in the Greco-Roman World.* 1971.

The Rise of Rome

c. 753–44 B.C.

Temple of Castor and Pollux in the Roman Forum
One of the most prominent temples in the center of Rome, this building was originally constructed in the forum in the fifth century B.C. to honor the divine twins Castor and Pollux for their help in battle. It was rebuilt several times; the remains seen today date to the time of Augustus (c. 27 B.C.–A.D. 14). The temple served important state functions: the Senate often met inside, and it held the official standards for weights and measures as well as treasuries for the emperors and wealthy individuals. Its architectural detail is famous for its elegance; notice the sculpted capitals atop the forty-feet-high columns.
Sonia Halliday Photographs.

THE ANCIENT ROMANS TREASURED the many legends describing their state's long and often violent transformation from a tiny village to a world power. They especially loved stories about their legendary first king, Romulus, who was remembered as a hot-tempered but shrewd leader. According to the legend later known as the "Rape of the Sabine Women," Romulus's Rome was a community so tiny that it lacked enough women to bear children to increase its population and help defend it from enemies. The king therefore asked the surrounding peoples of central Italy for permission for his subjects to intermarry with them. Everyone turned him down, scorning Rome's poverty and weakness. Enraged, Romulus hatched a plan to use force where diplomacy had failed. Inviting the neighboring Sabines to a festival honoring the gods, he had his men kidnap the unmarried women and fight off their relatives' frantic attempts at rescue. The kidnappers promptly married the women, fervently promising to cherish them as beloved wives and new citizens. When the neighbors' armies returned to attack Rome, the women rushed into the midst of the bloody battle, begging their brothers, fathers, and new husbands either to stop slaughtering one another or to kill them to end the war. The men immediately made peace and agreed to merge their populations under Roman rule.

This legend emphasizes that Rome, unlike the city-states of Greece, expanded by absorbing outsiders into its citizen body, sometimes violently, sometimes peacefully. Rome's growth became the ancient world's most dramatic expansion of population and territory, as a people originally housed in a few huts gradually created a state that

753 B.C.	509 B.C.	400 B.C.	275 B.C.	160 B.C.	44 B.C.

Politics and War

Traditional date of Rome's founding

First Punic war between Rome and Carthage

Civil war; Caesar the victor

Roman Republic established

Caesar appointed dictator; assassinated by republican "liberators"

Rome begins to expand its power outside Italy

Society and Economy

Creation of the Twelve Tables, Rome's first written laws

Struggle of the orders

Roman imperialism leads to social unrest

Rome becomes the richest and most powerful Mediterranean society

Culture, Religion, and Intellectual Life

Romans follow Greek models in religion and education

Livius Andronicus writes Latin poetry, the first Roman literature

Plautus and Terence compose Roman "situation comedies" based on Greek models

Cato writes the first Roman history in Latin

Cicero becomes renowned for his Latin oratory and rhetorical system

swallowed up most of Europe, North Africa, Egypt, and the eastern Mediterranean lands. The social, cultural, political, legal, and economic traditions that Roman society and government developed in ruling this vast area created closer interconnections between its diverse peoples than ever before or since. Unlike the Greeks and Macedonians, the Romans maintained the unity of their state for centuries. Alexander the Great's conquests won him everlasting fame as the ancient world's most fearless hero, but even he failed to equal the Romans in affecting the course of Western civilization: the history of Europe and its colonies, including the United States, has deep roots in Rome.

Roman culture sprang from the traditions of ancient Italy's many peoples, but Greek literature, art, and thought profoundly influenced the culture of Rome as the once tiny village grew into a world power. This does not mean that Romans mindlessly took over the traditions of the older civilization and changed them only in superficial ways, such as giving Latin names to Greek gods. As is always true in cross-cultural influence, whatever they took over from other people they adapted to their own purposes in complex ways. That is, they changed what they took to suit themselves and thus made it their own. It is more accurate to think of the cross-cultural contact that so deeply influenced Rome as a kind of competition in innovation between equals rather than as imagining Greek culture to have been "superior" and improving "inferior" Roman culture. Romans, like other ancient peoples, learned from their neighbors, but they determined their own cultural identity.

The kidnapping legend belongs to the earliest period of Rome, when kings ruled (c. 753–509 B.C.), but the most important history of Rome falls into two major periods of about five hundred years each—the republic and the empire. These terms refer only to the system of government in place at the time: under the republic (founded 509 B.C.), an oligarchy dominated by the elite governed; under the empire, monarchs once again ruled. Rome's greatest expansion came during the republic. The confidence that fueled this amazing process came above all from Romans' belief in a divine destiny: the gods willed that the Romans should rule the world by military might and law and improve it through social and moral values. Their unshakable faith that heaven backed them is illustrated by the foundation legend in which the earliest Romans used a religious festival as a ruse to kidnap women. Their firm belief that values should drive politics showed in their determination to persuade the captives that loyalty and love would wipe out the crime that had forcibly turned them into wives and Romans.

In addition to the devotion to family that this story implies, Roman values under the republic emphasized selfless service to the community, individual honor and public status, the importance of the laws, and shared decision making. By the late republic, these values seriously conflicted with one another, especially when powerful and successful individuals placed their personal and family interests ahead of the common good. During most of the republic, these conflicts never became fierce enough to threaten Rome's stability. By the first century B.C., however, power-hungry politician-generals such as Sulla and Julius Caesar had plunged Rome into civil war and destroyed the republic by putting their personal ambition before the good of the state.

❖ Social and Religious Traditions

To understand the history of the Roman republic, we need always to keep in mind the social and religious institutions that shaped the attitudes and behaviors of the Romans. They self-consciously saw their lives as governed by eternal moral and social values interconnecting them in complex ways and by their duties to and support from the gods. Hi-

erarchy touched every aspect of their lives: in society, people related to one another as patron or client, each with obligations to the other; in families, power was distributed unequally; in religion, the magnificent superiority of the gods meant that people had to pray for their favor for the protection of the community and the family. The Roman value system provided the foundation for all these institutions.

Roman Values

Romans believed that the values by which they lived had been handed down from ancient times. They referred to those values as *mos maiorum*, "the way of the ancestors." The Romans treasured their values' antiquity because, for Romans, *old-fashioned* meant "good" and *newfangled* meant "dangerous." Roman morality emphasized what we might in very broad terms call uprightness, faithfulness, and respect; status was the valuable reward for right conduct. These values took many particular forms, depending on the context, and often they overlapped. In their most significant forms, they concerned relationships with others and with the gods.

Uprightness largely defined how a person related to others. In the second century B.C., the Roman poet Lucilius defined this as *virtue*:

Virtue is to know the human relevance of each
  thing,
To know what is humanly right and useful and
  honorable,
And what things are good and what are bad, useless, shameful, and dishonorable. . . .
Virtue is to pay what in reality is owed to honorable status
To be an enemy and a foe to bad people and bad
  values
But a defender of good people and good values. . . .
And, in addition, virtue is putting the country's
  interests first,
Then our parents', with our own interests third
  and last.

Faithfulness had many forms, for women as well as for men. Basically, it meant to keep one's obligations no matter the cost, whether the obligation was formal or informal. To fail to meet an obligation was to offend the community and the gods.

"A Mother's Gift"

This engraved bronze urn, cast near the end of the fourth century B.C. and decorated with scenes from the story of the Argonauts seeking the Golden Fleece, held toiletries and personal articles. Two inscriptions indicate who crafted it, who bought it, and why: "Novios Plautus made me in Rome" and "Dindia Malconia gave this to her daughter." Containers made of metal, which was expensive, ranked as luxury items, so Dindia and her child were obviously wealthy. Alainari/Art Resource, NY.

Faithful women remained virgins before marriage and monogamous afterward. Men demonstrated faithfulness by never breaking their word, paying their debts, and treating everyone with justice— which did not mean treating everyone the same, but rather treating them appropriately according to whether they were equal, superior, or inferior.

Respect was an even more multifaceted concept. In some ways, faithfulness (*fides,* from which our word *fidelity* derives) was one aspect of respect. Showing devotion to the gods and to one's family was the supreme form of this value. Women and men alike respected the superior authority of the gods and of the elders and ancestors of their families. Performing religious rituals properly and regularly was also crucial. Maintaining the divine favor protecting the community required that Romans faithfully and piously worship the gods. Respect for

one's self as an upright person demanded that each person maintain self-control and limit displays of emotion. So strict was this expectation that not even wives and husbands could kiss in public without seeming emotionally out of control. It also meant that a person should never give up no matter how hard the situation. Persevering and adhering to duty under all conditions were thus basic Roman values.

The reward for living these values was status. Women earned respect most of all by bearing legitimate children and educating them morally; their reward was a good reputation. Rewards for men included concrete honors, especially election to high public office and public commemoration of their military bravery and other contributions to the common good. A man who had earned very high status commanded so much respect that others would obey him regardless of whether he exercised formal power over them. A man with this much prestige was said to enjoy "authority."

Finally, Romans believed that family lineage had a bearing on a person's values. High birth therefore was a two-edged sword. It automatically entitled a person to greater status, but at the same time it imposed a harsher standard for measuring up to the demands of the Roman system of values. In theory, wealth had nothing to do with moral virtue. Over time, however, money became overwhelmingly important to the Roman elite, not to hoard but to spend in displays of conspicuous consumption, social entertainments, and public gifts to the community. In this way, wealth became intertwined with status. By the later centuries of the Roman republic, ambitious men required ample sums of money to buy respect, and they became more willing to trample on other values to acquire wealth and the status it now conveyed. Thus did the Romans come to have values that did not always harmonize.

The Patron-Client System

The differences in status so key in Roman society were institutionalized in the patron-client system. Under this pervasive system, Roman society developed an interlocking network of personal relationships that obligated people to one another morally and legally. A patron was a man of superior status who could provide *benefits,* as they were called, to those people of lower status who paid him special attention. These were his clients, who in return for benefits owed him *duties*. Both sets of obligations centered on financial and political help to the other party. The system's hierarchy had multiple levels: a patron of others was often himself the client of a more distinguished man. The Romans spoke of the hierarchy as "friendship"—with clearly defined roles for each party. A sensitive patron would greet a social inferior as "my friend," not as "my client." A client, however, would honor his superior by addressing him as "my patron."

Benefits and duties took various forms. A patron might help a client get started in a political career by supporting his candidacy or might provide gifts or loans in hard times. A patron's most important obligation was to support a client and his family if they got into legal difficulties, such as lawsuits involving property, which were common. Clients had to aid their patrons' campaigns for public office by swinging votes their way. They also had to lend money when patrons serving as officials incurred large expenses to provide public works and fund their daughters' lavish dowries. Furthermore, because it was a mark of great status to have numerous clients thronging around like a swarm of bees, a patron expected them to gather at his house early in the morning and accompany him to the forum, the city's public center. A Roman leader needed a large, fine house to hold this throng and to entertain his social equals; a crowded house signified social success.

These mutual obligations were supposed to be stable and long-lasting, enduring over generations. Ex-slaves, who automatically became the clients for life of the masters who freed them, often passed on this relationship to their children. Romans with contacts abroad could acquire clients among foreigners; particularly distinguished and wealthy Romans sometimes had entire foreign communities obligated to them. With its emphasis on duty and permanence, the system epitomized the Roman view that social stability and well-being were achieved by faithfully maintaining the ties that linked people to one another.

The Roman Family

The family was the bedrock institution of Roman society because it taught values and determined the ownership of property. Men and women shared the duty of teaching values to their children, though

by law the father possessed the *patria potestas* ("power of a father") over his children, no matter how old, and his slaves. This power made him the sole owner of all the property acquired by his dependents. As long as he was alive, no son or daughter could own anything, accumulate money, or possess any independent legal standing—in theory at least. In practice, however, adult children could acquire personal property and money, and favored slaves might build up some savings. Fathers also held legal power of life and death over these members of their households, but they rarely exercised this power on anyone except newborns. Abandoning unwanted babies so that they would die, be adopted, or be raised as slaves by strangers was an accepted practice to control the size of families and dispose of physically imperfect infants. Baby girls probably suffered this fate more often than boys— a family enhanced its power by investing its resources in its sons.

Since their values had a strong communal aspect, Romans in private life regularly conferred with others on important family issues to seek a consensus. Each Roman man had a circle of friends and relatives, his "council," whom he consulted before making significant decisions. A man contemplating the drastic decision to execute an adult member of his household, for example, would not have made the decision on his own. A father's council of friends would certainly have advised him to think again if he proposed killing his adult son, except for an extremely compelling reason. One outraged Roman had his son put to death in 63 B.C. because the youth had committed treason by joining a conspiracy to overthrow the government. Such violent exercises of a father's power happened very rarely.

The *patria potestas* did not allow a husband to control his wife because "free" marriages—in which the wife formally remained under her father's power as long as he lived—eventually became the most common. But in the ancient world, few fathers lived long enough to oversee the lives of their married daughters or sons; four out of five parents died before their children reached thirty. A woman without a living father was relatively independent. Legally she needed a male guardian to conduct business for her, but, by the first century B.C., guardianship was largely an empty formality. Upper-class women could even on occasion demonstrate to express their opinions; in 195 B.C., for example, a

Sculpted Tomb of a Family of Ex-Slaves
The husband and wife depicted on this tomb, which may date to the first century B.C., had started life as slaves but gained their freedom and thus became Roman citizens; their son, shown in the background holding a pet pigeon, was a free person. One of the remarkable features of Roman civilization, and a source of its demographic strength, was the wholesale incorporation of ex-slaves into the citizen body. This family had done well enough financially to afford a sculpted tomb; the tablets the man is holding and the carefully groomed hairstyle of the woman are meant to show that their family was literate and stylish.
German Archeological Institute/Madeline Grimoldi.

group of women blocked Rome's streets for days, until the men rescinded a wartime law that had tried to reduce tensions between rich and poor by limiting the amount of gold jewelry and fine clothing women could wear and where they could ride in carriages. A later jurist commented on women's freedom of action: "The common belief, that because of their instability of judgment women are often deceived and that it is only fair to have them controlled by the authority of guardians, seems more specious than true. For women of full age manage their affairs themselves."

Regardless of her legal independence, a woman had to grow up fast in Roman society to assume her duties as teacher of values to her children and manager of her household's resources. Tullia (c. 79–45 B.C.), daughter of the renowned politician and orator Marcus Tullius Cicero (106–43 B.C.), was engaged at twelve, married at sixteen, and widowed by twenty-two. Like any married woman of wealth, she oversaw the household slaves, monitored the nurturing of the young children by wet nurses, kept account books to track the property she personally owned, and accompanied her husband to dinner parties—something a Greek wife never did.

A mother's power in shaping the moral outlook of her children was especially valued in Roman society and constituted a major component of female virtue. Women like Cornelia, a famous aristocrat of the second century B.C., won enormous respect for their accomplishments both in managing property and in raising outstanding citizens. When her distinguished husband died, Cornelia refused an offer of marriage from the Ptolemaic king of Egypt so she could instead oversee the family estate and educate her surviving daughter and two sons. (Her other nine children had died.) The boys, Tiberius and Gaius Gracchus, grew up to be among the most influential and controversial tribunes of the late republic. The number of children she bore exemplified the fertility and stamina required of a Roman wife to ensure the survival of her husband's family line. Cornelia became renowned for entertaining important people and for her stylish letters, which were still being read by the educated public a century later.

Wealthy women like Cornelia could wield political influence, but only indirectly, by expressing their opinions privately to the male members of their families: husbands, male children, and other

Sculpture of a Woman Running a Store
This relief sculpture portrays a woman selling food from behind the counter of a small shop, while customers make purchases or hold a conversation with each other. Since Roman women could own property, it is possible that the woman is the store owner. The man immediately to her right behind the counter could be her husband or a servant. The market areas in Roman towns were packed with small, family-run stores like this that sold everything imaginable, much like malls of today.
Art Resource, NY.

relatives. Marcus Porcius Cato (234–149 B.C.), a famous politician and author, hinted at the limited, behind-the-scenes reality of women's power in public life with a biting comment directed at his fellow leaders: "All mankind rule their wives, we rule all mankind, and our wives rule us."

Women helped themselves and their families by accumulating property in diverse ways, from inheritance to entrepreneurship; recent archaeological discoveries suggest that by the end of the republic some women owned large businesses. Most poor women, like poor men, had to toil for a living; usually they had to settle for small-scale jobs selling vegetables or amulets or colorful ribbons from a stand. Even if women's families produced goods such as furniture or clothing at home, the predominant form of manufacturing in the Roman economy, they normally sold rather than made the products the family manufactured. The men in these families usually worked the raw materials, cutting, fitting, and polishing wood, leather, and metal. Those women with the worst luck or from the poorest families often could earn money only as prostitutes. Prostitution was legal but considered disgraceful. Because both women and men could

control property, prenuptial agreements to outline the rights of both partners in the marriage were common. Legally, divorce was a simple matter, with fathers usually keeping the children.

Education for Public Life

The education of both women and men had the goal of making them exponents of traditional values and, for different purposes, effective speakers. As in Greece, most children received their education in the family; only the well-to-do could afford to pay teachers. Wealthy parents bought literate slaves to tend their children and help with their education; by the late republic, they often chose Greek slaves so their children could be taught to speak that language and read its literary classics, which most Romans regarded as the world's best. Parents might also send their children, from about seven years old, to classes offered by independent schoolmasters in their lodgings. Repetition was the usual teaching technique, with corporal punishment frequently used to keep pupils attentive. In upper-class families, both daughters and sons learned to read; the girls were also taught literature, perhaps some music, and, especially, how to make educated conversation at dinner parties. Another principal aim of the education of women was to prepare them for the important role of instilling traditional social and moral values in their children.

Fathers carefully instructed their sons in masculine values, especially physical training, fighting with weapons, and courage, but the principal aim of a boy's education was to teach him rhetoric—the skill of persuasive public speaking. Rhetorical training dominated an upper-class Roman boy's curriculum because it was crucial to a successful public career. A boy would hear rhetoric in action by accompanying his father, a male relative, or a family friend to public meetings, assemblies, and court sessions. By listening to the speeches, he would learn to imitate winning techniques. Cicero, the most famous orator of the republic, agreed with his brother's advice that young men must learn to "excel in public speaking. It is the tool for controlling men at Rome, winning them over to your side, and keeping them from harming you. You fully realize your own power when you are a man who can cause your rivals the greatest fears of meeting you in a trial."

Wealthy parents paid advanced teachers to instruct their sons in the skills and general knowledge an effective speaker required, the same sort of education that sophists had offered in Greece. Roman rhetoric owed much to Greek techniques, and many Roman orators studied with Greek teachers. When Roman textbooks on rhetoric began to be written in the second century B.C., they reflected material derived from Greek works. This was only one of the crucial ways in which Greek culture influenced Rome.

Religion for Public and Private Interests

As in education, Romans followed Greek models in religion, worshiping many divinities identified directly with those of Greece. Romans viewed their chief deity, Jupiter, who corresponded to the Greek god Zeus, as a powerful, stern father. Juno (Greek Hera), queen of the gods, and Minerva (Greek Athena), goddess of wisdom, joined Jupiter to form the central triad of the state cults. These three deities shared Rome's most revered temple on the Capitoline, its acropolis.

Guarding Rome's physical safety and prosperity was the gods' major function in Roman religion. Above all, they were supposed to help defeat ene-

Household Shrine from Pompeii
This colorfully painted shrine stood inside the entrance to a house at Pompeii known as the House of the Vettii from the name of its owners. Successful businessmen, they spared no expense in decorating their home: with 188 frescoes (paintings done by applying pigments to damp plaster) adorning its walls, the interior blazed in a riot of color. This type of shrine, found in every Roman house, is called a lararium *after the* lares *(deities protecting the household), who are shown here flanking a central figure. He portrays the spirit (genius) of the father of the family. The snake below, which is about to drink from a bowl probably holding milk set out for it, also symbolizes a protective force ("the good daimon"). The whole scene sums up the role Romans expected their gods to play: staving off harm and bad luck.*
Scala/Art Resource, NY.

mies in war, but divine support for agriculture was also indispensable. Many official prayers therefore requested the gods' aid in ensuring good crops, warding off disease, and promoting healthy reproduction for both domestic animals and people. In times of crisis, Romans even sought foreign gods to protect them, such as when the government imported the cult of the healing god Asclepius from Greece in 293 B.C., hoping he would save Rome from a plague. Similarly, in 204 B.C., the Senate voted to bring to Rome the pointed black stone that represented Cybele ("the Great Mother"), whose chief sanctuary was in Phrygia in Asia Minor (the

Roman term for Anatolia). Her cult was believed to promote fertility.

The republic supported many other cults with special guardian features. The shrine of Vesta (Greek Hestia), the goddess of the hearth and therefore a protector of the family, housed the official eternal flame of Rome, which guaranteed the state's permanent existence. The Vestal Virgins, six unmarried women sworn to chastity at age six to ten for terms of thirty years, tended Vesta's shrine. In this cult, female chastity symbolized the safety and protection of the Roman family structure and thus the preservation of the republic itself. As Rome's only female priesthood, the Vestals earned high status and freedom from their fathers' control by performing their most important duty: keeping the flame from going out. As the Greek historian Dionysius of Halicarnassus reported in the first century B.C., "The Romans dread the extinction of the fire above all misfortunes, looking upon it as an omen which portends the destruction of the city." Should the flame happen to go out, the Romans assumed that one of the women had broken her vow of chastity and that a Vestal had to be buried alive as the penalty.

Reverence for the cult of Vesta was only one way in which Roman religion was associated with the family as well as the state. Each family maintained a sacred space in its home for small shrines housing its Penates (spirits of the household stores) and Lares (spirits of the ancestors), who were connected with keeping the family well and its moral traditions alive. The statuettes representing these spirits signified respect for the family's heritage. Upper-class families kept death masks of distinguished ancestors hanging on the walls of the main room in their homes and wore them at funerals to commemorate the ancestral ideals of the family and the current generation's responsibility to live up to those virtuous standards. The strong sense of family tradition instilled by these practices and by instruction from parents (especially mothers) represented the principal source of Roman morality. The shame of losing public esteem by tarnishing this tradition, not the fear of divine punishment, was the strongest deterrent to immoral behavior.

Because Romans believed that divine spirits participated in crucial moments of life, such as birth, marriage, and death, they performed many rituals in search of protection in a world fraught with dangers and uncertainties. Special rituals accompanied activities as diverse and commonplace as breast-feeding babies and fertilizing crops. Many public religious gatherings had the goal of promoting the health and stability of the community. For example, during the February 15 Lupercalia festival (whose name recalled the wolf, *luper* in Latin, who legend said had reared Romulus and his twin, Remus), naked young men streaked around the Palatine hill, lashing any woman they met with strips of goatskin. Women who had not yet borne children would run out to be struck, believing this would help them to become fertile. The December 17 Saturnalia festival, honoring the Italian deity of liberation, Saturnus, temporarily turned the social order topsy-turvy to release tensions caused by the inequalities between masters and slaves. As the playwright and scholar Accius (c. 170–80 B.C.) described the occasion, "People joyfully hold feasts all through the country and the towns, each owner acting as a waiter to his slaves." This inversion of roles reinforced the slaves' ties to their owners by symbolizing a benefit from the latter, which the former had to repay with faithful service.

Like the Greek gods, those of Rome had few direct connections with human morality because Roman tradition did not regard the gods as the originators of the society's moral code. Cicero's description of Jupiter's official titles explained public religion's closer ties to national security and prosperity than to individual morality: "We call Jupiter the Best (*Optimus*) and Greatest (*Maximus*) not because he makes us just or sober or wise but, rather, healthy, unharmed, rich, and prosperous." Therefore, every official action was preceded by "taking the auspices"—seeking Jupiter's approval to proceed by observing natural "signs" such as the direction of the flights of birds, their eating habits, or the appearance of thunder and lightning. Romans embedded their values in religion by regarding abstract moral qualities such as faithfulness (*fides*) as special divine beings or forces. Also regarded as divine was piety (*pietas*), which meant a sense of devotion and duty to family, to friends, to the republic, and to keeping one's word. Rome's temple to *pietas* housed a statue of this moral quality personified as a female divinity in human form. This personification of abstract moral qualities provided a focus for cult rituals. Another revered quality was virtue (*virtus*), a primarily masculine value stressing courage, strength, and loyalty. But *virtus* also included wisdom and moral purity, qualities that members of the social elite were expected to display in their public and private lives. In this broader sense, *virtus* applied to women as well as men. The religious aura attached to the cults of moral qualities emphasized that they were ideals to which every Roman should aspire.

Roman government and public religion were inextricably intertwined: both were intended to serve and defend the community. As in Greek public religion, the duty of priesthoods was to ensure the gods' goodwill toward the state, a crucial relationship the Romans called the *pax deorum* ("peace of/with the gods"). Men and women from the top of the social hierarchy served as priests and priestesses by conducting frequent sacrifices, festivals, and other rituals conforming strictly to ancestral tradition. These people were not professionals devoting their lives solely to religious activity; rather, they were citizens performing public service in keeping with Roman values. The most important official, the *pontifex maximus* ("highest priest"), served as the head of state religion and the ultimate authority on religious matters affecting government; this priesthood's political powers motivated Rome's most prominent men to seek it.

Disrespect for religious tradition brought punishment. Naval commanders, for example, took the auspices by feeding sacred chickens on their ships: if the birds ate energetically before a battle, Jupiter favored the Romans and an attack could begin. In 249 B.C., the commander Publius Claudius Pulcher grew frustrated when his chickens, probably seasick, refused to eat; determined to attack, he finally hurled them overboard in a rage, sputtering, "Well then, let them drink!" When he promptly suffered a huge defeat, he was fined very heavily by a tribunal at Rome.

❖ From Monarchy to Republic, c. 753–287 B.C.

The communal values of Roman social and religious institutions provided the unity and stability necessary for Rome's astounding growth from a tiny settlement into the Mediterranean's greatest power. This process took centuries, as the Romans reinvented their government and expanded their territory and population. Politically, they began with

rule by kings from the eighth through the sixth century B.C., adopting the most common kind of regime in the ancient world. Disturbed by the later kings' violence, members of the social elite overthrew the monarchy to create a new political system that lasted from the fifth through the first century B.C. The republic, from the Latin *res publica* ("the people's matter" or "the public business"), distributed power more widely by providing for election of officials in open meetings of male citizens, though the elite dominated politics. Rome gained land and population by winning aggressive wars and by absorbing others. Its economic and cultural growth depended on contact with many other peoples around the Mediterranean.

The Monarchy, c. 753–509 B.C.

Legend taught that Rome's original government had seven kings, ruling in succession from 753 (the most commonly given date for the city's founding) to 509 B.C.; in truth, little reliable evidence exists for this period and its dates. It does seem clear, however, that the kings created the Senate, a body of advisers chosen from the city's leading men to serve as a personal council, in keeping with the Roman principle that decisions should be thoroughly discussed with one's wisest friends. This remarkable institution endured in the same role—advising government leaders—for two thousand years, as Rome changed from a monarchy to a republic and back to a monarchy (the empire).

The kings also laid the foundation for the city's expansion by fighting enemies and taking in outsiders whom they conquered; this tradition was reflected, for example, in the story of Romulus's plot to kidnap the Sabine women and the eventual absorption of the women's relatives into the Roman state. The policy of assimilating others promoted ethnic diversity in early Rome and contrasted sharply with the exclusionary laws of the contemporary Greek city-states. Another important part of Roman policy—also different from Greek practice—was to grant citizenship to freed slaves. These "freedmen" and "freedwomen," as they were called, still owed special obligations to their former owners, and they could not hold elective office or serve in the army. In all other ways, however, ex-slaves enjoyed full civil rights, such as legal marriage.

MAP 5.1 Ancient Italy, c. 500 B.C.
When the Romans ousted the monarchy to found a republic in 509 B.C., they inhabited a relatively small territory in central Italy between the western coast and the mountain range that bisects the peninsula from north to south. Many different peoples lived in Italy at this time, with the most prosperous occupying fertile agricultural land and sheltered harbors on the peninsula's west side. The early republic's most urbanized neighbors were the Etruscans to the north and the Greeks in the city-states to the south, including on the island of Sicily.

Their children possessed citizenship without any limitations. By the late republic, many Roman citizens were descendants of freed slaves.

Expansion and Cross-Cultural Contact.   Over the 250 years of the monarchy, Rome's inclusionary policy produced tremendous expansion. By around 550 B.C., the Romans controlled three hundred square miles of the area around Rome, called Latium—

enough agricultural land to support a population of thirty thousand to forty thousand people. This growth under the kings foreshadowed Rome's future as a powerful, imperialist state.

The physical factors of geography and contact with other cultures, especially Greek, helped propel the process by which early Rome consistently expanded its population and its territory. The city's location played a large part in its rise to power because it lay at the natural center of both Italy and the Mediterranean world. The historian Livy (59 B.C.– A.D. 17), who became famous for depicting Rome's early history as heroic, summed up the city's geographical advantages: "With reason did gods and men choose this site: all its advantages make it of all places in the world the best for a city destined to grow great." These advantages were fertile farmland, control of a river crossing on the major north–south route in the peninsula, a nearby harbor on the Mediterranean Sea, and—compared with Greece—more open terrain that made political expansion easier, at least physically. Most important, Rome was ideally situated for contact with the outside world. Italy stuck so far out into the Mediterranean that east–west traffic naturally encountered it (Map 5.1).

The early Romans' contact with their neighbors profoundly influenced their cultural development. Ancient Italy was home to a diverse population. The people of Latium were poor villagers like the Romans and spoke the same Indo-European language, an early form of Latin. To the south, however, lived Greeks, and contact with them had the greatest effect on the development of Roman culture. Greeks had established colonies on the Campanian plain as early as the 700s B.C. These settlements, such as Naples, grew prosperous and populous thanks to their location in a fertile area and their participation in international trade. Greek culture reached its most famous flowering in the fifth century B.C., at the time when the republic was just taking shape after the end of the monarchy and centuries before Rome had its own literature or theater or monumental architecture. Romans developed a love-hate relationship with Greece, admiring its literature and art but despising its lack of military unity. They adopted many elements from Greek culture— from ethical values to deities for their national cults, from the model for their poetry and prose to architectural design and style.

Banquet Scene Painted in an Etruscan Tomb
Painted about 480–470 B.C., this brightly colored fresco decorated a wall in an Etruscan tomb (known today as the "Tomb of the Leopards" from the animals painted just above this scene) at Tarquinia. Wealthy Etruscans filled their tombs with pictures such as these, which simultaneously represented the funeral feasts held to celebrate the life of the dead person and also the social pleasures experienced in this life and expected in the next. The banqueters recline on their elbows in Greek style, one of the many ways in which Etruscans were influenced by Hellenic culture; the Greeks themselves had probably adopted their dining customs from Near Eastern precedents.
Scala/Art Resource, NY.

The Etruscans. Cross-cultural influence flowed to Rome also from the Etruscans, a people living north of Rome. The relationship between Etruscan and Roman culture remains a controversial topic. Until recently, scholars viewed Etruscan cultural influence on early Rome as huge, even speculating that Etruscans conquered Rome and dominated it politically in the sixth century B.C. The Etruscans were also seen as more culturally refined than early Romans, mainly because so much Greek art has been found at Etruscan sites; they were therefore assumed to have completely reshaped Roman culture during this period of supposed domination. New scholarship, however, stresses the independence of Romans in developing their own cultural traditions: they borrowed from Etruscans, as from Greeks, whatever appealed to them and revised it to fit their local circumstances.

Etruscan origins and culture remain obscure because their language has not yet been fully deciphered. They became a prosperous people living in independent towns nestled on central Italian hilltops. Magnificently colored wall paintings, which survive in some of their tombs, portray funeral

banquets and games testifying to the splendor of their society. While producing their own fine artwork, jewelry, and sculpture, they nevertheless had a passion for importing luxurious objects from Greece and other Mediterranean lands. Most of the intact Greek vases known today, for example, were found in Etruscan tombs. Etruscans' international contacts encouraged cultural interaction: gold tablets inscribed in Etruscan and Phoenician and discovered in 1964 at the port of Pyrgi (thirty miles northwest of Rome) reveal that at about 500 B.C. the Etruscans dedicated a temple to the Phoenician goddess Astarte, whom they had learned about from trade with Carthage. That rich city, founded in western North Africa (modern Tunisia) by Phoenicians about 800 B.C., dominated seaborne commerce in the western Mediterranean.

Scholars agree that Romans adopted ceremonial features from the Etruscans, such as magistrates' elaborate garments, musical instruments, and procedures for religious rituals. They also learned from them to divine the will of the gods by looking for clues in the shapes of the vital organs of slaughtered animals. And they may have adopted from

Etruscan society the tradition of wives joining husbands at dinner parties.

Many features of Roman culture formerly seen as deriving from Etruscan influence were probably part of the ancient Mediterranean's shared cultural environment. Rome's first political system, monarchy, was widespread in that world. The organization of the Roman army, a citizen militia of heavily armed infantry troops (hoplites) fighting in formation, reflected not just Etruscan precedent but that of many other peoples in the region. The alphabet, which the Romans certainly first learned from the Etruscans and used to write their own language, was actually Greek; the Greeks had gotten it through their contact with the earlier alphabets of eastern Mediterranean peoples. Trade with other areas of the Mediterranean and civil engineering leading to urbanization are other features of Etruscan life that Romans are said to have assimilated, but it is too simplistic to assume that cultural developments of this breadth resulted from one superior culture "instructing" another, less developed one. Rather, at this time in Mediterranean history, similar cultural developments were under way in many places. The Romans, like so many others, found their own way in navigating through this common cultural sea.

The Early Roman Republic, 509–287 B.C.

The social elite's distrust of monarchy motivated the creation of the Roman republic as a new political system. The suspicion was that a sole ruler and his family would inevitably become tyrannical and misuse their rule, a belief enshrined in Livy's story of the rape of Lucretia, the most famous legend about the birth of the republic. Like most of Livy's stories about Roman history, it stressed the role of moral virtue in the republic's founding. The tragedy of Lucretia, a chaste wife in the social elite, took place when the swaggering son of King Tarquin the Proud violently raped her to demonstrate his superior power. Despite pleas from her husband and father not to blame herself, she committed suicide after denouncing her attacker.

Declaring themselves Rome's liberators from tyranny, her relatives and their friends, led by Lucius Junius Brutus, drove out Tarquin in 509 B.C. to prevent royal abuse of power. They then installed the republic to ensure the sharing of power and to block the rule of one man or family. Thereafter, the

Romans prided themselves on having created a freer political system than that of many of their neighbors. The legend of the warrior Horatius at the bridge, for example, advertised the republic's dedication to national freedom. As Livy told the story, Horatius single-handedly blocked the Etruscan army's access to Rome over a bridge crossing the Tiber River when at the beginning of the republic they tried to reimpose a king on the city. While hacking at his opponents, Horatius berated them as slaves who had lost their freedom because they were ruled by haughty kings. This legend made clear

Bronze Bust of Lucius Junius Brutus, the "Liberator"
Brutus was a Roman hero for his role in ousting the monarchy and liberating Rome by founding the republic in 509 B.C. This bust was probably sculpted in the fourth or third century B.C. Its striking portrayal of the Liberator's face, emphasizing his piercing gaze and calm resolution, expressed the dignified way in which his family wanted him remembered, to emphasize their own distinguished heritage and status. As usual with metal busts, paste and colored glass were used to make the eyes look lifelike.
Scala/Art Resource, NY.

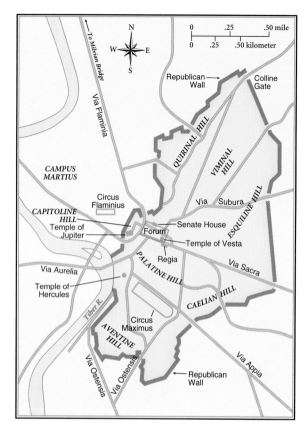

MAP 5.2 The City of Rome during the Republic
*Roman tradition said that King Servius Tullius had built
Rome's first defensive wall in the sixth century B.C., but
archaeology seems to show that the first wall completely encircling the city's center and seven hills on the east bank of
the Tiber River belongs to the fourth century B.C. and covered
a circuit of about seven miles. By the second century, the wall
had been extended to soar fifty-two feet high and had been
fitted with catapults to protect the large gates. Like the open
agora surrounded by buildings at the heart of a Greek city,
the forum remained Rome's political and social heart.*

that the compelling reason to found the republic as
a new system of government was to prevent one-
man rule and its abuses (Map 5.2).

The Struggle of the Orders. It took until the third
century B.C. for the Romans to work out a stable and
equitable system guaranteed by law in the republic.
Bitter turmoil between a closed circle of elite families (called the *patricians*) and the rest of Rome's citizen population (the *plebeians*), the republic's two
"orders," recurred for more than two hundred years
following the foundation of the republic. In 287 B.C.,
the plebeians finally won the right to make laws in

their own assembly. Historians therefore refer to this
period as "the struggle of the orders."

Social and economic issues fueled the struggle.
The patricians inherited their status as members of
a limited number of families, which had become
distinguished by controlling important religious activities. Patricians constituted only a tiny percentage of the population, but a generation after the
founding of the republic they began to monopolize
political offices. At this period, patricians were much
wealthier than most citizens. Some plebeians, however, were also rich, and they especially resented the
arrogance of the patricians, who proudly advertised
their status by sporting red shoes to set themselves
apart; later they changed to black shoes adorned
with a small metal crescent. Patricians also banned
intermarriage between the orders as a way to sustain their social superiority.

Turmoil arose because plebeians united to resist patrician power and demand improvements in
their situations: rich members of the order clamored for the right to marry patricians as social
equals, while the poor insisted on relief from crushing debts and a more equitable distribution of
farmland. To pressure the patricians, the plebeians
periodically resorted to the drastic measure of physically withdrawing from the city to a temporary settlement; the men then refused military service. This
tactic of secession worked because Rome's army was
minuscule without plebeians: the patricians numbered only about 130 families in the early republic
and could not defend Rome by themselves.

Forced to capitulate to plebeian demands, the
patricians agreed to a series of written laws to guarantee greater equality and social mobility. The earliest code of Roman law, called the Twelve Tables,
from the bronze tablets on which it was engraved
for display, was enacted between 451 and 449 B.C.
in response to a secession brought on by a patrician's violence against a plebeian woman. The
Tables encapsulated the prevailing legal customs of
early Rome's agricultural society in simply worded
provisions such as "If plaintiff calls defendant to
court, he shall go" and "If a wind causes a neighbor's tree to be bent and lean over your farm, action may be taken to have that tree removed."
In Livy's words, these laws prevented the patrician
public officials who judged most legal cases from
"arbitrarily giving the force of law to their own
preferences." So important did the Twelve Tables

become as a symbol of the Roman commitment to justice for all citizens that children were required to memorize the laws for the next four hundred years. The Roman belief in clear, fair laws as the best protection against unrest helped keep social hostilities from undermining the republic until the murderous turmoil of the late second century B.C. surrounding Tiberius and Gaius Gracchus.

The Consuls, Other Officials, and the Senate. Elected officials ran the republican government; they were chosen as panels, numbering from two to more than a dozen, so that shared, not sole, rule would be the norm. The highest officials were called *consuls*. Two were elected each year to support the principle of sharing power. Their foremost duties were leading the army's officers and commanding in battle. Winning a consulship was the highest political honor a Roman man could achieve, and it bestowed high status on his descendants forever.

To gain the consulship, a man traditionally had to work his way up a "ladder" of offices. After ten years of military service from about age twenty to thirty, he would start by seeking election as a *quaestor*, a financial administrator. Continuing to climb the ladder, he would be elected as one of Rome's *aediles*, who had the irksome duty of caring for the city's streets, sewers, aqueducts, temples, and markets. Each higher rung on the ladder was more competitive, and few men reached the next level, the office of *praetor*. The board of praetors performed judicial and military duties. The most successful of these then reached for the gold ring of Roman public office, the consulship. Ex-consuls could also compete to become one of the *censors*, prestigious senior officials elected very five years to conduct censuses of the citizen body and select new senators to keep the Senate membership at about three hundred men; to be eligible for selection to the Senate, a man had to have won election as a quaestor.

The struggle of the orders extended to control of these offices. The patricians tried to monopolize the highest ones, but the plebeians resisted fiercely. Through violent struggle from about 500 to 450 B.C., they forced the patricians to yield another important concession besides the Twelve Tables: the creation of a special panel of ten annually elected officials, called *tribunes*, whose only responsibility was to stop actions that would harm plebeians and their property. The tribunate's focus made it stand apart from the regular ladder offices. Tribunes, who had to be plebeians, derived their power from the sworn oath of the other plebeians to protect them against all attacks; this inviolability, called *sacrosanctity*, allowed tribunes the right to use a *veto* (a Latin word meaning "forbid") to block the actions of officials, prevent the passage of laws, suspend elections, and even counter the advice of the Senate. The tribunes' extraordinary power to stop government action could make them the catalysts for bitter political disputes.

Roman values motivated men to compete for status and glory, not money, by pursuing a public career; by 367 B.C., the plebeians had pushed their way fully into this competition by forcing passage of a law requiring that at least one consul every year must be a plebeian. Only well-off men could run for election because officials earned no salaries. On the contrary, they were expected to spend large sums to win popular support by entertaining the electorate with, for example, lavish shows that featured gladiators (trained fighters) and wild beasts, such as lions imported from Africa. Financing such exhibitions could put a candidate deeply in debt. Once elected, a magistrate had to help the treasury pay for public works, such as roads, aqueducts, and temples, that benefited the populace.

The only rewards for officials in the early republic were the status their positions carried and the esteem they could win by service to "the people's matter." As the Romans gradually came to control more and more overseas territory through warfare, however, their desire for the glory that money could buy in financing successful election campaigns overcame their values of faithfulness and honesty. By the second century B.C., military officers could enrich themselves by seizing booty from enemies in successful foreign wars and by extorting bribes from the local people while administering conquered territory. They could then use these profits of war to finance their political careers at home. In this way, acquiring money became more important in the late republic than winning status by upright public service.

To try to guide officials in making good decisions and deter them from bad conduct, the Senate retained the role it had enjoyed under the monarchy: giving advice on all matters of public interest. In keeping with the Roman tradition that prestige should be visible, the senators proclaimed their office by wearing special black high-top shoes and robes embroidered with a broad purple stripe. The senators' high social standing and the Roman respect for ancient traditions gave their opinions the moral force—though not the official status—of law. The Senate thus guided the republic's government in every area: decisions on war, domestic and foreign policy, state finance, official religion, and all types of legislation.

The Assemblies. The passage of laws, government policies, elections, and certain trials took place in a complicated system of differing assemblies— outdoor meetings of adult male citizens. Assemblies took place in various forms, but they were only for voting, not discussion; every assembly concerning laws and policies was preceded by a public gathering for speeches by leading men about the issues. Everyone, including women and noncitizens, could listen to these speeches. The crowd would loudly express its agreement or disagreement with the speeches by applauding or hissing. Speakers therefore had to pay close attention to public opinion in forming proposals that they would put before the men who would vote them up or down in the assemblies. A significant restriction on this democratic aspect of assembly procedure, however, was that each assembly was divided into different groups, whose size was determined by status and wealth. Voting took place by groups, with each group, not each individual, having a vote; a small group had the same vote as a large group.

The long process of political struggle led to a complex organization of the assemblies. Legend dated the earliest major one, the Centuriate Assembly, to the time of Servius Tullius, Rome's fifth king, in the sixth century b.c. The hierarchy of its voting groups reflected the organization of the army and left the huge group of people too poor to afford military weapons, the *proletarians,* in one group holding only one out of the total of 193 votes; the assembly was therefore dominated by the groups of patricians and richer citizens. Its main function under the republic became holding the elections to choose consuls and praetors.

As a counterweight to this assembly, the plebeians in the fifth century b.c. created another meeting, the Plebeian Assembly, in which they excluded patricians and assigned themselves to one of thirty-five groups according to where they lived; this assembly elected tribunes. As the plebeians gradu-

ally gained the upper hand in the struggle of the orders, their assembly became more important; in 287 b.c., its resolutions, called *plebiscites,* were officially recognized as legally binding on all Romans. Soon after the creation of the Plebeian Assembly, the patricians were allowed to join the plebeians in the Tribal Assembly, which also grouped voters by domicile. This assembly, in which plebeians greatly outnumbered patricians, eventually became the republic's most important institution for making policy, passing laws, and, until separate courts were created, conducting judicial trials.

The Judicial System. The republic's judicial system, like its other governmental institutions, developed slowly and with overlapping features. The praetors originally decided many legal cases, after listening to the advice of their personal council of friends and clients; especially serious trials could be transferred to the assemblies. A separate jury system started to be put in place only in the second century b.c., and senators repeatedly clashed with other upper-class Romans over whether these juries should be manned only by Senate members.

As in Greece, Rome had no state-sponsored prosecutors or defenders or any lawyers to hire. Both accusers and accused had to speak for themselves in court or have friends speak for them. People of lower social status suffered a distinct disadvantage if they lacked a patron well versed in public speaking to plead their case. Priests dominated in knowledge of the law and legal procedures until the third century b.c. At that time, prominent men, usually senators with expertise in law, began to play a central role in the Roman judicial system. Although jurists, as they were called (from the Latin *jus, juris,* "law"), frequently developed their expertise by serving in Roman elective office, they operated as private citizens, not officials, giving legal advice to other citizens and magistrates. This reliance on jurists in Roman republican justice reflected the tradition of consulting councils of advisers to make decisions. Romans had a simple criminal law, but they formulated sophisticated civil law to regulate disputes over property and personal interests; developed over centuries and gradually incorporating laws from other peoples, it became the basis for many later Western legal codes still in use today.

The republic's political and judicial systems, with their jumbled network of institutions, lacked an overall structure to consolidate them. Many different political bodies enacted laws or, in the Senate's case, opinions that amounted to laws, and legal cases could be heard in varying ways. Yet Rome had no highest judicial authority, such as the U.S. Supreme Court, that could resolve disputes about the validity of conflicting laws or cases. The republic's well-being and stability therefore depended on a reverence for tradition, the "way of the ancestors." This reliance on tradition ensured that the most socially prominent and the richest Romans dominated government and society—because they defined the "way of the ancestors."

❖ Roman Imperialism and Its Consequences, Fifth to Second Centuries B.C.

Expansion through war propelled republican domestic and foreign policy and made conquest and military service central to the lives of Romans. During the fifth, fourth, and third centuries B.C., the Romans fought war after war in Italy until they became the most powerful state on the peninsula. In the third and second centuries B.C., they also warred far from home in the west, the north, and the east, but above all they battled Carthage to the south. Their success in these campaigns made Rome the premier power in the Mediterranean.

Two principal motivations dominated Roman imperialism under the republic: fear and ambition. The senators' worries about national security made them recommend preemptive attacks against others perceived as enemies who might attack Rome, while everyone longed to capture wealth on foreign military campaigns. Poorer soldiers hoped their gains would pull their families out of poverty; the elite expected to increase their riches and acquire glory as commanders, to promote their public careers.

The consequences of repeated wars in Italy and abroad transformed Romans culturally and socially. Astonishingly, they had no literature before about 240 B.C.; the increased contact with others that accompanied expansion stimulated their first history and poetry and deeply influenced their art, especially portraiture. Endless military service away from home created stresses on family life and small farmers and undermined the stability of Roman so-

ciety, as did the importation of huge numbers of war captives to work as slaves on the estates of the rich. The conquests and spoils of war from Rome's great victories in the third and second centuries B.C. thus turned out to be a two-edged sword: they brought expansion and wealth, but their unexpected social and political consequences disrupted traditional values and the community's stability.

Expansion in Italy

The Romans believed they were successful militarily because they respected the will of the gods. Reflecting on the republic's earlier history, Cicero claimed, "We have overcome all the nations of the world, because we have realized that the world is directed and governed by the gods." Believing that the gods supported defensive wars as just, the Romans always insisted they fought only in self-defense, even when they attacked first.

After a victory over their Latin neighbors in the 490s B.C., the Romans spent the next hundred years warring with the Etruscan town of Veii, a few miles north of the Tiber River. Their 396 B.C. victory doubled Roman territory. By the fourth century B.C., the Roman infantry legion had surpassed the Greek and Macedonian phalanx as an effective fighting force. A devastating sack of Rome in 387 B.C. by marauding Gauls (Celts) from beyond the Alps proved only a temporary military setback, though it made Romans forever fearful of foreign invasion. By around 220 B.C., Rome controlled all of the peninsula south of the Po River.

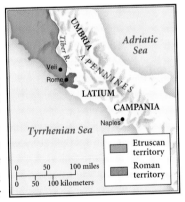

Rome and Central Italy, Fifth Century B.C.

Brutality marked the conduct of these wars of conquest. The Romans sometimes enslaved the defeated or forced them to give up large parcels of land. Yet they also regularly struck generous peace terms with former enemies. Some defeated Italians immediately became Roman citizens; others gained limited citizenship without the right to vote; still other communities received treaties of alliance. No conquered Italian peoples had to pay taxes to

Aqueduct at Nîmes in France

Like the Greeks, the Romans met the challenge of supplying drinkable water to towns by constructing aqueducts; they excelled at building complex delivery systems of tunnels, channels, and bridges to transport it from far away. One of the best-preserved sections of a major aqueduct is the so-called Pont-du-Gard near Nîmes (ancient Nemausus) in France, erected in the late first century B.C. to serve the flourishing town there. Built of stones fitted together without clamps or mortar, the span soars 160 feet high and 875 feet long, carrying water from thirty-five miles away in a channel constructed to fall only one foot in height for every 3,000 feet in length, so that the flow would remain steady but gentle.
Hubertus Kanus/Photo Researchers, Inc.

Rome. All, however, had to render military aid in future wars. These new allies then received a share of the booty, chiefly slaves and land, from victorious campaigns against a new crop of enemies. In this way, the Romans adroitly co-opted their former opponents by making them partners in the spoils of conquest, an arrangement that in turn enhanced Rome's wealth and authority.

To buttress Italy's security, the Romans planted colonies of citizens and constructed roads up and down the peninsula to allow troops to march faster. These roads also connected the diverse peoples of Italy, hastening the creation of a more unified culture dominated by Rome. Latin, for example, came to be the common language, although local tongues lived on, especially Greek in the south. The wealth won in the first two centuries of expansion attracted hordes of people to the capital because it financed new aqueducts to provide fresh, running water—a rarity in the ancient world—and a massive building program that employed the poor. By around 300 B.C., perhaps 150,000 people lived within Rome's walls. Outside the city, about 750,000 free Roman citizens inhabited various parts of Italy on land taken from local peoples. Much conquered territory was declared public land, open to any Roman to use for grazing herds of cattle.

Rich patricians and plebeians cooperated to exploit the expanding Roman territories; the old distinction between the orders had

Roman Roads, c. 110 B.C.

become largely a technicality. This merged elite derived its wealth mainly from agricultural land and plunder acquired during military service. Since Rome levied no regular income or inheritance taxes, financially prudent families could pass down this wealth from generation to generation. Families at the top of this highest social stratum consisted of those who at some point had a consul in the family. They called themselves "the nobles" to set themselves apart from the rest of the elite.

Wars with Carthage

Since most of Rome's leaders, remembering the attack of the Gauls, feared foreign invasions and also saw imperialism as the route to riches, it is hardly surprising that the Roman republic fought its three

most famous wars against the powerful and wealthy city of Carthage. Governed, like Rome, as a republic, by the third century B.C. Carthage controlled an empire encompassing the northwest African coast, part of Libya, Sardinia, Corsica, Malta, and the southern portion of Spain. Geography therefore meant that an expansionist Rome would sooner or later infringe on Carthage's interests, which depended on the sea; the city had a strong fleet but had to hire mercenaries to field a sizable infantry. To Romans, Carthage seemed both a dangerous rival and, potentially, a fine prize because it had grown so prosperous from agriculture and international trade. Roman hostility was also fueled by horror at the Carthaginian tradition of incinerating infants in the belief it would placate their gods in times of trouble.

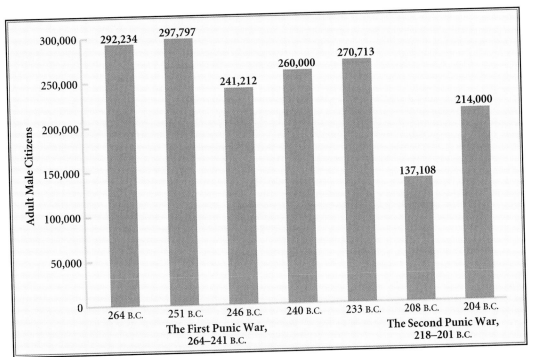

TAKING MEASURE Census Records of Adult Male Roman Citizens during the First and Second Punic Wars

Livy (59 B.C.–A.D. 17) and Jerome (c. A.D. 347–420) provide these numbers from the censuses, which counted only adult male citizens (the men eligible for Rome's regular army), conducted during and between the first two wars against Carthage. The drop in the total for 246 B.C., compared with the total for 264 B.C., reflects losses in the First Punic War. The low total for 208 B.C. reflects both losses in battle and defections of communities such as Capua in 216 B.C. Since the census did not include the Italian allies fighting on Rome's side, the census numbers understate the wars' total casualties; scholars estimate that they took the lives of nearly a third of Italy's adult male population, which would have meant perhaps a quarter of a million soldiers killed.

Tenney Frank, *An Economic Survey of Ancient Rome, Vol. I* (New York: Farrar, Straus, and Giroux, 1959), 56.

War Abroad. A coincidence finally ignited open conflict with Carthage, taking Roman troops outside Italy and across the sea for the first time; the three wars that ensued are called the Punic Wars, from the Roman term for Phoenicians, *Punici*. The First Punic War (264–241 B.C.) began when a beleaguered band of mercenaries in Messana at Sicily's northeastern tip appealed to Rome and Carthage simultaneously to aid them against their neighbors. Both states sent troops. The Carthaginians wanted to protect their revenue from Sicilian trade; the Romans wanted to keep Carthaginian troops from moving close to their territory and to reap the rewards of conquest. The clash between them exploded into a war that lasted a generation. Its agonizing battles revealed why the Romans so consistently conquered their rivals: in addition to being able to draw on the Italian population for reserves of manpower, they were prepared to spend as much money, sacrifice as many troops, and fight as long as necessary to prevail. Previously unskilled at naval warfare, they expended vast sums to build warships to combat Carthage's experienced navy; they lost more than five hundred ships and 250,000 men while learning how to win at sea. (See "Taking Measure," page 175.)

Their victory in the First Punic War made the Romans masters of Sicily, where they set up their first province, a foreign territory ruled and taxed by Roman officials. This innovation proved so profitable that they soon seized the islands of Sardinia and Corsica from the Carthaginians to create an-other province. These first successful foreign conquests whetted their appetite for more (Map 5.3). They also feared a renewal of Carthage's power; pressing their advantage, they next made alliances with local peoples in Spain, where the Carthaginians were expanding from their original trading posts in the south.

A Roman ultimatum to Carthage against further expansion convinced the Carthaginians that another war was inevitable, so they decided to strike back. In the Second Punic War (218–201 B.C.), the daring Carthaginian general Hannibal (247–182 B.C.) flabbergasted the Romans by marching troops and war elephants from Carthaginian territory in Spain over the snowy Alps into Italy. Slaughtering more than thirty thousand at Cannae in 216 B.C. in the bloodiest Roman loss in history, he tried to provoke widespread revolts among the numerous Italian cities allied to Rome. But disastrously for him, most Italians remained loyal to Rome. His alliance in 215 B.C. with King Philip V of Macedonia (238–179 B.C.) forced the Romans to fight on a second front in Greece, but they refused to crack despite Hannibal's ravaging Italy from 218 to 203 B.C. The Romans finally won by turning the tables: invading the Carthaginians' homeland, the Roman general Scipio crushed them at the battle of Zama in 202 B.C. and was dubbed "Africanus" to commemorate the victory. The Senate imposed a punishing settlement on the enemy in 201 B.C., forcing Carthage to scuttle its navy, pay huge war indemnities scheduled to last fifty years, and hand over its lucrative holdings in Spain, which Rome made into provinces famous for their mines.

Dominance in the Mediterranean. The Third Punic War (149–146 B.C.) broke out when the Carthaginians, who had finally revived financially, retaliated against the aggression of their neighbor and Roman ally the Numidian king Masinissa. After winning the war, the Romans heeded the advice "We must destroy Carthage," which the crusty senator Cato had repeatedly intoned: they razed the city and converted its territory into a province. This disaster did not obliterate Punic social and cultural ways, however, and under the Roman Empire this part of North Africa became distinguished for its economic and intellectual vitality, which emerged from a synthesis of Roman and Punic traditions.

Imported "Surprise" Lamp Found in Carthage

The Phoenician settlers of Carthage (Tunis in modern Tunisia) became the foremost traders of the western Mediterranean. This sculpted lamp was imported to Carthage, probably from Alexandria in Egypt. Ancient lamps were candles burning liquid fuel, usually olive oil lit with a flax wick; the upper part of this lamp, made to resemble a bearded man or god, served as the oil reservoir. The eyes in the face glinted naturalistically with gold inlaid in blue glass. When turned over, the lamp offered a surprise: its lower side was a frog, perhaps a sly hint of its origin in the marshy region at the mouth of the Nile River.
Martha Cooper/Peter Arnold, Inc.

MAP 5.3 Roman Expansion, c. 500–44 B.C.

During the first two centuries of its existence, the Roman republic used war and diplomacy to extend its power north and south in the Italian peninsula. In the third and second centuries B.C., conflict with Carthage in the south and west and the Hellenistic kingdoms in the east extended Roman power far outside Italy and led to the creation of provinces from Spain to Greece. The first century B.C. saw the conquest of Syria by Pompey and of Gaul by Julius Caesar (d. 44 B.C.).

With the conquests of the Punic Wars, Rome extended its power not just to Spain and North Africa but also to Macedonia, Greece, and part of Asia Minor. King Philip's alliance with Hannibal had brought Roman troops east of Italy for the first, but not the last, time. After thrashing Philip for revenge and to prevent any threat of his invading Italy, the Roman commander Flamininus had proclaimed the "freedom of the Greeks" in 196 B.C. to show respect for Greece's distinguished past. The Greek cities and federal leagues naturally understood the proclamation to mean they could behave as they liked. They misunderstood. The Romans meant them to behave as clients and follow their new patrons' advice, while the Greeks thought, as "friends"

of Rome, that they were truly free. Trouble then developed because the two parties failed to realize that common and familiar words like *freedom* and *friendship* could carry very different implications in different societies. The Romans continued their military interventions to make the kingdom of Macedonia and the Greeks observe their obligations as clients; faced with continuing resistance, the Senate in 146 B.C. ordered the destruction of Corinth for asserting its independence and converted Macedonia and Greece into a province. In 133 B.C., the Attalid king Attalus III of Pergamum increased Roman power with an astonishing gift: he left his Asia Minor kingdom to Rome in his will. In 121 B.C., the lower part of Gaul across the Alps (modern France)

Plate Decorated with a War Elephant
This third-century plate from southern Italy depicts a cow Indian elephant followed by her calf; the adult animal is equipped with a fortified compartment on its back that could hold archers. War elephants had been introduced to the Mediterranean after Alexander the Great had confronted them in his campaigns in India; commanders tried to use them mostly to frighten and confuse the enemy with their size and loud bellowing. This plate most likely depicts one of the twenty beasts that the Epirote mercenary general Pyrrhus (319–272 B.C.) transported by sea to southern Italy in 280 B.C. when the Greek cities there hired him to fight the Romans on their behalf. In 218 B.C., the famous Carthaginian general Hannibal, who studied Pyrrhus's tactics, shocked the Romans by leading a force of thirty-seven elephants (and thousands of troops) over the treacherous passes of the Alps to invade Italy. In the long run, however, armies gave up on elephants because they were too expensive to maintain and too difficult to control when confused or wounded in battle.
Scala/Art Resource, NY.

was made into a province. By this date, then, Rome governed and profited from two-thirds of the Mediterranean region; only the easternmost Mediterranean lay outside its control (see Map 5.3).

Hellenism in Roman Literature and Art

Roman imperialism set in motion a great deal of cross-cultural contact, especially with Greece. Although Romans looked down on Greeks for their military impotence, they felt awe before Hellenic literature and art. Roman authors and artists looked to Greek models in all that they did. A vivid proof of the depth of their respect is revealed by the language in which the first Roman historian, Fabius Pictor, worked: about 200 B.C., he published his narrative of Rome's foundation and the wars with Carthage—in Greek. Greece also directly inspired the earliest literature in Latin: the adaptation of Homer's *Odyssey* by a Greek ex-slave, Livius Andronicus, written sometime after the First Punic War. Unfortunately, very little of their work has survived.

Greek Influences on Roman Literature. Roman literature expressed its vitality by combining the foreign and the familiar. Many of the most famous early Latin authors were not native Romans; their widespread origins testified to the intermingling of cultures already well under way in the Roman world. The poet Naevius (d. 201 B.C.) came from Campania; the poet Ennius (d. 169 B.C.) from even farther south, in Calabria; the comic playwright Plautus (d. 184 B.C.) from north of Rome, in Umbria; his fellow comedy writer Terence (c. 190–159 B.C.) from North Africa. They all found inspiration in Greek literature. Roman comedies, for example, took their plots and stock characters from Hellenistic Greek comedy, which raised laughs from family life and stereotyped personalities, such as the braggart warrior and the obsessed lover.

Not all Romans applauded Greek influence. Cato, although he studied Greek himself, repeatedly thundered against the deleterious effect the "effete" Greeks had on the "sturdy" Romans. He established Latin as an appropriate language for prose by publishing a history of Rome, *The Origins* (written between 168 and 149 B.C.), and instructions on running a large farm, *On Agriculture* (published about 160 B.C.). Glumly he predicted that if the Romans ever became infected with Greek literature, they would lose their dominions. In fact, despite its debt to Greek literature, early Latin literature reflected traditional Roman values. Ennius, for example, was inspired by Greek epic poetry to compose his path-breaking Latin epic *Annals*, a poetic version of Roman history. Its contents praised ancestral tradition, as a famous line demonstrates: "On the ways and the men of old rests the Roman commonwealth."

Later Roman writers routinely took inspiration from Greek literature in both content and style. The poet Lucretius (c. 94–55 B.C.), for example, wrote a long poem, entitled *On the Nature of Things* and probably published in the early 50s B.C., to argue that people should have no fear of death, which only inflamed "the running sores of life." His work's content followed closely the "atomic theory" of the nature of existence of the great Greek philosopher Epicurus (341–270 B.C.) and explained matter as composed of tiny, invisible particles. Dying, the poem taught, simply meant the dissolution of the union of atoms, which had come together temporarily to make up a person's body. There could be no eternal punishment or pain after death, indeed no existence at all, because a person's soul, itself made up of atoms, perished along with the body.

The style of early Hellenistic authors inspired Catullus (c. 84–54 B.C.), whose concise and witty poems alternately savaged prominent politicians for their sexual behavior and lamented his own disastrous love life. His most famous series of love poems detailed his passion for a married woman named Lesbia, whom he begged to think only of immediate pleasures: "Let us live, my Lesbia, and love; the gossip of stern old men is not worth a cent. Suns can set and rise again; we, when once our brief light has set, must sleep one never-ending night. Give me a thousand kisses, then a hundred, then a thousand more."

The great orator Cicero wrote not only speeches and letters but also many prose works on political science, philosophy, ethics, and theology that built on the work of Greek philosophers. He adapted their ideas to Roman life and infused his writings on these topics with a deep understanding of the need to appreciate the uniqueness of each human personality. He wrote his most influential philosophical works in one period of furious activity while in political exile in 45 and 44 B.C. His doctrine of *humanitas* ("humanness, the quality of humanity") combined various strands of Greek philosophy, especially Stoicism, to express an ideal for human life based on generous and honest treatment of others and an abiding commitment to morality derived from natural law (the right that exists for all people by

Wall Painting Depicting Actors in a Comedy
This painting found in the excavation of Pompeii shows actors portraying characters in one of the various kinds of comedy popular during the Roman republic. In this variety, the actors wore masks designating stock personality types and strove for broad, farcical effects. The plots were often burlesques of famous mythological stories.
Scala/Art Resource, NY.

nature, independent of the differing laws and customs of different societies). What he passed on to later ages was perhaps the most attractive ideal to come from ancient Greece and Rome: the spirit of *humanitas.*

Realistic Portraiture. Greece influenced Rome in all areas of art and architecture, from the style of sculpture and painting to the design of public buildings. Romans firmly adapted Greek models to their own purposes; the most striking example of this adaptation came in portrait sculpture. Hellenistic artists had pioneered the sculpting of realistic statues that showed the ravages of age and infirmity on the human body. Such works, however, portrayed human stereotypes (the "old man," the "drunken woman"), not specific people. Individual portrait sculpture tended to present its subjects in the best possible light, much like a retouched photograph today.

Roman artists in the later republic applied the tradition of realistic sculpture to portraiture busts, as contemporary Etruscan sculptors did also. Their sculptures of specific men did not try to hide unflattering features: long noses, receding chins, deep wrinkles, bald heads, careworn looks. Portraits of women, by contrast, were generally more idealized, perhaps to represent the traditional vision of the bliss of family life; portraits of children were not popular during the republic, perhaps because offspring were not seen as contributing to public life until they were grown. Because either the men depicted in the portraits or their families paid for the busts, they presumably wanted the faces sculpted realistically—showing the toll of age and effort—to emphasize how hard the men had worked to serve "the people's matter" that was the republic.

Stresses on Society

The republic faced grave social and economic difficulties when the successful wars of the third and second centuries B.C. ironically turned out to be disastrous for many small farmers and their families throughout Italy. The new kind of warfare required for the Punic Wars and the numerous interventions in Macedonia and Greece had the unintended consequence of disrupting the traditional forms of agricultural life in the Roman countryside and forcing many poor people to move to the capital. Before this time, Roman warfare, like Greek, had followed a pattern of short campaigns timed not to interfere with the fluctuating labor needs of farming.

The prolonged campaigns of wars abroad disrupted the agricultural system, the basis of the Roman economy. For centuries, farmers working little plots had formed the backbone of the system; they also constituted the principal source of soldiers. A farmer absent on long military expeditions had two choices: rely on a hired hand or slave to manage his crops and animals, or have his wife try to take on what was traditionally man's work in the fields in addition to her usual domestic tasks. The story of the consul Regulus, who led a Roman army to victory in Africa in 256 B.C., revealed the severe problems a man's absence could cause. When the man who managed his 4$\frac{1}{3}$-acre farm died while the consul was away fighting Carthage, a hired hand absconded with all the farm's tools and livestock. Regulus implored the Senate to send a general to replace him so he could return home to prevent his wife and children from starving. The senators responded to save Regulus's family and property from ruin because they wanted to keep him as a commander in the field, but ordinary soldiers could expect no such special aid. Many of them failed in their dreams to win riches by fighting abroad; their wives and children in the same plight as Regulus's family faced disaster.

The Poor. These troubles caused by prolonged wars hit the poor particularly hard. Many farmers and their families fell into debt and were forced to sell their land. Not all regions of Italy suffered as severely as others, and some impoverished farmers and their families managed to remain in the countryside by working as day laborers for others. Many displaced people, however, migrated to Rome, where the men looked for work as menial laborers and women sought piecework making cloth—but often were forced into prostitution.

This influx of desperate people swelled the poverty-level urban population, and the difficulty these landless poor had supporting themselves made them a potentially explosive element in Roman politics. They were willing to back any politician who promised to address their need for sustenance, and the state had to feed them to avert riots. Like Athens in the fifth century B.C., Rome by the late second century B.C. needed to import grain to feed its swollen urban population. The poor's demand for at least partial rations of low-priced

Dishes of Carbonized Food

When the volcano Mount Vesuvius erupted in A.D. 79, it buried the Roman towns of Pompeii and Herculaneum on the southwestern Italian coast, near Naples. People evidently left their meals on the table when they fled, and in some cases the heat preserved the form of the food by carbonizing it, as with these dishes. They contain typical ancient Roman fare: eggs, nuts, dates, and a loaf of bread, here cut into wedges for serving. Leonhard von Matt/Photo Researchers, Inc.

(and eventually free) food distributed at the state's expense became one of the most contentious issues in late republican politics.

The Rich.   Rome's elite reaped rich political and material rewards from imperialism. The increased need for commanders to lead military campaigns abroad created opportunities for successful generals to enrich themselves and their families. By using their gains to finance public buildings, the elite could enhance their reputations while benefiting the general population. Building new temples, for example, was thought to increase everyone's security because the Romans believed it pleased their gods to have more shrines in their honor; in 146 B.C., a previously victorious general, Caecilius Metellus, paid for Rome's first temple built of marble, finally bringing this Greek style to the capital city.

The distress of farmers in Italy suited rich landowners because they could buy bankrupt small farms to create large estates. They further increased their holdings by illegally occupying public land carved out of the territory of defeated peoples. The rich worked their large estates, called *latifundia*, with slaves as well as free laborers. They had a ready supply of slaves because of the huge number of captives taken in the same wars that displaced Italy's small farmers; as it turned out, the victories won by poor Roman soldiers created a workforce with

which they could not compete. The growing size of the slave crews working on *latifundia* was a mixed blessing for their wealthy owners because the presence of so many slave workers in one place led to periodic revolts that required the army to suppress.

The elite profited from Rome's expansion because they filled the governing offices in the new provinces and could get much richer if they ignored the traditional value of uprightness. Since provincial officials ruled by martial law, no one in the provinces could curb a greedy governor's appetite for graft, extortion, and plunder. Not all governors were corrupt, of course, but some did use their unsupervised power to squeeze all they could from the provincials. Normally such offenders faced no punishment because their colleagues in the Senate excused one another's crimes.

The new opportunities for luxurious living financed by the fruits of expansion abroad strained the traditional values of moderation and frugality. Before, a man like Manius Curius (d. 270 B.C.) was enshrined in legend: despite his glorious military victories, he was said to have boiled turnips for his meals in a humble hut. Now, the elite acquired ostentatious luxuries, such as large and showy country villas for entertaining friends and clients, to proclaim their social superiority. Money had become more valuable to them than the good of the "people's matter."

❖ Upheaval in the Late Republic, c. 133–44 B.C.

Placing their own interests ahead of traditional communal values by competing for individual success instead of devoting themselves to public service, some ambitious members of the Roman elite set the republic on the road to war with itself instead of with others. When Tiberius and Gaius Gracchus used their powers as tribunes to agitate for reforms to help small farmers, the backbone of the army, their opponents in the Senate resorted to murder to curb them. When a would-be member of the elite, Gaius Marius, opened military service to the poor to boost his personal status, his creation of "client armies" undermined faithfulness to the general good of the community. When the people's unwillingness to share citizenship with Italian allies sparked a war in Roman territory and the clashing ambitions of the "great men" Sulla, Pompey, and Julius Caesar burst into civil war, the republic fractured and did not recover.

The Gracchi and Factional Politics

The upper-class brothers Tiberius and Gaius Sempronius Gracchus based their political careers on advocating that the rich make concessions to help strengthen the state. This stance set them at odds with many of the elite into whose order they had been born: their grandfather was the Scipio who had defeated Hannibal, and their mother was the Cornelia whom the Ptolemaic king of Egypt had courted after their father died. Tiberius, the older of the Gracchi (the plural of *Gracchus*), eloquently dramatized the tragic circumstances that motivated them politically, according to the biographer Plutarch (c. A.D. 50–120):

> The wild beasts that roam over Italy have their dens. . . . But the men who fight and die for Italy enjoy nothing but the air and light; without house or home they wander about with their wives and children. . . . They fight and die to protect the wealth and luxury of others; they are styled masters of the world, and have not a clod of earth they call their own.

In 133 B.C., Tiberius won election as a tribune, and he energetically pursued the role of protecting the people. When his opponents blocked his attempts at reform using conventional channels, he overrode the wishes of the Senate by having the plebeian assembly pass reform laws to redistribute public land to landless Romans. He further broke with tradition by circumventing the senators' will on financing this agrarian reform. Before they could decide on whether to accept the bequest of his kingdom made by the recently deceased ruler of Pergamum, Tiberius had the people pass a law that the gift be used to equip the new farms that were to be established on the redistributed land.

Tiberius then announced his intention to stand for reelection as tribune for the following year, violating the prohibition of the "way of the ancestors" against consecutive terms. His senatorial opponents boiled over: Tiberius's cousin Scipio Nasica, an ex-consul, led a band of senators and their clients in a sudden attack on him to, as they shouted, "save the republic." Pulling up their togas over their left arms so they would not trip in a fight, these illustrious Romans clubbed to death the tribune and many of his followers. Their assault began the sorry history of murder as a political tactic in the republic.

Gaius, whom the people elected tribune for 123 B.C. and, contrary to tradition, again for the next year, followed his brother's lead by pushing measures that outraged the reactionary members of the elite: more agrarian reform, subsidized prices for grain, public works projects throughout Italy to provide employment for the poor, and colonies abroad with farms for the landless. His most revolutionary proposals were to grant Roman citizenship to many Italians and to establish new courts that would try senators accused of corruption as provincial governors. The new juries would be manned not by senators but by *equites* ("equestrians" or "knights"). These were landowners from outside the city who, in the earliest republic, had been what the word suggests—men rich enough to provide horses for cavalry service—but were now wealthy businessmen, whose choice of commerce over a public career set them at odds with senators. Because they did not serve in the Senate, the equestrians could convict criminal senators free of peer pressure. Gaius's proposal marked the emergence of the equestrians as a political force in Roman politics, to the dismay of the Senate.

When the senators blocked his plans, Gaius in 121 B.C. assembled an armed group to threaten them. They responded by telling the consuls "to take all measures necessary to defend the republic," meaning the use of force. To escape arrest and certain execution, Gaius had one of his slaves cut his throat; hundreds of his supporters were then killed by the senators and their supporters and servants.

The violent deaths of the Gracchi and so many of their followers introduced factions into Roman politics. From now on, members of the elite positioned themselves either as supporters of the people, referred to as *populares,* or of "the best," referred to as *optimates.* Some identified with one faction or the other from genuine allegiance to its policies; others based their choice on political expediency, supporting whichever side better promoted their own political advancement. In any case, this division of the elite into hostile factions persisted as a source of friction and violence until the end of the first century B.C.

Gaius Marius and the Origin of Client Armies

The republic continued to need effective commanders to combat slave revolts and foreign invasions in the late second and early first centuries B.C. In response to the disarray of the elite and constant military threats, a new kind of leader arose in Roman politics: men without a consul among their ancestors, though always members of the upper classes, who relied on sheer ability to force their way to fame, fortune, influence, and—their ultimate goal—the consulship. Called "new men," they challenged the political dominance of the traditional elite.

The man who set this new political force in motion, Gaius Marius (c. 157–86 B.C.), came not from Rome's elite but rather from the equestrian class of Arpinum in central Italy. Ordinarily, a man of Marius's origins and status had little chance of cracking the ranks of Rome's ruling oligarchy of noble families, who virtually monopolized the office of consul. Fortunately for Marius, however, Rome at the end of the second century B.C. had a pressing need for men who could lead an army to victory. Capitalizing on his military record as a junior officer and on popular dissatisfaction with the nobles' war leadership, Marius won election as one of the consuls for 107 B.C. In Roman terms this election

made him a "new man"—that is, the first man in the history of his family to become consul, a rare achievement. Marius's continuing success as a commander in great crises, first in North Africa and next against German tribes who attacked southern France and then Italy, led the people to elect him consul for an unprecedented six terms, including consecutive service, by 100 B.C.

So celebrated was Marius that the Senate voted him a triumph, Rome's ultimate military honor. On the day of triumph, the general who had earned this award rode through the streets of Rome in a chariot. His face was painted red for reasons Romans could no longer remember. Huge crowds cheered him, while his army pricked him with off-color jokes, perhaps to ward off the evil eye at this moment of supreme glory. For a similar reason, a slave rode behind him in the chariot and kept whispering in his ear, "Look behind you, and remember that you are a mortal." For a former small-town equestrian like Marius to be granted a triumph was a supreme social coup.

Despite his triumph, the optimates faction never accepted Marius because they viewed him as an upstart and a threat to their preeminence. His support came mainly from the common people, for whom his reform of entrance requirements for the army made him intensely popular. Previously, only men with property could enroll as soldiers. Marius opened the ranks even to proletarians, men who owned virtually nothing. For them, serving in the army under a successful general meant an opportunity to better their lot by acquiring booty and a grant of land to retire on.

This change created armies more loyal to their commander than to the state. That is, proletarian troops felt immense goodwill toward a commander who led them to victory and then divided the spoils with them generously. The crowds of poor Roman soldiers thus began to behave like an army of clients following their patron, the commander, whose personal ambitions they naturally supported. Marius was merely the first to promote his own career in this way. He lost his political importance after 100 B.C. when he was no longer consul and stopped commanding armies and tried to insinuate himself among the optimates. When other commanders after Marius used client armies to advance their political careers more ruthlessly than even he had, the disintegration of the republic accelerated.

Sulla and Civil War

An unscrupulous noble named Lucius Cornelius Sulla (c. 138–78 B.C.) took advantage of uprisings in Italy and Asia Minor in the early first century B.C. to use his client army to seize the highest offices and compel the Senate to follow his wishes. His career revealed the dirty secret of politics in the late re-

public: traditional values no longer restrained commanders who prized their own advancement and the enrichment of their troops above peace and the good of the community.

The Social War. The uprisings in Italy occurred because Rome's Italian allies mostly lacked Roman citizenship and therefore had no voice in decisions concerning domestic or foreign policy, even when their interests were directly involved. They became increasingly unhappy as wealth from conquests piled up in the late republic; their upper classes especially wanted a greater share of the luxurious prosperity that war had brought the citizen elite. Romans rejected the allies' demand for citizenship, from fear that sharing that status would lessen their economic and political power.

The Italians' discontent finally erupted in 91–87 B.C. in the Social War (so named because the Latin word for *ally* is *socius*). Forming a confederacy to fight Rome, the allies demonstrated their commitment by the number of their casualties—300,000 dead. Although Rome's army eventually prevailed, the rebels won the political war: the Romans granted citizenship to all the freeborn peoples of Italy south of the Po River. Most important, their men could come to Rome to vote in the assemblies. Sadly, it took the bloodshed of the Social War to reestablish Rome's principle of gaining strength by granting citizenship to outsiders. The other significant outcome of this war was that it propelled Sulla to prominence: his successful generalship against the allies won him election as consul for 88 B.C.

Plunder Abroad and Violence at Home. The foreign uprising that Sulla took advantage of erupted in Asia Minor in 88 B.C. The king of Pontus on the southern coast of the Black Sea, Mithridates VI (120–63 B.C.), instigated a murderous rebellion against Rome's control of the region, especially its rapacious tax collectors, who tried to make provincials pay much more than was required. After denouncing the Romans as "the common enemies of all mankind," he persuaded the people of Asia Minor to kill all the Italians there—tens of thousands of them—in a single day.

As retaliation for this treachery, the Senate advised a military expedition; victory would mean

Bust of the General Lucius Cornelius Sulla
Sulla (c. 138–78 B.C.) was the Roman commander who lit the match to the dynamite that was the political situation in the late republic. When he marched on Rome in 88 B.C., employing violence against his own countrymen to make the Senate give him the command in Asia Minor, he smashed beyond repair the Roman tradition that leading citizens should put the interests of the commonwealth ahead of their private goals. This bust, now in the Venice Archaeological Museum, is usually identified as Sulla—its harsh gaze at least corresponds to what the ancient sources report of his personality.
Scala/Art Resource, NY

unimaginable booty because Asia Minor held many wealthy cities. Born to a patrician family that had lost much of its status and all of its money, Sulla craved the command against Mithridates. When the Senate gave it to him, his jealous rival Marius, now an old man, immediately connived to have it transferred to himself by plebiscite. Outraged, Sulla marched his client army against Rome itself. All his officers except one deserted him in horror at this unthinkable outrage. His common soldiers followed him to a man. Neither they nor their commander shrank from starting a civil war. After capturing Rome, Sulla killed or exiled his opponents and let his men rampage through the city. He then led them off to fight Mithridates, ignoring a summons to stand trial and sacking Athens on the way to Asia Minor.

The Kingdom of Mithridates VI, c. 88 B.C.

Sulla's unprecedented violence only bred more. After gathering forces, Marius and his friends embarked on their own reign of terror in Rome. In 83 B.C., Sulla returned after defeating Mithridates, having allowed his soldiers to strip Asia Minor bare. Civil war recommenced for two years until Sulla crushed his Roman enemies and their Italian allies. The climactic battle of the war took place in late 82 B.C. before the gates of Rome. An Italian general whipped his troops into a frenzy by shouting, "The last day is at hand for the Romans! These wolves that have made such ravages upon our liberty will never vanish until we have cut down the forest that harbors them."

This passionate cry for freedom failed to carry the day. Sulla won and proceeded to exterminate everyone who had opposed him. To speed the process, he devised a horrific procedure called *proscription*—posting a list of those supposedly guilty of treasonable crimes so that anyone could hunt them down and execute them. (See "Contrasting Views," page 186.) Because the property of those proscribed was confiscated, the victors fraudulently added to the list the name of anyone whose wealth they desired. The Senate in terror appointed Sulla

dictator—an emergency office supposed to be held only temporarily—without any limitation of term. He used the office to reorganize the government in the interest of "the best people"—his social class—by making senators the only ones allowed to judge cases against their colleagues and forbidding tribunes to offer legislation on their own or hold any other office after their term.

The Effects of Sulla's Career. Convinced by an old prophecy that he had only a short time to live, Sulla surprised everyone by retiring to private life in 79 B.C. and indeed dying the next year. His bloody career had starkly underlined the strengths and weaknesses of the social and political values of the republic. First, success in war had long ago changed its meaning from defense of the community to acquiring profits for common soldiers and commanders alike, primarily by selling prisoners of war into slavery and looting captured territory. Second, the patron-client system led poor soldiers to feel stronger ties of obligation to their generals than to their republic; Sulla's men obeyed his order to attack Rome because they owed obedience to him as their patron and could expect benefits from him in return. He fulfilled his obligations to them by permitting the plundering of domestic and foreign opponents alike.

Finally, the traditional desire to achieve status worked both for and against political stability. When that value motivated men from distinguished families to seek office to promote the welfare of the population as well as the standing of their families—the traditional ideal of a public career—it exerted a powerful force for social peace and general prosperity. But pushed to its extreme, as in the case of Sulla, the concern for prestige and wealth could overshadow all considerations of public service. Sulla in 88 B.C. simply could not bear to lose the personal glory that a victory over Mithridates would bring, preferring to initiate a civil war rather than to see his cherished status diminished.

The republic was doomed once its leaders and its followers forsook the "way of the ancestors" that valued respect for the peace, prosperity, and traditions of the republic above personal gain. Sulla's career helps to reveal how the social and political structure of the republic contained the seeds of its own destruction.

The Proscription Edict of 43 B.C.

Lucius Cornelius Sulla (c. 138–78 B.C.) initiated the brutal punishment known by the misleadingly neutral name of proscription (from the Latin for "publishing a notice"). To take revenge on his enemies and raise money after capturing Rome in 82 B.C., he posted lists of Romans who were declared outlaws and whose property could therefore be confiscated. Those named in these notices could be killed by anyone with impunity, rewards were offered for their deaths, and their descendants were barred from public office. Sulla's associates added the names of innocent people to settle grudges or seize valuable properties. The victors in the civil wars of the later first century B.C. continued this practice (Document 1), making it difficult to achieve a secure peace because proscription caused such bitterness among its victims' families (Documents 2 and 3).

1. The Winners in the Civil War Justify Their Proscription Edict of 43 B.C.

Following the assassination of Julius Caesar in 44 B.C., Octavius (the future Augustus), Mark Antony, and Lepidus eventually joined to control Rome. As victors over the Senate's supporters, they formed a triumvirate (rule of three men); their most infamous action was launching a proscription. Here, the second-century A.D. historian Appian reports the triumvirate's public justification for proscribing fellow citizens.

The proscription edict was in the following words: 'Marcus Lepidus, Marcus Antonius, and Octavius Caesar, chosen by the people to set in order and regulate the Republic, declare as follows:

'Had not perfidious traitors begged for mercy and when they had obtained it become the enemies of their benefactors and conspired against them, neither would Gaius Caesar have been slain by those whom he saved by his clemency after capturing them in war, whom he admitted to his friendship, and upon whom he heaped offices, honors, and gifts, nor should we have been compelled to use this widespread severity against those who have insulted us and declared us public enemies. Now, seeing that the malice of those who have conspired against us and by whose hands [Gaius] Julius Caesar perished cannot be mollified by kindness, we prefer to anticipate our enemies rather than suffer at their hands. Let no one who sees what both Caesar and we ourselves have suffered consider our action unjust, cruel, or immoderate. . . .

'Some of them we have punished already; and by the aid of divine providence you shall presently see the rest punished. Although the chief part of this work has been finished by us or is well under control, namely the settlement of Spain and Gaul as well as matters here in Italy, one task still remains, and that is to march against Caesar's assassins beyond the sea. On the eve of undertaking this foreign war for you, we do not consider it safe, either for you or for us, to leave other enemies behind to take advantage of our absence and watch for opportunities during the war; nor again do we think that in such great urgency we should delay on their account, but that we ought rather to sweep them out of our pathway once and for all, seeing that they began the war against us when they voted us and the armies under us public enemies.

'What vast numbers of citizens have they, on their part, doomed to destruction with us, disregarding the vengeance of the gods and the reprobation of mankind! We shall not deal harshly with any multitude of men, nor shall we count as enemies all who have opposed or plotted against us, or those distinguished for their riches merely, their abundance or their high position, or as many as another man slew who held the supreme power before us when he too was regulating the commonwealth in civil convulsions, and whom you named the Fortunate on account of his success; and yet necessarily three persons will have more enemies than one. We shall take vengeance only on the worst and most guilty. This we shall do for your interest no less than for our own, for while we keep up our conflicts you will all be involved necessarily in great dangers, and it is necessary for us also to do something to quiet the army, which has been insulted, irritated, and decreed a public enemy by our common foes. Although we might arrest on the spot whomsoever we had determined on, we prefer to proscribe rather than seize them unawares—and this too on your account, so that it may not be in the power of enraged soldiers to exceed their orders against persons not responsible, but that they may be restricted to a certain number designated by name and spare the others according to order.

'So be it then! Let no one harbor anyone of those whose names are appended to this edict, or conceal them, or send them away anywhere, or be corrupted by their money. Whoever shall be detected in saving, aiding, or conniving with them we will put on the list of the proscribed without allowing any excuse or pardon. Let those who kill the proscribed bring us their heads and receive the following rewards: to a free man 25,000 Attic drachmas per head, to a slave his freedom and 10,000 Attic drachmas and his master's right of citizenship. Informers shall receive the same rewards. In order that they may remain unknown the names of those who receive the rewards shall not be inscribed in our records.'

Source: Appian, *Civil Wars*, Book 4.2.8.–11, Loeb Classical Library (Cambridge: Harvard University Press, 1913).

2. The Future Augustus Betrays Cicero

The most famous victim of the proscription of 43 B.C. was the orator and politician Cicero, who had helped Octavius to power. Cicero had desperately underestimated Octavius's determination and ruthlessness when he planned to use the young man to promote the Senate's interest against Antony and then discard him. When Antony and Octavius unexpectedly united in the triumvirate, Cicero lost his gamble, with fatal consequences.

But after Antony had been defeated and, both consuls having died after the battle, the forces had united under [Caesar,] the senate became afraid of a young man who had enjoyed such brilliant good fortune, and endeavoured by honours and gifts to call his troops away from him and to circumscribe his power, on the ground that there was no need of defensive armies now that Antony had taken to flight. Under these circumstances Caesar took alarm and secretly sent messengers to Cicero begging and urging him to obtain the consulship for them both, but to manage affairs as he himself thought best, after assuming the office, and to direct in all things a youthful colleague who only craved name and fame. And Caesar himself admitted afterwards that it was the fear of having his troops disbanded and the dangers of finding himself left alone which led him to make use in an emergency of Cicero's love of power, by inducing him to sue for the consulship with his cooperation and assistance in the canvass.

Here, indeed, more than at any other time, Cicero was led on and cheated, an old man by a young man. He assisted Caesar in his canvass and induced the senate to favour him. For this he was blamed by his friends at a time, and shortly afterwards he perceived that he had ruined himself and betrayed the liberty of the people. For after the young man had waxed strong and obtained the consulship, he gave Cicero the go-by, and after making friends with Antony and Lepidus and uniting his forces with theirs, he divided the sovereignty with them, like any other piece of property. And a list was made out by them of men who must be put to death, more than two hundred in number. The proscription of Cicero, however, caused most strife in their debates, Antony consenting to no terms unless Cicero should be the first man to be put to death, Lepidus siding with Antony, and Caesar holding out against them both. They held secret meetings by themselves near the city of Bononia for three days, coming together in a place at some distance from the camps and surrounded by a river. It is said that for the first two days Caesar kept up his struggle to save Cicero, but yielded on the third and gave him up. The terms of their mutual concessions were as follows. Caesar was to abandon Cicero, Lepidus his brother Paulus, and Antony Lucius Caesar, who was his uncle on the mother's side. So far did anger and fury lead them to renounce their human sentiments, or rather, they showed that no wild beast is more savage than man when his passion is supplemented by power.

Source: Plutarch, *Life of Cicero*, 45.4–46.4, Loeb Classical Library (Cambridge: Harvard University Press, 1919).

3. A Grieving Husband Describes His Dead Wife's Valor

This eulogy emotionally describes the loss a husband felt at the death of his wife, who had literally saved his life during the proscription, first by helping him escape and then by confronting Lepidus when he tried to void her husband's pardon. Their story shows the victim's side of this notorious episode.

The day before our wedding you were suddenly left an orphan when both your parents were murdered. Although I had gone to Macedonia and your sister's husband, Gaius Cluvius, had gone to the province of Africa, the murder of your parents did not remain unavenged. You carried out this act of piety with such great diligence—asking questions, making inquiries, demanding punishment—that if we had been there, we could not have done better. You and that very pious woman, your sister, share the credit for success. . . .

Rare indeed are marriages of such long duration, which are ended by death, not divorce. We had the good fortune to spend forty-one years together with no unhappiness. I wish that our long marriage had come finally to an end by *my* death, since it would have been more just for me, who was older, to yield to fate.

Why should I mention your personal virtues—your modesty, obedience, affability, and good nature, your tireless attention to wool-working, your performance of religious duties without superstitious fear, your artless elegance and simplicity of dress? Why speak about your affection toward your relatives, your sense of duty toward your family (for you cared for my mother as well as you cared for your parents)? Why recall the countless other virtues which you have in common with all Roman matrons worthy of that name? The virtues I claim for you are your own special virtues; few people have possessed similar ones or been known to possess them. The history of the human race tells us how rare they are. . . .

When my political enemies were hunting me down, you aided my escape by selling your jewelry; you gave me all the gold and pearls which you were wearing and added a small income from household funds. We deceived the guards of my enemies, and you made my time in hiding an "enriching" experience. . . .

Why should I now disclose memories locked deep in my heart, memories of secret and concealed plans? Yes, memories—how I was warned by swift messages to avoid present and imminent dangers and was therefore saved by your quick thinking; how you did not permit me to be swept away by my foolhardy boldness; how, by calm consideration, you arranged a safe place of refuge for me and enlisted as allies in your plans to save me your sister and her husband, Gaius Cluvius, even though the plans were dangerous to all of you. If I tried to touch on all your actions on my behalf, I could go on forever. For us let it suffice to say that you hid me safely.

Yet the most bitter experience of my life came later. . . . I was granted a pardon by Augustus, but his colleague Lepidus opposed the pardon. When you threw yourself on the ground at his feet, not only did he not raise you up, but in fact he grabbed you and dragged you along as if you were a slave. You were covered with bruises, but with unflinching determination you reminded him of Augustus Caesar's edict of pardon. . . . Although you suffered insults and cruel injuries, you revealed them publicly in order to expose him as the author of my calamities. . . .

When the world was finally at peace again and order had been restored in the government, we enjoyed quiet and happy days.

Source: H. Dessau, ed., *Inscriptiones Latinae Selectae*, No. 8393 (Berlin, 1892–1916).

QUESTIONS FOR DEBATE

1. Is violence justified if it is meant to bring peace?
2. What controls are possible to prevent the victors in war from abusing their defeated enemies?

The Downfall of the Republic

The great generals whose names dominate the history of the republic after Sulla all took him as their model: while professing allegiance to the state, they relentlessly pursued their own advancement. Their motivation—that a Roman noble could never have too much glory or too much wealth—was a corruption of the finest ideals of the republic. Their fevered pursuit of self-aggrandizement ignored the honored tradition of public service to the commonwealth. Two Roman nobles, Pompey and Caesar, gained glory and prodigious amounts of money for themselves, but the brutal civil war they eventually fought against each other ruined the republic and opened the way for the return of monarchy after an absence of nearly five hundred years.

Pompey's Irregular Career. Gnaeus Pompey (106–48 B.C.) first forced his way onto the scene in 83 B.C. during Sulla's return from defeating Mithridates. The course of his career shows how the traditional restraints on an individual's power ceased operating in the first century B.C. At only twenty-three years old, Pompey gathered a private army from his father's clients to fight for Sulla. So splendid were his victories that his astonishing demand for a triumph could not be refused. Awarding the supreme honor to such a young man, who had held not a single public post, shattered an ancient tradition of the republic. But his personal power made him irresistible. As Pompey told Sulla, "People worship the rising, not the setting, sun."

Beginning his career at the top, Pompey went on from success to success. After helping suppress a major rebellion in Spain led by a renegade Roman commander, in 71 B.C. he piggybacked onto the final victories in a massive slave rebellion led by Spartacus, stealing the glory from the real victor, the commander Marcus Licinius Crassus (c. 115–53 B.C.). (For two years, the fugitive gladiator Spartacus had terrorized southern Italy and defeated consuls with his army of 100,000 escaped slaves.) Pompey demanded and won election to the consulship in 70 B.C., well before he had reached the legal age of forty-two or even held any other office. Three years later, he received a command with unlimited powers to exterminate the pirates currently infesting the Mediterranean; he smashed them in a matter of months. This success made him wildly popular with the urban poor, who depended on a steady flow of imported grain; with the wealthy commercial and shipping interests, which depended on safe sea lanes; and with coastal communities that had suffered from the pirates' raids. In 66 B.C., he received the command against Mithridates, who was still stirring up trouble in Asia Minor, and went on to win the first Roman victories in the Levant. By annexing Syria as a province in 64 B.C., he ended the Seleucid Kingdom and extended Rome's power to the eastern edge of the Mediterranean. He marched as far south as Jerusalem, capturing it in 63 B.C. Jews had lived in Rome since the second century B.C., but most Romans knew little about their religion; Pompey inspected the Jerusalem temple to satisfy his curiosity and remove its treasures.

Pompey's success in the East was so spectacular that people compared him to Alexander the Great and referred to him as *Magnus* ("the Great"). No fan of modesty, he boasted that he had increased Rome's provincial revenues by 70 percent and distributed spoils equal to twelve and a half years' pay each to his soldiers. The extent to which foreign policy had become the personal business of "great men" was evident: during his time in the east he operated on his own initiative and ignored the tradition of commanders consulting the Senate to decide on new political arrangements for conquered territories. For all practical purposes, he behaved more like an independent king than a Roman magistrate. Even early in his career he pithily expressed his attitude when replying to some foreigners after they had objected to his actions as unjust: "Stop quoting the laws to us," he told them. "We carry swords."

Fearing his power, Pompey's enemies at Rome tried to strengthen their own positions by proclaiming their concern for the plight of the common people. And there was much cause for concern. By the 60s B.C., Rome's population had soared to over half a million people. Hundreds of thousands of them lived crowded together in shabby apartment buildings no better than slums and depended on subsidized food. Work was hard to find. Danger haunted the crowded streets because the city had no police force. Even the propertied class was in trouble: Sulla's confiscations had caused land values to plummet and produced a credit crunch by flooding the real estate market with properties for sale. Overextended investors were trying to borrow their way back to liquidity, with no success.

The "First Triumvirate." Pompey's return from the east in 62 B.C. lit the fuse to this political time bomb. The Senate, eager to bring "the Great" down a notch, shortsightedly refused to approve his arrangements in the Levant or his reward of land to the veterans of his army. This setback forced Pompey to negotiate with his fiercest political rivals, Crassus and Julius Caesar (100–44 B.C.). In 60 B.C., these three allied with one another in an unofficial arrangement usually called the "First Triumvirate" ("coalition of three men"). Their combined influence proved unstoppable: Pompey had laws passed to confirm his eastern arrangements and provide land for his veterans, thus affirming his status as a glorious patron; Caesar gained the consulship for 59 B.C. along with a special command in Gaul, giving him a chance to build his own client army financed with barbarian booty; and Crassus received financial breaks for the Roman tax collectors in Asia Minor, whose support gave him political clout and in whose business he had a stake.

This unprecedented coalition of former political enemies shared no common philosophy of governing; its only cohesion came from the personal connection of its members. To cement his bond with Pompey, Caesar married his daughter, Julia, to him in 59 B.C., even though she had been engaged to another man. Pompey soothed Julia's jilted fiancé by having him marry his own daughter, who had been engaged to yet somebody else. Through these marital machinations, the two powerful antagonists now had a common interest: the fate of Julia, Caesar's only daughter and Pompey's new wife. (He had earlier divorced his second wife after Caesar allegedly seduced her.) Pompey and Julia apparently fell deeply in love in their arranged marriage. As long as Julia lived, Pompey's affection for her helped restrain him from an outright break with her father. With the triumvirate, these private relationships blatantly replaced communal values as the glue of republican politics.

Caesar's Civil War. Caesar cemented the affection of his client army with year after year of victories and plunder in central and northern Gaul, which he added to the Roman provinces; he awed his troops with his daring by crossing the channel to Britain for brief campaigns. His political enemies at Rome dreaded him even more as his military successes

Coin Portrait of Julius Caesar

Julius Caesar (100–44 B.C.) was the first living Roman to have his portrait depicted on a coin. Roman republican coinage had annually changing "types" (the pictures and words placed on the front and back of coins) determined by the officials in charge of minting (the "moneyers"), but tradition mandated that only dead persons could be shown (the same rule applies to United States currency). After he won the civil war in 45 B.C., Caesar broke that tradition, as he did many others, to show that he was Rome's supreme leader. Here he wears the laurel wreath of a conquering general (a triumphator); the portrait conforms to late republican style, in which the subject is shown realistically. Caesar's wrinkled neck and careworn expression emphasize the suffering he had endured—and imposed on others—to reach the pinnacle of success.
Bibliothèque Nationale, Paris.

mounted, and the bond linking him to Pompey dissolved in 54 B.C. when Julia died in childbirth. As his supporters in Rome worked to win popular support for his eventual return to politics in the capital, the two sides' rivalry exploded into violence. By the mid-50s B.C., political gangs of young men regularly combed the streets of Rome in search of opponents to beat up or murder. Street fighting reached such a pitch in 53 B.C. that it was impossible to hold elections; no consuls could be chosen until the year was half over. The triumvirate completely dissolved that same year with the death of Crassus in battle at Carrhae in northern Mesopotamia; in an attempt to win the military glory he felt had been stolen from him, without authorization he had taken a Roman army across the Euphrates River to fight the Parthians, an Iranian people who ruled a vast territory stretching from the Euphrates to the Indus River. A year later, Caesar's most determined enemies took the extraordinary step of having Pompey appointed as sole consul. The traditions of republican government had plainly fallen into the dust.

When the Senate ordered Caesar to surrender his command and thus open himself to prosecution by his enemies, like Sulla before him he led his army against Rome in a bitter civil war. As he crossed the Rubicon River, the official northern boundary of Italy, in early 49 b.c., he uttered the famous words signaling that he had made an irrevocable choice: "The die is cast." His troops followed him without hesitation, and the people of the towns and countryside of Italy cheered him on enthusiastically. He had many backers in Rome, too, from the masses who looked forward to his legendary generosity to impoverished members of the elite hoping to recoup their fortunes through proscriptions of the rich.

This enthusiastic response induced Pompey and most senators to flee to Greece to prepare their forces. Caesar entered Rome peacefully, soon departed to defeat the army his enemies had raised in Spain, and then sailed to Greece in 48 b.c. There he nearly lost the war when his supplies ran out, but his loyal soldiers stuck with him even when they were reduced to eating bread made from roots. When Pompey saw what his opponent's troops were willing to subsist on, he lamented, "I am fighting wild beasts." Caesar exploited the high morale of his army and Pompey's weak generalship to gain a stunning victory at the battle of Pharsalus in 48 b.c. The loser fled to Egypt, where he was treacherously murdered by the ministers of the boy-king Ptolemy XIII (63–47 b.c.).

Caesar soon invaded Egypt, winning a difficult campaign that ended when the young pharaoh drowned in the Nile and Caesar restored Cleopatra VII (69–30 b.c.) to the throne of Egypt. As ruthless as she was intelligent, Cleopatra charmed the invader into sharing her bed and supporting her rule. This attachment shocked the general's friends and enemies alike: they thought Rome should seize power from foreigners, not yield it to them. Still, so effective were Cleopatra's powers of persuasion that Caesar maintained the love affair and acknowledged her personal dominion over a rich land that his army otherwise would have conquered for Roman gain.

Caesar's Rule and Murder. By 45 b.c., Caesar had defeated the final holdouts in the civil war and faced the intractable problem of ruling a shattered republic. The predicament had deep roots. Sad experience had shown that only a sole ruler could end the chaotic violence of factional politics, but the oldest tradition of the republic was its abhorrence

of monarchy. The second-century b.c. senator Cato, famous for his advice about destroying Carthage, had best expressed the Roman elite's views on monarchy: "A king," he quipped, "is an animal that feeds on human flesh."

Caesar's solution was to rule as king in everything but name. First, he had himself appointed dictator in 48 b.c., with his term in the traditionally temporary office extended to a lifetime tenure around 44 b.c. "I am not a king," he insisted. But the distinction was meaningless. As dictator, he controlled the government despite the appearance of normal procedures. Elections for offices continued, for example, but Caesar manipulated the results by recommending candidates to the assemblies, which his supporters dominated. Naturally his recommendations were followed.

Caesar's policies as Rome's ruler were ambitious and broad: a moderate cancellation of debts; a limitation on the number of people eligible for subsidized grain; a large program of public works, including the construction of public libraries; colonies for his veterans in Italy and abroad; the rebuilding of Corinth and Carthage as commercial centers; and a revival of the ancient policy of strengthening the

Ides of March Coin Celebrating Caesar's Murder

Roman coins, which were the most widely distributed form of art and communication in the Roman world, carried messages in their types. Usually the messages expressed the mint officials' pride in their own ancestry, but during the crisis of the late republic, types became topical and contemporary. Caesar's assassins, led by Marcus Junius Brutus (85–42 b.c.), issued this coin celebrating the murder and their claim to be liberators. The daggers refer to the method they used, while the conical cap stands for liberation (it was the kind of headgear worn by slaves who had won their freedom). The inscription gives the date of the assassination, the Ides of March (March 15), according to the Roman calendar.
British Museum.

IMPORTANT DATES

753 B.C. Traditional date of Rome's founding as a monarchy

509 B.C. Roman republic established

509–287 B.C. Struggle of the orders

451–449 B.C. Creation of the Twelve Tables, Rome's first written law code

396 B.C. Defeat of the Etruscan city of Veii; first great expansion of Roman territory

387 B.C. Sack of Rome by Gauls

264–241 B.C. First Punic War between Rome and Carthage

c. 220 B.C. Rome controls Italy south of the Po River

218–201 B.C. Second Punic War between Rome and Carthage

168–149 B.C. Cato writes *The Origins*, the first history of Rome in Latin

149–146 B.C. Third Punic War between Rome and Carthage; destruction of Carthage and Corinth in 146 B.C.

133 B.C. Tiberius Gracchus elected tribune; assassinated in same year

91–87 B.C. Social War between Rome and its Italian allies

60 B.C. First Triumvirate of Caesar, Pompey, and Crassus

49–45 B.C. Civil war, with Caesar the victor

45–44 B.C. Cicero writes his philosophical works on *humanitas*

44 B.C. Caesar appointed dictator for life; assassinated in same year

state by giving citizenship to non-Romans, such as the Cisalpine Gauls (those on the Italian side of the Alps). He also admitted non-Italians to the Senate when he expanded its membership from six hundred (the number after Sulla) to nine hundred. Unlike Sulla, he did not proscribe his enemies. Instead he prided himself on his clemency, the recipients of which were, by Roman custom, bound to be his grateful clients. In return, he received unprecedented honors, such as a special golden seat in the Senate house and the renaming of the seventh month of the year after him (our July). He also reg-

ularized the Roman calendar by having each year include 365 days, a calculation based on an ancient Egyptian calendar that roughly forms the basis for our modern one.

His office and his honors pleased most Romans but outraged the narrow circle of optimates. These men resented their exclusion from power and their domination by one of their own, a "traitor" who had deserted to the people's faction in the republic's perpetual conflict between rich and poor. A band of senators conspired against Caesar, led by his former close friend Marcus Junius Brutus and inspired by their memory of the leadership of Brutus's ancestor Lucius Junius Brutus in violently expelling Rome's early monarchy. They cut Caesar to pieces with daggers in a hail of blood in the Senate house on March 15 (the Ides of March in the Roman calendar), 44 B.C. When his friend Brutus stabbed him, Caesar, according to some ancient reports, gasped his last words—in Greek: "You, too, child?" One of the ironies noted of his murder is that he collapsed dead at the foot of a statue of Pompey.

The "liberators," as they styled themselves, had no concrete plans for governing Rome. They apparently believed that the traditional political system of the republic would somehow reconstitute itself without any action on their part and without further violence; in their profound naiveté, they ignored the grisly reality of the previous forty years and the complete imbalance that reigned in Roman values, with ambitious individuals putting their own interests and those of their clients far ahead of the community's. Distraught at the loss of their patron, the masses rioted at Caesar's funeral to vent their anger against the upper class that had robbed them of their benefactor. Far from presenting a united front, the elite resumed their vendettas with one another to secure personal political power. By 44 B.C., the republic had suffered damage beyond repair.

Conclusion

The most intriguing features of the Roman republic were its phenomenal expansion and its equally remarkable disintegration. From its beginnings in 509 B.C., the republic flourished because it incorporated outsiders, its small farmers produced agricultural surpluses, and its values stressed the common

MAPPING THE WEST The Roman World at the End of the Republic, c. 44 B.C.
When Octavius (the future Augustus) finished Julius Caesar's plan for expansion by conquering Egypt in 30 B.C., the territory that would form the Roman Empire was essentially complete. Geography and distance were the primary factors inhibiting further expansion, which Romans never stopped thinking of as desirable, even when practical difficulties rendered this goal purely theoretical. The deserts of Africa and the Near East worked against expansion southward or eastward against the often formidable powers located beyond, while trackless forests and fierce resistance from local inhabitants made expansion into central Europe and the British Isles impossible to maintain.

good. Its surpluses supported a growth in population that supplied the soldiers for a strong army of citizens and allies. The Roman willingness to endure great losses of life and property—the proof of their value of faithfulness—helped make their army invincible in prolonged conflicts: Rome might lose battles, but never wars. Because wars initially brought profits, peace seemed a wasted opportunity. Elite commanders especially liked war because they could win glory and riches to enhance their status in Rome's social hierarchy.

But the continued wars of the republic against Carthage and in Macedonia and Greece had unexpected consequences that spelled disaster. Long military service ruined many of the small landowners

on whom Italy's prosperity depended. When the dispossessed flocked to Rome, they created a new, unstable political force: the urban mob demanding subsidized food. Members of the upper class escalated their competition with each other for the increased career opportunities presented by constant war. These rivalries became unmanageable when successful generals began to extort advantages for themselves instead of the republic by acting as patrons to their client armies of poor troops. In this dog-eat-dog atmosphere, violence and murder became the preferred means of settling political disputes. But violent actions provoked violent responses; communal values were drowned in the blood of civil war. No reasonable Roman could have been optimistic about the chances for an enduring peace in the aftermath of Caesar's assassination in 44 B.C.; that another "great man" would forge such a peace less than fifteen years later would have seemed an impossible dream.

Suggested References

Social and Religious Traditions

Historians have long appreciated that to understand Roman history one must understand Roman values, but recent scholarship emphasizes how those values related to religion. In addition, study of legends about the foundation of Rome shows how Romans much later in the republic relied on those stories to define their national identity.

Beard, Mary, et al. *Religions of Rome*. 2 vols. 1998.

Bradley, Keith. *Slavery and Society at Rome*. 1994.

Daily life (and more): http://vroma.rhodes.edu/~bmcmanus/romanpages.html.

Dowden, Ken. *Religion and the Romans*. 1992.

Earl, Donald. *The Moral and Political Tradition of Rome*. 1967.

Gardner, Jane. *Women in Roman Law and Society*. 1986.

Miles, Gary B. *Livy: Reconstructing Early Rome*. 1992.

Potter, T. W. *Roman Italy*. 1987.

Rawson, Beryl, ed. *The Family in Ancient Rome: New Perspectives*. 1986.

Tellegen-Couperus, Olga. *A Short History of Roman Law*. 1993.

From Monarchy to Republic, c. 753–287 B.C.

Instead of seeing early Rome as shaped largely by Etruscan influence, contemporary scholarship stresses the Romans' own efforts at shaping their state and culture, as clearly explained in Cornell's book. Recent interpretation of the struggle of the orders has concentrated on the effects of the overlapping interests of patricians and plebeians rather than merely on the division between the orders.

Boëthius, Axel. *Etruscan and Early Roman Architecture*. 2nd ed. 1978.

Bonfante, Larissa, ed. *Etruscan Life and Afterlife: A Handbook of Etruscan Studies*. 1986.

Brunt, P. A. *Social Conflicts in the Roman Republic*. 1971.

Cornell, T. J. *The Beginnings of Rome: Italy and Rome from the Bronze Age to the Punic Wars (c. 1000–264 B.C.)*. 1995.

Crawford, Michael. *The Roman Republic*. 2nd ed. 1993.

Ladder of offices (*cursus honorum*): http://vroma.rhodes.edu/~bmcmanus/romangvt.html.

MacNamara, Ellen. *The Etruscans*. 1991.

Timeline of Roman history: http://acs.rhodes.edu/~jruebel/timeline.

Watson, Alan. *Rome of the XII Tables: Persons and Property*. 1975.

————. *International Law in Archaic Rome: War and Religion*. 1993.

Wiseman, T. P. *Remus: A Roman Myth*. 1995.

Roman Imperialism and Its Consequences, Fifth to Second Centuries B.C.

Scholarly debate about the causes and effects of Roman imperialism remains vigorous. Interpretations now tend to stress a multiplicity of causes and the complicated ways in which conquered peoples responded to and resisted Roman power, even after their defeat. Continuing archaeological excavation at Carthage has revealed much about the history of that extremely successful Phoenician foundation.

Alcock, Susan. *Graecia Capta: The Landscapes of Roman Greece*. 1993.

Astin, Alan E. *Cato the Censor*. 1978.

Badian, E. *Roman Imperialism in the Late Republic*. 2nd ed. 1968.

————. *Publicans and Sinners: Private Enterprise in the Service of the Roman Republic*. 1972.

Conte, Gian Biagio. *Latin Literature: A History*. Trans. Joseph B. Solodow. Rev. Don Fowler and Glenn W. Most. 1994.

Errington, R. M. *The Dawn of Empire: Rome's Rise to World Power*. 1972.

Etruscan realistic portraiture (second century B.C.): http://www.worcesterart.org/Collection/Ancient/1926.19.html.

Gabba, Emilio. *Republican Rome: The Army and the Allies*. Trans. P. J. Cuff. 1976.

Gruen, Erich S. *The Hellenistic World and the Coming of Rome*. 2 vols. 1984.

Harris, William V. *War and Imperialism in Republican Rome, 327–70 B.C.* 1985.

Lancel, Serge. *Carthage: A History*. Trans. Antonia Nevill. 1995.

Lazenby, J. F. *The First Punic War: A Military History*. 1996.

Nicolet, Claude. *The World of the Citizen in Republican Rome*. 1980.

Ogilvie, R. M. *Roman Literature and Society*. 1980.

Salmon, E. T. *Roman Colonization under the Republic*. 1970.

Scullard, H. H. *From the Gracchi to Nero: A History of Rome, 133 B.C. to A.D. 68*. 5th ed. 1982.

Strong, Donald. *Roman Art*. 2nd ed. 1988.

Taylor, Lilly Ross. *Roman Voting Assemblies: From the Hannibalic War to the Dictatorship of Caesar*. 1966.

Toynbee, J. M. C. *Roman Historical Portraits*. 1978.

Upheaval in the Late Republic, c. 133–44 B.C.

It is only with the history of the late republic that the surviving written sources become more than scanty, with contemporary documents such as the many letters and speeches of Cicero and the memoirs of Caesar to supplement the ancient narrative accounts (which date to the later period of empire). Arguments about the failure of the republic now tend to reject the traditional view that destructive rivalries were based more on family and group loyalties than on political differences; instead, deep divisions about political issues are seen to be primary, in addition to the emergence of new forms of elite competition.

Beard, Mary, and Michael Crawford. *Rome in the Late Republic.* 1985.

Bradley, Keith R. *Slavery and Rebellion in the Roman World, 140 B.C.–70 B.C.* 1998.

Greenhalgh, Peter. *Pompey the Roman Alexander.* 1981.

———. *Pompey the Republican Prince.* 1982.

Keaveney, Arthur. *Sulla: The Last Republican.* 1982.

Meier, Christian. *Caesar: A Biography.* Trans. David McLintock. 1995.

Roman archaeological sites: http://www.ukans.edu/history/index/europe/ancient_rome/E/Roman/RomanSites*Topics/Archaeology.html.

Shotter, David. *The Fall of the Roman Republic.* 1994.

Southern, Pat. *Cleopatra.* 1999.

Stockton, David. *The Gracchi.* 1979.

Ward, Allen. *Marcus Crassus and the Late Roman Republic.* 1977.

CHAPTER

6

The Roman Empire

c. 44 B.C.–A.D. 284

Portrait of a Married Couple from Pompeii

This twenty-six-inch-high wall painting of a woman and her husband was found in an alcove off the central room of a comfortable house in Pompeii, the town in southern Italy buried by a volcanic explosion in A.D. 79. The couple may have owned the bakery that adjoined the house. Both are depicted with items meant to indicate that they were fashionable and educated. She holds the notepad of the time, a hinged wooden tablet filled with wax for writing on with the stylus (thin stick) that she touches to her lips; he holds a scroll, the standard form for books in the early Roman Empire. Her hairstyle was one popular in the mid-first century A.D., which hints that this picture was painted not many years before Mount Vesuvius erupted and covered Pompeii in twelve feet of ash.
Scala/Art Resource, NY.

IN A.D. 203, VIBIA PERPETUA, wealthy and twenty-two years old, nursed her infant in a Carthage jail while awaiting execution; she had received the death sentence for refusing to sacrifice to the gods for the Roman emperors' health and safety. One morning the jailer dragged her off to the city's main square, where a crowd had gathered. Perpetua described in a journal what happened when the local governor made a last, public attempt to get her to save her life: "My father came carrying my son, crying 'Perform the sacrifice; take pity on your baby!' Then the governor said, 'Think of your old father; show pity for your little child! Offer the sacrifice for the welfare of the imperial family.' 'I refuse,' I answered. 'Are you a Christian?' asked the governor. 'Yes.' When my father would not stop trying to change my mind, the governor ordered him flung to the earth and whipped with a rod. I felt sorry for my father; it seemed they were beating me. I pitied his pathetic old age." The brutality of Perpetua's later punishment failed to break her: gored by a wild bull and stabbed by a gladiator, she died professing her faith.

A clash over the traditional Roman values of faithfulness and loyalty had condemned Perpetua: she believed that her faith in Christ required her to refuse the state's demand for loyalty to the "way of the elders" in public religion as well as to look beyond her family obligations. This conflict echoed in a different form the divided loyalties that had destroyed the republic, when ambitious commanders fought civil wars because they valued their individual goals above service to the

197

44 B.C.	A.D. 20	A.D. 85	A.D. 150	A.D. 215	A.D. 284

Politics and War

- Augustus inaugurates the principate
- Political Golden Age of the principate
- Domitian's campaigns against Germanic bands
- Germanic attacks on northern frontiers
- Civil wars, fiscal instability lead to political crisis
- Expansion of imperial army

Society and Economy

- Peace and prosperity under the principate
- Collapse of the Roman economy
- Civil war during the "Year of the Four Emperors"
- Caracalla extends Roman citizenship to most free inhabitants
- Augustan reforms restore stability, transform republican Rome into inperial Rome
- Fiscal strains caused by military expansion
- Sassanid capture of the emperor Valerian

Culture, Religion, and Intellectual Life

- Latin Golden Age authors, including Virgil, Horace, Livy, Ovid
- New Testament Gospels written down
- Christians persecuted under Decius
- Crucifixion of Jesus of Nazareth
- Latin Silver Age authors, including Juvenal, Tacitus
- Paul's travels to win Christian converts begin
- Christian ministries of the prophetesses Prisca and Maximilla in Asia Minor

common good. Following Julius Caesar's assassination in 44 B.C., Augustus (63 B.C.–A.D. 14) eventually developed a special kind of monarchy to restore stability by reorienting communal loyalty toward the ruling family. This refocusing of trust restored the peace that the civil wars of the first century B.C. had squandered. Remembering the violent history of the late republic, Rome's rulers feared disloyalty. Perpetua's refusal to sacrifice was considered treason and impiety because it threatened to punish the entire community by angering the gods.

The Roman Empire, the usual modern name applied to the period from Augustus onward, opened with a bloodbath: seventeen years of civil war followed Caesar's funeral. Finally, in 27 B.C., Augustus created his new monarchical government—the *principate*—to end the violence. He ingeniously disguised his creation as a restoration of the republic because officially abandoning the tradition of shared governing would have seemed too radical. He retained old institutions—the Senate, the consuls, the courts—while fundamentally reshaping the distribution of power by making himself sole ruler in practice. He masked his monarchy with deft propaganda: instead of calling himself "king" (Latin *rex*), he used "first man" (*princeps,* hence the term *principate*), a traditional honorary title designating the leading senator. *Princeps* became the office that today we call "emperor" (from the Latin *imperator*, "commander"). Augustus's arrangement made Rome into a monarchy on the Hellenistic model, without the name but with an untested principle of succession calling for the *princeps* to groom a successor approved by the Senate.

Except for a few brief political struggles for the throne, this transformed system of government brought stability for two hundred years. Worn out by war with each other, Romans welcomed this period of tranquillity and calm prosperity, which historians call the *Pax Romana* ("Roman peace"). In the third century A.D., however, violent rivalry for the throne reignited long civil wars that generated fiscal and then economic crisis. By the end of that century, Roman government desperately needed to refocus its values and again transform its political institutions to keep its society from disintegrating. The most pressing question remained how to balance the traditional values of official loyalty and public service by the wealthy. Winning the throne in A.D. 284, the emperor Domitian began that process.

❖ Creating "Roman Peace"

Inventing tradition takes time. Augustus founded his new political system gradually; as the biographer Suetonius (c. 70–130) expressed it, Augustus "made haste slowly." In the long run, the principate created an extended period of peace inside its borders, although its rulers periodically fought to expand imperial territory, suppress rebellions, or repel invaders. Its founder succeeded because he won the struggle for power, reinvented government, and found new ways to build loyalty by communicating an image of himself as a dedicated leader. The extent of his changes and the length of his reign implanted monarchy permanently in Rome's future.

From Republic to Principate, 44–27 B.C.

The gruesome infighting to fill the political vacuum created by Caesar's assassination in 44 B.C. transformed the republic into the principate. The main competitors for power were prominent generals,

above all Mark Antony, and Caesar's ambitious eighteen-year-old grandnephew and heir Octavian (the future Augustus). The youthful Octavian won the support of Caesar's soldiers by promising them rewards from their murdered general's wealth. Marching these men to the capital, the youth demanded to be made consul in 43 B.C. without ever having held any public office. As with Pompey's irregular career, fearful senators granted Octavian the consulship, disregarding the tradition that required a man to progress gradually to reach the pinnacle of power. Civil war had made acquiescence to the demands of powerful military men standard practice rather than a rare exception to tradition.

Octavian, Antony, and a general named Lepidus joined forces to eliminate other rivals, especially the self-styled liberators, condemned as assassins of Caesar, and their supporters. In late 43 B.C., the trio formed the so-called Second Triumvirate, which they forced the Senate to recognize as an official emergency arrangement for reconstituting the state. With no check on their power, they ruthlessly instituted a proscription to murder their enemies and confiscate their property. (See "Contrasting Views," page 186.) Echoing the course of the First Triumvirate, Octavian and Antony eventually forced Lepidus into retirement and, too ambitious to cooperate indefinitely, began civil war anew. Antony made the eastern Mediterranean his base, joining forces with Cleopatra VII (69–30 B.C.), the remarkable Ptolemaic queen who had earlier allied with Caesar. Impressed with her wit and intelligence, Antony became her ally and her lover. Skillfully playing on Romans' fear of foreigners, Octavian rallied support by claiming that Antony planned to make Cleopatra their ruler. He shrewdly persuaded the residents of Italy and the western provinces to swear a personal oath of allegiance to him, effectively making them all his clients. His victory at the naval battle of Actium in northwest Greece in 31 B.C. won the war. Cleopatra and Antony fled to Egypt, where they both committed suicide in 30 B.C., following the Greek and Roman tradition of choosing one's own death to deprive a victorious enemy of a celebrity hostage. The general first stabbed himself, bleeding to death in his lover's embrace. The queen then fittingly ended her life by allowing a poisonous serpent, a symbol of Egyptian royal authority, to bite her. Octavian's capture of Egypt made him Rome's richest citizen and its unrivaled leader.

Augustus's "Restoration," 27 B.C.–A.D. 14

After distributing land to army veterans and creating colonies in the provinces, Octavian formally announced in 27 B.C. that he had restored the republic. It was up to the Senate and the Roman people, he proclaimed, to decide how to preserve it thereafter. Recognizing that Octavian possessed overwhelming power in this unprecedented display of political theater, the Senate promptly implored him to do whatever was necessary to safeguard the restored republic, granted him special civil and military powers, and bestowed on him the honorary name Augustus, meaning "divinely favored." Octavian had considered changing his name to Romulus, after Rome's legendary first king, but as the historian Cassius Dio (c. A.D. 164–230) reported, "When he realized the people thought this preference meant he longed to be their king, he accepted the other title instead, as if he were more than human; for everything that is most treasured and sacred is called *augustus*."

Inventing the Principate. In the years following 27 B.C., the annual election of consuls and other officials, the continuation of the Senate, and the

Priests on the Altar of Augustan Peace

After four years of construction, Augustus dedicated the Altar of Augustan Peace in northwest Rome on his wife's birthday in 9 B.C. The altar itself resided inside a four-walled enclosure, open to sky, about thirty-four feet long, thirty-eight feet wide, and twenty-three feet high. Relief sculptures covered the walls. This section shows a religious procession, headed by the imperial family (out of the picture to the left) and completed by a representation of Rome's senators on the opposite side. The figures wearing leather caps with spikes are priests called flamines, whose special headgear was only part of the complex ritual of their positions. The hooded man at the right, veiled for performing sacrifice, is probably Marcus Agrippa, Augustus's greatest general. Mythological figures were also sculpted on the walls, expressing the same message as the Prima Porta statue (page 207): Augustus, with his divine family origins, was the patron who brought peace and prosperity to Rome while respecting its republican traditions. The altar can be seen today in its original form because it was reconstructed by Benito Mussolini, Fascist dictator of Italy from 1926 to 1943, who wanted to appropriate Augustan glory for his regime.
Art Resource, NY.

passing of legislation in public assemblies maintained the façade of republican government. Periodically, Augustus served as consul, the republic's premier official. To preserve the tradition that no official should hold more than one post at a time, he had the Senate grant him the powers of the tribunate without actually holding the office; that is, he possessed the authority to act and to compel as if he were a tribune protecting the rights of the people, but he left all the positions themselves open for members of the plebeian elite to occupy, just as they had under the republic. The ceremony of rule also remained republican: Augustus dressed and acted like a regular citizen, not a haughty monarch. In reality, Augustus exercised supreme power because he controlled the army and the treasury.

Augustus's choice of *princeps* as his only title of office was a cleverly calculated move. In the republic, the "first man" had guided Rome only by the respect (*auctoritas*) he commanded; he had no more formal power (*potestas*) than any other leader. By appropriating this title, Augustus appeared to carry on this valued tradition. In truth, he revised the basic power structure: no one previously could have exercised the powers of both consul and tribune simultaneously. The principate became in effect a monarchy disguised as a corrected and improved republic, headed by an emperor cloaked as a *princeps*.

Augustus used the military to back up his moral authority as the restorer of the republic, taking the final step of turning the republican army of citizens into a full-time professional force. He established regular lengths of service for soldiers and substantial payment upon retirement. His changes solidified the trend of generals making themselves their armies' patrons: henceforth soldiers' benefits were permanent and guaranteed. To pay for the added costs, Augustus imposed an inheritance tax on citizens. This measure directly affected the rich, who vehemently opposed it, but the army in gratitude for his reforms obeyed and protected the emperor. For the first time, soldiers—the *praetorian cohorts*—were stationed in Rome itself. These troops prevented rebellion in the capital and provided an imperial bodyguard, a visible reminder that the ruler's superiority was in reality guaranteed by the threat of force.

Communicating the Emperor's Image. To promote the stability of the new system, Augustus brilliantly communicated his image as patron and protector on objects as small as coins and as large as buildings. As the only mass-produced source of official messages, coins could function something like modern political advertising. They proclaimed slogans such as "Father of his Country" to remind Romans of their emperor's moral authority over them, or "Roads have been built" to emphasize his personal generosity in paying for highway construction.

Grandly following the tradition that rich politicians and generals should spend money for the public good, Augustus erected huge buildings in Rome paid for by the fortune he had inherited and increased in the civil wars. The huge Forum of Augustus he dedicated in 2 B.C. best illustrates his skill at sending messages with bricks and stone. It centered on a temple to Mars, the Roman god of war. Two-story colonnades stretched out from the temple like wings, sheltering statues of famous Roman heroes, who could serve as inspi-

Central Rome and the Forum of Augustus

rations to future leaders. Augustus's forum provided practical space for religious rituals and the ceremonies marking the passage into adulthood of upper-class boys, but it also stressed the themes Augustus wanted to communicate about his regime: peace restored through victory, the foundation of a new age, devotion to the gods who protected Rome in war, respect for tradition, and unselfishness in spending money for public purposes. These messages constituted Augustus's justification for his rule.

Augustus's Motives. Augustus never revealed his deepest motives in establishing the principate. Was he a cynical despot bent on suppressing the freedoms of the republic? Did he have no choice but to impose a veiled monarchy to stabilize a society crippled by anarchy? Or did his motives lie somewhere in between? Perhaps the answer is that he was a revolutionary bound by tradition. His problem had been the one always facing Roman politicians—how to balance society's need for peace, its traditional commitment to its citizens' freedom of action, and his own personal ambitions. Augustus's solution was to employ traditional values to make changes, as seen in his inspired reinvention of the meaning of "first man." Above all, he transferred the traditional paternalism of social relations—the patron-client system—to politics by making the emperor everyone's most important patron with the moral authority to guide their lives. This process culminated with his being named "Father of his Country" in 2 B.C. He proclaimed that this title was the greatest honor Rome could grant, to emphasize that the principate provided Romans with a sole ruler who governed them like a father: stern but caring, expecting obedience and loyalty from his children, and obligated to nurture them in return. The goal of such an arrangement was stability and order, not political freedom.

Despite frequent bouts of poor health, Augustus ruled as emperor until his death at age seventy-five in A.D. 14. The great length of his reign—forty-one years—helped institutionalize his changes in Roman government. As the Roman historian Tacitus (c. 56–120) later remarked, by the time Augustus died, "almost no one was still alive who had seen the republic." Through his longevity, command over the army, rapport with the capital's urban masses, and crafty manipulation of the traditional vocabulary of politics to disguise his power, Augustus restored stability to society and transformed republican Rome into imperial Rome.

Augustan Rome

A crucial factor in Augustus's success was his attention to the lives of Roman citizens. The most pressing social problems he faced were in the capital city, a teeming metropolis with a population probably well over half a million, many of whom had too little to eat and not enough jobs. A variety of archaeological and literary sources allow us to sketch a composite picture of life in Augustan Rome. Although some of the sources refer to times after Augustus and to cities other than Rome, they nevertheless help us understand this period; economic and social conditions were essentially the same in all Roman cities throughout the early centuries of the empire.

The population of Augustan Rome was vast for the ancient world. Indeed, no European city would have nearly this many people again until London in

the 1700s. The streets were packed: "One man jabs me with his elbow, another whacks me with a pole; my legs are smeared with mud, and from all sides big feet step on me" was the poet Juvenal's description of walking in Rome in the early second century. To ease congestion in the narrow streets, the city banned carts and wagons in the daytime. This regulation made nights noisy with the creaking of axles and the shouting of drivers caught in traffic jams.

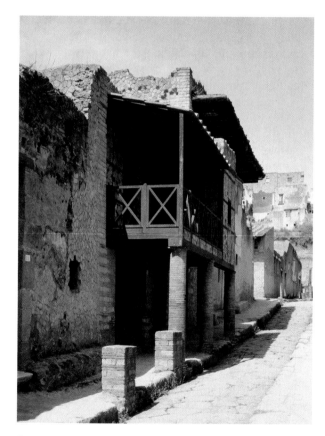

Downtown Street in Herculaneum
Like Pompeii, the prosperous town of Herculaneum on the shore of the Bay of Naples was frozen in time by the massive eruption of the neighboring volcano, Mount Vesuvius, in A.D. 79. A shower of ash from the eruption buried the town and preserved its buildings until they were excavated beginning in the eighteenth century. Typical of a Roman town, it had straight roads paved with large, flat stones and flanked by sidewalks. Balconies jutted from the upper stories of houses, offering residents a shady viewing point for the lively traffic in the urban streets. Instead of having yards in front or back, houses often enclosed a garden courtyard open to the sky.
Scala/Art Resource, NY.

The Precariousness of City Life. Most urban residents lived in small apartments in multistoried buildings called *insulae* ("islands," so named because in early times, before the city grew crowded, each building had an open strip around it). Outnumbering private houses by more than twenty to one, the apartment buildings' first floors usually housed shops, bars, and simple restaurants. Graffiti of all kinds—political endorsements, the posting

The Warm Room of a Public Bath
By the first century B.C., most sizable Roman towns had public bath buildings near their centers. Wealthy houses had private baths, but large public bathing establishments served the rest of the population. This vaulted room from a bath at Herculaneum displays the artful decoration that upper-class patrons in this luxury suburb of Naples expected. Outfitted with couches on which bathers could rest on cushions, this so-called warm room was the middle space in a set of linked chambers kept at differing temperatures from cold to hot, often equipped with pools for immersion, through which patrons proceeded as they warmed up. Bathing was a daily activity in Roman life, with socializing as important a goal as cleanliness.
Erich Lessing/Art Resource, NY.

of rewards, personal insults, and advertising—frequently decorated the exterior walls. The higher the floor, the cheaper the apartment. Well-off tenants occupied the lower stories, while the poorest people lived in single rooms rented by the day on the top floors. Aqueducts delivered a plentiful supply of fresh water, but because they had no plumbing, apartment dwellers had to lug buckets up the stairs from one of hundreds of public fountains. The wealthy few had piped-in water at ground level. Most tenants lacked bathrooms and had to use the public latrines or pots for toilets at home. Some buildings had cesspits, or buckets could be carried down to the streets to be emptied by people who made their living collecting excrement. Careless tenants haphazardly flung the foul-smelling contents of these containers out the window. Because the city generated about sixty tons of human waste every day, sanitation was an enormous problem.

To keep clean, residents used public baths. Because admission fees were low, almost everyone could afford to go to the baths daily. Scores of these establishments existed in the city, serving like modern health clubs as centers for exercising and socializing as well as washing. Bath patrons progressed through a series of increasingly warm, humid areas until they reached a sauna-like room. Bathers swam naked in their choice of hot or cold pools. Women had full access to the public baths, but men and women bathed apart, either in separate rooms or at different times of the day. Since bathing was thought to be particularly valuable for sick people, communal baths contributed to the spread of communicable diseases.

Roman officials made Herculean efforts to keep the city clean and orderly, but as in all ancient cities, public health was difficult to maintain. By 33 B.C., Augustus's general Agrippa had vastly improved the city's main sewer, but its contents emptied untreated into the Tiber River, which ran through the city. The technology for sanitary disposal of waste simply did not exist. People regularly left human and animal corpses in the streets, to be gnawed by vultures and dogs. The poor were not the only people affected by such conditions: a stray mutt once brought a human hand to the table where Vespasian, who would be emperor from 69 to 79, was eating lunch. Flies buzzing everywhere and a lack of mechanical refrigeration contributed to frequent gastrointestinal ailments: the most popular jewelry of the time was supposed to ward off stomach trouble. Although the wealthy could not eliminate such discomforts, they made their lives more pleasant with luxuries such as snow rushed from the mountains to ice their drinks and slaves to clean their airy houses, which were built around courtyards and gardens.

City residents faced unpredictable hazards beyond infectious disease. Broken crockery and other debris were routinely hurled out of the upper stories of apartment buildings, and rained down like missiles on unwary pedestrians. "If you are walking to a dinner party in Rome," Juvenal warned, "you would be foolish not to make out your will first. For every open window is a source of potential disaster." The *insulae* could be dangerous to their inhabitants as well as to passersby because they were in constant danger of collapsing. Roman engineers, despite their expertise in using concrete, brick, and stone as durable building materials, lacked the technology to calculate precisely how much stress their constructions could stand. Builders trying to cut costs paid little attention to engineering safeguards in any case, so Augustus imposed a height limit of seventy feet on new apartment buildings. Often built in valleys because the sunny hilltops were occupied by the homes of the rich, apartment buildings were also susceptible to floods. Fire presented an even greater risk; one of Augustus's many services to the urban masses was to provide Rome with the first public fire department in Western history. He also established the first police force in the west, despite his reported fondness for stopping to watch the frequent brawls that the crowding in Rome's streets encouraged.

Augustus also tried to aid the urban masses, many of whom could find only sporadic employment, by assuring them an adequate food supply. This service was his responsibility as Rome's foremost patron, and he freely drew upon his personal fortune to pay for imported grain. Distributing free grain to the capital's poor citizens had been a tradition for decades, but the scale of his dole system reached the immense number of 250,000 recipients. Because many of these poor citizens had families, this statistic suggests that perhaps 700,000 people depended on the government for their dietary staple. Poor Romans usually made this grain into a watery porridge, which they washed down with cheap wine. If they were lucky, they might have some beans, leeks, or cheese on the side. The rich, as we learn from an ancient cookbook, ate more delec-

table dishes, such as spiced roast pork or crayfish, often flavored with sweet-and-sour sauce concocted from honey and vinegar.

Some wealthy Romans had come to prefer spending money on luxuries and costly political careers instead of families. Fearing that lack of offspring would destroy the elite on which Rome relied for leadership, Augustus passed laws to strengthen marriages and encourage more births by granting special legal privileges to the parents of three or more children. Adultery became a criminal offense; so seriously did Augustus support these reforms that he exiled his own daughter—his only child—and a granddaughter after extramarital scandals. His legislation had little effect, however, and the prestigious old families dwindled over the coming centuries. Recent research suggests that up to three-quarters of senatorial families lost their official status or died out every generation. Equestrians and provincials who won imperial favor took their places in the social hierarchy and the Senate.

Roman Slavery. Slaves occupied the lowest rung in society's hierarchy and provided the basis of the imperial workforce. Unlike Greece, however, Rome gave citizenship to freed slaves. This policy made a crucial difference that deeply affected Roman society in the long term: all slaves could hope to acquire the rights of a free citizen, and their descendants, if they became wealthy, could become members of the social elite. This arrangement gave slaves reason to persevere and cooperate with their masters.

Conditions of slavery varied widely according to occupation. Slaves in agriculture and manufacturing had a grueling existence. Most such workers were men, although women might assist the foremen who managed gangs of rural laborers. The second-century novelist Apuleius penned this grim description of slaves at work in a flour mill: "Through the holes in their ragged clothes you could see all over their bodies the scars from whippings. Some wore only loincloths. Letters had been branded on their foreheads and irons manacled their ankles." Worse than the mills were the mines, where the foremen constantly flogged the miners to keep them working in such a dangerous environment.

Household slaves had an easier physical existence. Many, perhaps most, Romans owned slaves to work in their homes, from one or two in modestly well-off families to hordes of them in rich houses and, above all, the imperial palace. Domestic slaves were often women, working as nurses, maids, kitchen help, and clothes makers. Some male slaves ran businesses for their masters, and they were often allowed to keep part of the profits as an incentive and as savings to purchase their freedom someday. Women had less opportunity to earn money. Masters sometimes granted tips for sexual favors, and female prostitutes (many of whom were slaves) had more chances to make money for themselves. Slaves who managed to acquire funds would sometimes buy slaves themselves, thereby creating their own hierarchy. A man, for example, might buy a woman for a mate. They could then have a semblance of family life, though a normal marriage was impossible because they remained their master's property, as did their children. If truly fortunate, slaves could slowly accumulate enough to buy themselves from their masters or could be freed by their masters' wills. Some epitaphs on tombs testify to affectionate feelings of masters for slaves, but even household servants had to endure violent treatment if their masters were cruel. Slaves had no recourse; if they attacked their owners because of inhumane treatment, their punishment was death.

Violence in Public Entertainment. Potential violence was a defining characteristic of a slave's life; actual violence held a prominent place in Roman public entertainment. The emperors regularly provided mass spectacles featuring "hunters" killing fierce beasts, wild African animals such as lions mangling condemned criminals, mock naval battles in flooded arenas, gladiatorial combats, and chariot races. Spectators filled stadiums for these shows, seated according to their social rank and gender following an Augustan law; the emperor and senators sat close to the action, while women and the poor were relegated to the upper tiers. These shows had a political context, demonstrating that the rulers were generous in providing expensive entertainment for their subjects, powerful enough to command life-and-death exhibitions, and dedicated to preserving the social hierarchy.

Gladiators were men and, rarely, women who fought with various weapons in special shows; war captives, criminals, slaves, and free volunteers appeared as gladiators. Augustus made gladiatorial shows, which originated under the republic as part of the ceremony at extravagant funerals, so popular that they provided entertainment for public festivals before tens of thousands of spectators. Gladiatorial combat was bloody but usually fought to the death only for captives and criminals; professional fighters could have extended careers. To make the fights more exciting, gladiators brandished a variety of weapons. One favorite bout pitted a lightly armored fighter, called a "net man" because he used a net and a trident, against a more heavily armored "fish man," so named from the design of his helmet crest. Betting was a great attraction, and crowds could be rowdy. As the Christian theologian Tertullian

Violent Shows
This mosaic from about A.D. 300, found in the atrium (open-roofed entrance hall) of a large country home near Tusculum outside Rome, shows animals and gladiators in combat. Ninety-one feet long (heavily restored as seen today in Rome's Villa Borghese Museum), this giant picture, like others found in private homes, reminded the owner's guests that their host was the kind of virtuous citizen who paid for spectacular entertainments for the benefit of his community and his own status.
CORBIS/Roger Woods.

(c. 160–240) described: "Look at the mob coming to the show—already they're out of their minds! Aggressive, heedless, already in an uproar about their bets! They all share the same suspense, the same madness, the same voice."

Many gladiatorial champions won riches and celebrity but not social respectability. Early in the first century A.D., the senators became alarmed at what they regarded as the disgrace to the upper class caused by some of its members becoming gladiators. They therefore banned the elite and all freeborn women under twenty from appearing in gladiatorial shows. Daughters trained by their gladiator fathers had first competed during the republic, and women continued to compete occasionally until the emperor Septimius Severus (r. 193–211) banned their appearance.

From the start of Augustus's reign, mass gatherings featuring gladiatorial shows, chariot races, and theater productions became a way for ordinary citizens to express their wishes to the emperors, who were expected to attend. On more than one occasion, for example, poorer Romans rioted at festivals to protest a shortfall in the free grain supply. In this way, public entertainment served as a two-way form of communication between ruler and ruled.

Arts and Letters Fit for an Emperor

Elite culture changed in the Augustan age to serve the same goal as public entertainment: legitimizing and strengthening the transformed system of government. In particular, oratory—the highest attainment of Roman arts and letters—lost its bite. Under the republic, the ability to make stirring speeches criticizing political opponents had been such a powerful weapon that it could catapult a "new man" like Cicero, who lacked social and military distinction, to a leadership role. Under the principate, the emperor's supremacy ruled out freewheeling political debate and open decision making. Now ambitious men required rhetorical skills not just for the traditional functions of arguing legal cases and prosecuting government officials, but also to praise the emperor on the numerous public occasions that promoted his image as a competent and compassionate ruler. Political criticism, however, was out.

The Process of Education. Education leading to skill in oratory remained a privilege of the wealthy.

Rome had no free public schools, so the poor were lucky to pick up even rudimentary knowledge from their harried parents. Most people had time only for training in practical skills. A character in *Satyricon*, a satirical literary work of the first century by Petronius, expresses this utilitarian attitude toward education succinctly: "I didn't study geometry and literary criticism and worthless junk like that. I just learned how to read the letters on signs and how to work out percentages, and I learned weights, measures, and the values of the different kinds of coins."

Although the Roman ideal called for mothers to teach children right from wrong, servants usually looked after the offspring of rich families. Such children attended private elementary schools from age seven to eleven to learn reading, writing, and basic arithmetic. Teachers used rote methods in the classroom, with physical punishment for mistakes. Some children went on to the next three years of school, in which they were introduced to literature, history, and grammar. Only a few boys then proceeded to the study of rhetoric.

Advanced studies concerned literature, history, ethical philosophy, law, and dialectic (reasoned argument). Mathematics and science were rarely studied as discrete disciplines, but engineers and architects became extremely proficient at calculation. Rich men and women would pursue their interests by having slaves read aloud to them. Books were not sets of bound pages but rather were continuous scrolls made from papyrus or animal skin. Reading required manual dexterity as well as literacy because a reader had to unroll the scroll with one hand and simultaneously roll it up with the other.

Celebrated Ideals in Literature and Sculpture. So much literature blossomed at this time that modern critics call Augustus's reign the Golden Age of Latin literature. The emperor, who himself dabbled in composing verse and prose, supported the flourishing arts by serving as the patron of a circle of writers and artists. His favorites were Horace (65–8 B.C.) and Virgil (70–19 B.C.). Horace entranced audiences with the supple rhythms and subtle irony of his short poems on public and private subjects. His poem celebrating Augustus's victory at Actium became famous for its opening line "Now is the time for drinking a toast!"

Virgil later became the most popular Augustan poet for his epic poem *The Aeneid*, which he wrote not only to please but to criticize the emperor gently. He composed so painstakingly that the epic remained unfinished at his death and he wanted it burned; Augustus preserved it. An epic inspired by Homeric poetry, it told the legend of the Trojan Aeneas, the most distant ancestor of the Romans. Virgil tempered his praise of the state with a profound recognition of the price to be paid for success. *The Aeneid* therefore underscored the complex mix of gain and loss that followed Augustus's transformation of politics and society. Above all, it expressed a moral code for all Romans: no matter how tempting the emotional pull of revenge and pride, be merciful to the conquered but lay low the haughty.

Authors with a more independent streak had to be careful. The historian Livy (54 B.C.–A.D. 17) composed an enormous history of Rome in which he refused to hide the ruthless actions of Augustus and his supporters. The emperor chided but did not punish him because the history did proclaim that success and stability depended on traditional values of loyalty and self-sacrifice. The poet Ovid (43 B.C.–A.D. 17) fared worse. An irreverent wit, in *Art of Love* and *Love Affairs* he implicitly mocked the emperor's moral legislation with tongue-in-cheek tips for conducting love affairs and picking up other men's wives at festivals. His *Metamorphoses* ("Transformations") undermined the idea of hierarchy as natural and stable through bizarre stories of supernatural shape-changes, with people becoming animals and confusion between the human and the divine. In 8 B.C., after Ovid was embroiled in a scandal involving Augustus's daughter, the emperor exiled the poet to a bleak town on the Black Sea.

Public sculpture also responded to the emperor's wishes. When Augustus was growing up, portraits were characterized by the complexity of human experience and were starkly realistic. The sculpture that Augustus commissioned displayed a more idealized style, reminiscent of classical Greek and Hellenistic portraiture. In renowned works of art such as the Prima Porta ("First Gate") statue of himself or the sculpted frieze on his Altar of Peace (finished in 9 B.C.), Augustus had himself portrayed as serene and dignified, not careworn and sick, as he often was. As with his monumental architecture, Augustus used sculpture to project a calm and competent image of himself as the "restorer of the world" and founder of a new age for Rome.

❖ Maintaining "Roman Peace"

A serious problem confronted Augustus's "restored republic": how to avoid the violent struggles for supreme power that had characterized the late republic. The solution was to train an heir during the emperor's lifetime to take over as *princeps* at his death, with the Senate's blessing and awarding of

Marble Statue of Augustus from Prima Porta
At six feet eight inches high, this imposing sculpture of Rome's first emperor stood a foot taller than its subject. Found at his wife Livia's country villa at Prima Porta ("First Gate") just outside the capital, the marble statue was probably a copy of a bronze original sculpted about 20 B.C., when Augustus was in his early forties. The sculptor has depicted him as a younger man, using the idealizing techniques of classical Greek art. The sculpture is crowded with symbols communicating Augustus's image as he wished to be regarded: the bare feet hint he is a near-divine hero, the Cupid refers to the Julian family's descent from the goddess Venus, and the design on the breastplate shows a Parthian surrendering to a Roman soldier under the gaze of personified cosmic forces admiring the peace Augustus's regime has created.
Scala/Art Resource, NY.

the same powers conferred on Augustus. This strategy kept the throne in his family, called the Julio-Claudians, until the death of the infamous Nero in A.D. 68. Thus was established the tradition that family dynasties ruled imperial Rome.

Under the Augustan system, the *princeps* necessarily had as his main goals preventing unrest, building loyalty, and financing the administration while governing a vast territory of diverse provinces. Augustus set a pattern for effective rule that some of his successors emulated better than others: taking special care of the army, communicating the image of the *princeps* as a just and generous ruler, and promoting Roman law and culture as universal standards while allowing as much local freedom as possible. The citizens, in return for their loyalty, expected the emperors to be generous patrons, but the difficulties of long-range communication imposed practical limits on imperial intervention in the lives of the residents of the provinces, for better or worse.

Making Monarchy Permanent, A.D. 14–180

Augustus feared that peace would be lost after his death. He wanted to make monarchy the permanent government to avoid civil war, but his fiction that Rome remained a republic meant that he needed the cooperation of the Senate to give legitimacy to any succession. As early as the 20s B.C., he began looking for a relative to designate as his intended heir (he had no son), but one after another they died before he did. Finally, in A.D. 4, he adopted a relative who would survive him, Tiberius (42 B.C.–A.D. 37). Since Tiberius had a distinguished record as a general, the army supported recommending him to the Senate as the next "first man." The senators prudently accepted this recommendation when Augustus died in A.D. 14; the Julio-Claudian dynasty thus began.

The First Dynasty: The Julio-Claudians, 14–68. The stern and irascible Tiberius (r. 14–37) held power for twenty-three years because he had the most important qualification for succeeding as emperor: the respect of the army. A reluctant ruler, he paid a steep personal price for becoming "first man." To strengthen their family ties, Augustus had forced him to divorce his beloved wife Vipsania to marry Augustus's daughter, Julia, a marriage that proved disastrously unhappy. Tiberius's long reign provided the stable transition period that the principate needed, establishing the compromise between the elite and the emperor that would last as long as the empire did. On the one hand, the traditional offices of consul, senator, and so forth would continue and the elite would fill them and bask in their prestige; on the other hand, the emperors would decide who filled the offices and would control the making of law and policy. In this way, everyone saved face by pretending that the remaining traces of republican government still mattered. Tiberius's reign also revealed the problems that a disaffected *princeps* could create. When his personal torments and fear of rivals led him to spend the last decade of his rule away from Rome as a virtual recluse, his lack of involvement in governing opened the way for abuses by subordinates in Rome and kept him from preparing a successor effectively.

Tiberius designated Gaius (r. 37–41), better known as Caligula, as the next *princeps* because he was Augustus's great-grandson and a fawning supporter, not because he exhibited the personal qualities a worthy ruler needed or had received any training for rule. Still, the young emperor might have been successful because he knew about soldiering: Caligula means "baby boots," the nickname the soldiers gave him as a child because he wore little leather shoes like theirs as he was growing up in the military garrisons his father commanded. Unfortunately, he utterly lacked the virtues of leadership; what he did possess were enormous appetites. Ruling through cruelty and violence and giving no thought to the succession, he overspent from the treasury to humor his whims. Suetonius labeled him a "monster." He frequently outraged social conventions by fighting mock gladiatorial combats, and appearing in public in women's clothing or costumes imitating gods. His abuses soon went too far: two praetorian commanders murdered him in 41 to avenge personal insults.

Following Caligula's death, some senators debated the idea of truly restoring the republic by refusing to choose a new emperor. They capitulated, however, when Claudius (r. 41–54), Augustus's grandnephew and Caligula's uncle, obtained the backing of the praetorian guard with promises of money. The succession of Claudius under the threat of force made it abundantly clear that the soldiers would insist on having an emperor, a patron to promote their interests. It also revealed that any senatorial yearnings for the return of a genuine republic would never be fulfilled. Claudius set a crucial precedent for imperial rule by enrolling men from a province outside Italy (Transalpine Gaul) in the Senate. This change opened the way for provincial inhabitants to expand their participation in governing the principate; in return for help in keeping their regions peaceful and prosperous, they would receive offices at Rome and imperial patronage. Claudius also changed imperial government by employing freed slaves as powerful administrators; since they owed their great advancement to the emperor, they could be expected to be loyal.

When Claudius died at the relatively old age of sixty-four, the glorious temptations of absolute power corrupted his young successor. Only sixteen, Nero (r. 54–68) had a passion for music and acting, not governing. The spectacular public festivals he sponsored and the cash he distributed to the masses in Rome kept him popular with the poor. Among the wealthy, however, a giant fire in 64 (the incident that led to the legend of Nero "fiddling while Rome burned") aroused suspicions that he might have ordered the conflagration to clear the way for new building projects. Nero scandalized the senatorial class by repeatedly appearing onstage to sing to captive audiences, and he bankrupted the treasury by spending outrageous sums on such pleasures as a sumptuous palace (the Golden House) and a lavish trip to Greece. His unsavory methods of raising money included trumping up charges of treason against senators and equestrians to seize their property. When rebellious commanders in the provinces toppled his regime, he had a servant help him cut his own throat, after wailing, "To die! And such a great artist!"

The Flavian Dynasty and the Imperial Cult, 69–96.

After a year of civil war in which four rival generals tried to hold the throne (69, the "Year of the Four Emperors," as it is called today), Vespasian (r. 69–79) became emperor. His victory proved that the monarchy was permanent because the ruling class and the army demanded it. With the accession of Vespasian, who belonged to the Flavian family, a new dynasty began. To minimize uncertainty, Vespasian took two steps. First, he had the Senate publicly recognize him as ruler even though he was not a Julio-Claudian. This declaration made official what everybody already knew: the principate was controlled by dynasties. Second, he encouraged the

spread of the imperial cult (worship of the emperor as a living god and sacrifices for his household's welfare) in the provinces outside Italy, where most of the empire's population resided.

In promoting this worship, Vespasian was building on local traditions. In the eastern provinces, the Hellenistic kingdoms had long before established the precedent of worshiping the present ruler; provincials there had treated the emperor as a living god as early as Augustus. The imperial cult communicated the same image of the emperor to the people of the provinces as the city's architecture and sculpture did to the people of Rome: he was larger than life, worthy of loyal respect, and the source of benefactions as their patron. Because emperor worship was already well established in Greece and the ancient Near East, Vespasian concentrated on spreading it in the provinces of Spain, southern France, and North Africa. Italy, however, still had no temples to the living emperor. Traditional Romans scorned the imperial cult as a provincial aberration; Vespasian, known for his wit, even muttered as he lay dying in 79, "Oh me! I think I'm becoming a god."

Following their father's lead, the Flavian sons Titus (r. 79–81) and Domitian (r. 81–96) further restored imperial prestige with hardheaded fiscal policy, professional administration, and high-profile campaigns on the frontiers to forestall threats. Titus, for example, had finished his father's effort to suppress a revolt in Judea by capturing Jerusalem in 70. He sent relief to the populations of Pompeii and Herculaneum, towns buried by a massive volcanic eruption of Mount Vesuvius in 79, and provided a state-of-the-art site for lavish public entertainments by finishing Rome's Colosseum, outfitted with giant awnings to shade the crowd. The great amphitheater was deliberately constructed on the site of the former fish pond in Nero's Golden House to demonstrate the new dynasty's public-spiritedness. Domitian balanced the budget and led the army north to take decisive action against Germanic tribes threatening the frontier regions along the Rhine and Danube Rivers—an area that would prove to be a hot spot for military clashes for centuries to come.

Not everything Domitian did was successful. His arrogance inspired hatred among the senators, to whom he once sent a letter announcing, "Our lord god, myself, orders you to do this." Embittered by the rebellion of a general in Germany, he executed numerous upper-class citizens as conspirators. Fearful they, too, would become victims, his wife and members of his court murdered him in 96.

The Five "Good Emperors," 96–180.

As Domitian's fate showed, the principate had not solved the monarchy's enduring weakness: rivalry for rule that could explode into murderous conspiracy and make the transfer of power unstable. The danger of civil war always existed, whether generated by ambitious generals or by competition among the emperor's heirs. There was no way to guarantee that a good ruler would emerge from the struggle. As Tacitus

Roman Arch at Thamugadi in North Africa
The emperors fueled the process of Romanization in the provinces by building new settlements for military veterans. The best-preserved such town is Thamugadi (today Timgad in Algeria). Founded by the emperor Trajan in A.D. 100, it was laid out like a Roman military camp, a perfect square with a grid of straight streets and rectangular houses. The new town's architecture imitated Rome's, with a capacious theater for public entertainments and this mammoth arch, probably built toward the end of the second century A.D., as a spectacular entrance to a colonnaded boulevard. Romanization was a two-way process, with local peoples influencing the Roman settlers and vice versa. At Thamugadi, indigenous African religious cults, lightly adapted to Roman traditions, flourished alongside ancient Roman cults and attracted worshipers of all kinds.
SEF/Art Resource, NY.

acidly commented, emperors became like the weather: "We just have to wait for bad ones to pass and hope for good ones to appear." Fortunately for Rome, fair weather dawned with the next five emperors— Nerva (r. 96–98), Trajan (r. 98–117), Hadrian (r. 117–138), Antoninus Pius (r. 138–161), and Marcus Aurelius (r. 161–180). Following the lead of the influential eighteenth-century historian Edward Gibbon, historians have dubbed these reigns the empire's political Golden Age because they provided peaceful transfers of power for nearly a century. This period was, however, full of war and strife, as Roman history always was: Trajan fought fierce campaigns that expanded Roman power northward across the Danube River into Dacia (today Romania) and eastward into Mesopotamia (Map 6.1); Hadrian earned the hatred of the Senate by executing several senators as alleged conspirators and punished a Jewish revolt by turning Jerusalem into a military colony; and Aurelius spent many miserable years on campaign protecting the Danube region from outside attacks.

Still, there is much validity to the idea of a Golden Age under the "five good emperors." They succeeded one another without murder or conspiracy—indeed, the first four, lacking surviving sons, used adoption to find the best possible successor. Moreover, enough money was coming in through taxes to bolster their power, and the army remained obedient. It was no small blessing that their reigns marked the longest stretch without a civil war since the second century B.C.

Life in the Golden Age, 96–180

The peace and prosperity of the second century A.D. depended on defense by a loyal and efficient military, public-spiritedness among provincial elites in local administration and tax collection, the spread of common laws and culture throughout huge and diverse territories, and a healthy population reproducing itself. The size of the empire and the enduring conditions of ancient life meant that emperors had only limited control over these factors.

The Army and Imperial Military Aims.

In theory, Rome's military goal remained infinite expansion because conquest brought glory to the emperor. Virgil in *The Aeneid* had expressed this notion by portraying Jupiter, the king of the gods, as promising "imperial

MAP 6.1 The Expansion of the Roman Empire, 30 B.C.–A.D. 117

When Octavian (the future Augustus) captured Egypt in 30 B.C. after the suicides of Mark Antony and Cleopatra, he made a significant contribution to the economic strength of Rome. The land of the Nile yielded prodigious amounts of grain and gold; and Roman power now effectively encircled the Mediterranean Sea (though Mauretania was technically under the rule of indigenous kings with Roman approval until about A.D. 44 in the reign of Claudius). When the emperor Trajan took over the southern part of Mesopotamia in A.D. 114–117, imperial conquest reached its height: Rome's control had never extended so far east. Egypt remained part of the empire until the Arab conquest in A.D. 642, but Mesopotamia was immediately abandoned by Hadrian, Trajan's successor, probably because it seemed too distant to defend.

rule without limit." In reality, the emperors were mostly content to have other kingdoms and peoples recognize their authority and not disturb the frontier regions; imperial territory never expanded permanently much beyond what Augustus had controlled, encircling the Mediterranean Sea.

Stable and peaceful in the first two centuries after Augustus, most provinces had no need for garrisons of troops; soldiers were a rare sight in many places. Even Gaul, which had originally resisted im-

perial control with an almost suicidal frenzy, was, according to a contemporary witness, "kept in order by 1,200 troops—hardly more soldiers than it has towns." Most legions (a legion was a unit of five thousand to six thousand troops) were concentrated on the northern and eastern frontiers of the provinces, where hostile neighbors lived just beyond the boundaries and the distance from the center weakened the local residents' loyalty. The Roman peace guaranteed by the army allowed commerce to operate smoothly in imperial territory; the Golden Age's prosperity promoted long-distance trade for luxury goods, such as spices and silk, that established contacts as far away as India and China.

The lack of added conquests made paying for the army difficult. In the past, foreign wars had been an engine of prosperity because they brought in huge amounts of capital through booty and prisoners of war sold into slavery. Conquered territory also provided additional tax revenues. There were now no such new sources of income, but the standing army had to be paid regularly to maintain discipline. To fulfill their obligations as patrons of the army, emperors on their accession and other special occasions supplemented soldiers' regular pay with substantial bonuses. These rewards made a legionary career desirable, and enlistment counted as a privilege restricted to free male citizens. The army, however, also included auxiliary units of noncitizens from the provinces. Serving under Roman officers, they could pick up some Latin and Roman customs, and they contributed to improving life in the provinces by helping construct public works. Upon discharge, they received Roman citizenship. In this way the army served as an instrument for spreading a common way of life.

Financing Government and Defense. A tax on agricultural land in the provinces (Italy was exempt) provided the principal source of revenue for imperial government and defense. The administration consumed relatively little money because it was small compared with the size of the territory being governed: no more than several hundred top officials governed a population of about fifty million. Thus most locally collected taxes stayed in the provinces for expenditures there. Senatorial and equestrian governors with small staffs ran the provinces, which eventually numbered about forty. In Rome, the emperor employed a substantial palace staff, while equestrian officials called *prefects* managed the city itself.

The decentralized tax system required public service by the provincial elites; the central and local governments' financial well-being absolutely depended on it. As *decurions* (members of the municipal senate, later called *curiales*), the local officials were required to collect taxes and personally guarantee that their town's public expenditures were covered. If there was a shortfall in tax collection or local finances, these wealthy men had to make up the difference from their own pockets. Most emperors under the early principate attempted to keep taxes low. As Tiberius put it when refusing a request for tax increases from provincial governors, "I want you to shear my sheep, not skin them alive." This responsibility could make civic office expensive, but the prestige that the positions provided made the elite willing to take the risk. Some received priesthoods in the imperial cult as a reward, an honor open to both men and women. All could hope to catch the emperor's ear for special help for their area, for example, after an earthquake or a flood.

The system worked because it was deeply traditional: the local social elites were the patrons of their communities but the clients of the emperors. As long as there were enough rich, public-spirited provincials responding to this system, which offered nonmonetary rewards, the principate could function effectively by fostering the republican ideal of communal values.

The Impact of Roman Culture on the Provinces. The principate changed the Mediterranean world profoundly but not evenly. Its provinces contained a wide diversity of peoples speaking different languages, observing different customs, dressing in different styles, and worshiping different divinities (Map 6.2). In the remote countryside, Roman conquest had modest effect on local customs. Where new cities sprang up, however, Roman influence prevailed. These communities sprouted around Roman forts or grew from the settlements of army veterans the emperors had sprinkled throughout the provinces. They became particularly influential in western Europe, permanently rooting Latin (and the languages that would emerge from it) and Roman law and customs there. Prominent modern cities such as Trier and Cologne in Germany started as Roman towns. Over time, social and cultural distinctions lessened between the provinces and Italy. Eventually, emperors came from the provinces; Trajan, from Spain, was the first.

Romanization, as historians call the spread of Roman culture in the provinces, raised the standard of living for many provincials as roads and bridges improved, trade increased, and agriculture flourished under the peaceful conditions secured by the army. The troops' need for supplies meant new business for farmers and merchants. Living more

MAP 6.2 Natural Features and Languages of the Roman World

The environment of the Roman world included a large variety of topography, climate, and languages. The inhabitants of the Roman world, estimated to have numbered as many as 50 million, spoke dozens of different tongues, many of which survived well into the late empire. The two predominant languages were Latin in the western part of the empire and Greek in the eastern. Latin remained the language of law even in the eastern empire. Fields for growing grain were the most crucial topographical feature for agriculture because wheat and barley provided the basis for the ancient diet. Vineyards and olive groves were also important: wine was regarded as an essential beverage, and olive oil was the principal source of fat for most people, as well as being used to make soap, perfume, and other products for daily life.

prosperously under Roman rule than ever before made Romanization easier for provincials to take. In addition, Romanization was not a one-way street culturally. In western areas as diverse as Gaul, Britain, and North Africa, interaction between the local people and Romans produced new, mixed cultural traditions, especially in religion and art. Therefore, the process led to a gradual merging of Roman and local culture, not the unilateral imposition of the conquerors' way of life.

Romanization had less effect on the eastern provinces, which largely retained their Greek and Near Eastern character. In much of this region, daily life continued to follow traditional Greek models. When Romans had gradually taken over these areas during the second and first centuries B.C., they found urban cultures that had flourished for thousands of years. Huge Hellenistic cities such as Alexandria in Egypt and Antioch in Syria rivaled Rome in size and splendor. In fact, compared with Rome, they boasted more individual houses for the well-to-do, fewer blocks of high-rise tenements, and equally magnificent temples. While retaining their local languages and customs, the eastern social elites easily accepted the nature of Roman governance: the emperor was their patron, they his clients, with the mutual obligations this traditional relationship required. Provincial elites had long ago become accustomed to such a system through the paternalistic relationships that had underlain Hellenistic rule. Their willing cooperation in the task of governing the provinces was crucial for imperial stability and prosperity.

New Trends in Literature. The continuing vitality of Greek culture and language in bustling eastern cities contributed to a flourishing in literature. New trends, often harking back to classical literature, blossomed in Greek. Authors of the second century A.D. such as Chariton and Achilles Tatius wrote romantic adventure novels that opened the way to the popularity of that literary form. Lucian (c. 117–180) composed satirical dialogues fiercely mocking both stuffy people and superstitious religiosity. As part of his enormous and varied literary output, the essayist and philosopher Plutarch (c. 50–120) wrote *Parallel Lives,* biographies of matching Greek and Roman men. His keen moral sense and lively taste for anecdotes made him favorite reading for centuries; the great English dramatist William Shakespeare (1564–1616) based several plays on his work.

Latin literature thrived as well; in fact, scholars rank the late first and early second centuries A.D. as its "Silver Age," second only to the masterpieces of Augustan literature. Its most famous authors wrote with acid wit, verve, and imagination. Tacitus (c. 56–120) composed his *Annals* as a biting narrative of the Julio-Claudians, laying bare the ruthlessness of Augustus and the personal weaknesses of his successors. The satiric poet Juvenal (c. 65–130) skewered pretentious Romans and grasping provincials while hilariously

bemoaning the indignities of being broke in the city. Apuleius (c. 125–170) scandalized readers with his *Golden Ass,* a lusty novel about a man turned into a donkey who then regains his body and his soul by the kindness of the Egyptian goddess Isis.

Law and Order through Equity. Unlike Augustus, later emperors never worried that scandalous literature posed a threat to the social order they worked constantly to maintain. They did, however, share his belief that law was crucial. Indeed, Romans prided themselves on their ability to order their society through law. As Virgil said, their mission was "to establish law and order within a framework of peace." Roman law influenced most systems of law in modern Europe. One distinctive characteristic was the recognition of the principle of equity, which meant accomplishing what was "good and fair" even if the letter of the law had to be ignored to do so. This principle led legal thinkers to insist, for example, that the intent of parties in a contract outweighed the words of their agreement and that the burden of proof lay with the accuser rather than the accused. The emperor Trajan ruled that no one should be convicted on the grounds of suspicion alone because it was better for a guilty person to go unpunished than for an innocent person to be condemned. (See "Contrasting Views," page 220.)

Roman notions of propriety required making formal distinctions among the "orders" into which society was divided. As always, the elites constituted a tiny portion of the population. Only about one in every fifty thousand had enough money to qualify for the senatorial order, the highest-ranking class, while about one in a thousand belonged to the equestrian order, the second-ranking class. Different purple stripes on clothing identified these orders. The third-highest order consisted of decurions, the local officials in provincial towns.

Those outside the social elite faced greater disadvantages than mere snobbery. The old republican distinction between the "better people" and the "humbler people" hardened under the principate, and by the third century A.D. it pervaded Roman law. Law institutionalized such distinctions because an orderly existence was thought to depend on them. The "better people" included senators, equestrians, decurions, and retired army veterans. Everybody else—except slaves, who counted as property, not people—made up the vastly larger group of "humbler people." The latter faced their gravest disadvantage in court: the law imposed harsher penalties on them for the same crimes as committed by "better people." "Humbler people" convicted of capital crimes were regularly executed by being crucified or torn apart by wild animals before a crowd of spectators. "Better people" rarely suffered the death penalty; if they were condemned, they received a quicker and more dignified execution by the sword. "Humbler people" could also be tortured in criminal investigations, even if they were citizens. Romans regarded these differences as fair on the grounds that a person's higher status created a higher level of responsibility for the common good. As one provincial governor expressed it, "Nothing is less equitable than mere equality itself."

Reproduction and Marriage.   Law was necessary to maintain order, but nothing mattered more to the stability and prosperity of the empire than steady population levels. Concern about reproduction therefore permeated marriage. The upper-class government official Pliny, for example, sent the following report to the grandfather of his third wife, Calpurnia: "You will be very sad to learn that your granddaughter has suffered a miscarriage. She is a young girl and did not realize she was pregnant. As a result she was more active than she should have been and paid a high price."

Ancient medicine could do little to promote healthy childbirth and reduce infant mortality. Complications during and after delivery could easily lead to the mother's death because doctors could not stop internal bleeding or cure infections. They possessed carefully crafted instruments for surgery and for physical examinations, but they were badly mistaken about the process of reproduction. Gynecologists such as Soranus, who practiced in Rome during the reigns of Trajan and Hadrian, erroneously recommended the days just after menstruation as the best time to become pregnant, when the woman's body was "not congested." As in Hellenistic medicine, treatments were mainly limited to potions, poultices, and bleeding; Soranus recommended treating exceptionally painful menstruation by drawing blood "from the bend of the arm." Many doctors were freedmen from Greece and other provinces, usually with only informal training. People considered their occupation of low status, unless they served the upper class.

As in earlier times, girls often wed in their early teens or even younger and thus had as many years as possible to bear children. Because so many babies died young, families had to produce numerous

Midwife's Sign
Childbirth was exceptionally perilous for women because of the great danger of bleeding to death from an internal hemorrhage. This terra-cotta sign from Ostia, the ancient port city of Rome, probably hung outside a midwife's rooms to announce her expertise in aiding women in giving birth. It shows a pregnant woman clutching the sides of her chair, with an assistant supporting her from behind and the midwife crouched in front to help deliver the baby. Such signs were especially effective for people who were illiterate; a person did not have to read to understand the services that the specialist inside could provide.
Scala/Art Resource, NY.

offspring to keep from disappearing. The tombstone of Veturia, a soldier's wife married at eleven, tells a typical story: "Here I lie, having lived for twenty-seven years. I was married to the same man for sixteen years and bore six children, five of whom died before I did." The propertied classes usually arranged marriages between spouses who hardly knew each other, although they could grow to love each other in a partnership devoted to family.

The emphasis on childbearing in marriage brought many health hazards to women, but to remain single and childless represented social failure for Romans. Once children were born, they were cared for by both their mothers and servants in all but the more affluent families. Wealthier women routinely hired "wet nurses" to attend to and breast-feed their babies. When Romans wanted to control family size, they used female contraception by obstructing the female organs or by administering drugs. They also practiced exposure (abandoning imperfect and unwanted babies to be raised by others, usually as slaves, or to die), more frequently for infant girls than boys because sons were considered more valuable than daughters as future supporters and protectors of their families.

The emperors and some members of the social elite did their best to support reproduction. The emperors aided needy children to encourage larger families. Wealthy people often adopted children in their communities. One North African man gave enough money to support three hundred boys and three hundred girls each year until they grew up. The differing value afforded male and female children was also evident in these humanitarian programs: boys often received more aid than girls.

❖ The Emergence of Christianity

Christianity began as a kind of splinter group within Judaism in Judea, where, as elsewhere under Roman rule, Jews were allowed to practice their ancestral religion. The new faith did not soon attract large numbers; three centuries after the death of Jesus, Christians were still a small minority. Moreover, they faced constant suspicion and hostility; virtually every book of the New Testament refers to the resistance the emerging faith encountered. It grew,

if only gradually, because it had an appeal flowing from the charismatic career of Jesus, from its message of salvation, from its early believers' sense of mission, and from the strong bonds of community it inspired. Ultimately, the emergence of Christianity proved the most significant and enduring development during the Roman Empire.

Jesus of Nazareth and the Spread of His Teachings

The new religion sprang from the life and teachings of Jesus (c. 4 B.C.–A.D. 30; see "B.C./A.D. System for Dates" at the beginning of the book for an explanation of the apparent anomaly of the date of his birth "before Christ"). Its background lay, however, in Jewish history from long before. Harsh Roman rule in Judea had made the Jews restless and the provincial authorities anxious about rebellion. Jesus' career therefore developed in an unsettled environment. His execution reflected Roman readiness to eliminate perceived threats to peace and social order. In the two decades after his crucifixion, his devoted followers, particularly Paul of Tarsus, spread his teachings beyond the Jewish community of Palestine, and Christianity took its first step into an unwelcoming wider world.

Jewish Apocalypticism: The Setting for Christianity. Christianity offered an answer to a difficult question about divine justice that the Jews' experiences of political and economic oppression under the kingdoms of the ancient Near East and the Hellenistic period had raised: how could a just God allow the wicked to prosper and the righteous to suffer? Nearly two hundred years before Jesus' birth, persecution by the Seleucid king Antiochus IV (r. 175–164 B.C.) had provoked the Jews into a long and bloody revolt; this protracted struggle gave birth to a complex of ideas called *apocalypticism* (from the Greek for "revealing what is hidden"). According to this worldview, evil powers, divine and human, controlled the present world. This regime would soon end, however, when God and his agents would reveal their plan to conquer the forces of evil by sending an "anointed one" (Hebrew, *Mashia* or *Messiah;* Greek, *Christ*) to win the great battle. A final judgment would follow, to bestow eternal punishment on the wicked and eternal reward on the righteous. Apocalypticism proved influential, especially among many Jews living in Judea under Roman rule. Eventually, it inspired not only Jews but Christians and Muslims.

Apocalyptic doctrines had special appeal around the time of Jesus' birth because most Judean Jews were discontent with foreign rule and disagreed among themselves about what form Judaism should take in such troubled times. Some favored accommodation with their overlords, while others preached rejection of the non-Jewish world and its spiritual corruption. Their local ruler, installed by the Romans, was Herod the Great (r. 37–4 B.C.). His flamboyant taste for a Greek style of life, which flouted Jewish law, made him unpopular with many locals, despite his magnificent rebuilding of the holiest Jewish shrine, the great temple in Jerusalem. When a decade of unrest followed his death, Augustus responded to local petitions for help by installing provincial government to deal with squabbling dynasts and competing religious factions. Jesus' homeland had turned into a powderkeg by his lifetime.

The Life of Jesus. Born in Nazareth, Jesus began his career as a teacher and healer in his native Galilee, the northern region of Palestine, during the reign of Tiberius. The books that would later become the New Testament Gospels, composed between about 70 and 90, offer the earliest accounts of his life. Jesus himself, like Socrates, wrote nothing down, and, just as in the case of Athens's famous sage, others' accounts of his words and deeds are varied and controversial. Jesus taught not by direct instruction but by telling stories and parables that challenged his followers to ponder what he meant.

All of the Gospels begin the account of his public ministry with his baptism by John the Baptist, who preached a message of repentance before the approaching final judgment. John was executed by the Jewish ruler Herod Antipas, a son of Herod the Great whom the Romans supported; Herod feared that John's apocalyptic preaching might instigate riots. After John's death, Jesus continued his mission by traveling around Judea's countryside proclaiming the imminence of God's kingdom and the need to prepare spiritually for its coming. While many saw Jesus as the Messiah, his complex apocalypticism did not preach immediate revolt against the Romans. Instead, he taught that God's true kingdom was to be sought not on earth but in heaven. He stressed that this kingdom was open to believers regardless of their social status or apparent sinfulness. His emphasis on God's love for humanity and people's

Palestine in the Time of Jesus, A.D. 30

Catacomb Painting of Christ as the Good Shepherd
Catacombs (underground tombs), cut into soft rock outside various cities of the Roman Empire, served as vast underground burial chambers for Jews and Christians. Rome alone had 340 miles of catacombs. Painted in the third century A.D. on the wall of a Christian catacomb just outside Rome, this fresco depicts Jesus as the Good Shepherd (John 10:10–11). In addition to the tired or injured sheep, Jesus carries a pot of milk and perhaps honey, which new Christians received after their baptism as a symbol of their entry into the Promised Land of the Hebrew Bible. Such catacomb paintings were the earliest Christian art. By the fifth century A.D., the emperors' adoption of the new religion meant that Christians no longer had to make their tombs inconspicuous, and catacombs became sites of pilgrimage instead of burial.
Scala/Art Resource, NY.

overriding responsibility to love one another reflected Jewish religious teachings, as in the interpretation of the Scriptures by the first-century rabbinic teacher Hillel.

An educated Jew who probably knew Greek as well as Aramaic, the local tongue, Jesus realized that he had to reach the urban crowds to make an impact. Therefore, he left the Galilean villages where he had started and took his message to the Jewish population of Jerusalem, the region's main city. His miraculous healings and exorcisms combined with his powerful preaching to create a sensation. His popularity attracted the attention of the Jewish authorities, who automatically assumed he aspired to political power. Fearing he might ignite a Jewish revolt, the Roman governor Pontius Pilate (r. 26–36) ordered his crucifixion, the usual punishment for sedition, in Jerusalem in 30.

The Mission of Paul of Tarsus. In contrast to the fate of other suspected rebels whom the Romans executed, Jesus' influence endured after his execution. His followers reported that they had seen him in person after his death, proclaiming that God had miraculously raised him from the dead. They set about convincing other Jews that he was the promised savior who would soon return to judge the world and usher in God's kingdom. At this point, his closest disciples, the twelve Apostles (Greek for "messengers"), still considered themselves faithful Jews and continued to follow the commandments of Jewish law.

A radical change took place with the conversion of Paul of Tarsus (c. 10–65), a pious Jew of the Diaspora, a Roman citizen who had been violently opposed to those who accepted Jesus as the Messiah. A spiritual vision on the road to Damascus in Syria, which Paul interpreted as a divine revelation, inspired him to become a follower of Jesus as the Messiah or Christ—a Christian, as members of the movement came to be known. Paul taught that accepting Jesus as divine and his crucifixion as the ultimate sacrifice for the sins of humanity was the only way of becoming righteous in the eyes of God. In this way alone could one expect to attain salvation in the world to come.

Seeking to win converts outside Judea, beginning in about 46 Paul traveled to preach to the Jews of the Diaspora and Gentiles (non-Jews) who had adopted some Jewish practices in Syria, Asia Minor, and Greece. Although he stressed the necessity of ethical behavior along traditional Jewish lines, especially the rejection of sexual immorality and polytheism, he also taught that converts need not keep all the provisions of Jewish law. To make conversion easier, he did not require the males who entered the movement to undergo the Jewish initiation rite of circumcision. This tenet and his teachings that his congregations did not have to observe Jewish dietary restrictions or festivals led to tensions with Jewish authorities in Jerusalem as well as with the followers of Jesus living there, who still believed that Christians had to follow Jewish law. Roman authorities soon arrested Paul as a criminal troublemaker; he was executed in about 65.

Paul's mission was only one part of the turmoil afflicting the Jewish community in this period; hatred of Roman rule in Palestine finally provoked the Jews to revolt in 66, with disastrous results. After defeating the rebels in 70, Titus (who would become emperor in 79) destroyed the Jerusalem temple and sold most of the city's population into slavery. In the aftermath of this catastrophe, the distancing of Christianity from Judaism begun by Paul gained momentum, giving birth to a separate religion now that the Jewish community had lost its religious center. Paul's impact on the movement can be gauged by the number of letters—thirteen—attributed to him in the twenty-seven Christian writings that were put together as the New Testament by around 200. Followers of Jesus came to regard the New Testament as having equal authority with the Jewish Bible, which they then called the Old Testament. Since teachers like Paul preached mainly in the cities to reach large crowds, congregations of Christians began to spring up in urban areas. Women could sometimes be leaders in the movement, but not without arousing controversy; one view was that men should teach and women only listen. Still, early Christianity was diverse enough that the first head of a congregation named in the New Testament was a woman.

Growth of a New Religion

To develop as a new religion apart from Judaism, Christianity had to overcome serious hurdles. Imperial officials, suspecting it of being politically subversive, persecuted its adherents, such as Perpetua, for treason, especially for refusing to participate in the imperial cult. Christian leaders had to build an organization from scratch to administer their growing congregations. Finally, they had to address the controversial question of the leadership role of women in the movement.

The Rise of Persecution and Martyrdom. The emperors found Christians baffling and irritating. In contrast to Jews, Christians espoused a novel faith rather than a traditional religion handed down from their ancestors; they therefore enjoyed no special treatment under Roman law. Most Romans felt hostile toward Christians because they feared that tolerating them would offend the gods of the Roman religion. Their denial of the old gods and the emperor's divine associations seemed sure to provoke natural catastrophes. Christians furthermore aroused contempt because they proclaimed as divine king a man the imperial government had crucified as a criminal. Their secret rituals led to accusations of cannibalism amidst sexual promiscuity because they symbolically ate the body and drank the blood of Jesus during communal dinners, called "Love Feasts," which men and women attended together. In short, they seemed a dangerous new threat to peace with the gods and the social order.

Not surprisingly, then, Romans were quick to blame Christians for public disasters. When a large portion of Rome burned in 64, Nero punished them for arson. As Tacitus reports, Nero had Christians "covered with the skins of wild animals and mauled to death by dogs, or fastened to crosses and set on fire to provide light at night." The unusual cruelty of their punishment ironically earned Christians some sympathy from Rome's population.

After Nero's persecution, the government acted against Christians only intermittently. No law specifically forbade their religion, but they made easy prey for officials, who could punish them in the name of maintaining public order. The action of Pliny as a provincial governor in Asia Minor illustrated the predicament for both sides. (See "Contrasting Views," page 220.) In about 112, he asked some people accused of practicing this new religion if they were indeed Christians, urging those who admitted it to reconsider. He freed those who denied it as well as those who stated they no longer believed, after they sacrificed to the gods, vowed allegiance to the imperial cult, and cursed Christ. He executed those who persisted in their faith.

In response to persecution, defenders of Christianity such as Tertullian and Justin (c. 100–165) argued that Romans had nothing to fear from their faith. Far from spreading immorality and subversion, these writers insisted, Christianity taught an elevated moral code and respect for authority. It was not a foreign superstition but the true philosophy that combined the best features of Judaism and Greek thought and was thus a fitting religion for their diverse world. Tertullian pointed out that, although Christians could not worship the emperors, they did "pray to the true God for their [the emperors'] safety. We pray for a fortunate life for them, a secure rule, . . . a courageous army, a loyal Senate, a virtuous people, a world of peace."

Persecution did not stop Christianity; Tertullian indeed proclaimed that "the blood of the martyrs is the seed of the Church." Christians like Perpetua regarded public trials and executions as an opportunity to become witnesses (*martyrs* in Greek) to their faith and thus to strengthen Christians' sense of identity. Their firm conviction that their deaths would lead directly to heavenly bliss allowed them to face excruciating tortures with courage; some even courted martyrdom. Ignatius (c. 35–107), bishop of Antioch, begged Rome's congregation, which was becoming the most prominent Christian group, not to ask the emperor to show him mercy after his arrest: "Let me be food for the wild animals [in the arena] through whom I can reach God," he pleaded. "I am God's wheat, to be ground up by the teeth of beasts so that I may be found pure bread of Christ." Most Christians tried their best to avoid becoming martyrs by keeping a low profile, but stories recounting the martyrs' courage inspired the faithful to endure hostility from non-Christians and helped shape the identity of this new religion as a creed that gave its believers the spiritual power to overcome great suffering.

The Development of Christian Institutions. Many first-century Christians expected Jesus to return to pass judgment on the world during their lifetimes. When this hope was not met, they began transforming their religion from an apocalyptic Jewish sect expecting the immediate end of the world into one that could survive over the long term. To do this, they tried to achieve unity in their beliefs and to create a hierarchical organization that would impose order on the congregations.

Christians in the Empire: Conspirators or Faithful Subjects?

Ancient Romans worried that new religions might disrupt their long-standing "peace with the gods," on which their national safety and prosperity depended. Groups whose religious creed seemed likely to offend the traditional deities were therefore accused of treason, especially if they held private meetings that could be seen as opportunities for conspiracy (Document 1). Christians insisted that they were not disloyal just because they were different (Document 2). The early emperors faced a daunting challenge in trying to forge a policy that was fair both to Christian subjects and to those citizens who feared and detested them (Document 3).

1. A Denunciation of Christians, According to Minucius Felix (c. A.D. 200)

Not content with blasting Christians as sexually immoral, opponents also claimed they killed and ate babies in their religious rites—or at least that is how the Christian author Minucius Felix depicts them. The viciousness of the charges is consistent with the seriousness with which Romans searched for religious truth.

Is it not deplorable that a faction . . . of abandoned, hopeless outlaws makes attacks against the gods? They gather together ignorant persons from the lowest dregs, and credulous women, easily deceived as their sex is, and organize a rabble of unholy conspirators, leagued together in nocturnal associations and by ritual fasts and barbarous foods, not for the purpose of some sacred rite but for the sake of sacrilege—a secret tribe that shuns the light, silent in public but talkative in secret places. They despise the temples as if they were tombs, they spit upon the gods, they ridicule our sacred rites. . . .

Already . . . decay of morals spreads from day to day throughout the entire world, and the loathsome shrines of this impious conspiracy multiply. This plot must be completely rooted out and execrated. They recognize one another by secret signs and tokens; they love one another almost before they are acquainted. Everywhere a kind of religion of lust is also associated with them, and they call themselves promiscuously brothers and sisters, so that ordinary fornication, through the medium of a sacred name, becomes incest. And thus their vain and mad superstition glories in crimes. . . . What is told of the initiation of neophytes is as detestable as it is notorious. An infant covered with flour to deceive the unsuspecting is set before the one to be initiated in the rites. The neophyte is induced to strike what seem to be harmless blows on the surface of the covering, and this infant is killed by his random and unsuspecting blows. Its blood—oh, shocking!—they greedily lap up; the limbs they eagerly distribute; and by this victim they league themselves, and by this complicity in crime they pledge themselves to mutual silence. . . .

But you [Christians] meanwhile in anxious doubt abstain from wholesome pleasures; you do not attend the shows; you take no part in the processions; fight shy of public banquets; abhor the sacred games, meats from the sacrificial victims, drinks poured in libation on the altars.

Source: Minucius Felix, *Octavius*, 8.3–12.6.

2. Tertullian's Defense of His Fellow Christians, c. A.D. 197

An eloquent theologian from North Africa, Tertullian insisted that Christians did indeed support the empire. Even though they refused to pray to the emperor, they prayed for him and thus for the community's health and safety, he explained.

So that is why Christians are public enemies—because they will not give the emperors vain, false, and rash honors; because, being men of a true religion, they celebrate the emperors' festivals more in heart than in frolic. . . .

On the contrary, the name faction may properly be given to those who join to hate the good and honest, who shout for the blood of the innocent, who use as a pretext to defend their hatred the absurdity that they take the Christians to be the cause of every disaster to the state, of every misfortune of the people. If the Tiber reaches the walls, if the Nile does not rise to water the fields, if the sky does not move [i.e., if there is no rain] or the earth does, if there is famine, if there is plague, the cry at once arises: "The Christians to the lions!"

For we invoke the eternal God, the true God, the living God for the safety of the emperors. . . . Looking up to heaven, the Christians—with hands outspread, because innocent, with head bare because we do not blush, yes! and without a prompter because we pray from the heart—are ever praying for all the emperors. We pray for a fortunate life for them, a secure rule, a safe house, brave armies, a faithful senate, a virtuous people, a peaceful world. . . .

Should not this sect have been classed among the legal associations, when it commits no such actions as are commonly feared from unlawful associations? For unless I am mistaken, the reason for prohibiting associations clearly lay in forethought for public order—to save the state from being torn into factions, a thing very likely to disturb election assemblies, public gatherings, local senates, meetings, even the public games, with the clashing and rivalry of partisans. . . . We, however, whom all the passion for glory and rank leave cold, have no need to combine; nothing is more foreign to us than the state. One state we recognize for all—the universe.

Source: Tertullian, *Apology*, 10.1, 23.2–3, 35.1, 40.1–2.

3. Pliny on Early Imperial Policy toward Christians, c. A.D. 112

As governor of the province of Bithynia, Pliny had to decide the fate of Christians accused of crimes by their neighbors. With no precedent, he tried to be fair and wrote to the emperor Trajan to ask if he had acted correctly. The emperor's reply set out what passed for official policy concerning Christians in the early empire.

[Pliny to the emperor Trajan]

It is my practice, my lord, to refer to you all matters concerning which I am in doubt. For who can better give guidance to my hesitation or inform my ignorance? I have never participated in trials of Christians. I therefore do not know what offenses it is the practice to punish or investigate, and to what extent. . . .

In the case of those who were denounced to me as Christians, I have observed the following procedure: I interrogated these as to whether they were Christians; those who confessed I interrogated a second and a third time, threatening them with punishment; those who persisted I ordered executed. For I had no doubt that, whatever the nature of their creed, stubbornness and inflexible obstinacy surely deserve to be punished. There were others possessed of the same folly; but because they were Roman citizens, I signed an order for them to be transferred to Rome.

Soon accusations spread, as usually happens, because of the proceedings going on, and several incidents occurred. An anonymous document was published containing the names of many persons. Those who denied that they were or had been Christians, when they invoked the gods in words dictated by me, offered prayer with incense and wine to your image, which I had ordered to be brought for this purpose together with statues of the gods, and moreover cursed Christ—none of which those who are really Christians, it is said, can be forced to do—these I thought should be discharged. Others named by the informer declared that they were Christians, but then denied it, asserting that they had been but had ceased to be, some three years before, others many years, some as much as twenty-five years. They all worshiped your image and the statues of the gods, and cursed Christ.

They asserted, however, that the sum and substance of their fault or error had been that they were accustomed to meet on a fixed day before dawn and sing responsively a hymn to Christ as to a god, and to bind themselves by oath, not to some crime, but not to commit fraud, theft, or adultery, not to falsify their trust, nor to refuse to return a trust when called upon to do so. When this was over, it was their custom to depart and to assemble again to partake of food—but ordinary and innocent food. Even this, they affirmed, they had ceased to do after my edict by which, in accordance with your instructions, I had forbidden political associations. Accordingly, I judged it all the more necessary to find out what the truth was by torturing two female slaves who were called attendants. But I discovered nothing else but depraved, excessive superstition.

I therefore postponed the investigation and hastened to consult you. For the matter seemed to me to warrant consulting you, especially because of the number involved. For the contagion of this superstition has spread not only to the cities but also to the villages and farms. But it seems possible to check and cure it. It is certainly quite clear that the temples, which had been almost deserted, have begun to be frequented, that the established religious rites, long neglected, are being resumed, and that from everywhere sacrificial animals are coming, for which until now very few purchasers could be found. Hence it is easy to imagine what a multitude of people can be reformed if an opportunity for repentance is afforded.

[Trajan to Pliny]

You observed proper procedure, my dear Pliny, in sifting the cases of those who had been denounced to you as Christians. For it is not possible to lay down any general rule to serve as a kind of fixed standard. They are not to be sought out; if they are denounced and proved guilty, they are to be punished, with this reservation, that whoever denies that he is a Christian and really proves it—that is, by worshiping our gods—even though he was under suspicion in the past, shall obtain pardon through repentance. But anonymously posted accusations ought to have no place in any prosecution. For this is both a dangerous kind of precedent and out of keeping with [the spirit of] our age.

Source: Pliny, *Letters,* Book 10, nos. 96 and 97.

QUESTIONS FOR DEBATE

1. Should a society allow religious freedom if its members believe that divine goodwill—and the safety it ensures—demands only certain kinds of worship?

2. How should a society treat a minority of its members whose presence severely disturbs the majority?

Early Christians constantly and fiercely disagreed about what they should believe, how they should live, and who had the authority to decide these questions. Some, as had the followers of the Hellenistic philosopher Epicurus, insisted that it was necessary to withdraw from the everyday world to escape its evil, abandoning their families and shunning sex and reproduction. Others believed they could strive to live by Christ's teachings while retaining their jobs and ordinary lives. Many Christians questioned whether they could serve as soldiers without betraying their religious beliefs because the army participated in the imperial cult. This dilemma raised the further issue of whether they could remain loyal subjects of the emperor. Controversy over such matters raged in the many congregations that arose in the early empire around the Mediterranean, from Gaul to Africa to the Near East (Map 6.3).

The emergence of bishops with authority to define doctrine and conduct became the most impor-

tant institutional development to deal with this disunity in the later first and second centuries. Bishops received their positions through the principle later called *apostolic succession,* which states that Jesus' Apostles appointed the first bishops as their successors, granting these new officials the powers Jesus had originally given to the Apostles. Those designated by the Apostles in turn appointed their own successors, and so on. Bishops had the authority to ordain priests with the holy power to administer the sacraments, above all baptism and communion, which believers regarded as necessary for achieving eternal life. Bishops also controlled their congregations' memberships and finances; the money financing the early church flowed from members' gifts.

The bishops were expected to combat the splintering effect of the differing versions of the new religion. They had the power to define what was true doctrine (*orthodoxy*) and what was not (*heresy*). For all practical purposes, the meetings of the bishops of different cities constituted the church's organization, though it by no means displayed unity in this early period. Today it is common to refer to this loose organization as the early Catholic ("universal") church.

Women in the Church.   Early Christians disagreed about the role women should play in the church. In the first congregations, women held leadership positions in special circumstances. When bishops were established atop the hierarchy, however, women were usually relegated to inferior positions. This demotion reflected the view that in Christianity women should be subordinate to men, just as in Roman imperial society in general.

Some congregations took a long time to accept this development, however, and women still commanded positions of authority in some groups in the second and third centuries. Declaring themselves believers in the predictions of the imminent end of the world made by a mysterious preacher named Montanus, the late-second-century prophetesses Prisca and Maximilla, for example, claimed the authority to prophesy and baptize. They spread the apocalyptic message that the heavenly Jerusalem would soon descend in Asia Minor. Even when leadership posts were closed off to them, many women chose a life of celibacy to demonstrate their devotion to Christ. Their commitment to chastity gave these women the power to control their own bodies by removing their sexuality from the province of men. Women with a special closeness to God were judged holy and socially superior by other Christians. By rejecting the traditional roles of wife and mother in favor of spiritual excellence, celibate Christian women achieved a measure of independence and authority generally denied them in the outside world.

Parallel Belief Systems

Even three or four centuries after Jesus' death, the overwhelming majority of the population still practiced polytheism, which was never a unified religion (as the modern term *paganism,* under which diverse cults are often grouped, might suggest). The success and prosperity of the principate gave traditional believers confidence that the old gods favored and protected them and that the imperial cult only added to their safety. Even those who found a more intellectually satisfying understanding of the world in philosophies such as Stoicism respected the traditional cults.

Polytheism.   Polytheistic religion had as its goal worshiping and thus gaining the favor of all the divinities who could affect human life. Its deities ranged from the stalwarts of the state cults, such as

MAP 6.3 Christian Populations in the Late Third Century A.D.
Christians were still a distinct minority in the Roman world 300 years after the crucifixion of Jesus. Certain areas of the empire, however, especially Asia Minor (western Turkey), where Paul had preached, had a concentration of Christians. Most Christians lived in cities and towns, where the missionaries had gone to spread their message to crowds of curious listeners; paganus, a Latin word for "country person" or "rural villager," was appropriated to mean a believer in traditional polytheistic cults—hence the term pagan often found in modern works on this period.

Mithras Slaying the Bull

Hundreds of shrines to the mysterious god Mithras have been found in the Roman Empire, but the cult remains poorly known because almost no texts exist to explain it. To judge from the many representations in art, such as this wall painting of about A.D. 200 from the shrine at Marino south of Rome, the story of Mithras slaying a bull was a central part of the cult's identity. Scholars strenuously debate the symbolic meaning of the bull slaying, in which a snake and a dog lick the animal's blood while a scorpion pinches its testicles. Most agree, however, that Mithras was derived, perhaps as late as the early imperial period, from the ancient Persian divinity Mithra. Only men could be worshipers, and many were soldiers. Earlier scholarly claims of the cult's popularity were exaggerated; its members numbered no more than 1 or 2 percent of the population. Mithraism probably involved complex devotion to astrology, with devotees ranked in grades each protected by a different celestial body.
Scala/Art Resource, NY.

Jupiter and Minerva, to spirits traditionally thought to inhabit local groves and springs. Famous old cults such as the initiation rituals of Demeter and Persephone at Eleusis outside Athens remained popular; the emperor Hadrian was initiated at Eleusis in 125.

The Hellenized cult of the Egyptian goddess Isis clearly revealed how traditional rituals could provide believers with a religious experience arousing strong personal emotions and demanding a moral way of life. Her cult had already attracted Romans by the time of Augustus, who tried to suppress it because it was Cleopatra's religion. But Isis's stature as a kind, compassionate goddess who cared for the suffering of each of her followers made her cult too popular to crush: the Egyptians said it was her tears for famished humans that caused the Nile to flood every year and bring them good harvests. Her image was that of a loving mother, and in art she is often shown nursing her son. A central doctrine of her cult concerned the death and resurrection of her husband, Osiris; Isis promised her followers a similar hope for life after death.

Isis expected her adherents to behave righteously. Inscriptions put up for all to read expressed her standards by referring to her own civilizing accomplishments: "I broke down the rule of tyrants; I put an end to murders; I caused what is right to be mightier than gold and silver." The hero of Apuleius's novel *The Golden Ass*, whom Isis rescues from torturous enchantment, expresses his intense joy after being spiritually reborn: "O holy and eternal guardian of the human race, who always cherishes mortals and blesses them, you care for the troubles of miserable humans with a sweet mother's love. Neither day nor night, nor any moment of time, ever passes by without your blessings." Other cults also required their adherents to lead ethically upright lives. Numerous inscriptions from remote villages in Asia Minor, for example, record the confessions of peasants to sins such as sexual transgressions for which their local god had imposed severe penance.

Philosophy: Stoicism and Neoplatonism. Many upper-class Romans guided their lives by philosophy. Stoicism, derived from the teachings of the Greek Zeno (335–263 B.C.), was the most popular. Stoics believed in self-discipline above all, and their code of personal ethics left no room for riotous conduct. As the Stoic philosopher Seneca (4 B.C.–A.D. 65) put it, "It is easier to prevent harmful emotions from entering the soul than it is to control them once they have entered." Stoicism taught that the universe is guided by a single creative force incorporating reason, nature, and divinity. Humans share in the essence of this universal force and find happiness and patience by living in accordance with it and always doing their duty. The emperor Marcus Aurelius, in his memoirs entitled *Meditations*, emphasized the Stoic belief that people exist for each other: "Either make them better, or just put up with them," he advised.

Christian and polytheistic intellectuals energetically debated Christianity's relationship to traditional Greek philosophy. The theologian Origen (c. 185–255), for example, argued that Christianity was both true and superior to Hellenic philosophical doctrines as a guide to correct living. At about the same time, however, philosophic belief achieved its most intellectual formulation in the works of Plotinus (c. 205–270). Plotinus's spiritual philosophy, called *Neoplatonism* because it developed new doctrines based on Plato's philosophy, influenced many educated Christians as well as polytheists. Its religious doctrines focused on a human longing to return to the universal Good from which human existence derives. By turning away from the life of the body through the intellectual pursuit of philosophy, individual souls could ascend to the level of the universal soul, becoming the whole of which, as individuals, they formed a potential part. This mystical union with what the Christians would call God could be achieved only through strenuous self-discipline in personal morality as well as intellectual life. Neoplatonism's stress on spiritual purity gave it a powerful appeal to Christian intellectuals.

Like the cult of Isis or Stoicism, Neoplatonism provided guidance, comfort, and hope through good times or bad. By the third century, then, spiritually inclined people had various belief systems from which to choose to help them survive the harshness of ancient life.

❖ The Crisis of the Third Century A.D.

Life turned much grimmer for many people in the middle of the third century. Several factors combined to create a crisis for government and society. The invasions that outsiders had long been conducting on the northern and eastern frontiers had forced the emperors to expand the army for defense, but no new revenues came in to meet the additional costs. The emperors' desperate schemes to raise money to pay and equip the troops damaged the economy and public confidence. The ensuing unrest encouraged ambitious generals to imitate the behavior that had destroyed the republic: commanding personal armies to seize power. The worst trouble came when civil war once again infected Rome. Earthquakes and scattered epidemics added to the destruction caused by these struggles. By the end of the third century, this combination of troubles had shredded the "Roman peace."

Defending the Frontiers

Emperors had been leading campaigns to repel invaders since Domitian in the first century. The most aggressive attackers were the loosely organized Germanic bands that often crossed the Danube and Rhine rivers for raiding. They mounted especially dangerous invasions during the reign of Marcus Aurelius (161–180). Constant fighting against the Roman army forced these informally organized northerners to develop greater military skills. A major threat also appeared at the eastern edge of the empire, when a new dynasty, the Sassanids, defeated the Parthian Empire and reenergized the ancient Persian kingdom. By 227, Persia's military resurgence compelled the emperors to concentrate forces in the rich eastern provinces, at the expense of the defense of the northern frontiers.

Recognizing the skill of Germanic warriors, the emperors had begun hiring them as auxiliary soldiers for the Roman army as early as Domitian and settling them on the frontiers as buffers against other invaders. By around 200, the army had expanded to enroll perhaps as many as 450,000 legionary and auxiliary troops (the size of the navy remains unknown). As always in the Roman military, existence was demanding. Training constantly, soldiers had to be fit enough to carry forty-pound packs up to twenty miles in five hours, swimming rivers en route. Since the reign of Hadrian in the second century, the emperors had built many stone camps for permanent garrisons, but on the march an army constructed a fortified camp every night; soldiers transported all the makings of a wooden-walled city everywhere they went. As one ancient commentator noted during the republic, "Infantrymen were little different from loaded pack mules." At one temporary fort in a frontier area, for example, archaeologists found a supply of a million iron nails—ten tons' worth. The same encampment required seventeen miles of timber for its barracks' walls. To outfit a single legion of 5,000 to 6,000 men with tents required 54,000 calves' hides.

The increased requirement for pay and supplies strained imperial finances because successful conquests had dwindled over time. The army had become a source of negative instead of positive cash flow to the treasury, and the economy had not expanded sufficiently to make up the difference. To make matters worse, inflation had driven up prices.

A principal cause of inflation under the principate may have been, ironically, the long period of peace that promoted increased demand for the economy's relatively static production of goods and services.

Over time, some emperors responded to inflated prices by debasing imperial coinage in a vain attempt to cut government costs. By putting less silver in each coin without changing its face value, emperors hoped to create more cash with the same amount of precious metal. (See "Taking Measure,"

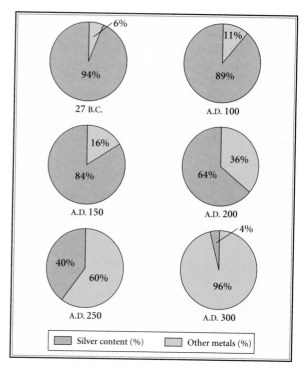

TAKING MEASURE The Value of Roman Imperial Coinage, 27 B.C.–A.D. 300

Ancient silver coinage derived its value from its metallic content; the less silver in a coin, the less the coin was worth. When they faced rising government and military expenses but had flat or falling revenues, emperors resorted to debasing the coinage by reducing the amount of silver and increasing the amount of other, cheaper metals in each coin. These pie charts reveal that there was a relatively gradual devaluation of the coinage until the third century, when military expenses apparently skyrocketed. By 300, only a trace amount of silver was left in coins. Debasement fueled inflation because merchants and producers had to raise their prices for goods and services when they were being paid with currency that was increasingly less valuable.

Adapted from Kevin Greene, *The Archeology of the Roman Empire* (London: B. T. Batsford, Ltd., 1986), 60. Reprinted with permission of Salamander Books Limited.

page 226.) But merchants simply raised prices to make up for the loss in value from the debased currency, increasing the momentum of the inflationary spiral. By 200, these pressures were ruining the imperial balance sheet. Still, the soldiers demanded that their patrons, the emperors, pay them well. The stage was set for a crisis; the financial system finally fell into full collapse in the 250s and 260s.

The Severan Emperors and Catastrophe

Septimius Severus (r. 193–211) and his sons put the catastrophe in motion: the father fatally drained the treasury to satisfy the army, while his sons' murderous rivalry and reckless spending destroyed the government's stability. A soldier's soldier who came from the large North African city of Lepcis Magna in what is today Libya, Severus became emperor in 193 when his predecessor proved hopelessly incompetent and set off a government crisis and civil war. To remedy the situation by restoring imperial prestige and acquiring money through foreign conquest, Severus vigorously pursued successful campaigns beyond the frontiers of the provinces in Mesopotamia and northern Britain.

The soldiers were desperate by this time because inflation had diminished the value of their wages to virtually nothing after the costs of basic supplies and clothing were deducted. They therefore routinely expected the emperors as their patrons to favor them with gifts of extra money. Severus spent large sums to do this and then set out to improve conditions fundamentally by raising the soldiers' pay by a third. The expanded size of the army made this raise more expensive than the treasury could handle and further increased inflation. The dire financial consequences of his military policy concerned Severus not at all. His deathbed advice to his sons in 211 was to "stay on good terms with each other, be generous to the soldiers, and pay no attention to anyone else."

Caracalla's Failure. Sadly for the principate, his sons followed this advice only on the last two points. Caracalla (r. 211–217) seized the throne for himself by murdering his brother Geta. Caracalla's violent and profligate reign signaled the end of the peace and prosperity of the Roman Golden Age. He increased the soldiers' pay by another 40–50 percent and spent gigantic sums on grandiose building

War Scenes on Trajan's Column
Much of our knowledge of Roman military equipment, such as the intricate construction of chain-mail armor, comes from close study of Trajan's Column in Rome. The sculpted band depicting Trajan's Dacian wars that spiraled up his column (detail shown here) contained some 2,500 figures. The scenes were about three feet high at the bottom but grew to four feet at the top to accommodate the distance and angle of vision for spectators. The spiral's beginning shows the landscape of Dacia, with the following narrative scenes blending into one another without formal frames to separate them. They show the emperor leading his troops and making sacrifices to the gods, while his soldiers appear preparing to march, crossing the Danube, building sturdy camps, being stormed in their encampments by bands of Dacians, and fighting fierce hand-to-hand battles.
Scala/Art Resource, NY.

projects, including the largest public baths Rome had ever seen, covering blocks and blocks of the city. His extravagant spending put unbearable pressure on the local provincial officials responsible for collecting taxes and on the citizens whom they squeezed for ever greater amounts.

In 212, Caracalla took his most famous step to try to fix the budget crisis: he granted Roman citizenship to almost every man and woman in imperial territory except slaves. Noncitizens were liable for other taxes, but only citizens paid inheritance taxes and fees for freeing slaves. Therefore, an increase in citizens meant an increase in revenues, most of which was earmarked for the army. But too much was never enough for Caracalla, who contemporaries whispered was insane. He soon wrecked the imperial budget and paved the way for absolutely ruinous inflation in the coming decades. Once when his mother upbraided him for his excesses he replied, as he drew his sword, "Never mind, we shall not run out of money as long as I have this."

The Threat of Fragmentation. Political instability accompanied the financial weakening of the empire. After Macrinus, the commander of the praetorians, murdered Caracalla in 217 to make himself emperor, Caracalla's female relatives convinced the army to overthrow Macrinus in favor of a young male relative. The restored dynasty did not last long, however, and the assassination of the last Severan emperor in 235 opened a half-century of civil wars that, compounded by natural disasters, broke the principate's back. For fifty years, a parade of emperors and pretenders fought over power; over two dozen men, often several at a time, held or claimed the throne during that period of near-anarchy. Their only qualification was their ability to command a frontier army and to reward the troops for loyalty to their general instead of the state.

The virtually constant civil war of the mid-third century exacted a tremendous toll on the population and the economy; insecurity combined with hyperinflation to make life miserable in many regions. Agriculture withered as farmers found it impossible to keep up normal production in wartime, when battling armies damaged their crops searching for food. City council members faced constantly escalating demands for tax revenues from the swiftly changing emperors; the constant financial pressure destroyed their enthusiasm for helping their communities.

Foreign enemies took advantage of the Roman civil wars to attack, especially from the east and the north. Roman fortunes hit bottom when Shapur I, king of the Sassanid Empire of Persia, captured the emperor Valerian (r. 253–260) while invading the province of Syria in 260. Imperial territory was in constant danger of splintering into breakaway empires in this period. Even the tough and experienced emperor Aurelian (r. 270–275) could do no more to ward off the danger than to recover Egypt and Asia Minor from Zenobia, the warrior queen of Palmyra in Syria. He also had to encircle Rome with a massive wall to ward off surprise attacks from Germanic tribes, who were already smashing their way into Italy from the north.

Territory of Zenobia, Queen of Palmyra, A.D. 269–272

MAPPING THE WEST The Roman Empire in Crisis, c. A.D. 284

By the 280s A.D., the principate had been torn apart by the fifty years of civil war following the end of the Severan dynasty. Imperial territory generally retained the outlines that had existed since the time of Augustus, except for the loss of Dacia to the Goths during Aurelian's reign (A.D. 270–275). Attacks from the north and the east had repeatedly penetrated into its frontiers, however. Shapur I, Sassanid king (c. 240–270), for example, temporarily held Antioch and captured the emperor Valerian in 260. The public humiliation and death in captivity of the elderly ruler symbolized the depth to which Roman fortunes had sunk in the crisis of the third century.

Historians dispute how severely these troubles were worsened by natural disasters, but devastating earthquakes and virulent epidemics did strike some of the provinces around the middle of the century. The population probably declined significantly as food supplies became less dependable, civil war killed soldiers and civilians alike, and infection flared over large regions. The loss of population meant fewer soldiers for the army, whose efficiency as a defense and police force had already deteriorated seriously from political and financial chaos. More frontier areas became vulnerable to raids, while roving bands of robbers also became increasingly common inside the borders.

Polytheists explained these horrible times in the traditional way: the state gods were angry about something. But what? The obvious answer seemed to be the presence of Christians, who denied the existence of the Roman gods and refused to participate in their worship. Therefore, violent and systematic persecutions began to eliminate this contaminated group and restore the goodwill of the gods. The emperor Decius (r. 249–251) launched his attack by styling himself "Restorer of the Cults" while proclaiming, "I would rather see a rival to my throne than another bishop of Rome." He ordered all inhabitants of the empire to prove their loyalty to the welfare of the state by participating in a sacrifice to its gods. Christians who refused to do so were killed.

These new persecutions did not stop the civil war, economic failure, and diseases that had precipitated the protracted crisis. By the 280s, no one could deny that the principate was near to fragmenting. Remarkably, it was to be dragged back to safety in the same way it had begun: by Diocletian's creation of a new form of authoritarian leadership to replace the principate, which had replaced the republic.

Conclusion

Augustus created the principate by substituting a cloaked monarchy for the political structure of the republic while insisting that he was restoring the republic to its traditional values. He succeeded above all because he retained the loyalty of the army and exploited the familiar tradition of the patron-client system. The principate made the emperor the patron of the army and of all the people. Most provincials, especially in the eastern Mediterranean, found this arrangement acceptable because it replicated the relationship between ruler and ruled that was familiar from the Hellenistic kingdoms.

So long as sufficient funds allowed the emperors to keep their millions of clients satisfied, stability prevailed. They spent money to provide food to the poor, build baths and arenas for public entertainment, and pay their troops. The emperors of the first and second centuries expanded the military to protect their distant territories stretching from Britain to North Africa to Syria. By the second century, peace and prosperity had created an imperial Golden Age. Long-term fiscal difficulties set in, however, because the army, concentrating on defense rather than conquest, no longer brought money into the treasury. Severe inflation made the situation worse. The wealthy elites found they could no longer meet the demand for increased taxes without draining their fortunes, and they lost their public-spiritedness and avoided their communal responsibilities. Loyalty to the state became too expensive.

The emergence of Christians added to the uncertainty by making officials doubtful of their dedication to the state. Their new religion evolved from Jewish apocalypticism to an increasingly hierarchical organization. Its adherents disputed with each other and with the authorities; martyrs such as Perpetua impressed and worried the government with the depth of their convictions. Citizens placing loyalty to a divinity ahead of loyalty to the state was a new and inexplicable phenomenon for Roman officialdom.

When financial ruin, civil war, and natural disasters combined to weaken the imperial system in the mid-third century, the emperors lacked the money and the popular support to end the crisis. Not even persecutions of Christians could convince the gods to restore Rome's good fortunes. The empire instead had to be transformed politically and religiously. Against all expectations, that process began with Diocletian in 284.

Suggested References

Creating "Roman Peace"

For decades scholars have debated Augustus's motives in contriving the principate and how to evaluate his rule; whether they label him tyrant or reformer, all agree that he was a brilliant visionary. Recent research on the ways Augustus and his successors communicated the meaning of empire to the public stresses the role of grandiose and often violent spectacles.

Auguet, Roland. *Cruelty and Civilization: The Roman Games.* 1972.

Bradley, Keith. *Slavery and Society at Rome.* 1994.

Conlin, Diane Atnally. *The Artists of the Ara Pacis: The Process of Hellenization in Roman Relief Sculpture.* 1997.

Futrell, Alison. *Blood in the Arena: The Spectacle of Roman Power.* 1997.

Galinsky, Karl. *Augustan Culture.* 1996.

Henig, Martin, ed. *A Handbook of Roman Art: A Comprehensive Survey of All the Arts of the Roman World.* 1983.

Horace's country house: http://www.humnet.ucla.edu/horaces-villa/contents.html.

Jackson, Ralph. *Doctors and Diseases in the Roman Empire.* 1988.

Potter, D. S., and D. J. Mattingly, eds. *Life, Death, and Entertainment in the Roman Empire.* 1999.

Roman emperors: http://www.roman-emperors.org.

Southern, Pat. *Augustus.* 1998.

Wallace-Hadrill, Andrew. *Augustan Rome.* 1993.

Wiedemann, Thomas. *Emperors and Gladiators.* 1995.

Zanker, Paul. *The Power of Images in the Age of Augustus.* Trans. Alan Shapiro. 1988.

Maintaining "Roman Peace"

The avoidance of civil war was the foremost marker of the period of "Roman peace" in the late first and second centuries. As various scholarly studies show, this interlude was made possible both by the devotion of duty of emperors such as Aurelius and by the general prosperity that emerged during the absence of war in imperial territory.

Birley, Anthony. *Marcus Aurelius: A Biography.* Rev. ed. 1987.

Garnsey, Peter, and Richard Saller. *The Roman Empire: Economy, Society, and Culture.* 1987.

Johnston, David. *Roman Law in Context.* 1999.

Lintott, Andrew. *Imperium Romanum: Politics and Administration.* 1993.

Mattern, Susan. *Rome and the Enemy: Imperial Strategy in the Principate.* 1999.

Roman towns and monuments: http://www.ukans.edu/history/index/europe/ancient_rome/E/Roman/home.html.

Treggiari, Susan. *Roman Marriage: Iusti Coniuges from the Time of Cicero to the Time of Ulpian.* 1991.

Webster, Graham. *The Roman Imperial Army of the First and Second Centuries A.D.* 3rd ed. 1985.

Wiedemann, Thomas. *The Julio-Claudian Emperors, A.D. 14–70.* 1989.

The Emergence of Christianity

Few fields in ancient history generate as much scholarly activity as does the study of early Christianity, and the disputes over how to understand it are lively; the significance of the role of women is especially controversial. The sources are relatively plentiful, compared with those for other periods in Greek and Roman history, but their meaning is hotly contested because both the authors and their interpreters usually have particular points of view.

Doran, Robert. *Birth of a World View: Early Christianity in Its Jewish and Pagan Contexts.* 1999.

Frend, W. H. C. *The Rise of Christianity.* 1984.

Kraemer, Ross Shephard. *Her Share of the Blessings: Women's Religion among Pagans, Jews, and Christians in the Greco-Roman World.* 1992.

MacMullen, Ramsay. *Christianizing the Roman Empire (A.D. 100–400).* 1984.

Meeks, Wayne A. *The First Urban Christians: The Social World of the Apostle Paul.* 1983.

Schurer, Emil. *The History of the Jewish People in the Age of Jesus Christ (175 B.C.–A.D. 135).* Rev. ed. 4 vols. 1973, 1979, 1986.

Stambaugh, John E., and David L. Balch. *The New Testament in Its Social Environment.* 1986.

Torjesen, Karen Jo. *When Women Were Priests: Women's Leadership in the Early Church and the Scandal of Their Subordination in the Rise of Christianity.* 1993.

Turcan, Robert. *The Cults of the Roman Empire.* Trans. Antonia Nevill. 1996.

Witt, R. E. *Isis in the Greco-Roman World.* 1971.

The Crisis of the Third Century A.D.

Unfortunately, our sources become fragmentary just during the period when the empire was in danger of splitting into pieces. The fundamental problem remained what it had always been: the Roman monarchy's propensity to generate civil war and the inevitably disastrous effects on the economy. Hence, scholarly study of the crisis must always begin with military and political history.

Elton, Hugh. *Frontiers of the Roman Empire.* 1996.

———. Military Aspects of the Collapse of the Roman Empire: http://www.unipissing.ca/department/history/orb/milex.htm.

Grant, Michael. *The Collapse and Recovery of the Roman Empire.* 1999.

Isaac, Benjamin. *The Limits of Empire: The Roman Army in the East.* 1989.

MacMullen, Ramsay. *Roman Government's Response to Crisis, A.D. 235–337.* 1976.

The Transformation of the Roman Empire

A.D. 284–c. 600

Late Byzantine Mosaic of Christ from Constantinople
This mosaic of Christ from the fourteenth-century Chora monastery in Constantinople (now Istanbul's Kariye Djamii Museum) attests to the enduring legacy of the late Roman Empire. Produced a thousand years after Constantine became the first Christian emperor, this portrait represents the potent combination of traditions that had transformed the empire. Christ's garment is reminiscent of elite Greek and Roman clothing, and Christ keeps his right arm decorously confined, just as classical orators had done. At the same time, he holds a codex of the Christian Scriptures, bedecked with jewels that recall the splendor of the imperial court, which was losing the struggle to prevent a Turkish takeover of the eastern Roman Empire but holding fast to the memory of its days of glory as the heir of Augustan Rome.
Erich Lessing/Art Resource, NY.

AN EGYPTIAN WOMAN NAMED ISIS wrote a letter to her mother in the third century (the precise date is unknown) that modern archaeologists found among the remains of a village near the Nile River. The letter, written in Greek on papyrus, offers a hint of some of the unsettling changes that affected the lives of many people in the Roman Empire during that tumultuous period.

Every day I pray to the lord Sarapis and his fellow gods to watch over you. I want you to know that I have arrived in Alexandria safely after four days. I send fond greetings to my sister and the children and Elouath and his wife and Dioscorous and her husband and children and Tamalis and her husband and son and Heron and Ammonarion and . . . Sanpat and her children. And if Aion wants to be in the army, let him come. For everybody is in the army.

Although tantalizing in its suggestions of the history of the time, the letter leaves us with basic questions unanswered, such as the relationship between Isis and most of the people she mentions, with their mixture of Greek and Semitic names. It also raises many others. Did Isis know how to write or, as was common, had she hired a scribe? Why did she go to Alexandria? Why did Aion want to become a soldier? Why was "everybody" in the army?

These questions reflect the many dimensions of the third-century crisis in the empire. Perhaps economic troubles forced Isis to leave her home to look for work in the largest city in her area. Perhaps Aion wanted to join the army to better his prospects. Perhaps it appeared that

233

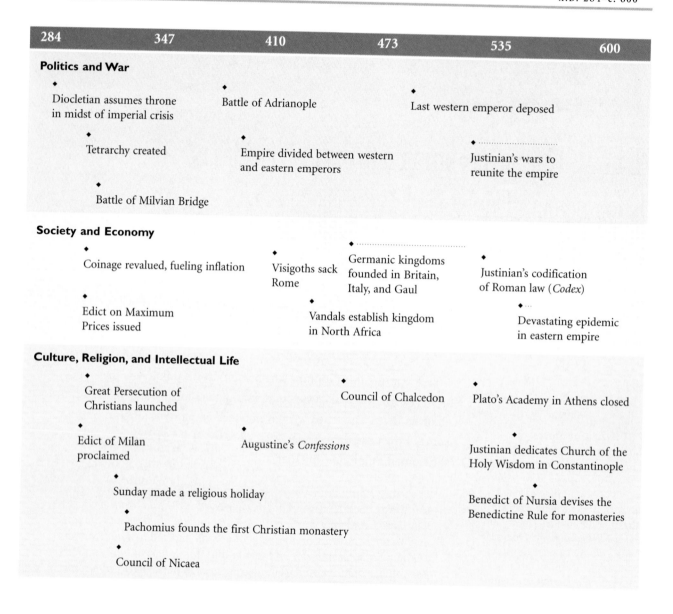

284	347	410	473	535	600

Politics and War

- Diocletian assumes throne in midst of imperial crisis
- Battle of Adrianople
- Last western emperor deposed
- Tetrarchy created
- Empire divided between western and eastern emperors
- Justinian's wars to reunite the empire
- Battle of Milvian Bridge

Society and Economy

- Coinage revalued, fueling inflation
- Visigoths sack Rome
- Germanic kingdoms founded in Britain, Italy, and Gaul
- Justinian's codification of Roman law (*Codex*)
- Edict on Maximum Prices issued
- Vandals establish kingdom in North Africa
- Devastating epidemic in eastern empire

Culture, Religion, and Intellectual Life

- Great Persecution of Christians launched
- Council of Chalcedon
- Plato's Academy in Athens closed
- Edict of Milan proclaimed
- Augustine's *Confessions*
- Justinian dedicates Church of the Holy Wisdom in Constantinople
- Sunday made a religious holiday
- Benedict of Nursia devises the Benedictine Rule for monasteries
- Pachomius founds the first Christian monastery
- Council of Nicaea

everybody was in the army because the political turmoil in the empire was generating decades of civil war. These answers seem plausible in the context of the desperate challenge facing imperial government by the 280s, after half a century of Roman armies fighting Roman armies over who should be emperor: how to reorganize the empire to restore its traditional function as the guarantor of peace and order through military force, government administration, ancestral religion, and economic prosperity. Diocletian, who became emperor in A.D. 284, turned out to be a leader tough enough to overcome this challenge and delay the political fragmentation of the empire.

Regaining social calm was difficult because religious tensions were growing between Christians and followers of traditional polytheistic cults like Isis the letter writer, whose faith was visible in her namesake, an Egyptian goddess. Polytheist emperors believed that Christians caused divine anger against their regimes, and they embarked on the worst persecutions yet. The emperor Constantine at the beginning of the fourth century unexpectedly initiated a resolution to this conflict by converting to Christianity and officially favoring it, yet it was the end of the fourth century before the new faith became the state religion. The social and cultural effects of this shift took even longer to settle, owing to the persistence of pre-Christian traditions and Christians' fierce disputes over doctrine.

The political rescue of the empire engineered by Diocletian and promoted by Constantine postponed but did not prevent the splintering of imperial territory: at the end of the fourth century, the empire fragmented permanently into two geographic divisions, west and east. In the west, various Germanic peoples subsequently migrated to the region and transformed it socially, culturally, and politically by replacing Roman provincial government with their own new kingdoms. There they lived side by side with Romans, the different groups keeping some customs of their heritage intact but merging other parts of their cultures. The growing strength of these new regimes and the consequent decentralization of authority in the fifth century transformed western Europe and set the pattern for later political divisions. In the east, the Roman provinces remained economically vibrant and politically united, becoming (in modern terminology) the Byzantine Empire in the sixth century. Despite financial pressures and loss of provincial territory, this Christian continuation of the Roman imperial structure endured until Turkish invaders conquered it in 1453. In this way, the empire lived on in the eastern Mediterranean for a thousand years beyond its transformation in the west.

❖ Reorganizing the Empire

The Roman Empire reemerged from its third-century crisis as a unified state ruled by a strong central authority. The penetration of the empire's borders by different invaders over several decades, however, had imposed a pressing need to reorganize its defenses and its system of collecting revenue. In the religious arena, the emperors confronted the thorny issue of a growing Christian church, whose presence was now felt throughout the Roman world. The definitive responses to these challenges came during the reign of the emperors Diocletian (r. 284–305) and Constantine (r. 306–337).

Imperial Reform and Fragmentation

No one could have predicted Diocletian's success: he was an uneducated military man from the rough region of Dalmatia (in what is now the former Yugoslavia). Yet his exceptional talent for leadership, his courage, and his intelligence propelled him through the ranks until the army made him emperor in 284. He ended the third-century anarchy by imposing the most autocratic system of rule the Roman world had yet seen.

The Power of the Dominate. Relying on the military's support, Diocletian had himself formally recognized as *dominus*, or "master"—the term slaves called their owners—to replace the republican title Augustus had chosen, *princeps* ("first man"). Roman imperial rule from Diocletian onward is therefore called the *dominate*. Its blatant autocracy—rule by

Miniature Portrait of Emperor Constantine
This eight-inch-high bust of Constantine is carved from chalcedony, a crystalline mineral prized for its milky translucence. The first Christian emperor is depicted as gazing upward, to link himself to his hero and model Alexander the Great, who had ordered his portrait done in this posture. Constantine also appears without a beard, a style made popular by Alexander and imitated by Augustus and Trajan, successful emperors with whose memory Constantine also wished to be associated. The cross at the top center of Constantine's breastplate makes the statuette one of the relatively few pieces of fourth-century Roman art to display overtly Christian symbols. The position of this unmistakable sign of the emperor's religious choice recalls the sculpture on the armor on the Prima Porta statue of Augustus (see p. 207); like the founder of the principate, Constantine communicated his image through art.
Bibliothèque Nationale.

absolute power—eliminated any reality of shared authority between the emperor and the elite, echoing the traditions of ancient Near Eastern monarchies. Senators, consuls, and other vestiges of the republic continued to exist, but in name only, wielding no power. Administrators were increasingly chosen from lower ranks of society based on their competence and loyalty to the emperor.

Over time, the emperors as "masters" developed new ways to display their supremacy: sitting on a dais, dressing in jeweled robes, and surrounding themselves with courtiers and ceremony. Constantine even began wearing a diadem, a purple headband sparkling with jewels, a symbol of kingship that earlier emperors had avoided. To demonstrate the difference between the master and ordinary mortals, a series of veils separated the palace's waiting rooms from the inner space where the ruler held audiences. Officials marked their rank in the fiercely hierarchical administration with grandiose titles such as "most perfect" and sported special shoes and belts. In its style and titles the dominate's imperial court resembled that of the Great King of Persia a thousand years earlier more closely than that of the first Roman emperors: the masters abandoned the principate's claim that the ruler was merely the most distinguished citizen and embraced instead the notion that citizens were the monarch's subjects. The architecture of the dominate also reflected the image of its rulers as all-powerful autocrats. Diocletian's public bath in Rome rivaled earlier emperors' buildings in the capital with its soaring vaults and domes covering a space more than three thousand feet long on each side.

The dominate also developed a theological framework for legitimating its rule that harked back to Hellenistic kingship. Religious language was used to mark the emperor's special status above everybody else. Recalling the emperor Domitian's initiative, which had failed to take hold in his time, the emperors now succeeded in adding the title *et deus* ("and God") to *dominus* as a mark of supreme honor. Diocletian also adopted the title *Jovius*, proclaiming himself descended from Jupiter (Jove), the chief Roman god. These titles expressed the sense of complete respect and awe emperors now expected from their subjects, demonstrated that government on earth replicated divine hierarchy, and promised greater control in a very insecure world recovering from the horrors of anarchy.

The dominate's emperors asserted their autocracy most aggressively in law and punishments as a solution to the disorder of the third century's civil wars. Their word alone made law; indeed, they came to be above the law because they were not bound even by the decisions of their predecessors. Relying on a personal staff that isolated them from the outside world, they rarely sought advice from the elite, as earlier rulers had done. Their concern to maintain order led them to increase the severity of punishment for crimes to brutal levels. For example, Constantine mandated that if officials did not keep their "greedy hands" off bribes, "they shall be cut off by the sword." Serious malefactors were dispatched with the traditional punishment of being tied in a leather sack with poisonous snakes and drowned in a river. The guardians of a young girl who allowed a lover to seduce her were punished by having molten lead poured into their mouths. Punishments grew especially harsh for the large segment of the population legally designated as "humbler people," but the laws excused the "better people" from most of the harshest treatments for comparable offenses. In this way, autocracy strengthened the divisions between the poor and the rich.

The Tetrarchy. Although a self-made autocrat, Diocletian realized that the situation had become too perilous to administer and defend imperial territory from a single center. To combat the danger of fragmentation raised by the third century's prolonged civil wars, he hit upon the expedient of subdividing the empire to try to hold it together. In a daring innovation in 293, he carved imperial territory into four loosely defined administrative districts, two in the west and two in the east. Because he had no sons as heirs, he appointed three "partners" to join him in governing cooperatively in two pairs, each consisting of a senior "Augustus" with a junior "Caesar" as his adopted son and designated successor. The partners, Diocletian and Maximian as "Augustuses" and Galerius and Constantius as "Caesars", each controlled one of the districts. To prevent disunity, the most senior partner—in this case Diocletian—served as supreme ruler and was supposed to enjoy the loyalty of the others. This *tetrarchy* ("rule by four"), as modern scholars call it, was Diocletian's attempt to keep imperial government from being isolated at a distance from the empire's elongated frontiers and to prevent civil war over the succession. For the same reasons, he sub-divided the provinces, nearly doubling their number to almost a hundred; he then grouped them in twelve dioceses under regional administrators, who reported to the four emperors' first assistants, the praetorian prefects (Map 7.1). Finally, he tried to prevent rebellion by beginning to separate civil and military authority, with administrators in control only of legal and financial affairs and generals only of defense; Constantine, Constantius's son, completed this process.

Although the tetrarchy and the geographical divisions changed under later rulers, Diocletian's creation of a hierarchical system of provincial administration endured. It also ended Rome's thousand years as the capital city. Diocletian—who lived in Nicomedia, in Asia Minor—did not even visit Rome until 303, nearly twenty years after becoming emperor. He chose his four new capitals for their utility as military command posts closer to the frontiers: Milan in northern Italy, Sirmium near the Danube River border, Trier near the Rhine River

MAP 7.1 Diocletian's Reorganization of 293

Anxious to avoid further civil war, Emperor Diocletian reorganized imperial territory for tighter control by placing the empire under the rule of the tetrarchy's four partners, each the head of a large district. He subdivided the preexisting provinces into smaller units and grouped them into twelve dioceses, each overseen by a regional administrator. The four districts as shown here reflect the arrangement mentioned by the imperial official Sextus Aurelius Victor in his book On the Caesars, *a biographically oriented history of the empire inspired by Suetonius's biographies from the early second century, which Victor published around 360.*

border, and Nicomedia. Italy became just another section of the empire, on an equal footing with the other provinces and subject to the same taxation system, except for the district of Rome itself—the last vestige of the city's former primacy.

Separate Spheres, East and West. Diocletian's reforms failed to prevent civil war. When he abdicated in 305, Constantius succeeded him but died in 306. Constantine then took his father's position and

fought until 324 to eliminate emperors outside his own family. At the end of his reign, he designated his three sons as joint heirs, admonishing them to continue the new imperial system of co-emperorship. They failed as bloodily as had the sons of Septimius Severus a century earlier, plunging into war with one another.

The Sections of the Empire, c. 395

When their gory rivalry ruined any chance of cooperative rule, geography led the opposing forces to take up positions roughly splitting the empire on a north–south line along the Balkan peninsula. This de facto territorial division followed the administrative division initiated by Diocletian; in 395, the territory was formally divided into a western and an eastern empire, with a co-emperor ruling each half. East and west were intended to cooperate, but the permanent division launched the empires on different courses that would endure.

Each empire featured its own capital city. Constantinople, near the mouth of the Black Sea, was the choice in the east. The ancient city of Byzantium (today Istanbul, Turkey), Constantinople had been reconstructed by Constantine in 324 as his "new Rome" in his own name. He had chosen it for its military and commercial possibilities: it lay on an easily fortified peninsula astride principal routes for trade and troop movements. To recall the glory of Rome and thus appropriate for himself the political legitimacy bestowed by the memory of the old capital, Constantine had graced his refounded city with a forum, an imperial palace, a hippodrome for

chariot races, and monumental statues of the traditional gods. The eastern emperors inherited Constantine's "new" city as their capital; eventually it gave its former name to what we call the Byzantine Empire.

Geography determined the site of the western capital as well. The western emperor Honorius (r. 395–423) wanted to keep the protective mass of the Alps between his territory and the marauding Germanic bands to the north while having a more strategic location than Rome. In 404, Honorius made Ravenna, a port on Italy's northeastern coast, the permanent capital because it housed a main naval base and was an important commercial center. City walls and marshes protected it from attack by land, while access to the sea kept it from being starved out in a siege. Ravenna never rivaled Constantinople in size or splendor; its most enduring marks of status were the great churches with dazzling multicolored mosaics that were erected there.

Financial Reform

Diocletian's rescue of the empire called for vast revenues, which the hyperinflation of the third century had made harder to acquire. The biggest expense stemmed from paying a large army. Diocletian used his power as sole lawmaker to dictate reforms meant to improve the financial situation: price controls and a new taxation system.

Edict on Maximum Prices of 301. Even though he tried to prevent debasing of the currency (using less silver in the coins) by issuing new money, Diocletian miscalculated in mandating values to the denominations and sparked a financial panic that fueled inflation in many regions after 293. As inflated costs caused people to hoard whatever they could buy, prices were driven even higher. "Hurry and spend all my money you have; buy me any kinds of goods at whatever prices they are available," wrote one official to his servant on hearing of another impending plan to reduce the value of the currency.

In 301, Diocletian tried to curb inflation by imposing an elaborate system of wage and price controls in the worst-hit areas. His Edict on Maximum Prices, which blamed high prices on profiteers' "unlimited and frenzied avarice," forbade hoarding and set ceilings on what could legally be charged or paid for about a thousand goods and services. The edict, promulgated only in the eastern part of the empire, soon became ineffective because merchants refused to cooperate and government officials were unable to enforce it, despite the threat of death or exile as the penalty for violations. Diocletian in his final years at last revalued the currency to restore sound money and stable prices, but civil wars initiated by Constantine quickly undermined this success.

Higher Taxes. The inability to control market forces left the empire's currency and the taxes paid with it virtually worthless. But an alternative way existed to increase revenue: collect taxes in goods. Recent research disputes whether this form of revenue actually displaced taxes in coin, as previous scholars believed, or only served as a way to impose higher tax rates on property, paid as much as possible in money. By the end of the fourth century, it is clear, payments were expected in gold and silver to make collection easier for the government. In any case, taxes rose, especially on the local elites. Taxes went mostly to support the army, which required enormous amounts of grain, meat, salt, wine, vegetable oil, horses, camels, and mules. The major sources of payments—the amounts varied by region—were a tax on land, assessed according to its productivity, and a head tax on individuals.

The tax system lacked consistency because the empire was too large to enforce regularity. In some areas, both men and women from the age of about twelve to sixty-five paid the full tax, but in others women paid only one-half the tax assessment or none at all. Workers in cities probably owed taxes only on their property. They periodically paid "in kind," that is, by laboring without pay on public works projects such as cleaning municipal drains or repairing buildings. Owners of urban businesses, from shopkeepers to prostitutes, still paid taxes in money; members of the senatorial class were exempt from ordinary taxes but had to pay special levies.

Social Consequences. The new tax system would work only if agricultural production remained stable and the government controlled the people liable for the head tax. (See "Taking Measure," below.) Hence Diocletian restricted the movement of the *coloni*, or tenant farmers, the empire's economic base. *Coloni* had traditionally been free to move to different farms under different landlords as long as their debts were paid. Now male tenant farmers, as well as their wives in areas where women were assessed for taxes, were increasingly tied to a particular plot. Their children were also bound to the family plot, and agriculture thus became a hereditary occupation.

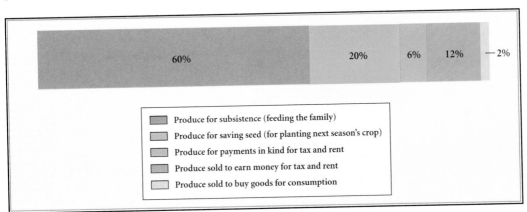

TAKING MEASURE Peasants' Use of Farm Produce in the Roman Empire

This graph offers a hypothetical model of how peasants during the Roman Empire may have used what they produced as farmers and herders to maintain their families, pay rent and taxes, and buy things they did not produce themselves. The amounts are speculative because reliable and comprehensive statistics of this kind do not exist for the ancient world. Individual families would have had widely varying experiences, and this estimate applies only to the population of peasant producers as a whole. Still, it is very likely that most families did have to use most of their production just to maintain a subsistence level—a description of poverty by modern standards.

Adapted from Keith Hopkins, *Conquerors and Slaves: Sociological Studies in Roman History* (New York: Cambridge University Press, 1978), 17. Reprinted with permission of Cambridge University Press.

The government also deemed some other occupations essential and prohibited changes in work. State bakers, for example, could not leave their jobs, and anyone who acquired a baker's property had to assume that occupation. The bakers were essential in producing free bread for Rome's poor, a tradition begun under the republic to prevent food riots. From Constantine's reign on, the military was a lifetime, hereditary career: the sons of military veterans had to serve in the army.

The emperors decreed equally oppressive regulations for the propertied class in the cities and towns, the *curiales*. In this period, almost all men in the *curial* class were obliged sooner or later to serve as unsalaried city council members, who had to use their own funds if necessary to support the community. Their financial responsibilities ranged from maintaining the water supply to feeding troops, but their most expensive duty was paying for shortfalls in tax collection. The emperors' demands for more and more revenue now made this a crushing blow, compounding the damage to the *curiales* that the third-century crisis had begun.

For centuries, the empire's welfare had depended on a steady supply of public-spirited members of the social elite enthusiastically filling these crucial local posts to win the admiration of their neighbors. Now this tradition broke down as wealthier people

avoided public service to escape financial ruin. So distorted was the situation that compulsory service on a municipal council became one of the punishments for a minor crime. Eventually, to prevent *curiales* from escaping their obligations, imperial policy forbade them to move away from the town where they had been born; they even had to ask official permission to travel. These laws made members of the elite feverish to win exemptions from public service by exploiting their connections to petition the emperor, by bribing higher officials, or by taking up an occupation that freed them from such obligations (the military, imperial administration, or church governance). The most desperate simply fled, abandoning home and property to avoid fulfilling their traditional duties.

The restrictions on freedom caused by the vise-like pressure for higher taxes thus eroded the communal values that had motivated wealthy Romans for so long. The attempt to stabilize the empire by increasing its revenues also produced social discontent among poorer citizens: when the tax rate on land eventually reached one-third of its gross yield, this intolerable burden impoverished the rural population. Conditions became so bad in fifth-century Spain, for example, that the peasants there initiated an open revolt against imperial control. Financial troubles, especially severe in the west,

Upper-Class Country Life
This fourth-century mosaic, fourteen by eighteen feet, covered a floor in a country villa at Carthage in North Africa. Like a set of cartoon strips, it portrays the life of an elite couple on their estate at different seasons of the year. Their home, resplendent with towers and a second story colonnade, stands as a fortified retreat at the center. Above, the lady of the house sits in parklike surroundings while her servants and tenants tend to animals; winter activities are at the left, summer at the right. In the middle, hunters pursue game. Below left, the lady appears in springtime; below right, her husband in autumn. The servant to his left hands him a roll addressed "to the master Julius," revealing his name. Estates such as these provided security and prosperity for their owners but also made desirable prizes for the Vandal invaders of North Africa.
Le Musee du Bardo, Tunis.

kept the empire from ever regaining the prosperity of its Golden Age and contributed to increasing friction between government and citizens.

Religious Reform

Ancient belief required religious explanations for disasters. Accordingly, Diocletian concluded that the gods' anger had caused the civil wars. To restore divine goodwill, he called on citizens to follow the traditional gods who had guided Rome to power and virtue in the past: "Through the providence of the immortal gods, eminent, wise, and upright men have in their wisdom established good and true principles. It is wrong to oppose these principles or to abandon the ancient religion for some new one." Christianity was the novel faith he meant.

From Persecution to Conversion. Blaming Christians' hostility to traditional religion for the empire's troubles, Diocletian in 303 launched a massive attack remembered as the Great Persecution. He expelled Christians from his administration, seized their property, tore down churches, and executed them for refusing to participate in official religious rituals. As often, policy was applied differently in different regions. In the western empire, the violence stopped after about a year; in the east, it continued for a decade. So gruesome were the public executions of martyrs that they aroused the sympathy of some polytheists. The persecution had a contrary effect: it undermined the peace and order of society while failing to stop the spread of Christianity.

Constantine changed the empire's religious history forever by converting to the new faith. He chose Christianity for the same reason that Diocletian had persecuted it: in the belief that he was securing divine protection for himself and the empire. During the civil war that he fought to succeed Diocletian, Constantine experienced a dream-vision promising him the support of the Christian God. His biographer, Eusebius (c. 260–340), later reported that Constantine had also seen a vision of Jesus' cross in the sky surrounded by the words "In this sign you shall be the victor." When Constantine finally triumphed over his rival Maxentius by winning the battle of the Milvian Bridge in Rome in 312, he proclaimed that God's miraculous power and goodwill needed no further demonstration. He therefore declared himself a Christian emperor.

Edict of Milan of 313. Following his conversion, Constantine did not outlaw polytheism or make Christianity the official religion. Instead, he decreed religious toleration. The best statement of this new policy survives in the Edict of Milan of 313. It proclaimed free choice of religion for everyone and referred to the empire's protection by "the highest divinity"—an imprecise term meant to satisfy both polytheists and Christians.

Constantine wanted to avoid angering traditional believers and creating discontent because they still greatly outnumbered Christians, but he nevertheless did all he could to promote his newly chosen religion. These goals called for a careful balancing act. For example, he returned all property seized during the Great Persecution to its Christian owners, but he had the treasury compensate those who had bought the confiscated property at auction. When in 321 he made the Lord's Day a holy occasion each week on which no official business or manufacturing work could be performed, he called it "Sunday" to blend Christian and traditional notions in honoring two divinities, God and the sun. When he adorned his new capital, Constantinople, he stationed many statues of traditional gods around the city. Most conspicuously, he respected tradition by continuing to hold the office of *pontifex maximus* ("chief priest"), which emperors had filled ever since Augustus.

❖ Christianizing the Empire

Constantine's brilliantly crafted religious policy set the empire on the path to Christianization. The process proved to be slow and sometimes violent: not until the end of the fourth century was Christianity proclaimed the official religion, and even thereafter many people long kept worshiping the traditional gods in private. Eventually, however, Christianity became the religion of the overwhelming majority because it solidified its hierarchical organization, drew believers from women as well as men of all classes, assured them of personal salvation, nourished a strong sense of community, and offered the social advantages and security of belonging to the emperors' religion. The transformation from polytheist empire into Christian state became by far the most influential legacy of Greco-Roman antiquity to later history.

Relief Sculpture of Saturn from North Africa

This sculpted and inscribed pillar depicts the solar divinity known to Romans as Saturn and to Carthaginians as Ba'al Hammon, from the cult of the Phoenician founders of Carthage. This syncretism (identifying deities as the same even though they carried different names in different places) was typical of ancient polytheism and allowed Roman and non-Roman cults to merge. The inscription dates the pillar to 323, a decade later than Constantine's conversion to Christianity; such objects testifying to the prevalence of polytheistic cults remained common until the end of the fourth century, when the Christian emperors succeeded in suppressing most public manifestations of traditional religion.

Copyright Martha Cooper/Peter Arnold, Inc.

Religious Change

The empire's Christianization provoked passionate responses because ordinary people cared fervently about religion, which provided their best hope for private and public salvation in a dangerous world over which they had little control. In this regard polytheists and Christians shared some similar beliefs. Both assigned a potent role to spirits and demons as ever-present influences on life. For some, it seemed safest to ignore neither faith. For example, a silver spoon used in the worship of the polytheist forest spirit Faunus has been found engraved with a fish, the common symbol whose Greek spelling (*ichthys*) was taken as an acronym for the Greek words "Jesus Christ the Son of God, the Savior."

The Persistence of Polytheism. The differences between polytheists' and Christians' beliefs far outweighed their similarities. People debated passionately about whether there was one God or many and about what kind of interest the divinity (or divinities) took in the world of humans. Polytheists still participated in frequent festivals and sacrifices to many different gods. Why, they asked, did these joyous occasions not satisfy everyone's yearnings for contact with divinity?

Equally incomprehensible to them was belief in a savior who had not only failed to overthrow Roman rule but had even been executed as a common criminal. The traditional gods, by contrast, had bestowed a world empire on their worshipers. Moreover, they pointed out, cults such as that of the goddess Isis, after whom the worried letter writer had been named, and philosophies such as Stoicism insisted that only the pure of heart and mind could be admitted to their fellowship. Christians, by contrast, embraced the impure. Why, wondered perplexed polytheists, would anyone want to associate with sinners? In short, as the Greek philosopher Porphyry (c. 234–305) argued, Christians had no right to claim they possessed the sole version of religious truth, for no doctrine that provided "a universal path to the liberation of the soul" had ever been devised.

The slow pace of religious change revealed how strong polytheism remained in this period, especially at the highest social levels. In fact, the emperor Julian (r. 361–363) rebelled against his family's Christianity—hence he was known as Julian the Apostate—and tried to impose his philosophical brand of polytheism as the official religion. Deeply religious, he believed in a supreme deity corresponding to the aspirations of Greek philosophers: "This divine and completely beautiful universe, from heaven's highest arch to earth's lowest limit, is tied together by the continuous providence of god, has existed ungenerated eternally, and is imperishable forever." Julian's restoration of the traditional gods ended with his unexpected death on a campaign in Persia. Even though Christians at Antioch had jeered at his philosopher's beard instead of listening to the emperor's message, Christian leaders learned how vulnerable was the new faith's position when imperial patronage was withdrawn.

Making Christianity Official. Christian emperors succeeding Julian attacked polytheism by slowly removing its official privileges. In 382, Gratian (r. 375–383 in the west), who had dropped the title *pontifex maximus*, took the highly charged step of removing the altar and statue of Victory, which had stood in the Senate house in Rome for centuries, and stopped government financing of traditional sacrifices. Symmachus (c. 340–402), a polytheist senator who held the prestigious post of prefect ("mayor") of Rome, objected to what he saw as an outrage to the state's tradition of religious diversity. Speaking eloquently in a last public protest against the new religious order, he argued: "We all have our own way of life and our own way of worship. . . . So vast a mystery cannot be approached by only one path."

Christianity replaced traditional polytheism as the state religion in 391 when the emperor Theodosius (r. 379–395 in the east) succeeded where his predecessors had failed: he enforced a ban on polytheist sacrifices, even if private individuals paid for the animals. Following Gratian in rejecting the emperor's traditional role as chief priest of the state's polytheist cults, he made divination by the inspection of entrails punishable as high treason and ordered that all polytheist temples be closed. But many shrines, such as the Parthenon in Athens, remained in use for a long time; only gradually were temples converted to churches during the fifth and sixth centuries. Christian emperors outlawed what they perceived as offensive beliefs, just as their polytheist predecessors had, but lacked the means to enforce religious uniformity. Non-Christian schools were not forced to close—the Academy, founded by Plato in Athens in the early fourth century B.C., endured for 140 years after Theodosius's reign—but Christians received advantages in official careers. Non-Christians became outsiders in an empire whose monarchs were devoted to the Christian deity.

Jews, neither polytheists nor Christians, posed a special problem for the Christian emperors. Like polytheists, Jews rejected the new official religion. Yet they seemed entitled to special treatment because Jesus had been a Jew and because previous emperors had allowed Jews to practice their religion, even after Hadrian's refounding of Jerusalem as a Roman colony after putting down a fierce revolt there (132–135). Fourth-century and later emperors loaded legal restrictions on Jews. For example, imperial decrees eventually banned Jews from holding government posts but still required them to assume

Illustration of November from the Codex-Calendar
This picture symbolizing the month of November derives from a manuscript recording the only calendar known from ancient Rome. Called the Codex-Calendar (A.D. 354), it was actually more like an almanac, recording a vast amount of historical and chronological information: polytheist holidays, imperial anniversaries, astrological phenomena, lists of the consuls, prefects and bishops of Rome, and more. The most famous calligrapher, Furius Dionysius Filocalus, made the calendar for a wealthy Christian named Valentinus, who would have used it to help plan his public life in the capital. The panel illustrating November shows a priest of Isis, whose festival took place in early November, surrounded by cultic implements, including a bust or mask of the Egyptian animal-headed god Anubis.

the financial burdens of *curiales* without receiving the honor of curial status. By the late sixth century, they barred Jews from making wills, receiving inheritances, or testifying in court, restrictions that increased the pressure on Jews to convert.

Although these developments began the long process that made Jews into second-class citizens in later European history, they did not disable Judaism. Magnificent synagogues continued to exist in Palestine, where a few Jews still lived; most had been dispersed throughout the cities of the empire and the lands to the east. The study of Jewish law and lore flourished in this period, culminating in the learned texts known as the Palestinian and the Babylonian Talmuds (collections of scholarly opinions on Jewish law) and the scriptural commentaries of the Midrash (explanation of the meaning of the Hebrew Bible). These works of religious scholarship laid the foundation for later Jewish life and practice.

Christianity's Growing Appeal. Christianity's official status attracted new believers, especially in the military. Soldiers now found it comfortable to convert and still serve in the army; previously, Christian soldiers had sometimes created disciplinary problems by renouncing their military oath. As one

senior infantryman had said at his court-martial in 298 for refusing to continue his duties, "A Christian serving the Lord Christ should not serve the affairs of this world." Once the emperors had become Christians, however, soldiers could justify military duty as serving the affairs of Christ.

But the main sources of Christianity's appeal were its religious and social values. Christianity offered believers a strong sense of community in this world as well as the promise of salvation in the next. Wherever they traveled or migrated, they could find a warm welcome in the local congregation (Map 7.2). The faith also won adherents by actively following the tradition of charitable works characteristic

MAP 7.2 The Spread of Christianity, 300–600
Christians were distinctly a minority in the Roman Empire in 300, although congregations existed in many cities and towns, especially in the eastern provinces. The emperor Constantine's conversion to Christianity in the early fourth century gave a boost to the new religion; it gained further strength during that century as the Christian emperors supported it financially and eliminated further subsidies for the polytheist cults that had previously made up the religion of the state. By 600, the preaching of the church's missionaries and the money of the emperors had spread Christianity from end to end of the empire's huge expanse of territory.
From Henry Chadwick and G.R. Evans, *Atlas of the Christian Church* (Oxford: Andromeda Oxford Ltd., 1987), 28. Reproduced by permission of Andromeda Oxford Limited.

of Judaism and some polytheist cults, which emphasized caring for the poor, widows, and orphans. By the mid-third century, for example, Rome's congregation was supporting fifteen hundred widows and other impoverished persons. Christians' practice of fellowship and philanthropy was enormously important because people at that time had to depend mostly on friends and relatives for help; state-sponsored social services were rare and limited.

Scholars continue to debate the role of women in the early growth of Christianity, but it is clear that they were deeply involved in the new faith. Augustine (354–430), bishop of Hippo in North Africa and perhaps the most influential theologian in Western history, eloquently recognized women's contribution to the strengthening of Christianity in a letter he wrote to the unbaptized husband of a baptized woman: "O you men, who fear all the burdens imposed by baptism. You are easily bested by your women. Chaste and devoted to the faith, it is their presence in large numbers that causes the church to grow." Some women earned exceptional renown and status by giving their property to their congregation or by renouncing marriage to dedicate themselves to Christ. Consecrated virgins and widows who chose not to remarry thus joined large donors as especially respected women. These women's choices presented a stark challenge to the traditional social order, in which women were supposed to devote themselves to raising families. But even these sanctified women were excluded from leadership positions as the church's organization evolved into a hierarchy more and more resembling the male-dominated world of imperial rule.

Solidifying Hierarchy. Perhaps the most crucial part of Christianity's expansion was its success in consolidating a formal leadership hierarchy: a rigid organization based on the authority of male bishops, who replaced early Christianity's relatively loose, communal form in which women were also leaders. Bishops had the right to select priests to conduct the church's sacraments, such as baptism and communion, the rituals that guaranteed eternal life. They also oversaw their congregations' memberships and finances; much of the funds came from believers' gifts and bequests. Over time, the bishops replaced the *curiales* as the emperors' partners in local rule and in return earned the favor of controlling the distribution of imperial sub-

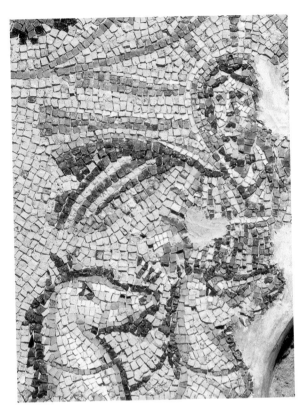

Christ as Sun God

This heavily damaged mosaic comes from a burial chamber in Rome that is now in the Vatican under the basilica of St. Peter built by Constantine. It perhaps dates to the mid-third century. Christ appears in a guise traditional for polytheistic representations of the Sun god, especially the Greek Apollo: riding in a chariot pulled by horses with rays of light shining forth around his head. This symbolism—God is light—had a long history reaching back to ancient Egypt; Christian artists used it to portray Jesus because he had said "I am the light of the world" (John 8:12). Here the mosaic artist has carefully arranged the sunbeams to suggest the shape of the Christian cross. The cloak flaring from Christ's shoulder suggests the spread of his motion across the heavens. Scala/Art Resource, NY.

sidies in the empire's cities and towns. Regional councils of bishops exercised supreme authority in appointing new bishops and deciding the doctrinal disputes that increasingly arose. The bishops in the largest cities became the most powerful leaders in the church. The main bishop of Carthage, for example, oversaw at least one hundred local bishops in the surrounding area. But it was the bishop of Rome who eventually emerged as the church's supreme leader in the western empire. The eastern church never agreed that this status entitled the bishop of Rome to control the entire Christian world, but his dominance in the west won him pre-eminent use there of the title previously applied to many bishops: *pope* (from *pappas*, Greek for "father"), the designation still used for the head of the Roman Catholic church.

The bishops of Rome found a scriptural basis for their leadership over other bishops in the New Testament, where Jesus speaks to the Apostle Peter: "You are Peter, and upon this rock I will build my church. . . . I will entrust to you the keys of the kingdom of heaven. Whatever you bind on earth shall be bound in heaven. Whatever you loose on earth shall be loosed in heaven" (Matt. 16:18–19). Because Peter's name in Greek means "rock" and because Peter was believed to have been the first bishop of Rome, later bishops in Rome claimed that this passage recognized their direct succession from Peter and thus their supremacy in the church.

Seeking Religious Truth

Jesus himself had written nothing down, and the earliest Christians frequently argued over what their savior had meant them to believe. The church's expanding hierarchy pushed hard for uniformity in belief and worship to ensure its members' spiritual purity and to maintain its authority over them. Bishops as well as congregation members often disagreed about theology, however, and Christians never achieved uniformity in their doctrines.

Disputes centered on what constituted *orthodoxy* (the official doctrines proclaimed by councils of bishops, from the Greek for "correct thinking") as opposed to *heresy* (dissent from official thinking, from the Greek for "private choice"). After Christianity became official, the emperor was ultimately responsible for enforcing orthodox creed (a summary of beliefs) and could use force to compel agreement if disputes became such that they provoked violence.

A Bitter Dispute: Arianism. Subtle theological questions about the nature of the Trinity of Father, Son, and Holy Spirit, seen by the orthodox as a unified, co-eternal, and identical divinity, caused the deepest divisions. *Arianism* generated fierce controversy for centuries. Named after its founder, the priest Arius (c. 260–336) from Alexandria, this doctrine maintained that Jesus as God's son had not existed eternally; rather, God the Father had "begot" (created) his son from nothing and bestowed on him his special status. Thus Jesus was not co-eternal with God and not identical in nature with his father. This view implied that the Trinity was divisible and that Christianity's monotheism was not absolute. Arianism found widespread support, perhaps because it eliminated the difficulty of understanding how a son could be as old as his father and because its subordination of son to father corresponded to the norms of family life. Arius used popular songs to make his views known, and people everywhere became engrossed in the controversy. "When you ask for your change from a shopkeeper," one observer remarked in describing Constantinople, "he harangues you about the Begotten and the Unbegotten. If you inquire how much bread costs, the reply is that 'the Father is superior and the Son inferior.'"

Many Christians became so incensed over this apparent demotion of Jesus that Constantine had to intervene to try to restore ecclesiastical peace and lead the bishops in determining religious truth. In 325, he convened 220 bishops at the Council of Nicaea to settle the dispute over Arianism. The majority of bishops voted to come down hard on the heresy: they banished Arius to Illyria, a rough Balkan region, and declared that the Father and the Son were indeed "of one substance" and co-eternal. So difficult were the issues, however, that Constantine later changed his mind twice, first recalling Arius from exile and then reproaching him again not long after. The doctrine lived on: Constantine's third son, Constantius II (r. 337–361), favored Arianism, and his missionaries converted many of the Germanic peoples who later came to live in the empire.

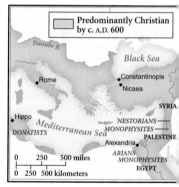

Original Areas of Christian Splinter Groups

Monophysitism, Nestorianism, and Donatism.

Numerous other disputes about the nature of Christ persistently fractured attempts to build unity, especially in the east. The orthodox position held that Jesus' divine and human natures commingled within his person but remained distinct. Monophysites (a Greek term for "single-nature believers") argued that the divine took precedence over the human and that Jesus had essentially only a single nature. They split from the orthodox hierarchy in the sixth century to found independent churches in Egypt (the Coptic church), Ethiopia, Syria, and Armenia.

Nestorius, who became bishop of Constantinople in 428, disagreed with the orthodox version of how Jesus' human and divine natures were related to his birth, insisting that Mary gave birth to the human that became the temple for the indwelling divine. Nestorianism enraged orthodox Christians by rejecting the designation *theotokos* (Greek for "bearer of God") as an appellation of Mary. The bishops of Alexandria and Rome had Nestorius deposed and his doctrines officially rejected at councils held in 430 and 431; they condemned his writings in 435. Nestorian bishops in the eastern empire refused to accept these decisions, however, and they formed a separate church centered in Persia, where for centuries Nestorian Christians flourished under the benign tolerance of non-Christian rulers. They later became important agents of cultural diffusion by establishing communities that still endure in Arabia, India, and China.

No heresy better illustrates the ferocity of Christian disunity than Donatism. A dispute arose in North Africa in the fourth century over whether to readmit to their old congregations those Christians who had cooperated with imperial authorities and had thus escaped martyrdom during the Great Persecution. Some North African Christians felt these lapsed members should be forgiven, but the Donatists (followers of the North African priest Donatus) insisted that the church should not be polluted with such "traitors." Most important, Donatists insisted, unfaithful priests and bishops could not administer the sacraments. So bitter was the clash that it even sundered Christian families. A son threatened his mother thus: "I will join Donatus's followers, and I will drink your blood."

With emotions at a fever pitch, the church urgently strove to provide convincing explanations of orthodoxy as religious truth. The Council of Chalcedon (an outskirt of Constantinople), at which the empress Pulcheria and her consort Marcian brought together more than five hundred bishops in 451, was the most important attempt to forge agreement on

Mosaic of a Family from Edessa
This mosaic, found in a cave tomb, depicts an upper-class family of Edessa in the late Roman Empire. Their names are given in Syriac, the dialect of Aramaic spoken in their region, and their colorful clothing reflects local Iranian traditions. Edessa was the capital of the small kingdom of Osrhoëne, between the Taurus Mountains and the Syrian desert. Rome annexed the kingdom in 216, and it became famous in Christian history because its king Agbar (r. 179–216) was remembered as the first monarch to convert to Christianity, well before Constantine. By the early fourth century, the story had emerged that after his death Jesus had sent one of his disciples to Edessa; the disciple painted a picture of Jesus that served as a talisman to protect the city from its enemies. The Byzantine emperors proclaimed themselves the heirs of King Agbar and the city's grant of divine protection.
Photo courtesy of Thames & Hudson Ltd., London, from *Vanished Civilizations.*

orthodoxy. Its conclusions form the basis of what most Christians in the West still accept as doctrine. At the time, it failed to create unanimity, especially in the eastern empire, where Monophysites were many.

Augustine and Order. No one person had a stronger impact on the establishment of the western church's orthodoxy and therefore on later Catholicism than Augustine (354–430). Born to a Christian mother and a polytheist father, Augustine began his career by teaching rhetoric at Carthage, where he fathered a son by a mistress, and was befriended by the prominent polytheist noble Symmachus after moving to Italy. In 386, he converted to Christianity under the influence of his mother and Ambrose (c. 339–397) the powerful bishop of Milan; in 395, he himself was appointed bishop of Hippo. His tremendous reputation rests not on his official career but on his writings. By around 500, Augustine and other influential theologians such as Ambrose and Jerome (c. 345–420) had earned the informal title "church fathers" because their views were cited as authoritative in disputes over orthodoxy. Of this group of patristic (from the Greek for "father," *pater*) authors, Augustine became the most famous, and for the next thousand years his works would be the most influential texts in western Christianity, save for the Bible. He wrote so prolifically in Latin about religion and philosophy that a later scholar was moved to declare: "The man lies who says he has read all your works."

Augustine deeply affected later thinkers with his views on authority in human life. His most influential exposition of the proper role of secular authority came in his *City of God*, a "large and arduous work," as he called it, written between 413 and 426. The book's immediate purpose was to refute those who expected that Christianity, like the traditional cults it had replaced, would guarantee Christians earthly success and to counter those who rejected any place for the state in a Christian world. For example, some polytheists asserted that the sack of Rome by Germanic marauders in 410 was divine retribution for the official abandonment of the Roman gods; Augustine sought to reassure Christians that their faith had not caused Rome's defeat. His larger aim, however, was to redefine the ideal state as a society of Christians. Not even Plato's doctrines offered a true path to purification, Augustine asserted, because the real opposition for humans was not between emotion and reason but between desire for earthly pleasures and spiritual purity. Emotion, especially love, was natural and desirable, but only when directed toward God. Humans were misguided to look for value in life on earth. Earthly life was transitory. Only life in God's city had meaning.

Nevertheless, Augustine wrote, secular law and government were required because humans are inherently imperfect. God's original creation in the Garden of Eden was full of goodness, but humans lost their initial perfection by inheriting a permanently flawed nature after Adam and Eve had disobeyed God. The doctrine of original sin—a subject of theological debate since at least the second century—meant that people suffered from a hereditary moral disease that turned the human will into a disruptive force. This corruption required governments to use coercion to suppress vice. Although desperately inferior to the divine ideal, civil government was necessary to impose moral order on the chaos of human life after the fall from grace in the Garden of Eden. The state therefore had a right to compel people to remain united to the church, by force if necessary.

Order in society was so valuable, Augustine argued, that it could even turn to comparatively good purposes such inherently evil practices as slavery. Augustine detested slavery, but he acknowledged that well-treated slaves in rich homes were better off than destitute free laborers. Social institutions like slavery, in his view, were lesser evils than the violent troubles that would follow if disorder were to prevail. Christians therefore had a duty to obey the emperor and participate in political life. Soldiers, too, had to follow their orders. Torture and capital punishment as judicial procedures, by contrast, had no place in a morally upright government. The purpose of secular authority was to maintain a social order based on a moral order.

In *City of God*, Augustine sought to show a divine purpose, not always evident to humans, in the events of history. All that Christians could know with certainty was that history progressed toward an ultimate goal, but only God could know the meaning of each day's events. What could not be doubted was God's guiding power:

> To be truthful, I myself fail to understand why God created mice and frogs, flies and worms. Nevertheless, I recognize that each of these creatures is beautiful in its own way. For when I contemplate the body and limbs of any living creature, where do I not find proportion, number, and order exhibiting the unity of concord? Where one discovers proportion, number, and order, one should look for the craftsman.

The repeated *I* in this example exemplifies the intense personal engagement Augustine brought to matters of faith and doctrine. Many other Christians shared this intensity, a trait that energized their disagreements over orthodoxy and heresy.

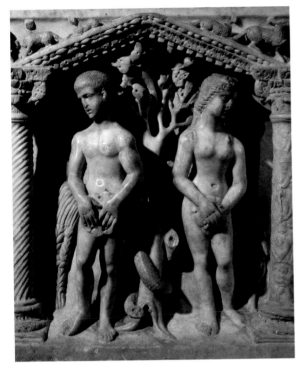

Adam and Eve on the Sarcophagus of Junius Bassus
This scene of the biblical first man and woman in the Garden of Eden was one image on the most spectacular Christian sarcophagus to survive. It holds the remains of Junius Bassus, the son of a consul who himself became prefect of Rome in 359. Carved from marble in a classical style, pictures are all taken from the Bible and center on the story of Christ. The exclusion of scenes from polytheistic mythology, which had been standard on Christian sarcophaguses, illustrates Christians' growing confidence in their religious traditions.
Erich Lessing/Art Resource, NY.

Augustine and Sexual Desire. Next to the nature of Christ, the question of how to understand and regulate sexual desire presented Christians with the thorniest problem in the search for religious truth. Augustine became the most influential source of the enduring doctrine that sex automatically enmeshed human beings in evil and that they should therefore strive for *asceticism* (the practice of strict self-denial, from the Greek *askesis*, meaning "training"). Augustine knew from personal experience how difficult it was to accept this doctrine. In fact, he revealed in his autobiographical work *Confessions*, written about 397, that he felt a deep conflict between his sexual desire and his religious philosophy. Only after a long period of reflection and doubt, he

explained, did he find the inner strength to pledge his future chastity as part of his conversion to Christianity.

He advocated sexual abstinence as the highest course for Christians because he believed that Adam and Eve's disobedience in the Garden of Eden had forever ruined the original, perfect harmony God created between the human will and human passions. According to Augustine, God punished his disobedient children by creating an eternal conflict: sexual desire would forever remain a disruptive force because humans could never completely control it through their will. Although he reaffirmed the value of marriage in God's plan, he added that sexual intercourse even between loving spouses carried the melancholy reminder of humanity's fall from grace. A married couple should "descend with a certain sadness" to the task of procreation, the only acceptable reason for sex; sexual pleasure could never be a human good.

This doctrine ennobled virginity and sexual renunciation as the highest virtues; in the words of the ascetic biblical scholar Jerome, they counted as "daily martyrdom." Such self-chosen holiness earned women benefits beyond status in the church: they could, for example, demand more education in Hebrew and Greek to read the Bible. By the end of the fourth century, the centrality of virginity as a Christian virtue had grown so large that congregations began to call for virgin priests and bishops.

The Beginning of Christian Monasticism

Christian asceticism reached its peak with the development of monasticism. The word *monk* (from the Greek *monos*, for "single, solitary") described the essential experience of monasticism: men and women withdrawing from everyday society to live a life of extreme self-denial imitating Jesus' suffering, demonstrating their complete devotion to God, and praying for divine mercy on the world. At first, monks lived alone, but eventually they formed communities for mutual support in the pursuit of holiness.

Monks as Models of Excellence. Christians were far from the first to choose to live conspicuously as ascetics; polytheists and Jewish ascetics had long been doing so, motivated by philosophy and religion. What made Christian monasticism distinctive were the huge numbers of people drawn to it and

Monastery of St. Catherine at Mount Sinai

The Byzantine emperor Justinian (r. 527–565) built a wall to enclose the buildings of this monastery in the desert at the foot of Mount Sinai (on the peninsula between Egypt and Arabia). Justinian supported the monastery to promote orthodoxy in a region dominated by Monophysite Christians. The monastery gained its name in the ninth century when the story was circulated that angels had recently brought the body of Catherine of Alexandria there. Catherine was said to have been martyred in the fourth century for refusing to marry the emperor because, in her words, she was the bride of Christ; no contemporary sources record her story.
Erich Lessing/Art Resource, NY.

the high status that they earned in the eyes of the general population. Monks' renown came from their complete shunning of ordinary pleasures and comforts. They left their families and congregations, renounced sex, worshiped almost constantly, wore the roughest clothes, and ate barely enough to survive. They hoped by their ascetic living to obtain an inner peace detached from daily concerns. The reality of monastic life, however, was constant spiritual struggle, especially against fantasies of earthly delights—monks frequently dreamed of plentiful, tasty food, more often even than of sex, to judge from their accounts of their personal struggles.

The earliest Christian ascetics emerged in the second half of the third century in Egypt. Antony (c. 251–356), the son of a well-to-do family, was among the first to renounce regular existence. One day, Antony abruptly abandoned all his property after hearing a sermon based on Jesus' admonition to a rich young man to sell his possessions and give the proceeds to the poor (Matt. 19:21). Placing his sister in a home for unmarried women, Antony spent the rest of his life alone in barren territory to demonstrate his excellence through worshiping God.

Monasticism appealed for many reasons, but above all because it gave ordinary people a way to achieve excellence and recognition, which had always been an ideal in the ancient world. This opportunity seemed all the more valuable in the aftermath of Constantine's conversion and the end of the persecutions. Becoming a monk, a living martyrdom, served as the substitute for a martyr's death and emulated the sacrifice of Christ. Individual or *eremetic* (hence *hermit*) monks went to great lengths to secure fame for their dedication. In Syria, for example, "holy women" and "holy men" attracted great attention with feats of pious endurance; Symeon the Stylite (390–459), for one, lived atop a tall pillar (*stylos* in Greek) for thirty years, preaching to the people gathered at the foot of his perch. Egyptian Christians came to believe that their monks' supreme piety made them living heroes who ensured the annual flooding of the Nile, the duty once associated with the magical power of the ancient pharaohs.

Ascetics with reputations for exceptional holiness exercised even greater influence after death. Their relics—body parts or clothing—became treasured sources of protection and healing. Functioning as the living power of saints (people venerated after their deaths for their special holiness), relics gave believers faith in divine favor. Christian reverence for relics continued a very long tradition: the fifth-century B.C. Athenians, to recall one example, had rejoiced at the good fortune they believed would follow from recovering bones identified as the remains of Theseus, their legendary founder and hero.

The Rise of Monastic Communities. The earliest monks followed Antony's example in living alone. In about 323, however, Pachomius in Upper Egypt organized the first monastic community, setting a precedent for such single-sex settlements that assembled groups of male and female monks together to encourage one to share the harsh road to supreme holiness. These monasteries began the form of austere communal life ("coenobitic," or "life in common," monasticism) that would dominate Christian asceticism ever after. Communities of men and women were often built close together to divide their labor, with women making clothing, for example, while men farmed.

All monastic groups imposed military-style discipline, but they differed in their attitudes about contact with the outside world and in the degree of austerity enforced internally. Some strove for complete self-sufficiency to avoid transactions with the outside world. The most isolationist and ascetic groups were in the eastern empire, but the followers of Martin of Tours (c. 316–397), an ex-soldier famed for his pious deeds, founded communities in the west as austere as any in the east. Basil ("the Great") of Caesarea in Asia Minor (c. 330–379) started a competing tradition of monasteries in service to society. Basil required monks to perform charitable deeds, such as ministering to the sick, a development that led to the foundation of the first hospitals, attached to monasteries.

A milder code of monastic conduct became the standard in the west and later influenced almost every area of Catholic worship. Called the Benedictine rule after its creator, Benedict of Nursia in central Italy (c. 480–553), the monastic code prescribed the monks' daily routine of prayer, scriptural readings, and manual labor. The rule divided the day into seven parts, each with a compulsory service of prayers and lessons. The required worship for each part of the day was called the *office*. Unlike the harsh regulations of other monastic communities, Benedict's code did not isolate the monks from the outside world or deprive them of sleep, adequate food, or warm clothing. Although it gave the abbot (the head monk) full authority, it instructed him to lis-

ten to what every member of the community, even the youngest monk, had to say before deciding important matters. He was not allowed to beat them for lapses in discipline, as sometimes happened under other, stricter systems. Communities of women, such as those founded by Basil's sister Macrina and Benedict's sister Scholastica, usually followed the rules of the male monasteries, with an emphasis on the decorum thought necessary for women.

The thousands upon thousands of Christians who joined monasteries from the fourth century onward left the outside world for social as well as theological reasons. Some had been given as babies to monasteries by parents who could not raise them or were fulfilling pious vows, a practice called *oblation*. Jerome, a monk in a monastery for men that was located next to one for women, once gave this advice to a mother who decided to send her young daughter to a monastery:

> Let her be brought up in a monastery, let her live among virgins, let her learn to avoid swearing, let her regard lying as an offense against God, let her be ignorant of the world, let her live the angelic life, while in the flesh let her be without the flesh, and let her suppose that all human beings are like herself.

When she reaches adulthood as a virgin, he added, she should avoid the baths so she would not be seen naked or give her body pleasure by dipping in the warm pools. Jerome enunciated traditional values favoring males when he promised that God would reward the mother with the birth of sons in compensation for the dedication of her daughter.

Monastic communities also attracted some men evading civic or military obligations and some women seeking to sidestep social expectations, especially marriage. Jerome explained this latter attraction: "[As monks] we evaluate people's virtue not by their gender but by their character, and deem those to be worthy of the greatest glory who have renounced both status and riches." This openness to all helped monasticism attract a steady stream of adult adherents eager to serve God in this world and be saved in the next.

Not all Christians approved of the growth of monasticism. In particular, the monasteries' prickly independence set them at odds with the church hierarchy. Bishops resented devoted members of their congregations withdrawing into monasteries, not least because they bestowed their gifts and bequests on their new community rather than on their local churches. Moreover, monks represented a threat to bishops' authority because holy men and women earned their special status not by having it bestowed from the church hierarchy but through their own actions; strengthening the bishops' right to discipline monks who resisted their authority was one of the goals of the Council of Chalcedon. At bottom, however, bishops and monks did share a spiritual goal—salvation and service to God. While polytheists had enjoyed immediate access to their gods, who were thought to visit the earth constantly, Christians worshiped a transcendent God removed from this world. Monks bridged the chasm between the human and the divine by interceding with God to show mercy on the faithful.

❖ Germanic Kingdoms in the West

The regional differences between western and eastern monasticism found a parallel in the diverging social and political characteristics of the divided empire. The fragmentation of the empire had especially significant cultural consequences for the west, where the migrations of Germanic peoples into the empire transformed European politics, society, and economy. These diverse groups had two strong desires propelling them westward into Roman territory: to flee the constant attacks of the Huns and to join in the empire's prosperity. By the 370s their influx had swollen to a flood and had provoked widespread violence in the western empire, where the imperial government's ability to maintain order had gravely weakened. In a remarkable transition, Germanic peoples transformed themselves from vaguely defined and organized tribes into kingdoms with separate ethnic identities. By the 470s, one of their commanders ruled Italy—the political change that has been said to mark the so-called fall of the Roman Empire. In fact, the lasting effects of the interactions of these Germanic peoples with the diverse peoples of western Europe and North Africa are better understood as a political, social, and cultural transformation that made them the heirs of the western Roman Empire and led to the formation of medieval Europe.

Germanic Migrations

Fourth-century emperors encouraged the initial migrations: just as earlier emperors had done, they recruited Germanic men to serve in the Roman army. This time, they wished to fill out the army's reduced ranks after its losses in the third-century civil wars. By the late fourth century, a flood of noncombatants had followed these warriors into the empire (Map 7.3). The inability of the western government either to absorb the newcomers or to mount a strong defense against them would prove its undoing.

Economic failure rooted in the third-century political crisis underlay this weakness. To pay for civil war, the emperors had demanded higher taxes, forcing landowners to demand higher payments from their *coloni*. Many of these tenants responded by illegally running away; their masters had to follow if they could not pay their taxes. This flight left farms deserted; as much as 20 percent of arable territory lay unfarmed in the most seriously affected areas. The financial consequences were twofold: the government had to increase its demands for revenues from the farmers who remained, and the loss of revenue crippled the government's ability to pay for soldiers to keep more Germanic peoples from migrating into the empire.

Germanic bands crossed into imperial territory not in carefully planned invasions but often fleeing for their lives; fourth-century raids by the Huns, nomads from the steppes of central Asia, had forced them from their traditional homelands east of the Rhine and north of the Danube. Groups of men, women, and children crossed the Roman border as hordes of refugees. Their prospects looked grim because they came with no political or military unity, no clear plan, and not even a shared sense of identity. Loosely organized at best as vaguely democratic and often warring tribes, they really shared only the Germanic origins of their languages (hence the term used to designate them as a whole) and their terror of the Huns. The migrating Germanic peoples developed their respective ethnic identities only after they were unable to assimilate into Roman life and society and instead settled in groups forming new states within the Roman imperial frontiers.

Germanic Society.   Their quest for new homes forced the Germanic bands to change their way of life: they had to develop a more tightly structured

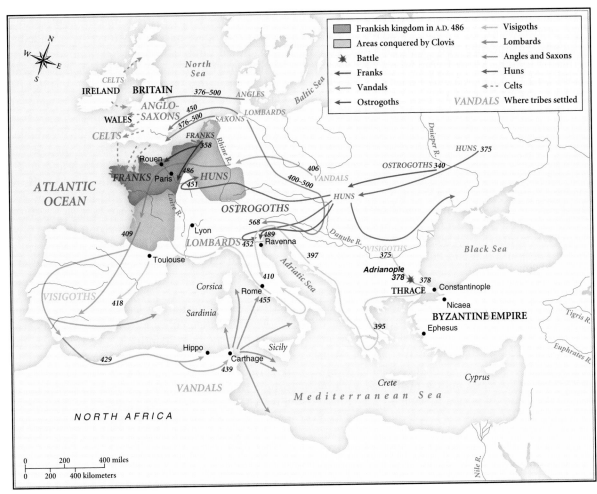

MAP 7.3 Germanic Migrations and Invasions of the Fourth and Fifth Centuries
The movements of Germanic peoples into imperial territory transformed the Roman Empire. This phenomenon had begun as early as the reign of Domitian (r. 81–96), but in the fourth century it became a pressing problem for the emperors when the Huns' attacks pushed Germanic bands from their homelands in eastern Europe into the empire's northern provinces. Print maps can offer only a schematic representation of dynamic processes such as the Germanic migrations and invasions, but this map does convey a sense of the variety of peoples involved, the wide extent of imperial territory that they affected, and the concentration of their effects in the western section of the empire.

society to govern their new lands. The traditions they brought with them from their homelands in eastern Europe had ill prepared them for ruling others. There they had lived in small settlements whose economies depended on farming, herding, and ironworking; they had no experience with running kingdoms.

The Germanic groups were led by men averse to strong central authority. Even groups with clearly defined leaders were constituted as chiefdoms, whose members could be only persuaded, not compelled, to follow the chief. The chiefs maintained their status by giving gifts to their followers and by leading warriors on frequent raids to seize cattle and slaves. Germanic society was patriarchal: men headed households and exercised authority over women, children, and slaves. Germanic women were valued above all for their ability to bear children, and rich men could have more than one wife and perhaps concubines as well. A clear division of labor made women responsible for agriculture, pottery making, and the production of textiles, while men worked iron and herded cattle. Warfare and its accompaniments preoccupied Germanic men, as their ritual sacrifices of weapons preserved in northern European bogs have shown. Women had certain rights of inheritance and could control property, and married women received a dowry of one-third of their husbands' property.

Households were grouped into clans on kinship lines based on maternal as well as paternal descent. The members of a clan were supposed to keep peace among themselves, and violence against a fellow clan member was the worst possible offense. Clans in turn grouped themselves into tribes, very loose and fluctuating multiethnic coalitions that non-Germans could join. Different tribes identified themselves primarily by their clothing, hairstyles, jewelry, weapons, religious cults, and oral stories.

Assemblies of free male warriors provided the tribes' only traditional form of political organization. Their leaders' functions were restricted mostly to religious and military matters. Tribes could be very unstable and prone to internal conflict—clans frequently feuded, with bloody consequences. Tribal law tried to set boundaries to the violence acceptable in seeking revenge, but Germanic law was oral, not written, and thus open to wide dispute.

The Huns, Catalysts of Migration. The Germanic migrations began in earnest when the Huns invaded eastern Europe in the fourth century. Distantly related to the Hiung-nu who had attacked China and Persia, they arrived on the Russian steppes shortly before 370 as the vanguard of Turkish-speaking nomads. Huns excelled as raiders, launching cavalry attacks far and wide. Their warriors' appearance terrified their targets, who reported skulls elongated from having been bound between boards in infancy, faces grooved with decorative scars, and arms fearsome with elaborate tattoos. Their prowess as horsemen made them legendary; they could shoot their powerful bows while riding full tilt and stay mounted for days, sleeping atop their horses and carrying snacks of raw meat between their thighs and the animal's back.

The Huns' repeated incursions against central Asian kingdoms finally caused these states to push them out with large-scale military campaigns. The Huns turned west to attack the Germanic peoples north of the Danube and east of the Rhine. Moving into the Hungarian plain in the 390s, they began raiding southward into the Balkans.

When the emperors in Constantinople bribed the Huns to spare eastern territory, they decided to change their rambling way of life dramatically and permanently: from nomads they turned into landlords, cooperating to create an empire north of the Danube that subjected farming peoples and siphoned off their agricultural surplus. Their most ambitious leader, Attila (r. c. 440–453), extended their domains from the Alps to the Caspian Sea. In 451, he led his forces as far west as Paris and in 452 into northern Italy. At Attila's death in 454, the Huns lost their fragile cohesiveness and faded from history. By this time, however, the damage had been done: the pressure that they had put on the Germanic peoples had already set in motion the migrations that would further transform the western empire.

Setting the Pattern: The Visigoths. The people who would, after entering imperial territory, coalesce to create their identity as Visigoths were the first to experience what would become the common pattern of the migrations: some desperate Germanic people in barely organized groups would petition for asylum and the empire would accept them in return for service. Shredded by constant Hunnic raids, in 376 they begged the eastern emperor Valens (r. 364–378) to let them migrate into the Balkans. They received permission on condition that their warriors enlist in the Roman army to help repel the Huns.

As events proved, the final part of the pattern was for such deals to fall apart disastrously. The plight of the Visigoths started this dismal trend. When greedy and incompetent Roman officers charged with helping the refugees neglected them, they approached starvation; the officials forced them to sell some of their own people into slavery in return for dogs to eat. In desperation, the Visigoths rebelled. In 378 they defeated and killed Valens at Adrianople in Thrace. His successor, Theodosius I (r. 379–395), then had to renegotiate the deal from a position of weakness. His concessions established the terms that other bands would seek for themselves and that would create new, self-conscious identities for them: permission to settle permanently inside the borders, freedom to establish a kingdom under their own laws, large annual payments from the emperors, and designation as "federates" (allies) expected to help protect the empire.

Soon realizing they could not afford to keep this agreement, the eastern emperors decided to force the newcomers to the west; this would be their strategy henceforth. They cut off the subsidies and threatened full-scale war unless the refugees decamped. Following the path of least resistance, the disgruntled Visigoths entered the western empire; neither the western empire nor they would ever be the same. In 410, they stunned the world by sacking Rome itself. For the first time since the Gauls eight hundred years before, a foreign force occupied the ancient capital. They terrorized the population: when their commander Alaric demanded all the city's gold, silver, movable property, and foreign slaves, the Romans asked, "What will be left to us?" "Your lives," he replied.

Too weak to fend off the invaders indefinitely, the western emperor Honorius (r. 395–423) in 418 reluctantly agreed to settle the Visigoths in southwestern Gaul (present-day France), saving face by calling them federates. The Visigoths then completed their remarkable transition from a tribal society to a formal kingdom by doing what no Germanic group had done before: establishing an ethnic identity and organizing a state. They followed the model of Roman monarchy by emphasizing mutually beneficial relations with the social elite. Romans could join that elite and use time-tested ways of flattering their superiors to gain advantages. Sidonius Apollinaris, for example, a well-connected noble from Lyons (c. 430–479), once purposely lost a backgammon game to the Visigothic king as a way of gaining a favor from the ruler. Honorius tried, without much success, to limit Germanic influence on Roman citizens by ordering them not to adopt Visigothic clothing styles, such as furs.

How the new Germanic kingdoms such as that of the Visigoths financed their states has become a much debated question. The older view is that the newcomers became landed proprietors by forcing Roman landowners to redistribute a portion of their lands, slaves, and movable property to them. Recent scholarship argues that Roman taxpayers in the kingdoms did not have to give up their lands but were instead made directly responsible for paying the expenses of the Germanic soldiers, who lived mostly in urban garrisons. Whatever the new arrangements were, the Visigoths found them profitable enough to expand into Spain within a century of establishing themselves in southwestern Gaul.

Violence in Western Europe: The Vandals. The western government's settlement with the Visigoths emboldened other groups to seize territory and create new kingdoms and identities if they could not get all they wanted through negotiation. An especially dramatic episode began in 406 when the Vandals, fleeing the Huns, crossed the Rhine into Roman territory. This huge group cut a swath through Gaul all the way to the Spanish coast. (The modern word *vandal*, meaning "destroyer of property," perpetuates their reputation for warlike ruthlessness.)

In 429, eighty thousand Vandals ferried to North Africa, where they soon broke their agreement to become federates and captured the region. They further weakened the western emperors by seizing the region's traditional tax payments of grain and vegetable oil and disrupting the importation of grain to Rome; they frightened the eastern empire with a navy strong enough to threaten the eastern Mediterranean. In 455, they set the western government tottering by plundering Rome. Their kingdom caused tremendous hardship for local Africans by confiscating property rather than (like the Visigoths) allowing owners to make regular payments to "ransom" their land.

On the Fringes of the Empire: The Anglo-Saxons. Small groups far less powerful than the Vandals took advantage of the disruption caused by bigger bands to break off distant pieces of the weakened western empire. The most significant such population for later history was the Anglo-Saxons. Composed of Angles from what is now Denmark and Saxons from northwestern Germany, this mixed group invaded Britain in the 440s after the Roman army had been recalled from the province to defend Italy against the Visigoths. They established their kingdoms by wresting territory away from the indigenous Celtic peoples and the remaining Roman inhabitants. Gradually, their culture replaced the local traditions of the island's eastern regions: the Celts there lost most of their language and Christianity, which survived only in Wales and Ireland.

The Ostrogoths and the "Fall of Rome." By the time Theodoric (r. 493–526) established the Ostrogothic kingdom in Italy, there was no longer a formally recognized western Roman emperor and never would be again—the change that has traditionally, but simplistically, been called the "fall of

Looking for the Decline and Fall of the Roman Empire

In 1776, the Englishman Edward Gibbon (1737–1794) became a celebrity by publishing the first installment of the best-selling, multi-volume work *The Decline and Fall of the Roman Empire*. The reading public loved his writing for its stinging style, though some people found Gibbon himself irritating for his flashy vanity and conceit.

Ironically, historians have found his title aggravating for its enduring renown: the phrase grew so famous that, if there is anything commonly "known" about the Roman Empire, it is that it declined and fell. The trouble is that this idea is woefully misleading. Gibbon himself lived to regret his choice of a title because his work continued telling the empire's story far beyond A.D. 476, the year when a Germanic general ruled in the west without a Roman emperor on the throne there. His final volume (published in 1788) reached A.D. 1453, when the Turks toppled the Byzantine Empire by taking Constantinople.

Various sources of new information and analysis have revealed the inadequacies of the idea that the Roman Empire "fell" once and for all in 476. This is not to say that nothing bad happened in the fourth and fifth centuries: clearly some conditions of life—economic security and prosperity, opportunities for leisure and entertainment, and even nutrition—got worse for many people as Germanic peoples entered the western empire and the center of power shifted to its eastern half. So, too, the Byzantine emperors regarded the political division of the old empire as a problem they wanted to remedy by conquering the new Germanic king-

doms to reunite west and east. Still, these changes are far from the full story. To tell all that story today, it is more accurate to describe the empire's fate as a complex transformation rather than as a simple decline and fall.

Art and archaeology have provided some of the most intriguing sources for this perspective, either from looking at long-known objects in new ways or from discovering new objects. Byzantine art, for example, is not a recent discovery, but valuing it as a sophisticated visual historical source is. Gibbon simply ignored it in his history. When eighteenth- and nineteenth-century observers considered it, they mostly saw art in decline compared with what they judged to be the perfection of classical times. Recent scholarship takes a different view: ancient classicism had emphasized realism

The Eyes of Byzantine Art
Erich Lessing/Art Resource, NY.

Rome" under the influence of Edward Gibbon's famous work. (See "New Sources, New Perspectives," above.) The story's details reveal the complexity of the political transformation of the western empire under new Germanic regimes. The deep background is familiar: the weakness of the western em-

perors' army obliged them to hire numerous Germanic officers to lead the defense of the Roman heartland in Italy. By the middle of the fifth century, one Germanic general after another decided who would serve as puppet emperor under his control. The employees were running the company.

Eagle *fibulae* (brooches) from Gothic Spain
Walters Art Gallery, Baltimore.

in depicting human beings, aiming to make paintings and sculptures look as close as possible to "real," almost like a photograph in paint or stone or metal. The artists of the Byzantine Empire, however, opted for expressionism: they portrayed people not as we ordinarily perceive them, which is to say the way they "really" look. Instead, they painted and sculpted faces so that their outer appearance expressed their inner being. For this reason, they made the eyes larger than life-size, not because they could not depict realistic-looking faces but because they believed that the eyes represented the mirror of the soul. This same expressionist approach reappears in some modern art.

Similarly, Germanic art was considered inferior because, unlike classical art, its designs did not emphasize the human figure or symmetry. Instead, it focused on animal motifs and abstract patterns. This tendency did not mean that it could not communicate as powerfully as classical art; it just

meant that observers had to be able to understand the art's conventions and goals. Recent archaeological research has shown that Goths used everyday art objects to convey crucial meanings—in particular, assertions of the growing sense of ethnic identity that emerged during their migrations into the Roman Empire. When in the fifth century A.D. Visigoths took up permanent residence in Spain, the women expressed their Germanic identity by emphasizing an old custom from their traditional Danube region: wearing two artfully crafted brooches to fasten their clothes at the shoulders instead of just one. Previously, this style had not served to identify separate groups; now it said, "I am a Visigothic woman."

Above all, Germanic art expressed the transformation of the empire. A clear example comes in the spectacular eagle pins that elite Goths favored. Dazzlingly fashioned in gold and semiprecious stones, these small works of art took their inspiration from the traditions of the Huns and the Romans, both of whom highlighted the eagle as a symbol of power. Goths had never previously used eagles this way, but now they adapted the traditions of others to express their own transformation into powerful members of imperial politics and society. From their perspective, the empire's fate was hardly a decline and fall.

QUESTIONS FOR DEBATE
1. How do historical and aesthetic appreciations of art differ? What are the advantages of each approach?
2. How do people determine whether art is "superior" or "inferior"? Are such judgments important to make?

FURTHER READING
Greene, K. "Gothic Material Culture." In Ian Hodder, ed. *Archaeology as Long-Term History.* 1987, 117–42.

Heather, Peter. *The Goths.* 1996, Chapter 10.

Hoxie, Albert. "Mutations in Art." In Lynn White Jr., ed. *The Transformation of the Roman World: Gibbon's Problem after Two Centuries.* 1966, 266–90.

The last such unfortunate puppet was a usurper; his father, Orestes, a former aide to Attila, had rebelled from the emperor Julius Nepos in 475 and raised his young son to the throne. He gave the boy emperor the name Romulus Augustulus, diminutives appropriate to his tender age and meant to recall both Rome's founder and its first emperor. In 476, following a dispute over pay, the Germanic soldiers murdered Orestes and deposed the boy; pitied as an innocent child, Romulus was provided with safe refuge and a generous pension. The rebels' leader, Odoacer, did not appoint another emperor.

Mausoleum of Theodoric at Ravenna

Theodoric, king of the Ostrogoths in Italy from 493 until his death in 526 and self-appointed heir of the western Roman Empire, conducted a major building program in Ravenna, the western capital, to demonstrate that he was ruling in the grand imperial tradition of Rome. To perpetuate his memory, he constructed this massive mausoleum just outside the city's wall. Two stories high, it appears circular on the inside but is decagonal (ten-sided) on the outside, fulfilling the Roman architectural tradition of creatively mixing shapes to make buildings visually interesting. It was constructed of marble blocks, the largest of which weighed three hundred tons. By building on this scale, Theodoric was communicating his power as well as his respect for the empire's past.
Hirmer Fotoarchiv.

Instead, seeking to block Nepos's campaign to regain the throne, he had the Roman Senate petition Zeno, the eastern emperor, to recognize his leadership in return for his acknowledging Zeno as sole emperor. Odoacer thereafter oversaw Italy nominally as the eastern emperor's viceroy, but in fact he ruled as he liked.

In 488, Zeno plotted to rid himself of another ambitious Germanic general then resident in Constantinople—Theodoric—by sending him to fight Odoacer, whom the emperor had found too independent. Successful in eliminating Odoacer by 493, Theodoric went on to establish his own state to rule Italy from the traditional capital at Ravenna until his death in 526. Thus the Ostrogothic kingdom was founded.

Theodoric and his Ostrogothic nobles wanted to enjoy the luxurious life of the empire's elite, not destroy it, and to preserve the empire's prestige and status. They therefore left the Senate and consulships intact. An Arian Christian, Theodoric followed Constantine's example by announcing a policy of religious toleration: "No one can be forced to believe against his will." He, like other Germanic rulers, appropriated the traditions of the Roman past that would support the stability of his own rule. For this reason, modern scholars consider it more accurate to speak of the western empire's "transformation" than its "fall."

The Enduring Kingdom of the Franks. The Franks were the Germanic people who transformed Roman Gaul into Francia (from which the name *France* comes). Roman emperors had allowed some of them to settle in a rough northern border region (now in the Netherlands) in the early fourth century; by the late fifth century they were a major presence in Gaul. Their king Clovis (r. 485–511) in 507 overthrew the Visigothic king in southern Gaul with support from the eastern Roman emperor. When the emperor named him an honorary consul, Clovis celebrated this ancient honor by having himself crowned with a diadem in the style of the emperors since Constantine. He carved out western Europe's largest Germanic kingdom in what is today mostly France, overshadowing the neighboring and rival kingdoms of the Burgundians and Alemanni in eastern Gaul. Probably persuaded by his wife Clotilda, a Christian, to believe that God had helped him defeat the Alemanni, Clovis proclaimed himself an orthodox Christian and renounced Arianism, which he had reportedly embraced previously. To build stability, he carefully fostered good relations with the bishops as the regime's intermediaries with the population.

Clovis's dynasty, called *Merovingian* after the legendary Frankish ancestor Merovech, foreshadowed

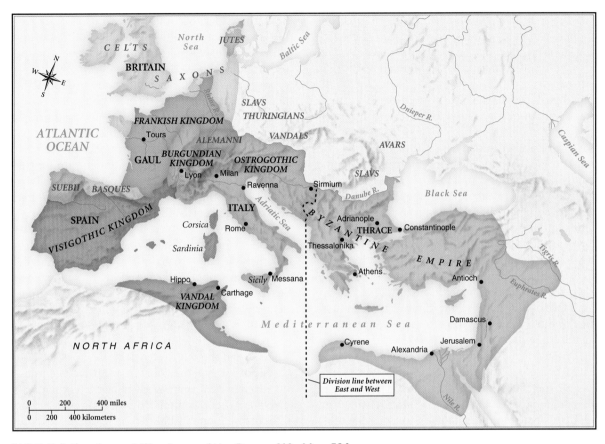

MAP 7.4 Peoples and Kingdoms of the Roman World, c. 526

The provinces of the Roman Empire had always been home to a population diverse in language and ethnicity. By the early sixth century, the territory of the western empire had become a welter of diverse political units as well. Italy and most of the former western provinces were ruled by kingdoms organized by different Germanic peoples, who had moved into former imperial territory over the past several centuries. The eastern empire, which we call the Byzantine Empire, remained under the political control of the emperor in Constantinople (formerly Byzantium until refounded by Constantine in 330).

the kingdom that would emerge much later as the forerunner of modern France. The dynasty endured for another two hundred years, far longer than most other Germanic royalty in the west. The Merovingians survived so long because they created a workable symbiosis between Germanic military might and Roman social and legal traditions.

Mixing Roman and Germanic Traditions

Western Europe's political transformation—the replacement of imperial government by Germanic kingdoms—set in motion an equally innovative social and cultural transformation (Map 7.4). The Germanic newcomers and the former Roman provincials cre-

ated new ways of life based on a combination of the old. This process proved particularly potent in developing new law codes and, in a far more negative development, altering the economic landscape.

Some of these changes happened unexpectedly, but others were intentional. The Visigoth king Athaulf (r. 410–415) married a Roman noblewoman and explicitly stated his goal of integrating their diverse traditions:

At the start I wanted to erase the Romans' name and turn their land into a Gothic empire, doing myself what Augustus had done. But I have learned that the Goths' free-wheeling wildness will never accept the rule of law, and that state with no law is no state. Thus, I have more wisely chosen another path to glory: reviving the Roman name with Gothic vigor. I pray that future generations will remember me as the founder of a Roman restoration.

This spirit fueled the fire of social and cultural transformation in postmigration western Europe.

Visigothic and Frankish Law.   Roman law was the most influential precedent for the new Germanic kings in their efforts to construct stable states. In their homeland tribal societies, they had never had written laws; now that they had transformed themselves into monarchs ruling Romans as well as their own people, they required legal codes to create a sense of justice and keep order. The Visigothic kings were the first leaders in Germanic history to develop a written law code. Composed in Latin and heavily influenced by Roman legal traditions, it made fines and compensation the primary method for resolving disputes. Clovis also emphasized written law for the Merovingian kingdom. His code, published in Latin, promoted social order through clear penalties for specific crimes. In particular, he formalized a system of fines intended to defuse feuds and vendettas between individuals and clans. The most prominent component of this system was *Wergild*, the payment a murderer had to make as compensation for his crime. Most of the money was paid to the victim's kin, but the king received perhaps one-third of the amount.

Since law codes enshrine social values, the differing amounts of Wergild imposed offer a glimpse of the relative values of different categories of people in Clovis's kingdom. Murdering a woman of childbearing age, a boy under twelve, or a man in the king's retinue incurred a massive fine of six hundred gold coins, enough to buy six hundred cattle. A woman past childbearing age (specified as sixty years), a young girl, or a freeborn man was valued at two hundred. Ordinary slaves rated thirty-five.

A Transformed Economic Landscape.   The migrations that transformed the west harmed its already weakened economy. The Vandals' violent sweep severely damaged many towns in Gaul, hastening the decline of urban communities that had been in progress for some time as economic activity increasingly shifted to the countryside. Especially in the countryside, now outside the control of any central government, wealthy Romans built sprawling villas on extensive estates, staffed by tenants bound to the land like slaves. These establishments strove to operate as self-sufficient units by producing all they needed, defending themselves against raids, and keeping their distance from any authorities. Craving isolation, the owners shunned municipal offices and tax collection, the public services that had supplied the lifeblood of Roman administration. The vestiges of provincial government disappeared, and the new kingdoms never matured sufficiently to replace their services fully.

The situation only grew grimmer as the effects of these changes multiplied one another. The infrastructure of trade—roads and bridges—fell into disrepair with no public-spirited elite to maintain them. Nobles holed up on their estates could take care of themselves and their fortresslike households because they could be astonishingly rich. The very wealthiest boasted an annual income rivaling that of an entire region in the old western empire.

In some cases, these fortunate few helped transmit Roman learning to later ages. Cassiodorus (c. 490–585), for example, founded a monastery on his ancestral estate in Italy in the 550s after a career in imperial administration. He gave the monks the task of copying manuscripts to keep their contents alive as old ones disintegrated. His own book *Institutions*, composed in the 550s to guide his monks, encapsulated the respect for tradition that kept classical traditions alive: in prescribing the works a person of superior education should read, it included ancient secular texts as well as Scripture and Christian literature. But the most strenuous effort to perpetuate the Roman past came in the eastern empire.

❖ Byzantine Empire in the East

The eastern empire avoided the massive transformations that reshaped western Europe. The trade routes and diverse agriculture of the east kept it richer than the west, and by shrewdly employing force, diplomacy, and bribery, its emperors minimized the effect of the Germanic migrations on their territory and blunted the aggression of the

Sassanid kingdom in Persia. In this way, they largely maintained their region's ancient traditions and demography. By the early sixth century, the old empire's eastern half had achieved such power, riches, and ambition that historians have given it a new name, the Byzantine Empire. Its emperors would rule in Constantinople for nearly a thousand years.

These rulers confidently saw themselves as perpetuating the Roman Empire and guarding its culture against barbarism; they regarded themselves as protectors of Constantine's "new Rome." The most famous early Byzantine emperor, Justinian (r. 527–565), took this mission so seriously that he nearly bankrupted the east with wars to reunify the empire by recovering the west. Like Diocletian—though he would have abhorred a comparison to a polytheist emperor who persecuted Christians—Justinian strengthened the autocracy of his rule and tried to purify religion to provide what he saw as the strict leadership and divine favor needed in unsettled times. One especially significant contribution of the early Byzantine Empire to later history was its crucial role in preserving classical literature while western Europe was struggling through the effects of its transformations.

Byzantine Society

The sixth-century Byzantine Empire enjoyed a vitality that had vanished in the west. Its elite spent freely on luxury goods imported from China and India: silk, precious stones, and prized spices such as pepper. The markets of its large cities, such as Constantinople, Damascus, and Alexandria, teemed with merchants from far and wide. Its churches' soaring domes testified to its self-confidence in its devotion to God as its divine protector.

As in the earlier Roman Empire, the Byzantine emperors sponsored religious festivals and entertainments on a massive scale to rally public support. Rich and poor alike crowded city squares, theaters, and hippodromes to bursting on these spirited occasions. Chariot racing aroused the hottest passions. Constantinople's residents, for example, divided themselves into competitive factions called Blues and Greens after the racing colors of their favorite charioteers. These high-energy fans mixed religious competition with their sports rivalry: orthodox Christians joined the Blues, while Monophysites

were Greens. When they mingled at the track, they frequently brawled with one another over theological arguments as well as race results. This tendency toward divisiveness pressured the government to try to impose unity on its subjects, with limited success.

Preserving "Romanness." The emperors ardently believed they had to maintain tradition to support the health and longevity of Roman civilization. They therefore did everything they could to preserve "Romanness," fearing that contact with Germanic peoples would "barbarize" their empire just as it had the west. Like the western emperors, they hired many Germanic and Hunnic mercenaries, but they tried to keep the foreign traditions from influencing the empire's residents. Styles of dress, for example, figured prominently in this struggle to maintain ethnic identity. Just as Honorius had tried to do in the early fifth century in the western empire, eastern emperors sought to control the sartorial habits of the capital's residents by forbidding them to wear Germanic-style clothing (especially heavy boots and clothing made from animal furs) instead of traditional Roman garb (sandals or light shoes and robes).

Preserving any sort of unitary Romanness was in reality a hopeless quest because the empire was thoroughly multilingual and multiethnic. Many heterogeneous yet intertwining traditions interacted in Byzantine society. Most of its inhabitants regarded themselves as the heirs of ancient Roman culture: they customarily referred to themselves as "Romans." At the same time, they spoke Greek as their native language and used Latin only for government and military communication. (For this reason, people in the western empire referred to them as "Greeks.") A significant number of people retained their traditional languages, such as Phrygian and Cappadocian in western Asia Minor, Armenian farther east, and Syriac and other Aramaic dialects in the Levant. Travelers around the empire therefore heard many different languages, observed many styles of dress, and encountered various ethnic groups.

Romanness definitely included Christianity, but the Byzantines' theological diversity nearly matched their ethnic complexity. Frequent, bitter controversies over doctrine divided eastern Christians and disrupted society. The emperors fruitlessly joined forces with church officials in trying to impose

MAXIMIANVS

Justinian and His Court in Ravenna

This mosaic scene dominated by the Byzantine emperor Justinian (r. 527–565) stands across the chancel from Theodora's mosaic in St. Vitale's church in Ravenna. Justinian and Theodora had finished building the church, which the Ostrogothic king Theodoric had started, to commemorate their successful campaign to restore Italy to the Roman empire and reassert control of the western capital, Ravenna. The soldiers at left remind viewers of the monarchs' aggressive military policy in service of imperial unity. The inclusion of the portrait of Maximianus, bishop of Ravenna, standing on Justinian's left and identified by name, stresses the theme of cooperation between bishops and emperors in ruling the world. Scala/Art Resource, NY.

orthodoxy. Emperors generally preferred words to swords in convincing heretics to return to orthodox theology and the hierarchy of the church, but they resolutely applied violence when persuasion failed. They had to resort to such extreme measures, they believed, to save lost souls and preserve the empire's religious purity and divine goodwill. The persecution of Christian subjects by Christian emperors symbolized the disturbing consequences that the quest for a unitary identity could cause.

Women in Society and at Court. In the patriarchal society of the Byzantine Empire, most women contributed to social order according to ancient Mediterranean precedent: they concentrated on the support of their households and minimized contact with men outside that circle. Law barred them from fulfilling many public functions, such as witnessing wills. Subject to the authority of their fathers and husbands, women veiled their heads (though not their faces) to show modesty. Since Christian theologians generally went beyond Roman tradition in restricting sexuality and reproduction, divorce be-

came more difficult and remarriage discouraged even for widows. Stiffer legal penalties for sexual offenses also became normal. Female prostitution remained legal, but emperors raised the penalties for those who forcibly made prostitutes of women under their control (children or slaves). Nevertheless, female prostitutes, often poor women desperate for income, continued to abound in the streets and inns of eastern cities, just as in earlier days.

Women in the imperial family were the exception to the rule: they could sometimes achieve a prominence unattainable for their workaday contemporaries. Theodora (d. 548), wife of the emperor Justinian, dramatically showed the influence women could achieve in Byzantine monarchy. Uninhibited by her humble origins (she was the daughter of a bear trainer and had been an actress with a scandalous reputation), she came to rival anyone in influence and wealth. Some ancient sources suggest that she had a hand in every aspect of Justinian's rule, advising him on personnel choices for his administration, pushing for her religious views in the continuing disputes over Christian doctrine, and

Theodora and Her Court in Ravenna

This resplendent mosaic shows the empress Theodora (c. 500–548) and her court. It was placed on one wall of the chancel of the church of St. Vitale in Ravenna, facing the matching scene of her husband Justinian and his attendants. Theodora wears the jewels, pearls, and rich robes characteristic of Byzantine monarchs. She extends in her hands a gem-encrusted bowl, evidently a present to the church; her gesture imitates the gift-giving of the Magi to the baby Jesus, the scene illustrated on the hem of her garment. The circle around her head, called a nimbus (Latin for "cloud"), indicates special holiness.
Scala/Art Resource, NY.

rallying his courage at time of crisis. John Lydus, a contemporary government official and high-ranking administrator, judged her "superior in intelligence to any man."

Social Class and Government Services. Byzantine government aggravated social divisions because it provided services according to people's wealth. Its complicated hierarchy required reams of paperwork and fees for countless aspects of daily life, from commercial permits to legal grievances. Without bribery, nothing got done. People with money and status found this process easy: they relied on their social connections to get a hearing from the right official and on their wealth to pay bribes to move matters along quickly. Whether seeking preferential treatment or just spurring administrators to do what they were supposed to do, the rich could make the system work.

Those of limited means, by contrast, found that their poverty put them at a grave disadvantage because they could not afford the large bribes that government officials routinely expected to carry out

their duties. Interest rates were high, and people could incur backbreaking debt trying to raise the cash to pay high officials to act on important matters. This system saved the emperors money to spend on their own projects: they could pay their civil servants paltry salaries because the public supplemented their incomes. John Lydus, for example, reported that he earned thirty times his annual salary in payments from petitioners during his first year in office. To keep the system from destroying itself through limitless extortion, the emperors published an official list of the maximum bribes that their employees could exact. Overall, however, this approach to government service generated enormous hostility among poorer subjects and did nothing to encourage public morale for the emperors' ambitious plans in pursuit of glory and conquest.

The Reign of Justinian, 527–565

Justinian, the most famous early Byzantine emperor, eagerly pursued these prizes of war. Born to a Latin-speaking family in a small Balkan town, he rose rapidly in imperial service until 527, when he succeeded his uncle as emperor. During his reign he launched enormous military expeditions to try to reclaim the western Germanic kingdoms and resurrect the old Roman Empire. His desire to perpetuate imperial glory also led him to embellish Constantinople with magnificent and costly architecture. The first intellectual on the throne since Julian in the 360s, Justinian was motivated by his deep interest in the law and theology to impose reforms with the same aims as all his predecessors, whether Christian or polytheist: to preserve social order based on hierarchy and maintain heaven's favor for himself and his subjects. But the financial strains of his campaigns and programs instead led to social unrest.

Financial Distress and Social Unrest. From the beginning of his reign, Justinian faced bitter resistance to his reform program and the cost of his bold plans. So heavy and unpopular were his taxes and so notorious was his tax collector, the ruthless John of Cappadocia, that they provoked a major riot in 532. Known as the "Nika Riot," it arose when the Blue and Green factions gathering in Constantinople's hippodrome to watch chariot races unexpectedly united against the emperor, shouting "Nika! Nika!" ("Win! Win!") as their battle cry. After nine days of violence that left much of Constantinople in ashes, Justinian was ready to abandon his throne and flee in panic. But Theodora sternly rebuked him: "Once born, no one can escape dying, but for one who has held imperial power it would be unbearable to be a fugitive. May I never take off my imperial robes of purple, nor live to see the day when those who meet me will not greet me as their sovereign." Her husband then sent in troops, who quelled the disturbance by slaughtering thirty thousand rioters trapped in the racetrack.

Justinian's most ambitious mission was to reunite the eastern and western empires to bring back the unified territory, religion, and culture of Constantine's rule. Pursuing the restoration of Roman rule in the former western provinces, his brilliant generals Belisarius and Narses defeated the Vandals and Ostrogoths after campaigns that in some cases took decades to complete. With enormous effort and expense, imperial armies reoccupied Italy, the Dalmatian coast, Sicily, Sardinia, Corsica, part of southern Spain, and western North Africa by 562.

These successes indeed restored the old empire's geography temporarily: Justinian's territory stretched from the Atlantic to the western edge of Mesopotamia.

But Justinian's military triumphs came at a tragic cost: they destroyed the west's infrastructure and the east's finances. Italy endured the most physical damage; the war there against the Goths spread death and destruction on a massive scale. The east suffered because Justinian squeezed even more taxes out of his already overburdened population to finance the western wars and bribe the Sassanids in Mesopotamia not to attack while his home defenses were depleted. The tax burden crippled the economy, leading to constant banditry in the countryside. Crowds poured into the capital from rural areas, seeking relief from poverty and robbers.

Natural disaster compounded Justinian's troubles. In the 540s, a horrific epidemic killed a third of his empire's inhabitants; a quarter of a million succumbed in Constantinople alone, half the capital's population. This was only the first onslaught in a long series of pandemics that erased millions of people in the eastern empire over the next two centuries. The loss of so many people created a shortage of army recruits, required the hiring of expensive mercenaries, and left countless farms vacant, reducing tax revenues.

Strengthening Monarchy. The strains constantly threatening his regime made Justinian crave stability; to strengthen his authority he emphasized his closeness to God and increased the autocratic nature of his rule. These traits became characteristic of Byzantine monarchy. His artists brilliantly recast the symbols of rule in a Christian context. A gleaming mosaic in his church at San Vitale in Ravenna, for example, displayed a dramatic vision of the emperor's role: Justinian standing at the center of the cosmos shoulder to shoulder with both the ancient Hebrew patriarch Abraham and Christ. Moreover, Justinian proclaimed the emperor the "living law," reviving a Hellenistic royal doctrine.

His building program in Constantinople concretely communicated an image of his overpowering supremacy and religiosity. Most spectacular of all was his magnificent reconstruction of Constantine's Church of the Holy Wisdom (Hagia Sophia). Its location facing the palace announced Justinian's interlacing of imperial and Christian authority. Creating a new design for churches, the architects erected a huge building on a square plan capped by a dome 107 feet across and soaring 160 feet above the floor. Its interior walls glowed like the sun from the light reflecting off their four acres of gold mosaics. Imported marble of every color added to the sparkling effect. When he first entered his masterpiece, dedicated in 538, Justinian exclaimed, "Solomon, I have outdone you," claiming to have bested the glorious temple that ancient king built for the Hebrews.

The new autocracy increasingly concentrated attention on the capital to the detriment of the provinces. Most seriously, it reduced the autonomy of the empire's cities. Their councils ceased to govern; imperial officials took over instead. Provincial elites still had to ensure full payment of their area's taxes, but they lost the compensating reward of deciding local matters. Now the imperial government determined all aspects of decision making and social status. Men of property from the provinces who aspired to power and prestige knew they could satisfy their ambitions only by joining the imperial administration.

Constantinople during the Rule of Justinian

Law and Religion.

To solidify his authority, Justinian acted swiftly to codify the laws of the empire to bring uniformity to the often confusing welter of decisions that earlier emperors had enacted. The first edition of his *Codex* appeared in 529; the second, expanded version completed the task in 534. A team of scholars also condensed millions of words of regulations to produce the *Digest* in 533, intended to expedite legal cases and provide a syllabus for law schools. This collection, like the others written in the traditional Latin and therefore readable in the western empire, influenced legal scholars for centuries. Justinian's experts also compiled a textbook for students, the *Institutes*, which appeared in 533 and remained on law school reading lists until modern times.

To fulfill his sacred duty to secure the welfare of the empire, Justinian acted to guarantee its religious purity. Like the polytheist and Christian em-

perors before him, he believed his world could not flourish if its divine protector became angered by the presence of religious offenders. As emperor, Justinian decided who the offenders were. Zealously enforcing laws against polytheists, he compelled them to be baptized or forfeit their lands and official positions. Three times he purged heretical Christians whom he could not reconcile to his version of orthodoxy. In pursuit of sexual purity, his laws made male homosexual relations illegal for the first time in Roman history. Homosexual marriage, apparently not uncommon earlier, had been officially prohibited in 342, but civil sanctions had never before been imposed on men engaging in homosexual activity. All the previous emperors, for example, had simply taxed male prostitutes. The legal status of homosexual activity between women is less clear; it probably counted as adultery when married women were involved and thus constituted criminal behavior.

A brilliant theologian in his own right, Justinian labored mightily to reconcile orthodox and Monophysite Christians by having the creed of the Council of Chalcedon revised. But the church leaders in Rome and Constantinople had become too bitterly divided and too jealous of the others' prominence to agree on a unified church; the eastern and western churches were by now firmly launched on the diverging courses that would result in formal schism five hundred years later. Justinian's own ecumenical council in Constantinople ended in disaster in 553 when he jailed Rome's defiant Pope Vigilius while also managing to alienate Monophysite bishops. Perhaps no one could have done better, but his efforts at religious unity only drove Christians further apart and undermined his vision of a restored Roman world.

Preserving Classical Literature

Christianization of the empire put the survival of classical literature—from plays and histories to speeches and novels—at risk because these works were polytheist and therefore potentially subversive of Christian belief. The real danger to the classical tradition, however, stemmed not so much from active censorship as from potential neglect. As Christians became authors, which they did in great numbers and with a passion, their works displaced the ancient texts of Greece and Rome as the most

IMPORTANT DATES

284 Diocletian assumes throne in midst of imperial crisis

293 Diocletian creates the tetrarchy

303 Great Persecution of Christians launched

312 Constantine converts to Christianity

c. 323 Pachomius in Upper Egypt establishes the first monasteries for men and women

324 Constantine refounds Byzantium as Constantinople, the "new Rome"

325 Council of Nicaea

378 Visigoths defeat Romans at battle of Adrianople

391 Theodosius bans pagan sacrifice and closes temples

395 Empire divided into western and eastern spheres

c. 397 Augustine writes *Confessions*

410 Visigoths sack Rome

451 Council of Chalcedon

476 German commander Odoacer deposes the final western emperor, Romulus Augustulus

493–526 Ostrogothic kingdom in Italy

507 Clovis establishes Frankish kingdom in Gaul

c. 530 Plato's Academy in Athens closes

538 Justinian dedicates Church of the Holy Wisdom

c. 540 Benedict devises his Rule for monasteries

540s Epidemic sweeps through Byzantine Empire, killing about one-third of the population

565 Death of Justinian

important literature of the age. Fortunately for later times, however, the Byzantine Empire played a crucial role in preserving these brilliant intellectual legacies, too.

Christian Education and Classical Literature. Of central importance to the survival of classical texts was the rooting of elite Christian education and literature in distinguished polytheist models, Latin as well as Greek. In the eastern empire, the region's original Greek culture remained the dominant influence, but Latin literature continued to be read because the administration was bilingual, with official documents and laws published in Rome's ancient tongue along with Greek translations. Latin scholarship in the east received a boost when Justinian's Italian wars impelled Latin-speaking scholars to flee for safety to Constantinople. Their labors in the cap-

ital helped to conserve many works that might otherwise have disappeared, because conditions in the west were hardly conducive to safekeeping ancient learning, except in such rare instances as Cassiodorus's private effort.

Byzantine scholars valued and preserved classical literature because they regarded it as a crucial part of a high-level education, an attitude reflecting their deep regard for elite tradition. Much of the classical literature available today survived because it served as schoolwork for Byzantine Christians. They received at least a rudimentary knowledge of some pre-Christian classics as a requirement for a good career in government service, the goal of every ambitious student. In the words of an imperial decree from 360, "No person shall obtain a post of the first rank unless it shall be shown that he excels in long practice of liberal studies, and that he is so polished in literary matters that words flow from his pen faultlessly."

Another factor promoting the preservation of classical literature was that the principles of classical rhetoric provided the guidelines for the most effective presentation of Christian theology. When Ambrose, bishop of Milan from 374 to 397, composed the first systematic description of Christian ethics for young priests, he consciously imitated the great classical orator Cicero. Theologians employed the dialogue form pioneered by Plato to refute heretical Christian doctrines, and polytheist traditions of laudatory biography survived in the hugely popular genre of saints' lives. Similarly, Christian artists incorporated polytheist traditions in communicating their beliefs and emotions in paintings, mosaics, and carved reliefs. A favorite artistic motif of Christ with a sunburst surrounding his head, for example, took its inspiration from polytheist depiction of the radiant Sun as a god.

The proliferation of Christian literature generated a technological innovation whose effects spilled over in the preservation of classical literature. Polytheist scribes had written books on sheets made of thin animal skin or paper made from papyrus. They then glued the sheets together and attached rods at both ends to form a scroll. Readers faced a cumbersome task in unrolling them to read. For ease of use, Christians produced their literature in the form of the *codex*—a book with bound pages. Eventually the codex became the standard form of book production in the Byzantine world. Because it was less susceptible to damage from rolling and unrolling and could contain text more efficiently than scrolls, which were cumbersome for long works, the codex aided the preservation of literature. This technological innovation greatly increased the chances of survival of classical texts.

Dangers and Possibilities. Despite the continuing importance of classical Greek and Latin literature in Byzantine education and rhetoric, its survival remained precarious in a war-torn world dominated by Christians. Knowledge of Greek in the turbulent west faded so drastically that almost no one could read the original versions of Homer's *Iliad* and *Odyssey*, the traditional foundations of a polytheist literary education. Latin fared better, and scholars such as Augustine and Jerome knew Rome's ancient literature extremely well. But they also saw its classics as potentially too seductive for a pious Christian because the enormous pleasure that came from reading them could be a distraction from the worship of God. Jerome in fact once had a nightmare of being condemned on Judgment Day for having been a Ciceronian instead of a Christian.

The closing around 530 of the Academy founded in Athens by Plato more than nine hundred years earlier vividly demonstrated the dangers for classical learning lurking in the Byzantine world. This most famous of classical schools finally shut its doors when many of its scholars emigrated to Persia to escape harsher restrictions on polytheists and its revenues dwindled because the Athenian elite, its traditional supporters, were increasingly Christianized. The Neoplatonist school at Alexandria, by contrast, continued; its leader John Philoponus (c. 490–570) was a Christian. In addition to Christian theology, Philoponus wrote commentaries on the works of Aristotle; some of his ideas anticipated those of Galileo a thousand years later. With his work, he achieved the kind of synthesis of old and new that was one of the fruitful possibilities in the ferment of the late Roman world—that is, he was a Christian subject of the Byzantine Empire in sixth-century Egypt, heading a school founded long before by polytheists, studying the works of an ancient Greek philosopher as the inspiration for his forward-looking scholarship. The strong possibility that the present could learn from the past would continue as Western civilization once again remade itself in medieval times.

Conclusion

The history of the late Roman Empire reveals a contest between the forces of unity and division. The third-century civil wars brought the empire to a turning point. Military activity was so prominent that, as Isis wrote to her mother, it seemed as if everybody was in the army. Diocletian's autocratic reorganization delayed the empire's fragmentation but opened the way to its eventual separation in 395 into western and eastern halves. From this time on, its history more and more divided into two regional streams, even though emperors as late as Justinian in the sixth century retained the dream of reuniting it and restoring it to the glory of its Golden Age.

A complex of forces interacted to destroy the unity of the Roman world, beginning with the catastrophic losses of property and people during the third-century crisis, which hit the west harder than the east. The late fourth century brought pressures on the central government created by migrations of Germanic peoples fleeing the Huns. When the Roman authorities proved unequal to the task of absorbing the Germanic tribes without disturbance, the newcomers created kingdoms that eventually replaced imperial government in the west. This change transformed not only the west's politics, society, and economy but also the Germanic tribes themselves, as they had to develop a sense of ethnic identity while organizing themselves into kingdoms on a new model. The economic deterioration accompanying these transformations drove a stake into the heart of the elite public-spiritedness that had been one of the foundations of imperial stability, as wealthy nobles retreated to self-sufficient country estates and shunned municipal office.

The eastern empire fared better economically and avoided the worst of the violent effects of the Germanic migrations. As the Byzantine state, it self-consciously continued the empire not only politically but also culturally by seeking to preserve "Romanness." The financial drain of pursuing the goal of unity through war against the Germanic kingdoms ironically increased social discontent by driving tax rates to punitive levels, while the concentration of power in the capital weakened the local communities that had made the empire robust.

This period of increasing political and social division saw the official religious unification of the empire under the banner of Christianity. Constantine's

MAPPING THE WEST **The Byzantine Empire and Western Europe, c. 600**

The Byzantine emperor Justinian employed brilliant generals and expended huge sums of money to reconquer Italy, North Africa, and part of Spain to reunite the western and eastern halves of the former Roman Empire. His wars to regain Italy and North Africa eliminated the Ostrogothic and Vandal kingdoms, respectively, but at a huge cost in effort, time—the war in Italy took twenty years—and expense. The resources of the eastern empire were so depleted that his successors could not maintain the reunification. By the early seventh century, the Visigoths had taken back all of Spain. Africa, despite serious revolts by indigenous Berber tribes, remained under imperial control until the Arab conquest of the seventh century, but within five years of Justinian's death the Lombards had set up a new kingdom controlling a large section of Italy. Never again would anyone attempt to reestablish a universal Roman empire.

conversion in 312 marked an epochal turning point in Western history, though Romans at the time did not know it. Christianization of the Roman world was far from complete, and Christians disagreed among themselves, even to the point of violence, over fundamental doctrines of faith. The church developed a hierarchy to prevent disunity, but believers proved remarkably recalcitrant in the face of authority. Many of them abandoned everyday society to live as monks attempting to come closer to God personally and praying daily for mercy

for the world. Monastic life redefined the meaning of holiness by creating communities of God's heroes who withdrew from this world to devote their service to glorifying the next. In the end, then, the imperial vision of unity faded before the divisive forces of the human spirit combined with the powerful dynamics of political and social transformation. Nevertheless, the memory of Roman power and culture remained potent and present, providing an influential inheritance to the peoples and states that would become Rome's heirs.

Suggested References

Reorganizing the Empire

In addition to trying to reconcile the sources' sometimes conflicting information about the events of the late third and fourth centuries, scholars continue to debate the personalities and motives of Diocletian and Constantine. Understanding these emperors is challenging because their religious sensibilities, markedly different from those of most modern believers, so deeply influenced their political actions.

Barnes, Timothy D. *Constantine and Eusebius.* 1981.

Bowersock, G. W., Peter Brown, and Oleg Grabar, eds. *Late Antiquity: A Guide to the Postclassical World.* 1999.

Diocletian's biography: http://www.salve.edu/~romanemp/dioclet.htm.

Elsner, Jaś. *Imperial Rome and Christian Triumph: The Art of the Roman Empire* A.D. *100–450.* 1998.

Harl, Kenneth W. *Coinage in the Roman Economy 300* B.C. *to* A.D. *700.* 1996.

Jones, A. H. M. *The Later Roman Empire.* 1964.

Salzman, Michele Renee. *On Roman Time: The Calendar of 354 and the Rhythms of Urban Life in Late Antiquity.* 1990.

Southern, Pat, and Karen R. Dixon. *The Late Roman Army.* 1996.

Whittaker, C. R. *Frontiers of the Roman Empire: A Social and Economic Study.* 1994.

Williams, Stephen. *Diocletian and the Roman Recovery.* 1985.

Christianizing the Empire

Recent research has deepened our appreciation of the complexity of the religious transformation of the Roman Empire and the emotional depths that the process reached for polytheists and Christians. People's ideas about the divine changed, as well as their ideas about themselves, even at the most intimate levels and activities of human life.

Bowersock, G. W. *Julian the Apostate.* 1978.

———. *Martyrdom and Rome.* 1995.

Brown, Peter. *Augustine of Hippo.* 1967.

———. *The Body and Society: Men, Women, and Sexual Renunciation in Early Christianity.* 1988.

Drake, H. A. *Constantine and the Bishops: The Politics of Intolerance.* 2000.

Early Christian literature: http://www.ocf.org/OrthodoxPage/reading/St.Pachomius/Welcome.html.

Herrin, Judith. *The Formation of Christendom.* Rev. ed. 1989.

MacMullen, Ramsay. *Christianity and Paganism in the Fourth to Eighth Centuries.* 1997.

McLynn, Neil B. *Ambrose of Milan: Church and Court in a Christian Capital.* 1994.

Raven, Susan. *Rome in Africa.* New ed. 1984.

Rousseau, Philip. *Pachomius: The Making of a Community in Fourth-Century Egypt.* 1985.

Rousselle, Aline. *Porneia: On Desire and the Body in Antiquity.* Trans. Felicia Pheasant. 1988.

Wills, Garry. *Saint Augustine.* 1999.

Germanic Kingdoms in the West

Debate still thrives over how to categorize the social and cultural transformation of the Roman world in the fourth and fifth centuries after the large-scale incursions of Germanic peoples. It is becoming increasingly clear that those people underwent a process of ethnogenesis (developing a separate ethnic identity) in constructing their new kingdoms on imperial territory in western Europe, but it is less clear how to measure the extent of the trauma inflicted on Romans and Roman culture.

Barnwell, P. S. *Emperor, Prefects, and Kings: The Roman West, 395–565.* 1992.

Burns, Thomas. *Barbarians within the Gates of Rome: A Study of Roman Military Policy and the Barbarians, ca. 375–425* A.D. 1994.

———. *A History of the Ostrogoths.* 1984.

Drew, Katherine Fischer. *The Laws of the Salian Franks.* 1991.

Geary, Patrick J. *Before France and Germany: The Creation and Transformation of the Merovingian World.* 1988.

Heather, Peter. *The Goths and Romans.* 1996.

King, Anthony. *Roman Gaul and Germany.* 1990.

Matthews, John. *Western Aristocracies and Imperial Court* A.D. *364–425.* 1975.

Wolfram, Herwig. *The Roman Empire and Its Germanic Peoples.* Trans. Thomas Dunlap. 1997.

Byzantine Empire in the East

Scholars today recognize the "Byzantine Empire" as the continuation of the eastern Roman Empire, emphasizing the challenge posed to its rulers in trying to maintain order and prosperity for their distinctly multicultural and multilingual population. The story of the Byzantine emperors poses provocative questions because the inclusiveness of their regimes was made possible by a political rigor that some would say approached tyranny.

Bowersock, G. W. *Hellenism in Late Antiquity.* 1990.

Byzantine history: http://thoughtline.com/byznet/.

Cameron, Averil. *The Mediterranean World in Late Antiquity,* A.D. *395–600.* 1993.

Cavallo, Guglielmo, ed. *The Byzantines.* 1997.

Mathews, Thomas F. *Byzantium: From Antiquity to the Renaissance.* 1998.

Rice, Tamara Talbot. *Everyday Life in Byzantium.* 1967.

Women in Byzantine history bibliography: http://www.wooster.edu/Art/wb.html.

8

The Heirs of the Roman Empire

600–750

A CCORDING TO A WRITER who was not very sympathetic to the Byzantines, one night Emperor Heraclius (r. 610–641) had a dream: "Verily [he was told] there shall come against thee a circumcised nation, and they shall vanquish thee and take possession of the land." Heraclius thought the vision foretold an uprising of the Jews, and he ordered mass baptisms in all his provinces. "But," continued the story,

after a few days there appeared a man of the Arabs, from the southern districts, that is to say, from Mecca or its neighborhood, whose name was Muhammad; and he brought back the worshipers of idols to the knowledge of the One God. . . . And he took possession of Damascus and Syria, and crossed the Jordan and dammed it up. And the Lord abandoned the army of the Romans before him.

Mosque at Damascus
Islam conquered the Byzantines, then Islam was "conquered" in turn by Byzantine culture. For the grand mosque at Damascus, his capital city, the Umayyad caliph al-Walid employed Byzantine mosaicists, who depicted classical motifs—buildings, animals, vegetation—in a style that harked back to the classical past. However, the artists scrupulously avoided depicting human beings, in this way conforming to one strain of Islamic thought that argued against figural representations.
(Detail) Jean-Louis Nou.

This tale, however fanciful, recalls the most astonishing development of the seventh century: the Arabs conquered much of the Roman Empire and became one of its heirs. The western and eastern parts of the empire, both diminished, were now joined by yet a third power—Arab and Muslim. The resulting triad has endured in various guises to the present day: the western third of the old Roman Empire became western Europe; the eastern third, occupying what is now Turkey, Greece, and some of the Balkans, became part of eastern Europe and helped to create Russia; and North Africa, together with the ancient Near East (now called the Middle East), remains the Arab world.

271

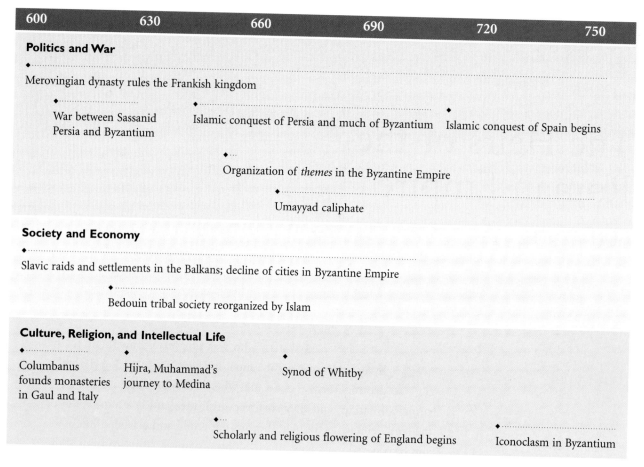

	600	630	660	690	720	750

Politics and War

Merovingian dynasty rules the Frankish kingdom

War between Sassanid Persia and Byzantium

Islamic conquest of Persia and much of Byzantium

Islamic conquest of Spain begins

Organization of *themes* in the Byzantine Empire

Umayyad caliphate

Society and Economy

Slavic raids and settlements in the Balkans; decline of cities in Byzantine Empire

Bedouin tribal society reorganized by Islam

Culture, Religion, and Intellectual Life

Columbanus founds monasteries in Gaul and Italy

Hijra, Muhammad's journey to Medina

Synod of Whitby

Scholarly and religious flowering of England begins

Iconoclasm in Byzantium

As diverse as these cultures are today, they share many of the same roots. All were heirs of Hellenistic and Roman traditions. All adhered to monotheism. The western and eastern halves of the empire had Christianity in common, although they differed at times in interpreting it. The Arab world's religion, Islam, accepted the same one God that Christians did but considered Jesus one of God's prophets rather than his son.

The history of the seventh and eighth centuries is a story of adaptation and transformation. Historians consider the changes important enough to signal the end of one era—antiquity—and the beginning of another—the Middle Ages. (See "Terms of History," page 274.) The seventh century is considered the early Middle Ages, a period in which, in their different ways, all three heirs of the Roman Empire combined elements of their heritage with new values, interests, and conditions. The divergences among them resulted from disparities in geographical and climatic conditions, material and human resources, skills, and local traditions. But these differences should not obscure the fact that the Byzantine, Muslim, and western European worlds were sibling cultures.

✦ Byzantium: A Christian Empire under Siege

Emperor Justinian had tried to re-create the old Roman Empire. On the surface he succeeded. His empire once again included Italy, North Africa, and the Balkans. Vestiges of old Roman society persisted: an educated elite maintained its prestige, town governments continued to function, and old myths and legends were retold in poetry and depicted on silver plates and chests. By 600, however, the eastern empire began to undergo a transformation as striking as the one that had earlier remade the western half. Historians call this reorganized empire the Byzantine Empire, or Byzantium, after the Greek name for the city of Constantinople. From the last third of the sixth century, Byzantium was almost constantly at war, and its territory shrank drastically. Cultural and political change came as well. Cities—except for a few such as Constantinople—decayed, and the countryside became the focus of government and military administration. In the wake of these shifts, the old elite largely disappeared, and classical learning gave way to new forms of education, mainly religious in content. The traditional styles of urban life, dependent on public gathering places and community spirit, faded away.

Byzantium at War, c. 600–750

From about 570 to 750, the Byzantine Empire waged war against invaders. Its first major challenge came from the Sassanid Empire of Persia. Its second came from new groups—Lombards, Slavs, Avars, Bulgars, and Muslims—who pushed into the empire. In the wake of these onslaughts, Byzantium was transformed.

Challenge from Persia. The Sassanid Empire of Persia was the "superpower" on the Byzantine doorstep. Since the third century, the Sassanid kings and Roman emperors had fought sporadically but never with decisive effect on either side. But in the middle of the sixth century, the Sassanids chose to concentrate their activities on their western half, Mesopotamia (today Iraq), nearer the Byzantine border (Map 8.1). They began to collect land taxes from the prosperous farmers of the region, assuring their government of a steady, predictable income. Furthermore, they turned Persia into a center of trade, while maintaining control over most of it. Reforming the army, which previously had depended on nobles who could supply their own arms, the Sassanid kings began to pay and arm new warriors, drawn from the lower nobility. Called *dekkans*, these heavily armored soldiers on horseback were precursors of the medieval knight. They were paid not only in coin and movable property but in whole villages and thereby became important landowners.

MAP 8.1 Byzantine and Sassanid Empires, c. 600
Justinian's grand design to regain the Roman Empire produced something new: the Byzantine Empire, with a capital at Constantinople and heartlands in the Balkans and the eastern Mediterranean. To its east was the Sassanid Empire, equally powerful and ambitious. In 600, the two faced each other uneasily. Three years later, the Sassanid king attacked Byzantine territory. The resulting wars, which lasted until 627, exhausted both empires and left them open to invasion by the Arabs.

Medieval

How did the word *medieval* come into being, and why is it used today as the equivalent of *barbaric*? No one who lived in the Middle Ages thought of herself as "medieval." No one thought he lived in the "Middle Ages." The whole idea of the "Middle Ages" began after the period it refers to, in the sixteenth century. At that time, writers decided that their own age, known as the *Renaissance* (French for "rebirth"), and the ancient Greek and Roman civilizations were much alike. They dubbed the period "in between"—the whole thousand-year period from about 600 to about 1400—with a Latin term: the *medium aevum,* or the "middle age." It was not a flattering term. Renaissance writers considered the "middle age" a single unfortunate, barbaric, and ignorant period.

Only with the Romantic movement of the nineteenth century and the advent of history as an academic discipline did writers begin to divide that "Middle Age" into several "ages." Often, they divided it into three periods: early (c. 600–1100), high (c. 1100–1300), and late (c. 1300–1400). This categorization revealed a bias: the "high Middle Ages" was clearly considered more important—"higher"—than what came before or after. In the view of nineteenth-century historians, the high Middle Ages was important for two reasons. First, it saw the beginnings of modern institutions such as the common law, universities, and centralized states. Second, it fostered the development of typically "medieval" yet highly regarded institutions such as the Crusades, Gothic cathedrals, and scholasticism.

The period *before* the high Middle Ages was sometimes called the "Dark Ages," a term that immediately brings to mind doom and gloom. The period *after* the high Middle Ages was more problematic for historians because the fourteenth century was not just the end of the Middle Ages but also the period in which the Renaissance began. Historians tended (and still tend) to ignore this fact. Instead, they fix on certain events, developments, and ideas within the period. If these seem modern and new—such as the rise of humanism and the development of diplomacy—historians call them part of the Renaissance. But if they seem retrograde or old—such as the ecstasies of mystics or knightly warfare—historians tend to call them late medieval.

One of the most radical recent developments in historians' view of the Middle Ages concerns the early Middle Ages. Since cultures in the period from about 400 to about 1100, with few exceptions, lacked centralized governments, organized institutions of higher learning, and well-developed legal systems, historians of the old school found little to praise in that time. However, in the 1960s, in the wake of the civil rights struggles, protests against the war in Vietnam, and a sense of loss of local community spirit, some historians came to see the early Middle Ages differently. Rather than applaud the high Middle Ages for its bureaucratic states and its laws, they relished the variety of peoples, the informal methods of government, and the community involvement evident in the society of the early Middle Ages.

Today, newspaper reporters and others still sometimes use *medieval* as a derogatory term, for example, by calling a primitive prison system "medieval." Little do they know that using the term in this way is as out of date as the sixteenth century.

FURTHER READING

Freedman, Paul, and Gabrielle Spiegel. "Medievalisms Old and New: The Rediscovery of Alterity in North American Medieval Studies." *American Historical Review* 103 (1998): 677–704.

Little, Lester K., and Barbara H. Rosenwein. *Debating the Middle Ages: Issues and Readings.* 1998.

At Ctesiphon, the capital city the Sassanid rulers constructed on the model of the great Byzantine city Antioch (in fact, they gave it the title "Better-than-Antioch"), they set up a bureaucracy of scribes tied to them by job and loyalty. They cultivated other writers and writings as well and thus opened their court to Byzantine and other Western influences and teachings. This openness accorded with their policy of maintaining good relations with the native population in Mesopotamia, many of whom were Nestorian Christians, even though the kings still adhered to Zoroastrianism.

The Sassanid kings promoted an exalted view of themselves and organized their court accordingly. They took the title "king of kings" and gave the men at their court titles such as "priest of priests" and "scribe of scribes." The practice emphasized hierarchy. The art that the kings patronized—as well as art not done explicitly for king or court—was stylized, with monograms and heraldic devices that immediately communicated a symbolic meaning. There was no room for ambiguity in this clearly graded society that admitted only four classes under the king: first the priests, then the scribes, next the warriors, and finally the common people.

Royal glory was accompanied by military and imperial dreams. The Sassanid king Chosroes II (r. 591–628) wanted to re-create the Persian empire of Xerxes and Darius, which had extended down through Syria all the way to Egypt. He began by invading the Byzantine Empire in 603. By 613, he had taken Damascus; he conquered Jerusalem the following year and Egypt in 619. Byzantine emperor Heraclius reorganized his army and inspired his troops to avenge the sack of Jerusalem; by 627, the Byzantines had regained all their lost territory.

Attack on All Fronts.   Because Byzantium was pre-occupied by war with the Sassanids, it was ill equipped to deal with other groups pushing into parts of the empire at about the same time (see Map 8.1). The Lombards, a Germanic people, arrived in northern Italy in 568 and by 572 had taken over most of southern Italy as well, leaving the Byzantines only Bari, Calabria, and Sicily as well as Rome and a narrow swath of land through the middle called the Exarchate of Ravenna.

The Byzantine army could not contend any more successfully with the Slavs and other peoples just beyond the Danube River. The Slavs conducted lightning raids on the Balkan countryside (part of Byzantium at the time) and, joined by the Avars, nomadic pastoralists and warriors, they attacked Byzantine cities as well. In fact, in 626 the Avars laid siege to Constantinople itself, though they could not, in the end, breach its walls.

Finally came the Bulgars, who entered what is now Bulgaria in the 670s. They defeated the Byzantine army and in 681 forced the emperor to recognize the state they carved out of formerly Byzantine

A Sassanid King
His head topped by a mighty horned headdress, this representation of a Sassanid ruler evokes the full majesty of the Kings of Kings. Traditional Persian sculpture was not, as here, in the round; the influence of Greek and Roman classical styles is evident in this sixth- or seventh-century bronze figure, despite the enmity between Sassanid Persia and Byzantium (heir of Greece and Rome) at the time.
Louvre/Agence Photographique de la réunion des musées nationaux.

The Walls of Constantinople
The thick walls put up by Emperor Theodosius II (408–450) are still visible at Istanbul today. A huge ring of stone forts, the walls incorporated not only the urban center but rural fields and gardens as well. Thus the city could support and feed itself even under siege. The walls of Constantinople helped protect it from the onslaughts of invaders for more than a thousand years.
Sonia Halliday Photographs.

territory. This Bulgar state crippled the Byzantines' influence in the Balkans and helped further isolate them from the West.

At the same time as the Byzantine Empire was being attacked on all fronts, its power was being whittled away by more peaceful means. For example, as Slavs and Avars settled in the Balkans, they often intermingled with the indigenous population, absorbing local agricultural techniques and burial practices while imposing their language and religious cults.

Consequences of Constant Warfare.   The loss of Byzantine control over the Balkans through both peaceful and military means meant further shrinking of its empire. More important over the long term

was that the Balkans could no longer serve, as they had previously, as a major conduit between Byzantium and the West. The loss of the Balkans exacerbated the increasing separation of the eastern and western halves of the former Roman Empire. The political division between the Greek-speaking East and the Latin-speaking West had already begun in the fourth century. The events of the seventh century, however, made the split both physical and cultural. Avar and Slavic control of the Balkans effectively cut off trade and travel between Constantinople and the cities of the Dalmatian coast, and the Bulgar state threw a political barrier across the Danube. Perhaps as a result of this physical separation, Byzantine historians ceased to be interested in the West, and its scholars no longer bothered to learn Latin. The two halves of the Roman Empire, once united, communicated very little in the seventh century.

The principal outcome of Byzantium's wars with the Sassanid Empire was the sapping of both Persian and Byzantine military strength. Exhausted, these empires were now vulnerable to attack by the Arabs, whose military prowess would create a new empire and spread a new religion, Islam. In the hundred years between 630 and 730, the Arabs succeeded in conquering much of the Byzantine Empire, at times attacking the very walls of Constantinople itself. No wonder the patriarch of Jerusalem, chief bishop of the entire Levant, saw in the Arab onslaught the impending end of the world: "Behold," he said, "the Abomination of Desolation, spoken of by the Prophet Daniel, that standeth in the Holy Place."

From an Urban to a Rural Way of Life

Though still viewing itself as the Roman Empire, by the eighth century Byzantium was quite small. Conquered Byzantine subjects in Syria and Egypt now were under Arab rule. For them, despite their new overlords, daily life remained essentially unchanged. Non-Muslims paid a special tax to their conquerors, but they could practice their Christian and Jewish religions in peace. In the countryside they were permitted to keep and farm their lands, and their cities remained centers of government, scholarship, and business.

Ironically, the most radical transformations for seventh- and eighth-century Byzantines occurred not in the territories lost but in the shrunken empire itself. Under the ceaseless barrage of invaders, many towns, formerly bustling nodes of trade and centers of the imperial bureaucratic network, vanished or became unrecognizable in their changed way of life. The public activity of marketplaces, theaters, and town squares gave way to the family table and hearth. City baths, once places where people gossiped, made deals, and talked politics and philosophy, disappeared in most Byzantine towns—with the significant exception of Constantinople. Warfare reduced some cities to rubble, and when they were rebuilt, the limited resources available went to construct thick city walls and solid churches instead of marketplaces and baths. Marketplaces

moved to overcrowded streets that looked much like the open-air bazaars of the modern Middle East. People under siege sought protection rather than community pastimes. In the Byzantine city of Ephesus, for example, the citizens who built the new walls in the seventh century enclosed not the old public edifices but rather their homes and churches (Map 8.2). Despite the new emphasis on church buildings, many cities were too impoverished even to repair their churches. (See "Taking Measure," page 279.)

The pressures of war against the Arabs brought a change in Byzantine society parallel to that in the West a few centuries before, spelling the end of the class of town councilors (the *curiales*), the elite that for centuries had mediated between the emperor and the people. But an upper class nevertheless remained: as in the West, bishops and their clergy continued to form a rich and powerful upper stratum even within declining cities.

Despite the general urban decline, Constantinople and a few other urban centers retained much of their old vitality. Some industry and trade continued, particularly the manufacture of fine silk textiles. These were the prestige items of the time, and

A New Rural Ideal
While incessant wars led to the depopulation of the Byzantine Empire and the decline of its cities, rural life gained importance both in reality and as a pastoral ideal. This mosaic on the floor of the imperial palace at Constantinople, probably made in the seventh century, shows an idyllic view of farm life. The Walker Trust, University of St. Andrew's Library, Scotland.

As urban life declined, agriculture, always the basis of the Byzantine economy, became the center of its social life as well. But unlike the West, where an extremely rich and powerful elite dominated the agricultural economy, the Byzantine Empire of the seventh century was principally a realm of free and semifree peasant farmers, who grew food, herded cattle, and tended vineyards on small plots of land. In the shadow of decaying urban centers, the social world of the farmer was narrow. Two or three neighbors were enough to ratify a land transfer. Farmers interacted mostly with their families or with monasteries. The buffer once provided by the curial class was gone; these families now felt directly the impact of imperial rule.

In turn, the emperors of the seventh and eighth centuries tried to give ordinary family life new institutional importance. Imperial legislation narrowed the grounds for divorce and set new punishments for marital infidelity. Husbands and wives who committed adultery were whipped and fined, and their noses were slit. Abortion was prohibited, and new protections were set in place against incest with children. Mothers were given equal power with fathers over their offspring and, if widowed, became the legal guardians of their minor children and controlled the household property.

MAP 8.2 Diagram of the City of Ephesus
The center of classical Ephesus had been the agora and the embolos (a wide street paved with marble and rimmed by shops and monuments). After the seventh century, the city was partially destroyed, its population declined, and the rebuilt city—without agora or embolos—was located to the north and protected by walls.

New Military and Cultural Forms

The transformations of the countryside went hand in hand with military, political, and cultural changes. On the military front, the Byzantine navy found a potent weapon in "Greek fire," a combustible oil that floated on water and burst into flames upon hitting its target. Determined to win wars on land as well, the imperial government exercised greater autocratic control, hastening the decline of the curial class, wresting power from other elite families, and encouraging the formation of a middle class of farmer-soldiers.

In the seventh century an emperor, possibly Heraclius, divided the empire into military districts called *themes* and put all civil matters in each district into the hands of one general, a *strategos* (plural, *strategoi*). This new organization effectively countered frontier attacks. Landless men were lured to join the army with the promise of land and low taxes; they fought side by side with local farmers,

their production and distribution were monitored by the government. State-controlled factories produced the very finest fabrics, which legally could be worn only by the emperor, his court, and his friends. In private factories, merchants, spinners, and weavers turned raw silk into slightly less luxurious cloth for both internal consumption and foreign trade. Even though Byzantium's economic life became increasingly rural and barter-based in the seventh and eighth centuries, the skills, knowledge, and institutions of urban workers made possible long-distance trade and the domestic manufacture of luxury goods. The full use of these resources, however, had to await the end of centuries of debilitating wars.

who provided their own weapons and horses. The *strategoi* not only led the local troops into battle but also served as the emperor's regional tax collectors. They soon became the vanguard of a new elite and began to dominate the rural scene. Nevertheless, between about 650 and 800 the reorganization of the countryside worked to the peasants' advantage while helping to strengthen the empire against the Arabs.

The military and social changes brought about by the new network of *themes* went hand in hand with changes in values; these were reflected, in turn, in education and culture. Whereas the old curial elite had cultivated the study of the pagan classics, sending their children (above all, their sons) to schools or tutors to learn to read the works of Greek poets and philosophers, eighth-century parents showed far more interest in giving their children,

both sons and daughters, a religious education. Even with the decay of urban centers, cities and villages often retained an elementary school. There teachers used the Book of Psalms as their primer. Throughout the seventh and eighth centuries, secular, classical learning remained decidedly out of favor, whereas dogmatic writings, saints' lives, and devotional works took center stage. In one popular tale of the time, for example, a prostitute arriving at an inn with a group of young men was attracted to a monk reading the Bible. "Unfortunate one, you are very impudent; are you not ashamed of coming over here and sitting next to us?" asked the monk. "No, Father . . . I have hope in the Son of the living God that after today I shall not remain in sin," replied the penitent woman. Thereupon she followed the monk and entered a monastery for women.

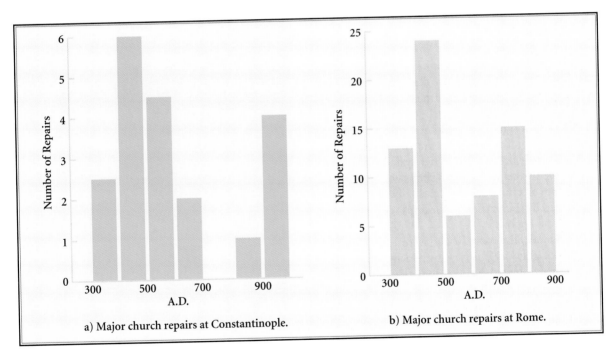

a) Major church repairs at Constantinople.

b) Major church repairs at Rome.

TAKING MEASURE Church Repair, 600–900

The impoverishment of the period 600–750 is clear from graph (a), which shows a major slump in church repair at Constantinople during the period. If there had been any money to spend on building repairs, it would undoubtedly have gone to the churches first. By contrast, graph (b) shows that Rome was not so hard hit as Constantinople, even though it was part of the Byzantine Empire. There was, to be sure, a dramatic reduction in the number of church repairs in the period 500–600. But from 700 to 800, there was a clear, if small, increase. Taken together, the two graphs help show the toll taken by the invasions and financial hardships of the period 600–750.

Data adapted from Klavs Randsborg, "The Migration Period: Model History and Treasure," *The Sixth Century: Production, Distribution and Demand,* eds. Richard Hodges and William Bowden (Leiden: Brill, 1998).

Religion, Politics, and Iconoclasm

The importance placed on religious learning and piety complemented both the autocratic imperial ideal and the powers of the bishops in the seventh century. Since the spiritual and secular realms were understood to be inseparable, the bishops wielded political power in their cities, while Byzantine emperors ruled as religious as well as political figures. In theory, imperial and church power were separate but interdependent. In fact, the emperor functioned as the head of the church hierarchy, appointing the chief religious official, the patriarch of Constantinople; formulating Christian doctrine; calling church councils to determine dogma; and setting out the criteria for bishops to be ordained. Beginning with Heraclius (r. 610–641), the emperors considered it one of their duties to baptize Jews forcibly, persecuting those who would not convert. In the view of the imperial court, this was part of the ruler's role in upholding orthodoxy.

Bishops and Monks.   Bishops functioned as state administrators in their cities. They acted as judges and tax collectors. They distributed food in times of famine or siege, provisioned troops, and set up military fortifications. As part of their charitable work, they cared for the sick and the needy. Byzantine bishops were part of a three-tier system: they were appointed by *metropolitans*, bishops who headed an entire province; and the metropolitans, in turn, were appointed by the patriarchs, bishops with authority over whole regions.

Theoretically, monasteries were under limited control of the local bishop, but in fact they were enormously powerful institutions that often defied the authority of bishops and even emperors. Because monks commanded immense prestige as the holiest of God's faithful, they could influence the many issues of church doctrine that racked the Byzantine church.

Conflict over Icons.   The most important issue of the Byzantine church revolved around icons. Icons are images of holy people—Christ, the Virgin, and the saints. To Byzantine Christians, they were far more than mere representations. Icons were believed to possess holy power that directly affected people's daily lives as well as their chances for salvation.

Many seventh-century Byzantines made icons the focus of their religious devotion. To them, icons were like the incarnation of Christ; they turned spirit into material substance. Thus an icon manifested in physical form the holy person it depicted. Some Byzantines actually worshiped icons; others, particularly monks, considered icons a necessary part of Christian piety. As the monk St. John of Damascus put it in a vigorous defense of holy images, "I do not worship matter, I worship the God of matter, who became matter for my sake, and

Icon of Virgin and Child
Surrounded by two angels in the back and two soldier saints at either side, the Virgin Mary and the Christ Child are depicted with still, otherworldly dignity. Working with hot pigmented beeswax, the sixth-century artist gave the angels transparent halos to emphasize their incorporeality while depicting the saints as earthly men, with hair, beards, and feet planted firmly on the ground. Icons such as this were used in private worship as well as in the religious life of Byzantine monasteries.

deigned to inhabit matter, who worked out my salvation through matter."

Other Byzantines abhorred icons. Most numerous of these were the soldiers on the frontiers. Shocked by Arab triumphs, they found the cause of their misfortunes in the biblical injunction against graven images. When they compared their defeats to Muslim successes, they could not help but notice that Islam prohibited all representations of the divine. To these soldiers and others who shared their view, icons revived pagan idolatry and desecrated Christian divinity. As iconoclastic (anti-icon or, literally, icon-breaking) feeling grew, some churchmen became outspoken in their opposition to icons, and church councils condemned them.

Byzantine emperors shared these religious objections, but they also had important political reasons for opposing icons. In fact, the issue of icons became a test of their authority. Icons diffused loyalties, setting up intermediaries between worshipers and God that undermined the emperor's exclusive place in the divine and temporal order. In addition, the emphasis on icons in monastic communities made the monks potential threats to imperial power; the emperors hoped to use this issue to break the power of the monasteries. Above all, though, the emperors opposed icons because the army did, and they wanted to support their troops.

The controversy climaxed in 726, after Emperor Leo III the Isaurian (r. 717–741) had defeated the Arabs besieging Constantinople in 717 and 718 and turned his attention to consolidating his political position. In the wake of the victory, officers of the imperial court tore down the great golden icon of Christ at the gateway of the palace and replaced it with a cross. In protest, a crowd of women went on a furious rampage in support of icons. This event marked the beginning of the period of *iconoclasm* (icon-smashing); soon afterward, Leo ordered all icons destroyed, a ban that remained in effect, despite much opposition, until 787. A modified ban would be revived in 815 and last until 843.

Iconoclasm had an enormous impact on daily life. At home, where people had their own portable icons, it forced changes in private worship: the devout had to destroy their icons or worship them in secret. Iconoclasm meant ferocious attacks on the monasteries: splendid collections of holy images were destroyed; vast properties were confiscated;

and monks, who were staunch defenders of icons, were ordered to marry. In this way iconoclasm destroyed communities that might otherwise have served as centers of resistance to imperial power. Reorganized and reoriented, the Byzantine rulers were able to maintain themselves against the onslaught of the Arabs, who attacked under the banner of Islam.

❖ Islam: A New Religion and a New Empire

The Bedouin tribal society from which Islam sprang was not united. It seemed hardly suited to a new religion that called for all to submit to the will of one God. Yet the very word *Islam*, meaning "submission," reveals that this is precisely what happened. Islam was founded by Muhammad, a merchant turned holy man from the Arabian city of Mecca. He recognized only one God, that of the Jews and the Christians. He saw himself as God's last prophet, the person to receive and in turn repeat God's final words to humans. Invited by the disunited and pagan people of the city of Medina to come and act as a mediator for them, Muhammad exercised the powers of both a religious and a secular leader. This dual role became the model for his successors (*caliphs*) as well. Through a combination of persuasion and force, Muhammad and his

Arabia in Muhammad's Lifetime

co-religionists, the Muslims, converted most of the Arabian peninsula. By the time he died in 632, this conquest and conversion had begun to move northward, into Byzantine and Persian territories. In the next generation, the Arabs conquered most of Persia and all of Egypt and were on their way across North Africa to Spain. Yet within the territories they conquered, daily life went on much as before.

Bedouin Tribal Society

Before the seventh century, the Arabian peninsula was sparsely populated by Bedouins, who lived in tribes—loose confederations of clans, or kin groups—that herded flocks for meat and milk and traded (or raided) for grain, dates, and slaves. Poor tribes herded sheep, whereas richer ones kept camels—extremely hardy animals, splendid beasts of burden, and good producers of milk and meat. (*Arab* was the name camel nomads called themselves.)

The Bedouins' world contained few cities and placed little emphasis on the political and cultural institutions of a *polis*-centered life. Whereas Greco-Roman civilization, based as it was on the Mediterranean Sea, took water for granted, Arabian life was inland, in the desert, where water was the very source of life: "The heavens and the earth were an integrated mass, then We split them and made every living thing from water," says God in the Qur'an, the holy book of Islam that serves Muslims much as the Bible does Christians and Jews.

Tribal, nomadic existence produced its own culture, including a common spoken language of extraordinary delicacy, precision, and beauty. In the absence of written language, the Bedouins used oral poetry and storytelling to transmit their traditions, simultaneously entertaining, reaffirming values, and teaching new generations.

Even in city oases—fertile, green areas where permanent settlements arose—the clan was the key social institution and focus of loyalties. Clans grouped together in tribes, their makeup shifting as kin groups joined or left. These associations, however changing, nevertheless saw outsiders as rivals, and tribes constantly fought with one another. Yet clan rivalry was itself an outgrowth of the values the various tribes shared. Bedouin men prized "manliness," which meant far more than sexual prowess. They strove to be brave in battle and feared being shamed. Manliness also entailed an obligation to be generous, to give away the booty that was the goal of intertribal warfare. Women were often part of this booty; a counterpart to Bedouin manliness was therefore the practice of polygyny (having more than one wife at the same time). Bedouin wars rarely involved much bloodshed; their main purpose was to capture and take belongings. It was not a big step from this booty-gathering to trading and from that to the establishment of commercial centers.

Mecca, a major oasis near the Red Sea, was one such commercial center. Meccan caravans were organized to sell Bedouin products—mainly leather goods and raisins—to more urbanized areas in the north, at the border between Arabia and Syria. More important, Mecca played an important religious role because it contained a shrine, the Ka'ba. Long before Muhammad was born, the Ka'ba, hedged about with 360 idols, served as a sacred place within which war and violence were prohibited. The tribe that dominated Mecca, the Quraysh, controlled access to the shrine and was able to tax the pilgrims who flocked there as well as sell them food and drink. In turn, plunder was transformed into trade as the visitors bartered with one another on the sacred grounds, assured of their security.

The Prophet Muhammad and the Faith of Islam

Thus Mecca, the birthplace of Muhammad (c. 570–632) was a center with two important traditions—one religious, the other commercial. Muhammad's early years were inauspicious: orphaned at the age of six, he spent two years with his grandfather and then came under the care of his uncle, a leader of the Quraysh tribe. Eventually, Muhammad became a trader. At the age of twenty-five, he married Khadija, a rich widow who had once employed him. They had at least four daughters and lived (to all appearances) happily and comfortably. Yet Muhammad sometimes left home and spent a few days in a nearby cave in prayer and contemplation, practicing a type of piety also practiced by early Christians.

Beginning in 610 and continuing until he died in 632, Muhammad heard a voice speaking what he came to identify as the words of God, or Allah (*Allah* means "God" in Arabic). "Recite!" began the voice, and to Muhammad it entrusted a special mission: to speak God's words, to live by them, eventually to preach them, and to convert others to follow them. The holy book of Islam, the Qur'an, means "recitation"; each of its chapters, or *suras*, is understood to be God's revelation as told to Muhammad by the angel Gabriel, then recited in turn by Muhammad to others. The earliest revelations emphasized the greatness, mercy, and goodness of God; the obligations of the rich to the poor; and the certainty of Judgment Day. In time they covered the gamut of human experience and the life to

Qur'an
More than a "holy book," the Qur'an represents for Muslims the very words of God that were dictated to Muhammad by the angel Gabriel. Generally the Qur'an was written on pages wider than long, perhaps to differentiate it from other books. This example dates from the seventh or eighth century. It is written in Kufic script, a formal and majestic form of Arabic that was used for the Qur'an until the eleventh century. The round floral decoration on the right-hand page marks a new section of the text.

come. For Muslims the Qur'an contains the sum total of history, prophecy, and the legal and moral code by which men and women should live: "Do not set up another god with God. . . . Do not worship anyone but Him, and be good to your parents. . . . Give to your relatives what is their due, and to those who are needy, and the wayfarers."

The Qur'an emphasizes the nuclear family—a man, his wife, and children—as the basic unit of Muslim society. Hence it cut the Bedouin tribespeople adrift from the protection and particularism of the tribe but gave them in return an identity as part of the *ummah,* the community of believers, who shared both a belief in one God and a set of religious practices. Islam depends entirely on individual belief and adherence to the Qur'an. Muslims have no priests, no mass, no intermediaries between the divine and the individual. Instead, Islam stresses the relationship between the individual and God, a relationship characterized by gratitude to and worship of God, by the promise of reward or punishment on Judgment Day "when the sky is cleft asunder," and by exhortations to human kindness— "Do not oppress the orphan. And do not drive the

beggar away." The Ka'ba, with its many idols, had gathered together tribes from the surrounding vicinity. Muhammad, with his one God, forged an even more universal religion.

Growth of Islam, c. 610–632

First to convert to Muhammad's faith was his wife, Khadija, and then a few friends and members of his immediate family. Discontented young men, often commercial failures, joined his converts, as did some wealthy merchants. Soon, however, the new faith polarized Meccan society. Muhammad's insistence that all pagan cults be abandoned in favor of his one faith brought him into conflict with leading clan members of the Quraysh tribe, whose positions of leadership and livelihood were threatened. Lacking political means to expel him, they insulted Muhammad and harassed his adherents.

Hijra: Journey to Medina. Disillusioned and angry with his own tribe and with Mecca, where he had failed to make much of an impact, Muhammad tried to find a place and a population receptive to his message. Most important, he expected support from Jews, whose monotheism, in Muhammad's view, prepared them for his own faith. When a few of Muhammad's converts from Medina promised to protect him if he would join them there, he eagerly accepted the invitation, in part because Medina had a significant Jewish population. In 622, Muhammad made the *Hijra,* or emigration, to Medina, an oasis about two hundred miles north of Mecca. This journey proved a crucial event for the fledgling movement. At Medina, Muhammad found followers ready to listen to his religious message and to regard him as the leader of their community. They expected him, for example, to act as a neutral and impartial judge in their interclan disputes. Muhammad's political position in the community set the pattern by which Islamic society would be governed afterward; rather than add a church to political and cultural life, Muslim political and religious institutions were inseparable. After Muhammad's death, the year of the Hijra was named the first year of the Islamic calendar; it marked the beginning of the new Islamic era.*

At Medina, Muhammad established the ummah, a single community distinct from other people. But the Muslims were not content to confine themselves to a minor outpost at Medina. Above all, it was essential for the success of the new religion to control Mecca, still a potent holy place. In 624, Muhammad led a small contingent to ambush a huge Meccan caravan brimming with goods; at the battle of Badr, aided by their position near an oasis, he and his followers killed forty-nine of the Meccan enemy, took numerous prisoners, and confiscated rich booty. This was a major turning point for the fledgling religion. With the battle of Badr, traditional Bedouin plundering was grafted on to the Muslim duty of *jihad* (literally "striving," but often translated as "holy war").

The battle of Badr was a great triumph for Muhammad, who was now able to consolidate his position at Medina, gaining new adherents and silencing all doubters. For example, the Jews at Medina, whom Muhammad had at first seen as allies, had not converted to Islam as he had expected. Right

after the battle of Badr, suspecting them of supporting hostile tribes, Muhammad attacked the Jews at Medina, eventually expelling, executing, or enslaving them.

Defining the Faith. At the same time Muhammad broke with the Jews, he distanced himself from Judaism and instituted new practices to define Islam as a unique religion. Among these were the *zakat,* a tax on possessions to be used for alms; the fast of Ramadan, which took place during the ninth month of the Islamic year, the month in which the battle of Badr had been fought; the *hajj,* a yearly pilgrimage to Mecca; and the *salat,* formal worship at least three times a day (later increased to five), which could include the *shahadah,* or profession of faith— "There is no divinity but God, and Muhammad is the messenger of God." Emphasizing his repudiation of Jewish traditions, Muhammad now had the Muslims physically turn themselves while praying away from Jerusalem, the center of Jewish worship, toward Mecca and the Ka'ba. Detailed regulations for these practices, sometimes called the "five pillars of Islam," were worked out in the eighth and early ninth centuries.

Meanwhile, the fierce rivalry between Mecca's clans and Medina's Muslims began to spill over into the rest of the Arabian peninsula as both sides strove to win converts. Muhammad sent troops to subdue Arabs north and south. In 630, he entered Mecca with ten thousand men and took over the city, assuring the Quraysh of leniency and offering alliances with its leaders. By this time the prestige of Islam was enough to convince clans elsewhere to convert. Through a combination of force, conversion, and negotiation, Muhammad was able to unite many, though by no means all, Arabic-speaking tribes under his leadership by the time of his death two years later.

In so doing, Muhammad brought about important social transformations. As they "submitted" to Islam, Muhammad's converts formed not a clan or tribe but rather a community bound together by the worship of God. Women were accepted into this community and their status enhanced. Islam prohibited all infanticide, for example, a practice that had long been used largely against female infants; and at first, Muslim women joined men during the prayer periods that punctuated the day. Men were allowed to have up to four wives at one time, but

---

*Thus 1 A.H. (1 *anno Hegirae*) on the Muslim calendar is equivalent to A.D. 622 (*anno Domini,* "year of the Lord," 622) on the Christian calendar.

they were obliged to treat them equally; their wives received dowries and had certain inheritance rights. But beginning in the eighth century, women began to pray apart from the men. Like Judaism and Christianity, Islam retained the practices of a patriarchal society in which women's participation in community life was circumscribed.

Even though Islamic society was a new sort of community, in many ways it did function as a tribe, or rather a "supertribe," obligated to fight common enemies, share plunder, and resolve peacefully any internal disputes. Muslims participated in group rituals, such as the salat and public recitation. The Qur'an was soon publicly sung by professional reciters, much as the old tribal poetry had been. Most significant for the eventual spread of Islam, Muslim men continued to be warriors. They took up where Meccan traders had been forced to leave off; along the routes once taken by caravans to Syria, their armies reaped profits at the point of a sword. But this differed from intertribal fighting; it was the

"striving" (jihad) of people who were carrying out the injunction of God against unbelievers. "Strive, O Prophet," says the Qur'an, "against the unbelievers and the hypocrites, and deal with them firmly. Their final abode is Hell: And what a wretched destination!"

Muhammad's Successors, 632–750

In founding a new political community in Arabia, Muhammad reorganized traditional Arab society as he cut across clan allegiances and welcomed converts from every tribe. He forged the Muslims into a formidable military force, and his successors, the caliphs, assaulted the Roman and Persian worlds, taking them by storm.

War and Conquest. To the west, the Muslims attacked Byzantine territory in Syria with ease and moved into Egypt in the 640s (Map 8.3). To the east, they invaded the Sassanid Empire, defeating the

MAP 8.3 Expansion of Islam to 750
In little more than a century, Islamic armies conquered a vast region that included numerous different people, cultures, climates, and living conditions. Yet under the Umayyads, these disparate territories were administered by one ruler from his capital city at Damascus. The uniting force was the religion of Islam, which gathered all believers into one community, the ummah.

Persians at the very gates of their capital, Ctesiphon, in 637. The whole of Persia was in Muslim hands by 651. During the last half of the seventh and the beginning of the eighth century, Islamic warriors extended their sway from Spain to India.

How were such conquests possible, especially in so short a time? First, the Islamic forces came up against weakened empires. The Byzantine and Sassanid states were exhausted from fighting one another. The cities of the Middle East that had been taken by the Persians and retaken by the Byzantines were depopulated, their few survivors burdened with heavy taxes. Second, the Muslims were welcomed into both Byzantine and Sassanid territories by discontented groups. Many Monophysite Christians in Syria and Egypt had suffered persecution by the Byzantines and were glad to have new, Islamic overlords. In Persia, Jews, Monophysites, and Nestorian Christians were at best irrelevant to the Zoroastrian King of Kings and his regime. These were the external reasons for Islamic success. There were also internal reasons. Arabs had long been used to intertribal warfare; now, under the banner of jihad, Muslims united as a supertribe, exercising their skills as warriors not against one another but rather against unbelievers. Fully armed, on horseback, and employing camels as convoys, they seemed almost a force of nature. Where they conquered, the Muslims

Arab Coin
The Arabs learned coinage and minting from those whom they conquered — the Persians and the Byzantines. The ruler depicted on this silver coin is wearing a headdress that echoes the one worn by the Sassanid ruler depicted on page 275. But the word for this type of coin, dirham, is not Persian but rather Greek, from drachma. The Umayyad Islamic fiscal system, which retained the old Roman land tax, was administered by Syrians who had often served Byzantine rulers in the same capacity.
The British Museum.

built garrison cities from which soldiers requisitioned taxes and goods. Sometimes whole Arab tribes, including women and children, were imported to settle conquered territory, as happened in parts of Syria. In other regions, such as Egypt, a small Muslim settlement at Fustat sufficed to gather the spoils of conquest.

The Politics of Succession. Struck down by an illness in the midst of preparations for an invasion of Syria, Muhammad died quietly at Medina in 632. His death marked a crisis in the government of the new Islamic state and the origin of tension between Shi'ite and Sunni Muslims that continues today. The choice of caliphs to follow Muhammad was difficult. They came not from the traditional tribal elite but rather from a new inner circle of men close to Muhammad and participants in the Hijra. The first two caliphs ruled without serious opposition, but the third caliph, Uthman (r. 644–656), a member of the Umayyad family and son-in-law (by marriage to two daughters) of Muhammad, aroused discontent among other clan members of the inner circle and soldiers unhappy with his distribution of high offices and revenues. Accusing Uthman of favoritism, they supported his rival, Ali, a member of the Hashim clan (to which Muhammad had belonged) and the husband of Muhammad's only surviving child, Fatimah. After a group of discontented soldiers murdered Uthman, civil war broke out between the Umayyads and Ali's faction. It ended when Ali was killed by one of his own erstwhile supporters, and the caliphate remained in Umayyad hands from 661 to 750.

Nevertheless, the *Shi'at Ali*, the faction of Ali, did not fade away. Ali's memory lived on among groups of Muslims (the Shi'ites) who saw in him a symbol of justice and righteousness. For them Ali's death was the martyrdom of the only true successor to Muhammad. They remained faithful to his dynasty, shunning the "mainstream" caliphs of the other Muslims (Sunni Muslims, as they were later called). The Shi'ites awaited the arrival of the true leader—the *imam*—who in their view could come only from the house of Ali.

Under the Umayyads the Muslim world became a state with its capital at Damascus, the historic capital of Syria—and today's as well. Borrowing from the institutions well known to the civilizations they had just conquered, the Muslims issued coins and hired former Byzantine and Persian officials. They made Arabic a tool of centralization, imposing it as the language of government on regions not previously united linguistically. For Byzantium this period was one of unparalleled military crisis, the prelude to iconoclasm. For the Islamic world, now a multiethnic society of Muslim Arabs, Syrians, Egyptians, Iraqis, and other peoples, it was a period of settlement, new urbanism, and literary and artistic flowering.

Peace and Prosperity in Islamic Lands

Ironically, the Islamic warriors brought peace. While the conquerors stayed within their fortified cities or built magnificent hunting lodges in the deserts of Syria, the conquered went back to work, to study, to play, and—in the case of Christians and Jews, who were considered "protected subjects"—to worship as they pleased in return for the payment of a special tax. At Damascus, local artists and craftspeople worked on the lavish decorations for a mosque in a neoclassical style at the very moment Muslim armies were storming the walls of Constantinople. Leaving the Byzantine institutions in place, the Muslim conquerors allowed Christians and Jews to retain their posts and even protected dissidents.

During the seventh and eighth centuries, Muslim scholars wrote down the hitherto largely oral Arabic literature. They determined the definitive form for the Qur'an and compiled pious narratives about Muhammad (*hadith* literature). Scribes composed these works in exquisite handwriting; Arab calligraphy became an art form. A literate class, composed mainly of the old Persian and Syrian elite now converted to Islam, created new forms of prose writing in Arabic—official documents as well as essays on topics ranging from hunting to ruling. Umayyad poetry explored new worlds of thought and feeling. Patronized by the caliphs, who found in written poetry an important source of propaganda and a buttress for their power, the poets also reached a wider audience that delighted in their clever use of words, their satire, and their invocations of courage, piety, and sometimes erotic love:

> I spent the night as her bed-companion,
>   each enamored of the other,
> And I made her laugh and cry, and stripped
>   her of her clothes.

> I played with her and she vanquished me;
>   I made her happy and I angered her.
> That was a night we spent, in my sleep,
>   playing and joyful,
> But the caller to prayer woke me up.

Such poetry scandalized conservative Muslims, brought up on the ascetic tenets of the Qur'an. But this love poetry was a product of the new urban civilization of the Umayyad period, where wealth, cultural mix, and the confidence born of conquest inspired diverse and experimental literary forms. By the close of the Umayyad period in 750, Islamic civilization was multiethnic, urban, and sophisticated, a true heir of Roman and Persian traditions.

❖ The Western Kingdoms

With the demise of Roman imperial government in the West, the primary foundations of power and stability in Europe were kinship networks, church patronage, royal courts, and wealth derived from land and plunder. In contrast to Byzantium, where an emperor still ruled as the successor to Augustus and Constantine, drawing upon an unbroken chain of Roman legal and administrative traditions, political power in the West was more diffuse. Churchmen and rich magnates, sometimes one and the same, held sway. Power derived as well from membership in royal dynasties, such as that of the Merovingian kings, who traced their ancestry back to a sea monster whose magic ensured the fertility and good fortune of the Franks. Finally, people believed that power lodged in the tombs and relics of saints, who represented and wielded the divine forces of God. Although the patterns of daily life and the procedures of government in the West remained recognizably Roman, they were also in the process of change, borrowing from and adapting local traditions.

Frankish Kingdoms with Roman Roots

The core of the Frankish kingdoms was Roman Gaul. During the sixth century, the Franks had established themselves as dominant in Gaul, and by the seventh century the limits of their kingdoms roughly approximated the eastern borders of present-day France, Belgium, the Netherlands, and

MAP 8.4 The Merovingian Kingdoms in the Seventh Century
By the seventh century, there were three powerful Merovingian kingdoms: Neustria, Austrasia, and Burgundy. The important cities of Aquitaine were assigned to one of these major kingdoms, while Aquitaine as a whole was assigned to a duke or other governor. Kings did not establish capital cities; they did not even stay in one place. Rather, they continually traveled throughout their kingdoms, making their power felt in person.

Luxembourg (Map. 8.4). Moreover, their kings, the Merovingians (the name of the dynasty derived from Merovech, a reputed ancestor), had subjugated many of the peoples beyond the Rhine, foreshadowing the contours of modern Germany. These northern and eastern regions were little Romanized, but the inhabitants of the rest of the Frankish kingdoms lived with the vestiges of Rome at their door.

Roman Ruins. Travelers making a trip to Paris in the seventh century, perhaps on a pilgrimage to the tomb of St. Denis, would probably have relied on river travel, even though some Roman roads were still in fair repair. (They would have preferred water routes because land travel was very slow and because even large groups of travelers on the roads were vulnerable to attacks by robbers.) Like the roads, other structures in the landscape would have seemed familiarly Roman. Coming up the Rhône from the south, voyagers would have passed Roman amphitheaters and farmlands neatly and squarely laid out by Roman land surveyors. The great stone palaces of villas would still have dotted the countryside.

What would have been missing, if the travelers had been very observant, were thriving cities. Hulks of cities remained, of course, and they served as the centers of church administration; but gradually during the late Roman period, many urban centers had lost their commercial and cultural vitality. Depopulated, many survived as mere skeletons, with the exception of such busy commercial centers as Arles and Marseilles. Moreover, if the travelers had approached Paris from the northeast, they would have passed through dense, nearly untouched forests and land more often used as pasture for animals than for cereal cultivation. These areas were not much influenced by Romans; they represented far more the farming and village settlement patterns of the Franks. Yet even on the northern and eastern fringes of the Merovingian kingdoms some structures of the Roman Empire remained. Fortresses were still standing at Trier (near Bonn, Germany, today), and great stone villas, such as the one excavated by archaeologists near Douai (today in France, near the Belgian border), loomed over the more humble wooden dwellings of the countryside.

Amphitheater at Arles
In what is today southern France the ruins of an amphitheater built by the Romans still dwarfs the surrounding buildings of the modern city of Arles. This huge stadium must have been even more striking in the seventh century, when the city was impoverished and depopulated. Plague, war, and the dislocation of Roman trade networks meant that most people abandoned the cities to live on the land. Only the bishop and his clergy— and those who could make a living servicing them — remained in the cities.
Jean Dieuzaide.

The Social Scale. In the south, gangs of slaves still might occasionally be found cultivating the extensive lands of wealthy estate owners, as they had done since the days of the late republic. Scattered here and there, independent peasants worked their own small plots as they had for centuries. But for the most part, seventh-century travelers would have found semi-free peasant families settled on small holdings, their *manses*—including a house, a garden, and cultivable land—for which they paid dues and owed labor services to a landowner. Some of these peasants were descendants of the *coloni* (tenant farmers) of the late Roman Empire; others were the sons and daughters of slaves, now provided with a small plot of land; and a few were people of free Frankish origin who for various reasons had come down in the world. At the lower end of the social scale, the status of Franks and Romans had become identical.

At the upper end of the social scale, Romans (or, more precisely, Gallo-Romans) and Franks had also merged. Although people south of the Loire River continued to be called Romans and people to the north Franks, their cultures were strikingly similar: they shared language, settlement patterns, and religious sensibilities. (See "New Sources, New Perspectives," page 292). There were many dialects in the Frankish kingdoms in the seventh century, but most were derived from Latin, though no longer the Latin of Cicero. "Though my speech is rude," Gregory, bishop of Tours (r. 573–c. 594), wrote at the end of the sixth century,

I have been unable to be silent as to the struggles between the wicked and the upright; and I have been especially encouraged because, to my surprise, it has often been said by men of our day, that few understand the learned words of the rhetorician but many the rude language of the common people.

Thus Gregory began his *Histories,* a valuable source for the Merovingian period (c. 500–751). He was trying to evoke the sympathies of his readers, a traditional Roman rhetorical device; but he also expected that his "rude" Latin—the plain Latin of everyday speech—would be understood and welcomed by the general public.

Whereas the Gallo-Roman aristocrat of the fourth and fifth centuries had lived in isolated villas with his *familia*—his wife, children, slaves, and servants—aristocrats of the seventh century lived in more populous settlements: in small villages surrounded by the huts of peasants, shepherds, and artisans. The early medieval village, constructed mostly out of wood or baked clay, was generally built near a waterway or forest or around a church for protection. Intensely local in interests and outlook, the people in the Frankish kingdoms of the seventh and eighth centuries clustered in small groups next to protectors, whether rich men or saints.

The Living and the Dead. Tours—the place where Gregory was bishop—exemplified this new-style settlement. Once a Roman city, Tours's main focus was now outside the city walls, where a church had been

Early Medieval Accounting

In the seventh century, peasants were lucky to produce more grain than they sowed. To make sure that it got its share of this meager production, at least one enterprising landlord, the monastery of St.-Martin at Tours, kept a kind of ledger. This extremely unusual parchment sheet, dating from the second half of the seventh century, lists the amount of grain and wood owed to St.-Martin by its tenants.
Bibliothèque Nationale, Paris.

built. The population of the surrounding countryside was pulled to this church as if to a magnet, for it housed the remains of the most important and venerated person in the locale: St. Martin. This saint, a fourth-century soldier-turned-monk, was long dead, but his relics—his bones, teeth, hair, and clothes—could be found at Tours, where he had served as bishop. There, in the succeeding centuries, he remained a supernatural force: a protector, healer, and avenger through whom God manifested divine power. In Gregory's view, for example, Martin's relics (or rather God *through* Martin's relics) had prevented armies from plundering local peasants. Martin was not the only human thought to have great supernatural power; all of God's saints were miracle workers.

Tours, c. 600
Nancy Gauthier and Henri Galinié, eds., *Gregoire de Tours et l'espace gaulois* (Tours: Actes du congrés internationale, 1997), 70.

Whereas in the classical world the dead had been banished from the presence of the living, in the medieval world the holy dead held the place of highest esteem. The church had no formal procedures for proclaiming saints in the early Middle Ages, but holiness was "recognized" by influential local people and the local bishop. When, for example, miracles were observed at the site of a tomb in Dijon, the common people went there regularly to ask for help. But the nearby bishop was convinced that St. Benignus inhabited the tomb only after the martyr himself came to visit the bishop in a vision. At St. Illidius's tomb in Clermont, it was reported that "the blind are given light, demons are chased away, the deaf receive hearing, and the lame the use of their limbs." Even a few women were so esteemed: "[Our Savior] gave us as models [of sanctity] not only men, who fight [against sinfulness] as they should, but also women, who exert themselves in the struggle with success," wrote Gregory as a preface to his story of the nun Monegund, who lived with a few other ascetic women and whose miracles included curing tumors and prompting paralyzed limbs to work again. No one at Tours doubted that Martin had been a saint, and to tap into the power of his relics the local bishop built his church in the cemetery directly over his tomb. For a man like Gregory of Tours and his flock, the church building was above all a home for the relics of the saints.

Economic Activity in a Peasant Society

As a bishop, Gregory was aware of some of the sophisticated forms of economic activity in seventh- and eighth-century Europe, such as long-distance trade. Yet most people lived on the very edge of survival. Studies of Alpine peat bogs show that from the fifth to the mid-eighth century glaciers advanced and the mean temperature in Europe dropped. This climatic change spelled shortages in crops. Chronicles, histories, and saints' lives also describe crop shortages, famines, and diseases as a normal part of life. For the year 591 alone, Gregory reported that

> *a terrible epidemic killed off the people in Tours and in Nantes. . . . In the town of Limoges a number of people were consumed by fire from heaven for having profaned the Lord's day by transacting business. . . . There was a terrible drought which destroyed all the green pasture. As a result there were great losses of flocks and herds.*

Subsistence and Gift Economies. An underlying reason for these calamities was the weakness of the agricultural economy. Even the meager population of the Merovingian world was too large for its productive capacities. The dry, light soil of the Mediterranean region was easy to till, and wooden implements were no liability. But the northern soils of most of the Merovingian world were heavy, wet, and difficult to turn and aerate. These technological limitations meant a limited food supply, and agricultural work was not equitably or efficiently allocated and managed. A leisure class of landowning warriors and churchmen lived off the work of peasant men, who tilled the fields, and peasant women, who gardened, brewed, baked, and wove cloth.

Occasionally surpluses developed, either from peaceful agriculture or plunder in warfare, and these were traded, although not in an impersonal, commercial manner. Most economic transactions of the seventh and eighth centuries were part of a gift economy, a system of give and take: booty was taken, tribute demanded, harvests hoarded, and coins minted, all to be redistributed to friends, followers,

Reliquary
The cult of relics necessitated housing the precious parts of the saints in equally precious containers. This reliquary, made of cloisonné enamel (bits of enamel framed by metal), garnets, glass gems, and a cameo, is in the shape of a miniature sarcophagus. On the back is the inscription "Theuderic the priest had this made in honor of Saint Maurice." Theuderic probably gave the reliquary to the monastery of St. Maurice d'Agaune, today in Switzerland, which was renowned for its long and elaborate liturgy—its daily schedule of prayer—in the late seventh century.
Photo courtesy Thames and Hudson Ltd., London, from *The Dark Ages,* 1975.

and dependents. Kings and other rich and powerful men and women amassed gold, silver, ornaments, and jewelry in their treasuries and grain in their storehouses to mark their power, add to their prestige, and demonstrate their generosity. Those benefiting from this largesse included religious people and institutions: monks, nuns, and bishops, monasteries and churches. We still have a partial gift economy today. At holidays, for example, goods change hands for social purposes: to consecrate a holy event, to express love and friendship, to "show off" wealth and status. In the Merovingian world, the gift economy was the dynamic behind most of the moments when goods and money changed hands.

Trade and Traders. Some economic activity in the seventh century was purely commercial and impersonal, especially long-distance trade, in which the West supplied human and raw materials like slaves,

Anthropology, Archaeology, and Changing Notions of Ethnicity

At the end of the nineteenth century, scholars argued that ethnicity was the same as race and that both were biological. They measured skeletal features and argued that different human groups—blacks, whites, Jews, and Slavs, for example—were biologically distinct and that some were better than others according to "scientific" criteria.

It was not long before some anthropologists challenged this view. In the early 1900s, for example, the anthropologist Franz Boas showed that American Indians were not biologically different from any other human group; their "ethnicity" was cultural. Boas meant that the characteristics that made Indians "Indian" were not physical but rather a combination of practices, beliefs, language, dress, and sense of identity. Influenced by Boas, the husband-and-wife research team of Melville and Frances Herskovits showed how African tribal groups differed from one another not "essentially" but rather culturally. Ethnicity was not genetic, they asserted.

Historians were slow to take up this new, anthropological point of view. Until very recently they spoke of the various Germanic groups who entered the Roman Empire—Franks, Visigoths, Saxons, Lombards—as if these people were biologically different from Romans and from one another. For example, they thought that there was a real biological group called "the Lombards" that had migrated into the Roman Empire and set up the "Lombard kingdom" in Italy by conquering another real biological group called "the Romans."

This view does not square with the facts, as a number of recent scholars, many of them associated with the University of Vienna, are showing. They approach ethnicity as a cultural entity that is shaped by human activity and will.

Walter Pohl, for example, has demonstrated how ethnic groups like the Lombards and Franks were made up of men and women from all sorts of backgrounds. Their sense of belonging to one distinct group was a product of such cultural factors as common dress, weapons, and hairstyles, not of descent. An artifact or style produced or adopted by the group was important for defining a group's identity. Just as there are American "team colors" and "gang signs," for example, so in the early Middle Ages cultural practices and objects identified a person as a "Frank," say, and not as a "Lombard." Moreover, these common practices and objects could change over time.

Applied to archaeological remains, this new approach brings new insights as well. No physical difference distinguishes a Frankish skeleton from a Lombard or a Roman one. Evidence of cultural practices and artifacts are the only clue to ethnicity. Even then, archaeologists cannot be sure that the same artifact points to one ethnic group. For example, a number of ornamental clasps called

furs, and honey and in return received luxuries and manufactured goods such as silks and papyrus from the East. Trade was a way in which the Byzantine, Islamic, and western European descendants of the Roman Empire kept in tenuous contact with one another. Seventh- and eighth-century sources speak of Byzantines, Syrians, and Jews as the chief intermediaries, many of them living in the still-thriving port cities of the Mediterranean. Gregory of Tours associated Jews with commerce, complaining that they sold things "at a higher price than they were worth."

Contrary to Gregory's view, Jews were not involved only, or even primarily, in trade but were almost entirely integrated into every aspect of secular life in many regions of Europe. They used Hebrew in worship, but otherwise they spoke the same languages as Christians and used Latin in their legal documents. Their children were often given the same names as Christians (and, in turn, Christians often took Old Testament biblical names); they dressed as everyone else dressed; and they engaged in the same occupations. Many Jews planted and tended vineyards, in part because of the importance "imperial fibulae" were found in widely scattered excavations. Should archaeologists conclude that one ethnic group lived in scattered settlements? Historians of the Vienna school argue that they should not: different groups could use the same fibulae in different ways.

This approach also means looking at old texts in a newly critical manner. For example, Roman writers referred to the Germans as long-haired and fair. (This became a stereotypical description used by the Nazis and remains so even today.) Yet other ancient writers called the Germans "red-heads," which is exactly what they called the Celts, who were not German. In short, naming the hair color may have been a strategy—a way for the Romans to set themselves apart from the German barbarians—rather than a factual description. Interestingly, some Germans found it to their advantage to feed the stereotype: they took up the challenge and dyed their hair red.

Historians used to consider the names of tribes to be clues to ethnicity. But even these names were not fixed, and they did not always refer to ethnic identity. The word *Frank* originally meant "the brave" but later came to mean "the free." The word *Lombard* meant "long beard." But, as Pohl points out, some Lombards did not wear beards, while many who were not Lombards sported facial hair. Depictions of Lombards on coins and other objects are inconclusive; some have beards and some do not. Clearly, even the very meaning of their name was not essential to their sense of identity. Rather, it more likely was connected to their gender relations. The Lombards believed that their name came from a trick played by their women, who tied their long hair around their chins, humoring the war god Woden into calling them "Longbeards" and giving their men victory in battle. External beards were not signs of ethnicity but rather ingredients in a myth about women and valor.

Seeing ethnicity as cultural rather than biological allows historians to understand the origin of European states not as the result of the conquest of one genetically determined group by another but rather as a historical process. France, Germany, and England were not created by fixed entities known for all time as, respectively, the Franks, the Germans, and the Angles. Rather, they were created and shaped by the will and imagination of men and women who intermingled, interacted, and adapted to one another over time.

QUESTIONS FOR DEBATE

1. How might the biological notion of ethnicity have led to Nazi racist ideology and even to the recent drive toward "ethnic cleansing" in the former Yugoslavia?

2. How do the new cultural notions of ethnicity change the way that historians select and study their evidence?

FURTHER READING

Hines, John, ed. *The Anglo-Saxons, from the Migration Period to the Eighth Century: An Ethnographic Perspective.* 1997.

Pohl, Walter, with Helmut Reimitz. *Strategies of Distinction: The Construction of Ethnic Communities, 300–800.* 1998.

Wolfram, Herwig. "The Shaping of the Early Medieval Kingdom." *Viator* 1 (1970): 1–20.

of wine in synagogue services, in part because the surplus could easily be sold. Some Jews were rich landowners, with slaves and dependent peasants working for them; others were independent peasants of modest means. Whereas some Jews lived in towns with a small Jewish quarter where their homes and synagogues were located, most Jews, like their Christian neighbors, lived on the land. Only much later, in the tenth century, would their status change, setting them markedly apart from Christians.

Nor were women as noticeably set apart from men in the Merovingian period as they had been in Roman times. As in the Islamic world, western women received dowries and could inherit property. In the West, they could be entrepreneurs as well: documents reveal at least one enterprising peasant woman who sold wine at Tours to earn additional money.

The Powerful in Merovingian Society

Monarchs and aristocrats were the powerful people of Merovingian society. Merovingian aristocrats—who included monks and bishops as well as laypeople—did not form a separate legal group but held power through hereditary wealth, status, and political influence.

The Aristocrats. Many aristocrats lived in leisurely abundance. At the end of the sixth century, for example, one of them, Nicetius, inhabited a palace that commanded a view of his estates overlooking the Moselle River:

> From the top [of the palace] you can see boats gliding by on the surface of the river in summertime; orchards with fruit-trees growing here and there fill the air with the perfume of their flowers.

York Helmet

This fine helmet, once belonging to a very wealthy warrior living near York, England, in the second half of the eighth century, was intended for both display and real battle. The helmet, made of iron, and the back flap, made of flexible chain mail, gave excellent protection against sword blades. The cheek pieces were probably originally pulled close to the warrior's face by a leather tie. The nose piece, decorated with interlaced animals, protected his nose. Over the top, two bands of copper sheets meet at the middle. They were inscribed "In the name of our Lord Jesus, the Holy Spirit, God, and with all, we pray. Amen. Oshere. Christ."
York Castle Museum/City of York Museum Services.

Along with tending their estates, male aristocrats of the period spent their time honing their skills as warriors. To be a great warrior in Merovingian society, just as in the otherwise very different world of the Bedouin, meant more than just fighting: it meant perfecting the virtues necessary for leading armed men. Aristocrats affirmed their skills and comradeship in the hunt; they proved their worth in the regular taking of booty; and they rewarded their followers afterward at generous banquets. At these feasts, following the dictates of the gift economy, the lords combined fellowship with the redistribution of wealth, as they gave abundantly to their retainers.

Merovingian aristocrats also spent a good deal of time in bed. The bed—and the production of children—was the focus of their marriage. Because of its importance to the survival of aristocratic families and to the transmission of their property and power, marriage was an expensive institution, especially the most formal kind of marriage. The man had to pay a dowry to his bride, and after the marriage was consummated, he gave her a morning gift consisting of money, slaves, and heads of cattle. A less formal marriage, practiced by very wealthy men who could—and wanted to—support more than one wife at a time, was *Friedelehe.* This was a second-class marriage that did not involve a dowry, though the husband did give each of these lesser wives a morning gift and set her up in a separate household. In this period, churchmen had many ideas about the value of marriages, but in practice they had little to do with the matter: no one was married in a church.

Sixth-century aristocrats with wealth and schooling like Nicetius still patterned their lives on those of Romans, teaching their children Latin poetry and writing to one another in phrases borrowed from Virgil. Less than a century later, however, aristocrats no longer adhered to the traditions of the classical past. Most important, their spoken language was now very different from literary Latin and they paid little attention to Latin poetry. Some still learned Latin, but they cultivated it mainly to read the Psalms. A religious culture emphasizing Christian piety over the classics was developing in the West at the same time as in Byzantium.

The new religious sensibility was given powerful impetus by the arrival (c. 591) on the continent of the Irish monk St. Columbanus (d. 615). The Merovingian aristocracy was much taken by Columbanus's brand of monasticism, which stressed exile, devotion, and discipline. The monasteries St. Columbanus established in both Gaul and Italy attracted local recruits from the aristocracy, some of them grown men and women. Others were young children, given to the monastery by their parents. This practice, called *oblation*, was not only accepted but also often considered essential for the spiritual well-being of both the children and their families. Irish monasticism introduced aristocrats on the continent to a deepened religious devotion. Those aristocrats who did not join or patronize a monastery still often read (or listened to others read) books about penitence, and they chanted the Psalms.

Growth of Columbanian Monasticism

Bishops, generally aristocrats, ranked among the most powerful men in Merovingian society. Gregory of Tours, for example, considered himself the protector of "his citizens" at Tours. When representatives of the king came to collect taxes, Gregory stopped them in their tracks, warning them that St. Martin would punish anyone who tried to tax his people. "That very day," Gregory reported, "the man who had produced the tax rolls caught a fever and died." Gregory then obtained a letter from the king, "confirming the immunity from taxation of the people of Tours, out of respect for Saint Martin."

Like other aristocrats, many bishops were married even though church councils demanded celibacy. As the overseers of priests, however, bishops were expected to be moral supervisors and refrain from sexual relations with their wives. Since bishops were ordinarily appointed late in life, long after they had raised a family, this restriction did not threaten the ideal of a procreative marriage.

Women of Power. Noble parents determined whom their daughters were to marry, for such unions bound together whole extended families rather than simply husbands and wives. As was true for brides of the lower classes, aristocratic wives received a dowry (usually land) over which they had some control; if they were widowed without children, they were allowed to sell, give away, exchange, or rent out their dowry estates as they wished. Moreover, men could give their women kinfolk property outright in written testaments. Fathers so often wanted to share their property with their daughters that an enterprising author created a formula for scribes to follow when drawing up such wills. It began:

> For a long time an ungodly custom has been observed among us that forbids sisters to share with their brothers the paternal land. I reject this impious law: I make you, my beloved daughter, an equal and legitimate heir in all my patrimony [inheritance].

Because of such bequests, dowries, and other gifts, many aristocratic women were very rich. Childless widows frequently gave grand and generous gifts to the church from their vast possessions. But a woman need not have been a widow to control enormous wealth: in 632, for example, the nun

Reading Desk of St. Radegund
Radegund was a Thuringian princess captured and taken prisoner during a war with the Franks. Soon thereafter she became King Clothar I's queen. But Radegund was not happy at court. She founded a monastery at Poitiers, appointed an abbess there, and lived within its walls for the rest of her life. Famous for obtaining a precious relic of the Holy Cross for her convent (named Holy Cross in its honor), Radegund made her monastery an important part of royal politics. This reading desk is itself a pious object: it depicts the Lamb of God in the center, the symbols of the evangelists (the authors of the four Gospels) in the corners, and other symbols of Christ in the remaining squares.
Musée de Poitiers.

Burgundofara, who had never married, drew up a will giving her monastery the land, slaves, vineyards, pastures, and forests she had received from her two brothers and her father. In the same will, she gave other property near Paris to her brothers and sister. Aristocratic women maintained close ties with their relatives. They tried to find powerful husbands for their sisters and prestigious careers for their brothers; in turn, they relied on their relatives for support.

Though legally under the authority of her husband, a Merovingian woman often found ways to take control of her life and of her husband's life as well. Tetradia, wife of Count Eulalius, left her husband, taking all his gold and silver, because

> he was in the habit of sleeping with the women-servants in his household. As a result he neglected his wife. . . . As a result of his excesses, he ran into serious debt, and to meet this he stole his wife's jewelery and money.

In a court of law, Tetradia was sentenced to repay Eulalius four times the amount she had taken from him, but she was allowed to keep and live on her own property. Other women were able to exercise behind-the-scenes control through their sons. Artemia, for example, used the prophecy that her son Nicetius would become a bishop to prevent her husband from taking the bishopric himself. Although the prophecy eventually came to pass, Nicetius remained at home with his mother well into his thirties, working alongside the servants and teaching the younger children of the household to read the Psalms.

Some women exercised direct power. Rich widows with fortunes to bestow wielded enormous influence. Some Merovingian women were abbesses, rulers in their own right over female monasteries and sometimes over "double monasteries," with separate facilities for men and women. These could be very substantial centers of population: the convent at Laon, for example, had three hundred nuns in the seventh century. Because women lived in populous convents or were monopolized by rich men able to support several wives or mistresses at one time, unattached aristocratic women were scarce in society and therefore valuable.

The Power of Kings.   Atop the aristocracy were the Merovingian kings, rulers of the Frankish kingdoms

Relic of Queen Balthild
A slave, purchased in England by a Frankish mayor of the palace, Balthild soon caught the eye of the Frankish king himself, who made her his queen. This seventh-century Cinderella story did not end with marriage: when her husband died, Balthild played an important role as regent for her young son. Later she retired to a monastery, where she was revered as a saint. This shirt is one of her relics. Tradition has it that, rather than wear real jewels, Balthild distributed them to the poor and contented herself with their images in embroidery.
Musée de Chelles/photographers: E. Mittard and N. Georgieff.

from about 486 to 751. The dynasty owed its longevity to good political sense: it had allied itself with local lay aristocrats and ecclesiastical authorities. The kings relied on these men to bolster their power derived from other sources: their tribal war leadership and access to the lion's share of plunder; their quasi-magical power over crops and fertility; and their takeover of the taxation system, public lands, and the legal framework of Roman administration. The kings' courts functioned as schools for the sons of the aristocracy, tightening the bonds between royal and aristocratic families and loyalties. And when kings sent officials—counts and dukes—to rule in their name in various regions of their kingdoms, these regional governors worked with and married into the aristocratic families who had long controlled local affairs.

Both kings and aristocrats had good reason to want a powerful royal authority. The king acted as arbitrator and intermediary for the competing interests of the aristocrats while taking advantage of local opportunities to appoint favorites and garner prestige by giving out land and privileges to supporters and religious institutions. Gregory of Tours's history of the sixth century is filled with stories of bitter battles between Merovingian kings, as royal brothers fought continuously over territories, wives, and revenues. Yet what seemed like royal weakness and violent chaos to the bishop was in fact one way the kings focused local aristocratic enmities, preventing them from spinning out of royal control. By the beginning of the seventh century, three relatively stable Frankish kingdoms had emerged: Austrasia to the northeast; Neustria to the west, with its capital city at Paris; and Burgundy, incorporating the southeast (see Map 8.4). These divisions were so useful to local aristocrats and the Merovingian dynasty alike that even when royal power was united in the hands of one king, Clothar II (r. 613–623), he made his son the independent king of Austrasia.

The very power of the kings in the seventh century, however, gave greater might to their chief court official, the mayor of the palace. In the following century, allied with the Austrasian aristocracy, one mayoral family would displace the Merovingian dynasty and establish a new royal line, the Carolingians.

Christianity and Classical Culture in England and Ireland

The Merovingian kingdoms exemplify some of the ways in which Roman and non-Roman traditions combined. Anglo-Saxon England shows still another way in its formation of a learned monastic culture. The impetus for this culture came not from native traditions but from Rome and Ireland. After the Anglo-Saxon conquest (440–600), England gradually emerged politically as a mosaic of about a dozen kingdoms ruled by separate kings. They found no strong Christian aristocracy with which to ally, for the British Christians who remained had been either absorbed into the pagan culture of the invaders or pushed west into Wales or north into Scotland, where Christianity survived.

Two Forms of Christianity. Christianity was reintroduced in England from two directions. In the north of England, Irish monks brought their own brand of Christianity. Converted in the fifth century by St. Patrick and other missionaries, the Irish had rapidly evolved a church organization that corresponded to its rural clan organization. Abbots and abbesses, generally from powerful dynasties, headed monastic *familiae*, communities composed of blood relatives, servants, slaves, and, of course, monks or nuns. Bishops were often under the authority of abbots, and the monasteries rather than cities were the centers of population settlement in Ireland. The Irish missionaries to England were monks, and they set up monasteries on the model of those at home.

In the south of England, Christianity came via missionaries sent by Gregory the Great (r. 590–604) in 597. The missionaries, under the leadership of Augustine (not the same Augustine as the bishop of Hippo), intended to convert the king and people of Kent, the southernmost kingdom, and then work their way northward. But Augustine and his party brought with them Roman practices at odds with those of Irish Christianity, stressing ties to the pope and the organization of the church under bishops rather than abbots. Using the Roman model, they divided England into territorial units called *dioceses* headed by an archbishop and bishops. Augustine, for example, became archbishop of Canterbury. As he was a monk, he set up a monastery right next to his cathedral, and it became a peculiar characteristic of the English church to have a community of monks attached to the bishop's church.

A major bone of contention between the Roman and Irish churches involved the calculation of the date of Easter. The Roman church insisted that Easter fall on the first Sunday after the spring equinox. The Irish had a different method of determining when Easter should fall, and therefore they celebrated a different Easter. As everyone agreed that

Lindisfarne Gospels

At the end of the seventh century, the monks of Lindisfarne, in the extreme north of England, produced the lavishly illuminated manuscript of the Gospels from which this photograph is taken. For the Lindisfarne monks and many others of the time, the book was a precious object, to be decorated much like a piece of jewelry. To introduce each of the four Gospels, the artist, the monk Eadfrith, produced three elaborate pages: the first was a "portrait" of the evangelist, the second a decorative "carpet" page, and the third the beginning of the text. The page depicted here is the beginning of the Gospel according to St. Matthew, which begins with the words "Liber generationis." Note how elaborately Eadfrith treated the first letter, L, and how the decoration gradually recedes, so that the last line, while still very embellished, is quite plain in comparison with the others. In this way Eadfrith led the reader slowly and reverently into the text itself. British Library.

believers could not be saved unless they observed Christ's resurrection properly and on the right day, the conflict over dates was bitter. It was resolved by Oswy, king of Northumbria. In 664, he organized a meeting of churchmen, the Synod of Whitby, which chose the Roman calculation. He was convinced that Rome spoke with the voice of St. Peter, who was said in the New Testament to hold the keys of the Kingdom of Heaven. Oswy's decision paved the way for the triumph of the Roman brand of Christianity in England.

Literary Culture. St. Peter was not the only reason for favoring Rome. To many English churchmen, Rome had great prestige because it was a treasure trove of knowledge, piety, and holy objects. Benedict Biscop (c. 630–690), the founder of two important English monasteries, made many arduous trips to Rome, bringing back relics, liturgical vestments, and even a cantor to teach his monks the proper melodies in a time before written musical notation. Above all, he went to Rome to get books. At his monasteries in the north of England, he built up a grand library. In Anglo-Saxon England as in Ireland, both of which lacked a strong classical tradition from Roman times, a book was considered a precious object, to be decorated as finely as a garnet-studded brooch.

The Anglo-Saxons and Irish Celts had a thriving oral culture but extremely limited uses for writing. Books became valuable only when these societies converted to Christianity. Just as Islamic reliance on the Qur'an made possible a literary culture under the Umayyads, so Christian dependence on the Bible, written liturgy, and patristic thought helped make England and Ireland centers of literature and learning in the seventh and eighth centuries. Archbishop Theodore (r. 669–690), who had studied at Constantinople and was one of the most learned men of his day, founded a school at Canterbury where students mined Latin and even some Greek manuscripts to comment on biblical texts. Men like Benedict Biscop soon sponsored other centers of learning, using the texts from the classical past. Although women did not establish famous schools, many abbesses ruled over monasteries that stressed Christian learning. Here as elsewhere, Latin writings, even pagan texts, were studied diligently, in part because Latin was so foreign a language that mastering it required systematic and formal study. One of Benedict Biscop's pupils was Bede (673–735), an Anglo-Saxon monk and a historian of extraordinary breadth. Bede in turn taught a new generation of monks who became advisers to eighth-century rulers.

The vigorous pagan Anglo-Saxon oral tradition was only partially suppressed; much of it was adapted to Christian culture. Bede told the story of Caedmon, a layman who had not wanted to sing and make up poems, as he was expected to do at the convivial feasts of warriors. One night Caedmon had a dream: he was commanded by an unknown man to sing about Creation. In his sleep Caedmon dreamed an Anglo-Saxon poem that praised God as author of all things. He became a kind of celebrity, joined a monastery, and spent the rest of his days turning passages of Scripture into poetry in his own language, English. Although Bede translated Caedmon's poem into Latin when he wrote down the tale, he encouraged and supported the use of Anglo-Saxon, urging Christian priests, for example, to use it when they instructed their flocks. In contrast to other European regions, where the vernacular was rarely written, Anglo-Saxon came to be a written language used in every aspect of English life, from government to entertainment.

After the Synod of Whitby, the English church was tied by doctrine, friendship, and conviction to the church of Rome. An influential Anglo-Saxon monk and bishop, Wynfrith, even changed his name to the Latin Boniface to symbolize his loyalty to the Roman church. Preaching on the continent, Boniface (680–754) worked to set up churches in

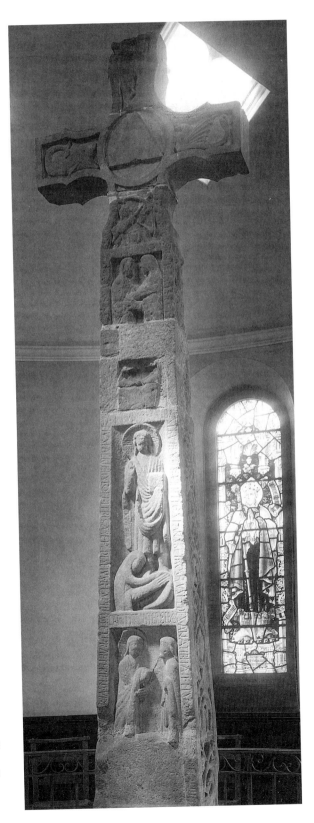

Ruthwell Cross

The Ruthwell Cross is one of a number of monumental stone pillars and crosses that sculptors in the north of England began to produce in the eighth century. It is a fascinating (and still not fully understood) mixture of Latin and runic inscriptions, vinescrolls, and biblical scenes. Art historians are astonished by the monument because it presents figures in half-round at a time when sculptors elsewhere were working only in flat relief. The runes on the edges of the cross give the text of the poem "Dream of the Holy Rood," which purports to be the "dream" of the wood on which Christ was crucified. The cross at the top was probably added later. What purposes might have been served by monuments such as this?
Edwin Smith.

Germany and Gaul that, like those in England, looked to Rome for leadership and guidance. His zeal would give the papacy new importance in the West.

Visigothic Unity and Lombard Division

In contrast to England, southern Gaul, Spain, and Italy had long been part of the Roman Empire and preserved many of its traditions. Nevertheless, as they were settled and fought over by new peoples, their histories came to diverge dramatically. When

the Merovingian king Clovis defeated the Visigoths in 507, their vast kingdom, which had sprawled across southern Gaul into Spain, was dismembered. By midcentury, the Franks came into possession of most of the Visigothic kingdom in southern Gaul.

In Spain the Visigothic king Leovigild (r. 569–586) established territorial control by military might. But no ruler could hope to maintain his position there without the support of the Hispano-Roman population, which included both the great landowners and leading bishops; and their backing

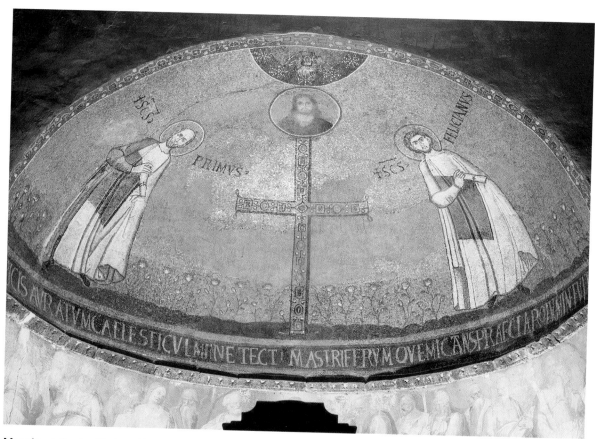

Mosaic at Santo Stefano Rotondo
The church of Santo Stefano, built by Pope Simplicius (r. 468–483), was round, like a classical temple. It made up part of the papal Lateran palace complex, in the southeastern zone of Rome. Later popes continued to beautify and adorn Santo Stefano, drawing on the artistic styles of their own time. Pope Theodore (r. 642–649) moved the relics of two Roman martyrs, Primus and Felician, from a small church outside of Rome to Santo Stefano. To celebrate the event, he commissioned the mosaic shown here, in which the figures of Primus and Felician flank a giant cross. The heavy outlines and gold surroundings echo mosaics done at Byzantium around the same time, attesting to political, cultural, and theological links between Rome and Constantinople.
Madeline Grimoldi.

was unattainable while the Visigoths remained Arian. Leovigild's son Reccared (r. 586–601) took the necessary step in 587, converting to Catholic Christianity. Two years later, at the Third Council of Toledo, most of the Arian bishops followed their king by announcing their conversion to Catholicism, and the assembled churchmen enacted decrees for a united church in Spain.

Thereafter the bishops and kings of Spain cooperated to a degree unprecedented in other regions. While the king gave the churchmen free rein to set up their own hierarchy (with the bishop of Toledo at the top) and to meet regularly at synods to regulate and reform the church, the bishops in turn supported their Visigothic king, who ruled as a minister of the Christian people. Rebellion against him was tantamount to rebellion against Christ. The Spanish bishops reinforced this idea by anointing the king, daubing him with holy oil in a ritual that paralleled the ordination of priests and demonstrated divine favor. Toledo, the city where the highest bishop presided, was also where the kings were "made" through anointment. While the bishops in this way made the king's cause their own, their lay counterparts, the great landowners, helped supply the king with troops, allowing him to maintain internal order and repel his external enemies.

Ironically, it was precisely the centralization and unification of the Visigothic kingdom that proved its undoing. When the Arabs arrived in 711, they needed only to kill the king, defeat his army, and capture Toledo to deal it a crushing blow.

By contrast, in Italy the Lombard king constantly faced a hostile papacy in the center of the peninsula and virtually independent dukes in the south. Theoretically royal officers, in fact the dukes of Benevento and Spoleto ruled on their own behalf. Although many Lombards were Catholics, others, including important kings and dukes, were Arian. The "official" religion varied with the ruler in power. Rather than signal a major political event, the conversion of the Lombards to Catholic Christianity occurred gradually, ending only around the mid-seventh century. Partly as a result of this slow development, the Lombard kings, unlike the Visigoths, Franks, or even the Anglo-Saxons, never enlisted the wholehearted support of any particular group of churchmen.

Lacking strong and united ecclesiastical favor, Lombard royal power still had bulwarks. Chief among these were the traditions of leadership associated with the royal dynasty, the kings' military ability and their control over large estates in northern Italy, and the Roman institutions that survived in Italy. Although the Italian peninsula had been devastated by the wars between the Ostrogoths and the Byzantine Empire, the Lombard kings took advantage of the still-urban organization of Italian society and economy, assigning dukes to city bases and setting up a royal capital at Pavia. Recalling emperors like Constantine and Justinian, the kings built churches, monasteries, and other places of worship in the royal capital, maintained the walls, and minted coins. Revenues from tolls, sales taxes, port duties, and court fines filled their coffers, although their inability to revive the Roman land tax was a major weakness. Like other Germanic kings, the Lombards issued law codes that revealed a great debt to Roman legal collections, such as those commissioned by Justinian. While individual provisions of the law code promulgated by King Rothari (r. 636–652), for example, reflected Lombard traditions, the code also suggested the Roman idea that the law should apply to all under his rule, not just Lombards. "We desire," Rothari wrote,

Lombard Italy, Early Eighth Century

> that these laws be brought together in one volume so that everyone may lead a secure life in accordance with the law and justice, and in confidence thereof will willingly set himself against his enemies and defend himself and his homeland.

Unfortunately for the Lombard kings, the "homeland" they hoped to rule was not united under them. As soon as they began to make serious headway into southern Italy against the duchies of Spoleto and Benevento, the pope began to fear for his own position in Rome in the middle of the country and called on the Franks for help.

IMPORTANT DATES

c. 570–632 Life of Muhammad, prophet of Islam

590–604 Papacy of Gregory the Great

c. 591 Columbanus, an Irish monk, arrives on the continent

596–597 Augustine sent to England by Pope Gregory the Great to convert the Anglo-Saxons

610–641 Reign of Emperor Heraclius

622 Muhammad's Hijra to Medina and beginning of Islamic calendar

630–730 Period of Islamic conquests

661 Death of Ali; origins of Sunni/Shi'ite split

661–750 Umayyad caliphate

664 Synod of Whitby; English king opts for Roman Christianity

718–719 Major Arab attack on Constantinople repulsed

726–843 Period of iconoclasm at Byzantium

Political Tensions and Reorganization at Rome

By 600, the pope's position was ambiguous: he was both a ruler and a subordinate. On the one hand, believing he was the successor of St. Peter and head of the church, he wielded real secular power. Pope Gregory the Great (r. 590–604) in many ways laid the foundations for the papacy's later spiritual and temporal ascendancy. During his tenure, the pope became the greatest landowner in Italy; he organized the defenses of Rome and paid for its army; he heard court cases, made treaties, and provided welfare services. The missionary expedition he sent to England was only a small part of his involvement in the rest of Europe. For example, Gregory maintained close ties with the churchmen in Spain who were working to convert the Visigoths from Arianism to Catholicism. A prolific author of spiritual works and biblical commentaries, Gregory digested and simplified the ideas of church fathers like St. Augustine of Hippo, making them accessible to a wider audience. His practical handbook for the clergy, *Pastoral Rule*, was matched by practical reforms within the church: he tried to impose in Italy regular elections of bishops and to enforce clerical celibacy.

On the other hand, the pope was not independent. He was only one of many bishops in the Roman Empire, which was now ruled from Constantinople; and he was therefore subordinate to the emperor and Byzantium. For a long time the emperor's views on dogma, discipline, and church administration prevailed at Rome. This authority began to unravel in the seventh century. In 691, Emperor Justinian II convened a council that determined 102 rules for the church, and he sent them to Rome for papal endorsement. Most of the rules were unobjectionable, but Pope Sergius I (r. 687 or 689–701) was unwilling to agree to the whole because it permitted priestly marriages (which the Roman church did not want to allow) and it prohibited fasting on Saturdays in Lent (which the Roman church required). Outraged by Sergius's refusal, Justinian tried to arrest the pope, but Italian armies (theoretically under the emperor) came to the pontiff's aid, while Justinian's arresting officer cowered under the pope's bed. The incident reveals that some local forces were already willing to rally to the side of the pope against the emperor. By now Constantinople's influence and authority over Rome was tenuous at best. Sheer distance, as well as diminishing imperial power in Italy, meant the popes were in effect the leaders of the parts of Italy not controlled by the Lombards.

The gap between Byzantium and the papacy widened in the early eighth century as Emperor Leo III tried to increase the taxes on papal property to pay for his all-consuming war against the Arab invaders. The pope responded by leading a general tax revolt. Meanwhile, Leo's fierce policy of iconoclasm collided with the pope's tolerance of images. In the West, Christian piety focused not so much on icons as on relics, but the papacy was not willing to allow sacred images and icons to be destroyed. The pope argued that holy images could and should be venerated—but not worshiped. His support of images reflected popular opinion as well. A later commentator wrote that iconoclasm so infuriated the inhabitants of Ravenna and Venice that "if the pope had not prohibited the people, they would have attempted to set up a [different] emperor over themselves."

These difficulties with the emperor were matched by increasing friction between the pope

MAPPING THE WEST Europe and the Mediterranean, c. 750
The major political fact of the period 600–750 was the emergence of Islam and the conquest of an Islamic state that reached from Spain to the Indus River. The Byzantine Empire, once a great power, was dwarfed—and half swallowed up—by its Islamic neighbor. To the west were fledgling barbarian kingdoms, mere trifles on the world stage. The next centuries, however, would prove their resourcefulness and durability.

and the Lombards. The Lombard kings had gradually managed to bring under their control the duchies of Spoleto and Benevento as well as part of the Exarchate of Ravenna. By the mid-eighth century, the popes feared that Rome would fall to the Lombards, and Pope Zachary (r. 741–752) looked northward for friends. He created an ally by sanctioning the deposition of the last Merovingian king and his replacement by the first Carolingian king, Pippin III the Short (r. 751–768). In 753, a subsequent pope, Stephen II (r. 752–757), called on Pippin to march to Italy with an army to fight the Lombards. Thus events at Rome had a major impact on the history not only of Italy but of the Frankish kingdom as well.

Conclusion

The three heirs of the Roman Empire—Byzantines, Muslims, and the peoples of the West—built upon three distinct legacies. Byzantium directly inherited the central political institutions of Rome; its people called themselves Romans; its emperor was the Roman emperor; and its capital, Constantinople, was the new Rome. Sixth-century Byzantium also inherited the cities, laws, and religion of Rome. The changes of the seventh and eighth centuries—contraction of territory, urban decline, disappearance of the old elite, a ban on sacred images—whittled away at this Roman character. By 750, Byzantium was less Roman than it was a new, resilient political and cultural entity, a Christian polity on the borders of the new Muslim empire.

Muslims were the newcomers to the Roman world, with Islam influenced by Jewish monotheism and only indirectly by Roman Christianity. Under the guidance of the Prophet Muhammad, Islam became both a coherent theology and a tightly structured way of life with customs based on Bedouin tribal life and defined in the Qur'an. Once the Muslim Arabs embarked on military conquests, however, they too became heirs of Rome, preserving its cities, hiring its civil servants, and adopting its artistic styles. Drawing upon Roman and Persian traditions, the Muslims created a powerful Islamic state, with a capital city in Syria, regional urban centers elsewhere, and a culture that tolerated a wide variety of economic, religious, and social institutions so long as the conquered paid taxes to their Muslim overlords.

The West also inherited Roman institutions and transformed them with great diversity. Frankish Gaul built on Roman traditions that had long been transformed by provincial and Germanic custom. In Italy and at Rome itself, the traditions of the classical past remained living parts of the fabric of life. The roads remained, the cities of Italy survived (although depopulated), and both the popes and the Lombard kings ruled in the traditions of Roman government. In Spain, the Visigothic kings allied themselves with a Hispano-Roman elite that maintained elements of the organization and vigorous intellectual traditions of the late empire. In England, however, once the far-flung northern summit of the Roman Empire, the Roman legacy had to be reimported in the seventh century.

All three heirs to Rome suffered the ravages of war. In all three societies the social hierarchy became simpler, with the loss of "middle" groups like the *curiales* at Byzantium and the near-suppression of tribal affiliations among Muslims. As each of the three heirs shaped Roman institutions to its own uses and advantages, each also strove to create a religious polity. In Byzantium, the emperor was a religious force, presiding over the destruction of images. In the Islamic world, the caliph was the successor to Muhammad, a religious and political leader. In the West, the kings allied with churchmen in order to rule. Despite their many differences, all

these leaders had a common understanding of their place in a divine scheme: they were God's agents on earth, ruling over God's people.

Suggested References

Byzantium: A Christian Empire under Siege

While some scholars (Ousterhout and Brubaker, Weitzmann) concentrate on religion, culture, and the role of icons, others (Treadgold, Whittow) tend to stress politics and war.

The Byzantine Studies Page: http://www.bway.net/~halsall/byzantium.html.

*Geanakoplos, Deno John, ed. and trans. *Byzantium: Church, Society, and Civilization Seen through Contemporary Eyes.* 1986.

Haldon, J. F. *Byzantium in the Seventh Century: The Transformation of a Culture.* 1990.

Norwich, John Julius. *Byzantium: The Early Centuries.* 1989.

Ousterhout, Robert, and Leslie Brubaker. *The Sacred Image East and West.* 1995.

Treadgold, Warren. *A History of the Byzantine State and Society.* 1997.

Weitzmann, Kurt. *The Icon: Holy Images, Sixth to Fourteenth Century.* 1978.

Whittow, Mark. *The Making of Byzantium, 600–1025.* 1996.

Islam: A New Religion and a New Empire

The classic (and as yet unsurpassed) discussion is in Hodgson. Crone's book is considered highly controversial; Kennedy's is useful to consult for basic facts.

Ahmed, Leila. *Women and Gender in Islam: Historical Roots of a Modern Debate.* 1992.

Crone, Patricia. *Meccan Trade and the Rise of Islam.* 1987.

Donner, Fred McGraw. *The Early Islamic Conquests.* 1981.

Hodgson, Marshall G. S. *The Venture of Islam: Conscience and History in a World Civilization.* Vol. 1, *The Classical Age of Islam.* 1974.

Islamic Sourcebook: http://www.fordham.edu/halsall/islam/islamsbook.html.

Kennedy, Hugh. *The Prophet and the Age of the Caliphates: The Islamic Near East from the Sixth to the Eleventh Century.* 1986.

Lapidus, Ira. *A History of Islamic Societies.* 1988.

*Lewis, Bernard, ed. and trans. *Islam: From the Prophet Muhammad to the Capture of Constantinople.* 2 vols. 1987.

*Primary sources.

Ruthven, Malise. *Islam in the World.* 1984.

Waddy, Charis. *Women in Muslim History.* 1980.

The Western Kingdoms

Wood and Geary provide complementary guides to the Merovingian world. Goffart suggests important ways to read primary sources from the period. Recent keen historical interest in the role of the cults of the saints in early medieval society is reflected in Van Dam.

*Bede. *A History of the English Church and People.* Trans. Leo Sherley-Price. 1991.

Collins, Roger. *Early Medieval Spain: Unity in Diversity, 400–1000.* 1983.

*Fouracre, Paul, and Richard A. Gerberding. *Late Merovingian France: History and Hagiography, 640–720.* 1996.

Geary, Patrick. *Before France and Germany: The Creation and Transformation of the Merovingian World.* 1988.

Goffart, Walter. *The Narrators of Barbarian History* (A.D. 550–800): *Jordanes, Gregory of Tours, Bede, and Paul the Deacon.* 1988.

*Gregory of Tours. *The History of the Franks.* Trans. Lewis Thorpe. 1976.

Gregory of Tours: http://www.unipissing.ca/department/history/4505/show.htm.

Riché, Pierre. *Education and Culture in the Barbarian West: Sixth through Eighth Centuries.* Trans. by John J. Contreni. 1975.

Van Dam, Raymond. *Saints and Their Miracles in Late Antique Gaul.* 1993.

Wood, Ian. *The Merovingian Kingdoms, 450–751.* 1994.

Unity and Diversity in Three Societies

750–1050

Ivory Situla

This situla was carved out of ivory to hold the holy water that was used in the consecration of the emperor, probably Otto III, who became emperor in 996. The carving depicts important personages. At the top is the crowned emperor, holding the symbols of his universal power, the scepter and orb; looking out from the left is the pope, giving his blessing; in the other niches are archbishops, bishops, and an abbot. Below are armed guards. The whole ensemble suggests equality and concord between the emperor and the church.
Ann Munchow/Das Domkapital.

IN 841, A FIFTEEN-YEAR-OLD BOY NAMED WILLIAM went to serve at the court of the king of the Franks, Charles the Bald. William's father was Bernard, an extremely powerful noble. His mother was Dhuoda, a well-educated, pious, and able woman; she administered the family's estates in the south of France while her husband occupied himself in court politics and royal administration. In 841, however, politics had become a dangerous business. King Charles, named after his grandfather Charlemagne, was fighting with his brothers over his portion of the Carolingian Empire, and Bernard (who had been a supporter of Charles's father, Louis the Pious) held a precarious position at the young king's court. In fact, William was sent to Charles's court as a kind of hostage, to ensure Bernard's loyalty. Anxious about her son, Dhuoda wanted to educate and counsel him, so she wrote a handbook of advice for William, outlining what he ought to believe about God, about politics and society, about obligations to his family, and, above all, about his duties to his father, which she emphasized even over loyalty to the king:

> In the human understanding of things, royal and imperial appearance and power seem preeminent in the world, and the custom of men is to account those men's actions and their names ahead of all others. . . . But despite all this . . . I caution you to render first to him whose son you are special, faithful, steadfast loyalty as long as you shall live.

William heeded his mother's words, with tragic results: when Bernard ran afoul of Charles and was executed, William died in a failed attempt to avenge his father.

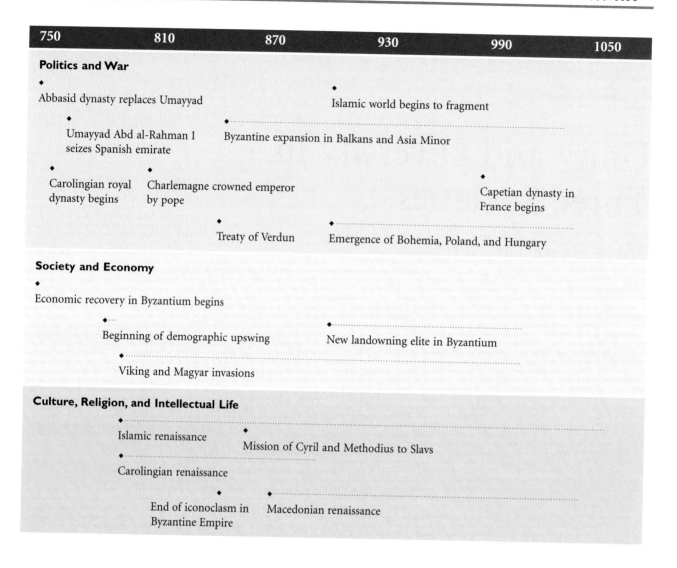

750	810	870	930	990	1050

Politics and War

Abbasid dynasty replaces Umayyad

Islamic world begins to fragment

Umayyad Abd al-Rahman I seizes Spanish emirate

Byzantine expansion in Balkans and Asia Minor

Carolingian royal dynasty begins

Charlemagne crowned emperor by pope

Capetian dynasty in France begins

Treaty of Verdun

Emergence of Bohemia, Poland, and Hungary

Society and Economy

Economic recovery in Byzantium begins

Beginning of demographic upswing

New landowning elite in Byzantium

Viking and Magyar invasions

Culture, Religion, and Intellectual Life

Islamic renaissance

Mission of Cyril and Methodius to Slavs

Carolingian renaissance

End of iconoclasm in Byzantine Empire

Macedonian renaissance

Dhuoda's handbook reveals the volatile political atmosphere of the mid-ninth century, and her advice to her son points to one of its causes: a crisis of loyalty. Loyalty to emperors, caliphs, and kings—all of whom were symbols of unity cutting across regional and family ties—competed with allegiances to local authorities; and those, in turn, vied with family loyalties. The period 600–750 had seen the startling rise of Islam, the whittling away of Byzantium, and the beginnings of stable political and economic development in an impoverished West. The period 750–1050 would see all three societies contend with internal issues of diversity even as they became increasingly conscious of their unity and uniqueness. At the beginning of this period,

rulers built up and dominated strong and united polities. By the end, these realms had fragmented into smaller, more local, units. While men and women continued to feel some loyalty toward faraway kings, caliphs, or emperors, their most powerful allegiances often focused on authorities closer to home.

At Byzantium, the military triumphs of the emperors brought them enormous prestige. A renaissance of culture and art took place at Constantinople. Yet at the same time the *strategoi*, the new-style military generals whose positions had been created in the seventh century, began to increase their power and dominate the Byzantine countryside. In the Islamic world, a dynastic revolution in 750 ousted the Umayyads from the caliphate and replaced them with a new family, the Abbasids. The new caliphs moved their capital to the east and adopted some elements of the persona of the Sassanid King of Kings. Yet their power too began to ebb as regional Islamic rulers came to the fore. In the West, Charlemagne—a Frankish king from a new dynasty, the Carolingians—forged an empire that embraced most of Europe. Yet this new unified polity, like the others, turned out to be fragile, disintegrating within a generation of his death. Indeed, in the West, even more than in the Byzantine and Islamic worlds, power fell into the hands of local strongmen.

All along the fringes of these realms, new political entities began to develop, conditioned by the religion and culture of their more dominant neighbors. Russia grew up in the shadow of Byzantium, as did Bulgaria and Serbia. The West was more crucial in the development of central Europe. By the year 1050, the contours of modern Europe and the Middle East were dimly visible.

❖ Byzantium: Renewed Strength and Influence

In the hundred years between 750 and 850, Byzantium staved off Muslim attacks in Asia Minor and began to rebuild itself. After 850, it went on the attack, and by 900 it had reconquered some of the territory it had lost. Military victory brought new wealth and power to the imperial court, and the emperors supported a vast program of literary and artistic revival—the Macedonian renaissance—at Constantinople. But while the emperor dominated at the capital, a new landowning elite began to control the countryside. On its northern front, Byzantium helped create new Slavic realms.

Imperial Might

The seventh-century imperial reorganization of the Byzantine army into *themes* proved effective against Islamic armies. Avoiding battles in the field, the Byzantines allowed Muslim warriors to enter their territory, but they evacuated the local populations and burned any extra food. Then they waited in their fortified strongholds for the Muslims to attack.

In this way they fought from a position of strength. If the Muslims decided to withdraw, other Byzantine troops were ready at the border to ambush them.

Beginning around 850 and lasting until 1025, the Byzantines turned the tables. They began advancing on all fronts. By the 1020s, they had regained Antioch, Crete, and Bulgaria (Map 9.1). They had not controlled so much territory since their wars with the Sassanids four hundred years earlier.

Victories such as these gave new prestige to the army and to the imperial court. New wealth matched this prestige. The emperors drew revenues from vast and growing imperial estates. They could tax and demand services from the general population at will—requiring them to build bridges and roads, to offer lodging to the imperial retinue, and to pay taxes in cash. These taxes increased over time, partly because of fiscal reforms and partly because of population increases (the approximately seven million people who lived in the empire in 780 had swelled to about eight million less than a century later).

The emperor's power extended over both civil administration and military command. The only check on imperial authority was the possibility of an uprising, either at court or in the army. For this reason, among others, emperors surrounded themselves with eunuchs—castrated men who were believed unfit to become emperors themselves and who were unable to have sons to challenge the imperial dynasty. Eunuchs were employed in the civil service; they held high positions in the army; and they were important palace officials. Eunuchs had a privileged place in Byzantine administrations because they were less likely than others to have an independent power base.

Emperors, supported by their wealth and power, negotiated from a position of strength with other rulers. Ambassadors were exchanged, and the Byzantine court received and entertained diplomats with elaborate ceremonies. One such diplomat, Liutprand, bishop of the Northern Italian city of Cremona, reported on his audience with Emperor Constantine VII Porphyrogenitos (r. 913–959):

Leaning upon the shoulders of two eunuchs I was brought into the emperor's presence. At my approach [mechanical] lions began to roar and birds to cry out, each according to its kind. . . . After I

MAP 9.1 The Expansion of Byzantium, 860–1025
In 860, the Byzantine Empire was a shrunken hourglass. To the west, it had lost most of Italy, to the east, it held only part of Asia Minor. On its northern flank, the Bulgarians had set up an independent state. By 1025, however, it had become a barbell, its western half embracing the whole Balkans, its eastern arm extending around the Black Sea, and its southern fringe reaching nearly to Tripoli. The year 1025 marked the Byzantine Empire at its greatest extent after the rise of Islam.

had three times made obeisance to the emperor with my face upon the ground, I lifted my head, and behold! the man whom just before I had seen sitting on a moderately elevated seat had now changed his raiment and was sitting on the level of the ceiling. How it was done I could not imagine, unless perhaps he was lifted up by some such sort of device as we use for raising the timbers of a wine press.

Although this elaborate court ceremonial clearly amused Liutprand, its real function was to express the serious, sacred, concentrated power of imperial majesty. Liutprand missed the point because he was a westerner unaccustomed to such displays.

The emperor's wealth relied on the prosperity of an agricultural economy organized for trade. State regulation and entrepreneurial enterprise were delicately balanced in Byzantine commerce. Although the emperor controlled craft and commercial guilds (such as those of the silk industry) to ensure imperial revenues and a stable supply of valuable and useful commodities, entrepreneurs organized most of the fairs held throughout the empire. Foreign merchants traded within the empire, either at Constantinople or in some border cities. Because this international trade intertwined with foreign policy, the Byzantine government considered trade a political as well as an economic matter. Emperors issued privileges to certain "nations" (as, for example, the Venetians, Russians, and Jews were called), regulating the fees they were obliged to pay and the services they had to render. At the end of the tenth century, for example, the Venetians bargained to reduce their customs dues per ship from thirty *solidi* (coins) to two; in return they promised to transport Byzantine soldiers to Italy whenever the emperor wished.

Merchants from each nation were lodged at state expense within the city for about three months to transact their business. The Syrians, although Muslims, received special privileges: their merchants were allowed to stay at Constantinople for six months. In return, Byzantine traders were guaranteed protection in Syria, and the two governments split the income from the taxes on the sales Byzantine merchants made there. Thus Byzantine trade flourished in the Levant (the region bordering the southeastern Mediterranean) and, thanks to Venetian intermediaries, with the Latin West.

Equally significant was trade to the north. Byzantines may have mocked the "barbarians," dressed in animal skins, who lived beyond the Black Sea. Nevertheless, many Byzantines wore furs from Russia and imported Russian slaves, wax, and honey. Some Russians even served as mercenaries in the Byzantine army. The relationship between the two peoples became even closer at the end of the tenth century.

The Macedonian Renaissance, c. 870–c. 1025

Flush with victory, reminded of Byzantium's past glory, the emperors now revived classical intellectual pursuits. Basil I (r. 867–886) from Macedonia founded the imperial dynasty that presided over the so-called Macedonian renaissance (c. 870–c. 1025). The *renaissance* (French for "rebirth") was made possible by an intellectual elite, who came from families that, even in the anxious years of the eighth century, had persisted in studying the classics in spite of the trend toward a simple religious education.

Now, with the empire slowly regaining its military eminence and with icons permanently restored in 843, this scholarly elite thrived again. Byzantine artists produced new works of art, and emperors and other members of the new court society, liberated from sober taboos, sponsored sumptuous artistic productions. Emperor Constantine Porphyrogenitos wrote books of geography and history and financed the work of other scholars and artists. He even supervised the details of his craftspeople's products, insisting on exacting standards: "Who could enumerate how many artisans the Porphyrogenitos corrected? He corrected the stonemasons, the carpenters, the goldsmiths, the silversmiths, and the blacksmiths," wrote a historian supported by the same emperor's patronage.

Silk Chasuble
The crimson silk of this garment was woven at Constantinople around 972, a good example of the fine silk production characteristic of the Byzantine capital during this period. Its history illustrates both the close relationship between east and west and the ways in which gifts of precious items were used to cement diplomatic relations. The Byzantine princess Theophanu took the silk as part of her dowry when she went west to marry Emperor Otto II. Then either she, her husband, or one of his successors gave it to Albuin (975–1006), the powerful and saintly bishop of Bressanone (today in Italy). He had it made into a chasuble, the sleeveless tunic worn by priests during church services.
Diozesanmuseum, Brixen

The Crowning of Constantine Porphyrogenitos
This ivory plaque was carved at Constantinople in the mid-tenth century. The artist wanted to emphasize hierarchy and symbolism, not nature. Christ is shown crowning Emperor Constantine Porphyrogenitos (r. 913–959). What message do you suppose the artist wanted to telegraph by making Christ higher than the emperor by having the empire slightly incline his head and upper torso to receive the crown?
Hirmer Fotoarchiv, München.

Other members of the imperial court also sponsored writers, philosophers, and historians. Scholars wrote summaries of classical literature, encyclopedias of ancient knowledge, and commentaries on classical authors. Others copied manuscripts of religious and theological commentaries, such as homilies, liturgical texts, Bibles, and Psalters. They hoped to revive the intellectual and artistic achievements of the heyday of imperial Roman rule. But the Macedonian renaissance could not possibly succeed

in this endeavor: too much had changed since the time of Justinian. Nevertheless, the renaissance permanently integrated classical forms into Byzantine political and religious life.

The merging of classical and Christian traditions is clearest in manuscript illuminations (painted illustrations or embellishments in hand-copied manuscripts). Both at Byzantium and in the West, artists chose their subjects by considering the texts they were to illustrate and the ways in which previous artists had handled particular themes. They drew upon traditional models to make their subjects identifiable. As a modern illustrator of Santa Claus relies on a tradition dictating a plump man with a bushy white beard—Santa's "iconography"—medieval artists depended on particular visual cues. For example, to illustrate King David, the supposed poet of the Psalms, an artist illuminating a Psalter turned to a model of Orpheus, the enchanting musician of Greek mythology.

A New Landowning Elite

Alongside the revived imperial court and the scholarly and artistic upper class at Constantinople, a vital new elite group, tied to the countryside, developed in the eighth century. This rural elite was an unanticipated outcome of the *theme* organization. The heirs of some of the peasant-soldiers settled on virtually tax-free land, adding to their holdings and forming a new class of large landowners. Many smaller peasants, unable or unwilling to pay their taxes, were compelled to give up their small freeholds to become dependents of these great landlords. Subjugated to their overlords, they still tilled the soil, but they no longer owned it.

The most powerful of the large landowners were the generals, the *strategoi,* who had been set up as imperial appointees to rule the *themes* and who now found their prestige enhanced by victory. The *strategoi* took orders from the imperial palace, which did not always mean from the emperor, for within the period 756–1054 three powerful women ruled, generally as regents for their young sons. The *strategoi* also exercised considerable power on their own. One *strategos,* Michael Lachanodracon, disbanded the monasteries in his *theme* and sold off their property on his own initiative, sending the proceeds to the imperial treasury as a gesture of camaraderie. Although individual *strategoi* could be demoted or dismissed by irate emperors, most *strategoi* formed a powerful hereditary class of landowners. In these ways, the social hierarchy of Byzantium began to resemble that of western Europe, where grand estates owned by aristocrats were farmed by a subject peasantry whose tax and service obligations bound them to the fields that they cultivated.

New States under the Influence of Byzantium

The shape of modern eastern European states— Bulgaria, Serbia, and Russia—grew out of the Slavic polities created during the period 850–950. By 800, Slavic settlements dotted the area from the Danube River down to Greece and from the Black Sea to Croatia. The Bulgar khagan ruled over the largest realm, populated mostly by Slavic peoples and situated northwest of Constantinople. Under Khagan Krum (r. c. 803–814) and his son, Slavic rule stretched west all the way to the Tisza River in modern Hungary. At about the same time as Krum's triumphant expansion, however, the Byzantine Empire began its own campaigns to conquer, convert, and control these Slavic regions.

The Balkans, c. 850–950

Bulgaria and Serbia. The Byzantine offensive began under Emperor Nicephorus I (r. 802–811), who waged war against the Slavs of Greece in the Peloponnesus, set up a new Christian diocese there, organized it as a new military *theme,* and forcibly resettled Christians in the area to counteract Slavic paganism. The Byzantines followed this pattern of conquest as they pushed northward. By 900, Byzantium ruled all of Greece.

Still under Nicephorus, the Byzantines launched a massive attack against the Bulgarians, took the chief city of Pliska, plundered it, burned it to the ground, and then marched against Krum's encampment in the Balkan mountains. Krum took advantage of his position, however, attacked the imperial troops, killed Nicephorus, and brought home the emperor's skull in triumph. Cleaned out and lined with silver, the skull served as the victorious Krum's drinking goblet. In 816, the two sides agreed to a peace that lasted for thirty years. But hostility remained, and wars between the Bulgarians and Byzantines broke out with increasing intensity. Intermittent skirmishes gave way to longer wars throughout the tenth century. The Byzantines advanced, at first taking Bulgaria's eastern territory. Then, in a slow and methodical conquest (1001– 1018) led by Emperor Basil II (r. 976–1025), aptly called the "Bulgar-Slayer" (Bulgaroctonos), they subjected the entire region to Byzantine rule and forced its ruler to accept the Byzantine form of Christianity. Similarly the Serbs, encouraged by Byzantium to oppose the Bulgarians, began to form the state that would become Serbia, in the shadow of Byzantine interest and religion.

Religion played an important role in the Byzantine offensive. In 863, two brothers, Cyril and Methodius, were sent as missionaries from Byzantium to the Slavs. Well-educated Greeks, they spoke one Slavic dialect fluently and devised an alphabet for Slavic (until then an oral language) based on Greek forms. It was the ancestor of the modern Cyrillic alphabet used in Bulgaria, Serbia, and Russia.

Kievan Russia. Russia in the ninth and tenth centuries lay outside the sphere of direct Byzantine rule, but like Serbia and Bulgaria, it came under increasingly strong Byzantine cultural and religious influence. Vikings—Scandinavian adventurers who ranged over vast stretches of ninth-century Europe seeking trade, booty, and land—had penetrated Russia from the north and imposed their rule over the Slavs inhabiting the broad river valleys connecting the Baltic Sea with the Black Sea and thence with Constantinople. Like the Bulgars in Bulgaria, the Scandinavian Vikings gradually blended into the larger Slavic population. At the end of the ninth century, one Dnieper valley chief, Oleg, established control over most of the tribes in southwestern Russia and forced peoples farther away to pay tribute. The tribal association he created formed the nucleus of Kievan Russia, named for the city that had become the commercial center of the region and is today the capital of Ukraine.

Kievan Russia and Byzantium began their relationship with war, developed it through trade agreements, and finally sustained it by religion. Around 905, Oleg launched a military expedition to

Constantinople, forcing the Byzantines to pay a large indemnity and open their doors to Russian traders in exchange for peace. At the time, only a few Christians lived in Russia, along with Jews and probably some Muslims. The Russians' conversion to Christianity was spearheaded by a Russian ruler later in the century. Vladimir (r. c. 980–1015), the grand prince of Kiev and all Russia, and the Byzantine emperor Basil II agreed that Vladimir should adopt the Byzantine form of Christianity. Vladimir took a variant of the name Basil in honor of the emperor and married the emperor's sister Anne; then he reportedly had all the people of his state baptized in the Dnieper River.

Vladimir's conversion represented a wider pattern. Along with the Christianization of Slavic realms such as Old Moravia, Serbia, and Bulgaria under the Byzantine church, the rulers and peoples of Poland, Hungary, Denmark, and Norway were converted under the auspices of the Roman church. Russia's conversion to Christianity was especially significant, because Russia was geographically as close to the Islamic world as to the Christian and could conceivably have become an Islamic land. By converting to Byzantine Christianity, Russians made themselves heir to Byzantium and its church, customs, art, and political ideology. Adopting Christianity linked Russia to the Christian world, but choosing Byzantine rather than Roman Christianity served to isolate Russia later from western Europe, because in time the Greek and Roman churches would become estranged.

Four Daughters of Iaroslav the Wise

Imitating the Byzantines, who had a church of St. Sophia (Holy Wisdom) in their capital at Constantinople, Iaroslav the Wise built his own church of Holy Wisdom at Kiev. Iaroslav was in contact with Europe as well as with Byzantium, and his church contains a hint of those interests. On its walls are frescoes (paintings on fresh plaster) of his daughters, portrayed as pious members of the church. But they were also pawns of diplomacy. Just as silks could cement good relations (see page 311), so too could marriages. Iaroslav had his oldest daughter marry the king of Norway; the second married the king of France, Henry I; and the third married the king of Hungary.
Photo courtesy Thames and Hudson Ltd., London, from *The Dark Ages*, 1975.

Russian rulers at times sought to cement relations with central and western Europe, which were tied to Rome. Prince Iaroslav the Wise (r. 1019–1054) forged such links through his own marriage and those of his sons and daughters to rulers and princely families in France, Hungary, and Scandinavia. Iaroslav encouraged intellectual and artistic developments that would connect Russian culture to the classical past. According to an account written about a half-century after his death, Iaroslav

> applied himself to books and read them continually day and night. He assembled many scribes to translate from the Greek into Slavic. He caused many books to be written and collected, through which true believers are instructed and enjoy religious education.

At his own church of St. Sophia, at Kiev, which copied the one at Constantinople, Iaroslav created a major library.

When Iaroslav died, his kingdom was divided among his sons. Civil wars broke out between the brothers and eventually between cousins, shredding what unity Russia had known. Massive invasions by outsiders, particularly from the east, further weakened Kievan rulers, who were eventually displaced by princes from northern Russia. At the crossroads of East and West, Russia could meet and adopt a great variety of traditions; but its situation also opened it to unremitting military pressures.

❖ From Unity to Fragmentation in the Islamic World

A new dynasty of caliphs—the Abbasids—first brought unity and then, in their decline, fragmentation to the Islamic world. Caliphs continued to rule in name only, while regional rulers took over the real business of government in Islamic lands. Local traditions based on religious and political differences played an increasingly important role in people's lives. Yet, even in the eleventh century, the Islamic world had a clear sense of its own unity, based on language, commercial life, and vigorous intellectual give-and-take across regional boundaries.

The Abbasid Caliphate, 750–c. 950

In 750, a civil war ousted the Umayyads and raised the Abbasids to the caliphate. The Abbasids found support in an uneasy coalition of Shi'ites (the faction loyal to Ali's memory) and non-Arabs who had been excluded from Umayyad government and now demanded a place in political life. The new regime signaled a revolution. The center of the Islamic state shifted from Damascus, with its roots in the Roman tradition, to Baghdad, a new capital city, built by the Abbasids right next to Ctesiphon, which had been the Sassanid capital. Here the Abbasid caliphs imitated the Persian King of Kings and adopted the court ceremony of the Sassanids. Their administration grew more and more centralized: the caliph controlled the appointment of regional governors; his staff grew, and their jobs became more complex. Although some Shi'ites were reconciled to this new regime, a minority continued to tend the flame of Ali's memory and the justice and purity it stood for.

The Abbasid caliph Harun al-Rashid (r. 786–809) presided over a flourishing empire from Baghdad. (He and his court are immortalized in *Thousands and One Nights,* a series of anonymous stories about Scheherezade's efforts to keep her husband from killing her by telling him a story each night for 1,001 nights.) Charlemagne, Harun's contemporary, was very impressed with the elephant Harun sent him as a gift, along with monkeys, spices, and medicines. But these items were mainstays of everyday commerce in Harun's Iraq. For example, a mid-ninth-century list of imports inventoried "tigers, panthers, elephants, panther skins, rubies, white sandal, ebony, and coconuts" from India; "silk, chinaware, paper, ink, peacocks, racing horses, saddles, felts [and] cinnamon" from China.

The Abbasid dynasty began to decline after Harun's death, mostly because of economic problems. Obliged to support a huge army and increasingly complex civil service, the Abbasids found their tax base inadequate. They needed to collect revenues from their provinces, such as Syria and Egypt, but the governors of those regions often refused to send the revenues. After Harun's caliphate, ex-soldiers, seeking better salaries, recognized different caliphs and fought for power in savage civil wars. The caliphs tried to bypass the regular army, made up largely of free Muslim foot soldiers, by turning to slaves, bought and armed to serve as mounted cavalry. This tactic failed, however, and in the tenth century the caliphs became figureheads only, as independent rulers established themselves in the various Islamic regions. To support themselves militarily, many of these new rulers came to depend on independent military commanders who led armies of Mamluks—Turkish slaves or freedmen trained as professional mounted soldiers. Mamluks were well paid to maintain their mounts and arms, and many gained renown and high positions at the courts of regional rulers.

Thus in the Islamic world, as in the Byzantine Empire, a new military elite arose. But the Muslim

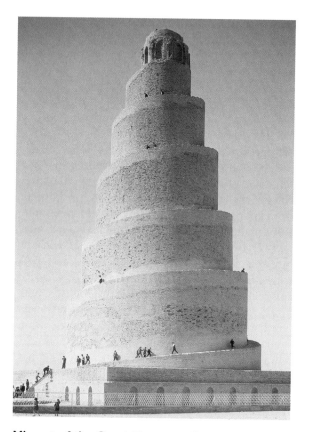

Minaret of the Great Mosque at Samarra
In 836 the Abbasid caliphs moved their capital from Baghdad to Samarra, about seventy miles north. In part, this was a response to the very tensions that produced the separate Islamic states of the tenth century. At Samarra, the Abbasid court created a cultural center, with the Great Mosque, begun in 847, the largest ever built. Shown here is its minaret (the tower from which Muslims are summoned to prayer) looming over the mosque some distance from its outer wall. Scholars are still debating the reasons for its spiral shape. Bildarchiv Preußischer Kulturbesitz.

and Byzantine elites differed in key ways. Whereas the Byzantine *strategoi* were rooted in particular regions, the Mamluks were highly mobile. They were not tied to specific estates but rather were paid from rents collected by the local government. Organized into tightly knit companies bound together by devotion to a particular general and by a strong camaraderie, they easily changed employers, moving from ruler to ruler for pay.

Regional Diversity

A faraway caliph could not command sufficient allegiance from local leaders once he demanded more in taxes than he gave back in favors. The forces of fragmentation were strong in the Islamic world: it was, after all, based on the conquest of many diverse regions, each with its own deeply rooted traditions and culture. The Islamic religion, with its Sunni/Shi'ite split, also became a source of polarization. Western Europeans knew almost nothing about Muslims and called them all *Saracens* (from the Latin for "Arabs") without distinction. But, in fact, Muslims were of different ethnicities, practiced different customs, and identified with different regions. With the fragmentation of political and religious unity, each of the tenth- and early-eleventh-century Islamic states built upon local traditions under local rulers (Map 9.2).

The Fatimid Dynasty. In the tenth century, one group of Shi'ites, calling themselves the Fatimids (after Fatimah, wife of Ali and Muhammad's only surviving child), began a successful political movement. Allying with the Berbers in North Africa, the Fatimids established themselves in 909 as rulers in the region now called Tunisia. The Fatimid Ubayd Allah claimed to be not only the true imam, descendant of Ali, but also the *mahdi*, the "divinely guided" messiah, come to bring justice on earth. In 969, the Fatimids declared themselves rulers of Egypt. Their dynasty lasted for about two hundred years. Fatimid leaders also controlled North Africa, Arabia, and even Syria for a time.

The Spanish Emirate. Whereas the Shi'ites dominated Egypt, Sunni Muslims ruled al-Andalus, the Islamic central and southern heart of Spain. Unlike the other independent Islamic states, which were forged during the ninth and tenth centuries, the

MAP 9.2 Islamic States, c. 1000
A glance back at Map 8.3 on page 285 will quickly demonstrate the fragmentation of the once united Islamic caliphate. In 750, one caliph ruled territory stretching from Spain to India. In 1000, there was more than one caliphate as well as several other ruling dynasties. The most important were the Fatimids, who began as organizers of a movement to overthrow the Abbasids. By 1000, they had conquered Egypt and claimed hegemony over all of North Africa and even Sicily.

Spanish emirate of Córdoba (so called because its ruler took the secular title *emir,* "commander," and fixed his capital at Córdoba) was created near the start of the Abbasid caliphate, in 756. During the Abbasid revolution, Abd al-Rahman—a member of the Umayyad family—fled to Morocco, gathered an army, invaded Spain, and was declared emir after only one battle. He and his successors ruled a broad range of peoples, including many Jews and Christians. After the initial Islamic conquest of Spain, the Christians adopted so much of the new language and so many of the customs that they were called *Mozarabs,* that is, "like Arabs." The Arabs allowed them freedom of worship and let them live according to their own laws. Some Mozarabs were content with their status; others converted to Islam; still others intermarried—most commonly, Christian women married Muslim men and raised their children as Muslims.

Under Abd al-Rahman III (r. 912–961), who took the title caliph in 929, members of all religious groups in al-Andalus were given absolute freedom of worship and equal opportunity to rise in the civil service. Abd al-Rahman initiated important diplomatic contracts with Byzantine and European rulers. He felt strong enough not to worry much about the weak and tiny Christian kingdoms squeezed into northern Spain. Yet al-Andalus, too, experienced the same political fragmentation that was occurring everywhere else. In 1031, the caliphate of Córdoba broke up, as rulers of small, independent regions, called *taifas,* took power.

Unity of Commerce and Language

Although the regions of the Islamic world were diverse, they maintained a measure of unity through trade networks and language. Their principal bond was Arabic, the language of the Qur'an. At once poetic and sacred, Arabic was also the language of commerce and government from Baghdad to Córdoba. Moreover, despite political differences, borders were open: an artisan could move from Córdoba to Cairo; a landowner in Morocco might very well own property in al-Andalus; a young man from North Africa would think nothing of going to Baghdad to find a wife; a young girl purchased as a slave in Mecca might become part of a prince's

Dome of the Mihrab of the Great Mosque at Córdoba *The mihrab is the prayer niche of the mosque, located across from the entrance, in such a way that the worshiper facing it is thereby facing Mecca. For the one at Córdoba, built between 961 and 976 by the Andalusian caliph al-Hakam, Byzantine mosaicists were imported to produce a decoration that would recall the mosaics of the Great Mosque at Damascus (see page 270). Why would this caliph, a Umayyad, be particularly interested in reminding Andalusians of the Damascus mosque?* Institut Amatller d'Art Hispanic, Barcelona.

harem in Baghdad. With no national barriers to trade and few regulations (though every city and town had its own customs dues), traders regularly dealt in far-flung, various, and often exotic goods.

Although the primary reason for this internationalism was Islam itself, open borders extended to non-Muslims as well. The Tustari brothers, Jewish merchants from southern Iran, typified the commercial activity in the Arabic-speaking world. By 1026, they had established a flourishing business in Egypt. The Tustaris did not have "branch offices," but informal contacts allowed them many of the same advantages and much flexibility: friends and family in Iran shipped them fine textiles to sell in Egypt, and the Tustaris exported Egyptian fabrics to sell in Iran. (See "New Sources, New Perspectives," page 320.) Dealing in fabrics could yield fabulous wealth, for cloth was essential not only for clothing but also for home decoration: textiles covered walls; curtains separated rooms. The Tustari brothers held the highest rank in Jewish society and had contacts with Muslim rulers. The son of one of the brothers converted to Islam and became *vizier* (chief minis-

ter) to the Fatimids in Egypt. But the sophisticated Islamic society of the tenth and eleventh centuries supported networks even more vast than those represented by the Tustari family. Muslim merchants brought tin from England; salt and gold from Timbuktu in west-central Africa; amber, gold, and copper from Russia; and slaves from every region.

The Islamic Renaissance, c. 790–c. 1050

The dissolution of the caliphate into separate political entities multiplied the centers of learning and intellectual productivity. Unlike the Macedonian renaissance of Byzantium, which was concentrated in Constantinople, a "renaissance of Islam" occurred throughout the Islamic world. It was particularly dazzling in urban court centers such as Córdoba, where tenth-century rulers presided over a brilliant court culture. They patronized scholars, poets, and artists, and their library at Córdoba contained the largest collection of books in Europe.

Elsewhere, already in the eighth century, the Abbasid caliphs endowed research libraries and set up centers for translation where scholars culled the writings of the ancients, including the classics of Persia, India, and Greece. Scholars read, translated, and commented on the works of neo-Platonists and Aristotle. Others worked on mathematical matters. Al-Khwarizmi wrote a book on equation theory in about 825 that became so well known in the West that the word *al-jabr* in the title of his book became the English word *algebra*. Other scholars, such as Al-hazen ('Ali al-Hasan, c. 1000), wrote studies on cubic and quadratic equations. Muhammad ben Musa (d. 850) used Hindu numerals in his treatise on arithmetical calculations, introducing the crucial number zero. No wonder that the numbers 1, 2, 3, and so on, though invented in India, were known as "Arabic numerals" when they were introduced into western Europe in the twelfth century.

The newly independent Islamic rulers supported science as well as mathematics. Unusual because she was a woman was al-Asturlabi, who followed her father's profession as a maker of astrolabes for the Syrian court. Astrolabes measured the altitude of the sun and stars to calculate time and latitude. More typical were men like Ibn Sina (980–1037), known in the West as Avicenna, who wrote books on logic, the natural sciences, and physics. His *Canon of Medicine* systematized earlier treatises and reconciled them with his own experience as a physician. Active in the centers of power, he served as vizier to various rulers. In his autobiography he spoke with pleasure and pride about his intellectual development:

> One day I asked permission [of the ruler] to go into [his doctors'] library, look at their books, and read the medical ones. He gave me permission, and I went into a palace of many rooms, each with trunks full of books, back-to-back. In one room there were books on Arabic and poetry, in another books on jurisprudence, and similarly in each room books on a single subject.... When I reached the age of eighteen, I had completed the study of all these sciences.

Long before there were universities in the West, there were important institutions of higher learning in the Islamic world. In Islam all law and literature was understood to derive from God's commands as contained in the Qur'an or as revealed to the ummah, the community of believers. For this reason, the study of the Qur'an and related texts held

a central place in Islamic life. By the ninth century, rich Muslims, generally of the ruling elite, demonstrated their piety and charity by establishing schools for professors and their students. Each school, or *madrasa*, was located within or attached to a mosque. Visiting scholars often arrived at the madrasas to dispute, in a formal and scholarly way, with the professors there. Such events of intellectual sparring attracted huge audiences. On ordinary

Andromeda C
The study of sciences such as medicine, physics, and astronomy flourished in the tenth and eleventh centuries in the cosmopolitan Islamic world. This whimsical depiction of Andromeda C, a constellation in the Northern Hemisphere, illustrates the Book of Images of the Fixed Stars, *an astronomical treatise written around 965 by al-Sufi at the request of his "pupil," the ruler of Iran. Since the Muslim calendar was lunar and the times of Muslim prayer were calculated by the movement of the sun, astronomy was important for religious as well as secular purposes. Al-Sufi drew from classical treatises, particularly the* Almagest *by Ptolemy. This copy of his book, probably made by his son in 1009, also draws on classical models for the illustrations; but instead of Greek clothing, Andromeda wears the pantaloons and skirt of an Islamic dancer.*
Bodleian Library, Oxford.

The Cairo Geniza

What can historians know about the daily life of ordinary people in the tenth and eleventh centuries? Generally speaking, very little. We have writings from the intellectual elite and administrative documents from monasteries, churches, and courts. But these rarely mention ordinary folk; and if they do, it is always from the standpoint of those who are not ordinary themselves. The material culture of people well down on the social scale can sometimes be deduced from archaeological excavations, which, for example, can ascertain the postholes that anchored the wooden houses of villagers. Researchers can tell from such evidence how large the houses were and perhaps even how sturdy. But to glimpse beyond that, to the concerns, occupations, and family relations of tenth- and eleventh-century people as they went about their daily lives is very difficult—except at medieval Cairo, in Egypt.

Cairo is exceptional because of a cache of unusual sources that were discovered in the *geniza,* or "depository" of the Jewish synagogue near the city. By tradition and religious belief, the members of the Jewish community were obliged to leave all their writings, including their notes, letters, and even shopping lists, in the *geniza* to await ceremonial burial. Cairo was not the only place where this was the practice. But by chance at Cairo, the papers were left untouched in the depository and not buried. In 1890, when the synagogue was remodeled, workers tore down the walls of the *geniza* and discovered literally heaps of documents.

Many of these documents were purchased by American and English collectors and ended up in libraries in New York, Philadelphia, and Cambridge, England, where they remain. As is often the case in historical research, the questions that scholars ask are more important than the sources themselves. At first, historians did not ask what the documents could tell them about everyday life. They wanted to know how to transcribe and read them; they wanted to study the evolution of their writing style (the study of *paleography*). They also needed to organize the material. Dispersed among various libraries, the documents were a hodgepodge of lists, books, pages, and fragments. For example, the first page of a personal letter might be in one library, the second page in a completely different location. For decades scholars were busy simply transcribing the documents with a view to printing and publishing their contents. Not until 1964 was a bibliography of these published materials was made available.

Only then, when they knew where to find the sources and how to piece them together, did historians, most notably S. D. Goitein, begin to work through the papers for their historical interest. What Goitein learned through the remains of the *geniza* amplified historians' understanding of the everyday life of much of the Mediterranean world. He discovered a cosmopolitan community, occupied with trade, schooling, marriages, divorces,

days, though, the professors held regular classes. A professor might, for example, begin his day with a class interpreting the Qur'an, following it with a class on other interpretations, and ending with a class on literary or legal texts. Students, all male, attended the classes that suited their achievement level and interest. Most students paid a fee for learning, but there were also scholarship students, such as one group of lucky students who were given annual funds by a tenth-century vizier. He was so solicitous for the welfare of all scholars that each day he set out for them iced refreshments, candles, and paper in his own kitchen.

The use of paper, made from flax and hemp or rags and vegetable fiber, points up a major difference among the Islamic, Byzantine, and (as we shall see) Carolingian renaissances. Byzantine scholars worked to enhance the prestige of the ruling classes. Their work, written on expensive parchment, kept manuscripts out of the hands of all but the very rich. This was true of scholarship in the West as well. By contrast, Islamic scholars had goals that cut across all classes: to be physicians to the rich, teachers to the young, and contributors to passionate religious debates. Their writings, on less expensive paper, were widely available.

Jews under Muslim Rule
This letter written about 1000 in Hebrew, ended up among the geniza *documents near Cairo. It illustrates the far-flung connections of Jewish merchants: the writer, who lived in Tunisia, writes to an acquaintance in Egypt about business matters in Spain.*
Bayerische Staatsbibliothek, München.

poetry, litigation—all the common issues and activities of a middle-class society. For example, some documents showed that middle-class Jewish women disposed of their own property and that widows often reared and educated their children on their own.

The *geniza* documents also shed light on commercial activity in the Arabic-speaking world. Consider the Tustari brothers, the Jewish merchants from southern Iran who by 1026 had established a flourishing business in Egypt. Despite their importance, we would know almost nothing about the Tustaris had it not been for the chance discovery of the Cairo *geniza*.

So think twice the next time you throw away a piece of paper. If a historian of the year 3000 were to read your notes, lists, or letters, what would he or she learn about your culture?

QUESTIONS FOR DEBATE
1. Why do the documents in the *geniza* tell us about Muslim as well as Jewish life in medieval Cairo?
2. Why was it impossible for historians to begin to write about daily life in medieval Cairo immediately after the discovery of the *geniza*?

FURTHER READING
Constable, Olivia Remie. *Trade and Traders in Muslim Spain: The Commercial Realignment of the Iberian Peninsula, 900–1500.* 1994.

Goitein, S. D. *A Mediterranean Society: The Jewish Communities of the Arab World as Portrayed in the Documents of the Cairo Geniza.* 6 vols. 1967–1983.

❖ The Creation and Division of a New Western Empire

Just as in the Byzantine and Islamic worlds, so too in the West, the period 750–1050 saw first the formation of a strong empire, ruled by one man, and then its fragmentation, as local rulers took power into their own hands. A new dynasty, the Carolingians, came to rule in the Frankish kingdom at almost the very moment that the Abbasids gained the caliphate. Charlemagne, the most powerful Carolingian monarch, conquered new territory, took

the title of emperor, and presided over a revival of Christian classical culture known as the "Carolingian renaissance." He ruled at the local level through counts and other military men who were faithful to him—he called them his *fideles*, or "loyal men." Nevertheless, the unity of this empire, based largely on conquest, a measure of prosperity, and personal allegiance to Charlemagne, was shaky. Its weaknesses were exacerbated by attacks from invaders— Vikings, Muslims, and Magyars. Charlemagne's successors divided his empire among themselves and saw it divided further as local strongmen took defense—and rule—into their own hands.

The Rise of the Carolingians

The Carolingians were among many aristocratic families on the rise during the Merovingian period. Like the others, they were important landowners, and they gained exceptional power by monopolizing the position of "palace mayor" in the kingdom of Austrasia and, after 687, the kingdom of Neustria as well. As mayors, the Carolingians traveled with the Merovingian kings, signed their documents, and helped them formulate and carry out policies. They also cemented alliances with other aristocrats on their own behalf and, by patronizing monasteries and supporting churchmen in key positions, they garnered additional prestige and influence. In the first half of the eighth century, many of the Merovingian kings were children, and the mayors took over much of the responsibility and power of kings themselves.

Charles Martel gave the name Carolingian (from *Carolus,* the Latin for "Charles") to the dynasty. He was palace mayor from 714 to 741. Although he spent most of his time fighting vigorously against opposing aristocratic groups, later generations would recall with nostalgia his defeat of a contingent of Muslims between Poitiers and Tours in about 732. In contending against regional aristocrats who were carving out independent lordships for themselves, Charles and his family turned aristocratic factions against one another, rewarded supporters, crushed enemies, and dominated whole regions by controlling monasteries that served as focal points for both religious piety and land donations. Allying themselves with these influential religious and political institutions, the Carolingians brought both lay and clerical aristocrats into their allegiance.

The Carolingians chose their allies well. Anglo-Saxon missionaries like Boniface, who went to Frisia (today the Netherlands) and Germany, helped them expand their control, converting the population as a prelude to conquest. Many of the areas Boniface reached had long been Christian, but the churches there had followed local or Irish models rather than Roman. Boniface, who came to Germany from England as the pope's ambassador, set up a hierarchical church organization and founded monasteries dedicated to the rule of St. Benedict. His newly appointed bishops were loyal to Rome and the Carolingians, not to regional aristocracies. They knew that their power came from papal and royal fiat rather than from local power centers.

Although at first men like Boniface worked indirectly to bring about the Carolingian alliance with the papacy, Pippin III, Charles Martel's son (d. 768), and his supporters cemented the partnership by deposing the Merovingian king in 751. They petitioned Pope Zachary to legitimize their actions and he agreed. The Carolingians readily returned the favor a few years later when the pope asked for their help in defense against hostile Lombards. The request signaled a major shift. Before 754, the papacy had been part of the Byzantine Empire; after that it turned to the West. In that year the papacy and the Franks formed a close, tight alliance based, as their agreement put it, on *amicitia, pax et caritas* ("mutual friendship, close relations, and Christian love"). Pippin launched a successful campaign against the Lombard king that ended in 756 with the so-called Donation of Pippin, a peace accord between the Lombards and the pope. The treaty gave back to the pope cities that had been ruled by the Lombard king. The new arrangement recognized what the papacy had long ago created: a territorial "republic of St. Peter" ruled by the pope, not by the Byzantine emperor. Henceforth the fate of Italy would be tied largely to the policies of the pope and the Frankish kings to the north, not to the emperors of the East.

The Carolingian partnership with the Roman church gave the dynasty a Christian aura, expressed in symbolic form by anointment. Carolingian kings, as Visigothic kings had been, were rubbed with holy oil on their foreheads and on their shoulders in a ceremony that, to contemporaries, harked back to the Old Testament kings who had been anointed by God.

Charlemagne and His Kingdom, 768–814

The most famous Carolingian king was Charles (r. 768–814), called "the Great" ("le Magne" in Old French) by his contemporaries. Epic poems portrayed Charlemagne as a just, brave, wise, and warlike king. In a biography written by Einhard, his friend and younger contemporary, and patterned closely on Suetonius's *Lives of the Caesars,* Charlemagne was the very model of a Roman emperor. Some scholars at his court described him as another David, the anointed Old Testament king. Modern historians are less dazzled than his contemporaries were, noting that he was complex, contradictory, and sometimes brutal. He loved listening to St. Augustine's *City of God* and supported major scholarly enterprises; yet he never learned to write. He was devout, building a beautiful chapel at his major residence at Aachen in Austrasia; yet he flouted the advice of churchmen when they told him to convert pagans rather than force baptism on them. He admired Roman emperors, yet Einhard described him as furious when the pope placed the imperial crown on his head. He waged many successful wars, yet he thereby destroyed the buffer states surrounding the Frankish kingdoms, unleashing a new round of invasions even before his death.

Behind these contradictions, however, lay a unifying vision. Charlemagne dreamed of an empire that would unite the martial and learned traditions of the Roman and Germanic worlds with the legacy of Christianity. This vision lay at the core of his political activity, his building programs, and his active support of scholarship and education.

Territorial Expansion. Charlemagne spent the early years of his reign conquering lands in all directions and subjugating the conquered peoples (Map 9.3). He invaded Italy, seizing the crown of the Lombard kings and annexing northern Italy in 774. He then moved northward and began a long and difficult war against the Saxons, concluded only after more than thirty years of fighting, during which he forcibly annexed Saxon territory and converted the Saxon people to Christianity through mass baptisms at the point of the sword. To the southeast, Charlemagne waged a campaign against the Avars, the people who had fought the Byzantines almost two centuries before. His biographer Einhard exulted, "All the money and treasure that had been amassed over many years was seized, and no war in which the Franks have ever engaged within the memory of man brought them such riches and such booty." To the southwest, Charlemagne led an expedition to al-Andalus. Although suffering a notable but local defeat at Roncesvalles in 778 (immortalized later in the medieval epic *The Song of Roland*), he did set up a *march*, or military buffer region, between al-Andalus and his own realm.

By the 790s, Charlemagne's kingdom stretched eastward to the Saale River (today in eastern Germany), southeast to what is today Austria, and south

to Spain and Italy. Such hegemony in the West was unheard of since the time of the Roman Empire. Charlemagne began to act according to the old Roman model, sponsoring building programs to symbolize his authority, standardizing weights and measures, and acting as a patron of intellectual and artistic efforts. He built a capital city at Aachen, complete with a church patterned on one built by Justinian at Ravenna. He even dismantled the columns, mosaics, and marble from the church at Ravenna and carted them northward to use in constructing his new church. He initiated a revival of Christian and classical learning.

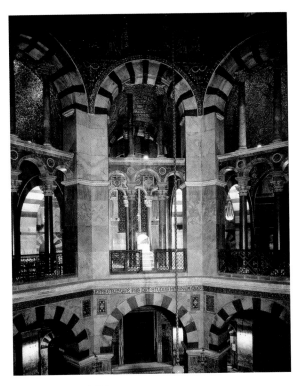

Charlemagne's Throne

Charlemagne was the first Frankish king to build a permanent capital city. The decision to do so was made in 789, and the king chose Aachen because of its natural warm springs. There he built a palace complex that included a grand living area for the king and his retinue and a church, still standing today, modeled on the Byzantine church of San Vitale in Ravenna. In the balcony above the altar of the church, Charlemagne placed his throne. Consider that Charlemagne had conquered northern Italy in 774. What aspirations might Charlemagne have been expressing by imitating a northern Italian Byzantine church? What idea of himself was he promulgating by placing his own throne above the main altar? Ann Munchow/Das Domkapital, Aachen.

MAP 9.3 Expansion of the Carolingian Empire under Charlemagne
The conquests of Charlemagne temporarily united almost all of western Europe under one government. Although this great empire broke apart (see the insert showing the divisions of the Treaty of Verdun), the legacy of that unity remained, even serving as one of the inspirations behind today's European Union.

To discourage corruption, Charlemagne appointed special officials, called *missi dominici* (meaning "those sent out by the lord king"), to oversee his regional governors—the counts—on the king's behalf. The *missi*—lay aristocrats or bishops—traveled in pairs to make a circuit of regions of the kingdom. As one of Charlemagne's capitularies (summaries of royal decisions) put it, the *missi* "are to make diligent inquiry wherever people claim that someone has done them an injustice, so that the *missi* fully carry out the law and do justice for everyone everywhere, whether in the holy churches of God or among the poor, orphans, or widows."

Imperial Coronation. While Charlemagne was busy imitating Roman emperors through his conquests, his building programs, his legislation, and his efforts at church reform, the papacy was beginning to claim imperial power for itself. At some point, perhaps in the mid-750s, members of the papal chancery, or writing office, forged a document, called the Donation of Constantine, that declared the pope the recipient of the fourth-century emperor Constantine's crown, cloak, and military rank along with "all provinces, palaces, and districts of the city of Rome and Italy and of the regions of the West." The tension between the imperial claims of the Carolingians and those of the pope was heightened by the existence of an emperor at Constantinople who also had rights in the West.

Pope Hadrian I (r. 772–795) maintained a balance among these three powers. But Hadrian's successor, Leo III (r. 795–816), tipped the balance. In 799, accused of adultery and perjury by a faction of the Roman aristocracy, Leo narrowly escaped being blinded and having his tongue cut out. He fled northward to seek Charlemagne's protection. Charlemagne had him escorted back to Rome under royal protection and arrived there himself in late November 800 to an imperial welcome orchestrated by Leo. On Christmas Day of that year, Leo put an imperial crown on Charlemagne's head and the clergy and nobles who were present acclaimed the king Augustus, the title of the first Roman emperor. The pope hoped in this way to exalt the king of the Franks, to downgrade the Byzantine ruler, and to enjoy the role of "emperor maker" himself.

About twenty years later, when Einhard wrote about this coronation, he said that the imperial title at first so displeased Charlemagne "so much that he stated that, if he had known in advance of the pope's plan, he would not have entered the church that day." In fact, Charlemagne did not use any title but king for more than a year afterward. But it is unlikely that Charlemagne was completely surprised by the imperial title; his advisers certainly had been thinking about claiming it. He might have hesitated because he feared the reaction of the Byzantines, as Einhard went on to suggest, or he might well have objected to the papal role in his crowning rather than to the crown itself. When he finally did call himself emperor, after establishing a peace with the Byzantines, he used a long and revealing title: "Charles, the most serene Augustus, crowned by God, great and peaceful Emperor who governs the Roman Empire and who is, by the mercy of God, king of the Franks and the Lombards." According to this title, Charlemagne was not the Roman emperor crowned by the pope but rather God's emperor, who governed the Roman Empire along with his many other duties.

Charlemagne's Successors, 814–911

Charlemagne's son Louis the Pious (r. 814–840) was also crowned emperor, and he took his role as guarantor of the Christian empire even more seriously.

He brought the monastic reformer Benedict of Aniane to court and issued a capitulary in 817 imposing a uniform way of life, based on the rule of St. Benedict, on all the monasteries of the empire. Although some monasteries opposed this legislation, and in the years to come the king was unable to impose his will directly, this moment marked the effective adoption of the Benedictine rule as the monastic standard in the West. Louis also standardized the practices of his notaries, who issued his documents and privileges, and he continued to use *missi* to administer justice throughout the realm.

In a new development of the coronation ritual, Louis's first wife, Ermengard, was crowned empress by the pope in 816. In 817, their firstborn son, Lothar, was given the title emperor and made co-ruler with Louis. Their other sons, Pippin and Louis (later called "the German"), were made subkings under imperial rule. Louis the Pious hoped in this way to ensure the unity of the empire while satisfying the claims of all his sons. Should any son die, only his firstborn could succeed him, a measure intended to prevent further splintering. But Louis's hopes were thwarted by events. Ermengard died, and Louis married Judith, the daughter of one of the most powerful families in the kingdom. In 823, she and Louis had a son, Charles (later known as "the Bald," to whose court Dhuoda's son William was sent). The sons of Ermengard, bitter over the birth of another royal heir, rebelled against their father and fought one another. A chronicle written during this period suggests that nearly every year was filled with family tragedies. In 830, for example, Pippin and his brother Lothar plotted to depose their father and shut Judith up in a convent. Louis regained control, but three years later his sons by Ermengard once again banded together and imprisoned him. Louis was lucky that the brothers began quarreling among themselves. Their alliance broke apart, and he was released.

Family battles such as these continued, both during Louis's lifetime and, with great vigor, after his death in 840. In 843, the Treaty of Verdun divided the empire among the three remaining brothers (Pippin had died in 838) in an arrangement that would roughly define the future political contours of western Europe (see Map 9.3). The western third, bequeathed to Charles the Bald (r. 843–877), would eventually become France; the eastern third, handed to Louis the German (r. 843–876), would become Germany. The "Middle Kingdom," which was given to Lothar (r. 840–855) along with the imperial title, had a different fate: parts of it were absorbed by France and Germany, and the rest eventually formed the modern states of the Netherlands, Belgium, Luxembourg, Switzerland, and Italy.

In 843, the European-wide empire of Charlemagne had dissolved. Forged by conquest, it had been supported by a small group of privileged aristocrats with lands and offices stretching across the whole of it. Their loyalty, based on shared values, real friendship, expectations of gain, and sometimes formal ties of vassalage and fealty (see page 334), was crucial to the success of the Carolingians. The empire had also been supported by an ideal, shared by educated laymen and churchmen alike, of imperialism and Christian belief working together to bring good order to the earthly state. But powerful forces operated against the Carolingian Empire. Once the empire's borders were fixed and it could no longer expand, the aristocrats could no longer hope for new lands and offices. They put down roots in particular regions and began to gather their own followings. Powerful local traditions such as different languages also undermined imperial unity. Finally, as Dhuoda revealed, some people disagreed with the imperial ideal. Asking her son to put his father before the emperor, she demonstrated her belief in the primacy of the family and the intimate and personal ties that bound it together. Dhuoda's ideal did not eliminate the emperor (European emperors would continue to reign until World War I), but it represented a new sensibility that saw real value in the breaking apart of Charlemagne's empire into smaller, more intimate local units.

Land and Power

The Carolingian economy, based on trade and agriculture, contributed to both the rise and the dissolution of the Carolingian Empire. At the onset its wealth came from land and plunder. After the booty from war ceased to pour in, the Carolingians still had access to money and goods. To the north, in Viking trading stations such as Haithabu (today Hedeby, in northern Germany), archaeologists have found Carolingian glass and pots alongside Islamic coins and cloth, which tells us that the Carolingian economy intermingled with that of the Abbasid caliphate. Silver from the Islamic world probably

Two Cities Besieged

In about 900, the monks of the monastery of St. Gall produced a Psalter with numerous illuminations. This illustration for Psalm 59, which tells of King David's victories, used four pages. This page was the fourth. On the top level, David's army besieges a fortified city from two directions. On the right are foot soldiers, one of whom holds a burning torch to set the city afire; on the left are horsemen—led by their standard-bearer—with lances and bows and arrows. Note their chain-mail coats and their horses' stirrups. Within the city, four soldiers protect themselves with shields, but another has fallen and hangs upside down from the city wall. The dead and wounded on the ground are bleeding. Four other men seem to be cowering behind the city. In the bottom register, a different city burns fiercely (note the burning towers). This city lacks defenders; the people within it are unarmed. Although this illumination purports to show David's victories, in fact it nicely represents the equipment and strategies of ninth-century warfare. Stiftsbibliothek St. Gallen, Switzerland.

came north up the Volga River through Russia to the Baltic Sea. There the coins were melted down, the silver traded to the Carolingians in return for wine, jugs, glasses, and other manufactured goods. The Carolingians turned the silver into coins of their own, to be used throughout the empire for small-scale local trade. The weakening of the Abbasid caliphate in the mid-ninth century, however, disrupted this far-flung trade network and contributed to the weakening of the Carolingians at about the same time.

Land provided the most important source of Carolingian wealth and power. Like the landholders of the late Roman Empire and the Merovingian period, Carolingian aristocrats held many estates, scattered throughout the Frankish empire. But in the Carolingian period these estates were reorganized and their productivity carefully calculated. Modern historians often call these estates *manors.*

Typical was the manor called Villeneuve St.-Georges, which belonged to the monastery of St.-Germain-des-Prés (today in Paris) in the ninth century. Villeneuve consisted of arable fields, vineyards, meadows where animals could roam, and woodland, all scattered about the countryside rather than connected in a compact unit. The land was not tilled by slave gangs, as had been the custom on great estates of the Roman Empire, but by peasant families, each one settled on its own *manse,* which consisted of a house, a garden, and small pieces of the arable land. They farmed the land that belonged to them and also worked the *demesne,* the very large manse of the lord (in this case the abbey of St.-Germain).

These peasant farms, cultivated by households, marked a major social and economic development. Slaves had not been allowed to live in family units. By contrast, the peasants on Villeneuve and on other Carolingian estates could not be separated involuntarily from their families or displaced from their manses. In this sense, the peasant household of the Carolingian period was the precursor of the modern nuclear family.

Peasants at Villeneuve practiced the most progressive sort of plowing, known as the *three-field system,* in which they farmed two-thirds of the arable land at one time. They planted one-third with winter wheat and one-third with summer crops and left one-third fallow, to restore its fertility. The crops sown and the fallow field then rotated, so that land use was repeated only every three years. This method of organizing the land produced larger yields (because two-thirds of the land was cultivated each year) than the still prevalent two-field system, in which only half of the arable land was cultivated one year, the other half the next.

All the peasants at Villeneuve were dependents of the monastery and owed dues and services to St.-Germain. Their obligations varied enormously, depending on the status of the peasants and the manse they held. One family, for example, owed four silver coins, wine, wood, three hens, and fifteen eggs every year, and the men had to plow the fields of the demesne land. Another family owed the intensive labor of working the vineyards. One woman was required to weave cloth and feed the chickens. Peasant women spent much time at the lord's house in the *gynaeceum*—the women's workshop, where they made and dyed cloth and sewed garments—or in the kitchens, as cooks. Peasant men spent most of their time in the fields.

Estates organized on the model of Villeneuve were profitable. Like other lords, the Carolingians benefited from their extensive estates. Nevertheless, farming was still too primitive to return great surpluses, and as the lands belonging to the king were divided up in the wake of the partitioning of the empire and new invasions, Carolingian dependence on manors scattered throughout their kingdom proved to be a source of weakness.

The Carolingian Renaissance, c. 790–c. 900

At the height of their power, with wealth coming in from trade and profits from their estates, the Carolingians supported a revival of learning designed to enhance their glory, educate their officials, reform the liturgy, and purify the faith. The revival began in the 790s and continued for about a century. Parallel in some ways to the renaissances of the Byzantine and Islamic worlds, the Carolingian renaissance resuscitated the learning of the past. Scholars studied Roman imperial writers such as Suetonius and Virgil; they read and commented on the works of the church fathers; and they worked to establish complete and accurate texts of everything they read and prized.

The English scholar Alcuin (c. 732–804), a member of the circle of scholars whom Charlemagne recruited to form a center of study, brought with him the traditions of Anglo-Saxon scholarship that had been developed by men such as Benedict Biscop and Bede. Invited to Aachen, Alcuin became Charlemagne's chief adviser, writing letters on the king's behalf, counseling him on royal policy, and tutoring the king's household, including the women. Charlemagne's sister and daughter, for example, often asked Alcuin to explain passages from the Gospel to them. Charlemagne entrusted Alcuin with

St. Matthew

The Carolingian renaissance produced art of extraordinary originality. The artist of this picture was certainly inspired by the same sort of classical models that interested Byzantine artists. But his frenetic, emotional lines and uncanny colors are something new. This illustration, a depiction of St. Matthew writing (with an ink horn in his left hand and a quill in his right hand), precedes the text of St. Matthew's Gospel in a book of Gospels made around 820 for Ebbo of Reims. Ebbo had been born a serf but was freed and educated by Charlemagne. Later he was appointed to one of the highest positions in the empire, the archbishopric of Reims. Artistic patronage by a former serf was very unusual in this period.

La Médiathèque, Ville d'Epernay.

the task of preparing an improved edition of the Vulgate, the Latin Bible read in all church services.

The Carolingian renaissance depended on an elite staff of scholars such as Alcuin, yet its educational program had broader appeal. In one of his capitularies, Charlemagne ordered that the cathedrals and monasteries of his kingdom teach reading and writing to all who were able to learn. Some churchmen expressed the hope that schools for children (perhaps they were thinking also of girls) would be established even in small villages and hamlets. Although this dream was never realized, it shows that at just about the same time as the Islamic world was organizing the madrasa system of schools, the Carolingians were thinking about the importance of religious education for more than a small elite.

Scholarship complemented the alliance between the church and the king symbolized by Charlemagne's anointment. In the Carolingian world, much as in the Islamic and Byzantine, there was little distinction between politics and religion: kings considered themselves appointed by the grace of God, often based their laws on biblical passages, involved themselves in church reform, appointed churchmen on their own initiative, and believed their personal piety a source of power.

Just as in the Byzantine renaissance, Carolingian artists often illuminated texts using earlier pictures as models. But their imitation was not slavish. To their models Carolingian artists added exuberant decoration and design, often rendering architectural elements as bands of color and portraying human figures with great liveliness. Some models came from Byzantium, and perhaps some Carolingian artists themselves came originally from Greece, refugees from Byzantium during its iconoclastic period. Models from Italy provided the kings' artists with examples of the sturdy style of the late Roman Empire. In turn, Carolingian art became a model for later illuminators. The Utrecht Psalter, for example, made at Reims in about 820, was copied by artists in eleventh-century England.

The Carolingian program was ambitious and lasting, even after the Carolingian dynasty had faded to a memory. The work of locating, understanding, and transmitting models of the past continued in a number of monastic schools. In the materials they studied, the questions they asked, and the answers they suggested, the Carolingians offered a mode of inquiry fruitful for subsequent generations. In the

Oseberg Ship
Excavated in 1904 from a burial mound at Oslofjord, Norway, this ninth-century ship, here shown reconstructed and displayed at the Viking Ship Museum at Bygdøy, is much finer and more highly carved than the typical longships used by the Vikings in their far-flung voyages across the seas. This must have been a ceremonial ship, and it is there-fore not surprising that in its center was the burial chamber of a royal lady.
Universitetet: Oslo, Oldsakamlingen, Oslo, Norway.

twelfth century, scholars would build on the foundations laid by the Carolingian renaissance. The very print of this textbook depends on one achievement of the period: modern letter fonts are based on the clear and beautiful letter forms, called Caroline minuscule, invented in the ninth century to standardize manuscript handwriting and make it more readable.

Invasion on the Borders

Like the Roman emperors they emulated, Carolingian kings and counts confronted new groups along their borders (Map 9.4). The new peoples—Vikings to the north, Muslims to the south, and Magyars to the east—were feared and hated; but like the Germanic tribes that had entered the Roman Empire, they also served as military allies. As royal sons fought one another and as counts and other powerful men sought to carve out their own principalities, their alliances with the newcomers helped integrate the outsiders swiftly into European politics. The impact of these foreign groups hastened, but did not cause, the dissolution of the empire. The Carolingian kings could not muster troops quickly or efficiently enough to counter the lightning attacks of the raiders. Defense fell into the hands of

local authorities who, building on their new prestige and the weakness of the king, became increasingly independent rulers themselves.

Vikings. At the same time as they made their forays into Russia, the Vikings moved westward. The Franks called them Northmen; the English called them Danes. They were, in fact, much less united than their victims thought. When they began their voyages at the end of the eighth century, they did so in independent bands. Merchants and pirates at the same time, Vikings followed a chief, seeking profit, prestige, and land. Many traveled as families: husbands, wives, children, and slaves.

The Vikings perfected the art of navigation. In their longships they crossed the Atlantic, settling Iceland and Greenland and (about A.D. 1000) landing on the coast of North America. Other Viking bands navigated the rivers of Europe. The Vikings were pagans, and to them monasteries and churches—with their reliquaries, chalices, and crosses—were storehouses of booty. "Never before," wrote Alcuin, who experienced one attack, "has such terror appeared in Britain as we have now suffered from a pagan race. . . . Behold the church of St. Cuthbert spattered with the blood of the priests of God, despoiled of all its ornaments."

MAP 9.4 Muslim, Viking, and Magyar Invasions of the Ninth and Tenth Centuries
Bristling with multicolored arrows, this map suggests that western Europe was continually and thoroughly pillaged by outside invaders for almost two centuries. That impression is only partially true; it must be offset by several factors. First, not all the invaders came at once. The Viking raids were nearly over when the Magyar attacks began. Second, the invaders were not entirely unwelcome. The Magyars were for a time enlisted as mercenaries by the King of Italy, and some Muslims were allied to local lords in Provence. Third, the invasions, though widespread, were local in effect. Note, for example, that the Viking raids were largely limited to rivers or coastal areas.

England confronted sporadic attacks by the Vikings in the 830s and 840s. By midcentury, Viking adventurers regularly spent winters there. The Vikings did not just destroy. In 876, they settled in the northeast of England, plowing the land and preparing to live on it. The region where they settled and imposed their own laws was later called the *Danelaw*.

In Wessex, the southernmost kingdom of England, King Alfred the Great (r. 871–899) bought time and peace by paying tribute and giving hostages. Such tribute, later called *Danegeld*, was collected as a tax that eventually became the basis of a relatively lucrative taxation system in England. Then in 878, Alfred led an army that, as his biographer put it, "gained the victory through God's will. He destroyed the Vikings with great slaughter and pursued those who fled . . . hacking them down." Thereafter the pressures of invasion eased as Alfred reorganized his army, set up strongholds, and deployed new warships.

Vikings invaded Ireland as well, setting up fortified bases along the coast from which they attacked and plundered churches and monasteries. But they also established Dublin as a commercial center and, in the tenth century, began to intermarry with the Irish and convert to Christianity.

On the continent, too, the invaders set up trading emporia and settled where originally they had raided. Beginning about 850, their attacks became well-organized expeditions for regional control. At the end of the ninth century, one contingent settled in the region of France that soon took the name Normandy, the land of the Northmen. The new inhabitants converted to Christianity during the tenth century. Rollo, the Viking leader in Normandy, accepted Christianity in 911, at the same time Normandy was formally ceded to him by the Frankish king Charles the Simple (or Straightforward).

Normandy was not the only new Christian polity created in the north during the tenth and eleventh centuries. Scandinavia itself was transformed with the creation of the powerful kingdom of Denmark. There had been kings in Scandinavia before the tenth century, but they had been weak, their power challenged by nearby chieftains. The Vikings had been led by these chieftains, each competing for booty to win prestige, land, and power back home. During the course of their raids, they and their followers came into contact with new cultures and learned from them. Meanwhile the Carolingians and the English supported missionaries in Scandinavia. By the middle of the tenth century, the Danish kings and their people had become Christian. And, following the model of the Christian kings to their south, they built up an effective monarchy, with a royal mint and local agents who depended on them. By about 1000, the Danes had extended their control to parts of Sweden, Norway, and even, under King Cnut (r. 1017–1035), England.

Although most Vikings adopted the sedentary ways of much of the rest of Europe, some of their descendants continued their voyages and raids. In southern Italy the popes first fought against and then made peace with the Normans, who in the early eleventh century traveled southward from Normandy to hire themselves out as warriors. They fought for the Byzantines or the Muslims, siding with whoever paid them best.

Muslims. Although Muslim armies had entered western Europe in the eighth century, the ninth-century Muslims were a different breed: they were freebooters, working independently of any caliph or other ruler. Taking advantage of Byzantium's initial weakness, in 827 they began the slow conquest of Sicily, which took nearly one hundred years. During the same century, Muslim pirates set up bases on Mediterranean islands and strongholds in Provence (in southern France) and near Naples (in southern Italy). Liutprand of Cremona reported on the activities of one such group:

> [*Muslim pirates from al-Andalus*], *disembarking under cover of night, entered the manor house unobserved and murdered—O grievous tale!—the Christian inhabitants. They then took the place as their own . . . [fortified it and] started stealthy raids on all the neighboring country.*

The Muslims at this base, set up in 891, robbed, took prisoners, and collected ransoms. But they were so useful to their Christian neighbors, who called on them to support their own feuds, that they were not ousted until 972. Only then, when they caused a scandal by capturing the holiest man of his era, Abbot Maieul of Cluny, did the count of Provence launch a successful attack against their lair.

Magyars. The Magyars, a nomadic people and latecomers to the West, arrived around 899 into the Danube basin. Until then the region had been predominantly Slavic, but the Magyars came from the East and spoke a language unrelated to any other in Europe (except Finnish). Their entry drove a wedge between the Slavs near the Frankish kingdom and those bordering on Byzantium; those near Byzantium, such as the Bulgarians, Serbs, and Russians, were driven into the Byzantine orbit, while those nearer the Frankish kingdom came under the influence of Germany.

From their bases in present-day Hungary, the Magyars raided far to the west, attacking Germany, Italy, and even southern Gaul frequently between 899 and 955. Then in the summer of 955, one marauding party of Magyars was met at the Lech River by the German king Otto I (r. 936–973), whose army decimated them in the battle of Lechfeld. Otto's victory, his subsequent military reorganization of his eastern frontiers, and the cessation of Magyar raids around this time made Otto a great hero to his contemporaries. However, historians today think the containment of the Magyars had more to do with their internal transformation from nomads to farmers than with their military defeat.

The Viking, Muslim, and Magyar invasions were the final onslaught western Europe experienced from outsiders. In some ways they were a continuation of the invasions that had rocked the Roman Empire in the fourth and fifth centuries. Loosely organized in warbands, the new groups entered western Europe looking for wealth but, apart from the Muslims, stayed on to become absorbed in its new post-invasion society.

❖ The Emergence of Local Rule in the Post-Carolingian Age

Despite implementing some of their visions, the Carolingians could not hold their empire together. Fundamentally, it was too diverse to cohere. Latin was a universal language, but few people spoke it; instead they used a wide variety of different languages and dialects. The king demanded loyalty from everyone, but most people knew only his representative, the local count. The king's power ulti-mately depended on the count's allegiance, but as the empire ceased to expand and was instead attacked by outsiders, the counts and other powerful men stopped looking to the king for new lands and offices and began to develop and exploit what they already had. They became powerful lords, commanding followings of vassals, building castles, setting up markets, collecting revenues, keeping the peace, and seeing themselves as independent regional rulers. They dominated the local peasantry. In this way, a new warrior class of lords and vassals came to dominate post-Carolingian society.

Yet it would be wrong to imagine that all of Europe came under the control of rural warlords. In Italy, where cities had never lost their importance, urban elites ruled over the surrounding countryside. Everywhere kings retained a certain amount of power; indeed, in some places, such as Germany and England, they were extremely effective. Central European monarchies formed under the influence of Germany.*

Public Power and Private Relationships

The key way in which both kings and less powerful men commanded others was by ensuring personal loyalty. While today citizens pledge allegiance to a flag, in the Carolingian and post-Carolingian periods, loyalty was gained less through public institutions and symbols than through private, personal relationships. In the ninth century, the Carolingian kings had their *fideles*, their "faithful men." Among these were the counts. In addition to a share in the revenues of their administrative district, the *county,* the counts received benefices, later also called *fiefs,* temporary grants of land given in return for service. These short-term arrangements often became permanent, however, once a count's son inherited the job and the fiefs of his father. By the end of the ninth century, fiefs were often properties that could be passed on to heirs.

Lords and Vassals. In the wake of the invasions, more and more warriors were drawn into similar networks of dependency, but not with the king: they became the faithful men—the *vassals*—of local lords.

---

*Terms such as "Germany," "France," and "Italy" are used here for the sake of convenience. They refer to regions, not the nation-states that would eventually become associated with those names.

Feudalism

Feudalism is a modern word, like *capitalism* and *communism*. No one in the Middle Ages used it, nor any of its related terms, such as *feudal system* or *feudal society*. Many historians today think that it is a misleading word and should be discarded. The term poses two serious problems. First, historians have used it to mean different things. Second, it implies that one way of life dominated the Middle Ages, when in fact there were numerous varieties of social, political, and economic arrangements.

Consider the many different meanings that *feudalism* has had. Historians influenced by Karl Marx's powerful communist theory used (and still use) *feudalism* to refer to an economic system in which nobles dominated subservient peasant cultivators. When they speak of feudalism, they are speaking of manors, lords, and serfs. Other historians, however, call that system *manorialism*. They reserve the term *feudalism* for a system consisting of vassals (who never did agricultural labor but only military service), lords, and fiefs. For example, in an influential book written in the mid-1940s, *Feudalism*, F. L. Ganshof considered the tenth to the thirteenth centuries to be the "classical age of feudalism" because during this period lords regularly granted fiefs to their vassals, who fought on their lord's behalf in return.

But, writing around the same time, Marc Bloch included in *his* definition of *feudalism* every aspect of the political and social life of the Middle Ages, including peasants, fiefs, knights, vassals, the fragmentation of royal authority and yet the survival of the state, which "was to acquire renewed strength" in the course of the feudal period. Some historians, reacting to this broad definition, have tried to narrow it by considering *feudalism* to be a political term that refers to the decline of the state and the dispersal of political power. Others, while also trying to narrow the definition, use *feudalism* to mean a system by which kings controlled their men. These definitions are opposites.

Whatever the definition, they all stress certain institutions that some recent historians argue were very peripheral to medieval life. The fief, for example, a word whose Latin form (*feodum*) gave rise to the word *feudalism*, was by no means important everywhere. And even where it was important, it did not necessarily have anything to do with lords, vassals, or military obligations. "Nobles and free men," writes the historian Susan Reynolds, "did not generally owe military service before the twelfth century because of the grant of anything like fiefs to them or their ancestors. . . . They owed whatever service they owed, not because they were vassals of a lord, but because they were subjects of a ruler" (477). For Reynolds, feudalism is a myth.

Mythical or not, all these views, even that of Reynolds, have one thing in common: a stress on vertical hierarchies, such as lords over peasants or kings over their subjects. Some recent historians, however, point out that not all of medieval society was hierarchical. Horizontal relations—such as those that created peasant communities, urban corporations, and the comradeship of knightly troops—were equally, if not more, important.

For all of these reasons, many historians have stopped using the word *feudalism*, preferring to stress the variety of medieval social and political arrangements. How many times have you encountered the term in this history book?

FURTHER READING

Bloch, Marc. *Feudal Society.* 2 vols. Trans. L. A. Manyon, 1961.

Ganshof, F. L. *Feudalism.* Trans. Philip Grierson, 1961.

Reynolds, Susan. *Fiefs and Vassals: The Medieval Evidence Reinterpreted.* 1994.

From the Latin word for *fief* comes the word *feudal*, and historians often use the term *feudalism* to describe the social and economic system created by the relationship among vassals, lords, and fiefs. (See "Terms of History," above.)

It was frequently said by medieval people that their society consisted of three groups: those who prayed, those who fought, and those who worked. All of these people were involved in a hierarchy of dependency and linked by personal bonds, but the upper classes—the prayers (monks) and the fighters (the knights)—were free. Their brand of dependency was prestigious, whether they were vassals, lords, or both. In fact, a typical warrior was lord of several vassals and the vassal of another lord. Monasteries normally had vassals to fight for them; and their abbots in turn were often vassals of a king or other powerful lord.

Vassalage grew up as an alternative to public power and at the same time as a way to strengthen what little public power there was. Given the impoverished economic conditions of the West, its primitive methods of communication, and its lack of unifying traditions, kings came to rely on vassals personally loyal to them to muster troops, collect taxes, and administer justice. When in the ninth century the Frankish empire broke up politically and power fell into the hands of local lords, they too needed "faithful men" to protect them and carry out their orders. And vassals needed lords. At the low end of the social scale, poor vassals looked to their lords to feed, clothe, house, and arm them. They hoped that they would be rewarded for their service with a fief of their own, with which they could support themselves and a family. At the upper end of the social scale, vassals looked to lords to enrich them further.

A few women were vassals, and some were lords (or, rather, "ladies," the female counterpart); and many upper-class laywomen participated in the society of fighters and prayers as wives and mothers of vassals and lords. Other aristocratic women entered convents and became members of the social group that prayed. Through its abbess or a man standing in for her, convents often had vassals as well.

Becoming the vassal of a lord often involved both ritual gestures and verbal promises. In a ceremony witnessed by others, the vassal-to-be knelt and, placing his hands between the hands of his lord, said, "I promise to be your man." This act, known as *homage*, was followed by the promise of *fealty*—fidelity, trust, and service—which the vassal swore with his hand on relics or a Bible. Then the vassal and the lord kissed. In an age when many people could not read, a public ceremony such as this represented a visual and verbal contract. Vassalage bound the lord and vassal to one another with reciprocal obligations, usually military. Knights, as the premier fighters of the day, were the most desirable vassals.

Lords and Peasants.   At the bottom of the social scale were those who worked—the peasants. In the Carolingian period, many peasants were free; they did not live on a manor or, if they did, they owed very little to its lord. But as power fell into the hands of local rulers, fewer and fewer peasants remained free. Rather, they were made dependent on lords, not as vassals but as serfs. Serfdom was a dependency separate from and completely unlike that of a vassal. It was not voluntary but rather inherited. No serf did homage or fealty to his lord; no serf kissed his lord as an equal. And the serf's work as a laborer was not prestigious. Unlike knights, who were celebrated in song, peasants, who constituted the majority of the population, were nevertheless barely noticed by the upper classes—except as a source of revenue.

New methods of cultivation and a burgeoning population helped transform the rural landscape and make it more productive. With a growing number of men and women to work the land, the lower classes now had more mouths to feed and faced the hardship of food shortage. Landlords began reorganizing their estates to run more efficiently. In the tenth century, the three-field system became more prevalent; heavy plows which could turn the heavy northern soils came into wider use; and horses (more effective than oxen) were harnessed to pull the plows. The result was surplus food and a better standard of living for nearly everyone.

In search of greater profits, some lords lightened the dues and services of peasants temporarily to allow them to open up new lands by draining marshes and cutting down forests. Some landlords converted dues and labor services into money payments, a boon for both lords and peasants. Lords now had money to spend on what they wanted rather than hens and eggs they might not need or want. Peasants benefited because their tax was fixed despite inflation. Thus, as the prices of their hens and eggs went up, they could sell them, reaping a profit in spite of the dues they owed their lords.

By the tenth century, many peasants lived in populous rural settlements, true villages. In the midst of a sea of arable land, meadow, wood, and wasteland, these villages developed a sense of community. Boundaries—sometimes real fortifications, sometimes simple markers—told nonresidents to keep out and to find shelter in huts located outside the village limits.

Hard Work in January
During the cold month of January, peasants had to put on their warm clothes, harness their oxen to the plow, and turn over the heavy soil to loosen and aerate it for planting. This illustration of January's peasant labor comes from a Calendar — a text useful to clergy because it listed the saints' feasts for each day of each month. In this case the artist was an Anglo-Saxon working in the second quarter of the eleventh century. Normally medieval artists followed painted models rather than nature; nevertheless, this miniature probably represents contemporary reality fairly well. One peasant guides the heavy plow as it makes a deep furrow, another drives the animals, and a third drops the seeds. Farmwork was cooperative, and peasant solidarity was an important aspect of village life.
British Library.

The church often formed the focal point of local activity. There people met, received the sacraments, drew up contracts, and buried their parents and children. Religious feasts and festivals joined the rituals of farming to mark the seasons. The church dominated the village in another way: men and women owed it a tax called a *tithe* (equivalent to one-tenth of their crops or income, paid in money or in kind), which was first instituted on a regular basis by the Carolingians.

Village peasants developed a sense of common purpose based on their practical interdependence, as they shared oxen or horses for the teams that pulled the plow or turned to village craftsmen to fix their wheels or shoe their horses. A sense of solidarity sometimes encouraged people to band together to ask for privileges as a group. Near Verona, in northern Italy, for example, twenty-five men living around the castle of Nogara in 920 joined together to ask their lord, the abbot of Nonantola, to allow them to lease plots of land, houses, and pasturage there in return for a small yearly rent and the promise to defend the castle. The abbot granted their request.

Village solidarity could be compromised, however, by conflicting loyalties and obligations. A peasant in one village might very well have one piece of land connected with a certain manor and another bit of arable field on a different estate; and he or she might owe several lords different kinds of dues. Even peasants of one village working for one lord might owe him varied services and taxes.

Layers of obligations were even more striking across the regions of Europe than in particular villages. The principal distinction was between free peasants, such as small landowners in Saxony and other parts of Germany, and unfree peasants, who were especially common in France and England. In Italy, peasants ranged from small independent landowners to leaseholders (like the tenants at Nogara); most were both, owning a parcel in one place and leasing another nearby.

As the power of kings weakened, this system of peasant obligations became part of a larger system of local rule. As landlords consolidated their power over their manors, they collected not only dues and services but also fees for the use of their flour mills, bake houses, and breweries. Some built castles, fortified strongholds, and imposed the even wider powers of the *ban:* the rights to collect taxes, hear court cases, levy fines, and muster men for defense.

In France, for example, as the king's power waned, political control fell into the hands of counts and other princes. By 1000, castles had become the key to their power. In the south of France, power was so fragmented that each man who controlled a castle—a *castellan*—was a virtual ruler, although often with a very limited reach. In northwestern France, territorial princes, basing their rule on the control of *many* castles, dominated much broader regions. For example, Fulk Nera, count of Anjou (987–1040), built more than thirteen castles and captured others from rival counts. By the end of his life, he controlled a region extending from Blois to Nantes along the Loire valley.

Castellans extended their authority by subjecting everyone near their castle to their ban. Peasants, whether or not they worked on a castellan's estates, had to pay him a variety of dues for his "protection" and judicial rights over them. Castellans also established links with the better-off landholders in the region, tempting or coercing them to become vassals. Lay castellans often supported local monasteries and controlled the appointment of local priests. But churchmen themselves sometimes held the position of territorial lord, as for example the archbishop of Milan in the eleventh century.

The development of virtually independent local political units, dominated by a castle and controlled by a military elite, marks an important turning point in western Europe. Although this development did not occur everywhere simultaneously (and in some places it hardly occurred at all), the social, political, and cultural life of the West was now dominated by landowners who saw themselves as military men and regional leaders. This phenomenon paralleled certain changes in the Byzantine and Islamic worlds; at just about the same time, the Byzantine *strategoi* were becoming a landowning elite and Muslim provincial rulers were employing Mamluk warriors. But crucial differences existed. The *strategoi* were still largely under the emperor's command, whereas Muslim dynasties were dependent on mercenaries. In contrast, castellans acted as quasi-kings; they were the lords of their vassals, whom they had kissed in token of their sworn bond of mutual service.

Warriors and Warfare

All warriors were not alike. At the top of the elite were the kings, counts, and dukes. Below them, but "on the rise," were the castellans; and still farther down the social scale were ordinary knights. Yet all shared in a common lifestyle.

Knights and their lords fought on horseback. High astride his steed, wearing a shirt of chain mail and a helmet of flat metal plates riveted together, the knight marked a military revolution. The war season started in May, when the grasses were high enough for horses to forage. Horseshoes allowed armies to move faster than ever before and to negotiate rough terrain previously unsuitable for battle. Stirrups, probably invented by Asiatic nomadic tribes, allowed the mounted warrior to hold his seat. This made it possible for knights to thrust at their enemy with heavy lances. The light javelin of ancient warfare was abandoned.

Lords and their vassals often lived together. In the lord's great hall they ate, listened to entertainment, and bedded down for the night. They went out hunting together, competed with one another in military games called *tournaments,* and went off to the battlefield as a group as well. Of course there were powerful vassals—counts, for example. They lived on their own fiefs and hardly ever saw their lord (probably the king), except when doing homage and fealty—once in their lifetime—or serving him in battles, for perhaps forty days a year. But they themselves were lords of knightly vassals who were not married and who lived and ate and hunted with them.

No matter how old they might be, unmarried knights who lived with their lords were called "youths" by their contemporaries. Such perpetual bachelors were something new, the result of a profound transformation in the organization of families and inheritance. Before about 1000, noble families had recognized all their children as heirs and had divided their estates accordingly. In the mid-ninth century, Count Everard and his wife, for example, willed their large estates, scattered from Belgium to Italy, to their four sons and three daughters (although they gave the boys far more than the girls, and the oldest boy far more than the others).

By 1000, however, adapting to diminished opportunities for land and office and wary of fragmenting the estates they had, French nobles changed both their conception of their family and the way property passed to the next generation. Recognizing the overriding claims of one son, often the eldest, they handed down their entire inheritance to him. (In cases where the heir is indeed the eldest son, this system of inheritance is called *primogeniture.*) The heir, in turn, traced his lineage only through the male line, backward through his father and forward through his own eldest son. Such *patrilineal* families left many younger sons without an inheritance and therefore without the prospect of marrying and founding a family; instead the younger sons lived at the courts of the great as "youths," or they joined the church as clerics or monks. The development of territorial rule and patrilineal families went hand in hand, as fathers passed down to one son undiminished not only manors but titles, castles, and the authority of the ban.

Patrilineal inheritance tended to bypass daughters and so worked against aristocratic women, who lost the power that came with inherited wealth. In families without sons, however, widows and daughters did inherit property; land given out as a fief, normally for military service, was not usually given to a woman. Thus a major source of control over land, people, and revenues was often denied to women. Yet they played an important role in this warrior society. A woman who survived childbirth and the death of her husband could marry again and again, becoming a peace broker as she forged alliances between great families and powerful "lords" on behalf of her younger sons. And wives often acted as lords of estates when their husbands were at war.

Efforts to Contain Violence

Warfare benefited territorial rulers in the short term, but in the long run their revenues suffered as armies plundered the countryside and sacked walled cities. Bishops, who were themselves from the class of lords and warriors, worried about the dangers to church property. Peasants cried out against wars that destroyed their crops or forced them to join regional infantries. Monks and religious thinkers were appalled at violence that was not in the service of an anointed king. By the end of the tenth century, all classes clamored for peace.

Sentiment against local violence was united in a movement called the Peace of God, which began in the south of France and by 1050 had spread over a wide region. Meetings of bishops, counts, and lords and often crowds of lower-class men and women set forth the provisions of this peace: "No man in the counties or bishoprics shall seize a horse, colt, ox, cow, ass, or the burdens which it carries. . . . No one shall seize a peasant, man or woman," ran the decree of one council held in 990. Anyone who violated this peace was to be excommunicated: cut off from the community of the faithful, denied the services of the church and the hope of salvation.

The peace proclaimed at local councils like this limited some violence but did not address the problem of conflict between armed men. A second set of agreements, the Truce of God, soon supplemented the Peace of God. The truce prohibited fighting between warriors at certain times: on Sunday because it was the Lord's Day, on Saturday because it was a reminder of Holy Saturday, on Friday because it symbolized Good Friday, and on Thursday because it stood for Holy Thursday. Enforcement of the truce fell to the local knights and nobles, who swore over saints' relics to uphold it and to fight anyone who broke it.

The Peace of God and Truce of God were only two of the mechanisms that attempted to contain or defuse violent confrontations in the tenth and eleventh centuries. At times, lords and their vassals mediated wars and feuds in assemblies called *placita*. In other instances, monks or laymen tried to find solutions to disputes that would leave the honor of both parties intact. Rather than try to establish guilt or innocence, winners or losers, these methods of adjudication often resulted in compromises on both sides.

Life in the early Middle Ages did not become less contentious because of these expedients, but the attempts to contain violence did affect society. Some aggressiveness was channeled into the church-sanctioned militias mandated by the Truce of God. Sometimes disputes prodded neighbors to readjust their relationships and become friends. Churchmen made the rituals of swearing to uphold the peace part of church ceremony, the oaths backed by the power of the saints. In this way any bloodshed involved in apprehending those who violated the peace was made holy.

Urban Power in Italy

In Italy the power structure was somewhat different. Still reflecting, if feebly, the political organization of ancient Rome, Italian cities were the centers of power. Whereas in France great landlords built their castles in the countryside, in Italy they often constructed their family seats within the walls of cities such as Milan and Lucca. Churches, as many as fifty or sixty, were also built within the city walls, the proud work of rich laymen and laywomen or of bishops. From their perch within the cities, the great landholders, both lay and religious, dominated the countryside.

Italian cities also functioned as important marketplaces. Peasants sold their surplus goods there; artisans and merchants lived within the walls; foreign traders offered their wares. These members of the lower classes were supported by the noble rich, who depended, even more than elsewhere, on cash to satisfy their desires. In the course of the ninth and tenth centuries, both servile and free tenants became renters who paid in currency.

The social and political life in Italy was conducive to a familial organization somewhat different from the patrilineal families of France. To stave off the partitioning of their properties among heirs, families organized themselves by formal contract into *consorteria,* in which all male members shared the profits of the family's inheritance and all women were excluded. The consorterial family became a kind of blood-related corporation, a social unit upon which early Italian businesses and banks would later be modeled.

In some ways, Rome in the tenth century closely resembled other central Italian cities. Large and powerful families who built their castles within its walls and controlled the churches and monasteries in the vicinity dominated and fought continually over it. The urban area of Rome had shrunk dramatically in the early Middle Ages, and it no longer commanded an international market: the population therefore depended on local producers for their food, and merchants brought their wares to sell within its walls. Yet the mystique of Rome remained. Although it was no longer the hub of a great empire, it was still the *see,* the center of church authority, of the pope. Rome was the goal of many pilgrims, and the papacy was the prize of powerful families there.

Regional Kingship in the West

As a consequence of the splintering of the Carolingian Empire, the western king of the Franks—who would only later receive the territorial title of king of France—was a relatively weak figure in the tenth and eleventh centuries. The German and English kings had more power, controlling much land and wealth and appointing their followers to both secular and ecclesiastical offices.

England. In the face of the Viking invasions in England, King Alfred of Wessex (r. 871–899) developed new mechanisms of royal government, instituting reforms that his successors continued. He fortified settlements throughout Wessex and divided the army into two parts, one with the duty of defending these fortifications (or *burhs*), the other operating as a mobile unit. Alfred also started a navy. These military innovations cost money, and the assessments fell on peasants' holdings.

Alfred sought to strengthen his kingdom's religious integrity as well as its regional fortifications. In the ninth century, people interpreted invasions as God's punishment for sin, which therefore was the real culprit. Hence Alfred began a program of religious reform by bringing scholars to his court to write and to educate others. Above all, Alfred wanted to translate key religious works from Latin into Anglo-Saxon (or Old English). He was determined to "turn into the language that we can all understand certain books which are the most necessary for all men to know." Alfred and scholars under his guidance translated works by church fathers such as Gregory the Great and St. Augustine. Even the Psalms, until now sung only in Hebrew, Greek, and Latin, were rendered into Anglo-Saxon. Whereas in the rest of ninth- and tenth-century Europe, Latin remained the language of scholarship

Kingdom of Alfred
Dependent on Wessex
To Alfred in 878

North Sea

Northumbria

DANELAW

Mercia   East Anglia

Wales

Wessex

England in the Age of King Alfred, 871–899

The Alfred Jewel

About two and a half inches long, this jewel consists of a gold drop-shaped frame around an enamel plaque that depicts a man enthroned holding two flowering rods. Rock crystal encloses the plaque in the frame. Along the side of the frame are gold letters in Anglo-Saxon, that mean "Alfred had me made." Below the head of a beast at the bottom is a hollow tube probably meant to hold a wooden or ivory pointer. If this jewel belonged to King Alfred, as is likely, then it may have been much like one of the "pointers" that Alfred wanted distributed to all the bishops in the kingdom along with his translation of Gregory the Great's Pastoral Care. *Such pointers were used to point to passages in manuscripts.* Ashmolean Museum, Oxford.

and writing, separate from the language people spoke, in England the vernacular—the common spoken language—was also a literary language. With Alfred's work giving it greater legitimacy, Anglo-Saxon came to be used alongside Latin for both literature and administration. It was the language of royal *writs*, which began as terse directives from the king and queen to their officials.

Alfred's reforms strengthened not only defense, education, and religion but also royal power. He consolidated his control over Wessex and fought the Danish kings, who by the mid-870s had taken Northumbria, northeastern Mercia, and East Anglia. Eventually, as he harried the Danes who were pushing south and westward, he was recognized as king of all the English not under Danish rule. He issued a law code, the first by an English king since 695. Unlike earlier codes, drawn up for each separate

TAKING MEASURE **Viking Coin Hoards, c. 865–895**

We know from chronicles and other texts that the Vikings invaded and settled in England. But it is very hard to know from such sources exactly where they settled and how many people were involved. Counting buried coins from the period can help answer these questions. Before safe-deposit boxes and banks, people buried their money in times of trouble. From Viking coin hoards in England archaeologists can see that the area called Danelaw was fairly thickly populated by Vikings, with a scattering in other regions as well. The Viking impact on England was not so much political—no Viking chief took it over—as demographic. After 900, England was as much Scandinavian as it was Anglo-Saxon. The lack of Viking coin hoards in Ireland suggests that the Scandinavians did not settle there permanently.
From David Hill, *An Atlas of Anglo-Saxon England* (Toronto, 1981).

kingdom of England, Alfred drew his laws from and for all of the English kingdoms. In this way Alfred became the first king of all the English.

Alfred's successors rolled back the Danish rule in England. "Then the Norsemen departed in their nailed ships, bloodstained survivors of spears," wrote one poet about a battle the Vikings lost in 937. But many Vikings remained. (See "Taking Measure," page 339.) Converted to Christianity, their great men joined Anglo-Saxons in attending the English king at court. As peace returned, new administrative subdivisions were established throughout England: *shires* and *hundreds,* districts for judicial and taxation purposes. The powerful men of the kingdom swore fealty to the king, promising to be enemies of his enemies, friends of his friends. England was united and organized to support a strong ruler.

Alfred's grandson Edgar (r. 957–975) commanded all the possibilities early medieval kingship offered. He was the sworn lord of all the great men of the kingdom. He controlled appointments to the English church and sponsored monastic reform. In 973, following the continental fashion, he was anointed. The fortifications of the kingdom were in his hands, as was the army, and he took responsibility for keeping the peace by proclaiming certain crimes—arson and theft—to be under his special jurisdiction and mobilizing the machinery of the shire and hundred to find and punish thieves.

Despite its apparent centralization, England was not a unified state in the modern sense, and the king's control was often tenuous. Many royal officials were great landowners who (as on the continent) worked for the king because it was in their best interest. When it was not, they allied with different claimants to the throne.

The kingdom built by Alfred and his successors could fragment easily, and it was easily conquered. At the beginning of the eleventh century, the Danes invaded England, and the Danish king Cnut (or Canute) became king of England (r. 1017–1035). Yet under Cnut, English kingship did not change much. He kept intact much of the administrative, ecclesiastical, and military apparatus already established. By Cnut's time Scandinavian traditions had largely merged with those of the rest of Europe, and the Vikings were no longer an alien culture.

France. French kings had a harder time coping with the invasions than English kings because their realm was much larger. They had no chance to build up their defenses slowly from one powerful base. During most of the tenth century, Carolingian kings alternated on the throne with kings from a family that would later be called the *Capetian.* As the Carolingian dynasty waned, the most powerful men of the kingdom—dukes, counts, and important bishops—prevented serious civil war by electing Hugh

Capet (r. 987–996). This event marked the end of Carolingian rule and the beginning of the new Capetian dynasty that would hand down the royal title from father to son until the fourteenth century.

In the eleventh century, the reach of the Capetian kings was limited by territorial lordships in the vicinity. The king's scattered but substantial estates lay in the north of France, in the region around Paris—the Île-de-France (literally "island of France"). His castles and his vassals were there. Independent castellans, however, controlled areas nearby, such as Montmorency, less than ten miles from Paris. In the sense that he was a neighbor of castellans and not much more powerful militarily than they, the king of France was just another local strongman. Yet the Capetian kings had considerable prestige. They were anointed with holy oil, and they represented the idea of unity inherited from Charlemagne. Most of the counts, at least in the north of France, became their vassals, swearing fealty and paying homage as feudal lords. As vassals they did not promise to obey the king, but they did vow not to try to kill or depose him.

The Kingdom of the Franks under Hugh Capet, 987–996

Germany. In contrast with the development of territorial lordships in France, Germany's fragmentation hardly began before it was reversed. Five *duchies* (regions dominated by dukes) emerged

The Ottonian Empire, 936–1002

in Germany in the late Carolingian period, each much larger than the

Otto III Receiving Gifts

This triumphal image is in a book of Gospels made for Otto III. The crowned women on the left are personifications of the four parts of Otto's empire: Sclavinia (the Slavic lands), Germania (Germany), Gallia (Gaul), and Roma (Rome). Each offers a gift in tribute and homage to the emperor, who sits on a throne holding the symbols of his power (orb and scepter) and flanked by representatives of the church (on his right) and of the army (on his left). Why do you suppose that the artist separated the image of the emperor from that of the women? What does the body language of the women indicate about the relations Otto wanted to portray between himself and the parts of his empire? Can you relate this manuscript, which was made in 997–1000, to Otto's conquest over the Slavs in 997?

Pro Biblioteca Academiae Scientiarum, Hungaricae.

counties and castellanies of France. With the death in 911 of the last Carolingian king in Germany, Louis the Child, the dukes elected one of themselves as king. Then, as the Magyar invasions increased, the dukes gave the royal title to the duke of Saxony, Henry I (r. 919–936), who proceeded to set up fortifications and reorganize his army, crowning his efforts with a major defeat of a Magyar army in 933.

Otto I, the son of Henry I, was an even greater military hero. His defeat of the Magyar forces in 955 gave him prestige and helped solidify his dynasty. In 951, he marched into Italy and took the Lombard crown. Against the Slavs, with whom the Germans shared a border, Otto set up marches from which he could make expeditions and stave off counterattacks. After the pope crowned him emperor in 962, he claimed the Middle Kingdom carved out by the

Treaty of Verdun and cast himself as the agent of Roman imperial renewal.

Otto's victories brought tribute and plunder, ensuring him a following but also raising the German nobles' expectations for enrichment. He and his successors, Otto II (r. 973–983), Otto III (r. 983–1002)—not surprisingly the dynasty is called the Ottonian—and Henry II (r. 1002–1024), were not always able or willing to provide the gifts and inheritances their family members and followers expected. To maintain centralized rule, for example, the Ottonians did not divide their kingdom among their sons: like castellans in France, they created a patrilineal pattern of inheritance. But the consequence was that younger sons and other potential heirs felt cheated, and disgruntled royal kin led revolt after revolt against the Ottonian kings. The

IMPORTANT DATES

750 Abbasid caliphate begins

751 Pippin III deposes the last Merovingian king; beginning of the Carolingian monarchy

756 Spanish emirate at Córdoba begins

768–814 Charlemagne rules as king of the Franks

786–809 Caliphate of Harun al-Rashid

c. 790–c. 900 Caolingian renaissance

800 Charlemagne crowned emperor by Pope Leo III

843 End of iconoclasm at Byzantium; Treaty of Verdun divides Frankish kingdom

c. 870–c. 1025 Macedonian renaissance at Byzantium

871–899 Reign of King Alfred the Great in England

955 Otto I defeats Magyars

969–1171 Fatimid dynasty in Egypt

976–1025 Reign of Byzantine emperor Basil II Bulgaroctonos

c. 1000 Age of the castellans in France

rebels found followers among the aristocracy, where the trend toward the patrilineal family prompted similar feuds and thwarted expectations.

Relations between the Ottonians and the German clergy were more harmonious. With a ribbon of new bishoprics along his eastern border, Otto I appointed bishops, gave them extensive lands, and subjected the local peasantry to their overlordship. Like Charlemagne, Otto believed that the well-being of the church in his kingdom depended on him. The Ottonians placed the churches and many monasteries of Germany under their control. They gave bishops the powers of the ban, allowing them to collect revenues and call men to arms. Answering to the king and furnishing him with troops, the bishops became royal officials, while also carrying out their pastoral and religious duties. German kings claimed the right to select bishops, even the pope at Rome, and to "invest" them by participating in the ceremony that installed them in office. The higher clergy joined royal court society. Most came to the court to be schooled; in turn, they taught the kings, princes, and noblewomen there.

Like all the strong rulers of the day, whether in the West or the Byzantine and Islamic worlds, the Ottonians presided over a renaissance of learning.

For example, the tutor of Otto III was Gerbert, the best-educated man of his time. Placed on the papal throne as Sylvester II (r. 999–1003), Gerbert knew how to use the abacus and to calculate with Arabic numerals. He "used large sums of money to pay copyists and to acquire copies of authors," as he put it. He studied the classics as models of rhetoric and argument, and he loved logic and debate. Not only did churchmen and kings support Ottonian scholarship, but to an unprecedented extent noblewomen in Germany also acquired an education and participated in the intellectual revival. Aristocratic women spent much of their wealth on learning. Living at home with their kinfolk and servants or in convents that provided them with comfortable private apartments, noblewomen wrote books and occasionally even Roman-style plays. They also supported other artists and scholars.

Despite their military and political strength, the kings of Germany faced resistance from dukes and other powerful princes, who hoped to become regional rulers themselves. The Salians, the dynasty that succeeded the Ottonians, tried to balance the power among the German dukes but could not meld them into a corps of vassals the way the Capetian kings tamed their counts. In Germany vassalage was considered beneath the dignity of free men. Instead of relying on vassals, the Salian kings and their bishops used *ministerials*, men who were legally serfs, to collect taxes, administer justice, and fight on horseback. Ministerials retained their servile status even though they often rose to wealth and high position. Under the Salian kings, ministerials became the mainstay of the royal army and administration.

The Emergence of Central Europe. Supported by their prestige, their churchmen, and their ministerials, the German kings expanded their influence eastward, into the region from the Elbe River to Russia. Otto I was so serious about expansion that he created an extraordinary "elastic" archbishopric: it had no eastern boundary, so it could increase as far as future conquests and conversions to Christianity would allow. Hand in hand with the papacy, the German kings fostered the emergence of Christian monarchies aligned with the Roman church in the regions that today constitute the Czech and Slovak Republics, Poland, and Hungary.

The Czechs, who lived in the region of Bohemia, converted under the rule of Václav (r. 920–929),

MAPPING THE WEST Europe and the Mediterranean, c. 1050

In 1050, it seemed that the future would lie with the four great political entities that dominated the west. In Europe, the German king presided over an empire that reached from Rome to the North Sea. To the east a new state, Kievan Russia, was being forged from a mix of Scandinavian and Slavic populations, leavened by Greek Orthodox Christianity. To the south was the Byzantine Empire, still celebrating its successes over the Bulgarians. And on the other side of the Mediterranean was the Muslim world, united by religion if not by rulers. The next centuries, however, would show how weak these large states actually were.

who thereby gained recognition in Germany as the duke of Bohemia. He and his successors did not become kings, remaining politically within the German sphere. Václav's murder by his younger brother made him a martyr and the patron saint of Bohemia, a symbol around which later movements for independence rallied.

The Poles gained a greater measure of independence than the Czechs. In 966, Mieszko I (r. 963–992), the leader of the Slavic tribe known as the Polanians, accepted baptism to forestall the attack that the Germans were already mounting against pagan Slavic peoples along the Baltic coast and east of the Elbe River. Busily engaged in bringing the other Slavic tribes of Poland under his control, he adroitly shifted his alliances with various German princes as they suited his needs.

In 991, Mieszko placed his realm under the protection of the pope, establishing a tradition of Polish loyalty to the Roman church. Mieszko's son Boleslaw the Brave (r. 992–1025) greatly extended Poland's boundaries, at one time or another holding sway from the Bohemian border to Kiev. In 1000, he gained a royal crown with papal blessing.

Hungary's case is similar to that of Poland. The Magyars settled in the region known today as Hungary. They became landowners, using the native Slavs to till the soil and imposing their language. At the end of the tenth century, the Magyar ruler Stephen I (r. 997–1038) accepted Christianity. In return, German knights and monks helped him consolidate his power and convert his people. According to legend, the crown placed on Stephen's head in 1001, like Boleslaw's, was sent to him by the pope.

To this day, the crown of St. Stephen remains the most hallowed symbol of Hungarian nationhood. Symbols of rulership such as crowns, consecrated by Christian priests and accorded a prestige almost akin to saints' relics, were among the most vital institutions of royal rule in central Europe. The economic basis for the power of central European rulers gradually shifted from slave raids to agriculture. This change encouraged a proliferation of regional centers of power that challenged monarchical rule. From the eleventh century onward, all the medieval Slavic states would face a constant problem of internal division.

Conclusion

In 800, the three heirs of the Roman Empire all appeared to be organized like their "parent": centralized, monarchical, imperial. Byzantine emperors writing their learned books, Abbasid caliphs holding court in their new resplendent palace at Baghdad, and Carolingian emperors issuing their directives for reform to the *missi dominici* all mimicked the Roman emperors. Yet they confronted tensions and regional pressures that tended to decentralize political power. Byzantium felt this fragmentation least, yet even there the emergence of a new elite, the *strategoi*, led to decentralization and the emperor's loss of control over the countryside.

In the Islamic world, economic crisis, religious tension, and the ambitions of powerful local rulers decisively weakened the caliphate and opened the way to separate successor states. In the West, powerful independent landowners strove with greater or lesser success (depending on the region) to establish themselves as effective rulers. By 1050, the states that would become those of modern Europe began to form.

In western Europe, local conditions determined political and economic organizations. Between 900 and 1000, for example, French society was transformed by the development of territorial lordships, patrilineal families, and ties of vassalage. These factors figured less prominently in Germany, where a central monarchy remained, buttressed by churchmen, ministerials, and conquests to the east.

After 1050, however, the German king lost his supreme position as a storm of church reform whirled around him. The economy changed, becoming more commercial and urban, and new learning, new monarchies, and new forms of religious expression came to the fore.

Suggested References

Byzantium: Renewed Strength and Influence

Recent studies of Byzantium stress the revival in the arts and literature, but Treadgold is interested in political developments. Almost nothing was available in English on eastern Europe and Russia until the 1980s.

Byzantine art: http://gallery.sjsu.edu/artH/byzantine/mainpage.html.

Davies, Norman. *God's Playground: A History of Poland.* Vol. 1. 1982.

Fine, Jon V. A., Jr. *The Early Medieval Balkans: A Critical Survey from the Sixth to the Late Twelfth Century.* 1983.

Franklin, Simon, and Jonathan Shepard. *The Emergence of Rus, 750–1200.* 1996.

Head, Constance. *Imperial Byzantine Portraits: A Verbal and Graphic Gallery.* 1982.

Jenkins, Romilly. *Byzantium: The Imperial Centuries,* A.D. *610–1071.* 1966.

Manteuffel, Tadeusz. *The Formation of the Polish State: The Period of Ducal Rule, 963–1194.* Trans. A. Gorski. 1982.

*Psellus, Michael. *Fourteen Byzantine Rulers: The Chronographia.* Trans. E. R. A. Sewter. 1966.

*Primary sources.

Treadgold, Warren. *The Byzantine Revival, 780–842.* 1988.

Wilson, N. G. *Scholars of Byzantium.* 1983.

From Unity to Fragmentation in the Islamic World

The traditional approach to the Islamic world is political (Kennedy). Glick is unusual in taking a comparative approach. The newest issue for scholars is the role of women in medieval Islamic society (Spellberg).

Ashtor, E. *A Social and Economic History of the Near East in the Middle Ages.* 1976.

Glick, Thomas. *Islamic and Christian Spain in the Early Middle Ages: Comparative Perspectives on Social and Cultural Formation.* 1979.

Kennedy, Hugh. *The Prophet and the Age of the Caliphates: The Islamic Near East from the Sixth to the Eleventh Century.* 1986.

Makdisi, George. *The Rise of Colleges.* 1981.

Spellberg, Denise. *Politics, Gender, and the Islamic Past.* 1994.

The Creation and Division of a New Western Empire

Huge chunks of the primary sources for the Carolingian world are now available in English translation, thanks in large part to the work of Paul Dutton. Hodges and Whitehouse provide the perspective of archaeologists. The Carolingian renaissance is increasingly recognized as a long-term development rather than simply the achievement of Charlemagne.

Carolingian studies: http://orb.rhodes.edu/encyclop/religion/hagiography/carol.htm.

*Dutton, Paul Edward. *Carolingian Civilization: A Reader.* 1993.

*_____. *Charlemagne's Courtier: The Complete Einhard.* 1998.

*Einhard and Notker the Stammerer. *Two Lives of Charlemagne.* Trans. Lewis Thorpe. 1969.

Hodges, Richard, and David Whitehouse. *Mohammed, Charlemagne, and the Origins of Europe.* 1983.

McKitterick, Rosamond. *Carolingian Culture: Emulation and Innovation.* 1994.

Nelson, Janet. *Charles the Bald.* 1987.

Riche, Pierre. *Daily Life in the World of Charlemagne.* Trans. J. A. McNamara. 1978.

The Emergence of Local Rule in the Post-Carolingian Age

Historians used to lament the passing of the Carolingian Empire. More recently, however, they have come to appreciate the strengths and adaptive strategies of the post-Carolingian world. Duby speaks of the agricultural "takeoff" of the period, while Head and Landes explore new institutions of peace.

Duby, Georges. *The Early Growth of the European Economy: Warriors and Peasants from the Seventh to the Twelfth Century.* Trans. H. B. Clark. 1974.

Fell, Christine E., Cecily Clark, and Elizabeth Williams. *Women in Anglo-Saxon England, and the Impact of 1066.* 1984.

Frantzen, Allen. *King Alfred.* 1986.

Head, Thomas, and Richard Landes, eds. *The Peace of God: Social Violence and Religious Response in France around the Year 1000.* 1992.

Jones, Gwyn. *A History of the Vikings.* Rev. ed. 1984.

Medieval and Renaissance manuscripts: http://www.columbia.edu/cu/libraries/indiv/rare/images.

Medieval studies: http://www.georgetown.edu/labyrinth/labyrinth-home.html.

Medieval studies: http://argos.evansville.edu.

Reuter, Timothy. *Germany in the Early Middle Ages, c. 800–1056.* 1991.

Sweeney, Del, ed. *Agriculture in the Middle Ages: Technology, Practice, and Representation.* 1995.

*Whitelock, Dorothy, ed. *English Historical Documents.* Vol. 1. 2nd ed. 1979.

Wilson, David. *The Vikings and Their Origins: Scandinavia in the First Millennium.* 1970.

Renewal and Reform

1050–1150

BRUNO OF COLOGNE WAS ENGAGED in a promising career in the church. He was an esteemed teacher at the prominent French cathedral school of Reims and a likely choice for promotion to bishop or even archbishop. But around 1084, he abandoned it all. He was disgusted with the new archbishop of Reims, Manasses, who had purchased his office and was so uninterested in religious matters that he once reportedly said, "The archbishopric of Reims would be a good thing, if one did not have to sing Mass for it." Bruno quit his post at the school and left the city. But he did not do what ethical and morally outraged men of the time were expected to do—join a monastery. Rejecting both the worldly goals of secular clerics like Manasses and the communal goals of Benedictine monks, Bruno set up a hermitage at Chartreuse, high in the Alps. The hermits who gathered there lived in isolation and poverty. One of Bruno's contemporaries marveled: "They do not take gold, silver, or ornaments for their church from anyone." This unworldliness was matched, however, with keen interest in learning: for all its poverty, Chartreuse had a rich library.

Thus began La Chartreuse, the chief house of the Carthusian order, an order still in existence. The Carthusian monks lived as hermits, eschewed material wealth, and emphasized learning. In some ways their style of life was a reaction against the monumental changes rumbling through their age: their reclusive solitude ran counter to the burgeoning cities, and their austerity contrasted sharply with the opulence and power of princely courts. Their reverence for the written word, however, reflected the growing interest in scholarship and learning.

Church over State
Around 1140, Gratian, an expert in canon law, wrote a concordance of Church laws that soon became authoritative. This illumination by a late-twelfth-century artist in a copy of Gratian's book puts a saint, symbolizing the church, above the crossbar of the initial H *and a king underneath. The scroll, which represents the voice of the church, says, "I am the King of kings; I make you king."* Berlin, Staatsbibliothek zu Berlin—Preußisher Kulturbesitz-Handschriftenabteilung.

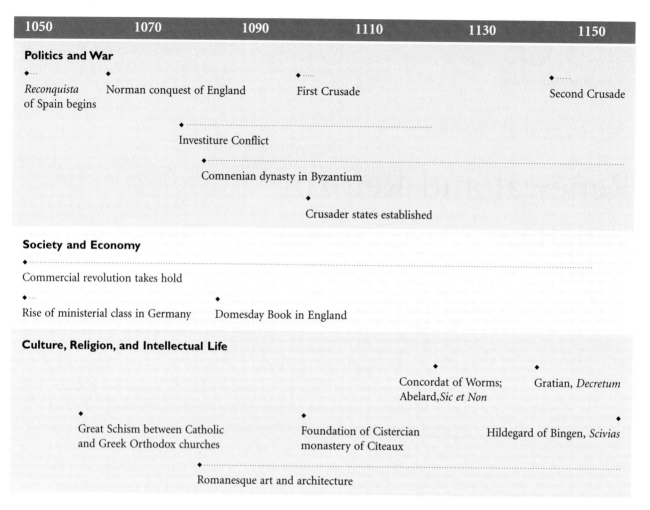

1050	1070	1090	1110	1130	1150

Politics and War

Reconquista of Spain begins

Norman conquest of England

First Crusade

Second Crusade

Investiture Conflict

Comnenian dynasty in Byzantium

Crusader states established

Society and Economy

Commercial revolution takes hold

Rise of ministerial class in Germany

Domesday Book in England

Culture, Religion, and Intellectual Life

Concordat of Worms; Abelard, *Sic et Non*

Gratian, *Decretum*

Great Schism between Catholic and Greek Orthodox churches

Foundation of Cistercian monastery of Cîteaux

Hildegard of Bingen, *Scivias*

Romanesque art and architecture

The most salient feature of the period 1050–1150 was increasing wealth. Cities, trade, and agricultural production swelled. The resulting worldliness met with a wide variety of responses. Some people, like Bruno, fled the world; others tried to reform it; and still others embraced, enjoyed, or tried to understand it.

Within one century, the development of a profit economy transformed western European communities. Many villages and fortifications became cities where traders, merchants, and artisans conducted business. Although most people still lived in less-populated, rural areas, their lives were touched in many ways by the new cash economy. Economic concerns drove changes within the church, where a movement for reform gathered steam. Money helped redefine the role of the clergy and, elaborating new political ideas, popes, kings, and princes came to exercise new forms of power.

At the same time, city dwellers began to demand their own governments. Monks and clerics reformulated the nature of their communities and, like Bruno of Cologne, sought intense spiritual lives. All of these developments inspired (and in turn were inspired by) new ideas, forms of scholarship, and methods of inquiry. The rapid pace of religious, political, and economic change was matched by new developments in thought, learning, and artistic expression.

❖ The Commercial Revolution

As the population of Europe continued to expand in the eleventh century, cities, long-distance trade networks, local markets, and new business arrangements meshed to create a profit-based economy.

With improvements in agriculture and more land in cultivation, the great estates of the eleventh century produced surpluses that helped feed—and therefore make possible—a new urban population.

Commerce was not new to the history of the West, of course, but the commercial economy of the Middle Ages spawned the institutions that would be the direct ancestors of western businesses: corporations, banks, accounting systems, and, above all, urban centers that thrived on economic vitality. Whereas ancient cities had primarily religious, social, and political functions, medieval cities were primarily centers of production and economic activity. Wealth meant power: it allowed city dwellers to become self-governing.

Commercial Centers

Commercial centers developed around castles and monasteries and within the walls of ancient towns. Great lords in the countryside—and this included monasteries—were eager to take advantage of the profits that their estates generated. In the late tenth century, they had reorganized their lands for greater productivity, encouraged their peasants to cultivate new land, and converted services and dues to money payments. Now with ready cash, they not only fostered the development of sporadic markets where they could sell their surpluses and buy luxury goods but even encouraged traders and craftspeople to settle down near them. The lords gained at each step: their purchases brought them an enhanced lifestyle and greater prestige, while they charged merchants tolls and sales taxes, in this way profiting even more from trade.

Trade did not benefit only great lords. The vassals who lived with them enjoyed a better standard of living. Peasants, too, participated in the new economy, selling their meager surpluses at local markets. Commerce sometimes opened up unexpected opportunities for enrichment. Former servants of the bishop of Mâcon (today in France), for example, set up a bakery near the bridge of the city and sold bread to travelers. They soon grew prosperous.

At Bruges (today in Belgium), the local lord's castle became the magnet around which a city formed. As a medieval chronicler observed:

> To satisfy the needs of the people in the castle at Bruges, first merchants with luxury articles began

to surge around the gate: then the wine-sellers came; finally the innkeepers arrived to feed and lodge the people who had business with the prince. . . . So many houses were built that soon a great city was created.

Other commercial centers clustered around Benedictine monasteries, which by the eleventh century had become large communities of several hundred monks with many needs to supply. Still other markets formed just outside the walls of older cities; these gradually merged into new and enlarged urban

Medieval Conques
Conques in medieval France was a major pilgrimage center. Housed in its monastery church was the powerful relic of Ste. Foy (St. Faith), whose miracle-working cures were famous across Europe. People went to Conques directly to seek help from Ste. Foy or as part of a multistop journey that took them across the south of France and the north of Spain to Santiago de Compostela, where they sought the relics of St. James. A whole city of shopkeepers, hoteliers, and craftspeople grew up around the monastery at Conques to serve the throngs of pilgrims.
Jean Dieuzaide.

communities as town walls were built around them to protect their inhabitants. Sometimes informal country markets might eventually be housed in permanent structures. To the north, in places like Frisia, the Vikings had already established centers of wealth and trade, and these settlements became permanent, thriving towns. Along the Rhine and in other river valleys, cities sprang up to service the merchants who traversed the route between Italy and the north.

Merchants and Markets.   Merchants were a varied lot. Some were local traders, like one Benedictine monk who supervised a manor twenty miles to the south of his monastery in France and sold its surplus horses and grain at a local market. Others—mainly Jews and Italians—were long-distance traders, in great demand because they supplied the fine wines, spices, and fabrics beloved by lords and ladies, their families, and their vassals. Jews had often been involved at least part-time in long-distance trade as vintners; and as lords reorganized the countryside, driving out Jewish landowners, most Jews were forced to turn to commerce full-time. Other long-distance traders came

from Italy, where urban mercantile activities at places like Venice and Genoa had never quite ceased. Contact with the great commercial center Byzantium and opportunities for plunder and trade on the high seas and in Muslim and Byzantine ports provided the background to Italy's early commercial growth (Map 10.1).

At Reims, the city Bruno left, the middle of a forum dating back to the Roman Empire became a new commercial center. As early as 1067, the king of France was writing about the many fairs in his realm—great markets held at regular intervals that attracted large crowds. Around the marketplace at Reims grew a network of streets whose names (many of which still exist) revealed their essentially commercial functions: Street of the Butchers, Street of the Wool Market, Street of the Wheat Market.

The Building Boom.   The look and feel of such developing cities varied enormously. Nearly all included a marketplace, a castle, and several churches, however. And most had to adapt to increasingly crowded conditions. Archaeologists have discovered that at the end of the eleventh century in Winchester, England, city plots were still large enough to

Medieval Workshops
In this eleventh-century miniature combining two workshops, the artist portrays two carpenters sawing a piece of wood, while a blacksmith works alone on the right-hand side. Above the anvil, the blacksmith holds a piece of hot iron with his tongs as he gets ready to strike with his hammer. Why were blacksmiths important to village survival? What other workshops might you expect to find in prosperous villages and towns?
A.M. Rosati/Art Resource NY.

MAP 10.1 Medieval Trade Routes in the Eleventh and Twelfth Centuries
This spider's web of lines showing the major trade routes of the medieval world obscures the simple pattern: bulk goods from the north (furs, fish, wood) were traded for luxury goods from the south (ivory and spices, including medicines, perfumes, and dyes). Already regions were beginning to specialize. England, for example, supplied raw wool, but Flanders (Ypres, Ghent) specialized in turning that wool into cloth and shipping it farther south, to the fairs of Champagne (whose capital was Troyes) or Germany. Italian cities channeled goods from the Muslim and Byzantine worlds northward and exported European goods southward and eastward.

accommodate houses parallel to the street; but the swelling population soon necessitated destroying these houses and building instead long, narrow, hall-like tenement houses, constructed at right angles to the thoroughfare. These were built on a frame made from strips of wood filled with wattle and daub—twigs woven together and covered with clay. If they were like the stone houses built in the late twelfth century (a period about which we know a good deal), they had two stories: a shop or ware-

house on the lower floor and living quarters above. Behind this main building was the kitchen and perhaps also enclosures for livestock, as archaeologists have found at Southampton, England. Even city dwellers clung to rural pursuits, living largely off the food they raised themselves.

The construction of wattle and daub houses, churches, castles, and markets was part of a building boom that began in the tenth century and continued at an accelerated pace through the thirteenth.

Specialized buildings for trade and city government were put up—charitable houses for the sick and indigent, community houses, and warehouses. In addition to individual buildings the new construction involved erecting masses of walls. Medieval cities were ringed by walls. By 1100, Speyer (today in Germany) had three: one around its cathedral, the next just beyond the parish church of St. Moritz, the third still farther out to protect the marketplace. Within the walls lay a network of streets, often narrow, dirty, dark, and winding, made of packed clay or gravel. In English towns the main street broadened as it approached a rectangular or V-shaped marketplace. Bridges spanned the rivers; on the Meuse, for example, six new bridges were built during the eleventh century alone. Before the eleventh century, Europeans had depended on boats and waterways for bulky long-distance transport; now carts could haul items overland because new roads through the countryside linked the urban markets.

Although commercial centers developed throughout western Europe, they grew fastest and became most dense in regions along key waterways: the Mediterranean coasts of Italy, France, and Spain; northern Italy along the Po River; the river system of the Rhône-Saône-Meuse; the Rhineland; the English Channel; the shores of the Baltic Sea. During the eleventh century these waterways became part of a single interdependent economy.

Business Arrangements

The development of commercial centers reflected changing attitudes toward money. The new mode of commerce transformed the social relations involved in economic transactions. In the gift economy, exchanges of coins, gold, and silver were components of ongoing relationships. Kings offered treasures to their followers, peasants gave dues to their lords, and pious donors presented land to the saintly patrons of churches, all in the expectation of long-term relationships. In the new market economy, which thrived on the profit motive, arrangements were less personal. They often relied on written contracts and calculations of the profitability of a particular business venture. Even largely social associations, such as the new collective organizations called *guilds*, betrayed participation in the commercial economy through their regulations concerning the manufacture, pricing, and distribution of their products.

Partnerships, Contracts, and the Rise of Industry. In the course of the eleventh and twelfth centuries, people created new kinds of business arrangements through partnerships, contracts, and large-scale productive enterprises. Although they took many forms, all new business agreements had the common purpose of bringing people together to pool their resources and finance larger enterprises. The *commenda*, for example, an Italian invention, was a partnership established for commerce by sea. In a common arrangement, one or more investors furnished the money, and the other partners undertook the risks of the actual voyage. If a trip proved successful, the investors received three-quarters of the profit and the travelers the rest. But if the voyage failed, the investors lost their outlay, and the travelers expended their time and labor to no profit. The impermanence of such partnerships (they lasted for only one voyage) meant that capital could be shifted easily from one venture to another and could therefore be used to support a variety of enterprises.

Land trade often involved a more enduring partnership. In Italy this took the form of a *compagnia*, formed when family property was invested in trade. Unlike the *commenda*, in which the partners could lose no more than they had put into the enterprise, the *compagnia* left its members with joint and unlimited liability for all losses and debts. This provision enhanced family solidarity, because each member was responsible for the debts of all the others; but it also risked bankrupting entire households.

The commercial revolution also fostered the development of contracts for sales, exchanges, and loans. Loans were the most problematic. In the Middle Ages, as now, interest payments were the chief inducement for an investor to supply money. To circumvent the church's ban on usury (profiting from loans), interest was often disguised as a penalty for "late payment" under the rules of a contract. The new willingness to finance business enterprises with loans signaled a changed attitude toward credit: risk was acceptable if it brought profit.

Contracts and partnerships made large-scale productive enterprises possible. In fact, light industry began in the eleventh century. Just as in the Industrial Revolution of the eighteenth and nineteenth centuries, one of the earliest products to benefit from new industrial technologies was cloth. Water mills powered machines such as flails to clean and thicken cloth and presses to extract oil from fibers. Machines were also used to exploit raw materials more efficiently: new deep-mining technology provided Europeans with hitherto untapped sources of metals. At the same time, forging techniques improved, and iron was for the first time regularly used for agricultural tools and plows. This, in turn, made for better farming, and better farming fed the commercial revolution. Metals were also used for weapons and armor or fashioned into ornaments or coins.

Guilds. Whether fashioned by machines or hand-workers, production relied on the expertise of artisans able to finish the cloth, mint the coins, and forge the weapons. To regulate and protect their products and trades, craftspeople and others involved in commerce formed *guilds*: local social, religious, and economic associations whose members plied the same trade. One guild in the Italian city of Ferrara began as a prayer confraternity, an association whose members gathered and prayed for one another. If a member or his wife died, the others would bear the body to the church, bury it with honors, and offer money for Masses to be said for the salvation of the dead person's soul. In time this guild's membership came to be limited to shoemakers. Although mothers, wives, daughters, and female apprentices often knew how to make shoes, weave cloth, or sell goods, women did not ordinarily join guilds. While partly social and convivial fraternities, guilds also undertook to regulate their members' work hours, materials, and prices and to set quality standards. Although not eliminating all competition among craftspeople in the same field, the guild prevented any one artisan from gaining unfair advantages over another. Most important, the guild guaranteed each member a place in the market by controlling the production of shoes, fabrics, candles, and other items in each city.

Clearly the legitimacy and enforceability of the regulations of guilds and other trade and crafts organizations depended on the guilds' recognition by the political powers that ruled each city. Guild rules could not supersede city and church laws. But in most cities guilds and the city rulers had comfortable relationships based on mutual benefit. For example, when in 1106, twenty-three fishermen at Worms in Germany wanted exclusive rights to the wholesale fish market there, they petitioned the lo-cal bishop to give them the privilege and impose penalties on anyone who violated it. In return, they promised to give him two salmon every year and the local count one salmon a year.

Self-Government for the Towns

Guilds were one way townspeople expressed their mutual concerns and harnessed their collective energies. Movements for self-government were another. Townspeople banded together for protection and freedom.

Both to themselves and to outsiders, townspeople seemed different. Tradespeople, artisans, ship captains, innkeepers, and money changers did not fit into the old categories of medieval types—those who pray, those who fight, and those who labor. Just knowing they were different gave townspeople a sense of solidarity with one another. But practical reasons also contributed to their feeling of common purpose: they lived in close quarters with one another, and they shared a mutual interest in reliable coinage, laws to facilitate commerce, freedom from servile dues and services, and independence to buy and sell as the market dictated. Already in the early twelfth century, the king of England granted to the citizens of Newcastle-upon-Tyne the privilege that

Shoemaker
By the twelfth century, a fortified village (a burg) had developed around the monastery of Cluny to cater to the monks' material needs. This carving of a shoemaker at his bench, which was displayed above his shop at Cluny, is an example of the sorts of signs that merchants used to advertise their services. Musée Ochier, Cluny, France.

any unfree peasant who lived there unclaimed by his lord for a year and a day would thereafter be a free person. To townspeople, freedom meant having their own officials and law courts. They petitioned the political powers that ruled them—bishops, kings, counts, castellans—for the right to govern themselves. Often they formed *communes*, sworn associations of townspeople that generally cut across the boundaries of rich and poor, merchants and craftspeople, clergy and laity.

Collective movements for urban self-government emerged especially in Italy, France, and Germany. Italian cities were centers of regional political power even before the commercial revolution. Castellans constructed their fortifications and bishops ruled the countryside from such cities. The commercial revolution swelled the Italian cities with tradespeople, whose interest in self-government was often fueled by religious as well as economic concerns. At Milan in the second half of the eleventh century, popular discontent with the archbishop, who effectively ruled the city, led to numerous armed clashes. In 1097, the Milanese succeeded in transferring political power from the archbishop and his clergy to a government of leading men of the city, who called themselves "consuls." The title recalled the government of the ancient Roman republic, affirming the consuls' status as representatives of the people. Like the archbishop's power before, the consuls' rule extended beyond the town walls, into the *contado*, the outlying countryside.

Outside of Italy, movements for city independence took place within the framework of larger kingdoms or principalities. Such movements were sometimes violent, as at Milan, but at other times they were peaceful. For example, William Clito, who claimed the county of Flanders (today in Belgium), willingly granted the citizens of St. Omer the rights they asked for in 1127 in return for their support of his claims: he recognized them as legally free, gave them the right to mint coins, allowed them their own laws and courts, and lifted certain tolls and taxes. Although the merchant guild profited the most, as it alone gained freedom from tolls throughout Flanders, all the citizens of St. Omer benefited from these privileges. Here as elsewhere the men and women who created new forms of business and political associations to meet their needs gained a measure of self-rule in towns and cities.

❖ Church Reform and Its Aftermath

The commercial revolution affected the church because the church too was part of the world. Bishops ruled over many cities. Kings appointed many bishops. Local lords installed priests in their parish churches. Churchmen gave gifts and money to these secular powers for their offices. The impulse to free the church from "the world" was as old as the origins of monasticism, but, beginning in the tenth century and increasing to fever pitch in the eleventh, reformers demanded that the church as a whole remodel itself and become free of secular entanglements.

This freedom was from the start as much a matter of power as of religion. Most people had long believed that their ruler—whether king, duke, count, or castellan—reigned by the grace of God and had the right to control the churches in his territory. But by the second half of the eleventh century, more and more people saw a great deal wrong with secular power over the church. They looked to the papacy to lead the movement of church reform. The most important moment came in 1075, when Pope Gregory VII called upon the emperor, Henry IV, to end his appointment of churchmen. This ushered in a major civil war in Germany and a great upheaval in the distribution of power everywhere. By the early 1100s, a reformed church—with the pope at its head—had become institutionalized, penetrating into areas of life never before touched by churchmen. Church reform began as a way to free the church from the world; but in the end the church was equally involved in the new world it had helped to create.

Beginnings of Reform

The idea of freeing the church from the world began in the tenth century with no particular program and only a vague idea of what it might mean. A program took shape in the eleventh century, in the hands of reformers in the empire. The program was not fully worked out, however, until it was taken up by the papacy and turned into a recipe for reorganizing the church under papal leadership. The movement to "liberate the church" in fact began in unlikely circles: with the very rulers who were controlling churches and monasteries, appointing churchmen, and using bishops as their administrators.

Cluniac Reform.   The Benedictine monastery of Cluny is a good example of the reform movement before it became an organized program. The monastery was founded in 910 by the duke and duchess of Aquitaine, who endowed it with property but then gave it and its worldly possessions to Saints Peter and Paul. In this way they put control of the monastery into the hands of the two most powerful heavenly saints. They designated the pope, as the successor of St. Peter, to be the monastery's worldly protector if anyone should bother or threaten it. The whole notion of "freedom" at this point was very vague. But Cluny's prestige was great because of its status as St. Peter's property and the elaborate round of prayers that the monks carried out there with scrupulous devotion. The Cluniac monks fulfilled the role of "those who pray" in a way that dazzled their contemporaries. Through their prayers they seemed to guarantee the salvation of all Christians. Rulers, bishops, rich landowners, and even serfs (if they could) gave Cluny donations of land, joining their contributions to the land of St. Peter. Powerful men and women called on the Cluniac monks to reform new monasteries along the Cluniac model.

The abbots of Cluny came to see themselves as reformers of the world as well. They believed in clerical celibacy, preaching against the prevailing norm in which parish priests and even bishops were married. They also thought that the laity could be reformed, become more virtuous, and cease its oppression of the poor.

In the eleventh century, the Cluniacs began to link their program of internal monastic and external worldly reform to the papacy. They called on the popes to help them when their lands were encroached upon by bishops and laypeople at the same time as the papacy itself was becoming interested in reform.

Church Reform in the Empire.   Calls for a program of reform began with a small group of clerics and monks in the empire. They buttressed their arguments with new interpretations of canon law—the laws decreed over the centuries at church councils and by bishops and popes. They concentrated on two breaches of those laws: nicolaitism (clerical marriage) and simony (buying church offices). Most of the men who promoted these ideas lived in the most commercialized regions of the empire: the Rhineland (the region along the northern half of the Rhine River) and Italy. Their familiarity with the impersonal practices of a profit economy led them to interpret as crass purchases the gifts that churchmen were used to giving in return for their offices.

Emperor Henry III (r. 1039–1056) supported the reformers. Taking seriously his position as the anointed of God, Henry felt responsible for the well-being of the church in his empire. He denounced simony and personally refused to accept money or gifts when he appointed bishops to their posts. When in 1046 three men, each representing a different faction of the Roman aristocracy, claimed to be pope, Henry, as ruler of Rome, traveled to Italy to settle the matter. The Synod of Sutri (1046), over which he presided, deposed all three popes and elected another. In 1049, Henry appointed Leo IX (r. 1049–1054), a bishop from the Rhineland, to the papacy. But this appointment marked an unanticipated turning point for the emperor when Leo set out to reform the church under papal control.

Leo IX and the Expansion of Papal Power.   During Leo's tenure, the pope's role expanded and the Catholic church changed irrevocably. Leo knew canon law. He insisted, for example, that he be elected by the clergy and people of Rome before assuming the papal office. During his five years as pope, he traveled to Germany and France and held church councils. Before this time, popes had made the arduous journey across the Alps from Italy to the rest of Europe only rarely. They were, after all, mainly the bishops of Rome. But under Leo, the pope's role expanded. He sponsored the creation of a canon lawbook—the *Collection in 74 Titles*—which emphasized the pope's power. To the papal court Leo brought the most zealous reformers of his day: Humbert of Silva Candida, Peter Damian, and Hildebrand (later Gregory VII).

At first, Leo's claims to new power over the church hierarchy were complacently ignored by clergy and secular rulers alike. The Council of Reims, which he called in 1049, for example, was attended by only a few bishops and boycotted by the

Leo IX

This eleventh-century manuscript shows not so much a portrait of Leo IX as an idealized image of his power and position. What does the halo signify? Why do you suppose he stands at least three heads taller than the other figure in the picture, Warinus, the abbot of St. Arnulf of Metz? What is Leo doing with his right hand (hint: look at the image of the pope on page 306). With his left hand he holds a little church (symbol of a real one) that is being presented to him by Warinus. Compare these figures to those of emperor and Christ on page 312. What did the artist intend to convey about the relationship of this church to papal power? Burgerbibliothek Bern cod. 292f.#72r.

king of France. Nevertheless, Leo made it into a forum for exercising his authority. Placing the relics of St. Remegius (the patron saint of Reims) on the altar of the church, he demanded that the attending bishops and abbots say whether or not they had purchased their offices. A few confessed they had; some did not respond; others gave excuses. The new and

extraordinary development was that all present felt accountable to the pope and accepted his verdicts. One bishop was stripped of his episcopal office; another was summoned to Rome to explain himself. The power of St. Peter had come to match the force of a king's, but with a scope that encompassed the western half of Europe.

In 1054, Leo sent Humbert of Silva Candida to Constantinople on a diplomatic mission to argue against the patriarch of Constantinople on behalf of the new, lofty claims of the pope. Furious at the contemptuous way he was treated, Humbert ended his mission by excommunicating the patriarch. In retaliation the Byzantine emperor and his bishops excommunicated Humbert and his party, threatening them with eternal damnation. Clashes between the two churches had occurred before and had been patched up, but this one, called the Great Schism, proved insurmountable.* Thereafter the Roman Catholic and the Greek Orthodox churches were largely separate.

Following the Great Schism, the papacy intervened in many venues to protect itself; demonstrate its primacy, or leadership of the church; and (in its view) ensure the salvation of all Christians. For example, when military adventurers from Normandy began carving out states for themselves in southern Italy, the popes in nearby Rome felt threatened. After waging unsuccessful war against the interlopers, the papacy made the best of a bad situation by granting the Normans Sicily and parts of southern Italy as a fief, turning its former enemies into vassals.

As leader of the Christian people, the papacy also participated in wars in Spain, where it supported Christians against the dominant Muslims. The political fragmentation of al-Andalus into small and weak *taifas* (see page 317) made it fair game to the Christians to the north. Slowly the idea of the *reconquista*, the Christian reconquest of Spain, took shape, fed by religious fervor as well as worldly ambition. Pope Alexander II (r. 1061–1073) helped turn the reconquista into a holy war by relieving Christians on their way to battle of their duty to do penance and forgiving their sins.

---

*Despite occasional thaws and liftings of the sentences, the mutual excommunications of pope and patriarch largely remained in effect until 1965, when Pope Paul VI and the Greek Orthodox patriarch, Anthenagoras I, publicly deplored them.

The Gregorian Reform, 1073–1085

For all the importance of Leo IX and Alexander II, the papal reform movement is above all associated with Pope Gregory VII (r. 1073–1085). He began as a lowly Roman cleric with the job of administering the papal estates and rose slowly in the hierarchy. A passionate advocate of papal primacy (the theory that the pope was the head of the church), he was not afraid to clash head on with Emperor Henry IV (r. 1056–1106) over leadership of the church. In his view—and it was astonishing at the time, given the religious and spiritual roles associated with rulers—the emperor was just a layman who had no right to meddle in church affairs.

Gregory was and remains an extraordinarily controversial figure. He certainly thought that he was acting as the vicar, or representative, of St. Peter on earth. Describing himself, he declared, "I have labored with all my power that Holy Church, the bride of God, our Lady Mother, might come again to her own splendor and might remain free, pure, and Catholic." He thought the reforms he advocated and the upheavals he precipitated were necessary to free the church from the Satanic rulers of the world. But his great nemesis Henry IV had a very different view of Gregory. He considered him an ambitious and evil man who "seduced the world far and wide and stained the Church with the blood of her sons." Not surprisingly, modern historians are only a bit less divided in their assessment of Gregory. Few deny his sincerity and deep religious devotion, but many speak of his pride, ambition, and single-mindedness. He was not an easy man.

Henry IV was less complex. He was brought up in the traditions of his father, Henry III, a pious church reformer who considered it part of his duty to appoint bishops and even popes to ensure the well-being of church and state together. The emperor believed that he and his bishops—who were, at the same time, his most valuable supporters and administrators—were the rightful leaders of the church. He had no intention of allowing the pope to become head of the church.

The Investiture Conflict. The great confrontation between Gregory and Henry began over the appointment of the archbishop of Milan. Gregory disputed Henry's right to "invest" the archbishop (put him

into his office). In the investiture ritual, the emperor or his representative symbolically gave the church and the land that went with it to the priest or bishop or archbishop chosen for the job. In 1075, Gregory prohibited lay investiture, thereby denying the emperor's right to invest churchmen. When Henry defied this prohibition and invested a new archbishop of Milan, the two men hurled unceasing denunciations at each other. The next year Henry called a council of German bishops who demanded that Gregory, that "false monk," resign. In reply Gregory called a synod that both excommunicated and suspended Henry from office:

> *I deprive King Henry, son of the emperor Henry, who has rebelled against [God's] Church with unheard-of audacity, of the government over the whole kingdom of Germany and Italy, and I release all Christian men from the allegiance which they have sworn or may swear to him, and I forbid anyone to serve him as king.*

The last part of this decree gave it a secular punch because it authorized anyone in Henry's kingdom to rebel against him. Henry's enemies, mostly German princes (as German aristocrats were called), now threatened to elect another king. They were motivated partly by religious sentiments, as many had established links with the papacy through their support of reformed monasteries, and partly by political opportunism, as they had chafed under the strong German king, who had tried to keep their power in check. Some bishops joined forces with Gregory's supporters, however. This was a great blow to royal power because Henry desperately needed the troops supplied by his churchmen.

The World of the Investiture Conflict, c. 1070–1122

Attacked from all sides, Henry traveled to intercept Gregory, who was journeying northward to visit the rebellious princes. In early 1077, king and pope met at Canossa, high in central Italy's snowy

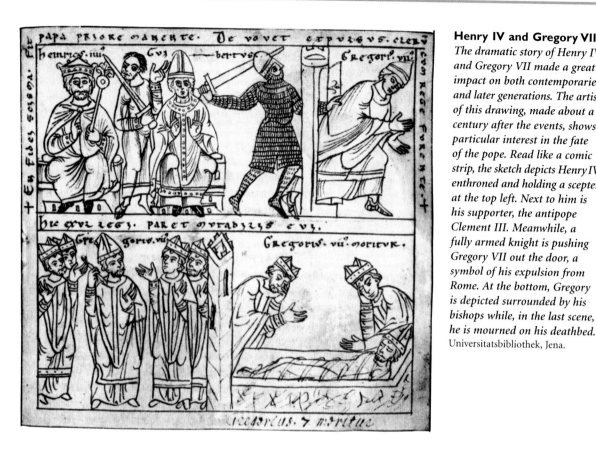

Henry IV and Gregory VII
The dramatic story of Henry IV and Gregory VII made a great impact on both contemporaries and later generations. The artist of this drawing, made about a century after the events, shows particular interest in the fate of the pope. Read like a comic strip, the sketch depicts Henry IV enthroned and holding a scepter at the top left. Next to him is his supporter, the antipope Clement III. Meanwhile, a fully armed knight is pushing Gregory VII out the door, a symbol of his expulsion from Rome. At the bottom, Gregory is depicted surrounded by his bishops while, in the last scene, he is mourned on his deathbed. Universitatsbibliothek, Jena.

Apennine Mountains. Gregory was inside a fortress there; Henry stood outside as a penitent. This posture was an astute move by Henry because no priest could refuse absolution to a penitent; Gregory had to lift the excommunication and receive Henry back into the church. But Gregory now had the advantage of the king's humiliation before the majesty of the pope. Gregory's description of Henry suggests that the pope indeed believed himself to have triumphed:

> There, on three successive days, standing before the castle gate, laying aside all royal insignia, barefooted and in coarse attire, he did not cease, with many tears, to beseech the apostolic help and comfort.

Although Henry was technically back in the fold, nothing of substance had been resolved, and civil war began. The princes elected an antiking (a king chosen illegally), and Henry and his supporters elected an antipope. From 1077 until 1122, Germany was ravaged by civil war.

Outcome of the Investiture Conflict. The Investiture Conflict was finally resolved long after Henry IV and Gregory VII had died. The Concordat of Worms of 1122 ended the fighting with a compromise that relied on a conceptual distinction between two parts of investiture—the spiritual (in which a man received the symbols of his clerical office) and the secular (in which he received the symbols of the material goods that would allow him to function). Under the terms of the concordat, the ring and staff, the symbols of church office, would be given by a churchman in the first part of the ceremony. The emperor or his representative would touch the bishop with a scepter, a symbolic gesture that stood for the land and other possessions that went with his office, in the second part of the ceremony. Elections of bishops in Germany would take place "in the presence" of the emperor—that is, under his influence. In Italy, the pope would have a comparable role.

Thus in the end secular rulers continued to have a part in choosing and investing churchmen, but few people any longer claimed the king was the head of the church. Just as the new investiture ceremony broke the ritual into spiritual and secular parts, so too it implied a new notion of kingship that separated it from priesthood. The Investiture Conflict did not produce the modern distinction between church and state—that would develop only very slowly—but it set the wheels in motion. At the time, its most important consequence was to strengthen the papacy.

Thus the Investiture Conflict and the civil war it generated shattered the delicate balance among political and ecclesiastical powers in Germany and Italy. In Germany, the princes consolidated their lands and their positions at the expense of royal power. They became virtual monarchs within their own principalities, whereas the emperor, though retaining his title, became a figurehead.

As overlord of northern Italy, the emperor also lost power to the communes and other movements for local self-government, which developed in the late eleventh and early twelfth centuries. The rise of the Italian communes in a time of war between the emperor and the pope left an indelible mark on these new political entities. Conflict between the supporters of the emperor and those of the pope caused friction throughout the twelfth century. The ongoing hostilities of popes and emperors mirrored fierce communal struggles in which factions, motivated in part by local grievances, claimed to fight on behalf of the papal or the imperial cause.

The Sweep of Reform

Church reform involved much more than the clash of popes, emperors, and their supporters. It penetrated into the daily lives of ordinary Christians, both lay and clerical; inspired new forms of legal scholarship; and changed the way the church worked.

New Emphasis on the Sacraments.   Since the time of the early church, Christians believed that the sacraments were the regular means by which God's heavenly grace infused mundane existence. But this did not mean that Christians were clear about how many sacraments there were, how they worked, or even their significance. Eleventh-century church reformers began the process—which would continue into the thirteenth century—of emphasizing the importance of the sacraments and the special nature of the priest, whose chief role was to administer them.

In the sacrament of marriage, for example, the effective involvement of the church in the wedding of man and wife came only after the Gregorian reform. Not until the twelfth century did people regularly come to be married by a priest in church, and only then did churchmen assume jurisdiction over marital disputes, not simply in cases involving royalty but also in those of lesser aristocrats. The clergy's prohibition of marriage partners as distant as seventh cousins (marriage between such cousins was considered incest) had the potential to control dynastic alliances. Because many noble families kept their inheritance intact through a single male heir, the heirs' marriages took on great significance. The church's incest prohibitions gave the clergy a measure of power over all European states. For example, when King Henry I of England (r. 1100–1135) wanted to marry one of his daughters to William of Warenne, earl of Surrey (his good friend, adviser, and important political ally), he asked Anselm, the archbishop of Canterbury, for his advice. Anselm warned against the union on the grounds that William and his prospective bride shared two ancestors several generations back. The match was broken off.

At the same time, churchmen began to stress the sanctity of marriage. Hugh of St. Victor, a twelfth-century scholar, dwelled on the sacramental meaning of marriage:

> Can you find anything else in marriage except conjugal society which makes it sacred and by which you can assert that it is holy? . . . Each shall be to the other as a same self in all sincere love, all careful solicitude, every kindness of affection, in constant compassion, unflagging consolation, and faithful devotedness.

Hugh saw marriage as a matter of love.

The reformers also proclaimed the special importance of the sacrament of the Mass, holy communion through the body and blood of Christ. Gregory VII called the Mass "the greatest thing in the Christian religion." No layman, no matter how powerful, and no woman of any sort at all could perform anything equal to it, for the Mass was the key to salvation.

Clerical Celibacy. The new emphasis on the sacraments, which were now more thoroughly and carefully defined, along with the desire to set priests clearly apart from the laity, led to vigorous enforcement of an old element of church discipline: the celibacy of priests. The demand for a celibate clergy had far-reaching significance for the history of the church. It distanced western clerics even further from their eastern Orthodox counterparts (who did not practice celibacy), exacerbating the Great Schism of 1054. It also broke with traditional local practices, as clerical marriage was customary in some places. In eleventh-century Normandy, for example, even the highest clergymen had wives: one archbishop of Rouen was married and had three sons, and a bishop of Sées was the father of a different archbishop. Gregorian reformers exhorted every cleric in higher orders, from the humble parish priest to the exalted bishop, to refrain from marriage or to abandon his wife. Naturally many churchmen resisted. The historian Orderic Vitalis (1075–c. 1142) reported that one zealous archbishop

> *fulfilled his duties as metropolitan with courage and thoroughness, continually striving to separate immoral priests from their mistresses [wives]: on one occasion when he forbade them to keep concubines he was stoned out of the synod.*

Undaunted, the reformers persisted, and in 1123 the pope proclaimed all clerical marriages invalid. No wonder a poem of the twelfth century had a lady repulse a cleric's offer of love with the reply "I refuse to commit adultery; I want to get married." Clearly clerics were no longer suitable candidates for matrimony.

The "Papal Monarchy." The newly reformed and strengthened papacy enhanced its position by consolidating and imposing canon law. Canon law originated at meetings of churchmen at church councils and synods held since the fourth century. But not until the Gregorian reform were these decrees compiled in a great push for systematization. Reformers began to study church canons in the same formal and orderly manner that legal scholars were beginning to use for Roman and other secular laws. A landmark in canon law jurisprudence was the *Concordance of Discordant Canons*, also known as the *Decretum*, compiled in about 1140 by Gratian, a monk who taught law at Bologna in northern Italy. Gratian gathered thousands of passages from the decrees of popes and councils with the intention of showing their harmony. To make conflicting canons conform to one another, he adopted the principle that papal pronouncements superseded the laws of church councils and all secular laws.

At the time Gratian was writing, the papal *curia*, or government, centered in Rome, resembled a court of law with its own collection agency. The papacy had developed a bureaucracy to hear cases and rule on petitions, such as disputed elections of bishops. Hearing cases cost money: lawyers, judges, and courtroom clerks had to be paid. Churchmen not involved in litigation went to Rome for other sorts of benefits: to petition for privileges for their monasteries or to be consecrated by the pope. These services were also expensive, requiring hearing officers, notaries, and collectors. The lands owned by the papacy were not sufficient to support the growing administrative apparatus, and the petitioners and litigants themselves had to pay, a practice they resented. A satire written about 1100, in the style of the Gospels, made bitter fun of papal greed:

> *There came to the court a certain wealthy clerk, fat and thick, and gross, who in the sedition [rebellion] had committed murder. He first gave to the dispenser, second to the treasurer, third to the cardinals. But they thought among themselves that they should receive more. The Lord Pope, hearing that his cardinals had received many gifts, was sick, nigh unto death. But the rich man sent to him a couch of gold and silver and immediately he was made whole. Then the Lord Pope called his cardinals and ministers to him and said to them: "Brethren, look, lest anyone deceive you with vain words. For I have given you an example: as I have grasped, so you grasp also."*

The pope, with his law courts, bureaucracy, and financial apparatus, had become a monarch.

The First Crusade, 1096–1099

The papacy, asserting itself as the head of the Christian church and leader of its reform movement, sometimes supported and proclaimed holy wars to further the cause of Christianity. Alexander II forgave the sins of those who fought in the reconquista,

A Crusader and His Wife
How do we know that the man on the left is a crusader? On his shirt is a cross, the sign worn by all men going on the crusades. In his right hand is a pilgrim's staff, a useful reminder that the crusades were sometimes considered less a matter of war than of penance and piety. What does the crusader's wife's embrace imply about marital love in the twelfth century?
Musée Lorrain, Nancy/photo: P. Mignot.

for example. Even while the Investiture Conflict was raging, Pope Urban II (r. 1088–1099) launched a far more ambitious war, the First Crusade.

The crusades were a combination of war and pilgrimage, the popular practice of making a pious voyage to a sacred shrine to petition for help or cure. Authorized by the papacy, the crusades sent armed European Christians into battle against non-Christians, especially Muslims in the Holy Land, the place where Christ lived and died. The First Crusade was called in response to a new wave of Muslim invasions that threatened the Byzantine Empire and led the Byzantine emperor to ask for military help from the West.

Although the crusades ultimately failed in the sense that the crusaders did not succeed in permanently retaining the Holy Land for Christendom, they were a pivotal episode in Western civilization. They marked the first stage of European overseas expansion, of what later would become imperialism.

The Setting. The events that led to the First Crusade began in Asia Minor (Map 10.2). In the 900s, the Muslim world had splintered into numerous small states; by the 1050s, the fierce, nomadic Sunni Muslim Seljuk Turks had captured Baghdad, subjugated the caliphate, and begun to threaten Byzantium. The difficulties the Byzantine emperor Romanus IV had in pulling together an army to attack the Turks in 1071 reveal how weak his position had become. Unable to muster Byzantine troops—the *strategoi* were busy defending their own districts, and provincial nobles were wary of sending support to the emperor—Romanus had to rely on a mercenary army made up of Normans, Franks, Slavs, and even Turks. This motley force met the Seljuks under Sultan Alp Arslan at Manzikert in what is today eastern Turkey. The battle was a disaster for Romanus: the Seljuks routed his army and captured him. Manzikert marked the end of Byzantine domination in the region.

The Turks, gradually settling in Asia Minor, extended their control across the empire and beyond, all the way to Jerusalem, which had been under Muslim control since the seventh century. In 1095, the Byzantine emperor Alexius I appealed for help to Pope Urban II, hoping to get new mercenary troops for a fresh offensive.

Urban II chose to interpret the request differently. At the Council of Clermont (in France) in

MAP 10.2 The First Crusade, 1096–1098

The First Crusade was a major military undertaking that required organization, movement over both land and sea, and enormous resources. Four main groups were responsible for the conquest of Jerusalem. One began at Cologne, in northern Germany; a second group started out from Blois, in France; the third originated just to the west of Provence; and the fourth launched ships from Brindisi, at the heel of Italy. All joined up at Constantinople, where their leaders negotiated with Alexius for help and supplies in return for a pledge of vassalage to the emperor.

1095, after finishing the usual business of proclaiming the Truce of God (prohibition of fighting on various days of the week for various reasons) and condemning simony among the clergy, Urban moved outside the church and addressed an already excited throng:

> *Oh, race of Franks, race from across the mountains, race beloved and chosen by God. . . . Let hatred depart from among you, let your quarrels end, let wars cease, and let all dissensions and controversies slumber. Enter upon the road to the Holy Sepulcher; wrest that land from the wicked race, and subject it to yourselves.*

The crowd reportedly responded with one voice: "God wills it." Historians remain divided over Ur-

ban's motives for his massive call to arms. Certainly he hoped to win Christian control of the Holy Land. He was also anxious to fulfill the goals of the Truce of God by turning the entire "race of Franks" into a peace militia dedicated to holy purposes, an army of God. Just as the Truce of God mobilized whole communities to fight against anyone who broke the truce, so the First Crusade mobilized armed groups sworn to free the Holy Land of its enemies. Finally, Urban's call placed the papacy in a new position of leadership, one that complemented in a military arena the position the popes had gained in the church hierarchy.

The Crusaders. The early crusades involved many people. Both men and women, rich and poor, young and old participated. They abandoned their homes and braved the rough journey to the Holy Land to fight for their God. They also went—especially younger sons of aristocrats, who could not expect an inheritance because of the practice of primogeniture—because they wanted land. Some knights took the cross because in addition to their pious duty they were obligated to follow their lord. Others hoped for plunder. Although women were discouraged from going on the crusades (one, who begged permission from her bishop, was persuaded to stay home and spend her wealth on charity instead), some crusaders were accompanied by their wives. These women went partly to be with their husbands and partly to express their own militant piety. We know the names of a few of them, such as Emma, who came from England, and Florina, who was Burgundian. We know of a crusading nun as well; she was captured by the Turks, released, and (if her chronicler can be believed) scandalously eloped with her captor. Other women went as servants; a few may have been fighters. Children and old men and women, not able to fight, made the cords for siege engines—giant machines used to hurl stones at enemy fortifications. As more crusades were undertaken during the twelfth century, the transport and supply of these armies became a lucrative business for the commercial classes of maritime Italian cities such as Venice.

The armies of the First Crusade were organized not as one military force but rather as separate militias, each commanded by a different individual. Fulcher of Chartres, an eyewitness, reported: "There grew armies of innumerable people coming together from everywhere. Thus a countless multitude speaking many languages and coming from many regions was to be seen." Fulcher was speaking of the armies led by nobles and authorized by the pope. One band, not authorized by the pope, consisted of commoners. This People's Crusade, which started out before the others under the leadership of an eloquent but militarily unprepared French preacher, Peter the Hermit, was butchered as soon as it reached Asia Minor.

In some crusaders' minds the "wicked races" were much closer to home: some armies stopped along their way to the Holy Land to kill Jews. By this time, most Jews lived in cities, many in the flourishing commercial region of the Rhineland. Under Henry IV, the Jews in Speyer and elsewhere in the empire had gained a place within the government system by receiving protection from the local bishop (an imperial appointee) in return, of course, for paying a tax. Within these cities the Jews lived in their own neighborhoods—Bishop Rudiger even built walls around the one at Speyer—and their tightly knit communities focused around the

Jewish Cemetery at Worms
There was a large Jewish community at Worms in the eleventh century, and Emperor Henry IV granted the Jews there the right to travel and trade within the empire. He also exempted them from various tolls and taxes. Lured by the size and wealth of its Jewish population, one crusading contingent massacred about eight hundred Jews at Worms in 1096. The slaughtered men, women, and children were no doubt buried in this cemetery, which dates to the completion of the synagogue in 1034. It contains about two thousand gravestones; the oldest one extant was put up in 1076.
Erich Lessing/Art Resource, NY.

synagogue, which was a school and community center as well as a place of worship. Nevertheless, Jews also participated in the life of the larger Christian community. Archbishop Anno of Cologne dealt with Jewish moneylenders, and other Jews in Cologne were allowed to trade their wares at the fairs there.

Although officials pronounced against the Jews from time to time and Jews were occasionally expelled from cities like Mainz, they were not persecuted systematically until the First Crusade. Then, as one commentator put it, the crusaders considered it ridiculous to attack Muslims when other infidels lived in their own backyards: "That's doing our work backward." A number of crusade leaders threatened Jews with forced conversion or death but relented when the Jews paid them money. Others, however, attacked. Jews sometimes found refuge with bishops or in the houses of Christian friends, but in many cities—Metz, Speyer, Worms, Mainz, and Cologne—they were massacred. Laden with booty from the Jewish quarters, the crusaders continued on their way to Jerusalem, the most holy of all the places in the Holy Land because Christ died there. (See "Contrasting Views," page 366.)

The main objective of the First Crusade—to wrest the Holy Land from the Muslims and subject it to Christian rule—was accomplished largely because of Muslim disunity. After nearly a year of ineffectual attacks, the crusaders took Antioch on June 28, 1098, killing every Turk in the city; on July 15, 1099, they seized Jerusalem. The leaders of the First Crusade set up four states—collectively called Outremer, the lands "beyond the sea"—on the coastal fringe of the Muslim west. They held on to them, tenuously, until 1291.

Jewish Communities Attacked during the First Crusade
Adapted from Angus Mackay with David Ditchburn, eds., *Atlas of Medieval Europe* (New York: Routledge, 1997).

❖ The Revival of Monarchies

Even as the papacy was exercising new authority, kings and other rulers were enhancing and consolidating their own power. They created new and old ideologies to justify their hegemony; they hired officials to work for them; and they found vassals and churchmen to support them. Money gave them increased effectiveness, and the new commercial economy supplied them with increased revenues.

A Byzantine Revival

The First Crusade was an unanticipated result of a monarchical revival at Byzantium. In 1081, ten years after the disastrous battle at Manzikert, the energetic soldier Alexius Comnenus seized the throne. He faced considerable unrest in Constantinople, whose populace suffered from a combination of high taxes and rising living costs; and on every side the empire was under attack—from Normans in southern Italy, Seljuk Turks in Asia Minor, and new groups in the Balkans. But Alexius I (r. 1081–1118) managed to turn actual and potential enemies against one another, staving off immediate defeat.

When Alexius asked Urban II to supply him with some western troops to fight his enemies, he was shocked and disappointed to learn that crusaders rather than mercenaries were on the way. His daughter, Anna Comnena (1083–c. 1148), later wrote an account of the crusades from the Byzantine perspective in a book about her father, the *Alexiad*. To her, the crusaders were barbarians and her father the consummate statesman and diplomat:

> *The emperor sent envoys to greet them as a mark of friendship. . . . It was typical of Alexius: he had an uncanny prevision [foresight] and knew how to seize a point of vantage before his rivals. Officers appointed for this particular task were ordered to provide victuals on the journey—the pilgrims must have no excuse for complaint for any reason whatever.*

To wage all the wars he had to fight, Alexius relied less on the peasant farmers and the *theme*

Alexius Comnenus Stands before Christ

In this twelfth-century manuscript illumination, the Byzantine emperor Alexius is shown in the presence of Christ. Note that both are almost exactly the same height, and the halos around their heads are the same size. What do you suppose is the significance of Christ's being on a throne while the emperor is standing? Compare this image of the emperor with that on page 312. What statement is the twelfth-century artist making about the relationship between Christ and Alexius?
Biblioteca Apostolica Vaticana.

system than on mercenaries and great magnates armed and mounted like western knights and accompanied by their own troops. In return for their services he gave these nobles *pronoia*, lifetime possession of large imperial estates and their dependent peasants. The *theme* system, under which peasant soldiers in earlier centuries had been settled on imperial lands, gradually disappeared. Alexius conciliated the great families by giving the provincial nobility *pronoia* and satisfied the urban elite by granting them new offices. The emperor normally got on well with the patriarch and Byzantine clergy, for emperor and church depended on each other to suppress heresy and foster orthodoxy.

The emperors of the Comnenian dynasty (1081–1185) thus gained a measure of increased imperial power, but at the price of important concessions to the nobility. The distribution of *pronoia* made the Byzantine Empire resemble a kingdom like England, where the great barons received fiefs in return for military service. However, at first the *pronoia* could not be inherited, nor could holders subdivide their possessions to give to their own warriors. In this way the emperor retained more direct authority over every level of the Byzantine populace than did any ruler in Europe.

Constantinople in the eleventh and early twelfth centuries remained a rich, sophisticated, and highly cultured city. Sculptors and other artists strove to depict ideals of human beauty and elegance. Churches built during the period were decorated with elaborate depictions of the cosmos.

Significant innovations occurred in the realm of Byzantine scholarship and literature. The neo-Platonic tradition of late antiquity had always influenced Byzantine religious and philosophical thought, but now scholars renewed their interest in the wellsprings of classical Greek philosophy, particularly Plato and Aristotle. The rediscovery of ancient culture inspired Byzantine writers to reintroduce old forms into the grammar, vocabulary, and rhetorical style of Greek literature. Anna Comnena wrote her *Alexiad* in this newly learned Greek and prided herself on "having read thoroughly the treatises of Aristotle and the dialogues of Plato." The revival of ancient Greek writings, especially Plato's, in eleventh- and twelfth-century Byzantium had profound consequences for both eastern and western European civilization in centuries to come as their ideas slowly penetrated European culture.

England under Norman Rule

In Europe, the twelfth-century kings of England were the most powerful monarchs because they ruled the whole kingdom by right of conquest. When the Anglo-Saxon king Edward the Confessor (r. 1042–1066) died childless in 1066, three main contenders desired the English throne: Harold, earl of Wessex, an Englishman close to the king but not of royal blood; Harald Hardrada, the king of Norway, who had unsuccessfully attempted to conquer the Danes and now turned hopefully to England;

The First Crusade

When Urban II preached the First Crusade at Clermont in 1095, he unleashed a movement that was seen and interpreted in many different ways. Document 1 is an early and almost "official" account begun around 1100 by Fulcher of Chartres, who considered the crusade a wonderful historical movement and participated in it himself. Jews in the Rhineland who experienced the virulent attacks of some of the crusading forces had a very different view (Document 2). The final document presents an Arab view of the crusaders' capture of Jerusalem (Document 3).

1. The Chronicle of Fulcher of Chartres

Fulcher of Chartres, a chaplain for one of the crusade leaders, wrote his account of the First Crusade for posterity. His chronicle is ordinarily very accurate, and he is careful to note the different experiences of different participants. It is all the more significant, therefore, that he expresses the public view of the First Crusade by making liberal use of biblical quotations and imagery to describe the event. He saw it as the fulfillment of God's plan for humanity.

In March of the year 1096 from the Lord's Incarnation, after Pope Urban had held the Council, which has been described, at Auvergne in November, some people, earlier prepared than others, hastened to begin the holy journey. Others followed in April or May, June or July, and also in August, September, or October, whenever the opportunity of securing expenses presented itself.

In that year, with God disposing, peace and a vast abundance of grain and wine overflowed through all the regions of the earth, so that they who chose to follow Him with their crosses according to His commands did not fail on the way for lack of bread.

Since it is appropriate that the names of the leaders of the pilgrims at that time be remembered, I name Hugh the Great, brother of Philip, King of France. The first of the heroes crossing the sea, he landed at the city of Durazzo in Bulgaria with his own men, but having imprudently departed with a scant army, he was seized by the citizens there and brought to the Emperor of Constantinople [Alexius Comnenus], where he was detained for a considerable time not altogether free.

After him, Bohemond, an Apulian of Norman race, the son of Robert Guiscard, went along the same route with his army.

Next, Godfrey, Duke of Lorrain, went through Hungary with many people.

Raymond, Count of the Provençals, with Goths and Gascons; also, Ademar, Bishop of Puy, crossed through Dalmatia.

A certain Peter the Hermit, after many people on foot and a few knights had joined him, first made his way through Hungary. . . .

So, with such a great band proceeding from western parts, gradually from day to day on the way there grew armies of innumerable people coming together from everywhere. Thus a countless multitude speaking many languages and coming from many regions was to be seen. However, all were not assembled into one army until we arrived at the city of Nicaea.

What more shall I tell? The islands of the seas and all the kingdoms of the earth were so agitated that one believed that the prophecy of David was fulfilled, who said in his Psalm: "All nations whom Thou hast made shall come and worship before Thee O Lord" [Ps. 86:9]; and what those going all the way there later said with good reason: "We shall worship in the place where His feet have stood" [Ps. 132:7]. We have read much about this in the Prophets which it is tedious to repeat.

Source: Edward Peters, ed., *The First Crusade: The Chronicle of Fulcher of Chartres and Other Source Materials* (Philadelphia: University of Pennsylvania Press, 1971), 35–37.

2. The Jewish Experience as Told by Solomon Bar Simson

Around 1140, Solomon Bar Simson, a Jew from Mainz, published a chronicle of the First Crusade. This excerpt shows that the Jewish community interpreted the coming of the crusaders as a punishment from God; hence their prayers and fasting and their conviction that those killed by the crusaders were martyrs for God.

I will now recount the event of this persecution in other martyred communities as well—the extent to which they clung to the Lord, God of their fathers, bearing witness to His Oneness to their last breath.

In the year four thousand eight hundred and fifty-six, the year one thousand twenty-eight of our exile, in the eleventh year of the cycle Ranu, the year in which we anticipated salvation and solace, in accordance with the prophecy of Jeremiah: "Sing with gladness for Jacob, and shout at the head of the nations," etc.—this year turned instead to sorrow and groaning, weeping and outcry. Inflicted upon the Jewish People were the many evils related in all the admonitions; those enumerated in Scripture as well as those unwritten were visited upon us.

At this time arrogant people, a people of strange speech, a nation bitter and impetuous, Frenchmen and Germans, set out for the Holy City, which had been desecrated by barbaric nations, there to seek their house of idolatry and banish the Ishmaelites [Muslims] and other denizens of the land and conquer the land for themselves. . . . Now it came to pass that as they passed through the towns where Jews dwelled, they said to one another: "Look now, we are going a long way to seek out the profane shrine and to avenge ourselves on the Ishmaelites, when here, in our very midst, are the Jews—they whose forefathers murdered and crucified [Christ] for no reason. Let us first avenge ourselves on them and exterminate them from among the nations so that the name of Israel will no longer be remembered, or let them adopt our faith and acknowledge the offspring of promiscuity."

When the Jewish communities became aware of their intentions, they resorted to the custom of our ancestors, repentance, prayer, and charity. The hands of the Holy Nation turned faint at this time, their hearts melted, and their strength flagged. They hid in their innermost rooms to escape the swirling sword. They subjected themselves to great endurance, abstaining from food and drink for three consecutive days and nights, and then fasting many days from sunrise to sunset, until their skin was shriveled and dry as wood upon their bones. And they cried out loudly and bitterly to God. . . .

On the eighth day of Iyar, on the Sabbath, the foe attacked the community of Speyer and murdered eleven holy souls who sanctified their Creator on the holy Sabbath and refused to defile themselves by adopting the faith of their foe. There was a distinguished, pious woman there who slaughtered herself in sanctification of God's name. She was the first among all the communities of those who were slaughtered. The remainder were saved by the local bishop without defilement [baptism], as described above.

On the twenty-third day of Iyar they attacked the community of Worms. The community was then divided into two groups; some remained in their homes and others fled to the local bishop seeking refuge. Those who remained in their homes were set upon by the steppe-wolves who pillaged men, women, and infants, children and old people. They pulled down the stairways and destroyed the houses, looting and plundering; and they took the Torah Scroll, trampled it in the mud, and tore and burned it.

Source: Patrick J. Geary, ed., *Readings in Medieval History* (Peterborough, Ont.: Broadview Press, 1989), 433–34.

3. The Seizure of Jerusalem as Told by Ibn Al-Athir

Ibn Al-Athir (1160–1233) was an Arab historian who drew on earlier accounts for this recounting of the crusaders' conquest of Jerusalem. He stresses the greed and impiety of the crusaders, who pillaged Muslim holy places, and their pitiless slaughter.

After their vain attempt to take Acre by siege, the Franks moved on to Jerusalem and besieged it for more than six weeks. They built two towers, one of which, near Sion, the Muslims burnt down, killing everyone inside it. It had scarcely ceased to burn before a messenger arrived to ask for help and to bring the news that the other side of the city had fallen. In fact Jerusalem was taken from the north on the morning of Friday 22 sha'ban 492 [July 15, 1099]. The population was put to the sword by the Franks who pillaged the area for a week. A band of Muslims barricaded themselves into the Oratory of David and fought on for several days. They were granted their lives in return for surrendering.

The Franks honored their word, and the group left by night for Ascalon. In the Masjid al-Aqsa [a mosque] the Franks slaughtered more than 70,000 people, among them a large number of Imams and Muslim scholars, devout and ascetic men who had left their homelands to live lives of pious seclusion in the Holy Place. The Franks stripped the Dome of the Rock [a place holy to the Muslims, upon which was built the mosque that the Crusaders plundered] of more than forty silver candelabra, each of them weighing 3,600 drams, and a great silver lamp weighing forty-four Syrian pounds, as well as a hundred and fifty smaller silver candelabra and more than twenty gold ones, and a great deal more booty. Refugees from Syria reached Baghdad in ramadan [the month of fasting]. . . . They told the Caliph's ministers a story that wrung their hearts and brought tears to their eyes. On Friday they went to the Cathedral Mosque and begged for help, weeping so that their hearers wept with them as they described the sufferings of the Muslims in that Holy City: the men killed, the women and children taken prisoner, the homes pillaged. Because of the terrible hardships they had suffered, they were allowed to break the fast.

Source: Patrick J. Geary, ed., *Readings in Medieval History* (Peterborough, Ont.: Broadview Press, 1989), 443.

QUESTIONS FOR DEBATE

1. Which commonalities, if any, do you detect between the religious ideas of the crusaders and those whom they attacked?

2. Compare the experiences of the Jews in Rhineland cities and the Arabs in Jerusalem.

3. What were the motives of the crusaders?

---

and William, duke of Normandy, who claimed that Edward had promised him the throne fifteen years earlier. On his deathbed, Edward had named Earl Harold to succeed him, and the witan, a royal advisory committee that had the right to choose the king, had confirmed the nomination.

The Norman Invasion, 1066. When he learned that Harold had been anointed and crowned, William (1027–1087) prepared for battle. Appealing to the pope, he received the banner of St. Peter, and with this symbol of God's approval William launched the invasion of England, filling his ships with warriors recruited from many parts of France. About a week before William's invasion force landed, Harold defeated Harald Hardrada at Stamford Bridge, near York, in the north of England. When he heard of William's arrival, Harold wheeled his forces south, marching them 250 miles and picking up new soldiers along the way to meet the Normans.

The two armies clashed at Hastings on October 14, 1066, in one of history's rare decisive battles. Both armies had about seven or eight thousand men, Harold's in defensive position on a slope, William's attacking from below. All the men were crammed into a very small space as they began the fight. Most of the English were on foot, armed with battle-axes and stones tied to sticks, which could be thrown with great force. William's army consisted of perhaps three thousand mounted knights, a thousand archers, and the rest infantry. At first William's knights broke rank, frightened by the fiercely thrown battle-axes of the English; but then some of the English also broke rank as they pursued the knights. William removed his helmet so his men would know him, rallying them to surround and cut down the English who had broken away. Similar skirmishes lasted the entire afternoon, and gradually Harold's troops were worn down, particularly by William's archers, whose arrows flew a hundred yards, much farther than an English battle-ax could be thrown. By dusk, King Harold was dead and his army utterly defeated. No other army gathered to oppose the successful claimant.

Some people in England gladly supported William; in fact, the first to come forward was a most illustrious woman, Queen Edith, Harold's sister and the widow of Edward the Confessor. Those English who backed William considered his victory a verdict from God, and they hoped to be granted a place in the new order themselves. But William—known to posterity by the epithet "the Conqueror"— wanted to replace, not assimilate, the Anglo-Saxons. In the course of William's reign, families from the continent almost totally supplanted the English aristocracy. And although the English peasantry remained—now with new lords—they were severely shaken. A twelfth-century historian claimed to record William's death-bed confession:

> I have persecuted [England's] native inhabitants beyond all reason. Whether gentle or simple, I have cruelly oppressed them; many I unjustly disinherited; innumerable multitudes, especially in the county of York, perished through me by famine or the sword.

Modern historians estimate that one out of five people in England died as a result of the Norman conquest and its immediate aftermath.

Norman Conquest of England, 1066

Bayeux "Tapestry"
This famous "tapestry" is misnamed; it is really an embroidery, 231 feet long and 20 inches wide, that was made to tell the story of William's conquest of England from his point of view. In this detail, the Norman archers are lined up along the lower margin, in a band below the armies. In the central band, English warriors, on foot and carrying long battle-axes, are attacked by Norman knights on horseback. Who seems to be winning? Compare the armor and fighting gear shown here with that shown on page 326.
Tapisserie de Bayeux.

Institutions of Norman Kingship. Although the Normans destroyed a generation of English men and women, they preserved and extended many Anglo-Saxon institutions. For example, the new kings used the writ to communicate orders, and they retained the old administrative divisions and legal system of the shires (counties) and hundreds. The peculiarly English system of royal district courts continued. The king appointed a sheriff to police the shire, muster military levies, and haul criminals into court. William and his successors intended to control conflicts. If disagreements involved their barons (their great vassals), they expected the litigants to come to the personal court of the king. But other disputes were to be heard in shire courts presided over by the sheriff. These courts had a popular as well as a royal component, since the free men of the shire were summoned to attend them. Although great lords in England set up their own private law courts (just as counts and castellans did on the continent), the county courts eventually encroached on them and extended the king's law across all of England, to create English "common law."

Not all of the institutions of the new dynasty came from Anglo-Saxon precedents. The Norman kings also drew from continental institutions. They set up a graded political hierarchy, culminating in the king and buttressed by his castles, just as French kings were trying to do at about the same time (see page 371). But because all of England was the king's by conquest, he could treat it as his booty; William kept about 20 percent of the land for himself and divided the rest, distributing it in large but scattered fiefs to a relatively small number of his barons and family members, lay and ecclesiastical, as well as to some lesser men, such as personal servants and soldiers. In turn these men maintained their own vassals; they owed the king military service (and the service of a fixed number of their vassals) along with certain dues, such as reliefs (money paid upon inheriting a fief) and aids (payments made on important occasions).

Domesday Book. Some revenues and rights came from the nobles, but the king of England commanded the peasantry as well. In 1086, twenty years after his conquest, William ordered a survey and census of England, popularly called "Domesday" because, like the records of people judged at dooms-day, it provided facts that could not be appealed. It was the most extensive inventory of land, livestock, taxes, and population that had ever been compiled in Europe. (See "Taking Measure," below.) The king

sent his men over all England into every shire and had them find out how many hundred hides [a measure of land] there were in the shire, or what land and cattle the king himself had in the country, or what dues he ought to receive every year

TAKING MEASURE Distribution of Slaves in England in 1086 as Reported in Domesday
Domesday did not report on all of England, but for the regions it surveyed, it provided important data not only for the English king in 1086 but for historians today. We can see from this distribution map, for example, that slavery was an important institution in England. The slaves had no land of their own, were maintained by their lord, and were used by him to cultivate his demesne land. They could be bought and sold. Although the precise numbers given in Domesday—hence the precise percentages given here—are suspect (it is likely that slaves formed between 2 and 10 percent of the population), the distribution here is correct. It shows that slaves were used most in the west of England, while free peasants dominated in the east.
Adapted from H.C. Darby, *Domesday England* (Cambridge: Cambridge University Press, 1977). Reprinted with the permission of Cambridge University Press.

from the shire. . . . So very narrowly did he have the survey to be made that there was not a single hide or yard of land, nor indeed . . . an ox or a cow or a pig left out.

The king's men conducted local surveys by consulting Anglo-Saxon tax lists and by taking testimony from local jurors, men sworn to answer a series of formal questions truthfully. From these inquests scribes wrote voluminous reports filled with facts and statements from villagers, sheriffs, priests, and barons. These reports were then summarized in Domesday itself, a concise record of England's resources that supplied the king and his officials with information such as how much and what sort of land England had, who held it, and what revenues—including the lucrative Danegeld, which was now in effect a royal tax—could be expected from it.

England and the Continent. The Norman conquest tied England to the languages, politics, institutions, and culture of the continent. Modern English is an amalgam of Anglo-Saxon and Norman French, the language the Normans spoke. English commerce was linked to the wool industry in Flanders. The continental movement for church reform had its counterpart in England, with a controversy similar to the Investiture Conflict: in 1097 and again from 1103 to 1107, the archbishop of Canterbury, St. Anselm (1033–1109), and the sons of William clashed over the king's rights over churchmen and church offices, the same issues that had engaged Henry IV and Pope Gregory VII. The English compromise of 1107 anticipated the provisions of the Concordat of Worms of 1122 by rescinding the king's right to bestow the staff and ring but leaving him the right to receive the homage of churchmen before their consecration.

The English Channel served as a bridge rather than a barrier to the interchange of goods and culture. St. Anselm, the most brilliant intellect of his day, was born in Italy, became abbot of the Norman monastery of Bec, and was then appointed archbishop in England. The barons of England retained their estates in Normandy and elsewhere, and the kings of England often spent more time on the continent than they did on the island. The story of England after 1066 is, in miniature, the story of Europe.

Praising the King of France

The twelfth-century kings of France were much less obviously powerful than their English and Byzantine counterparts. Yet they too took part in the monarchical revival. Louis VI the Fat (r. 1108–1137), so heavy that he had to be hoisted onto his horse by a crane, was a tireless defender of royal power. We know a good deal about him and his reputation because a contemporary and close associate, Suger (1081–1152), abbot of St. Denis, wrote Louis's biography. Suger also tutored Louis's son Louis VII (r. 1137–1180) and acted as regent of France when Louis VII left to lead the Second Crusade in 1147.

Suger was a chronicler and propagandist for Louis the Fat. When Louis set himself the task of consolidating his rule in the Île-de-France, Suger portrayed the king as a righteous hero. He thought of the king as the head of a political hierarchy in which Louis had rights over the French nobles because they were his vassals or because they broke the peace. Suger also believed that Louis had a religious role: to protect the church and the poor. He viewed Louis as another Charlemagne, a ruler for all society, not merely an overlord of the nobility. Louis waged war to keep God's peace. Of course, the Gregorian reform had made its mark: Suger did not claim Louis was the head of the church, but he emphasized the royal dignity and its importance to the papacy. When a pope happened to arrive in France, Louis, not yet king, and his father, Philip I (r. 1052–1108), bowed low, but "the pope lifted them up and made them sit before him like devout sons of the apostles. In the manner of a wise man acting wisely, he conferred with them privately on the present condition of the church." Here the pope was shown needing royal advice. Meanwhile, Suger stressed Louis's piety and active defense of the faith:

> *Helped by his powerful band of armed men, or rather by the hand of God, he abruptly seized the castle [of Crécy] and captured its very strong tower as if it were simply the hut of a peasant. Having startled those criminals, he piously slaughtered the impious.*

When Louis VI died in 1137, Suger's notion of the might and right of the king of France reflected reality in an extremely small area. Nevertheless,

Louis laid the groundwork for the gradual extension of royal power in France. As the lord of vassals, the king could call upon his men to aid him in times of war (though the great ones sometimes disregarded his wishes and chose not to help). As a king and landlord, he could obtain many dues and taxes. He also drew revenues from Paris, a thriving city not only of commerce but also of scholarship. Officials, called *provosts*, enforced his royal laws and collected taxes. With money and land, Louis could dispense the favors and give the gifts that added to his prestige and his power. Louis VI and Suger together created the territorial core and royal ideal of the future French monarchy.

The Crusader States: A Western European Outpost

Like Norman England, the crusader states of Outremer were created by conquest. The crusaders carved out four tiny regions around Edessa, Antioch, Jerusalem, and (after a major battle in 1109) Tripoli. Like England, these states were lordships. The ruler granted fiefs to his own vassals, and some of these men in turn gave portions of their holdings as fiefs to some of their own vassals. Many other vassals simply lived in the households of their lords.

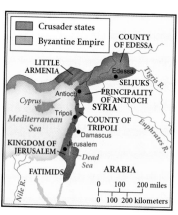

The Crusader States of Outremer in 1109

Thus the crusader states were western European outposts where foreign knights imposed their rule on indigenous populations with vastly different customs and religions. In Europe, peasants clearly differed from knights and nobles by occupation, dress, and style of life, but they were not separate from the upper classes, since the two classes lived on the same estates and shared the same religion. By contrast, in Outremer, the Europeans lived in towns and had little in common with the Muslims, Jews, and even native Arab-speaking Christians who tilled the soil.

The Christians of Outremer largely kept themselves aloof not only from the peasants at their doorstep but also from the Islamic states that surrounded them. Good trade relations and numerous declared truces reveal times of peaceful and neighborly coexistence. However, the settlers of the crusader states thought of themselves as living on a slender beach threatened by a vast Islamic sea. Their leaders feared attack at any time, and the countryside bristled with their defensive stone castles and towers.

So organized for war was this society that it produced a new and militant kind of monasticism: the Knights Templar. Like Bruno's Carthusians, the Templars vowed themselves to poverty and chastity. But rather than withdraw to a hermitage on a mountaintop, the Templars, whose name came from their living quarters in the area of the former Jewish Temple at Jerusalem, devoted themselves to warfare. Their first mission—to protect the pilgrimage routes from Palestine to Jerusalem—soon diversified. They manned the town garrisons of the crusader states, and they transported money from Europe to the Holy Land. Since relatively few Europeans permanently settled in Outremer, the Templars were essential to the area's military and economic survival.

The Templars became enormously popular and wealthy, with branches in major cities across Europe, where they stored gold bullion before escorting it to Outremer. Numerous knights joined their ranks, and, until 1128, women were allowed to become "sisters" in the order, giving it their property and living under its rule, though in separate quarters. After 1128, when they were no longer allowed to join the order (the Templars were afraid that contact with women would compromise their purity), women linked themselves to it in other ways, such as through prayer associations.

The presence of the Templars did not prevent a new Seljuk chieftain, Zengi, from taking Edessa in 1144. The slow but steady shrinking of the crusader states began. The Second Crusade (1147–1149) came to a disastrous end. After only four days of besieging the walls of Damascus, the crusaders, whose leaders could not keep the peace among themselves, gave up and went home. Thereafter, despite numerous new crusades, most Europeans were simply not willing to commit the vast resources and personnel that would have been necessary to maintain outposts in Outremer. The crusader states fell to the Muslims permanently in 1291.

The crusader states were the creation of a movement that brought together all the contradictory

Krak-des-Chevaliers
This imposing castle was built in 1142 on the site of a Muslim fortification in Syria by the Hospitallers, a religious military order much like the Templars. A large community of perhaps fifty monk-knights and their hired mercenaries lived there. To the northeast (in back of the complex seen here) was a fortified village that in part served the needs of the castle. Peasants raised grain, which was ground by a windmill on one wall of the castle. For water, there were reservoirs to catch the rain, wells, and an aqueduct (on the right). Twelve toilets connected to a common drain. The monks worshiped in a chapel within the inner walls. The outer walls, built of masonry, completely enclosed the inner buildings, making Krak one of the most important places for refuge and defense in the crusader states.
Maynard Williams/NGS Image Collection.

impulses of the late eleventh century. Called by a reforming pope, the First Crusade asked warriors to give up their petty quarrels and domestic comforts to undertake a work of piety. The initial popular response was unexpected and enormous. People were ready to reform their own lives—to give up the world for a cause. Yet this meant mobilizing tremendous resources and in the end setting up new polities in Outremer that were protected by the most worldly yet unworldly of all institutions: knight-monks.

❖ New Forms of Scholarship and Religious Expression

The commercial revolution, the newly organized church, and the revived monarchies of the eleventh and twelfth centuries set the stage for the growth of schools and for new forms of scholarship. Money and career opportunities attracted unheard-of numbers of students to city schools. Worldly motivations were, however, equaled by spiritual ones. The movement for church reform stressed the importance of the church and its beliefs. Many students and teachers in the twelfth century sought knowledge to make their faith clearer and deeper. "Nothing can be believed unless it is first understood," said one of the period's greatest scholars, Peter Abelard (1079–1142).

Other people in the twelfth century, however, sought to avoid the cities and the schools. Some found refuge in the measured ceremonies and artistic splendor of Benedictine monasteries such as Cluny. Others considered these vast monastic complexes to be ostentatious and worldly. Rejecting the opulence of cities and the splendor of well-endowed monasteries alike, they pursued a monastic life of poverty.

But many people did not choose definitively one place or the other. Some shuttled back and forth between monasteries and city schools. Others, such as Bruno of Cologne, imported the learning of the schools into their religious life. Others decidedly did not, and yet the new learning, like the new commerce, had a way of seeping into the cracks and crannies of even the most resolutely separate institutions.

Schools and the Liberal Arts

Schools had been connected to monasteries and cathedrals since the Carolingian period. They served to train new recruits to become either monks or priests. Some were better endowed with books and masters (or teachers) than others; a few developed a reputation for a certain kind of theological approach or specialized in a branch of learning, such as literature, medicine, or law. By the end of the eleventh century, the best schools were generally in the larger cities: Reims, Paris, Bologna, Montpellier.

Eager students sampled nearly all of them. The young monk Gilbert of Liège was typical: "Instilled with an insatiable thirst for learning, whenever he heard of somebody excelling in the arts, he rushed immediately to that place and drank whatever delightful potion he could draw from the master there." For Gilbert and other students, a good lecture had the excitement of theater. Teachers at cathedral schools found themselves forced to find larger halls to accommodate the crush of students. Other teachers simply declared themselves "masters" and set up shop by renting a room. If they could prove their mettle in the classroom, they had no trouble finding paying students.

"Wandering scholars" like Gilbert were probably all male, and because schools had hitherto been the training ground for clergymen, all students were considered clerics, whether or not they had been ordained. Wandering became a way of life as the consolidation of castellanies, counties, and kingdoms made violence against travelers less frequent. Urban centers soon responded to the needs of transients with markets, taverns, and lodgings. Using Latin, Europe's common language, students could drift from, say, Italy to Spain, Germany, England, and France, wherever a noted master had settled. Along with crusaders, pilgrims, and merchants, students made the roads of Europe very crowded indeed.

What the students sought, above all, was knowledge of the seven liberal arts. Grammar, rhetoric, and logic (or dialectic) belonged to the "beginning" arts, the so-called *trivium*. Logic, involving the tech-

A Teacher and His Students
This miniature expresses the hierarchical relationship between students and teachers in the twelfth century. But there is more. The miniature appears in a late-twelfth-century manuscript of a commentary written by Gilbert (d. 1154), bishop of Poitiers. Gilbert's ideas in this commentary provoked the ire of St. Bernard, who accused Gilbert of heresy. But Gilbert escaped condemnation. This artist asserts Gilbert's orthodoxy by depicting Gilbert with a halo, in the full dress of a bishop, speaking from his throne. Below Gilbert are three of his disciples, also with halos. The artist's positive view of Gilbert is echoed by modern historians, who recognize Gilbert as a pioneer in his approach to scriptural commentary.
Bibliothèque Municipale de Valenciennes.

nical analysis of texts as well as the application and manipulation of mental constructs, was a transitional subject leading to the second, higher part of the liberal arts, the *quadrivium*. This comprised four areas of study that we might call theoretical math and science: arithmetic, geometry, music (theory rather than practice), and astronomy. Of all these, logic excited the most intense interest. Medieval students and masters were convinced that logic clarified every issue, even questions about their own subjectivity and the nature of God. With logic, they thought, one could prove that what one believed on faith was in fact true.

The key logical breakthrough of the twelfth century involved the question of "universals": whether individual things were real or just accidental manifestations of a reality beyond them. Peter Abelard broke through this conundrum by elaborating a theory that focused on the observer rather than the thing.

At the heart of the debate over universals was the nature of the individual. The *nominalist* position held that each individual was unique. In the nominalist view, Tom and Harry (and Carol, for that matter) may be called "man" (a word that includes both males and females), but that label is merely a convenience, a manner of speaking. In reality Tom and Harry and Carol are so unlike that each can be truly comprehended only as separate and irreducible entities. Only very few people in Abelard's time argued this position, in part because it led to clearly heretical results: applied to the Trinity, it shattered the unity of the Father, Son, and Holy Ghost, leaving the idea of the Trinity an empty name. (The word *name* in Latin is *nomen,* from which *nominalist* was derived.)

The *realist* position, argued by Abelard's teacher William of Champeaux, was more acceptable in the twelfth century. Realists argued that the "real," the essential, aspect of the individual was the universal quality of his or her group. Thus Tom and Harry and Carol were certainly different, but their differences were inessential "accidents." In truth all three people must be properly comprehended as "man." This view also raised theological problems—if taken to an extreme, the Trinity would melt into one. And it certainly did not satisfy a man like Abelard, who was adamant about his individuality.

Abelard created his own position, called *modified realism*, by focusing on the observer, who sees "real" individuals and who abstracts "real" universals from them. The key for Abelard was the nature of the knower: the concept of "man" was formed by the knower observing the similarities of Tom, Harry, and Carol and deriving a universal concept that allowed him or her to view individuals properly in its light.

Later in the twelfth century, scholars discovered that Aristotle had once elaborated a view parallel to

Abelard's, but until midcentury, very little of Aristotle's work was available in Europe because it had not been translated from Greek into Latin. By the end of the century, however, that situation had been rectified by translators who traveled to Islamic cities, where Aristotle was already translated into Arabic and closely studied. (See "Did You Know?," page 376.) In a sense, early-twelfth-century scholars, with their pioneering efforts in logic, opened the way for Christian Europe to welcome Aristotle. By the thirteenth century, Aristotle had become the primary philosopher for scholastics, the scholars of the European medieval universities.

After studying the liberal arts, students went on to study medicine (the great school for that was at Montpellier), theology, or law. Schools of law, for example, began in Italy in the eleventh century. At Bologna, Irnerius (d. c. 1129) was the guiding light of a law school where students studied Lombard, Roman, or canon law. Men skilled in canon law served popes and bishops; popes, kings, princes, and communes all found that Roman law, which claimed the emperor as its fount, justified their claims to power.

Scholars of the New Learning

The remarkable renewal of scholarship in the twelfth century had an unexpected benefit: we know a great deal about the men involved in it—and a few of the women—because they wrote so much, often about themselves. Three important figures typify the scholars of the period: Abelard and Heloise, who embraced the new learning wholeheartedly and retired to monasteries only when forced to do so; and Hildegard, who happily spent most of her life in a cloister yet wrote knowingly about the world.

Abelard and Heloise. Born into a family of the petty (lesser) French Breton nobility and destined for a career as a warrior and lord, Peter Abelard instead became one of the twelfth century's greatest thinkers. In his autobiographical account, *Historia calamitatum* ("Story of My Calamities"), Abelard describes his shift from the life of the warrior to the life of the scholar:

> *I was so carried away by my love of learning, that I renounced the glory of a soldier's life, made over*

Translations

Tłumaczenie! Do you know what that means? If you don't, it's easy enough to find out. Today there are many dictionaries, translators, and interpreters for almost every one of the world's three thousand languages. But for most of history, this has not been the case. In the Middle Ages, dictionaries and interpreters were very rare. The great writings of the three heirs of the Roman Empire—the Byzantine, Muslim, and European—were largely unavailable across cultures. This kept these societies from knowing about and benefiting from one another. And of the three, Europe was the most isolated.

In the twelfth century this began to change. The same Europeans who flocked to the city schools knew vaguely about Arabic philosophical learning, and they ached to know more. Some of them traveled to the peripheries of Europe, in particular, to Palermo, in Sicily, where Greek, Arabic, and Latin were all official languages, as the illustration shows. Palermo was unique as a European city that supported a diversity of languages and people who could read and write in a number of them. Some people from France, Germany, England, and northern Italy who wanted to read books in languages other than Latin went to Palermo to learn how to become translators themselves or to find others to do the job. In the illustration, each scribe is writing in a different language.

Others headed to Spain, where they worked with Jewish converts to Christianity. Rather than learn Arabic, they relied on these converts to translate from Arabic into Spanish. Then the Europeans translated from Spanish into Latin. It was in this roundabout way that Aristotle's works were rediscovered in Arabic translation, that Arabic medical treatises were read, that Arabic love poetry came to inspire medieval songwriters, and that Arabic mathematical breakthroughs, including the discovery of algebra and the use of "Arabic" numerals, came to the Latin-speaking West.

By the way, the word *tłumaczenie* (pronounced "twoo-ma-c*hain*-yeh") means "translation" in Polish.

Scribes at Palermo
This manuscript illustration depicts the scribes at the royal court at Palermo (in Sicily), each writing in a different language. Palermo was practically unique as a European city that supported a diversity of languages and people who could read and write in a number of them. Some people from France, Germany, England, and Northern Italy who wanted to read books in languages other than Latin went to Palermo to learn how to become translators themselves or to find others to do the job.
Burgerbibliothek Bern cod. 120/II#f.101.

my inheritance and rights of the eldest son to my brothers, and withdrew from the court of Mars [war] in order to kneel at the feet of Minerva [learning].

Arriving eventually at Paris, Abelard studied with William of Champeaux and then challenged his teacher's scholarship. Later Abelard began to lecture and to gather students of his own.

Around 1122–1123, Abelard prepared a textbook for his students, the *Sic et Non* ("Yes and No"). It was unusual because it arranged side-by-side opposing positions on 156 subjects, among them "That God is one and the contrary," "That all are permitted to marry and the contrary," "That it is permitted to kill men and the contrary." Arrayed on both sides of each question were the words of authorities such as the Bible, the church fathers, and the letters of popes. The juxtaposition of authoritative sentences was nothing new; what was new was calling attention to their contradictions. Abelard's students loved the challenge: they were eager to find the origins of the quotes, consider the context of each one carefully, and seek a reconciliation of the opposing sides. Abelard wrote that his method "excite[d] young readers to the maximum of effort in inquiring into the truth." In fact, in Abelard's view the inquiring student would follow the model of Christ himself, who as a boy sat among the rabbis, questioning them.

Abelard's fame as a teacher was such that a Parisian cleric named Fulbert gave Abelard room and board and engaged him as tutor for Heloise (c. 1100–c. 1163/1164), Fulbert's niece. Heloise is one of the few learned women of the period who left traces. (Hildegard is another.) Brought up under Fulbert's guardianship, Heloise had been sent as a young girl to a convent school, where she received a thorough grounding in literary skills. Her uncle had hoped to continue her education at home by hiring Abelard. Abelard, however, became her lover as well as her tutor. "Our desires left no stage of lovemaking untried," wrote Abelard in his *Historia.* At first their love affair was kept secret. But Heloise became pregnant, and Abelard insisted they marry. They did so clandestinely to prevent damaging Abelard's career, for the new emphasis on clerical celibacy meant that Abelard's professional success and prestige would have been compromised if news

of his marriage were made public. After they were married, Heloise and Abelard rarely saw one another. Fulbert, suspecting foul play, plotted a cruel punishment: he paid a servant to castrate Abelard. Soon after, both husband and wife entered separate monasteries.

For Heloise, separation from Abelard was a lasting blow. Although she became a successful abbess, carefully tending to the physical and spiritual needs of her nuns, she continued to call on Abelard for "renewal of strength." In a series of letters addressed to him, she poured out her feelings as "his handmaid, or rather his daughter, wife, or rather sister":

You know, beloved, as the whole world knows, how much I have lost in you, how at one wretched stroke of fortune that supreme act of flagrant treachery robbed me of my very self in robbing me of you. . . . You alone have the power to make me sad, to bring me happiness or comfort.

For Abelard, however, the loss of Heloise and even his castration were not the worst disasters of his life. The cruelest blow came later, and it was directed at his intellect. He wrote a book that applied "human and logical reasons" (as he put it) to the Trinity; the book was condemned at the Council of Soissons in 1121, and he was forced to throw it, page by page, into the flames. Bitterly weeping at the injustice, Abelard lamented, "This open violence had come upon me only because of the purity of my intentions and love of our Faith which had compelled me to write."

Abelard had written the treatise on the Trinity for his students, maintaining that "words were useless if the intelligence could not follow them, [and] that nothing could be believed unless it was first understood." For Abelard, logic was the key to knowledge, and knowledge the key to faith.

Hildegard of Bingen. Unlike Abelard and Heloise, Hildegard (1098–1179) did not actively seek to become a scholar. Placed in a German convent at age eight, she received her schooling there and took vows as a nun. In 1136, she was elected abbess of the convent. Shortly thereafter, very abruptly, she began to write and to preach. She was probably the only woman authorized by the church to preach in her day.

Hildegard of Bingen
The illustrations that Hildegard commissioned for her
Scivias *have been lost since the end of World War II, but
a hand-drawn copy from 1920 has survived. This image
from the copy shows Hildegard at the beginning of the book,
where, she writes, "Heaven was opened and a fiery light . . .
came and permeated my whole brain. . . . And immediately
I knew the meaning of the . . . Scriptures." In the miniature,
the fiery light comes down like giant fingers to cover Hildegard's head, while she holds a wax tablet and stylus to write
with. The monk peeking through the door is Volmar, who
served as Hildegard's secretary.*
Photograph by Erich Lessing/Art Resource.

Writing and preaching were the sudden external manifestations of an inner life that had been extraordinary from the beginning. Even as a child,
Hildegard had had visions—of invisible things, of
the future, and (always) of a special kind of light.
These visions were intermingled with pain and sickness. Only in her forties did Hildegard interpret her
sickness and her visions as gifts from God: her
fragility made the visions possible. In her *Scivias*

("Know the Ways of the Lord," 1151), Hildegard describes some of her visions and explains what they
meant. She interprets them as containing nothing
less than the full story of creation and redemption,
a *summa*, or compendium, of church doctrine.

The *Scivias* was not just a text. Accompanying
Hildegard's words were vivid illustrations of her visions, probably painted by a nun under her supervision. For the final vision of the book, Hildegard
added fourteen pieces of music. And at the conclusion of the entire *Scivias*, Hildegard appended a play,
the leading roles taken by the Virtues, the Soul, and
the Devil. She later expanded this and set it to music.

Hildegard's inventiveness was not confined to
religious and artistic matters. During the 1150s,
she wrote two scientific treatises, one focused on
diseases and herbal remedies, the other on subjects
ranging from animals and plants to gemstones and
metallurgy. For Hildegard, knowledge of God made
the world intelligible.

Benedictine Monks and Artistic Splendor

Hildegard's appreciation of worldly things as expressions of God's splendor was typical of Benedictine monks and nuns in the twelfth century. They
spent nearly their entire day in large and magnificently outfitted churches singing an expanded and
complex liturgy. Hildegard's music was added to the
liturgical round at her convent, for example.

In the context of the new monastic movements stressing poverty, the Benedictines were
old-fashioned. Yet the "black monks"—so called
because they dyed their robes black—reached the
height of their popularity in the eleventh century.
Monasteries often housed hundreds of monks; convents for nuns were usually less populated. Cluny
was one of the largest monasteries, with some four
hundred brothers in the mid-eleventh century.

The chief occupation of the monks, as befitted
(in their view) citizens of heaven, was prayer. The
black monks and nuns devoted themselves to
singing the Psalms and other prayers specified in the
rule of St. Benedict, adding to them still more
Psalms. The rule called for chanting the entire
Psalter—150 psalms—over the course of a week,
but some monks, like those at Cluny, chanted that
number in a day.

Gregorian Chant. Prayer was neither private nor silent. Black monks had to know not only the words but also the music that went with their prayers; they had to be musicians. The music of the Benedictine monastery was *plainchant*, also known as *Gregorian chant*, which consisted of melodies, each sung in unison, without accompaniment. Although chant was rhythmically free, lacking a regular beat, its melodies ranged from extremely simple to highly ornate and embellished. By the twelfth century, a large repertoire of melodies had grown up, at first through oral composition and transmission and then in written notation, which first appeared in manuscripts of the ninth century.

The melodies preserved by this early notation probably originated in Rome and had been introduced into northern Europe at the command of Charlemagne, who wanted to unify the liturgical practices of his empire. Musical notation was developed to help monks remember unfamiliar melodies and to ensure that the tunes were sung in approximately the same way in all parts of the Carolingian realm. The melodies were further mastered and organized at this time by fitting them into the Byzantine system of eight modes, or *scales*. This music survived the dissolution of the Carolingian Empire and remained the core music of the Catholic church into the twentieth century. At Cluny, where praying and singing occupied nearly the entire day and part of the night, the importance of music was made visible—the scales were personified and depicted in sculpture on some of the columns circling the choir of the church.

Romanesque Style. The church of Cluny was part of the building boom that saw the construction or repair of town walls, dwellings, mills, castles, monasteries, and churches. The style of many of these buildings, like the church of Cluny, rebuilt around 1100, was Romanesque. Cluny was particularly enormous. Constructed of stone, it must have reverberated with the voices of the hundreds of monks who sang there. Although they varied greatly, most Romanesque churches, like Cluny, had massive stone and masonry walls decorated on the interior with paintings in bright colors. The various parts of the church—the chapels in the *chevet* (the east end), for example—were handled as discrete units, retaining the forms of cubes, cones, and cylinders

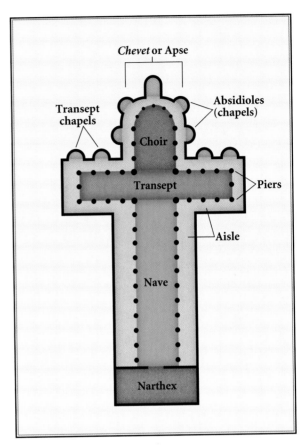

FIGURE 10.1 Floor Plan of a Romanesque Church
As churchgoers entered a Romanesque church, they passed through the narthex, an anteroom decorated with sculptures depicting important scenes from the Bible. Walking through the portal of the narthex, they entered the church's nave, at the east end of which—just after the crossing of the transept and in front of the choir—was the altar. Walking down the nave, they passed massive, tall piers leading up to the vaulting (the ceiling) of the nave. Each of these piers was decorated with sculpture, and the walls were brightly painted. Romanesque churches were both lively and colorful (because of their decoration) and solemn and somber (because of their heavy stones and massive scale).

(Figure 10.1). Inventive sculptural reliefs, both inside and outside the church, enlivened these pristine geometrical forms. Emotional and sometimes frenzied, Romanesque sculpture depicted themes ranging from the beauty of Eve to the horrors of the Last Judgment.

In such a setting, gilded reliquaries and altars made of silver, precious gems, and pearls were the fitting accoutrements of worship. Prayer, liturgy, and

St.-Savin-sur-Gartempe

The nave of the church of St.-Savin was built between 1095 and 1115. Its barrel (or tunnel) vault is typical of Romanesque churches, as is its sense of liveliness, variety, and color. The columns, decorated with striped or wavy patterns, are topped by carved capitals, each different from the next. The entire vault is covered with frescoes painted in shades of browns, ochers, and yellows depicting scenes from the Old Testament. Try to pick out the one that shows Noah's ark. Were such scenes meant to delight the worshipers? How would St. Bernard have answered this question?
Giraudon/Art Resource, NY.

Eberbech

Compare the nave of Eberbech, a Cistercian church built between 1170 and 1186, with that of St.-Savin. What at St.-Savin was full of variety and color is here subdued by order and calm. There are no wall paintings in a Cistercian church, no variegated columns, no distractions from the interior life of the worshiper. Yet, upon closer look, there are subtle points of interest. How has the architect played with angles, planes, and light in the vaulting? Are the walls utterly smooth? Can you see any decorative elements on the massive piers between the arches?
AKG London/Stefan Drechsel.

music in this way complemented the gift economy: richly clad in vestments of the finest materials, intoning the liturgy in the most splendid of churches, monks and priests offered up the gift of prayer to God; in return they begged for the gift of salvation of their souls and the souls of all the faithful.

New Monastic Orders of Poverty

Not all agreed that such opulence pleased or praised God. At the end of the eleventh century, the new commercial economy and the profit motive that fueled it led many to reject wealth and to embrace poverty as a key element of religious life. The Carthusian order founded by Bruno of Cologne was one such group. Each monk took a vow of silence and lived as a hermit in his own small hut. Monks occasionally joined others for prayer in a common prayer room, or *oratory*. When not engaged in prayer or meditation, the Carthusians copied manuscripts. They considered this task part of their religious vocation, a way to preach God's word with their hands rather than their mouths. The Carthusian order grew slowly. Each monastery was limited to only twelve monks, the number of the Apostles.

The Cistercians, in contrast, expanded rapidly. Rejecting even the conceit of blackening their robes, they left them the original color of wool (hence their nickname, the "white monks"). The Cistercian order began as a single monastery, Cîteaux (in Latin, *Cistercium*) in France, founded in 1098. It grew to include more than three hundred monasteries spread throughout Europe by the middle of the twelfth century. Despite the Cistercian order's official repudiation of female houses, many convents followed its lead and adopted its customs. Women were as eager as men to live the life of simplicity and poverty that they believed the Apostles had enjoyed and endured.

The guiding spirit and preeminent Cistercian abbot was St. Bernard (c. 1090–1153), who arrived at Cîteaux in 1112 along with about thirty friends and relatives. But even before Bernard's arrival, the program of the new order had been set. A chronicle of the order reports that:

They rejected anything opposed to the [Benedictine] Rule: frocks, fur tunics, linsey-woolsey shirts and cowls [hooded robes], straw for beds and various dishes of food in the refectory, as well as lard and all other things which ran counter to the letter of the Rule.

Although they held up the rule of St. Benedict as the foundation of their customs, the Cistercians elaborated a style of life all their own, largely governed by the goal of simplicity.

Cistercian churches, though built of stone, were initially unlike the great Romanesque churches of the Benedictines. They were remarkably standardized; the church and the rest of the buildings of any Cistercian monastery were almost exactly like those of any other (Figure 10.2). The churches were small, made of smoothly hewn, undecorated stone. Wall paintings and sculpture were prohibited. St. Bernard wrote a scathing attack on Romanesque sculpture in which he acknowledged, in spite of himself, its exceptional allure:

What is the point of ridiculous monstrosities in the cloister where there are brethren reading—I mean those extraordinary deformed beauties and beautiful deformities? What are those lascivious apes doing, those fierce lions, monstrous centaurs, halfmen and spotted leopards? . . . It is more diverting to decipher marble than the text before you.

The Cistercians had no such diversions, but the simplicity of their buildings and of their clothing also had its beauty. Illuminated by the pure white light that came through clear glass windows, Cistercian houses were luminous, cool, and serene.

True to this emphasis on purity, the communal liturgy of the Cistercians was simplified and shorn of the many additions that had been tacked on in the houses of the black monks. Only the liturgy as prescribed in the rule of St. Benedict plus one daily Mass was allowed. Even the music for the chant was changed; the Cistercians rigorously suppressed the B flat, even though doing so made the melody discordant, because of their insistence on strict simplicity.

With their time partly freed from the choir, the white monks dedicated themselves to private prayer and contemplation and to monastic administration. In some ways these activities were antithetical— one internal and the other external. The Cistercian Charter of Charity, in effect a constitution of the

FIGURE 10.2 Floor Plan of a Cistercian Monastery

*Cistercian monasteries seldom deviated much from this standard plan, which perfectly suited their
double lifestyle—one half for the lay brothers, who worked in the fields, the other half for the
monks, who performed the devotions. This plan shows the first floor. Above were the dormitories.
The lay brothers slept above their cellar and refectory, the monks above their chapter house, common
room, and room for novices. No one had a private bedroom, just as the rule of St. Benedict prescribed.*

Adapted from Wolfgang Braunfels, *Monasteries of Western Europe* (Princeton, N.J.: Princeton University Press, 1972), 75.

order, provided for a closely monitored network of
houses, and each year the Cistercian abbots met to
hammer out legislation for all the monasteries. The
abbot of the mother house (or founding house) visited the daughter houses annually to make sure the
legislation was being followed. Each house, whether
mother or daughter, had large and highly organized
farms and grazing lands called *granges*. Cistercian
monks spent much of their time managing their estates and flocks, both of which yielded handsome
profits by the end of the twelfth century. Clearly part
of the agricultural and commercial revolutions of
the Middle Ages, the Cistercian order made managerial expertise a part of the monastic life.

At the same time, the Cistercians elaborated a
spirituality of intense personal emotion. As Bernard
said:

*Often enough when we approach the altar to pray
our hearts are dry and lukewarm. But if we perse-*

*vere, there comes an unexpected infusion of grace,
our breast expands as it were, and our interior is
filled with an overflowing love.*

The Cistercians emphasized not only human emotion but also Christ's and Mary's humanity. While
pilgrims continued to stream to the tombs and reliquaries of saints, the Cistercians dedicated all their
churches to the Virgin Mary (for whom they had no
relics) because for them she signified the model of
a loving mother. Indeed, the Cistercians regularly
used maternal imagery (as Bernard's description
invoking the metaphor of a flowing breast illustrates) to describe the nurturing care provided to
humans by Jesus himself. The Cistercian God was
approachable, human, protective, even mothering.

Similar views of God were held by many who
were not members of the Cistercian order; their
spirituality signaled wider changes. For example,
around 1099, St. Anselm wrote a theological treatise

entitled *Why God Became Man* in which he argued that since man had sinned, only a sinless man could redeem him. St. Anselm's work represented a new theological emphasis on the redemptive power of human charity, including that of Jesus as a human being. The crusaders had trodden the very place of Christ's crucifixion, making his humanity both more real and more problematic to people who walked in the holy "place of God's humiliation and our redemption," as one chronicler put it. Yet this new stress on the loving bonds that tied Christians together also led to the persecution of others, like Jews and Muslims, who lived outside the Christian community.

Conclusion

The commercial revolution and the building boom it spurred profoundly changed the look of Europe. Thriving cities of merchants and artisans brought trade, new wealth, and new institutions to the West. Mutual and fraternal organizations like the commune, the *compagnia*, and the guilds expressed and reinforced the solidarity and economic interest of city dwellers.

Political consolidation accompanied economic growth, as kings and popes exerted their authority and tested its limits. The Gregorian reform pitted the emperor against the pope, and two separate political hierarchies emerged, the secular and the ecclesiastical. The two might cooperate, as Suger and Louis VI showed in their mutual respect, admiration, and dependence; but they might also clash, as Anselm did with the sons of William the Conqueror. Secular and religious leaders developed new and largely separate systems of administration, reflecting in political life the new distinctions that differentiated clergy and laity, such as clerical celibacy and allegiance to the pope. Although in some ways growing apart, the two groups never worked so closely as in the crusades, military pilgrimages inspired by the pope and led by lay lords.

The commercial economy, political stability, and ecclesiastical needs fostered the growth of schools and the achievements of new scholarship. Young men like Abelard, who a generation before would have become knights, now sought learning to enhance their careers and bring personal fulfill-

IMPORTANT DATES

1054 Great Schism between Roman Catholic and Greek Orthodox churches
1066 Norman conquest of England; Battle of Hastings
1077 Henry IV does penance before Gregory VII at Canossa
1086 Domesday Book commissioned by William I of England
c. 1090–1153 Life of St. Bernard, leader of Cistercian order
1095 Urban II preaches the First Crusade at Clermont
1097 Commune of Milan established
1122 Concordat of Worms ends the Investiture Conflict
c. 1122 Abelard writes *Sic et Non*
1130 Norman kingdom of Sicily established
1140 Gratian's *Decretum* published
1151 Hildegard of Bingen's *Scivias* published

ment. Elite women like Heloise could gain an excellent basic education in a convent and then go on to higher studies, as Heloise did, with a tutor. Logic fascinated students because it seemed to clarify what was real about themselves, the world, and God. Churchmen such as St. Bernard, who felt that faith could not be analyzed, rejected scholarship based on logic.

While Benedictine monks added to their hours of worship, built lavish churches, and devoted themselves to the music of the plainchant, a reformer such as St. Bernard insisted on an intense, interior spiritual life in a monastery austerely and directly based on the rule of St. Benedict. Other reformers, such as Bruno of Cologne, sought the high mountaintop for its isolation and hardship. These reformers repudiated urban society yet unintentionally reflected it: the Cistercians were as interested as any student in their interior state of mind and as anxious as any tradesman in the success of their granges, and the Carthusians were dedicated to their books.

The early twelfth century saw a period of renaissance and reform in the church, monarchies, and scholarship. The later twelfth century would be an age when people experimented with and rebelled against the various forms of authority.

MAPPING THE WEST Major Religions in the West, c. 1150
The broad washes of color on this map tell a striking story: by 1150, there were three major religions, each corresponding to a broad region. To the west, north of the Mediterranean Sea, Catholic Christianity held sway; to the east, the Greek Orthodox Church was ascendant; all along the southern Mediterranean, Islam triumphed. Only a few places defied this logic: one was Outremer, a tiny outpost of Catholic crusaders who ruled over a largely Muslim population. What this map does not show, however, are the details: Jewish communities in many cities; lively varieties of Islamic beliefs within the Muslim world; communities of Coptic Christians in Egypt; and scattered groups of heretics in Catholic lands.

Suggested References

The Commercial Revolution

The idea of a commercial revolution in the Middle Ages originated with Lopez. Little discusses some religious consequences. Hyde explores the society and government of the Italian communes.

Hyde, J. K. *Society and Politics in Medieval Italy: The Evolution of Civil Life, 1000–1350.* 1973.

Little, Lester K. *Religious Poverty and the Profit Economy in Medieval Europe.* 1978.

Lopez, Robert S. *The Commercial Revolution of the Middle Ages, 950–1350.* 1976.

*_____ ; and Irving W. Raymond, *Medieval Trade in the Mediterranean World.* 1955.

*Primary sources.

Church Reform and Its Aftermath

The Investiture Conflict, which pitted the pope against the emperor, has been particularly important to German historians. Blumenthal gives a useful overview. The consequences of church reform and the new papal monarchy included both the growth of canon law (see Brundage) and the crusades (see Erdmann and Riley-Smith).

Blumenthal, Uta-Renate. *The Investiture Controversy: Church and Monarchy from the Ninth to the Twelfth Century.* 1991.

Brundage, James A. *Medieval Canon Law.* 1995.

Crusades: http://orb.rhodes.edu/bibliographies/crusades. html.

Duby, Georges. *Medieval Marriage: Two Models from Twelfth-Century France.* Trans. Elborg Forster. 1978.

Erdmann, Carl. *The Origins of the Idea of Crusade.* Trans. Marshall W. Baldwin and Walter Goffart. 1977.

*Peters, Edward, ed. *The First Crusade: The Chronicle of Fulcher of Chartres and Other Source Materials.* 1971.

Riley-Smith, Jonathan. *The Crusades. A Short History.* 1987.

_____. *The First Crusaders, 1095–1131.* 1997.

*Tierney, Brian, ed. *The Crisis of Church and State, 1050–1300.* 1964.

The Revival of Monarchies

The growth of monarchical power and the development of state institutions are topics of keen interest to historians. Clanchy points to the use of writing and recordkeeping in government. Suger shows the importance of the royal image. Douglas and Hallam discuss different aspects of the Norman conquest of England.

Chibnall, Marjorie. *Anglo-Norman England, 1066–1166.* 1986.

Clanchy, Michael. *From Memory to Written Record: England 1066–1307.* 2nd ed. 1993.

Douglas, David C. *William the Conqueror: The Norman Impact upon England.* 1967.

Dunbabin, Jean. *France in the Making, 843–1180.* 1985.

Hallam, Elizabeth M. *Domesday Book through Nine Centuries.* 1986.

*Suger. *The Deeds of Louis the Fat.* Trans. Richard C. Cusimano and John Moorhead. 1992.

New Forms of Scholarship and Religious Expression

The new learning of the twelfth century was first called a "renaissance" by Haskins. Clanchy's more recent study looks less at the revival of the classics, stressing instead the social and political context of medieval teaching and learning. Recent research on religious developments include discussions of women in the new monastic movements of the twelfth century (Venarde), challenges to old views about the participation of monks in local economies (Bouchard), and new interpretations of the religious fervor of the period as a whole (Constable).

Abelard's *History of My Calamities:* http://www.fordham. edu/halsall/basis/abelard-histcal.html.

Benson, Robert L., and Giles Constable, eds., with the assistance of Carol Lanham. *Renaissance and Renewal in the Twelfth Century.* 1982.

Bouchard, Constance B. *Holy Entrepreneurs: Cistercians, Knights, and Economic Exchange in Twelfth-Century Burgundy.* 1991.

Clanchy, Michael. *Abelard: A Medieval Life.* 1997.

Constable, Giles. *The Reformation of the Twelfth Century.* 1996.

Haskins, Charles Homer. *The Renaissance of the Twelfth Century.* 1927.

Hildegard of Bingen: http://www.uni-mainz.de/~horst/ hildegard/links.html.

Hildegard von Bingen: Ordo virtutum, Deutsche Harmonia Mundi CD, 77394 (music from Hildegard's *Scivias* and the expanded play at its end).

Letters of Abelard and Heloise. Trans. Betty Radice. 1974. Includes *History of My Calamities.*

Murray, Alexander. *Reason and Society in the Middle Ages.* 1978.

Venard, Bruce L. *Women's Monasticism and Medieval Society: Nunneries in France and England, 890–1215.* 1997.

An Age of Confidence

1150–1215

IN 1155, KING FREDERICK BARBAROSSA OF GERMANY met representatives of the fledgling Roman commune on his way to Rome, where he intended to be crowned emperor. Recalling the glory of the Roman Empire, these ambassadors of the "senate and people of Rome" claimed that they alone could make Frederick emperor. To deliver the imperial title, they demanded five thousand pounds of gold "as expense money." Frederick, "inflamed with righteous anger," according to his uncle and biographer, Otto of Freising, interrupted them. The Roman imperial title was not theirs to give, he retorted. The spotlight of history in which Rome had once basked as capital city of the empire had shifted to Germany: "Do you wish to know the ancient glory of your Rome? The worth of senatorial dignity? . . . Behold our state. . . . All these things have descended to us, together with the empire."

Frederick's confident self-assertion characterized an age in which participants in emerging institutions of government, commerce, and religion commanded enhanced authority. Although at odds with the ambassadors of the Roman commune, Frederick shared with them a newly precise and proud notion of his rights and goals. In the second half of the twelfth century, kings, princes, popes, city dwellers, and even heretics were acutely conscious of themselves as individuals and as members of like-minded groups with identifiable objectives and plans to promote and perpetuate their aims. For example, by about 1200, many schools, which in the early twelfth century had crystallized around charismatic teachers like Peter Abelard, became permanent institutions

Man at the Center of the Universe
In this thirteenth-century miniature, a man representing humankind stands with arms outstretched at the very center of the universe. The universe, in turn, is embraced by nature (her arms encircle the globe), while crowning nature is the head of wisdom. The whole image expresses confidence in human capacity and its harmony with nature.
Biblioteca Statale di Lucca.

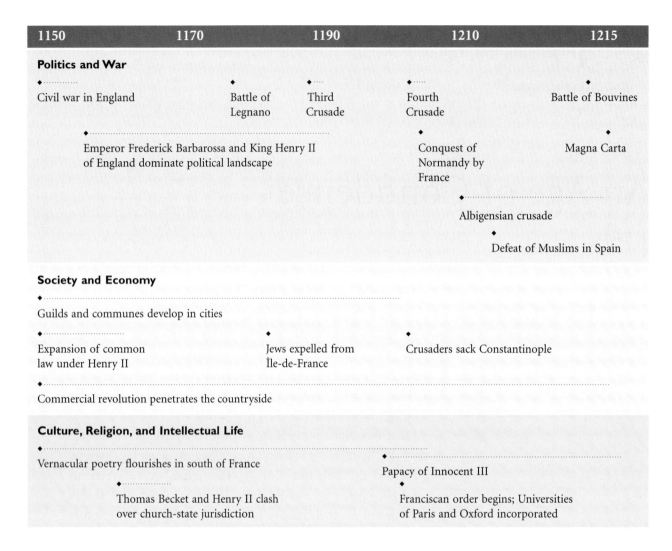

1150	1170	1190	1210	1215

Politics and War

Civil war in England

Battle of Legnano

Third Crusade

Fourth Crusade

Battle of Bouvines

Emperor Frederick Barbarossa and King Henry II of England dominate political landscape

Conquest of Normandy by France

Magna Carta

Albigensian crusade

Defeat of Muslims in Spain

Society and Economy

Guilds and communes develop in cities

Expansion of common law under Henry II

Jews expelled from Île-de-France

Crusaders sack Constantinople

Commercial revolution penetrates the countryside

Culture, Religion, and Intellectual Life

Vernacular poetry flourishes in south of France

Papacy of Innocent III

Thomas Becket and Henry II clash over church-state jurisdiction

Franciscan order begins; Universities of Paris and Oxford incorporated

called universities. Staffs of literate government officials now preserved both official documents and important papers; lords reckoned their profits with the help of accountants; craft guilds and religious associations defined and regulated their membership with increased exactitude.

The period 1150–1215 was characterized by confidence buttressed by new organizations and institutions. Well-organized rulers exercised control over whole territories through institutions of government that could—if need be—function without them. In the cultural arena, new-style poets boldly used the common language of everyday life, rather than Latin, to write literature of astonishing beauty, humor, and emotional range. Laypeople and those who devoted themselves to religion participated in newly articulate and well-organized groups. But increased confidence and more clearly defined group and individual identities brought with them increased intolerance toward and aggression against those perceived as deviants.

❖ Governments as Institutions

By the end of the twelfth century, Europeans for the first time spoke of their rulers not as kings of a people (for example, king of the Franks) but as kings of a territory (for example, king of France). This new designation reflected an important change in medieval rulership. However strong earlier rulers had been, their political power had been personal (depending on ties of kinship, friendship, and vassalage) rather than territorial (touching all who lived within the borders of their state). Noble and regal families were organized to pass along inheritances directly from father to son. That new organization, along with renewed interest in Roman legal concepts, served as a foundation for strong, central rule. The process of state building began to encompass clearly delineated regions, most strikingly in western Europe but in central and eastern Europe as well.

Western European rulers now began to employ professional administrators; sometimes, as in England, the system was so institutionalized that government did not require the king's personal presence to function. Even when the king left England (as often happened, since he had continental possessions to attend to), his government ran smoothly under his subordinates and appointees. In other regions, such as Germany, bureaucratic administration did not develop so far. In eastern Europe it hardly began at all.

Reviving the German Monarchy

The Investiture Conflict and the civil war it generated (1075–1122) strengthened the German princes and weakened the kings, Henry IV and Henry V, who were also the emperors. For decades, the princes enjoyed near independence, building castles on their properties and establishing control over whole territories. To ensure that the emperors who succeeded Henry V (r. 1106–1125) would be weak, the princes supported only rulers who agreed to give them new lands and powers. A ruler's success depended on balancing the many conflicting interests of his own royal and imperial offices, his family, and the German princes. He also had to contend with the increasing influence of the papacy and the Italian communes, which forged alliances with one another and with the German princes, preventing the consolidation of power under a strong German monarch during the first half of the twelfth century.

During the civil war in Germany, the two sides were represented by two noble families: fighting for the imperial party were the Staufer, or Hohenstaufen clan; their opponents, the princely-papal party, were the Welfs. (Two later Italian factions, the Ghibellines and the Guelphs, corresponded respectively to the Hohenstaufens and the Welfs.) The enmity between these families was legendary, and warfare between the groups raged even after the Concordat of Worms

in 1122. Exhausted from constant battles, by 1152 all parties longed for peace. In an act of rare unanimity, they elected as king Frederick I Barbarossa (r. 1152–1190). In Frederick they seemed to have a candidate who could end the strife: his mother was a Welf, his father a Staufer. Contemporary accounts of the king's career represented Frederick in the image of Christ as the "cornerstone" that joined two houses and reconciled enemies.

New Foundations of Power.   Frederick's appearance impressed his contemporaries—the name *Barbarossa* referred to his red-blond hair and beard. But beyond appearances, Frederick inspired those around him by his firmness. He affirmed royal

Frederick Barbarossa
In a thirteenth-century manuscript about imperial honor, Frederick Barbarossa is remembered for his firmness. At the top Frederick takes leave of his sons before going on the Third Crusade. They bow in deference to his authority and dignity. At the bottom, Frederick mounts his horse, gesturing a command with his left hand. The caption in Latin reads, "Frederick orders his men to cut down the forest in Hungary." Did Frederick fear retaliation from the Hungarian king? What sort of vision of imperial might did the artist of this miniature want to suggest?
Burgerbibliothek Bern, Cod. 120, II, f. #143r.

rights, even when he handed out duchies and allowed others to name bishops, because in return for these political powers Frederick required the princes to concede formally and publicly that they held their rights and territories from him as their lord. By making them his vassals, although with near royal rights within their principalities, Frederick defined the princes' relationship to the German king: they were powerful yet personally subordinate to him. In this way Frederick hoped to save the monarchy and to coordinate royal and princely rule, thus ending Germany's chronic civil wars. Frederick used the lord-vassal relationship to give him a free hand to rule while placating the princes.

As the king of Germany, Frederick had the traditional right to claim the imperial crown. Historians often date the Holy Roman Empire to this period. (Sometimes they even attribute the foundation of the Holy Roman Empire to Charlemagne.) In fact, the term was used first only in 1254, more than a half-century after Frederick's death. But Frederick did think of his empire as holy. He called it *sacer*, "sacred." By using this term, he asserted that his empire was in its own way as precious, worthwhile, and God-given as the church.

This is why Frederick would not listen to the "ambassadors" of Rome. They had no right to give him the imperial title. Frederick buttressed his high view of imperial right with very worldly power. He married Beatrice of Burgundy, whose vast estates in Burgundy and Provence enabled Frederick to establish a powerful political and territorial base centered in Swabia (today southwestern Germany).

Frederick and Italy. Since the Investiture Conflict, the emperor had ruled Italy in name only. The communes of the northern cities guarded their liberties jealously, while the pope considered Italy his own sphere of influence. Frederick's territorial base just north of Italy threatened those interests (Map 11.1). Moreover, his words to the "ambassadors" of Rome antagonized Pope Hadrian IV (r. 1154–1159), who thought that the papacy, not Frederick, represented the glory of Rome. The pope claimed jurisdiction over Rome and, since the ninth century, the right to anoint the emperor. In Frederick's day a fresco on one wall of the Lateran Palace (the pope's residence) went further: it showed the German king Lothar III receiving the imperial crown from the pope as if the empire were the pope's gift, as the papacy would

have liked the world to believe. In 1157, soon after Frederick's imperial coronation, Hadrian's envoys arrived at a meeting called by the emperor with a letter detailing the dignities, honors, and other *beneficia* the pope had showered on Frederick. The word *beneficia* incensed the assembled company of Frederick's supporters because it meant not only "benefits" but also "fiefs," casting Frederick as the pope's vassal. The incident opened old wounds from the Investiture Conflict and revealed the gulf between papal and imperial conceptions of worldly authority.

Although papal claims meant that conquering Italy would not be easy, no emperor could possibly leave Italy alone. Some historians have faulted Frederick for "entangling" himself in Italy. But Frederick's title was emperor, a position that demanded he intervene in Italy. To fault him for not concentrating on Germany is to blame him for lacking modern wisdom, which knows from hindsight that European polities developed into nation-states, such as France, Germany, and Italy. There was nothing inevitable about the development of nation-states, and Frederick should not be criticized simply because he did not see into the future.

In addition, control of Italy made sense even for Frederick's effectiveness in Germany. His base in Swabia together with northern Italy would give him a compact and central territory. Moreover, the flourishing commercial cities of Italy would make him rich. Taxes on agricultural production there alone would yield thirty thousand silver talents annually, an incredible sum equal to the annual income of the richest ruler of the day, the king of England.

By alternately negotiating with and fighting against the great cities of northern Italy, especially Milan, Frederick achieved military control there in 1158. No longer able to make Italian bishops royal governors, as German kings had done earlier—the Investiture Conflict had effectively ended that practice—Frederick insisted that the communes be governed by magistrates (called *podestà*) from outside the commune who were appointed (or at least authorized) by the emperor and who would collect revenues on his behalf. Here is where Frederick made his mistake. The heavy hand of these officials, many of them from Germany, created enormous resentment. For example, the *podestà* at Milan immediately ordered an inventory of all taxes due the

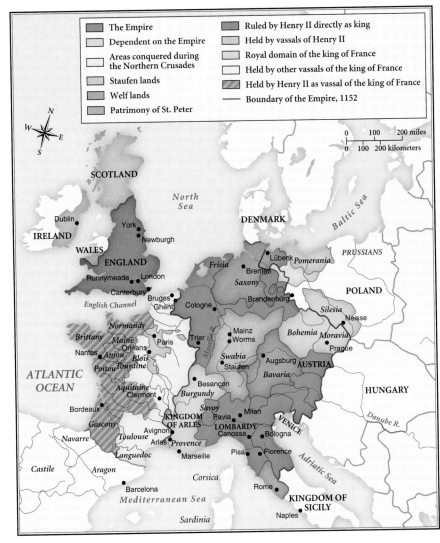

MAP 11.1 Europe in the Age of Frederick Barbarossa and Henry II, 1150–1190

The second half of the twelfth century was dominated by two men, Emperor Frederick Barbarossa and King Henry II. Not just king of England, Henry also held northwestern France by inheritance and southwestern France through his wife, Eleanor of Aquitaine. A few hundred miles to the east were the borders of Frederick Barbarossa's empire, a huge territory, but much of it held by him only weakly. Only the Staufen lands were directly under his control.

emperor and levied new and demeaning labor duties, even demanding that citizens carry the wood and stones of their plundered city to Pavia, twenty-five miles away, for use in constructing new houses there. By 1167, most of the cities of northern Italy had joined with Pope Alexander III (r. 1159–1181) to form the Lombard League against Frederick. Defeated at the battle of Legnano in 1176, Frederick made peace with Alexander and withdrew most of his forces from Italy. The battle marked the triumph of the city over the crown in Italy, which would not have a centralized government until the nineteenth century; its political history would instead be that of its various regions and their dominant cities.

Frederick Barbarossa was the victim of traditions that were rapidly being outmoded. He based much of his rule in Germany on the bond of lord and vassal at the very moment when rulers elsewhere were relying less on such personal ties and more on salaried officials. He lived up to the meaning of emperor, with all its obligations to rule Rome and northern Italy, when other leaders were consolidating their territorial rule bit by bit. In addition, as "universal" emperor, he did not recognize the importance of local pride, language, customs, and traditions; he tried to rule Italian communes with henchmen from the outside, and he failed.

Henry the Lion: Lord and Vassal. During Frederick I Barbarossa's reign, many princes of Germany enjoyed near royal status, acting as independent rulers of their principalities, though acknowledging

Frederick as their feudal lord. One of the most powerful was Henry the Lion (c. 1130–1195). Married to Matilda, daughter of the English king Henry II and Eleanor of Aquitaine, Henry was duke of Saxony and Bavaria, which gave him important bases in both the north and the south of Germany. A self-confident and aggressive ruler, Henry dominated his territory by investing bishops (usurping the role of the emperor as outlined in the Concordat of Worms), collecting dues from his estates, and exercising judicial rights over his duchies. He also actively extended his rule, especially in Slavic regions, pushing northeast past the Elbe River to reestablish dioceses and to build the commercial emporium of Lübeck.

Lord of many vassals, commander of a large army composed chiefly of ministerials (knights with much prestige but of unfree status) along with some Slavic reinforcements, Henry took advantage of government institutions to enforce his authority and help him maintain control of his territories. Ministerials acted not only as his soldiers but as his officials; they collected Henry's taxes and his share of profits from tolls, markets, and mints (like kings, Henry took a percentage of the silver that was minted into coins). At court his steward, treasurer, and stable marshal were all ministerials. Other officials were notaries, normally clerics, who wrote and preserved some of his

legal acts. Thus Henry the Lion created a small staff to carry on the day-to-day administration of his principality without him. Here, as elsewhere, administration no longer depended entirely on the personal involvement of the ruler.

Yet like kings, princes could fall. Henry's growing power so threatened other princes and even Frederick that in 1179 Frederick called Henry to the king's court for violating the peace. When Henry chose not to appear, Frederick exercised his authority as Henry's lord and charged him with violating his duty as a vassal. Because Henry refused the summons to court and avoided serving his lord in Italy, Frederick condemned him, confiscated his holdings, and drove him out of Germany in 1180. Although he wished to retain Henry's duchy for himself, Frederick had to divide and distribute it to supporters whose aid he needed to enforce his decrees against Henry.

Late-twelfth-century kings and emperors often found themselves engaged in this balancing act of ruling yet placating their powerful vassals. The process almost always was a gamble. Successfully challenging one recalcitrant prince-vassal meant negotiating costly deals with the others, since their support was vital. Monarchs such as Frederick often lost as much as they gained in such actions, usually defeating the targeted truant but ending up with little to show for it after paying off all the favors required to win.

Henry the Lion

In 1166, when Henry the Lion was under especially heavy attack by his enemies, he had this giant lion cast out of iron mined in his duchy. A symbol of justice and also of Henry himself, the lion "guarded" Henry's castle at Brunswick. Its pose is probably modeled on that of the she-wolf of Rome, which Henry must have seen near the Lateran Palace when he accompanied Frederick Barbarossa to Rome in 1155. Its snarling mouth was meant to suggest ferocity. This lion is the first large freestanding sculpture of the Middle Ages. Compare it with the crusader on page 361 and the shoemaker on page 353.
Erich Lessing/Art Resource.

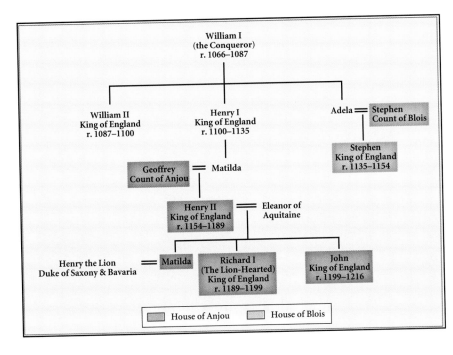

FIGURE 11.1 Genealogy of Henry II

King William I of England was succeeded by his sons William II and Henry I. When Henry died, the succession was disputed by two women and their husbands. One was William I's daughter Adela, married to the count of Blois; the other was Henry's daughter Matilda, wife of the count of Anjou. Although the English crown first went to the house of Blois, it reverted in mid-century to the house of Anjou, headed by Matilda's son Henry. He thus began the Angevin dynasty in England.

England: Unity through Law

In the mid-twelfth century, the government of England was by far the most institutionalized in Europe. The king hardly needed to be present: royal government functioned by itself, with officials handling all the administrative matters and record keeping. The English government reflected both the Anglo-Saxon tradition of using writs (royal orders conveyed in writing) and the Norman tradition of retaining the ruler's control over his officials, over taxes (paid in cash), and over court cases involving all capital crimes. The very circumstances of the English king favored the growth of an administrative staff: his frequent travels to and from the continent meant that officials needed to work in his absence, and his enormous wealth meant that he could afford them. King Henry II (r. 1154–1189) was the driving force in extending and strengthening the institutions of English government.

Accession of Henry II, 1154. Henry II became king in the wake of a civil war that threatened the new Norman dynasty in England. Henry I (r. 1100–1135), son of William the Conqueror, had no male heir. Before he died, he called on the great barons to swear that his daughter Matilda would rule after

him. The effort failed; the Norman barons could not imagine a woman ruling them, and they feared her husband, Geoffrey of Anjou, their perennial enemy. The man who succeeded to the throne, Stephen of Blois (r. 1135–1154), was the son of Henry's sister, Adela. With Matilda's son, the future Henry II, only two years old when Stephen took the crown, the struggle for control of England during Stephen's reign became part of a larger territorial contest between the house of Anjou (Henry's family) and the house of Blois (Stephen's family) (Figure 11.1). Continual civil war in England, as in Germany, benefited the English barons and high churchmen, who gained new privileges and powers as the monarch's authority waned. Newly built private castles, already familiar on the continent, now appeared in England as symbols of the rising power of the English barons. But Stephen's coalition of barons, high clergymen, and townsmen eventually fell apart, causing him to agree to the accession of Matilda's son, Henry of Anjou. Thus began what would be known as the *Angevin* (from *Anjou*) dynasty.*

---

*Henry's father, Geoffrey of Anjou, was nicknamed "Plantagenet" from the *genet,* a shrub he liked. Historians sometimes use the name to refer to the entire dynasty, so Henry II was the first *Plantagenet* as well as the first *Angevin* king of England.

The English Royal Family

Tranquil together in death as they had never been in life, the remains of Eleanor of Aquitaine, King Henry II, and other members of their family lie side by side in tombs at Fontevrault, near Poitiers, France. Their generous patronage of Fontevrault, a double monastery for both monks and nuns, is an important reminder that in the second half of the twelfth century, the "English" royalty also ruled much of France. In fact, the choice of Fontevrault as his resting place suggests that Henry considered it the spiritual center of his dominions. Life-size tomb sculptures such as these were just coming into vogue at the time. They were in part effigies, in part idealized representations. Why do you suppose Eleanor was given a book to read?

Collection Roger-Viollet.

Henry's marriage to Eleanor of Aquitaine in 1152 brought the enormous inheritance of the duchy of Aquitaine to the English crown. Although he remained the vassal of the king of France for his continental lands, Henry in effect ruled a territory that stretched from England to southern France.

Not only did Eleanor bring to Henry the duchy of Aquitaine, but she bore him sons to maintain his dynasty. Before her marriage to Henry, Eleanor had been married to King Louis VII of France; Louis had the marriage annulled because Eleanor had borne him only daughters. Nevertheless, as queen of France, Eleanor had enjoyed an important position: she disputed with St. Bernard, the Cistercian abbot who was the most renowned churchman of the day; she accompanied her husband on the Second Crusade, bringing more troops than he did; and she determined to separate from her husband even before he considered leaving her. But she lost much of her power under her English husband, for Henry dominated her just as he came to dominate his

barons. Turning to her offspring in 1173, Eleanor, disguised as a man, tried to join her eldest son, Henry the Younger, in a plot against his father. But the rebellion was put down, and she spent most of her years thereafter, until her husband's death in 1189, confined under guard at Winchester Castle.

Royal Authority and Common Law. When Henry II became king of England, he immediately sought to reassert royal authority over the barons newly ensconced in their castles. He destroyed or confiscated their strongholds and regained crown lands. Then he proceeded to extend monarchical power, imposing royal justice by expanding his system of courts. "Throughout the realm," wrote a contemporary admirer, "he appointed judges and legal officials to curb the audacity of wicked men and dispense justice to litigants according to the merits of their case." Henry enlarged the role of the crown in both criminal and civil cases through a system of judicial visitations called *eyres* (from the Latin *iter*, "journey").

Under this system, royal justices made regular trips to every locality in England. Henry declared that some crimes, such as murder, arson, and rape, were so heinous as to violate the "king's peace," no matter where they were committed. The king required local representatives of the knightly class to meet during each eyre and either give the sheriff the names of those suspected of committing crimes in the vicinity or arrest the suspects themselves and hand them over to the royal justices. This system gave the king an important role in local law and order. At the same time, it increased his income with confiscated lands and fines collected from criminals.

At the eyres, the justices heard what we now call civil cases, cases between individuals. Free men and women (that is, people of the knightly class or above) could bring their disputes over such matters as inheritance, dowries, and property claims to the king's justices. Earlier courts had generally relied on duels between litigants to determine verdicts. Henry's new system offered a different option, an inquest under royal supervision. It also gave the king a new source of control and revenue. For example, a widow named Mabel might dispute the possession of a parcel of land at Stoke with a man named Ralph. By purchasing a royal writ, she could set the wheels of the king's new justice in motion. The writ would order the sheriff to summon a jury of twelve free men from Stoke to declare in front of the justices whether Ralph or Mabel had the better right to possess the land. The power of the king would then back the verdict.

In this way the Angevin kings made local business royal business. There was a system of common law—law that touched all the free people in England—before Henry II. The Anglo-Saxon king Alfred the Great (r. 871–899) had promulgated a common-law code for the English more than 250 years earlier, and Norman kings had established a system of royal district courts. But Henry's reforms made the king's justice felt everywhere on a regular basis.

The new system was praised for its efficiency, speed, and conclusiveness by a contemporary legal treatise known as *Glanvill* (after its presumed author): "This legal institution emanates from perfect equity. For justice, which after many and long delays is scarcely ever demonstrated by the duel, is advantageously and speedily attained through this institution." *Glanvill* might have added that the king also speedily gained a large treasury. The exchequer, as the financial bureau of England was called, recorded all the fines paid for judgments and the sums collected for writs. The amounts, entered on parchment sewn together and stored as rolls, became the Receipt Rolls and Pipe Rolls, the first of many such records of the English monarchy and an indication that writing had become a mechanism for institutionalizing royal power in England.

Hanging Thieves
The development of common law in England meant mobilizing royal agents to bring charges and arrest people throughout the land. In 1124, the royal justice Ralph Basset hanged forty-four thieves. It could not have been very shocking in that context to see, in this miniature from around 1130, eight thieves hanged for breaking into the shrine of St. Edmund. Under Henry II all cases of murder, arson, and rape were considered crimes against the king himself. The result was not just the enhancement of the king's power but also new definitions of crime, more thorough policing, and more systematic punishments. Even so, hanging was probably no more frequent than it had been before.
Pierpont Morgan Library/Art Resource, NY.

The stiffest opposition to Henry's extension of royal courts came from the church, where a separate system of trial and punishment had long been available to the clergy and to others who enjoyed church protection. The punishments for crimes meted out by these courts were generally quite mild. Jealous of their prerogatives, churchmen refused to submit to the jurisdiction of Henry's courts, and the ensuing contest between Henry II and his appointed archbishop, Thomas Becket (1118–1170), became the greatest battle between the church and the state in the twelfth century. The conflict over jurisdiction simmered for six years, until Henry's henchmen murdered Thomas, unintentionally turning him into a martyr. Although Henry's role in the murder remained ambiguous, he had to do public penance for the deed largely because of the general outcry. In the end both church and royal courts expanded to address the concerns of an increasingly litigious society.

Henry II was an English king with an imperial reach. He was lord over almost half of France, though much of this territory was in the hands of his vassals, and he was, at least theoretically, a vassal to the French king. In England, he made the king's presence felt everywhere through his system of royal courts that traveled the length and breadth of the country. On the continent, he maintained his position through a combination of war and negotiation, dogged as he was throughout his life by rebellions, which were often fomented by one of his sons aided by the king of France.

Henry's Successors. Under Henry and his sons Richard I (r. 1189–1199) and John (r. 1199–1216), the English monarchy was omnipresent and rich. Its omnipresence derived largely from its eyre system of justice and its administrative apparatus. Its wealth came from court fees, income from numerous royal estates both in England and on the continent, taxes from cities, and customary feudal dues (called *aids*) collected from barons and knights. These aids were paid on such occasions as the knighting of the king's eldest son and the marriage of the king's eldest daughter. Enriched by the commercial economy of the late twelfth century, the English kings encouraged their knights and barons not to serve them personally in battle but instead to pay the king a tax called *scutage* in lieu of service. The monarchs preferred to hire mercenaries both as troops to fight external enemies and as police to enforce the king's will at home.

Richard I was known as the Lion-Hearted for his boldness. But historians have often criticized him for being an "absentee" king. He went on the Third Crusade the very year he was crowned; on his way home, he was captured and held for a long time for ransom by political enemies; and he died defending his possessions on the continent. Yet it is hard to see what he might have done differently. He could hardly ignore the lure of the crusade when every great European king was participating in one. And he could not ignore his territory on the continent; it was the source of both power and wealth. Richard's real tragedy was that he died young.

Henry II Doing Penance

King Henry II's henchmen murdered Archbishop Thomas Becket within his own church at Canterbury. Becket was immediately considered a martyr, and the outcry was so great and widespread that Henry had to do penance for the act. Here, in stained glass made very soon after the archbishop's death, Henry is depicted bowing down in front of Becket's tomb, hands raised in prayer for forgiveness. Is it surprising that this quatrefoil glass was made for the Trinity chapel of Canterbury Cathedral? Sonia Halliday and Laura Lushington.

Richard's successor, John, has also been widely faulted. Even in his own day, he was accused of asserting his will in a high-handed way. But to understand John, it is necessary to appreciate how desperate he was to keep his continental possessions. In 1204, the king of France, Philip II (r. 1180–1223), confiscated the northern French territories held by John. Between 1204 and 1214, John did everything he could to add to the crown revenues so he could pay for an army to fight Philip. He forced his vassals to pay ever-increasing scutages and extorted money in the form of new feudal aids. He compelled the widows of his vassals to marry men of his choosing or pay him a hefty fee if they refused. Despite John's heavy investment in this war effort, his army was defeated in 1214 at the battle of Bouvines. The defeat caused discontented English barons to rebel openly against the king. At Runnymede in June 1215, John was forced to agree to the charter of baronial liberties that has come to be called *Magna Carta,* or "Great Charter."

Magna Carta, 1215. The English barons intended Magna Carta (so named to distinguish it from a smaller charter issued around the same time concerning the royal forests) to be a conservative document defining the "customary" obligations and rights of the nobility and forbidding the king to break from these customs without consulting his barons. It also maintained that all free men in the land had certain customs and rights in common and that the king must uphold those customs and rights. (See "Contrasting Views," page 398.) In this way, Magna Carta documented the subordination of the king to custom; it implied that the king was not above the law. The growing royal power was matched by the self-confidence of the English barons, certain of their rights and eager to articulate them. In time, as the definition of "free men" expanded to include all the king's subjects, Magna Carta came to be seen as a guarantee of the rights of Englishmen in general.

The Consolidation of France

Whereas the power of the English throne led to a baronial movement to curb it, the weakness of the French monarchy ironically led to its expansion. In 1180, the French monarchy passed from the Capetian king Louis VII (first husband of Eleanor of Aquitaine) to his son, Philip II (who would eventually defeat King John at Bouvines). When Philip II came to the throne, the royal domain, the Île-de-France, was sandwiched between territory controlled by the counts of Flanders, Champagne, and Anjou. By far the most powerful ruler on the continent was King Henry II of England, who was both the count of Anjou and the duke of Normandy and who also held the duchy of Aquitaine through his wife, while exercising hegemony over Poitou and Brittany.

Henry and the counts of Flanders and Champagne vied to control the newly crowned fourteen-year-old king of France. Philip, however, quickly learned to play them off against one another, in particular by setting the sons of Henry II against their father. For example, Philip helped Henry the Younger rebel against his father in 1183 by sending the young man a contingent of mercenary troops.

John's Seal on Magna Carta
When the rebels at Runnymede got John to assent to their charter, later known as Magna Carta, he did not sign it; he sealed it. From the thirteenth through the fifteenth century, seals were used by kings, queens, aristocrats, guilds, communes, and many other people at all levels of society to authenticate their charters— what we would call "legal documents." The seal itself was made out of wax or lead, melted and pressed with a matrix of hard metal, such as gold or brass, that was carved with an image in the negative, designed to produce a raised image. These images reminded the public of the status as well as the name of the sealer. Note the image that John chose to place on his seal.
British Museum.

Magna Carta

Magna Carta, today considered a landmark of constitutional government, began as a demand for specific rights and privileges. When, in 1215, the English barons and churchmen could no longer tolerate King John's demands, they insisted on getting a "charter of liberties" from the king. The document that they drafted for John to seal is called the "Great Charter" (Magna Carta, Document 1). It set forth the customs that the king was expected to observe and, in its sixty-first clause, in effect allowed the king's subjects to declare war against him if he failed to carry out the charter's provisions.

About ten years later, a biographer of one of the few barons who had remained loyal to the king still feared the wrath of the rebels (Document 2). By that time, several new versions of Magna Carta had been issued by John's son Henry III. All of them lacked the original sixty-first clause, though other clauses were expanded and clarified. In 1225, Henry issued a definitive version of the charter. By then it had become more important as a symbol of liberty than for its specific provisions. It was, for example, invoked by the barons in 1242 when they were summoned to one of the first Parliaments (Document 3).

1. Magna Carta, 1215

In these excerpts, the provisions that were dropped in the definitive version of 1225 are starred. Explanatory notes are in brackets. The original charter had sixty-three clauses. In every clause John refers to himself by the royal "we."

1. First of all [we, i.e., John] have granted to God, and by this our present charter confirmed for us and our heirs for ever that the English church shall be free, and shall have its rights undiminished and its liberties unimpaired. . . .

8. No widow shall be forced to marry so long as she wishes to live without a husband, provided that she gives security [a pledge or deposit] not to marry without our consent if she holds [her land] from us, or without the consent of her lord of whom she holds, if she holds of another.

9. Neither we nor our bailiffs will seize for any debt any land or rent, so long as the chattels [property] of the debtor are sufficient to repay the debt. . . .

*10. If anyone who has borrowed from the Jews any sum, great or small, dies before it is repaid, the debt shall not bear interest as long as the heir is under age, of whomsoever [lord] he holds [his land]; and if the debt falls into our hands [which might happen, as Jews were serfs of the crown], we will not take anything except the principal mentioned in the bond.

*12. No scutage or aid [money payments owed by a vassal to his lord] shall be imposed in our kingdom unless by common counsel of our kingdom, except for ransoming our person, for making our eldest son a knight, and for once marrying our eldest daughter; and for these only a reasonable aid shall be levied. . . .

30. No sheriff, or bailiff of ours, or anyone else shall take the horses or carts of any free man [for the most part, a member of the elite] for transport work save with the agreement of that freeman.

31. Neither we nor our bailiffs will take, for castles or other works of ours, timber which is not ours, except with the agreement of him whose timber it is. . . .

39. No free man shall be arrested or imprisoned or disseised [deprived of his land] or outlawed or exiled or in any way victimized, neither will we attack him or send anyone to attack him, except by the lawful judgment of his peers or by the law of the land.

*61. Since . . . we have granted all these things aforesaid . . . we give and grant [the barons] the under-written security, namely, that the barons shall choose any twenty-five barons of the kingdom they wish, who must with all their might observe, hold, and cause to be observed, the peace and liberties which we have granted and confirmed to them by this present charter of ours, so that if we, or our justiciar [the king's chief minister], or our bailiffs or any one of our servants offend in any way against anyone or transgress any of the articles of the peace or the security . . . , [the barons] shall come to us . . . and laying the transgression before us, shall petition us to have that transgression corrected without delay. And if we do not correct the transgression . . . within forty days . . . those twenty-five barons together with the community of the whole land shall distrain and distress us in every way they can, namely, by seizing castles, lands, possessions, and in such other ways as they can, saving [not harming] our person.

Source: *English Historical Documents*, vol. 3, ed. Harry Rothwell (London: Eyre & Spottiswoode, 1975), 317–23.

2. The History of William the Marshal, c. 1226

William the Marshal was one of the few barons who, for reasons of both conviction and personal advantage, remained loyal to John during the barons' revolt. The following excerpt from William's biography shows that although Magna Carta had patched up a peace, resentments still simmered.

I must pass rapidly over the war that broke out between the king and his barons, because there were too many circumstances that are not creditable to relate. Harm might come to me because of them. The barons having formed a league came to the king and demanded of him their liberties. He refused: then they made it known that if they did not obtain their liberties they would withdraw from his service and do him all the harm they could. They kept their word and betook themselves to London to act against him. But note well that the Marshal took no part whatever in this movement. He grieved for the excesses into which those on both sides had allowed themselves to be drawn.

Source: *English Historical Documents*, 3:81.

3. The Barons at Parliament Refuse to Give the King an Aid, 1242

Henry III convoked the barons to a meeting (parliament), expecting them to ratify his request for money to wage war for his French possessions. As this document makes clear, the barons considered his request an excessive imposition. Magna Carta

thus became a justification for their flat rejection of the king's request.

Since he had been their ruler they had many times, at his request, given him aid, namely, a thirteenth of their movable property, and afterwards a fifteenth and a sixteenth and a fortieth. . . . Scarcely, however, had four years or so elapsed from that time, when he again asked them for aid, and, at length, by dint of great entreaties, he obtained a thirtieth, which they granted him on the condition that neither that exaction nor the others before it should in the future be made a precedent of. And regarding that he gave them his charter. Furthermore, he then [at that earlier time] granted them that all the liberties contained in Magna Carta should thenceforward be fully observed throughout the whole of his kingdom. . . .

Furthermore, from the time of their giving the said thirtieth, itinerant justices have been continually going on eyre [moving from place to place] through all parts of England, alike for pleas of the forest [to enforce the king's monopoly on forests] and all other pleas, so that all the counties, hundreds, cities, boroughs, and nearly all the vills of England are heavily amerced [fined]; wherefore, from that eyre alone the king has, or ought to have, a very large sum of money, if it were paid, and properly collected. They therefore say with truth that all in the kingdom are so oppressed and impoverished by these amercements and by the other aids given before that they have little or no goods left. And because the king had never, after the granting of the thirtieth, abided by his charter of liberties, nay had since then oppressed them more than usual . . . they told the king flatly that for the present they would not give him an aid.

Source: *English Historical Documents*, 3:355–56.

QUESTIONS FOR DEBATE
1. From the clauses of Magna Carta that say what will henceforth *not* be done, speculate about what the king *had been* doing.
2. Why would the biographer of William the Marshal fear the anger of the barons who had revolted in 1215?
3. How did the barons of 1242 use Magna Carta as a symbol of liberty?

Despite his apparent political competence, contemporaries were astounded when Philip successfully gained territory: he wrested Vermandois and Artois from Flanders in the 1190s and Normandy, Anjou, Maine, Touraine, and Poitou from King John of England in 1204. After these feats a contemporary chronicler dubbed him Philip Augustus, the augmenter.

Nevertheless, before 1204 the French king's territory was minuscule compared with the vast regions held by the English king. Although it seems logical today that the French king would rule all of France, twelfth-century observers would not necessarily have agreed.

Pivotal forces led to the extension of the French king's power and the territorial integrity of France. The Second Crusade brought together many French lords as vassals of the king and united them against a common foe. The language they spoke was becoming increasingly uniform and "French." Nevertheless, this in itself did not create a larger French kingdom. That came about through royal strategy. In 1204, having declared his vassal the duke of Normandy (who was also the English king, John) disobedient for not coming to court when summoned, Philip confiscated most of John's continental territories. He confirmed this triumph decisively ten years later at the battle of Bouvines, in which, mainly by luck, Philip's armies routed his major opponents and took others prisoner. Though the English still held Aquitaine, the French monarch could boast that he was the richest and most powerful ruler in France. Unlike Frederick I Barbarossa, who was compelled to divide the territory he had seized from Henry the Lion among the German princes, Philip had sufficient support and resources to keep a tight hold on Normandy. He received homage and fealty from most of the Norman aris-

The Consolidation of France under Philip Augustus, 1180–1223

tocracy; his officers carefully carried out their work there in accordance with Norman customs. For ordinary Normans the shift from duke to king brought few changes.

As impressive as Philip's conquests were, even more extraordinary was his ability to keep and administer his new territories.* Rather than give them out as fiefs, Philip set out to govern them himself. He instituted a new kind of French administration, run, as in England, by officials who kept accounts and files. Before Philip's day most royal arrangements were committed to memory rather than to writing. If decrees were recorded at all, they were saved by the recipient, not by the government. For example, when a monastery wanted a confirmation of its privileges from the king, its own scribes wrote the document for its archives to preserve it against possible future challenges. The king did keep some documents, which generally followed him in his travels like personal possessions. But in 1194, in a battle with the king of England, Philip lost his meager cache of documents along with much treasure when he had to abandon his baggage train. After 1194, the king had all his decrees written down, and he established permanent repositories in which to keep them.

Whereas German rulers employed ministerials to do the daily work of government, Philip, like the English king, relied largely on members of the lesser nobility—knights and clerics, many of whom were "masters" educated in the city schools of France. They served as officers of his court; as *prévôts*, who oversaw the king's estates and collected his taxes; and as *baillis* (or *sénéchaux* in the south), who not only supervised the *prévôts* but also functioned as regional judges, presiding over courts that met monthly and making the king's power felt locally as never before.

Fragmenting Realms in Eastern Europe and Byzantium

The importance of institutions such as those developed in England and France is made clear by the experience of regions where they were not estab-

---

*Philip was particularly successful in imposing royal control in Normandy; later French kings gave most of the other territories to collateral members of the royal family.

lished. In eastern Europe the characteristic pattern was for states to form under the leadership of one great ruler and then to fragment under his successor. For example, King Béla III of Hungary (r. 1172–1196) built up a state that looked superficially like a western European kingdom. He married a French princess, employed at least one scholar from Paris, and built his palace in the French Romanesque style. He enjoyed an annual income from his estates, tolls, dues, and taxes equal to that of the richest western monarchs. But he did not set up enduring government institutions, and in the decades that followed his death, wars between Béla's sons splintered his monarchical holdings, and aristocratic supporters divided the wealth.

Russia underwent a similar process. Although twelfth-century Kiev was politically fragmented, autocratic princes to the north constructed Suzdal, the nucleus of the later Muscovite state. The borders of Suzdal were clearly defined; well-to-do towns prospered; monasteries and churches dotted the countryside; and the other princes of Russia recognized its ruler as the "grand prince." Yet in 1212 this nascent state began to crumble as the sons of Grand Prince Vsevolod III (r. 1176–1212) fought one another for territory, much as Béla's sons had done in Hungary.

Eastern Europe and Byzantium, c. 1200

Although the Byzantine Empire was already a consolidated, bureaucratic state, after the death of John II (r. 1118–1143) it gradually began to show weakness. Traders from the west—the Venetians especially—dominated its commerce. The Byzantine emperors who ruled during the last half of the twelfth century downgraded the old civil servants, elevated their relatives to high offices, and favored the military elite. As Byzantine rule grew more personal and western rule became more bureaucratic, the two gradually became more like one another.

❖ The Growth of a Vernacular High Culture

With the consolidation of territory, wealth, and power in the last half of the twelfth century, kings, barons, princes, and their wives and daughters supported new kinds of literature and music. For the first time on the continent, though long true in England, poems and songs were written in the vernacular, the spoken language, rather than in Latin. They celebrated the lives of the nobility and were meant to be read aloud or sung, sometimes with accompanying musical instruments. Although not overtly political, they provided a common experience under the aegis of the court. Whether in the cities of Italy or the more isolated courts of northern Europe, patrons and patronesses, enriched by their estates and by the commercial growth of the twelfth century, now spent their profits on the arts. Their support helped develop and enrich the spoken language while it heightened their prestige as aristocrats.

Poets of Love and Play: The Troubadours

Already at the beginning of the twelfth century, Duke William IX of Aquitaine (1071–1126), the grandfather of Eleanor, had written lyric poems in Occitan, the vernacular of southern France. Perhaps influenced by love poetry in Arabic and Hebrew from al-Andalus, his own poetry in turn provided a model for poetic forms that gained popularity through repeated performances. The final four-line stanza of one such poem demonstrates the composer's skill with words:

Per aquesta fri e tremble,	*For this one I shiver and tremble,*
quar de tan bon' amor l'am;	*I love her with such a good love;*
qu'anc no cug qu'en nasques semble	*I do not think the like of her was ever born*
en semblan de gran linh n'Adam.	*in the long line of Lord Adam.*

The rhyme scheme of this poem appears to be simple—*tremble* goes with *semble, l'am* with *n'Adam*—but the entire poem has five earlier verses, all six lines long and all containing the *-am, -am* rhyme in the fourth and sixth lines, while every other line within each verse rhymes as well.

Troubadours, lyric poets who wrote in Occitan, varied their rhymes and meters endlessly to dazzle their audiences with brilliant originality. Most of their rhymes and meters resemble Latin religious poetry of the same time, indicating that the vernacular and Latin religious cultures overlapped. Such similarity is also evident in the troubadours' choice of subjects. The most common topic, love, echoed the twelfth-century church's emphasis on the emotional relationship between God and humans.

The troubadours invented new meanings for old images. When William IX sang of his "good love" for a woman unlike any other born in the line of Adam, the words could be interpreted in two ways. They reminded listeners of the Virgin, a woman unlike any other, but they also referred to William's lover, recalled in another part of the poem, where he had complained

> *If I do not get help soon*
> *and my lady does not give me love,*
> *by Saint Gregory's holy head I'll die*
> *if she doesn't kiss me in a chamber or under a tree.*

His lady's character is ambiguous: she is like Mary, but she is also his mistress.

Troubadours, both male and female, expressed prevalent views of love much as popular singers do today. The Contessa de Dia (flourished c. 1160), probably the wife of the lord of Die in France, wrote about her unrequited love for a man:

> *So bitter do I feel toward him*
> *whom I love more than anything.*
> *With him my mercy and fine manners [cortesia]*
> *are in vain.*

The key to troubadour verse is the idea of *cortesia*. It refers to *courtesy*, the refinement of people living at court, and to their struggle to achieve an ideal of virtue.

Historians and literary critics used to use the term *courtly love* to emphasize one of the themes of courtly literature: the poet expresses overwhelming love for a beautiful married noblewoman who is far above him in status and utterly unattainable. But this was only one of many aspects of love that the

Troubadour Song

Raimon de Miraval flourished between 1191 and 1229, very late for a troubadour. He was a petty knight who became a poet and was welcomed at the courts of rulers such as those of Toulouse, Aragon, and Castile. More than forty of his poems have survived, twenty-two of them with written music. The song here, beginning "A penas," is set to music with a five-line staff. Notice that some of the notes are single, while others are in groups. The grouped notes are to be sung, one right after the other, on the same syllable or word.

troubadours sang about: some boasted of sexual conquests; others played with the notion of equality between lovers; still others preached that love was the source of virtue. The real overall theme of this literature is not courtly love; it is the power of women. No wonder Eleanor of Aquitaine and other aristocratic women patronized the troubadours: they enjoyed the image that it gave them of themselves. Until recently historians thought that the image was a delusion and that twelfth-century aristocratic women were valuable mainly as heiresses to marry and as mothers of sons. But new research reveals that there were many powerful female lords in southern France. They owned property, had vassals, led battles, decided disputes, and entered into and broke political alliances as their advantage dictated. Both men and women appreciated troubadour poetry, which recognized and praised women's power even as it eroticized it.

Music was part of troubadour poetry, which was always sung, typically by a *jongleur* (musician). Unfortunately, no written troubadour music exists from before the thirteenth century, and even then we have music for only a fraction of the poems. By the thirteenth century, music was written on four- and five-line staves, so scholars can at least determine relative pitches, and modern musicians can sing some troubadour songs with the hope of sounding reasonably like the original. This is the earliest popular music that can be re-created authentically (Figure 11.2).

From southern France the lyric love song spread to Italy, northern France, England, and Germany—regions in which Occitan was a foreign language. Here instruments probably accompanied performances for audiences who did not understand the words. Similar poetry appeared in other vernacular languages: the *minnesingers* (literally, "love singers") sang in German; the *trouvères* sang in the Old French of northern France. One *trouvère* was the English king Richard the Lion-Hearted, son of Henry II and Eleanor of Aquitaine. Taken prisoner on his return from the Third Crusade, Richard wrote a poem expressing his longing not for a lady but for the good companions of war, the knightly "youths" he had joined in battle:

They know well, the men of Anjou and
    Touraine,
those bachelors, now so magnificent and
    safe,
that I am arrested, far from them, in
    another's hands.
They used to love me much, now they love
    me not at all.
There's no lordly fighting now on the barren
    plains,
because I am a prisoner.

The Literature of Epic and Romance

The yearning for the battlefield was not as common a topic in lyric poetry as love, but long narrative poems about heroic deeds (*chansons de geste*) appeared frequently in vernacular writing. Such poems followed a long oral tradition and appeared at about the same time as love poems. Like the songs of the troubadours, these epic poems implied a code of behavior for aristocrats, in this case on the battlefield.

By the end of the twelfth century, warriors wanted a guide for conduct and a common class

FIGURE 11.2 Troubador Song: "I Never Died for Love"

This music is the first part of a song that the troubadour poet Peire Vidal wrote sometime between 1175 and 1205. It has been adapted here for the treble clef. There is no time signature, but the music may easily be played by calculating one beat for each note, except for the two-note slurs, which fit into one beat together, a half-beat for each note.

From Samuel N. Rosenberg, Margaret Switten, and Gerard Le Vot, eds. *Songs of the Troubadours and Trouvères*, Copyright © 1997 by Samuel N. Rosenberg, Margaret Switten, and Gerard Le Vot. Reprinted by permission of Taylor & Francis/Garland Publishing, http://www.taylorandfrancis.com.

identity. Nobles and knights had begun to merge into one class because they felt threatened from below by newly rich merchants and from above by newly powerful kings. Their ascendancy on the battlefield, where they unhorsed one another with lances and long swords and took prisoners rather than kill their opponents, was also beginning to wane in the face of mercenary infantrymen who wielded long hooks and knives that ripped easily through chain mail. A knightly ethos and sense of group solidarity emerged in the face of these social, political, and military changes.

Thus the protagonists of heroic poems yearned not for love but for battle:

> The armies are in sight of one another. . . . The cowards tremble as they march, but the brave hearts rejoice for the battle.

Examining the moral issues that made war both tragic and inevitable, poets played on the contradictory values of their society, such as the conflicting loyalties of friendship and vassalage or a vassal's right to a fief versus a son's right to his father's land.

These vernacular narrative poems, later called *epics,* focused on war. Other long poems, later called *romances,* explored the relationships between men and women. Romances reached their zenith of popularity during the late twelfth and early thirteenth centuries. The legend of King Arthur inspired a romance by Chrétien de Troyes (c. 1150–1190) in which a heroic knight, Lancelot, in love with Queen Guinevere, the wife of his lord, comes across a comb bearing some strands of her radiant hair:

> Never will the eye of man see anything receive such honour as when [Lancelot] begins to adore these tresses. . . . Even for St. Martin and St. James he has no need.

At one level Chrétien is evoking the familiar imagery of relics, such as bits of hair or the bones of saints, as items of devotion. Making Guinevere's hair an object of adoration not only conveys the depth of Lancelot's feeling but also pokes a bit of fun at him. Like the troubadours, the romantic poets delighted in the interplay between religious and amorous feelings. Just as the ideal monk merged his will in God's will, Chrétien's Lancelot loses his will to Guinevere. When she sees Lancelot—the great-

est knight in Christendom—fighting in a tournament, she tests him by asking him to do his "worst." The poor knight is obliged to lose all his battles until she changes her mind.

Lancelot was the perfect chivalric knight. The word *chivalry* derives from the French word *cheval* ("horse"); the fact that the knight was a horseman marked him as a warrior of the most prestigious sort. Perched high on his horse, his heavy lance couched in his right arm, the knight was an imposing and menacing figure. Chivalry made him gentle—except to his enemies on the battlefield. The chivalric hero was a knight constrained by a code of refinement, fair play, piety, and devotion to an ideal. Historians debate whether real knights lived up to the codes implicit in epics and romances. But there is no doubt that knights saw themselves that way. They were the poets' audience. Sometimes they were the poets' subject as well. For example, when the knight William the Marshal died, his son commissioned a poet to write his biography. In it, William was depicted as a model knight, courteous with the ladies and brave on the battlefield.

❖ New Lay and Religious Associations

The new vernacular culture was merely one reflection of the growing wealth, sophistication, and self-confidence of twelfth-century society. At every level, people were creating new and well-defined institutions to implement their goals. Great lords hired estate managers; townspeople increasingly joined guilds that regulated their lives according to impersonal rules; and students and teachers joined to form universities. Many of these associations reflected the developing commercial society.

The Penetration of the Commercial Revolution

By 1150, rural life was increasingly organized for the marketplace. The commercialization of the countryside opened up opportunities for both peasants and lords, but it also burdened some with unwelcome obligations.

Great lords hired trained, literate agents to administer their estates, calculate profits and losses, and make marketing decisions. Aristocrats needed money not only because they relished luxuries but also because their honor and authority continued to depend on their personal generosity, patronage, and displays of wealth. In the late twelfth century, when some townsmen could boast fortunes that rivaled the riches of the landed aristocracy, the economic pressures on the nobles increased as their extravagance exceeded their income. Most went into debt.

The lord's need for money changed peasant life, as peasants too became more integrated into the developing commercial economy. The population continued to increase in the twelfth century, and the greater demand for food required more farmland. By the middle of the century, isolated and sporadic attempts to cultivate new land had become a regular and coordinated activity. Great lords offered special privileges to peasants who would do the backbreaking work of plowing marginal land. In 1154, the bishop of Neisse (today in Germany) called for settlers from Flanders and established a village for them. Experts in drainage, these new settlers got rights to the land they reclaimed and owed only light monetary obligations to the bishop, who nevertheless expected to reap a profit from their tolls and tithes. Similar encouragement came from lords throughout Europe, especially in northern Italy, England, Flanders, and Germany. In Flanders, where land was regularly inundated by seawater, the great monasteries sponsored drainage projects; and canals linking the cities to the agricultural regions let boats ply the waters to virtually every nook and cranny of the region. With its dense population, Flanders provided not only a natural meeting ground for long-distance traders from England and France but also numerous markets for local traders.

Sometimes free peasants acted on their own to clear land and relieve the pressure of overpopulation, as when the small freeholders in England's Fenland region cooperated to build banks and dikes to reclaim the land that led out to the North Sea. Villages were founded on the drained land, and villagers shared responsibility for repairing and maintaining the dikes even as each peasant family farmed its new holding individually.

On old estates the rise in population strained to the breaking point the manse organization that had developed in Carolingian Europe, where each household was settled on the land that supported it.

Now in the twelfth century, twenty peasant families might live on what had been, in the tenth century, the manse of one family. With the manse supporting so many more people, labor services and dues had to be recalculated, and peasants and their lords often turned services and dues into money rents, payable once a year. With this change, peasant men gained more control over their plots—they could sell them, will them to their sons, or even designate a small portion for their daughters. However, for these privileges, they had either to pay extra taxes or, like communes, to join together to buy their collective liberty for a high price, paid out over many years to their lord. Peasants, like town citizens, gained a new sense of identity and solidarity as they bargained with a lord keen to increase his income at their expense.

Peasants now owed more taxes to support the new administrative apparatuses of monarchs and princes. Kings' demands for money from their subjects filtered to the lowest classes either directly or indirectly. In Italy the cities themselves often imposed and enforced dues on the peasants, normally tenant farmers who leased their plots in the countryside surrounding each city. In the mid-twelfth century at Florence the urban officials, working closely with the bishop, dominated the countryside, collecting taxes from its cultivators, calling up its men to fight, and importing its food into the city. Therefore peasants' gains from rising prices, access to markets, greater productivity, and increased personal freedom were partially canceled out by their cash burdens. Peasants of the late twelfth century ate better than their forebears, but they also had more responsibilities.

Urban Corporations

The relatively informal arrangements of city dwellers in the first half of the twelfth century gave way to clearly defined and regulated institutions in the second half. Guilds—originally associations for religious devotion, convivial feasting, charitable activities, and regulation of crafts or trade—became corporations defined by statutes and rules. They negotiated with lords and town governments, set standards, and controlled membership. Universities were also a kind of guild. They too were defined by statutes created and strengthened through political negotiations, and they too were devoted to setting standards and controlling membership. But in the case of the universities, standards concerned scholarship, and members consisted of masters (teachers) and students.

Guilds. As guilds became formally organized, they drew up statutes to determine dues, working hours, fix wages, and set standards for materials and products. Sometimes they came into conflict with town government, as for example in Italy, where some communes considered bread too important a commodity to allow bakers to form a guild. At other times the communes supported guild efforts to control wages, reinforcing guild regulations with

A Weaving Workshop
A series of pen-and-ink drawings of various crafts was made in an early-thirteenth-century manuscript produced at the Austrian Cistercian monastery of Reun. In this depiction of a weavers' workshop, a woman (at left) works a carpet loom. She holds a spindle in her left hand and a beater in her right. Two men nearby use other implements of the weaver's trade: shuttles, scissors, and a beater.
Österreichische Nationalbibliothek, Vienna.

statutes of their own. When great lords rather than communes governed a city, they too tried to control and protect the guilds. King Henry II of England, for example, eagerly gave some guilds in his Norman duchy special privileges so that they would depend on him.

The manufacture of finished products often required the cooperation of several guilds. Producing wool cloth involved numerous guilds—shearers, weavers, fullers (people who beat the cloth to make it bulkier), dyers—generally working under the supervision of the merchant guild that imported the raw wool. Some guilds were more prestigious than others: in Florence, for example, professional guilds of notaries and judges ranked above craft guilds. Within each guild of artisans or merchants existed another kind of hierarchy. Apprentices were at the bottom, journeymen and -women in the middle, and masters at the top. Apprentices were boys and occasionally girls placed under the tutelage of a master for a number of years to learn a trade. (See "Taking Measure," page 407.) Normally the child's parents made the formal contract; but sometimes the children themselves took the initiative, as did a young man named John at Genoa in 1180 when he apprenticed himself to a turner, an expert in the use of the lathe. John promised to serve his master faithfully for five years, do whatever was expected of him, and not run away. In turn, his master promised to give him food, clothing, shelter, and a small salary; to teach him the turner's art; and to give him a set of tools at the end of the five years.

It would take many more years for a young person like John to become a master, however. First he would likely spend many years as a day laborer, a journeyman, hired by a master who needed extra help. Unlike apprentices, journeymen and -women did not live with their masters; they worked for them for a wage. This marked an important stage in the economic history of the West. For the first time, many workers were neither slaves nor dependents but free and independent wage earners. Although we know more about journeymen than journeywomen, we know that at least a few day workers were female; invariably they received wages far lower than their male counterparts. Sometimes a married couple worked at the same trade and hired themselves out as a team. Often journeymen and -women had to be guild members—for their dues and so their masters could keep tabs on them.

Lengths of Apprenticeships (years)	Occupation: Paris	Occupation: Genoa
4	Baker, carpenter	Draper, spinner
5	Fur hatter	Horseshoer, barber, cobbler, mason
6	Hatter, cutler, mason	Dyer, tailor
7	Felt hatter	Turner, smith, carpenter, coppersmith, carder
8	Tanner, locksmith, lace and silk maker	Locksmith, cutler, butcher
9		Harness maker
10	Buckle maker, tapestry maker, crucifix maker, table maker, goldsmith	Silversmith, armorer, saddler, cooper
11	Harness maker	Chest maker

TAKING MEASURE
Lengths of Apprentice-ships in the Thirteenth Century
An apprenticeship was a form of schooling, and, as this table indicates, most lasted from four to eleven years and none less than four years. The table also shows how local standards differed. To be a harness maker in Paris required eleven years of apprenticeship, but only nine years in Genoa.
From Steven A. Epstein, *Wage Labor and Guilds in Medieval Europe.* Copyright © 1991 by the University of North Carolina Press. Used by permission of the publisher.

Masters occupied the top of the guild hierarchy. Almost exclusively men, they dominated the offices and policies of the guild, hired journeymen, and recruited and educated apprentices. They drew up the guild regulations and served as chief overseers, inspectors, and treasurers. Because the number of masters was few and the turnover of official posts frequent, most masters eventually had a chance to serve as guild officers. Occasionally they were elected, but more often they were appointed from among the masters of the craft by the ruler—whether a prince or a commune—of the city.

During the late twelfth century, women's labor in some trades gradually declined in importance. In Flanders, for example, as the manufacture of woolen cloth shifted from rural areas to cities, women participated less in the process. Only isolated manors still needed a *gynaeceum*, the women's quarter where female dependents spun, wove, and sewed garments. Instead, new-style large looms in cities like Ypres and Ghent were run by men working in pairs. They produced a heavy-weight cloth superior to the fabric made on the lighter looms that women had worked. Similarly, women once ground grain into flour tediously by hand; but water mills and animal-powered mills gradually took the place of female labor, and most millers who ran the new machinery were male. Some women were certainly artisans and traders, and their names occasionally appeared in guild memberships. But they did not become guild officers, and they played no official role in town government. Women of the late twelfth century worked, but were increasingly dominated by men. Bernarda Cordonaria ("Shoemaker") was not the only woman in Toulouse at the beginning of the thirteenth century who took her last name not from her own trade but from her husband's craft.

Universities. Guilds of masters and students developed at the beginning of the thirteenth century at places such as Paris, Bologna, and Oxford. Each guild (*universitas* in Latin) was so tightly connected to the schools at which the masters taught and the students learned that eventually the term *university* came to include the school as well as the guild.

The universities regulated student discipline, scholastic proficiency, and housing while determining the masters' behavior in equal detail. For example, at the University of Paris the masters were required to wear long black gowns, follow a particular order in their lectures, and set the standards by which students could become masters themselves. The University of Bologna was unique in having two guilds, one of students and one of masters. At Bologna, the students participated in the appointment of masters and paid their salaries.

The University of Bologna was unusual because it was principally a school of law, where the students were often older men, well along in their careers and used to wielding power. The University of Paris, however, attracted younger students, drawn particularly by its renown in the liberal arts and theology. The Universities of Salerno and Montpellier specialized in medicine. Oxford, once a sleepy town where students clustered around one or two masters, became a center of royal administration, and its university soon developed a reputation for teaching the liberal arts, theology, science, and mathematics.

The curriculum at each university differed in content and duration. At the University of Paris in the early thirteenth century, for example, a student had to spend at least six years studying the liberal arts before he could begin to teach. If he wanted to continue his studies with theology, he had to attend lectures on the subject for at least another five years. Lectures were clearly the most important way in which material was conveyed to students. Books were very expensive and not readily available, so students committed their teachers' lectures to memory. The lectures were organized around important texts: the master read an excerpt aloud, delivered his commentary on it, and disputed any contrary commentaries that rival masters might have proposed.

Within the larger association of the university, students found more intimate groups with which to live. These groups, called *nations,* were linked to the students' place of origin. At Bologna, for example, students incorporated themselves into two nations, the Italians and the non-Italians. Each nation protected its members, wrote statutes, and elected officers.

With few exceptions, masters and students were considered clerics. This had two important consequences. First, there were no university women. And second, university men were subject to church courts rather than the secular jurisdiction of towns or lords. Many universities could also boast generous privileges from popes and kings, who valued the services of scholars. The combination of clerical status and special privileges made universities virtually self-governing corporations within the towns. This sometimes led to friction. For example, when a student at Oxford was suspected of killing his mistress and the townspeople tried to punish him, the masters protested by refusing to teach and leaving town. Incidents such as this explain why historians speak of the hostility between "town" and "gown." Yet university towns depended on scholars to patronize local restaurants, shops, and hostels. Town and gown normally learned to negotiate with one another to their mutual advantage.

Religious Fervor and Dissent

Around the same time as universities were forming, renewed religious fervor led to the formation of new religious movements that galvanized individual piety and involved great numbers of laywomen and -men. While the Cistercians and other reformed orders of the early twelfth century had fled the cities, the new religious groups of the late twelfth century embraced (and were embraced by) urban populations. Rich and poor, male and female joined these movements. They criticized the existing church as too wealthy, ritualistic, and impersonal. Intensely and personally focused on the life of Christ, men and women in the late twelfth century made his childhood, agony, death, and presence in the Eucharist—the bread and wine that became the body and blood of Christ in the Mass—the most important experiences of their own lives.

For women in particular, common involvement in new sorts of piety was unprecedented, even in the monasteries of the past. Now beckoning to women of every age and every walk of life, the new piety spread beyond the convent, punctuating the routines of daily life with scriptural reading, fasting, and charity. Some of this intense religious response developed into official, orthodox movements within the church; other religious movements so threatened established doctrine that church leaders declared them heretical.

Francis and the Franciscans.   St. Francis (c. 1182–1226) founded the most famous orthodox religious movement—the Franciscans. Francis was a child of the commercial revolution. Although expected to follow his well-to-do father in the cloth trade at Assisi in Italy, Francis began to experience doubts, dreams, and illnesses, which spurred him to religious self-examination. Eventually he renounced his family's wealth, dramatically marking the decision by casting off all his clothes and standing naked before his father, a crowd of spectators, and the bishop of Assisi. Francis then put on a simple robe and went about preaching penance to anyone who would listen. Clinging to poverty as if, in his words, "she" was his "lady" (and thus borrowing the vocabulary of chivalry), he accepted no money, walked without shoes, wore only one coarse tunic, and refused to be cloistered. Intending to follow the model of Christ, he received, as his biographers put it, a miraculous gift of grace: the stigmata, bleeding sores corresponding to the wounds Christ suffered on the cross.

By all accounts Francis was a spellbinding speaker, and he attracted many followers. Recognized as a religious order by the pope, the Brothers of St. Francis (or friars, from the Latin term for "little brothers") spent their time preaching, ministering to lepers, and doing manual labor. Eventually they dispersed, setting up fraternal groups throughout Italy and then in France, Spain, the Holy Land, Germany, and England. Unlike Bruno of Cologne and the Cistercians, who had rejected cities, the friars sought town life, sleeping in dormitories on the outskirts of cities and becoming part of urban community life, preaching to crowds and begging for their daily bread. St. Francis converted both men and women. In 1212 an eighteen-year-old noblewoman, Clare, formed the nucleus of a community of pious women, which became the Order of the Sisters of St. Francis. At first the women worked alongside the friars; but the church disapproved of their activities in the world, and soon Franciscan sisters were confined to cloisters under the rule of St. Benedict.

The Beguines. Clare was one of many women who sought a new kind of religious expression. Some women joined convents; others became recluses, living alone, like hermits; still others sought membership in new lay sisterhoods. In northern Europe at the end of the twelfth century, laywomen who lived together in informal pious communities were called Beguines. Without permanent vows or an established rule, the Beguines chose to be celibate (though they were free to leave and marry) and often made their living by weaving cloth or working with the sick and old. Although their daily occupations were ordinary, the Beguines' private, internal lives were often emotional and ecstatic, infused with the combined imagery of love and religion so pervasive in both monasteries and courts.

One renowned Beguine, Mary of Oignies (1177–1213), who like St. Francis was said to have received stigmata, felt herself to be a pious mother entrusted with the Christ child. As her biographer, Jacques de Vitry, wrote:

> Sometimes it seemed to her that for three or more days she held [Christ] close to her so that He nestled between her breasts like a baby, and she hid Him there lest He be seen by others.

Heresies. In addition to the orthodox religious movements that formed at the end of the twelfth century, there was a veritable explosion of ideas and doctrines that contradicted those officially accepted by church authorities and were therefore labeled heresies. Heresies were not new in the twelfth century. But the eleventh-century Gregorian reform had created for the first time in the West a clear church hierarchy headed by a pope who could enforce a single doctrine, discipline, and dogma. Such clearly defined orthodoxy meant that only now would people in western Europe perceive heresy as a serious problem. The growth of cities, commerce, and intellectual life fostered a new sense of community for many Europeans. But when intense religious feeling led to the fervent espousal of new religious ideas, established authorities often felt threatened and took steps to preserve their power.

Among the most visible heretics were *dualists*, who saw the world torn between two great forces, one good, the other evil. Already important in Bulgaria and Asia Minor, dualism became a prominent ingredient in religious life in Italy and the Rhineland by the end of the twelfth century. Another center of dualism was Languedoc, an area of southern France; there the dualists were called Albigensians, a name derived from the Languedoc town of Albi.

Described collectively as Cathars, or "Pure Ones," these groups believed that the devil had created the material world. Therefore they renounced the world, abjuring wealth, sex, and meat. Their repudiation of sex reflected some of the attitudes of eleventh-century church reformers (whose orthodoxy, however, was never in doubt), while their rejection of wealth echoed the same concerns that moved Bruno of Cologne to forswear city life and St. Francis to embrace poverty. In many ways the dualists simply took these attitudes to an extreme;

but unlike orthodox reformers, they also challenged the efficacy and value of the church hierarchy. Attracting both men and women and giving women access to the highest positions in their hierarchy, Cathars young and old, literate and unlettered, saw themselves as followers of Christ's original message. But the church called them heretics.

The church also condemned other, nondualist groups as heretical not on doctrinal grounds but because these groups allowed their lay members to preach, challenging the authority of the church hierarchy. In Lyon (in southeastern France) in the 1170s, for example, a rich merchant named Waldo decided to take literally the Gospel message "If you wish to be perfect, then go and sell everything you have, and give to the poor" (Matt. 19:21). The same message had inspired countless monks and would worry the church far less several decades later, when St. Francis established his new order. But when Waldo went into the street and gave away his belongings, announcing "I am not really insane, as you think," he scandalized not only the bystanders but the church as well. Refusing to retire to a monastery, Waldo and his followers, men and women called Waldensians, lived in poverty and went about preaching, quoting the Gospel in the vernacular so that everyone would understand. But the papacy rebuffed Waldo's bid to preach freely; and the Waldensians—denounced, excommunicated, and expelled from Lyon—wandered to Languedoc, Italy, northern Spain, and the Moselle valley, just across the French border into Germany.

❖ European Aggression Within and Without

New associations and allegiances gave European men and women a greater sense of identity, confidence, and assertiveness. Those perceived as different, however, became the focus of prejudice, intolerance, and aggression. The legacy of this period of aggression lasted long past the Middle Ages. It marked the beginning of systematic anti-Semitism and the weakening of Byzantium.

Classifying a particular group as a threat to society was a common method of asserting political and religious control within Europe in the second half of the twelfth century. Segregated from Chris-

tian society, vilified, and persecuted, those who were singled out, principally Jews and heretics, provided a rallying point for popes, princes, and Christian armies. Taking the offensive against those defined as different also meant launching campaigns to defeat people on Christendom's borders, a trend begun earlier with the First Crusade and the reconquista of Spain. In the early thirteenth century, wars against the Muslims to the south, the pagans to the north, and the Byzantine Empire to the east made crusading a permanent feature of medieval life. Even western Europe did not escape: the crusade waged against the Albigensians starting in 1208 in southern France replaced the ruling class and eclipsed the court culture of the troubadours there.

Jews as Strangers

The sentiment against Jews grew over time. Ever since the Roman Empire had become Christian, Jews had been seen as different from Christians, and imperial law had prohibited them, for example, from owning Christian slaves or marrying Christian women. Church laws had added to these restrictions, and in the twelfth century intellectuals elaborated objections against Jewish doctrine. Socially isolated and branded as outcasts, Jews served as scapegoats who helped define the larger society as orthodox. Like lepers, whose disease cut them off from ordinary communities, Jews were believed to threaten the health of those around them. Lepers had to wear a special costume, were forbidden to touch children, could not eat with those not afflicted, and were housed in hospices called leprosaria. Jews were similarly segregated from emerging Christian institutions, though they were not confined to hospices.

Forced off their lands during the eleventh century, most ended up in the cities as craftsmen, merchants, or moneylenders, providing capital for the developing commercial society, whose Christian members were prohibited from charging interest as usury forbidden by the Gospel. The growing monopoly of the guilds, which prohibited Jewish members, pushed Jews out of the crafts and trades: in effect, Jews were compelled to become "usurers" because other fields were closed to them. Even with Christian moneylenders available (for some existed despite the prohibitions), lords, especially kings, borrowed from Jews and encouraged others to do so because, along with their newly asserted powers, European rulers claimed the Jews as their serfs and Jewish property as their own. In England a special royal exchequer of the Jews created in 1194 collected unpaid debts due after the death of a Jewish creditor.

Even before 1194, Henry II had imposed new and arbitrary taxes on the Jewish community. Similarly in France, persecuting Jews and confiscating their property benefited both the treasury and the authoritative image of the king. For example, early in his reign Philip Augustus's agents surprised Jews at Sabbath worship in their synagogues and seized their goods, demanding that they redeem their own property for a large sum of money. Shortly thereafter, Philip declared forfeit 80 percent of all debts owed to Jews; the remaining 20 percent was to be paid directly to the king. About a year later, in 1182, Philip expelled the Jews from the Île-de-France:

> The king gave them leave to sell each his movable goods.... But their real estate, that is, houses, fields, vineyards, barns, winepresses, and such like, he reserved for himself and his successors, the kings of the French.

When he allowed the Jews to return, in 1198, he intended for them to be moneylenders or money changers exclusively, and their activities were to be taxed and monitored by officials.

Limiting Jews to moneylending in an increasingly commercial economy also served the interests of lords in debt to Jewish creditors. For example, in 1190, local nobles orchestrated a brutal attack on the Jews of York (in England) to rid themselves of their debts and of the Jews to whom they owed money. Churchmen too used credit in a money economy but resented the fiscal obligations it imposed. With their drive to create centralized territorial states and their desire to make their authority known and felt, powerful rulers of Europe—churchmen and laymen alike—exploited and coerced the Jews while drawing upon and encouraging a wellspring of elite and popular anti-Jewish feeling. Although Jews must have looked exactly like Christians in reality, Jews now became clearly identified in sculpture and in drawings by markers such as conical hats and, increasingly, by demeaning features.

Attacks against Jews were inspired by more than resentment against Jewish money and the desire for power and control. They also, ironically, grew out

The Jew as the Other
In medieval art, people were often portrayed not as individuals but rather as "types" who could be identified by physical markers. In the second half of the twelfth century, Jews were increasingly portrayed as looking different from Christians. In this illustration, clerics are shown borrowing money from a Jew. What physical features do all the clerics have in common? (Be sure to look at the clothes as well as the hairstyle.) What distinguishes the laymen from the clerics? How do you know who is meant to be the Jew? In fact, Jews did not regularly wear this type of pointed hat until they were forced to do so in some regions of Europe in the late thirteenth century.
Bayerische Staatsbibliothek.

of the codification of Christian religious doctrine and Christians' anxiety about their own institutions. For example, in the twelfth century, a newly rigorous definition of the Eucharist was promulgated. This held that when the bread and wine were blessed by the priest during Mass, they became the true body and blood of Christ. For some this meant, in effect, that Christ, wounded and bleeding, lay upon the altar. Miracle tales sometimes reported that the Eucharist bled. Reflecting Christian anxieties about real flesh upon the altar, sensational stories, originating in clerical circles but soon widely circulated, told of Jews who secretly sacrificed Christian children in a morbid revisiting of the crucifixion of Jesus. This charge, called "blood libel" by historians, led to massacres of Jews in cities in England, France, Spain, and Germany. Jews had no rituals involving blood sacrifice at all, but they were convenient and vulnerable scapegoats for Christian guilt and anxiety.

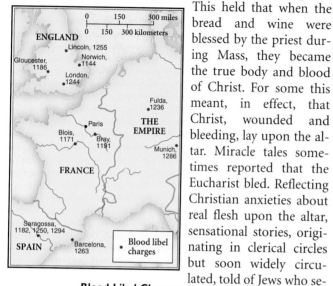

Blood Libel Charges in France and England, c. 1100–1300
Adapted from Angus Mackay with David Ditchburn, eds., *Atlas of Medieval Europe* (New York: Routledge, 1997).

Heretics as Threats

Attacks against Jews coincided with campaigns against heretics, whose beliefs spread in regions where political control was less centralized, as, for example, in southern France. By the end of the twelfth century, church and secular powers combined to stamp out heresies.

Papal missions to Languedoc to address the heretical Albigensians led to the establishment of the Dominican order. Its founder, St. Dominic (1170–1221), recognized that preachers of Christ's word who came on horseback, followed by a crowd of servants and wearing fine clothes, had no moral leverage with their audience. Dominic and his followers, like their adversaries the Albigensians, rejected material riches and instead went about on foot, preaching and begging. They resembled the Franciscans both organizationally and spiritually and were also called friars.

Sometimes the church resorted to armed force in its campaign against heretics. In 1208, the murder of a papal legate in southern France prompted Pope Innocent III (r. 1198–1216) to demand that northern princes take up the sword, invade Languedoc, wrest the land from the heretics, and populate it with orthodox Christians. This Albigensian Crusade (1209–1229) marked the first time the pope offered warriors fighting an enemy in Christian Europe all the spiritual and temporal benefits of a crusade to the Holy Land. Innocent suspended crusaders' monetary debts and promised that their sins would be forgiven after forty days' service. Like all crusades, the Albigensian Crusade had political as well as religious dimensions. It pitted southern French princes, with Cathar connections, like Raymond VI, count of Toulouse, against northern leaders like Simon IV de Montfort l'Amaury, a castellan from the Île-de-France eager to demonstrate piety and win new possessions. After twenty years of fighting, leadership of the crusade was taken over in 1229 by the Capetian kings of France. Southern resistance was broken, and Languedoc was brought under the French crown.

The Albigensian Crusade, 1209–1229

More Crusades to the Holy Land

The second half of the twelfth century saw new crusades outside western Europe (Map 11.2). Following the crushing defeat of the crusaders in the Second Crusade, the Muslim hero Nur al-Din united Syria under his command and presided over a renewal of Sunni Islam. His successor, Saladin (1138–1193), became well known to Europeans at the time of the Third Crusade.

Saladin and the Christian king of Jerusalem fought over Egypt, which Saladin ruled by 1186 together with Syria. Caught in a pincer, Jerusalem fell to Saladin's armies in 1187. The Third Crusade, called to retake Jerusalem, marked a military and political watershed for the crusader states. The European outpost of Outremer survived, but it was reduced to a narrow strip of land. Christians could continue to enter Jerusalem as pilgrims, but Islamic hegemony over the Holy Land would remain a fact of life for centuries.

The Third Crusade, 1189–1192. Called by the pope and led by the greatest rulers of Europe— Emperor Frederick I Barbarossa, Philip II of France, Leopold of Austria, and Richard I of England—the

MAP 11.2 Crusades and Anti-Heretic Campaigns, 1150–1204
Europeans aggressively expanded their territory during the second half of the twelfth century. To the north, German knights pushed into Pomerania; to the south, Spanish warriors moved into the remaining strip of Islamic Iberia; to the east, new crusades were undertaken to shore up the tiny European outpost in the Holy Land. Although most of these aggressive activities had the establishment of Christianity as at least one motive, the conquest of Constantinople in 1204 had no such justification. It grew in part out of general European hostility toward Byzantium but mainly out of Venice's commercial ambitions.

Third Crusade reflected political tensions among the European ruling class. Richard in particular seemed to cultivate enemies. The most serious of these was Leopold, whom he offended at the siege of Acre. But the apparent personal tensions indicated a broader hostility between the kings of England and France. Leopold, for example, was Philip's ally. On his return home, Richard was captured by Leopold and held for a huge ransom. He had good reason to write his plaintive poem bemoaning his captivity and the lost "love" of former friends.

The Third Crusade accomplished little and exacerbated tensions with Byzantium. Frederick I went overland on the crusade, passing through Hungary and Bulgaria and descending into the Byzantine Empire. Before his untimely death by drowning in Turkey, he spent most of his time harassing the Byzantines.

The Fourth Crusade, 1202–1204. The hostilities that surfaced during the Third Crusade made it a dress rehearsal for the Fourth Crusade, called by Pope Innocent III in 1202 as part of his more general plan to define, invigorate, and impose his brand of Christianity on both believers and nonbelievers. From the first, Innocent intended to direct a new crusade that would reverse the failures of the past. But attitudes and circumstances beyond the pope's control took over the Fourth Crusade. Prejudices, religious zeal, and self-confidence had become characteristic of western European attitudes toward the Byzantine Greeks.

Such attitudes help explain the course of events from 1202 to 1204. The crusading army turned out to be far smaller than had been expected. Its leaders could not pay the Venetians, who had fitted out a large fleet of ships in anticipation of carrying multitudes of warriors across the water to Jerusalem. The Venetians seized the opportunity to enhance Venice's commercial hegemony and convinced the crusade's leaders to pay for the fleet by attacking Zara, a Christian city but Venice's competitor in the Adriatic. The Venetians then turned their sights toward Constantinople, hoping to control it and gain a commercial monopoly there. They persuaded the crusaders to join them on behalf of a member of the ousted imperial family, Alexius, who claimed the Byzantine throne and promised the crusaders that he would reunite the eastern with the western church and fund the expedition to the Holy Land.

Most of the crusaders convinced themselves that the cause was noble. "Never," wrote a contemporary, "was so great an enterprise undertaken by any people since the creation of the world." The siege took nearly a year, but on April 12, 1204, Constantinople fell to the crusaders. The deal with Alexius had broken down, and the crusaders brutally sacked the city, killing, plundering, and ransacking it for treasure and relics. When one crusader discovered a cache of relics, a chronicler recalled, "he plunged both hands in and, girding up his loins, he filled the folds of his gown with the holy booty of the Church." The Byzantines, naturally enough, saw the same events as a great tragedy. The bishop of Ephesus wrote:

> And so the streets, squares, houses of two and three stores, sacred places, nunneries, houses for nuns and monks, sacred churches, even the Great Church of God and the imperial palace, were filled with men of the enemy, all of them maddened by war and murderous in spirit. . . . [T]hey tore children from their mothers and mothers from their children, and they defiled the virgins in the holy chapels, fearing neither God's anger nor man's vengeance.

Pope Innocent decried the sacking of Constantinople, but he also took advantage of it, ordering the crusaders to stay there for a year to consolidate their gains. The crusade leaders chose one of themselves—Baldwin of Flanders—to be Byzantine emperor, and he, the other princes, and the Venetians parceled out the empire among themselves. This new Latin empire of Constantinople lasted until 1261, when the Byzantines recaptured the city and some of its outlying territory. No longer a strong heir to the Roman Empire, Byzantium in 1204 became overshadowed and hemmed in by the stronger military might of both the Muslims and the Europeans.

Popes continued to call crusades to the Holy Land until the mid-fifteenth century, but the Fourth Crusade marked the last such major mobilization of men and leaders. Working against these expeditions were the new values of the late twelfth century, which placed a premium on the *interior* pilgrimage of the soul and valued rulers who stayed home to care for their people. The crusades served as an outlet for religious fervor, self-confidence, ambition, prejudice, and aggression and were a dress rehearsal

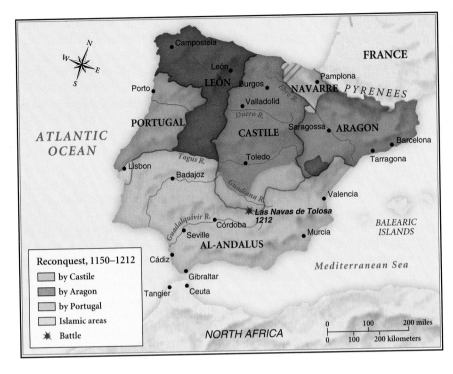

MAP 11.3 The Reconquista, 1150–1212

Slowly but surely the Christian kingdoms of Spain encroached on al-Andalus, taking Las Navas de Tolosa, deep in Islamic territory, in 1212. At the center of this activity was Castile. It had originally been a tributary of León, but in the course of the twelfth century it became a power in its own right. (In 1230, León and Castile merged into one kingdom.) Meanwhile, the ruler of Portugal, who had also been dependent on León, began to claim the title of king, which was recognized officially in 1179, when he put Portugal under the protection of the papacy.

for the next wave of European colonization, which began in the sixteenth century. But they had in themselves very little lasting positive effect. They marginally stimulated the European economy, taught Europeans about the importance of stone fortifications, and inspired a vast literature of songs and chronicles. Such achievements must be weighed against the lives lost (on both sides) and the religious polarization and prejudices that the crusades fed upon and fortified. The bitterest fruit of the crusades was the destruction of Byzantium. The Latin conquest of Constantinople in 1204 irrevocably weakened the one buffer state that stood between Europe and Islam.

Crusades at the Borders of Europe

Armed expeditions against those perceived as infidels were launched not only against the Holy Land but also much nearer to home. In the second half of the twelfth century, the Spanish reconquista continued with increasing success and virulence while new wars of conquest were waged at the northern edge of Europe.

The Reconquista Triumphs, 1212. In the second half of the twelfth century, Christian Spain achieved

the political configuration that would last for centuries, dominated to the east by the kingdom of Aragon; in the middle by Castile, whose ruler styled himself emperor; and in the southwest by Portugal, whose ruler similarly transformed his title from prince to king. The three leaders competed for territory and power, but above all they sought an advantage against the Muslims to the south (Map 11.3).

Muslim disunity aided the Christian conquest of Spain. The Muslims of al-Andalus were themselves beset from the south by a new group of Muslims from North Africa, the Almohades. Claiming religious purity, the Almohades declared their own holy war against the Andalusians. These simultaneous threats caused alliances in Spain to be based on political as well as religious considerations. The Muslim ruler of Valencia, for example, declared himself a vassal of the king of Castile and bitterly opposed the Almohades' expansion.

But the crusading ideal held no room for such subtleties. During the 1140s, armies under the command of the kings of Portugal, Castile, and Aragon scored resounding victories against Muslim cities. Enlisting the aid of crusaders on their way to the Holy Land in 1147, the king of Portugal promised land, plunder, and protection to all who would help him attack Lisbon. His efforts succeeded, and

Lisbon's Muslim inhabitants fled or were slain, its Mozarabic bishop (the bishop of the Christians under Muslim rule) was killed, and a crusader from England was set up as bishop. In the 1170s, when the Almohades conquered the Muslim south and advanced toward the cities taken by the Christians, their exertions had no lasting effect. In 1212, a Christian crusading army of Spaniards led by the kings of Aragon and Castile defeated the Almohades decisively at Las Navas de Tolosa. "On their side 100,000 armed men or more fell in the battle," the king of Castile wrote afterward, "but of the army of the Lord . . . incredible though it may be, unless it be a miracle, hardly 25 or 30 Christians of our whole army fell. O what happiness! O what thanksgiving!" The decisive turning point in the reconquista was reached.

The Northern Crusades. Christians flexed their military muscle along Europe's northern frontiers as well. By the twelfth century, the peoples living along the Baltic coast—partly pagan, mostly Slavic- or Baltic-speaking—had learned to glean a living and a profit from the inhospitable soil and climate. Through fishing and trading, they supplied the rest of Europe and Russia with slaves, furs, amber, wax, and dried fish. Like the earlier Vikings, they com-

bined commercial competition with outright raiding, so that the Danes and the Saxons (that is, the Germans in Saxony) both benefited and suffered from their presence. When St. Bernard began to preach the Second Crusade in Germany, he discovered that the Germans were indeed eager to attack the infidels—the ones right next door, that is. St. Bernard pressed the pope to add these northern heathens to the list of those against whom holy war should be launched and urged their conversion or extermination. Thus began the Northern Crusades, which continued intermittently until the early fifteenth century.

The Danish king Valdemar I (r. 1157–1182) and the Saxon duke Henry the Lion led the first phase of the Northern Crusades. Their initial attacks on the Slavs were uncoordinated—in some instances they even fought each other. But in key raids in the 1160s and 1170s, the two leaders worked together briefly to bring much of the region west of the Oder River under their control. They took some land outright—Henry the Lion apportioned conquered territory to his followers, for example—but more often the Slavic princes surrendered and had their territories reinstated once they became vassals of the Christian rulers. Meanwhile, churchmen arrived: the Cistercians came long before the first phase of

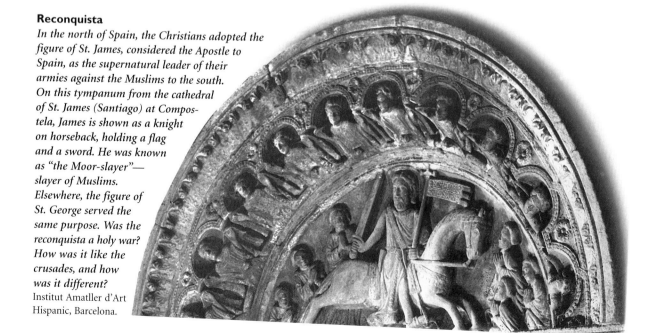

Reconquista

In the north of Spain, the Christians adopted the figure of St. James, considered the Apostle to Spain, as the supernatural leader of their armies against the Muslims to the south. On this tympanum from the cathedral of St. James (Santiago) at Compostela, James is shown as a knight on horseback, holding a flag and a sword. He was known as "the Moor-slayer"—slayer of Muslims. Elsewhere, the figure of St. George served the same purpose. Was the reconquista a holy war? How was it like the crusades, and how was it different?
Institut Amatller d'Art Hispanic, Barcelona.

fighting had ended, confidently building their monasteries to the very banks of the Oder River. Slavic peasants surely suffered from the conquerors' fire and pillage, but the Slavic ruling classes ultimately benefited from the crusades. Once converted to Christianity, they found it advantageous for both their eternal salvation and their worldly profit to join new crusades to areas still farther east.

Although less well known than the crusades to the Holy Land, the Northern Crusades had far more lasting effects: they settled the Baltic region with German-speaking lords and peasants and forged a permanent relationship between the very north of Europe and its neighbors to the south and west. With the Baltic dotted with churches and monasteries and its peoples dipped into baptismal waters, the region would gradually adopt the institutions of western medieval society—cities, guilds, universities, castles, and manors. The Livs (whose region was eventually known as Livonia) were conquered by 1208, and their bishop sent knights northward to conquer the Estonians. The Prussians would be conquered with the cooperation between the Polish and German aristocracy; German peasants eventually settled Prussia. Only the Lithuanians managed to successfully resist western conquest, settlement, and conversion.

IMPORTANT DATES	
1135–1154	Reign of King Stephen and civil war in England
1152–1190	Reign of Emperor Frederick Barbarossa
1154–1189	Reign of Henry II of England
1176	Battle of Legnano; Frederick Barbarossa defeated in northern Italy
1180–1223	Philip II Augustus rules as king of France
1182–1226	Life of St. Francis
1189–1192	Third Crusade
1198–1216	Papacy of Innocent III
c. 1200	Incorporation of University of Paris
1202–1204	Fourth Crusade
1204	Sack of Constantinople
1215	Magna Carta

Conclusion

The second half of the twelfth century saw the consolidation of Europe's new political configuration, reaching the limits of a continental expansion that stretched from the Baltic to the Straits of Gibraltar. European settlements in the Holy Land, by contrast, were nearly obliterated. When western Europeans sacked Constantinople in 1204, Europe and the Islamic world became the dominant political forces in the West.

Powerful territorial kings and princes expressed their new self-confidence by supporting a lay vernacular culture that celebrated their achievements and power. They also began to establish institutions of bureaucratic authority. They hired staffs to handle their accounts, record acts, collect taxes, issue writs, and preside over courts. Flourishing cities, a growing money economy, and trade and manufacturing provided the finances necessary to support the personnel offices now used by medieval governments. Clerical schools and, by the end of the twelfth century, universities became the training grounds for the new administrators.

Rulers were not alone in their quest to document, define, and institutionalize their power. The second half of the twelfth and the early thirteenth

Valdemar's Penny
Valdemar I, king of Denmark, had his image in profile cast on this penny. How can you tell immediately that this is the portrait of a king? On the reverse (bottom) he indicates that he wants to be associated with the Northern Crusades by depicting a flag with a cross. How does this coin compare with a royal seal? See page 397.
National Museum, Copenhagen, The Royal Collection of Coins and Medals.

MAPPING THE WEST Europe and Byzantium, c. 1215

The major transformation in the map of the West between 1150 and 1215 was the conquest of Constantinople and the setting up of European rule there until 1261. The Byzantine Empire was now a mere shell. A new state, Epirus, emerged in the power vacuum to dominate Thrace. Bulgaria once again gained its independence. If Venice had hoped to control the Adriatic by conquering Constantinople, it must have been disappointed, for Hungary became its rival over the ports of the Dalmatian coast.

centuries were a great age of organization. Associations, which had earlier been fluid, now solidified into well-defined corporations—craft guilds and universities, for example—with statutes providing clearly specified rights, obligations, and privileges to their members. Developing out of the commercial revolution, such organizations in turn made commercial activities a permanent part of medieval life.

Religious associations also formed. The Franciscans, Dominicans, Waldensians, and Cathars—however dissimilar their beliefs—all articulated specific creeds and claimed distinctiveness. In rejecting wealth and material possessions, they revealed how deeply the commercial revolution had affected the

moral life of some Europeans, who could not accept the profit motive inherent in a money economy. In emphasizing preaching, these religious associations showed that a lay population, already Christian, now yearned for a more intense and personal spirituality.

New piety, new exclusivity, and new power arose in a society both more confident and less tolerant. Crusaders fought more often and against an increasing variety of foes, not only in the Holy Land but in Spain, in southern France, and on Europe's northern frontiers. With heretics voicing criticisms and maintaining their beliefs, the church, led by the papacy, now defined orthodoxy and declared dissenters its enemies. The Jews, who had once been fairly well integrated into the Christian community, were treated ambivalently, alternately used and abused. The Slavs and Balts became targets for new evangelical zeal; the Greeks became the butt of envy, hostility, and finally enmity. European Christians still considered Muslims arrogant heathens, and the deflection of the Fourth Crusade did not stem the zeal of popes to call for new crusades to the Holy Land.

Confident and aggressive, the leaders of Christian Europe in the thirteenth century would attempt to impose their rule, legislate morality, and create a unified worldview impregnable to attack. But this drive for order would be countered by unexpected varieties of thought and action, by political and social tensions, and by intensely personal religious quests.

Suggested References

Governments as Institutions

The medieval origins of modern state institutions is a traditional interest of historians studying the medieval period. Clanchy's important book concentrates on England but provides insight into the process of bureaucratization in general. Hudson explores the growth of royal institutions of justice. Baldwin gives a carefully focused account of the French experience.

Baldwin, John W. *The Government of Philip Augustus: Foundations of French Royal Power in the Middle Ages.* 1986.

Clanchy, Michael T. *From Memory to Written Record, 1066–1307.* 2nd ed. 1993.

Fuhrmann, Horst. *Germany in the High Middle Ages, c. 1050–1200.* Trans. T. Reuter. 1986.

Hudson, John. *The Formation of the English Common Law: Law and Society in England from the Norman Conquest to Magna Carta.* 1996.

Jordan, Karl. *Henry the Lion: A Biography.* Trans. P. S. Falla. 1986.

*Otto of Freising. *The Deeds of Frederick Barbarossa.* Trans. C. C. Mierow. 1953.

The Growth of a Vernacular High Culture

Chrétien de Troyes's *Yvain* is a good example of a twelfth-century romance, while troubadour poetry is collected in Goldin's anthology. New and important research on women's power in the period is presented in Evergates's book.

Bouchard, Constance B. *"Strong of Body, Brave and Noble": Chivalry and Society in Medieval France.* 1998.

*Chrétien de Troyes. *Yvain: The Knight of the Lion.* Trans. Burton Raffel. 1987.

Crouch, David. *William Marshal: Court, Career, and Chivalry in the Angevin Empire, 1147–1219.* 1990.

Evergates, Theodore, ed. *Aristocratic Women in Medieval France.* 1999.

Gold, Penny S. *The Lady and the Virgin: Image, Attitude, and Experience in Twelfth-Century France.* 1985.

*Goldin, Frederick. *Lyrics of the Troubadors and Trouvères: Original Texts, with Translations.* 1973.

*The Song of Roland. Trans. P. Terry. 1965.

New Lay and Religious Associations

The Little Flowers of Saint Francis gives a good idea of Franciscan spirituality, while the Franciscans are explored as part of wider religious, social, and economic movements in Little's study. Reynolds gives a broad overview of associations of every sort, from the community of the parish to representative institutions.

Epstein, Steven. *Wage Labor and Guilds in Medieval Europe.* 1991.

Ferruolo, Stephen C. *The Origins of the University: The Schools of Paris and Their Critics, 1100–1215.* 1985.

*The Little Flowers of Saint Francis. Trans. L. Sherley-Price. 1959.

Little, Lester K. *Religious Poverty and the Profit Economy in Medieval Europe.* 1978.

Reynolds, Susan. *Kingdoms and Communities in Western Europe, 900–1300.* 1984.

European Aggression Within and Without

Bartlett looks at expansion on all the frontiers of Europe, connecting movement outward with the creation of internal identity. Christiansen's book is the essential source for the Northern Crusades, Wakefield's for the Albigensian Crusade. There are numerous books on the crusades to the east; Riley-Smith gives a good overview.

Bartlett, Robert. *The Making of Europe: Conquest, Colonization, and Cultural Change, 950–1350.* 1993.

Blood libel: http://www.fordham.edu/halsall/source/1173williamnorwich.html.

Christiansen, Eric. *The Northern Crusades.* 2nd ed. 1998.

Crusade bibliography: http://orb.rhodes.edu/encyclop/religion/crusades/crux-bib.html.

Queller, Donald E., and Thomas F. Madden. *The Fourth Crusade: The Conquest of Constantinople, 1201–1204.* 2nd ed. 1999.

Riley-Smith, Jonathan. *The Crusades: A Short History.* 1987.

Wakefield, Walter L. *Heresy, Crusade, and Inquisition in Southern France, 1100–1250.* 1974.

*Primary sources.

tudines. qñ similia accidunt fantasmata eis q̄ i aq̄ s̄ vꝛ
sicut z pꝛi9 dictũ9. Ibi vo si mī q̄s fuit mot9: tñ sili
sit apparitio z ycolar̄ ei9. Simpꝛ eum sigicanata̅l
iudicare eiit9q̄ pot ato senate z inspice ѡisa z ѡistoꝛ
ta ycoloꝛ q̄ntum est huϯ hõt l̄ eq̄u aut aut ai q̄
Et sibi q̄ndã simuł potest sompniũ h̄. odoꝛ eni i
pedit sompniũ rectũ Q̄d q̄ndã sompn̄ z sꝑ somp
niũ z sꝑ qñ cãm utriuml̄ hoꝛs sit. Amp. aũ z de ea q̄
ex sompnis diuina rõne cãm sit.

e eo autem qd est ee alia
q̄ndã longe uite. alia ѡo
breuis. z de uite tota longi
tudie z breuitate ꝯsidand̄
Pꝛincipiũ autem inten
cõnis nrãm est pꝛiũ expo
nere de ipsis. Non autem ma
nifm̄ est utrum una z ea
dem cã sit oĩbus aĩalibz z plantis. H q̄ndã ee longe
uite alia ѡo breuis. Et plantaꝛ q̄ndã alie breuem
alie mͽto tempꝛ hn̄t uitã Amp. utrum eab sunt
q̄ sunt longe uite z q̄ sm̄ naturã sunt sana. loꝛ
que sm̄ naturã subsistunt sana. aut diuisa sunt
q̄ sunt breui uite aut egrotancia. aut q̄ sunt sm̄
quasõ egritudines imutant egrotancia natam
coꝛpa breui uita. Sedm̄ quasõ autem nich phībꝛ
z egrotancia ee longe uite. D e sompno auϯ z de
uigilia tñ est pꝛi9. sz z de egritudie l̄ sanitate in q̄m
tum ѡfeꝛt phice. Sunt auϯ ẽ causal̄ h q̄ndã ee lon
ge uite illa ѡo breuis sicut dm̄ est pꝛi9 spectand̄ e.
unt aũ z hanc hentia dr̄am totaq̄ ad tota gr̄a z
q̄ sunt sb una sꝑ alia ad alta. Dico aũ sm̄ gen

The Elusive Search for Harmony

1215–1320

I N THE SECOND HALF of the thirteenth century, a Parisian workshop that specialized in manuscript illuminations got an unusual request from a wealthy patron: illustrate the opening of Aristotle's *On the Length and Shortness of Life*. Most Parisian illuminators knew very well how to illustrate the Bible, liturgical books, and patristic writings. But Aristotle had been an ancient Greek. He had lived before the time of Christ, and he was skeptical about the possibility of an afterlife. His treatise on the "length of life" ended with death. The workshop's artists could not accept that fact. They proceeded to illustrate Aristotle's work as if he had been a Christian and had believed in the immortal soul. In the first initial of the book (the large, highly decorated letter that opened the text), the artists enclosed a depiction of the Christian Mass for the dead, a rite that is performed for the eternal salvation of Christians. In this way, the artists subtly but surely forced Aristotle's treatise into the prevailing system of Christian belief and practice.

In the period 1215 to 1320, people at all levels, from workshop artisans to kings and popes, expected to find harmony, order, and unity in a world they believed was created by God. Sometimes, as in the case of the illumination made for Aristotle's work or in the Gothic cathedrals built in the cities, such harmony was made manifest. But often its achievement was elusive. For example, kings and popes disputed about the limits of their power, while theologians fought over the place of reason in matters of faith. Discord continually threatened expectations of harmony and unity.

Christianizing Aristotle
This illumination was created for a thirteenth-century translation of Aristotle. Artists placed a depiction of the Christian Mass for the dead, harmonizing the ancient teachings of Aristotle with Christian practice.
Biblioteca Apostolica Vaticana.

421

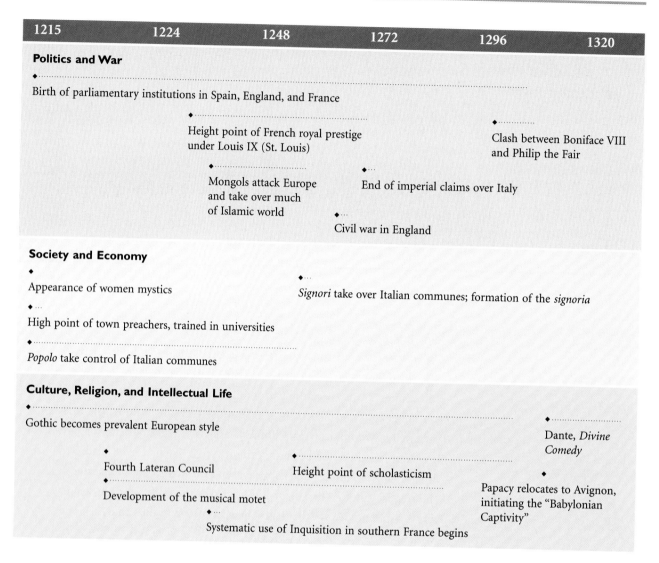

1215	1224	1248	1272	1296	1320

Politics and War

Birth of parliamentary institutions in Spain, England, and France

Height point of French royal prestige under Louis IX (St. Louis)

Clash between Boniface VIII and Philip the Fair

Mongols attack Europe and take over much of Islamic world

End of imperial claims over Italy

Civil war in England

Society and Economy

Appearance of women mystics

Signori take over Italian communes; formation of the *signoria*

High point of town preachers, trained in universities

Popolo take control of Italian communes

Culture, Religion, and Intellectual Life

Gothic becomes prevalent European style

Dante, *Divine Comedy*

Fourth Lateran Council

Height point of scholasticism

Papacy relocates to Avignon, initiating the "Babylonian Captivity"

Development of the musical motet

Systematic use of Inquisition in southern France begins

Expectations of harmony also undergirded new institutions of power and control. The church created tribunals of inquisition to root out religious dissidents, and kings and other rulers extended their influence over their subjects. Yet these tribunals did not end heresy, and kings did not gain all the power that they wanted. Diversity and opposition continually threatened attempts at control from above.

❖ The Church's Mission

Ever since the Gregorian reform of the eleventh century, the papacy had considered its mission to include reforming the secular world. In the Gregorian period, this task had focused on the king, because,

in the view of the popes of the period, a godless king threatened the redemption of all his subjects. In the thirteenth century, however, the popes focused on the reform of clergy and laity alike. They wanted to purify all of society through church councils such as the Fourth Lateran Council, which sought to regulate Christian life. They looked to strengthened institutions of justice to combat heresy and heretics; and they supported preachers who would bring the official views of the church to the streets. In this way, the church attempted to reorder the world in the image of heaven. It meant for all of society to follow one rule of God in order and harmony. To some degree, it was successful in this endeavor; but it also came up against the limits of control, as dissident voices and forces clashed with its vision.

Innocent III and the Fourth Lateran Council of 1215

Innocent III (r. 1198–1216) was the most powerful, respected, and prestigious of medieval popes. He was the pope who allowed St. Francis's group of impoverished followers to become a new church order, and he was the pope who called the Fourth Crusade, the last to mobilize a large force drawn from every level of European society. Innocent was the first pope trained at the city schools; during his youth he studied theology at Paris and law at Bologna. From theology, he learned to tease new meaning out of the pope's position: he thought of himself as ruling in the place of Christ the King. In his view, secular kings and emperors existed to help the pope. From law, Innocent gained his conception of the pope as lawmaker and of law as an instrument of moral reformation.

Innocent utilized the traditional method of declaring church law: through a council, which he convened in 1215 at the pope's Lateran Palace in Rome.

Innocent III
Pope Innocent III appears young, aristocratic, and impassive in this thirteenth-century fresco in the lower church of Sacro Speco, Subiaco, about thirty miles east of Rome and not far from Innocent's birthplace. Innocent claimed full power over the whole church, in any region. Moreover, he thought the pope had the right to intervene in any issue where sin might be involved—and that meant most matters. While these were only theoretical claims, difficult to put into practice given his meager resources and inefficient staff, Innocent was a major force through his sometimes deadly dealings with secular leaders, through his calling of the Fourth Crusade, and above all through the Fourth Lateran Council, which set the standard for the behavior of all Christians.
Scala/Art Resource, NY.

Presided over by Innocent, the Fourth Lateran Council labored to regulate all aspects of Christian life. The comprehensive legislation it produced in only three days (mainly because the pope and his committees had prepared it beforehand) included canons, or provisions, aimed at reforming not only the clergy but also the laity. Innocent and the other assembled churchmen hoped in this way to create a society united under the authority of the church and appreciative of the priesthood. They expected that Christians, lay and clerical alike, would work together harmoniously to achieve the common goal of salvation. They did not anticipate both the sheer variety of responses to their message and the persistence of those who defied it altogether.

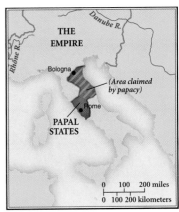

The World of Pope Innocent III, r. 1198–1216

The Laity and the Sacraments. For laymen and laywomen, perhaps the most important canons of the Fourth Lateran Council concerned the sacraments, the rites the church fathers believed Jesus had instituted to confer sanctifying grace. One canon required Christians to attend Mass and to confess their sins to a priest at least once a year. Others codified the traditions of marriage, in which the church had involved itself more and more since the twelfth century. The council declared marriage a sacrament and claimed jurisdiction over marital disputes. In addition, it decreed that marriage banns (announcements) had to be made publicly by local priests to ensure that people from the community could voice any objections to a marriage. (For example, the intended spouses might be more closely related than the church allowed.) Priests now became responsible for ferreting out this information and identifying any other impediments to the union. The canons further insisted that children conceived within clandestine or forbidden marriages were illegitimate; they could not inherit from their parents or become priests.

Nevertheless, there is good reason to think that the impact of these provisions was less dramatic

Host Mold

One of the most important decisions of the Fourth Lateran Council was to declare that the body and blood of Christ were "transubstantiated" in the Eucharist: that is, they were transformed into the actual body and blood of Christ. Veneration of the host began to supplant veneration of saints, and increasingly people desired to see the host, to gaze at it. Albert the Great wrote: "Showing the host to good people impels them to the good." Molds such as the one shown here, made in the fourteenth century, impressed inspiring images into the bread, in this case the image of Christ surrounded by the twelve apostles.

than the church leaders hoped. Well-to-do London fathers included their bastard children in their wills. On English manors, sons conceived out of wedlock regularly took over their parents' land. The requirement to read out the marriage banns publicly was meant to prevent secret marriages; nevertheless such marriages continued to take place. Even churchmen had to admit that the consent of both parties made a marriage valid.

The Meaning of the Eucharist.   A very important canon of the Fourth Lateran Council concerned the transformation of bread and wine (the Eucharist) in the Mass. In the twelfth century a newly rigorous understanding of this transformation had already been promulgated, according to which Christ's body and blood were truly contained in the sacrament that looked like bread and wine on the altar. The Fourth Lateran Council not only declared this to be dogma (authoritative) but also explained it by using a technical term coined by twelfth-century scholars. The bread and wine were *transubstantiated*: though the Eucharist continued to *look* like bread and wine, after the consecration during the Mass the bread became the actual flesh and the wine the real blood of Christ. The council's emphasis on this potent event strengthened the role of the priest, for only he could celebrate this mystery (that is,

transform the bread and wine into Christ's body and blood), through which God's grace was transmitted to the faithful.

The Labeling of the Jews.   Innocent III had wanted the council to condemn Christian men who had intercourse with Jewish women and then claimed "ignorance" as their excuse. But the council went even further, requiring all Jews to advertise their religion by some outward sign: "We decree that [Jews] of either sex in every Christian province at all times shall be distinguished from other people by the character of their dress in public."

As with all church rules, these took effect only when local rulers enforced them. In many instances, they did so with zeal, not so much because they were eager to humiliate Jews but rather they could make money selling exemptions to Jews who were willing to pay to avoid the requirements. Nonetheless, sooner or later Jews almost everywhere had to wear a badge as a sign of their second-class status.

In southern France and in a few places in Spain, Jews were supposed to wear round badges. In England, Oxford required a badge, while Salisbury demanded that Jews wear special clothing. In Vienna they were told to put on pointed hats.

The Suppression of Heretics.   The Fourth Lateran Council's longest decree blasted heretics: "Those condemned as heretics shall be handed over to the secular authorities for punishment." If the secular authority did not "purge his or her land of heretical filth," the heretic was to be excommunicated, his vassals released from their oaths of fealty, and his land taken over by orthodox Christians.

Rulers heeded these warnings. Already some had taken up arms against heretics in the Albigensian Crusade (1209–1229). After the crusade, southern France, which had been the home of most Albigensians, came under French royal control. The continuing presence of heretics there and elsewhere led church authorities inspired by the Fourth Lateran Council to set up the Inquisition.

The Inquisition

An *inquisition* was simply an inquiry, a method long used by secular rulers to summon people together, either to discover facts or to uncover and punish crimes. In its zeal to end heresy and save souls, the thirteenth-century church used the Inquisition to ferret out "heretical depravity." Calling suspects to testify, inquisitors, aided by secular authorities, rounded up virtually entire villages and interrogated everyone. (See "New Sources, New Perspectives," page 426.)

First the inquisitors typically called the people of a district to a "preaching," where they gave a sermon and promised clemency to those who confessed their heresy promptly. Then, at a general inquest, they questioned each man and woman who seemed to know something about heresy: "Have you ever seen any heretics or Waldenses [followers of Peter Waldo]? Have you heard them preach? Attended any of their ceremonies? Adored heretics?" The judges assigned relatively lenient penalties to those who were not aware that they held heretical beliefs and to heretics who quickly recanted. But unrepentant heretics were burned at the stake, because the church believed that such people threatened the salvation of all. Their ashes were sometimes tossed into the water so they could not serve as diabolical relics. Anyone who died while still a heretic could not be buried in consecrated ground. Raymond VII, the count of Toulouse, saw the body of his father—who died excommunicate—rot in its coffin as the pope denied all requests for its burial. Houses where heretics had resided or even simply entered were burned, and the sites were turned into garbage dumps. Children of heretics could not inherit any property or become priests, even if they adopted orthodox views.

In the thirteenth century, for the first time, long-term imprisonment became a tool to repress heresy, even if the heretic confessed. "It is our will," wrote one tribunal, "that [Raymond Maurin and Arnalda, his wife,] because they have rashly transgressed against God and holy church . . . be thrust into perpetual prison to do [appropriate] penance, and we command them to remain there in perpetuity." The inquisitors also used imprisonment to force people to recant, to give the names of other heretics, or to admit a plot. Guillaume Agasse, for example, confessed to participating in a wicked (and imagined) meeting of lepers who planned to poison all the wells. As the quest for religious control spawned wild fantasies of conspiracy, the inquisitors pinned their paranoia on real people.

The Inquisition also created a new group—penitent heretics—who lived on as marginal people. Forced, like Jews, to wear badges as a mark of dis-grace, penitent heretics were stigmatized by huge yellow fabric crosses sewn on the front and back of their shirts. So that the crosses would be visible, penitents were forbidden to wear yellow clothing. Moreover, every Sunday and every feast day penitent heretics had to attend church twice; and during religious processions these men and women were required to join with the clergy and the faithful, carrying large branches in their hands as a sign of their penance. (See "Taking Measure," below.)

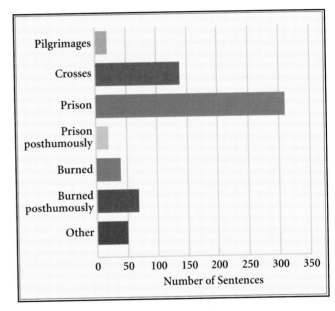

TAKING MEASURE Sentences Imposed by an Inquisitor, 1308–1323

How harsh was the Inquisition? Did its agents regularly burn people alive? How frequently did they imprison people or order them to wear crosses on their clothing? Statistical data to answer these sorts of questions are normally lacking for the medieval period. But there are exceptions. One comes from a register of offenses and punishments kept by the Languedocian inquisitor Bernard Gui from 1308 to 1323. Of 633 punishments handed down by Gui's tribunal, only a relatively small number of people were burned alive. (Those "burned posthumously" would have been burned alive, but they died before that could happen.) Nearly half of the guilty were sentenced to prison, usually for life. (Some were sent to prison posthumously; that is, they would have gone to prison had they not died in the meantime.) Many historians conclude that the Inquisition was not particularly harsh, for capital punishment at the time was regularly meted out to criminals under secular law.

From J. Given, "A Medieval Inquisitor at Work," in S.K. Cohn and S.A. Epstein, *Portraits of Medieval and Renaissance Living* (Ann Arbor: University of Michigan Press, 1996), 215.

The Peasants of Montaillou

While historians have fairly easily discovered how medieval peasants lived and worked, it is nearly impossible to find out what they thought. Almost all of our sources come from the elite classes who, if they noticed peasants at all, certainly did not care about their ideas. How, then, can historians hear and record the voices of peasants themselves? Until the 1960s, historians did not much care to hear those voices. They wanted to know about economic structures rather than peasant mentalities.

That is why historians did not notice an extremely important source of peasant voices, the Inquisition register made at the command of Bishop Fournier of Pamiers in the years 1318–1325. Fournier was a zealous anti-heretic, and when he became bishop of a diocese that harbored many Albigensians, he put the full weight of his office behind rounding them up. He concentrated on one particularly "heretic-infested" village, Montaillou, in the south of France near the Spanish border. Interrogating a total of 114 people, including 48 women, over seven years, he committed their confessions and testimony to parchment with a view to imprisoning and burning those who were heretics. Fournier was not interested in the peasants' "voices": he wanted to know their religious beliefs and every other detail of their lives and thoughts. However, the long-term result of Fournier's zealous inquest—though he would not be happy to hear it—was to preserve the words of a whole village of peasants, shepherds, artisans, and shopkeepers.

Fournier's register sat in the Vatican archives for centuries, gathering dust, until it was tran-

Peasant Life in the Fourteenth Century
This page from a German manuscript dated around 1330 shows the wide variety of tasks in which peasants engaged. Note the overlord on horseback with a whip in the lower right corner.
Universitatsbibliothek Heidelberg.

scribed and published in 1965. Only in 1975 was its great potential for peasant history made clear when Emmanuel Le Roy Ladurie published *Montaillou: The Promised Land of Error*, which for the first time made a medieval peasant village come to life.

Le Roy Ladurie's book reveals the myths, beliefs, rivalries, tensions, love affairs, tendernesses, and duplicities of a small peasant community where all the people, even those who were better off, worked with their hands; where wealth was calculated by the size of a family's herd of livestock;

Religious Institutions and Town Life

Dominican and Franciscan friars actively participated in the church's mission to regulate and Christianize lay behavior. The Dominicans were es-

pecially involved in the Inquisition. Both orders insisted on travel, preaching, and poverty, vocations that pulled the friars into cities and towns, where laypeople eagerly listened to their words and supported them with food and shelter.

and where the church's demands for tithes seemed outrageously unfair. For example, one weaver complained that "the priests and the clerks . . . extort and receive from the people the first-fruits and the tithes of products for which they have not done the smallest stroke of work."

The register shows a community torn apart by the opportunities the Inquisition gave to informers. The village priest, who belonged to a well-off family, was very clear about why he was denouncing his parishioners. He liked the Albigensians, he said (he was probably one himself), but "I want to be revenged on the peasants of Montaillou, who have done me harm, and I will avenge myself in every possible way." But the register also shows a community united by blood ties (the villagers married among themselves) and love. Love for children is a striking feature of this community, especially since some historians claim that such sentiments were lacking until the modern period. Love between husbands and wives figures as well. One villager reported that "more than 12 years ago, during the summer, I was madly in love with Raymonde, who is now my wife." And there was illicit love, too. One passionate affair took place between the village priest and Béatrice, a woman of somewhat higher rank. The priest courted her for half a year, and after she gave in, they met two or three nights a week. In the end, though, Béatrice decided to marry someone else and left the village.

Béatrice was not the only independent-minded person in Montaillou. Many people there were indeed heretics in the sense that their beliefs defied the teachings of the church. But they called themselves "good Christians." Other villagers remained in the Catholic fold. And still others had their own ideas. One peasant, for example, didn't believe in God at all. Another argued: "When a man dies, the soul dies too. It is just the same as with animals. The soul is only blood."

Fournier's register became a "new" source because Le Roy Ladurie had new questions and sought a way to answer them, treating his evidence the way ethnographers treat reports by native peoples they have interviewed. Today some historians question Le Roy Ladurie's approach, arguing that an Inquisition record cannot be handled the way ethnographers consider information from their informants. For example, they point out that the words of the peasants were translated from Occitan, the language they spoke, to Latin for the official record. What readers hear are not the voices of the peasants but rather their ideas filtered through the vocabulary of the elite. Moreover, the peasants called before the tribunal were held in prison and feared for their lives. When they were forced to talk about events that had taken place ten or more years earlier, to what extent can their testimony be a direct window onto their lives? Nevertheless, the register remains a precious source for learning at least something about what ordinary people thought and felt in a small village about seven hundred years ago.

QUESTIONS FOR DEBATE

1. In what ways are modern court cases like the Inquisition register of Fournier? In what ways are they unlike such a source? Could you use modern court cases to reconstruct the life of a community?

2. What are the advantages and the pitfalls of using a source such as the register for historical research?

FURTHER READING

Boyle, Leonard. "Montaillou Revisited: *Mentalité* and Methodology." In J. A. Raftis, ed. *Pathways to Medieval Peasants*. 1981.

Le Roy Ladurie, Emmanuel. *Montaillou: The Promised Land of Error*. 1978. The original French version was published in 1975.

Resaldo, Renato. "From the Door of His Tent: The Fieldworker and the Inquisitor." In James Clifford and George E. Marcus, eds. *Writing Culture: The Poetics and Politics of Ethnography*. 1986.

The Ministry of the Friars.   Although St. Francis had wanted his followers to sleep wherever they found themselves, by the second quarter of the thirteenth century most Franciscans and Dominicans lived in houses called *convents* just outside cities. Nearly every city, even those of moderate size, had these convents outside its walls. Some Franciscan convents housed nuns, who, unlike their male counterparts, lived in strict seclusion. Yet they too ministered to the world by taking in the sick. The

Friars and Usurers

As the illustration on page 411 reveals, clerics sometimes borrowed money. The friars had a different attitude. St. Francis, son of a merchant, refused to touch money altogether. Instead, he and his friars begged for food and shelter. Even when their numbers grew and they began forming communities and living in monasteries, the friars still insisted on personal poverty, while ministering to city dwellers, who had to deal with money in some way to make a living. In this illumination from about 1250, a Franciscan (in light-colored robes) and a Dominican (in black) reject offers from two usurers, whose profession they are thus shown to condemn. Other friars, including Thomas Aquinas, worked out justifications for some kinds of money-making professions. Bibliothèque Nationale, Paris.

mendicant (or "begging") orders further tied their members to the community through the "tertiaries," affiliated laymen and -women who adopted many Franciscan practices—prayer and works of charity, for example—while continuing to live in the world, raising families and tending to the normal tasks of daily life, whatever their occupation. Even kings became tertiaries.

The thirteenth century was an age of preaching: large numbers of friars and others trained in the universities took to the road to speak to throngs of townsfolk. When Berthold, a Franciscan who traveled the length and breadth of Germany giving sermons, came to a town, a high tower was set up for

him outside the city walls. A pennant advertised his presence and let people know which way the wind would blow his voice. St. Anthony of Padua preached in Italian to huge audiences lined up hours in advance to be sure they would have a place to hear him.

Townspeople flocked to such preachers because they wanted to know how the Christian message applied to their daily lives. They were concerned, for example, about the ethics of moneymaking, sex in marriage, and family life. In turn, the preachers represented the front line of the church. They met the laity on their own turf and taught them to bend their activities to church teachings.

The Piety of Women. All across Europe, women in the thirteenth century sought outlets for their intense piety. As in previous centuries, powerful families founded new nunneries, especially within towns and cities. On the whole, these were set up for the daughters of the very wealthy. Ordinary women found different modes of religious expression. Some sought the lives of quiet activity and rapturous mysticism of the Beguines, others the lives of charity and service of women's mendicant orders, and still others domestic lives of marriage and family punctuated by religious devotions. Elisabeth of Hungary, who married a German prince at the age of fourteen, raised three children. At the same time, she devoted her life to fasting, prayer, and service to the poor.

Many women were not as devout as Elisabeth. In the countryside, they cooked their porridge, brewed their ale, and raised their children. They attended church regularly, on major feast days or for churching—the ritual of purification after a pregnancy—but not extravagantly. In the cities, workingwomen scratched out a meager living. They sometimes made pilgrimages to relic shrines to seek help or cures. Religion was a part of these women's lives, but it did not dominate them.

For some women, however, religion was the focus of life, and the church's attempt to define and control the Eucharist had some unintended results. The new emphasis on the holiness of the transformed wine and bread induced some of these pious women to eat nothing but the Eucharist. One such woman, Angela of Foligno, reported that the consecrated bread swelled in her mouth, tasting sweeter than any other food. For these women, eating the Eucharist was literally eating God. This is how they understood the church's teaching that the consecrated bread was actually Christ's body. In the minds of these holy women, Christ's crucifixion was the literal sacrifice of his body, to be eaten by sinful men and women as the way to redeem themselves. Renouncing all other foods became part of a life of service to others, because many of these devout women gave the poor the food that they refused to eat.

Such women lived in every sort of urban setting. They might be laywomen—daughters, wives, and mothers living at home—or they might be Beguines or nuns living in cloistered or semicloistered communities. Even if not engaged in community service, holy women felt their suffering itself was a work of charity, helping to release souls from purgatory, the place the church taught where souls were cleansed of their sins.

These women both accepted and challenged the pronouncements of the Fourth Lateran Council about the meaning of the Eucharist. For example, they accepted that only priests could say Mass; but some of them bypassed their own priests, receiving the Eucharist (as they explained) directly from Christ in the form of a vision. Although men dominated the institutions that governed political, religious, and economic affairs, these women found ways to control their own lives and to some extent the lives of those around them. Typically involved with meal preparation and feeding, like other women of the time, these holy women found a way to use their control over ordinary food to gain new kinds of social and religious power that could force the clergy to confront female piety.

❖ Harmony of Heaven and Earth

Just as the church saw itself as regulating worldly life in accordance with God's plan for salvation, so contemporary thinkers, writers, musicians, and artists sought to harmonize the secular with the sacred. Scholars wrote treatises that reconciled faith with reason; poets and musicians sang of the links between heaven and human life on earth; artists expressed the same ideas in stone and sculpture. Even in the face of many contradictions, they were largely successful in communicating this harmonious image of the world.

Scholasticism

Scholasticism was the logical method of inquiry and exposition pioneered by Abelard and other twelfth-century teachers. In the thirteenth century, the method was used to summarize and reconcile all knowledge. Many of the thirteenth-century scholastics (the name given to the scholars who used this method) were members of the Dominican and Franciscan orders and taught in the universities. They were confident that knowledge obtained through the senses and by logical reasoning was entirely compatible with the knowledge known through faith and revelation. One of their goals was to demonstrate this harmony. The scholastic *summa*, or summary of knowledge, was a systematic exposition of the answer to every possible question about human morality, the physical world, society, belief, action, and theology. Another goal

Embroidery
Whether at home or in the convent, many women embroidered. The opus Anglicanum, *or "English specialty" was the exquisite embroidery done in England. Fabrics were worked with needle and fine silk, gold, and silver threads, often incorporating pearls and gemstones. Pictured here is a cope—a capelike vestment used by cantors on great feast days—made by English nuns and featuring the figures of saints, angels, and scenes from Christ's life. It might take several years to make just one such piece of fine embroidery.*
Victoria and Albert Museum, London.

of the scholastics was to preach the conclusions of these treatises. As one scholastic put it, "First the bow is bent in study, then the arrow is released in preaching": first you study the *summa* and then you hit your mark—convert people—by preaching. Many of the preachers who came to the towns were students and disciples of scholastic university teachers.

The method of the *summa* derived from the *sic et non* (also called the "dialectical") method of Abelard, in which different positions on a given topic were juxtaposed. However, rather than leave the questions open, as Abelard had done, the scholastics gave their own considered opinions. Their arguments borrowed much of the vocabulary and rules of logic long ago outlined by Aristotle. Even though Aristotle was a pagan, scholastics considered his coherent and rational body of thought the most perfect that human reason alone could devise. Because they had the benefit of Christ's reve-lations, the scholastics considered themselves able to take Aristotle's philosophy one necessary step fur-ther and reconcile human reason with Christian faith. Full of confidence in their method and conclusions, scholastics embraced the world and its issues.

Some scholastics considered questions about the natural world. Albertus Magnus (c. 1200–1280), a major theologian, also contributed to the fields of biology, botany, astronomy, and physics. His reconsideration of Aristotle's views on motion led the way to distinctions that helped scientists in the sixteenth and seventeenth centuries arrive at the modern notion of inertia.

One of Albertus's students was St. Thomas Aquinas (c. 1225–1274), perhaps the most famous scholastic. Huge of build, renowned for his composure in debate, Thomas came from a noble Neapolitan family that had hoped to see him become a powerful bishop rather than a poor university professor. When he was about eighteen years old, he thwarted his family's wishes and joined the Dominicans. Soon he was studying at Cologne with Albertus. At thirty-two he became a master at the University of Paris.

Like many other scholastics, Thomas considered Aristotle "the Philosopher," the authoritative voice of human reason, which he sought to reconcile with divine revelation in a universal and harmonious scheme. In 1273, he published his monumental *Summa Theologiae* (sometimes called the *Summa Theologica*), which covered all impor-

Thomas Aquinas in Glory
In this fourteenth-century painting (probably by Francesco Traini) from Santa Caterina, Pisa, Thomas Aquinas is pictured as a philosopher-saint. Beneath him and to his right is Aristotle, who holds up a book, symbol of the philosophy that Thomas has harvested; to his left is Plato, the second great influence behind scholastic philosophy. Above are other learned saints, and at the top is Christ, source of the Word and hence of all philosophy. Compare this representation of a great teacher with that of Gilbert of Poitiers on page 374. Scala/Art Resource, NY.

tant topics, human and divine. He divided these topics into questions, exploring each one thoroughly and systematically with the *sic et non* method. Thomas concluded each question with a decisive position and a refutation of opposing views.

Many of Thomas's questions spoke to the keenest concerns of his day. He asked, for example, whether it was lawful to sell something for more than its worth. Thomas arranged his argument systematically, quoting first authorities that seemed to declare every sort of selling practice, even deceptive ones, to be lawful. This was the *sic* (or "yes") position. Then he quoted an authority that opposed selling something for more than its worth. This was the *non*. Following that, he gave his own argument, prefaced by the words *I answer that*. Unlike Abelard, whose method left differences unresolved, Thomas wanted to harmonize the two points of view, and so he pointed out that price and worth depended on the circumstances of the buyer and seller and concluded that charging more than a seller had originally paid could be legitimate at times.

For townspeople engaged in commerce and worried about biblical prohibitions on moneymaking, Thomas's ideas about selling practices addressed burning questions. Hoping to go to heaven as well as reap the profits of their business ventures, laypeople listened eagerly to preachers who delivered their sermons in the vernacular but who based their ideas on the Latin *summae* of Thomas and other scholastics. Thomas's conclusions aided townspeople in justifying their worldly activities.

In his own day, Thomas Aquinas was a controversial figure, and his ideas, emphasizing reason, were by no means universally accepted. Yet even Thomas departed from Aristotle, who had explained the universe through human reason alone. In Thomas's view, God, nature, and reason were in harmony, so Aristotle's arguments could be used to explore both the human and the divine order, but with some exceptions. "Certain things that are true about God wholly surpass the capability of human reason, for instance that God is three and one," Thomas wrote. But he thought these exceptions rarely occurred.

The work of the thirteenth-century scholastics to unite the secular with the sacred continued for another generation after Thomas. Yet at the beginning of the fourteenth century, fissures began to appear. In the *summae* of John Duns Scotus (c. 1266–1308), for example, the world and God were less compatible. John, whose name "Duns Scotus" betrays his Scottish origin, was a Franciscan who taught at both Oxford and Paris. For John, human reason could know truth only through the "special illumination of the uncreated light," that is, by divine illumination. But unlike his predecessors, John believed that this illumination came not as a matter of course but only when God chose to intervene. John—and others—now sometimes experienced God as willful rather than reasonable. Human reason could not soar to God; God's will alone determined whether or not a person could know Him. In this way, John separated the divine and secular realms.

Scholastics like Thomas were enormous optimists. They believed that everything had a place in God's scheme of things, that the world was orderly, and that human beings could make rational sense of it. This optimism filled the classrooms, spilled into the friars' convents, and found its way to the streets where artisans and shopkeepers lived and worked. Scholastic philosophy helped give ordinary people a sense of purpose and a guide to behavior. Yet even among scholastics, unity was elusive. In his own day, Thomas was accused of placing too much emphasis on reason, and later scholastics argued pessimistically that reason could not find truth through its own faculties and energies. Once again, harmony was challenged by discord.

New Syntheses in Writing and Music

Thirteenth-century writers and musicians, like scholastics and preachers, presented complicated ideas and feelings as harmonious and unified within a Christian worldview. Writers explored the relations between this world and the next; musicians found ways to bridge sacred and secular forms of music.

The Growth of Vernacular Literature. Dante Alighieri (1265–1321), perhaps the greatest medieval vernacular poet, harmonized the scholastic universe with the mysteries of faith and the poetry of love. Born in Florence in a time of political turmoil, Dante incorporated the heroes and villains of his day into his most famous poem, the *Commedia*, written between 1313 and 1321. Later known as the *Divine Comedy*, Dante's poem describes the poet taking an imaginary journey from Hell to Purgatory and finally to Paradise.

The poem is an allegory in which every person and object must be read at more than one level. At the most literal level, the poem is about Dante's travels. At a deeper level, it is about the soul's search for meaning and enlightenment and its ultimate discovery of God in the light of divine love. Just as Thomas Aquinas thought that Aristotle's logic could lead to important truths, so Dante used the pagan poet Virgil as his guide through Hell and Purgatory. And just as Thomas believed that faith went beyond reason to even higher truths, so Dante found a new guide representing earthly love to lead him through most of Paradise. This guide was Beatrice, a Florentine girl with whom Dante had fallen in love as

The Last Judgment
Satan sits in the center of hell devouring souls in this mid-thirteenth-century mosaic on the vault of the
baptistery at Florence. The horrors of hell are graphically depicted, partly because mosaics allow for greater
detail than stone carving and partly because of the vivid and expressive visions of the afterlife that poets
like Dante, a Florentine, were promulgating around the time this mosaic was executed.
Scala/Art Resource, NY.

a boy and whom he never forgot. But only faith, in the form of the divine love of the Virgin Mary, could bring Dante to the culmination of his journey—a blinding and inexpressibly awesome vision of God:

> *What I then saw is more than tongue can say.*
> *Our human speech is dark before the vision.*
> *The ravished memory swoons and falls away.*

Dante's poem electrified a wide audience. By elevating one dialect of Italian—the language that ordinary Florentines used in their everyday life—to a language of exquisite poetry, Dante was able to communicate the scholastics' harmonious and optimistic vision of the universe in an even more exciting and accessible way. So influential was his work that it is no exaggeration to say that modern Italian is based on Dante's Florentine dialect.

Other writers of the period used different methods to express the harmony of heaven and earth. The anonymous author of the *Quest of the Holy Grail* (c. 1225), for example, wrote about the adventures of some of the knights of King Arthur's Round Table to convey the doctrine of transubstantiation and the wonder of the vision of God. In *The Romance of the Rose*, begun by one author (Guillaume de Lorris, a poet in the romantic tradition) and finished by another (Jean de Meun, a poet in the scholastic tradition), a lover seeks the rose,

his true love. In the long dream that the poem describes, the narrator's search for the rose is thwarted by the personifications of love, shame, reason, abstinence, and so on. They present him with arguments for and against love, not incidentally commenting on people of the poets' own day. In the end, sexual love is made part of the divine scheme—and the lover plucks the rose.

New Musical Forms. Musicians, like poets, developed new forms that bridged sacred and secular subjects in the thirteenth and fourteenth centuries. This connection appears in the most distinctive musical form of the thirteenth century, the *motet* (from the French *mot*, meaning "word"). The motet is an example of polyphony, music that consists of two or more melodies performed simultaneously. Before about 1215, most polyphony was sacred; purely secular polyphony was not common before the fourteenth century. The motet, a unique merging of the sacred and the secular, evidently originated in Paris, the center of scholastic culture as well.

The typical thirteenth-century motet has three melody lines (or "voices"). The lowest, usually from a liturgical chant melody, has no words and may have been played on an instrument rather than sung. The remaining melodies have different texts, either Latin or French (or one of each), which are sung simultaneously. Latin texts are usually sacred, whereas French ones are secular, dealing with themes such as love and springtime. In one example the top voice chirps in quick rhythm about a lady's charms ("Fair maiden, lovely and comely; pretty maiden, courteous and pleasing, delicious one"); the middle voice slowly and lugubriously laments the "malady" of love; and the lowest voice sings a liturgical melody. The motet thus weaves the sacred (the chant melody in the lowest voice) and the secular (the French texts in the upper voices) into a sophisticated tapestry of music. Like the scholastic *summae*, the motets were written by and for a clerical elite. Yet they incorporated the music of ordinary people, such as the calls of street vendors and the boisterous songs of students. In turn they touched the lives of everyone, for polyphony influenced every form of music, from the Mass to popular songs that entertained and diverted laypeople and churchmen alike.

Complementing the motet's complexity was the development of a new notation for rhythm. By the eleventh century, musical notation could indicate pitch but had no way to denote the duration of the notes. Music theorists of the thirteenth century, however, developed increasingly precise methods to indicate rhythm. Franco of Cologne, for example, in his *Art of Measurable Song* (c. 1280), used different shapes to mark the number of beats each note should be held. His system became the basis of modern musical notation. Because each note could now be allotted a specific duration, written music could express new and complicated rhythms. The music of the thirteenth century reflected both the melding of the secular and the sacred and the possibilities of greater order and control.

The Order of High Gothic

Just as polyphonic music united the sacred with the secular, so Gothic architecture, sculpture, and painting expressed the order and harmony of the universe. The term "Gothic" refers to much of the art and architecture of the twelfth to fifteenth centuries. It is characterized by pointed arches, which began as architectural motifs but were soon adopted in every art form. Gothic churches appealed to the senses the way that scholastic argument appealed to human reason: both were designed to lead people to knowledge that touched the divine. Being in a Gothic church was a foretaste of heaven.

Architecture. Gothic architecture began around 1135, with the project of Abbot Suger, the close associate of King Louis the Fat (see page 371), to remodel portions of the church of St. Denis. Suger's rebuilding of St. Denis was part of the fruitful melding of royal and ecclesiastical interests and ideals in the north of France. At the west end of his church, the point where the faithful entered, Suger decorated the portals with figures of Old Testament kings, queens, and patriarchs, signaling the links between the present king and his illustrious predecessors. Within the church, Suger rebuilt the *chevet*, or choir area, using pointed arches and stained glass to let in light, which Suger believed would transport

Musicians on a Psalter
On the margins of a Psalter, fanciful musicians play their instruments. At the top is a bell ringer; down the right-hand side is a woman playing a small organ, and farther down is a bagpipe player; at the bottom, a monkeylike creature plays a hurdy-gurdy (with a monkey head peeking out), while another musician bangs on drums. These were all typical and noisy instruments. Why were Psalters associated with music?
British Library.

the worshiper from the "slime of earth" to the "purity of Heaven." Suger believed that the Father of lights, God himself, "illuminated" the minds of the beholders through the light that filtered through the stained-glass windows.

Soon the style that Suger pioneered was taken up across northern France and then, as French culture gained enormous prestige under Louis IX (see page 440), all across Europe. Gothic was an urban architecture, reflecting—in its grand size, jewel-like windows, and bright ornaments—the aspirations, pride, and confidence of rich and powerful merchants, artisans, and bishops. A Gothic church, usually a cathedral (the bishop's principal church), was the religious, social, and commercial focal point of a city. Building Gothic cathedrals was a community project, enlisting the labor and support of an entire urban center. New cathedrals required a small army of quarrymen, builders, carpenters, and glass cutters. Bishops, papal legates, and clerics planned and helped pay for these grand churches, but townspeople also generously financed them and filled them to attend Mass and visit relics. Guilds raised money to pay for stained-glass windows that depicted and celebrated their own patron saints. In turn, towns made money when pilgrims came to visit relics and sightseers arrived to marvel at their great churches. At Chartres, near Paris, for example, which had the relic of the Virgin's robe, crowds thronged the streets, the poor buying small lead figures of the Virgin, the rich purchasing wearable replicas of her robe. Churches were centers of commercial activity. In their basements, wine merchants plied their trade; vendors sold goods outside.

The technologies that made Gothic churches possible were all known before the twelfth century. But Suger's church showed how they could be used together to achieve a particularly dazzling effect. Gothic techniques included ribbed vaulting, which gave a sense of precision and order; the pointed arch, which produced a feeling of soaring height; and flying buttresses, which took the weight of the vault off the walls (Figure 12.1). The buttresses permitted much of the wall to be cut away and the open spaces to be filled with glass.

Unlike Romanesque churches, whose exteriors prepare visitors for what they would see within them, Gothic cathedrals surprise. The exterior of a Gothic church has an opaque, bristling, and forbidding look owing to the dark surface of its stained glass and its flying buttresses. The interior, however, is just the opposite. It is all soaring lightness, harmony, and order. Just as a scholastic presented his argument with utter clarity, so the interior of a Gothic church revealed its structure through its skeleton of ribbed vaults and piers. And just as a scholastic bridged the earthly and celestial realms, so the cathedral elicited a response beyond reason, evoking a sense of awe.

By the mid-thirteenth century, Gothic architecture had spread from France to other European countries. Yet the style varied by region, most dramatically in Italy. The outer walls of the cathedral at Orvieto, for example, alternate bricks of light and dark color, providing texture instead of glass and

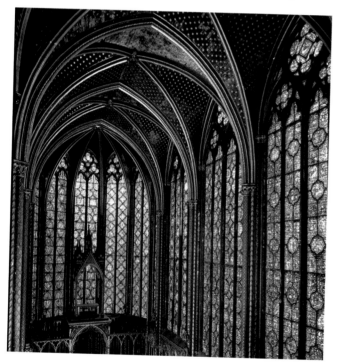

French Gothic: Ste.-Chapelle
Gothic architecture opened up the walls of the church to windows. Filled with "stained" glass—actually the colors were added to the ingredients of the glass before they were heated, melted, and blown—the windows glowed like jewels. Moreover, each had a story to tell: the life of Christ, major events from the Old Testament, the lives of saints. Ste.-Chapelle, commissioned by King Louis IX (St. Louis) and consecrated in 1248, was built to house Christ's crown of thorns and other relics of the Passion. Compare the use of windows, walls, vault, and piers here to that of a Romanesque church such as St.-Savin (see page 380).
Giraudon/Art Resource, NY.

boss

high vault

transverse rib

diagonal rib

springing

clerestory

flying buttress

mullion

light

string course

triforium

gargoyle

spandrel

arcade arch

capital

buttress

main arcade

pier

base

aisle

central or main vessel

FIGURE 12.1 Elements of a Gothic Cathedral

Bristling on the outside with stone flying buttresses, Gothic cathedrals were lofty and serene on the inside. The buttresses, which held the weight of the vault, allowed Gothic architects to pierce the walls with windows running the full length of the church. Within, thick piers anchored on sturdy bases became thin columns as they mounted over the triforium and clerestory, blossoming into ribs at the top. Whether plain or ornate, the ribs gave definition and drew attention to the high pointed vault.

Figure adapted from Michael Camille, *Gothic Art: Glorious Visions* (New York: Abrams, 1996).

light; and the vault over the large nave is round rather than pointed, recalling the Roman aqueducts that could still be seen in Italy when the builders were designing the cathedral. With no flying buttresses and relatively little portal sculpture, Italian Gothic churches convey a spirit of austerity.

Art. Gothic art, both painting and sculpture, echoed and decorated the Gothic cathedral. Gothic sculpture differed from earlier church sculpture by its naturalism and monumentality. Romanesque sculpture played upon a flat surface; Gothic figures were liberated from their background. Sculpted in the round, they turned, moved, and interacted with one another. They also sometimes smiled.

Gothic sculpture often depicted complex stories or scenes. The positions of the figures, the people they represented, and the ways in which they interacted were meant to be "read" like a scholastic *summa*. The south portal complex of Chartres

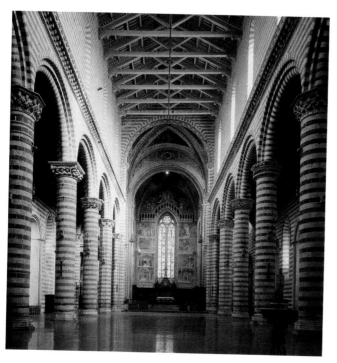

Italian Gothic: Orvieto

The cathedral at Orvieto was begun about forty years after Ste.-Chapelle (see page 434). While in France the Gothic style—with its high vaults, pointed arches, and large stained-glass windows—spread quickly and decisively, this did not always happen elsewhere. Orvieto, a typical central Italian inland town, adopted very few "French" Gothic elements for its cathedral. Instead, its builders used round arches and small windows, allowing in only enough of the hot Italian sun to illuminate the walls' variegated texture of dark and light.
Scala/Art Resource, NY.

cathedral is a good example. Each massive doorway tells a separate story through sculpture: the left depicts the martyrs, the right the confessors, and the center the Last Judgment. Like Dante's *Divine Comedy*, these portals taken together show the soul's pilgrimage from the suffering of this world to eternal life.

Gothic sculpture began in France and was adopted, with many variations, elsewhere in Europe during the thirteenth century. The Italian sculptor Nicola Pisano (c. 1220–1278?), for example, was very interested in classical forms. German sculptors, in contrast, created excited, emotional figures that sometimes gestured dramatically to one another.

By the early fourteenth century, the expansive sculptures so prominent in architecture were reflected in painting as well. This new style is evident in the work of Giotto (1266–1337), a Florentine artist who changed the emphasis of painting, which had been predominantly symbolic, decorative, and intellectual. For example, Giotto filled the walls of a private chapel at Padua with paintings depicting scenes of Christ's life. Here he experimented with the illusion of depth. Giotto's figures, appearing weighty and voluminous, express a range of emotions as they seem to move across interior and exterior spaces. In bringing sculptural realism to a flat surface, Giotto stressed three-dimensionality, illusional space, and human emotion. By melding earthly sensibilities with religious themes, Giotto found yet another way to bring together the natural and divine realms.

German Gothic: Strasbourg

The Virgin is mourned in this tympanum over the portal of the Strasbourg cathedral's south transept (the arm that crosses the church from north to south). Here, in German Gothic, the emphasis is on emotion and expressivity. Compare the depiction of Mary—with her bedclothes agitated and her body contorted—with the depiction of Gregory VII on page 358. Why do you suppose that Christ stands in the center of the tympanum, as if he is one of the mourners? What is he holding in the crook of his arm? (Hint: The souls of the dead are often shown as miniature people.)
Bildarchiv Foto Marburg.

❖ The Politics of Control

The quest for order, control, and harmony also became part of the political agendas of princes, popes, and cities. These rulers and institutions imposed—or tried to impose—their authority more fully and systematically through taxes, courts, and sometimes representative institutions. The ancestors of modern European parliaments and of the U.S. Congress can be traced to this era. In the thirteenth century, both secular and church rulers endeavored to expand their spheres of power and eliminate opposition.

The Clash of Imperial and Papal Aims

During the thirteenth century, the popes and emperors sought to dominate Italy. In the end, the emperor lost control not only of Italy but of Germany as well. The papacy, while temporarily the victor in the struggle, soon found itself embroiled in a conflict with the kings of France and England that left it tottering.

The clash of emperor and papacy had its origins in Frederick Barbarossa's failure to control northern Italy. Italy was crucial to imperial policy. The model of Charlemagne required his imperial successors to exercise hegemony there. Moreover, Italy's prosperous cities beckoned as rich sources of income. When Barbarossa failed in the north, his son, Henry VI (r. 1190–1197), tried a new approach to gain Italy: he married the heiress of Sicily, Constance. From this base near the southern tip of Italy, Henry hoped to make good his imperial title. But Henry died suddenly, leaving a three-year-old son, Frederick II, to take up his plan. It was a perilous moment.

While Frederick was a child, the imperial office became the plaything of the German princes and the papacy. Both wanted an emperor, but they wanted him to be virtually powerless. Thus, when Frederick's uncle Duke Philip of Swabia attempted to become interim king until Frederick reached his majority, many princes and the papacy blocked the move. They supported Otto of Brunswick, the son of Henry the Lion and an implacable foe of Frederick's Staufer family. Otto promised the pope that he would not intervene in Italy, and in return the pope—Innocent III, revealing yet another side of his policy—crowned him emperor.

But this time Innocent had miscalculated. No emperor worthy of the name could leave Italy alone. Almost immediately after his coronation, Otto invaded Sicily, and Innocent excommunicated him in 1211. In 1212, Innocent gave the imperial crown to Frederick II (r. 1212–1250), now a young man ready to take up the reins of power.

Frederick was an amazing ruler: the "stupor mundi"—"wonder of the world"—his contemporaries called him. Heir to two cultures, Sicilian on his mother's side and German on his father's, he cut a worldly and sophisticated figure. In Sicily he moved easily within a diverse culture of Jews, Muslims, and Christians. Here he could play the role of all-powerful ruler. In Germany he was less at home. There Christian princes, often churchmen with ministerial retinues, were acutely aware of their crucial role in royal elections and jealously guarded their rights and privileges.

Both emperor and pope needed to dominate Italy to maintain their power and position (Map 12.1). The papacy under Innocent III was expansionist, gathering money and troops to make good its claim to the Papal States. From this region the pope expected dues and taxes, military service, and the profits of justice. To ensure its survival, the pope refused to tolerate any imperial claims to Italy.

Frederick, in turn, could not imagine ruling as an emperor unless he controlled Italy. He attempted to do this throughout his life, as did his heirs. Frederick had a three-pronged strategy. First, to ensure that he would not be hounded by opponents in Germany, he granted the princes important concessions, finalized in 1232. These privileges allowed the German princes to turn their principalities into virtually independent states. Second, Frederick revamped the government of Sicily to give him more control and yield greater profits. His *Constitutions of Melfi* (1231), an eclectic body of laws, set up a system of salaried governors who worked according to uniform procedures. The *Constitutions* called for nearly all court cases to be heard by royal courts, regularized commercial privileges, and set up a system of taxation. Third, Frederick sought to enter Italy through Lombardy, as his grandfather had done.

The pope followed Frederick's every move, and he excommunicated the emperor a number of times. The most serious of these came in 1245, when the pope and other churchmen, assembled at the Council of Lyon, excommunicated and deposed

MAP 12.1 Europe in the Time of Frederick II, r. 1212–1250

King of Sicily and Germany and emperor as well, Frederick ruled over territory that encircled—and threatened—the papacy. Excommunicated several times, Frederick spent much of his career fighting the pope's forces. In the process he conceded so many powers to the German princes that the emperor thenceforth had little power in Germany. Meanwhile rulers of smaller states, such as England, France, and León-Castile, were increasing their power and authority.

Frederick, absolving his vassals and subjects of their fealty to him and, indeed, forbidding anyone to support him. By 1248, papal legates were preaching a crusade against Frederick and all his followers. Two years later, Frederick died.

The fact that Frederick's vision of the empire failed is of less long-term importance than the way it failed. His concessions to the German princes meant that Germany would not be united until the nineteenth century. The political region now called Germany was simply a geographical expression, divided under many independent princes. Between 1254 and 1273, the princes kept the German throne empty. Splintered into factions, they elected two different foreigners, who spent their time fighting each other. In one of history's great ironies, it was dur-

ing this low point of the German monarchy that the term "Holy Roman Empire" was coined. In 1273, the princes at last united and elected a German, Rudolph (r. 1273–1291), whose family, the Habsburgs, was new to imperial power. Rudolf used the imperial title to help him consolidate control over his own principality, Swabia (in southern Germany), but he did not try to fulfill the meaning of the imperial title elsewhere. For the first time, the word *emperor* was freed from its association with Italy and Rome. For the Habsburgs, the title Holy Roman Emperor was a prestigious but otherwise meaningless honorific.

The Staufer failure in Italy meant that the Italian cities would continue their independent course. In Sicily, the papacy ensured that the heirs of Frederick would not continue their rule by calling successively upon other rulers to take over the island—first Henry III of England and then Charles of Anjou. Forces loyal to the Staufer family turned to the king of Aragon (Spain). The move left two enduring claimants to Sicily's crown: the kings of Aragon and the house of Anjou. And it spawned a long war impoverishing the region.

In the struggle between pope and emperor, the pope had clearly won, at a moment that marked a high point in the political power of the medieval papacy. Nevertheless, some agreed with Frederick II's view that by tampering with secular matters the popes had demeaned and sullied their office: "These men who feign holiness," Frederick sneered, referring to the popes, are "drunk with the pleasures of the world." Scattered throughout Germany were people who believed that Frederick was a divine scourge sent to overpower a materialistic papacy.

The papacy won the war against Frederick, but at a cost. Even the king of France criticized the popes for doing "new and unheard of things."

Louis IX and a New Ideal of Kingship

From hindsight, we can see that Frederick's fight for an empire that would stretch from Germany to Sicily was doomed. The successful rulers of medieval Europe were those content with smaller, more compact, more united polities. The future was reserved for "national" states, like France, Spain, and Germany. (Of course, that too may just be one phase of Western civilization.) In France the new ideal of a "stay-at-home" monarch started in the thirteenth century with the reign of Louis IX (r. 1226–1270) and his mother, Blanche of Castile, who ruled on his behalf until 1234 and continued to rule for him when he was absent on crusades until her death in 1252.

Louis was revered not because he was a military leader but because he was an administrator, judge, and "just father" of his people. On warm summer days, he would sit under a tree in the woods near his castle at Vincennes on the outskirts of Paris, hearing disputes and dispensing justice personally. Through his administrators, he vigorously imposed his laws and justice over much of France. At Paris he appointed a salaried officer who could be

[map labels:] Drava R. · Danube R. · Milan · Verona · Venice · ...ardy · HUNGARY · Florence · Claimed by papacy · Adriatic Sea · Rome · PAPAL STATES · Naples · KINGDOM OF NAPLES (Anjou after 1265) · Sardinia (Aragon) · KINGDOM OF SICILY (Aragon after 1282) · ...RTH ...RICA · 0 100 200 miles · 0 100 200 kilometers · ...y at the End of the ...rteenth Century

Louis IX and Blanche of Castile

This miniature probably shows St. Louis, portrayed as a young boy, sitting opposite his mother, Blanche of Castile. Blanche served as regent twice in Louis's lifetime, once when he was too young to rule and a second time when he was away on crusade. The emphasis on the equality of queen and king may be evidence of Blanche's influence on and patronage of the artist. Note that the artist has set both royal figures in a Gothic windowlike setting.
The Pierpont Morgan Library/Art Resource, NY.

supervised and fired if necessary. During his reign the influence of the Parlement* of Paris, the royal court of justice, increased significantly. Originally a changeable and movable body, part of the king's personal entourage when he dealt with litigation, it was now permanently housed in Paris and staffed by professional judges who heard cases and recorded their decisions. The king's subjects came to look to him for justice and equity.

Unlike his grandfather Philip Augustus, Louis did not try to expand his territory. He inherited a large kingdom that included Poitou and Languedoc (Map 12.2), and he was content. Although Henry III, the king of England, attacked him continually to try to regain territory lost under Philip Augustus, Louis remained unprovoked. Rather than prolong the fighting, he conceded and made peace in 1259.

While always respectful of the church and the pope, Louis vigorously maintained the dignity of the king and his rights. He accepted limits on his power in relation to the church and never claimed power over spiritual matters. He expected royal and ecclesiastical power to work in harmony. At the same time, however, he refused to let the church dictate how he should use his temporal authority. For example, French bishops wanted royal officers to support the church's sentences of excommunication. But Louis declared that he would authorize his officials to do so only if he were able to judge each case for himself, to see if the excommunication had been justly pronounced or not. The bishops refused, and Louis held his ground. Royal and ecclesiastical power would work side by side, neither subservient to the other.

Louis saw himself as chivalrous, pious, and just. His contemporaries went further: they considered him a saint. They praised his care for the poor and sick, the pains and penances he inflicted on himself, and his regular participation in church services. In 1297, he was canonized as St. Louis. The result was enormous prestige for the French monarchy. This

*Although *Parlement* and *Parliament* are very similar words, both deriving from the French word *parler* ("to speak"), the institutions they named were very different. The Parlement of France was a law court, whereas the English Parliament, although beginning as a court to redress grievances, had by 1327 become above all a representative institution. The major French representative assembly, the Estates General, first convened at the beginning of the fourteenth century.

MAP 12.2 France under Louis IX, r. 1226–1270
Louis IX did not expand his kingdom as dramatically as his grandfather Philip Augustus had done. He was greatly admired nevertheless, for he was seen by contemporaries as a model of Christian piety and justice. After his death, he was recognized as a saint and thus posthumously enhanced the prestige of the French monarchy in a new way.

prestige, joined with the renown of Paris as the center of Gothic architecture and scholastic thought and the repute of French courts as the hubs of chivalry, made France the cultural model of Europe. In many ways, it retains that allure today.

Many modern historians fault Louis for his policies toward the Jews. His hatred of them was well known. He did not exactly advocate violence against them, but he sometimes subjected them to arrest, canceling the debts owed to them (but collecting part into the royal treasury), and confiscating their belongings. In 1253, he ordered them to live "by the labor of their hands" or leave of France. He meant that they should no longer lend money. In effect, he took away their livelihood.

Other than some outspoken Jews, most of Louis's contemporaries did not condemn him for these policies. To the contrary, they sometimes took his antagonism much further than he intended. In Bourges, for example, they burned the synagogue. What they did criticize, however, were Louis's two unsuccessful crusades to the Holy Land. One of Louis's biographers complained that before the king left for his second expedition in 1270, all was peaceful and prosperous in France, but "ever since King Louis went away the state of the kingdom has done nothing but go from bad to worse." Louis died in the course of this, the Eighth Crusade.

The Birth of Representative Institutions

As thirteenth-century monarchs and princes expanded their powers, they devised a new political tool to enlist more broadly based support: all across Europe, from Spain to Poland, from England to Hungary, rulers summoned parliaments. These grew out of the ad hoc advisory sessions kings had held with their nobles and clergy, men who informally represented the two most powerful classes, or "orders," of medieval society. In the thirteenth century, the advisory sessions turned into solemn, formal meetings of representatives of the orders to the kings' chief councils, the origin of parliamentary sessions. Although these bodies differed from place to place, the impulse behind their creation was similar. Beginning as assemblies where kings celebrated their royal power and prestige and where the "orders" simply assented to royal policy, they eventually became organs through which people not ordinarily at court could articulate their wishes.

The orders, which evolved from the tenth-century categories (those who pray, those who fight, and those who work), consisted of the clergy, nobles, and commoners of the realm. Unlike modern "classes," which are defined largely by economic status, medieval orders cut across economic boundaries. The order of clerics, for example, embraced the clergy from the most humble parish priest to the most exalted archbishop and the pope. The order of commoners theoretically included both rich merchants and poor peasants. But the notion of orders was an idealized abstraction; in practice, thirteenth-century kings did not so much command representatives of the orders to come to court as they simply summoned the most powerful members of their realm, whether clerics, nobles, or important townsmen, to support their policies. In thirteenth-century León (part of present-day Spain), for example, the

king sometimes called only the clergy and nobles; sometimes, especially when he wanted the help of their militias, he sent for representatives of the towns. As townsmen gradually began to participate regularly in advisory sessions, kings came to depend on them and their support. In turn commoners became more fully integrated into the work of royal government.

Spanish Cortes. The *cortes* of Castile-León were among the earliest representative assemblies called to the king's court and the first to include townsmen. As the reconquista pushed southward across the Iberian peninsula during the twelfth century, Christian kings called for settlers to occupy new frontiers. Enriched by plunder, fledgling villages soon burgeoned into major commercial centers. Like the cities of Italy, Spanish towns dominated the countryside. Their leaders—called *caballeros villanos*, or "city horsemen," because they were rich enough to fight on horseback—monopolized municipal offices. In 1188, when King Alfonso IX (r. 1188–1230) summoned townsmen to the *cortes*, the city *caballeros* served as their representatives, agreeing to Alfonso's plea for military and financial support and for help in

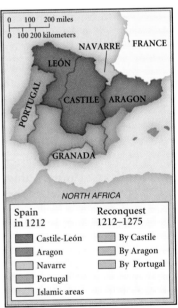

Spain in the Thirteenth Century

Spain in 1212	Reconquest 1212–1275
Castile-León	By Castile
Aragon	By Aragon
Navarre	By Portugal
Portugal	
Islamic areas	

consolidating his rule. Once convened at court, these wealthy townsmen joined bishops and noblemen in formally counseling the king and assenting to royal decisions. Beginning with Alfonso X (r. 1252–1284), Castilian monarchs regularly called on the *cortes* to participate in major political and military decisions and to assent to new taxes to finance them.

English Parliament. The English Parliament also developed as a new tool of royal government. In this case, however, the king's control was complicated by the power of the barons, manifested, for example, when Magna Carta was drawn up in 1215.

In the twelfth century, King Henry II had consulted prelates and barons at Great Councils, using these parliaments as his tool to ratify and gain support for his policies. Though Magna Carta had nothing to do with such councils, the barons thought the document gave them an important and permanent role in royal government as the king's advisers and a solid guarantee of their customary rights and privileges. When Henry III (r. 1216–1272) was crowned at the age of nine, he was king in name only for the first sixteen years of his reign. Instead, England was governed by a council consisting of a few barons, professional administrators, and a papal legate. Although not quite "government by Parliament," this council set a precedent for baronial participation in government.

A parliament that included commoners came only in the midst of war and as a result of political weakness. Henry so alienated nobles and commoners alike by his wars, debts, choice of advisers, and demands for money that the barons threatened to rebel. At a meeting at Oxford in 1258, they forced Henry to dismiss his foreign advisers; rule with the advice of a Council of Fifteen chosen jointly by the barons and the king; and limit the terms of his chief officers. However, this new government was itself riven by strife among the barons, and civil war erupted in 1264. At the battle of Lewes in the same year, the leader of the baronial opposition, Simon de Montfort (c. 1208–1265), routed the king's forces, captured the king, and became England's de facto ruler. Because only a minority of the barons followed Simon, he sought new support by convening a parliament in 1265, to which he summoned not only the earls, barons, and churchmen who backed him but also representatives from the towns, the "commons"—and he appealed for their help. Thus for the first time the commons were given a voice in government. Even though Simon's brief rule ended that very year and Henry's son Edward I (r. 1272–1307) became a rallying point for royalists, the idea of representative government in England had emerged, born out of the interplay between royal initiatives and baronial revolts.

Boniface and Philip Collide

In France, the development of representative government originated in the conflict between Pope Boniface VIII (r. 1294–1303) and King Philip IV

(r. 1285–1314), known as Philip the Fair. At the time, this confrontation seemed to be just one more episode in the ongoing struggle between medieval popes and rulers for power and authority. But in fact, at the end of the thirteenth century kings had more power, and the standoff between Boniface and Philip became a turning point that weakened the papacy and strengthened the monarchy.

Taxing the Clergy. Unlike his grandfather St. Louis, Philip the Fair did not hesitate to fight the king of England, Edward I, over territory. The two kings financed their wars by taxing the clergy along with everyone else, as if they were preparing for a crusade and could expect church support. Without even pretending any concern for clerical autonomy, Edward's men, for example, forced open church vaults to confiscate money for the royal coffers.

For the kings of both England and France, the principle of national sovereignty meant they could claim jurisdiction over all people, even churchmen, who lived within their borders. For the pope, however, the principle at stake was his role as head of the clergy. Boniface asserted that only the pope could authorize the taxation of clerics. He threatened to excommunicate kings who taxed prelates without papal permission, and he called upon clerics to disobey any such royal orders.

Edward and Philip reacted swiftly. Taking advantage of the important role English courts played in protecting the peace, Edward declared that all clerics who refused to pay his taxes would be considered outlaws—literally "outside the law." Clergymen who were robbed, for example, would have no recourse against their attackers; if accused of crimes, they would have no defense in court. Relying on a different strategy, Philip forbade the exportation of precious metals, money, or jewels, effectively sealing French borders. Immediately the English clergy cried out for legal protection, while the papacy itself cried out for the revenues it had long enjoyed from French pilgrims, litigants, and travelers. Boniface was forced to back down, conceding in 1297 that kings had the right to tax their clergy in emergencies. But this did not end the confrontation.

The King's New Tools: Propaganda and Popular Opinion. In 1301, Philip the Fair tested his jurisdiction in southern France by arresting Bernard Saisset, the bishop of Pamiers, on a charge of treason for slandering the king by comparing him to an owl, "the handsomest of birds which is worth absolutely nothing." Saisset's imprisonment violated the principle, maintained both by the pope and by French law, that a clergyman was not subject to lay justice. Boniface reacted angrily, suggesting that the pope was the king's superior in matters both temporal and spiritual.

Philip quickly seized the opportunity to deride and humiliate Boniface, directing his agents to forge and broadly circulate a new papal letter, a parody of the original, which declared (as Boniface had never done) that the king was subject to the pope. At the same time, Philip convened representatives of the clergy, nobles, and townspeople to explain, justify, and propagandize his position. This new assembly, which met at Paris in 1302, was the ancestor of the Estates General, which would meet sporadically for centuries thereafter—for the last time in 1789, at the beginning of the French Revolution. (In France the various orders—clergy, nobles, and commoners—were called "estates.") Most of those present at the assembly of 1302 supported Philip, wrote letters of protest to the cardinals, and referred to Boniface not as pope but as "he who now presides over the government of the Church."

Boniface's reply, the bull* *Unam Sanctam* (1302), intensified the situation to fever pitch with the words "Therefore we declare, state, define and pronounce that it is altogether necessary to salvation for every human creature to be subject to the Roman Pontiff." At meetings of the king's inner circle, Philip's agents declared Boniface a false pope and accused him of sexual perversion, various crimes, and heresy: "He has a private demon whose advice he follows in all things. . . . He is a Sodomite and keeps concubines. . . . He has had many clerics killed in his presence, rejoicing in their deaths," and so on. The king sent his commissioners to the various provinces of France to convene local meetings to popularize his charges against Boniface and gain support. These meetings, including clergy, local nobles, townspeople, and even villagers, almost unanimously denounced the pope. Perhaps the most striking support came from the clergy, who began to view themselves as members of a free, national French church largely independent of the papacy.

*An official papal document is called a bull, from the *bulla*, or seal, that was used to authenticate it.

Boniface III

For the sculptor who depicted Pope Boniface III, Arnolfo di Cambio (d. 1302), not much had changed since the time of Innocent III. Look at the picture of Innocent on page 423 and compare the two popes: both are depicted as young, majestic, authoritative, sober, and calm. Yet Boniface could not have been very calm, for his authority was challenged at every turn. He was forced to withdraw his opposition to royal taxation of the clergy. He tried to placate the French king, Philip the Fair, by canonizing Philip's grandfather, St. Louis. Even so, Philip arrested the bishop of Pamiers and brought him to trial. When Boniface protested, he was proclaimed a heretic by the French. A few months later he was dead.
Scala/Art Resource, NY.

Papal Defeat. In 1303, royal agents, acting under Philip's orders, invaded Boniface's palace at Anagni (southeast of Rome) to capture the pope, bring him to France, and try him. Fearing for the pope's life, however, the people of Anagni joined forces and drove the French agents out of town. Yet even after such public support for the pope, the king made his power felt. Boniface died very shortly thereafter, and the next two popes quickly pardoned Philip and his agents for their actions.

Just as Frederick II's defeat showed the weakness of the empire, so Boniface's humiliation showed the limits of papal control. The two powers that claimed "universal" authority had very little weight in the face of the new, limited, but tightly controlled national states. After 1303, popes continued to fulminate against kings and emperors, but henceforth their words had less and less impact. In the face of newly powerful medieval states such as France, Spain, and England—undergirded by vast revenues, judicial apparatuses, representative institutions, and even the loyalty of churchmen—the papacy could make little headway. The delicate balance between church and state, a hallmark of the years of St. Louis that reflected a search for harmony as well as a drive for power, broke down by the end of the thirteenth century. The quest for control led not to harmony but to confrontation and extremism.

In 1309, forced from Rome by civil strife, the papacy settled at Avignon, a city technically in the Holy Roman Empire but very close to, and influenced by, France. Here the popes remained until 1378. The period from 1309 to 1378 came to be called the Babylonian Captivity by Europeans sensitive to having the popes live far from Rome, on the Rhône River. The Avignon popes, many of them French, established a sober and efficient organization that took in regular revenues and gave the papacy more say than ever before in the appointment of churchmen. They would, however, slowly abandon the idea of leading all of Christendom and would tacitly recognize the growing power of the secular states to regulate their internal affairs.

Power Shift in the Italian Communes

During the thirteenth century, the Italian communes continued to extend their control over the surrounding countryside as independent city-states. While generally presenting a united front to out-siders, factions within the communes fought for control and its spoils. In the early thirteenth century, these factions largely represented noble families. However, in the course of the century, newer groups, generally from the nonnoble classes, attempted to take over the reins of power in the communes. The *popolo* ("people"), as such groups were called, incorporated members of city associations such as craft and merchant guilds, parishes, and the commune itself. In fact, the *popolo* was a kind of alternative commune, a sworn association in each city that dedicated itself to upholding the interests of its members. Armed and militant, the *popolo* demanded a share in city government, particularly to gain a voice in matters of taxation. In 1222 at Piacenza, for example, the *popolo*'s members won half the government offices; a year later they and the nobles worked out a plan to share the election of their city's *podestà*, or governing officials. Such power sharing often resulted from the *popolo*'s struggle. In some cities, nobles overcame and dissolved the *popolo*; but in others, the *popolo* virtually excluded the nobles from government. Constantly confronting one another, quarreling, feuding, and compromising, such factions turned Italian cities into centers of civil discord.

Weakened by this constant friction, the communes were tempting prey for great regional nobles who, allying with one or another faction, tried to establish themselves as *signori* (singular *signore*, "lord") of the cities, keeping the peace at the price of repression. In these circumstances, the commune gave way to the *signoria* (a state ruled by a *signore*), with one family dominating the government. The fate of Piacenza over the course of the thirteenth century was typical: first dominated by nobles, its commune granted the *popolo* a voice by 1225; but then by midcentury the *signore*'s power eclipsed both the nobles and the *popolo*. The communes were no more, and many Italian cities fell under control of despots.

The Mongol Invasions in Eastern Europe

Outside western Europe the fragmentation of political power left eastern Europe and Russia vulnerable to invasions from Asia. One of the most important of these was the Mongol invasions. At the beginning of the thirteenth century, on the northern border of China in present-day Mongolia,

MAP 12.3 The Mongol Invasions to 1259
The Mongols were the first people to tie the eastern world to the west. Their conquest of China, which took place at about the same time as their invasions of Russia and Iran, created a global economy, opening up trade relations across regions that had formerly been separated by language, religion, and political regimes.

various tribes of mixed ethnic origins and traditions fused into an aggressive army under the leadership of Chingiz (or Genghis) Khan (c. 1162–1227). In part, economic necessity impelled them: climatic changes had reduced the grasslands that sustained their animals and their nomadic way of life. But their advance out of Mongolia also represented the political strategy of Chingiz, who reckoned that military offensives would keep the tribes united under him. By 1215, the Mongols (also called the Tatars or Tartars) held Beijing and most of northern China. Some years later they moved through central Asia and skirted the Caspian Sea.

Russia and Eastern Europe under Attack. In the 1230s, the Mongols began concerted attacks in Europe—in Russia, Poland, and Hungary, where weak native princes were no match for the Mongols' formidable armies and tactics. Only the death of their Great Khan, Chingiz's son Ogodei (1186–1241)—styled the khagan, or khan of khans—and disputes over his succession prevented a concentrated assault on Germany. In the 1250s, the Mongols took Iran, Baghdad, and Damascus, stopped in their conquest of the Muslim world only by the Egyptian armies (Map 12.3).

The Mongols' sophisticated and devastating military tactics contributed to their overwhelming success. Organizing their campaigns at meetings held far in advance of a planned attack, they devised two- and three-flank operations. The invasion of Hungary, for example, was two-pronged: one division of their army arrived from Russia while the other moved through Poland and Germany. Many

Hungarians perished in the assault as the Mongols, fighting mainly on horseback, with heavy lances and powerful bows and arrows whose shots traveled far and penetrated deeply, crushed the Hungarian army of mixed infantry and cavalry.

The Mongols' attack on Russia had the most lasting impact. At Vladimir in Suzdal, the strongest Russian principality, they broke through the defensive walls of the city and burned the populace huddled for protection in the cathedral. Their most important victory in Russia was the capture of Kiev in 1240. Making the mouth of the Volga River the center of their power in Russia, the Mongols dominated all of Russia's principalities for about two hundred years.

The Mongol Empire in Russia, later called the Golden Horde (*golden* probably from the color of their leader's tent; *horde* from a Turkish word meaning "camp"), adopted much of the local government apparatus. The Mongols standardized the collection of taxes and the recruitment of troops by basing them on a population census, and they allowed Russian princes to continue ruling as long as they paid homage and tribute to the khan. The Mongol overlords even exempted the Russian church from taxes.

Opening of China to Europeans. The Mongol invasion changed the political configuration of Europe and Asia. Because the Mongols were willing to deal with westerners, one effect of their conquests was to open China to Europeans for the first time. Some missionaries, diplomats, and merchants traveled overland to China; others set sail from the Persian Gulf (controlled by the Mongols) and rounded India before arriving in China. Some hoped to enlist the aid of the Mongols against the Muslims; others expected to make new converts to Christianity; still others dreamed of lucrative trade routes.

The most famous of these travelers was Marco Polo (1254–1324), son of a merchant family from Venice. Marco's father and uncle had already been to China and met Khubilai, Chingiz's grandson and the new khagan, who used them as envoys to ask the pope to send "men able to show by clear reasoning that the Christian religion is better than [that of the Mongols]," according to Marco's later account. The delegation sent back to China, however, consisted not of missionaries but, Marco wrote, of himself, his father, and his uncle. Marco stayed for nearly two years. As conquerors in China, the Mongols trusted foreigners more than native Chinese did and willingly received Europeans. In fact, evidence suggests that an entire community of Venetian traders—women, men, and children—lived in the city of Yangzhou in the mid-fourteenth century.

Merchants paved the way for missionaries. Friars, preachers to the cities of Europe, became missionaries to new continents as well. In 1289, the pope made the Franciscan John of Monte Corvino his envoy to China. Preaching in India along the way, John arrived in China four or five years after setting out, converted one local ruler, and built a church. A few years later, now at Beijing, he boasted that he had converted six thousand people, constructed two churches, translated the New Testament and Psalms into the native language, and met with the khagan.

The long-term effect of the Mongols on the West was to open up new land routes to the East that helped bind the two halves of the known world together. Travel stories such as Marco Polo's stimulated others to seek out the fabulous riches—textiles, ginger, ceramics, copper—of China and other regions of the East. In a sense, the Mongols initiated the search for exotic goods and missionary opportunities that culminated in the European "discovery" of a new world, the Americas.

MAPPING THE WEST Europe, c. 1320
The empire, now called the Holy Roman Empire, still dominated the map of Europe in 1320, but the emperor himself had little power. Each principality—often each city—was ruled separately and independently. To the east, the Ottoman Turks were just beginning to make themselves felt. In the course of the next century they would disrupt the Mongol hegemony and become a great power.

Conclusion

The thirteenth century sought harmony but discovered how elusive it could be. Theoretically, the universal papacy and empire were supposed to work together; instead they clashed in bitter warfare, leaving the government of Germany to the princes and northern Italy to its communes. Theoretically, faith and reason were supposed to arrive at the same truths. In the hands of scholastics they sometimes did so, but not always. Theoretically, all Christians should practice the same rites and follow the teachings of the church. In practice, local enforcement determined which church laws took effect—and to

what extent. In addition, the quest for harmony was never able to bring together all the diverse peoples, ideas, and interests of thirteenth-century society. Far from integrating, Jews found themselves set apart from everyone else through legislation and visible markers. Heretics were pursued with zeal; there was no question here of unity.

The quest for harmony worked more surely in the arts. Artists and architects integrated sculpture, stone, and glass to depict religious themes and fill the light-infused space of Gothic churches. Musicians wove together disparate melodic and poetic lines into motets. Writers melded heroic and romantic themes with theological truths and mystical visions.

Political leaders also aimed at order and control: to increase their revenues, expand their territories, and enhance their prestige. The kings of England and France and the governments of northern and central Italian cities partially succeeded in achieving these goals. The king of Germany failed bitterly, and Germany remained fragmented until the nineteenth century. Within the new, compact governments, however, the quest for harmony was somewhat successful. Kings and representative institutions worked well together on the whole, and clergy and laymen came to feel that they were part of the same political entity, whether that entity was France or a German principality.

But the harmonies became discordant at the end of the thirteenth century. The balance between church and state achieved under St. Louis in France, for example, disintegrated into irreconcilable claims to power in the time of Pope Boniface and Philip the Fair. The carefully constructed tapestry of St. Thomas's *summae*, which wove together Aristotle's secular philosophy and divine Scripture, began to unravel in the teachings of John Duns Scotus. The eclectic Italian Gothic style, which gathered indigenous as well as northern elements, gave way to a new artistic style, that of Giotto, whose work would be the foundation of Renaissance art in the fourteenth century.

Suggested References

The Church's Mission

While historians continue to explore the traditional and important political figures behind the thirteenth-century church (Sayers), the most recent work looks at the impact of new church doctrine on the laity and the way the laity actively interpreted it (Bynum).

Bynum, Caroline Walker. *Holy Feast and Holy Fast: The Religious Significance of Food to Medieval Women.* 1987.

Fourth Lateran Council: http://abbey.apana.org.au/councils/ecum12.htm.

Partner, Peter. *The Lands of St. Peter: The Papal State in the Middle Ages and the Early Renaissance.* 1972.

Sayers, Jane. *Innocent III: Leader of Europe, 1198–1216.* 1994.

*Wood, Charles T. *Philip the Fair and Boniface VIII: State vs. Papacy.* 2nd ed. 1971.

*Primary sources.

Harmony of Heaven and Earth

While most studies of the art and thought of the period specialize in one or the other, the pioneering synthesis by Panofsky demonstrates that a wider view is possible. Duby attempts to place Gothic architecture in the context of the culture and society that produced it.

Amiens cathedral: http://www.learn.columbia.edu/MCAHweb/index-frame.html.

*Dante. *The Divine Comedy.* Many editions; recommended are translations by Mark Musa and John Ciardi and Robert Pinsky's translation of the *Inferno.*

Duby, Georges. *The Age of the Cathedrals: Art and Society, 980–1420.* Trans. Eleanor Levieux and Barbara Thompson. 1981.

Katzenellenbogen, Adolf. *The Sculptural Programs of Chartres Cathedral.* 1959.

Panofsky, Erwin. *Gothic Architecture and Scholasticism.* 1951.

Sargent, Steven D., ed. and trans. *On the Threshold of Exact Science: Selected Writings of Anneliese Maier on Late Medieval Natural Philosophy.* 1982.

Smart, Alastair. *The Dawn of Italian Painting, 1250–1400.* 1978.

Thomas Aquinas: http://www.newadvent.org/summa/.

The Politics of Control

Thirteenth-century states used to be seen as harbingers of modern ones, but the newest history suggests that this is anachronistic. Thus Abulafia argues that Frederick II followed models of medieval rulership, and O'Callaghan shows how different medieval representative institutions were from their modern counterparts. Only in the last ten or so years have historians studied the prelude to Columbus's voyages by looking at medieval precedents.

Abulafia, David. *Frederick II: A Medieval Emperor.* 1988.

Campbell, Mary B. *The Witness and the Other World: Exotic European Travel Writing, 400–1600.* 1989.

Fernández-Armesto, Felipe. *Before Columbus: Exploration and Colonization from the Mediterranean to the Atlantic, 1229–1492.* 1987.

*Joinville, Jean de, and Geoffroy de Villehardouin. *Chronicles of the Crusades.* Trans. M. R. B. Shaw. 1963.

Jordan, William Chester. *The French Monarchy and the Jews: From Philip Augustus to the Late Capetians.* 1989.

Morgan, David. *The Mongols.* 1986.

O'Callaghan, Joseph F. *The Cortes of Castille-Léon, 1188–1350.* 1989.

Phillips, J. R. S. *The Medieval Expansion of Europe.* 1988.

Richard, Jean. *Saint Louis: Crusader King of France.* Trans. Jean Birrell. 1992.

Strayer, Joseph R. *The Reign of Philip the Fair.* 1980.

Tandē p̄ stragem loim maximā luct̄ ieuinia et
p̄nas graues iṗ processionalr eunt̄ p̄ romā cum
uniuersa plebe et clero apparet angelus sanguino
lentū ensē inagina reponens sup̄ palacui magi᷑

The Crisis of Late Medieval Society

1320–1430

"IN THE YEAR OF OUR LORD 1349," so began the chronicle kept by the Nuremberg citizen Ulman Stromer, "the Jews resided in the middle of the square, and their houses lined its sides as well as a street behind where Our Lady's now stands. And the Jews were burned on the evening of St. Nicholas's as it has been described." These terse words belie the horror experienced by the Jewish community. Robbed of their belongings in an uprising, the Jews of Nuremberg were later rounded up by the city magistrates, and those who refused to convert to Christianity were burned at the stake. A new church dedicated to Our Lady went up on the site where their synagogue was razed.

Nuremberg in central Germany was but one of numerous sites of anti-Jewish furor in 1349. After decades of increasing control through religious and political institutions, the violence of 1349 represented the breakdown of authority in the face of widespread warfare, catastrophic losses of population, and unprecedented challenges to religious authority. The coming together of these political, demographic, and religious developments resulted in a general crisis of late medieval society.

The first crisis was a political one, centering on the conflict between the English and the French that came to be called the Hundred Years' War (1337–1453). The war not only laid waste to large areas of France but also pushed neighboring countries into the maelstrom of violence. High taxes and widespread devastation also led to popular revolts that shook political society.

In society at large, order gave way to chaos and violence. Groups of flagellants, who whipped themselves as a form of penance, roamed central

The Last Days of the Plague
In this scene from the Book of Hours *of the Duke de Berry, the burial of Roman victims of the plague takes place. The angel in heaven heralds God's mercy after his chastisement of sins. Books of Hours were prayer books for individual use. This scene is a reminder of the imminence of death for all Christians and the need to lead a pious life: sudden death does not spare even those in the holy city of Rome. The* Book of Hours of the Duke de Berry, *located in the Chateau de Chantilly, north of Paris, is the best-known text of its kind.* The Metropolitan Museum of Art, The Cloisters Collection, 1954. (54.1.1) Photograph © 1987 The Metropolitan Museum of Art (detail).

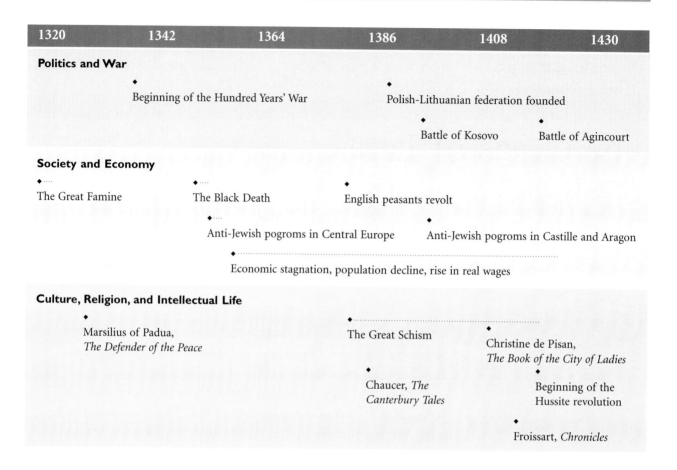

1320	1342	1364	1386	1408	1430

Politics and War

Beginning of the Hundred Years' War

Polish-Lithuanian federation founded

Battle of Kosovo

Battle of Agincourt

Society and Economy

The Great Famine

The Black Death

English peasants revolt

Anti-Jewish pogroms in Central Europe

Anti-Jewish pogroms in Castille and Aragon

Economic stagnation, population decline, rise in real wages

Culture, Religion, and Intellectual Life

Marsilius of Padua, *The Defender of the Peace*

The Great Schism

Christine de Pisan, *The Book of the City of Ladies*

Chaucer, *The Canterbury Tales*

Beginning of the Hussite revolution

Froissart, *Chronicles*

Europe. Jews were persecuted on a scale not surpassed until the twentieth century. Anti-Jewish persecutions, or pogroms, broke out in the Holy Roman Empire, southern France, Aragon, and Castile, ravaging the once-flourishing Jewish culture of the Middle Ages.

Both the flagellant movement and the anti-Semitic violence were manifestations of the general crisis. In the mid-fourteenth century a series of disasters—famine, climatic changes, and disease—scourged a society already weakened by overpopulation, economic stagnation, social conflicts, and war. The plague, or Black Death, wiped out at least a third of Europe's population. With recurring plagues and continuous warfare through the second half of the fourteenth century, population density would not reach thirteenth-century levels again until the sixteenth, and in many areas not until the eighteenth, century.

Dynastic conflicts, popular uprisings, and an external menace to the Christian nobility as the Muslim Ottoman Turks advanced steadily in southeastern Europe. All undermined political authority and threat-

ened the social order. During the later Middle Ages, the idea of universal Christendom that had fueled and sustained the Crusades receded, while loyalties to state, community, and social groups deepened. The papacy, the very symbol of Christian unity and authority, remained divided by the claims of rival popes and challenged by heretical movements.

The word *crisis* implies a turning point, a decisive moment, and during the hundred-plus years between 1320 and 1430, European civilization faced such a time. Departing from the path of expansion, it entered a period of uncertainty, disunity, and contraction.

❖ Political Crises across Europe

The crises of the fourteenth century affected political allegiances as well as social and religious tensions. Just as many people no longer accepted the church's dictates, so did citizens refuse to trust rulers to serve the ordinary person's best interests. The idea of Christian solidarity, always stronger in theory than in practice, dissolved in the face of national rivalries, urban and rural revolts, and the military resurgence of the Muslims. The conflict between the English and the French known as the Hundred Years' War destroyed the lives of countless thousands of noncombatants as well as soldiers. Commoners—town residents and peasants—challenged the political status quo, wanting a share of the power their rulers wielded over them or at least a voice in how they were governed. The Ottoman Turks battled Christian Europe in a bloody war to reclaim the land westerners had conquered in the Crusades. The political crises of the later Middle Ages shaped the pattern of conflicts for the next two hundred years.

The Changing Nature of Warfare

The nobility continued to dominate European society in the later Middle Ages, but their social and political roles were gradually but fundamentally transformed. Although the ranks of the nobility encompassed a wide range of people—from powerful magnates whose wealth rivaled that of kings to humble knights who lived much like peasants—two developments in the later Middle Ages affected all of them: an agrarian crisis and the changing nature of warfare.

Traditionally the nobles had been the warrior class and had lived on the profits from the land they owned. In the wake of the Black Death, their income from their land dwindled as food prices declined because of the dramatic drop in population. Forced to seek additional revenues, knights turned enthusiastically to war. Noblemen from many nations served willingly in foreign campaigns, forming units at their own expense, motivated solely by material gain. The English knight John Hawkwood put it best: "Do you not know that I live by war, and peace would be my undoing?" Captain of an army that sold its services to various Italian states vying for power, Hawkwood represented the new soldier: the mercenary who lived a life of violence and whose loyalty was given to the side that paid the most.

As if to compensate for the cynical reality of mercenary warfare, the European nobility emphasized the traditional knightly codes of behavior in an effort to bolster their authority. Romances associated with King Arthur and his round table of

chivalrous knights became a vogue, not only in reading but also in life. Edward III of England, for example, created the Order of the Garter in 1344 to revive the idea of chivalry. During truces in the Hundred Years' War, English and French knights jousted, glorifying mock combat according to the rules of chivalry. The French chronicler Jean Froissart noted that English and French knights scorned their German counterparts for ignoring the rules and rituals of war that masked the exercise of violence and power.

Yet chivalric combat waged by knights on horseback was quickly yielding to new military realities. By the last decades of the fourteenth century, cannons were becoming common in European warfare. New military technologies—firearms, siege equipment,

Siege Warfare
Siege warfare during the Hundred Years' War pitted cannons against fortifications. As cannons grew in caliber, walls became thicker, and protruding battlements and gun emplacements were added to provide counter-firepower. Late-medieval sieges were time-consuming affairs that often lasted for years. Bibliothèque Nationale de France.

and fortification, for example—undermined the nobility's preeminence as a fighting force. Well-equipped fighting forces counted more than valor and often determined the outcome of battles. Commoners, criminals, and adventurers often joined the ranks. To maintain their social eminence, the nobles were forced to become entrepreneurs as either military captains or estate managers. Many turned to state service to reinforce their social stations. Kings and princes welcomed such service. By appointing nobles to the royal household, as military commanders and councilors, kings and princes could further consolidate the power of emerging states.

The Hundred Years' War, 1337–1453

The Hundred Years' War was a protracted struggle in western Europe that involved the nobility of almost every nation. It was sparked by conflicting French and English interests in southwestern France. As part of the French royal policy of centralizing jurisdiction, Philip VI in 1337 confiscated the southwestern province of Aquitaine, which had been held by the English monarchs as a fief of the French crown. To recover his lands, Edward III of England in turn laid claim to the French throne.

The Combatants.   To rally Englishmen to their cause, English kings spread anti-French propaganda throughout their realm. Yeomen (freemen farmers) as well as the nobility rallied to serve their king, fired by patriotism and the lust for plunder. The spectacular victories won by various English kings at Crécy, Poitiers, and Agincourt further fueled popular fervor for war, as knights, yeomen, and adventurers returned home with booty, hostages, and tales of bloody slaughter and amorous conquests. War became its own engine. Mercenary companies came to replace levies of freemen archers in the English army. These companies remained in France during the long intervals of armistice between short, destructive campaigns punctuated by a few spectacular battles. For the English soldier, in time the lush, green, and fertile French countryside, with its wealthy towns and fabulous chateaux and its riches and beautiful women, represented the rewards of war far more promising than peaceful poverty.

Elaborate chivalric behavior, savage brutality, and unabashed profiteering permeated the fighting in the Hundred Years' War. Warfare in this era involved definite rules whose application depended on social status. English and French knights took one another prisoner and showed all the formal courtesy required by chivalry—but they slaughtered captured common soldiers like cattle. Overall the pattern of war was not pitched battles but a series of raids in which English fighters plundered cities and villages, causing terrible destruction. English knights financed their own campaigns, and war was expected to turn a profit, either in captured booty or in ransom paid to free noble prisoners of war.

Ruling over a more populous realm and commanding far larger armies, the French kings were, nevertheless, hindered in the war by the independent actions of their powerful barons. Against the accurate and deadly English freemen archers, the French knights met repeated defeats. Yet the French nobility despised their own peasants, fearing them and the urban middle classes more perhaps than they did their noble English adversaries. Their fears were not unfounded, for a deep chasm separated the warrior class from their social inferiors in medieval Europe.

The Course of the War.   Historians divide the Hundred Years' War into three periods: the first marked by English triumphs, the second in which France slowly gained the upper hand, and the third ending in the English expulsion from France (Map 13.1). In the first period (1338–1360), the English won several famous victories such as Crécy, in which the vastly outnumbered English knights and long-bowmen routed the French cavalry. In another victory at Poitiers (1356), Edward the Black Prince (heir to the English throne, named for his black armor) defeated a superior French army and captured the French king John and a host of important noblemen, whom they ransomed for hefty sums. Divided and demoralized, the French signed the peace treaty of Brétigny in 1360, ceding vast territories in the southwest to England.

The second phase of the war lasted from 1361 to 1413. In Charles V (r. 1364–1380) and his brother Philip the Bold (the duke of Burgundy), the French finally found energetic leaders who could resist the English. In 1372, aided by a Castilian fleet, a French force took La Rochelle, long an English stronghold in Gascony. In 1386, in the aftermath of a peasant revolt in England, the French even assembled a fleet to conquer England. Although unsuccessful in landing an

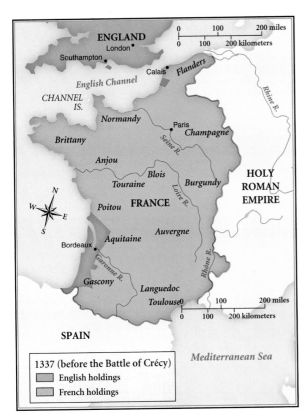

1337 (before the Battle of Crécy)
- English holdings
- French holdings

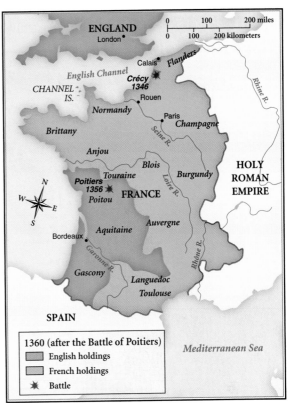

1360 (after the Battle of Poitiers)
- English holdings
- French holdings
- ✳ Battle

c.1429 (after the Siege of Orléans)
- English holdings
- French holdings
- Burgundian lands allied with England to 1435
- ✳ Battle
- ← Route taken by Joan of Arc, 1429–31

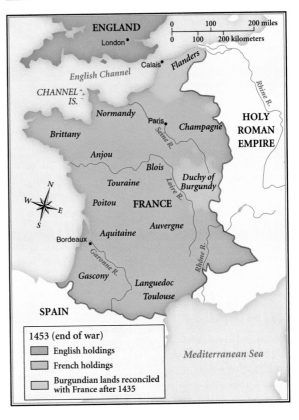

1453 (end of war)
- English holdings
- French holdings
- Burgundian lands reconciled with France after 1435

MAP 13.1 The Hundred Years' War, 1337–1453

As rulers of Aquitaine, English kings contested the French monarchy for the domination of France. Squeezed between England and Burgundy, the effective possession of the French kings was vastly reduced after the battle of Poitiers.

The Spoils of War
This illustration from Jean Froissart's Chronicles *depicts soldiers pillaging a conquered city. Looting in the Hundred Years' War became the main income for mercenary troops and contributed to the general misery of late medieval society. Food, furniture, even everyday household items were looted. War had come to feed on itself.*
Bibliothèque Nationale de France.

army, the French raided English ports into the early fifteenth century.

At the turn of the century a new set of players entered the political stage. In 1399, the English noble Henry Bolingbroke forced Richard II (grandson of Edward III) to abdicate. The coup made Bolingbroke Henry IV of England (r. 1399–1413), whose story was later made famous (and much distorted) by Shakespeare's plays. Factional strife poisoned French political unity. The struggle for power began in 1392 after Charles VI (r. 1380–1422), called the Mad King of France, suffered his first bout of insanity. Two factions then began to coalesce—one around John of Burgundy (the son of Philip the Bold) and the other around the duke of Orléans. In 1407, Burgundian agents assassinated the duke, whose followers, called the Armagnacs, sought vengeance and plunged France into civil war. When both parties appealed for English support in 1413, the young King Henry V (r. 1413–1422), who had just succeeded his father, Henry IV, launched a full-scale invasion of France.

The third phase of the war (1413–1453) began when Henry V crushed the French at Agincourt (1415). Unlike the earlier battles of Crécy and Poitiers, however, this isolated victory achieved little in the long run. Three parties now struggled for domination. Henry occupied Normandy and claimed the French throne; the dauphin (son of Charles VI and heir apparent to the French throne), later Charles VII of France (r. 1422–1461),* ruled central France with the support of the Armagnacs; and the duke of Burgundy held a vast territory in the northeast that included the Low Countries. Burgundy was thus able to broker war or peace by shifting support first to the English and then to the French. But even with Burgundian support the English could not establish firm control. In Normandy, a savage guerrilla war harassed the English army. Driven from their villages by pillaging and murdering soldiers, the Norman peasants retreated

---

*Although the dauphin was not crowned until 1429, he assumed the title Charles VII in 1422, following the death of his father.

into forests, formed armed bands, and attacked the English. The miseries of war inspired prophecies of miraculous salvation; among the predictions was the belief that a virgin would deliver France from the English invaders.

Joan of Arc.   At the court of the dauphin, in 1429, a sixteen-year-old peasant girl presented herself and her vision to save France. Born in a village in Lorraine, Joan of Arc, La Pucelle ("the Maid"), as she always referred to herself, grew up in a war-ravaged country that longed for divine deliverance. (See "Contrasting Views," page 458.) The young maid had first presented herself as God's messenger to the local noble, who was sufficiently impressed to equip Joan with horse, armor, and a retinue to send her to the dauphin's court. (According to her later testimony, Joan ran away from home when her father threatened to drown her because she refused an arranged marriage.) Joan of Arc's extraordinary appearance inspired the beleaguered French to trust in divine providence. In 1429, she accompanied the French army that laid a prolonged but successful siege on Orléans, was wounded, and showed great courage in battle. Upon her urging, the dauphin traveled deep into hostile Burgundian territory to be anointed King Charles VII of France at Reims cathedral, thus strengthening his legitimacy by following the traditional ritual of coronation.

Joan's fortunes declined after Reims. She promised to capture Paris, then in Anglo-Burgundian hands, and in 1430 attacked the city on the feast of the Virgin Mary, thus violating one of the holiest religious feast days. After the Anglo-Burgundian defenders drove back her troops, the French began to lose faith in the Maid. When the Burgundians captured her in 1430 during a minor skirmish, Charles and his forces did little to save her. Still, Joan was a powerful symbol, and the English were determined to undermine her claim to divine guidance. In a trial conducted by French theologians in Anglo-Burgundian service, Joan was accused of false prophecy, suspected of witchcraft because she wore male clothes and led armies, and tricked into recanting her prophetic mission. Almost immediately, however, she retracted her confessions, returned the female attire given her after an English soldier had raped her in prison, and reaffirmed her divine mission. The English then burned her at the stake as a relapsed heretic in 1431.

Joan the Warrior
Joan of Arc's career as a charismatic military leader was an extraordinary occurrence in fifteenth-century France. In this manuscript illumination, Joan, in full armor, directs French soldiers as they besiege the English at Orléans. The victory she gained here stunned the French people.
Erich Lessing/Art Resource, NY.

After Joan's death, the English position slowly crumbled when their alliance with the Burgundians fell apart in 1435. The duke of Burgundy recognized Charles VII as king of France, and Charles entered Paris in 1437. Skirmish by skirmish, the English were driven from French soil, retaining only the port of Calais when hostilities ceased in 1453. Two years later, the French church rescinded the 1431 verdict that had condemned Joan of Arc as a heretic. Some five centuries later, she was canonized and declared the patron saint of France.

Consequences of the War.   The Hundred Years' War profoundly altered the economic and political landscape of western Europe. It had three major impacts. First, the long years of warfare aggravated the demographic and economic crises of the fourteenth century. In addition to recurrent plagues, the population was further ravaged by pillage and warfare. Constant insecurity caused by marauding bands of soldiers prevented the cultivation of fields even in times of truce. In a region such as Normandy in France, perhaps up to half the population had perished by the end of the war, victims of disease, famine, and warfare.

Joan of Arc: Who Was "the Maid"?

Looming above the confused events and personalities of the Hundred Years' War, the figure of Joan of Arc gained eternal fame when she was canonized in 1921 and remembered as the heroine who saved France. But who was this slender young woman from the Lorraine? Calling herself "the Maid," Joan left home after she was instructed in a vision to present herself as God's messenger at the court of Charles, the dauphin of France (Document 1). Initial skepticism turned to adulation when in 1430 Joan led the French army that lifted the siege of Orléans and dealt the English a crushing blow. Either captivated by her piety and bravery or threatened by her power and actions, contemporaries labeled Joan everything from a divine symbol to a relapsed heretic (Documents 2–4). Her capture by the Burgundians, her year-long imprisonment, torture, interrogation, and subsequent execution generated documentation and ensured her immortality (Document 5).

1. Joan's Vision

Joan first spoke of her visions at length after her capture by her enemies, who were eager to prove that she was inspired by the devil. This document is the only information we have from Joan herself about her childhood. Notice three things about the document: first, the description of the vision refers to light and voice, a standard representation by medieval visionaries; second, Joan was instructed not to tell her father about her mission, which implied that she actually left home without his consent; and third, the reference to the siege of Orléans might have been an addition to her memory after the momentous events of her career. It was likely that she thought of her mission in a more general way of saving France.

When I was thirteen years old, I had a voice from God to help me govern my conduct. And the first time I was very fearful. And came this voice, about the hour of noon, in the summer-time, in my father's garden; I had not fasted on the eve preceding that day. I heard the voice on the right-hand side, towards the church; and rarely do I hear it without a brightness. This brightness comes from the same side as the voice is heard. It is usually a great light. When I came to France, often I heard this voice. . . . The voice was sent to me by God and, after I had thrice heard this voice, I knew that it was the voice of an angel. This voice has always guarded me well and I have always understood it clearly. . . .

It has taught me to conduct myself well, to go habitually to church. It told me that I, Joan, should come into France. . . . This voice told me, twice or thrice a week, that I, Joan, must go away and that I must come to France and that my father must know nothing of my leaving. The voice told me that I should go to France and I could not bear to stay where I was. The voice told me that I should raise the siege laid to the city of Orléans. . . . And me, I answered it that I was a poor girl who knew not how to ride nor lead in war.

Source: Régine Pernoud, ed., *Joan of Arc: By Herself and Her Witnesses* (Lanham, Md.: Scarborough House, 1994), 30.

2. Messenger of God?

When Joan appeared at the court of the dauphin, her reputation as the messenger of God had preceded her. The French court received her with a mixture of wonder, curiosity, and outright skepticism. The political and military situation looked so desperate that many had been hoping for a divine deliverance when Joan made her arrival in history. There was debate among the dauphin's counselors whether Joan should be taken seriously, however, and the dauphin referred the case to a panel of theologians to determine whether Joan's mission was divine in origin. The following account of Joan's first visit to the dauphin was recorded by Simon Charles, president of the Chamber of Accounts.

I know that, when Joan arrived in [the castle and town of] Chinon, there was deliberation in counsel to decide whether the King should hear her or not. To start with they sent to ask her why she was come and what she was asking for. She was unwilling to say anything without having spoken to the King, yet was she constrained by the King to say the reasons for her mission. She said that she had two [reasons] for which she had a mandate from the King of Heaven; one, to raise the siege of Orléans, the other to lead the King to Rheims for his [coronation]. Which being heard, some of the King's counsellors said that the King should on no account have faith in Joan, and the others that since she said that she was sent by God, and that she had something to say to the King, the King should at least hear her.

Source: Pernoud, 48–49.

3. Normal Girl?

This memoir, written by Marguerite la Touroulde, one of the women who lived with Joan and took care of her after the dauphin had accepted Joan's services to save France, testifies to Joan's ordinariness. The messenger of God appears in these words as a normal, devout young girl, whose only remarkable quality seems to be her physical and martial prowess.

"I did not see Joan until the time when the King returned from Rheims where he had been crowned. He came to the town of Bourges where the Queen was and me with her. . . . Joan was then brought to Bourges and, by command of the lord d'Albret, she was lodged in my house. . . . She was in my house for a period of three weeks, sleeping, drinking and eating, and almost every day I slept with Joan and I neither saw in her nor perceived anything of any kind of unquietness, but she behaved herself as an honest and Catholic woman, for she went very often to confession, willingly heard mass and often asked me to go to Matins. And at her instance I went, and took her with me several times.

"Sometimes we talked together and some said to Joan that doubtless she was not afraid to go into battle because she knew well that she would not be killed. She answered that she was no safer than any other combatant. And sometimes Joan told how she had been examined by the clerks and that she had answered them: 'In Our Lord's books there is more than in yours. . . .' Joan was very simple and ignorant and knew absolutely nothing, it seems to me, excepting in the matter of war. I remember that several women came to my house while Joan was staying there, and brought paternosters [rosary beads] and other objects of piety that she might touch them, which made her laugh and say to me, 'Touch them yourself, they will be as good from your touch as from mine.' She was open-handed in almsgiving and most willingly gave to the indigent and to the poor, saying that she had been sent for the consolation of the poor and the indigent.

"And several times I saw her at the bath and in the bath-houses, and so far as I was able to see, she was a virgin, and from all that I know she was all innocence, excepting in arms, for I saw her riding on horseback and bearing a lance as the best of soldiers would have done it, and at that the men-at-arms marvelled."

Source: Pernoud, 64–65.

4. Relapsed Heretic?

After her capture, Joan was interrogated for more than a year by a panel of theologians, who were determined to destroy her reputation. Headed by Pierre Cauchon, the judges cast doubt on the divine origins of Joan's visions, suggesting that they had come instead from the devil. They also accused her of disobedience to the church and of violating social and religious norms by dressing in man's clothing. Worn down by her long imprisonment and abandoned to her enemies, Joan recanted and admitted that the voices had not come from God. But after Joan was raped in jail by English soldiers, she retracted her confession, reverted to dressing in man's clothing, and reasserted her divine mission. This occasion provided the legal pretext for condemning Joan as a lapsed heretic. The following document recounts the long judgment condemning Joan.

Cauchon wasted no time in bringing Joan to trial for her "relapse." After the interrogation . . . , on May 28th, he summoned the principal assessors to meet on the 29th, and gave them a brief *exposé* of the state of her case: after the solemn preaching and admonitions addressed to her, Joan had renounced the error of her ways and signed an abjuration [retraction] with her own hand. . . . However, at the suggestion of the devil she had started saying again that her voices and spirits had come to her, and having rejected woman's clothes, had resumed the wearing of male attire. Which was why he was now asking the assessors to give their opinion on what should now be done.

The first asked to speak happened to be Master Nicolas de Venderès. . . . As may well be imagined, his opinion was clear: Joan must be held to be a heretic and without further delay handed over to the secular arm, "with a recommendation to be gentle with her." This was a conventional formula [employed by Inquisition courts] and everyone knew what it implied.

But Giles de Duremort, abbot of Fécamp, asked next to give his opinion, introduced a request which must have made Cauchon uneasy. "It seems to me," he said, "that she is a relapsed heretic and that the word of God should be preached to her; that the abjuration which was read to her shall be read to her again and explained; that done, the judges will have to declare her a heretic and abandon her to secular justice." . . .

Whereupon—we are still quoting the official proceedings—"Having heard the opinion of each one, we, the judges, thanked them and thereafter concluded that the said Joan be proceeded against as a relapsed heretic according to law and reason."

Source: Pernoud, 223–24.

5. Sacred Martyr?

Condemned to burn at the stake, Joan went to her death in 1431 clutching a crucifix and uttering the name of Christ. Her actions and demeanor moved many to remember the event. Their testimonies ten years later provided the evidence for judges to overturn her conviction. Her good name restored, Joan would live on in the memory of France as its greatest heroine. Pierre Cusquel, a stonemason from Orléans, offered this testimony.

"I heard say that Master Jean Tressard, secretary to the King of England, returning from Joan's execution afflicted and groaning, wept lamentably over what he had seen in that place and said indeed: 'We are all lost, for we have burnt a good and holy person,' and that he believed that her soul was in God's hands and that, when she was in the midst of the flames, she had still declaimed the name of the Lord Jesus. That was common repute and more or less all the people murmured that a great wrong and injustice had been done to Joan. . . . After Joan's death the English had the ashes gathered up and thrown into the Seine because they feared lest she escape or lest some say she had escaped."

Source: Pernoud, 233.

QUESTIONS FOR DEBATE

1. What was Joan's vision? Was her vision understood differently by the French king, by her inquisitors, and by herself during her trial?

2. How did her judges try to frame a charge against her during her captivity? Why?

3. What was the source of Joan's charisma? Why did she inspire such a wide range of responses?

Second, the war prevented a quick resolution of the crisis in spiritual authority. As we will see, the collapse of papal authority known as the Great Schism owed much to the fact that rival popes could call on the respective belligerents to support their own claim. Locked in combat, the French, English, and Burgundian rulers could not put aside their political differences to restore papal authority.

The third long-term consequence of the war was the changing political landscape of western Europe.

The necessity of mobilization strengthened the hand of the French monarchy. Under Charles VII a standing army was established to supplement the feudal noble levies, an army financed by increased taxation and expanded royal judicial claims. By 1500, the French monarchy would emerge as one of the leading powers of Europe, ready to battle Burgundy and the empire for the domination of Europe.

Burgundy also emerged as a strong power from the Hundred Years' War. By absorbing the Low

Countries, this French duchy was evolving into an independent state, a rich power situated between France and Germany and commanding the fabulous wealth of Flemish cities. The Burgundian dukes became rivals of French kings after about 1450 and established a brilliant court and civilization.

Defeated in war, the English monarchy suffered through decades of disunity and strife. Defeat abroad spread discontent at home. From the 1460s to 1485, England was torn by civil war—the War of the Roses between the red rose of Lancaster and the rival white rose of York. A deposed king (Henry VI), a short reign (Edward IV), and the murder of two princes by their uncle (Richard III) followed in quick succession in a series of conflicts that decimated the leading noble families of England. When Henry Tudor succeeded to the throne in 1485, England was exhausted from years of confusion. Henry managed to end the civil war and unite the houses of Lancaster and York, but only slowly did England begin to recover strength.

The heavy financial burden of warfare also destabilized the banking system. Default on war loans by the English king, Edward III, precipitated the collapse of several of the largest banks in Europe, all based in Italy. The political crisis of the Hundred Years' War thus had a direct impact on the economic crisis of the fourteenth century.

Popular Uprisings

English and French knights waged war at the expense of the common people. While French peasants and townsfolk were taxed, robbed, raped, and murdered by marauding bands of mercenaries, their English counterparts had to pay ever higher taxes to support their kings' wars. Widespread resentment fueled popular uprisings, which contributed to the general disintegration of political and social order. In 1358, a short but savage rebellion erupted in the area around Paris, shocking the nobility. And in 1381, a more widespread and broadly based revolt broke out in England.

Jacquerie Uprising in Paris, 1358. Historians have traditionally described the 1358 Jacquerie—named after the jacket (*jacque*) worn by serfs—as a "peasant fury," implying that it represented simply a spontaneous outburst of aimless violence. More recent research, however, reveals the complex social origins

of the movement. The revolt broke out after the English captured King John at the battle of Poitiers, when the estates of France (the representatives of the clergy, nobility, and the cities) met in Paris to discuss monarchical reform and national defense. Unhappy with the heavy war taxes and the incompetence of the warrior nobility, the townspeople, led by Étienne Marcel, the provost of the merchants of Paris, sought greater political influence. Through merchants' and artisans' guilds, the citizens and government of Paris now assumed a new political importance. In the absence of royal authority, the common people vied with the nobles for control of government, and a clash between peasants and nobles near Paris led to a massive uprising.

The rebels began to destroy manor houses and castles near Paris, massacring entire noble families in a savage class war. Contemporaries were astonished at the intensity and violence of the Jacquerie. The chronicler Jean Froissart, sympathetic to the nobility, reflected the views of the ruling class in

The English Peasant Uprising, 1381
In this manuscript illumination, depicting a much more orderly scene than ever must have been the reality, a host of rebellious peasants led by John Ball (on horseback) confronts troops gathered under the royal banners of England and St. George. Such confrontations, frequent in late-medieval and early modern Europe, always ended with the same result, as well-armed soldiers mowed down desperate village folk.
British Library, London/The Bridgeman Art Library.

describing the rebels as "small, dark, and very poorly armed." As for the violence, Froissart continued, "They thought that by such means they could destroy all the nobles and gentry in the world." Repression by nobles was even more savage, as thousands of rebels died in battles or were executed. In Paris the rebel leader Marcel was killed in factional strife, but urban rebellions continued until the fifteenth century.

English Peasant Revolt of 1381. In England, rural and urban discontent intensified as landlords, peasants, and workers pursued increasingly opposing interests. The trigger for outright rebellion was the imposition of a poll tax passed by Parliament in 1377 to raise money for the war against France, a war that peasants believed benefitted only the king and the nobility. Unlike traditional subsidies to the king, the poll tax was levied on everyone. In May 1381, a revolt broke out to protest the taxes. Rebels in Essex and Kent joined bands in London to confront the king. The famous couplet of the radical preacher John Ball, who was executed after the revolt, expresses the rebels' egalitarian, antinoble sentiment:

When Adam delved [dug] *and Eve span
Who was then a gentleman?*

Forced to address the rebels, young King Richard II agreed to abolish serfdom and impose a ceiling on land rent, concessions immediately rescinded after the rebels' defeat.

Unrest in Flanders. Popular uprisings also took place in the Low Countries, especially in the cities of Flanders, the most densely populated and urbanized region of Europe. For over a century, Flanders had been Europe's industrial and financial heartland, importing raw wool from England, manufacturing fine cloth in cities, and exporting woolen goods to all parts of Europe.

Because the region depended on trade for food and goods, Flanders was especially sensitive to the larger political and economic changes. Between 1323 and 1328, unrest spread from rural Flanders to Bruges and Ypres, as citizens refused to pay the tithe to the church or taxes to the count of Flanders. Later, the Hundred Years' War undermined the woolen industry as Edward III of England declared a trade embargo, thus halting shipments of raw ma-

terials to Flemish industries. Although Flanders was a French fief, weavers and other artisans opposed their count's pro-French policy as they depended on English wool. From 1338 to 1345, the citizens of the large industrial city of Ghent rebelled against their prince. In the tumultuous years 1377–1383, the townspeople of Ghent sought an alliance with the citizens of Paris, fielded an army to battle the count, and held out into the fifteenth century despite their disastrous defeat by the French army in 1382. Thus the urban insurrections in Flanders became part of the economic and political struggles of the Hundred Years' War.

Urban Insurrections in Italy. Revolts in Rome and Florence resulted in part from the long absence of the popes during the Avignon papacy. Factional violence between powerful noble clans in Rome fueled popular hatred of local magnates and provided the background for the dramatic episode of the Roman commune. The Florentine chronicler Giovanni Villani narrates that "on May 20, 1347 . . . a certain Cola di Rienzo had just returned to Rome from a mission on behalf of the Roman people to the court of the Pope, to beg him to come and live, with his court, in the see of St. Peter, as he should do." Although unsuccessful in his mission to Avignon, Rienzo so impressed the Romans with his speech that they proclaimed him "tribune of the people," a title harking back to the plebeians' representatives in the ancient Roman republic. "Certain of the Orsini and the Colonna," continues Villani, "as well as other nobles, fled from the city to their lands and castles to escape the fury of the tribune and the people." Inspired by his reading of ancient Roman history, Rienzo and his followers took advantage of the nobles' flight and tried to remake their city in the image of classical Roman republicanism. But like the revolts in Paris and Ghent, the Roman uprising (1347–1354) was suppressed by the nobility.

The pattern of social conflict behind these three failed urban revolts is best exemplified by the Ciompi uprising in Florence. Florence was one of the largest European cities in the fourteenth century and a center of banking and the woolen industry in southern Europe. There the large populations of woolworkers depended on the wool merchants, who controlled both the supply of raw material and the marketing of finished cloth. Unlike artisans in other trades, woolworkers were prohibited from forming their own guild and thus constituted a politically unrepresented wage-earning working class. As the wool industry declined because of falling demand, unemployment became an explosive social problem. During the summer of 1378, the lower classes, many of them woolworkers, rose against the regime, demanding a more egalitarian social order. A coalition of artisans and merchants, supported by woolworkers, demanded more equitable power sharing with the bankers and wealthy merchants who controlled city government. By midsummer, crowds thronged the streets, and woolworkers set fire to the palaces of the rich and demanded the right to form their own guild. The insurrection was subsequently called the Ciompi uprising, meaning "uprising by the little people." Alarmed by the radical turn of events, the guild artisans turned against their worker allies and defeated them in fierce street battles. The revolt ended with a restoration of the patrician regime, although Ciompi exiles continued to plot worker revolts into the 1380s.

The Ciompi rebellion, like the uprisings in Paris, Ghent, and Rome, signaled a pattern of change in late medieval Europe. Although they represented a continuation of the communal uprisings of the eleventh and twelfth centuries, which helped establish town governments in some parts of Europe, the primary causes in the fourteenth century were the disruptions of the Black Death and the subsequent economic depression. But as significant as their motivations was their failure. Urban revolts did not redraw the political map of Europe, nor did they significantly alter the distribution of power. Instead they were subsumed by larger political transformations from which the territorial states would emerge as the major political forces.

Fragmentation and Power in Central and Eastern Europe

While England and France struggled for domination in western Europe, the Holy Roman Empire, unified in name only, became an arena where princes and cities assumed more power in their own hands. This political fragmentation, together with a stronger orientation toward the Slavic lands of eastern Europe, signified a growing separation between central and western Europe (Map 13.2). Within the empire the four most significant developments were the shift of political focus from the south and west to the east, the changing balance of power between the emperor and the princes, the development of cities, and the rise of self-governing communes in the Alps.

Three of the five emperors in this period belonged to the House of Luxembourg: Charles IV (r. 1347–1378), Wenceslas (r. 1378–1400), and Sigismund (r. 1410–1437). Having obtained Bohemia by marriage, the Luxembourg dynasty based its power in the east, and Prague became the imperial capital. This move initiated a shift of power within the Holy Roman Empire, away from the Rhineland and Swabia toward east central Europe.

The Seven Electors
This miniature from a German manuscript in Koblenz shows the seven electors of the Holy Roman Empire in 1308. They were the archbishops of Cologne, Mainz, and Trier; the electors of the Palatinate, Saxony, and Brandenburg; and the king of Bohemia, identifiable through their coat of arms on the shields hanging above them. Hence the electors were composed of three clergymen and four secular princes.
Mary Evans Picture Library.

MAP 13.2 Central and Eastern Europe, c. 1400
Through the Holy Roman Empire and the Teutonic Knights, Germanic influence extended far into eastern Europe including Bohemia, Moravia, and the Baltic coast. The Polish-Lithuanian Commonwealth, united in 1386, and the Kingdom of Hungary were the other great powers in eastern Europe.

Except for a continuous involvement with northern Italy, theoretically a part of the Holy Roman Empire, German institutions became more closely allied with eastern rather than western Europe. For example, the Holy Roman Empire's first university, Charles University (named after its royal founder, Charles IV), was established in 1348 in Prague. Bohemians and Hungarians also began to exert more influence in imperial politics.

Another development that separated central from western Europe was the fragmentation of political authority in the empire at a time when French, English, and Castilian monarchs were consolidating their power. Charles IV's coronation as emperor in 1355 did not translate into more power at home. The Bohemian nobility refused to recognize his supreme authority, and the German princes secured from him

a constitutional guarantee for their own sovereignty. In 1356, Charles was forced to agree to the Golden Bull, a document that required the German king to be chosen by seven electors: the archbishops of Mainz, Cologne, and Trier and four princes, namely, the king of Bohemia, the elector of Saxony, the count of the Palatinate, and the margrave of Brandenburg. The imperial electoral college also guaranteed the existence of numerous local and regional power centers, a distinctive feature in German history that continued into the modern age.

Although no single German city rivaled Paris, London, Florence, or Ghent in population, its large number of cities made Germany the economic equal of northern Italy and the Low Countries. But rivalry among powerful princes prevented the urban communes from evolving into city republics like those in Italy. In 1388, for example, the count of Würt-temberg defeated the Swabian League of cities, formed in 1376. Nevertheless, the cities were at the forefront of economic growth. Nuremberg and Augsburg became centers of the north-south trade, linking Poland, Bohemia, and the German lands with the Mediterranean. In northern Germany the Hanseatic League, under the leadership of Lübeck, united the many towns trading between the Baltic and the North Sea. At its zenith in the fifteenth century, the Hanseatic fleet controlled the Baltic, and the league was a power to be reckoned with by kings and princes.

Another sign of political fragmentation was the growth of self-governing peasant and town communes in the high Alpine valleys that united in the Swiss Confederation. In 1291, the peasants of Uri, Schwyz, and Unterwalden had sworn a perpetual alliance against their oppressive Habsburg overlord. After defeating a Habsburg army in 1315, these free peasants took the name "Confederates" and developed a new alliance that would become Switzerland. In the process, the Swiss enshrined their freedom in the legend of William Tell, their national hero who was forced by a Habsburg official to prove his archery skills by shooting an apple placed on the head of his own son. This act so outraged the citizens that they rose up in arms against the Habsburg rule. By 1353, Lucerne, Zurich, and Bern had joined the confederation. The Swiss Confederation continued to acquire new members into the sixteenth century, defeating armies sent by different princes to undermine its liberties.

Growth of the Swiss Confederation to 1353

Also in the mid-fourteenth century, two large monarchies took shape in northeastern Europe—Poland and Lithuania. In the early twelfth century, Poland had splintered into petty duchies, and the Mongol invasion of the 1240s had caused frightful devastation. But recovery was under way by 1300, and unlike almost every other part of Europe, Poland experienced an era of demographic and economic expansion in the fourteenth century. Both Jewish and German settlers, for example, helped build thriving towns like Cracow. Monarchical consolidation followed. King Casimir III (r. 1333–1370) won recognition in most of the country's regions for his royal authority, embodied in comprehensive law codes. A problem that persisted throughout his reign, however, was conflict with the neighboring princes of Lithuania, Europe's last pagan rulers, who for centuries fiercely resisted Christianization by the German crusading order, the Teutonic Knights. After the Mongols overran Russia, Lithuania extended its rule southward, offering western Russian princes protection against Mongol and Muscovite rule. By the late fourteenth century, a vast Lithuanian principality had arisen, embracing modern Lithuania, Belarus, and Ukraine.

Casimir III died in 1370 without a son; the failure of a new dynasty to take hold opened the way for the unification of Poland and Lithuania. In 1386, the Lithuanian prince Jogailo accepted Roman Catholic baptism, married the young queen of Poland, and later assumed the Polish crown. Under the Jagiellonian dynasty, Poland and Lithuania kept separate legal systems. Catholicism and Polish culture prevailed among the principality's upper class, while most native Lithuanian village folk remained pagan for several centuries. With only a few interruptions, the Polish-Lithuanian federation would last for five centuries.

Multiethnic States on the Frontiers

While some Christian princes were battling one another within Christendom, others fought Muslim foes at the frontiers of Christian Europe. Two regions at opposite ends of the Mediterranean—Spain and the Ottoman Empire—were unusual in medieval Europe for their religious and ethnic diversity. As a result of the Spanish reconquista of the twelfth and thirteenth centuries, the Iberian Christian kingdoms contained large religious and ethnic minorities. In Castile, where historians estimate the population before the outbreak of the plague in 1348 at four to

Christian Territory in Iberia, c. 1350

five million, 7 percent of the inhabitants were Muslims or Jews. In Aragon, of the approximately 1 million people at midcentury, perhaps 3 to 4 percent belonged to these two religious minorities. In the Iberian peninsula, the Christian kingdoms consolidated their gains against Muslim Granada through internal colonization, bringing sizable minority populations into newly Christian regions. At the same time, the orthodox Byzantine Empire, hardly recovered from the Fourth Crusade, fought for survival against the Ottoman Turks. In the Balkans and Anatolia, the Ottomans created a multiethnic state, but one different from the model of the Hispanic kingdoms.

The Iberian Peninsula. In the mid-fourteenth century, the Iberian peninsula encompassed six areas: Portugal, Castile, Navarre, Aragon, and Catalonia—all Christian—and Muslim Granada. Among these territories, Castile and Aragon were the most important, both politically and economically. The Muslim population was concentrated in the south: from the Algarve in Portugal eastward across Andalusia to Murcia and Valencia. Initially, the Iberian Muslims (called Moors) could own property, practice their religion, and elect their own judges, but conditions worsened for them in the fifteenth century as fears of rebellions and religious prejudices intensified among Christians. As Christian conquerors and settlers advanced, most Muslims were driven out of the cities or confined to specific quarters. Many Muslims were captured and enslaved by Christian armies. These slaves worked in Christian households or on large estates called *latifundia*, which were granted by the Castilian kings to the crusading orders, the church, and powerful noble families. Slavery existed on a fairly large scale at both ends of the Mediterranean, where Christian and Muslim civilizations confronted one another: in Iberia, North Africa, Anatolia, and the Balkans.

Unlike the Muslims, Jews congregated exclusively in cities, where they practiced many urban professions. Prior to 1391, they encountered few social obstacles to advancement. Jewish physicians and tax collectors made up part of the administration of Castile, but the Christian populace resented their social prominence and wealth. Moreover, the religious fervor and sense of crisis in the later fourteenth century intensified the ever-present intolerance toward Jews. In June 1391, incited by the

sermons of the priest Fernandon Martínez, a mob attacked the Jewish community in Seville, plundering, burning, and killing all who refused baptism. The anti-Semitic violence spread to other cities in Andalusia, Castile, Valencia, Aragon, and Catalonia. Sometimes the authorities tried to protect the Jews, who were legally the king's property. In Barcelona the city government tried to suppress the mob, but the riot became a popular revolt that threatened the rich and the clergy. About half of the two hundred thousand Castilian Jews converted to Christianity to save themselves; another twenty-five thousand were murdered or fled to Portugal and Granada. The survivors were to face even more discrimination and violence in the fifteenth century.

The Ottoman and Byzantine Empires. The fourteenth century also saw a great power rise at the other end of the Mediterranean. Under Osman I (r. 1280–1324) and his son Orhan Gazi (r. 1324–1359), the Ottoman dynasty became a formidable force in Anatolia and the Balkans, where political disunity opened the door for Ottoman advances (Map 13.3). The Ottomans were one of several Turkish

MAP 13.3 Ottoman Expansion in the Fourteenth and Fifteenth Centuries
The Balkans were the major theater of expansion for the Ottoman Empire, whose conquests also included Egypt and the North African coast. The Byzantine Empire was long reduced to the city of Constantinople and surrounded by the Ottomans before its final fall in 1453.

Janissaries in the Ottoman Army
Literally "new infantry," Janissaries were recruited from among Christian boys raised by the sultan.
They were distinguished by their ornamental, high headgear and their use of firearms, which made
them a particularly effective component of the Ottoman forces. Here a squad of Janissaries is shown
on parade, with a model of a Turkish war galley.
Österreichische Nationalbibliothek.

tribal confederations in central Asia. As converts to Islam and as warriors, the Ottoman cavalry raided Byzantine territory in an Islamic *jihad,* or holy war.

Under Murat I (r. 1360–1389), the Ottomans reduced the Byzantine Empire to the city of Constantinople and the status of a vassal state. In 1364, Murat defeated a joint Hungarian-Serbian army at the Maritsa River, alerting Europe for the first time to the threat of an Islamic invasion. Pope Urban V called for a crusade, but the Christian kingdoms in the west were already fighting in the Hundred Years' War. In the Balkans the Ottomans skillfully exploited Christian disunity, playing Serbian, Albanian, Wallachian, Bulgarian, and Byzantine interests against one another. Moreover, Venice, Genoa, and Ragusa each pursued separate commercial interests. Thus an Ottoman army allied not only with the Bulgarians but even with some Serbian princes won the battle of Kosovo (1389), destroying the last orga-

nized Christian resistance south of the Danube. The Ottomans secured control of southeastern Europe after 1396, when at Nicopolis they crushed a crusading army summoned by Pope Boniface IX.

The Ottoman invasion was more than a continuation of the struggle between Christendom and Islam. The battle for territory transcended the boundaries of faith. Christian princes also served the Ottoman Empire as vassals to the sultan. The Janissaries, Christian slave children raised by the sultan as Muslims, constituted the fundamental backbone of the Ottoman army. They formed a service class, the *devshirme,* which was both dependent on and loyal to the ruler.

At the sultan's court, Christian women were prominent in the harem; thus many Ottoman princes had Greek or Serbian mothers. In addition to the Janissaries, Christian princes and converts to Islam served in the emerging Ottoman administration. In areas conquered, existing religious and social structures remained intact when local people accepted Ottoman overlordship and paid taxes. Only in areas of persistent resistance did the Ottomans drive out or massacre the inhabitants, settling Turkish tribes in their place. A distinctive pattern of Balkan history was thus established at the beginning of the Ottoman conquest: the extreme diversity of ethnic and religious communities were woven together into the fabric of an efficient central state.

By the mid-fourteenth century, the territory of the Byzantine Empire consisted of only Constantinople, Thessalonika, and a narrow strip of land in modern-day Greece. During the fourteenth century, the Black Death, three civil wars between rivals to the throne, and numerous Ottoman incursions devastated Byzantine land and population. Constantinople was saved in 1402 from a five-year Ottoman siege only when Mongol invaders crushed another Ottoman army near Ankara in Anatolia. Although the empire's fortunes declined, Byzantium experienced a religious and cultural ferment, as the elites compensated for their loss of power in a search for past glory. The majority asserted the superiority of the Greek orthodox faith and opposed the reunion of the Roman and Greek churches, the political price for western European military aid. Many adhered to tradition, attacking any departures from ancient literary models and Byzantine institutions. A handful, such as the scholar George Gemistos (1353–1452), abandoned Christianity and embraced Platonic philosophy. Gemistos even changed his name (meaning "full" in Greek) to Plethon, its classical equivalent. The scholar Manuel Chrysoloras became professor of Greek in Florence in 1397, thus establishing the study of ancient Greece in western Europe. This revival of interest in Greek antiquity would eventually blossom into the broad cultural movement known as the Renaissance.

❖ The Plague and Society

Confronted with the rise of the Muslim Ottoman Empire to the east, Latin Christendom faced internally a series of crises that wrought havoc on its population and economy. In the fifty years after 1348, Europe lost one-third of its population to repeated outbreaks of the bubonic plague, which originated in central Asia and inflicted epidemic outbreaks in

China and the Middle East before it reached Europe. A healthy population could have resisted the plague. But Europeans were far from healthy: because food production failed to keep up with the great population increase of the thirteenth century, they had been suffering from famines and hunger for two generations before the first outbreak of the plague. In the face of massive deaths, a new climate of fear settled on the landscape. Some people tried to avert the "scourge of God" in rituals of religious fanaticism; others searched out scapegoats, killing Jews and burning synagogues.

Beyond these immediate reactions of fear, the demographic crisis also had important consequences for the economy. The catastrophic reduction in population caused falling demands for food and goods, leading to economic contraction, as farms and settlements were abandoned. Further symptoms of this social and economic crisis were social unrest, labor strife, rising wages, and falling investments. A mood of uncertainty prevailed in business, and women were excluded more and more from the urban economy.

Rise and Spread of the Plague

Well before the plague struck, European economic growth had slowed and then stopped. By 1300, the economy could no longer support Europe's swollen population. Having cleared forests and drained swamps, the peasant masses now divided their plots into ever smaller parcels and farmed marginal lands; their income and the quality of their diet eroded. In the great urban centers, where thousands depended on steady employment and cheap bread, a bad harvest, always followed by sharply rising food prices, meant hunger and eventual famine. A cooling of the European climate also contributed to the crisis in the food supply. Modern studies of tree rings indicate that fourteenth-century Europe entered a colder period, with a succession of severe winters beginning in 1315. The extreme cold upset an ecological system already overtaxed by human civilization. Crop failures were widespread. In many cities of northwestern Europe, the price of bread tripled in a month, and thousands starved to death. Some Flemish cities, for example, lost 10 percent of their population. But the Great Famine of 1315–1317 was only the first in a series of catastrophes confronting the overpopulated and undernourished society of fourteenth-century Europe. In midcentury death, in the form of an epidemic, mowed down masses of weakened bodies.

From its breeding ground in central Asia, the bubonic plague passed eastward into China, where it decimated the population and wiped out the remnants of the tiny Italian merchant community in Yangzhou. Bacteria-carrying fleas, living on black rats, transmitted the disease. They traveled back to Europe alongside valuable cargoes of silk, porcelain, and spices. In 1347, the Genoese colony in Caffa in the Crimea contracted the plague from the Mongols.

Fleeing by ship in a desperate but futile attempt to escape the disease, the Genoese in turn communicated the plague to other Mediterranean seaports. By January 1348, the plague had infected Sicily, Sardinia, Corsica, and Marseilles. Six months later the plague had spread to Aragon, all of Italy, the Balkans, and most of France. The disease then crept northward to Germany, England, and Scandinavia, reaching the Russian city of Novgorod in 1350 (Map 13.4).

Nothing like the Black Death, as this epidemic came to be called, had struck Europe since the great plague of the sixth century. The Italian writer

MAP 13.4 Advance of the Plague, 1347–1350
The gradual but deadly spread of the plague followed the roads and rivers of Europe. Note the earlier transmission by sea from the Crimea to the ports of the Mediterranean before the general spread to northern Europe.

Giovanni Boccaccio (1313–1375) reported the plague

first betrayed itself by the emergence of certain tumors in the groin or the armpits, some of which grew as large as a common apple, others as an egg . . . . From the two said parts of the body this . . . began to propagate and spread itself in all directions indifferently; after which the form of the malady began to change, black spots or livid making their appearance in many cases on the arm or the thigh or elsewhere, now few and large, now minute and numerous.

Inhabitants of cities, where crowding and filth increased the chances of contagion, died in massive numbers. Florence lost almost two-thirds of its population of ninety thousand; Siena lost half its people. Paris, the largest city of western Europe, came off relatively well, losing only a quarter of its two hundred thousand inhabitants. Most cities the plague visited on its deadly journey lost roughly half their population in less than a year. Rural areas seem to have suffered fewer deaths, but regional differences were pronounced. (See "Taking Measure," below.)

Helplessness and incomprehension worsened the terror wrought by the plague. The Black Death was not particular: old and young, poor and rich were equally affected, although the wealthy had a better chance of avoiding the disease if they escaped to their country estates before the epidemic hit their city. Medical knowledge of the time could not explain the plague's causes. The physicians at the University of Paris blamed the calamity on the stars. In a report prepared for King Philip VI of France in 1348, the professors of medicine described a conjunction of Saturn, Mars, and Jupiter in the house of Aquarius in 1345, resulting in widespread death and pestilence on earth. Various treatments were used in an attempt to combat the plague, ranging from bloodletting, a traditional cure to balance the body's four humors, to the commonsense remedy of lying quietly in bed and the desperate suggestion of breathing in the vapors of latrines. Many people believed that poisoned air caused the disease, and upon hearing of an outbreak, they walled in their neighbors, hoping in vain to contain the epidemic.

The devastation of 1348 was only the beginning. The plague cut down Europeans repeatedly. Further outbreaks occurred in 1361, 1368–1369, 1371, 1375, 1390, and 1405; they continued, with longer dormant intervals, into the eighteenth century. Together with wars, plagues caused a significant long-term decrease in population. Although

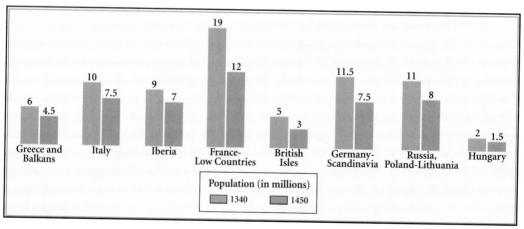

TAKING MEASURE Population Losses and the Plague

The bar chart represents dramatically the impact of the Black Death and the recurrent plagues between 1340 and 1450. More than a century after the Black Death, none of the regions of Europe had made up for the losses of population. The population of 1450 stood at about 75–80 percent of the pre-plague population. The hardest hit areas were France and the Low Countries, which also suffered from the devastations of the Hundred Years' War.

From Carlo M. Cipolla, ed., *Fontana Economic History of Europe: The Middle Ages.* (Great Britain: Collins/Fontana Books, 1974), 36.

general figures are unavailable, detailed local studies convey the magnitude of the destruction wreaked by the Black Death and war. In eastern Normandy, for example, the population in 1368 was only 42 percent of its height in 1314; and it declined still further in the fifteenth century.

Responses to the Plague: Flagellants, Preachers, and Jews

Some believed the plague was God's way of chastising a sinful world and sought to save themselves by repenting their sins. In 1349, bands of men and women wearing tattered clothes, marching in pairs, carrying flags, and following their own leaders appeared in southern Germany. When they reached a town or village, they visited the local church and, to the great astonishment of the congregation and the alarm of the clergy, sang hymns while publicly whipping themselves, according to strict rituals, until blood flowed. The flagellants, as they soon came to be called, cried out to God for mercy and called upon the congregation to repent their sins.

From southern Germany the flagellants moved throughout the Holy Roman Empire. In groups of several dozen to many hundred, they traveled and attracted great excitement. The flagellants' flamboyant piety moved many laypeople, but most of the clergy distrusted a lay movement that did not originate within the church hierarchy. At the inception of the movement, the flagellants recruited only from respectable social groups, such as artisans and merchants. Converts who joined the wandering bands, however, often came from the margins of society, and discipline began to break down. In 1350, the church declared the flagellants heretical and suppressed them.

In some communities the religious fervor aroused by the flagellants spawned violence against Jews. From 1348 to 1350, anti-Semitic persecutions, beginning in southern France and spreading through Savoy to the Holy Roman Empire, destroyed many Jewish communities in central and western Europe. Sometimes the clergy incited the attacks against the Jews, calling them Christ-killers, accusing them of poisoning wells and kidnapping and ritually slaughtering Christian children, and charging them with stealing and desecrating the host (the communion wafer that Catholics believed became the body of Christ during Mass). In towns throughout Europe,

Flagellant Procession
Flagellants hoping to stave off the Black Death are depicted in this German manuscript from Munich. The text describes their ritual of self-inflicted tortures during processions of penance, when they would call out loudly for the forgiveness of sins.
Bayerische Staatsbibliothek, Munich.

economic resentment fueled anti-Semitism as those in debt turned on creditors, often Jews who became rich from the commercial revolution of the thirteenth century. Perhaps most cynical were the nobility of Alsace, heavily indebted to Jewish bankers, who sanctioned the murder of Jews to avoid repaying money they had borrowed.

Many anti-Semitic incidents were spontaneous, with mobs plundering Jewish quarters and killing anyone who refused baptism. Authorities seeking a focus for the widespread anger and fear orchestrated some of the violence. Relying on chronicles, historians have long linked the arrival of the Black Death with anti-Jewish violence. More recent historical research shows that in some cities the anti-Semitic violence actually preceded the epidemic. This revised chronology of events demonstrates official

The Burning of Jews
While knights and noblewomen watch, an executioner carries more firewood to the pyre of Jews. There were many incidents of anti-Jewish violence in the fourteenth century because Christians suspected Jews of desecrating the Eucharist and of kidnapping and murdering Christian children. This religious violence, arising out of the confrontation between Christianity and Judaism, had the opposite effect to that intended by Christians. Instead of converting, most Jews honored their martyrs and felt less incentive to accept the faith of their oppressors.
Bibliothèque Royale Albert 1er, Brussels.

complicity and even careful premeditation in the destruction of some Jewish communities. For example, the magistrates of Nuremberg obtained approval from Emperor Charles IV before organizing the 1349 persecution directed by the city government. Thousands of German Jews were slaughtered. Many fled to Poland, where the incidence of plague was low and where the authorities welcomed Jews as productive taxpayers. In western and central Europe, however, the persecutions destroyed the financial power of the Jews.

Consequences of the Plague

Although the Black Death took a horrible human toll, the disaster actually profited some people. In an overpopulated society with limited resources, massive death opened the ranks for advancement. For example, after 1350, landlords had difficulty acquiring new tenant farmers without making concessions in land contracts; fewer priests now competed for the same number of benefices (ecclesiastical offices funded by an endowment), and workers received much higher wages because the supply of laborers had plummeted. The Black Death and the resulting decline in urban population meant a lower demand for grain relative to the supply and thus a drop in cereal prices. All across Europe noble landlords, whose revenues dropped as prices dropped, had to adjust to these new circumstances. Some revived seigneurial demands for labor services; others looked to their central government for legislation to regulate wages; and still others granted favorable terms to peasant proprietors, often after bloody peasant revolts. Many noblemen lost a portion of their wealth and a measure of their autonomy and political influence. Consequently, European nobles became more dependent on their monarchs and on war to supplement their incomes and enhance their power.

For the peasantry and the urban working population, the higher wages generally meant an improvement in living standards. To compensate for the lower demand and price for grain, many peasants and landlords turned to stock breeding and grape and barley cultivation. As European agriculture diversified, peasants and artisans consumed more beer, wine, meat, cheese, and vegetables, a better and more varied diet than their thirteenth-century forebears had eaten. The reduced cereal prices also stimulated sheep raising in place of farming, so that a portion of the settled population, especially in the English Midlands and in Castile, became migratory.

Because of the shrinking population and decreased demand for food, cultivating marginal fields was no longer profitable, and many settlements were simply abandoned. By 1450, for example, some 450 large English villages and many smaller hamlets had disappeared. In central Europe east of the Elbe River, where German peasants had migrated, large tracts of cultivated land reverted to forest. Estimates suggest that some 80 percent of all villages in parts of Thuringia (Germany) vanished.

Also as a result of the plague, production shifted from manufacturing for a mass market to a highly lucrative, if small, luxury market. The drastic loss in urban population had reduced the demand for such mass-manufactured goods as cloth. Fewer people now possessed proportionately greater concentrations of wealth. In the southern French city of Albi, for example, the proportion of citizens possessing more than 100 livres in per capita income doubled between 1343 and 1357, while the number of poor people, those with less than 10 livres, declined by half.

Faced with the possibility of imminent and untimely death, some of the urban populace sought immediate gratification. The Florentine Matteo Villani described the newfound desire for luxury in his native city in 1351. "The common people . . . wanted the dearest and most delicate foods . . . while children and common women clad themselves in all the fair and costly garments of the illustrious who had died." Those with means increased their consumption of luxuries: silk clothing, hats, doublets (snug-fitting men's jackets), and boots from Italy; expensive jewelry and spices from Asia became fashionable in northwestern Europe. Whereas agricultural prices continued to decline, prices of manufactured goods, particularly luxury items, remained constant and even rose as demand for them outstripped supply.

The long-term consequences of this new consumption pattern spelled the end for the traditional

Deserted Fields

Aerial photography has revealed the outlines of cultivated fields and old settlements in many areas of northern Europe invisible from the ground. These are the signs marking the expansion and contraction of human settlement and cultivation in fourteenth-century Europe before and after the Black Death. As the plague swept through the land, and as whole populations of smaller settlements died off, villages were deserted and cultivated fields reverted back to nature. In England, for example, of about 900 medieval churches, more than 225 were abandoned and nearly 250 were in ruins in the later half of the fourteenth century. This photograph shows the former cultivated fields of the village of Tusmore, Oxfordshire, whose inhabitants all died of the plague. Copyright reserved Cambridge University, Collection of Air Photographs.

woolen industry that had produced for a mass market. Diminishing demand for wool caused hardships for woolworkers, and social and political unrest shook many older industrial centers dependent on the cloth industry. In the Flemish clothing center of Ypres, for example, production figures fell from a high of ninety thousand pieces of cloth in 1320 to fewer than twenty-five thousand by 1390. In Ghent, where 44 percent of all households were woolworkers and where some 60 percent of the working population depended on the textile industry, the woolen market's slump meant constant labor unrest.

Much more difficult to measure was the sense of economic insecurity. One trend, however, seemed clear: the increasingly restrictive labor market for women in the urban economy in this age of crisis. In the German city of Cologne, for example, more and more artisan guilds excluded women from their ranks. By the late fifteenth century the independent women's guilds had become a relic of the past. Everywhere, fathers favored sons and sons-in-law to succeed them in their crafts. Daughters and widows resisted this patriarchal regime in the urban economy. They were most successful in industries with the least regulations, such as in beer-brewing—where in Munich, for example, women held productive positions in this climate of economic recession.

❖ Challenges to Spiritual Authority

The crises of confidence and control that swept late medieval Europe extended to the papacy, the very symbol of Christian unity and authority. The popes' claim to supremacy in Christendom had never been unchallenged. Kings and princes contested the popes' dual authority as spiritual and temporal rulers; friars and preachers questioned their wealth and power; theologians doubted the monarchical pretensions of popes over general church councils; heretics and dissenters denied outright their claims of apostolic succession. While some voices opposed papal authority within the church, other movements offered alternative visions and institutions for the faithful's guidance and salvation.

Papal Monarchy and Its Critics

Papal government continued to grow even after the papal residence moved to Avignon in 1309. In the fourteenth century, the papacy's government and institutions were more sophisticated than those of secular states. A succession of popes, all lawyers by training, concentrated on consolidating the financial and legal powers of the church, mainly through appointments and taxes. Claiming the right to assign all benefices, the popes gradually secured authority over the clergy throughout western and central Europe. Under the skillful guidance of John XXII (r. 1316–1334), papal rights increased incrementally without causing much protest. By 1350, the popes had secured the right to appoint all ma-

jor benefices and many minor ones. To gain these lucrative positions, potential candidates often made gifts to the papal court. The imposition of papal taxes on all benefice holders developed from taxation to finance the Crusades. Out of these precedents the papacy instituted a regular system of papal taxation that produced the money it needed to consolidate papal government.

Papal government, the curia, consisted of the pope's personal household, the College of Cardinals, and the church's financial and judicial apparatus. Combining elements of monarchy and oligarchy, the curia developed a bureaucracy that paralleled the organization of secular government. The pope's relatives often played a major role in his household; many popes came from extended noble lineages, and they often gave their family members preferential treatment.

After the pope, the cardinals, as a collective body, were the most elevated entity in the church. Like great nobles in royal courts, the cardinals, many of them nobles themselves, advised and aided the pope. They maintained their own households, employing scores of scribes, servants, and retainers. Most posts in the papal bureaucracy went to clerics with legal training, thus accentuating the juristic and administrative character of the highest spiritual authority in Christendom. During the fourteenth and fifteenth centuries, the papal army also grew, as the popes sought to restore and control the Papal States in Italy.

This growing papal monarchy was sharply criticized by members of the mendicant orders, who denounced the papal pretension to worldly power and wealth. William of Ockham (c. 1285–1349), an English Franciscan who was one of the most eminent theologians of his age, believed that church power derived from the congregation of the faithful, both laity and clergy, not from the pope or the church council. Rejecting the confident synthesis of Christian doctrine and Aristotelian philosophy by Thomas Aquinas, Ockham believed that universal concepts had no reality in nature but instead existed only as mere representations, names in the mind—a philosophy that came to be called *nominalism*. Perceiving and analyzing such concepts as "man" or "papal infallibility" offered no assurance that the concepts expressed truth. Observation and human reason were limited as the means to understand the universe and to know God. Consequently, God might be capricious, contradictory, or many rather than one. Denying the possibility of an evil or erratic God, Ockham emphasized the covenant between God and his faithful. God promises to act consistently—for example, to reward virtue and punish vice. Ockham stressed simplicity in his explanations of universal concepts. His insistence that shorter explanations were superior to wordy ones became known as "Ockham's razor." Imprisoned by Pope John XXII for heresy, Ockham escaped in 1328 and found refuge with Emperor Louis of Bavaria.

Another antipapal refugee at the imperial court was Marsilius of Padua, a citizen of an Italian commune, a physician and lawyer by training, and rector of the University of Paris. Marsilius attacked the very basis of papal power in *The Defender of the Peace* (1324). The true church, Marsilius argued, was constituted by the people, who had the right to select the head of the church, either through the body of the faithful or through a "human legislator." Papal power, Marsilius asserted, was the result of historical usurpation, and its exercise represented tyranny. In 1327, John XXII, the living target of the treatise, decreed the work heretical.

The Great Schism, 1378–1417

By the second half of the fourteenth century, the Avignon papacy had taken on a definitive French character. All five popes elected between 1305 and 1378 were natives of southern France, as were many of the cardinals and most of the curia. Moreover, French parishes provided half of the papacy's income. Subjected to pressure from the French monarchy and turning increasingly secular in its opulence and splendor, the papacy was lambasted by the Italian poet Francesco Petrarch as being "in Babylonian Captivity," like the Jews of ancient Israel who were exiled by their Babylonian conquerors. Nonetheless, Gregory XI, elected pope in 1371, was determined to return to Rome, where he expected to exert greater moral force to organize a crusade against the Muslim Ottomans. Before he could carry out his plans, however, Florence declared war against the Papal States in 1375, and Gregory hastened to Rome to prevent the collapse of his territorial power in Italy.

When Gregory died in 1378, sixteen cardinals—one Spanish, four Italian, and eleven French—met in Rome to elect the new pope. Although many in the curia were homesick for Avignon, the Roman people, determined to keep the papacy and its revenues in Rome, clamored for the election of a Roman. An unruly crowd rioted outside the conclave, drowning out the cardinals' discussions. Fearing for their lives, the cardinals elected the archbishop of Bari, an Italian, who took the title Urban VI. If the cardinals thought they had elected a weak man who would both do their bidding and satisfy the Romans, they were wrong: Urban immediately tried to curb the cardinals' power. In response, thirteen cardinals elected another pope, Clement VII, and returned to Avignon.

Thus began the Great Schism, which was perpetuated by political divisions in Europe (Map 13.5). Charles V of France, who did not want the papacy to return to Rome, immediately recognized Clement, his cousin, as did the rulers of Sicily, Scotland, Castile, Aragon, Navarre, Portugal, Ireland, and Savoy. An enemy of Charles V, Richard II of England, professed allegiance to Urban and was followed by the rulers of Flanders, Poland, Hungary, most of the empire, and central and northern Italy. Faithful Christians were equally divided in their loyalties. Even the greatest mystic of the age—Catherine of Siena (1347–1380), who told of her mystical unions with God and spiritual ecstasies in more than 350 letters and was later canonized a saint—found herself forced to take sides. Catherine supported Urban. But another holy man, Vincent Ferrer (1350–1419), a popular Dominican preacher, supported Clement. All Christians theoretically found themselves deprived of the means of salvation, as bans from Rome and Avignon each placed a part of Christian Europe under interdict, or censure from participation in most sacraments and from Christian burial. Because neither pope would step down willingly, the leading intellectuals in the church tried to end the schism. Success would elude them for nearly forty years.

The Conciliar Movement

According to canon law, only a pope could summon a general council of the church, a sort of parliament of all Christians. But given the state of confusion in Christendom, many intellectuals argued that the crisis justified calling a general council to represent the body of the faithful, over and against the head of the church. Jean Gerson, chancellor of the

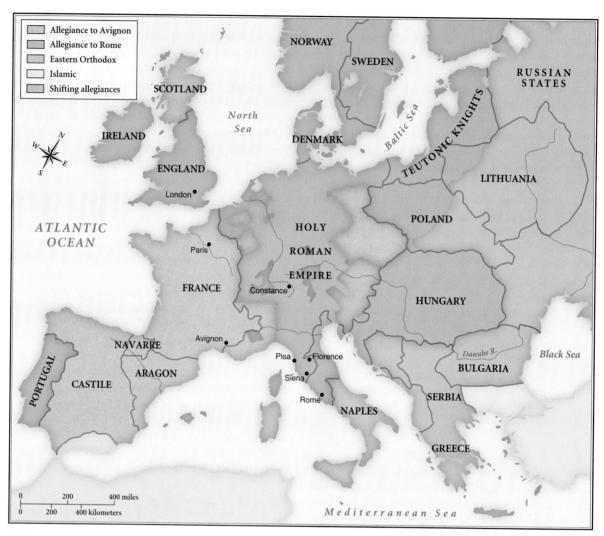

MAP 13.5 The Great Schism, 1378–1417
The allegiances to Roman and Avignon popes followed the political divisions between the European monarchs. The Great Schism weakened the Latin West during a period of Islamic expansion through the Ottoman Empire.

University of Paris, asserted that "the pope can be removed by a general council celebrated without his consent and against his will." He justified his claim by reasoning that "normally a council is not legally . . . celebrated without papal calling. . . . But, as in grammar and in morals, general rules have exceptions. . . . Because of these exceptions a superior law has been ordained to interpret the law."

The first attempt to resolve the question of church authority came in 1409, at the Council of Pisa, attended by cardinals who had defected from the two popes. The council asserted its supremacy by declaring both popes deposed and electing a new

pontiff, Alexander V. When the popes at Rome and Avignon refused to yield to the authority of the council, Christian Europe found itself in the embarrassing position of choosing among three popes. Pressure to hold another council then came from central Europe, where a new heretical movement, ultimately known as Hussitism, undermined orthodoxy from Bohemia to central Germany. Threatened politically by challenges to church authority, Emperor Sigismund pressed Pope John XXIII, the successor to Alexander (who had died ten months after being elected), to convene a church council at Constance in 1414.

The cardinals, bishops, and theologians assembled in Constance felt compelled to combat heresy, heal the schism, and reform the church. They ordered Jan Hus, the Prague professor and inspiration behind the Hussite movement, burned at the stake in spite of an imperial safe conduct he had been promised, but this act failed to suppress dissent. They deposed John XXIII, the "Pisan pope," because of tyrannical behavior, condemning him as an antipope. The Roman pope, Gregory XII, accepted the council's authority and resigned in 1415 (having been elected in 1406). At its closing in 1417, the council also deposed Benedict XIII (Clement's successor), the "Spanish mule," who refused to abdicate the Avignon papacy and lived out his life in a fortress in Spain, still regarding himself as pope and surrounded by his own curia. The rest of Christendom, however, hailed Martin V, the council's appointment, as the new pope, thus ending the Great Schism. The council had taken a stand against heresy and had achieved unity under one pope.

Dissenters and Heretics

Religious conflict in the later Middle Ages took a variety of forms. The papacy struggled with its critics within the church but found religious dissension outside the church even more threatening.

Free Spirits, Beguines, and Beghards. One movement of dissent, the Free Spirits, did not oppose the pope, yet the church still labeled them heretics. The Free Spirits, found mostly in northern Europe, practiced an extreme form of mysticism. They asserted that humans and God were of the same essence and that individual believers could attain salvation, even sanctity, without the church and its sacraments. In the fourteenth century, the Free Spirits found converts among the Beguines, pious laywomen who lived together, and the Beghards, men who did not belong to a particular religious order but who led pious lives and begged for their sustenance. Living in community houses (*beguinages*), the Beguines imitated the convent lives of nuns but did not submit to clerical control. First prevalent in northern Europe, beguinages sprang up rapidly in the Low Countries and the Rhineland, regions of heavy urbanization. This essentially urban development represented the desire by many urban women to achieve salvation through piety and good works, as many began to feel that the clergy did not adequately address their spiritual needs.

For the church, the existence of Free Spirits among the Beghards and Beguines raised the larger question of ecclesiastical control, for this development threatened to eliminate the boundary between the laity and the clergy. In the 1360s, Emperor Charles IV and Pope Urban V extended the Inquisition to Germany in a move to crush this heresy. In the cities of the Rhineland, fifteen mass trials took place, most around the turn of the fifteenth century. By condemning the "heretics" and requiring beguinages to be under the control of the mendicant orders, the church contained potential dissent. Throughout the fifteenth century the number of beguinages continued to drop.

Lollards. In England, intellectual dissent, social unrest, and nationalist sentiment combined to create a powerful anticlerical movement that the church hierarchy labeled Lollardy (from *lollar*, meaning "idler"). John Wycliffe (c. 1330–1384), who inspired the movement, was an Oxford professor. Initially employed as a royal apologist in the struggle between state and church, Wycliffe gradually developed ideas that challenged the very foundations of the Roman church. His treatise *On the Church*, composed in 1378, advanced the view that the true church was a community of believers rather than a clerical hierarchy. In other writings, Wycliffe repudiated monasticism, excommunication, the Mass, and the priesthood, substituting reliance on Bible reading and individual conscience in place of the official church as the path to salvation. Responsibility for church reform, Wycliffe believed, rested with the king, whose authority he claimed exceeded that of the pope.

At Oxford, Wycliffe gathered around him likeminded intellectuals, and together they influenced and reflected a widespread anticlericalism in late medieval England. Wycliffe actively promoted the use of English in religious writing. He and his disciples attempted to translate the Bible into English and to popularize its reading throughout all ranks of society, although he died before completing the project. His supporters included members of the gentry, but most were artisans and other humbler people who had some literacy. Religious dissent was key in motivating the 1381 peasant uprising in England, and the radical preacher John Ball was only

Burning of a Heretic
Execution by fire was the usual method of killing heretics. This illustration shows the burning of a Lollard, a follower of the teachings of Wycliffe, who opposed the established church. While heretics were condemned by the Church, their executions were at the hands of secular authorities, who are present here.
Hulton Getty/Liaison Agency.

one of the many common priests who supported the revolt. Real income for parish priests had fallen steadily after the Black Death, and as a result the sympathy of the impoverished clergy lay with the common folk against the great bishops, abbots, and lords of the realm.

After Wycliffe's death, the English bishops suppressed intellectual dissent at Oxford. In 1401, Parliament passed a statute to prosecute heretics. The only Lollard revolt occurred when John Oldcastle, a knight inspired by Wycliffe's ideas, plotted an assault on London. It was crushed in 1414. But in spite of persistent persecutions, Lollardy survived underground during the fifteenth century, to resurface during the convulsive religious conflict of the early sixteenth century known as the Reformation.

The Hussite Revolution

The most profound challenge to papal authority in the later Middle Ages came from Bohemia. Here the spiritual, intellectual, political, and economic criticisms of the papacy that sprang up in other countries fused in one explosive spark. Religious dissent quickly became the vehicle for a nationalist uprising and a social revolution.

Under Emperor Charles IV the pace of economic development and social change in the Holy Roman Empire had quickened in the mid-fourteenth century. Prague, the capital, became one of Europe's great cities: the new silver mine at Kutná Hora boosted Prague's economic growth, and the first university in the empire was founded there in 1348. Prague was located in Bohemia, a part of the Holy Roman Empire settled by a Slavic people, the Czechs, since the early Middle Ages. Later, many German merchants and artisans migrated to Bohemian cities, and Czech peasants, uprooted from the land, flocked to the cities in search of employment. This diverse society became a potentially explosive mass when heightened expectations of commercial and intellectual growth collided with the grim realities of the plague and economic problems in the late fourteenth century. Tax protests, urban riots, and ethnic conflicts signaled growing unrest, but it was religious discontent that became the focus for popular revolt.

Critics of the clergy, often clergy themselves, decried the moral conduct of priests and prelates who held multiple benefices, led dissolute lives, and ignored their pastoral duties. How could the clergy, living in a state of mortal sin, legitimately perform the sacraments? critics asked. Advocating greater lay participation in the Mass and in the reading of Scripture, religious dissenters drew some of their ideas from the writings of the English intellectual John Wycliffe. Among those influenced by Wycliffe's ideas were Jan Hus (d. 1415) and his follower Jerome of Prague (d. 1416), both Prague professors, ethnic Czechs, and leaders of a reform party in Bohemia. Although the reform party attracted adherents from all Czech-speaking social groups, the German minority, who dominated the university and urban elites in Prague, opposed it out of ethnic rivalry. The Bohemian nobility protected Hus; the common clergy rebelled against the bishops; and the artisans and workers in Prague were ready to back the reform party by force. These disparate social interests all focused on one symbolic but passionately felt religious demand: the ability to receive the Eucharist as both bread and wine at Mass. In traditional Roman liturgy, the chalice was reserved for the clergy; the Utraquists, as their opponents called them (from *utraque*, Latin for "both"), also wanted to drink wine from the chalice, to achieve a measure of equality between laity and clergy.

Despite a guarantee of safety from Emperor Sigismund, Hus was burned at the stake while attending the Council of Constance in 1415. Hus's death caused a national uproar, and the reform movement, which had thus far focused only on religious issues, burst forth as a national revolution.

The Hussite Revolution, 1415–1436

Sigismund's initial repression of the revolt in the provinces was brutal, and many dissenters were massacred. To organize their defense, Hussites gathered at a mountain in southern Bohemia, which they called Mount Tabor after the mountain in the New Testament where the transfiguration of Christ took place. Now called Taborites, they began to restructure their community according to biblical injunctions. Like the first Christian church, they initially practiced communal ownership of goods and thought of themselves as the only true Christians awaiting the return of Christ and the end of the world. As their influence spread, the Taborites compromised with the surrounding social order, collecting tithes from peasants and retaining magistrates in towns under their control. Taborite leaders were radical priests who ministered to the community in the Czech language, exercised moral and judicial leadership, and even led the people into battle.

Modeling themselves after the Israelites of the Old Testament and the first Christians of the New Testament, the Taborites impressed even their enemies. Aeneas Sylvius Piccolomini, the future Pope Pius II (r. 1458–1464), observed that "among the Taborites you will hardly find a woman who cannot demonstrate familiarity with the Old and New Testaments." The Taborite army, drawn from many social classes and led by priests, repelled five attacks by the "crusader" armies from neighboring Germany, triumphing over their enemies using a mixture of religious fervor and military technology, such as a wagon train to protect the infantry from cavalry charges. Resisting all attempts to crush them, the Czech revolutionaries eventually gained the right from the papacy to receive the Eucharist as both bread and wine, a practice that continued until the sixteenth century.

❖ The Social Order and Cultural Change

An abundance of written and visual records documenting the lives of all social groups has survived from the fourteenth century. Sources ranging from chronicles of dynastic conflicts and noble chivalry to police records of criminality paint a vivid picture of late medieval society, showing the changed relations between town and country, noble and commoner, and men and women. These sources reveal Europeans' struggles to adjust to uncertainties and changes related to the plague, war, and religious dissent. New material wealth allowed some to enjoy more comfortable lives, but the disruptions and dislocations caused by various crises forced many on the margins of society—the poor, beggars, and prostitutes—into a violent underworld of criminality.

One response to the upheavals of the later Middle Ages was the blossoming of a broad cultural movement. As the Byzantines recovered their appreciation of Greek antiquity, so did Italians revive ancient Roman culture. This movement focused initially on imitating classical Latin rhetoric, but it later extended to other disciplines, such as the study of history. The brilliant achievements in the visual arts and vernacular literature realized at this time were the beginnings of the great movement known as the *Renaissance* (French for "rebirth").

The Household

Family life and the household economy formed the fabric of late medieval society. In contrast to the nobility and great merchants, whose power rested on their lineages, most Europeans lived in a more confined social world, surrounded by smaller families and neighbors. The focus of their lives was the house, where parents and children, and occasionally a grandparent or other relative, lived together. This pattern generally characterized both urban and rural society. In some peasant societies, such as in Languedoc (southern France), brothers and their families shared the same roof; but the nuclear family was by far the norm.

For artisans and peasants of medium wealth, the family dwelling usually consisted of a two-to-three-story building in the city and a single farmhouse in the countryside. For these social groups the household generally served as both work and private space; shopkeepers and craftspeople used their ground floors as workshops and storefronts, reserving the upper stories for family life. By today's standards, late medieval urban life was intolerably crowded, with little privacy. Neighbors could easily spy on each other from adjoining windows or even come to blows, as did two Florentine neighbors who argued over the installation of a second-story latrine that emptied from one's property to the other's. In rural areas the family house served a variety of purposes, not least to shelter the farm animals during the winter.

In a society with an unequal distribution of power between women and men, the worlds of commerce and agriculture were those in which women came closest to partnership with their husbands. As a consequence of the plague and labor shortages, women found themselves in relatively favorable working positions. In cities all over Europe, women worked in retail trade. They sold dairy products,

June
Real farmwork in fourteenth-century France was never as genteel as in this miniature painting, part of a series illustrating the months of the year in the beautiful devotional book, the Book of Hours *of the Duke de Berry. Nevertheless, the scene does faithfully represent haying and suggests the gendered division of village labor, as the men swing their scythes and the women wield rakes.*
Giraudon/Art Resource, NY.

meat, cloth, salt, flour, and fish; brewed beer; spun and wove cloth; and often acted informally as their husbands' business partners. Although excluded from many crafts and professions and barred from all but a few guilds, fourteenth-century women played a crucial role in the urban economy.

The degree to which women participated in public life, however, varied with class and region.

February

As in all the miniatures in the Duke de Berry's prayer book, this cozy scene shows that the late-medieval nobility liked to imagine their peasants and livestock securely housed in warm, separate shelters, while the customary work of rural society goes on peacefully. But in reality, peasants led a hard life, faced with the uncertainties of weather and the depredations of war.
Giraudon/Art Resource, NY.

Women in Mediterranean Europe, especially in upper-class families, lived more circumscribed lives than their counterparts in northern Europe. In the southern regions, for example, women could not dispose of personal property without the consent of males, be they fathers, husbands, or grown sons. In the north, women regularly represented themselves in legal transactions and testified in court.

Partnership in marriage characterized the peasant household. Although men and women performed different tasks, such as plowing and spinning, many chores required mutual effort. During harvests, all family members were mobilized. The men usually reaped with sickles, while the women gleaned the fields. Viticulture (the cultivation of grapes for wine making) called for full cooperation between the sexes: both men and women worked equally in picking grapes and trampling them to make wine.

Because the rural household constituted the basic unit of agricultural production, most men and women remarried quickly after a spouse died. The incidence of households headed by a single person, usually a poor widow, was much lower in villages than in cities. Studies of court records for fourteenth-century English villages show relatively few reports of domestic violence, a result perhaps of the economic dependency between the sexes. Violence against women was more visible in urban societies, where many women worked as servants and prostitutes.

The improved material life of the middle classes was represented in many visual images of the later Middle Ages. Italian and Flemish paintings of the late fourteenth and early fifteenth centuries depict the new comforts of urban life such as fireplaces and private latrines and show an interest in material objects: beds, chests, rooms, curtains, and buildings provide the ubiquitous background of Italian paintings of the period. An illustration in *The Book of Hours* (1416), commissioned by the duke of Berry, brother of the French king, depicts a romanticized view of country life that might have characterized the peasant elite. Surrounded by a low fence, the family compound includes a house, a granary, and a shed. Animals and humans no longer intermingle, as they did in the thirteenth century and still did in poorer peasant households. The picture shows peasants warming themselves and drying their laundry in front of the fire, while the sheep are safe and warm in the shed.

The Underclass

If family life and the household economy formed the fabric of late medieval society, the world of poverty and criminality represented its torn fringes. Indeed, the boundary between poor and criminal was very thin. Fourteenth-century society rested on a broad base of underclass—poor peasants and laborers in the countryside, workers and servants in the cities. Lower still were the marginal elements of society, straddling the line between legality and criminality.

Men populated the violent criminal underworld. Organized gangs prowled the larger cities. In Paris, a city teeming with thieves, thugs, beggars, prostitutes, and vagabonds, the Hundred Years' War led to a sharp rise in crime. Gang members were mostly artisans who vacillated between work and crime. Sometimes disguised as clerics, they robbed, murdered, and extorted from prostitutes. Often they served as soldiers. War was no longer an occupation reserved for knights but had become a vocation that absorbed young men from poor backgrounds. Initiated into a life of plunder and killing, soldiers adjusted poorly to civilian life after discharge; between wars, these men turned to crime.

A central feature of social marginality was mobility. Those on society's fringes were mostly young, lacking stable families; they wandered extensively, begging and stealing. Criminals were even present among the clergy. While some were laymen who assumed clerical disguises to escape the law, others were bona fide clerics who turned to crime to make ends meet during an age of steadily declining clerical income. "Decent society" treated these marginal elements with suspicion and hatred. During the later Middle Ages, attitudes concerning poverty hardened. Townspeople and peasants distrusted travelers and vagabonds. New laws restricted vagabonds and begging clerics, although cities and guilds also began building hospitals and almshouses to deal with these social problems.

Women featured prominently in the underclass, reflecting the unequal distribution of power between the sexes. In Mediterranean Europe, some 90 percent of slaves were women in domestic servitude. Their actual numbers were small—several hundred in fourteenth-century Florence, for example—because only rich households could afford slaves. They came from Muslim or Greek Orthodox countries and usually served in upper-class households in the great commercial city republics of Venice, Florence, and Ragusa. Urban domestic service was also the major employment for girls from the countryside, who worked to save money for their dowries. In addition to the usual household chores, women also worked as wet nurses.

Given their exclusion from many professions and their powerlessness, many poor women found prostitution the only available way to make a living. Male violence also forced some women into prostitution: rape stripped away their social respectability and any prospects for marriage. Condemned by the church, prostitutes were tolerated throughout the Middle Ages, but in the fourteenth and fifteenth centuries the government intensified its attempts to control sexuality by institutionalizing prostitution. Restricted to particular quarters in cities, supervised by officials, sometimes under direct government management, prostitutes found themselves confined to brothels, increasingly controlled by males. In legalizing and controlling prostitution, officials aimed to maintain the public order. In Florence such state sponsorship was intended to check homosexuality and concubinage by offering female sexuality to young men who did not have the means to hire prostitutes on their own. Female sexuality directed by the state in this way also helped define and limit the role of women in society at large.

Hard Times for Business

Compared with the commercial prosperity of the twelfth and thirteenth centuries, the later Middle Ages was an age of retrenchment for business. As the fourteenth-century crises afflicted the business community, a climate of pessimism and caution permeated commerce, especially during the second half of the century.

The first major crisis that undermined Italian banks was caused by the Hundred Years' War, during which the English king Edward III borrowed heavily from the largest Italian banking houses, the Bardi and Peruzzi of Florence. With many of their assets tied up in loans to the English monarchy, the Italian bankers had no choice but to extend new credits, hoping vainly to recover their initial investments. In the early 1340s, however, Edward defaulted. Adding to their problems, the Florentine bankers were forced to make war loans to their own government. These once-illustrious and powerful banks could not rebound from the losses they incurred, and both of them fell.

This breakdown in the most advanced economic sector reflected the general recession in the European economy. Merchants were less likely to take risks and more willing to invest their money in government bonds than in production and commerce. Fewer merchants traveled to Asia, partly because of the danger of attack by Ottoman Turks on the overland routes that had once been protected by the Mongols. The Medici of Florence, who would dominate Florentine politics in the next century, stuck close to home, investing part of their banking profits in art and politics and relying mostly on business agents to conduct their affairs in other European cities.

Historians have argued that this fourteenth-century economic depression diverted capital away from manufacturing and into investments in the arts and luxuries for immediate consumption. Instead of plowing their profits back into their businesses, merchants acquired land, built sumptuous townhouses, purchased luxury items, and invested in bonds. During the last decades of the fourteenth century, the maritime insurance rates in the great merchant republics of Venice and Genoa rose, also reflecting the general lack of confidence in business.

The most important trade axis continued to link Italy with the Low Countries. Italian cities produced silk, wool, jewelry, and other luxury goods that northern Europeans desired, and Italian merchants also imported spices, gold, and other coveted products from Asia and Africa. Traveling either by land through Lyons or by sea around Gibraltar, these products reached Bruges, Ghent, and Antwerp, where they were shipped to England, northern Germany, Poland, and Scandinavia. The reverse flow carried raw materials and silver, the latter to help balance the trade between northern Europe and the Mediterranean. Diminished production and trade eventually caused turmoil in northern Europe and a crisis for financiers in the Low Countries. Bruges, the financial center for northwestern Europe, saw its power fade during the fifteenth century when a succession of its money changers went bankrupt. The Burgundian dukes eventually enacted a series of monetary laws that undermined Bruges's financial and banking community and, by extension, the city's political autonomy as well.

The Flourishing of Vernacular Literature and the Birth of Humanism

From the epics and romances of the twelfth and thirteenth centuries, vernacular literature blossomed in the fourteenth. Poetry, stories, and chronicles composed in Italian, French, English, and other national languages helped articulate a new sense of aesthetics. No longer did Latin and church culture dominate the intellectual life of Europe, and no longer were writers principally clerics or aristocrats.

Middle-Class Writers and Noble Patrons. The great writers of late medieval Europe were of urban middle-class origins, from families that had done well in government or church service or commercial enterprises. Unlike the medieval troubadours, with their aristocratic backgrounds, the men and women who wrote vernacular literature in this age typically came from the cities, and their audience was the literate laity. Francesco Petrach (1304–1374), the poet laureate of Italy's vernacular literature, and his younger contemporary and friend Giovanni Boccaccio (1313–1375) were both Florentine. Petrarch was born in Arezzo, where his father, a notary, lived in political exile from Florence. Boccaccio's father worked for the Florentine banking firm of Bardi in Paris, where Boccaccio was born. Geoffrey Chaucer (c. 1342–1400) was the first great vernacular poet of medieval England. His father was a wealthy wine merchant; Chaucer worked as a servant to the king and controller of customs in London. Even writers who celebrated the life of the nobility were children of commoners. Although born in Valenciennes to a family of moneylenders and merchants, Jean Froissart (1333?–c. 1405), whose chronicle vividly describes the events of the Hundred Years' War, was an ardent admirer of chivalry. Christine de Pisan (1364–c. 1430), the official biographer of the French king, was the daughter of a Venetian municipal counselor.

Life in all its facets found expression in the flourishing vernacular literature, as writers told of love, greed, and salvation. Boccaccio's *Decameron* popularized the short story, as the characters in this novella tell sensual and bizarre tales in the shadow of the Black Death. These stories draw on Boccaccio's own experiences in banking and commerce. Members of different social orders parade themselves in Chaucer's *Canterbury Tales*, journeying together on a pilgrimage. He describes a merchant on horseback:

> A marchant was ther with a forked berd
> In mottelee, and hye on horse he sat
> up-on his heed a Flaundrish bever hat
> his botes clasped faire and fetisly . . .
> For sothe he was a worthy man withalle
> but sooth to seyn, I noot how men him calle.

Chaucer also vividly portrayed other social classes— yeomen, London guildsmen, and minor officials.

Noble patronage was crucial to the growth of vernacular literature, a fact reflected in the careers of the most famous writers. Perhaps closest to the model of an independent man of letters, Petrarch nonetheless relied on powerful patrons at various times. His early career began at the papal court in Avignon, where his father worked as a notary; during the 1350s, he enjoyed the protection and patronage of the Visconti duke of Milan. For Boccaccio, who started out in the Neapolitan world of commerce, the court of King Robert of Naples initiated him into the world of letters. Chaucer served in administrative posts and on many diplomatic missions, during which he met his two Italian counterparts. Noble patronage also shaped the literary creations of Froissart and Christine de Pisan. Com-

Poet and Queen
Christine de Pisan, kneeling, presents a manuscript of her poems to Isabelle of Bavaria, the queen of France. Isabelle's royal status is marked by the French coat of arms, the fleur-de-lis that decorates the bedroom walls. The sumptuous interior (chairs, cushions, tapestry, paneled ceiling, glazed and shuttered windows) was typical of aristocratic domestic architecture. Even in the intimacy of her bedroom, Queen Isabelle, like all royal personages, was constantly attended and almost never alone (note her ladies-in-waiting).
The British Library Picture Library, London.

missioned to write the official biography of King Charles V, Christine would have been unable to produce most of her writings without the patronage of women in the royal household. She presented her most famous work, *The Book of the City of Ladies* (1405), a defense of women's reputation and virtue, to Isabella of Bavaria, the queen of France and wife of Charles VI. Christine's last composition was a poem praising Joan of Arc, restorer of French royal fortunes and, like Christine herself, a distinguished woman in a world otherwise dominated by men.

Classical Revival. Vernacular literature blossomed not at the expense of Latin but alongside a classical revival. In spite of the renown of their Italian writings, Petrarch and Boccaccio, for example, took great pride in their Latin works. Latin represented the language of salvation and was also the international language of learning. Professors taught and wrote in Latin; students spoke it as best they could; priests celebrated Mass and dispensed sacraments in Latin; and theologians composed learned

Paradise Lost

This fourteenth-century painting by the Sienese Giovanni di Paolo depicts the expulsion of Adam and Eve from the Garden of Eden. At right, an angel chases away the ancestors of humanity. At left, Paradise is the core around which the seven celestial spheres rotate, propelled by the action of God. By positioning Adam and Eve to the right-hand side of the panel, Paolo dramatically represents their expulsion from the Garden of Eden. The Metropolitan Museum of Art, Robert Lehman Collection, 1975. (1975.1.31) Photograph © 1981 the Metropolitan Museum of Art.

treatises in Latin. Church Latin was very different from the Latin of the ancient Romans, both in syntax and in vocabulary. In the second half of the fourteenth century, writers began to imitate the rather antiquated "classical" Latin of Roman literature. In the forefront of this literary and intellectual movement, Petrarch traveled to many monasteries in search of long-ignored Latin manuscripts. For writers like Petrarch, medieval church Latin was an artificial, awkward language, whereas classical Latin and, after its revival, Greek were the mother tongues of the ancients. Thus the classical writings of Rome and Greece represented true vernacular literature, only more authentic, vivid, and glorious than the poetry and prose written in Italian and other contemporary European languages. Classical allusions and literary influences abound in the works of Boccaccio, Chaucer, Christine de Pisan, and others. The new intellectual fascination with the ancient past also stimulated translations of classical works into the vernacular.

This attempt to emulate the virtues and learning of the ancients gave rise to a new intellectual movement: humanism. For humanists the study of history and literature was the chief means of iden-

tifying with the glories of the ancient world. By the early fifteenth century, the study of classical Latin had become fashionable among a small intellectual elite, first in Italy and gradually throughout Europe. Reacting against the painstaking logic and abstract language of the scholastic philosophy that predominated in the medieval period, the humanists of the Renaissance preferred eloquence and style in their discourse, imitating the writings of Cicero and other great Roman authors.

Italian lawyers and notaries had a long-standing interest in classical rhetoric because eloquence was a skill essential to their professions. Gradually the imitation of ancient Roman rhetoric led to the absorption of ancient ideas. In the writings of Roman historians such as Livy and Tacitus, fifteenth-century Italian civic elites (many of them lawyers) found echoes of their own devout patriotism. Between 1400 and 1430 in Florence, a time of war and crisis, the study of the humanities evolved into a republican ideology that historians call "civic humanism." In the early fifteenth century, the Florentines waged a highly successful propaganda war on behalf of virtuous republican Florence against tyrannical Milan, invoking the memory of the overthrow of Etruscan

MAPPING THE WEST Europe, c. 1430

Two of the dynamic regions of expansion lie in the southeastern and southwestern sectors of this map: the Ottoman Empire, which continued its attacks into central Europe and the Mediterranean, and the Iberian countries that opposed Muslim advances by their own Crusades and maritime expansions. While England, France, Iberia, and the Balkans were consolidated into large political entities, central Europe and Italy remained fragmented. Yet it was these two fragmented regions that gave Europe the cultural and technological innovations of the age.

tyrants by the first Romans. Thus the study of ancient civilization was not only an antiquarian quest but a call to public service and political action.

Conclusion

Between 1320 and 1430, Europe was a civilization in crisis. The traditional order, achieved during the optimism and growth of the High Middle Ages, was undercut first—and most severely—by the Black Death and the Hundred Years' War, which combined to cause a drastic reduction in population and contraction of the economy. Faced with massive death and destruction, some people sought escape in rituals of religious fanaticism. Others searched out scapegoats, spawning a wave of anti-Jewish persecutions that reached from southern France to the extent of the Holy Roman Empire; the Nuremberg pogrom of 1349 was only one example. Empire and papacy, long symbols of unity, collapsed into political disintegration and spiritual malaise.

The disintegration of European order hastened the consolidation of some states, as countries such as England and France developed political, linguistic, and cultural boundaries that largely coincided. Other areas, such as Spain and the Ottoman Empire, included different linguistic and religious groups under one political authority. Still other regions, principally central Europe and Italy, remained divided into competing city-states characterized more by the sense of local differences than by their linguistic similarity.

In the eastern Mediterranean, European civilization retreated in the face of Ottoman Turk advances. Christian Europe continued to grow, however, in the Iberian peninsula; for the next three centuries the Mediterranean would be the arena for struggles between Christian and Islamic empires. The papacy would clamor for new crusades.

The conciliar movement, although instrumental in ending the Great Schism, failed to limit supreme papal power, identified by its critics as the source of spiritual discontent. Traumatized, perhaps by the crisis of authority, the next generations of popes would concentrate on consolidating their worldly power and wealth. Successful in repressing or compromising with the Lollard, Hussite, and other heretical movements, the church would focus its attention on control and would neglect, to its future regret, the spiritual needs of a laity increasingly estranged from a dominating clerical elite.

Suggested References

Political Crises across Europe

The scholarship on the political conflicts of late medieval Europe has shifted from narrative of military campaigns and diplomacy to focus on peasant uprisings, urban revolts, and their relationship to the larger struggles between dynasties and countries. In addition to the Hundred Years' War, southeastern Europe and Iberia have also come into focus.

Allmand, Christopher. *The Hundred Years' War: England and France at War, c. 1300–1450.* 1988.

Froissart, Jean. *Chronicles.* Trans. Geoffrey Brereton. 1968.

Hilton, R. H., and T. H. Aston, eds. *The English Rising of 1381.* 1984.

Index of Late Medieval Maps–Index of Cartographic Images Illustrating Maps of the Late Medieval Period 1300–1500 A.D. http://www.henry-davis.com/MAPS/LMwebpages/LML.html.

Joan of Arc: By Herself and Her Witnesses. Ed. Régine Pernoud. 1966.

Leuschner, Joachim. *Germany in the Late Middle Ages.* 1980.

Mollat, Michel, and Philippe Wolff. *The Popular Revolutions of the Late Middle Ages.* 1973.

Nichols, David. *The van Arteveldes of Ghent: The Varieties of Vendetta and the Hero in History.* 1988.

O'Callaghan, Joseph F. *A History of Medieval Spain.* 1975.

Shaw, Stanford J. *History of the Ottoman Empire and Modern Turkey.* Vol. 1, *Empire of the Gazia: The Rise and Decline of the Ottoman Empire, 1280–1808.* 1976.

Warner, Marina. *Joan of Arc: The Image of Female Heroism.* 1981.

Plague and Society

Recent scholarship stresses the social, economic, and cultural impact of the plague. One particularly exciting direction of research focuses on the persecution of religious minorities as a result of the Black Death.

Bois, Guy. *The Crisis of Feudalism: Economy and Society in Eastern Normandy, c. 1300–1550.* 1984.

Duby, Georges. *A History of Private Life.* Vol. 2, *Revelations of the Medieval World.* 1988.

Geremek, Bronislaw. *The Margins of Society in Late Medieval Paris.* 1987.

Hanawalt, Barbara A., ed. *Women and Work in Preindustrial Europe.* 1986.

Miskimim, Harry A. *The Economy of Early Renaissance Europe, 1300–1460.* 1975.

Nirenberg, David. *Communities of Violence: Persecution of Minorities in the Middle Ages.* 1996.

Rörig, Fritz. *The Medieval Town.* 1967.

Ziegler, Philip. *The Black Death.* 1970.

Plague and public health in Renaissance Europe: http://jefferson.village.virginia.edu/osheim/intro.html.

Challenges to Spiritual Authority

While there continues to be a great deal of interest in dissident thinkers who challenged the authority of the medieval church, much recent scholarship is devoted to the popular movements of dissent against papal and ecclesiastical authority.

Kaminsky, Howard. *A History of the Hussite Revolution.* 1967.

Leff, Gordon. *Heresy in the Later Middle Ages: The Relation of Heterodoxy to Dissent, c. 1250–1450.* 1967.

Oakley, Francis. *Council over Pope? Towards a Provisional Ecclesiology.* 1969.

Ozment, Steven. *The Age of Reform, 1250–1550: An Intellectual and Religious History of Late Medieval and Reformation Europe.* 1980.

Renouard, Yves. *The Avignon Papacy, 1305–1403.* 1970.

Renaissance Europe

1400–1500

Sacred and Social Body
The fifteenth-century Venetian state used lavish, dignified ceremony to impress citizens and visitors with its grandeur and to symbolize its divine protection. Here the great Venetian Renaissance painter Gentile Bellini depicts one such scene, a procession of the Eucharist across the Piazza San Marco uniting in common purpose the clergy and the Venetian governing elite.
Scala/Art Resource, NY.

I

N 1461, THE OTTOMAN RULER MEHMED II sent a letter to Sigismondo Malatesta, the Lord of Rimini, asking the Italian prince to lend him the Rimini court painter and architect Matteo de Pasti. The Ottoman sultan was planning to build a new palace in the recently conquered capital, Constantinople (modern Istanbul), as a fitting symbol of his imperial dominion, and he had heard of Matteo de Pasti's reputation. Not only had the Rimini painter produced illuminated manuscripts and portrait medals of Sigismondo's mistress for his patron, he had also designed a monument to the prince's military glory, modeled after the principles described in Vitruvius's treatise *On Architecture* (first century B.C.), a work rediscovered in 1414 in Italy.

Armed with a letter from Sigismondo, with maps and gifts, de Pasti set out for Constantinople, ready to court favors for his patron, who was eager to form an alliance with the Turkish ruler. Venetian authorities, however, intercepted the artist in Crete. Anxious to prevent a political connection between another Italian power and the sultan, the Venetians confiscated the gifts and sent de Pasti back to Rimini. Thus Mehmed's new palace was constructed without de Pasti's help, but with the aid of several Venetian painters instead. The palace came to be called the Topkapi Saray and still stands today looking across the Bosporus, the strait that divides European and Asian Turkey.

The story of Matteo de Pasti's failed mission illustrates the central theme of the Renaissance: the connection among power, culture, and fame in an age that was rediscovering the arts and worldview of

489

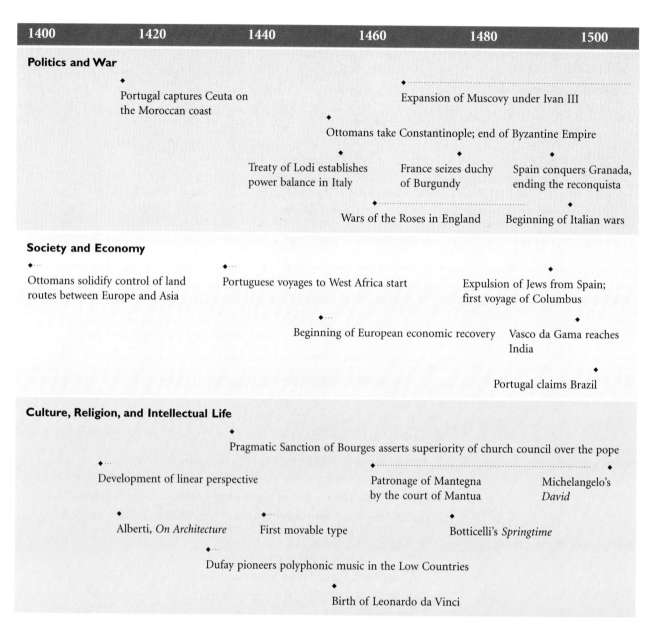

| 1400 | 1420 | 1440 | 1460 | 1480 | 1500 |

Politics and War

Portugal captures Ceuta on the Moroccan coast

Expansion of Muscovy under Ivan III

Ottomans take Constantinople; end of Byzantine Empire

Treaty of Lodi establishes power balance in Italy

France seizes duchy of Burgundy

Spain conquers Granada, ending the reconquista

Wars of the Roses in England

Beginning of Italian wars

Society and Economy

Ottomans solidify control of land routes between Europe and Asia

Portuguese voyages to West Africa start

Expulsion of Jews from Spain; first voyage of Columbus

Beginning of European economic recovery

Vasco da Gama reaches India

Portugal claims Brazil

Culture, Religion, and Intellectual Life

Pragmatic Sanction of Bourges asserts superiority of church council over the pope

Development of linear perspective

Patronage of Mantegna by the court of Mantua

Michelangelo's *David*

Alberti, *On Architecture*

First movable type

Botticelli's *Springtime*

Dufay pioneers polyphonic music in the Low Countries

Birth of Leonardo da Vinci

classical antiquity. This rediscovery, which scholars in the sixteenth century labeled the *Renaissance* (French for "rebirth"), signified the revival of forms of classical learning and the arts following the long interval they characterized as the Middle Ages. (See "Terms of History," page 492.) After the crisis of the fourteenth century, European civilization seemed to rise in the fifteenth like a phoenix from the ashes of the Black Death. This Renaissance of civilization had two main trajectories: a revolution in culture that originated in Italy and gradually expanded north to other countries of Europe and, an even more profound and far-reaching development, the expansion of European control to the non-European world.

The story of de Pasti's mission further illustrates three secondary themes. First, it shows how specific Renaissance artistic practices were based on the revival of classical learning. Second, it reflects the competition between Italian city-states set against a larger backdrop of changing relations between Christian Europe and the non-Christian world, in this case the rising Muslim Ottoman Empire. And third, it demonstrates a new and important use of culture by both Christian and non-Christian rulers to justify and glorify power and fame.

The Renaissance of culture took many forms: in learning, in the visual arts, in architecture, and in music. Much new work was created in praise of personal and public lives. Portraits, palaces, and poetry commemorated the glory of the rich and powerful, while a new philosophy called *humanism* advocated classical learning and argued for the active participation of the individual in civic affairs. Family, honor, social status, and individual distinction—these were the goals that fueled the ambitions of Renaissance men and women.

A new feeling of power characterized the spirit of the Renaissance, as Europeans recovered their sense of control of the world after the crisis of the fourteenth century. The quest for power by families and individuals duplicated on a smaller scale the enhanced power of the state. Like individuals, the Renaissance states competed for wealth, glory, and honor. While warfare and diplomacy channeled the restless energy of the Italian states, monarchies and empires outside of Italy also expanded their power through conquests and institutional reforms. The European world changed drastically as new powers such as the Ottoman Empire and Muscovy rose to prominence in the east, while the Iberian kingdoms of Portugal and Spain expanded European domination to Africa, Asia, and the Americas.

❖ Widening Intellectual Horizons

A revolution in the arts and learning was in the making. Europeans' rediscovery of Greek and Roman writers reflected an expanded interest in human achievements and glory. New secular voices celebrating human glory were added to the old prayers for salvation in the afterlife. While the intense study of Latin and Greek writings focused on rhetoric and eloquence in learning, revolutionary techniques in bookmaking, painting, architecture, and music created original forms and expressed a new excitement with the beauty of nature. In the center of this fascinating nature was humanity.

The Humanist Renewal

Europeans' fascination with the ancient past in turn gave rise to a new intellectual movement: *humanism,* so called because its practitioners studied and supported the liberal arts, the humanities. As a group the humanists were far from homogeneous, although they were overwhelmingly wellborn. Some were professional scholars, others high-ranking civil servants, still others rich patricians who had acquired a taste for learning. Many were notaries or government officials. Nonetheless, all humanists focused on classical history and literature in their attempt to emulate the glories of the ancient world.

By the early fifteenth century the study of classical Latin (which had begun in the late fourteenth century) as well as classical and biblical Greek had become fashionable among a small intellectual elite, first in Italy and, gradually, throughout Europe. The fall of Constantinople in 1453 sent Greek scholars to Italy for refuge, giving extra impetus to the revival of Greek learning in the West. Venice and Florence assumed leadership in this new field—the former by virtue of its commercial and political ties to the eastern Mediterranean, the latter thanks to the patronage of Cosimo de' Medici, who sponsored the Platonic Academy, a discussion group dedicated to the study of Plato and his followers under the intellectual leadership of Marsilio Ficino (1433–1499). Thinkers of the second half of the fifteenth century had more curiosity about Platonic and various mystical neo-Platonic ideas—particularly alchemy, numerology, and natural magic—than about the serious study of natural phenomena and universal principles.

Most humanists did not consider the study of ancient cultures a conflict with their Christian faith. In "returning to the sources"—a famous slogan of the time—philosophers attempted to harmonize the disciplines of Christian faith and ancient learning. Ficino, the foremost Platonic scholar of the Renaissance, was deeply attracted to natural magic and was also a priest. He argued that the immortality of the soul, a Platonic idea, was perfectly compatible with Christian doctrine and that much of ancient wisdom actually foreshadowed later Christian teachings.

In Latin learning, the fifteenth century continued in the tradition of Petrarch. Reacting against the

Renaissance

The term *Renaissance* originated with the Italian painter and architect Giorgio Vasari (1511–1574) in his *Lives of the Most Excellent Italian Architects, Painters, and Sculptors* (1550). Vasari argues that Greco-Roman art declined after the dissolution of the Roman Empire, to be followed by a long period of barbaric insensitivity to classical monuments. Only in the past generations had Italian artists begun to restore the perfection of the arts, according to Vasari, a development he called *rinascita*, the Italian for "rebirth." It was the French equivalent—*renaissance*—that stuck.

Referring initially to a rebirth in the arts and literature, the term *Renaissance* came to define a consciousness of modernity. The writings of the Florentines Petrarch and Boccaccio in the fourteenth century showed that they thought of themselves as living in an age distinct from a long preceding period—which they dubbed the "middle age"—with values different from those of the classical civilizations of Greece and Rome. Petrarch, Boccaccio, and other Florentines began to consider their civilization a revival of the classical model in art, architecture, and language, the latter evidenced by an increased interest in classical Latin and Greek. From Florence and Italy, the Renaissance spread to France, Spain, the Low Countries, and central Europe by the fifteenth century. It inspired a golden age of vernacular literature in those countries during the second half of the sixteenth century; scholars speak of a "Northern Renaissance" as late as 1600.

The term *Renaissance* acquired widespread recognition with the publication of Jakob Burckhardt's *The Civilization of the Renaissance in Italy* in 1860. A historian at the University of Basel, Burckhardt considered the Renaissance a watershed in Western civilization. For him, the Renaissance ushered in a spirit of modernity, freeing the individual from the domination of society and creative impulses from the repression of the church; the Renaissance represented the beginning of secular society and the preeminence of individual creative geniuses.

Dominant for a long time, Burckhardt's ideas have been strongly revised by scholars. Some point out the many continuities between the Middle Ages and the Renaissance; others argue that the Renaissance was not a secular but a profoundly religious age; and still others see the Renaissance as only the beginning of a long period of transition from the Middle Ages to modernity. The consensus among scholars is that the Renaissance represents a distinct cultural period lasting from the fourteenth to the sixteenth century, centered on the revival of classical learning and spreading from Italy to northern Europe. Historians disagree about the significance of this cultural rebirth for society at large, but they generally understand it to represent some of the complex changes that characterized the passing of medieval society to modernity.

FURTHER READING

Jakob Burckhardt, *The Civilization of the Renaissance in Italy.* 1860.

Wallace K. Ferguson, *The Renaissance in Historical Thought.* 1948.

Denis Hay, "Idea of Renaissance," in *Dictionary of the History of Ideas.* 1973.

Guido Ruggiero, ed., *The Blackwell Companion to the World of the Renaissance.* 2001.

painstaking logic and abstract language of scholastic philosophy, the humanists of the Renaissance advocated eloquence and style in their discourse, imitating the writings of Cicero and other great Roman authors. The Roman influence manifested itself especially in the transformation of historians' writings, as Italian humanists used the classical genre to explore the role of human agency in political affairs.

Between 1400 and 1430 in Florence, which at the time was at war with the duchy of Milan, the study of the humanities evolved into a republican ideology that historians call *civic humanism*. In the early fifteenth century, the Florentines waged a highly successful propaganda war on behalf of virtuous republican Florence against tyrannical Milan, invoking the memory of the overthrow of Etruscan tyrants by the first Romans. Whereas Florentine humanists modeled their praise of republicanism after the Romans Livy and Cicero, humanists serving the duke of Milan drew their inspiration from the writings of Suetonius's biographies of Roman emperors. Thus the study of ancient civilization was not only an antiquarian quest but a call to public service and political action.

Through their activities as educators and civil servants, professional humanists gave new vigor to the humanist curriculum of grammar, rhetoric, poetry, history, and moral philosophy. By the end of the fifteenth century, European intellectuals considered a good command of classical Latin, with perhaps some knowledge of Greek, as one of the requirements of an educated man. This humanist revolution would influence school curricula up to the middle of the nineteenth century and even beyond.

The Advent of Printing

The invention of mechanical printing aided greatly in making the classical texts widely available. Printing with movable type—a revolutionary departure from the old practice of copying by hand—was invented in the 1440s by Johannes Gutenberg, a German goldsmith (c. 1400–1470). Mass production of identical books and pamphlets made the world of letters more accessible to a literate audience. Two preconditions proved essential for the advent of printing: the industrial production of paper and the commercial production of manuscripts.

Increased paper production in the fourteenth and fifteenth centuries was the first stage in the rapid growth of manuscript books—hand-copied works bound as books—which in turn led to the invention of mechanical printing. Papermaking came to Europe from China via Arab intermediaries. By the fourteenth century, paper mills were operating in Italy, producing paper that was more fragile but much cheaper than parchment or vellum, the animal skins that Europeans had previously used for writing. To produce paper, old rags were soaked in a chemical solution, beaten by mallets into a pulp, washed with water, treated, and dried in sheets—a method that still produces good-quality paper today.

By the fifteenth century, a brisk industry in manuscript books was flourishing in Europe's university towns and major cities. Production was in

Printing Press

This illustration from a French manuscript of 1537 depicts typical printing equipment of the sixteenth century. To the left an artisan is using the screw press to apply the paper to the inked type. Also shown are the composed type secured in a chase, the printed sheet (four pages of text printed on one sheet) held by the seated proofreader, and the bound volume. When two pages of text are printed on one sheet, the bound book is called a folio. A bound book with four pages of text on one sheet is called in quarto ("in four"), and a book with eight pages of text on one sheet is called in octavo ("in eight"). The last is a pocket-size book, smaller than today's paperback.
Giraudon/Art Resource, NY.

the hands of stationers, who organized workshops known as *scriptoria*, where the manuscripts were copied, and acted as retail booksellers. The largest stationers, in Paris or Florence, were extensive operations by fifteenth-century standards. The Florentine Vespasiano da Bisticci, for example, created a library for Cosimo de' Medici by employing forty-five copyists to complete two hundred volumes in twenty-two months. Nonetheless, bookmaking in *scriptoria* was slow and expensive.

The invention of movable type was an enormous technological breakthrough that took bookmaking out of the hands of human copyists.

Printing—or "mechanically writing," as contemporaries called it—was not new: the Chinese had been printing by woodblock since the tenth century, and woodcut pictures made their appearance in Europe in the early fifteenth century. Movable type, however, allowed entire manuscripts to be printed. The process involved casting durable metal molds to represent the letters of the alphabet. The letters were arranged to represent the text on a page and then pressed in ink against a sheet of paper. The imprint could be repeated numerous times with only a small amount of human labor. In 1467, two German printers established the first press in Rome and produced twelve thousand volumes in five years, a feat that in the past would have required one thousand scribes working full time for the same number of years.

After the 1440s, printing spread rapidly from Germany to other European countries (Map 14.1). Cologne, Strasbourg, Nuremberg, Basel, and Augsburg had major presses; many Italian cities had established their own by 1480. In the 1490s, the German city of Frankfurt-am-Main became an international meeting place for printers and booksellers. The Frankfurt Book Fair, where printers from different nations exhibited their newest titles, represented a major international cultural event and remains an unbroken tradition to this day. Early books from the presses were still rather exclusive and inaccessible, especially to a largely illiterate population. Perhaps the most famous early book, Gutenberg's two-volume edition of the Latin Bible, was unmistakably a luxury item. Altogether 185 copies were printed. First priced at well over what a

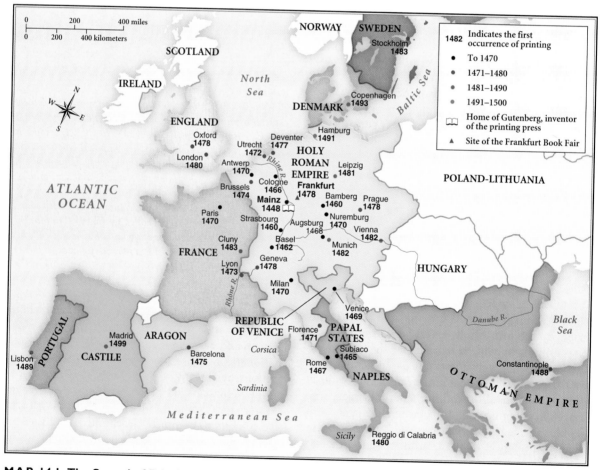

MAP 14.1 The Spread of Printing in the Fifteenth Century
The Holy Roman Empire formed the center of printing. Presses in other countries were often established by migrant German printers, especially in Italy. Printing did not reach Muscovy until the sixteenth century.

fifteenth-century professor could earn in a year, the Gutenberg Bible has always been one of the most expensive books in history, for both its rarity and its exquisite crafting.

Some historians argue that the invention of mechanical printing gave rise to a "communications revolution" as significant as, for example, the widespread use of the personal computer today. The multiplication of standardized texts altered the thinking habits of Europeans by freeing individuals from having to memorize everything they learned; it certainly made possible the relatively speedy and inexpensive dissemination of knowledge, and it created a wider community of scholars, no longer dependent on personal patronage or church sponsorship for texts. Printing facilitated the free expression and exchange of ideas, and its disruptive potential did not go unnoticed by political and ecclesiastical authorities. Emperors and bishops in Germany, the homeland of the printing industry, moved quickly to issue censorship regulations.

❖ Revolution in the Arts

The Renaissance was one of the most creative periods in the European arts. New techniques in painting, architecture, and musical performance fostered original styles and new subjects. Three transformations were particularly significant. First, artists, previously seen as artisans, acquired a more prominent social status, as individual talent and genius were recognized by a society hungry for culture. Second, artists developed a more naturalistic style, especially in representing the human body, in their sculpture and paintings. And finally, the use of perspective in Renaissance art reflected a new mathematical and scientific basis for artistic creation, which was manifest not only in the visual arts but also in architecture and musical composition.

From Artisan to Artist

Like the copyists before them, the printers who operated the new presses saw themselves as artisans practicing a craft. The result might be genuinely artistic, but the producer did not think of himself as an artist, uniquely gifted. The artist was a new social model in the Renaissance. In exalting the status of the artist, Leonardo da Vinci (1452–1519),

painter, architect, and inventor who was himself trained in the artisanal tradition, described his freedom to create, as a gentleman of leisure. "The painter sits at his ease in front of his work, dresses as he pleases, and moves his light brush with the beautiful colors . . . often accompanied by musicians or readers of various beautiful works." If this picture fits with today's image of the creative genius, so do the stories about Renaissance painters and their eccentricities: some were violent, others absentminded; some worked as hermits, others cared little for money. Leonardo was described by his contemporaries as "capricious," and his work habits (or lack of them) irritated at least one employer.

The point of stories about "genius," often told by Renaissance artists themselves, was to convince society that the artists' works were unique and their talents priceless. The artist, as opposed to the artisan, was an individual with innate talents who created works of art according to his imagination, rather than following the blueprints of a patron. During the fifteenth century, as artists began to claim the respect and recognition of society, however, the reality was that most relied on wealthy patrons for support. And although they wished to create as their genius dictated, not all patrons of the arts allowed artists to work without restrictions. While the duke of Milan appreciated Leonardo's genius, the duke of Ferrara paid for his art by the square foot. For every successful artist—such as the painter Andrea Mantegna (1431–1506), who was exalted by Pope Innocent VIII—there were many others who painted marriage chests and look-alike Madonnas for middle-class homes.

A successful artist who did fit the new vision of unfettered genius was the Florentine sculptor Donatello (1386–1466), one of the heroes in Giorgio Vasari's *Lives*. Not only did Donatello's sculptures evoke classical Greek and Roman models, but the grace and movement of his work inspired Cosimo de' Medici, the ruler of Florence, to excavate antique works of art. Moreover, Donatello transcended material preoccupations. According to Vasari:

> *Donatello was free, affectionate, and courteous . . . and more so to his friends than to himself. He thought nothing of money, keeping it in a basket suspended by a rope from the ceiling, so that all his workmen and friends took what they wanted without saying anything to him.*

A favorite artist of the most powerful man in fifteenth-century Florence, Donatello owed his ability to be generous in large part to Medici patronage.

Renaissance artists worked under any of three conditions: long-term service in princely courts, commissioned piecework, and production for the market. Mantegna, for example, worked from 1460 until his death in 1506 for the Gonzaga princes of Mantua. In return for a monthly salary and other gifts, he promised to paint panels and frescoes (paintings on a wet plaster surface). His masterpieces—fresco scenes of courtly life with vivid and accurate portraits of members of the princely family—decorated the walls of the ducal palace. In practice, however, Mantegna sometimes was treated more as a skilled worker in service to the prince than as an independent artist: he was once asked to adorn his majestic Gonzaga tapestries with life sketches of farm animals.

The workshop—the norm of production in Renaissance Florence and in northern European cities such as Nuremberg and Antwerp—afforded the artist greater autonomy. As heads of workshops, artists trained apprentices and negotiated contracts with clients, with the most famous artists fetching good prices for their work. Famous artists developed followings, and wealthy consumers came to pay a premium for work done by a master instead of apprentices. Studies of art contracts show that in the course of the fifteenth century artists gained greater control over their work. Early in the century clients routinely stipulated detailed conditions for works of art, specifying, for instance, gold paint or "ultramarine blue," which were among the most expensive pigments. Clients might also determine the arrangement of figures in a picture, leaving the artist little more than the execution. After midcentury, however, such specific directions became less common. In 1487, for example, the Florentine painter Filippo Lippi (1457–1504), in his contract to paint frescoes in the Strozzi chapel, specified that the work should be "all from his own hand and particularly the figures." The shift underscores the increasing recognition of the unique skills of individual artists.

A market system for the visual arts emerged in the Renaissance, initially in the Low Countries. In the fifteenth century, most large-scale work was commissioned by specific patrons, but the art market, for which artists produced works without prior arrangement for sale, was to develop into the major force for artistic creativity, a force that prevails in contemporary society. Limited at first to smaller altarpieces, woodcuts, engravings, sculpture, and pottery paintings, the art market began to extend to larger panel paintings. A vigorous trade in religious art sprang up in Antwerp, which was becoming the major market and financial center in Europe. Ready-made altarpieces were sold to churches and consumers from as far as Scandinavia, and merchants could buy small religious statues to take along on their travels. The commercialization of art celebrated the new context of artistic creation itself: artists working in an open, competitive, urban civilization.

The Human Figure

If the individual artist is a man of genius, what greater subject for the expression of beauty is there than the human body itself? From the fourteenth-century Florentine painter Giotto (see Chapter 12), Renaissance artists learned to depict ever more expressive human emotions and movements. The work of the short-lived but brilliant painter Masaccio (1401–1428) exemplifies this development. His painting *The Expulsion from Paradise* shows Adam and Eve grieving in shame and despair; another painting, *Naked Man Trembling*, demonstrates his skill in depicting a man trembling in the cold.

Feminine beauty also found many masterpiece representations in Renaissance art. They range from the graceful movements of classical pagan figures and allegories, as in Sandro Botticelli's (c. 1445–1510) *The Birth of Venus* and *Springtime*, to Raphael's (1483–1520) numerous tender depictions of the Virgin Mary and the infant Jesus. In addition to rendering homage to classical and biblical figures, Renaissance artists painted portraits of their contemporaries.

The increasing number of portraits in Renaissance painting illustrates the new, elevated view of human existence. Initially limited to representations of pontiffs, monarchs, princes, and patricians, portraiture of the middle classes became more widespread as the century advanced. Painters from the Low Countries such as Jan van Eyck (1390?–1441) distinguished themselves in this genre; their portraits achieved a sense of detail and reality unsurpassed until the advent of photography.

The ideal of a universal man was elaborated in the work of Giovanni Pico della Mirandola (1463–1494). Born to a noble family, Pico avidly studied Latin and Greek philosophy. He befriended Ficino, Florence's leading Platonic philosopher, and enjoyed the patronage of Lorenzo de' Medici (1449–1492), who provided him with a villa after the papacy condemned some of his writings. Pico's oration *On the Dignity of Man* embodied the optimism of Renaissance philosophy. To express his marvel at the human species, Pico imagined God's words at his creation of Adam: "In conformity with your free judgment, in whose hands I have placed them, you are confined by no bounds, and you will fix limits of nature for yourself." Pico's construct placed mankind at the center of the universe as the measure of all things and "the molder and maker of himself." In his efforts to reconcile Platonic and Christian philosophy, Pico stressed both the classical emphasis on human responsibility in shaping society and the religious trust in God's divine plan. For the first time after classical antiquity, sculptors again cast the human body in bronze, in life-size or bigger freestanding statues. Donatello's equestrian statue of a Venetian general was one of the finest examples of this new endeavor; consciously based on Roman statues of mounted emperors, it depicted a relatively minor but successful professional commander (ironically nicknamed "Honey Cat" for his failure to inspire awe). Free from fabric and armor, the human body was idealized in the eighteen-foot marble sculpture *David*, the work of the great Michelangelo Buonarroti (1475–1564).

Order through Perspective

Renaissance art was distinguished from its predecessors by its depiction of the world as the eye perceives it. The use of *visual perspective*—an illusory three-dimensional space on a two-dimensional surface and the ordered arrangement of painted objects from one viewpoint—became one of the distinctive features of Western art. Neither Persian, Chinese, Byzantine, nor medieval Western art—all of which had been more concerned with conveying symbolism than reality—expressed this aesthetic for order through the use of perspective. Underlying the idea of perspective was a new Renaissance worldview: humans asserting themselves over nature in painting and design by controlling space. Optics became the organizing principle of the natural world in that it detected the "objective" order in nature. The Italian painters were keenly aware of their new technique, and they criticized the Byzantine and the northern Gothic stylists for "flat" depiction of the human body and the natural world. The highest accolade for a Renaissance artist was to be described as an "imitator of nature": the artist's teacher was nature, not design books or master painters. Leonardo described how "painting . . . compels the mind of the painter to transform itself into the mind of nature itself and to translate between nature and art, setting out, with nature, the causes of nature's phenomena regulated by nature's laws." To imitate nature, Leonardo continued, required the technique of visual perspective.

The perspectival representation that now dominated artistry is illustrated aptly by the work of three artists: Lorenzo Ghiberti (c. 1378–1455), Andrea Mantegna, and Piero della Francesca (1420–1492). In 1401, the sculptor and goldsmith Ghiberti won a contest to design bronze doors for the San Giovanni Baptistry in Florence, a project that would occupy the rest of his life. Choosing stories from the Old and New Testaments as his themes, Ghiberti used linear perspective to create a sense of depth and space in his bronze panels. His representation of the sacrifice of Isaac, for example, created a majestic scene of movement and depth. His doors were so moving that Michelangelo in the sixteenth century described them as "the Gates of Paradise."

Mantegna's most brilliant achievement, his frescoes in the bridal chamber of the Gonzaga Palace, completed between 1465 and 1474, created an illusory extension of reality, a three-dimensional representation of life, as the actual living space in the chamber "opened out" to the painted landscape on the walls. By contrast, the painter Piero della Francesca set his detached and expressionless figures in a geometrical world of columns and tiles, framed by intersecting lines and angles. Human existence, if della Francesca's painting can be taken as a reflection of his times, was shaped by human design, in accordance with the faculties of reason and observation. Thus the artificially constructed urban society of the Renaissance was the ideal context in which to understand the ordered universe.

Masaccio's Trembling Man (above)

Renaissance paintings differ from medieval art in many ways, one of which is naturalism, in which subjects—human and nature—are depicted in a realistic rather than a symbolic way. Here, the important subject is baptism, but Masaccio's representation emphasizes the feeling of cold water, a naturalistic treatment intended to connect the subject of the painting and the viewer.
Erich Lessing/Art Resource, NY.

Madonna and Child (upper right)

Raphael's Madonna and Child flows with natural grace: Jesus and the Virgin Mary are unfrozen from their static representations in Byzantine and medieval art. This naturalistic portrayal reflects how religious feelings were permeated by the everyday in the Renaissance.
Scala/Art Resource, NY.

Botticelli's *Spring* (right)

This detail from Botticelli's Spring *depicts the graceful movements of dance and the beauty of the female body through the naturalistic technique of Renaissance art. Note the contrast between the stillness of the formal composition, with the figures anchored by the trees in the background, and the movement conveyed by the gently flowing robes and the swirling motion of the dancing figures.*
Scala/Art Resource, NY.

Michelangelo's *David* (upper left)

Commissioned of the great Florentine artist when he was twenty-six, David (1501–1504) represents a masterpiece of sculpture that equaled the glory of ancient human sculpture. This huge marble figure—the earliest monumental statue of the Renaissance—depicts David larger than life-size in the full beauty and strength of the male body.
Nimatallah/Art Resource, NY.

Equestrian Statue of Gattamelata (upper right)

The artist's largest freestanding work in bronze, Donatello's equestrian monument of a Venetian general (1445–1450) consciously imitates the examples of ancient Rome. Unlike triumphant Caesars and Roman generals, however, Gatta-melata, the recently deceased commander depicted, did not enjoy a particularly successful career in terms of victories.
Scala/Art Resource, NY.

The Sacrifice of Isaac (left)

Ghiberti's brilliant work (1401–1402) forms one of the panels on the door of the Baptistery of Florence. Technically difficult to execute, this bronze relief captures the violence of move-ment as the angel intervenes as Abraham is about to slit the throat of Isaac, a story told in the Hebrew Scriptures.
Scala/Art Resource, NY.

**Piero della Francesca,
*The Flagellation of Christ***
*Active in Urbino in the mid-
fifteenth century, the Tuscan
artist Piero della Francesca was
a master of dramatic perspective
and design, as exemplified in
this small panel painting. His
use of cool colors and his imaginative manipulation of geometric space have led many art
historians to regard Piero as the
earliest forebear of the abstract
artists of our own time.*
Scala/Art Resource, NY.

**Frescoes of the
Camera degli Sposi**
*Andrea Mantegna's frescoes in
the ducal palace depict members
of the Gonzaga family, together
with their court and animals,
in various festive scenes. In
masterly use of the perspective
techniques, four painted walls
lead to a vaulted ceiling decorated as heaven. The landscape
view to the left of the door reflects the Renaissance idea of
a painting as a window to the
real world.*
Scala/Art Resource, NY.

Perhaps even more than the visual artists, fifteenth-century architects embodied the Renaissance ideals of uniting artistic creativity and scientific knowledge. Among the greatest talents of the day was Filippo Brunelleschi (1377–1446), a Florentine architect whose designs included the dome of the city's cathedral, modeled after ancient Roman ruins; the Ospedale degli Innocenti (a hospital for orphans); and the interiors of several Florentine churches. Son of a lawyer and a goldsmith by train-

ing, Brunelleschi also invented machines to help with architectural engineering.

One of the first buildings designed by the Florentine architect Leon Battista Alberti (1404–1472), the Rucellai Palace in Florence, shows a strong classical influence and inaugurated a trend in the construction of urban palaces for the Florentine ruling elite. Although Alberti undertook architectural designs for many princes, his significance lies more in his theoretical works, which strongly influenced his contemporaries. In a book on painting dedicated to Brunelleschi, Alberti analyzed the technique of perspective as the method of imitating nature. In *On Architecture* (1415), modeled after the Roman Vitruvius, Alberti argued for large-scale urban planning, with monumental buildings set on open squares, harmonious and beautiful in their proportions. His ideas were put into action by Pope Sixtus IV (r. 1471–1484) and his successors in the urban renewal of Rome, and they served to transform that unruly medieval town into a geometrically constructed monument to architectural brilliance by recalling the grandeur of its ancient origins.

New Musical Harmonies

Italy set the standards for the visual arts in Europe, but in musical styles it was more influenced by the northern countries. Around 1430, a new style of music appeared in the Low Countries that would dominate composition for the next two centuries. Instead of writing pieces with one major melodic line, composers were writing for three or four instrumental or human voices, each equally important in expressing a melody in harmony with the others.

The leader of this new style, known as *polyphonic* ("many sounds") music, was Guillaume Dufay (1400–1474), whose musical training began in the cathedral choir of his hometown, Cambrai in the Low Countries. His successful career took him to all the cultural centers of the Renaissance, where nobles sponsored new compositions and maintained a corps of musicians for court and religious functions. In 1438, Dufay composed festive music to celebrate the completion of the cathedral dome in Florence designed by Brunelleschi. Dufay expressed the harmonic relationship among four voices in ratios that matched the mathematically precise dimensions of Brunelleschi's architecture. After a period of employment at the papal court, Dufay returned to his native north and composed music for the Burgundian and French courts.

Although his younger counterpart Johannes Ockeghem (c. 1420–1495), whose influence rivaled Dufay's, worked almost exclusively at the French court, Dufay's mobile career was typical. Josquin des Prez (1440–1521), another Netherlander, wrote music in Milan, Ferrara, Florence, and Paris and at the papal court. The new style of music was beloved by the elites: Lorenzo de' Medici sent Dufay a love poem to set to music, and the great composer maintained a lifelong relationship with the Medici family.

Within Renaissance polyphony were three main musical genres: the canon (central texts) of the Catholic Mass; the motet, which used both sacred and secular texts; and the secular *chanson*, often using the tunes of folk dances. Composers often adapted familiar folk melodies for sacred music, expressing religious feeling primarily through human voices instead of instruments. The tambourine and the lute were indispensable for dances, however, and small ensembles of wind and string instruments with contrasting sounds performed with singers in the fashionable courts of Europe. Also in use in the fifteenth century were new keyboard instruments—the harpsichord and clavichord—which could play several harmonic lines at once.

❖ The Intersection of Private and Public Lives

Paid for largely by the patronage of the ruling elites, Renaissance culture served not only for their enjoyment but also to glorify the republics, principalities, and kingdoms and to justify the legitimacy of their rulers. Just as lineage and descent shaped political power in dynastic states in the fourteenth century, the state itself, through its institutions and laws, now attempted to shape private life. Nowhere was this process more evident than at Florence, the leading center of Renaissance culture. Considerations of state power intruded into the most intimate personal concerns: sexual intimacy, marriage, and childbirth could not be separated from the values of the ruling classes. With a society dominated by upper-class, patriarchal households, Renaissance Italy specified rigid roles for men and women, subordinating women and making marriage a vehicle for consolidating social hierarchy.

Renaissance Social Hierarchy

To deal with a mounting fiscal crisis, in 1427 the government of Florence ordered that a comprehensive tax record of households in the city and territory be compiled. Completed in 1430, this survey represented the most detailed population census then taken in European history. From the resulting mass of fiscal and demographic data, historians have been able to reconstruct a picture of the Florentine state, particularly its capital—the most important city of the Renaissance and a city whose records for this period are unparalleled in their detail.

The state of Florence, roughly the size of Massachusetts, had a population of more than 260,000. Tuscany, the area in which the Florentine state was located, was one of the most urbanized regions of Europe. With 38,000 inhabitants, the capital city of Florence claimed 14 percent of the total population and an enormous 67 percent of the state's wealth. Straddling the Arno River, Florence was a beautiful, thriving city with a defined social hierarchy. In describing class divisions, the Florentines themselves referred to the "little people" and the "fat people." Some 60 percent of all households belonged to the "little people"—workers, artisans, small merchants. The "fat people" (roughly our middle class) made up 30 percent of the urban population and included the wealthier merchants, the leading artisans, notaries, doctors, and other professionals. At the very bottom of the hierarchy were slaves and servants, largely women employed in domestic service. Whereas the small number of slaves were of Balkan origin, the much larger population of domestic servants came to the city from the surrounding countryside as contracted wage earners. At the top, a tiny elite of patricians, bankers, and wool merchants controlled the state with their enormous wealth. In fact, the richest 1 percent of urban households (approximately one hundred families) owned more than one-quarter of the city's wealth and one-sixth of Tuscany's total wealth. The patricians in particular owned almost all government bonds, a lucrative investment guaranteed by a state they dominated.

Surprisingly, men seem to have outnumbered women in the 1427 survey. For every 100 women there were 110 men, unlike most past and present populations, in which women are the majority. In addition to female infanticide, which was occasionally practiced, the survey itself reflected the society's bias against women: persistent underreporting on women probably explained the statistical abnormality; and married daughters, young girls, and elderly widows frequently disappeared from the memories of householders. Most people, men and women alike, lived in households with at least six inhabitants, although the form of family unit—nuclear or extended—varied, depending mainly on wealth, with poor people rarely able to support

extended families. Among urban patricians and landowning peasants, the extended family held sway. The number of children in a family, it seems, reflected class differences as well. Wealthier families had more children; childless couples existed almost exclusively among the poor, who were also more likely to abandon the infants they could not feed.

Family Alliances

Wealth and class clearly determined family structure and the pattern of marriage and childbearing. In a letter to her eldest son, Filippo, dated 1447, Alessandra Strozzi announced the marriage of her daughter Caterina to the son of Parente Parenti. She described the young groom, Marco Parenti, as "a worthy and virtuous young man, and . . . the only son, and rich, 25 years old, and keeps a silk workshop; and they have a little political standing." The dowry was set at one thousand florins, a substantial sum—but for four to five hundred florins more, Alessandra admitted to Filippo, Caterina would have fetched a husband from a more prominent family.

The Strozzi belonged to one of Florence's most distinguished traditional families, but at the time of Caterina's betrothal the family had fallen into political disgrace. Alessandra's husband, an enemy of the Medici, was exiled in 1434; Filippo, a rich merchant in Naples, lived under the same political ban. Although Caterina was clearly marrying beneath her social station, the marriage represented an alliance in which money, political status, and family standing all balanced out. More an alliance between families than the consummation of love, an Italian Renaissance marriage was usually orchestrated by the male head of a household. In this case, Alessandra, as a widow, shared the matchmaking responsibility with her eldest son and other male relatives. Eighteen years later, when it came time to find a wife for Filippo, who had by then accumulated enough wealth to start his own household, Marco Parenti, his brother-in-law, would serve as matchmaker.

The upper-class Florentine family was patrilineal, that is, it traced descent and determined inheritance through the male line. Because the distribution of wealth depended on this patriarchal system, women occupied an ambivalent position in the household. A daughter could claim inheritance only through her dowry, and she often disappeared from family records after her marriage. A wife seldom emerged

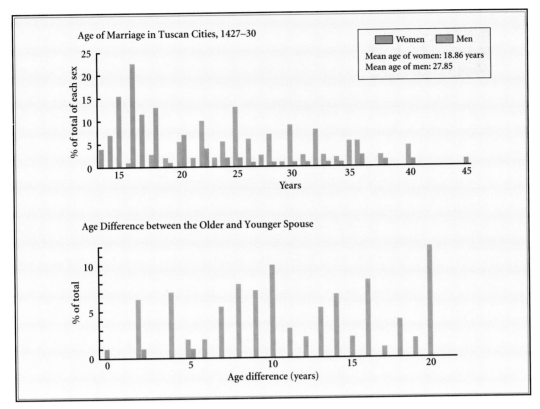

TAKING MEASURE Age of Marriage in Tuscan Cities, 1427–1430

The 1427–1430 Florentine tax and census records indicate two distinctly different marriage patterns for men and women. While the mean marriage age for women was 18.86 years, that for men was 27.85 years. This difference reflected the considerable difficulty for young men to amass enough wealth to start a household. More revealing is the chart showing the differences in age between the spouses. Some 12 percent of all spouses had a difference of twenty years. While the great majority of these marriages involved older, wealthier, established males, often in second marriages after the death of their first spouses, a small number involved younger men marrying up in the social ladder to widows of guild members to acquire a position. Together these charts give important information on gender relations and reflect the underlying class and gender inequalities in Renaissance society.
From David Herlihy and Christiane Klapisch-Zuber, *Tuscans and Their Families: A Study of Florentine Catasto of 1427* (New Haven: Yale University Press, 1985), 205. Reprinted by permission of Yale University Press.

from the shadow of her husband, and consequently the lives of many women have been lost to history.

In the course of a woman's life, her family often pressured her to conform to conventional expectations. At the birth of a daughter, most wealthy Florentine fathers opened an account at the Dowry Fund, a public fund established in 1425 to raise state revenues and a major investment instrument for the upper classes. In 1433, the fund paid annual interest of between 15 and 21 percent, and fathers could hope to raise handsome dowries to marry their daughters to more prominent men when the daughters became marriageable in their late teens. The

Dowry Fund supported the structure of the marriage market, in which the circulation of wealth and women consolidated the social coherence of the ruling classes. (See "Taking Measure," above.)

Women's subordination in marriages often reflected the age differences between spouses. The Italian marriage pattern, in which young women married older men, contrasted sharply with the northern European model, in which partners were much closer in age. Significant age disparity also left many women widowed in their twenties and thirties, and remarriage often proved a hard choice. A widow's father and brothers frequently pressed her to remarry to form a new family alliance. A widow, however, could not bring her children into her new marriage because they belonged to her first husband's family. Faced with the choice between her children and her paternal family, not to mention the question of her own happiness, a widow could hope to gain greater autonomy only in her old age, when, like Alessandra, she might assume matchmaking responsibilities to advance her family's fortunes.

In northern Europe, however, women enjoyed a relatively more secure position. In England, the Low Countries, and Germany, for example, women played a significant role in the economy—not only in the peasant household, in which everyone worked, but especially in the town, serving as peddlers, weavers, seamstresses, shopkeepers, midwives, and brewers. In Cologne, for example, women could join one of several artisans' guilds, and in Munich they ranked among some of the richest brewers. Women in northern Europe shared inheritances with their brothers, retained control of their dowries, and had the right to represent themselves before the law. Italian men who traveled to the north were appalled at the differences in gender relations, criticizing English women as violent and brazen and disapproving of the mixing of the sexes in German public baths.

The Regulation of Sexuality

Along with marriage patterns, child care and attitudes toward sexuality also reflected class differences in Renaissance life. Florentine middle- and upper-class fathers arranged business contracts with wet nurses to breast-feed their infants; babies thus spent prolonged periods of time away from their families. Such elaborate child care was beyond the reach of the poor, who often abandoned their children to strangers or to public charity.

By the beginning of the fifteenth century, Florence's two hospitals were accepting large numbers of abandoned children in addition to the sick and infirm. In 1445, the government opened the Ospedale degli Innocenti to deal with the large number of abandoned children. These unfortunate children came from two sources: poor families who were unable to feed another mouth, especially in times of famine, war, and economic depression; and women who had given birth out of wedlock. A large number of the latter were domestic slaves or servants who had been impregnated by their masters; in

1445, one-third of the first hundred foundlings at the new hospital were children of the unequal liaisons between masters and women slaves. For some women the foundling hospital provided an alternative to infanticide. Over two-thirds of abandoned infants were girls, a clear indicator of the inequality between the sexes. Although Florence's government employed wet nurses to care for the foundlings, the large number of abandoned infants overtaxed the hospital's limited resources. The hospital's death rate for infants was much higher than the already high infant mortality rate of the time.

Illegitimacy in itself did not necessarily carry a social stigma in fifteenth-century Europe. Most upper-class men acknowledged and supported their illegitimate children as a sign of virility, and illegitimate children of noble lineage often rose to social and political prominence. Any social stigma was borne primarily by the woman, whose ability to marry became compromised. Shame and guilt drove some poor single mothers to kill their infants, a crime for which they paid with their own lives.

In addition to prosecuting infanticide, the public regulation of sexuality focused on prostitution and homosexuality. Intended "to eliminate a worse evil by a lesser one," a 1415 statute established government brothels in Florence. Concurrent with its higher tolerance of prostitution, the Renaissance state had a low tolerance of homosexuality. In 1432, the Florentine state appointed magistrates "to discover—whether by means of secret denunciation, accusations, notification, or any other method—those who commit the vice of sodomy, whether actively or passively." The government set fines for homosexual acts and carried out death sentences against pederasts (men who have sex with boys).

Fifteenth-century European magistrates took violence against women less seriously than illegal male sexual behavior, as the different punishments indicate. In Renaissance Venice, for example, the typical jail sentence for rape and attempted rape was only six months. Magistrates often treated noblemen with great leniency and handled rape cases according to class distinctions. For example, Agneta, a young girl living with a government official, was abducted and raped by two millers, who were sentenced to five years in prison; several servants who abducted and raped a slave woman were sentenced to three to four months in jail; and a nobleman who abducted and raped Anna, a slave woman, was freed.

Whether in marriage, inheritance, illicit sex, or sexual crime, the Renaissance state regulated the behavior of men and women according to differing concepts of gender. The brilliant civilization of the Renaissance was experienced very differently by men and women.

❖ The Renaissance State and the Art of Politics

Among the achievements of the Renaissance, the state seemed to represent a work of art. For the Florentine political theorist Niccolò Machiavelli (1469–1527), the state was an artifice of human creation to be conquered, shaped, and administered by princes according to the principles of power politics. Machiavelli laid out these principles in his work, *The Prince*: "It can be observed that men use various methods in pursuing their own personal objectives, that is glory and riches. . . . I believe that . . . fortune is the arbiter of half the things we do, leaving the other half or so to be controlled by ourselves." *The Prince* was the first treatment of the science of politics in which the acquisition and exercise of power were discussed without reference to an ultimate moral or ethical end. Machiavelli's keen observations of power, scandalous to his contemporaries, were based on a careful study of Italian politics during the Renaissance. Though a republican at heart, Machiavelli recognized the necessity of power in founding a state, whose sustenance ultimately rested on republican virtue. Outside of Italy, other European states also furnished many examples to illustrate the ruthless nature of power politics and the artifice of state building. In general, a midcentury period of turmoil gave way to the restructuring of central monarchical power in the last decades of the fifteenth century. Many states developed stronger, institutionally more complex central governments in which middle-class lawyers played an increasingly prominent role. The expanded Renaissance state paved the way for the development of the nation-state in later centuries.

Republics and Principalities in Italy

The Italian states of the Renaissance can be divided into two broad categories: republics, which preserved the traditional institutions of the medieval

MAP 14.2 Italy, c. 1450
The political divisions of Italy reflected powerful city-centered republics and duchies in the north and the larger but economically more backward south. Local and regional identities remained strong into the modern age.

commune by allowing a civic elite to control political and economic life, and principalities, which were ruled by one dynasty. The most powerful and influential states were the republics of Venice and Florence and the principalities of Milan and Naples. In addition to these four, a handful of smaller states, such as Siena, Ferrara, and Mantua stood out as important cultural centers during the Renaissance (Map 14.2).

Venice. Venice, a city built on a lagoon, ruled an extensive colonial empire that extended from the Adriatic to the Aegean Sea. Venetian merchant ships sailed the Mediterranean, the Atlantic coast, and the Black Sea; Christian pilgrims to Palestine booked passage on Venetian ships; in 1430, the Venetian navy numbered more than three thousand ships. Symbolizing their intimacy with and dominion over the sea, the Venetians celebrated an annual

"Wedding of the Sea." Amid throngs of spectators and foreign dignitaries, the Venetian doge (the elected duke) sailed out to the Adriatic, threw a golden ring into its waters to renew the union, and intoned, "Hear us with favor, O Lord. We worthily entreat Thee to grant that this sea be tranquil and quiet for our men and all others who sail upon it."

In the early fifteenth century, however, Venetians faced threats on both sides. From 1425 to 1454, Venice fought the expanding duchy of Milan on land. The second and greater danger came from the eastern Mediterranean, where the Ottoman Turks finally captured Byzantine Constantinople in 1453. Faced by these external threats, Venice drew strength from its internal social cohesion. Under the rule of an oligarchy of aristocratic merchants, Venice enjoyed stability; and its maritime empire benefited citizens of all social classes, who joined efforts to defend the interests of the "Most Serene Republic," a contemporary name that reflected Venice's lack of social strife.

Florence. Compared with serene Venice, the republic of Florence was in constant agitation: responsive to political conflicts, new ideas, and artistic styles. Like Venice, Florence described its government in the humanist language of ancient Roman republicanism. Unlike Venice, Florentine society was turbulent as social classes and political factions engaged in constant civic strife. By 1434, a single family had emerged dominant in this fractious city: the Medici. Cosimo de' Medici (1388–1464), the head of the family, was ruthless. His contemporary Pope Pius II did not mince words in describing Medici power. "Cosimo, having thus disposed of his rivals, proceeded to administer the state at his pleasure and amassed wealth. . . . In Florence he built a palace fit for a king." As head of one of the largest banks of Europe, Cosimo de' Medici used his immense wealth to influence politics. Even though he did not hold any formal political office, he wielded influence in government through business associates and clients who were indebted to him for loans, political appointments, and other favors.

As the largest bank in Europe, the Medici Bank handled papal finances and established branch offices in many Italian cities and the major northern European financial centers. Backed by this immense private wealth, Cosimo became the arbiter of war and peace, the regulator of law, more master than

citizen. Yet the prosperity and security that Florence enjoyed made him popular as well. At his death, Cosimo was lauded as the "father of his country."

Cosimo's grandson Lorenzo (called "the Magnificent"), who assumed power in 1467, bolstered the regime's legitimacy with his lavish patronage of the arts. But opponents were not lacking. In 1478, Lorenzo narrowly escaped an assassination attempt. Two years after Lorenzo's death in 1494, partisans who opposed the Medici drove them from Florence. The Medici returned to power in 1512, only to be driven out again in 1527. In 1530, the republic fell and the Medici once again seized control, declaring Florence a duchy.

Milan. Unlike Florence, with its republican aspirations, the duchy of Milan had been under dynastic rule since the fourteenth century. The most powerful Italian principality, Milan was a military state relatively uninterested in the support of the arts but with a first-class armaments and textile industry in the capital city and rich farmlands of Lombardy. Until 1447, the duchy was ruled by the Visconti dynasty, a group of powerful lords whose plans to unify all of northern and central Italy failed from the combined opposition of Venice, Florence, and other Italian powers. In 1447, the last Visconti duke died without a male heir, and the nobility proclaimed Milan to be the Ambrosian republic (named after the city's patron saint, Ambrose), thus bringing the Visconti rule to a close.

For three years the new republic struggled to maintain Milan's political and military strength. Cities that the Visconti family had subdued rebelled against Milan, and the two great republics of Venice and Florence plotted its downfall. Milan's ruling nobility, seeking further defense, appointed Francesco Sforza, who had married the illegitimate daughter of the last Visconti duke, to the post of general. Sforza promptly turned against his employers, claiming the duchy as his own. A bitter struggle between the nobility and the townspeople in Milan further undermined the republican cause, and in 1450 Sforza entered Milan in triumph.

The power of the Sforza dynasty reached its height during the 1490s. In 1493, Duke Ludovico married his niece Bianca Maria to Maximilian, the newly elected Holy Roman Emperor, promising an immense dowry in exchange for the emperor's legitimization of his rule. But the newfound Milanese glory was soon swept aside by France's invasion of Italy in 1494, and the duchy itself eventually came under Spanish rule.

Naples. After a struggle for succession between Alfonso of Aragon and René d'Anjou, a cousin of the king of France, the kingdoms of Naples and Sicily came under Aragonese rule between 1435 and 1494. Unlike the northern Italian states, Naples was dominated by powerful feudal barons who retained jurisdiction and taxation over their own vast estates. Alfonso I (r. 1435–1458), called "the Magnanimous" for his generous patronage of the arts, promoted the urban middle class to counter baronial rule, using as his base the city of Naples, the only large urban center in a relatively rural kingdom. Alfonso's son Ferante I (r. 1458–1494) continued his father's policies: two of his chief ministers hailed from humble backgrounds. With their private armies and estates intact, however, the barons constantly threatened royal power, and in 1462 many rebelled against Ferante. More ruthless than his father, Ferante handily crushed the opposition. He kept rebellious barons in the dungeons of his Neapolitan castle and confiscated their properties. When his ministers plotted against him, siding with yet other rebel barons, Ferante feigned reconciliation and then arrested the ministers at a banquet and executed them and their families.

Embroiled in Italian politics, Alfonso and Ferante shifted their alliances among the papacy, Milan, and Florence. But the greater threat to Neapolitan security was external. In 1480, Ottoman forces captured the Adriatic port of Otranto, where they massacred the entire male population. And in 1494, a French invasion ended the Aragonese dynasty in Naples, although, as in Milan, France's claim would eventually be superseded by that of Spain.

The Papal States. In the violent arena of Italian politics, the papacy, an uneasy mixture of worldly splendor and religious authority, was a player like the other states. The vicars of Christ negotiated treaties, made war, and built palaces; a few led scandalous lives. Pope Alexander VI (r. 1492–1503), the most notorious pontiff, kept a mistress and fathered children, one of whom, Cesare Borgia, served as the model ruthless ruler for Machiavelli in *The Prince*.

The popes' concern with politics stemmed from their desire to restore papal authority, greatly undermined by the Great Schism and the conciliar movement. To that end, the popes used both politics and culture to enhance their authority. Politically, they curbed local power, expanded papal government, increased taxation, enlarged the papal army and navy, and extended papal diplomacy. Culturally, the popes renovated churches, created the Vatican Library, sponsored artists, and patronized writers to glorify their role and power as St. Peter's successors. In undertaking these measures, the Renaissance papacy merely exemplified the larger trend toward the centralization of power evident in the development of monarchies and empires outside of Italy as well.

Renaissance Diplomacy

Many features of diplomacy characteristic of today's nation-states first appeared in fifteenth-century Europe. By midcentury, competition between states and the extension of warfare raised the practice of diplomacy to nearly an art form. The first diplomatic handbook, composed in 1436 by Frenchman Bernard du Rosier, later archbishop of Toulouse, declared that the business of the diplomat was "to pay honor to religion . . . and the Imperial crown, to protect the rights of kingdoms, to offer obedience . . . to confirm friendships . . . make peace . . . to arrange past disputes and remove the cause for future unpleasantness."

The emphasis on ceremonies, elegance, and eloquence (Italians referred to ambassadors as "orators") masked the complex game of diplomatic intrigue and spying. In the fifteenth century, a resident ambassador was expected to keep a continuous stream of foreign political news flowing to the home government, not just to conduct temporary diplomatic missions, as earlier ambassadors had done. In some cases the presence of semiofficial agents developed into full-fledged ambassadorships: the Venetian embassy to the sultan's court in Constantinople developed out of the merchant-consulate that had represented all Venetian merchants, and Medici Bank branch managers eventually acted as political agents for the Florentine republic.

Foremost in the development of diplomacy was Milan, a state with political ambition and military might. Under the Visconti dukes, Milan sent ambassadors to Aragon, Burgundy, the Holy Roman Empire, and the Ottoman Empire. Under the Sforza dynasty, Milanese diplomacy continued to function as a cherished form of statecraft. For generations Milanese diplomats at the French court sent home an incessant flow of information on the rivalry between France and Burgundy. Francesco Sforza, founder of the dynasty, also used his diplomatic corps to extend his political patronage. In letters of recommendation to the papacy, Francesco commented on the political desirability of potential ecclesiastical candidates by using code words, sometimes supplemented with instructions to his ambassador to indicate his true intent regardless of the coded letter of recommendation. In more sensitive diplomatic reports, ciphers were used to prevent them from being understood by hostile powers.

As the center of Christendom, Rome became the diplomatic hub of Europe. During the 1490s, well over two hundred diplomats were stationed in Rome. The papacy sent out far fewer envoys than it received; only at the end of the fifteenth century were papal nuncios, or envoys, permanently established in the European states.

The most outstanding achievement of Italy's Renaissance diplomacy was the negotiation of a general peace treaty that settled the decades of warfare engendered by Milanese expansion and civil war. The Treaty of Lodi (1454) established a complex balance of power among the major Italian states and maintained relative stability in the peninsula for half a century. Renaissance diplomacy eventually failed, however, when more powerful northern European neighbors invaded in 1494, leading to the collapse of the whole Italian state system.

Monarchies and Empires

Locked in fierce competition among themselves, the Italian states paid little attention to large territorial states emerging in the rest of Europe that would soon overshadow Italy with their military power and economic resources. Whether in Burgundy, England, Spain, France, the Ottoman Empire, or Muscovy, the ruler employed various stratagems to expand or enhance his power. In Burgundy, the dukes staged lavish ceremonies to win the affection of their diverse subjects; in England, a strengthened monarchy emerged from a civil war that weakened the feudal nobility; in Spain, the monarchs repressed religious minorities in their newly unified land; in France, the kings raised taxes and established a per-

manent standing army; in the Balkans and Russia, autocratic princes enjoyed powers unheard of in western Europe in their expanding empires. In central Europe, by contrast, the rulers failed to centralize power.

Burgundy. The expansion of Burgundy during the fifteenth century was a result of military might and careful statecraft. The spectacular success of the Burgundian dukes—and the equally dramatic demise of Burgundian power—bear testimony to the artful creation of the Renaissance state, paving the way for the development of the European nation-state.

Part of the French royal house, the Burgundian dynasty expanded its power rapidly by acquiring land, primarily in the Netherlands. Between 1384 and 1476, the Burgundian state filled the territorial gap between France and Germany, extending from the Swiss border in the south to Friesland, Germany, in the north. Through purchases, inheritance, and conquests, the dukes ruled over French-, Dutch-, and German-speaking subjects, creating a state that resembled a patchwork of provinces and regions, each jealously guarding its laws and traditions. The Low Countries, with their flourishing cities, constituted the state's economic heartland, and the region of Burgundy itself, which gave the state its name, offered rich farmlands and vineyards. Unlike England, whose island geography made it a natural political unit; or France, whose borders were forged in the national experience of repelling English invaders; or Castile, whose national identity came from centuries of warfare against Islam, Burgundy was an artificial creation whose coherence depended entirely on the skillful exercise of statecraft.

Expansion of Burgundy, 1384–1476

At the heart of Burgundian politics was the personal cult of its dukes. Philip the Good (r. 1418–1467) and his son Charles the Bold (r. 1467–1477) were very different kinds of rulers, but both were devoted to enhancing the prestige of their dynasty and the security of their dominion. A bon vivant who fathered many illegitimate children, Philip was a lavish patron of the arts who commissioned numerous illuminated manuscripts, chronicles, tapestries, paintings, and music in his efforts to glorify Burgundy. Charles, by contrast, spent more time on war than at court, preferring to drill his troops rather than seduce noblewomen. Renowned for his courage (hence his nickname), he died in 1477 when his army was routed by the Swiss at Nancy.

The Burgundians' success depended in large part on their personal relationship with their subjects. Not only did the dukes travel constantly from one part of their dominion to another, they also staged elaborate ceremonies to enhance their power and promote their legitimacy. Their entries into cities and their presence at ducal weddings, births, and funerals became the centerpieces of a "theater" state in which the dynasty provided the only link among very diverse territories. New rituals became propaganda tools. Philip's revival of chivalry in the ducal court transformed the semi-independent nobility into courtiers closely tied to the prince.

In addition to sponsoring political propaganda, the Burgundian rulers controlled their geographically dispersed state by developing a financial bureaucracy and a standing army. But maintaining the army, one of the largest in Europe, left the dukes chronically short of money. They were forced to sell political offices to raise funds, a practice that led to an inefficient and corrupt bureaucracy. The demise of the Burgundian state had two sources: the loss of Charles the Bold, who died without a male heir, and an alliance between France and the Holy Roman Empire. When Charles fell in battle in 1477, France seized the duchy of Burgundy. The Netherlands remained loyal to Mary, Charles's daughter, and through her husband, the future Holy Roman Emperor Maximilian, some of the Burgundian lands and the dynasty's political and artistic legacy passed on to the Habsburgs.

England. In England, defeat in the Hundred Years' War was followed by civil war at home. Henry VI (r. 1422–1461), who ascended to the throne as a

The Burgundian Court
The ideals of late-medieval courtly style found fullest expression in the fifteenth-century Burgundy. This painting of the wedding of Philip the Good and Isabella of Portugal was executed in the workshop of the Flemish master Jan van Eyck. It conveys the atmosphere of chivalric fantasy in which the Burgundian dynasty enveloped itself.
Giraudon/Art Resource, NY.

child, proved in maturity to be a weak and, on occasion, mentally unstable monarch. He was unable to control the great lords of the realm, who wrought anarchy with their numerous private feuds; between 1450 and 1455, six of the thirty-six peers in the House of Lords were imprisoned at some time for violence. Henry was held in contempt by many, particularly his cousin Richard, the duke of York, who resented bitterly that the House of Lancaster had usurped the throne in 1399, depriving the House of York of its legitimate claim. In 1460, Richard rebelled; although he was killed in battle, his son defeated Henry and was then crowned Edward IV (r. 1461–1483). England's intermittent civil wars, later called the Wars of the Roses (after the white and red roses worn by the Yorkists and Lancastrians, respectively), continued until 1485, fueled at home by factions among nobles and regional discontent and abroad by Franco-Burgundian intervention. Edward IV crushed the Lancastrian claim in 1470, but the Yorkist succession ended in 1485 when Richard III (r. 1483–1485), Edward's younger brother, perished at the battle of Bosworth. The ultimate victor was Henry Tudor, who married Elizabeth of York, the daughter of Edward IV, and became Henry VII (r. 1485–1509). The Tudor claim benefited from Richard's notoriety; Richard was widely suspected of obtaining the throne by murdering his young nephews, two of Edward IV's sons—a sinister legend to which William Shakespeare would give even more fantastic proportions one century later in his famous play *Richard III*.

The Wars of the Roses did relatively little damage to England's soil. The battles were generally short, and, in the words of the French chronicler Philippe de Commynes (c. 1447–1511), "England enjoyed this peculiar mercy above all other kingdoms, that neither the country, nor the people nor the houses, were wasted, destroyed or demolished, but the calamities and misfortunes of the war fell only upon the soldiers, and especially on the nobility." As a result, the English economy continued to grow during the fifteenth century. The cloth industry expanded considerably, and the English now used much of the raw wool that they had been exporting to the Low Countries to manufacture goods at home. London merchants, taking a vigorous role in trade, also assumed greater political prominence not only in the governance of London but as bankers to kings and members of Parliament; they constituted a small minority in the House of Commons, which was dominated by the country gentry. In the countryside the landed classes—the nobility, the gentry, and the yeomanry (free farmers)—benefited from rising farm and land-rent income as the population increased slowly but steadily.

Spain.   In the Iberian monarchies, decades of civil war over the royal successions began to wane only in 1469, when Isabella of Castile and Ferdinand of Aragon married. Retaining their separate titles, the two monarchs ruled jointly over their dominions, each of which adhered to its traditional laws and privileges. Their union represented the first step toward the creation of a unified Spain out of two medieval kingdoms. Isabella and Ferdinand limited the privileges of the nobility and allied themselves with the cities, relying on the Hermandad (civic militia) to enforce justice and on lawyers to staff the royal council.

The united strength of Castile and Aragon brought the reconquista to a close with a final crusade against the Muslims. After more than a century of peace, war broke out in 1478 between Granada, the last Iberian Muslim state, and the Catholic royal forces. Weakened by internal strife, Granada finally fell in 1492. Two years later, in recognition of the crusade, Pope Alexander VI bestowed the title "Catholic monarchs" on Isabella and Ferdinand, ringing in an era in which

Unification of Spain, Late Fifteenth Century

militant Catholicism became an instrument of state authority and shaped the national consciousness.

The relative religious tolerance of the Middle Ages, in which Iberian Muslims, Jews, and Christians had lived side by side, now yielded to the demand for religious conformity. The practice of Catholicism became a test of one's loyalty to the church and to the Spanish monarchy. In 1478, royal jurisdiction introduced the Inquisition to Spain, primarily as a means to control the *conversos* (Jewish converts to Christianity), whose elevated positions in the economy and the government aroused widespread resentment from the so-called Old Christians. *Conversos* often were suspected of practicing their ancestral religion in secret while pretending to adhere to their new Christian faith. Appointed by the monarchs, the clergy (called "inquisitors") presided over tribunals set up to investigate those suspected of religious deviancy. The accused, who were arrested on charges often based on anonymous denunciations and information gathered by the inquisitors, could defend themselves but not confront their accusers. The wide spectrum of punishments ranged from monetary fines to the *auto de fé* (a ritual of public confession) to

Queen Isabella of Castile
In 1474 Isabella became queen of Castile, and in 1479 her husband Ferdinand took control of the kingdom of Aragon. This union of crowns would lead to the creation of a unified Spain. It would also promulgate a religious hegemony as the "Catholic monarchs" expelled Jews and Muslims from their kingdoms.
Laurie Platt Winfrey, Inc.

burning at the stake. After the fall of Granada, many Moors were forced to convert or resettle in Castile, and in 1492 Ferdinand and Isabella ordered all Jews in their kingdoms to choose between exile and conversion.

The single most dramatic event for the Jews of Renaissance Europe was their expulsion from Spain, the country with the largest and most vibrant Jewish communities, and their subsequent dispersion throughout the Mediterranean world. On the eve of the expulsion, approximately 200,000 Jews and 300,000 *conversos* were living in Castile and Aragon. Faced with the choice to convert or leave, well over 100,000 Jews chose exile. The priest Andrés Bernáldez described the expulsion:

Just as with a strong hand and outstretched arm, and much honor and riches, God through Moses had miraculously taken the other people of Israel from Egypt, so in these parts of Spain they had . . . to go out with much honor and riches, without losing any of their goods, to possess the holy promised land, which they confessed to have lost through their great and abominable sins which their ancestors had committed against God.

France. France, too, was recovering from war. Although France won the Hundred Years' War, it emerged from that conflict in the shadow of the brilliant Burgundian court. Under Charles VII (r. 1422–1461) and Louis XI (r. 1461–1483), the French monarchy began the slow process of expansion and recovery. Abroad, Louis fomented rebellion in England. At home, however, lay the more dangerous enemy, Burgundy. In 1477, with the death of Charles the Bold, Louis seized large tracts of Burgundian territory. France's horizons expanded even more when Louis inherited most of southern France after the Anjou dynasty died out. By the end of the century, France had doubled its territory, assuming close to its modern-day boundaries.

To strengthen royal power at home, Louis promoted industry and commerce, imposed permanent salt and land taxes (called the *gabelle* and the *taille*), maintained the first standing army in western Europe, and dispensed with the meeting of the General Estates, which included the clergy, the nobility, and the major towns of France. The French kings further increased their power with important concessions from the papacy. With the 1438 Pragmatic Sanction of Bourges, Charles asserted the superiority of a general church council over the pope. Harking back to a long tradition of the High Middle Ages, the Sanction of Bourges established what would come to be known as Gallicanism (after Gaul, the ancient Roman name for France), in which the French king would effectively control ecclesiastical revenues and the appointment of French bishops.

Central-Eastern Europe. The rise of strong, new monarchies in western Europe contrasted sharply with the weakness of state authority in central and eastern Europe, where developments in Hungary, Bohemia, and Poland resembled the Burgundian model of personal dynastic authority (Map 14.3). Under Matthias Corvinus (r. 1456–1490), the

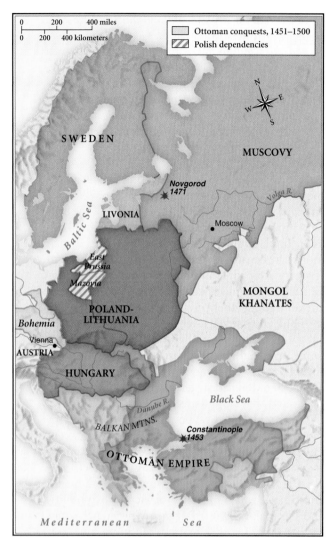

MAP 14.3 Eastern Europe in the Fifteenth Century
The rise of Muscovy and the Ottomans shaped the map of eastern Europe. Some Christian monarchies such as Serbia lost their independence. Others, such as Hungary, held off the Ottomans until the early sixteenth century.

In Poland, the nobility preserved their power under the monarchy by maintaining their right to elect kings. By selecting weak monarchs and fiercely defending noble liberties, the Polish nobility ruled a land of serfs and frustrated any attempt at the centralization of power and state building. Only in 1506 would Poland and Lithuania again form a loosely united "commonwealth" under a single king.

The Ottoman Empire. In the Balkans, the Ottoman Empire, under Sultan Mehmed II (r. 1451–1481), became a serious threat to all of Christian Europe. After Mehmed ascended the throne, he proclaimed a holy war and laid siege to Constantinople in 1453. A city of 100,000, the Byzantine capital could muster only 6,000 defenders (including a small contingent of Genoese) against an Ottoman force estimated at between 200,000 and 400,000 men. The city's fortifications, many of which dated from Emperor Justinian's rule in the sixth century, were no match for fifteenth-century cannons. The defenders held out for fifty-three days: while the Christians confessed their sins and prayed for divine deliverance, in desperate anticipation of the Second Coming, the Muslim besiegers pressed forward, urged on by the certainty of rich spoils and Allah's promise of a final victory over the infidel Rome. Finally the defenders were overwhelmed, and the last Byzantine emperor, Constantine Palaeologus, died in battle. Some 60,000 residents were carried off in slavery, and the city was sacked. Mehmed entered Constantinople in triumph, rendered thanks to Allah in Justinian's Church of St. Sophia, which had been turned into a mosque, and was remembered as "the Conqueror." In another sign of the times, however, the Muslim ruler would ask Italian court painter Matteo de Pasti to help create the imperial palace intended to communicate Ottoman power.

Muscovy. North of the Black Sea and east of Poland-Lithuania, a very different polity was taking shape. In the second half of the fifteenth century, the princes of Muscovy embarked on a spectacular path of success that would make their state the largest on earth. Subservient to the Mongols in the fourteenth century, the Muscovite princes began to assert their independence with the collapse of Mongol power. Ivan III (r. 1462–1505) was the first Muscovite prince to claim an imperial title, referring to himself as *tsar* (or *czar,* from the name *Caesar*). In

Hungarian king who briefly united the Bohemian and Hungarian crowns, a central-eastern European empire seemed to be emerging. A patron of the arts and a humanist, Matthias created a great library in Hungary. He repeatedly defeated the encroaching Austrian Habsburgs and even occupied Vienna in 1485. His empire did not outlast his death in 1490, however. The powerful Hungarian magnates, who enjoyed the constitutional right to elect the king, ended it by refusing to acknowledge his son's claim to the throne.

The Medieval Royal Castle of Visegrad

King Matthias Corvinus made Visegrad the political and cultural center of Hungary before it was destroyed in the Ottoman conquests. Situated on top of a hill commanding a strategic position over the road and the Danube River, Visegrad—shown here in a present-day reconstruction—was above all a fortification. Szabolcs Hámor/MTI/Eastfoto.

A View of Moscow

This image comes from the travel book of the Habsburg ambassador to Moscow, Sigismund von Herberstein, who engraved it himself in 1547. Note the representation of Muscovite soldiers with bows and arrows, weapons long since outdated in western Europe. Note also the domination of the Kremlin (in the middle of the city) over a city that consisted mostly of modest wooden houses. Giraudon/Art Resource, NY.

1471, Ivan defeated the city-state of Novgorod, whose territories encompassed a vast region in northern Russia. Six years later he abolished the local civic government of this proudly independent city, which had enjoyed individual trade with economically thriving cities of central Europe. To con- solidate his autocratic rule and wipe out memories of past freedoms, in 1484 and 1489 Ivan forcibly relocated thousands of leading Novgorod families to lands around Moscow. He also expanded his territory to the south and east when his forces pushed back the Mongols to the Volga River.

Unlike monarchies in western and central-eastern Europe, whose powers were bound by collective rights and laws, Ivan's Russian monarchy claimed absolute property rights over all lands and subjects. The expansionist Muscovite state was shaped by two traditions: religion and service. After the fall of the Byzantine Empire, the tsar was the Russian Orthodox church's only defender of the faith against Islam and Catholicism. Orthodox propaganda thus legitimized the tsar's rule by proclaiming Moscow the "Third Rome" (the first two being Rome and Constantinople) and praising the tsar's autocratic power as the best protector of the faith. The Mongol system of service to rulers also deeply informed Muscovite statecraft. Ivan III and his descendants considered themselves heirs to the empire of the Mongols. In their conception of the state as private dominion, their emphasis on autocratic power, and their division of the populace into a landholding elite in service to the tsar and a vast majority of taxpaying subjects, the Muscovite princes created a state more in the despotic political tradition of the central Asian steppes and the Ottoman Empire than of western Europe.

Hence in the intense competition and state building of the fifteenth century, Muscovy joined England, France, and Spain as examples of success, in sharp contrast to Burgundy and Poland. Yet far more significant was the expansion of the boundary of Europe itself, as maritime explorations brought Europeans into contact with indigenous civilizations in Africa, the Americas, and Asia.

❖ On the Threshold of World History: Widening Geographic Horizons

The fifteenth century constituted the first era of world history. The significance of the century lies not so much in the European "discovery" of Africa and the Americas as in the breakdown of cultural frontiers inaugurated by European colonial expansion. Before the maritime explorations of Portugal and Spain, Europe had remained at the periphery of world history. Fourteenth-century Mongols had been more interested in conquering China and Persia—lands with sophisticated cultures—than in invading Europe; Persian historians of the early

fifteenth century dismissed Europeans as "barbaric Franks"; and China's Ming dynasty rulers, who sent maritime expeditions to Southeast Asia and East Africa around 1400, seemed unaware of the Europeans, even though Marco Polo and other Italian merchants had appeared at the court of the preceding Mongol Yuan dynasty. In the fifteenth century, Portuguese and Spanish vessels, followed a century later by English, French, and Dutch ships, sailed across the Atlantic, Indian, and Pacific Oceans, bringing with them people, merchandise, crops, and diseases in a global exchange that would shape the modern world. For the first time the people of the Americas were brought into contact with a larger historical force that threatened to destroy not only their culture but their existence. European exploitation, conquest, and racism defined this historical era of transition from the medieval to the modern world, as Europeans left the Baltic and the Mediterranean for wider oceans.

The Divided Mediterranean

In the second half of the fifteenth century, the Mediterranean Sea, which had dominated medieval maritime trade, began to lose its preeminence to the Atlantic Ocean. To win control over the Mediterranean, the Ottomans embarked upon an ambitious naval program to transform their empire into a major maritime power. War and piracy disrupted the flow of Christian trade: the Venetians mobilized all their resources to fight off Turkish advances, and the Genoese largely abandoned the eastern Mediterranean for trade opportunities presented by the Atlantic voyage.

The Mediterranean states used ships made with relatively backward naval technology, compared with that of Portugal and Spain. The most common ship, the galley—a flat-bottomed vessel propelled by sails and oars—dated from the time of ancient Rome. Most galleys could not withstand open-ocean voyages, although Florentine and Genoese galleys still made long journeys to Flanders and England, hugging the coast for protection. The galley's dependence on human labor was a more serious handicap. Because prisoners of war and convicted criminals toiled as oarsmen in both Christian and Muslim ships, victory in war or the enforcement of criminal penalties was crucial to a state's ability to float large numbers of galleys. Slavery, too, a traditional Mediterranean institution, sometimes provided the necessary labor.

Although the Mediterranean was divided into Muslim and Christian zones, it still offered a significant opportunity for exchange. Sugarcane was transported to the western Mediterranean from western Asia. From the Balearic Islands off Spain (under Aragonese rule), the crop then traveled to the Canary Islands in the Atlantic, where the Spanish enslaved the native population to work the new sugar plantations. In this way, slavery was exported from the western Mediterranean to the Atlantic, and then on to the Americas.

Engraving of Katharina, an African Woman
Like other artists in early-sixteenth-century Europe, Albrecht Dürer would have seen in person Africans who went to Portugal and Spain as students, servants, and slaves. Note Katharina's noble expression and dignified attire. Before the rise of the slave trade in the seventeenth century, most Africans in Europe were household servants of the aristocracy. Considered prestigious symbols, such servants were not employed primarily for economic production.
Foto Marburg/Art Resource, NY.

Different ethnic groups also moved across the maritime frontier. After Granada fell in 1492, many Muslims fled to North Africa and continued to raid the Spanish coast. When Castile expelled the Jews, some of them settled in North Africa, more in Italy, and many in the Ottoman Empire, Greek-speaking Thessalonika, and Palestine. Conversant in two or three languages, Spanish Jews often served as intermediaries between the Christian West and Muslim East. Greeks occupied a similar position. Most Greeks in the homeland adhered to the Greek Orthodox church under Ottoman protection, but some converted to Islam and entered imperial service, making up a large part of the Ottoman navy. The Greeks on Crete, Chios, and other Aegean islands, however, lived under Italian rule, some of them converting to Roman Catholicism and entering Venetian, Genoese, and Spanish service. A region with warring states and competing religions, the Mediterranean remained a divided zone as more and more Europeans turned instead to the unknown oceans.

Portuguese Explorations

The first phase of European overseas expansion began in 1433 with Portugal's systematic exploration of the west African coast and culminated in 1519–1522 with Spain's circumnavigation of the globe (Map 14.4). Looking back, the sixteenth-century Spanish historian Francisco López de Gómora described the Iberian maritime voyages to the East and West Indies as "the greatest event since the creation of the world, apart from the incarnation and death of him who created it." (See "New Sources, New Perspectives," page 518.)

In many ways a continuation of the struggle against Muslims in the Iberian peninsula, Portugal's maritime voyages displayed that country's mixed motives of piety, glory, and greed. The Atlantic explorations depended for their success on several technological breakthroughs, such as the lateen sail adapted from the Arabs (it permitted a ship to tack against headwinds), new types of sailing vessels, and better charts and instruments. But the sailors themselves were barely touched by the expanding intellectual universe of the Renaissance; what motivated these explorers was a combination of crusading zeal against Muslims and medieval adventure stories, such as the tales of the Venetian traveler Marco Polo (1254–1324) and John Mandeville, a fourteenth-

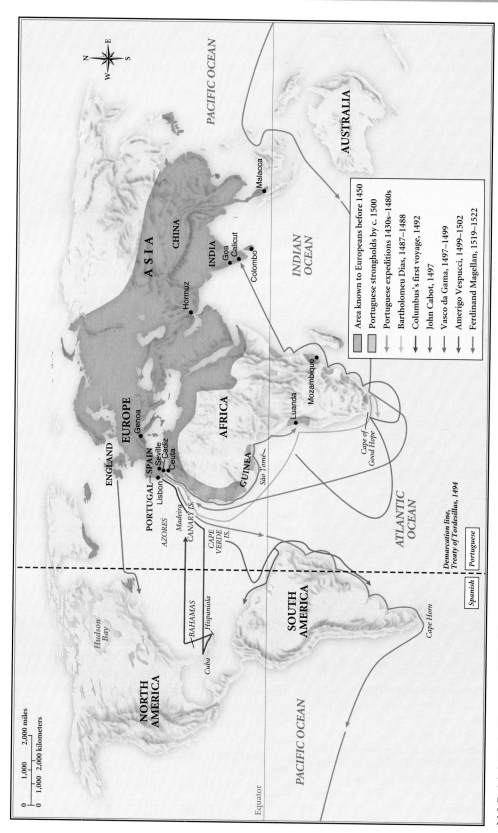

MAP 14.4 Early Voyages of World Exploration

Over the course of the fifteenth and early sixteenth centuries, the Atlantic Ocean was dominated by European shipping following the pioneering voyages of the Portuguese, who also first sailed around the Cape of Good Hope to the Indian Ocean and the Cape Horn to the Pacific. The search for spices and the need to circumnavigate the Ottoman Empire inspired these voyages.

Legend:
- Area known to Europeans before 1450
- Portuguese strongholds by c. 1500
- Portuguese expeditions 1430s–1480s
- Bartholomeu Dias, 1487–1488
- Columbus's first voyage, 1492
- John Cabot, 1497
- Vasco da Gama, 1497–1499
- Amerigo Vespucci, 1499–1502
- Ferdinand Magellan, 1519–1522

Demarcation line, Treaty of Tordesillas, 1494

Spanish | Portuguese

century English knight who in *Travels of Sir John Mandeville* transfixed readers with his stirring and often fantastic stories. Behind the spirit of the crusade lurked vistas of vast gold mines in West Africa (the trade across the Sahara was controlled by Arabs) and a mysterious Christian kingdom established by Prester John (actually the Coptic Christian kingdom of Abyssinia, or Ethiopia, in East Africa). The Portuguese hoped to reach the spice-producing lands of South and Southeast Asia by sea to bypass the Ottoman Turks, who controlled the traditional land routes between Europe and Asia.

By 1415, the Portuguese had captured Ceuta on the Moroccan coast, thus establishing a foothold in Africa. Thereafter Portuguese voyages sailed farther and farther down the West African coast. By mid-century, the Portuguese chain of forts had reached Guinea and could protect the gold and slave trades. At home the royal house of Portugal financed the fleets, with crucial roles played by Prince Peter, regent of the throne between 1440 and 1448; his more famous younger brother Prince Henry the Navigator; and King John II (r. 1481–1495). As a governor of the Order of Christ, a noble crusading order, Henry financed many voyages out of the order's revenues. Private monies also helped, as leading Lisbon merchants participated in financing the gold and slave trades off the Guinea coast.

In 1455, Pope Nicholas V (r. 1447–1455) sanctioned Portuguese overseas expansion, commending King John II's crusading spirit and granting him and his successors the monopoly on trade with inhabitants of the newly "discovered" regions. By 1478–1488, Bartholomeu Dias could take advantage of the prevailing winds in the South Atlantic to reach the Cape of Good Hope. A mere ten years later (1497–1499), under the captainship of Vasco da Gama, a Portuguese fleet rounded the cape and reached Calicut, India, the center of the spice trade. Twenty-three years later, in 1512, Ferdinand Magellan, a Portuguese sailor in Spanish service, led the first expedition to circumnavigate the globe. By 1517, a chain of Portuguese forts dotted the Indian Ocean: at Mozambique, Hormuz (at the mouth of the Persian Gulf), Goa (in India), Colombo (in modern Sri Lanka), and Malacca (modern Malaysia).

After the voyages of Christopher Columbus, Portugal's interests clashed with Spain's. Mediated by Pope Alexander VI, the 1494 Treaty of Tordesillas settled disputes between Portugal and Spain by dividing the Atlantic world between the two royal houses. A demarcation 370 leagues west of the Cape Verdes Islands divided the Atlantic Ocean, reserving for Portugal the west African coast and the route to India and giving Spain the oceans and lands to the west (see Map 14.4). Unwittingly, this agreement also allowed Portugal to claim Brazil in 1500, which was accidentally "discovered" by Pedro Alvares Cabral (1467–1520) on his voyage to India. The Iberian maritime expansion drew on a mixture of religious zeal and greed that would mark the beginnings of European colonialism in the rest of the world.

The Voyages of Columbus

Historians agree that Christopher Columbus (1451–1506) was born of Genoese parents; beyond that, we have little accurate information about this man who brought together the history of Europe and the Americas. In 1476, he arrived in Portugal, apparently a survivor in a naval battle between a Franco-Portuguese and a Genoese fleet; in 1479, he married a Portuguese noblewoman. He spent the next few years mostly in Portuguese service, gaining valuable experience in regular voyages down the west coast of Africa. In 1485, after the death of his wife, Columbus settled in Spain.

Fifteenth-century Europeans already knew that Asia lay beyond the vast Atlantic Ocean, and *The Travels of Marco Polo*, written more than a century earlier, still exerted a powerful hold on European images of the East. Columbus read it many times, along with other travel books, and proposed to sail west across the Atlantic to reach the lands of the khan, unaware that the Mongol Empire had already collapsed in eastern Asia. Vastly underestimating the distances, he dreamed of finding a new route to the East's gold and spices and partook of the larger European vision that had inspired the Portuguese voyages. (His critics had a much more accurate idea of the globe's size and of the difficulty of the venture.) But after the Portuguese and French monarchs rejected his proposal, Columbus found royal patronage with the recently proclaimed Catholic monarchs Isabella of Castile and Ferdinand of Aragon.

In August 1492, equipped with a modest fleet of three ships and about ninety men, Columbus set sail across the Atlantic. His contract stipulated that he would claim Castilian sovereignty over any new land and inhabitants and share any profits with the

Portuguese Voyages of Discovery

The quincentennial celebration of Vasco da Gama's 1499 voyage to India took place in the same year (1998) that Lisbon staged a World Exposition—thus inspiring the theme of "Discoveries of the Oceans" in Portugal's presentation of its historical past and contributions to civilization. The celebration of Portugal and the oceans strengthened interest in Portuguese maritime history and traditions but it also inspired examination of that country's historical memory and criticism of that history. The result has been a rich mix of new sources and perspectives, presented in publications and exhibitions.

A Nautical Tide Calendar
A high-tide chart, showing at which hour and at which fifth (the hour is divided into twelve minute segments) high tide will recur from the day of the new moon. The left column in black starts with the date of the new moon and day. The red columns indicate first the hour and then the fifth of high tide.

A Nautical Solar Guide
From the codex of Bastiao Lopes (c. 1568), this guide shows the declination angle of the sun for different days in the months of April, May, and June.

The more traditional historical approach emphasizes the technical innovations of Portuguese seamanship. Inventions of new sailing vessels, such as the *caravel*, a high-sided ship capable of carrying a large load and maintaining balance in rough seas, enabled Portuguese sailors to venture ever farther into the oceans. Other nautical instruments reflected a cumulative knowledge of seamanship and geography that reduced the risks of long-distance travel. Sailors compiled nautical guides showing the time of tides (Figure 1) and the position of the sun in the sky at different latitudes at different seasons (Figure 2). Most valuable of all were the pilots' books, or *roteiros* (books of sailing directions), often accompanied by detailed maps of maritime regions and coasts. These books of routes and maritime charts lessened but did not eliminate the dangers of the oceans. The *roteiro* of Diogo Alfonso (1535), for example, gave these directions for the voyage to India:

Setting forth from Lisbon you steer to the south-west until you catch sight of the island of Porto Santo or the island of Madeira. And from thence go southward in search of the Canaries; and as soon as you pass the Canaries set course south-west and south until you reach 15 degrees, that is 50 leagues from Cape Verde.

After passing through the mid-Atlantic, Alfonso advised the pilots to seek the most important landmark of all:

If you come 35 degrees more or less, seeking the Cape of Good Hope, when you come upon cliff-faces, you may know that they are those of the Cape of Good Hope. . . . From hence you should set course northeast by north to 19¼ degrees. Then north-northeast, until you reach the latitude of 16¾ degrees (59).

Portugal's historical memory, solidified in the centuries since its earliest explorers, has celebrated its national heroes and discoverers as it mourned the numerous ships and men lost at sea. But much of this commemoration developed as a justification for Portuguese colonialism in the late nineteenth and early twentieth centuries, a fact now being examined by scholars in the wake of the Vasco da Gama quincentennial. How did Muslims and Indians see the arrival of the Portuguese, for example? The Indian historian Sanjay Subrahmanyam has argued that Vasco da Gama brought a new level of maritime violence to the Indian Ocean in 1499 by his attacks on Muslim shipping. Still other scholars, such as Antonio Manuel Hespanha, director of the Scientific Committee of the Discoveries, has called upon Portuguese scholars to examine their own past with a critical eye. The many volumes and expositions sponsored by the committee have highlighted the multicultural aspects of the Portuguese encounter with Asia, America, and Africa, one that was too complex and ambivalent to be reduced to a simple heroic mode.

QUESTIONS FOR DEBATE

1. What do the two documents suggest about the dangers faced by Portuguese sailors?

2. What were the motives behind the Portuguese voyages to India?

FURTHER READING

Russell-Wood, A. J. R. *A World on the Move: The Portuguese in Africa, Asia, and America, 1415–1800.* 1992.

Subrahmanyam, S. *The Career and Legend of Vasco da Gama.* 1997.

Portuguese Ships
Maritime voyagers in Portugal were sponsored by the highest authorities in the land, the best known of whom was Prince Henry, nicknamed "the Navigator." This detail from the Altarpiece of Santa Ana depicts monarchs, noblemen, and bishops against a backdrop of different types of sailing vessels. The caravel, the largest ship in the background, was the main type of vessel for Portuguese voyages in the fifteenth and sixteenth centuries.

IMPORTANT DATES

1415 Portugal captures Ceuta, establishing foothold in Africa

1438 Pragmatic Sanction of Bourges

1440s Gutenberg introduces the printing press

c. 1450–1500 Height of Florentine Renaissance

1453 Fall of Constantinople; end of Byzantine Empire

1454 Treaty of Lodi; power balance in Italy

1460–1485 Wars of the Roses; Tudor dynasty ascendant

1462 Ivan III of Muscovy claims imperial title "tsar"

1471–1484 Reign of Pope Sixtus IV; Renaissance in Rome

1474–1516 Spain unified under Isabella of Castile and Ferdinand of Aragon

1477 Death of Charles the Bold; end of Burgundy

1478 Inquisition established in Spain

1492 Columbus's first voyage; Christians conquer Muslim Granada and expel Jews from Spain

1499 Vasco da Gama reaches India

1500 Portugal claims Brazil

crown. Reaching what is today the Bahamas on October 12, Columbus mistook the islands to be part of the East Indies, not far from Japan and "the lands of the Great Khan." As the Castilians explored the Caribbean islands, they encountered communities of peaceful Indians, the Arawaks, who were awed by the Europeans' military technology, not to mention their appearance. Exchanging gifts of beads and broken glass for Arawak gold—an exchange that convinced Columbus of the trusting nature of the Indians—the crew established peaceful relationships with many communities. Yet in spite of many positive entries in the ship's log referring to Columbus's personal goodwill toward the Indians, the Europeans' objectives were clear: find gold, subjugate the Indians, and propagate Christianity.

Excited by the prospect of easy riches, many flocked to join Columbus's second voyage. When

Columbus in the Caribbean

Columbus departed Cádiz in September 1493, he commanded seventeen ships that carried between 1,200 and 1,500 men, many believing all they had to do was "to load the gold into the ships." Failing to find the imaginary gold mines and spices, however, the colonial enterprise quickly switched its focus to finding slaves. Columbus and his crew first enslaved the Caribs, enemies of the Arawaks; in 1494, Columbus proposed a regular slave trade based in Hispaniola. The Spaniards exported enslaved Indians to Spain, and slave traders sold them in Seville. Soon the Spaniards began importing sugarcane from Madeira, forcing large numbers of Indians to work on plantations to produce enough sugar for export to Europe. Columbus himself was edged out of this new enterprise. When the Spanish monarchs realized the vast potential for material gain that lay in their new dominions, they asserted direct royal authority by sending officials and priests to the Americas, which were named after the Italian Amerigo Vespucci, who led a voyage across the Atlantic in 1499–1502.

Columbus's place in history embodies the fundamental transformations of his age. A Genoese in the service of Portuguese and Spanish employers, Columbus had a career illustrating the changing balance between the Mediterranean and the Atlantic. As the fifteenth-century Ottomans drove Genoese merchants out of the eastern Mediterranean, the Genoese turned to the Iberian peninsula. Columbus was one of many such adventurers who served the Spanish and Portuguese crowns. The voyages of 1492–1493 would eventually draw the triangle of exchange among Europe, the Americas, and Africa, an exchange gigantic in its historical impact and its human cost.

A New Era in Slavery

The European voyages of discovery initiated a new era in slavery, both in expanding the economic scale of slave labor and in attaching race and color to servitude. Slavery had existed since antiquity. During the Renaissance, slavery was practiced in many diverse forms. Nearly all slaves arrived as strangers in the Mediterranean ports of Barcelona, Marseille, Venice, and Genoa. Some were captured in war or by piracy; others—Africans—were sold by other Africans and Bedouin traders to Christian buyers; in western Asia, parents sold their children into servitude out of poverty; and many in the Balkans became slaves when their land was devastated by Ottoman invasions. Slaves were Greek, Slav, European, African, and Turk. Many served as domestic slaves in the leading European cities of the Mediterranean. Others sweated as galley slaves in Ottoman and Christian fleets. Still others worked as agricultural laborers on Mediterranean islands. In the Ottoman army, slaves even formed an important elite contingent.

The Portuguese maritime voyages changed this picture. From the fifteenth century, Africans increasingly filled the ranks of slaves. Exploiting warfare in West Africa, the Portuguese traded in gold and "pieces," as African slaves were called, a practice condemned at home by some conscientious clergy. One, Manoel Severim de Faria, observed that "one cannot yet see any good effect resulting from so much butchery; for this is not the way in which commerce can flourish and the preaching of the gospel progress." Critical voices, however, could not deny the enormous profits that the slave trade brought to Portugal. Most slaves toiled in the sugar plantations of the Portuguese Atlantic islands and

in Brazil. A fortunate few labored as domestic servants in Portugal, where African freedmen and slaves, some 35,000 in the early sixteenth century, constituted almost 3 percent of the population, a percentage that was much higher than in other European countries. In the Americas, slavery would truly flourish as an institution of exploitation.

Europeans in the New World

In 1500, on the eve of European invasion, the native peoples of the Americas were divided into many sedentary and nomadic societies. Among the settled peoples, the largest political and social organizations centered in the Mexican and Peruvian highlands. The Aztecs and the Incas ruled over subjugated Indian populations in their respective empires. With an elaborate religious culture and a rigid social and political hierarchy, the Aztecs and Incas based their civilizations in large, urban capitals.

The Spanish explorers organized their expeditions to the mainland from a base in the Caribbean (Map 14.5). Two prominent leaders, Hernán Cortés

MAP 14.5 European Explorations in the Americas in the Sixteenth Century
While Spanish and Portuguese explorers claimed Central and South America for the Iberian crowns, there were relatively few voyages to North America. The discovery of precious metals fueled the explorations and settlements of Central and South America, establishing the foundations of European colonial empires in the New World.

(1485–1547) and Francisco Pizarro (c. 1475–1541), gathered men and arms and set off in search of gold. Catholic priests accompanied the fortune hunters to bring Christianity to allegedly uncivilized peoples and thus to justify brutal conquests. His small band swelled by peoples who had been subjugated by the Aztecs, Cortés captured the Aztec capital, Tenochtitlán, in 1519. Two years later Mexico, then named New Spain, was added to Charles V's empire. To the south, Pizarro conquered the Andean highlands, exploiting a civil war between rival Incan kings.

By the mid-sixteenth century the Spanish empire, built on greed and justified by its self-proclaimed Catholic mission, stretched unbroken from Mexico to Chile. In addition to the Aztecs and Incas, the Spaniards also subdued the Mayas on the Yucatán peninsula, a people with a sophisticated knowledge of cosmology and arithmetic. The gold and silver mines in Mexico proved a treasure trove for the Spanish crown, but the real prize was the discovery of vast silver deposits in Potosí (today in Bolivia).

Not to be outdone by the Spaniards, other European powers joined the scramble for gold in the New World. In 1500, a Portuguese fleet landed at Brazil, but Portugal did not begin colonizing until 1532, when it established a permanent fort on the coast. In North America, the French went in search of a "northwest passage" to China. By 1504, French fishermen had appeared in Newfoundland. Thirty years later Jacques Cartier led three voyages that explored the St. Lawrence River as far as Montreal. An early attempt in 1541 to settle Canada failed because

MAPPING THE WEST   Renaissance Europe, c. 1500

By 1500, the shape of early modern Europe was largely consolidated and would remain stable until the eighteenth century. The only exception was the disappearance of an independent Hungarian kingdom after 1529.

of the harsh winter and Indian hostility, and John Cabot's 1497 voyage to find a northern route to Asia also failed. More permanent settlements in Canada and the present-day United States would succeed only in the seventeenth century.

Conclusion

The Renaissance was a period of expansion: in the intellectual horizons of Europeans through the rediscovery of classical civilization and a renewed appreciation of human potential and achievement; in the greater centralization and institutionalization of expanded power of the state; and, finally, in the widened geographic horizons of an age of maritime exploration. Above all, the Renaissance was one of the most brilliant periods in artistic activity, one that glorified both God and humanity. A new spirit of confidence spurred Renaissance artists to a new appreciation for the human body and a new visual perspective in art and to apply mathematics and science to architecture, music, and artistic composition.

Highlighting the intensity of cultural production was the competition between burgeoning states and between Christian Europe and the Muslim Ottoman Empire. That competition fostered an expansion of the frontiers of Europe first to Africa and then across the Atlantic Ocean to the Americas. While centered in Italy, the Renaissance was also the first period of global history, which would eventually shift the center of European civilization from the Mediterranean to the Atlantic seaboard. But while Europeans of the Renaissance recovered from the deprivations of the later Middle Ages, they would soon enter yet another period of turmoil, one brought about not by demographic and economic collapse but by a profound crisis of conscience that the brilliance of Renaissance civilization had tended to obscure.

Suggested References

Widening Intellectual Horizons

In addition to the study of great artists and writers, recent scholarship has turned its attention to the "consumption" of cultural goods. Its focus has been on issues of education, readership, art markets, and the different habits of reading and seeing in the past.

Baxandall, Michael. *Painting and Experience in Fifteenth Century Italy: A Primer in the Social History of Pictorial Style.* 1972.

Burke, Peter. *The Italian Renaissance: Culture and Society in Italy.* 1986.

Grafton, Anthony, and Lisa Jardine. *From Humanism to the Humanities: Education and the Liberal Arts in Fifteenth and Sixteenth Century Europe.* 1986.

Jardine, Lisa. *Worldly Goods.* 1996.

http://www.lincolnu. edu/~kluebber/euroart.htm. Renaissance art links.

Martin, Henri-Jean, and Lucien Febvre. *The Coming of the Book: The Impact of Printing, 1450–1800.* 1976.

The Intersection of Private and Public Lives

Much scholarship has focused on Italy and the Low Countries, where historical sources from this period are abundant. The investigation of legal records, population censuses, and tax rolls have yielded fascinating insights into the daily life of the period and the relationship between private life and the political process.

Brucker, Gene A., ed. *The Society of Renaissance Florence: A Documentary Study.* 1971.

Herlihy, David, and Christiane Klapisch-Zuber. *Tuscans and Their Families: A Study of the Florentine Catasto of 1427.* 1978.

Martines, Lauro. *Power and Imagination: City-States in Renaissance Italy.* 1979.

Pitkin, Hanna Fenichel. *Fortune Is a Woman: Gender and Politics in the Thought of Niccolò Machiavelli.* 1984.

Po-chia Hsia, R. *Trent 1475: Stories of a Ritual Murder Trial.* 1992.

Prevenier, Walter, and Wim Blockmans. *The Burgundian Netherlands.* 1986.

Ruggiero, Guido. *Boundaries of Eros: Sex Crime and Sexuality in Renaissance Venice.* 1985.

On the Threshold of World History

The recent celebrations of the overseas voyages of Christopher Columbus and Vasco da Gama have inspired studies with new perspectives. The traditional view of "Europe discovers the world" has been replaced by a more nuanced and complex picture that takes in non-European views and uses Asian, African, and Mesoamerican sources.

Boxer, Charles R. *Four Centuries of Portuguese Expansion, 1415–1826.* 1969.

Fuson, Robert H., ed. *The Log of Christopher Columbus.* 1987.

Russell-Wood, A. J. R. *A World on the Move: The Portuguese in Africa, Asia, and America, 1415–1808.* 1992.

Subrahmanyam, Sanjay. *The Career and Legend of Vasco da Gama.* 1997.

15

The Struggle for Reformation Europe

1500–1560

Brueghel the Elder, **Struggle between Carnival and Lent**
In this allegorical painting, Pieter Brueghel the Elder depicts the struggle for Christians between the temptations of Carnival and the observance of Lent, the season of repentance before Easter when the church prescribes fasting and other acts of penitence. At the same time, this picture vividly represents the lively street scenes from the towns of the Low Countries, the most densely urbanized region of sixteenth-century Europe. Carnival revelry still characterizes town festivities in Belgium today.
Erich Lessing/Art Resource, NY.

H
ILLE FEIKEN LEFT THE CITY of Münster, Germany, on June 16, 1534, elegantly dressed, bedecked with jewels, and determined to kill. Münster, which religious radicals had declared a holy city, lay under siege by armies loyal to its bishop, Franz von Waldeck. Hille was attempting to rescue her city by imitating an ancient Israelite heroine named Judith, who according to the Book of Judith delivered Jerusalem from an invading Assyrian army. The Assyrian commander Holofernes, charmed by Judith's beauty, tried to seduce her; but after he had fallen into a drunken sleep, Judith cut off his head. Terrified, the Assyrian forces fled Jerusalem. Obsessed with this story, Hille crossed enemy lines and tried to persuade the commander of the besieging troops to take her to the bishop, promising to reveal a secret means of capturing the city without further fighting. Unfortunately, a defector recognized Hille and betrayed her. She was beheaded, in her own words, for "going out as Judith and trying to make the Bishop of Münster into a Holofernes."

Hille Feiken and the other radicals in Münster were Anabaptists, part of a sect whose members believed they were a community of saints amid a hopelessly sinful world. The Anabaptists' efforts to form a holy community separate from society tore at the foundations of the medieval European order, and they met merciless persecution from the political and religious authorities. Anabaptism was only one dimension of the Protestant Reformation, which had been set in motion by the German friar Martin Luther in 1517 and had become a sweeping

525

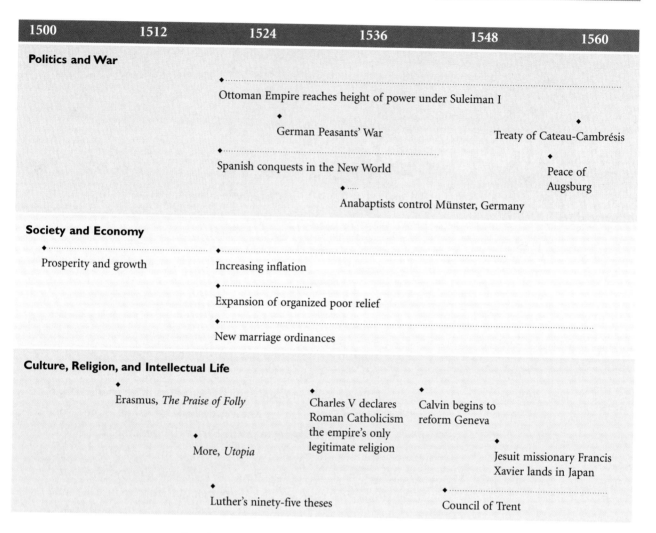

1500	1512	1524	1536	1548	1560

Politics and War

Ottoman Empire reaches height of power under Suleiman I

German Peasants' War

Treaty of Cateau-Cambrésis

Spanish conquests in the New World

Peace of Augsburg

Anabaptists control Münster, Germany

Society and Economy

Prosperity and growth

Increasing inflation

Expansion of organized poor relief

New marriage ordinances

Culture, Religion, and Intellectual Life

Erasmus, *The Praise of Folly*

Charles V declares Roman Catholicism the empire's only legitimate religion

Calvin begins to reform Geneva

More, *Utopia*

Jesuit missionary Francis Xavier lands in Japan

Luther's ninety-five theses

Council of Trent

movement to uproot church abuses and restore early Christian teachings. When Luther first criticized the practices and doctrines of the Catholic church, he had not wished to break away from Rome. As the breach widened, however, Luther and his followers referred to their camp as the "evangelical movement," emphasizing its adherence to the Bible. Supporters of Luther were called "evangelicals" until 1529, when German princes and city delegates lodged a formal protest against imperial authorities who had declared Luther's cause criminal. They were called "protestants," those who protested, and the term quickly stuck to supporters of the Reformation.

Hille Feiken's story was a sign of the times. Inspired by Luther—but often going far beyond what he would condone—ordinary men and women attempted to remake their heaven and earth. Their

stories intertwined with bloody struggles among princes for domination in Europe, an age-old conflict now complicated by the clash of rival faiths. In the end the princes would prevail over both a divided Christendom and a restless people. Protestant or Catholic, European monarchs expanded their power at the expense of the church and disciplined their subjects in the name of piety and order.

❖ A New Heaven and a New Earth

The last book of the Bible, Revelation (also known as the Apocalypse), foretells the passing of the old world and the coming of a new heaven and earth presided over by Christ. In 1500, some Europeans expected the Last Judgment to arrive soon. Indeed, the times seemed desperate. Muslim Turks were advancing on Europe while Christian princes fought among themselves. Some critics of the church labeled the pope as none other than the terrifying Antichrist, whose evil reign (according to Revelation) would end with Christ's return to earth.

It was in this frightening atmosphere that many people intensified their search for religious comfort. Popular pilgrimages, devotional acts, and reported miracles multiplied in an atmosphere of fear and hope. Alongside this fervor for religious certainty, important intellectuals within the Catholic church sharply criticized the shortcomings of its leaders and the clergy, who failed to provide the authority sought for by the people. Committed to a gradual reform rather than a drastic break with the Roman church, these intellectuals, known as Christian humanists for their devotion to both Christian and pagan antiquity, envisioned a better world based on education.

The Crisis of Faith

It was the established church, not Christian religion, that proved deficient to believers in Europe. Numerous signs pointed to an intense spiritual anxiety among the laity. People went on pilgrimages; new shrines sprang up, especially ones dedicated to the Virgin Mary and Christ; prayer books printed in vernacular languages as well as Latin sold briskly. Alongside the sacraments and rituals of the official church, laypeople practiced their own rituals for healing and salvation.

The worst excesses in popular piety resulted in a religious intolerance not seen in Christian Europe since the Middle Ages. In the generation before the Reformation, Jews were frequently accused of ritually slaughtering Christian children and defiling the host, the consecrated bread that Catholics believed was the body of Christ. In 1510, a priest in Brandenburg, Germany, accused local Jews of stealing and stabbing the host. When, according to legend, the host bled, the Jews were imprisoned and killed. A shrine dedicated to the bleeding host attracted thousands of pilgrims seeking fortune and health.

Some of the most flagrant abuses occurred within the church itself. Only a thin line separated miracles, which the church accepted, and magic, which it rejected. Clerics who wanted to reform the

church denounced superstitions, but other clergy readily exploited gullible laypeople. Perhaps the most notorious scandal prior to the Reformation occurred in the Swiss city of Basel. There, in 1510, several Dominicans claimed that the Virgin Mary had worked "miracles," which they themselves had in fact concocted. For a while their plot brought in crowds of pilgrims, but when the deception was uncovered, the perpetrators were burned at the stake.

Often the church gave external behavior more weight than spiritual intentions. On the eve of the Reformation, numerous regulations defined the gradations of human sinfulness. For example, even married couples could sin by having intercourse on one of the church's many holy days or by making love out of "lust" instead of for procreation. The church similarly regulated other kinds of behavior, such as prohibiting the eating of meat on certain days and censoring blasphemous language.

In receiving the sacrament of penance—one of the central pillars of Christian morality and of the Roman church—sinners were expected to examine their consciences, sincerely confess their sins to a priest, and receive forgiveness. In practice, however, confession proved highly unsatisfactory to many Christians. For those with religious scruples, the demands of confession intensified their anxiety about salvation. Some believers were not sure they had remembered to confess all their sins; others trembled before God's anger and doubted his mercy. Also, some priests abused their authority by demanding sexual or monetary favors in return for forgiveness. They seduced or blackmailed female parishioners and excommunicated debtors who failed to pay church taxes or loans. Such reported incidents, although by no means widespread, seriously compromised the sanctity of the priestly office and the sacrament.

Although a sincere confession saved a sinner from hell, he or she still faced doing penance, either in this life or the next. To alleviate suffering after death in purgatory, a person could earn what is called an *indulgence* by performing certain religious tasks—going on pilgrimage, attending mass, doing holy works. The common church practice of selling indulgences as a substitution for performing good works suggested that the church was more interested in making money than in saving souls.

Another way to diminish time in purgatory was to collect and venerate holy relics. A German prince,

Frederick the Wise of Saxony, amassed the largest collection of relics outside of Italy. By 1518, his castle church contained 17,443 holy relics, including what were thought to be a piece of Moses's burning bush, parts of the holy cradle and swaddling clothes, thirty-five fragments of the True Cross, and the Virgin Mary's milk. A diligent and pious person who rendered appropriate devotion to each of these relics could earn exactly 127,799 years and 116 days of remission from purgatory.

Dissatisfaction with the official church and its inflexible rules prompted several reform efforts by bishops and leading clerics prior to the Reformation; these were, however, limited to certain monastic houses and dioceses. More important, there existed a gulf between clerical privileges and the religious sensibilities of the laypeople. Urban merchants and artisans yearned for a religion more meaningful to their daily lives and for a clergy more responsive to their needs. They wanted priests to preach edifying sermons, to administer the sacraments conscientiously, and to lead moral lives. They criticized the church's rich endowments that provided income for children of the nobility. And they generously donated money to establish new preacherships for university-trained clerics, overwhelmingly from urban backgrounds and often from the same social classes as the donors. Most of these young clerics, who criticized the established church and hoped for reform, were schooled in Christian humanism.

Christian Humanism

Outraged by the abuse of power, a generation of Christian humanists dreamed of ideal societies based on peace and morality. Within their own Christian society, these intellectuals sought to realize the ethical ideals of the classical world. Scholarship and social reform became inseparable goals. Two men, the Dutch scholar Desiderius Erasmus (c. 1466–1536) and the English lawyer Thomas More (1478–1535), stood out as representatives of these Christian humanists, who, unlike Italian humanists, placed their primary emphasis on Christian piety.

Erasmus.   Erasmus dominated the humanist world of early-sixteenth-century Europe, just as Cicero had dominated the glory of ancient Roman letters.

He was on intimate terms with kings and popes and his reputation extended across Europe. Following a brief stay in a monastery as a young man, Erasmus dedicated his life to scholarship. After studying in Paris, Erasmus traveled to Venice and served as an editor with Aldus Manutius, the leading printer of Latin and Greek books.

Through his books and letters, disseminated by Manutius's printing press, Erasmus's fame spread. In the *Adages* (1500), a collection of quotations from ancient literature offering his witty and wise commentaries on the human experience, Erasmus established a reputation as a superb humanist dedicated to educational reform. Themes explored in the *Adages* continued in the *Colloquies* (1523), a compilation of Latin dialogues intended as language-learning exercises, in which Erasmus exerted his sharp wit to criticize the morals and customs of his time. Lamenting poor table manners, for example, Erasmus advised his cultivated readers not to pick their noses at meals, not to share half-eaten chicken legs, and not to speak while stuffing their mouths. Turning to political matters, he mocked the clergy's corruption and Christian princes' bloody ambitions.

Only through education, Erasmus believed, could individuals reform themselves and society. His goal was a unified, peaceful Christendom in which charity and good works, not empty ceremonies, would mark true religion and in which learning and piety would dispel the darkness of ignorance. He elaborated many of these ideas in his *Handbook of the Militant Christian* (1503), an eloquent plea for a simple religion devoid of greed and the lust for power. In *The Praise of Folly* (1509), Erasmus satirized values held dear by his contemporaries. Modesty, humility, and poverty represented the true Christian virtues in a world that worshiped pomposity, power, and wealth. The wise appeared foolish, he concluded, for their wisdom and values were not of this world.

Erasmus devoted years to translating a new Latin edition of the New Testament from the original Greek; it was published in 1516 by the Froben Press in Basel. Moved by the pacifism of the apostolic church, Erasmus instructed the young future emperor Charles V to rule as a just Christian prince. He vented his anger by ridiculing the warrior-pope Julius II and expressed deep sorrow for the brutal warfare that had been ravaging Europe for decades.

Albrecht Dürer, *The Knight, Death, and the Devil*
Dürer's 1512 engraving of the knight depicts a grim and determined warrior advancing in the face of devils, one of whom holds out an hourglass with a grimace while another wields a menacing pike. An illustration for Erasmus's The Handbook of the Militant Christian, *this scene is often interpreted as portraying a Christian clad in the armor of righteousness on a path through life beset by death and demonic temptations. Yet the knight in early-sixteenth-century Germany had become a mercenary, selling his martial skills to princes. Some waylaid merchants, robbed rich clerics, and held citizens for ransom. The most notorious of these robber-knights, Franz von Sickingen, was declared an outlaw by the emperor and murdered in 1522.*
Giraudon/Art Resource, NY.

A man of peace and moderation, Erasmus found himself challenged by angry younger men and radical ideas once the Reformation took hold; he eventually chose Christian unity over reform and schism. His dream of Christian pacifism shattered, he lived to see dissenters executed—by Catholics and Protestants alike—for speaking their conscience. Erasmus spent his last years in Freiburg and died in Basel, isolated from the Protestant community and his writings condemned by many in the Catholic church, which was divided over the intellectual legacy of its famous son.

Thomas More.   If Erasmus found himself abandoned by his times, his good friend Thomas More, to whom *The Praise of Folly* was dedicated,* met with even greater suffering. Having attended Oxford and the Inns of Court, where English lawyers were trained, More had legal talents that served him well in government. As a member of Parliament and then a royal ambassador, he proved a competent and loyal servant to Henry VIII. In 1529, this ideal servant to the king became lord chancellor, the chief official in government, but, tired of court intrigue and in protest against Henry's control of the clergy, More resigned his position in 1532. He would later pay with his life for upholding conscience over political expediency.

Inspired by the recent voyages of discovery, More's best-known work, *Utopia* (1516), describes an imaginary land and was intended as a critique of his own society. A just, equitable, and hard-working community, Utopia (meaning both "no place" and "best place" in Greek) was the opposite of England. In Utopia everyone worked the land for two years; and since Utopians enjoyed public schools, communal kitchens, hospitals, and nurseries, they had no need for money. Greed and private property disappeared in this world. Dedicated to the pursuit of knowledge and natural religion, with equal distribution of goods and few laws, Utopia knew neither crime nor war. But in the real world, unlike More's "Nowhereland," social injustice bred crime and warfare. Desperate men, deprived of their livelihoods, became thieves, and "thieves do make quite efficient soldiers, and soldiers make quite enterprising thieves." More believed that politics, property, and war fueled human misery, whereas for his Utopians, "fighting was a thing they absolutely loathe. They say it's a quite subhuman form of activity, although human beings are more addicted to it than any of the lower animals."

More's tolerant and rational society did have a few oddities—voluntary slavery, for instance, and strictly controlled travel. Although premarital sex

---

*The Latin title, *Encomium Moriae* ("The Praise of Folly"), was a pun on More's name and the Latin word for *folly.*

brought severe punishment, prospective marriage partners could examine each other naked before making their final decisions. Men headed Utopia's households and exercised authority over women and children. And Utopians did not shy away from declaring war on their neighbors to protect their way of life. Nevertheless, this imaginary society was paradise compared with a Christian Europe battered by division and violence. The Christian humanists dreamed beautiful visions for a better future, but they lived in a time that called for violent and radical changes to solve a profound crisis of faith.

❖ Protestant Reformers

Since the mid-fifteenth century, many clerics had tried to reform the church from within, criticizing clerical abuses and calling for moral renewal, but their efforts came up against the church's inertia and resistance. At the beginning of the sixteenth century, widespread popular piety and anticlericalism existed side by side, fomenting a volatile mixture of need and resentment. A young German friar, tormented by his own religious doubts, was to become the spokesman for a generation. From its origins as a theological dispute in 1517, Martin Luther's reform movement sparked explosive protests. By the time he died in 1546, half of western Europe had renounced allegiance to the Roman Catholic church.

While Luther opened the first act of the Reformation in Germany, Huldrych Zwingli extended the Reformation to Switzerland. The French theologian John Calvin continued the work of religious reform in a later generation. Calvin's challenge to the Catholic church extended far beyond the German-speaking lands of central Europe, eventually shaping Protestantism in England, Scotland, the Low Countries, France, and eastern Europe.

Martin Luther and the German Nation

Son of a miner and entrepreneur, Martin Luther (1483–1546) began his studies in the law, pursuing a career open to ambitious young men from middle-class families and urged on him by his father. His true calling, however, lay with the church. Caught in a storm on a lonely road one midsummer's night, the young student grew terrified by the thunder and lightning. He implored the help of St. Anne, the

mother of the Virgin Mary, and promised he would enter a monastery if she protected him. To the chagrin of his father, Luther abandoned law for a religious life and entered the Augustinian order.

In the monastery the young Luther, finding no spiritual consolation in the sacraments of the church, experienced a religious crisis. Appalled at his own sense of sinfulness and the weakness of human nature, he lived in terror of God's justice in spite of frequent confessions and penance. A pilgrimage to Rome only deepened his unease with the institutional church. A sympathetic superior came to Luther's aid and sent him to study theology, a discipline that gradually led him to experience grace and gain insight into salvation. Luther recalled his monastic days shortly before his death:

> Though I lived as a monk without reproach, I felt that I was a sinner before God with an extremely disturbed conscience. I could not believe that he was placated by my satisfaction [in penance]. I did not love, yes, I hated the righteous God who punishes sinners, and secretly . . . I was angry with God. . . . Nevertheless, I beat importunately upon Paul [in Romans 1:17]. . . . At last, by the mercy of God, meditating day and night, I gave heed to the context of the words, namely, "In [the gospel] the righteousness of God is revealed, as it is written, 'He who through faith is righteous shall live.'" There I began to understand that the righteousness of God is that by which the righteous live by a gift of God, namely by faith.

Luther followed this tortuous and private spiritual journey while serving as a professor of theology at the University of Wittenberg. But subsequent events made Luther a public figure. In 1516, the new archbishop of Mainz, Albrecht of Brandenburg, commissioned a Dominican friar to sell indulgences in his archdiocese (which included Saxony); the proceeds would help cover the cost of constructing St. Peter's Basilica in Rome and also partly defray Archbishop Albrecht's expenses in pursuing his election. Such blatant profiteering outraged many, including Luther. In 1517, Luther composed ninety-five theses—propositions for an academic debate—that questioned indulgence peddling and the purchase of church offices. Once they became public, the theses unleashed a torrent of pent-up resentment and frustration among the laypeople.

What began as a theological debate in a provincial university soon engulfed the Holy Roman Empire. (See "Contrasting Views," page 532.) Two groups predominated among Luther's earliest supporters: younger humanists and those clerics who shared Luther's critical attitude toward the church establishment. They called themselves "evangelicals," after the Gospels.* None of the evangelicals came from the upper echelons of the church; many were from urban middle-class backgrounds, and most were university-trained and well educated. As a group, their profile differed from that of the poorly educated rural clergy or from

Luther's World in the Early Sixteenth Century

their noble clerical superiors, who often owed their ecclesiastical positions to family influence rather than theological learning. The evangelicals also stood apart in that they represented those social groups most ready to challenge clerical authority—merchants, artisans, and literate urban laypeople.

Initially, Luther presented himself as the pope's "loyal opposition." In 1520, he composed three treatises. In *Freedom of a Christian,* which he wrote in Latin for the learned and addressed to Pope Leo X, Luther argued that the Roman church's numerous rules and its stress on "good works" were useless. He insisted that faith, not good works, would save sinners from damnation, and he sharply distinguished between true Gospel teachings and invented church doctrines. Luther argued that Christ, by his suffering on the cross, had freed humanity from the guilt of sin and that only through faith in God's justice and mercy could believers be saved. Thus the church's laws governing behavior had no place in the search for salvation. Luther suggested instead "the priesthood of all believers," arguing that the Bible provided all the teachings necessary for Christian living and that a professional caste of clerics should not hold sway over laypeople. *Freedom of a Christian* was immediately translated into German and was circulated widely. Its principles "by faith

alone," "by Scripture alone," and "the priesthood of all believers" became central features of the reform movement.

In his second treatise, *To the Nobility of the German Nation,* which he wrote in German, Luther appealed to German nationalism. He denounced the corrupt Italians in Rome who were cheating and exploiting his compatriots and called upon the German princes to defend their nation and reform the church. Luther's third major treatise, *On the Babylonian Captivity of the Church,* which he composed in Latin mainly for a clerical audience, condemned the papacy as the embodiment of the Antichrist.

From Rome's perspective, the "Luther Affair," as church officials called it, was essentially a matter of clerical discipline. Rome ordered Luther to obey his superiors and keep quiet. But the church establishment had seriously misjudged the extent of Luther's influence. Luther's ideas, published in numerous German and Latin editions, spread rapidly throughout the Holy Roman Empire, unleashing forces that Luther could not control. Social, nationalist, and religious protests fused into an explosive mass very similar to the Czech revolution that Jan Hus had inspired a century earlier. Like Hus, Luther appeared before an emperor: in 1521, he defended his faith before Charles V (r. 1520–1558), the newly elected Holy Roman Emperor who at the age of nineteen was the ruler of the Low Countries, Spain, Spain's Italian and New World dominions, and the Austrian Habsburg lands. At the Imperial Diet of Worms, the formal assembly presided over by this powerful ruler, Luther shocked Germans by declaring his admiration for the Czech heretic. But unlike Hus, Luther did not suffer martyrdom because he enjoyed the protection of Frederick the Wise, the elector of Saxony (one of the seven German princes entitled to elect the Holy Roman Emperor) and Luther's lord.

Essentially, the early Reformation was an urban movement: during the 1520s, the anti-Roman evangelicals included many German princes, city officials, professors, priests, and ordinary men and women, particularly in the cities. As centers of publishing and commerce, German towns became natural distribution points for Lutheran propaganda. Moreover, urban people proved particularly receptive to Luther's teachings. Many were literate and were eager to read the Scriptures, and merchants and artisans resented the clergy's tax-exempt status and

---

*The word *gospel,* meaning "good tidings," comes from the Old English translation of the Greek word *evangelion.*

Martin Luther: Holy Man or Heretic?

When Martin Luther criticized the papacy and the Catholic church, he was hailed as a godly prophet by some and condemned as a heretic by others. Both Protestants and Catholics used popular propaganda to argue their cause. They spread their message to a largely illiterate or semiliterate society through pamphlets, woodcuts, and broadsheets in which visual images took on increasing importance, to appeal to a wide public. These polemical works were produced in the thousands and distributed to cities and market towns throughout the Holy Roman Empire. A few were even translated into Latin to reach an audience outside of Germany.

The 1521 woodcut by Matthias Gnidias represents Luther standing above his Catholic opponent, the Franciscan friar Thomas Murner, who is depicted here as a crawling dragon, Leviathan, the biblical monster (Document 1). Another positive image of Luther, also published in 1521, depicts him as inspired by the Holy Spirit (Document 2). A few years later, an anti-Luther image represents him as a seven-headed monster (Document 3), signifying that the reformer is the source of discord within Christianity. This image appeared in the 1529 book published by the Dominican friar Johannes Cochlaeus, one of Luther's strongest opponents, in which Cochlaeus also accused Luther of inciting the 1525 peasants' uprising (Document 4). The Catholic attack on Luther stood in sharp contrast with his image among Protestants. For the English Protestant church historian John Foxe (1516–1587), Luther was more than a courageous hero who exposed the corruption of the Roman Catholic church; he was a prophet and a holy man specially blessed by God (Document 5).

◄ 1. Matthias Gnidias's Representation of Luther and Leviathan, 1521

Dressed in a friar's robes, the Murner-Leviathan monster breathes "ignis, sumus, & sulphur"—fire, smoke, and sulphur. The good friar, Luther, holds the Bible in his hands, and is represented here as a prophet (foretelling the end of the world). The vertical Latin caption declares that the Lord will visit the earth with his sword and kill the Leviathan monster; he will trample underfoot lions and dragons; and the dragon, with a halter around its nostrils, will be dragged away on a hook.

2. Luther as Monk, Doctor, Man of the Bible, and Saint, 1521 ►

This woodcut by an anonymous artist appeared in a volume that the Strasbourg printer Johann Schott published in 1521. In addition to being one of the major centers of printing, Strasbourg was also a stronghold of the reform movement. Note the use of traditional symbols to signify Luther's holiness: the Bible in his hands, the halo, the Holy Spirit in the form of a dove, and his friar's robes.

LVTHERVS.

Luther and Leviathan

Although the cult of saints and monasticism came under severe criticism during the Reformation, the representation of Luther in traditional symbols of sanctity stressed his conservative values instead of his radical challenge to church authorities.

3. The Seven-Headed Martin Luther by Johannes Cochlaeus, 1529

The seven heads are, from left to right: doctor, Martin, Luther, ecclesiast, enthusiast, visitirer, and Barrabas. The term enthusiast *represented a name of abuse, applied usually by the Catholic church to Anabaptists and religious radicals of all sorts.* Visitirer *is a pun in German on the word* Tier, *meaning "animal." Cochlaeus also mocks the new practice of Protestant clergy visiting parishes to enforce Christian discipline. From left to right Luther's many heads gradually reveal him to be a*

rebel, as Barrabas was condemned to die as a rabble-rouser by the Romans but instead was freed and his place taken by Jesus at the crucifixion. The number seven also alludes to the seven deadly sins.

4. Johannes Cochlaeus on Luther and the Peasants' War, 1529

Although Luther eventually condemned the peasants' uprising of 1525, he was at first sympathetic to their cause and blamed the oppression of the princes for the peasants' misery. For Catholics such as Cochlaeus, Luther remained the source of all disorder by challenging established church authority.

There were many peasants slain in the uprising, many fanatics banished, many false prophets hanged, burned, drowned, or beheaded who perhaps

Luther as Monk
The Granger Collection

Seven-Headed Luther
The Granger Collection

would still all live as good obedient Christians had Luther not written. . . . There are still many Anabaptists, assailants of the Sacrament, and other mob-spirits awakened by Luther to rebellion and error. . . . I'd lay you odds, however, that among all the peasants, fanatics, and mob-spirits not one could be found who has written more obscenely, more disdainfully, and more rebellously than Luther has.

Source: Mark U. Edwards, *Printing, Propaganda, and Martin Luther* (1994), 84.

5. John Foxe on Martin Luther as Prospective Saint, 1563

Foxe's work, Actes and Monuments of These Latter and Perillous Days Touching Matters of the Church, *describes the persecutions of Christians in England from the early church to the time of Mary Tudor. A Protestant, Foxe was inspired by the martyrdoms of his fellow believers under Queen Mary (r. 1555–1559), who tried to restore Catholicism to England with widespread persecutions. The compilation of* Actes and Monuments *occupied Foxe during his lifetime and became the most famous work in English church history. In it, Luther occupied a central role, as the founder of the Protestant Reformation. For Foxe, Luther was more than a prophet and hero; he was no less than a man of God, a holy man, a saint, in short, chosen by God for cleansing Christianity.*

Those who write the lives of saints use to describe and extol their holy life and godly virtues, and also to set forth such miracles as be wrought in them by God; whereof there lacketh no plenty in Martin Luther, but rather time lacketh to us, and opportunity to tarry upon them, having such haste to other things. Otherwise what a miracle might this seem to be, for one man, and a poor friar, creeping out of a blind cloister, to be set up against the pope, the universal bishop, and God's mighty vicar on earth; to withstand all his cardinals, yea, and to sustain the malice and hatred of almost the whole world being set against him; and to work that against the said pope, cardinals, and church of Rome, which no king nor emperor could ever do, yea, durst ever attempt, nor all the learned men before him could ever compass: which miraculous work of God, I account nothing inferior to the miracle of David overthrowing the great Goliath. Wherefore if miracles do make a saint (after the pope's definition), what lacketh in Martin Luther, but age and time only, to make him a saint? who, standing openly against the pope, cardinals, and prelates of the church, in number so many, in power so terrible, in practice so crafty, having emperors and all the kings of the earth against him; who, teaching and preaching Christ the space of nine and twenty years, could, without touch of all his enemies, so quietly in his own country where he was born, die and sleep in peace. In which Martin Luther, first to stand against the pope was a great miracle; to prevail against the pope, a greater; so to die untouched, may seem greatest of all, especially having so many enemies as he had. Again, neither is it any thing less miraculous, to consider what manifold dangers he escaped besides: as when a certain Jew was appointed to come to destroy him by poison, yet was it so the will of God, that Luther had warning thereof before, and the face of the Jew sent to him by picture, whereby he knew him, and avoided the peril.

Source: John Foxe, *Actes and Monuments*, vol. 4 (London, 1837), 818–819.

QUESTIONS FOR DEBATE
1. Why did Johannes Cochlaeus condemn Martin Luther? How did he construct a negative image of Luther?
2. Evaluate the visual and the textual representations of Luther as a godly man: which medium is more effective?

the competition from monasteries and nunneries that produced their own goods. Magistrates began to curtail clerical privileges and subordinate the clergy to municipal authority. Luther's message—that each Christian could appeal directly to God for salvation—spoke to townspeople's spiritual needs and social vision. Thus inspired, many reform priests led their urban parishioners away from Roman liturgy. From Wittenberg, the reform movement quickly emerged into a torrent of many streams.

Huldrych Zwingli and the Swiss Confederation

While Luther provided the religious leadership for northern Germany, the south came under the strong influence of the Reformation movement that had emerged in the poor, mountainous country of Switzerland. In the late fifteenth and early sixteenth centuries, Switzerland's chief source of income was the export of soldiers; hardy Swiss peasants fought as mercenaries in papal, French, and imperial armies, earning respect as fierce pikemen. Military captains recruited and organized young men from village communes; the women stayed behind to farm and tend animals. Many young Swiss men died on the battlefields of Italy, and many others returned maimed for life. In 1520, the chief preacher of the Swiss city of Zurich, Huldrych Zwingli (1484–1531), criticized his superior, Cardinal Matthew Schinner, for sending the country's young men off to serve in papal armies.

The son of a Swiss village leader, Zwingli became a reformer independent of Martin Luther. After completing his university studies, Zwingli was ordained a priest and served as an army chaplain for several years. Deeply influenced by Erasmus, whom he met in 1515, Zwingli adopted the Dutch humanist's vision of social renewal through education. In 1520, he openly declared himself a reformer and attacked corruption among the ecclesiastical hierarchy as well as the church rituals of fasting and clerical celibacy.

Under Zwingli's leadership, Zurich served as the center for the Swiss reform movement. Guided by his vision of a theocratic (church-directed) society that would unite religion, politics, and morality, Zwingli refused to draw any distinction between the ideal citizen and the perfect Christian—an idea radically different from Luther's—and rooted out internal dissent. Luther and Zwingli also differed in their views of the role of the Eucharist, or holy communion. Luther insisted that Christ was both truly and symbolically present in this central Christian sacrament; Zwingli, influenced by Erasmus, viewed the Eucharist as simply a ceremony symbolizing Christ's union with believers.

In 1529, troubled by these differences and other disagreements, evangelical princes and magistrates assembled the major reformers at Marburg, in central Germany. After several days of intense discus-

The Progress of the Reformation

1517 Martin Luther disseminates ninety-five theses attacking the sale of indulgences and other church practices
1520 Reformer Huldrych Zwingli breaks with Rome
1525 Radical reformer Thomas Müntzer killed in Peasants' War
1529 Lutheran German princes protest the condemnation of religious reform by Charles V; genesis of the term *Protestants*
1529 The English Parliament establishes King Henry VIII as head of the Anglican church, severing ties to Rome
1534–1535 Anabaptists control the city of Münster, Germany, in a failed experiment to create a holy community
1541 John Calvin establishes himself permanently in Geneva, making that city a model of Christian reform and discipline

sions, the north German and Swiss reformers managed to resolve many doctrinal differences, but Luther and Zwingli failed to agree on the meaning of the Eucharist. Thus the German and Swiss reform movements continued on separate paths. The issue of the Eucharist would later divide Lutherans and Calvinists as well.

John Calvin and Christian Discipline

Under the leadership of John Calvin (1509–1564), another wave of reform pounded at the gates of Rome. Born in Picardy, in northern France, to the secretary of the bishop of Noyon, Calvin benefited from his family connections and received a scholarship to study in Paris and Orléans, where he took a law degree. A gifted intellectual who was attracted to humanism, Calvin could have enjoyed a brilliant career in government or church service. Instead, experiencing a crisis of faith, like Luther, he sought eternal salvation through intense theological study.

Influenced by the leading French humanists who sought to reform the church from within, Calvin gradually crossed the line from loyal opposition to questioning fundamental Catholic teachings. His conversion came about after a lengthy and anxious intellectual battle. Unlike Luther, who described his life in vivid detail, Calvin generally revealed nothing about personal matters.

During Calvin's long religious gestation, the Reformation steadily gained adherents in France. On Sunday, October 18, 1534, Parisians found church doors posted with ribald broadsheets denouncing the Catholic Mass. Smuggled into France from the Protestant and French-speaking parts of Switzerland, the broadsheets unleashed a wave of royal repression in the capital. Rumors of a Protestant conspiracy and massacre circulated, and magistrates swiftly promoted a general persecution of reform groups throughout France, including the hitherto unmolested religious dissidents. This so-called Affair of the Placards provoked a national crackdown on church dissenters. Hundreds of French Protestants were arrested, scores were executed, and many more, including Calvin, fled abroad.

On his way to Strasbourg, Germany, a haven for religious dissidents, Calvin detoured to Geneva— the French-speaking city-republic where he would find his life's work. Ge-

Calvin's World in the Mid-Sixteenth Century

neva had renounced allegiance to its bishop, and the local reformer Guillaume Farel threatened Calvin with God's curse if he did not stay and labor in Geneva. This frightening appeal succeeded. Under Calvin and Farel, the reform party became embroiled in a political struggle between two civic factions: their supporters, many of whom were French refugees, and the opposition, represented by the leading old Genevan families, who resented the moralistic regulations of the new, foreign-born clerical regime. A political setback in 1538 drove Calvin and Farel from Geneva, but Calvin returned in 1541, after his supporters triumphed. He remained there until his death in 1564.

Under Calvin's inspiration and moral authority, Geneva became a disciplined Christian republic, modeled after the ideas in Calvin's *The Institutes of the Christian Religion*, first published in 1536. No reformer prior to Calvin had expounded on the doctrines, organization, history, and practices of Chris-

John Calvin
This painting of the reformer (c. 1538) is attributed to the German artist Hans Holbein the Younger, one of the most famous portraitists of the early sixteenth century. Note the serene and learned character conveyed by the painting.
Calvin College and Calvin Theological Seminary/H. Henry Meedon Center.

tianity in such a systematic, logical, and coherent manner. Calvin followed Luther's doctrine of salvation to its ultimate logical conclusion: if God is almighty and humans cannot earn their salvation by good works, then no Christian can be certain of salvation. Developing the doctrine of *predestination*, Calvin argued that God had ordained every man, woman, and child to salvation or damnation—even before the creation of the world. Thus the "elect," in Calvinist theology, were known only to God. In practice, however, Calvinist doctrine demanded rigorous discipline: the knowledge that a small group of "elect" would be saved should guide the actions of the godly in an uncertain world. Fusing church and society into what followers named the "Reformed church," Geneva became a single moral community, a development strongly supported by its very low rate of extramarital births in the sixteenth century. Praised by advocates as a community less troubled by crime and sin than other cities and attacked by critics as despotic, Geneva under Calvin exerted a powerful influence on the course of the Reformation.

Like Zwingli, Calvin did not tolerate dissenters. While passing through Geneva in 1553, the Spanish physician Michael Servetus was arrested because he had published books attacking Calvin and questioning the doctrine of the Trinity, the belief that God exists in three persons—the Father, Son (Christ), and Holy Spirit. Upon Calvin's advice,

Servetus was executed by the authorities. (Calvin did not approve, however, of the method of execution: burning at the stake.) Although Calvin came under criticism for Servetus's death, Geneva became the new center of the Reformation, the place where pastors trained for mission work and from which books propagating Calvinist doctrines were exported. The Calvinist movement spread to France, the Netherlands, England, Scotland, Germany, Poland, Hungary, and eventually New England, becoming the established form of the Reformation in many of these countries (Map 15.1).

MAP 15.1 Spread of Protestantism in the Sixteenth Century

The Protestant Reformation divided northern and southern Europe. From its heartland in the Holy Roman Empire, the Reformation won the allegiance of Scandinavia, England, and Scotland and made considerable inroads in the Low Countries, France, eastern Europe, Switzerland, and even parts of northern Italy. While the Mediterranean countries remained loyal to Rome, a vast zone of confessional divisions and strife characterized the religious landscape of Europe from Britain in the west to Poland in the east.

❖ Reshaping Society through Religion

The religious upheavals of the sixteenth century reshaped European society in two major ways. First, those who challenged the social order were crushed by the political and religious authorities. Such was the fate of the Anabaptists and peasant rebels in the Holy Roman Empire, who tried in vain to establish biblically inspired new social orders in the early years of the Reformation. As a result of these radical movements, both Protestant and Catholic authorities became alarmed by the subversive political potential of religious reforms. They viewed religious reforms, instead, as ways of instilling greater discipline in Christian worship and in social behavior. Hence, the second and most lasting impact of the Reformation was in the realm of church discipline

and piety. Through reading the Bible, indoctrinating the young, relieving the poor, revising laws of marriage, and performing sacred music, Protestant reformers and their supporters tried to create a God-fearing, pious, and disciplined Christian society out of corrupt human nature.

Challenging the Social Order

The freedom of the Christian proclaimed by Luther resonated with those who suffered oppression; and the corruption of sin decried by the reformers inspired others to seek Christian perfection. During the early 1520s, two movements emerged in the Holy Roman Empire to challenge the foundations of religious and political order. While peasants and urban artisans staged massive revolts against church and nobility, the Anabaptists attempted to re-create the perfect Christian community on earth.

Pillage of the Abbey of Weissenbau
In the Peasants' War of 1525, monasteries were the first target of rebellious German peasants, who resented them for owning vast tracts of land and ruling over large numbers of serfs. When Luther attacked monks as enemies of Christ, the peasants enthusiastically attacked these institutions of spiritual and material oppression. This engraving from the Chronicle of the Peasants' War *by Abbot Murer reveals the Catholic interpretation of the peasants' revolt.*
© Artephoto/T. Schneiders.

MAP 15.2 The Peasants' War of 1525

The centers of uprisings clustered in southern and central Germany, where the density of cities encouraged the spread of discontent and allowed for alliances between urban masses and rural rebels. The proximity to the Swiss Confederation, a stronghold of the Reformation movement, also inspired anti-establishment uprisings.

The Peasants' War of 1525. Between 1520 and 1525, many city governments, often under intense popular pressure and sometimes in sympathy with the evangelicals, allowed the reform movement to sweep away church authority. Local officials appointed new clerics who were committed to reforming Christian doctrine and ritual. The turning point came in 1525, when the crisis of church authority exploded in a massive rural uprising that threatened the entire social order (Map 15.2).

The church was the largest landowner in the Holy Roman Empire: about one-seventh of the empire's territory consisted of ecclesiastical principalities in which bishops and abbots exercised both secular and churchly power. Luther's anticlerical message struck home with peasants who were paying taxes to both their lord and the church. In the spring of 1525, many peasants in southern and central Germany rose in rebellion, sometimes inspired by wandering preachers. The princes of the church, the rebels charged, were wolves in sheep's clothing, fleecing Christ's flock to satisfy their greed. Some urban workers and artisans joined the peasant bands, plundering monasteries, refusing to pay church taxes, and demanding village autonomy, the abolition of serfdom, and the right to appoint their own pastors. The more radical rebels called for the destruction of the entire ruling class. In Thuringia, the rebels were led by an ex-priest, Thomas Müntzer (1468?–1525), who promised to chastise the wicked and thus clear the way for the Last Judgment.

The revolution of 1525, known as the Peasants' War, split the reform movement. Princes and city authorities turned against the rebels. In Thuringia, Catholic and evangelical princes joined hands to crush Müntzer and his supporters. All over the

Persecution of the Anabaptists

A large number of the more than one thousand martyrs killed for their faith in the Low Countries were Anabaptists. Until persecutions stopped in the 1580s, the authorities executed hundreds of Anabaptist men by beheading and women by drowning. This drawing is from the 1685 Dutch Anabaptist martyrology (a collection of books dedicated to the study and remembrance of martyrs), The Bloody Theater, *compiled by Tilleman van Bracht.*
Beinecke Rare Book and Manuscript Library, Yale University.

empire, princes defeated peasant armies, hunted down their leaders, and uprooted all opposition. By the end of the year, more than 100,000 rebels had been killed and others maimed, imprisoned, or exiled. Luther had tried to mediate the conflict, criticizing the princes for their brutality toward the peasants but also warning the rebels against mixing religion and social protest. Luther believed that rulers were ordained by God and thus must be obeyed even if they were tyrants. The Kingdom of God belonged not to this world but to the next, he insisted, and the body of true Christians remained known only to God. Luther considered Müntzer's mixing of religion and politics the greatest danger to the Reformation, nothing less than "the devil's work." When the rebels ignored Luther's appeal and continued to follow more radical preachers, Luther called on the princes to restore the divinely ordained social order and slaughter the rebels. Fundamentally conservative in its political philosophy, the Lutheran church would henceforth depend on established political authority for its protection.

Emerging as the champions of an orderly religious reform, many German princes eventually confronted Emperor Charles V, who supported Rome. In 1529, Charles declared the Roman Catholic faith the empire's only legitimate religion. Proclaiming

their allegiance to the reform cause, the Lutheran German princes protested, and thus came to be called Protestants.

Anabaptists. Common people, however, did not disappear from the Reformation movement. While Zwingli was challenging the Roman church, some laypeople in Zurich were secretly pursuing their own path to reform. Taking their cue from the New Testament's descriptions of the first Christian community, these men and women believed that true faith was based on reason and free will. How could a baby knowingly choose Christ? Only adults could believe and accept baptism; hence the invalidity of Catholic infant baptism and the need for a new rite. These people came to be called Anabaptists—those who were rebaptized. The practice of rebaptism symbolized the Anabaptists' determination to withdraw from a social order corrupted (as they saw it) by power and evil. As pacifists who rejected the authority of courts and magistrates, they considered themselves a community of true Christians unblemished by sin. The Anabaptist movement drew its leadership primarily from the artisan class and its members from the middle and lower classes— men and women attracted by a simple message of peace and salvation.

Zwingli immediately attacked the Anabaptists for their refusal to bear arms and swear oaths of allegiance, sensing accurately that they were repudiating his theocratic order. When persuasion failed to convince the Anabaptists, Zwingli urged Zurich magistrates to impose the death sentence. Thus the Reformation's first martyrs of conscience were victims of its evangelical reformers.

Nevertheless, Anabaptism spread quickly from Zurich to many cities in southern Germany, despite the Holy Roman Empire's general condemnation of the movement in 1529. In 1534, one incendiary Anabaptist group, believing that the end of the world was imminent, seized control of the northwestern German city of Münster. Proclaiming themselves a community of saints and imitating the ancient Israelites, they were initially governed by twelve elders and later by Jan of Leiden, a Dutch Anabaptist tailor who claimed to be the prophesied leader—a second "King David." During this short-lived social experiment, the Münster Anabaptists abolished private property in imitation of the early Christian church and dissolved traditional marriages, allowing men, like Old Testament patriarchs, to have multiple wives, to the chagrin of many women. Besieged by a combined Protestant and Catholic army, messengers like Hille Feiken left Münster in search of relief while the leaders exhorted the faithful to remain steadfast in the hope of the Second Coming of Christ. But with food and hope exhausted, a soldier betrayed the city to the besiegers in June 1535. The leaders of the Münster Anabaptists died in battle or were horribly executed.

The Anabaptist movement in northwestern Europe nonetheless survived under the determined pacifist leadership of the Dutch reformer Menno Simons (1469–1561). Defeated in their bid for a socioreligious revolution, the common people became the subject of religious reforms and discipline. The Reformation strengthened rather than loosened social control in a vast effort to instill religious conformity and moral behavior orchestrated by secular rulers and a new clerical elite.

New Forms of Discipline

The emergence of a new urban, middle-class culture was one result of the religious cataclysms of the sixteenth century. Appearing first in Protestant Europe, it included marriage reforms, an emphasis on literacy, a new educational agenda, and a new work ethic, which came together as a watershed in European civilization. Other changes, although sparked by the Protestant Reformation, represented the culmination of developments that stretched back to the Middle Ages: the advent of public relief for the poor, the condemnation of vagrancy, and a general disciplining of society, from marriage reforms to changes in musical composition.

Reading the Bible. Prior to the Reformation, the Latin Vulgate was the only Bible authorized by the church, although many vernacular translations of parts of the Bible circulated. The Vulgate contains errors of translation from the Greek and Hebrew, as humanists such as Erasmus pointed out. Nevertheless, textual authority was predicated on church authority, and textual revisions were potentially subversive. The challenges to the Roman church from the Hussite and Lollard movements from previous centuries drew their legitimacy from the Scriptures; one of their chief aims was to translate the Bible into the vernacular. Although most sixteenth-century Europeans were illiterate, the Bible assumed for them a new importance because biblical stories were transmitted by pictures and the spoken word as well as through print. The Bible had the potential to subvert the established order.

In 1522, Martin Luther translated Erasmus's Greek New Testament into German, the first full vernacular translation in that language. Illustrated with woodcuts, more than 200,000 copies of Luther's New Testament were printed over twelve years, an immense number for the time. In 1534, Luther completed a translation of the Old Testament. Peppered with witty phrases and colloquial expressions, Luther's Bible was a treasure chest of the German language. Because of a huge appetite for the story of salvation, the popular reception of Luther's Bible was virtually assured. Between 1466 and 1522, more than twenty translations of the Bible had appeared in the various German dialects. Widespread among urban households, the German Bible occupied a central place in a family's history. Generations passed on valuable editions; pious citizens often bound the Scriptures with family papers or other reading material. To counter Protestant success, Catholic German Bibles appeared, thus authorizing and encouraging Bible reading by the Catholic laity, a sharp departure from medieval church practice.

The relationship between Scripture reading and religious reform also highlighted the history of early French and English Bibles. In the same year that Luther's German New Testament appeared in print, the French humanist Jacques Lefèvre d'Étaples (c. 1455–1536) translated the Vulgate New Testament into French. Sponsored by Guillaume Briçonnet, the bishop of Meaux, who wanted to distribute free copies of the New Testament to the poor of the region, the enterprise represented an early attempt to reform the French church without breaking with Rome.

Sensing a potentially dangerous association between the vernacular Bible and heresy, England's church hierarchy reacted swiftly against English-language Bibles. In a country with few printing presses, the first English Protestants could not publish their writings at home. Inspired by Luther's Bible during a visit to Wittenberg, the Englishman William Tyndale (1495–1536) translated the Bible into English. After he had his translation printed in Germany and the Low Countries, Tyndale smuggled copies into England. Later, following Henry VIII's break with Rome and adoption of the Reformation, the government promoted an English Bible based on Tyndale's translation, but Tyndale himself was burned at the stake as a hated heretic.

Although the vernacular Bible occupied a central role in Protestantism, Bible reading did not become widespread until the early seventeenth century. Educational reform and the founding of new schools proceeded slowly throughout the sixteenth century, thus limiting the number of literate people. Furthermore, the complete Bible was a relatively expensive book inaccessible to poorer households. Perhaps most important of all, the Protestant clergy, like their Catholic counterparts, grew suspicious of unsupervised Bible reading. Just as the first reformers cited Scripture against Rome, ordinary men and women drew their own lessons from the vernacular Bible, questioning and challenging the authority of the new Protestant establishment.

Indoctrinating the Young. To realize the Kingdom of God, Luther warned the princes and magistrates of the Holy Roman Empire that they must change hearts and minds. He encouraged them to establish schools, supported by confiscated church property, to educate children in the knowledge and fear of God. The ordinance for a girls' school in Göttingen spelled out that the school's purpose was "to initiate and hold girls in propriety and the fear of God. To fear God, they must learn their catechism, beautiful psalms, sayings, and other fine Christian and holy songs and little prayers."

The Protestant Reformation replaced late medieval church schools with a state school system. Controlled by state officials who examined, appointed, and paid teachers, the new educational system aimed to train obedient, pious, and hardworking Christian citizens. Discipline, not new ideas, informed sixteenth-century pedagogy. Teachers frequently used the rod to enforce discipline while students memorized their catechisms, prayers, and other short Christian texts. In addition to reading and writing, girls' schools included domestic skills in their curriculum.

A two-tier system existed in Protestant education. Every parish had its primary school for children between six and twelve. To train future pastors, scholars, and officials, the Protestant church developed a secondary system of humanist schools. These higher schools for boys, called *gymnasia* (from the Greek *gymnasion*), were intended to prepare students for university study. Greek and Latin classics constituted the core of the curriculum, to which was added religious instruction.

In Catholic Europe, educational reforms at the primary level proceeded unevenly. In northern and central Italian cities, most girls and boys received some education, in a strong pedagogic tradition dating to at least the thirteenth century. Concerning other Catholic territories, such as Spain, France, and southern Germany, our knowledge is fragmentary. But if Catholics lagged behind Protestants in promoting primary education, they did succeed in developing an excellent system of secondary education through the colleges established by the new Society of Jesus (known as the Jesuits), the most important religious order of Catholic Europe in the sixteenth century. Established to compete with the Protestant *gymnasia,* hundreds of Jesuit colleges dotted the landscape of Spain, Portugal, France, Italy, Germany, Hungary, Bohemia, and Poland by the late sixteenth century. Among their alumni would be princes, philosophers, lawyers, churchmen, and officials— the elite of Catholic Europe. The existence of different Christian schools helped to perpetuate the religious divisions of Reformation Europe for many generations.

Public Relief for the Poor. In the early sixteenth century, secular governments began to take over institutions of public charity from the church. This broad development, which took place in both Catholic and Protestant Europe, marked two trends that had become apparent during the later Middle Ages: the rise of a work ethic simultaneous with a growing hostility toward the poor and the widespread poverty brought about by population growth and spiraling inflation. (See "Taking Measure," right.)

Based on an agrarian economy that had severe technological limitations, European society again felt the pressure of population growth on its food resources. By 1500, the cycle of demographic collapse and economic depression triggered by the Black Death of 1348 had passed. Between 1500 and 1560, a new cycle of rapid economic and population growth created prosperity for some and stress —caused or heightened by increased inflation—for many. Wandering and begging in cities were by no means novel, but the reaction to poverty was new.

Sixteenth-century moralists decried the crime and sloth of vagabonds. Rejecting the notion that the poor played a central role in the Christian moral economy and that charity and prayers united rich and poor, these moralists cautioned against charlatans and criminals who brought disease in their wake. Instead, they said, people should distinguish between the genuine poor, or "God's Poor," and vagabonds; the latter, who were able-bodied, should be forced to work.

The Reformation provided an opportunity to restructure relief for the poor. In Nuremberg (1522) and Strasbourg (1523), magistrates centralized poor relief with church funds. Instead of using decentralized, private initiative, magistrates appointed officials to head urban agencies that would certify the genuine poor and distribute welfare funds to them. This development progressed rapidly in urban areas, where poverty was most visible, and transcended religious divisions. During the 1520s, cities in the Low Countries and Spain passed ordinances that prohibited begging and instituted public charity. In 1526, the Spanish humanist Juan Luis Vives wrote *On the Support of the Poor,* a Latin treatise urging authorities to establish public poor relief; the work was soon translated into French, Italian, German, and English. National measures followed urban initiatives. In 1531, Henry VIII asked justices of the peace (unpaid local magistrates) to license the

TAKING MEASURE Population Growth in Early Modern Europe

Only in the last quarter of the fifteenth century did Europe experience a sustained population growth, which took on a quick pace during most of the sixteenth century, especially during the first fifty years. The populations of Castile and the Kingdom of Naples doubled, for example. The most spectacular growth occurred in the city of Constantinople, the capital of the far-flung Ottoman Empire.

From Harry K. Miskimin, *The Economy of Later Renaissance Europe, 1460–1600* (Cambridge: Cambridge University Press, 1977) 26. Reprinted by permission of Cambridge University Press.

poor in England and to differentiate between those capable of working and those who could not. In 1540, Charles V (who ruled Spain as Charles I) imposed a welfare tax in Spain to augment that country's inadequate system of private charity.

More prevalent in Protestant areas, public relief for the poor became a permanent feature of Protestant governments once private charity ceased to be

Twelve Characteristics of an Insanely Angry Wife
This 1530 broadsheet depicts with a woodcut and accompanying text "the twelve properties of an insanely angry wife." The negative representation of female anger reflects the values dominant in Reformation society: a harmonious household ruled by a patriarch.
Schlossmuseum, Gotha.

considered a good work necessary to earn salvation. In fact, the number of voluntary donations took a significant drop once poor relief was introduced. The new work ethic acquired a distinctly Protestant aura in that it equated laziness with a lack of moral worth (and frequently associated laziness with Catholics) and linked hard work and prosperity with piety and divine providence. In Catholic lands, by contrast, collective charity persisted, supported by a theology of good works, by societies (in Italy and Spain, for example) more sharply divided between the noble rich and the poor, and by the elites' sense of social responsibility. These new changes in poor relief began to distinguish Protestant social order from traditional Catholic society.

New Marriage Ordinances. In their effort to establish order and discipline in worship and in society, the Protestant reformers decried sexual immorality and glorified the family. The idealized patriarchal family provided a bulwark against the forces of disorder. Protestant magistrates established marital courts, promulgated new marriage laws, closed brothels, and inflicted harsher punishments for sexual deviance.

Prior to the Reformation, marriages had been private affairs between families; some couples never even registered with the church. Under canon law, the Catholic church recognized any promise made between two consenting adults (with the legal age of twelve for females, fourteen for males) as a valid marriage. In rural areas and among the urban poor, most couples simply lived together as common-law husband and wife. The problem with the old marriage laws had been their complexity and the difficulties of enforcement. Often young men readily promised marriage in a passionate moment only to renege later. The overwhelming number of cases in Catholic church courts involved young women seeking to enforce promises after they had exchanged their personal honor—that is, their virginity—for the greater honor of marriage.

The Reformation proved more effective than the late medieval church in suppressing common-law marriages. Protestant governments asserted greater official control over marriage, and Catholic governments followed suit. A marriage was legitimate only if it had been registered by an official and a pastor. In many Protestant countries, the new marriage ordinances also required parental consent, thus giving householders immense power in regulating marriage and the transmission of family property.

Enjoined to become obedient spouses and affectionate companions in Christ, women approached this new sexual regime with ambivalence. The new laws stipulated that women could seek divorce for desertion, impotence, and flagrant abuse, although in practice the marital courts encouraged reconciliation. These changes from earlier laws came with a price, however: a woman's role took on the more limited definition of obedient wife, helpful companion, and loving mother. Now the path to religious power was closed to women. Unlike Catherine of Siena and Teresa of Ávila (later acknowledged as saints) or other pious Catholic women, Protestant women could not renounce family, marriage, and sexuality to attain recognition and power in the church.

In the fervor of the early Reformation years, the first generation of Protestant women attained greater marital equality than subsequent generations. For example, Katharina Zell, who had married the reformer Matthew Zell, defended her equality by citing Scripture to a critic. The critic had invoked St. Paul to support his argument that women should remain silent in church; Katharina retorted, "I would remind you of the word of this same apostle that in Christ there is no male nor female." Further quoting the Book of Joel, she recited the prophecy that "[God] will pour forth [his] spirit upon all flesh and your sons and daughters will prophesy."

Katharina was much more than the ideal pastor's wife, however. In 1525, she helped feed and clothe the thousands of refugees who flooded Strasbourg after their defeat in the Peasants' War. In 1534, she published a collection of hymns. She encouraged her husband to oppose Protestant persecution of dissenters. After Matthew's death in 1548, Katharina continued to feed the sick, the poor, and the imprisoned. Outraged by the intolerance of a new breed of Protestant clergy, she reprimanded the prominent Lutheran pastor Ludwig Rabus for his persecution of dissenters: "You behave as if you had been brought up by savages in a jungle." Comparing the Anabaptists to beasts pursued by hunters and wild animals, she praised them for bearing witness to their faith "in misery, prison, fire, and water." Rebuking Rabus, she wrote: "You young fellows tread on the graves of the first fathers of this church in Strasbourg and punish all who disagree with you, but faith cannot be forced."

A more typical role model for the average Protestant woman was Katharina von Bora (1499–1550), who married Martin Luther in 1525. Sent to a Catholic nunnery at the age of ten, the adult Katharina responded to the reformers' calls attacking monasticism. With the help of Luther, she and other nuns escaped by hiding in empty barrels that had contained smoked herring. After their marriage, the couple lived in the former Augustinian cloister in Wittenberg, which the elector of Saxony had given to Luther. Katie, as Luther affectionately called her, ran the establishment, feeding their children, relatives, and student boarders. Although she deferred to Luther—she addressed him as "Herr Doktor"—Katharina defended a woman's right as an equal in marriage. When Luther teased her about Old Testament examples of polygamy, Katharina retorted, "Well, if it comes to that, I'll leave you and the children and go back to the cloister." Accepting her prescribed role in a patriarchal household—one of the three estates in the new Christian society of politics, household, and church—Katharina von Bora represented the ideal Protestant woman.

The Sacred and Secular Patronage of Music. Religious reform left its imprint on musical composition as it did on other aspects of social and cultural life. In Catholic Europe the church and, to a lesser extent, the princely courts still employed and commissioned musicians. The two leading composers of the sixteenth century, Orlando de Lassus (1532–1594) and Giovanni Pierluigi da Palestrina (1525–1594), were both in papal service as choirmasters. Lassus, a Fleming by birth, went to Munich in 1556 to enter the service of the court of Bavaria, the most important German Catholic principality in the Holy Roman Empire. A prolific composer, Lassus left 390 secular songs in Italian, French, and German, as well as approximately 500 motets and other substantial sacred vocal works. The Italian Palestrina is remembered for his sacred music, especially for his polyphonies that accompanied the liturgy of the Mass, in which he reaffirmed Catholic tradition by using themes from Gregorian chants.

In Protestant Europe the chorale—or harmonized hymn—emerged as a new musical form. Unlike Catholic services, for which professional musicians sang in Latin, Protestant services enjoined the entire congregation to sing in unison. To encourage participation, Martin Luther, an accomplished lute player, composed many hymns in German. Drawing from Catholic sacred music as well as secular folk tunes, Luther and his collaborators wrote words to accompany familiar melodies.

The best known of Luther's hymns, "Ein' feste Burg," became the beloved English Protestant hymn "A Mighty Fortress" and inspired many subsequent variations.

Protestants sang hymns to signify their new faith. During the Peasants' War of 1525, for example, Thomas Müntzer and the peasant rebels implored God's intercession by singing the hymn "Oh Come, Thou Holy Spirit" before they were mowed down by the knights and mercenaries in a one-sided slaughter. Eyewitnesses also reported Protestant martyrs singing hymns before their executions. In Lutheran Germany, hymnals and prayer books adorned many urban households; the intimate relationship among religious devotion, bourgeois culture, and musical literacy would become a characteristic of Germany in later centuries.

❖ A Struggle for Mastery

In the sixteenth century, new patterns of conflicts generated by the Reformation superimposed themselves on traditional dynastic strife. Two developments came together to create instability: the ambitions of powerful princes and the passions of religious reformers. Almost everywhere in Europe, the conflicts of religious differences accentuated civil and dynastic wars. And almost everywhere, violence failed to settle religious differences. By 1560, an exhausted Europe found itself in a state of compromised peace, but a peace sown fraught with the seeds of future conflict.

The Court

At the center of this politics of dynasty and religion was the court, the focus of princely power and intrigue. European princes used the institution of the royal court to bind their nobility and impress their subjects. Briefly defined, the court was the prince's household. Around the ruling family, however, a small community coalesced, made up of household servants, noble attendants, councilors, officials, artists, and soldiers. During the sixteenth century, this political elite developed a sophisticated culture.

The French court of Francis I (r. 1515–1547) became the largest in Europe after the demise of the Burgundian dukes. In addition to the prince's household, the royal family set up households for other members: the queen and the queen mother each had her own staff of maids and chefs, as did each of the royal children. The royal household employed officials to handle finances, guard duty, clothing, and food; in addition, physicians, librarians, musicians, dwarfs, animal trainers, and a multitude of hangers-on bloated its size. By 1535, the French court numbered 1,622 members, excluding the nonofficial courtiers.

Although Francis built many palaces (the most magnificent at Fontainebleau), the French court was often on the move. It took no fewer than eighteen thousand horses to transport the people, furniture, and documents—not to mention the dogs and falcons for the royal hunt. Hunting, in fact, was a passion for the men at court; it represented a form of mock combat, essential in the training of a military elite. Francis himself loved war games. He staged a mock battle at court involving twelve hundred "warriors," and he led a party to lay siege to a model town during which several players were accidentally killed. Once Francis almost lost his own life when, storming a house during another mock battle, he was hit on the head by a burning log.

Italy gave Europe the ideological justification for court culture. Two writers in particular were the most eloquent spokesmen for the culture of "courtesy": Ludovico Ariosto (1474–1533), in service at the Este court in Ferrara, and Baldassare Castiglione (1478–1529), a servant of the duke of Urbino and the pope. Considered one of the greatest Renaissance poets, Ariosto composed a long epic poem, *Orlando Furioso* ("The Mad Roland"), which represented court culture as the highest synthesis of Christian and classical values. Set against the historic struggle between Charlemagne and the Arabs, the poem tells the love story of Bradamente and Ruggiero. Before the separated lovers are reunited, the reader meets scores of characters and hundreds of adventures. Modeled after Greek and Roman poetry, especially the works of Virgil and Ovid, *Orlando Furioso* also followed the tradition of the medieval chivalric romance. The tales of combat, valor, love, and magic captivated the court's noble readers, who, through this highly idealized fantasy, enjoyed a glorified view of their own world. In addition, the poem's characters represent the struggle between good and evil and between Christianity and Islam that was so much a part of the crusading spirit of the early sixteenth century.

Equally popular was *The Courtier* by the suave diplomat Castiglione. Like Ariosto, Castiglione tried to represent court culture as a synthesis of military virtues and literary and artistic cultivation. Speaking in eloquent dialogues, Castiglione's characters debate the qualities of an ideal courtier. The true courtier, Castiglione asserts, is a gentleman who speaks in a refined language and carries himself with nobility and dignity in the service of his prince and his lady. Clothing assumes a significant symbolism in *The Courtier;* in the words of one character, "I am not saying that clothes provide the basis for making hard and fast judgments about a man's character. . . . But I do maintain that a man's attire is also no small evidence for what kind of personality he has." The significance of outward appearance in court culture reflected the rigid distinctions between the classes and the sexes in sixteenth-century Europe. In Castiglione's words, the men at court had to display "valor" and the women "feminine sweetness." All the

formalities of court culture, however, could not mask the smoldering religious passions within, and the chivalry of Ariosto's *Mad Roland* had its real-life counterpart in the savage wars between Christianity and Islam in the sixteenth century.

Art and the Christian Knight

Through their patronage of artists, the Habsburg emperors and the Catholic popes created idealized self-images, representations of their era's hopes. The use of art for political glorification was nothing new, but below the surface of sixteenth-century art flowed an undercurrent of idealism. For all his political limitations, Emperor Maximilian I (r. 1493–1519), for example, was a visionary who dreamed of restoring Christian chivalry and even toyed with

Titian, *Charles V at Mühlberg*
The Venetian artist Titian was commissioned by Charles V to paint a series of portraits of the emperor at four stages of his career to show events in his long life for which he wished to be remembered. Titian here captures the emperor's sense of victory at having finally crushed the German Protestant princes in battle in 1547. Charles's triumph was to be short-lived.
Scala/Art Resource, NY.

Titian, *Gloria*
All military glory and earthly power is doomed to fade away, as this detail of Titian's Gloria *vividly depicts. Among the multitude turning to the Trinity in the heavens is the Emperor Charles V, dressed in a white robe. Painted after his abdication in 1556,* Gloria *is a reminder to Charles of the transience of earthly glory, for white is both the color of newborn innocence and that of the burial shroud.*
Institut Amatller d'Art Hispanic.

the idea of ruling as pope and emperor. He appointed the Nuremberg artist Albrecht Dürer (1471–1528) as court painter, to represent the Habsburg vision of universal Christian emperorship. Dürer's design for Maximilian's triumphal carriage in 1518 positioned the figures of Justice, Temperance, Prudence, and Fortitude at a level above the seated emperor, with other important allegorical figures—Reason, Nobility, and Power—also in attendance.

For many artists and humanists, such as Erasmus, Emperor Charles V embodied the ideal Christian knight. The Venetian painter Titian (1477–1576) captured the emperor's life on canvas four times. His 1532 portrait depicts a grand prince in his early thirties. Two portraits from 1548 and 1550 show him victorious over Protestants. Charles's favorite was the final portrait, *Gloria,* one of two Titians he took with him to his monastic retirement: it shows the kneeling emperor wrapped in a white death shroud joining the throng of the saved to worship the Trinity.

The Habsburg dynasty did not monopolize artistic self-glorification, however. The Florentine Michelangelo Buonarroti (1475–1564) matured his multiple talents in the service of the Medici family. After the overthrow of the Medici, he became Pope Julius II's favorite artist, painting with furious energy the Sistine Chapel (including the ceiling) and working on a never-finished tomb and sculpture for that same warrior-pope. Later Michelangelo was commissioned by Pope Paul III to design palaces in Rome; in 1547, he became the chief architect of St. Peter's Basilica. Michelangelo's work signified the transition from the Renaissance to the age of religious conflicts. His artistic talents served to glorify a papacy under siege, just as Titian lent his hand in defending the Habsburg cause against infidels and heretics.

The Field of the Cloth of Gold
This painting by an unknown artist shows the meeting of Henry VIII of England and Francis I of France near Calais for the sealing of an Anglo-French alliance. Note the prominent figure of Henry on horseback among his entourage. The meeting was a scene of ritual display of power and pomp, with carpets laid out over a vast area for the royal receptions, hence the name of the painting,
The Field of the Cloth of Gold.
The Queen Royal Collection © 1999 Her Majesty Queen Elizabeth II.

MAP 15.3 Habsburg-Valois-Ottoman Wars, 1494–1559
As the dominant European power, the Habsburg dynasty fought on two fronts: a religious war against the Islamic Ottoman Empire and a political war against the French Valois, who challenged Habsburg hegemony. The Mediterranean, the Balkans, and the Low Countries all became theaters of war.

Wars among Habsburgs, Valois, and Ottomans

While the Reformation was taking hold in Germany, the great powers of Spain and France fought each other for the domination of Europe (Map 15.3). French claims over Italian territories provided the fuse for this conflict. The Italian Wars, started in 1494, escalated into a general conflict that involved most Christian monarchs and the Muslim Ottoman sultan as well. There were two patterns to this struggle. First, from 1494 to 1559 the Valois and Habsburg dynasties remained implacable enemies; only in 1559 did the French king acknowledge defeat and sign the Treaty of Cateau-Cambrésis that established peace. Second, this basic Franco-Spanish (Valois-Habsburg) struggle drew in many other belligerents, who fought on one side or the other for their own benefits. Some acted purely out of power considerations, such as England, first siding with France and then with Spain. Others fought for their indepen-

dence, such as the papacy and the Italian states, who did not want any one power, particularly Spain, to dominate Italy. Still others chose sides for religious reasons, such as the Protestant princes in Germany, who exploited the Valois-Habsburg conflict to extract religious liberties from the emperor in 1555. Finally, the Ottoman Turks considered the religious schism in Christendom an opportunity to further their territorial expanse.

In this arena of struggle, Christian and Muslim armies clashed in Hungary and the Mediterranean. The Ottoman Empire reached its height of power under Sultan Suleiman I "the Magnificent" (r. 1520–1566). In 1526, a Turkish expedition destroyed the Hungarian army at Mohács. Three years later, the Ottoman army laid siege to Vienna; though unsuccesful, the siege sent shock waves throughout Christian Europe. In 1535, Charles V led a campaign to capture Tunis, the lair of North African pirates under Ottoman suzerainty. Desperate to overcome Charles's superior forces, Francis I eagerly forged an

The Battle at Mohács
This Ottoman painting shows the 1529 victory of the sultan's army over the Hungarians at Mohács. The battle resulted in the end of the Hungarian kingdom, which would be divided into three realms under Ottoman, Habsburg, and Transylvanian rule. Note the prominence of artillery and the Janissaries with muskets. The Ottomans commanded a vast army with modern equipment, a key to their military prowess in the sixteenth century.
Topkapi Palace Museum.

alliance with the Turkish sultan. Coming to the aid of the French, the Turkish fleet besieged Nice, on the southern coast of France, which was occupied by imperial troops. Francis even ordered all inhabitants of nearby Toulon to vacate their town so that

he could turn it into a Muslim colony for eight months, complete with a mosque and slave market.

Although the Turks eventually evacuated Toulon, many Christians were scandalized that France would ally itself with the Turks to make war on another Christian king. This brief Franco-Turkish alliance, however, reflected the spirit of the times: the age-old idea of the Christian crusade against Islam was in competition with a new political strategy that saw religion as but one factor in power politics.

While the Mediterranean served as the theater of war between Habsburgs and Ottomans, most battles between the Valoises and the Habsburgs were fought in Italy and the Low Countries. There were spectacular and bloody victories, but none led to a speedy and decisive end to the war. During the 1520s, the Habsburgs seemed triumphant. In 1525, the troops of Charles V crushed the French army at Pavia, Italy, counting among their captives the French king, Francis I. Treated with great honor by Charles, Francis was kept in Spain until he agreed to a treaty renouncing all claims to Italy. Furious at this humiliation, Francis repudiated the treaty the moment he reached France, reigniting the conflict. In 1527, Charles's troops captured Rome because the pope had allied with the French. Many of the imperial troops were German Protestant mercenaries, who delighted in tormenting the Catholic clergy. Protestants and Catholics alike interpreted the sack of Rome by imperial forces as a punishment of God; this disaster shocked the Catholic church out of its apathy and turned it toward reform.

The 1530s and 1540s saw more indecisive battles. Constantly distracted by the challenges of the Ottomans and the German Protestants, Charles V could not crush France in one swift blow. Years of conflict drained the treasuries of all monarchs because warfare was becoming more expensive.

The Finance and Technologies of War

The sixteenth century marked the beginning of superior Western military technology. Fueled by warfare, all armies grew in size, and their firepower became ever more deadly. With new weapons and larger armies, the costs of war soared. For example, heavier artillery pieces meant that the rectangular walls of medieval cities had to be transformed into fortresses with jutting forts and gun emplacements.

England had a war expenditure more than double its royal revenues in the 1540s. To pay these bills, the government devalued its coinage (the sixteenth-century equivalent of printing more paper money), causing prices to rise rapidly during those years.

Other European powers fell into similar predicaments. Charles V boasted the largest army in Europe—but he also sank deeper into debt. Between 1520 and 1532, Charles borrowed 5.4 million ducats, primarily to pay his troops; from 1552 to 1556, his war loans soared to 9.6 million ducats. Francis I, his opponent, similarly overspent. On his death in 1547, Francis owed the bankers of Lyon almost 7 million French pounds—approximately the entire royal income for that year.

The European powers literally fought themselves into bankruptcy. France and Spain had to pay 14 to 18 percent interest on their loans. Taxation, the sale of offices, and outright confiscation failed to bring in enough money to satisfy the war machine. Both the Habsburg and the Valois kings looked to their leading bankers to finance their costly wars.

Foremost among the financiers of the warring princes was the Fugger bank, the largest such enterprise in sixteenth-century Europe. Based in the southern German imperial city of Augsburg, the Fugger family and their associates built an international financial empire that helped to make kings. The enterprise began with Jakob Fugger (1459–1525), nicknamed "the Rich," who became personal banker to Charles V's grandfather Maximilian I. Constantly short of cash, Maximilian had granted the Fugger family numerous mining and minting concessions. The Fugger enterprise reaped handsome profits from its Habsburg connections: in addition to collecting interest and collateral, the Fugger banking house, with branches in the Netherlands, Italy, and Spain, transferred funds for the emperor across the scattered Habsburg domains. To pay for the service of providing and accepting bills of exchange, the Fuggers charged substantial fees. By the end of his life, Maximilian was so deeply in debt to Jakob Fugger that he had to pawn the royal jewels.

In 1519, Fugger assembled a consortium of German and Italian bankers to secure the election of Charles V as Holy Roman Emperor. For the next three decades, the alliance between Europe's largest international bank and its largest empire tightened.

Between 1527 and 1547, the Fugger bank's assets grew from 3 million guldens (German currency) to over 7 million; roughly 55 percent of the assets were from loans to the Habsburgs, with the Spanish dynasty taking the lion's share. Nothing revealed the power of international banking more than a letter Jakob Fugger wrote to Charles V in 1523 to recoup his investment in the 1519 election, asking the emperor "[to] graciously recognize my faithful, humble service, dedicated to the greater well-being of Your Imperial Majesty, and that you will order that the money which I have paid out, together with the interest upon it, shall be reckoned up and paid, without further delay."

Charles barely stayed one step ahead of his creditors, and his successor in Spain gradually lost control of the Spanish state finances. To service debts, European monarchs sought revenues in war and tax increases. But paying for troops and crushing rebellions took more money and more loans. The cycle of financial crises and warfare persisted until the late eighteenth century. It forced Spain and France to sign the Treaty of Cateau-Cambrésis in 1559, thus ending more than sixty years of warfare.

The Divided Realm

Throughout Europe, rulers viewed religious divisions as a dangerous challenge to the unity of their realms and the stability of their rule. A subject could very well swear greater allegiance to God than to his lord. Moreover, the Peasants' War of 1525 showed that religious dissent could lead to rebellion. In addition, religious differences intensified the formation of noble factions, which exploited the situation when weak monarchs or children ruled.

France. In France, Francis I tolerated Protestants until the Affair of the Placards in 1534. Persecutions of Huguenots—as the followers of John Calvin were called in France—were only sporadic, however, and the Reformed church grew steadily in strength. During the 1540s and 1550s, many French noble families converted to Calvinism. Under noble protection, the Reformed church was able to organize openly and hold synods (church meetings), especially in southern and western France. Some of the most powerful noble families, such as the Montmorency and the Bourbon, openly professed Protestantism.

The French monarchy tried to maintain a balance of power between Catholic and Huguenot and between hostile noble factions. Francis and his successor, Henry II (r. 1547–1559), both succeeded to a degree. But after Henry's death the weakened monarchy could no longer hold together the fragile realm. The real drama of the Reformation in France took place after 1560, when the country plunged into decades of religious wars, whose savagery was unparalleled elsewhere in Europe.

England. The English monarchy played the central role in shaping that country's religious reform. During the 1520s, English Protestants were few in number—a handful of clerical dissenters (particularly at Cambridge University) and, more significantly, a small but influential noble faction at court and a mercantile elite in London. King Henry VIII (r. 1509–1547) changed all that.

Until 1527, Henry firmly opposed the Reformation, even receiving the title "Defender of the Faith" from Pope Leo X for a treatise Henry wrote against Luther. A robust, ambitious, and well-educated man, Henry wanted to make his mark on history and, with the aid of his chancellors Cardinal Thomas Wolsey and Thomas More, he vigorously suppressed Protestantism and executed its leaders.

But by 1527, the king wanted to divorce his wife, Catherine of Aragon (d. 1536), the daughter of Ferdinand and Isabella of Spain and the aunt of Charles V. The eighteen-year marriage had produced a daughter, Princess Mary (known as Mary Tudor), but Henry desperately needed a male heir to consolidate the rule of the still new Tudor dynasty, begun by Henry's father, Henry VII. Moreover, he was in love with Anne Boleyn, a lady-in-waiting at court and a strong supporter of the Reformation. Henry claimed that his marriage to Catherine had never been valid because she was the widow of his older brother, Arthur. Arthur and Catherine's marriage, which apparently was never consummated, had been annulled by Pope Julius II so that the marriage between Henry and Catherine could take place to cement the dynastic alliance between England and Spain. Now, in 1527, Henry asked the reigning pope, Clement VII, to declare his marriage to Catherine invalid.

Around "the king's great matter" unfolded a struggle for political and religious control. When

Henry failed to secure a papal dispensation for his divorce, he chose two Protestants as his new loyal servants: Thomas Cromwell (1485–1540) as chancellor and Thomas Cranmer (1489–1556) as archbishop of Canterbury. Under their leadership the English Parliament passed a number of acts between 1529 and 1536 that severed ties between the English church and Rome. The Act of Supremacy of 1529 established Henry as the head of the so-called Anglican church (the Church of England), invalidated the claims of Catherine and Princess Mary to the throne, recognized Henry's marriage to Anne Boleyn, and allowed the English crown to confiscate the properties of the monasteries.

By 1536, Henry had grown tired of Anne Boleyn, who had given birth to the future Queen Elizabeth I but had produced no sons. The king, who would go on to marry four other wives but father only one son, Edward (by his third wife, Jane Seymour), had Anne beheaded on the charge of adultery, an act that he defined as treason (Figure 15.1). Thomas More also had gone to the block in 1535 for treason—in his case, for refusing to recognize Henry as "the only supreme head on earth of the Church of England"—and Cromwell suffered the same fate in 1540 when he lost favor. When Henry died in 1547, the Anglican church, nominally Protestant, still retained much traditional Catholic doctrine and ritual. But the principle of royal supremacy in religious matters would remain a lasting feature of Henry's reforms.

Under Edward VI (r. 1547–1553) and Mary Tudor (r. 1553–1558), official religious policies oscillated between Protestant reforms and Catholic restoration. The boy-king Edward furthered the Reformation by welcoming prominent religious refugees from the continent. With Mary Tudor's accession, however, Catholicism was restored and Protestants persecuted. Close to three hundred Protestants perished at the stake, and more than eight hundred fled to Germany and Switzerland. Finally, after Anne Boleyn's daughter, Elizabeth, succeeded her half-sister Mary to the throne in 1558, the Anglican cause again gained momentum; it eventually defined the character of the English nation.

Scotland. Still another pattern of religious politics unfolded in Scotland, where powerful noble clans directly challenged royal power. Until the 1550s,

FIGURE 15.1 The Wives of Henry VIII
Henry's increasingly urgent desire for a son to solidify the nascent Tudor dynasty caused him to enter into six marriages. In the process he dissolved all formal English ties to the Roman Catholic church and established the Anglican church.

Protestants had been a small minority in Scotland; they were easy to suppress if they did not enjoy the protection of sympathetic local lords. The most prominent Scottish reformer, John Knox (1514–1572), spent many of his early years in exile in England and on the continent. For Knox, God's cause was obstructed by a woman, who became his greatest enemy.

The queen regent Mary of Guise (d. 1560) stood at the center of Scotland's conflict. After the death of her husband, James V, in 1542, Mary of Guise, a Catholic, cultivated the support of her native France. Her daughter and heir to the throne, Mary Stuart (also a Catholic), had been educated in France and was married to the French dauphin Francis, son of Henry II. The queen regent surrounded herself with French advisers and soldiers. Alienated by this pro-French atmosphere, many Scottish noblemen had joined the pro-English, anti-French Protestant cause.

The era's suspicion of female rulers and regents also played a part in Protestant propaganda. In 1558, John Knox published *The First Blast of the Trumpet against the Monstrous Regiment [Rule] of Women,* a diatribe against both Mary Tudor of England and Mary of Guise. Knox declared that "to promote a woman to bear rule, superiority, dominion, or empire above any realm, nation, or city is repugnant to nature, contumely to God, a thing most contrary to his revealed will and approved ordinance and, finally, it is the subversion of good order, of all equality and justice." In 1560, the Protestants assumed control of the Scottish Parliament, and Mary of Guise fled to England.

The German States. In the German states, the Protestant princes and cities formed the Schmalkaldic League. Headed by the elector of Saxony and Philip of Hesse (the two leading Protestant princes), the league included most of the imperial cities, the chief source of the empire's wealth. On the other side, allied with Emperor Charles V, were the bishops and the few remaining Catholic princes. Although Charles had to concentrate on fighting the French and the Turks during the 1530s, he had by now temporarily secured the western Mediterranean; thus he turned to central Europe to try to resolve the growing religious differences there.

In 1541, Charles convened an Imperial Diet at Regensburg to patch up the theological differences between Protestants and Catholics, only to see negotiations between the two sides break down rapidly. The schism threatened to be permanent. Vowing to crush the Schmalkaldic League, the emperor secured French neutrality in 1544 and papal support in 1545. Luther died in 1546. In the following year, war broke out. Using seasoned Spanish veterans and German allies, Charles occupied the German imperial cities in the south, restoring Catholic patricians and suppressing the Reformation. In 1547, he defeated the Schmalkaldic League armies at Mühlberg and captured the leading Lutheran princes. Jubilant, Charles proclaimed a decree, the "Interim," which restored Catholics' right to worship in Protestant lands while permitting Lutherans to consecrate holy communion as both bread and wine. Protestant resistance to the Interim was deep and widespread: many pastors went into exile, and riots broke out in many cities.

For Charles V, the reaction of his former allies proved far more alarming than Protestant resistance. His success frightened some Catholic powers. With Spanish troops controlling Milan and Naples, Pope Julius III (r. 1550–1552) feared that papal authority would be subjugated by imperial might. In the Holy Roman Empire, Protestant princes spoke out against "imperial tyranny." Jealously defending their traditional liberties against an over-mighty emperor, the Protestant princes, led by Duke Maurice of Saxony, a former imperial ally, raised arms against Charles. The princes declared war in 1552, chasing a surprised, unprepared, and practically bankrupt emperor back to Italy.

Forced to construct an accord, Charles V agreed to the Peace of Augsburg in 1555. The settlement recognized the Evangelical (Lutheran) church in the empire, accepted the secularization of church lands but "reserved" the existent ecclesiastical territories (mainly the bishoprics) for Catholics, and, most important, established the principle that all princes, whether Catholic or Lutheran, enjoyed the sole right to determine the religion of their lands and subjects. Significantly, Calvinist, Anabaptist, and other dissenting groups were excluded from the settlement. The religious revolt of the common people had culminated in a princes' Reformation. As the constitutional framework for the Holy Roman Empire, the Augsburg settlement preserved a fragile peace in central Europe until 1618, but the exclusion of Calvinists would plant the seed for future conflict.

Exhausted by decades of war and disappointed by the disunity in Christian Europe, Emperor Charles V resigned his many thrones in 1555 and 1556, leaving his Netherlandish-Burgundian and Spanish dominions to his son, Philip II, and his Austrian lands to his brother, Ferdinand (who was also elected Holy Roman Emperor to succeed Charles). Retiring to a monastery in southern Spain, the most powerful of the Christian monarchs spent his last years quietly seeking salvation (Figure 15.2).

❖ A Continuing Reformation

Reacting to the waves of Protestant challenge, the Catholic church mobilized for defense. Drawing upon traditions of fervor prior to the Reformation, Catholicism offered hopes of renewal in the 1540s and 1550s: the Council of Trent defined the beliefs and practices of the Catholic church and condemned Protestant beliefs, while new religious orders, most notably the Society of Jesus, began a vigorous campaign for the reclamation of souls.

Christian Europe was transformed. Not only had the old religious unity passed forever, but new earth emerged under the canopy of a new heaven, as missionaries from Catholic Europe traveled to other parts of the world to win converts who might compensate for the millions lost to the Protestant Reformation.

Catholic Renewal

Many voices for reform had echoed within the Catholic church long before Luther, but the papacy had failed to sponsor any significant change. Nevertheless, a Catholic reform movement gathered

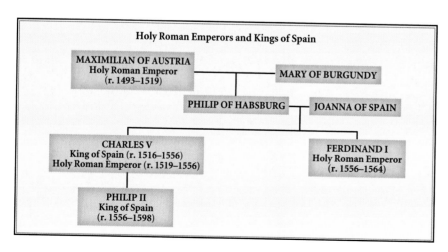

FIGURE 15.2 The Habsburg Succession, 1493–1556
The reign of Charles V ended with the splintering of the largest empire in Europe. Saddled with debts inherited from his grandfather and accrued from perpetual warfare, Charles ceded the Holy Roman Empire to his brother Ferdinand and gave Spain to his son Philip.

momentum in Italy during the 1530s and 1540s. Drawn from the elite, especially the Venetian upper class, the Catholic evangelicals stressed biblical ethics and moral discipline. Gian Matteo Giberti, bishop of Verona from 1524 to 1543, resigned his position in the Roman curia to concentrate on his pastoral duties. Gasparo Contarini (1483–1542), who was descended from a Venetian noble family and had served the republic as ambassador to Charles V, subsequently was elevated to cardinal, in which position he labored to heal the schism within the church.

Under Pope Paul III (r. 1534–1549) and his successors, the papacy finally took the lead in church reform. The Italian nobility also played a leading role, and Spaniards and Italians of all classes provided the backbone for this movement, sometimes called the Counter-Reformation. The Counter-Reformation's crowning achievements were the calling of a general church council and the founding of new religious orders.

The Council of Trent, 1545–1563.

In 1545, Pope Paul III and Charles V convened a general church council at Trent, a town on the border between the Holy Roman Empire and Italy. The Council of Trent, which met sporadically over the next seventeen years and finally completed its work in 1563, shaped the essential character of Catholicism until the 1960s. It reasserted the supremacy of clerical authority over the laity and stipulated that bishops reside in their dioceses and that seminaries be established in each diocese to train priests. The council also confirmed and clarified church doctrine and sacraments. On the sacrament of the Eucharist, the council reaffirmed that the bread actually *becomes* Christ's body—a rejection of all Protestant positions on this issue sufficiently emphatic as to preclude compromise. For the sacrament of marriage, the council stipulated that all weddings must henceforth take place in churches and be registered by the parish clergy; it further declared that all marriages remain valid, explicitly rejecting the Protestant allowance for divorce.

The Council of Trent marked a watershed; henceforth, the schism between Protestant and Catholic remained permanent and all hopes of reconciliation faded. The focus of the Catholic church turned now to rolling back the tide of dissent.

The Society of Jesus.

The energy of the Counter-Reformation expressed itself most vigorously in the founding of new religious orders. The most important of these, the Society of Jesus, or Jesuits, was established by a Spanish nobleman, Ignatius of Loyola (1491–1556). Imbued with tales of chivalric romances and the national glory of the Reconquista, Ignatius eagerly sought to prove his mettle as a soldier. In 1521, while defending a Spanish border fortress against French attack, he sustained a severe injury. During his convalescence, Ignatius read lives of the saints; once he recovered, he abandoned his quest for military glory in favor of serving the church.

Attracted by his austerity and piety, young men gravitated to this charismatic figure. Thanks to

Death Mask of Ignatius
This death mask of Ignatius of Loyola was executed immediately after his death in 1556 by his close associates in the Society of Jesus. The preservation of the aura of the founder by the early Jesuits was a vigorous effort that ultimately resulted in the canonization of Ignatius.
Leonard von Matt/Photo Research, Inc.

The Portuguese in Japan

In this sixteenth-century Japanese black-lacquer screen painting of Portuguese missionaries, the Jesuits are dressed in black and the Franciscans in brown. At the lower right corner is a Portuguese nobleman depicted with exaggerated "Western" features. The Japanese considered themselves lighter in skin color than the Portuguese, whom they classified as "barbarians." In turn, the Portuguese classified Japanese (and Chinese) as "whites." The perception of ethnic differences in the sixteenth century depended less on skin color than on clothing, eating habits, and other cultural signals. Color classifications were unstable and changed over time: by the late seventeenth century, Europeans no longer regarded Asians as "white."
Laurie Platt Winfrey, Inc.

Ignatius's noble birth and Cardinal Contarini's intercession, Ignatius gained a hearing before the pope, and in 1540 the church recognized his small band. With Ignatius as its first general, the Jesuits became the most vigorous defenders of papal authority. The society quickly expanded; by the time of Ignatius's death in 1556, Europe had one thousand Jesuits. Jesuits established hundreds of colleges throughout the Catholic world, educating future generations of Catholic leaders. Jesuit missionaries played a key role in the global Portuguese maritime empire and brought Roman Catholicism to Africans, Asians, and native Americans. Together with other new religious orders, the Jesuits restored the confidence of the faithful in the dedication and power of the Catholic church.

Missionary Zeal

To win new souls, Catholic missionaries set sail throughout the globe. They saw their effort as proof of the truth of Roman Catholicism and the success of their missions as a sign of divine favor, both particularly important in the face of Protestant challenge. But the missionary zeal of Catholics brought different messages to indigenous peoples: for some the message of a repressive and coercive alien religion, for others a sweet sign of reason and faith. Frustrated in his efforts to convert Brazilian Indians, a Jesuit missionary wrote to his superior in Rome in 1563 that "for this kind of people it is better to be preaching with the sword and rod of iron." This attitude was common among Christian missionaries in the Americas and Africa, despite the isolated missionary voices that condemned Europeans' abuse of native populations.

The Dominican Bartolomé de Las Casas (1474–1566) was perhaps the most severe critic of colonial brutality in Spanish America, yet even he argued that Africans were constitutionally more suitable for labor and should be imported to the plantations in the Americas to relieve the indigenous peoples, who were being worked to death. Under the influence of Las Casas and his followers, the Spanish crown tried to protect the indigenous peoples against exploitation by European settlers, a policy whose success was determined by the struggle among missionaries, *conquistadores* (Spanish conquerors in the Americas), and royal officials for the bodies and souls of native populations.

To ensure rapid Christianization, European missionaries focused initially on winning over local elites. The recommendation of a Spanish royal official in Mexico City was typical. He wrote to the crown in 1525:

> In order that the sons of caciques [chiefs] and native lords may be instructed in the faith, Your Majesty must command that a college be founded wherein they may be taught . . . to the end that they may be ordained priests. For he who shall become such among them, will be of greater profit in attracting others to the faith than will fifty [European] Christians.

Nevertheless, this recommendation was not adopted and the Catholic church in Spanish America re-

IMPORTANT DATES

1494 Start of the Italian Wars
1517 Martin Luther criticizes sale of indulgences and other church practices; the Reformation begins
1520 Reformer Huldrych Zwingli breaks with Rome
1520–1558 Reign of Charles V as Holy Roman Emperor
1526 Ottomans defeat Hungarians at Mohács
1529 Imperial Diet of Speyer; genesis of the term *Protestants*
1529 Henry VIII is declared head of the Anglican church
1532–1536 Spanish conquest of Peru
1534–1535 Anabaptists take control of Münster, Germany
1541 John Calvin established permanently in Geneva
1545–1563 Council of Trent
1546–1547 War of Schmalkaldic League
1555 Peace of Augsburg
1559 Treaty of Cateau-Cambrésis

mained overwhelmingly European in its clerical staffing.

The Portuguese were more willing to train indigenous peoples as missionaries. A number of young African nobles went to Portugal to be trained in theology, among them Dom Henry, a son of King Afonso I of Kongo, a Portuguese ally. In East Asia, Christian missionaries under Portuguese protection concentrated their efforts on the elites, preaching the Gospel to Confucian scholar-officials in China and to the samurai (the warrior aristocracy) in Japan. Measured in numbers alone, the missionary enterprise seemed highly successful: by the second half of the sixteenth century, vast multitudes of native Americans had become Christians at least in name, and thirty years after Francis Xavier's 1549 landing in Japan the Jesuits could claim over 100,000 Japanese converts.

After an initial period of relatively little racial discrimination, the Catholic church in the Americas and Africa adopted strict rules based on color. For example, the first Mexican Ecclesiastical Provincial Council in 1555 declared that holy orders were not to be

MAPPING THE WEST Reformation Europe, c. 1560

The fortunes of Roman Catholicism were at their lowest point around 1560. Northern Germany and Scandinavia owed allegiance to the Lutheran church, England broke away under a national church headed by its monarchs, and the Calvinist Reformation would extend across large areas of western, central, and eastern Europe. Southern Europe remained solidly Catholic.

conferred on Indians, *mestizos* (people of mixed European-Indian parentage), and *mulattos* (people of mixed European-African heritage); along with descendants of Moors, Jews, and persons who had been sentenced by the Spanish Inquisition, these groups were deemed "inherently unworthy of the sacerdotal [priestly] office." Europeans reinforced their sense of racial superiority with their perception of the "treachery" that native Americans and Africans exhibited whenever they resisted domination.

A different conversion tactic applied to Asia. There, European missionaries, who admired Chinese and Japanese civilization and were not backed by military power, used the sermon rather than the sword to win converts. The Jesuit Francis Xavier preached in India and Japan, his work vastly assisted by a network of Portuguese trading stations. He died in 1552, while awaiting permission to travel to China. A pioneer missionary in Asia, Xavier had prepared the ground for future missionary successes in Japan and China.

Conclusion

Mocking the warlike popes, the Dutch humanist Erasmus compared his times to those of the early Christian church. In *The Praise of Folly*, he satirized Christian prelates and princes, who "continued to shed Christian blood," the same blood as that of the martyrs who had built the foundations of Christianity. Turning from the papacy to the empire, Erasmus and many intellectuals and artists of his generation saw in Emperor Charles V the model Christian prince. As the most powerful ruler in all Europe, Charles was hailed as the harbinger of peace, the protector of justice, and the foe of the infidel Turks. For the generation that came of age before the Reformation, Christian humanism—and its imperial embodiment—represented an ideal for political and moral reform that would save Christendom from corruption and strife.

The Reformation changed this dream of peace and unity. Instead of leading a crusade against Islam—a guiding vision of his life—Charles V wore himself out in ceaseless struggle against Francis I of France and the German Protestants. Instead of the Christian faith of charity and learning that Erasmus had envisioned, Christianity split into a number of hostile camps that battled one another with words and swords. Instead of the intellectual unity of the generation of Erasmus and Thomas More, the mid-sixteenth-century cultural landscape erupted in a burst of conflicting doctrinal statements and left in its wake a climate of censorship, repression, and inflexibility.

After the brutal suppression of popular revolts in the 1520s and 1530s, religious persecution be-

came a Christian institution: Luther called on the princes to kill rebellious peasants in 1525, Zwingli advocated the drowning of Anabaptists, and Calvin supported the death sentence for Michael Servetus. Meanwhile, in Catholic lands persecutions and executions provided Protestants with a steady stream of martyrs. The two peace settlements in the 1550s failed to provide long-term solutions: the Peace of Augsburg gradually disintegrated as the religious struggles in the empire intensified, and the Treaty of Cateau-Cambrésis was but a brief respite in a century of crisis. In the following generations, civil war and national conflicts would set Catholics against Protestants in numerous futile attempts to restore a single faith.

Suggested References

A New Heaven and a New Earth

Recent scholarship on the Reformation era has emphasized the connected nature of religious, political, social, economic, and cultural history. Another new direction is to connect the study of Christian reform movements with Christian-Jewish relations prior to the Reformation.

Brady, Thomas A. *Turning Swiss: Cities and Empire, 1450–1550.* 1985.

Essential Works of Erasmus. Ed. W. T. H. Jackson. 1965.*

Hsia, R. Po-chia. *The Myth of Ritual Murder: Jews and Magic in the Reformation.* 1988.

Protestant Reformers

While continuing to refine our understanding of the leading Protestant reformers, recent scholars have also offered new interpretations that take into consideration the popular impact of the reformers' teachings.

Bouwsma, William J. *John Calvin: A Sixteenth-Century Portrait.* 1988.

Hillerbrand, Hans J., ed. *The Protestant Reformation.* 1969.*

http://www.puritansermons.com/poetry.htm. Puritan and Reformed sermons and other writings.

http://www.wsu.edu/~dee/REFORM/LUTHER.HTM. The life and thought of Martin Luther.

Oberman, Heiko A. *Luther: Man between God and Devil.* 1990.

Scribner, R. W. *For the Sake of Simple Folk: Popular Propaganda for the German Reformation.* 1981.

*Primary sources.

Reshaping Society through Religion

The most important trend in recent scholarship has been the consideration of the impact of the Reformation on society and culture. Many studies have shown the limited influence of the ideas of reformers; others document the persistence of traditional religious habits and practices well past the sixteenth century.

Bainton, Roland. *Women of the Reformation in Germany and Italy.* 1971.

Blickle, Peter. *The Revolution of 1525.* 1981.

Elton, G. R. *Reformation Europe, 1517–1559.* 1963.

Hsia, R. Po-chia. *The German People and the Reformation.* 1988.

Ozment, Steven E. *The Reformation in the Cities.* 1975.

Strauss, Gerald. *Luther's House of Learning: Indoctrination of the Young in the German Reformation.* 1978.

A Struggle for Mastery

Still focused on the struggle between the Habsburg and Valois dynasties, historical scholarship has also moved out in the direction of cultural and military history. Recent works have studied military innovations and artistic representations of the sixteenth-century monarchs.

Elliott, J. H. *The Old World and the New, 1492–1650.* 1970.

Guicciardini, Francesco. *The History of Italy.* Trans. Sidney Alexander. 1969.*

Knecht, R. J. *Francis I.* 1982.

Parker, Geoffrey. *The Military Revolution: Military Innovation and the Rise of the West, 1500–1800.* 1988.

Partridge, Loren, and Randolph Starn. *A Renaissance Likeness: Art and Culture in Raphael's Julius II.* 1980.

Trevor-Roper, Hugh. *Princes and Artists: Patronage and Ideology at Four Habsburg Courts, 1517–1633.* 1976.

A Continuing Reformation

Current scholarship suggests that by comparing the Protestant and Catholic Reformations, we can gain insight into the underlying social and cultural changes that affected all of Christian Europe. Another new direction of research brings the study of Christianity into the non-European realm by focusing on missions.

Crosby, Alfred W. *The Colombian Exchange: Biological and Cultural Consequences of 1492.* 1972.

Evennet, Henry Outram. *The Spirit of the Counter-Reformation.* 1968.

Hsia, R. Po-chia. *The World of the Catholic Renewal.* 1997.

Prodi, Paolo. *The Papal Prince, One Body and Two Souls: The Papal Monarchy in Early Modern Europe.* 1982.

Wars over Beliefs

1560–1648

I N MAY 1618, Protestants in the kingdom of Bohemia furiously protested the Holy Roman Emperor's attempts to curtail their hard-won religious freedoms. Protestants wanted to build new churches; the Catholic emperor wanted to stop them. Tensions boiled over when two Catholic deputy-governors tried to dissolve the meetings of Protestants. On May 23, a crowd of angry Protestants surged up the stairs of the royal castle in Prague, trapped the two Catholic deputies, dragged them screaming for mercy to the windows, and hurled them to the pavement below. One of the rebels jeered: "We will see if your [Virgin] Mary can help you!" But because they landed in a dung heap, the Catholic deputies survived. One of the two limped off on his own; the other was carried away by his servants to safety. Although no one died, this "defenestration" (from the French for "window," *la fenêtre*) of Prague touched off the Thirty Years' War (1618–1648), which eventually involved almost every major power in Europe. Before it ended, the fighting had devastated the lands of central Europe and produced permanent changes in European politics and culture.

The Thirty Years' War grew out of the religious conflicts initiated by the Reformation. When Martin Luther began the Protestant Reformation in 1517, he had no idea that he would be unleashing such dangerous forces, but religious turmoil and warfare followed almost immediately upon his break with the Catholic church. Until the early 1600s, the Peace of Augsburg of 1555 maintained relative calm in the lands of the Holy Roman Empire by granting each ruler the right to

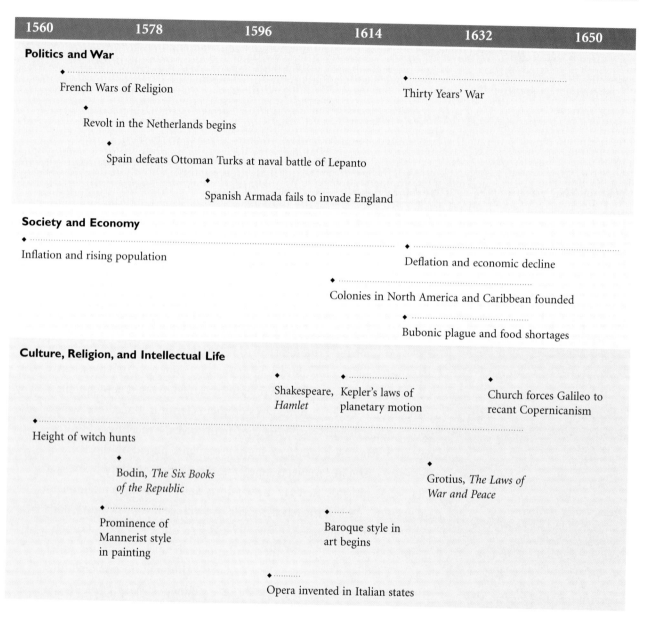

1560	1578	1596	1614	1632	1650

Politics and War

French Wars of Religion

Thirty Years' War

Revolt in the Netherlands begins

Spain defeats Ottoman Turks at naval battle of Lepanto

Spanish Armada fails to invade England

Society and Economy

Inflation and rising population

Deflation and economic decline

Colonies in North America and Caribbean founded

Bubonic plague and food shortages

Culture, Religion, and Intellectual Life

Shakespeare, Kepler's laws of *Hamlet* planetary motion

Church forces Galileo to recant Copernicanism

Height of witch hunts

Bodin, *The Six Books of the Republic*

Grotius, *The Laws of War and Peace*

Prominence of Mannerist style in painting

Baroque style in art begins

Opera invented in Italian states

determine the religion of his territory. But in western Europe, religious strife increased dramatically after 1560 as Protestants made inroads in France, the Spanish-ruled Netherlands, and England. All in all, nearly constant warfare marked the century between 1560 and 1648. These struggles most often began as religious conflicts, but religion was never the sole motive; political power entered into every equation and raised the stakes of conflict. The Bohemian Protestants, for example, wanted both freedom to practice their religion as Protestants and national independence for the Czechs, the largest ethnic group in Bohemia. Since Bohemia had many Catholics, religious and political aims inevitably came into conflict.

The Thirty Years' War brought the preceding religious conflicts to a head and by its very violence effectively removed religion from future international disputes. Although religion still divided people *within* various states, after 1648 religion no longer provided the rationale for wars *between* European states. The orgy of mutual destruction in the Thirty Years' War left no winners in the religious struggle, and the cynical manipulation of religious issues by both Catholic and Protestant leaders showed that political interests eventually outweighed those of religion. In addition, the violence of religious conflict pushed rulers and political thinkers to seek other, nonreligious grounds for governmental authority. Few would argue for genuine toleration of religious differences, but many began to insist that the interests of states had to take priority over the desire for religious conformity.

Although particularly dramatic and deadly, the church-state crisis was only one of a series of upheavals that shaped this era. In the early seventeenth century, a major economic downturn led to food shortages, famine, and disease in much of Europe. These hit especially hard in the central European lands devastated by the fighting of the Thirty Years' War and helped shift the balance of economic power to northwestern Europe, away from the Mediterranean and central Europe. An upheaval in worldviews was also in the making, catalyzed by increasing knowledge of the new worlds discovered overseas and in the heavens. The development of new scientific methods of research would ultimately reshape Western attitudes toward religion and state power, as Europeans desperately sought alternatives to wars over religious beliefs.

❖ Religious Conflicts and State Power, 1560–1618

The Peace of Augsburg of 1555 made Lutheranism a legal religion in the predominantly Catholic Holy Roman Empire, but it did not extend recognition to Calvinists. Although the followers of Martin Luther (Lutherans) and those of John Calvin (Calvinists) similarly refused the authority of the Catholic church, they disagreed with one another about religious doctrine and church organization. Lutheranism flourished in the northern German states and Scandinavia; Calvinism spread from its headquarters in the Swiss city of Geneva. The rapid expansion of Calvinism after 1560 threatened to alter the religious balance of power in much of Europe. Calvinists challenged Catholic dominance in France, the Spanish-ruled Netherlands, Scotland, and Poland-Lithuania. In England they sought to influence the new Protestant monarch, Elizabeth I. Calvinists were not the only source of religious

contention, however. While trying to suppress the revolt of Calvinists in the Netherlands, Philip II of Spain also fought the Muslim Ottoman Turks in the Mediterranean and expelled the remnants of the Muslim population in Spain. To the east, the Russian tsar Ivan IV fought to make Muscovy the center of an empire based on Russian Orthodox Christianity. He had to compete with Lutheran Sweden and Poland-Lithuania, itself divided by conflicts among Catholics, Lutherans, and Calvinists.

French Wars of Religion, 1562–1598

Calvinist inroads in France had begun in 1555, when the Genevan Company of Pastors took charge of missionary work. Supplied with false passports and often disguised as merchants, the Calvinist pastors moved rapidly among their growing congregations, which gathered in secret in towns near Paris or in the south. Calvinist nobles provided military protection to local congregations and helped set up a national organization for the French Calvinist—or Huguenot—church. In 1562, rival Huguenot and Catholic armies began fighting a series of wars that threatened to tear the French nation into shreds (Map 16.1).

Religious Division in the Nobility.   Conversion to Calvinism in French noble families often began with the noblewomen, some of whom sought intellectual independence as well as spiritual renewal in the new faith. Charlotte de Bourbon, for example, fled from a Catholic convent and eventually married William of Orange, the leader of the anti-Spanish resistance in the Netherlands. Jeanne d'Albret, mother of the future French king Henry IV, became a Calvinist and convinced many of her clan to convert, though her husband died fighting for the Catholic side. Calvinist noblewomen protected pastors, provided money and advice, and helped found schools and establish relief for the poor.

Religious divisions in France often reflected political disputes among noble families. At least one-third of the nobles—a much larger proportion than in the general population—joined the Huguenots, who usually followed the lead of the Bourbon family. The Bourbons were close relatives of the French king and stood first in line to inherit the throne if the Valois kings failed to produce a male heir. The most militantly Catholic nobles took their cues from

MAP 16.1 Protestant Churches in France, 1562
Calvinist missionaries took their message from their headquarters in Geneva across the border into France. The strongest concentration of Protestants was in southern France. The Bourbons, leaders of the Protestants in France, had their family lands in southwestern France in Navarre, a region that had been divided between France and Spain.

the Guise family, who aimed to block Bourbon ambitions. The Catholic Valois were caught between these two powerful factions, each with its own military organization. The situation grew even more volatile when King Henry II was accidentally killed during a jousting tournament in 1559 and his fifteen-year-old son Francis died soon after. Ten-year-old Charles IX (r. 1560–1574) became king, with his mother, Catherine de Medicis, as regent. Catherine, an Italian and a Catholic, urged limited toleration for the Huguenots in an attempt to maintain political stability, but her influence was severely limited. As one ambassador commented, "It is sufficient to say that she is a woman, a foreigner, and a Florentine to boot, born of a simple house, altogether beneath the dignity of the Kingdom of

France." In the vacuum created by the death of Henry II, the Bourbon and Guise factions consolidated their forces, and civil war erupted in 1562. Both sides committed terrible atrocities. Priests and pastors were murdered, and massacres of whole congregations became frighteningly commonplace.

St. Bartholomew's Day Massacre, 1572. Although a Catholic herself, Catherine aimed to preserve the throne for her son by playing the Guise and Bourbon factions off each other. To this end she arranged the marriage of the king's Catholic sister Marguerite de Valois to Henry of Navarre, a Huguenot and Bourbon. Just four days after the wedding in August 1572, assassins tried but failed to kill one of the Huguenot nobles allied with the Bourbons, Gaspard de Coligny. Panicked at the thought of Huguenot revenge and perhaps herself implicated in the botched plot, Catherine convinced her son to order the killing of leading Huguenots. On St. Bartholomew's Day, August 24, a bloodbath began, fueled by years of growing animosity between Catholics and Protestants. The duke of Guise himself killed Coligny. Each side viewed the other as less than human, as a source of moral pollution that had to be eradicated. In three days, Catholic mobs murdered three thousand Huguenots in Paris. Ten thousand died in the provinces over the next six weeks. The pope joyfully ordered the church bells rung throughout Catholic Europe; Spain's Philip II wrote Catherine that it was "the best and most cheerful news which at present could come to me."

The massacre settled nothing. Huguenot pamphleteers now proclaimed their right to resist a tyrant who worshiped idols (a practice that Calvinists equated with Catholicism). This right of resistance was linked to a notion of contract; upholding the true religion was part of the contract imagined as binding the ruler to his subjects. Both the right of resistance and the idea of a contract fed into the larger doctrine of constitutionalism—that a government's legitimacy rested on its upholding a constitution or contract between ruler and ruled. Constitutionalism justified resistance movements from the sixteenth century onward. Protestants and Catholics alike now saw the conflict as an international struggle for survival that required aid to coreligionists in other countries. In this way, the French Wars of Religion paved the way for wider international conflicts over religion in the decades to come.

Henry IV and the Edict of Nantes. The religious division in France grew even more dangerous when, two years after the massacre, Charles IX died and his brother Henry III (r. 1574–1589) became king. Like his brothers before him, Henry III failed to produce an heir. Next in line to the throne was none other than the Protestant Bourbon leader Henry of Navarre. Yet because Henry III and Catherine de

Massacre Motivated by Religion
The Italian artist Giorgio Vasari painted St. Bartholomew's Night: The Massacre of the Huguenots *for a public room in Pope Gregory XIII's residence. The pope and his artist intended to celebrate a Catholic victory over Protestant heresy.* Scala/Art Resource.

Henry IV's Paris
This painting of the Pont Neuf (new bridge) over the Seine River in Paris dates from about 1635 and shows the statue of Henry IV that was erected after his assassination in 1610. Henry IV built the bridge, the first one in Paris to have no houses on it, to link an island in the river with the two banks. This bridge is still one of the most beautiful in Paris.
Giraudon/Art Resource, NY.

Medicis saw an even greater threat to their authority in the Guises and their newly formed Catholic League, which had requested Philip II's help in rooting out Protestantism in France, they cooperated with Henry of Navarre. The Catholic League, believing that Henry III was not taking a strong enough stand against the Protestants, began to encourage disobedience. Henry III responded with a fatal trick: in 1588 he summoned the two Guise leaders to a meeting and had his men kill them. A few months later a fanatical monk stabbed Henry III to death, and Henry of Navarre became Henry IV (r. 1589–1610), despite Philip II's attempt to block his way with military intervention.

The new king soon concluded that to establish control over the war-weary country he had to place the interests of the French state ahead of his Protestant faith. In 1593, Henry IV publicly embraced Catholicism, reputedly explaining his conversion with the phrase "Paris is worth a Mass." Within a few years he defeated the ultra-Catholic opposition and drove out the Spanish. In 1598, he made peace with Spain and issued the Edict of Nantes, in which he granted the Huguenots a large measure of religious toleration. The approximately 1.25 million Huguenots became a legally protected minority within an officially Catholic kingdom of some 20 million people. Protestants were free to worship in specified towns and were allowed their own troops, fortresses, and even courts. The Edict of Nantes pacified a religious minority too large to ignore and impossible to eradicate. Few believed in religious toleration, but Henry IV followed the advice of those neutral Catholics and Calvinists called *politiques* who urged him to give priority to the development of a durable state. Although their opponents hated them for their compromising spirit, the *politiques* believed that religious disputes could be resolved only in the peace provided by strong government. The Edict of Nantes ended the French Wars of Religion.

But the new king needed more than a good theory to strengthen state power. To ensure his own safety and the succession of his heirs, Henry had to reestablish monarchical authority. Shrewdly mixing his famous charm with bravado and cunning, Henry created a splendid image of monarchy and extended his government's control. He used paintings, songs, court festivities, and royal processions to rally subjects and officials around him. Henry also developed a new class of royal officials to counterbalance the fractious nobility. For some time the French crown had earned considerable revenue by selling offices to qualified bidders. Now, in exchange for an annual payment, officeholders could not only own their offices but also pass them to heirs or sell them to someone else. Because these offices carried prestige and often ennobled their holders, rich middle-class merchants and lawyers with aspirations to higher social status found them attractive. By buying offices they could become part of a new social elite known as the "nobility of the robe" (named after the robes that magistrates wore, much like those judges wear today). The monarchy acquired a growing bureaucracy, though at the cost of granting broad autonomy to new officials who could not be dismissed. Nonetheless, new income raised by the increased sale of offices reduced the state debt and helped Henry build the base for a strong monarchy. His efforts did not, however, prevent his own assassination in 1610 after nineteen unsuccessful attempts.

Challenges to Spanish Power

Although he failed to prevent Henry IV from taking the French throne, Philip II of Spain (r. 1556–1598) was the most powerful ruler in Europe (Map 16.2). In addition to the western Habsburg lands in

MAP 16.2 The Empire of Philip II, r. 1556–1598
Spanish king Philip II drew revenues from a truly worldwide empire. In 1580 he was the richest European ruler, but the demands of governing such far-flung territories eventually drained many of his resources.

Spain and the Netherlands, he had inherited from his father, Charles V, all the Spanish colonies recently settled in the New World of the Americas. Gold and silver funneled from the colonies supported his campaigns against the Ottoman Turks and French and English Protestants. But all of the money of the New World could not prevent his eventual defeat in the Netherlands, where Calvinist rebels established an independent Dutch Republic that soon vied with Spain, France, and England for commercial supremacy.

Philip II, the Catholic King. A deeply devout Catholic, Philip II came to the Spanish throne at age twenty-eight. He built a great gray granite structure, half-palace, half-monastery, called the Escorial, in the mountains near Madrid. There he lived in a small room and dressed in somber black, while amassing an impressive collection of books and paintings. His austere personal style hid a burning ambition to restore Catholic unity in Europe and lead the Christian defense against the Muslims. In his quest Philip benefited from a series of misfortunes. He had four wives, who all died, but through them he became part of four royal families: Portuguese, English, French, and Austrian. His brief marriage to Mary Tudor (Mary I of England) did not produce an heir, but it and his subsequent marriage to Elisabeth de Valois, the sister of Charles IX and Henry III of France, gave him reason enough for involvement in English and French affairs. In 1580, when the king of Portugal died without a direct heir, Philip took over this neighboring realm with its rich empire in Africa, India, and the Americas.

Philip insisted on Catholic unity in his own possessions and worked to forge an international Christian coalition against the Ottoman Turks. In 1571, he achieved the single greatest military victory of his reign when he joined with Venice and the papacy to defeat the Turks in a great sea battle off the Greek coast at Lepanto. Fifty thousand sailors and soldiers fought on the allied side, and eight thousand died. Spain now controlled the western Mediterranean. But Philip could not rest on his laurels. Between 1568 and 1570, the Moriscos—Muslim converts to Christianity who remained secretly faithful to Islam—had revolted in the south of Spain, killing 90 priests and 1,500 Christians. The victory at Lepanto destroyed any prospect that the Turks might come to their aid, yet Philip took stern

measures against the Moriscos. He forced 50,000 to leave their villages and resettle in other regions. In 1609, his successor, Philip III, ordered their expulsion, and by 1614 some 300,000 Moriscos had been forced to relocate to North Africa.

The Revolt of the Netherlands. The Calvinists of the Netherlands were less easily intimidated than the Moriscos: they were far from Spain and accustomed to being left alone. In 1566, Calvinists in the Netherlands attacked Catholic churches, smashing stained-glass windows and statues of the Virgin Mary. Philip sent an army, which executed more than 1,100 people during the next six years. Prince William of Orange (whose name came from the lands he owned in southern France) took the lead of the anti-Spanish resistance. He encouraged adventurers and pirates known as the Sea Beggars to invade the northern ports. The Spanish responded with more force, culminating in November 1576 when Philip's long-unpaid mercenary armies sacked Antwerp, then Europe's wealthiest commercial city. In eleven days of horror known as the Spanish Fury, the Spanish soldiers slaughtered seven thousand people. Shocked into response, the ten largely Catholic southern provinces formally allied with the seven largely Protestant northern provinces and expelled the Spaniards.

Important religious, ethnic, and linguistic differences promoted a federation rather than a union of Dutch states. The southern provinces remained Catholic, French-speaking in parts, and suspicious of the increasingly strict Calvinism in the north. In 1579, the southern provinces returned to the Spanish fold. Despite the assassination in 1584 of William of Orange, after he had been outlawed as "an enemy of the human race" by Philip II, Spanish troops never regained control in the north. Spain would not formally recognize Dutch independence until 1648, but by the end of the sixteenth century the Dutch Republic was a self-governing state sheltering a variety of religious groups.

The Netherlands during the Revolt, c. 1580

Rembrandt's Depiction of Dutch Life
Rembrandt's painting known as The Night Watch *(1642) shows members of a voluntary militia company in action. In fact, it is a group portrait, probably commissioned by the guardsmen themselves. Once responsible for defending the city, the militia companies had become eating and drinking clubs for prosperous businessmen. The painting demonstrates Rembrandt's interest in every aspect of daily life in the Dutch Republic.*
Rijksmuseum, Amsterdam.

The Dutch Republic. The princes of Orange resembled a ruling family in the Dutch Republic (sometimes incorrectly called "Holland" after the most populous of the seven provinces), but their powers paled next to those of local interests. Urban merchant and professional families known as "regents" controlled the towns and provinces. This was no democracy: governing explicitly included "the handling and keeping quiet of the multitude." In the absence of a national bureaucracy, a single legal system, or a central court, each province governed itself and sent delegates to the one common institution, the States General, which carried out the wishes of the strongest individual provinces and their ruling families.

Well situated for maritime commerce, the Dutch Republic developed a thriving economy based on shipping and shipbuilding. Whereas elites in other countries focused on their landholdings, the Dutch looked for investments in trade. After the

Dutch gained independence, Amsterdam became the main European money market for two centuries. The city was also a primary commodities market and a chief supplier of arms—to allies, neutrals, and even enemies. Dutch entrepreneurs produced goods at lower prices than anyone else and marketed them more efficiently. Dutch merchants favored free trade in Europe because they could compete at an advantage. They controlled many overseas markets thanks to their preeminence in seaborne commerce: by 1670, the Dutch commercial fleet was larger than the English, French, Spanish, Portuguese, and Austrian fleets combined.

Since the Dutch traded with anyone anywhere, it is perhaps not surprising that Dutch society tolerated more religious diversity than the other European states. One-third of the Dutch population remained Catholic, and the secular authorities allowed them to worship as they chose in private. Because Protestant sects could generally count on toleration from local regents, they remained peaceful. The Dutch Republic also had a relatively large Jewish population because many Jews had settled there after being driven out of Spain and Portugal; from 1597, Jews could worship openly in their synagogues. This openness to various religions helped make the Dutch Republic one of Europe's chief intellectual and scientific centers in the seventeenth and eighteenth centuries.

Elizabeth I's Defense of English Protestantism

As the Dutch revolt unfolded, Philip II became increasingly infuriated with Elizabeth I (r. 1558–1603), who had succeeded her half-sister Mary Tudor as queen of England. Philip had been married to Mary and had enthusiastically seconded Mary's efforts to return England to Catholicism. When Mary died in 1558, Elizabeth rejected Philip's proposal of marriage and promptly brought Protestantism back to England. Eventually she provided funds and troops to the Dutch Protestant cause. As Elizabeth moved to solidify her personal power and the authority of the Anglican church (Church of England), she had to squash uprisings by Catholics in the north and at least two serious plots against her life. In the long run, however, her greater challenges came from the Calvinist Puritans and Philip II.

Puritanism and the Church of England. The Puritans were strict Calvinists who opposed all vestiges of Catholic ritual in the Church of England. After Elizabeth became queen, many Puritans returned from exile abroad, but Elizabeth resisted their demands for drastic changes in church ritual and governance. She had assumed control as "supreme governor" of the Church of England, replacing the pope as the ultimate religious authority, and appointed all bishops. The Church of England's Thirty-Nine Articles of Religion, issued in 1563, incorporated elements of Catholic ritual along with Calvinist doctrines. Puritan ministers angrily denounced the Church of England's "popish attire and foolish disguising, . . . tithings, holy days, and a

Glorifying the Ruler
This exquisite miniature (c. 1560) attributed to Levina Teerlinc, a Flemish woman who painted for the English court, shows Queen Elizabeth I dressed in purplish blue, participating in an Easter Week ceremony at which the monarch washed the feet of poor people before presenting them with money, food, and clothing. The ceremony was held to imitate Christ's washing of the feet of his disciples; it showed that the queen could exercise every one of the ruler's customary roles.
Private collection.

thousand more abominations." To accomplish their reforms, Puritans tried to undercut the bishops' authority by placing control of church administration in the hands of a local presbytery made up of the minister and the elders of the congregation. Elizabeth rejected this Calvinist "presbyterianism."

Even though Puritans lost on almost every national issue about church organization, their influence steadily increased in local parishes. Known for their emphasis on strict moral lives, the Puritans opposed traditional forms of merrymaking such as maypole festivals and dances and regarded Sunday fairs as an insult to the Sabbath (observed by Puritans as the day of rest and worship). They abhorred the "hideous obscenities" that took place in theaters and tried to close them down. Every Puritan father—with the help of his wife—was to "make his house a little church" by teaching the children to read the Bible. At Puritan urging, a new translation of the Bible, known as the King James Bible after Elizabeth's successor, James I, was authorized in 1604. Believing themselves God's elect and England an "elect nation," the Puritans also pushed Elizabeth to help Protestants on the continent.

Triumph over Spain.   Although enraged by Elizabeth's aid to the Dutch rebels, Philip II bided his time as long as she remained unmarried and her Catholic cousin Mary, Queen of Scots (Mary Stuart), stood next in line to inherit the English throne. In 1568, Scottish Calvinists forced Mary to abdicate the throne of Scotland in favor of her year-old son James (eventually James I of England), who was then raised as a Protestant. Mary spent nearly twenty years under house arrest in England, fomenting plots against Elizabeth. In 1587, when Mary's letter offering her succession rights to Philip was discovered, Elizabeth overcame her reluctance to execute a fellow monarch and ordered Mary's beheading. In response, Pope Sixtus V decided to subsidize a Catholic crusade under Philip's leadership against the heretical queen, "the English Jezebel."

At the end of May 1588, Philip II sent his *armada* (Spanish for "fleet") of 130 ships from Lisbon toward the English Channel. The Spanish king's motives were at least as much political and economic as they were religious; he now had an excuse to strike at the country whose pirates raided his shipping and encouraged Dutch resistance, and he hoped to use his fleet to ferry thousands of troops from the Netherlands across the channel to invade England itself. After several inconclusive engagements, the English scattered the Spanish Armada by sending blazing fire ships into its midst. A gale then forced the Spanish to flee around Scotland. When the Armada limped home in September, half the ships had been lost and thousands of sailors were dead or starving. Protestants throughout Europe rejoiced; Elizabeth struck a medal with the words "God blew, and they were scattered." In his play *King John* a few years later (1596), William Shakespeare wrote, "This England never did, nor never shall, Lie at the proud foot of a conqueror." Philip and Catholic Spain suffered a crushing psychological blow. A Spanish monk lamented, "Almost the whole of Spain went into mourning."

By the time Philip II died in 1598, his great empire had begun to lose its luster. The Dutch revolt ground on, and Henry IV seemed firmly established in France. The costs of fighting the Dutch, the English, and the French mounted, and in the 1590s pervasive crop failures and an outbreak of the plague made hard times even worse. An overburdened peasantry could no longer pay the taxes required to meet rising expenses. In his novel *Don Quixote* (1605), the Spanish writer Miguel de Cervantes captured the sadness of Spain's loss of grandeur. Cervantes himself had been wounded at Lepanto, been held captive in Algiers, and then served as a royal tax collector. His hero, a minor nobleman, wants to understand "this

Retreat of the Spanish Armada, 1588

thing they call reason of state," but he reads so many romances and books of chivalry that he loses his wits and wanders the countryside hoping to re-create the heroic deeds of times past. He refuses to believe that these books are only fantasies: "Books which are printed under license from the king . . . can such be lies?" Don Quixote's futile adventures incarnated the thwarted ambitions of a declining military aristocracy.

England could never have defeated Spain in a head-to-head battle on land, but Elizabeth made the most of her limited means and consolidated the country's position as a Protestant power. In her early years, she held out the prospect of marriage to many political suitors but never married. She cajoled Parliament with references to her female weaknesses, but she knew Latin, French, and Italian and showed steely-eyed determination in protecting the monarchy's interests. Her chosen successor, James I (r. 1603–1625), came to the throne as king of both Scotland and England. Shakespeare's tragedies *Hamlet* (1601), *King Lear* (1605), and *Macbeth* (1606), written about the time of James's succession, might all be read as commentaries on the uncertainties faced by Elizabeth and James. In each play, family relationships are linked to questions about the legitimacy of government, just as they were for Elizabeth and James. But Elizabeth's story, unlike those of Shakespeare's tragedies, had a happy ending; she left James secure in a kingdom of growing weight in world politics.

The Clash of Faiths and Empires in Eastern Europe

State power in eastern Europe was also tied up with religion, but in less predictable ways than in western Europe. In the east, the most contentious border divided Christian Europe from the Islamic realm of the Ottoman Turks. After their defeat at Lepanto in 1571, the Ottomans were down but far from out. Even in the Mediterranean, they continued their attacks, seizing Venetian-held Cyprus in 1573. Ottoman rule went unchallenged in the Balkans, where the Turks allowed their Christian subjects to cling to the Orthodox faith rather than forcibly converting them to Islam. Orthodox Christians thus enjoyed relative toleration and were unlikely to look to western Europe for aid. Even less inclined to turn westward were the numerous and prosperous Jewish communities of the Ottoman Empire, augmented by Jews expelled from Spain.

Orthodox Christians in Russian lands received official protection from the Muscovite tsars, but on occasion some suffered the effects of official displeasure. Building on the base laid by his grandfather Ivan III, Tsar Ivan IV (r. 1533–1584) stopped

at nothing in his endeavor to make Muscovy the center of a mighty Russian empire. Given to unpredictable fits of rage, Ivan tortured priests, killed numerous *boyars* (nobles), and murdered his own son with an iron rod during a quarrel. His epithet "the Terrible" reflects not only the terror he unleashed but also the awesome impression he evoked. Cunning, intelligent, morbidly suspicious, and cruel, Ivan came to embody barbarism in the eyes of westerners. An English visitor wrote that Ivan's actions had bred "a general hatred, distreccion [distraction], fear and discontentment throw [throughout] his kingdom. . . . God has a great plague in store for this people." Such warnings did not keep away the many westerners drawn to Moscow by opportunities to buy furs and sell western cloth and military hardware.

Ivan brought the entire Volga valley under Muscovite control and initiated Russian expansion eastward into Siberia. In 1558, he struck out to the west, vainly attempting to seize the decaying state of the German crusader (Teutonic) knights in present-day Estonia and Latvia to provide Russia direct access to the Baltic Sea. Two formidable foes blocked Ivan's plans for expansion: Sweden (which then included much of present-day Finland) and Poland-Lithuania. Their rulers hoped to annex the eastern Baltic provinces themselves. Poland and the grand duchy of Lithuania

Russia, Poland-Lithuania, and Sweden in the Late 1500s

united into a single commonwealth in 1569 and controlled territory stretching from the Baltic Sea to deep within present-day Ukraine and Belarus. It was the largest state lying wholly within the boundaries of Europe.

Poland-Lithuania, like the Dutch Republic, constituted one of the great exceptions to the general trend in early modern Europe toward greater monarchical authority; the Polish and Lithuanian nobles elected their king and severely circumscribed his authority. Noble converts to Lutheranism or Calvinism feared religious persecution by the Catholic majority, so the Polish-Lithuanian nobility insisted that their kings accept the principle of religious toleration as a prerequisite for election. The numerous Jewish communities prospered under the protection of the king and nobles.

Poland-Lithuania threatened the rule of Ivan's successors in Russia. After Ivan IV died in 1584, a terrible period of chaos known as the Time of Troubles ensued, during which the king of Poland-Lithuania tried to put his son on the Russian throne. In 1613, an army of nobles, townspeople, and peasants finally drove out the intruders and put on the throne a nobleman, Michael Romanov (r. 1613–1645), who established an enduring new dynasty. With the return of peace, Muscovite Russia resumed the process of state building. Reorganizing tax gathering and military recruitment and continuing to create a service nobility to whom the peasantry was increasingly subject, the first Romanovs laid the foundations of the powerful Russian empire that would emerge in the late seventeenth century under Peter the Great.

❖ The Thirty Years' War and the Balance of Power, 1618–1648

Although the eastern states managed to avoid civil wars over religion, the rest of Europe was drawn into the final and most deadly of the wars of religion, the Thirty Years' War. It began in 1618 with conflicts between Catholics and Protestants within the Holy Roman Empire and eventually involved most European states. By its end in 1648, many central European lands lay in ruins and the balance of power had shifted away from the Habsburg powers—Spain and Austria—toward France, England, and the Dutch Republic. Constant warfare created immediate turmoil, but it also fostered the growth of armies and the power of the bureaucracies that fed them with men and money. Out of the carnage would emerge centralized and powerful states that made increasing demands on ordinary people.

The Course of the War

The fighting that devastated central Europe had its origins in a combination of political weakness, ethnic competition, and religious conflict. The Austrian Habsburgs officially ruled over the huge Holy Roman Empire, which comprised eight major ethnic groups, but they could govern only with local cooperation. The emperor and four of the seven electors who chose him were Catholic; the other three electors were Protestants. The Peace of Augsburg of 1555 was supposed to maintain the balance between Catholics and Lutherans, but it had no mechanism for resolving conflicts; tensions rose as the new Catholic religious order, the Jesuits, won many Lutheran cities back to Catholicism and as Calvinism, unrecognized under the Peace, made inroads into Lutheran areas. By 1613, two of the three Protestant electors had become Calvinists. The long and complex war that grew out of these tensions took place in four phases: Bohemian (1618–1625), Danish (1625–1630), Swedish (1630–1635), and French (1635–1648).

Bohemian Phase. War first broke out in Bohemia after the defenestration of Prague in May 1618. The Austrian Habsburgs held not only the imperial crown of the Holy Roman Empire but also a collection of separately administered royal crowns, of which Bohemia was one. When the Catholic Habsburg heir Archduke Ferdinand was crowned king of Bohemia in 1617, he began to curtail the religious freedom previously granted to Protestants and thereby set in motion a fatal chain of events. After the defenestration, the Czechs, the largest ethnic group in Bohemia, established a Protestant assembly to spearhead resistance. A year later, when Ferdinand was elected emperor (as Ferdinand II, r. 1619–1637), the rebellious Bohemians deposed him and chose in his place the young Calvinist Frederick V of the Palatinate (r. 1616–1623). A quick series of clashes ended in 1620 when the imperial armies defeated the outmanned Czechs at the Battle of White Mountain, near Prague. Like the martyrdom of the religious reformer Jan Hus in 1415, White Mountain became an enduring symbol of the Czechs' desire for self-determination. They would not gain their independence until 1918.

White Mountain did not end the war. Private mercenary armies (armies for hire) began to form during the fighting, and the emperor had virtually no control over them. The meteoric rise of one commander, Albrecht von Wallenstein (1583–1634), showed how political ambition could trump religious conviction. A Czech Protestant by birth, Wallenstein offered in 1625 to raise an army for the Catholic emperor and soon had in his employ

125,000 soldiers, who occupied and plundered much of Protestant Germany with the emperor's approval.

Danish and Swedish Phases. The Lutheran king of Denmark Christian IV (r. 1596–1648) responded to Wallenstein's depredations by invading northern Germany to protect the Protestants and to extend his own influence. Despite Dutch and English encouragement, Christian lacked adequate military support, and Wallenstein's forces defeated him. Emboldened by his general's victories, Ferdinand issued the Edict of Restitution in 1629, which outlawed Calvinism in the empire and reclaimed Catholic church properties confiscated by the Lutherans.

With Protestant interests in serious jeopardy, Gustavus Adolphus (r. 1611–1632) of Sweden marched into Germany in 1630. Declaring his support for the Protestant cause, he clearly intended to gain control over trade in northern Europe, where he had already ejected the Poles from present-day Latvia and Estonia. His highly trained army of some 100,000 soldiers made Sweden, with a population of only one million, the supreme power of northern Europe. Now the primacy of political motives became obvious: the

Catholic French government under the leadership of Cardinal Richelieu offered to subsidize the Lutheran Gustavus. Richelieu hoped to block Spanish intervention in the war and win influence and perhaps territory in the Holy Roman Empire. The agreement between the Lutheran and Catholic powers to fight the Catholic Habsburgs showed that state interests now outweighed all other considerations.

Gustavus defeated the imperial army and occupied the Catholic parts of southern Germany before he was killed at the battle of Lützen in 1632. Once again the tide turned, but this time it swept Wallenstein with it. Because Wallenstein was rumored to be negotiating with Protestant powers, Ferdinand dismissed his general and had his henchmen assassinate him.

French Phase. France openly joined the fray in 1635 by declaring war on Spain and soon after forged an alliance with the Calvinist Dutch to aid them in their struggle for independence from Spain. The French king Louis XIII (r. 1610–1643) and his chief minister Richelieu (1585–1642) had hoped to profit from the troubles of Spain in the Netherlands and from the conflicts between the Austrian

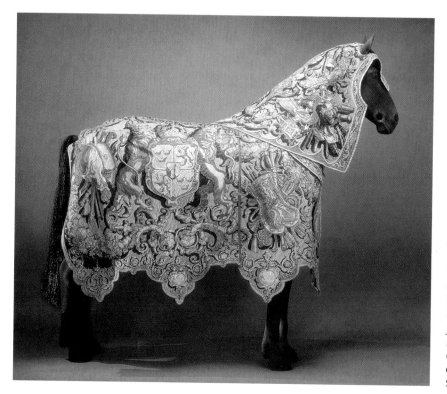

A Ruler Rides in Majesty
This caparison (ornamental covering) of wool and silk was decorated with the arms of Gustavus Adolphus of Sweden. It was manufactured in 1621 for the king's official entry into Stockholm.
© LSH Fotoavdelnigen. Foto Goran Schmidt/Livrustkammaren, Stockholm.

The Horrors of the Thirty Years' War
The French artist Jacques Collot produced this engraving of the Thirty Years' War as part of a series called The Miseries and Misfortunes of War *(1633). The actions depicted resemble those in Hans Grimmelshausen's novel* The Adventures of a Simpleton, *based on Grimmelshausen's personal experience of the Thirty Years' War.*
The Granger Collection.

emperor and his Protestant subjects. Religion took a backseat as the two Catholic powers France and Spain pummeled each other. The Swedes kept up their pressure in Germany, the Dutch attacked the Spanish fleet, and a series of internal revolts shook the cash-strapped Spanish crown. In 1640, peasants in the rich northeastern province of Catalonia rebelled, overrunning Barcelona and killing the viceroy; the Catalans resented government confiscation of their crops and demands that they house and feed soldiers on their way to the French frontier. The Portuguese revolted in 1640 and proclaimed independence like the Dutch. In 1643, the Spanish suffered their first major defeat at French hands. Although the Spanish were forced to concede independence to Portugal (part of Spain only since 1580), they eventually suppressed the Catalan revolt.

France too faced exhaustion after years of rising taxes and recurrent revolts. In 1642 Richelieu died. Louis XIII followed him a few months later and was succeeded by his five-year-old son Louis XIV. With an Austrian queen mother serving as regent and an Italian cardinal, Mazarin, providing advice, French politics once again moved into a period of instability, rumor, and crisis. All sides were ready for peace.

The Effects of Constant Fighting

When peace negotiations began in the 1640s, they did not come a moment too soon for the ordinary people of Europe. Warfare left much of central Europe in shambles and taxed to the limit the resources of people in all the countries involved. The desperate efforts of rulers to build up bigger and bigger armies left their mark on the new soldiers and eventually on state structures as well.

The Experience of Ordinary People. People caught in the paths of rival armies suffered most. Some towns had faced up to ten or eleven prolonged sieges during the fighting. In 1648, as negotiations dragged on, a Swedish army sacked the rich cultural capital Prague, plundered its churches and castles, and effectively eliminated it as a center of culture and learning. Even worse suffering took place in the countryside. Peasants fled their villages, which were often burned down. At times, desperate peasants revolted and attacked nearby castles and monasteries. War and intermittent outbreaks of plague cost some German towns one-third or more of their population. One-third of the inhabitants of Bohemia also perished.

One of the earliest German novels, *The Adventures of a Simpleton* (1669) by Hans Grimmelshausen, recounts the horror of the Thirty Years' War. In one scene, the boy Simplicius looks up from his bagpipe to find himself surrounded by unidentified enemy cavalrymen, who drag him back to his father's farm; ransack the house; rape the maid, his mother, and his sister; force water mixed with dung (called "the Swedish drink" after the Swedish armies) down the hired farmhand's throat; and hold the feet of Simplicius's father to the fire until he tells where he hid his gold and jewels. The invaders then torture neighbors with thumbscrews, throw one alive into the oven, and strangle another with a crude noose. Simplicius hides in the woods but can still hear the cries of the suffering peasants and see his family's house burn down.

The Growth of Armies.   Soldiers did not fare all that much better than peasants as rulers sought to expand their armies by any means possible. Governments increasingly short of funds often failed to pay the troops, and frequent mutinies, looting, and pillaging resulted. Armies attracted all sorts of displaced people desperately in need of provisions. In the last year of the Thirty Years' War, the Imperial-Bavarian Army had 40,000 men entitled to draw rations—and more than 100,000 wives, prostitutes, servants, children, maids, and other camp followers forced to scrounge for their own food. The bureaucracies of early-seventeenth-century Europe simply could not cope with such demands: armies and their hangers-on had to live off the countryside. The result was scenes like those witnessed by Simplicius.

The Thirty Years' War accelerated developments in military armament and tactics. To get more firepower, commanders followed the lead of Gustavus Adolphus in spreading out the soldiers firing guns; rather than bunching those firing muskets together, they set up long, thin lines of three to five ranks firing in turn. Tightly packed formations of pike-carrying foot soldiers pushed the battle forward. Everywhere, the size of armies increased dramatically. Most armies in the 1550s had fewer than 50,000 men, but Gustavus Adolphus had 100,000 men under arms in 1631; by the end of the seventeenth century, Louis XIV of France could count on 400,000 soldiers. The cost of larger armies and weapons such as cannon and warships strained the resources of every state. Maintaining discipline in

these huge armies required harsher methods. Drill, combat training, and a clear chain of command became essential. Newly introduced "uniforms" created—as their name suggests—standardization, but uniforms soon lost their distinctiveness in the conditions of early modern warfare. An Englishman who fought for the Dutch army in 1633 described how he slept on the wet ground, got his boots full of water, and "at peep of day looked like a drowned ratt."

Although foreign mercenaries still predominated in many armies, rulers began to recruit more of their own subjects. Volunteers proved easiest to find in hard times, when the threat of starvation induced men to accept the bonus offered for signing up. A Venetian general explained the motives for enlisting: "To escape from being craftsmen [or] working in a shop; to avoid a criminal sentence; to see new things; to pursue honour (though these are very few) . . . all in the hope of having enough to live on and a bit over for shoes, or some other trifle."

The Peace of Westphalia, 1648

The comprehensive settlement provided by the Peace of Westphalia—named after the German province where negotiations took place—would serve as a model for resolving conflict among warring European states. For the first time, a diplomatic congress addressed international disputes, and the signatories to the treaties guaranteed the resulting settlement. A method still in use, the congress was the first to bring *all* parties together, rather than two or three at a time.

The Winners and Losers.   France and Sweden gained most from the Peace of Westphalia. Although France and Spain continued fighting until 1659, France acquired parts of Alsace and replaced Spain as the prevailing power on the continent. Baltic conflicts would not be resolved until 1661, but Sweden took several northern territories from the Holy Roman Empire (Map 16.3).

The Habsburgs lost the most. The Spanish Habsburgs recognized Dutch independence after eighty years of war. The Swiss Confederation and the German princes demanded autonomy from the Austrian Habsburg rulers of the Holy Roman Empire. Each German prince gained the right to establish Lutheranism, Catholicism, or Calvinism in his state,

MAP 16.3 The Thirty Years' War and the Peace of Westphalia, 1648
The Thirty Years' War involved many of the major continental European powers. The arrows marking invasion routes show that most of the fighting took place in central Europe in the lands of the Holy Roman Empire. The German states and Bohemia sustained the greatest damage during the fighting. None of the combatants emerged unscathed because even ultimate winners such as Sweden and France depleted their resources of men and money.

a right denied to Calvinist rulers by the Peace of Augsburg in 1555. The independence ceded to German princes sustained political divisions that would remain until the nineteenth century and prepared the way for the emergence of a new power, the Hohenzollern Elector of Brandenburg, who increased his territories and developed a small but effective standing army. After losing considerable territory in the west, the Austrian Habsburgs turned eastward to concentrate on restoring Catholicism to Bohemia and wresting Hungary from the Turks.

The Peace of Westphalia permanently settled the distributions of the main religions in the Holy Roman Empire: Lutheranism would dominate in the north, Calvinism in the area of the Rhine River,

and Catholicism in the south. Most of the territorial changes in Europe remained intact until the nineteenth century. In the future, international warfare would be undertaken for reasons of national security, commercial ambition, or dynastic pride rather than to enforce religious uniformity. As the *politiques* of the late sixteenth century had hoped, state interests now outweighed motivations of faith in political affairs.

The Growth of State Authority. Warfare increased the reach of states: to field larger armies, governments needed more revenue and more officials to supervise the supply of troops, the collection of taxes, and the repression of resistance to higher taxes. In France the rate of land tax paid by peasants doubled in the eight years after France joined the war. In addition to raising taxes, governments frequently resorted to currency depreciation, which often resulted in inflation and soaring prices; the sale of new offices; forced loans to raise money in emergencies; and manipulation of the embryonic stock and bond markets. When all else failed, they declared bankruptcy; the Spanish government, for example, did so three times in the first half of the seventeenth century.

Poor peasants and city workers could hardly bear new demands for money, and the governments' creditors and high-ranking nobles resented monarchical intrusions. Opposition to royal taxation often set off uprisings. From Portugal to Muscovy, ordinary people resisted new impositions by forming makeshift armies and battling royal forces. With their colorful banners, unlikely leaders, strange names (the Nu-Pieds, or "Barefooted," in France, for instance), and crude weapons, the rebels usually proved no match for state armies, but they did keep officials worried and troops occupied.

As the demand for soldiers and for the money to supply them rose, the number of state employees multiplied, paperwork proliferated, and appointment to office began to depend on university education in the law. Monarchs relied on advisers who now took on the role of modern prime ministers. Axel Oxenstierna, for example, played a central part in Swedish governments between 1611 and 1654; continuity in Swedish affairs, especially after the death of Gustavus Adolphus, largely depended on him. As Louis XIII's chief minister, Richelieu arranged support for the Lutheran Gustavus even though Richelieu was a cardinal of the Catholic church. His priority was *raison d'état* ("reason of state"), that is, the state's interest above all else. He silenced Protestants within France because they had become too independent and crushed noble and popular resistance to Louis's policies. He set up *intendants*—delegates from the king's council dispatched to the provinces—to oversee police, army, and financial affairs.

To justify the growth of state authority and the expansion of government bureaucracies, rulers carefully cultivated their royal images. James I of England explicitly argued that he ruled by divine right and was accountable only to God: "The state of monarchy is the supremest thing on earth; for kings are not only God's lieutenant on earth, but even by God himself they are called gods." He

The Arts and State Power
Diego Velázquez painted King Philip IV of Spain and many members of his court. This painting of 1634–1635 shows Philip on horseback. In the seventeenth century, many rulers hired court painters to embellish the image of royal majesty. Philip IV commissioned this painting for his new palace called Buen Retiro.

advised his son to maintain a manly appearance (his own well-known homosexual liaisons did not make him seem less manly to his subjects): "Eschew to be effeminate in your clothes, in perfuming, preening, or such like, and fail never in time of wars to be galliardest and bravest, both in clothes and countenance." Clothes counted for so much that most rulers regulated who could wear which kinds of cloth and decoration, reserving the richest and rarest such as ermine and gold for themselves.

Just as soldiers had to learn new drills for combat, courtiers had to learn to follow precise rituals at court. In Spain, court regulations set the wages, duties, and ceremonial functions of every official. Hundreds, even thousands, of people made up such a court. The court of Philip IV (r. 1621–1665), for example, numbered seventeen hundred. In the 1630s he built a new palace near Madrid. There the courtiers lived amid extensive parks and formal gardens, artificial ponds and grottoes, an iron aviary (which led some critics to call the whole thing a "chicken coop"), a wild animal cage, a courtyard for bullfights, and rooms filled with sculptures and paintings. State funerals, public festivities, and court display, like the acquisition of art and the building of sumptuous palaces, served to underline the power and glory of the ruler.

❖ Economic Crisis and Realignment

The devastation caused by the Thirty Years' War deepened an economic crisis that was already under way. After a century of rising prices, caused partly by massive transfers of gold and silver from the New World and partly by population growth, in the early 1600s prices began to level off and even to drop, and in most places population growth slowed. With fewer goods being produced, international trade fell into recession. Agricultural yields also declined. Just when states attempted to field ever-expanding standing armies, peasants and townspeople alike were less able to pay the escalating taxes needed to finance the wars. Famine and disease trailed grimly behind economic crisis and war, in some areas causing large-scale uprisings and revolts. Behind the scenes, the economic balance of power gradually shifted as northwestern Europe began to

dominate international trade and broke the stranglehold of Spain and Portugal in the New World.

From Growth to Recession

Population grew and prices rose in the second half of the sixteenth century. Even though religious and political turbulence led to population decline in some cities, such as war-torn Antwerp, overall rates of growth remained impressive: in the sixteenth century, parts of Spain doubled in population and England's population grew by 70 percent. The supply of precious metals swelled too. Improvements in mining techniques in central Europe raised the output of silver and copper mines, and in the 1540s new silver mines had been discovered in Mexico and Peru. Spanish gold imports peaked in the 1550s, silver in the 1590s. (See "Taking Measure," below). This flood of precious metals combined with population

TAKING MEASURE The Rise and Fall of Silver Imports to Spain, 1550–1660
Gold and silver from the New World enabled the king of Spain to pursue aggressive policies in Europe and around the world. At what point did silver imports reach their highest level? Was the fall in silver imports precipitous or gradual? What can we conclude about the resources available to the Spanish king?
From Earl J. Hamilton, *American Revolution and the Price Revolution in Spain, 1501–1650* (Cambridge, Harvard University Press, 1934).

growth to fuel an astounding inflation in food prices in western Europe—400 percent in the sixteenth century—and a more moderate rise in the cost of manufactured goods. Wages rose much more slowly, at about half the rate of the increase in food prices. Governments always overspent revenues and by the end of the century most of Europe's rulers faced deep deficits.

Recession did not strike everywhere at the same time, but the warning signs were unmistakable. From the Baltic to the East Indies, foreign trade slumped as war and an uncertain money supply made business riskier. After 1625, silver imports to Spain declined, in part because so many of the native Americans who worked in Spanish colonial mines died from disease and in part because the ready supply of precious metals was progressively exhausted. Textile production fell in many countries and in some places nearly collapsed, largely because of decreased demand and a shrinking labor force. Even the relatively limited trade in African slaves stagnated, though its growth would resume after 1650 and skyrocket after 1700. African slaves were first transported to the new colony of Virginia in 1619, foreshadowing a major transformation of economic life in the New World colonies.

Demographic slowdown also signaled economic trouble. Overall, Europe's population may actually have declined, from 85 million in 1550 to 80 million in 1650. In the Mediterranean, growth apparently stopped in the 1570s. The most sudden reversal occurred in central Europe as a result of the Thirty Years' War: one-fourth of the inhabitants of the Holy Roman Empire perished in the 1630s and 1640s. The population continued to increase only in England and Wales, the Dutch Republic and the Spanish Netherlands, and Scandinavia.

Crop production eventually reflected these differences. Where the population stagnated or declined, agricultural prices dropped because of less demand, and farmers who produced for the market suffered. Many reacted by converting grain-growing land to pasture or vineyards (the prices of other foods fell less than the price of grain). Interest in improvement of the land diminished. In some places peasants abandoned their villages and left land to waste, as had happened during the plague epidemic of the late fourteenth century. The only country that emerged unscathed from this downturn was the Dutch Republic, principally because it had

long excelled in agricultural innovation. Inhabiting Europe's most densely populated area, the Dutch developed systems of field drainage, crop rotation, and animal husbandry that provided high yields of grain for both people and animals. Their foreign trade, textile industry, crop production, and population all grew. After the Dutch, the English fared best; unlike the Spanish, the English never depended on New World gold and silver, and unlike most continental European countries, England escaped the direct impact of the Thirty Years' War.

Historians have long disagreed about the causes of the early-seventeenth-century recession. Some cite the inability of agriculture to support a growing population by the end of the sixteenth century; others blame the Thirty Years' War, the states' demands for more taxes, the irregularities in money supply resulting from rudimentary banking practices, or the waste caused by middle-class expenditures in the desire to emulate the nobility. To this list of causes, recent researchers have added climatic changes. (See "New Sources, New Perspectives," page 584.) Cold winters and wet summers meant bad harvests, and these natural disasters ushered in a host of social catastrophes. When the harvest was bad, prices shot back up and many could not afford to feed themselves.

Consequences for Daily Life

The recession of the early 1600s had both short-term and long-term effects. In the short term it aggravated the threat of food shortages and increased the outbreaks of famine and disease. In the long term it deepened the division between prosperous and poor peasants and fostered the development of a new pattern of late marriages and smaller families.

Famine and Disease. Outside of England and the Dutch Republic, grain had replaced meat as the essential staple of most Europeans' diets because meat had become too expensive. Most people consumed less butter, eggs, poultry, and wine and more grain products, ranging from bread to beer. The average adult European now ate more than four hundred pounds of grain per year. Peasants lived on bread, soup with a little fat or oil, peas or lentils, garden vegetables in season, and only occasionally a piece of meat or fish. In most places the poor existed on the verge of starvation; one contemporary observed that "the fourth part of the inhabitants of the parishes of England are miserable people and (harvest time excepted) without any subsistence."

The threat of food shortages haunted Europe whenever harsh weather destroyed crops. Local markets were vulnerable to problems of food distribution: customs barriers inhibited local trade, overland transport moved at a snail's pace, bandits disrupted traffic, and the state or private contractors commandeered available food for the perpetually warring armies. Usually the adverse years differed from place to place, but from 1594 to 1597 most of Europe suffered from shortages; the resulting famine triggered revolts from Ireland to Muscovy. To head off social disorder, the English government drew up a new Poor Law in 1597 that required each community to support its poor. Many other governments also increased relief efforts.

Most people, however, did not respond to their dismal circumstances by rebelling or mounting insurrections. They simply left their huts and hovels and took to the road in search of food and charity. Overwhelmed officials recorded pitiful tales of suffering. Women and children died while waiting in line for food at convents or churches. Husbands left their wives and families to search for better conditions in other parishes or even other countries. Those left behind might be reduced to eating chestnuts, roots, bark, and grass. In eastern France in 1637, a witness reported, "The roads were paved with people. . . . Finally it came to cannibalism." Eventually compassion gave way to fear as these hungry vagabonds, who sometimes banded together to beg for bread, became more aggressive, occasionally threatening to burn a barn if they were not given food.

Successive bad harvests led to malnutrition, which weakened people and made them more susceptible to such epidemic diseases as the plague, typhoid fever, typhus, dysentery, smallpox, and influenza. Disease did not spare the rich, although many epidemics hit the poor hardest. The plague was feared most: in one year it could cause the death of up to half of a town's or village's population, and it struck with no discernible pattern. Nearly 5 percent of France's entire population died just in the plague of 1628–1632.

The Changing Status of the Peasantry.

Other effects of economic crisis were less visible than famine and disease, but no less momentous. The most im-

The Life of the Poor
This mid-seventeenth-century painting by the Dutch artist Adriaen Pietersz van de Venne depicts the poor peasant weighed down by his wife and child. An empty food bowl signifies their hunger. In retrospect, this painting seems unfair to the wife of the family; she is shown in clothes that are not nearly as tattered as her husband's and is portrayed entirely as a burden, rather than as a help in getting by in hard times. In reality, many poor men abandoned their homes in search of work, leaving their wives behind to cope with hungry children and what remained of the family farm.
Allen Memorial Art Museum, Oberlin College, Oberlin, Ohio, Mrs. F. F. Prentiss Fund, 1960.

portant was the peasantry's changing status. Peasants faced many obligations, including rent and various fees for inheriting or selling land and tolls for using mills, wine presses, or ovens. States collected direct taxes on land and sales taxes on such consumer goods as salt, an essential preservative.

NEW SOURCES, NEW PERSPECTIVES

Tree Rings and the Little Ice Age

The economic crisis of the seventeenth century had many causes, and historians disagree about what they were and which were more important. One cause that has inspired intense debate is global cooling. Glaciers advanced, average temperatures fell, and winters were often exceptionally severe. Canals and rivers essential to markets froze over. Great storms disrupted ocean traffic (one storm changed the escape route of the Spanish Armada). Entire villages were demolished by glacier advance. Even in the valleys far from the mountains, cooler weather meant lower crop yields, which quickly translated into hunger and greater susceptibility to disease, leading in turn to population decline. Some historians of climate refer to the entire period 1600–1850 as the little ice age because glaciers advanced during this time and retreated only after 1850; others argue for the period 1550–1700 as the coldest, but either time frame includes the seventeenth century. Since systematic records of European temperatures were kept only from the 1700s onward, how do historians know that the weather was cooler? Given the current debates about global warming, how can we sift through the evidence to come up with a reliable interpretation?

Information about climate comes from various sources. The advance of glaciers can be seen in letters complaining to the authorities. In 1601, for example, panic-stricken villagers in Savoy (in the French Alps) wrote, "We are terrified of the glaciers . . . which are moving forward all the time and have just buried two of our villages." Yearly temperature fluctuations can be determined from the dates of wine harvests; growers harvested their grapes earliest when the weather was warmest and latest when it was coolest. Scientists study ice cores taken from Greenland to determine temperature variations; such studies seem to indicate that the coolest times were the periods 1160–1300; the 1600s; and 1820–1850. The period 1730–1800 appears to have been warmer. Recently, scientists have developed techniques for sampling corals in the tropics and sediments on oceanic shelves.

But most striking are data gathered from tree rings (the science is called *dendrochronology* or *dendroclimatology*). Timber samples have been taken from very old oak trees and also from ancient beams in buildings and archaeological digs and from logs left long undisturbed in northern bogs and riverbeds. In cold summers, trees lay down thinner growth rings; in warm ones, thicker rings.

Protestant and Catholic churches alike exacted a tithe (a tax equivalent to one-tenth of the parishioner's annual income); often the clergy took their tithe in the form of crops and collected it directly during the harvest. Any reversal of fortune could force peasants into the homeless world of vagrants and beggars, who numbered as much as 1 to 2 percent of the total population.

In the seventeenth century the mass of peasants in western Europe became more sharply divided into prosperous and poor. In England, the Dutch Republic, northern France, and northwestern Germany, the peasantry was disappearing: improvements gave some peasants the means to become farmers who rented substantial holdings, produced for the market, and in good times enjoyed relative comfort and higher status. Those who could not afford to plant new crops such as maize (American corn) or buckwheat or to use techniques that ensured higher yields became simple laborers with little or no land of their own. The minimum plot of land needed to feed a family varied depending on the richness of the soil, available improvements in agriculture, and distance from markets. For example,

The Frozen Thames

This painting by Abraham Hondius of the frozen Thames River in London dates to 1677. In the 1670s and 1680s the Thames froze several times. Hondius himself depicted another such view in 1684. Diarists recorded that shopkeepers even set up their stalls on the ice. In other words, the expected routines of daily life changed during the cooling down of the seventeenth century. Contemporaries were shocked enough by the changes to record them for posterity. Museum of London.

Information about tree rings confirms the conclusions drawn from wine harvest and ice core samples: the seventeenth century was relatively cold. Recent tree ring studies have shown that some of the coldest summers were caused by volcanic eruptions; according to a study of more than one hundred sites in North America and Europe, the five coldest summers in the past four hundred years were in 1601, 1641, 1669, 1699, and 1912 (four out of five in the seventeenth century), and all but the summer of 1699 came in years following recorded eruptions.

QUESTIONS FOR DEBATE

1. What were the historical consequences of global cooling in the seventeenth century?

2. Why would trees be especially valuable sources of information about climate?

FURTHER READING

H. H. Lamb, *Climate, History and the Modern World*, 2nd ed., 1995.

Patrick R. Galloway, "Long-Term Fluctuations in Climate and Population in the Preindustrial Era," *Population and Development Review* 12 (1986): 1–24.

only two acres could support a family in Flanders, as opposed to ten acres in Muscovy. One-half to four-fifths of the peasants did not have enough acreage to support a family. They descended deeper into debt during difficult times and often lost their land to wealthier farmers or to city officials intent on developing rural estates.

As the recession deepened, women lost some of their economic opportunities. Widows who had been able to take over their late husbands' trade now found themselves excluded by the urban guilds or limited to short tenures. Many women went into

domestic service until they married, some for their entire lives. When town governments began to fear the effects of increased mobility from country to town and town to town, they carefully regulated women's work as servants, requiring them to stay in their positions unless they could prove mistreatment by a master.

Effects on Marriage and Childbearing. Demographic historians have shown that European families reacted almost immediately to economic crisis. During bad harvests they postponed marriages and

The Figure Explained:

Being a Dissection of the WOMB, with the usual manner how the CHILD lies therein near the time of its Birth.

B B. The inner parts of the *Chorion* extended and branched out.

C. The *Amnios* extended.

D D. The Membrane of the Womb extended and branched.

E. The Fleshy substance call'd the *Cake* or *Placenta*, which nourishes the Infant, it is full of Vessels.

F. The Vessels appointed for the Navel string.

G. The Navel string carrying nourishment from the *Placenta* to the Navel.

H H H. The manner how the Infant lieth in the Womb near the time of its Birth.

I. The Navel string how it enters into the Navel.

The *Midwives Book* (1671)
The English woman Jane Sharp wrote the first book on midwifery by a woman. She endeavored to provide as much scientific information about the female body as was available at the time.
British Library.

had fewer children. When hard times passed, more people married and had more children. But even in the best of times, one-fifth to one-quarter of all children died in their first year, and half died before age twenty. In 1636, an Englishman described his grief when his twenty-one-month-old son died: "We both found the sorrow for the loss of this child, on whom we had bestowed so much care and affection . . . far to surpass our grief for the decease of his three elder brothers, who dying almost as soon as they were born, were not so endeared to us as this [one] was."

Childbirth still carried great risks for women, about 10 percent of whom died in the process. Even in the richest and most enlightened homes, childbirth often occasioned an atmosphere of panic. To allay their fears, women sometimes depended on magic stones and special pilgrimages and prayers. Midwives delivered most babies; physicians were scarce, and even if they did attend a birth they were generally less helpful. The Englishwoman Alice Thornton described in her diary how a doctor bled her to prevent a miscarriage after a fall; her son died anyway in a breech birth that almost killed her too.

It might be assumed that families would have more children to compensate for high death rates, but beginning in the early seventeenth century and continuing until the end of the eighteenth, families in all ranks of society started to limit the number of children. Because methods of contraception were not widely known, they did this for the most part by marrying later; the average age at marriage dur-

ing the seventeenth century rose from the early twenties to the late twenties. The average family had about four children. Poorer families seem to have had fewer children, wealthier ones more. Peasant couples, especially in eastern and southeastern Europe, had more children than urban couples because cultivation still required intensive manual labor.

The consequences of late marriage were profound. Young men and women were expected to put off marriage (*and* sexual intercourse) until their mid- to late twenties—if they were among the lucky 50 percent who lived that long and not among the 10 percent who never married. Because both the Reformation and Counter-Reformation had stressed sexual fidelity and abstinence before marriage, the number of births out of wedlock was relatively small (2–5 percent of births); premarital intercourse was generally tolerated only after a couple had announced their engagement.

The Economic Balance of Power

Just as the recession produced winners and losers among ordinary people, so too it created winners and losers among the competing states of Europe. The economies of southern Europe declined, whereas those of the northwest emerged stronger. Competition in the New World reflected and reinforced this shift as the English, Dutch, and French rushed to establish trading outposts and permanent settlements to compete with the Spanish and Portuguese.

Regional Differences. The crisis of the seventeenth century ended the dominance of Mediterranean economies, which had endured since the time of the Greeks and Romans, and ushered in the new powers of northwestern Europe with their growing Atlantic economies. With expanding populations and geographical positions that promoted Atlantic trade, England and the Dutch Republic vied with France to become the leading mercantile powers. Northern Italian industries were eclipsed; Spanish commerce with the New World dropped. Amsterdam replaced Seville, Venice, Genoa, and Antwerp as the center of European trade and commerce. The plague also had differing effects. Whereas central Europe and the Mediterranean countries took generations to recover from its ravages, northwestern Europe quickly replaced its lost population, no doubt because this area's people had suffered less from the effects of the Thirty Years' War and from the malnutrition related to the economic crisis.

East-west differences would soon overshadow those between northern and southern regions. Because labor shortages coincided with economic recovery, peasants in western Europe gained more independence and all but the remnants of serfdom disappeared. By contrast, from the Elbe River east to Muscovy, nobles reinforced their dominance over peasants, thanks to cooperation from rulers and lack of resistance from villagers, whose community traditions had always acknowledged nobles' rights of lordship.

The price rise of the sixteenth century prompted Polish and eastern German nobles to increase their holdings and step up their production of grain for western markets. To raise production, they demanded more rent and dues from their peasants, whom the government decreed must stay in their villages. Although noble landlords lost income in the economic downturn of the first half of the seventeenth century, their peasants gained nothing. Those who were already dependent became serfs—completely tied to the land. A local official might complain of "this barbaric and as it were Egyptian servitude," but he had no power to fight the nobles. In Muscovy the complete enserfment of the peasantry would eventually be recognized in the Code of Laws in 1649. Although enserfment produced short-term profits for landlords, in the long run it retarded economic development in eastern Europe and kept most of the population in a stranglehold of illiteracy and hardship.

Competition in the New World. Many European states, including Sweden and Denmark, rushed to join the colonial competition because they considered it a branch of mercantilist policy. According to the doctrine of mercantilism, governments should sponsor policies to increase national wealth. To this end, they chartered private joint-stock companies to enrich investors by importing fish, furs, tobacco, and precious metals, if they could be found, and to develop new markets for European

"Savages" of the New World
Europeans found the "savages" of the New World fascinating and terrifying. Both sides are captured in Paolo Farinati's 1595 painting America. *The half-dressed savage appears much like a noble Italian; he holds a crucifix in his right hand, signifying his conversion to Christianity. But to his right his comrades are roasting human flesh. Europeans were convinced that many native peoples were cannibals.*
Villa della Torre, Mezzane de Sotto, Verona.

products. Because Spain and Portugal had divided among themselves the rich spoils of South America, other prospective colonizers had to carve niches in seemingly less hospitable places, especially North America and the Caribbean (Map 16.4). Eventually the English, French, and Dutch would dominate commerce with these colonies.

English settlement policies had an unfortunate precedent in Ireland, where in the 1580s English armies drove the Irish clans from their strongholds and claimed the land for English and Scottish Protes-

tant colonists. When the Irish resisted with guerrilla warfare, English generals waged total war, destroying harvests and burning villages; one general lined the path to his headquarters with Irish heads. A few decades later, the English would use the same tactics against another group of "savages," this time in the New World.

Some colonists in North America justified their mission by promising to convert the native population to Christianity. As the English colonizer John Smith told his followers in Virginia, "The growing

MAP 16.4 European Colonization of the Americas, c. 1640
Europeans established themselves first in coastal areas. The English, French, and Dutch set up most of their colonies in the Caribbean and North America because the Spanish and Portuguese had already colonized the easily accessible regions in South America. Vast inland areas still remained unexplored and uncolonized in 1640.

provinces addeth to the King's Crown; but the reducing heathen people to civility and true religion bringeth honour to the King of Heaven." Catholic France and Spain were more successful, however, than Protestant England in their efforts to convert American natives. Protestantism did not mesh well with native American cultures because it demanded an individual conversion experience based on a Christian notion of sin. Catholicism, in contrast, stressed shared rituals, which were more accessible to the native populations.

In establishing permanent colonies, the Europeans created whole new communities across the Atlantic. Careful plans often fell afoul of the hazards of transatlantic shipping, however. Originally, the warm climate of Virginia made it an attractive destination for the Pilgrims, a small English sect that, unlike the Puritans, attempted to separate from the Church of England. But the *Mayflower*, which had sailed for Virginia with Pilgrim emigrants, landed far to the north in Massachusetts, where in 1620 the settlers founded New Plymouth Colony. As the religious situation for English Puritans worsened, wealthier people became willing to emigrate, and in 1629 a prominent group of Puritans incorporated themselves as the Massachusetts Bay Company. They founded a virtually self-governing colony headquartered in Boston.

Colonization gradually spread. Migrating settlers, including dissident Puritans, soon founded new settlements in Connecticut and Rhode Island. Catholic refugees from England established a much smaller colony in Maryland. By the 1640s, the British North American colonies had more than fifty thousand people—not including the Indians, whose numbers had been decimated in epidemics and wars—and the foundations of representative government in locally chosen colonial assemblies. By contrast, French Canada had only about three thousand European inhabitants by 1640. Because the French government refused to let Protestants emigrate from France and establish a foothold in the New World, it denied itself a ready population for the settling of permanent colonies abroad. Both England and France turned their attention to the Caribbean in the 1620s and 1630s when they occupied the islands of the West Indies after driving off the native Caribs. These islands would prove ideal for a plantation economy of tobacco and sugar cane.

❖ A Clash of Worldviews

The countries that moved ahead economically in this period—England, the Dutch Republic, and to some extent France—turned out to be the most receptive to new secular worldviews. Although *secularization* did not entail a loss of religious faith, it did prompt a search for nonreligious explanations for political authority and natural phenomena. During the late sixteenth and early seventeenth centuries, art, political theory, and science all began to break some of their bonds with religion. The visual arts, for example, more frequently depicted secular subjects. Scientists and scholars sought laws in nature to explain politics as well as movements in the heavens and on earth. A "scientific revolution" was in the making. Yet traditional attitudes did not disappear. Belief in magic and witchcraft pervaded every level of society. People of all classes accepted supernatural explanations for natural phenomena, a view only gradually and partially undermined by new ideas.

The Arts in an Age of Religious Conflict

Two new forms of artistic expression—professional theater and opera—developed to express secular values in an age of conflict over religious beliefs. The greatest playwright of the English language, William Shakespeare, never referred to religious disputes in his plays, and he always set his most personal reflections on political turmoil and uncertainty in faraway times or places. Religion played an important role in the new Mannerist and baroque styles of painting, however, even though many rulers commissioned paintings on secular subjects for their own uses.

Theater in the Age of Shakespeare. Permanent professional theater companies appeared for the first time in Europe in the last quarter of the sixteenth century. In previous centuries, traveling companies made their living by playing at major religious festivals and by repeating their performances in small towns and villages along the way. In London, Seville, and Madrid, the first professional acting companies performed before paying audiences in the 1570s. A huge outpouring of playwriting followed. The Spanish playwright Lope de Vega (1562–1635) alone wrote more than fifteen hundred plays. Between 1580 and 1640, three hundred English playwrights produced works for a hundred different acting companies. Theaters did a banner business despite Puritan opposition in England and Catholic objections in Spain. Shopkeepers, apprentices, lawyers, and court nobles crowded into open-air theaters to see everything from bawdy farces to profound tragedies.

The most enduring and influential playwright of the time was the Englishman William Shakespeare (1564–1616), son of a glovemaker, who wrote three dozen plays and acted in one of the chief troupes. Although Shakespeare's plays were not set in contemporary England, they reflected the concerns of his age: the nature of power and the crisis of authority. His greatest tragedies—*Hamlet* (1601), *King Lear* (1605), and *Macbeth* (1606)—show the uncertainty and even chaos that result when power is misappropriated or misused. In each play, family relationships are linked to questions about the legitimacy of government, just as they were for Elizabeth I herself. Hamlet's mother marries the man who murdered his royal father and usurped the crown; two of Lear's daughters betray him when he tries to divide his kingdom; Macbeth's wife persuades him to murder the king and seize the throne. Some of Shakespeare's female characters, like Lady Macbeth, are as driven, ambitious, powerful, and tortured as the male protagonists; others, like Queen Gertrude in *Hamlet*, reflect the ambiguity of women's role in public life—they were not expected to act with authority, and their lives were subject to men's control.

Shakespeare's stories of revenge, exile, political instability, broken families, betrayal, witchcraft, madness, suicide, and murder clearly mirror the anxieties of the period. One character in the final act describes the tragic story of Prince Hamlet as one "Of carnal, bloody, and unnatural acts; Of accidental judgments, casual slaughters; Of deaths put on by cunning and forced cause." Like many real-life people, Shakespeare's tragic characters found little peace in the turmoil of their times.

Mannerism and the Baroque in Art. New styles of painting reflected similar concerns less directly, but they too showed the desire for changed standards. In the late sixteenth century the artistic style

Mannerist Painting
With its distortion of perspective, crowding of figures, and mysterious allusions, El Greco's painting The Dream of Philip II *(1577) is a typical mannerist painting. Philip II can be seen in his usual black clothing with a lace ruffle as his only decoration.*
© National Gallery, London.

known as Mannerism emerged in the Italian states and soon spread across Europe. Mannerism was an almost theatrical style that allowed painters to distort perspective to convey a message or emphasize a theme. The most famous Mannerist painter, called El Greco because he was of Greek origin, trained in Venice and Rome before he moved to Spain in the

Baroque Painting
The Flemish baroque painter Peter Paul Rubens used monumental canvases to glorify the French queen Marie de Medici, wife of Henry IV and mother of Louis XIII. Between 1622 and 1625, Rubens painted twenty-four panels like this one to decorate Marie's residence in Paris. Their gigantic size (some were more than twenty feet wide), imposing figures captured in rich colors, and epic settings characterized the use of the baroque to exalt secular rulers. In this scene, Henry is shown handing over government to his wife on behalf of his young son (Henry was assassinated in 1610). Giraudon/Art Resource, NY.

1570s. His paintings encapsulated the Mannerist style: he crowded figures or objects into every available space, used larger-than-life or elongated figures, and created new and often bizarre visual effects. This style departed abruptly from precise Renaissance perspective. The religious intensity of El Greco's pictures shows that faith still motivated many artists, as it did much political conflict.

The most important new style in seventeenth-century high art was the baroque, which, like Mannerism, originated in the Italian states. As is the case with many historical categories, *baroque* was not used as a label by people living at the time; in the eighteenth century, art critics coined the word to

mean shockingly bizarre, confused, and extravagant, and until the late nineteenth century, art historians and collectors largely disdained the baroque. Stylistically, the baroque rejected Renaissance classicism: in place of the classical emphasis on line, harmonious design, unity, and clarity, the baroque featured curves, exaggerated lighting, intense emotions, release from restraint, and even a kind of artistic sensationalism.

In church architecture and painting the baroque melodramatically reaffirmed the emotional depths of the Catholic faith and glorified both church and monarchy. The Catholic church encouraged the expression of religious feeling through art because its emotional impact helped strengthen the ties between the faithful and the Counter-Reform church (the label given the Catholic church in the aftermath of the Protestant Reformation, when it offered its own internal reforms). As an urban and spectacular style, the baroque was well suited to public festivities and display. Along with religious festivals, civic processions, and state funerals that served the interests of the church and state, baroque portraits, such as the many portraits of Philip IV by Diego Velázquez, celebrated authority.

Closely tied to the Counter-Reformation, the baroque style spread from Rome to other Italian states and then into central Europe. The Catholic Habsburg territories, including Spain and the Spanish Netherlands, embraced the style. The Spanish built baroque churches in their American colonies as part of their massive conversion campaign. Within Europe, Protestant countries largely resisted the baroque, as we can see by comparing Flemish painters from the Spanish Netherlands with Dutch artists. The first great baroque painter was an Italian-trained Fleming, Peter Paul Rubens (1577–1640). A devout Catholic, Rubens painted vivid, exuberant pictures on religious themes, packed with figures. His was an extension of the theatrical baroque style, conveying ideas through broad gestures and dramatic poses. The great Dutch Protestant painters of the next generation, such as Rembrandt van Rijn (1606–1669), sometimes used biblical subjects, but their pictures were more realistic and focused on everyday scenes. Many of them suggested the Protestant concern for an inner life and personal faith rather than the public expression of religiosity.

Church Music and Opera. As in the visual arts, differences in musical style during the late sixteenth and early seventeenth centuries reflected religious divisions. The new Protestant churches developed their own distinct music, which differentiated their worship from the Catholic Mass and also marked them as Lutheran or Calvinist. Lutheran composers developed a new form, the strophic hymn, or chorale, a religious text set to a tune that is then enriched through harmony. Calvinist congregations, in keeping with their emphasis on simplicity and austerity, avoided harmony and more often sang in unison, thereby encouraging participation.

A new secular musical form, the opera, grew up parallel to the baroque style in the visual arts. First influential in the Italian states, opera combined music, drama, dance, and scenery in a grand sensual display, often with themes chosen to please the ruler and the aristocracy. Operas could be based on typically baroque sacred subjects or on traditional stories. Like Shakespeare, opera composers often turned to familiar stories their audiences would recognize and readily follow. One of the most innovative composers of opera was Claudio Monteverdi (1567–1643), whose work contributed to the development of both opera and the orchestra. His earliest operatic production, *Orfeo* (1607), was the first to require an orchestra of about forty instruments and to include instrumental as well as vocal sections.

The Natural Laws of Politics

In reaction to the wars over religious beliefs, jurists and scholars not only began to defend the primacy of state interests over those of religious conformity but also insisted on secular explanations for politics. Machiavelli had pointed in this direction with his prescriptions for Renaissance princes in the early sixteenth century, but the intellectual movement gathered steam in the aftermath of the religious violence unleashed by the Reformation. Religious toleration could not take hold until government could be organized on some principle other than one king, one faith. The French *politiques* Michel de Montaigne and Jean Bodin started the search for those principles. During the Dutch revolt against Spain, the jurist Hugo Grotius gave new meaning to the notion of "natural law"—laws of nature that give legitimacy to government and stand above the actions of any particular ruler or religious group. His ideas would influence John Locke and the American revolutionaries of the eighteenth century.

Montaigne and Bodin. Michel de Montaigne (1533–1592) was a French magistrate who resigned his office in the midst of the wars of religion to write about the need for tolerance and open-mindedness. Although himself a Catholic, Montaigne painted on the beams of his study the words "All that is certain is that nothing is certain." To capture this need for personal reflection in a tumultuous age of religious discord, he invented the essay as a short and pithy form of expression. He revived the ancient doctrine of skepticism, which held that total certainty is never attainable—a doctrine, like toleration of religious differences, that was repugnant to Protestants and Catholics alike, both of whom were certain that their religion was the right one. He also questioned the common European habit of calling newly discovered peoples in the New World barbarous and savage: "Everyone gives the title of barbarism to everything that is not in use in his own country."

The French Catholic lawyer Jean Bodin (1530–1596) sought systematic secular answers to the problem of disorder in *The Six Books of the Republic* (1576). Comparing the different forms of government throughout history, he concluded that there were three basic types of sovereignty: monarchy, aristocracy, and democracy. Only strong monarchical power offered hope for maintaining order, he insisted. Bodin rejected any doctrine of the right to resist tyrannical authority: "I denied that it was the function of a good man or of a good citizen to offer violence to his prince for any reason, however great a tyrant he might be" (and, it might be added, whatever his ideas on religion). Bodin's ideas helped lay the foundation for absolutism, the idea that the monarch should be the sole and uncontested source of power. Nonetheless, the very discussion of types of governments in the abstract implied that they might be subject to choice rather than simply being God-given, as most rulers maintained.

Grotius and Natural Law. Hugo Grotius (1583–1645) argued that natural law stood beyond the reach of either secular or divine authority; it would be valid even if God did not exist. Natural law should govern politics, by this account, not Scripture, religious authority, or tradition. Not surprisingly, these ideas got Grotius into trouble. His work *The Laws of War and Peace* (1625) was condemned by the Catholic church. The Dutch Protestant government arrested him for his part in religious controversies; his wife helped him escape prison by hiding him in a chest of books. He fled to Paris, where he got a small pension from Louis XIII and served as his ambassador to Sweden. The Swedish king Gustavus Adolphus claimed that he kept Grotius's book under his pillow even while at battle. Grotius was one of the first to argue that international conventions should govern the treatment of prisoners of war and the making of peace treaties.

At the same time that Grotius expanded the principles of natural law, most jurists worked on codifying the huge amount of legislation and

jurisprudence devoted to legal forms of torture. Most states and the courts of the Catholic church used torture when the crime was very serious and the evidence seemed to point to a particular defendant but no definitive proof had been established. The judges ordered torture—hanging the accused by the hands with a rope thrown over a beam, pressing the legs in a leg screw, or just tying the hands very tightly—to extract a confession, which had to be given with a medical expert and notary present and had to be repeated without torture. Children, pregnant women, the elderly, aristocrats, kings, and even professors were exempt.

Grotius's conception of natural law directly challenged the use of torture. To be in accord with natural law, Grotius argued, governments had to defend natural rights, which he defined as life, body, freedom, and honor. Grotius did not encourage rebellion in the name of natural law or rights, but he did hope that someday all governments would adhere to these principles and stop killing their own and one another's subjects in the name of religion. Natural law and natural rights would play an important role in the founding of constitutional governments from the 1640s forward and in the establishment of various charters of human rights in our own time.

The Origins of the Scientific Revolution

Although the Catholic and Protestant churches encouraged the study of science and many prominent scientists were themselves clerics, the search for a secular, scientific method of determining the laws of nature eventually challenged the traditional accounts of natural phenomena. (See "Did You Know?" page 594.) Christian doctrine had incorporated the scientific teachings of ancient philosophers, especially Ptolemy and Aristotle; now these came into question. A revolution in astronomy challenged the Ptolemaic view, endorsed by the Catholic church, which held that the sun revolved around the earth. Startling breakthroughs took place in medicine, too, which laid the foundations for modern anatomy and pharmacology. By the early seventeenth century, a new scientific method had been established based on a combination of experimental observation and mathematical deduction. Conflicts between the new science and religion followed almost immediately.

The Gregorian Calendar: 1582

The Catholic church relied on the work of astronomers when it undertook a major reform of the calendar in 1582. Every culture has some kind of calendar by which it groups days to mark time, but the length of the day, the week, and the month have varied throughout much of human history. At different moments in the past, West Africans, for example, used four-day weeks, central Asians five-day weeks, and Egyptians ten-day weeks. These different systems became uniform when most of the world's countries adopted the Gregorian calendar. The spread of the use of the Gregorian calendar, which happened only very gradually after its introduction in 1582, marked the extension of Western influence in the world.

The Gregorian calendar got its name from Pope Gregory XIII, who ordered calendar reform to compute more accurately the exact date on which Easter—the Christian holiday commemorating the resurrection of Jesus—should fall. Easter was supposed to fall on the first Sunday after the first full moon after the vernal equinox. But over the years the dates had become confused because no one had been able to calculate the exact length of a solar year (365.242199 days). As a result, the calendar had become increasingly out of phase with the seasons; by 1545, the vernal (spring) equinox had moved ten days from its proper date. In 1582, when the reform took effect, October 5 became October 15, thus omitting ten days and setting the vernal equinox straight—but causing any number of legal complications.

Although the Gregorian calendar was based on a truer calculation of the length of a year and thus required less adjustment than previous calendars, it was not immediately adopted, even in Christian Europe, in part because any change would have been difficult to enforce given the state of communications at the time. Because the pope had sponsored the reform, the Catholic countries embraced it first; Protestant countries used it only after 1700. England accepted it in 1752. Adoption followed in Japan in 1873, Egypt in 1875, Russia in 1918, and Greece in 1923. The Greek Orthodox church never accepted it, so Easter in that church is about one week later than elsewhere in Christianity.

Even though the Gregorian calendar is astronomically correct, it still has bothersome defects: the months are different in length, and holidays do not fall on the same day in each year. Two other calendars have been proposed. The International Fixed Calendar would divide the year into thirteen

The Revolution in Astronomy. The traditional account of the movement of the heavens derived from the second-century Greek astronomer Ptolemy, who put the earth at the center of the cosmos. Above the earth were fixed the moon, the stars, and the planets in concentric crystalline spheres; beyond these fixed spheres dwelt God and the angels. The planets revolved around the earth at the command of God. In this view, the sun revolved around the earth; the heavens were perfect and unchanging, and the earth was "corrupted." Ptolemy insisted that the planets revolved in perfectly circular orbits (because circles were more "perfect" than other figures). To account for the actual elliptical paths that could be observed and calculated, he posited orbits within orbits, or epicycles.

In 1543, the Polish clergyman Nicolaus Copernicus (1473–1543) began the revolution in astronomy by publishing his treatise *On the Revolution of the Celestial Spheres.* Copernicus attacked the Ptolemaic account, arguing that the earth and planets revolved around the sun, a view known as *heliocentrism* (a

Calendar
This painting by Aldo Durazzi shows Gregory XIII presiding over the council of 1582 that reformed the calendar. The Catholic church sponsored the work of many astronomers and other scientists.
Archivio di Stato, Siena. Photo Lensini Fabrio.

months of twenty-eight days with an additional day at the end. The World Calendar would divide the year into four quarters of ninety-one days each with an additional day at the end of the year; the first month in each quarter would have thirty-one days and the second and third thirty days each. Neither has been adopted. Logic does not always win this kind of argument, for changing the length of the months seems almost equivalent to changing which side of the road you drive on; once a system is learned, no one really wants to give it up and start all over again. The same is true for the numbering of the years, which was set by the Council of Nicea in 325. The year 1 was designated as the year it was believed Jesus was born. Today scholars have determined that the date was wrong by several years, and many object in any case to the use of a calendar based on the birth of Jesus. But if that dating system were eliminated, what would replace it? Where should a common calendar begin?

sun-centered universe). He discovered that by placing the sun instead of the earth at the center of the system of spheres, he could eliminate many epicycles from the calculations. In other words, he claimed that the heliocentric view simplified the mathematics. Copernicus died soon after publishing his theories, but when the Italian monk Giordano Bruno (1548–1600) taught heliocentrism, perhaps with the aim of establishing a new religion, the Catholic Inquisition (set up to seek out heretics) arrested him and burned him at the stake.

For the most part, however, Copernicus's ideas attracted little sustained attention until the early seventeenth century, when astronomers systematically collected evidence that undermined the Ptolemaic view. A leader among them was the Danish astronomer Tycho Brahe (1546–1601), who was educated in Copenhagen and Leipzig. While at university he lost part of his nose in a duel and for the rest of his life he wore a metal insert to replace the missing part. Brahe designed and built new instruments for observing the heavens and trained a whole

The Trial of Galileo

In this anonymous painting of the trial held in 1633, Galileo appears seated on a chair in the center facing the church officials who accused him of heresy for insisting that the sun, not the earth, was the center of the universe (heliocentrism). Catholic officials forced him to recant or suffer the death penalty, but the trial did more damage in the long term to the Catholic church's reputation than it did to Galileo's.
Private collection, New York.
© Photograph by Erich Lessing/ Art Resource.

generation of astronomers. His observation of a new star in 1572 and a comet in 1577 called into question the Aristotelian view that the universe was unchanging. Brahe still rejected heliocentrism, but the assistant he employed when he moved to Prague in 1599, Johannes Kepler (1571–1630), was converted to the Copernican view. Kepler continued Brahe's collection of planetary observations and used the evidence to develop his three laws of planetary motion, published between 1609 and 1619. Kepler's laws provided mathematical backing for heliocentrism and directly challenged the claim long held, even by Copernicus, that planetary motion was circular. Kepler's first law stated that the orbits of the planets are ellipses, with the sun always at one focus of the ellipse.

The Italian Galileo Galilei (1564–1642) provided more evidence to support the heliocentric view and also challenged the doctrine that the heavens were perfect and unchanging. In 1609, he learned that two Dutch astronomers had built a telescope. He quickly invented a better one and observed the earth's moon, four satellites of Jupiter, the phases of Venus (a cycle of changing physical appearances), and sunspots. The moon, the planets, and the sun were no more perfect than the earth,

he insisted, and the shadows he could see on the moon could only be the product of hills and valleys like those on earth. Galileo portrayed the earth as a moving part of a larger system, only one of many planets revolving around the sun, not as the fixed center of a single, closed universe.

Because he recognized the utility of the new science for everyday projects, Galileo published his work in Italian, rather than Latin, to appeal to a lay audience of merchants and aristocrats. But he meant only to instruct an educated elite. The new science, he claimed, suited "the minds of the wise," not "the shallow minds of the common people." After all, his discoveries challenged the commonsensical view that it is the sun that rises and sets while the earth stands still. If the Bible were wrong about motion in the universe, as Galileo's position implied, the error came from the Bible's use of common language to appeal to the lower orders. The Catholic church was not mollified by this explanation. In 1616 the church forbade Galileo to teach that the earth moves and in 1633 accused him of not obeying the earlier order. Forced to appear before the Inquisition, he agreed to publicly recant his assertion that the earth moves to save himself from torture and death. Afterward he lived under house arrest and could publish his work only in the Dutch Republic, which had become a haven for iconoclastic scientists and thinkers.

Breakthroughs in Medicine. Until the mid-sixteenth century, medical knowledge in Europe had been based on the writings of the second-century Greek physician Galen, who was a contemporary of Ptolemy. Galen derived his knowledge of the anatomy of the human body from partial dissections. In the same year that Copernicus challenged the traditional account in astronomy (1543), the Flemish scientist Andreas Vesalius (1514–1564) did the same for anatomy. He published a new illustrated anatomical text, *On the Construction of the Human Body*, that revised Galen's work. Drawing on public dissections in the medical faculties of European universities, Vesalius at first hesitated to entirely reject Galen, but in his second edition of 1555 he explicitly refuted his predecessor. Theophrastus Bombastus von Hohenheim, better known as Paracelsus (1493–1541), went even further than Vesalius. He burned Galen's text at the University of Basel, where he was a professor of medicine. Paracelsus experimented with new drugs, performed operations (at the time most academic physicians taught medical theory, not practice), and pursued his interests in magic, alchemy, and astrology. He helped establish the modern science of pharmacology.

The Englishman William Harvey (1578–1657) also used dissection to examine the circulation of blood within the body, demonstrating how the heart worked as a pump. The heart and its valves were "a piece of machinery," Harvey insisted. They obeyed mechanical laws just as the planets and earth revolved around the sun in a mechanical universe. Nature could be understood by experiment and rational deduction, not by following traditional authorities.

Scientific Method: Bacon and Descartes. In the 1630s, the European intellectual elite began to accept the new scientific views. Ancient learning, the churches and their theologians, and even cherished popular beliefs seemed to be undermined by a new standard of truth—scientific method, which was based on systematic experiments and rational deduction. Two men were chiefly responsible for spreading the prestige of scientific method: the English politician Sir Francis Bacon (1561–1626) and the French mathematician and philosopher René

Descartes (1596–1650). They represented the two essential halves of scientific method: respectively, inductive reasoning through observation and experimental research and deductive reasoning from self-evident principles.

In *The Advancement of Learning* (1605), Bacon attacked reliance on ancient writers and optimistically predicted that scientific method would lead to social progress. The minds of the medieval scholars, he said, had been "shut up in the cells of a few authors (chiefly Aristotle, their dictator) as their persons were shut up in the cells of monasteries and colleges," and they could therefore produce only "cobwebs of learning" that were "of no substance or profit." Advancement would take place only through the collection, comparison, and analysis of information. Knowledge, in Bacon's view, must be empirically based (that is, gained by observation and experiment). Bacon ardently supported the scientific method over popular beliefs, which he rejected as "fables and popular errors." Claiming that God had called the Catholic church "to account for their degenerate manners and ceremonies," Bacon looked to the Protestant English state, which he served as lord chancellor, for leadership on the road to scientific advancement.

Although he agreed with Bacon's denunciation of traditional learning, Descartes saw that the attack on tradition might only replace the dogmatism of the churches with the skepticism of Montaigne—that nothing at all was certain. A Catholic who served in the Thirty Years' War, Descartes aimed to establish the new science on more secure philosophical foundations, those of mathematics and logic (Descartes invented analytic geometry). In his *Discourse on Method* (1637), he argued that mathematical and mechanical principles provided the key to understanding all of nature, including the actions of people and states. All prior assumptions must be repudiated in favor of one elementary principle: "I think, therefore I am." Everything else could—and should—be doubted, but even doubt showed the certain existence of someone thinking. Begin with the simple and go on to the complex, he asserted, and believe only those ideas that present themselves "clearly and distinctly." Descartes believed that rational individuals would see the necessity of strong state power and that only "meddling and restless spirits" would plot against it. He insisted that human reason could not only unravel the secrets of nature but also prove the existence of God. Although he hoped to secure the authority of both church and state, his reliance on human reason alone irritated authorities, and his books were banned in many places. He moved to the Dutch Republic to work in peace. Scientific research, like economic growth, became centered in the northern, Protestant countries, where it was less constrained by church control.

Magic and Witchcraft

Despite the new emphasis on clear reasoning, observation, and independence from past authorities, science had not yet become separate from magic. Many scholars, like Paracelsus, studied alchemy alongside other scientific pursuits. Elizabeth I maintained a court astrologer who was also a serious mathematician, and many writers distinguished between "natural magic," which was close to experi-

Persecution of Witches

This engraving from a pamphlet account of witch trials in England in 1589 shows three women hanged as accused witches. At their feet are frogs and toads, which were supposed to be the witches' "familiars," sent by the devil to help them ruin the lives of their neighbors by causing disease or untimely deaths among people and livestock. The ferret on the woman's lap was reported to be the devil himself in disguise.
Lambeth Palace Library.

mental science, and demonic "black magic." The astronomer Tycho Brahe defended his studies of alchemy and astrology as part of natural magic. For many of the greatest minds, magic and science were still closely linked.

In a world in which most people believed in astrology, magical healing, prophecy, and ghosts, it is hardly surprising that many of Europe's learned people also firmly believed in witchcraft, the exercise of magical powers gained by a pact with the devil. The same Jean Bodin who argued against religious fanaticism insisted on death for witches—and for those magistrates who would not prosecute them. In France alone, 345 books and pamphlets on witchcraft appeared between 1550 and 1650. Trials of witches peaked in Europe between 1560 and 1640, the very time of the celebrated breakthroughs of the new science. Montaigne was one of the few to speak out against executing accused witches: "It is taking one's conjectures rather seriously to roast someone alive for them," he wrote in 1580.

Belief in witches was not new in the sixteenth century. Witches had long been thought capable of almost anything: passing through walls, flying through the air, destroying crops, and causing personal catastrophes from miscarriage to demonic possession. What was new was the official persecution, justified by the notion that witches were agents of Satan whom the righteous must oppose. In a time of economic crisis, plague, warfare, and the clash of religious differences, witchcraft trials provided an outlet for social stress and anxiety, legitimated by state power. At the same time, the trials seem to have been part of the religious reform movement itself. Denunciation and persecution of witches coincided with the spread of reform, both Protestant and Catholic. The trials concentrated especially in the German lands of the Holy Roman Empire, the boiling cauldron of the Thirty Years' War.

The victims of the persecution were overwhelmingly female: women accounted for 80 percent of the accused witches in about 100,000 trials in Europe and North America during the sixteenth and seventeenth centuries. About one-third were sentenced to death. Before 1400, when witchcraft trials were rare, nearly half of those accused had been men. Explanations for this gender difference have raised many controversies. Some historians argue that the trials expressed a fundamental hatred of women that came to a head during conflicts over the Reformation. Official descriptions of witchcraft oozed lurid details of sexual orgies, incest, homosexuality, and cannibalism, in which women acted as the devil's sexual slaves. In this view, Catholic and Protestant reforming clergy attacked the presumably wild and undisciplined sexuality of women as the most obvious manifestation of popular unruliness and heretical tendencies. Lawyers and judges followed their lead.

Other historians see in the trials a social dimension that helps explain the prominence of women. Accusers were almost always better off than those they accused. The poorest and most socially marginal people in most communities were elderly spinsters and widows. Because they were thought likely to hanker after revenge on those more fortunate, they were singled out as witches. Another commonly accused woman was the midwife, who was a prime target for suspicion when a baby or mother died in childbirth. Although sometimes venerated for their special skill, midwives also numbered among the thousands of largely powerless women persecuted for their supposed consorting with the devil.

Witchcraft trials declined when scientific thinking about causes and effects raised questions about the evidence used in court: how could judges or jurors be certain that someone was a witch? The tide turned everywhere at about the same time, as physicians, lawyers, judges, and even clergy came to suspect that accusations were based on popular superstition and peasant untrustworthiness. As early as the 1640s, French courts ordered the arrest of witch-hunters and released suspected witches. In 1682, a French royal decree treated witchcraft as fraud and imposture, meaning that the law did not recognize anyone as a witch. In 1693, the jurors who had convicted twenty witches in Salem, Massachusetts, recanted, claiming: "We confess that we ourselves were not capable to understand. . . . We justly fear that we were sadly deluded and mistaken." The Salem jurors had not stopped believing in witches; they had simply lost confidence in their ability to identify them. This was a general pattern. Popular attitudes had not changed; what had changed was elites' attitudes. When physicians and judges had believed in witches and persecuted them officially, with torture, witches had gone to their deaths in record numbers. But when the same groups distanced themselves from popular beliefs, the trials and the executions stopped.

IMPORTANT DATES

1562	French Wars of Religion begin
1566	Revolt of Calvinists in the Netherlands against Spain begins
1569	Formation of commonwealth of Poland-Lithuania
1571	Battle of Lepanto marks victory of West over Ottomans at sea
1572	St. Bartholomew's Day Massacre of French Protestants
1588	Defeat of the Spanish Armada by England
1598	French Wars of Religion end with Edict of Nantes
1601	William Shakespeare, *Hamlet*
1618	Thirty Years' War begins
1625	Hugo Grotius publishes *The Laws of War and Peace*
1629	English Puritans set up the Massachusetts Bay Company and begin to colonize New England
1633	Galileo Galilei is forced to recant his support of heliocentrism
1635	French join the Thirty Years' War by declaring war on Spain
1648	Peace of Westphalia ends the Thirty Years' War

Conclusion

The witchcraft persecutions reflected the traumas of these times of religious war and economic decline. Marauding armies combined with economic depression, disease, and the threat of starvation to shatter the lives of many ordinary Europeans. Some people blamed the poor widow or upstart midwife for their problems; others joined desperate revolts; still others emigrated to the New World to seek a better life. Even rulers confronted frightening choices: forced abdication, death in battle, or assassination often accompanied their religious decisions, and economic shocks could threaten the stability of their governments.

Religious conflicts shaped the destinies of every European power in this period. These conflicts came to a head in 1618–1648 in the Thirty Years' War, which cut a path of destruction through central Europe and involved most of the European powers.

MAPPING THE WEST The Religious Divisions of Europe, c. 1648

The Peace of Westphalia recognized major religious divisions within Europe that have endured for the most part to the present day. Catholicism dominated in southern Europe, Lutheranism had its stronghold in northern Europe, and Calvinism flourished along the Rhine River. In southeastern Europe, the Islamic Ottoman Turks accommodated the Greek Orthodox Christians under their rule but bitterly fought the Catholic Austrian Habsburgs for control of Hungary.

Repulsed by the effects of religious violence on international relations, European rulers agreed to a peace that effectively removed disputes between Catholics and Protestants from the international arena. The growing separation of political motives from religious ones did not mean that violence or conflict had ended, however. Struggles for religious uniformity within states would continue, though on a smaller scale. Bigger armies required more state involvement, and almost everywhere rulers emerged from these decades of conflict with expanded powers. The growth of state power directly changed the lives

of ordinary people: more men went into the armies and most families paid higher taxes. The constant extension of state power is one of the defining themes of modern history; religious warfare gave it a jump start.

For all their power, rulers could not control economic, social, or intellectual trends, much as they often tried. The economic downturn of the seventeenth century produced unexpected consequences for European states even while it made life miserable for many ordinary people; economic power and vibrancy shifted from the Mediterranean world to the northwest because the countries of northwestern Europe—England, France, and the Dutch Republic especially—suffered less from the fighting of the Thirty Years' War and recovered more quickly from the loss of population and production during bad times.

In the face of violence and uncertainty, some began to look for secular alternatives in art, politics, and science. Although it would be foolish to claim that everyone's mental universe changed because of the clash between religious and secular worldviews, a truly monumental shift in attitudes had begun. Secularization combined a growing interest in nonreligious forms of art, such as theater and opera, the search for nonreligious foundations of political authority, and the establishment of scientific method as the standard of truth. Proponents of these changes did not renounce their religious beliefs or even hold them less fervently, but they did insist that attention to state interests and scientific knowledge could serve as a brake on religious violence and popular superstitions.

Suggested References

Religious Conflicts and State Power, 1560–1618

The personalities of rulers such as Elizabeth I of England and Philip II of Spain remain central to the religious and political conflicts of this period. Recent scholarship also highlights more structural factors, especially in the French Wars of Religion and the rise of the Dutch Republic.

Cameron, Euan, ed. *Early Modern Europe: An Oxford History.* 1999.

Holt, Mack P. *The French Wars of Religion, 1562–1629.* 1995.

Israel, Jonathan. *The Dutch Republic: Its Rise, Greatness, and Fall, 1477–1806.* 1995.

Kamen, Henry. *Philip of Spain.* 1997.

Mattingly, Garrett. *The Defeat of the Spanish Armada.* 2nd ed. 1988.

Roberts, Penny. *A City in Conflict: Troyes during the French Wars of Religion.* 1996.

Strong, Roy. *The Cult of Elizabeth: Elizabethan Portraiture and Pageantry.* 1977.

The Thirty Years' War and the Balance of Power, 1618–1648

As ethnic conflicts erupt again in eastern Europe, historians have traced their roots back to the intertwined religious, ethnic, and dynastic struggles of the Thirty Years' War.

Asch, Ronald G. *The Thirty Years War: The Holy Roman Empire and Europe, 1618–48.* 1997.

Lee, Stephen J. *The Thirty Years War.* 1991.

Parker, Geoffrey. *The Military Revolution: Military Innovation and the Rise of the West, 1500–1800.* 1988.

———, ed. *The Thirty Years' War.* 2nd ed. 1997.

*Rabb, Theodore K. *The Thirty Years' War.* 2nd ed. 1972.

Economic Crisis and Realignment

Painstaking archival research has enabled historians to reconstruct the demographic, economic, and social history of this period. Recently, attention has focused more specifically on women, the family, and the early history of slavery.

Ashton, Trevor H., ed. *Crisis in Europe.* 1965.

Braudel, Fernand. *The Mediterranean and the Mediterranean World in the Age of Philip the Second.* 2 vols. Trans. Siân Reynolds. 1972–1973.

De Vries, Jan. *The Economy of Europe in an Age of Crisis, 1600–1750.* 1982.

Parry, J. H. *The Age of Reconnaissance.* 1981.

Pouncy, Carolyn Johnston, ed. and trans. *The "Domostroi": Rules for Russian Households in the Time of Ivan the Terrible.* 1994.

Spierenburg, Pieter. *The Broken Spell: A Cultural and Anthropological History of Preindustrial Europe.* 1991.

Wiesner, Merry E. *Women and Gender in Early Modern Europe.* 1993.

A Clash of Worldviews

The transformation of intellectual and cultural life has long fascinated scholars. Recent works have developed a new kind of study called "microhistory," focused on one person (like Ginzburg's Italian miller) or a series of individual stories (as in Roper's analysis of witchcraft in the German states).

Baroque architecture: http://www.lib.virginia.edu:80/dic/colls/arh102/index.html.

*Drake, Stillman, ed. *Discoveries and Opinions of Galileo.* 1957.

The Galileo Project: http://riceinfo.rice.edu/Galileo.

Ginzburg, Carlo. *The Cheese and the Worms: The Cosmos of a Sixteenth-Century Miller.* Trans. John and Anne Tedeschi. 1992.

Jacob, James. *The Scientific Revolution.* 1998.

Roper, Lyndal. *Oedipus and the Devil: Witchcraft, Sexuality, and Religion in Early Modern Europe.* 1994.

Skinner, Quentin. *The Foundations of Modern Political Thought.* Vol. 2, *The Age of Reformation.* 1978.

Thomas, Keith. *Religion and the Decline of Magic.* 1971.

Zagorin, Perez. *Francis Bacon.* 1998.

*Primary sources.

State Building and the Search for Order

1648–1690

Louis XIV in Roman Splendor
Images of Louis appear everywhere in his chateau at Versailles. This plaster relief by Antoine Coysevox in the Salon de la Guerre *(War Hall) represents Louis as Mars, the Roman god of war, riding roughshod over his enemies.*
Giraudon/Art Resource, NY.

I N ONE OF HER HUNDREDS OF LETTERS to her daughter, the French noblewoman Marie de Sévigné told a disturbing story about a well-known cook. The cook got upset when he did not have enough roast for several unexpected guests at a dinner for King Louis XIV. Early the next morning, when the fish he had ordered did not arrive on time, the cook felt personally dishonored. He rushed up to his room, put his sword against the door, and ran it through his heart on the third try. The fish arrived soon after. The king regretted the trouble his visit had caused, but others soon filled in for the chief cook. That evening, Sévigné wrote, there was "a very good dinner, light refreshments later, and then supper, a walk, cards, hunting, everything scented with daffodils, everything magical."

Reading this account now produces puzzlement and shock. It is difficult to comprehend how anyone could care that much about a shipment of fish. The story nonetheless reveals an important aspect of state building in the seventeenth century: to extend state authority, which had been challenged during the wars over religion and threatened by economic recession, many rulers created an aura of overwhelming power and brilliance around themselves. Louis XIV, like many rulers, believed that he reigned by divine right. He served as God's lieutenant on earth and even claimed certain godlike qualities. The great gap between the ruler and ordinary subjects accounts for the extreme reaction of Louis's cook, and even leading nobles such as Sévigné came to see the king and his court as somehow "magical."

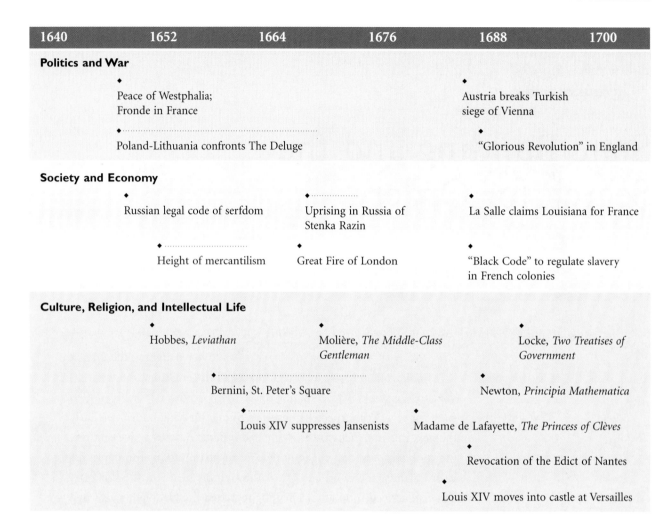

1640	1652	1664	1676	1688	1700

Politics and War

Peace of Westphalia; Fronde in France

Poland-Lithuania confronts The Deluge

Austria breaks Turkish siege of Vienna

"Glorious Revolution" in England

Society and Economy

Russian legal code of serfdom

Height of mercantilism

Uprising in Russia of Stenka Razin

Great Fire of London

La Salle claims Louisiana for France

"Black Code" to regulate slavery in French colonies

Culture, Religion, and Intellectual Life

Hobbes, *Leviathan*

Bernini, St. Peter's Square

Louis XIV suppresses Jansenists

Molière, *The Middle-Class Gentleman*

Madame de Lafayette, *The Princess of Clèves*

Locke, *Two Treatises of Government*

Newton, *Principia Mathematica*

Revocation of the Edict of Nantes

Louis XIV moves into castle at Versailles

Louis XIV's model of state building was known as *absolutism,* a system of government in which the ruler claimed sole and uncontestable power. Although absolutism exerted great influence, especially in central and eastern Europe, it faced competition from *constitutionalism,* a system in which the ruler had to share power with parliaments made up of elected representatives. Constitutionalism led to weakness in Poland-Lithuania, but it provided a strong foundation for state power in England, the British North American colonies, and the Dutch Republic. Constitutionalism triumphed in England, however, only after one king had been executed as a traitor and another had been deposed.

Although the differences between absolutism and constitutionalism turned out to be very significant in the long run, these two methods of state building faced similar challenges in the mid-seventeenth century. Competition in the international arena required resources, and all states raised taxes in this period, provoking popular protests and rebellions. The wars over religion that culminated in the Thirty Years' War left many economies in dire straits, and, even more significant, they created a need for new explanations of political authority. Monarchs still relied on religion to justify their divine right to rule, but they increasingly sought secular defenses of their powers too. Absolutism and constitutionalism were the two main responses to the threat of disorder and breakdown left as a legacy of the wars over religion.

The search for order took place not only at the level of states and rulers but also in intellectual, cultural, and social life. In science, the Englishman Isaac Newton explained the regular movement of the universe with the law of gravitation and thereby consolidated the scientific revolution. Artists sought means of glorifying power and expressing order and symmetry in new fashion. As states consolidated their power, elites endeavored to distinguish themselves more clearly from the lower orders. The upper classes emulated the manners developed at court and tried in every way to distance themselves from anything viewed as vulgar or lower class. Officials, clergy, and laypeople all worked to reform the poor, now seen as a major source of disorder. Whether absolutist or constitutionalist, seventeenth-century states all aimed to extend control over their subjects' lives.

❖ Louis XIV: Model of Absolutism

French king Louis XIV (r. 1643–1715) personified the absolutist ruler who shared his power with no one. Louis personally made all important state decisions and left no room for dissent. In 1651, he reputedly told the Paris high court of justice, "*L'état, c'est moi*" ("I am the state"), emphasizing that state authority rested in him personally. Louis cleverly manipulated the affections and ambitions of his courtiers, chose as his ministers middle-class men who owed everything to him, built up Europe's largest army, and snuffed out every hint of religious or political opposition. Yet the absoluteness of his power should not be exaggerated. Like all rulers of his time, Louis depended on the cooperation of many others: local officials who enforced his decrees, peasants and artisans who joined his armies and paid his taxes, creditors who loaned crucial funds, and nobles who might stay home and cause trouble rather than join court festivities organized to glorify the king.

The Fronde, 1648–1653

Absolutism was not made in a day. Louis XIV built on a long French tradition of increasing centralization of state authority, but before he could extend it he had to weather a series of revolts known as the *Fronde*. Derived from the French word for a child's slingshot, the term was used by critics to signify that the revolts were mere child's play. In fact, however, they posed an unprecedented threat to the French crown. Louis was only five when he came to the

throne in 1643 upon the death of his father, Louis XIII, who with his chief minister Cardinal Richelieu had steered France through increasing involvement in the Thirty Years' War, rapidly climbing taxes, and innumerable tax revolts. Louis XIV's mother, Anne of Austria, and her Italian-born adviser and rumored lover Cardinal Mazarin (1602–1661) ruled in the young monarch's name. French nobles and magistrates suspected the motives of the foreign-born Anne and Mazarin. Some of them hoped to use the crisis created by Louis XIII's death to move France toward a constitutional government.

To meet the financial pressure of fighting the Thirty Years' War, Mazarin sold new offices, raised taxes, and forced creditors to extend loans to the government. In 1648, a coalition of his opponents presented him with a charter of demands that, if granted, would have given the parlements (high courts) a form of constitutional power with the right to approve new taxes. Mazarin responded by arresting the leaders of parlements. He soon faced a series of revolts that at one time or another involved nearly every social group in France.

The Fronde posed an immediate menace to the young king. Fearing for his safety, his mother and

Anne of Austria
Wife of Louis XIII and mother of Louis XIV, Anne served as regent during her son's youth but delegated most authority to Cardinal Mazarin, her Italian-born adviser. She is shown here praying with Louis and his younger brother Philippe. The painting emphasizes her religious devotion.
Laurie Platt Winfrey, Inc.

members of his court took Louis and fled Paris. With civil war threatening, Mazarin and Anne agreed to compromise with the parlements. The nobles saw an opportunity to reassert their claims to power against the weakened monarchy and renewed their demands for greater local control, which they had lost when the religious wars ended in 1598. Leading noble-women often played key roles in the opposition to Mazarin, carrying messages and forging alliances, especially when male family members were in prison. While the nobles sought to regain power and local influence, the middle and lower classes chafed at the constant tax increases. Conflicts erupted throughout the kingdom as nobles, parlements, and city councils all raised their own armies to fight either the crown or each other, and rampaging soldiers devastated rural areas and disrupted commerce. In places, such as the southwestern city of Bordeaux, the urban poor revolted as well.

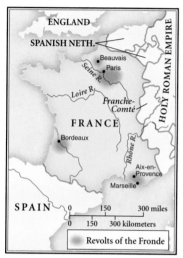

The Fronde, 1648–1653

Despite the glaring weakness of central power, the monarchy survived. Neither the nobles nor the judges of the parlements really wanted to overthrow the king; they simply wanted a greater share in power. But Louis XIV never forgot the humiliation and uncertainty that marred his childhood. Years later he recalled an incident in which a band of Parisians invaded his bedchamber to determine whether he had fled the city, and he declared the event an affront not only to himself but also to the state. His own policies as ruler would be designed to prevent the repetition of any such revolts.

Court Culture as a Form of State Power

When Cardinal Mazarin died in 1661, Louis XIV decided to rule without a first minister. He described the dangers of his situation in memoirs he wrote later for his son's instruction: "Everywhere was disorder. My Court as a whole was still very far removed from the sentiments in which I trust you will find it." Louis listed many other problems in the kingdom, but none occupied him more than his attempts to control France's leading nobles, some of whom came from families that had opposed him militarily during the Fronde.

Typically quarrelsome, the French nobles had long exercised local authority by maintaining their own fighting forces, meting out justice on their estates, arranging jobs for underlings, and resolving their own conflicts through dueling. Louis set out to domesticate the warrior nobles by replacing violence with court ritual. Using a systematic policy of bestowing pensions, offices, honors, gifts, and the threat of disfavor or punishment, he induced the nobles to cooperate with him and made himself the center of French power and culture. At Louis's court the great nobles vied for his favor, attended the ballets and theatricals he put on, and learned the rules of etiquette he supervised—in short, became his clients, dependent on him for advancement. Access to the king was the most valued commodity at court. Nobles competed for the honor of holding his shirt when he dressed; foreign ambassadors squabbled for places near him; and royal mistresses basked in the glow of his personal favor.

Participation at court required constant study. The preferred styles changed without notice, and the tiniest lapse in attention to etiquette could lead to ruin. Madame de Lafayette described the court in her novel *The Princess of Clèves* (1678): "The Court gravitated around ambition. Nobody was tranquil or indifferent—everybody was busily trying to better his or her position by pleasing, by helping, or by hindering somebody else." Occasionally the results were tragic, as in the suicide of the cook recounted by Marie de Sévigné. Elisabeth Charlotte, duchess of Orléans, the German-born sister-in-law of Louis, complained that "everything here is pure self-interest and deviousness," but she gloried in the special privileges of her closeness to the king, which included the right to a military honor guard and a special cloth to stand on during daily Mass.

Politics and the Arts. Louis XIV appreciated the political uses of every form of art. Mock battles, extravaganzas, theatrical performances, even the king's dinner—Louis's daily life was a public performance designed to enhance his prestige. Calling himself the Sun King, Louis adorned his court with statues of Apollo, Greek god of the sun. He also emulated the style and methods of ancient Roman emperors. At a celebration for the birth of his first son in 1662, Louis dressed in Roman attire, and many engravings and paintings showed him as a Roman emperor. Sculpture and paintings adorned his palace; commissioned histories vaunted his achievements; and coins and medals spread his likeness throughout the realm.

The king's officials treated the arts as a branch of government. The king gave pensions to artists who worked for him and sometimes protected writers from clerical critics. The most famous of these was the playwright Molière, whose comedy *Tartuffe* (1664) made fun of religious hypocrites and was loudly condemned by church leaders. Louis forced Molière to delay public performances of the play but resisted calls for his dismissal. Louis's ministers set up royal academies of dance, painting, architecture, and music and took control of the Académie française (French Academy), which to this day decides on correct usage of the French language. A royal furniture workshop at the Gobelins tapestry works in Paris turned out the delicate and ornate pieces whose style bore the king's name. Louis's government also regulated the number and locations of theaters and closely censored all forms of publication.

Music and theater enjoyed special prominence. Louis commissioned operas to celebrate royal marriages, baptisms, and military victories. His favorite composer, Jean-Baptiste Lully, an Italian who began as a cook's assistant and rose to be virtual dictator of French musical taste, wrote sixteen operas for court performances as well as many ballets. Louis himself danced in the ballets if a role seemed especially important. Playwrights presented their new plays directly to the court. Pierre Corneille and Jean-Baptiste Racine wrote tragedies set in Greece or Rome that celebrated the new aristocratic virtues which Louis aimed to inculcate: a reverence for order and self-control. All the characters were regal or noble, all the language lofty, all the behavior aristocratic. The king's sister-in-law called the plays of Corneille "the best entertainment I have."

The Palace of Versailles. Louis glorified his image as well through massive public works projects. Military facilities, such as veterans' hospitals and new fortified towns on the frontiers, represented his military might. Urban improvements, such as the reconstruction of the Louvre palace in Paris, proved his wealth. But his most remarkable project was the construction of a new palace at Versailles, twelve miles from the turbulent capital.

Building began in the 1660s. By 1685, the frenzied effort engaged 36,000 workers, not including

Palace of Versailles

In this defining statement of his ambitions, Louis XIV emphasized his ability to impose his own personal will, even on nature itself. The sheer size and precise geometrical design of the palace underlined the presence of an all-powerful personality, that of the Sun King. The palace became a national historical monument in 1837 and was used for many momentous historical occasions, including the signing of the peace treaty after World War I.

Giraudon/Art Resource, NY.

Louis XIV Visits the Royal Tapestry Workshop
This tapestry was woven at the Gobelins tapestry workshop between 1673 and 1680. It shows Louis XIV (wearing a red hat) and his minister Colbert (dressed in black, holding his hat) visiting the workshop on the outskirts of Paris. The artisans of the workshop scurry around to show Louis all the luxury objects they manufacture. Louis bought the workshop in 1662 and made it a national enterprise for making tapestries and furniture.
Giraudon/Art Resource, NY.

the thousands of troops who diverted a local river to supply water for pools and fountains. Royal workshops produced tapestries, carpets, mirrors, and porcelains. Even the gardens designed by landscape architect André Le Nôtre reflected the spirit of Louis XIV's rule: their geometrical arrangements and clear lines showed that art and design could tame nature and that order and control defined the exercise of power. Le Nôtre's geometrical landscapes were imitated in Spain, the Italian states, Austria, the German states, and later as far away as St. Petersburg in Russia and Washington, D.C. Versailles symbolized Louis's success in reining in the nobility and dominating Europe, and other monarchs eagerly mimicked French fashion and often conducted their business in French.

Yet for all its apparent luxury and frivolity, life at Versailles was often cramped and cold. Fifteen thousand people crowded into the palace's apartments, including all the highest military officers, the ministers of state, and the separate households of each member of the royal family. Refuse collected in the corridors during the incessant building, and thieves and prostitutes overran the grounds.

By the time Louis actually moved from the Louvre to Versailles in 1682, he had reigned as monarch for thirty-nine years. After his wife's death in 1683, he secretly married his mistress, Françoise d'Aubigné, marquise de Maintenon, and conducted most state affairs from her apartments at the palace.

Her opponents at court complained that she controlled all the appointments, but her efforts focused on her own projects, including her favorite: the founding in 1686 of a royal school for girls from impoverished noble families. She also inspired Louis XIV to pursue his devotion to Catholicism.

Enforcing Religious Orthodoxy

Louis believed that as king he must defend the Catholic faith against Protestants and dissident Catholics; orthodox Catholicism was an essential pillar of his rule. One of his advisers, Bishop Jacques-Benigne Bossuet (1627–1704), explained the principle of divine right that justified the king's actions: "We have seen that kings take the place of God, who is the true father of the human species. We have also seen that the first idea of power which exists among men is that of the paternal power; and that kings are modeled on fathers." The king, like a father, should instruct his subjects in the true religion, or at least make sure that others did so. Some questioned Louis's understanding of the finer points of doctrine: according to his sister-in-law, Louis himself "has never read anything about religion, nor the Bible either, and just goes along believing whatever he is told."

Louis's campaign for religious conformity first focused on the Jansenists, Catholics whose doctrines and practices resembled some aspects of

Protestantism. Following the posthumous publication of the book *Augustinus* (1640) by the Flemish theologian Cornelius Jansen (1585–1638), the Jansenists stressed the need for God's grace in achieving salvation. They emphasized the importance of original sin; and, in their austere religious practice, resembled the English Puritans. Prominent among the Jansenists was Blaise Pascal (1623–1662), a mathematician of genius, who wrote his *Provincial Letters* (1656–1657) to defend Jansenism against charges of heresy. Many judges in the parlements likewise endorsed Jansenist doctrine.

Louis feared any doctrine that gave priority to considerations of individual conscience over the demands of the official church hierarchy. He preferred teachings that stressed obedience to authority. Therefore, in 1660 he began enforcing various papal bulls (decrees) against Jansenism and closed down Jansenist theological centers. Jansenists were forced underground for the rest of his reign.

After many years of escalating pressure on the Calvinist Huguenots, Louis revoked the Edict of Nantes in 1685 and eliminated all of the Calvinists' rights. Louis considered the Edict (1598), by which his grandfather Henry IV granted the Protestants religious freedom and civil rights, a temporary measure, and he fervently hoped to reconvert the Huguenots to Catholicism. He closed their churches and schools, banned all their public activities, and exiled those who refused to embrace the state religion. Thousands of Huguenots emigrated to England, Brandenburg-Prussia, or the Dutch Republic. Many now wrote for publications attacking Louis XIV's absolutism. Protestant European countries were shocked by this crackdown on religious dissent and would cite it when they went to war against Louis.

Extending State Authority at Home and Abroad

Louis XIV could not have enforced his religious policies without the services of a nationwide bureaucracy. *Bureaucracy*—a system of state officials carrying out orders according to a regular and routine line of authority—comes from the French word *bureau,* for "desk," which came to mean "office," both in the sense of a physical space and a position of authority. Louis personally supervised the activities of his bureaucrats and worked to ensure his

supremacy in all matters. The ultimate goal of developing absolute power at home was the pursuit of French glory abroad.

Bureaucracy and Mercantilism. Louis extended the bureaucratic forms his predecessors had developed, especially the use of intendants, officials who held their positions directly from the king rather than owning their offices, as crown officials had traditionally done. Louis handpicked them to represent his will against entrenched local interests such as the parlements, provincial estates, and noble governors. The intendants reduced local powers over finances and insisted on more efficient tax collection. Despite the doubling of taxes in Louis's reign, the local rebellions that had so beset the crown from the 1620s to the 1640s subsided in the face of these better-organized state forces.

Louis's success in consolidating his authority depended on hard work, an eye for detail, and an ear to the ground. In his memoirs he described how he operated:

> to learn each hour the news concerning every province and every nation, the secrets of every court, the mood and weaknesses of each Prince and of every foreign minister; to be well-informed on an infinite number of matters about which we are supposed to know nothing; to elicit from our subjects what they hide from us with the greatest care; to discover the most remote opinions of our courtiers and the most hidden interests of those who come to us with quite contrary professions [claims].

To gather all this information, Louis relied on a series of talented ministers, usually of modest origins, who gained fame, fortune, and even noble status from serving the king. Most important among them was Jean-Baptiste Colbert (1619–1683), the son of a wool merchant turned royal official. Colbert had managed Mazarin's personal finances and worked his way up under Louis XIV to become head of royal finances, public works, and the navy. Like many of Louis's other ministers, he founded a family dynasty that eventually produced five ministers of state, an archbishop, two bishops, and three generals.

Colbert used the bureaucracy to establish a mercantilist policy. According to the economic doctrine of *mercantilism*, governments must intervene to increase national wealth by whatever means

Wars of Louis XIV

1667–1668 War of Devolution
Enemies: Spain, Dutch Republic, England, Sweden
Ended by Treaty of Aix-la-Chapelle in 1668, with France gaining towns in Spanish Netherlands (Flanders)

1672–1678 Dutch War
Enemies: Dutch Republic, Spain, Holy Roman Empire
Ended by treaty of Nijmegen, 1678–1679, which gave several towns in Spanish Netherlands and Franche-Comté to France

1688–1697 War of the League of Augsburg
Enemies: Holy Roman Empire, Sweden, Spain, England
Ended by treaty of Rijswijk, 1697, with Louis returning all his conquests made since 1678 except Strasbourg

possible. Such government intervention inevitably increased the role and eventually the number of bureaucrats needed. Under Colbert, the French government established overseas trading companies, granted manufacturing monopolies, and standardized production methods for textiles, paper, and soap. A government inspection system regulated the quality of finished goods and compelled all craftsmen to organize into guilds, in which masters could supervise the work of the journeymen and apprentices. To protect French production, Colbert rescinded many internal customs fees but enacted high foreign tariffs, which cut imports of competing goods. To compete more effectively with England and the Dutch Republic, Colbert also subsidized shipbuilding, a policy that dramatically expanded the number of seaworthy vessels. Such mercantilist measures aimed to ensure France's prominence in world markets and to provide the resources needed to fight wars against the increasingly long list of enemies. Although later economists questioned the value of this state intervention in the economy, virtually every government in Europe embraced mercantilism.

Colbert's mercantilist projects extended to Canada, where in 1663 he took control of the trading company that had founded New France. He transplanted several thousand peasants from western France to the present-day province of Quebec, which France had claimed since 1608. To guard his investment, Colbert sent fifteen hundred soldiers to join the settlers. Of particular concern to the French government were the Iroquois, who regularly interrupted French fur-trading convoys. Shows of French military force, including the burning of Indian villages and winter food supplies, forced the Iroquois to make peace with New France, and from 1666 to 1680, French traders moved westward with minimal interference. In 1672, fur trader Louis Jolliet and Jesuit missionary Jacques Marquette reached the upper Mississippi River and traveled downstream as far as Arkansas. In 1684, French explorer Sieur de La Salle went all the way down to the Gulf of Mexico, claiming a vast territory for Louis XIV and calling it Louisiana after him. Louis and Colbert encouraged colonial settlement as part of their rivalry with the English and the Dutch in the New World.

The Army and War. Colonial settlement occupied only a small portion of Louis XIV's attention, however, for his main foreign policy goal was to extend French power in Europe. In pursuing this purpose, he inevitably came up against the Spanish and Austrian Habsburgs, whose lands encircled his. To expand French power Louis needed the biggest possible army. His powerful ministry of war centralized the organization of French troops. Barracks built in major towns received supplies from a central distribution system. The state began to provide uniforms for the soldiers and to offer veterans some hospital care. A militia draft instituted in 1688 supplemented the army in times of war and enrolled 100,000 men. Louis's wartime army could field a force as large as that of all his enemies combined.

Absolutist governments always tried to increase their territorial holdings, and as Louis extended his reach, he gained new enemies. In 1667–1668, in the first of his major wars after assuming personal control of French affairs, Louis defeated the Spanish armies but had to make peace when England, Sweden, and the Dutch Republic joined the war. In the Treaty of Aix-la-Chapelle in 1668, he gained control of towns on the border of the Spanish Netherlands. Pamphlets sponsored by the Habsburgs accused Louis of aiming for "universal monarchy," or domination of Europe. The chorus of denunciation would only grow over the years.

In 1672, Louis XIV opened hostilities against the Dutch because they stood in the way of his acquisition of more territory in the Spanish Netherlands. He declared war again on Spain in 1673. By now the Dutch had allied themselves with their former Spanish masters to hold off the French. Louis also marched his troops into territories of the Holy Roman Empire, provoking many of the German princes to join with the emperor, the Spanish, and the Dutch in an alliance against Louis, now denounced as a "Christian Turk" for his imperialist ambitions. But the French armies more than held their own. Faced with bloody but inconclusive results on the battlefield, the parties agreed to the Treaty of Nijmegen of 1678–1679, which ceded several Flemish towns and Franche-Comté to Louis, linking Alsace to the rest of France. These territorial additions were costly: French government deficits soared, and increases in taxes touched off the most serious antitax revolt of Louis's reign, in 1675.

Louis had no intention of standing still. Heartened by the Habsburgs' seeming weakness, he pushed eastward, seizing the city of Strasbourg in 1681 and invading the province of Lorraine in 1684. In 1688,

he attacked some of the small German cities of the Holy Roman Empire and was soon involved again in a long war against a Europe-wide coalition. As Louis's own mental powers diminished with age, he seems to have lost all sense of measure. His armies laid waste to German cities such as Mannheim; his government ordered the local military commander to "kill all those who would still wish to build houses there." Between 1689 and 1697, a coalition made up of England, Spain, Sweden, the Dutch Republic, the Austrian emperor, and various German princes fought Louis XIV to a stalemate. When hostilities ended in the Peace of Rijswijk in 1697, Louis returned many of his conquests made since 1678 with the exception of Strasbourg (Map 17.1). Louis never lost his taste for war, but his allies learned how to set limits on his ambitions.

Louis was the last French ruler before Napoleon to accompany his troops to the battlefield. In later generations, as the military became more professional, French rulers left the fighting to their generals. Although Louis had eliminated the private armies

MAP 17.1 Louis XIV's Acquisitions, 1668–1697

Every ruler in Europe hoped to extend his or her territorial control, and war was often the result. Louis XIV steadily encroached on the Spanish Netherlands to the north and the lands of the Holy Roman Empire to the east. Although coalitions of European powers reined in Louis's grander ambitions, he nonetheless incorporated many neighboring territories into the French crown.

of his noble courtiers, he constantly promoted his own military prowess in order to keep his noble officers under his sway. He had miniature battle scenes painted on his high heels and commissioned tapestries showing his military processions into cities, even those he did not take by force. He seized every occasion to assert his supremacy, insisting that other fleets salute his ships first.

War required money and men, which Louis obtained by expanding state control over finances, conscription, and military supply. Thus absolutism and warfare fed each other, as the bureaucracy created new ways to raise and maintain an army and the army's success in war justified further expansion of state power. But constant warfare also eroded the state's resources. Further administrative and legal reform, the elimination of the buying and selling of offices, and the lowering of taxes—all were made impossible by the need for more money.

The playwright Corneille wrote, no doubt optimistically, "The people are very happy when they die for their kings." What is certain is that the wars touched many peasant and urban families. The people who lived on the routes leading to the battlefields had to house and feed soldiers; only nobles were exempt from this requirement. Everyone, moreover, paid the higher taxes that were necessary to support the army. By the end of Louis's reign, one in six Frenchmen had served in the military.

❖ Absolutism in Central and Eastern Europe

Central and eastern European rulers saw in Louis XIV a powerful model of absolutist state building, yet they did not blindly emulate the Sun King, in part because they confronted conditions peculiar to their regions. The ruler of Brandenburg-Prussia had to rebuild lands ravaged by the Thirty Years' War and unite far-flung territories. The Austrian Habsburgs needed to govern a mosaic of ethnic and religious groups while fighting off the Ottoman Turks. The Russian tsars wanted to extend their power over an extensive but relatively impoverished empire. The great exception to absolutism in eastern Europe was Poland-Lithuania, where a long crisis virtually destroyed central authority and sucked much of eastern Europe into its turbulent wake.

Brandenburg-Prussia and Sweden: Militaristic Absolutism

Brandenburg-Prussia began as a puny, landlocked state on the Elbe River, but it had a remarkable future. In the nineteenth century, it would unify the disparate German states into modern-day Germany. The ruler of Brandenburg was an elector, one of the seven German princes entitled to select the Holy Roman Emperor. Since the sixteenth century the ruler of Brandenburg had also controlled the duchy of East Prussia; after 1618 the state was called Brandenburg-Prussia. Through marriages and alliances, including French support in the Thirty Years' War, Brandenburg-Prussia slowly added lands on the Rhine and the Baltic coast. Each territory had its own laws and representative institutions, called *estates*. Despite meager resources, Frederick William of Hohenzollern, the Great Elector of Brandenburg-Prussia (r. 1640–1688), succeeded in welding these scattered lands into an absolutist state.

Pressured first by the necessities of fighting the Thirty Years' War and then by the demands of reconstruction, Frederick William set four main tasks for himself: establishing his personal authority at the expense of the estates, founding a strong standing army, creating an efficient bureaucracy, and extending his territory. To force his territories' estates to grant him a dependable income, the Great Elector struck a deal with the Junkers (nobles) of each land: in exchange for allowing him to collect taxes, he gave them complete control over their enserfed peasants and exempted them from taxation. The tactic worked. By the end of his reign the estates met only on ceremonial occasions.

Supplied with a steady income, Frederick William could devote his attention to military and bureaucratic consolidation. Over forty years he expanded his army from eight thousand to thirty thousand men. (See "Taking Measure," page 613.) The army mirrored the rigid domination of nobles over peasants that characterized Brandenburg-Prussian society: peasants filled the ranks, and Junkers became officers. Each group learned discipline and obedience, with peasants serving the nobles and nobles serving the elector. Nobles also served the elector by taking positions as bureaucratic officials, but military needs always had priority. The elector named special war commissars to take charge not only of military affairs but also of tax collection. To

State	Soldiers		Population	Ratio of soldiers/ total population
France		300,000	20 million	1:66
Russia		220,000	14 million	1:64
Austria		100,000	8 million	1:80
Sweden		40,000	1 million	1:25
Brandenburg-Prussia		30,000	2 million	1:66
England		24,000	10 million	1:410

*Figures for the end of the seventeenth century, ranging from 1688 for Prussia to 1710 for France

TAKING MEASURE
The Seventeenth-Century Army

The figures in this chart are only approximate, but an important story. What conclusions can be drawn about the relative weight of the military in the different European states? Why would England have such a smaller army than the others? Is the absolute or the relative size of the military the most important indicator? From André Corvisier. *Armées et sociétés en Europe de 1494 à 1789.* (Paris: Presses Universitaires de France, 1976), 126.

hasten military dispatches, he also established one of Europe's first state postal systems.

As a Calvinist ruler, Frederick William avoided the ostentation of the French court, even while following the absolutist model of centralizing state power. He boldly rebuffed Louis XIV by welcoming twenty thousand French Huguenot refugees after Louis's revocation of the Edict of Nantes. In pursuing foreign and domestic policies that promoted state power and prestige, Frederick William adroitly switched sides in Louis's wars and would stop at almost nothing to crush resistance at home. In 1701, his son Frederick I (r. 1688–1713) persuaded Holy Roman Emperor Leopold I to grant him the title "king in Prussia." Prussia had arrived as an important power.

Across the Baltic, Sweden also stood out as an example of absolutist consolidation. In the Thirty Years' War, King Gustavus Adolphus's superb generalship and highly trained army had made Sweden the supreme power of northern Europe. The huge but sparsely populated state included not only most of present-day Sweden but also Finland, Estonia, half of Latvia, and much of the Baltic coastline of modern Poland and Germany. The Baltic, in short, was a Swedish lake. After Gustavus Adolphus died, his daughter Queen Christina (r. 1632–1654) conceded much authority to the estates. Absorbed by religion and philosophy, Christina eventually abdicated and converted to Catholicism. Her successors temporarily made Sweden an absolute monarchy.

In Sweden (as in neighboring Denmark-Norway), absolutism meant simply the estates standing aside while the king led the army in lucrative foreign campaigns. The aristocracy went along because it staffed the bureaucracy and reaped war profits. Intrigued by French culture, Sweden also gleamed with national pride. In 1668, the nobility demanded the introduction of a distinctive national costume: should Swedes, they asked, "who are so glorious and renowned a nation . . . let ourselves be led by the nose by a parcel of French dancing-masters"? Sweden spent the forty years after 1654 continuously warring with its neighbors. By the 1690s, war expenses began to outrun the small Swedish population's ability to pay, threatening the continuation of absolutism.

An Uneasy Balance: Austrian Habsburgs and Ottoman Turks

Holy Roman Emperor Leopold I (r. 1658–1705) ruled over a variety of territories of different ethnicities, languages, and religions, yet in ways similar to his French and Prussian counterparts, he gradually consolidated his power. Like all the Holy Roman emperors since 1438, Leopold was an Austrian Habsburg. He was simultaneously duke of Upper and Lower Silesia, count of Tyrol, archduke of Upper and Lower Austria, king of Bohemia, king of Hungary and Croatia, and ruler of Styria and Moravia (Map 17.2). Some of these territories were provinces in the

MAP 17.2 State Building in Central and Eastern Europe, 1648–1699
The Austrian Habsburgs had long contested the Ottoman Turks for dominance of eastern Europe, and by 1699, they had pushed the Turks out of Hungary. In central Europe, the Austrian Habsburgs confronted the growing power of Brandenburg-Prussia, which had emerged from relative obscurity after the Thirty Years' War to begin an aggressive program of expanding its military and its territorial base. As emperor of the Holy Roman Empire, the Austrian Habsburg ruler governed a huge expanse of territory, but the emperor's control was in fact only partial because of guarantees of local autonomy.

Holy Roman Empire; others were simply ruled from Vienna as Habsburg family holdings. Leopold needed to build up his armies and state authority in order to defend the Holy Roman Empire's international position, which had been weakened by the Thirty Years' War, and to push back the Ottoman Turks who steadily encroached from the southeast.

The Austrian Version of Absolutism. To forge a powerful central state, Leopold had to modernize his army and gain control over far-flung provinces that cherished their independent ways. The emperor and his closest officials took control over recruiting, provisioning, and strategic planning and worked to replace the mercenaries hired during the Thirty Years' War with a permanent standing army that promoted

professional discipline. When Leopold joined the coalition against Louis XIV in 1672, his new imperial troops fought well; and thanks to the emperor's astute diplomacy, the Austrians played a critical role in keeping Louis XIV's ambitions in check.

To pay for the army and staff his growing bureaucracy, Leopold had to gain the support of local aristocrats and chip away at provincial institutions' powers. As punishment for rebelling against Austrian rule, the Bohemians lost their right to elect a monarch; the Austrians named themselves hereditary rulers of Bohemia. To replace Bohemian nobles who had supported the 1618 revolt against Austrian authority, the Habsburgs promoted a new nobility made up of Czechs, Germans, Italians, Spaniards, and even Irish who used German as their common tongue, professed Catholicism, and loyally served the Austrian dynasty. Bohemia became a virtual Austrian colony. "You have utterly destroyed our home, our ancient kingdom, and have built us no new one in its place," lamented a Czech Jesuit in 1670, addressing Leopold. "Woe to you! . . . The nobles you have oppressed, great cities made small. Of smiling towns you have made straggling villages." Austrian censors prohibited publication of this protest for over a century.

Battle for Hungary. In addition to holding Louis XIV in check on his western frontiers, Leopold had to confront the ever-present challenge of the Ottoman Turks to his east. Hungary was the chief battle zone between Austria and the Turks for more than 150 years. In 1682, when war broke out again, Austria controlled the northwest section of Hungary; the Turks occupied the center; and in the east, the Turks demanded tribute from the Hungarian princes who ruled Transylvania. In 1683, the Turks pushed all the way to the gates of Vienna and laid siege to the Austrian capital; after reaching this high-water mark, however, Turkish power ebbed. With the help of Polish cavalry, the Austrians finally broke the siege and turned the tide in a major counter-offensive. By the Treaty of Karlowitz of 1699, the Ottoman Turks had to surrender almost all of Hungary to the Austrians.

Hungary's "liberation" from the Turks came at a high price. The fighting laid waste vast stretches of Hungary's central plain, and the population may have declined as much as 65 percent since 1600. To repopulate the land, the Austrians settled large communities of foreigners: Romanians, Croats, Serbs, and Germans. Magyar (Hungarian) speakers became a minority, and the seeds were sown for the poisonous nationality conflicts in nineteenth- and twentieth-century Hungary, Romania, and Yugoslavia.

Once the Turks had been beaten back, Austrian rule over Hungary tightened. In 1687, the Habsburg dynasty's hereditary right to the Hungarian crown was acknowledged by the Hungarian diet, a parliament revived by Leopold in 1681 to gain the support of Hungarian nobles. The diet was dominated by nobles who had amassed huge holdings in the liberated territories. They formed the core of a pro-Habsburg Hungarian aristocracy that would buttress the dynasty until it fell in 1918. As the

Turks retreated from Hungary, Leopold systematically rebuilt churches, monasteries, roadside shrines, and monuments in the flamboyant Austrian baroque style.

Ottoman State Authority. The Ottoman Turks also pursued state consolidation, but in a very different fashion from the Europeans. The Ottoman state centralized its authority through negotiation with and incorporation of bandit armies, which European rulers typically suppressed by armed force. In the seventeenth century, mutinous army officers often deposed the Ottoman ruler, or sultan, in a palace coup, but because the Ottoman state had learned to manage constant crises, the state itself survived and rarely faced peasant revolts. Rather than remaining in their villages and resisting state authorities, Ottoman peasants often left to become bandits who periodically worked for the state as

The Siege of Vienna, 1683
In this stylized rendition by Frans Geffels, the Ottoman Turks bombard the city, which had been surrounded for two months. The forces commanded by Polish king Jan Sobieski are arriving in the foreground to help lift the siege.
Museen der Stadt, Wien (detail).

mercenaries. Leaders of bandit gangs entered into negotiation with the Ottoman sultan, sometimes providing thousands of bandit mercenaries to the sultan's armies and even taking major official positions. Similarly, the Ottomans avoided revolt by the elites by playing them off against each other, absorbing some into the state bureaucracy and pitting one level of authority against another. This constantly shifting social and political system explains how the coup-ridden Ottoman state could appear "weak" in Western eyes and still pose a massive military threat on Europe's southeastern borders. In the end, the Ottoman state lasted longer than Louis XIV's absolute monarchy.

Russia: Foundations of Bureaucratic Absolutism

Superficially, seventeenth-century Russia seemed a world apart from the Europe of Louis XIV. Straddling Europe and Asia, it stretched across Siberia to the Pacific Ocean. Western visitors either sneered or shuddered at the "barbarism" of Russian life, and Russians reciprocated by nursing deep suspicions of everything foreign. But under the surface, Russia was evolving along paths much like the rest of absolutist Europe; the tsars wanted to claim unlimited autocratic power, but they had to surmount internal disorder and come to an accommodation with noble landlords.

Serfdom and the Code of 1649.   When Tsar Alexei (r. 1645–1676) tried to extend state authority by imposing new administrative structures and taxes in 1648, Moscow and other cities erupted in bloody rioting. The government immediately doused the fire. In 1649, Alexei convoked the Assembly of the Land (consisting of noble delegates from the provinces) to consult on a sweeping law code to organize Russian society in a strict social hierarchy that would last for nearly two centuries. The code of 1649 assigned all subjects to a hereditary class according to their current occupation or state needs. Slaves and free peasants were merged into a serf class. As serfs they could not change occupations or move; they were tightly tied to the soil and to their noble masters. To prevent tax evasion, the code also forbade townspeople to move from the community where they resided. Nobles owed absolute obedience to the tsar and were required to serve in the army, but in return no other group could own estates worked by serfs. Serfs became the chattel of their lord, who could sell them like horses or land. Their conditions of life differed little from those of the slaves on the plantations in the Americas.

Some peasants resisted enserfment. In 1667, Stenka Razin, a Cossack from the Don region in southern Russia, led a rebellion that promised liberation from "the traitors and bloodsuckers of the peasant communes"—the great noble landowners, local governors, and Moscow courtiers. Captured

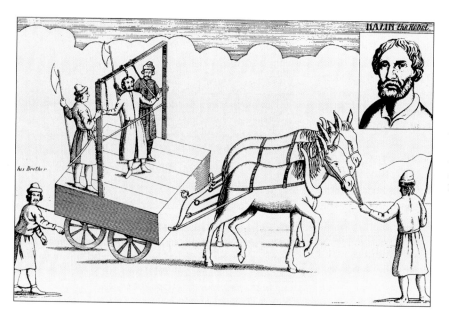

Stenka Razin in Captivity
After leading a revolt of thousands of serfs, peasants, and members of non-Russian tribes of the middle and lower Volga region, Razin was captured by Russian forces and led off to Moscow, as shown here, where he was executed in 1671. He has been the subject of songs, legends, and poems ever since. Novosti Photo Library (London).

four years later by the tsar's army, Razin was dismembered, his head and limbs publicly displayed, and his body thrown to the dogs. Thousands of his followers also suffered grisly deaths, but his memory lived on in folk songs and legends. Landlords successfully petitioned for the abolition of the statute of limitations on runaway serfs, the use of state agents in searching for runaways, and harsh penalties against those who harbored runaways. The increase in Russian state authority went hand in hand with the enforcement of serfdom.

The Tsar's Absolute Powers. To extend his power and emulate his western rivals, Tsar Alexei wanted a bigger army, exclusive control over state policy, and a greater say in religious matters. The size of the army increased dramatically from 35,000 in the 1630s to 220,000 by the end of the century. The Assembly of the Land, once an important source of noble consultation, never met again after 1653. Alexei also imposed firm control over the Russian Orthodox church. In 1666, a church council reaffirmed the tsar's role as God's direct representative on earth. The state-dominated church took action against a religious group called the Old Believers, who rejected church efforts to bring Russian worship in line with Byzantine tradition. Old Believer leaders, including the noblewoman Fedosia Morozova, endured exile, prison, and torture; whole communities of Old Believers starved or burned themselves to death rather than submit. Religious schism opened a gulf between the Russian people and the crown.

Nevertheless, modernizing trends prevailed. As the state bureaucracy expanded, adding more officials and establishing regulations and routines, the government intervened more and more in daily life. Decrees regulated tobacco smoking, card playing, and alcohol consumption and even dictated how people should leash and fence their pet dogs. Western ideas began to seep into educated circles in Moscow. Nobles and ordinary citizens commissioned portraits of themselves instead of only buying religious icons. Tsar Alexei set up the first Western-style theater in the Kremlin, and his daughter Sophia translated French plays. The most adventurous nobles began to wear German-style clothing. Some even argued that service and not just birth should determine rank. A long struggle over Western influences had begun.

Poland-Lithuania Overwhelmed

Unlike the other eastern European powers, Poland-Lithuania did not follow the absolutist model. Decades of war weakened the monarchy and made the great nobles into virtually autonomous warlords. They used the parliament and demands for constitutionalism to stymie monarchical power. The result was a precipitous slide into political disarray and weakness.

In 1648, Ukrainian Cossack warriors revolted against the king of Poland-Lithuania, inaugurating two decades of tumult known as the Deluge. Cossack bands had formed from runaway peasants and poor nobles in the no man's land of southern Russia and Ukraine. The Polish nobles who claimed this potentially rich land scorned the Cossacks as troublemakers; but to the Ukrainian peasant population they were liberators. In 1654, the Cossacks offered Ukraine to Russian rule, provoking a Russo-Polish war that ended in 1667 when the tsar annexed eastern Ukraine and Kiev. Neighboring powers tried to profit from the chaos in Poland-Lithuania; Sweden, Brandenburg-Prussia, and Transylvania sent armies to seize territory.

Poland-Lithuania in the Seventeenth Century

Many towns were destroyed in the fighting, and as much as a third of the Polish population perished. The once prosperous Jewish and Protestant minorities suffered greatly: some 56,000 Jews were killed either by the Cossacks, Polish peasants, or Russian troops, and thousands more had to flee or convert to Christianity. One rabbi wrote, "We were slaughtered each day, in a more agonizing way than cattle: they are butchered quickly, while we were being executed slowly." Surviving Jews moved from towns to *shtetls* (Jewish villages), where they took up petty trading, moneylending, tax gathering, and tavern leasing—activities that fanned peasant anti-Semitism. Desperate for protection amid the war, most Protestants backed the violently anti-Catholic Swedes, and the victorious Catholic majority branded them as traitors. Some Protestant refugees fled to the Dutch Republic and England. In Poland-Lithuania it came to be assumed that a good Pole was a Catholic. The commonwealth had ceased to be an outpost of toleration.

The commonwealth revived briefly when a man of ability and ambition, Jan Sobieski (r. 1674–1696), was elected king. He gained a reputation throughout Europe when he led 25,000 Polish cavalrymen into battle in the siege of Vienna in 1683. His cavalry helped rout the Turks and turned the tide against the Ottomans. Married to a politically shrewd French princess, Sobieski openly admired Louis XIV's France. Despite his efforts to rebuild the monarchy, he could not halt Poland-Lithuania's decline into powerlessness.

Elsewhere the ravages of war had created opportunities for kings to increase their power, but in Poland-Lithuania the great nobles gained all the advantage. They dominated the Sejm (parliament), and to maintain an equilibrium among themselves, they each wielded an absolute veto power. This "free veto" constitutional system soon deadlocked parliamentary government. The monarchy lost its room to maneuver, and with it much of its remaining power. An appalled Croat visitor in 1658 commented on the situation:

> Among the Poles there is no order in the state, and the subjects are not afraid either of the king or the judge. Everybody who is stronger thinks to have the right to oppress the weaker, just as the wolves and bears are free to capture and kill cattle. . . . Such abominable depravity is called by the Poles "aristocratic freedom."

The Polish version of constitutionalism fatally weakened the state and made it prey to neighboring powers.

❖ Constitutionalism in England

In the second half of the seventeenth century, western and eastern Europe began to move in different directions. The farther east one traveled, the more absolutist the style of government and the greater the gulf between landlord and peasant. In eastern Europe, nobles lorded over their serfs but owed almost slavish obedience in turn to their rulers. In western Europe, even in absolutist France, serfdom had almost entirely disappeared and nobles and rulers alike faced greater challenges to their control. The greatest challenges of all would come in England.

This outcome might seem surprising, for the English monarchs enjoyed many advantages compared with their continental rivals: they needed less money for their armies because they had stayed out of the Thirty Years' War, and their island kingdom was in theory easier to rule because the population they governed was only one-fourth the size of France's and relatively homogeneous ethnically. Yet the English rulers failed in their efforts to install absolutist policies. The English revolutions of 1642–1660 and 1688–1689 overturned two kings, confirmed the constitutional powers of an elected parliament, and laid the foundation for the idea that government must guarantee certain rights under the law.

England Turned Upside Down, 1642–1660

Disputes about the right to levy taxes and the nature of authority in the Church of England had long troubled the relationship between the English crown and Parliament. For over a hundred years, wealthy English landowners had been accustomed to participating in government through Parliament and expected to be consulted on royal policy. Although England had no one constitutional document, a variety of laws, judicial decisions, charters and petitions granted by the king, and customary procedures all regulated relations between king and parliament. When Charles I tried to assert his authority over Parliament, a civil war broke out in 1642. It set in motion an unpredictable chain of events, which included an extraordinary ferment of religious and political ideas. Some historians view the English civil war of 1642–1646 as the last great war of religion because it pitted Puritans against those trying to push the Anglican church toward Catholicism; others see in it the first modern revolution because it gave birth to democratic political and religious movements.

Charles I versus Parliament. When Charles I (r. 1625–1649) succeeded his father, James I, he faced an increasingly aggressive Parliament that resisted new taxes and resented the king's efforts to extend his personal control. In 1628, Parliament

Artemisia Gentileschi, *Painting*
(an allegorical self-portrait)
*Like all monarchs of his time, King Charles I of England
spent lavishly on clothing, furniture, and art. Among the
many paintings commissioned by him was this painting by
the Italian woman artist Gentileschi (1630s), which shows
the artist herself at work. Gentileschi lived at the English
court and worked for Charles between 1638 and 1641. She
painted as well for King Philip IV of Spain and for many
Italian patrons. Coming from the hand of a woman, the painting must be seen as a kind of wry commentary on women's
exclusion from most cultural endeavors. The figure supposedly
represents an allegory of painting. Most allegories—symbolic
figures standing for abstract concepts—relied on female figures, not because women did these things but because women
could be imagined as symbols. The Italian word for* painting,
*moreover, like many Romance-language words for abstrac-
tions, is gendered female* (la pittura). *But Gentileschi portrays herself, not an abstract female figure, as if to say that
real women can paint too.*
The Royal Collection. © 1998 Her Majesty Queen Elizabeth II.

forced Charles to agree to a Petition of Right by
which he promised not to levy taxes without its consent. Charles hoped to avoid further interference
with his plans by simply refusing to call Parliament
into session between 1629 and 1640. Without it, the
king's ministers had to find every loophole possible
to raise revenues. They tried to turn "ship money,"
a levy on seaports in times of emergency, into an
annual tax collected everywhere in the country. The
crown won the ensuing court case, but many subjects still refused to pay what they considered to be
an illegal tax.

Religious tensions brought conflicts over the
king's authority to a head. The Puritans had long
agitated for the removal of any vestiges of Catholicism, but Charles, married to a French Catholic,
moved in the opposite direction. With Charles's
encouragement, the archbishop of Canterbury,
William Laud (1573–1645), imposed increasingly
elaborate ceremonies on the Anglican church. Angered by these moves toward "popery," the Puritans
poured forth vituperative pamphlets and sermons.
In response Laud hauled them before the feared
Court of Star Chamber, which the king personally
controlled. The court ordered harsh sentences for
Laud's Puritan critics; they were whipped, pilloried,
branded, and even had their ears cut off and their
noses split. When Laud tried to apply his policies to
Scotland, however, they backfired completely: the
stubborn Presbyterian Scots rioted against the imposition of the Anglican prayer book—the Book of
Common Prayer—and in 1640 they invaded the
north of England. To raise money to fight the war,
Charles called Parliament into session and unwittingly opened the door to a constitutional and religious crisis.

The Parliament of 1640 did not intend revolution, but reformers in the House of Commons (the
lower house of Parliament) wanted to undo what
they saw as the royal tyranny of the 1630s. Parliament removed Laud from office, ordered the execution of an unpopular royal commander, abolished
the Court of Star Chamber, repealed recently levied
taxes, and provided for a parliamentary assembly at
least once every three years, thus establishing a constitutional check on royal authority. Moderate reformers expected to stop there and resisted Puritan
pressure to abolish bishops and eliminate the Anglican prayer book. But their hand was forced in January 1642, when Charles and his soldiers invaded

Parliament and tried unsuccessfully to arrest those leaders who had moved to curb his power. Faced with mounting opposition within London, Charles quickly withdrew from the city and organized an army. The stage was set for a civil war between king and parliament.

Civil War and the Challenge to All Authorities.   The war lasted four years (1642–1646) and divided the country. The king's army of royalists, known as Cavaliers, enjoyed most support in northern and western England. The parliamentary forces, called Roundheads because they cut their hair short, had their stronghold in the southeast, including London. Although Puritans domi-

nated on the parliamentary side, they were divided among themselves about the proper form of church government: the Presbyterians wanted a Calvinist church with some central authority, whereas the Independents favored entirely autonomous congregations free from other church government (hence the term *congregationalism*, often associated with the Independents). Putting aside their differences for the sake of military unity,

England during the Civil War

the Puritans united under an obscure member of the House of Commons, the country gentleman Oliver Cromwell (1599–1658), who sympathized with the Independents. After Cromwell skillfully reorganized the parliamentary troops, his New Model Army defeated the Cavaliers at the battle of Naseby in 1645. Charles surrendered in 1646.

Although the civil war between king and Parliament had ended in victory for Parliament, divisions within the Puritan ranks now came to the fore: the Presbyterians dominated Parliament, but the Independents controlled the army. Both factions' leaders belonged to the social and political elite, but the Independents favored more far-reaching political and religious changes than the Presbyterians. Their disputes drew lower-class groups into the debate. (See "Contrasting Views," page 622.) The most

important were the Levellers, who emerged among disgruntled soldiers when Parliament tried to disband the New Model Army. In 1647, the Levellers honed their ideas about the nature of political authority in a series of debates between soldiers and officers at an army camp near London. They insisted that Parliament meet annually, that members be paid so as to allow common people to participate, and that all male heads of households be allowed to vote. Their proposed democracy excluded servants, the propertyless, and women but nonetheless "leveled" social differences (hence their name) by offering political access to artisans, shopkeepers, and modest farmers. Cromwell and other army leaders rejected the Levellers' demands as threatening to property owners. Cromwell insisted, "You have no other way to deal with these men but to break them in pieces. . . . If you do not break them they will break you."

Just as political differences between Presbyterians and Independents helped spark new democratic political movements, so too their conflicts over church organization fostered the emergence of new religious doctrines. The new sects had in common only their emphasis on the "inner light" of individual religious inspiration and a disdain for hierarchical authority. Their emphasis on equality before God and democracy within the church appealed to the middle and lower classes. The Baptists, for example, insisted on adult baptism because they believed that Christians should choose their own church and that every child should not automatically become a member of the Church of England. The Quakers demonstrated their beliefs in equality and the inner light by refusing to doff their hats to men in authority. Manifesting their religious experience by trembling, or "quaking," the Quakers believed that anyone—man or woman—inspired by a direct experience of God could preach.

Parliamentary leaders feared that the new sects would overturn the whole social hierarchy. Rumors abounded, for example, of naked Quakers running through the streets waiting "for a sign." Some sects did advocate sweeping change. The Diggers promoted rural communism—collective ownership of all property. Seekers and Ranters questioned just about everything. One notorious Ranter, John Robins, even claimed to be God. A few men advocated free love. These developments convinced the political elite that tolerating the new sects would lead to skepticism, anarchism, and debauchery.

One Evins a welch-man was lately comited to New-gate for saying hee was Christ

Iesuit

Heer's one blasphemously That hee was christ did say Such spirits were foretold To rise ith latter daye

Arminian

Libertin

Ante Scripturian

Soule Sleeper

Anabaptist

Diuorcer

Religious Radicals

The Puritans in Parliament had opposed the Catholic leanings of the Church of England (shown as the Arminian here) and worried that Catholic missionary groups, such as the Jesuits (top left), might gain access to England. But they also detested the nonconformist Protestant sects that sprang up during the civil war: some individuals, called Ranters or Seekers, supposedly claimed they were Jesus come again; Arians rejected the doctrine of the Trinity; libertines attacked all sacramental objects of religion, anti-scriptarians rejected the authority of the Bible; soul sleepers denied the afterlife; Anabaptists refused infant baptism; the family of love did not keep the sabbath; and some advocated easier divorce. It should be remembered that pamphlets such as this one represented the views of those who opposed these tendencies. It is questionable, for example, whether Arians believed in free love, libertines attacked religious objects, or those in favor of easier divorce beat their wives.
British Library.

In keeping with their notions of equality and individual inspiration, many of the new sects provided opportunities for women to become preachers and prophets. The Quakers thought women especially capable of prophecy. One prophet, Anna Trapnel, explained her vocation: "For in all that was said by me, I was nothing, the Lord put all in my mouth, and told me what I should say." Women presented petitions, participated prominently in street demonstrations, distributed tracts, and occasionally even dressed as men, wearing swords and joining armies. The duchess of Newcastle complained in 1650 that women were "affecting a Masculinacy . . . practicing the behaviour . . . of men." The outspoken women in new sects like the Quakers underscored the threat of a social order turning upside down.

Oliver Cromwell. At the heart of the continuing political struggle was the question of what to do with the king, who tried to negotiate with the Presbyterians in Parliament. In late 1648, Independents

The English Civil War

The civil war between Charles I and Parliament (1642–1646) excited furious debates about the proper forms of political authority, debates that influenced political thought for two centuries or more. The Levellers, who served in the parliamentary army, wanted Parliament to be more accountable to ordinary men like themselves (Document 1). When the king came to trial in January 1649, he laid out the royalist case for the supremacy of the king (Document 2). After the restoration of the monarchy in 1660, Lucy Hutchinson wrote a memoir in which she complained that *Puritan* had become a term of political slander. Her memoir shows how religious terms had been politicized by the upheaval (Document 3). Thomas Hobbes in his famous political treatise *Leviathan* (1651) develops the consequences of the civil war for political theory (Document 4).

1. The Levellers, "The Agreement of the People, as Presented to the Council of the Army" (October 28, 1647)

Note especially two things about this document: (1) it focuses on Parliament as the chief instrument of reform and demands proportional or democratic representation; and (2) it claims that government depends on the consent of the people.

. . . Since, therefore, our former oppressions and scarce-yet-ended troubles have been occasioned, either by want of frequent national meetings in Council [Parliament], or by rendering those meetings ineffectual, we are fully agreed and resolved to provide that hereafter our representatives be neither left to an uncertainty for the time nor made useless to the ends for which they are intended. In order whereunto we declare:—

That the people of England, being at this day very unequally distributed by Counties, Cities, and Borough for the election of their deputies in Parliament, ought to be more indifferently [equally] proportioned according to the number of the inhabitants. . . .

That the power of this, and all future Representatives of this Nation, is inferior only to theirs who choose them, and doth extend, without the consent or concurrence of any other person or persons [the king], to the enacting, altering, and repealing of laws, to the erecting and abolishing of offices and courts, to the appointing, removing, and calling to account magistrates and officers of all degrees, to the making war and peace, to the treating with foreign States [in other words, Parliament is the supreme power, not the king]. . . .

These things we declare to be our native rights, and therefore are agreed and resolved to maintain them with our utmost possibilities against all opposition whatsoever. . . .

Source: Samuel Rawson Gardiner, *The Constitutional Documents of the Puritan Revolution, 1625–1660* (1906), 333–35.

2. Charles I's Refusal of the Jurisdiction of the Court Appointed to Try Him (January 21, 1649)

Charles argued that his trial was illegal. He cast himself as the true defender of English liberties and accused Parliament of going against both the Bible and English law.

The duty I owe to God in the preservation of the true liberty of my people will not suffer me at this time to be silent: for, how can any free-born subject of England call life or anything he possesseth his own, if power without right daily make new, and abrogate the old fundamental laws of the land which I now take to be the present case? . . . Now I am most confident this day's proceeding cannot be warranted by God's laws; for, on the contrary, the authority of obedience unto Kings is clearly warranted, and strictly commanded in both the Old and New Testament. . . .

Then for the law of this land, I am no less confident, that no learned lawyer will affirm that an impeachment can lie against the King, they all going in his name: and one of the maxims is, that the King can do no wrong.

Thus you see that I speak not for my own right alone, as I am your King, but also for the true liberty of all my subjects, which consists not in the power of government, but in living under such laws, such a government, as may give themselves the best assurance of their lives, and property of their goods.

Source: Stuart E. Prall, ed., *The Puritan Revolution: A Documentary History* (Gloucester, Mass.: Peter Smith, 1973), 186–88.

3. Lucy Hutchinson, Memoirs of the Life of Colonel Hutchinson *(1664–1671)*

Lucy Hutchinson wrote her memoir to defend her Puritan husband, who had been imprisoned upon the restoration of the monarchy.

If any were grieved at the dishonour of the kingdom, or the griping of the poor, or the unjust oppressions of the subject by a thousand ways invented to maintain the riots of the courtiers and the swarms of needy Scots the king had brought in to devour like locusts the plenty of this land, he was a puritan; if any showed favour to any godly, honest person, kept them company, relieved them in want, or protected them against violent and unjust oppression, he was a puritan. . . . In short, all that crossed the views of the needy courtiers, the proud encroaching priests, the thievish projectors, the lewd nobility and gentry . . . all these were puritans; and if puritans, then enemies to the king and his government, seditious, factious hypocrites, ambitious disturbers of the public peace, and finally the pest of the kingdom.

Source: Christopher Hill and Edmund Dell, eds., *The Good Old Cause: The English Revolution of 1640–1660, Its Causes, Course and Consequences* (London: Lawrence and Wishart, 1949), 179–80.

4. Thomas Hobbes, Leviathan *(1651)*

In this excerpt, Hobbes depicts the anarchy of a society without a strong central authority, but he leaves open the question of whether that authority should be vested in "one Man" or "one Assembly of men," that is, a king or a parliament.

During the time men live without a common Power to keep them all in awe, they are in that condition which is called Warre; and such a warre, as is of every man, against every man. . . . In such condition, there is no place for Industry; because the fruit thereof is uncertain: and consequently no Culture of the Earth; no Navigation, nor use of the commodities that may be imported by Sea; no commodious Building; no Instrument of moving, and removing such things as require much force; no Knowledge of the face of the Earth; no account of Time; no Arts; no Letters; no Society; and which is worst of all, continuall feare, and danger of violent death; And the life of man, solitary, poore, nasty, brutish, and short.

The only way to erect such a Common Power, as may be able to defend them from the invasion of Forraigners, and the injuries of one another, and thereby to secure them in such sort, as that by their owne industrie, and by the Fruites of the Earth, they may nourish themselves and live contentedly; is, to conferre all their power and strength upon one Man, or upon one Assembly of men, that may reduce all their wills, by plurality of voices, unto one Will. . . . This is more than Consent, or Concord; it is a reall Unitie of them all, in one and the same Person, made by Covenant of every man with every man. . . . This done, the Multitude so united in one Person, is called a COMMON-WEALTH, in latine CIVITAS. This is the Generation of that great LEVIATHAN, or rather (to speake more reverently) of that *Mortall God,* to which wee owe under the *Imortall God,* our peace and defence.

Source: Thomas Hobbes, *Leviathan,* ed. Richard E. Flathman and David Johnston (New York: Norton, 1997), 70, 95.

QUESTIONS FOR DEBATE
1. Which of these views do you find most persuasive?
2. Why did Hobbes's arguments about political authority upset supporters of both monarchy and Parliament?

Death Warrant of Charles I
Parliament voted to try Charles I for treason, and the trial began in January 1649. A week later the court found Charles to be a "tyrant, traitor, murderer, and public enemy" and ordered his execution. When the monarchy was restored in 1660, everyone who signed Charles I's death warrant was hunted down and executed.
Mary Evans Picture Library.

Silk Shirt Worn by Charles I at His Execution
The blood is still visible on the shirt worn by Charles I for his beheading. After his head was severed, many people rushed forward to dip their handkerchiefs in the blood, which some believed to have miraculous qualities. His wife and son fled to France.
Museum of London Photographic Library.

in the army purged the Presbyterians from Parliament, leaving a "rump" of about seventy members. This Rump Parliament then created a high court to try Charles I. The court found him guilty of attempting to establish "an unlimited and tyrannical power" and pronounced a death sentence. On January 30, 1649, Charles was beheaded before an enormous crowd, which reportedly groaned as one when the axe fell. Although many had objected to Charles's autocratic rule, few had wanted him killed. For royalists, Charles immediately became a martyr, and reports of miracles, such as the curing of blindness by the touch of a handkerchief soaked in his blood, soon circulated.

The Rump Parliament abolished the monarchy and the House of Lords (the upper house of Parliament) and set up a Puritan republic with Oliver Cromwell as chairman of the Council of State. Cromwell did not tolerate dissent from his policies. He saw the hand of God in events and himself as God's agent. Pamphleteers and songwriters ridiculed his red nose and accused him of wanting to be king, but few challenged his leadership. When his agents discovered plans for mutiny within the army, they executed the perpetrators; new decrees silenced the Levellers. Although Cromwell allowed the various Puritan sects to worship rather freely and permitted Jews with needed skills to return to England for the first time since the thirteenth century, Catholics could not worship publicly, nor could Anglicans use the Book of Common Prayer. The elites—many of them were still Anglican—were troubled by Cromwell's religious policies but pleased to see some social order reestablished.

The new regime aimed to extend state power just as Charles I had before. Cromwell laid the foundation for a Great Britain made up of England, Ireland, and Scotland by reconquering Scotland and subduing Ireland. Anti-English rebels in Ireland had seized the occasion of troubles between king and Parliament to revolt in 1641. When his position was secured in 1649, Cromwell went to Ireland with a large force and easily defeated the rebels, massacring whole garrisons and their priests. He encouraged expropriating the lands of the Irish "barbarous wretches," and Scottish immigrants resettled the northern county of Ulster. This seventeenth-century English conquest left a legacy of bitterness that

Oliver Cromwell
Shown here preparing for battle, Cromwell lived an austere life but believed fiercely in his own personal righteousness. As leader he tolerated no opposition. When he died, he was buried in Westminster Abbey, but in 1661 his body was exhumed and hanged in its shroud. His head was cut off and displayed outside Westminster Hall for nearly twenty years.
Courtesy of the National Portrait Gallery, London.

the Irish even today call "the curse of Cromwell." In 1651, Parliament turned its attention overseas, putting mercantilist ideas into practice in the first Navigation Act, which allowed imports only if they were carried on English ships or came directly from the producers of goods. The Navigation Act was aimed at the Dutch, who dominated world trade; Cromwell tried to carry the policy further by waging naval war on the Dutch from 1652 to 1654.

At home, however, Cromwell faced growing resistance. His wars required a budget twice the size of Charles I's, and his increases in property taxes and customs duties alienated landowners and merchants. The conflict reached a crisis in 1653: Parliament considered disbanding the army, whereupon Cromwell abolished the Rump Parliament in a military coup and made himself Lord Protector. He now silenced his critics by banning newspapers and using networks of spies and mail readers to keep tabs on his enemies. Although he assumed some trappings of royalty, he refused the crown. When he died in 1658, one opponent claimed, "There were none that cried but dogs." Cromwell intended that his son should succeed him, but his death only revived the prospect of civil war and political chaos. In 1660, a newly elected, staunchly Anglican Parliament invited Charles II, the son of the executed king, to return from exile.

The "Glorious Revolution" of 1688

Most English welcomed back the king in 1660. According to one royalist, throughout the realm "the ways were strewed with flowers, the bells ringing, the streets hung with tapestry, fountains running with wine." The restoration of royal authority in 1660 whisked away the more austere elements of Puritan culture and revived old traditions of celebration—drinking, merrymaking, and processions of young maidens in royalist colors. But the religious policies of Charles II and his successor, James II, ensured that conflicts between king and Parliament would erupt once again.

The Restored Monarchy.   In 1660, the traditional monarchical form of government was reinstated, restoring the king to full partnership with Parliament. Charles II (r. 1660–1685) promised "a liberty to tender consciences" in an attempt to extend religious toleration, especially to Catholics, with whom

Great Fire of London, 1666

This view of London shows the three-day fire at its height. The writer John Evelyn described the scene in his diary: "All the sky was of a fiery aspect, like the top of a burning oven, and the light seen above 40 miles round about for many nights. God grant mine eyes may never behold the like, who now saw above 10,000 houses all in one flame; the noise and cracking and thunder of people, the fall of towers, houses, and churches, was like an hideous storm." Everyone in London at the time felt overwhelmed by the catastrophe, and many attributed it to God's punishment for the upheavals of the 1640s and 1650s.
Museum of London Photographic Library.

he sympathized. Yet more than a thousand Puritan ministers lost their positions, and after 1664, attending a service other than one conforming with the Anglican prayer book was illegal.

Natural disasters marred the early years of Charles II's reign. The plague stalked London's rat-infested streets in May 1665 and claimed more than thirty thousand victims by September. Then in 1666, the Great Fire swept the city. Diarist Samuel Pepys described its terrifying progress: "It made me weep to see it. The churches, houses, and all on fire and flaming at once, and a horrid noise the flames made, and the cracking of houses at their ruine." The crown now had a city as well as a monarchy to rebuild.

The restoration of monarchy made some in Parliament fear that the English government would come to resemble French absolutism. This fear was not unfounded. In 1670, Charles II made a secret agreement, soon leaked, with Louis XIV in which he promised to announce his conversion to Catholicism in exchange for money for a war against the Dutch. Charles never proclaimed himself a Catholic, but in his Declaration of Indulgence (1673) he did suspend all laws against Catholics and Protestant dissenters. Parliament refused to continue funding the Dutch war unless Charles rescinded his Declaration of Indulgence. Asserting its authority further, Parliament passed the Test Act in 1673, requiring all government officials to profess allegiance to the Church of England and in effect disavow Catholic doctrine. Then in 1678, Parliament precipitated the so-called Exclusion Crisis by explicitly denying the throne to a Roman Catholic. This action was aimed at the king's brother and heir, James, an open convert to Catholicism. Charles refused to allow it to become law.

The dynastic crisis over the succession of a Catholic gave rise to two distinct factions in Parliament: the Tories, who supported a strong, hereditary monarchy and the restored ceremony of the Anglican church, and the Whigs, who advocated parliamentary supremacy and toleration for Protestant dissenters such as Presbyterians. Both labels were originally derogatory: *Tory* meant an Irish Catholic bandit; *Whig* was the Irish Catholic designation for a Presbyterian Scot. The Tories favored James's succession despite his Catholicism, whereas the Whigs opposed a Catholic monarch. The loose moral atmosphere of Charles's court also offended some Whigs, who complained tongue in cheek that Charles was father of his country in much too literal a fashion (he had fathered more than one child by his mistresses but produced no legitimate heir).

Parliament's Revolt against James II. Upon Charles's death, his brother, James, succeeded to the throne as James II (r. 1685–1688). James pursued pro-Catholic and absolutist policies even more aggressively than his brother. When a male heir—who would take precedence over James's two adult Protestant daughters and be reared a Catholic—was born, Tories and Whigs banded together. They invited the Dutch ruler William, prince of Orange and the husband of James's older daughter, Mary, to invade England. James fled to France and hardly any blood was shed. Parliament offered the throne jointly to William (r. 1689–1702) and Mary (r. 1689–1694) on the condition that they accept a bill of rights guaranteeing Parliament's full partnership in a constitutional government.

In the Bill of Rights, William and Mary agreed not to raise a standing army or to levy taxes without Parliament's consent. They also agreed to call meetings of Parliament at least every three years, to guarantee free elections to parliamentary seats, and to abide by Parliament's decisions and not suspend duly passed laws. The agreement gave England's constitutional government a written, legal basis by formally recognizing Parliament as a self-contained, independent body that shared power with the rulers. Victorious supporters of the coup declared it the "Glorious Revolution." Constitutionalism had triumphed over absolutism in England.

The propertied classes who controlled Parliament eagerly consolidated their power and prevented any resurgence of the popular turmoil of the 1640s. The Toleration Act of 1689 granted all Protestants freedom of worship, though non-Anglicans were still excluded from the universities; Catholics got no rights but were more often left alone to worship privately. In Ireland the Catholics rose to defend James II, but William and Mary's troops brutally suppressed them. With the Whigs in power and the Tories in opposition, wealthy landowners now controlled political life throughout the realm. The factions' differences, however, were minor; essentially, the Tories had less access to the king's patronage. A contemporary reported that King William had said "that if he had good places [honors and land] enough to bestow, he should soon unite the two parties."

❖ Constitutionalism in the Dutch Republic and the Overseas Colonies

When William and Mary came to the throne in England in 1689, the Dutch and the English put aside the rivalries that had brought them to war against each other in 1652–1654, 1665–1667, and 1672–1674. Under William, the Dutch and the English together led the coalition that blocked Louis XIV's efforts to dominate continental Europe. The English and Dutch had much in common: oriented toward commerce, especially overseas, they were the successful exceptions to absolutism in Europe. Also among the few outposts of constitutionalism in the seventeenth century were the British North American colonies, which developed representative government while the English were preoccupied with their revolutions at home. Constitutionalism was not the only factor shaping this Atlantic world; as constitutionalism developed in the colonies, so too did the enslavement of black Africans as a new labor force.

The Dutch Republic

When the Dutch Republic gained formal independence from Spain in 1648, it had already established a decentralized, constitutional state. The individual provinces granted power over foreign policy to the Estates General, an assembly made up of deputies from each province, but local authorities jealously guarded most of the power. Rich merchants called *regents* effectively controlled the internal affairs of each province and through the Estates General named the *stadholder*, the executive officer responsible for defense and for representing the state at all ceremonial occasions. They almost always chose one of the princes of the house of Orange, but the prince of Orange resembled a president more than a king. One foreign visitor observed that the Dutch "behave as if all men were created equal," but in fact real power remained in the hands of the regents, not the common people.

The decentralized state encouraged and protected trade, and the Dutch Republic soon became Europe's financial capital. The Bank of Amsterdam offered interest rates less than half those available in England and France. Praised for their industriousness, thrift, and cleanliness—and maligned as greedy, dull "butter-boxes"—the Dutch dominated overseas commerce with their shipping (Map 17.3). They imported products from all over the world: spices, tea,

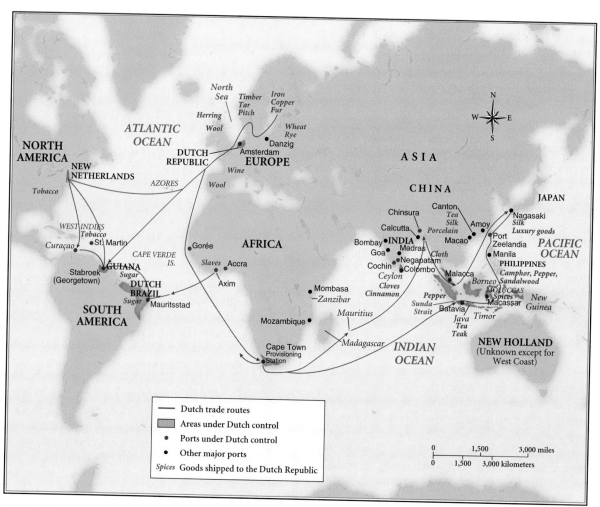

MAP 17.3 Dutch Commerce in the Seventeenth Century

Even before gaining formal independence from the Spanish in 1648, the Dutch had begun to compete with the Spanish and Portuguese all over the world. In 1602, a group of merchants established the Dutch East India Company, which soon offered investors an annual rate of return of 35 percent on the trade in spices with countries located on the Indian Ocean. Global commerce gave the Dutch the highest standard of living in Europe and soon attracted the envy of the French and the English.

and silk from Asia; sugar and tobacco from the Americas; wool from England and Spain; timber and furs from Scandinavia; grain from eastern Europe. (See "Did You Know?", page 630.) One English traveler in 1660 described the riches of Amsterdam as superior to those of Venice and called the Hague "the most pleasant place in the world." A widely reprinted history of Amsterdam that appeared in 1662 described the city as "risen through the hand of God to the peak of prosperity and greatness. . . . The whole world stands amazed at its riches and from east and west, north and south they come to behold it."

The Dutch rapidly became the most prosperous and best-educated people in Europe. Middle-class people supported the visual arts, especially painting, to an unprecedented degree. Artists and engravers produced thousands of works, and Dutch artists were among the first to sell to a mass market. Whereas in other countries kings, nobles, and churches bought art, Dutch buyers were merchants, artisans, and shopkeepers. Engravings, illustrated histories, and oil paintings, even those of the widely acclaimed Rembrandt van Rijn (1606–1669), were all relatively inexpensive. One foreigner commented that "pictures are very common here, there being scarce an ordinary tradesman whose house is not decorated with them." The pictures reflected the Dutch interest in familiar daily details: children at play, winter landscapes, and ships in port.

The family household, not the royal court, determined the moral character of this intensely commercial society. Dutch society fostered public enterprise in men and work in the home for women, who were expected to filter out the greed and materialism of commercial society by maintaining domestic harmony and virtue. Relative prosperity decreased the need for married women to work, so Dutch society developed the clear contrast between middle-class male and female roles that would become prevalent elsewhere in Europe and in America more than a century later. As one contemporary Dutch writer explained, "The husband must be on the street to practice his trade; the wife must stay at home to be in the kitchen."

Extraordinarily high levels of urbanization and literacy created a large reading public. Dutch presses printed books censored elsewhere (printers or authors censored in one province simply shifted operations to another), and the University of Leiden attracted students and professors from all over Eu-

A Typical Dutch Scene from Daily Life
Jan Steen painted The Baker Arent Oostward and His Wife *in 1658. Steen ran a brewery and tavern in addition to painting, and he was known for his interest in the details of daily life. Dutch artists popularized this kind of "genre" painting, which showed ordinary people at work and play.*
Rijksmuseum, Amsterdam.

rope. Dutch tolerance extended to the works of Benedict Spinoza (1633–1677), a Jewish philosopher and biblical scholar who was expelled by his synagogue for alleged atheism but left alone by the Dutch authorities. Spinoza strove to reconcile religion with science and mathematics, but his work scandalized many Christians and Jews because he seemed to equate God and nature. Like nature, Spinoza's God followed unchangeable laws and could not be influenced by human actions, prayers, or faith.

Dutch learning, painting, and commerce all enjoyed wide renown in the seventeenth century, but this luster proved hard to maintain. The Dutch lived in a world of international rivalries in which strong central authority gave their enemies an advantage. Though inconclusive, the naval wars with England drained the state's revenues. Even more dangerous

Tobacco and the Invention of "Smoking"

In the early seventeenth century, a "new astonishing fashion," wrote a German ambassador, had come to the Dutch Republic from the New World. For a long time there was no word for what you did with tobacco; *smoking* came to be commonly used as a term only in the seventeenth century. Until then one spoke of "a fog-drinking bout," "drinking smoke," or "drinking tobacco." One Jesuit preacher called it "dry drunkenness." The analogy to inebriation is not entirely far-fetched, for nicotine (named after the French ambassador to Portugal, Jean Nicot, who brought tobacco to France in the mid-sixteenth century) does have an effect more comparable to alcohol than to caffeine; nicotine is a nerve toxin that dulls the nervous system. It is not known exactly where in the Americas tobacco had its birthplace, but its use was widespread by the time the Europeans arrived. Mayans and Aztecs smoked ceremonial pipes, Incas used tobacco as a medicine, and Indians in Brazil took snuff.

Spain began exporting tobacco to other European countries in the sixteenth century. The Spanish did not exploit the possibilities of producing tobacco on plantations; tobacco growing began in earnest in the seventeenth century only with the spread of black slavery. Virginia and Maryland expanded their exports of tobacco sixfold between 1663 and 1699. Until 1700, Amsterdam dominated the curing process; half the tobacco factories in Amsterdam were owned by Jewish merchants of Spanish or Portuguese descent.

Smoking spread geographically from western to eastern Europe, socially from the upper classes downward, and from men to women. At first the Spanish preferred cigars, the British pipes, and the French snuff. In the eighteenth century, both upper- and middle-class women took snuff, which was considered an aristocratic taste. Before the end of the nineteenth century, women did not regularly take tobacco in any form other than snuff. A woman smoking a pipe or cigar was a favorite target of cartoonists in the eighteenth and nineteenth centuries. This changed with the Russian invention of the cigarette in the mid-nineteenth century. Women began to smoke cigarettes in the late 1800s as a sign of emancipation.

Source: Wolfgang Schivelbusch, *Tastes of Paradise: A Social History of Spices, Stimulants, and Intoxicants,* trans. David Jacobson, 1993.

The Vice of Tobacco
In this engraving of 1628, The Vice of Tobacco, *the Dutch artist Gillis van Scheyndel portrays smoking as similar to excessive drinking, a habit that makes people sick and leads them astray. Pipes often symbolized the folly and futility of a life given over to materialistic pleasures. The company of revelers is led on by a pipe-smoking ape who has features like a devil.* Koninklijke Bibliotheek.

were the land wars with France, which continued into the eighteenth century. The Dutch survived these challenges but increasingly depended on alliances with other powers, such as England. At the end of the seventeenth century, the regent elite became more exclusive, more preoccupied with ostentation, less tolerant of deviations from strict Calvinism, and more concerned with imitating French styles. Dutch architecture, painting, and intellectual life eventually came under French influence.

Freedom and Slavery in the New World

The French and English also increasingly overshadowed the Dutch in the New World colonies. While the Dutch concentrated on shipping, including the slave trade, the seventeenth-century French and English established settler colonies that would eventually provide fabulous revenues to the home countries. Many European governments encouraged private companies to vie for their share of the slave trade, and slavery began to take clear institutional form in the New World in this period. Even while slavery offered only a degrading form of despotism to black Africans, whites found in the colonies greater political and religious freedom than in Europe.

The Rise of the Slave Trade.   After the Spanish and Portuguese had shown that African slaves could be transported and forced to labor in South and Central America, the English and French endeavored to set up similar labor systems in their new Caribbean island colonies. White planters with large tracts of land bought African slaves to work fields of sugarcane, and as they gradually built up their holdings, the planters displaced most of the original white settlers, who moved to mainland colonies. After 1661, when Barbados instituted a slave code that stripped all Africans of rights under English law, slavery became codified as an inherited status that applied only to blacks. The result was a society of extremes: the very wealthy whites, about 7 percent of the population in Barbados; and the enslaved, powerless black majority. The English brought little of their religious or constitutional practices to the Caribbean. Other Caribbean colonies followed a similar pattern of development. Louis XIV promulgated a "black code" in 1685 to regulate the legal status of slaves in the French colonies. Although one

of his aims was to prevent non-Catholics from owning slaves in the French colonies, the code had much the same effect as the English codes on the slaves themselves: they had no legal rights.

The highest church and government authorities in Catholic and Protestant countries alike condoned the gradually expanding slave trade; the governments of England, France, Spain, Portugal, the Dutch Republic, and Denmark all encouraged private companies to traffic in black Africans. The Dutch West India Company was the most successful of them. In 1600, about 9,500 Africans were exported from Africa to the New World every year; by 1700, this had increased nearly fourfold to 36,000 annually. Historians advance several different factors for the increase in the slave trade: some claim that improvements in muskets made European slavers more formidable; others cite the rising price for slaves which made their sale more attractive for Africans; still others focus on factors internal to Africa such as the increasing size of African armies and their use of muskets in fighting and capturing other Africans for sale as slaves. Whatever the reason, the way had been prepared for the development of an Atlantic economy based on slavery.

Constitutional Freedoms in the English Colonies. Virtually left to themselves during the upheavals in England, the fledgling English colonies in North America developed representative government on their own. Almost every colony had a governor and a two-house legislature. The colonial legislatures constantly sought to increase their power and resisted the efforts of Charles II and James II to reaffirm royal control. William and Mary reluctantly allowed emerging colonial elites more control over local affairs. The social and political elite among the settlers hoped to impose an English social hierarchy dominated by rich landowners. Ordinary immigrants to the colonies, however, took advantage of plentiful land to carve out their own farms using white servants and, later, in some colonies, African slaves.

For native Americans, the expanding European presence meant something else altogether. They faced death through disease and warfare and the accelerating loss of their homelands. Unlike white settlers, native Americans believed that land was a divine gift provided for their collective use and not subject to individual ownership. As a result,

Europeans' claims that they owned exclusive land rights caused frequent skirmishes. In 1675–1676, for instance, three tribes allied under Metacomet (called King Philip by the English) threatened the survival of New England settlers, who savagely repulsed the attacks and sold their captives as slaves. Whites portrayed native Americans as conspiring villains and sneaky heathens, who were akin to Africans in their savagery.

❖ The Search for Order in Elite and Popular Culture

The early success of constitutionalism in England, the Dutch Republic, and the English North American colonies would help to shape a distinctive Atlantic world in the eighteenth century. Just how constitutionalism was linked to the growing commerce with the colonies remains open to dispute, however, since the constitutional governments, like the absolutist ones, avidly pursued profits in the burgeoning slave trade. Freedom did not mean liberty for everyone. One of the great debates of the time—and of much of the modern world that followed—concerned the meaning of freedom: for whom, under what conditions, with what justifiable limitations could freedom be claimed?

There was no freedom without order to sustain it, and most Europeans feared disorder above all else. In 1669, the English writer Margaret Cavendish, duchess of Newcastle, cataloged some of the sources of disorder in her time: "I wish Men were as Harmless as most Beasts are, then surely the World would be more Quiet and Happy than it is, for then there would not be such Pride, Vanity, Ambition, Covetousness, Faction, Treachery, and Treason, as is now." Cavendish wrote not long after the restoration of the monarchy in England, and her thoughts echoed the titanic struggles that had taken place over the nature of authority, not only in England but throughout Europe. Political theories, science, poetry, painting, and architecture all reflected in some measure the attempts to ground authority—to define the relation between freedom and order—in new ways. Authority concerned not just rulers and subjects but also the hierarchy of groups in society. As European states consolidated their powers,

elites worked to distinguish themselves from the lower classes. They developed new codes of correct behavior for themselves and tried to teach order and discipline to their social inferiors.

Social Contract Theory: Hobbes and Locke

The turmoil of the times prompted a major rethinking of the foundations of all authority. Two figures stood out prominently amid the cacophony of voices: Thomas Hobbes and John Locke. Their writings fundamentally shaped the modern subject of political science. Hobbes justified absolute authority; Locke provided the rationale for constitutionalism. Yet both argued that all authority came not from divine right but from a "social contract" between citizens.

Hobbes. Thomas Hobbes (1588–1679) was a royalist who sat out the English civil war of the 1640s in France, where he tutored the future king Charles II. Returning to England in 1651, he published his masterpiece, *Leviathan* (1651), in which he argued for unlimited authority in a ruler. Absolute authority could be vested in either a king or a parliament; it had to be absolute, he insisted, in order to overcome the defects of human nature. Believing that people are essentially self-centered and driven by the "right to self-preservation," Hobbes made his case by referring to science, not religion. To Hobbes, human life in a state of nature—that is, any situation without firm authority—was "solitary, poor, nasty, brutish, and short." He believed that the desire for power and natural greed would inevitably lead to unfettered competition. Only the assurance of social order could make people secure enough to act according to law; consequently, giving up personal liberty, he maintained, was the price of collective security. Rulers derived their power, he concluded, from a contract in which absolute authority protects people's rights.

Hobbes's notion of rule by an absolute authority left no room for political dissent or nonconformity, and it infuriated both royalists and supporters of Parliament. He enraged royalists by arguing that authority came not from divine right but from the social contract between citizens. Parliamentary supporters resisted Hobbes's claim that rulers must possess absolute authority to prevent the greater evil of anarchy; they believed that a constitution should guarantee shared power between king and parliament and protect individual rights under the law. Like Machiavelli before him, Hobbes became associated with a cynical, pessimistic view of human nature, and future political theorists often began their arguments by refuting Hobbes.

Locke. Rejecting both Hobbes and the more traditional royalist defenses of absolute authority, John Locke (1632–1704) used the notion of a social contract to provide a foundation for constitutionalism. Locke experienced political life firsthand as physician, secretary, and intellectual companion to the earl of Shaftesbury, a leading English Whig. In 1683, during the Exclusion Crisis, Locke fled with Shaftesbury to the Dutch Republic. There he continued work on his *Two Treatises of Government*, which, when published in 1690, served to justify the Glorious Revolution of 1688. Locke's position was thoroughly anti-absolutist. He denied the divine right of kings and ridiculed the common royalist idea that political power in the state mirrored the father's authority in the family. Like Hobbes, he posited a state of nature that applied to all people. Unlike Hobbes, however, he thought people were reasonable and the state of nature peaceful.

Locke insisted that government's only purpose was to protect life, liberty, and property, a notion that linked economic and political freedom. Ultimate authority rested in the will of a majority of men who owned property, and government should be limited to its basic purpose of protection. A ruler who failed to uphold his part of the social contract between the ruler and the populace could be justifiably resisted, an idea that would become crucial for the leaders of the American Revolution a century later. For England's landowners, however, Locke helped validate a revolution that consolidated their interests and ensured their privileges in the social hierarchy. Although he himself owned shares in the Royal African Company and justified slavery, Locke's writings were later used by abolitionists in their campaign against slavery.

Locke defended his optimistic view of human nature in the immensely influential *Essay Concerning Human Understanding* (1690). He denied the existence of any innate ideas and asserted instead that each human is born with a mind that is a tabula rasa (blank slate). Everything humans know, he claimed, comes from sensory experience, not from anything inherent in human nature. Locke's views promoted the belief that "all men are created equal," a belief that challenged absolutist forms of rule and ultimately raised questions about women's roles as well. Not surprisingly, Locke devoted considerable energy to rethinking educational practices; he believed that education crucially shaped the human personality by channeling all sensory experience.

The Scientific Revolution Consolidated

New breakthroughs in science lent support to Locke's optimistic view of human potential. Building on the work of Copernicus, Kepler, and Galileo (see Chapter 16), the English scientist Isaac Newton finally synthesized astronomy and physics with his law of gravitation. His work further enhanced the prestige of science, but he sought no conflict with religious authorities. Indeed, many clergy applauded his refutation of atheism and his success in explaining the orderliness of God's creation. Some rulers supported scientific activity as another form of mercantilist intervention to enhance state power. Science also gained a broader audience among upper-class men and women.

Newton. A Cambridge University student at the time of Charles II's restoration, Isaac Newton (1642–1727) was a pious Anglican who aimed to reconcile faith and science. By proving that the physical universe followed rational principles, Newton argued, scientists could prove the existence of God and so liberate humans from doubt and the fear of chaos. Newton applied mathematical principles to formulate three physical laws: (1) in the absence of force, motion continues in a straight line; (2) the rate of change in the motion of an object is a result of the forces acting on it; and (3) the action and reaction between two objects are equal and opposite. The basis of Newtonian physics thus required understanding mass, inertia, force, velocity, and acceleration—all key concepts in modern science.

Extending these principles to the entire universe in his masterwork, *Principia Mathematica* (1687), Newton united celestial and terrestrial mechanics—astronomy and physics—with his law of gravitation. This law held that every body in the universe exerts over every other body an attractive force directly proportional to the product of their masses and inversely proportional to the square of the distance between them. The law of gravitation explained Kepler's elliptical planetary orbits just as it accounted for the motion of ordinary objects on earth. Once set in motion, the universe operated like clockwork, with no need for God's continuing intervention. Gravity, although a mysterious force, could be expressed mathematically. In Newton's words, "From the same principles [of motion] I now demonstrate the frame of the System of the World." The English poet Alexander Pope later captured the intellectual world's appreciation of Newton's accomplishment:

Nature and Nature's laws lay hid in night
God said, Let Newton be! and all was light.

Newton's science was not just mathematical and deductive; he experimented with light and helped establish the science of optics. Even while making these fundamental contributions to scientific method, Newton carried out alchemical experiments in his rooms at Cambridge University and spent long hours trying to calculate the date of the beginning of the world and of the second coming of Jesus. Not all scientists accepted Newton's theories immediately, especially on the continent, but within a couple of generations his work was preeminent, partly because of experimental verification. His "frame of the System of the World" remained the basis of all physics until the advent of relativity theory and quantum mechanics in the early twentieth century.

Public Interest in Science. Absolutist rulers saw science as a means for enhancing their prestige and glory. Frederick William, the Great Elector of Brandenburg-Prussia, for example, set up agricultural experiments in front of his Berlin palace, and various German princes supported the work of Gottfried Wilhelm Leibniz (1646–1716), one of the inventors of calculus. A lawyer, diplomat, and scholar who wrote about metaphysics, cosmology, and history, Leibniz helped establish scientific societies in the German states. Government involvement in science was greatest in France, where it became an arm of mercantilist policy; in 1666, Colbert founded the Royal Academy of Sci-

ences, which supplied fifteen scientists with government stipends.

Constitutional states supported science less directly but nonetheless provided an intellectual environment that encouraged its spread. The English Royal Society, the counterpart to the Royal Academy of Sciences in France, grew out of informal meetings of scientists at London and Oxford rather than direct government involvement. It received a royal charter in 1662 but maintained complete independence. The society's secretary described its business to be "in the first place, to scrutinize the whole of Nature and to investigate its activity and powers by means of observations and experiments; and then in course of time to hammer out a more solid philosophy and more ample amenities of civilization." Whether the state was directly involved or not, thinkers of the day now tied science explicitly to social progress.

Because of their exclusion from most universities, women only rarely participated in the new scientific discoveries. In 1667, nonetheless, the English Royal Society invited Margaret Cavendish, a writer of poems, essays, letters, and philosophical treatises, to attend a meeting to watch the exhibition of experiments. She attacked the use of telescopes and microscopes because she detected in the new experimentalism a mechanistic view of the world that exalted masculine prowess and challenged the Christian belief in freedom of the will. She also urged the formal education of women, complaining that "we are kept like birds in cages to hop up and down in our houses." "Many of our Sex may have as much wit, and be capable of Learning as well as men," she insisted, "but since they want Instructions, it is not possible they should attain to it."

Freedom and Order in the Arts

Even though Newtonian science depicted an orderly universe, most artists and intellectuals had experienced enough of the upheavals of the seventeenth century to fear the prospect of chaos and disintegration. The French mathematician Blaise Pascal vividly captured their worries in his *Pensées* ("Thoughts") of 1660: "I look on all sides, and I see only darkness everywhere. Nature presents to me nothing which is not a matter of doubt and concern. . . . It is incomprehensible that God should exist, and incomprehensible that He should not exist." Poets, painters, and architects all tried to make sense of the individual's place within what Pascal called "the eternal silence of these infinite spaces."

Milton. The English Puritan poet John Milton (1608–1674) gave priority to individual liberty. In 1643, in the midst of the civil war between king and Parliament, he published writings in favor of divorce. When Parliament enacted a censorship law aimed at such literature, Milton responded in 1644 with one of the first defenses of freedom of the press, *Areopagitica* ("Tribunal of Opinion"). Milton served as secretary to the Council of State during Cromwell's rule and earned the enmity of Charles II by writing a justification for the execution of his father, Charles I, based on biblical precedents.

In forced retirement and now totally blind, in 1667 Milton published his epic poem *Paradise Lost*, which some have read as a veiled commentary on English affairs. The poet used Adam and Eve's Fall to meditate on human freedom and the tragedies of rebellion. Although Milton wanted to "justify the ways of God to man," his Satan, the proud angel who challenges God, is so compelling as to be heroic. In the end, Adam and Eve learn to accept moral responsibility and face the world "all before them." Individuals learn the limits to their freedom, yet personal liberty remains essential to their definition as human.

The Varieties of Artistic Style. The dominant artistic styles of the time—the baroque and the classical—both submerged the individual in a grander design. The baroque style proved to be especially suitable for public displays of faith and power that overawed individual beholders. The combination of religious and political purposes in baroque art is best exemplified in the architecture and sculpture of Gian Lorenzo Bernini (1598–1680), the papacy's official artist. His architectural masterpiece was the gigantic square facing St. Peter's Basilica in Rome (1656–1671). His use of freestanding open colonnades and a huge open space is meant to impress the individual observer with the power of the popes and the Catholic religion. Bernini also sculpted tombs for the popes and a large statue of Constantine, the first Christian emperor of Rome—perfect examples of the marriage of power and religion.

Gian Lorenzo Bernini,
Ecstasy of St. Teresa of Ávila (c. 1650)
This ultimate statement of baroque sculpture captures all the drama and even sensationalism of a mystical religious faith. Bernini based his figures on a vision reported by St. Teresa in which she saw an angel: "In his hands I saw a great golden spear, and at the iron tip there appeared to be a point of fire. This he plunged into my heart several times so that it penetrated my entrails. When he pulled it out I felt that he took them with it, and left me utterly consumed by the great love of God." Scala/Art Resource, NY.

In 1665, Louis XIV hired Bernini to plan the rebuilding of the Louvre palace in Paris but then rejected his ideas as incompatible with French tastes. The one tangible result of his visit to Paris, a marble bust of Louis XIV, captured the king's strength and dynamism.

Although France was a Catholic country, French painters, sculptors, and architects, like their

French Classicism
In his 1638 painting Moses Saved from the Floods of the Nile, *the French painter Nicolas Poussin sets a biblical story in an antique Roman landscape, with a pyramid serving as the sole reference to Egypt. The austerity and statuesque poses of the figures convey the ideals of classicism rather than the exuberance of the baroque style.*
Giraudon/Art Resource, NY.

patron Louis XIV, preferred the standards of classicism to those of the baroque. French artists developed classicism to be a French national style, distinct from the baroque style that was closely associated with France's enemies, the Austrian and Spanish Habsburgs. As its name suggests, classicism reflected the ideals of the art of antiquity; geometric shapes, order, and harmony of lines took precedence over the sensuous, exuberant, and emotional forms of the baroque. Rather than being overshadowed by the sheer power of emotional display, in classicism the individual could be found at the intersection of converging, symmetrical, straight lines. These influences were apparent in the work of the leading French painters of the period,

Nicolas Poussin (1594–1665) and Claude Lorrain (1600–1682), both of whom worked in Rome and tried to re-create classical Roman values in their mythological scenes and Roman landscapes.

Dutch painters found the baroque and classical styles less suited to their private market, where buyers sought smaller-scale works with ordinary subjects. Dutch artists came from common stock themselves—Rembrandt's father was a miller, and the father of Jan Vermeer (1632–1675) was a silk worker. Their clients were people like themselves who purchased paintings much as they bought tables and chairs. Rembrandt occasionally worked on commission for the prince of Orange but even he painted ordinary people, suffusing his canvases with a radiant, otherworldly light that made the plainest people and objects appear deeply spiritual. Vermeer's best-known paintings show women working at home, and, like Rembrandt, he made ordinary activities seem precious and beautiful. In Dutch art, ordinary individuals had religious and political significance.

Art might also serve the interests of science. One of the most skilled illustrators of insects and flowers was Maria Sibylla Merian (1646–1717), a German-born painter-scholar whose engravings were widely celebrated for their brilliant realism and microscopic clarity. Merian eventually separated from her husband and joined a sect called the Labadists (after their French founder, Jean de Labadie), who did not believe in formal marriage ties and established a colony in the northern Dutch province of Friesland. After moving there with her daughters, Merian went with missionaries from the sect to the Dutch colony of Surinam in South America and painted watercolors of the exotic flowers, birds, and insects she found in the jungle around the cocoa and sugarcane plantations. In the seventeenth century, many women became known for their still-lifes and especially their paintings of flowers. Paintings by the Dutch artist Rachel Ruysch, for example, fetched higher prices than those received by Rembrandt.

Women and Manners

Poetry and painting imaginatively explored the place of the individual within a larger whole, but real-life individuals had to learn to navigate their own social worlds. Manners—the learning of individual self-discipline—were essential skills of social navigation, and women usually took the lead in teaching them. Women's importance in refining social relationships quickly became a subject of controversy.

The Cultivation of Manners. The court had long been a central arena for the development of individual self-discipline. Under the tutelage of their mothers and wives, nobles learned to hide all that was crass and to maintain a fine sense of social distinction. In some ways, aristocratic men were expected to act more like women; just as women had long been expected to please men, now aristocratic men had to please their monarch or patron by displaying proper manners and conversing with ele-

European Fascination with Products of the New World

In this painting of a banana plant, Maria Sybilla Merian offers a scientific study of one of the many exotic plants and animals found by Europeans who traveled to the colonies overseas. Merian was fifty-one when she traveled to the Dutch South American colony of Surinam with her daughter. Courtesy of Hunt Institute for Botanical Documentation, Carnegie Mellon University, Pittsburgh, PA.

gance and wit. Men as well as women had to master the art of pleasing—foreign languages (especially French), dance, a taste for fine music, and attention to dress.

As part of the evolution of new aristocratic ideals, nobles learned to disdain all that was lowly. The upper classes began to reject popular festivals and fairs in favor of private theaters, where seats were relatively expensive and behavior was formal. Clowns and buffoons now seemed vulgar; the last king of England to keep a court fool was Charles I.

Music and the Refinement of Manners

In Emanuel de Witte's Woman at the Clavecin, *the artist celebrates the importance of music in the Dutch home. The woman herself remains a mystery, but the sumptuous setting of heavy curtains, mirrors, and chandeliers signals that clavichord music was associated with refinement.*
The Netherlands Institut of Cultural Heritage, Rijswijk, the Netherlands; Museum Boijmans-Van Beuningen, Rotterdam.

Chivalric romances that had entranced the nobility down to the time of Cervantes's *Don Quixote* (1605) now passed into popular literature.

The greatest French playwright of the seventeenth century, Molière (the pen name of Jean-Baptiste Poquelin, 1622–1673), wrote sparkling comedies of manners that revealed much about the new aristocratic behavior. Son of a tradesman, Molière left law school to form a theater company, which eventually gained the support of Louis XIV. His play *The Middle-Class Gentleman* first performed at the royal court in 1670, revolves around the yearning of a rich, middle-class Frenchman, Monsieur Jourdain, to learn to act like a *gentil-homme* (meaning both "gentleman" and "nobleman" in French). Monsieur Jourdain buys fancy clothes, hires private instructors in dancing, music, fencing, and philosophy, and lends money to a debt-ridden noble in hopes of marrying his daughter to him. Only his sensible wife and his daughter's love for a worthier commoner stand in his way. The

women in the family, including the servant girl Nicole, are reasonable, sincere, and keenly aware of what behavior is appropriate to their social station, whereas Jourdain stands for social ambition gone wild. The message for the court seemed to be a reassuring one: Only true nobles by blood can hope to act like nobles. But the play also showed how the middle classes were learning to emulate the nobility; if one could learn to *act* nobly through self-discipline, could not anyone with some education and money pass himself off as noble?

As Molière's play demonstrated, new attention to manners trickled down from the court to the middle class. A French treatise on manners from 1672 explained:

> If everyone is eating from the same dish, you should take care not to put your hand into it before those of higher rank have done so. . . . Formerly one was permitted . . . to dip one's bread into the sauce, provided only that one had not already bitten it.

Nowadays that would be a kind of rusticity. Formerly one was allowed to take from one's mouth what one could not eat and drop it on the floor, provided it was done skillfully. Now that would be very disgusting.

The key words *rusticity* and *disgusting* reveal the association of unacceptable social behavior with the peasantry, dirt, and repulsion. Similar rules now governed spitting and blowing one's nose in public. Ironically, however, once the elite had successfully distinguished itself from the lower classes through manners, scholars became more interested in studying popular expressions. They avidly collected proverbs, folktales, and songs—all of these now curiosities. In fact, many nobles at Louis XIV's court read fairy tales.

Debates about Women's Roles. Courtly manners often permeated the upper reaches of society by means of the *salon,* an informal gathering held regularly in private homes and presided over by a socially eminent woman. In 1661, one French author claimed to have identified 251 Parisian women as hostesses of salons. Although the French government occasionally worried that these gatherings might be seditious, the three main topics of conversation were love, literature, and philosophy. Hostesses often worked hard to encourage the careers of budding authors. Before publishing a manuscript, many authors would read their compositions to a salon gathering. Corneille, Racine, and even Bishop Bossuet sought female approval for their writings.

Some women went beyond encouraging male authors and began to write on their own, but they faced many obstacles. Marie-Madeleine de La Vergne, known as Madame de Lafayette, wrote several short novels that were published anonymously because it was considered inappropriate for aristocratic women to appear in print. Following the publication of *The Princess of Clèves* in 1678, she denied having written it. Hannah Wooley, the English author of many books on domestic conduct, published under the name of her first husband. Women were known for writing wonderful letters (Marie de Sévigné was a prime example), many of which circulated in handwritten form; hardly any appeared in print during their authors' lifetimes. In the 1650s, despite these limitations, French women began to turn out best-sellers in a new type of literature, the novel. Their success prompted the philosopher Pierre Bayle to remark in 1697 that "our best French novels for a long time have been written by women."

The new importance of women in the world of manners and letters did not sit well with everyone. Although the French writer François Poulain de la Barre (1647–1723), in a series of works published in the 1670s, used the new science to assert the equality of women's minds, most men resisted the idea. Clergy, lawyers, scholars, and playwrights attacked women's growing public influence. Women, they complained, were corrupting forces and needed restraint. Only marriage, "this salutary yoke," could control their passions and weaknesses. Salons drew fire as promoting unrestrained social ambition; women were accused of raising "the banner of prostitution in the salons, in the promenades, and in the streets." Some feared the new manners would make men effeminate: "Thus, the entire nation, formerly full of courage, grows soft and becomes effeminate, and the love of pleasure and money succeeds that of virtue." Molière wrote plays denouncing women's pretension to judge literary merit. English playwrights derided learned women by creating characters with names such as Lady Knowall, Lady Meanwell, and Mrs. Lovewit. A real-life target of the English playwrights was Aphra Behn (1640–1689), one of the first professional woman authors, who supported herself by journalism and wrote plays and poetry. Her short novel *Oroonoko* (1688) told the story of an African prince wrongly sold into slavery. The story was so successful that it was adapted by playwrights and performed repeatedly in England and France for the next hundred years. Behn responded to her critics by demanding that "the privilege for my masculine part, the poet in me" be heard and by arguing that there was "no reason why women should not write as well as men."

Reforming Popular Culture

The illiterate peasants who made up most of Europe's population had little or no knowledge of the law of gravity, upper-class manners, or novels, no matter who authored them. Their culture had three main elements: the knowledge needed to work at farming or in a trade; popular forms of entertainment such as village fairs and dances; and their religion, which shaped every aspect of life and death. What changed most noticeably in the seventeenth century was the social elites' attitude toward lower-class culture. The division between elite and popular culture widened as elites insisted on their difference from the lower orders and tried to instill new forms of discipline in their social inferiors. Historians have learned much of what they know about popular culture from the attempts of elites to change it.

Popular Religion. In the seventeenth century, Protestant and Catholic churches alike pushed hard to change popular religious practices. Their campaigns against popular "paganism" began during the sixteenth-century Protestant Reformation and Catholic Counter-Reformation but reached much of rural Europe only in the seventeenth century. Puritans in England tried to root out maypole dances, Sunday village fairs, gambling, taverns, and bawdy ballads because they interfered with sober observance of the Sabbath. In Lutheran Norway, pastors denounced a widespread belief in the miracle-working powers of St. Olaf. *Superstition* previously meant "false religion" (Protestantism was a superstition for Catholics, Catholicism for Protestants). In the seventeenth century it took on its modern meaning of irrational fears, beliefs, and practices, which anyone educated or refined would avoid. *Superstition* became synonymous with popular or ignorant beliefs.

The Catholic campaign against superstitious practices found a ready ally in Louis XIV. While he reformed the nobles at court through etiquette and manners, Catholic bishops in the French provinces trained parish priests to reform their flocks by using catechisms in local dialects and insisting that parishioners attend Mass. The church faced a formidable challenge. One bishop in France complained in 1671, "Can you believe that there are in this diocese entire villages where no one has even heard of Jesus Christ?" In some places, believers sacrificed animals to the Virgin, prayed to the new moon, and worshiped at the sources of streams as in pre-Christian times.

Like its Protestant counterpart, the Catholic campaign against ignorance and superstition helped extend state power. Clergy, officials, and local police worked together to limit carnival celebrations, to regulate pilgrimages to shrines, and to replace "indecent" images of saints with more restrained and decorous ones. In Catholicism, the cult of the Virgin Mary and devotions closely connected with Jesus, such as the Holy Sacrament and the Sacred Heart, took precedence over the celebration of more popular saints who seemed to have pagan origins or were credited with unverified miracles. Reformers everywhere tried to limit the number of feast days on the grounds that they encouraged lewd behavior.

New Attitudes toward Poverty. The campaign for more disciplined religious practices helped generate a new attitude toward the poor. Poverty previously had been closely linked with charity and virtue in Christianity; it was a Christian duty to give alms to the poor, and Jesus and many of the saints had purposely chosen lives of poverty. In the sixteenth and seventeenth centuries, the upper classes, the church, and the state increasingly regarded the poor as dangerous, deceitful, and lacking in character. "Criminal laziness is the source of all their vices," wrote a Jesuit expert on the poor. The courts had previously expelled beggars from cities; now local leaders, both Catholic and Protestant, tried to reform their character. Municipal magistrates collected taxes for poor relief, and local notables organized charities; together they transformed hospitals into houses of confinement for beggars. In Catholic France, upper-class women's religious associations, known as *confraternities*, set up asylums that confined prostitutes (by arrest if necessary) and rehabilitated them. Confraternities also founded hospices where orphans learned order and respect. Such groups advocated harsh discipline as the cure for poverty.

Although hard times had increased the numbers of poor and the rates of violent crime as well, the most important changes were attitudinal. The elites wanted to separate the very poor from society either to change them or to keep them from contaminating others. Hospitals became holding pens for society's unwanted members, where the poor joined the disabled, the incurably diseased, and the insane. The founding of hospitals demonstrates the connection between these attitudes and state building. In 1676, Louis XIV ordered every French city to establish a hospital, and his government took charge of their finances. Other rulers soon followed the same path.

MAPPING THE WEST Europe at the End of the Seventeenth Century
A map can be deceiving. Although Poland-Lithuania looks like a large country on this map, it had been fatally weakened by internal conflicts. In the next century it would disappear entirely. The Ottoman Empire still controlled an extensive territory, but outside of Anatolia its rule depended on intermediaries. The Austrian Habsburgs had pushed the Turks out of Hungary and back into the Balkans. At the other end of the scale, the very small Dutch Republic had become very rich through international commerce. Size did not always prove to be an advantage.

Conclusion

The search for order took place on various levels, from the reform of the disorderly poor to the establishment of more regular bureaucratic routines in government. The biggest factor shaping the search for order was the growth of state power.

Whether absolutist or constitutionalist in form, seventeenth-century states all aimed to penetrate more deeply into the lives of their subjects. They wanted more men for their armed forces, higher taxes to support their projects, and more control over foreign trade, religious dissent, and society's unwanted.

IMPORTANT DATES

1642–1646 Civil war between King Charles I and Parliament in England

1648 Peace of Westphalia ends Thirty Years' War; the Fronde revolt challenges royal authority in France; Ukrainian Cossack warriors rebel against the king of Poland-Lithuania

1649 Execution of Charles I of England; new Russian legal code

1651 Thomas Hobbes publishes *Leviathan*

1660 Monarchy restored in England

1661 Slave code set up in Barbados

1667 Louis XIV begins first of many wars that continue throughout his reign

1670 Molière's play, *The Middle-Class Gentleman*

1678 Marie-Madeline de La Vergne (Madame de Lafayette) anonymously publishes her novel *The Princess of Clèves*

1683 Austrian Habsburgs break the Turkish siege of Vienna

1685 Louis XIV revokes toleration for French Protestants granted by the Edict of Nantes

1687 Isaac Newton publishes *Principia Mathematica*

1688 Parliament deposes James II and invites his daughter, Mary, and her husband, William of Orange, to take the throne

1690 John Locke's *Two Treatises of Government*, *Essay Concerning Human Understanding*

Some tearing had begun to appear, however, in the seamless fabric of state power. In England, the Dutch Republic, and the English North American colonies, property owners successfully demanded constitutional guarantees of their right to participate in government. In the eighteenth century, moreover, new levels of economic growth and the appearance of new social groups would exert pressures on the European state system. The success of seventeenth-century rulers created the political and economic conditions in which their critics would flourish.

Suggested References

Louis XIV: Model of Absolutism

Recent studies have examined Louis XIV's uses of art and imagery for political purposes and have also rightly insisted that absolutism could never be entirely absolute because the king depended on collaboration and cooperation to enforce his policies. Some of the best sources for Louis XIV's reign are the letters written by important noblewomen. The Web site of the Château of Versailles includes views of rooms in the castle.

Beik, William. *Absolutism and Society in Seventeenth-Century France: State Power and Provincial Aristocracy in Languedoc.* 1985.

Burke, Peter. *The Fabrication of Louis XIV.* 1992.

Collins, James B. *The State in Early Modern France.* 1995.

*Forster, Elborg, trans. *A Woman's Life in the Court of the Sun King: Elisabeth Charlotte, Duchesse d'Orléans.* 1984.

Ranum, Oreste. *The Fronde: A French Revolution, 1648–1652.* 1993.

*Sévigné, Madame de. *Selected Letters.* Trans. Leonard Tancock. 1982.

Versailles: http://www.chateauversailles.com.

Absolutism in Central and Eastern Europe

Too often central and eastern European forms of state development have been characterized as backward in comparison with those of western Europe. Now historians emphasize the patterns of ruler-elite cooperation shared with western Europe, but they also underscore the weight of serfdom in eastern economies and political systems.

Barkey, Karen. *The Ottoman Route to State Centralization.* 1994.

Davies, Norman. *God's Playground: A History of Poland.* Vol. 1, *The Origins to 1795.* 1981.

Dukes, Paul. *The Making of Russian Absolutism, 1613–1801.* 1990.

Kivelson, Valerie A. *Autocracy in the Provinces: The Muscovite Gentry and Political Culture in the Seventeenth Century.* 1996.

Vierhaus, Rudolf. *Germany in the Age of Absolutism.* Trans. Jonathan B. Knudsen. 1988.

Wilson, Peter H. *German Armies: War and German Politics, 1648–1806.* 1998.

Constitutionalism in England

Though recent interpretations of the English revolutions emphasize the limits on radical change, Hill's portrayal of the radical ferment of ideas remains fundamental.

Carlin, Norah. *The Causes of the English Civil War.* 1999.

Cust, Richard, and Ann Hughes, eds. *The English Civil War.* 1997.

*Primary sources.

*Graham, Elspeth, et al., eds. *Her Own Life: Autobiographical Writings by Seventeenth-Century English Women.* 1989.

*Haller, William, and Godfrey Davies, eds. *The Leveller Tracts, 1647–1653.* 1944.

Hill, Christopher. *The World Turned Upside Down: Radical Ideas during the English Revolution.* 1972.

Israel, Jonathan, ed. *The Anglo-Dutch Moment: Essays on the Glorious Revolution and Its World Impact.* 1991.

Mack, Phyllis. *Visionary Women: Ecstatic Prophecy in Seventeenth-Century England.* 1992.

Manning, Brian. *Aristocrats, Plebeians, and Revolution in England, 1640–1660.* 1996.

*Pincus, Steven Carl Anthony. *England's Glorious Revolution and the Origins of Liberalism: A Documentary History of Later Stuart England.* 1998.

Constitutionalism in the Dutch Republic and the Overseas Colonies

Studies of the Dutch Republic emphasize the importance of trade and consumerism. Recent work on the colonies has begun to explore the intersecting experiences of settlers, native Americans, and African slaves.

*Campbell, P. F. *Some Early Barbadian History.* 1993.

Delâge, Denys. *Bitter Feast: Amerindians and Europeans in Northeastern North America, 1600–64.* Trans. Jane Brierley. 1993.

*Foster, William C., ed. *The La Salle Expedition to Texas: The Journal of Henri Joutel, 1684–1687.* Trans. Johanna S. Warren. 1998.

Israel, Jonathan. *Dutch Primacy in World Trade, 1585–1740.* 1989.

Merrell, James Hart. *Into the American Woods: Negotiators on the Pennsylvania Frontier.* 1999.

Price, J. L. *The Dutch Republic in the Seventeenth Century.* 1998.

Schama, Simon. *The Embarrassment of Riches: An Interpretation of Dutch Culture in the Golden Age.* 1988.

Thornton, John. *Africa and Africans in the Making of the Atlantic World, 1400–1800.* 1992.

The Search for Order in Elite and Popular Culture

Historians do not always agree about the meaning of popular culture: was it something widely shared by all social classes or a set of activities increasingly identified with the lower classes, as Burke argues? The central Web site for Dutch museums allows the visitor to tour rooms and see paintings in scores of Dutch museums, many of which have important holdings of paintings by Rembrandt and Vermeer. The website on Isaac Newton links to many other sites on his scientific and mathematical discoveries.

Burke, Peter. *Popular Culture in Early Modern Europe.* 1978.

Davis, Natalie Zemon. *Women on the Margins: Three Seventeenth-Century Lives.* 1995.

DeJean, Joan E. *Tender Geographies: Women and the Origins of the Novel in France.* 1991.

Dobbs, Betty Jo Teeter and Margaret C. Jacob. *Newton and the Culture of Newtonianism.* 1994.

Dutch Museums: http://www.hollandmuseums.nl.

Elias, Norbert. *The Civilizing Process: The Development of Manners.* Trans. by Edmund Jephcott. 1978.

*Fitzmaurice, James, ed. *Margaret Cavendish: Sociable Letters.* 1997.

Isaac Newton: http://www.newtonia.freeserve.co.uk.

Todd, Janet M. *The Secret Life of Aphra Behn.* 1997.

The Atlantic System and Its Consequences

1690–1740

J OHANN SEBASTIAN BACH (1685–1750), composer of mighty organ fugues and church cantatas, was not above amusing his Leipzig audiences, many of them university students. In 1732 he produced a cantata about a young woman in love—with coffee. Her old-fashioned father rages that he won't find her a husband unless she gives up the fad. She agrees, secretly vowing to admit no suitor who will not promise in the marriage contract to let her brew coffee whenever she wants. Bach offers this conclusion:

> *The cat won't give up its mouse,*
> *Girls stay faithful coffee-sisters*
> *Mother loves her coffee habit,*
> *Grandma sips it gladly too—*
> *Why then shout at the daughters?*

Bach's era might well be called the age of coffee. European travelers at the end of the sixteenth century had noticed Middle Eastern people drinking a "black drink," *kavah*. Few Europeans sampled it at first, and the Arab monopoly on its production kept prices high. This changed around 1700 when the Dutch East India Company introduced coffee plants to Java and other Indonesian islands. Coffee production then spread to the French Caribbean, where African slaves provided the plantation labor. In Europe, imported coffee spurred the development of a new kind of meeting place: the first coffeehouse opened in London in 1652, and the idea spread quickly to other European cities. The coffeehouses became

London Coffeehouse

This gouache (a variant on watercolor painting) from about 1725 depicts a scene from a London coffeehouse located in the courtyard of the Royal Exchange (merchants' bank). Middle-class men (wearing wigs) read newspapers, drink coffee, smoke pipes, and discuss the news of the day. The coffeehouse draws them out of their homes into a new public space.
British Museum, Bridgeman Art Library, NY.

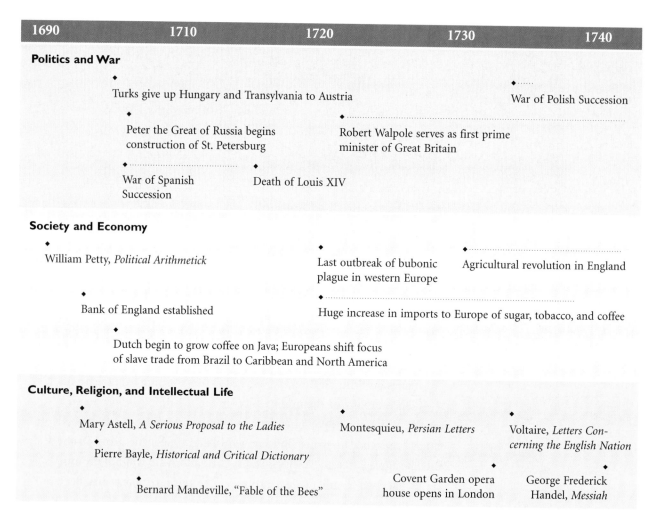

1690	1710	1720	1730	1740

Politics and War

Turks give up Hungary and Transylvania to Austria

War of Polish Succession

Peter the Great of Russia begins construction of St. Petersburg

Robert Walpole serves as first prime minister of Great Britain

War of Spanish Succession

Death of Louis XIV

Society and Economy

William Petty, *Political Arithmetick*

Last outbreak of bubonic plague in western Europe

Agricultural revolution in England

Bank of England established

Huge increase in imports to Europe of sugar, tobacco, and coffee

Dutch begin to grow coffee on Java; Europeans shift focus of slave trade from Brazil to Caribbean and North America

Culture, Religion, and Intellectual Life

Mary Astell, *A Serious Proposal to the Ladies*

Montesquieu, *Persian Letters*

Voltaire, *Letters Concerning the English Nation*

Pierre Bayle, *Historical and Critical Dictionary*

Bernard Mandeville, "Fable of the Bees"

Covent Garden opera house opens in London

George Frederick Handel, *Messiah*

gathering places for men to drink, read newspapers, and talk politics. As a London newspaper commented in 1737, "There's scarce an Alley in City and Suburbs but has a Coffeehouse in it, which may be called the School of Public Spirit, where every Man over Daily and Weekly Journals, a Mug, or a Dram . . . devotes himself to that glorious one, his Country."

European consumption of coffee, tea, chocolate, and other novelties increased dramatically as European nations forged worldwide economic links. At the center of this new world economy was an "Atlantic system" that bound together western Europe, Africa, and the Americas. Europeans bought slaves in western Africa, transported and sold them in their colonies in North and South America and the Caribbean, bought the commodities such as coffee and sugar that were produced by the new colonial plantations, and then sold the goods in European ports for refining and reshipment. This Atlantic system first took clear shape in the early eighteenth century; it was the hub of European expansion all over the world.

Coffee was one example among many of the new social and cultural patterns that took root between 1690 and 1740. Improvements in agricultural production at home reinforced the effects of trade overseas; Europeans now had more disposable income for "extras," and they spent their money not only in the new coffeehouses and cafés that sprang up all over Europe but also on newspapers, musical concerts, paintings, and novels. A new middle-class public began to make its presence felt in every domain of culture and social life.

Although the rise of the Atlantic system gave Europe new prominence in the global context, European rulers still focused most of their political, diplomatic, and military energies on their rivalries within Europe. A coalition of countries succeeded in containing French aggression, and a more balanced diplomatic system emerged. In eastern Europe, Prussia and Austria had to contend with the rising power of Russia under Peter the Great. In western Europe, both Spain and the Dutch Republic declined in influence but continued to vie with Britain and France for colonial spoils in the Atlantic. The more evenly matched competition among the great powers encouraged the development of diplomatic skills and drew attention to public health as a way of encouraging population growth.

In the aftermath of Louis XIV's revocation of the Edict of Nantes in 1685, a new intellectual movement known as the Enlightenment began to germinate. French Protestant refugees began to publish works critical of absolutism in politics and religion. Increased prosperity, the growth of a middle-class public, and the decline in warfare after Louis XIV's death in 1715 all fostered the development of this new critical spirit. Fed by the popularization of science and the growing interest in travel literature, the Enlightenment encouraged greater skepticism about religious and state authority. Eventually the movement would question almost every aspect of social and political life in Europe. The Enlightenment began in western Europe in those countries—Britain, France, and the Dutch Republic—most affected by the new Atlantic system. It too was a product of the age of coffee.

❖ The Atlantic System and the World Economy

Although their ships had been circling the globe since the early 1500s, Europeans did not draw most of the world into their economic orbit until the 1700s. Western European trading nations sent ships loaded with goods to buy slaves from local rulers on the western coast of Africa; then transported the slaves to the colonies in North and South America and the Caribbean and sold them to the owners of plantations producing coffee, sugar, cotton, and tobacco; and bought the raw commodities produced in the colonies and shipped them back to Europe, where they were refined or processed and then sold to other parts of Europe and the world. The Atlantic system and the growth of international trade helped create a new consumer society.

Slavery and the Atlantic System

Spain and Portugal had dominated Atlantic trade in the sixteenth and seventeenth centuries, but in the eighteenth century European trade in the Atlantic rapidly expanded and became more systematically interconnected (Map 18.1, inset). By 1630, Portugal had already sent 60,000 African slaves to Brazil to work on the new plantations (large tracts of lands farmed by slave labor), which were producing some 15,000 tons of sugar a year. Realizing that plantations producing staples for Europeans could bring fabulous wealth, the European powers grew less interested in the dwindling trade in precious metals and more eager to colonize. Large-scale planters of sugar, tobacco, and coffee displaced small farmers who relied on one or two servants. Planters and their plantations won out because slave labor was cheap and therefore able to produce mass quantities of commodities at low prices.

State-chartered private companies from Portugal, France, Britain, the Dutch Republic, Prussia, and even Denmark exploited the 3,500-mile coastline of West Africa for slaves. Before 1675, most blacks taken from Africa had been sent to Brazil, but by 1700 half of the African slaves landed in the Caribbean (Figure 18.1). Thereafter, the plantation economy began to expand on the North American mainland. The numbers stagger the imagination. Before 1650, slave traders transported about 7,000 Africans each year across the Atlantic; this rate doubled between 1650 and 1675, nearly doubled again in the next twenty-five years, and kept going until the 1780s (Figure 18.2). In all, more than 11 million Africans, not counting those who died at sea or in Africa, were transported to the Americas before the slave trade began to wind down after 1850. Many traders gained spectacular wealth, but companies did not always make profits. The English Royal African Company, for example, delivered 100,000 slaves to the Caribbean, imported 30,000 tons of sugar to Britain, yet lost money after the few profitable years following its founding in 1672.

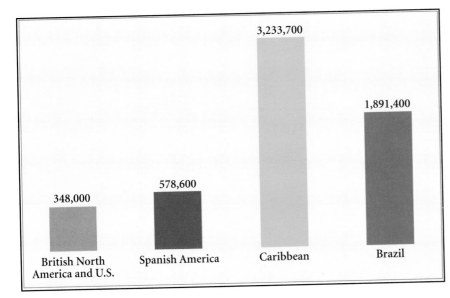

FIGURE 18.1 African Slaves Imported into American Territories, 1701–1810

During the eighteenth century, planters in the newly established Caribbean colonies imported millions of African slaves to work the new plantations that produced sugar, coffee, indigo, and cotton for the European market. The vast majority of African slaves transported to the Americas ended up in either the Caribbean or Brazil. Adapted from Philip D. Curtin, *The Atlantic Slave Trade: A Census* (Madison: University of Wisconsin Press, 1969).

The Life of the Slaves. The balance of white and black populations in the New World colonies was determined by the staples produced. New England merchants and farmers bought few slaves because they did not own plantations. Blacks—both slave and free—made up only 3 percent of the population in eighteenth-century New England, compared with 60 percent in South Carolina. On the whole, the British North American colonies contained a higher proportion of African Americans from 1730 to 1765 than at any other time in American history. The imbalance of whites and blacks was even more extreme in the Caribbean; in the early 1700s, the British sugar islands had a population of about 150,000 people, only 30,000 of them Europeans. The rest were African slaves, as most indigenous people died fighting Europeans or the diseases brought by them.

The slaves suffered terrible experiences. Most had been sold to European traders by Africans from the west coast who acquired them through warfare or kidnapping. The vast majority were between fourteen and thirty-five years old. Before being crammed onto the ships for the three-month trip, their heads were shaved, they were stripped naked, and some were branded with red-hot irons. The men and women were separated and the men shack-led with leg irons. Sailors and officers raped the women whenever they wished and beat those who refused their advances. In the cramped and appalling conditions of the voyage, as many as one-fourth of the slaves died in transit.

Once they landed, slaves were forced into degrading and oppressive conditions. As soon as masters bought slaves, they gave them new names, often only first names, and in some colonies branded them as personal property. Slaves had no social identities of their own; they were expected to learn their master's language and to do any job assigned. Slaves worked fifteen- to seventeen-hour days and were fed only enough to keep them on their feet. Brazilian slaves consumed more calories than the poorest Brazilians do today, but that hardly made them well fed. The manager of a plantation in Barbados insisted in 1711, "It is the greatest misfortune in this island that few planters give [the slaves] . . . a bellyful" of corn. The death rate among slaves was high, especially in Brazil, where quick shifts in the weather, lack of clothing, and squalid living conditions made them susceptible to a variety of deadly illnesses.

Not surprisingly, despite the threat of torture or death on recapture, slaves sometimes ran away. (See

◀ MAP 18.1 European Trade Patterns, c. 1740

By 1740, the European powers had colonized much of North and South America and incorporated their colonies there into a worldwide system of commerce centered on the slave trade and plantation production of staple crops. Europeans still sought spices and luxury goods in China and the East Indies, but outside of Java, few Europeans had settled permanently in these areas.

Conditions on Slave Ships

Although the viewer cannot tell if the slaves are lying down or standing, this engraving, inspired by the campaign to abolish slavery, has a clear message: the slaves had to endure crowded conditions on their long passage across the Atlantic. Most slaves (like crew members, who also died in large numbers) fell victim to dysentery, yellow fever, measles, or smallpox; a few committed suicide by jumping overboard. North Wind Picture Archive.

"New Sources, New Perspectives," page 652). In Brazil, runaways hid in *quilombos* (hideouts) in the forests or backcountry. When it was discovered and destroyed in 1695, the *quilombo* of Palmares had thirty thousand fugitives who had formed their own social organization complete with elected kings and councils of elders. Outright revolt was uncommon, especially before the nineteenth century, but other forms of resistance included stealing food, breaking tools, and feigning illness or stupidity. Slaveholders' fears about conspiracy and revolt lurked beneath the surface of every slave-based society. In 1710, the royal governor of Virginia reminded the colonial legislature of the need for unceasing vigilance: "We are not to Depend on Either Their Stupidity, or that Babel of Languages among 'em; freedom Wears a Cap which Can Without a Tongue, Call Togather all Those who Long to Shake off the fetters of Slavery." Masters defended whipping and other forms of physical punishment as essential to maintaining discipline. Laws called for the castration of a slave who struck a white person.

Effects on Europe. Plantation owners often left their colonial possessions in the care of agents and collected the revenue to live as wealthy landowners back home, where they built opulent mansions and gained influence in local and national politics. William Beckford, for example, had been sent from Jamaica to school in England as a young boy. When he inherited sugar plantations and shipping companies from his father and older brother, he moved the headquarters of the family business to London in the 1730s to be close to the government and financial markets. His holdings formed the single most powerful economic interest in Jamaica, but he preferred to live in England where he could collect art for his many luxurious homes, hold political office (he served as lord mayor of London and in Parliament), and even lend money to the government.

The slave trade permanently altered consumption patterns for ordinary people. Sugar had been prescribed as medicine before the end of the sixteenth century, but the development of plantations in Brazil and the Caribbean made it a standard food item. By 1700, the British sent home 50 million pounds of sugar a year, a figure that doubled by 1730. During the French Revolution of the 1790s, sugar shortages would become a cause for rioting in Paris. Equally pervasive was the spread of tobacco; by the 1720s, Britain imported two hundred shiploads of tobacco from Virginia and Maryland every year, and men of every country and class smoked pipes or took snuff.

The Origins of Racism. The traffic in slaves disturbed many Europeans. As a government memorandum to the Spanish king explained in 1610: "Modern theologians in published books commonly report on, and condemn as unjust, the acts of enslavement which take place in provinces of this Royal Empire." Between 1667 and 1671, the French Dominican monk Father Du Tertre published three volumes in which he denounced the mistreatment of slaves in the French colonies.

In the 1700s, however, slaveholders began to justify their actions by demeaning the mental and spiritual qualities of the enslaved Africans. White Europeans and colonists sometimes described black slaves as animal-like, akin to apes. A leading New England Puritan asserted about the slaves: "Indeed their *Stupidity* is a *Discouragement*. It may seem, unto as little purpose, to *Teach*, as to *wash an Aethiopian* [Ethiopian]." One of the great paradoxes of this time was that talk of liberty and self-evident rights, especially prevalent in Britain and its North American colonies, coexisted with the belief that some people were meant to be slaves. Although Christians believed in principle in a kind of spiritual equality between blacks and whites, the churches often defended or at least did not oppose the inequities of slavery.

World Trade and Settlement

The Atlantic system helped extend European trade relations across the globe. The textiles that Atlantic shippers exchanged for slaves on the west coast of Africa, for example, were manufactured in India and exported by the British and French East India Companies. As much as one-quarter of the British exports to Africa in the eighteenth century were actually re-exports from India. To expand its trade in the rest of the world, Europeans seized territories and tried to establish permanent settlements. The eighteenth-century extension of European power prepared the way for western global domination in the nineteenth and twentieth centuries.

The Americas.   In contrast to the sparsely inhabited trading outposts in Asia and Africa, the colonies in the Americas bulged with settlers. The British North American colonies, for example, contained about 1.5 million nonnative (that is, white settler and black slave) residents by 1750. While the Spanish competed with the Portuguese for control of South America, the French competed with the British for control of North America. Spanish and

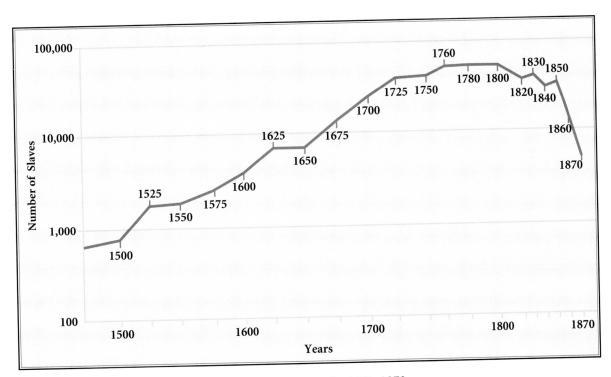

FIGURE 18.2 Annual Imports in the Atlantic Slave Trade, 1450–1870
The importation of slaves to the American territories reached its height in the second half of the eighteenth century and began to decline around 1800. Yet despite the abolition of the slave trade by the British in 1807, commerce in slaves did not seriously diminish until after the revolutions of 1848.
Adapted from Philip D. Curtin, *The Atlantic Slave Trade: A Census* (Madison: University of Wisconsin Press, 1969). Reprinted by permission of the University of Wisconsin Press.

Oral History and the Life of Slaves

Because slaves imported from Africa to the New World did not speak the language of their captors, historians have found it difficult to reconstruct slave life from the point of view of the slaves themselves. Ship records provide information about the number of slaves captured and transported, the deaths on the voyages across the Atlantic, and the prices paid for slaves when they finally arrived. This information comes from the point of view of slave traders, and it says very little about the realities of life on board ship or at the plantations. Scholars have attempted to fill in this blank by using a variety of overlapping sources. The most interesting and controversial of them are oral histories taken from descendants of slaves. In some former slave societies, descendants of slaves still tell stories about their ancestors' first days under slavery. The controversy comes from using twentieth-century memories to get at eighteenth-century lives.

One of the regions most intensively studied in this fashion is Dutch Surinam, on the northeast coast of South America between present-day Guyana and French Guiana. It is a good source of oral histories because 10 percent of the African slaves transported there between the 1680s and the 1750s escaped from the plantations and fled into the nearby rain forests. There they set up their own societies and developed their own language in which they carried on the oral traditions of the first runaway slaves. The twentieth-century descendants of the runaway slaves recount:

In slavery, there was hardly anything to eat. It was at the place called Providence Plantation. They

Slaves of Surinam in the 1770s

John Gabriel Stedman published an account of his participation in a five-year expedition against the runaway slaves of Surinam that took place in the 1770s. He provided drawings such as the one reproduced here, which shows Africans who have just come off a slave ship. Schomburg Center for Research in Black Culture/New York Public Library.

whipped you there till your ass was burning. Then they would give you a bit of plain rice in a calabash [a bowl made from the tropical American tree known as calabash]. . . . And the gods told them that this is no way for human beings to live. They would help them. Let each person go where he could. So they ran.

British settlers came to blows over the boundary between the British colonies and Florida, which was Spanish.

Local economies shaped colonial social relations; men in French trapper communities in Canada, for example, had little in common with the men and women of the plantation societies in Barbados or Brazil. Racial attitudes also differed from place to place. The Spanish and Portuguese tolerated intermarriage with the native populations in both America and Asia. Sexual contact, both inside and outside marriage, fostered greater racial variety in the Span-

From other sources, historians have learned that there was a major slave rebellion at Providence Plantation in 1693.

By comparing such oral histories to written accounts of plantation owners, missionaries, and Dutch colonial officials, historians have been able to paint a more richly detailed picture not only of slavery but also of runaway slave societies, which were especially numerous in South America. At the end of the eighteenth century, a Portuguese-speaking Jew wrote his own history of plantation life based on records from the local Jewish community that are now lost. Because the Dutch, unlike most other Europeans, allowed Jews to own slaves, Portuguese-speaking Jews from Brazil owned about one-third of the plantations and slaves in Surinam. This eighteenth-century chronicler, David de Ishak Cohen Nassy, wrote his version of Surinam's first slave revolt:

There was in the year 1690 a revolt on a plantation situated on the Cassewinica Creek, behind Jews Savannah, belonging to a Jew named Imanuël Machado, where, having killed their master, they fled, carrying away with them everything that was there. . . . The Jews . . . in an expedition which they undertook against the rebels, killed many of them and brought back several who were punished by death on the very spot.

The oral histories told about the revolt from the runaway slaves' perspective:

There had been a great council meeting [of runaway slaves] in the forest. . . . They decided to burn a different one of his plantations from the place where he had whipped Lanu [one of the runaway slaves] because they would find more tools there. This was the Cassewinica Plantation, which had many slaves. They knew all about this plantation from slavery times. So, they attacked.

It was at night. They killed the head of the plantation, a white man. They took all the things, everything they needed.

The runaway slaves saw the attack as part of their ongoing effort to build a life in the rain forest, away from the whites.

Over the next decades, the runaway slaves fought a constant series of battles with plantation owners and Dutch officials. Finally in 1762, the Dutch granted the runaway slaves their freedom in a peace agreement; offered them tools, gunpowder, and other necessities; and allowed them to trade in the main town of the colony in exchange for agreeing to return all future runaways. The runaways had not destroyed the slave system, but they had gained their own independence alongside it. From their oral histories it is possible to retrace their efforts to build new lives in a strange place, in which they combined African practices with New World experiences.

Source: Richard Price, *Alabi's World* (Baltimore: Johns Hopkins University Press, 1990), 17, 9.

QUESTIONS FOR DEBATE

1. What did runaway slaves aim to accomplish when they attacked plantations?

2. Why would runaway slaves make an agreement with the Dutch colonial officials to return future runaways?

3. Can oral histories recorded in the twentieth century be considered accurate versions of events that took place in the eighteenth century? How can they be tested?

FURTHER READING

Richard Price, *Alabi's World*. 1990.

John Gabriel Stedman, *Narrative of a Five Years' Expedition Against the Revolted Negroes of Surinam*, edited, and with an introduction and notes, by Richard Price and Sally Price. 1988.

ish and Portuguese colonies than in the French or the English territories (though mixed-race people could be found everywhere). By 1800, *mestizos*, children of Spanish men and Indian women, accounted for more than a quarter of the population in the Spanish colonies, and many of them aspired to join the local elite. Greater racial diversity seems not to have improved the treatment of slaves, however, which was probably harshest in Portuguese Brazil.

Where intermarriage between colonizers and natives was common, conversion to Christianity proved most successful. Although the Indians

India Cottons and Trade with the East
This brightly colored cotton cloth was painted and embroidered in Madras in southern India sometime in the late 1600s. The male figure with a mustache may be a European, but the female figures are clearly Asian. Europeans— especially the British— discovered that they could make big profits on the export of Indian cotton cloth to Europe. They also traded Indian cottons in Africa for slaves and sold large quantities in the colonies.
Victoria and Albert Museum, London.

maintained many of their native religious beliefs, many Indians in the Spanish colonies had come to consider themselves devout Catholics by 1700. Indian carpenters and artisans in the villages produced innumerable altars, retables (painted panels), and sculpted images to adorn their local churches, and individual families put up domestic shrines. Yet the clergy remained overwhelmingly Spanish: the church hierarchy concluded that the Indians' humility and innocence made them unsuitable for the priesthood.

In the early years of American colonization, many more men than women emigrated from Europe. Although the sex imbalance began to decline at the end of the seventeenth century, it remained substantial; two and one-half times as many men as women were among the immigrants leaving Liverpool, England, between 1697 and 1707, for example. Women who emigrated as indentured servants ran great risks: if they did not die of disease during the voyage, they might end up giving birth to illegitimate children (the fate of at least one in five servant women) or being virtually sold into marriage. Many upper-class women were kept in seclusion, especially in the Spanish and Portuguese colonies.

The uncertainties of life in the American colonies provided new opportunities for European women and men willing to live outside the law,

however. In the 1500s and 1600s, the English and Dutch governments had routinely authorized pirates to prey on the shipping of their rivals, the Spanish and Portuguese. Then, in the late 1600s, English, French, and Dutch bands made up of deserters and crews from wrecked vessels began to form their own associations of pirates, especially in the Caribbean. Called *buccaneers* from their custom of curing strips of beef, called *boucan* by the native Caribs of the islands, the pirates governed themselves and preyed on everyone's shipping without regard to national origin. In 1720, the trial of buccaneers associated with Calico Jack Rackham in Jamaica revealed that two women had dressed as men and joined the pirates in looting and plundering English ships. Mary Read and Anne Bonny escaped death by hanging only because they were pregnant. After 1700, the colonial governments tried to stamp out piracy. As one British judge argued in 1705, "A pirate is in perpetual war with every individual and every state. . . . They are worse than ravenous beasts."

Africa and Asia.   White settlements in Africa and Asia remained small and almost insignificant, except for their long-term potential. Europeans had little contact with East Africa and almost none with the continent's vast interior. A few Portuguese trading posts in Angola and Dutch farms on the Cape of Good Hope provided the only toeholds for future expansion. In China the emperors had welcomed Catholic missionaries at court in the seventeenth century, but the priests' credibility diminished as they squabbled among themselves and associated with European merchants, whom the Chinese considered pirates. "The barbarians [Europeans] are like wild beasts," one Chinese official concluded, "and are not to be ruled on the same principles as citizens." In 1720, only one thousand Europeans resided in Guangzhou (Canton), the sole place where foreigners could legally trade for spices, tea, and silk.

Europeans exercised more influence in Java in the East Indies and in India. Dutch coffee production in Java and nearby islands increased phenomenally in the early 1700s, and many Dutch settled there to oversee production and trade. In India, Dutch, English, French, Portuguese, and Danish companies competed for spices, cotton, and silk; by the 1740s the English and French had become the leading rivals in India, just as they were in North America. Both countries extended their power as India's Muslim rulers lost control to local Hindu princes, rebellious Sikhs, invading Persians, and their own provincial governors. A few thousand Europeans lived in India, though many thousand more soldiers were stationed there to protect them. The staple of trade with India in the early 1700s was calico—lightweight, brightly colored cotton cloth that caught on as a fashion in Europe.

Europeans who visited India were especially struck by what they viewed as exotic religious practices. In a book published in 1696 of his travels to western India, an Anglican minister described the fakirs (religious mendicants or beggars of alms), "some of whom show their devotion by a shameless appearance, walking naked, without the least rag of clothes to cover them." Such writings increased European interest in the outside world but also fed a European sense of superiority that helped excuse the more violent forms of colonial domination.

The Birth of Consumer Society

Worldwide colonization produced new supplies of goods, from coffee to calico, and population growth in Europe fueled demand for them. Beginning first in Britain, then in France and the Italian states,

and finally in eastern Europe, population surged, growing by about 20 percent between 1700 and 1750. The gap between a fast-growing northwest and a more stagnant south and central Europe now diminished, as regions that had lost population during the seventeenth-century downturn recovered. Cities, in particular, grew. Between 1600 and 1750, London's population more than tripled, and Paris's more than doubled.

Although contemporaries could not have realized it then, this was the start of the modern "population explosion." It appears that a decline in the death rate, rather than a rise in the birthrate, explains the turnaround. Three main factors contributed to this decline in the death rate: better

The Exotic as Consumer Item
In this painting by the Venetian woman Rosalba Carriera (1675–1757), Africa *(the title of the work) is represented by a young black girl wearing a turban. Carriera was known for her use of pastels. In 1720, she journeyed to Paris where she became an associate of Antoine Watteau and helped inaugurate the rococo style in painting.*
Staatliche Kunstsammlungen Dresden, Gemäldegalerie Alte Meister.

weather and hence more bountiful harvests, improved agricultural techniques, and the plague's disappearance after 1720.

By the early eighteenth century, the effects of economic expansion and population growth brought about a consumer revolution. The British East India Company began to import into Britain huge quantities of calicoes. British imports of tobacco doubled between 1672 and 1700; at Nantes, the center of the French sugar trade, imports quadrupled between 1698 and 1733. Tea, chocolate, and coffee became virtual necessities. In the 1670s, only a trickle of tea reached London, but by 1720 the East India Company sent 9 million pounds to England—a figure that rose to 37 million pounds by 1750. By 1700, England had two thousand coffeehouses; by 1740, every English country town had at least two. Paris got its first cafés at the end of the seventeenth century; Berlin opened its first coffeehouse in 1714; Bach's Leipzig boasted eight by 1725.

The birth of consumer society did not go unnoticed by eye witnesses. In the English economic literature of the 1690s, writers began to express a new view of humans as consuming animals with boundless appetites. Such opinions gained a wide audience with the appearance of Bernard Mandeville's poem "Fable of the Bees" (1705), which argued that private vices might have public benefits. In the poem a hive of bees abolishes evil in its society, only to discover that the society has also disappeared. Mandeville insisted that pride, self-interest, and the desire for material goods (all Christian vices) in fact promoted economic prosperity: "every part was full of Vice, Yet the whole mass a Paradise." Many authors attacked the new doctrine of consumerism, and the French government banned the poem's publication. But Mandeville had captured the essence of the emerging market for consumption.

❖ New Social and Cultural Patterns

The impact of the Atlantic system and world trade was most apparent in the cities, where people had more money for consumer goods. But rural changes also had significant long-term influence, as a revolution in agricultural techniques made it possible to feed more and more people with a smaller agricultural workforce. As population increased, more people moved to the cities, where they found themselves caught up in innovative urban customs such as attending musical concerts and reading novels. Along

Agricultural Revolution
This English painting of a manor in Gloucestershire from about 1730 demonstrates the concrete effects of the agricultural revolution. Fields are enclosed as far as the eye can see, and large groups of men and women work together to farm the consolidated plots of land owned by the wealthy local landlord. The individual peasant family working its own small plot of land has disappeared in favor of a new and more hierarchical labor structure.
Cheltenham Art Gallery & Museums, Gloucestershire. Bridgeman Art Library, NY.

with a general increase in literacy, these activities helped create a public that responded to new writers and artists. Social and cultural changes were not uniform across Europe, however; as usual, people's experiences varied depending on whether they lived in wealth or poverty, in urban or rural areas, or in eastern or western Europe.

Agricultural Revolution

Although Britain, France, and the Dutch Republic shared the enthusiasm for consumer goods, Britain's domestic market grew most quickly. In Britain, as agricultural output increased 43 percent over the course of the 1700s, the population increased by 70 percent. The British imported grain to feed the growing population, but they also benefited from the development of techniques that together constituted an agricultural revolution. No new machinery propelled this revolution—just more aggressive attitudes toward investment and management. The Dutch and the Flemish had pioneered many of these techniques in the 1600s, but the British took them further.

Four major changes occurred in British agriculture that eventually spread to other countries. First, farmers increased the amount of land under cultivation by draining wetlands and by growing crops on previously uncultivated common lands (acreage maintained by the community for grazing). Second, those farmers who could afford it consolidated smaller, scattered plots into larger, more efficient units. Third, livestock raising became more closely linked to crop growing, and the yields of each increased. (See "Taking Measure," opposite.) For centuries, most farmers had rotated their fields in and out of production to replenish the soil. Now farmers planted carefully chosen fodder crops such as clover and turnips that added nutrients to the soil, thereby eliminating the need to leave a field fallow (unplanted) every two or three years. With more fodder available, farmers could raise more livestock, which in turn produced more manure to fertilize grain fields. Fourth, selective breeding of animals combined with the increase in fodder to improve the quality and size of herds. New crops had only a slight impact; potatoes, for example, were introduced to Europe from South America in the 1500s, but because people feared they might cause leprosy, tuberculosis, or fevers, they were not grown in quantity until the late 1700s. By the 1730s and 1740s,

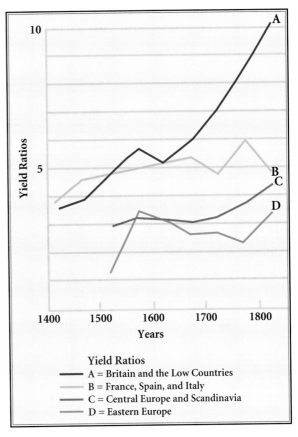

TAKING MEASURE Relationship of Crop Harvested to Seed Used, 1400–1800

The impact and even the timing of the agricultural revolution can be determined by this figure, based on yield ratios (the number of grains produced for each seed planted). Britain, the Dutch Republic, and the Austrian Netherlands all experienced huge increases in crop yields after 1700. Other European regions lagged behind right into the 1800s.
From Peter J. Hugill, *World Trade since 1431: Geography, Technology, and Capitalism* (Johns Hopkins University Press, 1995), p. 56. Reprinted by permission of Johns Hopkins University Press.

agricultural output had increased dramatically, and prices for food had fallen because of these interconnected innovations.

Changes in agricultural practices did not benefit all landowners equally. The biggest British landowners consolidated their holdings in the "enclosure movement." They put pressure on small farmers and villagers to sell their land or give up their common lands. The big landlords then fenced off ("enclosed") their property. Because enclosure eliminated community grazing rights, it frequently sparked a struggle between the big landlords and villagers, and in Britain it normally required an act of Parliament. Such acts became increasingly common in the second half of the eighteenth century, and by the century's end six million acres of common lands had been enclosed and developed. "Improvers" produced more food more efficiently and thus supported a growing population.

Contrary to the fears of contemporaries, small farmers and cottagers (those with little or no property) were not forced off the land all at once. But most villagers could not afford the litigation involved in resisting enclosure, and small landholders consequently had to sell out to landlords or farmers with larger plots. Landlords with large holdings leased their estates to tenant farmers at constantly increasing rents, and the tenant farmers in turn employed the cottagers as salaried agricultural workers. In this way the English peasantry largely disappeared, replaced by a more hierarchical society of big landlords, enterprising tenant farmers, and poor agricultural laborers.

The new agricultural techniques spread slowly from Britain and the Low Countries (the Dutch Republic and the Austrian Netherlands) to the rest of western Europe. Outside a few pockets in northern France and the western German states, however, subsistence agriculture (producing just enough to get by rather than surpluses for the market) continued to dominate farming in western Europe and Scandinavia. In southwestern Germany, for example, 80 percent of the peasants produced no surplus because their plots were too small. Unlike the populations of the highly urbanized Low Countries (where half the people lived in towns and cities), most Europeans, western and eastern, eked out their existence in the countryside.

In eastern Europe, the condition of peasants worsened in the areas where landlords tried hardest to improve their yields. To produce more for the Baltic grain market, aristocratic landholders in Prussia, Poland, and parts of Russia drained wetlands, cultivated moors, and built dikes. They also forced peasants off lands the peasants worked for themselves, increased compulsory labor services (the critical element in serfdom), and began to manage their estates directly. Some eastern landowners grew fabulously wealthy. The Potocki family in the Polish Ukraine, for example, owned three million

Treatment of Serfs in Russia

Visitors from western Europe often remarked on the cruel treatment of serfs in Russia. This drawing by one such visitor shows the punishment that could be inflicted by landowners. Serfs could be whipped for almost any reason, even for making a soup too salty or neglecting to bow when the lord's family passed by. Their condition actually deteriorated in the 1700s, as landowners began to sell serfs much like slaves. New decrees made it illegal for serfs to contract loans, enter into leases, or work for anyone other than their lord. Some landlords kept harems of serf girls. Although the Russian landlords' treatment of serfs was even more brutal than that in the German states and Poland, upper classes in every country regarded the serfs as dirty, deceitful, brutish, and superstitious. New York Public Library Slavonic Division.

acres of land and had 130,000 serfs. The Eszterházy family of Hungary owned seven million acres; and the Lithuanian magnate Karol Radziwill controlled six hundred villages. In parts of Poland and Russia the serfs hardly differed from slaves in status, and their "masters" ran their huge estates much like American plantations.

Social Life in the Cities

Because of emigration from the countryside, cities grew in population and consequently exercised more influence on culture and social life. Between 1650 and 1750, cities with at least ten thousand inhabitants increased in population by 44 percent. From the eighteenth century onward, urban growth would be continuous. Along with the general growth of cities, an important south-to-north shift occurred in the pattern of urbanization. Around 1500, half of the people in cities of at least ten thousand residents could be found in the Italian states, Spain, or Portugal; by 1700, the urbanization of northwestern and southern Europe was roughly equal. Eastern Europe, despite the huge cities of Istanbul and Moscow, was still less urban than western Europe. London was by far the most populous European city, with 675,000 inhabitants in 1750; Berlin had 90,000 people, Warsaw only 23,000.

Urban Social Classes. Many landowners kept a residence in town, so the separation between rural and city life was not as extreme as might be imagined, at least not for the very rich. At the top of the ladder in the big cities were the landed nobles. Some of them filled their lives only with conspicuous consumption of fine food, extravagant clothing, coaches, books, and opera; others held key political, administrative, or judicial offices. However they spent their time, these rich families employed thousands of artisans, shopkeepers, and domestic servants. Many English peers (highest-ranking nobles) had thirty or forty servants at each of their homes.

The middle classes of officials, merchants, professionals, and landowners occupied the next rung down on the social ladder. London's population, for example, included about 20,000 middle-class families (constituting, at most, one-sixth of the city's population). In this period the middle classes began to develop distinctive ways of life that set them apart from both the rich noble landowners and the lower classes. Unlike the rich nobles, the middle classes lived primarily in the cities and towns, even if they owned small country estates. They ate more moderately than nobles but much better than peasants or laborers. For breakfast the British middle classes ate toast and rolls and, after 1700, drank tea. Dinner, served midday, consisted of roasted or boiled beef or mutton, poultry or pork, and vegetables. Supper was a light meal of bread and cheese with cake or pie. Beer was the main drink in London, and many families brewed their own. Even children drank beer because of the lack of fresh water.

In contrast to the gigantic and sprawling country seats of the richest English peers, middle-class

houses in town had about seven rooms, including four or five bedrooms and one or two living rooms, still many more than the poor agricultural worker. New household items reflected society's increasing wealth and its exposure to colonial imports: by 1700, the middle classes of London typically had mirrors in every room, a coffeepot and coffee mill, numerous pictures and ornaments, a china collection, and several clocks. Life for the middle classes on the continent was quite similar, though wine replaced beer in France.

Below the middle classes came the artisans and shopkeepers (most of whom were organized in professional guilds), then the journeymen, apprentices, servants, and laborers. At the bottom of the social scale were the unemployed poor, who survived by intermittent work and charity. Women married to artisans and shopkeepers often kept the accounts, supervised employees, and ran the household as well. Every household from the middle classes to the upper classes employed servants; artisans and shopkeepers frequently hired them too. Women from poorer families usually worked as domestic servants until they married. Four out of five domestic servants in the city were female. In large cities such as London, the servant population grew faster than the population of the city as a whole.

Signs of Social Distinction. Social status in the cities was readily visible. Wide, spacious streets graced rich districts; the houses had gardens and the air was relatively fresh. In poor districts the streets were narrow, dirty, dark, humid, and smelly, and the houses were damp and crowded. The poorest people were homeless, sleeping under bridges or in abandoned homes. A Neapolitan prince described his homeless neighbors as "lying like filthy animals, with no distinction of age or sex." In some districts, rich and poor lived in the same buildings, with the poor having to clamber to the shabby, cramped apartments on the top floors.

Like shelter, clothing was a reliable social indicator. The poorest workingwomen in Paris wore woolen skirts and blouses of dark colors over petticoats, bodice, and corset. They also donned caps of various sorts, cotton stockings, and shoes (probably their only pair). Workingmen dressed even more drably. Many occupations could be recognized by their dress: no one could confuse lawyers in their dark robes with masons or butchers in their special

The Seedy Side of City Life
The English painter and engraver William Hogarth chronicled every aspect of social life in London. In Night *(1738), he completes a cycle of engravings about greed and carelessness in city life. The Salisbury Flying Coach has overturned in Charing Cross Road, narrowly missing a bonfire. Despite the statue of King Charles I in the background, this is a sordid street filled with taverns, a quack pulling teeth, and urchins up to no good. About to be showered with the contents of a chamber pot is a drunken magistrate known for his anti-alcohol legislation. He is oblivious to the ills of the city that surround him, but Hogarth knew them well.*
Carole Frohlich Archive.

aprons, for example. People higher on the social ladder were more likely to sport a variety of fabrics, colors, and unusual designs in their clothing and to own many different outfits. Social status was not an abstract idea; it permeated every detail of daily life.

The Growth of a Literate Public

The ability to read and write also reflected social differences. People in the upper classes were more literate than those in the lower classes; city people were more literate than peasants. Protestant countries appear to have been more successful at promoting education and literacy than Catholic

countries, perhaps because of the Protestant emphasis on Bible reading. Widespread popular literacy was first achieved in the Protestant areas of Switzerland and in Presbyterian Scotland, and rates were also very high in the New England colonies and the Scandinavian countries. In France, literacy doubled in the eighteenth century thanks to the spread of parish schools, but still only one in two men and one in four women could read and write. Despite the efforts of some Protestant German states to encourage primary education, primary schooling remained woefully inadequate almost everywhere in Europe: few schools existed, teachers received low wages, and no country had yet established a national system of control or supervision.

Despite the deficiencies of primary education, a new literate public arose especially among the middle classes of the cities. More books and periodicals were published than ever before. Britain and the Dutch Republic led the way in this powerful outpouring of printed words. The trend began in the 1690s and gradually accelerated. In 1695, the British government allowed the licensing system, through which it controlled publications, to lapse, and new newspapers and magazines appeared almost immediately. The first London daily newspaper came out in 1702, and in 1709 Joseph Addison and Richard Steele published the first literary magazine, *The Spectator*. They devoted their magazine to the cultural improvement of the increasingly influential middle class. By the 1720s, twenty-four provincial newspapers were published in England, and by the 1730s the new *Gentleman's Magazine*, a kind of *Reader's Digest* of news, literature, and humor, enjoyed a large national circulation. In the London coffeehouses, an edition of a single newspaper might reach ten thousand male readers. Women did their reading at home. Newspapers on the continent lagged behind and often consisted mainly of advertising with little critical commentary. France, for example, had no daily paper until 1777.

New Tastes in the Arts

The new literate public did not just read newspapers; its members now pursued an interest in painting, attended concerts, and besieged booksellers in search of popular novels. Because increased trade and prosperity put money into the hands of the growing middle classes, a new urban audience began to compete with the churches, rulers, and courtiers as chief patrons for new work. As the public for the arts expanded, printed commentary on them emerged, setting the stage for the appearance of political and social criticism. New artistic tastes thus had effects far beyond the realm of the arts.

Rococo Painting. Developments in painting reflected the tastes of the new public, as the rococo style challenged the hold of the baroque and classical schools, especially in France. Like the baroque, the rococo emphasized irregularity and asymmetry, movement and curvature, but it did so on a much smaller, subtler scale. Many rococo paintings depicted scenes of intimate sensuality rather than the monumental, emotional grandeur favored by classical and baroque painters. Personal portraits and pastoral paintings took the place of heroic landscapes and grand, ceremonial canvases. Rococo

paintings adorned homes as well as palaces and served as a form of interior decoration rather than as a statement of piety. Its decorative quality made rococo art an ideal complement to newly discovered materials such as stucco and porcelain, especially the porcelain vases now imported from China.

Rococo, like *baroque,* was an invented word (from the French word *rocaille,* meaning "shell-work") and originally a derogatory label, meaning "frivolous decoration." But the great French rococo painters, such as Antoine Watteau (1684–1721) and François Boucher (1703–1770), were much more than mere decorators. Although both emphasized the erotic in their depictions, Watteau captured the melancholy side of a passing aristocratic style of life, and Boucher painted middle-class people at home during their daily activities. Both painters thereby contributed to the emergence of new sensibilities in art that increasingly attracted a middle-class public.

Rococo Painting
Painted originally as a shop sign for an art merchant, Gersaint's Shopsign *(1721) by Antoine Watteau demonstrates the new rococo style. The colors are muted and the atmosphere is light and airy. The subject matter—the sale of art, gilded mirrors, and toiletries to the new urban aristocrats and middle classes—is entirely secular and even commercial. The canvas reflects the new urban market for art and slyly notes the passing of a era: a portrait of the recently deceased Louis XIV is being packed away on the left-hand side of the painting. Watteau painted the sign in eight days while suffering from the tuberculosis that would kill him just a few months later.*
Erich Lessing/Art Resource, NY.

Music for the Public. The first public music concerts were performed in England in the 1670s, becoming much more regular and frequent in the 1690s. City concert halls typically seated about two hundred, but the relatively high price of tickets limited attendance to the better-off. Music clubs provided entertainment in smaller towns and villages. On the continent, Frankfurt organized the first regular public concerts in 1712; Hamburg and Paris began holding them within a few years. Opera continued to spread in the eighteenth century; Venice had sixteen public opera houses by 1700, and in 1732 Covent Garden opera house opened in London.

The growth of a public that appreciated and supported music had much the same effect as the extension of the reading public: like authors, composers could now begin to liberate themselves from court patronage and work for a paying audience. This development took time to solidify, however, and court or church patrons still commissioned much eighteenth-century music. Bach, a German Lutheran, wrote his *St. Matthew Passion* for Good Friday services in 1729 while he was organist and choirmaster for the leading church in Leipzig. He composed secular works (like the "Coffee Cantata") for the public and a variety of private patrons.

The composer George Frederick Handel (1685–1759) was among the first to grasp the new directions in music. He began his career playing second violin in the Hamburg opera orchestra and then moved to Britain in 1710. After distinguishing himself with operas and music composed for the British court, he turned to composing oratorios, a form he introduced in Britain. The oratorio combined the drama of opera with the majesty of religious and ceremonial music and featured the chorus over the soloists. Handel's most famous oratorio, *Messiah* (1741), reflected his personal, deeply felt piety but also his willingness to combine musical materials into a dramatic form that captured the enthusiasm of the new public. In 1740, a poem published in the *Gentleman's Magazine* exulted: "His art so modulates the sounds in all, / Our passions, as he pleases, rise and fall." Music had become an integral part of the new middle-class public's culture.

Novels. Nothing captured the imagination of the new public more than the novel, the literary genre whose very name underscored the eighteenth-century taste for novelty. Over three hundred French novels appeared between 1700 and 1730. During this unprecedented explosion, the novel took on its modern form and became more concerned with individual psychology and social description than with the picaresque adventures popular earlier (such as Cervantes's *Don Quixote*). The novel's popularity was closely tied to the expansion of the reading public, and novels were available in serial form in periodicals or from the many booksellers who popped up to serve the new market.

Women figured prominently in novels as characters, and women writers abounded. The English novel *Love in Excess* (1719) quickly reached a sixth printing, and its author, Eliza Haywood (1693?–1756), earned her living turning out a stream of novels with titles such as *Persecuted Virtue, Constancy Rewarded,* and *The History of Betsy Thoughtless*—all showing a concern for the proper place of women as models of virtue in a changing world. Heywood had first worked as an actress when her husband deserted her and her two children, but she soon turned to writing plays and novels. In the 1740s, she began publishing a magazine, *The Female Spectator*, which argued in favor of higher education for women.

Haywood's male counterpart was Daniel Defoe (1660?–1731), a merchant's son who had a diverse and colorful career as a manufacturer, political spy, novelist, and social commentator. Defoe wrote about schemes for national improvement, the state of English trade, the economic condition of the countryside, the effects of the plague, and the history of pirates, as well as such novels as *Robinson Crusoe* (1719) and *Moll Flanders* (1722). The story of the adventures of a shipwrecked sailor, *Robinson Crusoe* portrayed the new values of the time: to survive, Crusoe had to meet every challenge with fearless entrepreneurial ingenuity. He had to be ready for the unexpected and be able to improvise in every situation. He was, in short, the model for the new man in an expanding economy. Crusoe's patronizing attitude toward the black man Friday now draws much critical attention, but his discovery of Friday shows how the fate of blacks and whites had become intertwined in the new colonial environment.

Religious Revivals

Despite the novel's growing popularity, religious books and pamphlets still sold in huge numbers, and most Europeans remained devout, even as their religions were changing. In this period a Protestant revival known as Pietism rocked the complacency of the established churches in the German Lutheran states, the Dutch Republic, and Scandinavia. Pietists believed in a mystical religion of the heart; they wanted a more deeply emotional, even ecstatic religion. They urged intense Bible study, which in turn promoted popular education and contributed to the increase in literacy. Many Pietists attended catechism instruction every day and also went to morning and evening prayer meetings in addition to regular Sunday services.

As a grassroots movement, Pietism appealed to both Lutherans and Calvinists, some of whom left their churches to form new sects. One of the most remarkable disciples of Pietism was the English woman Jane Leade (1623–1704), who founded the sect of Philadelphians (from the Greek for "brotherly love"), which soon spread to the Dutch Republic and the German states. Leade's visions and studies of mysticism led her to advocate a universal, nondogmatic church that would include all reborn Christians. Philadelphic societies maintained only loose ties to one another, however, and despite Leade's organizational aims they soon went off in different directions.

Catholicism also had its versions of religious revival, especially in France. A French woman, Jeanne Marie Guyon (1648–1717), attracted many noblewomen and a few leading clergymen to her own Catholic brand of Pietism, known as Quietism. Claiming miraculous visions and astounding prophecies, she urged a mystical union with God through prayer and simple devotion. Despite papal condemnation and intense controversy within Catholic circles in France, Guyon had followers all over Europe.

Even more influential were the Jansenists, who gained many new adherents to their austere form of Catholicism despite Louis XIV's harassment and repeated condemnation by the papacy. Under the pressure of religious and political persecution, Jansenism took a revivalist turn in the 1720s. At the funeral of a Jansenist priest in Paris in 1727, the crowd who flocked to the grave claimed to witness a series of miraculous healings. Within a few years a cult formed around the priest's tomb, and clandestine Jansenist presses reported new miracles to the reading public. When the French government tried to suppress the cult, one enraged wit placed a

sign at the tomb that read, "By order of the king, God is forbidden to work miracles here." Some believers fell into frenzied convulsions, claiming to be inspired by the Holy Spirit through the intercession of the dead priest. Although the Catholic church, the French state, and even some Jansenists ultimately repudiated the new cult, its remarkable emotional power showed that popular expressions of religion could not be easily contained. After midcentury, Jansenism became even more politically active as its adherents joined in opposition to crown policies on religion.

❖ Consolidation of the European State System

The spread of Pietism and Jansenism reflected the emergence of a middle-class public that now participated in every new development, including religion. The middle classes could pursue these interests because the European state system gradually stabilized. Warfare settled three main issues between 1690 and 1740: a coalition of powers held Louis XIV's France in check on the continent; Great Britain emerged from the wars against Louis as the preeminent maritime power; and Russia defeated Sweden in the contest for supremacy in the Baltic. After Louis XIV's death in 1715, Europe enjoyed the fruits of a more balanced diplomatic system, in which warfare became less frequent and less widespread. States could then spend their resources establishing and expanding control over their own populations, both at home and in their colonies.

The Limits of French Absolutism

When the seventy-six-year-old Louis XIV lay on his deathbed suffering from constipation and gangrene in 1715, he must have felt depressed by the unraveling of his accomplishments. Not only had his plans for territorial expansion been thwarted, but his incessant wars had exhausted the treasury, despite new taxes. In 1689, Louis's rival, William III, prince of Orange and king of England and Scotland (r. 1689–1702), had set out to forge a European alliance that eventually included Britain, the Dutch Republic, Sweden, Austria, and Spain. The allies fought Louis to a stalemate in the War of the League of Augsburg, sometimes called the Nine Years' War (1689–1697), but hostilities resumed four years later in the War of the Spanish Succession, which brought France's expansionist ambitions to a grinding halt.

The War of the Spanish Succession, 1701–1713. When the mentally and physically feeble Charles II (r. 1665–1700) of Spain died in 1700 without a direct heir, all of Europe poised for a fight over the spoils. The Spanish succession could not help but be a burning issue, given Spain's extensive territories in Italy and the Netherlands and colonies overseas. It seemed a plum ripe for picking. Spanish power had declined steadily since its golden age in the sixteenth century: the gold and silver of the New World had been exhausted, and the Spanish kings neglected manufactures, debased their coinage, and failed to adopt the new scientific ideas and commercial practices developed by the Dutch and the British. As a consequence, they lacked the resources for international competition.

Before Charles died, he named Louis XIV's second grandson, Philip, duke of Anjou, as his heir, but his bequest resolved nothing. Louis XIV and the Austrian emperor Leopold I had competing dynastic claims to the Spanish crown, and Leopold refused to accept Charles's deathbed will. The ensuing War of the Spanish Succession proved disastrous for the French because most of Europe once again allied against them, fearing the consequences of French control over Spanish territories. The French lost several major battles and had to accept disadvantageous terms in the Peace of Utrecht of 1713–1714 (Map 18.2). Although Philip was recognized as king of Spain, he had to renounce any future claim to the French crown, thus barring unification of the two kingdoms. Spain surrendered its territories in Italy and the Netherlands to the Austrians and Gibraltar to the British; France ceded possessions in North America (Newfoundland, the Hudson Bay area, and most of Nova Scotia) to Britain. France no longer threatened to dominate European power politics.

The Death of Louis XIV and the Regency. At home, Louis's policy of absolutism had fomented bitter hostility. Nobles fiercely resented his promotions of commoners to high office. The duke of Saint-Simon complained that "falseness, servility, admiring glances, combined with a dependent and cringing attitude, above all, an appearance of being nothing without him, were the only ways of pleasing him." Even some of the king's leading servants, such as Archbishop Fénelon, who tutored the king's grandson, began to call for monarchical reform. An admirer of Guyon's Quietism, Fénelon severely criticized the court's excesses: the "steady stream of extravagant adulation, which reaches the point of idolatry"; the constant, bloody wars; and the misery of the people.

On his deathbed, Louis XIV gave his blessing and some sound advice to his five-year-old great-grandson and successor, Louis XV (r. 1715–1774): "My child, you are about to become a great King. Do not imitate my love of building nor my liking for war." Squabbling over control of the crown began immediately. The duke of Orléans (1674–1723), nephew of the dead king, was named regent. He revived some of the parlements' powers and tried to give leading nobles a greater say in political affairs as a way to restore confidence and appease aristocratic critics. The regent also moved the court back to Paris, away from the atmosphere of moral rigidity and prudery that Louis had enforced in his last years at Versailles.

Financial problems plagued the Regency as they would beset all succeeding French regimes in the eighteenth century. In 1719, the regent appointed the Scottish adventurer and financier John Law to the top financial position of controller-general. Law founded a trading company for North America and a state bank that issued paper money and stock (without them trade depended on the available supply of gold and silver). The bank was supposed to offer lower interest rates to the state, thus cutting the cost of financing the government's debts. The value of the stock rose rapidly in a frenzy of speculation, only to crash a few months later. With it vanished any hope of establishing a state bank or issuing paper money for nearly a century.

France finally achieved a measure of financial stability under the leadership of Cardinal Hercule de Fleury (1653–1743), the most powerful member of the government after the death of the regent. Fleury aimed to avoid adventure abroad and keep social peace at home; he balanced the budget and carried out a large project for road and canal construction. Colonial trade boomed. Peace and the acceptance of limits on territorial expansion inaugurated a century of French prosperity.

MAP 18.2 Europe, c. 1715

Although Louis XIV succeeded in putting his grandson Philip on the Spanish throne, France emerged considerably weakened from the War of Spanish Succession. France ceded large territories in Canada to Britain, which also gained key Mediterranean outposts from Spain, as well as a monopoly on providing slaves to the Spanish colonies. Spanish losses were catastrophic. Philip had to renounce any future claim to the French crown and give up considerable territories in the Netherlands and Italy to the Austrians.

British Rise and Dutch Decline

The British and the Dutch had joined in a coalition against Louis XIV under their joint ruler William III, who was simultaneously stadholder of the Dutch Republic and, with his English wife, Mary (d. 1694), ruler of England, Wales, and Scotland. After William's death in 1702, the British and Dutch went their separate ways. Over the next decades, the English monarchy incorporated Scotland and subjugated Ireland, becoming "Great Britain." At the same time Dutch imperial power declined; even though Dutch merchants still controlled a substantial portion of world trade, by 1700 Great Britain dominated the seas and the Dutch, with their small population of less than two million, came to depend on alliances with bigger powers.

From England to Great Britain.   English relations with Scotland and Ireland were complicated by the problem of succession: William and Mary had no children. To ensure a Protestant succession, Parliament ruled that Mary's sister, Anne, would succeed William and Mary and that the Protestant House of Hanover in Germany would succeed Anne if she had no surviving heirs. Catholics were excluded. When Queen Anne (r. 1702–1714) died leaving no children, the elector of Hanover, a Protestant great-grandson of James I, consequently became King George I (r. 1714–1727). The House of Hanover— it was renamed the House of Windsor during World War I—still occupies the British throne.

Support from the Scots and Irish for this solution did not come easily because many in Scotland and Ireland supported the claims to the throne of the deposed Catholic king, James II, and, after his death in 1701, his son James Edward. Out of fear of this "Jacobitism" (from the Latin *Jacobus* for "James"), Scottish Protestant leaders agreed to the Act of Union of 1707, which abolished the Scottish Parliament and affirmed the Scots' recognition of the Protestant Hanoverian succession. The Scots agreed to obey the Parliament of Great Britain, which would include Scottish members in the House of Commons and the House of Lords. A Jacobite rebellion in Scotland in 1715, aiming to restore the Stuart line, was suppressed. The threat of Jacobitism nonetheless continued into the 1740s.

The Irish—90 percent of whom were Catholic— proved even more difficult to subdue. When James

II had gone to Ireland in 1689 to raise a Catholic rebellion against the new monarchs of England, William III responded by taking command of the joint English and Dutch forces and defeating James's Irish supporters. James fled to France, and the Catholics in Ireland faced yet more confiscation and legal restrictions. By 1700, Irish Catholics, who in 1640 had owned 60 percent of the land in Ireland, owned just 14 percent. The Protestant-controlled Irish Parliament passed a series of laws limiting the rights of the Catholic majority: Catholics could not bear arms, send their children abroad for education, establish Catholic schools at home, or marry Protestants. Catholics could not sit in Parliament, nor could they vote for its members unless they took an oath renouncing Catholic doctrine. These and a host of other laws reduced Catholic Ireland to the status of a colony; one English official commented in 1745, "The poor people of Ireland are used worse than negroes." Most of the Irish were peasants who lived in primitive housing and subsisted on a meager diet that included no meat.

The Parliament of Great Britain was soon dominated by the Whigs. In Britain's constitutional system, the monarch ruled with Parliament. The crown chose the ministers, directed policy, and supervised administration, while Parliament raised revenue, passed laws, and represented the interests of the people to the crown. The powers of Parliament were reaffirmed by the Triennial Act in 1694, which provided that Parliaments meet at least once every three years (this was extended to seven years in 1716, after the Whigs had established their ascendancy). Only 200,000 propertied men could vote, out of a population of more than 5 million people, and, not surprisingly, most members of Parliament came from the landed gentry. In fact, a few hundred families controlled all the important political offices.

George I and George II (r. 1727–1760) relied on one man, Sir Robert Walpole (1676–1745), to help them manage their relations with Parliament. From his position as First Lord of the Treasury, Walpole made himself into first or "prime" minister, leading the House of Commons from 1721 to 1742. Although appointed initially by the king, Walpole established an enduring pattern of parliamentary government in which a prime minister from the leading party guided legislation through the House of Commons. Walpole also built a vast patronage machine that dispensed government jobs to win

Sir Robert Walpole at a Cabinet Meeting
Sir Robert Walpole and George II developed government by a cabinet, which consisted of Walpole as first lord of the treasury, the two secretaries of state, the lord chancellor, the chancellor of the exchequer, the lord privy seal, and the lord president of the council. Walpole's cabinet was the ancestor of modern cabinets in both Great Britain and the United States. Its similarities to modern forms should not be overstated, however. The entire staff of the two secretaries of state, who had charge of all foreign and domestic affairs other than taxation, numbered twenty-four in 1726.
The Fotomas Index, U.K.

support for the crown's policies. Some complained that his patronage system corrupted politics, but Walpole successfully used his political skills to convince the ruling class not to rock its own boat. Walpole's successors relied more and more on the patronage system and eventually alienated not only the Tories but also the middle classes in London and even the North American colonies.

The partisan division between the Whigs, who supported the Hanoverian succession and the rights of dissenting Protestants, and the Tories, who had backed the Stuart line and the Anglican church, did not hamper Great Britain's pursuit of economic, military, and colonial power. In this period, Great Britain became a great power on the world stage by virtue of its navy and its ability to finance major military involvement in the wars against Louis XIV. The founding in 1694 of the Bank of England—which, unlike the French bank, endured—enabled the government to raise money at low interest for foreign wars. The bank's success can be measured by the amount of money it lent in wartime: by the 1740s, the government could borrow more than four times what it could in the 1690s.

The Dutch Eclipse. When William of Orange (William III of England) died in 1702, he left no heirs, and for forty-five years the Dutch lived without a stadholder. The merchant ruling class of some two thousand families dominated the Dutch Republic more than ever, but they presided over a country that counted for less in international power politics. In some areas, Dutch decline was only relative: the Dutch population was not growing as fast as others, for example, and the Dutch share of the Baltic trade decreased from 50 percent in 1720 to less than 30 percent by the 1770s. After 1720, the Baltic countries—Prussia, Russia, Denmark, and Sweden—began to ban imports of manufactured goods to protect their own industries, and Dutch trade in particular suffered. The output of Leiden textiles dropped to one-third of its 1700 level by 1740. Shipbuilding, paper manufacturing, tobacco processing, salt refining, and pottery production all dwindled as well. The Dutch East India Company saw its political and military grip loosened in India, Ceylon, and Java.

The biggest exception to the downward trend was trade with the New World, which increased with escalating demands for sugar and tobacco. The Dutch shifted their interest away from great power rivalries toward those areas of international trade and finance where they could establish an enduring presence.

Russia's Emergence as a European Power

Dutch and British commerce and shipbuilding so impressed Russian tsar Peter I (r. 1689–1725) that he traveled incognito to their shipyards in 1697 to learn their methods firsthand. But the tsar intended to build a strong absolutist state in Russia, avoiding the weaknesses of decentralization that plagued the Dutch. As Britain gained dominance on the seas in the West, Peter aimed for dominance on land in the East. Known to history as Peter the Great, he dragged Russia kicking and screaming all the way to great power status. Although he came to the throne while still a minor (on the eve of his tenth birthday), grew up under the threat of a palace coup, and enjoyed little formal education, his accomplishments soon matched his seven-foot-tall stature. Peter transformed public life in Russia and established an absolutist state on the western model. His westernization efforts ignited an enduring controversy: did Peter set Russia on a course of inevitable westernization required to compete with the West, or did he forever and fatally disrupt Russia's natural evolution into a distinctive Slavic society?

Peter the Great's Brand of Absolutism.   Peter reorganized government and finance on western models; he streamlined the ministries and assigned each a foreign adviser. Like other absolute rulers, he strengthened his army. With ruthless recruiting methods, which included branding a cross on every recruit's left hand to prevent desertion, he forged an army of 200,000 men and equipped it with modern weapons. He created schools for artillery, engineering, and military medicine and built the first navy in Russian history. Not surprisingly, taxes tripled.

The tsar allowed nothing to stand in his way. He did not hesitate to use torture and executed thousands. He allowed a special guards regiment unprecedented power to expedite cases against those suspected of rebellion, espionage, pretensions to the throne, or just "unseemly utterances" against him. Opposition to his policies reached into his own family: because his only son, Alexei, had allied himself with Peter's critics, he threw him into prison, where the young man mysteriously died.

To control the often restive nobility, Peter insisted that all noblemen engage in state service. A Table of Ranks (1722) classified them into military, administrative, and court categories, a codification of social and legal relationships in Russia that would last for nearly two centuries. All social and material advantages now depended on serving the crown. Because the nobles lacked a secure independent status, Peter could command them to a degree that was unimaginable in western Europe. State service was

Peter the Great Modernizes Russia

In this popular print, a barber forces a protesting noble to conform to Western fashions. (The barber is sometimes erroneously identified as Peter himself.) Peter ordered all nobles, merchants, and middle-class professionals to cut off their beards or pay a huge tax to keep them. An early biographer of Peter, the French writer Jean Rousset de Missy (1730), claimed that those who lost their beards saved them to put in their coffins, in fear that they would not enter heaven without them. Most western Europeans applauded these attempts to change Russian customs, but many Russians deeply resented the attack on traditional ways.
Carole Frohlich Archive.

not only compulsory but also permanent. Moreover, the male children of those in service had to be registered by the age of ten and begin serving at fifteen. To increase his authority over the Russian Orthodox church, Peter allowed the office of patriarch (supreme head) to remain vacant, and in 1721 he replaced it with the Holy Synod, a bureaucracy of laymen under his supervision. To many Russians, Peter was the Antichrist incarnate.

Westernization.   With the goal of Westernizing Russian culture, Peter set up the first greenhouses, laboratories, and technical schools and founded the

Russian Academy of Sciences. He ordered translations of western classics and hired a German theater company to perform the French plays of Molière. He replaced the traditional Russian calendar with the western one,* introduced Arabic numerals, and brought out the first public newspaper. He ordered his officials and the nobles to shave their beards and dress in western fashion, and he even issued precise regulations about the suitable style of jacket, boots, and cap (generally French or German). He published a book on manners for young noblemen and experimented with dentistry on his courtiers.

Peter did not undertake these reforms alone. Elite men who were eager for social mobility and willing to adopt Western values cooperated with him. Peter encouraged foreigners to move to Russia to offer their advice and skills, especially for building the new capital city, St. Petersburg. The new capital, named after Peter, was meant to symbolize Russia's opening to the West. Construction began in 1703 in a Baltic province that had been recently conquered from Sweden. By the end of 1709, forty thousand recruits a year found themselves assigned to the work. Peter ordered skilled workers to move to the new city and commanded all landowners possessing more than forty serf households to build houses there. In the 1720s, a German minister described the city "as a wonder of the world, considering its magnificent palaces, . . . and the short time that was employed in the building of it." By 1710, the permanent population of St. Petersburg reached eight thousand. At Peter's death in 1725, it had forty thousand residents.

As a new city far from the Russian heartland around Moscow, St. Petersburg represented a decisive break with Russia's past. Peter widened that gap by every means possible. At his new capital he tried to improve the traditionally denigrated, secluded status of women by ordering them to dress in European styles and appear publicly at his dinners for diplomatic representatives. Imitating French manners, he decreed that women attend his new social salons of officials, officers, and merchants for con-

Russian Rococo
Peter the Great's insistence on incorporating western European influences extended even to tableware. This silver tureen might have been fashioned in Paris or any other western European center of decorative art. Its motifs and trim reveal rococo influences. State Historical Museum, St. Petersburg.

versation and dancing. A foreigner headed every one of Peter's new technical and vocational schools, and for its first eight years the new Academy of Sciences included no Russians. Upper-class Russians learned French or German, which they often spoke even at home. Such changes affected only the very top of Russian society, however; the mass of the population had no contact with the new ideas and ended up paying for the innovations either in ruinous new taxation or by building St. Petersburg, a project that cost the lives of thousands of workers. Serfs remained tied to the land, completely dominated by their noble lords.

Despite all his achievements, Peter could not ensure his succession. In the thirty-seven years after his death in 1725, Russia endured six different rulers: three women, a boy of twelve, an infant, and an imbecile. Recurrent palace coups weakened the monarchy and enabled the nobility to loosen Peter's rigid code of state service. In the process the serfs' status only worsened. They ceased to be counted as legal subjects; the criminal code of 1754 listed them as property. They not only were bought and sold like cattle but also had become legally indistinguishable from them. Westernization had not yet touched the lives of the serfs.

The Balance of Power in the East

Peter the Great's success in building up state power changed the balance of power in eastern Europe. Overcoming initial military setbacks, Russia eventually defeated Sweden and took its place as the

---

*Peter introduced the Julian calendar, then still used in Protestant but not Catholic countries. Later in the eighteenth century, Protestant Europe abandoned the Julian for the Gregorian calendar. Not until 1918 was the Julian calendar abolished in Russia, at which point it had fallen thirteen days behind Europe's Gregorian calendar.

leading power in the Baltic region. Russia could then turn its attention to eastern Europe, where it competed with Austria and Prussia. Once mighty Poland-Lithuania became the playground for great power rivalries.

The Decline of Sweden. Sweden had dominated the Baltic region since the Thirty Years' War and did not easily give up its preeminence. When Peter the Great joined an anti-Swedish coalition in 1700 with Denmark, Saxony, and Poland, Sweden's Charles XII (r. 1697–1718) stood up to the test. Still in his teens at the beginning of the Great Northern War, Charles first defeated Denmark, then destroyed the new Russian army, and quickly marched into Poland and Saxony. After defeating the Poles and occupying Saxony, Charles invaded Russia. Here Peter's rebuilt army finally defeated him at the battle of Poltava (1709).

The Russian victory resounded everywhere. The Russian ambassador to Vienna reported, "It is commonly said that the tsar will be formidable to all Europe, that he will be a kind of northern Turk." Prussia and other German states joined the anti-Swedish alliance, and war resumed. Charles XII died in battle in 1718, and complex negotiations finally ended the Great Northern War. By the terms of the Treaty of Nystad (1721), Sweden ceded its eastern Baltic provinces—Livonia, Estonia, Ingria, and southern Karelia—to Russia. Sweden also lost territories on the north German coast to Prussia and the other allied German states (Map 18.3). An aristocratic reaction against Charles XII's incessant demands for war supplies swept away Sweden's absolutist regime, essentially removing Sweden from great power competition.

Prussian Militarization. Prussia had to make the most of every military opportunity, as it did in the Great Northern War, because it was much smaller in size and population than Russia, Austria, or France. King Frederick William I (r. 1713–1740) doubled the size of the Prussian army; though much smaller than those of his rivals, it was the best-trained and most up-to-date force in Europe. By 1740, Prussia had Europe's highest proportion of men at arms (1 of every 28 people, versus 1 in 157 in France and 1 in 64 in Russia) and the highest proportion of nobles in the military (1 in 7 noblemen, as compared with 1 in 33 in France and 1 in 50 in Russia).

The army so dominated life in Prussia that the country earned the label "a large army with a small state attached." So obsessed was he with his soldiers

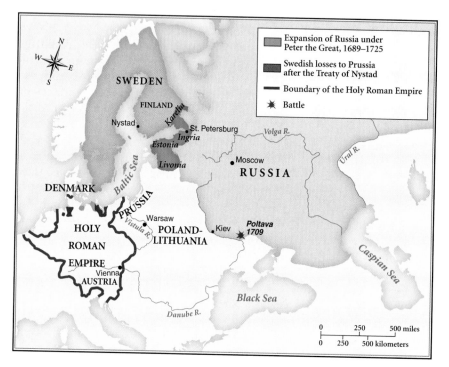

MAP 18.3 Russia and Sweden after the Great Northern War, 1721
After the Great Northern War, Russia supplanted Sweden as the major power in the north. Although Russia had a much larger population from which to draw its armies, Sweden made the most of its advantages and gave way only after a great military struggle.

that the five-foot-five-inch-tall Frederick William formed a regiment of "giants," the Grenadiers, composed exclusively of men over six feet tall. Royal agents scoured Europe trying to find such men and sometimes kidnapped them right off the street. Frederick William, the "Sergeant King," was one of the first rulers to wear a military uniform as his everyday dress. He subordinated the entire domestic administration to the army's needs. He also installed a system for recruiting soldiers by local district quotas. He financed the army's growth by subjecting all the provinces to an excise tax on food, drink, and manufactured goods and by increasing rents on crown lands. Prussia was now poised to become one of the major players on the continent.

The War of Polish Succession, 1733–1735. Prussia did not enter into military conflict foolishly. During the War of Polish Succession it stood on the sidelines, content to watch others fight. The war showed how the balance of power had changed since the heyday of Louis XIV: France had to maneuver within a complex great power system that now included Russia, and Poland-Lithuania no longer controlled its own destiny. When the king of Poland-Lithuania died in 1733, France, Spain, and Sardinia went to war against Austria and Russia, each side supporting rival claimants to the Polish throne. After Russia drove the French candidate out of Poland-Lithuania, France agreed to accept the Austrian candidate; in exchange, Austria gave the province of Lorraine to the French candidate, the father-in-law of Louis XV, with the promise that the province would pass to France on his death. France and Britain went back to pursuing their colonial rivalries. Prussia and Russia concentrated on shoring up their influence within Poland-Lithuania. Austria did not want to become mired in a long struggle in Poland-Lithuania because its armies still faced the Turks on

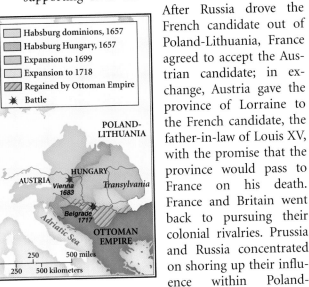

Habsburg dominions, 1657
Habsburg Hungary, 1657
Expansion to 1699
Expansion to 1718
Regained by Ottoman Empire
Battle

POLAND-
LITHUANIA

AUSTRIA HUNGARY
Vienna Transylvania
1683
Belgrade
1717
Adriatic Sea OTTOMAN
EMPIRE

250   500 miles
250   500 kilometers

Austrian Conquest of Hungary, 1657–1730

its southeastern border. Even though the Austrians had forced the Turks to recognize their rule over all of Hungary and Transylvania in 1699 and occupied Belgrade in 1717, the Turks did not stop fighting. In the 1730s, the Turks retook Belgrade, and Russia now claimed a role in the struggle against the Turks. Moreover, Hungary, though "liberated" from Turkish rule, proved less than enthusiastic about submitting to Austria. In 1703, the wealthiest Hungarian noble landlord, Ferenc Rákóczi (1676–1735), led a combined noble and peasant revolt against the Austrians. Rákóczi raised an army of seventy thousand men who pledged to fight for "God, Fatherland, and Liberty." Although the rebels did not win the ensuing war, which lasted until 1711, they forced the Austrians to recognize local Hungarian institutions, grant amnesty, and restore confiscated estates in exchange for confirming hereditary Austrian rule. Austria had more than sufficient reason to avoid committing itself to a long war against France.

The Power of Diplomacy

No single power emerged from the wars of the first half of the eighteenth century clearly superior to the others, and the idea of maintaining a balance of power guided both military and diplomatic maneuvering. The Peace of Utrecht had explicitly declared that such a balance was crucial to maintaining peace in Europe, and in 1720 a British pamphleteer wrote, "There is not, I believe, any doctrine in the law of nations, of more certain truth . . . than this of the balance of power." It was the law of gravity of European politics. This system of equilibrium often rested on military force, such as the leagues formed against Louis XIV or the coalition against Sweden. All states counted on diplomacy, however, to resolve issues even after fighting had begun.

To meet the new demands placed on it, the diplomatic service, like the military and financial bureaucracies before it, had to develop regular procedures. The French set a pattern of diplomatic service that the other European states soon imitated. By 1685, France had embassies in all the important capitals. Nobles of ancient families served as ambassadors to Rome, Madrid, Vienna, and London, whereas royal officials were chosen for Switzerland, the Dutch Republic, and Venice. Most held their appointments for at least three or four years, and all went off with elaborate written instructions that included explicit statements of policy as well as full accounts of the political conditions of the country to which they were posted. The ambassador selected and paid for his own staff. This practice could make the journey to a new post very cumbersome, because the staff might be as large as eighty people, and they brought along all their own furniture, pictures, silverware, and tapestries. It took one French ambassador ten weeks to get from Paris to Stockholm.

By the early 1700s, French writings on diplomatic methods were read everywhere. François de Callières's manual *On the Manner of Negotiating with Sovereigns* (1716) insisted that sound diplomacy was based on the creation of confidence, rather than deception: "The secret of negotiation is to harmonize the real interests of the parties concerned." Callières believed that the diplomatic service had to be professional—that young attachés should be chosen for their skills, not their family connections. These sensible views did not prevent the development of a dual system of diplomacy, in which rulers issued secret instructions that often negated the official ones sent by their own foreign offices. Secret diplomacy had some advantages because it allowed rulers to break with past alliances, but it also led to confusion and, sometimes, scandal, for the rulers often employed unreliable adventurers as their confidential agents. Still, the diplomatic system in the early eighteenth century proved successful enough to ensure a continuation of the principles of the Peace of Westphalia (1648); in the midst of every crisis and war, the great powers would convene and hammer out a written agreement detailing the requirements for peace.

The Power of Numbers

Successful diplomacy could smooth the road toward peace, but success in war still depended on sheer numbers—of men and muskets. Because each state's strength depended largely on the size of its army, the growth and health of the population increasingly entered into government calculations. The publication in 1690 of the Englishman William Petty's *Political Arithmetick* quickened the interest of government officials everywhere; Petty offered statistical estimates of human capital—that is, of population and wages—to determine Britain's national wealth. This "political arithmetic" inevitably drew attention to public health issues. Although hospitals were transformed in this period from public charities into medical institutions focused more narrowly on disease, health care remained precarious at best.

Political Arithmetic. A large, growing population could be as vital to a state's future as access to silver mines or overseas trade, so government officials devoted increased effort to the statistical estimation of total population and rates of births, deaths, marriages, and fertility. In 1727, Frederick William I of Prussia founded two university chairs to encourage population studies, and textbooks and handbooks advocated state intervention to improve the population's health and welfare.

Physicians used the new population statistics to explain the environmental causes of disease, another new preoccupation in this period. Petty devised a quantitative scale that distinguished healthy from unhealthy places largely on the basis of air quality, an early precursor of modern environmental studies. After investigating specific cities, German medical geographers urged government campaigns to improve public sanitation. Everywhere, environmentalists gathered and analyzed data on climate, disease, and population, searching for correlations to help direct policy. As a result of these efforts, local governments undertook such measures as draining low-lying areas, burying refuse, and cleaning wells, all of which eventually helped lower the death rates from epidemic diseases.

Public Hygiene and Health Care. Urban growth made public hygiene problems more acute. Cities were the unhealthiest places because excrement (animal and human) and garbage accumulated where people lived densely packed together. A traveler described the streets of Madrid in 1697 as "always very dirty because it is the custom to throw all the rubbish out of the window." Paris seemed to a visitor "so detestable that it is impossible to remain there" because of the smell; even the facade of the Louvre palace in Paris was soiled by the contents of night commodes that servants routinely dumped out of windows every morning. Only the wealthy could escape walking in mucky streets, by hiring men to carry them in sedan chairs or to drive them in coaches.

Founded originally as charities concerned foremost with the moral worthiness of the poor, hospitals gradually evolved into medical institutions that defined patients by their diseases. The process of diagnosis changed as physicians began to use specialized Latin terms for illnesses. The gap between medical experts and their patients increased, as physicians now also relied on postmortem dissections in the hospital to gain better knowledge, a practice most patients' families resented. Press reports of body snatching and grave robbing by surgeons and their apprentices outraged the public well into the 1800s.

Despite the change in hospitals, individual health care remained something of a free-for-all in which physicians competed with bloodletters, itinerant venereal-disease doctors, bonesetters, druggists, midwives, and "cunning women," who specialized in home remedies. Physicians often followed popular prescriptions for illnesses because they had nothing better to offer. Recipes for cures were part of most people's everyday conversation. The various "medical" opinions about childbirth highlight the confusion people faced. Midwives delivered most babies, though they sometimes encountered criticism, even from within their own ranks. One consulting midwife complained that ordinary midwives in Bristol, England, made women in labor drink a mixture of their husband's urine and leek juice. By the 1730s, female midwives faced competition from male midwives, who were known for using instruments such as forceps to pull the baby out of the birth canal. Women rarely sought a physician's help in giving birth, however; they preferred the advice and assistance of trusted local midwives. In any case, trained physicians were few in number and almost nonexistent outside cities.

Public and private hygiene improved only gradually. Patients were as likely to die of diseases caught in the hospital as to be cured there. Antiseptics were virtually unknown. The wealthy preferred treatment at home, sometimes by private physicians. The medical profession, with nationwide organizations and licensing, had not yet emerged, and no clear line separated trained physicians from quacks. For example, if a woman of the prosperous classes had breast cancer, she could have a doctor remove the breast tumors in a short, painful operation without anesthesia; but many opted instead to use folk remedies such as a plaster of mutton suet, beeswax, and flaxseed. Unfortunately, usually neither the surgery nor the concoctions proved effective.

Insanity was treated as a physical rather than an emotional ailment. Doctors believed most madness was caused by "melancolia," a condition they attributed to disorders in the system of bodily "humors." Their prescribed treatments included blood transfusions; ingestion of bitter substances such as coffee, quinine, and even soap; immersion in water; various forms of exercise; and burning or cauterizing the body to allow black vapors to escape.

Hardly any infectious diseases could be cured, though inoculation against smallpox spread from the Middle East to Europe in the early eighteenth century, thanks largely to the efforts of Lady Mary Wortley Montagu, who learned about the technique while living in Constantinople. (See "Did You Know?," page 674.) After 1750, physicians developed successful procedures for wide-scale vaccination, although even then many people resisted the idea of inoculating themselves with a disease. Other diseases spread quickly in the unsanitary conditions of urban life. Ordinary people washed or changed clothes rarely, lived in overcrowded housing with poor ventilation, and got their water from contaminated sources, such as refuse-filled rivers.

Until the mid-1700s, most people considered bathing dangerous. Public bathhouses had disappeared from cities in the sixteenth and seventeenth centuries because they seemed a source of disorderly behavior and epidemic illness. In the eighteenth century, even private bathing came into disfavor because people feared the effects of contact with water. Fewer than one in ten newly built private mansions in Paris had baths. Bathing was hazardous, physicians insisted, because it opened the body to disease. One manners manual of 1736 admonished, "It is correct to clean the face every morning by using a white cloth to cleanse it. It is less good to wash with water, because it renders the face susceptible to cold in winter and sun in summer." The upper classes associated cleanliness not with baths but with frequently changed linens, powdered hair, and perfume, which was thought to strengthen the body and refresh the brain by counteracting corrupt and foul air.

Lady Mary Wortley Montagu and Inoculation for Smallpox

The Scourge of Smallpox
This engraving from a hospital report of 1750 shows a patient being tended in a smallpox hospital for the poor in London. The patient's face has been disfigured by the disease.
British Museum.

Daughter of a duke, wife of an ambassador, and mother-in-law of a prime minister, Lady Mary Wortley Montagu (1689–1762) might have confined herself to socializing in the highest circles and managing a large household. But her life changed as a result of two unexpected circumstances: in 1715 she caught smallpox, which left her disfigured by pitted skin and the loss of her eyelashes (her brother died of the dread disease); and in 1716 her husband was named the British ambassador to the Ottoman Empire. She undertook the long voyage with him and wrote letters filled with vivid descriptions of life in eastern Europe and the Ottoman Empire. She returned from Constantinople in 1718, determined to introduce a Turkish invention, inoculation against smallpox. Lady Mary studied inoculation in several Turkish towns and tried it on her son while still in the Ottoman Empire. In 1717, she wrote a friend describing how inoculation was carried out by old women who used needles to prick the skin with smallpox "venom." The children fell ill after eight days but recovered completely.

In 1721, when a new smallpox epidemic threatened England, Lady Mary called on her physician to inoculate her daughter with two additional physicians attending as witnesses. One of the observers immediately inoculated his own son: the newspapers picked up the story, and within a few weeks six convicted criminals had volunteered to serve as guinea pigs in front of a crowd of witnesses including scientists from the English Royal Society. All six survived, but when two new patients died after inoculation in the following months, clergymen and physicians attacked the practice. One physician denounced "an Experiment practiced only by a few *Ignorant Women,* amongst an illiterate and unthinking People." Montagu printed a stinging rejoinder under the anonymous signature "Turkey Merchant." Although she won this battle as inoculation spread in use, she never published anything under her own name in her lifetime.

Ridiculed by some male contemporaries for her meddling in public affairs, Montagu had the last word after her death when her letters about the Ottoman Empire were published, revealing her as a correspondent with a talent for description of foreign customs and a wide-ranging interest in philosophical and literary matters. Lady Mary incarnated the new perspective gained by travel, in which close study of another culture challenged preconceptions and might even suggest important innovations to bring back home.

❖ The Birth of the Enlightenment

Economic expansion, the emergence of a new consumer society, and the stabilization of the European state system all generated optimism about the future. The intellectual corollary was the *Enlightenment*, a term used later in the eighteenth century to describe the loosely knit group of writers and scholars who believed that human beings could apply a critical, reasoning spirit to every problem they encountered in this world. The new secular, scientific, and critical attitude first emerged in the 1690s, scrutinizing everything from the absolutism of Louis XIV to the traditional role of women in society. After 1740, criticism took a more systematic turn as writers provided new theories for the organization of society and politics, but even by the 1720s and 1730s, established authorities realized they faced a new set of challenges.

Popularization of Science and Challenges to Religion

The writers of the Enlightenment glorified the geniuses of the new science and championed scientific method as the solution for all social problems. (See "Terms of History," page 676.) One of the most influential popularizations was the French writer Bernard de Fontenelle's *Conversations on the Plurality of Worlds* (1686). Presented as a dialogue between an aristocratic woman and a man of the world, the book made the Copernican, sun-centered view of the universe available to the literate public. By 1700, mathematics and science had become fashionable pastimes in high society, and the public flocked to lectures explaining scientific discoveries. Journals complained that scientific learning had become the passport to female affection: "There were two young ladies in Paris whose heads had been so turned by this branch of learning that one of them declined to listen to a proposal of marriage unless the candidate for her hand undertook to learn how to make telescopes." Such writings poked fun at women with intellectual interests, but they also demonstrated that women now participated in discussions of science.

The New Skepticism.   Interest in science spread in literate circles because it offered a model for all forms of knowledge. As the prestige of science increased, some developed a skeptical attitude toward attempts to enforce religious conformity. A French Huguenot refugee from Louis XIV's persecutions, Pierre Bayle (1647–1706), launched an internationally influential campaign against religious intolerance from his safe haven in the Dutch Republic. His *News from the Republic of Letters* (first published in

A Budding Scientist
In this engraving, Astrologia, *by the Dutch artist Jacob Gole (c. 1660–1723), an upper-class woman looks through a telescope to do her own astronomical investigations. Women with intellectual interests were often disparaged by men, yet some middle- and upper-class women managed to pursue serious interests in science. One of the best known of these was the Italian Laura Bassi (1711–1778), who was a professor of physics at the University of Bologna. Such a position was all but impossible to attain since women were not allowed to attend university classes in any European country. Yet because many astronomical observatories were set up in private homes rather than public buildings or universities, wives and daughters of scientists could make observations and even publish their own findings.*
Bibliotèque Nationale de France.

Progress

Believing as they did in the possibilities of improvement, many Enlightenment writers preached a new doctrine about the meaning of human history. They challenged the traditional Christian belief that the original sin of Adam and Eve condemned human beings to unhappiness in this world and offered instead an optimistic vision: human nature, they claimed, was inherently good, and progress would be continuous if education developed human capacities to the utmost. Science and reason could bring happiness in this world. The idea of novelty or newness itself now seemed positive rather than threatening. Europeans began to imagine that they could surpass all those who preceded them in history, and they began to think of themselves as more "advanced" than the "backward" cultures they encountered in other parts of the world.

More than an intellectual concept, the idea of progress included a new conception of historical time and of Europeans' place within world history. Europeans stopped looking back, whether to a lost Garden of Eden or to the writings of Greek and Roman antiquity. Growing prosperity, European dominance overseas, and the scientific revolution oriented them toward the future. Europeans began to call their epoch "modern" to distinguish it from the Middle Ages (a new term), and they considered their modern period superior in achievement. Consequently, Europeans took it as their mission to bring their modern, enlightened ways of progress to the areas they colonized.

The economic and ecological catastrophes, destructive wars, and genocides of the twentieth century cast much doubt on this rosy vision of continuing progress. As the philosopher George Santayana (1863–1952) complained, "The cry was for vacant freedom and indeterminate progress: Vorwarts! Avanti! Onward! Full Speed Ahead!, without asking whether directly before you was a bottomless pit." In the movement toward *postmodernism*, which began in the 1970s, critics argued that we should no longer be satisfied with the modern; the modern brought us calamity and disaster, not reason and freedom. They wanted to go beyond the modern, hence "postmodernism." The most influential postmodern historian, the Frenchman Michel Foucault, argued in the 1970s and 1980s that history did not reveal a steady progress toward enlightenment, freedom, and humanitarianism but rather a descent into greater and greater social control, what he called a "carceral [prisonlike] society." He analyzed the replacement of torture with the prison, the birth of the medical clinic, and the movements for sexual liberation and declared that all simply ended up teaching people to watch themselves more closely and to cooperate in the state's efforts to control their lives.

Historians are now chastened in their claims about progress. They would no longer side with the German philosopher Georg W. F. Hegel who proclaimed in 1832, "The history of the world is none other than the progress of the consciousness of freedom." They worry about the nationalistic claims inherent, for example, in the English historian Thomas Babington Macaulay's insistence that "the history of England is emphatically the history of progress" (1843). But most would not go so far as Foucault in denouncing modern developments. As with many other historical questions, the final word is not yet in: is there a direction in human history? Or is history, as many in ancient times thought, a set of repeating cycles?

FURTHER READING

Bury, J. B. *The Idea of Progress: An Inquiry into Its Origin and Growth.* 1932.

Foucault, Michel. *Discipline and Punish: The Birth of the Prison.* Trans. Alan Sheridan. 1977.

1684) bitterly criticized the policies of Louis XIV and was quickly banned in Paris and condemned in Rome. After attacking Louis XIV's anti-Protestant policies, Bayle took a more general stand in favor of religious toleration. No state in Europe officially offered complete tolerance, though the Dutch Republic came closest with its tacit acceptance of Catholics, dissident Protestant groups, and open Jewish communities. In 1697, Bayle published the *Historical and Critical Dictionary*, which cited all the errors and delusions that he could find in past and present writers of all religions. Even religion must meet the test of reasonableness: "Any particular dogma, whatever it may be, whether it is advanced on the authority of the Scriptures, or whatever else may be its origins, is to be regarded as false if it clashes with the clear and definite conclusions of the natural understanding [reason]."

Although Bayle claimed to be a believer himself, his insistence on rational investigation seemed to challenge the authority of faith. As one critic complained, "It is notorious that the works of M. Bayle have unsettled a large number of readers, and cast doubt on some of the most widely accepted principles of morality and religion." Bayle asserted, for example, that atheists might possess moral codes as effective as those of the devout. Bayle's *Dictionary* became a model of critical thought in the West.

Other scholars challenged the authority of the Bible by subjecting it to historical criticism. Discoveries in geology in the early eighteenth century showed that marine fossils dated immensely farther back than the biblical flood. Investigations of miracles, comets, and oracles, like the growing literature against belief in witchcraft, urged the use of reason to combat superstition and prejudice. Comets, for example, should not be considered evil omens just because such a belief had been passed on from earlier generations. Defenders of church and state published books warning of the dangers of the new skepticism. The spokesman for Louis XIV's absolutism, Bishop Bossuet, warned that "reason is the guide of their choice, but reason only brings them face to face with vague conjectures and baffling perplexities." Human beings, the traditionalists held, were simply incapable of subjecting everything to reason, especially in the realm of religion.

State authorities found religious skepticism particularly unsettling because it threatened to undermine state power too. The extensive literature of criticism was not limited to France, but much of it was published in French, and the French government took the lead in suppressing the more outspoken works. Forbidden books were then often published in the Dutch Republic, Britain, or Switzerland and smuggled back across the border to a public whose appetite was only whetted by censorship.

The Young Voltaire Challenges Church and State. The most influential writer of the early Enlighten-

ment was a French man born into the upper middle classes, François Marie Arouet, known by his pen name, Voltaire (1694–1778). Voltaire took inspiration from Bayle: "He gives facts with such odious fidelity, he exposes the arguments for and against with such dastardly impartiality, he is so intolerably intelligible, that he leads people of only ordinary common sense to judge and even to doubt." In his early years Voltaire suffered arrest, imprisonment, and exile, but he eventually achieved wealth and acclaim. His tangles with church and state began in the early 1730s, when he published his *Letters Concerning the English Nation* (the English version appeared in 1733), in which he devoted several chapters to Newton and Locke and used the virtues of the British as a way to attack Catholic bigotry and government rigidity in France. Impressed by British toleration of religious dissent (at least among Protestants), Voltaire spent two years in exile in Britain when the French state responded to his book with yet another order for his arrest.

Voltaire also popularized Newton's scientific discoveries in his *Elements of the Philosophy of Newton* (1738). The French state and many European theologians considered Newtonianism threatening because it glorified the human mind and seemed to reduce God to an abstract, external, rationalistic force. So sensational was the success of Voltaire's book on Newton that a hostile Jesuit reported, "The great Newton, was, it is said, buried in the abyss, in the shop of the first publisher who dared to print him. . . . M. de Voltaire finally appeared, and at once Newton is understood or is in the process of being understood; all Paris resounds with Newton, all Paris stammers Newton, all Paris studies and learns Newton." The success was international too. Before long, Voltaire was elected a fellow of the Royal Society in London and in Edinburgh, as well as to twenty other scientific academies. Voltaire's fame continued to grow, reaching truly astounding proportions in the 1750s and 1760s (see Chapter 19).

Travel Literature and the Challenge to Custom and Tradition

Just as scientific method could be used to question religious and even state authority, a more general skepticism also emerged from the expanding knowledge about the world outside of Europe. During the seventeenth and eighteenth centuries, accounts of travel to exotic places dramatically increased as travel writers used the contrast between their home societies and other cultures to criticize the customs of European society.

Travel and Relativism in Morals.   In their travels to the new colonies, visitors sought something resembling "the state of nature," that is, ways of life that preceded sophisticated social and political organization—although they often misinterpreted different forms of society and politics as having no organization at all. Travelers to the Americas found "noble savages" (native peoples) who appeared to live in conditions of great freedom and equality; they were "naturally good" and "happy" without taxes, lawsuits, or much organized government. In China, in contrast, travelers found a people who enjoyed prosperity and an ancient civilization. Christian missionaries made little headway in China, and visitors had to admit that China's religious systems had flourished for four or five thousand years with no input from Europe or from Christianity. The basic lesson of travel literature in the 1700s, then, was that customs varied: justice, freedom, property, good government, religion, and morality all were relative to the place. Europe—and Christianity— might be seen as just one of many options, as relatively and not absolutely true.

Europeans from all countries began to travel more, though most limited their itineraries to Europe. Philosophers and scientists traveled to exchange thoughts; even monarchs such as Peter the Great journeyed in search of new ideas. One critic complained that travel encouraged free thinking and the destruction of religion: "Some complete their demoralization by extensive travel, and lose whatever shreds of religion remained to them. Every day they see a new religion, new customs, new rites."

From Travel Account to Political Commentary. Travel literature turned explicitly political in Montesquieu's *Persian Letters* (1721). Charles-Louis de Secondat, baron of Montesquieu (1689–1755), the son of an eminent judicial family, was a high-ranking judge in a French court. He published *Persian Letters* anonymously in the Dutch Republic, and the book went into ten printings in just one year—a best-seller for the times. Montesquieu tells the story of two Persians, Rica and Usbek, who leave

their country "for love of knowledge" and travel to Europe. They visit France in the last years of Louis XIV's reign, writing of the king: "He has a minister who is only eighteen years old, and a mistress of eighty. . . . Although he avoids the bustle of towns, and is rarely seen in company, his one concern, from morning till night, is to get himself talked about." Other passages ridicule the pope. Beneath the satire, however, was a serious investigation into the foundation of good government and morality. Montesquieu chose Persians for his travelers because they came from what was widely considered the most despotic of all governments, in which rulers had life and death powers over their subjects. In the book, the Persians constantly compare France to Persia, suggesting that the French monarchy might verge on despotism itself.

The paradox of a judge publishing an anonymous work attacking the regime that employed him demonstrates the complications of the intellectual scene in this period. Montesquieu's anonymity did not last long, and soon Parisian society lionized him. In the late 1720s, he sold his judgeship and traveled extensively in Europe, including an eighteen-month stay in Britain. In 1748, he published a widely influential work on comparative government, *The Spirit of Laws*. The Vatican soon listed both *Persian Letters* and *The Spirit of Laws* in its index of forbidden books.

Raising the Woman Question

Many of the letters exchanged in *Persian Letters* focused on women, marriage, and the family because Montesquieu considered the position of women a sure indicator of the nature of government and morality. Although Montesquieu was not a feminist, his depiction of Roxana, the favorite wife in Usbek's harem, struck a chord with many women. Roxana revolts against the authority of Usbek's eunuchs and writes a final letter to her husband announcing her impending suicide: "I may have lived in servitude, but I have always been free, I have amended your laws according to the laws of nature, and my mind has always remained independent." Women writers used the same language of tyranny and freedom to argue for concrete changes in their status. Feminist ideas were not entirely new, but they were presented systematically for the first time and represented a fundamental challenge to the ways of traditional societies.

The most systematic of these women writers was the English author Mary Astell (1666–1731), the daughter of a businessman and herself a supporter of the Tory party and the Anglican religious establishment. In 1694, she published *A Serious Proposal to the Ladies,* in which she advocated founding a private women's college to remedy women's lack of education. Addressing women, she asked, "How can you be content to be in the World like Tulips in a Garden, to make a fine *shew* [show] and be good for nothing?" Astell argued for intellectual training based on Descartes' principles, in which reason, debate, and careful consideration of the issues took priority over custom or tradition. Her book was an immediate success: five printings appeared by 1701. In later works, Astell criticized the relationship between the sexes within marriage: "If absolute sovereignty be not necessary in a state, how comes it to be so in a family? . . . If all men are born free, how is it that all women are born slaves?" Her critics accused her of promoting subversive ideas and of contradicting the Scriptures.

Astell's work inspired other women to write in a similar vein. The anonymous *Essay in Defence of the Female Sex* (1696) attacked "the Usurpation of Men; and the Tyranny of Custom," which prevented women from getting an education. In 1709, Elizabeth Elstob published a detailed account of the prominent role women played in promoting Christianity in English history. She criticized men who "would declare openly they hated any Woman who knew more than themselves." Other women wrote poetry about the same themes. In the introduction to the work of one of the best-known poets, Elizabeth Singer Rowe, a friend of the author, complained of the "notorious Violations on the Liberties of Freeborn English Women" that came from "a plain and an open design to render us meer [mere] Slaves, perfect Turkish Wives."

Most male writers unequivocally stuck to the traditional view of women. Throughout the 1700s, male commentators complained about women's interest in reading novels, which they thought encouraged idleness and corruption. The French theologian Drouet de Maupertuis published an essay, *Dangerous Commerce between the Two Sexes* (1715), in which he harped once again on the traditional theme of women's self-centeredness: "Women love neither their husbands nor their children nor their lovers," he concluded. "They love themselves." Although the French writer François Poullain de la

IMPORTANT DATES

1690s Beginning of rapid development of plantations in Caribbean

1694 Bank of England established; Mary Astell's *A Serious Proposal to the Ladies* argues for the founding of a private women's college

1697 Pierre Bayle publishes *Historical and Critical Dictionary,* detailing errors of religious writers

1699 Turks forced to recognize Habsburg rule over Hungary and Transylvania

1703 Peter the Great of Russia begins construction of St. Petersburg, founds first Russian newspaper

1713–1714 Peace of Utrecht

1714 Elector of Hanover becomes King George I of England

1715 Death of Louis XIV

1719 Daniel Defoe publishes *Robinson Crusoe*

1720 Last outbreak of bubonic plague in western Europe

1721 Treaty of Nystad; Montesquieu publishes *Persian Letters* anonymously in the Dutch Republic

1733 War of the Polish Succession; Voltaire's *Letters Concerning the English Nation* attacks French intolerance and narrow-mindedness

1741 George Frederick Handel composes the *Messiah*

Barre (1647–1723) had asserted the equality of women's minds in a series of works published in the 1670s, most men resisted this idea. Bayle argued, for example, that women were more profoundly tied to their biological nature than were men; by nature less capable of discernment but for this very reason, more inclined to conform to God's wishes.

Such opinions about women often rested on biological suppositions. In the absence of precise scientific knowledge about reproduction, scientists of the time argued heatedly with one another about women's biological role. In the long-dominant Aristotelian view, only the male seed carried spirit and individuality. At the beginning of the eighteenth century, more physicians and surgeons began to champion the doctrine of *ovism*—that the female egg was essential in making new humans. During the decades that followed, male Enlightenment writers would continue to debate women's nature and appropriate social roles.

MAPPING THE WEST Europe in 1740

By 1740, Europe had achieved a kind of diplomatic equilibrium in which no one power predominated. But the relative balance should not deflect attention from important underlying changes: Spain, the Dutch Republic, Poland-Lithuania, and Sweden had all declined in power and influence while Great Britain, Russia, Prussia, and Austria had solidified their positions, each in a different way. France's ambitions had been thwarted, but its combination of a big army and rich overseas possessions made it a major player for a long time to come.

Conclusion

Europeans crossed a major threshold in the first half of the eighteenth century. They moved silently but nonetheless momentously from an economy governed by scarcity and the threat of famine to one of ever increasing growth and the prospect of continuing improvement. Expansion of colonies overseas and economic development at home created greater wealth, longer life spans, and higher expectations for the future. In these better times for many, a spirit of optimism prevailed. People could now spend money on newspapers, novels, and travel literature as well as on coffee, tea, and cotton cloth. The growing literate public avidly followed the latest trends in religious debates, art, and music. Everyone did not share equally in the benefits: slaves toiled in abjection in the Americas; serfs in eastern Europe found themselves ever more closely bound to their noble lords; and rural folk almost everywhere tasted fewer fruits of consumer society.

Politics changed too as population and production increased and cities grew. Experts urged government intervention to improve public health, and states found it in their interest to settle many international disputes by diplomacy, which itself became more regular and routine. The consolidation of the European state system allowed a tide of criticism and new thinking about society to swell in Great Britain and France and begin to spill throughout Europe. Ultimately, the combination of the Atlantic system and the Enlightenment would give rise to a series of Atlantic revolutions.

Suggested References

The Atlantic System and the World Economy

It is easier to find sources on individual parts of the system than on the workings of the interlocking trade as a whole, but work has been rapidly increasing in this area. The Dunn book nonetheless remains one of the classic studies of how the plantation system took root. Eze's reader should be used with caution, as it sometimes distorts the overall record with its selections.

Blackburn, Robin. *The Making of New World Slavery: From the Baroque to the Modern, 1492–1800*. 1997.

Dunn, Richard S. *Sugar and Slaves: The Rise of the Planter Class in the English West Indies, 1624–1713*. 1972.

*Eze, Emmanuel Chukwudi. *Race and the Enlightenment: A Reader*. 1997.

Jordan, Winthrop D. *The White Man's Burden: Historical Origins of Racism in the United States*. 1974.

Mintz, Sidney W. *Sweetness and Power: The Place of Sugar in Modern History*. 1985.

Morgan, Philip D. *Slave Counterpoint: Black Culture in the Eighteenth-Century Chesapeake and Low Country*. 1998.

Slave movement during the eighteenth and nineteenth centuries: http://dpls.dacc.wisc.edu/slavedata/.

Smith, Alan K. *Creating a World Economy: Merchant Capital, Colonialism, and World Trade, 1400–1825*. 1991.

New Social and Cultural Patterns

Many of the novels of the period provide fascinating insights into the development of new social attitudes and customs. In particular, see Daniel Defoe's *Robinson Crusoe* (1719) and *Moll Flanders* (1722); the many novels of Eliza Heywood; and Antoine François Prévost's *Manon Lescaut* (1731), a French psychological novel about a nobleman's fatal love for an unfaithful woman, which became the basis for an opera in the nineteenth century.

Artwork of Boucher, Chardin, and Watteau: http://mistral.culture.fr/lumiere/documents/peintres.html.

De Vries, Jan. *European Urbanization, 1500–1800*. 1984.

Earle, Peter. *The Making of the English Middle Class: Business, Society, and Family Life in London, 1660–1730*. 1989.

Handel's Messiah: The New Interactive Edition (CD-ROM). 1997.

Raynor, Henry. *A Social History of Music, from the Middle Ages to Beethoven*. 1972.

Roche, Daniel. *The People of Paris: An Essay in Popular Culture in the Eighteenth Century*. Trans. Marie Evans. 1987.

Consolidation of the European State System

Studies of rulers and states can be supplemented by work on "political arithmetic" and public health.

Aspromourgos, Tony. *On the Origins of Classical Economics: Distribution and Value from William Petty to Adam Smith*. 1996.

Black, Jeremy, ed. *Britain in the Age of Walpole*. 1984.

Brewer, John. *The Sinews of Power: War, Money, and the English State, 1688–1783*. 1990.

Brockliss, Laurence, and Colin Jones. *The Medical World of Early Modern France*. 1997.

Campbell, Peter R. *Power and Politics in Old Regime France, 1720–1745*. 1996.

Hughes, Lindsey. *Russia in the Age of Peter the Great*. 1998.

Frey, Linda, and Marsha Frey. *Societies in Upheaval: Insurrections in France, Hungary, and Spain in the Early Eighteenth Century*. 1987.

Lawrence, Susan C. *Charitable Knowledge: Hospital Pupils and Practitioners in Eighteenth-Century London*. 1996.

Raeff, Marc. *Understanding Imperial Russia: State and Society in the Old Regime*. Trans. Arthur Goldhammer. 1984.

The Birth of the Enlightenment

The definitive study of the early Enlightenment is the book by Hazard, but many others have contributed biographies of individual figures or, more recently, studies of women writers.

Besterman, Theodore. *Voltaire*. 1969.

Grendy, Isobel. *Lady Mary Wortley Montagu*. 1999.

Hazard, Paul. *The European Mind: The Critical Years, 1680–1715*. 1990.

*Hill, Bridget, ed. *The First English Feminist: Reflections upon Marriage and Other Writings by Mary Astell*. 1986.

*Jacob, Margaret C. *The Enlightenment: A Brief History with Selected Readings*. 2000.

Rothkrug, Lionel. *The Opposition to Louis XIV: The Political and Social Origins of the French Enlightenment*. 1966.

Smith, Hilda L. *Reason's Disciples: Seventeenth-Century English Feminists*. 1982.

*Primary sources.

The Promise of Enlightenment

1740–1789

I N THE SUMMER OF 1766, Empress Catherine II ("the Great") of Russia wrote to Voltaire, one of the leaders of the Enlightenment:

It is a way of immortalizing oneself to be the advocate of humanity, the defender of oppressed innocence. . . . You have entered into combat against the enemies of mankind: superstition, fanaticism, ignorance, quibbling, evil judges, and the powers that rest in their hands. Great virtues and qualities are needed to surmount these obstacles. You have shown that you have them: you have triumphed.

Catherine the Great
At the time of this portrait by Johann Baptist Edler von Lampi of 1793, the Russian empress Catherine the Great had ruled for thirty-one years and was only three years from her death. Born Sophia Augusta Frederika of Anhalt-Zerbst in 1729, she was the daughter of a minor German prince. When she married the future tsar Peter III in 1745, she promptly learned Russian and adopted Russian Orthodoxy. Peter, physically and mentally frail, proved no match for her, and she took his place on his death in 1762. The painter of this portrait was a native of northern Italy who had worked at the Austrian court in Vienna before being summoned to St. Petersburg. He painted many portraits of the Russian court and royal family between 1792 and 1797.
Art Resource, NY.

Over a fifteen-year period Catherine corresponded regularly with Voltaire, a writer who, at home in France, found himself in constant conflict with authorities of church and state. Her admiring letter shows how influential Enlightenment ideals had become by the middle of the eighteenth century. Even an absolutist ruler such as Catherine endorsed many aspects of the Enlightenment call for reform; at this same time, Catherine set up a commission to write a new law code, and she introduced reforms in favor of education and religious toleration. She too wanted to be an "advocate of humanity."

Catherine's letter aptly summed up Enlightenment ideals: progress for humanity could be achieved only by rooting out the wrongs left by superstition, religious fanaticism, ignorance, and outmoded forms of justice. Enlightenment writers used every means at their disposal—from encyclopedias to novels to personal interaction with rulers—to argue for reform. Everything had to be examined in the cold light of reason,

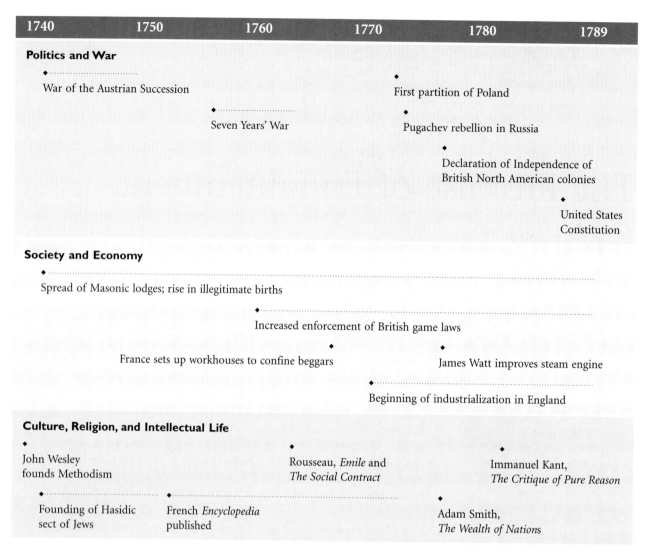

| 1740 | 1750 | 1760 | 1770 | 1780 | 1789 |

Politics and War

War of the Austrian Succession

Seven Years' War

First partition of Poland

Pugachev rebellion in Russia

Declaration of Independence of British North American colonies

United States Constitution

Society and Economy

Spread of Masonic lodges; rise in illegitimate births

Increased enforcement of British game laws

France sets up workhouses to confine beggars

James Watt improves steam engine

Beginning of industrialization in England

Culture, Religion, and Intellectual Life

John Wesley founds Methodism

Rousseau, *Emile* and *The Social Contract*

Immanuel Kant, *The Critique of Pure Reason*

Founding of Hasidic sect of Jews

French *Encyclopedia* published

Adam Smith, *The Wealth of Nations*

and if it did not promote the improvement of humanity, it should be jettisoned. As a result, Enlightenment writers attacked the legal use of torture to extract confessions and supported religious toleration. They favored the spread of education to eliminate ignorance and criticized censorship by state or church. These ideas spread far and wide through the book trade, some of it clandestine; coffeehouses; lending libraries; local academies; Masonic lodges (social clubs organized with the rituals of masons' guilds); and salons, sophisticated evening discussions organized by upper-class women.

Catherine's correspondence with Voltaire should not blind us to the limitations of Enlightenment. While a new elite of middle- and upper-class men and women embraced the Enlightenment, the lower classes had little contact with the new ideas. The continuing rise in population, the start of industrialization, and wars between the great powers shaped their lives more profoundly. States had to balance conflicting social pressures: on the one hand, rulers pursued those Enlightenment reforms that might enhance state power; and on the other hand, they feared changes that might unleash popular discontent. Catherine herself felt pulled in different directions. She had staged a coup against her husband Tsar Peter III; when he was killed, she succeeded him. German-born and educated, she aimed to bring Western ideas, culture, and reforms to Russia, but above all she intended to maintain and even extend her authority. When faced with a massive uprising of the serfs, she not only suppressed the revolt but also increased the powers of the nobles over their serfs. All reform-minded rulers faced similar potential challenges to their authority.

Even if the movement for reform had its limits, Catherine's letter should not be read as a cynical ploy. It reflected a very real shift in the basis of authority. Governments, almost all of them still ruled by hereditary monarchs, now had to respond to a new force known as "public opinion." The Russian educated public was minuscule, but Catherine nevertheless felt the need to justify her policies to her broader public, the intellectuals of western Europe. Other rulers confronted a much more aggressive, home-grown public that now read newspapers and closely followed political developments. Rulers had to portray themselves as modern, open to reform, and responsive to this public. By 1789, when revolution erupted in France, public opinion had begun to demand democracy—that is, government by, for, and of the people. Most Enlightenment writers did not embrace democracy, however; between the 1740s and the 1780s, they still looked to rulers to effect reform and addressed the educated classes as their audience. Writers such as Voltaire expressed little interest in the future of peasants or lower classes; they favored neither revolution nor political upheaval. Yet their ideas paved the way for something much more radical and unexpected. The American Declaration of Independence in 1776 showed how Enlightenment ideals could be translated into democratic political practice. After 1789, democracy would come to Europe as well.

❖ The Enlightenment at Its Height

The Enlightenment emerged as an intellectual movement before 1740 but reached its peak only in the second half of the eighteenth century. The writers of the Enlightenment called themselves *philosophes* (French for "philosophers"), but that term is somewhat misleading. Whereas philosophers concern themselves with abstract theories, the philosophes were public intellectuals dedicated to solving the real problems of the world. They wrote on subjects ranging from current affairs to art criticism, and they wrote in every conceivable format. The Swiss philosophe Jean-Jacques Rousseau,

for example, wrote a political tract, a treatise on education, a constitution for Poland, an analysis of the effects of the theater on public morals, a best-selling novel, an opera, and a notorious autobiography. The philosophes wrote for a broad educated public of readers who snatched up every Enlightenment book they could find at their local booksellers', even when rulers or churches tried to forbid their publication. Between 1740 and 1789, the Enlightenment acquired its name and, despite heated conflicts between the philosophes and state and religious authorities, gained support in the highest reaches of government. (See "Terms of History," page 687.)

The Men and Women of the Republic of Letters

Although *philosophe* is a French word, the Enlightenment was distinctly cosmopolitan; philosophes could be found from Philadelphia to Moscow and from Edinburgh to Naples. The philosophes considered themselves part of a grand "republic of letters" that transcended national political boundaries. They were not republicans in the usual sense, that is, people who supported representative government and opposed monarchy. Many, like Voltaire, warmly endorsed reform programs proposed by monarchs. What united them were the ideals of reason, reform, and freedom. The French editors of the *Encyclopedia* (published from 1751 to 1772) declared that they would "overturn the barriers that reason never erected" and "give back to the arts and sciences the liberty that is so precious to them." In 1784, the German philosopher Immanuel Kant summed up the program of the Enlightenment in two Latin words: *sapere aude*, "dare to know"—have the courage to think for yourself.

The philosophes used reason to attack superstition, bigotry, and religious fanaticism, which they considered the chief obstacles to free thought and social reform. Voltaire took religious fanaticism as his chief target: "Once fanaticism has corrupted a mind, the malady is almost incurable. . . . The only remedy for this epidemic malady is the philosophical spirit." Enlightenment writers did not necessarily oppose organized religion, but they strenuously objected to religious intolerance. They believed that the systematic application of reason could do what religious belief could not: improve the human

Bookbinding

In this plate from the Encyclopedia, *the various stages in bookbinding are laid out from left to right. Binding was not included in the sale of books; owners had to order leather bindings from a special shop. The man at (a) is pounding the pages to be bound on a marble block. The woman at (b) is stitching the pages with a special frame. The worker at (c) cuts the pages, and at (d) the volumes are pressed to prevent warping. This illustration is typical of the hundreds of plates in the* Encyclopedia *in its effort to represent precisely and thoroughly every stage in artisanal production.*

condition by pointing to needed reforms. Reason meant critical, informed, scientific thinking about social issues and problems. In the multivolume *Encyclopedia*, scores of collaborators gathered knowledge about every aspect of economic, social, and cultural life, from the secrets of manufacturing to theories of music. The chief editor of the *Encyclopedia*, Denis Diderot (1713–1784), explained their purpose: "All things must be examined, debated, investigated without exception and without regard for anyone's feelings."

The philosophes believed that the spread of knowledge would encourage reform in every aspect of life, from the grain trade to the penal system. Chief among their desired reforms was intellectual freedom, the freedom to use one's own reason and to publish the results. The philosophes wanted freedom of the press and freedom of religion, which they considered "natural rights" guaranteed by "natural law." In their view, progress depended on these

freedoms. As Voltaire asserted, "I quite understand that the fanatics of one sect slaughter the enthusiasts of another sect . . . [but] that Descartes should have been forced to flee to Holland to escape the fury of the ignorant . . . these things are a nation's eternal shame."

Most philosophes, like Voltaire, came from the upper classes, yet Rousseau's father was a modest watchmaker in Geneva, and Diderot was the son of a cutlery maker. Although it was a rare phenomenon, some women were philosophes, such as the French noblewoman Émilie du Châtelet (1706–1749), who wrote extensively about the mathematics and physics of Leibniz and Newton. (Her lover Voltaire learned much of his science from her.) Few of the leading writers held university positions, except those who were German or Scottish. Universities in France were so dominated by the clergy and unreceptive to Enlightenment ideals that they took the lead in banning Enlightenment books.

Enlightenment

In 1784, in an essay titled "What Is Enlightenment?," the German philosopher Immanuel Kant gave widespread currency to a term that had been in the making for several decades. The existence of an online database of French literature enables us to trace the actual appearance of the equivalent terms in French: *siècle de lumière(s)* or *siècle éclairé*—"century of light(s)" or "enlightened century." The term *enlightened century* became common beginning only in the 1760s. The even more common term *century of light(s)* first appeared in the inaugural volume of the *Encyclopedia* in 1751 and was soon taken up by all the major French Enlightenment writers. Closely related to Enlightenment was the French term *philosophe*, which was first used to mean "proponent of Enlightenment" in the 1740s. A clandestine tract of 1743 titled *Le Philosophe* explained that the philosophe was the man who saw through popular errors.

The Enlightenment gave itself its own name, and the name clearly had propaganda value. The philosophes associated Enlightenment with philosophy, reason, and humanity; religious tolerance; natural rights; and criticism of outmoded customs and prejudices. They tied Enlightenment to "progress" and to the "modern," and it came into question, just as these other terms did, when events cast doubt on the benefits of progress and the virtues of modernity. Although some opposed the Enlightenment from the very beginning as antireligious, undermining of authority, and even atheistic and immoral, the French Revolution of 1789 galvanized the critics of Enlightenment who blamed every excess of revolution on Enlightenment principles. Some critics believed that a conspiracy of Masonic lodges lay behind both the Enlightenment and the French Revolution.

For most of the nineteenth century, condemnation of the Enlightenment came from right-wing sources: those who opposed modernity, secularization, revolution, and sometimes any form of liberalization viewed the Enlightenment with distrust and even disdain. Some of the more extreme of these critics denounced a supposed "Jewish-Masonic conspiracy," believing that Jews and Freemasons benefited most from the spread of Enlightenment principles and worked secretly to jointly undermine Christianity and established monarchical authorities. Adolf Hitler and his followers shared these suspicions, and during World War II the Germans confiscated the records of Masonic lodges in every country they occupied. They sent the documents back to Berlin so that a special office could trace the links of this supposed conspiracy. They found nothing.

After the catastrophes of World War II, the Enlightenment came under attack for the first time from left-wing critics, those who had previously supported modernity, secularization, and even revolution. In a book published right after World War II, *Dialectic of Enlightenment*, Max Horkheimer and Theodor W. Adorno, two German Jewish refugees from Hitler's regime who had fled to the United States, denounced the Enlightenment as "self-destructive" and even "totalitarian" because its belief in reason led not to freedom but to greater bureaucratic control. They asked "why mankind, instead of entering into a truly human condition, is sinking into a new kind of barbarism," and they answered, because we have trusted too much in the Enlightenment and its belief in reason and science. Reason and science might have been tools of criticism of church and state in the eighteenth century, but in the twentieth century, Horkheimer and Adorno insisted, they resulted in concentration camps, ecological disasters, and a deadening mass culture incarnated by Hollywood films. Reason provided the technology to transport millions of Jews to their deaths in scientifically sound gas chambers. Reason invented the atomic bomb and gave us the factories that pollute the atmosphere. The masses did not rise up against these uses of reason because they were distracted by a mass culture that emphasized entertainment rather than reflection. These criticisms of the Enlightenment, however extreme and sometimes outlandish, show how central the Enlightenment remains to the very definition of modern history.

Sources: ARTFL (American Resource, Treasury of the French Language): http://humanities.uchicago.edu/ARTFL/ARTFL.html, Max Horkheimer and Theodor W. Adorno, *Dialectic of Enlightenment*, trans. John Cumming (New York: Continuum, 1993; first published 1947), xi, 6.

Enlightenment ideas developed instead through personal contacts; letters that were hand-copied, circulated, and sometimes published; salon readings of manuscripts; and letters to the editor and book reviews in periodicals. Commenting on the exchanges found in French and Italian newspapers, one writer exclaimed, "Never have new ideas had such rapid circulation at long distance." The salons gave intellectual life an anchor outside the royal court and the church-controlled universities. The best known was the Parisian salon of Madame Marie-Thérèse Geoffrin (1699–1777), a wealthy middle-class widow who had been raised by her grandmother and married off at fourteen to a much older man. Creating a salon was her way of educating herself and participating directly in the movement for reform. She brought together the most exciting thinkers and artists of the time; her social gatherings provided a forum for new ideas and an opportunity to establish new intellectual contacts. In the salon the philosophes could discuss ideas they might hesitate to put into print and thus test public opinion and even push it in new directions. Madame Geoffrin corresponded extensively with influential people across Europe, including Catherine the Great and King Stanislaw August Poniatowski of Poland-Lithuania. One Italian visitor commented, "There is no way to make Naples resemble Paris unless we find a woman to guide us, organize us, *Geoffrinize* us."

Women's role in creating salons provoked criticism from men who resented their power. (See "Contrasting Views," page 690.) Nevertheless, women's salons helped galvanize intellectual life and reform movements all over Europe. Wealthy Jewish women created nine of the fourteen salons in Berlin at the end of the eighteenth century, and in Warsaw, Princess Zofia Czartoryska gathered around her the reform leaders of Poland-Lithuania. Middle-class women in London used their salons to raise money to publish women's writings. Salons could be tied closely to the circles of power: in France, for example, Louis XV's mistress, Jeanne-Antoinette Poisson, first made her reputation as hostess of a salon frequented by Voltaire and Montesquieu. When she became Louis XV's mistress in 1745, she gained the title Marquise de Pompadour and turned her attention to influencing artistic styles by patronizing architects and painters.

Conflicts with Church and State

Madame Geoffrin did not approve of discussions that attacked the Catholic church, but elsewhere voices against organized religion could be heard.

Madame Geoffrin's Salon in 1755

This 1812 painting by Anicet Charles Lemonnier claims to depict the best-known Parisian salon of the 1750s. Lemonnier was only twelve years old in 1755 and so could not have based his rendition on firsthand knowledge. Madame Geoffrin is the figure in blue on the right facing the viewer. The bust is of Voltaire. Rousseau is the fifth person to the left of the bust (facing right) and behind him (facing left) is Raynal.
Giraudon/Art Resource, NY.

Criticisms of religion required daring because the church, whatever its denomination, wielded enormous power in society, and most influential people considered religion an essential foundation of good society and government. Defying such opinion, the Scottish philosopher David Hume (1711–1776) boldly argued in *The Natural History of Religion* (1755) that belief in God rested on superstition and fear rather than on reason. Hume soon met kindred spirits while visiting Paris; he attended a dinner party consisting of "fifteen atheists, and three who had not quite made up their minds."

Before the scientific revolution, virtually every European believed in God. After Newton, however, and despite Newton's own deep religiosity, people could conceive of the universe as an eternally existing, self-perpetuating machine, in which God's intervention was unnecessary. In short, such people could become either *atheists*, who did not believe in any kind of God, or *deists*, who believed in God but gave him no active role in earthly affairs. For the first time, writers claimed the label *atheist* and disputed the common view that atheism led inevitably to immorality.

Deists continued to believe in a benevolent, all-knowing God who had designed the universe and set it in motion. But deists usually rejected the idea that God directly intercedes in the functioning of the universe, and they often criticized the churches for their dogmatic intolerance of dissenters. Voltaire was a deist, and in his popular *Philosophical Dictionary* (1764) he attacked most of the claims of organized Christianity, both Catholic and Protestant. Christianity, he argued, had been the prime source of fanaticism and brutality among humans. Throughout his life, Voltaire's motto was *Ecrasez l'infâme*—"Crush the infamous thing" (the "thing" being bigotry and intolerance). The French authorities publicly burned his *Philosophical Dictionary*.

Criticism of religious intolerance involved more than simply attacking the churches. Critics also had to confront the states to which churches were closely tied. In 1761, a judicial case in Toulouse provoked an outcry throughout France that Voltaire soon joined. When the son of a local Calvinist was found hanged (he had probably committed suicide), authorities accused the father, Jean Calas, of murdering him to prevent his conversion to Catholicism. (Since Louis XIV's revocation of the Edict of Nantes in 1685, it had been illegal to practice Calvinism

Voltaire

In this marble bust by Jean-Antoine Houdon (1741–1828), Voltaire seems the same age as he does in the Lemonnier painting on page 688. However, Houdon began turning out a series of busts of eminent people only in 1771, so it seems likely that Lemonnier imported a later sculpture into his painting of Madame Geoffrin's salon in 1755. This bust shows Voltaire in his old age (he died in 1778).
Art Resource, NY.

publicly in France.) The all-Catholic parlement of Toulouse tried to extract a confession using torture—breaking all Calas's bones—and then executed him when he still refused to confess. Voltaire launched a successful crusade to rehabilitate Jean Calas's good name and to restore the family's properties, which had been confiscated after his death. Voltaire's efforts eventually helped bring about the extension of civil rights to French Protestants and encouraged campaigns to abolish the legal use of torture.

Critics also assailed state and church support for European colonization and slavery. One of the most popular books of the time was the *Philosophical and Political History of European Colonies and Commerce in the Two Indies*, published in 1770 by Abbé Guillaume Raynal (1713–1796), a French Catholic clergyman. Raynal and his collaborators described in excruciating detail the destruction of native populations by Europeans and denounced the inhumanity and irrationality of European ways.

Women and the Enlightenment

During the Enlightenment, women's roles in society became the subject of heated debates. Some men resented what they saw as the growing power of women, especially in the salons. Rousseau railed against their corrupting influence: "Every woman at Paris gathers in her apartment a harem of men more womanish than she." Male writers were divided in their attitudes. Many argued for greater education for women and for women's equality with men in marriage, but others still insisted on the natural weakness of women and their unsuitability for public affairs. Rousseau's *Emile* (Document 1) offered his own influential answer to the question of how women should be educated. The *Encyclopedia* ignored the contributions of salon women and praised women who stayed at home; in the words of one typical contributor, women "constitute the principal ornament of the world. . . . May they, through submissive discretion and through simple, adroit, artless cleverness, spur us [men] on to virtue." Many women objected to these characterizations. The editor of a prominent newspaper for women, Madame de Beaumer, wrote editorials blasting the masculine sense of superiority (Document 2). Many prominent women writers specifically targeted Rousseau's book because it proved to be the most influential educational treatise of the time (Document 3). Their ideas formed the core of nineteenth-century feminism.

1. Jean-Jacques Rousseau, Emile (1762)

Rousseau used the character of Emile's wife-to-be, Sophie, to discuss his ideas about women's education. "Woman is made to please and to be subjugated to man," he claimed. Sophie is educated for a domestic role as wife and mother, and she is taught to be obedient, always helpful to her husband and family, and removed from any participation in the public world. Despite his insistence on the differences between men's and women's roles, many

women enthusiastically embraced Rousseau's ideas, for he placed great emphasis on maternalism, breastfeeding, and childrearing. Many women not only took to heart Rousseau's ideas about childrearing, some began to publish manuals for mothers. Rousseau's own children, however, suffered the contradictions that characterized his life. By his own admission, he abandoned to a foundling hospital all the children he had by his lower-class common-law wife because he did not think he could support them properly; if their fate was like that of most abandoned children of the day, they met an early death.

There is no parity between man and woman as to the importance of sex. The male is only a male at certain moments; the female all her life, or at least throughout her youth, is incessantly reminded of her sex and in order to carry out its functions she needs a corresponding constitution. She needs to be careful during pregnancy; she needs rest after childbirth; she needs a quiet and sedentary life while she nurses her children; she needs patience and gentleness in order to raise them; a zeal and affection that nothing can discourage. . . .

The relative duties of the two sexes are not and cannot be equally rigid. When woman complains about the unjust inequalities placed on her by man she is wrong; this inequality is by no means a human institution or at least it is not the work of prejudice but of reason. She to whom nature has entrusted the care of the children must hold herself accountable for them. . . .

On the good constitution of mothers depends primarily that of the children; on the care of women depends the early education of men; and on women, again, depend their morals, their passions, their tastes, their pleasures, and even their happiness. Thus the whole education of women ought to be relative to men. To please them, to be useful to them, to make themselves loved and honored by them, to educate them when young, to care for them when grown, to counsel them, to console them, and to make life agreeable and sweet to them—these are the duties of women at all times, and should be taught them from their infancy.

Source: Susan Groag Bell and Karen M. Offen, *Women, the Family, and Freedom: The Debate in Documents*, vol. 1, 1750–1880 (Stanford: Stanford University Press, 1983), 46–49.

2. Madame de Beaumer, editorial in Le Journal des Dames ("The Ladies' Journal"), 1762

Madame de Beaumer (d. 1766) was the first of three women editors of Le Journal des Dames. *She ran it for two years and published many editorials defending women against their male critics.*

The success of the *Journal des Dames* allows us to triumph over those frivolous persons who have regarded this periodical as a petty work containing only a few bagatelles suited to help them kill time. In truth, Gentlemen, you do us much honor to think that we could not provide things that unite the useful to the agreeable. To rid you of your error, we have made our Journal historical, with a view to putting before the eyes of youth striking images that will guide them toward virtue.... An historical *Journal des Dames*! these Gentlemen reasoners reply. How ridiculous! How out of character with the nature of this work, which calls only for little pieces to amuse [ladies] during their toilette.... Please, Gentlemen *beaux esprits* [wits], mind your own business and let us write in a manner worthy of our sex; I love this sex, I am jealous to uphold its honor and its rights. If we have not been raised up in the sciences as you have, it is you who are the guilty ones.

Source: Bell and Offen, 27–28.

3. Catharine Macaulay, Letters on Education (1787)

Catharine Sawbridge Macaulay-Graham (1731–1791) was one of the best-known English writers of the 1700s. She wrote immensely popular histories of England and also joined in the debate provoked by Rousseau's Emile.

There is another prejudice ... which affects yet more deeply female happiness, and female importance; a prejudice, which ought ever to have been confined to the regions of the east, because [of the] state of slavery to which female nature in that part of the world has been ever subjected, and can only suit with the notion of a positive inferiority in the intellectual powers of the female mind. You will soon perceive, that the prejudice which I mean, is that degrading difference in the culture of the understanding, which has prevailed for several centuries in all European societies.... Be no longer niggards [misers], then O ye parents, in bestowing on your offspring, every blessing which nature and fortune renders them capable of enjoying! Confine not the education of your daughters to what is regarded as the ornamental parts of it, nor deny the graces to your sons.... Let your children be brought up together; let their sports and studies be the same....

Among the most strenuous asserters of a sexual difference in character, Rousseau is the most conspicuous, both on account of that warmth of sentiment which distinguishes all his writing, and the eloquence of his compositions: but never did enthusiasm and the love of paradox, those enemies of philosophical disquisition, appear in more strong opposition to plain sense than in Rousseau's definition of this difference. He sets out with a supposition, that Nature intended the subjection of the one sex to the other; that consequently there must be an inferiority of intellect in the subjected party; but as man is a very imperfect being, and apt to play the capricious tyrant, Nature, to bring things nearer to an equality, bestowed on the woman such attractive graces, and such an insinuating address, as to turn the balance on the other scale....

The situation and education of women ... is precisely that which must necessarily tend to corrupt and debilitate both the powers of mind and body. From a false notion of beauty and delicacy, their system of nerves is depraved before they come out of the nursery; and this kind of depravity has more influence over the mind, and consequently over morals, than is commonly apprehended.

Source: Bell and Offen, 54–55.

QUESTIONS FOR DEBATE

1. Why would women in the eighteenth century read Rousseau with such interest and even enthusiasm?
2. Why does Madame de Beaumer address herself to male readers if the *Journal des Dames* is intended for women?
3. Why would Macaulay focus so much of her analysis on Rousseau? Why does she not just ignore him?
4. Was the Enlightenment intended only for men?

The book strongly opposed slavery and predicted the appearance of a black hero who would lead a rebellion of slaves "against the blind avarice of European and American colonists." Raynal was forced into exile as soon as the book appeared; like many other Enlightenment books, his work was banned by both the Catholic church and the French government.

The Enlightenment belief in natural rights led many to denounce slavery. An article in the *Encyclopedia* proclaimed, "There is not a single one of these hapless souls . . . who does not have the right to be declared free . . . since neither his ruler nor his father nor anyone else had the right to dispose of his freedom." Some Enlightenment thinkers, however, took a more ambiguous or even negative view. Montesquieu, for example, ridiculed arguments in favor of slavery yet argued that it was less irrational in hot climates because no one would work there without being compelled. Writing on national character, Hume judged blacks to be "naturally inferior to the whites," concluding, "There never was a civilized nation of any other complexion than white." Efforts to study the types of animals in nature led some scientists to rank humans according to their race, with European whites on top and African blacks at the bottom of the scale.

Enlightenment critics of church and state advocated reform, not revolution. Although he lived near the French-Swiss border in case he had to flee arrest, Voltaire, for example, made a fortune in financial speculations, wrote a glowing history called *The Age of Louis XIV* (1751), and lived to be celebrated in his last years as a national hero even by many former foes. Other philosophes also lived respectably, believing that published criticism, rather than violent action, would bring about necessary reforms. As Diderot said, "We will speak against senseless laws until they are reformed; and, while we wait, we will abide by them." Those few who lived long enough to see the French Revolution in 1789 resisted its radical turn, for the philosophes generally regarded the lower classes—"the people"—as ignorant, violent, and prone to superstition, hence in need of leadership from above. They pinned their hopes on educated elites and enlightened rulers.

Despite the philosophes' preference for reform, in the long run their books often had a revolutionary impact. For example, Montesquieu's widely reprinted *Spirit of the Laws* (1748) warned against the dangers of despotism, opposed the divine right of kings, and favored constitutional government. In his somewhat rosy view, Great Britain was "the one nation in the world which has political liberty as the direct object of its constitution." His analysis of British constitutionalism inspired French critics of absolutism and would greatly influence the American revolutionaries.

The Individual and Society

The controversy created by the most notorious conflicts between the philosophes and the various churches and states of Europe drew attention away from a subtle but profound transformation in worldviews. In previous centuries, questions of theological doctrine and church organization had been the main focus of intellectual and even political interest. The Enlightenment writers shifted attention away from religious questions toward the secular study of society and the individual's role in it. Religion did not drop out of sight, but the philosophes tended to make religion a private affair of individual conscience, even while rulers and churches still considered religion very much a public concern.

The Enlightenment interest in secular society produced two major results: it advanced the secularization of European political life that had begun after the Wars of Religion of the sixteenth and seventeenth centuries, and it laid the foundations for the social sciences of the modern era. Not surprisingly, then, many historians and philosophers consider the Enlightenment to be the origin of "modernity," which they define as the belief that human reason, rather than theological doctrine, should set the patterns of social and political life. This belief in reason as the sole foundation for secular authority has often been contested, but it has also proved to be a powerful force for change.

Although most of the philosophes believed that human reason could understand and even remake society and politics, they disagreed about what that reason revealed. Among the many different approaches were two that proved enduringly influential, those of the Scottish philosopher Adam Smith and the Swiss writer Jean-Jacques Rousseau. Smith provided a theory of modern capitalist society and devoted much of his energy to defending free markets as the best way to maximize individual efforts. The modern discipline of economics took shape around the questions raised by Smith. Rousseau set out the principles of a more communitarian philosophy, one that emphasized the needs of the community over those of the individual. His work led both toward democracy and toward communism and continues to inspire heated debate in political science and sociology.

Adam Smith. Adam Smith (1723–1790) optimistically believed that individual interests naturally harmonized with those of the whole society. He claimed, "The study of his own [the individual's] advantage necessarily leads him to prefer what is most advantageous to the society." To explain how this natural harmonization worked, he published *An Inquiry into the Nature and Causes of the Wealth of Nations* in 1776. Like Bernard Mandeville before him but much more systematically, Smith insisted that individual self-interest, even greed, was quite compatible with society's best interest: the laws of supply and demand served as an "invisible hand" ensuring that individual interests would be synchronized with those of the whole society. Market forces—"the propensity to truck, barter, and exchange one thing for another"—naturally brought individual and social interests in line.

Smith rejected the prevailing mercantilist views that the general welfare would be served by accumulating national wealth through agriculture or the hoarding of gold and silver. Instead, he argued that the division of labor in manufacturing increased productivity and generated more wealth for society and well-being for the individual. By performing a manufacturing task over and over again, a person functioned as a part in a well-running machine. In his much-cited example of the manufacture of pins, Smith showed that when the manufacturing process was broken down into separate operations—one man to draw out the wire, another to straighten it, a third to cut it, a fourth to point it, and so on— workers who could make only one pin a day on their own could make thousands working together.

To maximize the effects of market forces and the division of labor, Smith endorsed a concept called *laissez-faire* (that is, "to leave alone") to free the economy from government intervention and control. He insisted that governments eliminate all restrictions on the sale of land, remove restraints on the grain trade, and abandon duties on imports. He believed that free international trade would stimulate production everywhere and thus ensure

Major Works of the Enlightenment

1748 Charles-Louis de Secondat, baron of Montesquieu, *Spirit of Laws*
1751 Beginning of publication of the French *Encyclopedia*
1755 David Hume, *The Natural History of Religion*
1762 Jean-Jacques Rousseau, *The Social Contract* and *Emile*
1764 Voltaire, *Philosophical Dictionary*
1770 Abbé Guillaume Raynal, *Philosophical and Political History of European Colonies and Commerce in the Two Indies*
1776 Adam Smith, *An Inquiry into the Nature and Causes of the Wealth of Nations*
1781 Immanuel Kant, *The Critique of Pure Reason*

the growth of national wealth. He insisted: "The natural effort of every individual to better his own condition, when suffered to exert itself with freedom and security, is so powerful a principle, that it is alone, and without any assistance, not only capable of carrying the society to wealth and prosperity, but of surmounting a hundred impertinent obstructions with which the folly of human laws too often encumbers its operations." Governments should restrict themselves to providing "security," that is, national defense, internal order, and public works. Smith recognized that government had an important role in providing a secure framework for market activity, but he placed most emphasis on freeing individual endeavor from what he saw as excessive government interference.

Jean-Jacques Rousseau. Much more pessimistic about the relation between individual self-interest and the good of society was Jean-Jacques Rousseau (1712–1778). In Rousseau's view, society itself threatened natural rights or freedoms: "Man is born free, and everywhere he is in chains." Rousseau first gained fame by writing a prize-winning essay in 1749 in which he argued that the revival of science and the arts had corrupted social morals, not improved them. This startling conclusion seemed to oppose some of the Enlightenment's most cherished beliefs. Rather than improving society, he claimed, science and art raised artificial barriers between

Rousseau's Worries

Jean-Jacques Rousseau's novel The New Heloise *(1761) sold better than any other work in French in the second half of the eighteenth century. But Rousseau himself was deeply concerned about the effects of novel reading, especially on young women. The first of these illustrations for the novel (on the left) by Moreau the Younger, was rejected by Rousseau because the couple (Julie and Saint Preux) are shown in direct physical contact. He accepted the engraving on the right, by Gravelot, because it only hinted at passion.* Bibliothèque Nationale.

people and their natural state. Rousseau's works extolled the simplicity of rural life over urban society. Although he participated in the salons and contributed to the *Encyclopedia*, Rousseau always felt ill at ease in high society, and he periodically withdrew to live in solitude far from Paris. Paradoxically, his "solitude" was often paid for by wealthy upper-class patrons, who lodged him on their estates, even as his writings decried the upper-class privilege that made his efforts possible.

Rousseau explored the tension between the individual and society in various ways. In his best-selling novel *The New Heloise* (1761), he told the story of Julie, who gives up her penniless lover Saint Preux to marry someone else to please her father. Rousseau completely transformed the medieval story of Heloise and Abelard to focus on the conflict between social demands for virtue in marriage and Julie's intensely personal feelings. Julie learns to live a virtuous, domestic life with her husband and sacrifices her feelings for Saint Preux; her death at the end of the novel makes her into a saintly heroine, but it also raises questions about the cost to the individual of social virtue. In his work on education, *Emile* (1762), Rousseau tried to find a less tragic solution to the conflict between the individ-

ual and society. Without relying solely on books and free from the supervision of the clergy, who controlled most schools, the boy Emile works alone with his tutor to develop practical skills and independent ways of thinking. After developing his individuality, Emile joins society through marriage to Sophie, who received the education Rousseau thought appropriate for women. (See "Contrasting Views," page 690.)

In *The Social Contract* (1762), Rousseau proposed a political solution to the tension between the individual and society. Whereas earlier he had argued that society corrupted the individual by taking him out of nature, in this work Rousseau insisted that the right kind of political order could make people truly moral and free. In other words, he hoped to generalize the solution advanced in *Emile* to all of society. Individual moral freedom could be achieved only by learning to subject one's individual interests to "the general will," that is, the good of the community. Individuals did this by entering into a social contract not with their rulers, but with one another. If everyone followed the general will, then all would be equally free and equally moral because they lived under a law to which they had all consented.

These arguments threatened the legitimacy of eighteenth-century governments. Rousseau derived his social contract from human nature, not from history, tradition, or the Bible. He implied that people would be most free and moral under a republican form of government with direct democracy, and his abstract model included no reference to differences in social status. He roundly condemned slavery: "To decide that the son of a slave is born a slave is to decide that he is not born a man." Not surprisingly, authorities in both Geneva and Paris banned *The Social Contract* for undermining political authority. Rousseau's works became a kind of political bible for the French revolutionaries of 1789, and his attacks on private property inspired the communists of the nineteenth century such as Karl Marx. Rousseau's rather mystical concept of the general will remains controversial. The "greatest

good of all," according to Rousseau, was liberty and equality, but he also insisted that the individual could be "forced to be free" by the terms of the social contract. He provided no legal protections for individual rights. Rousseau's particular version of democracy might not preserve the individual freedoms so important to Adam Smith.

Spreading the Enlightenment

The spread of the Enlightenment followed a distinct geographic and social pattern: it flourished in places where an educated middle class provided an eager audience for ideas of constitutionalism and reform. It therefore found its epicenter in the triangle formed by London, Amsterdam, and Paris and diffused outward to eastern and southern Europe and North America (Map 19.1). Where constitutionalism and

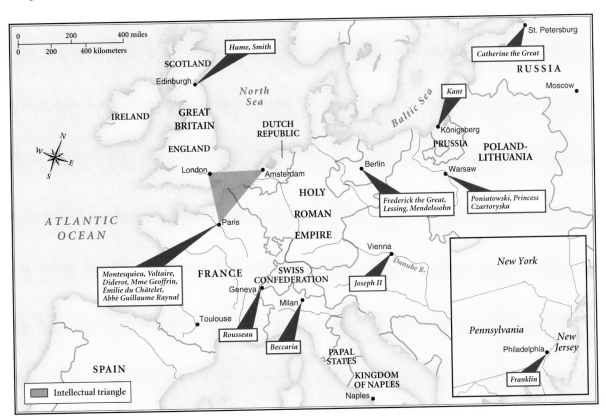

MAP 19.1 Centers of the Enlightenment
Paris was the heart of the Enlightenment because most philosophes, whatever their nationality, spoke and wrote French. Both Catherine the Great and Frederick the Great corresponded in French with their favorite French philosophes. Many French philosophes traveled to London where they met with their English and Scottish counterparts. Montesquieu and Voltaire wrote extensively about English customs. Dutch printers published books censored in France and made them available throughout Europe and the American colonies.

the guarantee of individual freedoms were most advanced, as in Great Britain and the Dutch Republic, the movement had less of an edge because there was, in a sense, less need for it. Scottish and English writers concentrated on economics, philosophy, and history rather than politics or social relations. Dutch printers made money publishing the books that were forbidden in France. In British North America, Enlightenment ideas helped stiffen growing colonial resistance to British rule after 1763. In places with small middle classes, such as Spain, the Italian states, and Russia, governments successfully suppressed writings they did not like. Italian philosophes, such as the Milanese penal reformer Cesare Beccaria (1738–1794), got moral support from their French counterparts in the face of stern censorship at home.

The French Enlightenment. The hot spot of the Enlightenment was France. French writers published the most daring critiques of church and state and suffered the most intense harassment and persecution. Voltaire, Diderot, and Rousseau all faced arrest, exile, or even imprisonment. The Catholic church and royal authorities routinely forbade the publication of their books, and the police arrested publishers who ignored their warnings. Yet the French monarchy was far from the most autocratic in Europe, and Voltaire, Diderot, and Rousseau all ended their lives as cultural heroes. France seems to have been curiously caught in the middle during the Enlightenment: with fewer constitutional guarantees of individual freedom than Great Britain, it still enjoyed much higher levels of prosperity and cultural development than most other European countries. In short, French elites had reason to complain, the means to make their complaints known, and a government torn between the desires to censor dissident ideas and to appear open to modernity and progress. The French government controlled publishing—all books had to get official permissions—but not as tightly as in Spain, where the Catholic Inquisition made up its own list of banned books, or in Russia, where Catherine the Great allowed no opposition.

By the 1760s, the French government regularly ignored the publication of many works once thought offensive or subversive. In addition, a growing flood of works printed abroad poured into France and circulated underground. In the Dutch Republic and Swiss cities, private companies made fortunes smuggling illegal books into France over mountain passes and back roads. Foreign printers provided secret catalogs of their offerings and sold their products through booksellers who were willing to market forbidden books for a high price. Among such books were not only the philosophical treatises of the Enlightenment but also pornographic books and pamphlets (some by Diderot) lampooning the Catholic clergy and leading members of the royal court. In the 1770s and 1780s, lurid descriptions of sexual promiscuity at the French court helped undermine the popularity of the throne.

The German Enlightenment. In the German states the Enlightenment followed a very different course. Whereas the French philosophes often took a violently anticlerical and combative tone, their German counterparts avoided direct political confrontations with authorities. Gotthold Lessing (1729–1781) complained in 1769 that Prussia was still "the most slavish society in Europe" in its lack of freedom to criticize government policies. As a playwright, literary critic, and philosopher, Lessing promoted religious toleration for the Jews and spiritual emancipation of Germans from foreign, especially French, models of culture, which still dominated. Lessing also introduced the German Jewish writer Moses Mendelssohn (1729–1786) into Berlin salon society. Mendelssohn labored to build bridges between German and Jewish culture by arguing that Judaism was a rational and undogmatic religion. He believed persecution and discrimination against the Jews would end as reason triumphed.

Reason was also the chief focus of the most influential German thinker of the Enlightenment, Immanuel Kant (1724–1804). Kant, a university professor who lectured on everything from economics to astronomy, wrote one of the most important works in the history of Western philosophy, *The Critique of Pure Reason* (1781). Kant admired Adam Smith and especially Rousseau, whose portrait he displayed proudly in his lodgings. Just as Smith founded modern economics and Rousseau modern political theory, Kant in *Critique of Pure Reason* set the foundations for modern philosophy. In this complex book, Kant established the doctrine of *idealism*, the belief that true understanding can come only from examining the ways in which ideas are formed in the mind. Ideas are shaped, Kant argued, not just by sensory information (a position central to *empiricism*, a philosophy based on John Locke's writings) but also by the operation on that information of mental categories such as space and time. In Kant's philosophy these "categories of understanding" were neither sensory nor supernatural; they were entirely ideal and abstract and located in the human mind. For Kant the supreme philosophical questions—Does God exist? Is personal immortality possible? Do humans have free will?—were unanswerable by reason alone. But like Rousseau, Kant insisted that true moral freedom could be achieved only by living in society and obeying its laws.

The Limits of Reason: Roots of Romanticism and Religious Revival

As Kant showed, reason had its limits: it could not answer all of life's pressing questions. In reaction to what some saw as the Enlightenment's excessive reliance on the authority of human reason, a new artistic movement called *romanticism* took root. Although it would not fully flower until the early nineteenth century, romanticism traced its emphasis on individual genius, deep emotion, and the joys of nature to thinkers like Rousseau who had scolded the philosophes for ignoring those aspects of life that escaped and even conflicted with the power of reason. Rousseau's autobiographical *Confessions*, published posthumously in 1782, caused an immediate sensation because it revealed so much about his inner emotional life, including his sexual longings and his almost paranoid distrust of other Enlightenment figures.

The appeal to feelings and emotions also increased interest in the occult. In the 1780s, a charismatic Austrian physician turned "experimenter," Franz Mesmer, awed crowds of aristocrats and middle-class admirers with his Paris demonstrations of "animal magnetism." He passed a weak electrical current through tubs filled with water or iron filings, around which groups of his disciples sat, holding hands; with this process of "mesmerism" he claimed to cure their ailments. (The word *mesmerize*, meaning "hypnotize" or "hold spellbound," is derived from Mesmer's name.)

A novel by the young German writer Johann Wolfgang von Goethe (1749–1832) captured the early romantic spirit with its glorification of emo-

tion. *The Sorrows of Young Werther* (1774) told of a young man who resembles Rousseau's Julie in many respects: he loves nature and rural life and is unhappy in love. When the woman he loves marries another, he falls into deep melancholy and eventually kills himself. Reason cannot save him. The book spurred a veritable Werther craze: there were Werther costumes, Werther engravings and embroidery, medallions, a perfume called Eau de Werther, and, unfortunately, a few imitations of Werther's suicide. The young Napoleon Bonaparte, who was to build an empire for France, claimed to have read Goethe's novel seven times.

Religious revivals underlined the limits of reason in a different way. Much of the Protestant world experienced an "awakening" in the 1740s. In the German states, Pietist groups founded new communities; and in the British North American colonies, revivalist Protestant preachers drew thousands of fervent believers in a movement called the Great Awakening. In North America bitter conflicts between revivalists and their opponents in the established churches prompted the leaders on both sides to set up new colleges to support their beliefs. These included Princeton, Columbia, Brown, and Dartmouth, all founded between 1746 and 1769.

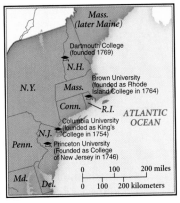

New Colleges in North America

Revivalism also stirred eastern European Jews at about the same time. Israel ben Eliezer (c. 1700–1760), later known as Ba'al Shem Tov (or the Besht, from the initials), laid the foundation for the Hasidic sect in the 1740s and 1750s. Teaching outside the synagogue system, Ba'al Shem Tov traveled the Polish countryside offering to cure men of their evil spirits. He invented a new form of popular prayer, in which the believer aimed to annihilate his own personality in order to let the supernatural speak through him. His followers, the *Hasidim* (Hebrew for "most pious" Jews), often prayed at the top of their lungs, joyfully swaying and clapping their hands. They scorned the formality of the regular synagogues in favor of their own prayer houses, where they gathered in rustic clothing and broad fur

A Hasid and His Wife
The followers of Ba'al Shem Tov were known as Hasidim ("most pious Jews"). They insisted on wearing Polish peasant-style clothing even if they themselves were not peasants. The Hasidim stressed devotion to the rebbe *("teacher and spiritual guide").*
Encyclopedia of Jewish History.

hats to emphasize their piety and simplicity. Their practices soon spread all over Poland-Lithuania.

Most of the waves of Protestant revivalism ebbed after the 1750s, but in Great Britain the movement known as *Methodism* continued to grow through the end of the century. John Wesley (1703–1791), the Oxford-educated son of an Anglican cleric, founded Methodism, a term evoked by Wesley's insistence on strict self-discipline and a methodical approach to religious study and observance. In 1738, Wesley had a mystical experience in which he felt the need to submit his life totally to Christ. Immediately afterward, he began to travel all over the British Isles, preaching a new brand of Protestantism that emphasized an intense personal experience of salvation and a life of thrift, abstinence, and hard work. In meadows and brickyards, in mine pits and copperworks, wherever ordinary people played or worked, Wesley would mount a table or a box to speak or begin a hymn. He slept in his followers' homes, ate their food, and treated their illnesses with various remedies, including small electric shocks for nervous diseases (Wesley eagerly followed Benjamin Franklin's experiments with electricity). In fifty years, Wesley preached forty thousand sermons, an average of fifteen a week. Not surprisingly, his preaching disturbed the Anglican authorities, who refused to let him preach in the churches. In response, Wesley began to ordain his

own clergy. Nevertheless, during Wesley's lifetime the Methodist leadership remained politically conservative; Wesley himself wrote many pamphlets urging order, loyalty, and submission to higher authorities. He denounced political agitation in the 1770s because he said it threatened to make Great Britain "a field of blood" ruled by "King Mob."

✦ Society and Culture in an Age of Enlightenment

Religious revivals and the first stirrings of romanticism show that all intellectual currents did not flow in the same channel. Similarly, some social and cultural developments manifested the influence of Enlightenment ideas but others did not. The traditional leaders of European societies—the nobles—responded to Enlightenment ideals in contradictory fashion: many simply reasserted their privileges and resisted the influence of the Enlightenment, but an important minority embraced change and actively participated in reform efforts. The expanding middle classes saw in the Enlightenment a chance to make their claim for joining society's governing elite. They bought Enlightenment books, joined Masonic lodges, and patronized new styles in art, music, and literature. The lower classes had much less contact with the Enlightenment. Economic growth affected them much more. Continuing population increase contributed to a rise in prices for basic goods, but the industrialization of textile manufacturing, which began in this period, made cotton clothing more accessible to those at the bottom of the social scale. Social change, however, was neither uniform nor painless. Most peasants remained tied to the land and their lords; those who moved to the cities in search of work did not always find their situations better.

The Nobility's Reassertion of Privilege

Nobles made up about 3 percent of the European population, but the proportion and their way of life varied greatly from country to country. At least 10 percent of the population in Poland was noble and 7 to 8 percent in Spain, in contrast to only 2 percent in Russia and between 1 and 2 percent in the rest of western Europe. Polish and Spanish nobles in particular often lived in poverty; titles did not guarantee wealth. The wealthiest European nobles luxuriated in almost unimaginable opulence. Many of the English peers, for example, owned more than ten thousand acres of land (the average western European peasant owned about five acres), invested widely in government bonds and trading companies, kept several country residences with scores of servants as well as houses in London, and occasionally even had their own private orchestras as well as libraries of expensive books, greenhouses for exotic plants, kennels of pedigree dogs, and collections of antiques, firearms, and scientific instruments.

In the face of the commercialization of agriculture and inflation of prices, European aristocrats converted their remaining legal rights (called *seigneurial dues*, from the French *seigneur*, for "lord") into money payments and used them to support an increasingly expensive lifestyle. Peasants felt the squeeze as a result. French peasants, for instance, paid a wide range of dues to their landlords, including payments to grind grain at the lord's mill, bake bread in his oven, press grapes at his winepress, and various inheritance taxes on the land. In addition, peasants had to work without compensation for a specified number of days every year on the public roads. They also paid taxes to the government on salt, an essential preservative, and on the value of their land; customs duties if they sold produce or wine in town; and the tithe on their grain (one-tenth of the crop) to the church.

In Britain, the landed gentry could not claim these same onerous dues from their tenants, but they tenaciously defended their exclusive right to hunt game. The game laws kept the poor from eating meat and helped protect the social status of the rich. The gentry enforced the game laws themselves by hiring gamekeepers who hunted down poachers and even set traps for them in the forests. According to the law, anyone who poached deer or rabbits while armed or disguised could be sentenced to death. After 1760, the number of arrests for breaking the game laws increased dramatically. In most other countries, too, hunting was the special right of the nobility and a cause of deep popular resentment.

Even though Enlightenment writers sharply criticized nobles' insistence on special privileges, most aristocrats maintained their marks of distinction. The male court nobility continued to sport swords, plumed hats, makeup, and powdered hair, while middle-class men wore simpler and more somber clothing. Aristocrats had their own seats in church and their own quarters in the universities. Frederick II ("the Great") of Prussia (r. 1740–1786) made sure that nobles dominated both the army officer corps and the civil bureaucracy. Catherine II of Russia (r. 1762–1796) granted the nobility vast tracts of land, the exclusive right to own serfs, and exemption from personal taxes and corporal punishment. Her Charter of the Nobility of 1785 codified these privileges in exchange for the nobles' political subservience to the state. In many countries, including Spain and France, the law prohibited aristocrats from engaging directly in retail trade. In Austria, Spain, the Italian states, Poland-Lithuania, and Russia, most nobles consequently cared little about Enlightenment ideas; they did not read the books of the philosophes and feared reforms that might challenge their dominance of rural society.

In France, Britain, and the western German states, however, the nobility proved more open to the new ideas. Among those who personally corresponded with Rousseau, for example, half were nobles, as were 20 percent of the 160 contributors to the *Encyclopedia*. It had not escaped their notice that Rousseau had denounced inequality. In his view, it was "manifestly contrary to the law of nature . . . that a handful of people should gorge themselves with superfluities while the hungry multitude goes in want of necessities."

The Middle Class and the Making of a New Elite

Enlightenment ideals helped break down the traditional barriers between the aristocracy and the middle class in western Europe and were in turn further energized by this development. The Enlightenment offered middle-class people an intellectual and cultural route to social improvement; it gave them the chance to join with nobles in a new mixed elite, united by common interests in reform and new cultural tastes. Intermarriage, the spread of businesslike attitudes among the nobility, and the middle-class emulation of noble ways encouraged this intermixing of the elite. Although middle-class people had many reasons to resent the nobles, they also aspired to be like them. The richest hoped to buy themselves a title and share all the special privileges accorded nobles.

The term *middle class* referred to the middle position on the social ladder; it comprised the families who did not have legal titles like the nobility above them but who did not work with their hands like the peasants, artisans, or workers below them. Most middle-class families lived in towns or cities and earned their living in some professional capacity—as doctors, lawyers, or lower-level officials or through investment in land, trade, or manufacturing. In the eighteenth century, the ranks of the middle class—also known as the *bourgeoisie* after *bourg*, the French word for "town," or *bourgeois*, the French word for "city dweller"—grew steadily in western Europe as a result of economic expansion. In France, for example, the overall population grew by about one-third in the 1700s, but the bourgeoisie nearly tripled in size.

Lodges and Learned Societies. Nobles and middle-class professionals mingled in Enlightenment salons and joined the new Masonic lodges and local learned societies. The Masonic lodges began as social clubs with elaborate secret rituals based on those of the masons' guilds. Their members were known as *freemasons* because that was the term given to apprentice masons when they were deemed "free" to practice as masters of their guild. Although not explicitly political in aim, the lodges encouraged equality among members, and both aristocrats and middle-class men could join. In France, women set up their own Masonic lodges. Members wrote constitutions for their lodges and elected their own officers, thus promoting a direct experience of constitutional government.

Freemasonry arose in Great Britain and spread eastward: the first French and Italian lodges opened in 1726; Frederick II of Prussia founded a lodge in 1740; and after 1750, freemasonry spread in Poland, Russia, and British North America. Despite the papacy's condemnation of freemasonry in 1738 as subversive of religious and civil authority, lodges continued to multiply throughout the eighteenth century because they offered a place for socializing outside of the traditional channels and a way of declaring one's interest in the Enlightenment and reform. In short, freemasonry offered a kind of secular religion. After 1789 and the outbreak of the French Revolution, conservatives would blame the lodges for every kind of political upheaval, but in the 1700s many high-ranking nobles became active members and saw no conflict with their privileged status.

Nobles and middle-class professionals also met in local learned societies, which greatly increased in number in this period. They gathered to discuss such practical issues as new scientific innovations

Neoclassical Style

In this Georgian interior of Syon House on the outskirts of London, various neoclassical motifs are readily apparent: Greek columns, Greek-style statuary on top of the columns, and Roman-style mosaics in the floor. The Scottish architect Robert Adams created this room for the duke of Northumberland in the 1760s. Adams had spent four years in Italy and returned in 1758 to London to decorate homes in the "Adams style," meaning the neoclassical manner. Fotomas Index, UK.

or methods to eliminate poverty. The societies, or academies, brought the Enlightenment down from the realm of books and ideas to the level of concrete reforms. They sponsored essay contests, such as the one won by Rousseau in 1749, or the one set by the society in Metz in 1785 on the question "Are there means for making the Jews happier and more useful in France?" The Metz society approved essays that argued for granting the Jews civil rights.

New Cultural Styles. Shared tastes in travel, architecture, and the arts helped solidify the intermingled elite of nobility and middle class. "Grand tours" of Europe often led upper-class youths to recently discovered Greek and Roman ruins at Pompeii, Herculaneum, and Paestum in Italy. These excavations aroused enthusiasm for the neoclassical style in architecture and painting, which began pushing aside the rococo and the long dominant baroque. Urban residences and new government buildings soon reflected the neoclassical emphasis on purity and clarity of forms. As one German writer noted, with considerable exaggeration, "Everything in Paris is in the Greek style." In the 1760s and 1770s in Britain, the upper classes began building magnificent houses in the neoclassical style called Georgian (after the reigning king, George III), and pottery, furniture, fabrics, cutlery, and even wallpaper incorporated classical themes and allowed middle-class people to emulate the richest aristocrats.

This period also supported artistic styles other than neoclassicism. Frederick II of Prussia built himself a palace in the earlier rococo style and gave it a French name, *Sans-souci* ("worry-free"), and filled it with the works of French masters of the rococo. The new emphasis on emotion and family life, represented in Rousseau's *The New Heloise*, was reflected in a growing taste for moralistic family scenes in painting. The paintings of Jean-Baptiste Greuze (1725–1805), much praised by Diderot, depicted ordinary families at moments of domestic crisis. Such subjects appealed in particular to the middle-class public, which now attended the official painting exhibitions in France that were held regularly every other year after 1737. Court painting nonetheless remained much in demand. Marie-Louise-Elizabeth Vigée-Lebrun (1755–1842), who painted portraits at the French court, reported that in the 1780s "it was difficult to get a place on my waiting list. . . . I was the fashion."

The English engraver and painter William Hogarth (1697–1764) ranged from noble portraits to popular moralistic print series. He sold his engravings to the middle class but he still hoped to have his work taken seriously as high art. The English potter Josiah Wedgwood (1730–1795) almost

Jean-Baptiste Greuze, *The Beloved Mother* (1765)
Greuze made his reputation as a painter of moralistic family scenes. In this one, a mother has just finished breast-feeding her infant, a practice urgently advocated at just this time by Rousseau. The contented mother is surrounded by adoring children and an admiring husband. Diderot praised Greuze's work as "morality in paint," but in later years Greuze began to depict much more ambiguous scenes, often with an erotic subtext. Art Resource, NY.

single-handedly created a mass market for domestic crockery by appealing to middle-class desires to emulate the rich and royal. His designs of special tea sets for the British queen, for Catherine the Great of Russia, and for leading aristocrats allowed him to advertise his wares as fashionable. As he said, "Few ladies dare venture at anything out of the common stile 'till authorized by their betters." By 1767, he claimed that his Queensware pottery had "spread over the whole Globe," and indeed by then his pottery was being marketed in France, Russia, Venice, the Ottoman Empire, and British North America.

Although wealthy nobles still patronized Europe's leading musicians, music too began to reflect the broadening of the elite and the spread of Enlightenment ideals as classical forms replaced the baroque style. Complex polyphony gave way to melody, which made the music more accessible to ordinary listeners. The violin's tone became stronger and more resonant, and it overcame a reputation as fit only for village dances. Mass sections of string instruments became the backbone of professional orchestras, which now played to large audiences of well-to-do listeners in sizable concert halls. The public concert gradually displaced the private recital, and a new attitude toward "the classics" developed: for the first time in the 1770s and 1780s, concert groups began to play older music rather than simply playing the latest commissioned works.

This laid the foundation for what we still call *classical* music today, that is, a repertory of the greatest music of the eighteenth and early nineteenth centuries. Because composers now created works that would be performed over and over again as part of a classical repertory, rather than occasional pieces for the court or noble patrons, they deliberately attempted to write lasting works. As a result, the major composers began to produce fewer symphonies: the Austrian composer Franz Joseph Haydn (1732–1809) wrote more than one hundred symphonies, but his successor Ludwig van Beethoven (1770–1827) would create only nine.

The two supreme masters of the new musical style of the eighteenth century show that the transition from noble patronage to classical concerts was far from complete. The Austrians Haydn and Wolfgang Amadeus Mozart (1756–1791) both wrote for noble patrons, but by the early 1800s their compositions had been incorporated into the canon of concert classics all over Europe. Incredibly prolific, both excelled in combining lightness, clarity, and profound emotion. Both also wrote numerous Italian operas, a genre whose popularity continued to grow: in the 1780s, the Papal States alone boasted forty opera houses. Haydn spent most of his career working for a Hungarian noble family, the Eszterházys. Asked why he had written no string quintets (at which Mozart excelled), he responded simply: "No one has ordered any."

Reading Matters. The Enlightenment created a new public for reading that extended far beyond the narrow confines of standard secondary and higher education. In secondary school, whether lay- or church-run, boys studied Latin, Greek, philosophy, and logic but spent little time on mathematics, science, history, or modern languages. Girls learned domestic skills, some music, and one or two foreign languages, but they did not receive the classical education considered essential for government service or intellectual life. Boys and girls read Enlightenment books at home, not in school. The universities of many countries appeared rigid and behind the times. As an Austrian reformer complained about the universities in his country, "Critical history, natural sciences—which are supposed to make enlightenment general and combat prejudice—were neglected or wholly unknown."

Shaped by coffeehouses, Masonic lodges, and public concerts more than by formal schooling, the new reading public fed a frenzied increase in publication. By the end of the eighteenth century, six times as many books were being published in the German states, for instance, as at the beginning. One Parisian author commented that "people are certainly reading ten times as much in Paris as they did a hundred years ago." Although religious books still predominated, books on history, the arts, and the sciences proliferated. Provincial towns in Britain, France, the Dutch Republic, and the German states published their own newspapers; by 1780, thirty-seven English towns had local newspapers. Newspapers advertised arithmetic, dancing, and drawing lessons, and they did not always stick to high-minded subjects; they also advertised cures for venereal disease and abortifacients. Lending libraries multiplied, and, in England especially, even small villages housed secular book clubs. Women benefited as much as men from the spread of print. As one Englishman observed, "By far the greatest part of ladies now have a taste for books." Catherine Macaulay (1731–1791) published best-selling histories of Britain, and in France Stéphanie de Genlis (1746–1830) wrote children's books—a genre that was growing in importance as middle-class parents became more interested in education.

The novel had become a respectable and influential genre. Among the most widely read novels were those of the English printer and writer Samuel Richardson (1689–1761). In *Clarissa Harlowe* (1747–1748), a long novel in eight volumes, Richardson told the story of a young woman from a heartless upper-class family who is torn between her family's choice of a repulsive suitor and her attraction to Lovelace, an aristocratic rake. Although she runs off with Lovelace to escape her family, she resists his advances; after being drugged and raped by Lovelace—despite the frantic pleas of readers of the first volumes to spare her—Clarissa dies of what can only be called a broken heart. One woman complained to Richardson, "I verily believe I have shed a pint of tears, and my heart is still bursting." The French writer Diderot compared Richardson to Moses, Homer, Euripides, and Sophocles.

Novels aroused criticism, however, because they sympathetically portrayed characters from the lower classes. Even Richardson attacked his fellow English novelist Henry Fielding: "I found the characters and situations so wretchedly low and dirty, that I imagined I could not be interested for any one of them. . . . It is beyond my conception, that a man of family, and who had some learning, and who really is a writer, should descend so excessively low, in all his pieces. Who can care for any of his people?" Although Richardson wrote *Clarissa* as a kind of manual of virtuous female conduct, critics worried that novels undermined morals with their portrayals of low-life characters, the seductions of virtuous women, and other examples of immoral behavior.

Spotlight on Children. As the rates of child mortality gradually declined in the 1700s, children became the focus of much new attention. Rousseau's *Emile* attracted so many readers because it offered an educational approach for gently drawing the best out of children rather than repressing their natural curiosity and love of learning. The book helped change attitudes in the new elite toward children, who were no longer viewed only as little sinners in need of harsh discipline. Paintings now showed individual children playing at their favorite activities rather than formally posed with their families. Books about and for children became popular. *The Newtonian System of the Universe Digested for Young Minds*, by "Tom Telescope," was published in Britain in 1761 and reprinted many times. In 1730, no shops specialized in children's toys in Britain; by 1780, such shops could be found throughout the country. In 1762, John Spilsbury, a London engraver and mapmaker, invented the jigsaw puzzle when he mounted a map on a sheet of wood and cut around the borders of the countries using a fine-bladed saw. Babies' and children's clothing now differed in style from adult clothing: childhood was seen as a separate stage of life, and children were no longer considered miniature adults.

The Enlightenment's emphasis on reason, self-control, and childhood innocence made parents increasingly anxious about their children's sexuality. Moralists and physicians wrote books about the evils of masturbation, "proving" that it led to physical and mental degeneration and even madness. One English writer linked masturbation to debility of body and of mind; infertility; epilepsy; loss of memory, sight, and hearing; distortions of the eyes, mouth, and face; a pale, sallow, and bluish complexion; wasting of the limbs; idiotism; and death itself. The Enlightenment taught the middle and upper classes to value their children and to expect their improvement through education, but at the same time it encouraged excessive concern about children being left too much to their own devices.

Life on the Margins

The upper and middle classes worried most about the increasing numbers of poor people. Although booming foreign trade—French colonial trade increased tenfold in the 1700s—fueled a dramatic economic expansion, the results did not necessarily trickle all the way down the social scale. The population of Europe grew by nearly 30 percent, with especially striking gains in England, Ireland, Prussia, and Hungary. (See "Taking Measure," page 704.) Even though food production increased, shortages and crises still occurred periodically. Prices went up in many countries after the 1730s and continued to

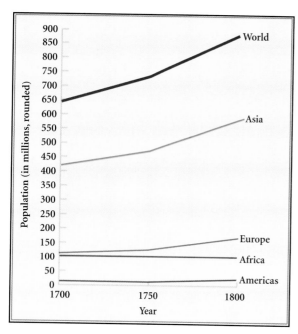

TAKING MEASURE World Population Growth, 1700–1800

Asia had many more people than Europe, and both Asia and Europe were growing much more rapidly in the 1700s than Africa or the Americas. The population stagnation in Africa has been the subject of much scholarly controversy. What are the advantages of a growing population? What are the disadvantages?

Adapted from Andre Gundar Frank, *Reorient: Global Economy in the Asian Age* (Berkeley: University of California Press), 1998.

rise gradually until the early nineteenth century; wages in many trades rose as well, but less quickly than prices. Peasants who produced surpluses to sell in local markets and shopkeepers and artisans who could increase their sales to meet growing demand prospered. But those at the bottom of the social ladder—day laborers in the cities and peasants with small holdings—lived on the edge of dire poverty, and when they lost their land or work, they either migrated to the cities or wandered the roads in search of food and work. In France alone, 200,000 workers left their homes every year in search of seasonal employment elsewhere. At least 10 percent of Europe's urban population depended on some form of charity.

The growing numbers of poor overwhelmed local governments. In some countries, beggars and vagabonds had been locked up in workhouses since the mid-1600s. The expenses for running these overcrowded institutions increased 60 percent in England between 1760 and 1785. After 1740, most German towns created workhouses that were part workshop, part hospital, and part prison. Such institutions also appeared for the first time in Boston, New York, and Philadelphia. To supplement the inadequate system of religious charity, offices for the poor, public workshops, and workhouse-hospitals, the French government created *dépôts de mendicité*, or beggar houses, in 1767. The government sent people to these new workhouses to labor in manufacturing, but most were too weak or sick to work, and 20 percent of them died within a few months of incarceration. The ballooning number of poor people created fears about rising crime. To officials, beggars seemed more aggressive than ever. The handful of police assigned to keep order in each town or district found themselves confronted with increasing incidents of rural banditry and crimes against property.

Persistence of Popular Culture. An increase in literacy, especially in the cities, allowed some lower-class people to participate in new tastes and ideas. One French observer insisted, "These days, you see a waiting-maid in her backroom, a lackey in an anteroom reading pamphlets. People can read in almost all classes of society." In France, however, only 50 percent of men and 27 percent of women could read and write in the 1780s (although that was twice the rate of a century earlier). Literacy rates were higher in England and the Dutch Republic, but much lower in eastern Europe. About one in four Parisians owned books, but the lower classes overwhelmingly read religious books, as they had in the past.

Whereas the new elite might attend salons, concerts, or art exhibitions, peasants enjoyed their traditional forms of popular entertainment, such as fairs and festivals, and the urban lower classes relaxed in cabarets and taverns. Sometimes pleasures were cruel. In Britain, bullbaiting, bearbaiting, dogfighting, and cockfighting were all common forms of entertainment that provided opportunities for organized gambling. Even "gentle" sports frequented by the upper classes had their violent side, showing that the upper classes had not become so different as they sometimes thought. Cricket matches, whose rules were first laid down in 1744, were often accompanied by brawls among fans (not unlike soccer matches today, though on a much smaller scale). Many Englishmen enjoyed what one observer called a "battle royal with sticks, pebbles and hog's dung."

Changes in Sexual Behavior. As population increased and villagers began to move to cities to better their prospects, sexual behavior changed too. The rates of births out of wedlock soared, from less than 5 percent of all births in the seventeenth century to nearly 20 percent at the end of the eighteenth. Historians have disagreed about the causes and meaning of this change. Some detect in this pattern a sign of sexual liberation and the beginnings of a modern sexual revolution: as women moved out of the control of their families, they began to seek their own sexual fulfillment. Others view this change more bleakly, as a story of seduction and betrayal: family and community pressure had once forced a man to marry a woman pregnant with his child, but now a man could abandon a pregnant lover, just by moving away.

Increased mobility brought freedom for some women, but it also aggravated the vulnerability of those newly arrived in cities from the countryside. For them, desperation, not reason, often ruled their choices. Women who came to the city as domestic servants had little recourse against masters or fellow servants who seduced or raped them. The result was a startling rise in abandoned babies. Most European cities established foundling hospitals in the 1700s, but infant and child mortality was 50 percent higher in such institutions than for children brought up at home. Some women tried herbs, laxatives, or crude surgical means of abortion; a few, usually servants who would lose their jobs if their employers discovered they had borne a child, resorted to infanticide.

European states had long tried to regulate sexual behavior but without much consistent success. Every country had laws against prostitution, adultery, fornication, sodomy, and infanticide. Despite official denunciations, sexual entertainment for men grew increasingly commercialized in this period of economic growth, and houses of prostitution became more specialized, developing into flagellation clubs and bagnios, which combined brothel and bathhouse. Reformers advocated lessening of punishments for fornication, which often included some form of public humiliation, and they criticized the harshness of laws against infanticide, but they showed no mercy for "sodomites" (as male homosexuals were called), who in some places, in particular the Dutch Republic, were systematically persecuted and imprisoned or even executed. Male homosexuals attracted the attention of authorities because they had begun to develop networks and special meeting places. The stereotype of the effeminate, exclusively homosexual male seems to have appeared for the first time in the eighteenth century, perhaps as part of a growing emphasis on separate roles for men and women.

Roots of Industrialization

Although it was only starting to take hold, industrialization would eventually transform European society. The process began in England in the 1770s and 1780s and included four interlocking trends: (1) population increased dramatically, by more than 50 percent in England in the second half of the eighteenth century; (2) manufacturers introduced steam-driven machinery to increase output; (3) they established factories to concentrate the labor of their workers; and (4) the production of cotton goods, which were lighter and more versatile than woolens, increased tenfold. Together these factors sparked the Industrial Revolution, which would change the face of Europe—indeed, of the entire world—in the nineteenth century.

Innovations in the technology of cotton production permitted manufacturers to make use of the growing supply of raw cotton shipped from the plantations of North America and the Caribbean. In 1733, the Englishman John Kay patented the flying shuttle, which weavers operated by pulling a cord that drove the shuttle to either side, enabling them to "throw" yarn across the loom rather than draw it back and forth by hand. When the flying shuttle came into widespread use in the 1760s, weavers began producing cloth more quickly than spinners could produce the thread. The shortage of spun thread propelled the invention of machines to speed the process of spinning: the spinning jenny and the water frame, a power-driven spinning machine, were introduced in the 1760s. In the following decades, water frames replaced thousands of women spinners working at home by hand. In 1776, the Scottish engineer James Watt developed an improved steam engine, and, in the 1780s, Edmund

Handloom Weaving
This plate from the Encyclopedia *demonstrates handloom weaving of gold-threaded fabrics (tassels, trims, fringes, borders). Fancy threads could not be used on the early mechanical looms, which were suitable only for basic cotton thread. This kind of handloom weaving continued well into the 1800s.*
Stock Montage, Inc.

Cartwright, an English clergyman and inventor, designed a mechanized loom, which when perfected could be run by a small boy and yield fifteen times the output of a skilled adult weaver working a handloom. By the end of the century, all the new power machinery was assembled in large factories that hired semiskilled men, women, and children to replace skilled weavers.

Historians have no single explanation for why England led the Industrial Revolution. Some have emphasized England's large internal market, increasing population, supply of private investment capital from overseas trade and commercial profits, or natural resources such as coal and iron. Others have cited England's greater opportunities for social mobility, its relative political stability in the eighteenth century, or the pragmatism of the English and Scottish inventors who designed the necessary machinery. These early industrialists hardly had a monopoly on ingenuity, but they did come out of a tradition of independent capitalist enterprise. They

also shared a culture of informal scientific education through learned societies and popular lectures (one of the prominent forms of the Enlightenment in Britain). For whatever reasons, the combination of improvements in agricultural production, growth in population and foreign trade, and willingness to invest in new machines and factories appeared first in this relatively small island.

Although the rest of Europe did not industrialize until the nineteenth century, textile manufacturing—long a linchpin in the European economy—expanded dramatically in the eighteenth century even without the introduction of new machines and factories. Textile production increased because of the spread of the "putting-out" or "domestic" system. Hundreds of thousands of families manufactured cloth in every country from Britain to Russia. Under the putting-out system, manufacturers supplied the families with raw materials, such as woolen or cotton fibers. Working at home in a dimly lit room, a whole family labored together. The mother and her children washed the fibers and carded and combed them. Then the mother and oldest daughters spun them into thread. The father, assisted by the children, wove the cloth. The cloth was then finished (bleached, dyed, smoothed, and so on) under the supervision of the manufacturer in a large workshop, located either in town or in the countryside. This system had existed in the textile industry for hundreds of years, but in the eighteenth century it expanded immensely, drawing in thousands of peasants in the countryside, and it included not only textiles but also the manufacture of such products as glassware, baskets, nails, and guns. The spread of the domestic system of manufacturing is sometimes called *proto-industrialization* to signify that the process helped pave the way for the full-scale Industrial Revolution.

All across Europe, thousands of people who worked in agriculture became part-time or full-time textile workers. Peasants turned to putting-out work because they did not have enough land to support their families. Men labored off-season and women often worked year-round to augment their meager incomes. At the same time, population growth and general economic improvement meant that demand for cloth increased because more people could afford it. Studies of wills left by working-class men and women in Paris at the end of the eighteenth century show that people owned more clothes of greater variety. Working-class men in Paris began to wear underclothes, something rare at the beginning of the century. Men and women now bought night-clothes; before, Europeans had slept naked except in cold weather. And white, red, blue, yellow, green, and even pastel shades of cotton now replaced the black, gray, or brown of traditional woolen dress.

❖ State Power in an Era of Reform

All rulers recognized that manufacturing created new sources of wealth, but the start of industrialization had not yet altered the standard forms of competition between states: commerce and war. The diffusion of Enlightenment ideas of reform had a more immediate impact on the ways European monarchs exercised power than did industrialization. Historians label many of the sovereigns of this time "enlightened despots" or "enlightened absolutists," for they aimed to combine Enlightenment reforms with absolutist powers. Catherine the Great's admiring relationship with Voltaire showed how even the most absolutist rulers championed reform when it suited their own goals. Voltaire considered the nobles and the established churches the real obstacles to reform, and, like many other Enlightenment writers, he looked to monarchs such as Catherine and Frederick the Great of Prussia to overcome their resistance.

Every European ruler tried to introduce reforms in this period, including improvements in the condition of the peasantry in Austria, freer markets in grain in France, extension of education in Prussia, and new law codes almost everywhere. Success or failure in the competition for trade and territory directly affected these reform efforts. French losses in the Seven Years' War, for example, prompted the French crown to introduce far-reaching reforms that provoked violent resistance and helped pave the way for the French Revolution of 1789. Reform proved to be a two-edged sword.

War and Diplomacy

Europeans no longer fought devastating wars over religion that killed hundreds of thousands of civilians; instead, professional armies and navies battled for control of overseas empires and for dominance on the European continent. Rulers continued to expand their armies: the Prussian army, for example, nearly tripled in size between 1740 and 1789. Widespread use of flintlock muskets required deployment in long lines, usually three men deep, with each line in turn loading and firing on command. Military strategy became cautious and calculating, but this did not prevent the outbreak of hostilities. The instability of the European balance of power resulted in two major wars, a diplomatic reversal of alliances, and the partition of Poland-Lithuania among Russia, Austria, and Prussia. By 1789, Prussia had confirmed its rise to great-power status, the British had eclipsed the French overseas, and once-great Poland-Lithuania had been reduced in size and importance.

War of the Austrian Succession, 1740–1748. The difficulties over the succession to the Austrian throne typified the dynastic complications that

Maria Theresa and Her Family
In this portrait by Martin van Meytens (1695–1770), Austrian empress Maria Theresa is shown with her husband, Francis I, and eleven of their sixteen children. Their eldest son eventually succeeded to the Austrian throne as Joseph II, and their youngest daughter, Maria Antonia, or Marie-Antoinette, became the queen of France.
Giraudon/Art Resource, NY.

repeatedly threatened the European balance of power. In 1740, Holy Roman Emperor Charles VI died without a male heir. Most European rulers recognized the emperor's chosen heiress, his daughter Maria Theresa, because Charles's Pragmatic Sanction of 1713 had given a woman the right to inherit the Habsburg crown lands. The new king of Prussia, Frederick II, who had just succeeded his father a few months earlier in 1740, saw his chance to grab territory and immediately invaded the rich Austrian province of Silesia. France joined Prussia in an attempt to further humiliate its traditional enemy Austria, and Great Britain allied with Austria to prevent the French from taking the Austrian Netherlands (Map 19.2). The War of the Austrian Succession (1740–1748) soon expanded to the overseas colonies of Great Britain and France as well. Maria Theresa (r. 1740–1780) survived only by conceding Silesia to Prussia in order to split the Prussians off from France. The Peace of Aix-la-Chapelle of 1748 recognized Maria Theresa as the heiress to the Austrian lands, and her husband, Francis I, became Holy Roman Emperor, thus reasserting the integrity of the Austrian Empire.

The fighting between France and Great Britain quickly extended to India, where a series of naval battles left the British in control of the seas. The peace of 1748 failed to resolve the colonial conflicts, and British and French trading companies continued to fight unofficially for domination in India. French and British colonials in North America also fought each other all along their boundaries, enlisting native American auxiliaries. Britain tried but failed to isolate the French Caribbean colonies during the war, and hostilities and suspicions continued unabated.

Seven Years' War, 1756–1763.   In 1756, a major reversal of alliances—what historians call the "Diplomatic Revolution"—reshaped relations among the great powers. Prussia and Great Britain signed a defensive alliance, prompting Austria to overlook two centuries of hostility and ally with France. Russia and Sweden soon joined the Franco-Austrian

MAP 19.2 War of the Austrian Succession, 1740–1748

The accession of a twenty-three-year-old woman, Maria Theresa, to the Austrian throne gave the new king of Prussia, Frederick II, an opportunity to invade the province of Silesia. France joined on Prussia's side, Great Britain on Austria's. In 1745, the French defeated the British in the Austrian Netherlands and helped instigate a Jacobite uprising in Scotland. The rebellion failed and British attacks on French overseas shipping forced the French to negotiate. The peace treaties guaranteed Frederick's conquest of Silesia, which soon became the wealthiest province of Prussia. France came to terms with Great Britain to protect its overseas possessions; Austria had to accept the peace settlement after a formal public protest.

STATE POWER IN AN ERA OF REFORM **709**

1740–1789

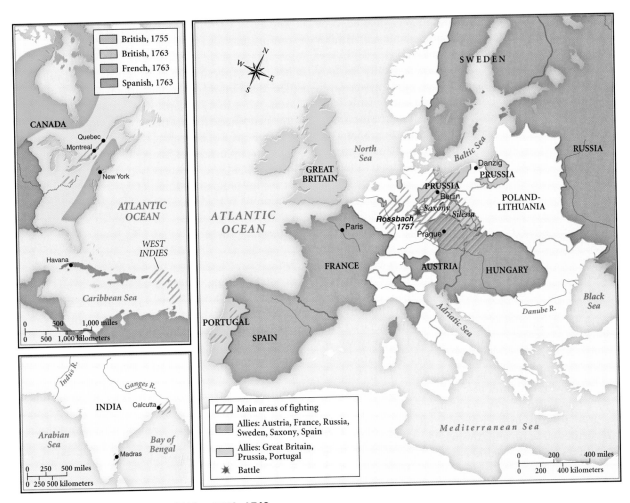

MAP 19.3 The Seven Years' War, 1756–1763

In what might justly be called the first worldwide war, the French and British fought each other on the European continent, in the West Indies, and in India. Their international struggle coincided with a realignment of forces within Europe caused by the desire of Austria, France, and Russia to check Prussian growth. Fearing, with reason, a joint Austrian-Russian attack, Frederick II of Prussia invaded Saxony in August 1756. Despite overwhelming odds, Frederick managed time and again to emerge victorious, until the Russians withdrew and the coalition against Prussia fell apart. The treaty between Austria and Prussia simply restored the status quo. The changes overseas were much more dramatic. Britain gained control over Canada and India but gave back to France the West Indian islands of Guadeloupe and Martinique. Britain was now the dominant power on the seas.

alliance. When Frederick II invaded Saxony, an ally of Austria, with his bigger and better-disciplined army, the long-simmering hostilities between Great Britain and France over colonial boundaries flared into a general war that became known as the Seven Years' War (1756–1763).

Fighting soon raged around the world (Map 19.3). The French and British battled on land and sea in North America (where the conflict was called the French and Indian War), the West Indies, and India. The two coalitions also fought each other in central Europe. At first, in 1757, Frederick the Great surprised Europe with a spectacular victory at Rossbach in Saxony over a much larger Franco-Austrian army. But in time, Russian and Austrian armies encircled his troops. Frederick despaired: "I believe all is lost. I will not survive the ruin of my country." A fluke of history saved him. Empress Elizabeth of

Russia (r. 1741–1762) died and was succeeded by the mentally unstable Peter III, a fanatical admirer of Frederick and things Prussian. Peter withdrew Russia from the war. (This was practically his only accomplishment as tsar. He was soon mysteriously murdered, probably at the instigation of his wife, Catherine the Great.) In a separate peace treaty Frederick kept all his territory, including Silesia.

Although Prussia suffered great losses in the fighting—some 160,000 Prussian soldiers died either in action or of disease—the army helped vault Prussia to the rank of leading powers. In 1733, Frederick II's father, Frederick William I, had instituted the "canton system," which enrolled peasant youths in each canton (or district) in the army, gave them two or three months of training annually, and allowed them to return to their family farms the rest of the year. They remained "cantonists" (reservists) as long as they were able-bodied. In this fashion, the Prussian military steadily grew in size; by 1740, Prussia had the third or fourth largest army in Europe even though it was tenth in population and thirteenth in land area. Under Frederick II, Prussia's military expenditures rose to two-thirds of the state's revenue. Virtually every nobleman served in the army, paying for his own support as officer and buying a position as company commander. Once retired, the officers returned to their estates, coordinated the canton system, and served as local officials. In this way, the military permeated every aspect of rural society, fusing army and agrarian organization. The army gave the state great power, but the militarization of Prussian society also had a profoundly conservative effect: it kept the peasants enserfed to their lords and blocked the middle classes from access to estates or high government positions.

The Anglo-French overseas conflicts ended more decisively than the continental land wars. British naval superiority, fully achieved only in the 1750s, enabled Great Britain to decisively defeat the French in their competition for colonial supremacy; the British routed the French in North America, India, and the West Indies. In the Treaty of Paris of 1763, France ceded Canada to Great Britain and agreed to remove its armies from India, in exchange for keeping its rich West Indian islands. Eagerness to avenge this defeat would motivate France to support the British North American colonists in their War of Independence just fifteen years later.

The First Partition of Poland, 1772. Eighteenth-century Poland-Lithuania was large but weak, and it became prey to the absolutist powers that surrounded it. Under Catherine the Great, Russia successfully battled the Ottoman Empire in intermittent fighting from 1768 to 1774 and promoted Greek efforts at independence from the Turks. Fearful of increasing Russian influence in the Balkans and the prospect of complete Russian domination of Poland, in 1772 Frederick the Great of Prussia proposed that large chunks of Polish-Lithuanian territory be divided among Austria, Prussia, and Russia. Despite the protests of the Austrian empress Maria Theresa that the partition would spread "a stain over my whole reign," she agreed to split one-third of Poland-Lithuania's territory and half of its people among the three powers. Conflicts between Catholics, Protestants, and Orthodox Christians were used to justify this cynical move. Russia took over most of Lithuania, effectively ending the Polish-Lithuanian commonwealth.

The First Partition of Poland, 1772

State-Sponsored Reform

In the aftermath of the Seven Years' War, all the belligerents faced pressing needs for more money to fund their growing armies, to organize navies to wage overseas conflicts, and to counter the impact of inflation. Rather than simply raise taxes as they had in the past, the enlightened absolutists—Frederick II in Prussia, Catherine II in Russia, Maria Theresa and Joseph II (r. 1780–1790) in Austria, Louis XV (r. 1715–1774) and Louis XVI (r. 1774–1792) in France—all proposed similar programs to increase economic and military power by modernizing society. In short, they tried to make tax increases more palatable by promising general social reforms. To harness Enlightenment ideals to their own ends, they appointed reform-minded ministers and gave them a mandate to inventory the country's resources in order to make taxes more equitable and standardize their collection, establish state independence from the church, make the legal system more predictable and accessible, and, in some instances, extend education and religious toleration. As one adviser to Joseph II put it, "A properly constituted state must be exactly analogous to a machine . . . and the ruler must be the foreman, the mainspring . . . which sets everything else in motion." Such reforms always threatened the interests of traditional groups, however, and the spread of Enlightenment ideas aroused sometimes unpredictable desires for more change.

Administrative and Legal Reforms.

The reforming monarchs did not invent government bureaucracy, but in Austria and Prussia especially they insisted on greater attention to merit, hard work, and professionalism, which made bureaucrats more like modern civil servants. As Joseph II of Austria explained, government must be organized according to "uniform principles," and it must unite "a single mass of people all subject to impartial guidance." In this view, the ruler should be a benevolent, enlightened administrator who worked for the general well-being of his or her people. Frederick II of Prussia, who drove himself as hard as he drove his officials, boasted, "I am the first servant of the state."

Legal reform, both of the judicial system and of the often disorganized and irregular law codes, was central to the work of many reform-minded monarchs. Although Frederick II favored all things French in culture—he insisted on speaking French in his court and prided himself on his personal friendship with Voltaire—he made Prussian justice the envy of Europe. His institution of a uniform civil justice system created the most consistently administered laws and efficient judiciary of the time. Joseph II also ordered the compilation of a unified law code, a project that required many years for completion. Catherine II of Russia began such an undertaking even more ambitiously. In 1767, she called together a legislative commission of 564 deputies and asked them to consider a long document called the *Instruction*, which represented her hopes for legal reform based on the ideas of Montesquieu and the Italian writer Cesare Beccaria. Montesquieu had insisted that punishment should fit the crime; he criticized the use of torture and brutal corporal punishment. In his influential book *On Crimes and Punishments* (1764), Beccaria argued

Dividing Poland, 1772
In this contemporary depiction, Catherine the Great, Joseph II, and Frederick II point on the map to the portion of Poland-Lithuania each plans to take. The artist makes it clear that Poland's fate rested in the hands of neighboring rulers, not its own people.
Mansell/Time, Inc.

that laws should be printed for everyone to read and administered in rational procedures, that torture should be abolished as inhumane, and that the accused should be presumed innocent until proven guilty. Despite much discussion and hundreds of petitions and documents about local problems, little came of Catherine's commission because the monarch herself—despite her regard for Voltaire and his fellow philosophes—was not very committed to reform.

The Church and Education.

Rulers everywhere wanted more control over church affairs, and they used Enlightenment criticisms of the organized churches to get their way. In Catholic countries, many government officials resented the influence of the Jesuits, the major Catholic teaching order. The

Jesuits trained the Catholic intellectual elite, ran a worldwide missionary network, enjoyed close ties to the papacy, and amassed great wealth. Critics mounted campaigns against the Jesuits in many countries, and by the early 1770s the Society of Jesus had been dissolved in Portugal, France, and Spain. In 1773, Pope Clement XIV (r. 1769–1774) agreed under pressure to disband the order, an edict that held until a reinvigorated papacy restored the society in 1814. Joseph II of Austria not only applauded the suppression of the Jesuits but also required Austrian bishops to swear fidelity and submission to him. Under Joseph, the Austrian state supervised seminaries, reorganized diocesan boundaries, abolished comtemplative monastic orders, and confiscated their property to pay for education and poor relief.

Enlightened absolutists tried to gain greater state authority over education, even while extending education to the lower classes. Joseph II launched the most ambitious educational reforms of the period. In 1774, once the Jesuits had been disbanded, a General School Ordinance in Austria ordered state subsidies for local schools, which the state would regulate. By 1789, one-quarter of the school-age children attended school. In Prussia the school code of 1763 required all children between the ages of five and thirteen to attend school. Although not enforced uniformly, the Prussian law demonstrated Frederick II's belief that modernization depended on education. Catherine II of Russia also tried to expand elementary education—and the education of women in particular—and founded engineering schools.

Religious Toleration. Many rulers favored religious toleration, but no one achieved more than Joseph II of Austria, who had become Holy Roman Emperor and co-regent with his mother, Maria Theresa, in 1765. Joseph was able to carry out his most radical policies only when he ruled alone after 1780, but then he acted swiftly and sometimes brutally. His own brother described him as "imbued with arbitrary, brutal principles and the most severe, brutal and violent despotism." These qualities nevertheless enabled Joseph to push through reforms that might otherwise have been resisted. In 1781, he granted freedom of religious worship to Protestants, Orthodox Christians, and Jews. For the first time

these groups were allowed to own property, build schools, enter the professions, and hold political and military offices.

The efforts of other rulers to extend religious toleration proved more limited. The French state regarded Protestants as heretics until 1787, when Louis XVI signed an edict of toleration restoring their civil rights—but still they could not hold political office. Great Britain continued to deny Catholics freedom of open worship and the right to sit in Parliament. Most European states limited the rights and opportunities available to Jews. In Russia, only wealthy Jews could hold municipal office, and the Polish and Lithuanian Jews in the territory incorporated into Russia were restricted to certain places of residence. In Prussia, Frederick the Great called the Jews "useless to the state" and imposed special taxes on them. Even in Austria, where Joseph encouraged toleration, the laws forced Jews to take German-sounding names, and in the Papal States, the pope encouraged forced baptism. The leading philosophes opposed persecution of the Jews in theory but often treated them with undisguised contempt. Diderot's comment was all too typical: the Jews, he said, bore "all the defects peculiar to an ignorant and superstitious nation."

Limits of Reform

When government leaders introduce reforms, they often run into resistance from groups who feel threatened by innovation. Such was the experience of the absolutist rulers, who on many occasions faced upsurges of reaction that forced a quick backpedal. The most contentious area of reform was agricultural policy. Whereas Frederick II and Catherine II reinforced the authority of nobles over their serfs, Joseph II tried to remove the burdens of serfdom in the Habsburg lands. In 1781, he abolished the personal aspects of serfdom: serfs could now move freely, enter trades, or marry without their lords' permission. Joseph abolished the tithe to the church, shifted more of the tax burden to the nobility, and converted peasants' labor services into cash payments.

The Austrian nobility furiously resisted these far-reaching reforms. When Joseph died in 1790, his brother Leopold II had to revoke most reforms to appease the nobles. On his deathbed, Joseph recognized the futility of many of his efforts; as his epitaph he suggested, "Here lies Joseph II, who was unfortunate in all his enterprises." Prussia's Frederick II, like Joseph, encouraged such agricultural innovations as planting potatoes and turnips (new crops that could help feed a growing population), experimenting with cattle breeding, draining swamplands, and clearing forests. But Prussia's noble landlords, the Junkers, continued to expand their estates at the expense of poorer peasants, and Frederick did nothing to ameliorate serfdom except on his own domains.

Reforming ministers also tried to stimulate agricultural improvement in France. Unlike most other western European countries, France still had about 100,000 serfs; though their burdens weighed less heavily than those in eastern Europe, serfdom did not entirely disappear until 1789. A group of economists called the *physiocrats* urged the French government to deregulate the grain trade and make the tax system more equitable to encourage agricultural productivity. In the interest of establishing a free market, they also insisted that urban guilds be abolished because they prevented free entry into the trades. Their proposed reforms applied the Enlightenment emphasis on individual liberties to the

economy; Adam Smith took up many of the physiocrats' ideas in his writing in favor of free markets. The French government heeded some of this advice and gave up its system of price controls on grain in 1763, but it had to reverse this decision in 1770 when grain shortages caused a famine.

French reform efforts did not end there. To break the power of the parlements, the thirteen high courts of law that had led the way in opposing royal efforts to increase and equalize taxation, Louis XV appointed a reform-minded chancellor who replaced the parlements with courts in which the judges no longer owned their offices and thus could not sell them or pass them on as an inheritance. Justice would then be more impartial. Nevertheless, the judges of the displaced parlements aroused widespread opposition to what they portrayed as tyrannical royal policy. The furor calmed down only when Louis XV died in 1774 and his successor, Louis XVI, yielded to aristocratic demands and restored the old parlements. Louis XV died one of the most despised kings in French history, resented both for his highhanded reforms and his private vices. Underground pamphlets lampooned Louis, describing his final mistress, Madame Du Barry, as a prostitute who pandered to the elderly king's well-known taste

Russian Peasants

This engraving from the 1700s shows Russian peasants in their one-room hut. Two or more married brothers, their wives, children, and parents would share the space with poultry and livestock. Cooking took place in one corner, which was always diagonally across from the icon corner (left), where socializing took place. The fathers and younger men slept on benches, the rest of the family in the loft (right). In the winter, everyone slept near the oven.

Fotomas Index, UK.

for young girls. This often pornographic literature linked despotism to the supposedly excessive influence of women at court. Rousseau was not alone in attacking the feminizing influence of powerful women.

Louis XVI tried to carry out part of the program suggested by the physiocrats, and he chose one of their disciples, Jacques Turgot (1727–1781), as his chief minister. A contributor to the *Encyclopedia*, Turgot pushed through several edicts that again freed the grain trade, suppressed many guilds, converted the peasants' forced labor on roads into a money tax payable by all landowners, and reduced court expenses. He also began making plans to introduce a system of elected local assemblies, which would have made government much more representative. Faced with broad-based resistance led by the parlements and his own courtiers, as well as with riots against rising grain prices, Louis XVI dismissed Turgot, and one of the last possibilities to overhaul France's government collapsed.

The failure of reform in France paradoxically reflected the power of Enlightenment ideas; everyone now endorsed Enlightenment ideals but used them for different ends. The nobles in the parlements blocked the French monarchy's reform efforts using the very same Enlightenment language spoken by the crown's ministers. But unlike Austria, the other great power that faced persistent aristocratic resistance to reform, France had a large middle-class public that was increasingly frustrated by the failure to institute social change, a failure that ultimately helped undermine the monarchy itself. Where Frederick II, Catherine II, and even Joseph II used reform to bolster the efficiency of absolutist government, attempts at change in France backfired. French kings found that their ambitious programs for reform succeeded only in arousing unrealistic hopes.

❖ Rebellions against State Power

Although traditional forms of popular discontent had not disappeared, Enlightenment ideals and reforms changed the rules of the game in politics. Governments, especially in western Europe, now had to respond to public opinion; they had become accountable for their actions to a much wider range of people than ever before. In Britain and France, ordinary people rioted when they perceived government as failing to protect them against shortages created by free trade in grains. Monarchs justified their policies by appealing to the public, but they could not always control the consequences of the intensification of political interest. The growth of informed public opinion had its most dramatic consequences in the North American colonies, where a struggle over the British Parliament's right to tax turned into a full-scale war for independence. The American War of Independence showed that once put into practice, Enlightenment ideals could have revolutionary implications.

Food Riots and Peasant Uprisings

Population growth, inflation, and the extension of the market system put added pressure on the already beleaguered poorest classes of people. Seventeenth-century peasants and townspeople had rioted to protest new taxes. In the eighteenth century, they reacted violently when they feared that officials might fail to protect them from food shortages, either by freeing the grain market, which would benefit big farmers, or by requisitioning grain for the armies or the big cities. Other eighteenth-century forms of collective violence included riots against religious minorities, against militia recruiting, against turnpikes and tollgates, against attempts to arrest smugglers, and against enclosures of common fields. People sometimes rioted to express fear and anger in reaction to unexplained epidemics or to protest the execution of criminals who had captured the popular imagination.

In the last half of the eighteenth century, the food supply became the focus of political and social conflict. The poorer people in the villages and the towns believed it was the government's responsibility to ensure enough food for them, and in fact many governments did stockpile grain to make up for the occasional bad harvest. At the same time, in keeping with Adam Smith's and the French physiocrats' free market proposals, governments wanted to allow grain prices to rise with market demand, because higher profits would motivate producers to increase the overall supply of food.

But free trade in grain also meant selling to the highest bidder, even if that bidder was a foreign merchant. In the short run, in times of scarcity, big landowners and farmers could make huge profits by selling grain outside their hometowns or villages. This practice enraged poor farmers, agricultural workers, and city wageworkers, who could not afford the higher prices. Lacking the political means to affect policy, they could enforce their desire for old-fashioned price regulation only by rioting. Most did not pillage or steal grain but rather forced the sale of grain or flour at a "just" price and blocked the shipment of grain out of their villages to other markets. Women often led these "popular price fixings," as they were called in France, in desperate attempts to protect the food supply for their children.

Such food riots occurred regularly in Britain and France in the last half of the eighteenth century. One of the most turbulent was the so-called Flour War in France in 1775. Turgot's deregulation of the grain trade in 1774 caused prices to rise in several provincial cities. Rioting spread from there to the Paris region, where villagers attacked grain convoys heading to the capital city. Local officials often ordered merchants and bakers to sell at the price the rioters demanded, only to find themselves arrested by the central government for overriding free trade. The government brought in troops to restore order and introduced the death penalty for rioting.

Frustrations with serfdom and hopes for a miraculous transformation provoked the Pugachev rebellion in Russia beginning in 1773. An army deserter from the southeast frontier region, Emelian Pugachev (1742–1775) claimed to be Tsar Peter III, the dead husband of Catherine II. Pugachev's appearance seemed to confirm peasant hopes for a "redeemer tsar" who would save the people from oppression. He rallied around him Cossacks like himself who resented the loss of their old tribal independence. Now increasingly enserfed or forced to pay taxes and endure army service, these nomadic bands joined with other serfs, rebellious mineworkers, and Muslim minorities. Catherine dispatched a large army to squelch the uprising, but

The Pugachev Rebellion, 1773

Pugachev eluded them and the fighting spread. Nearly three million people eventually participated, making this the largest single rebellion in the history of tsarist Russia. When Pugachev urged the peasants to attack the nobility and seize their estates, hundreds of noble families perished. Foreign newspapers called it "the revolution in southern Russia" and offered fantastic stories about Pugachev's life history. Finally, the army captured the rebel leader and brought him in an iron cage to Moscow, where he was tortured and executed. In the aftermath, Catherine tightened the nobles' control over their serfs and harshly punished those who dared to criticize serfdom.

Public Opinion and Political Opposition

Peasant uprisings might briefly shake even a powerful monarchy, but the rise of public opinion as a force independent of court society caused more enduring changes in European politics. Across much of Europe and in the North American colonies, demands for broader political participation reflected Enlightenment notions about individual rights. Aristocratic bodies such as the French parlements, which had no legislative role like that of the British Parliament, insisted that the monarch consult them on the nation's affairs, and the new educated elite wanted more influence too. Newspapers began to cover daily political affairs, and the public learned the basics of political life, despite the strict limits on political participation in most countries.

Monarchs turned to public opinion to seek support against aristocratic groups that opposed reform. Gustavus III of Sweden (r. 1771–1792) called himself "the first citizen of a free people" and promised to deliver the country from "insufferable aristocratic despotism." Shortly after coming to the throne, Gustavus proclaimed a new constitution that divided power between the king and the legislature, abolished the use of torture in the judicial process, and assured some freedom of the press.

In France both the parlements and the monarch appealed to the public through the printed word. The crown hired writers to make its case; the magistrates of the parlements wrote their own rejoinders. French-language newspapers published in the Dutch Republic provided many people in France with detailed accounts of political news and also gave voice to pro-parlement positions. One of the

IMPORTANT DATES

1740–1748   War of the Austrian Succession: France, Spain, and Prussia versus Austria and Great Britain

1751–1772   *Encyclopedia* published in France

1756–1763   Seven Years' War fought in Europe, India, and the American colonies

1762   Jean-Jacques Rousseau, *The Social Contract* and *Emile*

1764   Voltaire, *Philosophical Dictionary*

1770   Louis XV of France fails to break the power of the French law courts

1772   First partition of Poland

1773   Pugachev rebellion of Russian peasants

1776   American Declaration of Independence from Great Britain; James Watt improves the steam engine, making it suitable for new industrial projects; Adam Smith, *The Wealth of Nations*

1780   Joseph II of Austria undertakes a wide-reaching reform program

1781   Immanuel Kant, *The Critique of Pure Reason*

1785   Catherine the Great's Charter of the Nobility grants nobles exclusive control over their serfs in exchange for subservience to the state

1787   Delegates from the states draft a new United States Constitution

---

new French-language newspapers printed inside France, *Le Journal des Dames* ("The Ladies' Journal"), was published by women and mixed short stories and reviews of books and plays with demands for more women's rights.

The Wilkes affair in Great Britain showed that public opinion could be mobilized to challenge a government. In 1763, during the reign of George III (r. 1760–1820), John Wilkes, a member of Parliament, attacked the government in his newspaper, *North Briton*, and sued the crown when he was arrested. He won his release as well as damages. When he was reelected, Parliament denied him his seat, not once but three times.

The Wilkes episode soon escalated into a major campaign against the corruption and social exclusiveness of Parliament, complaints the Levellers had first raised during the English Revolution of the late 1640s. Newspapers, magazines, pamphlets, handbills, and cheap editions of Wilkes's collected works

all helped promote his cause. Those who could not vote demonstrated for Wilkes. In one incident eleven people died when soldiers broke up a huge gathering of his supporters. The slogan "Wilkes and Liberty" appeared on walls all over London. Middle-class voters formed a Society of Supporters of the Bill of Rights, which circulated petitions for Wilkes; they gained the support of about one-fourth of all the voters. The more determined Wilkesites proposed sweeping reforms of Parliament, including more frequent elections, more representation for the counties, elimination of "rotten boroughs" (election districts so small that they could be controlled by one big patron), and restrictions of pensions used by the crown to gain support. These demands would be at the heart of agitation for parliamentary reform in Britain for decades to come.

Popular demonstrations did not always support reforms. In 1780, the Gordon riots devastated London. They were named after the fanatical anti-Catholic crusader Lord George Gordon, who helped organize huge marches and petition campaigns against a bill the House of Commons passed to grant limited toleration to Catholics. The demonstrations culminated in a seven-day riot that left fifty buildings destroyed and three hundred people dead. Despite the continuing limitation on voting rights in Great Britain, British politicians were learning that public opinion could be ignored only at their peril.

Political opposition also took artistic forms, particularly in countries where governments restricted organized political activity. A striking example of a play with a political message was *The Marriage of Figaro* (1784) by Pierre-Augustin Caron de Beaumarchais (1732–1799), a watchmaker, a judge, a gunrunner in the American War of Independence, and a French spy in Britain. *The Marriage of Figaro* was first a hit at court, when Queen Marie-Antoinette had it read for her friends. But when her husband, Louis XVI, read it, he forbade its production on the grounds that "this man mocks at everything that should be respected in government." When finally performed publicly, the play caused a sensation. The chief character, Figaro, is a clever servant who gets the better of his noble employer. When speaking of the count, he cries, "What have you done to deserve so many rewards? You went to the trouble of being born, and nothing more." Two years later, Mozart based an equally famous but somewhat tamer opera on Beaumarchais's story.

Revolution in North America

Oppositional forms of public opinion came to a head in Great Britain's North American colonies, where the result was American independence and the establishment of a republican constitution that stood in stark contrast to most European regimes. The successful revolution was the only blow to Britain's increasing dominance in world affairs in the eighteenth century, and as such it was another aspect of the power rivalries existing at that time. Yet many Europeans saw the American War of Independence, or the American Revolution, as a triumph for Enlightenment ideas. As one German writer exclaimed in 1777, American victory would give "greater scope to the Enlightenment, new keenness to the thinking of peoples and new life to the spirit of liberty."

The American revolutionary leaders had been influenced by a common Atlantic civilization; they participated in the Enlightenment and shared political ideas with the opposition Whigs in Britain.

Supporters demonstrated for Wilkes in South Carolina and Boston, and the South Carolina legislature donated a substantial sum to the Society of Supporters of the Bill of Rights. In the 1760s and 1770s, both British and American opposition leaders became convinced that the British government was growing increasingly corrupt and despotic, and both were concerned with the lack of representation in Parliament. British radicals wanted to reform Parliament so the voices of a broader, more representative segment of the population would be heard. The colonies had no representatives in Parliament, and colonists claimed that "no taxation without representation" should be allowed. Indeed, they denied that Parliament had any jurisdiction over the colonies, insisting that the king govern them through colonial legislatures and recognize their traditional British liberties. The failure of the "Wilkes and Liberty" campaign to produce concrete results convinced many Americans that Parliament was hopelessly tainted and that they would have to stand up for their rights as British subjects.

Overthrowing British Authority
The uncompromising attitude of the British government went a long way toward dissolving long-standing loyalties to the home country. During the American War of Independence, residents of New York City pulled down the statue of the hated George III.
Lafayette College Art Collection, Easton, Pennsylvania.

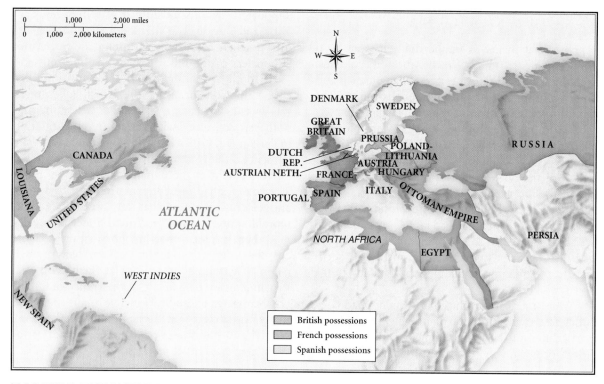

MAPPING THE WEST Europe and the World, c. 1780
Although Great Britain lost control over the British North American colonies, which became the new United States, European influence on the rest of the world grew dramatically in the eighteenth century. The slave trade linked European ports to African slave-trading outposts and to plantations in the Caribbean, South America, and North America. The European countries on the Atlantic Ocean benefited most from this trade. Yet almost all of Africa, China, Japan, and large parts of India still resisted European incursion, and the Ottoman Empire, with its massive territories, still towered over most European countries.

The British colonies remained loyal to the crown until Parliament's encroachment on their autonomy and the elimination of the French threat at the end of the Seven Years' War transformed colonial attitudes. Unconsciously, perhaps, the colonies had begun to form a separate nation; their economies generally flourished in the eighteenth century, and between 1750 and 1776 their population almost doubled. With the British clamoring for lower taxes and the colonists paying only a fraction of the tax rate paid by the Britons at home, Parliament passed new taxes, including the Stamp Act in 1765, which required a special tax stamp on all legal documents and publications. After violent rioting in the colonies, the new tax was repealed, but in 1773 a new Tea Act revived colonial resistance, which culminated in the so-called Boston Tea Party of 1773. Colonists dressed as Indians boarded British ships and dumped the imported tea (by this time an enormously popular beverage) into Boston's harbor. The British government tried to clamp down on the unrest, but British troops in the colonies soon found themselves fighting locally organized militias.

Political opposition in the American colonies turned belligerent when Britain threatened to use force to maintain control. In 1774, the First Continental Congress convened, composed of delegates from all the colonies, and unsuccessfully petitioned the crown for redress. The next year the Second Continental Congress organized an army with George Washington in command. After actual fighting had begun, in 1776, the congress proclaimed the Declaration of Independence. An eloquent statement of the American cause written by Thomas Jefferson, the Declaration of Independence was couched in the language of universal human rights, which enlightened Europeans could be expected to understand. George III denounced the American "traitors and rebels," calling them "misled by dangerous and ill-designing men." But European newspapers enthusiastically reported on every American response to "the cruel acts of oppression they have been made to suffer." In the War of Independence (1775–1783), France boosted the American cause by entering on the colonists' side in 1778. Spain too saw an opportunity to check the growing power of Britain, though without actually endorsing American independence out of fear of the response of its Latin American colonies. Spain declared war on Britain in 1779; in 1780, Great Britain declared war on the Dutch Republic in retaliation for Dutch support of the rebels. The worldwide conflict that resulted was more than Britain could handle. The American colonies achieved their independence in the peace treaty of 1783.

The newly independent states still faced the challenge of republican self-government. The Articles of Confederation, drawn up in 1777 as a provisional constitution, proved weak because they gave the central government few powers. In 1787, a constitutional convention met in Philadelphia to draft a new constitution. It established a two-house legislature, an indirectly elected president, and an independent judiciary. The Constitution's preamble insisted explicitly, for the first time in history, that government derived its power solely from the people and did not depend on divine right or on the tradition of royalty or aristocracy. The new educated elite of the eighteenth century had now created government based on a "social contract" among male, property-owning, white citizens. It was by no means a complete democracy, and women and slaves were excluded from political participation. But the new government represented a radical departure from European models. In 1791, a Bill of Rights was appended to the Constitution outlining the essential rights (such as freedom of speech) that the government could never overturn. Although slavery continued in the American republic, the new emphasis on rights helped fuel a movement for its abolition in both Britain and the United States.

Interest in the new republic was greatest in France. The United States Constitution and various state constitutions were published in French with commentary by leading thinkers. Even more important in the long run were the effects of the American war. Dutch losses to Great Britain aroused a widespread movement for political reform in the Dutch Republic, and debts incurred by France in supporting the American colonies would soon force the French monarchy to the edge of bankruptcy and then to revolution. Ultimately, the entire European system of royal rule would be challenged.

Conclusion

The American Revolution was the most profound practical result of the general European movement known as the Enlightenment. When he looked back many years later on the Declaration of Independence, Thomas Jefferson said he hoped it would be "the signal of arousing men to burst the chains under which monkish ignorance and superstition had persuaded them to bind themselves." What began as a cosmopolitan movement of a few intellectuals in the first half of the eighteenth century reached a relatively wide audience among the educated elite of men and women. The spirit of reform swept from the salons and coffeehouses into the halls of government. Reasoned, scientific inquiry into the causes of social misery and laws defending individual rights and freedoms gained adherents everywhere.

For most Europeans, however, Enlightenment remained a promise rather than a reality. Rulers such as Catherine the Great had every intention of retaining their full, often unchecked, powers, even as they corresponded with leading philosophes, announced support for their causes, and entertained them at their courts. Moreover, would-be reformers often found themselves thwarted by the resistance of nobles, by the priorities rulers gave to waging wars, or by popular resistance to deregulation of trade that stripped away protection against the uncertainties of the market. Yet even the failure of reform contributed to the ferment in Europe after 1770. Peasant rebellions in eastern Europe, the "Wilkes and Liberty" campaign in Great Britain, the struggle over reform in France, and the revolution in America all occurred at about the same time, and their conjunction convinced many Europeans that the world was in fact changing. Just how much it had changed, and whether the change was for better or for worse, would become more evident in the next ten years.

Suggested References

The Enlightenment at Its Height

The interpretive study by Gay remains useful even though it is over thirty years old. Starobinski's intellectual biography of Rousseau shows the unities in the life and work of this enduringly controversial figure. Much more emphasis has been placed in recent studies on the role of women; on this point see Goodman and Landes. Equiano, an ex-slave, offers one of the earliest firsthand views of the experience of slavery. Voltaire's *Candide* is an accessible introduction to the thought of the philosophes.

*Equiano, Olaudah. *The Interesting Narrative and Other Writings*. Ed. Vincent Carretta. 1995.

Gay, Peter. *The Enlightenment: An Interpretation*. 2 vols. 1966, 1969.

Goodman, Dena. *The Republic of Letters: A Cultural History of the French Enlightenment*. 1994.

Griswold, Charles. *Adam Smith and the Virtues of Enlightenment*. 1999.

Jacob, Margaret C. *Living the Enlightenment: Freemasonry and Politics in Eighteenth-Century Europe*. 1991.

Landes, Joan B. *Women and the Public Sphere in the Age of the French Revolution*. 1988.

Starobinski, Jean. *Jean-Jacques Rousseau: Transparency and Obstruction*. Trans. Arthur Goldhammer. 1988.

*Voltaire. *Candide*. Ed. and trans. Daniel Gordon. 1999.

Voltaire Foundation: http://www.voltaire.ox.ac.uk.

Society and Culture in an Age of Enlightenment

Recent work has drawn attention to the lives of ordinary people. The personal journal of the French glassworker Ménétra is a rarity: it offers extensive documentation of the inner life of an ordinary person during the Enlightenment. Ménétra claimed to have met Rousseau. Even if not true, the claim shows that Rousseau's fame was not limited to the upper classes.

Darnton, Robert. *The Great Cat Massacre and Other Episodes in French Cultural History*. 1984.

Gullickson, Gay L. *Spinners and Weavers of Auffay: Rural Industry and the Sexual Division of Labor in a French Village, 1750–1850*. 1986.

Hull, Isabel V. *Sexuality, State, and Civil Society in Germany, 1700–1815*. 1996.

Jarrett, Derek. *England in the Age of Hogarth*. 1986.

McManners, John. *Death and the Enlightenment*. 1981.

*Ménétra, Jacques Louis. *Journal of My Life*. Trans. Arthur Goldhammer. Introd. Daniel Roche. 1986.

Mozart Project: http://www.frontiernet.net/~sboerner/mozart/biography/.

Stone, Lawrence. *The Family, Sex, and Marriage in England, 1500–1800*. Abridged ed. 1979.

Trumbach, Randolph. *Sex and the Gender Revolution*. 1998.

State Power in an Era of Reform

Biographies and general histories of this period tend to overemphasize the individual decisions of rulers. Although these are incontestably important, side-by-side reading of Büsch, Frederick II's writings on war, and Showalter's book on the wars themselves offers a broader view that puts Frederick II's policies into the context of military growth and its impact on society.

Blanning, T. C. W. *Joseph II and Enlightened Despotism*. 1970.

Büsch, Otto. *Military System and Social Life in Old Regime Prussia, 1713–1807: The Beginnings of the Social Militarization of Prusso-German Society*. Trans. John G. Gagliardo. 1997.

Crankshaw, Edward. *Maria Theresa*. 1996.

Cronin, Vincent. *Catherine, Empress of All the Russias*. 1996.

*Frederick II, King of Prussia. *Frederick the Great on the Art of War*. Ed. and trans. Jay Luvaas. 1999.

Showalter, Dennis E. *The Wars of Frederick the Great*. 1996.

Venturi, Franco. *The End of the Old Regime in Europe, 1768–1776: The First Crisis*. Trans. R. Burr Litchfield. 1989.

Rebellions against State Power

Exciting work has focused on specific instances of riot and rebellion. One of the most interesting studies is Thompson's work on the British repression of poaching and its significance for British social and political history. Palmer's overview remains valuable, especially for its comparative aspects.

Alexander, John T. *Autocratic Politics in a National Crisis: The Imperial Russian Government and Pugachev's Revolt, 1773–1775*. 1969.

Palmer, R. R. *The Age of Democratic Revolution: A Political History of Europe and America, 1760–1800*. Vol. 1, *The Challenge*. 1959.

*Rakove, Jack N. *Declaring Rights: A Brief History with Documents*. 1998.

Thomas, P. D. G. *John Wilkes: A Friend to Liberty*. 1996.

Thompson, E. P. *Whigs and Hunters: The Origin of the Black Act*. 1975.

Wood, Gordon S. *The Radicalism of the American Revolution*. 1992.

*Primary sources.

20

The Cataclysm of Revolution

1789–1800

O N OCTOBER 5, 1789, AN INCIDENT OCCURRED in France that reflected the trauma and unpredictability of revolutionary times. As tensions mounted over the rising price of bread and uncertainties about the future direction of the country, rumors spread that officers guarding the king at his palace at Versailles had stomped in drunken fury on the red, white, and blue cockades that adorned the hats of supporters of the emerging revolutionary movement. Outraged at this insult and determined to get the king's help in securing more grain for the hungry, a crowd of several thousand women marched in a drenching rain twelve miles from the center of Paris to Versailles. They sent delegates to talk with the king and demanded an audience with the deputies of the newly formed National Assembly, which met nearby. Before the evening was over, thousands of men had marched from Paris to reinforce the women. The atmosphere turned ominous as the crowd camped out all night near the palace.

Early the next morning, an angry mob forced its way into the palace grounds and broke into the royal family's private apartments. To prevent further bloodshed—two of the royal bodyguards had already been killed and their heads paraded on pikes—the king agreed to move his family and his government back to Paris. A dramatic procession guarded by thousands of ordinary men and women made its way back to Paris. The people's proud display of cannons and pikes underlined the fundamental transformation that was occurring. Ordinary people had forced the king of France to respond to their grievances. The French

Fall of the Bastille

The Bastille prison is shown here in all its imposing grandeur. The moment depicted is that of the surrender of the fortress's governor, Bernard René de Launay. Because so many of the besieging citizens had been killed (only one of the defenders died), popular anger ran high and de Launay was to be the sacrificial victim. As the hastily formed citizens' guard marched him off to city hall, huge crowds taunted and spat at him. When he lashed out at one of the men nearest him, he was immediately stabbed and shot. A pastry cook cut off the governor's head, which was promptly displayed as a trophy on a pike held high above the crowd. Royal authority had been successfully challenged and even humiliated.
Chateau de Versailles, France/
Bridgeman Art Library, NY.

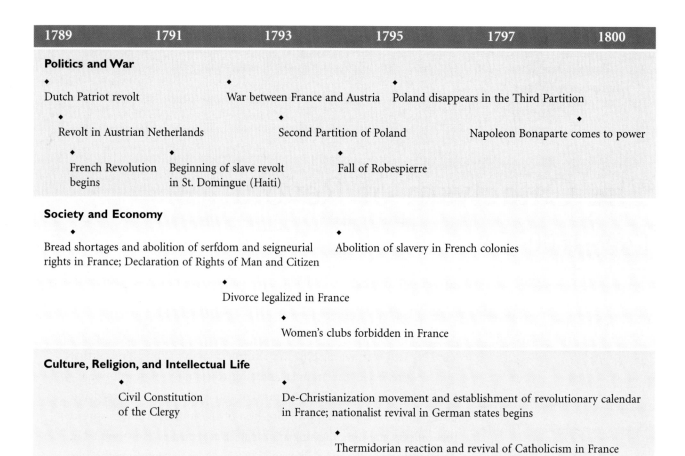

1789	1791	1793	1795	1797	1800

Politics and War

Dutch Patriot revolt

Revolt in Austrian Netherlands

French Revolution begins

Beginning of slave revolt in St. Domingue (Haiti)

War between France and Austria   Poland disappears in the Third Partition

Second Partition of Poland

Fall of Robespierre

Napoleon Bonaparte comes to power

Society and Economy

Bread shortages and abolition of serfdom and seigneurial rights in France; Declaration of Rights of Man and Citizen

Abolition of slavery in French colonies

Divorce legalized in France

Women's clubs forbidden in France

Culture, Religion, and Intellectual Life

Civil Constitution of the Clergy

De-Christianization movement and establishment of revolutionary calendar in France; nationalist revival in German states begins

Thermidorian reaction and revival of Catholicism in France

monarchy was now in danger, and if such a powerful and long-lasting institution could come under fire, then could any monarch of Europe rest easy?

Although entirely unpredicted when it erupted in 1789, the French Revolution followed a series of upheavals that began in the 1770s with the American fight for independence from Great Britain. In 1787 in the Dutch Republic and in 1788 in the Austrian Netherlands and Poland, protesters mounted campaigns for political reform that threatened the very existence of the governments in place. Unlike these protest movements, all of which failed in achieving their aims, the French Revolution exceeded everyone's expectations. It had its immediate origins in a constitutional crisis provoked by a growing government deficit, traceable to French involvement in the American War of Independence. The constitutional crisis came to a head on July 14, 1789, when armed Parisians captured the Bastille, a royal fortress and symbol of monarchical authority in the center of the capital. In the march to Versailles

of October 1789—soon known as "the October days"—the common people of Paris showed once again their determination to shape unfolding events.

In its early days, the French Revolution grabbed the attention of the entire world because it seemed to promise universal human rights, constitutional government, and broad-based political participation. In the words of its most famous slogan, it pledged "liberty, equality, and fraternity." Many Europeans greeted 1789 as the dawn of a new era. Wrote an enthusiastic German, "One of the greatest nations in the world, the greatest in general culture, has at last thrown off the yoke of tyranny." Others expressed horror at the violence that accompanied the dramatic events. In 1790, the British politician Edmund Burke denounced the "vilest of women" and the "cruel ruffians and assassins" who participated in the march to Versailles. He saw anarchy and terror where others saw liberation.

As events unfolded with astonishing rapidity after 1789, the French Revolution became *the* model

Women's March to Versailles, October 5, 1789
This anonymous engraving shows a crowd of armed women marching to Versailles to confront the king. The sight of armed women frightened many observers and demonstrated that the Revolution was not only men's affair. Note the middle-class woman in a hat at the far left. She is obviously reluctant to join in but is being pulled along by the market women in their simple caps.
Musée de la Ville de Paris/Musée Carnavalet, Paris/Giraudon/Art Resource, NY.

of modern revolution and in the process set the enduring patterns of all modern politics. Republicanism, democracy, terrorism, nationalism, and military dictatorship all took their modern forms during the French Revolution. The revolutionaries used a blueprint based on the Enlightenment idea of reason to remake all of society and politics: they executed the king and queen, established a republic for the first time in French history, abolished nobility, and inaugurated bold programs for political reeducation that included reforming the calendar, introducing the metric system, and celebrating festivals of reason to replace Christianity. When they encountered resistance to their programs, they set up a government of terror to compel obedience. As a result, the Revolution became linked in some minds with violence and intimidation, and some see in it the origins of modern *totalitarianism*—that is, governments that try to control every aspect of life, including daily activities, while limiting all forms of political dissent.

The Revolution might have remained a strictly French affair if war had not involved the rest of Europe. After 1792, huge French republican armies, fueled by patriotic nationalism, marched across Europe, promising liberation from traditional monarchies but often delivering old-fashioned conquest and annexation. French victories spread revolutionary ideas far and wide, from the colonies in the Caribbean, where the first successful slave revolt established the republic of Haiti, to Poland and Egypt. The army's success ultimately undermined the republic and made possible the rise of Napoleon Bonaparte, a remarkable young general who brought France more wars, more conquests, and a form of military dictatorship.

The breathtaking succession of regimes in France between 1789 and 1799 and the failure of the republican experiment after ten years of upheaval raised disturbing questions about the relationship between rapid political change and violence. Do all revolutions inevitably degenerate into terror or wars of conquest? Is a regime democratic if it does not allow poor men, women, or blacks to vote? The French Revolution raised these questions and many more. The questions resonated in many countries because the French Revolution seemed to be only the most extreme example of a much broader political and social movement at the end of the eighteenth century.

❖ The Revolutionary Wave, 1787–1789

From Philadelphia to Warsaw, the new public steeped in Enlightenment ideas now demanded to be heard. In 1787, at the same time the recently independent United States of America was preparing a new constitution, a broad-based Dutch Patriot movement challenged the powers of the ruling Dutch stadholder. In the Austrian Netherlands (present-day Belgium and Luxembourg), the upper classes resisted, in the name of constitutional liberties, the reforms of Emperor Joseph II of Austria. In Warsaw, patriotic reformers hoped to lead Poland out of the quagmire of humiliating political impotence, dependence on Russia, and large territorial losses in the partition of 1772. All these movements included calls for more representative government, but only the French revolt developed into a full-fledged revolution.

Europe on the Eve of Revolution

In the early spring of 1787, few felt the tremors forewarning a cataclysm. Many Europeans enthusiastically greeted the American experiment in republican government, but most did not consider the changes taking place far away in a former colony a likely model for their much older, more populous, and traditional states. The Enlightenment had spread into most of the circles of high society in western Europe without affecting the social prominence of aristocrats or the political control of kings and queens. In fact, the European monarchies seemed more securely established than ever, and the French monarchy appeared as sturdy as any. Montesquieu and Rousseau, the leading political theorists of the Enlightenment, taught that republics suited only small countries, not big ones like France or Austria.

After suffering humiliation at the hands of the British in the Seven Years' War (1756–1763), the French had regained international prestige by supporting the victorious Americans, and the monarchy had shown its eagerness to promote reforms. In 1787, for example, the French crown granted civil rights to Protestants.

Europeans in general were wealthier, healthier, more numerous, and better educated than they had ever been before. They had more newspapers and books to read, more concerts to attend, and more coffeehouses to enjoy, all subtle signs of economic growth and development. Ironically, political agitation would be most dramatic in some of the wealthiest and best-educated societies within Europe, such as the Low Countries. The eighteenth-century revolutions were a product of long-term prosperity and high expectations; the short-term downturn and depression after 1786 seemed all the more disappointing after the preceding decades of robust growth.

Historians have sometimes referred to the revolts of the 1780s as the *Atlantic revolutions* because so many protest movements arose in countries on both shores of the North Atlantic in the late 1700s. Most scholars agree now, however, that the French Revolution differed greatly from the others: not only was France the richest, most powerful, and most populous state in western Europe, but its revolution was also more violent, more long-lasting, and more influential in its effects. (See "Terms of History," page 728.)

Interpretation of the Revolutionary Outbreak

Many different explanations for the French Revolution have been offered. The Marxist interpretation, presented by the nineteenth-century revolutionary philosopher Karl Marx and his modern followers, was one of the most influential. Marx saw the French Revolution as the classic example of a *bourgeois*, that is, middle-class, revolution. According to the Marxist interpretation, the *bourgeoisie* (middle class) overthrew the monarchy because of its association with the remnants of feudalism. French revolutionaries used the term *feudalism* to refer to everything that seemed outdated in their nation's economic and social systems, particularly the legal privileges long held by the aristocracy and the seigneurial rights of landowners, such as the many dues landlords levied on their tenants—payments for the use of the lord's baking oven or winepress, for example. Marxists believed the remains of the feudal order needed to be swept away to facilitate the development of capitalism.

Recent historians have successfully challenged many aspects of the Marxist interpretation, especially the link between revolution and capitalism. They argue that the French Revolution did not foster the development of capitalism and that a capitalist middle class composed of merchants and manufacturers did not lead the revolt. A kind of middle class did play an important role in the protest movements of the 1780s across Europe, but this middle class comprised lawyers, journalists, intellectuals, and lower-ranking officials rather than capitalist manufacturers. Moreover, the middle classes did not start most protest movements, which began only when aristocratic elites themselves challenged their rulers' powers. Once the uprisings began, the participation of men and women from the urban lower classes propelled the movements, just as it had during the English Revolution of the mid-seventeenth century. The volatility of this combination of upper, middle, and lower classes ultimately defeated each revolution. The appeal to "the people" as the source of legitimacy pitted one group against another and opened the way to new and sometimes dangerous forms of political mobilization. According to this interpretation, concerns about politics and power completely overshadowed interests in economic change.

Protesters in the Low Countries and Poland

If the eighteenth-century revolutions began in the British North American colonies with the War of American Independence, they took their next step on the other side of the Atlantic. Political protests in the Dutch Republic attracted European attention because Dutch banks still controlled a hefty portion of the world's capital at the end of the eighteenth century, even though the Dutch Republic's role in international politics had diminished. Revolts also broke out in the neighboring Austrian Netherlands and Poland. Although none of these movements ultimately succeeded, they showed how quickly political discontent could boil over in this era of rising economic and political expectations.

The Dutch Patriot Revolt, 1787. The Dutch Patriots, as they chose to call themselves, wanted to follow the American example and reduce the powers of the kinglike stadholder, the prince of Orange, who favored close ties with Great Britain. Government-sponsored Dutch banks owned 40 percent of the British national debt, and by 1796 they held the entire foreign debt of the United States. Relations with the British deteriorated during the American War of Independence, however, and by the middle of the 1780s, agitation in favor of the Americans had boiled over into an attack on the stadholder.

The Patriots began their protest in the relatively restricted circles of middle-class bankers, merchants, and writers who supported the American cause. They soon gained a more popular audience by demanding political reforms in a petition campaign and forming armed citizen militias of men, called Free Corps. Parading under banners that read "Liberty or Death," they forced local officials to set up new elections to replace councils that had been packed with Orangist supporters through patronage or family connections. The future American president John Adams happened to be visiting Utrecht when such a revolt occurred. He wrote admiringly to Thomas Jefferson that "in no instance, of ancient or modern History, have the People ever asserted more unequivocally their own inherent and unalienable Sovereignty."

In 1787, the protest movement coalesced when a national assembly of the Free Corps joined with a group of Patriot Regents (the upper-class officials who ran the cities) to demand "the true republican form of government in our commonwealth," that is, the reduction of stadholder powers. The Free Corps fought the prince's troops and soon got the upper hand. In response, Frederick William II of Prussia, whose sister had married the stadholder, intervened

The Low Countries in 1787

with tacit British support. Thousands of Prussian troops soon occupied Utrecht and Amsterdam, and the House of Orange regained its former position.

Revolution

Many of our most important political labels and concepts—*left* and *right*, *terrorist*, and even *revolution* itself—come from the French Revolution. *Left* and *right* correlated spatial locations in the hall of the National Assembly with political positions. Those deputies who favored extensive change sat in the seats on the speaker's left hand; the Jacobins became the most prominent group on the left. On the right were the deputies who preferred a more cautious and conservative stance; royalists were most consistently on the right. A *terrorist* was someone who supported the revolutionary regime of the Terror (1793–1794), but it came to mean anyone who used terror to achieve his or her political ends.

Revolution provided the context for all these changes in meaning. It had previously meant cyclical change that brought life back to a starting point, as a planet makes a revolution around the sun. Revolutions could come and go, by this definition, and change nothing fundamental in the structure of society. After 1789, *revolution* came to mean a self-conscious attempt to leap into the future by reshaping society and politics and even the human personality. A revolutionary official analyzed the meaning of the word in 1793: "A revolution is never made by halves; it must either be total or it will abort. . . . *Revolutionary* means outside of all forms and all rules; *revolutionary* means that which affirms, consolidates the revolution, that which removes all the obstacles which impede its progress." In short, *revolution* soon had an all-or-nothing meaning; you were either for the revolution or against it. There could be no in between.

Revolution still has the same meaning given it by the French revolutionaries, but it is now an even more contested term because of its association with communist theory. In the nineteenth century, Karl Marx incorporated the French Revolution into his new doctrine of communism. In his view, the middle-class French revolutionaries had overthrown the monarchy and the "feudal" aristocracy to pave the way for capitalist development. In the future, the proletariat (industrial workers) would overthrow the capitalist middle class to install a communist government that would abolish private property. Since Marxists claimed the French Revolution as the forerunner of the communist revolution in the nineteenth and twentieth centuries, it was perhaps inevitable that those who opposed communism would also criticize the French Revolution.

The Patriots fell to the fatal combination of outside intervention and their own internal social divisions. Many of the Patriot Regents from the richest merchant families resisted the growing power of the Free Corps. The Free Corps wanted a more democratic form of government and encouraged the publication of pamphlets and cartoons attacking the prince and his wife, the rapid spread of clubs and societies made up of common people, and crowd-pleasing public ceremonies, such as parades and bonfires, that sometimes turned into riots. As divisiveness within the Patriot ranks increased, the prince of Orange was able to muster his own popular support. In the aftermath of the Prussian invasion in September 1787, the Orangists got their revenge: lower-class mobs pillaged the houses of prosperous Patriot leaders, forcing many to flee to the United States, France, or the Austrian Netherlands. Those Patriots who remained nursed their grievances until the French republican armies invaded in 1795.

The Belgian Independence Movement. If Austrian emperor Joseph II had not tried to introduce reforms, the Belgians of the ten provinces of the Austrian Netherlands might have remained tranquil. Yet Joseph, inspired by Enlightenment ideals, made changes that both extended civil rights and enhanced his own power. He abolished torture, decreed toleration for Jews and Protestants (in this resolutely Catholic area), and suppressed monasteries. His 1787 reorganization of the administrative and judicial systems eliminated many offices that belonged to nobles and lawyers. The upper classes felt their power was being usurped.

Belgian resistance to Austrian reforms consequently began as a reactionary movement, which was intended to defend historic local liberties against an

The most influential example of this view is that of the French scholar François Furet. An ex-communist, Furet argues that the French Revolution can be seen as the origin of totalitarianism: "Today the Gulag [the Soviet system of prison camps for dissidents] is leading to a rethinking of the Terror precisely because the two undertakings are seen as identical." The Soviet Gulag and the Terror were identical systems for repressing all avenues of dissent. The French Revolution ended up in totalitarianism during the Terror because it incarnated what Furet calls "the illusion of politics," that is, the belief that people can transform social and economic relationships through political revolution. The French revolutionaries became totalitarian, in Furet's view, however, because they wanted to establish a kind of political and social utopia (a perfect society), in which reason alone determined the shape of political and social life. Because this dream was impossible given human resistance to rapid change, the revolutionaries had to use force to achieve their goals. In other words, revolution itself was a problematic idea, according to Furet.

Controversy about the relationship between the French Revolution and totalitarianism continues. Critics of Furet argue that he focuses too narrowly on the Terror, which, after all, lasted only about one year, from mid-1793 to mid-1794. The French Revolution included many different political experiments: constitutional monarchy (1789–1792), a democratic republic (which preceded and succeeded the period of the Terror), and, later, a more authoritarian republic and then an empire under Napoleon Bonaparte. Is the central meaning of the French Revolution to be found in any single one of these periods or in the very fact of the succession of different phases? France went on in the nineteenth and twentieth centuries to have another constitutional monarchy, one more empire, and four more republics—and never another period of terror. Which kind of experiment was more significant in its lasting effects? Since the French government today is a democratic republic, might it not be argued that this tradition—democratic republicanism—was the most lasting outcome of the French Revolution? In short, *revolution* as a term remains as contested as the events that gave rise to it.

FURTHER READING

Furet, François. *Interpreting the French Revolution.* Trans. Elborg Forster. 1981.

Hunt, Lynn. *Politics, Culture, and Class in the French Revolution.* 1984.

---

overbearing reform-minded government. The upper classes initiated the resistance. The countess of Yves, for example, wrote pamphlets against Joseph's reforms and provided meeting places for the rebels. The movement nonetheless soon attracted democrats, who wanted a more representative government and organized clubs to give voice to their demands. At the end of 1788, a secret society formed armed companies to prepare an uprising. By late 1789, each province had separately declared its independence, and the Austrian administration had collapsed. Delegates from the various provinces declared themselves the United States of Belgium, a clear reference to the American precedent.

Once again, however, internal squabbling doomed the rebels. The democrats denounced aristocratic authority. "The nobles have no acquired right over the people," one writer proclaimed. In the face of increasing democratic ferment, aristocratic leaders drew to their side the Catholic clergy and peasants, who had little sympathy for the democrats of the cities. Every Sunday in May and June 1790, thousands of peasant men and women, led by their priests, streamed into Brussels carrying crucifixes, nooses, and pitchforks to intimidate the democrats and defend the church. Faced with the choice between the Austrian emperor and "our current tyrants," the democrats chose to support the return of the Austrians under Emperor Leopold II (r. 1790–1792), who had succeeded his brother.

Polish Patriots. A reform party calling itself the Patriots also emerged in Poland, which had been shocked by the loss of a third of its territory in the First Partition of 1772. The Patriots sought to overhaul the weak commonwealth along modern western European lines. Reformers included a few leading aristocrats; middle-class professionals and clergy who espoused Enlightenment ideas; and King Stanislaw August Poniatowski (r. 1764–1795). A nobleman who owed his crown solely to the dubious honor of being Catherine the Great's discarded lover but who was also a favorite correspondent of the Parisian salon hostess Madame Geoffrin, Poniatowski saw in moderate reform the only chance for his country to escape the consequences of a century's misgovernment and cultural decline. Ranged against the Patriots stood most of the aristocrats and the formidable Catherine the Great, determined to uphold imperial Russian influence.

Watchful but not displeased to see Russian influence waning in Poland, Austria and Prussia allowed the reform movement to proceed. In 1788, the Patriots got their golden chance. Bogged down in war with the Ottoman Turks, Catherine could not block the summoning of a reform-minded parliament, which with King Stanislaw's aid outmaneuvered the antireform aristocrats. Amid much oratory denouncing Russian overlordship, the parliament enacted the constitution of May 3, 1791, which established a hereditary monarchy with somewhat strengthened authority, at last freed the two-house legislature from the individual veto power of every aristocrat, granted townspeople limited political rights, and vaguely promised future Jewish emancipation. Abolishing serfdom was hardly mentioned. Modest though they were, the Polish reforms did not endure. Catherine II could not countenance the spread of revolution into eastern Europe and within a year engineered the downfall of the Patriots and further weakened the Polish state.

The Beginning of the French Revolution, 1787–1789

The French Revolution began with a fiscal crisis caused by a mounting deficit. After trying every available avenue to raise needed funds, Louis XVI (r. 1774–1792) was forced to call a meeting of the Estates General, a body which had not met since 1614. After the Estates General opened in May 1789, a constitutional stalemate soon pitted deputies of the commons against deputies of the nobility. Fear of a noble-led conspiracy inspired the people of Paris to revolt and attack the Bastille prison on July 14, 1789. Unlike the revolts elsewhere in Europe, the fall of the Bastille would open the way to a rev-

olutionary movement that lasted ten years and reshaped modern European, even world, politics.

Fiscal Crisis. France's fiscal problems stemmed from its support of the Americans against the British in the American War of Independence. About half of the French national budget went to paying interest on the debt that had accumulated. In contrast to Great Britain, which had a national bank to help raise loans for the government, the French government lived off relatively short-term, high-interest loans from private sources including Swiss banks,

Marie-Antoinette
In this gouache of 1775 by T. Gautier d'Agoti, Marie-Antoinette Playing the Harp, *the queen is shown playing music and surrounded by figures of the court. At the time she was only twenty years old, having married the future Louis XVI at age fifteen in 1770. Her mother, Maria Theresa, frequently wrote to advise her on her behavior at court and expressed disapproval because Marie-Antoinette had a reputation for being frivolous and flirtatious.*
Photo Bulloz.

government annuities, and advances from tax collectors.

For years the French government had been trying unsuccessfully to modernize the tax system to raise more revenue and respond to widespread criticism that the system was unfair. The peasants bore the greatest burden of taxes, whereas the nobles and clergy were largely exempt. Tax collection was also far from systematic: private contractors collected many taxes and pocketed a large share of the proceeds. The failure of the crown's various reform efforts left it at the mercy of its creditors at the end of the American War of Independence. With the growing support of public opinion, the bond and annuity holders from the middle and upper classes now demanded a clearer system of fiscal accountability. Declaring bankruptcy, as many rulers had in the past, was no longer an option.

In a monarchy the ruler's character is always crucial. Louis XVI was the model of a virtuous husband and father, but he took a limited view of his responsibilities in this time of crisis. Many complained that he showed more interest in hunting or in his hobby of making locks than in the problems of government. His wife, Marie-Antoinette, was blond, beautiful, and much criticized for her extravagant taste in clothes, elaborate hairdos, and supposed indifference to popular misery. "The Austrian bitch," as underground writers called her, had been the target of an increasingly nasty pamphlet campaign in the 1780s. By 1789, the queen had become an object of popular hatred; when confronted by the inability of the poor to buy bread, she was mistakenly reported to have replied, "Let them eat cake." The king's ineffectiveness and the queen's growing unpopularity helped undermine the monarchy as an institution.

Faced with a mounting deficit, in 1787 Louis called an Assembly of Notables, a group of hand-picked nobles, clergymen, and officials that had last met in 1626. After considering royal proposals for a more uniform land tax, the abolition of internal tariffs, and the establishment of a state bank, the assembly refused to cooperate. Next the king tried his old rival the parlement of Paris. When it too refused to agree to his proposals, he ordered the parlement judges into exile in the provinces. Overnight, the judges (members of the nobility because of the offices they held) became popular heroes for resisting the king's "tyranny"; in reality, however, the judges, like the notables, wanted reform only on their own terms. Nobles in the parlement and in the Assembly

REVEIL DU TIERS ETAT.

Ma feinte, il étoit tems que je me réveillasse, car l'oppression de mes fers me donnoit le cochemar un peu trop fort.

The Third Estate Awakens
This print, produced after the fall of the Bastille (note the heads on pikes outside the prison), shows a clergyman (First Estate) and a noble (Second Estate) alarmed by the awakening of the commoners (Third Estate). The Third Estate breaks the chains of oppression and arms itself to battle for its rights. The message is that social conflicts lay behind the political struggles in the Estates General.
Musée Carnavale/Photo Bulloz.

of Notables saw an opportunity to make themselves partners in running France. Louis finally gave in to their demands that he call a meeting of the Estates General, which had last met 175 years before.

The Estates General. The calling of the Estates General galvanized public opinion. Who would determine the fate of the nation? There were three estates, or orders, in the Estates General. The deputies in the First Estate represented some 100,000 clergy of the Catholic church, which owned about 10 percent of the land and collected its own taxes (the tithe) on peasants. The deputies of the Second Estate represented the nobility, about 400,000 men and women who owned about 25 percent of the land, enjoyed many tax exemptions, and collected seigneurial dues and rents from their peasant tenants. The deputies of the Third Estate represented everyone else, at least 95 percent of the nation. In 1614, at the last meeting of the Estates General, each order had voted separately, and either the clergy or the nobility could therefore veto any decision of the Third Estate. Before the elections to the Estates General in 1789, the king agreed to double the number of deputies for the Third Estate (making them equal in number to the other two combined), but he left it to the Estates General to decide whether the estates would continue to vote separately by order rather than by individual head. Voting by order would conserve the traditional powers of the clergy and nobility; voting by head would give the Third Estate an advantage since many clergymen and even some nobles sympathized with the Third Estate.

As the state's censorship apparatus broke down, pamphleteers by the hundreds denounced the traditional privileges of the nobility and clergy and called for voting by head rather than order. Critics charged that the interests of the Third Estate clashed with those of the nobility; the clergy were caught in between because most ordinary clergy were not nobles but many bishops and archbishops were. The middle class, made more self-confident by the boom in trade and its participation in the Enlightenment, would no longer settle for crumbs from the political table. In the most vitriolic of all the pamphlets, *What Is the Third Estate?*, the middle-class clergyman Abbé Emmanuel-Joseph Sieyès charged that the nobility contributed nothing at all to the nation's well-being; they were "a malignant disease which preys upon and tortures the body of a sick man."

In the winter and spring of 1789, thousands of men (and a few women by proxy) held meetings to elect deputies and write down their grievances. The effect was electric. Although educated men dominated the meetings at the regional level, the humblest peasants also voted in their villages and burst forth with complaints, especially about taxes. As one villager lamented, "The last crust of bread has been taken from us." The long series of meetings raised expectations that the Estates General would help the king to solve all the nation's ills.

These new hopes soared just at the moment France experienced an increasingly rare but always dangerous food shortage. (See "Taking Measure," below.) Bad weather damaged the harvest of 1788, causing bread prices to rise in many places in the spring and summer of 1789 and threatening starvation for the poorest people. A serious slump in textile production had been causing massive unemployment since 1786, when France signed a free-trade treaty with Great Britain, opening the door to the more rapidly industrializing—and therefore cheaper—British suppliers. In the biggest French

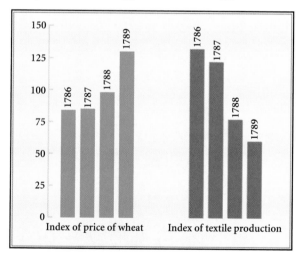

TAKING MEASURE Wheat Prices and Textile Production in France, 1786–1789
This chart, comparing yearly averages against an index set at 100 (based on the average of all four years), shows the dramatic change over time in wheat prices and textile production. The price of wheat steadily increased in the years just prior to the French Revolution, while the production of textiles dramatically declined. What would be the consequences of this movement in opposite directions? Which groups in the French population would be especially at risk?
From Ernest Labrousse et al., *Historie économique et sociale de la France* (Paris: Presses Universitaries de France, 1970), 553.

MAP 20.1 Revolutionary Paris, 1789
The French Revolution began with the fall of the Bastille prison on July 14, 1789. The huge fortified prison was located on the eastern side of the city in a neighborhood of working people. Before attacking the Bastille, crowds had torn down many of the customs booths located in the wall of the Farmers General (the private company in charge of tax collection), and taken the arms stored in the Hôtel des Invalides, a veterans hospital on the western side of the city where the upper classes lived. In other words, the crowds had roamed throughout the city.

cities, thousands of textile workers were out of work and hungry, adding another volatile element to an already tense situation.

In May 1789, some 1,200 deputies journeyed to the king's palace of Versailles for the opening of the Estates General. Many readers avidly followed the developments in newspapers that sprouted overnight. Although most nobles insisted on voting by order, the deputies of the Third Estate refused to proceed on that basis. After six weeks of stalemate, on June 17, 1789, the deputies of the Third Estate took unilateral action and declared themselves and whoever would join them the "National Assembly," in which each deputy would vote as an individual. Two days later the clergy voted by a narrow margin to join them. A constitutional revolution was under

way, for now the elected deputies of "the nation" displaced the old estates in which nobles and clergy dominated. As one new newspaper asserted, "The day of the seventeenth will be forever memorable." Barred from their meeting hall on June 20, the deputies met on a nearby tennis court and swore an oath not to disband until they had given France a constitution that reflected their newly declared authority. This "tennis court oath" expressed the determination of the Third Estate to carry through a constitutional revolution.

July 14, 1789: The Fall of the Bastille.   At first Louis appeared to agree to the new representative assembly, but he also ordered thousands of soldiers to march to Paris (Map 20.1). The deputies who supported the new National Assembly feared a plot by the king and high-ranking nobles to arrest them and disperse the assembly. "Everyone is convinced that the approach of the troops covers some violent design," one deputy wrote home. Their fears were confirmed when on July 11 the king fired Jacques Necker, the Swiss Protestant finance minister and the one high official regarded as sympathetic to the deputies' cause.

The popular reaction in Paris to Necker's dismissal and the threat of military force changed the course of the French Revolution. When the news spread, the common people in Paris began to arm themselves and attack places where either grain or arms were thought to be stored. A deputy in Versailles reported home: "Today all of the evils overwhelm France, and we are between despotism, carnage, and famine." On July 14, 1789, an armed crowd marched on the Bastille, a fortified prison that symbolized royal authority. After a chaotic battle in which one hundred armed citizens died, the prison officials surrendered. The angry crowd hacked to death the governor of the prison and flaunted his head on a pike.

The fall of the Bastille (an event now commemorated as the French national holiday) set an important precedent. The common people showed themselves willing to intervene violently at a crucial

The Great Fear, 1789

political moment. All over France, food riots turned into local revolts. The officials in one city wrote of their plight: "Yesterday afternoon [July 19] more than seven or eight thousand people, men and women, assembled in front of the two gates to the city hall. . . . We were forced to negotiate with them and to promise to give them wheat . . . and to reduce the price of bread." Local governments were forced out of power and replaced by committees of "patriots" loyal to the revolutionary cause. The patriots relied on newly formed National Guard units composed of civilians. One of their first du-

ties was to calm the peasants in the countryside, who feared that the beggars and vagrants crowding the roads might be part of an aristocratic plot to starve the people by burning crops or barns. In some places, the Great Fear (the term used by historians to describe this rural panic) turned into peasant attacks on aristocrats or on seigneurial records of peasants' dues kept in the lord's château. The king's government began to crumble. One of Louis XVI's brothers and many other leading aristocrats fled into exile. In Paris, the marquis de Lafayette, a hero of the American War of Independence and a noble deputy in the National Assembly, became commander of the new National Guard. The Revolution thus had its first heroes, its first victims, and its first enemies.

❖ From Monarchy to Republic, 1789–1793

Until July 1789, the French Revolution followed a course much like that of the protest movements in the Low Countries. Unlike the Dutch and Belgian uprisings, however, the French Revolution did not come to a quick end. The French revolutionaries first tried to establish a constitutional monarchy based on the Enlightenment principles of human rights and rational government. The constitutional monarchy failed, however, when the king tried to raise a counter-revolutionary army. When war broke out in 1792, new tensions culminated in a second revolution that deposed the king and established a republic in which all power rested in an elected legislature.

The Revolution of Rights and Reason

For two years after July 1789, the deputies of the National Assembly strove to establish an enlightened, constitutional monarchy. The National Assembly included the lawyers and officials who had represented the Third Estate in 1789 as well as most of the deputies from the clergy and a substantial number of nobles. Their first goal was to write a constitution, but they faced more immediate problems. In the countryside, peasants refused to pay seigneurial dues to their landlords, and the persistence of peasant violence raised alarms about the potential for a general peasant insurrection.

Major Events of the French Revolution

1789
May 5   The Estates General opens at Versailles
June 17   The Third Estate decides to call itself the National Assembly
June 20   "Tennis court oath" shows determination of deputies to carry out a constitutional revolution
July 14   Fall of the Bastille
August 4   Night session of the National Assembly abolishes "feudalism"
August 26   National Assembly passes Declaration of the Rights of Man and Citizen
October 5–6   Women march to Versailles and join with men in bringing the royal family back to Paris

1790
July 12   Civil Constitution of the Clergy

1791
June 20   Louis and Marie-Antoinette attempt to flee in disguise and are captured at Varennes

1792
April 20   Declaration of war on Austria
August 10   Insurrection in Paris and attack on Tuileries palace lead to suspension of the king
September 2–6   Murder of prisoners in "September massacres" in Paris
September 22   Establishment of the republic

1793
January 21   Execution of Louis XVI
March 11   Beginning of uprising in the Vendée
May 31–June 2   Insurrection leading to arrest of the Girondins
July 27   Robespierre named to the Committee of Public Safety
September 29   Convention establishes General Maximum on prices and wages
October 16   Execution of Marie-Antoinette

1794
February 4   Slavery abolished in the French colonies
March 13–24   Arrest, trial, and executions of so-called ultrarevolutionaries
March 30–April 5   Arrest, trial, and executions of Danton and his followers
July 27   "The Ninth of Thermidor" arrest of Robespierre and his supporters (executed July 28–29)

1795
October 26   Directory government takes office
April 1796–October 1797   Succession of Italian victories by Bonaparte
May 1798–October 1799   Bonaparte in Egypt and Middle East

1799
November 9   Bonaparte's coup of 18 Brumaire

The Night of August 4, 1789.   In response to peasant unrest, the National Assembly decided to make sweeping changes. On the night of August 4, 1789, noble deputies announced their willingness to give up their tax exemptions and seigneurial dues, thereby freeing the peasants from some of their most pressing burdens. By the end of the night, amid wild enthusiasm, dozens of deputies had come to the podium to relinquish the tax exemptions of their own professional groups, towns, or provinces. The National Assembly decreed the abolition of what it called "the feudal regime"—that is, it freed the few remaining serfs and eliminated all special privileges in matters of taxation, including all seigneurial dues on the land (a few days later the deputies insisted on financial compensation for some of these dues, but most peasants refused to pay). Peasants had

achieved their goals, and most now turned conservative. The Assembly also mandated equality of opportunity in access to official posts. Talent, rather than birth, was to be the key to success. Enlightenment principles were beginning to become law.

The Declaration of the Rights of Man and Citizen.   Passed three weeks later, the Declaration of the Rights of Man and Citizen, was the National Assembly's most stirring statement of Enlightenment principles. In words reminiscent of the American Declaration of Independence, whose author Thomas Jefferson was in Paris at the time, it proclaimed, "Men are born and remain free and equal in rights." The Declaration granted freedom of religion, freedom of the press, equality of taxation, and equality before the law. It established the principle of national sovereignty: since "all sovereignty rests essentially in the nation," the king derived his authority henceforth from the nation rather than from tradition or divine right. By pronouncing all "men" free and equal, the Declaration immediately created new dilemmas. Did women have equal rights with men? What about free blacks in the colonies? How could slavery be justified if all men were born free? Did religious toleration of Protestants and Jews include equal political rights? Women never received the right to vote during the French Revolution, though Protestant and Jewish men did. Women were theoretically citizens under civil law but without the right to full political participation.

Some women did not accept their exclusion, viewing it as a betrayal of the promised new order.

In addition to joining demonstrations, such as the march to Versailles in October 1789, women wrote petitions, published tracts, and organized political clubs to demand more participation. In her Declaration of the Rights of Women of 1791, Olympe de Gouges (1748–1793) played on the language of the official Declaration to make the point that women should also be included. In Article I, she announced, "Woman is born free and lives equal to man in her rights." She also insisted that since "woman has the right to mount the scaffold," she must "equally have the right to mount the rostrum." De Gouges linked her complaints to a program of social reform in which women would have equal rights to property and public office and equal responsibilities in taxes and criminal punishment.

French Provinces, 1789

French Departments, 1791

MAP 20.2 Redrawing the Map of France, 1789–1791

Before 1789, France had been divided into provinces, each with its own administration. Some provinces had their own law codes. As it began its deliberations, the new National Assembly determined to install uniform administrations and laws for the entire country. Discussion of the administrative reforms began in October 1789 and was completed on February 15, 1790, when the Assembly voted to divide the provinces into eighty-three departments, with names based on their geographical characteristics: Basses-Pyrenees for the Pyrenees mountains, Haute-Marne for the Marne River, and so on. By eliminating the old names of provinces, with their historical associations, and supplanting them with geographical ones, the Assembly aimed to show that reason would now govern all French affairs.

Que ce jour est heureux mes Sœurs, oui les doux nom de mere et d'épouse est bien préferable a celui de none il vous rend tous les droits de la Nature ainsi qu'a nous

Decret de l'Assemblée National qui Supprime les Ordres Religieux et Religieuses. Le Mardi 16 Fevr. 1790.

Anticlerical Sentiments
This satirical anti-Catholic engraving celebrates the National Assembly's decree of February 16, 1790, which abolished all religious orders. Nuns and monks are depicted as overjoyed at being released from their religious vows and encouraged to marry. In fact, many resisted the destruction of their way of life. Actions taken against the Catholic church alienated a considerable number of French people from the Revolution.
Snark/Art Resource, NY.

The Constitution and the Church. Unresponsive to calls for women's equality, the National Assembly turned to preparing France's first written constitution. The deputies gave voting rights only to white men who passed a test of wealth. The Constitution defined them as the "active citizens"; all others were "passive." Despite this limitation, the Constitution produced fundamental changes in French government. France became a constitutional monarchy in which the king was simply the leading state functionary. A one-house legislature was responsible for making laws. The king could hold up enactment of laws but could not veto them absolutely. The deputies abolished all the old administrative divisions of the provinces and replaced them with a national system of eighty-three departments (*départements*) with identical administrative and legal structures (Map 20.2). All officials were elected; no offices could be bought and sold. The deputies also abolished the old taxes and re-

placed them with new ones that were supposed to be uniformly levied. The new government had difficulty collecting taxes, however, because many people had expected a substantial cut in the tax rate. The new administrative system survived, nonetheless, and the departments are still the basic units of the French state today.

When the deputies turned to reforming the Catholic church, they created conflicts that would erupt again and again over the next ten years. Following a long tradition of state involvement in church affairs but with the new aim of countering aristocratic domination of high church offices, the National Assembly passed a Civil Constitution of the Clergy in July 1790. The constitution set pay scales for the clergy and provided that the voters elect their own parish priests and bishops just as they elected other officials. Motivated partly by the ongoing financial crisis, the National Assembly confiscated all the church's property and promised to pay clerical salaries in return. The impounded property served as a guarantee for the new paper money, called *assignats*, issued by the government. The *assignats* soon became subject to inflation because the government began to sell the church lands to the highest bidders in state auctions. The sales increased the landholdings of wealthy city dwellers and prosperous peasants but cut the ground out from under the *assignats*.

The government's offensive on the church did not stop at confiscation of church lands. Convinced that monastic life encouraged idleness and a decline in the nation's population, the deputies outlawed any future monastic vows and encouraged monks and nuns to return to private life on state pensions. Many monks took the opportunity, but few nuns did; for nuns, the convent was all they knew. As the Carmelite nuns of Paris responded, "If there is true happiness on earth, we enjoy it in the shelter of the sanctuary."

In November 1790, the National Assembly required all clergy to swear an oath of loyalty to the Civil Constitution of the Clergy. Pope Pius VI in Rome condemned the constitution, and half of the French clergy refused to take the oath. The oath of allegiance permanently divided the Catholic population, which had to choose between loyalty to the old church and commitment to the Revolution with its "constitutional" church. The revolutionary government lost many supporters by passing laws against the clergy who refused the oath and by forcing them into exile, deporting them forcibly, or executing them as traitors. Riots and demonstrations led by women greeted many of the oath-taking priests who showed up to replace those who refused.

The End of Monarchy

Louis XVI was reluctant to recognize the new limits on his powers, and the reorganization of the Catholic church particularly offended him. On June 20, 1791, the royal family escaped in disguise from the Tuileries palace in Paris and fled to the eastern border of France, where they hoped to gather support to overturn the Revolution from Austria, whose emperor, Leopold II, was the brother of Marie-Antoinette. The plans went awry when a postmaster recognized the king from his portrait on the new French money, and the royal family was arrested at Varennes, forty miles from the Austrian border. The National Assembly tried to depict this incident as a

kidnapping, but the "flight to Varennes" touched off demonstrations in Paris against the royal family, whom some now regarded as traitors. Cartoons circulated depicting the royal family as animals being returned "to the stable."

War with Austria and Prussia. The Constitution that Louis finally endorsed in 1791 provided for the immediate election of a new Legislative Assembly. In a rare act of self-denial, the deputies of the National Assembly declared themselves ineligible for the new Assembly. Those who had experienced the Revolution firsthand now departed from the scene, opening the door to men with little previous experience in national politics. The status of the king might have remained uncertain if war had not intervened, but by early 1792 everyone seemed intent on war with Austria. Louis and Marie-Antoinette hoped that war would lead to the definitive defeat of the Revolution, whereas the deputies who favored a republic hoped that war would reveal the king's treachery and lead to his downfall. On April 21, 1792, Louis declared war on Leopold. Prussia immediately entered on the Austrian side. Thousands of French aristocrats, including two-thirds of the army officer corps, had already emigrated, including both the king's brothers, and they were gathering along France's eastern border in expectation of joining Leopold's counterrevolutionary army.

When fighting broke out in 1792, all the powers expected a brief and relatively contained war. Instead, it would continue despite brief interruptions for the next twenty-three years. In 1792, the French were woefully unprepared, and in the first battles the Austrians promptly routed the French armies, joking that the new French motto was "Conquer or Run."

The Second Revolution of August 10, 1792. As the French frantically reorganized their armies to replace the thousands of aristocratic officers who had emigrated, the authority of the Legislative Assembly came under fire. In June 1792, an angry crowd invaded the hall of the Assembly in Paris and threatened the royal family. In response, Lafayette left his command on the eastern front and came to Paris to insist on punishing the demonstrators. His appearance only fueled distrust of the army commanders, which increased to a fever pitch when the Prussians crossed the border and advanced on Paris. The Prussian commander, the duke of Brunswick, issued

The Guillotine

Before 1789 only nobles were decapitated if condemned to death; commoners were usually hanged. Equalization of the death penalty was first proposed by J. I. Guillotin, a professor of anatomy and a deputy for the Third Estate in the National Assembly. He also suggested that a mechanical device be constructed for decapitation, leading to the instrument's association with his name. The Assembly decreed decapitation as the death penalty in June 1791 and another physician, A. Louis, actually invented the guillotine. Its use began in April 1792 and did not end until 1981, when the French government abolished the death penalty. Although it was invented to make death equal and painless, the guillotine disturbed many observers; its mechanical operation and efficiency — the executioner only pulled up the blade by a cord and then released it — seemed somehow inhuman. Nonetheless, the guillotine fascinated much as it repelled. Reproduced in miniature, painted onto snuffboxes and china, worn as jewelry, and even serving as a toy, the guillotine became a part of popular culture, celebrated as the people's avenger by supporters of the Revolution and vilified as the preeminent symbol of the Terror by opponents.
Musée Carnavalet/Photo Bulloz.

wives and daughters, had followed every twist and turn in revolutionary fortunes. Political clubs had multiplied since the founding in 1789 of the first and most influential of them, the Jacobin Club (named after the former monastery in Paris where the first club met). Newspapers, pamphlets, posters, and cartoons proliferated. Every local district in Paris had its club, where men and women listened to the news of the day and discussed their options.

Faced with the threat of military retaliation and frustrated with the inaction of the Legislative Assembly, on August 10, 1792, leaders of the local district governments of Paris (called *sections*) organized an insurrection and attacked the Tuileries palace, where the king resided. The king and his family had to escape into the meeting room of the Legislative Assembly, where the frightened deputies ordered new elections—this time by universal male suffrage (no wealth qualifications as in the Constitution of 1791)—for a National Convention that would write yet another constitution. When it met, the Convention abolished the monarchy and on September 22, 1792, established the first republic in French history. The republic would answer only to the people, not to any royal authority. Lafayette and other liberal aristocrats who had supported the constitutional monarchy fled into exile.

Violence soon exploded again. Early in September 1792, as the Prussians approached Paris, hastily gathered mobs stormed the overflowing prisons to seek out traitors who might help the enemy. In an atmosphere of near hysteria, eleven hundred inmates were killed, including many ordinary and completely innocent people. The princess of Lamballe, one of the queen's favorites, was hacked to pieces and her mutilated body displayed beneath the windows where the royal family was kept under guard. These "September massacres" showed the dark side of popular revolution, in which the common people demanded instant revenge on supposed enemies and conspirators.

Republican Rivals and the Execution of the King.
The National Convention faced a dire situation. It needed to write a new constitution for the republic while fighting a war with external enemies and confronting increasing resistance at home. The Revolution had divided the population: for some it had not gone far enough toward providing food, land, and retribution against enemies; for others it had

a manifesto—the Brunswick Manifesto—announcing that Paris would be totally destroyed if the royal family suffered any violence.

The ordinary people of Paris did not passively await their fate. Known as *sans-culottes* ("without breeches")—because men who worked with their hands wore long trousers rather than the knee breeches of the upper classes—tailors, shoemakers, cabinetmakers, and shopkeepers, along with their gone too far by dismantling the church and the monarchy. The French people had never known any government other than monarchy. Only half the population could read and write at even a basic level. In this situation, symbolic actions became very important. Any public sign of monarchy was at risk, and revolutionaries soon pulled down statues of kings and burned reminders of the former regime.

The fate of Louis XVI and the future direction of the republic divided the deputies elected to the National Convention. The deputies came from very similar social backgrounds and shared many political beliefs; most of them were middle-class lawyers and professionals who had developed their ardent republican beliefs in the national network of Jacobin Clubs. After the fall of the monarchy in August 1792, however, the Jacobins divided into two factions. The Girondins (named after a department in southwestern France, the Gironde, which provided some of its leading orators) met regularly at the salon of Jeanne Roland, the wife of a minister. They resented the growing power of Parisian militants and tried to appeal to the departments outside of Paris. The Mountain (so called because its deputies sat in the highest seats of the Convention), in contrast, was closely allied with the Paris militants.

The first showdown between the Girondins and the Mountain occurred during the trial of the king in December 1792. Although the Girondins agreed that the king was guilty of treason, many of them argued for clemency, exile, or a popular referendum on his fate. After a long and difficult debate, the Convention supported the Mountain and voted by a very narrow majority to execute the king. Louis XVI went to the guillotine on January 21, 1793, sharing the fate of Charles I of England in 1649. "We have just convinced ourselves that a king is only a man," wrote one newspaper, "and that no man is above the law."

✤ The Terror and the Republic of Virtue

The execution of the king did not end the new regime's problems. The continuing war required even more men and money, and the introduction of a national draft provoked massive resistance in some parts of France. In response to growing pressures,

the National Convention set up a highly centralized government designed to provide food, direct the war effort, and punish counterrevolutionaries. Thus began "the Terror," in which the guillotine became the most frightening instrument of a government that suppressed almost every form of dissent. The leader of this government, Maximilien Robespierre, aimed to create a "Republic of Virtue," in which the government would teach, or force, citizens to become virtuous republicans through a massive program of political reeducation. These policies only increased divisions, which ultimately led to Robespierre's fall from power and to a dismantling of government by terror.

Robespierre and the Committee of Public Safety

The conflict between the Girondins and the Mountain did not end with the execution of Louis XVI. Militants in Paris agitated for the removal of the deputies who had proposed a referendum on the king, and in retaliation the Girondins tried to single out Parisian leaders for punishment. First the Girondins engineered the arrest of Jean-Paul Marat, a deputy who styled himself in his newspaper "the friend of the people" and urged violent measures against enemies of the republic. Marat was acquitted. Then the Girondins devised a special commission to investigate the situation in Paris, ordering the arrest of various local leaders. In response, Parisian militants organized an armed demonstration and invaded the National Convention on June 2, 1793, forcing the deputies to decree the arrest of their twenty-nine Girondin colleagues. The Convention agreed to the establishment of paramilitary bands called "revolutionary armies" to enforce the distribution of grain and hunt down hoarders and political suspects and to the increased use of revolutionary courts to try political suspects and execute the guilty. In a series of decrees over the next few months, the Convention also tried to stabilize prices; on September 29, 1793, it established a General Maximum on the prices of thirty-nine essential commodities and on wages.

Setting the course for government and the war increasingly fell to the Committee of Public Safety, set up by the Convention on April 6, 1793. Composed of twelve deputies elected by the Convention, the committee gradually established its paramount

An Anti-Jacobin Satire
In The Purifying Pot of the Jacobins *(1793), the anonymous artist makes fun of the Jacobin Club's penchant for constantly examining the political correctness of its members. Those who failed the test suffered harsh, sometimes fatal consequences.* Art Resource, NY.

authority. When Maximilien Robespierre (1758–1794) was named to the committee on July 27, 1793, he became in effect its guiding spirit and the chief spokesman of the Revolution. A lawyer from northern France known as "the incorruptible" for his stern honesty and fierce dedication to democratic ideals, Robespierre remains one of the most controversial figures in world history because of his association with the Terror. In September 1793, again in response to popular pressure, the deputies of the Convention voted to "put Terror on the agenda." Robespierre took the lead in implementing this decision. Although he originally opposed the death penalty and the war, he was convinced that the emergency situation of 1793 required severe measures, including death for those, such as the Girondins, who opposed the committee's policies.

Robespierre was the theorist of the Terror and the chief architect of the Republic of Virtue. Like many other educated eighteenth-century men, he had read all the classics of republicanism from Tacitus and Plutarch to Montesquieu and Rousseau. But he took them a step further. He spoke eloquently about "the theory of revolutionary government" as "the war of liberty against its enemies." He defended the people's right to democratic government, while in practice he supported many emergency measures

that restricted their liberties. He personally favored a free market economy, as did almost all middle-class deputies, but in this time of crisis he was willing to enact price controls and requisitioning. Like Rousseau, he believed the republic would have to reform its citizens by establishing a new civic religion. In a famous speech to the Convention, he insisted: "The first maxim of your policies must be to lead the people by reason and the people's enemies by terror . . . without virtue, terror is deadly; without terror, virtue is impotent." *Terror* was not an idle term; it seemed to imply that the goal of democracy justified what we now call totalitarian means, that is, the suppression of all dissent.

Through a series of desperate measures, the Committee of Public Safety set the machinery of the Terror in motion. It sent deputies out "on mission" to purge unreliable officials, work with local leaders of the Jacobin Clubs and other popular societies to uncover dissidents, and organize the war effort. In the first universal draft of men in history, every unmarried man and childless widower between the ages of eighteen and twenty-five was declared eligible for conscription into the army. Revolutionary tribunals set up in Paris and provincial centers tried political suspects. In October 1793, the Revolutionary Tribunal in Paris convicted Marie-Antoinette of treason and sent her to the guillotine. The Girondin leaders and Madame Roland were also guillotined, as was Olympe de Gouges. The government confiscated all the property of convicted traitors.

The Terror won its greatest success on the battlefield. As of April 1793, France faced war with Austria, Prussia, Great Britain, Spain, Sardinia, and the Dutch Republic—all fearful of the impact of revolutionary ideals on their own populations. The execution of Louis XVI, in particular, galvanized European governments; according to William Pitt, the British prime minister, it was "the foulest and most atrocious act the world has ever seen." To face this daunting coalition of forces, the French republic tapped a new and potent source of power, nationalist pride, in decrees mobilizing young and old alike:

> *The young men will go to battle; married men will forge arms and transport provisions; women will make tents and clothing and serve in hospitals; children will make bandages; old men will get themselves carried to public places to arouse the courage of warriors and preach hatred of kings and unity of the republic.*

Scientists contributed improvements in iron production, forges were set up in the parks and gardens of Paris to produce thousands of guns, and citizens everywhere helped collect saltpeter for gunpowder. By the end of 1793, the French nation in arms had stopped the advance of the allied powers, and in the summer of 1794 it invaded the Austrian Netherlands and crossed the Rhine River. The army was ready to carry the gospel of revolution and republicanism to the rest of Europe.

The Republic of Virtue, 1793–1794

The program of the Terror went beyond pragmatic measures to fight the war and internal enemies to include efforts to "republicanize everything"—in other words, to effect a cultural revolution. The government utilized every possible means to transform the old subjects of the monarchy into virtuous republican citizens. While censoring writings deemed counterrevolutionary, the government encouraged republican art, set up civic festivals, and in some places directly attacked the churches in a campaign known as *de-Christianization*. In addition to drawing up plans for a new program of elementary ed-

ucation, the republic set about politicizing every aspect of daily life, from the naming of babies to the measurement of space and time.

Republican Culture. Refusing to tolerate opposition, the republic left no stone unturned in its endeavor to get its message across. Songs—especially the new national anthem, "La Marseillaise"—placards, posters, pamphlets, books, engravings, paintings,

Representing Liberty
Liberty was represented by a female figure because in French the noun is feminine (la liberté). *This painting by a woman, Jeanne-Louise Vallain, from 1793–1794 captures the usual attributes of liberty: she is soberly seated, wearing a Roman-style toga, and holding a pike with a Roman liberty cap on top. Her Roman appearance signals that she is the representation of an abstract quality. The fact that she holds an instrument of battle suggests that women might be active participants. Liberty is holding the Declaration of the Rights of Man and Citizen as it was revised in 1793. This painting was most likely hung in a central location in the Paris Jacobin Club.* Musée de la Revolution Française, Vizille.

sculpture, even everyday crockery, chamberpots, and playing cards conveyed revolutionary slogans and symbols. Foremost among them was the figure of Liberty (an early version of the Statue of Liberty now in New York harbor), which appeared on coins and bills, letterheads and seals, and as statues in festivals. Hundreds of new plays were produced and old classics revised. To encourage the production of patriotic and republican works, the government sponsored state competitions for artists. Works of art were supposed to "awaken the public spirit and make clear how atrocious and ridiculous were the enemies of liberty and of the Republic."

At the center of this elaborate cultural campaign were the revolutionary festivals modeled on Rousseau's plans for a civic religion. The festivals first emerged in 1789 with the spontaneous planting of liberty trees in villages and towns. The Festival of Federation on July 14, 1790, marked the first anniversary of the fall of the Bastille. Under the Convention, the well-known painter Jacques-Louis David (1748–1825), who was a deputy and associate of Robespierre, took over festival planning. David aimed to destroy the mystique of monarchy and to make the republic sacred. His Festival of Unity on August 10, 1793, for example, celebrated the first anniversary of the overthrow of the monarchy. In front of the statue of Liberty built for the occasion, a bonfire consumed the crowns and scepters of royalty while a cloud of three thousand white doves rose into the sky. This was all part of preaching the "moral order of the Republic . . . that will make us a people of brothers, a people of philosophers."

De-Christianization. Some revolutionaries hoped the festival system would replace the Catholic church altogether. They initiated a campaign of de-Christianization that included closing churches (Protestant as well as Catholic), selling many church buildings to the highest bidder, and trying to force even those clergy who had taken the oath of loyalty to abandon their clerical vocations and marry. Some of the greatest churches in Christendom became storehouses for arms or grain, or their stones were sold off to contractors. The medieval statues of kings on the facade of Notre Dame cathedral were beheaded. Church bells were dismantled and church treasures melted down for government use.

In the ultimate step in de-Christianization, extremists tried to establish a Cult of Reason to sup-

plant Christianity. In Paris in the fall of 1793, a goddess of Liberty, played by an actress, presided over a Festival of Reason in Notre Dame cathedral. Local militants in other cities staged similar festivals, which alarmed deputies in the Convention, who were wary of turning rural, devout populations against the republic. The Committee of Public Safety halted the de-Christianization campaign, and Robespierre with David's help tried to institute an alternative, the Cult of the Supreme Being, in June 1794. Robespierre objected to the de-Christianization campaign's atheism; he favored a Rousseau-inspired deistic religion without the supposedly superstitious trappings of Catholicism. Neither cult attracted many followers, but both show the depth of the commitment to overturning the old order and all its traditional institutions.

Politicizing Daily Life. In principle the best way to ensure the future of the republic was through the education of the young. The deputy Georges-Jacques Danton (1759–1794), Robespierre's main competitor as theorist of the Revolution, maintained that "after bread, the first need of the people is education." The Convention voted to make primary schooling free and compulsory for both boys and girls. It took control of education away from the Catholic church and tried to set up a system of state schools at both the primary and secondary levels, but it lacked trained teachers to replace those the Catholic religious orders provided. As a result, opportunities for learning how to read and write may have diminished. In 1799, only one-fifth as many boys enrolled in the state secondary schools as had studied in church schools ten years earlier.

Although many of the ambitious republican programs failed, almost all aspects of daily life became politicized. Already in 1789, the colors one wore had political significance. The tricolor—the combination of red, white, and blue that was to become the flag of France—was devised in July 1789, and by 1793 everyone had to wear a cockade with the colors. Using the formal forms of speech (in French, *vous* for "you") or the title Monsieur or Madame might identify someone as an aristocrat; true patriots used the informal *tu* and Citizen instead. Some people changed their names or gave their children new kinds of names; biblical and saints' names such as Jean, Pierre, Joseph, or Marie gave way to names recalling heroes of the ancient

The Revolutionary Tricolor
This painting by an anonymous artist probably shows a deputy in the uniform prescribed for those sent to supervise military operations. His dress prominently displays the revolutionary tricolor — red, white, and blue — both on his official sash and on the trim of his hat. Plumes had once been reserved to nobles; now nonnobles could wear them on their hats, but they still signaled dignity and importance. Dress became a contested issue during the Revolution, and successive governments considered prescribing some kind of uniform, at least for the deputies in the legislature.
Louvre/Reunion des Musées Nationaux.

Roman republic (Brutus, Gracchus, Cornelia), revolutionary heroes, or flowers and plants. Such changes symbolized adherence to the republic and to Enlightenment ideals rather than to Catholicism.

Even the measures of time and space were revolutionized. In October 1793, the Convention introduced a new calendar to replace the Christian one. Its basis was reason and republican principles. Year I dated from the beginning of the republic on September 22, 1792. Twelve months of exactly thirty days each received new names derived from nature: Pluviôse (roughly equivalent to February), for example, recalled the rain of late winter (*la pluie* is French for "rain"). Instead of seven-day weeks, ten-day *décades* provided only one day of rest every ten days and pointedly eliminated the Sunday of the Christian calendar. The five days left at the end of the calendar year were devoted to special festivals called *sans-culottides*. The calendar remained in force for twelve years despite continuing resistance to it. More enduring was the new metric system based on units of ten that was invented to replace the hundreds of local variations in weights and measures. Other countries in Europe and throughout the world eventually adopted the metric system.

Successive revolutionary legislatures had also changed the rules of family life. The state took responsibility for all family matters away from the Catholic church: birth, death, and marriage registration now happened at city hall, not the parish church. Marriage became a civil contract and as such could be broken. The new divorce law of September 1792 was the most far-reaching in the West: a couple could divorce by mutual consent or for reasons such as insanity, abandonment, battering, or criminal conviction. Thousands of men and women took advantage of the law to dissolve unhappy marriages, even though the pope had condemned the measure. (In 1816, the government revoked the right to divorce, and not until the 1970s did French divorce laws return to the principles of the 1792 legislation.) The revolutionary government also limited fathers' rights over their children; they could not imprison them without cause or control their lives after the age of twenty-one. In one of its most influential actions, the National Convention passed a series of laws that created equal inheritance among all children in the family, including girls. The father's right to favor one child, especially the oldest male, was considered aristocratic and hence antirepublican.

Resisting the Revolution

By intruding into religion, culture, and daily life, the republic inevitably provoked resistance. Shouting curses against the republic, uprooting liberty trees, carrying statues of the Virgin Mary in procession,

Charlotte Corday
In this anonymous painting, Charlotte Corday has just stabbed Marat to death in his bath. Her gaily decorated hat seems incongruous in the gruesome setting. Corday stabbed Marat when she gained admission to his bathroom, where he spent hours every day writing and even receiving visitors. The twenty-five-year-old Corday was tried the next day and amazed even her opponents by remaining absolutely calm and convinced of the rightness of her act.
Musée Carnavalet/Laurie Platt Winfrey, Inc.

hiding a priest who would not take the oath, singing a royalist song—all these expressed dissent with the new symbols, rituals, and policies. Resistance also took more violent forms, from riots over food shortages or religious policies to assassination and full-scale civil war.

Women's Resistance. Many women, in particular, suffered from the hard conditions of life that persisted in this time of war, and they had their own ways of voicing discontent. The long bread lines in the cities exhausted the patience of women already overwhelmed by the demands of housekeeping, childrearing, and working as shop assistants, fishwives, laundresses, and textile workers. Police spies reported their constant grumbling, which occasionally turned into spontaneous demonstrations or riots over high prices or food shortages.

Other forms of resistance were more individual. One young woman, Charlotte Corday, assassinated Jean-Paul Marat in July 1793. Corday fervently supported the Girondins, and she considered it her patriotic duty to kill the deputy who, in the columns of his paper *The Friend of the People,* had constantly demanded more heads and more blood. Marat was immediately eulogized as a great martyr: Corday went to the guillotine vilified as a monster but confident that she had "avenged many innocent victims."

Rebellion and Civil War. Violent resistance broke out for various reasons in many parts of France. In the early years of the Revolution, Catholics rioted in places with large Protestant or Jewish populations, which tended to support the Revolution and the religious toleration and civil rights it promised. The arrest of the Girondin deputies in June 1793 sparked insurrections in several departments. After the government retook the city of Lyon, one of the centers of the revolt, the deputy on mission ordered sixteen hundred houses demolished. Special courts sentenced almost two thousand people to death. The name of the city was changed to Ville Affranchie (Liberated Town).

Nowhere was resistance to the republic more persistent and violent than in the Vendée region of western France. Between March and December 1793, peasants, artisans, and weavers joined under noble leadership to form a "Catholic and Royal Army." One rebel group explained its motives: "They [the republicans] have killed our king, chased away our priests, sold the goods of our church, eaten everything we have and now they want to take our bodies [in the draft]." The uprising took two different forms: in the Vendée itself, a counterrevolutionary army organized to fight the republic; in nearby Brittany, resistance took the form of guerrilla bands, which united to attack a target and then quickly melted into the countryside. Great Britain provided money and underground contacts for these attacks, which were almost always aimed at towns. Town officials sold church lands, enforced measures against the clergy, and supervised conscription. In many ways this was a civil war between town and country, for the townspeople were the ones who supported the Revolution and bought church lands for themselves. The peasants had gained most of what they wanted in 1789 with the abolition of seigneurial dues, and they resented the government's demands for money and manpower and actions taken against their local clergy.

For several months in 1793, the Vendée rebels stormed the largest towns in the region. Both sides committed horrible atrocities. At the small town of Machecoul, for example, the rebels massacred five hundred republicans, including administrators and National Guard members; many were tied together, shoved into freshly dug graves, and shot. By the fall, however, republican soldiers had turned back the rebels. A republican general wrote to the Committee of Public Safety claiming, "There is no more Vendée, citizens, it has perished under our free sword along with its women and children. . . . Following the orders that you gave me I have crushed children under the feet of horses, massacred women who at least . . . will engender no more brigands." "Infernal columns" of republican troops marched through the region to restore control, military courts ordered thousands executed, and republican soldiers massacred thousands of others. In one especially gruesome incident, the deputy Jean-Baptiste Carrier supervised the drowning of some two thousand Vendée rebels, including a number of priests. Barges loaded with prisoners were floated into the Loire River near Nantes and then sunk. Controversy still rages about the rebellion's death toll. Estimates of rebel deaths alone range from about 20,000 to 250,000 and higher. Many thousands of republican soldiers and civilians also lost their lives. Even the low estimates reveal the carnage of this catastrophic confrontation between the republic and its opponents.

The Vendée Rebellion, 1793

The Fall of Robespierre and the End of the Terror, 1794–1799

In an atmosphere of fear of conspiracy that was fueled by overt resistance in places like the Vendée, Robespierre tried simultaneously to exert the Convention's control over popular political activities and to weed out opposition among the deputies. As a result, the Terror intensified until July 1794, when a group of deputies joined within the Convention to order the arrest and execution of Robespierre and his followers. The Convention then ordered elections and drew up a new republican constitution that gave executive power to five directors. This Directory government maintained power during four years of seesaw battles between royalists and former Jacobins. Ultimately it gave way to Napoleon Bonaparte.

The Revolution Devours Its Own. In the fall of 1793, the Convention cracked down on popular clubs and societies. First to be suppressed were women's political clubs. Founded in early 1793, the Society of Revolutionary Republican Women played a very active part in *sans-culottes* politics. The society agitated for harsher measures against the republic's enemies and insisted that women have a voice in politics even if they did not have the vote. Women set up their own clubs in many provincial towns and also attended the meetings of local men's organizations. The closing of women's clubs marked an important turning point in the Revolution. From then on the *sans-culottes* and their political organizations came increasingly under the thumb of the Jacobin deputies in the National Convention.

The Convention severely limited women's participation in the public sphere because the deputies associated women's groups with political disorder and social upheaval. As one deputy stated, women's clubs consisted of "adventuresses, knights-errant, emancipated women, amazons." Another deputy continued, "Women are ill suited for elevated thoughts and serious meditations." In subsequent years physicians, priests, and philosophers amplified such opinions by formulating explanations for women's "natural" differences from men to justify their inferior status.

In the spring of 1794, the Committee of Public Safety moved against its critics among leaders in Paris and deputies in the Convention itself. First a handful of men labeled "ultrarevolutionaries"—in fact a

A Women's Club
In this gouache by the Lesueur brothers, The Patriotic Women's Club, *the club president urges the members to contribute funds for poor patriot families. Women's clubs focused on philanthropic work but also discussed revolutionary legislation and the debates in the National Assemblies. The colorful but sober dress indicates that the women are middle class.* Musée de la Ville de Paris/Musée Carnavalet, Paris/Giraudon/Art Resource, NY.

motley collection of local Parisian politicians—were arrested and executed. Next came the other side, the "indulgents," so called because they favored a moderation of the Terror. Included among them was the deputy Danton, himself once a member of the Committee of Public Safety and a friend of Robespierre, despite the striking contrast in their personalities. Danton was the Revolution's most flamboyant orator and, unlike Robespierre, a high-living, high-spending, excitable politician. At every critical turning point in national politics, his booming voice had swayed opinion in the National Convention. Now, under government pressure, the Revolutionary Tribunal convicted him and his friends of treason and sentenced them to death.

With the arrest and execution of these leaders in Paris, the prophecies of doom for the Revolution seemed about to be realized. "The Revolution," as one of the Girondin victims of 1793 had remarked, "was devouring its own children." The middle-class leaders were killing each other. Even after the major threats to the committee's power had been eliminated, the Terror continued and even worsened. A law passed in June 1794 denied the accused the right of legal counsel, reduced the number of jurors necessary for conviction, and allowed only two judgments: acquittal or death. The category of political crimes expanded to include "slandering patriotism" and "seeking to inspire discouragement." Ordinary

people risked the guillotine if they expressed any discontent. (Ironically, the guillotine had been introduced just a few months before the king's execution as a way of making capital punishment more humane and uniform.) The rate of executions in Paris rose from five a day in the spring of 1794 to twenty-six a day in the summer. The political atmosphere darkened even though the military situation improved. At the end of June, the French armies decisively defeated the main Austrian army and advanced through the Austrian Netherlands to Brussels and Antwerp. The emergency measures for fighting the war were working, yet Robespierre and his inner circle had made so many enemies that they could not afford to loosen the grip of the Terror.

The Terror hardly touched many parts of France. But overall the experience was undeniably traumatic. Across the country the official Terror cost the lives of at least 40,000 French people, most of them living in the regions of major insurrections or near the borders with foreign enemies, where suspicion of collaboration ran high. As many as 300,000 people went to prison as suspects between March 1793 and August 1794 (that is, one out of every fifty French). The toll for the aristocracy and the clergy was especially high. Many leading nobles perished under the guillotine, and thousands emigrated. Thirty thousand to forty thousand clergy who refused the oath emigrated, at least two thousand (including many nuns) were executed, and thousands were imprisoned. The clergy were singled out in particular in the civil war zones: 135 priests were massacred at Lyon in November 1793 and 83 shot in one day during the Vendée revolt. Yet many victims of the Terror were peasants or ordinary working people.

The final crisis of the Terror came in July 1794. Conflicts within the Committee of Public Safety and the National Convention left Robespierre isolated. On July 27, 1794 (the ninth of Thermidor, Year II, according to the revolutionary calendar), Robespierre appeared before the Convention with yet another list of deputies to be arrested. Many feared they would be named, and they shouted him down and ordered him arrested along with his followers on the committee, the president of the Revolutionary Tribunal in Paris, and the commander of the Parisian National Guard. An armed uprising led by the Paris city government failed to save Robespierre when most of the Parisian *sections* and two-thirds of the National Guard took the side of the Convention. Robespierre tried to kill himself with a pistol but only broke his jaw. The next day he and scores of followers went to the guillotine.

The Thermidorian Reaction and the Directory, 1794–1799. The men who led the attack on Robespierre in Thermidor (July 1794) did not intend to reverse all his policies, but that happened nonetheless. Newspapers attacked the Robespierrists as "tigers thirsting for human blood." The new government released hundreds of suspects and arranged a temporary truce in the Vendée. It purged Jacobins from local bodies and replaced them with their opponents. It arrested some of the most notorious "terrorists" in the National Convention, such as Carrier, and put them to death. Within the year the new leaders abolished the Revolutionary Tribunal and closed the Jacobin Club in Paris. Popular demonstrations met severe repression. In southeastern France, in particular, a "White Terror" replaced the Jacobins' "Red Terror." Former officials and local Jacobin leaders were harassed, beaten, and often murdered by paramilitary bands who had tacit support from the new authorities. Those who remained in the National Convention prepared yet another constitution in 1795, setting up a two-house legislature and an executive body—the Directory, headed by five directors.

The Directory regime tenuously held on to power for four years, all the while trying to fend off challenges from the remaining Jacobins and the resurgent royalists. The puritanical atmosphere of the Terror gave way to the pursuit of pleasure—low-cut dresses of transparent materials, the reappearance of prostitutes in the streets, fancy dinner parties, and "victims balls" where guests wore red ribbons around their necks as reminders of the guillotine. Bands of young men dressed in knee breeches and rich fabrics picked fights with known Jacobins and disrupted theater performances with loud antirevolutionary songs. All over France people banded together and petitioned to reopen churches closed during the Terror. If necessary they broke into a church to hold services with a priest who had been in hiding or a lay schoolteacher who was willing to say Mass.

Although the Terror had ended, the revolution had not. In 1794, the most democratic and most repressive phases of the Revolution ended both at once. Between 1795 and 1799, the republic endured in France, but it directed a war effort abroad that would ultimately bring to power the man who would dismantle the republic itself.

❖ Revolution on the March

Beginning in 1792, war raged almost constantly until 1815. At one time or another, and sometimes all at once, France faced every principal power in Europe. The French republic—and later the French Empire under its supreme commander, Emperor Napoleon Bonaparte—proved an even more formidable opponent than the France of Louis XIV. New means of mobilizing and organizing soldiers enabled the French to dominate Europe for a generation. The influence of the Revolution as a political model and the threat of French military conquest combined to challenge the traditional order in Europe.

Arms and Conquests

The allied powers had a chance to defeat France in 1793, when the French armies verged on chaos because of the emigration of noble army officers and the problems of integrating new draftees. At that moment, however, Prussia, Russia, and Austria were preoccupied with clamping down on Poland. For France, this diversion meant a reprieve.

Because of the new national draft, the French had a huge and powerful fighting force of 700,000 men by the end of 1793. But the army faced many problems in the field. As many as a third of the recent draftees deserted before or during battle. Uniforms fashioned out of rough cloth constricted movements, tore easily, and retained the damp of muddy battlefields, exposing the soldiers to the elements and the spread of disease. At times the soldiers were fed only moldy bread, and if their pay was late, they sometimes resorted to pillaging and looting. Generals might pay with their lives if they lost a key battle and their loyalty to the Revolution came under suspicion. France nevertheless had one overwhelming advantage: its soldiers, drawn largely from the peasantry and the lower classes of the

cities, fought for a revolution that they and their brothers and sisters had helped make. The republic was their government, and the army was in large measure theirs too; many officers had risen through the ranks by skill and talent rather than by inheriting or purchasing their positions. One young peasant boy wrote to his parents, "Either you will see me return bathed in glory, or you will have a son who is a worthy citizen of France who knows how to die for the defense of his country."

When the French armies invaded the Austrian Netherlands and crossed the Rhine in the summer of 1794, they proclaimed a war of liberation. But as they annexed more and more territory, "liberated" people in many places began to view them as an army of occupation (Map 20.3). Those just across the northern and eastern borders of France reacted most positively to the French invasion. In the

MAP 20.3 French Expansion, 1791–1799

The influence of the French Revolution on neighboring territories is dramatically evident in this map. The French directly annexed the papal territories in southern France in 1791, Nice and Savoy in 1792, and the Austrian Netherlands in 1795. They set up a series of sister republics in the former Dutch Republic and in various Italian states. Local people did not always welcome these changes. For example, the French made the Dutch pay a huge war indemnity, support a French occupying army of 25,000 soldiers, and give up some southern territories. One of the generals who invaded the Dutch Republic wrote, "Holland has done nothing to avoid being classed among the general order of our conquests. . . . It follows from this that there can be no reason to treat her any differently from a conquered country." The sister republics faced a future of subordination to French national interests.

Austrian Netherlands, Mainz, Savoy, and Nice, French officers organized Jacobin Clubs that attracted middle-class locals. The clubs petitioned for annexation to France, and French legislation was then introduced, including the abolition of seigneurial dues. Despite resistance, especially in the Austrian Netherlands, these areas remained part of France until 1815, and the legal changes were permanent. Like Louis XIV a century before, most deputies in the National Convention considered the annexed territories within France's "natural frontiers"—the Rhine, the Alps, and the Pyrenees.

The Directory government that came to power in 1795 was torn between defending the new frontiers and launching a more aggressive policy of creating semi-independent "sister" republics wherever the armies succeeded. When Prussia declared neutrality in 1795, the French armies swarmed into the Dutch Republic, abolished the stadholderate, and, with the revolutionary penchant for renaming, created the new Batavian Republic, a satellite of France. The brilliant young general Napoleon Bonaparte defeated the Austrian armies in northern Italy in 1797 and created the Cisalpine Republic. Next he overwhelmed Venice and then handed it over to the Austrians in exchange for a peace agreement that lasted less than two years. After the French attacked the Swiss cantons in 1798, they set up the Helvetic Republic and curtailed many of the Catholic church's privileges. They conquered the Papal States in 1798 and installed a Roman Republic; the pope fled to Siena.

The same year, 1798, Bonaparte took a great army, originally raised to invade England, across the Mediterranean Sea to Egypt. The Directory government hoped that an occupation of Egypt would strike a blow at British trade by cutting the route to India and thus compensate France for its losses there years before. Once the army disembarked, however, the British admiral Horatio Nelson destroyed the French fleet while it was anchored in Aboukir Bay. In the face of determined resistance and an outbreak of the bubonic plague, Bonaparte's armies retreated from a further expedition in Syria. But the French occupation of Egypt lasted long enough for that largely Muslim country to experience the same kinds of Enlightenment-inspired legal reforms that had been introduced in Europe: the French abolished torture, introduced equality before the law, eliminated religious taxes, and proclaimed religious toleration.

The revolutionary wars had an immediate impact on European life at all levels of society. Thousands of men died in every country involved, with perhaps as many as 200,000 casualties in the French armies alone in 1794 and 1795. No accurate statistics documenting casualties in these wars exist, but we do know that more soldiers died in hospitals as a result of their wounds than on the battlefields. Constant warfare hampered world commerce and especially disrupted French overseas shipping. (The abolition of slavery in the French colonies in 1794 also cut off one lucrative market for the French port cities.) In contrast to the prosperous times that preceded the French Revolution, times were now hard almost everywhere, because the dislocations of internal and external commerce provoked constant shortages.

European Reactions to Revolutionary Change

The French Revolution profoundly transformed European politics and social relations. (See "Contrasting Views," page 752.) In 1789, an English supporter, the Unitarian minister Richard Price, wrote enthusiastically about the Revolution's prospects: "Behold, the light . . . after setting AMERICA free, reflected to FRANCE, and there kindled into a blaze that lays despotism in ashes, and warms and illuminates EUROPE." The governing elites of Europe became alarmed, however, when the revolutionaries abolished monarchy and nobility and encouraged popular participation in politics. Democrats and reformers from many countries flooded to Paris to witness events firsthand. Supporters of the French Revolution in Great Britain, like the earlier reformers of the 1760s and 1770s, joined constitutional and reform societies that sprang up in many cities. The most important of these societies, the London Corresponding Society, founded in 1792, corresponded with the Paris Jacobin Club and served as a center for reform agitation in England. The British government quickly suppressed the societies and harassed their leaders, charging that their ideas and their contacts with the French were seditious.

Pro-French feeling ran even stronger in Ireland. Catholics and Presbyterians, both excluded from the vote, came together in 1791 in the Society of United Irishmen, which eventually pressed for secession from England. In 1798, the society timed a rebellion

FRENCH LIBERTY.   BRITISH SLAVERY.

The English Rebuttal
In this caricature, James Gillray satirizes the French version of liberty. Gillray, a supporter of the Tories in Britain, produced thousands of political caricatures. British Museum.

to coincide with a French invasion, but the French sent too few soldiers and the British mercilessly repressed the revolt. Thirty thousand people were killed. Twice as many regular British troops (seventy thousand) as fought in any of the major continental battles were required to put down the rebellion.

Those countries near France with a substantial middle class and access to newspapers and other publications generally sympathized the most with French ideas. Yet even countries close to France sometimes fiercely resisted French occupation, often in the form of banditry. In the German Rhineland, for example, gangs of bandits preyed on the French and on Jews. One German traveler reported, "It is characteristic of the region in which the bandits are based that these two nations [the French and the Jews] are hated. So crimes against them are motivated not just by a wish to rob them but also by a variety of fanaticism which is partly political and partly religious." Because the French offered the Jews religious toleration and civil and political rights wherever they conquered, anti-French groups sometimes attacked Jews.

Many leading intellectuals in the German states, including the philosopher Immanuel Kant, initially supported the revolutionary cause, but after 1793 most of them turned against the popular violence and military aggressiveness of the Revolution. One of the greatest writers of the age, Friedrich Schiller

(1759–1805), typified the turn in sentiment against revolutionary politics:

Freedom is only in the realm of dreams
And the beautiful blooms only in song.

The German states, still run by many separate rulers, experienced a profound artistic and intellectual revival, which eventually connected with anti-French nationalism. This renaissance included a resurgence of intellectual life in the universities, a thriving press (1,225 journals were launched in the 1780s alone), and the multiplication of Masonic lodges and literary clubs.

Not surprisingly, the areas farthest from France—Russia, the Ottoman Empire, the Balkans, Austria, Hungary, and the Scandinavian states—were generally least affected by the French Revolution. One exception was the United States, where opinion fiercely divided on the virtues of the French Revolution. Sweden was a second exception. Gustavus III (r. 1771–1792) was assassinated in Stockholm by a nobleman who claimed that "the king has violated his oath . . . and declared himself an enemy of the realm." The king's murder changed little in Sweden's power structure, however; his son Gustavus IV (r. 1792–1809) was convinced that the French Jacobins had sanctioned his father's assassination, and he insisted on avoiding "licentious liberty." Although just across the border from France, Spain's royal

Consequences of the French Revolution

Contemporaries instantly grasped the cataclysmic significance of the French Revolution and began to argue about its lessons for their own countries. A member of the British Parliament, Edmund Burke, ignited a firestorm of controversy with his *Reflections on the Revolution in France* (Document 1). He condemned the French revolutionaries for attempting to build a government on abstract reasoning rather than taking historical traditions and customs into account; his book provided a foundation for the doctrine known as *conservatism*, which argued for "conserving" the traditional foundations of society and avoiding the pitfalls of radical or revolutionary change. Burke's views provoked a strong response from the English political agitator Thomas Paine. Paine's pamphlet *Common Sense* (1776) helped inspire the British North American colonies to demand independence from Great Britain. In *The Rights of Man* (Document 2), written fifteen years later, Paine attacked the traditional order as fundamentally unjust and defended the idea of a revolution to uphold rights. Joseph de Maistre, an aristocratic opponent of both the Enlightenment and the French Revolution, put the conservative attack on the French Revolution into a deeply religious and absolutist framework (Document 3). In contrast, Anne-Louise-Germaine de Staël, an opponent of Napoleon and one of the most influential intellectuals of the early nineteenth century, took the view that the violence of the Revolution had been the product of generations of superstition and arbitrary rule, that is, rule by an absolutist Catholic church and monarchical government (Document 4).

1. Edmund Burke, Reflections on the Revolution in France *(1790)*

Born in Ireland and a supporter of the American colonists in their opposition to the British Parliament, Edmund Burke (1729–1797) opposed the French Revolution, warning his countrymen against the dangerous abstractions of the French. He argued the case for tradition, continuity, and gradual reform based on practical experience— what he called "a sure principle of conservation."

Can I now congratulate the same nation [France] upon its freedom? Is it because liberty in the abstract may be classed amongst the blessings of mankind, that I am seriously to felicitate a madman, who has escaped from the protecting restraint and wholesome darkness of his cell, on his restoration to the enjoyment of light and liberty? Am I to congratulate an highwayman and murderer, who has broke prison, upon the recovery of his natural rights? . . .

Government is not made in virtue of natural rights, which may and do exist in total independence of it; and exist in much greater clearness, and in a much greater degree of abstract perfection: but their abstract perfection is their practical defect. By having a right to every thing they want every thing. Government is a contrivance of human wisdom to provide for human *wants*. . . .

The science of constructing a commonwealth, or renovating it, or reforming it, is, like every other experimental science, not to be taught *a priori* [based on theory rather than on experience]. Nor is it a short experience that can instruct us in that practical science; because the real effects of moral causes are not always immediate; but that which in the first instance is prejudicial may be excellent in its remoter operation; and its excellence may arise even from the ill effects it produces in the beginning. . . .

All the pleasing illusions, which made power gentle, and obedience liberal, which harmonized the different shades of life, and which, by a bland assimilation, incorporated into politics the sentiments which beautify and soften private society, are to be dissolved by this new conquering empire of light and reason. All the decent drapery of life is to be rudely torn off. All the super-added ideas, furnished from the wardrobe of a moral imagination, which the heart owns, and the understanding ratifies, as necessary to cover the defects of our naked shivering nature, and to raise it to dignity in our own estimation, are to be exploded as a ridiculous, absurd, and antiquated fashion.

On this scheme of things, a king is but a man; a queen is but a woman; a woman is but an animal; and an animal not of the highest order. All homage paid to the sex in general as such, and without distinct views, is to be regarded as romance and folly. Regicide, and parricide, and sacrilege, are but fictions of superstition. . . .

In the groves of *their* academy, at the end of every visto [vista], you see nothing but the gallows. Nothing is left which engages the affections on the part of the commonwealth. . . . To make us love our country, our country ought to be lovely.

Source: *Two Classics of the French Revolution: Reflections on the Revolution in France (Edmund Burke) and The Rights of Man (Thomas Paine)* (New York: Doubleday Anchor Books, 1973), 19, 71–74, 90–91.

2. *Thomas Paine,* The Rights of Man *(1791)*

In his reply to Burke, The Rights of Man, *which sold 200,000 copies in two years, Thomas Paine (1737–1809) defended the idea of reform based on reason, advocated a concept of universal human rights, and attacked the excesses of privilege and tradition in Great Britain. Elected as a deputy to the French National Convention in 1793 in recognition of his writings in favor of the French Revolution, Paine narrowly escaped condemnation as an associate of the Girondins.*

Before anything can be reasoned upon to a conclusion, certain facts, principles, or data, to reason from, must be established, admitted, or denied. Mr. Burke, with his usual outrage, abuses the *Declaration of the Rights of Man,* published by the National Assembly of France, as the basis on which the Constitution of France is built. This he calls "paltry and blurred sheets of paper about the rights of man."

Does Mr. Burke mean to deny that *man* has any rights? If he does, then he must mean that there are no such things as rights any where, and that he has none himself; for who is there in the world but man? . . .

Hitherto we have spoken only (and that but in part) of the natural rights of man. We have now to consider the civil rights of man, and to show how the one originates from the other. Man did not enter into society to become *worse* than he was before, nor to have fewer rights than he had before, but to have those rights better secured. His natural rights are the foundation of all his civil rights. . . .

Every civil right has for its foundation some natural right pre-existing in the individual, but to the enjoyment of which his individual power is not, in all cases, sufficiently competent. Of this kind are all those which relate to security and protection. . . .

A constitution is not a thing in name only, but in fact. It has not an ideal, but a real existence; and wherever it cannot be produced in a visible form, there is none. A constitution is a thing *antecedent* to a government, and a government is only the creature of a constitution. The constitution of a country is not the act of its government, but of the people constituting a government. . . .

Can then Mr. Burke produce the English Constitution? If he cannot, we may fairly conclude, that though it has been so much talked about, no such thing as a constitution exists, or ever did exist, and consequently that the people have yet a constitution to form.

Source: *Two Classics of the French Revolution: Reflections on the Revolution in France (Edmund Burke) and The Rights of Man (Thomas Paine)* (New York: Doubleday Anchor Books, 1973), 302, 305–306, 309.

3. *Joseph de Maistre,* Considerations on France *(1797)*

An aristocrat born in Savoy, Joseph de Maistre (1753–1821) believed in reform but he passionately opposed both the Enlightenment and the French Revolution as destructive to good order. He believed that Protestants, Jews, lawyers, journalists, and scientists all threatened the social order because they questioned the need for absolute obedience to authority in matters both religious and political. De Maistre set the foundations for reactionary conservatism, a conservatism that defended throne and altar.

In a word, if there is no moral revolution in Europe, if the religious spirit is not reinforced in this part of the world, the social bond will dissolve. Nothing can be predicted, and anything must be expected, but if there is to be improvement in this matter, either France is called upon to produce it, or there is no more analogy, no more induction, no more art of prediction.

This consideration especially makes me think that the French Revolution is a great epoch and that its consequences, in all kinds of ways, will be felt far beyond the time of its explosion and the limits of its birthplace. . . .

There is a satanic quality to the French Revolution that distinguishes it from everything we have ever seen or anything we are ever likely to see in the future. Recall the great assemblies, Robespierre's speech against the priesthood, the solemn apostasy [renunciation of vows] of the clergy, the desecration of objects of worship, the installation of the goddess of reason, and that multitude of extraordinary actions by which the provinces sought to outdo Paris. All this goes beyond the ordinary circle of crime and seems to belong to another world.

Source: Joseph de Maistre, *Considerations on France*, trans. Richard A. Lebrun (Cambridge: Cambridge University Press, 1994), 21, 41.

4. Anne-Louise-Germaine de Staël, Considerations on the Main Events of the French Revolution *(1818)*

De Staël published her views long after the Revolution was over, but she had lived through the events herself. She was the daughter of Jacques Necker, Louis XVI's Swiss Protestant finance minister. Necker's dismissal in July 1789 had sparked the attack on the Bastille. De Staël published novels, literary tracts, and memoirs and became one of

the best-known writers of the nineteenth century. In her writings she defended the Enlightenment; though she opposed the violence unleashed by the Revolution, she traced it back to the excesses of monarchical government.

Once the people were freed from their harness there is no doubt that they were in a position to commit any kind of crime. But how can we explain their depravity? The government we are now supposed to miss so sorely [the former monarchy] had had plenty of time to form this guilty nation. The priests whose teaching, example, and wealth were supposed to be so good for us had supervised the childhood of the generation that broke out against them. The class that revolted in 1789 must have been accustomed to the privileges of feudal nobility which, as we are also assured, are so peculiarly agreeable to those on whom they weigh [the peasants]. How does it happen, then, that the seed of so many vices was sown under the ancient institutions? . . . What can we conclude from this, then?—That no people had been as unhappy for the preceding century as the French. If the Negroes of Saint-Domingue have committed even greater atrocities, it is because they had been even more greatly oppressed.

Source: Vivian Folkenflik, ed. *An Extraordinary Woman: Selected Writings of Germaine de Staël* (New York: Columbia University Press, 1987), 365–66.

QUESTIONS FOR DEBATE
1. Which aspect of the French Revolution most disturbed these commentators?
2. How would you align each of these writers on a spectrum running from extreme right to extreme left in politics?
3. How would each of these writers judge the Enlightenment that preceded the French Revolution?

government suppressed all news from France, fearing that it might ignite the spirit of revolt. This fear was not misplaced because even in Russia, for instance, 278 outbreaks of peasant unrest occurred between 1796 and 1798. One Russian landlord complained, "This is the self-same . . . spirit of insubordination and independence, which has spread through all Europe."

Poland Extinguished, 1793–1795

The spirit of independence made the Poles and Lithuanians especially discontent, for they had already suffered a significant loss of territory and population. "I shall fight Jacobinism, and defeat it in Poland," vowed Catherine the Great in 1792. Frightened by reports of a few friends of the

French Revolution cropping up throughout eastern Europe—even in St. Petersburg—Catherine determined to smite the moderate reformers in Warsaw. Prussia joined her, fearing a regenerated, pro-French Poland. While Prussian and Austrian troops battled the French in the west, a Russian army easily crushed Polish resistance. In effect for barely a year, Poland's constitution of May 3, 1791, was abolished, and Prussia and Russia helped themselves to generous new slices of Polish territory in the Second Partition of 1793 (Map 20.4).

Poland's reform movement became even more pro-French. Some leaders fled abroad, including Tadeusz Kościuszko (1746–1817), an officer who had been a foreign volunteer in the War of American Independence and who now escaped to Paris. In the spring of 1794, Kościuszko returned from

MAP 20.4 The Second and Third Partitions of Poland, 1793 and 1795

In 1793, after Russian armies invaded Poland, Russia and Prussia agreed to another partition of Polish territories. Prussia took over territory that included 1.1 million Poles while Russia gained 3 million new inhabitants. Austria gave up any claims to Poland in exchange for help from Russia and Prussia in acquiring Bavaria. When Kościuszko's nationalist uprising failed in 1794, Russia, Prussia, and Austria agreed to a final division. Prussia absorbed an additional 900,000 Polish subjects, including those in Warsaw; Austria incorporated 1 million Poles and the city of Cracow; Russia gained another 2 million Poles. The three powers determined never to use the term "Kingdom of Poland" again.

France as "dictator," empowered by his fellow conspirators to lead a national revolt. He incited an uprising at Cracow, which then spread to Warsaw and the old Lithuanian capital, Vilnius. Kościuszko faced an immediate, insoluble dilemma. He could win only if the peasants joined the struggle—highly unlikely unless villagers could be convinced that serfdom would end. But such a drastic step risked alienating the nobles who had started the revolt. So Kościuszko compromised. In his proclamation of May 7, 1794, he summoned the peasantry to the national cause and promised a reduction of their obligations as serfs, but not freedom itself. He received an equally equivocal response. Armed with scythes, a few peasant bands joined the insurrection, but most let their lords fight it out alone. Urban workers displayed more enthusiasm; at Warsaw, for example, a mob hanged several Russian collaborators, including an archbishop in his full regalia.

The uprising failed. Kościuszko led his troops to a few victories over the surprised Russians, but when Catherine's forces regrouped, they routed the Poles and Lithuanians. Kościuszko and other Patriot leaders languished for years in Russian and Austrian prisons. Taking no further chances, Russia, Prussia, and Austria wiped Poland completely from the map in the Third Partition of 1795. "The Polish question" would plague international relations for more than a century as Polish rebels flocked to any international upheaval that might undo the partitions. Beyond all this maneuvering lay the unsolved problem of Polish serfdom, which isolated the nation's gentry and townspeople from the rural masses.

Revolution in the Colonies

The Caribbean colonies lay far from France, but inevitably they felt the effects of revolution. From the beginning, political leaders in Paris feared the potential for conflict in the colonies, as aspirations for broader political rights might threaten French authority. The Caribbean colonies were crucial to the French economy. Twice the size in land area of the neighboring British colonies, they also produced nearly twice as much revenue in exports. The slave population had doubled in the French colonies in the twenty years before 1789. St. Domingue (present-day Haiti) was the most important French colony, with its approximately 465,000 slaves, 30,000 whites, and 28,000 free people of color, who were employed primarily to apprehend runaway slaves and assure plantation security.

Despite the efforts of a Paris club called the Friends of Blacks, most French revolutionaries did

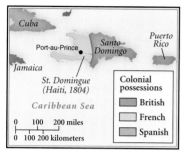

St. Domingue on the Eve of the Revolt, 1791

not consider slavery a pressing problem. As one deputy explained, "This regime [in the colonies] is oppressive, but it gives a livelihood to several million Frenchmen. This regime is barbarous but a still greater barbarity will result if you interfere with it without the necessary knowledge."

In August 1791, however, the slaves in northern St. Domingue organized a large-scale revolt with the slogan "Listen to the voice of Liberty which speaks in the hearts of all." To restore authority over the slaves, the Legislative Assembly in Paris granted civil and political rights to the free blacks—an action that alienated the white planters and merchants, who in 1793 signed an agreement with Great Britain, now France's enemy in war, declaring British sovereignty over the island. To complicate matters further, Spain, which controlled the rest of the island and had entered on Great Britain's side in the war, offered freedom to individual slave rebels who joined the Spanish armies as long as they agreed to maintain the slave regime for the other blacks.

The few thousand French republican troops on the island were outnumbered, and to prevent complete military disaster the French commissioner freed all the slaves in his jurisdiction in August 1793 without permission from the government at home. In February 1794, the National Convention formally abolished slavery and granted full rights to all black men in the colonies. These actions had the desired effect. One of the ablest black generals allied with the Spanish, the ex-slave François Dominique Toussaint L'Ouverture (1743–1803), changed sides and committed his troops to the French. The French eventually appointed Toussaint governor of St. Domingue as a reward for his efforts. The vicious fighting and flight of whites left the island's economy in ruins; in 1800, the plantations produced one-fifth of what they had in 1789. In the zones Toussaint controlled, army officers or officials took over the great estates and kept all those working in

Toussaint L'Ouverture

The leader of the St. Domingue slave uprising appears in his general's uniform, sword in hand. This portrait appeared in one of the earliest histories of the revolt, Marcus Rainsford's Historical Account of the Black Empire of Hayti *(London, 1805). Toussaint, a former slave who educated himself, fascinated many of his contemporaries in Europe as well as the New World by turning a chaotic slave rebellion into an organized and ultimately successful independence movement.* North Wind Picture Archives.

agriculture under military discipline. The former slaves were bound to their estates like serfs and forced to work the plantations in exchange for an autonomous family life and the right to maintain personal garden plots.

Toussaint remained in charge until 1802, when Napoleon sent French armies to regain control of the island. They arrested Toussaint and transported him to France, where he died in prison. The arrest prompted the English poet William Wordsworth to write of him:

There's not a breathing of the common wind
That will forget thee; thou hast great allies;
Thy friends are exultations, agonies,
And love, and man's unconquerable mind.

Toussaint became a hero to abolitionists everywhere, a potent symbol of black struggles to win freedom. Napoleon attempted to restore slavery, sending Polish volunteers to do much of the grueling work, but the remaining black generals defeated his armies and in 1804 proclaimed the Republic of Haiti.

The Rise of Napoleon Bonaparte

Toussaint had followed with interest Napoleon's rise to power in France; he once wrote to Bonaparte, "From the First of the Blacks to the First of the Whites." He was not alone in his fascination, for the story of the rise of Napoleon Bonaparte (1769–1821) is one of the most remarkable in Western history. It would have seemed astonishing in 1795 that the twenty-six-year-old son of a noble family from the island of Corsica off the Italian coast would within four years become the supreme ruler of France and one of the greatest military leaders in world history. In 1795, he was a penniless artillery officer, only recently released from prison as a presumed Robespierrist. Thanks to some early military successes and links to Parisian politicians, he was named commander of the French army in Italy in 1796.

Bonaparte's astounding success in the Italian campaigns of 1796–1797 launched his meteoric career. With an army of fewer than fifty thousand men, he defeated the Piedmontese and the Austrians. In quick order he established client republics dependent on his own authority; he negotiated with the Austrians himself; and he molded the army into his

Bonaparte in Egypt
This engraving, based on Antoine Jean Gros's painting Napoleon Visiting the Victims of the Plague at Jaffa *(1804), is meant to glorify Bonaparte's courage: he is not afraid to touch the victims of the plague. Yet it also signals a terrible problem in Bonaparte's campaign for domination in the western Mediterranean. He has won many battles at this moment in 1799, but he is losing the war through attrition, disease, and mounting resistance.*
National Library of Medicine, Bethesda/Visual Image Presentations.

IMPORTANT DATES

1787 Dutch Patriot revolt is stifled by Prussian invasion

1788 Beginning of resistance of Austrian Netherlands against reforms of Joseph II; opening of reform parliament in Poland

1789 French Revolution begins

1790 Internal divisions lead to collapse of resistance in Austrian Netherlands

1791 Beginning of slave revolt in St. Domingue (Haiti)

1792 Beginning of war between France and the rest of Europe; second revolution of August 10 overthrows monarchy

1793 Second Partition of Poland by Austria and Russia; Louis XVI of France executed for treason

1794 France annexes the Austrian Netherlands; abolition of slavery in French colonies; Robespierre's government by terror falls

1795 Third (final) Partition of Poland

1797–1798 Creation of "sister" republics in Italian states and Switzerland

1799 Napoleon Bonaparte comes to power in a coup that effectively ends the French Revolution

personal force by paying the soldiers in cash taken as tribute from the newly conquered territories. He mollified the Directory government by sending home wagonloads of great Italian masterpieces of art, which were added to Parisian museum collections after being paraded in victory festivals. (Most are still there.) Even the failures of the Egyptian campaign did not dull his luster. Bonaparte had taken France's leading scientists with him on the expedition, and his soldiers had discovered a slab of black basalt dating from 196 B.C. written in both hieroglyphic and Greek. Called the *Rosetta stone* after a nearby town, it enabled scholars to finally decipher the hieroglyphs used by the ancient Egyptians. When his army was pinned down after its initial successes, Napoleon slipped out of Egypt and made his way secretly across the Mediterranean to southern France.

In October 1799, Bonaparte arrived home at just the right moment. The war in Europe was going badly; the departments of the former Austrian Netherlands had revolted against new conscription laws; deserters swelled the ranks of the rebels in

western France; a royalist army had tried to take the city of Toulouse in the southwest; and many government leaders wanted to revise the Constitution of 1795. Amidst increasing political instability, generals in the field had become virtually independent, and the troops felt more loyal to their units and generals than to the republic. As one army captain wrote, "In a conquering people the military spirit must prevail over other social conditions." Its victories had made the army a parallel and rival force to the state.

Disillusioned members of the government saw in Bonaparte's return an occasion to overturn the Constitution of 1795. On November 9, 1799 (18 Brumaire, Year VIII by the revolutionary calendar), the conspirators persuaded the legislature to move out of Paris to avoid an imaginary Jacobin plot. But when Bonaparte marched into the meeting hall the next day and demanded changes in the Constitution, he was greeted by cries of "Down with the dictator." His quick-thinking brother Lucien, president of the Council of Five Hundred (the lower house), saved Bonaparte's coup by summoning troops guarding the hall and claiming that the deputies had tried to assassinate the popular general. The soldiers ejected the deputies, and a hastily assembled rump legislature voted to abolish the Directory and establish a new three-man executive called the consulate. Bonaparte became First Consul, a title revived from the ancient Roman republic.

Shortly after the coup, a new constitution was submitted to the voters. Millions abstained from voting, and the government falsified the results to give an appearance of even greater support to the new regime. Altogether it was an unpromising beginning; yet within five years Bonaparte would crown himself Napoleon I, emperor of the French. A new order would rise from the ashes of the republic, and the French armies would recover from their reverses of 1799 to push the frontiers of French influence even farther eastward.

Conclusion

In 1799, no one knew what course Napoleon Bonaparte would follow. Inside France, political apathy had overtaken the original enthusiasm for revolutionary ideals. Yet the political landscape had been permanently altered by the revolutionary cataclysm.

MAPPING THE WEST Europe in 1800

France's expansion during the revolutionary wars threatened to upset the balance of power in Europe. A century earlier the English and Dutch had allied and formed a Europe-wide coalition to check the territorial ambitions of Louis XIV. Thwarting French ambitions after 1800 would prove to be even more of a challenge to the other European powers. The Dutch had been reduced to satellite status, as had most of the Italian states. After 1800, even Austria and Prussia would suffer devastating losses to the French on the battlefield. Only a new coalition of European powers could stop France in the future.

Between 1789 and 1799, monarchy as a form of government had given way to a republic whose leaders were elected. Aristocracy based on rank and birth had been undermined in favor of civil equality and the promotion of merit. The people who marched in demonstrations, met in clubs, and, in the case of men, voted in national elections for the first time had insisted that government respond to them. Thousands of men had held elective office.

A revolutionary government had tried to teach new values with a refashioned calendar, state festivals, and a civic religion. Its example would inspire future revolutionaries.

But the French Revolution also had its darker side. The divisions created by the Revolution within France endured in many cases until after World War II. Even now, French public-opinion surveys ask if it was right to execute the king in 1793 (most believe Louis XVI was guilty of treason but should not have been executed). The revolutionaries proclaimed human rights and democratic government as a universal goal, but they also explicitly excluded women, even though they admitted Protestant, Jewish, and eventually black men. They used the new spirit of national pride to inspire armies that conquered other peoples. Their ideals of universal education, religious toleration, and democratic participation could not prevent the institution of new forms of government terror to persecute, imprison, and kill dissidents. These paradoxes created an opening for Napoleon Bonaparte, who rushed in with his remarkable military and political skills to push France—and with it all of Europe—in new directions.

Suggested References

The Revolutionary Wave, 1787–1789

In the 1950s and 1960s, historians debated vehemently about whether the French Revolution should be considered part of a more general phenomenon of Atlantic revolutions, as R. R. Palmer argues. Recent work on the Dutch Republic and the Austrian Netherlands has developed nuanced comparisons that show both similarities with and differences from the French Revolution. Historians of France have focused more single-mindedly on the French origins of revolution. The most influential book on the meaning of the French Revolution is still the classic study of Tocqueville, who insisted that the Revolution continued the process of state centralization undertaken by the monarchy.

*Baker, Keith Michael, ed. *The Old Regime and the French Revolution.* University of Chicago Readings in Western Civilization, vol. 7. 1987.

Chartier, Roger. *The Cultural Origins of the French Revolution.* Trans. Lydia G. Cochrane. 1991.

Lefebvre, Georges. *The Coming of the French Revolution.* Trans. with a new preface, R. R. Palmer. 1989.

Palmer, R. R. *The Age of the Democratic Revolution: A Political History of Europe and America, 1760–1800.* Vol. 2, *The Struggle.* 1964.

Polasky, Janet L. *Revolution in Brussels, 1787–1793.* 1987.

Te Brake, Wayne. *Regents and Rebels: The Revolutionary World of an Eighteenth-Century Dutch City.* 1989.

Tocqueville, Alexis de. *The Old Regime and the French Revolution.* Trans. Stuart Gilbert. 1955. Originally published 1856.

From Monarchy to Republic, 1789–1793

From 1789 onward, commentators on the French Revolution have differed over its meaning: was it a revolution for human rights and democracy (the positions of Paine and Wollstonecraft) or a dangerous experiment in implementing reason and destroying religion and tradition (Burke and Tocqueville)? The collections edited by Blanning and Kates sample some of the newer versions of these enduring controversies. Among the most important additions to the debate have been new works on women, Jews, Protestants, and slaves.

Blanning, T. C. W., ed. *The French Revolution: Class War or Culture Clash?* 2nd ed. 1998.

*Hunt, Lynn, ed. *The French Revolution and Human Rights: A Brief Documentary History.* 1996.

Images of the French Revolution: http://chnm.gmu.edu/revolution.

Kates, Gary, ed. *The French Revolution: Recent Debates and New Controversies.* 1998.

*Levy, Darline Gay, Harriet Branson Applewhite, and Mary Durham Johnson, eds. *Women in Revolutionary Paris, 1789–1795.* 1979.

Schama, Simon. *Citizens: A Chronicle of the French Revolution.* 1989.

Two Classics of the French Revolution: Reflections on the Revolution in France (*Edmund Burke*) *and* The Rights of Man (*Thomas Paine*). 1973.

*Wollstonecraft, Mary. *A Vindication of the Rights of Woman.* Ed. Miriam Brody. 1992.

The Terror and the Republic of Virtue

The most controversial episode in the French Revolution has not surprisingly provoked conflicting interpretations. Soboul offers the Marxist interpretation, which Furet specifically opposes. Very recently interest has shifted from these broader interpretive issues back to the principal actors themselves: Robespierre, the Jacobins, and women's clubs have all attracted scholarly attention.

Desan, Suzanne. *Reclaiming the Sacred: Lay Religion and Popular Politics in Revolutionary France.* 1990.

Furet, François. *Interpreting the French Revolution.* Trans. Elborg Forster. 1981.

Godineau, Dominique. *The Women of Paris and Their French Revolution.* Trans. Katherine Streip. 1998.

Haydon, Colin, and William Doyle, eds. *Robespierre.* 1999.

Higonnet, Patrice L. R. *Goodness beyond Virtue: Jacobins during the French Revolution.* 1998.

*Primary sources.

Hunt, Lynn. *Politics, Culture, and Class in the French Revolution.* 1984.

Palmer, R. R. *Twelve Who Ruled: The Year of the Terror in the French Revolution.* 1989.

Soboul, Albert. *The Sans-Culottes: The Popular Movement and Revolutionary Government, 1793–1794.* Trans. Remy Inglis Hall. 1980.

Sutherland, D. M. G. *France, 1789–1815: Revolution and Counterrevolution.* 1986.

Revolution on the March

In the past, controversy about the Revolution in France raged while its influence on other places was relatively neglected. This imbalance is now being redressed in studies of the colonies and the impact of the revolutionary wars on areas from Egypt to Ireland. Recent work pays close attention to the social background of soldiers as well as their experiences in warfare.

Beaucour, Fernand Emile, Yves Laissus, and Chantal Orgogozo. *The Discovery of Egypt.* Trans. Bambi Ballard. 1990.

Blackburn, Robin. *The Overthrow of Colonial Slavery, 1776–1848.* 1988.

Blanning, T. C. W. *The French Revolutionary Wars, 1787–1802.* 1996.

Elliot, Marianne. *Partners in Revolution: The United Irishmen and France.* 1982.

Forrest, Alan I. *The Soldiers of the French Revolution.* 1990.

James, C. L. R. *Black Jacobins: Toussaint L'Ouverture and the San Domingo Revolution*, 2nd ed. 1989.

CHAPTER
21

Napoleon and the Revolutionary Legacy

1800–1830

Napoleon as Military Hero
In this painting from 1800–1801,
Napoleon Crossing the Alps at
St. Bernard, *Jacques-Louis David
reminds the French of Napoleon's
heroic military exploits. Napoleon
is a picture of calm and composure while his horse shows the
fright and energy of the moment.
David painted this propagandistic
image shortly after one of his
former students went to the
guillotine on a trumped-up charge
of plotting to assassinate the
new French leader. The former
organizer of republican festivals
during the Terror had become
a kind of court painter for the
new regime.*
© Photo RMN/Herve Lewandowski.

I N HER NOVEL *FRANKENSTEIN* (1818), the prototype for modern
thrillers, Mary Shelley tells the story of a Swiss technological genius who creates a humanlike monster in his pursuit of scientific
knowledge. The monster, "so scaring and unearthly in his ugliness," ter-
rifies all who encounter him and ends by destroying Dr. Frankenstein's
own loved ones. Despite desperate chases across deserts and frozen landscapes, Frankenstein never manages to trap the monster, who is last seen
hunched over his creator's deathbed.

Frankenstein's monster can be taken as a particularly horrifying
incarnation of the fears of the postrevolutionary era, but just what did
Shelley intend? Did the monster represent the French Revolution, which
had devoured its own children in the Terror? Shelley was the daughter
of Mary Wollstonecraft, an English feminist who had defended the
French Revolution and died in childbirth when Mary was born. Did the
monster stand for the dangerous possibilities that might be unleashed
by science and industry in the new age of industrial growth? She was
also the wife of the romantic poet Percy Bysshe Shelley, who often wrote
against the ugliness of contemporary life and celebrated nature and the
"beautiful idealisms of moral excellence." Whatever the meaning—and
Mary Shelley may well have intended more than one—the novel makes
the forceful point that humans cannot always control their own creations. The Enlightenment and the French Revolution had celebrated the
virtues of human creativity, but Shelley shows that innovation often has
a dark and uncontrollable side.

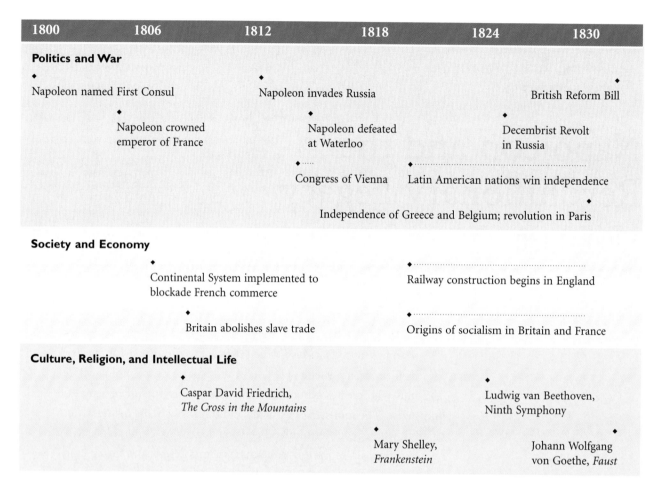

1800	1806	1812	1818	1824	1830

Politics and War

Napoleon named First Consul

Napoleon crowned emperor of France

Napoleon invades Russia

Napoleon defeated at Waterloo

Congress of Vienna

British Reform Bill

Decembrist Revolt in Russia

Latin American nations win independence

Independence of Greece and Belgium; revolution in Paris

Society and Economy

Continental System implemented to blockade French commerce

Britain abolishes slave trade

Railway construction begins in England

Origins of socialism in Britain and France

Culture, Religion, and Intellectual Life

Caspar David Friedrich, *The Cross in the Mountains*

Mary Shelley, *Frankenstein*

Ludwig van Beethoven, Ninth Symphony

Johann Wolfgang von Goethe, *Faust*

Those who witnessed Napoleon Bonaparte's stunning rise to European dominance after 1800 might have cast him as either Frankenstein or his monster. Though short and physically unimpressive, like the scientist Frankenstein, Bonaparte created something dramatically new: the French Empire with himself as emperor. Like the former kings of France, he ruled under his first name. This Corsican artillery officer who spoke French with an Italian accent ended the French Revolution even while maintaining some of its most important innovations. Bonaparte transformed France from a democratically elected republic to an empire with a new aristocracy based on military service. But he kept the revolutionary administration and most of its laws that ensured equal treatment to all citizens. Although he tolerated no opposition at home, he prided himself on bringing French-style changes to peoples elsewhere.

Bonaparte continued the revolutionary policy of conquest and annexation until it reached grotesque dimensions. His foreign policies made many see him as a monster hungry for dominion; he turned the sister republics of the revolutionary era into kingdoms personally ruled by his relatives, and he exacted tribute from subject peoples wherever he triumphed. Eventually resistance to the French armies and the ever-mounting costs of military glory toppled Napoleon. The powers allied against him met and agreed to restore the monarchical governments that had been overthrown by the French, shrink France back to its prerevolutionary boundaries, and maintain this settlement against future demands for change.

Although the people of Europe longed for peace and stability in the aftermath of the Napoleonic whirlwind, they lived in a world that was deeply unsettled by two parallel revolutions: the Industrial

Revolution and the French Revolution. The Industrial Revolution spread from Great Britain to the continent in the early 1800s in the form of factories and railroads. Even those who resisted the impact of the French Revolution with its Napoleonic sequel had to confront the underlying changes in social and economic structures that resulted from industrialization. These changes inevitably reinforced the legacy of the French Revolution, which included equality before the law, religious toleration, and, eventually, nationalism. Profoundly affected by French military occupation, many peoples organized to demand ethnic and cultural autonomy, first from Napoleon and then from the restored governments after 1815. Alongside nationalism, other new ideologies such as liberalism and socialism emerged under the impact of the Industrial and French Revolutions. These offered their adherents a doctrine that explained social change and advocated political transformation. In 1830, the development of liberalism, socialism, and nationalism shocked Europe with a new round of revolutions in France, Belgium, Poland, and some of the Italian states. By then the spread of industry, the growing awareness of social problems, and aspirations for national self-determination had reinvigorated the force of the revolutionary legacy.

❖ From Consulate to Empire: The Napoleonic State

When Napoleon Bonaparte came to power in 1799, his coup d'état appeared to be just the latest in a long line of upheavals in revolutionary France. Within the year, however, he had effectively ended the French Revolution and set France on a new course toward an authoritarian state. As emperor after 1804, he dreamed of European integration in the tradition of Augustus and Charlemagne, but he also mastered the details of practical administration. To achieve his goals, he compromised with the Catholic church and with exiled aristocrats willing to return to France. His most enduring accomplishment, the new Civil Code, tempered the principles of the Enlightenment and the Revolution with an insistence on the powers of fathers over children, husbands over wives, and employers over workers.

His influence spread into many spheres as he personally patronized scientific inquiry and encouraged artistic styles in line with his vision of imperial greatness.

The End of the French Republic

Napoleon had no long-range plans to establish himself as emperor and conquer most of Europe. Yet by seizing every opportunity, he first gained control over the new French government and then eliminated the republic and put an empire in its place. The deputies of the legislature who engineered the coup d'état of November 1799 picked him as one of three provisional consuls (the title drew on the ancient Roman precedent) only because he was a

Francisco de Goya, *The Colossus* (1808–1812)
The Spanish painter Goya might be imagined as capturing Frankenstein's monster or Napoleon himself as the new giant overwhelming much of Europe. Goya painted for the Spanish court before Napoleon invaded and occupied the country; after an illness left him deaf, he turned toward darkly imaginative works such as this one.
Museo del Prado, Madrid.

Napoleon's Coronation as Emperor
In The Coronation of Napoleon and Josephine *(1805–1807), Jacques-Louis David shows Napoleon crowning his wife at the ceremony of 1804. Napoleon orchestrated the entire event and took the only active role in it: Pope Pius VII gave his blessing to the ceremony, but Napoleon crowned himself.*
Scala/Art Resource, NY.

famous general. Napoleon immediately asserted his leadership over the other two consuls in the process of drafting another constitution—the fourth since 1789 and the third for the republic established in 1792.

Toward Empire. The constitution of 1799 made Napoleon the First Consul with the right to pick the Council of State, which drew up all laws. He quickly exerted control by choosing men loyal to him. Government was no longer representative in any real sense: the new constitution eliminated direct elections for deputies and granted no independent powers to the three houses of the legislature. Napoleon and his advisers chose the legislature's members out of a small pool of "notables." Almost all men over twenty-one could vote in the plebiscite (referendum) to approve the constitution, but their only option was to choose Yes or No.

Napoleon's most urgent task was to reconcile to his regime Catholics who had been alienated by revolutionary policies. Although nominally Catholic, Napoleon held no deep religious convictions. "How can there be order in the state without religion?" he asked cynically. "When a man is dying of hunger beside another who is stuffing himself, he cannot accept this difference if there is not an authority who tells him: 'God wishes it so.'" In 1801, a concordat with Pope Pius VII (r. 1800–1823) ended a decade of church-state conflict. The pope validated all sales of church lands, and the government agreed to pay the salaries of bishops and priests who would swear loyalty to the state. Catholicism was officially recognized as the religion of "the great majority of French citizens." (The state also paid Protestant pastors' salaries.) The pope thus brought the huge French Catholic population back into the fold and Napoleon gained the pope's support for his regime.

Napoleon continued the centralization of state power that had begun under the absolutist monarchy of Louis XIV and resumed under the Terror. As First Consul he appointed prefects who directly supervised local affairs in every *département*, or region. He created the Bank of France to facilitate government borrowing and relied on gold and silver coinage rather than paper money. He made good use of budgets and improved tax collection, but he also frequently made ends meet by exacting tribute from the territories he conquered. The government directly managed every aspect of education: at the new *lycées*, the state-run secondary schools for boys from better-off families, students wore military uniforms, and drumrolls signaled the beginning and end of classes. (Without the military trappings, the lycées are now coeducational and still the heart of the French educational system.) Napoleon took little interest in girls' education, believing that they should spend most of their time at home learning religion, manners, and such "female occupations" as sewing and music.

Napoleon promised order and an end to the upheavals of ten years of revolutionary turmoil, but his regime severely limited political expression. He never relied on mass executions to achieve control, but he refused to allow those who opposed him to meet in clubs, influence elections, or publish newspapers. A decree reduced the number of newspapers in Paris from seventy-three to thirteen (and then finally to four), and the newspapers that remained became government organs. Government censors had to approve all operas and plays, and they banned "offensive" artistic works even more frequently than their royal predecessors. The minister of police, Joseph Fouché, once a leading figure in the Terror of 1793–1794, could impose house arrest, arbitrary imprisonment, and surveillance of political dissidents. Political contest and debate shriveled to almost nothing. When a bomb attack on Napoleon's carriage failed in 1800, Fouché suppressed the evidence of a royalist plot and instead arrested hundreds of former Jacobins. More than one hundred of them were deported and seven hundred imprisoned.

Napoleon feared the influence of fervent supporters of the republic more than that of supporters of the monarchy. In 1802, his intentions became clear: he planned to eliminate the republic. He named himself First Consul for life, and in 1804,

Empire Style
Philibert-Louis Debucourt made a reputation with paintings and engravings of everyday life such as this one, Frascati Café. Napoleon admired neoclassicism, and its influence can be seen in the Greek columns and archways of the room as well as in the high empire waists of the women's dresses. Note that some men now wear pantaloons—the forebears of modern trousers—rather than the knee breeches of the Old Regime aristocracy.
The Metropolitan Museum of Art, Harris Brisbane Dick Fund, 1935. (35.100.31)

with the pope's blessing, he crowned himself emperor. Once again, plebiscites approved his decisions, but no alternatives were offered.

The Civil Code.   This was government from the top down, yet it was government based on law. The revolutionary governments had tried to unify and standardize France's multiple legal codes, but only Napoleon successfully established a new one, partly because he personally presided over the commission that drafted the new Civil Code, completed in 1804. Called the Napoleonic Code as a way of further exalting his image, it defined and assured property rights, guaranteed religious liberty, and established a uniform system of law that provided equal treatment for all adult males and affirmed the right of men to choose their professions.

The code sharply curtailed women's rights in almost every aspect of public and private life. Napoleon wanted to restrict women to the private sphere of the home. One of his leading jurists remarked, "There have been many discussions on the equality and superiority of the sexes. Nothing is more useless than such disputes. . . . Women need protection because they are weaker; men are free because they are stronger." The law obligated a husband to support his wife, but he alone controlled any property held in common; a wife could not sue in court, sell or mortgage her own property, or contract a debt without her husband's consent.

The Civil Code modified even those few revolutionary laws that had been favorable to women and in some instances denied women rights they had had under the monarchy. Divorce was still possible but severely restricted, especially for women. Adultery was an acceptable grounds for divorce, but the law considered a wife's infidelity more reprehensible than a husband's. A wife could petition for divorce only if her husband brought his mistress to live in the family home. In contrast, a wife convicted of adultery could be imprisoned for up to two years. The code's framers saw these discrepancies as a way to reinforce the family and make women responsible for private virtue, while leaving public decisions to men. The French code was imitated in many European and Latin American countries and the French colony of Louisiana, where it had a similar negative effect on women's rights. Not until 1965 did French wives gain legal status equal to that of their husbands.

Imperial Rule

Napoleon's charismatic personality dominated the new regime. He worked hard at establishing his reputation as an efficient administrator with broad intellectual interests: he met frequently with scientists, jurists, and artists, and stories abounded of his unflagging energy. He set an example by rising at 2:00 A.M., after only four or five hours' sleep, and working for three hours before going back to bed from 5:00 to 7:00 A.M. When not on military campaigns, he worked on state affairs, usually until 10:00 P.M., taking only a few minutes for each meal. "Authority," declared his adviser Sieyès, "must come from above and confidence from below."

As emperor, Napoleon cultivated personal symbolism to enhance his image as a hero. His face and name adorned coins, engravings, histories, paintings, and public monuments. His favorite painters embellished his legend by depicting him as a warrior-hero of mythic proportions. In his imperial court, Napoleon staged his entrances carefully to maximize his personal presence: his wife and courtiers were dressed in regal finery, and he was announced with great pomp—but he usually arrived dressed in a simple military uniform with no medals.

Believing that "what is big is always beautiful," Napoleon embarked on ostentatious building projects that would outshine even those of Louis XIV. Government-commissioned architects built the Arc de Triomphe, the Stock Exchange, fountains, and even slaughterhouses. Most of his new construction reflected his neoclassical taste for monumental buildings set in vast empty spaces. Old, winding streets with their cramped houses were demolished to make way for Napoleon's grand designs.

Despite appearances, Napoleon did not rule alone. Among his most trusted officials were men who had served with him in Italy and Egypt. His chief of staff Alexandre Berthier, for example, became minister of war, and the chemist Claude Berthollet, who had organized the scientific part of the expedition to Egypt, became vice president of the Senate in 1804. Napoleon's bureaucracy was based on a patron-client relationship, with Napoleon as the ultimate patron. Some of Napoleon's closest associates married into his family.

Napoleon reinstituted a social hierarchy in France by rewarding merit and talent, regardless of social origins. He used the Senate to dispense his patronage and personally chose as senators the nation's most illustrious generals, ministers, prefects, scientists, rich men, and former nobles. Intending to replace both the old nobility of birth and the republic's strict emphasis on equality, in 1802 he took the first step toward creating a new nobility by founding a Legion of Honor. (Members of the legion received lifetime pensions along with their titles.) Napoleon usually equated honor with military success. By 1814, the legion had 32,000 members, only 5 percent of them civilians.

In 1808, Napoleon introduced a complete hierarchy of noble titles, ranging from princes down to barons and chevaliers. All Napoleonic nobles had served the state. Titles could be inherited but had to be supported by wealth—a man could not be a duke without a fortune of 200,000 francs, or a chevalier without 3,000 francs. To go along with their new titles, Napoleon gave his favorite generals huge fortunes, often in the form of estates in the conquered territories.

Napoleon's own family reaped the greatest benefits. He made his older brother, Joseph, ruler of the newly established kingdom of Naples in 1806, the same year he installed his younger brother Louis as king of Holland. He proclaimed his twenty-three-year-old stepson Eugène de Beauharnais viceroy of Italy in 1805 and established his sister Caroline and brother-in-law General Murat as king and queen of Naples in 1808 when he moved Joseph to the throne of Spain. Napoleon wanted to establish an imperial

succession, but he lacked an heir. In thirteen years of marriage, his wife Josephine had borne no children, so in 1809 he divorced her and in 1810 married the eighteen-year-old Princess Marie-Louise of Austria. The next year she gave birth to a son to whom Napoleon immediately gave the title king of Rome.

The New Paternalism

Since Napoleon shared the rewards of rule with his own family, it is perhaps not surprising that he brought a familial model of power to his empire, instilling his personal version of paternalism. The Civil Code not only reasserted the Old Regime's patriarchal system of male domination over women but also insisted on a father's control over his children, which revolutionary legislation had limited. For example, if children under age sixteen refused to follow their fathers' commands, they could be sent to prison for up to a month with no hearing of any sort. At the same time, the code required fathers to provide for their children's welfare. Napoleon himself encouraged the foundation of private charities to help indigent mothers, and one of his decrees made it easier for women to abandon their children anonymously to a government foundling hospital. Napoleon hoped such measures would discourage abortion and infanticide, especially among the poorest classes in the fast-growing urban areas.

In periods of economic crisis the government opened soup kitchens, but in time-honored fashion it also arrested beggars and sent them to newly established workhouses. The state also intervened in prostitutes' lives. Migration from the countryside and wartime upheavals had caused a surge of prostitution in French cities. The authorities arrested prostitutes who worked on their own, but they tolerated brothels, which could be supervised by the police, and required the women in them to have monthly medical examinations for venereal disease.

The new paternalism extended to relations between employers and employees. The state required all workers to carry a work card attesting to their good conduct, and it prohibited all workers' organizations. The police considered workers without cards as vagrants or criminals and could send them to workhouses or prison. After 1806, arbitration boards settled labor disputes, but they took

Medal of the Legion of Honor
"Men are led through baubles," Napoleon once remarked, but "a little cash does not hurt." He gave this medal to members of the Legion of Honor and added a small pension. Never missing an occasion to glorify his own image, Napoleon had his portrait installed in the center of the star and garland.
© Photo Musée de L'Armee, Paris.

employers at their word while treating workers as minors, demanding that foremen and shop superintendents represent them. Occasionally strikes broke out, led by secret, illegal journeymen's associations, yet many employers laid off employees when times were hard, deducted fines from their wages, and dismissed them without appeal for being absent or making errors. These limitations on workers' rights won Napoleon the support of French business.

Patronage of Science and Intellectual Life

Napoleon did everything possible to promote French scientific inquiry, especially that which could serve practical ends. (See "Did You Know?," page 771.) He closely monitored the research institutes established during the Revolution, sometimes intervening personally to achieve political conformity. An impressive outpouring of new theoretical and practical scientific work rewarded the state's efforts. Experiments with balloons led to the discovery of laws about the expansion of gases, and research on fossil shells prepared the way for new theories of evolutionary change later in the nineteenth century. The surgeon Dominique-Jean Larrey developed new techniques of battlefield amputation and medical care during Napoleon's wars, winning an appointment as an officer in the Legion of Honor and becoming a baron with a pension.

Napoleon had his own forward-looking vision for modernizing French society through science and central administration, but to maintain his control he stifled dissent. Napoleon considered most writers useless or dangerous, "good for nothing under any government." Some of the most talented French writers of the time had to live in exile. The best-known expatriate was Germaine de Staël (1766–1817), known as Madame de Staël, the daughter of Louis XVI's chief minister Jacques Necker. When explaining his desire to banish her, Napoleon exclaimed, "She is a machine in motion who stirs up the salons." While exiled in the German states, Madame de Staël wrote a novel, *Corinne* (1807), whose heroine is a brilliant woman thwarted by a patriarchal system, and *On Germany* (1810), an account of the important new literary currents east of the Rhine. Her books were banned in France.

Although Napoleon restored the strong authority of state and religion in France, many royalists and

Germaine de Staël
One of the most fascinating intellectuals of her time, Anne-Louise Germaine de Staël seemed to irritate Napoleon more than any other person did. Daughter of Louis XVI's Swiss Protestant finance minister, Jacques Necker, and wife of a Swedish diplomat, Madame de Staël frequently criticized Napoleon's regime. She published best-selling novels and influential literary criticism and whenever allowed to reside in Paris she encouraged the intellectual and political dissidents from Napoleon's regime.
Photographie Bulloz.

Catholics still criticized him as an impious usurper. (See "Contrasting Views," page 778.) François-René de Chateaubriand (1768–1848) admired Napoleon as "the strong man who has saved us from the abyss," but he preferred monarchy. In his view, Napoleon had not properly understood the need to defend Christian values against the Enlightenment's excessive reliance on reason. Chateaubriand wrote his *Genius of Christianity* (1802) to draw attention to the power and mystery of faith. He warned, "It is to the vanity of knowledge that we owe almost all our misfortunes. . . . The learned ages have always been followed by ages of destruction."

How the Orient Became Oriental

As a result of Napoleon's expedition to conquer Egypt in 1798, Europeans began to study systematically what they named "the Orient" (from *oriēns*, Latin for "rising sun"), meaning the lands east of Europe. Napoleon took with him 151 French scientific experts in everything from architecture to mineralogy. Their mission was to discover and record the natural and human history of Egypt. While some set up the Institute of Egypt in Cairo to conduct scientific experiments, others traveled with army units, collecting information and data on Egypt.

Of course, Europeans had visited the Middle East before, but they had never so rigorously studied its cultures. Although Napoleon's occupation of Egypt eventually failed, enthusiasm for "Orientalism" spread far and wide; scholarly societies set up professorships and periodicals dedicated to Oriental studies, and before long romantic poets, novelists, and painters flocked to North Africa and the Middle East in search of new themes for their work.

Europeans viewed the Orient as exotic but also backward. In the introduction to the twenty-three-volume *Description of Egypt* published by French scholars of the Institute of Egypt between 1809 and 1828, Jean-Baptiste Fourier wrote, "Napoleon wanted to offer a useful European example to the Orient, and finally also to make the inhabitants' lives more pleasant, as well as to procure for them all the advantages of a perfect civilization." According to Fourier, "This country [Egypt], which has transmitted its knowledge to so many nations, today is plunged into barbarism." Civilization vs. barbarism; advancement vs. backwardness, science vs. superstition: before long Europeans had set up a series of mutually reinforcing categories to distinguish their culture from that of the Orient. It is probably fair to say that Orientalism led to much new knowledge but also to many unpleasant stereotypes of non-Western peoples and cultures.

It is important to remember, moreover, that *West* and *East* are relative terms; they can be defined only in relation to each other. Americans sometimes call Japan, for instance, the "Far East," following European usage, but it is closest to the western, not the eastern, half of the United States. For Japan, in fact, the United States is the "Far East."

Source: Edward W. Said, *Orientalism* (New York: Pantheon Books, 1978), quote from page 85.

Eugène Delacroix, *The Death of Sardanapalus* (1826–1827)
All of the exoticism, violence, and erotic imagery of the East are on view in this romantic painting that aims to recapture a moment in ancient history when the Assyrian king Sardanapalus first killed his harem before killing himself. Delacroix was presumably influenced by a play by Byron on the subject, though Delacroix's rendition is much less favorable to the king than Byron's.
© Photo RMN/Herve Lewandowski.

❖ "Europe Was at My Feet": Napoleon's Conquests

Napoleon left an indelible stamp on French institutions and political life, yet his fame and much of his power rested on his military conquests. Building on innovations introduced by the republican governments before him, Napoleon revolutionized the art of war with tactics and strategy based on a highly

mobile army. By 1812, he ruled an empire more extensive than any since the time of ancient Rome (Map. 21.1). Yet that empire had already begun to crumble, and with it went Napoleon's power at home. Napoleon's empire failed because it was based on a contradiction: Napoleon tried to reduce virtually all of Europe to the status of colonial dependents when Europe had long consisted of independent states. The result, inevitably, was a great upsurge in nationalist feeling that has dominated European politics to the present.

MAP 21.1 Napoleon's Empire at Its Height, 1812

In 1812, Napoleon had at least nominal control of almost all of western Europe. Even before he made his fatal mistake of invading Russia, however, his authority had been undermined in Spain and seriously weakened in the Italian and German states. His efforts to extend French power sparked resistance almost everywhere: as Napoleon insisted on French domination, local people began to think of themselves as Italian, German, or Dutch. Thus Napoleon inadvertently laid the foundations for the nineteenth-century spread of nationalism.

Following the Wars
Louis-Léopold Boilly's Reading of the XIth and XIIth Bulletins of the Grand Army *shows ordinary people on the home front eagerly reading Napoleon's own bulletins of the army's progress.*
Collection Privée/Photo Bulloz.

The Grand Army and Its Victories, 1800–1807

Napoleon attributed his military success "three-quarters to morale" and the rest to leadership and superiority of numbers at the point of attack. Conscription provided the large numbers: 1.3 million men age twenty to twenty-four were drafted between 1800 and 1812, another million in 1813–1814. So many willingly served because the republic had taught them to identify the army with the nation. Military service was both a patriotic duty and a means of social mobility. The men who rose through the ranks to become officers were young, ambitious, and accustomed to the new ways of war. Consequently, the French army had higher morale than the armies of other powers, most of which rejected conscription as too democratic and continued to restrict their officer corps to the nobility. Only in 1813–1814 did French morale plummet, as the military tide turned against Napoleon.

When Napoleon came to power in 1799, France had been at war for almost seven years, and its military position was precarious. Desertion was rampant, and the generals competed with one another for predominance. Napoleon ended this squabbling

by uniting all the armies into one Grand Army under his personal command. By 1812, he commanded 700,000 troops; while 250,000 soldiers fought in Spain, others remained garrisoned in France. In any given battle, between 70,000 and 180,000 men, not all of them French, fought for France. Life on campaign was no picnic—ordinary soldiers slept in the rain, mud, and snow and often had to forage for food—but Napoleon nonetheless inspired almost fanatical loyalty. A brilliant strategist who carefully studied the demands of war, he outmaneuvered virtually all his opponents. He fought alongside his soldiers in some sixty battles and had nineteen horses shot from under him. One opponent said that Napoleon's presence alone was worth 50,000 men.

Napoleon had a pragmatic and direct approach to strategy: he went for the main body of the opposing army and tried to crush it in a lightning campaign. He gathered the largest possible army for one great and decisive battle and then followed with a relentless pursuit to break enemy morale altogether. His military command, like his domestic role, was personal and highly centralized. He essentially served as his own operations officer: "I alone know what I have to do," he insisted. This style worked as long as Napoleon could be on the battlefield, but he failed to train independent subordinates to take over in his absence. He also faced constant difficulties in supplying a rapidly moving army, which could not always live off the land.

One of Napoleon's greatest advantages was the lack of coordination among his enemies. Britain dominated the seas but did not want to field huge land armies. On the continent, the French republic had already set up satellites in the Netherlands and Italy, which served as a buffer against the big powers to the east, Austria, Prussia, and Russia. By maneuvering diplomatically and militarily, Napoleon could usually take these on one by one. After reorganizing the French armies in 1799, for example, Napoleon won striking victories against the Austrians at Marengo and Hohenlinden in 1800, forcing them to agree to peace terms. Once the Austrians had withdrawn, Britain agreed to the Treaty of Amiens in 1802, effectively ending hostilities on the continent. Napoleon considered the peace with Great Britain merely a truce, however, and it lasted only until 1803.

Napoleon used the breathing space not only to consolidate his position before taking up arms again but also to send an expeditionary force to St. Domingue to regain control of the island. Continuing resistance among the black population and an epidemic of yellow fever forced Napoleon to withdraw his troops from St. Domingue and abandon his plans to extend his empire to the Western Hemisphere. As part of his retreat, he sold the Louisiana Territory to the United States in 1803.

France's Retreat from America

When war resumed in Europe, the British navy once more proved its superiority by blocking an attempted French invasion and by defeating the French and their Spanish allies in a huge naval battle at Trafalgar in 1805. France lost many ships; the British lost no vessels, but their renowned admiral Lord Horatio Nelson died in the battle. On land, Napoleon remained invincible. In 1805, Austria took up arms again when Napoleon demanded that it declare neutrality in the conflict with Britain. Napoleon promptly captured 25,000 Austrian soldiers at Ulm in Bavaria in 1805. After marching on to Vienna, he again trounced the Austrians, who had been joined by their new ally, Russia. The battle of Austerlitz, often considered Napoleon's greatest victory, was fought on December 2, 1805, the first anniversary of his coronation.

After maintaining neutrality for a decade, Prussia now declared war on France. In 1806, the French promptly destroyed the Prussian army at Jena and Auerstadt. In 1807, Napoleon defeated the Russians at Friedland. Personal negotiations between Napoleon and the young tsar Alexander I (r. 1801–1825) resulted in a humiliating settlement imposed on Prussia, which paid the price for temporary reconciliation between France and Russia; the Treaties of Tilsit turned Prussian lands west of the Elbe River into the kingdom of Westphalia under Napoleon's brother Jerome, and Prussia's Polish provinces became the duchy of Warsaw. Alexander recognized Napoleon's conquests in central and western Europe and promised to help him against the British in exchange for Napoleon's support against the Turks. Neither party kept the bargain. Napoleon once again had turned the divisions among his enemies in his favor.

The Impact of French Victories

Wherever the Grand Army conquered, Napoleon's influence soon followed. By annexing some territories and setting up others as satellite kingdoms with much reduced autonomy, Napoleon attempted to colonize large parts of Europe (see Map 21.1). But even where he did not rule directly or through his relatives, his startling string of victories forced the other powers to reconsider their own methods of rule.

Rule in the Colonized Territories. Napoleon brought the disparate German and Italian states together to rule them more effectively and to exploit their resources for his own ends. In 1803, he consolidated the tiny German states by abolishing some of them and attaching them to larger units. In July 1806, he established the Confederation of the Rhine, which soon included almost all the German states except Austria and Prussia. The Holy Roman Emperor gave up his title, held since the thirteenth century, and became simply the emperor of Austria. Napoleon established three units in Italy: the territories directly annexed to France and the satellite kingdoms of Italy and Naples. Italy had not been so unified since the Roman Empire.

Napoleon forced French-style reforms on both the annexed territories, which were ruled directly from France, and the satellite kingdoms, which were usually ruled by one or another of Napoleon's relatives but with a certain autonomy. French reforms included abolishing serfdom, eliminating seigneurial dues, introducing the Napoleonic Code, suppressing monasteries, and subordinating church to state, as well as extending civil rights to Jews and other religious minorities. The experience in the kingdom of Westphalia was typical of a French satellite. When Jerome Bonaparte and his wife Catherine arrived as king and queen in 1807, they relied on French experts who worked with a hand-picked committee of Germans to write a constitution and install legal reforms. The Westphalian army had the first Jewish officers in the German states, and the army, administration, and judiciary were all opened to the middle classes. As time passed, however, the German subjects began to chafe under French rule. German officials enforced French decrees only halfheartedly, and the French army had to forbid its soldiers to frequent local taverns and shops because their presence often started fights.

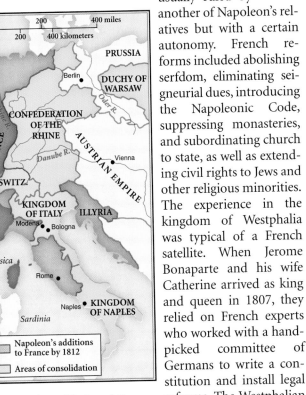

Consolidation of German and Italian States, 1812

As the example of Westphalia shows, reactions to Napoleonic innovations were mixed. Napoleon's chosen rulers often made real improvements in roads, public works, law codes, and education. The removal of internal tariffs fostered economic growth by opening up the domestic market for goods, especially textiles. By 1814, Bologna had five hundred factories and Modena four hundred. Yet almost everyone had some cause for complaint. Republicans regretted Napoleon's conversion of the sister republics into kingdoms after his coronation. Tax increases and ever-rising conscription quotas also fomented discontent. The annexed territories and satellite kingdoms paid half the French war expenses.

Almost everywhere, conflicts arose between Napoleon's desire for standardized, central government and local insistence on maintaining customs and traditions. Sometimes his own relatives sided with the countries they ruled. Napoleon's brother Louis, for instance, would not allow conscription in the Netherlands because the Dutch had never had compulsory military service. When Napoleon tried to introduce an economic policy banning trade with Great Britain, Louis's lax enforcement prompted the frustrated emperor to complain that "Holland [the leading province in the Netherlands] is an English province." In 1810, Napoleon annexed the satellite kingdom because his brother had become too sympathetic to Dutch interests.

Pressure for Reform in Prussia and Russia. Napoleon's victories forced defeated rulers to rethink their political and cultural assumptions. After the crushing defeat of Prussia in 1806 left his country much reduced in territory, Frederick William III (r. 1797–1840) appointed a reform commission, and on its recommendation he abolished serfdom and allowed nonnobles to buy and enclose land. Peasants gained their personal independence from their noble landlords, who could no longer sell them to pay gambling debts, for example, or refuse them permission to marry. Yet the lives of the former serfs remained bleak; they were left without land and their landlords no longer had to care for them in hard times. The king's advisers also overhauled the army to make the high command more efficient and to open the way to the appointment of middle-class officers. Prussia instituted these reforms to try to compete with the French, not to promote democracy. As one reformer wrote to Frederick William, "We must do from above what the French have done from below."

Reform received lip service in Russia. Tsar Alexander I had gained his throne after an aristocratic coup deposed and killed his autocratic and capricious father, Paul (r. 1796–1801), and in the early years of his reign the remorseful young ruler created Western-style ministries, lifted restrictions on importing foreign books, and founded six new universities; reform commissions studied abuses; nobles were encouraged voluntarily to free their serfs (a few actually did so); and there was even talk of drafting a constitution. But none of these efforts reached beneath the surface of Russian life, and by the second decade of his reign Alexander began to reject the Enlightenment spirit that his grandmother Catherine the Great had instilled in him.

The Continental System. The one power always standing between Napoleon and total dominance of Europe was Great Britain. The British ruled the seas and financed anyone who would oppose Napoleon. In an effort to bankrupt this "nation of shopkeepers" by choking its trade, Napoleon inaugurated the Continental System in 1806. It prohibited all commerce between Great Britain and France, as well as between Great Britain and France's dependent states and allies. At first the system worked: British exports dropped 20 percent in 1807–1808, and industrial production declined 10 percent; unemployment and a strike of 60,000 workers in northern England resulted. The British retaliated by confiscating merchandise on ships, even those of powers neutral in the wars, that sailed to or from ports from which the British were excluded by the Continental System.

In the midst of continuing wars, moreover, the system proved impossible to enforce, and widespread smuggling brought British goods into the European market. British industrial growth continued, despite some setbacks; calico-printing works, for example, quadrupled their production, and imports of raw cotton increased 40 percent. At the same time, French and other continental industries benefited from the temporary protection from British competition.

Resistance to French Rule, 1807–1812. Smuggling British goods was only one way of opposing the French. Almost everywhere in Europe, resistance began as local opposition to French demands for money or draftees, but it eventually prompted that patriotic defense of the nation known as nationalism (see page 791). In southern Italy, gangs of bandits harassed the French army and local officials; 33,000 Italian bandits were arrested in 1809 alone. But resistance continued via a network of secret societies, called the *carbonari* ("charcoal-burners"), which got its name from the practice of marking each new member's forehead with a charcoal mark. Throughout the nineteenth century the *carbonari* played a leading role in Italian nationalism. In the

German states, intellectuals wrote passionate defenses of the virtues of the German nation and of the superiority of German literature.

No nations bucked Napoleon's reins more than Spain and Portugal. In 1807, Napoleon sent 100,000 troops through Spain to invade Portugal, Great Britain's ally. The royal family fled to the Portuguese colony of Brazil, but fighting continued, aided by a British army. When Napoleon got his brother Joseph named king of Spain in place of the senile Charles IV (r. 1788–1808), the Spanish clergy and nobles raised bands of peasants to fight the French occupiers. Even Napoleon's taking personal command of the French forces failed to quell the Spanish, who for six years fought a war of national independence that pinned down thousands of French soldiers. Germaine de Staël commented that Napoleon "never understood that a war might be a crusade.... He never reckoned with the one power that no arms could overcome— the enthusiasm of a whole people."

The Spanish War for Independence, 1807–1813

More than a new feeling of nationalism was aroused in Spain. Peasants hated French requisitioning of their food supplies and sought to defend their priests against French anticlericalism. Spanish nobles feared revolutionary reforms and were willing to defend the old monarchy in the person of the young Ferdinand VII, heir to Charles IV, even while Ferdinand himself was congratulating Napoleon on his victories. The Spanish Catholic church spread anti-French propaganda that equated Napoleon with heresy. As the former archbishop of Seville wrote to the archbishop of Granada in 1808, "You realize that we must not recognize as king a free-mason, heretic, Lutheran, as are all the Bonapartes and the French nation." In this tense atmosphere, the Spanish peasant rebels, assisted by the British, countered every French massacre with atrocities of their own. They tortured their French prisoners (boiling one general alive) and lynched collaborators.

Napoleon's Mamelukes Massacre the Spanish
In one of the paintings he produced to criticize Napoleon's occupation of Spain, Second of May 1808
*at the Puerta del Sol (1814), Goya depicts the brutal suppression of the Spanish revolt in Madrid
against Napoleon. Napoleon used Mamelukes, Egyptian soldiers descended from freed Turkish slaves.
For the Spanish Christians—and for European viewers of the painting—use of these mercenaries
made the event even more horrifying. Europeans considered Muslims, and Turks in particular, as
menacing because the Europeans had been fighting them for centuries.*
Museo del Prado, Madrid.

From Russian Winter to Final Defeat, 1812–1815

Despite opposition, Napoleon ruled over an extensive empire by 1812. He controlled more territory than any European ruler had since Roman times. Only two major European states remained fully independent—Great Britain and Russia—but once allied they would successfully challenge his dominion and draw many other states to their side. Britain sent aid to the Portuguese and Spanish rebels, while Russia once again prepared for war. Tsar Alexander I made peace with Turkey and allied himself with Great Britain and Sweden. In 1812, Napoleon invaded Russia with 250,000 horses and 600,000 men, including contingents of Italians, Poles, Swiss, Dutch, and Germans. This daring move proved to be his undoing.

Invasion of Russia, 1812. Napoleon followed his usual strategy of trying to strike quickly, but the Russian generals avoided confrontation and retreated eastward, destroying anything that might be useful to the invaders. In September, on the road to Moscow, Napoleon finally engaged the main Russian force in the gigantic battle of Borodino (see Map 21.1). French casualties were 30,000 men, including 47 generals; the Russians lost 45,000. The French soldiers had nothing to celebrate around their campfires: as one soldier wrote, "Everyone . . . wept for some dead friend." Once again the Russians retreated, leaving Moscow undefended. Napoleon entered the deserted city, but the victory turned hollow because the departing Russians had set the wooden city on fire. Within a week, three-fourths of it had burned to the ground. Still Alexander refused to negotiate, and French morale plunged with

Napoleon: For and Against

Napoleon and Hitler are the two most controversial figures in all of modern Western history, and they are often compared with each other. What they shared was a desire to dominate Europe by military force, and they both came very close to achieving that goal. But they differed entirely in ideas: to take just the most important example, Napoleon offered emancipation to the Jews wherever he ruled, whereas Hitler tried to eliminate them as a group, ultimately by murdering as many as he could.

Napoleon enthralled Europe. The Prussian philosopher Georg W. F. Hegel dubbed him "world history on horseback." After his final exile, Napoleon presented himself as a martyr to the cause of liberty whose goal was to create a European "federation of free people." Few were convinced by this "gospel according to St. Helena" (Document 1). Followers such as Emmanuel de Las Cases burnished the Napoleonic legend (Document 2), but detractors such as Benjamin Constant viewed him as a tyrant (Document 3). For all his defects, Napoleon fascinated even those who were too young to understand his rise and fall. The French romantic poet Victor Hugo celebrated both the glory and the tragedy of Napoleonic ambitions (Document 4).

1. Napoleon's Own View from Exile

As might be expected, Napoleon put the most positive possible construction on his plans for France. In exile he wrote letters and talked at length to Emmanuel de Las Cases (1766–1842), an aristocratic officer in the royal navy who rallied to Napoleon in 1802, served in the Council of State, and later accompanied him to St. Helena. Much of what we know about Napoleon's views comes from a book published by Las Cases in 1821.

March 3, 1817:

In spite of all the libels, I have no fear whatever about my fame. Posterity will do me justice. The truth will be known; and the good I have done will be compared with the faults I have committed. I am not uneasy as to the result. Had I succeeded, I would have died with the reputation of the greatest man that ever existed. As it is, although I have failed, I shall be considered as an extraordinary man: my elevation was unparalleled, because unaccompanied by crime. I have fought fifty pitched battles, almost all of which I have won. I have framed and carried into effect a code of laws that will bear my name to the most distant posterity. I raised myself from nothing to be the most powerful monarch in the world. Europe was at my feet. I have always been of the opinion that the sovereignty lay in the people. In fact, the imperial government was a kind of republic. Called to the head of it by the voice of the nation, my maxim was, *la carrière est ouverte aux talents* ["careers open to talent"] without distinction of birth or fortune, and this system of equality is the reason that your oligarchy hates me so much.

Source: R. M. Johnston, *The Corsican: A Diary of Napoleon's Life in His Own Words* (Boston: Houghton Mifflin, 1921), 492.

2. Napoleon's Own History of France

Las Cases included in his book parts of a history of France that Napoleon himself had undertaken to write. Napoleon here argues that his ascent to the throne was legitimate, though he did not come from the Bourbon family of kings, and that he reconciled the old nobles to the new regime by creating a new standard of nobility in the Legion of Honor. In short, he offered something for everyone.

No prince mounted the throne with more legitimate rights than Napoleon. The throne was tendered to Hugh Capet by some bishops and some nobles; the imperial throne was given to Napoleon by the will of all the citizens, verified three times in a solemn manner. Pope Pius VII, chief of the Roman, Catholic, and Apostolic religion, the religion of the majority of Frenchmen, crossed the Alps to anoint the Emperor with his own hands, surrounded by all the bishops of France, by all the cardinals of the Roman Church, and by the deputies of all the cantons of the Empire. . . .

The Emperor bound up the wounds of the Revolution; all the émigrés returned and that list of proscribed persons was destroyed. The prince performed the most kindly glorious act, that of recalling to their country, and thus reestablishing, more than twenty thousand families. Their unsold property was returned to them; and wiping clean the slate of the past, he welcomed equally to all employments individuals of all the classes, whatever their conduct had been. . . . All titles were forgotten; there were no longer aristocrats or Jacobins, and the establishment of the Legion of Honor, which was the reward for military, civil, and judicial service, united side by side the soldier, the scholar, the artist, the prelate, and the magistrate; it was a symbol of reunion of all the estates, of all the parties.

Source: Emmanuel de Las Cases, *Le Mémorial de Sainte-Hélène* (Paris: Garnier Frères, n.d.) 3:430–34, translated and excerpted by David H. Pinkney, *Napoleon, Historical Enigma* (Lexington: D. C. Heath, 1969), 1–2.

3. Benjamin Constant, Spokesman for the Liberal Opposition to Napoleon

Benjamin Constant (1767–1830) came from an old French Calvinist family that had fled to Switzerland to escape persecution. Constant spent the early years of the French Revolution in a minor post at a minor German court. He moved to Paris in 1795 and became active in French politics during the Directory. Under Napoleon he went into exile, where he published a romantic novel (Adolphe, 1806) and pamphlets like this one attacking Napoleon. He reconciled to Napoleon during the Hundred Days and then opposed the restored Bourbon monarchy. In this selection, written during his exile, he expresses his hostility to Napoleon as a usurper dependent on war to maintain himself in power.

Surely, Bonaparte is a thousand times more guilty than those barbarous conquerors who, ruling over barbarians, were by no means at odds with their age. Unlike them, he has chosen barbarism; he has preferred it. In the midst of enlightenment, he has sought to bring back the night. He has chosen to transform into greedy and bloodthirsty nomads a mild and polite people: his crime lies in this premeditated intention, in his obstinate effort to rob us of the heritage of all the enlightened generations who have preceded us on this earth. But why have we given him the right to conceive such a project?

When he first arrived here, alone, out of poverty and obscurity, and until he was twenty-four, his greedy gaze wandering over the country around him, why did we show him a country in which any religious idea was the object of irony? [Constant refers here to de-Christianization during the French Revolution.] When he listened to what was professed in our circles, why did serious thinkers tell him that man had no other motivation than his own interest? . . .

[Napoleon] judged France by her own words, and the world by France as he imagined her to be. Because immediate usurpation was easy, he believed it could be durable, and once he became a usurper, he did all that usurpation condemns a usurper to do in our century.

It was necessary to stifle inside the country all intellectual life: he banished discussion and proscribed the freedom of the press.

The nation might have been stunned by that silence: he provided, extorted or paid for acclamation which sounded like the national voice. . . . War flung onto distant shores that part of the French nation that still had some real energy. It prompted the police harassment of the timid, whom it could not force abroad. It struck terror into men's hearts, and left there a certain hope that chance would take responsibility for their deliverance: a hope agreeable to fear and convenient to inertia. How many times have I heard men who were pressed to resist tyranny postponing this, during wartime till the coming of peace, and in peacetime until war commences!

I am right therefore in claiming that a usurper's sole resource is uninterrupted war. Some object:

what if Bonaparte had been pacific? Had he been pacific, he would never have lasted for twelve years. Peace would have re-established communication among the different countries of Europe. These communications would have restored to thought its means of expression. Works published abroad would have been smuggled into the country. The French would have seen that they did not enjoy the approval of the majority of Europe.

Source: Benjamin Constant, "Further Reflections on Usurpation," in *Political Writings*, trans. Biancamaria Fontana (Cambridge: Cambridge University Press, 1988), 161–63.

4. Victor Hugo, "The Two Islands," 1825

Victor Hugo (1802–1885) was France's greatest romantic poet and novelist, author of The Hunchback of Notre Dame *and* Les Misérables. *His father was a Napoleonic general, but his mother was an equally ardent royalist. In this early poem, Hugo compares Napoleon to one of Napoleon's favorite icons, the eagle, symbol of empire. The two islands of the title are Corsica, Napoleon's birthplace, and St. Helena, his place of final exile and death.*

These Isles, where Ocean's shattered spray
    Upon the ruthless rocks is cast,
Seem like two treacherous ships of prey,
    Made by eternal anchors fast.
The hand that settled bleak and black
Those shores on their unpeopled rack,
And clad in fear and mystery,
    Perchance thus made them tempest-torn,

That Bonaparte might there be born,
And that Napoleon there might die.
. . . .
He his imperial nest hath built so far and high,
He seems to us to dwell within that tranquil sky,
Where you shall never see the angry tempest break.
    'Tis but beneath his feet the growling storms are sped,
      And thunders to assault his head
Must to their highest source go back.
The bolt flew upwards: from his eyrie [nest] riven,
Blazing he falls beneath the stroke of heaven;
    Then kings their tyrant foe reward—
They chain him, living, on that lonely shore;
And earth captive giant handed o'er
    To ocean's more resistless guard.
. . . .
Shame, hate, misfortune, vengeance, curses sore,
On him let heaven and earth together pour:
    Now, see we dashed the vast Colossus low.
    May he forever rue, alive and dead,
    All tears he caused mankind to shed,
    And all the blood he caused to flow.

Source: Henry Carrington, *Translations from the Poems of Victor Hugo* (London: Walter Scott, 1885), 34–41.

QUESTIONS FOR DEBATE

1. Which of these views of Napoleon has the most lasting value as opposed to immediate dramatic effect?
2. Based on these selections, what was Napoleon's greatest accomplishment? His greatest failure?
3. Victor Hugo called Napoleon "the vast Colossus." Why did he pick this larger-than-life metaphor even when writing lines critical of Napoleon's legacy of tears and bloodshed?

---

worsening problems of supply. Weeks of constant marching in the dirt and heat had worn down the foot soldiers, who were dying of disease or deserting in large numbers.

In October Napoleon began his retreat; in November came the cold. Napoleon himself reported that on November 14 the temperature fell to −4 degrees Fahrenheit. A German soldier in the Grand Army described trying to cook fistfuls of raw bran with snow to make something like bread. For him the retreat was "the indescribable horror of all possible plagues." Within a week the Grand Army lost 30,000 horses and had to abandon most of its artillery and food supplies. Russian forces harassed the retreating army, now more pathetic than grand. By December only 100,000 troops remained, one-sixth the original number, and the retreat had turned into a rout: the Russians had captured 200,000 soldiers, including 48 generals and 3,000 other officers.

Napoleon had made a classic military mistake that would be repeated by Adolf Hitler in World War II: fighting a war on two distant fronts simultaneously. The Spanish war tied down 250,000 French troops and forced Napoleon to bully Prussia and Austria into supplying soldiers of dubious loyalty for the Moscow campaign. They deserted at the first opportunity. The fighting in Spain and Portugal also exacerbated the already substantial logistical and communications problems involved in marching to Moscow.

The End of Napoleon's Empire. Napoleon's humiliation might have been temporary if the British and Russians had not successfully organized a coalition to complete the job. Napoleon still had resources at his command; by the spring of 1813 he had replenished his army with another 250,000 men. With British financial support, Russian, Austrian, Prussian, and Swedish armies met the French outside Leipzig in October 1813 and defeated Napoleon in the Battle of the Nations. One by one, Napoleon's German allies deserted him to join the German nationalist "war of liberation." The Confederation of the Rhine dissolved, and the Dutch revolted and restored the prince of Orange. Joseph Bonaparte fled Spain, and a combined Spanish-Portuguese army under British command invaded France. In only a few months the allied powers crossed the Rhine and marched toward Paris. In March 1814, the French Senate deposed Napoleon, who abdicated when his remaining generals refused to fight. Napoleon went into exile on the island of Elba off the Italian coast. His wife Marie-Louise refused to accompany him. The allies restored to the throne Louis XVIII (r. 1814–1824), the brother of Louis XVI (whose son was known as Louis XVII even though he died in prison in 1795 without ever ruling).

Napoleon had one last chance to regain power because Louis XVIII lacked a solid base of support. The new king tried to steer a middle course through a charter that established a British-style monarchy with a two-house legislature and guaranteed civil rights. But he was caught between returning emigré nobles who demanded a complete restoration of their lands and powers and those who had supported either the republic or Napoleon during the previous twenty-five years. Sensing an opportunity, Napoleon escaped from Elba in early 1815 and, landing in southern France, made swift and unimpeded progress to Paris. Although he had left in ignominy, now crowds cheered him and former soldiers volunteered to serve him. The period known as the "Hundred Days" (the length of time between his escape and his final defeat) had begun. Louis XVIII fled across the border, waiting for help from France's enemies.

Napoleon quickly moved his reconstituted army into present-day Belgium. At first it seemed that he might succeed in separately fighting the two armies arrayed against him—a Prussian army and a joint force of Belgian, Dutch, German, and British troops led by Sir Arthur Wellesley (1769–1852), duke of Wellington. But the Prussians evaded him and joined with Wellington at Waterloo. Completely routed, Napoleon had no choice but to abdicate again. This time the victorious allies banished him permanently to the remote island of St. Helena, far off the coast of West Africa, where he died in 1821 at the age of fifty-two.

The cost of Napoleon's rule was high: 750,000 French soldiers and 400,000 others from annexed and satellite states died between 1800 and 1815. Yet no other military figure since Alexander the Great had made such an impact on world history. (See "Contrasting Views," page 778.) His plans for a united Europe, his insistence on spreading the legal reforms of the French Revolution, his social welfare programs, and even his inadvertent awakening of national sentiment set the agenda for European history in the modern era.

❖ The "Restoration" of Europe

Even while Napoleon was making his last desperate bid for power, his enemies were meeting in the Congress of Vienna (1814–1815) to decide the fate of postrevolutionary Europe. Although interrupted by the Hundred Days, the Congress of Vienna settled the boundaries of European states, determined who would rule each nation, and established a new framework for international relations based on periodic meetings, or congresses, between the major powers. This congress system, or "concert of Europe," helped prevent another major war until the 1850s, and no conflict comparable to the Napoleonic wars would occur again until 1914.

Many of Europe's rulers hoped to nullify revolutionary and Napoleonic reforms and thus

The Congress of Vienna

An unknown French engraver caricatured the efforts of the diplomats at the Congress of Vienna, complaining that they used the occasion to divide the spoils of European territory. At the far left is Metternich preparing to take Venice and Lombardy (northern Italy).
Historisches Museum der Stadt Wien.

"restore" their old regimes. Some of the returning rulers so detested French innovations that they tore French plants out of their gardens and threw French furniture out of their palaces. The most successful rulers compromised between old traditions and new ideas. Total negation of the revolutionary legacy might work for a time, but in the long run, accommodation was unavoidable.

The Congress of Vienna, 1814–1815

The Vienna settlement established a new equilibrium that relied on cooperation among the major powers while guaranteeing the status of smaller states. The revolutionary and Napoleonic wars had produced a host of potentially divisive issues. In addition to determining the boundaries of France, the congress had to decide the fate of Napoleon's duchy of Warsaw, the German province of Saxony, the Netherlands, the states once part of the confederation of the Rhine, and various Italian territories. All had either changed hands or been created during the wars. These issues were resolved by face-to-face negotiations among representatives of the five major powers: Austria, Russia, Prussia, Britain, and France. With its aim to establish a long-lasting,

negotiated peace endorsed by all parties, both winners and losers, the Congress of Vienna provided a model for the twentieth-century League of Nations and United Nations.

Austria's chief negotiator, Prince Klemens von Metternich (1773–1859), took the lead in devising the settlement. A well-educated nobleman who spoke five languages, Metternich served as a minister in the Austrian cabinet from 1809 to 1848. More than anyone else, he shaped the post-Napoleonic order. Although his penchant for womanizing made him a security risk in the eyes of the British Foreign Office (he even had an affair with Napoleon's younger sister), he worked with the British prime minister Robert Castlereagh (1769–1822) to ensure a moderate agreement that would check French aggression and yet maintain its great-power status. Metternich and Castlereagh believed that French aggression must be contained because it had threatened the European peace since the days of Louis XIV, but that France must remain a major player precisely so that no one European power might dominate the others. In this way France could help Austria and Britain counter the ambitions of Prussia and Russia. Castlereagh hoped to make Britain the arbiter of European affairs, but he knew this could be accomplished only through adroit diplomacy because the British constitutional monarchy had little in common with most of its more absolutist continental counterparts.

The task of ensuring France's status at the congress fell to Prince Charles Maurice de Talleyrand (1754–1838), an aristocrat and former bishop who had embraced the French Revolution, served as Napoleon's foreign minister, and ended as foreign minister to Louis XVIII after helping to arrange the emperor's overthrow. Informed of Talleyrand's betrayal, Napoleon called him "excrement in silk stockings." When the French army failed to oppose Napoleon's return to power in the Hundred Days, the allies took away all territory conquered since 1790 and required France to pay an indemnity and support an army of occupation until it had paid. Talleyrand nonetheless successfully argued that the restored French monarchy could succeed only if it retained its great-power status and fully participated in the negotiations.

The goal of the congress was to achieve postwar stability by establishing secure states with guaranteed borders (Map 21.2). Where possible, the

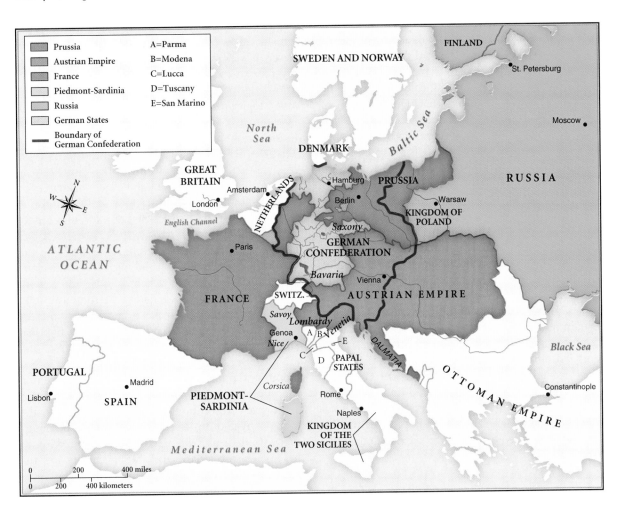

MAP 21.2 Europe after the Congress of Vienna, 1815
The diplomats meeting at the Congress of Vienna could not simply "restore" Europe to its prerevolutionary borders. Too much had changed since 1789. France was forced to return to its 1789 borders and Spain and Portugal regained their former rulers. The Austrian Netherlands and the Dutch Republic were united in a new kingdom of the Netherlands, the German states were joined in a Germanic Confederation that built upon Napoleon's Confederation of the Rhine, and Napoleon's Grand Duchy of Warsaw became the kingdom of Poland with the tsar of Russia as king.

congress simply restored traditional rulers, as in Spain and the Italian states. Where restoration was impossible, it rearranged territory to balance the competing interests of the great powers. Thus the congress turned the duchy of Warsaw into a new Polish kingdom but made the tsar of Russia its king. (Poland would not regain its independence until 1918.) The former Dutch Republic and the Austrian Netherlands, both annexed to France, now united as the new kingdom of the Netherlands under the restored stadholder. Prussia gained territory in Saxony and on the left bank of the Rhine to compensate for its losses in Poland. To make up for its losses in Poland and Saxony, Austria reclaimed the Italian provinces of Lombardy and Venetia and the Dalmatian coast. Austria now presided over the German Confederation, which replaced the defunct Holy Roman Empire and also included Prussia. The lesser powers were not forgotten. The kingdom of Piedmont-Sardinia took Genoa, Nice, and part of Savoy. Sweden obtained Norway from Denmark but had to accept Russia's conquest of Finland. Finally, various international trade issues were also resolved. At the urging of Great Britain, the congress agreed to condemn in principle the slave trade, abolished by Great Britain in 1807. In reality, however, the slave trade continued in many places until the 1840s.

To impart spiritual substance to this very calculated settlement of political affairs, Tsar Alexander proposed a Holy Alliance that would ensure divine assistance in upholding religion, peace, and justice. Prussia and Austria signed the agreement, but Great Britain refused to accede to what Castlereagh called "a piece of sublime mysticism and nonsense." Pope Pius VII also refused on the grounds that the papacy needed no help in interpreting the Christian truth. Despite the reassertion of traditional religious principle, the congress had in fact given birth to a new diplomatic order: in the future, the legitimacy of states depended on the treaty system, not on divine right.

The Emergence of Conservatism

The French Revolution and Napoleonic domination of Europe had shown contemporaries that government could be changed overnight, that the old hierarchies could be overthrown in the name of reason, and that even Christianity could be written off or at least profoundly altered with the stroke of a pen. The potential for rapid change raised many questions about the proper sources of authority. Kings and churches could be restored and former revolutionaries locked up or silenced, but the old order no longer commanded automatic obedience. The old order was now merely *old*, no longer "natural" and "timeless." It had been ousted once and therefore might fall again. People insisted on having reasons to believe in their "restored" governments. The political doctrine that justified the restoration was *conservatism*.

Conservatives benefited from the disillusionment that permeated Europe after 1815. In the eyes of most Europeans, Napoleon had become a tyrant who ruled in his own interests. Conservatives believed it was crucial to analyze the roots of such tyranny so established authorities could use their knowledge of history to prevent its recurrence. They saw a logical progression in recent history: the Enlightenment based on reason led to the French Revolution, with its bloody guillotine and horrifying Terror, which in turn spawned the authoritarian and militaristic Napoleon. Conservative intellectuals therefore either rejected Enlightenment principles or at least subjected them to scrutiny and skepticism.

The most influential spokesman of conservatism was Edmund Burke (1729–1799), the British critic of the French Revolution. He argued that the revolutionaries erred in thinking they could construct an entirely new government based on reason. Government, Burke said, had to be rooted in long experience, which evolved over generations. All change must be gradual and must respect national and historical traditions.

Like Burke, later conservatives believed that religious and other major traditions were an essential foundation for any society. Conservatives blamed the French Revolution's attack on religion on the skepticism and anticlericalism of such Enlightenment thinkers as Voltaire, and they defended both hereditary monarchy and the authority of the church, whether Catholic or Protestant. The "rights of man," according to conservatives, could not stand alone as doctrine based simply on nature and reason. The community too had its rights, more important than those of any individual, and established institutions best represented those rights. The church, the state, and the patriarchal family would provide an enduring social order for everyone. Faith, sentiment, history, and tradition must fill the vacuum left by the failures of reason and excessive belief in individual rights. Across Europe these views were taken up and elaborated by government advisers, professors, and writers. Not surprisingly, they had their strongest appeal in ruling circles and guided the politics of men such as Metternich in Austria and Alexander I in Russia.

The restored monarchy in France provided a major test for conservatism because the returning Bourbons had to confront the legacy of twenty-five years of upheaval. Louis XVIII tried to ensure a measure of continuity by maintaining Napoleon's Civil Code. He also guaranteed the rights of ownership to church lands sold during the revolutionary period and created a parliament composed of a Chamber of Peers nominated by the king and a Chamber of Deputies elected by very restricted suffrage (fewer than 100,000 voters in a population of 30 million, or about 3 percent). In making these concessions, the king tried to follow a moderate course of compromise, but the Ultras (ultraroyalists) pushed for complete repudiation of the revolutionary past. When Louis returned to power after Napoleon's final defeat, armed royalist bands attacked and murdered hundreds of Bonapartists and former revolutionaries. In 1816, the Ultras insisted on abolishing divorce and set up special courts to punish opponents of the regime. More extreme measures were to come.

The Revival of Religion

The experience of revolutionary upheaval and nearly constant warfare prompted many to renew their religious faith once peace returned. In France, the Catholic church sent missionaries to hold open-air "ceremonies of reparation" to express repentance for the outrages of revolution. In Rome, the papacy reestablished the Jesuit order, which had been disbanded during the Enlightenment. In the Italian states and Spain, governments used religious societies of laypeople to combat the influence of reformers and nationalists such as the Italian *carbonari*.

Revivalist movements, especially in Protestant countries, could on occasion challenge the status quo, not support it. In parts of Protestant Germany and Britain, religious revival had begun in the eighteenth century with the rise of Pietism and Methodism, movements that stressed individual religious

experience rather than reason as the true path to moral and social reform. The English Methodists followed John Wesley (1703–1791), who preached an emotional, morally austere, and very personal "method" of gaining salvation. The Methodists, or Wesleyans, gradually separated from the Church of England and in the early decades of the nineteenth century attracted thousands of members in huge revival meetings that lasted for days.

Shopkeepers, artisans, agricultural laborers, miners, and workers in cottage industry, both male and female, flocked to the new denomination, even though at first Methodism seemed to emphasize conservative political views: Methodist statutes of 1792 had insisted that "none of us shall either in writing or in conversation speak lightly or irreverently of the government." In their hostility to rigid doctrine and elaborate ritual and their encouragement of popular preaching, however, the Methodists fostered a sense of democratic community and even a rudimentary sexual equality. From the beginning, women preachers traveled on horseback to preach in barns, town halls, and textile dye houses. The Methodist Sunday schools that taught thousands of poor children to read and write eventually helped create greater demands for working-class political participation.

The religious revival was not limited to Europe. In the United States, the second "Great Awakening" began around 1790 with huge camp meetings that brought together thousands of worshippers and scores of evangelical preachers, many of them Methodist. (The original Great Awakening took place in the 1730s and 1740s, sparked by the preaching of George Whitefield, a young English evangelist and follower of John Wesley.) Men and women danced to exhaustion, fell into trances, and spoke in "tongues." During this period, Protestant sects began systematic missionary activity in other parts of the world, with British and American missionary societies taking the lead in the 1790s and early 1800s. In the British colony of India, for example, Protestant missionaries argued for the reform of Hindu customs. *Sati*—the burning of widows on the funeral pyres of their husbands—was abolished by the British administration of India in 1829. Missionary activity by Protestants and Catholics would become one of the arms of European imperialism and cultural influence in the nineteenth century.

❖ Forces for Social and Cultural Change

Conservatives hoped to clamp a lid on European affairs, but the lid kept threatening to fly off. In France in 1820, an assassin killed Louis XVIII's nephew, inspiring a like-minded group to try, unsuccessfully, to blow up Britain's Tory cabinet. Rapid urban growth and the spread of industry created new social tensions and inspired new political doctrines to explain the meaning of economic and social changes. These doctrines soon galvanized opponents of the conservative Vienna settlement. Cutting across and drawing on the turmoil in society and politics was romanticism, a new international movement in the arts and literature that originated in reaction to the Enlightenment in the eighteenth century and dominated artistic expression in the first half of the nineteenth.

Industrial and Urban Growth in Britain

Historians today use the term *Industrial Revolution* to describe the set of changes that brought steam-driven machinery, large factories, and a new working class first to Britain, then to the rest of Europe, and eventually to the rest of the world. French and English writers of the 1820s introduced the term to capture the drama of contemporary change and to draw a parallel with the French Revolution. But we should not take the comparison too literally. Unlike the French upheaval, the Industrial Revolution was not over in a decade. From Great Britain in the second half of the eighteenth century it spread slowly; even by the 1830s it had little effect on the continent outside of northern France, Belgium, and the Rhineland. Most Europeans were still peasants working in the old ways.

Factories and Workers. Steam-driven machines first brought workers together in factories in the textile industry. By 1830, more than one million people in Britain depended on the cotton industry for employment, and cotton cloth constituted 50 percent of the country's exports. Factories quickly sprang up in urban areas, where the growing population provided a ready source of labor. The rapid expansion of the British textile industry had as its colonial corollary the destruction of the hand manufacture of textiles in India. The British put high import duties on Indian cloth entering Britain and kept such duties very low for British cloth entering India. The figures are dramatic: in 1813, the Indian city of Calcutta exported to England £2,000,000 of cotton cloth; by 1830, Calcutta was importing from England £2,000,000 of cotton cloth. When Britain abolished slavery in its Caribbean colonies in 1833, British manufacturers began to buy raw cotton in the southern United States, where slavery still flourished. (See "Taking Measure," page 787.)

Factories drew workers from the urban population surge, which had begun in the eighteenth century and now accelerated. The reasons for urban growth are not entirely clear. The population of such new industrial cities as Manchester and Leeds increased 40 percent in the 1820s alone. Historians long thought that factory workers came from the countryside, pushed off the land by the field enclosures of the 1700s. But recent studies have shown that the number of agricultural laborers actually increased during industrialization in Britain, suggesting that a growing birthrate created a larger population and fed workers into the new factory system.

The new workers came from several sources: families of farmers who could not provide land for all their children, soldiers demobilized after the Napoleonic wars, artisans displaced by the new machinery, and children of the earliest workers who had moved to the factory towns. A system of employment that resembled family labor on farms or in cottage industry also developed in the new factories. Entire families came to toil for a single wage, although family members performed different tasks. Workdays of twelve to seventeen hours were typical, even for children, and the work was grueling. Community ties remained important as workers migrated from rural to urban areas to join friends and family from their original villages.

As urban factories grew, their workers gradually came to constitute a new socioeconomic class with a distinctive culture and traditions. Like *middle class*, the term *working class* came into use for the first time in the early nineteenth century. It referred to the laborers in the new factories. In the past, workers had labored in isolated trades: water and wood carrying, gardening, laundry, and building. In contrast, factories brought working people together with machines, under close supervision by their employers. They soon developed a sense of

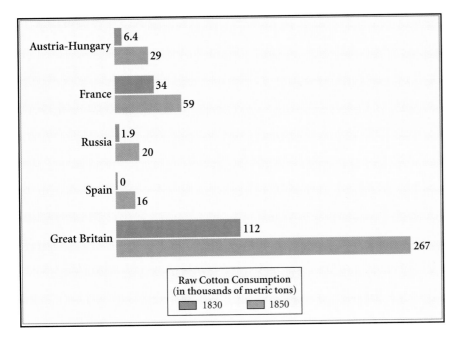

TAKING MEASURE
**Raw Cotton Consumption,
1830–1850**

The consumption of raw cotton correlates with the level of industrialization in the textile industry. Great Britain already imported more raw cotton in 1830 than any other country in Europe, and it widened the gap in the next generation. But the rate of increase was even greater in Austria-Hungary, Russia, and Spain (but not France). Can you calculate the rate of increase between 1830 and 1850?
From B. R. Mitchell, *European Historical Statistics 1750–1970* (New York: Columbia University Press, 1975), FD13.

common interests and organized societies for mutual help and political reform. From these would come the first labor unions.

The new factories and new technology threatened some people's very existence, especially in hard times. To protect livelihoods at risk from the introduction of new technology, bands of handloom weavers, fearing their displacement by machines, wrecked factory machinery and burned mills in the Midlands, Yorkshire, and Lancashire. To restore order and protect industry, the government sent in an army of twelve thousand regular soldiers and made machine wrecking punishable by death. The rioters were called *Luddites* after the fictitious figure Ned Ludd, whose signature appeared on their manifestos. (The term is still used to describe those who resist new technology.)

Other workers focused their organizing efforts on reforming Parliament, whose members were chosen in elections dominated by the landowning elite. One reformer complained that the members of the House of Commons were nothing but "toad-eaters, gamblers, public plunderers, and hirelings." Reform clubs held large open-air meetings, and ordinary people eagerly bought cheap newspapers that clamored for change. In August 1819, sixty thousand people attended an illegal meeting held in St. Peter's Fields in Manchester. When the local authorities sent the cavalry to arrest the speaker,

panic resulted; eleven people were killed and many hundreds injured. Punsters called it the Battle of Peterloo or the Peterloo Massacre. An alarmed government passed the Six Acts, which forbade large political meetings and restricted press criticism, suppressing the reform movement for a decade.

The Rise of the Railroad. Steam-driven engines were not limited to factory production. They appeared in the 1820s in a dramatic new form when the English engineer George Stephenson perfected an engine to pull wagons along rail tracks. Suddenly, railroad building became a new industry. (See "Taking Measure," page 788.) The idea of a railroad was not new: iron tracks had been used since the seventeenth century to haul coal from mines in wagons pulled by horses. A railroad system as a mode of transport, however, developed only after Stephenson's invention of a steam-powered locomotive.

New companies soon manufactured rails and laid track, with Parliament's permission. In 1830, the Liverpool and Manchester Railway line opened to the cheers of crowds and the congratulations of government officials, including the duke of Wellington, the hero of Waterloo and now prime minister. In the excitement, some of the dignitaries gathered on a parallel track. Another engine, George Stephenson's famous Rocket, approached at high speed. Most of the gentlemen scattered to safety, but

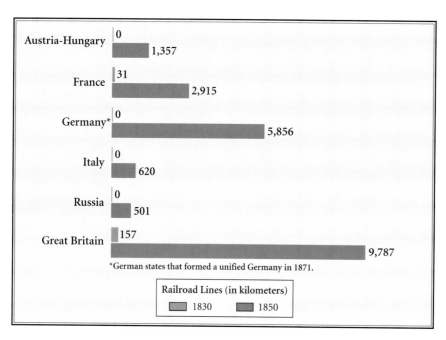

Austria-Hungary 0 / 1,357

France 31 / 2,915

Germany* 0 / 5,856

Italy 0 / 620

Russia 0 / 501

Great Britain 157 / 9,787

*German states that formed a unified Germany in 1871.

Railroad Lines (in kilometers)
1830   1850

TAKING MEASURE
Railroad Lines, 1830–1850
Great Britain quickly extended its lead in the building of railroads. The extension of commerce and, before long, the ability to wage war would depend on the development of effective railroad networks. These statistics might be taken as predicting a realignment of power within Europe after 1850. What do the numbers say about the relative position of Germany (the German states, including Prussia but excluding Austria) and Austria-Hungary and Germany and France?
From B. R. Mitchell, *European Historical Statistics* 1750–1970 (New York: Columbia University Press, 1975), F1.

former cabinet minister William Huskisson fell and was hit. In a few hours he died, the first official casualty of the newfangled railroad. Despite the tragedy, the line was an immediate success, carrying up to 110 passengers and freight in each direction. One of the many commentators described it as "a kind of miracle exhibited before my astonished eyes."

Railroads were dramatic and expensive—the most striking symbol of the new industrial age. Placed on the new tracks, steam-driven carriages could transport people and goods to the cities and link coal and iron deposits to the new factories. They gave industrialization a big push forward as every European country soon tried to set up its own railroad system.

The New Ideologies

Although traditional ways of life still prevailed in much of Europe, new modes of thinking about the changes in the social and political order arose in direct response to what some have called the "dual revolution" of the French Revolution and the Industrial Revolution. The 1820s and 1830s were an era of "isms"—conservatism, liberalism, nationalism, romanticism, and, newest on the scene, socialism. The French Revolution had caused people to

ask questions about the best possible form of government, and its effects had made clear that people acting together could change their political system. The events of the 1790s and the following decades, however, also produced enormous differences of opinion over what constituted the ideal government. Similarly, the Industrial Revolution, first in Britain and then in western Europe, posed fundamental questions about changes in society and social relations: How did the new social order differ from the earlier one, which was less urban and less driven by commercial concerns? Who should control this new order? Should governments try to moderate or accelerate the pace of change? Answers to these questions about the social and political order were called *ideologies*, a word coined during the French Revolution. An *ideology* is a coherent set of beliefs about the way a society's social and political order should be organized. In the 1830s and 1840s, new political and social movements organized around these ideologies.

Liberalism. As an ideology, liberalism traced its origins to the writings of John Locke in the seventeenth century and the Enlightenment philosophy of the eighteenth. The adherents of *liberalism* defined themselves in opposition to conservatives on one end of the political spectrum and revolutionaries on the other. Unlike conservatives, liberals supported the Enlightenment ideals of constitutional guarantees of personal liberty and free trade in economics, believing that greater liberty in politics and economic matters would promote social improvement and economic growth. For that reason, they also generally applauded the social and economic changes produced by the Industrial Revolution, while opposing the violence and excessive state power promoted by the French Revolution. The leaders of the rapidly expanding middle class composed of manufacturers, merchants, and professionals favored liberalism.

Liberals' demands varied from country to country. In divided countries like Italy, liberals allied with movements for national unification. In France and Britain, liberals agitated largely for parliamentary reforms, including more middle-class representation, but also wanted economic changes, notably free trade, because they believed lifting tariffs would

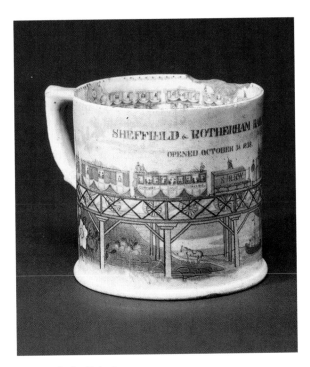

Railroads in Britain
A commemorative mug shows an early railway carriage. The mug was manufactured to celebrate the opening of the Sheffield and Rotherham line on October 31, 1838. Items such as this spread awareness of railroads to people who lived far from the places first linked together.
Fitzwilliam Museum, University of Cambridge.

lower prices, increase consumption, and consequently stimulate economic activity. Economic liberalism was much less important in countries such as Spain, where commercial and industrial change had not yet affected much of society. Nowhere did liberals favor democracy, however, because they feared that extending the vote to all men (let alone women) would lead to anarchy and disorder.

The foremost exponent of early-nineteenth-century liberalism was the English philosopher and jurist Jeremy Bentham (1748–1832). He called his brand of liberalism *utilitarianism* because he held that the best policy is the one that produces "the greatest good for the greatest number" and is thus the most useful, or utilitarian. Liberalism and utilitarianism were closely identified in England. Such views clearly challenged aristocratic dominance, which relied on policies that defended the privileges of a small minority. Bentham's criticisms spared no institution; he railed against the injustices of the British parliamentary process, the abuses of the prisons and the penal code, and the educational system. In his zeal for social engineering, he proposed elaborate schemes for managing the poor and model prisons that would emphasize rehabilitation through close supervision rather than corporal punishment. British liberals like Bentham wanted government involvement, including deregulation of trade, but they shied away from any association with revolutionary violence.

Bentham and many other liberals joined the abolitionist, antislavery movement that intensified between the 1790s and 1820s. One English abolitionist put the matter in these terms: "[God] has given to us an unexampled portion of civil liberty; and we in return drag his rational creatures into a most severe and perpetual bondage." The contradiction between calling for more liberty at home and maintaining slavery in the West Indies seemed intolerable to British liberals and to many religious groups, especially the Quakers, who since the 1780s had taken the lead in forming antislavery societies in both the United States and Great Britain. Agitation by such groups as the London Society for Effecting the Abolition of the Slave Trade succeeded in gaining a first victory in 1807 when the British House of Lords voted to abolish the slave trade. Throughout the 1820s, antislavery activism expanded in the United States, Great Britain, and France because the slave trade still continued in some countries and because slavery itself had not been abolished. As one disappointed British abolitionist explained in 1830:

> We supposed that when by the abolition of the slave trade the planters could get no more slaves, they would not only treat better those whom they then had in their power, but that they would gradually find it to their advantage to emancipate them. . . . We did not sufficiently take into account the effect of unlimited power.

The abolitionists' efforts would bear fruit in 1833 when Britain abolished slavery in all its colonies.

Socialism. The newest ideology of the 1820s, *socialism*, took up where liberalism left off: socialists believed that the liberties advocated by liberals benefited only the middle class, the owners of factories and businesses, not the workers. They sought to reorganize society totally rather than to reform it piecemeal through political measures. Many were *utopians* who believed that ideal communities are based on cooperation rather than competition. Like Thomas More, whose book *Utopia* (1516) gave the movement its name, the utopian socialists believed that society would benefit all its members only if private property did not exist.

Socialists criticized the new industrial order for dividing society into two classes: the new middle class, or *capitalists*, who owned the wealth; and the working class, their downtrodden and impoverished employees. Such divisions tore the social fabric, and, as their name suggests, the socialists aimed to restore harmony and cooperation through social reorganization. Robert Owen (1771–1858), a successful Welsh-born manufacturer, founded British socialism. In 1800, he bought a cotton mill in New Lanark, Scotland, and began to set up a model factory town, where workers labored only ten hours a day (instead of seventeen, as was common) and children between the ages of five and ten attended school rather than working in the factory. Owen moved to the United States in the 1820s to put his principles once more into action in the community in Indiana he named New Harmony. The experiment collapsed after three years, a victim of internal squabbling. But out of Owen's experiments and writings, such as *The Book of the New Moral World*

(1820), would come the movement for producer cooperatives (businesses owned and controlled by their workers), consumers' cooperatives (stores in which consumers owned shares), and a national trade union.

Owen's utopian counterparts in France were Claude Henri de Saint-Simon (1760–1825) and Charles Fourier (1772–1837). Saint-Simon was a noble who had served as an officer in the War of American Independence and lost a fortune speculating in national property during the French Revolution. Fourier traveled as a salesman for a Lyon cloth merchant. Both shared Owen's alarm about the effects of industrialization on social relations. Saint-Simon—who coined the terms *industrialism* and *industrialist* to define the new economic order and its chief animators—believed that work was the central element in the new society and that it should be controlled not by politicians but by scientists, engineers, artists, and industrialists themselves. To correct the abuses of the new industrial order, Fourier urged the establishment of utopian communities that were part garden city and part agricultural commune; all jobs would be rotated to maximize happiness. Fourier hoped that a network of small, decentralized communities would replace the state. The emancipation of women was essential to Fourier's vision of a harmonious community: "The extension of the privileges of women is the fundamental cause of all social progress." Fourier's projects sometimes included outlandish predictions; he envisioned a world in which the oceans would turn into lemonade and the population would include 37 million poets equal to Homer, 37 million mathematicians equal to Newton, and 37 million dramatists equal to Molière.

After Saint-Simon's death in 1825, some of his followers established a quasi-religious cult with elaborate rituals and a "he-pope" and "she-pope," or ruling father and mother. Saint-Simonians lived and worked together in cooperative arrangements and scandalized some by advocating free love. They set up branches in the United States and Egypt. In 1832, Saint-Simonian women founded a feminist newspaper, *The Free Woman*, asserting that "with the emancipation of woman will come the emancipation of the worker." These early utopian socialists were lonely voices. Their emphasis on community and cooperation gained more adherents after 1830.

Nationalism. Nationalists could be liberals, socialists, or even conservatives. Their ability to cross political lines helped nationalism to influence the course of modern world history more than any other ideology. *Nationalism* holds that all peoples derive their identities from their nations, which are defined by common language, shared cultural traditions, and sometimes religion. When such "nations" do not coincide with state boundaries, as they often did not in the nineteenth and twentieth centuries, nationalism can produce violence and warfare as different national groups compete for control over territory.

The French showed the power of national feeling in their revolutionary and Napoleonic wars, but they also provoked nationalism in the people they conquered. Once Napoleon and his satellite rulers departed, nationalist sentiment turned against other outside rulers—the Ottoman Turks in the Balkans, the Russians in Poland, and the Austrians in Italy. Intellectuals took the lead in demanding unity and freedom for their peoples. They collected folktales, poems, and histories and prepared grammars and dictionaries of their native languages. Students, middle-class professionals, and army officers formed secret societies to promote national independence and constitutional reform.

Nationalist aspirations were especially explosive for the Austrian Empire, which included a variety of peoples united only by their enforced allegiance to the Habsburg emperor. The empire included three main national groups: the Germans, who made up one-fourth of the population; the Magyars of Hungary (which included Transylvania and Croatia); and the Slavs, who together formed the largest group in the population but were divided into different nationalities such as Poles, Czechs, Croats, and Serbs. The empire also included Italians in Lombardy and Venetia and Romanians in Transylvania. Efforts to govern such diverse peoples preoccupied Metternich, chief minister to the weak Habsburg emperor Francis I (r. 1792–1835). Metternich's domestic policy aimed to restrain nationalist impulses, and it largely succeeded until the 1840s.

As a conservative, Metternich believed that the experience of the French Revolution proved the superiority of monarchy and aristocracy as forms of government and society. But he did not hesitate to use new methods of governing when necessary.

Consequently, he set up a secret police on the Napoleonic model. The secret police opened letters of even the highest officials, reported any "suspicious" conversations, and followed travelers. Censorship in the Italian provinces was so strict that even the works of Dante were expurgated, and Metternich announced that "the Lombards must forget that they are Italians."

In reaction, novelists, playwrights, and poets used their pens to arouse nationalist sentiment. Membership grew in secret societies such as the *carbonari*; before the fall of Napoleon, many had been anti-French, but now the societies turned anti-Austrian and supported political rights and national self-determination. The societies had no common program across Italy and no central organization, but they attracted tens of thousands of members, including physicians, lawyers, officers, and students.

The new Germanic Confederation had a federal assembly, but it largely functioned as a tool of Metternich's policies. The only sign of resistance came from university students, who formed nationalist student societies, or *Burschenschaften*. In 1817, they held a mass rally at which they burned books they did not like, including Napoleon's Civil Code. One of their leaders, Friedrich Ludwig Jahn, spouted such xenophobic (antiforeign) slogans as "If you let your daughter learn French, you might just as well train her to become a whore." Metternich was convinced that the *Burschenschaften* in the German states and the *carbonari* in Italy were linked in an international conspiracy; in 1820, when a student assassinated the playwright August Kotzebue because he ridiculed the student movement, Metternich convinced the leaders of the biggest German states to pass the Karlsbad Decrees dissolving the student societies and more strictly censoring the press. No evidence for a conspiracy was found.

Tsar Alexander faced similar problems in Poland, his "congress kingdom" (so called because the Congress of Vienna had created it), which in 1815 was one of Europe's most liberal states. The tsar reigned in Poland as a limited monarch, having bestowed a constitution that provided for an elected parliament, a national army, and guarantees of free speech and a free press. But by 1818, Alexander had begun retracting his concessions. Polish students and military officers responded by forming secret nationalist societies to plot for change by illegal means. The government then cracked down, arresting student leaders and dismissing professors who promoted reforms. By the 1820s, Polish nationalists and the Russian imperial government were on a collision course.

Romanticism

More of an artistic movement than a true ideology, *romanticism* glorified nature, emotion, genius, and imagination. It proclaimed these as antidotes to the Enlightenment and to classicism in the arts, challenging the reliance on reason, symmetry, and cool geometric spaces. Classicism idealized models from Roman history; romanticism turned to folklore and medieval legends. Classicism celebrated orderly, crisp lines; romantics sought out all that was wild, fevered, and disorderly. Chief among the arts of romanticism were poetry, music, and painting, which captured the deep-seated emotion characteristic of romantic expression. Romantics might take any political position, but they exerted the most political influence when they expressed nationalist feelings.

Romantic Poetry. Romantic poetry celebrated overwhelming emotion and creative imagination. George Gordon, Lord Byron (1788–1824) explained his aims in writing poetry:

> For what is Poesy but to create
> From overfeeling, Good and Ill, and aim
> At an external life beyond our fate,
> And be the new Prometheus of new man.

Prometheus was the mythological figure who brought fire from the Greek gods to human beings. Byron did not seek the new Prometheus among the men of industry; he sought him within his own "overfeeling," his own intense emotions. Byron became a romantic hero himself when he rushed off to act on his emotions by fighting and dying in the Greek war for independence from the Turks. An English aristocrat, Byron nonetheless claimed, "I have simplified my politics into a detestation of all existing governments."

Romantic poetry elevated the wonders of nature almost to the supernatural. In a poem that became one of the most beloved exemplars of romanticism, "Tintern Abbey" (1798), the English poet William Wordsworth (1770–1850) compared

Lord Byron

George Gordon, Lord Byron (1788–1824), lived a short, tumultuous life, wrote enduring romantic poetry, loved both women and young men, and died a heroic death fighting for Greek independence. In the midst of the Napoleonic wars, he left Britain in 1809 for a two-year trip through Spain and Portugal, Greece, Turkey, and Turkish-controlled Albania. He visited the Turkish rulers in Greece and Albania and collected souvenir costumes, such as that worn in this portrait by Thomas Philips (1813). As a result of this trip, he became passionately involved in things Greek; when the Greek rebellion broke out, he promptly joined the British Committee that gathered aid for the Greeks. He died of a fever in Greece where he had gone to distribute funds. National Portrait Gallery, London.

himself to a deer even while making nature seem filled with human emotions:

> I came among these hills; when like a roe
> I bounded o'er the mountains, by the sides
> Of the deep rivers, and the lonely streams,
> Wherever nature led.

Nature, wrote Wordsworth, "to me was all in all." It allowed him to sing "the still, sad music of humanity" and was "a presence that disturbs me with the joy of elevated thoughts; a sense sublime." Like many poets of his time, Wordsworth greeted the French Revolution with joy; in his poem "French Revolution" (1809), he remembered his early enthusiasm: "Bliss was it in that dawn to be alive." But gradually he became disenchanted with the revolutionary experiment and celebrated British nationalism instead; in 1816, he published a poem to commemorate the "intrepid sons of Albion [England]" who died at the battle of Waterloo.

Their emphasis on authentic self-expression at times drew romantics to exotic, mystical, or even reckless experiences. Such transports drove one leading German poet to the madhouse and another to suicide. Some romantics depicted the artist as possessed by demons and obsessed with hallucinations. This more nightmarish side was captured, and perhaps criticized, by Mary Shelley in *Frankenstein*. The aged German poet Johann Wolfgang von Goethe (1749–1832) likewise denounced the extremes of romanticism, calling it "everything that is sick." In his epic poem *Faust* (1832), he seemed to warn of the same dangers Shelley portrayed in her novel. In Goethe's retelling of a sixteenth-century legend, Faust offers his soul to the devil in return for a chance to taste all human experience—from passionate love to the heights of power—in his effort to reshape nature for humanity's benefit. Faust's striving, like Frankenstein's, leaves a wake of suffering and destruction. Goethe did not make the target of his warning explicit, but the French revolutionary legacy and industrialization both seemed to be releasing "faustian" energies that could turn destructive.

Romantic Painting and Music. Romanticism in painting also idealized nature and often expressed anxiety about the coming industrial order. These concerns came together in an emphasis on natural landscape. The German romantic painter Caspar David Friedrich (1774–1840) depicted scenes—often in the mountains, far from any factory—that captured the romantic fascination with the sublime power of nature. His melancholy individual figures looked lost in the vastness of an overpowering nature. Friedrich hated the new modern world and considered industrialization a disaster. His landscapes often had religious meaning as well, as in his controversial painting *The Cross in the Mountains* (1808), which showed a Christian cross standing alone in a mountain scene. It symbolized the steadfastness of faith but seemed to separate religion from the churches and attach it to mystical experience.

Many other artists developed similar themes. The English painter Joseph M. W. Turner (1775–1851) depicted his vision of nature in mysterious, misty seascapes, anticipating later artists by blurring

William Blake, *The Circle of the Lustful* (1824)
An English romantic poet, painter, engraver, and printmaker, Blake always sought his own way. Self-taught, he began writing poetry at age twelve and apprenticed to an engraver at fourteen. His works incorporate many otherworldly attributes; they are quite literally visionary— imagining other worlds. In this engraving of hell, the figures twist and turn and are caught up in a kind of spiritual ether. Blake, "Circle of the Lustful"/ Birmingham Museums and Art Gallery.

Caspar David Friedrich, *Wanderer above the Sea of Fog* (1818)
Friedrich, a German romantic painter, captured many of the themes most dear to romanticism: melancholy, isolation, and individual communion with nature. He painted trees reaching for the sky and mountains stretching into the distance. Nature to him seemed awesome, powerful, and overshadowing of human perspectives. The French sculptor David d'Angers said of Friedrich, "Here is a man who has discovered the tragedy of landscape."
Co Elke Walford, Hamburg/Hamburger Kunsthalle.

the outlines of objects. The French painter Eugène Delacroix (1798–1863) chose contemporary as well as medieval scenes of great turbulence to emphasize light and color and break away from what he saw as "the servile copies repeated *ad nauseum* in academies of art." Critics denounced the new techniques as "painting with a drunken broom." To broaden his experience of light and color, Delacroix traveled in the 1830s to North Africa and painted many exotic scenes in Morocco and Algeria.

The towering presence of the German composer Ludwig van Beethoven (1770–1827) in early nineteenth-century music helped establish the direction for musical romanticism. His music, ac-

cording to one leading German romantic, "sets in motion the lever of fear, of awe, of horror, of suffering, and awakens just that infinite longing which is the essence of Romanticism." Beethoven transformed the symphony into a connected work with recurring and evolving musical themes. Romantic symphonies conveyed the impression of growth, a metaphor for the organic process with an emphasis on the natural that was dear to the romantics. For example, Beethoven's Sixth Symphony, the *Pastoral* (1808), used a variety of instruments to represent sounds heard in the country. Beethoven's work showed remarkable diversity ranging from religious works to symphonies, sonatas, and concertos. Some of his work was explicitly political; his Ninth Symphony (1824) employed a chorus to sing the German poet Friedrich Schiller's verses in praise of universal human solidarity.

Romantic Nationalism. If romantics had any common political thread, it was the support of nationalist aspirations, especially through the search for the historical origins of national identity. In the German states, the Austrian Empire, Russia and other Slavic lands, and Scandinavia, romantic poets and writers collected old legends and folktales that expressed a shared cultural and linguistic heritage stretching back to the Middle Ages. These collections showed that Germany, for example, had always existed even if it did not currently take the form of a single unified state. Romantic nationalism permeated the enormously popular historical novels of Sir Walter Scott (1771–1832) and *The Betrothed* (1825–1827), a novel by Alessandro Manzoni (1785–1873) that constituted a kind of bible for Italian nationalists.

Scott's career incorporates many of the strands of romanticism. He translated Goethe and published Scottish ballads that he heard as a child. After achieving immediate success with his poetry, he switched to historical novels, but he also wrote a nine-volume life of Napoleon and edited historical memoirs. His novels are almost all renditions of historical events, from *Rob Roy* (1817), with its account of Scottish resistance to the English in the early eighteenth century, to *Ivanhoe* (1819), with its tales of medieval England. The influence of Scott's historical novels was immense. One historian claimed that *Ivanhoe* was more historically true than any scholarly work: "There is more history in the novels of Walter Scott than in half of the historians."

❖ Political Challenges to the Conservative Order

As the spread of romanticism shows, the challenges to the conservative order ran deep but not always in the same political direction. Yet in many places, discontent with the conservative Vienna settlement threatened to rise over its banks as liberals, nationalists, and socialists expressed their exasperation. The revolutionary legacy kept coming to the surface to challenge Europe's rulers. Isolated revolts threatened the hold of some conservative governments in the 1820s, but most of them were quickly bottled up. Then in 1830, successive uprisings briefly overwhelmed the established order. Across Europe, angry protesters sought constitutional guarantees of individual liberties and national unity and autonomy.

Political Revolts in the 1820s

Combinations of liberalism and nationalism fueled political upheavals in the 1820s in Spain and Italy, Russia, Greece (Map 21.3), and across the Atlantic in the Spanish and Portuguese colonies of Latin Amer-

ica. Most revolts failed, but those in Greece and Latin America succeeded, largely because they did not threaten the conservative order in Europe.

Uprisings in Spain and Italy. The restoration of regimes after Napoleon's fall disappointed those who dreamed of constitutional freedoms. When Ferdinand VII regained the Spanish crown in 1814, he quickly restored the prerevolutionary nobility, church, and monarchy. He had foreign books and newspapers confiscated at the frontier and allowed the publication of only two newspapers. Not surprisingly, such repressive policies disturbed the middle class, especially the army officers who had encountered French ideas. Many responded by joining secret societies. In 1820, disgruntled soldiers demanded that Ferdinand proclaim his adherence to the Constitution of 1812, which he had abolished in 1814. When the revolt spread, Ferdinand convened the *cortes* (parliament), which could agree on virtually nothing. Ferdinand bided his time, and in 1823 a French army invaded and restored him to absolute power. The French acted with the consent of the other great powers, who had met to discuss the Spanish situation and agree on a course of

MAP 21.3 Revolutionary Movements of the 1820s
The revolts of the 1820s took place on the periphery of Europe, in Spain, Italy, Greece, Russia, and in the Spanish and Portuguese colonies of Latin America. Rebels in Spain and Russia wanted national independence. Although the Italian revolts failed, as did the uprisings in Spain and Russia, the Greek and Latin American independence movements succeeded.

action. The restored Spanish government tortured and executed hundreds of rebels; thousands were imprisoned or forced into exile.

The uprising in Spain proved contagious. Hearing of the Spanish struggles, rebellious soldiers in the kingdom of Naples joined forces with the *carbonari* and demanded a constitution. When a new parliament met, it too broke down over internal disagreements. The promise of reform sparked rebellion in the northern Italian kingdom of Piedmont-Sardinia, where rebels urged Charles Albert, the young heir to the Piedmont throne, to fight the Austrians for Italian unification. He vacillated; but in 1821, after the rulers of Austria, Prussia, and Russia met and agreed on intervention, the Austrians defeated the rebels in Naples and Piedmont. Liberals were arrested in many Italian states, and the pope condemned the secret societies as "at heart only devouring wolves." Despite the opposition of Great Britain, which condemned the "indiscriminate" suppression of revolutionary movements, Metternich convinced the other powers to agree to his muffling of the Italian opposition to Austrian rule.

The Decembrist Revolt in Russia. Aspirations for constitutional government surfaced in Russia when Alexander I died suddenly in 1825. On the December day that the troops assembled in St. Petersburg to take an oath of loyalty to Alexander's brother Nicholas as the new tsar, rebel officers insisted that the crown belonged to another brother, Constantine, whom they hoped would be more favorable to constitutional reform. Constantine, though next in the line of succession after Alexander, had refused the crown. The soldiers nonetheless raised the cry "Long live Constantine, long live the Constitution." (Some troops apparently thought that "the Constitution" was Constantine's wife.) Soldiers loyal to Nicholas easily suppressed the Decembrists (so called after the month of their uprising), who were so outnumbered that they had no realistic chance to succeed. The subsequent trial, however, made the rebels into legendary heroes. Of their imprisonment at hard labor, the Russian poet Alexander Pushkin (1799–1837) wrote:

> The heavy-hanging chains will fall,
> The walls will crumble at a word,
> And Freedom greet you in the light,
> And brothers give you back the sword.

Pushkin would not live to see this freedom. For the next thirty years, Nicholas I (r. 1825–1855) used a new political police, the Third Section, to spy on potential opponents and stamp out rebelliousness.

Greek Independence from the Turks. The Greek movement for independence eventually succeeded, largely because it was a nationalist movement against the Ottoman Turks, who enjoyed little support in Christian Europe and whose authority had been declining steadily. As the French ambassador explained to Chateaubriand when the writer visited Istanbul in 1807, "To make an alliance with Turkey is the same as putting your arms around a corpse to make it stand up!" Serbs revolted against Turkish rule in the Balkans and won virtual independence by 1817. A Greek general in the Russian army, Prince Alexander Ypsilanti, tried to lead a revolt against the Turks in 1820, but he failed when the tsar, urged on by Metternich, disavowed him. Metternich feared rebellion even by Christians against their Turkish rulers.

Nationalistic Movements in the Balkans, 1815–1830

A second revolt, this time by Greek peasants, sparked a wave of atrocities in 1821 and 1822. The Greeks killed every Turk who did not escape; in retaliation the Turks hanged the Greek patriarch of Constantinople, and in the areas they still controlled they pillaged churches, massacred thousands of men, and sold the women into slavery. Western opinion turned against the Turks; Greece, after all, was the home of Western civilization. While the great powers negotiated, Greeks and pro-Greece committees around the world sent food and military supplies; like the English poet Byron, a few enthusiastic European and American volunteers joined the Greeks.

The Greeks held on until the great powers were willing to intervene. In 1827, a combined force of British, French, and Russian ships destroyed the Turkish fleet at Navarino Bay; and in 1828, Russia

Greek Independence
From 1836 to 1839 the Greek painter Panagiotis Zographos worked with his two sons on a series of scenes from the Greek struggle for independence from the Turks. Response was so favorable that one Greek general ordered lithographic reproductions for popular distribution. Nationalistic feeling could be thus encouraged even among those who were not directly touched by the struggle. Here Turkish sultan Mehmet the Conqueror, exulting over the fall of Constantinople in 1453, views a row of Greeks under the yoke, a sign of submission. Collection, Visual Connection.

declared war on Turkey and advanced close to Istanbul. The Treaty of Adrianople of 1829 gave Russia a protectorate over the Danubian principalities in the Balkans and provided for a conference among representatives of Britain, Russia, and France, all of whom had broken with Austria in support of the Greeks. In 1830, Greece was declared an independent kingdom under the guarantee of the three powers; in 1833, the son of King Ludwig of Bavaria became Otto I of Greece. Nationalism, with the support of European public opinion, had made its first breach in Metternich's system.

Wars of Independence in Latin America. Across the Atlantic, national revolts also succeeded after a series of bloody wars of independence. Taking advantage of the upheavals in Spain and Portugal that began under Napoleon, restive colonists from Mexico to Argentina rebelled. Their leader was Simon Bolívar, son of a slave owner, who was educated in Europe on the works of Voltaire and Rousseau. Although Bolívar fancied himself a Latin American Napoleon, he had to acquiesce to the formation of a series of independent republics between 1821 and 1823, even in Bolivia, which is named after him. At the same time, Brazil (then still a monarchy) separated from Portugal (Map 21.4). The United States recognized the new states, and in 1823 President James Monroe announced his Monroe Doctrine, closing the Americas to European intervention—a

prohibition that depended on British naval power and British willingness to declare neutrality. Great Britain dominated the Latin American economies, which had suffered great losses during the wars for independence. The new Latin American states would be politically unstable for years to come.

Revolution and Reform, 1830–1832

In 1830 a new wave of liberal and nationalist revolts broke against the bulwark of conservatism. The revolts of the 1820s served as warning shots, but the earlier uprisings had been largely confined to the peripheries of Europe. Now revolution once again threatened the established order in western Europe.

The French Revolution of 1830. Louis XVIII's younger brother and successor, Charles X (r. 1824–1830), brought about his own downfall by steering the monarchy in an increasingly repressive direction. In 1825, a Law of Indemnity compensated nobles who had emigrated during the Revolution for the loss of their estates, and a Law of Sacrilege in the same year imposed the death penalty for such offenses as stealing religious objects from churches. Charles enraged liberals when he dissolved the legislature, removed many wealthy and powerful voters from the rolls, and imposed strict censorship. Spontaneous demonstrations in Paris led to fighting on July 26, 1830. After three days of street battles in

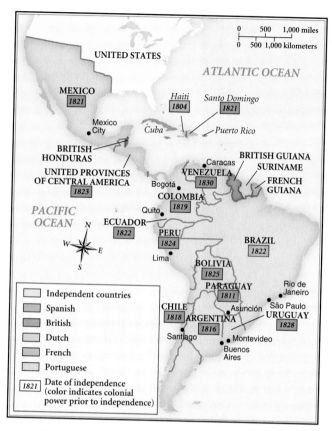

MAP 21.4 Latin American Independence, 1804–1830

The French lost their most important remaining American colony in 1804 when St. Domingue declared its independence as Haiti. But the impact of the French Revolution did not end there. Napoleon's occupation of Spain and Portugal seriously weakened those countries' hold on their Latin American colonies. Despite the restoration of the Spanish and Portuguese rulers in 1814, most of their colonies successfully broke away in a wave of rebellions between 1811 and 1830. Meanwhile a revolt in Spain in 1820–1823 led to a constitutional regime. For example, the Spanish general sent to suppress the revolt in Mexico ended up joining the rebels' cause and helping them establish independence in 1821.

which 500 citizens and 150 soldiers died, a group of moderate liberal leaders, fearing the reestablishment of a republic, agreed to give the crown to Charles X's cousin Louis-Philippe, duke of Orléans.

Charles X went into exile in England, and the new king extended political liberties and voting rights. Although the number of voting men nearly doubled, it remained minuscule—approximately 170,000 in a country of 30 million, between 5 and 6 percent. Such reforms did little for the poor and

working classes, who had manned the barricades in July. Dissatisfaction with the 1830 settlement boiled over in Lyon in 1831, when a silk-workers' strike over wages turned into a rebellion that died down only when the army arrived. Revolution had broken the hold of those who wanted to restore the pre-1789 monarchy and nobility, but it had gone no further this time than installing a more liberal, constitutional monarchy.

Belgian Independence from the Dutch. The success of the July Revolution in Paris ignited the Belgians, whose country had been annexed to the kingdom of the Netherlands in 1815. Differences in traditions, language, and religion separated the largely Catholic Belgians from the Dutch. An opera about a seventeenth-century insurrection in Naples provided the spark, and students in Brussels rioted, shouting "Down with the Dutch."

The riot turned into revolt. King William of the Netherlands appealed to the great powers to intervene; after all, the Congress of Vienna had established his kingdom. But Great Britain and France opposed intervention and invited Russia, Austria, and Prussia to a conference that guaranteed Belgium independence in exchange for its neutrality in international affairs. Belgian neutrality would remain a cornerstone of European diplomacy for a century. After much maneuvering, the crown of the new kingdom of Belgium was offered to a German prince, Leopold of Saxe-Coburg, in 1831. Belgium, like France and Britain, now had a constitutional monarchy.

Revolts in Italy and Poland. The Russian tsar and the Austrian emperor would have supported intervention in Belgium had they not been preoccupied with their own revolts. Anti-Austrian uprisings erupted in a handful of Italian states, but they fizzled without the hoped-for French aid. The Polish revolt was more serious. Once again, in response to news of revolution in France, students raised the banner of rebellion, this time in Warsaw in November 1830. Polish aristocrats soon formed a provisional government. Despite some victories on the battlefield, the provisional government got no support from Britain or France and was defeated. In reprisal, Nicholas abolished the Polish constitution that Alexander had granted and ordered thousands of Poles executed or banished.

IMPORTANT DATES

799 Coup against Directory government in France; Napoleon Bonaparte named First Consul

801 Napoleon signs a concordat with the pope

804 Napoleon crowned as emperor of France; issues new Civil Code

805 British naval forces defeat the French at the battle of Trafalgar; Napoleon wins his greatest victory at the battle of Austerlitz

812 Napoleon invades Russia

814–1815 Congress of Vienna

815 Napoleon defeated at Waterloo and exiled to island of St. Helena, where he dies in 1821

818 Mary Shelley, *Frankenstein*

820 Robert Owen, *The Book of the New Moral World*; revolt of liberal army officers against the Spanish crown; the Karlsbad Decrees abolish German student societies and tighten press censorship

824 Ludwig van Beethoven, Ninth Symphony

825 Russian army officers demand constitutional reform in the Decembrist Revolt

830 The Manchester and Liverpool Railway opens in England; Greece gains its independence from Ottoman Turks; rebels overthrow Charles X of France and install Louis-Philippe

832 English Parliament passes Reform Bill; Johann Wolfgang von Goethe, *Faust*

The British Reform Bill of 1832. The British had long been preoccupied with two subjects: the royal family and elections for control of Parliament. In 1820, the domestic quarrels between the new king George IV (r. 1820–1830) and his German wife Caroline seemed to threaten the future of the monarchy. When George IV came to the throne, he tried to divorce Caroline, and he refused to have her crowned queen. He hoped to use rumors of her love affairs on the continent to win his case, but the divorce trial provoked massive demonstrations in support of Caroline. Women's groups gathered thousands of signatures on petitions supporting her, and popular songs and satires portrayed George as a fat, drunken libertine. Caroline's death a few months after George's coronation ended the Queen Caroline Affair. The monarchy survived but with a tarnished reputation.

The 1820s had brought into British government new men who were open to change. Sir Robert Peel (1788–1850), the secretary for home affairs, revised the criminal code to reduce the number of crimes punishable by death and introduced a municipal police force in London, called the *Bobbies* after him. In 1824, the laws prohibiting labor unions were repealed, and though restrictions on strikes remained, workers could now organize themselves legally to confront their employers collectively. In 1828, the appointment of the duke of Wellington, the hero of Waterloo, as prime minister kept the Tories in power, and his government pushed through a bill in 1829 allowing Catholics to sit in Parliament and hold most public offices.

When in 1830, and again in 1831, the Whigs in Parliament proposed an extension of the right to vote, Tory diehards, principally in the House of Lords, dug in their heels and predicted that even the most modest proposals would doom civilization itself. Even though the proposed law would not grant universal male suffrage, mass demonstrations in favor of it took place in many cities. One supporter of reform described the scene: "Meetings of almost every description of persons were held in cities, towns, and parishes; by journeymen tradesmen in their clubs, and by common workmen who had no trade clubs or associations of any kind." In this "state of diseased and feverish excitement" (according to its opponents), the Reform Bill of 1832 passed, after the king threatened to create enough new peers to obtain its passage in the House of Lords.

Although the Reform Bill altered Britain's political structure in significant ways, the gains were not revolutionary. One of the bill's foremost backers, historian and member of Parliament Thomas Macaulay, explained, "I am opposed to Universal Suffrage, because I think that it would produce a destructive revolution. I support this plan, because I am sure that it is our best security against a revolution." Although the number of male voters increased by about 50 percent, only one in five Britons could now vote, and voting still depended on holding property. Nevertheless, the bill gave representation to new cities in the industrial north for the first time and set a precedent for further widening suffrage. Exclusive aristocratic politics now gave way to a mixed middle-class and aristocratic structure that would prove more responsive to the problems of a

MAPPING THE WEST Europe in 1830

By 1830, the fragilities of the Congress of Vienna settlement had become apparent. Rebellion in Poland failed, but Belgium won its independence from the kingdom of the Netherlands, and a French revolution chased out the Bourbon ruler and installed Louis-Philippe, who promised constitutional reform. Most European rulers held on to their positions in this period of ferment, but they had to accommodate to some extent the new demands created by industrialization, desires for constitutional guarantees of rights, and growing nationalist sentiment.

fast-growing industrial society. Those disappointed with the outcome would organize with renewed vigor in the 1830s and 1840s.

Conclusion

The agitations and uprisings of the 1820s and early 1830s showed that the revolutionary legacy still smoldered and might erupt into flames again at any moment. The efforts of the great powers to maintain the European peace by shoring up established governments and damping down aspirations for constitutional freedoms and national

autonomy sometimes failed. Belgium separated from the Netherlands, Greece achieved independence from the Turks, Latin American countries shook off the rule of Spain and Portugal, and the French installed a more liberal monarchy than the one envisioned by the Congress of Vienna. Yet Metternich's vision of a conservative Europe still held: Russia clamped down on Poland, Austria stifled any sign of Italian nationalism, and the elites of Britain and France managed to maintain their hold by compromising at the right moment.

In her novel *Frankenstein*, Mary Shelley had captured some of the deepest worries of the age; human creativity might have an unpredictably destructive side in spite of every good intention. Although she did not intend her novel as a brief in support of political conservatism—she hated what Metternich stood for—she did tap into European fears about the changes taking place. The French and Industrial Revolutions promised to transform European life, for better or worse. Napoleon Bonaparte had used the French revolutionary legacy to propel his attempted colonization of much of Europe. Others used the revolutionary legacy to argue for new ideologies that would become even more important in the future. The machines of industrialization seemed to some Europeans just as horrible as Frankenstein's monster; others welcomed them as promising a brighter future. In the years to come industrialization would proceed even faster, and revolution would return to shatter the order so carefully nurtured by Metternich and his colleagues.

Suggested References

From Consulate to Empire: The Napoleonic State

Much has been written about Napoleon as a military leader, but only recently has his regime within France attracted interest. Historians now emphasize the mixed quality of Napoleon's rule. He carried forward some revolutionary innovations and halted others.

*Arnold, Eric A., Jr., ed. *A Documentary Survey of Napoleonic France*. 1994.

Crook, Malcolm. *Napoleon Comes to Power: Democracy and Dictatorship in Revolutionary France, 1795–1804*. 1998.

Ellis, Geoffrey James. *Napoleon*. 1996.

Kafker, Frank A., and James M. Laux. *Napoleon and His Times: Selected Interpretations*. 1989.

Lyons, Martyn. *Napoleon Bonaparte and the Legacy of the French Revolution*. 1994.

Napoleon Foundation: http://www.napoleon.org.

Wilson-Smith, Timothy. *Napoleon and His Artists*. 1996.

"Europe Was at My Feet": Napoleon's Conquest

Recent work shows how powerfully Napoleon's armies affected every European state. Whether annexed, allied, or simply defeated, every nation had to come to terms with this dynamo of activity.

*Brunn, Geoffrey. *Napoleon and His Empire*. 1972.

Connelly, Owen. *Napoleon's Satellite Kingdoms*. 1965.

Dallas, Gregor. *The Final Act: The Roads to Waterloo*. 1997.

Gates, David. *The Napoleonic Wars, 1803–1815*. 1997.

Simms, Brendan. *The Impact of Napoleon: Prussian High Politics, Foreign Policy, and the Crisis of the Executive, 1797–1806*. 1997.

The "Restoration" of Europe

New visions of diplomacy are emerging in recent scholarship, but internal affairs are relatively understudied. As a consequence, Artz's book is still a good introduction.

Artz, Frederick B. *Reaction and Revolution, 1814–1832*. 1934.

Johnson, Paul. *The Birth of the Modern: World Society, 1815–1830*. 1991.

Schroeder, Paul W. *The Transformation of European Politics, 1763–1848*. 1994.

Seward, Desmond. *Metternich: The First European*. 1991.

Forces for Social and Cultural Change

The new ideologies have been the subject of a steady stream of excellent work, ranging from individual figures such as Fourier to the antislavery movement and the origins of working-class activism. The Web site Romantic Chronology provides access to a wealth of information about every aspect of romanticism.

Beecher, Jonathan. *Charles Fourier: The Visionary and His World*. 1986.

Berlin, Sir Isaiah. *The Roots of Romanticism*. 1999.

Davis, David Brion. *The Problem of Slavery in the Age of Revolution, 1770–1823*. 1975.

*Hugo, Howard E., ed. *The Romantic Reader*. 1957.

Romantic Chronology: http://english.ucsb.edu:591/rchrono/.

Thompson, E. P. *The Making of the English Working Class*. 1964.

Wright, Beth S. *Painting and History during the French Restoration: Abandoned by the Past*. 1997.

Political Challenges to the Conservative Order

Recent work in British history has been particularly impressive, but in general this is an understudied period of European history. Unsuccessful revolts attract less attention than successful ones, but even the Greek, Latin American, and Belgian independence movements need to be better integrated into European history.

Clark, Anna. "Queen Caroline and the Sexual Politics of Popular Culture in London, 1820," *Representations* 31 (1990): 47–68.

Colley, Linda. *Britons: Forging the Nation, 1707–1837*. 1992.

Di Scala, Spencer. *Italy: From Revolution to Republic, 1700 to the Present*. 2nd ed. 1998.

Spitzer, Alan B. *The French Generation of 1820*. 1987.

*Primary sources.

22

Industrialization, Urbanization, and Revolution

1830–1850

Drink and the Working Classes
The title of this lithograph (c. 1830) by the German artist Franz Burchard Dörbeck seems to be simply descriptive. He called it Two Drunken Day Laborers. *Like many lithographs about social types, however, this one cuts more than one way. On the one hand, it seems to criticize workingmen's propensity to drink. The Prussian government supported anti-alcohol campaigns because it feared that the rapidly growing lower classes would turn to drink, prostitution, and crime as they moved to the cities. On the other hand, the lithograph was intended to be humorous, and the artist seems to treat his working-class subjects with affection and understanding. The lower classes themselves used humor to soften the edges of their often harsh lives.*
Stadtmuseum Berlin; photo: Hans-Joachim Bartsch, Berlin.

A POPULAR GERMAN LITHOGRAPH published around 1830 shows two drunken workingmen standing in front of a water pump in Berlin. In the lithograph's caption, one says, "What'd you think, Schulze, what if that were Kümmel [the Berlin liqueur made with caraway]?" His comrade responds, "Yeah, that would be my first wish if I could wish three times." "So, and the second?" "That all [water] pumps were full of Kümmel."* The lithograph quickly cuts to the core of social life in the turbulent 1830s and 1840s, in particular fears of lower-class behavior. Rapid industrial and urban growth created unprecedented social problems as peasants and workers streamed into the cities. For example, the population of Berlin more than doubled between 1819 and 1849, reaching 412,000. By 1840, more than half the residents of Berlin had been born outside the city. Many feared that these newcomers would precipitate the disintegration of traditional lifestyles. Overcrowding, disease, prostitution, crime, and drinking all seemed to be on the increase. The lithograph focused on drink because it was an issue the censors agreed could be aired for public discussion. In 1832, the king of Prussia ordered all local authorities to promote temperance societies, and within fifteen years, 600,000 German men had taken the pledge to abstain from alcohol.

---

*Translation from Mary Lee Townsend, *Forbidden Laughter: Popular Humor and the Limits of Repression in Nineteenth-Century Prussia* (Ann Arbor: University of Michigan Press, 1992), 10.

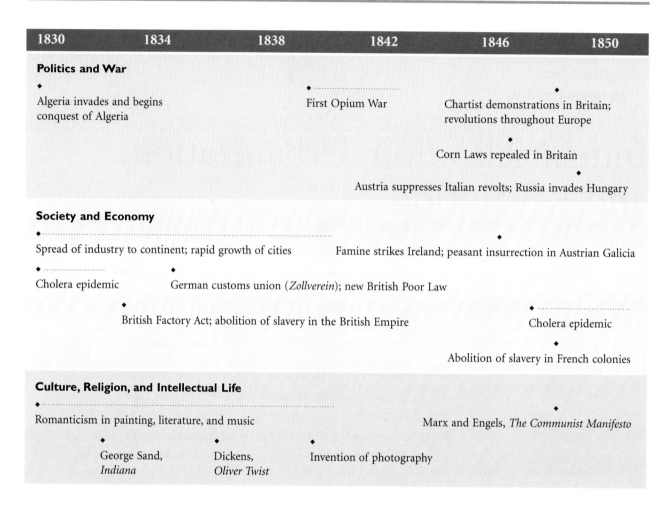

In this case, the medium was part of the message, for lithography was a new artistic technology and consequently a sign of the increasing influence of technology on social life. Lithography (from the Greek *lithos,* "stone") was invented by a German engraver in 1798, but, like the steam engine perfected in 1776, its use spread across Europe only in the nineteenth century. In lithography, an artist used a greasy crayon to trace an image on a flat stone; the grease attracted the ink while the blank areas repelled it. The inked stone was embedded in a printing press that could produce thousands of identical images. By creating pictures of every class in society and their problems and by publishing their images in daily and weekly newspapers, artists enlightened a mass audience about social and political problems created by industrial and urban growth. Even criticisms of modern ways relied on modern forms to make their point.

Lithographs helped ordinary people make sense, even while making fun, of the changes taking place around them. Industrial and urban growth unleashed profound and sometimes frightening transformations in everyday life. Seeing the advantages of Great Britain's burgeoning railway network, other European countries soon hurried to lay down their own iron tracks. Factory machinery groaned and growled, dark clouds of grit billowed out of smokestacks, and men, women, and children trudged out to labor for twelve, fourteen, sometimes seventeen hours a day. Even without factories, cities ballooned in size as peasants left their villages to seek a better life. Builders could not keep up, and overcrowding soon provided a receptive environment for epidemic diseases such as cholera, tuberculosis, and typhus. To many commentators, the cities seemed a cesspool of crime, corruption, and degradation, dangerous places that required close police supervision.

The shock of industrial and urban growth generated an outpouring of commentary on the need for social reforms. Lithographs played a vital role in creating sympathy for the downtrodden. The French artist Honoré Daumier, for example, published no fewer than four thousand prints and caricatures criticizing the social inequalities exacerbated by economic development. Painters, poets, and especially novelists joined in the chorus warning about rising tensions. Many who wrote on social issues expected middle-class women to organize their homes as a domestic haven from this heartless process of upheaval. Yet despite the emphasis on

Life as a Married Couple
In this 1846 lithograph by Honoré Daumier titled All That One Would Want, *the wife follows meekly behind her husband. Daumier is criticizing the provision of Napoleon's Civil Code which required the wife to go to live wherever her husband chose. In his lithographs, Daumier satirized landlords, judges, lawyers, politicians, and even King Louis-Philippe himself. In the early 1830s, his political satires landed him in prison with a six-month sentence. His work always took the side of the lowly and downcast and made most fun of the high and mighty in society. His massive output of caricatures typifies an era of preoccupation with the consequences of rapid social change.*
Jean-Loup Charmet.

domesticity, middle-class women participated in public issues too: they set up reform societies that fought prostitution and helped poor mothers, and they agitated for temperance (abstention from alcohol) and joined the campaigns to abolish slavery. Middle-class men and women frequently denounced the lower classes' appetites for drink, tobacco, and cockfighting, but they remained largely silent when British traders received government support in forcing the Chinese to accept imports of opium.

Social and economic changes kept the ideological pots boiling. One German entrepreneur confidently predicted, "The locomotive is the hearse which will carry absolutism and feudalism to the graveyard." In fact, however, the consequences of industrialization and urbanization proved less than straightforward. Nationalists, liberals, socialists, and communists offered competing visions of a new social order: they all agreed that change was necessary, but they disagreed about both the means and the ends of change.

In 1848, the rapid transformation of European society provided the combustible material for a new set of revolutionary outbreaks, more consuming than any since 1789. As in 1789, food shortages and constitutional crises acted as the tinderbox, but now class tensions and nationalist impulses ignited outbreaks in capitals across Europe, not only in Paris. Some revolutionaries, such as Karl Marx, the theorist of communism, saw this as the beginning of a new age of class warfare. Because of internal quarrels and conflicts, the revolutionaries of 1848 eventually went down to defeat.

❖ The Advance of Industrialization and Urbanization

Industrialization and urbanization transformed Europe and eventually most of the world in the nineteenth and twentieth centuries. Because they are not single events but rather long-term processes that continue to the present, it is impossible to give them precise beginning and ending dates. Nevertheless, historians have shown that both processes accelerated quite suddenly in the first half of the nineteenth century and touched off loud complaints about their effects. Great Britain led the way in both industrialization and urbanization, but contemporaries did not fully understand their linkage; even today, scholars debate the connection between industrial and urban growth. Rulers quickly saw the advantages in industrialization, and in the 1830s and 1840s many of them encouraged railroad construction and the mechanization of manufacturing. States exercised little control over the consequences of industrial and urban growth, and many officials, preachers, and intellectuals worried that unchecked growth would destroy traditional social relationships and create disorder. Some held out the constancy of rural life as an antidote to the ravages of industrialization and urbanization, but population growth produced new tensions in the countryside too.

MAP 22.1 Industrialization in Europe, c. 1850

Industrialization first spread in a band across northern Europe that included Great Britain, northern France, Belgium, the northern German states, the region around Milan in northern Italy, and Bohemia. Much of Scandinavia and southern and eastern Europe were left out of this first phase of industrial development. Although railroads were not the only factor in promoting industrialization, the map makes clear the interrelationship between railroad building and the development of new industrial sites of coal mining and textile production.

	Austria	Belgium	France	German states (including Prussia)	Great Britain
1830	214	*	1,863	1,800	22,800
1835	251	2,639	2,506	2,100	28,100
1840	473	3,930	3,003	3,200	34,200
1845	689	4,919	4,202	4,400	46,600
1850	877	5,821	4,434	5,100	50,200

Output of coal (in thousands of metric tons)

*Data not available

TABLE 22.1 Coal Output, 1830–1850
Like the quantities for railroad mileage and raw cotton consumption provided pages 787–788, these figures for coal production show the economic dominance of Great Britain throughout the period 1830–1850. As long as coal remained the essential fuel of industrialization, Britain enjoyed a clear advantage. Although it produced more coal than any other European country, rates of increase in the production of coal were comparable or even higher in other countries, showing that some countries were starting to catch up with Britain.
From B. R. Mitchell, *European Historical Statistics, 1750–1970* (New York: Columbia University Press, 1975), D2.

Engines of Change

Great Britain had led the way in the development of factories and railroads since the late eighteenth century. In the 1830s and 1840s, industrialization spread to continental Europe, first to Belgium, northern France, and northern Italy and then eastward to Prussia, Austria, and eventually Russia. Despite striking industrial growth, factory workers remained a minority everywhere. In the 1840s, factories in England employed only 5 percent of the workers; in France, 3 percent; in Prussia, 2 percent. But these small figures hide a broader transformation as the nature of work changed in many sectors even without the introduction of factories.

Railroads and Steam. In the 1840s alone, railroad track mileage more than doubled in Great Britain, and British investment in railways jumped tenfold. The British also began to build railroads in India. Canal building waned in the 1840s: the railroad had won out.

Britain's success with rail transportation led other countries to develop their own projects. Railroads grew spectacularly in the United States in the 1830s and 1840s. Belgium, newly independent in 1830, opened the first continental European railroad with state bonds backed by British capital in 1835. By 1850, France had 2,000 miles of railroad and the German states nearly twice as many; Great Britain had 6,000 miles and the United States 9,000 miles. In all, the world had 23,500 miles of track by midcentury.

Railroad building spurred both industrial development and state power (Map 22.1). Governments everywhere participated in the construction of railroads, which depended on private and state funds to pay for the massive amounts of iron, coal, heavy machinery, and human labor required to build and run them. Demand for iron products accelerated industrial development. Until the 1840s, cotton had led industrial production; between 1816 and 1840, cotton output more than quadrupled in Great Britain. But from 1830 to 1850, Britain's output of iron and coal doubled (Table 22.1). Similarly, Austrian output of iron doubled between the 1820s and the 1840s. One-third of all investment in the German states in the 1840s went into railroads.

As railroads created new transportation networks for raw materials and finished goods, the steam engine provided power for textile factories, mining, locomotives, and steamboats. The number of steamboats in Great Britain increased from two in 1812 to six hundred in 1840. Between 1840 and 1850, steam-engine power doubled in Great Britain and increased even more rapidly elsewhere in Europe, as those adopting British inventions strove to catch up. The power applied in German manufacturing, for example, rose from 60,000 to 360,000 hp (units horsepower) during the 1840s but still amounted to only a little more than a quarter of the British figure. German coal and iron output were only 6 or 7 percent of the British output. Steam-powered engines made Britain the world leader in manufacturing. By midcentury, more than half of Britain's national income came from manufacturing and trade.

Industrialization Moves Eastward. Industrialization spread slowly east from key areas in Prussia (near Berlin), in Saxony, and in Bohemia. The Austrian Empire, with industrialization centered in Bohemia, produced more cotton cloth than either Prussia or Saxony. Cotton production in the Austrian Empire tripled between 1831 and 1845, with Bohemia accounting for half of the empire's mechanized cotton spinning and three-fourths of its cotton weaving. By 1847, coal production, also concentrated in Bohemia, had increased fourfold in just over twenty years.

The advance of industrialization in eastern Europe was slow, in large part because serfdom still survived there, hindering labor mobility and tying up investment capital: as long as peasants were legally tied to the land as serfs, they could not migrate to the new factory towns, and landlords felt little incentive to invest their income in manufacturing. The problem was worst in Russia, where industrialization had hardly begun and would not take off until the end of the nineteenth century. Nevertheless, even in Russia signs of industrialization could be detected: raw cotton imports (a sign of a growing textile industry) increased sevenfold between 1831 and 1848, and the number of factories doubled along with the size of the industrial workforce.

Although Great Britain consciously strove to protect its industrial supremacy, thousands of British engineers defied laws against the export of machinery or the emigration of artisans. The best known of them, John Cockerill, set up a machine works in Belgium that was soon selling its products as far east as Poland and Russia. Cockerill claimed to know of every innovation within ten days of its appearance in England. Only slowly, thanks to such pirating of British methods and to new technical schools, did most continental countries begin closing the gap. Belgium became the fastest-growing industrial power on the continent: between 1830 and 1844, the number of steam engines in Belgium quadrupled, and Belgians exported seven times as many steam engines as they imported. Even so, by 1850, continental Europe still lagged almost twenty years behind Great Britain in industrial development.

The Formation of the Working Class. As industrialization proceeded, factories increasingly became the workplace of laboring people, replacing the dispersed households of preindustrial artisans. But this process stretched over years, indeed decades. Many peasants kept their options open by combining factory work with agricultural labor. From Switzerland to Russia, people worked in agriculture during the spring and summer and in manufacturing in the fall and winter. In this way, workers and their families ensured their food supply and maintained the rhythms of life on the land. Unstable industrial wages made such arrangements essential. Some new industries idled periodically: for example, iron forges stopped for several months when the water level in streams dropped, and blast furnaces shut down for repairs several weeks every year. In hard times, factory owners simply closed their doors until demand for their goods improved.

In addition, workers continued to toil at home in putting-out, or cottage, industries. In the 1840s, for example, two-thirds of the manufacturing workers in Prussia and Saxony labored at home for contractors or merchants who supplied raw materials and then sold the finished goods. Women worked in the putting-out system as much as or even more than men—they plaited straw and embroidered in Hungary, made pots in Denmark, fashioned lace in Great Britain and France, and spun cotton almost everywhere.

Some of the old forms of putting-out work changed during this period, even when factories did not supplant cottage industries. Little or no technological innovation prompted the change; instead, labor was organized in a different way. Tailoring, for example, which had been the province of male artisans preparing entire garments in small shops, was now broken up into piecework that was farmed out to women working at home for much lower "piece rates."

Even though factories employed only a small percentage of the population, they attracted much attention. Factories produced wealth without regard to the pollution they caused or the exhausted state of their workers; industry created unheard-of riches and new forms of poverty all at once. "From this foul drain the greatest stream of human industry flows out to fertilize the whole world," wrote the French aristocrat Alexis de Tocqueville after visiting the new English industrial city of Manchester in the 1830s. "From this filthy sewer pure gold flows. Here humanity attains its most complete development and its most brutish, here civilization works its miracles and civilized man is turned almost into a savage." Studies by physicians set the life expectancy of workers in Manchester at just seventeen years (partly because of high rates of infant mortality), whereas the average life expectancy in England was forty years in 1840. (See "New Sources, New Perspectives," page 810.) In some parts of Europe, city leaders banned factories, hoping to insulate their towns from the effects of industrial growth. Visitors invariably complained about the smoke and soot. One American visitor in Britain in the late 1840s described how "in the manufacturing town, the fine soot or *blacks* darken the day, give white sheep the color of black sheep, discolor the human saliva, contaminate the air, poison many plants, and corrode monuments and buildings."

As factory production expanded, local and national governments collected information about the workers. Investigators detailed the pitiful condition of factory workers. A French physician in the eastern town of Mulhouse described the "pale, emaciated women who walk barefooted through the dirt" to reach the factory. The young children who worked in the factory appeared "clothed in rags which are greasy with the oil from the looms and frames." A report to the city government in Lille, France, in 1832 described "dark cellars" inhabited by the cotton workers, where "the air is never renewed, it is infected; the walls are plastered with garbage. . . . If a bed exists, it is a few dirty, greasy planks; it is damp and putrescent straw."

Authorities worried in particular about the effects on families. A doctor in the Prussian town of Breslau (population 111,000 in 1850), for example, reported that in working-class districts "several persons live in one room in a single bed, or perhaps a whole family, and use the room for all domestic duties, so that the air gets vitiated [polluted]. . . . Their diet consists largely of bread and potatoes. These are clearly the two main reasons for the scrofula [a disease related to tuberculosis] which is so widespread here; the diet is also the cause of the common malformation of limbs."

Government inquiries often focused on women and children. In Great Britain, the Factory Act of 1833 outlawed the employment of children under the age of nine in textile mills (except in the lace and silk industries) and limited the workdays of children age nine to thirteen to nine hours a day and those age thirteen to eighteen to twelve hours. These figures give some sense of the drudgery of factory work: adults worked even longer hours. Reports on conditions in other industries prompted further legislation. When investigating commissions showed that women and young children, sometimes under age six, were hauling coal trucks through low, cramped passageways in coal mines, the British Parliament passed a Mines Act in 1842 prohibiting the employment of women and girls underground. One nine-year-old girl, Margaret Gomley, described her typical day in the mines as beginning at 7:00 A.M. and ending at 6:00 P.M.: "I get my dinner at 12 o'clock, which is a dry muffin, and sometimes butter on, but have no time allowed to stop to eat it, I eat it while I am thrusting the load. . . . They flog us down in the pit, sometimes with their hand upon my bottom, which hurts me very much." In 1847, the Central Short Time Committee, one of Britain's many social reform organizations, successfully pressured Parliament to limit the workday of women and children to ten hours. The continental countries followed the British lead, but since most did not insist on government inspection, enforcement was lax.

Urbanization and Its Consequences

Industrial development spurred urban growth wherever factories were located in or near cities, yet cities grew even with little industry. Here, too, Great Britain led the way: half the population of England and Wales lived in towns by 1850, while in France and the German states the urban population was only about a quarter of the total. Both old and new cities teemed with growing population in the 1830s and 1840s. In the 1830s alone, London grew by 130,000 people, Manchester by 70,000, and Birmingham by 40,000. Paris grew by 120,000 just

Statistics and the Standard of Living of the Working Class

From the very beginning of industrialization, experts argued about whether industrialization improved or worsened the standard of living of the working class. For every claim, there was a counterclaim, and most often these claims came in the form of statistics. Some experts argued that factories offered higher-paying jobs to workers; others countered that factories took work away from artisans such as handloom weavers and left them on the verge of starvation. Supporters of industrialization maintained that factories gave women paying work; opponents insisted that factories destroyed the family by taking women away from the home. Through mass production, industrialization made goods cheaper and therefore more available; by polluting the air, it destroyed health, lowered life expectancy, and ruined the environment. Karl Marx and Friedrich Engels would give the debate even more of an edge by tying it to the ideology of communism. In 1844, Engels described to Marx his aim in writing *The Condition of the Working Class in England*: "I shall present the English with a fine bill of indictment. At the bar of world opinion I charge the English middle classes with mass murder, wholesale robbery and all the other crimes in the calendar."* The stakes of the argument were not small.

---

*Quoted in R. M. Hartwell et al., *The Long Debate on Poverty* (Surrey, England: Institute of Economic Affairs, 1972), 185.

The controversy about the benefits and costs of industrialization has continued in different forms right down to the present, in part because it is an argument directly inspired by the ideologies—liberalism, socialism, communism—that emerged as explanations of and blueprints for economic and social change. In the 1830s and 1840s, liberals insisted that industrialization would promote greater prosperity for everyone, whereas conservatives complained that it destroyed traditional ways of life and socialists warned that it exaggerated inequality and class division. In the 1950s and 1960s, defenders of capitalist free enterprise still advanced the argument about prosperity, but now they were opposed by communists who argued that state control of production could sidestep the horrors of early capitalist exploitation. Newly developing countries looked to the history of the 1830s and 1840s for lessons about the likely impact of industrialization on their countries in the 1950s and beyond. The scholarly debates therefore attracted worldwide attention, and all sides called on statistics to make their competing cases.

Unfortunately, the statistics can be interpreted in many different ways. Did it matter more that wages for factory workers went up or that life expectancy went down? If an increase in sugar consumption in Great Britain from 207,000 tons in 1844 to 290,000 tons in 1847 meant an overall increase in the standard of living, how does that square with the hundreds of thousands of deaths in Ireland at the same time or the increasing disparity throughout Great Britain between rich and poor? Some convergence of opinion has taken place, however. Most now agree that by sometime between 1820 and 1845 (the exact date depending on the scholar), conditions in Great Britain had become better than before the Industrial Revolution. And there is no doubt that the debate itself

between 1841 and 1846, Vienna by 125,000 between 1827 and 1847, and Berlin by 180,000 between 1815 and 1848. (See "Taking Measure," page 812.)

Massive rural emigration, not natural increase (births to women already living in cities), accounted for this remarkable increase. Agricultural improvements had increased the food supply and hence the rural population, but the land could no longer support the people living on it. City life and new factories beckoned those faced with hunger and poverty. They also attracted emigrants from other lands: thousands of Irish emigrated to English cities, Italians went to French cities, and Poles flocked to German cities. Settlements sprang up outside the old city limits but gradually became part of the urban area. As cities grew, their medieval walls came down.

has had one major positive effect: since making one's point depends on having statistics to prove it, the debate itself has encouraged a staggering amount of research into quantitative measures of just about everything imaginable, from measures of wages and prices to rates of mortality and even average heights (height being correlated, it is thought, to economic well-being). British soldiers in the nineteenth century were taller on average than those in any other country except the United States, and people who believe that industrialization improved the standard of living are happy to seize on this as evidence for their case.

One example of a recently developed statistic shows both how powerful and how debatable such sources can be. This table adapted from a recent study by Jeffrey G. Williamson, provides a simple measure—based on complex calculations—of the gap in wages between British farm and nonfarm laborers for the period 1797 to 1851. The index measures the attractiveness of nonfarm (basically city, mining, and factory) work. It shows that nonfarm wages rose faster than farm wages, but only after 1820 or so. By 1851, nonfarm wages had far outstripped those on the farm. What can we conclude? Although these data seem to support the view that the standard of living of workers improved sometime in the 1820s and continued to do so afterward, Williamson does not conclude that factory workers were better off than farmers; instead, he argues that the gap indicates that farm people did not migrate quickly enough to the city to satisfy urban labor demands. In short, he seems to consider the gap between farm and nonfarm wages to be a problem of "labor-market disequilibrium." The lesson to be learned is that all historians' conclusions depend on the questions they ask and the sources they use—and few sources are as open to different interpretations as statistics.

Trends in the British Nominal-Wage Gap, 1797–1851 (1797=100)

Year	Index
1797	100
1805	86.6
1810	96.7
1815	105.1
1827	132.4
1835	134.7
1851	148.3

The gap is calculated as the difference between the weighted average of nonfarm unskilled earnings (common laborers, porters, police, guards, watchmen, coal miners, and so on) and the farm-earnings rate, divided by the farm-earnings rate. Thus, it is the percentage differential by which nonfarm unskilled wages exceeded farm wages.

Source: Jeffrey G. Williamson, "Leaving the Farm to Go to the City: Did They Leave Quickly Enough?" in John A. James and Mark Thomas, *Capitalism in Context: Essays on Economic Development and Cultural Change in Honor of R. M. Hartwell* (Chicago: University of Chicago Press, 1994), 159–183, table p. 182.

QUESTIONS FOR DEBATE

1. What is a good measure of the standard of living in the first half of the nineteenth century? How would you measure it today?

2. How do you explain the initial decline in nonfarm wages relative to farm wages and the subsequent rise?

3. What are the virtues of using statistical measures to determine the standard of living? What are the defects?

FURTHER READING

Morgan, Kenneth. *The Birth of Industrial Britain: Economic Change 1750–1850.* 1999.

Thompson, Noel W. *The Real Rights of Man: Political Economies for the Working Class, 1775–1850.* 1998.

At the same time, cities incorporated parks, cemeteries, zoos, and greenways, all imitations of the countryside, which itself was being industrialized by railroads and factories. "One can't even go to one's land for the slightest bit of gardening," grumbled a French citizen, annoyed by new industrial potteries in town, "without being covered with a black powder that spoils every plant that it touches."

Overcrowding and Disease. The rapid influx of people caused serious overcrowding in the cities because the housing stock expanded much more slowly than population growth. In Paris, 30,000 workers lived in lodging houses, eight or nine to a room, with no separation of the sexes. One contemporary observed: "The difficulty of finding lodgings is for the worker a constant ordeal and a

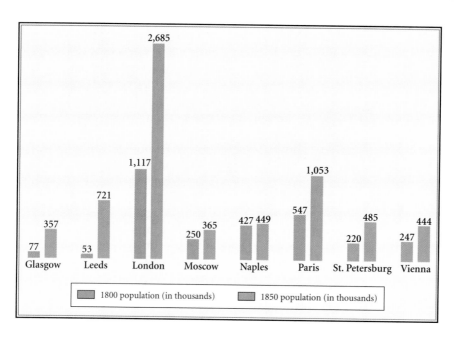

TAKING MEASURE
Population of Major European Cities, 1800–1850
Although London was by far the biggest city in mid-nineteenth-century Europe, it was not the fastest growing. According to these figures for population in 1800 and 1850, which city was the fastest growing? How much was population growth in these cities due to industrialization? What problems might have been created by especially rapid growth?
From B. R. Mitchell, *European Historical Statistics, 1750–1970* (New York: Columbia University Press, 1975), B4.

perpetual cause of misery." In 1847 in St. Giles, the Irish quarter of London, 461 people lived in just twelve houses. Men, women, and children huddled together on piles of filthy rotting straw or potato peels because they had no money for fuel to keep warm.

Severe crowding worsened already dire sanitation conditions. Garbage and refuse littered the unpaved streets of poor districts, and smog, smoke, and putrid smells fouled the air. Water was scarce and had to be fetched daily from nearby fountains. Despite the diversion of water from provincial rivers to Paris and a tripling of the number of public fountains, Parisians had enough water for only two baths annually per person (the upper classes enjoyed more baths, of course; the lower classes, fewer). In London, private companies that supplied water turned on pumps in the poorer sections for only a few hours three days a week. Sewage removal was practically nonexistent. Residents dumped refuse into streets or courtyards, and human excrement collected in cesspools under apartment houses. At mid-century, London's approximately 250,000 cesspools were emptied only once or twice a year. In rapidly growing British industrial cities such as Manchester, one-third of the houses contained no latrines. Human waste ended up in the rivers that supplied drinking water. The horses that provided transportation inside the cities left droppings everywhere, and city dwellers often kept chickens, ducks,

goats, pigs, geese, and even cattle, as well as dogs and cats, in their houses. The result was a "universal atmosphere of filth and stink."

Such conditions made cities prime breeding grounds for disease; those with 50,000 people or more had twice the death rates of rural areas. In 1830–1832 and again in 1847–1851, devastating outbreaks of cholera swept across Asia and Europe (touching the United States as well in 1849–1850). Today we know that a waterborne bacterium causes the disease, but at the time no one understood the disease and everyone feared it. The usually fatal disease induced violent vomiting and diarrhea and left the skin blue, eyes sunken and dull, and hands and feet ice cold. While cholera particularly ravaged the crowded, filthy neighborhoods of rapidly growing cities, it also claimed many rural as well as some well-to-do victims. In Paris, 18,000 people died in the 1832 epidemic and 20,000 in that of 1849; in London, 7,000 died in each epidemic; in Russia, the epidemic was catastrophic, claiming 250,000 victims in 1831–1832 and a million in 1847–1851 (Map 22.2).

Rumors and panic followed in the epidemics' wakes. Everywhere the downtrodden imagined conspiracies: in Paris in April 1832, a crowd of workers attacked a central hospital, believing the doctors were poisoning the poor but using cholera as a hoax to cover up the conspiracy. Eastern European peasants burned estates and killed physicians and officials.

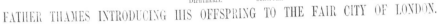

FATHER THAMES INTRODUCING HIS OFFSPRING TO THE FAIR CITY OF LONDON.

Lithograph of London
This English lithograph draws attention to the connection between contaminated water supplies—in this case the Thames River in London—and epidemic disease—diphtheria, scrofula, and cholera are cited at the bottom of the print. The title, Father Thames Introducing His Offspring to the Fair City of London, *is particularly jarring; a monsterlike figure drags a dead body out of the slime and presents it to the fair maiden who represents London. The sub-title, "A Design for a Fresco in the New Houses of Parliament" challenges the political leadership to recognize the social problems festering nearby.*
Hulton Getty/Liaison Agency.

Daguerreotype of Paris
Daguerre experimented extensively with producing an image on a metal plate before he came up with a viable photographic process in 1837. In 1839, the French government bought the rights and made the process freely available. This picture of a Parisian boulevard seems to depict empty streets because with the long exposure required to capture the image, moving objects did not register. The image is also reversed (as if seen in a mirror). Because of these technical problems, the early photographic process proved most suitable for portraits.
Bayrisches National Museum.

Although devastating, cholera did not kill as many people as tuberculosis, Europe's number-one deadly disease. But tuberculosis took its victims one by one and therefore had less impact on social relations.

Raging epidemics spurred a growing concern for public health. When news of the cholera out-break in eastern Europe reached Paris in 1831, the city set up commissions in each municipal district to collect information about lower-class housing and sanitation. In Great Britain, reports on sanitation conditions among the working class led to the passage of new public health laws.

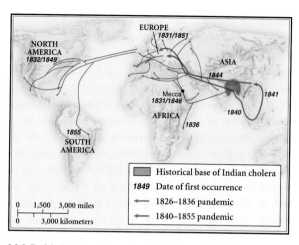

MAP 22.2 The Spread of Cholera, 1826–1855
Contemporaries did not understand the causes of the cholera epidemics in the 1830s and the 1840s in Europe. Western Europeans knew only that the disease marched progressively from east to west across Europe. Nothing seemed able to stop it. It appeared and died out for reasons that could not be grasped at the time. Nevertheless, the cholera epidemics prompted authorities in most European countries to set up public health agencies to coordinate the response and study sanitation conditions in the cities.

Middle-Class Fears. The middle and upper classes feared the urban threats to their settled, comfortable ways of life. The more prosperous classes lived in large, well-appointed apartments or houses with more light, more air, and more water than in lower-class dwellings. But the lower classes lived nearby, sometimes in the cramped upper floors of the same apartment houses. Middle-class reformers often considered the poor to be morally degenerate because of the circumstances of urban life. In their view, overcrowding led to sexual promiscuity and illegitimacy. They depicted the lower classes as dangerously lacking in sexual self-control. A physician visiting Lille, France, in 1835 wrote of "individuals of both sexes and of very different ages lying together, most of them without nightshirts and repulsively dirty. . . . The reader will complete the picture. . . . His imagination must not recoil before any of the disgusting mysteries performed on these impure beds, in the midst of obscurity and drunkenness."

Officials collected statistics on illegitimacy that seemed to bear out these fears: one-quarter to one-half of the babies born in the big European cities in the 1830s and 1840s were illegitimate, and alarmed medical men wrote about thousands of infanticides. Between 1815 and the mid-1830s in France, 33,000 babies were abandoned at foundling hospitals every year; 27 percent of births in Paris in 1850 were illegitimate, compared with only 4 percent of rural births. By collecting such statistics, physicians and administrators in the new public health movement hoped to promote legislation to better the living conditions for workers, but at the same time they helped stereotype workers as helpless and out of control.

Sexual disorder seemed to go hand in hand with drinking and crime. Beer halls and pubs dotted the urban landscape. By the 1830s, Hungary's twin cities of Buda and Pest had eight hundred beer and wine houses for the working classes. One London street boasted twenty-three pubs in three hundred yards. Police officials estimated that London had 70,000 thieves and 80,000 prostitutes. In many cities, nearly half the urban population lived at the level of bare subsistence, and increasing numbers depended on public welfare, charity, or criminality to make ends meet.

Everywhere reformers warned of a widening separation between rich and poor and a growing sense of hostility between the classes. The French poet Amédée Pommier wrote of "These leagues of laborers who have no work, / These far too many arms, these starving mobs." Clergy joined the chorus of physicians and humanitarians in making dire predictions. A Swiss pastor noted: "A new spirit has arisen among the workers. Their hearts seethe with hatred of the well-to-do; their eyes lust for a share of the wealth about them; their mouths speak unblushingly of a coming day of retribution." In 1848 it would seem that that day of retribution had arrived.

Agricultural Perils and Prosperity

Rising population created increased demand for food and spurred changes in life in the countryside too. Peasants and farmers planted fallow land and chopped down forests and drained marshes to open up more land for farming. Still, Europe's ability to feed its expanding population remained questionable: although agricultural yields increased by 30 to 50 percent in the first half of the nineteenth century, population grew by nearly 100 percent.

Railroads and canals improved food distribution, but much of Europe—particularly in the east—remained isolated from markets and vulnerable to famines.

Most people still lived on the land, and the upper classes still dominated rural society. Successful businessmen bought land avidly, seeing it not only as the ticket to respectability but also as a hedge against hard times. Hardworking, crafty, or lucky commoners sometimes saved enough to purchase holdings that they had formerly rented or slowly acquired slivers of land from less fortunate neighbors. In France at midcentury, almost two million economically independent peasants tended their own small properties. But in England, southern Italy, Prussia, and eastern Europe, large landowners, usually noblemen, consolidated and expanded their estates by buying up the land of less successful nobles or peasants. As agricultural prices rose, the big landowners pushed for legislation to allow them to continue converting common land to private property.

Wringing a living from the soil under such conditions put pressure on traditional family life. For example, men often migrated seasonally to earn cash in factories or as village artisans, while their wives, sisters, and daughters did the traditional "men's work" of tending crops. The threat of subdivision of the land encouraged rudimentary forms of birth control. In France, for instance, the Napoleonic Code provided for an equal distribution of inheritance among all heirs; as a result, land was divided over generations into such small parcels that less than 25 percent of all French landowners could support themselves. In the past, population growth had been contained by postponing marriage (leaving fewer years for childbearing) and by high rates of death in childbirth and infant mortality. Now, as child mortality declined outside the industrial cities and people without property began marrying earlier, Europeans became more aware of birth control methods. Contraceptive techniques improved; for example, the vulcanization of rubber in the 1840s made condoms more reliable. When such methods failed and population increase left no options open at home, people emigrated, often to the United States. Some 800,000 Germans had moved out of central Europe by 1850, while in the 1840s famine drove tens of thousands of Irish abroad. Between 1816 and 1850, five million Europeans left their home countries for new lives overseas. When France colonized Algeria in the 1830s and 1840s, officials

Bearbaiting
This colored engraving from 1821 of Charley's Theater in London shows that bearbaiting did not attract only the lower classes, as reformers often implied. Top hats were most often worn by middle-class men, who seem to be enjoying the spectacle of dogs taunting the bear as much as the working-class men present. At this time, bearbaiting, like bullbaiting, began to come under fire as cruel to animals.
Mary Evans Picture Library.

tried to attract settlers by emphasizing the fertility of the land; they offered the prospect of agricultural prosperity in the colony as an alternative to the rigors of industrialization and urbanization at home.

Despite all the challenges to established ways of life, rural political power remained in the hands of traditional elites. The biggest property owners dominated their tenants and sharecroppers, often demanding a greater yield without contributing to improvements that would enhance productivity. They also controlled the political assemblies and often personally selected the parish clergy and local officials. Such power not surprisingly provoked resentment. As one Italian critic wrote, "Great landowner is often the synonym for great ignoramus." Nowhere did the old rural social order seem more impregnable than in Russia. Most Russian serfs remained tied to the land, and troops easily suppressed serfs' uprisings in 1831 and 1842. By midcentury, peasant emancipation remained Russia's great unresolved problem.

❖ Reforming the Social Order

In the 1830s and 1840s, Europeans organized to reform the social evils created by industrialization and urbanization. They acted in response to the outpouring of government reports, medical accounts, and literary and artistic depiction of new social problems. Middle-class women often took the lead in establishing new charitable organizations that tried to bring religious faith, educational uplift, and the reform of manners to the lower classes. Middle-class men and women too expected women to soften the rigors of a rapidly changing society, but this expectation led to some confusion about women's proper role: should they devote themselves to social reform in the world or to their own domestic spaces? Many hoped to apply the same zeal for reform to the colonial peoples living in places administered by Europeans.

Cultural Responses to the "Social Question"

The "social question," an expression reflecting the deeply shared concern about social changes, pervaded all forms of art and literature. The dominant artistic movement of the time, romanticism, generally took a dim view of industrialization. The English-born painter Thomas Cole (1801–1848) complained in 1836: "In this age . . . a meager utilitarianism seems ready to absorb every feeling and sentiment, and what is sometimes called improvement in its march makes us fear that the bright and tender flowers of the imagination shall all be crushed beneath its iron tramp." When Cole went to the United States to paint, he depicted "primeval forests, virgin lakes and waterfalls"—that is, a landscape untouched by machinery. Yet culture itself underwent important changes as the growing capitals of Europe attracted flocks of aspiring painters and playwrights; the 1830s and 1840s witnessed an explosion in culture as the number of would-be artists increased dramatically and new technologies such as photography and lithography brought art to the masses. Many of these new intellectuals would support the revolutions of 1848.

Romantic Concerns about Industrial Life. Because romanticism tended to glorify nature and reject industrial and urban growth, romantics often gave vivid expression to fears of economic and social transformation. The English poet Elizabeth Barrett Browning, best known for her love poems, decried child labor in "The Cry of the Children" (1843):

> For, all day, we drag our burden tiring
> Through the coal-dark underground,
> Or, all day, we drive the wheels of iron
> In the factories, round and round

Architects of the period sought to recapture a preindustrial world. When the British Houses of Parliament were rebuilt after they burned down in 1834, the architect Sir Charles Barry constructed them in a Gothic style reminiscent of the Middle Ages. This medievalism was taken even further by A. W. N. Pugin, who prepared the Gothic details for the Houses of Parliament. In his polemical book *Contrasts* (1836), Pugin denounced modern conditions and compared them unfavorably with those in the 1400s. To underline his view, Pugin wore medieval clothes at home.

Romantic painters specialized in landscape as a way of calling attention to the sublime wonders of nature, but sometimes even landscapes showed the power of new technologies. In *Rain, Steam, and*

Joseph M. W. Turner, *The Fighting Téméraire Tugged to Her Last Berth to Be Broken Up* (1838)
Turner's painting captures the clash of old and new as a steamer belching smoke tows a wooden sailing ship
to its last berth, where it will be destroyed. Turner muses about the passing of old ways but also displays his
mastery of color in the final blaze of sunset, itself another sign of the passing of time. Turner considered
painting to be closely related to poetry; he was an avid reader of the romantic poets, especially Byron.
National Gallery, London.

Speed: The Great Western Railway (1844), the leading English romantic painter, Joseph M. W. Turner (1775–1851), portrayed the struggle between the forces of nature and the means of economic growth. Turner was fascinated by steamboats: in *The Fighting "Téméraire" Tugged to Her Last Berth to Be Broken Up* (1838), he featured the victory of steam power over more conventional sailing ships. An admirer described it as an "almost prophetic idea of smoke, soot, iron, and steam, coming to the front in all naval matters."

The Depiction of Social Conditions in Novels.
The novel was the art form best suited to presenting social problems. Thanks to increased literacy, the spread of reading rooms and lending libraries, and serialization in newspapers and journals, novels reached a large reading public. Unlike the fiction of the eighteenth century, which had focused on indi-

vidual personalities, the great novels of the 1830s and 1840s specialized in the portrayal of social life in all its varieties. Manufacturers, financiers, starving students, workers, bureaucrats, prostitutes, underworld figures, thieves, and aristocratic men and women filled the pages of works by popular writers such as Honoré de Balzac and Charles Dickens. Pushing himself to exhaustion and a premature death to get out of debt, the French writer Balzac (1799–1850) cranked out ninety-five novels and many short stories. He aimed to catalog the social types that could be found in French society. Many of his characters, like himself, were driven by the desire to climb higher in the social order.

Charles Dickens (1812–1870) worked with a similar frenetic energy and for much the same reasons. When his father was imprisoned for debt in 1824, the young Dickens took a job in a shoe-polish factory. In 1836, he published a series of literary sketches of daily life in London to accompany a volume of caricatures by the artist George Cruikshank, whose work resembled the lithograph that opens this chapter. Dickens then produced a series of novels that appeared in monthly installments and attracted thousands of readers. In them he paid close attention to the distressing effects of industrialization and urbanization. In *The Old Curiosity Shop* (1841), for example, he depicts the Black Country, the manufacturing region west and northwest of Birmingham, as a "cheerless region," a "mournful place," in which tall chimneys "made foul the melancholy air." In addition to publishing such enduring favorites as *Oliver Twist* (1838) and *A Christmas Carol* (1843), he ran charitable organizations and pressed for social reforms. For Dickens, the ability to portray the problems of the poor went hand in hand with a personal commitment to reform.

Novels by women often revealed the bleaker side of women's situations. *Jane Eyre* (1847), a novel by Charlotte Brontë, describes the difficult life of an orphaned girl who becomes a governess, the only occupation open to most single middle-class women. Although in an economically weak position, Jane Eyre refuses to achieve respectability and security through marriage, the usual option for women. The French novelist George Sand (Amandine-Aurore Dupin, 1804–1876) took her social criticism a step further. She announced her independence in the 1830s by dressing like a man and smoking cigars. Like many other women writers of the time, she published her work under a male pseudonym while creating female characters who prevail in difficult circumstances through romantic love and moral idealism. Sand's novel *Indiana* (1832), about an unhappily married woman, was read all over Europe. Her notoriety—she became the lover of the Polish pianist Frédéric Chopin, among others, and threw herself into socialist politics—made the term *George-Sandism* a common expression of disdain for independent women.

The Explosion of Culture. As artists became more interested in society and social relations, ordinary citizens crowded cultural events. Museums opened to the public across Europe, and the middle classes began collecting art. Popular theaters in big cities drew thousands from the lower and middle classes every night; in London, for example, some

George Sand

In this lithograph by Alcide Lorentz of 1842, George Sand is shown in one of her notorious male costumes. Sand published numerous works, including novels, plays, essays, travel writing, and an autobiography. She actively participated in the revolution of 1848 in France, writing pamphlets in support of the new republic. Disillusioned by the rise to power of Louis-Napoleon Bonaparte, she withdrew to her country estate and devoted herself exclusively to her writing. The Granger Collection.

24,000 people attended eighty "penny theaters" nightly. The audience for print culture also multiplied. In the German states, for example, the production of new literary works doubled between 1830 and 1843, as did the number of periodicals and newspapers and the number of booksellers. Thirty or forty private lending libraries offered books in Berlin in the 1830s, and reading rooms in pastry shops stocked political newspapers and satirical journals. Young children and ragpickers sold cheap prints and books door to door or in taverns.

The advent of photography in 1839 provided an amazing new medium for artists. Daguerreotypes, named after their inventor, French painter Jacques Daguerre (1787–1851), prompted one artist to claim that "from today, painting is dead." Although this prediction was highly exaggerated, photography did open up new ways of portraying reality. Visual images, whether in painting, on the stage, or in photography, heightened the public's awareness of the effects of industrialization and urbanization.

The number of artists and writers swelled. Estimates suggest that the number of painters and sculptors in France, the undisputed center of European art at the time, grew sixfold between 1789 and 1838. Not everyone could succeed in this hothouse atmosphere as writers and artists furiously competed for public attention. Their own troubles made some of them more keenly aware of the hardships faced by the poor. In one of many bitingly critical journals and booklets published in Berlin appeared the following "Lies Chronicle": "In Ipswich in England a mechanical genius has invented a stomach, whose extraordinary efficient construction is remarkable. This artificial stomach is intended for factory workers there and is adjusted so that it is fully satisfied with three lentils or peas; one potato is enough for an entire week."

The Varieties of Social Reform

Lithographs, novels, even joke booklets helped drive home the need for social reform, but religious conviction also inspired efforts to help the poor. Moral reform societies, Bible groups, Sunday schools, and temperance groups all aimed to turn the poor into respectable people. In 1844, for example, 450 different relief organizations operated in London alone. States supported these efforts by encouraging education and enforcing laws against the vagrant poor.

The Religious Impulse for Social Reform. Religiously motivated reformers first had to overcome the perceived indifference of the working classes. Protestant and Catholic clergy complained that workers had no interest in religion; less than 10 percent of the workers in the cities attended religious services. In a report on the state of religion in England and Wales in 1851, the head of the census Horace Mann commented that "the masses of our working population . . . are *unconscious secularists.* . . . These are never, or but seldom seen in our religious congregations." To combat such indifference, British religious groups launched the Sunday school movement, which reached its zenith in the 1840s. By 1851, more than half of all working-class chil-

dren between five and fifteen were attending Sunday school, even though very few of their parents regularly went to religious services. The Sunday schools taught children how to read at a time when few working-class children could go to school during the week.

Women took a more prominent role than ever before in charitable work. Catholic religious orders, which by 1850 enrolled many more women than men, ran schools, hospitals, leper colonies, insane asylums, and old-age homes. New Catholic orders, especially for women, were established, and Catholic missionary activity overseas increased. Protestant women in Great Britain and the United States established Bible, missionary, and female reform societies by the hundreds. Chief among their concerns was prostitution, and many societies dedicated themselves to reforming "fallen women" and castigating men who visited prostitutes. As a pamphlet of the Boston Female Moral Reform Society explained, "Our mothers, our sisters, our daughters are sacrificed by the thousands every year on the altar of sin, and who are the agents in this work of destruction: Why, our fathers, our brothers, and our sons." Elizabeth Fry, an English Quaker minister, toured Europe in the 1830s helping set up institutions for female prisoners modeled on the school and manufacturing shop she had organized at Newgate Prison in London.

Catholics and Protestants alike promoted the temperance movement. In Ireland, England, the German states, and the United States, temperance societies organized to fight the "pestilence of hard liquor." The first societies had appeared in the United States as early as 1813, and by 1835 the American Temperance Society claimed 1.5 million members. The London-based British and Foreign Temperance Society, established in 1831, matched its American counterpart in its opposition to all alcohol. In the northern German states, temperance societies drew in the middle and working classes, Catholic as well as Protestant. Temperance advocates saw drunkenness as a sign of moral weakness and a threat to social order. Industrialists pointed to the loss of worker productivity, and efforts to promote temperance often reflected middle- and upper-class fears of the lower classes' lack of discipline. One German temperance advocate insisted, "One need not be a prophet to know that all efforts to combat the widespread and rapidly spreading

Temperance Broadsheet
This broadsheet from the 1830s linked the temperance movements in Ireland, where it was established in 1829, England, and Scotland. Queen Victoria became patron of the British and Foreign Temperance Society upon her accession to the throne in 1837. The account is melodramatic: drink leads to crime, disease, and even hanging.
Mansell Collection/Time Inc.

pauperism will be unsuccessful as long as the common man fails to realize that the principal source of his degradation and misery is his fondness of drink." Yet temperance societies also attracted working-class people who shared the desire for respectability.

Education and Reform of the Poor.   Social reformers saw education as one of the main prospects for uplifting the poor and the working class. In addition to setting up Sunday schools, British churches founded organizations such as the National Society for the Education of the Poor in the Principles of the Established Church and the British and Foreign School Society. Most of these emphasized Bible reading. More secular in intent were the Mechanics Institutes, which provided education for workers in the big cities.

In 1833, the French government passed an education law that required every town to maintain a primary school, pay a teacher, and provide free education to poor boys. As the law's author, François Guizot, argued, "Ignorance renders the masses turbulent and ferocious." Girls' schools were optional, although hundreds of women taught at the primary level, most of them in private, often religious schools. Despite these efforts, only one out of every thirty children went to school in France, many fewer than in Protestant states such as Prussia, where 75 percent of children were in primary school by 1835. Popular education remained woefully undeveloped in most of eastern Europe. Peasants were specifically

excluded from the few primary schools in Russia, where Tsar Nicholas I blamed the Decembrist Revolt of 1825 on education.

Above all else, the elite sought to impose discipline and order on working people. Popular sports, especially blood sports such as cockfighting and bearbaiting, suggested a lack of control, and long-standing efforts in Great Britain to eliminate these recreations now gained momentum through organizations such as the Society for the Prevention of Cruelty to Animals. By the end of the 1830s, bull-baiting had been abandoned in Great Britain. "This useful animal," rejoiced one reformer in 1839, "is no longer tortured amidst the exulting yells of those who are a disgrace to our common form and nature." The other blood sports died out more slowly, and efforts in other countries generally lagged behind those of the British.

When private charities failed to meet the needs of the poor, governments often intervened. Great Britain sought to control the costs of public welfare by passing a new poor law in 1834, called by its critics the "Starvation Act." The law required that all able-bodied persons receiving relief be housed together in workhouses, with husbands separated from wives and parents from children. Workhouse life was designed to be as unpleasant as possible so that poor people would move on to regions of higher employment. British women from all social classes organized anti–poor law societies to protest the separation of mothers from their children in the workhouses.

Domesticity and the Subordination of Women.

Many women viewed charitable work as the extension of their domestic roles: they promoted virtuous behavior and morality and thus improved society. In one widely read advice book, Englishwoman Sarah Lewis suggested in 1839 that "women may be the prime agents in the regeneration of mankind." But women's social reform activities concealed a paradox. According to the set of beliefs that historians call the doctrine or ideology of domesticity, women should live their lives entirely within the domestic sphere; they should devote themselves to the home. The English poet Alfred, Lord Tennyson, captured this view in a popular poem published in 1847: "Man for the field and woman for the hearth; / Man for the sword and for the needle she. . . . All else confusion." Many believed that maintaining proper and distinct roles for men and women was critically important to maintaining social order in general.

Most women had little hope of economic independence. The notion of a separate, domestic sphere for women prevented them from pursuing higher education, work in professional careers, or participation in politics through voting or holding office, all activities deemed appropriate only to men. Laws everywhere codified the subordination of women. Many countries followed the model of Napoleon's Civil Code, which classified married women as legal incompetents along with children, the insane, and criminals. In Great Britain, which had no national law code, the courts upheld the legality of a husband's complete control. For example, in 1840 a court ruled that "there can be no doubt of the general dominion which the law of England attributes to the husband over the wife." In some countries, such as France and Austria, unmarried women enjoyed some rights over property, but elsewhere laws explicitly defined them as perpetual minors under paternal control.

Distinctions between men and women were most noticeable in the privileged classes. Whereas boys attended secondary schools, most middle- and upper-class girls still received their education at home or in church schools, where they were taught to be religious, obedient, and accomplished in music and languages. As men began to wear practical clothing—long trousers and short jackets of solid, often dark colors, no makeup (previously common for aristocratic men), and simply cut hair—women continued to dress for decorative effect, now with tightly corseted waists that emphasized the differences between female and male bodies. Middle- and upper-class women had long hair that required hours of brushing and pinning up, and they wore long, cumbersome skirts. Advice books written by women detailed the tasks that such women undertook in the home: maintaining household accounts, supervising servants, and organizing social events.

Scientists reinforced stereotypes. Once considered sexually insatiable, women were now described

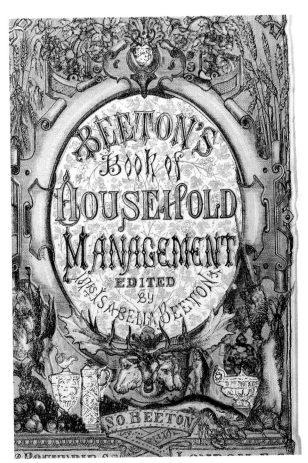

A Manual of Domesticity
Beeton's Book of Household Management *appeared in book form in 1861 after it had been published in* The Englishwoman's Domestic Magazine *by Mrs. Beeton's husband in the 1850s. In more than a thousand pages, it codified the domestic expectations of middle-class women. Mrs. Beeton, who died in childbirth at age twenty nine, advised women on almost every aspect of domestic life, from the management of servants to how to spend evenings at home (the lady does needlework; the man reads aloud from an edifying work).*
Pix Producers, Inc.

as incapacitated by menstruation and largely uninterested in sex, an attitude that many equated with moral superiority. Thus was born the "Victorian woman," a figment of the largely male medical imagination. Physicians and scholars considered women mentally inferior. In 1839, Auguste Comte, an influential early French sociologist, wrote, "As for any functions of government, the radical inaptitude of the female sex is there yet more marked . . . and limited to the guidance of the mere family."

Some women denounced the ideology of domesticity; according to the English writer Ann Lamb, for example, "the duty of a wife *means* the obedience of a Turkish slave." Middle-class women who did not marry, however, had few options for earning a living; they often worked as governesses or ladies' companions for the well-to-do. Most lower-class women worked because of financial necessity; as the wives of peasants, workers, or shopkeepers, they had to supplement the family's meager income by working on the farm, in a factory, or in a shop. For them, domesticity might have been an ideal; rarely a reality. Families crammed into small spaces had no time or energy for "separate spheres."

Abuses and Reforms Overseas

Like the ideals of domesticity, the ideals of colonialism often conflicted with the reality of economic interests. In the first half of the nineteenth century, those economic interests changed as European colonialism underwent a subtle but momentous transformation. Colonialism became *imperialism*—a word coined only in the mid-nineteenth century—as Europeans turned their interest away from the plantation colonies of the Caribbean toward the new colonies in Asia and Africa. Whereas colonialism most often led to the establishment of settler colonies, direct rule by Europeans, the introduction of slave labor from Africa, and the wholesale destruction of indigenous peoples, imperialism usually meant more indirect forms of economic exploitation and political rule. Europeans still profited from their colonies, but now they also aimed to reform colonial peoples in their own image—when it did not conflict too much with their economic interests to do so.

Abolition of Slavery. Colonialism—as opposed to imperialism—rose and fell with the enslavement

Abolitionism

In 1807, Charles James Fox introduced a bill prohibiting British participation in the slave trade. This statue of a black slave kneeling in gratitude was included in Fox's memorial in Westminster Abbey. Although Parliament passed Fox's bill, other countries proved less eager to give up the slave trade, which actually expanded in the 1830s and 1840s. Britain abolished slavery in its colonies in 1833, France in 1848. Human bondage continued in the United States and Brazil until 1863 and 1888, respectively.
National Monuments Record © Crown Copyright NMR.

of black Africans. The antislavery movement spread slowly but decisively following the British withdrawal from the slave trade in 1807. The new Latin American republics abolished slavery in the 1820s and 1830s after they defeated the Spanish with armies that included many slaves. British missionary and evangelical groups condemned the conquest, enslavement, and exploitation of native

African populations and successfully blocked British annexations in central and southern Africa in the 1830s. British reformers finally obtained the abolition of slavery in the British Empire in 1833. Anti-slavery petitions to Parliament bore 1.5 million signatures, including those of 350,000 women on one petition alone. In France, the new government of Louis-Philippe took strong measures against clandestine slave traffic, virtually ending French participation during the 1830s. Slavery was abolished in the remaining French Caribbean colonies in 1848.

Slavery did not disappear immediately just because the major European powers had given it up. The transatlantic trade in slaves actually reached its peak numbers in the early 1840s. Human bondage continued unabated in Brazil, Cuba (still a Spanish colony), and the United States. Some American reformers supported abolition, but it remained a minority movement. Like serfdom in Russia, slavery in the Americas involved a quagmire of economic, political, and moral problems that worsened over time.

Historians debate the causes of the end of the African slave trade and of African slavery as a form of labor in the New World. Some argue that industrialization made slavery superfluous because with steam-driven machinery free labor proved itself more productive in the long run. Yet the British textile manufacturers relied heavily on imports of cotton from the southern slave states of the United States. Others place more emphasis on the anti-slavery campaign itself, arguing that slavery was incompatible with the humanitarian values of a reforming era. This explanation has trouble, however, in accounting for the fact that the French and Dutch governments also abolished slavery even though neither faced major public reform campaigns. Whatever the reason for abolition, slavery, and with it the old-style colonialism, was on the wane.

Economic and Political Imperialism.   Despite the abolition of slavery, Britain and France had not lost interest in overseas colonies. Using the pretext of an insult to its envoy, France invaded Algeria in 1830 and after a long military campaign established political control over most of the country in the next two decades. By 1850, more than seventy thousand French, Italian, and Maltese colonists had settled there, often confiscating the lands of native peoples. The new French administration of the colony made

efforts to balance native and settler interests, however, and eventually France would not only incorporate Algeria into France but also try to assimilate its native population to French culture. France also imposed a protectorate government over the South Pacific island of Tahiti.

The British likewise increased their holdings overseas. Although they granted Canada greater self-determination in 1839, they annexed Singapore (1819) and New Zealand (1840). They also extended their control in India through the administration of the East India Company, a private group of merchants chartered by the British crown. The British educated a native elite to take over much of the day-to-day business of administering the country and used native soldiers to augment their military control. By 1850, only one in six soldiers serving Britain in India was European.

The East India Company also tried to establish a regular trade with China in opium, a drug long known for its medicinal uses but increasingly bought in China as a recreational drug. (See "Did You Know?," page 824.) The Chinese government did its best to keep the highly addictive drug away from its people, both by forbidding western merchants to venture outside the southern city of Guangzhou (Canton) and by banning the export of precious metals and the import of opium. These measures failed. By smuggling opium into China and bribing local officials, British traders built up a flourishing market, and by the mid-1830s they were pressuring the British government to force an expanded opium trade on the Chinese. When in 1839 the Chinese authorities expelled British merchants from southern China, Britain retaliated by bombarding Chinese coastal cities. In 1842, it dictated to a defeated China the Treaty of Nanking, by which the British forced the opening of four more Chinese ports to Europeans, took sovereignty over the island of Hong Kong, received a substantial war indemnity, and were assured of a continuation of

The First Opium War, 1839–1842

Opium Addiction in Nineteenth-Century Britain

Great Britain fought two opium wars with China (1839–1842 and 1856–1858) that drew world attention to the problem of Chinese drug addiction. In Great Britain itself, the government did not regulate or restrict opium use until 1868. Pharmacists and grocers sold pills, lozenges, enemas, vinegars, and wines prepared with opium, which came from the heads of poppy plants imported first from the Ottoman Empire and, after 1750, from India. Tincture of opium (opium dissolved in alcohol), known as *laudanum*, was widely used as a sedative, and even children's opiates could be bought almost anywhere. Laudanum mixed with egg yolk was sold as a cure for hemorrhoids, and opiates were a popular remedy for toothache and diarrhea. Most doctors considered opium a good cure for delirium tremens, caused by alcohol abuse.

Death by overdose was a well-known phenomenon, but public opinion turned against the drug only when it became associated with abuse by the lower classes. Parliamentary inquiries in the 1830s denounced the use of opiates by working-class mothers, who gave their children Godfrey's Cordial or Street's Infant Quietness to make them sleep while they worked. Officials also worried that workers took opium and laudanum as a cheap substitute for alcohol, whose use was widely and loudly denounced by temperance societies. The concern about opiates followed from the general trend toward "reforming" lower-class behavior.

Well-known cases of addiction among writers and poets also attracted attention. The writer Thomas De Quincey stirred up controversy when he published his *Confessions of an English Opium-Eater* in 1821, but it was reissued many times during the nineteenth century. In the book, De Quincey discusses his and the romantic poet Samuel Taylor Coleridge's addiction. De Quincey calls himself the "pope" of the "true church" of opium and describes weaning himself from the drug in 1819 to escape the hallucinatory dreams

Opium Den in London ▶

This woodcut by Gustave Doré (c. 1870) shows that opium smoking persisted in Britain at least to the 1870s. Doré was a French book illustrator who came to London in 1869–1871 and produced illustrations of the poorer neighborhoods in the city. His taste for the grotesque is apparent in the figures watching the smokers. Doré also illustrated a book of Coleridge's poetry.
Print Collection, Miriam and Ira D. Wallach Division of Arts, Prints and Photographs. New York Public Library. Astor, Lenox and Tilden Foundation.

the opium trade. In this case, reform took a backseat to economic interest, despite the complaints of religious groups in Britain.

❖ The Ferment of Ideologies

Although reform organizations grew rapidly in the 1830s and 1840s, many Europeans found them insufficient to solve the problems created by industrialization and urbanization. They turned to movements inspired by the new political ideologies that had taken shape in the aftermath of the French Revolution. Liberals sought constitutional guarantees of rights and economic growth through free trade. Socialists developed new organizations to speak for the working classes and demand changes in the nature of work itself. But the most potent ideology—nationalism—looked past social problems to concentrate on achieving political autonomy and self-determination for groups identified by common languages and cultures rather than by class.

The Spell of Nationalism

Nationalists sought political autonomy for their ethnic group—a people linked by language and shared traditions. Although nationalism was still nascent in the first half of the nineteenth century among the peasants and workers of most countries, ethnic heritage was increasingly a major determinant of personal and political identity. Poles, that haunted him. He had terrifying nightmares of living in China in houses in which tables and sofas turned into crocodiles multiplied ten thousand times. But he relapsed and soon took bigger and bigger doses right into the 1840s. De Quincey and Coleridge were only the best-known cases of opium addiction: Byron, Shelley, Elizabeth Barrett Browning, Walter Scott, and Charles Dickens all took opiates at one time or another, as did many leading doctors and preachers.

The history of opium use in the nineteenth century raises significant questions: why did British authorities condemn its use at home even while forcing opium on the Chinese? Why was lower-class use of opiates especially disturbing to officials? Why did so many writers experiment with the drug? The history of opium is a fascinating example of the West's interaction with the rest of the world: it was first cultivated by ancient Sumerians and passed on to the Assyrians, Babylonians, Egyptians, and then Greeks; the Portuguese brought it to Europe in the sixteenth century as part of their trade with China; and its modern derivative heroin is now the subject of worldwide smuggling and official regulation.

Sources: Virginia Berridge and Griffith Edwards, *Opium and the People: Opiate Use in Nineteenth-Century England* (New York: St. Martin's Press, 1981); Thomas De Quincey, *The Confessions of an English Opium-Eater and Other Essays* (London: Macmillan, 1924).

Italians, Germans, Irish, and Russians all pursued nationalist goals (Map 22.3).

Polish nationalism became more self-conscious after the collapse of the revolt in 1830 against Russian domination. Ten thousand Poles, mostly noble army officers and intellectuals, fled Poland in 1830 and 1831. Most of them took up residence in western European capitals, especially Paris, where they mounted a successful public relations campaign for worldwide support. Their intellectual hero was the poet Adam Mickiewicz (1798–1855), whose mystical writings portrayed the Polish exiles as martyrs of a crucified nation with an international Christian mission: "Your endeavors are for all men, not only for yourselves. You will achieve a new Christian civilization."

Mickiewicz formed a Polish Legion to fight for national restoration, but rivalries and divisions among the Polish nationalists prevented united action until 1846, when Polish exiles in Paris tried to launch a coordinated insurrection for Polish independence. Poles in Cracow responded, and in a manifesto the rebels proclaimed, "All free nations of the world are calling on us not to let the great principle of nationality fail." Plans for an uprising in the Polish province of Galicia in the Austrian Empire collapsed, however, when peasants instead revolted against their noble Polish masters. Slaughtering some two thousand aristocrats, a desperate rural population served the Austrian government's end by defusing the nationalist challenge. Class interests and national identity were not always the same.

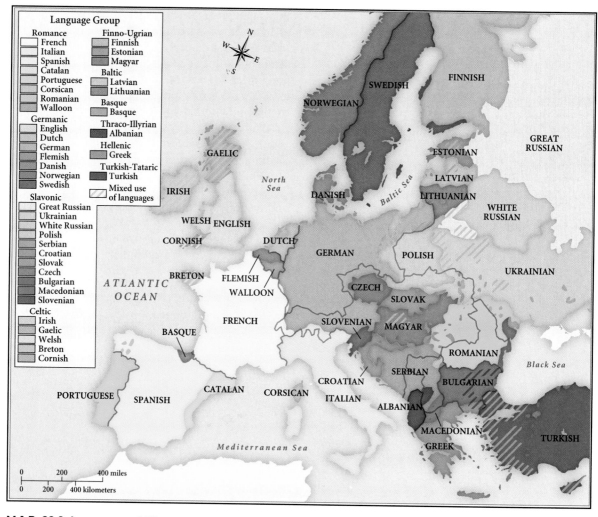

MAP 22.3 Languages of Nineteenth-Century Europe
Even this detailed map of linguistic diversity understates the number of different languages and dialects spoken in Europe. In Italy, for example, few Italians spoke Italian as their first language. Instead, they spoke local dialects such as Piedmontese or Ligurian, and some might speak better French than Italian if they came from the regions bordering France. The map does underline the inherent contradictions of nationalism in eastern Europe, where many linguistic regions incorporated other languages, and the result was constant conflict. But even in Spain, France, and Great Britain, linguistic diversity continued right up to the beginning of the 1900s.

One of those most touched by Mickiewicz's vision was Giuseppe Mazzini (1805–1872), a fiery Italian nationalist and republican journalist. Exiled in 1831 for his opposition to Austrian rule in northern Italy, Mazzini founded Young Italy, a secret society that attracted thousands with its message that Italy would touch off a European-wide revolutionary movement. The conservative order throughout Europe felt threatened by Mazzini's charismatic leadership and conspiratorial scheming, but he lacked both European allies against Austria and widespread support among the Italian masses.

Nationalism was an especially volatile issue in the Austrian Empire because Austria ruled over so many different nationalities (Map 22.3). The 1830s and 1840s saw the spread of nationalism among Magyars, Czechs, Slovaks, Serbs, Slovenes, Croats, and Romanians, in addition to Poles and Italians, all ethnic groups within the empire. Each of these peoples produced leaders who called for a cultural revival in language, literature, and education, as well as political rights. Scholars compiled dictionaries and created standard literary languages to replace peasant dialects; writers used the rediscovered vernacular instead of Latin or German; and historians glorified the national past. During the revolutions of 1848, however, it would become evident that these different ethnic groups disliked each other as much as they disliked their Austrian masters.

In the German states, teachers of German language, literature, law, and history embraced nationalism. German economic unification took a step forward with the foundation in 1834, under Prussian leadership, of the *Zollverein,* or "customs union," of most of the German states. Economist Friedrich List argued for external tariffs that would promote industrialization and cooperation across the boundaries of the German states so that an economically united Germany might compete with the rest of Europe. German nationalists sought a government uniting German-speaking peoples, but they could not agree on its boundaries. Austria was not part of the Customs Union: would the unified German state include both Prussia and the Austrian Empire? If it included Austria, what about the non-German territories of the Austrian Empire? And could the powerful and conservative kingdom of Prussia coexist in a unified German state with other, more liberal but smaller states? These questions would vex German history for decades to come.

In Russia, nationalism took the form of opposition to western ideas. Russian nationalists, or "Slavophiles" (lovers of the Slavs), opposed the "Westernizers," who wanted Russia to follow western models of industrial development and constitutional government. The Slavophiles favored maintaining rural traditions infused by the values of the Russian Orthodox church. Only a return to Russia's basic historical principles, they argued, could protect the country against the corrosion of rationalism and materialism. Slavophiles sometimes criticized the regime, however, because they believed the state exerted too much power over the church. The conflict between Slavophiles and Westernizers continues to shape Russian cultural and intellectual life to the present day.

Although nationalism was a more potent force in eastern Europe, nationalist movements arose in western Europe as well. The most significant of these was in Ireland. The Irish had struggled for centuries against English occupation, but Irish nationalists developed strong organizations only in the 1840s. In 1842, a group of writers founded the Young Ireland movement that aimed to recover Irish history and preserve the Gaelic language (spoken by at least one-third of the peasantry). Daniel O'Connell (1775–1847), a Catholic lawyer and landowner who sat in the British House of Commons, hoped to force the British Parliament to repeal the Act of Union of 1801, which had made Ireland part of Great Britain. In 1843, London newspapers reported "monster meetings" that drew crowds of as many as 300,000 people in support of repeal of the union. In response the British government arrested O'Connell and convicted him of conspiracy. Although his sentence was overturned, O'Connell withdrew from politics, partly because of a terminal brain disease. More radical leaders, who preached insurrection against the English, replaced him.

Liberalism in Economics and Politics

Nationalism overshadowed liberalism in eastern Europe, but liberalism had a strong base in the industrializing countries of western Europe. British liberals emphasized free markets, in part because they already enjoyed constitutional guarantees and in part because British industry no longer needed direct government protection. On the continent, liberals gave priority to constitutional reform. Free trade was in fact unthinkable in most other European countries because the British, dominant in technology and industrial production, could swamp rivals unprotected by tariffs.

British liberals wanted government to limit its economic role to maintaining the currency, enforcing contracts, and financing major enterprises like the military and the railroads. As historian and member of Parliament Thomas Macaulay (1800–1859) explained in 1830:

Our rulers will best promote the improvement of the nation by strictly confining themselves to their own legitimate duties, by leaving capital to find its most lucrative course, commodities their fair price, industry and intelligence their natural reward, idleness and folly their natural punishment, by maintaining peace, by defending property, by diminishing the price of law, and by observing strict economy in every department of the State.

Liberals of the 1830s sought to lower or eliminate British tariffs, especially through repeal of the Corn Laws, which benefited landowners by preventing the import of cheap foreign grain. They also advocated noninterference in employer-employee relations. This hands-off policy caused workers to feel ambivalent about liberalism: although food would cost less if tariffs on grain imports were cut, they would face unemployment and low wages should the government not protect them from their employers.

Liberals had widely supported the Reform Bill of 1832, hoping to gain more votes in Parliament for their economic program. When landholders in the House of Commons thwarted efforts to lower grain tariffs, two Manchester cotton manufacturers set up an Anti–Corn Law League. They appealed to the middle classes against the landlords, whom they labeled "a bread-taxing oligarchy" and "blood-sucking vampires," and attracted working-class backing by promising lower food prices. The league established local branches, published newspapers and the journal *The Economist* (founded in 1843 and now one of the world's most influential periodicals), and campaigned in elections. They eventually won the support of the Tory prime minister Sir Robert Peel, whose government repealed the Corn Laws in 1846.

Unlike their British counterparts, continental liberals focused on political, not economic, reform. Landowners, iron and steel manufacturers, and sugar interests fiercely resisted a French free-trade association founded in 1845. Liberals on the continent did not oppose a strong state or state intervention in the economy; they usually supported freeing internal trade while maintaining tariffs against imports.

Before 1848, continental liberals failed to win political reforms, a failure that opened the way to more radical groups. In France, Louis-Philippe's government brutally repressed working-class and republican insurrections in Lyon and Paris in the early 1830s and forced the republican opposition underground. But the French king's increasingly restrictive governments also thwarted liberals' hopes for reforms by suppressing many political organizations and reestablishing censorship. The

regime antagonized all manner of opponents: supporters of the old monarchy, nostalgic Bonapartists, die-hard republicans, and newly organizing workers and artisans.

Repression muted criticism in most other European states as well. Nevertheless, the rulers of Prussia, the smaller German states, and the Austrian Empire all encountered reform movements. In the pockets of industrialization in those countries, industrialists wanted more political clout. Metternich's government allowed liberal societies to form; indeed, in the Austrian Empire even some state bureaucrats favored economic liberalism, especially university-trained middle-class officials. Members of the societies scrutinized British institutions and economic writings, hoping to apply their ideas at home. The British example occasionally attracted noble landowners, as the remarkable career of the Hungarian count Stephen Széchenyi (1791–1860) illustrates. As an army officer, Széchenyi had spent years abroad, where he had come into contact with British liberalism. Back in Hungary, he introduced British agricultural techniques on his own lands and wrote books criticizing the social system. He advocated eliminating seigneurial burdens and equalizing taxation. In the 1830s, he helped establish projects to start up steamboat traffic on the Danube, to import machinery and technicians for steam-driven textile factories, and to construct Hungary's first railway line, from Budapest to Vienna.

In the 1840s, however, Széchenyi's efforts paled before those of the flamboyant Magyar nationalist Lajos Kossuth (1802–1894). After spending four years in prison for sedition, Kossuth grabbed every opportunity to publicize American democracy and British political liberalism, all in a fervent nationalist spirit. In 1844, he founded the Protective Association, whose members bought only Hungarian products; to Kossuth, boycotting Austrian goods was crucial to ending "colonial dependence" on Austria. Born of a lesser landowning family without a noble title, Kossuth did not hesitate to attack "the cowardly selfishness of the landowner class."

Even in Russia, stereotyped in the West as corrupt, lifeless, and dominated by "regimented Tatars," signs of liberal, even socialist, opposition appeared in the 1830s and 1840s. Small "circles" of young noblemen serving in the army or bureaucracy met in cities, especially Moscow, to discuss the latest western ideas and to criticize the Russian state: "The world is undergoing a transformation, while we vegetate in our hovels of wood and clay," wrote one. Out of these groups came such future revolutionaries as Alexander Herzen (1812–1870), described by the police as "a daring free-thinker, extremely dangerous to society." Tsar Nicholas I (r. 1825–1855) banned Western liberal writings as well as all books about the United States. He sent nearly ten thousand people a year into exile in Siberia as punishment for their political activities.

Socialism and the Early Labor Movement

Socialism had many variants in the 1830s and 1840s, but all railed against the inequalities caused by industrialization and considered liberalism an inadequate response. Socialists envisioned a future society in which workers would share a harmonious, cooperative, and prosperous life. They built on the theoretical and practical ideas laid out in the early nineteenth century by Count Henri de Saint-Simon, Charles Fourier, and Robert Owen, whose moralistic reform fervor they shared. They saw the positive potential of industrialization and hoped that economic planning and working-class organization would solve the problems caused by industrial growth, including the threat of increasingly mechanical, unfeeling social relations.

Socialism and Women. Given the focus on reconstructing social relationships, women not surprisingly participated actively in the socialist movements of the day, even though socialist men often shared the widespread prejudice against women's political activism. In Great Britain many women joined the Owenites and helped form cooperative societies and unions. They defended women's working-class organizations against the complaints of men in the new societies and trade unions. As one woman wrote, "Do not say the unions are only for men . . . 'tis a wrong impression, forced on our minds to keep us slaves!" Women's influence in the Owenite movement helped turn it toward community experimentation. Socialism no longer concentrated exclusively on work and consumer organization; Owenites now became interested in free religious thought, women's rights, marriage reform, and popular education. Rousing speakers such as Emma Martin (1812–1851) forcefully put the case: "One great evil is the depraved

and ignorant condition of woman; this evil can only be removed by Socialism." Martin's speeches often stirred turbulent opposition as clergymen urged their congregations to shout her down. Occasionally, she was jeered, chased, and even stoned by mobs, so much did her ideas and very presence challenge conventional expectations.

The French activist Flora Tristan (1801–1844) devoted herself to reconciling the interests of male and female workers. She had seen the "frightful reality" of London's poverty and made a reputation reporting on British working conditions. Tristan published a stream of books and pamphlets urging male workers to address women's unequal status, arguing that "the emancipation of male workers is *impossible* so long as women remain in a degraded state." Influenced by Fourier and Owen, Tristan advocated a Universal Union of Men and Women Workers and proposed workers' palaces to educate children and care for aged and injured laborers. Despite political harassment, she traveled around France speaking out for her beliefs and attempting to organize workers.

Collectivists and Communists. Tristan's advocacy of working-class associations reflected a general trend within socialism, even though most male socialists ignored her plea for women's participation. The French socialist Louis Blanc (1811–1882) explained the importance of working-class associations in *Organization of Labor* (1840), which deeply influenced the French labor movement. Similarly, Pierre-Joseph Proudhon (1809–1865) urged workers to form producers' associations so that the workers could control the work process and eliminate profits made by capitalists. His 1840 book *What Is Property?* argues that property is theft: labor alone is productive, and rent, interest, and profit unjust.

After 1840, some socialists began to call themselves "communists," emphasizing their desire to replace private property by communal, collective ownership. The Frenchman Étienne Cabet (1788–1856) first used the word *communist*. In 1840, he published *Travels in Icaria*, a novel describing a communist utopia in which a popularly elected dictatorship efficiently organized work, reduced the workday to seven hours, and made work tasks "short, easy, and attractive."

French socialist ideas circulated throughout Europe, from Belgium and the German states to

Russia. They evoked most response in areas of incipient industrialization where artisans and workers felt intensely threatened by the prospect of change. The German tailor Wilhelm Weitling (1808–1871) developed an influential variant of socialism that had deeply religious overtones. His book *Guarantees of Harmony and Freedom* (1842) argues for a communal society but also emphasizes faith as necessary to life. In his view, "Jesus, too, was a communist." Weitling made a profound impression on workers' societies in the western German states.

Out of the churning of socialist ideas of the 1840s emerged two men whose collaboration would change the definition of socialism and remake it into an ideology that would shake the world for the next 150 years. Karl Marx (1818–1883) and Friedrich Engels (1820–1895) seemed unlikely revolutionaries. Both were the sons of prosperous German-Jewish families that had converted to Christianity. Marx studied philosophy at the University of Berlin and then edited a liberal newspaper until the Prussian government suppressed it. He left for Paris, where he met Engels. While working in the offices of his wealthy family's cotton manufacturing interests in Manchester, England, Engels had been shocked into writing *The Condition of the Working Class in England in 1844* (1845), a sympathetic depiction of industrial workers' dismal lives. In Paris, where German and eastern European intellectuals could pursue their political interests more freely than at home, Marx and Engels threw themselves into organizing German workers living outside the German states. Marx read voraciously, especially histories of the French Revolution, and promptly earned a reputation as a fearsome critic of other socialists and would-be reformers. He attacked Weitling, destroyed much of his influence, and set up the Communist League, in whose name he and Engels published the *Communist Manifesto* (1848). It eventually became the touchstone of Marxist and communist revolution all over the world. In declaring himself a communist, Marx wanted to differentiate his ideology from that of what he called "utopian socialists," whom he considered mere fanciful dreamers.

Negligible as was Marx's and Engels's influence in the 1840s, they had already begun their lifework of scientifically understanding the "laws" of capitalism and fostering revolutionary organizations. Their principles and analysis of history were in place: communists, the *Manifesto* declared, must aim for "the downfall of the bourgeoisie [capitalist class] and the ascendancy of the proletariat [working class], the abolition of the old society based on class conflicts and the foundation of a new society without classes and without private property." Unlike many utopian socialists, Marx and Engels embraced industrialization because they believed it would eventually bring on the proletarian revolution and lead inevitably to the abolition of exploitation, private property, and class society.

Working-Class Organization. Socialism accompanied, and in some places incited, an upsurge in working-class organization in western Europe. British workers founded cooperative societies, local trade unions, and so-called friendly societies for mutual aid, associations that frightened the middle classes. A newspaper exclaimed in 1834, "The trade unions are, we have no doubt, the most dangerous institutions that were ever permitted to take root."

Even when not unionized, British workers joined in the political campaigns of the huge Chartist movement. Called *Chartism* because its members endorsed a document known as the People's Charter, the new movement brought together thousands of workers, poor people, and middle-class radicals who wanted a democratic government. They demanded universal manhood suffrage, vote by secret ballot, equal electoral districts, annual elections, and the elimination of property qualifications for and the payment of stipends to members of Parliament. They denounced their opponents as seeking "to keep the people in social slavery and political degradation." Many women took part by founding female political unions, setting up Chartist Sunday schools, organizing boycotts of unsympathetic shopkeepers, and joining Chartist temperance associations. Nevertheless, the People's Charter refrained from calling for woman suffrage because the movement's leaders feared that doing so would alienate potential supporters.

The Chartists organized a massive campaign during 1838 and 1839, with large public meetings, fiery speeches, and torchlight parades. Presented with petitions for the People's Charter signed by more than a million people, the House of Commons refused to act. In response to this rebuff from middle-class liberals, the Chartists allied themselves in the 1840s with working-class strike movements in the manufacturing districts and associated with various European revolutionary movements. But at the same time they—like their British and continental allies—distanced themselves from women workers. Chartists complained that workingwomen undermined men's manhood, taking men's jobs and turning the men into "women-men" or "eunuchs." Continuing agitation and organization prepared the way for a last wave of Chartist demonstrations in 1848.

Continental workers were less well organized because trade unions and strikes were illegal everywhere except Great Britain. Nevertheless, artisans and skilled workers in France formed mutual aid societies that provided insurance, death benefits, and education. Workers in new factories rarely organized, but artisans in the old trades, such as the silk workers of Lyon, France, created societies to resist mechanization and wage cuts.

The new workers' press, such as the Saint-Simonian *People's Beehive* (1839), spread the ideas of socialist harmony and economic reform among the working classes. In eastern and central Europe, however, socialism and labor organization—like liberalism—had less impact than in western Europe. Guild-based organizations survived in the German states, for example, but cooperative societies and workers' newspapers did not appear until 1848. Farther east, the working classes were even smaller, and labor organizing reached few people.

The New Historical Imagination

In an age of competing ideologies, every ideology offered its own reading of history as a way to buttress its analysis of the direction change should take. Nationalism, in particular, fostered an enthusiasm for history, because history substantiated claims for a common national identity. German nationalists, for example, avidly read such massive books as Friedrich C. Schlosser's eighteen-volume *General History for the German People* (1844–1856). In Great Britain the equally famous histories by Thomas Macaulay described the British people as "the greatest and most highly civilized people that the world ever saw." Macaulay aimed to broaden history to include everyday life as well as politics, war, and diplomacy.

History entered the lifeblood of literature and painting as well. Romanticism had given history a special glamour, opening the way for a commercially successful genre, the historical novel. Readers devoured novels like Alexandre Dumas's *The Three Musketeers* (1844), set in the reign of Louis XIII in the 1620s. Dumas, the grandson of a Haitian slave, recounts the adventures of four soldiers who valiantly serve the queen of France and foil the plots of Cardinal Richelieu. Governments appreciated the value of paintings with a historical theme in reinforcing their own legitimacy. To link himself to the growing cult of Napoleon, for example, Louis-Philippe commissioned four paintings of the emperor's victories for the new Gallery of Battles at Versailles, now transformed into a museum. This effort culminated in 1840 when the government, led by the new prime minister Adolphe Thiers (himself a noted historian of the French Revolution), arranged to return Napoleon's ashes to the Invalides church in Paris. Although the spectacular public funeral showed Louis-Philippe's eagerness to establish his connections to Napoleonic history, it would not succeed in its goal of stifling demands for reform.

Nationalism and the new historical imagination also influenced musical romanticism. The Polish composer and pianist Frédéric Chopin (1810–1849) became a powerful champion in the West for the cause of his native land, with music that incorporated Polish folk rhythms and melodies. Opera, long a favorite with the public, experienced an abrupt transformation about 1830. Before this time, operatic plots had generally derived from classical mythology or had been contemporary social satires; now the public demanded passionate tragedy, usually with a picturesque medieval or Renaissance setting. The operatic portrayal of heroines as sexually pure, noble-minded, emotionally vulnerable, and tragic victims mirrored the redefinition of women's character in contemporary middle-class opinion.

Alongside the burst of interest in the political and artistic uses of history came a new trend in historical writing that valued professional training above literary skill. The foremost practitioner of this new scholarship was Leopold von Ranke (1795–1886), a professor at the University of Berlin who taught many of the leading German historians of the nineteenth century. Ranke tried to understand the past objectively, on its own terms, rather than as lessons for present-day purposes. He organized small seminars of young men for the close study of documents. His reliance on source materials instead of legend or tradition helped reshape the study of history into a discipline based on critical methods. The most immediate response to this approach came in the history of religion. In 1835, the German scholar David Friedrich Strauss published the two-volume *Life of Jesus*, in which he argues that the Gospels were not history but only imaginative stories that reflected Jewish myths in Roman times. Widely reprinted, Strauss's book caused a storm of controversy. In the 1840s, a series of new books followed Strauss's lead; some of them ended with proclamations that Jesus never existed.

The study of geology prompted the examination of other religious doctrines. A three-volume work published in 1830–1833 by the British geologist Charles Lyell (1797–1875) with the bland title *Principles of Geology* ignited debate. Lyell argues that the earth is much older than the dating of the biblical story of creation (assumed by many to be 4004 B.C.). Questioning religious assumptions enraged those whose beliefs rested on biblical certainty. Un-

der Lyell's influence, Charles Darwin (1809–1882) would begin to sketch out the essentials of his theory of evolution by natural selection. Geology, opera, nationalist histories, and historical novels all helped foster new forms of historical sensibility. But a sense of history did nothing to quiet the storm of ideological discontent. Liberals, socialists, and nationalists all vied for public support for their answers to the political and social questions raised by industrialization, urbanization, and the demand for national self-determination.

❖ The Revolutions of 1848

Food shortage, overpopulation, and unemployment helped turn ideological turmoil into revolution. In 1848, demonstrations and uprisings toppled governments, forced rulers and ministers to flee, and offered revolutionaries an opportunity to put liberal, socialist, and nationalist ideals into practice (Map 22.4). Of the major powers only Great Britain

MAP 22.4 The Revolutions of 1848
The attempts of rulers to hold back the forces of change collapsed suddenly in 1848 when once again the French staged a revolution that inspired many others in Europe. This time, cities all over central and eastern Europe joined in as the spirit of revolt inflamed one capital after another. Although all of these revolutions eventually failed because of social and political divisions, the sheer scale of rebellion forced rulers to reconsider their policies.

Territories with revolts
Revolts and centers of revolutionary activity
Boundary of German Confederation

0   200   400 miles
0 200   400 kilometers

and Russia remained untouched, the former because it already had constitutional government and the latter because its autocratic government had stamped out all signs of dissent. In the end, all the revolutions failed because liberal, socialist, and nationalist movements quarreled with one another, leaving an opening for rulers and their armies to return to power.

The Hungry Forties

In 1845, an airborne blight destroyed Europe's potato crop. The next year, other crops failed when drought gripped southern Europe and excessive rain fell on northern Europe. Farmers who could produce something got higher prices, but marginal cultivators and farm laborers starved. Urban workers lost their jobs because rural people could no longer afford industrial goods. At the same time, workers faced escalating food prices. (In the best of times urban workers paid 50 to 80 percent of their income for a diet consisting largely of bread; now even bread

was beyond their means.) An aristocrat from Silesia, a province in Prussia, described the political consequences: "As long as there was a sure, and honest livelihood, none of the Silesian weavers paid any attention to communistic agitation . . . despair was aroused among them by hunger."

Overpopulation hastened famine in some places, especially Ireland, where even in years of good harvest the food supply had barely kept pace with explosive population growth. Potatoes were the principal food for Irish peasants, and the poor ate little else. Potatoes yielded more food value per acre than grains: a family of four might live off one acre of potatoes but would require at least two acres of grain. As potato cultivation increased, greater food production spurred population growth as peasants, assured of a food supply, had more children. Irish peasants often sought security in large families, trusting that their children might help work the land and care for them in old age. Thus Irish population growth surpassed that of the rest of Europe. By the 1840s, Ireland was especially

The Potato Blight and Irish Famine

In this painting by Daniel McDonald, The Discovery of the Potato Blight *(1852), a family is shown digging up its potato crop only to find that the potatoes had rotted from blight. This discovery spelled disaster for this family and thousands like it. The blight spores were airborne. After they landed on potato plants they killed the leaves, which fell to the ground. The spores were washed into the earth, where they infected the underground tubers. The crop could even look normal and still be infected.*

vulnerable to the potato blight, which returned in 1846, 1848, and 1851. Out of a population of 8 million, as many as 1 million people died of starvation and disease. Corpses lay unburied on the sides of roads, and whole families were found dead in their cottages, half-eaten by dogs. Hundreds of thousands emigrated to England, the United States, and Canada.

Throughout Europe, famine jeopardized social peace. In age-old fashion, rumors circulated about large farmers selling to other localities or hoarding grain to drive up prices. Believing that governments should ensure fair prices that would make food accessible, crowds took over village and town streets to protest, often attacking markets or bakeries. In villages across Europe they threatened officials with retribution. "If the grain merchants do not cease to take away grains . . . we will go to your homes and cut your throats and those of the three bakers . . . and burn the whole place down." So went one threat from French villagers in the hungry winter of 1847. Although harvests improved in 1848, by then many people had lost their land or become hopelessly indebted, and they strongly resented those who had prospered from high prices.

Had the crisis affected only the food supply, rural and urban people might have found outwork such as spinning, weaving, or other artisan-type production to make up for what the land failed to yield. But high food prices also drove down the demand for manufactured goods resulting in increased unemployment. Industrial workers' wages had been rising—in the German states, for example, wages rose an average of 5.5 percent in the 1830s and 10.5 percent in the 1840s—but the cost of living rose about 16 percent each decade, canceling out wage increases. Seasonal work and regular unemployment were already the norm when the crisis of the late 1840s exacerbated the uncertainties of urban life. "The most miserable class that ever sneaked its way into history" is how Friedrich Engels described underemployed and starving workers in 1847.

Another French Revolution

The specter of hunger tarnished the image of established rulers and amplified voices critical of them. Louis-Philippe's government had blocked all moves for electoral reform, and, beginning in 1847,

opposition leaders in France sponsored political meetings under the cover of banquets at which they demanded liberalization of Louis-Philippe's regime. In February 1848, the banquet campaign turned into a revolution as the people of Paris took to the streets. They demanded and got the establishment of a republic, which soon came under pressure from those who favored greater democracy and even socialism. In June 1848, the republican army crushed an uprising by workers in Paris. In the midst of this class conflict and political turmoil, an overwhelmingly rural electorate chose as president Louis-Napoleon Bonaparte, nephew of Emperor Napoleon. His election marked the end of the revolution of 1848 in France and the opening of a new period in French history.

The February Revolution. Demonstrations began on the rainy, chilly morning of February 22, 1848. At first the police and the army dispersed the students, workers, and the unemployed who gathered to build barricades. The next day, however, the crowd came back in a fighting mood. Forty or fifty people died when panicky soldiers opened fire on the crowd. On February 24, faced with fifteen hundred barricades and a furious populace, Louis-Philippe abdicated and fled to England. A hastily formed provisional government declared France a republic once again. Its most noteworthy leader was Alphonse de Lamartine (1790–1869), a romantic poet, eloquent orator, and historian of the French Revolution. Lamartine's conviction that he was destined to lead the people enabled him to face down the crowds who demanded immediate responses to hunger and unemployment.

The new republican government issued liberal reforms—an end to the death penalty for political crimes, the abolition of slavery in the colonies, and freedom of the press—and agreed to introduce universal adult male suffrage despite misgivings about political participation by peasants and unemployed workers. For middle-class liberals, these measures more than sufficed. Many in the lower classes, however, wanted more. To address the gnawing problem of unemployment and appease the one socialist in the provisional government, Louis Blanc, the government allowed Paris officials to organize a system of "national workshops" to provide the unemployed with construction work and wages of two francs a day. This was not a living wage, but the workshops did attract many desperately poor men to Paris. When women protested their exclusion, the city set up a few workshops for women workers, with even lower wages. To meet a mounting deficit, the provisional government then levied a 45 percent surtax on property taxes, alienating peasants and landowners.

The establishment of the republic politicized many segments of the population. Outside Paris, city after city announced support for the reforms and established similar workshops for the unemployed. Priests showed solidarity with the republic by blessing hundreds of liberty trees, reminders of the French Revolution of 1789. Scores of newspapers and political clubs inspired grassroots democratic fervor. Meeting in concert halls, theaters, and government auditoriums, clubs became a regular evening attraction for the citizenry. Women also formed clubs, published women's newspapers, and demanded representation in national politics. In a twist on domestic ideology, some argued that political activity followed naturally from motherhood. "This holy function of motherhood," one activist claimed, "gives women the right to intervene not only in all acts of civic life, but also in all acts of political life."

The June Days. Street-corner activism alarmed middle-class liberals and conservatives. To ensure its control, the republican government paid some unemployed youths to join a mobile guard with its own uniforms and barracks. Tension between the government and the workers in the national workshops rose. Soon competing groups paraded for their causes in massive demonstrations. The communist Étienne Cabet led one demonstration of 150,000 workers. Faced with rising radicalism in Paris and other big cities, the voters elected a largely conservative National Assembly in April 1848; most of the deputies chosen were middle-class professionals or landowners, who favored either a restoration of the monarchy or a moderate republic.

The Assembly immediately appointed a five-man executive committee to run the government and pointedly excluded known supporters of workers' rights. Suspicious of all demands for rapid change, the deputies dismissed a petition to restore divorce and voted down women's suffrage, 899 to 1.

The Vésuviennes, 1848
This lithograph satirizes women's political ambitions, referring to a women's club named the Vésuviennes (after the recent eruption of Mount Vesuvius in Italy). The artist implies that women have left their children at home in the care of their hapless husbands so that they can actively participate in politics. Some scholars claim that this particular club was invented by the police to ridicule women. Meetings of feminist clubs were often disrupted by men hostile to their aims. Bibliothèque National de France.

When the numbers enrolled in the national workshops in Paris rocketed from a predicted 10,000 to 110,000, the government ordered the workshops closed to new workers, and on June 21 it directed that those already enrolled move to the provinces or join the army.

The workers of Paris responded to these measures on June 23 by taking to the streets in the tens of thousands. In the June Days, as the following week came to be called, the government summoned the army, the National Guard, and the newly recruited mobile guard to fight the workers. Provincial volunteers came to help put down the workers, who had been depicted to them as lazy ruffians intent on destroying order and property. One observer breathed a sigh of relief: "The Red Republic [red being associated with demands for socialism] is lost forever; all France has joined against it. The National Guard, citizens, and peasants from the remotest parts of the country have come pouring in." The republic's army crushed the workers; more than 10,000, most of them workers, were killed or injured, 12,000 were arrested, and 4,000 eventually were convicted and deported.

Louis-Napoleon Bonaparte.   When the National Assembly adopted a new constitution calling for a presidential election in which all adult men could vote, the electorate chose Louis-Napoleon Bonaparte, nephew of the dead emperor. Lamartine's moment of glory had passed: he came in fifth with less than 18,000 votes. (Bonaparte got more than 5.5 million votes out of some 7.4 million cast.) Bonaparte had lived most of his life outside of France, and the leaders of the republic expected him to follow their tune. In uncertain times, the name promised something to everyone. Even many workers supported him because he had no connection with the blood-drenched June Days.

In reality, Bonaparte's election had spelled the end of the Second Republic, just as his uncle had dismantled the first one established in 1792. In 1852, on the forty-eighth anniversary of Napoleon I's coronation as emperor, Louis-Napoleon declared himself Emperor Napoleon III. (Napoleon I's son died and never became Napoleon II, but Napoleon III wanted to create a sense of legitimacy and so used the Roman numeral III.) Political division and class conflict had proved fatal to the Second Republic. Although the revolution of 1848 never had a period of terror like that in 1793–1794, it nonetheless ended in similar fashion, with an authoritarian government that tried to play monarchists and republicans off against each other.

Nationalist Revolution in Italy

Italian nationalists hoped to unite a diverse collection of territories: the kingdom of Piedmont-Sardinia, ruled by King Charles Albert; Lombardy and Venetia under Austrian control; the principalities

Uprising in Milan, 1848
In this painting by an unknown artist, Fighting at the Tosa Gate, *the Milanese are setting up barricades to oppose their Austrian rulers. Whole families are involved. The flag of green, white, and red is the flag of the Cisalpine Republic of the Napoleonic period whose capital was Milan. The three colors would be incorporated into the national flag of Italy after unification.*
Scala/Art Resource, NY.

of central Italy, including the Papal states; and the kingdom of the Two Sicilies, comprising Naples and Sicily and governed by a branch of the Bourbons.

When Giuseppe Verdi's opera *Macbeth* was performed in Venice in 1847, audiences leaped to their feet at the words "The fatherland has been betrayed . . . brothers we must hasten to save it." In January 1848, a revolt broke out in Palermo, Sicily, against the Bourbon ruler. Then came the electrifying news of the February Revolution in Paris. In Milan a huge nationalist demonstration quickly degenerated into battles between Austrian forces and armed demonstrators. In Venice an uprising drove out the Austrians. Peasants in the south occupied large landowners' estates. Across central Italy revolts mobilized the poor and unemployed against local rulers. Peasants demanded more land, and artisans and workers called for higher wages, restrictions on the use of machinery, and unemployment relief.

The Divisions of Italy, 1848

But class divisions and regional differences stood in the way of national unity. Property owners, businessmen, and professionals wanted liberal reforms and national unification under a conservative regime; intellectuals, workers, and artisans dreamed of democracy and social reforms. Some nationalists favored a loose federation; others wanted a monarchy under Charles Albert of Piedmont-Sardinia; still others urged rule by the pope; a few shared Mazzini's vision of a republic with a strong central government. Many leaders of national unification spoke Italian only as a second language; most Italians spoke regional dialects.

As king of the most powerful Italian state, Charles Albert inevitably played a central role. After some hesitation caused by fears of French intervention, he led a military campaign against Austria. It soon failed, partly because of dissension over goals and tactics among the nationalists. Determined republicans in Milan, for example, wanted an independent Lombard republic, not union with conservative, monarchical Piedmont. The pope refused to join the war on Austria, and Charles Albert proved unwilling to press beyond his initial successes.

Although Austrian troops defeated the rebels in the north in the summer of 1848, democratic and nationalist forces prevailed at first in the south. In the fall the Romans drove the pope from the city and declared Rome a republic. For the next few months republican leaders, such as Mazzini and Giuseppe Garibaldi (1807–1882), congregated in Rome to organize the new republic. These efforts eventually faltered when foreign powers intervened. The new president of republican France, Louis-Napoleon Bonaparte, sent an expeditionary force to secure the papal throne for Pius IX. Mazzini and Garibaldi fled. Although revolution had been defeated in Italy, the memory of the Roman republic and the commitment to unification remained, and they would soon emerge again with new force.

Revolt and Reaction in Central Europe

News of the February Revolution in Paris sparked popular demonstrations in the "three Germanies"—Prussia, Austria, and the "third Germany," comprising the other thirty-six kingdoms, duchies, and city-states included in the German Confederation of 1815. "My heart beat with joy. The monarchy had fallen. Only a little blood had been shed for such a high stake, and the great watchwords Liberty, Equality, Fraternity were again inscribed on the banner of the movement." So responded one Frankfurt woman to Louis-Philippe's overthrow. Most German rulers lost their nerve in

The "Three Germanies," 1848

the face of popular revolts in March 1848. But revolutionaries did not succeed in filling the vacuum. Middle-class leaders feared lower-class demands for democracy and social reform and were quickly distracted by nationalist aspirations and ethnic conflicts. In the end, all the rulers returned to power.

Revolutions of 1848

1848

January   Uprising in Palermo, Sicily

February   Revolution in Paris; proclamation of republic

March   Insurrections in Vienna, German cities, Milan, and Venice; autonomy movement in Hungary; Charles Albert of Piedmont-Sardinia declares war on Austrian Empire

May   Frankfurt parliament opens

June   Austrian army crushes revolutionary movement in Prague; June Days end in defeat of workers in Paris

July   Austrians defeat Charles Albert and Italian forces

November   Insurrection in Rome

December   Francis Joseph becomes Austrian emperor; Louis-Napoleon elected president in France

1849

February   Rome declared a republic

April   Frederick William of Prussia rejects crown of united Germany offered by Frankfurt parliament

July   Roman republic overthrown by French intervention

August   Russian and Austrian armies combine to defeat Hungarian forces

Prussia and the Frankfurt Parliament.   At first, the German revolutions looked much like the French, with different social groups combining in giant marches to demand political liberalization. The Prussian army's efforts to clear the square in front of Berlin's royal palace on March 18, 1848, provoked panic and street fighting around hastily assembled barricades. The next day the crowd paraded wagons loaded with dead bodies under King Frederick William IV's window, forcing him to salute the victims killed by his own army. In a state of near collapse, the king promised to call an assembly to draft a constitution and adopted the German nationalist flag of black, red, and gold.

The goal of German unification soon took precedence over social reform or constitutional changes within the separate states. One noble official wrote, "The lightning has struck, and Germany will not allow itself to be lulled back to sleep." In March and April, most of the German states agreed to elect delegates to a federal parliament at Frankfurt that would attempt to unite Germany. Local princes and even the more powerful kings of Prussia and Bavaria seemed to totter. In Bavaria, students marched to the "Marseillaise" and called for a republic. Yet the revolutionaries' weaknesses soon became apparent. The eight hundred delegates to the Frankfurt parliament had little practical political experience: "a group of old women," one socialist called them; a "Professors Parliament" was the common sneer. These delegates had no access to an army, and they dreaded the demands of the lower classes for social reforms. Unemployed artisans and workers smashed machines; peasants burned landlords' records and occasionally attacked Jewish moneylenders; women set up clubs and newspapers to demand their emancipation from "perfumed slavery."

The advantage lay with the princes, who retained legal authority and control over the armed forces. The most powerful German states, Prussia and Austria, expected to determine whether and how Germany should unite. While the Frankfurt parliament laboriously prepared a liberal constitution for a united Germany—one that denied self-determination to Czechs, Poles, and Danes within its proposed German borders—the Prussian king Frederick William IV (r. 1840–1860) recovered his confidence. First his army crushed the revolution in Berlin in the fall of 1848. Prussian troops then intervened to help other local rulers put down the last wave of democratic and nationalist insurrections in the spring of 1849. When the Frankfurt parliament finally concluded its work, offering the emperorship of a constitutional, federal Germany to the king of Prussia, Frederick William contemptuously refused this "crown from the gutter."

Ethnic Divisions in the Austrian Empire.   By the summer of 1848, the Austrian Empire had reached the verge of complete collapse. Just as Italians were driving the Austrians out of their lands in northern Italy and Magyar nationalists were demanding political autonomy for Hungary, on March 13, 1848, in Vienna, a student-led demonstration for political reform turned into rioting, looting, and machine-breaking. Metternich resigned, escaping to England in disguise. Emperor Ferdinand promised a constitution, an elected parliament, and the end of censorship. The beleaguered authorities in Vienna could not refuse Magyar demands for home rule, and Széchenyi and Kossuth both became ministers in the new Hungarian government. The Magyars were the largest ethnic group in Hungary but still did not make up 50 percent of the population, which included Romanians, Slovaks, Croats, and Slovenes who preferred Austrian rule to domination by local Magyars.

The ethnic divisions in Hungary foreshadowed the many political and social divisions that would doom the revolutionaries. Fears of peasant insurrection prompted the Magyar nationalists around Kossuth to abolish serfdom. This measure alienated the largest noble landowners. In Prague, Czech nationalists convened a Slav congress as a counter to the Germans' Frankfurt parliament and called for a reorganization of the Austrian Empire that would recognize the rights of ethnic minorities. Such assertiveness by non-German peoples provoked German nationalists to protest on behalf of German-speaking people in areas with a Czech or Magyar majority.

Revolution of 1848 in Eastern Europe
This painting by an unknown artist shows Ana Ipatescu leading a group of Romanian revolutionaries in Transylvania in opposition to Russian rule. The Transylvanian provinces of Moldavia and Walachia had been under Russian domination since the 1770s and occupied directly since 1829. In April 1848, local landowners began to organize meetings. Paris-educated nationalists spearheaded the movement, which demanded the end of Russian control and various legal and political reforms. By August the movement had split between those who wanted independence only and those who pushed for the end of serfdom and for universal manhood suffrage. In response, the Russians invaded Moldavia and the Turks moved into Walachia. By October the uprising was over. Russia and Turkey agreed to control the provinces jointly.
The Art Archive.

The Austrian government slowly took advantage of these divisions. To quell peasant discontent and appease liberal reformers, it abolished all remaining peasant obligations to the nobility in March 1848. Rejoicing country folk soon lost interest in the revolution. Class conflicts flared in Vienna, where the middle classes had little sympathy for the starving artisans and workers. The new Hungarian government alienated the other nationalities when it imposed the Magyar language on them. Similar divisions sapped national unity in the Polish and Czech lands of the empire.

Military force finally broke up the revolutionary movements. The first blow fell in Prague in June 1848; General Prince Alfred von Windischgrätz, the military governor, bombarded the city into submission when a demonstration led to violence (including the shooting death of his wife, watching from a window). After another uprising in Vienna a few months later, Windischgrätz marched 70,000 soldiers into the capital and set up direct military rule. In December the Austrian monarchy came back to life when the eighteen-year-old Francis Joseph (r. 1848–1916), unencumbered by promises extracted by the revolutionaries from his now feeble uncle Ferdinand, assumed the imperial crown after intervention by leading court officials. In the spring of 1849, General Count Joseph Radetsky defeated the last Italian challenges to Austrian power in northern Italy, and his army moved east, joining with Croats and Serbs to take on the Hungarian rebels. The Austrian army teamed up with Tsar Nicholas I, who marched into Hungary with more than 300,000 Russian troops. Hungary was put under brutal martial law. Széchenyi went mad, and Kossuth found refuge in the United States. Social conflicts and ethnic divisions weakened the revolutionary movements from the inside and gave the Austrian government the opening it needed to restore its position.

Aftermath to 1848

Although the revolutionaries of 1848 failed to achieve most of their goals, their efforts left a profound mark on the political and social landscape. Between 1848 and 1851, the French served a kind of republican apprenticeship that prepared the population for another, more lasting republic after 1870.

No French government could henceforth rule without extensive popular consultation. In Italy, the failure of unification did not stop the spread of nationalist ideas and the rooting of demands for democratic participation. In the three Germanies, the revolutionaries of 1848 turned nationalism from an idea of professors and writers into a popular enthusiasm. The very idea of a Frankfurt parliament and the insistence on brandishing a German national flag at demonstrations showed that German nationalism had become a practical reality. The initiation of artisans, workers, and journeymen into democratic clubs increased political awareness in the lower classes and helped prepare them for broader political participation. Almost all the German states had a constitution and a parliament after 1850. The spectacular failures of 1848 thus hid some important underlying successes.

The absence of revolution in 1848 was just as significant as its presence. No revolution occurred in Great Britain, the Netherlands, or Belgium, three places where industrialization and urbanization had developed most rapidly. In Great Britain the prospects for revolution actually seemed quite good: the Chartist movement took inspiration from the European revolutions in 1848 and mounted several gigantic demonstrations to force Parliament into granting all adult males the vote. But Parliament refused and no uprising occurred, in part because the government had already proved its responsiveness. The middle classes in Britain had been co-opted into the established order by the Reform Bill of 1832, and the working classes had won parliamentary regulation of children's and women's work.

The other notable exception to revolution among the great powers was Russia, where Tsar Nicholas I maintained a tight grip through police surveillance and censorship. The Russian schools, limited to the upper classes, taught Nicholas's three most cherished principles: autocracy (the unlimited power of the tsar), orthodoxy (obedience to the church in religion and morality), and nationality (devotion to Russian traditions). These provided no space for political dissent. Social conditions also fostered political passivity: serfdom continued in force and the slow rate of industrial and urban growth created little discontent.

For all the differences between countries, some developments touched all of them in similar manner.

The Crystal Palace, 1851

This color lithograph by George Baxter provides a good view of the exterior of the main building for the Exhibition of the Works of Industry of All Nations in London. The building was designed by Sir Joseph Paxton (1801–1865) to gigantic dimensions: 1,848 feet long by 456 feet wide; 135 feet high; 772,784 square feet of ground floor area covering no less than 18 acres.

© The Bridgeman Art Library International Ltd.

The Crystal Palace and the Colonies

This colored lithograph by Peter Mabuse offers a view of one of the colonial displays at the Crystal Palace exhibition of 1851. The tented room and ivory carved throne are meant to recall India, Britain's premier colony. In a sermon given on the occasion of the opening of the exhibition, Reverend George Clayton attributed Britain's national greatness to its colonial presence: "Great she [Britain] truly is—great in her trade and commerce—great in her laws and constitution—great in her freedom, both civil and religious—great in the power, the character, and the virtues of her queen . . . great in the resources of her wealth, in the number and extent of her colonial possessions—great in the multitude of her subjects—great in the moral and Christian bearing of a large proportion of her people—great in the cultivation of the mind and morals of the rising population of her inhabitants—great in the distribution of her Bibles, in her mission to the heathen, in the emancipation of the slave, and in the circulation of her countless tracts for the instruction of universal man."

© The Bridgeman Art Library International Ltd.

IMPORTANT DATES

1830–1832 Cholera epidemic sweeps across Europe

1830 France invades and begins conquest of Algeria

1831 British and Foreign Temperance Society established

1832 George Sand, *Indiana*

1833 Factory Act regulates work of children in Great Britain; abolition of slavery in the British Empire

1834 German customs union (*Zollverein*) established under Prussian leadership

1835 Belgium opens first continental railway built with state funds

1839 Beginning of Opium War between Britain and China; invention of photography

1841 Charles Dickens, *The Old Curiosity Shop* (1841)

1846 Famine strikes Ireland; Corn Laws repealed in England; peasant insurrection in Austrian province of Galicia

1847 Charlotte Brontë, *Jane Eyre* (1847)

1848 Last great wave of Chartist demonstration in Britain; Karl Marx and Friedrich Engels, *The Communist Manifesto*; revolutions of 1848 throughout Europe; abolition of slavery in French colonies; end of serfdom in Austrian Empire

1851 Crystal Palace exhibition in London

European states continued to expand their bureaucracies. For example, in 1750 the Russian government employed approximately 10,500 functionaries; a century later it needed almost 114,000. In Great Britain a swelling army of civil servants produced parliamentary studies on industrialization, foreign trade, and colonial profits, while new agencies such as the British urban police forces (10,000 strong in the 1840s) intruded increasingly in ordinary people's lives. States wanted to take children out of the fields and factories where they worked with their families and educate them. In some German cities the police reported people who cleared snow off their roofs after the permitted hour or smoked in the street. A few governments even prescribed the length of sermons.

Although much had changed, the aristocracy remained the dominant power almost everywhere. As army officers, aristocrats put down revolutionary forces. As landlords, they continued to dominate the rural scene and control parliamentary bodies. They also held many official positions in the state bureaucracies. One Italian princess explained, "There are doubtless men capable of leading the nation . . . but their names are unknown to the people, whereas those of noble families . . . are in every memory." Aristocrats kept their authority by adapting to change: they entered the bureaucracy and professions, turned their estates into moneymaking enterprises, and learned how to invest shrewdly.

The reassertion of conservative rule hardened gender definitions. Women everywhere had participated in the revolutions, especially in the Italian states, where they joined armies in the tens of thousands and applied household skills toward making bandages, clothing, and food. Schoolgirls in Prague had thrown desks and chairs out of windows and helped build students' barricades. Many women in Paris had supported the new republic and seized the occasion of greater political openness to demand women's rights, only to experience isolation as their claims were denied by most republican men. Men in the revolutions of 1848 almost always defined universal suffrage as a male right. When workingmen gained the vote and women did not, the notion of separate spheres penetrated even into working-class life: political participation became one more way to distinguish masculinity from femininity. As conservatives returned to power, all signs of women's political activism disappeared. The French feminist movement, the most advanced in Europe, fell apart after the June Days when the increasingly conservative republican government forbade women to form political clubs and arrested and imprisoned two of the most outspoken women leaders for their socialist activities.

In May 1851, Europe's most important female monarch presided over a midcentury celebration of peace and industrial growth that helped dampen the still-smoldering fires of revolutionary passion. Queen Victoria (r. 1837–1901), who herself promoted the notion of domesticity as women's sphere, opened the international Exhibition of the Works of Industry of All Nations in London on May 1. A monument of modern iron and glass architecture had been built to house the display; the building was more than a third of a mile long and so tall that it was built over the trees of its Hyde Park site. Soon

MAPPING THE WEST Europe in 1850

This map of population growth between 1800 and 1850 reveals important trends that would not otherwise be evident. Population growth correlated for the most part with industrialization; industrializing areas such as England, Belgium, and northern Italy also experienced great increases in population compared with places with little or no industrialization, such as Spain, Portugal, and southern Italy. Population also grew, however, in more agricultural regions such as East Prussia, Poland, and Ireland. Ireland's rapid population growth does not appear on this map because by 1850 more than a million people had died or emigrated because of the famine of 1846–1851.

people referred to it as the "Crystal Palace"; its nine hundred tons of glass created an aura of fantasy, and the abundant goods from all nations inspired satisfaction and pride. One German visitor described it as "this miracle which has so suddenly appeared to dazzle the inhabitants of our globe." In the place of revolutionary fervor, the Crystal Palace offered a government-sponsored spectacle of what industry, hard work, and technological imagination could produce.

Conclusion

Many of the six million people who visited the Crystal Palace display had not forgotten the threat of disease, fears of overpopulation, popular resentments, and political upheavals that had been so prominent in the 1830s and 1840s. Even though industrial growth brought railroads, cheaper clothing, and access to exhibitions like the Crystal Palace, it also brought in its train urban overcrowding and miserable working conditions. The Crystal Palace presented the rosy view, but the housing shortages, inadequacy of water supplies, and recurrent epidemic diseases had not disappeared. Social reform organizations still drew attention to prostitution, child abandonment, alcohol abuse, and other problems associated with burgeoning cities.

Although the revolutions of 1848 brought to the surface the profound tensions within a European society in transition toward industrialization and modernization, they did not definitively resolve those tensions. Industrialization and urbanization continued, workers developed more extensive organizations, and liberals and socialists fought over the pace of reform. The revolutions produced their most striking impact negatively rather than positively: confronted with the menace of revolution, elites now sought alternatives that would be less threatening to the established order and still permit some change. This search for alternatives became immediately evident in the question of national unification in Germany and Italy. National unification would hereafter depend on what the Prussian leader Otto von Bismarck would call "blood and iron," not speeches and parliamentary resolutions.

Suggested References

The Advance of Industrialization and Urbanization

The spread of industrialization has elicited much more historical interest than the process of urbanization because the analysis of industrialization occupied a central role in Marxism. Some of the best recent work on urbanization, such as Kudlick's book on cholera, combines an interest in urban history with an interest in the history of public health. The

Spartacus Internet Encyclopedia has an excellent section on the textile industry and its transformation.

Ashton, T. S. *The Industrial Revolution, 1760–1830.* 1997.

Engerman, Stanley. "Reflections on 'The Standard of Living Debate.'" In John A. James and Mark Thomas, *Capitalism in Context: Essays on Economic Development and Cultural Change in Honor of R. M. Hartwell.* 1994.

Hobsbawm, E. J. *The Age of Revolution, 1789–1848.* 1996.

Kudlick, Catherine J. *Cholera in Post-Revolutionary Paris: A Cultural History.* 1996.

Mokyr, Joel, ed. *The British Industrial Revolution: An Economic Perspective.* 2nd ed. 1999.

Pinkney, David H. *Decisive Years in France, 1840–1847.* 1986.

*Pollard, S., and C. Holmes. *Documents of European Economic History.* Vol. 1, *The Process of Industrialization, 1750–1870.* 1968.

Spartacus Internet Encyclopedia, British History 1700–1950: http://www.spartacus.schoolnet.co.uk/Britain.html.

Reforming the Social Order

Although romanticism remains a focus of interest for cultural historians, the history of women and the origins of feminism have attracted attention in recent years. The Web site Gallica, produced by the National Library of France, offers a wealth of imagery and information on French cultural history.

Davidoff, Leonore, and Catherine Hall. *Family Fortunes: Men and Women of the English Middle Class, 1780–1850.* 1987.

The Dickens Project: http://humwww.ucsc.edu/dickens/index.html.

Gallica: Images and Texts from Nineteenth-Century French-Speaking Culture: http://gallica.bnf.fr/.

Lees, Lynn. *The Solidarities of Strangers: The English Poor Laws and the People, 1700–1948.* 1998.

Moses, Claire Goldberg. *French Feminism in the Nineteenth Century.* 1984.

*Murray, Janet Horowitz. *Strong-Minded Women and Other Lost Voices from Nineteenth-Century England.* 1982.

Roberts, James S. *Drink, Temperance, and the Working Class in Nineteenth-Century Germany.* 1984.

Rodner, William S. *J. M. W. Turner: Romantic Painter of the Industrial Revolution.* 1997.

Townsend, Mary Lee. *Forbidden Laughter: Popular Humor and the Limits of Repression in Nineteenth-Century Prussia.* 1992.

*Primary sources.

The Ferment of Ideologies

Ideologies are too often studied in an exclusively national context, so broader generalizations are difficult. The important exception to this national focus in the wide-ranging study by Anderson. The works by Clark and Taylor show how gender entered in to working-class organization and socialist ideology.

Anderson, Benedict. *Imagined Communities: Reflections on the Origin and Spread of Nationalism.* 1983.

Clark, Anna. *The Struggle for the Breeches: Gender and the Making of the British Working Class.* 1995.

*Mather, F. C., ed. *Chartism and Society: An Anthology of Documents.* 1980.

Sewell, William H., Jr. *Work and Revolution in France: The Language of Labor from the Old Regime to 1848.* 1980.

Taylor, Barbara. *Eve and the New Jerusalem: Socialism and Feminism in the Nineteenth Century.* 1983.

The Revolutions of 1848

Interest in the revolutions of 1848 has revived of late, perhaps because the recent upsurge of ethnic violence in the Balkans has prompted scholars to look again at this critical period. Not to be overlooked is the excellent treatment of the Irish famine by O'Grada.

Blackbourn, David. *The Long Nineteenth Century: A History of Germany, 1780–1918.* 1998.

Lincoln, W. Bruce. *Nicholas I: Emperor and Autocrat of All the Russias.* 1978.

O'Grada, Cormac. *The Great Irish Famine.* 1989.

Randers-Pehrson, Justine Davis. *Germans and the Revolution of 1848–1849.* 1999.

Sperber, Jonathan. *The European Revolutions, 1848–1851.* 1994.

Spira, Gyorgy. *The Nationality Issue in the Hungary of 1848–49.* 1992.

*Walker, Mack. *Metternich's Europe.* 1968.

Politics and Culture of the Nation-State

c. 1850–1870

IN 1859, THE NAME VERDI SUDDENLY APPEARED scrawled on walls across the disunited cities of the Italian peninsula. The graffiti seemed to celebrate the composer Giuseppe Verdi, whose operas thrilled crowds of Europeans. Verdi was a particular hero among Italians, however, for his stories of downtrodden groups struggling against tyrannical government seemed to refer specifically to their plight. As his operatic choruses thundered out calls to rebellion in the name of the nation, Italian audiences were sure that Verdi meant for them to throw off Austrian and papal rule and unite in a new version of the ancient Roman Empire. Yet the graffiti was doubly political, a call to arms in the days before mass media. For VERDI also formed an acronym for *Vittorio Emmanuele Re* ("king") *d'Italia*, and in 1859 it summoned Italians to unite immediately under Victor Emmanuel II, king of Sardinia and Piedmont—the one leader with a nationalist, modernizing profile. The graffiti did its work, for the very next year Italy united as a result of warfare, popular uprisings, and hard bargaining by political realists.

In the wake of the failed revolutions of 1848, European statesmen and the politically conscious public increasingly rejected the politics of idealism in favor of *Realpolitik*—a politics of tough-minded realism aimed at strengthening the state and tightening social order. Claiming to distrust the romanticism and high-minded ideologies of the revolutionaries and hoping to control nationalism and other movements for reform, Realpolitikers believed in playing power politics, establishing a strong government, and using violence to attain their goals. Two

Aïda Poster
Aïda (1871), Giuseppe Verdi's opera of human passion and state power, became a staple of Western culture, bringing people across Europe into a common cultural orbit. Written to celebrate the opening of the Suez Canal, Aïda *also celebrated Europe's better access to Asian resources provided by the new waterway. As the poster shows, the opera ushered in another wave of Egyptomania.*
Madeline Grimoldi.

1850	1854	1858	1862	1866	1870

Politics and War

Continuing Russian expansion into Asia

Taiping rebellion ends

Franco-Prussian War

Second Empire in France

Crimean War

Italy unified

Meiji Restoration begins in Japan

Sepoy Mutiny in India

U.S. Civil War

German Empire established; Paris Commune

Austro-Hungarian monarchy established; Second Reform Bill in Britain

Society and Economy

Urban improvements and expansion of government bureaucracy and services; Britain continues to pursue free-trade policies

International Workingmen's Association formed in London

Abolition of serfdom in Russia

Suez Canal opened

Culture, Religion, and Intellectual Life

Positivism and Darwinism become popular theories among middle classes; Wagner's musical compositions

Pope Pius IX issues *The Syllabus of Errors*

Verdi's *Aïda* debuts in Cairo

Realism in literature and painting

Crystal Palace exhibition in Britain

Universal Exposition in Paris

particularly skilled practitioners of Realpolitik, the Italian Camillo di Cavour and the Prussian Otto von Bismarck, succeeded in unifying Italy and Germany, respectively, not by consensus but by war and diplomacy. Most leading figures of these decades, enmeshed like Verdi's operatic heroes in violent political maneuverings, advanced state power by harnessing the forces of nationalism and liberalism that had led to earlier romantic revolts.

Many ingredients went into making modern nation-states and empires during these momentous decades. Continued economic development was crucial, as was a growing sense of national identity and common purpose forged by both culture and government policy. As productivity and wealth increased, governments took vigorous steps to im-

prove the urban environment, monitor public health, and promote national sentiment. State support for cultural developments ranging from public schools to opera productions helped establish a common fund of knowledge and even shared political beliefs. Authoritarian leaders such as Bismarck and the new French emperor Napoleon III believed that a better quality of life would not only calm revolutionary impulses, ensure social order, and build state power but also keep political liberals at bay.

Culture also built a sense of belonging. Reading novels, attending art exhibitions, keeping up-to-date at the newly fashionable world's fairs, and attending theater and opera created a greater sense of being French or German or British but also of being European. Cultural works increasingly rejected romanticism, featuring instead realistic aspects of ordinary people's lives. Artists painted nudes in shockingly blunt ways, eliminating romantic hues and poses. Verdi's celebrated opera *La Traviata* showed a frolicking courtesan menacing a middle-class family. The Russian author Leo Tolstoy depicted the bleak life of soldiers in the Crimean War while his countryman Fyodor Dostoevsky wrote of criminals and murders in urban neighborhoods.

Realpolitik cared less for the costs than for the outcomes of state building. Advancing state power entailed stamping out resistance to colonial expansion. At home it uprooted neighborhoods in favor of public buildings, roads, and parks. The process of national expansion was often brutal, bringing war, arrests, protests, and outright civil war—all of these the centerpieces of Verdi's operas as well. As the wars of German unification drew to a close in 1871, an uprising of Parisians threw the new terms of nation building into question as citizens challenged the central government's intrusion into everyday life and its failure to count the costs. For the most part, the powerful Western state did not take shape automatically during these years. Instead, its growth occasioned warfare and dislocation, shrewd policy and heated debate. Realpolitik produced all of these, as well as a general climate of modern opinion that valued realism and hard facts.

❖ The End of the Concert of Europe

The revolutions of 1848 had weakened the concert of Europe, driving out its architect Metternich and allowing the forces of nationalism to flourish. It became more difficult for countries to control their competing ambitions and act together. In addition, the dreaded resurgence of Bonapartism in the person of Napoleon III (Louis-Napoleon, the nephew of Napoleon I) added to the volatility in international politics as France sought to reassert itself. One of Napoleon's targets was Russia, formerly a mainstay of the concert of Europe. While Russia pursued its own goals of expanded borders, France helped engineer the Crimean War of 1854–1856. Taking a huge toll in human life, the war weakened Russia and Austria and made way for a massive shift in the distribution of European power.

Napoleon III and the Quest for French Glory

Louis-Napoleon Bonaparte encouraged the resurgence of French grandeur and the cult of his famous uncle as part of nation building. "There are certain men who are born to serve as a means for the march of the human race," he wrote. "I consider myself to be one of these." On December 2, 1851, the anniversary of Napoleon I's coronation in 1804, he staged a political coup that allowed him to revise the constitution and declare himself eligible for a second presidential term, provided male voters approved. Napoleon won easily, partly because he promised not to restrict voter eligibility, as monarchists in the Assembly had proposed. Exactly one year later he declared himself Emperor Napoleon III (r. 1852–1870) and proclaimed the Second Empire. The French traded in dreams of political liberty for a strong man's promises of order and national glory.

Napoleon III acted as Europe's schoolmaster, showing its leaders how to combine economic liberalism and nationalism with authoritarian rule. Under the banner of "Order and Progress," he ruthlessly repressed opposition in small towns and cities alike, deporting, sometimes with no provocation, thousands of Parisians who appeared suspicious to harsh prison colonies outside of France. For example, Pauline Roland, a former Saint-Simonian who had become a newspaper editor, was convicted of opposing the coup in Paris and sent to a penal colony even though she had been far from the capital when the coup took place. Pro-republican professors were thrown out of work, cafés where men might discuss politics were closed, and a rubber-stamp legislature (the *Corps législatif*) reduced representative government to a facade. Imperial style replaced republican rituals. Napoleon's opulent court dazzled the public, and the emperor cultivated a masculine image of strength and majesty by wearing military uniforms (like his namesake) and by conspicuously maintaining mistresses. Napoleon's wife, Empress Eugénie, however, followed middle-class conventions such as separate spheres for men and women by serving as a devoted mother to her only son and supporting many volunteer charities. The authoritarian, apparently old-fashioned order imposed by Napoleon satisfied the many peasants who opposed urban radicals.

Napoleon III and Eugénie Receive the Siamese Ambassadors
At a splendid gathering of their court, the emperor Napoleon III, his consort Eugénie, and their son and heir greet ambassadors from Siam, whose exoticism and servility before the imperial family are the centerpiece of this depiction. Amidst the grandeur of the Napoleonic dynasty, the West towers above the East.
Giraudon/Art Resource, NY.

Yet Napoleon III was simultaneously a modernizer, and he promoted a strong economy, public works programs, and jobs, which lured the middle and working classes away from radical politics. International trade fairs, artistic expositions, and the magnificent rebuilding of Paris helped sustain French prosperity as Europe recovered from the hard times of the late 1840s. Empress Eugénie wore lavish gowns, encouraging French silk production and keeping Paris at the center of the lucrative fashion trade. The emperor's policies advanced commerce, most notably in a free-trade agreement with England, the Cobden-Chevalier Treaty (1860). The regime also launched a major financial innovation by backing an investment bank, the Crédit Mobilier. Such new institutions led the way in financing railroad expansion, and railway mileage increased fivefold during Napoleon III's reign.

When an economic recession struck in the late 1850s, the regime was once again subject to criticism and Napoleon III was forced to seek new alliances. Conservatives opposed Napoleon's free-trade and foreign policies, so he tried to woo political liberals by introducing democratic features into his governing methods. He encouraged the

formation of working-class organizations and in the following years allowed the Corps législatif more power of deliberation. Although some historians have judged Napoleon III to be enigmatic and shifty because of these abrupt changes, his maneuvers were pragmatic responses to the fluid economic and political conditions.

On the international scene, Napoleon III's main goals were to overcome the containment of France imposed by the Congress of Vienna, realign continental politics to benefit France, and acquire international glory like a true Bonaparte. To realign European politics, Napoleon pitted France first against Russia in the Crimean War, then against Austria in the War of Italian Unification, and finally against Prussia in the Franco-Prussian War of 1870. Beyond Europe, Napoleon's army continued to enforce French rule in Algeria and Southeast Asia and tried to install Habsburg emperor Francis Joseph's brother Maximilian as ruler of Mexico and ultimately of all Central America—an assault that ended in 1867 with Maximilian's execution. Napoleon's foreign policy transformed relations among the great powers by causing a breakdown in the international system of peaceful diplomacy established at the Congress of Vienna. While his encouragement of projects like the Suez Canal to connect the Mediterranean and the Red Seas proved visionary, this push for worldwide influence eventually destroyed him: the French overthrew him after Prussia easily defeated his army in 1870.

The Crimean War, 1853–1856: Turning Point in European Affairs

Napoleon first flexed his diplomatic muscle in the Crimean War (1853–1856), which began as a conflict between the Russian and Ottoman Empires but ended as a war with long-lasting consequences for much of Europe. While professing to uphold the concert of Europe, Russia continued to build state power by making further inroads into Asia and the Middle East. In particular Tsar Nicholas I wanted to absorb much of the Ottoman Empire, fast becoming known as "the sick man of Europe" because of its disintegrating authority. To this end, Russia claimed an official right to protect Orthodox Christians within the declining empire. Nevertheless Napoleon III maneuvered Tsar Nicholas to be more aggressive in Russia's claims when he suddenly declared the rights of France as protector of Christians in the Ottoman Empire. As Russia became increasingly belligerent, war erupted in October 1853 between the two eastern empires (Map 23.1).

Behind the widening war lay the question of Europe's balance of power. The other great powers feared that increased Russian authority in Ottoman-controlled southeastern Europe would adversely affect their interests. To protect its Mediterranean routes to East Asia, Britain prodded the Ottomans to stand up to Russia. The Austrian government still resented its dependence on Russia in putting down Hungarian revolutionaries in 1849 and felt threatened by continuing Russian expansion into the Balkans. This anxiety helped Napoleon III gain a promise of Austrian neutrality during the war, thus fracturing the conservative Russian-Austrian coalition that had quashed French ambitions since 1815. In the fall of 1853, the Russians blasted the wooden Turkish ships to bits at the Ottoman port of Sinope on the Black Sea; in 1854, France and Great Britain, enemies in war for more than a century, declared war on Russia to defend the Ottoman Empire's sovereignty and territory.

Faced with attacking the massive Russian Empire, the opposition settled for limited military goals focused on capturing the Russian naval base at Sevastopol on the Black Sea in the Crimea. Even so, the Crimean War was spectacularly bloody. British and French troops landed in the Crimea in September 1854 and waged a long siege of the fortified city, but it fell only after a year of savage and costly combat. Generals on both sides demonstrated their incompetence; and governments failed to provide combatants with even minimal supplies, sanitation, or medical care. Russian military leadership proved most inept, but the British was not much better: the British commander in chief, a veteran of Waterloo, still harangued his troops to beat "the French." Like many of his fellow officers and soldiers, he would die of cholera during the war. The war claimed a massive toll. Three-quarters of a million men died, more than two-thirds from disease and starvation.

In the midst of this unfolding catastrophe, Alexander II (r. 1855–1881) ascended the Russian

MAP 23.1 The Crimean War, 1853–1856
The most destructive war in Europe between the Napoleonic Wars and World War I, the Crimean War drew attention to the conflicting ambitions around territories of the declining Ottoman Empire. Importantly for state building in these decades, the war fractured the alliance of conservative forces from the Congress of Vienna, allowing Italy and Germany to come into being as unified states and permitting Napoleon III to pursue his ambitions for France.

throne following the death of his father, Nicholas I, in 1855. The new tsar hoped for some minimal Russian triumph so he could negotiate peace from a position of strength, but as the casualties mounted and the possibility of victory dwindled, he yielded. As a result of the Peace of Paris, signed on March 30, 1856, Russia lost the right to base its navy in the Straits of Dardanelles and the Black Sea, which were declared neutral waters. Moldavia and Walachia (which soon merged to form Romania) became autonomous Turkish provinces under the victors' protection.

Some historians have called the Crimean War one of the most senseless conflicts in modern history because competing claims in southeastern Europe could have been settled by diplomacy had it not been for Napoleon III's driving ambition. Yet the war was full of consequence. New technologies were introduced into warfare, though their use was not yet perfected: the railroad, shell-firing cannon,

breech-loading rifles, the telegraph, and steam-powered ships. The relationship of the home front to the battlefront was beginning to change with the use of the telegraph and increased press coverage. Home audiences received news from the Crimean front lines more rapidly and in more detail than ever before. The news stunned even those who longed for the excitement of battle: reports of incompetence, poor sanitation, and the huge death toll outraged the public, and some people went to the front to help out or take photographs. One admirable figure rose above the carnage—Florence Nightingale (1820–1910). She seized the moment to escape the confines of middle-class domesticity by organizing a battlefield nursing service to care for the British sick and wounded. Through her tough-minded organization of nursing units, she secured additional personnel and medical supplies for her hospital and improved the sanitary conditions of the troops. (See "Did You Know?,"

The Mission of Mercy
Florence Nightingale organized British health care services during the Crimean War, inspiring a committed cadre of women volunteers to leave domestic life for the battlefront. As disease took its heavy toll, Nightingale introduced sanitary measures into the care of the wounded and sick. This romantic portrayal of her greeting the wounded at Scutari hardly captures the strenuous and tough-minded efforts involved in her work.
National Portrait Gallery, London.

Mrs. Seacole: The Other Florence Nightingale

Another highly skilled medical worker besides Florence Nightingale made an impact on the battlefields in Crimea. Mary Seacole (1805–1881), daughter of a free-black Jamaican woman and a Scottish army officer, had learned about medicine from her mother and from doctors who passed through Kingston, staying at the family boardinghouse. In addition to having a gift for healing, especially curing tropical diseases and cholera, Mrs. Seacole (as she was always called) had a passion for travel. She supported her visits to the southern United States, Panama, Europe, and elsewhere by healing and by provisioning hospitals, travelers, and the sick. Before any trip, she spent weeks preserving fruits and meats, preparing homeopathic treatments, and stitching garments—all to sell to her fellow travelers. In England when the Crimean War broke out, she chafed—like Nightingale herself—to be at the battlefront. "Now, no sooner had I heard of a war somewhere, than I longed to witness it," she wrote, and in 1855 arrived in Crimea.

Nineteenth-century armies relied on informal groups of camp followers and local provisioners to supply the ill with food, clothing, and medicine. With contagious diseases rampant among the troops, Mrs. Seacole used her healing arts to save lives. Her efforts, however, ruined her financially, and, unlike Nightingale, she was not wealthy. Returning to England, she became highly decorated, and grateful veterans tried to help her out. Resourceful as ever, Mrs. Seacole wrote her autobiography, a wonderful saga of travel, hardship, and devotion to medicine and curing the ill.

Mrs. Seacole in the Crimean War
Until well into the nineteenth century, armies lacked well-organized supply and medical units. Women, often called "camp followers" and long considered to be prostitutes, actually did much of the service work that in the twentieth-century army would be regularized as part of military service. Mary Seacole was part of a group who made a business from provisioning the forces. Mary Evans Picture Library.

above.) Back in England following the war, she spearheaded the campaign for military reform and pioneered nursing as a profession.

More immediately, the war accomplished Napoleon III's goal of severing the alliance between the Habsburgs and Russia, the two conservative powers on which the Congress of Vienna peace settlement had rested since 1815. It thus ended Austria's and Russia's grip on European affairs and undermined their ability to contain the forces of liberalism and nationalism. The defeat was cataclysmic for Russia, as its autocracy was forced to abolish serfdom, embark on long-overdue internal reforms, and strive to renovate the empire.

Spirit of Reform in Russia

Defeat in the Crimean War not only thwarted Russia's territorial ambition but also forced it on the path of reform. Hundreds of peasant insurrections had erupted during the decade before the Crimean War. Serf defiance ranged from malingering while at forced labor to boycotting vodka to protest its heavy taxation. "Our own and neighboring households were gripped with fear," one aristocrat reported, because everyone expected "a serf rising at any minute."

Although industrial development and liberal ideology spread in eastern Europe, the Russian economy stagnated compared with western Europe's. Old-fashioned farming techniques led to depleted soil and food shortages, and the nobility was often contemptuous of ordinary people's suffering. Nonetheless, through sympathetic portrayals of serfs and frank depiction of brutal masters, such as in novelist Ivan Turgenev's *A Hunter's Sketches* (1852), a spirit of reform grew. A Russian translation of Harriet Beecher Stowe's antislavery novel *Uncle Tom's Cabin* (1852) also appeared in the 1850s and struck a responsive chord. When Russia

lost the Crimean War, the educated public, including some government officials, found the poor performance of serf-conscripted armies a disgrace and the system of serf labor an intolerable liability.

Emancipation of the Serfs.   Confronted with the need for change, Alexander proved more flexible than his father Nicholas I. Well educated and more widely traveled, he ushered in what came to be known as the age of Great Reforms, granting Russians new rights from above as a way of ensuring that change would not be forced from below through violent action. The most dramatic reforms were the emancipation of 22 million privately owned serfs in 1861 and 25 million state-owned peasants a few years later. Other important innovations included the creation of a judicial system that limited landowners' rights to mete out justice arbitrarily and the establishment of regional self-governing councils, or *zemstvos*, in 1864 to promote local government. Realistic officials knew, however, that these reforms were not designed to introduce democracy but rather to preserve the social hierarchy. One aristocratic landowner described the serfs' emancipation as "even more necessary for the welfare of our class than for the serfs."

By the terms of emancipation, communities of former serfs, headed by male village elders, received grants of land. The community itself, called a *mir*, had full power to allocate this land among

Emancipation of the Russian Serfs

The Crimean War came as a harsh warning that the Russian Empire sorely needed social reform in an age of growing state power. The plight of tens of millions of serfs was often dire compared with the condition of western Europeans, and the emancipation of 1861 was seen as key to stabilizing both state and society.
Hulton Getty/Liaison.

individuals and to direct their economic activity. Thus, although emancipation partially laid the groundwork for a modern labor force in Russia, communal landowning and decision making prevented unlimited mobility and the development of a pool of free labor. The condition attached to these so-called land grants was that peasants were not *given* land along with their personal freedom: they were forced to "redeem" the land they farmed by paying the government through long-term loans, which in turn compensated the original landowners. With much land going to the nobility, most peasants ended up owning less land than they had tilled as serfs. These conditions, especially the huge burden of debt and communal regulations, blunted Russian agricultural development for decades. But idealistic reformers believed the emancipation of the serfs, once treated by the nobility virtually as livestock, produced miraculous results. As one of them put it, "The people are without any exaggeration transfigured from head to foot. . . . The look, the walk, the speech, everything is changed."

As with serf emancipation in Prussia in 1810 and in Austria in 1848, landowners benefited most from the change because they received the best land. Fearful of alienating the nobility, the tsar's government compensated them not only for the loss of land but also for the loss of peasant services. Through the *zemstvos*, the aristocrats could provide considerable leadership in neglected local matters such as education, public health, and welfare. Generally dominated by the nobility, some of whom were expanding their political involvement, *zemstvos* were essentially a conservative structure, but they became a countervailing political force to the distant central government. Some nobles profited from the relaxation of censorship, of restrictions on travel, and of controls on university teaching to continue the trend of Westernization begun under Peter the Great, even coming to agree with liberals in western Europe that the Russian system of political autocracy and religious orthodoxy had grave disadvantages.

Another reform swept away much of Russia's abuse-ridden judicial system. One conservative writer exclaimed, "At the mere recollection of it [the old court system] one's hair stands on end and one's flesh begins to creep." Judicial reform gave all Russians, even former serfs, access to modern civil courts, rather than leaving them at the mercy of a landowner's version of justice or secret, blatantly preferential practices. The Western principle of equality of all persons before the law, regardless of social rank, was introduced in Russia for the first time.

Military reform followed in 1874 when the government ended the twenty-five-year period of conscription that had kept the army both inefficient and too small for modern needs. A six-year term and attention to education, efficiency, and humane treatment of recruits made the Russian army more competitive with those in western Europe. Service in the army had formerly been so like a lifetime sentence that villages had held funerals for its conscripts. Soldiers returned home from the reduced term somewhat more educated and patriotic.

From Reform to Rebellion. Alexander's reforms assisted modernizing and market-oriented landowners just as enclosures and emancipation had done much earlier in western Europe. Other landowners, unprepared for modern competition, mortgaged or sold their estates and remained confined within the traditional mindset of provincial life. The changes diminished the personal prerogatives of the nobility, leaving their authority weakened and sparking intergenerational rebellion. "An epidemic seemed to seize upon [noble] children . . . an epidemic of fleeing from the parental roof," one observer noted.

A new sense of an expanding public life took shape. Rejecting aristocratic leisure, youthful rebels from the upper class valued practical activity and sometimes identified with peasants and workers. Some formed communes where they hoped to do humble manual labor or start small businesses, whereas others turned to higher education, especially the sciences. Rebellious daughters of the nobility flouted parental expectations by cropping their hair short, wearing black, and escaping from home through phony marriages so they could study in European universities. This repudiation of traditional society led Turgenev to label radical youth as *nihilists* (from the Latin for "nothing"), a term that meant a lack of belief in any values whatsoever.

The atmosphere of reform also produced resistance among Russian-dominated nationalities, including an uprising by the Poles in 1863. Although Alexander II had begun extending his reforms to the Congress Kingdom of Poland (the part of Poland that came under Russian control after the Congress of Vienna), aristocratic and middle-class nationalists revolted for full independence. By 1864, Alexander II's army regained control of the Russian section of the former Poland, having used reforms to buy peasant loyalty and support in defeating the rebels. In the Caucasus and elsewhere Alexander responded to nationalist unrest with repression and programs of intensive Russification—a tactic meant to reduce the threat of future rebellion by national minorities within the empire by forcing them to adopt Russian language and culture.

In this era of the Great Reforms, the tsarist regime only partially succeeded in transforming itself into a modern authoritarian state. Political pragmatism in Russia produced a hybrid: economic growth and the spread of liberal ideas accompanied the evolution of a bureaucratic autocracy ruling over a multinational state. Elsewhere the sense of citizenship took shape in the nineteenth century, but in imperial Russia the persistence of autocracy and the abuse of large numbers of the population hurt this development.

❖ War and Nation Building

With the concert of Europe a thing of the past and with Russia absorbed by its own crises, nationalist ambitions flourished in other parts of the West. Politicians in the German and Italian states used the opportunity to unify their countries quickly and violently through warfare. When disunity threatened, the United States also waged a bloody civil war to ensure continued expansion and the consolidation of its national borders. Historians sometimes treat the rise of Italy, Germany, and a powerful United States as seemingly inevitable, but underneath the ferment lay incredible uncertainty. And for all the winners, there were as many losers and even more unpersuaded: the Austrian Empire, Ireland, and millions of individuals whose allegiances were local rather than national or imperial.

Cavour, Garibaldi, and the Process of Italian Unification

The disunited states of the Italian peninsula were tiny compared with Russia and France, but after the Crimean War the disintegrating diplomatic equilibrium in Europe allowed a unified Italy to emerge as a potential power. Despite the failure of

the revolutions of 1848, the issue of *Risorgimento* (literally meaning "rebirth" but associated with the movement for Italian unification) continued to percolate. This time the clear leader of Risorgimento would be the kingdom of Piedmont-Sardinia, in the economically modernizing north of Italy. The kingdom rallied to the operas of Verdi, but it was fortified with railroads, a modern army, and the support of France against the Austrian Empire, which still dominated the peninsula.

Cavour.   The architect of the new Italy was the pragmatic Camillo di Cavour (1810–1861), prime minister of the kingdom of Piedmont-Sardinia from 1852 until his death. A rebel, economic liberal, and gambler in his youth, the young Cavour also conducted agricultural experiments on his aristocratic father's land. He organized steamship companies, played the stock market, and inhaled the heady air of modernization during his travels to Paris and London. Verdi called Cavour "the man whom every Italian will call the father of his country"—although like 90 percent of the peninsula's residents Cavour did not speak Italian, but Piedmontese, a dialect.

Cavour had begun his quest for a united Italy by making economic development rather than democratic uprising the means to his end. As prime minister to the capricious and scheming king, Victor Emmanuel II (r. 1861–1878), he capitalized on favorable conditions to develop a healthy Piedmontese economy, a modern army, and a liberal political climate through reforms such as freedom of the press. Gradually, he focused most of his immense energy on plotting the expansion of Piedmont so it would dominate the unification process (Map 23.2).

To unify Italy, however, Piedmont would have to confront Austria, which governed the provinces of Lombardy and Venetia and exerted strong influence over most of the peninsula. Cavour turned for help to Napoleon III. He admired French success in advancing the liberal economic goals that he saw as essential for Italian independence. Napoleon, in turn, championed national self-determination when it might weaken powers like Austria. In the summer of 1858 at a meeting in the French mountain spa of Plombières, Cavour promised Napoleon the city of Nice and the region of Savoy in exchange for French help in driving the Austrians out of Italy. Napoleon III expected that once the

MAP 23.2 Unification of Italy, 1859–1870

The many states of the Italian peninsula had different languages, ways of life, and economic interests. In the north, the kingdom of Sardinia, which included the commercially advanced state of Piedmont, had much to gain from a unified market and a more extensive pool of labor. Although King Victor Emmanuel's and Garibaldi's armies brought these states together as a single country, it would take decades to construct a culturally, socially, and economically unified nation.

Austrians were gone, he, not they, would influence the peninsula. Sure of French help, Cavour provoked the Austrians to invade northern Italy in April 1859, and using the newly built Piedmontese railroad to move troops, the French joined the Piedmontese army. Once war broke out, the cause of Piedmont became the cause of nationalist Italians everywhere, even those who had supported romantic republicanism in 1848. Putting aside their former aspirations, political liberals in Tuscany and other central Italian states rose up on the side of Piedmont. "During the war of independence, I do not want liberty," said one, "but dictatorship: the dictatorship of a soldier."

Napoleon III was not a reliable ally, however. In June 1859, French and Piedmontese troops soundly defeated the Habsburg forces at Solferino and Magenta. Hoping to prevent a sweeping Piedmontese victory that might lessen his own control, Napoleon signed a peace treaty with Habsburg emperor Francis Joseph one month later. Its terms gave Lombardy but not Venetia to Piedmont, and the rest of Italy remained disunited. The treaty allowed both France and Austria to avoid the financial and political losses a prolonged war would entail. It enraged Cavour, but events proved that Napoleon's anxiety over growing Piedmontese strength was well founded.

Garibaldi. Napoleon's plans for controlled liberation of Lombardy and Venetia and a partitioned Italy were derailed as support for Piedmont continued to swell inside Italy and as a financially strapped Austria stood by helplessly. Ousting their rulers, citizens of Parma, Modena, Tuscany, and the Papal States (except Rome, which French troops had occupied) elected to join Piedmont. In May 1860, Giuseppe Garibaldi (1807–1882), a committed republican, inspired guerrilla fighter, and veteran of the revolutions of 1848, set sail from Genoa with a thousand red-shirted volunteers (many of them teenage boys) to liberate Sicily, where peasant revolts against landlords and the corrupt government were under way. Garibaldi's rallying cry was "Italy and Victor Emmanuel," but he was also known as a democratic populist. Garibaldi's expedition to Sicily forced Cavour to expand his vision of Piedmont's leadership to include poor and agrarian southern Italy. Rapid victories on the island followed by the Red Shirts' invasion of the southern mainland alarmed Cavour, who dispatched the Piedmontese army south to keep Garibaldi from reaching Rome, where he would surely confront the French with his ragtag army.

In the autumn of 1860, the forces of King Victor Emmanuel and Garibaldi finally met in Naples. Although some of his supporters still clamored for social reform and a republic, Garibaldi threw his support to the king, and the two unlikely allies rode together through the streets to the wild cheering of the crowd. Public celebrations and holidays were becoming increasingly important to nation building, and, after warfare had done its work, this parade bound rulers and ruled in support of the nation-state. In 1861, the kingdom of Italy was proclaimed with Victor Emmanuel as king.

Exhausted by a decade of overwork, Cavour died within months of leading the unification, leaving lesser men to organize the new Italy. Consensus among Italy's elected political leaders was often elusive once the war was over, and admirers of Cavour, such as Verdi (who had been made senator), fled the heated political scene. The wealthy commercial north and impoverished agricultural south remained at odds, as they do even today. Many southern peasants continued to rebel against the old, inequitable patterns of landholding, whereas the northern politicians who dominated the government concentrated economic benefits in their own area. Italian borders did not yet seem final because Venetia and Rome remained outside them, under Austrian and French control, respectively. But

Seamstresses of the Red Shirts
Sewing uniforms and making battle flags, European women like these Italian volunteers saw themselves as contributors to the nation. Donating their domestic skills and raising the next generation of citizens to be patriotic, many nineteenth-century women participated in nation building as "republican mothers."

the legend of an Italian struggle for freedom symbolized by the figure of Garibaldi and his Red Shirts papered over these defects and sentimentalized the Realpolitik that had made unification possible.

Bismarck and the Realpolitik of German Unification

The most momentous act of nation building for the future of Europe and of the world was the creation of a united Germany in 1871. This too was the work of Realpolitik, undertaken once the concert of Europe was smashed and the champions of the status quo defeated. Employing the old military order to wage war, yet with the support of economic modernizers who saw profits in one huge national market, the Prussian state brought a vast array of cities and kingdoms under its control within a single decade. From then on, Germany prospered, continuing to consolidate its economic and political might. By the end of the nineteenth century it would be the foremost continental power.

Bismarck's Rise to Power.   The architect of a unified Germany was Otto von Bismarck (1815–1898), the Prussian minister-president. Bismarck came from a traditional Junker (Prussian landed nobility) family on his father's side; his mother's family included high-ranking bureaucrats and literati of the middle class. Obeying his mother's wishes, the young Bismarck had gone to the university, but he spent his time there gambling and womanizing. Only a course on the economic foundations of politics interested him academically. After failing in the civil service he worked to modernize operations on his landholdings and read widely. Otherwise, by his own admission he led a loutish life.

In 1846, Bismarck experienced a religious conversion, married a pious Lutheran woman, and acquired a seriousness of purpose. In 1851, he became the Prussian representative to the restored assembly of the various German states. There Prussia's impotence and the Habsburg domination of German affairs repelled him. He learned a formative lesson in Realpolitik: despite ideological similarities between the Prussian and Austrian monarchies and past alliances to contain revolutionary France, the multinational Habsburg Empire, with its overbearing diplomacy, blocked the full flowering of the Prussian state.

In 1862, William I (king of Prussia, r. 1861–1888; German emperor, r. 1871–1888) appointed Bismarck prime minister in hopes that he would quash the growing power of the liberals in the Prussian parliament. The liberals, representing the prosperous professional and business classes, had gained parliamentary strength at the expense of conservative landowners during the decades of industrial expansion. Indeed, the liberals' wealth was crucial to the Prussian state's ability to augment its power. Desiring Prussia to be like western Europe, Prussian liberals advocated the extension of political rights, increased civilian control of the military, and other reforms. William I, along with members of the traditional Prussian elite, rejected the west-

ern European model. In fact, William wanted to consolidate state control by ending the citizen militia system, integrating the militia into the regular army, and lengthening the term of military service.

The issue of the military, on which Prussian bureaucratic and political strength had depended, gave Bismarck his first critical victory. When the liberals rejected the tax increase needed to expand the army, Bismarck announced that the king's agents would collect taxes despite parliament, and he proceeded with the military buildup. He also gave his own appraisal of contemporary politics, specifically his view of liberal ideals: "Germany looks not to Prussia's liberalism, but to its power," he preached. "The great questions of the day will not be settled by speeches and majority decisions— that was the great mistake of 1848 and 1849—but by blood and iron."

Wars of Unification.   After his triumph over the parliament, Bismarck led Prussia into a series of wars, against Denmark in 1864, against Austria in 1866, and, finally, against France in 1870. Using war as a political tactic, he kept the disunited German states from choosing Austrian leadership and instead united them around Prussia, forcing what was known as a *kleindeutsch*, or "small German," alternative that did not include Austria. The war with Denmark was a prelude to imposing the *kleindeutsch* solution and finally resolving the Austro-Prussian rivalry that had existed since the eighteenth century. When the Danish king suggested incorporating into Denmark the provinces of Schleswig and Holstein, with their mixed Danish and German populations, Bismarck drew Austria into a joint war with Prussia against Denmark in 1864. The allied victory resulted in an agreement that Prussia would administer Schleswig, and Austria, Holstein. Such an arrangement stretched Austria's geographic interests far from its central European base.

Austria proved weaker than Prussia. By the time France and Piedmont defeated the Habsburgs in 1859, Austria's state debt had swollen to five times its annual revenues, and because economic development did not grow at the same pace, Austria could not afford Prussian-style military modernization. Internally the empire had to contend with disaffected nationalities, particularly the Magyars, whose oppression after 1849 fueled their nationalism. Despite these problems, the Austrian government still behaved as if it had the same power and prestige as in the days of Metternich. Bismarck encouraged these pretensions. Then, fomenting disputes over the administration of Schleswig and Holstein, he goaded Austria into declaring war on Prussia itself. In the summer of 1866, Austria went to war with the support of most small states in the German Confederation. Within seven weeks the modernized Prussian army, using railroads and breech-loading rifles against the out-

dated Austrian military, had won decisively. Victory allowed Bismarck to drive Austria from the German Confederation and to create a North German Confederation led by Prussia. This confederation subsequently adopted a common political and economic program, permitting it to compete more effectively in the growing industrial marketplace and to spearhead reform. Bavaria and the other independent southern German states found themselves clients of Prussia, and some clamored for annexation (Map 23.3).

MAP 23.3 Unification of Germany, 1862–1871

In a complex series of diplomatic maneuvers, Bismarck welded disunited kingdoms and small states into a major continental power independent of the other dominant German dynasty, the Habsburg monarchy. Prussia's use of force unified Germany politically, and almost immediately that unity unleashed the new nation's economic potential. An aristocratic and agrarian elite remained firmly in power, but a rapidly growing working class would soon become a political force to be reckoned with.

Emperor William I of Germany, 1871
The defeat of France in the Franco-Prussian War of 1870 –1871 ended with the proclamation of the king of Prussia as emperor of a unified Germany. Otto von Bismarck, who had orchestrated the wars of unification, appropriately appears in this artistic rendering as the central figure attired in heroic white. But the event in the French palace of Versailles symbolized the militaristic and antagonistic side of state building, especially the Franco-German rivalry that would disastrously motivate European politics in the future.
AKG London.

To bring the remaining German states into the rapidly developing nation, Bismarck next moved to entrap France in a war with Prussia. During the Austro-Prussian War, Bismarck had suggested to Napoleon III that his neutrality would bring France territory, but the emperor's actual announcement of such expansion whipped up German nationalism. The atmosphere was charged, and in 1868 an issue arose that would precipitate war between France and Prussia. A military coup in Spain sent that country's leaders shopping for a new king from among Europe's royal families. They chose a German prince of the minor branch of the Prussian ruling family. His candidacy threatened the French with Prussian rulers on two of their borders. As pressure mounted, the candidacy was withdrawn, but the French remained furious. In the summer of 1870, the French ambassador accosted William I at the German spa of Ems and demanded both an apology and promises that Prussia would never again make such a claim on the Spanish throne. "If he refuses, it's war," the French foreign minister remarked. When William sent a telegram to Bismarck about the incident, Bismarck saw his opportunity to stir up nationalist

journalism in both countries. Although William's message contained only complaints about the French ambassador's public harangue, Bismarck edited the so-called Ems telegram to make it look as if William had insulted France and then released the revised version to journalists. The inflamed French public demanded war. The parliament gladly declared it.

The French declaration of war on July 19, 1870, set in motion the alliances Prussia had created with the other German states. Bonapartism and Bismarck's diplomacy had isolated France from such potential allies as Austria, Russia, and Great Britain, and all three states sat by as the Prussians captured Napoleon III with his army on September 2, 1870. "Thank God," remarked Alexander II of Russia on hearing of Napoleon's defeat. "Sevastopol is now avenged."

The Second Empire fell on September 4, 1870. With Prussian forces still besieging Paris and the French political future uncertain, in January 1871 in the Hall of Mirrors at Versailles, King William of Prussia was proclaimed the kaiser of a new, imperial Germany. The terms of the peace signed in May 1871 required France to cede the rich industrial provinces of Alsace and Lorraine to Germany and to pay a multibillion-franc indemnity. Without French protection for the papacy, Rome became part of Italy. Germany was now poised to dominate continental politics.

The German Nation Takes Shape. Prussian military might served as the foundation for German state building, and a complex constitution ensured the continued political dominance of the aristocracy and monarchy. The kaiser, who remained Prussia's king, controlled the military and appointed Bismarck to the powerful position of Reich's chancellor. The German states balanced monarchical authority somewhat through the Bundesrat, a body composed of representatives from each state. The Reichstag, an assembly elected by universal male suffrage, ratified all budgets. In framing this constitutional settlement, Bismarck accorded rights such as suffrage in the belief that the masses would uphold autocracy out of their fear of "the domination of finance capital"—shorthand for "liberal power." He balanced this move, however, with an electoral system in which the votes from the upper classes counted more than those from the lower.

Bismarck had little to fear from the liberals, who became dizzy with German military success. The new National Liberal Party came to blend its belief in economic progress and constitutionalism with militaristic nationalism and support for the Prussian social hierarchy that Bismarck represented. Once associated with demands for political rights and constitutional reform to protect ordinary people from abuses by monarchs and aristocrats, German nationalism came more to connote military superiority. Bismarck, who later instituted many social welfare programs that benefited the German people, did nothing to discredit a vision of Prussia as a military nation led by powerful heroes like himself: "The old women, when they hear my name, fall upon their knees and beg me for their lives," he wrote to his wife during one of his wars. "Attila was a lamb compared with me." During the next decades, German ascendancy was fostered by Bismarck's flexible leadership in foreign and domestic affairs, the continuing expansion of industry, and the flowering of German culture and national pride.

Francis Joseph and the Creation of the Austro-Hungarian Monarchy

There was no blueprint for nation building. Just as the Crimean War left Russia searching for solutions to its social and political problems, so the confrontation with Cavour and Bismarck left the Habsburg Empire at bay. At first, the Habsburg Empire emerged from the revolutions of 1848 and 1849 renewed by the ascension of Francis Joseph (r. 1848–1916), who favored absolutist rule. Francis Joseph took charge of the government, working tirelessly on policies and documents and enhancing his authority through stiff, formal court ceremonies. Because the emperor insisted on grandeur and decorum, the Viennese became expert in recognizing degrees of nobility according to symbols such as insignia on carriages or one's position in funeral processions. Francis Joseph ruled by playing to the popular fascination with the trappings of power; he also stubbornly resisted change, compromising only under duress.

Despite the emperor's adherence to tradition, some changes occurred. Official standards of honesty and efficiency improved, and the government promoted local education. Although the German language was used by the administration and taught by the schools, the government respected the rights of national minorities—the Czechs and Poles, for instance—to receive education and to communicate with officials in their native tongue. Above all, the government abolished most internal customs barriers, freed trade with Germany, and sold off much of the state railway system, giving impetus to a boom in private railway construction. Foreign investment flowed into Austria; the capital city of Vienna underwent extensive rebuilding; and people found jobs as industrialization progressed.

In a fast-paced age, the emperor could not match Bismarck in advancing the power of the state. Francis Joseph's rigid adherence to absolutism often frustrated the modernizing bureaucrats. Prosperous liberals resented the swarm of police informers, the virtually free hand of the Catholic church in education and in civil institutions such as marriage, and their own lack of representation in such important policy matters as taxation and finance. Money for military modernization and warfare dried up, and Francis Joseph was forced to modify his absolutist system. He created a more modern parliament, the Reichsrat, in which German liberals predominated and which almost immediately imposed rigid economies on the military similar to those demanded by Prussian liberals in Berlin. However, the emperor lacked Bismarck's craftiness to override the liberals.

After Prussia's victory over Francis Joseph's scaled-back armies in 1866, the most disaffected but wealthy part of the empire, Hungary, became the key to stability, even to the empire's existence.

The Austro-Hungarian Monarchy, 1867

The leaders of the Hungarian agrarian elites made a simple demand: Magyar home rule over the Hungarian kingdom. Negotiating from a position of strength, the Magyar leadership forced the emperor to accept a "dual monarchy." This agreement restored the Hungarian parliament, gave it control of internal policy (including the right to decide how to treat Hungary's national minorities), and made the Hungarian contribution to the joint army a matter of negotiation every decade. Although the Habsburg emperor Francis Joseph was crowned king of Hungary and Austro-Hungarian foreign policy was coordinated from Vienna, the Hungarians mostly ruled themselves after 1867 and hammered out any policies of joint interest, such as taxation and tariffs, in cumbersome and acrimonious negotiations with Vienna.

The dual monarchy of Austria-Hungary was designed specifically to address the Hungarian demands, but in so doing it strengthened the voices of Czechs, Slovaks, and at least half a dozen additional national groups in the Habsburg Empire wanting the same kind of consideration and self-rule. Czechs who helped the empire advance industrially failed to gain Hungarian-style liberties, and no one achieved the full range of reforms desired by the middle class of every nationality. For some of the dissatisfied ethnic groups, Pan-Slavism—that is, the transnational loyalty of all ethnic Slavs—became a rallying cry as the various Slav peoples saw themselves as having a common heritage. Instead of looking toward Vienna, they turned to the largest Slavic country—Russia—as a focal point for potential national unity. As the nation-state grew in strength, transnational movements like Pan-Slavism in Austria-Hungary would emerge to provide alternative allegiances for those not

Muslim Quarter and Bazaar

Nineteenth-century Europeans were a diverse people, composed of many religions, ethnicities, and ways of life. In the Balkans, many were Muslims, as this marketplace in Sarajevo, Bosnia, illustrates. The goal of finding a common cultural ground eluded the peoples of the Balkans. The Habsburg monarchy, which annexed Bosnia-Herzegovina in 1908, exerted its influence in the area to keep peoples divided and to play one against the other. Graphische Sammlung Albertina, Wien.

recognized as equal citizens in their home countries. Although a growing sense of national identity contributed to nation building during this period, it was increasingly a divisive and destabilizing concept.

Political Stability through Gradual Reform in Great Britain

In contrast to the turmoil on the continent, Britain appeared the epitome of liberal progress. By the 1850s, the monarchy symbolized domestic tranquillity and propriety. Unlike their predecessors, Queen Victoria (r. 1837–1901) and her husband, Prince Albert, were considered models of morality, emblematic of British stability and middle-class virtues. Britain's parliamentary system incorporated new ideas and steadily brought more men into the political process. Economic prosperity further fortified ongoing political reform, resulting in relative social peace, at least in England itself.

Whereas some countries were powder kegs of antagonistic political interests and others (such as Italy and Germany) were just being born, Great Britain was united under a single government, despite Ireland's continued suffering and its growing demands for reform. Smooth governmental decision making was fostered by an ever-changing party system. Some historians believe that the presence of a woman on the British throne allowed the monarchical system slowly to lose its prerogatives to a male electorate. Strained by the repeal of the Corn Laws in 1846, the Tory Party evolved into the Conservatives, who favored a more status-oriented politics but still went along with the developing liberal consensus around economic development and representative government. The Whigs changed names, too, and became the Liberals; the inclusion of radical members of Parliament in the government built new levels of support for liberalism. In 1867, the Conservatives, led by Benjamin Disraeli (1804–1881), passed the Second Reform Bill, which made a million more men eligible to vote. After 1867, the Conservatives and Liberals developed into more efficient political organizations with recognized platforms that targeted a wider variety of male voters.

Political parties supported reforms because pressure groups now influenced the party system.

The Law Amendment Society and the Social Science Association, for example, lobbied for laws to improve social conditions, and groups like the Reform Union and the Reform League worked for a broader male franchise. Under pressure from women's groups, the government addressed family and marital issues with the Matrimonial Causes Act of 1857, which facilitated divorce, and the Married Women's Property Act of 1870, which allowed married women to own property and keep the wages they earned. Reformist activism, much of it by the middle class, added to the political process a continuous and extensive network of groups that

Queen Victoria and Prince Albert
Mid-nineteenth-century rulers started using the new photographic technology to make themselves respectable and celebrated figures. Queen Victoria and her consort Prince Albert were expert publicists, often posing as an ordinary middle-class couple and the epitome of domestic order. Their photos were sold or given away on small cards called carte de visites, *a means used by many leaders to spread their fame.*
The Royal Archives © Her Majesty Queen Elizabeth II.

rejected the revolutionary politics common on the continent and instead pressed for change from within the British political structure.

Not everyone favored reform, especially reforms aimed at expanding the electorate. Lower-class voters, charged an angry critic, were full of "blockheadism, gullibility, bribability, amenability to beer and balderdash." But the government overlaid liberalism with plush ceremonies that united critics and activists and, more important, different social classes. Whereas previous monarchs' sexual infidelities had inspired bawdy songs and incited crowds to riot, the monarchy of Queen Victoria and Prince Albert, with its newly devised celebrations of royal marriages, anniversaries, and births, drew respectful, though still exuberant crowds. The scheme promoting the monarchy in this way was so successful that the term *Victorian* came to symbolize almost the entire century and could refer to anything from manners to political institutions. Recalling the royal past, the aristocracy began building gigantic country houses in such traditional English architectural styles as Queen Anne and Georgian. Other building projects used a refurbished design of the thatched-roof cottage associated with the rural countryside. Like the ubiquitous monuments to Garibaldi that suggested unity, not political tensions, in the new Italy, these symbols of Merrie Olde England evoked a common past to harmonize the dislocations of rapid urbanization and industrialization. As one poet expressed it:

> *Forget the spreading of the hideous town;*
> *Think rather of the pack-horse on the down,*
> *And dream of London, small, and white,*
> *   and clean.*

Britain's politicians were as devoted to Realpolitik as were those in Germany, Italy, or France, but robust industry, a liberal consensus, and an expanding overseas empire underwrote Britain's special success in creating the sense of a shared political destiny. Acquiring its expanding empire inflicted the same toll of violence as did German, Italian, and U.S. nation building. The violence was far beyond the view of most British people, however, allowing them to imagine their nation as peaceful, advanced, and united.

Civil War and Nation Building in the United States and Canada

In North America, increasing nationalism and powerful economic growth characterized the nation-building experience. The United States entered a midcentury period of upheaval with a more democratic political culture than Europe had. Virtually universal white male suffrage, a rambunctiously independent press, and mass political parties endorsed the accepted view that sovereignty derived from the people.

The United States continued to expand its territory to the west (Map 23.4). In 1848, victory in its war with Mexico almost doubled the size of the country: Texas was officially annexed, and large portions of California and the Southwest extended U.S. borders into former Mexican land. Politicians and citizens alike favored banning the native Indian peoples from these western lands. Complicating matters, however, was the question of whether the West would be settled by free white farmers or whether southern slaveholders could bring in their slaves.

The issue polarized the country. In the North, the new Republican Party emerged to demand "free soil, free labor, free men," although few Republicans endorsed the abolitionists' demand to end slavery. With the 1860 election of Republican Abraham Lincoln to the presidency, most of the slaveholding states seceded to form the Confederate States of America. Between 1861 and 1865, the United States was torn apart by a devastating civil war.

Under Lincoln's leadership, the North fought to uphold the Union. Lincoln did not initially aim to abolish slavery, but in January 1863 his Emancipation Proclamation came into force as a wartime measure, officially freeing all slaves in the Confederate states and turning the war into a fight not only for union but also for liberation from slavery. After the summer of 1863, the North's superior industrial strength and military might overpowered and physically destroyed much of the South. By April 1865, the North had prevailed, even though a Confederate sympathizer had assassinated Lincoln. Distancing the United States still further from the colonial, plantation model, constitutional amendments ended slavery and promised free African American men full political rights.

Battle of Fredericksburg, 1863

President Abraham Lincoln cemented North and South by military means in the U.S. Civil War, which destroyed large sections of the Southeast. A war with huge casualties inflicted by the industrial development of modern weaponry, the Civil War took place on farmlands and in cities and towns. This depiction by a local artist captures the disorderly setting of the battle of Fredericksburg in the summer of 1863.
Corbis/Bettmann.

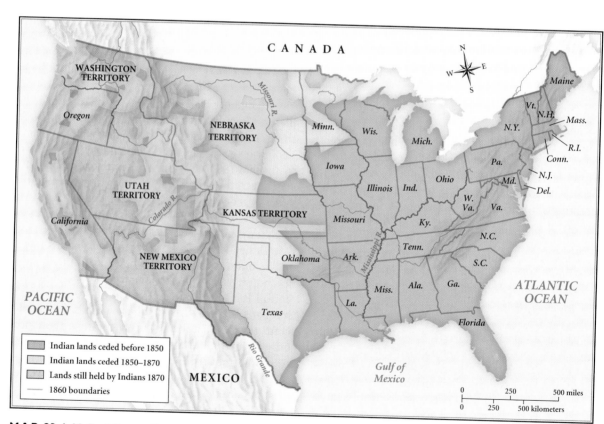

MAP 23.4 United States Expansion, 1850–1870

Like Russia, the United States expanded into adjacent regions to create a continental nation-state. Conquering indigenous peoples and taking over their territories, the United States differed from Russia, however, by herding native peoples into small confined spaces called reservations so that settlers could acquire thousands of square miles for farming and other enterprises. Gradually some Native Americans acquired the right to vote, and the United States government granted full citizenship for all in 1925.

Northerners hailed their victory as the triumph of American values, but racism remained entrenched throughout the Union. By 1871, northern interest in promoting African American political rights was waning, and southern whites began regaining control of state politics, often by organized violence and intimidation. The end of northern occupation of the South in 1877 put on hold for nearly a century the promise of rights for blacks.

The North's triumph had profound effects elsewhere in North America. It allowed the reunited United States to contribute to Napoleon III's defeat in Mexico in 1867. The United States also demanded the annexation of Canada in retribution for Britain's partiality to the Confederacy because of its dependence on cotton. To head off this threat, the British government allowed Canadians to form a united, self-governing dominion. According dominion status answered Canadian appeals for home rule and lessened domestic opposition to Britain's owning Canada in the first place.

❖ Instituting Social Order

In this age of nation building, government officials developed mechanisms to forge internal social unity and order that served to clean up or offset the violence by which the state was expanding. Confronted with growing populations and crowded cities, governments throughout Europe intervened in more areas of everyday life. (See "Taking Measure," page 868.) Many liberal theorists advocated a laissez-faire government that left social and economic life largely to private enterprise. But waves of revolution and epidemics convinced officials that the state needed to guard social peace by attending to the health and safety of its citizens. Along with continuing industrial development, expanding public institutions in Europe during the 1850s and 1860s affected the psychological, physical, and social life of ordinary citizens. Nevertheless, having confidence in the benefits of European institutions in general, bureaucrats, missionaries, and explorers pressed European influence beyond the nation-state's boundaries into the farthest reaches of the globe.

Bringing Order to the Cities

Dramatic changes in the urban environment made many European cities the backdrop for displays of state power and national solidarity. Efforts to improve sanitation and control disease also redounded to the state's credit. Governments focused their refurbishing efforts on their capital cities, although many noncapital cities acquired handsome parks, widened streets, and erected stately museums and massive city halls. In 1857, Francis Joseph ordered the destruction of the old Viennese city walls and their replacement with concentric boulevards lined with major public buildings such as the opera house and government offices. Napoleon III initiated similar embellishment of Paris, making it the symbol of his regime's grandeur. Opera houses and ministries tangibly represented national wealth and power, and the broad boulevards allowed crowds to observe royal pageantry. These wider roads were also easier for troops to navigate than the twisted, narrow medieval streets that in 1848 had concealed insurrectionists in cities like Paris and Vienna—an advantage that convinced some otherwise reluctant officials to approve the expense. Impressive parks and public gardens showed the state's control of nature, while they helped order people's leisure time. The revamped city inspired awe for the nation-state or empire.

One effect of refurbished cities was to highlight class differences. Construction first required destruction; buildings and entire neighborhoods of housing for the poor disappeared, and thousands of city dwellers were dislocated. The boulevards often served as boundaries marking rich and poor sections of the city. In Vienna, wealthy inhabitants even suggested walling off major streets so they might obtain a more secure separation from the poor. In Paris, the process of urban change was called *Haussmannization*, named for the prefect Georges-Eugène Haussmann, who implemented a grand design that included eighty-five miles of new city streets, many lined with showy dwellings for the wealthy. Tens of thousands of poor people lost their homes, as old buildings were torn down. London experienced more piecemeal urban development. British city planners nonetheless saw advantages in rebuilding for an industrial nation, and large commercial streets replaced slums and lower-class neighborhoods.

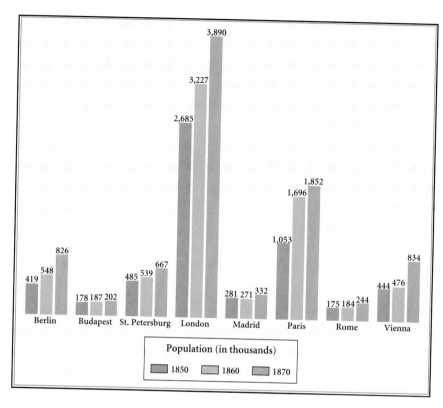

TAKING MEASURE
Urban Population Growth, 1850–1870

As state building and industrialization advanced, population grew in capital, commercial, and manufacturing cities and towns. As this graph shows, major cities gained hundreds of thousands of new inhabitants, and the outdated urban environment was usually strained beyond its capacity. Industrial and commercial cities like Leeds, Essen, Düsseldorf, and Lodz doubled and even quintupled in size, however.

B.R. Mitchell, *International Historical Statistics, 1750–1993* (New York: Macmillan, 1998), 74–76.

Other improvements in London seemed only decorative: old building facades, for example, were given a new look with graceful plasterwork and pillars. Those who undertook these embellishments, which often strike twentieth-century observers as manifestations of Victorian excess and bad taste, believed that ornamentation would blot out the ugliness of commerce and industry. Public beauty would enhance pedestrians' lives and lift their spirits. Moreover, the size and spaciousness of the many new banks and insurance companies built in London "help[ed] the impression of stability," as an architect put it, and this would foster social order.

Amid signs of economic prosperity, the devastation caused by repeated epidemics of diseases such as cholera debilitated city dwellers and gave the strong impression of social decay. Poor sanitation allowed typhoid bacteria to spread through sewage and into water supplies, infecting rich and poor alike. In 1861, Britain's Prince Albert reputedly died of typhus, commonly known as a "filth disease." Unregulated urban slaughterhouses and

tanneries; heaps of animal excrement in chicken coops, pigsties, and stables; human waste alongside buildings; open cesspools; and garbage everywhere facilitated the spread of disease. The many corpses that had to be buried during epidemics also posed health problems. As society grew more prosperous, the stench, diseases, and "morbid air" of cities indicated such a degree of failure, disorder, and danger that sanitation became a government priority.

Scientific research, increasingly undertaken in public universities and hospitals, provided the means to promote public health and control disease. Initial efforts to improve public sanitation relied on the *miasmatic theory* of disease, which traced sickness to breathing in putrid odors. The germ theory advanced by France's Louis Pasteur (1822–1895), whose three young daughters had died of typhus, was not only more accurate but also had widespread sanitary application. Seeking a method to prevent wine from spoiling, Pasteur began his work in the mid-1850s by studying fermentation. He found that the growth of living organisms caused fermentation, and he suggested that certain organisms—bacteria and parasites—might be responsible for human and animal diseases. Pasteur further demonstrated that heating foods such as wine and milk to a certain temperature, a process that soon became known as *pasteurization*, killed these organisms and made food safe. In the mid-1860s, the English surgeon Joseph Lister (1827–1912) applied the germ theory in medicine. He connected Pasteur's theory of bacteria to infection and developed antiseptics for treating wounds. Using carbolic acid for sterilization, as Lister suggested, hastened the decline of puerperal fever, a condition that was caused by the dirty hands of physicians and midwives and that killed innumerable women after childbirth.

Even though the germ theory proved that "morbid air" did not cause disease, air pollution still bothered city dwellers, prompting the most fastidious to move to elegant suburbs, where they could breathe fresher air and also escape the sight of their poorer neighbors. Land development and new roads also gave workers displaced by urban renewal a chance to live outside the city. By the mid-1860s, the Viennese, like residents of other capitals, could travel the city and reach rings of inner and outer suburbs by streetcar or horse-drawn omnibuses.

Meanwhile, governments undertook projects to improve sewer systems and drainage. In Paris, huge underground collectors provided a watertight terminus for accumulated sewage. In addition, Haussmann was determined to provide fresh water for every Parisian dwelling. To do so, he piped in water from less-contaminated sources in the countryside. Such ventures were imitated throughout Europe: the Russian Empire's port city Riga (now in Latvia), for example, organized its first water company in 1863. Improved sanitation testified to progress and a more active role for the state. Modernization of the city also encouraged new values. Citizens came to prize these material improvements

Vienna Opera House
The era of nation building saw the construction of architectural monuments in the center of capital cities to display cultural power and to bring music, art, and science to the people. Vienna's center was rebuilt around imposing facades like that of the Imperial Opera House, which opened in 1869.
Hulton Getty/Liaison Agency.

Paris Sewer

The Paris sewers were rebuilt in Napoleon III's Second Empire as models of modern hygiene sponsored by the state. Their construction was part of the effort to eliminate smells and signs of germs from both public and private life. As society opted for hygiene, sewers became emblematic of dangerous and diseased peoples who were threats to social well-being and order.
Corbis/Bettmann.

and came to develop a deeper feeling of national and local pride.

Ordinary people often supported better public works despite the governmental expansion and higher taxes such improvements entailed. Shop-keepers agitated for paved streets to end the diffi-culties of transporting goods along muddy or flooded roadways. When public toilets for men be-came a feature of modern Paris, women petitioned the government unsuccessfully for decades for sim-ilar facilities. On the lookout for disease and sani-tary dangers, the average person became more aware of smells and the foul air that had been an accepted part of daily life for thousands of years. A citizen of Voronezh in central Russia reported to the Moscow papers that "an enormous cloud of white dust [hung] constantly over the city," injur-ing the lungs and eyes. To show that they were becoming more "civilized," the middle and lower-middle classes bathed more regularly and even per-fumed themselves, something aristocrats had been doing for centuries. Middle-class concerns for re-finement and health coincided with the quest of governments for order.

Expanding the Reach of Bureaucracy

Central to enacting new programs to build social order and enhance the nation was an expansion of state bureaucracies. The nation-state required citi-zens to follow a growing catalog of regulations, as government authority reached further into the realm of everyday life. The regular censuses that Britain, France, and the United States had begun early in the nineteenth century became routine in most other countries as well. Censuses provided the state with such personal details of its citizens' lives as age, occupation, marital status, residential patterns, and fertility. Governments then used these data for a variety of endeavors, ranging from setting quotas for military conscription to predict-ing needs for new prisons. Reformers like Florence Nightingale, who gathered medical and other sta-tistics to support sanitary and military reform, be-lieved that such quantitative information made government less susceptible to corruption, special deals, and inefficiency. In 1860, Sweden introduced taxation based on income, which opened an area of private life—one's earnings from work or invest-ment—to government scrutiny. The extension of bureaucracy pleased those who thought centralized policies would help society operate more fairly and efficiently than the capricious rule of local nota-bles, but those who believed in laissez-faire often opposed such "intrusions."

To bring about their vision of social order, most governments, including those of Britain, Italy, Austria, and France, also expanded their regulation and investigation of prostitution. Venereal disease, especially syphilis, was a scourge of the era that, like typhus, infected individuals and whole fami-lies. Officials blamed prostitutes for its spread. The police picked up any suspect woman on the street and passed her to public health doctors who exam-ined her for syphilis. If the woman was infected with the disease she was sent to a medical institu-tion for mandatory treatment, which usually meant a period of incarceration. To control prosti-tution in cities, French public planners stipulated that brothels could be built only in designated neighborhoods. As states began monitoring prosti-tution and other social matters like public health and housing, they had to add new departments and agencies. In 1867, Hungary's bureaucracy handled fewer than 250,000 individual cases, ranging from health to poverty issues; twenty years later it dealt with more than a million.

As government bureaucracies grew, new jobs opened. The looming question was who would get these influential, relatively secure, and higher-status positions. Would the old aristocracy and their clients fill them? Or would the government hire people based on merit and skill? In the Austro-Hungarian monarchy, an effort to open bureaucratic posts to native speakers prompted various nationalities to demand that their language replace German as the official language of local administration. The middle classes in the empire lobbied to eliminate aristocrats' stranglehold on the top positions and to keep civil service jobs from becoming a reward for political loyalty. In Britain, a civil service law passed in 1870 required competitive examinations for government posts—an idea in the air since the West had come in contact with the Chinese examination system. The push for reform in Sweden transformed the bureaucracy from an aristocratic bastion to a civil service in which more than two-thirds of all jobs went to members of the middle class. Not only did government impose new standards of order, but citizens also insisted that the state itself conform to middle-class ideas of competence and opportunity.

Schooling Society

Bureaucrats and reformers called for radical changes in the scope, curriculum, and personnel of schools—from kindergarten to university—to make the general population more fit for citizenship and useful in furthering economic progress. Ongoing expansion of the electorate along with lower-class activism prompted one British aristocrat to exclaim, "We must now educate our masters!" The growth of commerce and the state was partly behind a craze for learning, which made traveling lecturers, public forums, reading groups, and debating societies popular among the middle and working classes. Governments also introduced compulsory schooling to reduce illiteracy (more than 70 percent in Italy and Spain in the 1870s and even higher in eastern than in western Europe).

Even a few hours of lessons each day were said to teach important social habits and the responsi-

bilities of citizenship, along with practical knowledge. The impulse to strengthen the educational system came from a variety of quarters: liberals, nationalists, conservatives, and radicals all believed in bettering educational opportunities. However, the ends differed: to train people for the civil service or industry, to encourage civic loyalty, to instill patterns of obedience, to develop "modern" attitudes.

Primary education had traditionally emphasized religious instruction, with church doctrine, biblical maxims, and obedience at the core of the curriculum. Initially, various denominations had supervised schools and charged tuition, making primary education an option chosen only by prosperous or religious parents. Curricular changes in the 1850s and 1860s aimed at introducing secular and scientific instruction, because many leaders felt that liberal rationalism should supplant religiosity as a guiding principle. In 1861, an English commission on education concluded that instead of the Bible, "the knowledge most important to a labouring man is that of the causes which regulate the amount of his wages, the hours of his work, the regularity of his employment, and the prices of what he consumes."

Accomplishing this instruction was another matter. For example, the Netherlands and Switzerland had fully functioning systems of public primary schools in the 1830s, and Sweden ordered towns and parishes to provide primary schooling after 1842. Yet school attendance was virtually impossible to enforce, because it often conflicted with family interests. Rural parents depended on their children to perform farm chores and believed that they would gain useful knowledge in the fields or the household. Urban homemakers needed their children to help with domestic tasks such as fetching water, disposing of waste, tending the younger children, and scavenging for household necessities such as stale bread from bakers or soup from local missions. Secondary and university education was even more of a luxury, reserved for the top echelons of society, and officials argued endlessly about the curriculum of higher education. In many countries people debated whether future leaders should have traditional education in religion, a classical education based on Latin and Greek, or a liberal arts education grounded in science, mathematics, and modern languages. In Russia, for example, the government considered technical subjects and science potentially subversive and closely monitored university professors.

Amid the controversy over the best kind of education, the secondary school became more systematized, reflecting the demands of both an industrial society and a bureaucratic state. In Prussia, a system of secondary schools (*Gymnasia*) offered a liberal arts curriculum that trained students for a variety of careers. Those who left after a few years entered the lower ranks of the bureaucracy; higher-level positions in government and the professions were reserved for graduates and those who went to the university. In the 1860s, however, new *Realschulen*, less prestigious at the time, emphasized math, science, and modern languages for those who would not attain a Gymnasium degree or go on to attend the university. Typically, those trying for a business or technical career pursued the Realschulen education. Like many other countries, Prussia ultimately developed an intricate educational system to track the various career paths and social strata of its students.

Girls and young women were educated separately from boys, just as they were prepared for separate spheres in their adult lives. Reformers pushed for more advanced and more complex courses for young women than the fare they were initially offered. In France and Russia, for example, government leaders themselves saw that "public education has had in view only half the population—the male sex," as the Russian minister of education wrote to Tsar Alexander II in 1856. Both Napoleon III and Alexander II sponsored secondary- and university-level courses for women as part of their program to control the modernization of society. Nonetheless, higher education for women remained a hotly contested issue because religion, sewing, deportment, and writing appeared more than adequate. Yet reformers from across the political spectrum concurred that well-educated mothers—those who knew some science, history, and literature—would rear their children better and prove more satisfactory companions to their husbands.

Young women who attended universities in Zurich and Paris in the 1860s, where medical training was open to them, often aspired to an education that would qualify them to move into social roles other than those of wife and mother. The expansion of the medical profession and the opportunities in

public health appealed to women's reforming zeal. By joining a profession only men had previously entered, these women appeared to weaken the system of separate spheres. Yet many women wanted to practice medicine to protect female patients' modesty and to bring feminine values to health care. Women doctors claimed to perform examinations and treatments with more discretion and concern for female patients than shown by male doctors. In Britain the founders of two women's colleges, Girton (1869) and Newnham (1871) at Cambridge University, believed that exacting standards in women's higher education would provide an example of a modern curriculum in this stronghold of traditional learning. Reformers maintained that low standards of scholarship prevalent in the men's colleges of Cambridge and Oxford reinforced the gentlemanly ideal that education served primarily as a mark of social status. Rewarding merit and competition in women's education, they hoped, would lead to improved education for men too. As in primary-school reform, better education for women served a variety of ends.

The expansion of preschool education offered an opportunity for large numbers of women to enter teaching, a field once dominated by men. Influenced by the German reformer Friedrich Froebel, hundreds of women founded nurseries, kindergartens, primary schools, and day-care centers. Education in many of these institutions was based on Enlightenment ideas, which held that instruction and supervision by mothers from an early age started developmental processes on the right footing. In Italy, women founded schools as a way to expand knowledge and teach civics lessons, thus providing a service to the fledgling state. Yet the idea of women theorizing about educational development and teaching citizenship also aroused intense opposition: "I shudder at philosophic women," wrote one critic of female kindergarten teachers. Seen as radical because it enticed middle-class women out of the home, the cause of early childhood education, or the "kindergarten movement," was as controversial as most other educational reforms.

Spreading Western Order beyond the West

In an age of nation building, colonies took on new importance, adding a political dimension, including direct rule from the homeland, to the economic role that global trade already played in national prosperity. Great-power jockeying and securing colonial trade provided motives for continued global expansion as the 1850s opened. Gaining strategic commercial and military advantages remained an important motivation for some European overseas ventures in this age of Realpolitik. The Crimean War had shown the great powers that the Mediterranean basin was pivotal in European trade. Napoleon III, remembering his uncle's campaign in Egypt, took an interest in building the Suez Canal, which would connect the Mediterranean with the Red Sea and the Indian Ocean and thus dramatically shorten the route to Asia. The canal was completed in 1869 and formally opened by Empress Eugénie with a gala celebration. Canal fever spread: Verdi composed the opera *Aïda* (set in ancient Egypt), but the Franco-Prussian War of 1870 delayed its premiere.

After midcentury, however, Great Britain, France, and Russia revised their colonial policies by instituting direct rule, expanding colonial bureaucracies, and in many cases providing a wider array of social and cultural services such as schools. In the 1850s and 1860s, provincial governors and local officials promoted the extension of Russian borders to gain control over many nomadic tribes in central and eastern Asia. As in areas like Poland and the Ukraine, they instituted educational and religious policies that they felt were central to social order. The state redefined its self-interest as it expanded the quest for order far beyond its borders.

Imperial expansion was a matter of push, pull, and paradox. The French government pushed to establish its dominion over Cochin China (modern southern Vietnam) in the 1860s. But missionaries in the area, ambitious French naval officers stationed in Asia, and even some local peoples pulled the French government to commit resources to successive attacks in the region. Likewise, driving into the North African hinterland, the French army occupied all of Algeria by 1870; Napoleon established a governmental agency for "Algeria and the colonies," and the number of immigrants reached one-quarter million by 1870. There was also a pull: French rule in Algeria, like European rule in many other parts of the non-European world, was aided by the attraction of European goods, technology, and institutions to the local peoples. Merchants and local leaders cooperated in building railroads,

sought bank loans and trade from the French, and sent their children to schools that provided a European education. Like the rural and working classes at home, many local peoples resisted the invasions, died from European-spread diseases, or did not benefit from this expansion. By 1872, the native population in Algeria had declined by more than 20 percent from five years earlier.

Great Britain, the era's mightiest colonial power, made a dramatic change of course toward direct political rule during these decades. Before the 1850s, British liberals desired the commercial opportunities offered by colonies, but, believing in laissez-faire, they also wanted to spend as few public resources as possible in governing them. Thus, political involvement in colonial affairs remained minimal, whereas trading treaties multiplied. In India, for example, the British government exercised control indirectly through the East India Company, and many regional rulers maintained their thrones by awarding the company commercial advantages. Since the eighteenth century, the East India Company had expanded its dominion over various kingdoms on the Indian subcontinent whenever a regional throne fell vacant and built railroads throughout the countryside. Contrary to strict laissez-faire beliefs, British institutions gradually arose in India, inspired in part by historian Thomas Macaulay, who two decades earlier in the House of Commons had called for an activist colonial policy to form "a class of persons, Indians in blood and colour, but English in taste, in opinion, in morals, and in intellect." An expanding British bureaucratic and economic presence allowed some Indian merchants to grow wealthy

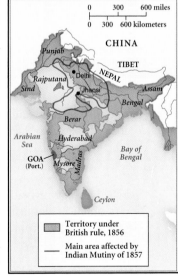

Indian Resistance, 1857

and send their children to British schools. Other local men enlisted in the British-run Indian army.

Resistance and resentment grew as British institutions became more widespread. In 1857, Indian troops, both Muslim and Hindu, violently

Photographs and Their Messages

After almost a century of experimentation, photography was invented in France and Britain in 1839, by a handful of different men, working independently. Photography immediately expanded people's access to visual information. Ordinary people were quick to have their photographs taken to send to distant relatives or to make visual records for themselves. Governments also understood photography to be an important resource. In the Crimean War, photographers began to substitute for official illustrators and mapmakers who customarily sketched out the vistas of towns and roads, including the placement of public buildings, natural lines of defense, and fortifications necessary for army maneuvers. Army illustrators flocked to this unrecorded region, but so did photographers. One was Carol Popp de Szathmari of Budapest, who took photos of both Russian and Turkish camps; he later sold a photo album of the war containing more than two hundred pictures. It was in this war that newspapers also began printing lithographs of wartime destruction to buildings. As in many wars, photographs of human carnage were not generally shown. An eager public bought both newspapers and albums and strengthened their allegiance to the nation-state and its wars.

Since the Crimean War, historians have recognized the importance of photography for the data it provides. Photographers recorded the vast interest in Asia and the Middle East as evidenced in the thousands of extant photographs of monuments of Egypt, Turkey, and Japan taken in the second half of the nineteenth century. *Social Life of the Chinese: A Daguerreotype of Daily Life in China* was a popular album of photos published in 1868. Historians have also believed that images of the great personages made the study of the past more vivid and more knowable. Using photos of furniture and fashions that salesmen carried from city to city in the 1850s and 1860s, historians have been able to visualize everyday life better. Individual portraits of ordinary people taken in intricately designed photography studios have similarly given a sense of what constituted people's physical reality or their fantasies of what it should be.

Recently, however, photography in this period has come to yield new interpretations, especially about people's values. The earliest photos started inching the West toward its modern celebrity cult. Photos of renowned professors were sold right outside their classroom doors, while great poets, kings and queens, businessmen, and public figures had their likenesses taken. The widespread distribution of these photos in magazines, in books, and on individual cards, called *cartes de visites*, made all of these personalities more popular. Political knowledge was spread on these little cards. The execution of Maximilian in 1867, for example, was memorialized in photos of

rebelled against regulations that violated their religious practices. Ignoring the Hindu ban on beef and the Muslim prohibition on pork, the British forced Indian soldiers to use cartridges greased with cow and pig fat. The infuriated soldiers stormed and conquered Delhi and declared the independence of the Indian nation—an uprising that became known as the Sepoy Mutiny. Simultaneously the Rani Lakshmibai, widow of the ruler of the state of Jhansi in central India, led a separate military revolt when the East India Company tried to take over her lands after her husband died. Brutally put down by the British as the record of pho-

tography would show, the Sepoy Mutiny and the Jhansi revolt gave birth to Indian nationalism. (See "New Sources, New Perspectives," above.) They also persuaded the British government to take direct control of India rather than work through the East India Company. "Despotism is a legitimate mode of government . . . with barbarians, provided the end be improvement," the liberal thinker John Stuart Mill proclaimed after the rebellions. The Government of India Act of 1858 redefined India as the concern of the British cabinet in London; the resulting colonial civil service reinforced the trend to direct governmental control of all colonies.

his dead body that were affixed to cards and sold to the public. The British royal family had *cartes de visites* made of the Prince of Wales and Princess Alexandra on their marriage to build allegiance to the monarchy.

Photography allowed people to manipulate reality. Historians have recently seen the genius of Queen Isabella II of Spain, whose chaotic administration was made to look orderly by her official photographer's expert shots of tidy parts of cities and public buildings. The queen had set this publicist to work as early as 1852 to change the image of her reign. Even battlefield shots, historians have recently admitted, were often staged after the fact. Whereas once historians might have looked at images of mid-nineteenth-century Balkan peasants for the information about costumes, now they see further: that these photos were taken to build allegiance to Balkan liberation from Ottomans and Habsburgs. The photograph—on the surface a portrayal of a single reality—may have still more to yield the imaginative viewer.

In China, Christian missionaries from European countries, carrying their message of Christian salvation, provided an opening for Western powers to enhance their position there. Directing the Christian message to a population that had almost doubled during the preceding century and now numbered about 430 million, missionaries spread Christianity among people already disturbed by demographic growth, defeat in the Opium War, and economic pressures from European trade. These contacts with the West had helped generate the mass movement known as the Taiping (Heavenly Kingdom). The leader, Hung Hsui-ch'uan (Hong Xinquan), who believed he was the younger brother of Jesus Christ, attracted millions of followers by preaching an end to the ruling Qing dynasty, the reform of morals, the elimination of foreigners, more equal treatment of women, and land reform. By the mid-1850s, the Taiping controlled half of China. The Qing regime, its dynasty threatened, promised the British and French greater economic and political influence in exchange for aid. The result was a bloody civil war that lasted until 1864 with some 30–60 million Chinese killed (compared with 600,000 dead in the U.S. Civil War, 1861–1865). When peace finally came, Western governments controlled much of the Chinese customs service and had virtually unlimited access to the country.

Japan alone was able to escape European domination. Through Dutch traders at Nagasaki, the Japanese had become keenly aware of the rising Western challenge to China but also of the important industrial, military, and commercial innovations of European society. Thus in 1854, when American commodore Matthew Perry declared that he had "opened" Japan to trade, contacts with Europe had already given the Japanese a healthy appetite for Western goods and knowledge. Curiosity, ambition, and fear that the United States would attack its cities with superior weapons motivated the trade agreements that followed Perry's arrival, but relations with the West became increasingly tense. In 1867, the ruling Tokugawa shogun (the dominant military leader) abdicated under pressure from reformers, who restored the emperor to full power. The goal of the Meiji Restoration was to establish Japan as a modern, technologically powerful state free from Western control. Even the word *Meiji*, chosen by the new emperor to name his reign, meant "enlightened rule," as the regime professed to combine "Western science and Eastern values" as a way of "making new"—hence, *restoration*. The Meiji Restoration ultimately inspired other countries to resist the intensifying pressure of Europeans.

❖ Artistic and Intellectual Visions of Social Order

Artists and writers helped build the age of realism and social order with their complex reactions to the rising nation-state and its expanding reach. After 1848, many artists and writers expressed profound grievances, notably about the brutal repression of revolutionary activists, and real concerns about the effect of enfranchising working-class men. Infused with commercial values and organized by officials, daily life seemed tawdry and hardly bearable to many artists. Unlike the romantics of the first half of the century, however, artists of the 1850s and 1860s often had difficulty depicting heroic alternatives or recapturing an ideal past. "How tired I am of the ignoble workman, the inept

bourgeois, the stupid peasant, and the odious priest," wrote the French novelist Gustave Flaubert, frustrated by his inability to romanticize these figures as previous generations had done. Such disenchantment promoted the literary and artistic style called *realism*. In contrast, intellectuals proposed theories called *positivism* and *Darwinism*, which appraised social change and even political upheaval as part of human progress. Realism, positivism, and Darwinism shared a claim to look at society with a detached eye and to depict social order starkly.

The Arts Confront Social Reality

The quest for national power enlisted culture in its cause. A hungry reading public devoured biographies of political leaders, past and present, and credited heroes with creating the triumphant nation-state. Energetic and commanding figures such as the Italian Garibaldi ultimately served as substitutes for both the divine-right king and the active democratic citizen. As literacy spread through schooling, all classes of readers responded to the mid-nineteenth-century novel and to an increasing number of artistic, scientific, and natural history exhibitions. Whether reading the same novels or attending musical events together, citizens came to be schooled in a common artistic style called *realism*.

The Realist Novel. A well-financed press and commercially minded publishers produced an age of best-sellers out of the craving for realism. The novels of Charles Dickens (1812–1870) appeared in serial form in magazines and periodicals, and each installment attracted eager buyers for the latest plot twist. His characters came from contemporary English society and included starving orphans, grasping lawyers, heartless bankers, and ruthless opportunists. *Hard Times* (1854) depicted the difficult life of sensitive members of the middle class as well as the grinding poverty and ill health of workers. *Bleak House* (1852) used dark humor to portray the judicial bureaucracy's intrusion into private life, while Dickens's other novels linked social ills to poorhouses and other bureaucratic institutions. Professing to depict ordinary reality, popular novels like Dickens's helped form a shared culture among people in distant parts of a nation much as state institutions did.

The novelist George Eliot (the pseudonym of Mary Ann Evans, 1819–1880) was also celebrated and widely read. Her novels examined contemporary moral values and deeply probed private dilemmas: works like *The Mill on the Floss* (1860) and *Middlemarch* (1871–1872) showed heroines vacillating between a world of imagination and the "real" world of family. Depicting rural society—high and low—Eliot allowed Britons to see one another's predicaments, wherever they lived. Eliot knew the pain of ordinary life from her own experience: she was a social outcast because she lived with a married man. Despite her fame, she was not received in polite society. Her depictions of social order emphasized the fragility and torment of institutions such as the family and marriage—conventionally upheld as the bulwark of stability.

French writers scorned dreams of political utopias and ideals of transcendent beauty, preferring instead to show the world as it was. In *Madame Bovary* (1857), Gustave Flaubert (1821–1880) told the story of a bored doctor's wife who, full of romantic longings and eager for distraction, has one love affair after another and becomes so hopelessly indebted that she commits suicide. Serialized in a Paris journal, *Madame Bovary* scandalized French society for its brutal depiction of marriage and frank picture of women's sexuality. The poet Charles-Pierre Baudelaire (1821–1867), called "Satanic" by his critics, wrote explicitly about sex, gaining shocked attention from the buying public on whom writers now depended. In *Les Fleurs du mal* ("Flowers of Evil," 1857), he expressed sexual passion, described drug- and wine-induced fantasies, and spun out visions condemned as perverse. Both Flaubert and Baudelaire attacked a range of social conventions, but the French authorities fought back, successfully prosecuting the two writers on obscenity charges. The issue was social and artistic order: "Art without rules is no longer art," the prosecutor maintained.

During the era of the Great Reforms, Russian writers debated whether western European values were insidiously transforming their culture. Rather than dividing the nation, this discussion about the nature of Russian culture united people around a national issue. From one viewpoint, Ivan Turgenev (1818–1883) created a powerful novel of Russian life, *Fathers and Sons* (1862), a story of nihilistic

An Age of Great Books

1851	Auguste Comte, *System of Positive Politics*
1852	Harriet Beecher Stowe, *Uncle Tom's Cabin*
1854	Charles Dickens, *Hard Times*
1857	Gustave Flaubert, *Madame Bovary*
	Charles Baudelaire, *Les Fleurs du mal*
1859	Charles Darwin, *On the Origin of Species*
	John Stuart Mill, *On Liberty*
1866	Fyodor Dostoevsky, *Crime and Punishment*
1867	Karl Marx, *Das Kapital*
1869	John Stuart Mill, *The Subjection of Women*
1871–1872	George Eliot, *Middlemarch*

children rejecting the older, romantic generation's spiritual values and espousing science instead. Popular in the West, Turgenev aroused anger in Russian readers for the way he criticized both romantics and the new generation of hardheaded "materialists." From another point of view, Fyodor Dostoevsky (1821–1881) satirized Turgenev's writing in *The Possessed* (1871–1872) and other works by showing the dark, ridiculous, and neurotic side of nihilists and thus holding up Turgenev as a soft-headed romantic. Dostoevsky was exiled to Siberia late in the 1840s for participating in a political study group; there his contact with many common criminals provided him with models for his brand of literary antihero featured in *Notes from the Underground* (1864) and *Crime and Punishment* (1866). His highly intelligent characters are often personally tormented and condemned to lead absurd lives. Dostoevsky used these antiheroes to emphasize spirituality and traditional Russian values, but with a "realistic" spin by planting such values in ordinary people, not elevated, noble, unrealistic types.

Painting and Sculpture. Unlike writers, visual artists across Europe depended on government commissions, and government-sponsored exhibitions drew a more limited set of buyers. Prince Albert of England was an active patron of the arts, purchasing works for official collections and for himself until his death in 1861. Having artwork

Gustave Courbet, *Wrestlers* (1850)
Courbet painted his dirty, grunting wrestlers in the realist style, which rejected the hazy romanticism of revolutionary Europe. These muscular men summed up the resort to physical struggle during the state-building decades as well as conveyed the art world's recognition that Realpolitik had taken over the governance of society.
Museum of Fine Arts, Budapest/The Bridgeman Art Library, NY.

displayed at government-sponsored exhibitions (called *salons* in Paris, the center of the art world) was the best way for an artist to gain prominence and earn a living. Officially appointed juries selected works of art to appear in the salon and then chose prize winners from among them. By the Second Empire, thousands of paintings were shown annually, with hundreds of thousands of people from all classes in attendance. Nearly a million people visited the art portion of the international exposition held in Paris in 1855.

After 1848, the repression of political opposition lessened the romantic glorification of workers, country folk, and nature. Instead of idealizing their subjects, artists took the lead of novelists in realistically depicting society. French painter Gustave Courbet (1819–1877) portrayed groaning laborers at backbreaking work because he believed an artist should "never permit sentiment to overthrow logic." Art could foster "democracy" by showing the world as it was and hiding neither the shabbiness nor the depravity of life.

These realist painters also rejected grand historic scenes and instead traced the course of social change, particularly the reconstruction of cities. Paris, artists found, had become a visual spectacle, a place of grand boulevards where urban residents performed as part of the cityscape. The artists' canvases showed the renovated city as a stage for individual ambition and display. *Universal Exhibition* (1867) by Édouard Manet (1823–1883) used the world's fair of 1867 as the background; figures from all social classes in the foreground were separated from one another by the planned urban spaces as they promenaded, gazing at the Paris scene and watching one another to learn the new social rules of modern life.

Manet's work removed the rose-colored glasses through which polite society seemed to view women and sexuality. His famous *Déjeuner sur l'herbe* ("Luncheon on the Grass," 1863) was deemed scandalous because it portrayed two women, one naked and the other half-dressed, on a picnic in a woods with fully clothed contemporary men. Manet's *Olympia* (1865) depicted a white courtesan lying on her bed, attended by a black woman. Both nudes shocked audiences because they showed women's bodies in realistic settings instead of mythologizing and romanticizing them. This disregard for the classical traditions of the fine arts was too much for the critics: "A sort of female gorilla," one wrote of *Olympia*. "Her greenish, bloodshot eyes appear to be provoking to the public," wrote another. Shocking at first, graphic portrayals that shattered comforting illusions became a feature of modern art.

Opera.   Unlike most of the visual arts, opera was commercially profitable, accessible to most classes of society, and thus effective artistically for reaching the nineteenth-century public. Verdi used musical theater to contrast noble ideals with the corrosive effects of power, love of country with the

Édouard Manet, *Déjeuner sur l'herbe* ("Luncheon on the Grass," 1863)
The leading painters of the Parisian art world rejected the highly idealized paintings of nudes and romanticized historical scenes. In Manet's portrayal of a picnic, the clothed men made the nude and seminude women, with their garments tossed about, seem out of place and even lewd. Such critical art annoyed many genteel citizens in the art-viewing public.
Giraudon/Art Resource, NY.

inevitable call for sacrifice and death, and the lure of passion with the need for social order. His *La Traviata* (1853) stunned audiences with the tragedy of a tubercular Parisian courtesan who falls in love with a respectable middle-class man. In a series of lyrical arias, the characters express the lure of a heartfelt passion at odds with the need for stable families.

The German Richard Wagner (1813–1883) was the most flamboyant and musically innovative composer of this era. Wagner hoped to revolutionize opera by fusing music and drama to arouse the audience's fear, awe, and engagement with his vision. His music was lush and harmonically daring, and it strove for overpowering emotional climaxes. Exiled from most German states because of his revolu-

tionary activities in 1848, Wagner spent much of the 1850s working on a gigantic cycle of four operas, *Der Ring des Nibelungen*, which reshaped ancient German myths into a modern, nightmarish allegory of a world doomed by its obsessive pursuit of money and power and redeemable only through unselfish love. Despairing of seeing *The Ring* actually staged, Wagner produced other operas, most notably the comedy *Die Meistersinger* (1862–1867), a nationalistic tribute to German art. Wagner's flair for publicity, musical innovation and dramatization, and nationalistic themes ultimately made him a major force in philosophy, politics, and the arts. He thus excelled in fulfilling the nationalizing and unifying potential of literature, art, music, and other cultural works.

No matter how controversial, opera, like the other arts, helped unite isolated individuals into a community or public with a shared, if debated, cultural experience. The arts provided visions of social structure, political values, and real life—visions that themselves were ordered by the realist style.

Religion and Secular Order

Organized religion formed one bulwark of traditional social and political order after the revolutions of 1848, but the expansion of state power set the stage for clashes over influence. Should religion have the same hold on government and public life as in the past, thus competing with the national loyalty? The views were mixed and would remain so. In the 1850s, many politicians supported religious institutions and attended public church rituals because they were another source of order. Simultaneously, some nation builders, intellectuals, and economic liberals came to reject the competing jurisdiction and religious worldview of established churches, particularly Roman Catholicism. Bismarck would later be one of these. "Do not interfere with what we teach and write," one intellectual proposed to the clergy in still another view of the relationship between religion and society, "and we will not question your control over the people." Protestant churches claimed limited authority over secular life, though they inspired social reform. The Roman Catholic church, however, insisted on its political influence and explicitly attacked nineteenth-century visions of progress and reform embodied in such institutions as secular public schools. Competition between church and state for power and influence heated up in this age of Realpolitik.

Catholic Reaction.   The Catholic church felt assaulted by a growing rationalism that replaced religious faith for many people and by the state building of Italy and Germany that competed for people's traditional loyalty. Conversely, rulers of these new countries found that the loyalty demanded by the church drained patriotism. In addition, nation building had resulted in the extension of liberal rights to Jews, whom Christians often considered enemies. Provocatively attacking reform and changing values, Pope Pius IX (r. 1846–1878) issued *The Syllabus of Errors* (1864), which put the

church and the pope at odds "with progress, with liberalism, and with modern civilization." In 1870, the First Vatican Council approved the dogma of papal infallibility. This teaching proclaimed that the pope, under certain circumstances, must be regarded by Catholics as speaking divinely revealed truth on issues of morality and faith. Liberal-minded Catholic intellectuals and clergy found themselves obliged either to submit to the new dogma or to be excommunicated.

Religious doctrine continued to have powerful popular appeal, but the place of organized religion in society at large was changing. On the one hand, church attendance declined among workers and artisans; on the other, many in the upper and middle classes and most of the peasantry remained faithful. The Orthodox church of Russia and eastern Europe with its Pan-Slavic appeal fostered nationalism among oppressed Serbs and became a rallying point. Other churches did the same for ethnic minorities in other, scattered rural areas. Women's spiritual beliefs became more intense, with both Roman Catholic and Russian Orthodox women's religious orders increasing in size and number; men, by contrast, were falling away from religious devotion. In 1854, the pope's announcement of the doctrine of the Immaculate Conception (stating that Mary, alone among all humans, had been born without original sin) was followed by an outburst of popular religious fervor, especially among women. In 1858, a peasant girl from Lourdes in southern France, Bernadette Soubirous, began having visions of the Virgin Mary. According to Bernadette, Mary, calling herself "the Immaculate Conception," told the young girl to drink from the ground, at which point a spring appeared. Crowds, mostly of women, besieged the area to be cured of ailments by the waters of Lourdes. In 1867, less than ten years later, a railroad track was laid to Lourdes to enable millions of pilgrims to visit the shrine on church-organized trips. The Catholic church thus showed that it was not passé but that it could use such modern means as railroads, medical verifications of miraculous cures, journalism, and political lobbying to make Lourdes itself the center of a brisk commercial as well as religious culture.

The Challenge of Natural Science.   Almost contemporaneously with Bernadette's vision, the English naturalist Charles Darwin (1809–1882) published

On the Origin of Species (1859), a challenge to the Judeo-Christian worldview that humanity was a unique creation of God. Darwin argued that life had taken shape over countless millions of years before humans existed and that human life was but the result of this slow development, or evolution.

Darwin Ridiculed, c. 1860
Charles Darwin's theories claimed that humans evolved from animal species and rejected the long-standing explanation of a divine human origin. His scientific ideas so diverged from people's beliefs that cartoonists lampooned both the respectable Darwin and his theory. Despite the controversy, evolution withstood the test of further scientific study.
Hulton Getty/Liaison.

Science thus called into question the divine character of both natural and human order, much as Enlightenment thinkers and French revolutionaries had done more than half a century earlier.

Evolutionary theory was in the air before Darwin's book appeared: Charles Lyell's *Principles of Geology* (1832–1834) had suggested that the earth's geological structure had developed over an immense span of time. As a young scientist on an expedition to South America, Darwin had read Lyell's work and had begun to consider various scientific puzzles in the environments he visited. Why, he pondered, did species of animals vary from one tropical island to another even though climate and other natural conditions were roughly the same? As early as the 1840s, Darwin was applying theories of evolution to biological life and suggesting that new biological forms arise from older ones as the most fit forms survive and reproduce.

Darwin's thought also reflected the gloomy predictions of the economist Thomas Malthus (1766–1834) that population growth would outstrip the food supply unless checked by famine or disease. Instead of the Enlightenment vision of nature and society as harmonious, Darwin saw the constant turmoil of all species, including humans, struggling to survive. In this fight, only the hardiest prevail and in the selection of sexual partners pass their natural strength to the next generation. That generation in turn might face harsh conditions. In this perpetual challenge to meet the forces of nature, Darwin suggested, some species die out whereas those with better-adapted characteristics survive in a new environment.

Darwin's theories angered adherents of traditional Christianity because the idea of evolution undercut the story of creation described in Genesis. Instead of God miraculously bringing the universe and all life into being in six days, Darwin held that life developed from lower forms through a primal battle for survival and through the sexual selection of mates—processes called *natural selection*. An eminently respectable Victorian gentleman, Darwin announced that the Bible gave a "manifestly false history of the world." Darwin's theories also undermined certain liberal, secular beliefs. Enlightenment principles, for example, had glorified nature as tranquil and noble and had viewed human nature as essentially rational. The theory of natural selection, in which the fittest survive, suggested a different kind of human society, one based in a hostile environment where combative individuals and groups constantly fight one another.

The mechanisms by which characteristics are passed from generation to generation eluded Darwin, but the Austrian monk and botanist Gregor Mendel (1822–1884) was laying the foundation for this understanding in Darwin's lifetime. Working in obscurity on pea plants in his monastery garden, Mendel discovered the principles of heredity in the 1860s from which the science of genetics developed. His discoveries received little attention at the time, but would prove momentous in the twentieth century.

Darwin's findings and other innovative biological research provoked further studies and influenced contemporary beliefs. Investigation into the female reproductive cycle led German scientists to discover the principle of spontaneous ovulation—the automatic release of the egg by the ovary whether sexual intercourse took place or not. This discovery caused theorists to conclude that men had aggressive and strong sexual drives because reproduction depended on their sexual arousal. In contrast, the spontaneous and cyclical release of the egg independent of arousal indicated that women were passive and lacked sexual feeling. Scientists now vied with the clergy in making weighty pronouncements on social roles.

Darwin, who shared the stereotypical social assumptions of his age, was among those who used his findings to explain the social order. The legal, political, and economic privilege of white European men in the nineteenth century, he maintained, naturally derived from their being more highly evolved than white women or people of color. Although Darwin pointed to a common ancestor for all races, he held that people of color, or "lower races," were far behind whites in intelligence and civilization. As for women, "the chief distinction in the intellectual powers of the two sexes," Darwin declared, "is shewn by man's attaining to a higher eminence in whatever he takes up." The body of his thought came to be known as *Darwinism*. As others applied Darwin's theories to explain social life, they emphasized white, middle-class, and male superiority. A school of Social Darwinism arose to lobby for public policy based on this vulgarized version of evolution and natural selection.

From Natural Science to Social Science

Darwin's thought accelerated the search for alternatives to the religious understanding of social order as being divinely ordained. Even before *Origin of Species* appeared, select members of the English middle class had formed the National Association for the Advancement of Social Science in 1857, and the French Society for Sociology was founded in 1872. The impulse for such new organizations came partly from the theories of the French social philosopher Auguste Comte (1798–1857), whose ideas formed the basis of a "positive science" of society and politics. *Positivism* claimed that careful study of facts would generate accurate, or "positive," laws of society. Comte's *System of Positive Politics, or Treatise on Sociology* (1851) proposed that social scientists construct knowledge of the political order as they would an understanding of the natural world, that is, according to informed investigation. This idea inspired people to believe they could solve the problems spawned by economic and social change. Comte also promoted women's participation in reform because he deemed "womanly" compassion and love as equally fundamental to social harmony as was scientific public policy. Positivism led not only to women's increased social and political activism but to the fields of anthropology, psychology, economics, and sociology, which developed during this period, largely under the banner of positivism.

For a time, the influential English philosopher John Stuart Mill (1806–1873) became an enthusiast of Comte, whose theories led Mill to espouse widespread reform and mass education and to support the complete enfranchisement of women. His political treatise *On Liberty* (1859) couched his aspiration for a general social improvement in a concern that superior people not be brought down or confined by the will of the masses. *On Liberty* also argued for individual liberties protected from state intrusion and for freedom of expression for those whose views ran counter to state interests. Mill's writings reflected anxiety for the status of the individual in a nation with a growing electorate of differing interests and a multiracial empire.

Stretching liberal principles to embrace an array of issues, Mill became notorious for advocating the extension of rights and freedom to women. On this subject Mill felt the profound influence of his wife, Harriet Taylor Mill (1808–1858), with whom he studied marriage, women's rights, and divorce. After his wife's death, Mill intensified his activities on behalf of women's rights, notably by introducing a woman suffrage bill into the House of Commons. The bill's defeat prompted Mill to publish *The Subjection of Women* (1869), a work recapitulating his studies with his wife. Translated into many languages and influential in eastern Europe, Scandinavia, and the western hemisphere, *The Subjection of Women* presented the family as maintaining an older kind of politics devoid of modern concepts of rights and freedom. Mill also proposed that the aura of women's voluntary obedience and love in marriage was necessary to mask gross marital inequality. According to Mill, to create "not a forced slave, but a willing one," society trained women "from the very earliest years in the belief that their ideal of a character is the very opposite to that of men; not self-will and government by self-control, but submission and yielding to the control of others." Critiquing the century's most basic beliefs about men's and women's roles, *The Subjection of Women* became a respected guide for a growing women's movement committed to expanding liberal rights.

The more progressive side of Mill's social thought was soon lost in the flood of Social Darwinist theories. Even before *Origin of Species*, Herbert Spencer's *Social Statics* (1851) advocated the study of society from many intellectual perspectives to arrive at a true picture of its workings. Spencer promoted laissez-faire and unadulterated competition, and his claim that the "unfit" should be allowed to perish in the name of progress was greatly reinforced by Darwin's work. Spencer's opposition to public education, social reform, and any other attempt to soften the harshness of the struggle for existence struck a receptive chord among the middle and upper classes and contributed to the surge of Social Darwinism in the next decades.

These various visions of social order would become dominant in future national debates over policy in the West. The influence of Darwinism and Mill's liberalism, like that of the arts, religion, and science, would be to shape the public, giving it common subjects for discussion and setting the terms of social and political thought. In an age of nation building, culture often enhanced the political call for realistic, hardheaded thinking about social order.

❖ Contesting the Political Order of the Nation-State

By the end of the 1860s, the unchecked growth of the state and the ongoing process of economic change had led to palpable tensions in European society. Protests abounded, but in France anger at defeat in the Franco-Prussian War and at economic hardship made these tensions erupt into a bitter if brief civil war. In the spring of 1871, the people of Paris—blaming the centralized state for the French surrender to the Germans—declared Paris a *commune*, a community of equals without bureaucrats and pompous politicians. The economist and philosopher Karl Marx heard of the bloody struggle between the people of Paris and the new republican government while living in England and produced his *Civil War in France* (1871). Translated along with his other writings, it provided workers with a popular and politically galvanizing account of events. From the 1870s on, these two phenomena— the writings of Karl Marx and the fury of working people—renewed fear among the middle classes that both nation-state and society might be violently destroyed.

Marxist Ideas and the Working-Class Movement

After a period of repression in the 1850s, workers' organizations slowly reemerged as a political force in the West. Like other interest groups, workers' organizations were part of a pattern of *horizontal allegiances*, in which people with similar backgrounds or with similar goals came together to shape the political process. Such allegiances replaced or coexisted with the *vertical allegiances* that reflected not similarity and equality but hierarchy and subordination. The family was one example of a vertical structure increasingly displaced as a source of social identity by peer groups in schools, factories, and clubs.

IMPORTANT DATES

1850s–1860s   Positivism and Darwinism become popular in social and political thought

1850s–1870s   Realism in the arts

1852   The Second Empire begins in France

1854–1856   Britain and France clash with Russia in the Crimean War

1857   Sepoy Mutiny in India

1861   Victor Emmanuel declared king of a unified Italy; abolition of serfdom in Russia

1861–1865   Civil War in the United States

1867   Second Reform Bill, increasing the ranks of male voters, passed by English Parliament; Austro-Hungarian monarchy established

1868   The Meiji Restoration begins in Japan

1869–1871   Women's colleges founded at Cambridge University

1870   Bismarck manipulates the Ems telegram and sparks the Franco-Prussian War

1871   Franco-Prussian War ends; German Empire proclaimed at Versailles; Parisians form Commune in March to oppose the central government; the French army crushes the Commune in May

In the 1850s, governments often outlawed unions, fearing they would challenge the established political order. Unions that existed were thus secret, poorly coordinated, and shaped by a wide range of programs for change, including the ideas of former printer Pierre-Joseph Proudhon (1809–1865). In the 1840s, Proudhon had coined the explosive phrase "Property is theft," suggesting that ownership robbed propertyless people of their rightful share of the earth's benefits. He opposed the centralized state and proposed that society be organized instead around natural groupings of men (but not women) in artisans' workshops. These workshops and a central bank crediting each worker for his labor would replace government and would lead to a *mutualist* social organization. Proudhon heartily opposed any mingling of men and women in political life; he believed the mutualist organization of men in public should be matched by the seclusion of their wives laboring at home for their husbands' comfort.

In 1864, a London meeting of German, Italian, British, and French workers formed the International Workingmen's Association. One leader, Russian nobleman Mikhail Bakhunin (1814–1876), argued that the existence of the state was the root of social injustice. According to Bakhunin, the slightest infringement on freedom, especially by the central state and its laws, was unacceptable. These ideas were the fundamental tenets of the political theory of *anarchism*, which advocated the destruction of all state power. Besides Bakhunin, another of the new organization's sponsors was Karl Marx (1818–1883), who constantly battled mutualism and anarchism. These doctrines, Marx insisted, were emotional and wrongheaded, lacking the sound, scientific basis of his own theory, subsequently called *Marxism*.

Marx's analysis, expounded most notably in *Das Kapital* ("Capital"), adopted the liberal idea, dating back to John Locke in the seventeenth century, that human existence was defined by the requirement to work as a way of fulfilling basic needs such as food, clothing, and shelter. Marx and Engels's *Communist Manifesto* of 1847 had many romantic ingredients, but *Capital*, published between 1867 and 1894, was based on mathematical calculations of production and profit that would justify a Realpolitik for the working classes. Marx held that the fundamental organization of any society, including its politics and culture, derived from the relationships arising from work or production. This idea, known as *materialism*, meant that the foundation of a society rested on class relationships—such as those between serf and medieval lord, slave and master, or worker and capitalist. Marx called the class relationships that developed around work the *mode of production*: for instance, feudalism, slavery, or capitalism. Rejecting the liberal focus on individual rights, he emphasized the unequal class relations caused by feudal lords, slaveholders, and the capitalists or bourgeoisie—that is, those who took control of the "means of production" in the form of the capital, land, tools, or factories necessary to fulfill basic human needs. When capitalist control disappeared, a classless society of workers—that is, a *socialist* one—would arise.

Economic liberals saw the free market ultimately producing balance and a harmony of interests, but Marx saw social organization and productive life not as harmonious but in conflict because of economic oppression. He believed that workers' awareness of their oppression would produce class consciousness among those in the same predicament and ultimately lead them to revolt against their exploiters. Such revolt, not reform or legislation, would be the mechanism for historical change. Capitalism would be overthrown by these workers—the *proletariat*—and the reign of socialism would ensue. Tough-minded theories that social conflict was necessary for progress were common to Marx and Darwin.

Marx was never precise about what socialism would entail, except that it would involve workers' control of production in large factories. A socialist utopia meant an end to private ownership of the means of production, which would in turn end class conflict and the need for a state to prop up the propertied classes. Like many male intellectuals at midcentury, Marx accorded little analytical importance to inequalities based on race and sex, concluding, for example, that the condition of women would automatically improve in a socialist utopia. The possibility of this socialist utopia continued to inspire many working-class men to organize, and some governments came to recognize an advantage in unions: they could render worker protests more predictable and more controllable.

The conditions of working-class life remained harsh, and a wave of strikes erupted in the late 1860s. In France alone, 40,000 workers participated in strikes in 1869, followed by more than 85,000 in 1870. The strikers included artisans and industrial workers who felt overworked and underpaid because of the continuing pace and expense of technological innovation. More often than not, the strikes focused on economic issues. But at times, such as in the Paris Commune, protest questioned the entire political system.

The Paris Commune versus the French State

The bloody and bitter struggle over the Paris Commune developed from mutualist and socialist political ideas that churned to the surface in Paris as the Franco-Prussian War ended. The weaknesses of the French state first became apparent in the late 1860s when Napoleon III was forced to grant liberal re-

forms such as freedom of the press and a more independent legislature. But the Haussmannization of Paris, which had displaced workers from their homes in the heart of the city, embittered many Parisians against the state. As the Prussians pressed on to Paris in 1870, the besieged Parisians demanded new republican liberties and a more balanced distribution of power between the central government and localities.

By the winter of 1870–1871, the Parisian population was suffering from the harsh weather and a Prussian siege that deprived them of sufficient food to feed more than 2 million people. As rumors of coups filled the air, Parisians demanded to elect their own local government to handle the emergency (Map 23.5). Given the threat to the nation, the temporary head of state, Adolphe Thiers, called the Parisians a "vile multitude" and sent the army into Paris in mid-March. For Parisians, this

MAP 23.5 The Paris Commune, 1871
The war between the French government and the Paris Commune took place on the streets of Paris and resulted in widespread destruction of major buildings, most notably the Tuileries Palace adjacent to the Louvre. Many government records were destroyed in what some saw as a civil war; bitterness, like destruction of property, was great on both sides. The government defeat of the Communards brought the execution of thousands of people.

Woman Incendiary

The Paris Commune galvanized women activists, many of whom hoped to reform social conditions. For the short time of the Commune's existence they implemented cooperative programs for work and engaged in public political debate — something women were forbidden by law to do. However, in the aftermath of the Commune, their public image was changed from seriousness of purpose to one of half-clothed degeneracy as a way of illustrating the disorderliness of the Commune's resistance to the state.
Jean Loup Charmet.

decision revealed the utter despotism of the centralized government, and they declared themselves a self-governing commune on March 28, 1871. Other French municipalities would do the same, in an attempt to form a decentralized state of independent, confederated units.

In the Paris Commune's two months of existence, its forty-member council, its National Guard, and its many other improvised offices found themselves at cross-purposes. Trying to

maintain "communal" instead of "national" values, Parisians quickly developed a wide array of political clubs, local ceremonies, and self-managed, cooperative workshops. Women workers, for example, banded together to make National Guard uniforms on a cooperative rather than a profitmaking basis. Beyond liberal political equality, the Commune proposed to liberate the worker and ensure "the absolute equality of women laborers." Thus a *commune* in contrast to a *republic* was meant to entail a social revolution. But Communards often disagreed on what specific route to take to change society: mutualism, anticlericalism, feminism, international socialism, and anarchism were but a few of the proposed avenues to social justice.

In the meantime, the provisional government at Versailles struck back to reinstitute national order. It quickly stamped out similar uprisings in other French cities. On May 21, the army entered Paris. In a week of fighting, both Communards and the army set the city ablaze (the Communards did so to slow the progress of government troops). Both sides executed hostages, and in the wake of victory the army shot tens of thousands of citizens found on the streets. Just to be in the city meant treason: Parisian insurgents, one citizen commented, "deserved no better judge than a soldier's bullet." The Communards had fatally promoted a kind of antistate in an age of growing national power, and the French establishment saw all Parisians as traitors.

This reaction soon succumbed to a different interpretation of the Commune as the work of the *pétroleuse*, or "woman incendiary." Adolphe Thiers roused the French to battle by describing the Commune as basically a case of women run mad, crowding the streets in frenzy and fury. Other writers portrayed women of the Commune as sexually depraved: "They tossed much more than their caps over windmills. . . . Soon all the rest of their clothing followed." Within a year, writers were blaming the burning of Paris on women—"shameless slatterns, half-naked women, who kindled courage and breathed life into arson." Revolutionary men often became heroes in the history books, but women in political situations were characterized as "sinister females, sweating, their clothing undone, their bosoms almost bare, [who] passed from man to man."

Defeat in the Franco-Prussian War, the Commune, and the civil war were all horrendous blows

MAPPING THE WEST Europe and the Mediterranean, 1871

European nation-states consolidated their power by building unified state structures and by developing the means for the diverse peoples within their borders to became socially and culturally integrated. They were also rapidly expanding outside their boundaries, extending the economic and political reach of the nation-state. North Africa and the Middle East—parts of the declining Ottoman Empire—had particular appeal because of their resources and their potential for further European settlement. They offered a gateway to the rest of the world.

from which the French state struggled to recover. Key to restoring order in France after 1870 were instilling family virtues, fortifying religion, and claiming that the Commune had resulted from the collapsed boundaries between the male political sphere and the female domestic sphere. Karl Marx disagreed: he analyzed the Commune as a class struggle of workers attacking bourgeois interests, which were embodied in the centralized state. Executions and deportations by the thousands virtually shut down the French labor movement and kept resentment smoldering. The French would spend the next decades struggling to rebuild political and social unity.

Conclusion

Throughout modern history the development of nation-states has been neither inevitable nor uniform nor peaceful. This was especially true in the nineteenth century, when ambitious politicians, resilient monarchs, and determined bureaucrats transformed very different countries into various kinds of states by a variety of methods and policies. Nation building was most dramatic in Germany and Italy, where states unified through military force and where people of many political tendencies ultimately agreed that national unity surpassed most other causes. Compelled by military defeat to shake off centuries of tradition, the Austrian and Russian monarchs instituted reforms as a way of keeping their systems viable. In eastern Europe, the middle class was far less powerful than in western Europe, and reform came from above to preserve autocratic power rather than from popular agitation to democratize it.

After decades of romantic fervor idealizing society, politics, and culture, hardheaded realism became a much-touted norm, often with unexpected consequences. Darwin and Marx breathed the air of realism and their theories were disturbing to those who maintained an Enlightenment faith in social and political harmony. Realist novels and art jarred polite society, and, like the operas of Verdi, they also portrayed dilemmas of the times. The internal policies of the growing state apparatus that were meant to bring order often brought disorder. When the ordinary people of the Paris Commune rose up to protest the loss of French power and prestige but also to defy the trend toward state building, their actions raised difficult questions. How far should the power of the state extend in both domestic and international affairs? Would nationalism be a force for war or for peace? As these issues ripened, the next decades saw extraordinary economic advance and an unprecedented surge in European global power.

Suggested References

The End of the Concert of Europe

The inglorious Crimean War has often been left behind in historiography despite its impact on European politics. Much of the best new literature focuses not only on politi-cal changes but on the war's social impact in Russia. Engel and the Kingston-Mann and Mixter anthology give searching looks at Russian peasant life in this age of transition.

Edgerton, Robert B. *Death or Glory: The Legacy of the Crimean War.* 1999.

Engel, Barbara Alpern. *Between the Fields and the City: Women, Work, and Family in Russia, 1861–1914.* 1994.

Hazareesingh, Sudhir. *From Subject to Citizen: The Second Empire and the Emergence of Modern French Democracy.* 1998.

Kingston-Mann, Esther, and Timothy Mixter, eds. *Peasant Economy, Culture, and Politics of European Russia, 1800–1921.* 1991.

*Seacole, Mary. *Wonderful Adventures of Mrs. Seacole in Many Lands.* 1857.

Wortman, Richard S. *Scenarios of Power: Myth and Ceremony in Russian Monarchy.* 1995.

War and Nation Building

Nation building has produced a varied literature ranging from biographies to studies of ceremonials and the presentation of royalty as celebrities and unifying figures. Two Web sites show the complexities of this process. Brown University's Victorian Web demonstrates the connections among royalty, politicians, religion, and culture. Bucknell University's Russian Studies site opens to the strains of the Russian national anthem, composed in the reign of Nicholas I to foster reverence for the dynasty and homeland.

Blackbourn, David. *Fontana History of Germany, 1780–1918: The Long Nineteenth Century.* 1997.

Breuilly, John. *The Formation of the First German Nation-State, 1800–1871.* 1996.

DiScala, Spencer. *Italy: From Revolution to Republic, 1700 to the Present.* 1995.

Homans, Margaret. *Royal Representations: Queen Victoria and British Culture, 1837–1876.* 1998.

Russian Studies: http://www.departments.bucknell.edu/Russian/.

Smith, Paul. *Disraeli: A Brief Life.* 1996.

The Victorian Web: http://landow.stg.brown.edu/victorian/victov.html.

Instituting Social Order

Nation building entailed state-sponsored activities stretching from promoting education to rebuilding cities. New histories show the process of creating a sense of nationality through government management of people's environment, so that citizenship became part of seemingly nonpolitical life.

*Primary sources.

Eley, Geoff, and Ronald Grigor Suny. *Becoming National: A Reader.* 1996.

Hamm, Michael F. *Kiev: A Portrait, 1800–1917.* 1993.

Johanson, Christine. *Women's Struggle for Higher Education in Russia, 1855–1900.* 1987.

Jordan, David. *Transforming Paris: The Life and Labor of Baron Haussmann.* 1995.

Lebra-Chapman, Joyce. *The Rani of Jhansi: A Study in Female Heroism in India.* 1986.

Rotenberg, Robert. *Landscape and Power in Vienna.* 1995.

Slezkine, Yuri. *Arctic Mirrors: Russia and the Small Peoples of the North.* 1994.

Wohl, Anthony. *Endangered Lives: Public Health in Victorian Britain.* 1983.

Artistic and Intellectual Visions of Social Order

Like the biographies of politicians, the lives of artists and intellectuals have proven crucial to understanding this period of realism and Realpolitik. They show artists, intellectuals, and scientists addressing the central issues of their day amidst dramatic social change.

Bordenheimer, Rosemarie. *The Real Life of Mary Ann Evans: George Eliot, Her Letters and Fiction.* 1994.

*Darwin, Charles. *Autobiography.* 1969.

Gieson, Gerald L. *The Private Science of Louis Pasteur.* 1996.

Kaufman, Suzanne. "Lourdes, Popular Religion, and Tourism." In Shelley Baranowski and Ellen Furlough, eds. *Being Elsewhere: Tourism, Consumer Culture, and Identity in Modern Europe and North America.* 2000.

Mayr, Ernst. *One Long Argument: Charles Darwin and the Genesis of Modern Evolutionary Thought.* 1991.

*Turgenev, Ivan. *A Hunter's Sketches.* 1852.

Contesting the Political Order of the Nation-State

The teachings of Karl Marx and the story of the Paris Commune haunted Europeans at the time, and have since fascinated historians. The following works capture the fear of the working classes that shaped middle-class thought in the nineteenth century, and they show the energy that working- and middle-class people alike put into politics and into developing political theories, especially in this period of political transformation.

Gullickson, Gay. *Unruly Women of Paris: Images of the Commune.* 1996.

McClellan, David. *Karl Marx: His Life and Thought.* 1978.

Nord, Philip. *The Republican Moment: Struggles for Democracy in Nineteenth-Century France.* 1995.

CHAPTER

24

Industry, Empire, and Everyday Life

1870–1890

ETWEEN 1870 AND 1890, MARIANNE NORTH, an unmarried English woman, traveled the globe several times. The end of the nineteenth century was a time of vast migration, some of it in search of a better life, some of it for imperial conquest, and some of it, as in the case of Marianne North, in pursuit of knowledge. North was a botanical illustrator and "plant hunter," one of those avid Europeans who on their own or under government sponsorship searched the world over for plants to classify, grow, and put to commercial use. North ventured to North and South America, India, Java, Borneo, South Africa, and many other distant points setting up her easel and making scientific drawings of plants. She discovered at least five new species (officially named after her) and a new type of tree as well as collecting thousands of plants to send back to botanical gardens in England. When she became too frail to travel, she organized a permanent museum in London to display her botanical drawings to the public. Her goal was promoting ordinary people's knowledge of the British Empire: "I want them to know," she announced, "that cocoa doesn't come from the coconut."

Historians have aptly labeled the decades from 1870 to 1890 an era of industry and empire in the West. Empires were spreading rapidly, and this expansion was knit into the fabric of industrial growth and the everyday life of all social classes. Industrial output soared in the West, as industrialization spread from Britain to central and eastern Europe and new products kept appearing on the market. A growing appetite

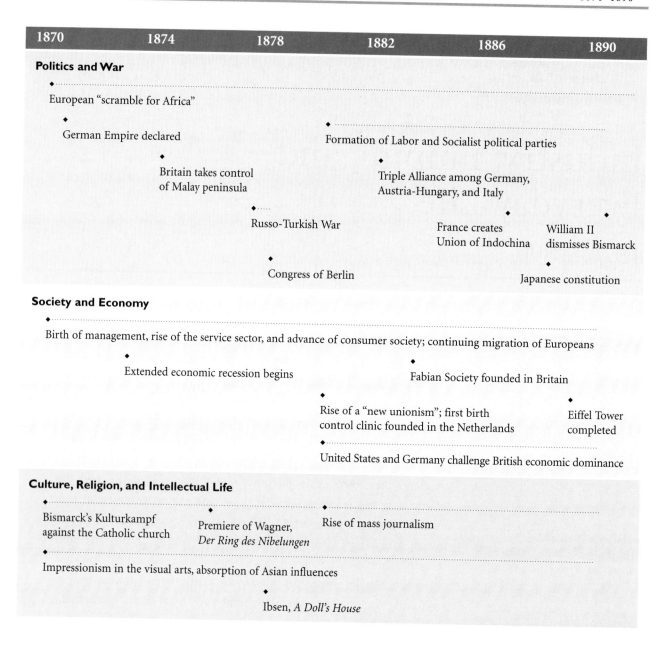

| 1870 | 1874 | 1878 | 1882 | 1886 | 1890 |

Politics and War

European "scramble for Africa"

German Empire declared

Britain takes control
of Malay peninsula

Formation of Labor and Socialist political parties

Triple Alliance among Germany,
Austria-Hungary, and Italy

Russo-Turkish War

France creates
Union of Indochina

William II
dismisses Bismarck

Congress of Berlin

Japanese constitution

Society and Economy

Birth of management, rise of the service sector, and advance of consumer society; continuing migration of Europeans

Extended economic recession begins

Fabian Society founded in Britain

Rise of a "new unionism"; first birth
control clinic founded in the Netherlands

Eiffel Tower
completed

United States and Germany challenge British economic dominance

Culture, Religion, and Intellectual Life

Bismarck's Kulturkampf
against the Catholic church

Premiere of Wagner,
Der Ring des Nibelungen

Rise of mass journalism

Impressionism in the visual arts, absorption of Asian influences

Ibsen, *A Doll's House*

for these goods, many of them for household consumption, was partly responsible for an intensified search for raw materials around the globe. Informal educators like Marianne North made people more knowledgeable about the connections among industry, empire, and their own lives.

Those connections were tight, as many Europeans benefited from the enforced labor of millions of Asians and Africans under the "new imperialism"—one name for the accelerated race for empire. Beginning in these decades, the "new im-

perialism" was merely the final gulp of global territory that Europeans had been acquiring since the late fifteenth century. They explored and took political control of the interior of Africa and worked to dominate even more of Asia until by the beginning of the twentieth century they controlled more than 80 percent of the world's surface. Control was not narrowly political: Europeans tried to stamp other continents with European-style borders, place-names, architecture, clothing, languages, domestic customs, and other cultural features.

As Europeans forced open the globe, millions seized the opportunity to move vast distances, still another change in everyday life. Some movement was temporary migration to the colonies to serve in the colonial civil service, for instance, and some was permanent—to North and South America or Australia in search of work or personal safety. Some was simply to other cities or regions in Europe. The costs of this unprecedented imperial migration were also part of everyday life: among them social dislocation for tens of millions of people and violence against indigenous peoples in European colonies.

The intertwined progress of industry and empire affected politics in paradoxical ways. As urban people became more educated and more united by common experiences of neighborhood and work life, they came to share political interests and make greater demands for participation. Politics became part of their everyday lives because governments, growing bigger as their territories, economies, and population expanded, intervened more in daily affairs. At the same time, political participation of ordinary citizens increased, with suffrage opening up to more men from all social classes. Bureaucrats organized both ordinary citizens and the colonized with programs intended to unify: social reform, education, and public ceremonials. Citizens were also unified by pride in their nations' conquests and their common access to a mushrooming array of colonial goods. Europe officially brimmed with confidence and hope, while the paradoxes of industrial and imperial progress played themselves out in distant colonies, urban slums, and declining standards of living in rural areas.

❖ The Advance of Industry

The end of the Franco-Prussian War and the Paris Commune in 1871 saw an initial burst of prosperity. Paris, Berlin, Vienna, and Rome experienced a frenzy of building, and many workers' wages increased. Industry turned out a cornucopia of products that improved people's material well-being. Beginning in 1873, however, a series of downturns in business threatened both entrepreneurs and the working class. Business people sought remedies in further innovation, in new managerial techniques, and in revolutionizing marketing, most visibly in the development of the department store. Governments played their part by changing business law and supporting the drive for global profits. The steady advance of industry and the rise of a consumer economy further transformed the work lives of millions of people.

Industrial Innovation

Industrial, technological, and commercial innovation together characterized nineteenth-century Europe. New products ranging from the bicycle, typewriter, and telephone to the internal combustion

Marianne North, Pitcher Plant
Migration by wealthy Europeans increasingly occurred in the quest for knowledge and adventure, and as the West prospered travel and world tourism did too. As a woman amateur, Marianne North initially gained an official audience for her scientific drawings, reports, and specimens only because she traveled in the "best circles." Once seen, however, her canvases, like this one of a pitcher plant, were prized by scientists and curators alike.
Trustees of the Royal Botanic Gardens, Kew.

engine provided dizzying proof of industrial progress. Many independent tinkerers or inventor-manufacturers created new products, but sophisticated engineers also invented revolutionary technologies. For example, in 1885 the German engineer Karl Benz devised a workable gasoline engine; six years later France's Armand Peugeot constructed a car and tested it by chasing a bicycle race. Electricity became more widely used after 1880, providing power to light everything from private drawing rooms to government office buildings. The Eiffel Tower in Paris, constructed for the International Exhibit of 1889, stood as a monument to the age's engineering wizardry; visitors rode to its summit in electric elevators.

To fuel this explosive industrial growth, the leading industrial nations mined and produced massive quantities of coal, iron, and steel during the 1870s and 1880s; production of iron increased from 11 million to 23 million tons. (Even in relatively underdeveloped Spain, iron-ore mining unearthed a total of 6 million tons in 1890, up from 130,000 tons in 1861—an almost 5,000 percent increase.) Steel output grew just as impressively in the industrial nations, increasing from 500,000 to 11 million tons in the 1870s and 1880s. Manufacturers used the metal to build the more than 100,000 locomotives that pulled trains during these years—trains that transported 2 billion people annually.

Historians used to contrast a "second" Industrial Revolution, with its concentration on heavy industrial products, to the "first" revolution of the eighteenth and early nineteenth centuries, in which innovations in textile making and the use of steam energy predominated. But many historians now believe this distinction applies mainly to Britain: in countries where industrialization came later, the two stages occurred simultaneously. Numerous textile mills were installed on the continent later than in Britain, for instance, at the same time as blast furnaces were constructed. Although industrialization led to the decline of cottage production in traditional crafts like weaving, home industry—or *outwork*—persisted in garment making, metalwork, and such "finishing trades" as porcelain painting and button polishing. The coexistence of home and factory enterprise continued through all the changes in manufacturing, to the present day.

Industrial innovations also transformed agriculture. Chemical fertilizers boosted crop yields,

Universal Exposition of 1889
French politicians launched the Universal Exposition, or World's Fair, of 1889 in Paris to celebrate what they called the "progress resulting from one hundred years of freedom." The exposition featured the latest industrial inventions as well as musical and artistic displays from the cultures France had conquered. The greatest attraction, however, was the Eiffel Tower, constructed in two years to much criticism. Tens of thousands flocked to ascend this masterpiece of engineering technology—the same technology Gustave Eiffel had used to provide the iron skeleton supporting the Statue of Liberty. Jean-Loup Charmet.

and reapers and threshers mechanized harvesting. In the 1870s, Sweden produced a cream separator, a first step toward mechanizing dairy farming. Wire fencing and barbed wire replaced wooden fencing and stone walls, both of which were labor-intensive to create. Refrigeration, developed during this period, allowed fruits, vegetables, and meat to be transported without spoiling, thus diversifying and increasing the urban food supply. Tin from colonial trade facilitated large-scale commercial canning, which made many foods available year-round to people in the cities.

Challenge to British Dominance.   During these decades, Britain's rate of industrial growth slowed, as its entrepreneurs remained wedded to older, successful technologies. Although Great Britain maintained its high output of industrial goods and profited from a multitude of worldwide investments, two countries began surpassing it in research, technical education, innovation, and rate of growth: Germany and the United States.

In the aftermath of the Franco-Prussian War, Germany received the territories of Alsace and Lorraine, which had textile industries as well as rich iron deposits. Investing heavily in research, German businesses rapidly devised new industrial processes and began to mass-produce goods that other countries had originally manufactured. Germany also spent as much money on education as on its military in the 1870s and 1880s. This investment resulted in highly skilled engineers and technical workers whose productivity enabled Germany's electrical and chemical engineering capabilities to soar.

The United States began an intensive exploitation of its vast natural resources, including coal, ores, gold, and oil. The value of U.S. industrial goods spurted from $5 billion in 1880 to $13 billion two decades later. Whereas German accomplishments rested more on state promotion of industrial efforts, U.S. growth often involved innovative entrepreneurs, such as Andrew Carnegie in iron and steel and John D. Rockefeller in oil. The three-way industrial rivalry created by Germany and the United States challenging Britain's dominance would soon have political and diplomatic repercussions.

Areas of Slower Industrialization.   With the exception of Belgium, the first continental country to industrialize, other countries trailed the three leaders in the pervasiveness of industry. French industry grew steadily, but French businesses remained smaller than those in Germany and the United States: although France had some huge mining, textile, and metallurgical establishments, many businessmen retired early to imitate the still-enviable aristocratic way of life. Industrial development in Spain, Austria-Hungary, and Italy was primarily a local phenomenon. Austria-Hungary had densely industrialized areas around Vienna and in Styria and Bohemia, but the rest of the country remained tied to traditional, unmechanized agriculture. Italy's economy continued to industrialize in the north while remaining rural and agricultural in the south. The Italian government spent more on building Rome into a grand capital than it invested in economic growth. A mere 1.4 percent of Italy's 1872 budget went to education and science, compared with 10.8 percent in Germany. The commercial use of electricity helped Scandinavians, who were poor in coal and ore, to industrialize in the last third of the nineteenth century. Sweden and Norway became leaders in the use of hydroelectric power and the development of electrical products; Denmark developed a major commercial sector in animal and dairy products. Despite these innovations, however, Scandinavia retained its mostly rural character, at a time when traditional farm life was becoming increasingly difficult.

Russia's road to industrialization was torturous, slowed partly by its relatively small urban labor force. Many Russian peasants who may have

Trans-Siberian Railroad
Begun in 1892, the Trans-Siberian railroad, the major east–west transportation line across the Russian Empire, took several decades to complete. From farms in western Siberia the line brought goods to markets in major cities, and in the more sparsely populated east the railroad mostly served to transport troops to secure imperial conquests and guard frontiers. The railroad also became a feature of around-the-world tourism; voyagers traveled in luxurious, if very slow, trans-Siberian railway coaches.
Sovfoto. ·

wished to take advantage of the opportunities of industrialization were tied to the *mir*, or landed community, by the terms of the serf emancipation. Some villages sent men and women to cities, but on the condition that they return for plowing and harvesting. Nevertheless, by the 1890s, Moscow, St. Petersburg, and a few other cities had substantial working-class populations. Minister of Finance Sergei Witte attracted foreign capital, entrepreneurs, and engineers and used them to construct railroads, including the Trans-Siberian Railroad (1891–1916), which upon completion stretched 5,787 miles from Moscow to Vladivostok. The burgeoning of the railroads combined with growth in metallurgical and mining operations lifted Russia as an industrial and military power. As in most of eastern Europe, the peasants bore the main burden of financing Russia's industrial growth, especially in the form of higher taxes on vodka. Thus neither they nor the underpaid Russian workers could afford to buy the goods their country produced. Russia was a prime example of the complexities of industrialization and its uneven benefits.

Facing Economic Crisis

Although innovations and business expansion often conveyed a sense of optimism, economic conditions were far from rosy throughout the 1870s and 1880s. Within two years of the end of the Franco-Prussian War, prosperity abruptly gave way to a severe economic depression in many industrial countries. The crisis of 1873 was followed by almost three decades of economic fluctuations, most alarmingly a series of sharp downturns whose severity varied from country to country. People of all classes lost their jobs or businesses and faced consequences ranging from long stretches of unemployment to bankruptcy. Economists of the day were stunned by the relentlessness and pervasiveness of the slump. Because economic ties bound industrialized western Europe to international markets, recession affected the economies of such diverse regions as Australia, South Africa, California, Newfoundland, and the West Indies.

These dramatic fluctuations differed from the economic cycles that were the rule before 1850, in which failure on the land led to higher food prices and then to failure in manufacturing. Although suffering problems of its own, agriculture was no

longer so dominant that its fate determined the welfare of other sectors of the economy. By the 1870s, industrial and financial setbacks were sending businesses into long-term tailspins. In France, for example, the textile industry slumped early in the 1870s and revived only in the late 1880s; facing growing competition from Asian imports, the vital Italian silk industry did not recover until the 1890s. Innovation created new or modernized industries on an unprecedented scale, but economic disaster constantly loomed. Politicians, economists, and bureaucrats struggled in vain to understand this paradox and control its impact.

As industrialization advanced, entrepreneurs encountered fundamental problems. First, the start-up costs of new enterprises skyrocketed. Textile mills had required relatively modest amounts of capital in comparison to factories producing steel and iron. Industrialization had become what modern economists call *capital-intensive* rather than *labor-intensive*: its growth required the purchase of expensive machinery, not merely the hiring of more workers. Second, the distribution and consumption of goods were inadequate to sustain industrial growth. Increased productivity in both agriculture and industry led to rapidly declining prices. Wheat, for example, dropped to one-third its 1870 price by the 1890s. Consumers, however, did not always benefit from this deflation as wages were slashed and unemployment rose during the economic downturns; nor could they always afford the new goods. Industrialists had made their fortunes by emphasizing production, not consumption. The series of slumps refocused entrepreneurial policy on finding ways to enhance sales and distribution and to control markets and prices.

In response to nervous business owners and to those fearful of potential social unrest, governments took steps to foster economic prosperity. New laws spurred the development of the limited-liability corporation, which protected investors from personal responsibility for the firm's debt. Before limited liability, businesses drew the necessary capital primarily from their own family assets, and financial backers were individually responsible for the firm's financial difficulties. In one case in England, a former partner who had failed to have his name removed from a legal document after leaving the business remained responsible to creditors when the company went bankrupt. He lost everything he owned except a watch and the equivalent of $100. The end of personal liability greatly increased investor confidence about financing business ventures.

Public financing in stocks and bonds promised wider opportunity to gain high profits. Stock markets had existed prior to the changes in liability laws, but they had dealt mainly in government bonds and in government-sponsored enterprises such as railroads. By the end of the century, stock markets traded heavily in industrial corporate stock owned by many individuals, and investors thus raised money from a larger pool of private capital than before. At the center of an international economy linked by telegraph, telephone, railways, and steamships, the London Stock Exchange in 1882 traded industrial shares worth £54 million, a value that surged to £443 million by 1900. Banks competed with the stock exchange in financing industry.

Less personal financial liability and new sources of capital did not eliminate business difficulties, however. In another adaptive move, firms in the same industry banded together in cartels and trusts to control prices and competition. Cartels flourished particularly in German chemical, iron, coal, and electric industries. For example, the Rhenish-Westphalian Coal Syndicate, founded in 1893, eventually dominated more than 95 percent of coal production in Germany. Although business owners might continue to advocate free trade, cartels broke with free-trade practices by restricting output and setting prices. Smaller businesses trying to compete and consumers had no effective means of resisting these new business techniques.

Trusts appeared first in the United States. In 1882, John D. Rockefeller created the Standard Oil Trust by acquiring stock from many different oil companies and placing it under the direction of trustees. The trustees then controlled so much of the companies' stock that they could set prices for the entire industry. They could even dictate to the railroads the rates for transporting the oil. Trusts and cartels also oversaw the *vertical integration* of industries, in which, for example, a steel company acquired mining operations in ore and coal as well as railroads to distribute its output. Such acquisitions ensured access to raw materials, lower production costs, and greater control of product distribution.

Like the practices of cartels and trusts, government imposition of tariffs expressed declining faith in classical liberal economics. Much of Europe had adopted free trade after midcentury, but during the recessions of the 1870s huge trade deficits—caused when imports exceed exports—had soured many Europeans on the concept. A country with a trade deficit had less capital available to invest internally; fewer jobs were created, and the chances of social unrest increased. Farmers in many European countries were hurt when improvements in transportation made it possible to import perishable food, such as grain from the United States and Ukraine. France and Germany were particularly vulnerable to trade deficits in the last three decades of the century. In response, governments in both countries approved tariffs throughout these decades. Farmers, capitalists, and even many workers supported these taxes on imports to prevent competition from foreign goods. Governments in the West responded to calls for economic nationalism, and by the early 1890s all but Belgium, Britain, and the Netherlands had ended free trade.

Revolution in Business Practices

Industrialists tried to minimize the damage of economic downturns by revolutionizing the everyday conduct of their businesses. A generation earlier, a factory owner was directly involved in every aspect of his business and often learned to run the firm through trial and error. In the late 1800s, industrialists began to hire managers to run their increasingly complex day-to-day operations. Managers who specialized in sales and distribution, finance, and purchase of raw materials made decisions and oversaw the implementation of their policies. Lower-level managers supervised workers to ensure productivity. One German steel magnate told his managers to hire "supervisors and supervisors of supervisors to watch what our men are doing." The managerial class formed a useful buffer between owners and workers.

The White-Collar Sector. The rise of the manager was accompanied by the emergence of a "white-collar" service sector of office workers. Businesses employed secretaries, file clerks, and typists to guide the flow of business information. Banks that accepted savings from the general

Remington Typewriter Company Office
The typewriter symbolized the beginnings of the service revolution, which would take almost a century to unfold, as a sector of work developed that was performed neither by owners nor by factory workers. Like these typists, service workers processed information, dealt with managerial knowledge, or performed various service tasks such as health care. Typing was seen as the perfect work for genteel ladies, both because it was comparatively clean and because women's nimble fingers were seen as best suited for the skill.
The Granger Collection.

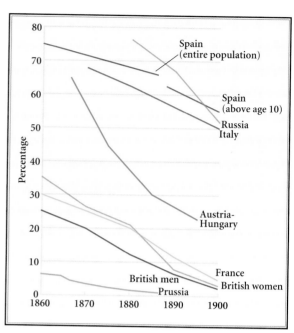

TAKING MEASURE The Decline of Illiteracy
The development of mass politics and the consolidation of the nation-state depended on building a cohesive group of citizens, informed about the progress of the nation. Increasing literacy was thus a national undertaking but one with national variations ranging from low levels of illiteracy in Prussia to high levels in Austria-Hungary and Russia. Even in regions of high illiteracy, however, governments successfully encouraged people to read.
Theodore Hamerow, *The Birth of New Europe: State and Society in the Nineteenth Century* (Chapel Hill: University of North Carolina Press, 1983), 85.

public and that invested those funds heavily in business needed tellers and clerks; railroads, insurance companies, and government-run telegraph and telephone companies all needed armies of white-collar employees.

Workers with mathematical skills and literacy acquired in the new public primary schools staffed this service sector, which provided in particular clean work for educated, middle-class women. (See "Taking Measure," above right.) Female employees eventually predominated in service jobs. In Paris the number of women in white-collar work tripled between 1866 and 1886. Early in the century, middle-class women had tended businesses with their husbands, but then the ideology of domesticity had dictated that middle-class women should not work

outside the home. By the late nineteenth century, however, the costs of middle-class family life, especially children's education, were becoming a burden. Many middle-class people could not even afford to marry. So whether to help pay family expenses or to support themselves, unmarried and a greater number of married women of the respectable middle class took jobs. Employers, as one put it, found in the new women workers a "quickness of eye and ear, and the delicacy of touch" essential to office work. By hiring women for newly created clerical jobs, business and government contributed to a dual labor market in which certain categories of jobs were predominantly male and others were overwhelmingly female. In the absence of competition, businesses in the service sector saved significantly by paying women chronically low wages—much less than they would have had to pay men for the same work.

The Department Store. Finally, the rise of consumer capitalism transformed the scale of consumption the way industrial capitalism had transformed the scale of production. The principal institution of this change was the department store. Founded after midcentury in the largest cities, department stores gathered such an impressive variety of goods in one place that consumers popularly called them "marble palaces" or "the eighth wonder of the world." Created by daring entrepreneurs such as Aristide and Marguerite Boucicaut of the Bon Marché in Paris and John Wanamaker of Wanamaker's in Philadelphia, department stores eventually replaced the single-item stores that people entered knowing clearly what they wanted to purchase.

These modern palaces sought to stimulate consumer whims and desires with luxurious fabrics, delicate laces, and richly embellished tapestries. The items spilled over railings and counters, not in the calculated order inherent in rational ideals of the nineteenth century, but in intentional and glorious disarray. Shoppers no longer bargained over prices; instead they reacted to sales, a new marketing technique that could incite a buy-

ing frenzy. As most men lacked the time for shopping expeditions, department stores appealed mostly to women, who came out of their domestic sphere into a new public role. Women explained their forays outside the home as necessary to enhance their home and family lives. Attractive salesgirls, another variety of service workers, were hired to inspire customers to buy. Shopping was not only an urban phenomenon: glossy mail-order catalogs from the Bon Marché or Sears, Roebuck arrived regularly in rural areas, replete with all the luxuries and household items contained in the exotic, far-away dream world of the city.

Consumerism joined hands with empire. Wealthy travelers like Marianne North traveled on well-appointed oceanliners, carrying quinine, antiseptics, and other medicines as well as cameras, revolvers, and the latest in rubber goods and apparel. Coffee, tea, sugar, tobacco, cocoa, and cola were stimulants from the colonies whose consumption became more widespread. Tons of palm oil from Africa were turned into both margarine, adding fat to the European diet, and fine soap, allowing Westerners to see themselves as cleaner and more civilized. Industry and empire jointly shaped everyday life as a voracious desire to consume and own—whether industrial goods or colonies—took root in Western culture.

Crespin and Dufayel Department Store
The department store marked the definitive transition of European society from one of subsistence and scarcity to one of relative abundance. Centralizing the sale of all varieties of goods, department stores displayed more consumer items than any single person could possibly use. This particular Parisian department store was relatively subdued in its displays, but others ran sales and so seductively arranged goods that Europe's uninitiated consumers were often tempted into irrational purchasing.
Jean-Loup Charmet.

❖ The New Imperialism

In the last third of the nineteenth century, industrial demand and rampant business rivalry added fuel to the contest for territory in Africa and Asia. A "new imperialism"—unlike the trader-based domination of preceding centuries—brought direct rule of these two continents by European nations. The race to imperial conquest constituted an integral component of European nation building, whose champions came to connect industrial prosperity and imperial expansion with national identity. "Nations are not great except for the activities they undertake," declared a French advocate of huge imperial acquisitions in 1885. Conquering foreign territory appeared to heap glory on the nation-state. While the "new imperialism" aimed to advance Western religions and culture, simultaneously the expansion of the West increased the subjection of local peoples, inflicting violence and altering everyday life. Said to benefit all, it paradoxically intensified discord among the European powers and even among ordinary citizens.

Taming the Mediterranean

European countries eyed the African and Asian shores of the Mediterranean for reasons based on the old imperialism: the chance to profit through trade. Great Britain and France were especially eager to do business with Egypt, where the combined value of imports and exports had jumped from 3.5 million Egyptian pounds in 1838 to 21 million in 1880 (and would grow to 60 million in 1913). European capital investment in the region also rose, first in ventures such as the Suez Canal in the 1860s and then in the laying of thousands of miles of railroad track and the creation of telegraph systems. Improvement-minded rulers in Asia and Africa paid dearly for modernization: whereas European bankers charged 5 percent interest on loans at home, they charged non-Europeans 12 percent or more, a difference they justified by determining foreign investments to be a greater risk. High rates of return on loans made foreign investments very attractive, and the completion of harbors, dams, canals, and railroads increased the Middle East's desirability as a market for European exports and as an intermediate stop on the way to trade with Asia.

After India fell to direct British rule in 1858, Egypt felt the next blow of Britain. Britain and France had pursued a stake in Egypt since the Napoleonic Wars, and in 1875 British prime minister Benjamin Disraeli bought a massive share in the Suez Canal for Britain. This purchase gave the khedive Ismail (r. 1863–1879), Egypt's profligate ruler, money to make payments on high-interest loans to European creditors. In 1879, the British and the French took over the Egyptian treasury to secure their own financial investments. Nationalist groups protested this heavy-handed encroachment on Egyptian sovereignty. By this time some

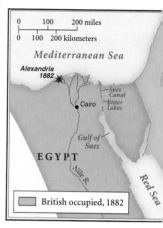

The Suez Canal and British Invasion of Egypt, 1882

88 percent of the India trade was using the Suez Canal, and to protect European interests Britain used the nationalist threat as an excuse to bombard Alexandria and invade Egypt in 1882.

After defeating the nationalist forces, however, the British did not restore the khedive's independent rule but instead ran the government from behind the scenes. Despite heated parliamentary opposition at home, the British reshaped the Egyptian economy to their own needs. In keeping with the demands of modernization, they brought in new agricultural machinery, created irrigation systems, and abolished forced labor. They also reorganized agriculture, changing the system from one based on multiple crops that maintained the country's self-sufficiency to one that emphasized the production of a few crops—mainly cotton, raw silk, wheat, and rice, which were especially useful to European manufacturing. Colonial powers, local landowners, and moneylenders profited from these agricultural changes, while the bulk of the rural population barely eked out an existence.

The rest of the Mediterranean and the Ottoman Empire felt the heightened presence of the European powers. With Algeria increasingly dominated by the French military, French settlers now moved onto land taken from indigenous people. As a further guarantee of their Mediterranean claims, the French occupied neighboring Tunisia in 1881. Elsewhere, businessmen from Britain, France, and Germany flooded Asia Minor with cheap goods, driving artisans from their trades and into low-paid work building railroads or processing tobacco. Instead of basing wage rates on gender (as they did at home), Europeans used ethnicity and religion, paying Muslims less than Christians, and Arabs less than other ethnic groups. Such practices, as well as contact with European technology and nationalism, planted the seeds for anticolonial movements.

Scramble for Africa

Sub-Saharan Africans also felt the heavier hand of European ambition after the British takeover of the Egyptian government. Economic relations between Africans and Europeans were not new, but contact between the two continents had principally involved the trade of African slaves for European manufactured goods. The slave trade had drastically diminished by this time, and Europeans' principal objective was expanding trade in Africa's raw materials, such as palm oil, cotton, diamonds, cocoa, and rubber. Additionally, with its industrial and naval supremacy and its empire in India, Britain hoped to keep the southern and eastern coasts of Africa secure for stopover ports on the route to Asia.

Except for the French conquest of Algeria, commerce had rarely involved direct political control in Africa. Yet in the 1880s, European influence turned into direct control as one African territory after another fell to European military force (Map 24.1). The French, Belgians, Portuguese, Italians, and Germans jockeyed to dominate peoples, land, and resources—"the magnificent cake of Africa," as King Leopold II of Belgium (r. 1865–1909) put it. Driven by insatiable greed, Leopold claimed the Congo region of central Africa, thereby initiating competition with France for that territory and inflicting on its peoples unparalleled acts of cruelty. German chancellor Otto von Bismarck, who saw colonies mostly as political bargaining chips, sent out explorers in 1884 and established German control over Cameroon and a section of East Africa. Faced with competition, the British poured millions of pounds into preserving their position by dominating the continent "from Cairo to Cape Town," as the slogan went, and the French cemented their hold on large portions of western Africa.

The Violence of Colonization
King Leopold, ruler of the Belgian Congo, was so greedy that his agents squeezed the last drop of rubber and other resources from local peoples. Missionaries reported such atrocities as the killing of workers whose quotas were even slightly short or the amputation of hands for the same offense. Belgian agents collected amputated hands and sent them to government officials to show Leopold that they were enforcing his kind of discipline.
Anti-Slavery International.

The scramble for Africa escalated tensions in Europe and prompted Bismarck to call a conference of European nations at Berlin. The fourteen nations at the conference, held in a series of meetings in 1884 and 1885, decided that settlements along the African coast guaranteed rights to internal territory. This agreement led to the strictly linear dissection of the continent; geographers and diplomats cut across indigenous boundaries of

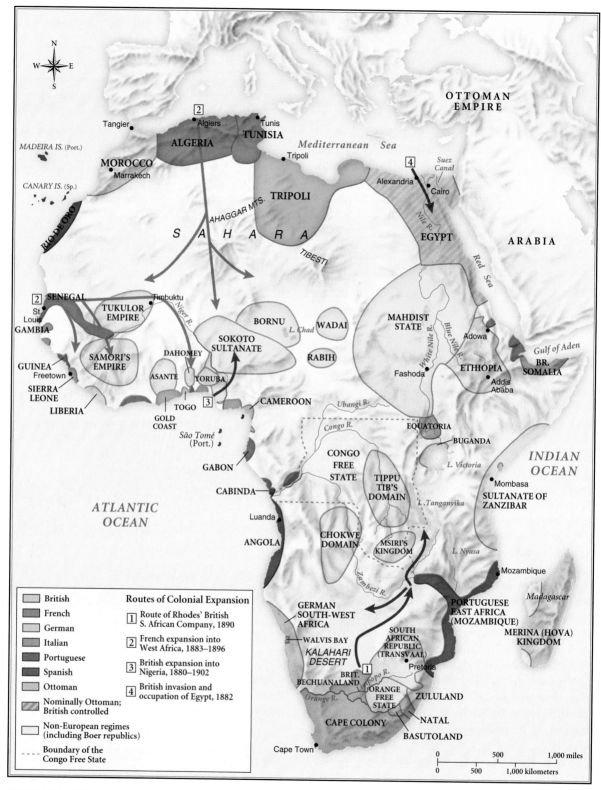

MAP 24.1 Africa, c. 1890

The "scramble for Africa" entailed a real reversal of European trading practices, which were generally limited to the coastline. Trying to conquer, economically penetrate, and rule the interior resulted in a map of the continent that made sense only to the imperial powers, for it divided ethnic groups and made territorial unities that had nothing to do with Africans' sense of geography or patterns of settlement. Nor did it conform in any way to Africans' own political organization.

African culture and ethnic life. The Berlin conference also banned the sale of alcohol and controlled the sale of arms to native peoples. In theory the meeting was supposed to reduce bloodshed and temper ambitions in Africa, but in reality European leaders were intent on maintaining and expanding their power, and utterly rapacious individuals like King Leopold continued to plunder the continent and terrorize its people. The news from Berlin only whetted the popular appetite for more imperialist ventures.

Technological development of powerful guns, railroads, steamships, and medicines dramatically expanded and facilitated Western domination, accelerating the penetration of all the continents after more than three centuries of exploration and trade. The gunboats that forced the Chinese to open their borders to opium played a part in forcing African ethnic groups to give up their independence. Quinine and guns were also an important factor in African conquest. Before the development of medicinal quinine in the 1840s and 1850s, the deadly tropical disease malaria had threatened to decimate any European party embarking on exploration or military conquest, giving Africa the nickname "White Man's Grave." The use of quinine, extracted from cinchona bark from the Andes, to treat malaria sent death rates among missionaries, adventurers, traders, and bureaucrats plummeting. A Dutch cartel, successfully experimenting with cinchona cultivation in Indonesia, broke the South American hold on quinine production and cornered the market until World War II.

While quinine saved white lives, technology to take lives was also advancing. Improvements to the breech-loading rifle and the development of the machine gun, or "repeater," between 1862 and the 1880s dramatically increased firepower. Europeans carried on a brisk trade selling inferior guns to Africans on the coast, but peoples of the interior used bows and arrows. Muslim slave traders and European Christians alike crushed African resistance with blazing gunfire: "The whites did not seize their enemy as we do by the body, but thundered from afar," claimed one local African resister. "Death raged everywhere—like the death vomited forth from the tempest."

Nowhere did this destructive capacity have greater effect than in southern Africa, where farmers of European descent and prospectors, rather than military personnel, battled the Xhosa, Zulu, and other African peoples for control of the frontier regions of Transvaal, Natal, the Orange Free State, Rhodesia, and the Cape Colony. Although the Dutch originally settled the area in the seventeenth century, the British had gained control by 1815. Thereafter descendants of the Dutch, called *Boers* (Dutch for "farmers"), were joined by British immigrants in their fight to wrest farmland and mineral resources from natives. British businessman and politician Cecil Rhodes (1853–1902), sent to South Africa for his health just as diamonds were being discovered in 1870, cornered the diamond market and claimed a huge amount of African territory with the help of official charters from the British government, all before he turned forty. Pushing hundreds of miles into the interior of southern Africa (a region soon to be named Rhodesia after him), Rhodes moved into gold mining too. His ambition for Britain and for himself was boundless: "I contend that we are the finest race in the world," he explained, "and that the more of the world we inhabit the better it is." Although notions of

Malian Young Men's House
Europeans claimed that sub-Saharan Africans had no culture and especially no technical knowledge. Skilled road builders, textile designers, and manufacturers of weapons, these Africans had also constructed intricate mosques, private dwellings, and communal buildings such as this one for young men in Mali. European painters, architects, and sculptors soon adapted features from African styles and even wholly modeled their designs on those of artists beyond the West.
Carollee Pelos/Jean-Louis Bourgeois.

European racial superiority had been advanced before, racist attitudes now justified converting trade with Africans into conquest and political control of their lands. Within just a few decades Darwinism had evolved from a contribution to science to a racist justification for imperialism.

Wherever necessary to ensure profit and domination, Europeans destroyed African economic and political systems or transformed them into instruments of their rule. A British governor of the Gold Coast put the matter succinctly in 1886: the British would "rule the country as if there were no inhabitants," as if local traditions of political and economic life did not exist. Indeed, most Europeans considered Africans barely civilized despite the wealth local rulers and merchants accumulated in their international trade in raw materials and slaves and despite individual African people's accomplishments in dyeing, road building, and architecture. Unlike the Chinese and Indians, whom Europeans credited with a scientific and artistic heritage, Africans were seen as valuable only for manual labor. By confiscating Africans' land, Europeans forced native peoples to work for them to earn a living and to pay the taxes they imposed. Subsistence agriculture, often performed by women and slaves, thus declined in favor of mining and farming cash crops. Standards of living dropped for Africans who lost their lands without realizing the Europeans were claiming permanent ownership. Systems of family and community unity provided support networks for Africans during this upheaval in everyday life.

Acquiring Territory in Asia

Britain justified the invasion of African countries as strategically necessary to preserve control of India's quarter of a billion people, but in reality from the 1870s on, the expansion of European power was occurring around the world. Much of Asia, with India as the centerpiece, was integrated into Western empires.

After two centuries of British authority, a system of rule emerged in which close to half a million Indians governed a region the British called *India* under the supervision of a few thousand British men. Indians also collected taxes and distributed patronage. As in Africa, colonial rule meant attaching subordinated peoples to the government not only through such mechanisms as native armies and civil service but also through intervention in everyday life. Thus, ordinary Indians benefited in some places from improved sanitation and medicine, which allowed the population to surge. Upper-class Indians attended British-style schools and served in a British-style bureaucracy, often coming to reject Indian customs such as infanticide, child marriage, and *sati*—a widow's self-immolation on her husband's funeral pyre. British notions of a scientific society attracted some in these upper classes, while the unity that British rule gave to what were once small localities and princedoms with separate allegiances promoted nationalism among the new, Western-educated elite.

Domination was also blatant: in 1876, the British Parliament declared Queen Victoria the empress of India. British policy forced the end to indigenous production of finished goods such as cotton textiles that would compete with Britain's own manufactures. Instead the British wanted cheaper raw materials such as wheat, cotton, and jute to supply their industries. Enclaves of British civil servants, who sought prosperity and social advancement for governing the vast subcontinent, enforced segregation and an inferior status on all classes of Indians. Discriminated against but educated, the Indian elite in 1885 founded the Indian National Congress, which challenged Britain's right to rule. In the next century, the Congress would develop into a mass movement.

British Colonialism in the Malay Peninsula and Burma, 1826–1890

To the east, British military forces took control of the Malay peninsula in 1874 and of the interior of Burma in 1885. In both areas, political instability often threatened secure trade. The British depended on the region's tin, oil, rice, teak, and rubber as well as its access to the interior trade routes of China. The presence of British troops guaranteed the order necessary to expand railroads for more efficient export of raw materials and the development of Western systems of communication. Once secured, the relative tranquillity also allowed the British to build factories and from there to create an industrial base in China.

The British rapidly added to their holdings in Asia partly to counter Russian and French annexations. Since 1865, Russia had been absorbing the small Muslim states of central Asia, including Turkestan and provinces of Afghanistan (Map 24.2). Besides extending into the Ottoman Empire, Russian tentacles reached Persia, India, and China, often encountering British ambition. The Trans-Siberian Railroad allowed Russia to begin integrating Siberia—considered a colony in the eighteenth and early nineteenth centuries. Using favorable treaties backed by the threat of military action, in 1887 France created the Union of Indochina from the ancient states of Cambodia, Tonkin, Annam, and

The Union of Indochina, 1893

Cochin China (the latter three now constitute Vietnam). Laos was added to Indochina in 1893.

Like the British, the French brought some Western programs to the societies they brutally conquered. Modern projects in the Mekong Delta, for example, increased the amount of cultivated land and spurred rapid growth in the food supply; the French also improved sanitation and public health in Indochina. Such changes proved a mixed blessing, however, because they led to population growth that strained the societies' other resources. Furthermore, landowners and French imperialists siphoned off most of the profits from economic improvement. The French also undertook a cultural mission to transform Saigon and other cities into centers of French civilization. Tree-lined boulevards that emulated Paris were constructed in an urban building program. French literature, theater, and art diverted not only colonial officials but also upper-class Indochinese. Nonetheless, contact with Western culture would eventually spawn Indochinese nationalism, influenced by Western models but rejecting Western rule.

Japan's Imperial Agenda

Japan escaped the "new" European imperialism by its rapid transformation into a modern industrial nation with its own imperial agenda. A Japanese print of the 1880s illustrates both traditional ways

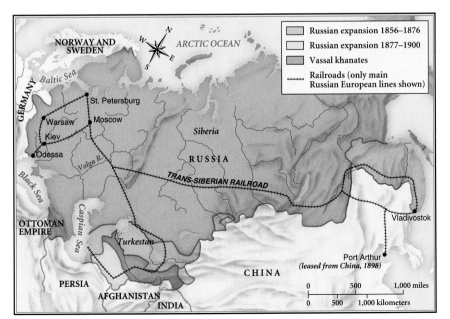

MAP 24.2 Expansion of Russia in Asia, 1865–1895
Russian administrators and military men continued enlarging Russia, bringing in Asians of many different ethnicities, ways of life, and religions. Simultaneously, land-hungry peasants in western Russia followed the path of expansion into Siberia and Muslim territories in the south. In some cases they drove native peoples from their lands, but in others they settled unpopulated frontier areas. As in all cases of imperial expansion, local peoples resisted any expropriation of their livelihood.

Modernization in Japan

Japan modernized with breathtaking speed, as this view of a railroad station demonstrates. Japan both borrowed from the West and loyally supported its own traditions. Thus, while many Japanese donned Western clothes, others remained wedded to local costumes and to native scenery such as cherry trees. In this woodcut by Ando Hiroshige II—son of the artist imitated by many in the West—the train schedule appears across the top of the depiction.
Laurie Platt Winfrey Inc.

and the Western influence behind Japan's burgeoning power. The picture's costumed women, strolling with their parasols amidst flowering cherry trees, might have been rendered centuries earlier; but a steaming locomotive in the background symbolizes change. The Japanese embraced foreign trade and industry under the leadership of the Satcho Hito clan, whose accession to power in 1868 ushered in the Meiji Restoration. "All classes high and low shall unite in vigorously promoting the economy and welfare of the nation," ran one of the first pronouncements of the new regime. The Japanese had long acquired knowledge from other countries. Unlike China, which had rejected it, Japan had endorsed the challenge from the West.

In the 1870s, Japanese government officials traveled to Europe and the United States to study technological and industrial developments. Western dress became the rule at the imperial court, and when fire destroyed Tokyo in 1872 a European directed the rebuilding in Western architectural style. Opposition to such changes was not tolerated, as the new central government, led by some of the old *samurai*, or warrior elite, crushed mas-

sive rebellions by any who resisted modernization. The Japanese adapted samurai traditions such as spiritual discipline and the drive to excel to a large, technologically modern military, which was filled by universal conscription. By 1894, Japan had become powerful enough to force traders to accept its terms for commerce and diplomatic relations.

The Japanese government instigated the turn toward industry. Japanese legal scholars, following German models, helped draft a constitution in 1889 that emphasized state power rather than individual rights. The state also stimulated economic development by building railroads and shipyards and establishing financial institutions. Then in the 1880s, when the cost of modernization had drained resources, the government auctioned off its businesses to private entrepreneurs, thereby collecting essential revenue to stabilize its finances. State support led daring innovators like Iwasaki Yataro, founder of the Mitsubishi firm, to develop heavy industries such as mining and shipping. In Japan, unlike the rest of Asia, the adaptation of Western-style enterprises became a patriotic goal. Like its Western models, Japan started intervening in nationalist and imperialist struggles elsewhere in Asia. This interference ultimately provoked war with its traditionally more powerful neighbors China and Russia.

The Paradoxes of Imperialism

Imperialism ignited constant, sometimes heated debate because of the many paradoxes in its meaning and scope. Although it was meant to stabilize great-power status, imperialism intensified distrust in international politics. New countries vied with old ones for a share of world influence. In securing India's borders, for example, the British faced Russian expansion in Afghanistan and along the borders of China. Moreover, imperial competition made areas of Europe, such as the Balkans, more volatile than ever as states sought status and national security in the control of disputed territory.

Politicians debated the economic value of empire. The search for new markets often proved more costly than profitable to societies. Britain, for example, spent enormous amounts of tax revenues to maintain its empire even as its industrial base began to decline. Yet for certain businesses, colonies provided crucial markets: late in the century, French colonies bought 65 percent of France's exports of soap and 41 percent of its metallurgical exports. Imperialism provided huge numbers of jobs

to people in European port cities, but—whether they benefited or not—taxpayers in all parts of a nation paid for colonial armies, increasingly costly weaponry, and administrators.

Motives for imperialism were equally paradoxical. Goals such as fostering national might, boosting national loyalty, and the centuries-old effort to Christianize peoples often proved unattainable or difficult to measure. Many believed that through imperialist ventures, "a country exhibits before the world its strength or weakness as a nation," as one French politician announced. Governments worried that imperialism—because of its expense and the constant possibility of war—might weaken rather than strengthen them. Another French statesman argued that France "must keep its role as the soldier of civilization." But, as French rule in Indochina showed, it was unclear if imperialists should emphasize soldiering—that is, conquest and conflict—or the more encompassing goal of exporting culture and religion.

Hoping to Christianize colonized peoples, European missionaries ventured to newly secured areas of Africa and Asia. A woman missionary working among the Tibetans reflected a common view when she remarked that the native peoples were "going down, down into hell, and there is no one but me . . . to witness for Jesus amongst them." Europeans were confident in their religious and

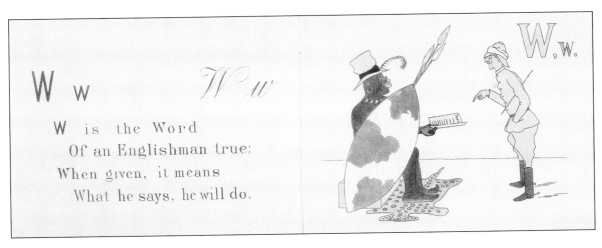

An ABC for Baby Patriots (1899)
Pride in empire began at an early age, when learning the alphabet from this kind of book helped develop an imperial sensibility. The subject of geography became important in schools during the decades between 1870 and 1890 and helped young people know what possessions they could claim as citizens. In British schools, the young celebrated the holiday Empire Day with ceremonies and festivities emphasizing imperial power.
Bodleian Library, Oxford.

cultural superiority. In the judgment of many, Asians and Africans were a class beneath Europeans, variously characterized as lying, lazy, self-indulgent, or irrational. One English official pontificated that "accuracy is abhorrent to the Oriental mind." At the height of imperialism, such beliefs offered still another justification for conquest and dominion: the civilizing process of colonization would eventually make conquered peoples grateful for what Europe had brought them. Viewing other races as "degenerate" helped promote Western notions of progress, but this cultural pride prompted "civilizers" such as missionaries paradoxically to collaborate with the most brutal military measures to accomplish their goals.

Western scholars and travelers had long gathered ideas and knowledge about Asian and African languages and cultures, and they claimed during these years to have garnered a totally objective and scientific view of history and society. Yet even the best scholars generally considered foreign cultures in terms of their own biases, characterizing Islam's Muhammad as a mere imitation of Jesus, for example. Alternatively, some Europeans—from novelists to military men—considered conquered peoples better than Europeans because they were unspoiled by civilization. "At last some local color," enthused one colonial officer, fresh from industrial cities of Europe, on seeing Constantinople. This romantic, misinformed, "orientalizing" vision of an ancient center of culture, similar to eighteenth-century condescension toward the "noble savage," had little to do with the reality of conquered peoples' lives. A look back at these paradoxical efforts suggests that Europe itself became conflicted as it underwent profound changes in the course of further industrialization and imperial expansion.

❖ The Transformation of Culture and Society

Advancing industrialization and empire not only made the world an interconnected marketplace but transformed everyday culture and society. Success in manufacturing and foreign ventures created millionaires, and the expansion of a professional middle class and development of a service sector resulted in more people affluent enough to own property, see some of the world, and provide their children a more cosmopolitan education. Price deflation caused by industrial success and imperial conquest changed everyday life: consumers in the West could purchase goods that poured in from around the world. Many Europeans grew healthier, partly because of improved diet and partly because of the efforts of reformers who sponsored government programs aimed at promoting the fitness necessary for citizens of imperial powers.

Industrial and imperial advance simultaneously challenged many working-class people in the West, buffeting them with the threat of replacement with machinery while offering new opportunities for mobility as European societies opened up the globe. Their experience of the internationalizing force of imperialism was different from that of the middle class: from the mid-nineteenth century on, millions migrated to the United States, Canada, Australia, Argentina, Brazil, and Siberia and, as frequently, from country to city and back. In the process they transported and imported culture. Artists captured the imperial and industrial spectacle in increasingly iconoclastic works influenced by styles from beyond the West. Their art, like the everyday lives of those they depicted, was transformed in the industrial, imperial crucible.

The "Best" Circles

The profits from industry and empire added new members to the upper class, or "best" circles, so called at the time because of their members' wealth, education, and social status. People in the best circles often came from the aristocracy, which retained much of its power and was still widely emulated. Increasingly, however, aristocrats had to share their social position with new millionaires from the ranks of the bourgeoisie. In fact, the very distinction between aristocrat and bourgeois became blurred, as monarchs gratefully endowed millionaire industrialists and businesspeople with aristocratic titles, in thanks for their contributions to the national wealth. Moreover, down-at-the-heels aristocrats were only too willing to offer their children in marriage to families from the newly rich. Such arrangements brought a much-needed infusion of funds to old, established families and the cachet of an aristocratic title to upstart families. Thus the American heiress Winaretta Singer (of Singer sewing machine fame) married Prince Edmond de Polignac of France, and Jeanette

Lord and Lady Curzon on a Tiger Shoot
Big-game hunting became the imperial sport of choice, and real adventurers came to see fox hunting and other traditional pastimes of the elites as effeminate if not decadent. European hunters took the sport over from local Africans and Asians who had previously depended on the hunt for their livelihood. Now these Africans and Asians served the European amateurs, many of whom were in wretched physical shape. Some women enjoyed hunting too. As a gesture of chivalry, men would let the woman issue the coup de grace, or death shot, if a tiger materialized during a hunt.
India Office Library/British Library.

Jerome, daughter of a wealthy New York financier, married England's Lord Randolph Churchill (their son Winston later became England's prime minister). Even millionaires without official connections to the aristocracy discarded the modest ways of a century earlier to build palatial country homes and villas, engage in conspicuous displays of wealth, and wall themselves off from the poor in suburbs or new sections of town inhabited only by the rich. To justify their success, the wealthy often appealed to Social Darwinist principles, which indicated that their accumulation of money demonstrated the natural superiority of the rich over the poor.

Sport and leisure brought upper-class men together in their favorite activity—hunting—as this activity was reshaped by imperial contact. Fox and bird hunting had been aristocratic pastimes in parts of Europe for centuries, but big-game hunting in Asia and Africa now became the rage. European hunters forced native Africans, who had depended on hunting for income or food and for group unity, to work as guides, porters, and domestics on hunts instead. Mastering foreign games like polo or activities like big-game hunting demonstrated that Europeans could conquer both territory and the more intangible things like culture. (See "Did You Know?," page 910.) Collectors on the hunts brought exotic specimens back to Eu-

rope for zoological exhibits, natural history museums, and traveling displays, all of which flourished during this period. Stags' heads, elephant tusks, and animal skins also decorated European homes.

Members of the upper class did their best to exclude others by controlling their children's social lives. Marriageable women in the upper and middle classes were closely watched to preserve their chastity and to keep them from socializing with lower-class men. Upper-class men had liaisons with lower-class women—part of the double standard that saw promiscuity as normal for men and as immoral for women—but few thought of marrying them. Parents still arranged many marriages directly, but other marriages were initiated during visiting days, on which occasions prominent hostesses held an open house under rather formal conditions. Such regular social contact sometimes provided the foundation for matrimonial decisions.

Ritualistic visits filled the everyday lives of upper-class women. Instead of working for pay, they devoted themselves to having children, directing staffs of servants, and maintaining standards of etiquette and social conduct. Women took their role seriously by keeping detailed accounts of their expenditures and monitoring their children's religious and intellectual development. The pursuit of fashion in home furnishing took on imperial

Polo and Social Class

Today's historians often see the implantation of sports by the imperial powers in colonized regions as a form of domination. By organizing teams of cricket or rugby players in West Africa, India, or the Caribbean, for instance, the British were said to be inventing identities and traditions that were based on Western ideas of what sports and sportsmen were. In this interpretation, imperialists replaced local cultures with their own.

But imperialism has always been a two-way street despite great differences in power. While planting cricket in the colonies, the British upper classes became hooked on polo, an Asian sport that imperial forces picked up in India. Played on horseback, *puhluh* was a team sport that allowed a cavalry-based fighting force (both men and horses) to stay in shape during long, idle intervals. Chutneys, curries, verandahs, jodphurs, and the game of pachisi were some of the many borrowings from India by the West in the nineteenth century. It was polo, however, that has lost most of its associations with imperial borrowing, seeming to many the essence of Britain's celebrated, aristocratic way of life.

Anglo-Indian Polo Team
Team sports underwent rapid development during the imperial years, as spectators rooted for the success of their football team in the same spirit they rooted for their armies abroad. Some educators believed that team sports formed the male character so that men could be more effective soldiers against peoples of other races. Thus this mixed team of polo players was uncharacteristic. In cricket, soccer, and other sports, city challenged city, nation challenged nation, and race often challenged race.
Hulton Getty Collection/Liaison Agency.

motifs in these decades, featuring Persian-inspired designs in textiles, Oriental carpets, wicker furniture, and Chinese porcelains. With the importation of plants such as azaleas and rhododendrons from around the world, gardens replaced parks and lawns—another domestic element for upper-class women to oversee. Being an active consumer of fashion in clothing was time-consuming. In contrast to men's plain garments, upper-class women's costumes were elaborate, ornate, and dramatic, featuring constricting corsets, long voluminous skirts, bustles, and low-cut necklines for evening wear. Upper-class women, symbols of elite leisure, fervently tried to offset the drabness of industrial life

with the rigorous practice of art and music. One Hungarian observer wrote, "The piano mania has become almost an epidemic in Budapest as well as Vienna." Some women were also quite active outside the home, engaging in religious and philanthropic activities and taking a particular interest in the welfare of lower-class women.

The Rise of Middle-Class Professionals

Below the richest best circles or "upper crust," the "solid" middle class was expanding, most notably in western and central Europe: the Russian government often sought out foreigners from Germany and other parts of central Europe to build its professional and entrepreneurial classes. Growing numbers of doctors, lawyers, managers, professors, and successful journalists found their positions enhanced by the prestige of science and information, and they established their position as masters of a complex body of knowledge. Government legislation began to allow professional people to determine who would and would not be admitted to "the professions." Such legislation had both positive and negative effects: groups could set their own standards, but otherwise qualified people were sometimes prohibited from working because they lacked the established credentials. The German medical profession, for example, was granted authority to control licensing, which led to more rigorous university training for future doctors but also pushed midwives out of medicine and caused the arrest of healers not trained in medical school. Science, too, became the province of the trained specialist rather than the amateur genius; scientists were likely to be employed by universities and institutes, funded by the government, and provided with equipment and assistants. Like other members of the middle class, professors of science were intensely patriotic, often interpreting their work as part of an international struggle for prestige and excellence. Without more staff and equipment, one French scientist threatened in 1880, "we will be far behind the German and Dutch laboratories."

Although professionals could sometimes mingle with those at the apex of society, their lives remained more modest. They employed at least one servant, to give the appearance of leisure to the middle-class woman in the home. Professional men working at home did so from the best-appointed, if not lavish, room. Middle-class domesticity substituted cleanliness and polish for upper-class conspicuous consumption. The soap and tea used in the middle-class home were becoming signs—along with hard work—of a racial superiority and higher status not accessible to the colonized peoples who actually produced those goods.

Professional Sports and Organized Leisure

As nations competed for territory and economic markets, male athletes banded together to organize team sports that eventually replaced village games. Large audiences now backed a particular team, as soccer, rugby, and cricket drew mass followings and integrated migrants as well as the lower and higher classes into a common culture. The heightened emphasis on group competition also found favor with the reading public; newspapers reported the results of all sorts of contests, including the Tour de France bicycle race, sponsored by tire makers who wanted to prove the superiority of their product.

Victorian Women's Bicycle Race

The bicycle represented freedom for millions of young people, and many credit it with changes in social customs that gradually appeared in these decades. In clubs or groups of friends, the young went off riding for miles; for young women the bicycle was particularly liberating, giving them exercise and a chance to see a bit more of the world. Their clothing changed subtly too as full skirts and abundant petticoats were soon found cumbersome and even unsafe. The bicycle also provided easier transportation for working people.
Collection of Sally Fox.

Tests of speed measured by clocks and involving the use of machines like bicycles and cars replaced older forms of competition such as cockfighting and sack racing. Competitive sports began to be seen as valuable to national strength and spirit. "The Battle of Waterloo was won on the playing fields of Eton," ran the wisdom of the day, suggesting that the games played in school could mold the strength and character of an army.

Team sports—like civilian military service—helped differentiate male and female spheres and thus promoted social order based on distinction between the sexes. Some team sports for women emerged, such as soccer, field hockey, and rowing, but in general women were encouraged to engage in individual sports. "Riding improves the temper, the spirits and the appetite," wrote one sportswoman. "Black shadows and morbid fancies disappear from the mental horizon." Rejecting the idea of women's natural frailty, reformers introduced exercise and gymnastics into schools for girls, often with the idea that these would strengthen them for motherhood and thus help build the nation-state. So-called Swedish exercises for young women spread through respectable homes across Europe, while more sophisticated women practiced yoga.

The middle classes believed their leisure pursuits should be edifying as well as fun. Thus mountain climbing became a popular middle-class hobby. As the editor of a Swedish publication of 1889 explained, "The passion for mountain-climbing can only be understood by those who realize that it is the step-by-step achievement of a goal which is the real pleasure of the world." Working-class people adopted middle-class habits by joining clubs for such pursuits as bicycling, touring, and hiking. Laborers and their families also sought the benefits of fresh air and exercise by visiting the beach, taking the train into the countryside, and enjoying day trips on river steamships. Clubs that sponsored trips often had such names as the Patriots or the Nationals, again associating physical fitness with national strength. The new emphasis on healthy recreation gave individuals a greater sense of individual freedom and power and thereby contributed to a developing sense of citizenship based less on constitutions and rights than on an individual nation's exercise of raw power. A farmer's son in the 1890s boasted that with a bicycle, "I was king of the road, since I was faster than a horse."

Working People's Strategies

Working people had for centuries migrated from countryside to city and from country to country to make a living. After the middle of the nineteenth century, empire and industry were powerful factors in migration. Older cities of Europe like Riga, Marseille, and Hamburg offered secure ports of entry and jobs—now in industry—and global trade, while new colonies provided land, posts for soldiers and administrators, and the possibility of unheard-of wealth in diamonds, gold, and other natural resources. City workers adapted to new conditions as industry made further inroads into the social and economic fabric.

Migration. Some Europeans followed an imperialist pattern of migration, moving well beyond their national borders. (See "Contrasting Views," page 914.) In parts of Europe, the land simply could not produce enough to support a rapidly expanding population. For example, the vast forests of Sicily that had once supplied the Greek navies with wood to build ships had been replaced by nearly worthless, eroded soil. By the end of the nineteenth century, hundreds of thousands of Sicilians were leaving, often temporarily, to find work in the industrial cities of northern Europe or the United States. The British Isles, especially Ireland, yielded one-third of all European emigrants between 1840 and 1920, first because of the potato famine and then because of uncertain farm tenancy and periodic economic crisis. Between 1886 and 1900, half a million Swedes out of a population of 4.75 million quit their country (Figure 24.1). Millions of rural Jews, especially those of eastern Europe, left their villages for economic reasons, but Russian Jews also fled in the face of vicious anti-Semitism. Russian mobs brutally attacked Jewish communities, destroying homes and businesses and even murdering some Jews. "People who saw such things never smiled anymore, no matter how long they lived," recalled one Russian Jewish woman who migrated to the United States in the early 1890s.

Commercial and imperial prosperity determined destinations. Most migrants went to North and South America, Australia, and New Zealand, as news of opportunity reached Europe. Moreover, the railroad and steamship made journeys across and out of Europe more affordable, more comfortable,

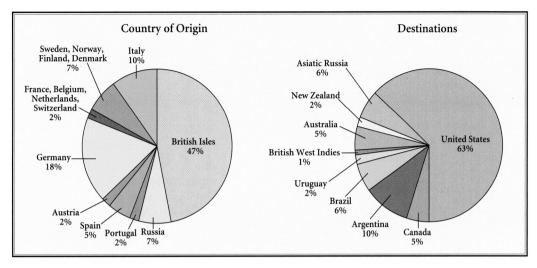

FIGURE 24.1 European Emigration, 1870–1890

The suffering caused by economic change and by political persecution motivated people from almost every European country to leave their homes for greater security elsewhere. North America attracted more than two-thirds of these migrants, many of whom followed reports of vast quantities of available land in both Canada and the United States. Both countries were known for following the rule of law and for economic opportunity in urban as well as rural areas.

Theodore Hamerow, *The Birth of New Europe: State and Society in the Nineteenth Century* (Chapel Hill: University of North Carolina Press, 1983), 169.

and faster, even though most travel was in steerage, with baggage and supplies and few amenities. Once established elsewhere, migrants frequently sent money back home and thus remained part of the family economy; European farm families often received a good deal of their income from sons and daughters who had left. Nationalist commentators in Slovakia, Poland, Hungary, and other parts of eastern and central Europe bemoaned the loss of ethnic vigor, but peasants themselves welcomed the arrival of "magic dollars" from their kin. Migrants appreciated the chance to begin anew without the deprivation and social constrictions of the old world. One settler in the United States was relieved to escape the meager peasant meal of rye bread and herring: "God save us from . . . all that is Swedish," he wrote home sourly.

Migration out of Europe often meant the end to the old way of life. Workingmen and -women immediately had to learn new languages and civic practices and to compete for jobs in growing cities where they formed the cheapest pool of labor, often in factories or sweatshops. Women who stayed at home, however, tended to associate with others like themselves, preserving traditional ways. More insulated at home, they might never learn the new

language or never put their peasant dresses away. Their children and husbands more often devalued their pasts as they were forced to build a life in schools and factories of the new world.

Simultaneously, rapid industrial development accelerated the urbanization of Europe. More common than international migration was internal migration from rural areas to European cities. Cities of more than 100,000 grew the most, but every urban area attracted migrants seeking employment. However, more people still lived in rural areas of under 2,000 people than lived in towns and cities. Migration back to those rural areas occurred at harvest time. The most urbanized countries were Great Britain and Belgium, followed by Germany, France, and the Netherlands. In Russia, only 7 percent of the population lived in cities of 10,000 or more; in Portugal the figure was 12 percent. But migration of all types continued unabated, whatever the population density. Ongoing modernization meant that peasants and city workers had to adapt to survive and to preserve their life. Temporary migrants to the cities worked as masons, cabdrivers, or factory hands to supplement declining income from agriculture; in the winter, those remaining on the land turned to cottage industry

Experiences of Migration

Migration helped to shape Europe long before the nineteenth century, but in this particular century millions of migrants moved thousands of miles from the lands of their birth. The accelerated pace of movement, the vast distances traveled, and the permanent relocation of this wave of migration generated a wide range of responses, from acceptance and enthusiasm to opposition and anger. The conflicting reactions to migration appeared in official reports, local newspapers, poems, and very personal letters. While many government officials could point with relief at the economic benefits of emigration (Document 1), people left behind were often heart-broken and suffered destitution (Document 2). Migrants themselves had vastly differing experiences, provoking a great debate over migration that continues today (Documents 3 and 4).

1. The Government View

The preamble to the Hungarian census for 1890 was blunt and unambiguous on the subject. It saw emigration exclusively in financial terms:

Emigration has proved to be a veritable boom. The impoverished populace has been drawn off to where it has found lucrative employment; the position of those left behind, their work opportunities and standard of living, have undoubtedly improved thanks to the rise in wages, and thanks to the substantial financial aid coming into the country: sums of from 300,000 to 1,500,000 florints.

Source: Quoted in Julianna Puskas, "Consequences of Overseas Migration for the Country of Origin: The Case of Hungary," in *Roots of the Transplanted: Late 19th Century East Central and Southeastern Europe*, Dirk Hoerder and Inge Blank, eds. (Boulder: East European Monographs, 1994), I: 397.

2. Those Left Behind

Teofila Borkowska from Warsaw, Poland, reacted to her husband's resettlement in the United States in two letters from 1893 and 1894. Stripped of a family group, Teofila had a difficult time surviving, and her husband never did return.

1893. Dear Husband: Up to the present I live with the Rybickis. I am not very well satisfied, perhaps because I was accustomed to live for so many years quietly, with you alone. And today you are at one end of the world and I at the other, so when I look at strange corners [surroundings], I don't know what to do from longing and regret. I comfort myself only that you won't forget me, that you will remain noble as you have been. . . . I have only the sort of friends who think that I own thousands and from time to time someone comes to me, asking me to lend her a dozen roubles.

1894. Up to the present I thought and rejoiced that you would still come back to Warsaw, but since you write that you won't come I comply with the will of God and with your will. I shall now count the days and weeks [until you take me to America]. May our Lord grant it to happen as soon as possible, for I am terribly worried. Such a sad life! I go almost to nobody, for as long as you were in Warsaw everything was different. Formerly we had friends, and everybody was glad to see us, while now, if I go to anybody, they are afraid I need something from them and they show me beforehand a different face. . . . They all do it, even those who were so good formerly. Now they show themselves as they are. You write me to try to earn something with Wladzia [a cousin owning a dressmaking shop]. But I have not earned yet a grosz from her.

Source: Letter from Teofila Borkowska to Wladyslaw Borkowski, in William Thomas and Florian Znaniecki, *The Polish Peasant in Europe and America* (New York: Dover, 1958), July 21, 1893, April 12, 1894, II: 874–75.

3. Migration Defended

In some cases emigrants were said to be unpatriotic and cowardly for leaving their homeland just to avoid hard economic times. Sweden, which more than a million left because of bad economic conditions in the countryside, saw accusation and counteraccusation fly. To charges against Swedish emigrants, one journalist, Isador Kjelberg, wrote:

Patriotism? Let us not misuse so fine a word! Does patriotism consist of withholding the truth from the workingman by claiming that "things are bad in America"? I want nothing to do with such patriotism! If patriotism consists of seeking, through lies, to persuade the poorest classes to remain under the yoke, like mindless beasts, so that we others should be so much better off, then I am lacking in patriotism. I love my country, as such, but even more I love and sympathize with the human being, the worker. . . . Among those who most sternly condemn emigration are those who least value the human and civic value of the workingman. . . . They demand that he remain here. What are they prepared to give him to compensate the deprivations this requires? . . . It is only cowardly, unmanly, heartless, to let oneself become a slave under deplorable circumstances which one *can* overcome.

Source: Quoted in H. Arnold Barton, *A Folk Divided: Homeland Swedes and Swedish Americans, 1840–1940* (Carbondale: Southern Illinois University Press, 1994), 72–73.

An anonymous Swedish poem joined the political defense of migration along with an economic motivation:

I'm bound for young America,
Farewell old Scandinavia.
I've had my fill of cold and toil,
All for the love of mother soil.
You poets with your rocks and rills
Can stay and starve—on words, no frills.

Me, I've got a stomach 'neath my hide,
No bonds can keep me on this side.
There, out west, a man breathes free,
While here one slaves, a tired bee,
Gathering honey to fill the hive
Of wise old rulers, on us they thrive.

In toil we hover before their thrones,
While they take to slumber, like lazy drones.
Drunk with our nectar they've set us afright,
But opportunity has knocked, and we'll take our flight.

Source: Quoted in ibid., 137.

4. The Perils of Migration

A contrasting view of emigration to the United States appeared in a Slovak song:

My fellow countryman, Rendek from Senica,
   the son of poor parents
Went out into the wide world. In Pittsburgh
   he began to toil.
From early morning till late at night he filled
   the furnaces with coal.
Faster, faster, roared the foreman, every day.
A letter came from home:
I want to board the ship,
Wrote his young wife.

Rendek toiled harder
So as to see his wife.
But alas! He was careless
And on Saturday evening late
He received his injuries.

At home his widow waited
For the card which would never come.
I, his friend, write this song
To let you know
What a hard life we have here.

Source: Quoted in Frantisek Bielik, Horst Hogh and Anna Stvrtecka, "Slovak Images of the New World: 'We Could Pay Off Our Debts'" in Hoerder and Blank, eds., *Roots of the Transplanted*, I:388.

QUESTIONS FOR DEBATE

1. Did the vast nineteenth-century migration ultimately enrich or diminish European culture and society?

2. How would you characterize the experience of migration for families and individuals?

3. How did migration affect the national identity of both receiving countries and European countries of origin?

making bricks, pottery, sieves, shawls, lace, locks, and samovars. To maintain their status as independent artisans, handweavers sent their wives and daughters to towns to work in factories.

Adaptation to Industrial Change. Changes in technology and management practices eliminated outmoded jobs and often made the work of those who survived job cuts more difficult. Workers complained that new machinery sped up the pace of work to an unrealistic level. For example, new furnaces at a foundry in suburban Paris required workers to turn out 50 percent more metal per day than they had produced using the old furnaces. Stepped-up productivity demanded much more physical exertion to tend and repair machines, often at a faster pace, but workers did not receive additional pay for their extra efforts. Workers also grumbled about the proliferation of managers; many believed that foremen, engineers, and other supervisors interfered with their work. For women, supervision sometimes brought on-the-job harassment, as in the case of female workers in a German food-canning plant who kept their jobs only in return for granting sexual favors to the male manager.

As new machines replaced old, managers established formal skill levels, from the most knowledgeable machinist to the untrained carrier of supplies. On the one hand, the introduction of machinery "deskilled" some jobs—traditional craft ability was not a prerequisite for operating many new machines. Employers could increasingly use untrained workers, often women, and pay them less than skilled workers. On the other hand, inventions always demanded new skills, especially for those who had to understand work processes or repair machinery. Employers began to use the concept of skill (based in the old craft traditions) to segment the labor force, but sometimes the designations were arbitrary.

Already prevalent in such trades as garment making, the trend toward breaking down and separating work processes into discrete tasks continued. For example, builders employed excavators, scaffolders, and haulers to do the "dirty work," hiring fewer highly paid carpenters. Those filling unskilled jobs could not count on regular employment and spent much of their time searching out temporary jobs. On the other end of the scale, foremen were no longer the most skilled workers,

but supervisors chosen, as one worker complained, for the "pushing powers . . . of driving fellow men."

Many in the urban labor force continued to do outwork at home. Every branch of industry, from metallurgy to toy manufacturing to food processing, employed women at home—and their work was essential to the family economy. They painted tin soldiers, wrapped chocolate, made cheese boxes, decorated porcelain, and polished metal. Factory owners liked to employ outworkers because their low piece rates made them desperate for work under any conditions, and they were willing to work extremely long days. A German seamstress at her new sewing machine reported that she "pedaled at a stretch from six o'clock in the morning until midnight. . . . At four o'clock I got up and did the housework and prepared meals." Owners could lay off women at home during slack times and rehire them whenever needed with less fear of organized protest.

Economic change and the periodic recurrence of hard times had uneven consequences for people's everyday lives. In the late nineteenth century, joblessness and destitution always threatened. Some city workers prospered by comparison to those left behind in rural areas, though a growing number lost the steadiness of traditional artisanal work. By and large, however, the urban working class was better informed, more visible, and more connected to the progress of industry and empire.

Reform Efforts for Working-Class People

The cycle of boom and bust, the uneven prosperity of industrialism, and the upheaval of migration caused social problems that many in the middle and upper classes sought to address through reform organizations and charities. Settlement houses, clinics, and maternal and child wellness societies seemed to rise overnight in cities, quickly becoming a common sight. Young men and women, often from universities, flocked to staff these new organizations, especially the settlement houses, where the reformers took up residence in poor neighborhoods to study and help the people. Believing in the scientific approach to social problems, they thought that study would uncover the causes of social ills and point the way to solutions. One group devoted to this enterprise was the Fabian Society in London, a small organization established in 1884. Committed to a socialism based on reform and state planning rather than revolution, the Fabians helped found the Labour Party in 1893 as a way of incorporating social improvement into politics. Still other reformers were motivated by a strong religious impulse. "There is Christ's own work to be done," wrote one woman who volunteered to inspect workhouse conditions. Religious fervor added a moral component to reform efforts.

Impelled as well by a Social Darwinist fear that Europeans would lack the fitness to survive in a competitive world, philanthropists, industrialists, and government agencies intervened more and more in the lives of working-class families. They sponsored health clinics and milk centers to provide good medical care and food for children and instructed mothers in child-care techniques, including breast-feeding—an important way, reformers maintained, to promote infant health. Some schools distributed free lunches, medicine, and clothing and inspected the health and appearance of their students. These attempts to improve urban life had their downside, however, as when government officials or private reformers deemed themselves the overseers of the working-class family and entered apartments with impunity. Such intrusions pressured poor, overworked mothers to conform to standards for their children—such as finding them respectable shoes and other clothing—that they often could not afford.

To counteract the burdens facing the working-class family, some professionals began to make available birth-control information in the belief that small families were more likely to survive the rigors of urban life. In the 1880s, Aletta Jacobs (1851–1929), a Dutch physician, opened the first birth-control clinic, which specialized in promoting the new, German-invented diaphragm. Jacobs was moved to act by the plight of women in Amsterdam slums who were worn out by numerous pregnancies and whose lives, she believed, would be greatly improved by limiting their fertility. But reformers were sharply divided over whether birth control was moral. Some also believed that contraception would increase the sexual exploitation of women if the threat of pregnancy and its responsibilities were overcome so easily.

Reproductive issues framed another significant government reform in these decades: legislation that would "protect" women from certain kinds of work. In such cases the fear was not that families were too large but that women were not producing healthy enough children and were stealing jobs from men. Moreover, protective legislation was considered crucial to national development; as one French official put it, such laws provided the foundation on which a nation could "achieve the plenitude of its economic and political power." Protection further divided work into jobs for men and jobs for women, which paid less. Women across Europe were barred from night work and from such "dangerous" trades as pottery allegedly for health reasons, even though medical statistics demonstrated that women became sick on the job less often than men. But lawmakers and workingmen claimed that women's work in potteries endangered reproduction, and women who had worked in the trade were forced to find other, lower-paying jobs or remain at home. The new laws did not prevent women from earning their livelihood, but they made the task harder by limiting their access to well-paying jobs.

Artistic Responses to Industrial and Imperial Change

In the 1870s and 1880s, the arts explored the consequences of global expansion and economic innovation, often in the same Darwinistic and gloomy terms that fed reformers' anxieties. Despite expansion and innovation, Darwin's theory held out the possibility that strong civilizations could fail to keep up with changing conditions and could thus decay and collapse. French writer Émile Zola (1840–1902), influenced by fears of social degeneration, produced a series of novels set in industrializing France about a family plagued by alcoholism and madness. Zola's protagonists, who led violent strikes and once even castrated an oppressive grocer, raised real anxieties about the future of civilization. Zola had less concern for exploring character than for describing the effects of industrial society on individuals: his *Au bonheur des dames* (*Women's Paradise*, 1883) depicts the supposedly refined upper-class shopper as a "queen drunk with love," all too quickly abandoning decorum to the "seductions" of the new department stores of Paris.

Other writers envisioned a widespread deterioration that threatened all of society—men and women, aristocrats and peasants, rural folk and urbanites, peasants and imperialists. Emilia Pardo Bazán (1859–1921) penned dramas of incest and murder among wealthy landowning families in rural Spain. In *The Mayor of Casterbridge* (1886), English novelist Thomas Hardy traced the path of a common man who sells his wife at a country fair and later rises to a position of power, only to find that he cannot escape his murky past. Hardy's vision was fatalistic; his characters battle forces beyond their control. Earlier urban writers such as Dickens had already brought attention to working-class lives, and now authors like Hardy examined rural conditions under the microscope of realism.

Some heroines were becoming more tough-minded. Norwegian playwright Henrik Ibsen (1828–1906) created the character of Nora, a woman who shocked audiences of *A Doll's House* (1879) by leaving a loveless and oppressive marriage. Olive Schreiner (1855–1920) went even further: in *The Story of an African Farm* (1889), the heroine rejects the role of submissive wife and describes the British Empire as a "dirty little world, full of confusion." By questioning British institutions, Schreiner, like Ibsen, helped launch a critical mindset about a range of social issues.

Creating new traditions or reviving old ones was another cultural response to the rapid, often disorienting pace of industrial and imperial change. Often these traditions served a unifying or nationalizing end. Country people used mass-produced textiles to design traditional-looking costumes and developed ceremonies based on a mythical past. Such customs amused city dwellers and brought tourist business to villages. So-called folk motifs also interested urban architects and industrial designers, who turned to rural artistic styles for models of household goods, decorative objects, and clothing. In the last decades of the century, architects copied Swiss chalets or Russian country homes to achieve a rustic look. Borrowing from Indian motifs, English designers William Morris (1834–1896) and his daughter May Morris (1862–1938) designed fabrics, wallpaper, and household items from such natural styles as the silhouettes of plants. Replacing what seemed "dead" and "ornate" styles of the early industrial years, "living flowers should inspire a living ornament," as May Morris explained. Some designers were inspired by socialist ideas and hoped the enthusiasm for handcrafted products would improve conditions for struggling artisans and help preserve unique styles in an age of increasing mass production.

Painters and sculptors, although patronized by wealthy collectors, continued to depend on the fancies of official taste. Government purchases of art for museums and government-sponsored exhibits of new works still determined an artist's success. But even artists in the government's good graces felt intense competition from a popular industrial invention—the camera. Photographers could produce cheap copies of paintings and create more realistic portraits than painters could, at affordable prices. In response, painters altered their style, at times trying to make their work look as different from photographs as possible.

As art departed from photographic realism, it nonetheless commented on the changing economic scene, especially the fact that a growing segment of service workers did less physical work and had more energy for leisure. The works of French painter Georges Seurat (1859–1891), for example, depicted the newly created parks with their walking paths and Sunday bicyclists; white-collar workers in their store-bought clothing, carrying books or newspapers, paraded like the well-to-do. Another French artist, Edgar Degas (1834–1917), focused on portraying women—from ballet dancers to laundry women—in various states of exertion and fatigue. Fatigue marked almost a romantic nostalgia for a past that was seen to require relentless physical labor from sunrise to sunset. When depicting the bleak outskirts of cities where industries were often located and where the desperately poor lived, Dutch-born Vincent Van Gogh (1853–1890) avoided the intense colors he typically used for the countryside.

Degas, Van Gogh, and Seurat, although their styles varied, have been characterized as avant-garde and impressionist. French artist Édouard Manet (1832–1883) used the term *impressionist* to emphasize the artist's attempt to capture a single moment by focusing on the ever-changing light and color found in everyday vision. Using splotches and dots, impressionists moved away from the precise realism of earlier painters; their challenge to the norm made impressionists simultaneously avant-garde. Claude Monet (1840–1926), for example, was fascinated by the way light transformed an object, and he often portrayed the same place—a bridge or a railroad station—at different times of day. Van Gogh used vibrant colors in great swirls to

Mary Cassatt, *In the Loge* (1879)
Cassatt patterned her work on artistic styles from East Asia. Sprigs of cherry blossoms and hairstyles that looked Chinese or Japanese often appeared in her paintings of mothers, children, and society women. Cassatt incorporated the color schemes from Japan, which poster artists were also using to advertise everything from world's fairs to cabarets and steamship travel. The arts of Asia and Africa were brightening the European public sphere.
The Hayden Collection, courtesy, Museum of Fine Arts, Boston.

capture sunflowers, corn stacks, and the starry evening sky. Such distortions of reality made the impressionists' visual style seem outrageous to those accustomed to realism, but others enthusiastically greeted impressionism's luminous quality. Industry contributed to the new style, as factories produced a range of pigments that allowed artists to use a wider, more intense spectrum of colors.

In both composition and style, impressionists borrowed heavily from Asian art and architecture. The concept of the fleetingness of situations came from a centuries-old and well-developed Japanese concept—*mono no aware* (serenity before and sensitivity to the fleetingness of life). The color, line, and delicacy of Japanese art (which many impressionists collected) is evident, for example, in Monet's later paintings of water lilies, his studies of wisteria, and even his re-creation of a Japanese gar-

den at his home in France as the subject for artistic study. Similarly, the American expatriate Mary Cassatt (1845–1926) used the two-dimensionality of Japanese art in her *In the Loge* (1879) and other paintings. Other artists, like Degas, imitated Asian art's use of wandering and conflicting lines to orchestrate space on a canvas, and Van Gogh filled the background of portraits with copies of intensely colored Japanese prints.

Music would soon be saturated with Asian influence too, but for the moment, like material culture, it was more likely to explore folk themes from hard-pressed rural life and to tout cultural nationalism. Czech composer Antonín Dvořák (1841–1904) employed popular national melodies in his *Moravian Duets* (1876) and *Slavonic Dances* (1878), and Norwegian composer Edvard Grieg's (1843–1907) music for Ibsen's play *Peer Gynt* (1875) integrated rural legends into music for urban audiences. In 1876, the most important operatic composer of the day, the anti-Semitic and increasingly reactionary Richard Wagner premiered his monumental cycle of four music dramas, *Der Ring des Nibelungen*. Although Wagner was steeped in Asian philosophy, the *Ring* was hailed as a triumphal celebration of German nationalism. While claiming to present universal beauty, music and the other arts were increasingly promoted as a national accomplishment, like empire. The work of Beethoven was now said to have made German unification possible by serving as a magnificent "call to battle." Thus the arts participated in nationalizing peoples thrown together by migration, technological change, and the forces of empire.

❖ The Birth of Mass Politics

Struggles for political voice, especially through the vote, accompanied imperial and economic expansion. The growth of industry and urban development heightened networks of political communication and consciousness, continuing the work of nationalizing institutions such as schools, urban agencies, and government bureaucracy. As national consciousness grew among workers, western European governments continued to allow more men to vote; even high-ranking politicians such as William Gladstone, the prime minister of Great Britain, had to campaign by railroad to win votes from a far-flung electorate. Although only men profited from electoral reform, the era's expanding franchise marked the beginning of mass politics—a hallmark of the twentieth-century West. Germany had manhood suffrage, but in more autocratic monarchies to the east—notably Russia and the Ottoman Empire—violence and ethnic conflict resulted from attempts to dominate minorities in ways that often resembled rule of colonized peoples.

Workers, Politics, and Protest

Despite widespread migration and social dislocation, workers coalesced politically to exert pressure on governments and businesses. Strikes and activism came in reaction to industrial innovation and an uneven economy, but community bonds forged by homemakers and neighborhood groups were a necessary precondition for collective worker action. School officials or police looking for truant children and delinquents met a phalanx of housewives ready to hide the children or to lie for their neighbors. When landlords evicted tenants, women would gather in the streets and replace household goods as fast as they were removed from the rooms of ousted families. Meeting on doorsteps or at fountains, laundries, pawnshops, and markets, women initiated rural newcomers into urban ways and developed a unity similar to that created by workers in the factory. Like strikes, other political activism grew not just from the shop floor but also in neighborhoods and on city streets.

Unions and Strikes. As the nineteenth century entered its final decades, the uncertainties of economic life led workers to organize formal unions, which attracted the allegiance of millions. Instead of simply gathering workers' contributions and paying out assistance in hard times, as the mutual aid societies had done early in the century, unions demanded a say in working conditions and aimed, as one union's rule book put it, "to ensure that wages never suffer illegitimate reductions and that they always follow the rises in the price of basic commodities." Strikes had occurred before the late nineteenth century, but in the wake of the revolutions of 1848 and the Paris Commune, businesses and governments viewed massive numbers of striking workers as the first step to political unrest and destructive violence. Even so, strong unions appealed to some industrialists because a union could make strikes more predictable (or even prevent them), present demands more coherently, and provide a liaison for labor-management relations.

From the 1880s on, the pace of collective action for more pay, lower prices, and better working conditions accelerated. In 1888, for example, hundreds of young women who made matches, the so-called London matchgirls, struck to end the fining system, under which they could be penalized an entire day's wage for being a minute or two late to work. This system, the matchgirls maintained, helped companies reap profits of more than 20 percent. Newspapers and philanthropists picked up the strikers' story, helping them win their case. Soon after, London dockworkers and gasworkers protested their precarious working conditions. Across Europe the number of strikes and demonstrations rose from 188 in 1888 to 289 in 1890. On May 1, 1890, sixty thousand workers took to the streets of Budapest to agitate for suffrage and safer working conditions. Day laborers on Hungarian farms struck in 1891.

Housewives, who often demonstrated in support of strikers, carried out their own protests against high food prices. In keeping with centuries of women's protest, they confiscated merchants' goods and sold them at what they considered a just price. "There should no longer be either rich or poor," argued organized Italian peasant women. "All should have bread for themselves and for their children. We should all be equal." Fearing threats to industrial and agricultural productivity, governments increasingly responded with force, even though most strikes were about the conditions of everyday life for workers and not about political revolution.

Craft-based unions of skilled artisans, such as carpenters and printers, were the most active and cohesive, but from the mid-1880s on, a *new unionism* attracted transport workers, miners, matchgirls, and dockworkers. These new unions were nationwide groups with salaried managers who could plan massive general strikes across the trades, focusing on such common goals as the eight-hour workday, and thus paralyze an entire nation. Although they never totally eliminated vibrant local or single-craft unions or religiously affiliated organizations, the large unions of the industrialized countries of western Europe, like cartels and trusts, increasingly influenced business practices and society's views of workers.

Political Parties. New political parties also engaged the masses in political life by addressing working-class issues. Workingmen helped create the Labour Party in England, the Socialist Party in France, and the Social Democratic Parties of Sweden, Hungary, Austria, and Germany—most of them inspired by Marxist theories. Germany was home to the largest socialist party in Europe after 1890. Historians attribute the extraordinary strength of the German Social Democratic Party, with its millions of voters, to the lack of middle-of-the-road alternatives to the conservative parties.

Workingwomen joined these parties, but in much smaller numbers than men. Not able to vote in national elections and usually responsible for housework in addition to their paying jobs, women had little time for party meetings. Furthermore, their low wages hardly allowed them to survive, much less to pay party or union dues. Many workingmen opposed their presence, fearing women would dilute the union's masculine camaraderie. Contact with women would mean "suffocation," one Russian workingman believed, and end male union members' sense of being "comrades in the revolutionary cause." The shortage of women's voices in unions and political parties paralleled women's exclusion from government; it helped make the middle-class belief in separate spheres part of a working-class ideology that glorified the heroic struggles of a male proletariat against capitalism. Marxist leaders continued to maintain that injustice to women was caused by capitalism and would disappear in the socialist society following the coming revolution. As a result, although the new political organizations encouraged women's support, they downplayed women's concerns about lower wages and sexual coercion.

Socialist parties attracted workingmen because they promised the triumph of new male voters who could become a powerful collective force in national elections. Those who accepted Marx's assertion that "workingmen have no country," however, wanted an international movement that could address workers' common interests. In 1889, some four hundred socialists from across Europe (joined by many onlookers and unofficial participants) met in Paris to form the Second International, a federation of working-class organizations and political parties replacing the First International founded by Marx before the Paris Commune. In

disarray after the bloody end to the Paris Commune and the outlawing of socialist parties in Germany between 1878 and 1890, socialists had nonetheless gained enormous strength from the growth of working-class organizations. Unlike the First International, this meeting adopted a Marxist revolutionary program from the start, but it also advocated suffrage where it still did not exist and better working conditions in the immediate future.

Members of the Second International determined to rid the organization of anarchists, who flourished in the less industrial parts of Europe—Russia, Italy, and Spain. In these countries anarchism attracted some industrial workers, but it got heavy support from peasants, small property owners, and agricultural day laborers, for whom the industrially based theories of Marx had less appeal. In an age of crop failures and stiff international competition in agriculture, many rural people looked to the possibility of life without the domination of large landowners and government. Many advocated extreme tactics, including physical violence and even murder. "We want to overthrow the government . . . with violence since it is by the use of violence that they force us to obey," wrote one Italian anarchist. In the 1880s, anarchists bombed stock exchanges, parliaments, and businesses and were punished for violence even without proof—as in the Haymarket Riot in Chicago in 1886, where political hysteria over anarchism caused the trial and execution of innocent anarchists and labor activists. "There are no innocents in bourgeois society," said one anarchist, echoing in reverse the general feeling toward his kind. Members of the Second International felt such random violence was counterproductive.

Outside the informal ties of neighborhoods and of the factory, a range of organizations forged worker solidarity through popular community activities that intertwined politics with everyday life. The gymnastics and choral societies that had once united Europeans in nationalistic fervor now served working-class goals. Songs emphasized worker freedom, progress, and eventual victory. "Out of the dark past, the light of the future shines forth brightly," went one Russian workers' song. Socialist gymnastics, bicycling, and marching societies rejected competition and prizes as middle-class preoccupations, but they valued physical fitness for what it could do to the "outer and inner organism" and for helping workers in the "struggle for existence"—a reflection of Darwinian thinking about "survival of the fittest." Workers also held festivals and gigantic parades, most notably on May 1, proclaimed by the Second International as a labor holiday. Like religious processions of an earlier time, parades were rituals that fostered unity. European governments at the time frequently prohibited such public gatherings, fearing they were tools for agitators.

Expanding Political Participation in Western Europe

Western European countries moved toward mass politics more rapidly than did countries to the east. Ordinary people everywhere in the West were becoming aware of politics through newspapers, which, combined with industrial and imperial progress, were an important nationalizing force. In western Europe in particular, people's access to newspapers and their political participation meant that politicians depended for election more on the will of the people and less on the power of small cliques.

Mass Journalism.   The rise of mass journalism after 1880 gave Europeans ready access to information (and misinformation) about politics and world events. The invention of automatic typesetting and the production of newsprint from wood pulp lowered the costs of printing; the telephone allowed reporters to communicate news to their papers almost instantly. Once philosophical and literary in content, daily newspapers now emphasized the sensational, using banner headlines, dramatic pictures, and gruesome or lurid details—particularly about murders and sexual scandals—to sell papers as well as their political point of view, whether it was liberal, conservative, or socialist. In the hustle and bustle of industrial society, one editor wrote, "you must strike your reader right between the eyes." A series of articles in 1885 in London's *Pall Mall Gazette* on the "white slave trade" warned the innocent not to read further. The author then proceeded to describe how young women were "snared, trapped," and otherwise forced into prostitution through sexual violation and drugs. Stories of imperial adventurers and exaggerated accounts of wasted women pottery or mine workers and their unborn babies similarly drew ordinary people to a mass, daily, and highly commercial press.

Journalism created a national community of up-to-date citizens, whether they could vote or not. Stories of crime and corruption appealed to the growing body of publicly educated, critical readers. Newspapers were not meant for quiet reflection at home or in the upper-class club but for quick reading on mass transportation and on the streets. Elites grumbled that the sensational press was itself a sign of social decay. But for up-and-coming people from the working and middle classes it provided an avenue to success. As London, Paris, Vienna, Berlin, and St. Petersburg became centers not only of politics but of news, a number of European politicians got their start working for daily newspapers. In this context of growing political literacy, politicians in western Europe sought to incorporate more people into the political process.

British Political Reforms.   In the fall of 1879, William Gladstone (1809–1898), leader of the British Liberals, whose party was then out of power, waged an experimental campaign in northern England and in Scotland for a seat in the House of Commons. During this campaign, Gladstone spoke before thousands of workingmen and -women, calling for greater self-determination in India and Africa and summoning his audiences to "honest, manful, humble effort" in the middle-class tradition of "hard work." Newspapers around the country highlighted his trip, and their reports along with mass meetings fueled public interest in politics. Queen Victoria bristled at Gladstone's speaking tour and at his attacks on her empire and vowed that he would never again serve as prime minister. Gladstone's Liberals won, however, and he did become prime minister.

Gladstone's campaign exemplified the trend toward expanded participation in Britain's political life. The process had begun with the Reform Bill of 1832, which extended the franchise to middle-class men. The Ballot Act of 1872 made voting secret, a reform supported by those who wished to limit the influence of landlords and employers, who without secrecy would know how everyone voted. Most significant, the Reform Act of 1884 doubled the electorate, to around 4.5 million men, enfranchising many urban workers and artisans and thus diminishing traditional aristocratic influence in the countryside.

As many British men entered political life as voters for the first time, Liberals and Conservatives alike found it necessary to establish national political clubs as a means to gain party loyalty. These clubs competed with the insular groups of parliamentary elites, who ruled through "wire-pulling," as one member of the House of Lords put it. These small cliques had heretofore determined the course of party politics. In contrast, broadly based interest groups such as unions, businessmen's associations, and national political clubs began to open up politics by appealing to many more voters.

British political reforms immediately affected Irish politics by arming disaffected tenant farmers with the secret ballot, making them less like colonized peoples than before. The political climate in Ireland was explosive mainly because of the repressive tactics of absentee landlords, many of them English and Protestant. These landlords evicted unsuccessful and prosperous tenants alike so they could raise rents for newcomers. In 1879, opponents formed the Irish National Land League and launched protests that charged the tense political atmosphere. Irish tenants elected a solid bloc of nationalist representatives to the British Parliament.

The Irish members of Parliament, voting as a group, had sufficient strength to defeat legislation proposed by either the Conservatives or the Liberals. Irish leader Charles Parnell (1846–1891) demanded support for home rule—a system giving Ireland its own parliament—in return for Irish votes. Gladstone, who served four nonconsecutive terms as prime minister between 1868 and 1894, accommodated Parnell with bills on home rule and tenant security. But Conservatives called home rule "a conspiracy against the honor of Britain." When they were in power (1885–1886 and 1886–1892), they cracked down on Irish activism. Scandals reported in the press ultimately ended Parnell's political career. The first came late in the 1880s, when journalists at the London *Times* fabricated letters implicating Parnell in the assassination of English officials. Parnell was cleared of this charge, but in 1890 the news broke of his affair with a married woman, and he died in disgrace soon after. Following his death, Irish home rule remained as divisive an issue as ever among the British.

France's Third Republic. In France, the Third Republic was a hotly contested political institution from its beginning in 1870 to its collapse seventy years later. Inflamed by the press, intrigue and scandal threatened popular politics in France,

Charles Parnell, Irish Hero
Charles Parnell gained the support of both the moderates and the radicals working for Irish home rule. Many saw Ireland as the first of England's colonial conquests—a land that was both ruled and exploited economically like a colony. Son of a landowning Protestant and a skilled parliamentary politician, Parnell threw himself into the Irish cause by paralyzing the British Parliament's conduct of business and was even able to bring down the government. In retaliation the government used forgeries and other unsavory means to destroy Parnell, but in the end scandal in his personal life lost him the vital support of the public.
Mary Evans Picture Library.

where universal manhood suffrage already existed as a result of classical liberalism's expansion to politics but where effective participation was still not secured. Following the Second Empire's defeat in the Franco-Prussian War, the Third Republic began shakily with monarchist political factions—Bonapartist, Orléanist, and Bourbon—struggling to control the National Assembly and to restore their respective families to power. But the republican form of government, which French supporters had been trying to solidify for almost a century, was saved when the compromise candidate of the monarchists, the comte de Chambord, stubbornly refused to accept the tricolored flag. Associating the tricolor with revolution, he would accept only the flag of the Bourbons and thus lost the chance to revive the monarchy. In 1875, a new constitution created a ceremonial presidency and a premiership dependent on support from an elected Chamber of Deputies. An alliance of businessmen, shopkeepers, professionals, and rural property owners hoped the new system would prevent the kind of strong-arm politics that had ended previous republics.

Fragile constitutional compromises, menaced by a highly partisan press, kept the Third Republic on shaky ground in the midst of destabilizing economic downturns, widespread corruption, and growing anti-Semitism. Support for the government was rocked by newspaper stories about members of the Chamber of Deputies selling their votes to business interests, and the press contributed to unrest by linking economic swings to the alleged machinations of Jewish businessmen. As a result, public sentiment turned against Jews for the failures of republican government and the economy. Confidence in republican politics plummeted in 1887 when the president's son-in-law was discovered to have sold memberships in the Legion of Honor. An aborted coup by the dashing and highly popular general Georges Boulanger soon thereafter showed the fragility of the republic, and thus of political liberalism. Had Boulanger not lost his will at the last moment, his followers might have thrust him into power, replacing a republic with a strongman yet again.

Republican leaders attempted to coalesce citizens by fortifying civic institutions, most notably by instituting compulsory and free public education through legislation in the 1880s. In public schools, secular, republican-minded teachers supplanted

Catholic clergy, who often favored a restored monarchy, and a centralized curriculum featured patriotic primers and courses in French geography, literature, and history. To perpetuate a republican ethos, the government established secular public high schools for young women, seen as the educators of future citizens. Mandatory military service for men inculcated the values of national identity and pride in place of regional and rural identities. In short, it turned peasants into Frenchmen.

Political Liberalism Refused. Although many western European leaders believed in economic liberalism, constitutionalism, and efficient central government, these ideals did not always translate into universal manhood suffrage and other forms of political liberalism in the less powerful western European countries. Spain and Belgium abruptly awarded suffrage to all men in 1890 and 1893, respectively, but both governments remained monarchies. Denmark and Sweden continued to limit political participation, and reform in the Netherlands in 1887 and 1896 increased manhood suffrage to only 14 percent. An 1887 law in Italy gave the vote to all men who had a primary school education, but this affected only 14 percent of the men.

In Italy the accession of liberals to power under the constitutional monarchy ironically led to decades of political and economic insecurity. The process of unification left a towering debt and massive pockets of discontent, including Catholic supporters of the pope and impoverished citizens in the south. Without receiving the benefits of nation building—the common experiences of compulsory education, urban improvements, industrial progress, and the vote—the average Italian feared the devastating effects of national taxes and the draft on the family economy.

Power Politics in Central and Eastern Europe

Germany, Austria-Hungary, and Russia diverged from the political paths taken by western European countries. These countries industrialized at varying rates—Germany rapidly and Russia far more slowly. Literacy and the development of a civic, urban culture were more advanced in Germany and Austria-Hungary than in Russia. Even Russia, however, saw the development of a modern press, although with a far smaller readership than elsewhere. Nonetheless in all three countries, agrarian political forces remained powerful, often working to block political, social, and economic change.

Bismarck's Germany. Bismarck had upset the European balance of power, first by humiliating France in the Franco-Prussian War and then by creating a powerful, unified Germany, exemplified in explosive economic growth and in rapid development of every aspect of the nation-state, from transport to its thriving capital city, Berlin (Map 24.3). His goals achieved, he now desired stability and a respite from war and so turned to diplomacy. Fearing that France would soon seek revenge against the new Reich and needing peace to consolidate the nation, he pronounced Germany "satisfied," meaning that it sought no new territory. To ensure Germany's long-term security in Europe, in 1873 Bismarck forged an alliance with Austria-Hungary and Russia, called the Three Emperors' League. The three conservative powers shared a strong interest in maintaining the political status quo.

MAP 24.3 Expansion of Berlin to 1914

"A capital city is essential for the state to act as a pivot for its culture," the German historian Heinrich von Treitschke asserted. No capital city grew as dramatically as Berlin after German unification in 1871. Industrialists and bankers set themselves up in the new capital, while workers migrated there for jobs, swelling the population. The city was newly dotted with military monuments and with museums to show off its culture.

At home, Bismarck, who owned land and invested heavily in industry, joined with the liberals to create a variety of financial institutions such as a central bank to further German commerce and industry. Bismarck aggressively opposed the Catholic church because its influence, especially in southern Germany and among ethnic minorities, impeded the growth of nationalist sentiment. Watching with alarm as the new Catholic Center Party made overtures to workers, he mounted a full-blown *Kulturkampf* (culture war). The government expelled the Jesuits in 1872, increased state power over the clergy in Prussia in 1873, and introduced obligatory civil marriage in 1875. Urged on by German liberals, Bismarck had miscalculated his own ability to manipulate politics. Both conservatives and Catholics rebelled against policies of religious repression.

The Kulturkampf ended during the pontificate of Leo XIII (r. 1878–1903), a cultured scholar and humanist who confronted the skeptical intellectual climate inhospitable to Catholicism and to religion in general. Encouraging up-to-date scholarship in Catholic institutes and universities, he also tried to develop an effective niche for Catholic politics by accepting aspects of democracy while opposing socialism. Because Catholicism had identified itself so strongly with monarchism, Leo's ideas marked a dramatic turn. His encyclical *Rerum Novarum* (1891), which articulated his political principles, urged Catholics to develop a social conscience that would allow for a rebirth of religious and political unity among the classes. During these dark days of war on Catholic culture, Leo's pontificate fortified beleaguered Catholics across Europe.

In a climate of economic crisis after the mid-1870s, Bismarck reevaluated Germany's situation and decided that the most pressing problems came not from Catholics but from social unrest and liberal economic policies. He stopped persecuting Catholics and turned his attention to socialists and liberals. He used unsuccessful assassination attempts on Emperor William I as a pretext to outlaw the Social Democratic Party in 1878. Simultaneously, hoping to wean the working class from socialism, Bismarck sponsored an accident and disability insurance program—the first of its kind in Europe and an important step in broadening the mandate of government to encompass social welfare. In 1879, he assembled a conservative

IMPORTANT DATES

1860s–1890s Impressionism flourishes in the arts; absorption of Asian influences

1870s–1890s Vast emigration from Europe continues; the new imperialism

1872 Bismarck begins the Kulturkampf against Catholic influence

1873 Extended economic recession begins; the impact is global

1876 Invention of the telephone

1882 The Triple Alliance formed between Germany, Austria-Hungary, and Italy

1882–1884 Bismarck sponsors social welfare legislation

1884 British Parliament passes the Second Reform Act, doubling the size of the male electorate

1884–1885 European nations carve up Africa at the Berlin conference

1888 Japan adopts constitution based on European models

1889 Socialists meet in Paris and establish the Second International

Reichstag coalition that put through tariffs protecting German agriculture and industry from foreign competition but also raising the prices of consumer goods. Ending his support for laissez-faire economics, Bismarck also severed his working relationship with political liberals.

Authoritarian Austria-Hungary. Like Germany, Austria-Hungary frequently relied on liberal economic policies and for a time in the 1870s even had political liberals in power. From the 1860s, liberal businessmen succeeded in industrializing parts of the empire, and the prosperous middle classes erected conspicuously large homes, giving themselves a prominence in urban life that rivaled the aristocracy's. They persuaded the government to enact free-trade provisions in the 1870s and to search out foreign investment to build up the infrastructure, such as railroads.

Yet despite such influences, Austria-Hungary remained resolutely monarchist and authoritarian. Liberals in Austria—most of them ethnic Germans—saw their influence eroded under the leadership of Count Edouard von Taaffe, Austrian

prime minister from 1879 to 1893. Taaffe built a coalition of clergy, conservatives, and Slavic parties and used its power to weaken the liberals. In Bohemia, for example, he designated Czech as an official language of the bureaucracy and school system, thus breaking the German speakers' monopoly on officeholding. Reforms outraged people at whose expense other ethnic groups received benefits, and those who won concessions, such as the Czechs, continued to clamor for even greater autonomy. In this way the government played nationalities off against one another and ensured the monarchy's predominance as the central mechanism for holding competing interest groups together in an era of rapid change.

Despite the success of these divide-and-rule tactics, Emperor Francis Joseph and his ministers feared the influence of the most powerful Slavic nation—Russia—on the ethnic minorities living within Austria-Hungary. Following its defeat in the Crimean War, Russia wanted to refurbish its tattered reputation as a great power, and to accomplish this goal it stirred up the emotions of discontented Slavs living in Austria-Hungary and in the Balkans under Ottoman rule. Slavophile Russian officials and journalists spread the gospel of Pan-Slavism, which could mean anything from loose cultural cooperation among Slavs to outright political union. Francis Joseph considered the Pan-Slavic movement dangerous to the stability of his empire.

The Balkans, where the competing forces of modernization and Ottoman decay aroused political ambition, became the scene of the next European struggle. Slavs of Bulgaria and Bosnia-Herzegovina revolted against Turkish rule in 1876, killing Ottoman officials. As the Ottomans slaughtered thousands of Bulgarians, two other small Balkan states, Serbia and Montenegro, rebelled against the sultan. Russian Pan-Slavic organizations sent aid to the Balkan rebels and so pressured the tsar's government that Russia declared war on Turkey in 1877, supposedly to protect Orthodox Christians. With help from Romania and Greece, Russia defeated the Ottomans and by the Treaty of San Stefano (1878) created a large, pro-Russian Bulgaria.

The Russo-Turkish War and the ensuing treaty sparked an international uproar that almost resulted in general war. Austria-Hungary and Britain feared that an enlarged Bulgaria would become a

Russian satellite that would enable the tsar to dominate the Balkans. British prime minister Disraeli moved warships into position against Russia. The public was drawn into foreign policy: the music halls and newspapers of England echoed a new *jingoism*, or political sloganeering that throbbed with sentiments of war. "We don't want to fight, but by Jingo if we do, We've got the ships, we've got the men, we've got the money too!"

The other great powers, however, did not want a European-wide war, and in 1878 they attempted to revive the concert of Europe by meeting at Berlin under the auspices of Bismarck, who saw this potential war as inopportune. The Congress of Berlin rolled back the Russian victory by partitioning the large Bulgarian state that Russia had carved out of Ottoman territory and denying any part of Bulgaria full independence from the Ottomans (Map 24.4). Austria occupied (but did not annex) Bosnia and Herzegovina as a way of gaining clout in the Balkans, and Britain received the island of Cyprus. Serbia and Montenegro became fully independent.

Nonetheless, the Congress failed to resolve the question of Slavic movements and Russian influence over them, and the Balkans remained a site of political unrest and great-power rivalries.

Following the Congress of Berlin, the European powers attempted to guarantee stability through a complex series of alliances and treaties. Anxious about Balkan instability and Russian aggression, Austria-Hungary forged a defensive alliance with Germany in 1879. The Dual Alliance, as it was called, offered protection against Russia, whose threat to Hungarian control of its Slavic peasantry, a German diplomat wrote, "was on [the Hungarian government's] mind day and night." In 1882, Italy joined this partnership (henceforth called the Triple Alliance), largely because of Italy's imperial rivalries with France. Trying to rebuild monarchical solidarity, Bismarck convinced both Austria-Hungary and Russia to join Germany in a revived Three Emperors' League, which lasted from 1881 to 1887. Because tensions between Russia and Austria-Hungary remained high, Bismarck signed

MAP 24.4 The Balkans, c. 1878

After mid-century, the map of the Balkans would almost constantly be redrawn. This resulted in part from the weakness of the dominant Ottoman Empire, but also from the ambitions of inhabitants themselves and from great power rivalry. In tune with the growing sense of national identities based on shared culture, history, and ethnicity, various Balkan peoples sought to emphasize small-group identities rather than merging around a single dominant group such as the Serbs.

the Reinsurance Treaty (1887) with Russia to stifle Habsburg illusions about having a free hand against rivals for Slavic loyalty.

Unrest in Russia. Although Russia enjoyed some international success during these decades, its internal affairs were in disarray. By 1871, the era of Great Reforms had run its course, and Russia remained almost the only European country without a constitutional government. Reform-minded youth increasingly turned to revolutionary groups for solutions to political and social problems. One such group, the Populists, wanted to rouse the debt-ridden peasantry to revolt. Other people formed tightly coordinated terrorist bands with the goal of assassinating public officials and thus forcing change. The secret police, relying on informers among the peasantry and the revolutionaries, rounded up hundreds of members of one of the largest groups, Land and Liberty, and subjected them to torture, show trials, and imprisonment. When in 1877 a young radical, Vera Zasulich, tried unsuccessfully to assassinate the chief of the St. Petersburg police, the people of the capital city applauded her act and acquittal, so great was their horror at the brutal treatment of young radicals from respectable families.

Writers added to the intense debate over Russia's future. Novelists Leo Tolstoy, author of the

Vera Zasulich
A radical activist, Vera Zasulich launched the violent phase in Russian protest when in 1877 she shot the governor-general of St. Petersburg after he ordered the beating of a political prisoner for not raising his cap to the governor. The religiously inspired daughter of a military official, Zasulich, like her two activist sisters, worked to mitigate the brutal conditions in her country. As reformers began to match the violence of the government, the assassination of Tsar Alexander II followed in 1881.
ItarTass/Sovfoto.

MAPPING THE WEST **The West and the World, c. 1890 ▶**

European influence was reaching its height in the late nineteenth century as European trade and political reach spanned the globe. Needing markets for the vast quantities of goods that poured from European factories and equally needing the raw materials to produce the goods, governments asserted that the Western way of life should be spread to the rest of the world and that resources would be best used by Europeans. Explorations and scientific discoveries continued both to build the knowledge base of European peoples and to enhance their ability for greater conquest. Simultaneously, millions of Europeans left their homes to find a better life elsewhere.

epic *War and Peace* (1869), and Fyodor Dostoevsky both opposed the revolutionaries' desire to overturn the social order; they believed that Russia above all required spiritual regeneration. Tolstoy's novel *Anna Karenina* (1877) tells the story of an impassioned, adulterous love affair, but it also weaves in the spiritual quest of Levin, a former "progressive" landowner who, like Tolstoy, eventually rejects modernization and idealizes the peasantry's tradition of stoic endurance. Dostoevsky had a different outlook and satirized Russia's radicals in *The Possessed* (1871), a novel in which a group of revolutionaries carries out one central act: the murder of one of its own members. In Dostoevsky's view the radicals could only act destructively and were incapable of offering any positive solution to Russia's ills.

The more radical revolutionary groups sought to change Russia by violent action rather than by spiritual uplift. In 1881, the People's Will, a splinter group of Land and Liberty impatient with its failure to mobilize the peasantry, killed Tsar Alexander II in a bomb attack. His death, however, failed to provoke the general uprising the terrorists expected. Instead the peasants thought the assassination of the "tsar liberator" was directed against them. Alexander III (r. 1881–1894), rejecting further liberal reforms that his father had proposed on the eve of his death, unleashed a new wave of oppression against religious and ethnic minorities and gave the police virtually unchecked power. Intensified Russification aggravated old grievances among oppressed nationalities such as the Poles, but it also turned the once-loyal German middle and upper classes of the Baltic provinces against Russian rule, with serious long-term consequences.

Colonial Empires. c. 1890

British
French
Portuguese
Italian
German
Spanish
Dutch
Russian

United States
Danish
Belgian
Japanese
Ottoman
Other countries

European migrations,
c. 1820–1910

ARCTIC OCEAN

PACIFIC OCEAN

INDIAN OCEAN

ATLANTIC OCEAN

ATLANTIC OCEAN

PACIFIC OCEAN

RUSSIA

Russians

CHINA

JAPAN

KOREA

Hong Kong (Br.)

PHILIPPINES

DUTCH EAST INDIES

SIAM
FR. INDO-CHINA

BURMA

INDIA

AFGHANISTAN

PERSIA

ARABIA

OTTOMAN EMPIRE

AUSTRIA-HUNGARY

GERMANY

ITALY

FRANCE

GREAT BRITAIN

NETHERLANDS

BELGIUM

DEN.

NORWAY AND SWEDEN

ICELAND

SPAIN

PORT.

TUN.

ALG.

TRIPOLI

EGYPT

RIO DE ORO

SENEGAL

GAMBIA

FR. GUINEA

SIERRA LEONE

LIBERIA

GOLD COAST

TOGO

SOKOTO SULTANATE

CAMEROON

GABON

CABINDA

ANGOLA

WALVIS BAY

GERMAN SOUTH-WEST AFRICA

CAPE COLONY

ORANGE FREE STATE

SOUTH AFRICAN REPUBLIC

PORTUGUESE EAST AFRICA (MOZAMBIQUE)

MADAGASCAR

SULTANATE OF ZANZIBAR

WITU

EQUATORIA

BR. SOMALIA

ETHIOPIA

NYINO

MAHDIST STATE

GREENLAND

CANADA

UNITED STATES

Alaska

MEXICO

BR. HON.

CUBA

VENEZUELA

COLOMBIA

ECUADOR

PERU

BOLIVIA

BRAZIL

FR. GUIANA

BR. GUIANA

DUTCH GUIANA

CHILE

ARGENTINA

FALKLAND IS. (Br.)

AUSTRALIA

NEW ZEALAND

New Caledonia (Fr.)

Fiji (Br.)

British

Scandinavians, Germans, British, Irish, Italians, Russians

Spanish, German, Italians

French

3,000 miles

0   1,500   3,000 kilometers

0   1,500   3,000 miles

The five million Russian Jews, confined to the eighteenth-century Pale of Settlement (the name for the restricted territory in which they were permitted to live), endured particularly severe oppression. Local officials instigated pogroms against Jews, whose distinctive language, dress, and isolation in ghettos made them easy targets in an age when the Russian government was enforcing cultural uniformity and national identity. Government officials encouraged people to blame Jews for escalating taxes and living costs—though the true cause was the policy of making the peasantry pay for industrialization by raising taxes.

Russia: The Pale of Settlement in the Nineteenth Century

As the tsar responded to internal turmoil with even greater repression, Bismarck's delicate alliance of the three conservative powers was unraveling. A brash but deeply insecure young kaiser, William II (r. 1888–1918), mounted the German throne in 1888. William chafed under Bismarck's tutelage, and his advisers flattered the young man into thinking that his own personal talent made Bismarck a hindrance, even a rival. William dismissed Bismarck in 1890 and, because he ardently supported German nationalism, let the alliance with Russia lapse in favor of a strong relationship with the supposedly kindred Austria-Hungary. Fatefully, he had opened the door to a realignment of the great powers. Unsettled internal politics in eastern Europe and the Balkans made the international scene more dangerous and unpredictable while imperial rivalries intensified antagonisms among the European nation-states and empires.

Conclusion

The period from the 1870s to the 1890s has been called the age of industry and empire because Western society pursued both these ends in a way that rapidly transformed Europe and the world. In these decades the West appeared at the top of its form. Industrial innovation and national growth caused much of Europe to thrive and become more populous and urban. Europeans proudly spread their "superior" culture globally and, like Marianne North, searched out whatever other peoples and places could offer by way of knowledge, experience, and wealth. The great powers undertook a new imperialism, and as they tightened connections with the rest of the globe, European culture, society, and everyday life also changed under the influence of other civilizations. In politics, reformers drew lower-class men into active citizenship by extending suffrage; humanitarian commitment prompted the development of philanthropic agencies and promoted the development of a more activist state that worked to make citizens of imperial countries more fit.

Yet as workers struck for improved wages and conditions and the impoverished migrated to find a better life, Western society showed its fissures and divisions. While newspapers, novels, and the arts helped inform people of profound social and international changes, they also raised questions about poverty and hopelessness. By the 1890s, the advance of industry and empire was bringing unprecedented tensions to national politics, the international scene, and everyday life around the globe. Racism, anti-Semitism, and ethnic chauvinism were spreading, sanctioned in most strata of society, and the costs of empire to conquered peoples were beyond measure.

Suggested References

The Advance of Industry

Industry advanced on every front, from the development of new products and procedures to the reorganization of work life and consumption. Trebilcock's classic work on the creation of an economic infrastructure contrasts with more recent studies (such as Rappaport's) on the impact of consumers and taste in driving economic change.

Coffin, Judith. *The Politics of Women's Work: The Paris Garment Trades, 1750–1915*. 1996.

Crossick, Geoffrey, and Serge Jaumin, eds. *Cathedrals of Consumption: The European Department Store, 1850–1939*. 1999.

Franzoi, Barbara. *At the Very Least She Pays the Rent: Women and German Industrialization*. 1985.

Good, David. *The Economic Rise of the Habsburg Empire.* 1984.

Marks, Steven G. *Road to Power: The Trans-Siberian Railroad and the Colonization of Asian Russia, 1850–1917.* 1991.

Rappaport, Erika. *Shopping for Pleasure: Women in the Making of London's West End.* 2000.

Trebilcock, Clive. *The Industrialization of the Continental Powers.* 1981.

The New Imperialism

New studies of imperialism show not only increasing conquest and the creation of an international economy but also the social and cultural impulses behind it. The University of Pennsylvania's African studies Web site offers an exciting look at African history, politics, and culture—some of it from this era. Depictions of African art and architecture, such as that confiscated for Western museums, are especially vivid.

African Studies Center: http://www.sas.upenn.edu/African _Studies/AS.html.

Baumgart, Winfried. *Imperialism: The Idea and Reality of British and French Colonial Expansion.* 1989.

Comaroff, Jean, and John Comaroff. *Of Revelation and Revolution: Christianity, Colonialism, and Consciousness in South Africa.* 1991.

Crosby, Alfred W. *Ecological Imperialism: The Biological Expansions of Europe, 900–1900.* 1993.

Ferro, Marc. *Colonization: A Global History.* 1997.

Hane, Mikiso. *Modern Japan: A Historical Survey.* 1992.

Harrison, Robert T. *Gladstone's Imperialism in Egypt: Techniques of Domination.* 1995.

Headrick, Daniel R. *The Tools of Empire: Technology and European Imperialism in the Nineteenth Century.* 1981.

Rotberg, R. I. *The Founder: Cecil Rhodes and the Pursuit of Power.* 1988.

Wesseling, H. L. *Divide and Rule: The Partition of Africa, 1880–1914.* 1996.

The Transformation of Culture and Society

Historians have come to see that industrial development and the spread of imperialism affected the smallest details of everyday life as well as the larger phenomena of class formation and massive regional and global migration. Beckles, Stodart, and Blakely give particularly rich portrayals of cultural mixture, exploitation, and resistance under the colonial regime.

Beckles, Hilary McD., and Brian Stodart, eds. *Liberation Cricket: West Indies Cricket Culture.* 1995.

Blakely, Allison. *Blacks in the Dutch World: The Evolution of Racial Imagery in Modern Society.* 1993.

*Bonnell, Victoria, ed. *The Russian Worker.* 1983.

MacKenzie, John. *The Empire of Nature: Hunting, Conservation, and British Imperialism.* 1988.

Maynes, Mary Jo. *Taking the Hard Road: Life Course in French and German Workers' Autobiographies in the Era of Industrialization.* 1995.

McKlintock, Anne. *Imperial Leather: Race, Gender, and Sexuality in the Colonial Contest.* 1995.

Moch, Leslie Page. *Moving Europeans: Migration in Western Europe since 1650.* 1993.

Worobec, Christine D. *Peasant Russia: Family and Community in the Post-Emancipation Period.* 1991.

The Birth of Mass Politics

Historical study of politics in this period entails looking at both government policies and the activism based on neighborhood solidarity, the growth of unions, and the rise of the mass media. The Avalon Project at the Yale Law School provides access to major treaties and conventions, making it an excellent resource for this period.

Applegate, Celia. *A Nation of Provincials: The German Idea of Heimat.* 1990.

Avalon Project at Yale Law School: http://www.yale.edu/ lawweb/avalon/avalon.htm.

Hoppen, K. Theodore. *Ireland since 1800: Conflict and Conformity.* 1999.

McReynolds, Louise. *The News under Russia's Old Regime.* 1991.

Rogger, Hans. *Jewish Policies and Right-Wing Politics in Imperial Russia.* 1986.

Ross, Ellen. *Love and Toil: Motherhood in Outcast London, 1870–1918.* 1993.

Todorova, Maria. *Imagining the Balkans.* 1997.

*Verga, Giovanni. *The House by the Medlar Tree.* 1981.

Weiner, Joel H., ed. *Papers for the Millions: The New Journalism in Britain, 1850s to 1914.* 1988.

---

*Primary sources.

Modernity and the Road to War

c. 1890–1914

I N THE FIRST DECADE OF THE TWENTIETH CENTURY, a wealthy young Russian man traveled from one country to another to find relief from neurasthenia, a common malady in those days. Its symptoms included fatigue, lack of interest in life, depression, and sometimes physical sickness. In 1910, the young man encountered Sigmund Freud, a Viennese physician whose unconventional treatment—eventually called *psychoanalysis*—took the form of a conversation about the patient's dreams, sexual experiences, and everyday life. Over the course of four years, Freud uncovered his patient's deeply rooted fear of castration disguised as a phobia for wolves—thus the name Wolf-Man by which he comes down to us. Freud worked his cure, as the Wolf-Man himself put it, "by bringing repressed ideas into consciousness." Freud's theories laid the groundwork for an understanding of the human psyche that has endured, with modifications and some controversy, to our own time.

The Wolf-Man was symptomatic of the age. Born into a family that owned vast estates, he reflected the growing prosperity of Europeans, albeit on a grander scale than most. Simultaneously, countless individuals seemed anguished and mentally disturbed, and suicides abounded—the Wolf-Man's own sister and father died from intentional drug overdoses. European society as a whole subjected itself to agonized questioning about the family, gender relationships, empire, religion, and the consequences of technology and progress. "Ours is a society ceaselessly racked," the novelist Émile Zola wrote in 1896: "We are sickened by our industrial progress, by science; we live in a fever, and we like to dig

Heading into War
In this colorful poster from 1907, itself a product of improved technology, a Belgian munitions factory displays all its peacetime wares, including a motorcycle. Dogs and rifles in tow, a group of men takes off to hunt in the latest automobile. The road to modernity was speedy and laden with new weaponry, as was the road to World War I.
Musée Communal de Herstal, Belgique.

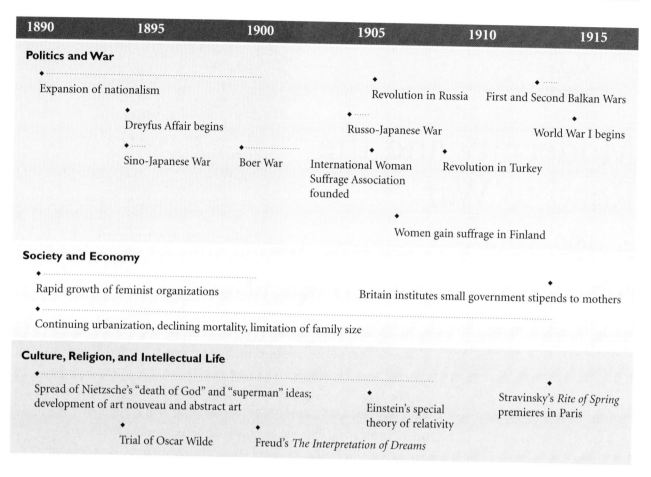

1890	1895	1900	1905	1910	1915

Politics and War

Expansion of nationalism

Dreyfus Affair begins

Sino-Japanese War   Boer War

Revolution in Russia   First and Second Balkan Wars

Russo-Japanese War   World War I begins

International Woman Suffrage Association founded   Revolution in Turkey

Women gain suffrage in Finland

Society and Economy

Rapid growth of feminist organizations

Britain institutes small government stipends to mothers

Continuing urbanization, declining mortality, limitation of family size

Culture, Religion, and Intellectual Life

Spread of Nietzsche's "death of God" and "superman" ideas; development of art nouveau and abstract art

Einstein's special theory of relativity

Stravinsky's *Rite of Spring* premieres in Paris

Trial of Oscar Wilde   Freud's *The Interpretation of Dreams*

deeper into our sores." Every sign of imperial wealth brought on an apparently irrational sense of Europe's decline. British writer H. G. Wells saw in this era "humanity upon the wane . . . the sunset of mankind."

Conflict reigned throughout Europe. Governments expanded the male electorate during this period in the hope of making politics more harmonious and manageable. Ethnic chauvinism, anti-Semitism, and militant nationalism only increased the violence of political rhetoric, however. Women suffragists along with politically disadvantaged groups such as the Slavs and Irish demanded full rights, but the liberal ethos of tolerance receded before a wave of political assassinations and public brutality. Colonized peoples developed a variety of liberation movements, many of them matching the progressive values but also the violence of the colonizing powers. At the same time, imperial competition among the great powers grew more heated, fueling an arms race that threatened to turn Europe, the "most civilized" continent in

the world according to its leaders, into a savage battleground.

These were just some of the conflicts associated with *modernity*—a term often used to describe the accelerated pace of life, the rise of mass politics, and the decline of a rural social order that were so visible in the West from the late nineteenth century on. (See "Terms of History," page 936.) *Modernity* also refers to the response of artists and intellectuals to this rapid change. The celebrated "modern" art, music, science, and philosophy of this period still resonate for their brilliant, innovative qualities. Yet these same innovations were often considered offensive at the time: cries of outrage at the new music echoed in concert halls, while educated people were utterly shocked at Freud's ideas that sexual drives motivate even the smallest children. Every advance in science and the arts simultaneously had consequences that undermined the middle-class faith in artistic and scientific progress.

When the heir to the Austro-Hungarian throne was assassinated in June 1914, few gave any thought to the global significance of the event, least of all Wolf-Man, whose treatment with Freud was just ending and who viewed that fateful day of June 28 simply as the day he "could now leave Vienna a healthy man." Yet the assassination was the catalyst for an eruption of political and societal discord that had simmered for several decades, as the nations of Europe lurched from one diplomatic crisis to another. The consequences of the resulting war, World War I, like the insights of Freud, would shape modern life.

❖ Private Life in an Age of Modernity

Transformations in private life accompanied industrialization, an improved standard of living, and the spread of democratic politics. A falling birthrate, a rising divorce rate, and growing activism for marriage reform provoked intense debate by the turn of the century. With relations between men and women changing, some imagined that distinct gender roles were disappearing. Women's visibility in

public life prompted one British songwriter in the late 1890s to write:

> Rock-a-bye baby, for father is near
> Mother is "biking" she never is here!
> Out in the park she's scorching all day
> Or at some meeting is talking away!

Some saw women's emergence into the public sphere as progress, others as decay. Homosexuality became a distinct way of life and a major political topic. This trend was seen as a sign of either modern enlightenment or sin, depending on one's point of view. Freud and other scientists tried to study such phenomena dispassionately and eventually formulated new theories of the human personality. Public discussions of private life—which often found their way into political rhetoric and social programs—demonstrated the interconnections of private and public concerns.

The Population Dilemma

Urgent population concerns clogged the agendas of politicians and reformers in the 1890s. (See "Taking Measure," below.) The staggering population

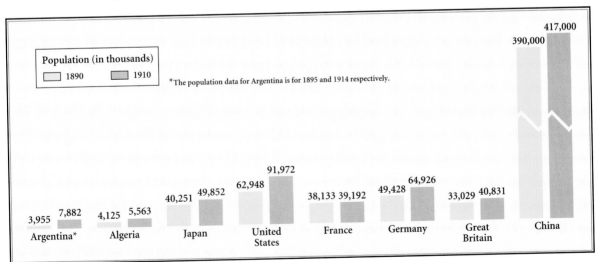

TAKING MEASURE Population Growth Worldwide, 1890–1910
Countries in the West were undergoing a demographic revolution in these decades as birthrates declined sharply. Yet population in many countries soared because of improved health, while other nations such as Argentina and the United States also received vast numbers of immigrants. Exceptions were China and other regions suffering the effects of imperialism; France's growth stagnated because the French had drastically curtailed reproduction beginning early in the century.

B. R. Mitchell, *International Historical Statistics: Africa, Asia, and Oceania, 1750–1993*, Third Edition (London: Macmillan Reference, 1998), 3, 56, 57; Mitchell, *International Historical Statistics: the Americas, 1750–1993*, Fourth Edition (London: Macmillan Reference, 1998), 6, 24; Mitchell, *International Historical Statistics: Europe, 1750–1993*, Fourth Edition (London: Macmillan Reference, 1998), 4, 8.

Modern

In one of his earliest writings from the first century, the Roman author Tacitus claimed that he could "hardly keep from laughing at some of the ancients, and from falling asleep at others."* He was advocating the distinct writing style of "our own day" and thus championing what we might call a "modern" approach to literature. But although he had the concept, there was not yet a word. *Modernus* was introduced into Latin only in the sixth century. After that, the idea of the "modern" can be found everywhere in the culture of the West. Shakespeare referred to "modern" ideas in his plays, and a huge quarrel erupted in the seventeenth century between the "ancients and the moderns" over whether people of earlier millennia should be imitated in their learning and style. By the second half of the nineteenth century, historians were heatedly debating where "modern" history began: with Abraham? with Charlemagne? with the Renaissance or the scientific revolution?

Despite the many claims to being "modern," the term has fastened itself most firmly around the period from the end of the nineteenth century through the first half of the twentieth. Its most specific historical use has been to describe the art, music, and dance that flourished at that time. When used in this sense, *modern* indicates a sharp break with lyrical romantic and classical music and dance and also with the conventions for representing objects in the arts. The blurred images of the impressionists and the jarring music of Schoenberg are part of modern art. The sexual rawness of *Madame Bovary* and *Les Fleurs du mal* (see Chapter 23) initiated a further ingredient into the multifaceted meanings of the word *modern* in the arts. Sometimes this intellectual break with the cultural past is referred to as *modernism*.

Simultaneously the term *modern* referred at the end of the nineteenth century to social phenomena. At this same historical moment, women who went to work or entered universities or began careers in the new field of social work were called "modern" women. They believed that by showing themselves capable and rational they could attain social progress and the end of

*"A Dialogue on Oratory," in *The Complete Works of Tacitus* (New York: Modern Library, 1942), 751.

---

increases of the eighteenth century had continued through the nineteenth. At the turn of the century, cities looked chaotic, filled with unwanted peoples of many ethnicities and races, as empire and industry changed the urban landscape. Influenced by Social Darwinist warnings of racial decay and armed with new types of statistical data, Western leaders faced a dramatic population dilemma.

Rising Population.   Across Europe, population in cities and countries soared. Germany increased in size from 41 million people in 1871 to 64 million in 1910; tiny Denmark, from 1.7 million in 1870 to 2.7 million in 1911. Such growth resulted from improvements in sanitation and public health that extended longevity and reduced infant mortality.

As people lived longer, cities struggled to cope with their burgeoning populations. Urban building, which disrupted the day-to-day life of millions, had consumed Paris and Vienna in the 1860s–1880s, and now Berlin, Budapest, and Moscow were torn apart and rebuilt. William II pulled down eighteenth-century Berlin and reconstructed the city with modern business and government buildings; the completion of new roadways and mass-transport systems helped push Berlin's population to over 4 million. In Moscow, an estimated 100,000 immigrants arrived each year from the countryside, and the Russian government undertook massive renovations. "Moscow has been transformed," reported a guidebook in 1903, becoming "overstimulating, full of bright colors that strike the eye and involuntarily attract attention." Rebuilding for population growth was not confined to capitals of the most powerful states: Balkan cities like Sofia, Belgrade, and Bucharest gained tree-lined boulevards, public buildings, and improved sanitation.

Falling Birthrate.   There was, however, a countertrend: while the absolute size of the population restrictions placed on them. Feminists were also called "modern" when they worked optimistically for improvement in the condition of women. Some of them lived different lives from those women who had large families and confined themselves to the domestic sphere. This departure from tradition also made them appear "modern."

In seeking an education and hoping for progress toward rationality and uniformity in the law, these women were invoking a meaning of the "modern" dating back to the Enlightenment. Progress, rational thought, and science have also been taken as the bedrock of the modern. Modern social theory, such as that of Freud, Weber, or Nietzsche, was so rationally oriented it even calculated the limitations in the attainment of social progress or the achievement of rational thought.

Modernization—another derivative of the term *modern*—refers to the kind of scientific and technological progress that came with industrialization and the rise of commercial agriculture as they began to shape the nineteenth and twentieth centuries. Indoor plumbing, electricity, telephones, and automobiles were signs of "modernity." As a result, "modern" artists painted teeming cities, industrial workers, world's fairs, and other scenes associated with "modernization" of the late nineteenth century. In the second decade of the twentieth century, other artists started converting parts of industrial products like the toilet and the automobile into works of art.

Modern may be so popular a term because it contains paradoxical meanings that make it multipurpose. While associated with the triumph of industry and rational thought at the turn of the century, cultural modernism brought a glorification of the so-called primitive and non-Western, whether in representational art, music, literature, or philosophy. The great innovative composer Richard Wagner gained his inspiration from Indian philosophy, while the philosopher Nietzsche read deeply in Asian religious writings. Picasso derived much of his "modern" style from African art, while the clean lines of "modern" architecture—the turn away from Victorian curlicues and gaudy colors—were modeled on the pure forms of native American, African, and Middle Eastern dwellings. Freud, it is suggested, gained his ideas for psychoanalysis from the various therapies of African and Asian peoples.

Complex, paradoxical, and dense with meaning, *modern* may not always be precise enough to be useful. But its very breadth explains why *modern* remains a crucial—and contested—term of history.

was rising in much of the West, the birthrate (measured in births per thousand people) was falling. The birthrate had been decreasing in France since the eighteenth century; other European countries began experiencing the decline late in the nineteenth century. The Swedish rate dropped from thirty-five births per thousand people in 1859 to twenty-four per thousand in 1911 and would fall even more in the next two decades. England and Wales experienced a similar slump, and even populous Germany went from forty births per thousand in 1875 to twenty-seven per thousand in 1913.

Community norms more than individual decision making had traditionally limited the size of families. For example, hard-pressed agrarian communities of early modern Europe often called for couples to postpone marriage until they were too old to produce large numbers of children. This group control had balanced population with resources, but rapid economic and social change broke the grip of community decision making. In an age of agricultural industrialization, farm families needed fewer hands and individual couples increasingly practiced birth control to limit their family's size. Abstinence was a common method, but the spread of new birth-control practices that would encompass most of the globe by the end of the twentieth century mainly accounted for modern Europe's ebbing birthrate. In cities, pamphlets and advice books for those with enough money and education spread information about coitus interruptus—the withdrawal method of preventing pregnancy. Technology also played a role in curtailing reproduction: diaphragms and condoms, improved after the vulcanization of rubber in the 1840s, proved fairly reliable in preventing conception. Abortions were legion in cities, with the most conservative figures showing that in Paris some 100,000 were performed annually during these decades.

Large German Family
Improved medicine, hygiene, and diet at the turn of the century helped more people survive infancy and childhood. Thus in many cases family size grew larger, as this photo from a working-class apartment suggests. Even those opposed to birth control were appalled that lower-class families were becoming larger than those of the "best circles," where family limitation was increasingly practiced.
AKG London.

The wider use of birth control stirred controversy. Critics accused middle-class women, whose fertility was falling most rapidly, of holding a "birth strike." Others thought women were creating an identity "independent of love"—that is, independent of men and motherhood. Anglican bishops, meeting early in the twentieth century, deplored family limitation, especially by artificial means, as "demoralizing to character and hostile to national welfare." In France, where fertility decline was startling, politicians worried about a crisis in masculinity. They suggested that men of the "best" classes were failing to produce new generations of leaders, and many feared that a declining population would keep France from competing militarily with Germany. As schools and industry took over the father's role of teaching sons a trade, moreover, critics charged that men had abandoned the family hearth for taverns or radical political activism. In response to these perceived problems, physicians, statisticians, and reformers founded the National Alliance for Increasing the French Population in 1896. At the same time German activists started the German League for the Preservation of the People.

The Social Darwinist focus on national peril in a menacing world converted the debate on family issues into anxieties over class and race. A falling birthrate among the middle and upper classes was seen as leading to social decay and national catastrophe. United States president Theodore Roosevelt (1858–1919), for example, warned that women's refusal to have large families "form[ed] one of the most unpleasant and unwholesome features of modern life." The "quality" of those being born worried activists and politicians: if the "best" classes had fewer children, they asked, what would society look like when peopled mostly by the "worst" classes? The decline in fertility, one German nationalist warned, would make the country a "conglomerate of alien peoples, above all Slavs and probably East European Jews as well."

The fear that one's nation or "race" was being polluted by the presence of "aliens," the mentally ill, the severely disabled, and "nonproductive" elderly was a feature of *eugenics*, a pseudoscience popular among wealthy, educated Europeans at the turn of the century. As a famed Italian criminologist put it, such classes were not people but "orangutans"; thus "the more reason for us to destroy them as soon as one is sure that they are and will remain orangutans." Applying Darwin's idea of the survival of the fittest to humans, eugenicists favored increased fertility for "the fittest" and limitations on the fertility of "degenerates," leading even to their sterilization or elimination. Politicians worked eugenicist rhetoric into electoral campaigns, inflaming fears of ethnic minorities and the poor where once they had sought consensus among all groups.

Reforming Marriage

An array of politicians, feminists, and population experts saw marriage reform as one way to address the problems of declining birthrates and a potentially "degenerate" population. Women, they felt, would be more inclined to reproduce if the shackles in the traditional system of marriage were removed and wives were no longer treated as second-class citizens. To win support for the passage of new laws, activists pointed out that for more than a century outmoded relationships such as those of master and slave or lord and serf had been eliminated but that married women still lacked basic rights. "Give birth, give birth, without stopping," one French woman complained, "but if married, your child will be the *property* of its father."

Feminists and reform-minded men successfully lobbied for changes in the legal relationships of married men and women. Across most of Europe, married women gained the legal right to their wages and to their own property. Sweden, which made men's and women's control over property equal in marriage, allowed women to work without a husband's permission. The German law code of 1900 eliminated phrases about women owing obedience to their husbands and about men's paternal power, although it limited divorce more than the earlier laws of some individual German states. Other countries, among them France (1884), legalized divorce and made it less complicated, and thus less costly, to obtain.

Reformers had good reason to believe that these legal changes would result in an upswing of the birthrate. Given the existing constraints of motherhood—no financial resources to leave the home, no legal rights to their own children, little recourse in the event of an abusive or miserable marriage—women were reluctant to have more than two or three, if any, children. Divorce would allow unhappy couples to separate and undertake a

new, more loving, and thus more fertile marriage. Greater financial parity in marriage was seen as a way to promote better health and a higher standard of living for women and their children. Swedish reformer Ellen Key (1849–1926) thought financially secure motherhood was a basic right of all women, married and single. Key, one of the most widely read reformers of the time, appealed both to "populationists" and to feminists in her advocacy of better living conditions for mothers and their children. By the early twentieth century, several countries had passed legislation that provided government subsidies to needy mothers. Great Britain, for example, mandated small maternal allowances in 1913. Like the earlier development of social security legislation in Germany and other countries, the system of subsidizing indigent mothers helped lay the foundations of the modern welfare state—a state concerned not only with war and diplomacy but with the everyday life of its citizens.

The conditions of marriage, motherhood, and other aspects of women's lives varied throughout Europe: women could get university degrees in Austrian universities long before they could at Oxford or Cambridge. A greater number of legal reforms occurred in western Europe, however. In much of rural eastern Europe the father's power over the extended family remained almost dictatorial. According to a survey of family life in eastern Europe in the early 1900s, fathers married off their children so young that 25 percent of women in their early forties had been pregnant more than ten times. A woman in Russia could obtain a divorce only if witnesses would testify that they had seen her husband having sex with another woman. Yet reform of everyday customs occurred, as community control gave way to individual practice in places, even though the pace of such change was slower than it was in western Europe. For instance, in some Balkan villages, a kind of extended-family system called the *zadruga* survived from earlier times, in which all the nuclear families shared a common great house, but now individual couples developed a degree of privacy by building one-room sleeping dwellings surrounding the great house. Among the middle and upper classes of eastern Europe, many grown children were coming to believe they had a right to select a marriage partner, not just to accept the spouse their parents chose for them based on economic or social reasons.

New Women, New Men, and the Politics of Sexual Identity

Rapid economic and institutional change set the stage for even bolder behaviors among some middle-class women, and the increasing availability of white-collar jobs for the educated meant that more European women could afford to adopt an independent way of life. So-called new women dressed more practically, with fewer petticoats and looser corsets, biked and hiked through city streets and down country lanes, lived apart from the family in women's clubs or apartments, and supported themselves. The growing number of women living on their own and freely moving in public spaces was a shocking phenomenon to the middle classes.

Many women acted in ways that further challenged accepted views of women's economic dependence and relative seclusion in the traditional middle-class family. Italian educator Maria Montessori (1870–1952), for example, went to medical school and secretly gave birth to an illegitimate child. Artists like the German painter Gabriele Münter lived openly with their lovers. Some writers portrayed these unconventional women sympathetically. Norwegian novelist and Nobel laureate Sigrid Undset in *Jenny* (1911) described an unmarried woman's reflections on her pregnancy: "She could provide for the child. . . . She had had enough of this sickly desire of clinging to somebody, to be cuddled and petted and called little girl." But in this time of social transformation, others protested the threat to gender roles: the new woman, German philosopher Friedrich Nietzsche wrote, had led to the "uglification of Europe."

Not just gendered behavior but sexual identity fueled discussion. Among books in the new field of "sexology," which studied sex scientifically from a clinical and medical point of view, *Sexual Inversion* (1894) by Havelock Ellis was popular. Ellis, a British medical doctor, postulated a new personality type—the homosexual—identifiable by such traits as effeminate behavior and a penchant for the arts in males and physical passion for members of their own sex in both males and females. Homosexuals joined the discussion, calling for recognition that they composed a legitimate and natural "third sex" and were not just people behaving sinfully. Much of this debate remained confined to physicians, psychologists, and intellectuals, but it

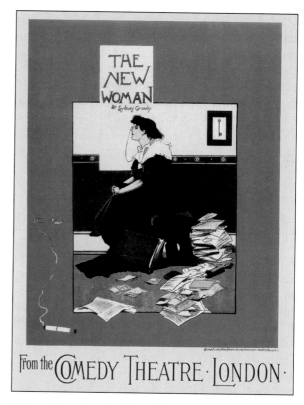

Sydney Grundy, *The New Woman* (1900)
By the opening of the twentieth century the "new woman" had become a much-discussed phenomenon. Artists painted portraits of this independent creature, while novelists and playwrights like Henrik Ibsen and Nobel Prize winner Sigrid Undset depicted her ambition to throw off the wifely role—or at least to shape that role more to her own personality. The new woman was also well educated: she had been to university, or wrote as a journalist, or entered professions such as law and medicine.
Jean-Loup Charmet.

began the trend toward considering sexuality in general as a fundamental part of human identity.

Sexual identity, including male homosexuality, became a wider public issue via the press. In the spring of 1895, reporters covered the trial of Irish playwright Oscar Wilde (1854–1900), who was sentenced to two years in prison for indecency—a charge that referred to his sexual affairs with young men. After Wilde's conviction one newspaper rejoiced, "Open the windows! Let in the fresh air!" The reading public lapped up such sensational stories. Beyond the infamous Wilde case, journalists revealed that married men of the ruling classes sometimes had sexual relations with other men. Between 1907 and 1909, for example, German newspapers publicized the courts-martial of men in Kaiser William II's closest circle who were condemned for homosexuality and transvestitism.

Attention to sexual behavior intensified concerns about falling birthrates and the solidity of the family. During the scandals over the kaiser's entourage, the public received assurances from the government itself that William's own family life "provides the entire country with a fine model." In a time of growing nationalism, sexuality took on patriotic overtones: the accused homosexual elite in Germany were said by journalists to be out to "emasculate our courageous master race." Although these cases paved the way for growing sexual openness in the next generations, sexual issues would simultaneously become regular weapons in politics.

Sciences of the Modern Mind

Scientists also found cause for alarm when they looked at population and the conditions of everyday life in industrial society and discovered a host of complaints such as fatigue and irritability. Most of these illnesses originated in the "nerves," they reasoned, which were troubled by the hectic pace and demands of urban living. Sciences of the mind such as psychology and psychoanalysis arose to treat everyone, not just the insane.

New Approaches to Mental Ailments. Nervous illness was yet another cause of national decline, according to Social Darwinists. A rash of books in the 1890s expounded on this subject. The most widely translated of them, *Degeneration*, written by Hungarian-born physician Max Nordau (1849–1923), blamed overstimulation for both individual and national deterioration. According to Nordau, increasingly bizarre modern art, male lethargy, and female hysteria were all symptoms of overstimulation and reflected a general downturn in the human species. The standard Social Darwinist cure for such mental decline was imperial adventure, renewed virility, and increased childbearing.

Medical scientists promised new and better approaches to nervous ailments. Some researchers attempted to classify and quantify mental characteristics. Italian psychiatrist Cesare Lombroso (1836–1909) devised typologies for criminal minds by evaluating the physical features of deviants and created the field of criminology. The French psychologist Alfred Binet (1857–1911) designed intelligence tests that he maintained could measure the capacity of the human mind more accurately than schoolteachers could. In Russia, physiologist Ivan Pavlov (1849–1936) proposed that conditioning

Oscar Wilde
The Irish-born writer Oscar Wilde symbolized the sufferings experienced by homosexuals in the late nineteenth century. Tried for and convicted of having sexual relations with another man, Wilde served time in prison—a humiliation for a husband, father, acclaimed author, and witty playwright. Wilde's writings aimed to suggest that the complexities of human society made narrow moral codes harmful.
Library of Congress.

mental reflexes—that is, causing a subject to associate a desired response with a previously unrelated stimulus—could modify behavior. His most famous case involved a dog. Knowing that the dog would begin to salivate after seeing its food, Pavlov rang a bell to announce dinner. Once he established the connection between the sound of the bell and the sight of the food, Pavlov withdrew the food and found that the dog would still salivate (the desired response) when the bell rang (the previously unrelated stimulus). Such experiments formed the basis of modern psychology.

Freud and Psychoanalysis. Sigmund Freud (1856–1939) devised an approach to modern anxieties that, he claimed, avoided traditional moral evaluations of human behavior. He became convinced that the human psyche was far from rational. Dreams, he explained in *The Interpretation of Dreams* (1900), reveal a repressed part of personality—the

"unconscious"—where all sorts of desires are more or less hidden. These desires appear only involuntarily, in the form of dreams, symptoms of physical illness, and abnormal behavior. Freud also believed that the human psyche is made up of three competing parts: the ego, the part that is most in touch with external reality; the id (or libido), the part that contains instinctive drives and sexual energies; and the superego, the part that serves as the force of conscience. Like Darwin's ideas, Freud's notions challenged accepted liberal belief in a unified, rational self that acted in its own interest. They also undermined the social implications of this belief, namely, that society would move in a consistently progressive direction.

Freud shocked many contemporaries by insisting that all children have sexual drives from the moment of birth, but he also believed that many of these sexual impulses have to be repressed for children to attain maturity and for society to remain

Freud's Office

Sigmund Freud's therapy room, where his patients experienced the "talking cure," was filled with imperial trophies such as Oriental rugs and African art objects. Freud himself was fascinated by cures brought about through shamanism, trances, and other practices of non-Western medicine as well as through drug-induced mental states. In 1938, Freud fled to England to escape the Nazis. This photo shows his office in London.

Mary Evans Picture Library/Sigmund Freud copyrights.

civilized. Attaining one's adult sexual identity is always a painful process because it depends on repressing infantile urges, which include bisexuality and incest. Thus, the Wolf-Man's nightmare of white wolves outside his window symbolized his unresolved sexual feelings for members of his family. Freud claimed that certain aspects of gender roles—such as motherhood—are normal and that throughout their lives women in general achieve far less than men do. At the same time, he believed that adult gender identity results not from anatomy alone (motherhood is not the only way to be female) but from inescapable mental processing of life experiences as well. He thus made gender more complicated than simple biology would suggest. Finally, Freud's psychoanalytic theory maintained that girls and women have powerful sexual feelings, an assertion that broke with ideas of women's passionlessness.

The influence of psychoanalysis became pervasive in the twentieth century. For example, free association of ideas and interpretation of dreams are mainstays in psychoanalysis: the "talking cure," as it was quickly labeled, gave rise to a general acceptance of talking out one's problems. (Ironically, Freud always had his patients lie on a couch facing away from him because he did not like to be looked at by his patients when they spoke.) As psychoanalysis became a respected means of recovering mental health, terms such as *neurosis, unconscious,* and *libido* came into widespread use, and patients faced little social stigma.

Yet despite its revolutionary content and impact, psychoanalysis reflected the many contradictions at work in turn-of-the-century Europe. For example, Freud attributed girls' complaints about unwanted sexual advances or abuse to fantasy caused by "penis envy," an idea that led members of the new profession of social work to believe that most instances of such abuse had not actually occurred. On the one hand, Freud was a meticulous scientist, examining symptoms, urging attention to the most minute evidence from everyday life, and demanding that sexual life be regarded with a rational rather than a religious eye. On the other hand, he was a pessimistic visionary who had abandoned the optimism of the Enlightenment and pre-Darwinian science by claiming that humans were motivated by irrational drives toward death and destruction and

that these shaped society's collective mentality. Freud would later interpret World War I's vast devastation of humanity as bearing out his bleak conclusions. (See "New Sources, New Perspectives," page 944.)

❖ Modernity and the Revolt in Ideas

Although the intellectuals and artists who participated in the turmoil of turn-of-the-century society did not know it at the time, their rejection of accepted values, beliefs, and artistic forms announced a new era. Philosophers who emphasized the role of the irrational and the accidental in day-to-day life challenged the belief that fundamental social laws could be discovered. In science, theories that time is relative and that energy and mass are interchangeable rocked established truths about time, space, matter, and energy. Art and music became unrecognizable. Artists and musicians who deliberately produced shocking, lurid works were, like Freud, heavily influenced by advances in science and critical thinking. Amidst contradictions such as the blending of the scientific and the irrational, intellectuals and artists helped launch the disorienting revolution in ideas and creative expression that we now identify collectively as *modernism.*

The Challenge to Positivism

Late in the nineteenth century, many philosophers and social thinkers rejected the century-old faith that in science one could discover enduring social laws based on rationally determined principles. This belief, called *positivism,* had emphasized the permanent nature of fundamental laws and had motivated reformers' attempts to perfect legislation based on studies of society. Challenging positivism, the philosophers Wilhelm Dilthey (1833–1911) in Germany and John Dewey (1859–1952) in the United States declared that human understanding was founded on the conditions of day-to-day existence. Because experience is ever changing, theories and standards cannot be constant or enduring. And just as scientific theory was modified over time, so must social theories and practice react pragmatically to the immediate conditions at hand.

Psychohistory and Its Lessons

In the nineteenth century, history books mostly told about the workings of public officials, religious institutions, and dynasties. They recounted the deeds of kings and emperors, discussed royal genealogy, and described wars and peace treaties. Determined to be factual, historians laid out the fine points of laws, charters, and treaties along with battles, strategies, and territorial gains whose records lay in official state archives.

Much has changed since then, partly because of the rise of psychology and psychoanalysis as the twentieth century opened. Confronted with strikes, mass demonstrations, anarchist deeds, anti-Semitism, and other forms of political violence, some observers tried to explain a phenomenon they called *crowd psychology*. According to this view, neither political ideas alone nor the actions of a politician as described in parliamentary records gives the full account of the past. Instead, new social observers suggested that psychic states are important factors in shaping some public events.

Not surprisingly, Sigmund Freud studied great historic figures like Leonardo da Vinci from a psychoanalytic perspective, exploring the person's work in relation to repressed childhood fantasies. Freud also explained the outbreak of World War I as more of a psychic than a diplomatic event. He showed the ways in which the war's pursuit could be connected to a form of collective death wish. In his studies, both individual and national histories were susceptible to psychoanalytic accounts.

It was not until the 1950s, however, that prominent historians turned to psychoanalysis, devising from it a genre called *psychohistory*. In 1957, William Langer, president of the American Historical Association, charged his fellow scholars with using a foolish conservatism in their methods. Unlike scientists, he claimed, historians did not experiment in their historical work, for instance by adopting new ideas like psychoanalysis that might advance their understanding of the past. Others joined the debate, finding the traditional history that ascribed actions to ambition, greed, hate, and great intelligence as superficial in its argument and lacking in explanatory force. Or they criticized it for attributing historical events to social forces and thereby discounting any kind of personal agency. A third criticism of history by those interested in psychology and psychoanalysis was that, if it did take human agency into account, it usually saw historical figures as acting rationally in their self-interest. Trauma, the irrational, uncontrollable drives, and unconscious motivations had no role to play in understanding historical figures.

Soon thereafter a major study by the German-born psychoanalyst Erik Erikson, *Young Man Luther* (1958), announced that the Protestant Reformation originated in the childhood traumas of Martin Luther. Identity crises stemming from his relationship with his father caused Luther to search for and reject father figures, not only his own father but the pope. Erikson's book caused a stir among historians, changing the way people approached Luther but also causing resistance. Not only did one need to know a great deal of psychology to duplicate Erikson's effort, one almost had to exclude other influences that historians considered important.

Not surprisingly, some of the most compelling examples of psychohistory have focused on the lives of individuals and the development of political movements that occurred during the period when Freud was setting the terms for psychoanalysis, roughly from the end of the nineteenth century to the beginning of World War II. Historians interested in psychoanalysis have tried to find in Kaiser William II's childhood answers to his rejection of Bismarck, his turn to an aggressive foreign policy, and his participation in World War I. Nietzsche's and Freud's intimate friend Lou Andreas-Salomé, a powerful intellectual during these years, was seen as having a "bisexual" personality because she published her writing, an occupation that suggested a masculine nature.

Kaiser William and Edward VII's Family

Psychotherapy aimed to cure the individual in good part by discussing family relationships and the fantasies built around them. Psychohistory often draws its analyses from these same relationships, as in the case of Martin Luther, for example, and his father. The royal families of Europe are ripe for such analysis because, as the photo shows, German and British monarchs (Edward VII, right; and William, second from right) were closely related; so too were the Russians, Germans, and British. These relationships raise potential questions about the outbreak of World War I.
Hulton Getty Picture Library/Liaison Agency.

On a collective level, analyses of Hitler's and Mussolini's followers have seen mass psychic needs and traumas as motivating their blind worship of these vicious dictators. But the intense nationalism that most people in the modern world have increasingly felt for their countries has also become a phenomenon that psychohistorians examine.

Psychohistory remains controversial to this day. While its practitioners expand the field of historical explanation, its critics find that it can be formulaic by fitting the behavior of historical characters into Freud's schema. Other critics find that psychohistory is too imprecise and speculative because it is not based on the same kinds of hard, documentary evidence that historians have been trained to use. Nonetheless, psychohistorians have made a good case that if we are going to look at personalities, character, and relationships, we should do so in the most informed way possible. Their rationale makes psychohistory a necessity.

QUESTIONS FOR DEBATE

1. What are the advantages and disadvantages of psychohistory?

2. How would you set out to investigate the psychological reasons for the actions of William II, Emmeline Pankhurst, Marie Curie, or Gavrilo Princip? Would you look at their character, their childhood, their social background, or other parts of their lives?

3. Can we write history without investigating psychology? Should we avoid "psychologizing" when thinking about the past?

FURTHER READING

Rudolph Binion, *Frau Lou: Nietzsche's Wayward Disciple.* 1968.

Erik Erikson, *Young Man Luther: A Study in Psychoanalysis and History.* 1958.

Journal of Psychohistory.

Thomas A. Kohut, *Wilhelm II and the Germans: A Study in Leadership.* 1991.

The turn-of-the-century thinkers, called *relativists* and *pragmatists*, influenced thinking about society throughout the twentieth century.

In the same vein, German sociologist and political theorist Max Weber (1864–1920) was pessimistic about the ability of government bureaucracy—once seen as a rational alternative to monarchy—to deal effectively with all the variables of modern society. Watching government and the electorate expand, Weber maintained that the sheer numbers involved in policymaking would often make decisive action impossible—especially in times of crisis, when a charismatic leader might usurp power because of his ability to make flexible and instinctive decisions. Thus the development of impartial forms of government such as bureaucracy carried the potential for undermining the rule of law and for eroding the modern commitment to constitutional government.

The most radical and influential of these scholars was the German philosopher Friedrich Nietzsche (1844–1900). Early in his career he developed one of his most challenging ideas, based on the distinction between the "Apollonian," or rational, side of human existence and the "Dionysian" side, with its expression of more primal urges. Nietzsche believed that people generally cling to the rational, Apollonian explanations of life because Dionysian ideas about nature, death, and love such as those found in Greek tragedy are too disturbing. Nietzsche maintained that all assertions of scientific fact and theory were mere illusions. Knowledge of nature had to be expressed in mathematical, linguistic, or artistic representation; truth thus existed only in the representation itself, for humans could never experience unfiltered knowledge of nature or reality. This aspect of Nietzsche's philosophy would lead to the late-twentieth-century school of thought called *postmodernism*.

Much of Nietzsche's writing took the form of aphorisms—short, disconnected statements of truth or opinion—a form that broke with the logical rigor of traditional Western philosophy. Nietzsche used aphorisms to convey the impression that his ideas were a single individual's unique perspective, not universal truths that thinkers since the Enlightenment had claimed were attainable. Influenced by a range of Asian philosophy, Nietzsche was convinced that late-nineteenth-century Europe was witnessing the decline of dogmatic truth, most notably in religion—hence his announcement that

"God is dead, we have killed him." Far from arousing dread, the death of God, according to Nietzsche, would give birth to a joyful quest for new "poetries of life" to replace worn-out religious rules. Not the rule-bound bourgeois but the untethered "superman" was Nietzsche's highly influential model.

Nietzsche's thought was inspiring from the outset, but over time it would be used for destructive ends. As a teacher he was so compelling that his first students thought they were hearing another Socrates. But after he contracted syphilis and became insane for the last eleven years of his life, his sister endeavored to spread his fame. Most important for twentieth-century politics, she edited Nietzsche's diatribes against middle-class values into attacks on Jews. She revised his concepts about each individual's "will to power" and of "superman" so as to advocate displays of military might. The popular teachings of French philosopher Henri Bergson (1859–1941) were similarly distorted. Bergson proposed the existence of an *élan vital*, or intuitive creative force, that could spark individuals and nations to superior accomplishments. Racists, nationalists, and militarists reduced these very complicated philosophies to simple-minded creeds that justified violent anti-Semitism and competition for empire.

Revolutionizing Science

While philosophers questioned the ability of science to provide timeless truths, scientific inquiry itself flourished. The scientific method gained authority beyond the traditional sciences, especially in fields such as history and psychology, and many people still held to positivist assumptions that natural laws could be understood and the universe consequently mastered. Technological breakthroughs, improvements in hygiene, and other fruits of scientific inquiry earned science great prestige with the public. Around the turn of the century, however, discoveries by pioneering researchers shook the foundations of traditional scientific certainty and challenged accepted knowledge about the nature of the universe.

Some scientists' findings undermined the principles of time, space, matter, energy, and the immutability of physical entities on which science had rested since Isaac Newton two centuries earlier. In 1896, Antoine Becquerel (1852–1908) discovered

Marie Curie and Her Daughter
Recipient of two Nobel Prizes, Marie Curie came from Poland to western Europe to study science. Curie's extraordinary career made her the epitome of new womanhood; her daughter Irene Joliot-Curie followed her mother into the field and also won a Nobel Prize. Both women died of leukemia caused by their exposure to radioactive materials. Today a reconstruction of the Curie laboratory as a museum contains a display of the intense radioactivity still in scientific instruments they used a century ago. ACJC–Archives Curie et Joliot-Curie.

radioactivity and suggested the mutability of elements by the rearrangement of their atoms. French chemist Marie Curie (1867–1934) and her husband, Pierre Curie (1859–1906), isolated the elements polonium and radium, which are more radioactive than the uranium Becquerel used. From these and other discoveries, scientists concluded that atoms are composed of subatomic particles moving about a core. Instead of being solid, as scientists had believed since ancient times, atoms are largely empty space and act not as a concrete substance but as an intangible electromagnetic field. German physicist Max Planck (1858–1947) announced his influential quantum theorem in 1900; it demonstrated that energy is emitted in irregular packets, not in a steady stream.

New research transformed astronomy as well as physics. Scientists had already demonstrated that light has a uniform velocity regardless of the direction it travels from the earth and that the velocity is not relative to the motion of the earth. Thus older theories of light on which scientists had relied were no longer tenable. It was in this unsettled situation that physicist Albert Einstein (1879–1955) published his special theory of relativity in 1905. Einstein, who had been expelled from high school as a disruptive influence on other students, had later studied physics with teachers ignorant of the intellectual transformation taking place in sci-

entific thought. But on his own, working in a Swiss patent office, he proclaimed in his 1905 paper that space and time are not absolute categories but instead vary according to the vantage point of the observer. Only the speed of light is constant. That same year he also suggested that the solution to problems in Planck's quantum theorem lay in considering light both as little packets *and* as waves. These theories continued to undercut Newtonian physics as well as commonsense understanding.

Einstein later proposed yet another blurring of two distinct physical properties, mass and energy. He expressed this equivalence in the formulation of $E = mc^2$, or energy equals mass times the square of the speed of light. In 1916, his general theory of relativity connected the force, or gravity, of an object with its mass and postulated a fourth mathematical dimension to the universe. Much more lay ahead, once Einstein's theories of energy were developed: television, nuclear power, and, within forty years, nuclear bombs.

The findings of Planck, Einstein, and others revolutionized the physical sciences, but these theories were often not accepted immediately largely because power and time-honored beliefs were at stake. Einstein struggled against mainstream science and its professional institutions. Even Planck, who had excellent university positions because of family connections, tried desperately for years to get senior researchers to accept his findings. Marie Curie faced such resistance that even after she became the first person ever to receive a second Nobel Prize (1911), the prestigious French Academy of Science turned down her candidacy for membership that year.

These prejudices ultimately broke down. Max Planck institutes were established in German cities, streets across Europe were named after Marie Curie and other scientific pioneers, and Einstein's name became synonymous with genius. These scientists achieved what historians call a *paradigm shift*—that is, in the face of understandable resistance they transformed the foundations of science and came themselves to supersede other names.

Religion Confronts Modernity

A growing acceptance of scientific and social scientific accounts of human society led to a decline in religious fervor among urban elites and the working class alike. Migration and urbanization also loosened the churches' social power. "The educated middle class, especially the young people, are losing touch altogether with the House of God," one Protestant clergyman wrote in 1911. Wealthy Catholic men often tended their businesses or played sports rather than attending Mass. Religion, for some men, was best left to women.

Churches fought secularization. Some theologians wanted to modernize religion by applying scholarly methods to the Bible, although many, especially papal policymakers, opposed liberalization to regain lost prestige and active church members. Pius X (r. 1903–1914) condemned Catholic modernists who wanted Catholicism to reconcile with scientific claims. Some Protestants and Catholics took a different approach by countering intellectual and political challenges to their authority through increased missionary efforts abroad and among the urban poor. Pope Leo XIII (r. 1878–1903) called for a more active ministry among the working classes; in response, the church in Hungary channeled some of its efforts away from its traditional constituency in villages and toward ministering to workers in cities. In Austria-Hungary, Francis Joseph and his officials, faced with mounting discontent, strictly observed the rituals of their Catholic faith hoping they would draw the masses away from spectacles such as the annual workers' May Day parade. In Orthodox Russia, the reactionary policies of Alexander III (r. 1881–1894) and his son Nicholas II (r. 1894–1917) opposed freethinking in both intellectual and religious matters. They equated the Orthodox religion with political loyalty.

Modern Art

The same conflicts between traditional values and new ideas raged in the arts, as artists distanced themselves from classical Western norms and from the conventions of polite society. Their rebellion, however, was far more disorganized than the

Pablo Picasso, *Les Demoiselles d'Avignon* (1907)
Impressionists had borrowed heavily from Asian art, but many artists in Pablo Picasso's generation leaned on Africa for inspiration. In Les Demoiselles d'Avignon, *Picasso used the elongated, angular limbs found in African carvings, while the faces resemble African masks. The artists Amadeo Modigliani, Barbara Hepworth, and Constantin Brancusi excelled in sculpture featuring the smooth forms and lively compositions of African wooden statuary.*
PICASSO, Pablo. *Les Demoiselles d'Avignon*. Paris (June – July 1907). Oil on canvas, 8' × 7'8". The Museum of Modern Art, New York. Acquired through the Lillie P. Bliss Bequest. Photograph © The Museum of Modern Art, New York © 2001 Estate of Pablo Picasso/ Artists Rights Society, NY.

impressionist revolt a generation earlier. Many new, almost incomprehensible types of visual art emerged to challenge the historic and realistic scenes still favored, for example, by the powerful German monarchy and by some buyers for museums and important collections. Modernism in the arts ushered in a proliferation of competing artistic styles and disagreement about art's relationship to society.

Art for Industrial Society. Some modern artists tried both to challenge and to comfort urbanites caught up in the rush of modern life. Abandoning the soft colors of impressionism as too subtle for a dynamic industrial society, a group of Parisian artists exhibiting in 1905 combined blues, greens, reds, and oranges so intensively that they were called *fauves*, or "wild beasts." A leader of the short-lived fauvism, Henri Matisse (1869–1954), soon struck out in a new direction, targeting the expanding class of white-collar workers. Matisse dreamed of "an art . . . for every mental worker, be he businessman or writer, like an appeasing influence, like a mental soother, something like a good armchair in which to rest from physical fatigue."

The mathematical, scientific tenor of the day appeared in the French artist Paul Cézanne's (1839–1906) focus on structure in painting. Cézanne used rectangular daubs of paint in his scenes of nature and portraits of people to capture a geometric vision of his subjects. Accentuating the lines and planes found in nature, Cézanne's art, like science, was removed from the realm of ordinary perception. The dishes, fruit, and drapery of his still lifes of the 1890s took geometric form, as did the human body. With Cézanne one of the most powerful new trends in the visual arts took shape.

Following in Cézanne's footsteps, Spanish artist Pablo Picasso (1881–1973) initiated *cubism*, a style with a radical emphasis on planes and surfaces that converted people into bizarre, inhuman, almost unrecognizable forms. Picasso's painting *Les Demoiselles d'Avignon* (1907) depicted the bodies of the *demoiselles*, or young ladies (prostitutes in this case), as fragmented and angular, with their heads modeled on African masks. Continuing along the path of impressionism and fauvism, Picasso's work showed the profound influences of African, Asian, and South American arts, but his depiction of these features was less decorative and more brutal than those by Matisse, for example. Like explorers, botanists, and foreign journalists, he was bringing knowledge of the empire into the imperial homeland, this time in a distinctly disturbing form.

Art as Political Criticism. Political critique also shaped painting. "Show the people how hideous is their actual life, and place your hands on the causes of its ugliness" was the anarchist challenge at the time. Picasso, who had spent his youth in the heart of working-class Barcelona, a hotbed of anarchist thought, aimed to replace middle-class sentimentality in art with truth about industrial society. In 1912, Picasso and French painter Georges Braque (1882–1963) devised a new kind of collage that incorporated bits of newspaper, string, and other artifacts. The effect was a canvas that appeared to be cluttered with refuse. The newspaper clippings Picasso included described battles and murders, suggesting the shallowness of Western pretensions to high civilization.

Although Paris was still the center of the art world, artists in the thriving cities of central and eastern Europe and Scandinavia also combined radical stylistic change with political critique. They formed associations (*secessions*) to express their own rebellion against officially approved styles. "The whole empire is littered with monuments to soldiers and monuments to Kaiser William of the same conventional type," one artist complained. Such groups as the Berlin Secession and the Vienna Workshop were at the forefront in experimenting with form and in portraying the psychological complexity of the self. Their joint exhibits of work by ethnically diverse artists criticized the growing nationalism that determined official purchases of sculpture and painting.

Scandinavian and eastern European artists produced anguished works. Like the vision of Freud, their style of portraying inner reality—called *expressionism*—broke with middle-class optimism. Norwegian painter Edvard Munch (1863–1944), who participated in German exhibitions, aimed "to make the emotional mood ring out again as happens on a gramophone." His painting *The Scream* (1895) used twisting lines and a depiction of tortured skeletal human form to convey the horror of modern life that many artists perceived. German avant-garde artist Gabriele Münter

(1877–1962) and Russian painter Wassily Kandinsky (1866–1944) opened their "Blue Rider" exhibit in Munich featuring "expressive" work that made use of geometric forms and striking colors. The artists of the Blue Rider group imitated the paintings of children and the mentally ill to achieve their depiction of psychological reality. Kandinsky, who employed these forms and colors to express an inner, spiritual truth, is often credited with producing the first fully abstract paintings.

The expressionism of Oskar Kokoschka (1886–1980) was even more intense, displaying ecstasy, horror, and hallucinations. As a result, his work—like that of other expressionists and cubists before World War I—was a commercial failure in an increasingly complex marketplace. Alongside government purchases arose a system of dealers who sponsored exhibits of "their" artists' work and who relied on favorable reviews by professional art critics. With styles changing rapidly, the "old masters" of Renaissance and baroque art gained status as classics, selling for ever higher prices. Experts in authenticating and judging these older works of art, among them the American art critic and historian Bernard Berenson (1865–1959), who set himself up outside Florence, Italy, as the ultimate arbiter, made it possible for international buyers to purchase with confidence. Trade in art became professionalized, as had medicine and government work before it, even as modern artists sought to shatter traditional norms.

Art Nouveau. Only one innovative style emerged an immediate commercial success: *art nouveau* ("new style") won approval from government, critics, and the masses. Creating everything from dishes and advertising posters to streetlamps and even entire buildings in this new style, designers manufactured beautiful things for the general public. As one French official said about the first version of art nouveau coins issued in 1895, "Soon even the most humble among us will be able to have a masterpiece in his pocket."

Like the earlier arts and crafts movement in Britain, art nouveau featured intertwined vines and flowers; women with long, wavy hair; and other similar motifs. Adapted from Asian design, the organic and natural elements of art nouveau were meant to offset the fragmentation of factory and office work with images depicting the unified forms of nature. The impersonality of machines was replaced by softly curving bodies of female nudes that would psychologically soothe the individual viewer—an idea that directly contrasted with Picasso's artistic vision. Gustav Klimt (1862–1918), son of a Czech goldsmith, flourished in Viennese high society because his paintings captured the psychological essence of dreamy, sensuous women, their bodies Eastern-inspired mosaics liberally dotted with gold. Art nouveau was the notable exception to the public outcries over innovations in the visual arts.

Musical Iconoclasm

"Astonish me!" was the motto of modern dance and music, both of which shocked audiences in the concert halls of Europe. American dancer Isadora Duncan (1877–1927) took Europe by storm at the turn of the century when, draped in a flowing garment, she danced barefoot in the first performance of modern dance. Drawing on sophisticated Japanese practices, hers was nonetheless called a primitive style that "lifted from their seats people who had never left theater seats before except to get up and go home." Similarly, experimentation with forms of bodily expression animated the Russian Ballet's performance in 1913 of *Rite of Spring* by Igor Stravinsky (1882–1971), the tale of an orgiastic dance to the death performed to ensure fertile soil and a bountiful harvest. The star, Vaslav Nijinsky (1890–1950), was noted for his grace and meticulous execution of classical ballet steps, but his choreography of *Rite of Spring* created a scandal. Nijinsky and the troupe struck awkward poses and danced to rhythms intended to sound primitive. At the work's premiere in Paris, one journalist reported that "the audience began shouting its indignation. . . . Fighting actually broke out among some of the spectators." Such controversy made *Rite of Spring* a box-office hit, although its choreographer was called a "lunatic" and the music itself "the most discordant composition ever written."

Music had been making this turn for several decades. Having heard Asian musicians at international expositions, French composers like Claude Debussy (1862–1918) transformed their style to reflect non-European musical patterns and themes. The twentieth century opened with *Scheherazade* by Frenchman Maurice Ravel (1875–1937) and

**Léon Bakst, *Nijinsky in L'Après-Midi d'un Faune*
("Nijinsky in The Afternoon of a Faun," 1912)**
*Theater sets, costume designs, and performance itself reso-
nated with the experimental climate of early-twentieth-
century Europe. Léon Bakst, a Russian painter and set
designer, used the art nouveau style to capture the faunlike
character of ballet star Vaslav Nijinsky. Yet on the eve of
World War I Nijinsky was part of a revolution in ballet that
introduced jerky, awkward, pounding movements to indicate
the primal nature of dance.*
Wadsworth Atheneum, Hartford. The Ella Gallup Sumner and Mary
Catlin Sumner Collection Fund.

Madame Butterfly by the Italian composer Giacomo
Puccini (1858–1924), both with non-Western subject matter.

Sound became jarring to many listeners. Austrian composer Richard Strauss (1864–1949) upset
convention by using several keys simultaneously in
his compositions. Like the fragmented representation of reality in cubism, atonality or several tonalities at once distorted familiar harmonic patterns
for the audience. Strauss's operas *Salome* (1905)
and *Elektra* (1909) took biblical and classical heroines and expressed through them the modern fascination with violence and obsessive passion. A
newspaper critic claimed that Strauss's dissonant
works "spit and scratch and claw each other like
enraged panthers." The Hungarian pianist Béla
Bartók (1881–1945) incorporated folk melodies
into his compositions as Edvard Grieg and other
nationalist composers had before him, but he composed so that two folk melodies could be played simultaneously in different keys. Bartók's aim was to
elevate the virtues of Hungarian ethnicity above
the Habsburg Empire's unifying multinationalism.
His music disturbed some audiences because of its
nationalism and others because of its dissonance.

The early orchestral work of Austrian composer Arnold Schoenberg (1874–1951), who also
wrote cabaret music to earn a living, shocked even
Strauss. In *Theory of Harmony* (1911) he proposed
eliminating tonality altogether; a decade later he
devised a new twelve-tone scale. "I am aware of
having broken through all the barriers of a dated
aesthetic ideal," Schoenberg wrote of his music.

Modernists in music, like modernists in other
arts, felt they were shattering old norms and values
with their concern for abstract forms. But new aesthetic models distanced these artists from their audiences, separating high from low culture even
more and ending the support of many in the upper
classes, who found this music not only incomprehensible but unpleasant. The artistic elite and the
social elite parted ranks. "Anarchist! Nihilist!"
shouted Schoenberg's audiences, showing their
contempt for modernism and bringing the language of politics into the arts.

❖ Politics in a New Key

New political challenges accompanied the revolution in intellectual life. To some observers, Queen
Victoria's death in 1901 after a reign of more than
sixty years symbolized the uncertainties that lay
ahead in European politics. "It isn't only the Queen
who has disappeared," commented a diplomat's
wife. "It is the century." The Crystal Palace exhibit

Queen Victoria had opened in 1851 had exemplified people's unshakable faith in progress. Now, fifty years later, that optimism had been tempered by an apprehensive, even pessimistic feeling about the future, especially among the upper classes. Cracks in the political consensus and changing political tactics had undermined upper-class control of politics. Liberalism had opened the door to expanded political representation and tolerance for diverse opinions. Political activists, however, were no longer satisfied with the liberal rights sought by reformers a century earlier. Militant nationalists, anti-Semites, socialists, suffragists, and many others demanded changes that alarmed traditional liberals. Mass politics soon threatened social unity, especially in central and eastern Europe, where governments often answered reformers' demands with refusal and repression.

The Growing Power of Labor

European leaders watched with dismay the rise of working-class political power late in the century. Unions gained members among factory workers, while Labor and Socialist Parties won seats in parliaments as men in the lower classes received the vote. In Germany, Kaiser William II had allowed antisocialist laws to lapse after dismissing Bismarck as chancellor in 1890. Through continuous grassroots organizing, the Social Democratic Party (SPD), founded by socialists in 1875, became the largest parliamentary group in the Reichstag by 1912. In France, competing political parties merged in 1905 to form the French Section of the Workers' International (SFIO). These massive workers' parties in central and western Europe voted representatives favorable to labor into parliaments, where they focused on passing legislation that benefited laborers and their families.

Electoral victories raised issues for socialists. Some felt uncomfortable sitting with the upper classes in parliaments. Others worried that their participation in cabinets would produce reform but compromise their ultimate goal of revolution. Often these deputies refused seats in the government. Between 1900 and 1904, the Second International wrestled with the issue of reformism. The International hotly debated the "revisionist" theories of Eduard Bernstein, who criticized many Marxist tenets and proposed that socialism be

achieved by evolutionary rather than revolutionary means. German Marxists responded that reformism only buttressed capitalism. The topic touched off stormy discussions, sometimes pitting delegates from France, England, and Belgium who had attained some political authority and favored reform against more intransigent German socialists who were denied ministerial posts by military and aristocratic statesmen or refused them.

Russian socialists had even less political power than their German counterparts and could gain no ground against a rigidly authoritarian government. Most of these socialists operated in exile because the Russian government outlawed political parties until 1905 and persecuted activists. The foremost activist, V. I. Lenin (1870–1924), became a radical after his brother was executed for plotting to assassinate the tsar. Jailed and sent to Siberia during the 1890s for his left-wing politics, Lenin migrated to western Europe after his release and earned his reputation among Russian Marxists there with his hard-hitting journalism and political intrigue. Lenin advanced the theory that a highly disciplined party elite would lead a lightly industrialized Russia immediately into socialism. At a 1903 party meeting of Russian Marxists, he briefly gained the upper hand when a group of his opponents walked out of the proceedings. In ensuing votes, Lenin's supporters eked out slim victories for control of the party. Thereafter his faction of Bolsheviks, so named after the Russian word for *majority* (which they had temporarily formed), constantly struggled to suppress the Mensheviks, the dominant voice in Russian Marxism. Neither of these groups, however, had as large a constituency within Russia as the Socialist Revolutionaries, whose objective was to politicize peasants rather than industrial workers as the prelude to a populist revolution. All these groups prepared for the revolutionary moment through study, propaganda efforts, and organizing.

During this period some trade union members, known as *syndicalists*, and anarchists kept Europe in a panic with terrorist acts; they also antagonized Marxists. Demonstrating their theory that all forms of government should be abolished, anarchists assassinated Spanish premier Antonio Canovas del Castillo in 1897, Empress Elizabeth of Austria-Hungary in 1898, King Umberto of Italy in 1900, and President William McKinley of the United States in 1901, to name a few famous victims. Syndicalists advocated the use of direct action, such as general strikes and sabotage, to bring industry and government under the control of labor unions. Their ideas were set forth most clearly in French engineer Georges Sorel's *Reflections on Violence* (1908), which explained how a general strike of workers could paralyze the industrial economy and how widespread violence could transform society. By the time of the book's publication, syndicalists had aroused some worker support for their goals. In Italy, for example, sporadic strikes among agricultural and industrial workers in the 1890s were followed by a general strike in 1904. Elsewhere anarchist plots, strikes, and protests over the high cost of living revealed rising worker activism.

Working people's voices had never been so powerful as in these two decades, and the power caused the upper and middle classes grave anxiety. Despite growing acceptance of representative institutions and despite the spread of education, most people in the "best circles" still believed that they alone should hold political power. Politicians from the old landowning and military elites of eastern and central Europe were often the most adamant in their rejection of mass politics, and many of them hoped to reverse the trend toward constitutionalism, worker activism, and reform.

Rights for Women and the Battle for Suffrage

Women did not benefit from the gains of liberalism such as parliamentary representation and equal access to the free press. They often could not vote, exercise free speech, or own property. In Austria and Germany they could not attend political meetings or belong to political groups. In France during the Third Republic, the police often prohibited women's political meetings and talks, citing laws dating from the French Revolution that forbade women to gather publicly. British women could serve on school councils but were deprived of most other representation.

Such restrictions strengthened the movement committed to gaining rights for women. Throughout the nineteenth century, women singly and in groups had struggled for rights, and by the end of the century their efforts involved millions of activists with a variety of goals. German women, in-

fluenced by the cultural ideal of *Bildung* (the belief that proper education can build strength of character and that this individual development has public importance), agitated to reform education and to acquire teaching positions more forcefully than they sought the vote. In several countries women continued to monitor the regulation of prostitution. Their goal was to prevent prostitutes from being imprisoned on suspicion of having syphilis when men with syphilis faced no such incarceration or inspection. Other women took up pacifism as their special cause. Many of them were inspired by Bertha von Süttner's popular book, *Lay Down Your Arms* (1889), which emphasized the terror inflicted on women and families by the ravages of war. (Later von Süttner would influence Alfred Nobel to institute a peace prize and then win the prize herself in 1903.)

By the 1890s, however, many activists concluded that only the right to vote would correct the problems they were combating in piecemeal fashion. Thus they launched a suffrage movement with the express purpose of reducing male privilege by giving women an equal say in society. They argued that men had promised to protect disfranchised women but that this system of supposed chivalry had led to exploitation and abuse. Power and privilege—no matter how couched in expressions of goodwill—worked to the detriment of those without them. "So long as the subjection of women endures, and is confirmed by law and custom, . . . women will be victimized," a leading suffragist claimed. Other activists believed that women had attributes needed to counterbalance masculine qualities in the running of society. The characteristics that came from mothering should shape a country's destiny as much as qualities that stemmed from work in industry and trade, they asserted.

Women's rights activists were predominantly, though not exclusively, from the middle class. Those whose husbands or fathers could afford servants and other conveniences simply had more time to be activists, and a higher level of education allowed them to read the works of feminist theorists such as Harriet Taylor and John Stuart Mill. Working-class women, especially socialists, felt conflicted over whether to engage in women's rights campaigns. Most distrusted middle-class men and women and saw suffrage for women as subordinate to economic concerns. Although some workingwomen, such as those in the textile industries of Manchester, England, put together a vigorous suffrage movement connecting the vote to improved working conditions, socialists and suffragists usually differed over issues of class and gender.

In the 1890s, major suffrage organizations with paid officials and permanent offices emerged out of the voluntary reform groups and women's clubs that had existed earlier in the century. From charity work performed as part of their mission, women had acquired skills in fundraising, public speaking, and organization building. They also devoted their lives to "the Cause" for personal reasons. British suffrage leader Millicent Garrett Fawcett (1847–1929) vowed to change things after enduring the humiliation of having her stolen purse officially labeled her husband's property. Fawcett pressured members of Parliament for the vote, recruited new members, and participated in national and international congresses on behalf of suffrage. Similarly, American Susan B. Anthony (1820–1906) traveled throughout the United States, organized suffrage societies, edited a newspaper, raised money for the movement, and founded the International Woman Suffrage Association in 1904.

In 1906 in Finland, suffragists achieved their first major victory when the Finnish parliament granted women the vote. But the failure of parliaments elsewhere in Europe to enact similar legislation provoked some suffragists to violence and bold public activism. Part of the British suffragist movement adopted a militant political style when Emmeline Pankhurst (1858–1928) and her daughters founded the Women's Social and Political Union (WSPU) in the belief that women would accomplish nothing unless they threatened men's property. Starting in 1907, members of the WSPU held parades in English cities, and in 1909 they began a campaign of violence, blowing up railroad stations, slashing works of art, and chaining themselves to the gates of Parliament. Easily disguising themselves as ordinary shoppers, they carried little hammers in their muffs to smash the plate-glass windows of department stores and shops. Parades and demonstrations made suffrage a public spectacle, resulting in violent attacks on the marchers by outraged men. Arrested for disturbing the peace, the marchers went on hunger strikes in prison. Like striking workers, these women were willing to use

Woman Suffrage in Finland

In 1906, Finnish women became the first in Europe to receive the vote in national elections when the socialist party— usually opposed to feminism as a middle-class rather than a working-class project—supported woman suffrage. The Finnish vote elated activists in the West, now linked together by many international organizations and ties, because it showed that more than a century of lobbying for reform could lead to gains.
Mary Evans Picture Library.

confrontational tactics to obtain rights. As politicians hedged the question of the vote for women, militant suffragists added to the tensions of conflict-ridden urban life.

Liberalism Modified

Governments in western Europe, where liberal institutions were seemingly well entrenched, sought to control the conflicts of the late nineteenth century with pragmatic policies that often (and paradoxically) struck at liberalism's very foundations. After ending laissez-faire in trade by instituting protective tariffs, some politicians and reformers decided that government needed to intervene in more than economic matters to maintain productivity and peace. The scope of social welfare programs broadened, giving government officials more access to information about the family, public health, and domestic relations so they could devise protective legislation, administer disability plans, and establish food and medical programs for needy children. Officials hoped these policies would guarantee a contented workforce and better productivity, which in turn would counter economic uncertainty and political unrest. Although many programs addressed urban needs insufficiently, they added to the growing apparatus of the welfare state in which government actively promoted social well-being.

Testing Liberalism in Britain. In 1905, the British Liberal Party won a solid majority in the House of Commons and seemed determined to enact social legislation to gain working-class support. "We are keenly in sympathy with the representatives of Labour," one Liberal politician announced. "We have too few of them in the House of Commons." Liberal chancellor of the exchequer David Lloyd George (1863–1945) wanted to make a "new departure" in social policy and initiated a system of relief for the unemployed in the National Insurance Act of 1911. Conservatives in the House of Lords resisted higher taxation on the wealthy to pay for this and other social programs, leading to a Liberal threat to create more peers (lords) and thus dilute the power and prestige of the nobility. The newcomers could be counted on to vote for reform. Under this threat the lords approved the Parliament Bill of 1911, which eliminated their veto power. Many wealthy businessmen deserted the Liberal Party because of its alliance with Labour, however.

A modified liberalism advanced in Britain on social issues, but the Irish question tested British commitment to such values as self-determination and individual rights. The House of Lords had blocked previous bills granting home rule to Ireland, and after the fall of their leader Charles Parnell Irish nationalists began to rebuild their organization using methods similar to those of activists in the colonies. In the 1890s, groups formed to foster Irish culture. In 1901, the circle around the modernist poet William Butler Yeats (1865–1939) and the charismatic patriot and actress Maud Gonne (1865–1953) founded the Irish Na-

tional Theater. Gonne took Irish politics into everyday life by opposing British efforts to woo the young. Every time an English monarch visited Ireland, he or she held special receptions for children. Gonne and other Irish volunteers sponsored competing events, handing out candies and other treats for patriotic youngsters. "Dublin never witnessed anything so marvelous," enthused one home rule supporter, "as the procession . . . of thirty thousand school children who refused to be bribed into parading before the Queen of England."

Speaking Gaelic instead of English, singing Gaelic songs, using Catholicism as a rallying point, and generally reconstructing an "Irish way of life," the promoters of Irish culture threw into question the educated class's preference for everything English. This cultural agenda took political shape with the founding in 1905 of Sinn Fein ("Ourselves Alone"), a group that strove for complete Irish independence. In 1913, Parliament approved home rule for Ireland, but the outbreak of World War I prevented the legislation from taking effect and cut short dreams of independence.

Political Troubles in Italy. While British Liberals modified their policies to enhance social cohesion, their Italian counterparts drifted more rapidly from liberalism's moorings. After the struggles of the 1840s, '50s, and '60s, the newly unified Italy faced unexpected political troubles, with the north–south split and the consequences of economic modernization foremost among them. Corruption plagued Italy's constitutional monarchy, which had not yet developed either the secure parliamentary system of England or the authoritarian monarchy of Germany to guide its growing industrial economy. To forge a national consensus in the 1890s, Prime Minister Francesco Crispi (r. 1887–1891, 1893–1896) used patriotic rhetoric, bribes to gain support from the press, and imperial adventure, culminating in an attempt to conquer Ethiopia in 1896 after an earlier failure to do so. But at the battle of Adowa, the spirited Ethiopian army delivered a humiliating defeat and forced the Italians out. Crispi's attempts to unite the public behind him through imperialism failed and led instead to riots and strikes, followed by armed government repression.

A new prime minister, Giovanni Giolitti, who held office for three terms between 1903 and 1914, followed a policy known as *trasformismo* (from the word for "transform"), by which he used bribes, public works programs, and other benefits to localities to influence their deputies in parliament in the absence of well-developed political parties. Political opponents called Giolitti the "Minister of the Underworld" and accused him of preferring to buy the votes of local bosses rather than to spend money to develop the Italian economy. Giolitti's attempt to achieve consensus met instead with unrest in the rapidly industrializing cities of Turin and Milan and in the depressed agrarian south. Urban and rural workers alike demanded change, especially of the restricted suffrage that allowed only three million of more than eight million adult men to vote. Giolitti appeased the protesters by instituting social welfare programs and, in 1912, virtually complete manhood suffrage.

Anti-Semitism and Nationalism in Mass Politics

In the two decades leading up to World War I, anti-Semitism and nationalism suggested pat answers to complex questions. Leaders invoked these concepts to maintain interest-group support, to direct hostility away from themselves, and to win elections. The public responded vehemently, coming to see Jews as villains responsible for the perils of modern society and the nation-state as the hero in the struggle to survive. In both republics and monarchies, anti-Semitism and nationalism played key roles in mass politics by providing a focus for the creation of a radical right increasingly committed to combating the radical left of social democracy. Adopting the imperiled nation as its theme and using the Social Darwinist category of race to identify threats to the nation, the right fundamentally changed the older notion of nationalism based on liberal ideas of rights. Liberals had hoped that voting by the masses would make politics more harmonious as parliamentary debate and compromise smoothed out class differences. But anti-Semites and nationalists, scorning tolerant liberal values as effete, often preferred fights in the street to consensus building in parliaments.

Russification. The Russian tsar Nicholas II confronted modern life with an unswerving belief in orthodoxy in religion, autocracy in politics, and anti-Semitism and Russification in social policy. In this he followed the lead of his father, Alexander III, whose reign had opened in 1881 with an outbreak of vicious pogroms against Jews. Taught as a child to hate Jews, Nicholas stepped up the persecutions, and in his reign many high officials eagerly endorsed anti-Semitism to gain his favor. Pogroms became a regular feature of the Easter holiday in Russia, and Nicholas increasingly limited where Jews could live and how they could earn a living. He tightened restrictions on other groups and supported even more severe Russification, under which Poles, Ukranians, Tatars, and the empire's many other minorities were coerced into learning and speaking Russian, converting to the Russian Orthodox religion, and ignoring, at least publicly, their own cultural heritage.

The Dreyfus Affair in France. Violence toward Russian Jews shocked liberals in western Europe, but anti-Semitism was worming its way into mass politics across the West. The most notorious instance occurred in France and quickly was labeled the Dreyfus Affair. In 1894, a French army captain, Alfred Dreyfus, was charged with spying for Germany. Dreyfus had attended the elite École Polytechnique in Paris and become an officer in the French military, whose upper echelons were traditionally aristocratic, Catholic, and monarchist. Evidence that documents were being passed to Germany led the military command, amidst much other blundering, to fix on a Jewish officer—Dreyfus. His conviction and harsh exile to Devil's Island (off French Guiana in South America) failed to stop the espionage, but his plight aroused little immediate notice, either in the Jewish community or among the public at large.

Dreyfus's family protested his innocence, but the republican government maintained, "There is no Dreyfus Affair." Then several newspapers received proof that the army had used perjured testimony and fabricated documents to convict Dreyfus. In 1898, the celebrated French novelist Émile Zola published "J'accuse" ("I accuse") on the front page of a Paris daily. Zola cited a list of military lies and cover-ups perpetrated by highly placed government officials to create an illusion of Dreyfus's guilt. The article was explosive because it named names; but it was also a ringing defense of liberal principles in government. "I have but one passion, that of Enlightenment," wrote Zola.

opposition fought out the Dreyfus Affair, socialists made inroads into local government, winning control of mayoralties and city councils. The government finally pardoned Dreyfus in 1899 and then ousted from office the aristocratic and Catholic officers held responsible for what increasingly appeared a humiliation of the republic. Early in the twentieth century it ended religious teaching orders to ensure a public school system that was secular and that taught liberal values of tolerance. When the smoke cleared, republicans had gained control as well over the army. They had secured their triumph, however, by fanning the flames of anticlericalism and hatred. The Dreyfus Affair made anti-Semitism a standard tool of politics by producing hate-filled slogans that would be used repeatedly to blame Jews for various dissatisfactions, whether social, economic, or political. The racial side of Social Darwinism had passed from being part of social and imperial policy to the mainstream of politics.

The Right in Germany.   The ruling elites in Germany also used anti-Semitism as a political weapon to garner support from those who feared the consequences of Germany's sudden and overwhelming industrialization. These elites, unlike French conservatives, still controlled the highest reaches of government and influenced the kaiser's policy. But the basis of their power was rapidly eroding, as agriculture, from which they drew their fortunes and social prestige, declined as a percentage of gross national product from 37 percent in the 1880s to only 25 percent early in the 1900s. As new opportunities lured rural people away from the land and as industrialists grew wealthier than they, the agrarian elites came to loathe industry and the working class. As a Berlin newspaper noted, "The agrarians' hate for cities . . . blinds them to the simplest needs and the most natural demands of the urban population." In contrast to Bismarck's astute wooing of the masses through social programs, William II's aristocracy often encouraged anti-Semitism, both in the corridors of power and in the streets.

Conservatives and a growing radical right claimed that Jews, who made up less than 1 percent of the German population, were responsible for the disruption of traditional society and charged them with being the main beneficiaries of economic

Public Opinion in the Dreyfus Affair: "Ah! The Dirty Beast!"

The French army used forged documents and perjured testimony to convict Captain Alfred Dreyfus of espionage. In a climate of escalating anti-Semitism, the conviction of a Jew struck many in the public as yet another narrow escape for the country. Only intense detective work by pro-Dreyfus activists and lobbying by Dreyfus's family convinced republican leaders that the system of equal rights was imperiled not by Dreyfus but by the bigotry of the army and those right-wing politicians who had trumped up the case against him. Photothèque des Musées de la Ville de Paris.

"J'accuse" caused the public to become violently divided over the question of Dreyfus's guilt or innocence.

Public riots, quarrels among families and friends, and denunciations of the army eroded public confidence in the republic and in French institutions. While republicans and the conservative change. In the 1890s, nationalist and anti-Semitic pressure groups flourished, spewing diatribes against Jews and "new women" but also against Social Democrats, whom they branded as internationalist, socially destructive, and unpatriotic. In the German elections of 1893, the new Agrarian League played to the fears of small farmers by accusing Jews of causing agricultural booms and busts. Candidates from other parties noted the popular response to these charges and made anti-Semitism and hate-filled speeches against an array of groups a regular feature of their campaigns, too.

These antiliberal movements profoundly affected German political life. First, instead of working for parliamentary compromise among various interests, they fueled extremist hatreds and violent feelings of nationalism. Second, instead of meeting the problems of rapid economic change with some measure of social unity and a rational program, these movements created classes of enemies whose defeat would allegedly cure all modern ills. Finally, the other great powers, facing severe economic competition from Germany for the first time and watching the increased saber rattling of its politicians, began to fear an outbreak of war at German hands and to prepare for it.

Ethnic Politics in Austria-Hungary. People in the Dual Monarchy also expressed their political and economic discontent in militantly nationalistic and anti-Semitic terms, but here nationalism had a different effect because of the presence of so many competing ethnic groups. Foremost among the nationalists were the Hungarians, who wanted autonomy for themselves while forcibly imposing Hungarian language and culture on all other ethnic groups in Hungary. The demands for greater Hungarian influence (or *Magyarization*, from Magyars, the principal ethnic group) seemed only just to them: Budapest was a thriving industrial city, and the export of Hungarian grain from the vast estates of the Hungarian nobility balanced the monarchy's foreign trade deficit. With vociferous nationalism and separatism mounting, the Independence Party provoked a series of crises in the Hungarian parliament that made a shambles of regular government processes.

Although capable of causing trouble for the empire, Hungarian nationalists, who mostly represented agrarian wealth, were vulnerable both to the resistance of other nationalities and to the demands of a growing industrial proletariat. On the land, the policy of Magyarization resulted in the formation of strong political groups among Slovaks, Romanians, and Ruthenians. Strikes erupted to protest horrendous labor conditions, and in the fall of 1905, one hundred thousand activists demonstrated in front of the Hungarian parliament for the vote. In the face of this resistance, Hungarians intensified Magyarization, even decreeing that all tombstones be engraved in Magyar. Emperor Francis Joseph temporarily brought the Hungarian nationalists to bay by threatening them with the introduction of universal manhood suffrage,

Principal Ethnic Groups in Austria-Hungary, c. 1900

which would allow the Magyars' lower-class opponents to vote. Although numerous nationality groups and the many Jews who settled in Budapest assimilated Magyar ways, the uncompromising and chauvinist nature of Hungarian policies toward both imperial government in Vienna and different ethnic groups within the empire made for instability throughout Austria-Hungary.

The insurgency of Hungary further changed the course of Habsburg politics by arousing other nationalists to intensify their demands for rights. Croats, Serbs, and other Slavic groups in the south organized and called for equality with the Hungarians. The central government gave more privileges to the Czechs and allowed them to increase the proportion of Czech officials in the government simply because growing industrial prosperity in their region gave them more influence. But every step toward recognition of Czech ethnicity provoked outrage from the traditionally dominant ethnic Germans, causing more tensions in the empire. When in 1897 Austria-Hungary decreed that government officials in the Czech region of the empire would have to know Czech as well as German, the Germans rioted.

Tensions mounted as politicians in Vienna linked the growing power of Hungarian and Czech politicians to Jews. A prime instigator of this "politics of the irrational"—as historians often label this ultranationalist and anti-Semitic phenomenon—was Karl Lueger (1844–1910), whose newly formed Christian Social Party attracted members from among the aristocracy, Catholics, artisans, shopkeepers, and white-collar workers. Thus Lueger used hatred to appeal to those groups for whom modern life meant a loss of privilege and security; in 1895, he was elected mayor of Vienna after using rough language and verbal abuse against Jews and ethnic groups in his campaign. Lueger's ethnic nationalism and anti-Semitism destabilized the multinational coexistence upon which Austria-Hungary was based.

By the turn of the century, influential parties of the right, built on aggressive nationalism and anti-Semitism, had appeared in Germany as well as Austria-Hungary. Jewishness became a symbol that Austrian and German politicians often harped on in their election campaigns, calling Jews the "sucking vampire" of modernity and blaming them for the unevenness of economic well-being, the tumult of migration and social dislocation, and just about anything else other people did not like. Rabid nationalism also inflamed the atmosphere, making politics a thing not of parliaments but of the streets, bloated with rhetoric and racism.

Jewish Responses to Modernity

Throughout the nineteenth century, the prevailing view in the West was that a Jewish identity was inferior to a Christian one, but this view provoked varying responses from Jews themselves. Jews in western Europe had responded to the spread of legal emancipation that followed in the wake of the Enlightenment by adopting liberal political and cultural values, intermarrying with Christians, and in some cases converting to Christianity. Such assimilation gave Jews the opportunity to give up the cultural ways that the dominant Christian culture saw as inferior. By contrast, Jews in Russia and Romania were increasingly singled out for persecution, legally disadvantaged, and forced to live in ghettos. If Jews wanted refuge, the cities of central and eastern Europe provided the best opportunity to succeed. They often adopted the cosmopolitan culture of Vienna or Magyar ways in Budapest. By 1900, Jews were both prominent in cultural and economic affairs in cities across the continent and discriminated against, even victimized, elsewhere.

Historians have debated why Jews disproportionately made such significant contributions to almost all fields of cultural and professional endeavor. Using the case of Jews in central Europe, some scholars maintain that in German culture such professions as medicine, the law, and the arts offered Jews a chance to demonstrate their acquisition of *Bildung*, which Germans prized above political participation. Many Jews also favored the German Empire because classical German culture seemed more appealing than the Catholic ritual they saw promoted by the Dual Monarchy of Austria-Hungary. Even escalating anti-Semitism did not stop Jews from dominating cultural achievement in Vienna, Budapest, and Prague. The celebrated composer Gustav Mahler, the budding writer Franz Kafka, and the pioneer of psychoanalysis Sigmund Freud were shaped in the crucible of Habsburg society.

Most Jews, however, were not so accomplished or prosperous as these cultural giants, and their escalating migration to the United States and other countries, in reaction to both pogroms and economic change, filled towns and cities with poor day laborers and struggling artisans (Map 25.1). Amidst this vast migration and continued persecution, a spirit of Jewish nationalism arose. "Why should we be any less worthy than any other . . . people," one leader asked. "What about our nation, our language, our land?" Jews began organizing resistance to pogroms and anti-Semitic politics, and intellectuals drew upon Jewish folklore, philology, and history to establish a national identity parallel to that of other Europeans.

In the 1880s, the Ukrainian physician Leon Pinsker, seeing the Jews' lack of national territory as fundamental to the persecution heaped on them, advocated the migration of Jews to Palestine. In 1896, Theodor Herzl (1860–1904), strongly influenced by Pinsker, published *The Jewish State*, which called not simply for migration but for the creation of a Jewish nation-state. A Hungarian-born Jew, Herzl experienced anti-Semitism firsthand as a Viennese journalist and a writer in Paris during the Dreyfus Affair. As an alternative to shedding Jewish identity, he became driven to found a Jewish state, searching Europe for financial backing, technical advice, and a political structure for the venture. His constituency should have been prosperous Jews, but many of them had assimilated and thought his ideas mad. However, with the

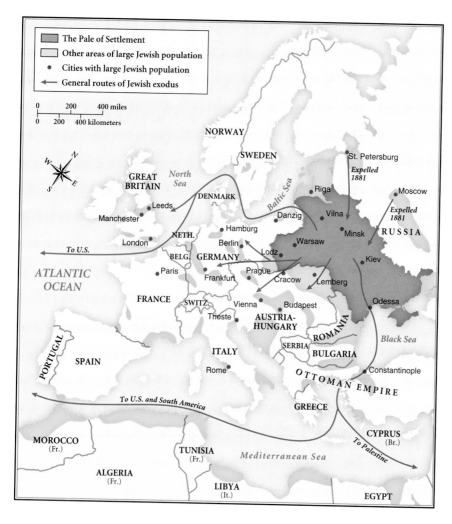

MAP 25.1 Jewish Migrations in the Late Nineteenth Century

Pogroms in eastern Europe, increasingly violent anti-Semitism across the continent, and the search for opportunity led Jews to many parts of the world. They migrated to European cities and, as Zionism progressed, to Palestine. The development of manufacturing in the United States offered a wealth of new opportunities, especially the chance to live where the rule of law was somewhat better established than in Russia.

support of poorer eastern European Jews, he succeeded in calling the first International Zionist Congress (1897), which endorsed settlement in Palestine and helped gain financial backing from the Rothschild banking family. By 1914, some 85,000 Jews had resettled in Palestine. Nonetheless, from many perspectives European domestic politics remained explosive.

❖ European Imperialism Challenged

Inflamed nationalism across the West made it difficult for nations to calm domestic politics and the traumas of modern industrial life. In 1897, the poet Rudyard Kipling marked the fiftieth anniver-

sary of Queen Victoria's reign with "Recessional," a somber poem comparing the British Empire to ancient cities whose glory had long since faded:

> *Far-called our navies melt away—*
> *On dune and headland sinks the fire—*
> *Lo, all our pomp of yesterday*
> *Is one with Nineveh and Tyre.*

Kipling's turn to pessimistic sentimentalism was apt, first because holding imperial territory was aggravating relations among the European powers and second because colonized peoples were challenging European control. Japan had become an Asian power, and nationalist movements for independence were gaining strength, a development that eventually led to new rebellions against European rule.

The Trials of Empire

After centuries of global expansion, imperial adventure soured for Britain and France as the twentieth century opened, and being an imperial power proved difficult for such newcomers as Italy and Germany. "Where thirty years ago there existed one sensitive spot in our relations with France, or Germany, or Russia," the British economist J. A. Hobson wrote in 1902, "there are a dozen now; diplomatic strains are of almost monthly occurrence between the Powers." Increasing competition among a greater number of nations for colonies and escalating tensions between the French and British in Africa and elsewhere had raised serious questions about the future of imperialism. For their part, colonized people were fighting back with stubborn vigor.

Boer War. Accustomed to crushing resistance to their imperial ambitions, the British experienced a bloody defeat in 1896, when Cecil Rhodes, prime minister of the Cape Colony in southern Africa, directed his right-hand man, Dr. Leander Jameson, to lead a raid into the neighboring territory of the Transvaal. The foray was intended to stir up trouble between the Boers, descendants of early Dutch settlers, and the more recent immigrants from Britain and elsewhere who had come to southern Africa in search of gold and other riches. Rhodes hoped the raid would justify a British takeover of the Transvaal and the Orange Free State, which the Boers independently controlled. The Boers, however, easily routed the raiders, forcing Rhodes to resign in disgrace. The defeat was a blow to the British public, whose patriotism featured imperial pride as a cornerstone.

Other Europeans gloated over the British loss. Kaiser William II telegraphed his congratulations to Transvaal president Paul Kruger for "maintaining the independence of the country against attacks from without." The British were not accustomed to, nor did they accept defeat easily: for the next three years they fought the Boer War directly against the Transvaal and the Orange Free State. Britain finally annexed the area after defeating the Boers in 1902, but the cost of war—in money, destruction, and loss of life—horrified many Britons and caused them to see imperialism as a burden (Map 25.2).

Setbacks and Newcomers. Almost simultaneously, Spain lost Cuba, Puerto Rico, and the Philippines as a result of its defeat in the Spanish-American War of 1898. Urged on the United States by the expansionist-minded Theodore Roosevelt, then assistant secretary of the navy, and the inflammatory daily press, this war revealed the fragility of established European empires and the unpredictability of imperial fortunes. Even the triumphant United States, encouraged by Kipling to "take up the white man's burden" by bringing the benefits of Western civilization to those liberated from Spain, had to wage a bloody war against the Filipinos, who wanted independence, not just another imperial ruler. Reports of American brutality in the Philippines further disillusioned the European public, who liked to imagine native peoples joyously welcoming the bearers of civilization.

Despite these setbacks, emerging powers had an emotional stake in gaining colonies. In the early twentieth century, Italian public figures bragged about the Italians becoming Nietzschean supermen by conquering Africa and restoring Italy to its ancient position of world domination. After its disastrous war against Ethiopia in 1896, Italy won a costly victory over Turkey in Libya. But these wars roused Italian hopes for national grandeur only to dash them.

Germany likewise demanded a place at the imperial table and an end to the virtual British-French monopoly of colonial power. Foremost among the new competitors for empire, German bankers and businessmen were ensconced throughout Asia, the Middle East, and Latin America. Colonial skirmishes Germany had once ignored became matters of utmost concern. But Germany, too, instead of winning unalloyed glory, met humiliation and constant problems, especially in its dealings with Britain and France. As Italy and Germany aggressively pursued new

The Struggle for Ethiopia, 1896

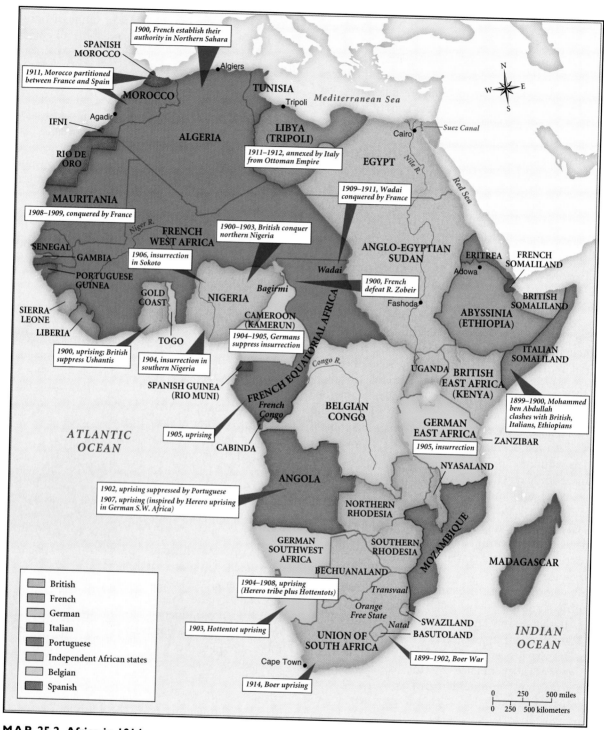

MAP 25.2 Africa in 1914

Uprisings intensified in Africa in the early twentieth century as Europeans tried both to consolidate their rule through bureaucratization and military action and to extract more wealth from the Africans. At the same time as Europeans were putting down the rebellions against their rule, a pan-African movement arose, attempting to unite Africans as one people. As in Asia and the Middle East, the more the colonial powers tried to impose their will, the greater the political forces—including the force of political ideas—that took shape against them.

territory, the rules set for imperialism at the Congress of Berlin a generation earlier gave way to increasingly heated rivalry and nationalist fury.

Japan Victorious. Europeans' confident approach to imperialism was also eroded by the rise of Japan as a power. The Japanese had started building an empire by invading the Chinese island of Formosa (present-day Taiwan) in 1874 and continued by forcing trading treaties on Korea in 1876 (Map 25.3). In 1894, Japan sparked the Sino-Japanese War, which ended China's domination of Korea. The Eu-

ropean powers, alarmed at Japan's victory, forced it to relinquish other gains, a move that outraged and affronted the Japanese. Japan's insecurity had risen with Russian expansion to the east and south in Asia. Pushing into eastern Asia, the Russians had built the Trans-Siberian Railroad through Manchuria and sponsored anti-Japanese groups in Korea, making the peninsula appear, as a Japanese military leader put it, like "a dagger thrust at the heart of Japan." Angered by the continuing presence of Russian troops in Manchuria, the Japanese attacked tsarist forces at Port Arthur in 1904.

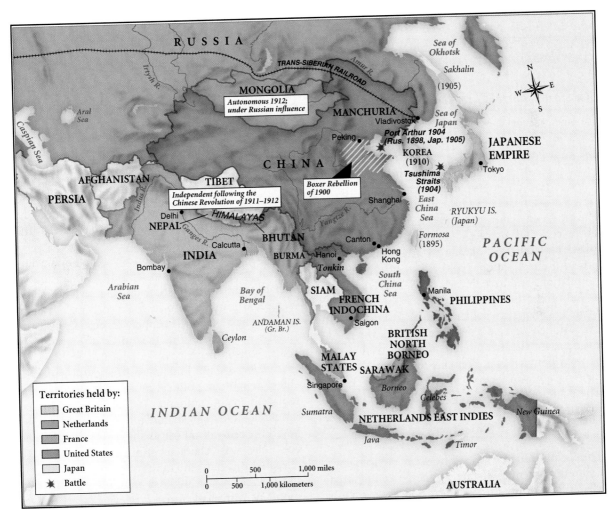

MAP 25.3 Imperialism in Asia, 1894–1914
Most of the modernizing states converged on Asia. The established imperialists came to blows in East Asia as they struggled for influence in China and as they met a formidable new rival—Japan. Simultaneously liberation movements like the Boxers were taking shape, committed to throwing off restraints imposed by foreign powers. Ultimately in 1911, Sun Yat-Sen overthrew the Qing dynasty that had left China unprepared to resist foreign takeover and started the country on a different course.

The conservative Russian military proved inept in the ensuing Russo-Japanese War, even though it often had better equipment or strategic advantage. In an astonishing display of poor leadership, Russia's Baltic Fleet sailed halfway around the globe only to be completely destroyed in the battle of Tsushima Straits (1905). Opening an era of Japanese domination in East Asian politics, the victory was the first by a non-European nation over a European great power in the modern age, and it gave the West an additional reason to fear the future. As one English general ominously observed of the Russian defeat: "I have today seen the most stupendous spectacle it is possible for the mortal brain to conceive—Asia advancing, Europe falling back." Japan went on to annex Korea in 1910 and to eye other areas in which to challenge the West.

Russian Empire Threatened

Russia, a mighty empire that had expanded southward in Asia and settled much of Siberia during the nineteenth century, concealed its weaknesses well. In reality it tottered on the brink of chaos in 1905 as revolution erupted alongside military defeat. State-sponsored industrialization in the 1890s had made the country appear modern to outside observers, and the Russification policy imitated Western-style state building by attempting to impose a unified, national culture on Russia's diverse population. Industrialization, however, also produced urban unrest as Marxist and union activists incited workers to demand better conditions. In 1903, skilled workers led strikes in Baku, where Armenians and Tatars united in a demonstration that showed how urbanization and Russification could facilitate political action among the lower classes. These and other worker protests challenged the autocratic regime.

The Revolution of 1905.   The secret police kept a lid on discontent by spying on people and by organizing its own unions staffed by police informants. In January 1905, a crowd led by one of these informants gathered one Sunday outside the tsar's Winter Palace in St. Petersburg to try to make Nicholas aware of brutal working conditions. Instead of allowing the demonstration to pass, troops guarding the palace shot into the crowd, killing hundreds and wounding thousands.

Thus began the Revolution of 1905, and news of Bloody Sunday spurred other urban workers to rebel. In almost a year of turmoil across Russia, workers struck over wages, hours, and factory conditions and demanded political representation in the government. Delegates from revolutionary parties such as the Social Democrats and the Socialist Revolutionaries encouraged more direct blows against the central government, but workers rejected their leadership and organized their own councils, called *soviets*. In February, Grand Duke Sergei, the tsar's uncle, was assassinated; in June sailors on the battleship *Potemkin* mutinied; in October a massive railroad strike ground rail transportation to a halt and the Baltic states and Transcaucasia rebelled; and in November uprisings broke out in Moscow. The tsar's Cossack troops kept killing strikers across the country, but their deaths only fueled the protest.

Russian Revolution of 1905

Because Nicholas II, almost alone among European monarchs, ruled his empire as an absolutist unhampered by a constitution, the revolution coalesced artisans and industrial workers, peasants, professionals, and the upper classes against the Russian nobility. Using the unrest to press their goals, liberals from *zemstvos* (local councils) and the *intelligentsia* (a Russian word for well-educated elites) demanded political reform, in particular the replacement of autocracy with a constitutional monarchy and representative legislature. They believed the reliance on censorship and the secret police that was characteristic of Romanov rule relegated Russia to the ranks of the most backward states. Preferring a military solution, Nicholas responded with half-hearted reforms—a response that triggered more street fighting. In the words of one protester, the tsar's attitude turned "yesterday's benighted slaves into decisive warriors."

Attempts at Political Reform.   Impelled by the continuing violence, the tsar created a representative body—the Duma. Although very few could vote for representatives to the Duma, its mere existence, coupled with the right of public political debate, liberalized government and allowed people to present their grievances to a responsive body. As important, during this time political parties took shape. After these constitutional parties threw their support to the reorganized government, revolutionary activity abated and the tsar's troops crushed the remaining pockets of resistance.

People soon began to wonder, however, if anything had really changed. From 1907 to 1917, the Duma convened, but twice when the tsar disliked its recommendations he sent the delegates home and forced new elections. Prime Minister Pyotr Stolypin (1863–1911), a successful administrator and landowner, was determined to eliminate the sources of discontent by ending the *mir* system of communal farming and taxation and canceling the land redemption payments that had burdened the peasants since their emancipation in 1861. He also made government loans available to peasants, who were then able to purchase land and to own farms outright. Although these reforms did not eradicate rural poverty, they did allow people to move to the cities in search of jobs and created a larger group of independent peasants. By 1917, some two-thirds of the peasantry had taken steps to gain title to their land, and 10 percent had acquired consolidated holdings.

Stolypin succeeded only partially in his other goal of restoring law and order. He clamped down on revolutionary organizations, executing their members by hanging them with "Stolypin neckties." The government urged more pogroms and stifled ethnic unrest by stepping up Russification. But rebels continued to assassinate government officials—four thousand were killed or wounded in 1906–1907—and Stolypin himself was assassinated in 1911. Stolypin's reforms had promoted peasant well-being, which encouraged what one historian has called a "new peasant assertiveness." The industrial proletariat also grew, and another round of strikes broke out, culminating in a general strike in St. Petersburg in 1914.

Despite the creation of the Duma and other reforms, the imperial government and the conservative nobility had no solution to the ongoing social turmoil and felt little inclination to share power. Their ineffectual response to the Revolution of 1905 would foster an even greater revolution in 1917.

Growing Resistance to Colonial Domination

The Japanese military victory over two important dynasties—the Qing in China and the Romanov in Russia—within a single decade had repercussions in the colonies, further eroding the security Westerners had once found in imperialism. The Japanese victories and the ability of Russian revolutionaries to force a great European power to reform inspired nationalist-minded opponents to European imperialism. The success of a non-Western, constitutional government fed protest throughout the globe.

Boxers in China. Uprisings began in China after its 1895 defeat by Japan forced the ruling Qing dynasty to grant more economic concessions to Western powers. Humiliated by these events, peasants organized into secret societies to restore Chinese integrity. One organization, based on beliefs in the spiritual values of boxing, was the Society of the Righteous and Harmonious Fists (or Boxers), whose members maintained that ritual boxing would protect them from a variety of evils, including bullets. Encouraged by the Qing ruler Dowager Empress Tz'u-hsi (Cixi) (1835–1908) and desperate because of worsening economic conditions, the Boxers rebelled in 1900, massacring the missionaries and Chinese Christians to whom they attributed China's troubles. The colonial powers put down the Boxer Rebellion and encouraged the Chinese troops in their service to ravage the areas in which the Boxers operated. Defeated once more, the Chinese were compelled to pay a huge indemnity, to destroy many of their defensive fortifications, and to allow more extensive foreign military occupation.

The Boxer Rebellion thoroughly discredited the Qing dynasty; in 1911 a successful group of revolutionaries finally overthrew the dynasty and the next year declared China a republic. Their leader, Sun Yat-Sen (1866–1925), who had been educated in Hawaii and Japan, used Western concepts to express traditional Chinese values while simultaneously promoting a cluster of Western programs: "nationalism, democracy, and socialism." Together they added up to freedom from the Qing dynasty, revival of the Chinese tradition of correctness in behavior between governors and the governed, modern economic reform, and a threat to European channels of trade and domination.

Boxer Rebellion
The Boxers sought to fortify the Chinese government against the many powers threatening its survival. They used brightly colored placards to spread information about their mission and its importance and to build support. The placards also depicted battles with imperialist forces and showed Boxer triumphs over foreign missionaries and other menacing groups.
Photo courtesy Thames & Hudson, Ltd., London.

Sun's stirring leadership and the changes brought about by China's revolution seriously derailed the course of Western imperialism.

Nationalists in India. In India, the Japanese victory over Russia and the Revolution of 1905 stimulated politicians to take a more radical course than that offered by the Indian National Congress. A Hindu leader, B. G. Tilak (1856–1920), fervently anti-British and less moderate than Congress reformers, preached blatant noncooperation: "We shall not give them assistance to collect revenue and keep peace. We shall not assist them in fighting beyond the frontiers or outside India with Indian blood and money." Tilak promoted Hindu customs, asserted their distinctiveness from British ways, and inspired violent rebellion in his followers. This brand of nationalism broke with that based on assimilating to British culture and promoting gradual change. Trying to repress Tilak, the British sponsored the Muslim League, a rival nationalist group favored for its restraint and its potential to divide Muslim nationalists from Hindus in the Congress.

Faced with political activism on many fronts, however, Britain conceded the right to vote based on property ownership and to representation in ruling councils. Because the independence movement had not fully reached the masses, these small concessions temporarily maintained British power by appeasing the best-educated and most influential dissidents among the upper and middle classes. But the British hold on India was weakening.

Young Turks in the Ottoman Empire. Revolutionary nationalism was simultaneously sapping the Ottoman Empire, which for centuries had controlled much of the Mediterranean. In the nineteenth century, several rebellions had plagued Ottoman rule, and more erupted early in the twentieth century because of growing resistance to the empire and to European influence. Just as the Habsburgs used the transnational appeal of Catholicism to quash nationalist aspirations, similarly Sultan Abdul Hamid II (r. 1876–1909) tried to revitalize the multiethnic empire by using Islam to counteract the rising nationalism of the Serbs, Bulgarians, and Macedonians. Instead he unwittingly provoked a burgeoning Turkish nationalism in Constantinople itself. Turkish nationalists rejected the sultan's pan-Islamic solution and built their movement on the uniqueness of their culture, history, and language, as many European ethnic groups were doing. Using the findings of Western scholarship, they first traced the history of the group they called Turks to change the word *Turk* from one of derision to one of pride. Nationalists also tried to purge their language of words from Arabic and Persian, and they popularized the folklore of rural Turkish peoples scattered across territories from eastern Europe through Asia. The events of 1904–1905 electrified these nationalists with the vision of a modern Turkey becoming "the Japan of the Middle East," as they called it. In 1908, a group of nationalists called the Young Turks took control of the government in Constantinople, which had been fatally weakened by nationalist agitation and by the empire's economic dependence on Western financiers and businessmen.

The Young Turks' triumph motivated other groups in the Middle East and the Balkans to demand an end to Ottoman domination in their regions as well. These groups adopted Western values and platforms, and some, such as the Egyptians, had strong contingents of feminist-nationalists who mobilized women to work for independence. But the Young Turks, often aided by European powers with financial and political interests in the region, brutally tried to repress the uprisings in Egypt, Syria, and the Balkans that their own success had encouraged.

Their rebellions became part of the tumult shaping international relations in the decade before World War I. Empires, whether old or young, were the scene of growing resistance in the wake of Japanese, Russian, and Turkish events. In German East Africa, colonial forces countered native resistance in 1905 with a scorched-earth policy, which eventually killed more than 100,000 Africans. The French closed the University of Hanoi, executed Indochinese intellectuals, and deported thousands of suspected nationalists merely to maintain a tenuous grip on Indochina. A French general stationed there summed up the fears of many colonial rulers in the new century: "The gravest fact of our actual political situation in Indochina is not the recent trouble in Tonkin [or] the plots undertaken against us but in the muted but growing hatred that our subjects show toward us more and more."

❖ Roads to War

These international developments simultaneously aggravated competition among the great powers and caused Western nationalism in its many varieties to swell. In the spring of 1914, U.S. president Woodrow Wilson (1856–1924) sent his trusted adviser Colonel House abroad to assess the tensions among the European powers. "It is militarism run stark mad," House reported, adding that he foresaw an "awful cataclysm" ahead. Government spending on what people called the "arms race" had stimulated European economies; but arms were not stockpiled only for economic growth. As early as the mid-1890s, the socialist Eduard Bernstein had called the situation a "cold war" because the hostile

atmosphere made physical combat seem imminent. By 1914, the air was even more charged, with militant nationalism in the Balkan states and conflicts in domestic politics also setting the stage for war. Although historians have long debated whether World War I could have been avoided, they have never reached a consensus. Considering the feverish background of prewar change, they have had to content themselves with tracing the steps Europeans took along the road toward mass destruction.

Competing Alliances and Clashing Ambitions

As the twentieth century opened, the Triple Alliance that Bismarck had negotiated among Germany, Austria-Hungary, and Italy confronted an opposing alliance between France and Russia, created in the 1890s. The wild card in the diplomatic scenario was Great Britain, traditional enemy of France, nowhere more than in the contest for colonial power. Constant rivals in Africa, Britain and France edged to the brink of war in 1898 at Fashoda in the Sudan. The French government, however, backed away and both nations were frightened into getting along for mutual self-interest. To prevent another Fashoda, they entered into secret agreements, the first of which (1904) guaranteed British claims in Egypt and French claims in Morocco. This agreement marked the beginning of the British-French alliance called the *Entente Cordiale*. Despite the alliance, Britain's response to a European war remained in question; even French statesmen feared that their ally might remain neutral.

Germany's Imperial Demands. From being a "satisfied" nation under Bismarck, who had worked to balance great-power interests and had spared Germany from the draining fight for colonies, Germany under William II became dissatisfied with its international status and inflamed rather than calmed the diplomatic atmosphere. Convinced of British hostility toward France and emboldened by Germany's growing industrial might, the kaiser used the opportunity presented by the defeat of France's ally Russia to contest French claims in Morocco. A man who boasted and blustered and was easily prodded to rash actions by his advisers, William landed in Morocco in 1905, thus challenging French predominance in what became known as the First Moroccan Crisis.

To resolve the situation, an international conference met in Spain in 1906, where Germany confidently expected to gain concessions and new territories. Instead the powers, now including the United States, decided to support French rule. The French and British military, faced with German aggression in Morocco, drew closer together.

Germany found itself weak diplomatically and strong economically, a situation that made its leaders more determined to compete for territory abroad. When the French finally took over Morocco in 1911, Germany triggered the Second Moroccan Crisis by sending a gunboat to the port of Agadir and demanding concessions from the French. This time no power—not even Austria-Hungary—backed the German move. No one acknowledged this dominant country's might, nor

did the constant demands for recognition encourage anyone to do so. The British and French now made binding military provisions for the deployment of their forces in case of war, thus strengthening the Entente Cordiale. Smarting from its setbacks on the world stage, Germany refocused its sights on its role on the continent and on its own alliances.

Crises in the Balkans. Germany's stream of territorial claims along with public uncertainty about the binding force of alliances unsettled Europe, particularly the Balkans. German statesmen began envisioning the creation of a *Mitteleuropa* that included central Europe, the Balkans, and Turkey under their sway. The Habsburgs, now firmly backed by Germany, judged that expansion into the

MAP 25.4 The Balkans, 1908–1914
Balkan peoples—mixed in religion, ethnicity, and political views—were successful in developing and asserting their desire for independence, especially in the First Balkan War, which claimed territory from the Ottoman Empire. Their increased autonomy sparked rivalries among them and continued to attract attention from the great powers. Three empires in particular—the Russian, Ottoman, and Austro-Hungarian—simultaneously sought greater influence for themselves in the region, which became a powderkeg of competing ambitions.

Balkans and the resulting addition of even more ethnic groups would weaken the claims of any single ethnic minority in the Dual Monarchy. Russia, however, saw itself as the protector of Slavs in the region and wanted to replace the Ottomans as the dominant Balkan power, especially after Japan had crushed its hopes for expansion to the east. Austria's swift annexation of Bosnia-Herzegovina during the Young Turk revolt in 1908 enraged not only the Russians but the Serbs as well, because these southern Slavs wanted Bosnia as part of an enlarged Serbia. The Balkans thus whetted many appetites (Map 25.4).

Even without the greedy eyes cast on the Balkans by outside powers, the situation would have been extremely complex given the tensions created by political modernity. The nineteenth century had seen the rise of nationalism and ethnicity as the basis for the unity of the nation-state, and by late in the century ethnic loyalty challenged dynastic power in the Balkans. Greece, Serbia, Bulgaria, Romania, and Montenegro emerged as autonomous states, almost all of them composed of several ethnicities as well as Orthodox Christians, Roman Catholics, and Muslims. All these states sought more Ottoman and Habsburg territory that included their own ethnic group—a complicated desire given the complex ethnic structure everywhere.

In the First Balkan War, in 1912, Serbia, Bulgaria, Greece, and Montenegro joined forces to gain Macedonia and Albania from the Ottomans. The victors divided up their booty, with Bulgaria gaining the most territory, but soon they turned against one another. Serbia, Greece, and Montenegro contested Bulgarian gains in the Second Balkan War in 1913. Much to Austrian dismay, these allies won a quick victory, though Austria-Hungary managed in the peace terms to prevent Serbia from annexing parts of Albania. Grievances between the Habsburgs and the Serbs now seemed irreconcilable. Moreover, the peace conditions did not demilitarize the region, and Balkan peoples, especially angry Slavs who continued to look to Russia for help, imagined further challenges to Austria-Hungary. The Balkans had become a perilous region along whose borders both Austria-Hungary, as ruler of many Slavs, and Russia as their protector stationed increasing numbers of troops. The situation tempted strategists to think that a quick war there—something like Bismarck's wars—could resolve tension and uncertainty.

Gute Freunde, getreue Nachbarn.

Good Friends, Trusted Neighbors (1909)
This cartoon provides a vision of European countries turning from neighborliness to warfare. By trying to keep up with one another's stock of arms, they have soon utterly destroyed the neighborhood—a sober warning from a German newspaper that within five years would prove to be an accurate prediction. The war would do more than physical damage, but this was not to be foreseen.
Mary Evans Picture Library.

The Race to Arms

Between the Napoleonic Wars of the early nineteenth century and World War I a hundred years later, technology, nationalism, and imperialism transformed the practice of and rationale for war. During that period global rivalries, aspirations for national greatness, and in some cases even the struggle for independence made constant readiness for war seem necessary. On the seas and in foreign lands the colonial powers battled to establish control, and they developed railroad, telegraph, and telephone networks everywhere to link their conquests and to move troops as well as commerce. Governments began to conscript ordinary citizens for periods of two to six years into large standing armies, in contrast to smaller eighteenth-century forces that had served the more limited military goals of the time.

By 1914, escalating tensions in Europe boosted the annual intake of conscripts: Germany, France, and Russia called up 250,000 or more troops each year; Austria-Hungary and Italy, about 100,000. The per capita expenditure on the military rose in all the major powers between 1890 and 1914; the proportion of national budgets devoted to defense in 1910 was lowest in Austria-Hungary at 10 percent and highest in Germany at 45 percent.

The modernization of weaponry also transformed warfare. Swedish arms manufacturer Alfred Nobel patented dynamite and developed a kind of gunpowder that improved the accuracy of guns and produced a less clouded battlefield environment by reducing smoke from the process of firing. The industrial revolution in chemicals affected long-range artillery, which by 1914 could fire on targets as far as six miles away. Greater accuracy and heavy firepower made military offensives more difficult to win than in the past because neither side could overcome such weaponry by attacking on foot or on horseback. Military leaders devised strategies to protect their armies from overwhelming firepower; in the Russo-Japanese War, trenches and barbed wire blanketed the front around Port Arthur. New weapons were used in that conflict and in the Boer War, including howitzers, Mauser rifles, and Hotchkiss machine guns. Vickers in Britain, Creusot in France, Krupp in Germany, and Skoda in Austria-Hungary manufactured ever-growing stockpiles of these weapons.

Naval construction also played a sensational role in nationalist politics. To defend against more powerful, accurate weaponry, ships were made out of metal rather than wood after the mid-nineteenth century. In 1905, the English launched the H.M.S. *Dreadnought*, a warship with unprecedented firepower and the centerpiece of a program

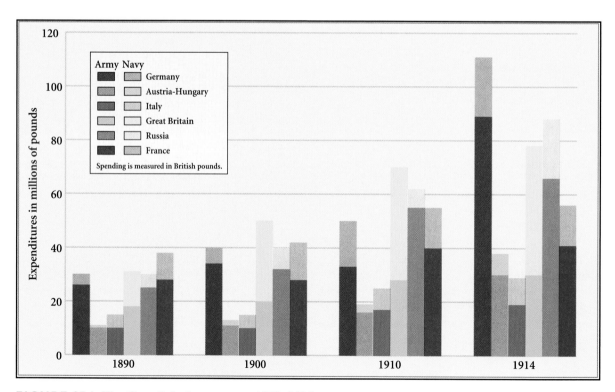

FIGURE 25.1 The Growth in Armaments, 1890–1914
The turn of the century saw the European powers engaged in a massive arms race. Several comparisons offer themselves, particularly the resources newly devoted to navies and the soaring defense spending of the Germans. Historians often ask whether better diplomacy could have prevented the outbreak of world war in 1914. The enormous military buildup, however, made some people living in the early twentieth century as well as some later historians see war as inevitable.
The Hammond Atlas of the Twentieth Century. (London: Times Books, 1996) 29.

to update the navy by constructing at least seven battleships per year. Germany had been following British navy building step by step and had made itself not just a land but a sea power. Grand Admiral Alfred von Tirpitz (1849–1930) encouraged the insecure William II to see the navy as the essential ingredient in making Germany a world power and oversaw the modernization and immense buildup of the fleet. Tirpitz admired the American naval theorist Alfred Thayer Mahan (1840–1914) and planned to build bases as far away as the Pacific, following Mahan's conclusion that command of the seas had historically been the key factor in determining international power. German ambitions, especially Tirpitz's drive to build battleships, alarmed the British and further motivated them to ally with France in the Entente Cordiale. Britain raised its naval spending from $50 million per year in the 1870s to $130 million in 1900; Germany, from $8.75 million to $37.5 million; France, from $37 million to $62.5 million (Figure 25.1). The Germans announced the fleet buildup as "a peaceful policy," but, like the British buildup, it led only to a hostile international climate and intense competition in weapons manufacture.

Because military buildup could help a country's social and economic stability by providing jobs and profit, military policy was made with an eye to internal politics. When critics of the arms race suggested a temporary "naval holiday" to stop British and German building, British officials opposed the moratorium by warning that it "would throw innumerable men on the pavement." Colonial leagues, nationalist organizations, and other patriotic groups lobbied for military spending, while enthusiasts in government publicized large navies as beneficial to international trade and domestic industry.

Public relations campaigns helped generate popular support for the arms race as they had for colonial expansion. When Tirpitz wanted to enlarge the German fleet, he made sure the press connected the buildup to the cause of national power and pride. The press accused Social Democrats, who wanted an equitable tax system more proportionate to wealth, of being unpatriotic. The Conservative Party in Great Britain, eager for more battleships, made popular the slogan "We want eight and we won't wait."

Despite the massive expenditures needed to establish military might in 1914, most of the public was convinced of the relationship between military power and national prestige and believed war was on its way to settle lingering international tensions. The remarks of Marshall Joseph Joffre (1852–1931) of France typified the sentiments of many military men of the time. When asked in 1912 if he thought about war, he said that he did constantly. "We shall have war," he maintained. "I will make it. I will win it."

1914: War Erupts

June 28, 1914, began as an ordinary day for Austrian Archduke Francis Ferdinand (1863–1914) and his wife, Sophie, as they ended a state visit to Sarajevo in Bosnia. The archduke, in full military regalia, was riding in a motorcade to bid farewell to various officials when a group of young Serb nationalists threw bombs in an unsuccessful assassination attempt. The full danger did not register,

Archduke Francis Ferdinand and His Wife in Sarajevo, June 1914
Archduke Francis Ferdinand, heir to the Austro-Hungarian monarchy, was a thorn in the side of many politicians because he did not want to favor Hungarian interests over other ethnic ones in his kingdom. His own family life was also unusual for royalty in those days in that his wife, Sophie, and he had married for love and did not like to be apart. Thus the couple were traveling together to Bosnia in 1914 and were jointly assassinated—the immediate prelude to the outbreak of World War I.
Mary Evans Picture Library.

IMPORTANT DATES

1894–1895 Japan defeats China in the Sino-Japanese War

1894–1899 Dreyfus Affair lays bare anti-Semitism in France

1899–1902 Boer War fought between Dutch descendants and the British in South African states

1900 Sigmund Freud publishes *The Interpretation of Dreams*

1901 Irish National Theater established by Maud Gonne and William Butler Yeats; death of Queen Victoria

1903 Emmeline Pankhurst founds the Women's Social and Political Union to fight for woman suffrage in Great Britain

1904–1905 Japan defeats Russia in the Russo-Japanese War

1905 Revolution erupts in Russia; violence forces Nicholas II to establish an elected body, the Duma; Albert Einstein publishes his "Special Theory of Relativity"

1906 Women receive the vote in Finland

1907 Pablo Picasso launches cubist painting with *Les Demoiselles d'Avignon*

1908 Young Turks revolt against rule by the sultan in the Ottoman Empire

1911–1912 Revolutionaries overthrow the Qing dynasty and declare China a republic

1914 Assassination of the Austrian archduke Francis Ferdinand and his wife by a Serbian nationalist precipitates World War I

and after a stop the archduke and his wife set out again. In the crowd was another nationalist, Gavrilo Princip, who for several weeks had traveled clandestinely to reach this destination, dreaming of reuniting his homeland of Bosnia-Herzegovina with Serbia and smuggling weapons with him to accomplish his end. The unprotected and unsuspecting couple became Princip's victims, as he shot both dead.

Some in the Habsburg government saw an opportunity to put down the Serbians once and for all. Evidence showed that Princip had received arms and information from Serbian officials, who directed the terrorist organization Black Hand from within the government. Endorsing a quick defeat of Serbia, German statesmen and military

leaders urged the Austrians to be unyielding and reiterated promises of support in case of war. While many heads of state and politicians were vacationing, the Austrians sent an ultimatum to the Serbian government, demanding public disavowals of terrorism, suppression of terrorist groups, and the participation of Austrian officials in an investigation of the crime. The ultimatum was severe. "You are setting Europe ablaze," the Russian foreign minister remarked of the humiliating demands made upon a sovereign state. Yet the Serbs were conciliatory, accepting all the terms except the presence of Austrian officials in the investigation. Kaiser William was pleased: "A great moral success for Vienna! All reason for war is gone." His relief proved unfounded. Austria-Hungary, confident of German backing, used the Serbs' resistance to only one of the ultimatum's terms as the pretext for declaring war against Serbia on July 28.

Complex and ineffectual maneuvering now consumed statesmen, some of whom tried very hard to avoid war. The tsar and the kaiser sent pleading letters to one another not to start a European war. Sir Edward Grey, British foreign secretary, proposed an all-European conference to no avail. The German chancellor as well as the kaiser displayed firm support for Austria in hopes of convincing the French and British to shy away from the war. The failure of either to fight, German officials believed, would subsequently keep Russia from mobilizing. At the same time, German military leaders had become fixed on fighting a short, preemptive war that would provide territorial gains leading toward the goal of a *Mitteleuropa*; simultaneously they hoped that martial law would justify arresting the leadership of the German Social Democratic Party, which threatened conservative rule.

The European press caught the war fever of the expansionist, imperialist, and other pro-war organizations, even as many governments were torn over what to do. Likewise, military leaders, especially in Germany and Austria-Hungary where there was less supervision of the military by the civilian government, promoted mobilization rather than diplomacy in the last days of July. The Austrians declared war and then ordered mobilization on July 31 without fear of a Russian attack. They did so in full confidence of German military aid, because as early as 1909 the German chief of staff Helmuth von Moltke had promised that his government would defend Austria-Hungary, believing

MAPPING THE WEST Europe at the Outbreak of World War I, August 1914

*All the powers expected a great, swift victory when war broke out. Sharing borders, many saw a
chance to increase their territories; and as rivals for trade and empire, they were almost all convinced
that war would bring them many advantages. But if European nations appeared well prepared and
invincible at the start of the war, relatively few would survive the conflict intact.*

Russia would not dare intervene. But Nicholas II ordered the Russian army to mobilize in defense of Russia's Slavic allies the Serbs. Encouraging the Austrians to attack Serbia, the German general staff mobilized on August 1.

German strategy was based on the Schlieffen Plan, named after its author, Alfred von Schlieffen (1833–1913), a former chief of the general staff. The plan essentially outlined a way to combat antagonists on two fronts by concentrating on one foe at a time. It called for a rapid and concentrated blow to the west against Russia's ally France, which would lead to that nation's defeat in six weeks, accompanied by a light holding action to the east.

The western armies would then be deployed against Russia, which, it was believed, would mobilize far more slowly. The attack on France was to proceed through Belgium, whose neutrality was guaranteed by the European powers.

The Schlieffen Plan

But German strategy hit an unexpected snag when the Belgian government rejected an ultimatum to allow the uncontested passage of the German army through the country. Now the riddle of Britain's position was solved. The subsequent violation of Belgian neutrality brought Britain into the war on the side of Russia and France, which was simultaneously mobilizing as part of its alliance with Russia. Although the kaiser at the last minute demanded a war limited to Russia to avoid fighting the British, the military vetoed him because of its unalterable plan for a two-front war. "Who rules in Berlin?" one statesman wondered upon viewing the German government's attempts at peace and the military's push toward war.

Conclusion

Rulers soon forgot their last-minute hesitations in the general celebration that erupted with the war. "Old heroes have reemerged from the books of legends," wrote a Viennese actor after watching the troops march off. "A mighty wonder has taken place, we have become *young*." Both sides exulted, believing in certain victory. A short conflict, people maintained, would resolve tensions ranging from the rise of the working class to political problems caused by global imperial competition.

The arms race had stimulated militant nationalism and brought many Europeans to favor war over peace. The crisis of modernity had helped blaze the path to war: the *Rite of Spring* ballet that opened in Paris in 1913 had taken as its theme the ritualistic attraction of death. Facing continuing violence in politics, incomprehensibility in the arts,

and problems in the industrial order, Europeans had come to believe that war would set events back on course and save them from the perils of modernity. "Like men longing for a thunderstorm to relieve them of the summer's sultriness," wrote one Austrian official, "so the generation of 1914 believed in the relief that war might bring." Such a possibility caused Europeans to rejoice. But tragically, their elation was short-lived. Instead of bringing the refreshment of summer rain, war opened an era of political turmoil, widespread suffering, massive human slaughter, and even greater doses of modernity.

Suggested References

Private Life in an Age of Modernity

Historians are engaged in serious study of the transformations of everyday life that industrial and imperial advance had brought about by the early twentieth century. In particular, personal and domestic life, as seen in the works of Hull, Walkowitz, and Duberman et al., have taken on greater importance as components of social movements and political developments.

Accampo, Elinor A., Rachel G. Fuchs, and Mary Lynn Stewart, eds. *Gender and the Politics of Social Reform in France, 1870–1914.* 1995.

Duberman, Martin, Martha Vicinus, and George Chauncey Jr. *Hidden from History: Reclaiming the Gay and Lesbian Past.* 1989.

Engelstein, Laura. *The Keys to Happiness: Sex and the Search for Modernity in Fin-de-Siècle Russia.* 1992.

Gillis, John. *A World of Their Own Making: Myth, Ritual, and the Quest for Family Values.* 1996.

Hull, Isabell. *The Entourage of Kaiser Wilhelm II, 1888–1918.* 1982.

Walkowitz, Judith. *City of Dreadful Delight: Narratives of Sexual Danger in Late-Victorian London.* 1993.

Modernity and the Revolt in Ideas

Some of the most controversial historiography sees the road to World War I as paved with cultural conflict. Many of the studies here suggest that new forms of art, music, dance, and philosophy were as central to the challenges Europe faced as were ethnic, economic, and international turmoil.

Eksteins, Modris. *Rites of Spring: The Great War and the Birth of the Modern Age.* 1989.

Everdell, William R. *The First Moderns. Profiles in the Origins of Twentieth-Century Thought.* 1997.

Jensen, Robert. *Marketing Modernism in Fin-de-Siècle Europe.* 1994.

Kern, Steven. *The Culture of Space and Time, 1880–1918.* 1983.

*Mann, Thomas. *Buddenbrooks.* 1901.

Nehamas, Alexander. *Nietzsche: Life as Literature.* 1985.

Nineteenth- and twentieth-century philosophy: http://www.epistemelinks.com/index.asp.

Silverman, Debora L. *Art Nouveau in Fin-de-Siècle France: Politics, Psychology, and Style.* 1989.

Politics in a New Key

Historians are uncovering the dramatic changes in political life and assessing the consequences of the rise of mass politics across Europe, including the development of suffragist movements. Some studies cited here investigate a second major political phenomenon: the formation of a politics of hatred and the rise of aggressive, warlike nationalism to replace nationalism based on rights and constitutional values.

Burns, Michael. *Dreyfus: A Family Affair.* 1992.

Chickering, Roger. *We Men Who Feel Most German: A Cultural Study of the Pan-German League, 1886–1914.* 1984.

Dennis, David B. *Beethoven in German Politics, 1870–1989.* 1996.

Kent, Susan. *Gender and Power in Britain, 1640–1990.* 1999.

Kornberg, Jacques. *Theodor Herzl: From Assimilation to Zionism.* 1993.

MacKenzie, David. *Violent Solutions: Revolutions, Nationalism, and Secret Societies in Europe to 1918.* 1996.

Schorske, Carl E. *Fin-de-Siècle Vienna: Politics and Culture.* 1981.

Scott, Joan. *Only Paradoxes to Offer: French Feminism and the Rights of Man.* 1996.

European Imperialism Challenged

In the midst of raucous political and social debate, the European powers faced growing resistance to their domination and increasingly serious setbacks. Many historians now judge Europe to have played a less commanding role in the rest of the world than the leading empires claimed. Imperial instability, as some studies show, paved the road to war. The fascination with the major non-Western contender—Japan—can be traced on the Japanese history Web site.

*Primary sources

Cohen, Paul A. *History in Three Keys: The Boxers as Event, Experience, and Myth.* 1997.

Gouda, Frances. *Dutch Culture Overseas: Colonial Practice in the Netherlands Indies, 1900–1942.* 1995.

Japanese history: http://www.csuohio.edu/history/japan/index.html.

Kansu, Aykut. *The Revolution of 1908 in Turkey.* 1997.

McDonald, David MacLaren. *United Government and Foreign Policy in Russia, 1900–1914.* 1992.

Meyers, Ramon H., and Mark R. Peattie, eds. *The Japanese Colonial Empire, 1895–1945.* 1984.

*Pruitt, Ida. *A Daughter of Han: The Autobiography of a Chinese Working Woman.* 1945.

Sinha, Mrinalini. *Colonial Masculinity: The "Manly Englishman" and the "Effeminate Bengali" in the Late Nineteenth Century.* 1995.

Weeks, Theodore R. *Nation and State in Late Imperial Russia: Nationalism and Russification on the Western Frontier.* 1996.

Roads to War

The question of why World War I broke out remains widely debated. There are always newcomers to the discussion devoted to assessing the responsibility for the war's beginning, but while these historians fix on a single country, other historians like to look at the full range of diplomatic, military, social, and economic conditions.

Ascher, Abraham. *The Revolution of 1905: Russia in Disarray.* 1988.

Berghahn, Volker. *Germany and the Approach of War.* 1993.

Cecil, Lamar. *Wilhelm II, Prince and Emperor, 1859–1900.* 1989.

Fenyvesi, Charles. *When the World Was Whole.* 1990.

Ferguson, Niall. *The Pity of War: Explaining World War I.* 1999.

Hoensch, Jorg K. *A History of Modern Hungary, 1867–1986.* 1988.

Lambi, Ivo. *The Navy and German Power Politics.* 1984.

Manning, Roberta. *The Crisis of the Old Order in Russia.* 1982.

Tech, Mikulás, and Roy Porter, eds. *The National Question in Europe in Historical Context.* 1993.

Williamson, Samuel. *Austria-Hungary and the Origins of the First World War.* 1991.

CHAPTER
26

War, Revolution, and Reconstruction

1914–1929

Grieving Parents
Before World War I the German artist Kaethe Köllwitz gained her artistic reputation with wood-cuts of handloom weavers whose livelihoods were threatened by industrialization. From 1914 on, she depicted the suffering and death that swirled around her and never with more sober force than in these two monuments to her son Peter, who had died on the western front in the first months of battle. Today one can still travel to his burial place in Vladslo, Belgium, to see this father and mother mourning their loss, like millions across Europe in those heartbreaking days.
The John Parker Picture Library.

JULES AMAR FOUND HIS TRUE VOCATION in World War I. A French expert on making industrial work more efficient, Amar switched his focus after 1914 as hundreds of thousands of men returned from the battlefront missing body parts. Plastic surgery developed rapidly, as did the construction of masks and other devices to hide deformities. But Amar, who designed artificial limbs and appendages in these traumatic years, sought to devise prostheses that would allow the wounded soldier to return to normal life by "mak[ing] up for a function lost, or greatly reduced." So the arms that he designed used hooks, magnets, and other mechanisms with which the veteran could hold a cigarette, play a violin, and most important work with tools such as typewriters. Mangled by the weapons of modern technological warfare, the survivors of World War I would be made whole, it was thought, by skills and technology such as Amar's.

Amar dealt with the human tragedy of the "Great War," so named by contemporaries because of its staggering human toll—forty million wounded or killed in battle. The Great War was also what historians call a "total war," meaning one built on full mobilization of soldiers, civilians, and the technological capacities of the most highly industrialized nations. The Great War did not settle problems or restore social order as the European powers hoped it would. Instead, the war produced political cataclysm and social and cultural upheaval. In Russia, revolutionaries overturned the tsarist regime even before the war ended. In Germany, defeat and rebellion forced the kaiser to

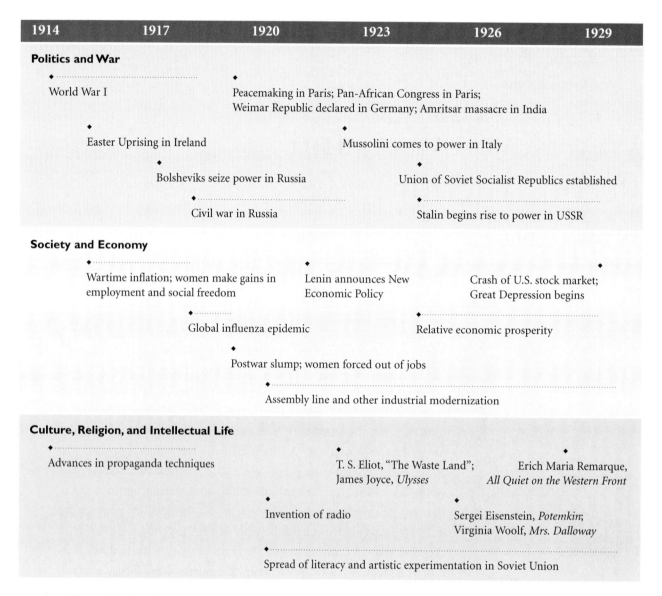

1914	1917	1920	1923	1926	1929

Politics and War

World War I

Peacemaking in Paris; Pan-African Congress in Paris;
Weimar Republic declared in Germany; Amritsar massacre in India

Easter Uprising in Ireland

Mussolini comes to power in Italy

Bolsheviks seize power in Russia

Union of Soviet Socialist Republics established

Civil war in Russia

Stalin begins rise to power in USSR

Society and Economy

Wartime inflation; women make gains in
employment and social freedom

Lenin announces New
Economic Policy

Crash of U.S. stock market;
Great Depression begins

Global influenza epidemic

Relative economic prosperity

Postwar slump; women forced out of jobs

Assembly line and other industrial modernization

Culture, Religion, and Intellectual Life

Advances in propaganda techniques

T. S. Eliot, "The Waste Land";
James Joyce, *Ulysses*

Erich Maria Remarque,
All Quiet on the Western Front

Invention of radio

Sergei Eisenstein, *Potemkin*;
Virginia Woolf, *Mrs. Dalloway*

Spread of literacy and artistic experimentation in Soviet Union

---

abdicate, leaving that once proud nation starving, demoralized, and buffeted by the winds of political extremism. Through ethnic uprisings and peace treaties, the long-lived Ottoman and Austro-Hungarian Empires were dismembered at the war's end. The crushing burden of war on the European powers accelerated the rise of the United States to global leadership, while service in the war intensified the demands of colonized peoples for autonomy.

For all the vast changes that the Great War ushered in, it also hastened transformations under way before it started. Nineteenth-century optimism, already tinged with a sense of decline, gave way to a more pervasive postwar cynicism. Many

Westerners turned their backs on politics and attacked life with frenzied gaiety in the Roaring Twenties, snapping up new consumer goods, drinking in entertainment provided by films and radio, and enjoying personal freedoms that Victorianism had forbidden. Others found reason for hope in the new political systems the war made possible: Soviet communism and Italian fascism. Building on prewar trends, communist and fascist leaders sought to mobilize the masses for political, even radical, ends. Modern communication technologies such as radio, film, and the press gave them the means to ally themselves with the cultural avant-garde to promote a utopian mass politics that paradoxically was antidemocratic, militaristic, and eventually totalitarian. Already weakening during the prewar period, the "gentlemanly" political tone of William Gladstone's day had been devastated by total war.

Seen as a solution to the conflicts of modernity, a war that was long anticipated and even welcomed in some quarters destabilized Europe and the world far into the next decades. From statesmen to ordinary citizens, many Europeans like Amar would spend their best peacetime efforts to make war-ravaged society function normally, while others saw that task as utterly futile, given the globally transformative force of the Great War. During the 1920s, both types were looking backward, constructing the future from the haunting fragments of an unforgettable past.

❖ The Great War, 1914–1918

When war erupted in August 1914, the ground had been prepared with long-standing alliances, the development of strategies for war, and the buildup of military technologies such as heavy artillery, machine guns, and the airplane. Seeing precedents in Prussia's rapid victories over Denmark, the Austrian Empire, and France in the 1860s and 1870 and the swift blows that Japan dealt Russia in 1904–1905, most people felt that this would be a short, decisive conflict. But the unforeseen happened: this war would last for more than four years, and it would be a total war, mobilizing soldiers, civilians, and the entire industrial capacity of the West. Although some British leaders with

A French Regiment Leaves for the Front, August 1914
Bands played, crowds cheered, and bicyclists led the way as bayonet-equipped soldiers marched eagerly to war. The mood changed quickly as machine guns and poison chemicals brought the bravest men down. People in cities, working to provide munitions and supplies, soon felt the pinch of inflation and later many lacked food. Men returned permanently disabled, even mentally deranged from their experience. And as four major empires—Ottoman, Russian, Austro-Hungarian, and German— collapsed, the war's bright beginnings disappeared from memory.
© Collection Viollet.

experience of the Boer War suggested that "the next war" would be an especially "nasty business," most of society did not anticipate the horror that lay ahead. It was precisely the unprecedented horror that made World War I "great."

Blueprints for War

World War I pitted two sets of opponents formed roughly out of the alliances developed during the previous fifty years. On one side stood the Central Powers (Austria-Hungary and Germany), which had evolved from Bismarck's Triple Alliance, and on the other the Allies (France, Great Britain, and Russia), which had emerged as a bloc from the Entente Cordiale between France and Great Britain and the 1890s treaties between France and Russia. In 1915, Italy, originally part of the Triple Alliance, joined the Allies in hopes of postwar gain. The two sides expanded globally almost from the start: in late August 1914, Japan, eager to extend its empire into China, went over to the Allies, while in the fall Turkey united with the Central Powers against its traditional enemy, Russia.

Joined by other, smaller countries, the antagonists fought with the same ferocious hunger for power, prestige, and prosperity that had inspired imperialism. Of the Central Powers, Germany aspired to a far-flung empire to be gained by annexing Russian territory and incorporating parts of Belgium, France, and Luxembourg. Some German leaders wanted to annex Austria-Hungary as well. Austria-Hungary hoped to retain its great-power status, threatened by the different nationalisms within its borders that were based on ethnicity rather than loyalty to the Habsburg crown.

Among the Allies, Russia wanted to reassert its status as a great power and as the protector of the Slavs by adding a reunified Poland to the Russian Empire, annexing the Austro-Hungarian territory peopled by Ukrainians, and reorganizing the rest of Austria-Hungary into a triple monarchy that recognized Slavic political claims. The French too craved territory, especially the return of Alsace and Lorraine, taken from them after the Franco-Prussian War, and wanted new, more secure boundaries with Germany. The British sought to keep the North Sea coast from falling to another great power and to cement their hold on Egypt and the Suez Canal, as well as to secure the rest of their world empire. By the Treaty of London (1915), France and Britain promised Italy territory in Africa, Asia Minor, the Balkans, and elsewhere in return for joining the Allies.

All the powers with colonies enlisted or conscripted tens of thousands of colonized men into their service. Britain deployed Indian regiments in western Europe in the first days of the war and enlisted Arabs against the Turks. The French relied heavily on Senegalese and North African recruits, promising them citizenship for their service. The Germans used colonial soldiers in Europe and later in Africa and Asia.

By August 1914, machine guns and rifles, airplanes, battleships, submarines, and motorized transport—cars and railroads—were at the disposal of armies; new technologies like chlorine gas, tanks, and bombs would develop between 1914 and 1918. Countries differed, however, in their experience with and quantities of weapons of war as well as knowledgeable in their use. British generals who had fought in the Boer War knew the destructive capacity of these weapons, while the Germans were far more advanced in strategy and weaponry than either the Russians or the Austrians. The war itself became a lethal testing ground, as both new and old weaponry were used, often ineffectively.

One military concept prevailed on both sides: officers believed in a "cult of the offensive," in which spirited attacks and high troop morale would be decisive. Despite the availability of newer, more powerful war technology, an old-fashioned vision of war made officers unwilling to abandon the more familiar sabers, lances, and bayonets. Given the technological potential of European industrialization, the war thus opened on a completely unrealistic note, with Napoleonic weaponry and strategy, uniforms, polished swords, and cheerful military plans seen as central to victory. The "cult of the offensive" would cost millions of lives.

The Battle Fronts

The first months of the war crushed hope of quick victory. All the major armies mobilized rapidly. The Germans, guided by the Schlieffen Plan (see page 973), reached Luxembourg on August 2 and Belgium on August 4, 1914. The plan counted on unchallenged passage through these small countries. Meanwhile, the main body of French troops,

MAP 26.1 The Fronts of World War I, 1914–1918

Because the western front remained relatively stationary, devastation of land and resources was intense. All fronts, however, destroyed segments of Europe's hard-won industrial and agricultural capacity, while the immobile trenches increased military casualties. Men engaged in trench warfare for so long developed an intense camaraderie based on their incredible suffering and deprivation.

tricked by German diversionary tactics, attacked the Germans in Alsace and Lorraine instead of meeting the invasion from the north. In the late summer heat, both the Schlieffen Plan and the French offensive disintegrated because of bad planning and worse luck.

1914–1915: Indecisive Offensives.   The Belgians unexpectedly resisted, slowing the German advance and allowing British and French troops to reach the northern front (Map 26.1). In September, the British and French armies engaged the Germans along the Marne River in France (Map 26.2).

Neither side could defeat the other, and the fighting continued late into the autumn along the Marne and up to Ypres in Belgium. Casualties were shocking: in the first three months of war, more than 1.5 million men fell on the western front alone. Firepower turned what was supposed to be an offensive war of movement into a stationary, defensive impasse. For the next four years the two sides faced off along a line that stretched from the North Sea through Belgium and northern France to Switzerland. Soldiers dug in, excavating parallel lines of trenches up to thirty feet deep that would serve millions of men as nightmarish homes.

On the eastern front, the "Russian steamroller"—so named because of the number of men mobilized, some twelve million in all—drove far more quickly than expected, into East Prussia on

August 17 and into parts of Austria-Hungary, while Russia's Serbian allies repelled Austria-Hungary's troops in Serbia. The Russians believed that no army could stand up to their massive numbers, no matter how ill equipped and poorly trained they were. Their success was short-lived. The Germans crushed the tsar's army in East Prussia at Tannenberg and in campaigns around the Masurian Lakes. The Germans then turned south to Galicia, where Russian and Austro-Hungarian armies were fighting costly battles. Although the Russian army was capable of fighting the dual monarchy's armed forces, the technologically superior German army often stopped the Russians cold. Victory boosted German morale and made heroes of the military leaders Paul von Hindenburg (1847–1934) and Erich Ludendorff (1865–1937), who thereupon

MAP 26.2 The Western Front

The western front occupied some of the richest parts of France, with long-lasting consequences. Destruction of French villages, roads, bridges, livestock, and property was the worst in Europe, while the trauma of the French people endured for generations. The effects of horrendous casualties, ever-present artillery fire, provisioning and hospital needs, and the demands of military and medical personnel changed everyone's way of life and made most people fear another war more than anything else.

The Toll of Trench Warfare
On both sides the war took an enormous toll in male lives, leaving politicians and citizens alike concerned about society's future. Depictions of shattered bodies that heavy firepower ripped to bits, however, hardly reached the home front and thus the illusion remained that the war was about individual prowess and that individual soldiers had a fighting chance of survival. Simultaneously troops from the colonies were often depicted as bringing an innate savagery to the battlefront, though these soldiers had even less chance of surviving because they were often placed in the front lines.
Left: Imperial War Museum, London; right: Robert Hunt Library.

demanded more troops for the eastern front. Despite heartening victories, by year's end German triumphs in the east had failed to knock out the Russians and had also misdirected the Schlieffen Plan, which called for only light holding action to the east until the western front had been won.

War at sea proved equally indecisive. Confident in Britain's superior naval power, the Allies blockaded the entries to the Mediterranean and North Seas to prevent supplies from reaching Germany and Austria-Hungary. William II and his advisers planned a massive submarine, or U-boat (*Unterseeboot*, "underwater boat"), campaign against Allied and neutral shipping around Britain and France. In May 1915, German submarines sank the British passenger ship *Lusitania* and killed 1,198 people, including 124 Americans. Although the atmosphere in the United States crackled with outrage, Woodrow Wilson (1856–1924; president 1913–1921) maintained a policy of neutrality. The Germans, not willing to provoke Wilson further, called off unrestricted submarine warfare. In May 1916, the navies of Germany and Britain finally

clashed in the battle of Jutland. Although inconclusive, the battle demonstrated that the German fleet could not dislodge the British as rulers of the sea.

Ideas of a negotiated peace were discarded while the cult of the offensive remained unmodified. "No peace before England is defeated and destroyed," the kaiser railed against his cousin King George V. "Only amidst the ruins of London will I forgive Georgy." Politician and powerful journalist Georges Clemenceau (1841–1929), who would become premier of France for the second time in 1917, called for a "war to the death." General staffs continued to prepare fierce attacks several times a year. Campaigns opened with heavy artillery pounding enemy trenches and gun emplacements. Troops then scrambled "over the top" of their trenches, usually to be mowed down by machine-gun fire from defenders secure in their own trenches.

Indecisive offensives continued. On the western front, the French desperately wanted to oust the Germans from their northern industrial regions. Throughout 1915, they assaulted the enemy at Ypres, Loos, and Artois; but they accomplished little, and casualties of 100,000 and more for a single campaign became commonplace. On the eastern front, troops on both sides fared no better than their counterparts in Belgium and France. In the spring of 1915, Russian armies captured parts of Galicia and lumbered toward Hungary. The Central Powers struck back in Poland later that year, bringing the front closer to Petrograd (formerly St. Petersburg), the Russian capital. The Austro-Hungarian armies routed the Serbs in 1915 and then engaged the newly mobilized Italian army.

1916: Mounting Catastrophe. The next year was even more disastrous. When the Germans judged that a definitive blow against the French would induce the British to withdraw from the war, they turned their attention in early 1916 to the fortress at Verdun. (See Map 26.2.) The fall of the fortress, they calculated, would cripple French morale. Launching massive assaults from February through April, the Germans fired as many as a million shells in a single day. Combined French and German losses totaled close to a million men. Nonetheless the French held.

Hoping to relieve their allies, the British unleashed an artillery pounding of German trenches in the Somme region in June 1916 that was supposed to ensure a bloodless victory for Britain. But on July 1, twenty thousand British soldiers died going "over the top"—the artillery had failed to penetrate the deeply dug German fortifications. In several months of battle at the Somme, 1.25 million men were killed or wounded, but the final result was stalemate. By the end of 1916, the French had absorbed more than 3.5 million casualties. To help the Allies engaged at Verdun and the Somme, the Russians struck again, driving once more into the Carpathians, recouping territory, and menacing the Habsburg Empire. Only the German army stopped the Russian advance. Amidst the huge losses, the Habsburg army recruited men in their mid-fifties and the German general staff was impelled to take over Austrian military operations. The war was sapping Europe's strength and individual sovereignty.

The View from the Trenches. Had the military leaders thoroughly dominated the scene, historians judge, all armies would have been utterly demol-

ished in nonstop offensives by the end of 1915. Yet historians have recently come to see that ordinary soldiers in this war were not automatons in the face of what seemed to them suicidal orders. Whereas governments and officers tended to see war as "kill or be killed," troops at the front often put into effect their own practice of "live and let live." Some battalions went for long stretches with hardly a casualty, a far cry from the common historical picture of relentless bloodshed. Diaries show that throughout the war, and despite the increasing threat of punishment, these low rates stemmed from agreements among troops to avoid battles. Enemies facing each other across the trenches frequently ate their meals in peace, for example, even though the trenches were within hand grenade reach. A German soldier described trenches "where friend and foe alike go to fetch straw from the same rick [stack] to protect them from cold and rain—and never a shot is fired." Throughout the war, soldiers fraternized on both fronts. They played an occasional game of soccer, yelled across the trenches, sang together at Christmas and Easter, exchanged mementos, and made gestures of agreement not to fight. A British veteran of the trenches explained to a new recruit that the Germans "don't want to fight any more than we do, so there's a kind of understanding between us. Don't fire at us and we'll not fire at you." Burying enemy dead in common graves with their own fallen comrades, many ordinary soldiers came to feel more warmly toward enemies who shared the trench experience than toward civilians back home. One infantryman wrote: "It is only on the home front that the atmosphere is still warlike. . . . At the [battle]front there is far too much mutual understanding of one for the other."

Newly forged bonds of male camaraderie alleviated some of the misery of trench life and aided survival. Sharing the danger of death and the deprivations of front-line experience weakened traditional class distinctions. In some cases upper-class officers and working-class draftees became friends in that "wholly masculine way of life uncomplicated by women," as one soldier put it. According to diaries and letters, soldiers picked lice from one another's bodies and clothes, revered section leaders who tended their blistered feet, and came to love one another, sometimes even passionately. Positive memories of this front-line community survived the war and influenced postwar politics.

Troops of colonized soldiers from Asia and Africa had different experiences of the trenches, especially as they were often put in the very front ranks where the risks were greatest. European observers noted that these soldiers suffered particularly from the rigors of a totally unfamiliar climate, strange food, and the ruin inflicted by Western war technology. Yet, as with class divisions, racial barriers sometimes fell, for instance, whenever a European understood enough to alleviate the distress that cold inflicted. Colonial troops' perspectives changed too, for in this war they got to see their "masters" completely undone and "uncivilized."

When the men in the trenches did fight one another, they lived in a veritable hell of shelling and sniping, flying body parts, rotting cadavers, and blinding gas. Some were reduced to hysteria or succumbed to shell shock through the sheer stress and violence of battle. Under these conditions many soldiers felt alienated from civilization and became cynical: "It might be me tomorrow," a young British soldier wrote his mother in 1916. "Who cares?" War was "so damned impersonal," depending less on swords and spirit than on wire cutters, artillery shells, gas masks, and tanks. Having gone to war often to escape ordinary life in industrial society, soldiers learned, as one German put it, "that in the modern war . . . the triumph of the machine over the individual is carried to its most extreme form." They took this hard-won knowledge into battle, pulling their comrades back when an offensive seemed lost or too costly.

The Home Front

World War I was taking place off the battlefield too. Even before the war had reached the stage of catastrophic impasse, it had become "total." Total war meant the indispensable involvement of civilians in the war industry: manufacturing the shells and bullets, machine guns and artillery, poisonous gases, cars and trains, bombs and airplanes, and eventually tanks that were the backbone of technological warfare. Increased production of artificial limbs, crutches, canes, wheelchairs, and coffins was also a wartime necessity. Because soldiers would have utterly failed without them, civilians had to work overtime for, believe in, and sacrifice for victory. To keep the war machine operating smoothly, governments directed the political, cultural, and

economic lives of citizens in unprecedented ways. They oversaw factories, transportation systems, and resources ranging from food to coal to textiles. Such control would have outraged many liberals before the war but was accepted as a necessary condition for victory.

Politics Suspended. At the outset, many socialists and working-class people who had formerly criticized the military buildup announced their support for the war. For decades socialist parties had preached that "the worker has no country" and that nationalism was an artificial ideology meant to keep workers disunited and subjected to the will of their employers. Socialists of the Second International had envisioned that their deputies would vote against military budgets and that their members would refuse to fight. But workers had joined in the euphoria of imperialism and the arms race before the war, and in August 1914 the socialist rank and file, along with most of the party leaders, were as patriotic as the rest of society. Their eager support of wartime governments ended the Second International's role as the vanguard of socialist leadership.

Initially political parties also put aside their differences; all-party solidarity was known in Germany as the *Burgfriede* ("domestic peace") and in France as the *union sacrée* ("sacred union"). Feminists divided over whether to maintain their traditional condemnation of militarism or to support the war. Although many feminists actively opposed the conflict, Emmeline Pankhurst and her daughter Christabel were among those who became militant nationalists, even changing the name of their suffrage paper to *Britannia*. Still other women flocked to philanthropic organizations assisting the war effort. Parties representing the middle classes shelved their distrust of the socialists and working classes to present a united front. In the name of victory, national leaders wanted to end political division of all kinds: "I no longer recognize [political] parties," William II declared on August 4, 1914. "I recognize only Germans."

Mobilizing for Total War. Governments took charge of the economy, as the lack of long-range planning hampered armies across Europe. All countries were caught without ready replacements for their heavy losses of weapons and military equipment, and governments soon stepped in to ensure steady production of war supplies and their timely arrival at the front. War ministries set up boards to allocate labor on the home front and the battlefront, sponsor efficiency studies of individual industries, oversee the regulation of factory work, and give industrialists financial incentives to encourage productivity. In Austria-Hungary, the Hungarian Emergency Measures Act allowed the drafting of both men and women for military or industrial service; in Germany, all men between the ages of seventeen and sixty could be drafted. In 1916, the National Service Act made all British citizens eligible for war service. The conscription of civilians into the labor force further blurred distinctions between military and civilian life.

Governments mobilized the home front with varying degrees of success. The Russian bureaucracy reluctantly and ineffectively cooperated with industrialists and other groups that could aid the war effort. Desperate for factory workers, the Germans forced Belgian citizens to move to Germany, housing them in prison camps until they could be rotated into factory work. In Germany, Austria, France, and Britain, officials eventually controlled food allocations through rationing because the war had curtailed farming and cut off trade. Municipal governments arranged for local workshops to organize sewing and other essential tasks; they also set up canteens and day-care centers so men and women could focus fully on war production. Rural Russia, Austria-Hungary, Bulgaria, and Serbia, where youths, women, and old men struggled to sustain farms, had no such relief programs. Simultaneously, governments and industrialists retreated from the trend toward protective legislation by ignoring laws that limited the length of women's workday, the kind of work they were allowed to do, and their performance of dangerous tasks. But this was one of the few steps away from big government that politicians took in World War I.

Governments throughout Europe passed sedition laws that made it a crime to criticize official policies. To ensure civilian acceptance of longer working hours and shortages of consumer goods, governments created propaganda agencies to tout the war as a patriotic mission to resist villainous enemies. British propagandists fabricated atrocities the German "Huns" supposedly committed against Belgians, and they invented statements—for example, the kaiser's remark that British soldiers formed

War Propaganda, 1915
"Never Forget!" screams the headline of this propaganda poster depicting an assaulted woman in despair. Intended to incite sentiment against the Germans, the poster suggested what German passage through neutral Belgium came to be called—"the rape of Belgium." Propaganda offices for the Allies sent out reports of women attacked and children massacred as the German armies moved through Belgian territories. Mary Evans Picture Library.

a "contemptible little army"—to incite the troops. British soldiers ridiculed the propaganda film *Battle of the Somme* (1916), with its staged scenes of war obviously filmed in a studio. The film drew packed civilian audiences, however, and its fake screen images bolstered the desire to smash the Germans. German propaganda warned that French African troops would rape German women if Germany was defeated. In Russia, Nicholas II changed the German-sounding name of St. Petersburg to the Russian Petrograd in 1914. But propaganda sometimes backfired. Worried about the loyalty of their many ethnic minorities, the Russians plastered Polish towns with posters promising national independence if the Poles would help fight the

Germans. But by mistakenly printing the Polish flag upside down on the posters, the Russians weakened rather than strengthened their cause.

Playing on fears and arousing hatred, propaganda rendered a compromise peace unlikely. Nonetheless, some individuals sought to shatter the nationalist consensus supporting the war. Activists in the international women's movement met in The Hague in 1915, determined to end the war. "We can no longer endure . . . brute force as the only solution of international disputes," declared Dutch physician Aletta Jacobs in her opening speech. Governments on both sides prevented many women from attending, because the slightest public moves toward a negotiated peace were seen as "defeatism." Those who reached The Hague, however, spent the remainder of the war urging statesmen to work out a peace settlement.

In Austria-Hungary, nationalist groups agitating for ethnic self-determination hampered the empire's war effort. The Czechs undertook a vigorous anti-Habsburg campaign at home, while in Paris, Thomas Masaryk (1850–1937) and Edouard Beneš (1884–1948) established the Czechoslovak National Council from which they lobbied Western governments for recognition of Czech rights. For Poles the war had finally split the powers that had partitioned their country in the eighteenth century. Jozef Pilsudski (1867–1935) set up the Polish Military Organization in Austrian Galicia, which he trained as the basis for an independent Polish army. In the Balkans, Croats, Slovenes, and Serbs formed a committee to plan a South Slav state carved from Habsburg possessions and other Balkan territory. The Allies encouraged such independence movements as part of their strategy to defeat the Habsburgs.

Society at War.   The war restructured the workforce. In the war's early days many women had lost their jobs when luxury shops, textile factories, and other nonessential establishments closed. With men at the front, many women headed households with little support and few opportunities to work. But governments and businesses soon recognized the amount of labor it would take to wage technological war. As more and more men left for the trenches, women who had lost their jobs in nonessential businesses as well as many low-paid domestic workers took over higher-paying jobs in formerly restricted munitions and metallurgical

German Welder Being Trained
As men were siphoned off to the battlefront in World War I, women took their places in factories, transportation, and services—all of them working overtime to supply the insatiable needs of modern, technological warfare. Women thus gained higher pay and learned new productive skills such as welding. A new working-class woman emerged from the experience of war.
Ullstein Bilderdienst.

industries. In Warsaw they drove trucks, and in London they conducted streetcars. Some young women drove ambulances and nursed the wounded near the front lines.

The press praised women's patriotism in adopting new roles, but women's assumption of men's jobs suggested not just social change but social disorder. From the start, a steady flood of wounded and weak men returned home to women who had adapted resourcefully and taken full charge. Some women demonstrated uncustomary strength and enthusiasm for war: "Oh, it's you that have all the luck, out there in the blood and muck," went one woman author's jingle. Workingmen commonly protested that women, in the words of one metalworker, were "sending men to the slaughter." Men feared that when the war was over women would remain in the workforce, robbing men of work and usurping their role as breadwinner. Many people, even some women, objected to women's loss of femininity. "The feminine in me decreased more and more, and I did not know whether to be sad or glad about this," wrote one Russian nurse about learning to wear rough male clothing near the battlefield. The factory woman emerged from long hours working with toxic substances looking like something that "makes you afraid with her hands and face turned yellow, her colourless hair and the corpse-like look which the handling of explosives gives her," as one male worker complained. Some criticized young female munitions workers for squandering their pay on ribbons, furs, and jewelry. These wartime tensions over traditional gender roles echoed prewar changes in relations between the sexes and presaged rifts to come.

Although many soldiers from different social backgrounds felt bonds of solidarity in the trenches, wartime conditions increasingly pitted civilians against one another along class lines. Workers toiled longer hours eating less, while many in the upper classes bought abundant food and fashionable clothing on the black market (outside the official system of rationing) and lived conspicuously well. Governments allowed many businesses high rates of profit, a step that resulted in a surge in the cost of living and thus contributed to social strife. Shortages of staples like bread, sugar, and meat grew worse, as the brutal "turnip winter" of 1916–1917—when turnips were often the only available food—progressed. A German roof workers' association pleaded for relief: "We can no longer go on. Our children are starving. . . . It is simply beyond our strength." Craftspeople producing nonessential consumer goods suffered the most. Civilians held governments responsible for these everyday difficulties; ultimately some of their bitterness festered into revolution.

Civilians in occupied areas and in the colonies suffered the most oppressive working conditions. The combatants deported or conscripted able-bodied people in territories they occupied, the Germans, for instance, sent civilians from Belgium and northern France to Germany to work. The French forcibly transported some 100,000 Vietnamese to work in France for the war effort.

Africans were made to do grueling labor for the armies in the African colonies. Of the million Kenyans and Tanzanians so conscripted, at least 100,000 died from disease and overwork. Colonized people also saw their taxes skyrocket and prices rise. All such actions, like increasing class divisions, led to further politicization.

❖ 1917–1918: Protest, Revolution, and War's End

By 1917, the situation was becoming desperate for politicians, the military, and civilians, and discontent on the home front started shaping the course of the war. Neither patriotic slogans before the war nor propaganda during it had prepared people for wartime suffering. Cities across Europe experienced civilian revolt, nationalist struggles continued to plague Britain and Austria-Hungary, and soldiers mutinied. In Petrograd, the combined protest of soldiers and civilians turned into the Russian Revolution, toppling the tsar's dynasty for good. Nor would revolt stop when the war did: instead it continued to spread in the military and among workers.

War Protest

On February 1, 1917, the German government, hard-pressed by the public clamor over mounting casualties and by the military's growing control over decision making, resumed unrestricted submarine warfare. Despite politicians' fear of bringing in the United States, Generals Ludendorff and Hindenburg, whose prestige was on the rise, bullied the kaiser into unleashing the U-boats. The military made the irresistible promise to end the war in six months by cutting off imported food and military supplies to Britain and thus forcing the island nation to surrender before the United States could come to its rescue. The British responded by mining harbors and the seas and by developing depth charges, antisubmarine bombs that exploded underwater. But the most effective measure was the convoy system of shipping, in which a hundred or more warships and freighters traveling the seas together could drive off the

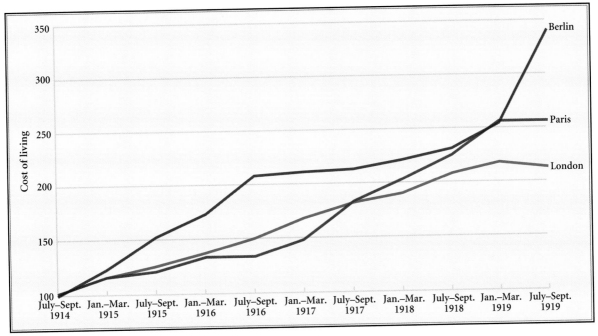

FIGURE 26.1 The Rising Cost of Living during World War I

The diversion of resources to the military resulted in a soaring cost of living for civilians. As men went to the front and as some remaining agricultural workers could find higher pay in factories, a decline in agricultural output led to scarcity and thus rising prices for food. Finally, housing came to be in short supply as resources were directed to the war effort rather than used to construct needed buildings. Even after the war prices rose in Germany because the Allies maintained their blockade to keep the pressure on the peacemaking process.

Jay Winter and Jean-Louis Robert, *Capital Cities at War: Paris, London, Berlin 1914 –1919* (Cambridge: Cambridge University Press, 1997), 259.

submarines. The Germans' submarine gamble failed to thwart the British. Moreover, unrestricted submarine warfare brought the United States into the war in April 1917, after German U-boats had sunk several American ships.

Political opposition increased in Europe, and deteriorating living conditions sparked outright revolt by civilians. "We are living on a volcano," warned an Italian politician in the spring of 1917. High prices and food shortages plagued everyday life (Figure 26.1). "Wages are not rising [but] food prices have risen by 100 and 200 percent," a Budapest paper complained in the summer of 1915. "We cannot bear this any longer!" Food shortages in cities of Italy, Russia, and Germany as well as in Vienna provoked riots by women who were unable to feed their families. As inflation mounted, tenants conducted rent strikes, factory hands and white-collar workers alike walked off the job, and female workers protested the skyrocketing cost of living and their fatigue from overwork.

Combatant countries were rife with dissension and conflicting goals. By 1917, the war had strengthened nationalist movements and the new emperor of Austria-Hungary secretly asked the Allies for a negotiated peace to avoid a total collapse of his empire. In the summer of 1917, the German Reichstag announced its desire for a "peace of understanding and permanent reconciliation of peoples." Woodrow Wilson further weakened civilian resolve in Germany and Austria-Hungary in January 1918 by issuing his Fourteen Points, a blueprint for a new international order that held out the promise of a nonvindictive peace settlement to war-weary citizens of the Central Powers. The Allies faced dissent too. In the spring of 1917, French soldiers mutinied, refusing to participate in any more bloody and fruitless offensives. And in Russia, wartime protest turned into outright revolution.

Revolution in Russia

Of all the warring nations, Russia sustained the greatest number of casualties—7.5 million by 1917. Slaughter on the eastern front had driven hundreds of thousands of peasants into the Russian

Revolution in Russia

1917

March 8   International Women's Day, strikes and demonstrations

March 12   Establishment of Provisional Government

March 15   Nicholas II abdicates

April 17   Lenin and other Bolshevik leaders return to Russia

May 14   Resignation of Milyukov, first head of Provisional Government

May 16   Kerensky takes over Provisional Government

Late June–early July   Russian offensive against Germany fails

Mid-July   Attempted popular uprising fails

September 9–14   Kornilov military coup d'état fails

November 6–7   Bolshevik seizure of power on behalf of soviets

November 25   Constituent assembly elections held

1918

January 18   Constituent assembly closed down by Bolsheviks

1918–1922   Civil war

1924   Union of Soviet Socialist Republics formally established

1928–1929   Stalin takes full power

---

interior, where officials were unprepared to deal with the refugees' hunger, homelessness, and disease. In March 1917,* crowds of workingwomen swarmed the streets of Petrograd demanding relief from harsh conditions. As these women were turned away from stores, they fell in with other protesters commemorating International Women's Day and began looting shops for food. Factory workers joined them in the streets, and the rioters enlisted support from other citizens and soldiers guarding the streets. Compared with the other great powers, Russia was industrially and commercially backward. Thus, the demands of the war

---

*Until February 1918, Russia remained on the Julian calendar, which was thirteen days behind the Gregorian calendar used by the rest of Europe. Hence the first phase of the revolution occurred in March according to the Gregorian or European calendar (but February in the Julian calendar), the later phase in November using the Gregorian calendar (October according to the Julian). All dates used in this book follow the Gregorian calendar.

---

overwhelmed the government's ability to provide basic necessities on the home front. In addition, many in the army, instead of remaining loyal to the tsar, were embittered by the massive casualties caused by their inferior weapons and their leaders' foolhardy tactics. The politicization that had evolved since the Revolution of 1905 combined with the government's incompetence during the war raised the voice of protest to a crescendo.

By 1917, the Russian monarchy commanded little respect because Nicholas was an inept leader in the best of circumstances. Unlike other heads of state, Nicholas failed to unify the bureaucracy, industrialists, workers, and peasants in a concerted effort to provision the military and home fronts. In addition, Grigori Rasputin, a combination of holy man and charlatan, held Nicholas and his wife, Alexandra, in his thrall by claiming to control the hemophilia of their son and heir. When government ministers challenged Rasputin's influence on state matters, Nicholas sided with Rasputin and dismissed his officials. "Is this stupidity or treason?" one member of the Duma asked of the corrupt, impotent wartime administration. Educated and influential leaders withdrew their support. When the riots erupted in February 1917, Nicholas was away, attempting to rally his forces at the front; but when railroad workers diverted his train on its way back to Petrograd, he knew the situation was hopeless. He abdicated, he and his family were taken into custody, and the three-hundred-year-old Romanov dynasty came to an end.

The Provisional Government. Politicians from the old Duma formed a new ruling entity called the Provisional Government, but continuing hardships and the competing aspirations of many groups—workers, homemakers, students, liberal politicians, and soldiers—made it difficult for the new body to govern. At first hopes were high, even utopian, that under the Provisional Government, as one revolutionary poet put it, "our false, filthy, boring, hideous life should become a just, pure, merry, and beautiful life." Composed essentially of moderates, the Provisional Government had to pursue the war successfully, manage internal affairs better, and set government on a firm constitutional footing to establish its credibility. However, it did not rule alone, as the Russian Revolution felt the tug of many different political forces.

Lenin Addressing the Second All-Russian Congress of Soviets
In the spring of 1917, the German government craftily let Lenin and other Bolsheviks travel from their exile in Switzerland back to the scene of the unfolding revolution in Russia. A committed revolutionary instead of a political reformer, Lenin used his oratory and skilled maneuvering to convince many in the soviets to follow him in overthrowing the Provisional Government, taking Russia out of the war, and implementing his brand of communism.
Novosti (London).

Spontaneously elected soviets—councils of workers and soldiers—competed with the government for political support and often challenged its policies. Soviets had sprung up during the Revolution of 1905 and quickly revived in 1917 to press for improved conditions and a speedy resolution of the war. Lively and informed, the soviets contrasted the people's needs with the privileges of the upper-class men in the Provisional Government. In the first euphoric rush of revolution, the soviets ended the deference society usually paid the wealthy and officers, urged respect for workers and the poor, and temporarily gave an air of celebration and carnival to this political cataclysm. The peasantry, another competing force for power, began to confiscate gentry estates and withheld produce from the market because of the lack of consumer goods for which to exchange food. Urban food shortages intensified.

In hopes of further destabilizing Russia, in April 1917 the Germans provided safe rail transportation for Lenin and other prominent Bolsheviks to return from their exile in Switzerland to Petrograd through German territory. Lenin, described by contemporaries as "humorless, uncompromising, and detached," had devoted his entire existence to bringing about socialism through the

force of his small band of Bolsheviks. As a political exile he had no parliamentary experience, but he had developed his position by maneuvering among socialist factions, by writing propaganda and theoretical works, and through the sheer strength of his will. Upon his return to Petrograd, Lenin issued the April Theses, a radical document that called for Russia to withdraw from the war, for the soviets to seize power on behalf of workers and poor peasants, and for all private land to be nationalized. The Bolsheviks challenged the legitimacy of the Provisional Government with the slogans "All power to the soviets" and "Peace, land, and bread." Committed to ending private property and to establishing Bolshevik leadership, Lenin wanted to block the success of the liberal policies of the Provisional Government.

By early summer the Provisional Government saw a battlefield victory as the only way to ensure its position against competitors at home and to bargain with the Central Powers for an advantageous peace. On July 1, the Russian army attacked the Austrians in Galicia but was defeated once again. The new prime minister, the Socialist Revolutionary Aleksandr Kerensky (1881–1970), used his commanding oratory to arouse patriotism, but he lacked the political skills needed to fashion an effective wartime government. In Petrograd groups of workers, soldiers, and sailors—many of them Bolsheviks—agitated for the soviets to replace the Provisional Government. So strong had the soviets grown under the coordination of the Petrograd soviet that they seemed to constitute a dual power along with the Provisional Government. To restore order, the government rounded up Bolshevik leaders and accused them of being German agents, forcing many others into hiding. Soon, however, the government needed the Bolsheviks to head off a military coup led by General Lavr Kornilov.

As Bolshevik popularity in the cities rose, the stature of other politicians fell. By fall 1917, Kerensky's Provisional Government was thoroughly discredited. Its leadership had failed both to enact a well-defined land reform and to call a constituent assembly to develop a permanent blueprint for government. Its conduct of the war had been disastrous, leaving the army, as one Russian critic put it, "a huge crowd of tired, poorly clad, poorly fed, embittered men."

The Bolshevik Takeover.   In November 1917, the Bolshevik leadership, urged on by Lenin, staged an uprising against Kerensky to prevent him from holding elections that might have stabilized the Provisional Government. The Bolsheviks took over key facilities (including the Winter Palace), drove out Kerensky's government, and seized power and placed it in the hands of a congress of soviets while claiming the right to form a government.

In January 1918, elections were finally held for a constituent assembly. Russian citizens, voting freely, elected representatives from a variety of political parties. The Bolsheviks, who by then had supported the elections, did not fare well, gaining fewer seats than the Socialist Revolutionaries. Within days, the Bolsheviks used troops to disrupt the assembly and took over the government by force. They seized town and city administrations, closing down the zemstvos (local councils) and other institutions in the countryside where Socialist Revolutionary support was keen. Soon after, the Bolsheviks asked Germany for peace.

The Germans agreed, but their idea of peace was the Treaty of Brest-Litovsk (March 1918), which placed vast regions of the old Russian Empire under German occupation. (See Map 26.1.) The treaty partially realized the German ideal of a

central European region, or *Mitteleuropa*, under German control. It also showed the remaining Allied powers how tough the Germans were as victors and how unreliable the Russians were as allies. Because the loss of millions of square miles put Petrograd at risk, the Bolsheviks relocated the capital to Moscow. Lenin agreed to the catastrophic terms of the treaty not only because he had promised to bring peace to Russia but also because he believed that the rest of Europe would soon rebel against war and overthrow the capitalist order. Signaling a new beginning, the congress that approved the Treaty of Brest-Litovsk formally adopted the name *Communist* (taken from Marx's writings) to distinguish itself from the socialists/social democrats who had voted for the disastrous war in the first place.

Civil War in Russia

Programs for rapid change and violent civil war soon followed the Bolshevik takeover. In the winter of 1918–1919, the Bolshevik government, observing Marxist doctrine, abolished private property. At the same time it allowed peasants to work the land they had seized in the first year of revolution to shift their allegiance away from the Socialist Revolutionary Party. The government also nationalized factories in order to restore production, which had fallen off precipitously even as factories came under the control of workers' councils. The Provisional Government had allowed both men and women to vote in 1917; Russia was thus the first great power to legalize universal suffrage. However, once the Bolsheviks limited slates to candidates from the Communist Party, the right to vote became a hollow privilege.

Resistance to Bolshevik policies mushroomed into full-fledged civil war (Map 26.3) with the pro-Bolsheviks (or "Reds") pitted against an array of antirevolutionary forces (the "Whites"). Among the Whites, the tsarist military leadership, composed of many landlords and supporters of aristocratic rule, took to the field whatever troops it could muster. Dispossessed businessmen and the liberal intelligentsia lent their support to the anti-Bolsheviks. The revolutionary picture was complicated by issues of nationality, class, and politics. Many non-Russian nationality groups, formerly incorporated into the empire through force, Russification, and other bureaucratic efforts, fought the Bolsheviks because they saw their chance for independence. Before World War I ended, Russia's former allies, notably the United States, Britain, France, and Japan, landed troops in the country. Motives for the invasion varied. Some wanted to keep Entente supplies out of German hands; others fought to help tsarist loyalists overturn the Bolsheviks. To compete with the Bolsheviks, the counterrevolutionary groups desperately needed a strong leader and unified goals. Instead, the groups competed with one another; the pro-tsarist forces, for example, alienated those aspiring to nation-state status, such as the Ukrainians, Estonians, and Lithuanians. Ultimately, without a common purpose, the opponents of revolution could not win.

The civil war shaped communism. Leon Trotsky (1879–1940), Bolshevik commissar of war, built a highly disciplined army by ending democratic procedures, such as the election of officers, that had originally attracted soldiers to Bolshevism.

Lenin and Trotsky introduced the policy of war communism, whereby urban workers and troops moved through the countryside, brutally confiscating grain from the peasantry to feed the army and workforce. The Cheka (secret police) set up detention camps for political opponents and black marketers and often shot them without trial. The expansion of the size and strength of the Cheka and the Red Army—the latter eventually numbered five million men—accompanied the expansion of the bureaucracy, making government more authoritarian and undermining the promise of Marxism that revolution would bring a "withering away" of the state.

As the Bolsheviks clamped down on opposition during the bloody civil war, they organized their supporters to foster revolutionary Marxism across Europe. In March 1919, they founded the Third International, also known as the Comintern (Communist International), for the explicit purpose of replacing the old International with a

MAP 26.3 The Russian Civil War, 1917–1922
Nationalists, aristocrats, middle-class citizens, and property-owning peasants tried to combine their interests to defeat the Bolsheviks, but they failed to create an effective political consensus. The result was more suffering for ordinary people, whose produce was confiscated to fight the civil war. The Western powers and Japan also sent in troops to put down this revolution that so threatened the economic and political order.

centralized organization dedicated to promoting communism. By mid-1921, the Red Army had successfully shored up Bolshevism in Russia and secured the Crimea, the Caucasus, and the Muslim borderlands. When the Japanese withdrew from Siberia in 1922, the civil war ended in central and east Asia. The Bolsheviks were now in charge of a state as multinational as the old Russian Empire had been.

The Russian Revolution, as led by the Bolsheviks, promised bold experiments in social and political leadership. But although the revolution had turned out the inept Romanovs and the privileged aristocracy, civil war turned Russia into a battlefield where disease, hunger, and death prevailed. Moreover, the brutal way the Bolsheviks came to power by crushing opposition of all stripes ushered in a political style and direction far different from earlier socialist hopes.

Ending the War: 1918

Having pulled Russia out of World War I, the Bolsheviks left the rest of Europe's leaders confronting a new balance of forces. Facing war protest as well, these leaders were also left fearing that communism might lie in their future.

German military leaders continued to uphold the cult of the offensive despite the groundswell of discontent. Indeed, the generals developed a new offensive strategy to break the stalemate. Instead of attacking along a front extending for miles, concentrated forces would pierce single points of the enemy's relatively thin defense lines and then wreak havoc from the rear. In the fall of 1917, the Central Powers overwhelmed the Italian army at Caporetto using these tactics. In the spring of 1918, they made one final attempt to smash through the Allied lines, but the offensive ground to a bloody halt within weeks. By then the British and French had started making limited but effective use of tanks supported by airplanes. Although the first tanks were cumbersome, their ability to withstand machine-gun fire made offensive attacks possible. In the summer of 1918, the Allies, now fortified by the Americans, pushed back the Germans all along the western front and headed toward Germany. The German armies, suffering more than two million casualties between spring and summer, rapidly disintegrated.

By October 1918, the desperate German command helped create a civilian government, hoodwinking inexperienced and weak politicians to take responsibility for the defeat and to sue for peace. This change in tactics acknowledged growing pressures for constitutionalism in Germany but also served to deflect blame from the military, whose generals proclaimed themselves still fully capable of winning the war. Weak-willed civilians, they could claim, had dealt the military a "stab in the back" and were, in the words of Ludendorff, "largely responsible for things having turned out as they have. . . . They must now eat the soup they have served us." Amidst this blatant political deceit and flux, naval officers called for a final sea battle. As rumors of the plans leaked, sailors at the naval base at Kiel mutinied against what they saw as a suicide mission. Their rebellion capped years of indignities at the hands of high-ranking officers whose champagne-filled diet contrasted with the sailors' meager fare of turnips and thin soup. The sailors' revolt spread to the workers, who demonstrated in Berlin, Munich, and other major cities. The uprisings provoked Social Democratic politicians to declare a German republic in an effort to prevent revolution. On November 9, 1918, Kaiser William II fled.

The Central Powers were collapsing on all fronts. Since the previous winter, Austria-Hungary had kept many combat divisions at home simply to maintain civil order. By the fall of 1918, crowds in Prague and other disaffected parts of the empire were vandalizing imperial insignia on public buildings. At the end of October, Czechs and Slovaks declared an independent state, and the Croatian parliament simultaneously announced Croatia's independence.

Finally, on November 11, 1918, at 5:00 A.M., an armistice was signed. The guns fell silent on the western front six hours later. In the course of four years, European civilization had been sorely tested, if not shattered. Conservative figures put the battlefield toll at a minimum of ten million deaths and thirty million wounded, incapacitated, or eventually to die of their wounds. In every European combatant country, industrial and agricultural production had plummeted from prewar output. Moreover, much of the reduced output had been put to military use, and food and supplies for civilians had often fallen below subsistence levels.

Asia, Africa, and the Americas, which depended on European trade, also felt the painful impact of Europe's declining production. From 1918 to 1919, the weakened global population suffered another devastating blow when an influenza epidemic rampaged around the world, leaving at least twenty million more dead.

Besides illness, hunger, and death, the war also provoked tremendous moral questioning. Soldiers returning home in 1918 and 1919 flooded the book market with their memoirs, trying to give meaning to their experiences. People had expressed a range of feelings about the Great War in prose and verse almost from the start: some 2,500 war poets published in Britain alone. Whereas many had begun by emphasizing heroism and glory, others were cynical and bitter by war's end. They insisted the fighting had been absolutely meaningless. Total war had drained society of resources and population and had inadvertently sown the seeds of future catastrophes.

❖ The Search for Peace in an Era of Revolution

Revolutionary fervor swept the continent, especially in the former empires of Germany and Austria-Hungary. In Moscow, Lenin welcomed the emperors' downfall as a phase of world revolution that would usher in an age of working-class internationalism. Indeed, until 1921 the triumph of socialism seemed plausible. Immediately following the war, many of the newly independent peoples of eastern and central Europe fervently supported socialist principles, and workers and peasants in Germany were in a revolutionary mood. Yet as revolutionaries attempted to realize their political program, they faced liberal and right-wing opponents. Many of the latter hoped for a political order based on military authority of the kind they had relied on during the war. Faced with a volatile mix of revolution and counterrevolution, diplomats from around the world arrived in Paris in January 1919 to negotiate the terms of peace. For eighteen months they planned Europe's reconstruction according to their own competing interests, often without recognizing the magnitude of the changes brought about by the war.

Europe in Turmoil

Urban people and returning soldiers ignited the protest that swept Europe in 1918 and 1919. In January 1919, the red flag of socialist revolution flew from city hall in Glasgow, Scotland, while in cities of the collapsing Austro-Hungarian Empire workers set up councils to direct factory production and to influence political events. As in Russia, many soldiers did not disband at the armistice but formed volunteer armies or paramilitary bands, making Europe ripe not for parliamentary politics but for revolution by force.

In November 1918, Germany was politically unstable, partly because of the shock of defeat. Germans initially took to the streets in droves to rally around the civilian politicians who were ending the war. By December, however, independent socialist groups and workers' councils were vying with the dominant Social Democrats for control of the government. Demonstrators, suffering under the Allies' continuation of the wartime blockade, demanded economic policies that would assuage workers' misery and give veterans their back pay. Whereas in 1848 revolutionaries had marched to city hall or the king's residence, these protesters took over newspapers and telegraph offices, thus controlling the flow of information. Some were inspired by one of the most radical socialist factions, the Spartacists, led by cofounders Karl Liebknecht (1871–1919) and Rosa Luxemburg (1870–1919). Unlike Lenin, the two Spartacist leaders favored political uprisings that would give workers political experience and thus eliminate the need for an all-knowing party leadership. They argued for *direct* worker control of institutions, but they shared Lenin's dislike for parliamentary politics.

Social Democratic leader Friedrich Ebert (1871–1925), who headed the new government, believed that the parliamentary republic would best realize Social Democratic objectives. Splitting with his former socialist allies, he called on the German army and the Freikorps—a roving paramilitary band of students, demobilized soldiers, and others—to suppress the workers' councils and demonstrators. He thus gave official credence to the idea that political differences could be settled with violence. "The enthusiasm is marvelous," wrote one young soldier. "No mercy's shown. We shoot even the wounded. . . . We were much more humane against the French in the field." Members of the Freikorps hunted down Luxemburg and Liebknecht and murdered them. A measure of calm returned to Berlin and other cities.

In February 1919, a constituent assembly met in the city of Weimar, where it approved a constitution and founded a parliamentary republic. The reaction could not have been worse. The military leadership dreamed of a restored monarchy and a return to the military prestige of imperial days. "As I love Germany, so I hate the Republic," wrote one officer. Contempt for republican institutions motivated Freikorps officers to attempt a coup (*putsch*), known as the Kapp Putsch after one of its right-wing leaders, in the spring of 1920. The military command refused to crush the coup: "Soldiers do not fire on soldiers." So Ebert called for a general strike that stopped the coup by showing its lack of popular support. Although revolutions from both the right and the left failed, the Weimar Republic's grip on power was far from solid, and it had set the dangerous precedent of relying on street violence, paramilitary groups, and protests to solve political problems.

In the late winter of 1919, leftists proclaimed soviet republics—governments led by workers' councils—in Bavaria and Hungary. The Hungarian regime, led by Béla Kun (1885–1937), gained some middle-class nationalist support by resisting Allied plans to reduce the size of Hungary drastically. But Kun's zeal to nationalize production and the brutality of his secret police alienated many Hungarians, and the soviet republic was overthrown in August. Meanwhile in Bavaria, leaders of the German soviets fell before the assault of the volunteer armies and Weimar troops.

The Bolsheviks tried to establish a Marxist regime in Poland in the belief that its people wanted a workers' revolution. Instead the Poles resisted and drove the Red Army back in 1920, while the Allied powers rushed supplies and advisers to Warsaw. Though this and other revolts failed, they provided further proof that total war had loosened political and social order.

Peacemaking

As political turmoil engulfed peoples from Berlin to Moscow, the Paris peace conference opened in January 1919. Visions of communism spreading westward haunted the assembled statesmen, but the desperation of millions of war-ravaged citizens, the status of Germany, and the reconstruction of a secure Europe topped their agenda. Leaders such as French Premier Georges Clemenceau had to satisfy their angry citizens, who demanded revenge or, at the very least, compensation for their suffering. France had lost 1.3 million people—almost an entire generation; and more than a million buildings, six thousand bridges, and thousands of miles of railroad lines and roads had been destroyed while the war was fought on its soil. Great Britain's representative, Prime Minister David Lloyd George, caught the mood of the British public by campaigning in 1918 with such slogans as "Hang the kaiser." Italians arrived on the scene unconditionally demanding the territory promised to them in the 1915 Treaty of London.

The stance of the United States further complicated the remaking of Europe. This new world power had helped achieve the Allied victory, and its presence at the conference indicated a dramatic realignment of power away from any individual European country. President Woodrow Wilson also had a special agenda. It was conciliatory, however, seeking to incorporate his Fourteen Points, on which the truce had been based, into the final settlement. Steeped in the language of freedom, the Fourteen Points called for open diplomacy, arms reduction, an "open-minded" settlement of colonial issues, and the self-determination of peoples.

This was no small ambition, for on top of the death and destruction on both sides, Allied propaganda had made the Germans seem like inhuman monsters. Many citizens demanded a harsh peace. Moreover, some experts feared that Germany was using the armistice only to regroup for more warfare. Indeed, Germans widely refused to admit that their army had lost the war. Eager for army support, Ebert had given returning soldiers a rousing welcome: "As you return unconquered from the field of battle, I salute you." Thus, conservative leaders among Wilson's former allies campaigned to make him look naive and deluded. "Wilson bores me with his Fourteen Points," Clemenceau complained. "Why, the good Lord himself has only ten."

Nevertheless, Wilson's Fourteen Points appealed to European moderates and convinced Germans that the settlement would not be vindictive. In fact, Wilson's commitment to *settlement* as opposed to *surrender* contained tough-minded stipulations, for he recognized that Germany was still

MAP 26.4 Europe and the Middle East after the Peace Settlements of 1919–1920
The political landscape of central, east, and east central Europe changed dramatically as a result of the Russian Revolution and the Peace of Paris. The Ottoman, German, Russian, and Austro-Hungarian Empires were either broken up altogether into multiple small states or territorially reduced in size. The settlement left resentments among Germans and Hungarians and created a group of weak, struggling nations in the heartland of Europe. The victorious powers took over much of the oil-rich Middle East.

the strongest state on the continent. He merely pushed for a treaty that balanced the strengths and interests of the various European powers. Many of the historians, economists, and other experts accompanying Wilson to Paris agreed that, harshly dealt with and humiliated, Germany might soon become vengeful and chaotic—a lethal combination that could lead to the growth of unsavory political sects.

The Peace of Paris, 1919–1920. After six months, the statesmen and their teams of experts produced the Peace of Paris, composed of a cluster of individual treaties (Map 26.4). These treaties shocked the countries that had to accept them, and in retrospect historians see how they destabilized eastern and east-central Europe. (See "Contrasting Views," page 998.) The treaties separated Austria from Hungary, reduced Hungary by almost

Arguing with the Victors

The end of World War I aroused hopes around the world. The conquered expected a fair-minded treaty based on Wilson's Fourteen Points, while a variety of other peoples saw in that same document the promise of "self-determination." In particular, men living under colonial domination, such as many in Africa and the Arab states, had taken part in the conflict because the Allies had promised new rights in return for fighting this bloody and destructive war. The emir Faisal had led troops to bring about freedom and Arab unity (Document 1). Like some representatives at the Pan-African Congress, even those Africans who had not fought saw peacemaking as a process that should forge a better future. Many wanted full political rights and parliamentary representation if not outright independence (Document 2).

Thus when the thousands of politicians and expert bureaucrats from the victorious powers gathered in Paris, they were besieged by numerous outsiders to Western government, each making a claim and taking a side for freedom, peace, rights, and special attention to their needs—right or wrong. Feminist-pacifists wanted to ensure the pacifist cause (Document 3), while a Polish representative articulated a concern that Jews had taken too many good jobs in the new Poland (Document 4). Caucuses and congresses were held simultaneously with the conference to present a variety of proposals to the peacemakers, but to very little avail.

1. Claiming Independence for the Middle East

Arabs had hotly debated whether to join with the colonizers in World War I, but promises of independence won them over. Some Arabs argued for independence of individual areas in the Middle East and for resolutions to competing claims of the Arabs and of new Jewish settlers in the region. Emir Faisal, who had commanded Arab forces in the war, presented the pan-Arab ideal.

The aim of the Arab nationalist movement is to unite the Arabs eventually into one nation. . . . I came to Europe on behalf of my father and the Arabs of Asia to say that they are expecting the powers at the Conference not to attach undue importance to superficial differences of condition among us and not to consider them only from the low ground of existing European material interests and supposed spheres of influence. They expect the powers to think of them as one potential people, jealous of their language and liberty, and they ask that no step be taken inconsistent with the prospect of an eventual union of these areas under one sovereign government.

Source: Stephen Bonsal, *Suitors and Suppliants: The Little Nations at Versailles* (Port Washington: Kennikat Press, 1969), 32–33.

2. The Voice of Pan-Africanists

African and African American leaders believed it would be opportune for them to meet in a Pan-African Congress while the Paris Peace Conference was going on. For some time an idea of a single African people had been forming among leading black intellectuals, and Pan-African meetings had taken place from the late nineteenth century on. The demands were legion, but above all the congress, by mid-February 1919, had resolved to seek better treatment from the colonial powers.

Resolved

That the Allied and Associated Powers establish a code of law for the international protection of the natives of Africa. . . .

The Negroes of the world demand that hereafter the natives of Africa and the peoples of African descent be governed according to the following principles:

1. The land: the land and its natural resources shall be held in trust for the natives and at all times they shall have effective ownership of as much land as they can profitably develop. . . .
3. Labor: slavery and corporal punishment shall be abolished and forced labor except in punishment for crime. . . .
5. The state: the natives of Africa must have the right to participate in the government as fast as

their development permits, in conformity with the principle that the government exists for the natives, and not the natives for the government.

Source: Quoted in W. E. B. Du Bois, *The World and Africa* (New York: International Publishers, 1946), 11–12.

3. Pacifists' Goals for the Peace Process

Pacifist women were angered that the peace conference would be held in Paris instead of in a noncombatant or neutral country. Situating it where wartime hatred was at a fevered pitch, they argued, would not allow the conquered to receive a fair hearing. The women themselves met in Switzerland to debate the shape of the peace so that German and Austrian women would attend. The German and Austrian representatives were crucial, the pacifists believed, for a continuing blockade of the Central Powers after the armistice was increasing suffering and causing deaths. The pacifist women speeded the dispatch of their resolutions to Paris when the Versailles portion of the Peace of Paris was announced.

The International Congress of Women regards the famine, pestilence, and unemployment extending throughout great tracts of central and eastern Europe and into Asia as a disgrace to civilization.

It therefore urges the Governments of all the Powers assembled at the Peace Conference immediately to develop the inter-allied organizations formed for purposes of war into an international organization for purposes of peace, so that the resources of the world—food, raw materials, finance, transport—shall be made available for the relief of the peoples of all countries from famine and pestilence.

To this end it urges that immediate action be taken . . . to raise the blockade.

The terms of the peace tacitly sanction secret diplomacy, deny the principles of self-determination, recognize the rights of victors to the spoils of war, and create all over Europe discords and animosities, which can only lead to future war. . . . By the financial and economic proposals a hundred million people of this generation in the heart of Europe are condemned to poverty, disease, and despair, which must result in the spread of hatred and anarchy within each nation.

Source: James Weber Linn, *Jane Addams: A Biography* (New York: Greenwood, 1968), 342–43.

4. Anti-Semitism at the Peacetable

A Polish leader lobbied the Allies to exercise a police power in the newly independent Poland, where major problems would be rural crowding and inability to make ends meet on the land.

We have too many Jews, and those who will be allowed to remain with us must change their habits. I recognize that this will be difficult and will take time. The Jew must produce and not remain devoted exclusively to what we regard as parasitical pursuits. Unless restrictions are imposed upon them soon, all our lawyers, doctors, and small merchants will be Jews. They must turn to agriculture, and they must at least share small business and retail stores with their Polish neighbors. I readily admit that there is some basis in the Jewish contention that in days past it was difficult for them to own land or even to work the fields of others as tenants; that they were often compelled by circumstances beyond their control to gain their livelihood in ways which are hurtful to Polish economy. Under our new constitution all this will be changed, and for their own good I hope the Jews will avail themselves of their new opportunities. I say this in their own interest as well as in the interest of restored Poland. Now, and I fear for decades to come, Poland will be too poor to permit one-tenth of its population to engage in pursuits which to say the least are not productive.

Source: Bonsal, *Suitors and Suppliants*, 124.

QUESTIONS FOR DEBATE

1. Describe the various contending claims beyond those of the official combatant powers. Did the victorious powers heed these voices when forging the peace?
2. How were the various demands at the peace conference related to the politics and conditions of World War I?
3. Do any of the demands seem more justifiable in addressing the peacetime needs of Europe and the world?

two-thirds of its inhabitants and three-quarters of its territory, broke up the Ottoman Empire, and treated Germany severely. They replaced the Habsburg Empire with a group of small, internally divided, and relatively weak states: Czechoslovakia, Poland, and the Kingdom of the Serbs, Croats, and Slovenes, later renamed Yugoslavia. Austria and Hungary were both left reeling at their loss of territory and resources and struggling for a sense of identity. Many Austrians, their multiethnic empire gone, desperately wanted to merge with Germany, but the settlement expressly forbade such a union.

After a century and a half of partition, Poland was reconstructed from parts of Russia, Germany, and Austria-Hungary, with one-third of its population ethnically non-Polish. The statesmen in Paris also created a Polish Corridor that connected Poland to the Baltic Sea and separated East Prussia from the rest of Germany. The Allies had high hopes that central and east-central Europe would be stable; however, many of the new states became rivals and were for the most part politically and economically weak.

The treaties with Austria and Hungary were crucial for the future of Europe. At the time, however, the Treaty of Versailles with Germany was the centerpiece of the Peace of Paris. This treaty only partially quenched the French thirst for revenge. France recovered Alsace and Lorraine, and the victors would temporarily occupy the left, or western, bank of the Rhine and the coal-bearing Saar basin. Wilson accepted his allies' expectations that Germany would pay substantial reparations for the civilian damage it inflicted in the war. The specific amount was established not by the peacemakers in 1919 but by Allied commissions, which only in 1921 agreed on the crushing sum of 132 billion gold marks. Germany also had to surrender the largest ships of its merchant marine, reduce its army, almost eliminate its navy, stop manufacturing offensive weapons, and deliver a large amount of free coal each year to Belgium and France. Furthermore, it was forbidden to have an air force and had to give up its colonies.

The average German saw in these terms an unmerited humiliation that was compounded by Article 231 of the treaty, which described Germany's "responsibility" for damage done during a conflict "imposed on [the Entente] by the aggression of Germany and her allies." The outraged German people interpreted this as a "war guilt" clause, and the government set up a special propaganda office to refute it and to contest the terms of what Germans came to call a *Diktat*, or dictated peace. Article 231 allowed the victors to collect reparations from economically viable Germany rather than from decimated Austria, which had deployed the first troops. War guilt also made Germany an outcast in the community of nations.

The League of Nations.   The Peace of Paris set up an organization called the League of Nations, whose responsibility for maintaining peace—a principle called *collective security*—was to replace the divisive secrecy of prewar power politics. As part of Wilson's vision, the league would guide the world toward disarmament, arbitrate its members' disputes, and monitor labor conditions around the world. Returning to prewar isolationism, the United States Senate, in a humiliating defeat for the president, failed to ratify the peace settlement and refused to join the league. Moreover, both Germany and Russia initially were excluded from the league and were thus blocked from acting in legal concert with other nations.

The covenant, or charter, of the League of Nations organized the administration of the colonies and territories of Germany and the Ottoman Empire—such as Togo, Cameroon, Tanganyika, Syria, and Lebanon—through a system of mandates. The European powers exercised political control over mandated territory, but local leaders retained limited authority. The league covenant justified the mandate system as providing governance by "advanced nations" over territories "not yet able to stand by themselves under the strenuous conditions of the modern world." The war, however, had depleted the great powers' financial resources and mental resolve to make a success of the mandate system. Their new responsibility was complicated by the fact that colonized and other people of color, who had served and fallen on the battlefield, began to challenge the claims of their European masters. They had seen how savage and degraded were these people who claimed to be racially superior, politically more advanced, and leaders of global culture. "Never again will the darker people of the world occupy just the place they had before," the African American leader W. E. B. Du Bois predicted in 1918. The mandate system continued the practice of apportioning the globe among European powers, but like the Peace of Paris it aroused anger and resistance. In the next decades, colonized peoples would rise up in greater numbers against this domination.

Economic and Diplomatic Consequences of the Peace

The financial and political settlement in the Peace of Paris had repercussions in the 1920s and beyond. Western leaders worried deeply about two intertwined issues in the aftermath of the war. The first was economic recovery and its relation to war debts, the conditions of international trade, and German reparations. The second was ensuring that peace lasted.

Economic Dilemmas. France, the hardest hit by wartime destruction and billions of dollars in debt to the United States, estimated that Germany owed it at least $200 billion. The British, by contrast, worried about maintaining their empire and restoring trade with Germany, not about exacting huge reparations. Nevertheless, both France and Britain depended on some monetary redress to pay their war debts to the United States because Europe's share of world trade had plunged during the war. Although the United States wanted the debts paid, it used a soft tone toward the fragile Weimar Republic and a harsh one toward its Allied debtors, for whom U.S. sympathy had dwindled.

Germany claimed that the demand for reparations strained its government, already beset by political upheaval. Indeed, as early as 1919 British economist John Maynard Keynes had predicted a chain of disasters if the German standard of living were to fall because of the financial burden of reparations. But hardship was not the result of the Peace of Paris alone. The kaiser had refused to raise taxes, especially on the rich, to pay for the war, so the new republic had to deal with the resulting inflation, to pay reparations, and to finance the staggering domestic war debt. As an experiment in democracy, the Weimar Republic needed to woo the citizenry, not alienate it by hiking taxes. In 1921, when Germans refused to present a realistic payment scheme, the French occupied several cities in the Ruhr. Germany then accepted a payment plan that appeared for the sake of voters in receiver

countries to amount to $33 billion but that really came to only $12.5 billion over thirty-six years.

Embroiled with powers to the west, the German government deftly sought economic and diplomatic relations in eastern Europe. It reached an agreement to foster economic ties with Russia, desperate for western trade, in the Treaty of Rapallo (1922, renewed in the Treaty of Berlin in 1926). Its relations with powers to the west, however, continued to deteriorate. In 1923, after Germany defaulted on coal deliveries, the French and Belgians sent troops into the Ruhr basin, planning to use its abundant resources to recoup their wartime expenditures. Urged on by the government, Ruhr citizens fought back, shutting down industry and services by staying home from work. The German government printed trillions of marks to support the workers, to provide funds to the closed industries, and to pay its own war debts with practically worthless currency. Soon Germany was in the midst of a staggering inflation that demoralized its citizens and gravely threatened the international economy: at one point a single U.S. dollar cost 4.42 trillion marks, and wheelbarrows of money were required to buy a turnip. Wreaking psychological havoc, the inflation also wiped out people's savings and ruined those living on fixed incomes.

The spirit of the League of Nations demanded a resolution to this economic chaos through negotiations. The Dawes Plan (1924) and eventually the Young Plan (1929) reduced payments to the victors and restored the value of German currency. These plans also evened the balance of Germany's trade between east and west, a balance the Treaty of Rapallo had threatened. Only the French were unhappy, but their postwar weakness forced them to accept the reductions.

Ensuring Peace. Following the Peace of Paris, statesmen recognized that ensuring peace entailed disarmament, bringing Germany back into the fold, and securing the new countries of eastern Europe. It took hard diplomatic bargaining outside the league to produce two plans in Germany's favor. At the Washington Conference in 1921, the United States, Great Britain, Japan, France, and Italy agreed to reduce their number of battleships and to stop constructing new ones for ten years. Four years later, in 1925, the league sponsored a meeting of the great powers, including Germany, at Locarno, Switzerland. The German diplomat Gustav Stresemann, who claimed that the Versailles treaty unfairly penalized Germany, negotiated a treaty at Locarno that provided Germany with a seat in the League of Nations as of 1926. In return, Germany agreed not to violate the borders of France and Belgium and to keep the nearby Rhineland demilitarized (unfortified by troops).

To the east, the door seemed open to a German attempt to regain territory lost to Poland, to form a merger with Austria, or to launch aggression against the states spun off from Austria-Hungary. To meet these unwelcome possibilities, Czechoslovakia, Yugoslavia, and Romania formed the "Little Entente" in 1920–1921. This was a collective security agreement to protect themselves from their two powerful neighbors Germany and Russia and to guard against Hungarian expansionism. Then, between 1924 and 1927, France allied itself with the Little Entente and with Poland. As diplomatic tensions relaxed, the major European powers, Japan, and the United States signed the Kellogg-Briand Pact (1928), which formally rejected international violence. The nations failed, however, to commit themselves to concrete action to prevent its outbreak.

The "Little Entente"

The publicity and planning that yielded the international agreements during the 1920s sharply contrasted with old-style diplomacy, which was conducted in secret and subject to little public scrutiny or democratic influence. The new openness suggested a diplomatic revolution and promised a peaceful age in international relations. Historians both praise and fault this era of apparent international cooperation. Some scholars praise it for promoting solid negotiations among the great powers, launching a system of collective security, reintegrating Germany into the community of nations, and showing an awareness that international politics and economics are related. Other scholars denounce the diplomats of this era who fed the press reports calculated to arouse the masses. For example,

much of the German populace was lashed into a nationalist frenzy by the press and opposing parties whenever Germany's diplomats, who were successfully working to undo the Treaty of Versailles, seemed to compromise. Although meetings such as the one at Locarno appeared to promote the goal of collective security, they also exposed the diplomatic process to nationalist demagogues who could rekindle political hatreds.

❖ A Decade of Recovery: Europe in the 1920s

Treaties ended the war but not the wartime spirit. Words and phrases from the battlefield punctuated everyday speech. Before the war the word *lousy* had meant "lice-infested"; but English-speaking soldiers returning from the trenches now applied it to anything bad. Raincoats became *trenchcoats*, and terms like *bombarded* and *rank and file* entered peacetime usage. Many feared the *Bolshies* and the *Reds* and wondered when rationing would end and they would have enough to eat. Maimed, disfigured veterans were present everywhere, and those without limbs were sometimes carried in baskets—hence the expression *basket case*. They overflowed hospitals, rest homes, and mental institutions, and family life centered on their care.

The 1920s was devoted to coming to terms with the social and political legacy of the war. A key question was how to restore civilian government when total war had generally strengthened military values, authoritarian government, and a controlled economy. Although people referred to the 1920s as the Roaring Twenties, the Jazz Age, and the Crazy Years, the sense of cultural release masked the serious problem of restoring social stability and implementing democracy. Three autocratic governments had collapsed as a result of the war, but how newly empowered citizens would react politically after the shock of war remained a burning question.

The Promise of Democratic Rebirth

The threat of revolution coexisted with a sense of democratic rebirth because of the League of Nations, the emergence of new nations from crumbled empires, and the formation of a constitutional

German republic. The extension of suffrage to women, widely granted at the war's end, also suggested the beginnings of a more democratic political order. Woman suffrage resulted in part from decades of activism; more immediately, many gov-

Women Gain Suffrage in the West

1906	Finland
1913	Norway
1915	Denmark, Iceland
1917	Netherlands, Russia
1918	Czechoslovakia, Great Britain (limited suffrage)
1919	Germany
1920	Austria, United States
1921	Poland
1925	Hungary (limited suffrage)
1945	Italy, France
1971	Switzerland

ernments gave women the vote to reward them for their war efforts and to make revolution less tempting. In the first postwar elections, women were voted into parliaments, and the impression grew that they had also made extraordinary gains in breaking down barriers in the workplace. French men pointedly denied women the vote, insisting they would use their vote to bring back the rule of kings and priests. Governments continued building the welfare state by expanding payments to families with children and insurance programs for workers. New government benefits attested to a spreading belief that more evenly distributed wealth—sometimes referred to as *economic democracy*—was important to social stability in postwar society.

In addition to bringing about political and economic changes, the war had blurred class distinctions, giving rise to expectations that life would be fairer afterward. The massive casualties had generated social mobility by allowing commoners to move up to the ranks of officers, positions often monopolized by the prewar aristocracy. Members of all classes had rubbed shoulders in the trenches. The identical, evenly spaced crosses of military cemeteries made all the dead seem equal, as did the mass "brothers' graves" at the battlefront where rich and poor lay side by side in a single burial pit. Middle-class daughters worked outside the home; their mothers did their own housework because servants could earn more money in factories. The "servant problem," born of wartime opportunities, thus made middle-class and working-class

Otto Dix, *The Sleepwalkers*
Artists in the defeated countries were especially attuned to the tragic absurdity of the war. German ex-soldier Otto Dix sketched smashed faces and corpses in varying states of decay, depicting people who had survived as grotesque or benumbed "sleepwalkers" who picked their way through the postwar wreckage. The simple horror of death and disfigurement made painted whores of those seeking a return to ordinary life.
"The Sleepwalkers" by Otto Dix from *The Nature of War* by John Keegan and Joseph Darracott. Holt, Rinehart and Winston, 1981. Private Collection, Essen.

households more similar. Finally, the Bolsheviks' refusal to honor prewar Russian bonds hurt tens of thousands of European investors, adding to the social leveling of war.

The slow trend toward economic democracy was not easy to maintain, however, because the cycles of boom and bust that had characterized the late nineteenth century reemerged. A short postwar boom prompted by rebuilding war-torn areas and filling consumer needs unsatisfied during the war was followed by an economic downturn that was most severe between 1920 and 1922. Skyrocketing unemployment led some to question the effectiveness of their governments and the fairness of society. By the mid-1920s, many of the economic opportunities for women had disappeared and they made up a smaller percentage of the workforce than in 1913.

Changes in the Political Landscape

Hard times especially corroded the new republics of eastern Europe, which were unprepared for independence in the sophisticated world market. Intensely nationalistic and competitive with one another, none but Czechoslovakia had a mature industrial sector, and agricultural techniques were often primitive. Like late-nineteenth-century politicians, leaders in these new countries reacted to adversity by enacting tariffs to protect domestic manufacturing and domestic markets.

Eastern Europe: Poland. The development of Poland exemplified the postwar political landscape in eastern Europe. Nationalism was increasingly defined in ethnic terms, and the reunified Poland consisted of one-third Ukrainians, Belorussians, Germans, and other ethnic minorities—many of whom had grievances against the dominant Poles. Moreover, varying religious, dynastic, and cultural traditions divided the Poles, who for 150 years had been ruled by three other powers. Polish reunification occurred without a common currency, political structure, or language—even the railroad tracks were not a standard size.

With virtually no economic or other support from the Allies, a constitutional government nonetheless took shape. Under a constitution that professed equal rights for all ethnicities and religions, the new democratic government, run by the Sejm

(parliament), tried to legislate the redistribution of large estates to the peasantry, but declining crop prices and overpopulation made life in the countryside difficult. Urban workers were better off than the peasantry (two-thirds of the population lived by subsistence farming) but worse off than laborers across Europe. The economic downturn brought strikes and violence in 1922–1923, and the inability of coalition parliaments to effect economic prosperity led to a coup in 1926 by strongman Jozef Pilsudski. Ultimately Pilsudski made it possible for a country choked by the endless debates of dozens of political parties and impaired by ethnic strife and anti-Semitism to function. Economic hardship and strong-arm solutions went hand in hand in east-central Europe. It was only with incredible difficulty that a reunified Poland survived the postwar years.

National Minorities in Postwar Poland

Map legend:
- Polish
- Czech
- Slovak
- Belorussian
- Ukranian
- German
- Latvian
- Lithuanian
- Magyar (Hungarian)
- Romanian

Central Europe: Germany. Germany was a different case. The industrially sophisticated Weimar Republic confronted daunting challenges to making Germany democratic, even after putting down the postwar revolution. Although the German economy picked up and Germany became a center of experimentation in the arts, political life remained precarious because so many people felt nostalgia for imperial glory and loathed the Versailles treaty's restrictions. On the surface, Weimar's political system—a bicameral parliament and a chancellor responsible to the lower house—appeared similar to the parliamentary system in Britain and France, but extremist politicians heaped daily abuse on Germany's leaders, and contempt for parliamentary politics was widespread. Anyone who cooperated with the parliamentary system, wrote a wealthy newspaper and film magnate, "is a moral cripple." Right-wing parties, supporting the defunct monarchy or envisioning a new authoritarian state, constituted a threat to

1914-1929

A DECADE OF RECOVERY: EUROPE IN THE 1920s **1005**

democracy instead of a healthy opposition. They favored violence rather than consensus building, and nationalist thugs murdered democratic leaders. One prominent victim was foreign minister Walter Rathenau, who had streamlined the German economy during the war; Rathenau, as a Jew and an industrialist, was part of two groups increasingly blamed for Germany's woes.

Support for the far right came from wealthy landowners and businessmen, white-collar workers whose standard of living had dropped during the war, and members of the lower-middle and middle classes hurt by inflation. Bands of disaffected youth and veterans proliferated, among them a group called Brown Shirts led by ex-soldier and political newcomer Adolf Hitler (1889–1945). In the wake of the Ruhr occupation of 1923, the Brown Shirts were one of the many elements that favored and even plotted the overthrow of the Weimar government. In November, Ludendorff and Hitler launched a coup d'état from a beer hall in Munich. Government troops suppressed the Beer Hall Putsch, but Hitler spent less than a year in jail and Ludendorff was acquitted. For conservative judges as for former aristocrats and most of the prewar bureaucrats who remained in government, such men were national heroes. After the mid-1920s, as the German economy surged, violent tactics and extreme political movements temporarily lost some of their appeal.

Western Europe: France and Britain. In France and Britain, parties of the right had less effect than elsewhere because parliamentary institutions were better established and the upper classes were not plotting to restore an authoritarian monarchy. In France, politicians from the conservative right and moderate left successively formed coalitions and rallied general support to rebuild war-torn regions and to force Germany to pay for the reconstruction. Hoping to stimulate population growth after the devastating loss of life, the French parliament made distributing birth-control information illegal and abortion a severely punished crime.

Britain encountered postwar boom and bust and continuing strife in Ireland. Ramsay MacDonald (1866–1937), elected the first Labour prime minister in 1924, represented the new-formed political ambitions of the working masses. Like other postwar British leaders, he had to swallow the

paradoxical fact that although Britain had the largest world empire, many of its industries were obsolete or in poor condition. A showdown came in the ailing coal industry, where prices fell and wages plummeted once the Ruhr mines reopened. On May 3, 1926, workers conducted a nine-day general strike against wage cuts and dangerous conditions in the mines. The strike provoked unprecedented middle-class resistance. University students, homemakers, and businessmen shut down the strike by driving trains, working on docks, and replacing workers in other jobs. The strike thus failed to help the miners, as citizens from many walks of life revived the wartime spirit to defend the declining economy.

In Ireland, the British government met bloody confrontation over the continuing failure to implement home rule. Irish republicans had attacked government buildings in Dublin on Easter Monday 1916 in an effort to wrest Irish independence from Britain. Leaders of the Easter Uprising were not prepared for full-scale revolt; their effort was easily defeated and many of them were hanged. The severity with which the British punished the rebels intensified demands for home rule, and in January 1919, republican leaders announced Ireland's independence from Britain and created a separate

The Irish Free State and Ulster, 1921

parliament called the Dail Eireann. The British government refused to recognize the parliament and sent in the Black and Tans, a volunteer army of demobilized soldiers so called for the color of their uniforms. Terror reigned in Ireland, as both the pro-independence forces and the Black and Tans waged guerrilla warfare, taking hostages, blowing up buildings, and even shooting into crowds at soccer matches.

By 1921, public outrage forced the British to negotiate. The treaty drawn up by the British government reversed the Irish declaration of independence and made the Irish Free State a self-governing dominion owing an oath of allegiance to the British crown. Ulster, a group of six northern counties containing a majority of Protestants, gained a separate status: it was self-governing but still had representation in the British Parliament. This division of Ireland and the terms of the division, though agreed upon at the time, subsequently led to new efforts for full independence of the Irish Free State. The rights of the Catholic minority in the north also became a major political issue there.

European powers encountered rebellion in overseas empires as well. Colonized peoples who had fought in the war expected more rights and even independence. Indeed, European politicians and military recruiters had actually promised the vote and many other reforms in exchange for support. But colonists' political activism, now enhanced by increasing education, trade, and experience with the West, mostly met a brutal response. Fearful of losing India, British forces massacred protesters at Amritsar in 1919 and put down revolts against the mandate system in Egypt and Iran in the early 1920s. The Dutch jailed political leaders in Indonesia; the French punished Indochinese nationalists. European politicians simultaneously began seeking compromises that would allow them to keep their empires intact. For many Western governments, maintaining empires abroad was crucial to ensuring democracy at home, as any hint of declining national prestige fed antidemocratic forces.

Reconstructing the Economy

For much of the West, worldwide economic competition was as big a challenge to recovery as were global political struggles. During the war the European economy had lost many of its international markets to India, Canada, Australia, Japan, and the United States. Nonetheless the war had forced European manufacturing to become more efficient and had expanded the demand for automotive and air transport, electrical products, and synthetic goods. The prewar pattern of mergers and cartels continued after 1918, giving rise to gigantic food-processing firms such as Nestlé in Switzerland and petroleum enterprises such as Royal Dutch Shell. Owners of these large manufacturing conglomerates wielded more financial and political power than entire small countries and hired rafts of public relations officials to perform a kind of indus-

trial diplomacy. By the late 1920s, Europe had overcome the wild economic swings of the immediate postwar years and was enjoying renewed prosperity.

Despite this growth, the United States was the trendsetter in economic modernization. Many European businessmen made pilgrimages to Henry Ford's Detroit assembly line, which by 1929 produced a Ford automobile every ten seconds. Ford touted this miracle of productivity as resulting in a lower cost of living and increased purchasing power for workers. Indeed, whereas French, German, and British citizens in total had under two million cars, some seventeen million cars were on U.S. streets in 1925.

Scientific management, sometimes called the science of work, also aimed to raise productivity. By timing and studying the motions workers used to accomplish tasks, the American efficiency expert Frederick Taylor demonstrated that people worked inefficiently. He developed methods to streamline workers' tasks and motions for maximum productivity. European industrialists adopted Taylor's methods during the war and after, but they were also influenced by European psychologists who emphasized the mental aspects of productivity and the need for a balance of work and leisure activities, such as cinema and sports, for both workers and managers.

The urgency behind this attention to productivity was both economic and political. Many industrial experts feared that Bolshevism would inspire class conflict, and they believed that increased productivity and prosperity would bind workers and management together. In theory, managers would reap enhanced output and profits, and workers would be rewarded with shorter hours, higher wages, and more consumer goods. In practice, streamlining did help reduce working hours in many industries, a result that encouraged union leaders to embrace modernization and the "cult of efficiency." For many workers, however, the emphasis on efficiency seemed inhuman, with restrictions on time and motion so severe that often they were allowed to use the bathroom only on a fixed schedule. "When I left the factory, it followed me," wrote one worker. "In my dreams I was a machine."

The managerial sector in industry had expanded during the war and continued to do so thereafter. Workers' initiative became devalued, with managers alone seen as creative and innovative. Managers reorganized work procedures and classified workers' skills. They categorized "female" jobs as those requiring less skill and therefore deserving of lower wages, thus adapting the old segmentation of the labor market to the new working conditions. With male workers' jobs increasingly threatened by labor-saving machinery, unions usually agreed that women should receive lower wages to keep them from competing with men for scarce high-paying jobs.

Union bureaucracy continued to balloon during World War I to help monitor labor's part in the war. Union leaders cooperated with their former antagonists in management and government to settle questions ranging from the creation of a lighter, less potent beer to plans for the reintegration of veterans into industry. Union bureaucracies became specialized, composed of negotiators, membership organizers, educators and propagandists, and political liaisons. Unions could mobilize masses of people, as they demonstrated when they blocked the 1920 Kapp Putsch against the Weimar government and organized the 1926 general strike in Great Britain. Although their lobbying efforts were often less successful than those of manufacturers' associations, unions played a key role in mass politics.

Restoring Society

With combined joy and trepidation, postwar society met the returning millions of brutalized, incapacitated, and shell-shocked veterans. Many veterans harbored hostility toward those who had remained home. Civilians had rebelled against wartime conditions, these soldiers charged, instead of patriotically enduring them. The world the veterans returned to differed from the home they left: women had cut their hair, wore tailored clothes, smoked, held jobs, and had money of their own. In contrast, veterans often had no jobs; and some soldiers found that their wives and sweethearts had abandoned them—a wrenching betrayal for those who had risked their lives to protect the homeland.

United by patriotism when the war erupted, civilians, especially women, sometimes felt estranged from these returning warriors, who had inflicted so much death and who had lived daily with filth, rats, and decaying animal and human

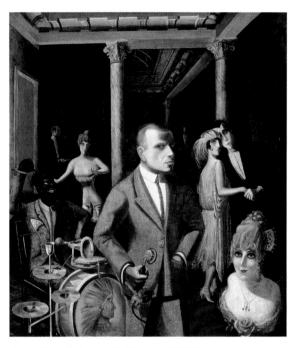

Otto Dix, *Cabaret: To Beauty* (1922)
Postwar fun, based on drinking, dancing, smoking, and sexual courting, took place in the newly popular cabaret or nightclub. Many cabarets in Berlin and elsewhere featured dramatic song and dance performances—sometimes of African American dancers and instrumentalists who represented the promise and exoticism of the United States. But continuing his theme of wartime trauma, Otto Dix in 1922 portrayed the cabaret as a setting for nothing more than further human alienation, no matter what the fancy garb or carefree activity.
Erich Lessing/Art Resource, NY.

flesh. Civilian anxieties were often valid. Tens of thousands of German, central European, and Italian soldiers refused to disband; a few British veterans even vandalized university classrooms and assaulted women streetcar conductors and factory workers. Women who had served on the front could empathize with the soldiers' woes. But many suffragists in England, for instance, who had fought for an end to separate spheres before the war, now embraced gender segregation, so shocked were they by the vision of brutalized veterans. Likewise, Social Democratic women in Germany began to de-emphasize political integration with men and to work instead for welfare organizations to aid women and families. Many feminist activists across the West eliminated rights for working and professional women from their agendas and

Le Corbusier's Paris of the Future
While the war profoundly disillusioned many in the West, peace aroused utopian hopes for a better future.
For modern architects like Swiss-born Le Corbusier (1887–1965), the "future city" and the "radiant city"
would organize space, and thus life, for ordinary people. Horizontal windows, roof gardens, and very plain
facades were hallmarks of this new design—a radical break with ornate prewar styles in building.
Fondation Le Corbusier/A.D.A.G.P.

instead fought for a separate, protected place in the family insured by welfare programs. Combined with the widespread victory of woman suffrage, this switch in emphasis caused commentators and even suffragists to pronounce feminism dead as a political issue.

Fearing the spread of Bolshevism, governments tried to make civilian life as comfortable as possible to reintegrate men into society and prevent revolution. Politicians believed in the stabilizing power of traditional family values and supported social programs to alleviate pent-up anger among veterans and civilians and reward their endurance. These programs included pension plans for veterans, stipends for war widows, benefits for out-of-work men, and housing for veterans—"homes for heroes," politicians called them.

The new housing was a vast improvement over nineteenth-century working-class tenements but most often benefited the more highly paid skilled workers. In Vienna, Frankfurt, Berlin, and Stockholm, modern housing projects provided collective laundries, day-care centers, and rooms for group socializing; they featured gardens, terraces, and balconies to provide a soothing, country ambiance

that offset the hectic nature of industrial life. Inside they boasted modern kitchens, indoor plumbing, central heating, and electricity. Borrowing the clean lines of East Asian and African dwellings to create a sense of modernity, domestic architects avoided ornate moldings, plasterwork, and curlicues—now seen as "old-fashioned." Architects for these projects became part of an intensive planning effort, and by the late 1920s some created housing developments on a gigantic scale to cut costs and to deal with the problem of urban crowding. German architect Ludwig Hilberseimer and Swiss-born French architect Le Corbusier favored "high-rise" apartments that adapted the principles of New York's skyscrapers to the domestic environment and satisfied the criterion of urban planning that called for an efficient use of space.

Despite government efforts to restore traditional family values, war had dissolved many middle-class conventions, among them attempts to keep unmarried young men and women apart. Freer relationships and more open discussions of sex occurred in the 1920s. Unmarried women of wealthy families no longer needed chaperones when on the streets or in the company of young men. Middle-class youth of both sexes visited jazz clubs together, attended movies, and began keeping company in cars. Revealing bathing suits, short skirts, and body-hugging clothing emphasized women's sexuality, seeming to invite men and women to join together and replenish the postwar population. Still, the context for sexuality remained marriage. In 1918, British scientist Marie Stopes published the best-seller *Married Love*, which featured frank discussions of sexual relations. In 1927, the wildly successful *Ideal Marriage: Its Physiology and Technique* by Dutch author Theodor van de Velde appeared. Translated into dozens of languages, van de Velde's book, as Stopes's had, described sex in rhapsodic terms and offered precise information about birth control and sexual physiology.

Changing ideas about sex were not limited to the middle and upper classes; one Viennese reformer described working-class marriage as "an erotic-comradely relationship of equals" rather than the economic partnership of past centuries. The flapper, a sexually liberated workingwoman, vied with the dedicated housewife to represent the ordinary woman in the public's eyes. Meanwhile such writers as the Briton D. H. Lawrence and the American Ernest Hemingway glorified men's sexual vigor in books like *Women in Love* (1920) and *The Sun Also Rises* (1926). Images of sexually compatible men and women served to bridge the gap between home and battlefront that had caused such anxiety as the war ended. Mass culture's focus on heterosexuality encouraged the return to normality after the gender disorder that troubled the prewar and war years.

As images of men and women changed, people paid more attention to bodily improvement. The increasing use of toothbrushes and toothpaste, safety and electric razors, and deodorants reflected new standards for personal hygiene and grooming. For Western women, a multibillion-dollar cosmetics industry sprang up almost overnight. Women went to beauty parlors regularly to have their short hair cut, set, dyed, conditioned, straightened, or curled. They also tweezed their eyebrows, applied makeup, and even submitted to cosmetic surgery. Ordinary women painted their faces as formerly only prostitutes had done and competed in beauty contests that judged physical appearance. Instead

of wanting to look plump and prosperous, people aimed to become thin and tan. The proliferation of boxers, hikers, gymnasts, and tap dancers spurred people to exercise and to participate in amateur sports. The consumer focus on personal health coincided with modern industry's need for a physically fit workforce.

As prosperity returned, people could afford to buy more consumer goods. Thanks to the gradual postwar increase in real wages, middle- and upper-class families snapped up sleek modern furniture, washing machines, and vacuum cleaners. Thousands of other modern conveniences such as electric irons, refrigerators, and stoves became standard in better-off working-class households. Installment buying, popularized from the 1920s on, helped ordinary people finance these purchases. Housework became more mechanized, and family intimacy increasingly depended on machines like radios, phonographs, and the less expensive automobiles. At the same time, these new domestic products that enhanced mass communication brought unforeseen changes in the public world of culture and mass politics.

❖ Mass Culture and the Rise of Modern Dictators

Wartime propaganda had aimed to unite all classes against a common enemy. In the 1920s, the process of incorporating diverse groups into a homogeneous Western culture, increasingly seen as a "mass culture," continued. The instruments of mass culture—primarily radio, film, and newspapers—expanded their influence in the 1920s. Whereas some intellectual leaders such as the Spanish poet José Ortega y Gasset urged elites to form an experimental avant-garde that refused to cater to "the drab mass of society," others wanted to use modern media and art to reach and even control the masses. Mass media had the potential for creating an informed citizenry and thus enhancing democracy. In the troubled postwar climate, however, mass media, coupled with political experimentation and outright brutality, also paved the road to dictatorship. Authoritarian rulers—Benito Mussolini, Joseph Stalin, and ultimately Adolf Hitler—aimed to control the masses in unprecedented ways.

Culture for the Masses

An array of media had received a big boost from the war. Bulletins from the battlefront had whetted the public's craving for news and real-life stories, and sales of nonfiction books soared. After years of deprivation, people were driven to achieve material success, and they devoured books that advised how to gain it. Henry Ford's biography, a story of social mobility and technological accomplishment, became a best-seller in Germany. With postwar readers avidly pursuing practical knowledge, institutes and night schools became popular, and school systems promoted reading in geography, science, and history. Photographs, the radio, and movies also contributed to the formation of national culture.

In the 1920s, filmmaking changed from an experimental medium to an international business. Since the mid-1890s, pioneering filmmakers had written, directed, produced, and starred in their own movies and hired little-known performers. The war years, when the U.S. film industry began to outstrip the European, gave rise to specialization: directors, producers, marketers, photographers, film editors, and many others subdivided the process. A star system turned film personalities into celebrities, highly admired and living like royalty. Stars and directors worked within a "studio," or large corporate structure, that set up theater chains and marketed films worldwide. To help sell films, fan magazines and paraphernalia like dolls and dishes bearing stars' faces made movies part of daily life. Films of literary classics and political events developed people's sense of a common heritage. The British government sponsored documentaries that articulated national goals. Bolshevik leaders also supported filmmaking, underwriting the innovative work of director Sergei Eisenstein (1898–1948). His films *Potemkin* (1925) and *Ten Days That Shook the World* (1927–1928) presented a Bolshevik view of history to Russian and international audiences.

Films incorporated familiar elements from other cultural forms. The piano accompaniment that went along with the action of silent films derived from music halls; comic characters, farcical plots, and slapstick humor were borrowed from street or burlesque shows and from new trends in postwar living. Thus popular comedies and romances of the 1920s satirized men and women

who botched the job of achieving emotional intimacy or featured the flapper and made her more visible to the masses. Movies attracted some 100 million weekly viewers, the majority of them women. Popular films and books crossed national borders easily, in the process enhancing cosmopolitanism and global culture for an international audience.

Cinematic portrayals also played to postwar fantasies and fears. In Germany, where filmmakers used expressionist sets and costumes to make films frightening, the influential hit *The Cabinet of Doctor Caligari* (1919) depicted events in an insane asylum as horrifying symbols of state power. Austrian-born Fritz Lang (1890–1976), who worked in Berlin and later Hollywood, showed technological forces in modern life as wildly and destructively out of control in films such as the classic *Metropolis* (1926). Popular detective and cowboy films portrayed heroes who could restore wholeness to the disordered world of murder, crime, and injustice. Depiction of the plight of gangsters appealed to war veterans, who had been exposed to the cheap value of life in the modern world. The films of German director G. W. Pabst awakened anxieties about cross-class sexual attraction; they also presented complex women characters, who did not fit such simple stereotypes as the flapper. English comedian, actor, and producer Charlie Chaplin (1889–1977) created the character of the "Little Tramp," who won international popularity as the defeated hero, the anonymous modern man, trying to keep his dignity in a mechanical world.

Film remained experimental well into the 1920s, but radio was even more so. Developed from Guglielmo Marconi's wireless technology, introduced at the turn of the century, radio broadcasts in the first half of the 1920s were heard by mass audiences in public halls (much like film theaters) and featured orchestras and song followed by audience discussion. The radio quickly became a relatively inexpensive consumer item, and the public concert or lecture could now penetrate the individual's private living space age. (See "Taking Measure," page 1011.) Specialized programming for men (such as sports reporting) and for women (such as advice on home management) soon followed. By the 1930s, radio was available for politicians to reach the masses wherever they might be—even alone at home.

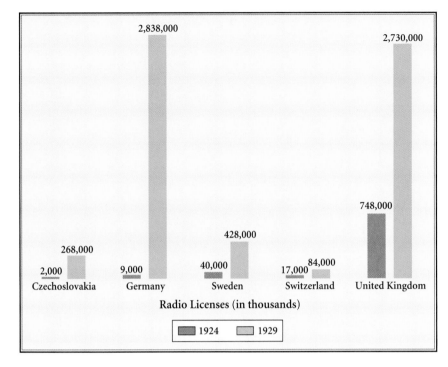

*The spread of radio technology,
like the earlier development of
printing, advanced the cultural
and political unity of citizens
in a nation-state. The most
industrially and commercially
developed societies witnessed the
most rapid diffusion of radios,
which were both programmed
and taxed by governments. Because of this centralized control,
historians can compare the
country-by-country use of radio
in Europe and in much of the
rest of the world.*

Cultural Debates over the Future

Cultural leaders in the 1920s either were obsessed
by the horrendous experience of war or—like the
modernists before the war—held high hopes for
creating a fresh, utopian future that would have little relation to the past. The vision of those haunted
by the war was bleak or violent, and this was especially a theme in German art. The German artist
Kaethe Köllwitz (1867–1945), whose son died in
the war, portrayed in her woodcuts bereaved parents, starving children, and other heart-wrenching,
antiwar images.

Other artists employed satire, irony, and flip-
pancy to express postwar rage and revulsion at civilization's apparent failure. George Grosz (1893–
1959), stunned by the carnage like so many other
German veterans, joined Dada, an artistic and literary movement that had emerged during the war.
Dada produced works marked by nonsense, in-
congruity, and shrieking expressions of alienation.
Grosz's paintings and cartoons of maimed soldiers
and brutally murdered women reflected his psychic
wounds and his self-proclaimed desire "to bellow
back." Dadaist bellowing continued the modernist
tradition of shocking audiences, but now the
shocks were more savage and often more hateful of

ordinary people. Avant-garde portrayals of seedi-
ness and perversion in everyday life flourished in
cabarets and theaters in the 1920s and reinforced
veterans' visions of civilian decadence.

A battle erupted in defeated Germany over the
war's lessons for postwar life. Popular writers such
as Ernst Jünger glorified life in the trenches and
called for the militarization of society to restore order. Erich Maria Remarque cried out for an end to
war in his controversial *All Quiet on the Western
Front* (1928). This international best-seller depicted the life shared by enemies on the battlefield,
thus dampening the national hatred stoked by
wartime propaganda. For the British, World War I
was the Great War, but the battle over the war's
meaning in German novels paralleled the Weimar
Republic's contentious politics.

Poets reflected on postwar conditions in more
general terms, using styles that rejected the comforting rhymes or accessible metaphors of earlier
verse. T. S. Eliot, an American-born poet who for a
time worked as a banker in Britain, portrayed postwar life as petty and futile in "The Waste Land"
(1922) and "The Hollow Men" (1925). The Irish
nationalist poet William Butler Yeats joined Eliot in
mourning the replacement of traditional society
with its moral conviction and religious values by a

new, superficial generation gaily dancing to jazz and engaging in promiscuous sex and vacuous conversation. Yeats's "Sailing to Byzantium" (1928) starts:

> *That is no country for old men. The young*
> *In one another's arms, birds in the trees*
> *—Those dying generations*

Both poets had an uneasy relationship with the modern world and at times advocated authoritarianism rather than democracy.

The postwar arts produced many a utopian fantasy turned upside down; *dystopias* of life in postrevolutionary, traumatized Europe proliferated. Franz Kafka, an employee of a large insurance company in Prague, saw the world as a vast, impersonal machine. His novels *The Trial* (1925) and *The Castle* (1926) evoked the hopeless condition of the individual confronting a relentless, coglike society; his theme seemed to capture for civilian life the helplessness that soldiers had felt at the front. Kafka's expressionistic and bizarre stories, such as "Metamorphosis," in which a salesman wakes up one morning to discover he has turned into a gigantic insect, resonated as nightmarish fables of postwar modernity.

It was especially hard to maintain social optimism and a sense of coherence as an old society collapsed so rapidly and as innovation in politics, technology, and cultural life accelerated dizzyingly. Some writers, picking up on the prewar turn to psychology, confined their work to depicting the complex inner life of individuals. French author Marcel Proust, in his multivolume novel *Remembrance of Things Past* (1913–1927), explored the workings of memory, the passage of time, and sexual modernity through the life of a narrator, eventually identified as the author. At the beginning of the first volume, the narrator is obsessed with his mother's company as he tries to fall asleep at night. He witnesses progressively disturbing obsessions, such as violent sexuality and personal betrayals of love. The haunted inner life analyzed by Freud was infiltrating fiction: for Proust redemption lay in producing beauty from the raw material of life, not in promoting outmoded conventions of decency and morality.

Irish writer James Joyce and British writer Virginia Woolf shared Proust's vision of an interior self built on memories and sensations. Joyce's

Virginia Woolf
Along with Marcel Proust and James Joyce, Virginia Woolf represented the peak of literary modernism with its emphasis on interior states of mind and disjointed, dreamlike slices of reality. Woolf's novels and essays also captured the unappreciated centrality of women, who provided an array of personal services to their more highly valued husbands. Woolf boldly announced that for a woman to be as creative as a man depended on her being partially relieved of the burdens of family—most notably having "a room of one's own."
Gisele Freund/Photo Researchers, Inc.

Ulysses (1922) and Woolf's *Mrs. Dalloway* (1925) illuminated the fast-moving inner lives of their characters in the course of a single day. In one of *Ulysses'* most celebrated passages, a long interior monologue traces a woman's lifetime of erotic and emotional sensations. For Woolf the war had dissolved the solid society from which absorbing stories and fascinating characters were once fashioned. Her characters experience fragmented conversations, momentary sensations, and incomplete relationships.

There was another side to the story, one based not on the interior life of traumatized society but on the promise of technology. Avant-garde artists before the war had celebrated the new, the futuristic, the utopian. Like Jules Amar crafting prostheses for shattered limbs, they were optimistic that technology could make an entire society whole after the slaughter. The aim of art, observed one of them, "is not to decorate our life but to organize it." The group of German artists called the Bauhaus (after the idea of a craft association, or *Bauhütte*) created streamlined office buildings and designed functional furniture, utensils, and decorative objects, many of them inspired by forms from "untainted" East Asia and Africa. Many artists worked in large collectives where, under the guidance of intellectuals such as the Bauhaus's Walter Gropius (1883–1969), they staged shows of modern products that also turned a profit. Before the war Russian artists had been in the vanguard of nonrepresentational and geometric art. Temporarily entranced by the Communist experiment, they optimistically wrote novels about cement factories and ballets about steel—the latter an element common to artificial limbs and advanced, utopian design.

Artists fascinated by technology and machinery were drawn to the most modern of all countries—the United States. Hollywood films, glossy advertisements, and the bustling metropolis of New York tempted careworn Europeans. They were especially attracted to jazz, the improvisational music that emanated from Harlem. African American jazz musicians showed a resiliency of spirit, although Europeans could still feel superior to those of dark skin color in "primitive" costumes. Performers like Josephine Baker (1906–1976) and Louis Armstrong (1900–1971) became international sensations when they toured Europe's capital cities. Like jazz, the New York skyscraper pointed to the future. Skyscrapers seemed to show how engineering and architectural genius could break the bounds of city space instead of being confined by it. Europeans found in New York a potent example of avant-garde expression that rejected a terrifying past and boldly shaped the future.

The Communist Utopia

Communism also promised a shining future and a modern, technological culture. But the Bolsheviks encountered powerful obstacles to consolidating their rule. In the early 1920s, peasant bands called Green Armies revolted against the policy of war communism that confiscated their agricultural produce. Industrial production stood at only 13 percent of its prewar output; the civil war had produced massive casualties; shortages of housing af-

fected the entire population; and millions of refugees clogged the cities and roamed the countryside. In the early spring of 1921, workers in Petrograd and sailors at the nearby naval base at Kronstadt revolted, protesting their short rations and the privileged standard of living that Bolshevik supervisors enjoyed and calling for "soviets without Communists"—that is, a return to the early promises of the Bolsheviks for a worker state.

Lenin raged that the rebels were merely reactionary "petit bourgeois" and Trotsky had many of them shot, but the Kronstadt revolt pushed Lenin to institute reform. During the revolt Lenin announced the first steps in his New Economic Policy (NEP), which imposed a fixed tax on production of grain rather than confiscating it. Subsequent laws returned parts of the economy to the free market, a temporary compromise with capitalist methods that allowed peasants to sell their grain freely and to profit from free trade in consumer goods. Although the state still controlled large industries and banking, the NEP encouraged people to produce, sell, and even, in the words of one leading Communist, "get rich." Consumer goods and more food to eat soon became available. Some peasants and merchants did indeed get rich, but many more remained impoverished. The rise of "NEPmen," who bought and furnished splendid homes and who cared only about conspicuous consumption, belied the Bolshevik credo of a classless utopia.

Protest erupted within Communist ranks. At the 1921 party congress, a group called the Worker Opposition objected to the party's usurpation of economic control from worker organizations and pointed out that the NEP was an agrarian program, not a proletarian one. Because of the NEP, critics complained, prostitutes, criminals, and bourgeois speculators thrived. In response to such charges of growing bureaucratization, Lenin suppressed the Worker Opposition faction in 1921 and set up procedures for purging dissidents.

Bolshevik leaders tightened their grip on politics by making the Communist revolution a cultural reality that would inform people's daily lives and reshape their thoughts. Party leaders invaded the countryside to set up classes in a variety of political and social subjects, and volunteers harangued the public about the importance of literacy—only 40 percent on the eve of World War I. To facilitate social equality between the sexes, as had been part of the Marxist vision of the future, the state made birth control, abortion, and divorce readily available. As commissar for public welfare, Alexsandra Kollontai (1872–1952) promoted birth-control education and programs to offer day care for children of working parents.

The bureaucracy swelled to bring modern culture to every corner of life, and *hygiene* and *efficiency* became watchwords, as they were in the rest of Europe. Such agencies as the Zhenotdel (Women's Bureau) sought to teach women about their rights under communism and about modern sanitary practices. "Americanization" was seen favorably because it had methods for sweeping away the past. Thus semiofficial institutes and associations brought the methods of Henry Ford and Frederick Taylor into factories, the army, the arts, and everyday life. *Timeists*, as efficiency experts were called, aimed to replace tsarist backwardness with technological modernity.

Journalists, writers, and artists argued heatedly about whether the old elite culture could be integrated into the Communist one, a strategy Lenin favored, or whether it had to be thrown out, as some avant-garde intellectuals believed. In the 1920s, Bolshevik culture maintained the rebelliousness of prewar experimental theater, abstract art, and free verse. The short-lived government agency Proletkult aimed to develop proletarian culture through such undertakings as workers' universities, a workers' encyclopedia, a workers' theater, and workers' publishing.

Many Russian artists experimented with blending high art, technology, and mass culture. Composers punctuated their music with the sound of train or factory whistles. The poet Vladimir Mayakovsky edited a journal advocating utilitarian art, wrote verse praising his Communist passport and essays promoting toothbrushing, and staged uproarious farces for ordinary citizens. Alexsandra Kollontai's novels about love and work in the new Communist society employed a direct, straightforward style so less-educated women might read them. The Bolsheviks confiscated mansions and imperial buildings and turned them into workers' clubs and galleries that displayed works of art to the masses.

As with war communism, many resisted the reshaping of culture to "modern" or "Western"

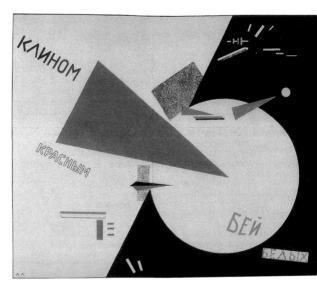

Eli Lissitsky, *Beat the Whites with the Red Wedge* (1919)
Russian artist Eli Lissitsky traveled Europe to bring news of Soviet experimentation. In particular the Soviets were taken with the new physics and their works of art surrounded the viewer with geometric forms. But abstract art was also political: in this 1919 painting, the "red" wedge uses the force of physical principles to defeat the objectively greater counterrevolutionary power of the "whites."
David King Collection.

standards. Bolsheviks threatened everyday customs and the distribution of power within the family. As Zhenotdel workers moved into the countryside, for example, they attempted to teach women to behave as men's equals. Peasant families were still strongly patriarchal, however, and Zhenotdel activists threatened gender relations. In Islamic regions incorporated from the old Russian Empire into the new Communist one, Bolsheviks urged Muslim women to remove their veils and change their way of life, but the Muslims often murdered or assaulted both Zhenotdel workers and women who followed their advice.

In the spring of 1922, Lenin suffered a debilitating stroke, and in January 1924, amidst ongoing cultural experimentation, factional fighting, and repression, the architect of the Bolshevik Revolution died. The party congress declared the day of his death a permanent holiday and changed the name of Petrograd to Leningrad. Lenin's funeral, stunning for its pomp, gave a new direction to Communist political life by elevating the deceased leader into a secular god. After Lenin's death, no one was allowed to criticize anything associated with Lenin's name, a situation that paved the way for future abuses of power by Communist leaders.

Joseph Stalin (1879–1953), who served in the powerful post of general secretary of the Communist Party, led the deification of Lenin. Both organizing the Lenin cult and dealing with thousands of local party officials gave him enormous national patronage, and his welding in 1924 of Russian and non-Russian regions into the Union of Soviet Socialist Republics gave him a claim to executive accomplishment. Lenin had become wary of Stalin's growing influence and ruthlessness and in his last will and testament asked that "the comrades find a way to remove Stalin." Stalin and the inner circle of the Communist Party, however, prevented Lenin's will from being publicized. Stalin proceeded to discredit his chief rival, Trotsky, as an unpatriotic internationalist who was unwilling to concentrate on the tough job of culturally and economically modernizing the Soviet Union. Bringing in several hundred thousand new party members who owed their positions in government and industry to him, Stalin by 1928–1929 had achieved virtually complete dictatorship in the USSR.

Fascism on the March

The political chaos and postwar discontent in Italy brought to power Benito Mussolini (1883–1945), who, like the Bolsheviks, promised an efficient utopia. Italian ire was first aroused when the Allies at Paris refused to honor the territorial promises of the Treaty of London. Domestic unrest swelled when peasants, who had made great sacrifices in the war, protested their serflike status in Italian society. Workers seized factories to draw attention to their economic plight, made worse by the slump of the early 1920s. Since the late nineteenth century, many Europeans had come to blame parliaments for their ills. So Italians were responsive when Mussolini, a socialist journalist who turned to the radical right, built a personal army (the Black Shirts) of veterans and the unemployed to overturn parliamentary government. In 1922, his supporters, known as Fascists, started a march on Rome, threatening a coup. Faced with the prospect of losing his crown, King Victor Emmanuel III (r. 1900–1946) asked the dynamic Mussolini to become prime minister and revive the country.

Mussolini and the Black Shirts
For movements like fascism the best society was one controlled by militarized politics that killed its critics and those of opposing political persuasions. Fascism saw parliamentary democracies as effeminate and doomed in the modern world, which would need dictators and obedient warriors to make it strong, efficient, and machinelike. Thus, in the name of promoting state power, Mussolini gained adherents both within and outside of Italy.
Farabolafoto.

IMPORTANT DATES

1914 August   World War I begins

1914–1925   Suffrage for women expands

1916   Irish nationalists stage Easter Uprising against British rule

1917 March   Revolution in Russia overturns tsarist autocracy

1917 April   The United States enters World War I

1917 November   Bolshevik Revolution in Russia

1918 November   Armistice ends fighting of World War I; revolutionary turmoil throughout Germany; a republic established at Weimar; the kaiser abdicates

1918–1922   Civil war in Russia

1919–1920   Paris Peace Conference redraws the map of Europe

1922   Ireland is split in two: the independent Irish Free State in the south and British-affiliated Ulster in the north; Fascists march on Rome; Mussolini becomes Italy's prime minister; T. S. Eliot publishes "The Waste Land"; James Joyce publishes *Ulysses*

1924   Lenin dies; Stalin and Trotsky contend for power

1924–1929   Period of general economic prosperity and stability

1929 October   Stock market crash in United States

The Fascist movement flourished in the soil of poverty, social unrest, and wounded national pride. It attracted to its bands of Black Shirts many young men who felt cheated of glory by the Allies and veterans who missed the vigor of military life. The *fasces*, an ancient Roman symbol depicting a bundle of sticks wrapped around an ax with the blade exposed, served as the movement's emblem; it represented both unity and force to Mussolini's supporters. Fascism offered a less-developed ideology than Marxism but fashioned its rejection of theory into a virtue. "Fascism is not a church," Mussolini announced upon taking power in 1922. "It is more like a training ground." Fascism was thus defined by its grounding of peacetime politics in an instinctual male violence and by what it opposed: the "antinationalist" socialist movement and parliamentary rule.

Mussolini consolidated his power by putting himself at the head of government departments, by making criticism of the state a criminal offense, and by violently steamrolling parliamentary opposition. His Fascist bands demolished socialist newspaper offices, attacked striking workers, and used their favorite tactic of forcing castor oil (which caused diarrhea) down the throats of socialists. They even murdered certain powerful opponents such as the moderate socialist parliamentary deputy Giacomo Matteotti.

Despite their brutality, the sight of the Black Shirts marching through the streets like disciplined soldiers signaled to many Italians that their country was ordered and modern. Large landowners and businessmen approved Fascist attacks on strikers, and they financially supported the movement. Their generous funding allowed Mussolini to build a large staff by hiring the unemployed and thus to make it look as if Fascists could spark the economy when no one else could.

In addition to violence, Mussolini used mass propaganda and the media to foster support for a kind of military campaign to remake Italy. Peasant men huddled around radios to hear him call for a "battle of wheat" to enhance farm productivity. Peasant women, responding to his praise for maternal duty, adulated him for appearing to value womanhood. In the cities the government launched modernist architecture projects, designed new statues and public adornments, and used public relations promoters to advertise its achievements. Some intellectuals liked the Fascists' avoidance of debate in favor of action and clamored to take part in Mussolini's promotion of avant-garde culture. Mussolini claimed that he made the trains run on time, and this one triumph of modern technology made people hopeful that he could restore order out of wartime and postwar chaos.

Mussolini added a strong dose of traditional values and prejudices to his modern order. Although an atheist, he recognized the importance of Catholicism to most Italians. In 1929, the Lateran Agreement between the Italian government and the church made the Vatican a state under papal

MAPPING THE WEST Europe and the World in 1929 ▶

The map reflects the partitions and nations that came into being as a result of war and revolution, while it obscures the increasing movement toward throwing off colonial rule. This was the true high point of empire: the drive for empire would diminish after 1929 except for Italy, which still craved colonies, and Japan, which continued searching for more land and resources to fuel its rapid growth.

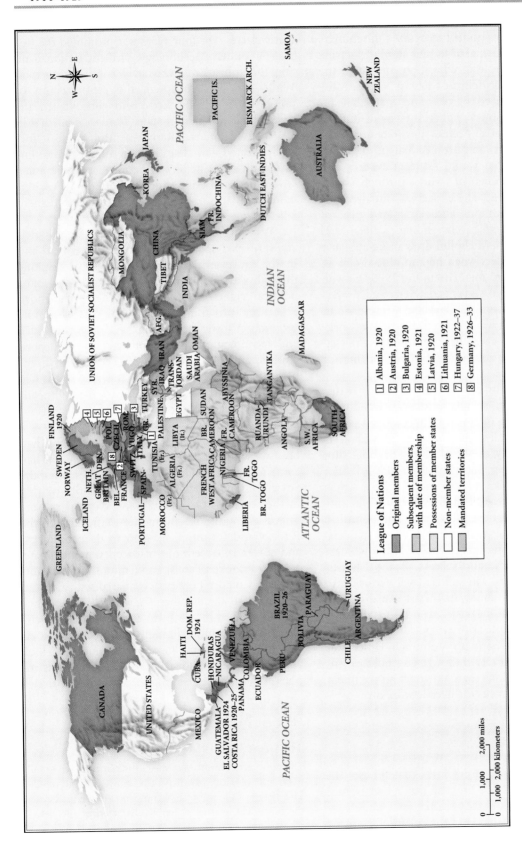

League of Nations

- Original members
- Subsequent members, with date of membership
- Possessions of member states
- Non-member states
- Mandated territories

1. Albania, 1920
2. Austria, 1920
3. Bulgaria, 1920
4. Estonia, 1921
5. Latvia, 1920
6. Lithuania, 1921
7. Hungary, 1922–37
8. Germany, 1926–33

sovereignty. The government recognized the church's right to determine marriage and family doctrine and endorsed its role in education. In return the church ended its criticism of Fascist tactics. Mussolini also introduced a "corporate" state that denied individual political rights in favor of duty to the state. Corporatist decrees in 1926 organized employers, workers, and professionals into groups or corporations that would settle grievances and determine conditions of work through state-controlled channels. These decrees outlawed independent labor unions and eliminated peasant political groups, effectively ending societal and workplace activism. Mussolini drew more applause from business leaders when he announced cuts in women's wages; and then late in the 1920s he won the approval of civil servants, lawyers, and professors by banning women from those professions. Mussolini did not want women out of the workforce altogether but wanted to ensure their relegation to low-paying jobs as part of his scheme for reinvigorating men.

Mussolini's admirers included Adolf Hitler, who throughout the 1920s had been building a paramilitary group of storm troopers and a political organization called the National Socialist German Workers' Party, or Nazis. During his brief stint in jail for the Beer Hall Putsch in 1923, Hitler wrote *Mein Kampf* ("My Struggle," 1925), which articulated a political psychology for manipulating the masses and worked the vicious anti-Semitism of prewar Viennese politics into a vision of racial annihilation. For practical purposes, Hitler was fascinated by the dramatic success of the Fascists' march on Rome, by Mussolini's legal accession to power, and by his ability to thwart socialists and trade unionists. But the austere conditions that had allowed Mussolini to rise to power in 1922 no longer existed in Germany. Although Hitler was welding the Nazi Party into a strong political instrument, the Weimar parliamentary government was actually working as the decade wore on.

Conclusion

The year 1929 was to prove just as fateful as 1914 had been. In 1914, an orgy of death had begun, leading to tens of millions of casualties, the destruction of major dynasties, and the collapse of aristo-

cratic classes. For four years war promoted the free play of military technology, virulent nationalism, and the control of everyday life by bureaucracy. While dynasties collapsed, the centralization of power increased the scope and consolidated the principles of the nation-state. The Peace of Paris in 1919 left Germans bitterly resentful, while it formally created new states in eastern and central Europe built on principles of nationalist ethnic unity. Given the intense intermingling of ethnicities, religions, and languages in the area, such a settlement failed to guarantee a peaceful future.

War furthered the development of mass society. It leveled social classes on the battlefield and in the graveyard, standardized political thinking through wartime propaganda, and extended many political rights to women for their war effort. Peacetime turned improved techniques of wartime production toward churning out consumer goods and technological innovations like air transport, cinema, and radio transmission for greater numbers of people. Modernity in the arts intensified after the war, exploring the recesses of the unconscious and probing the nightmarish battering endured by all segments of the population.

By the end of the 1920s, the legacy of war had been to so militarize politics that strongmen had come to power in Hungary, Poland, Romania, the Soviet Union, and Italy, with Adolf Hitler waiting in the wings in Germany. Many Westerners were impressed by the tough, modern efficiency of the Fascists and Communists who made parliaments and citizen rule seem out-of-date, even effeminate. Many overlooked Fascist and Communist commitment to violence because, compared with the war, it seemed so tame. When the United States stock market crashed in 1929 and economic disaster circled the globe, authoritarian solutions, technological culture, and militarism continued to look appealing. What followed was a series of catastrophes even more devastating than World War I.

Suggested References

The Great War, 1914–1918

The most recent histories of the Great War consider its military, technological, psychic, social, and economic aspects. This vision of the war as a phenomenon occurring beyond the battlefield as well as on it characterizes the newest scholarship.

Bourke, Joanna. *Dismembering the Male: Men's Bodies, Britain, and the Great War.* 1996.

*Brittain, Vera. *Testament of Youth.* 1933.

Downs, Laura Lee. *Manufacturing Inequality: Gender Division in the French and British Metalworking Industries, 1914–1939.* 1995.

Echenberg, Myron. *Colonial Conscripts: The "Tirailleurs Sénégalais" in French West Africa, 1857–1960.* 1990.

Ellis, John. *A Social History of the Machine-Gun.* 1986.

*Hasek, Jaroslav. *The Good Soldier Schweik.* 1920.

Leed, Eric J. *No Man's Land: Combat and Identity in World War I.* 1979.

Panchasi, Roxanne. "Reconstructions: Prosthetics and the Rehabilitation of the Male Body in World War I." *Differences.* 1995.

Roshwald, Aviel, and Richard Stites, eds. *European Culture in the Great War: The Arts, Entertainment, and Propaganda, 1914–1918.* 1999.

Schmitt, Bernadotte E., and Harold C. Vederler. *The World in the Crucible, 1914–1919.* 1984.

Winter, Jay, and Jean-Louis Robert, eds. *Capital Cities at War: Paris, London, Berlin, 1914–1919.* 1997.

World War I Documents Archive: http://www.lib.byu. edu/ %7Erdh/wwi/.

1917–1918: Protest, Revolution, and War's End

Histories of the war's end account for the cataclysmic setting: deprivation, ongoing mass slaughter, and the eruption of revolution. Peacemaking also occurred, and that too was complex. In all, the violence of the postwar scene has made historians call into question the idea that wars end with an armistice.

Lewis, David Levering. *W. E. B. Du Bois: Biography of a Race, 1868–1919.* 1993.

Neuberger, Joan. *Hooliganism: Crime, Culture, and Power in St. Petersburg.* 1994.

Pipes, Richard. *A Concise History of the Russian Revolution.* 1995.

Schwabe, Klaus. *Woodrow Wilson, Revolutionary Germany, and Peacemaking, 1918–1919: Missionary Diplomacy and the Realities of Power.* 1985.

Smith, Leonard. *Between Mutiny and Obedience: The Case of the French Fifth Infantry Division during World War I.* 1994.

Stites, Richard. *Revolutionary Dreams: Utopian Vision and Experimental Life in the Russian Revolution.* 1989.

Wohl, Robert. *A Passion for Wings: Aviation and the Western Imagination.* 1994.

A Decade of Recovery: Europe in the 1920s

Two themes shape the history of the 1920s: recovery from the trauma of war and revolution and ongoing modernization of work and social life. The great technological innovations of the prewar period such as films and airplanes receive sophisticated treatment by historians for their impact on people's imagination. The radio is another phenomenon just beginning to find its historians.

Grossman, Atina. *Reforming Sex: The German Movement for Birth Control and Abortion Reform, 1920–1930.* 1995.

Kah, Douglas, and Gregory Whitehead. *Wireless Imagination: Sound, Radio, and the Avant-Garde.* 1992.

Kent, Susan. *Making Peace: The Reconstruction of Gender in Postwar Britain.* 1994.

Miller, Michael. *Shanghai on the Metro: Spies, Intrigue, and the French between the Wars.* 1994.

Nolan, Mary. *Visions of Modernity: American Business and the Modernization of Germany.* 1994.

Rabinbach, Anson. *The Human Motor: Energy, Fatigue, and the Origins of Modernity.* 1990.

Roberts, Mary Louise. *Civilization without Sexes: Reconstructing Gender in Postwar France, 1917–1927.* 1994.

Schwartz, Vanessa, and Leo Charney, eds. *Cinema and the Invention of Modern Life.* 1995.

Mass Culture and the Rise of Modern Dictators

Mass communications advances in cinema and radio provided new tools for the rule of modern dictators who arose from the shambles of war and revolution. Many of the most interesting recent studies look at the cultural components of the consolidation of dictatorial power, while not forgetting the violence that was a particular feature of authoritarian rule in the postwar twentieth century.

Berghaus, Gunter. *Futurism and Politics: Between Anarchist Rebellion and Fascist Reaction, 1909–1944.* 1996.

De Grazia, Victoria. *How Fascism Ruled Women.* 1994.

Harsch, Donna. *German Social Democracy and the Rise of Nazism.* 1994.

*Kollontai, Alexsandra. *Love of Worker Bees.* 1923.

Lyttleton, Adrian. *The Seizure of Power: Fascism in Italy, 1919–1929.* 1987.

Schnapp, Jeffrey. *Staging Fascism: 18BL and the Theater of Masses for Masses.* 1996.

Tumarkin, Nina. *Lenin Lives! The Lenin Cult in Soviet Russia.* 1997.

*Primary sources.

An Age of Catastrophes

1929–1945

Nazis on Parade
By the time Hitler came to power in 1933, Germany was mired in the economic depression. Hated by Communists, Nazis, and conservatives alike, the republic had few supporters. To a nation still reeling from its defeat in World War I, the Nazis looked as if they would restore national power by defeating enemies—not the Allies but the Jews, Slavs, gypsies, and other groups both within and outside Germany's borders. Hitler took his cue from Mussolini by promising an end to democracy and tolerance.
Hugo Jaeger/LIFE/TimePix.

W HEN ETTY HILLESUM MOVED TO AMSTERDAM in the early 1930s to attend law school, an economic depression gripped the world. A resourceful young Dutch woman, Hillesum pieced together a living as a housekeeper and part-time language teacher. The pressures and pleasures of everyday life kept her from fully absorbing the headline accounts of Adolf Hitler's spectacular rise to power in Germany on a platform demonizing her fellow Jews for the economic slump. World War II, however, ruptured her normal existence. After the German army conquered the Netherlands in 1940, Dutch Jews suffered severe deprivation and persecution, a situation that forced Hillesum to the shattering realization she noted in her diary in July 1942: "What they are after is our total destruction." The Nazis occupied the Netherlands and started relocating Jews to camps in Germany and Poland. Hillesum went to work for Amsterdam's Jewish Council, which was compelled to organize the transportation of Jews to the east. Changing from self-absorbed student to heroine, she did what she could to help other Jews and minutely recorded the deportation. "I wish I could live for a long time so that one day I may know how to explain it." When she was taken prisoner, she smuggled out letters, witnessing the brutal treatment in the transit camps and serving as "the ears and eyes of a piece of Jewish history." Etty Hillesum never fulfilled her ambition to become a professional writer: she died in the Auschwitz death camp in November 1943.

1930	1933	1936	1939	1942	1945

Politics and War

Purges in the USSR; Sweden constructs welfare state; movement for Indian independence

World War II

Creation of British Commonwealth of Nations; Japan invades Manchuria

Japan bombs Pearl Harbor; United States enters World War II

Hitler comes to power in Germany; U.S. President Franklin Roosevelt begins the New Deal

Holocaust

Government of India Act

United States drops atomic bombs on Japan

Spanish Civil War

Society and Economy

Depression spreads around the world; collectivization of agriculture in USSR; continuing decline in European fertility; surging population in many non-Western countries

German rearmament

Wartime rationing and scarcity; rising employment

Culture, Religion, and Intellectual Life

Socialist realism becomes approved style in USSR; films with sound replace silent movies; Nazi campaign against "decadent art"; Anna Akhmatova's poetry critiques Stalinism

Charlie Chaplin, *Modern Times*

Virginia Woolf, *Three Guineas*

The U.S. stock market crash of 1929 opened a horrific era in world history. During the Great Depression of the 1930s, suffering was global, intensifying social grievances throughout the world. In Europe, many people turned to military-style strongmen for answers. Adolf Hitler roused the German masses to rededicate themselves to national greatness. Authoritarian, militaristic, and fascist regimes spread to Portugal, Spain, Poland, Hungary, Japan, China, and elsewhere, trampling on representative institutions. Joseph Stalin oversaw the Soviet Union's rapid industrialization, but in the process he justified the killing of millions of citizens as the necessary price of Soviet growth.

The international scene became doubly menacing because elected leaders in the democracies reacted cautiously to the simultaneous phenomena of the depression and fascist aggression. In an age of mass media, civilian leaders appeared weak and fearful of conflict, while dictators in uniform looked bold and decisive. Only the German invasion of Poland in 1939 finally roused the democracies to strong action.

But their efforts could not divert catastrophe. World War II erupted in Europe, and by 1941 the war had spread to the rest of the world. The United States, Great Britain, and the Soviet Union allied in combat against Germany, Italy, and Japan. Tens of millions would perish in this war because both technology and ideology had become more deadly than it had been just two decades earlier. Half the dead were civilians, among them Etty Hillesum, whose only crime was being a Jew.

❖ The Great Depression

The depression triggered by the U.S. stock market crash of 1929 was not the longest in history: many Europeans still labeled the brutal downturn that began in 1873 and lasted almost a quarter of a century the "Great Depression." However, as the slump threw tens of millions out of work and brought suffering to rural and urban folk alike, opinion changed. The whole world felt the depression's impact as commerce and investment in industry fell off, social life and gender roles were upset, and the birthrate plummeted. From peasants in Asia to industrial workers in Germany and the United States, the lives of large segments of the global population were ravaged.

Economic Disaster

In the 1920s, U.S. corporations and banks as well as millions of individual Americans had recklessly invested their money, or more often borrowed money to invest in the stock market, which seemed to churn out endless profits. Using readily available credit, they bought shares in popular new companies with complete confidence in a Yale economist's predictions that the stock market was on a "permanently high plateau." The Federal Reserve Bank—the nation's central bank, which controlled financial policy—tightened the availability of credit in an attempt to stabilize the market, however, and brokers demanded that their clients immediately pay back the money they had borrowed to buy stock. As stocks were sold to pay brokerage bills, the market collapsed. Between early October and mid-November 1929, the value of businesses listed on the U.S. stock market dropped from $87 billion to $30 billion.

The crash spawned a global depression because the United States, a leading international creditor, had financed the relative economic growth of the past five years in the West. Suddenly strapped for credit, U.S. financiers cut back on loans and called in short-term debts, undermining banks and industry at home and abroad. The fact that the United States had become the leading industrial power, producing 45 percent of the world's manufactured goods, compounded the collapse; in the interwar years, Japanese industry also took away business that had formerly been Europe's. From the aging industries of Britain to the fledgling factories of eastern Europe, a decline in consumer buying and overproduction further eroded the European economy. In particular, working-class wages, so central to a healthy economy, had not risen in proportion to the prosperity of the late 1920s. This was especially true in the United States; thus, despite its position as the world's leading

Italian Newspaper Depicts the Crash on Wall Street
The crash of the U.S. stock market was ultimately felt around the world, from Italian cities to the Asian countryside. Credit, on which modern industry and modern farming depended, dried up. Governments threw up huge tariff walls to protect national industries and thus curtailed trade, while they initially cut back on aid to unemployed people, which further reduced consumer purchasing and inflicted financial hardship and psychological pain.
Mary Evans Picture Library.

manufacturer, by 1932 U.S. steel production had slumped to only 12 percent of its level before the crash. The Great Depression left no sector of the world economy unscathed.

Government actions made the depression worse and longer than it might otherwise have been. To spur their economies, governments used standard tools such as budget cuts and high tariffs against foreign goods, but these policies further dampened trade and spending in the great industrial powers. (See "Taking Measure," below.) In 1933, an estimated 14 million U.S. workers were unemployed, and more than five thousand banks

had closed, wiping out savings and reserves. In Germany, almost 6 million workers, or about one-third of the workforce, were unemployed, and many others were underemployed. France had a more self-sufficient economy. Big businesses like the innovative Citroën car manufacturer began to fail, however, and by the mid-1930s more than 800,000 French people had lost their jobs. Great Britain, with its textile, steel, and coal industries near ruin because of out-of-date techniques and foreign competition, had close to 3 million unemployed in 1932—the worst year, by many British accounts, of this "devil's decade."

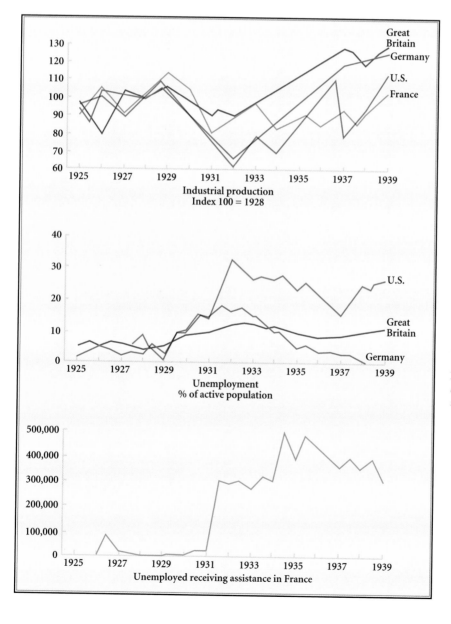

Industrial production
Index 100 = 1928

Unemployment
% of active population

Unemployed receiving assistance in France

TAKING MEASURE
Industrial Production and Unemployment, 1925–1939
The depression had many dimensions, both measurable and psychological. A calamitous fall in production in the most advanced industrial countries—Germany and the United States—was accompanied by rising unemployment. Whatever the resistance to providing government assistance, the trend toward the welfare state continued, moving from veterans' and old-age pensions to unemployment compensation, as the case of France demonstrates. Although less-industrialized countries around the world experienced smaller cuts in production, for them even the smallest decline was a setback on the road to modernizing their economy.
Based on *Atlas historique, histoire de l'humanité de la préhistoire à nos jours* (Paris: Hachette, 1987).

In the agricultural sector, where prices had been declining for several years because of abundant harvests and technological innovation, creditors confiscated farms and equipment. Millions of small farmers had no money to buy the chemical fertilizers and motorized machinery they needed to remain competitive, and they too went under. Eastern and southern European peasants, who had pressed for the redistribution of land after World War I, especially suffered because they could not afford to operate their newly acquired farms. The Polish Sejm (parliament), for example, had awarded more than six million acres from the vast estates of the Catholic church and nobility after World War I. Many of the 700,000 new landowners fell into debt trying to make their farms viable. Eastern European governments often ignored the farmers' plight and instead used scarce capital to start new industries in hopes that industrial prosperity would improve the entire economy. Most of the agricultural population were left to fend for themselves in these desperate times, a situation that increased tensions in rural society.

Social Effects of the Crash

The picture of society during the Great Depression was more complex than utter ruin, however. First, the situation was not uniformly bleak. Despite the slump, modernization proceeded. Bordering English slums, one traveler in the mid-1930s noticed, were "filling stations and factories that look like exhibition buildings, giant cinemas and dance halls and cafés, bungalows with tiny garages, cocktail bars, Woolworth's [and] swimming pools." Municipal and national governments continued road construction and sanitation projects. Running water, electricity, and sewage pipes were installed in many homes for the first time. New factories manufactured synthetic fabrics, electrical products such as stoves, and automobiles—all of them in demand. With government assistance, eastern European industry developed: Romanian industrial production, for example, increased by 55 percent between 1929 and 1939, and this increase looked like the beginning of a real success story. As war approached later in the decade, munitions production soared across Europe and helped create jobs.

Second, the majority of Europeans and Americans had jobs throughout the 1930s. Despite the depression, service workers, managers, and busi-

ness magnates often enjoyed considerable prosperity. Some members of the old aristocracy were able to maintain their high standards of living by selling their country estates and moving to the cities. Lower on the social scale, people with steady employment benefited from a drastic drop in prices.

Those with jobs, however, felt the threat of becoming unemployed and having to scrape, like thousands of others, for a bare existence. In towns with heavy industry, sometimes more than half the population was out of work. In England in the mid-1930s, close to 20 percent of the population lacked adequate food, clothing, or housing. "We was like animals, we was like animals at home, all of us hungry," a day laborer recalled of life in the 1930s. "I used to sit eating cabbage stalks cos I was that hungry." In a 1932 school assignment a German youth wrote: "My father has been out of work for two and a half years. He thinks that I'll never find a job because there are 700,000 young people alone unemployed in Germany." Despite the prosperity of many people, a thundercloud of fear and resentment settled over Western society.

Changing Roles for Men and Women. Economic catastrophe upset social life and strained gender relations. Sometimes unemployed men stayed home all day, increasing the tension in small, overcrowded apartments. Women could often find low-paying jobs doing laundry and cleaning house for others. While these women were out working, men who stayed at home sometimes took over housekeeping chores but often felt that this "women's work" demeaned their masculinity. As many women became breadwinners, men could be seen standing on street corners begging. This rearrangement of gender expectations fueled the discontent of unemployed men throughout Europe.

In cities the future looked especially grim for young men, who faced severe unemployment. Restlessness and enforced idleness led many of them to form gangs that rode the subways and seemed menacing to passengers. Others loitered in parks, intruding in areas usually frequented by mothers and their children and old people. Men who lived in rural areas saw their traditional roles erode as well. The percentage of farmworkers in the western European population decreased, and patriarchal authority, once central in overseeing farm labor and allocating property among inheritors, continued its decline. Demagogues everywhere berated parliamentary politicians for their failure to stop the collapse of traditional agrarian values. The climate was thus primed for Nazi and fascist politicians who promised to restore prosperity and male dignity.

The Population "Crisis." Politicians of all stripes did agree on one issue: the consequences of the falling birthrate. They forecast national collapse, as a declining birthrate combined with a declining economy to give the impression of social deterioration and lack of confidence in the national future.

After a brief postwar upturn, the birthrate had indeed dropped; in many industrial countries by the early 1930s, it stood at half or less than half of turn-of-the-century levels. The reason was clear: in difficult economic times, people chose to have fewer children. There were other reasons too. Mandatory education and more years of required schooling, enforced more strictly after World War I, resulted in greater expenses for parents. Working-class children no longer brought in wages to supplement the family's income; instead they cost money while they went to school. As knowledge of birth control spread to the working and lower-middle classes, cutting family size became more common. By 1939, Britain's Family Planning Association, founded by Maria Stopes and others, numbered more than sixty clinics. In the United States, Margaret Sanger, working with the medical profession, led a similar organization to make birth-control information and devices accessible.

The population "crisis" invigorated racist politics and rhetoric, which held that "superior" peoples were failing to breed, while "inferior" peoples were lurking to take their place. This racism took a violent form in eastern Europe, where the rural population rose because of increased life expectancy despite an overall drop in birthrate. But increased population compounded the burdens of eastern European farm families, who faced an unprecedented struggle for survival. Rural unrest weakened the fragile states created after World War I. Early in the 1930s, Polish peasants refused to pay new taxes and blockaded debt-laden farms about to be confiscated. Throughout eastern Europe, financial woes helped infect peasant political parties with anti-Semitism. The parties blamed Jewish bankers for farm foreclosures and Jewish civil servants (of whom there were actually very few) for new taxes and inadequate relief programs. They

maintained that Christians should fill the good jobs Jews held. Other minority peoples fared little better; the dominant nationality groups in Hungary, Yugoslavia, Romania, and elsewhere purged ethnic minorities from jobs. Thus population issues along with economic misery fueled ethnic hatred and anti-Semitism.

Global Dimensions of the Crash

The effects of declining purchasing power and ready credit extended beyond the West, further accelerating the pace of change and spread of discontent in European empires. World War I and postwar investment had generated economic growth in Asia, Africa, and Latin America. Economic expansion had brought profound demographic alterations not only in rising population but in high rates of rural emigration and explosive urban growth. Between 1920 and 1940, Shanghai ballooned from 1.7 million to 3.75 million residents, Calcutta from 1.8 million to 3.4 million, and Cairo from 865,000 to 1.5 million.

The depression affected both town and countryside beyond the West, cutting the demand for copper, tin, and other raw materials and for the finished products made in urban factories. It drove down the price of foodstuffs like rice and coffee, and this proved disastrous to people who had been forced to grow a single cash crop. However, the economic picture was uneven in the colonies as well as in Europe. For instance, established industrial sectors of the Indian economy like textiles gained strength, with India achieving virtual independence from British cloth, while fledgling industry like electrical energy usually suffered and per capita use remained low.

Economic distress added to other, smoldering grievances. Millions of African and Asian colonial troops had fought for Britain and France in World War I, but these countries had given little back to their colonial populations. In fact, the League of Nations charter had pointedly omitted any reference to the principle of racial equality demanded by people of color at the Versailles conference. Simultaneously, the growing economic power of Japan continued to provide colonized people a model of success by a non-Western power. Moved by the Wilsonian ideal of self-determination and inspired by Japan's example, colonial people increasingly set their sights on winning a Western-style autonomy—

at exactly the time that Western powers most needed to keep their colonies' allegiance *and* the profits of their economic development.

The British government loosened its formal political ties to its dominions (that is, those territories enjoying self-rule: Canada, New Zealand, Australia, the Irish Free State, and the Union of South Africa) with the Statute of Westminster (1931), which instituted the British Commonwealth of Nations. The commonwealth's tariffs against outsiders effectively created a beneficial group of trading partners. India was excluded from the commonwealth and became the arena for a momentous struggle against colonial domination.

Upper-class Indians, who had organized to gain rights from Britain in the late nineteenth century, were joined in the 1930s by millions of working people, including hundreds of thousands of returning soldiers. Mohandas ("Mahatma," or "great-souled") Gandhi (1869–1948) emerged as the charismatic leader for Indian independence. Of privileged birth and trained in England as a Western-style lawyer, Gandhi embraced Hindu self-denial, rejecting the elaborate trappings of British life in favor of simple clothing made of thread he had spun. He advocated *civil disobedience*—deliberately but peacefully breaking the law—which he professed to model on British suffragists' tactics and on the teachings of Jesus, Buddha, and other spiritual leaders. In 1930, he led a march to India's salt flats to protest the British monopolies in salt and other necessities that raised prices for Indians to boost colonial revenue. As Gandhi illegally picked up the forbidden salt, a nationalist-feminist poet shouted "Hail, lawbreaker." He encouraged all Indians to wear homespun clothing and thus boycott British-made textiles. Such "peaceful noncooperation" contrasted significantly with the deference Indians had traditionally shown the British.

Gandhi's tactics and leadership proved devastatingly effective in the long run, but the British did not surrender without a struggle. The colonial government jailed Gandhi repeatedly and tried to split the independence movement by encouraging the Muslim League, led by Mohammed Ali Jinnah. Hindu-Muslim antagonism, which the British had promoted since the nineteenth century, formed a counterpoint to Gandhi's campaign. By 1935, public pressure sympathetic to Gandhi led Parliament to pass the Government of India Act, which granted much of India internal self-government.

Gandhi Leading the Salt March
Mohandas Gandhi appealed to the masses, not just to the middle- and upper-class constituency of the Indian National Congress, which had emphasized reform and participation in government. Instead, Gandhi addressed the entire colonial system that prevented ordinary Indian people from using the country's national resources such as salt. Violating British laws, which prohibited Indians from gathering this natural product, Gandhi led the people in an act of civil disobedience—his march to the sea to touch the salt.
© Bettman/Corbis.

The drive for complete independence was momentarily checked.

In the Middle East, the economic and political ambitions of peoples of the old Ottoman Empire made quicker headway. Led by Westernizer Mustafa Kemal (1881–1938), or Atatürk ("first among Turks"), the Turks took advantage of European vulnerability both after World War I and during the depression to found an independent republic in 1923 and to craft a capitalist economy. In an effort to nationalize and modernize Turkish culture, Kemal moved the capital from Constantinople to Ankara in 1923, changed the ancient

Greek *Constantinople* to the Turkish *Istanbul* in 1930, mandated Western dress for men and women, introduced the Latin alphabet, and abolished polygamy. In 1936, women received the vote and were eligible to serve in the parliament. Persia similarly loosened the European grip on its economy by forcing the negotiation of oil contracts; at the same time it updated its government and in 1935 changed its name to Iran. Persistent uprisings compelled Britain to end its mandate in Iraq in 1930, although it retained crucial oil concessions. In 1936, Britain agreed to end its military occupation of Egypt (though not the Suez Canal), fulfilling the promise of self-rule granted in 1922. Conflict escalated in Palestine where British efforts to make a safe home for Zionist immigrants and to encourage the rights of native Arabs had created conditions for violence.

Obsessed by rising trade barriers in Europe and their own population decline, the French made fewer concessions to colonized people. Their trade with their colonies increased as that with Europe lagged, and the demographic surge in Asia and Africa bolstered French optimism; as one official put it, "One hundred and ten million strong, France can stand up to Germany." Western-educated native leaders such as Ho Chi Minh, founder of the Indochinese Communist Party, contested their people's subjection, but in 1930 the French government brutally crushed the peasant uprising he led. In Algeria, French settlers resisted a nationalist movement inspired by liberal values as well as Islamic and pan-Arab revivals advocated by other reform groups.

In general, British and French pursuit of economic recovery through empire split these two nations from their former allies in World War I. Preoccupied and divided, they let authoritarian and totalitarian forces spread unchecked throughout Europe during the crisis-ridden 1930s.

❖ Totalitarian Triumph

Representative government collapsed in many countries under the sheer weight of social and economic crisis. After 1929, Italy's Benito Mussolini, the Soviet Union's Joseph Stalin, and Germany's Adolf Hitler were able to mobilize vast support for their violent regimes. To some extent citizens had been conditioned to accept the military directives of wartime. But many people admired Mussolini and Hitler for the discipline they brought to social and economic life, and they overlooked the brutal side of dictatorship. Cultural leaders and working people around the world respected Stalin's administration in the USSR because it promised full employment, free social services, and education for the masses. In an age of crisis, utopian hopes also led many to support political violence. Unity and obedience—not freedom and rights—were seen as keys to rebirth.

Scholars often apply the term *totalitarianism* to the Fascist, Nazi, and Communist regimes of the 1930s. They use it to refer to highly centralized systems of government that attempt to control society and ensure conformity through a single party and police terror. (See "Terms of History," page 1030.) Forged in the crucible of war and its aftermath, totalitarian governments broke with liberal principles to wage war on their own citizens.

The Rise of Stalinism

In the 1930s, Joseph Stalin led the astonishing transformation of the USSR from a rural society into a formidable industrial power. Having taken firm control against Lenin's express wishes, Stalin ended the New Economic Policy (NEP), Lenin's temporary compromise between Marxism and capitalism. The Soviet Union became an industrial, Communist nation directed by a new generation of technocrats with few connections to the prewar socialist movement. The costs of industrialization and the consolidation of Stalin's power were staggering. Stalin became the unquestioned leader of a single-party state, while more than ten million people, by Stalin's own count, starved, were executed, or were worked to death in labor camps during the 1930s.

Rapid Industrialization. In the spring of 1929, Stalin presented the first of several five-year plans to the Communist Party congress. Outlining a program for massive increases in the output of coal, iron ore, steel, and industrial goods, Stalin called the plan, which laid out strict, meticulously calculated production goals, an emergency measure to end Soviet backwardness. He warned that without it, "the advanced countries . . . will crush us." He thus established central economic planning—a policy used on both sides in World War I by which government directed production, allocated resources, and mobilized the workforce. This policy had also helped Japan industrialize, and increasingly Western economists and industrialists favored some degree of economic planning. Between 1928 and 1940, the number of Soviet workers in industry, construction, and transport grew from 4.6 million to 12.6 million. From 1927 to 1937, production in metallurgy and machinery rose 1,400 percent. Stalin's first five-year plan had helped make the USSR a leading industrial nation.

Central planning helped create a new elite of bureaucrats and industrial officials; the number of managers in heavy industry grew by almost 500 percent between 1928 and 1935. Mostly party officials and technical experts, these managers dominated Soviet workers by limiting their ability to change jobs or move from place to place. Nonetheless, skilled workers as well as bureaucrats benefited substantially from the redistribution of privileges that accompanied industrialism and central planning. Compared with people working the land, those in industry and especially those with mechanical skills received better housing, higher wages, and access to the limited consumer goods. Communist officials, meanwhile, enjoyed perquisites such as country homes, better health care, foods unavailable to the masses, and luxurious vacations.

Unskilled workers, however, faced a grim plight. Newcomers from the countryside were often herded into barracklike dwellings, even tents, and subjected to dangerous factory conditions. Many took pride in the skills they acquired: "We mastered this profession—completely new to us—with great pleasure," a female lathe operator recalled. More often, however, workers lacked the technical education and even the tools necessary to accomplish goals prescribed by the five-year plan. Almost everyone, from workers and managers to inspectors and government overseers, falsified production figures and other supposedly scientific data to protect their jobs—and in some cases their lives. Because fulfilling the plan had top priority as a measure of progress toward Communist utopia, official lying and corruption became ingrained in the economic system.

In a single decade the Soviet Union went from being an illiterate peasant society to an advanced industrial economy, an extraordinary achievement that had taken other Western countries a century or more to accomplish. Suffering was intense but tolerated because Soviet workers, unlike their counterparts around the world, were employed and believed in the ethos of "constant struggle, struggle, and struggle" to achieve a Communist society, in the words of a worker. Youth in particular accepted the rigors of Stalin's industrialization as a heroic challenge. After the romance of the revolution and civil war, wrote one young man, "the older generation had left to our lot only a boring, prosaic life that was devoid of struggle and excitement." For workers, NEP had endorsed old-fashioned inequality; under Stalin, one maintained, "man himself is being rebuilt."

Collectivization of Agriculture. Stalinism, as this tough, even brutal vision of modernization came to be called, politicized work life in city and countryside alike as part of forced industrialization. Stalin demanded more grain from peasants (who had prospered under NEP), both to feed the urban workforce and to export as a way to finance industrialization. Peasants resisted government demands by cutting production or withholding produce from the market. Faced with such recalcitrance, Stalin called for the "liquidation of the kulaks." The name *kulak*, which literally means "fist," was a derogatory term for prosperous peasants, but in practice it applied to anyone who opposed his plans to end independent farming.

Stalin generated enthusiasm for the attack on the peasantry by presenting it as a revolutionary challenge. In the winter of 1929–1930, party workers armed with quotas scoured villages for produce; officials soon arrived and forced villagers to identify the kulaks among them. Propaganda units instilled hatred for anyone connected with kulaks. One Russian remembered believing they were "bloodsuckers, cattle, swine, loathsome, repulsive: they had no souls; they stank." Stalin ordered these "enemies of the state" evicted, imprisoned, exiled, or murdered. Whole families and even entire villages were robbed of their possessions and left to starve. "In the station square," one writer recalled, "Ukrainian kulaks . . . lay down and died. One got used to seeing the dead there in the morning, and the hospital stable-boy . . . would come along with his cart and pile the corpses in."

Totalitarianism

Totalitarianism is a term loaded with controversy, but when first introduced in Italy, Mussolini's government adopted it as a mark of pride. In 1923, Mussolini proposed a law by which the political party that garnered the most votes would seat 75 percent of the delegates in Italy's parliament. Italy had many political parties whose delegates formed coalitions that acted together to govern. Mussolini hoped to end that practice so that his small but powerful party could take most of the parliamentary seats and rule alone. Its temporary popularity would be transformed into real dominance.

The Italian journalist Giovanni Amendola cried foul, claiming that this proposal would eliminate both majority rule and minority coalitions in favor of a "totalitarian" system. Amendola, later beaten to death by Mussolini's thugs, warned that such a totalitarian system "denies you the right to possess a conscience—of your own, not one imposed by others."[1] Then, in a surprising turn, the Fascists embraced the term and proclaimed the superiority of an all-encompassing state led by a virile and forward-looking party. Their model was the "total state" under conditions of "total war" when the principles of conscience, rights, and freedom gave way to efficient military rule of the masses.

---

[1] Giovanni Amendola, quoted in Abbott Gleason, *Totalitarianism: The Inner History of the Cold War* (New York: Oxford University Press, 1995), 14.

The Nazis picked up on the term, hailing the effective totalitarian party that could mobilize workers and soldiers to make them like steel in body and in spirit. The flabby democratic state that had to respond to the wishes of a mass citizenry for programs such as insurance plans and workmen's compensation would disappear as it had during wartime. Some German theorists even looked admiringly at the Soviet Union with its five-year plans and forced industrialization as another model for "total mobilization" and the "total state." They pointed approvingly at its coercion in matters of political belief as a modern way to create state power.

As refugees fled Europe in the 1930s, they contributed another ingredient to the definition of totalitarianism, a system they professed to abhor. Refugee intellectuals saw totalitarianism as stemming from the rational thought of the eighteenth century and the aim of the scientific revolution and the Enlightenment to dominate nature. Analogously, to their mind, the system of free trade and capitalist industrialization aimed at domination of the economy and resources. By these arguments, the Soviets were less implicated in totalitarianism than the Fascists and Nazis; as the cold war took shape in 1945, people who defended the USSR and hailed its contribution in the war to defeat Hitler and Mussolini turned against the term's adequacy to describe these three towering dictatorships. In the cold war the United States wanted to view the Soviet system as identical to Nazism, while the USSR's defenders now envisioned the term *totalitarianism* as cold war propaganda and rejected its use. One modification that pleased some was the term *democratic totalitarianism*, used to distinguish Stalin's from Hitler's and

---

Confiscated kulak land formed the basis of the *kolkhoz*, or collective farm, where peasants were to create a Communist agricultural system using cooperative farming and modern machinery. Agricultural collectivization provoked resistance: some country men formed guerrilla bands, and women on the *kolkhoz* hid barnyard animals and preserved rural traditions that the modernizers detested. Many peasants deserted communism for good in the 1930s. Officials nonetheless announced that, as in the city, rural work life was becoming Communist.

The Purges. Once work life was politicized, economic failure took on political meaning. Factory workers, many newly arrived from the countryside, often were unable to meet the required quotas. In the countryside, party officials' ignorance of agriculture and a lack of equipment and scientific personnel made collectivization an utter disaster. Soviet citizens starved as the grain harvest declined from 83 million tons in 1930 to 67 million in 1934. Stalin blamed failure on "wreckers," saboteurs of communism, and he instituted purges—state

Mussolini's regimes. So heated became the debate over the concept and application of *totalitarianism* as a descriptive historical term, however, that many scholars ceased to use it.

Others, however, believe the term merits rethinking now that the cold war is over. A totalitarian state, as its definition evolved late in the twentieth century, was one that intensified government's concern with private life and individual thought, leaving no realm of existence outside the state's will. Censorship of speech, suppression of parliamentary and freely chosen representative rule, and violent elimination of disagreement were crucial ingredients of a totalitarian system. Because the state was seen as a unified, massively powerful entity, laws regulating reproduction and family life were central. Not only did the labor and armed forces expand, but through the control of fertility—especially by outlawing or enforcing birth control and abortion—the state showed its power to determine life's most intimate activity. Hitler, Mussolini, Stalin, and later Mao Zedong of China all made their control of reproduction pivotal to their regimes. Totalitarian regimes also relied on violence to forge unity: control of military or paramilitary weaponry and technology of modern communications allowed for the programming of thought and the elimination of enemies, including those whose thinking did not fall in line with the regime's ideas. Many believe that totalitarianism can work only in a society where the state uses advanced technology and advanced communications to dominate intimate behavior and control individual thought.

Nonetheless it is important to note the vast differences among totalitarian states: the socialist economy of the Soviet Union differed from the economies of both Nazi Germany and Fascist Italy. Moreover, systems lumped under the term *totalitarian* had different intellectual roots. Nationalism was key in the rise of fascism and Nazism, whereas communism began as an international workers' movement and forced people of many ethnicities to live together. Anti-Semitism also infected totalitarian societies in varying degrees: in Italy, Jews were rarely persecuted (and frequently protected from Nazis); Stalin purged individual Jews without singling out the entire race for extermination; Nazism had the elimination of the Jews as central to its mission. Even the democracies, like totalitarian countries, intervened more and more in daily life. Although not uniform in policy, the various states of the United States performed forced sterilization on many African American women in the pre–World War II period even as they outlawed birth control.

For all its limitations, the term *totalitarian* can help us think about the twentieth-century state in the context of total war, increasingly destructive technology, and sophisticated means of communication in an age of mass society. The implications of totalitarianism challenge a growing global commitment to individual and human rights—thus this historic term remains central to political concerns today.

FURTHER READING

Arendt, Hannah. *The Origins of Totalitarianism*. 1951.

Gleason, Abbott. *Totalitarianism: The Inner History of the Cold War*. 1995.

Tormey, Simon. *Making Sense of Tyranny: Interpretations of Totalitarianism*. 1995.

violence in the form of widespread arrests, imprisonments in labor camps, and executions—to rid society of these villains. These purges continued as long as Stalin lived and encompassed nearly all segments of society.

Bourgeois engineers were the first group condemned for causing low productivity. Soviet citizens expressed their relief that the wreckers had been punished, and they searched their own workplaces, as one young enthusiast believed, for "concrete bearers of evil . . . workers guilty of foul-ups, breakdowns, defects." Trials of prominent figures followed. When in 1934 Sergei Kirov, the popular first secretary of the Leningrad Communist Party, was murdered, Stalin used his death (which he may have instigated) as the pretext to try former Bolshevik leaders. The secret police soon claimed they had uncovered a massive conspiracy led by Stalin's old enemy Leon Trotsky to overthrow Soviet rule. At a series of "show trials" from 1936 to 1938—trials based on trumped-up charges, fabricated evidence, and confessions extracted after threats and torture—former Bolsheviks were coerced to confess that they had corresponded with the exiled Trotsky. Most of those found guilty were shot.

The spirit of purge swept society. One woman poet described the scene: "Great concert and lecture halls were turned into public confessionals. . . . People did penance for [everything]. . . . Beating their breasts, the 'guilty' would lament that they had 'shown political short-sightedness' and 'lack of vigilance' . . . and were full of 'rotten liberalism.'" Purges occurred in local bureaucracies, universities, technical schools, and other training grounds for political and technological jobs. As international tensions intensified later in the 1930s, Stalin convinced hesitant party members to accept more purges by pleading the dangers from "German-Japanese agents of Trotskyism." In 1937 and 1938, military leaders were arrested and executed without public trials; in some ranks every officer was killed. From industry and education to the party and the army, not even the Soviet power structure escaped the great purges.

Simultaneously the government developed an extensive system of prison camps over several thousand miles stretching from Moscow to Siberia. Called the *Gulag*—an acronym for the administrative arm of the camps—the system held as many as eight million prisoners, according to some estimates, during any one year in the 1930s. Of these, one million died annually as a result of the harsh conditions, which included insufficient clothing, food, and housing along with twelve- to sixteen-hour workdays at mining, heavy construction, and other crushing labor. Beatings and murder of prisoners rounded out Gulag life, as it became another aspect of Soviet violence.

This bloody period of Soviet history has provoked intense historical debate. Were the purges carefully planned and directed solely by Stalin, who watched the trials from a secret booth in the courtroom? Or were they initiated by the Communist Party's rank and file? Some historians view the purges as the machinations of a psychopath, whereas others see them as a clear-headed attempt on Stalin's part to eliminate barriers to total control. More recently, historians have judged the purges as discrete events that emanated from power struggles among party officials and were fueled by the treachery of those looking for a quick route to the top. People in the lower ranks denounced their superiors to cover the way they themselves had falsified statistics, been lenient on kulaks, or lacked the proper vigilance. Still other interpretations see many denunciations and confessions as sincere expressions of workers' commitment to rooting out enemies of their proletarian utopia. At stake in these debates is not only attributing responsibility for horrendous suffering and loss of life but for understanding the source of Communist policy in the 1930s and 1940s and thus the nature of the Soviet regime. At least we may be certain as to the outcome: ongoing arrests, incarcerations, and executions eliminated any rivals to Stalin's power.

Reshaping Soviet Society. The 1930s marked a sharp reversal of revolutionary experimentation in cultural and social life. This retreat curtailed, among other things, modernism in the arts, creativity in urban planning, and commitment to egalitarian gender ideals and sexual freedom. Much like the rest of Europe, the Soviet Union experienced a rapid decline in its birthrate in the 1930s. This drop, combined with the need to replace the millions lost since 1914, motivated Stalin to end the reproductive freedom of the early revolutionary years and turn state policy toward increasing the birthrate. Birth-control information, contraceptive devices, and abortions became difficult to obtain. Gold wedding rings and more lavish wedding ceremonies came back into fashion, and people were forced to remain married and encouraged to reproduce. The state criminalized homosexuality and touted motherhood as not only a joy but a patriotic duty. Whereas Bolsheviks had once derided the family as a "bourgeois" institution, propaganda now referred to the family unit as a "school for socialism"—that is, a miniature of the Soviet state.

Socialism under Stalin provided women a mixed experience. Those in rural areas made gains in literacy and in access to health-care facilities. They applauded new provisions for child support, as more and more men left the countryside for opportunities in factory work. Positions in the lower ranks of the party opened to women as the purges continued, and women increasingly were accepted into the professions. The stress on women, particularly those in the industrial workforce, increased however. Working long hours in factories, they also stood in long lines for scarce consumer goods and performed all household and child-care tasks under harsh conditions.

Cultural life was equally paradoxical under Stalin, as it simultaneously involved an end to avant-garde experimentation and a modern awareness of popular culture's power to shape a collective psyche. Modernist intellectuals continued to promote their ability to mobilize the masses by appealing to the unconscious and the emotions in their work. Stalin endorsed this role by calling artists and writers "engineers of the soul." In another form of central planning, he established the Union of Soviet Writers to control all matters related to the private and professional lives of writers. The union assigned housing, office space, supplies, equipment, and secretarial help and even determined the types of books authors could write.

N. J. Altman, *Anna Akhmatova* (1914)
This modernist painting portrays the poet Anna Akhmatova when she was a centerpiece of literary salon life in Russia and the subject of several avant-garde portraits. In the 1930s and 1940s, Akhmatova gave poetic voice to Soviet suffering, recording in her verse ordinary people's endurance of purges, deprivation, and warfare. As she encouraged people to resist the Nazis during World War II, Stalin allowed her to revive Russian patriotism instead of socialist internationalism.
State Russian Museum, St. Petersburg/The Bridgeman Art Library.

In return, the "comrade artist" adhered to the official style of "socialist realism," derived from the 1920s focus on the common worker as a type of social hero. This mandated style infused such monumental works as Mikhail Sholokhov's *And Quiet Flows the Don* (1928–1940), which explored the consciousness of a rural hero and his work on behalf of socialism. Painters, filmmakers, composers, and journalists aimed to "depict life in its revolutionary development," as union officials described the style. Some artists, such as the poet Anna Akhmatova (1889–1966), refused to accept this system.

> *Stars of death stood above us, and Russia,*
> *In her innocence, twisted in pain*
> *Under blood-spattered boots . . .*

wrote Akhmatova in those years. Many others, including the composer Sergei Prokofiev (1891–1953), found ways to accommodate their talents to the state's demands. Prokofiev composed the score for Sergei Eisenstein's 1938 film *Alexander Nevsky*, a work that transparently compared Stalin to the towering medieval rulers of the Russian people. When his ballet *Romeo and Juliet* was censored, Prokofiev wrote children's music, including the delightful *Peter and the Wolf*. Aided by adaptable artists, workers, and bureaucrats, Stalin stood triumphant as the 1930s drew to a close. Having brutally eliminated competitors, Stalin alone represented the revolutionary future.

Hitler's Rise to Power

Hitler ended German democracy. Since the early 1920s, he had tried to rouse the German masses to crush the fragile Weimar Republic. In his coup attempt, in his influential book *Mein Kampf* ("My Struggle," 1925), and in his leadership of the Nazi Party, he drummed at a message of anti-Semitism and the rebirth of the German "race." Hitler's message was hardly unique, but when the Great Depression struck Germany his party began to outstrip its rivals in elections. In the midst of financial collapse and unemployment, some big businessmen, notably film and press mogul Alfred Hugenberg, joined forces with Hitler to protest the restructuring of German reparations in the Young Plan. Hugenberg's press relentlessly attacked the

Weimar government, blaming it for the disastrous economy and inflaming wounded German pride over the defeat in World War I.

Simultaneously, parliamentary government virtually ground to a halt in the face of economic crisis. The conservative chancellor Heinrich Brüning (1885–1970) proposed to stabilize the economy with a balanced budget, reduced government expenditures, and increased taxes and protective tariffs, but the Reichstag failed to approve such emergency plans. Hitler's followers made parliamentary government look even more inept by rampaging through the streets, wrecking stores owned by Jews, and beating up Communists and Social Democrats. By targeting Social Democrats and Communists as a single, monolithic group of "Bolshevik" enemies, the Nazis won the approval of the middle classes, who feared Russian-style revolution and the loss of their property.

As a result of the publicity Hugenberg's media showered on it and of its own street tactics, Hitler's National Socialist German Workers' Party (NSDAP)—the Nazi Party—which had received little more than 2 percent of the vote in 1928, won almost 20 percent in the Reichstag elections of 1930 and more than doubled its representation in 1932. As newspapers vilified the Weimar Republic for its weakness, favorable press reports, brass-knuckle politics, and military parades gave the illusion of Nazi vigor. Many of Hitler's supporters, like Stalin's, were young and idealistic. In 1930, seventy percent of party members were under forty, a stark contrast to the image of Weimar politicians as aged and inef-

fectual. Although businessmen provided substantial sums of money, every class supported the Nazis. The largest number of supporters came from the industrial working class because they had the most voters, but white-collar workers and the lower-middle class joined the party in percentages out of proportion with their numbers in the population.

The elections of 1930 and 1932 stunned conservatives like Brüning because they showed the rising appeal of radicals—both Nazis and Communists made gains. Hitler's propaganda techniques had served him well with the masses against old-fashioned contenders. His propaganda chief, Joseph Goebbels, sent thousands of recordings of Hitler's speeches to the countryside and provided Nazi mementos to the citizenry. Teenagers painted their fingernails with swastikas, a symbol used by the Nazis, and in the German army, a bastion of traditional conservatism, soldiers flashed metal match covers with Nazi insignia.

Nazi rallies were masterpieces of political display in which Hitler mesmerized the crowds. He began by talking slowly until he had a sense of the audience; then, as one witness reported, "suddenly he bursts forth. His words go like an arrow to their target; he touches each private wound on the raw, liberating mass unconscious, expressing its innermost aspirations, telling it what it most wants to hear." Hitler fashioned himself the Führer, or leader, of the masses, to whom he appealed as a strong, vastly superior being. Frenzied and inspirational, he represented neither the calculating politician nor the rational bureaucrat but "the creative

Toys Depicting Nazis

As a totalitarian ideology, Nazism was part of everyday life. Nazi insignia decorated clothing, dishes, cigarette lighters, and even fingernails. People chose their loved ones according to Nazi rules, sent young people to Nazi clubs and organizations, and bought Nazi toys like these for their children's playtime. Nazi songs, Nazi parades and festivals, and Nazi art filled leisure hours.
Imperial War Museum, London.

element," one poet put it. In actuality, however, Hitler viewed the masses only as tools. In *Mein Kampf* he discussed his philosophy of how to deal with them:

> The receptivity of the great masses is very limited, their intelligence is small. In consequence of these facts, all effective propaganda must be limited to a very few points and must harp on those in slogans until the last member of the public understands what you want him to understand.

With Hitler, as with Stalin, mass politics had reached terrifying and cynical proportions.

The Communist and Nazi success in the 1932 Reichstag elections made the leader of one of those parties the logical choice as chancellor. Germany's conservative elites—from the military, industry, and the state bureaucracy—loathed the Communists and favored Hitler as a common type they could easily manipulate. Ultimately, elite leaders persuaded the aging president Paul von Hindenburg (1847–1934) to invite Hitler to become chancellor in January 1933.

The Nazification of German Politics

Vowing to uphold the Weimar constitution, Hitler took office amidst jubilation in Berlin, as tens of thousands of storm troopers holding blazing torches paraded through the streets. Millions celebrated Hitler's ascent to power. "My father went down to the cellar and brought up our best bottles of wine. . . . And my mother wept for joy," one German recalled. " 'To think that I should live to see this!' she said. 'Now everything will be all right.' " Hitler moved rapidly and brutally to fulfill his program by creating a new kind of antidemocratic state, crushing racial and other enemies, whom he saw as a menace to building a new, prosperous German order.

Terror in the Nazi State. Within a month of Hitler's taking power, the elements of Nazi political domination were in place. When the Reichstag building was gutted by fire in February 1933, he blamed the Communists and used the fire as the excuse for suspending civil rights, declaring censorship of the press, prohibiting meetings of opposition writers and artists, and disrupting the work of other political parties. Hitler had made clear throughout his career that *all* political parties except the NSDAP were his enemies. "Our opponents complain that we National Socialists, and I in particular, are intolerant and intractable," he declared. "They are right, we are intolerant! I have set myself one task, namely to sweep those parties out of Germany."

New elections were held in March. The Nazis won 288 Reichstag seats, but Social Democrats and Communists still retained more than 200 seats, and right and center parties claimed another 158. Storm troopers lashed out violently at this political failure, beating up opponents and destroying property. They prevented Communist delegates from attending Reichstag sessions and so intimidated the others that at the end of March, Hitler was able to pass the Enabling Act, which suspended the constitution for four years and allowed subsequent Nazi laws to take effect without parliamentary approval. Hitler had shown himself vigorous in meeting political crisis, and solid middle-class Germans approved the Enabling Act as a way to pull the country out of its economic and political morass.

Political violence became institutionalized to advance the creation of a *Volksgemeinschaft* ("people's community") of like-minded, racially pure Germans—"Aryans" in Nazi terminology. Heinrich Himmler, who headed the elite SS (*Schutzstaffel*) organization that protected Hitler and other Nazi leaders, commanded the Reich's political police system. The Gestapo, organized by Hermann Goering, and the Order of the Death's Head also enforced complete obedience to Nazism. These organizations had vast powers to arrest, execute, or imprison people in concentration camps, the first of which opened at Dachau near Munich in March 1933. The Nazis filled it and later camps with socialists, homosexuals, Jews, and others. They touted these camps as places where "antisocial" elements would be housed so that they could no longer interfere with the *Volksgemeinschaft*. In the muscular logic of the Nazis, individual rights interfered with the *Volksgemeinschaft*. One Nazi leader proclaimed:

> [National socialism] does not believe that one soul is equal to another, one man equal to another. It does not believe in rights as such. It aims to create the German man of strength, its task is to protect the German people, and all . . . must be subordinate to this goal.

Hitler deliberately blurred authority among the agencies of order and terror so that confusion and bitter competition reigned within the government and among the population at large. He thus prevented the emergence of coalitions against him and allowed himself to arbitrate the confusion.

At the same time, these rivalries threatened his regime, and Hitler responded with violence to discipline his closest followers as well as the masses. Ernst Roehm, leader of the SA (paramilitary troops), called for a "second revolution" to end the corrupt influence of the old business and military elites on the Nazi leadership, especially on Hitler. He hoped to make the SA the nucleus of a new German army. Despite their long-standing collaboration, Hitler ordered the assassination of Roehm, along with hundreds of SA leaders, individual enemies, and innocent civilians. The bloody Night of the Long Knives (June 30, 1934) eroded the SA's challenge to the army and the SS and led conservative business and military leaders to support Hitler yet again. Nazism's terroristic politics were in place as the foundation of his "Third Reich"—a German empire succeeding those of Charlemagne and William II. Further, massive violence was still to come.

Nazi Economic and Social Programs. Hitler continued his drastic reform of Germany with economic and social programs. Putting people back to work was crucial to the survival of his regime. Economic revival built popular support, strengthened military industries, and provided the basis for German expansion. The Nazi government pursued what economists call *pump priming*, that is, stimulating the economy through government spending. Under the guise of making farm equipment, Germany built tanks and airplanes; the Autobahn highway system was developed to serve military as well as civilian ends. From farms to factories, the government demanded high productivity and set goals for national economic independence and self-sufficiency. Skilled workers prospered in the drive to rearm; and unemployment declined from a peak of almost 6 million in 1932 to 1.6 million by 1936. As labor shortages began to appear in certain areas, the government conscripted single women into service as farmworkers and domestics.

The Nazi Party reorganized work life to increase efficiency and to curtail labor activism. Government officials and industrial managers classified jobs, determined work procedures, and set pay levels, rating women's jobs lower than men's regardless of the level of expertise required. In May 1933, the government closed down labor unions and seized their property. All workers, from the lowly unskilled to the top professionals, were compelled to join the Nazi-controlled German Labor Front, which was used to snuff out worker independence.

Imitating Stalin, Hitler announced a four-year plan in 1936 with the secret aim of preparing Germany for war by 1940. Government officials allocated raw materials, sponsored the production of synthetics, and intensified labor management; defense spending soared to 50 percent of all government expenditures by 1938. The four-year plan produced large trade deficits, which Hitler believed the spoils of future conquests would eliminate. Hitler had unprecedented power over the workings of everyday life, especially gender roles. In June 1933, a bill took effect that encouraged Aryans (those people defined as racially German) to marry and have children. The bill provided for loans to Aryan newlyweds, but only to those couples in which the wife left the workforce. The loans were forgiven on the birth of the pair's fourth child. Nazi marriage programs enforced a nineteenth-century ideal of femininity; females were supposed to be subordinate so men would feel tough and industrious despite military defeat and economic depression. Although some women complained about having to forfeit their jobs, others, remembering the miserable war and postwar years, believed that Hitler would elevate Nazi women, rewarding one, as a party leader put it, "who joyfully sacrifices and fulfills her fate."

Proposing to make life better for the German *Volk*, or people, Nazism in fact impoverished ordinary life. Although Goebbels, the minister of propaganda, ensured that 70 percent of households had "people's radios" by 1938, the programming broadcast was severely censored. Books like Remarque's *All Quiet on the Western Front* were banned, and in May 1933 a huge book-burning ceremony rid libraries of works by Jews, socialists, homosexuals, and modernist writers out of favor with the Nazis. Modern art in museums and private collections was either destroyed or confiscated. Civil servants, teachers, and other government officials were forced to adhere to Nazism. Another law took jobs from Jews and women and bestowed them on party members as rewards. In 1936, membership in the Hitler Youth, an organization that indoctrinated the young, became mandatory for all boys and girls over age ten. These children learned to report the names of adults they suspected of disloyalty to the regime, even their own parents. In public, citizens had to worry about the presence of informers—more than 100,000 were on the Nazi payroll—and so they employed what was called the "German look," a surreptitious glance around a public space for spies or party faithful.

Hitler partially fulfilled his promise to create a well-ordered national community. People boasted that they could leave their bicycles out at night without fear of robbery. And, in general, the improved economy led people to believe that Hitler was working an economic miracle while restoring pride in Germany, the prewar sense of authority, and the harmonious community of an imaginary past. For hundreds of thousands if not millions of Germans, however, Nazi rule in the 1930s brought anything but community.

Nazi Racism

The Nazis defined Jews as an inferior "race" dangerous to the superior Aryan or Germanic "race." According to Hitler, Jews were responsible for most of Germany's problems, including defeat in World War I and the intensity of the depression. Hitler attacked many ethnic and social groups, but he propelled the nineteenth-century politics of anti-Semitism to new and frightening heights. In the rhetoric of Nazism, Jews were "vermin," "abscesses," "parasites," and "Bolsheviks," whom the Germans would have to eliminate to become a true *Volksgemeinschaft*. By defining the Jews both as evil financiers and businessmen and as working-class Bolsheviks, Hitler fashioned an enemy for many segments of the population to hate passionately.

Nazi policy was called "racial," and it led to laws against "non-Aryans"—a group that, like "Aryans," was never defined. Racial classifications were made to appear scientific, however, by lists of physical and other characteristics that determined a person's "race." In 1935, the government enacted the Nuremberg Laws, legislation that specifically deprived Jews of citizenship, defined Jewishness according to a person's ancestry, ended special consideration for Jewish war veterans, and prohibited marriage between Jews and other Germans. To hold jobs, workers had to present their baptismal certificates and other evidence of their Aryan her-

itage. Whereas women defined as Aryan had increasing difficulty obtaining abortions or even birth-control information, these were readily available to the outcast groups, including Jews, gypsies, Slavs, and mentally or physically disabled people. By 1939, special courts forced Jews and other so-called inferior groups to undergo sterilization and reproductive experiments performed by Nazi doctors. In the name of improving the Aryan race, doctors helped organize the T4 project, which used carbon monoxide poisoning and other means to kill large numbers of people—200,000 handicapped and elderly—late in the 1930s, thus preparing the way for even larger mass exterminations that would occur later.

Some Jews thought the Nuremberg Laws would at least regularize their status and end street violence; instead the persecution escalated. One young Jewish woman fled her home in 1936 after being warned that the Gestapo had scheduled her arrest for daring to work in broadcasting, but her parents greeted this news with disbelief: "My mother thought I must be depressed over an unhappy love affair." Jews were forced into slave labor, evicted from their apartments, and prevented from buying most clothing and food. In 1938, a Jewish teenager, reacting to the harassment of his parents, killed a German official. In retaliation for this single murder, Nazis attacked some two hundred synagogues, smashed windows of Jewish-owned stores, broke into apartments of known or suspected Jews and stole or destroyed possessions, and threw more than twenty thousand Jews into prisons and camps. The night of November 9–10 became known as *Kristallnacht*, or the Night of Broken Glass.

Faced with this relentless persecution, which some historians have called a "social death," by the outbreak of World War II in 1939 more than half of Germany's 500,000 Jews had emigrated, often leaving behind all their possessions and paying huge fees to the government in exchange for exit visas. In the 1930s, Hitler's policies favored the migration of Jews rather than their extermination, and many emigrants—such as physicist Albert Einstein and filmmaker Fritz Lang—advanced the scientific, cultural, and scholarly accomplishments of their adopted countries, especially England and the United States. The confiscation of emigrants' property enriched their neighbors and individual Nazis; it also helped finance Germany's revival.

✦ Democracies on the Defensive

Nazism, communism, and fascism offered bold new approaches to modern politics and new kinds of economic and social policies. Their leaders' energetic, military style of mobilizing the masses challenged the other great powers to devise equally effective solutions to the problems created by the depression. However, leaders in the United States, France, and Great Britain also had to combat the political appeal of these new regimes, for Hitler, Mussolini, and Stalin had made representative government and democratic values appear effeminate, decadent signs of declining peoples. Thus the 1930s saw democracies on the defensive in a variety of arenas—economic, political, and cultural.

Confronting the Economic Crisis

As it wore on, the depression baffled as much as it alarmed politicians. Many favored tried and true remedies, but some governments undertook notable experiments to solve social and economic crises and still maintain democratic politics. The result across the West was to advance the trend toward the welfare state—that is, one that guarantees a certain level of economic well-being for individuals and businesses.

New Deal in the United States.   The Great Depression had struck first in the United States, where President Herbert Hoover (1874–1964) confidently predicted that the economic downturn was only temporary because of the fundamental health of American business. When his rosy forecast proved false, the conservative Hoover opposed direct help to the unemployed, believing that "handouts," as he called assistance, would weaken the nation's moral fiber. In June 1932, some ten thousand World War I veterans marched on Washington, D.C., demanding relief; Hoover ordered the army to drive them away with tanks.

With unemployment close to fifteen million, the situation was grim when a more innovative politician, Franklin Delano Roosevelt (1882–1945), the wealthy, patrician governor of New York, defeated Hoover in the presidential election of 1932. Fulfilling his promise to voters, in his first hundred days in office Roosevelt pushed through a torrent of legislation, some of it inspired by the central control of the economy achieved during World War I: relief for businesses and instructions for firms to cooperate in stabilizing prices; price supports for hard-pressed farmers; public works programs for unemployed youth; and refinancing agencies for homeowners' mortgages. The Social Security Act of 1935 set up a fund to which employers and employees contributed. It provided retirement benefits for workers, unemployment insurance, and payments to dependent mothers, their children, and people with disabling physical conditions.

Collectively announced as his New Deal, Roosevelt's programs angered business people and the wealthy, who saw them as "socialist." But even as the depression remained severe, Roosevelt (quickly nicknamed FDR) maintained widespread support. Like Mussolini, Hitler, and other successful politicians of the 1930s and thereafter, he was an expert at using the new mass media. His radio series of "fireside chats" to the American people developed technology's possibility for injecting a sense of intimacy into mass politics. In sharp contrast to Mussolini and Hitler, however, Roosevelt aimed in his public statements to sustain—not to denounce—faith in democratic rights and popular government. At his inauguration in 1933, he declared, "The only thing we have to fear is fear itself." Americans, he exhorted on accepting renomination in 1936, should focus not on their present miseries but on the greatness that lay before them: "This generation of Americans has a rendezvous with destiny." Eager to separate themselves from Hoover's position, First Lady Eleanor Roosevelt rushed to greet the next group of veterans marching on Washington and FDR received the delegation at the White House. The Roosevelts insisted that justice, human rights, and liberal values must not be surrendered in difficult times. "We Americans of today . . . are characters in the living book of democracy," FDR told a group of teenagers in 1939. "But we are also its author." Lynchings, racial violence, and harsh discrimination continued to cause enormous suffering in the United States during the Roosevelt administration, nor did the economy fully recover. But the president's media success and bold programs kept the masses committed to a democratic future.

Eleanor Roosevelt Talks to the Nation
Eleanor Roosevelt, the wife of FDR and mother of five children, gradually became a political activist in her own right. Her work on behalf of the poor and against discrimination earned her both incredible acclaim and real hatred. Using the print and radio media, she rallied citizens during the depression and the war and eventually worked for United Nations causes. Here she is shown on January 1, 1940, at the headquarters of the American Red Cross in Washington, D.C., appealing for donations to a war relief drive.
Hulton Getty Picture Library/Liaison Agency.

A Fireside Chat with FDR
President Franklin Delano Roosevelt was a master of words, uttering many memorable phrases that inspired Americans during the depression and World War II. Aware of growing media power in the making and breaking of politicians, the press never showed Roosevelt's disabilities even when he used crutches or fell down. Instead, FDR became a symbol of U.S. resolve, ingenuity, and growing power. Here he addresses the nation on August 23, 1938, over a radio hookup while Eleanor Roosevelt and the president's mother, Sarah, observe.
© Hulton Getty/Liaison Agency.

Sweden's Welfare State. While FDR's New Deal policies met resistance and demanded compromise, Sweden developed a coherent program for solving economic and population problems that gained world attention for the way it reconceived the government's role in promoting social welfare and economic democracy. Although Sweden had industrialized later than western Europe and the United States, it had a tradition of community responsibility for working through social and economic difficulties. Sweden succeeded in turning its economy around in the 1930s. A neutral power that had profited from World War I and then suffered post-war inflation, depression, and population decline, Sweden instituted central planning of the economy and social welfare programs. It also devalued the currency to make Swedish exports more attractive on the international market. Using pump-priming programs of public works to maintain consumer spending and to encourage modernization, the Social Democratic leaders saw Swedish productivity rise 20 percent between 1929 and 1935, a time when other democracies were still experiencing decline.

Sweden addressed the population problem with government programs, as did many other Western governments, but without the racist and antidemocratic coercion. Alva Myrdal (1902–1986), a social scientist and leading member of parliament, believed fertility rates were dependent on the economy and individual well-being. It was undemocratic, she maintained, "that the bearing of a child should mean economic distress to anybody in a country . . . who wants children." Acting on Myrdal's advice to promote "voluntary parenthood," the government started a loan program for married couples in 1937 and introduced prenatal care, free childbirth in a hospital, a food relief program, and subsidized housing for large families. By the end of the decade, almost 50 percent of all mothers received government aid. Long a concern of feminists and other social reformers, care of families became integral to the tasks of the modern state, which now saw itself as responsible for citizen welfare in hard times.

Liberalism Threatened in Britain and France. Unlike neutral Sweden, Britain and France emerged victorious but financially and morally exhausted from World War I. Because the most powerful democracy, the United States, had withdrawn from world leadership after the war by refusing to participate in the League of Nations, Britain and France had greater responsibility for international peace and well-being than their resources could sustain.

Britain was already mired in economic difficulties when the Great Depression hit. Faced with falling government revenues, Prime Minister Ramsay MacDonald, though leader of the Labour Party, reduced payments to the unemployed. At a time when married women were the first to be laid off and were often barred from holding any job, Parliament in 1931 effectively denied unemployment insurance to such women even though they had contributed to the unemployment fund. To protect jobs and domestic markets, the government imposed huge protective tariffs, setting duties on some goods at 100 percent of their value. The tariff discouraged a revival of international trade and did not relieve British misery.

Only in 1933, with the economy continuing to worsen, did the government begin to take effective steps. A massive program of slum clearance and new housing construction provided employment and infused money into the economy. By 1938, an extension of the National Insurance Act was providing minimal health benefits to twenty million workers and their families. The depression did not lift until Britain increased production to rearm in preparation for war late in the 1930s.

Depression struck later in France, but the country endured a decade of public strife in the 1930s. By 1932, severe postwar demoralization and stagnant population growth had joined with wage cuts and rising unemployment to create social and political turmoil. Deputies with opposing views on the economic crisis frequently came to blows in the Chamber of Deputies, and governments were voted in and out with dizzying rapidity. Parisians took to the streets to protest the government's belt-tightening policies, and the press trumpeted the disorderly mass rallies. Right-wing paramilitary groups mushroomed, attracting the unemployed, students, and veterans. They aimed to end representative government, which in their eyes was a "bastion of corruption."

In February 1934, the paramilitary groups joined Communists and other outraged citizens in riots around the parliament building. "Let's string up the deputies," chanted the crowd. "And if we can't string them up, let's beat in their faces, let's reduce them to a pulp." Hundreds of demonstrators were wounded and killed; inside the Chamber of Deputies, democratic representatives hurled ink bottles at one another. The antirepublican right lacked both substantial support outside Paris and a leader like Hitler or Mussolini capable of unifying its various groups. Thus France escaped the fate of Germany and Italy, but only for the present—the political chaos of the 1930s foreshadowed the fall of the Third Republic in 1940.

Mobilizing the Masses

Preserving representative government, the capitalist economy, and—for countries like Britain, France, the Netherlands, and Belgium—their empires motivated people in the democratic countries to mobilize mass support. In France, a coalition known as the "Popular Front" emerged to fight fascism and the effects of the depression. Across the democracies, writers and other intellectuals formed a kind of cultural front to brace the masses in hard, menacing times.

The Popular Front in France. Shocked into action by the force of fascism, French liberals, socialists, and Communists rallied in support of democracy. By 1936, these groups had established an antifascist coalition known as the Popular

Front. Until that time such a merging of groups had been impossible in democratic countries because of Stalin's strict opposition to Communist collaboration with liberals and socialists, who by this time disavowed Communist-style revolutions. As fascism spread throughout Europe, however, Stalin reversed course and allowed Communists to join such efforts.

For just over a year in 1936–1937 and again very briefly in 1938, the French Popular Front had enough electoral support to form a government, with the socialist leader Léon Blum (1872–1950) as premier. Like the American New Dealers and the Swedish Social Democrats, the Popular Front instituted long-overdue reforms. Blum extended family subsidies, state services, and welfare benefits, and he appointed women to his government (though women still were not allowed to vote). In June 1936, the government guaranteed workers two-week paid vacations, a forty-hour work week, and the right to collective bargaining. Working people would long remember Blum as the man who improved their living standards and provided them with benefits and vacations.

Family at Normandy Beach
In the midst of the depression of the 1930s, the working classes nonetheless gained a taste of leisure when the French government under Léon Blum mandated paid vacations for all workers. As other governments followed this lead, tourism became a booming business in the West. Citizens from all walks of life traveled to see their own country, witness its geographic differences, and visit its historic monuments.
Private Collection.

During its brief life the Popular Front made republicanism responsive to the masses by offering a youthful, but democratic, political culture. "In 1936 everyone was twenty years old," one man recalled, evoking the atmosphere of idealism. Local cultural centers sprang up for activities such as popular theater. Inspired to express their opposition to fascism, citizens celebrated democratic holidays like Bastille Day with new enthusiasm. Speakers at these events contrasted their spontaneous solidarity and good humor with fascist militarism and abuse of human rights.

Despite support from workers, the Popular Front governments were politically weak. Fearing for their investments, bankers and industrialists greeted Blum's appointment by sending their capital out of the country, leaving France financially strapped. "Better Hitler than Blum" was the slogan of the upper classes. Blum tried to win support from powerful financial interests by holding down taxes on the wealthy, in effect forcing the lower levels of society to pay for Popular Front programs. But Blum's government fell when it lost the left by refusing material support in the fight against fascism elsewhere, most notably Spain. As in Britain, memories of World War I caused leaders to block crucial support to foreign democratic forces and to keep the domestic military budgets small as a way of ensuring peace. The collapse of the antifascist Popular Front in late June 1937 showed the difficulties that pluralistic and democratic societies faced in crisis-ridden times.

Survival Strategies in Central Europe. Fledgling democracies to the east, hit hard by the depression, also fought the twin struggle for economic survival and representative government. In 1932, Engelbert Dollfuss (1892–1934) came to power in Austria; two years later he dismissed the parliament and ruled briefly as a dictator. Despite his authoritarian stance, Dollfuss would not submit to the Nazis, who assassinated him in 1934. In Hungary, where outrage over the Peace of Paris remained intense, a crippled economy resulted in right-wing general Gyula Gömbös (1886–1936) coming to power in 1932. Gömbös admired fascism and reoriented his country's foreign policy toward Mussolini and Hitler. He stirred up anti-Semitism and ethnic hatreds and left considerable pro-Nazi feeling after his death in 1936.

In democratic Czechoslovakia, the depression hit the primarily German population of the industrialized Sudeten region especially hard. As a result Nazism gained an enthusiastic following. The Slovaks, who were both poorer and less educated than the urbanized Czechs, built a strong Slovak Fascist Party. In Poland, Romania, Yugoslavia, and Bulgaria, ethnic tensions simmered and the appeal of fascism grew as the Great Depression lingered.

Cultural Vision in Hard Times

Just as culture had been mobilized in the war, postwar cultural leaders mobilized to meet the crisis of hard times and political menace. But the message was different: instead of turning away from public life as many had done in the 1920s, writers, filmmakers, and artists of the 1930s responded vigorously to the depression. Some empathized with the situations of factory workers, homemakers, and shopgirls struggling to support themselves or their families, others with the ever-growing number of unemployed and destitute. In 1931, French director René Clair's *À nous la liberté* ("Give Us Liberty") related prison life to work on a factory assembly line. Charlie Chaplin's film *Modern Times* (1936) showed the Little Tramp again, this time as a worker in a modern factory who was so molded by his monotonous job that he assumed anything he could see, even a co-worker's body, needed mechanical adjustment. These representations of the modern factory and hard times illuminated life in the 1930s with humor and sympathy that made Chaplin a hit even in the Soviet Union.

Media sympathy poured out to victims of the crisis, with women portrayed alternately as the cause and as the cure for society's problems. *The Blue Angel* (1930), a German film starring Marlene Dietrich, showed how a vital, modern woman could destroy men—and civilization. A woman's power was contrasted to the ineffectuality of an impractical professor. Although in dramas unemployment and the population crisis were often blamed on overpowering women, in comedies and musicals heroines behaved bravely, pulling their men out of the depths of despair and setting things right again. In such films as *Sally in Our Alley* (1931) and *Keep Smiling* (1938), the British comedienne Gracie Fields, for example, portrayed spunky working-class women who kept on smiling despite hard times.

Techniques of modern art like montage, which overlaid two or more photos or parts of photos, were used to grab visual and psychic attention in the cultural battles of the 1930s. Because of its urgency, however, the message came to take precedence over the form. Some intellectuals turned away from experimentation with nonrepresentational forms as they drove home their antifascist, pacifist, or pro-worker beliefs. Popular Front writers created realistic studies of human misery and the threat of war that haunted life in the 1930s. American novelist John Steinbeck (1902–1968) portrayed the desperate migration of ruined American farmers in *The Grapes of Wrath* (1939). The British writer George Orwell (1903–1950) described his experiences among the poor of Paris and London, wrote investigative pieces about the unemployed in the north of England, and published an account of atrocities committed by both sides during the Spanish Civil War (1936–1939). In some cases, the

Paul Klee, *Dancing with Fear* (1938)
Swiss-German artist Paul Klee explored modern art's ability to evoke universal truths behind surface reality. Delightful shapes and colors often marked his work, although he was always concerned with how technology would affect people's values. As the danger of Nazism's triumph mounted, Klee grew depressed and produced dark visions of fear and death.
"Tänze vor Angst," 1938, 90 (G 10) by Paul Klee. Paul-Klee-Stiftung, Kunstmuseum Bern, photo: Peter Lauri. © ARS, New York.

Soviet system inspired writers and artists, whether Communist or not, to adopt socialist realism for their depiction of working people.

Art became increasingly politicized. Some writers found it crucial to reaffirm their belief in Western values such as rationalism, rights, and concern for the poor. German writer Thomas Mann (1875–1955), a Christian, went into exile when Hitler came to power and began a series of novels based on the Old Testament hero Joseph to convey the struggle between humanist values and barbarism. The fourth volume, *Joseph the Provider* (1944), eulogized Joseph's welfare state, in which the granaries were full and the rich paid taxes so the poor might live decent lives. One of the last works of English writer Virginia Woolf, *Three Guineas* (1938), rejected experimental form for a direct attack on militarism, poverty, and the oppression of women, claiming they were interconnected parts of a single, devastating ethos undermining Europe in the 1930s.

While writers rekindled moral concerns, scientists in research institutes and universities continued to point out limits to human understanding—limits that seemed at odds with the megalomaniacal pronouncements of dictators. Astronomer Edwin Hubble (1889–1953) in California determined in the early 1930s that the universe was an expanding entity. Czech mathematician Kurt Gödel (1906–1978) maintained that any mathematical system contains some propositions that are undecidable. The German physicist Werner Heisenberg developed the "uncertainty," or "indeterminacy," principle in physics. Scientific observation of atomic behavior, according to this theory, actually disturbs the atom and thereby makes precise formulations impossible. Even scientists, Heisenberg asserted, had to settle for statistical probability. The attempt to learn the secrets of the universe led to doubts about human understanding itself. Viennese-born philosopher Ludwig Wittgenstein (1889–1951) explored the limits of language. He also questioned the traditional philosophical quest to find the essence of such terms as *thought, knowledge*, and *belief*.

Religious leaders also spurred many to recommit to religious activism. This impulse contested the violent secularization in Germany and the Soviet Union and helped foster a spirit of resistance to dictatorship among religious people. The Swiss theologian Karl Barth (1886–1968) encouraged rebellion against the Nazis, teaching that the faithful had to take seriously scriptural justifications of resistance to oppression. In his 1931 social encyclical, a letter addressed to the world on social issues, Pope Pius XI (r. 1922–1939) condemned the failure of modern societies to provide their citizens with a decent life and supported government intervention to create better moral and material conditions. The encyclical, *Quadragesimo Anno*, seemed to some an endorsement of the heavy-handed intervention of the fascists, but it also inspired some European theologians and pastors to ally themselves with the poor and politically oppressed. German Catholics frequently opposed Hitler, and religious commitment inspired many other individuals to resist fascism through the churches. During the 1930s, however, neither the traditional authority of the churches nor the cultural power of the art and mass media could block the ascendency of militarism and dictatorship.

❖ The Road to World War II

In the wake of economic catastrophe, Hitler, Mussolini, and Japan's military leaders marched the world toward another catastrophic war. Each of these leaders believed that his nation deserved to rule a far larger territory as part of its special destiny. At first many ordinary citizens and statesmen in Britain and France hoped that the League of Nations would be able to contain aggression by imposing embargoes or other sanctions. Others, believing that the powers had rushed into World War I, counseled the appeasement of Mussolini and Hitler. The widespread desire for peace in the 1930s sprang from fresh and painful memories: the destruction of World War I, the social and cultural chaos of the 1920s, and the economic turmoil of the Great Depression. But it left many people blind to Japanese actions in China and to Hitler's professed expansionist goals. By early 1938, Fascists were fighting to overthrow the Spanish republic, Japan had invaded the Asian mainland, and Hitler was menacing eastern Europe. Some historians claim that World War I, the turbulent interwar years, and World War II make up a single "Thirty Years' War" of the twentieth century. According to this view, the dramatic events of the 1930s, traditionally seen as the prelude to World War II, were actually the middle years of this conflict.

The Road to World War II

1929 Global depression begins with U.S. stock
      market crash
1931 Japan invades Manchuria
1933 Hitler comes to power in Germany
1935 Italy invades Ethiopia
1936 Civil war breaks out in Spain; Hitler remilitarizes
      the Rhineland
1937 Japan invades China
1938 Germany annexes Austria; European leaders meet
      in Munich to negotiate with Hitler
1939 Germany seizes Czechoslovakia; Hitler and Stalin
      sign nonaggression pact; Germany invades Poland;
      Britain and France declare war on Germany

Japan Strikes in Asia

Japan's military leaders chafed to control more of
Asia and saw China, Russia, and other powers as
obstacles to the empire's prosperity and the fulfillment of its destiny. Renewed military vigor was
seen as key to pulling agriculture and small business from the depths of economic depression. The
army took the lead: in September 1931, a railroad
train in the Chinese province of Manchuria blew
up, and Japanese officers used the explosion, which
they had actually set, as an excuse to invade the
territory. Setting up a puppet government in Manchuria, the army invaded more of China to push its
goal of political and economic penetration of the
Asian continent (Map 27.1).

Japanese leaders also believed that their society
had put up with interference and competition
from the Western powers long enough. During the
difficult years of the Great Depression, the Japanese press aroused public sentiment against the
kind of Western domination that had occurred at
the Washington Conference in 1921, when Japan
had been forced to agree to keep its fleet smaller
than Western navies. Journalists called for aggressive expansion to restore the economy. Businessmen wanted new markets and resources for their
burgeoning but wounded industries. In this uncertain time the military extended its influence in the
government, advocating Asian conquest as part of
Japan's "divine mission." By 1936–1937, Japan was
spending 47 percent of its budget on arms.

The situation in East Asia had international
repercussions. Great-power economic interests
were threatened, as Japanese aggression compounded the effect of the growing market in
Japanese goods. China asked the League of Nations
to adjudicate the question of Manchuria. The
league condemned the invasion, but it imposed no
sanctions that would have put economic teeth into
its condemnation. Meanwhile, the rebuff outraged
the Japanese public and goaded the government to
ally with Hitler and Mussolini. In 1933, China and
Japan agreed to a truce, with Japan occupying territory on the Asian mainland. In 1937, however,
Japan attacked China again, justifying its offensive
as a first step toward what it called "a new order" in
East Asia that would liberate the region from Western imperialism. Hundreds of thousands of Chinese were massacred in the "Rape of Nanjing"—an
atrocity so named because of the brutality toward
girls and women and the grim acts of torture perpetrated by the Japanese. The offensive set Japan
and the United States on a collision course. President Roosevelt immediately announced an embargo on U.S. export of airplane parts to Japan and
later enforced stringent economic sanctions on the
crucial raw materials that drove Japanese industry.
Nonetheless, the Western powers, including the Soviet Union, did not effectively resist Japan's territorial expansion in Asia and the Pacific.

Rejecting the Legacy of Versailles

Like Japanese leaders, Mussolini and Hitler called
their countries "have-nots." The Allies had reneged
on Britain's promise to hand over territories to
Italy after World War I, and Mussolini threatened
"permanent conflict" to right that wrong by expanding Italy's borders. Hitler's agenda, as stated in
Mein Kampf, included reestablishing control over
the Rhineland, breaking free from the Versailles
treaty's military restrictions, and bringing Germans
living in other nations into the Third Reich's orbit.
Superior "Aryans," moreover, needed *Lebensraum*,
or living space, to thrive. This space, according to
Nazi plans, would be taken from the "inferior"
Slavic peoples and Bolsheviks, who would be
moved to Siberia or would serve as slaves to
"Aryans." Both dictators portrayed themselves as
peace-loving men who resorted to extreme measures only to benefit their country and humanity.

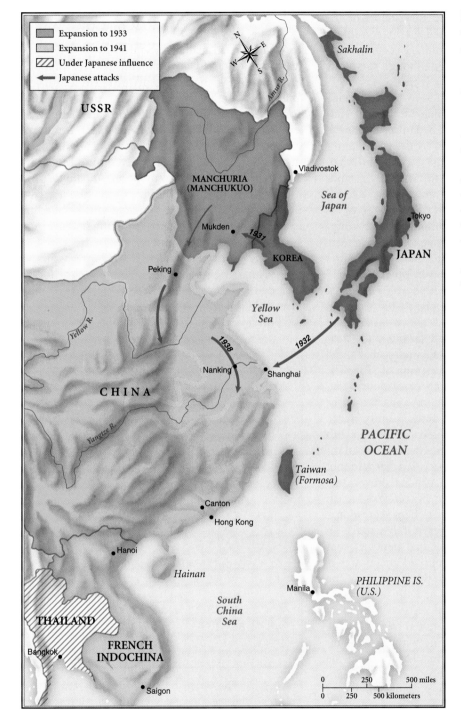

MAP 27.1 The Expansion of Japan, 1931–1941

Japanese expansion in the twentieth century approximated that of Russia and the United States in the nineteenth century: that is, it incorporated neighboring regions of Korea, Taiwan, and Manchuria with the vast area of China an inviting target. Governments of modernizing states believed that actual possession of territories was necessary for the resources, workforce, and markets they provided. But Japan's ambition fell afoul of the United States' own Pacific goals and made these two powers suddenly become deadly rivals.

Moreover, their anticommunism appealed to statesmen across Europe.

In the autumn of 1933, Hitler announced Germany's withdrawal from the League of Nations and from an international disarmament conference, which had been working fruitlessly for two years on proposals for limiting weapons. Hitler tried to unify Germany and Austria, but Austrian dictator Dollfuss resisted this first attempt at *Anschluss* (unification) and was assassinated for his obstruction.

In 1935, Hitler loudly rejected the clauses of the Treaty of Versailles that limited German military strength; he reintroduced military conscription and publicly started rearming, although Germany had been rearming in secret for years.

Mussolini also chose 1935 to assert Italian power: he invaded Ethiopia, one of the very few African states not overwhelmed by European imperialism. The attack was intended to demonstrate his regime's youth and vigor and to raise Italy's standing among the colonial powers. "A new cycle is beginning for our country," one soldier exclaimed. "The Roman legionnaires are again on the march." The poorly equipped Ethiopians resisted but could not withstand the Italian army, and their capital, Addis Ababa, fell in the spring of 1936. The League of Nations voted sanctions against Italy, but Britain and France opposed an embargo with teeth in it—one on oil—and thus kept the sanctions from being effective. The policy led to war, not peace, for the imposition of sanctions drove Mussolini into Hitler's arms, while British and French policy suggested a lack of resolve to fight aggression.

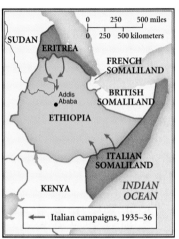

The Ethiopian War, 1935–1936

Profiting from the diversion of Italy's attack on Ethiopia, in March 1936 Hitler had defiantly sent his troops into what was supposed to be a permanently demilitarized zone in the Rhineland. The inhabitants greeted the Germans with wild enthusiasm, and the French, whose security was most endangered by this action, protested to the League of Nations instead of countering with an invasion as they had done in the Ruhr in 1923. Without the support of the British, who accepted the fait accompli, the French general staff, committed to a strategy of defense, counseled against an attack on Germany despite France's military superiority at the time. The two dictators thus appeared both as political leaders and as powerful military heroes forging, in Mussolini's muscular phrase, a "Rome-Berlin Axis." Next to them, the politicians of France and Great Britain looked not just cautious but timid.

The Spanish Civil War, 1936–1939

In what seemed like an exception to the trend toward authoritarian government, Spanish republicans overthrew their king in 1931. For centuries, Spain had declined economically and politically compared with the rest of Europe; large landowners and the Catholic clergy, who had the impoverished peasantry at their mercy, continued to dominate without modernizing the rural economy. The republicans hoped to modernize Spain by promoting industry and efficient, independent farming, but the government they established failed to enact land redistribution, which might have ensured popular loyalty and diminished the power of landowners and the church. This failure was all the more damaging because the antimonarchist forces included an array of liberals, anarchists, Communists, and other splinter groups constantly vying for power and harassing one another. In contrast,

MAP 27.2 The Spanish Civil War, 1936–1939
Pro-republican and antirepublican forces bitterly fought one another to determine whether Spain would be a democracy or an authoritarian state. Germany and Italy sent military assistance, notably airplanes to experiment with bombing civilians, while volunteers from around the world arrived to fight for the losing cause of the republic. Defeating these ill-organized groups, General Francisco Franco instituted a pro-fascist government that sent many to jail and into exile.

right-wing forces from the large landowners and clergy acted in concert and drew on their substantial financial resources.

In 1936, pro-republican forces temporarily banded together in a Popular Front coalition to win elections and prevent the republic from collapsing under the weight of internal squabbling and growing monarchist opposition. With the Popular Front victory, euphoria swept the country: prisoners were set free, unemployment abated, and coveted municipal jobs were doled out. But the right recovered and revolted under the leadership of General Francisco Franco (1892–1975). Franco had the support of a host of right-wing groups, including monarchists, clergy, landowners, and ultimately the fascist Falange Party.

The military uprising led to the Spanish Civil War, which pitted the republicans, or Loyalists, against the fascist Falangists and the far more powerful forces of the authoritarian right. In a war of ever shifting battle lines, republicans held Madrid, Barcelona, and other commercial and industrial areas, whereas the rebels found most support in the agricultural west and south (Map 27.2). The struggle became a rehearsal for World War II when Hitler and Mussolini sent military personnel in support of Franco and the right to test new weapons and to practice new tactics, particularly the terror bombing of civilians. In 1937, the German Condor Legion of aviation aces, who entered the country on tourist visas, attacked the town of Guernica with low-flying planes, mowing down civilians in the streets. This gratuitous slaughter inspired Pablo Picasso's memorial mural to the dead, *Guernica* (1937), in which the intense suffering is starkly displayed in monochromatic grays and whites to capture a sense of moral decay as well as physical death.

The Spanish republican government appealed everywhere for assistance. Only the Soviet Union answered, but Stalin withdrew his troops and tanks in 1938 as government ranks floundered. Britain and France again showed their war-wariness by refusing to provide aid despite the outpouring of popular support for the cause of democracy. Instead a few thousand volunteers from a variety of countries—including many students, journalists, and artists—fought for the republic. As these volunteers put it, "Spain was the place to stop fascism," while refugee-volunteers from Mussolini's

The Spanish Republic Appeals for Aid
The government of the Spanish Republic sent out modern advertising and propaganda to attract support from the remaining democracies—especially Great Britain and France. Antiwar sentiment remained high among the British and French, however. Thus, despite the horrifying and deliberate bombing of civilians by Franco's German allies, aid for the republic failed to arrive.
Imperial War Museum, London.

Italy found hope in thinking that their fighting meant, "Today in Spain, tomorrow in Italy." Besides being less well supplied than the Falangists and dependent on male and female volunteers, the republican ranks again splintered into competing groups of liberals, Trotskyites, anarchists, and Communists. In this bitter contest both sides committed widespread atrocities against civilians. The aid Franco received ultimately proved decisive, and his troops defeated the republicans in 1939. The ensuing dictatorship, which would remain in place until 1975, reinforced the European trend toward authoritarian government.

Hitler's Conquest of Central Europe, 1938–1939

The fall of central Europe that ultimately led to World War II began with Hitler's annexation of Austria in 1938. Many Austrians had actually wished for such a merger after the Paris peace settlement stripped them of their empire. In March 1938, Austrian Chancellor Kurt von Schuschnigg (1897–1977), hoping to maintain independence, called on Austrians to vote for or against Anschluss, or merging with the Third Reich. Fearing negative results, Hitler ordered an invasion.

His troops entered Austria as easily as tourists, and Austrian enthusiasm made the Anschluss appear to support the Wilsonian idea of "self-determination." The annexation fit into Hitler's plans in two ways: it began the unification of "Aryan peoples" into one greater German nation and it marked the first step in taking over the resources of central and eastern Europe. Austria was declared a German province, the Ostmark, and Hitler's thugs ruled once-cosmopolitan Vienna. An observer later commented on the scene:

> University professors were obliged to scrub the streets with their naked hands, pious white-bearded Jews were dragged into the synagogue by hooting youths and forced to do knee-exercises and to shout "Heil Hitler" in chorus. Innocent people in the streets were trapped like rabbits and herded off to clean the latrines in the S.A. barracks.

The Anschluss enhanced the image of German omnipotence, advancing Hitler's plan to "keep Europe gasping."

With Austria firmly in his grasp, Hitler turned to Czechoslovakia and its rich resources. Overpowering this democracy did not appear as simple a task as seizing Austria. Czechoslovakia had a large army and formidable border defenses and armament factories, and most Czech citizens were prepared to fight for their country. Hitler gambled correctly that the other Western powers would not interfere: many in the West thought that Czechoslovakia, a creation of the postwar peace settlement, unjustly denied Germans and other national minorities their right to self-determination.

Throughout the spring and summer of 1938, Hitler and his propaganda machine poured tremendous abuse on Czechoslovakia and its president, Edouard Beneš, for allegedly "persecuting" the German minority. Hitler wooed Czechoslovakia's neighbors into accepting his claims, partly by convincing the Poles and Hungarians that they had something to gain from the country's dismemberment. By October 1, 1938, he warned, Czechoslovakia would have to grant autonomy (amounting to Nazi rule) to the German-populated border region, the Sudetenland, or face German invasion.

As the October deadline approached, British Prime Minister Neville Chamberlain (1869–1940), eager to keep the peace, met with Hitler. Mussolini and French Premier Edouard Daladier (1884–1970) joined Hitler and Chamberlain at their last meeting in Munich and agreed not to oppose Germany's claim to the Sudetenland. Hitler topped off the Munich Conference by signing an agreement that Germany would never go to war with Great Britain. The strategy of preventing a war by making concessions for legitimate grievances (in this case, the alleged affront to Germans in the Peace of Paris) was called *appeasement*. At the time it was widely seen as a positive act, and the agreement between Germany and Great Britain prompted Chamberlain to announce that he had secured "peace in our time." Amidst great publicity, crowds lined the streets of European capitals and hailed their returning leaders for averting world war, despite the deal that in essence gave part of a sovereign country to Hitler. By contrast, the Czech ambassador to Germany wept. Stalin, excluded from the Munich deliberations, learned from the conference that the democracies were not going to fight to protect eastern Europe.

Hitler, meanwhile, was disgruntled that the agreement had thwarted his ambition to invade Czechoslovakia. Having portrayed himself as a man of peace, he waited another six months, until March 1939, and then sent German troops over the border (Map 27.3). Britain and France responded by promising military support to Poland, Romania, Greece, and Turkey in case of Nazi invasion. In May 1939, Hitler and Mussolini countered this agreement by signing a pledge of offensive and defensive support called the Pact of Steel.

Historians have sharply criticized the Munich Pact because it bought Hitler time to build his army and seemed to give him the green light for further aggression. Some historians believe that a

MAP 27.3 The Growth of Nazi Germany, 1933–1939
German expansion was rapid and surprising, as Hitler's forces and Nazi diplomacy brought the annexa-
tion of the new states of central and eastern Europe. Although committed to defending the sovereignty of
these states through the League of Nations, French and British diplomats were more concerned with satis-
fying Hitler in the mistaken belief that doing so would prevent his claiming more of Europe. In the process
Hitler acquired the human and material resources of adjacent countries to support his Third Reich.

confrontation might have stopped Hitler and that even if war had resulted, the democracies would have triumphed. According to this view, each military move by Germany, Italy, and Japan should have been met with stiff opposition, and the Soviet Union should have been made a partner to this resistance. Others counter that appeasement provided France and Britain precious time to beef up their own armies, which the Munich crisis caused them to do, and to prepare their citizens for an-

other war. Support for war was almost nonexistent, and even statesmen who knew of Hitler's ambitions respected, sometimes even admired, and almost always sought to pacify him in the belief that even though he was "mad" he could be dealt with rationally to meet Germany's just claims.

Such thinking received a final jolt on August 23, 1939, when Germany and the USSR signed a nonaggression agreement. The Nazi-Soviet Pact astonished public opinion in the West, given

Hitler's ambition to wipe the Bolsheviks off the face of the earth and official Soviet abhorrence of fascism. But Stalin needed extra time to reconstitute his military because he had just destroyed his officer corps in the purges. The pact provided that if one country became embroiled in war, the other country would remain neutral. Moreover, the two dictators secretly agreed to divide Poland and the Baltic States—Latvia, Estonia, and Lithuania—at some future date, with Hitler claiming western Poland and Stalin the Baltic States in addition to Finland and eastern Poland. The Nazi-Soviet Pact ensured that should war come, the democracies would be fighting a Germany with no fear of attack on its eastern borders. In the belief that Great Britain and perhaps even France would not fight because his aggression had met no resistance so far, Hitler now aimed his forces at Poland.

❖ World War II, 1939–1945

The global catastrophe that quickly came to be called the Second World War opened when Hitler launched an all-out attack on Poland on September 1, 1939. The Poles had rejected his demand that they return the free city of Danzig and yield to Germany the Polish Corridor—a strip of land to connect East Prussia with the rest of the Reich. Hitler had couched the ultimatum in nationalistic terms, claiming that Germans in Polish territory were in danger. "I needed an alibi," Hitler blatantly admitted, "especially with the German people." In contrast to 1914, no jubilation in Berlin accompanied the invasion; when Britain and France declared war two days later, the mood in other capitals was similarly grim. World War II began with dire predictions about its ultimate consequences: the British government had estimated in 1938 that the first two months of war would produce 1.8 million casualties and that London would be bombed daily by at least seven hundred tons of bombs. Although Japan, Italy, and the United States did not join the battle immediately, their participation eventually spread the fighting throughout the world. By the time World War II ended in 1945, many Europeans were starving, much of the continent lay in ruins, and unparalleled atrocities and genocide had killed 6 million Jews and countless others.

The German Onslaught

German ground forces quickly defeated the ill-equipped Polish troops by launching an overpowering *Blitzkrieg* ("lightning war"), in which the Germans concentrated airplanes, tanks, and motorized infantry to encircle Polish defenders and capture the capital, Warsaw, with overwhelming speed. Allowing the army to conserve supplies, Blitzkrieg assured Germans at home that the human costs of gaining Lebensraum, that is, sufficient "living space" for the full flowering of the Aryan race, would be low.

On September 17, 1939, the Soviets invaded Poland from the east to make their own conquest. By the end of the month, the Polish army was in shambles. Having divided the country according to the Nazi-Soviet Pact, Hitler issued a peace initiative in October so that future clashes would look like the fault of the democracies. The refusal of Britain and France to negotiate an immediate end to the conflict allowed Hitler to sell the war within the Reich as one of self-defense, especially from what propagandists called the "warlike menace" of world Jewry. Meanwhile, the USSR attacked Finland for refusing to provide a base for the Soviet military. As sympathy for the valiant Finns mounted, the League of Nations expelled the Soviet Union.

Hitler ordered an attack on France for November 1939, but his generals, who feared that Germany was ill prepared for total war, were able to postpone the offensive until the spring of 1940. During the period from November to April, known as the "phony war," the combatants engaged in little direct conflict. Then in April 1940, the Blitzkrieg crushed Denmark and Norway; the battles of Belgium, the Netherlands, and France followed in May and June.

In France, panic and defeatism infected the army. On June 5, Mussolini, eyeing future spoils for Italy, invaded France from the southeast. Much to the shock of the rest of the world, the French defense rapidly collapsed. Nor could the British army withstand the German onslaught. Trapped on the beaches of Dunkirk in northern France, 370,000 British and French soldiers were rescued in a heroic effort by an improvised fleet of naval ships, fishing boats, and pleasure craft. A dejected French government surrendered on June 22, 1940, leaving Germany to rule the northern half of the country, including Paris. In the south, named Vichy France after the spa town where the government sat, the reactionary and aged World War I hero Henri Philippe Pétain (1856–1951) was allowed to govern. Stalin used the diversion in western Europe to annex the Baltic States and to seize Bessarabia and Bukovina from Romania.

The Division of France, 1940

Britain now stood alone. Blaming Germany's rapid victories on Chamberlain's policy of appeasement, the British swept him out of office and installed as prime minister Winston Churchill (1874–1965), an early advocate of resistance to Hitler. After Hitler ordered the bombardment of Britain in the summer of 1940, Churchill rallied the nation by radio—now in more than nine million British homes—to reverse the pacifist spirit. Sacrifices to protect the ideals of liberty, he vowed, would yield Britain's "finest hour." He promised nothing, however, except "blood, toil, tears, and sweat."

In the battle of Britain, or Blitz as the British called it, the German air force (Luftwaffe) bombed public buildings and monuments, harbors and weapons depots, and military bases and industry. Refusing to negotiate, scorning surrender, and using the wealth of their colonies, the British held fast as the government poured resources into anti-aircraft weapons, its highly successful code-detecting group called Ultra, and development of its advantage in radar (a technology it had perfected in the 1930s). At year's end, the British air industry was outproducing the Germans by 50 percent.

By the fall of 1940, German air losses forced Hitler to abandon his plan for a naval invasion of Britain. He consoled himself by attacking British bases in the Mediterranean, Middle East, and North Africa and by forcing Hungary, Romania, and Bulgaria to join the Axis. This strategy gained Germany access to more food and oil for its army. Hitler then signed the Tripartite Pact with Italy and Japan (1940) and the Nonaggression Pact with Turkey (1941).

In spring 1941, Hitler, emboldened by his newly expanded power base, made his fatal decision to attack what he called the "center of judeobolshevism"—the Soviet Union. In June 1941, Operation Barbarossa began when the German army crossed the Soviet border. Hitler declared himself "happy to be delivered from [the] torment" of allying with Bolsheviks and promised to "raze Moscow and Leningrad to the ground."

Deployed along a two-thousand-mile front, 3 million German and other Axis troops quickly penetrated Soviet lines. When intelligence reports revealed troops massed on his border, Stalin simply disappeared for several days. Then he rallied to direct the defense; by July, however, the German army had rolled to within two hundred miles of Moscow and would eventually reach its suburbs. Using a strategy of rapid encirclement, German troops had killed, captured, and wounded more than half the 4.5 million Soviet soldiers defending the borders. Amidst success, Hitler blundered. Considering himself a military genius and the Slavic people inferior, he proposed attacking Leningrad, the Baltic States, and the Ukraine simultaneously, whereas his generals wanted to concentrate on Moscow. Following this cumbersome strategy lost precious time, and the German army got bogged down in the autumn rains. Driven by Stalin, local party members, and rising patriotic resolve, the Soviet people fought back in the winter, which turned Nazi soldiers to frostbitten wretches. In these early years of the war, Hitler feared that equipping his army for the Russian winter would suggest that the limits of Blitzkrieg had been reached and that a prolonged campaign lay in store—the scenario that did in fact materialize. Meanwhile his ill-supplied armies succumbed to the weather and disease. "What is all this for?" one German wrote in his diary in December 1941. "When will we ever get back home?"

War Expands: The Pacific and Beyond

As the German army entrenched in the Soviet Union, an all-out dramatic attack ignited war in the Pacific. On Sunday, December 7, 1941, Japanese navy planes bombed American naval and air bases at Pearl Harbor in Hawaii, seriously damaging or sinking all eight battleships there, and then decimated a fleet of airplanes in the Philippines. In an address to Congress Roosevelt pronounced it "a date which will live in infamy" and summoned the representatives to declare war on Japan. The outbreak of war in Europe intensified U.S.-Japanese competition, as Japan had taken control of parts of the British Empire, bullied the Dutch in Indonesia, and invaded Indochina to procure raw materials for its industrial and military expansion. Under Prime Minister Hideki Tojo (1884–1948), the militarist Japanese government decided it should settle matters with the West once and for all and forcibly unite Asians in a regional "coprosperity sphere." By spring 1942, the Japanese had conquered Guam, the Philippines, Malaya, Burma, Indonesia, Singapore, and much of the southwestern Pacific.

On December 11, 1941, Hitler, faithful to the Tripartite Pact, declared war on the United States—an appropriate enemy, he proclaimed, as it was "half Judaized and the other half Negrified." Mussolini followed suit. The United States was not prepared for a prolonged struggle: its armed forces numbered only 1.6 million, and no plan existed for producing the necessary guns, tanks, and airplanes. Earlier in 1941, Roosevelt had taken steps to assist Britain, notably with a program called Lend-Lease that provided supplies without immediate cash payment. American aid was crucial in the battle of the Atlantic—the struggle to protect vital British shipping from constant German attack. Fully 80 percent of Americans approved of the Lend-Lease plan.

But isolationist sentiment remained strong, led by the America First movement. Also working against war-preparedness was ambivalence toward the Soviet Union. Since the 1930s, many U.S. and British leaders and a good part of the general public had resisted joining forces with the USSR even against Hitler. Stalin himself reciprocated the mistrust. When Hitler declared war first on the USSR and then on the United States, his four enemies came together in the Grand Alliance of Great Britain, the Free French (an exile government led by General Charles de Gaulle and based in London), the Soviet Union, and the United States. The alliance evolved slowly over the course of the war through diplomatic negotiations and meetings of its leaders. Given the urgency of war and the partners' competing interests, the Grand Alliance and the larger coalition with twenty other countries—known collectively as the Allies—had much internal strife to overcome in their struggle against the Axis—Germany, Italy, and Japan.

The Holocaust

As the German army swept through eastern Europe, it slaughtered Jews, Communists, Slavs, and others deemed "racial inferiors" and enemies in Nazi ideology. In Poland, the SS murdered nobility, clergy, and intellectuals and relocated hundreds of thousands of Polish citizens to forced labor camps. Across the continent, the army rounded up civilians to work on German farms, in German industry, and in concentration and labor camps throughout the Reich—all to feed the voracious Nazi war machine. Herded into urban ghettos and living on minimal rations, many eastern European Jews were forced temporarily to work for the Nazis, but the Jews also became special targets of SS violence. Around Soviet towns, Jews were usually shot in pits, some of which they had been forced to dig themselves. After shedding their clothes and putting them in ordered piles for later Nazi use, ten thousand or more at a time were killed, often with the help of anti-Semitic Ukrainians or Lithuanians. More than thirty thousand were massacred at Babi Yar in the Ukraine after the fall of Kiev at the end of September 1941 (Map 27.4). However, the "Final Solution"—the Nazis' diabolical plan to exterminate all of Europe's Jews—was not yet fully under way.

In addition to the massacres, a bureaucratically organized and efficient technological system for rounding up Jews and transporting them to extermination sites had taken shape by the fall of 1941. On the eve of war in 1939, Hitler had predicted "the destruction of the Jewish race in Europe." In 1942, he exploded in rage before mass audiences: "There was a time when the Jews in Germany also laughed at my prophecies. . . . But take my word for it: they will stop laughing everywhere." Historians have demonstrated that although no clear order written by Hitler exists, he discussed the Final Solution's progress, issued oral directives for it, and from the beginning made lethal anti-Semitism a basis for Nazism.

The Holocaust was also a product of modern social and legal science and technology, managed by efficient scientists, doctors, lawyers, and government workers. Six camps in Poland were developed specifically for the purposes of mass murder—Auschwitz-Birkenau, Majdanek, Chelmno, Belzec,

Sobibor, and Treblinka. Some, like Auschwitz-Birkenau, served both as extermination and labor camps where inmates produced synthetic rubber and fuel. Others, such as Chelmno, existed solely for extermination. SS troops supervised all the camps. Improvising with sealed-up houses and trucks and using techniques developed in the T4 project in the late 1930s, Nazis and collaborators at Chelmno first gassed Christian Poles and Soviet prisoners of war. The Nazis burned the corpses in huge pits until the specially designed crematoria for mass burning started functioning in 1943. By then, Auschwitz had the capacity to burn 1.7 million bodies per year. About 60 percent of new arrivals—particularly children, women, and old people—were selected directly for murder in the gas chambers; the other 40 percent labored until, utterly used up, they too were sent to their deaths.

Extermination camps received their victims from across the continent. In the ghettos in various

MAP 27.4 Concentration Camps and Extermination Sites in Europe
This map shows the major extermination sites and concentration camps in Europe, but the entire continent was dotted with thousands of lesser camps to which the victims of Nazism were transported. Some of these lesser camps were merely way stations on the path to ultimate extermination. In focusing on the major camps historians often lose sight of the ways in which evidence of deportation and extermination blanketed Europe.

European cities, councils of Jewish leaders, such as the one in Amsterdam where Etty Hillesum worked, were ordered to determine those to be "resettled in the east." Many of them did so in the belief that life outside the ghetto could hardly be worse than life within. Effective resistance was nearly impossible, as Jews in the ghettos were weakened by hunger and disease and could not obtain enough necessary weapons. Moreover, the Jews who had emigrated outside Europe—mostly men and some younger women—left behind in the ghettos a surplus of women and older people. Any kind of resistance meant certain death. When Jews rose up against their Nazi captors in Warsaw in 1943, they were mercilessly butchered. The Nazis took pains to cloak their true purposes in the extermination camps. Bands played when trainloads of victims arrived; some were given postcards with reassuring messages to mail home. Then the selection process began, with men and women segregated. Many mothers, unaware that their children were automatically doomed, refused to be separated from them and thus went directly to the gas chamber. Those who avoided immediate selection had their heads shaved, were showered and disinfected, and were then given prison garments. So began life in "a living hell," as one survivor wrote.

Overworked inmates usually took in less than five hundred calories per day and experienced unimaginably bleak conditions, leaving them vulnerable to typhus and other diseases that swept through the camps. The brutality of inspections and roll calls, of mentally disturbed and criminal prison guards, and of inhumane medical experiments failed to crush the spirit of those like Etty Hillesum. Women observed religious holidays, celebrated birthdays, and re-created other sustaining aspects of domestic life. Language lessons or storytelling sessions maintained human culture in an inhuman setting. Prisoners forged new friendships that helped in the struggle for survival. An onion or part of a turnip could serve as a precious gift to someone sick with typhus. Thanks to those sharing a bread ration and doing him favors, wrote the Auschwitz survivor Primo Levi, "I managed not to forget that I myself was a man."

Historians debate what the Allies should have done about the Holocaust during the war. Some fault them for delaying the invasion of Europe or for failing to bomb the death camps about which they were informed. Others have calculated that many ordinary Germans knew of the genocide and ask why so few protested and why the Jews' own leaders cooperated in the deportations. Anti-Semitism had intensified since the end of the nineteenth century, and the Holocaust came about because of the high level of industrial, scientific, and legal organization that accompanied human hatred. Six million Jews, the vast majority from eastern Europe, along with an estimated five to six million gypsies, homosexuals, Slavs, and countless others were murdered. (See "New Sources, New Perspectives," page 1056.)

Societies at War

Even more than World War I, World War II depended on industrial productivity geared totally toward war and mass murder. The Axis countries remained at a disadvantage throughout the war despite their vast conquests. Although the war accelerated economic production some 300 percent between 1940 and 1944 in all belligerent countries, the Allies produced twice the armaments of the Axis powers in 1941 and more than three times Axis output in 1943. Even while its lands were occupied and many of its cities besieged, the Soviet Union increased its production of aircraft 40 percent between 1942 and 1943; by the spring of 1943 it was turning out 2,000 tanks per month (Figure 27.1).

Both Japan and Germany made the most of their lower capacity, most notably in the strategy of Blitzkrieg. Hitler had to avoid imposing wartime austerity because he had come to power promising

Persecution of Warsaw Jews
Hitler was determined to exterminate by violent means Jews, Slavs, gypsies, homosexuals, and others he deemed "undesirable"; he often enlisted community leaders to cooperate in deportation and even executions. In the 1930s, people fled Germany and then countries the Nazis conquered. In the city of Warsaw, where Jews were crowded into ghettos and deprived of food and fuel, the Jewish uprising brought massive retaliation.
© Bettman/Corbis.

	1939	1940	1941	1942	1943	1944	1945
Aircraft							
Great Britain	7,940	15,049	20,094	23,672	26,263	26,461	12,070
United States	5,856	12,804	26,277	47,826	85,998	96,318	49,761
USSR	10,382	10,565	15,735	25,436	34,900	40,300	20,900
Germany	8,295	10,247	11,776	15,409	24,807	39,807	7,540
Japan	4,467	4,768	5,088	8,861	16,693	28,180	11,066
Major Vessels							
Great Britain	57	148	236	239	224	188	64
United States	———	———	544	1,854	2,654	2,247	1,513
USSR	———	33	62	19	13	23	11
Germany (U-boats only)	15	40	196	244	270	189	0
Japan	21	30	49	68	122	248	51
Tanks							
Great Britain	969	1,399	4,841	8,611	7,476	5,000	2,100
United States	———	c. 400	4,052	24,997	29,497	17,565	11,968
USSR	2,950	2,794	6,590	24,446	24,089	28,963	15,400
Germany	c. 1,300	2,200	5,200	9,200	17,300	22,100	4,400
Japan	c. 200	1,023	1,024	1,191	790	401	142

FIGURE 27.1 Weapons Production of the Major Powers, 1939–1945

World War II devoured people and weapons, necessitating dramatic changes in the workforce and everyday life. As agricultural production was often hit hard by invading forces, people lived on reduced rations. Raw materials were channeled into the manufacture of weapons, and it was the real difference in productivity that spelled victory for the Allies: Germany and Japan were outproduced in almost every category. While the Allies filled their factories with women workers, German policies keeping women from well-paid industrial work could not be turned around in time to boost production. From *The Hammond Atlas of the Twentieth Century* (London: Times Books, 1996), 103.

to end economic suffering, not increase it. The use of millions of slave laborers and resources from occupied areas improved the German standard of living, but those benefits disappeared after Blitzkrieg failed in the Soviet Union. Although Japan's government had built public support for the war, it maintained the erroneous belief that a few costly attacks would discourage Americans from pursuing war so far from home. Neither Japan nor Germany took the resources and morale of its enemies into full account.

Allied governments were overwhelmingly successful in generating civilian participation, especially among women. In the Axis countries, where government policy encouraged large families and motherhood was particularly exalted, women followed the fascist doctrine of separate spheres, avoiding paid work in wartime even though they were desperately needed in offices and factories. "The weakening of the family system would be the weakening of the nation," Japanese leaders argued. In contrast, Soviet women constituted more than half the workforce by war's end. They dug massive antitank trenches around Moscow and other threatened cities, and 800,000 volunteered for the

military, even serving as pilots. As the Germans invaded, Soviet citizens moved entire factories eastward; some five hundred were moved from Moscow in October 1941 alone. Stalin encouraged a revival of Russian nationalism, allowing religious services because the Orthodox church provided people with hope and inspired patriotism and sacrifice.

The democracies used propaganda to mobilize loyalty; even more than in World War I, propaganda saturated society in movie theaters and on the radio. Accustomed to listening to politicians on the air, people were glued to their radios for war news. Films depicted aviation heroes and infantrymen as well as the workingwomen and wives left behind. Government agencies monitored filmmaking and allocated supplies to approved films. In the United States, military leaders loaned authentic props only if they could censor the scripts. Advertisers of consumer goods connected their products to the war effort: "If your dealer doesn't have your favorite LIFE SAVERS," read one advertisement, "please be patient. . . . It is because the shipment he would have received has gone to the Army and Navy."

Museums and Memory

Holocaust Memorial Museum
Designed to evoke a sense of awe at the unprecedented suffering caused by the mass murder of the Jews, the Holocaust Memorial Museum in Washington, D.C., displays pictures of thousands of Germany's victims. Other museums around the world focus on different aspects of Hitler's policy of extermination, emphasizing the many nationalities of his victims or the variety of reasons for their slaughter.
Johnson/Liaison.

W hat is the difference between history and memory? What is the difference between a historical monument and a history textbook? Or the difference between the history of the Holocaust and a Holocaust museum?

Recently historians have come to focus on the role of historical monuments and museums that house historical artifacts. Both of these institutions are testimonials to historical events because they provide records of those events and show that people were deeply moved by them. Monuments to World War I keep the memory of the Great War alive in villages and cities from which its fallen soldiers came, while Holocaust museums are found in dozens of countries, many far from the region where the Holocaust took place. Photographs and objects from the times make us feel as if we have had real and vivid contact with the past.

But is the impression conveyed by a tragic photo or the memory of an event the same as its history? Historians wrestle with this question and for the most part regard photographs and oral testimony as useful historical evidence. However, many judge such institutions as the Holocaust museum as only partially about the history of the Holocaust. Instead, the Holocaust museum tells a great deal about the nation or group that builds it. It tells about the "memory" that the nation or group wants average people to have of the Holocaust. Or it may convey a consensus view reached when officials from the government and survivors or their representatives come to an agreement about what the museum or monument should look like.

Holocaust memorials have had a complicated development that is instructive to historians. Some Holocaust memory sites sprang up sponta- neously in concentration camps as memorials consecrated by survivors themselves. Stones, writings, plaques, flowers and plants, and other objects were used to testify to what had happened in the camp. In many cases, these initial memorials

Between 1939 and 1945, people lost much of their privacy as governments organized many aspects of everyday life. Bureaucrats regulated the production and distribution of food, clothing, and household products, all of which were rationed and generally of lower quality. In England by 1943, the wartime Ministry of Food employed 39,000 people just to manage what people ate. These bureaucrats gave hints for meals without meat, sugar, fat, dairy products, and other staples and taught were replaced when local and national governments stepped in to take over the site, sometimes waiting years between destroying the spontaneous memorials and replacing them with an official museum. The concentration camp at Dachau, near Munich, is one that fell into disrepair until a group of survivors, including many Catholic clergy, demanded the camp be made into a permanent museum and memorial, with the crematorium and other grisly features preserved.

Although townspeople and local government resisted, Dachau and its crematorium became one of the most visited camps and indeed came to symbolize the Holocaust in all its horror. Yet Dachau was not primarily an extermination site for Jews, Slavs, and gypsies but a grim concentration camp where Hitler put political prisoners, many of them Catholic clergy. It is so often visited because it is on the tourist route, close to a beautiful city. Indeed, among the plaques in this "on-site" museum, one invites visitors to tour the other cultural institutions and scenery of the area while another asks them to remember that vast numbers of those interned were Polish and Catholic. All of these factors in the politics of memories—official and unofficial, competing and contested—need to be taken into account by historians.

Museums also serve to create an "official" memory for the people of a single nation-state who themselves have competing memories. The process of creating this memory provokes incredible public and private debate over what the museum should look like, what it should include, and even how it will fit with goals of tourism. The on-site museum at Auschwitz creates a Polish memory of the Holocaust by emphasizing the millions of Poles who died, while the museum at Buchenwald under the Communist East German regime emphasized the number of working-class people who died there and the uprising of its many socialist prisoners who ultimately liberated the camp.

In the case of Holocaust museums, official memories can clash with memories of actual survivors who, for instance, do not like what is often the most aesthetic or avant-garde in terms of art and architecture. They generally reject abstract art because a "realistic" depiction of their suffering seems most important. As for architectural design, the American Holocaust Museum was redone so that it would not look grimly "out-of-place" but rather fit in with the tranquil style of the central museum mall in Washington, D.C. Historians take into account these "official" memories, but they also look at the way certain objects like shoes or eyeglasses are displayed to create a certain memory effect. They note that costume designers puff up prison uniforms to make them look more lifelike and to make people feel emotionally that they are involved with the Holocaust.

Holocaust museums have offered a powerful, vivid, and emotionally charged experience of history. In contrast, history prides itself on eliminating emotions and biases in reaching historical judgments, ascertaining facts, and calculating cause and effect. Though each provides an important representation of the past, the relationship between memory and history remains fraught with questions—and never more so than in the case of the Holocaust.

QUESTIONS FOR DEBATE

1. Why do museums and public exhibitions of art and artifacts arouse more debate than do history books?

2. Do you trust a history book more than you trust a museum? How do we compare and evaluate the presentation of the past in either one?

FURTHER READING

Gillis, John R. *Commemorations: The Politics of National Identity.* 1994.

Sherman, Daniel J., and Irit Rogoff, eds. *Museum Culture: Histories, Discourses, Spectacles.* 1994.

Young, James Edward. *The Texture of Memory: Holocaust Memorials and Meaning.* 1993.

---

that women and children should embrace deprivation so their fighting men would survive. Governments hired more businessmen, economists, statisticians, and other specialists to influence civilian thought and behavior. Government-sponsored media directed people in techniques of home canning or growing "victory gardens" to add to the food supply. With governments standardizing such items as food, clothing, and entertainment, World War II furthered the development of mass society.

Propaganda and government policies promoted racial thinking and hatred on both sides. On the home front, homogenized news reports instilled hatred for the enemy. Since the early 1930s, the German government had drawn ugly caricatures of Jews, and anti-Semitic, anti-Slav, and anti-gypsy sentiment was a hallmark of Nazism. Similarly, Allied propaganda during the war depicted Germans as sadists and perverts and the "Japs" as uncivilized, insectlike fanatics. The U.S. government forced citizens of Japanese origin into concentration or internment camps in the western states. In the Soviet Union, Muslims and minority ethnic groups were uprooted and relocated as potential Nazi collaborators. In the Soviet-occupied parts of Poland, industrialists, union members, professionals, and thousands of others were sent to the Gulag, if not murdered outright. Soldiers and civilians on both sides were preoccupied with enemies, sharply depicted in stereotypical racial and ethnic terms.

Colonized peoples were drawn into the war, many of them against their will, through conscription into the armies and forced labor. Some two million Indian men served the Allied cause, as did several hundred thousand Africans. As the Japanese swept through the Pacific and parts of East Asia, they too conscripted men into their army. Both sides bombarded colonized societies with propaganda, as radio stations and newspapers proliferated during the war. Ironically this propaganda politicized colonized peoples in unprecedented numbers. Because of forced labor and artificially low wages and profits to native workers and entrepreneurs, politicization aroused interest not only in the war but also in postwar liberation.

From Resistance to Allied Victory

Professional armies ultimately defeated the Axis powers, but civilian resistance in Nazi-occupied areas also contributed to the Allied triumph. General Charles de Gaulle (1890–1970) directed the Free French government and its forces from his haven in England; some 20 percent of these were initially troops made up of colonized Asians and Africans. Other French resisters fought in Communist-dominated groups, some of whom gathered information to aid the Allied invasion of the continent. The Polish resistance was unified against the Nazis, whereas in Yugoslavia, Serbs and Croats often attacked each other as much as they did the fascists until the Communist forces of Josip Broz (known as Marshall Tito) came to dominate the resistance. Rural groups called partisans, or the *maquis*, planned assassinations, disrupted communications, and bombed bridges, rail lines, and military facilities and supplies.

People also fought back through everyday activities. Homemakers circulated newsletters telling how to foil the plans of the occupying powers through demonstrations at prisons where civilians were detained and marketplaces where food was rationed. In central Europe, hikers smuggled Jews and others over dangerous mountain passes. Danish villagers created vast escape networks. Resisters played on stereotypes of femininity: women often carried weapons to assassination sites in the correct belief that Nazis would rarely suspect or search them; they also seduced and murdered enemy officers. In Paris a woman chemist made explosives for the French resistance in her university laboratory. Other actions subtly undermined the demands of fascist leaders. Couples in Germany and Italy limited family size in defiance of pro-birth policies. German teenagers danced the forbidden American jitterbug, thus defying the Nazis and forcing the police to monitor their groups. Resistance underscored the importance of the liberal ideal of

Hidden Revolver
Resistance to Nazism took many forms, from the concerted uprising in Warsaw to small acts of protest to assassinations of Nazi officers and collaborators. In a militarized state with informers everywhere, retaliation against Nazis sparked human ingenuity, whether in obtaining enough food or killing the enemy. Weapons were hidden in baby carriages, under clothing, or in books—as in this example from the Dutch resistance.
Erich Lessing/Art Resource, NY.

Battle of Leningrad

In the face of Nazi invasion, Soviet citizens reacted heroically, moving entire factories to the interior of the country and building fortifications. Nowhere was their resolve so tested as in Leningrad (St. Petersburg), when hundreds of thousands died during a Nazi siege lasting more than two years. Before the invasion of Normandy in 1944, the people of the USSR bore the brunt of Nazi military might in Hitler's attempt to defeat what he called "judeobolshevism."
Sovfoto.

individual political action and helped rebuild the community solidarity that authoritarian rule had fractured.

The spirit of resistance produced renowned heroes such as Swedish diplomat Raoul Wallenberg (1912–1947?), whose dealings with Nazi officials saved thousands of Hungarian Jews. But traitors abounded—collaborators who contributed to the initial Nazi victories and who cooperated with the Nazis during the occupation for personal advantage. From Vidkun Quisling, a Norwegian promoter of Nazism and prime minister during the occupation of his country, to countless other individuals in all walks of life who betrayed Jews in hiding or informed on resistance networks, Nazi Germany profited from the services of collaborators.

The Axis Crushed. The Allies started tightening a noose around the Axis in mid-1942 (Map 27.5). A major turning point came in August when the German army began a siege on Stalingrad, a city whose capture would give access to Soviet oil and cut access to the country's interior. Months of ferocious fighting led to house-to-house combat, as neither side would surrender despite massive casualties. Finally, the Soviet army captured the ninety

thousand German survivors in February 1943. Meanwhile, the British army in North Africa held against the Germans in Egypt and Libya and together with U.S. forces invaded Morocco and Algeria in the autumn of 1942. In July 1943, Allied forces landed in Sicily, hoping for a quick victory over Italy as the king ousted Mussolini. However, the Germans came to their ally's aid, occupied northern Italy, and fought bitterly for the peninsula until April 1945, when Allied forces finally triumphed. After Italy's liberation, partisans shot Mussolini and his mistress and hanged their dead bodies for public display.

The victory at Stalingrad marked the beginning of the costly Soviet drive westward—during which the Soviets bore the brunt of the Nazi war machine. As the Americans and British invaded North Africa and Europe and pounded German cities with strategic bombing to demoralize civilians and destroy the war industry, coordination among the Allies became imperative. In November and December 1943, Roosevelt, Churchill, and Stalin met at Teheran, Iran, to agree on the opening of a western European front, for which Stalin had been pressing and which Churchill had resisted. On June 6, 1944, the combined Allied forces

Legend:

- Axis powers and their allies
- Axis-held, early November 1942
- Allied powers and their allies
- Neutral nations
- Greater Germany, 1942
- Axis offensives
- Allied offensives
- ★ Major battle

Besieged Aug. 21, 1942–Jan. 31, 1943 — Stalingrad

Meeting of Roosevelt, Churchill, and Stalin, Nov.–Dec. 1943 — Tehran

Besieged Sept. 1941–Jan. 1944 — Leningrad

Germans repulsed Dec. 1941 — Moscow

Surrendered May 8, 1945 — Berlin

Battle of Britain, 1940 — London

Normandy invasion, D-Day June 6, 1944 — Dunkirk

Battle of the Bulge Dec. 16, 1944–Jan. 31, 1945

Liberated Aug. 25, 1944 — Paris

Liberated June 4, 1944 — Rome

Monte Cassino May 1944

Salerno Sept. 1943

Kasserine Pass Feb. 1943 — Tunisia

Under Vichy government 1940–42 Joined Allies Nov. 1942

El Alamein Oct.–Nov. 1942

400 miles / 400 kilometers

USSR, FINLAND, SWEDEN, NORWAY, DENMARK, ESTONIA, LATVIA, LITHUANIA, POLAND, EAST PRUSSIA, GERMANY, NETH., BELG., LUX., FRANCE, VICHY FRANCE, SWITZ., ITALY, SLOVAKIA, HUNGARY, ROMANIA, BULGARIA, YUGOSLAVIA, ALBANIA (It.), GREECE, TURKEY, IRAN, IRAQ, SAUDI ARABIA, SYRIA (Fr.), LEBANON (Fr.), TRANSJORDAN (Br.), PALESTINE (Br.), EGYPT (Br.), LIBYA (It.), TUNISIA (Fr.), ALGERIA (Fr.), FRENCH NORTH AFRICA, MOROCCO (Fr.), SP. MOROCCO, SPAIN, PORTUGAL, GREAT BRITAIN, IRELAND, N. IRELAND

Cyprus (Br.), Rhodes (It.), Crete (Gr.), Sicily, Sardinia, Corsica

Caspian Sea, Black Sea, Mediterranean Sea, Adriatic Sea, Baltic Sea, North Sea, Atlantic Ocean

Volga R., Don R., Danube R., Oder R., Elbe R., Rhine R.

Bessarabia, Bukovina, Ukraine

Tehran, Yalta, Alexandria, Tunis, Danzig, Warsaw, Potsdam, Berlin, Paris, London

June 1941, Aug. 1943, Mar. 1944, July 1944, Sept. 1944, Aug. 1944, June 1941, April 1941, Dec. 1944, April 1941, May 1941, July 1943, April 1940, May 1940, June 1940, Aug. 1944, Nov. 1942, Nov. 1942

◀ **MAP 27.5 World War II in Europe and Africa**
World War II inflicted massive loss of life and destruction of property on civilians, armies, and all the infrastructure—including factories, equipment, and agriculture—needed to wage total war. Thus, the war swept the European continent as well as areas in Africa colonized by or allied with the major powers. Ultimately the Allies crushed the Axis by moving from east, west, and south to inflict a total defeat.

under the command of U.S. General Dwight Eisenhower reached the heavily fortified French coastline of Normandy. The Nazis had been deceived into concentrating their forces to the north. After taking the beaches, Allied troops fought their way through the Norman hedgerows as the air force pummeled the German-held cities of western France. In late July, Allied forces broke through German defenses and a month later helped liberate Paris, where rebellion had erupted against the Nazis. As the liberating armies marched through French cities, officials gave them the illusion of being ethnically French by moving to the rear the tens of thousands of troops from the colonies who had contributed to victory. British, Canadian, U.S., and other Allied forces then fought their way eastward to join the Soviets in squeezing the Third Reich to its final defeat.

In July 1944, a group of German military officers, fearing their country's military humiliation, attempted to assassinate Hitler by exploding a bomb at a meeting. The Führer was only wounded, and the conspirators and many hundred others were cruelly tortured and then killed. Despite crushing military defeat, Hitler continued to preach German victory, maintaining that the Allies were merely "stumbling into their ruin." Driven mad by his hate-filled ideology, he believed that Germans were proving themselves unworthy of his greatness and deserved to perish in a cataclysmic conflagration. He thus refused all negotiations that might have spared Germans further death and destruction. The Soviet armies entered Poland, pausing only to allow the Germans to put down a spontaneous uprising of the Polish resistance in August 1944. (The elimination of the Polish resistance would give the Soviets a freer hand after the war.) Facing more than twice as many troops as on the western front, Stalin's forces met fierce German fighting in Hungary during the winter of 1944–1945. Hitler's refusal to surrender resulted in mas-

sive bombing of Germany. As the Soviet army took Berlin, Hitler committed suicide with his wife, Eva Braun. Their bodies were burned in the courtyard of the German chancellery. Although many soldiers remained committed to the Third Reich, Germany finally surrendered on May 8, 1945.

Japan Defeated. In keeping with their "Europe first" strategy, the Allies had sent most men and material to the European theater. Following the German surrender, they were able to focus solely on the Pacific war (Map 27.6). In 1940 and 1941, Japan had ousted the Europeans from many colonial holdings in Asia, but in May 1942, the U.S. forces stopped the Japanese in the battle of the Coral Sea. In battles at Midway Island and Guadalcanal later that year the Allies turned the tide, despite their diminished forces, by destroying some of Japan's formidable naval power. Unlike the United States, Japan lacked the capacity to recoup losses of ships or of manpower. The Allies stormed one Pacific island after another, gaining more bases from which to cut off the import of supplies and to launch bombers toward Japan itself. The Japanese ruled out surrender even after the fall of Saipan in 1944 delivered a blow to the military government. The Japanese instead resorted to *kamikaze* tactics, in which pilots deliberately crashed their planes into American ships, killing themselves in the process.

The United States stepped up its bombing raids on the Japanese mainland. In the spring of 1945, its firebombing of Tokyo killed more than 100,000 civilians. Meanwhile a U.S.-based international team of more than 100,000 scientists, technicians, and other workers engaged in the Manhattan Project, which succeeded in developing the atomic bomb. The still controversial decision to use atomic weapons was based on cruel experience: in battles at Iwo Jima and Okinawa, Japanese troops had fought fiercely, inflicting horrendous losses and dying almost to the man rather than surrender. This suicidal and destructive strategy caused Allied military leaders to calculate that defeating Japan might cost hundreds of thousands of Allied lives and take months, if not years. To avoid this unacceptable toll and, some argue, to stop the war in the East before the Soviet Union could take territory, the U.S. government unleashed atomic weapons on Japan's civilian population. On August 6 and 9, 1945, U.S. pilots dropped atomic bombs

MAP 27.6 World War II in the Pacific

As in Europe, the early days of World War II gave the advantage to the Axis power, Japan, as it took the offensive in conquering islands in the Pacific and territories in Asia—many of them colonies of European states. Britain countered by mobilizing a vast Indian army, while the United States, after the disastrous losses at Pearl Harbor and in the Philippines, gradually gained the upper hand by costly assaults, island by island. The Japanese strategy of fighting to the last person instead of surrendering when a loss was in sight was one factor in President Truman's decision to drop the atomic bomb in August 1945.

Hiroshima Victim

On August 6 and 9, 1945, the United States dropped the first atomic weapons on Hiroshima and Nagasaki, Japan, killing tens of thousands instantly and leaving tens of thousands more to die of their injuries and the aftereffects. A few days later Japan surrendered, but controversy has swirled around the decision to drop the bomb ever since. Some see it as a racist act, no atomic weapons having been dropped on Germany, while others see it as a justified act of warfare in a conflict that threatened to cost countless more casualties because of Japan's policy of no surrender.
Gamma Liaison.

on Hiroshima and Nagasaki, respectively, killing 140,000 people instantly, with tens of thousands more deaths from burns, wounds, and other afflictions in the days and weeks to come. Although hardliners in the Japanese military wanted to continue the war, on August 14, 1945, Japan surrendered.

❖ Toward a Postwar Settlement

The Great Depression had inflicted global suffering, while the Second World War left fifty to sixty million dead, an equal number of refugees without homes, and probably the most tragic moral legacy in human history. Envisioning a postwar political, social, and cultural settlement was thus top priority. Unlike World War I, however, there would be neither a celebrated peace conference nor a definitive, formal agreement among all the Allies about the final resolution of the war. In fact, the victorious Allies distrusted one another in varying degrees, with the United States and the Soviet Union on the brink of another debilitating and dangerous war.

Wartime Agreements about the Peace

The Grand Alliance was composed of nations with vastly different political and economic systems, and wartime agreements reflected continuing differences about the shape of postwar Europe. Entered into during a catastrophic war, many agreements would later be contested or arouse intense political debate. In 1941, on a warship off Newfoundland, Roosevelt and Churchill had forged the Atlantic Charter, which condemned aggression, reaffirmed the ideal of collective security, and endorsed the right of all people to choose their governments. Not only did the Allies come to focus on these points, but so did colonized peoples to whom, Churchill said, the charter was not meant to apply.

In the heat of war, the Allied leaders kept meeting, hammering out wartime as well as postwar agreements. In October 1944, Churchill went to the USSR to plan with Stalin the postwar distribution of territories. The Soviet Union would control Romania and Bulgaria, Britain would control Greece, and they would jointly oversee Hungary and Yugoslavia. These agreements went against Roosevelt's faith in collective security and seemed to threaten American commitments to self-determination and open doors in trade. In February 1945, the "Big Three"—as Roosevelt, Churchill, and Stalin were quickly labeled—met in the Crimean town of Yalta. Roosevelt advocated the institution of the United Nations to replace the League of Nations as a global peace mechanism. He also supported future Soviet influence in Korea,

IMPORTANT DATES

1929   The U.S. stock market crashes; global depression begins; Soviet leadership initiates war against prosperous farmers, the kulaks; Germany's Thomas Mann wins the Nobel Prize for literature

1933   Hitler comes to power in Germany

1936   Show trials begin in the USSR; Stalin purges top Communist Party officials and military leaders; the Spanish Civil War begins

1938   Virginia Woolf publishes *Three Guineas*

1939   Germany invades Poland; World War II begins; the Spanish Civil War ends

1940   France falls to the German army

1940–1941   The British air force fends off German attacks in the battle of Britain

1941   Germany invades the Soviet Union; Japan attacks Pearl Harbor; the United States enters the war

1941–1945   The Holocaust

1944   Allied forces land at Normandy, France

1945   The fall of Berlin; United States drops atomic bombs on Hiroshima and Nagasaki; World War II ends

Francis Bacon, *Three Studies for Figures at Base of Crucifixion* (c. 1944), center panel
At the end of the war, English artist Francis Bacon depicted the traditional Western subject of the crucifixion, but in a way that converted the individual person into a grotesque monster. His figures often reflect horror, disgust, and debasement and thus seem to describe the human condition at the end of World War II and the Holocaust.
Tate Gallery, London/Art Resource, NY.

Manchuria, and the Sakhalin and Kurile Islands in return for Stalin's pledge of help against future Japanese aggression. The last meeting of the Allied leaders took place at Potsdam, Germany, in the summer of 1945. By this time, President Harry S. Truman (1884–1972) had succeeded Roosevelt, who had died in April; Prime Minister Clement Attlee (1883–1967), whose Labour Party had just won the British elections, replaced Churchill. At Potsdam the leaders agreed to give the Soviets control of eastern Poland, to cede a large stretch of eastern Germany to Poland, and to adopt a temporary four-way occupation of Germany that included France as one of the supervising powers. Yet as victory unfolded, the Allies scrambled to outmaneuver one another. Making peace proved a prolonged and bitter process—and one that was hardly over in 1945.

Europe's Uncertain Future

Allied leaders had more than the boundaries of Europe to account for. European dominion was at an end. Forced into armies or into labor camps for war production, colonial peoples were in full rebellion or close to it. For a second time in three decades, colonial peoples had seen their masters killing one another, slaughtered by the very technology that was supposed to make European civilization superior. The Japanese also inspired rebellion by organizing governments in Asia run by anti-Western, indigenous leaders. Deference to Europe was virtually finished, with independence a matter of time.

Western values were imperiled as well. Not only were normal liberal politics at a standstill, if not in chaos, in 1944–1945, but the high European standard of living had been replaced by wartime deprivation, even starvation. Rational, Enlightenment, democratic Europe had succumbed to

Percent of population killed
- Over 10%
- 5–10%
- 1–5%
- Under 1%

- ■ Military dead
- ▲ Civilian dead
- ✳ City substantially damaged

FINLAND
■ 79,047

NORWAY
■ 4,780

SWEDEN

Leningrad

ESTONIA

LATVIA

LITHUANIA

Königsberg

IRELAND

GREAT
BRITAIN
■ 271,311
▲ 60,595

North
Sea

DENMARK
■ 4,339

USSR
■ 14,500,000
▲ Over 7,000,000

Coventry

London

NETH.
■ 13,700
▲ 236,300

Hamburg

Bremen

Hanover

Berlin

Warsaw

POLAND
■ 850,000
(169,822 as Allies)
▲ 5,778,000

Kiev

Rotterdam

Düsseldorf

Dortmund

BELG.
■ 9,561
▲ 75,000

Cologne

GERMANY
■ 2,850,000
▲ 2,300,000

Dresden

Caen

Frankfurt

Würzburg

CZECHOSLOVAKIA
■ 6,683
▲ 310,000

FRANCE
■ 210,671
▲ 173,260

SWITZ.

Munich

AUSTRIA
■ 380,000
▲ 145,000

HUNGARY
■ ▲ 750,000

ROMANIA
■ 519,822
▲ 465,000

Ploesti

Milan

Genoa

Bologna

YUGOSLAVIA
■ ▲ 1,700,000

Black Sea

SPAIN
■ 4,500 (For Axis)
7,500 (For Allies)
■ ▲ 10,000
(in concentration camps)

Corsica

ITALY
■ 279,820
▲ 17,400 (as Allies)

BULGARIA
■ 18,500
▲ 1,500

Sardinia

GREECE
■ 16,357
▲ 155,300

0   200   400 miles
0   200   400 kilometers

MAPPING THE WEST Europe at War's End, 1945

While all of Europe was severely shocked during the age of catastrophe, wartime damage left scars that would last for decades. Major German cities were bombed to bits, while the Soviet Union suffered an unimaginable toll of perhaps twenty-five million deaths due to the war alone. Everything from politics to family life needed rebuilding. The chaos fueled postwar tensions stemming both from the quest to punish those held responsible for such suffering and from the superpowers' determination to gain the political allegiance of recovering countries in the cold war.
From *The Hammond Atlas of the Twentieth Century* (London: Times Books, 1996), 102.

permanent wartime values, and it was this Europe that George Orwell captured in his novel *1984* (1949). Poor food and worn clothing, grimy streets and dwellings, people prematurely aged and care-worn—all characterized both London of the 1940s and Orwell's fictional state, Oceania. Like his hero

Winston Smith, Orwell worked for the wartime Ministry of Information (called the Ministry of Truth in the novel) and churned out doctored news for wartime audiences. Information and truth hardly mattered, in the language Orwell called "Newspeak," where old words were replaced by sanitized ones. As in Orwell's novel, words had taken on new meaning during the war: *disengagement* replaced *retreat, battle fatigue* substituted for *insanity*, and *liberating* a country could mean invading it and slaughtering its army and civilians.

Millions rejoiced at the demise of Nazi evil in 1945, but Orwell saw as part of war's legacy the deadening of creativity, the intrusion of big government into everyday life, and the replacement of democracy by the rule of bureaucratic managers. For Orwell, bureaucratic power depended on the perpetuation of conflict, and fresh conflict was indeed brewing in the race for Berlin and Japan even before the war ended. As Allied powers competed for territory, a new struggle called the *cold war* was taking root.

Conclusion

The Great Depression brought massive social dislocation and fear. It provided a setting in which dictators thrived because they promised to restore national greatness, bring economic prosperity, and destroy the people's enemies. Enticed by the mass media, people turned from representative institutions toward dynamic, if brutal, leaders. Memories of World War I permitted Hitler and Mussolini to menace Europe unimpeded throughout the 1930s. When a coalition formed to stop them, it was an uneasy one among the imperial powers France and Britain, the Stalinist Soviet Union, and the industrial giant the United States.

The costs of a bloody war—one waged against civilians as much as armies—taught these powers different lessons. The United States, Britain, and France were convinced that a minimum of citizen well-being was necessary to prevent a recurrence of fascism. Soviet citizens hoped that life would become easier and more open for them. The devastation of the USSR's population and resources, however, made Stalin increasingly obsessed with national security and reparations. Britain and France confronted the final eclipse of their imperial might, underscoring Orwell's insight that the war had transformed society irrevocably. Neither the murder of millions of Jews, Slavs, and others in death camps nor the militarization of society would ever disappear from the European legacy. The deliberate, technological murder of innocents like Etty

Hillesum was a permanent blight on the human record. Nonetheless, backed by vast arsenals of sophisticated weaponry, the competing visions of former Allies on how to deal with Germany and eastern Europe led them to threaten one another—and the world—with yet another war.

Suggested References

The Great Depression

Historians look to the depression as a complex event with economic, social, and cultural consequences, but in addition they see its impact as yet another indication of the tightening of global economic connections. To follow some of the political implications for European empires, see in particular Columbia University's South Asia Web site, which explores Gandhi's economic resistance to British colonialism.

Brown, Ian. *The Economies of Africa and Asia in the Interwar Depression.* 1989.

Evans, Richard J., and Dick Geary. *The German Unemployed: Experiences and Consequences of Mass Unemployment from the Weimar Republic to the Third Reich.* 1987.

James, Harold. *The German Slump: Politics and Economics, 1924–1936.* 1986.

Johnson, H. Clark. *Gold, France, and the Great Depression, 1919–1932.* 1997.

Roszkowski, Wojciech. *Landowners in Poland, 1918–1939.* 1991.

Rothermund, Dietmar. *The Global Impact of the Great Depression, 1929–1939.* 1996.

South Asia and Gandhi: **http://www.columbia.edu/cu/libraries/indiv/area/sarai.**

Totalitarian Triumph

The vicious dictators Stalin, Hitler, and Mussolini are among the most popular subjects for historians and readers alike. Recent historical works have moved beyond this fascination to study their mobilization of art and the media and to consider people's reactions to totalitarian regimes. Historians are especially intrigued with the mixture of modernism and traditionalism or even antimodernism in the dictators' programs and policies.

Ades, Dawn, et al. *Art and Power: Europe under the Dictators, 1930–1945.* 1995.

Berezin, Mabel. *Making the Fascist Self: The Political Culture of Interwar Italy.* 1997.

Engel, Barbara Alpern, and Anastasia Posadskaya-Vanderbeck, eds. *A Revolution of Their Own: Voices of Women in Soviet History.* 1998.

Fest, Joachim. *Hitler.* 1974.

Fitzpatrick, Sheila. *Stalin's Peasants*. 1994.

Fritzsche, Peter. *Germans into Nazis*. 1998.

Groys, Boris. *The Total Art of Stalinism: Avant-Garde, Aesthetic Dictatorship, and Beyond*. 1992.

Hildebrand, K. *The Third Reich*. 1984.

Kaplan, Marion. *Between Dignity and Despair: Jewish Life in Nazi Germany*. 1998.

Koonz, Claudia. *Mothers in the Fatherland: Women, the Family, and Nazi Politics*. 1987.

Kotkin, Stephen. *Magnetic Mountain: Stalinism as Civilization*. 1995.

Kuromiya, Hiroaki. *Stalin's Industrial Revolution: Politics and Workers, 1928–1932*. 1988.

Democracies on the Defensive

The democracies attacked the depression from a variety of perspectives ranging from state policy to film and the arts, yet another indication of how complex politics can be. Further departure from liberal policies, whether in trade or in the development of the activist welfare state, also have attracted historical study.

Kalvemark, Ann-Sofie. *More Children or Better Quality? Aspects of Swedish Population Policy*. 1980.

Kennedy, David M. *Freedom from Fear: The American People in Depression and War, 1929–1945*. 1999.

Lavin, Maud, et al. *Montage and Modern Life, 1919–1942*. 1992.

Rearick, Charles. *The French in Love and War: Popular Culture in the Era of the World Wars*. 1997.

Richards, Jeffrey, ed. *The Unknown 1930s: An Alternative History of the British Cinema, 1929–39*. 1998.

The Road to World War II

The road to war encircled the globe, involving countries seemingly peripheral to the struggles among the antagonists. The perennial question for many historians is whether Hitler could have been stopped, but with globalization there is new attention to the beginnings of war beyond the West as a prelude to decolonization.

Crozier, Andrew. *The Causes of the Second World War*. 1997.

Iriye, Akira. *The Origins of the Second World War in Asia and the Pacific*. 1987.

Knight, Patricia. *The Spanish Civil War*. 1991.

*Mangini González, Shirley. *Memories of Resistance: Women's Voices from the Spanish Civil War*. 1995.

Watt, D. Cameron. *How War Came: The Immediate Causes of the Second World War*. 1989.

World War II, 1939–1945

In a vast literature historians have charted the war's innumerable and global horrors, with issues of the Holocaust, industrial killing, and the nature of racial thinking drawing particular attention. The United States Memorial Holocaust Museum provides online exhibits giving the history of the Holocaust in different locations. While looking at the social aspects of war, historians have intently debated the development of the cold war within the "hot" war.

Browning, Christopher. *The Path to Genocide: Essays on Launching the Final Solution*. 1992.

*Dawidowicz, Lucy S. *A Holocaust Reader*. 1976.

Dower, John W. *War without Mercy: Race and Power in the Pacific War*. 1986.

Fussell, Paul. *Wartime: Understanding and Behavior in the Second World War*. 1989.

Goodwin, Doris Kearns. *No Ordinary Time: Franklin and Eleanor Roosevelt, the Home Front in World War II*. 1994.

Holocaust Museum: http://usholocaustmuseum.org.

Lewis, Peter. *A People's War*. 1986.

Ofer, Dalia, and Lenore J. Weitzman, eds. *Women in the Holocaust*. 1998.

Rhodes, Richard. *The Making of the Atomic Bomb*. 1986.

*Vassiltchikov, Marie. *Berlin Diaries, 1940–1945*. 1988.

Weinberg, Gerhard. *A World at Arms: A Global History of World War II*. 1994

---

*Primary sources.

The Atomic Age

c. 1945–1960

The Atomic Age

The atomic bombs dropped on Hiroshima and Nagasaki in 1945 were followed by several decades of increasingly powerful detonations for testing purposes. The Soviet Union practiced underground testing, while the United States carried out atmospheric tests in the Pacific region. Protests against testing developed in the 1950s, many of them citing the hazards of radioactivity and the growing threat of nuclear annihilation. Simultaneously, nuclear power was converted to peacetime use, notably serving both as a source of energy and as a therapy for cancer.
Mark Meyer/Liaison Agency.

I N LATE AUGUST 1949, THE SOVIET UNION DETONATED its first atomic bomb. Two days after President Harry S. Truman announced the news of this test, Billy Graham, a young Baptist minister, based his sermon at a revival meeting on the fearsome event. Graham warned that U.S. officials believed "we have only five to ten years and our civilization will be ended." He announced that Russia had aimed bombs to strike New York, Chicago, and Los Angeles, where the revival was taking place. "Time is desperately short . . . . Prepare to meet thy God," he warned. People flocked to hear Graham, launching the evangelist's astonishing career of spiritual and political influence in the United States and around the globe.

Graham's message—"We don't know how soon, but we do know this, that right now the grace of God can still save a poor lost sinner"—captured the extremes of postwar sentiment in an atomic age. On the one hand, the postwar situation was tragic. Fifty million people had died globally; Europe and Japan were prostrate and their peoples starving; evidence of genocide and other inhumanity was everywhere; the menace of nuclear annihilation loomed. It was to this menace that Graham referred. The old international order was gone, replaced by the rivalry of the United States and the Soviet Union for control of a devastated Europe, whose political and economic systems had collapsed. The nuclear arsenals of these two "superpowers"—a term coined in 1947—grew massively in the 1950s, but they were enemies who did not fight outright. Thus their terrifying rivalry was called the *cold war*.

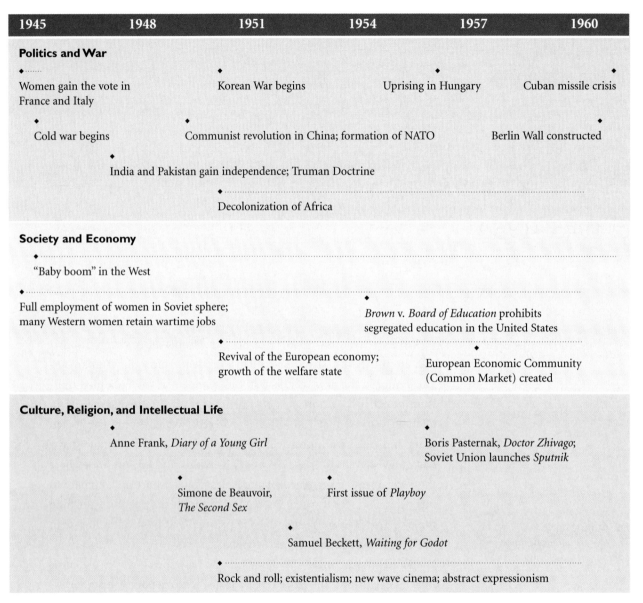

1945	1948	1951	1954	1957	1960

Politics and War

Women gain the vote in France and Italy

Korean War begins

Uprising in Hungary

Cuban missile crisis

Cold war begins

Communist revolution in China; formation of NATO

Berlin Wall constructed

India and Pakistan gain independence; Truman Doctrine

Decolonization of Africa

Society and Economy

"Baby boom" in the West

Full employment of women in Soviet sphere; many Western women retain wartime jobs

Brown v. *Board of Education* prohibits segregated education in the United States

Revival of the European economy; growth of the welfare state

European Economic Community (Common Market) created

Culture, Religion, and Intellectual Life

Anne Frank, *Diary of a Young Girl*

Boris Pasternak, *Doctor Zhivago*; Soviet Union launches *Sputnik*

Simone de Beauvoir, *The Second Sex*

First issue of *Playboy*

Samuel Beckett, *Waiting for Godot*

Rock and roll; existentialism; new wave cinema; abstract expressionism

The cold war divided the West politically, economically, and culturally, causing acute anxiety even for someone like Graham from the victorious and wealthy United States.

On the other hand, the defeat of Nazism inspired an upsurge of hope, a revival of religious feeling like Graham's, and a new commitment to humanitarian goals. Heroic effort had defeated fascism, and that defeat raised hopes that a new age would begin. Atomic science promised advances in medicine, and nuclear energy was trumpeted as a replacement for coal and oil. The creation of the United Nations heralded an era of international cooperation. Around the globe, colonial peoples won independence from European masters, while in the United States the civil rights movement gained new momentum. The welfare state expanded, and by the end of the 1950s economic rebirth, stimulated in part by the cold war, had made much of Europe more prosperous than ever before. An "economic miracle" had occurred.

Extremes of hope and fear infused the atomic age, as society, culture, and the international order were transformed. Gone was the definition of a West comprising Europe and its cultural offshoots such as the United States and an East comprising

Asian countries like India, China, and Japan. During the cold war, *West* came to stand for the United States and its client countries in western Europe, while *East* meant the Soviet Union and its tightly controlled bloc in eastern Europe. Still another terminology arose in the 1950s. The *first world* was the capitalist bloc of countries; the *second world*, the socialist bloc; and the *third world*, the countries emerging from imperial domination. As the world's people redefined themselves politically and culturally, they did so in an atmosphere of immense progress and equally immense peril. By the early 1960s, an array of new nations had arisen in Africa and Asia, and population growth soared. However, simultaneously millions were dying in wars of liberation, while the superpowers took the world to the brink of nuclear disaster when the United States discovered Soviet missile sites on its doorstep—ninety miles from Florida, on the island of Cuba. From the dropping of the atomic bomb on Japan in 1945 to the Cuban missile crisis of 1962, Graham's dread that "we are moving madly toward destruction" gripped much of the world.

❖ World Politics Transformed

The turmoil of wartime and the postwar years ended the global leadership of Europe. Many countries lay in ruins by the summer of 1945, and conditions would deteriorate before they got better. Bombed and bankrupt, victorious Britain could not feed its people. In contrast, the United States, whose territory was virtually untouched in the war, emerged as the world's sole economic giant, and the Soviet Union, despite suffering immense destruction, retained formidable military might. These two nations drew the entire world into a diplomatic battle of nerves that became known as the cold war. Having occupied Europe as part of the victorious alliance against Nazism and fascism, the two superpowers next used Germany—at the heart of the continent and its politics—to divide Europe in two. By the late 1940s, the USSR imposed Communist rule throughout most of eastern Europe and in the 1950s quashed rebellions against its dominance. Western Europeans found themselves at least partially constricted by the very U.S. economic power that helped them rebuild, as the United States maintained air bases and nuclear weapon sites across western Europe. The age of bipolar world politics had begun, with Europe as its testing ground.

Europe Prostrate

In contrast to World War I when devastation was limited to the front lines around the trenches, armies in World War II had fought a war of movement that leveled thousands of square miles of territory. Across the continent, whole cities were clogged with rubble; homeless survivors wandered the streets. In Sicily and on the Rhine River, almost no bridge remained standing; in France, motorized vehicles lacked the necessary parts to operate. In the Soviet Union, seventy thousand villages and more than a thousand cities lay in shambles.

Everywhere people were suffering. In the Netherlands, where both the Nazi occupation and the struggle for liberation had been unusually severe, the Dutch faced imminent death until a U.S. airlift of food provided some relief. In Britain, soap and other basic commodities were difficult to obtain, and many died in the bitterly cold winter of 1946–1947 because of a shortage of fuel. Italian bakers sold bread by the slice. When Allied troops passed through German towns, the famished inhabitants lined the roads in hopes that someone would toss them something to eat. "To see the children fighting for food," one British soldier noted, "was like watching animals being fed in a zoo." As Allied troops settled in to occupy the devastated continent, there were no uprisings as after World War I. Until the late 1940s, people were exhausted by the struggle for bare survival.

The tens of millions of refugees suffered the most. Many had been inmates of prisons and death camps; others, especially ethnic Germans, had fled westward to escape the victorious but destructive Red Army as it pushed toward Berlin. Native Germans in the Western-occupied zones viewed refugees as competitors for food and work. "Unwanted, even hated," they were treated "like dirt," one journalist on the scene reported. Many refugees ultimately found homes in countries that experienced little or no war damage, such as Denmark, Sweden, Canada, and Australia. Following the exodus of refugees from the east, western Europe became one of the world's most densely populated regions (Map 28.1).

Lost by Germany to Poland, 1945
Territory gained by Soviet Union
Allied occupation of Germany and Austria, 1945–55
Lost by Italy to Yugoslavia, 1945
Lost by Romania to Bulgaria, 1940–47

Zones of occupation
American
British
French
Soviet
Jointly occupied cities

Refugee movements and repatriated armed forces
Germans
Finns
Baltic peoples
Russians
Poles
Czechs
People settled by the International Refugee Organization

◀ **MAP 28.1 The Impact of World War II on Europe**
European governments, many of them struggling to provide food and other necessities for their populations, found themselves responsible for hundreds of thousands, if not millions, of new refugees. Simultaneously, millions of prisoners of war, servicemen, and slave laborers were returned to the Soviet Union, many of them by force. This situation unfolded amidst political instability and even violence.

The USSR drove many people from eastern Europe, yet it lobbied hard for the repatriation of several million Soviet prisoners of war and forced laborers. This was the first signal of Stalin's determination to revive Communist orthodoxy, which had weakened during the war. The Allies transported the majority of the Russian refugees back to the Soviet Union, where exile or execution for being "contaminated" by Western ideas awaited. As stories of executions filtered out, the Allies slowed the process, leaving hundreds of thousands of Soviet prisoners of war and former slave laborers to join the ocean of refugees in western Europe.

Survivors of the concentration camps also discovered that their suffering had not ended with Germany's defeat. In *The War* (1986), French author Marguerite Duras, drawing on her diary, described the returnees' arrival at Paris train stations: skeletal, diseased, and disoriented. Many surviving Jews often had no home to return to, as property had been confiscated and entire communities destroyed. Moreover, anti-Semitism had become official policy under the Nazis. In the summer of 1946, a vicious crowd in Kielce, Poland, rioted against returning Jewish survivors, killing at least 40 of the 250. Elsewhere in eastern Europe, such violence was common. Some Jewish survivors were not released from death camps for more than a year after the liberation because no one knew what to do with them. Meanwhile some officials across Europe even denied that unprecedented atrocities had been committed and wanted to refuse Jews any help.

Jews sought safety in various places. Some hoped to settle in the United States, but the federal government, fearing anti-Semitic backlash, let only about 12,000 Jews into the country. Many survivors crammed into the port cities of Italy and other Mediterranean countries, eventually to escape Europe for Palestine, where Zionists had been settling for half a century. As they had in the 1930s, the British balked at this vast migration to the Middle East, for they saw their interests threatened by likely Arab-Jewish conflict over control of the region. Unwilling or unable to help Hitler's most abused victims, many European countries had simply lost the capacity for moral and economic leadership.

New Superpowers: The United States and the Soviet Union

Only two powerful countries were left in 1945: the United States and the Soviet Union. The United States was now the richest country in the world. Its industrial output had increased a remarkable 15 percent annually between 1940 and 1944, a rate of growth that was reflected in workers' wages. By 1947, the United States controlled almost two-thirds of the world's gold bullion and more than half of its commercial shipping, up from almost one-fifth of the total in the 1930s. (Other countries had also profited from the war: Norwegian electrical output and Swedish exports to Nazi Germany were vast. India, Egypt, and Australia had made so much money supplying British war needs that they were able to buy out many British firms.) Continuing to spend heavily on industrial and military research, the United States enhanced its postwar economic position still more.

A confident mood swept the United States at the end of the war. Although some feared a postwar depression and many shared Billy Graham's worries about nuclear annihilation, a wave of suburban housing development and consumer spending kept the economy buoyant. Temporarily reversing the trend toward a lower birthrate, a "baby boom" exploded from the late 1940s through the early 1960s as couples responded to the economic abundance by having more children.

Casting aside the post–World War I policy of nonintervention, Americans embraced their position as global leaders. Many had learned about the world while tracking the war's progress; hundreds of thousands of soldiers, government officials, and relief workers had direct experience of Europe, Africa, and Asia. Leaders in the United States expressed trust in their ability to guide the rest of the world. "America must be the elder brother of nations in the brotherhood of man," *Life* magazine advised.

The Soviets also emerged from the war with a well-justified sense of accomplishment. Withstanding horrendous losses, they had resisted the most massive onslaught ever launched against a modern nation and thus earned an important position in world affairs. Instead of the international isolation dealt Russia after World War I, Soviet leadership expected equality in decision making with the United States, and indeed many Europeans and Americans had great respect for the Soviet contribution to Hitler's defeat. Ordinary Soviet citizens believed that a victory that had cost the USSR as many as 25 million lives would bring some improvement in the everyday conditions and a continuation of the war's relatively relaxed politics. "Life will become pleasant," one writer prophesied. "There will be much coming and going, and a lot of contacts with the West." Others foresaw the opening of private shops and restaurants as well as the distribution of plots of land to individual farmers. The Stalinist goals of industrialization and defense against Nazism had been won, and thus many Soviets expected an end to decades of hardship.

Stalin took a different view and chose to increase repression to bring about recovery. Mobilization for total war had encouraged individual responsibility while relaxing "Communist" oversight, and Stalin moved ruthlessly to reassert control. In 1946, his new five-year plan set increased production goals and mandated more stringent collectivization of agriculture. Although industrial production had doubled by 1950, per capita gross national product was still less than one-third that of the United States. Stalin cut back the army by two-thirds to beef up the labor force and also turned his attention to the low birthrate, a result of wartime male casualties and women's long, arduous working days, which discouraged them from adding child care to their already heavy responsibilities. He introduced an intense propaganda campaign emphasizing that workingwomen should hold down jobs and also fulfill their "true nature" by producing many children.

Origins of the Cold War

In the immediate postwar years, the United States and the Soviet Union engaged in a cold war that would afflict the world for more than four decades. How did these two titans, allies in the most colossal military victory of all times, turn against each other so quickly? Because no peace treaty officially ended the conflict with Germany as a written record of contest and compromise or of things gone wrong (as in the Peace of Paris), the origins of the cold war remain a matter of debate. Historians point to consistent U.S., British, and French hostility that began with the Bolshevik Revolution and continued through the war. Others point to Stalin's aggressive policies, notably the Nazi-Soviet alliance in 1939 and his quick claims on the Baltic states and Polish territory when World War II broke out. Although controversy continues, scholars today fault both sides. (See "New Sources, New Perspectives," page 1076.)

United States–Soviet Union Mistrust. Agreements during the war that held the Grand Alliance together were never reached easily, and Stalin felt that Churchill and Roosevelt were deliberately letting the USSR bear the brunt of Hitler's onslaught on the continent as part of their anti-Communist policy. Some Americans believed that dropping the atomic bomb on Japan would serve as a warning to Stalin not to try more land grabs. At war's end Stalin continued to see a world hostile to Soviet security, and indeed the new U.S. president, Harry Truman, was far more prepared than Roosevelt to refuse anything the Soviets wanted or needed. Given what Stalin interpreted as a menace from the West and his own country's exhausted condition, he saw the USSR as needing not just a temporary military occupation but a permanent "buffer zone" of European states loyal to the USSR as a safeguard. Across the Atlantic, Truman saw the initial Soviet occupation of eastern Europe as heralding an era of Communist expansion. By 1946, members of the U.S. State Department were describing Stalin as the final "neurotic" Asian ruler prepared to continue the centuries-old Russian thirst for "world domination."

The cold war thus became a series of moves and countermoves in an atmosphere of mutual suspicion that had deep roots. In retrospect it is hardly surprising that animosity developed, because the shared occupation of so rich an area as Europe by two such different countries as the United States and the Soviet Union was unprecedented. There were simply no rules, although some historians see the contest as in fact a case of traditional European or "Western" national rivalries. In line with its geopolitical needs, the USSR proceeded to repress democratic government in central and eastern Europe between 1945 and 1948. Coalition or popular-front type government, which included liberals, socialists, Communists, and peasant party leaders, at first predominated in Hungary, Poland, and Czechoslovakia. However, Stalin imposed Communist rule almost immediately in Bulgaria and Romania. In Romania, he cited citizen violence in 1945 as the excuse to demand an ouster of all non-Communists from the civil service and cabinet. When the Allies protested, a single member of the Peasant Party and another from the Liberal Party were allowed to join eighteen Communists in the government. In response to these events, party membership in Romania soared from 2,000 in 1945 to more than 800,000 a year later. In Poland the Communists fixed the election results of 1945 and 1946 to create the illusion of approval for communism. Nevertheless, the Communists had to share power between 1945 and 1947 with the popular Peasant Party of Stanisław Mikołajczyk, which had a large constituency of rural workers and peasant landowners.

Truman Doctrine and Marshall Plan.   The United States acknowledged Soviet influence in areas it occupied, but western European leaders worried that Communist power would spread even farther. The difficult conditions of postwar life made Communist programs promising better conditions and the confiscation of fascist property increasingly attractive to western European workers, while Communist leadership in the resistance gave the party a powerful allure. U.S. and British concern mounted when Communist insurgents threatened to overrun the right-wing monarchy the British had installed in Greece in 1944. The British propped up this repressive government until the terrible winter of 1946–1947 made it financially impossible for them to keep sending aid. Britain could no longer sustain its own people, let alone an unpopular foreign regime. U.S. leaders feared that Europe was on the brink of "going Communist."

The United States now put its new interventionist spirit to work. In March 1947, Truman reacted to the Communist threat by announcing what quickly became known as the *Truman Doctrine*, the countering of political crises with economic and military aid. The president requested $400 million in military aid for Greece and Turkey, where the Communists were also pressuring. Fearing that

The Cold War

1945–1949   USSR establishes satellite states in eastern Europe

1947   Truman Doctrine announces American commitment to contain communism; U.S. Marshall Plan provides massive aid to rebuild Europe

1948–1949   Soviet troops blockade Berlin; United States airlifts provisions to Berliners

1949   Western democracies form North Atlantic Treaty Organization (NATO); Soviet bloc establishes Council for Mutual Economic Assistance (COMECON); USSR tests its first nuclear weapon

1950–1953   Korean War

1950–1954   U.S. senator Joseph McCarthy leads hunt for American Communists

1953   Stalin dies

1955   USSR and Eastern bloc countries form military alliance, the Warsaw Pact

1956   Khrushchev denounces Stalin in "secret speech" to Communist Party Congress; Hungarians revolt unsuccessfully against Soviet domination

1959   Fidel Castro comes to power in Cuba

1961   Berlin Wall erected

1962   Cuban missile crisis

Americans would balk at backing Greece, U.S. congressmen would agree to the program only if Truman would "scare hell out of the country," as one put it. Truman thus publicized the aid program as necessary to fortify the world against a tide of global Soviet conquest. In the fall of 1948, the United States supplied the Greek government with 10,000 transport vehicles, close to 100,000 rifles, and 140 planes. The show of American support convinced the Communists to back off, and in 1949 the Greek rebels declared a cease-fire.

"The seeds of totalitarian regimes are nurtured by misery and want," the president warned in the same speech that introduced the Truman Doctrine. His linkage of poverty to the rise of dictatorship led to the *Marshall Plan*, a program of massive U.S. economic aid to Europe. Secretary of State George C. Marshall announced the plan in a Harvard commencement address in June 1947. He cited the deterioration of economic exchange during the war as a threat to political stability. By the early 1950s,

Government Archives and the Truth about the Cold War

The cold war involved a veritable battle of words over history. The United States alleged that Stalin was a monster perpetrating massacres even greater than those of Hitler and that the Soviet Union aimed for world domination. The Soviet Union claimed that the United States dropped the atomic bomb on Japan out of racist contempt for people of color and in preparation for a nuclear destruction of the Soviet Union and its allies. In those days, truth in history seemed to depend on whose side one favored or whose propaganda was most effective.

Government archives have enlightened some of these cold war accusations. As the modern nation-state grew in the nineteenth century, historians came increasingly to rely on official government archives to answer questions arising from such contests of words. Participants and eyewitnesses, it was believed, were not reliable because of their bias. Instead, trained scholars, ridding themselves of bias, would carefully examine government records, preserved in official repositories where tampering could not take place.

The opening of USSR archives in the late 1980s and 1990s after the fall of Soviet communism gave answers to many cold war questions. In 1956, in the midst of superpower rivalry, Nikita Khrushchev first threw official light on the slaughter connected with Stalin's regime. In his partial revelation of truths, Lenin and Stalin were seen as distinctly different political beings, with Lenin an ideologue and benefactor and Stalin a creature of excess. The Soviet archives, however, revealed a more vicious Lenin, one who demanded from the start of the Bolshevik regime the kind of brutality that Khrushchev had pinned on Stalin alone. Lenin and his contemporaries started the reliance on wholesale massacre of the upper classes, peasants, dissenters, and even ordinary citizens. At the same time, the archives discredited the U.S. claim that the Soviet Union in the 1950s was out to conquer the world. Instead, scholars found both Stalin and Khrushchev fearful of a U.S. nuclear attack and eager to come to terms. Their bluster and brinkmanship, the archives showed, often arose from a need to appear dominant to Soviet satellite states and to the new challenger for Communist leadership—the People's Republic of China.

Much official U.S. archival material still remains closed to scholars, but the Freedom of Information Act (1966, amended 1974) allows historians to press for access and at times to obtain it. Official U.S. documents have opened up debate about the dropping of the atomic bomb, with some scholars concluding that it was not merely a matter of ending the war with Japan in the most expeditious way. Instead, brandishing atomic weapons served U.S. cold war ends. Tapes released from the Kennedy administration have shown the president differing from his generals, most of whom wanted a nuclear war during the Cuban missile crisis. Kennedy, far from being the consistent cold warrior he sought to portray, pulled back from the brink.

For all that new archival evidence can reveal, reliance on this material has many pitfalls. One train of thought leads to the belief that if an archive contains no written evidence of an event, the event is open to question. For instance, if there is no written order from Hitler to start the Holocaust, some have argued, it means that he did not know about the event or even that it did not occur. Second, faith in archives also makes them susceptible to forgeries and the planting of

the United States had sent Europe more than $12 billion in food, equipment, and services.

The Marshall Plan claimed that it was not directed "against any country or doctrine but against hunger, poverty, desperation, and chaos." Stalin, however, saw it as a U.S. political ploy that caught him without similar economic aid to offer to his client countries in eastern Europe. The Soviet Union reacted by suppressing the remaining coalition governments and assuming political control in central and eastern Europe. In Poland, where the government found the possibility of Marshall Plan

Russian Secret Archives
The opening of archives across the former Soviet bloc had many consequences. In the former East Germany, for instance, names of secret police informers were made public and many people had their reputations utterly tarnished for their collaboration with the Communist government. The opening of the archives also exposed the cases of those convicted with trumped up evidence (some pictured here), most of them sent to camps and to their deaths long since. The probable existence of such secret archives and concealed official information around the world has made historians and the families of victims fight for access. ITAR-TASS/Sovfoto.

evidence. In a case of a former Soviet operative, Vasili Mitrokhin, who smuggled tens of thousands of hand-copied documents from Russia in the 1990s, questions arise as to how someone with a fairly low security clearance could have the prolonged access to top Soviet secrets that would enable him to do such extensive copying. Are these documents a plant of the Soviet secret police to show its virtuosity in global espionage?

Finally, excessive faith in archival documents, some critics say, skews history by suggesting that the most important kind of history comes from official government sources. These critics point out that important historical evidence lies as well in sources ranging from newspapers, family account books, diaries, and personal letters to novels, paintings, and architecture. The choice depends on the kind of history one believes most representative and influential.

QUESTIONS FOR DEBATE

1. Are archives overseen by government officials more or less likely to be biased than other sources? How can we know the extent to which they are telling the truth?

2. Make a list of the most reliable sources for discovering historical truth and provide reasons for your ranking these sources as reliable.

FURTHER READING

Christopher Andrew and Vasili Mitrokhin, *The Mitrokhin Archive: The KGB in Europe and the West.* 1999.

Stephane Courtois et al., *The Black Book of Communism: Crimes, Terror, Repression,* trans. Johnathan Murphy and Mark Kramer. 1999.

Vladislav Zubok and Constantine Pleshakov, *Inside the Kremlin's Cold War: From Stalin to Khrushchev.* 1996.

aid attractive, Stalin purged Mikołajczyk in 1947 in the name of creating a "people's government"—the code name for a Communist-controlled state. In Hungary, the prime minister and head of the popular Small-Holders Party was forced out while on a trip to Switzerland in 1947. Czechoslovakia, which by eastern European standards had prospered under a Communist-led coalition, welcomed the Marshall Plan as the beginning of East-West rapprochement. This illusion ended, however, during a purge of non-Communist officials that began in the autumn of 1947. By June 1948, the socialist president, Edouard

Beneš, had resigned and been replaced by a Communist figurehead. Nonetheless, the populace remained so passive that Communist leaders called the takeover "like cutting butter with a knife." The Soviet Union had successfully created a buffer of satellite states in eastern Europe directed by "people's governments." Stalin capped his victory by organizing the Cominform, a centralized association of Communist parties around the world under Moscow's direction.

The only exception to the Soviet sweep in eastern Europe came in Yugoslavia, under the Communist ruler Tito (Josip Broz, 1892–1980). During the war, Tito led the powerful anti-Nazi Yugoslav "partisans." After the war, he drew on support from Serbs, Croats, and Muslims to mount a Communist, but not a Soviet, revolution. Eager for Yugoslavia to develop industrially rather than simply serve Soviet needs, he remarked: "No matter how much each of us loves the land of Socialism, the USSR, he can, in no case love his country less. . . . We study and take as an example the Soviet system, but we are developing socialism in our country in somewhat different forms." Furious, Stalin ejected Yugoslavia from the Cominform. To Stalin, commitment to communism meant obedience to him.

Yugoslavia after the Revolution

Yugoslavia emerged from its Communist revolution as a federation of six republics and two independent provinces within Serbia. This settlement recognized the country's cultural diversity but was also based on the belief that only tough measures would quell ethnic and religious animosities. Tito's forceful personality held these groups together until his death in 1980; his strong organization also enabled Yugoslavia to hold the Soviets at bay.

The Division of Germany

The cold war became most menacing in the superpowers' struggle for control of Germany. The terms of the agreements reached at Yalta provided for Germany's occupation by troops divided among four zones, each of which was controlled by one of the four principal victors in World War II—the United States, the Soviet Union, Britain, and France. As the Soviet Union and the United States took firm stands over the future of this once rich and still potentially powerful country, at issue was the heart of the European continent.

The sides disagreed on fundamental matters in German history. Many in the United States had come to believe that there was something inherently wrong with the character of Germans, who had provoked two world wars and the Holocaust. At the height of the war, Roosevelt had often spoken of using desperate means to end their apparent militaristic tendencies. After the war, the U.S. occupation forces undertook a reprogramming of German cultural attitudes by controlling the press and censoring the content of all media in the U.S. zone to ensure that they did not express fascist or authoritarian values. Stalin took a different tack in the Soviet-occupied zone to suppress what he perceived as the "evils" of German society. He believed that Nazism was merely another form of advanced capitalism and he therefore confiscated and redistributed the estates of wealthy Germans.

A second disagreement arose over the use of Germany's economic potential. American leaders hoped for an economic coordination among the zones to benefit the occupying countries and to support Germany itself. According to their plan, surplus produce from the Soviet-occupied areas would feed urban populations in the western zones; in turn, industrial goods would be sent to the USSR. The Soviets upset this plan. The Grand Alliance had agreed that the USSR deserved reparations from German resources, so the Soviets immediately dismantled industries and sent machinery, vehicles, and other equipment to the Soviet Union. They transported skilled workers, engineers, and scientists to the USSR to work as virtual slave laborers. The Soviets also manipulated the currency in their zone, enabling the USSR to buy German goods at unrealistic prices.

Amidst these growing cold war tensions, the three Western Allies agreed to merge their zones into a West German state. Instead of continuing to curtail German power as wartime agreements called for, the United States embarked on an economic buildup under the Marshall Plan to make the western zone a buffer against the Soviets. By 1948, notions of a permanently weakened

Germany came to an end. To achieve the new government the United States enlisted many former Nazi officials as spies and rechanneled the hatred of Bolshevism that had been a keystone of Nazism into serving the cold war.

Stalin struck back at the Marshall Plan on July 24, 1948, when Soviet troops blockaded Germany's capital, Berlin. Like Germany as a whole, the city had been divided into four occupation zones, even though it was located more than one hundred miles deep into the Soviet zone and was thus cut off from Western territory. The Soviets declared that Berlin was now part of their zone of occupation and refused to allow vehicles to travel through the entire Soviet zone, including Berlin. They expected the West to capitulate to the new situation, as it had done elsewhere in eastern Europe.

Instead, the United States responded decisively, flying in millions of tons of provisions to the stricken city. During the winter of 1948–1949, the Berlin airlift—Operation Vittles, as U.S. pilots

called it—even funneled coal to the city to warm some two million isolated Berliners (Map 28.2). Reports of people's sufferings, of pilots' valiant deeds, and of Soviet belligerence transformed the cold war in the popular imagination, as many Westerners increasingly came to see the conflict as a moral crusade. By the time the Soviets ended the blockade on May 12, 1949, a divided Berlin had become the symbol of the cold war. By then, the reorganization of international politics after the collapse of Europe had become clear: over the security of an eastern European bloc of satellite states the Soviet Union would risk war, and the United States would do no less on behalf of a western Europe that ended at Berlin.

The logical consequence of the division of Germany and this new bipolarity was the formation of competing military alliances (Map 28.3). The United States, Canada, and their European allies formed the North Atlantic Treaty Organization, or NATO, in 1949. NATO provided a unified

MAP 28.2 Divided Germany and the Berlin Airlift, 1946–1949
Berlin, controlled by the United States, Great Britain, France, and the Soviet Union, was deep in the Soviet zone of occupation and became a major point of contention among the former allies. When the USSR blockaded the western half of the city, the U.S. responded with a massive airlift. To stop movement between the two zones, the USSR built a wall in 1961 and used troops to patrol it.

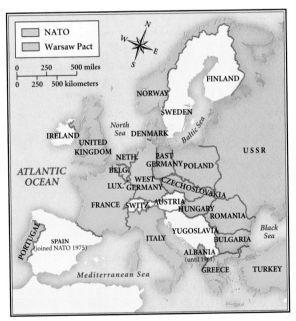

MAP 28.3 European NATO Members and the Warsaw Pact in the 1950s
The two superpowers intensified their rivalry by creating large military alliances: NATO, formed in 1949, and the Warsaw Pact, formed in 1955 after NATO invited West German membership. International politics revolved around these two alliances, which faced off in the heart of Europe. War games for the two sides often assumed a massive war concentrated in central Europe over control of Germany.

military force for the member countries, which also included Britain, France, Belgium, the Netherlands, Luxembourg, Italy, Denmark, Portugal, Iceland, and Norway. In 1955, after the United States forced France and Britain to invite West Germany to join NATO, the Soviet Union retaliated by establishing the military organization commonly called the Warsaw Pact, which included Albania, Bulgaria, Czechoslovakia, East Germany, Hungary, Poland, and Romania. These two massive regional alliances formed the military muscle for the new cold war politics. Replacing the individual might of the great European powers, the strength of each was seen to determine the fate of the world in the atomic age.

❖ The Political and Economic Recovery of Europe

The ideological clash between East and West served as a background to a remarkable economic and political recovery that took place between 1945 and 1960. The first order of business on the political front was a highly charged eradication of the Nazi past and an attempt to deal with its memories. western Europe revived its democratic political structures, its individualistic culture, and its productive capabilities. Eastern Europe restlessly endured a far less prosperous and far more repressive existence under Stalinism, although even these conditions of everyday life had improved as peasant societies were forced to modernize. By 1960, people across the continent had escaped the poverty of the depression, and Europeans had left behind wartime deprivation to enjoy a higher standard of living—an "economic miracle" it was even called—than ever before in human history. In both western and eastern Europe, the state took increasing responsibility for the health and well-being of citizens. The atomic age also became the age of the welfare state.

Dealing with the Nazi Past

In May 1945, Europeans lived under a complex system of political jurisdiction: local resistance leaders, Allied armies of occupation, international relief workers, and the remnants of bureaucracies often worked at odds to restore society. Amidst

confusion, starvation, and a thriving black market was an array of goals. While bureaucrats made feeding civilians a priority, international agencies dealt with the tens of millions of refugees. Resistance fighters' immediate purpose was to set up new governments, take over the collaborationist media, and purge Nazis, often by violent means. Occupying armies that covered much of the continent were often a law unto themselves: the Soviets were especially feared for inflicting rape and robbery. Distributing food and clothing, other armed forces tried to instill order.

The desire for revenge against Nazis hardened with the discovery of the death camps' skeletal survivors and the remains of the millions murdered in the camps as the Soviet army approached. Swift vigilante justice by civilians released pent-up rage and aimed to punish collaborators and fascist sympathizers for their complicity in the Holocaust and other occupation crimes. Villagers often shaved the heads of women suspected of associating with Germans and made them parade naked through the local streets. Members of the resistance did not wait for courtroom justice but executed tens of thousands of Nazi officers and collaborators on the spot. In this atmosphere of revenge and purge, crowds of men descended on village and town halls to get certification that they had been in the resistance. The celebration of resistance heroes—some of them self-proclaimed—and the purge of evildoers became the founding acts of a reborn European political community.

Government officials with clean records and Allied representatives undertook a more systematic "denazification." Investigators in Belgium identified 700,000 people suspected of collaboration out of a total population of 8 million. These investigations often showed how hard it was to draw a line between acts of collaboration with totalitarianism and cooptation in the name of survival. At a different level, the trials conducted at Nuremberg, Germany, by the victorious Allies in the fall of 1945 used the Nazis' own documents to provide a horrifying panorama of crimes by Nazi leaders. Each country contributed its most esteemed legal experts for these unusual trials, which underscored principles of justice and public accountability for crimes even in wartime. Although international law lacked a precedent for defining genocide as a crime, the judges at Nuremberg found sufficient

The Punishment of Collaborators
Women who had romantic involvements with Germans were called "horizontal" collaborators to
suggest that they were traitorous prostitutes. With heads shaved and often stripped of their clothing,
they were forced to parade through cities and towns enduring verbal and other abuse. The public
shaming of these women, a vivid part of the memory of the war, served as the background for the
film Hiroshima Mon Amour, *which gripped audiences late in the 1950s.*
Robert Capra/Magnum Photos Inc.

cause to sentence half of the twenty-four defendants to death, among them Hitler's closest associates such as Hermann Goering, and the remainder to prison terms. The Nuremberg trials introduced the notions, which have persisted to the present, of prosecution for crimes against humanity and an international politics based on demands for human rights.

After Nuremberg, Allied prosecution of Nazi and fascist leadership continued, but that huge task never succeeded completely. Some of the leaders most responsible for war crimes disappeared. Patriotic Germans, many of whom were brutalized by invading armies, were skeptical about denazification even as they were forced to march through concentration camps to acknowledge the inhumanity of Nazism. As women in Germany endured starvation and savage rape and additionally performed the arduous labor of clearing rubble, the belief took hold that Germans were the main victims of the war. German civilians also interpreted

the trials of Nazis as the characteristic retribution of victors rather than the well-deserved punishment of the guilty. Allied officials themselves, eager to restore government services, often relied on the expertise of high-ranking fascists and Nazis. Scientists of any political hue were welcomed in the United States to advance military capability, while many Nazi bureaucrats kept their jobs in the new West Germany to help the West wage the cold war more effectively. The Nazi past haunts European debates, cultural life, and politics to this day, yet political expediency led Westerners at the time to forgive some Nazis quite easily.

Rebirth of the West

Against all political and economic odds, western Europe revived. Reform-minded civilian governments reflected the coalitions that had opposed the Axis. They conspicuously emphasized democracy to show their rejection of the totalitarian

Women Clearing Berlin
The amount of destruction caused by World War II was staggering, requiring the mobilization of the civilian population in Berlin, where women were conscripted to sort the rubble and clear it away. Scenes like this were ultimately used as propaganda in the cold war to make it seem as if the Germans were the victims rather than the perpetrators of the war. Such depictions also made the Germans appear weak and helpless before a threatened menace, as in the photos of weak and ravaged Belgian women in World War I propaganda.
AKG Photo, London.

regimes that had earlier attracted so many Europeans—with such dire consequences. Rebuilding devastated towns and cities spurred industrial recovery, while bold projects for economic cooperation like the European Common Market and the conversion of wartime technological know-how to peacetime use produced a brisk trade in consumer goods and services in western Europe by the late 1950s.

The Challenge of Postwar Politics. Resistance leaders had the first claim on office in postfascist western Europe. In France the leader of the Free French, General Charles de Gaulle, governed briefly as chief of state; he quit over limitations on the president's power that were reminiscent of the Third Republic. The French approved a constitu-

tion in 1946 that established the Fourth Republic and finally granted the vote to French women. Meanwhile, Italy replaced its constitutional monarchy with a full parliamentary system that also allowed women the vote for the first time. As in France, a resistance-based socialist government initially governed. Then late in 1945 this was replaced by the conservative leadership of the Christian Democrats, who headed a coalition including Communists and socialists. Christian Democrats, who had a strong presence in postwar politics across western Europe, descended from the traditional Catholic centrist parties of the prewar period. They adopted this name to gain wider support that would include Protestants and workers and allow them to pursue liberal economic programs and democratic reform.

Tentative Steps toward Democracy. It was the Communist Party, however, that seemed to attract the most vocal loyalty of a consistently large segment of the western European population. Symbol of the common man, the ordinary Soviet soldier was a hero to many western Europeans outside occupied Germany, as were the resistance leaders — most of them Communist until late in the war when the impending Nazi collapse lured mainline politicians to join the anti-Nazi bandwagon. People still remembered the common man's plight in the depression of the 1930s. Thus, in Britain, despite the successes of Winston Churchill's Conservative Party leadership, the Labour government of Clement Attlee appeared more socialist by fulfilling promises that it would share prosperity equitably among the classes through expanded social welfare programs and the nationalization of key industries.

The political air became more charged as the cold war took hold. Increasingly urged on by Moscow, the French Communist chief called the French Fourth Republic a "reactionary dictatorship" and summoned the French people to overthrow it. Amidst ongoing hardship in everyday life, strikes broke out across the West, and de Gaulle responded by creating a new anti-Communist party, Rally of the French People (RPF). By the late 1940s, cooperation between ruling Christian Democrats and Communists in other countries fell apart. Rejecting the language of consensual politics, one intellectual called anyone who opposed communism "a dog." In the words of one French journalist, western Europe looked as if "blood was going to flow."

In West Germany, however, communism had no appeal. In 1949, centrist politicians helped create a new state, the German Federal Republic. Its first chancellor was the seventy-three-year-old Catholic anti-Communist Konrad Adenauer. Working with other democrats, Adenauer drafted a constitution that would prevent the emergence of a dictator and guarantee individual rights. Adenauer also allied himself with Ludwig Erhard, an economist who had stabilized the postwar German currency so that commerce could resume. Erhard used his academic expertise and commitment to the free market to "turn a lunar landscape into a flourishing beehive," in the words of one German commentator. The economist and the politician successsfully guided Germany away from both fas-

cism and communism and restored the representative government that Hitler had overthrown.

Paradoxically, it was in the United States, as it promoted democratic values against totalitarianism, that postwar politics most imperiled individual freedom and actually threatened peacetime democracy. The 1949, explosion of the Soviet atomic bomb and the successful Communist revolution in China brought to the fore Joseph McCarthy, a U.S. senator from Wisconsin, who announced that Communists were infiltrating American institutions. Facing a reelection struggle, McCarthy warned of a great conspiracy to overthrow the United States. His false claim to have

Hollywood Stars Protest in Washington
The appearance of top stars like Lauren Bacall and Humphrey Bogart to protest the persecution of writers, filmmakers, and actors late in the 1940s did not dampen the government's hunt for Communists. In the search for anyone critical of U.S. policy, people from many walks of life lost their jobs, were imprisoned, or endured public humiliation. Homosexuals of any political belief were special targets for what seemed to resemble the Soviet attempt to force everyone to hold the same political thoughts.
UPI/Corbis-Bettmann.

names of hundreds, even thousands, of conspirators led to a hysteria that curtailed free speech in the United States. As during the Soviet purges, people were called before panels to confess, testify against friends, think about whether they had ever had Communist thoughts or sympathies. The atmosphere was electric with fear because only five years before, such mass media as *Time* and *Life* magazines had run glowing stories about Stalin and the Soviet system. By 1952, more than six million people had been subpoenaed, investigated, or imprisoned or had lost their jobs. McCarthy had books like Thomas Paine's *Common Sense*, written in the eighteenth century to support the American Revolution, removed from government shelves, and he personally oversaw book burnings. Although the Senate finally voted to censure McCarthy in the winter of 1954, the assault on freedom had been devastating and anticommunism dominated political life.

Economic Miracles. Given the incredible devastation, the economic rebirth of western Europe was even more surprising than the revival of democracy. In the first weeks and months after the war, the job of rebuilding often involved menial physical labor that mobilized entire populations. With so many men dead, wounded, or detained as prisoners of war, German housewives, called "women of the ruins," earned their living clearing rubble by hand. The task was vast: up to 95 percent of major cities had been bombed to bits. Neighborhoods set up survival networks to provide daily necessities, and the resulting grassroots organizing, so at odds with Nazi practice, influenced German politics in the decades to come.

Initially governments diverted labor and capital into rebuilding infrastructure—transportation, communications, industrial capacity. However, the scarcity of goods sparked unrest and made communism attractive politically because it proclaimed less interest in the revival of big business than in the ordinary person's standard of living. But as the Marshall Plan sustained the initial recovery with American dollars, food and consumer goods became more plentiful, and demand for automobiles, washing machines, and vacuum cleaners boosted economies. The growth in production of all kinds wiped out most unemployment. Labor-short northern Europe even arranged for "guest" workers to migrate from impoverished regions like Sicily to help rebuild cities. The outbreak of war in Korea in 1950 further stimulated the European economy.

The 1950s witnessed astonishing rates of economic growth. (See "Taking Measure," below.) Between 1950 and 1954, the West German economy grew at an unmatched 8.2 percent annual rate. In the second half of the 1950s, France's economy

TAKING MEASURE
World Manufacturing Output, 1950–1970
During the "long boom" from the 1950s to the early 1970s, the world experienced increased industrial output, better agricultural production, and rising consumerism. This era of prosperity resulted not only from the demand generated by the need to rebuild Europe but also from the adaptation of war technology to peacetime uses. The General Agreement on Trade and Tariffs (GATT) was also implemented after the war, lowering tariffs and thus advancing trade.
Hammond Atlas of the Twentieth Century (London: Times Books, 1987), 127.

took off at an annual rate of 8 percent. Late in the 1950s, Italy likewise rebounded with new ventures in the production of oil and synthetic products. Britain's annual growth was a mere 3 percent because the country did not face massive reconstruction and merely repaired without modernizing its basic industries. More important, although Britain's immediate postwar capital investment was very high, its trade was oriented toward the less vigorous Commonwealth economies. Thus it missed out trading with the booming western European countries.

The postwar recovery also featured the adaptation of wartime technology to consumer industry and the continuation of military spending. Civilian travel expanded as nations organized their own air systems based on improved airplane technology. Developed to relieve wartime shortages, synthetic goods such as nylon now became part of peacetime civilian life. Factories churned out a vast assortment of plastic products, ranging from pipes to household goods and rainwear. In the climate of cold war, governments ordered bombs, fighter planes, tanks, and missiles; and they also continued to sponsor military research (Figure 28.1). Spending for armaments helped stabilize the economy by creating jobs, as it had in Germany and the United States in the late 1930s. The cold war ultimately prevented a repeat of the 1920s when reduced military spending threw people out of jobs and thus fed the growth of fascism.

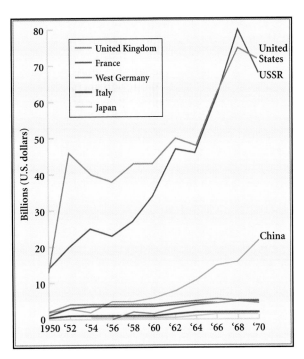

FIGURE 28.1 The Arms Race, 1950–1970
As soon as the war ended, the United States and the Soviet Union started a massive arms buildup that would continue into the 1980s. Because it had not suffered destruction during the war, the United States could afford spending hundreds of billions of dollars. The Soviet Union could not, and its citizens were comparatively deprived by these expenditures. By the end of the twentieth century, the United States and Russia held vast arsenals of nuclear and other weapons and along with France led the way in selling arms to the rest of the world.

The Common Market. International cooperation and planning that led to the creation of the Common Market and ultimately the European Union of the 1990s provided a final ingredient in recovery. The Bretton Woods Agreement of 1944, eventually signed by forty-four nations, with the Soviet Union a notable exception, envisioned a world bank and planned the International Monetary Fund (IMF). The IMF's goal was to ensure the stability of currencies by using pooled monies to prop up any weak currency and thus to further trade. One aim was to preempt the kind of economic instabilities that had led to social and political turmoil in the 1930s.

Drastic economic change was the order of the day. The Marshall Plan demanded as the condition for assistance that recipients cooperate in more far-reaching economic policy. In 1951, Italy, France, Germany, Belgium, Luxembourg, and the Nether-lands formed the European Coal and Steel Community (ECSC). This organization managed coal and steel production and prices and, most important, arranged for West German output to benefit western Europe. According to the ECSC's principal architect, Robert Schuman, the economic unity created by the organization would make another war "materially impossible." Simply put, the bonds of common productivity and trade would keep France and Germany from another cataclysmic war.

In 1957, the "six," as the ECSC members were called, took another major step toward regional prosperity when they signed the Treaty of Rome. The treaty provided for the sharing of atomic resources through a commission called EUROCOM and a trading partnership called the European Economic Community (EEC), known popularly as the Common Market. The EEC reduced tariffs among the six partners and worked to develop common trade policies. According to one of its founders, the EEC aimed to "prevent the race of nationalism, which is the true curse of the modern world." Increased cooperation produced great economic rewards for the six members. Britain pointedly refused to join the partnership; membership would have required that it surrender certain imperial trading rights. Since 1945, British statesmen had shunned the developing continental trading bloc because, as one of them put it, participation would make it "just another European country." As a result Britain continued its relative decline. By contrast, the Italian economy, which had also lagged behind that of France and Germany, boomed. The future lay with the new western Europe joined in the Common Market, which, besides prosperity, brought an end to the century-old national rivalries that had left Europe in ruins.

Behind the move to the Common Market stood the economic planning and coordination that had brought liberal economics under the government umbrella during wartime. Government experts (whether under Hitler or Roosevelt) had planned everything from transportation to the coordination of production in different regions. Called *technocrats* after 1945, these specialists were to base decisions on expertise rather than on personal interest; those working for the Common Market were to disregard the self-interest of any one nation. French economist Jean Monnet, who inspired and helped create the Common Market, believed that rational administration by supranational agencies composed of disinterested experts reduced the potential for irrationality and violence in politics, both domestic and international.

Cooperation and expert planning had an American aura that had also drawn Europeans to jazz and skyscrapers. Monnet attacked socially conservative government practices in favor of American ones. In summertime meetings he encouraged European government leaders to take the daring step of removing their jackets and rolling up their sleeves. "I'll do the same—it's a habit I picked up in America," he said. Some critics insisted, some even today, that expert planning diminished democracy by putting massive control in the hands of bureaucracy, not legislatures. Still others deplored the end of liberal economics and the free market, a development that to them smacked of socialism.

The Welfare State: Common Ground East and West

On both sides of the cold war, governments intervened forcefully to ameliorate social conditions. This policy of intervention became known as the *welfare state*, indicating that states were no longer interested solely in maintaining order and augmenting their power. The welfare state had been gradually building for almost a century, as in the creation of government pensions in Bismarck's newly created Germany or in the British national health-care system that began to give twenty million workers medical benefits during the depression. After World War II, governments further opened their purse strings to fund more and more social programs.

The welfare state encouraged population growth with direct financial aid. The European population had declined during the war, and almost all countries now desperately urged couples to reproduce. In France, where fertility had been dropping for more than a century, de Gaulle called on women to produce "twelve million healthy babies." Imitating the sweeping Swedish programs of the 1930s, nations expanded or created family allowances, health-care and medical benefits, and programs for pregnant women and new mothers. The French gave larger allowances for each birth after the first; for many French families this allowance provided as much as a third of the household income.

Britain's maternity benefits and child allowances, announced in a wartime report, favored women who did not work outside the home and provided little coverage of any kind to working-women. The West German government passed strict legislation that discouraged employers from hiring women. In fact, West Germans bragged about removing women from the workforce, claiming it distinguished democratic practices from Communist ones that were said to demand women's work outside the home. One result of the cutback in pensions and benefits to married women was their high rate of poverty in old age.

In eastern Europe and the Soviet Union, where wartime loss of life had been enormous, women worked nearly full time and usually outnumbered men in the workforce. Child-care programs, family allowances, and maternity benefits were designed to encourage pregnancies by such women. The scarcity of consumer goods, the housing shortages, and the lack of household conveniences in the Eastern bloc, however, discouraged workingwomen from having large families. Because women had sole responsibility for onerous domestic duties on top of their paying jobs, their already heavy workload increased with the birth of each additional child.

Other welfare-state programs aimed to improve people's health. State-funded medical insurance and subsidized medical care covered health-care needs everywhere except in the United States. Countries as diverse as Great Britain and the Soviet Union had nationalized health-care systems in which doctors and hospital employees worked for the state and the country's entire population was covered. In other nations, citizens' medical expenses were reimbursed through social security plans. The combination of better material conditions and state provision of health care dramatically extended life expectancy and lowered rates of infant mortality. Contributing to the overall progress, the number of medical doctors and dentists more than doubled between the end of World War I and 1950, and vaccines greatly reduced the death toll from such diseases as tuberculosis, diphtheria, measles, and polio. In England, schoolchildren stood on the average an inch taller than children the same age had a decade earlier. And as

people lived longer, governments began to establish programs for the elderly. All in all, per capita expenditures on civilian well-being shot up after the war. Belgium, for example, which had spent $12 per capita in 1930, led western European countries with $148 per capita in 1956; Britain, which had led in 1930 with welfare expenditures of $59, now lagged behind with $93 because of its near-bankrupt condition.

Welfare-state initiatives in other areas played a role in the higher standard of living. A growing network of government-built atomic power plants brought more thorough electrification of eastern Europe and the Soviet Union. Governments legislated better conditions and more leisure time for workers. Beginning in 1955, Italian workers received twenty-eight paid holidays annually; in Sweden they received twenty-nine vacation days, and the number grew in the 1960s. Planning also helped provide a more varied diet and more abundant food, with meat, fish, eggs, cheese, milk, and fresh fruit supplementing the older grain-based foods. In Czechoslovakia, annual per capita consumption of meat was 125 pounds in 1960 and in Hungary, 105.

Housing shortages posed a daunting challenge for both the welfare state and the individual. After three decades of economic depression and war, people had trouble finding a decent place to live. Because the war had been so destructive and had

Postwar Housing in Poland
Wartime devastation only added to the growing shortage of housing that had begun with the diversion of resources to fight World War I and that had increased during the depression of the 1930s, when housing construction almost entirely halted. In the post–World War II years, shortages were so grave that slapdash, cheap buildings with far less than one room per person went up from England to Eastern Europe. It was not until the 1960s that the Soviets began building anywhere near the housing units needed, some million or more per year.
Sovfoto.

diverted resources into military needs, postwar Europeans often lived with three generations sharing one or two rooms. Eastern Europeans faced the worst conditions, whereas Germans and Greeks fared better because only 20 to 25 percent of prewar housing had been lost. To rebuild, governments sponsored a postwar housing boom. In western Europe, they provided incentives to private builders but also, as in the Eastern bloc, the state itself undertook building projects. New cities formed around the edges of major urban areas in both East and West. Many buildings went up slapdash, and restored towns took on an undistinguished look and a constantly deteriorating condition. Westerners labeled the new apartments in Poland "environmentally horrible." Despite the building boom, housing shortages had not disappeared by the 1960s. Nevertheless the modernized appearance of many European cities suggested that the century's two cataclysmic wars had definitively swept away a good deal of the old Europe.

Recovery in the East

Creating a Soviet bloc according to Stalin's prewar vision of industrialization was an immense undertaking. Before the war, the economies of the successor states to Austria-Hungary such as Poland and Hungary had remained largely rural and dominated by small peasant farmers. Stalin called on the crushing methods that had served him before to transform these economies.

Stalin Unleashed. In eastern Europe, Stalin enforced collectivized agriculture and badly needed industrialization through the nationalization of private property. In Hungary, for example, where one thousand families owned more than one-quarter of the arable land, Communists seized and reapportioned all estates over twelve hundred acres. Having gained support of the poorer peasants through this redistribution, Communists later pushed them into cooperative farming. In the Transylvania area of Romania, Communists first seized the land of the German minority there and redistributed it to poorer Romanian farmers. Then they converted the property of wealthier peasants into collective farms. The process was brutal and slow, and rural Romanians would look back on the 1950s as "dreadful." Some of those same people

also felt that ultimately their lives and their children's lives had improved. "Before we peasants were dirty and poor, we worked like dogs. . . . Was that a good life? No sir, it wasn't. . . . I was a miserable sharecropper and my son is an engineer," said one Romanian peasant.

Stalin prodded all the socialist economies in his bloc to match U.S. productivity. An admirer of American industrial know-how, he once claimed that "the union of Russian revolutionary drive with American business ability" was "the essence of Leninism." The Soviet Union also formed regional organizations, instituting the Council for Mutual Economic Assistance (COMECON) to coordinate economic relations among the satellite countries and Moscow. Modernization of production in the Eastern bloc opened new technical and bureaucratic careers, and modernizers in the satellite states touted the virtues of steel plants and modern transport. The terms of the COMECON relationship thwarted development of the satellite states, for the USSR was allowed to buy goods from its clients at bargain prices and sell to them at exorbitant ones. Nonetheless these formerly peasant states became oriented toward technology and bureaucratically directed industrial economies. People moved to cities where they received better education, health care, and, ultimately, jobs.

Like Soviet industrialization in the 1930s, repression accompanied the drive for modernization. The Catholic clergy, which often protested the imposition of communism, was crushed. Old agrarian elites, professionals, intellectuals, and other members of the middle class were discriminated against, imprisoned, or executed. Prisoners in East German camps did hard labor in uranium and other dangerous mines; one imprisoned Romanian intellectual spent years in water up to his chin cutting bamboo for an aborted canal linking the Black Sea and the Danube. Although its Western allies often objected to the arrogance of the rich and powerful United States, the Soviet Union dominated its alliances through physical coercion along with state-instituted programs to build loyalty to the regime. Thus citizens in satellite countries found themselves obliged to attend adult education classes, women's groups, and public ceremonies.

Science and culture were the building blocks of Stalinism in the satellite countries as well as in the USSR. An intense program of Russification and

ELŐRE A BÉKE ÉS A SZOCIALIZMUS IFJU HARCOSAINAK KONGRESSZUSÁÉRT
1950. JUNIUS 17-18

Re-Creating Hungarian Youth

People across Europe focused on the well-being of young people after World War II, and in the Soviet sphere this took the form of education in Communist ways. Youth groups, such as those in the early Stalinist USSR, served this end, and vivid posters in the Soviet realist style carried inspirational messages: "Forward for the Congress of the Young Fighters of Peace and Socialism," reads this typical message to Hungarian youth in 1950.
Magyar Nemzeti Múzeum, Budapest (Hungarian National Museum).

de-Christianization began. The Soviets forced students in eastern Europe to read histories of the war that ignored native resistance and gave the Red Army sole credit for fighting the Nazis. They replaced national symbols with Soviet ones. For example, the Hungarians had to accept a new flag with a Soviet red star beaming rays onto a hammer and sickle; the Hungarian colors were reduced to a small band on the flag. Utter historical distortion, revivified anti-Semitism, and rigid censorship re-

sulted in what one staunchly socialist writer characterized as "a dreary torrent of colorless, mediocre literature." For information people had to rely on the *Great Soviet Encyclopedia*, started in 1949, which claimed the Russians to be forerunners in every field of endeavor from automobile technology to physics. Although modernization was a priority, Soviet ideology continued to take its toll by undercutting the potential for steady scientific advances.

In the USSR itself, Stalin instituted new purges to ensure obedience and conformity. Marshall Zhukov, a popular leader of the armed forces, was shipped to a distant command, while Anna Akhmatova, the great poet whose popular writing had emphasized perseverance and individual heroism during the war, died confined to a crowded hospital room because she refused to glorify Stalin in her postwar poetry. The tsarist tradition of Russification and anti-Semitism revived. Soviet agents rooted out "Jewish influences" and "bourgeois decadence" in the arts: they put writers and artists out of work, evicted them from their apartments, and denied them the privileges that came with artistic achievement.

After Stalin. In March 1953, while leading the rebuilding of the Soviet Union and planning more purges, Stalin died. As people openly mourned this man they considered their savior from backwardness and Nazism, troubles were already apparent in the empire he ruled so tyrannically. Political prisoners in the labor camps who had started rioting late in the 1940s now pressed their demands for reform. Consumer goods were much scarcer than in the West because of the government's high military spending and the enormous cost of recovery. Amid deprivation and discontent, Soviet leaders and bureaucrats enjoyed country homes, luxury goods, and plentiful food, but many of them had come to distrust Stalinism and were ready for some changes. The Stalinist system faced daunting challenges, but without Stalin.

It was a fateful time. A power struggle ensued within the Soviet government, and protests took place across the empire. Labor camp inmates stopped working to emphasize their need for better food and the right to receive letters. Amid turmoil some prisoners of the Gulag labor camps were freed and the production of consumer goods beefed up—a policy called "goulash communism" because in part it resulted in more food for ordinary people. The old ways could not hold. In 1955, Nikita Khrushchev (1894–1971), an illiterate coal miner before the revolution, outmaneuvered other rivals to emerge the undisputed leader of the Soviet Union, but he did so without the usual executions. The next year he attacked Stalinism. Addressing the Twentieth Party Congress, he listed what he called Stalin's "perversions" of the Communist revolution. Khrushchev denounced the "cult of personality" Stalin had built about himself and announced that Stalinism did not equal socialism. The "secret speech"—it was not published in the USSR but became widely known—sent tremors through Communist parties around the world and signaled that Stalin's death might bring a real change of direction.

In this climate of uncertainty, protest erupted once more in early summer 1956, when discontented Polish railroad workers struck for better wages. Popular support for their cause forced the return of Wladislaw Gomulka, a Communist victim of an earlier Stalinist purge. Gomulka initiated a more liberal Communist program. Inspired by the Polish example, Hungarians rebelled against forced collectivization in October 1956—"the golden October," they would call their uprising. As in Poland, economic issues, especially announcements of reduced wages, sparked some of the first outbreaks of violence, but the protest soon targeted the entire Communist system. Intellectuals and students turned universities into major political centers. Residents of Budapest filled the streets and smashed the huge statue of Stalin. Tens of thousands of protesters convinced the Hungarian army, sent to disperse them, to join the rebellion and succeeded in returning a popular hero, Imre Nagy, to power. When Nagy announced that Hungary might leave the Warsaw Pact, Soviet troops moved in, killing tens of thousands and causing hundreds of thousands more to flee to the West. Nagy was hanged. The U.S. refusal to intervene showed that, despite a rhetoric of "liberation," it would not risk World War III by militarily challenging the Soviet sphere of influence.

A Partial Thaw. The failure of eastern European uprisings overshadowed significant changes in Soviet policy. In the process of defeating his rivals, Khrushchev ended the Stalinist purges, reformed the courts (which came to function according to procedures, not like the stage for show trials of the past), and set a policy of more limited sentences for political offenders and criminals. The gates of the Gulag opened still farther, and the secret police lost many of its arbitrary powers. These reforms contributed to what came to be called the climate of "thaw" in the Soviet Union.

The thaw, however, was fragile. It depended not only on the death of Stalin but also on the Soviet sense of security acquired from increased productivity, military buildup, and stunning successes in aerospace development. In 1957, the Soviets successfully launched the first artificial earth satellite, *Sputnik*, and in 1961 they put the first cosmonaut, Yuri Gagarin, in orbit around the earth. The Soviets' edge in space technology shocked the Western bloc and motivated the creation of the U.S. National Aeronautics and Space Administration (NASA). Soviet successes indicated that the USSR was on the way to achieving Stalin's goals of Westernization and modernization. Nevertheless, Khrushchev continued to fear and bully dissidents. For example, he forced Boris Pasternak to refuse the 1958 Nobel Prize in literature because his novel *Doctor Zhivago* (1957) cast doubt on the glory of the revolution and affirmed the value of the individual.

Yet Khrushchev himself made several trips to the West and was more widely seen by the public than Stalin. More confident and more affluent, the Soviets took steps to reduce their diplomacy's paranoid style and concentrated their efforts on spreading the message of Leninism and socialist progress to the emerging nations of Asia, Africa, and Latin America.

❖ Decolonization in a Cold War Climate

World War II dealt the final blow to the ability of European powers to maintain their vast empires and their global influence. During the war the Allies had again relied heavily on Asian and African troops and had encouraged anti-Axis independence movements. In the postwar world, however, the Western powers attempted to stamp out nationalist groups and reimpose their control—with fatal results. As before, colonized peoples had been on the front lines defending the West; and as before, they had witnessed the full barbarism of Western warfare. Excluded from victory parades and other ceremonies so the powers could maintain the illusion of Western supremacy, adult men in the colonies still did not receive the political rights promised them. Instead, people in Asia, Africa, and the Middle East, often led by individuals steeped in Western values and experienced in war, embraced the cause of independence and often clashed with the West in bloody warfare.

The path to achieving a modern nation-state, however, was often fraught with conflict off the battlefield as well. In Africa, a continent whose peoples spoke more than five thousand languages, the European conquerors' need for convenient administrative units had led to regional designations such as Rhodesia and Nigeria, obliterating living arrangements that had relied on ethnic ties and local cultures. In addition, religion played a divisive role in independence movements. In India, Hindus and Muslims, both desiring independence, battled one another even though they shared the goal of eliminating the British. In the Middle East and North Africa, pan-Arab and pan-Islamic movements might seem to have been unifying forces. Yet many Muslims were not Arab, not all Arabs were Muslim, and Islam itself encompassed many competing beliefs and sects. Differences among religious beliefs, ethnic groups, and cultural practices—many of them invented or promoted by the colonizers to divide and rule—overlapped and undermined political unity. Despite these complications, peoples in what was coming to be called the third world succeeded in throwing off the imperial yoke imposed by Britain, France, Belgium, and the Netherlands.

Loss of empire threatened Europe's economy and upset a European sense of identity based on a belief in Western superiority. At the same time, the decolonizing world offered a new field for competition between the United States and the Soviet Union, thus increasing the possibility of nuclear war and magnifying the drama of decolonization. Many leaders of newly independent nations turned a cold shoulder to each of the global giants and envisioned instead a consortium of nonaligned countries exerting its own leverage in world affairs.

The End of Empire in Asia

By the end of World War II, leaders in Asia began to mobilize the mass discontent that had intensified during the war and were able to drive out foreign rulers. The biggest loser would be Britain, which by the 1960s would decline from a global imperial power to a small island nation. In need of postwar resources, Winston Churchill was determined not to let the colonies go their own way, but the victorious Labourites under Clement Attlee promoted decolonization as important to social justice. Such debate became moot as national liberation movements increasingly took matters into their own hands and as white settlers often resisted the independence of people they still wanted to rule.

Independence in South Asia. The British had promised to grant India its independence in the 1930s, but they postponed it when war broke out. They even declared war against the Nazis on the Indians' behalf. Some two million Indian men were mobilized, anchoring the war in the Middle East and Asia. Local industry became an important wartime supplier and Indian business leaders bought out British entrepreneurs short of cash. But during this period of economic prosperity for some, food shortages drove people to overcrowded cities, and political fissures between Hindus and Muslims, long encouraged by the British, widened.

When, after the war, the Labour government sent its statesmen to preside over the end of the British Empire in India, they decreed that two countries should emerge from the old colony, so great was the mistrust between the Congress and League Parties. Thus, in 1947 India was created for Hindus and Pakistan for Muslims. Yet during the independence year, political tensions exploded among opposing members of the two religions. Hundreds of thousands were massacred in the great shift of populations between the two nations. In 1948, a radical Hindu assassinated Gandhi, who though a Hindu himself had continued to champion religious reconciliation. Confronting nationalist movements elsewhere, Britain retained control of Hong Kong; but before two decades of the postwar era had passed, almost half a billion Asians had gained their freedom from the rule of fifty million British.

"People's Very Own Army"

Dramatic posters had spread the word during World War II of a range of Communist activities to help the Chinese people fight the Japanese invaders. In this depiction, Communists are neighbors, protectors, and providers of medical cures and supplies. They deal with all kinds of people, the poster claims, and are cheerfully helpful. As a result of their efforts, China would prosper.

Peasant Revolts in China (LWC Series), 1973. p. 106, ill. 41. Photo courtesy Thames & Hudson, Ltd., London.

Communist Revolution in East and Southeast Asia.

In 1949, a Communist takeover in China brought in a government that was no longer the plaything of the traditional colonial powers. Mao Zedong (1893–1976) led his army of Communists to victory over Jiang Jieshi's unpopular, corrupt Nationalist government, which the United States had bankrolled. Chinese communism in the new People's Republic of China emphasized above all the welfare of the peasantry rather than the indus-

trial proletariat and was thus distinct from Stalinism, Leninism, and Marxism. Mao instituted social reforms such as civil equality for women but at the same time copied Soviet collectivization, rapid industrialization, and brutal repression of the privileged classes. Although China began to distance itself from the USSR in the mid-1950s, the Western bloc saw only monolithic red from Leningrad to Beijing.

The United States and the Soviet Union were deeply interested in East Asia, the United States because of the region's economic importance and the USSR because of its shared borders. Thus the Chinese victory spurred both superpowers to increase their involvement in Asian politics. They faced off indirectly in Korea, which had been split at the thirty-eighth parallel after World War II. In 1950, the North Koreans, supported by the Soviet Union, invaded the U.S.-backed South. The United States maneuvered the UN Security Council into approving a "police action" against the North. The UN eventually deployed 400,000 troops from member nations to help the South Korean army repel the invaders. The combined military forces quickly drove well into North Korean territory, where they were met by the Chinese rather than the Soviet army. After two and a half years of stalemate, the opposing sides finally agreed to a settlement in 1953: Korea would remain split at its prewar border, the thirty-eighth parallel.

The United States lost more than 50,000 men—almost as many as would die in the Vietnam War—and increased its military spending from $10.9 billion in 1948 to almost $60 billion in 1953 to hold the line on Communist expansion. It outpaced Soviet expenditures by $10–$20 billion annually from 1951 to 1960. Communist potential in decolonizing areas led the American secretary of

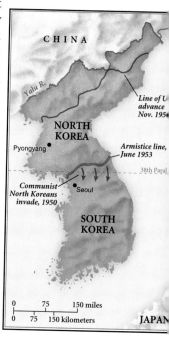

The Korean War, 1950–1953

state, John Foster Dulles, to characterize Asian countries as a row of dominoes: "You knock over the first one and what will happen to the last one is that it will go over [to communism] very quickly." The expansion of the cold war to Asia prompted the creation of an Asian counterpart to NATO. Established in 1954, the Southeast Asia Treaty Organization (SEATO) included Pakistan, Thailand, the Philippines, Britain, Australia, New Zealand, France, and the United States. One side effect was the rapid reindustrialization of Japan to provide the United States with supplies.

The cold war spread to Indochina, where nationalists had been struggling against the postwar

Indochina, 1954

revival of French imperialism. Their leader, the European-educated Ho Chi Minh (1890–1969), preached both nationalism and socialism and built a powerful organization, the Viet Minh, to fight colonial rule. He advocated the redistribution of land held by big landowners, especially in the rich agricultural area in southern Indochina where some six thousand owners possessed more than 60 percent of the land. The French army fought all efforts at independence, but the Viet Minh surprised the French with its tenacious resistance. Finally, these peasant guerrillas forced the technologically advanced French army to withdraw after the bloody battle of Dien Bien Phu in 1954.

The Geneva Convention of 1954 carved out an independent Laos and divided Vietnam into North and South, each free from French control. The Viet Minh was ordered to retreat to an area north of the seventeenth parallel. But superpower intervention undermined the peace treaty. President Truman had seen the Indochinese conflict as part of the anti-Communist crusade rather than as a nationalist issue; he began providing aid to the French well before their defeat at Dien Bien Phu. President

Eisenhower's advisers wanted him to drop an atomic bomb on the Viet Minh, and, although threatening to do so, the president refused direct military intervention. The decolonizing world was becoming a battleground not only for independence but also for the cold war. Avoiding major conflict in Europe, the superpowers and their allies volleyed back and forth, risking the nuclear brink while subjecting native peoples to the force of their military might. In fighting to prevent national liberation in the name of fighting communism, the United States in particular was acquiring a reputation as an "imperialist" power of the old school, nowhere more so than in Vietnam.

The Struggle for Identity in the Middle East

The power of oil and the ability of small countries to see the opportunity for maneuvering between antagonists in the cold war gave new impetus to independence struggles in the Middle East. The legacy of the Holocaust, however, complicated the political scene. As in the rest of the world after the war, Middle Eastern peoples renewed their commitment to independence and resisted attempts by the major powers to regain imperial control. Weakened by the war, British oil companies wanted to tighten their grip on profits, as the value of this energy source soared. The cold war gave Middle Eastern leaders an opening to bargain with the superpowers, playing them off one against another, especially over resources to re-establish war torn economies. The Western powers' commitment to secure a Jewish homeland in the Middle East further stirred up Arab determination to regain economic and political control of the region.

When World War II broke out, 600,000 Jewish settlers and twice as many Arabs lived, in intermittent conflict, in British-controlled Palestine. In 1947, an exhausted Britain ceded the area to the United Nations to work out a settlement between the Jews and the Arabs. In the aftermath of the Holocaust, the UN voted to partition Palestine into an Arab region and a Jewish one (Map 28.4). Conflicting claims, however, led to war, and Jewish military forces prevailed. On May 14, 1948, the state of Israel came into being. "The dream had come true," Golda Meir, the future president of Israel,

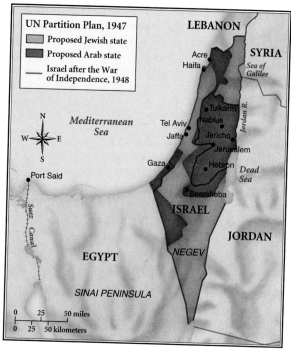

MAP 28.4 The Partition of Palestine and the Creation of Israel, 1947–1948
The creation of the Jewish state of Israel in 1948 against a backdrop of ongoing wars among Jews and indigenous Arab peoples made the Middle East a powder keg until the present day. The struggle for resources and for securing the borders of viable nation-states was at the heart of these bitter contests, threatening to pull the superpowers into a third world war.

remembered, but "too late to save those who had perished in the Holocaust." Israel opened its gates to immigrants, driving its ambitions against those of its Arab neighbors.

One of those neighbors, Egypt, had gained its independence from Britain at the end of the war. Britain, however, retained its control of Middle Eastern oil and its dominance of Asian shipping through the Suez Canal, which was owned by a British-run company. In 1952, Colonel Gamal Abdel Nasser became Egypt's president after the ouster of its king. Nasser's dreams for Egypt included economic modernization and true national independence. A prime goal was reclaiming the Suez Canal, "where 120,000 of our sons had lost their lives in digging it [by force]," he stated. In July 1956, Nasser nationalized the canal.

Britain immediately demanded the canal's return and won support from Israel and France. In October, the three countries attacked Egypt, bringing the Suez crisis to a head while the Hungarian revolt was in full swing. The British branded Nasser another Hitler and called on the United States for help. Anxious to avoid military conflict with the Soviet Union, which had threatened the British, French, and Israelis if they did not withdraw, the Americans declined. In refusing support, the United States struck an anti-imperialist posture for developing nations whose economic and political partnership it sought—unlike its response in Asia. American opposition made the British back down from what one British diplomat called "a squalid and most humiliating episode." Nasser's triumph inspired confidence that the Middle East could confront the West and win.

New Nations in Africa

In sub-Saharan Africa, nationalist leaders roused their people to challenge Europeans' increasing demand for resources and labor, which resulted in poverty for African peoples. "The European Merchant is my shepherd, and I am in want," went one African version of the Twenty-third Psalm. Disrupted in their traditional agricultural patterns, many Africans flocked to shantytowns in cities during the war, where they kept themselves alive through scavenging, craft work, and menial labor for whites. Protests multiplied, and underemployed city dwellers formed one power base for politicians committed to decolonization. Ironically, the ethnic groups fostered by the imperialist powers constituted another.

Already in 1945, delegates to the sixth Pan-African Congress had declared that "if the Western world is still determined to rule mankind by force, then Africans, as a last resort, may have to use force to achieve freedom." Kwame Nkrumah led the diverse inhabitants of the relatively prosperous, British-controlled West African Gold Coast in passive resistance, in imitation of Gandhian methods. After years of arresting and jailing the protesters, the British withdrew, allowing the state of Ghana to come into being in 1957. Nigeria, the most populous African region, became independent in 1960 after the leaders of its many regional groups and political organizations reached agreement on a federal-style government. In these and other African states where the population was mostly black, independence came less violently than in mixed-race territory (Map 28.5).

The eastern coast and southern and central areas of Africa had numerous European settlers, who violently resisted independence movements. In British East Africa, where white settlers ruled in splendor and where blacks lacked both land and economic opportunity, violence erupted in the 1950s. African men, almost all of whom had assisted the British as soldiers in World War II, formed rebel groups named the Land Freedom Army but known as Mau Mau. They maintained their solidarity through ceremonies, oaths, and rigid discipline. With women serving as provisioners, messengers, and weapon stealers, Mau Mau bands formed from the Kikuyu ethnic group tried to re-

cover land from whites. In 1964, after the British had slaughtered some ten to fifteen thousand Kikuyus, Kenya gained formal independence. In 1948, the Afrikaners took control of the South African government and formalized white supremacism in the brutal system of *apartheid* ("apartness"), which would last until the 1990s. Among the most urbanized and wealthiest of African nations, South Africa also had the most numerous Western-educated elites, many of whom formed the leadership of an ongoing and increasingly powerful resistance movement.

France—although eager to regain its great-power status after its humiliating defeat and occupation in World War II—easily granted certain demands for independence, such as those of Tunisia, Morocco, and West Africa, where there

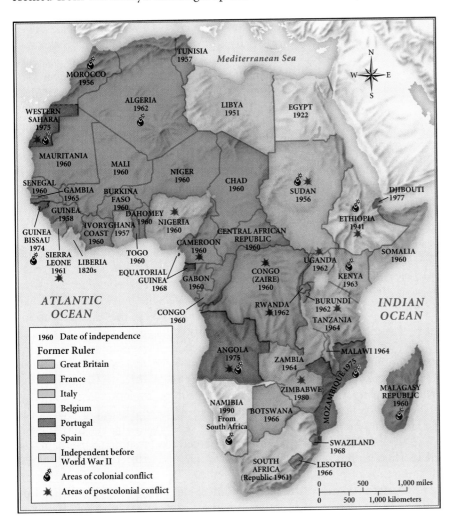

MAP 28.5 The Decolonization of Africa, 1951–1990
The liberation of Africa from European rule was an uneven process, sometimes occurring peacefully and at other times demanding armed struggle to drive out European settlers, governments, and armies. The difficult process of nation building following liberation involved setting up state institutions, including educational and other services. Creating national unity also took work, except where the struggle against colonialism had already brought people together.

Jomo Kenyatta, First President of the New Kenyan Nation

Jomo Kenyatta (1964–1978) had been educated in England and wrote Facing Mount Kenya, *a work that explained Kikuyu life as a distinct culture to Westerners. After a costly struggle that had resulted in his imprisonment by the British, Kenyatta became president of the new republic but closed down much political debate by outlawing opposition parties. His one-party government brought social calm, which made Kenya a good place for Western investments.*
© Bettman/CORBIS.

were fewer settlers, more limited economic stakes, and less military involvement. Elsewhere, French struggles against independence movements were costly, prolonged, and bloody. The ultimate test of the French empire came in Algeria. When Algerian nationalists rebelled against the restoration of French rule in the final days of World War II, the French army massacred tens of thousands of protesters. The liberation movement resurfaced as the Front for National Liberation in 1954. Those forces attacked European settlers and their Arab supporters

with ferocious intensity. Meanwhile the French dug in, sending more than 400,000 troops and fighting back savagely. Asked what would happen were France to grant Algeria independence without a fight, one general replied, "The army would rebel." Neither side fought according to the rules of warfare: the French tortured natives, while Algerian women, shielded by gender stereotypes, planted bombs in European clubs and cafés and carried weapons to assassination sites.

Shedding its colonies at a rapid rate, France drew the line at Algeria. "The loss of Algeria," warned one statesman, "would be an unprecedented national disaster." Although many agreed, the Algerian War also threatened French social stability, as protests in Paris greeted reports of the army's barbarous practices. French settlers in Algeria and the military met the antiwar movement with terrorism against citizens in France. They threatened coups, set off bombs, assassinated politicians, and promoted other kinds of violence in the name of *Algérie Française* (French Algeria).

France's Fourth Republic collapsed over Algeria. In 1958, Charles de Gaulle, supported by the army and approved by the Chamber of Deputies, came back to power. In return for leading France out of its Algerian quagmire, de Gaulle demanded the creation of a new republican government, one with a strong president who chose the prime minister and could exercise emergency power. From the strengthened presidential office of the Fifth Republic, de Gaulle led the French toward a new, postcolonial identity by paradoxically invoking images of French grandeur and the legacy of French culture as he planned to decolonize Algeria. Terrorism against him escalated, but by 1962 de Gaulle had negotiated independence with the Algerian nationalists. Hundreds of thousands of *pieds noirs* ("black feet"), as the French condescendingly called Europeans in Algeria, as well as their Arab supporters fled to France. The Dutch and Belgian empires also disintegrated. Violent resistance to the reimposition of colonial rule led to the establishment of the large independent states of Indonesia and Zaire.

As Europe received immigrants from former colonies, heated discussions over race and the rights of citizenship in the postcolonial era began reshaping political ideas. In the context of these tumultuous changes, structures emerged in which the new states could operate on the world stage.

The United Nations convened for the first time in 1945, and one notable change ensured it a greater chance of success than the League of Nations: both the United States and the Soviet Union were active members from the outset. The charter of the UN outlined a collective global authority that would adjudicate conflicts, provide military protection if any members were threatened by aggression, and oversee the fate of nonindependent states. Although the UN was a forum for cold war jockeying, notably in the transformation of the Belgian Congo into Zaire, many newly independent nations joined the General Assembly and eventually gained increasing global influence. In 1955, Achmed Sukarno, who succeeded in wrenching Indonesian independence from the Dutch, sponsored the Bandung Convention of nonaligned nations to set a common policy for achieving modernization and facing the major powers. Both the UN and the meetings of emerging nations began shifting global issues away from those of the Western powers. North-south inequities, ethnicity and human rights, and "postcolonialism" nudged their way into public consciousness alongside the "proletariat" and the fate of the West in the atomic age.

❖ Cultural Life on the Brink of Nuclear War

Both the Holocaust and the cold war shaped postwar leisure and political culture, as the responsibility for Nazism, the cause of ethnic and racial justice, and the merits of the two superpowers set people against one another. There was a veneer of normalcy in the baby boom and the apparent restoration of gender roles, and growing affluence sometimes papered over both the horrors of the Holocaust and the omnipresent threat of nuclear annihilation. Yet this was a time of intense self-scrutiny as Europeans debated decolonization and the Americanization that seemed to accompany the influx of U.S. dollars, consumer goods, and cultural media. Behind the prosperity, the cold war menaced. In October 1962, the world held its breath while the leaders of the Soviet Union and the United States provoked the real possibility of nuclear conflagration over the issue of missiles on the island of Cuba.

Restoring "Western" Values

After the depravity and inhumanity of Nazism, cultural currents in Europe and the United States reemphasized universal values, spiritual renewal, and political choice. Some, like Billy Graham, saw the churches as central to the restoration of values through an active commitment to "re-Christianizing" Europe and the United States. Their success was only partial, however, as the trend toward a more secular culture continued. Thus, in the early postwar years people emphasized the triumph of a Western heritage, a Western civilization, and Western values over fascism, and they characterized the war as one "to defend civilization [from] a conspiracy against man." This definition of *West* often emphasized the heritage of Greece and Rome and the rise of national governments in England, France, and western Europe as they encountered "barbaric" forces, be these nomadic tribes or Nazi armies. The West was a flexible entity, including those who could be shown to have aimed for common standards of constitutional or representative government and "civilized" behavior. The first Western civilization textbooks had appeared in the United States late in the 1930s to document the superiority of Western culture, threatened by fascists and by nationalist movements in Asia and Africa. University courses in Western civilization flourished after the war to reaffirm those values. At the same time, the postwar renewal of humanitarianism pushed issues of cultural pluralism and human rights to the forefront of culture.

Holocaust and Resistance Literature. Memoirs of the death camps became compelling reading material. Rescued from the Third Reich in 1940, Nelly Sachs won the Nobel Prize in literature in 1966 for her poetry about the Holocaust. Anne Frank's *Diary of a Young Girl* (1947), the poignant record of a teenager hidden with her family in the back of an Amsterdam warehouse, was emblematic of the survival of Western values in the face of Nazi persecution. Confronted with the small miseries of daily life and the grand evils of Nazism, Anne never stopped believing that "people are really good at heart." Some continued to admire the Nazis, so the flood of memoirs was doubly important in revealing the grim truth. This literature called for a new commitment to tolerance and pluralism.

Histories of the resistance also tapped into the public's need for inspiration after an orgy of savagery. Governments erected permanent plaques at spots where resisters had been killed; their biographies filled magazines and bookstalls; organizations of resisters commemorated their role in winning the war. Although resistance efforts were publicized, discussion of collaboration with Nazis was tacitly forbidden. French filmmakers, for instance, avoided the subject for decades after the war for fear of reopening wounds. Many a politician with a Nazi past moved into the new cultural mainstream even as the stories of resistance took on mythical qualities.

Existential Philosophy.   By the end of the 1940s, existential philosophy became the rage among the cultural elites and students and in universities. It explored the meaning (or lack of meaning) of human existence in a world where evil flourished. Two of its leaders, Albert Camus (1913–1960) and Jean-Paul Sartre (1905–1980), had written for the resistance during the war, although Nazi censors had also allowed the production of Sartre's plays. Taking their starting point from the German philosophers Friedrich Nietzsche (1844–1900) and Martin Heidegger (1889–1976), existentialists confronted the question of what "being" was about, given what they perceived as the absence of God and the breakdown of morality. Their answer was that "being," or existing, was not the automatic process either of God's creation or of birth into the natural world. One was not born with spiritual goodness in the image of a creator, but instead, through action and choice, one created an "authentic" existence. Camus's novels, such as *The Stranger* (1942) and *The Plague* (1947), dissected the evils of a corrupt political order and pondered human responsibility in such situations. Whereas Camus focused on mental attitudes and choices in the face of evil, Sartre's writings emphasized political activism. Sartre's idea of an activist existence validated resistance under totalitarianism. Despite the fact that they had never confronted the enormous problems of making choices while living under fascism, young people in the 1950s found existentialism compelling and made it the most fashionable philosophy of the day. A decade later the spirit of existentialism became part of the inspiration for

students who sought to reform society through political confrontation.

In 1949, Simone de Beauvoir (1908–1986), Sartre's lifetime companion, published the twentieth century's most important work on the condition of women, *The Second Sex*. Beauvoir believed that most women had failed to take the kind of action necessary to lead authentic lives. Instead they lived in the world of "necessity," devoting themselves exclusively to reproduction and motherhood. Failing to create an authentic self through considered action and accomplishment, they had become its opposite—an object or "Other." Moreover, instead of struggling to define themselves and assert their freedom, women passively accepted their own "Otherness" and lived as defined by men. In the 1960s, Beauvoir's theory would guide the women's movement beyond struggles for legal and political reform and underscore the powerful cultural and psychological components of women's experience.

Beauvoir's classic book was a smash hit, in large part because people thought Sartre had written it. Both were celebrities, for the intellectual world increasingly attracted media attention. The media spread the new commitment to humane values just as it had spread support for Nazism or for its wartime enemies. Photos in glossy magazines, a constant stream of articles in newspapers, and interviews on radio built a cohesive, enlightened sector of the public concerned with the death camp literature, stories of the resistance, or the latest trend in philosophy.

Race and Human Rights.   While Europeans debated decolonization among peoples of color in Africa and Asia, intellectuals spawned new theories of what liberation would mean for decolonized peoples. Already the first half of the century had witnessed the rise of pan-Africanism and theories exploring the distinctness of black culture forced to breed in the context of colonial rule. But it was in the 1950s and 1960s that the immensely influential writing of Frantz Fanon (1925–1961), a black psychiatrist from the French colony of Martinique, began analyzing liberation movements. He called the mental functioning of the colonized person "traumatized" by the violence and the brutal imposition of a culture other than one's own as the only standard

Jean-Paul Sartre and Simone de Beauvoir
The postwar period saw the rise of glossy, richly illustrated weekly magazines featuring news and
pop culture. The faces of even the most complex philosophers became well known to the public, while
their private lives intrigued readers. The public personae of these two existentialists, who were seen
to promote the revival of human values after the nightmare of fascism, hid the tortured relationship
Sartre and de Beauvoir actually had.
Editions Gallimard.

of value. Ruled by guns, the colonized person knew only violence and would thus naturally decolonize by means of violence. Translated into many languages, Fanon's *Black Skin, White Masks* (1952) and *The Wretched of the Earth* (1961) posed the question of how to "decolonize" one's mind.

Simone de Beauvoir had seen blacks in the United States as another example of an oppressed "Other," while African Americans had become only too aware of the cultural values common to both sides in the war: Nazis murdered those they considered of inferior "races" like Jews and blacks, while the United States dropped an atomic bomb on the Japanese people of color but not on the white race in Germany. In principle blacks had fought in the war to defeat the Nazi idea of white racial superiority. Thus, in the 1950s the commit-

ment to the civil rights cause embodied in such long-standing organizations as the National Association for the Advancement of Colored People (NAACP, founded 1909) intensified.

In 1954, the U.S. Supreme Court declared segregated education unconstitutional in *Brown* v. *Board of Education,* a case initiated by the NAACP. On December 1, 1955, in Montgomery, Alabama, Rosa Parks, an African American seamstress and part-time secretary for the local branch of the NAACP, boarded a bus and took the first available seat in the so-called white section at the front of the bus. When a white man found himself without a seat, the driver screamed at Parks, "Nigger, move back." Sitting in the front violated southern laws, which encompassed a host of inequitable, even brutal policies toward African Americans. Parks confronted that system through the studied practice of civil disobedience, and her action led to a boycott of public transportation that pushed the civil rights movement into the African American community as a whole.

The culture of rights and human values generated further organizing. Led by groups such as the Student Non-Violent Coordinating Committee (SNCC), the Southern Christian Leadership Conference (SCLC), and the NAACP, blacks and some white allies boycotted discriminatory businesses, "sat in" at segregated facilities, and registered black voters disfranchised by local regulations. Many talented leaders emerged, foremost among them Martin Luther King Jr. (1929–1968), a minister from Georgia whose oratorical power galvanized activists to Gandhian nonviolent resistance against brutal white retaliation, including bombings, arson, and murder. For a few years the postwar culture of nonviolence would shape the civil rights movement. Soon, however, the voices of postcolonial activists and thinkers like Fanon would merge with those of the African American civil rights movement to revolutionize thinking about race and rights.

Rising Consumerism and Shifting Gender Norms

Government spending on reconstruction, productivity, and welfare helped prevent the kind of social, political, and economic upheaval that had followed World War I. Nor did the same tensions prevail among men and women. A rising birthrate, bustling youth culture, and upsurge in consumerism edged out wartime behavior. Men returned from World War II much less frustrated than they had been in the 1920s, because of the decisive result of World War II. In England, for instance, where World War I veterans had wrecked some university classrooms and attacked working-women, faculty were surprised at how docilely young men returned to their studies after World War II.

Nonetheless the war affected men's roles and sense of themselves. Young men who had missed World War II adopted the rough, violent style of soldiers. The 1920s had seen the streets filled with illegal armies such as the German freikorps; in the

Zbigniew Cybulski, the Polish James Dean
Zbigniew Cybulski depicted a tortured young resistance fighter in Andrzej Wajda's film Ashes and Diamonds *(1958). On the last day of World War II Cybulski's character is to assassinate a Communist resistance leader, and his human dilemma around the act is set amidst the chaos in Poland at war's end. Like existentialist philosophers and other cinema directors at the time, Wajda captured the debate over human values and the interest in young heroes of the postwar era.*
Photofest.

1950s, roaming gangs merely posed as tough military types. Their delinquency did not necessarily involve actual crime but rather the swaggering control of urban space that occupying armies displayed. While Soviet youth admired aviator aces, elsewhere groups such as the "teddy boys" in England (named after their Edwardian style of dressing) and the gamberros in Spain took their cues from new forms of pop culture in music and film.

The leader of rock and roll style and substance was the American singer Elvis Presley. Sporting slicked-back hair and an aviator-style jacket, Presley bucked his hips and sang sexual lyrics to screaming and devoted fans. In a German nightclub late in the 1950s, members of a group of Elvis fans called the Quarrymen performed, fighting and yelling at one another as part of their show. They would soon become known as the Beatles. Rebellious young American film stars like James Dean in *Rebel without a Cause* and Marlon Brando in *The Wild One* created the beginnings of a conspicuous postwar youth culture.

The rebellious and rough masculine style appeared also in literature. In his autobiography explaining how he and Francis Crick had discovered the structure of the gene in 1953, James Watson portrayed himself as a fanatic bad boy. His book, *The Double Helix*, described how he had rifled people's desk drawers (among other dishonest acts) to become a scientific hero. Irish novelist and playwright Samuel Beckett's play *Waiting for Godot* (1952) has two tramps, perhaps like POWs, standing around talking nonstop while trusting that something—or someone—good will eventually come along. Beckett proposed that such hope was absurd. In the revival of West German literature, Heinrich Böll published *The Clown* (1963), a novel whose young hero takes to performing as a clown and begging in a railroad station. Böll protested that West Germany's postwar goal of respectability had allowed the resurgence of precisely those groups of people who had produced Nazism. Across the Atlantic, the American "Beat" poets, who looked dirty, bearded, and sometimes crazy, like prisoners or camp survivors, critiqued traditional ideals of the upright and rational male achiever.

Both high and low culture revealed that two horrendous world wars had weakened the Enlightenment view of men as rational, responsible breadwinners. The 1953 inaugural issue of the American magazine *Playboy* ushered in a widely imitated depiction of a changed male identity. *Playboy* differed from typical pornographic magazines: along with pictures of nude women, it featured serious articles, especially on the topic of masculinity. This segment of the media presented modern man as sexually aggressive and independent of dull domestic life—

just as he had been in the war. Breadwinning for a family only destroyed a man's freedom and sense of self. The notion of men's liberty had come to include not just political and economic rights but freedom of sexual expression; this definition would become increasingly integrated into political culture.

In contrast, Western society promoted a postwar model for women that differed from their experience of war as essential workers and heads of families in the absence of their men. Instead postwar women were made to symbolize the return to normalcy—a domestic, nonworking norm. Late in the 1940s, the fashion house of Christian Dior launched a clothing style called the "new look." It featured a pinched waist, tightly fitting bodices, and voluminous skirts. This restoration of the nineteenth-century female silhouette invited a renewal of clear gender roles. Women's magazines publicized the "new look" and urged a return to domesticity. Clad in crinolines, hats, gloves, and dainty shoes and reshaped by an array of constricting undergarments, "feminine" women portrayed the return to normalcy. Even in the hard-pressed Soviet Union, recipes for homemade face creams passed from woman to woman, and beauty parlors did a brisk business. New household products such as refrigerators and washing machines raised standards for women's accomplishment in the home by giving them the means to be "perfect" housewives.

However, "new look" propaganda did not mesh with reality. Dressmaking fabric was still being rationed in the late 1940s; even in the next decade women could not get enough of it to make voluminous skirts. In Europe, where people had barely enough to eat, the underwear needed for "new look" contours simply did not exist. Consumers had access only to standardized undergarments available with ration tickets. European women continued to work outside the home after the war; indeed, mature women and mothers were working more than ever before (Figure 28.2). The female workforce was going through a profound revolution as it gradually became less youthful and more populated by wives and mothers who would work outside the home all their lives. In the face of real women's long hours at work, heroines in Soviet fiction were still portrayed as ready to embrace a leisured version of femininity and maternal

The "New Look"

Immediately after the war, the French fashion industry swung into action to devise styles for the return to normal life. Cinched, even corseted waists and voluminous skirts suggested the nineteenth century rather than the depression and war years, when some women had started regularly wearing trousers. The highly restrictive femininity was also part of the cold war, as the leisured ideal demanded by the "new look" for middle-class Western women contrasted with the more practical styles in the Soviet Union, where women had to work to rebuild their devastated country. Liaison Agency.

subservience: "I can't be the boss forever," one woman said as she encouraged her husband to resume his prewar authority. "I'll be having children." Despite being bombarded with images of nineteenth-century middle-class femininity, women in Europe and the United States continued working to support their families.

The advertising business presided over the creation of cultural messages as well as over the rise of a new consumerism that accompanied recovery. Guided by marketing experts, western Europeans were imitating Americans, by driving some forty million motorized vehicles, including motorbikes, cars, buses, and trucks. The demand for cars made the automobile industry a leading economic sector. The number of radios in homes grew steadily—for example, by 10 percent a year in Italy between 1945 and 1950—and the 1950s marked a high tide of radio influence. The development of television in the 1920s and 1930s was interrupted by the war, but peacetime saw its rapid spread in the United States, which had twenty million sets by 1953. In Britain only 20 percent of the population owned TVs in the early 1950s, but 75 percent of all households owned one by 1961. Britain and the United States, however, were the great exceptions: the French had only sixty thousand sets in the mid-1950s; the Italians, only five thousand. Only in the 1960s did television become an important consumer item for most Europeans. In the 1950s, radio was still king.

The Culture of Cold War

Radio was at the center of the cold war. As superpower rivalry heated up, radio's propaganda function came to the fore. During the late 1940s and early 1950s, the Voice of America, with its main studio in Washington, D.C., broadcast in thirty-eight languages from one hundred transmitters and provided an alternative source of news for people in eastern Europe. The Soviet counterpart broadcast in Russian around the clock but initially spent much of its wattage jamming U.S. programming. Russian programs stressed a uniform Communist culture and values; the United States by contrast, emphasized diverse programming and promoted debate about current affairs.

Its issues and events conveyed by radio and other media, the cold war acquired a far-reaching

	Member Countries of Council of Mutual Economic Assistance[1]		Member Countries of European Economic Community[2]	
	1950	1960	1950	1960
Female as % of total population	54.9	53.9	51.8	51.6
Female labor force as % of total labor force	48.5	48.7	31.1	31.4
Distribution of female labor force (%):				
Agriculture	63.3	50.0	26.1	16.8
Industry	16.9	22.6	29.3	31.3
Services	19.8	27.4	44.6	51.9

[1] Albania, Bulgaria, Czechoslovakia, East Germany, Hungary, Poland, Romania, and USSR

[2] Belgium, Denmark, France, West Germany, Ireland, Italy, Luxembourg, Netherlands, and United Kingdom

FIGURE 28.2 Women in the Workforce, 1950–1960

In contrast to the situation after World War I, women did not leave the workforce in great numbers after World War II. In fact, Europe faced labor shortages. In countries of the Soviet bloc, women vastly outnumbered men because so many men had died in the war, and the task of rebuilding demanded every available worker. In Western Europe, women's workforce participation was lower, and countries like West Germany tried to keep women out of the labor pool to distinguish themselves from the Communist bloc. Note the increase in women's service-sector employment in just one decade.

World Employment 1996–1997: National Policies in a Global Context (Geneva: International Labour Office, 1996), 7.

emotional impact. The news featured reports about nuclear testing, military buildups, and hostile diplomatic incidents. The public heard tests of emergency power facilities that sent them scurrying for cover; in school, children rehearsed for nuclear war, and families built bomb shelters in their backyards. Reports of Soviet and American leaders facing one another down became part of everyday life. Amidst constant stories of the possibility of nuclear annihilation, mathematician and philosopher Bertrand Russell reported living daily in "confused agitation."

Popular culture centered on the cold war. Books like George Orwell's *1984* (1949) were claimed by ideologues on both sides as vindicating their beliefs. Ray Bradbury's popular *Fahrenheit 451* (1953), whose title indicated the temperature at which books would burn, condemned cold war

curtailment of intellectual freedom. In the USSR, official writers churned out spy stories, and espionage novels topped best-seller lists in the West. *Casino Royale* (1953) by the British author Ian Fleming introduced James Bond, who survived tests of wit and physical prowess at the hands of Communist and other political villains. Traveling to exotic places, Agent 007 brilliantly improvised with sophisticated, futuristic weaponry provided by government scientists—themselves employed in the cold war. Soviet pilots would not take off for flights when the work of Yulian Simyonov, the Russian counterpart of Ian Fleming, was playing on radio or television.

Consumer culture as a whole came under the cold war banner, as people debated the "Americanization" they saw taking place in Europe. While many Europeans were proponents of American

Bomb Shelter

Americans expressed their fear of nuclear annihilation by building tens of thousands of individual bomb shelters. Stocked with several months' supply of canned food and other goods, the shelters were to protect a family from the nuclear blast itself and from the disorder that might follow nuclear war. The government also prepared shelters to shield top officials and to ensure the continuation of civil society despite vast casualties and massive destruction.
Bettman/Corbis.

business practices, the Communist Party in France led a successful campaign to ban Coca-Cola for a time in the 1950s. A more widespread strategy involved producing elite consumer items. The French *new wave* cinema developed in reaction to mass-market Hollywood films. Directors like François Truffaut and Jean-Luc Godard focused on the maker, or *auteur*, of a film to contrast their work with movies concocted by anonymous studio executives. The *auteur* produced new wave films much as an author created a literary work. In addition, new wave directors introduced the history of film into their work in the form of film themes and symbols from the earliest days of film. In literature, French writers pioneered the *new novel* as an antidote to best-sellers that pumped up the U.S.-style mass market. Although the first in this genre, Nathalie Sarraute's *Tropismes,* was written in 1939,

most new novels appeared in the 1950s and thereafter. Sarraute wrote in terms of human "gestures," "subconversations," and fleeting glimpses of the interior of the human psyche.

Both sides tried to win the war by pouring vast sums of money into culture, though the United States did it by secretly channeling government money into foundations to promote U.S. symphonies, award fellowships to artists and writers, and start popular magazines around the world. As leadership of the art world passed to the United States, art became part of the cold war. *Abstract expressionism,* practiced by American artists such as Jackson Pollock, produced abstract works by dripping, spattering, and pouring paint in contrast to abstract works that still had elements of realism, such as those of Picasso. Abstract expressionists spoke of the importance of the artist's self-discovery, spiritual growth, and sensations in the process of painting. "If I stretch my arms next to the rest of myself and wonder where my fingers are, that is all the space I need as a painter," commented Dutch-born Willem de Kooning on his relationship with his canvas. Said to exemplify Western "freedom," such painters were given shows in Europe and awarded commissions at the direction of U.S. government agencies. Shrouded in a culture of secrecy and deception, information about both sides in the cold war is only now emerging from archives and memoirs.

The USSR openly promoted Communist culture around the world. When a show of abstract art opened in the Soviet Union, Khrushchev yelled

Mark Rothko, *Light Red over Black* (1957)
Lithuanian-born Mark Rothko spread large, luminous fields of color across his canvases in an attempt to capture universal spiritual values. Usually his paintings contained only two or three of these fields, prompting the viewer to experience long periods of contemplation. Rothko was part of a school of artists that aimed in the 1950s to reach enduring truths with such primal or "primitive" forms.
Tate Gallery, London/Art Resource, NY.

IMPORTANT DATES

1945	Cold war begins
1947	India and Pakistan win independence from Britain
1948	State of Israel established
1949	Mao Zedong leads Communist revolution in China; Simone de Beauvoir publishes *The Second Sex*
1950	Korean War begins
1953	Stalin dies; Korean War ends
1954	*Brown* v. *Board of Education* prohibits segregated schools in the United States; Vietnamese forces defeat the French at Dien Bien Phu
1956	Egyptian leader General Abdel Nasser nationalizes the Suez Canal; uprising in Hungary against USSR
1957	Boris Pasternak publishes *Doctor Zhivago*; USSR launches *Sputnik*
1958	Fifth Republic begins in France
1962	The United States and USSR face off in the Cuban missile crisis

that it was "dog shit." Pro-Soviet critics in western Europe saw U.S.-style abstract art as "an infantile sickness" and supported official socialist realist art with "human content," showing the condition of the workers and the oppressed races in the United States. In Italy, the *neorealist* technique was developed by filmmakers such as Roberto Rossellini in *Open City* (1945) and Vittorio De Sica in *The Bicycle Thief* (1948). Such works challenged Hollywood-style sets and costumes by using ordinary characters living in devastated, impoverished cities. By depicting stark conditions, neorealist directors conveyed their distance both from middle-class prosperity and from fascist bombast. "We are in rags? Let's show everyone our rags," said one Italian director. Values of the Communist resistance resonated not only in the post-fascist world but in the escalating climate of bipolarity. Reacting to the Soviet publicity of racial oppression in the United States, U.S. agents made certain that most films had African Americans as extras. Seen or unseen, the cold war entered the most unsuspected aspects of cultural life.

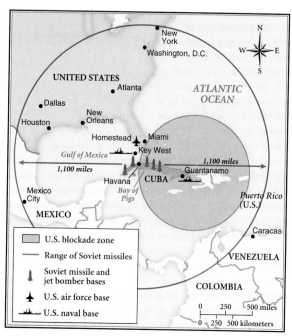

MAP 28.6 The Cuban Missile Crisis, 1962

Just off the coast of the southeastern United States, Cuba posed a threat to North American security once the Soviet Union began stocking the island with missiles. The United States reacted vigorously, insisting on the dismantling of missile sites and an end to the Soviets' supplying Cuba with further weaponry. Although his generals were prepared for nuclear war with the Soviet Union, President Kennedy refused to take this step despite his cold war stance on many other issues. Soviet Premier Khrushchev similarly backed down from a military confrontation.

Kennedy, Khrushchev, and the Atomic Brink

It was in this pervasive climate of cold war that John Fitzgerald Kennedy (1917–1963) became U.S. president in 1960. Kennedy represented American affluence and youth but also the nation's commitment to cold war. Kennedy's media advisers and ghostwriters recognized how perfect a match their articulate, good-looking president was to the power of television. A war hero and early fan of the fictional cold war spy James Bond, Kennedy intensified the arms race and escalated the cold war. In 1959, a revolution in Cuba had brought to power Fidel Castro, who allied his government with the Soviet Union. In the spring of 1961, Kennedy, assured by the Central Intelligence Agency (CIA) of success, launched an invasion of Cuba at the Bay of

Pigs to overthrow Castro. The invasion failed miserably and humiliated the United States. A few months later Kennedy had a chilling meeting with Khrushchev in Vienna, at which the Soviet leader brandished the specter of nuclear holocaust over the continuing U.S. presence in Berlin.

In the summer of 1961, East German workers, supervised by police and the army, stacked bales of barbed wire across miles of the city's east–west border to begin construction of the Berlin Wall. The divided city had served as an escape route by which some three million people had fled to the West. As a concrete wall replaced the barbed wire, people resorted to jumping through apartment windows to freedom and, when the windows were blocked, jumping from roofs. Kennedy responded at home with a call for more weapons and an enhanced civil defense program. In October 1962, matters came to a head when the CIA reported the installation of Soviet medium-range missiles in Cuba (Map 28.6). Kennedy now responded forcefully, calling for a blockade of ships headed for Cuba and threatening nuclear war if the missiles were not removed. For several days the world stood on the brink of nuclear disaster. Then, between October 25 and 27, Khrushchev and Kennedy negotiated an end to the crisis. The Soviets promised to remove the missile installations. Kennedy spent the remainder of his short life working to improve nuclear diplomacy; Khrushchev did the same. The two leaders, who had looked deeply into the nuclear future, clearly feared what they saw.

Conclusion

World War II began the atomic age and transformed international power politics. Two superpowers, the Soviet Union and the United States, each controlling atomic arsenals, replaced the former

MAPPING THE WEST The Cold War World, c. 1960 ▶

Superpower rivalry between the United States and the Soviet Union resulted in the division of much of the industrial world into cold war alliances. Simultaneously the superpowers vied for the allegiance of the newly decolonized countries of Asia and Africa by providing military, economic, and technological assistance. Wars such as those in Vietnam and Korea were also products of the cold war.

European leadership and engaged in a menacing cold war. The cold war saturated everyday life, giving birth to cold war religion in the preachings of the Reverend Billy Graham and to a secular culture of bomb shelters, spies, and witch-hunts. The postwar reconstruction of Europe created a cold war division into an Eastern bloc dominated by the Soviets and a freer West mostly allied with the United States.

Yet both halves of Europe recovered almost miraculously. The east, where wartime devastation was greatest, experienced less prosperity and achieved recovery at greater human cost than did western Europe. Wartime technology served as the basis for new consumer goods and improved health. Western Europe formed a successful Common Market that would become the foundation for the trend toward European unity. Yet as a result of the war Germany recovered as two countries, not one, and the former European powers shed their colonies. Newly independent nations emerged in Asia and Africa, opening the possibility for a more equitable distribution of global power.

As the West as a whole grew in prosperity, its cultural life focused on eradicating the evils of Nazism and on surviving the atomic rivalry of the superpowers. In the midst of consumerism and a heated cold war culture, many came to wonder whether cold war was really worth the threat of nuclear annihilation.

Suggested References

World Politics Transformed

In the past decade, the opening of Soviet archives and closer research in American records have allowed for more informed views of the diplomacy and politics of the cold war in Europe and around the world. Although few defend Stalin, we now benefit from balanced assessments of superpower rivalry. Two Web sites contain biographies of the main players, time lines, and miscellaneous details of cold war events.

Cold war: http://library.thinkquest.org/10826.mainpage .htm; http://history.acusd.edu/gen/20th/coldwarO.html.

Cronin, James. *The World the Cold War Made: Order, Chaos, and the Return of History.* 1996.

Eisenberg, Carolyn Woods. *Drawing the Line: The American Decision to Divide Germany, 1944–1949.* 1996.

Gaddis, John. *We Now Know: Rethinking Cold War History.* 1997.

Hogan, Michael J. *A Cross of Iron: Harry S Truman and the Origins of the National Security State, 1945–1954.* 1998.

*Pasternak, Boris. *Doctor Zhivago.* 1958.

Vadney, T. E. *The World Since 1945.* 1992.

Zubkova, Elena. *Russia after the War: Hopes, Illusions, and Disappointments, 1945–1957.* 1998.

Zubok, Vladislav, and Constantine Pleshakov. *Inside the Kremlin's Cold War: From Stalin to Khrushchev.* 1996.

The Political and Economic Recovery of Europe

Though painstaking and complex, recovery in its material and political forms yielded a distinctly new Europe whose characteristics historians are still uncovering. Because of the opening of the archives, historical attention has focused on charting Soviet occupation, recovery, and Communist takeover.

Herf, Jeffrey. *Divided Memory: The Nazi Past in the Two Germanies.* 1997.

Kenney, Padraic. *Rebuilding Poland: Workers and Communists, 1945–1950.* 1997.

Marrus, Michael. *The Unwanted: European Refugees in the Twentieth Century.* 1985.

Medvedev, Roy. *Khrushchev.* 1983.

Moeller, Robert, ed. *West Germany under Construction: Politics, Society, and Culture in the Adenauer Era.* 1997.

Naimark, Norman M. *The Russians in Germany: A History of the Russian Zone of Occupation, 1945–1949.* 1995.

Pinder, John. *European Community: The Building of a Union.* 1991.

Decolonization in a Cold War Climate

Novelists, philosophers, and historians debate the impact and issues of decolonization. Powerful evocations of the brutality of the process appear most often in novels such as *Cracking India*, recently made into the film *Earth*.

Brown, L. Carl. *International Politics and the Middle East.* 1984.

Dunbabin, J. P. D. *The Post-Imperial Age: The Great Powers and the Wider World.* 1994.

*Fanon, Frantz. *The Wretched of the Earth.* 1961.

Flaghan, Simha. *The Birth of Israel: Myths and Realities.* 1987.

Hargreaves, J. D. *Decolonization in Africa.* 1996.

---

*Primary source.

McIntyre, W. David. *British Decolonization, 1946–1997: When, Why, and How Did the British Empire Fall?* 1999.

*Sidhwa, Bapsi. *Cracking India: A Novel.* 1992.

Cultural Life on the Brink of Nuclear War

Cold war culture, including the growth of consumerism, make the 1950s a fertile field for research, especially as new sources become available. Historians like Saunders have focused on governments' direction of high culture to the point that some artists and writers were made "stars" because of government intervention.

*Beauvoir, Simone de. *The Mandarins.* 1956.

Boyer, Paul. *By the Bomb's Early Light: American Thought and Culture at the Dawn of the Atomic Age.* 1985.

Cohen-Solal, Annie. *Sartre.* 1987.

Heineman, Elizabeth D. *What Difference Does a Husband Make? Women and Marital Status in Nazi and Postwar Germany.* 1999.

Kuisel, Richard. *Seducing the French: The Dilemma of Americanization.* 1993.

Lapidus, Gail. *Women in Soviet Society: Equality, Development, and Social Change.* 1978.

McDowell, Colin. *Forties Fashion and the New Look.* 1997.

Marcus, Milicent. *Italian Film in the Light of Neorealism.* 1986.

Marling, Karal Ann. *As Seen on TV: The Visual Culture of Everyday Life in the 1950s.* 1994.

Saunders, Frances Stonor. *Who Paid the Piper?* 1999.

Swann, Abram de. *In Care of the State: Health Care, Education, and Welfare in Europe and the United States in the Modern Era.* 1988.

CHAPTER 29

Challenges to the Postindustrial West

1960–1980

Shrine to Jan Palach
Jan Palach was a martyr to the cause of an independent Czechoslovakia, free to pursue a non-Soviet destiny. His self-immolation on behalf of that cause roused the nation. As makeshift shrines sprang up and multiplied throughout the 1970s and 1980s, they served as common rallying points that ultimately contributed to the overthrow of Communist rule.
© Mark Garanger/Corbis.

I n January 1969, Jan Palach, a twenty-one-year-old philosophy student, drove to a main square in Prague, doused his body with gasoline, and set himself ablaze. In his coat—deliberately put to one side—was a paper demanding an end to Soviet-style repression in Czechoslovakia. It promised more such suicides unless the government lifted state censorship. The manifesto was signed: "Torch No. 1." Across a stunned nation black flags were flown, close to a million people flocked to Palach's funeral, and shrines to his memory seemed to spring up overnight. For the next months, as repression continued, more Czech youth followed Palach's grim example and became torches for freedom.

In an age of conspicuous technological growth, Jan Palach's self-immolation was a primal and horrifying scene. It was part of a massive uprising of youth, women, minorities, and many others in the 1960s and 1970s against repression, war, poverty, inequality, and technology itself. From Czechoslovakia to the United States and around the world, protests arose against the way in which industrial nations in general and the superpowers in particular were directing society.

Political repression outraged these activists, and they objected to the human consequences of technology's dizzying pace. Technological advances, reformers believed, had given enormous power to a handful of engineers, financiers, managers, and bureaucrats—the new (but unelected) leaders of a "postindustrial society." The term *postindustrial* indicated the emergence of the service sector—including finance, engineering, and

1960	1964	1968	1972	1976	1980

Politics and War

Test-ban treaty; assassination of U.S. president Kennedy

Nikita Khrushchev ousted in the USSR; U.S. Civil Rights Act

Willy Brandt becomes West German foreign minister and develops Ostpolitik

Revolution in Czechoslovakia; uprisings throughout Europe and the United States; Martin Luther King Jr. assassinated

Spread of political terrorism; growth of black power, environmental, gay rights, pacifist, and feminist movements

SALT I signed   Helsinki accords

Americans taken hostage in Iran

Treaty ending war in Vietnam; Yom Kippur War

Society and Economy

Emergence of multinational corporations; postindustrial society and economy in West

Migration from formerly colonized areas into the West; further decline in birthrate, rising rates of divorce, new family patterns; growth of Japanese economy

Launch of *Intelsat*

First successful human heart transplant

OPEC raises price of oil and imposes oil embargo in the West

First test-tube baby born

Miniaturization of computer

Culture, Religion, and Intellectual Life

English rock group the Beatles lead the way toward a new mass youth culture

Spread of TV culture in Europe; construction of new universities

Forum on "pop art" in New York City

U.S. astronauts walk on the moon; Sony produces first affordable color VCR

Vatican II   Christa Wolf, *Divided Heaven*

Aleksandr Solzhenitsyn, *Gulag Archipelago*

health care—as the dominant force in the economy in the West, replacing heavy industry. Many of the protesters were being educated to enter this service elite. As critics, however, they saw conformity, mindlessness, and bondage resulting from work in which the majority of people used neither mental nor physical skill but in many cases merely watched over an ever-growing number of machines. Protest in these postindustrial decades aimed at recovering human power and control.

While reformers questioned the values of technological society, whole nations challenged the superpowers' monopoly of international power. An agonizing war in Vietnam sapped the will and resources of the United States, and China confronted the Soviet Union with increasing belligerence and confidence. The oil-producing states of the Middle East formed a cartel and reduced the flow of oil to the leading industrial nations in the 1970s. The resulting price increases turned a slowdown in the postwar economy into a recession. Other third-world countries resorted not to economic leverage but to terrorism to achieve their ends; some countries deployed both. Even the wealth, military might, and technological leadership of the superpowers could not guarantee that they would always emerge victorious in this age of increasingly global competition. Nor during these decades could the superpowers prevent the erosion of their legitimacy—an erosion often brought on by the individual acts of citizens, like the human torches. In their economies, societies, and international and domestic politics, the superpowers faced challenges at virtually every turn.

❖ The Technology Revolution

Three decades after World War II, continuing technological advances steadily boosted prosperity and changed daily life in industrial countries. In Europe and the United States, people awoke to instantaneous radio and television news, worked with computers, and used revolutionary contraceptives to control reproduction. Satellites orbiting the earth reported weather conditions, relayed telephone signals, and collected military intelligence. Smaller gadgets—electric popcorn poppers, portable radios and tape players, automatic garage door openers—made life more pleasant. The reliance of humans on machines led one scientist and philosopher, Donna Haraway, to insist that people were no longer self-sufficient individuals, but rather *cyborgs*—that is, humans who needed machines to sustain ordinary life processes. However, as with the invention of textile machinery and the railroads in the eighteenth and nineteenth centuries, the full range of social implications would not take shape all at once.

The Information Age

Information technology catalyzed social change in these postindustrial decades just as innovations in textile making and the spread of railroads had in the nineteenth century. Some commentators have suggested that the development of information technology was even more revolutionary because of its

potential for conveying knowledge, culture, and politics globally. Mass journalism, film, and radio had begun to forge a more homogeneous society based on shared information and images in the first half of the twentieth century; in the last third of the century, television, computers, and telecommunications made information more accessible and, some critics said, culture more standardized. Politics and the economy felt the impact of information technology as well.

The Spread of Television Culture. Americans embraced television in the 1950s; following the postwar recovery, it was Europe's turn. Between the mid-1950s and the mid-1970s, Europeans rapidly adopted television as a major entertainment and communications medium. In 1954, one percent of French households had television; in 1964, nearly 40 percent did; and by 1974, almost 80 percent. With the average viewer tuning in about four and a half hours a day, the audience for newspapers and theater declined. "We devote more . . . hours per year to television than [to] any other single artifact," one sociologist commented in 1969. Virtually every Western home boasted a TV set. As with radio, European governments funded television broadcasting with tax dollars and controlled TV programming to avoid what they perceived as the substandard fare offered by American commercial TV; instead they featured drama, ballet, concerts, variety shows, and news. Governments believed this new medium should be used to preserve the humanist tradition by presenting viewers with "choice," as one British official put it, "the widest possible range of subjects treating the entire field and all the variety of the human conscience and experience." Thus the welfare state, in Europe at least, assumed a new obligation to fill its citizens' leisure time—and also gained more power to shape daily life.

With the emergence of communications satellites and video recorders in the 1960s, state-sponsored television encountered competition. Satellite technology allowed for the transmission of sports broadcasts and other programming to a worldwide audience. Feature films on videotape became readily available to television stations (although not yet to individuals) and competed with made-for-television movies and other programs. European governments continued to produce high-quality television, but they often found themselves outpaced by private pay stations that either churned out American-style sitcoms or bought American comedies and dubbed in the native language. The competition increased in 1969 when the Sony Corporation introduced the first affordable color videocassette recorder to the consumer market. What statesmen and intellectuals considered the junk programming of the United States—soap operas, game shows, sitcoms—amused a vast Western audience because it dealt with the joys, sorrows, tensions, and aspirations of daily life. Critics charged that both state-sponsored and commercial television avoided extremes to keep sponsors happy, instead spoon-feeding audiences only "official" or "moderate" opinions. They complained that although TV provided more information than had ever been available before, the resulting shared culture represented the lowest common denominator.

Soviet-bloc television also exercised a powerful, widespread cultural influence. Even in one rural area of the Soviet Union, 44 percent of the inhabitants watched television every day in the late 1970s; another 27 percent tuned in every three or four days; others continued to prefer radio. By the end of the 1970s, Soviet announcers were broadcasting government-approved news to some thirty million TV sets in both rural and urban areas, uniting a far-flung population. Educational programming also united the population of the USSR by broadcasting shows designed to advance Soviet culture. At the same time, with travel impossible or forbidden to many, shows about foreign lands were among the most popular—as were postcards from these lands, which became household decorations.

Governments used the media not only to disperse culture but also to achieve political ends. Heads of state could usually preempt regular programming. In the 1960s, French president Charles de Gaulle addressed his fellow citizens frequently, employing the grandiose gestures of an imperial ruler to stir patriotism. As electoral success increasingly depended on cultivating a successful media image, political staffs came to rely on media experts as much as they did policy experts. To ensure political neutrality in West Germany, an official committee regularly monitored state television announcers, watching for subtle signs of bias. Nonetheless, mere coverage on television news made national politics an ever-larger presence in daily life.

The Computer Age Opens. Just as revolutionary as television was the computer, which reshaped work in science, defense, and ultimately industry. Computers had evolved dramatically since the first electronic computer, Colossus, which the British used in 1943 to decode Nazi military and diplomatic messages. Awesome in its day, Colossus was primitive by later standards—gigantic, slow, able only to decode, and so noisy that it sounded like "a roomful of [people] knitting away with steel needles," in the words of one Western observer. With growing use in civilian industry and business after the war, computing machines shrank from the size of a

Venice Skyline
Television swept Europe in the 1960s and 1970s, increasingly uniting people by the daily news, theater, films, and game shows. Satellite transmission allowed programming to cross national boundaries, further welding peoples and cultures of the Common Market. In a divided Germany, the exchange of programming bridged even the Berlin Wall and was an early contributor to the erosion of cold war divisions.
Tom Bross/Stock Boston.

gymnasium in the 1940s to that of a small desk in the late 1970s. By the mid-1980s they would be no larger than an attaché case and fantastically more powerful than Colossus.

The expanding capabilities and tumbling prices of computers depended on the development of increasingly sophisticated digital electronic circuitry implanted on tiny silicon chips, which replaced the clumsy radio tubes used in 1940s and 1950s computers. Within a few decades the computer could perform hundreds of millions of operations per second and even respond to sound. The price of the integrated circuit at the heart of computer technology would eventually fall to less than a dollar; as a result, businesses and households would gain access to enormous amounts of information and computing ability at a reasonable cost. Commentators throughout the West spoke of an information revolution.

Computers changed the pace and patterns of work not only by speeding up and easing tasks but also by performing many operations that workers had once done themselves. In garment making, for example, experienced workers no longer painstakingly figured out how to arrange patterns on cloth for maximum efficiency and economy. Instead a computer specified instructions for the optimal positioning of pattern pieces, and trained workers, usually women, followed the machine's directions. By the end of the 1970s, the miniaturization of the computer had made possible a renewal of the eighteenth-century "cottage industry." As in earlier times, people could work in the physical isolation of their homes but be connected to a central mainframe. Some companies were even using electronic mail among employees in the late 1970s.

Did computers transform society for the better? Whereas the Industrial Revolution had seen physical power replaced by machine capabilities, the information revolution witnessed brainpower augmented by computer technology. Many believed computers would profoundly expand mental life, providing, in the words of one scientist, "boundless opportunities . . . to resolve the puzzles of cosmology, of life, and of the society of man." Others maintained that computers programmed people, reducing human capacity for inventiveness, problem solving, and initiative. As the 1970s closed, such predictions were still untested as this information revolution moved toward a more dramatic unfolding in the 1980s and 1990s.

The Space Age

1957 Soviet Union launches the first artificial satellite, *Sputnik*

1961 Soviet cosmonaut Yuri Gagarin orbits the earth; capsule carrying Alan Shepard Jr. makes first U.S. suborbital flight

1965 United States launches first commercial communications satellite, *Intelsat I*

1969 United States astronauts Neil Armstrong and Edwin Aldrin walk on moon's surface

1970s–present Soviet Union and United States individually and in collaboration with various countries perform space station experiments, lunar probes, and other scientific experiments

1971 Soviet Union attempts unsuccessfully to put *Salyut 1*, a space station, into orbit

1973 United States puts *Skylab*, an experimental space station, into orbit

1976 *Viking* spacecraft explores Mars

1979–1986 Spacecraft *Voyager* makes successful flybys of Jupiter, Saturn, and Uranus

The Space Age

When the Soviets launched the satellite *Sputnik* in 1957, they ignited competition with the United States that was quickly labeled the "space race." Although President Eisenhower had little interest in what he considered merely an expensive attempt to gain global status, his successor, John F. Kennedy, became obsessed by the idea of "beating" the Soviets in space. He proclaimed it an American goal to put a man on the moon by the end of the 1960s. Throughout the decade, increasingly complex space flights tested humans' ability to survive the process of space exploration, including weightlessness. Astronauts walked in space, endured weeks (and, later, months) in orbit, repaired malfunctioning equipment, docked with other craft, fixed satellites, and carried out experiments for the military and private industry. Meanwhile a series of unmanned rockets filled the earth's gravitational sphere with weather, television, intelligence, and other communications satellites.

In July 1969, a worldwide television audience watched as U.S. astronauts Neil Armstrong and

Valentina Tereshkova, Russian Cosmonaut

People sent into space were heroes, representing modern values of courage, strength, and well-honed skills. Insofar as the space age was part of the cold war race for superpower superiority, the USSR held the lead during the first decade. The Soviets trained both women and men, and the 1963 flight of Valentina Tereshkova—the first woman in space—supported Soviet claims of gender equality in contrast to the U.S. program.

Archive Photos.

Edwin "Buzz" Aldrin walked on the moon's surface—the climactic moment in the space race. As Armstrong stepped out of *Apollo 11*'s lunar module, he remarked, "That's one small step for man, one giant leap for mankind." Astronauts and cosmonauts were perhaps the era's most admired heroes. Beginning with Soviet cosmonaut Yuri Gagarin, these space explorers had to live up to high public expectations. American astronaut John Glenn later became a senator and presidential contender. The Soviets promoted the first woman in space, Valentina Tereshkova, as a role model for women—and never more so than when she married another cosmonaut and became a mother.

The space race also drove Western cultural developments. A whole new fantasy world developed.

Children's toys and games revolved increasingly around space. Science fiction writing, already a popular genre for several decades, reached ever-larger audiences. Films portrayed space explorers answering questions about life that were formerly the domain of church leaders. American filmmaker Stanley Kubrick's breathtaking 1968 hit movie based on Arthur C. Clarke's *2001: A Space Odyssey* explored human morality and intelligence through a prism of extraterrestrial life and space travel. Likewise, in the internationally popular television series *Star Trek*, members of the starship *Enterprise*'s diverse crew wrestled with the problems of maintaining humane values against less-developed, often menacing civilizations. In the Eastern bloc, Polish author Stanislaw Lem's novel *Solaris* (1971) similarly portrayed space age individuals engaged in personal quests and likewise drew readers and ultimately viewers into a futuristic fantasy.

This space age grew out of cold war concerns, but it also offered the possibility of more global political cooperation, for—like the U.S. atomic bomb project during World War II—the diffusion of rocket technology resulted from international efforts. From the 1960s on, U.S. spaceflights often involved the participation of other countries such as Great Britain and the Netherlands. In 1965, Western European nations established the European Space Research Organization to develop rocket technology in competition with the superpowers. Using rocket and other space technology, an international consortium headed by the United States launched the first commercial communications satellite, *Intelsat I*, in 1965, and by the 1970s more than four hundred stations worldwide and some 150 countries worked together to maintain global satellite communications. Interlocking space, computer, and other information technology systems still served cold war ends, but the international collaboration needed to sustain these systems also countered virulent nationalism.

Lunar landings and experiments in space advanced pure science despite space race hype. Astronomers, for example, previously dependent on remote sensing for their work, used mineral samples from the moon to calculate the age of the solar system more precisely. Unmanned spacecraft provided data on cosmic radiation, magnetic fields, and infrared sources. *Viking* transmitted stunning pictures of Mars in 1976, and *Voyager*, in its flyby of

Saturn, Jupiter, and Uranus beginning in 1979, supplied masses of new data about the earth's solar system. Such findings from outer space reinforced the "big bang" theory of the origins of the universe, first posited in the 1930s by American astronomer Edwin Hubble and given crucial support in the 1950s by the discovery of a low level of radiation permeating the universe in all directions. Based on the work of Einstein and Planck, the "big bang" theory explains the development of the universe from a condition of extremely high density and temperature some ten billion years ago. Nuclei emerged when these conditions dissipated in a rapid expansion of space—the so-called big bang.

Although the media touted the human conquerors of space, breakthroughs in space exploration and astronomy were utterly dependent on technology. As the first American astronauts themselves acknowledged, their chief role had been to rouse public interest. Scientists could gain accurate knowledge of the heavens only with the aid of mathematics and remarkable new instruments such as the radiotelescope, which depicted space by receiving, measuring, and calculating nonvisible rays. The scientific use of sophisticated technologies was not limited to astronomy and physics, moreover, but extended to the life sciences, which investigated the origins and evolution of life itself.

The Revolution in Biology

Advances in the biological sciences brought dramatic new health benefits, but they raised serious questions about scientific intervention in life processes. In 1952, scientists Francis Crick, an Englishman, and James Watson, an American, discovered the configuration of DNA, the material in a cell's chromosomes that carries hereditary information. Apparently solving the mystery of the gene and thus of biological inheritance, they showed how the "double helix" of the DNA molecule splits in cellular reproduction to form the basis of each new cell. This genetic material, biologists concluded, provides a chemical pattern for an individual organism's life. Beginning in the 1960s, genetics and the new field of molecular biology progressed rapidly. Growing understanding of nucleic acids and proteins permitted important progress in knowledge of viruses and bacteria and made possible a host of new antibiotics and antiviral serums to combat polio and

such dangerous childhood diseases as mumps and measles. Tetanus, syphilis, and tuberculosis no longer ravaged the West.

In the wake of this biological revolution came questions about the ethics of humans' tampering with the natural processes of life. For example, understanding how DNA works allowed scientists to bypass natural animal reproduction by a process called *cloning*—obtaining the cells of an organism and dividing or reproducing them (in an exact copy) in a laboratory. But *should* scientists interfere with so basic and essential a process as reproduction? ethicists and politicians asked. Similarly, the possibility of genetically altering species and even creating new ones (for instance, to control agricultural pests) led to concern about how such actions would affect the balance of nature. Thus, although science functioned on a theoretical plane, its consequences rippled through the social, cultural, and moral realms as well. Invoking Mary Shelley's *Frankenstein*, one critic noted that people still fear "that our scientists, well-intentioned and decent men and women all, will go on being titans who create monsters."

In a related medical field, Dr. Christiaan Barnard of South Africa performed the first successful heart transplant in 1967, and U.S. doctors later developed an artificial heart that allowed critically ill recipients to live for several years after a transplant, although often severely disabled. These medical miracles, however, prompted questions and even protests. For example, given the shortage of reusable organs, what criteria should doctors use in selecting recipients? Commentators also debated whether the enormous cost of new medical technology to save a few people would be better spent on helping the many who lacked even basic medical and health care. Such quandaries moved medicine further into the arena of social policy.

Reproductive Technologies and the Sexual Revolution

Technology also influenced the most intimate areas of human relations—sexuality and procreation. In traditional societies, community and family norms dictated marital arrangements and sexual practices, in large part because too many or too few children threatened the crucial balance between population size and agricultural productivity. As Western societies industrialized and urbanized, however, not only did these considerations become less urgent but the growing availability of reliable birth-control devices permitted young people to begin sexual relations earlier, with less risk of pregnancy. In the 1960s these trends accelerated. The birth-control pill, first produced in the United States and tested on women in developing areas, came on the Western market after U.S. and British health authorities approved it in the early 1960s. By 1970, "the pill" provided a more reliable means than condoms and diaphragms for controlling reproduction, and its use spread to all industrialized countries. Worldwide, millions sought out voluntary surgical sterilization through tubal ligations and vasectomies. New techniques brought abortion, traditionally performed by amateurs, into the hands of medical professionals, making it a safe procedure for the first time.

Childbirth and conception itself were similarly transformed. Whereas only a small minority of Western births took place in hospitals in 1920, more than 90 percent did by 1970. Obstetricians now performed much of the work midwives had once done. As pregnancy and birth became a medical process, innovative new procedures and equipment made it possible to monitor women and fetuses throughout pregnancy, labor, and delivery. The number of medical interventions rose: cesarean births increased 400

percent in the United States in the 1960s and 1970s, and the number of prenatal visits per patient in Czechoslovakia, for example, rose 300 percent between 1957 and 1976. In 1978, the first "test-tube baby," Louise Brown, was born to an English couple. She had been conceived when her mother's eggs were fertilized with her father's sperm in a laboratory dish and then implanted in her mother's uterus. This complex process, called *in vitro fertilization*, ultimately spared many couples the agony of unwanted childlessness. Donor-supplied "banks" provided sperm or eggs for the in vitro method if the couple who wanted to conceive could not produce their own. If a woman could not carry a child to term, the laboratory-fertilized embryo could be implanted in the uterus of a surrogate, or substitute, mother. Researchers even began working on an artificial womb to allow for reproduction entirely outside the body—from storage bank to artificial embryonic environment.

A host of disturbing ethical and political controversies—and some tragedies—accompanied these breakthroughs. In the early 1960s, a West German drug firm, without prior testing, distributed the tranquilizer thalidomide, claiming that it safely prevented miscarriages. Pregnant women used the drug widely, with disastrous results: thousands of disabled and mentally handicapped children were

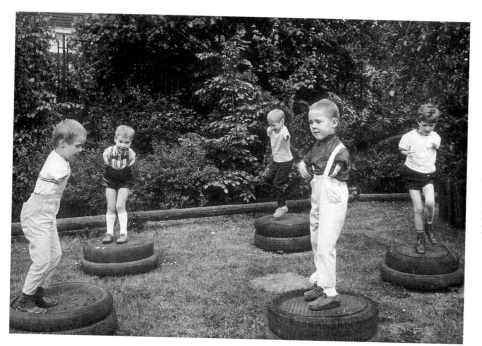

Thalidomide Children
In the last third of the century, increasingly destructive side effects of powerful medicines became apparent. Women who had taken the drug thalidomide gave birth to children with severe disabilities, and the public condemned companies selling untested products. The race to profit from scientific and technological developments sometimes ignored human well-being. Deutsche Press Agentur/Archive Photos.

born. The Catholic church firmly opposed all mechanical and chemical means of birth control as a sinful intervention in a sacred process. Many Catholics and other opponents of abortion maintained that life begins at conception, and they branded abortion as murder. In vitro fertilization also stirred disapproval, appearing to some as "playing God" with life.

The expanding media and medical professions meanwhile helped democratize knowledge of birth-control procedures after World War II and made public discussions of sexual matters explicit, technical, and widespread. Popular use of birth control allowed Western society to be saturated with highly sexualized music, literature, and journalism without a corresponding rise in the birthrate—impressive evidence of the increasing separation of sexuality from reproduction. Abundant statistical surveys showed that regular sexual activity began at an ever-younger age, and people talked more openly about sex—another component of cultural change. Finally, in a climate of increased publicity to sexuality, more open homosexual behavior became apparent, along with continued efforts to decriminalize it across the West. The Western media trumpeted the "commercialization of sex" and announced the arrival of a "sexual revolution." From the late nineteenth century to the 1960s, however, sexual revolution had been trumpeted with each advance in birth-control technology, showing once again the social and political impact of technological transformation.

❖ Postindustrial Society and Culture

Reshaped by soaring investments in science, the spread of technology, and growing prosperity, Western countries in the 1960s started on what social scientists labeled a *postindustrial* course. Instead of being centered on manufacturing and heavy industry, postindustrial society emphasized the distribution of such services as health care and education. The service sector was the leading force in the economy, and this meant that intellectual work, not industrial or manufacturing work, had become primary. Moreover, all parts of society and industry interlocked, forming a system constantly in need of complex analysis. Thus, unlike the preindustrial age

dominated by landlords or the industrial age dominated by manufacturers, postindustrial society brought to the fore highly educated professional and technical experts who could calculate needs, gather information, and make predictions. One Soviet scientist characterized his work as "not simply an act of creativity but a complex system of coordinati[on]" that demanded management. (See "Terms of History," page 1120.)

Postindustrial society changed the day-to-day lives and material conditions of millions of workers. Many working-class people, formerly cramped in tenements, could now afford to buy their own homes; by the 1970s, more than one-third of Western European workers owned homes. Corporations boosted workers' participation in management decisions and employed industrial psychologists to alleviate tensions. The rise of "industrial parks" at the edges of cities made room in city centers for corporate headquarters, banks, and university and government buildings. The postindustrial characteristics of individuals and society would carry over from the 1960s and 1970s into the next century.

Multinational Corporations

One of the major innovations of the postindustrial era was the rise of multinational corporations. These companies produced for a global market and conducted business worldwide, but unlike older kinds of international firms, they established major factories in countries other than their home base. For example, by 1970, Standard Oil of New Jersey employed about 150,000 people, some 90,000 (60 percent) of them outside the United States. Of the five hundred largest businesses in the United States in 1970, more than one hundred did over a quarter of their business abroad; IBM, for instance, operated in more than one hundred countries. Although U.S.-based corporations led the way, European and Japanese multinationals like Volkswagen, Shell, Nestlé, and Sony also had a broad global scope.

Some multinational corporations had bigger revenues than entire nations. They appeared to burst the bounds of the nation-state, as they set up shop in whatever part of the world offered cheap labor. Their interests differed starkly from those of ordinary people with a local or national outlook. In the first years after the war, multinationals preferred European employees, who constituted a highly

Postindustrial

In 1973, U.S. sociologist Daniel Bell's book *The Coming of Postindustrial Society* announced a momentous change in Western society. The economies of the major powers had stopped being predominantly manufacturing and had become instead "postindustrial." By this Bell meant not that there was no more industrial production of cars, household goods, and materials such as steel but rather that service industries like health care, education, banking, and other financial services had outstripped manufacturing. In terms of both number of employees and income generated, service industries were forming an ever larger sector of the economy, and Bell saw this postindustrial trend continuing. And, in fact, statistics from the 1990s testified to the accuracy of Bell's prediction: in the United States, for example, workers in manufacturing made up only 15 percent of the workforce.

Postindustrial society, in Bell's analysis, had a second component that has also been borne out over time. Like observers in Western Europe, Bell pointed to the critical importance of information and knowledge in the operation of society. Decisions in individual enterprises as well as in technological society as a whole could no longer spring from hunches and small bits of information. Instead the management of any entity depended on *systems analysis*, which took into account every factor pertinent to the system, be it a factory, a financial institution, or a government. Under these circumstances those who knew how to obtain, manipulate, and produce vast quantities of knowledge—even a single worker—could be far more important than the owner of a firm. Bell had captured the knowledge or information-based characteristics of the age.

The term *postindustrial* was part of a trend prevalent in these years to use the prefix *post* with an array of words, employed first in the term *postwar*. *Postwar* came to mean the period between the end of the war and economic recovery from it, 1945 to about 1960. On the one hand the term seemed simple enough to understand, but on the other hand some people found that the entire second half of the twentieth century was infused with the spirit of World War II, extending the meaning of postwar to encompass far more than a fifteen-year period and economic definition. Most notably, Europe and the world still reverberated with the legacy of the Holocaust and wartime devastation many decades later. *Posts* proliferated in these decades: *postmodern, post-historical, post-Marxist, post-Western,* and even *post-human,* to name a few of the most important uses.

The term *postmodern* arose after the various rebellions of the 1960s had challenged the rational,

educated labor pool, had a strong consumer tradition, and eagerly sought secure work. Then in the 1960s, multinationals moved more of their operations to the emerging economies of formerly colonized states. This development afforded new options for hiring should labor costs rise or taxes and regulations increase. Although multinational corporations provided jobs in developing areas, profits usually enriched foreign stockholders.

Initially critics denounced what they perceived as a new imperialism in the guise of corporate invasion. However, many European firms believed that they could stay competitive only by expanding, and they adeptly and aggressively reacted to the changing international business climate by stepping up mergers. In chemicals, glass, electrical products, transport, metallurgy, and many other industries, huge conglomerates came to dominate European production. In France, for example, a massive glass conglomerate merged with a metallurgical company to form a new group specializing in all phases of construction—a wise move given the postwar building boom. Whereas U.S. production had surpassed the combined output of West Germany, Great Britain, France, Italy, and Japan in the immediate postwar years, by the mid-1970s these countries had rebounded. By 1972, both the nationalized British Steel company and the privately owned and German-based Thyssen firm were approaching the revenues of U.S. Steel and Bethlehem Steel—giants of their time.

European firms were often backed and sometimes even owned by their governments. These companies increased their investment in research progressive, and technology-proud attitudes connected with the Enlightenment, the first wave of modernity. Enlightenment thinkers associated modernity with the triumph of science and Enlightenment faith that precise knowledge would yield an ever better future. In the 1960s, students and environmentalists maintained that bombs, pollution, and the rising tide of cancer—not progress—had been the most spectacular results of modernity. Over the next decades *postmodernity* would criticize even more aspects of the Enlightenment.

Post-human also began to emerge as an idea during these decades, associated at first with the development of artificial organs and body parts and the imminent development of robots to do factory work. Not only had machines replaced people in factories, critics observed, but ordinary people could not live without machines in their lives. The so-called "virtual reality" of the internet age contributed yet another sense of *post-human*, as people developed relationships that were purely electronic.

Post-Marxism can be dated to these years when socialist countries introduced elements of the market economy. Hungary was notable in opening the road to post-Marxism economically, while Czechoslovakia and Poland mounted continuing protests to Soviet rule. All of these set the stage for the collapse of communism in the 1980s and 1990s, ushering in a more thoroughly post-Marxist period. Some maintain that the challenges to Marxism from the 1950s on stemmed from the inability of the Communist system to meet the technological demands of the postindustrial age. As technology and information determined the well-being of industries, consumers, and social programs, ideology got in the way of efficiency, causing the government, the economy, and the social order to collapse.

The emergence of a postindustrial social and economic order may well leave us wondering what will succeed it as an organizing principle for human productivity. The emergence of such concepts as postmodern, post-human, and post-Marxist suggests that theorists are seeing further change already at hand. Historians, however, counterbalance these analyses by suggesting that most proclamations of change and most visions of the future have deep roots in the past.

FURTHER READING

Bell, Daniel. *The Coming of Post-Industrial Society: A Venture in Social Forecasting.* 1973.

Hayles, N. Katherine. *How We Became Posthuman: Virtual Bodies in Cybernetics, Literature, and Informatics.* 1999.

Seidman, Steven, ed. *The Postmodern Turn: New Perspectives on Social Theory.* 1994.

and used international cooperation to produce major new products. This new emphasis on research was a crucial ingredient in postindustrial society. Ventures like the British-French Concorde supersonic aircraft, which, beginning with its first flight in 1976, flew from London to New York in under four hours, and the Airbus, a more practical series of passenger jets inaugurated in 1972 by a consortium of European firms, attested to the strong relationship among government, business, and science (Map 29.1). Jointly pursuing technological and production innovations, European firms commanded large enough research budgets to compete successfully with U.S.-based multinational giants. "The prime function . . . of an industrial company," said one British executive, "[is] to spend every possible penny it can afford on technical development."

The New Worker

In its formative stage, industrial production had depended on workers who often labored to exhaustion, endured malnourishment, and lived in a state of poverty that sometimes led to violence. This scenario changed fundamentally in postwar Europe. To begin with, the proportion of people toiling in factories and mines and on farms dropped. Whereas the farm population had been declining as a percentage of the workforce for almost two centuries, the substantial reduction of the blue-collar workforce was new. It resulted from resource depletion in coal mines, the substitution of oil for coal and of plastics for steel, the growth of international competition, and automation in manufacturing processes.

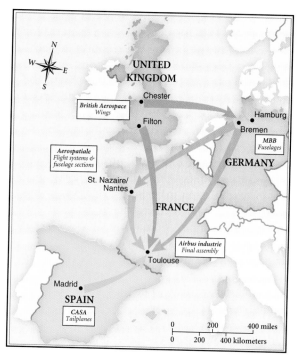

MAP 29.1 The Airbus Production System

The international consortium Airbus marked an important step in the economic and industrial integration of Europe. It also advanced the revitalization of the individual national economies by establishing new manufacturing centers away from capital cities and by modernizing older ones. Its formation presaged the international mergers and cooperative production that would characterize the late twentieth and early twenty-first centuries; today Airbus is a global enterprise with parts and service centers around the world, including the United States, China, and India.

Redefining Labor. Within firms the relationship of workers to bosses shifted. Managers increasingly blamed old-fashioned hierarchical decision making for diminished productivity. Following the lead of Swedish manufacturers, employers started grouping workers into teams that set their own production quotas, organized and assigned tasks, enforced their own quality standards, and competed with other teams to see who could produce more. As workers adopted attitudes and gained responsibilities that had once been managerial prerogatives, traditional definitions of labor became obsolete. Union membership declined along with blue-collar work, although strikes remained important for raising labor issues and unions continued to play a key role in factory organization (outside West Germany and most of the Soviet bloc, where unions were illegal).

When strikes occurred, however, they were often short-lived and symbolic.

In both U.S.-led- and Soviet-bloc countries, a new working class emerged, consisting of white-collar service personnel. Its rise undermined old social distinctions based on the way one worked: those who performed service work or had managerial functions were not necessarily better paid than blue-collar workers. The ranks of service workers swelled with researchers, health-care and medical workers, technicians, planners, and government functionaries. Scientists and technicians constituted 3.6 percent of the U.S. workforce in 1965, up 50 percent from a decade earlier. Employment in traditional parts of the service sector—banks, insurance companies, and other financial institutions—also surged because of the vast sums of money needed to finance technology and research. Entire categories of employees such as flight attendants devoted much of their skill to the psychological well-being of customers. The consumer economy provided more and more jobs in sales and repair, in restaurants and personal health, fitness, and grooming, and in hotels and tourism. By 1969, the percentage of service-sector employees had passed that of manufacturing workers in several industrial countries: 61.1 percent versus 33.7 percent in the United States; 49.8 percent versus 41.9 percent in the Netherlands; and 48.8 percent versus 41.1 percent in Sweden.

Postindustrial work life had some different ingredients in the Soviet bloc. Late in the 1960s, Communist leaders announced a program of "advanced socialism"—more social leveling, greater equality of salaries, and nearly complete absence of private production. The percentage of farmers remained higher in the Soviet bloc than in western Europe. A huge difference between professional occupations and those involving physical work remained as well in socialist countries. Less mobility existed between the two classifications, but much as in the U.S.-led bloc, gender also shaped the workforce into two groups, with men generally earning higher pay for better jobs and women relegated to lower pay and lesser jobs. Somewhere between 80 and 95 percent of women worked in socialist countries, but they generally held the most menial and worst-paying jobs.

As the postwar boom accelerated, West Germany and other Western nations absorbed immigrant,

United States

Japan

Average of 12 European Countries[1]

- Professional, technical, and related workers
- Administrative and managerial workers
- Clerical and related workers
- Sales and service workers
- Agricultural workers
- Production and transport workers, laborers
- Other

[1]Austria, Belgium, West Germany, Denmark, Spain, Finland, Greece, Ireland, Netherlands, Norway, Portugal, and Sweden

◀ **TAKING MEASURE** Postindustrial Occupational Structure, 1984

Striking changes occurred in the composition of the work-force in the postwar period. Agriculture continued its declining importance as a source of jobs, but by the 1980s the percentage of these workers in the most advanced industrial countries had dropped well below 10 percent. The most striking development was the expansion of the service sector, which came to employ more than half of all workers. In the United States, the agricultural and industrial sectors, which had dominated a century earlier, now offered less than a third of all jobs.

Yearbook of Labour Statistics (Geneva: International Labour Office, 1992), Table 2.7.

or "guest," laborers. Coming from Turkey, Greece, southern Italy, Portugal, and North Africa, these workers collected garbage, built roads, held factory jobs, and cleaned homes. In an environment where desirable work usually involved mental operations and clean conditions, these jobs appeared more lowly than before. Although males predominated among migrant workers, female migrants who worked performed similar chores for less pay. Often their menial work was "off the books," thus cutting them off from social security and other employee benefits. Migrants *looked* different from the native population and were thus pegged as lower class, although by the 1980s many had obtained better-paying, higher-status jobs and integrated themselves into the host culture. (See "Taking Measure," left.)

From Farming to Agribusiness. Farm life was updated, even bureaucratized. By the 1970s, one could travel for miles in Europe without seeing a farmhouse. Small landowners sold family plots to farmers engaged in *agribusiness*. Governments, farmers' cooperatives, and planning agencies took over decision making from the individual farmer; they set production quotas and handled an array of marketing transactions. Western European agriculture rebounded rapidly from its low productivity of the late 1940s, when refugees did much farm work without machinery or fertilizer. In the 1960s, agricultural output rose an average of 3 percent per year in Greece and Spain and 2.5 percent in the Netherlands, France, and Great Britain. Genetic research and the skyrocketing use of machinery contributed to growth. Between 1965 and 1979, the number of tractors in Germany more than tripled from 384,000 to 1,340,000 and in Spain rose from 22,000 to almost 250,000. The six Common Market countries used more than 8.3 million tons of chemical fertilizer in 1969. Although politicians continued to invoke the well-being of the family farmer to win elections, such appeals increasingly became successful exercises in nostalgia.

As farming modernized, it required constant adaptation to market trends and the newest technology. For example, in the 1970s a French farmer, Fernande Pelletier, with the help of her husband, son, and daughter-in-law, made a living on her hundred-acre farm in southwestern France in the new setting of international agribusiness. Advised by a government expert, Pelletier produced whatever foods might sell competitively in the Common Market—from lamb and veal to foie gras and walnuts. She also compared interest rates, whether on the purchase of machinery or of baby animals; learned how to diversify her labor-intensive farming; and joined with other farmers in her region to buy heavy machinery and to sell her products. Agricultural solvency required as much managerial and intellectual effort as did success in the industrial sector.

The Boom in Education and Research

Education and research were key to running postindustrial society and the means by which nations maintained their economic and military might. In the West, common sense, hard work, and creative intuition had launched the earliest successes of the Industrial Revolution. By the late twentieth century these qualities alone no longer sufficed. Rather, success in business or government demanded the humanistic or technological expertise of a highly educated manager and ever-growing staff of researchers. "Today one is educated and therefore powerful," one French official put it. "It's the accumulation of knowledge, not of wealth, that makes the difference."

Those corporations and governments that invested the most in research became military and industrial leaders. The United States funneled more than 20 percent of its gross national product into research in the 1960s, in the process siphoning off many of Europe's leading intellectuals and technicians in a so-called brain drain. Complex systems—for example, nuclear power generation with its

Shepherd and Nuclear Plant in Yugoslavia
Twentieth-century society continued to offer stark contrasts between the increasingly high-tech capabilities of government and business and the daily life of ordinary people. On the one hand, machines like TV sets filled the household, and the vast majority of people worked with mechanical tools. On the other hand, even working in the shadow of a vast nuclear installation, this shepherd symbolizes a simultaneous immunity to or escape from the spirit of the machine.
Steve McCurry/Magnum Photos, Inc.

many components, from scientific conceptualization to plant construction to the publicly supervised disposal of radioactive waste—required intricate professional oversight. Scientists and bureaucrats frequently made more crucial decisions than did elected politicians in the realm of space programs, weapons development, and economic policy. Soviet-bloc nations proved less adept at linking their considerable achievements in science to actual applications because of the bureaucratic red tape involved in getting an innovation approved. In the 1960s, some 40 percent of Soviet-bloc scientific findings became obsolete before the government approved them for application to technology.

The new criteria for success fostered unprecedented growth in education, especially in universities and scientific institutes (where most research was conducted) and other postsecondary institutions. The number of university students in the United States spurted from 1.2 million in 1950 to 7 million in 1969—an increase of nearly 600 percent. In Sweden it rose by about 580 percent and in West Germany 250 percent during that period. Great Britain established a new network of polytechnic universities to encourage the technical research that elite universities often scorned and to accommodate the baby boomers now coming of age. France set up administrative schools for future high-level bureaucrats. Khrushchev's successors tried to rid Soviet science of the priority Stalinism often gave to ideology over evidence from research. By the late 1970s, the Soviet Union had built its scientific establishment so rapidly that the number of its advanced researchers in the natural sciences and engineering surpassed that of the United States. Meanwhile, institutions of higher learning in the United States and Western Europe added courses in business and management, information technology, and systems analysis.

In principle, education made the avenues to success more democratic by basing them on talent instead of wealth. In fact, societal leveling did not occur in most western European universities. During these decades only about 10 percent of university students were the children of workers or peasants; thus to some extent a university degree certified that one was from the "right" social circles. Moreover, instruction often remained rigid and old-fashioned. Although eighteenth-century Europeans had pioneered educational reform, by the 1960s and 1970s U.S. innovations to foster creative teaching and learning had made little impact elsewhere. Students reported that teachers lectured even young children, who were required to take notes, and pupils spoke in class only to echo the teacher or to recite homework memorized the night before. At the university level, as one angry student put it, the professor was "a petty, threatened god" who puffed himself up "on the passivity and dependence of students." Such judgments would provoke young people to rebel late in the 1960s against the traditional authority of teachers, officials, and parents.

Redefining the Family

Just as education changed dramatically to meet the needs of postindustrial society, the contours of the family shifted from what they had been a century earlier: family roles were transformed, and the relationship between parents and children—long thought to be natural and unchangeable—looked alarmingly different. Even though television and media commentators often delivered messages about what the family should be, technology, consumer goods, and a constant flow of guest laborers and migrants from the former colonies made for enormous variety in what households actually were.

Changes in the Household. In the 1960s, the family appeared in many new forms: households were now headed by a single parent, by remarried parents merging two sets of unrelated children, by unmarried couples cohabitating, or by traditionally married parents who had fewer children. Households of same-sex partners also became more common. At the end of the 1970s, the marriage rate had fallen 30 percent in the West from its 1960s level. The average marriage lasted one-third longer than it had a century earlier because of increased longevity. The rate of divorce, especially in areas of northern Europe, nonetheless rose, suggesting yet another change in attitudes toward marriage.

After almost two decades of baby boom, the birthrate dropped significantly. On average, a Belgian woman, for example, bore 2.6 children in 1960 but only 1.8 by the end of the 1970s. Although the birthrate fell, the percentage of children born outside of marriage soared; in Switzerland, for example, it doubled during these years. Combined with high rates of abortion—435 per 1,000 live births in Czechoslovakia and 146 per 1,000 in Sweden—the new patterns of reproduction aroused social concern.

Daily life within the family changed. For one thing, technology became more readily available as consumer items saturated domestic space. Radio and television filled a family's leisure time and often formed the basis of its common social life. Machines such as dishwashers, washing machines, and clothes dryers became more affordable and more widespread, reducing (in theory) the time women had to devote to household work and raising standards of cleanliness. More women worked outside the home during these years to pay for the prolonged economic dependence of children. To advance in a knowledge-based society, these children did not enter the labor force until their twenties but instead attended school and required their parents' support. Some social scientists interpreted the phenomenon of mothers working outside the home to meet these rising costs as women's abandonment of the family. They charged that selfish and greedy women who worked caused many social problems and personal disorders.

Whereas the early modern family organized labor, taught craft skills, and monitored reproductive behavior, the modern family seemed to have a primarily psychological mission—bringing it more in line with the postindustrial nature of work. Parents were to provide emotional nurture while their children learned intellectual skills in school; spouses offered each other comfort after the grueling discipline of office or factory work. If families could not handle this responsibility alone, psychologists, social workers, and social service agencies were available to provide counseling and assistance. Television programs portrayed a variety of family experiences on soap operas, sitcoms, and family-oriented game shows and gave viewers an opportunity to see how other families dealt with the tensions of modern life. Postindustrial experts in media and health care reshaped the family as much as they changed the nature of work outside the home.

Youth and the Generation Gap. Postindustrial society transformed teenagers' lives. A century earlier, teens had been full-time wage earners; now most were students, financially dependent on their parents. The young sometimes remained financial "minors" into their twenties, a situation that produced new tensions for both young and old. Simultaneously youth gained new roles as consumers. Advertisers and industrialists saw the baby boomers as a huge market and wooed them with consumer items associated with rock music—records, portable radios, stereos. The rock music industry became a multibillion-dollar business. Pop music of the previous generation had described the route from youthful attraction to love and finally to adult marriage. In contrast, rock music celebrated youthful rebellion against adult culture in biting, critical, and often explicitly sexual lyrics. The mixture of high-tech music and pop-star marketing contributed to the growing "generation gap."

The new models for youth were themselves the products of advanced technology and savvy marketing. The Beatles were a little known English bar band in 1962 when they hired a new manager, Brian Epstein. Epstein remade their image and their music, booked them in major theaters across Europe and the United States, and encouraged them to produce tamer songs. Beatle John Lennon claimed to write two different kinds of music, one a formulaic kind for mass consumption and another, more innovative kind to please himself. "What's your message for American teenagers?" the Beatles were asked. "Buy some more Beatle records," they responded. Television and more sophisticated international marketing campaigns boosted the Beatles far beyond the popularity of earlier rock-and-roll stars, even Elvis. By the mid-1960s, public appearances of the Beatles summoned thousands of fans whose hysteria intensified during the group's performances.

Sex roles for the young did not change, however. Despite the popularity of a few individual women rockers, promoters focused on men, whom they depicted as surrounded by worshiping female "groupies." Targeting teenagers as avid consumers of sexuality and gender stereotypes, several recording empires sold billions of records and dominated rock music. Encouraged to see themselves as resisting adult values and their parents' demands, young people were financially part of families but bound emotionally to a commercial youth culture.

Art, Ideas, and Religion in a Technocratic Society

Cultural trends evolved with technology itself. Like modernists in the past, a new generation of artists addressed growing consumerism and technology with their art. Even as colonies continued officially to rip away from the old colonial powers, their influence on the Western mind remained powerful, leading musicians, scholars, and religious leaders to turn in their direction. Conversely, many of these intellectuals enjoyed growing international recognition and global markets—like the multinationals themselves—and they buttressed their prestige by employing statistical and other scientific methods.

Expanding Artistic Boundaries. "Pop art," whose leading practitioners were Richard Hamilton of Britain and Robert Rauschenberg of the United

Rolling Stones Tour Europe
The Rolling Stones took the youth revolution in music to a new level of raw energy and social critique. Much like the modernist avant-garde early in the twentieth century, they were dissonant and shocking. Unlike modernists, however, the Stones were commercially successful, all of them becoming multimillionaires, international celebrities, and models to youth around the world.
Dominique Berretty.

States, featured images from everyday life and employed the glossy techniques and products of what these artists called "admass," or mass advertising, society. "There's no reason," they maintained of modern society's commercialism, "not to consider the world as one gigantic painting." Rauschenberg sold little in the 1950s because his totally white paintings, executed with house paint, had no appeal; but he saw the reflections appearing in the monochromatic white as a new kind of art that broke down artistic boundaries. He eventually turned to collages made from comic strips, magazine clippings, and fabric to fulfill his vision that "a picture is more like the real world when it's made out of the real world."

In 1962, New York's Museum of Modern Art held a forum to consider the phenomenon of pop art. This event marked the beginning of the movement's acceptance and commercial success. By then such maverick American artists as Jasper Johns (b. 1930) and Andy Warhol (1927?–1987) had joined Rauschenberg. Pop art in the 1960s parodied modern commercialism. It showed, for example, how the female body, the classic form that attracted nineteenth-century male art buyers, was used to sell everything mass culture had to offer in the 1960s and 1970s. Swedish-born artist Claes Oldenburg (b. 1929) depicted the grotesque aspects of ordinary consumer products in *Giant Hamburger with Pickle Attached* (1962) and *Lipstick Ascending on Caterpillar Tractor* (1967).

"High" art picked up "low" objects to depict, but the effect was even more striking when the depictions were made of scraps of metal, cigarette butts, dirt, and, later, excrement. Artists again argued that these details were still another side of reality that they needed to capture. Such an attitude could have surprising results: the Swiss sculptor Jean

Niki de Saint-Phalle, *Fontaine Stravinsky* (1983)
Niki de Saint-Phalle's exuberant and playful art, seen in the fountains of Paris and cities around the
world, captured the accessibility of pop art. Her other work drew inspiration from Caribbean and
African styles and celebrated women of decolonizing countries. Living during the rebirth of activism,
de Saint-Phalle lined up suspended bags of paint and machine-gunned them to create a spattered
canvas—her answer to the alleged "macho" style of abstract expressionists like Jackson Pollock.
Barbara Alper/Stock Boston.

Tinguely (1925–1991) used rusted parts of old machines to make moving fountains. His partner Niki de Saint-Phalle then constructed huge, gaudy figures—many of them inspired by the folk traditions of the Caribbean and Africa—to decorate them. Their colorful fountains adorned main squares in Stockholm, Montreal, Paris, and other cities.

The American composer John Cage (1912–1992) had been working to the same ends when he added sounds produced by such everyday items as combs, pieces of wood, and radio noise into his musical scores. Buddhist influence led Cage also to incorporate silence in music and to compose by randomly tossing coins and then choosing notes by the corresponding numbers in the ancient Chinese *I Ching* ("Book of Changes"). Using silence was one way to capture the full range of sound and to continue the trend away from classical melody that had begun with modernism. Cage's orchestral scores allowed the players themselves to decide when and how they would participate in the musical production.

Other composers, called *minimalists*, simplified music by featuring repetition and sustained notes as well as by rejecting the "masterpiece" tradition of lush classical compositions. Some stressed modern technology; they introduced tape recordings into vocal pieces and used computers and synthesizers both to compose and to perform their works. German composer Karlheinz Stockhausen (b. 1928) introduced electronic music into classical composition in 1953, as did Cage soon after. Influenced by his own travels, Stockhausen continued the modern style of fully exploring non-Western tonalities in such 1970s pieces as *Ceylon*. But even though this music echoed the electronic and increasingly interconnected state of human society, its audiences diminished. By the 1970s, the amateur tradition of performing the latest style of music in the home had virtually disappeared, in part because of the technological demands. Some listeners found it difficult to appreciate the new patterns of sound, whether presented by amateurs or professionals. At the same time, improved recording technology and mass marketing brought music of all varieties to a wider home audience than ever before.

Heyday of Social Science. The social sciences reached the peak of their prestige during these decades, often because of their increasing use of statistical models and predictions. Sociologists and psychologists produced empirical studies that purported to demonstrate rules for understanding individual, group, and societal behavior. American psychologist B. F. Skinner (1904–1990) proposed to modify behavior through a system of accurately monitoring what people actually did, then rewarding positive behaviors and punishing negative ones. Critics worried that behaviorists trampled on concepts of human freedom in their advocacy of "social engineering" of ordinary people by so-called experts. Yet any promise of certainty in an age of rapid change was popular.

Sociologists, anthropologists, and psychologists also undermined some of the foundations for the belief that individuals had true freedom and for the assertion that Western civilization was any more sophisticated or just than non-Western societies. French anthropologist Claude Lévi-Strauss (b. 1908) developed a theory called *structuralism*. The theory insisted that all societies function within controlling structures—kinship and exchange, for example—that operate according to coercive rules similar to those of language. Structuralism challenged existentialism's tenet that humans could create a free existence and shook the social sciences' former faith in the triumph of rationality. In the 1960s and 1970s, the findings of the social sciences generally paralleled concerns that technology was creating a society of automatons and that complex managerial systems would eradicate individualism and human freedom.

Changes in Religion. Debates about free will coincided with new Christian preachings about the changing times. Responding to what he saw as a crisis in faith caused by affluence and secularism, Pope John XXIII (r. 1958–1963) in 1962 convened the Second Vatican Council, known as Vatican II. The bishops participating in Vatican II modernized the liturgy, democratized many church procedures, and at the last session in 1965 renounced church doctrine that Catholics should regard the Jewish

people as guilty of killing Jesus. These new policies countered elitist, authoritarian, and anti-Semitic aspects of traditional religion that many people interpreted as having buttressed fascism. The Catholic church thus opened itself to some new influences. Although Pope John's successor, Paul VI (r. 1963–1978), kept Catholic opposition to artificial birth control alive in the encyclical *Humanae Vitae* (1968), he became the first pontiff to visit Africa, Asia, and South America. He also encouraged Catholicism in the Soviet bloc, paving the way for religion to become a primary focal point for anticommunism there.

Simultaneously a Protestant revival occurred in the United States, and growing numbers of people joined sects that stressed the literal truth of the Scriptures. In western Europe, Christian churchgoing remained at a low ebb. In the 1970s, for example, only 10 percent of the British population went to religious services—about the same number that attended live soccer matches. The composition of the Western religious public was also metamorphosing because of immigration of people from the colonies, which increased the strength of the non-Christian religions. Muslims, Jews, and Hindus were among the major religious groups making their way to Europe and the United States to find economic opportunity and to escape the hardships of decolonization in an age of cold war.

❖ Contesting the Cold War Order in the 1960s

Affluence, scientific sophistication, and military might elevated the United States and the Soviet Union to the peak of their power early in the 1960s. By 1965, however, the six nations of the Common Market had replaced the United States as the leader in worldwide trade and often acted in their own self-interest by making overtures across the U.S.-Soviet divide. Communist China, along with countries in Eastern Europe, contested Soviet leadership, blurring the political boundary between the capitalist and Communist worlds. In the decolonizing regions, the superpowers had difficulty finding suitable and pliable allies. The struggle for Indochinese independence had never ended, and by the mid-1960s Marxist-Leninist ideology, peasant aspirations, and Western technological capitalism converged to produce a devastating war in Vietnam. But in some respects the most serious challenge to the cold war order came from rising citizen discontent within the West. Persistent injustice and repression so outraged people like Jan Palach that in the 1960s they rose up in protest against the consequences of technological development, the lack of fundamental rights, and the nuclear holocaust latent in the cold war.

Cracks in the Cold War Consensus

In the summer of 1963, less than a year after the shock of the Cuban missile crisis, the United States and the Soviet Union signed a test-ban treaty outlawing the explosion of nuclear weapons in the atmosphere and in the seas. The acceptance of the treaty suggested that the superpowers would reduce international tensions to focus on domestic politics. The new Soviet middle class of bureaucrats and managers demanded a better standard of living and a reduction in cold war animosity, and U.S.-led-bloc reformers called for more effective democracy and the more equal distribution of wealth. Amidst growing postindustrial prosperity clear signs emerged, particularly across Europe, that individuals and entire nations alike were not as interested as U.S. and Soviet leaders were in pursuing the cold war.

Western Europe.   In western European countries, voters elected politicians who promoted an increasing array of social programs designed to ensure economic democracy. A significant minority shifted their votes away from the Christian Democratic coalitions to Socialist, Labor, and Social Democratic Parties in hopes of placing more attention on ordinary people's needs during rapid change than on the cold war. In Britain, Harold Wilson, the Labour prime minister, came to power in 1964, calling for technical education and a focus on the needs of the expanding middle class of service workers. Wilson could not reverse the economy's half-century-long decline, however. British productivity remained the lowest among industrialized powers, and Commonwealth trading partners increasingly turned to Japanese and American goods.

Germany's leadership passed to Ludwig Erhard, who had guided the country's "economic miracle."

Here too Social Democratic politicians had enough influence to shift money from defense spending to domestic programs. Willy Brandt (1913–1992), the Socialist mayor of West Berlin, became foreign minister in a coalition government in 1966. Brandt pursued reconciliation with fellow Germans in Communist East Germany. This policy, known as *Ostpolitik*, ended frigid relations with the Soviet bloc and thus unsettled cold war thinking. With German and other markets saturated by goods from the economic resurgence, West German business leaders wanted, as one industrialist put it, "the depoliticization of Germany's foreign trade"—mainly the opening of the Soviet bloc to consumerism and new business opportunities.

French president Charles de Gaulle also moved to break the cold war stranglehold on Europe. Although France had but a 4 percent share of the world economy, de Gaulle forcefully advocated the interests of France and of a cooperative Europe in opposition to the superpowers. He poured more money into French nuclear development, and he steered a middle course between the United States and the Soviet Union. He withdrew French forces from NATO (after the United States tried to dissuade him from developing nuclear weapons independent of NATO) and signed trade treaties with the Soviet bloc. However, he also protected France's good relations with Germany to prevent further encroachments from the Soviet bloc. At home, de Gaulle's government mandated the cleaning of all Parisian buildings and sponsored the construction of modern housing. He described France as "the princess in the fairy story or the Madonna in the frescoes . . . dedicated to an exalted and exceptional destiny." With his haughty demeanor and stubborn pursuit of French grandeur, de Gaulle offered the European public an alternative to superpower toadying. Following his lead, western Europe began reasserting itself.

Eastern Europe.   Brandt's Ostpolitik and de Gaulle's assertiveness had their echoes in the Soviet bloc, where since 1953 the uneven progress of cold war thaw and hardening had stirred the winds of change. Pushing de-Stalinization, Khrushchev took the dangerous course of trying to reduce Communist officialdom's privileges, and he sanctioned the publication of dissident Aleksandr Solzhenitsyn's *One Day in the Life of Ivan Denisovitch* (1962), which revealed firsthand the terrible conditions in the labor camps. Khrushchev's blunders—notably his humiliation in the Cuban missile crisis, his ineffectual schemes to improve Soviet agriculture, and his inability to patch the rift with China—became intolerable to his Kremlin colleagues. In 1964 they ousted him in favor of two party bureaucrats, Leonid Brezhnev (1906–1982) and Alexei Kosygin (1904–1980). Nevertheless, attempts at reform continued. As premier, Kosygin encouraged plant managers to turn a profit. Soviet policy called for ratcheting up the defense budget while producing televisions, household appliances, and cheap housing to alleviate the discontent of a better-educated citizenry. The government also loosened restrictions to allow cultural and scientific meetings with Westerners, another move that relaxed the cold war atmosphere in the mid-1960s.

The Soviet satellites in eastern Europe grasped the opportunity presented by Moscow's relaxed pos-

ture. Members of COMECON (the Soviet bloc's economic organization) refused to become agricultural backwaters supporting Soviet growth. Romania promoted industrialization, Poland allowed private farmers greater freedom to make money, and Hungarian leader János Kádár (1912–1989) introduced elements of a market system into the national economy. East Germany, benefiting from economic ties to West Germany, strove to advance technological education. Each of these countries in its own way was differentiating itself from the Soviet model.

In the arts, Soviet-bloc writers continued for a time to thaw the frozen monolith of socialist realism. Ukrainian poet Yevgeny Yevtushenko (b. 1933) exposed Soviet complicity in the Holocaust in *Babi Yar* (1961), a passionate protest against the slaughter of tens of thousands of Jews near Kiev during World War II and the refusal of Soviet authorities to commemorate the tragedy. In East Berlin, Christa Wolf (b. 1929) challenged the

Hagop Hagopian, *No to the Neutron Bomb!* (1977)
In an era of ongoing cold war, culture continued to be on the front line, with the Soviets persecuting those who produced abstract or critical art. Artists were adept, however, at incorporating Soviet icons in work critical of the regime. They might, for instance, depict Lenin's portrait but with citizens turning their back on it instead of being inspired by it. Or, as in this painting, they bravely critiqued the course of the arms race.
The Jane Voorhees Zimmerli Art Museum. Rutgers, The State University of New Jersey. The Norton and Nancy Dodge Collection of Nonconformist Art from the Soviet Union. Photo: Jack Abraham.

celebratory nature of socialist art. Her novel *Divided Heaven* (1965) shows a couple divided by the Berlin Wall; the man chooses to escape to the West but the woman stays behind to support socialism and ultimately commits suicide.

Repression returned later in the 1960s, however, as the Soviet government took to bulldozing outdoor art shows and otherwise harassing artists. Visual artists held secret exhibitions in their apartments, even turning their living spaces into a new kind of art known as "installations." In installations, art includes the arrangement of many everyday objects in large spaces—a form very distinct from the space of a canvas or a sculpture. These artists' paintings depicted Soviet citizens as worn and tired in grays and other monochromatic color schemes instead of the brightly attired and heroic figures of socialist realism. Still victims of the cold war, writers relied on *samizdat* culture, in which uncensored publications were reproduced by hand or by mimeograph and passed from reader to reader. These cultural forms of resistance laid part of the foundation for the more successful movement against Soviet rule in the 1980s.

The United States.   Even in the United States, other issues challenged the cold war for front-page attention. The assassination of President John F. Kennedy in November 1963 shocked the nation and the world. But only momentarily did it still escalating demands for civil rights for African Americans and other minorities. White segregationists reacted with extraordinary violence to sit-ins at lunch counters, efforts to register black voters, and freedom marches. They firebombed black churches, schools, homes, and buses and murdered individual activists. This violent racism was a weak link in the American claim to moral superiority in the cold war, and in response to the murders and destruction, Kennedy had introduced civil rights legislation. Pressured by the growing momentum of African American activism, he forced the desegregation of schools and universities, calling civil rights for blacks "a moral issue . . . as old as the Scriptures" and appealing to Americans to end racism "in the Congress, in your state and local legislative body, and, above all, in our daily lives." In a massive rally in Washington, D.C., in August 1963, hundreds of thousands of marchers assembled around the Lincoln Memorial, where they heard the electrifying words of the African American minister Martin Luther King Jr.:

> *I have a dream that . . . all of God's children, black men and white men, Jews and Gentiles, Protestants and Catholics, will be able to join hands and sing in the words of the old Negro spiritual, "Free at last! Free at last! Thank God Almighty, we are free at last!"*

Lyndon B. Johnson (1908–1973), Kennedy's successor, turned rhetoric into reality when he steered the Civil Rights Act through Congress in

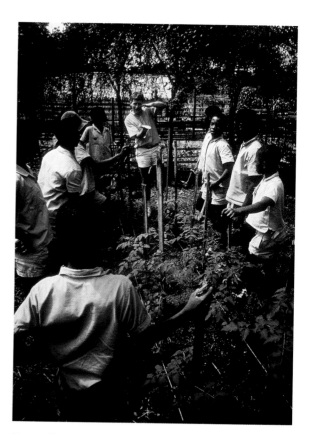

Peace Corps Volunteers in the Ivory Coast
The Peace Corps, founded by President Kennedy, tapped the idealism of young Americans in the 1960s; under the auspices of this program they went to all parts of the newly independent world and to regions where new economic development was taking place. Whether fostering literacy or working on agricultural projects, Peace Corps volunteers participated in the reformist spirit of the times, though their efforts were sometimes seen as a continuation of Western paternalism.
Jim Pickerell/Black Star.

1964. This legislation forbade segregation in public facilities and created the Equal Employment Opportunity Commission (EEOC) to fight job discrimination based on "race, color, national origin, religion, and sex." Southern conservatives had tacked on the provision against sex discrimination in the vain hope that it would doom the bill. Modeling himself on his hero Franklin Roosevelt, Johnson envisioned what he called a Great Society in which new government programs would give the forty million Americans living in poverty some share of American abundance. He sponsored myriad reform programs: Project Head Start for disadvantaged preschool children, the Job Corps for training youth, Volunteers in Service to America (VISTA) to support volunteers in poverty-stricken areas, and projects for urban development. These programs brought hope to many Americans, who agreed with black novelist Ralph Ellison that Johnson was "the greatest American president for the poor and the Negroes."

Vietnam and Turmoil in Asia

Outside the U.S.-led and Soviet blocs, some countries looked to the superpowers for military and economic support, playing the cold war card. Israel and Taiwan unequivocally depended on the United States to protect them; Cuba and certain African states turned to the Soviet Union. Yet elsewhere during the 1960s, third world nations increasingly distanced themselves from the superpowers. Many were still tied by technical systems such as radio and telephone networks and by trade to their former rulers; where the cold war was concerned, however, they sought to be nonaligned.

Communist China's independent way was the biggest surprise to both the Soviet Union and the United States. Mao Zedong, ever hostile to Western capitalism, also detested Soviet bureaucratization and claims to leadership. Moreover, he rebuked Khrushchev for backing down in Cuba. In 1966, Mao unleashed the Cultural Revolution, a movement to remake individual personality according to Mao's vision of socialism. Mao wanted the Chinese to experience revolution on a permanent basis instead of stagnating in Soviet-style bureaucratic corruption. China's youth were empowered to haul away people of every class for "reeducation"— which translated to personal humiliation, incarcer-

ation, and millions of deaths. Economic goals lost their importance as the Chinese became obsessed with reinventing revolutionary political culture.

Both superpowers had interests in East and Southeast Asia, but they often failed to see the complex changes under way in the region. American policymakers, for example, did not detect the growing dispute between the two Communist giants because they had an inflexible vision of monolithic communism. While China plunged into Mao's bloody cultural and economic experiments, the peoples of Southeast Asia were coming to grips with decades of demographic upheaval. Despite war and nationalist revolution, the region's population more than tripled between 1920 and 1970, reaching 370 million by the end of the 1970s. This explosive growth confounded nationalist leaders, typically military men with little experience in governing a booming population. Like the 85 percent of third world leaders who rose from the military, most East and Southeast Asian rulers were dictators without the technological expertise to make their countries economically viable.

Superpower intervention in this unstable part of the world was loaded with risk, and nowhere was this truer than in the tragic U.S. intervention in Vietnam (Map 29.2). Since the Geneva settlement in 1954, the United States had propped up corrupt and incompetent leaders, in the 1960s escalating its commitment to a non-Communist South Vietnam. North Vietnam, China, and the Soviet Union backed the rebel Vietcong, as the South Vietnamese Communists came to be called. Although Kennedy beefed up the U.S. military presence, the strength of the Vietcong seemed to grow daily.

In August 1964, Lyndon Johnson induced the U.S. Congress to pass a resolution endorsing the bombing of North Vietnam—the Vietcong's lifeline. By 1966, the United States had more than a half-million soldiers in South Vietnam. Before the war ended in 1975, the United States would drop more bombs on North Vietnam than the Allies had launched on Germany and Japan combined during World War II. Television reports carried the optimistic predictions of Johnson's advisers that each fresh attack and every new draft call-up revealed a "light at the end of the tunnel." Massive air attacks, some boasted, would "bomb North Vietnam back to the Stone Age." Yet the strategy failed. Despite regular announcements of enormous North

Vietnamese "body counts," American casualties also mounted relentlessly. The Vietcong escalated its guerrilla warfare and then melted away into jungles and cavernous hillsides.

Johnson offered massive aid to Indochina if the Vietcong and North Vietnamese would stop fighting. After decades of anticolonial struggle, the insurgents rejected a negotiated peace. North Vietnam's leaders calculated that the United States would give in first as the American public recoiled

MAP 29.2 The Vietnam War, 1954–1975
The local peoples of Southeast Asia had long resisted incursions by their neighbors. They also resisted French rule from the end of the nineteenth century, never more fiercely than in the war that liberated them after World War II. Ill prepared by comparison with the French, the Vietnamese nonetheless triumphed in the battle of Dien Bien Phu in 1954. But the Americans soon became involved, trying to stem what they saw as the tide of Communist influence behind the Vietnamese liberation movement. The ensuing war in Vietnam in the 1960s and 1970s spread into neighboring countries, making the region the scene of vast destruction.

from the horrors of televised slaughter: South Vietnamese officials casually executed people in the streets, and children screamed in mortal pain as they were engulfed by flaming napalm, a jellied gasoline that asphyxiated its victims while they burned. Branded as murderers by international opinion, American forces simultaneously looked inept before images of pajama-clad Asians on bicycles who held at bay the technologically advanced Yankees.

By 1968, a swelling American antiwar movement challenged the killing on humanitarian grounds. In an age of ideological war, lack of support at home spelled the beginning of the end for the U.S. war effort. Johnson abandoned his soaring political ambition and announced in March 1968 that he would not run for president again. As he left office in January 1969, peace remained elusive and the war's social and economic costs to the United States continued to mount. The U.S. superpower was tarnished, irreparably it seemed at the time; so too was the Soviet Union.

The Explosion of Civic Activism

In the midst of cold war, technological advance, and bloody conflict, a new social activism emerged in the West. Students, blacks and other racial minorities, women, antiwar protesters, environmentalists, and homosexuals raised their voices to demand that Western reality match its ideals. The civil rights movement in the United States ignited fiery protests in the streets, in universities, and in the halls of government. In the Soviet bloc dissident movements demanded political democratization and social change. These movements nearly swept up France and Czechoslovakia in revolution in 1968; they cast doubts on the superpower status of the United States and the Soviet Union; and they contested the cold war order.

Civil Rights. A broad cross section of Americans embraced the bold activism of the civil rights movement and transformed it. In 1965, César Chávez (1927–1993) led Mexican American migrant workers in the California grape agribusiness to strike for better wages and working conditions. Controversy swirled around the protest: "A hoax, a fantasy, a charade," one white columnist called the work action and the hunger strikes. Deeply religious and ascetic, Chávez helped Hispanic Americans define their identity and struggle against deportation, inferior schooling, and discrimination.

Meanwhile the African American civil rights movement took a dramatic turn as riots protesting police brutality erupted in Watts, a black district of Los Angeles, in the summer of 1965. City after city experienced similar outbursts of anger and frustration. Some activists transformed their struggle into a militant affirmation of racial differences. They urged blacks not to push for mere equality but for a celebration of their race under the banner "Black is beautiful." The issue they faced was one they felt they had in common with decolonizing people: how to shape an identity different from that of white oppressors. Imitating whites amounted to self-hatred, and thus blacks should celebrate their African heritage and work for "black power" by reclaiming rights instead of begging for them nonviolently. Some formerly pacifist black leaders turned their rhetoric to violence: "Burn, baby, burn," chanted rioters who destroyed the grim inner cities around them in the belief that civil rights legislation alone offered only slight relief to their plight.

Student Protest. As a result of the new turn in black activism, white American university students who had participated in the early stages of the civil rights movement found themselves excluded from leadership positions. Many soon joined the swelling protest against technological change, consumerism, sexual repression, the educational establishment, and the Vietnam War, including conscription into the U.S. forces fighting in Southeast Asia. European youth caught the fever. In the mid-1960s, university students in Rome occupied an administration building after right-wing opponents assassinated one of their number during a protest against the 200-to-1 student-teacher ratio. Polish high school and university students created Michnik Clubs, named for the outspoken dissident Adam Michnik, to study Western political theory, science, and economics but faced constant harassment by the secret police. In Prague in 1965, students held a carnival-like procession celebrating the American Beat poet Allen Ginsberg as their May King, and on May Day in 1966 they chanted, "The only good Communist is a dead one." In commemorating the tenth anniversary of the 1956 uprisings, some students were arrested and expelled from the university. The Federation of [West] German Socialist Students (SDS),

led by Rudi Dutschke and the "situationists" in Strasbourg, France, called on students to wake up from the slumbering pace of student life and reform the world. Situationists believed that bureaucratic, mass society numbed people, and they watched for opportunities or created "situations"—emblazoning university walls with challenging slogans, for example—to jolt individuals to action.

Students attacked the traditional university curriculum. They questioned how studying Plato or Dante would help them after graduation. They also took part in forcing from the curriculum required humanities courses in the arts, philosophy, and literature. Students turned the defiant rebelliousness of 1950s youth culture into a political style by mocking education: "How to Train Stuffed Geese," French students called the way universities taught them. "No professors over forty" and "Don't trust anyone over thirty" were powerful slogans of the day. Long hair, blue jeans, communal living, and a repudiation of personal hygiene announced students' rejection of middle-class values, as did their denunciation of sexual chastity. With the widespread use of the pill, abstinence became unnecessary as a method of birth control, and students made the sexual revolution explicit and public with open promiscuity and experimentation.

The young created a counterculture nourished with heavy doses of sex, rock and folk music, and drugs. Early in the 1960s, then Harvard professor Timothy Leary provided his students with the hallucinogen LSD. Marijuana use became common among student protesters, and amphetamines and barbiturates added to the drug culture, which had its own rituals, songs, and gathering places. Electronic rock music and mind-altering chemicals—produced by the very technology that youth culture scorned—induced new sensations, created a sense of personal creativity, and restored a belief in the individual experience. Businesses made billions of dollars selling blue jeans, dolls dressed as "hippies," natural foods, and drugs, as well as packaging and managing the stars of the counterculture.

Women's Protest. Women active in the civil rights and student movements soon realized that protest organizations devalued women just as society at large did. Male protesters adopted the leather-jacketed machismo style of their film and rock heroes, but women in the movements were often judged by the status of their male-protester lovers. "A woman was to 'inspire' her man," African American activist Angela Davis complained, adding that women aiming for equality supposedly "wanted to rob [male protesters] of their manhood." Such biting criticisms of masculine supremacy among African American activists elicited a response among white women, who admired the strength of African American women and also had their own grievances against the youth culture's exploitation of them. "We demand that our problems be discussed substantively," announced a speaker in Frankfurt, West Germany, interrupting a student meeting. "It is no longer enough that women are occasionally allowed to say a few words to which, as good antiauthoritarians, you listen—and then go on with the order of the day."

More politically conventional middle-class women eagerly responded to the international bestseller *The Feminine Mystique* (1963) by American journalist Betty Friedan. Friedan popularized Simone de Beauvoir's philosophy by focusing on the changes in middle-class women's lives wrought by technology and affluence. Friedan maintained that middle-class women led useless existences, allowing their talents to stagnate while laborsaving devices and their children's daily absence in school made them useless.

Throughout the West, middle-class activists were working on the legal aspects of reproductive and civil rights. In France they helped end the ban on birth control in 1965. In Sweden, where for decades generous welfare benefits and access to birth control had improved women's lives, the Frederika Bremer Association lobbied to make tasks both at home and in the workplace less gender-segregated. The National Organization for Women (NOW) was formed in the United States in 1966 "to bring women into full participation in the mainstream of American society now."

Whereas these organizations followed official procedures for contesting unequal rights, some middle-class women joined street activists on behalf of such issues as abortion rights or the decriminalization of gay and lesbian sexuality. Many flouted social conventions in their attire, language, and attitudes. Renouncing brassieres, hair curlers, high-heeled shoes, cosmetics, and other adornments, they spoke openly about taboo subjects such as their sexual feelings, explained the "politics of housework," and even announced that they had resorted to

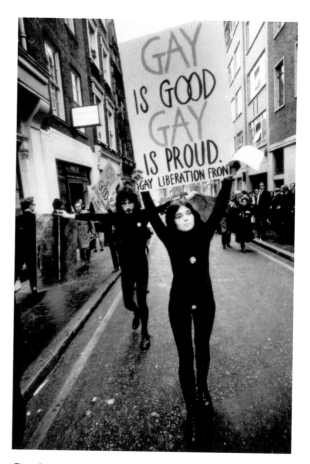

Gay Activists in London
The reformist spirit of the 1960s and 1970s changed the focus of homosexuals' activism. Instead of concentrating mostly on legal protection from criminal prosecution, gays and lesbians began affirming a special and positive identity. As other groups who had endured discrimination began making similar affirmations, "identity politics" was born. Critics charged that traditional universal values were sufficient and that homosexuals and others constituted "special-interest" groups. Gays, women, and ethnic or racial minorities countercharged that the universal values first put forth in the Enlightenment seemed to apply only to a privileged few.
© Hulton Getty/Liaison Agency.

illegal abortions. In France, for example, several hundred prominent women, including Simone de Beauvoir, went public with such information. This brand of feminist activity was meant to shock polite society—and it did. At a Miss America contest in 1968, women protesters crowned a sheep the new beauty queen. West German women students tossed tomatoes at male protest leaders in defiance of standards for ladylike behavior. Many women of color, however, broke with feminist solidarity and spoke out against the "double jeopardy" of being "black and female."

1968: Year of Crisis

The West seethed with protest and calls for reform; it erupted in 1968, propelled by forces on the other side of the world. In January, on the first day of Tet, the Vietnamese New Year, the Vietcong and the North Vietnamese attacked more than one hundred South Vietnamese towns and American bases, inflicting heavy casualties. The Tet offensive, as it came to be called, caused many Americans to conclude that the war might be unwinnable. The antiwar movement of students, clergy, and pacifists suddenly gained crucial momentum from a disillusioned public. Meanwhile in Czechoslovakia, a quieter movement against Soviet cold war domination had taken shape, but the atmosphere in that country, as elsewhere around the world, soon became explosive.

Violence Erupts.   On April 4, 1968, Martin Luther King Jr. was assassinated by a white racist, and more than a hundred cities in the United States erupted in violence as African Americans vented their anguish and rage. On campuses, strident confrontation over the intertwined issues of war, technology, racism, and sexism closed down classes. At Columbia University in New York City, where the administration had proposed destroying a Harlem neighborhood to build a gym, students took over buildings and suffered violent police attacks in order, as one student put it, "to recapture a school from business and war and rededicate it to learning and life."

At the same time, student protest was escalating in France. In January, students at Nanterre had gone on strike, invading administrative offices and demanding a say in university governance. They called themselves a "proletariat"—an exploited working class—and considered themselves part of a New Left. When students at the more prestigious Sorbonne in Paris showed solidarity with students of Nanterre in street demonstrations, the police arrested and assaulted hundreds of them. The Parisian middle classes reacted with unexpected sympathy to the student uprising because of their own resentment of bureaucracy. They were also horrified at

seeing the elite and brutal police force, the CRS, beating middle-class students and passersby who expressed their support.

By May the violence had accelerated into outright revolt, and French students handed out advice for evading tear gas and fragmentation grenades used by the CRS:

> VARIOUS PROTECTIVE MEASURES
> *Garbage can cover as a shield. . . . Lemon—wet a handkerchief with it, suck on it. Bicarbonate of soda around the eyes, in diluted form on a handkerchief. Goggles, motorcycle or ski, or a swimming mask.*

French workers joined in: some nine million went on strike, occupying factories and calling not only for higher wages but also for "participation" in everyday decision making. To some, the revolt of youth and workers looked as if it might spiral into another French revolution.

The normally decisive president Charles de Gaulle seemed paralyzed at first, but he soon took steps to undermine support for the student revolt. In June he announced a raise for workers, and businesses offered them a strengthened voice in decision making. Many citizens, having grown tired of the street violence, the destruction of private property, and the breakdown of social services (for example, garbage was not collected for weeks), were ready to dissociate themselves from the student protesters. After skillfully using the media to solidify the separation of students from the wider population, de Gaulle sent tanks into Paris. Although demonstrations continued throughout June, the student movement had been closed down.

Prague Spring.   The Soviets had weathered protests and even uprisings before, but the 1968 revolt began within the Czechoslovak Communist Party. In the autumn of 1967 at a Party congress, Alexander Dubček (1921–1992), head of the Slovak branch of the party, had called for more social and political openness. First Party Secretary Antonín Novotný (1904–1975) responded with ridicule: "We've had more than enough of democracy." In a culture where anti-Semitism and ethnic prejudice remained formidable political weapons, Novotný taunted Dubček as an inferior Slovak. Yet the call for reform struck a chord among frustrated party officials, technocrats, and intellectuals; Czechoslovaks

Prague Spring
When the Soviets and other Warsaw Pact members cracked down on the Prague Spring, they met determined citizen resistance. People refused assistance of any kind to the invaders. Indeed, despite dejection at the repression of Dubček's government, protest on a small and large scale was ongoing from then until the final fall of Communist rule two decades later.
Prache-Levin/Sygma.

began to dream of creating a new society—one based on "socialism with a human face." Party officials drove Novotný from power and replaced him with Dubček.

Dubček changed the Communist style of government, ending censorship, instituting the secret ballot for party elections, and allowing competing political groups to form. The "Prague Spring" had begun—"an orgy of free expression," one Czech journalist called it. People bought uncensored publications, packed uncensored theater productions, and engaged in almost nonstop political debate. "Nobody talks about football [soccer] . . . anymore," one taxi driver complained. Meanwhile, Dubček's new government faced the enormous problem of negotiating policies acceptable to the USSR and the entrenched party functionaries. Radicals pressed for fundamental change, but those with a vested

interest in the Communist system wanted more limited reform.

On top of the internal uncertainty, the Polish, East German, and Soviet regimes threatened the reform government daily. Announcing new recognition of civil rights and the separation of the Communist Party from the government, Dubček warned that democracy demanded "a conscious civic discipline" and "statesmanlike wisdom of all citizens." When Dubček failed to attend a meeting of Warsaw Pact leaders, Soviet threats became intense. Finally on the night of August 20–21, 1968, Soviet tanks rolled into Prague in a massive show of antirevolutionary force.

Citizens tried to halt the return to Communist orthodoxy by using free expression as sabotage. They painted graffiti on tanks and confused invading troops by removing street signs. Illegal radio stations broadcast testimonials of resistance, accounts of Soviet brutality, and warnings to people about to be arrested. They refused to sell food or other commodities to Soviet troops. As the Soviets gradually removed reformers from power, Jan Palach and other university students immolated themselves. Protest of one type or another never stopped, forcing the new Czechoslovak government to maintain repression. Meanwhile, Soviet determination to retain control over the Soviet bloc was expressed in the Brezhnev Doctrine, announced in November 1968. Reform movements, Brezhnev declared, were not merely domestic matters but rather "a common problem and concern of all socialist countries." Further moves toward change would meet similar repression.

Prague Spring, 1968

Protest in 1968 changed the style and direction of high politics in Western societies. It challenged superpower dominance on which the cold war was based. Whether burning draft cards in the United States or scribbling graffiti on public buildings in Europe, students made all government open to question. Yet change did not necessarily occur in the way reformers had hoped. Governments turned to conservative solutions, while disappointed reformers considered more radical avenues to social transformation.

❖ The Erosion of Superpower Mastery in the 1970s

The 1970s brought an era of *détente*—a lessening of cold war tensions—as the United States pulled out of the Vietnam War and as the superpowers negotiated to limit the nuclear arms race. Despite this relaxation in the cold war, the superpowers appeared to lose their dominance. By the early 1970s, student protest evolved into ongoing reform movements, while other groups, such as those for Basque independence in Spain and for Catholic rights in Northern Ireland, took violent action. This violence affected the superpowers as it threw their allies off

balance. Although the United States and the Soviet Union still controlled the balance of power, their grip was also loosening because of their own internal corruption, the challenge of terrorism, and competition from the oil-producing states, Japan, and the Common Market.

The Superpowers Tested

As the 1970s opened, both superpowers faced daunting internal and external challenges to their dominance, and both underwent crises of leadership as economic and political uncertainty mounted. Domestic politics remained heated during this decade; the uncertainties of economic modernization grew; and coalitions formed by other countries began to undermine superpower mastery. Neither superpower had leaders wholly competent to face these challenges.

The United States in Crisis. In November 1968, the conservative Richard Nixon (1913–1994) was elected president of the United States. Nixon claimed to have a "secret plan" to bring peace to Southeast Asia, but even as peace talks dragged on, warfare continued to ravage Vietnam and to mount up debt in the United States. In 1970, Nixon ordered U.S. troops to invade Cambodia, the site of North Vietnamese bases. Campuses erupted again in protest, and on May 4 the National Guard killed four students and wounded eleven others at a demonstration at Kent State University in Ohio. Nixon called the victims "bums," and a growing reaction against the counterculture made many Americans agree with him that the guardsmen "should have fired sooner and longer."

The United States and North Vietnam finally signed a peace treaty on January 27, 1973. By terms of the agreement, Nixon withdrew American troops, but he still continued to supply South Vietnam's forces. The Communists did not relent either, and in 1975 South Vietnam collapsed under a determined North Vietnamese offensive. Vietnam was forcibly reunified.

Small and great powers reeled from decades of conflicts in Southeast Asia. Tens of thousands of U.S. and South Vietnamese loyalists fled the region. In adjacent Cambodia the Communist Khmer Rouge government inflicted a horrendous reign of terror in which it slaughtered a million people in an attempt to turn the country back to an agrarian society. The Vietnam War had cost the United States billions of dollars, more than fifty thousand lives, and its moral authority. Many countries now viewed the United States not as a defender of liberty but as an oppressor of third world people. Moreover, the "domino theory," which had justified intervention since the 1950s, was proven false: although Cambodia and Laos went Communist, Thailand did not, and Communist Vietnam became Communist China's enemy.

Simultaneously the United States pulled off a foreign policy triumph when Henry Kissinger, Nixon's secretary of state and a believer—like Bismarck—in Realpolitik, decided to take advantage of the ongoing conflict between China and the USSR. In 1972, Kissinger's efforts to bring the United States and China closer resulted in Nixon's visiting the *other* Communist power. Pictures of Mao Zedong and Nixon shaking hands rocked the world, for they seemed to promise the possibility that diplomatic miracles would end the cold war. Within China the meeting helped stop the brutality and excesses of the Cultural Revolution, which had left the country prostrate. Gradually, Chinese pragmatists interested in technology, trade, and relations with the West replaced hard-line ideologues.

The world benefited from this diplomatic breakthrough. Fearful of the Chinese and of the cold war's economic toll, Soviet leader Brezhnev made overtures to the U.S.-led bloc. In 1972, the superpowers signed the Strategic Arms Limitation Treaty (SALT I), which set a cap on the number of antimissile defenses each country could have. In 1975, in the Helsinki accords on human rights, the Western bloc officially acknowledged Soviet territorial gains in World War II in exchange for the Soviet bloc's guarantee of basic human rights.

While pursuing a degree of mutual reconciliation with these foreign enemies, the enigmatic Nixon focused on reelection at any price. After his landslide victory in the 1972 presidential race, evidence came to light that Nixon's reelection committee had paid several men—caught in the act and arrested—to wiretap the telephones at Democratic Party headquarters in Washington's Watergate building. Televised congressional hearings revealed not only that the president's office had jeopardized the Constitution's guarantee of free elections but also

that Nixon himself had attempted to cover up the truth about the Watergate break-in. Between 1968 and 1972, Nixon had forged a powerful conservative consensus based on the idea that activist groups calling for expanded rights were but a minority. The so-called silent majority had supported Nixon in all but one state in 1972, but in the summer of 1974 the Watergate scandal forced Nixon to resign in disgrace—the first U.S. president ever to do so.

Dissent and Repression in the Soviet Bloc. The Soviet leadership also tried conservative solutions to meet mounting criticism. By the early 1970s, the hard-liner Brezhnev had eclipsed Kosygin's influence in the Soviet Union and freely clamped down on critics. Following the events in Czechoslovakia in 1968, the Soviet dissident movement was at a low ebb. "The shock of our tanks crushing the Prague Spring . . . convinced us that the Soviet colossus was invincible," explained one pessimistic liberal. Other voices persisted, however. In 1974, Brezhnev expelled Solzhenitsyn from the USSR after the publication of the first volume of *Gulag Archipelago* (1973–1976) in the U.S.-led bloc. Composed from myriad biographies, firsthand reports, and other sources of information about prison camp life, Solzhenitsyn's story of the Gulag (the Soviet system of internment and forced-labor camps) documented the brutal conditions Soviet prisoners endured under Stalin and his successors. The book appeared at a time when western European Ostpolitik was spreading dissatisfaction with the economy and the repression of free speech in the Eastern bloc. The expulsion of Solzhenitsyn showed that the Soviet hierarchy would severely punish revelations regarding the Gulag.

The Kremlin persecuted many ordinary people who did not have Solzhenitsyn's international reputation. Soviet psychologists, complying with the government, certified the "mental illness" of people who did not play by the rules; thus dissidents wound up as virtual prisoners in mental institutions. The crudest Soviet persecutions, however, involved anti-Semitism: Jews were subject to educational restrictions (especially in university admissions), severe job discrimination, and constant assault on their religious practice. It was "not dramatic" persecution, as one Jewish writer put it, "but daily . . . always present." A commonplace accusation by Soviet officials was that Jews were "unreliable, they think only of emigrating. . . . [T]heir allegiance is elsewhere. It's madness to give them an education, because it's state money wasted." Ironically, even dissidents blamed Jews for the Bolshevik Revolution, for the terror of Stalinist collectivization, and for the supposed destruction of Russian literature. As attacks intensified in the 1970s, Soviet Jews protested and sought to emigrate to Israel or the United States, but the government severely restricted emigration, often claiming that Jews who had finished their compulsory military service could not leave because they knew "state secrets."

Dissent persisted in satellite states. Throughout the 1970s, workers and intellectuals in Poland generated protest writing and formed activist groups. In an open letter to the Czechoslovak Communist Party leadership in 1975, playwright Václav Havel accused Marxist-Leninist rule of making people materialistic, not socialist, and indifferent to civic life. The only viable conduct under Communist repression, Havel wrote, was either to disengage from public life or to work for the special privileges awarded to successful technocrats. In 1977, Havel, along with a group of fellow intellectuals and workers, signed Charter 77, a public protest against the Communist regime. The police imprisoned and tormented many of the charter's signatories, including Havel; philosopher Jan Patocka died after his "interrogation."

By this time the brain drain of eastern European intellectuals had become significant. The modernist composer Gyorgy Ligeti had left Hungary in 1956, after which his work was celebrated in concert halls and in such classic films as *2001: A Space Odyssey*. From exile in Paris, Czech writer Milan Kundera enthralled audiences with *The Book of Laughter and Forgetting* and other novels that chronicled the lives of tortured characters caught in the grim realities of Communist institutions. The presence of these exiles and escapees to the United States and western European capitals helped erode any lingering support for communism. In France, for example, a group of "new philosophers" loudly demanded that leftists justify their commitment to Soviet communism in light of the brutal practices revealed by Solzhenitsyn and others. Communist parties in the West broke their last remaining ties to the Soviet Union, but even after declaring an independent path, their success at the polls dwindled.

The West, the World, and the Politics of Energy

While the superpowers wrestled with internal political embarrassments and the intricacies of nuclear diplomacy, other nations were developing new economic muscle. Since 1960, the six Common Market countries, led by West Germany, had surpassed the United States in percentage of gross world product. This achievement made the Common Market a countervailing economic power to the Soviet Union and the United States. Although the Common Market maintained the lead, its economic ascent slowed in the 1960s; by 1965, the rate of West German economic growth had fallen from a high of 9.4 percent between 1951 and 1955 to less than 5 percent—still a substantial rate. In the face of this downturn, which brought rising unemployment, politicians used pump-priming techniques to stimulate industrial investment and also put foreign "guest" laborers and married women out of work in favor of native-born men.

The opening of eastern European markets helped bolster western European prosperity; by the end of the decade, western European exports to the Soviet bloc totaled some $45 billion annually, producing a burden of debt that Communist countries could ill afford. In 1973, Britain joined the Common Market, followed by Ireland and Denmark. The market's exports now amounted to almost three times those of the United States.

Meanwhile, the United States, still the leading single producer in most fields, had become a major debtor. Rising purchases of military and imported goods brought inflation and a trade deficit. Dollars flooded the international currency markets, and in 1971, the Bretton Woods currency system, created during World War II to maintain stable international markets, collapsed. The international monetary crisis actually strengthened European integration still further as Common Market countries agreed to cooperate to prevent financial chaos. The Common Market's economic clout allowed it to force the United States to relinquish its single-handed direction of Western economic strategy.

Economic and geopolitical power spread not only beyond the United States but beyond the West. Japan emerged from its postwar reconstruction to challenge the United States and western Europe as

"AND ANYWHERE KHALID WENT, THE LAMB WAS SURE TO GO!"

The Middle East and the Politics of Oil

When Middle Eastern countries took control of the price and volume of oil they sold, Western leaders were taken aback, so thoroughly accustomed were the United States and its allies to setting the conditions of trade. OPEC leaders were lampooned in cartoons as the global economic crisis unfolded. Stagflation hit Western economies hard, while everyone came to terms with the new force of oil in international politics. Rosen-Albany Times-Union, NY/Rothco.

a manufacturing and exporting giant. In the 1960s, its rate of growth accelerated from an annual average of 9 percent in the 1950s to more than 11 percent, thanks in part to heavy buying by the United States for the wars in Korea and Vietnam. Even without oil and other key natural resources, Japan had become the world's largest shipbuilder by the 1970s, and only the United States and the Soviet Union surpassed it in iron and steel production.

In the 1970s, the Middle East's oil-producing nations also dealt Western dominance a critical blow. Tensions between Israel and the Arab world provided the catalyst. On June 5, 1967, Israeli forces, responding to Palestinian guerrilla attacks, seized Gaza and the Sinai peninsula from Egypt, the Golan Heights from Syria, and the West Bank from Jordan. Although Israel won a stunning victory in this Six-Day War, the Arab humiliation led the Arab states to try to forge a common political

Map: Israel after the Six-Day War, 1967

Legend:
- Israel after independence, 1948
- Israeli conquests, 1967

LEBANON, SYRIA, Golan Heights, Mediterranean Sea, Tel Aviv, West Bank, Jerusalem, Gaza, ISRAEL, JORDAN, Suez Canal, SINAI PENINSULA (returned to Egypt 1981), Gulf of Suez, EGYPT, SAUDI ARABIA, Red Sea

0   25   50 miles
0   50 kilometers

and economic strategy. This strategy ranged from the populist militancy of the defeated Egyptian leader Gamal Abdel Nasser to the more conservative and somewhat more pro-Western leadership in Saudi Arabia to the radical factions of the Palestine Liberation Organization (PLO), which used terrorism against Israel. In 1973, Egypt and Syria attacked Israel on Yom Kippur, the most holy day in the Jewish calendar. Egypt initially made headway, but Israel, with material assistance from the United States, stopped the assault and counterattacked.

Having failed militarily against Israel and the United States, the Arab nations turned decisively to economic clout. The Organization of Petroleum Exporting Countries (OPEC), a relatively loose consortium before the Yom Kippur War, quadrupled the price of its oil and imposed an embargo, cutting off all exports of oil to the United States in retaliation for its support of Israel. For the first time since imperialism's heyday, the *producers* of raw materials—not the industrial powers—controlled the flow of commodities and set prices to their own advantage. The West was now mired in an oil crisis.

Throughout the 1970s, oil-dependent Westerners watched in astonishment as OPEC upset the balance of economic power. Instead of being controlled by the Western powers, the oil-producing nations helped provoke an economic recession by restricting the flow of oil and charging more for it (Figure 29.1). These actions caused unemployment to rise by more than 50 percent in Europe and the United States. Economic policymakers found old theories ineffective. Whereas previous recessions had brought falling prices as goods went unsold, this recession resulted in soaring inflation. By the end of 1973, the inflation rate jumped to over 8 percent in West Germany, 12 percent in France, and 20 percent in Portugal; in 1974, it reached 13 percent in Britain and Italy and 8 percent in the United States. Eastern-bloc countries, dependent on Soviet oil, fared little better. Though formally outside the bloc, Yugoslavia felt the effects, with 40 percent inflation by the end of the decade. Skyrocketing interest rates in the U.S.-led bloc discouraged both industrial investment and consumer buying. With prices, unemployment, and interest rates soaring—the unusual combination of economic conditions was dubbed *stagflation*—a sense of discouragement settled over Westerners. They realized not only that energy resources were finite but also that their economic prosperity had limits.

Political Alternatives in Hard Times

The unprecedented economic situation and the changing global balance of power inspired new waves of citizen activism. Some of these movements took the cause of reform to shocking extremes. Frustrated by long-standing grievances or the slow pace of change, some turned to violence, including bombings, kidnapping, and murder—a politics of terror reminiscent of the late nineteenth century but devastating to the superpowers' goal of maintaining the status quo.

Environmental Politics. A sense of limits to global resources encouraged the formation of environmental political parties. An escapee from Nazi Germany, E. F. "Fritz" Schumacher, produced one of the bibles of the environmental movement, *Small Is Beautiful* (1973), which spelled out how technology and industrialization threatened the earth and its inhabitants. Environmentalists like Schumacher and the American Rachel Carson, author of *Silent Spring* (1962), advocated the immediate rescue of rivers, forests, and the soil from the ravages of factories and chemical farming. Instead of massive agribusiness, which required huge doses of chemical fertilizers and produced single crops for the market, they pleaded for small-scale, diverse, organic (pesticide-

FIGURE 29.1 Fluctuating Oil Prices, 1955–1985
Colonization allowed the Western imperial powers to obtain raw materials at advantageous prices. Even with decolonization, European and American firms often had such entrenched roots in newly independent economies that they were able to set the terms for trade. OPEC's oil embargo and price hikes of the 1970s were signs of change, which included the exercise of decolonized countries' control over their own resources. Not only did OPEC's action lead to a decade of painful economic downturn, it also encouraged some European governments to improve public transportation and to impose policies that would make individual consumers cut back on their dependence on oil.

free) farming. For industry, environmentalists demanded that factories be scaled back and made more environmentally responsible. These attitudes challenged almost two centuries of faith in industrial growth and in the infinite ability of humanity to extract progress from the natural world.

Initially the environmental movement had its greatest political effect in West Germany. As student protest subsided in the 1970s, environmentalism united members of older and younger generations around the 1960s political tactic called *citizen initiatives*, in which groups of people blocked everything from public transportation fare increases to plans for urban growth. In the 1970s, citizen initiative groups targeted nuclear power and nuclear installations; they took their cue from Chancellor Willy Brandt, whose Ostpolitik sought to extricate

West Germany from the threat of nuclear devastation. Demonstrations against nuclear power stations drew crowds in the tens of thousands, often armed with wirecutters to enter fenced-in areas.

In 1979, the Green Party was founded in West Germany and launched candidates for political office. Elsewhere in western Europe, environmentalists influenced mainstream politics, forcing candidates to voice their concern for the environment and leading governments to establish ministries for the environment. In the Soviet bloc, Communist commitment to industrial development blinded governments to environmental destruction and to the effects of pollution on people; citizen protest focused on basic needs and individual freedom.

Expansion of Feminism. Feminist activism made real gains in the 1970s. Environmental parties attracted many women angered at the birth of thalidomide babies and concerned about the chemical contamination of their family's food. Men could escape to the moon or into their careers, a West German ecologist maintained, but not women, "who must give birth to children, willingly or unwillingly, in this polluted world of ours." Other women's activism had notable successes in the 1970s. In Catholic Italy, feminists won the right to divorce, to gain access to birth-control information, and to obtain legal abortions. The demand for these rights as well as for equal pay, job opportunities, and protection from rape, incest, and battering framed the major legal struggles of thousands of women's groups in the 1970s.

In the U.S.-led bloc, personal change also became a goal for women. Consciousness-raising sessions in which groups of women shared individual experiences with marriage, with children, and in the workforce became popular. Such sessions alleviated

Soldiers and Civilians in Northern Ireland
Separatist, civil rights, and terrorist movements made everyday life unpredictably dangerous in the last third of the century, as activists increasingly directed their violence against ordinary people. The world wars had often targeted civilians, and those leading internal struggles did so even when the declared wars were over. In Belfast, Northern Ireland, British troops fought to put down the Irish Republican Army and restore unity. Civilians were often drawn into the conflict. It was only late in the 1990s that both sides called a halt to the killing and agreed to negotiate.
Brian Aris/Camera Press London.

some of the isolation women felt at home; participants realized that women shared many similar experiences. Soviet-bloc women, who often formed the majority of the workforce and shouldered responsibility for all domestic work, received inspiration from feminist stories spread through the *samizdat* network. The new camaraderie among many women in both the Soviet and U.S.-led blocs prepared them for political participation.

In 1977, fifteen thousand activist women from around the globe poured into Houston to mark the International Year of Women. The meeting brought together Westerners interested in political and economic rights and cultural equality and third world women who called for an end to violence, starvation, and disease. The utter poverty afflicting women in less-developed countries called into question the commonality on which Western feminist politics was based. The issue of sexual orientation also challenged many mainstream activists in Houston, as lesbians exposed the greater privileges heterosexual women enjoyed. After Houston the media publicized the "death of feminism," both because of the convention's relative calm and because of the invisible roots feminism had sunk into mainstream local, national, and global politics. In 1978, East German author Christa Wolf spoke of a confident new attitude pervading the movement: "[Women] feel that their new role has already begun to solidify; their lust for life is great, their hunger for reality insatiable." Organization, raised consciousness, and some economic gains backed women's entry into local and national government from the 1970s on. (See "Contrasting Views," page 1146.)

Politics by Violence. Terrorist bands took a radically different path, responding to the conservative political climate and worsening economic conditions with kidnappings, bank robberies, bombings, and assassinations. Disaffected and well-to-do youth, steeped in the most extreme theories of society's decay, often joined these groups. Eager to bring down the Social Democratic coalition that led West Germany throughout the 1970s, the Baader-Meinhof gang assassinated prominent businessmen as well as judges and other public officials. Practiced in assassinations of public figures and random shootings of pedestrians, Italy's Red Brigades kidnapped and then murdered the head of the dominant Christian Democrats in 1978. Advocates of

independence for the Basque nation in northern Spain assassinated Spanish politicians and police.

In Britain, nationalist and religious violence in the 1970s pitted the Catholics in Northern Ireland against the dominant Protestants. Catholics experienced job discrimination and a lack of civil rights. In 1969, Catholic student protest turned into demonstrations on behalf of union with the Irish Republic. As violence in Northern Ireland escalated, the British government sent in troops. On January 30, 1972, which became known as "Bloody Sunday," British troops fired at demonstrators and killed thirteen, setting off a cycle of violence that left five hundred dead in that single year. Protestants fearful of losing their dominant position combated a reinvigorated Irish Republican Army (IRA),

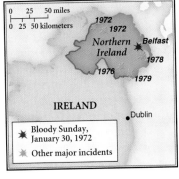

Nationalist Movements of the 1970s

which carried out bombings and assassinations to achieve the union of the two Irelands in order to end the oppression of Catholics.

Terrorists failed in their goal of overturning the existing democracies. In Italy, Christian Democrats and Communists managed to govern together throughout the terrorist crisis. In West Germany, Willy Brandt resigned in 1974 amidst a spy scandal within his government, the economic downturn, and ongoing terrorism. Another Social Democrat, the more pragmatic Helmut Schmidt, replaced him but continued Brandt's policies of rapprochement with East Germany and the Soviet Union.

Sorely tried as it was, parliamentary government scored some important successes in the 1970s. The Iberian Peninsula, suffering under dictatorship since the 1930s, regained its freedom and set out on a course of greater prosperity. The death of Spain's Francisco Franco (1892–1975) ended more than three decades of dictatorial rule. Franco's handpicked successor, King Juan Carlos (b. 1938), surprisingly steered his nation to Western-style

Feminist Debates

The new feminist movement of the late twentieth century provoked the most pronounced and widespread debate over gender in recorded history. Discussion often reached a heated pitch, much like other reform movements of the day. Hardly the single movement described by journalists, feminism had a variety of concerns often depending on nationality, ethnicity, sexual orientation, and class. These could produce conflict among activists and serious divisions on goals and policies, as the authors of the Combahee River Statement demonstrated (Document 1). At times, concerns over issues like equal opportunity in the workplace were directed at government policies, though secretly, as in the case of the Soviet worker (Document 2). Italian feminists saw all the disabilities imposed by government as characteristic of larger problems (Document 3), while Germans explicitly connected the cause of feminism to that of environmentalism (Document 4).

1. Criticizing Feminism

In the United States, black women, like several other minority groups, found themselves marginalized in both the feminist and civil rights movements. In 1977 some of them issued the Combahee River Statement.

A Black feminist presence has evolved most obviously in connection with the second wave of the American women's movement beginning in the late 1960s. Black, other third world, and working women have been involved in the feminist movement from its start, but both outside reactionary forces and racism and elitism within the movement itself have served to obscure our participation. . . .

Black feminist politics also have an obvious connection to movements for Black liberation, particularly those of the 1960s and 1970s. . . . It was our experience and disillusionment within these liberation movements, as well as experience on the periphery of the white male left, that led to the need to develop a politics that was antiracist, unlike those of white women, and antisexist, unlike those of Black and white men. . . .

Above all else, our politics initially sprang from the shared belief that Black women are inherently valuable, that our liberation is a necessity not as an adjunct to somebody else's but because of our need as human persons for autonomy.

Source: "The Combahee River Collective Statement" in *Feminism in Our Time: The Essential Writings, World War II to the Present,* Miriam Schneir, ed. (New York: Vintage, 1994), 177–179.

2. Criticizing Socialism

Official policy in the Soviet Union stated that socialism had brought women full equality, eliminating the need for feminism. Thus in 1930, the government abolished the women's bureau, or Zhenotdel, and had branded feminism "bourgeois." In the 1970s, however, Russian women in clusters announced their dissatisfaction with so-called equality under socialism. Tatyana Mamonova, the editor of a collection of Russian women's writings—which originally circulated in samizdat *form—was ultimately expelled from the country for publicizing views such as those of this railroad worker.*

Today a woman has no outlet for complaints because women's sections have been abolished as "unnecessary." It is becoming increasingly clear that the current equality means only giving women the right to perform heavy labor. . . . [I]n our day the woman, still not freed from the incredible burden of the family, strains herself even harder in the service of society. The situation . . . is true not only in large cities but also in villages. On collective and state farms, women do the hardest and most exhausting work while the men are employed as administrators, agronomists, accountants, warehouse managers, or high-paid tractor and combine drivers. In other words, men do the work that is more interesting and more profitable and does not damage their health.

Source: Tatyana Mamonova, ed., *Women and Russia: Feminist Writings from the Soviet Union* (Boston: Beacon Press, 1984), 8.

3. Policy and Patriarchy

In Italy, as in the Soviet Union, feminism had an underground quality to it involving mimeographed tracts and graffiti on buildings; women formed their own bookshops and published small newspapers. But women also lobbied hard to get legislation on divorce and abortion changed. With socialism powerful among some intellectuals and in unions, the Feminist Movement of Rome saw issues in theoretical terms and connected the disabilities imposed on women with both class and sexual customs in a 1976 article in its paper.

Patriarchal society is based on authoritarian-exploitative relationships, and its sexuality is sado-masochistic. The values of power, of the domination of man over the other [woman], are reflected in sexuality, where historically woman is given to man for his use. . . .

The idea of woman as man's property is fundamental to her oppression and she is often the only possession that dominant men allow exploited men to keep. . . .

In other words woman is given to the (exploited) man as compensation for his lack of possessions. . . .

We denounce as the latest form of woman's oppression the idea of a "sexual revolution" where woman is forced to go from being one man's object to being everybody's object, and where sado-masochistic pornography in films, in magazines, in all the forms of mass media that brutalize and violate woman, is bandied about as a triumph of sexual liberty.

Source: "Male Sexuality—Perversion," *Movimento Femminista Romano* (1976), quoted in *Italian Feminist Thought: A Reader*, ed. Paola Bono and Sandra Kemp (Oxford: Blackwell, 1991), 68–69.

4. Feminism and Environmentalism

"Green" feminists took a different approach, such as this announced by Delphine Brox-Brochot in "Manifesto of the 'Green' Women." Brox-Brochot was speaking in 1975 to people in Bremen, West Germany, in the context of men's landing on the moon and other accomplishments in space.

Man has actually landed on the moon—an admirable feat. . . . We "Green" women . . . believe that men belong to our environment. In order to rescue that environment for our children, we want to confront this man, this adventurer and moon explorer. A female cosmonaut from a so-called socialist republic doesn't justify this energy-wasting enterprise for us at a time when three-fourths of the earth's population is suffering from malnutrition.

Our inability to solve immediate problems may tempt us into escape—to the moon, into careerism, escape into ideologies, into alcohol or other drugs. But one group cannot escape completely: women, society's potential mothers, who must give birth to children, willingly or unwillingly, in this polluted world of ours.

Source: Delphine Brox-Brochot, "Manifesto of the 'Green' Women," in *German Feminism: Readings in Politics and Literature*, ed. Edith Hoshino Altbach et al. (Albany: State University of New York Press, 1984), 314.

QUESTIONS FOR DEBATE

1. To what extent should we see the feminist movements of the 1960s and 1970s as primarily an offshoot of other reform movements of the day and thus a product of their time?

2. Is it more appropriate to speak of feminism in these decades as a unified movement or as a set of multiple movements with multiple goals?

3. Were there distinctly national issues within feminism that made the movement more a product of national politics than of gender politics?

IMPORTANT DATES

1962 Forum on "pop art" at the Museum of Modern Art in New York City

1962–1965 Vatican II reforms Catholic ritual and dogma

1963 U.S. president John F. Kennedy assassinated

1964 Nikita Khrushchev ousted in the USSR, replaced by Leonid Brezhnev and Alexei Kosygin

1966 Willy Brandt becomes West German foreign minister and develops Ostpolitik, a policy designed to bridge tensions between the two Germanies

1967 South Africa's Dr. Christiaan Barnard performs first successful human heart transplant

1968 Revolution in Czechoslovakia against communism; student uprisings throughout Europe and the United States

1969 U.S. astronauts walk on the moon's surface

1972 SALT I treaty between the United States and Soviet Union

1973 North Vietnam and the United States sign treaty ending war in Vietnam; OPEC raises price of oil and imposes oil embargo on the West

1973–1976 Aleksandr Solzhenitsyn publishes *Gulag Archipelago*

1977 Feminists gather in Houston to mark the first International Year of Women

1978 The first test-tube baby is born in England

1979 Iranians take U.S. hostages in Teheran

constitutional monarchy, facing down threatened military coups. Portugal and Greece also ousted right-wing dictators, thus paving the way for their integration into western Europe and for substantial economic growth.

Yet the dominance of the West was deteriorating. In 1976, Jimmy Carter (b. 1924), a wealthy farmer and governor of Georgia, narrowly won the U.S. presidential election (the first after Watergate) by selling himself as an outsider to Washington corruption. Carter's domestic and foreign policies met with some success; but they did little to return the economy to its pre-Vietnam and pre–oil embargo prosperity or stem global terrorism.

The last two years of Carter's administration witnessed still another challenge to Western dominance in the form of Islamic militancy. Late in the 1970s, students, clerics, shopkeepers, and unem-

ployed men in Iran began a religious agitation that forced Shah Reza Pahlavi (1919–1980) into exile in January 1979. Repressively and brutally ruled by the U.S.-backed shah, Iran had enormous but unevenly distributed wealth and a large population of discontented, poor Shi'ite Muslims. The militants installed a fundamentalist Muslim leader, Ayatollah Ruhollah Khomeini (1900?–1989), whose political messages had arrived from his Parisian exile via cassette technology to consolidate opposition to the shah. Khomeini called for a transformation of the region into a truly Islamic society awaiting the coming of the Mahdi, or Messiah. Iran, he believed, could lead this transformation if it renounced the Western ways advocated by the shah and followed the strict rule of Islam. In the autumn of 1979, revolutionary supporters of Khomeini took hostages at the American embassy in Teheran and would not release them. The paralysis of the United States in the face of Islamic militancy along with the soaring inflation following another round of OPEC price hikes suggested that the 1980s and 1990s might cripple the West even more.

Conclusion

The 1960s and 1970s left the West with a sense of emergency. In these decades, an unprecedented level of technological development transformed businesses, the nature of warfare, the exploration of space, and the functioning of government. It also had an enormous impact on everyday life. Work changed, as society reached a stage called *postindustrial*, in which the service sector predominated. New patterns of family life, new relationships among the generations, and revised standards for sexual behavior also characterized these years. Optimism abounded in the potential of humans to perpetuate progress and affluence. Yet technological change produced stubborn problems: concentrations of bureaucratic and industrial power, social inequality, environmental degradation, even uncertainty about humankind's future.

A surge of rebellion among youth, ethnic and racial minorities, and women condemned these conditions along with the threats posed by the continued cold war. By the end of the 1970s, war in Vietnam, protests throughout the Soviet bloc, the power of oil-producing states, and the growing

Revolutionary Fervor in Iran

The installation of an Islamic government in Iran gained the real enthusiasm of citizens, for whom the rule of the shah had brought modernization and Westernization, but a clampdown on freedom and striking inequalities of wealth. Islamic rule meant distinctly different roles for men and women; women, for instance were required to wear more restrictive clothing and to adopt a more subservient demeanor after years of Westernization and liberalization. At the same time, the strict separation of the sexes brought new opportunity for jobs in medicine, teaching, and other professions as women were trained to treat an all-female clientele who could no longer use men's services.
Alfred/Liaison Agency.

political force of Islam had weakened superpower preeminence. The U.S.-led bloc also confronted terrorism, and the Soviet Union, long able to repress dissent in a growing economy, was putting more resources into military buildup than it could ultimately support. While the superpowers faltered, society approached the global age—one prepared by the array of technology of the 1960s and 1970s. The phenomena of rising citizen activism, globalism, and rapid technological advance posed real challenges to a world on the verge of a new millennium.

Suggested References

The Technology Revolution

Wartime technological development came to have profound consequences for the peacetime lives of individuals and for society. The works below describe the new technologies and analyze their importance, with authors divided on whether the new developments should be feared or embraced.

Hecht, Gabrielle. *The Radiance of France: Nuclear Power and National Identity after World War II.* 1998.

Kimbrell, Andrew. *The Human Body Shop: The Cloning, Engineering, and Marketing of Life.* 1997.

Mazlich, Bruce. *The Fourth Discontinuity: The Co-Evolution of Humans and Machines.* 1994.

*Rhodes, Richard, ed. *Visions of Technology: A Century of Vital Debate about Machines, Systems, and the Human World.* 1999.

Singer, Edward Nathan. *The Twentieth Century Revolution in Technology.* 1998.

*Stanworth, Michelle, ed. *Reproductive Technologies: Gender, Motherhood, and Medicine.* 1987.

Postindustrial Society and Culture

Changes in the way people worked became striking in the 1960s, causing social observers to analyze the meaning of the transformation. Many critics agree that technology's creation of a postindustrial workplace changed not only the way people worked but also how they lived in families and interacted with peers.

Bennett, Tony, ed. *Rock and Popular Music: Politics, Policies, Institutions.* 1993.

Evans, Christopher. *The Micro Millennium.* 1979.

Hochschild, Arlie. *The Time Bind: When Work Becomes Home and Home Becomes Work.* 1997.

Proctor, Robert. *Cancer Wars: The Politics behind What We Know and Don't Know about Causes and Trends.* 1994.

*Primary sources.

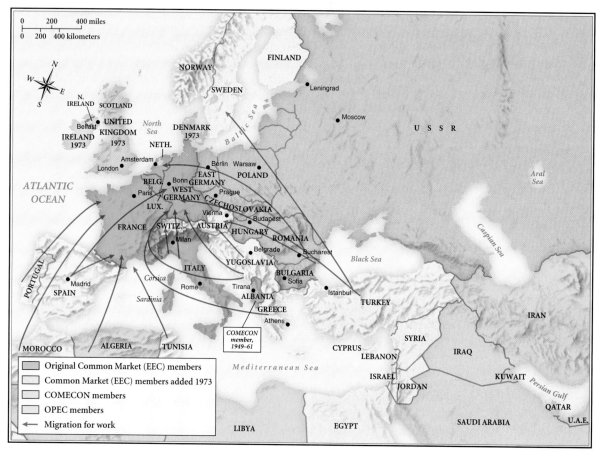

MAPPING THE WEST Europe and the Mediterranean, 1980

Despite the continuation of the cold war and the division of Europe into two antagonistic regions, the superpower grip diminished during the 1960s and 1970s. Within the Soviet bloc, several governments introduced features of a market economy and communications technology brought news of life in the U.S.-led bloc. U.S. allies protested American policies in Vietnam, with anti-American elements very much in evidence in the uprisings of 1968. Mediterranean countries played their role in the West's transformation during these decades, not only in the oil embargo but in sending tens of thousands of migrants to work in labor-short Europe and often to settle there permanently.

Sampson, Anthony. *The New Europeans.* 1968.

Sinfield, Alan. *Literature, Politics, and Culture in Post-war Britain.* 1989.

Contesting the Cold War Order in the 1960s

Historians look to domestic politics, international events, social change, and cultural life to capture the texture of this tumultuous decade. But the momentous changes on so many fronts still need synthetic treatment. A Martin Luther King Web site introduces visitors to the biography, speeches, sermons, and major life events of the slain civil rights leader.

Caute, David. *Sixty-Eight.* 1988.

*Dubček, Alexander. *Hope Dies Last: The Autobiography of Alexander Dubček.* 1993.

Fineberg, Jonathan. *Art since 1940: Strategies of Being.* 1995.

*Guy-Sheftall, Beverly, ed. *Words of Fire: An Anthology of African-American Feminist Thought.* 1995.

Katsiaficas, George. *The Subversion of Politics: European Autonomous Social Movements and the Decolonization of Everyday Life.* 1997.

*Lévi-Strauss, Claude. *Tristes Tropiques.* 1961.

The Martin Luther King, Jr. Papers Project at Stanford University: http://www.stanford.edu/group/King.

Tarrow, Sidney. *Democracy and Disorder: Protest Politics in Italy, 1965–1975.* 1989.

The Erosion of Superpower Mastery in the 1970s

As the superpowers continued their standoff, historians found that myriad global changes affected their status. Some of the most compelling reading is found in personal testimonies such as Chang's account of Maoism and the Cultural Revolution, while the dissident art of the Soviet Union is striking for its deft and moving critique of life under Communism. Many interesting Web sites explore the development of green parties over the past three decades, the most inclusive being that of the global organization with links to green parties of all continents and countries.

Battah, Abdalla M., and Yehuda Lukachs, eds. *The Arab-Israeli Conflict: Two Decades of Change.* 1988.

*Chang, Jung. *Wild Swans: Three Daughters of China.* 1991.

Green parties worldwide: http://www.greens.org.

Huelsberg, Werner. *The German Greens: A Social and Political Profile.* 1988.

Koshar, Rudy. *Germany's Transient Pasts: Preservation and National Memory in the Twentieth Century.* 1998.

Laqueur, Walter. *The Age of Terrorism.* 1987.

Olson, James S., and Randy Roberts. *Where the Domino Fell: America and Vietnam, 1945–1990.* 1996.

Rosenfeld, Alla, and Norton T. Dodge. *From Gulag to Glasnost: Nonconformist Art from the Soviet Union.* 1995.

Smith, Dennis B. *Japan since 1945: The Rise of an Economic Superpower.* 1995.

*Solzhenitsyn, Aleksandr Isaevich. *The Gulag Archipelago.* 1973–1976.

Swain, Geoffrey, and Nigel Swain. *Eastern Europe since 1945.* 1993.

CHAPTER 30

The New Globalism: Opportunities and Dilemmas

1980 to the Present

I N THE MID-1980S, THE SOVIET MAGAZINE OGONYOK ("Small Fires"), instead of making up patriotic "letters to the editor" as was the custom under communism, began printing actual reports from readers. Identifying herself as a "mother of two," one woman protested that the cost-cutting policy of reusing syringes in hospitals was spreading AIDS. "Why should little kids have to pay for the criminal actions of our Ministry of Health?" she asked. Other readers complained of corrupt factory managers, of "the radioactive sausages" foisted on the public after the disastrous explosion at the Chernobyl nuclear plant, and of endless lines at grocery stores and the lack of food. Sales of *Ogonyok* soared from a few hundred thousand to four million, and the experiment in printing real letters flooded the offices with hundreds of thousands of pieces of mail. The *Ogonyok* example was not unique: all across the Soviet bloc people were exploring political participation and resistance. They wrote, picketed, and protested; in so doing they created an unprecedented public activism that, with incredibly little bloodshed, toppled the Soviet empire in 1989 and ended the cold war.

The collapse of communism in Europe had unexpected repercussions, including the eruption of ethnic violence in the region, the deterioration of everyday life, and the decline of public services. The latter result was part of a general trend in the West, as Great Britain, the United States, and the other advanced industrial economies reversed the century-long trend toward the welfare state. Government support for citizens' health, housing, and social security diminished, as politicians

Paraguay-France Championship Soccer Match
Professional sports had become a force for global unity and national rivalry alike by the twenty-first century. The pool of highly paid and internationally celebrated athletes was a global melting pot of race, ethnicity, gender, and religion, while the diffusion of sports news and programming, such as the Paraguay-France soccer championship match, encouraged a common, global culture.
Owen Franken/Stock Boston.

1980	1984	1988	1992	1996	2000

Politics and War

Islamic revolution in Iran

Student uprising in Beijing's Tiananmen Square; collapse of Soviet empire

Retrenchment of the welfare state in Great Britain, the United States, other western nations

Germany reunified

International congress of women at Beijing

Rise of Solidarity in Poland

War in the Persian Gulf

First postapartheid elections in South Africa

Civil war in the former Yugoslavia

USSR formally dissolved

Society and Economy

Gorbachev's policy of perestroika; nuclear accident at Chernobyl

Genocide in Rwanda

AIDS epidemic reaches global proportions

Privatization and economic dislocation in post-Soviet economies; Internet revolution

Collapse of Thai currency and upset of Asian "tigers"

Euro becomes currency of the European Union; world population reaches six billion

Culture, Religion, and Intellectual Life

Growing influence of Islam in culture and politics; postmodernism in architecture, literature, and cultural theory; international diffusion of culture

looked back to the liberal values of the nineteenth century, not the liberalism of the twentieth. However, government increased subsidies and incentives for business, as the West found itself in a new struggle of global competition. This war targeted the rising economic power of Japan, China, and other Asian countries, and for a time it came to replace the cold war, at least in public rhetoric. As international business mergers accelerated in the 1990s and as the Internet connected enterprises around the world in a matter of seconds, however, international unity rather than competition became the order of the day among former rivals in business and politics alike.

The end of the cold war thus hastened the arrival of the "global age"—marked by the vast international and national migration of tens of millions of people, the expanding global marketplace, and an accelerated cultural exchange of popular music, books, films, and television entertainment. The global age also encompassed the international impact of disasters such as AIDS and environmental degradation. To some it signaled an end of superpower rivalry and the dominance of the United States. Others pointed to the rise of new forces that rivaled those of the West, such as the economic power of the Asian countries and the cultural might of Islam. Only as the century drew to a close did observers equate globalism with the revolutionary power of the Internet. Whatever the meaning of the many new phenomena, there is no question that the twenty-first century will bring extraordinary challenges that have worldwide resonance.

For historians, understanding the recent past is a challenge in itself. Every day of the past two decades has been filled with news—news that now receives virtually instantaneous reporting because of modern communications technology. Unlike journalists, historians do not attempt to choose from this mass the most talked-about story of the moment or the one that will attract the greatest readership. Rather, they are interested in judging what will be important in the long run and which items from the unfiltered mass of technologically transmitted news are actually true. Historians want to identify social, cultural, and political events that are uniquely important or generally significant for people's everyday lives. Historians make the most reliable evaluations when these phenomena are no longer "news"—that is, after a good period of time has shown their staying power and influence.

In the first edition of this book we held our breath in the face of rapidly changing events and judged that the fall of communism in Europe and the increasing interconnectedness of the world's peoples and cultures were the challenges not only of the moment but of history. In this second edition we persist in that judgment although the end of the Soviet Union and the coming of globalism have brought greater perils than we anticipated only five or six years ago. Other forces like the Internet missed our notice altogether, despite the fact that the system had been around for several decades. As an experiment in history, you might note the important events of the months in which you take this course, put your list away for several years or more, and then see if those events—along with the events discussed in this chapter—stand the test of time.

❖ Global Challenges

It is now a commonplace belief that we live in a global age, but once our historical vision widens to encompass the globe we see a picture of uneven development and much room for debate about the state of our planet and its peoples. Despite a rapidly changing economy, access to jobs, and prosperity for many, the end of the cold war ushered in many challenges. First, the health of the world's peoples and their environment encountered a multipronged attack as nuclear disaster, acid rain, and surging population threatened the planet's ecosystem. Second, economic prosperity and physical safety continued to elude great masses of people, especially in the southern half of the globe. Third, a greater number of states than ever before exercised economic and political power, especially through multinational agencies like the World Bank and the World Trade Organization—a shift from the bipolarism of the cold war when there were two reigning superpowers. Simultaneously, nonstate or transnational allegiances such as Islamic or ethnic movements also vied for power and influence, often calling into question not only the concept of national borders but the very nation-state on which modern history has focused.

Pollution and Population

Whereas industrialization and a growing population had once appeared wholly positive, people became aware of their dangers and limits. For each warning of imminent catastrophe—either from overcrowding or ecological disaster—some scientists and social theorists pointed to the solutions that humans had usually been able to devise for even the direst calamities.

Threats to the Environment. Despite the best efforts of the spreading ecology movement, technological development continued to threaten the environment. The dangers were laid bare starkly in 1986, when the nuclear plant at Chernobyl in the Soviet Union exploded and spewed radioactive dust into the atmosphere. The reactor, like most in the USSR, had been constructed with minimal safety features. Many plant workers died within the year; others perished more slowly from the effects of radiation. Levels of radioactivity rose for hundreds of miles in all directions, and by the 1990s cancer rates in the region were soaring, particularly among children.

Other environmental problems were more insidious but also had devastating global effects. Fossil-fuel pollutants such as those from natural gas, coal, and oil mixed with atmospheric moisture to

Chernobyl Memorial Demonstration
The explosion at the nuclear plant at Chernobyl in Ukraine caused death and illness and led to a regional surge in cancer cases that has lasted to the present day. Coming in the midst of reform in the Soviet Union, the explosion pointed to the dangers in the entire nuclear system, which had been built with minimal safety precautions to save money. Citizens protested more widely, revealing their anger at the condition of their daily lives.
Sovfoto/Eastfoto.

By the late 1980s, scientists from around the world had identified other challenges to the environment. The public's use of chlorofluorocarbons (CFCs), chemicals found in aerosol and refrigeration products, had blown a hole in the ozone layer. Part of the blanket of gases surrounding the earth, ozone prevents harmful ultraviolet rays from reaching the planet. Simultaneously, automobile and industrial emissions of chemicals were adding to the thermal blanket of which ozone was a part. The result was *global warming*, an increase in the temperature of the earth's lower atmosphere. Changes in temperature and dramatic weather cycles of drought or drenching rain indicated that a *greenhouse effect* might be permanently warming the earth. Some researchers forecast dire effects for the earth's future.

The global public stepped up pressure on governments to check pollution, and the affluent West possessed the resources to begin to undo some of the damage that had accompanied industrialization and technological change. Automobile manufacturers in western Europe and the United States began building cars with lower carbon monoxide emissions, and industrialists scaled back on factory pollution of air and waterways. Consumers began recycling such products as newspapers, glass and plastic containers, and cardboard. In Europe, municipal governments turned streets into automobile-free pedestrian zones, established more "green" areas in cities, and even banned cars altogether when ozone levels reached a danger point. European countries and Japan led the world in providing efficient public transportation, thus reducing the number of polluting automobiles on the streets. In the United States, the automobile industry's political influence blocked the expansion of mass transit, however, and prevented restrictions on automobile use.

produce acid rain, a poisonous brew that destroyed forests in industrial areas. Acid rain damaged more than 70 percent of Europe's Norway spruce trees. In eastern Europe, where fossil fuels were burned with virtually no safeguards, forests looked as if they had been ravaged by fire, and children suffered a range of ailments such as chronic bronchial disease. In less industrial areas, the world's rain forests were hacked down at an alarming rate, as people sought land to develop for cattle grazing or for growing cash crops. Clearing the forests depleted the global oxygen supply and threatened the biological diversity of the entire planet.

Population Growth. Nations with less-developed economies struggled with the pressing issue of surging population. Whereas by 1995 Europe was actually experiencing negative growth (that is, more deaths than births), the less industrially developed countries accounted for 98 percent of all population growth globally. The annual growth rate of world population had been about 2 percent since 1950. By late 1999, the globe's population had reached 6 billion and the growth rate was estimated at 1.5 percent, with a doubling at this rate forecast for 2045.

(See "Taking Measure," below.) Migration, urbanization, and social dislocation plagued nations without the industrial and commercial resources to feed these swelling numbers.

The population increased partly because the spread of Western medicine enabled people to live much longer. In nonindustrial countries, life expectancy rose by an average of sixteen years between 1950 and 1980. The superpowers did not fare particularly well by this measure of social health: life expectancy in the Soviet Union fell steadily in the 1970s to 1990s, from a peak of seventy years in the mid-1970s to fifty-three for Russian men in 1995; by 1995, the United States had fallen from the top twenty in longevity for both women and men. Meanwhile, fertility rates, which had been dropping in the West for decades, were also declining in the less-developed world by 1995, as some 58 percent of couples were estimated to use birth control. Women in North Africa, who had produced an average of 6.8 children in the 1950s and 1960s, were giving birth to an average of 5.6 by the mid-1980s. In China the number fell precipitously, from 6.2 to 2.0 in 1995, largely because of government restrictions on pregnancy. Nonetheless, the Chinese population skyrocketed. Where women entered the economic arena, as in South Korea, family limitation advanced. Many took heart at the slowdown in population increase as a sign of the potential for diverting calamitous growth.

Western medicine and better health found their way into the less-developed world in the form of vaccines and drugs for diseases such as malaria and smallpox. However, half of all Africans did not benefit from basic public health facilities such as safe drinking water. Drought and poverty, along with the maneuvers of politicians in some cases, spread famine in regions like the Sudan. Critics analyzed these conditions as the result of a growing divide not between East and West but among countries of the wealthy North and the far poorer South. Medical practice in the industrialized nations focused on high-tech solutions to health problems. Specialists performed heart bypass surgery, transplanted organs, and treated cancer with radiation and chemotherapy. Preventive care received less attention; for example, in the late 1970s the Netherlands spent less than 3 percent of its total medical expenditures on preventive medicine. Expensive, technological, in-hospital treatment of the sick became the rule in wealthy nations, and studies showed that a disproportionate amount of these services went to the upper classes, especially men. At the other end of the scale, the unemployed suffered more chronic illnesses than those who were better off, but they received less care. Within industrial countries as well

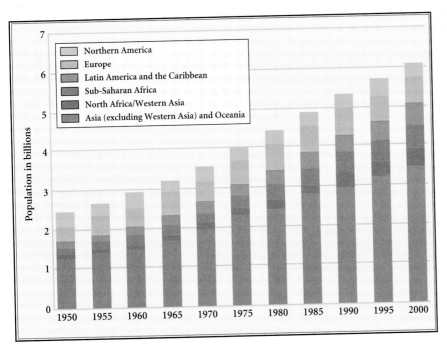

TAKING MEASURE
World Population Growth, 1950–2000

In the twenty-first century, a major question is whether the global environment can sustain billions of people indefinitely. In the early modern period, local communities had lived according to unwritten rules that balanced population size with the productive capacities of individual farming regions. Centuries later the same need for balance had reached global proportions. As fertility dropped around the planet because of contraception, population continued to grow because of improved health. The political, social, and environmental results remain unclear.

as outside them, the distribution of health services became a hotly debated issue in the general argument of whether technological solutions could remedy global problems.

North versus South?

During the 1980s and 1990s, world leaders tried to address the growing economic schism between the earth's northern and southern regions. Although Australians and New Zealanders were exceptions, southern peoples generally suffered lower living standards and measures of health than northerners. Recently emerging from colonial rule and economic exploitation by the North, citizens could not yet count on their new governments to provide welfare services or education. Latin American nations grappled with government corruption, multibillion-dollar debt, widespread crime, and grinding poverty. In Brazil, bands of homeless children roamed city streets. The drug trade plagued Colombia; illegal commerce diverted resources that might have been channeled toward investment, social reforms, and the development of democracy. Other countries, prominent among them Mexico, began to strengthen their economies by marketing their oil and other natural resources more effectively.

In sub-Saharan Africa, environmental destruction resulted from the conversion of land to the production of cash crops. The region suffered from drought, continuing famine, and civil war. In lands such as Rwanda, military rule, ideological factionalism, and ethnic antagonism encouraged under imperialism produced a lethal mixture of conflict and genocide in the 1990s. Millions perished; others were left starving and homeless. Although African countries began turning away from military dictatorship and toward parliamentary government, global economic advance was uneven on that continent.

In South Africa, native peoples struggled for political rights and economic opportunity against entrenched white racism. In 1990, the moderate South African leader F. W. de Klerk released the imprisoned political leader Nelson Mandela (b. 1918), who had been held for almost three decades because of his antiapartheid politics. By then the media had made Mandela's plight a focus of worldwide concern, and multinational corporations had reduced their economic activity in the segregated country. De Klerk's government followed Mandela's release

with a gradual dismantling of such aspects of apartheid as segregated parks and beaches. In 1993, the government and the African National Congress (ANC) agreed to a democratic constitution that granted the vote to the nonwhite majority while guaranteeing whites and other minorities civil liberties. The path to reform was complicated by divisions among African ethnic groups, most notably between the Xhosa, who held most of the positions of power in the ANC, and the Zulu, who opposed the ANC. Strong evidence suggested that conflict among Africans was fanned by white supremacists in the police and army and in paramilitary groups. In 1994, the ANC won a landslide victory and Mandela, the country's president, endorsed the tolerant new constitution, promoted a multiracial democracy in which international business flourished, and oversaw the election of a second postapartheid president in 1999.

Southern countries' drive to modernize could serve as a force for political stability, but sometimes internal struggles over national policy ignited turmoil. In India, Rajiv Gandhi (1944–1991), the grandson of India's first prime minister, Jawaharlal Nehru, worked for education, women's rights, and an end to bitter local rivalries; his assassination in 1991 by Tamil nationalists raised questions about whether India would continue to have the strong leadership necessary to attract investment and thus to continue modernization. That question was soon answered, as India developed its leadership in communications and other technology. In Pakistan and the Philippines, too, the impulse for modernization grew, but unstable social conditions and inept political systems discouraged investment. Moreover, the United Nations slapped both Pakistan and India with economic sanctions when they detonated nuclear weapons late in the 1990s. Because these emerging economies as a whole continued to increase their share of gross domestic product during the 1980s and 1990s, Western domination eroded proportionally. However, the hardships in the South by comparison with the North provided a new focus for global politics.

Islam Confronts the West

The Iran hostage crisis that began in 1979 showed that religion and nationalism could join with the power of oil to make the Middle East an arbiter of

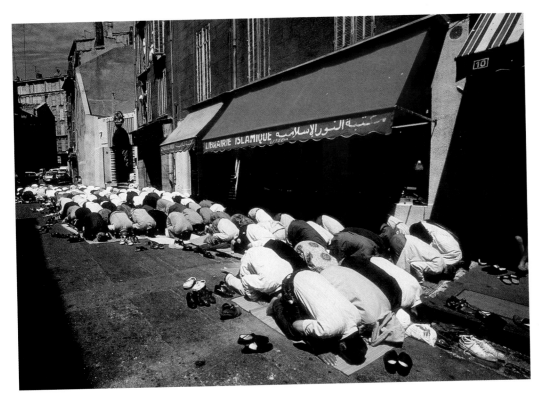

Muslims at Prayer in Marseille, France
As migration increased during the 1980s and 1990s, Europe became more ethnically and racially diverse than it had been for centuries. In most European countries, immigrants could eventually become citizens, while others such as Switzerland and Germany used the criterion of common ancestry to determine who would have political and civil rights. Cultural exchange and interaction accelerated during these decades, and debates over what constituted cultural values and cultural identity multiplied.
Steve McCurry/Magnum Photos, Inc.

international order. The charismatic leaders of the 1980s—Iran's Ayatollah Khomeini, Libya's Muammar Qaddafi, and Iraq's Saddam Hussein—despite important differences, all promoted a pan-Arabic or pan-Islamic world order that gathered increasing support. According to a Muslim intellectual, the capitalist West had used up "that stock of values which gave it its predominance. . . . The turn of Islam has come." Nor did the Soviet Union, before its demise, offer a useful alternative. Muslims should confront the superpowers, Khomeini urged, by taking the position "Neither East, nor West, only the Islamic Republic."

Khomeini's program had wide appeal. Turning from the Westernization that had flourished under the shah, his regime required women to cover their bodies almost totally in special clothing again, restricted their right to divorce, and eliminated a range of other rights. Such changes became a stand-

ard component of Islamic revolution because these restrictions were believed to restore the pride and Islamic identity that imperialism had stripped from Middle Eastern men. Khomeini built widespread support among the Shi'ite Muslims. Even though they constituted the majority in many Middle Eastern countries—72 percent of the population in Bahrain, 60 percent in Iraq, and 95 percent in Iran—they had long been ruled by the Sunnis. The tables turned when Khomeini proclaimed the ascendancy of the Shi'ite clergy in Islamic revolutionary society.

Power in the Middle East remained fragmented, however, and Islam did not achieve its unifying goals (Map 30.1). The Iranian Shi'ites expressed their newfound power and anti-Western feeling by refusing to release the hostages taken in 1979 from the U.S. embassy; their prolonging of the hostage crisis through 1980 contributed to the collapse of the Carter presidency and the election of Ronald

MAP 30.1 The Middle East, 1980–1991

Tensions among states in the Middle East, especially the ongoing conflict between Palestinians and Israelis, became more complicated in the 1980s. As Islam took center stage in politics, Middle Eastern populations additionally divided over such issues as the extent of religious determination of state policies, the rule of religion in everyday life, and access to human rights including freedom of speech and of movement. Conflicts erupted around some of these questions because, as elsewhere, they were also the vehicle for political ambition. The increasing demands of globalization in the 1990s pulled other citizens in the direction of secularization, high-tech international partnerships, and a reduction in the costly politics of violence.

Reagan. Meanwhile, in September 1980, Iraq's president, Saddam Hussein, launched an attack on Iran. Hussein feared that Iraq's Shi'ite minority might rebel against his regime, and he sought to channel their aggression through a patriotic crusade against the non-Arab Iranians. The Iraqi leader also coveted oil-rich territory in Iran. After eight years of com-

bat, the war's primary outcome was massive loss of life on both sides.

The Soviet Union became embroiled against the force of Islam when it supported a coup by a Communist faction against the Communist government in Afghanistan in 1979. The factionalism provided an opening for stiff resistance by Afghanis whose traditional way of life had been threatened by communism's modernizing thrust. By 1980, tens of thousands of Soviets were fighting in Afghanistan, using the USSR's most advanced missiles and artillery to overcome Muslim leaders. After the withdrawal of Soviet forces and the collapse of the USSR, power in Afghanistan remained contested, though by the late 1990s the fundamentalist Taliban party had succeeded in imposing a strict regime, creating millions of political and religious refugees.

As the USSR's empire fell apart, Saddam Hussein was the first to test the post–cold war waters. At the end of the Iran-Iraq war in 1988, Iraq staggered under a heavy debt, unresolved territorial disputes with Iran, the bitter loss of hundreds of thousands of soldiers and civilians, and a lowered standard of living. Hussein viewed the annexation of neighboring Kuwait, whose 600,000 citizens enjoyed the world's highest per capita income, as a solution to Iraq's troubles and a means of smothering internal discontent. In August 1990, he invaded the oil-rich country. While stirring fears among world leaders that he would take other nations, he appealed to the masses in the region as a pan-Arab hero.

Contrary to Hussein's expectations, the deployment of Iraqi troops on the Saudi Arabian border galvanized international resistance. The USSR joined the United Nations' effort to stop the Iraqi invasion, signaling a post–cold war shift in the winds of diplomacy whereby small warring nations would no longer be able to exploit superpower animosities. A multinational force led by the United States pummeled the Iraqi army. Iraq's defeat in the Persian Gulf War heightened pressure on all Middle Eastern leaders to negotiate a peaceful solution to their decades-long disputes.

Yet many of those same leaders used international terrorism to advance their causes. Assassinations and bombings of public buildings and transportation took their toll in lives, especially among the Western powers. Reaching Africa, Asia, and Latin America, terrorism reshaped international politics and perhaps even the definitions of the terms *war* and *peace*.

The Rise of the Pacific Economy

The last third of the twentieth century saw an incredible global diffusion of industry and technology, especially in Asia and some countries in Latin America such as Chile. Just as economic changes in the early modern period had redirected European affairs from the Mediterranean to the Atlantic, explosive productivity from Japan to Singapore in the 1980s began to spread economic power from the Atlantic region to the Pacific. In 1982, the Asian Pacific nations accounted for 16.4 percent of global gross domestic product, a figure that had doubled since the 1960s. More surprising, by the mid-1990s China was achieving economic growth rates of 8 percent and more, while Japan had developed the second largest national economy after the United States.

South Korea, Taiwan, Singapore, Hong Kong, and China were popularly called "tigers" for the ferocity of their growth. Japan, however, led the charge. Investment in high-tech consumer industries drove the Japanese economy. Thus in 1982, Japan had 32,000 industrial robots in operation; Western Europe employed only 9,000, the United States, 7,000. In 1989, the Japanese government and private businesses invested $549 billion to modernize industrial capacity, a full $36 billion more than American public and private investment combined. Such spending paid off substantially, as Japanese companies turned out high-quality consumer products that found an eager international market. Just as the U.S. military had done during its wars in Asia between 1950 and the 1970s, now U.S. buyers snapped up automobiles, televisions, videocassette recorders, cameras, and computers from Japanese or other Asian Pacific companies.

"Tigers" of the Pacific Rim, c. 1985

As the profits rolled in, Japanese enterprises bought large sections of American cities and swallowed up Western businesses, furthering globalization. Huge financial institutions flourished: by the end of the 1980s, Japan was home to the world's eight largest banks as well as a brokerage house that was twenty times larger than its nearest American competitor. Furthermore, whereas Japanese military expenses remained low by constitutional mandate, the United States throughout much of the 1980s poured mounting sums into its cold war military budget—but failed to raise taxes to pay for this expenditure. Thus the Japanese and other Asians who purchased U.S. government bonds actually financed America's ballooning national debt. Forty years after its total defeat in World War II, Japan was bankrolling its former conqueror.

Despite rising national prosperity, individual Asian workers, particularly outside of Japan, paid dearly for this newly created wealth. For example, women in South Korea and Taiwan labored in sweatshops to produce clothing for such U.S.-based companies as J. C. Penney and Calvin Klein. Using the lure of a low-paid and docile female workforce, governments were able to attract electronics and other industries. However, educational standards rose, along with access to birth control and other medical care for these women. Despite the persistent grip of authoritarian government, some of the tigers ranked high by UN standards for human development.

A single party that centralized decision making for the economy and much else in the society had dominated Japan's business-oriented government for most of the postwar period. The results were mixed. Japanese workers were expected to subordinate their interests to those of the business firm, just as business followed coordinated government instructions. The rewards for this discipline were great, and Japanese success was held up as a model to the West. Yet resistance to the patriarchal political elite developed: in 1989, Japanese women led the way in voting out of office a prime minister who kept a mistress. Women also entered the parliament and cabinet, long a bastion of elderly men. Government attempts to maintain cultural homogeneity brought charges of racism from abroad. The country also had to deal with the reality that hundreds of thousands of non-Japanese had illegally entered the country to perform the menial labor shunned by native workers. Critics began to express concern about environmental deterioration, the quality of life in overcrowded cities, and the growing menace of domestic terrorism.

Mounting economic difficulties plagued Japan and the other Asian tigers in the 1990s. Financial scandals and widespread corruption, long a problem in postwar Japanese politics, repeatedly brought down the political leadership. The stock market plunged, as did the value of the yen. Domestic consumers cut back, and those interested in saving sent their money abroad for higher returns. Japan's relations with its major trading partner, the United States, were often strained. From 1997 on, Japan's depressed economy threatened to pull the rest of the region, if not the world, into a deep recession. A severe business crisis struck the Pacific rim as currency speculation and irresponsible and corrupt financial practices first brought down the Thai currency in 1997 and then toppled politicians and industrial leaders in Indonesia, South Korea, and elsewhere in the region. Many Asian leaders vacillated amidst a growing recognition that for the first time in modern history global civilization's industrial and financial health depended on countries outside the West.

❖ The Welfare State in Question

Stagflation remained a powerful economic threat as the 1980s opened, and along with the realignment of global economic power it forced non-Communist governments in the West to put their economic houses in order. In the postwar world, the Keynesian practice of pump priming through government spending had been the spark that recharged a flagging economy. The unprecedented mix of the energy crisis, soaring unemployment, and double-digit inflation made new remedies imperative. Voters frustrated by threats of a declining standard of living elected conservative politicians, who maintained that decades of supporting a welfare state were at the heart of economic problems. Across the West, tough times intensified feelings that the unemployed and new migrants were responsible for the downturn. Nineteenth-century emphases on competitiveness, individualism, and revival of privilege for the "best circles'" replaced the twentieth-century trend toward advancing economic democracy to combat totalitarianism. The return of prosperity in the 1990s was accompanied by a measurable decline in the well-being of sectors of the working class and the poor. Whereas a few decades earlier, poverty was feared as a source of totalitarianism, the new politics dismissed it as a problem created by and restricted to the lower classes.

Thatcher Reshapes Political Culture

More than anyone else, Margaret Thatcher (b. 1925), the outspoken leader of Britain's Conservative Party from 1979 to 1990, reshaped the West's political and economic ideas. Coming to power amidst continuing economic decline, revolt in Northern Ireland, and labor unrest, the combative prime minister eschewed the politics of consensus building, vowing instead to transform Britain through the force of her own ideas. "I don't spend a lifetime watching which way the cat jumps," she announced. "I know really which way I want the cats to go." In parliamentary speeches, Thatcher lashed out at union leaders, Labour politicians, and people who received welfare-state benefits as enemies of British prosperity.

Thatcher believed that only a resurgence of private enterprise could revive the sluggish British economy. Her anti-welfare-state policies struck a revolutionary chord, and she called herself "a nineteenth-century liberal" in reference to the economic individualism of that age. In her view, business leaders and entrepreneurs were the key members of society. Although immigrants often worked for the lowest wages and contributed to profits, she characterized as inferior the unemployed and immigrants from Britain's former colonies, saying that neither group contributed to national wealth. More than two-thirds of the public read newspapers that expressed part or all of this general attitude; thus even members of the working class blamed labor leaders or newcomers for Britain's trauma.

The policies of "Thatcherism" were based on *monetarist* or *supply-side* theories associated most prominently with U.S. economist Milton Friedman. Monetarists contend that inflation results when government pumps money into the economy at a rate higher than a nation's economic growth rate. Thus they advocate a tight rein on the money supply to keep prices from rising rapidly. Supply-side economists maintain that the economy as a whole flourishes when business prosperity "trickles down" throughout the society. To implement such theories,

Margaret Thatcher

As British prime minister for more than a decade, Margaret Thatcher profoundly influenced European history by cutting back the welfare state. Thatcher was convinced and convinced others that the welfare state did not advance society and its citizens but made them lazy by rewarding those who had not contributed to the nation. Her tenure in office encouraged other politicians from Ronald Reagan to Helmut Kohl to execute similar cuts in programs; in this way, more than any other head of state she set the general course in domestic policy for the late twentieth century.
Stuart Franklin/Sygma.

the British government cut income taxes on the wealthy to spur new investment and pushed up sales taxes to compensate for the lost revenue; the result was an increased burden on working people, who bore the brunt of the sales tax. Thatcher vigorously pruned government intervention in the economy: she sold publicly owned businesses and utilities such as Britoil, British Airways, and Rolls-Royce; refused to prop up "outmoded" industries such as coal mining; and slashed education and health programs.

In the first three years of Thatcher's government, the British economy did not respond well to her shock treatment. The quality of universities, public transportation, highways, and hospitals deteriorated, and leading scholars and scientists left the country in a renewal of the brain drain. In addition, social unity fragmented—in 1981, blacks and Asians rioted in major cities—and Thatcher's popularity sagged. A turning point came in March 1982, when Argentina invaded the British Falkland Islands in the South Atlantic. Thatcher invoked patriotism to unify the nation and refused to surrender the islands without a fight, even though they were thousands of miles away. The gamble paid off, as the prime minister's public support soared. The appeal to national sentiment had replaced the progress of economic democratization as a unifying social force.

By the mid-1980s, inflation had dissipated in Britain. Historians and economists debate whether the change resulted from Thatcher's policies or from the lack of spending power that burdened the poor and unemployed. In any case, Thatcher's program became the standard. Even when the Labour Party gained power again late in the 1990s, it did so under the banner of competitiveness and "workfare" (a term suggesting that those receiving government benefits should work for them) instead of welfare. As enacted by Labour (and Democrats in the United States), the cutbacks traditionally associated with the right came to be called the "Third Way," which merged conservative and liberal programs into an alternative policy. Britain had been one of the pioneers of the welfare state, and now it pioneered in changing course.

The Reagan Revolution and Its Aftermath

Moved by the same social and political vision as Thatcher, Ronald Reagan (b. 1911; president 1981–1989) worked a similar revolution. The former actor was at his best in carefully planned television appearances. In front of the camera the "Great Communicator" furthered the idea that a so-called moral majority existed in the land that had somehow lost its grip on affairs to amoral, spendthrift forces. Reagan vowed to promote the values of the "moral majority," which included commitment to Bible-based religion, dedication to work, sexual restraint, and unquestioned patriotism.

In domestic affairs, Reagan pursued a radical course on a par with Thatcher's. His program of "Reaganomics" produced a whopping income tax cut of 25 percent between 1981 and 1983, combined with massive reductions in federal spending for student loans, school lunch programs, and mass transit. Like Thatcher, Reagan believed that tax cuts would lead to investment and a reinvigorated economy; federal outlays for welfare programs, which he felt only encouraged sloth, would generally be unnecessary thereafter.

In foreign policy, Reagan spent most of his time in office preoccupied with the Communist threat. The longtime cold warrior labeled the Soviet Union an "evil empire" and demanded huge military budgets to counter the Soviet arms buildup of the 1970s. Reagan announced the Strategic Defense Initiative (SDI, but known popularly as "Star Wars"), a costly plan to put lasers in space to defend the United States against a nuclear attack. The combination of tax cuts and military expansion had pushed the federal budget deficit to $200 billion by 1986.

The impact of Reagan's military buildup on U.S. global power and domestic health is a heatedly debated topic. Critics held Reaganomics accountable for the escalating violence and drug use in schools across the country and the growing numbers of homeless Americans sleeping on the streets. In his best-selling book *The Rise and Fall of the Great Powers* (1988), historian Paul Kennedy points out that nations at the top have always had trouble balancing military commitments with economic resources. Thus, although Reagan's administration spent less of the gross national product on the military than Eisenhower's had (7.5 percent as opposed to 10 percent), it did so at a time when the United States faced stiff competition from such global powers as Japan and West Germany. The system of military procurement itself took place outside the bounds of the competitive market system Reagan glorified. Citizens of both the United States and the USSR would feel the economic effects of policies based on "imperial overstretch," Kennedy predicted.

The election of Democrat Bill Clinton (b. 1946) as U.S. president in 1992 did not fundamentally change the move away from the welfare state. As in Britain, an ethic of workfare continued in the United States, and the goal of competitiveness in an increasingly global economy justified crumbling urban schools and the relative decline in the lower segments of society. In fact, the economy soared in the 1990s, lifting people in the professions and top management to ever greater wealth. From this vantage point, cuts in social programs were a real success, though others attributed rising wealth to technology's boosting worker productivity.

Alternatives to Thatcherism

Other Western European leaders found retrenchment of the welfare state necessary as well but did so with less politically divisive rhetoric. Facing welfare costs and the legacy of stagflation from the 1970s, the center-right West German leader Helmut Kohl (b. 1930), who took power in 1982, reduced welfare spending, froze government wages, and cut corporate taxes. By 1984, the inflation rate was only 2 percent, and West Germany had acquired a 10 percent share of world trade. Unlike Thatcher, Kohl did not fan class and racial hatreds. The politics of divisiveness was particularly unwise in Germany where terrorism on the left and on the right continued to flourish. Moreover, the legacy of Nazism loomed menacingly. "Let's gas 'em," said unemployed German youth of immigrant Turkish workers. The revival of Nazi language appalled many in Germany's middle class rather than gaining their support.

France took a different political path through the 1980s than either Germany or Britain but ended up in a similar position. By 1981, stagflation had put more than 1.5 million people out of work and reduced the economic growth rate to an anemic 1.2 percent. The French elected a socialist president, François Mitterrand (1916–1996), who nationalized banks and certain industries and stimulated the economy by wage increases and social spending—the opposite of Thatcherism. New public buildings like museums and libraries arose along with new subway lines and improved public transport. Financial leaders reacted by sending capital abroad rather than investing it at home, while many ordinary citizens continued to support the protections offered by state programs. In Mitterrand's second term, conservatives captured the majority of seats in the assembly, which entitled them to choose the prime minister. Until the end of the century, conservatives and socialists continued to share power. Thus French policy alternated between the need to encourage investment by cutting the costs of social

programs and the citizenry's commitment to social security programs and a vibrant public life. By 2000, the French economy was the most prosperous in Europe.

At the same time, France suffered continuing high unemployment as businesspeople refused to invest in new jobs laden with high costs such as social security. As elsewhere, political repercussions accompanied changing social and economic conditions, and political racism emerged as an expression

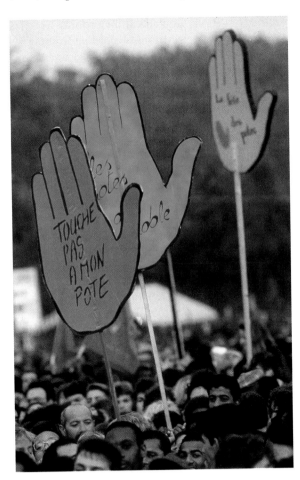

SOS-Racism

"Don't touch my pal" reads this slogan that was emblazoned on banners, posters, and buttons in France. As threats mounted to the safety of migrants across Europe, countermovements demanding tolerance and promoting their well-being grew. SOS-Racism was one of the most powerful, holding marches with hundreds of thousands of participants. Nonetheless, strongly racist political parties preaching hatred of all foreigners thrived and in Austria actually controlled the government by late 1999.
G. Merillon/Gamma Liaison.

of discontent. Beginning with the 1985 national elections, Jean-Marie Le Pen's National Front party, which promised to deport African and Muslim immigrants and cut French ties with nonwhite nations, won 10 percent or more of the vote. The class antagonisms that had once shaped politics changed to expressions of racial and ethnic hatred.

Meanwhile, a cluster of smaller states without heavy defense commitments enjoyed increasing prosperity after the recession of the early 1980s ended. In Spain, tourist dollars helped rebuild the southern cities of Granada and Córdoba. Under a moderate socialist prime minister, Felipe Gonzalez—who, like Mitterrand and other socialist leaders, supported the aspirations of the middle class—the country joined the Common Market in 1986. The Italian economy grew despite pervasive political corruption, and in Ireland a surge of investment in education for high-tech jobs combined with low wages to bring new business to the country. Prosperity and the increasingly unacceptable death toll led to a political rapprochement between Ireland and Northern Ireland in 1999. Austria prospered, too, in part by reducing government pensions and aid to industry and agriculture. Austrian chancellor Franz Vranitsky summed up the changed focus of government in the 1980s and 1990s: "In Austria, the shelter that the state has given to almost everyone—employee as well as entrepreneur—has led . . . a lot of people [to] think not only what they can do to solve a problem but what the state can do. . . . This needs to change." The century-long growth of the welfare state seemed to be over by the 1990s, but the future mission of government was unclear.

Maintaining a broad array of social programs despite the reigning mood, Sweden stood out as an exception. The government offered each immigrant a choice of subsidized housing in neighborhoods inhabited primarily by Swedes or primarily by people from the immigrant's native land. Such programs were expensive: the tax rate on income over $46,000 was 80 percent. When productivity flagged, the government denied benefits to unemployed workers who refused retraining or a job offer. The Swedes also reduced their costly dependence on foreign oil by cutting consumption in half between 1976 and 1986. Despite anti-inflationary success and a highly productive workforce, Sweden dropped from fourth to fourteenth place among nations in per capita income by 1998. Businesspeople were beginning to look to countries where taxation was far lower. Once Soviet communism was dead, Sweden's "middle way" came to seem extreme.

❖ The Collapse of Soviet Communism

The most consequential event of these decades was the breakup of the Soviet empire in 1989 followed by the collapse of the USSR itself in the 1990s. Emblematic of other trends, the end of bipolarity hastened globalization, while socialist collapse undermined the largest single system providing government benefits to citizens. But what most struck people at the time was the suddenness of it all. In 1979—a mere decade earlier—Communist leaders in eastern Europe and the Soviet Union held firmly to power and were wedded to the past. The fate of peoples in the USSR rested in the hands of Leonid Brezhnev and a group of elderly bureaucrats who had matured during Stalin's "construction of socialism" in the 1930s. Although Poland and Hungary experimented with limited economic reform, U.S.-led-bloc analysts found no reason to think that radical change would happen in the near future. In the United States the CIA erroneously reported that the bloc was in robust economic health.

Yet protest by workers, artists, and others had never really stopped across the Soviet realm despite repression of the Prague Spring. CIA reports to the contrary, the Soviet economy was not robust but deteriorating. Communications, international trade, and democratic movements were pulling apart a vast region that communism had structured for almost half a century. Ironically, the triumph of democracy in the former Soviet empire opened an era of painful adjustment, uncertainty, and violence for hundreds of millions of people.

Rebellion in Poland

Dissent against Soviet rule reached crisis stage in the summer of 1980, when Poles reacted furiously to government-increased food prices by going on strike. As the protest spread, workers at the Gdańsk shipyards, led by electrician Lech Walesa and crane operator Anna Walentynowicz, created an independent labor movement called Solidarity. The organization soon embraced much of the adult population, including a million members of the Communist Party.

The Poles had engaged in various forms of resistance to Communist rule for decades. The Catholic church, which numbered 28 million members out of a total population of 35 million, had long unified people around opposition to socialist secularization. Moreover, worker protest in the 1970s had been common, as steep energy prices, scarce consumer goods, inflation, and government ineptitude worsened the conditions of everyday life. In the summer of 1980, opposition to Poland's rulers, who directed both politics and the economy, coalesced. Intellectuals banded together in the Workers' Defense Committee (KOR) and joined the attack. Karol Wojtyła (b. 1920), the former archbishop of Cracow, had become Pope John Paul II in 1978, and he lent his authority to the anti-Communist cause. Solidarity workers occupied factories and waved Polish flags as well as giant portraits of the pope and the Virgin Mary.

Having achieved mass support at home and worldwide sympathy through media coverage, Solidarity pledged to support moderate economic reform. Its leaders insisted, however, that the government recognize it as an independent union—a radical demand under communism. As food became scarce and prices rose, tens of thousands of women marched in the streets crying, "We're hungry!" As the Communist Party teetered on collapse, the police and the army, with Soviet support, imposed a military government and in the winter of 1981 outlawed Solidarity. Continued efforts by reporters and dissidents, using global communications, kept Solidarity alive as a force both inside and outside of Poland.

Stern and puritanical, General Wojciech Jaruzelski took over as the head of Poland's new regime in 1981. Dissent persisted in various forms: in *Danton,* a 1982 film ostensibly about the French Revolution, Polish filmmaker Andrzej Wajda cast as Robespierre, the fanatic instigator of the Reign of Terror, an actor who looked just like the Polish leader. Jaruzelski insisted that "the place of People's Poland is and will remain among the socialist powers," but his hope was not so much to revive socialist enthusiasm at home as to ward off Soviet

intervention. The general could not push repression too far: he needed new loans from the U.S.-led bloc to keep the sinking Polish economy afloat. Instability infected Polish politics once Solidarity was born, and the stage was set for communism's downfall.

Reform in the Soviet Bloc

The rise of Solidarity exposed the economic woes of people living in the Soviet bloc. Far from insulating their citizens from the ups and downs of capitalism, Soviet-style economies suffered from rampant decay by the early 1980s and their people felt the full consequences. Years of stagnant and then negative growth led to a deteriorating standard of living. After working a full day, Soviet homemakers stood in long lines to obtain basic commodities; housing and food shortages necessitated the three-generation household, in which grandparents took over tedious homemaking tasks from their working children and grandchildren. "There is no special skill to this," a seventy-three-year-old grandmother and former garbage collector remarked. "You just stand in line and wait." Even so, they often went away empty-handed, and more than one foreign visitor complained that she had never eaten so many varieties of cabbage salad. Basic household supplies like soap disappeared instantly from stores, and the quality of medical care varied according to status. One cheap and readily available product—vodka—often formed the center of people's social lives. Alcoholism reached crisis levels, diminishing productivity and tremendously straining the nation's morale.

Economic stagnation had many other ramifications. Ordinary people decided not to have children, and fertility fell below replacement levels throughout the Soviet bloc, except for the Muslim areas of Soviet Central Asia. The country was forced to import massive amounts of grain because 20 to 30 percent of the grain that was produced in the USSR rotted before it could be harvested or shipped to market, so great was the inefficiency of the state-directed economy. Industrial pollution, spewed out by enterprises responsible only for meeting production quotas, reached scandalous dimensions. A massive and privileged party bureaucracy hobbled industrial innovation and failed to achieve socialism's professed goal of a decent standard of living for working people. To match American military growth, the Soviet Union diverted 15 to 20 percent of its gross national product (more than double the U.S. proportion) to armaments. As this combustible mixture of problems heated up, a new generation was coming of age that had no memory of World War II or Stalin's purges. One Russian observer found members of the younger generation "cynical, but less afraid." "They believe in nothing," a mother said of Soviet youth in 1984. "They won't be pushed around," added another.

In 1985 a new leader, Mikhail Gorbachev (b. 1931), opened an era of unexpected change. In 1956, Gorbachev, then only twenty-five, had attended the party congress at which Khrushchev had first condemned Stalin's excesses. Later, as a trusted official, he traveled widely in the Soviet bloc and got a first-hand glimpse of life in the West during trips to France, Italy, and West Germany. The son of peasants, Gorbachev had risen through the party ranks as an agricultural specialist, and he quickly proposed broad plans to reinvigorate the Soviet economy. His program of *perestroika* ("restructuring") aimed to streamline production and management. The economy had depended not on innovation but on labor-intensive production, and outmoded machinery hampered Soviet industrial output. Against the will of managers, who benefited from the status

quo, Gorbachev hoped to reverse economic decay by improving productivity, increasing the rate of capital investment, encouraging the use of up-to-date technology, and gradually introducing such market features as prices and profits.

Along with perestroika, Gorbachev proclaimed a policy of *glasnost* (usually translated as "openness" or "publicity"). For the Soviet leader, *glasnost* meant speaking "the language of truth," disseminating "wide, prompt, and frank information," and allowing Soviet citizens new measures of free speech. When officials complained that glasnost threatened their status, Gorbachev replaced more than a third of the party's leadership in the first months of his administration. The pressing need for glasnost became most evident after the Chernobyl catastrophe in 1986, when bureaucratic cover-ups delayed the spread of information about the accident, with lethal consequences for people living near the plant.

After Chernobyl even the Communist Party and Marxism-Leninism were opened to public criticism. Party meetings suddenly witnessed complaints about the highest leaders and their policies. Television shows such as *The Fifth Wheel* adopted the outspoken methods of American investigative reporting; one program showed an interview with an executioner of political prisoners and exposed the plight

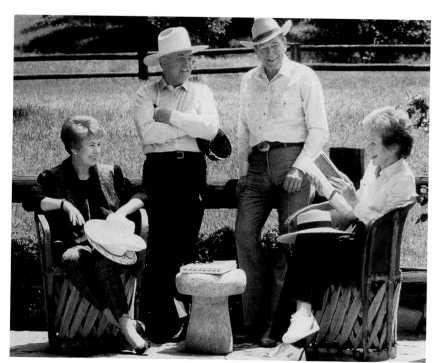

Gorbachevs and Reagans at the Ranch
Ronald Reagan raised the temperature of the cold war with a massive arms buildup in the 1980s that caused the U.S. budget deficit to soar. When Mikhail Gorbachev came to power in the USSR, he changed course, encouraging freer speech, seeking innovation in the economy, and reducing cold war tensions. The two leaders' regular meetings helped slow down the arms race.
Ruelas, L.A. Daily News/Sygma.

of Leningrad's homeless children. "Work is getting pretty easy around here," remarked TV censor Natalya Strepetova, who had less and less to do at her job.

Political factions arose, not only for and against Gorbachev, but across the political spectrum. In the fall of 1987, one of Gorbachev's erstwhile allies, Boris Yeltsin, quit the governing Politburo after denouncing perestroika as inadequate for real reform. Yeltsin's political daring, which in the past would have consigned him to oblivion (or Siberia), inspired others to organize in opposition to the crumbling ruling orthodoxy. By the spring of 1989, in a remarkably free balloting, not a single Communist was chosen for office in Moscow's local elections.

Glasnost and perestroika dramatically affected superpower relations as well. Recognizing how severely the cold war arms race was draining Soviet resources, Gorbachev almost immediately began scaling back missile production. His unilateral actions gradually won over Ronald Reagan. The two leaders met at Geneva, Switzerland, in the autumn of 1985 to initiate a personal relationship and begin defusing the cold war. "I bet the hard-liners in both our countries are bleeding when we shake hands," said the jovial Reagan at the summit's conclusion. Although future meetings did not go as smoothly, a major breakthrough from the U.S. point of view occurred in early 1989, when Gorbachev at last withdrew his country's forces from the debilitating war in Afghanistan. By the end of the year, the United States was beginning to cut back its own vast military buildup.

The End of Soviet Rule

Tremors shook the Communist world in the spring of 1989. Inspired by Gorbachev's visit to China's capital, Beijing, thousands of students massed in Tiananmen Square to demand democracy. They used telex machines and electronic mail to rush their messages to the international community, and they effectively conveyed their goals through the cameras that Western television trained on them. China's aged Communist leaders, while pushing economic modernization and even allowing market operations, refused to consider the introduction of democracy. As workers began joining the Democracy forces, the government crushed the movement and executed as many as a thousand rebels.

The End of Communism in Europe

June 1989   Solidarity defeats Communists in Polish elections

August 1989   Czechoslovakia opens borders to western Europe

October 1989   Hungary dismisses Communist Party as official party

November 1989   East German Politburo resigns; Berlin Wall opened; Alexander Dubček calls for the ouster of Stalinists and a reform government comes to power in Czechoslovakia

December 1989   Nicolae Ceauşescu driven from power and executed in Romania

Spring 1990   Lithuania announces its secession from the USSR and other Baltic States follow

October 1990   Germany reunited; Gorbachev announces transition to a market economy; Boris Yeltsin defeats Communist candidate to become president of the Russian Republic

August 1991   After coup attempt in Moscow, operations of Communist Party suspended

The "Velvet Revolution."   Despite the setback to the forces of democracy in China, the spirit of revolt advanced in eastern Europe in 1989 and brought decades of Communist rule to an end. Indeed, the year 1989 has been designated the twentieth century's *annus mirabilis* ("year of miracles") because of the sudden and unexpected disintegration of Communist power throughout the region (Map 30.2). Events in Poland took a dramatic turn first. In the spring the Polish government, weakened by its own bungling of the economy and lacking Soviet support for further repression, again legalized Solidarity and promised free elections. In parliamentary elections in June, Solidarity candidates drove out the Communists. "Our defeat," Jaruzelski admitted, "is total." By early 1990, Jaruzelski had been replaced as president by Walesa, who began Poland's rocky transition to a market economy.

As it became evident that the Soviet Union would not intervene in Poland, the fall of communism repeated itself in country after country. In Hungary, which had experimented with "market socialism" since the 1960s, popular demands for liberalization spread from economics to politics at the

MAP 30.2 The Collapse of Communism in Europe, 1989–1991

In one form or another, resistance to communism had been continuous since the 1940s; thus the 1989 overthrow of Communist government in the USSR satellite countries of Eastern Europe occurred with surprising rapidity. In 1991, Communist Yugoslavia began to break up into individual states composed of competing ethnicities and religions. Then the USSR itself fell apart, as the Baltic states seceded, followed by the official dissolution of the rest of the USSR on January 1, 1992.

beginning of 1989. Critical journals appeared, and the populace boycotted the traditional May Day parade. In the fall, the Parliament dismissed the Communist Party as the official ruling institution and people tore down Communist symbols throughout the country.

In Czechoslovakia, which after 1968 had been firmly restored to Soviet-style rule, people watched the progress of glasnost expectantly. Although they could see Gorbachev on television calling for free speech, he never mentioned reform in Czechoslovakia. In the spring of 1989, however, a petition campaign secured the release of dissident leader and playwright Václav Havel. Demonstrators protested in the streets for democracy, but the government cracked down by turning the police on them. The turning point came on November 24 when Alexander Dubček, leader of the Prague Spring of 1968, addressed the crowds in Prague's Wenceslas Square with a call for the ouster of Stalinists from the

government. Almost immediately, Communist leadership resigned. Capping the country's "velvet revolution," as it became known for its lack of bloodshed, the formerly Communist-dominated parliament elevated Havel to the presidency.

The most potent symbol of a divided Europe—the Berlin Wall—stood in the midst of a divided Germany. East Germans had attempted to escape over the wall for decades, despite their country's reputation as having the most dynamic economy in the socialist world. When Austria and Hungary opened their common border in August 1989, thousands of East Germans turned what looked like vacation travel to Hungary into escape. From Hungary they passed to Austria and on to West Germany, where the government had long promised citizenship to *all* Germans. But it was protest at home that ultimately toppled the regime, unsupported now by Soviet tanks. Throughout the fall, increasing crowds that ultimately reached half a million had rallied in East

Destroying the Berlin Wall
The most disturbing symbol of cold war, the Berlin Wall came down in 1989 as dramatically as it had gone up in 1961. The next decade saw not only the reunification of Germany but the massive rebuilding of Berlin as the nation's capital.
© Reuters Newmedia Inc./Corbis.

German cities, confusing politicians who on November 9 issued an ambiguous statement more or less permitting passage through the crossings in the Berlin Wall. The shock of suddenly free access was overwhelming, as guards allowed tens of thousands of Berliners to flood through, all of them celebrating the opening of the wall. Protest turned to festive holiday: West Berliners handed out bananas, a consumer good that had been in short supply in the Eastern zone, and that fruit became the unofficial symbol of reunion. Almost immediately Berliners released years of frustration at their division by assaulting the wall with sledgehammers and bringing home chunks as souvenirs. The government finished its complete destruction in the fall of 1990.

Almost as soon as the Berlin Wall tumbled, the world's attention fastened on the political drama in Romania. Since the mid-1960s, Nicolae Ceauşescu had ruled as the harshest dictator in Communist Europe since Stalin. In the name of modernization he destroyed whole villages; to build up the population he outlawed contraceptives and abortions, a restriction that led to the abandonment of tens of thousands of children. Most Romanians lived in utter poverty as Ceauşescu channeled almost all the country's resources into building himself an enormous palace in Bucharest. Yet in early December 1989, an opposition movement rose up, and when authorities moved to suppress it, the spirit of resistance spread. Most of the army turned against the government and crushed the forces loyal to Ceauşescu. On Christmas Day viewers watched on television as the dictator and his wife were tried by a military court and then executed. Soon after, Western photographers displayed what Ceauşescu had wrought, from orphanages packed with thousands of unwanted, uncared-for children to the mass graves of those who had earlier dared to dissent.

Reunification of Germany. The collapse of communism in Europe paved the way for the reunification of Germany. Chancellor Helmut Kohl of West Germany based the campaign for reunification on the promise of a more comfortable way of life. In July 1990, he arranged for East German currency to be exchanged on a one-to-one basis with West German marks. A shrewd politician, Kohl acted on what he called his "grass-roots instinct that the East Germans wanted their microwaves now, and not in three years." After the economic foundations were in place, full political union took place on October 3, 1990, far earlier than anyone had expected at the end of 1989.

German Reunification, October 1990

The realities of unification did not live up to the dream. East German industry passed into the hands of West German managers, whose efficiencies in downsizing the workforce caused unemployment to soar, especially among women and youth. As early as September 1990, many social services, such as day-care centers that allowed women to work to support their families, closed down. Imitating the capitalist U.S. and western European leaders meant eliminating institutions these countries did not favor. Although restoration of buildings and industrial modernization proceeded in the nation's former Communist half, social tensions flared. West Germans blamed their new co-citizens for the diversion of resources to the east, and East Germans took out their frustrations through murder, violent attacks, or hateful rhetoric against immigrants. As Germany tried to keep its high standard of living amidst these stresses, the economy declined late in the 1990s relative to others in Europe. Throughout the former Soviet bloc, the transition to democracy and free markets gave rise simultaneously to social instability, economic upheaval, and nationalist expressions of discontent.

The Breakup of Yugoslavia and the Soviet Union

After a few delirious months, the problems of post-Communist life intensified, turning events in ever more violent directions as first Yugoslavia and then the Soviet Union itself fell apart. Like Hungarians and Czechs in the nineteenth-century Habsburg Empire, nationality groups in the USSR began to demand political and cultural autonomy in the 1980s. The Soviet empire had held together more than one hundred ethnic groups, and the five republics of Soviet Central Asia were home to fifty million Muslims. Similarly in Yugoslavia, Communist rulers had enforced unity among religious and ethnic groups, and intermarriage among them occurred regularly. But ethnicity became an effective political slogan for ambitious politicians with the coming of democracy, and violent instability continued into the new millennium.

MAP 30.3 The Former Yugoslavia, c. 2000
After a decade of destructive civil war, UN forces and UN-brokered agreements attempted to protect the civilians of the former Yugoslavia from the brutal consequences of post-Communist rule. Ambitious politicians, most notably Slobodan Milosevic, used the twentieth-century Western strategy of fostering ethnic and religious hatred as a powerful tool to build support for themselves while making those favoring peace look softhearted and unfit to rule.

Yugoslavia in 1990, before Destruction of the Mostar Bridge (top) and after (bottom)
In modern history the construction of a nation-state has depended on the growth of institutions such as armies and bureaucracies and the promotion of a common national culture. In an effort to dominate Bosnia and Croatia, Serbs destroyed non-Serb architecture, books, and such ancient symbols as the Mostar Bridge.
Top: Sygma; bottom: Stephane Cardinale/Sygma.

Yugoslavia.   Ethnic tensions erupted in Yugoslavia in 1990 when a Serb Communist, Slobodan Milosevic, won the presidency of his republic and began to assert Serb ascendancy. Other nationalities resisted. "Slovenians . . . have one more reason to say they are in favor of independence," warned one of them. In the spring of 1991, first Slovenia and then Croatia seceded, but the Croats soon lost almost a quarter of their territory to the Serb-dominated Yugoslav army (Map 30.3). An even more devastating civil war engulfed Bosnia-Herzegovina, where the republic's Muslim majority tried to create a multicultural and multiethnic state. Many Bosnian Serb men formed a guerrilla army, backed by the covert support of Milosevic's government, and gained the upper hand; the Muslim Bosnians were prevented by a UN arms embargo from equipping their forces adequately to resist. Late in the 1990s, the Serb forces started attacking people of Albanian ethnicity living in the Yugoslav province of Kosovo. From 1997 to 1999, hundreds of thousands of Albanian Kosovars fled their homes as Serb militias and the Yugoslav army began attacking the civilian population. NATO pilots bombed the region in an attempt to drive back the army and Serb militias. Amidst incredible violence and suffering, UN peacekeeping forces stepped in to enforce an interethnic truce, but people throughout the world felt that this intervention came far too late, reflecting great-power self-interest rather than a true commitment to maintaining peace and protecting human rights.

During the 1990s, civilians died by the tens of thousands, as Yugoslav republics broke away and as Serbs pursued a policy they called "ethnic cleansing"—that is, genocide—against the other nationalities. They raped women as another form of "conquest" to leave them pregnant with Serb babies. Men and boys were often taken away and massacred. Each competing force also aimed at the cultural heritage of its opponent. Military units destroyed libraries and museums, architectural treasures like the Mostar Bridge, and cities rich with medieval history such as Dubrovnik. Ethnic cleansing thus entailed destroying actual people as well as all traces of their complex past. Many in the West explained violence in the Balkans as part of "age-old" blood feuds manifesting the backwardness of an almost "Asian" society. Others saw ethnic rivalry using genocide to achieve national power as a modern phenomenon, while still others blamed the former great powers for stirring up many of these tensions in the first place. Across both western and eastern Europe, the language of racial, ethnic, and religious hatred was shaping political agendas, nowhere more violently than in the former Communist states.

The Soviet Union. Horrendous as ongoing genocide was, the utter collapse of the Soviet Union in 1992 launched a string of secessions with the potential for widespread destabilization of regional and perhaps global politics. Perestroika had failed to revitalize the Soviet economy; people confronted soaring prices, the specter of unemployment, and even greater scarcity of goods than they had endured in the past. Although Gorbachev announced late in 1990 that there was "no alternative to the transition to the market," his plan was too little, too late and satisfied no one. The Russian parliament's election of Boris Yeltsin as president of the Russian Republic over a Communist candidate provoked a coup in 1991 by a group of eight antireform hard-liners, from the Soviet vice president to the powerful head of the Soviet secret police, or KGB. Holding Gorbachev under house arrest, coup leaders claimed to be rescuing the Soviet Union from the "mortal danger" posed by "extremist forces." Yeltsin, however, standing atop a tank outside the Russian Republic's

parliament building, called for mass resistance. Hundreds of thousands of residents of Moscow and Leningrad filled the streets, the heads of the other republics declared their support for Yeltsin and Gorbachev, and units of the army defected to protect Yeltsin's headquarters. People used fax machines and computers to coordinate internal resistance and send messages to the rest of the world. The coup was in complete disarray in the face of citizen determination not to allow a return of Stalinism, or indeed of any form of Soviet orthodoxy.

The Soviet Union disintegrated. People tore down statues of Soviet heroes; Yeltsin outlawed the party newspaper, *Pravda*, and sealed the KGB files. At the end of August the Soviet parliament suspended operations of the Communist Party itself. One republic after another followed the lead of the Baltic States, which declared their independence in September 1991. Blood was spilled throughout the disintegrating Communist world in a variety of ethnic conflicts. In the Soviet republic of Tajikistan, native Tajiks rioted against Armenians living there; in Azerbaijan, Azeris and Armenians clashed over contested territory; and in the Baltic States, anti-Semitism revived as a political tool. The USSR finally dissolved on January 1, 1992. Twelve of the fifteen former Soviet republics banded together in a Commonwealth of Independent States (CIS; Map 30.4).

The coup and drive for dissolution of the USSR so tainted Gorbachev's regime that he ceded power to Yeltsin. But increasingly plagued by corruption, the Russian economy went into an ever-deepening crisis. Yeltsin's political allies bought up national resources, stripped them of their value, and sent billions of dollars out of the country. By 1999, Yeltsin's own family appeared deeply implicated in stealing the wealth once seen as belonging to all the people. Ethnic and religious battles continued for the entire decade of the 1990s, as the government undertook disastrous policies. Military action against Muslim dissenters in the province of Chechnya inflicted destruction and massive casualties on both sides. In Russia, the political right appealed to nationalist sentiments and won increasing support. Political disorder was matched by social disarray, as organized crime interfered in the distribution of goods and services and assassinated legitimate entrepreneurs, legislators, and anyone who criticized them. As a result, western powers drastically reduced their aid to rebuild Russian infrastructure.

MAP 30.4 Countries of the Former Soviet Union, c. 2000

Following an agreement of December 1991, twelve of the countries of the former Soviet Union formed the Commonwealth of Independent States (CIS). Dominated by Russia and with Ukraine often disputing this domination, the CIS worked to bring about common economic and military policies. As nation-states dissolved rapidly in the late twentieth century, regional alliances and coordination were necessary to meet the political and economic challenges of the global age.

Developing a free market and a republican government brought suffering to Russia as it had more than a century earlier to other Western peoples. The conditions of everyday life grew increasingly dire as salaries went unpaid, food remained in short supply, and essential services disintegrated. People took drastic steps to stay alive. Hotel lobbies became clogged with women turning to prostitution

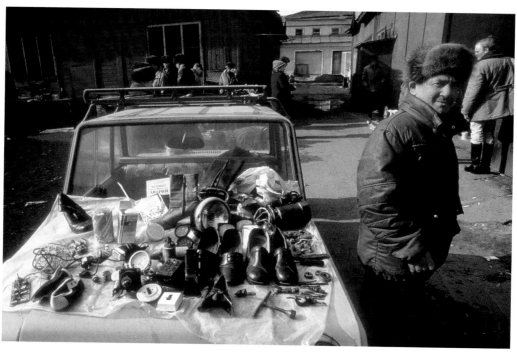

People Selling Belongings in the Former Soviet Union
The collapse of a state that not only employed and paid its citizens but also took responsibility for feeding, housing, and clothing them brought unbelievable hardship. Because the breakup of the USSR was total, no institutions existed to step in and hire or provision huge cities like Moscow and St. Petersburg. People desperately took to the streets selling dishes, clothes, and other possessions.
Swersey/Gamma Liaison.

because they were the first people fired as industry privatized and service jobs were cut back. Unpaid soldiers sold their services to the Mafia. Ordinary citizens stood on the sidewalks of major cities selling their household possessions. There were, of course, many plusses: people were able to travel freely for the first time and the media were more open than ever before in Russian history. Some, many of them young and highly educated, profited from contacts with technology and business. However, their frequent emigration to more prosperous parts of the world further depleted Russia's human resources.

The dismantling of communism was thus more complicated and painful than anyone had imagined. "I knew in my heart that it would collapse," said one ex-dissident, commenting sadly on the exodus of youth from his country, "but it never crossed my mind that the future would look like this." Alongside such human costs lay the question of who would control the massive Soviet arsenal of nuclear weapons and how global politics would shape up without cold war guidelines.

❖ Global Culture and Western Civilization at the Dawn of a New Millennium

As the final years of the millennium unfolded into a global age, thinkers began to posit a variety of scenarios for the future. On the one side was a view that the end of the cold war meant "an end of history" because the great ideological struggles were over and Western values and liberal democracy had triumphed. Attached to this view was a related one: the rest of the world was absorbing Western cultural values rapidly as it developed technologically and adopted more and more features of representative government and human rights. An opposing view predicted a "clash of civilizations" in which increasingly incompatible religions and cultures would lead to future global strife. For example, the power of Islam, as it gathered more than one billion followers, would confront Western values rather than absorb them. The latter view also seemed plausible given the growing number of small states populated by different ethnic and racial groups who refused to live under the same national and cultural umbrella.

The actual movement of peoples and cultures in the late twentieth century suggests that neither view holds. International migration, the movement of disease and climate, the information revolution, and the global sharing of culture have produced neither a successful Western homogenization nor a convincing argument for the cultural purity of any group. In the 1980s and 1990s, Western society changed as rapidly as it did when it came into intense contact with the rest of the globe hundreds of years earlier. Moreover, national boundaries in the traditional European center of the West were weakening politically and economically with the growing strength of the European Union and the simultaneous splintering of large nations into small states based on claims to ethnic uniqueness. Basque separatists of western France and separatist parties in different areas of Italy gained strength; Quebec threatened to secede from Canada. Culture respected national boundaries less as East, West, North, and South became saturated with one another's cultural products. Observers even labeled the new millennium an era of "denationalization." But there is no denying that even while the West absorbed peoples and cultures, it continued to exercise not only economic but also cultural power over the rest of the globe. (See "Contrasting Views," page 1178.)

Redefining the West: The Impact of Global Migration

The movement of people globally was massive in the last third of the twentieth century. Uneven economic development, political persecution, and warfare (which has claimed as many as 100 million victims worldwide since 1945) sent tens of millions in search of safety and opportunity. The most desperate of these migrants were displaced persons and refugees. (See "Taking Measure," right.) Many fled to the West. In the 1970s alone, more than 4.7 million people moved to the United States. By 1982, France had about 4.5 million foreign residents. But other parts of the world were as full as the West of people on the move. The oil-producing nations of the Middle East employed millions of foreign workers, who generally constituted one-third of the la-

bor force. Singapore and Nigeria were also home to millions of foreign-born inhabitants. The ongoing violence in Africa sent Rwandans, Zairians, and others to South Africa, as its government became dominated by blacks. War in Afghanistan made Iran one of the most popular asylums, with close to 2 million refugees in 1995.

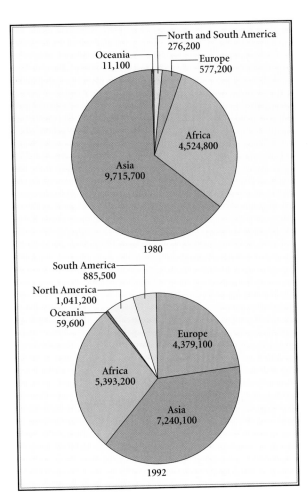

TAKING MEASURE World Refugee Population, 1980–1992

The global age has been characterized by widespread migration for both economic opportunity and physical safety from the wars, civil conflicts, and famine that menaced millions of people. As globalization advanced, migrants and refugees traveled greater distances, with North America and Europe receiving a larger percentage than they had in the 1980s and earlier. By the 1990s, some politicians began to realize that in losing large numbers of people their countries were sending vast human resources to other parts of the world. The Hammond Atlas of the Twentieth Century (London: Times Books, 1996) 183; David Levinson, ed., *Ethnic Relations: A Cross-Cultural Encyclopedia* (Santa Barbara: ABC-CLIO, 1994) 201.

The Debate over Globalization

Globalization has transformed the workings of government and industry, provoked the rise of thousands of organizations devoted to supporting and combating it, and expanded educational offerings to meet its needs. As part of the controversy over its value were hardheaded economic arguments on both sides: whereas a Harvard professor advocated the global scale of business (Document 1), two environmental scientists saw globalization as a disaster for the future of agriculture in India (Document 2). Another component of globalization—migration—aroused real opposition. According to a British newspaper editor, it led to political instability (Document 3). Rightist French politician Jean-Marie Le Pen preached "cultural diversity" for the world, by which he meant that the many peoples and cultures should be kept separate, with strict control of migration and of immigrants (Document 4).

1. Globalization Builds the Economic Future

Rosabeth Moss Kanter, a renowned management consultant and professor, cited the advantages of globalization in 1994.

[G]lobalization encourages the formation of alliances and partnerships—cooperative relationships that extend each partner's global reach while each contributes its local competence. . . . Some countries require local partners in order for companies to do business there. But even where this is not required, many companies recognize the benefits of establishing alliances to combine technologies or develop market access quickly. Connection to a global network allows smaller companies to gain the purchasing power or market clout of larger ones.

Source: Rosabeth Moss Kanter, afterword to *Global Strategies: Insights from the World's Leading Thinkers,* ed. Percy Barnevik and Rosabeth Moss Kanter (Cambridge: Harvard Business Review Books, 1994), 230.

2. Destruction of an Agricultural Way of Life

Scientists Vandana Shiva and Radha Holla-Bhar protested the ways in which economic globalization affected the environment and local farmers in their native India.

Until very recently in India, biodiversity was something held entirely in common by local communities of people. Resources and knowledge about forest or agricultural properties were freely shared. Whether it was seeds of the farm or plants of the forest, all were clearly understood to be part of the cultural, spiritual, and biological commons.

The idea that the commons could be divided up, purchased, and owned by individuals or companies for their own commercial purposes was unknown to Indian farmers until the early 1960s, when certain international conventions established "plant breeder's rights." These new "rights" allowed commercial plant breeders to take traditional indigenous varieties of seed, for example, "improve" them (often by very minor alterations of genetic structure), and then patent and commercialize them, eventually selling back the patented seeds to the communities that first provided them freely.

This globalization of the South's biodiversity commons was a windfall for northern corporations, which began a race to patent and privatize as much of this natural commons as possible, without ever paying royalties to the original breeders and farmers . . . who gathered all the knowledge about them.

The issue came to a crisis during the GATT [General Agreement on Tariffs and Trade] negotiations [1986], when the United States and other northern countries imposed their new rules of Trade-Related Intellectual Property Rights. . . . The northern countries argued that when southern farmers attempted to retain free use of their own seeds, developed by them over thousands of years, it was a form of piracy. . . .

Before GATT, Indian law excluded the private ownership of patent rights and biological materials. This helped ensure that entitlements to food and nutrition remained as broad-based as possible.

Source: Vandana Shiva and Radha Holla-Bhar, "Piracy by Patent: The Case of the Neem Tree," in *The Case against the Global Economy and for a Turn toward the Local*, ed. Jerry Mander and Edward Goldsmith (San Francisco: Sierra Club Books, 1996), 146–48.

3. The Perils of Global Migration

In 1995, Martin Woollacott, deputy editor of the influential British newspaper the Guardian, *found the global migration of peoples and their settlement in diasporas or communities of migrants from a different native land far from positive.*

Diasporas have many beneficial effects on both host and migrant communities, but they may also breed pathological attitudes among a small minority. Some may fight their own wars on foreign soil. Or diaspora communities can provide inadvertent cover, in their separateness from the main society, for terrorists and extremists from inside or outside who want to attack their hosts. . . . The global village can be a violent place. Its curse is that new combination of intimacy and aggression, with societies so penetrated by each other physically and culturally that awful damage can be wreaked at close quarters in a way that was not possible in the past.

Source: M. Woollacott, "Living in the Age of Terror," *Guardian*, August 22, 1995.

4. Guarding the Nation from Global Mixture

In France, Jean-Marie Le Pen led a popular political party, the National Front party, committed to renewed nationalism in the face of globalization. Here is an excerpt from his platform.

The French will have priority when it comes to being hired. In the event of group redundancies, they will be the first to keep their jobs. The immigrants who will be induced to going back to their country of origin will liberate numerous jobs for the French. Through the application of new protectionism, jobs will be protected against unauthorized competition from countries where wages and social protection are low. . . .

Foreigners whose resident's permit has expired and immigrant unemployed people with no more unemployment allowance rights will be repatriated to their country of origin in human and dignified conditions. Expulsions of illegal immigrants and delinquents will be effectively upheld. French people will be given priority for social allowances, housing and jobs. Family allowances and the Minimum Revenue for Insertion (RMI) will be reserved for our compatriots, and will therefore be revalued. In order to avoid all disguised immigration the right of asylum will be strictly limited, family regrouping will be abolished and French naturalization will become more difficult.

Source: mosaique@mosaique.worldnet.net. Copyright Mosaïque, March 1995.

QUESTIONS FOR DEBATE
1. Describe and analyze the areas in which globalization seems to raise the most questions.
2. In what ways are issues around globalization centuries-old points of contention?
3. Is it possible or desirable to change the course of globalization?
4. List the benefits of globalization and assess whether the benefits outweigh the costs, some of which are presented in these documents.

Post-decolonization turmoil produced millions of refugees who left their homelands in search of better work. Migrants often earned desperately needed income for family members who remained in the native country, and in some cases they propped up the economies of entire nations. In the southern African country of Lesotho, where the soil had been ruined by overuse during colonial rule, between 40 and 50 percent of national income came from migrant workers, particularly from those who toiled in the mines of South Africa. In countries as different as Yugoslavia, Egypt, Spain, and Pakistan, money sent home from abroad constituted up to 60 percent of national income. Many governments allowed foreigners to work in the host country for periods ranging from one or two to ten or more years. In places where immigration was restricted, millions of people nevertheless successfully crossed borders: from Mexico and China to the United States, over unguarded African frontiers, between European states. Such migrants, unprotected by law, risked exploitation and abuse of their human rights. Those at greatest risk were the eastern European and Asian prostitutes, many of whom were coerced into international sex rings that controlled their passports, wages, and lives.

Foreign workers were a convenient scapegoat for native peoples suffering from economic woes such as unemployment caused by downsizing. Political parties with racist programs came to life in Europe, where unemployment was in double digits at various times in the 1980s and 1990s. The National Front party in France, the Progress Party in Norway, and the Zentrum Party in the Netherlands thrived in the 1990s, while in Austria the party of the racist right became the dominant political force after its victory in the 1999 elections. These groups called for the elimination of blacks and Arabs from Europe in the name of creating racially and ethnically "pure" nations. Tensions between foreigners and natives often exploded in violence. In eastern Europe, which had accepted large numbers of Indochinese refugees, economic crisis brought outbursts against Vietnamese and other Asians. European countries rounded up illegal immigrants and deported them. Obtaining political asylum became more difficult despite worldwide violence.

Among migrants to the West, women had little to say in decisions about leaving home; a patriarchal head of the household generally made such choices.

Once abroad, migrant women suffered the most from unstable working conditions. West Germany, for example, prohibited them from working during economic crises. Even in prosperous times, foreign-born women usually obtained more menial, lower-paying jobs than migrant men or native Europeans. They formed the backbone of labor in oppressive sweatshops, whether in New York or Paris. Moreover, the host society often denigrated as "backward" or "primitive" the familial customs the migrants sought to uphold. Women were more likely than men to be refused political asylum. Rape and other violence against them, even during civil war, were classified as part of everyday life, not politics.

The offspring of immigrants also had a difficult time adjusting to their new surroundings. Young people generally struggled for jobs, and unemployment hit them especially hard because "whites" and "real" citizens received preference. They also struggled with questions of identity. To advance in school or at work, immigrant youth had to embrace their new society in varying degrees, and they often felt torn between two cultures. Young black immigrants in particular began to forge an international or transnational identity, one that combined elements of African, Caribbean, American, and European cultures. As tens of millions of people migrated in the 1980s and 1990s, the former belief in a national identity based on a single, unique culture was losing ground.

Uncertain Borders of the Nation-State

The Western nation-state had been an increasingly powerful source of identity for five hundred years, never more so than in the twentieth century. By the twenty-first century, however, the nature of European national borders was changing not only through the force of mass migration and decolonization but because of international cooperation, technology, transnational allegiances, and other factors that made the nation-state and excessive patriotism seem outmoded. The forces eroding the Western tradition of a single national identity affected not only immigrants but vast numbers of the world's peoples.

European Union. Regional alliances like NATO and the Warsaw Pact had appeared to override national interests, but nothing compared with the

MAP 30.5 The European Union in 2000

The European Union appeared to increase the economic health of its members despite the rocky start to the common currency—the euro. The EU decidedly helped end the traditional warfare its members had undertaken against one another for centuries, and common passports, common business laws, and borders open to member countries facilitated trade and migration of workers. But many critics feared the further loss of cultural distinctiveness among peoples in an age of mass communications if the economic union turned into a political one, while others predicted "Americanization" if political cooperation among European countries was lacking.

Map legend:
- Original members of the European Economic Union
- Became members in 1973
- Became a member in 1981
- Became members in 1986
- Became members in 1995
- Applying for membership

turn-of-the-millennium merging of individual nation-states into the European Union (Map 30.5). "[A united] Europe will not be created at a stroke [of a pen] or according to a single plan," Robert Schuman, an outspoken French promoter of European unity, had prophesied in the 1950s. Indeed, the experience of the European Community (EC) proved that a unified Europe remained an evolving entity with an unpredictable future. In 1992, the twelve countries of the EC ended national distinctions in the spheres of business activity, border controls, and transportation. Citizens of EC member countries carried a common burgundy-colored passport, and governments, whether municipal or national, had to treat all member nations' firms the same. In 1994 by the terms of the Maastricht Treaty, the EC became the European Union, and in 1999 a common currency, the European Currency Unit (ECU or euro) came into being. Common policies governed everything from the number of American soap operas aired on television to pollution controls on automobiles to standardized health warnings on cigarette packages.

Some national leaders opposed tighter integration as an infringement on national sovereignty. Margaret Thatcher, Britain's prime minister, warned that terrorists would pass freely across borders, opposed the use of a common currency, and criticized moves toward closer pan-European unity, but her forceful opposition seemed so out of step with the times that her own party forced her resignation in 1991. Meanwhile, intellectuals across the continent worried that an emerging "Eurospeak" jargon threatened the distinctiveness of national languages and portended a dull standardization of culture. But countries continued to join the original twelve. Sweden, Finland, and Austria joined the EU in 1995; Turkey and Cyprus were officially scheduled for entry. Most former Communist-run nations also sought inclusion. Though members initially balked

European Parliament
By the 1990s, the European Economic Community had evolved into a political body of more than a dozen members. Its parliament—the greatest symbol of the potential for complete unification of all Europe— met regularly in Strasbourg, France. Meanwhile, the countries of the former Soviet bloc applied virtually en masse for admission to the European Union.
AKG Photo, London.

at competing with the lower labor costs in the east, some of the former Communist countries were also promised future admission. Moreover, the splintering of Czechoslovakia into two states in 1993 along with the fragmentation of Yugoslavia and the former Soviet Union disturbed those who saw the European future in terms of one large region, not increasing numbers of small states. As union tightened, a highly advanced industrial megastate complete with its own bureaucracy overlaid the traditionally distinct individual nations of the western heartland. More diverse and multiethnic, European countries simultaneously grew more uniform.

The Challenge of the Internet. Rapid technological change in electronic communications also made traditional national borders appear easily permeable, if not obsolete. In 1969, the U.S. Department of Defense developed a computer network to carry communications in case of nuclear war. This system and others like it in universities, government, and business grew into an unregulated system of more than ten thousand networks globally. These came to be known as the *Internet*—shorthand for *inter-*

networking. By 1995, users in more than 137 countries were connected to the Internet.

The Internet created "communities" based on business needs, shared cultural interests, or other factors that transcended common citizenship in a particular nation-state. Communicating via the Internet allowed users often to escape state regulation such as censorship. A global marketplace in goods and services ranging from advanced weaponry to organ transplants opened up to the computer literate. With this technology, political and other causes could become transnational too. While enthusiasts claimed that this could promote world democracy, critics charged that communications technology favored elites and disadvantaged those without computer skills. They also argued that the ordinary person's most intimate records were now the easy prey not only of the state but of international forces.

Internet and other communications technology promoted business mergers on a vast international scale in the 1990s. Almost instantaneous information on inventory, wages, costs, and transportation could be accessed worldwide. This ease of access allowed businesses to move in and out of countries

Hong Kong Skyline

No longer could the East be used as an exotic foil to help those in the West lay claim to a superior civilization. The 1980s saw Hong Kong, Singapore, China, and other Pacific economies soar and develop the most modern technological capabilities. Skylines changed, reshaped by mountainous glass and steel skyscrapers, and cities like Hong Kong came to symbolize everything postmodern.
Jane Tyska/Stock Boston.

rapidly depending on wages and political conditions. As a result, the labor force gained an international quality, with workers of one country pitted against others in a similar job category on the other side of the globe. Moreover, high technology reduced those without computer skills to minimum-wage jobs as clerks and fast-food attendants. Such trends of the 1990s were creating a two-tiered labor market so reminiscent of the way women had traditionally been exploited that critics spoke of a new "feminization" of work around the world.

Operating on the Internet, global corporations, often seen as out of reach and out of touch, neither inspired nor displayed national loyalty, and mounting business scandals—ranging from Wall Street junk-bond scams to the corrupt dealings of much of the Italian elite—eroded confidence in the ethics of capitalism. "I don't care about ethics," said one German "cyberpunker" at his arraignment for infiltrating a variety of national computer banks. "If it's Russian interests or Western interests, I don't care about that stuff." As people questioned which values of Western civilization still held, some Westerners acknowledged their lack of compassion for the stateless migrant or a destitute fellow citizen. Without an

appreciation of face-to-face society, it was charged, technoculture dragged the Darwinian view of the struggle for survival to new depths of inhumanity.

Nonetheless, huge population centers arose precisely *because* of technoculture, and observers pointed to the growing importance of "global cities" like New York, Hong Kong, Tokyo, and London. These cities swelled in the 1990s; and their post-modernist architecture soared to new heights, drastically changing the modernist skylines of but a century earlier. In these cities, high-level information specialists such as lawyers, accountants, financiers, and a variety of analysts formed a decision-making loop in the technological network. Their financial power changed the complexion of most cities, making them unaffordable to lower levels of information management and service workers. Immigrants continued to flock to the global cities and generally filled the lowest levels of jobs.

The Spread of AIDS. Disease, like technology, operated on a global terrain. In the early 1980s both Western values and Western technological expertise were challenged by the spread of a global epidemic disease: acquired immune deficiency syndrome, or

An AIDS Educator in Thailand
AIDS spread rapidly around the world, demonstrating the mobility of both people and disease. Activism centered on forcing governments to support AIDS research and to fund AIDS treatment. Other activists, like this man instructing sex workers in Thailand, focused on prevention through education.
Peter Booker/Panos Pictures.

AIDS. An incurable, highly virulent killer, AIDS initially afflicted heterosexuals in central Africa; its first European victim, Danish physician Grethe Rask, died in 1977 after working among the sick in that region. The disease later turned up in Haitian immigrants to the United States and in homosexual men worldwide. As researchers focused attention on the mysterious ailment in the early 1980s, they discovered that it effectively shut down the body's entire immune system. By the late 1990s, no cure had yet been discovered, though protease-inhibiting drugs helped alleviate the disease.

The mounting death toll made some equate AIDS to a Black Death of the twentieth century, reinforcing prejudices and stereotypes about some of its most vulnerable victims. As millions contracted the disease in Africa, treatment was not forthcoming because the ill were too poor. In fact, the deadly Ebola virus and dozens of others smoldered like a global conflagration in the making. The failure of corporate and government "megasystems" to deal effectively with the important challenges of ad-

vanced technological society such as the spread of AIDS showed that while global forces could promote technological advance, they could not necessarily replace the nation-state's concern for its citizens' well-being.

The Global Diffusion of Culture

Culture has long transcended political boundaries, and in fact archaeologists point to its diffusion as a constant of tens of thousands of years of human history. In the ancient world, the Romans studied the work of Greek philosophers; in the nineteenth century, Western scholars immersed themselves in Eastern languages. Asian civilizations borrowed too as religions, agricultural products, and manufactured goods circulated strikingly in the last millennium. But in the postwar period cultural exchange accelerated vastly through new forms of transportation and communication: tourism, for instance, became the largest single industry in Britain and in many other Western countries by the early 1990s. Throngs of visitors from Japan and elsewhere testified to the powerful place the West still held in the world's imagination. Chinese students in Tiananmen Square had rallied around their own representation of the Statue of Liberty (which itself was a gift from France to the United States). In Japan, businesspeople wore Western-style clothing and watched soccer, baseball, and other Western sports using English terms. In Asia, ruling families became Western-style celebrities instead of sacred, godlike figures, while the Pacific Rim tigers became heavy borrowers of Western culture.

The Globalization of Pop Culture. Remarkable innovations in communications have also integrated cultures and made the earth seem a much smaller place, though one with a distinctly Western flavor. Videotapes and satellite-beamed telecasts transport American television shows to Hong Kong and Japanese movies to Europe and North America. American rock music sells briskly in Russia and elsewhere in the former Soviet bloc. When more than 100,000 Czechoslovakian rock fans, including President Václav Havel, attended a Rolling Stones concert in Prague in 1990, it was clear that despite a half-century of supposedly insular Communist culture, Czechs and Slovaks had tuned in to the larger world. Sports stars like the Brazilian soccer player Pelé and the American basketball hero Michael Jordan became better known to countless people than their own national leaders. In today's world, millions of people might even, at the same moment, be spectators at a "live" event anywhere on the planet, whether World Cup competition or an Academy Awards broadcast from Hollywood.

The political power of the United States and the Western presence in the global economy have given Western culture an edge. U.S. success in "marketing" culture, along with the legacy of British imperialism, helped make English the dominant international language. Such English words as *stop, shopping, parking, okay, weekend,* and *rock* infiltrated dozens of non-English vocabularies. With British and American pop music filling the airwaves worldwide, people anywhere could tune their radios to hear songs in English. English is the official language of the European Union and of the new Central European University in Budapest; unofficially, it is the language of travel. In the 1960s, French president de Gaulle, fearing the corruption of the French language, had banned such new words as *computer* in government documents; in the mid-1990s, the French government updated the ban. Neither directive, however, could stop the influx of English into scientific, technical, diplomatic, and daily life. Other European countries, among them Germany and the Netherlands, built on their polyglot traditions by rapidly assimilating new words.

Western Europe, the United States, and Australia boasted the largest publishing firms. The giant media empire of Australian-born Rupert Murdoch not only published books, magazines, and newspapers, but produced movies and television shows through its filmmaking and TV network subsidiaries. The news media concocted an extremely successful formula for "selling" news broadcasts that combined reports of late-breaking local, national, and international events with slice-of-life stories about ordinary people. Often focusing on third world suffering, whether because of war, famine, disease, or general underdevelopment, contemporary newscasts reinforced the apparent benefits of life in the West.

Globalism and the Arts. The West continued to devour material from others, as it had done since the age of expansion beginning in the late fifteenth century. Publishers successfully marketed the outpouring of written work by major non-Western artists and intellectuals, and Hollywood made many of their novels into internationally marketed films. Such literature won both popular and critical acclaim and exerted a strong influence on European and North American writers. The lush, exotic fantasies of Colombian-born Nobel Prize winner Gabriel García Márquez (b. 1928), for example, attracted a vast Western readership. His novels, including *One Hundred Years of Solitude* (1967) and *Love in the Time of Cholera* (1988), portray people of titanic ambitions and passions who endure war and all manner of personal trials. Whereas well-regarded European writers of the day, such as the philosopher and novelist Iris Murdoch (1919–1999) or the "new" novelist Nathalie Sarraute (1900–1999) often wrote fiction in a style that was inaccessible to a mass readership, García Márquez's *magical realism* continued an older tradition of comprehensible narrative with larger-than-life characters.

Another Nobel Prize recipient who won high regard in the West was Egyptian writer Naguib

Mahfouz (b. 1911). Having immersed himself in his youth in great Western literature, Mahfouz authored more than forty books. His celebrated *Cairo Trilogy*, written in the 1950s, describes a middle-class family—from its practice of Islam and seclusion of women to the business and cultural life of men in the family. British colonialism forms the trilogy's backdrop; it impassions the protagonists and shapes their lives and destinies. In the eyes of many Arab observers, Mahfouz was a "safe" choice for the Nobel Prize, not only because he produced a literature about the history of colonialism but also because he had adopted a European style. "He borrowed the novel from Europe; he imitated it," charged one fellow Egyptian writer. "It's not an Egyptian art form. Europeans . . . like it very much because it is their own form." The globally read Egyptian Nawal el-Saadawi was also accused of producing exotic accounts of women's oppression to appeal to Western feminists. Thus, although non-Western literature reshaped Western taste, it sometimes provoked charges of inauthenticity in its authors' homelands.

Immigrants to Europe described how the experience of Western culture felt to the transnational person. The popular writer Buchi Emecheta (b. 1944), in her novel *In the Ditch* (1972) and her autobiography *Head above Water* (1986), explored her experiences as a newcomer to Britain. Her *Joys of Motherhood* (1979) was an imaginary foray back in time to probe the nature of mothering under colonial rule in her native Lagos in West Africa. While critiquing colonialism and the welfare state from a non-Western perspective, Emecheta, like many writers and politicians from less-developed countries, felt the lure of Western education and Western values. International conflict around artistic expression became dangerous. Salman Rushdie (b. 1947), also an immigrant to Great Britain (from India), produced the novel *The Satanic Verses* (1988), which ignited outrage among Muslims around the world because it appeared to blaspheme the prophet Muhammad. From Iran the Ayatollah Khomeini promised both a monetary reward and salvation in the afterlife to anyone who would assassinate the writer. In a display of Western cultural unity, international leaders took bold steps to protect Rushdie until the threat was lifted a decade later.

The mainstream was widened and sometimes fraught with conflict as groups outside the accepted circles engaged in artistic production. From within the West, novelist Toni Morrison (b. 1931), who in 1993 became the first African American woman to win the Nobel Prize in literature, described the nightmares, daily experiences, and dreams of the descendants of men and women who had been brought as slaves to the United States. But many parents objected to the inclusion of Morrison's work in curricula. Critics charged that, unlike Shakespeare's universal Western truth, the writing of African Americans, Native Americans, and postcolonial authors represented only a partial vision, not great literature.

Cultural arbiters were often relieved when the novels of Eastern-bloc dissidents powerfully endorsed Western values. Many of these writers first published their works in the West, and their writings were eventually smuggled back to their homelands. Milan Kundera (b. 1929) left Czechoslovakia in 1975 after Communist police had harassed him for his rebellious writing. Settling in Paris, Kundera produced *The Book of Laughter and Forgetting* (1979) and *The Unbearable Lightness of Being* (1984). In these works he dwelt on the importance of remembering the oppressive climate of the Eastern bloc in the face of a natural tendency to repress and to forget. In Kundera's fictional world, life often drifts toward immateriality and a quest for ease. The culture of forgetting and an easy attitude toward life, however, were just what repressive governments wanted. Writers who remained in the Soviet bloc were often suspicious of those who found success in the West. In the land of prosperous book contracts, said one Polish writer, there was no such thing as literature; rather, writing was merely a "line of business." And indeed, the dissidents were often wildly successful.

Some dissident writers chose not to leave the Communist world, and they survived by turning out a literature that was acceptable, even if the government did not embrace it wholeheartedly. East German writer Christa Wolf (b. 1929) explored subjects, such as individuality, personal guilt, and the search for self-identity, that went against the grain of East Germany's Communist ideology. In such works as *The Quest for Christa T.* (1970), she touched on themes that appealed deeply to Westerners in the 1970s and 1980s. While probing Western values in the context of communism, however, Wolf never crossed the fine line that would have brought her

Toni Morrison Receiving Nobel Prize
The first African American woman to receive the Nobel Prize, Toni Morrison had used her literary talent to depict the condition of blacks under slavery and after emancipation. Morrison also published cogent essays on social, racial, and gender issues in the United States.
Pressens Bild/Gamma Liaison.

into open opposition to the government. Consequently, the East German regime allowed her to continue publishing. With the collapse of communism, Wolf was condemned for the privileges she had enjoyed under Communist rule and for her lack of forceful dissent.

Others in the Communist world mixed global cultures no matter how dangerous or unpopular. The acclaimed composer Sofia Gubaidulina (b. 1931)—a Tatar, granddaughter of a teacher of Islam, and herself a Christian strongly influenced by Asian mysticism—created music with electronic guitars, tam-tams, and accordion along with screams and whispers. Her music was tonal and atonal, like the chant of monks and like Wagner—a collage of sound and music from everywhere. Her music, however, lacked the harshness of modernists from the middle of the century and represented a turn toward accessibility in classical music.

Postmodernism. Some called this hyper-mixing of influences *postmodernism*, and one definition of postmodernism included multiplicity without a central unifying theme or privileged canon. Striking examples of postmodern art abounded in Western society, including the AT&T building in New York City, the work of architect Philip Johnson (b. 1906). Although the structure itself, designed in the late 1970s, looked sleek and modern, its entryway was a Roman arch, and its cloud-piercing top suggested the eighteenth-century Chippendale style. The blueprints of Johnson and other postmodernists appealed to the human past and drew from cultural styles that spanned millennia and continents without valuing one style above others. The Guggenheim Museum in Bilbao, Spain, designed by American Frank Gehry (b. 1929), was similarly bizarre by classical or even "modern" standards as it represented forms, materials, and perspectives that by rules of earlier decades did not belong together. These were aesthetic examples of the postmodern, which also gave rise to films and novels without the unity of a single narrative or plot.

Other intellectuals defined the postmodern in political terms as an outgrowth of the demise of the eighteenth-century ideals of human rights, individualism, personal freedom, and their guarantor—the Western nation-state. A structure like the Bilbao Guggenheim was just an international tourist attraction that had no Spanish roots or purpose; consumption, global technology, mass communications, and international migration made citizenship, nationalism, and rights irrelevant to its meaning. It was a rootless structure, unlike the Louvre in Paris. Moreover, the end of formal imperialism meant an end to the white privilege behind modern civil rights as defined in the eighteenth century. The 1982 American film *Blade Runner*, for example, depicted a dangerous, densely packed, multiethnic Los Angeles patrolled by police with high-tech gear—a metropolis with no place for national or personal identity or human rights. For postmodernists of a political bent, computers had replaced the autonomous, free self and bureaucracy had rendered

Christo and Jeanne-Claude, Umbrellas

Attuned to global differences and similarities in landscape, environment, and ways of life, the artists Christo and Jeanne-Claude created an art that enhanced people's sensual experience of the everyday world. Their installation of umbrellas in California (top) and Japan (bottom) featured colors that complemented distinctive rural terrain, just as their wrapping of the Reichstag in Berlin (1971–1995) had enhanced urban architecture. As global citizens, they recycled the vast quantities of materials once their works were dismantled.

Top: *Christo and Jeanne-Claude: The Umbrellas, Japan-USA, 1984–91. California site.* Photo: Wolfgang Volz. © Christo 1991; bottom: *Christo and Jeanne-Claude: The Umbrellas, Japan-USA, 1984–91. Ibaraki, Japan site.* Photo: Wolfgang Volz. © Christo 1991.

representative government obsolete—an international elite of the strong, technologically trained would replace the parliament.

A third definition of the postmodern involved investigating the "unfreedom" or irrationality that shaped human life. Thus French psychoanalyst Jacques Lacan, who deeply influenced Western literary criticism in the 1980s, maintained that people operate in an unfree, predetermined world of language. Patriarchal rules of language exist before we are born and are rooted in our psychic structure. In becoming social, communicating beings we must bow to these laws. Another prominent French thinker, Michel Foucault, professed to deplore the easy acceptance of such liberal ideas as the autonomous self, the progressive march of history, and the advance of freedom. For him the sexual revolution had not been liberating at all; rather, sexuality was merely a way in which humans expressed power over one another and through which society, by allowing greater sexual expression, actually controlled individuals. Freedom, in short, had lost credibility: even in the most intimate part of human experience, people were locked in a grid of social and individual constraint. For some people struggling with the legacy of colonialism, racism, and sexism, the message from these thinkers that the rational, independent, and superior Westerner was illusory was actually a hopeful one.

Conclusion: The Making of the West Continues

Although some postmodernists proclaimed an end to centuries of faith in progress, they themselves worked within the modern Western tradition of constant criticism and reevaluation. Moreover, said their critics, the daunting problems of contemporary life—population explosion, resource depletion, North-South inequities, nuclear power, global pollution, and ethnic hatred—demanded the exercise of humanistic values and the renewal of a rational commitment to progress now more than ever. Postmodernists and other philosophers countered with the question of "unintended consequences," that is, the question whether one could begin to know the consequences of an act. Who would have predicted, for example, the human misery resulting from the fall of the Soviet empire?

IMPORTANT DATES

1979 Islamic revolution in Iran

1980 An independent trade union, Solidarity, organizes resistance to Polish communism; Prime Minister Margaret Thatcher begins dismantling the welfare state in Britain

Early 1980s AIDS epidemic strikes the West; rise of the Pacific economy

1981 Ronald Reagan becomes U.S. president

1985 Mikhail Gorbachev comes to power in the USSR

1986 Explosion at Soviet nuclear plant at Chernobyl; Spain joins the Common Market

1989 Chinese students revolt in Tiananmen Square and government suppresses them; fall of the Berlin Wall

1990s Internet revolution

1990–1991 War in the Persian Gulf

1991 Civil war erupts in the former Yugoslavia

1992 Soviet Union is dissolved

1993 Toni Morrison becomes the first African American woman to win the Nobel Prize

1994 Postapartheid elections held in South Africa

1995 International congress of women at Beijing

1997 Collapse of Thai currency and upset of the Asian "tigers"

1999 Boris Yeltsin resigns as president of Russia; euro monetary system introduced in the European Union; world population reaches six billion

The years since 1980 proved both sides correct. The collapse of communism signaled at least the eclipse of an ideology that was perhaps noble in intent but deadly in practice. Events from South Africa to the Middle East to Northern Ireland indicated that certain long-feuding groups were wearying of conflict and groping for peace, even as other peoples took up arms against their neighbors. Yet the unintended consequences of communism's fall were bloodshed, sickness, and hardship, while the global age ushered in by the Soviet collapse has brought "denationalization" to many regions of the world. Africa and Asia also faced disease and the erosion of their economic and social fabric as they faced Westernization and the global age.

Peoples and cultures of the rest of the world have indeed played their roles in the making of the

MAPPING THE WEST The World at the Start of the New Millennium

By the twenty-first century, the Internet had transformed communications and economic organization into an interconnected global network. People in the so-called North had greater access to this network in 1999 and for the most part enjoyed greater wealth. Despite globalization, historians still find local and national conditions of political, social, and economic life important in telling the full story of peoples and cultures.

From www.mids.org (Austin: Matrix Information and Directory Services, Inc.)

The World's Wealth

Income bands
High
Middle
Low
No data available

Worldwide Internet Diffusion
Number of Internet hosts
(networked computers)
1,000,000
100,000
10,000
1,000
100
10
1

West—at some times more than others. At the dawn of the millennium, the West must look in many directions to find its way. Western traditions of democracy, human rights, and economic equality have much to offer. Given that these were usually intended only for certain people, global debates about their value abound. The nation-state, which protected those values for privileged Westerners, is another legacy that must be rethought in an age of transnationalism, when more people than ever are demanding the dignity of citizenship without its being attached to a specific ethnicity. At the same time, the West faces questions of its own cultural identity—an identity made from the far-flung cultural, natural, and human resources of Asia, Africa, and the Western Hemisphere. Non-Westerners have challenged, criticized, refashioned, and made enormous contributions to Western culture; they have also served the West's citizens as slaves, servants, and menial workers. One of the greatest challenges to the West and the world in this global millennium is to determine how peoples and cultures can live together on terms that are enriching for everyone.

A final challenge to the West is living with the inventive human spirit. In the past five hundred years the West has benefited from its scientific and technological advances. Longevity and improved material well-being have spread around the world. In the past century, communication and information technology brought people closer to one another than ever before. Simultaneously, through the use of technology the last century was the bloodiest in human history. War and genocide were among its hallmarks, and even now the world's leaders urge their scientific communities to search for ever more destructive weapons, posing perhaps the greatest challenge to the West and to the world. The making of the West has been a constantly inventive undertaking but also a deadly one. What mixture of peoples and cultures will face the paradoxical challenge of technology to protect the creativity of the human race in the twenty-first century?

Suggested References

Global Challenges

Historians see the challenges of the past two decades as enormously diverse, ranging from conditions in the environment to issues of leadership in international affairs. However, as Rives and Yousefi show, challenges such as the globalization of work have benefits as well as costs.

Appleyard, Reginald. *International Migration: Challenges for the Nineties.* 1991.

Feshbach, Murray. *Ecological Disaster: Cleaning Up the Hidden Legacy of the Soviet Regime.* 1995.

Keylor, William R. *The Twentieth-Century World: An International History.* 1992.

*Khadduri, Majid, and Edmund Ghareeb. *War in the Gulf, 1990–1991.* 1997.

Moin, Baqr. *Khomeini: Life of the Ayatollah.* 1999.

Rives, Janet, and Mahmood Yousefi. *Economic Dimensions of Gender Inequality: A Global Perspective.* 1997.

UN Population Data: http://www.unfpa.org/swp/swpmain .htm.

The Welfare State in Question

The transformation of the welfare state involved powerful political personalities and raised fundamental issues about the nature of citizenship. Much cutting-edge history concerns an analysis of citizens' relationship to their state and their relationship to one another in an age of global migration and dramatic economic change. The work of Paul Gilroy in particular has brought these questions to the fore.

Ash, Timothy Garton. *In Europe's Name: Germany and the Divided Continent.* 1993.

Caciagli, Mario, and David I. Kertzer, eds. *Italian Politics: The Stalled Transition.* 1996.

Gilroy, Paul. *"There Ain't No Black in the Union Jack": The Cultural Politics of Race and Nation.* 1987.

Sassen, Saskia. *Globalization and Its Discontents: Essays on the New Mobility of People and Money.* 1998.

Schaller, Michael. *Reckoning with Reagan: America and Its President in the 1980s.* 1992.

Thompson, Juliet S., and Wayne C. Thompson. *Margaret Thatcher: Prime Minister Indomitable.* 1994.

The Collapse of Soviet Communism

Historians will be telling and retelling this story, for the full consequences of communism's collapse are still unfolding. As new archives open, scholars, such as Kligman, focus on recounting some of the most horrendous aspects of Communist rule. Others, like Wachtel, explain the post-Communist situation in terms of very long-standing trends such as the obstacles to creating cultural unity among peoples of the former Yugoslavia.

Funk, Nanette, and Magda Mueller. *Gender Politics and Post-Communism: Reflections from Eastern Europe and the Former Soviet Union.* 1993.

*Primary sources.

Glenny, Misha. *The Fall of Yugoslavia: The Third Balkan War.* 1996.

*Gorbachev, Mikhail. *Memoirs.* 1996.

Jarausch, Konrad. *The Rush to German Unity.* 1994.

Kazanov, Anatoly M. *After the USSR: Ethnicity, Nationalism, and Politics in the Commonwealth of Independent States.* 1995.

Kligman, Gail. *The Politics of Duplicity: Controlling Reproduction in Ceauşescu's Romania.* 1998.

Sternhal, Suzanne. *Gorbachev's Reforms: De-Stalinization through Demilitarization.* 1997.

Strayer, Robert. *Why Did the Soviet Union Collapse?* 1998.

Wachtel, Andrew B. *Making a Nation, Breaking a Nation: Literature and Cultural Politics in Yugoslavia.* 1998.

Weigel, George. *Witness to Hope: The Biography of Pope John Paul II.* 1999.

Global Culture and Western Civilization at the Dawn of a New Millennium

The fate of cultural identity in an age of globalization engages a wide range of investigation and theorizing. From the nation-state to our individual relationships, as Applegate and Turkle, among others, suggest, long-standing identities are open to rethinking.

Agre, Philip. *Computation and Human Experience.* 1997.

Applegate, Celia. "A Europe of Regions: Reflections on the Historiography of Sub-National Places in Modern Times." *The American Historical Review.* 1999.

Bales, Kevin. *Disposable People: New Slavery in the Global Economy.* 1999.

Dery, Mark. *Escape Velocity: Cyberculture at the End of the Century.* 1996.

*Emecheta, Buchi. *The Joys of Motherhood.* 1979.

Huntington, Samuel P. *The Clash of Civilizations and the Re-making of the World Order.* 1996.

Iriye, Akira. *Cultural Internationalism and World Order.* 1997.

*Morrison, Toni. *Paradise.* 1998.

Piening, Christopher. *Global Europe: The European Union in World Affairs.* 1997.

Public Broadcasting: http://www.pbs.org.

Redmond, John, and Glenda S. Rosenthal. *The Expanding European Union: Past, Present, Future.* 1998.

Turkle, Sherry. *Life on the Screen: Identity in the Age of the Internet.* 1995.

APPENDIX

Useful Facts and Figures

PROMINENT ROMAN EMPERORS

Julio-Claudians

27 B.C.–14 A.D.	Augustus
14–37	Tiberius
37–41	Gaius (Caligula)
41–54	Claudius
54–68	Nero

Flavian Dynasty

69–79	Vespasian
79–81	Titus
81–96	Domitian

Golden Age Emperors

96–98	Nerva
98–117	Trajan
117–138	Hadrian
138–161	Antonius Pius
161–180	Marcus Aurelius

Severan Emperors

193–211	Septimius Severus
211–217	Antoninus (Caracalla)
217–218	Macrinus
222–235	Severus Alexander

Period of Instability

235–238	Maximinus Thrax
238–244	Gordian III
244–249	Philip the Arab
249–251	Decius
251–253	Trebonianus Gallus
253–260	Valerian
270–275	Aurelian
275–276	Tacitus
276–282	Probus
283–285	Carinus

Dominate

284–305	Diocletian
306	Constantius
306–337	Constantine I
337–340	Constantine II
337–350	Constans I
337–361	Constantius II

(Continued)

A-1

361–363	Julian
363–364	Jovian
364–375	Valentinian I
364–378	Valens
367–383	Gratian
375–392	Valentinian II
378–395	Theodosius I
	(the Great)

The Western Empire

395–423	Honorius
406–407	Marcus

407–411	Constantine III
409–411	Maximus
411–413	Jovinus
412–413	Sebastianus
423–425	Johannes
425–455	Valentinian III
455–456	Avitus
457–461	Majorian
461–465	Libius Severus
467–472	Anthemius
473–474	Glycerius
474–475	Julius Nepos
475–476	Romulus Augustulus

PROMINENT BYZANTINE EMPERORS

Dynasty of Theodosius

395–408	Arcadius
408–450	Theodosius II
450–457	Marcian

Dynasty of Leo

457–474	Leo I
474	Leo II
474–491	Zeno
475–476	Basiliscus
484–488	Leontius
491–518	Anastasius

Dynasty of Justinian

518–527	Justin
527–565	Justinian I
565–578	Justin II
578–582	Tiberius II
578–582	Tiberius II (I) Constantine
582–602	Maurice
602–610	Phocas

Dynasty of Heraclius

610–641	Heraclius
641	Heraclonas
641	Constantine III
641–668	Constans II
646–647	Gregory
649–653	Olympius
669	Mezezius

668–685	Constantine IV
685–695	Justinian II (banished)
695–698	Leontius
698–705	Tiberius III (II)
705–711	Justinian II (restored)
711–713	Bardanes
713–716	Anastasius II
716–717	Theodosius III

Isaurian Dynasty

717–741	Leo III
741–775	Constantine V Copronymus
775–780	Leo IV
780–797	Constantine VI
797–802	Irene
802–811	Nicephorus I
811	Strauracius
811–813	Michael I
813–820	Leo V

Phrygian Dynasty

820–829	Michael II
821–823	Thomas
829–842	Theophilus
842–867	Michael III

Macedonian Dynasty

867–886	Basil I
869–879	Constantine

887–912	Leo VI
912–913	Alexander
913–959	Constantine VII Porphygenitus
920–944	Romanus I Lecapenus
921–931	Christopher
924–945	Stephen
959–963	Romanus II
963–969	Nicephorus II Phocas
976–1025	Basil II
1025–1028	Constantine VIII (IX) alone
1028–1034	Romanus III Argyrus
1034–1041	Michael IV the Paphlagonian
1041–1042	Michael V Calaphates
1042	Zoe and Theodora
1042–1055	Constantine IX Monomchus
1055–1066	Theodora alone
1056–1057	Michael VI Stratioticus

Prelude to the Comnenian Dynasty

1057–1059	Isaac I Comnenos
1059–1067	Constantine X (IX) Ducas
1068–1071	Romanus IV Diogenes
1071–1078	Michael VII Ducas
1078–1081	Nicephorus III Botaniates
1080–1081	Nicephorus Melissenus

Comnenian Dynasty

1081–1118	Alexius I
1118–1143	John II
1143–1180	Manuel I
1180–1183	Alexius II

1183–1185	Andronieus I
1183–1191	Isaac, Emperor of Cyprus

Dynasty of the Angeli

1185–1195	Isaac II
1195–1203	Alexius III
1203–1204	Isaac II (restored) with Alexius IV
1204	Alexius V Ducas Murtzuphlus

Lascarid Dynasty in Nicaea

1204–1222	Theodore I Lascaris
1222–1254	John III Ducas Vatatzes
1254–1258	Theodore II Lascaris
1258–1261	John IV Lascaris

Dynasty of the Paleologi

1259–1289	Michael VIII Paleologus
1282–1328	Andronicus II
1328–1341	Andronicus III
1341–1391	John V
1347–1354	John VI Cantancuzenus
1376–1379	Andronicus IV
1379–1391	John V (restored)
1390	John VII
1391–1425	Manuel II
1425–1448	John VIII
1449–1453	Constantine XI (XIII) Dragases

PROMINENT POPES

314–335	Sylvester	1243–1254	Innocent IV
440–461	Leo I	1294–1303	Boniface VIII
590–604	Gregory I (the Great)	1316–1334	John XXII
687–701	Sergius I	1447–1455	Nicholas V
741–752	Zachary	1458–1464	Pius II
858–867	Nicholas I	1492–1503	Alexander VI
1049–1054	Leo IX	1503–1513	Julius II
1059–1061	Nicholas II	1513–1521	Leo X
1073–1085	Gregory VII	1534–1549	Paul III
1088–1099	Urban II	1555–1559	Paul IV
1099–1118	Paschal II	1585–1590	Sixtus V
1159–1181	Alexander III	1623–1644	Urban VIII
1198–1216	Innocent III	1831–1846	Gregory XVI
1227–1241	Gregory IX		

(Continued)

1846–1878	Pius IX
1878–1903	Leo XIII
1903–1914	Pius X
1914–1922	Benedict XV
1922–1939	Pius XI

1939–1958	Pius XII
1958–1963	John XXIII
1963–1978	Paul VI
1978	John Paul I
1978–	John Paul II

THE CAROLINGIAN DYNASTY

687–714	Pepin of Heristal, Mayor of the Palace
715–741	Charles Martel, Mayor of the Palace
741–751	Pepin III, Mayor of the Palace
751–768	Pepin III, King
768–814	Charlemagne, King
800–814	Charlemagne, Emperor
814–840	Louis the Pious

West Francia

840–877	Charles the Bald, King
875–877	Charles the Bald, Emperor
877–879	Louis II, King

879–882	Louis III, King
879–884	Carloman, King

Middle Kingdoms

840–855	Lothair, Emperor
855–875	Louis (Italy), Emperor
855–863	Charles (Provence), King
855–869	Lothair II (Lorraine), King

East Francia

840–876	Ludwig, King
876–880	Carloman, King
876–882	Ludwig, King
876–887	Charles the Fat, Emperor

GERMAN KINGS CROWNED EMPEROR

Saxon Dynasty

962–973	Otto I
973–983	Otto II
983–1002	Otto III
1002–1024	Henry II

Franconian Dynasty

1024–1039	Conrad II
1039–1056	Henry III
1056–1106	Henry IV
1106–1125	Henry V
1125–1137	Lothair II (Saxony)

Hohenstaufen Dynasty

1138–1152	Conrad III
1152–1190	Frederick I (Barbarossa)

1190–1197	Henry VI
1198–1208	Philip of Swabia
1198–1215	Otto IV (Welf)
1220–1250	Frederick II
1250–1254	Conrad IV

Interregnum, 1254–1273: Emperors from Various Dynasties

1273–1291	Rudolf I (Habsburg)
1292–1298	Adolf (Nassau)
1298–1308	Albert I (Habsburg)
1308–1313	Henry VII (Luxemburg)
1314–1347	Ludwig IV (Wittelsbach)
1347–1378	Charles IV (Luxemburg)
1378–1400	Wenceslas (Luxemburg)
1400–1410	Rupert (Wittelsbach)
1410–1437	Sigismund (Luxemburg)

Habsburg Dynasty

1438–1439	Albert II		1637–1657	Ferdinand III
1440–1493	Frederick III		1658–1705	Leopold I
1493–1519	Maximilian I		1705–1711	Joseph I
1519–1556	Charles V		1711–1740	Charles VI
1556–1564	Ferdinand I		1742–1745	Charles VII (not a Habsburg)
1564–1576	Maximilian II		1745–1765	Francis I
1576–1612	Rudolf II		1765–1790	Joseph II
1612–1619	Matthias		1790–1792	Leopold II
1619–1637	Ferdinand II		1792–1806	Francis II

RULERS OF FRANCE

Capetian Dynasty

987–996	Hugh Capet
996–1031	Robert II
1031–1060	Henry I
1060–1108	Philip I
1108–1137	Louis VI
1137–1180	Louis VII
1180–1223	Philip II (Augustus)
1223–1226	Louis VIII
1226–1270	Louis IX (St. Louis)
1270–1285	Philip III
1285–1314	Philip IV
1314–1316	Louis X
1316–1322	Philip V
1322–1328	Charles IV

Valois Dynasty

1328–1350	Philip VI
1350–1364	John
1364–1380	Charles V
1380–1422	Charles VI
1422–1461	Charles VII
1461–1483	Louis XI
1483–1498	Charles VIII
1498–1515	Louis XII
1515–1547	Francis I

1547–1559	Henry II
1559–1560	Francis II
1560–1574	Charles IX
1574–1589	Henry III

Bourbon Dynasty

1589–1610	Henry IV
1610–1643	Louis XIII
1643–1715	Louis XIV
1715–1774	Louis XV
1774–1792	Louis XVI

After 1792

1792–1799	First Republic, 1792–1799
1799–1804	Napoleon Bonaparte, First Consul
1804–1814	Napoleon I, Emperor
1814–1824	Louis XVIII (Bourbon Dynasty)
1824–1830	Charles X (Bourbon Dynasty)
1830–1848	Louis Philippe
1848–1852	Second Republic
1852–1870	Napoleon III, Emperor
1870–1940	Third Republic
1940–1944	Vichy government, Pétain regime
1944–1946	Provisional government
1946–1958	Fourth Republic
1958–	Fifth Republic

MONARCHS OF ENGLAND AND GREAT BRITAIN

Anglo-Saxon Monarchs

829–839	Egbert
839–858	Ethelwulf
858–860	Ethelbald
860–866	Ethelbert
866–871	Ethelred I
871–899	Alfred the Great
899–924	Edward the Elder
924–939	Ethelstan
939–946	Edmund I
946–955	Edred
955–959	Edwy
959–975	Edgar
975–978	Edward the Martyr
978–1016	Ethelred the Unready
1016–1035	Canute (Danish nationality)
1035–1040	Harold I
1040–1042	Hardicanute
1042–1066	Edward the Confessor
1066	Harold II

Norman Monarchs

1066–1087	William I (the Conqueror)
1087–1100	William II
1100–1135	Henry I

House of Blois

1135–1154	Stephen

House of Plantagenet

1154–1189	Henry II
1189–1199	Richard I
1199–1216	John
1216–1272	Henry III
1272–1307	Edward I
1307–1327	Edward II
1327–1377	Edward III
1377–1399	Richard II

House of Lancaster

1399–1413	Henry IV
1413–1422	Henry V
1422–1461	Henry VI

House of York

1461–1483	Edward IV
1483	Edward V
1483–1485	Richard III

House of Tudor

1485–1509	Henry VII
1509–1547	Henry VIII
1547–1553	Edward VI
1553–1558	Mary
1558–1603	Elizabeth I

House of Stuart

1603–1625	James I
1625–1649	Charles I

Commonwealth and Protectorate (1649–1660)

1653–1658	Oliver Cromwell
1658–1659	Richard Cromwell

House of Stuart (Restored)

1660–1685	Charles II
1685–1688	James II
1689–1694	William III and Mary II
1694–1702	William III (alone)
1702–1714	Anne

House of Hanover

1714–1727	George I
1727–1760	George II
1760–1820	George III
1820–1830	George IV
1830–1837	William IV
1837–1901	Victoria

House of Saxe-Coburg-Gotha

1901–1910	Edward VII

House of Windsor

1910–1936	George V
1936	Edward VIII
1936–1952	George VI
1952–	Elizabeth II

PRIME MINISTERS OF GREAT BRITAIN

Term	Prime Minister	Government
1721–1742	Sir Robert Walpole	Whig
1742–1743	Spencer Compton, Earl of Wilmington	Whig
1743–1754	Henry Pelham	Whig
1754–1756	Thomas Pelham-Holles, Duke of Newcastle	Whig
1756–1757	William Cavendish, Duke of Devonshire	Whig
1757–1761	William Pitt (the Elder), Earl of Chatham	Whig
1761–1762	Thomas Pelham-Holles, Duke of Newcastle	Whig
1762–1763	John Stuart, Earl of Bute	Tory
1763–1765	George Grenville	Whig
1765–1766	Charles Watson-Wentworth, Marquess of Rockingham	Whig
1766–1768	William Pitt, Earl of Chatham (the Elder)	Whig
1768–1770	Augustus Henry Fitzroy, Duke of Grafton	Whig
1770–1782	Frederick North (Lord North)	Tory
1782	Charles Watson-Wentworth, Marquess of Rockingham	Whig
1782–1783	William Petty FitzMaurice, Earl of Shelburn	Whig
1783	William Henry Cavendish Bentinck, Duke of Portland	Whig
1783–1801	William Pitt, the Younger	Tory
1801–1804	Henry Addington	Tory
1804–1806	William Pitt (the Younger)	Tory
1806–1807	William Wyndham Grenville (Baron Grenville)	Whig
1807–1809	William Henry Cavendish Bentinck, Duke of Portland	Tory
1809–1812	Spencer Perceval	Tory
1812–1827	Robert Banks Jenkinson, Earl of Liverpool	Tory
1827	George Canning	Tory
1827–1828	Frederick John Robinson (Viscount Goderich)	Tory
1828–1830	Arthur Wellesley, Duke of Wellington	Tory
1830–1834	Charles Grey (Earl Grey)	Whig
1834	William Lamb, Viscount Melbourne	Whig
1834–1835	Sir Robert Peel	Tory
1835–1841	William Lamb, Viscount Melbourne	Whig
1841–1846	Sir Robert Peel	Tory
1846–1852	John Russell (Lord)	Whig
1852	Edward Geoffrey–Smith Stanley Derby, Earl of Derby	Whig
1852–1855	George Hamilton Gordon Aberdeen, Earl of Aberdeen	Peelite
1855–1858	Henry John Temple Palmerston, Viscount Palmerston	Tory
1858–1859	Edward Geoffrey–Smith Stanley Derby, Earl of Derby	Whig
1859–1865	Henry John Temple Palmerston, Viscount Palmerston	Tory
1865–1866	John Russell (Earl)	Liberal
1866–1868	Edward Geoffrey–Smith Stanley Derby, Earl of Derby	Tory
1868	Benjamin Disraeli, Earl of Beaconfield	Conservative
1868–1874	William Ewart Gladstone	Liberal
1874–1880	Benjamin Disraeli, Earl of Beaconfield	Conservative
1880–1885	William Ewart Gladstone	Liberal
1885–1886	Robert Arthur Talbot, Marquess of Salisbury	Conservative
1886	William Ewart Gladstone	Liberal
1886–1892	Robert Arthur Talbot, Marquess of Salisbury	Conservative
1892–1894	William Ewart Gladstone	Liberal
1894–1895	Archibald Philip–Primrose Rosebery, Earl of Rosebery	Liberal

(Continued)

Term	Prime Minister	Government
1895–1902	Robert Arthur Talbot, Marquess of Salisbury	Conservative
1902–1905	Arthur James Balfour, Earl of Balfour	Conservative
1905–1908	Sir Henry Campbell-Bannerman	Liberal
1908–1915	Herbert Henry Asquith	Liberal
1915–1916	Herbert Henry Asquith	Coalition
1916–1922	David Lloyd George, Earl Lloyd-George of Dwyfor	Coalition
1922–1923	Andrew Bonar Law	Conservative
1923–1924	Stanley Baldwin, Earl Baldwin of Bewdley	Conservative
1924	James Ramsay MacDonald	Labour
1924–1929	Stanley Baldwin, Earl Baldwin of Bewdley	Conservative
1929–1931	James Ramsay MacDonald	Labour
1931–1935	James Ramsay MacDonald	Coalition
1935–1937	Stanley Baldwin, Earl Baldwin of Bewdley	Coalition
1937–1940	Neville Chamberlain	Coalition
1940–1945	Winston Churchill	Coalition
1945	Winston Churchill	Conservative
1945–1951	Clement Attlee, Earl Attlee	Labour
1951–1955	Sir Winston Churchill	Conservative
1955–1957	Sir Anthony Eden, Earl of Avon	Conservative
1957–1963	Harold Macmillan, Earl of Stockton	Conservative
1963–1964	Sir Alec Frederick Douglas-Home, Lord Home of the Hirsel	Conservative
1964–1970	Harold Wilson, Lord Wilson of Rievaulx	Labour
1970–1974	Edward Heath	Conservative
1974–1976	Harold Wilson, Lord Wilson of Rievaulx	Labour
1976–1979	James Callaghan, Lord Callaghan of Cardiff	Labour
1979–1990	Margaret Thatcher (Baroness)	Conservative
1990–1997	John Major	Conservative
1997–	Tony Blair	Labour

RULERS OF PRUSSIA AND GERMANY

1701–1713	*Frederick I
1713–1740	*Frederick William I
1740–1786	*Frederick II (the Great)
1786–1797	*Frederick William II
1797–1840	*Frederick William III
1840–1861	*Frederick William IV
1861–1888	*William I (German emperor after 1871)
1888	Frederick III
1888–1918	*William II
1918–1933	Weimar Republic
1933–1945	Third Reich (Nazi dictatorship under Adolf Hitler)
1945–1952	Allied occupation
1949–1990	Division of Federal Republic of Germany in west and German Democratic Republic in east
1990–	Federal Republic of Germany (united)

*King of Prussia

RULERS OF AUSTRIA AND AUSTRIA-HUNGARY

1493–1519	*Maximillian I (Archduke)
1519–1556	*Charles V
1556–1564	*Ferdinand I
1564–1576	*Maximillian II
1576–1612	*Rudolf II
1612–1619	*Matthias
1619–1637	*Ferdinand II
1637–1657	*Ferdinand III
1658–1705	*Leopold I
1705–1711	*Joseph I
1711–1740	*Charles VI
1740–1780	Maria Theresa
1780–1790	*Joseph II
1790–1792	*Leopold II
1792–1835	*Francis II (emperor of Austria as Francis I after 1804)
1835–1848	Ferdinand I
1848–1916	Francis Joseph (after 1867 emperor of Austria and king of Hungary)
1916–1918	Charles I (emperor of Austria and king of Hungary)
1918–1938	Republic of Austria (dictatorship after 1934)
1945–1956	Republic restored, under Allied occupation
1956–	Free Republic

*Also bore title of Holy Roman Emperor

LEADERS OF POST–WORLD WAR II GERMANY

West Germany (Federal Republic of Germany), 1949–1990

Years	Chancellor	Party
1949–1963	Konrad Adenauer	Christian Democratic Union (CDU)
1963–1966	Ludwig Erhard	Christian Democratic Union (CDU)
1966–1969	Kurt Georg Kiesinger	Christian Democratic Union (CDU)
1969–1974	Willy Brandt	Social Democratic Party (SPD)
1974–1982	Helmut Schmidt	Social Democratic Party (SPD)
1982–1990	Helmut Kohl	Christian Democratic Union (CDU)

East Germany (German Democratic Republic), 1949–1990

Years	Communist Party Leader
1946–1971	Walter Ulbricht
1971–1989	Erich Honecker
1989–1990	Egon Krenz

Federal Republic of Germany (reunited), 1990–

Years	Chancellor	Party
1990–1998	Helmut Kohl	Christian Democratic Union (CDU)
1998–	Gerhard Schroeder	Social Democratic Party (SPD)

RULERS OF RUSSIA, THE USSR, AND THE RUSSIAN FEDERATION

c. 980–1015	Vladimir
1019–1054	Yaroslav the Wise
1176–1212	Vsevolod III
1462–1505	Ivan III
1505–1553	Vasily III
1553–1584	Ivan IV
1584–1598	Theodore I
1598–1605	Boris Godunov
1605	Theodore II
1606–1610	Vasily IV
1613–1645	Michael
1645–1676	Alexius
1676–1682	Theodore III
1682–1689	Ivan V and Peter I
1689–1725	Peter I (the Great)
1725–1727	Catherine I
1727–1730	Peter II
1730–1740	Anna
1740–1741	Ivan VI
1741–1762	Elizabeth
1762	Peter III
1762–1796	Catherine II (the Great)
1796–1801	Paul
1801–1825	Alexander I
1825–1855	Nicholas I
1855–1881	Alexander II
1881–1894	Alexander III
1894–1917	Nicholas II

Union of Soviet Socialist Republics (USSR)*

1917–1924	Vladimir Ilyich Lenin
1924–1953	Joseph Stalin
1953–1964	Nikita Khrushchev
1964–1982	Leonid Brezhnev
1982–1984	Yuri Andropov
1984–1985	Konstantin Chernenko
1985–1991	Mikhail Gorbachev

Russian Federation

1991–1999	Boris Yeltsin
1999–	Vladimir Putin

*USSR established in 1922

RULERS OF SPAIN

1479–1504	Ferdinand and Isabella
1504–1506	Ferdinand and Philip I
1506–1516	Ferdinand and Charles I
1516–1556	Charles I (Holy Roman Emperor Charles V)
1556–1598	Philip II
1598–1621	Philip III
1621–1665	Philip IV
1665–1700	Charles II
1700–1746	Philip V
1746–1759	Ferdinand VI
1759–1788	Charles III
1788–1808	Charles IV
1808	Ferdinand VII
1808–1813	Joseph Bonaparte
1814–1833	Ferdinand VII (restored)
1833–1868	Isabella II
1868–1870	Republic
1870–1873	Amadeo
1873–1874	Republic
1874–1885	Alfonso XII
1886–1931	Alfonso XIII
1931–1939	Republic
1939–1975	Fascist dictatorship under Francisco Franco
1975–	Juan Carlos I

RULERS OF ITALY

1861–1878	Victor Emmanuel II
1878–1900	Humbert I
1900–1946	Victor Emmanuel III
1922–1943	Fascist dictatorship under Benito Mussolini (maintained in northern Italy until 1945)
1946 (May 9–June 13)	Humbert II
1946–	Republic

SECRETARIES-GENERAL OF THE UNITED NATIONS

		Nationality
1946–1952	Trygve Lie	Norway
1953–1961	Dag Hammarskjold	Sweden
1961–1971	U Thant	Myanmar
1972–1981	Kurt Waldheim	Austria
1982–1991	Javier Pérez de Cuéllar	Peru
1992–1996	Boutros Boutros-Ghali	Egypt
1997–	Kofi A. Annan	Ghana

UNITED STATES PRESIDENTIAL ADMINISTRATIONS

Term(s)	President	Political Party
1789–1797	George Washington	No party designation
1797–1801	John Adams	Federalist
1801–1809	Thomas Jefferson	Democratic-Republican
1809–1817	James Madison	Democratic-Republican
1817–1825	James Monroe	Democratic-Republican
1825–1829	John Quincy Adams	Democratic-Republican
1829–1837	Andrew Jackson	Democratic
1837–1841	Martin Van Buren	Democratic
1841	William H. Harrison	Whig
1841–1845	John Tyler	Whig
1845–1849	James K. Polk	Democratic
1849–1850	Zachary Taylor	Whig
1850–1853	Millard Filmore	Whig
1853–1857	Franklin Pierce	Democratic
1857–1861	James Buchanan	Democratic
1861–1865	Abraham Lincoln	Republican
1865–1869	Andrew Johnson	Republican
1869–1877	Ulysses S. Grant	Republican
1877–1881	Rutherford B. Hayes	Republican
1881	James A. Garfield	Republican
1881–1885	Chester A. Arthur	Republican
1885–1889	Grover Cleveland	Democratic
1889–1893	Benjamin Harrison	Republican
1893–1897	Grover Cleveland	Democratic
1897–1901	William McKinley	Republican
1901–1909	Theodore Roosevelt	Republican
1909–1913	William H. Taft	Republican
1913–1921	Woodrow Wilson	Democratic
1921–1923	Warren G. Harding	Republican
1923–1929	Calvin Coolidge	Republican
1929–1933	Herbert C. Hoover	Republican
1933–1945	Franklin D. Roosevelt	Democratic
1945–1953	Harry S. Truman	Democratic
1953–1961	Dwight D. Eisenhower	Republican
1961–1963	John F. Kennedy	Democratic
1963–1969	Lyndon B. Johnson	Democratic
1969–1974	Richard M. Nixon	Republican
1974–1977	Gerald R. Ford	Republican
1977–1981	Jimmy Carter	Democratic
1981–1989	Ronald W. Reagan	Republican
1989–1993	George H. W. Bush	Republican
1993–	William J. Clinton	Democratic

MAJOR WARS OF THE MODERN ERA

1546–1555	German Wars of Religion
1526–1571	Ottoman wars
1562–1598	French Wars of Religion
1566–1609, 1621–1648	Revolt of the Netherlands
1618–1648	Thirty Years' War
1642–1648	English Civil War
1652–1678	Anglo-Dutch Wars
1667–1697	Wars of Louis XIV
1683–1697	Ottoman wars
1689–1697	War of the League of Augsburg
1702–1714	War of Spanish Succession
1702–1721	Great Northern War
1714–1718	Ottoman wars
1740–1748	War of Austrian Succession
1756–1763	Seven Years' War
1775–1781	American Revolution
1796–1815	Napoleonic wars
1846–1848	Mexican-American War
1853–1856	Crimean War
1861–1865	United States Civil War
1870–1871	Franco-Prussian War
1894–1895	Sino-Japanese War
1898	Spanish-American War
1904–1905	Russo-Japanese War
1914–1918	World War I
1939–1945	World War II
1946–1975	Vietnam wars
1950–1953	Korean War
1990–1991	Persian Gulf War
1991–1997	Civil War in the former Yugoslavia

POPULATION OF MAJOR CITIES, 1750–1990

City	1750	1800	1850	1900	1950	1990
Amsterdam	210,000	217,000	224,000	511,000	804,000	713,000
Athens	10,000	12,000	31,000	111,000	565,000	772,000
Berlin	90,000	172,000	419,000	1,889,000	3,337,000	3,438,000
Brussels	60,000	66,000	251,000	599,000	956,000	954,000
Budapest	xxxxxxxx[1]	54,000	178,000	732,000	1,571,000	2,017,000
Dublin	90,000	165,000	272,000	373,000	522,000	920,000
Geneva	22,000	22,000	31,000	59,000	145,000	167,000
St. Petersburg	150,000	336,000	485,000	1,267,000	xxxxxxxx	4,437,000
Lisbon	148,000	180,000	240,000	356,000	790,000	678,000
London	675,000	1,117,000	2,685,000	6,586,000	8,348,000	6,803,000
Madrid	109,000	160,000	281,000	540,000	1,618,000	2,991,000
Moscow	130,000	250,000	365,000	989,000	xxxxxxxx	8,747,000
Paris	576,000	581,000	1,053,000	2,714,000	2,850,000	2,152,000
Prague	59,000	75,000	118,000	202,000	922,000	1,212,000
Rome	156,000	163,000	175,000	463,000	1,652,000	2,828,000
Stockholm	60,000	76,000	93,000	301,000	744,000	679,000
Warsaw	23,000	100,000	160,000	638,000	601,000	1,654,000
Zurich	11,000	12,000	17,000	151,000	390,000	342,000
New York	22,000	60,000	696,000	3,437,000	7,892,000	7,322,000
Montreal	6,000	xxxxxxxx	58,000	268,000	1,022,000	1,017,000
Mexico City	xxxxxxxx	137,000	170,000	345,000	2,234,000	8,235,000
Buenos Aires	11,000	40,000	99,000	664,000	2,981,000	2,960,000
Cairo	xxxxxxxx	211,000	267,000	570,000	2,091,000	6,452,000
Alexandria	xxxxxxxx	15,000	60,000	320,000	919,000	3,413,000
Istanbul	xxxxxxxx	600,000	xxxxxxxx	1,125,000	983,000	6,220,000
Damascus	xxxxxxxx	130,000	150,000	140,000	335,000	1,451,000
Jerusalem	xxxxxxxx	xxxxxxxx	xxxxxxxx	42,000	83,000	524,000
Tokyo	xxxxxxxx	xxxxxxxx	xxxxxxxx	1,819,000	6,778,000	8,163,000
Delhi	xxxxxxxx	xxxxxxxx	xxxxxxxx	209,000	914,000	8,419,000

[1] xxxxxxxx = population statistics unavailable

Source: B. R. Mitchell, ed. *International Historical Statistics* (1998).

Index

A note about the index:

Names of individuals appear in boldface; biographical dates are included for major historical figures.

Letters in parentheses following pages refer to:
(i)   illustrations, including photographs and artifacts
(f)   figures, including charts and graphs
(m)   maps
(b)   boxed features (such as "Contrasting Views")

continued

continued

continued

continued

continued

continued

continued

Elevation

Feet	Meters
Over 13,120	Over 4,001
6,561–13,120	2,001–4,000
1,641–6,560	501–2,000
661–1640	201–500
0–660	0–200
Below sea level	Below sea level

⊛ National capital
• Major city

0   150   300 miles
0   150   300 kilometers

NORWAY

Bergen

Oslo ⊛

SWED

Göteborg

North Sea

SCOTLAND

Glasgow   Edinburgh

NORTHERN
IRELAND

Belfast

Aarhus

DENMARK

Copenhagen

IRELAND   Dublin ⊛

UNITED

Liverpool

KINGDOM

WALES   Birmingham

ENGLAND
Thames R.

London ⊛

Elbe R.

NETHERLANDS

Amsterdam

Berlin ⊛

Rotterdam

Antwerp

Brussels ⊛

BELGIUM

Rhine R.

GERMANY

Prague ⊛

English Channel

Paris ⊛

Luxembourg ⊛

Frankfurt

CZECH

LUXEMBOURG

ATLANTIC
OCEAN

Loire R.

Seine R.

LIECHTENSTEIN

Munich

Vienna

Zürich   Vaduz ⊛

Danube R.

*Bay of
Biscay*

FRANCE

Bern ⊛

Innsbruck   AUSTRIA

SWITZERLAND

Graz

A L P S

Lyon

Milan

SLOVENIA

Rhône R.

Ljubljana ⊛

Po R.

CROATIA

Oporto

ANDORRA

Ebro R.

PYRENEES

Andorra
la Vella

San
Marino   SAN
MARINO   BOS
HERZ

A
P
E
N
N
I
N
E
S

Adriatic Sea

Marseille

MONACO

Split

PORTUGAL

Madrid ⊛

SPAIN

Barcelona

Corsica

Rome ⊛   ITALY

Naples

Lisbon ⊛

Seville

Sardinia

*Tyrrhenian
Sea*

BALEARIC IS.

Gibraltar
(Br.)

Palermo

Rabat ⊛

Algiers ⊛

Tunis ⊛

Sicily

Valletta ⊛

MALTA

MOROCCO

TUNISIA

ALGERIA

Tripoli ⊛

LIBYA